The Rough G **W9-CCR-795**

China

written and researched by

David Leffman, Simon Lewis and Jeremy Atiyah

with additional contributions by

Simon Foster, Travis Klingberg,
Mike Meyer and Xiaoshan Sun

ROUGH GUIDES

NEW YORK • LONDON • DELHI

www.roughguides.com

Contents

◄◄ Shanghai street ◄ Meili Xue Shan

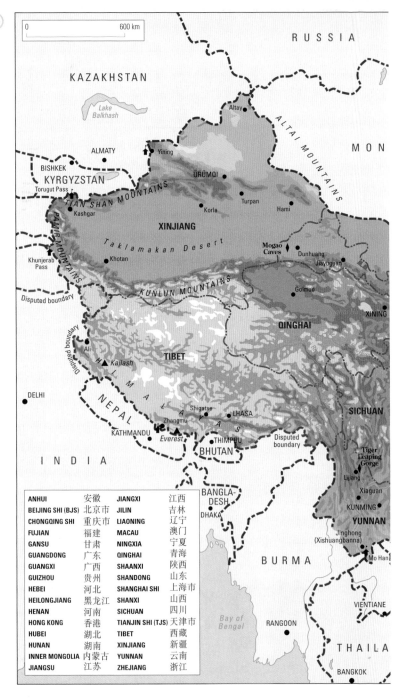

ANHUI	安徽	**JIANGXI**	江西
BEIJING SHI (BJS)	北京市	**JILIN**	吉林
CHONGQING SHI	重庆市	**LIAONING**	辽宁
FUJIAN	福建	**MACAU**	澳门
GANSU	甘肃	**NINGXIA**	宁夏
GUANGDONG	广东	**QINGHAI**	青海
GUANGXI	广西	**SHAANXI**	陕西
GUIZHOU	贵州	**SHANDONG**	山东
HEBEI	河北	**SHANGHAI SHI**	上海市
HEILONGJIANG	黑龙江	**SHANXI**	山西
HENAN	河南	**SICHUAN**	四川
HONG KONG	香港	**TIANJIN SHI (TJS)**	天津市
HUBEI	湖北	**TIBET**	西藏
HUNAN	湖南	**XINJIANG**	新疆
INNER MONGOLIA	内蒙古	**YUNNAN**	云南
JIANGSU	江苏	**ZHEJIANG**	浙江

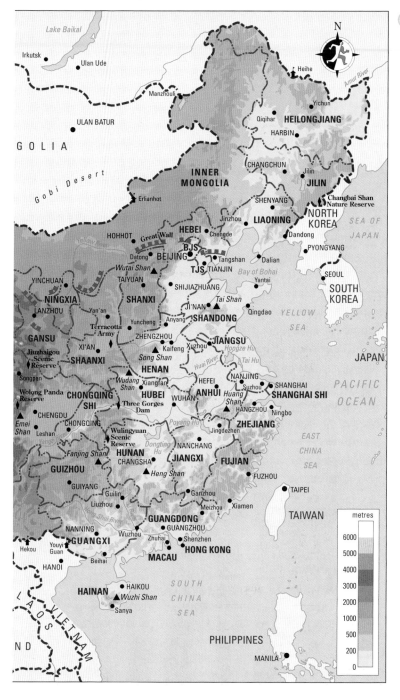

Introduction to
China

China has grown up alone and aloof, cut off from the rest of Eurasia by the Himalayas to the southwest and the Siberian steppe to the north. For the last three millennia, while empires, languages and peoples in the rest of the world rose, blossomed and disappeared without trace, China has been busy largely recycling itself. The ferocious dragons and lions of Chinese statuary have been produced for 25 centuries or more, and the script still used today reached perfection at the time of the Han dynasty, two thousand years ago. Until the late nineteenth century, the only foreigners China saw – apart from occasional ruling elites of Mongol and Manchu origin, who quickly became assimilated – were visiting merchants from far-flung shores or uncivilized nomads from the wild steppe: peripheral, unimportant and unreal.

 Today, while there is no sign of the Communist Party relinquishing power, the negative stories surrounding China – the runaway pollution, the oppression of dissidents and imperialist behaviour towards Tibet and other minority regions – are only part of the picture. As the Party moves ever further away from hard-line political doctrine and towards economic pragmatism, China is undergoing a huge commercial and creative upheaval. Hong Kong-style city skylines are rearing up across the country, and tens of millions of people are finding jobs that earn them a spending power their parents could never have known. Whatever the reasons you are attracted to China, the sheer

▲ Beijing Opera

pace of change, visible in every part of Chinese life, will ensure that your trip is a unique one.

The first thing that strikes visitors to China is the extraordinary density of its **population**. In central and eastern China, villages, towns and cities seem to sprawl endlessly into one another along the grey arteries of busy expressways. These are the **Han Chinese** heartlands, a world of chopsticks, tea, slippers, massed bicycles, shadow-boxing, exotic pop music, teeming crowds, chaotic train stations, smoky temples, red flags and the smells of soot and frying tofu. Move west or north away from the major cities, however, and the population thins out as it begins to vary: indeed, large areas of the People's Republic are inhabited not by the "Chinese", but by more than two hundred distinct **ethnic minorities**, ranging from animist hill tribes to urban Muslims. Here the landscape begins to dominate: green paddy fields and misty hilltops in the southwest, the scorched, epic vistas of the old Silk Road in the northwest, and the magisterial mountains of Tibet.

> China is undergoing a huge commercial and creative upheaval

While travel around the country itself is seldom problematic, it would be wrong to pretend that it is an entirely easy matter to penetrate modern China. The main tourist highlights – the Great Wall, the Forbidden City, the Terracotta Army, and Yangzi gorges – are relatively few considering the vast size of the country, and much of China's historic architecture has been deliberately destroyed in the rush to modernize. Added to this are the frustrations of travelling in a land where few people speak

7

Fact file

• With an **area** of 9.6 million square kilometres, China is the fourth largest country in the world – practically the same size as the United States – and the most populous nation on earth, with around 1.3 billion people. Of these, 92% are of the **Han** ethnic group, with the remainder comprising about sixty minorities such as Mongols, Uigurs and Tibetans. The main **religions** are Buddhism, Taoism and Confucianism, though the country is officially atheist. A third of China comprises fertile river plains, and another third arid deserts, plateaux or mountains. China's longest river is the **Yangzi** (6275km) and the highest peak is **Qomolongma** – Mount Everest (8850m), on the Nepalese border.

• China is a police state run by the **Chinese Communist Party**, the sole political organization, which is divided into Executive, Legislative and Judicial branches. The chief of state (President) and the head of government (Premier) are elected for five-year terms at the National People's Congress. After decades of state planning, the economy is now mixed, with state-owned enterprises on the decline and free-market principles ubiquitous. China's main **exports** are clothing, textiles, tea and fossil fuels, and its main trading partners are the US, Japan, South Korea and Europe.

English, the writing system is alien and foreigners are regularly viewed as exotic objects of intense curiosity, or as fodder for overcharging – though overall you'll find that the Chinese, despite a reputation for curtness, are generally hospitable and friendly.

Where to go

As China has opened up in recent years, so the emphasis on tourism has changed. Many well-known cities and sights have become so developed that their charm has become elusive; while in remoter regions – particularly Tibet, Yunnan and the northwest – previously

▼ Forbidden City, Beijing

Chinese cuisine

The Chinese can seem obsessed with eating, and each region boasts its own cuisine. Northern, Eastern, Cantonese and Sichuanese are the four major regional styles, but every area has its own specialities, including tear-jerkingly spicy tofu in Chengdu, salt-baked chicken in eastern Guangdong, boiled scorpions in Qufu, butter tea  in Tibet, handmade noodles and mutton soup in the northwest, elegant *dim sum* breakfasts in Guangzhou and Beijing duck in the capital. For snacking, noodle dishes, soups, and buns and dumplings stuffed with meats or vegetables are generally on sale at the nearest street corner. Eating is very much a social event: a selection of dishes is shared among family or friends, and most good restaurants are famously "hot and noisy". And despite the Western perception that all Chinese eat rice, in the north they favour wheat noodles and plain buns. For more on Chinese food, see p.57.

restricted or "undiscovered" places have become newly accessible. The following outline is a selection of both "classic" China sights and less-known attractions, which should come in handy when planning a schedule.

Inevitably, **Beijing** is on everyone's itinerary, and the Great Wall and the splendour of the Imperial City are certainly not to be missed; the capital also offers some of the country's best food and nightlife. **Chengde**, too, just north of Beijing, has some stunning imperial buildings, constructed by emperors when this was their favoured retreat for the summer.

South of the capital, the **Yellow River valley** is the cradle of Chinese civilization, where remnants of the dynastic age lie scattered in a unique landscape of loess terraces. The cave temples at **Datong** and **Luoyang** are magnificent, with huge Buddhist sculptures staring out impassively across their now industrialized settings.

Previously restricted or "undiscovered" places have become newly accessible

Of the historic capitals, **Xi'an** is the most obvious destination, where the celebrated Terracotta Army still stands guard over the tomb of Emperor Qin Shi Huang. Less visited ancient towns include sleepy **Kaifeng** in Henan and **Qufu**, the birthplace of Confucius in Shandong, both offering architectural treasures and an intimate, human scale that's missing in the large cities. The area is also well supplied with holy mountains, providing

Wildlife

Although China's varied geography and climate have created a wealth of wildlife habitats, the country's vast human population has put pressure on the environment, bringing some high-profile creatures to the edge of extinction. Most famous of these is the giant panda, which survives in pockets of high-altitude bamboo forest across the southwest. A few Siberian tigers haunt the northeastern highlands, while the critically endangered South China tiger numbers just thirty wild individuals. Less well-known rarities include the snub-nosed golden monkey, white-headed langur and Chinese alligator, all of which are possible – with a lot of luck – to see in the wild. Birdlife can be prolific, with freshwater lakes along the Yangzi and in western Guizhou, along with the vast saline Qinghai Lake, providing winter refuge for hosts of migratory wildfowl – including rare Siberian and black-necked cranes.

both beautiful scenery and a rare continuity with the past: **Tai Shan** is perhaps the grandest and most imperial of the country's pilgrimage sites; **Song Shan** in Henan sees followers of the contemporary kung-fu craze making the trek to the Shaolin Temple, where the art originated; and **Wutai Shan** in Shanxi features some of the best-preserved religious sites in the country.

Dominating China's east coast near the mouth of the Yangzi, **Shanghai** is the mainland's most Westernized city, a booming port where the Art Deco monuments of the old European-built Bund – the riverside business centre – rub shoulders with a hyper-modern metropolis, crowned with two of the world's tallest skyscrapers. It's interesting to contrast Shanghai's cityscape with that of rival business hub **Hong Kong**, off China's south coast. With its colonial heritage and refreshingly cosmopolitan outlook, there's almost nothing Hong Kong cannot offer in the way of tourist facilities, from fine beaches to great eating, drinking and nightlife. Nearby **Macau** is also worth a visit, if not for its casinos, then for its Baroque churches and fine Portuguese cuisine.

In the southwest of the country, Sichuan's **Chengdu** and Yunnan's **Kunming** remain two of China's most interesting and easy-going provincial capitals, and the entire region is, by any standards, exceptionally diverse, with landscapes encompassing everything from snowbound summits and alpine lakes to steamy tropical jungles. The karst (limestone peak) scenery is

Chinese script

Chinese characters are simplified images of what they represent, and their origins as pictograms can often still be seen, even though they have become highly abstract today. The earliest known examples of Chinese writing are predictions which were cut into "oracle bones" over three thousand years ago during the Shang

dynasty, though the characters must have been in use long before as these inscriptions already amount to a highly complex writing system. As the characters represent concepts, not sounds, written Chinese cuts through the problem of communication in a country with many different dialects. However, learning the writing system is ponderous, taking children an estimated two years longer than with an alphabet. Foreigners learning Mandarin use the modern *pinyin* transliteration system of accented Roman letters – used throughout this book – to help memorize the sounds. For more on language, see p.1227.

particularly renowned, especially along the Li River between **Yangshuo** and **Guilin** in Guangxi. In Sichuan, pilgrims flock to see the colossal Big Buddha at **Leshan**, and to ascend the holy mountain of **Emei Shan**; to the east, the city of **Chongqing** marks the start of river trips down the **Yangzi**, Asia's longest river, through the **Three Gorges**. As Yunnan and Guangxi share borders with Vietnam, Laos and Burma, while Sichuan rubs up against Tibet, it's not surprising to find that the region is home to near-extinct wildlife and dozens of ethnic autonomous regions; the attractions of the

▲ Tai ji students, Wudang Shan

latter range from the traditional Naxi town of **Lijiang** and Dai villages of **Xishuangbanna** in Yunnan, to the Khampa heartlands of western Sichuan, the exuberant festivals and textiles of Guizhou's Miao and the wooden architecture of Dong settlements in Guangxi's north.

The huge area of China referred to as the Northwest is where the people thin out and real wilderness begins. Inner Mongolia, just hours from Beijing, is already at the frontiers of Central Asia; here you can follow in the footsteps of Genghis Khan by going horse-riding on the endless grasslands of the steppe. To the south and west, the old **Silk Road** heads out of Xi'an right to and through China's western borders, via **Jiayuguan**, terminus of the Great Wall of China, and the lavish Buddhist cave art in the sandy deserts of **Dunhuang**.

West of here lie the mountains and deserts of vast Xinjiang, where China blends into old Turkestan and where simple journeys between towns become modern travel epics. The oasis cities of **Turpan** and **Kashgar**, with their bazaars and Muslim heritage, are the main attractions, though the blue waters of **Tian Chi**, offering alpine scenery in the midst of searing desert, are deservedly popular. Beyond Kashgar, travellers face some of the most adventurous routes of all, over the Khunjerab and Torugut passes to Pakistan and Kirgyzstan respectively.

Tibet remains an exotic destination, especially if you come across the border from Nepal or brave the long road in from Golmud in Qinghai province. Despite fifty years of Chinese rule, coupled with a mass migration of Han Chinese into the region, the manifestations of Tibetan culture remain intact – the Potala Palace in **Lhasa**, red-robed monks, lines of pilgrims turning prayer wheels, butter sculptures and gory frescoes decorating monastery halls. And Tibet's mountain scenery, which includes **Mount Everest**, is worth the trip in itself, even if opportunities for independent travel are more restricted than elsewhere in China.

When to go

China's **climate** is extremely diverse. The **south** is subtropical, with wet, humid summers (April to September) – when temperatures can approach 40°C – and a typhoon season on the southeast coast between July and September. Though it is often still hot enough to swim in the sea in December, the short winters, from January to March, can be surprisingly chilly.

Central China, around Shanghai and the Yangzi River, has brief, cold winters, with temperatures dipping below zero, and long, hot, humid

Urban pollution

A reliance on coal for power and heating, factories spewing untreated waste into the atmosphere, growing numbers of vehicles, and the sheer density of the urban population all conspire to make Chinese cities some of the most polluted on earth. Black sludge fills canals and streams; buildings are mired by soot; blue sky is only a memory; the population seem permanently stricken with bronchitis; and acid rain withers plants. In summer the worst spots are the Yangzi valley "furnaces" of Nanjing, Chongqing and Wuhan; winter in Xi'an, on the other hand, features black snow. The Chinese government is finally beginning to take pollution seriously, especially with the Beijing Olympics due in 2008: in the capital at least, factories are being relocated and elderly, fume-belching minibuses have been scrapped or foisted on other cities.

summers. It's no surprise that three Yangzi cities – Chongqing, Wuhan and Nanjing – are proverbially referred to as China's three "furnaces". Rainfall here is high all year round. Farther north, the **Yellow River basin** marks a rough boundary beyond which central heating is fitted as standard in buildings, helping to make the region's harsh

winters a little more tolerable. Winter temperatures in Beijing rarely rise above freezing from December to March, and freezing winds off the Mongolian plains add a vicious wind-chill factor. In summer, however, temperatures here can be well over 30°C. In **Inner Mongolia** and **Manchuria**, winters are at least clear and dry, but temperatures remain way below zero, while summers can be uncomfortably warm. **Xinjiang** gets fiercely hot in summer, though without the humidity of the rest of the country, and winters are as bitter as anywhere else in northern China. **Tibet** is ideal in midsummer, when its mountain plateaux are pleasantly warm and dry; in winter, however, temperatures in the capital, Lhasa, frequently fall below freezing.

Overall, the best time to visit China is **spring** or **autumn**, when the weather is at its most temperate. In the spring, it's best to start in the south and work north or west as summer approaches; in the autumn, start in the north and work south.

▼ Farmer, Yunnan

14

Average daily temperatures, and monthly rainfall

To convert °C to °F multiply by 1.8 and add 32. To convert mm to inches divide by 25.

	Jan	Feb	Mar	Apr	May	Jun	Jul	Aug	Sep	Oct	Nov	Dec
Beijing												
max °C	1	4	11	21	27	31	31	30	26	20	9	3
min °C	-10	-8	-1	7	13	18	21	20	14	6	-2	-8
rainfall mm	4	5	8	17	35	78	243	141	58	16	11	3
Chongqing												
max °C	9	13	18	23	27	29	34	35	28	22	16	13
min °C	5	7	11	16	19	22	24	25	22	16	12	8
rainfall mm	15	20	38	99	142	180	142	122	150	112	48	20
Guilin												
max °C	16	17	20	25	29	31	32	32	31	27	23	19
min °C	8	10	14	19	23	25	26	26	24	19	15	12
rainfall mm	33	56	97	160	206	193	160	178	84	43	38	37
Hong Kong												
max °C	18	17	19	24	28	29	31	31	29	27	23	20
min °C	13	13	16	19	23	26	26	26	25	23	18	15
rainfall mm	33	46	74	137	292	394	381	367	257	114	43	31
Jilin												
max °C	-6	-2	6	16	23	29	31	29	24	16	5	-4
min °C	-18	-14	-6	3	10	16	21	19	11	3	-6	-15
rainfall mm	8	8	18	28	69	84	183	170	64	36	28	15
Kunming												
max °C	20	22	25	28	29	29	28	28	28	24	22	20
min °C	8	9	12	16	18	19	19	19	18	15	12	8
rainfall mm	8	18	28	41	127	132	196	198	97	51	56	15
Lhasa												
max °C	7	9	12	16	19	24	23	22	21	17	13	9
min °C	-10	-7	-2	1	5	9	9	9	7	1	-5	-9
rainfall mm	0	13	8	5	25	64	122	89	66	13	3	0
Shanghai												
max °C	8	8	13	19	25	28	32	32	28	23	17	12
min °C	1	1	4	10	15	19	23	23	19	14	7	2
rainfall mm	48	58	84	94	94	180	147	142	130	71	51	36
Ürümqi												
max °C	-11	-8	-1	16	22	26	28	27	21	10	-1	-8
min °C	-22	-19	-11	2	8	12	14	13	8	-1	-11	-13
rainfall mm	15	8	13	38	28	38	18	25	15	43	41	10
Wuhan												
max °C	8	9	14	21	26	31	34	34	29	23	17	11
min °C	1	2	6	13	18	23	26	26	21	16	9	3
rainfall mm	46	48	97	152	165	244	180	97	71	81	48	28

35

things not to miss

It's not possible to see everything China has to offer in one trip – and we don't suggest you try. What follows is a selective and subjective taste of the country's highlights: gaudy temples, mouthwatering cuisine, exuberant festivals and beautiful landscapes. They're all arranged in five colour-coded categories to help you find the very best things to see, do and experience. All entries have a page reference to take you straight into the guide, where you can find out more.

01 The Great Wall Page **143** • Once the division between civilizations, this monumental barrier is still awe-inspiring.

03 Meili Xue Shan Page 846 • A wilderness area that offers great hiking, superlative views and a glimpse of the Tibetan world.

02 Li River scenery Page 740 • Take a boat trip here to admire the weird, contorted peaks of the sort you'll see on Chinese scroll paintings.

04 Huanglongxi Page 896 • This atmospheric Qing-dynasty village in Sichuan sports several old temples, and was used as a set in the film *Crouching Tiger, Hidden Dragon*.

05 Harbin Ice Festival Page 214 • "Lurid" and "outrageous" don't begin to describe the bizarre sculptures here – everything from life-size ice castles to fantastical snowy tableaux.

06 Colonial architecture, Xiamen Page 573 • Gulangyu Island here has some of the best architecture left by nineteenth-century Europeans.

17

07 Sisters' Meal festival Page **784** • Join tens of thousands of locals in Taijiang, Guizhou, as they participate in this annual three-day showcase of ethnic Miao culture.

09 Changbai Shan Nature Reserve Page **210** • Well worth a visit – though you'd have to be exceptionally lucky to spot its rare Siberian tigers.

08 Skiing at Yabuli Page **222** • The very idea of a Chinese skiing holiday sounds off-the-wall – and thus all the more worth trying.

10 Chengde Page **172** • The emperors' former retreat from the heat of summer holds a string of pretty temples.

11 **Mount Everest** Page **1148** • The sight of the mountain towering above ensures you won't regret the long journey up to Base Camp.

13 **Dim sum** Page **600** • The classic Cantonese breakfast; there's no better place to try it than Guangzhou.

14 **Dali** Page **822** • The capital of the Bai ethnic group is now a charming backpackers' oasis and host to the colourful Spring Fair festival.

12 **The Silk Road** Page **1055** • Abandoned cities here, such as Jiaohe, hint at the former importance of this ancient trading route.

15 **A cruise down the Yangzi River** Page **928** • Enjoy awesome scenery and a wealth of historic sights, despite rising water levels caused by the controversial Three Gorges Dam.

16 **Kashgar's Sunday Market** Page **1083** • Crowds from all over Central Asia descend to trade livestock, carpets, knives and clothes at this weekly event.

17 **The Jokhang, Lhasa** Page **1116** • Stuffed with gorgeous statuary and perpetually wreathed in juniper smoke and incense, this temple is one of the holiest in Tibet.

19 **Minority villages, Yunnan** Page **861** • The Xishuangbanna region, bordering Laos and Burma, is home to a range of ethnic groups with very different cultures and lifestyles.

18 **Confucius Temple** Page **333** • This lavish complex in Confucius's home town of Qufu shows the esteem in which China's great sage was held.

20 **Hong Kong's skyline** Page **660** • The drive of generations of the former colony's inhabitants is writ large in this electrifying cityscape.

21 **Labrang monastery, Xiahe** • Page **1009** • One of the most important Tibetan Buddhist monasteries, a riot of lavishly decorated halls, butter sculptures and ragged pilgrims.

22 **Jiayuguan fort** Page **1020** • A famously lonely outpost overlooking the desert at the western tail of the Great Wall.

23 **The Yellow River** Page **258** • One of the world's great rivers, offering a tantalizing range of vistas, including the turbid Hukou Falls.

24 **The Great Buddha (Dafo), Leshan** Page **910** • You'll feel a mere speck as you gaze up at the world's largest carved Buddha.

26 **Beijing duck** Page **126** • A northern Chinese culinary speciality and absolutely delicious – crisp skin and juicy meat eaten in a pancake.

25 **Tai Shan** Page **327** • The taxing ascent of this holy peak in Shandong is rewarded with some immaculate temples and pavilions.

28 **The Terracotta Army** Page **280** • Near the old capital of Xi'an, these 2200-year-old, life-size soldiers guard the tomb of China's first emperor.

27 **The Forbidden City** Page **105** • Once centre of the Chinese imperial universe and off limits to the hoi polloi, the emperor's impressive palace complex in Beijing is now open to all.

29 **Bird-watching, Cao Hai** Page **793** • Being punted around this shallow lake after rare birdlife is a wonderfully restful experience.

30 **The Hanging Temple and Yungang Caves** Page **236** • Near Datong in Shanxi are two incredible sights: a temple clinging to a precipice and a series of grottoes containing a panoply of Buddhist statuary.

31 Tiger Leaping Gorge Page
838 • One of China's great hikes, along a ridge above a dramatic gorge, with attractive homestays along the way.

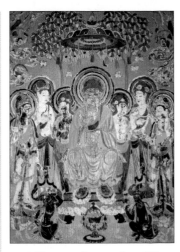

32 Mogao Caves Page **1025**
• These 1000-year-old man-made caves on the old Silk Road contain China's most impressive Buddhist heritage.

34 Sichuanese teahouses
Page **888** • Relaxed places to gossip, read or socialize for the price of a cup of tea.

35 The Bund, Shanghai
Page **372** • An elegant parade of colonial architecture, nestling incongruously at the heart of Shanghai's gaudy modernity.

33 Yonghe Gong, Beijing Page
120 • This charismatic Tibetan temple is an explosion of ornament and colour.

Basics

Basics

Getting there

China's most important long-haul international gateways are Beijing, Hong Kong, Guangzhou and Shanghai, though many other Chinese cities are served by international flights, operated mainly by airlines based in East Asia. There are also well-established overland routes into China – including road and rail links from its Southeast Asian neighbours, as well as the alluring Trans-Siberian train from Moscow.

Fares to Hong Kong are at their highest during the fortnight before Christmas, the fortnight before Chinese New Year (see p.67) and from mid-June to early October. The cheapest time to fly there is the months of February (after Chinese New Year), May and November. For Beijing, peak season is generally summertime. Note also that flying on weekends is slightly more expensive; price ranges quoted below assume midweek travel.

If China is only one stop on a much longer journey, you might want to consider buying a **Round-the-World** (**RTW**) ticket (around £1000/$1800). Some travel agents can sell you an "off-the-shelf" RTW ticket that will have you touching down in about half a dozen cities (Hong Kong is on many itineraries); others will have to assemble one for you, which can be tailored to your needs but is apt to be more expensive.

If your time is limited, you can't face the hassles of travelling on your own, or if you have a specialist interest such as cycling or bird-watching, then an **organized tour** of China, with flights, transport and accommodation included, might be worth considering. Though convenient, any tour including accommodation and internal travel is likely to work out more expensive per day than if you were travelling independently.

Booking flights online

Many airlines and discount travel websites offer you the opportunity to book your tickets, hotels and holiday packages online, cutting out the costs of agents and middlemen; these are worth going for, as long as you don't mind the inflexibility of non-refundable, non-changeable deals. There are some bargains to be had on auction sites too, if you're prepared to bid keenly. Almost all airlines have their own websites, offering flight tickets that can sometimes be just as cheap, and are often more flexible.

Online booking agents

Ⓦ **www.cheapflights.com** Flight deals, travel agents, plus links to other travel sites.
Ⓦ **www.cheaptickets.com** US discount flight specialists, also has deals on hotels and car hire.
Ⓦ **www.ebookers.com** Efficient, easy to use flight finder, with competitive fares.
Ⓦ **www.expedia.com** Discount airfares, all-airline search engine and daily deals.
Ⓦ **www.flynow.com** Simple to use independent travel site offering good-value fares.
Ⓦ **www.hotwire.com** US website with lots of last-minute deals, saving up to forty percent on regular published fares.
Ⓦ **www.lastminute.com** Offers good last-minute holiday package and flight-only deals.
Ⓦ **www.skyauction.com** Bookings from the US only. Auctions tickets and travel packages using a system similar to eBay.
Ⓦ **www.ticketplanet.com** California-based site that claims to be the first to sell consolidator fares over the Web. Especially good for round-the-world fares.
Ⓦ **www.travelocity.com**, Ⓦ **www.travelocity.co.uk** Good Web fares and deals on car rental, accommodation and lodging.
Ⓦ **www.travelshop.com.au** Australian website offering discounted flights, packages insurance and online bookings.

From the UK and Ireland

You can fly **direct** to China from London Heathrow with Air China, British Airways or Cathay Pacific to either Beijing (10hr), Hong Kong (12hr) or Shanghai (11hr). Other airlines flying via a change of planes in a hub city include Aeroflot, Air France, KLM, Singapore, Swiss and Thai. It's not a problem to fly to China from other UK airports or from the Republic of Ireland, though you'll end up either catching a connecting flight to London or flying via the airline's hub city.

From the UK, the lowest available fares to Beijing or Shanghai from London start from around £400 in low season, rising to £800 in high season; to Hong Kong the corresponding range is about £350–700. Unfancied airlines such as Air China and Aeroflot offer competitive fares, and even the more upmarket airlines such as British Airways run special offers or promotions – if you catch them at the right time you can enjoy the luxury of a nonstop flight at a budget price.

Airlines

Aeroflot UK ☎020/7355 2233, ✆www.aeroflot .co.uk.

Air China UK ☎020/7630 0919 or 7630 7678, ✆www.air-china.co.uk.

Air France UK ☎0845/359 1000, Republic of Ireland ☎01/605 0383, ✆www.airfrance.com.

British Airways UK ☎0870/850 9850, Republic of Ireland ☎1800/626 747, ✆www.ba.com.

Cathay Pacific UK ☎020/8834 8888, ✆www .cathaypacific.com/uk.

Emirates Airlines UK ☎0870/243 2222, ✆www .emirates.com.

Finnair UK ☎0870/241 4411, Republic of Ireland ☎01/844 6565, ✆www.finnair.com.

Gulf Air UK ☎0870/777 1717, ✆www.gulfairco .com. Daily from Heathrow to Hong Kong via Dubai.

KLM (Royal Dutch Airlines) UK ☎0870/507 4074, ✆www.klm.com.

Lufthansa UK ☎0845/773 7747, Republic of Ireland ☎01/844 5544, ✆www.lufthansa.com.

Malev Hungarian Airlines UK ☎0870/909 0577, Republic of Ireland ☎01/844 4303, ✆www .malev.hu.

Singapore Airlines UK ☎0870/608 8886, Republic of Ireland ☎01/671 0722, ✆www .singaporeair.com.

Swiss UK ☎0845/601 0956, Republic of Ireland ☎1890/200 515, ✆www.swiss.com.

Thai Airways UK ☎0870/606 0911, ✆www .thaiair.com.

Virgin Atlantic Airways UK ☎01293/747747, ✆www.virgin.com/atlantic.

Flight and travel agents

Aran Travel International Republic of Ireland ☎091/562 595, ✆homepages.iol.ie/~arantvl /aranmain.htm.

Bridge the World UK ☎0870/814 4400, ✆www .bridgetheworld.com.

Co-op Travel Care UK ☎0870/112 0085, ✆www .travelcareonline.com.

Flightcentre UK ☎0870/890 8099, ✆www .flightcentre.co.uk.

International Association of Air Travel Couriers UK ☎0800/0746 481, ✆www.aircourier .co.uk.

North South Travel UK ☎01245/608 291, ✆www.northsouthtravel.co.uk.

STA Travel UK ☎0870/1600 599, ✆www .statravel.co.uk.

Trailfinders UK ☎0845/0585 858, ✆www .trailfinders.co.uk; Republic of Ireland ☎01/677 7888, ✆www.trailfinders.ie.

Travel Bag UK ☎01/602 1904, ✆www.travelbag .co.uk.

usit NOW Republic of Ireland ☎01/602 1600, Northern Ireland ☎028/9032 7111; ✆www .usitnow.ie.

Organized tours

UK-based tour operators fall into two categories: those which offer a fully cosseted holiday and talk about the "romance" of China, and those which concern themselves with the "real" China – at the earthiest end of the market, these involve rugged overland trips in specially modified vehicles. The advantage of the latter tours is that they sometimes penetrate parts of China inaccessible by public transport.

A particularly good deal is the amazingly cheap off-season **flight-and-hotel** packages to Beijing which, at prices that often go below £500, provide six or seven nights in a four-star hotel effectively for free. Don't forget, though, that quoted prices in brochures usually refer to the low-season minimum, based on two people sharing – the cost for a single traveller in high season will always work out far more expensive.

Specialist tour operators

Birdfinders ☎01258/839066, ✆www .birdfinders.co.uk. Several trips per year to find rare and endemic species in mainland China and Tibet.

China Holidays ☎020/74872999, ⓦwww
.chinaholidays.co.uk. Aside from mainstream
packages to the Three Gorges, Shanghai and Guilin,
they also run a "Taste of China" gastronomic tour
sampling food between Beijing and Hong Kong.
CTS Horizons ☎020/7836 9911, ⓦwww
.ctshorizons.com. The China Travel Service's UK
branch, offering an extensive range of tours including
very cheap off-season hotel-and-flight packages to
Beijing, and tailor-made private tours.
Destinations Worldwide Holidays Republic of
Ireland ☎01/855 6641, ⓦwww.destinations.ie.
Undemanding two-week tours that include Hong Kong
and Beijing.
Exodus UK ☎020/8675 5550, ⓦwww.exodus
.co.uk. Offers some interesting and unusual overland
itineraries in the wilds of Tibet, Inner Mongolia and the
Northwest. Good-value three-week tours from £1700
including flights.
Explore Worldwide UK ☎01252/760 000,
ⓦwww.explore.co.uk. Big range of small-group
tours and treks, includingTibet tours and trips along
the Yangzi. Some supplements for single travellers.
Hayes & Jarvis UK ☎0870/898 9890, ⓦwww
.hayes-jarvis.com. Similar approach to Kuoni's,
though note that their Beijing flight-and-hotel-only
packages can be the cheapest around.
Intrepid Travel UK ☎020/8960 6333, ⓦwww
.intrepidtravel.com. Small-group tours with the
emphasis on cross-cultural contact and low-impact
tourism; visits some very out-of-the-way corners of
China.
Imaginative Traveller UK ☎020/8742 8612,
ⓦwww.adventurebound.co.uk. An emphasis on the
unusual, with cycling tours, a panda trek in Sichuan
and a Kathmandu–Lhasa–Kathmandu overland trip.
Kuoni Travel UK ☎01306/747 002, ⓦwww
.kuoni.co.uk. Packages China as a holiday
experience; often in conjunction with side-trips to Bali
or Bangkok.
Magic of the Orient UK ☎01293/537700,
ⓦwww.magic-of-the-orient.com. Tailor-made
holidays sometimes off the beaten track, in Yunnan
and along the Yangzi.
Regent Holidays UK ☎0117/921 1711,
ⓦwww.regent-holidays.co.uk. Offers interesting
Trans-Siberian packages for individual travellers in
either direction and with different possible stopover
permutations.
The Russia Experience UK ☎020/8566 8846,
ⓦwww.trans-siberian.co.uk. Besides detailing their
Trans-Siberian packages, their website is a veritable
mine of information about the railway.
World Expeditions UK ☎020/8870 2600,
ⓦwww.worldexpeditions.co.uk. Offers cycling and
hiking tours in rural areas.

From the US and Canada

There are more flights to **Hong Kong** from
North America than elsewhere in China,
though there's no shortage of flights to
Beijing. Airlines flying **direct** include Air
Canada (to Beijing), Air China (Beijing),
Cathay (Hong Kong) and United (Hong Kong,
Beijing and Shanghai). You can also choose
to fly to a Chinese provincial city – Chinese,
Japanese, Korean and Hong Kong airlines
offer services to cities throughout China via
their respective hubs. It takes around thirteen
hours' **flying time** to reach Beijing from the
West Coast; add seven hours or more to this
if you start from the East Coast (including a
stopover on the West Coast en route).

Round-trip fares to Hong Kong, Beijing
and Shanghai are broadly comparable: in
low season, expect to pay $750–1100/
CDN$1200–1400 from the West Coast (Los
Angeles, San Francisco, Vancouver), or
$900–1100/CDN$1250–2000 from the East
Coast (New York, Montreal, Toronto). To get
a good fare during high season it's important to buy your ticket as early as possible,
in which case you probably won't pay more
than $200/CDN$320 above what you would
have paid in low season.

Airlines

Air Canada ☎1-888/247-2262, ⓦwww
.aircanada.com.
Air China US ☎212/371-9898, Canada
☎416/581-8833, ⓦwww.airchina.com.cn.
American Airlines ☎1-800/433-7300, ⓦwww
.aa.com.
Asiana Airlines US ☎1-800/227-4262, ⓦwww
.flyasiana.com.
Cathay Pacific ☎1-800/233-2742, ⓦwww
.cathay-usa.com.
China Airlines ☎917/368-2000, ⓦwww.china
-airlines.com.
China Southern Airlines US ☎1-888/338-8988,
ⓦwww.cs-air.com.
EVA Air ☎1-800/695-1188, ⓦwww.evaair.com.
JAL (Japan Air Lines) ☎1-800/525-3663,
ⓦwww.japanair.com.
Korean Air ☎1-800/438-5000, ⓦwww.koreanair
.com.
Northwest/KLM ☎1-800/447-4747, ⓦwww
.nwa.com, ⓦwww.klm.com.
United Airlines ☎1-800/538-2929, ⓦwww
.united.com.

Travel and flight agents

Air Brokers International ☎1-800/883-3273, ⊛www.airbrokers.com.
Airtreks ☎1-877/AIRTREKS, ⊛www.airtreks.com.
Air Courier Association ☎1-800/282-1202, ⊛www.aircourier.org.
Flightcentre US ☎1-866/WORLD-51, ⊛www.flightcentre.us, Canada ☎1-888/WORLD-55, ⊛www.flightcentre.ca.
International Association of Air Travel Couriers ☎308/632-3273, ⊛www.courier.org.
STA Travel US ☎1-800/329-9537, Canada ☎1-888/427-5639, ⊛www.statravel.com.
Travel Avenue ☎1-800/333-3335, ⊛www.travelavenue.com.
Travel Cuts US ☎1-800/592-CUTS, Canada ☎1-888/246-9762, ⊛www.travelcuts.com.
Worldtek Travel ☎1-800/243-1723, ⊛www.worldtek.com.

Tour operators

Abercrombie & Kent ☎1-800/323-7308 or 630/954-2944, ⊛www.abercrombiekent.com. Luxury tours covering all the highlights, and can also cater for family groups.
Absolute Asia ☎1-800/736-8187, ⊛www.absoluteasia.com. Numerous tours of China lasting from between 6 and 23 days, in first-class accommodation, such as the 14-day "Art and History of China" tour.
Adventure Center ☎1-800/228-8747 or 510/654-1879, ⊛www.adventure-center.com. Dozens of tours in China and Tibet, from a week-long whizz around the highlights to a month of walking, hiking and biking expeditions.
Adventures Abroad ☎1-800/665-3998 or 360/775-9926, ⊛www.adventures-abroad.com. Small-group specialists with tours through China and Mongolia.
Asian Pacific Adventures ☎1-800/825-1680 or 818/886-5190, ⊛www.asianpacificadventures.com. Numerous tours of China, focusing on southwestern ethnic groups and often-overlooked rural corners.
Asia Transpacific Journeys ☎1-800/642-2742, ⊛www.southeastasia.com. Group and tailor-made tours visiting well-trodden sights but covering them in better depth than most.
Backroads ☎1-800/GO-ACTIVE or 510/527-1555, ⊛www.backroads.com. Cycling and hiking between Beijing and south China's Guangdong province.
Cross-Culture ☎1-800/491-1148 or 413/256-6303, ⊛www.crosscultureinc.com. Tours taking in Beijing, Xi'an, Shanghai, Guilin and the Yangzi, as well as parts of Tibet.

Geographic Expeditions ☎1-800/777-8183 or 415/922-0448, ⊛www.geoex.com. Adventurous travel amongst the ethnic groups of Guizhou, Tibet, western Sichuan, Xinjiang and Xishuangbanna, as well as more straightforward trips around Shanghai and Beijing.
Journeys International ☎1-800/255-8735 or 734/665-4407, ⊛www.journeys-intl.com. Several packages taking in east-coast highlights to remoter monasteries of Tibet.
Maupintour ☎1-800/255-4266, ⊛www.maupintour.com. Luxury tour operator offering city breaks in Beijing and Shanghai, escorted river trips, and Trans-Mongolian bookings.
Mir Corp ☎206-624-7289, ⊛www.mircorp.com. Specialists in Trans-Siberian rail travel, for small groups as well as individual travellers.
Mountain Travel Sobek ☎1-888/MTSOBEK or 510/687-6235, ⊛www.mtsobek.com. Adventure tours to Yunnan, the Yangzi and the Silk Road.
Pacific Delight Tours ☎1-800/221-7179 or 212/818-1781, ⊛www.pacificdelighttours.com. City breaks, cruises along the Li River and Yangzi, plus a range of tours to Tibet, the Silk Road and western Yunnan.
REI Adventures ☎1-800/622-2236, ⊛www.rei.com/travel. Cycling and hiking tours throughout China.
Worldwide Quest Adventures ☎1-800/387-1483 or 416/633-5666, ⊛www.worldwidequest.com. Small-group tours covering cycling, cultural and activity tours throughout China's wilder regions.

From Australia and New Zealand

The closest entry point into China from Australia and New Zealand is Hong Kong, though from Australia it's also possible to fly to Guangzhou, Shanghai and Beijing without changing planes. It's not a problem to fly elsewhere in China from either country if you catch a connecting flight along the way, though this can involve a long layover in the airline's hub city.

From eastern Australia, some of the cheapest fares to Hong Kong (A$750–900) are with Cathay Pacific, China Airlines, EVA Airlines or Singapore Airlines; to Shanghai (A$950–1100) with Royal Brunei, Singapore or Japanese Airlines (JAL); to Guangzhou (A$950–1100) with Singapore, Malaysian, JAL and Air China; and to Beijing (A$950–1100) with Singapore, JAL, Malaysian or China Eastern. Only Cathay and China

Eastern fly direct; the others require a stop-over in the airline's hub city. **From Perth**, fares to the above destinations are A$100–150 cheaper.

Flights **from New Zealand** are limited and therefore expensive: about the best deal is on Air New Zealand or Singapore from Auckland to Hong Kong (NZ$1850). Air New Zealand, Malaysian and other carriers also fly via other Southeast Asian hub cities to Hong Kong and elsewhere in China.

Airlines

Air China Australia ☏ 02/9232 7277, ⓦ www.airchina.com.cn.

Air New Zealand Australia ☏ 13 2476, New Zealand ☏ 0800 247 764; ⓦ www.airnewzealand.com.

Asiana ⓦ www.au.flyasiana.com.

Cathay Pacific Australia ☏ 13 1747, New Zealand ☏ 09/379 0861; ⓦ www.cathaypacific.com.

China Airlines Australia ☏ 02/9244 2121, New Zealand ☏ 09/308 3371, ⓦ www.china-airlines.com.

China Eastern Airlines Australia ☏ 02/9290 1148, ⓦ www.ce-air.com/cea/en_US/homepage.

EVA Air Australia ☏ 02/8338 0419, New Zealand ☏ 09/358 8300; ⓦ www.evaair.com.

Malaysia Airlines Australia ☏ 13 2627, New Zealand ☏ 0800/777 747 or 649/379 3743; ⓦ www.malaysiaairlines.com.

Qantas Australia ☏ 13 1313, New Zealand ☏ 09/357 8900 or 0800/808 767; ⓦ www.qantas.com.

Royal Brunei Australia ☏ 07/3017 5000, New Zealand ☏ 09/977 2240, ⓦ www.bruneiair.com.

Singapore Airlines Australia ☏ 13 1011 or ☏ 02/9350 0262, New Zealand ☏ 09/379 3209; ⓦ www.singaporeair.com.

Thai Airways Australia ☏ 1300 651 960, New Zealand ☏ 09/377 3886; ⓦ www.thaiair.com.

Flight and travel agents

Flight Centre Australia ☏ 13 31 33, ⓦ www.flightcentre.com.au; New Zealand ☏ 0800 243 544, ⓦ www.flightcentre.co.nz.

Holiday Shoppe New Zealand ☏ 0800/808 480, ⓦ www.holidayshoppe.co.nz.

OTC Australia ☏ 1300/855 118, ⓦ www.otctravel.com.au.

Plan It Holidays Australia ☏ 03/9245 0747, ⓦ www.planit.com.au.

STA Travel Australia ☏ 1300/733 035, ⓦ www.statravel.com.au; New Zealand ☏ 0508/782 872, ⓦ www.statravel.co.nz.

Student Uni Travel Australia ☏ 02/9232 8444, ⓦ www.sut.com.au, New Zealand ☏ 09/379 4224, ⓦ www.sut.co.nz.

Trailfinders Australia ☏ 1300/780 212, ⓦ www.trailfinders.com.au.

travel.com.au and **travel.co.nz** Australia ☏ 1300/130 482, ⓦ www.travel.com.au, New Zealand ☏ 0800/468 332, ⓦ www.travel.co.nz.

Specialist tour operators

The Adventure Travel Company New Zealand ☏ 09/379 9755, ⓦ www.adventuretravel.co.nz. NZ agent for Peregrine (see below). Trekking and just sightseeing in China, Mongolia and Tibet; also organizes Trans-Siberian rail trips.

Birding Worldwide Australia ☏ 03/9899 9303, ⓦ www.birdingworldwide.com.au. Organizes group trips to China – including Tibet – for those wanting to glimpse typical, unique and rare bird species.

China Travel Service Australia ☏ 02/9211 2633, New Zealand ☏ 09/309 6458, ⓦ www.chinatravel.com.au. Package tours to all the main sites in China, arranged through sister organizations in the country, plus hotel-only rates, train travel and independent excursions.

Gateway Travel Australia ☏ 02/9745 3333, ⓦ www.russian-gateway.com.au. Eastern European and Russian specialists; useful for Trans-Siberian bookings.

Intrepid Travel Australia ☏ 1300/360 667 or 03/9473 2626, ⓦ www.intrepidtravel.com. Small-group tours, with the emphasis on cross-cultural contact and low-impact tourism. Covers the staples – Beijing, Shanghai, Xi'an and the Yangzi – along with the Silk Road, Karakorum Highway and minor sights.

Passport Travel Australia ☏ 03/9867 3888, ⓦ www.travelcentre.com.au. A few city-based packages to Beijing and Shanghai in particular, plus Trans-Siberian bookings.

Peregrine Adventures Australia ☏ 03/9663 8611, ⓦ www.peregrine.net.au. In New Zealand, contact Adventure Travel Company ☏ 09/379 9755. Off-the-beaten-track excursions between Beijing and Xishuangbanna.

Sundowners Australia ☏ 03/9672 5300, ⓦ www.sundownerstravel.com. Tours of the Silk Road, plus Trans-Siberian rail bookings.

Travel Indochina Australia ☏ 1300/138 755, ⓦ www.travelindochina.com.au. Covers the obvious China sights but goes a bit beyond them too; also arranges cross-border visas for Thailand, Laos, Vietnam and Cambodia.

World Expeditions Australia ☏ 1300/720 000, ⓦ www.worldexpeditions.com.au, New Zealand ☏ 0800/350 354, ⓦ www.worldexpeditions.co.nz. Biking, hiking, eating and cultural tours all over the country, focusing on the southwest.

Overland routes

China has a number of **land borders** open to foreign travellers. When planning your trip, remember that Chinese visas must be used within three months of their date of issue, and so you may have to apply for one en route. Visas are obtainable in the capitals of virtually all European and Asian countries, and are likely to take several days to be issued (see p.34 for embassy addresses).

Via Russia and Mongolia

One of the classic overland routes to China is through Russia on the so-called **Trans-Siberian Express**. As a one-off trip, the journey is a memorable way to begin or end one's stay in China; views of stately birch forests, misty lakes and arid plateaus help time pass much faster than you'd think, and there are frequent stops during which you can wander the station platform for a few minutes, purchasing food and knick-knacks. The trains are comfortable and clean: second-class compartments contain four berths, while first-class have two and even boast a private shower.

There are actually two rail lines from Moscow to Beijing: the **Trans-Manchurian** line, which runs almost as far as the Sea of Japan before turning south through Dongbei (Manchuria) to Beijing; and the **Trans-Mongolian** express, which cuts through Mongolia from Siberia. The Manchurian train takes about six days, the Mongolian train about five; the latter is more popular with foreigners, not just because it's a little quicker but also because of the allure of Mongolia. Trans-Mongolian Chinese Train #4 is the most popular service for foreign tourists, a scenic route that rumbles past Lake Baikal and Siberia, the grasslands of Mongolia, and the desert of northwest China, skirting the Great Wall. At the Mongolia/China border, you can watch as the undercarriage is switched to a different gauge. The one drawback of this route is that you will need an additional visa for Mongolia.

Meals are included while the train is in China. In Mongolia, the dining car accepts payment in both Chinese and Mongolian currency; while in Russia, US dollars or Russian roubles can be used. It's worth having small denominations of US dollars as you can change these on the train throughout the journey, or use them to buy food from station vendors along the way – though experiencing the cuisine and people in the dining cars is part of the fun. Bring instant noodles and snacks as a backup, plenty of film, and that great long novel you've always wanted to read – such as the four-volume Chinese classic *Journey to the West*.

Tickets and packages

Booking tickets needs plenty of advance planning, especially during the popular summer months. Sorting out travel arrangements from abroad is also a complex business – you'll need transit visas for Russia, as well as for Mongolia if you intend to pass through there, and if you plan on reaching or leaving Moscow by rail via Warsaw, you'll have to get a transit visa for Belarus too. It's therefore advisable to use an experienced **travel agent** who can organize all tickets, visas and stopovers if required, in advance. Visa processing is an especially helpful time saver which agents can offer, given the ridiculous queues and paperwork required for visas along the route. One firm offering these services as well as rail packages that you can book from abroad is Monkey Business (Ⓦ www.monkeyshrine.com), who have offices in Hong Kong and Beijing; for details of companies **at home** which can sort out Trans-Siberian travel, see the lists of specialist travel agents earlier in this section. If you want to book a ticket yourself, reckon on paying the equivalent of at least US$200 for second-class travel from Moscow to Beijing. For information on taking the train **from Beijing**, see p.91.

Via the Central Asian republics

From Russia, you can also theoretically reach China through several Central Asian countries, though the obstacles can occasionally be insurmountable – Kyrgyzstan, for instance, was suffering serious civil unrest at the time of writing, and travel there was not recommended. Contact the in-country agents listed below, or Trans-Siberian operators listed earlier in this section, for up-to-date practicalities.

The main cities of **Kazakhstan** and **Kyrgyzstan** – Almaty and Bishkek – are both still linked by daily trains to Moscow (3 days), though getting Russian transit visas and booking berths on these trains is not easy. Kyrgyzstan-based Asia Silk Travel (ⓦwww .centralasiatravel.com) or Kyrgyz Concept (ⓦhttp://eng.concept.kg) are good sources of background information, including visa requirements, and can make bookings. It is also possible to get into Central Asia via **Turkmenistan**, and thence to the rest of Central Asia, via northeastern Iran or from Azerbaijan across the Caspian Sea, thus bypassing Russia completely. Ayan Travel, based in the Turkmenistan capital, Ashgabat (ⓦwww.ayan-travel.com), are the people to contact for this stage of the journey.

Once in the region, crossing into China from Kazakhstan is straightforward – there are comfortable twice-weekly trains from Almaty to Ürümqi, which take 35 hours and cost about US$75 for a berth in a four-berth compartment. There are also cheaper, faster, less comfortable buses (US$50; about 24hr). From Bishkek in Kyrgyzstan, Kashgar in the northwestern Chinese province of Xinjiang is only eleven hours' drive away (about US$50), and the two cities are linked by buses in summer months. Foreigners, however, have had difficulties in trying to use these and have usually had to resort to expensive private transport, run by local tour operators to help them across (see p.1058 in The Guide). You may well be expected to bribe the border guards US$20 or so.

From Pakistan and Nepal

The routes across the Himalayas to China are among the toughest in Asia. The first is from Pakistan into Xinjiang province over the **Karakoram Highway**, along one of the branches of the ancient Silk Road. This requires no pre-planning, except for the fact that it is open only from May to October, and closes periodically due to landslips. The Karakoram Highway actually starts at Rawalpindi (the old city outside the capital Islamabad), and in theory you can get from here to Kashgar in four days on public buses. From Rawalpindi, first take one of the daily minibuses which run the arduous fifteen-hour trip up the Indus gorge to the village of Gilgit, where you'll have to spend a night. From Gilgit, the next destination is the border town of Sust, a five-hour journey. There are a couple of daily buses on this route. Once in Sust, immediately book your ticket to Tashkurgan in China (7hr) for the next morning – it costs 1200 rupees (about US$30). A few travellers have managed to talk their way into being issued a visa at the border, but you're strongly advised to have one already. The route is popular with cyclists, but there's no guarantee that you will be allowed to bike across the border; you'll probably have to load your bike on a bus for this part of the trip. For more on crossing the Chinese border here, see p.1087.

Another formerly popular route was travelling **from Nepal into Tibet**, but at the time of writing Nepal's political situation was volatile, and you should check your government's travel advice on the latest situation – practical details are covered on p.1104.

From India itself there are, for political reasons, no border crossings to China. For years the authorities have discussed opening a bus route from Sikkim to Tibet, north from Darjeeling, but it has yet to materialize.

From Vietnam

Vietnam has three border crossings with China – **Dong Dang**, 60km northeast of Hanoi; **Lao Cai,** 150km northwest; and the little-used **Mong Cai**, 200km south of Nanning. All three are open daily between 8.30am and 5pm.

A twice-weekly **direct train** service from Hanoi is advertised as running all the way to **Beijing** (60hr), passing through **Kunming**, **Nanning** and **Guilin**. In practice, though, you'll have to leave the train at Dong Dang, walk across the border, and catch a minibus to the Chinese railhead, 15km away at Pingxiang, from where there's a connecting train for the 170-kilometre run northeast to Nanning, Guangxi's capital. Alternatively, there are good rail and road connections from Hanoi to Lang Son, from where a minibus can take you the last 5km to Dong Dang. Similarly, there are daily trains from Hanoi to Lao Cai, eleven hours away in Vietnam's mountainous and undeveloped northwest (near the pleasant resort of Sa Pa), from where you can cross into Yunnan province at

Hekou, and catch the daily train to Kunming. From Mong Cai, there are regular buses to Nanning.

From Laos and Burma (Myanmar)

Crossing into China **from Laos** also lands you in Yunnan, this time at Bian Mao Zhan in the Xishuangbanna region. Formalities are very relaxed and unlikely to cause any problems, though take some hard cash as you can't change traveller's cheques on the Chinese side. It's 220km on local buses north from here to the regional capital, Jinghong, with a likely overnight stop in the town of Mengla along the way (see p.872).

Entering China **from Burma** (Myanmar) is an interesting possibility too, with the old Burma Road cutting northeast from Rangoon (Yangon) to Lashio and the crossing at Wanding in Yunnan, just south of Ruili. At present this border is open to groups travelling with a tour agency, which will sort out all the necessary paperwork in Yangoon. Be aware that border regulations here are subject to change.

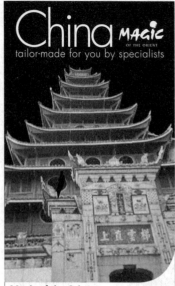

Magic of the Orient
Tel: 0117 311 6050 www.magicoftheorient.com
Email: info@magicoftheorient.com

Visas and red tape

All foreign nationals require a visa to enter mainland China, available from Chinese embassies and consulates worldwide. However, the greatest range of visas is available in Hong Kong, which (along with Macau) is open to most visitors with just a valid passport; you may want to apply for your mainland visa there – see p.668 for further details.

Visas

All visas must be used within three months of the date of issue. **Single-entry visas** (L-type) are valid for thirty days or three months, and are the type most likely to be issued to travellers by overseas consulates or embassies. **Multiple-entry visas** (F- or X-type), valid for either three months, six months, or longer, are theoretically only available with supporting documentation to business travellers or foreign students studying in China, but are increasingly issued on request to ordinary travellers by visa agents in Hong Kong. Be aware that **your nationality**, where you apply for a visa, and the type you're after, will affect the cost and which visas you are eligible for.

The **application form** asks for personal information, along with some details of your intended trip. Don't mention sensitive areas such as Tibet or Xinjiang, or admit to having a media-related job ("Computer operator" is a handy catch-all alternative), as doing so will prolong the application process – or even lead to your visa being rejected.

Chinese embassies and consulates

Australia 15 Coronation Drive, Yarralumla, ACT
2600 ☎02/6273 4780, ⓦwww.chinaembassy.org
.au. Also consulates at 77 Irving Rd, Toorak (visa
& passport enquiries ☎03/9804 3683) and 539
Elizabeth St, Surry Hills (☎02/9698 7929).
Canada 515 St Patrick St, Ottawa, Ontario K1N
5H3 ☎613/7893434 ⓦwww.chinaembassycanada
.org. Visas can also be obtained from the consulates
in Calgary, Toronto and Vancouver.
Ireland 40 Ailesbury Road, Dublin 4
☎053/12691707, ⓦwww.chinaembassy.ie.
Kazakhstan Furmanova Street 137, Almaty
☎07/3272 612482, ⓦkz.china-embassy.org
Kyrgyzstan ul. Toktogula 196, Bishkek
☎0312/610858, ⓔchinaemb_kg@mfa.gov.cn.
Laos Thanon Wat Nak Yai, Vientiane ☎021/315100,
ⓔembassyprc@laonet.net
Nepal Baluwatar, Toran Bhawan, Naxal, Kathmandu
☎071/4411740, ⓦwww.chinaembassy.org.np.
Visas available only through travel agents to those
travelling with a tour group.
New Zealand 2–6 Glenmore Street, Wellington
☎04/474 9631, ⓦwww.chinaembassy.org.nz; plus
a consulate in Auckland ☎09/525 1589, ⓦwww.
chinaconsulate.org.nz.
Pakistan Ramna 4, Diplomatic Enclave, Islamabad
☎051/2877279, ⓦpk.chineseembassy.org. Issues
only ten-day visas.
Russia ul. Druzhby 6, Moscow ☎095/9561168,
ⓦwww.chinaembassy.ru.
Thailand 57 Rachadapisake Rd, Huay Kwang,
Bangkok 10310 ☎02/245 7044; 111 Chang Lo Rd,
Chiang Mai ☎053/272197.
UK 49–51 Portland Place, London W1B 1JL
☎020/72994049, ⓦwww.chinese-embassy.
org.uk; Denison House, Denison Rd, Victoria Pk,
Manchester M14 5RX ☎0161/224 7480.
US 2300 Connecticut Ave NW, Washington, DC
20008 ☎202/3282500, ⓦwww.china-embassy
.org/eng. Also consulates in Chicago, Houston, Los
Angeles, New York and San Francisco.
Vietnam Tran Phu, Hanoi (round the corner from
the main embassy building at 46 Hoang Dieu)
☎04/8453736.

Visa extensions

Visa extensions are handled by the Foreign
Affairs section of the **Public Security
Bureau** (**PSB**), so you can apply for one in
any reasonably sized town. The amount of
money you'll pay for this, and the amount of
hassle you'll have, varies greatly depending
on where you are, your nationality, and what
season it is.

A first extension, valid for a month, is
easy to obtain and will cost around ¥160.
However, you're basically at the mercy of the
particular PSB office and they may decide to
levy charges on top. In some small towns the
charge may even be waived and the process take ten minutes; in cities it can take up
to a week. The worst place to apply is Tibet
(you'll be given a week at most); next worst
are Beijing and then Shanghai.

A second or third extension is harder to
get – in major cities you will probably be
turned away. PSB offices in small towns are
a much better bet, and you'd be unlucky to
come away without some kind of extension,
though it may only be for ten or twenty days.
You will be asked your reasons for wanting
an extension – simply saying you want to
spend more time in this wonderful country usually goes down well, or you could
cite illness or transport delays. Don't admit
to being low on funds. Fourth or even fifth
extensions are possible, but you'll need to
foster connections with a PSB office. Ask
advice from a local independent travel agent
– they often have the right sort of contacts.

Don't overstay your visa even for a few
hours – the fine is ¥500 a day, and if you're
caught at the airport with an out-of-date visa
the hassle that follows may mean you miss
your flight.

Customs

You're allowed to **import** into China up to
four hundred cigarettes and two litres of
alcohol. You can't take in more than ¥6000,
and amounts of foreign currency over
US$5000 or equivalent must be declared.
It's illegal to import printed matter, tapes or
videos critical of the country, but don't worry
too much about this, as confiscation is rare
in practice, except in sensitive areas such as
Tibet; here, some travellers have reported
books specifically about Tibet being taken off
them. Finally, note that **export restrictions**
apply on items which are more than 100
years old, for which you require an export
form available from Friendship Stores.

Information, websites and maps

The concept of a country promoting itself by giving out tourist information for free has not yet taken hold in China outside the biggest cities. There is a thin scattering of tourist promotion offices in foreign capitals, though these government organizations generally only recommend tour operators and are inexperienced in dealing with independent travellers. A more promising source of immediate information is the Internet.

Inside the People's Republic, tour operators such as the ubiquitous **CITS** (China International Travel Service), and slightly less widespread **CTS** (China Travel Service) and **CYTS** (China Youth Travel Service), are geared up to booking flight and train tickets, local tours and accommodation. All three have offices in major towns and cities – often with desks at hotels – but you'll also find branches in some quite obscure locations. Their value to individual travellers varies, but some staff are extremely helpful, and might be the only English-speakers in out-of-the-way places. Most leaflets, brochures and maps from these places will not be free. Other sources of information are hotel staff or tour desks (in upmarket places), or any local English-speakers you happen to meet. In certain tourist centres, restaurant proprietors have taken it upon themselves to act as the local information office, giving advice in exchange for custom.

In Beijing, Shanghai and Guangzhou you'll find English-language magazines with bar, restaurant and other **listings**, aimed at the resident expatriate population. These are usually distributed free in bars and upmarket hotels.

Hong Kong and Macau both have efficient and helpful tourist information offices, and several free listings magazines; see p.670 and p.717 for more on these.

Chinese tourist offices abroad

Australia 11th Floor, 234 George Street, Sydney, New South Wales, 2000 ☎02/9252-9838, ℻02/9252-2728; ⓦ www.cnto.org.au
Canada 480 University Ave, Suite 806, Toronto, Ontario M5G 1V2 ☎0416/5996636, ⓦwww .tourismchina-ca.com

UK 71 Warwick Road, London SW5 9HB ☎020 7373 0888.
USA 350 Fifth Avenue, Suite 6413, Empire State Building, New York, NY 10118 USA
Toll-free ☎1-888-760-8218, ℮ny@cnto.org
550 North Brand Boulevard, Suite 910, Glendale, CA 91203 USA
Toll free ☎1-800-670-2228,℮la@cnto.org

Online resources

Chinaetravel ⓦwww.chinaetravel.com. Online accommodation and tour booking service for all major destinations in the country.
China Tour ⓦwww.chinatour.com. Lightweight introduction to key sights and cities, and up-to-date visa information, tour and accommodation booking links, and cultural background.
China Travel ⓦwww.chinatravel.com. Online travel company with a host of links, booking services and advice for travellers.
China Travel News ⓦwww.chinatravelnews .com. The latest in travel information for tourists and business visitors, including details on border crossings.
China Vista ⓦwww.chinavista.com. China-based website with snippets about Chinese culture, history, attractions and food.
International Campaign for Tibet ⓦwww .savetibet.org. An authoritative source of current news from Tibet.
National Tourism Administration ⓦwww.cnta .com. Plenty of themed tour itineraries and cultural information, plus sketches of thousands of locations across the country.
That's China ⓦwww.thatschina.com. Webzine featuring articles on culture, heritage, travel, modern life, and expat accounts of living in the country.
Travel China ⓦwww.travelchinaguide.com. Unusual in covering obscure places and small-group tours, as well as the normal run of popular sites and booking links.

Travel advisories

Australian Department of Foreign Affairs ⓦ www.dfat.gov.au.
British Foreign & Commonwealth Office ⓦ www.fco.gov.uk.
Canadian Department of Foreign Affairs ⓦ www.dfait-maeci.gc.ca.
Irish Department of Foreign Affairs ⓦ www.irlgov.ie/iveagh.
New Zealand Ministry of Foreign Affairs ⓦ www.mft.govt.nz.
US State Department ⓦ travel.state.gov.

Maps

Street maps are available in China for almost every town and city. They are sold at street kiosks, hotel shops and Xinhua bookshops, and from vendors around train and bus stations. Most are in Chinese only, showing bus routes, hotels, restaurants and tourist attractions; local bus, train and flight timetables are often printed on the back as well. The same vendors also sell pocket-sized provincial **road atlases**, again in Chinese only.

Cities most commonly visited by foreign tourists also produce English-language maps, available at upmarket hotels, principal tourist sights, or tour operators' offices. In Beijing and Shanghai you'll find various editions of such maps, issued free in smart hotels and paid for by advertising. The situation is similar in Hong Kong and Macau, where the local tourist offices provide free maps which are adequate for most visitors' needs. For very detailed street maps of Hong Kong, have a look at the *Hong Kong Island Street Map* and the *Kowloon Street Map*, for sale in English-language bookshops.

Countrywide maps, which you should buy before you leave home, include the excellent 1:4,000,000 map from GeoCenter, which shows relief and useful sections of all neighbouring countries, and the Collins 1:5,000,000 map. For high-resolution maps showing details of terrain, especially useful for cyclists and trekkers in the wilderness parts of western China, the *Operational Navigation Charts* (Series ONC) – actually designed for pilots – are worth having a look at. One of the best maps of Tibet is *Stanfords Map of South-Central Tibet; Kathmandu–Lhasa Route Map*.

Map outlets

UK and Ireland

Stanfords 12–14 Long Acre, London WC2E 9LP ☎ 020/7836 1321, ⓦ www.stanfords.co.uk. Also at 39 Spring Gardens, Manchester ☎ 0161/831 0250, and 29 Corn St, Bristol ☎ 0117/929 9966.
Blackwell's Map and Travel Shop ⓦ maps.blackwell.co.uk/index.html. Branches all over the UK; check the website for details.
Easons Bookshop 40 Lower O'Connell St, Dublin 1 ☎ 01/858 3800, ⓦ www.eason.ie, plus other branches around Ireland; call or check the website for details.
John Smith & Son Glasgow Caledonian University Bookshop, 70 Cowcaddens Rd, Glasgow G4 0BA ☎ 0141/332 8173, ⓦ www.johnsmith.co.uk. For details of other branches in Scotland and England, call or check the website.
The Map Shop 30a Belvoir St, Leicester LE1 6QH ☎ 0116/247 1400, ⓦ www.mapshopleicester.co.uk.
National Map Centre 22–24 Caxton St, London SW1H 0QU ☎ 020/7222 2466, ⓦ www.mapsnmc.co.uk.
National Map Centre Ireland 34 Aungier St, Dublin ☎ 01/476 0471, ⓦ www.mapcentre.ie.
The Travel Bookshop 13–15 Blenheim Crescent, London W11 2EE ☎ 020/7229 5260, ⓦ www.thetravelbookshop.co.uk.

US and Canada

110 North Latitude US ☎ 336/369-4171, ⓦ www.110nlatitude.com.
Book Passage 51 Tamal Vista Blvd, Corte Madera, CA 94925 and in the historic San Francisco Ferry Building ☎ 1-800/999-7909 or ☎ 415/927-0960, ⓦ www.bookpassage.com.
Complete Traveller Bookstore 199 Madison Ave, New York, NY ☎ 212/685-9007, ⓦ www.completetravellerbooks.com
Globe Corner Bookstore 28 Church St, Cambridge, MA 02138 ☎ 1-800/358-6013, ⓦ www.globecorner.com.
Longitude Books 115 W 30th St #1206, New York, NY 10001 ☎ 1-800/342-2164, ⓦ www.longitudebooks.com.
Map Link 30 S La Patera Lane, Unit 5, Santa Barbara, CA 93117 ☎ 805/692-6777 or 1-800/962-1394, ⓦ www.maplink.com.
Map Town 400 5 Ave SW #100, Calgary, AB, T2P 0L6 ☎ 1-877/921-6277 or ☎ 403/266-2241, ⓦ www.maptown.com.
World of Maps 1235 Wellington St, Ottawa, ON, K1Y 3A3 ☎ 1-800/214-8524 or ☎ 613/724-6776, ⓦ www.worldofmaps.com.

Australia and New Zealand

Map Centre ⓦ www.mapcentre.co.nz.
Mapland (Australia) 372 Little Bourke St,
Melbourne ⓣ 03/9670 4383, ⓦ www.mapland
.com.au.
Map Shop (Australia) 6–10 Peel St, Adelaide
ⓣ 08/8231 2033, ⓦ www.mapshop.net.au.

Map World (Australia) 371 Pitt St, Sydney
ⓣ 02/9261 3601, ⓦ www.mapworld.net.au. Also
at 900 Hay St, Perth ⓣ 08/9322 5733, Jolimont
Centre, Canberra ⓣ 02/6230 4097 and 1981 Logan
Road, Brisbane ⓣ 07/3349 6633.
Map World (New Zealand) 173 Gloucester St,
Christchurch ⓣ 0800/627 967, ⓦ www.mapworld
.co.nz.

Insurance

Travel insurance is strongly advised for trips to China. However, it's worth checking whether you are already covered: some all-risks home insurance policies
may cover your possessions when overseas, and many private medical schemes
include cover when abroad.

If you're not already covered you should
contact a specialist travel insurance
company. A typical travel insurance policy
usually provides cover for the loss of
baggage, tickets and – up to a certain limit
– cash or cheques, as well as cancellation
or curtailment of your journey. Most of them
exclude so-called dangerous sports unless
an extra premium is paid: in China this can
mean scuba-diving, white-water rafting,
skiing, windsurfing and trekking, though
probably not kayaking or jeep safaris. Many
policies can be chopped and changed to
exclude coverage you don't need – for
example, sickness and accident benefits.
If you do take medical coverage, ascertain
whether benefits will be paid as treatment
proceeds or only after return home, and
whether there is a 24-hour medical emergency number. When securing baggage
cover, make sure that the per-article limit
– typically under £500/$750 – will cover
your most valuable possession. If you need
to make a claim, you should keep receipts
for medicines and medical treatment, and
in the event you have anything stolen, you
must obtain an official statement from the
police.

Rough Guides travel insurance

Rough Guides has teamed up with Columbus Direct to offer you travel insurance
that can be tailored to suit your needs. Readers can choose from many different
travel-insurance products, including a **low-cost backpacker** option for long stays;
a **short break** option for city getaways; a typical **holiday package** option, and
many others. There are also **annual multi-trip** policies for those who travel regularly,
with variable levels of cover available. Different sports and activities (trekking, skiing,
etc) can be covered if required on most policies.

Rough Guides travel insurance is available to the residents of 36 different
countries with different language options to choose from via our website – ⓦ www
.roughguidesinsurance.com – where you can also purchase the insurance.
Alternatively, call direct: UK residents ⓣ 0800 083 9507; US citizens ⓣ 1-800 749-
4922; Australians ⓣ 1 300 669 999; all other nationalities ⓣ +44 870 890 2843.

Health

Low standards of public hygiene, stress and overcrowded conditions are to blame for most of the health problems that beset travellers in China. If you do get ill, medical facilities, at least in the big cities, are adequate, and the largest cities have high-standard international clinics. For minor complaints, every town has a pharmacy which can suggest remedies, and doctors who can treat you with traditional Chinese or Western techniques. You'll need to take a phrasebook or a Chinese-speaker if you don't speak Chinese.

Before you go

No **vaccinations** are currently required for China, except for yellow fever if you're coming from an area where the disease is endemic. However, you should discuss with your doctor whether protection against the following health hazards are advisable.

Hepatitis A is a viral infection spread by contaminated food and water which causes an inflammation of the liver. The less common **hepatitis B** virus can be passed on through unprotected sexual contact, transfusions of unscreened blood and dirty needles, and is especially prevalent in parts of Asia. Hepatitis symptoms include yellowing of the eyes and skin, preceded by lethargy, fever and pains in the upper right abdomen.

Typhoid and cholera are spread by contaminated food or water, generally in localized epidemics. Symptoms of **typhoid** include headaches, high fever and constipation, followed by diarrhoea in the later stages. The disease is infectious and requires immediate medical treatment. **Cholera** begins with sudden but painless onset of watery diarrhoea, later combined with vomiting, nausea and muscle cramps. Rapid dehydration rather than the infection itself is the main danger, and should be treated with constant oral rehydration solutions if you can't get immediate medical help.

Meningitis (vectors unknown) and **rabies** (transmitted through bites from infected mammals) can be serious problems in parts of China. Remember also that a **tetanus** booster is required every ten years.

Visit a doctor as **early** as possible before you travel to allow time to complete any courses of vaccinations you need. You should have all your shots **recorded** on an International Certificate of Vaccination. If you have any longstanding medical conditions, or are travelling with small children, consult your doctor and take any necessary medicine with you. It's also wise to get a dental check-up.

It's worth taking a **first-aid kit** with you, particularly if you will be travelling extensively outside the cities, where the language barrier can make getting hold of the appropriate medicines difficult. Include bandages, plasters, painkillers, oral rehydration solution, medication to counter diarrhoea, vitamin pills and antiseptic cream. A sterile set of hypodermics may be advisable, as re-use of hypodermics does occur in China.

General precautions

There's no point in being overconcerned with your health in China, but it's an easy place to become stressed and exhausted, leaving yourself vulnerable to infections. Travel at an easy pace, and treat yourself occasionally to upmarket accommodation and food. Take vitamin pills (available in many cities) if you think your diet is lacking in variety.

Personal hygiene is one area you can control and it pays to be meticulous. Wash your hands often and don't share drinks or cigarettes. When in the shower, always wear flip-flops or shower shoes, provided free at most hotels (under the bed). The smallest cuts can become infected, so clean them thoroughly and apply an antiseptic cream, then keep them dry and covered.

With the majority of China's waterways highly contaminated, **water** is a potential cause of sickness. Don't drink unboiled tap water, or use it to clean your teeth; avoid ice in drinks, and the ice lollies sold by street-side entrepreneurs. The Chinese boil drinking water scrupulously, and every hotel room is equipped with a kettle or a vacuum flask, which the floor attendant will fill for you. **Bottled water** is available from supermarkets. If you stick to this and drink tea or carbonated drinks in restaurants, you should be fine. If you have to sterilize water yourself, boil it for at least ten minutes to kill microorganisms; at altitude, however, water boils below 100°C, so you'll have to use other methods. **Iodine tablets** are effective, but leave the water tasting rank, and are also unsafe for pregnant women, babies and people with thyroid complaints. If you've got the space, a **water purifier**, which removes contaminants by filtration, is ideal – they're available from specialist outdoor equipment stores before you leave home.

As for **food**, eat at places which look busy and clean, stick to fresh, thoroughly cooked food, and you'll have few problems. Beware of food that has been pre-cooked and kept warm for several hours. Shellfish are a potential hepatitis A risk in Asia, and best avoided. Fresh fruit you've peeled yourself is safe; other uncooked foods may have been washed in unclean water. The other thing to watch for is **dirty chopsticks**, though many restaurants provide disposable sets; if you want to be really sure, bring your own pair.

Intestinal troubles

Diarrhoea is the most common illness to affect travellers, usually in a mild form while your stomach gets used to unfamiliar food. The sudden onset of diarrhoea with stomach cramps and vomiting indicates food poisoning. In both instances, get plenty of rest, drink lots of water, and in serious cases replace lost salts with oral rehydration solution (ORS); this is especially important with young children. Take a few sachets with you, or make your own by adding half a teaspoon of salt and three of sugar to a litre of cool, previously boiled water. While down with diarrhoea, avoid milk, greasy or spicy foods, coffee and most fruit, in favour of bland foodstuffs such as rice, dumplings, noodles and soup. If symptoms persist, or if you notice blood or mucus in your stools, consult a doctor.

Dysentery is inflammation of the intestine, indicated by diarrhoea with blood or mucus and abdominal pain. There are two strains. Bacillary dysentery has an acute onset with discomfort, fever and vomiting, plus severe abdominal pains with bloody, watery diarrhoea. In mild cases recovery occurs spontaneously within a week, but a serious attack will require antibiotics. Amoebic dysentery is more serious as bouts last for several weeks and often recur. The gradually appearing symptoms are marked by bloody faeces accompanied by abdominal cramps, but no vomiting or fever. A prompt course of antibiotics should restore you to health.

Giardiasis is distinguished by smelly burps or farts, discoloured faeces without blood or pus, and fluctuating diarrhoea; left untreated, these symptoms disappear but recur around once a month. Again the disease is treatable with an antibiotic, Flagyl, under medical supervision. If you're heading for Tibet, where the disease is a particular problem, you will not be able to get the appropriate antibiotics there, so take some with you (you may need to get a prescription from your doctor for this).

Finally, if you're suffering from diarrhoea, remember that oral drugs such as anti-malarial and contraceptive pills may pass through your system too quickly to be absorbed effectively.

Mosquito-borne diseases

Summer outbreaks of **mosquito-borne diseases** are a serious, though not very common, threat in the tropical regions of Hainan Island and the southwestern provinces of Yunnan and Guangxi.

Carried by the *anopheles* mosquito, **malaria** is caused by a parasite which infects the blood and liver. Symptoms are flu-like fever with hammering headaches, shivering, and severe joint pain. If you're travelling in a high-risk area it is advisable to take **preventative tablets**, so talk the various options through with your doctor. Note that you need to start taking all anti-malarial medication some time before entering a malarial region, and then continue for a few weeks after leaving, as the parasite can lie dormant for a while. If you suspect you might have the disease a **blood test** will confirm the diagnosis and, if caught early, treatment can be quick and effective.

Aedes aegypti mosquitoes, identifiable by their black-and-white stripes, are responsible for transmitting **dengue fever**, a viral disease whose symptoms are similar to malaria, though there's sometimes also a rash spreading from the torso over the limbs and face. There's no cure, and though symptoms subside on their own after a week or so of rest, chronic fatigue can dog you for months afterwards. A more dangerous strain called **dengue haemorrhageic fever** primarily affects children. If you notice an unusual tendency to bleed or bruise, consult a doctor immediately.

The key measure with both diseases is to **avoid being bitten** in the first place. Mosquitoes are most active at dawn and dusk, so at these times wear long sleeves and trousers and avoid dark colours. Most hotels and guesthouses in affected areas provide **mosquito nets** (or you can buy your own before leaving home from specialist travel stores); tuck the edges in under the mattress at night, sleep away from the sides and make sure the mesh is not torn. **Mosquito coils** and insecticide sprays are also both highly effective and available in China, though rub- or spray-on **repellent** is not and again must be brought in with you. The most effective brands contain DEET (diethyltoluamide), but the chemical is toxic and prolonged use can cause side effects; keep it away from eyes and open wounds, and young children.

Respiratory infections

China is a hotbed of **respiratory infections**, compounded by overcrowded conditions, chain-smoking, intense pollution and the widespread habit of spitting, which rapidly spreads infection. In winter, most of the population seems stricken with common **colds** and **bronchitis**, best treated by drinking plenty of fluids and resting – though if symptoms persist, you should seek medical advice.

More serious is **tuberculosis**, a respiratory disease transmitted by inhalation, and spread by coughing and spitting – so it's not hard to see why China has a high incidence. It strikes at the lungs and in a small number of cases can be fatal. There is no need for visitors to be overly worried about the disease – many people are immune thanks to previous, mild infections or through childhood vaccinations. Especially if your trip will involve spending a lot of time on crowded trains and buses, it's worth consulting your doctor about your TB-immune status.

In 2002, there was a short-lived but unnerving outbreak of **SARS** (Severe Acute Respiratory Syndrome), an obscure, flu-like virus originating in China which killed several thousand people worldwide before vanishing in 2003. Equally worrying are persistent erruptions of **avian flu**, both in China and neighbouring countries such as Vietnam; this virus has been known to cross the species barrier from birds to humans, causing several fatalities. Both outbreaks illustrate China's potential as a reservoir of new, untreatable viruses which could spread rapidly around the globe – indeed, in 2005, migratory wildfowl in Qinghai were found to be carrying the avian flu virus.

Sexually transmitted diseases and AIDS

What with a burgeoning sexual revolution and the refusal of many men to use condoms, **sexually transmitted diseases** have flourished in modern China, **AIDS** among them. The government is becoming far more open about the problem, admitting to several million Chinese being infected with HIV (many through unscreened blood transfusions during the 1990s). The more common **gonorrhoea** and **syphilis**, identifiable by rashes around the genitals and painful discharge, are treatable with antibiotics, available from doctors.

As ever, it is extremely unwise to contemplate unprotected sex. Local Chinese **condoms** vary in quality, but imported brands are available in big cities. If it becomes essential for you to have an injection or blood transfusion in China, try to get to Hong Kong, where blood is reliably screened, and make sure that new, sterile needles are used – to be sure, bring your own. Similarly, don't undergo acupuncture unless you are sure that the equipment is sterile.

Environmental hazards

Parts of China are **tropical**, requiring a couple of weeks to acclimatize to the temperature and humidity, during which time you may feel listless and tire easily. Don't underestimate the strength of the sun in tropical areas such as Hainan Island, in desert regions such as Xinjiang or very high up, for example on the Tibetan plateau. **Sunburn** can be avoided by covering up and the liberal use of high-factor sunscreens, sometimes available in China.

Drinking plenty of water will prevent **dehydration**, but if you do become dehydrated – signified by infrequent or irregular urination – drink a salt-and-sugar solution (see p.40). **Heat stroke** is more serious and may require hospital treatment. Indications are a high temperature, lack of sweating, a fast pulse and red skin. Reducing your body temperature with a lukewarm shower will provide initial relief.

High humidity can cause **heat rashes**, **prickly heat** and **fungal infections**. Prevention and cure are the same: wear loose clothes made of natural fibres, wash frequently and dry off thoroughly afterwards. Talcum or anti-fungal powder and the use of mild antiseptic soap helps too.

At the other extreme, there are plenty of places in China – Tibet and the north in particular – that get very **cold** indeed. Watch out here for **hypothermia**, where the core body temperature drops to a point that can be fatal. Symptoms are a weak pulse, disorientation, numbness, slurred speech and exhaustion. To prevent the condition, wear lots of layers and a hat (most body heat is lost through the head), eat plenty of carbohydrates, and try to stay dry and out of the wind. To treat hypothermia, get the victim into shelter, away from wind and rain, give them hot drinks – but not alcohol – and easily digestible food, and keep them warm. Serious cases require immediate hospitalization.

Altitude sickness

You should be aware of the dangers posed by the **high altitude** in several regions of China, including Tibet and areas of Xinjiang, Sichuan and Yunnan. Reduced air pressure at altitude means that the blood does not absorb oxygen efficiently and so – until your body adapts after a week or two – you may suffer from **AMS** (acute mountain sickness); most people feel some effects above 3500m. Symptoms vary, but include becoming easily exhausted, headaches, shortness of breath, sleeping disorders and nausea; they're intensified if you ascend to altitude rapidly, for instance by flying direct from coastal cities to Lhasa. Relaxing for the first few days, drinking plenty of water, and taking painkillers will ease symptoms (some of Lhasa's hotels even have oxygen on hand). For most people the symptoms pass, although having acclimatized at one altitude you should still ascend slowly, or you can expect the symptoms to return.

If, for any reason, the body fails to acclimatize effectively, serious conditions can develop including **pulmonary oedema** (characterized by severe breathing trouble, a cough and frothy white or pink sputum), and **cerebral oedema** (causing severe headaches, loss of balance, other neurological symptoms and eventually coma). The only treatment for these is **rapid descent**: in Tibet, this means flying out to Kathmandu or Chengdu without delay. If symptoms have been serious, or persist afterwards, seek immediate medical treatment.

Getting medical help

Pharmacies (*yaodian*), found in all towns, can help with minor injuries or ailments. Larger ones sometimes have a separate counter offering diagnosis and advice, though it's unlikely that staff will speak anything but Chinese, so take along a phrasebook or a Chinese-speaker (see "Language", p.1237, for some useful phrases). The selection of reliable Asian and Western products available is improving (though always check expiry dates on brand-name products), and it's also possible to treat yourself for minor complaints with herbal medicines. Contraceptives are widely available, as are antibiotics. The staff will usually be able to help if you describe your symptoms.

Large hotels usually have a **clinic** for guests offering diagnosis, advice and prescriptions – ask an English-speaker from the reception desk to accompany you. Beijing, Shanghai, Guangzhou and Hong Kong and Macau have clinics specifically for foreigners where staff speak English. If you are seriously ill, head straight to a **hospital** – your accommodation or local CITS might be able to give you useful advice in an emergency. Addresses of clinics and hospitals can be found in the "Listings" sections of major towns and cities in the guide. You will be expected to pay for your treatment on the spot, but it should not be too expensive. Keep all medical bills and receipts so you can make an insurance claim when you get home.

If you're interested in being treated according to **Traditional Chinese Medicine** – of most use for minor and chronic complaints (see p.1183) – many hospitals and medical colleges have attached traditional institutes, while some hotels have their own massage or acupuncture services.

Travel health resources

Besides consulting the resources and clinics listed below, you can get practical information on staying healthy during your trip from the *Rough Guide to Travel Health*.

Websites

ⓦ **www.cdc.gov/travel** US government travel advice, listing precautions, diseases and preventive measures by region.

ⓦ **health.yahoo.com** Information on specific diseases and conditions, drugs and herbal remedies, as well as advice from health experts.

ⓦ **www.fitfortravel.scot.nhs.uk** Scottish NHS website carrying information about travel-related diseases and how to avoid them.

ⓦ **www.istm.org** The website of the International Society for Travel Medicine, with a list of clinics specializing in international travel health.

ⓦ **www.tmvc.com.au** Contains a list of all Travellers Medical and Vaccination Centres throughout Australia, New Zealand and Southeast Asia, plus general information on travel health.

ⓦ **www.travelvax.net** Everything you ever wanted to know about diseases and vaccines.

ⓦ **www.tripprep.com** A comprehensive database of necessary vaccinations for most countries, as well as destination and medical service provider information.

Travel clinics

In the UK and Ireland

British Airways Travel Clinics 213 Piccadilly, London W1G 9HQ (Mon–Fri 9.30am–5.30pm, Sat 10am–4pm, no appointment necessary); 101 Cheapside, London EC2 (Mon–Fri 9am–4.30pm, appointment required; ℡0845/600 2236); ⓦ www.britishairways.com/travel/healthclinintro.

Dun Laoghaire Medical Centre 5 Northumberland Ave, Dun Laoghaire, County Dublin ℡01/280 4996, ℻01/280 5603.

Glasgow Travel Clinic 3rd floor, 90 Mitchell St, Glasgow G1 3NQ ℡0141/221 4224.

Hospital for Tropical Diseases Travel Clinic 2nd floor, Mortimer Market Centre, off Capper St, London WC1E 6AU (Mon–Fri 9am–5pm by appointment only; ℡020/7388 9600, ⓦ www.masta.org).

Liverpool School of Tropical Medicine Pembroke Place, Liverpool L3 5QA ℡0151/708 9393 or premium-rate helpline ℡09067/010 095, ⓦ www.liv.ac.uk/lstm.

MASTA (Medical Advisory Service for Travellers Abroad) 40 regional clinics (call ℡0870/6062782 for the nearest). Also operates a pre-recorded 24-hour Travellers' Health Line (UK ℡0906/822 4100, 60p per min).

Nomad Pharmacy 52 Grosvenor Gdns, Victoria, London SW1W 0AG ℡020/78323/5823; 43 Bernard St, London, WC1N 1LE ℡020/7833 4114; and 3–4 Wellington Terrace, Turnpike Lane, London N8 0PX ℡020/8889 7014; ⓦ www.nomadtravel.co.uk.

Trailfinders Immunization clinic (no appointments necessary) at 194 Kensington High St, London W8 7RG (Mon–Fri 9am–5pm except Thurs to 6pm, Sat 10am–5.15pm; ℡020/7938 3999).

Travel Health Centre Department of International Health and Tropical Medicine, Royal College of Surgeons in Ireland, Mercers Medical Centre, Stephen's St Lower, Dublin 2 ℡01/402 2337.

In the US and Canada

Canadian Society for International Health 1 Nicholas St, Suite 1105, Ottawa, ON K1N 7B7 ℡613/241-5785, ⓦ www.csih.org.

International SOS Assistance 3600 Horizon Blvd, Suite 300, Trevose, PA 19053, US 19053-6956 ℡1-800/523-8930, ⓦ www.intsos.com.

MEDJET Assistance ℡1-800/963-3528, ⓦ www.medjetassistance.com.

Travel Medicine ℡1-800/TRAVMED, ⓦ www.travmed.com.

In Australia and New Zealand

Travellers' Medical and Vaccination Centres 27–29 Gilbert Place, Adelaide, SA 5000 ℡08/8212 7522. Vaccination and general travel health advice, and disease alerts; call ℡1-300/658 844 for details of travel clinics countrywide.

Ⓦ www.tmvc.com.au. 1/170 Queen St, Auckland ⓣ 09/373 3531; 5/247 Adelaide St, Brisbane, Qld 4000 ⓣ 07/3221 9066; 5/8–10 Hobart Place, Canberra, ACT 2600 ⓣ 02/6257 7156; 270 Sandy Bay Rd, Sandy Bay Tas, Hobart 7005 ⓣ 03/6223 7577; 2/393 Little Bourke St, Melbourne, Vic 3000 ⓣ 03/9602 5788; Level 7, Dymocks Bldg, 428 George St, Sydney, NSW 2000 ⓣ 02/9221 7133; Shop 15, Grand Arcade, 14–16 Willis St, Wellington ⓣ 04/473 0991.

Costs, money and banks

Compared to the rest of Asia, China is an expensive place to travel. Though it's possible to eat and move around fairly cheaply, accommodation costs can be relatively high, and daily expenses vary drastically, according to region.

In descending order, the three main price "zones" are Hong Kong and Macau, the eastern seaboard, and the interior provinces, with some variation within these categories. Basically, things get cheaper the farther west you go, though costs are always relatively more expensive in popular tourist spots.

Currency

The mainland **Chinese currency** is formally called **yuan** (¥), more colloquially known as **renminbi** (RMB, literally "the people's money") or **kuai**. One yuan breaks down into ten **jiao**, also known as **mao**. **Paper money** was invented in China and is still the main form of exchange, available in ¥100, ¥50, ¥20, ¥10, ¥5 and ¥1 notes, with a similar selection of mao. One mao, five mao, and ¥1 **coins** are increasingly common, though people in rural areas may never have seen them before. China suffers regular outbreaks of **counterfeiting**, some of it very sophisticated – check notes for watermarks, metal threads, and the feel of the paper.

The yuan floats within a narrow range set by a basket of currencies, keeping Chinese exports cheap (much to the annoyance of the US). At the time of writing, the **exchange rate** was approximately ¥18.1 to US$1, ¥14.3 to £1, ¥10 to €1, ¥6.6 to CAN$1 and ¥6.2 to AUS$1.

Hong Kong's currency is the Hong Kong dollar (HK$), divided into one hundred cents, while in **Macau** they use **pataca** (usually written MOP$), in turn broken down into 100 avos. Both currencies are roughly equivalent to the yuan, but while Hong Kong dollars are accepted in Macau and southern China's Special Economic Zones and can be exchanged internationally, neither yuan nor pataca is any use outside the mainland or Macau respectively. Tourist hotels in Beijing, Shanghai and Guangzhou also sometimes accept – even insist on – payment in Hong Kong or US dollars. Hong Kong dollars are available overseas, yuan and patacas are not, though both can be obtained in Hong Kong, and converted back at a bank before you leave the country.

Costs

Given the extreme regional variations, it's hard to make exact predictions of how much China costs on a daily basis. In general, however, by doing everything cheaply and sticking mostly to the less expensive interior provinces you can survive on £20/US$40 a day; travel a bit more widely and in better comfort from time to time and you're looking at £35/US$70 a day; while travelling in style and visiting only key places along the east coast, you're looking at daily expenses of £60/US$120 and above.

Price tiering, where foreigners are charged more than Chinese for services, was formerly widespread but has now been officially banned. This means that you should pay the same as everyone else for accommodation, transport, or to enter museums or famous sights. In practice, you might be sold the most expensive option for these things, without being informed of less costly alternatives; take comfort in the fact that Chinese tourists suffer the same treatment. **Student rates** are often available for entry fees, however, so it's worth getting hold of a **Chinese Student Card** – they are vaguely official-looking documents, adorned with your photograph and folded into a small plastic wallet. You can get one officially by studying, even briefly, in China; unofficially, budget tour agents geared up to foreign needs can often supply them for about ¥40. **ISIC cards** are also occasionally recognized, most likely in Beijing and Hong Kong.

Bargaining is another way to save costs, both at accommodation (where mid-range and upmarket places are often flexible over prices) and at markets, where you may initially be asked for up to ten times the going price for goods – find out what others are paying first and be prepared to haggle.

Costs in **Hong Kong** and **Macau** are higher than for comparable services on the mainland, particularly for upmarket accommodation – though food and drink are again pretty reasonable and transport expenses negligible.

Carrying your money

Credit cards and **debit cards** (also known as bank cards) are probably the best way to carry money in China; although of limited use for direct purchases outside of Hong Kong and Macau, both can be used to draw funds from your home bank account through most Bank of China **ATM**s. Visa is the most widely recognized credit card in China, Mastercard and Amex less so. In addition to using credit cards in ATMs, they can also be used for over-the-counter cash advances – though these incur interest accruing daily from the date of withdrawal. The Bank of China also charges a **three percent fee** on top of this, though Hong Kong banks do not.

Debit cards (or bank cards marked with the Cirrus/Maestro symbol) are not liable to interest payments, and are subject only to a flat fee per ATM transaction which is set by your bank – ask for details. Make sure you have a personal identification number (PIN) that's designed to work overseas.

Before leaving home, make a record of your card numbers and their emergency contact details and email them to your Webmail account, in case you have to contact the issuer if they are lost or stolen.

Traveller's cheques and cash

For backup purposes it's also wise to carry a certain quantity of **traveller's cheques**, available through banks and travel agents. Their advantages are that their exchange rate in China is fixed and actually better than for cash, and they can be replaced if lost or stolen – keep the **purchase agreement** and a list of the serial numbers separate from the cheques, and report any loss immediately to the issuing company. On the downside, you pay a fee when you buy them, another when you cash them, in **mainland China** they can be cashed only at major branches of the Bank of China and tourist hotels, and the process always involves lengthy paperwork. In **Hong Kong** and **Macau**, any bank or bureau de change will be happy to cash them, but watch out for poor exchange rates and/or high commissions.

When buying traveller's cheques, stick to brands such as Thomas Cook or American Express, as less familiar, bank-issued traveller's cheques won't be accepted in smaller places.

In case you find yourself in difficulties, it's worth taking along a small supply of **foreign currency** such as US, Canadian or Australian dollars, or British pounds, which are widely exchangeable in many banks on the mainland. There's a low-key and burgeoning **black market** in China for foreign currency, but the small differential in rates and the risks of getting ripped off or attracting police attention don't make it worthwhile.

Banks

Banks in major Chinese cities are sometimes open seven days a week, though foreign exchange is usually only available Monday to Friday, approximately between 9am and noon and again from 2pm to 5pm. All banks are closed for the first three days of the Chinese New Year, with reduced hours for the following eleven days, and at other holiday times. In Hong Kong, banks are generally open Monday to Friday from 9am to 4.30pm, until 12.30pm on Saturday, while in Macau they close thirty minutes earlier.

Wiring money

Wiring money from home basically involves someone paying money to you using an overseas branch of a money-transfer agent, allowing you to withdraw the same amount from their representative in China. The service isn't cheap or particularly convenient, however, so it should be considered a last resort. It's also possible to have money wired directly from a bank in your home country to a bank in China, although this is a more complex operation because it involves two separate institutions. If you go down this route, your home bank will need the address of the bank where you want to pick up the money and the address and telex number of the Beijing head office, which will act as the clearing house; money wired this way normally takes two working days to arrive, and costs around £25/$40 per transaction.

Money-wiring companies

Moneygram ⓦ www.moneygram.com.
Western Union ⓦ www.westernunion.com.

Getting around

China is huge, and unless you concentrate on a small area you're going to spend a good deal of your time just getting around. Fortunately, public transport is comprehensive and good value: you can fly to all regional capitals and many cities; the rail network extends to every province except Tibet (though that is soon to change); and you can reach China's remotest corners on local buses. Tibet is the one region where there are widespread restrictions on independent travel (see p.1093 for more details), though a few other localities around the country are officially off limits to foreigners.

While there are plenty of options, travel often requires planning, patience and stamina. You need to weigh up the mental and physical rigours involved if you insist on travelling the cheapest way all the time – it's well worth covering long distances in as much comfort as possible. **Tours** are one way of taking the pressure off, and in some cases are the only practical way of getting out to certain sights.

Public holidays (see p.67) are rotten times to travel, as half China is on the move between family and workplace: ticket prices rise (legally, by no more than fifteen percent, though often by up to fifty), bus and train station crowds swell insanely, and even flights become scarce.

Trains

China's rail network is vast and efficient, and the safest, most reliable way to get around the country. The country's first rail lines were laid in the nineteenth century, and China's leaders have always invested heavily in the network, seeing a healthy transport infrastructure as essential to economic growth – and political cohesion. Around US$42 billion was spent on rail development between 2002 and 2005, which saw 7000km of new track being laid; the most ambitious current project is a rail link **to Tibet**, due for completion some time in 2007.

Timetables and tickets

The first step in train travel is getting hold of a **timetable**. Usually on display somewhere in the ticket office, or sold from stalls around the station, timetables can be hard to decipher; you need to be able to recognize the characters for both where you are and your destination, then memorize the train number and how many services there are, in case your first choice isn't available.

Tickets – always **one-way** – show the date of travel and destination, along with the train number, carriage and seat or berth number. They become available up to five days in advance, though demand frequently outstrips supply, so it's wise to plan ahead. You can **book tickets online** at ⓦwww .china-train-ticket.com, a joint-venture operation with the CITS which delivers tickets to your hotel or address in China, and also has useful information for first-timers on China rail. Another easy option within China is to book tickets through an **agent**, such as the CITS or a hotel travel service, though you'll pay a commission of ¥30 or more per person.

Many cities also have downtown **advance purchase offices**, though some are so well hidden that even the locals don't seem to know about them; you pay a small commission (around ¥5 per ticket), and it makes sense to try these places first as train stations are often located far from city centres. Otherwise, head to the **train station ticket office**; most premises are computerized nowadays, and while queues can still tie you up for an hour, you'll generally get what you're after in the end. At the counter, state your destination, the day you'd like to travel, and the class you want, or have it written down (station staff rarely speak English, though you may strike it lucky in big cities). If there's nothing else available, you can ask the ticket office for an **unreserved ticket** (wuzuo, literally "no seat"), which doesn't give you an assigned seat but at least lets you on the train – though you might have to stand for the entire journey if you can't upgrade on board.

If you've bought a ticket but decide not to travel, you should be able to get most of the fare **refunded** by returning the ticket to a ticket office at least two hours before departure. If there's a window specifically for returned tickets (tuipiao), the people in the queue are actually a potential quick source of tickets – Chinese-speakers are best placed to take advantage.

Boarding the train

Even if you've bought your ticket in advance, you should still turn up at the station with time to spare before your train leaves. All luggage has to be passed through **x-ray machines** at the station entrance to check for dangerous goods such as firecrackers – though there's rarely anyone paying any attention to the monitors. Carry **film** through separately to avoid the possibility of getting it damaged. You then need to work out which platform your train leaves from – most stations have electronic departure boards in Chinese, or you can show your ticket to station staff who will point you in the right direction. Passengers are not allowed on to the platform until the train is in and ready to leave, which can result in some mighty stampedes when the gates open. All carriages are numbered on the outside, and your ticket is checked by a guard as you board. Once on the train, you can **upgrade** any ticket at the controller's booth, in the hard-seat carriage next to the restaurant car (usually #8), where you can sign up for beds or seats as they become available.

Types of train

There are several types of train in China, each given their own code on timetables. The best and fastest are **Z-class**; Express **trains** are marked T- (for tekuai); **fast** are K- (kuai); **ordinary** (putong che) have a number only and are the slowest option. Z, T- and K-trains reach 100–200kph and have modern fittings with text messages scrolled at the carriage's end announcing temperature, arrival time at next station, and speed. A few busy, short-haul express services, such as the Shenzhen-Guangzhou train, have double-decker carriages. **No-smoking** rules are often vigorously enforced. The numbered services, though older and stopping more frequently, can be well maintained, with smoking banned in sleeper carriages (leading to furtive huddles in the spaces in between). Some, however, are elderly plodders destined for the scrapheap whose interiors are crusty with cigarette smoke and sunflower-seed husks on the linoleum floor. As always in China, the faster services are slightly more expensive.

Classes

There are four train **classes**. The best is **soft sleeper** (ruanwo), which costs slightly less

Sample train fares

The fares below are for one-way travel on express trains.

	Hard seat	Hard sleeper	Soft sleeper
From Beijing			
Guangzhou	¥205	¥553	¥756
Hong Kong	¥215	¥595	¥925
Shanghai	¥135	¥375	¥515
Xi'an	¥140	¥390	¥531
From Xi'an			
Guangzhou	¥220	¥607	¥830
Turpan	¥215	¥585	¥805
Ürümqi	¥225	¥625	¥842

than flying and is patronized by foreigners, party officials and successful entrepreneurs. It's a nice experience; there's a plush waiting room at most stations, and on the train itself you get a four-berth compartment with a soft mattress, fan, optional radio, and a choice of Western- or Chinese-style toilets. If you've a long way to travel and can afford it, soft sleeper is well worth the money, allowing you to arrive rested and ready to enjoy your destination.

Hard sleeper (*yingwo*), about two-thirds the price of *ruanwo*, is the best value and hence is also the most difficult to book in advance. Carriages are divided into twenty sets of three-tiered **bunks**; the lowest bunk is the most expensive, but gets used as communal seating during the day and you may appreciate being able to withdraw to a higher level. The end tier of bunks is closest to night lights and the connecting space between carriages, where smokers congregate. Each set of six bunks has its own vacuum flask of boiled water (topped up from the urn at the end of each carriage) – bring your own mugs and tea bags etc. Every carriage also has a toilet and wash-basin, which can become unsavoury; do what the locals do and carry a face towel to keep clean on long journeys. There are fairly spacious **luggage racks**, though make sure you chain your bags securely while you sleep.

In either sleeper class, on boarding the carriage you will have your ticket exchanged for a metal tag by the attendant. The tag is swapped back for your ticket (so you'll be able to get through the barrier at the station) about half an hour before you arrive at your destination; you'll be woken up whatever hour of the day or night this happens to be.

Soft seat (*ruanzuo*) is increasingly available on services whose complete route takes less than a day. Seats are around the cost of an express-bus fare, have plenty of legroom, and are well padded. More common is **hard seat** (*yingzuo*), which is really only recommended for the impecunious – it costs around half the soft-seat fare – or on relatively short journeys. The basic hard-seat setup is a padded three-person bench with just enough room to sit, though more modern carriages are relatively comfortable. On older trains, the air is thick with cigarette smoke and every available inch of floorspace is crammed with travellers who were unable to book a seat – bear in mind that should you board a train with an unreserved ticket, you'll be standing with them. You'll often be the focus of intense and unabashed speculation from peasants and labourers who can't afford to travel in better style. The best way to cope is to join in as best you can, whether you can speak Chinese or not; you'll probably end up playing cards, sharing food and drinking with them.

Food, though expensive and ordinary, is always available on trains, either as polystyrene boxes of rice and stir-fries wheeled around along with snacks, or in the restaurant car between soft sleeper section and the rest of the train. You can also buy snacks from vendors at train stations during the longer station stops.

Buses and minibuses

Despite the ever-widening net thrown by the rail lines, there are still many parts of China unreachable by train – in which case **buses** are often the only means of getting there. Cities may have one central **main bus station**, several separate **suburban depots** (located on the side of town in which traffic is heading or arriving from), or both. **Private depots** – often with faster, more modern vehicles – are often located in the big squares outside train stations. Services are frequent, even to remote places, and some cities have so many competing depots it can be hard to find the right departure point.

Unlike train tickets, bus **tickets** are easy to buy: ticket offices at main stations are often computerized, queues are nowhere near as bad, and – with the exception of backroads routes, which might only run every other day – you don't need to book in advance and are guaranteed a seat. At private depots, you often buy tickets from a nearby booth, or pay on board. You'll do this too if you hail a bus in passing; destinations are always displayed (in Chinese characters) on the front of the vehicle. Bus-station **timetables** are often inaccurate; ticket staff are pretty helpful, however.

As with trains, there are various types of bus, though there's not always a choice available for particular routes. If there is, the station staff will assume that as a foreigner you'll want the fastest, most comfortable service – which will also be the most expensive. **Ordinary buses** (*putong che*) are cheap and basic, with wooden or lightly padded seats; they're never heated or air-conditioned, so dress accordingly. Seats can be cramped and luggage racks tiny; you'll have to put anything bulkier than a satchel on the roof, your lap, or beside the driver. They tend to stop off frequently, so don't count on an average speed of more than 50km an hour. **Sleeper buses** (*wopu che*) cost a bit more than ordinary, have basic bunks instead of seats, and can be either comfortable or excruciatingly cramped; it's worth remembering that there are more road accidents at night.

Lower bunks (*xiapu*) are a bit more expensive than upper bunks (*shangpu*), but are better because you don't get thrown out of bed every time the bus takes a corner. Bags can sometimes be stored, if you get in early, otherwise there's a shoebox-sized luggage rack per bed and nothing else. One advantage to sleeper buses is that if they reach their destination before dawn, passengers are left to sleep on board until sunrise, saving the price of a hotel room. They are also relatively quick, stopping off less along the way. **Express buses** (*kuai che*) are the most expensive and have good legroom, comfy seats which may well recline, air conditioning and video – usually playing the latest kung fu, pop or karaoke releases. Bulky luggage gets locked away in the belly of the bus, a fairly safe option as these buses operate on a speedy point-to-point basis, with no stops en route. The final option is **minibuses** (*xiao che*) seating up to twenty people, common on routes of less than 100km or so. Prices vary around the country, but they typically cost a little more than the same journey by ordinary bus. They can be extremely cramped, however, and often circuit the departure point for hours until they have filled up.

There are a few **downsides** to bus travel. **Roads** are not always in good condition, though the number of fast expressways is continually rising. Drivers, mobile phones in one hand, wheel in the other, have the dangerous habit of saving fuel by coasting down hills or mountainsides in neutral, with the engine off. **Airhorns** (banned in some places) can make the experience noisy, too, as drivers are obliged to announce their presence before overtaking anything, and so earplugs are seriously recommended. Take some **food** along, because though buses usually pull up at inexpensive roadhouses at mealtimes, they have been known to take two drivers and plough on for a full 24 hours without stopping. Only the most upmarket coaches have **toilets**; drivers generally pull up every few hours or if asked to do so by passengers (roadhouse toilets are some of the worst in the country, however). Owing to the frequent police checks on roads in China, buses are seldom illegally overcrowded.

Planes

China's airlines link all major cities. The main operators are Air China (Ⓦwww.airchina .com.cn/en/index.jsp), China Southern (Ⓦwww.cs-air.com/en) and China Eastern (Ⓦwww.ce-air.com), which – along with a few minor companies – are overseen by the Civil Aviation Administration of China, or **CAAC**. Flying is a luxury worth considering for long distances: prices compare with soft-sleeper train travel but journey times are obviously far less; planes are generally modern and well maintained; and service is good – soft drinks, biscuits and souvenir trinkets are handed out along the way, and sometimes there's even a raffle.

Buying tickets from the local CAAC office, hotel desk or tour agent is easy, and there seem to be enough flights along popular routes to cope with demand. Agents often give substantial discounts on advertised fares – their representatives can always be found standing outside the CAAC office, handing out flyers which list their prices, which are often less than those inside the office. **Timetables** are displayed at airline offices. **Fares** are based on one-way travel (so a return ticket is the price of two one-way tickets) and agents often give substantial discounts on advertised fares. As an illustration, from Beijing, expect to pay at least ¥620 to Xi'an; ¥690 to Shanghai; ¥935 to Chengdu; ¥1055 to Guangzhou; ¥1190 to Kunming, ¥1440 to Ürümqi and ¥1800 to Hong Kong.

Airlines frequently provide an **airport bus** running to and from the airport; as these can be 30km or more from city centres, it's worth finding out if a bus is available, if one isn't already mentioned in this guide. **Check-in time** for all flights is two hours before departure, and there's always a **departure tax** of ¥50 for internal flights, usually included in the ticket price.

Ferries

River and sea journeys are on the decline in China, with **passenger ferries** being made redundant by new and faster roads and rail lines. One of the world's great river journeys remains, however, namely the **Yangzi**, which is navigable for thousands of kilometres between the Sichuanese port of Chongqing and Wuhan in Hubei, a journey which takes you through the mighty **Three Gorges** – though the spectacle has been lessened by the construction of the giant Three Gorges Dam. Another favourite is the day-cruise down the **Li River** between Guilin and Yangshuo in southwestern Guangxi province, past a forest of pointy mountains looking just like a Chinese scroll painting. Other short ferry trips survive, mostly in rural areas – make use of them if you can, because doubtless they'll be gone in a few years. By sea, there are still passenger boats between Hong Kong, Macau and various towns through the Pearl River Delta.

Conditions on board are greatly variable, but on overnight trips there's always a choice of **classes** – sometimes as many as six – which can range from a bamboo mat on the floor, right through to the luxury of private cabins. Don't expect anything too impressive, however; many mainland services are cramped and overcrowded, and cabins, even in first class, are grimly functional.

Driving and car rental

Driving a car across China is an appealing idea, but an experience currently forbidden to foreign tourists – though the bilingual road signs going up along new expressways suggest that the notion is being considered. It is possible, however, to **rent vehicles** for local use in **Beijing**, **Shanghai** and **Hong Kong**, from rental companies at the airports. You need an international driving licence and a credit card to cover the deposit. Special licence plates make these rental vehicles easily identifiable to Chinese police, so don't try taking them beyond the designated boundaries. Rates are about ¥300 a day plus petrol.

The mainland Chinese drive **on the right**, although in practice drivers seem to drive wherever they like – through red lights, even on the left. They use their horns instead of the brake, and lorries and buses plough ahead regardless while smaller vehicles get out of the way. The exception is in Hong Kong, where they drive on the left, and actually take traffic regulations seriously.

Elsewhere the only option is to rent a **taxi**, **minibus** or Chinese **jeep**, complete with driver. Prices are set by negotiating and average ¥400 a day, and you'll be expected to provide lunch for the driver. It's cheapest to approach drivers directly, though if you can't speak Chinese your accommodation should be able to help, and some tour operators run vehicles too – and might include the services of an interpreter. In Tibet, renting a jeep with a driver is pretty much the only way to get to many destinations (see p.1105).

Bicycles

China has the highest number of **bicycles** of any country in the world, with about a quarter of the population owning one (despite many people ditching them in favour of motorbikes). Few cities have any hills and many have **bike lanes**, though **heavy traffic** can be a problem in big, congested metropolises such as Guangzhou and Beijing.

Rental shops or booths are common around the train stations, where you can rent a set of wheels for ¥5–10 a day. You will need to leave a deposit (¥200–400) and/or some form of ID, and you're fully responsible for anything that happens to the bike while it's in your care, so check brakes, tyre pressure and gearing before renting. Most rental bikes are bog-standard black rattletraps – the really de luxe models feature working bells and brakes. There are **repair shops** all over the place should you need a tyre patched or a chain fixed up (around ¥10). If the bike sustains any serious damage it's up to the parties involved to sort out responsibility and payment on the spot. To **avoid theft**, always use a bicycle chain or lock – they're available everywhere – and in cities, leave your vehicle in one of the ubiquitous designated **parking areas**, where it will be guarded by an attendant for a few yuan.

An alternative to renting is to **buy a bike**, a sensible option if you're going to be based anywhere for a while – foreigners don't need licences, all department stores stock them (from about ¥500), and demand is so high that there should be little problem reselling the bike when you leave. The cheapest are solid, heavy, unsophisticated machines such as the famous Flying Pigeon brand, though multigeared mountain-bikes are becoming very popular. You can also **take your own bike** into China with you; international airlines usually insist that the front wheel is removed, deflated and strapped to the back, and that everything is thoroughly packaged. Inside China, airlines, trains and ferries all charge to carry bikes, and the ticketing and accompanying paperwork can be baffling. Where possible, it's easier to stick to long-distance buses and stow it for free on the roof, no questions asked. Another option is to see China on a **specialized bike tour** such as those offered by Bike China (ⓦ www.bikechina.com) or Cycle China (ⓦ www.cyclechina.com); though by no means cheap, these can be an excellent start to a longer stay in China.

Hitching

Hitching around China is possible, and in remoter areas might save some time in reaching sights. However, drivers will usually charge you the going bus fare, and have been known to renegotiate en route, threatening to leave you stranded if you won't pay extra. Given the added personal risks inherent in hitching, and the fact that public transport is becoming ever more available, it's not recommended as a means of getting around.

If you must hitch, don't do it alone. The best places to try are on town and city exit roads. Get the driver's attention by waving your hand, palm down, at them. Expect to bargain for the fare, and make sure that you have your destination written down in Chinese characters.

A few travellers hitch **into Tibet** on trucks as a way to get around government travel restrictions. Be aware that if you do this you are putting yourself at some risk, as conditions can be very uncomfortable and sometimes extremely cold. If you are found, you might be arrested, have to pay a fine, and get kicked back the way you came, and your driver will be in serious trouble – some drivers have been severely beaten by police.

Organized tours

Chinese tour operators can almost always organize excursions, from local city sights to river cruises and multi-day cross-country trips. While you always pay for the privilege, sometimes these tours are not bad value: travel, accommodation and food – usually plentiful and excellent – are generally included, as might be the services of an interpreter and guide. And in some cases, tours are the most practical (if not the only) way to see something really worthwhile, saving endless bother organizing local transport and accommodation.

As regards **adventure tours**, it's worth checking out **WildChina** (🌐www.wildchina.com), or **Trax2** (🌐www.trax2.com), both of whom are based in-country and run excursions around the nation's fringes for individuals and groups, with trekking and hiking a focus of many trips, though some tours have an architectural or cultural emphasis.

On the downside, there are disreputable operators who'll blatantly overcharge for mediocre services, foist guides on you who can't speak local dialects or are generally unhelpful and spend three days on what could better be done in an afternoon. In general, it helps to make exhaustive enquiries about the exact nature of the tour, such as exactly what the price includes and the departure/return times, before handing any money over.

City transport

Most Chinese cities are spread out over areas which defeat even the most determined walker, but all have some form of **public transit system**. Hong Kong, Beijing, Guangzhou and Shanghai have efficient underground **metros**; elsewhere the **city bus** is the transport focus. These are cheap and run from around 6am to 9pm or later, but – Hong Kong's apart – are usually slow and crowded. Pricier **private minibuses** often run the same routes in similar comfort but at greater speed – they're either numbered or have their destination written up at the front.

If you're in a hurry or can't face another bus journey, you'll find **taxis** cruising the streets in larger towns and cities, or hanging around the main transit points and hotels. They're not bad value for a group, costing either a fixed rate within certain limits – ¥5 seems normal – or about ¥8 to hire and then ¥1–3 per kilometre. You'll also find (motorized- or cycle-) **rickshaws** and **motorbike taxis** outside just about every mainland bus and train station, whose highly erratic rates are set by bargaining beforehand.

Accommodation

Accommodation in China is generally disappointing. Acres of marble and chrome aside, the Chinese rarely seem to feel that a hotel can be more than just a functional place to stay, but could be an interesting or enjoyable place in itself. What's lacking is variety – characterful old family-run institutions of the kind that can be found all over Asia and Europe are rare in mainland China.

Despite the lack of variety, there is a vast **range of quality** in terms of comfort and service. A general rule is that newer hotels are almost always preferable, enjoying a honeymoon period of enthusiastic service and stain-free carpets before poor maintenance begins to take its toll. **Price**, however, is a poor guide to quality: eastern China, for example, is far more expensive than western China, and large cities are more expensive than small ones. Hotels seldom seem to revise their prices either, so a once upmarket place might still charge high rates long after the facilities have deteriorated to the point of no return. In any case, **room rates** on display at reception often turn out to be merely the starting point in negotiations; staff are almost always amenable to **bargaining**. Getting thirty percent off the advertised price isn't unusual, and you might get even more of a discount in low season or where there's plenty of competition. Conversely, at popular tourist destinations during peak season, hotels can charge considerably more. Polite enquiries might also persuade the receptionist to mention the existence of hitherto unsuspected cheaper rooms or a dormitory in another wing of the hotel.

One specific irritation for **foreigners** is the fact that plenty of hotels – normally the cheap ones – can't take them at all. Such hotels have not obtained police permission to do so, and if they are caught housing foreigners illegally they face substantial fines. The situation is always dependent on the local authorities, and can vary not just from province to province, but also from town to town. Nothing is ever certain in China, however: sometimes receptionists don't know that foreigners aren't allowed to stay, and if it is late at night, or if there is only one hotel in town, you will normally be allowed in anyway. Being able to speak Chinese greatly improves your chances – and if you can write your name in Chinese, or have it printed somewhere so that the receptionist can write it for you on the forms, then nobody need ever know that a foreigner stayed.

Hotels in China are reasonably **secure** places, although you would be foolish to leave money or valuables lying about in your room. If you lock valuables such as cameras inside your bag before going out you are unlikely to have problems.

Finding a room

For international-class rooms, **booking ahead** is a routine procedure and you will find receptionists who speak English to take your call. For any hotel below this category, however, the concept of booking ahead may be alien, and you won't make much headway without some spoken Chinese – though it's a good idea to call (or to ask someone to call for you) to see if vacancies exist before lugging your bag across town. One of the easier ways to book mid-range or better accommodation is to use a dedicated **website** – see "Online Resources" on p.36 for addresses to start looking – or contact the local CITS, who can wrangle excellent discounts, sometimes a lot more than you could get by bartering at the reception desk.

To find a room **upon arrival**, time things so that you reach your destination in broad daylight, then deposit your bag at a left-luggage office at the train or bus station and check out possible accommodation options. Always ask to see the room before deciding to take it.

In some places, **touts** with hotel brochures and name cards will approach you outside stations. They are paid directly by the hotels concerned, not by surcharges on your room price, so you won't lose much by following them. Sometimes, however, touts can inadvertently waste your time by taking you to hotels which turn out not to accept foreigners.

Checking in and out

The checking-in process involves filling in a detailed **form** giving details of your name, age, date of birth, sex and address, places where you are coming from and going to, how many days you intend staying and your visa and passport numbers. Filling in forms correctly is a serious business in bureaucratic China, and if potential guests are unable to carry out this duty the result is impasse. Upmarket hotels have English versions of these forms, and might fill them in for you, but hotels unaccustomed to foreigners usually have them in Chinese only, and might never have seen a foreign passport before – which explains the panic experienced by many hotel receptionists when they see a foreigner walk in the door. There's an example of this form in English and Chinese on p.54 to help you complete it correctly.

You are always asked to **pay** in advance and, in addition, leave a **deposit** which may amount to as much as twice the price of the room. Assuming you haven't broken anything – check that everything works properly when you check in – deposits are reliably refunded; just don't lose the receipt. Note that as the official **hotel day** begins at 6am, arriving before this time means you have to pay a portion of the rate for the previous night. If you're staying several nights, either pay the whole lot in advance, or check in again every day.

Except in upmarket places, you hardly ever get a **key** from reception; instead you'll get a piece of paper which you take to the appropriate floor attendant who will give

临时住宿登记表
REGISTRATION FORM FOR TEMPORARY RESIDENCE

请用正楷填写 Please write in block letters

英文姓 Surname	英文名 First name	性别 Sex
中文姓名 Name in Chinese	国籍 Nationality	出生日期 Date of birth
证件种类 Type of certificate (eg "Passport")	证件号码 Certificate no.	签证种类 Type of visa
签证有效期 Valid date of visa	抵店日期 Date of arrival	离店日期 Date of departure
由何处来 From	交通工具 Carrier	往何处 To
永久地址 Permanent address		停留事由 Object of stay
职业 Occupation		
接待单位 Received by		房号 Room no.

you a room card and open the door for you whenever you come in. Sometimes the floor attendant will offer you the key to keep, though if you want it you'll have to pay them another refundable deposit of ¥10–20. If your room has a **telephone**, disconnect it to avoid prostitutes calling up through the night.

Check-out time is noon, but if you have to leave early in the morning to catch a bus, for instance, you may be unable to find staff to refund your deposit, and might also encounter locked front doors or compound gates. This is most of a problem in rural areas, though often the receptionist sleeps behind the desk and can be woken up if you make enough noise.

Hotels

The different Chinese words for hotel are vague indicators of the status of the place – see the "Language" section (p.1236) for the *pinyin* and Chinese characters. Sure signs of upmarket pretensions are the modern-sounding **dajiulou** or **dajiudian**, which translate as something like "big wine bar". The term **binguan** is similarly used for smart new establishments, though it is also the name given to the older government-run hotels, many of which have now been renovated; foreigners can nearly always stay in these. **Fandian** (literally "restaurant") is used indiscriminately for top-class hotels as well as humble and obscure ones. Reliably downmarket – and rarely accepting foreigners – is **zhaodaisuo** ("guesthouse"), while the humblest of all is **lǚguan** ("inn"), where you might occasionally get to stay in some rural areas. These cheaper places are often simply signed **zhusu** ("accommodation").

Whatever type of hotel you are staying in, there are two things you can rely on. One is a pair of plastic or paper slippers under the bed, that you use for walking to the bathroom, and the other is a vacuum flask of drinkable hot water that can be refilled any time by the floor attendant – though upmarket places tend to provide electric kettles in the rooms. **Breakfast** is sometimes included in the price; nearly all hotels, even fairly grotty ones, will have a restaurant where at least a

Accommodation price codes

The accommodation listed in this book has been given one of the following price codes, which represent the price of the cheapest **double room**. In the cheaper hotels that have **dormitories** or that rent out individual beds in small rooms, we give the price of a bed in yuan.

It should generally be noted that in the **off season** – from October to June, excluding holidays such as Christmas and Chinese New Year – prices in tourist hotels are more flexible, and often lower, than during the peak summer months.

Note that the price codes do not take into account the **service charge** of fifteen percent added to bills in all mid-range and upmarket hotels.

❶ Up to ¥50	❹ ¥140–200	❼ ¥450–600
❷ ¥50–80	❺ ¥200–300	❽ ¥600–800
❸ ¥80–140	❻ ¥300–450	❾ Over ¥800

Chinese breakfast of buns, pickles and rice porridge is served between 7am and 9am.

Upmarket

In the larger cities – including virtually all provincial capitals – you'll find upmarket four- or five-star hotels. Conditions in such hotels are comparable to those anywhere in the world, with all the usual **international facilities** on offer – such as swimming pools, gyms and business centres – though the finer nuances of service will sometimes be lacking. Prices for standard doubles in these places are upwards of ¥800 (❾ in our price-code scheme) and go as high as ¥1500, with a fifteen percent **service charge** on top; the use of credit cards is routine. In **Hong Kong** and **Macau** the top end of the market is similar in character to the mainland, though prices are higher and service more efficient – price codes for these areas are found on p.674.

Even if you cannot afford to stay in the upmarket hotels, they can still be pleasant places to escape from the hubbub, and nobody in China blinks at the sight of a stray foreigner roaming around the foyer of a smart hotel. As well as air conditioning and clean toilets, you'll find cafés and bars (sometimes showing satellite TV), telephone and fax facilities and seven-days-a-week money changing (though this is not always open to non-guests).

Mid-range

Many urban Chinese hotels built nowadays are **mid-range**, and practically every town

in China has at least one hotel of this sort. Most rooms in these places are twin bed (*shuangrenfang*) or single (*danrenfang*); if you want a double bed, ask for a single with a "large bed" (*dachuan*).

In remote places you should get a twin or double in a mid-range establishment for ¥150–250, but expect to pay at least ¥350 in any sizeable city. Some mid-range hotels built during the dawn of tourism in 1980s, however, might retain older, **cheaper wings**. These are often well maintained, if threadbare, and cost ¥100–200 for a double with bathroom, and as low as ¥25 for a dorm bed – but as staff seldom allow foreigners to share with Chinese, you may be asked to pay for a whole room.

Budget hotels

Cheap hotels, with doubles costing less than ¥100, vary in quality from the dilapidated to the perfectly comfortable. In many cities, they're commonly located near the train station, though in the major cities such as Beijing or Shanghai you may end up far from the centre.

Where you do manage to find a budget hotel that takes foreigners, you'll notice that the Chinese routinely **rent beds** rather than rooms – doubling up with one or more strangers – as a means of saving money. Foreigners are seldom allowed to share rooms with Chinese people, but if there are three or four foreigners together it's often possible for them to share one big room. Otherwise, the main tourist centres, including large cities such as Beijing, Shanghai and Guangzhou, tend to have budget hotels with special **foreigners' dormitory** accommodation, costing around ¥20–50 per bed.

Hostels and guesthouses

There's an expanding network of **IYHA hostels** across China (all displaying the official blue triangular sign), from mainland cities to Hong Kong's islands, and places popular with backpackers, such as Yunnan. Details are given through the guide and booking ahead is always advisable – IYHA members get a small discount, and you can join at any mainland hostel for ¥60. Hong Kong, Macau and a few regions of China (mostly in southwestern provinces) also have a number of **privately run guesthouses** and hostels, whose variety comes as a relief after the dullness of mainland accommodation. Prices for double rooms in these guesthouses are generally cheaper than in hotels in most of eastern China, and very cheap dormitories are also plentiful.

A feature of some accommodation in northern China is a *kang*, a raised wooden platform warmed by being constructed over a pipe connected to the oven. During the day the platform is used as a dining area, and at night mattresses are rolled out on it. The platform is always on the west side of the room, the side where the ancestors are worshipped, and it's considered the most honoured place to sleep.

Youth hostel associations

China

YHA China ☎020/87345080, ☏87345428, ⓦwww.yhachina.com/english.

UK and Ireland

Youth Hostel Association (YHA) ☎0870/770 8868, ⓦwww.yha.org.uk.
Scottish Youth Hostel Association ☎0870/155 3255, ⓦwww.syha.org.uk.
Irish Youth Hostel Association ☎01/830 4555, ⓦwww.irelandyha.org.
Hostelling International Northern Ireland ☎028/9032 4733, ⓦwww.hini.org.uk.

US and Canada

Hostelling International-American Youth Hostels ☎301/495-1240, ⓦwww.hiayh.org.

Hostelling International Canada ☎1-800/663 5777 or 613/237 7884, ⓦwww.hihostels.ca.

Australia and New Zealand

Australia Youth Hostels Association ☎02/9261 1111, ⓦwww.yha.com.au.
Youth Hostelling Association New Zealand ☎0800/278 299 or 03/379 9970, ⓦwww.yha.co.nz.

University accommodation

Another budget possibility always worth trying is rooms in **universities**, as more and more of them are willing to accommodate foreign tourists. These will have a building on campus termed something like the "Foreigners' Guesthouse" (*waibing zhaodaisuo*) or the "Foreign Experts' Building" (*waiguo zhuanjia lou*), designed primarily to accommodate foreign students or teachers. You would be unlucky not to find some obliging English-speaking student to help you find the right block once you're inside the campus. These buildings act like simple hotels and you have to fill in all the usual forms. Expect to pay around ¥50 a night, though some places are now charging tourists substantially more. Sometimes you find yourself put in to share with a resident foreign student who may be less than gracious about having you – but this happens only if the student concerned has paid for only one of the two beds in their room, so you needn't feel guilty about it. Although universities are friendly places to stay, the communal washing and toilet facilities can be grim, and campuses are often located far out in the suburbs.

Camping and pilgrims' inns

Camping is only really feasible in the wildernesses of western China where you are not going to wake up under the prying eyes of thousands of local villagers. In parts of Tibet, Qinghai, Xinjiang, Gansu and Inner Mongolia there are places within reach of hikers or cyclists where this is possible, though don't bother actually trying to get permission for it. This is the kind of activity which the Chinese authorities do not really have any clear idea about, so if asked they will certainly answer "no". The only kind of regular, authorized camping in China is by the nomadic Mongolian and Kazakh peoples of the steppe who have their own highly sophisticated felt tents (*mengu bao*), which tourists can stay in under certain circumstances (see p.957).

An alternative to camping is the **pilgrims' inns** at important monasteries and lamaseries. These are an extremely cheap,

if rather primitive, form of accommodation, though vacancies disappear quickly. Foreigners are warmly welcomed in such places, and although the authorities are not particularly keen on you staying in them, you are most unlikely to be turned away if it is late in the day and you are really stuck.

Eating and drinking

The Chinese love to eat, and from market-stall buns and soup, right through to the intricate variations of regional cookery, China boasts one of the world's greatest cuisines. It's also far more complex than you might suspect from its manifestations overseas, though the inability to order effectively sees many travellers missing out, and they leave convinced that the bland stir-fries and dumplings served up in the cheapest canteens are all that's available. With a bit of effort you can eat well whatever your budget and ability with the language.

The **principles of Chinese cooking** are based on a desire for a healthy harmony between the qualities of different ingredients. For the Chinese, this extends right down to considering the *yin* and *yang* attributes of various dishes – for instance, whether food is "moist" or "dry", or "heating" or "cooling" in effect – but can also be appreciated in the use of ingredients with contrasting textures and colour, designed to please the eye as well as the palate. Recipes and ingredients themselves, however, are generally a response to more direct requirements. The chronic poverty of China's population is reflected in the traditionally scant quantity of meat used, while the need to preserve precious stocks of firewood led to the invention of quick cooking techniques, such as slicing ingredients into tiny shreds and stir-frying them. The reliance on eating whatever was immediately to hand also saw a readiness to experiment with anything edible; so, though you'd hardly

come across them every day, items such as bear's paw, shark's fin, fish lips and even jellyfish all appear in Chinese cuisine.

Meals are considered social events, and the process is accordingly geared to a group of diners sharing a variety of different dishes with their companions. Fresh ingredients are available from any market stall, though unless you're living long-term in the country there are few opportunities to cook for yourself.

Ingredients and cooking methods

In the south, **rice** in various forms – long and short grain, noodles, or as dumpling wrappers – is the staple, replaced in the cooler north by **wheat**, formed into buns or noodles. Keep an eye out for **lamian** – literally "pulled noodles" – a Muslim treat made as you wait by pulling out ribbons of dough between outstretched arms, and serving them in a spicy soup (see p.1053).

Meat is held to be invigorating and, ideally, forms the backbone of any meal – serving a pure meat dish is the height of hospitality. Pork is the most common meat used, except

For a comprehensive menu reader and useful phrases for ordering food and drink, see p.1238.

Vegetarian food

Vegetarianism has been practised for almost two thousand years in China for both religious and philosophical reasons, and its practitioners have included historical figures such as Cao Cao, the famous Three Kingdoms warlord, and the pious sixth-century emperor Wu. Vegetarian cooking takes at least three recognized forms: plain **vegetable dishes**, commonly served at home or in ordinary restaurants; **imitation meat** dishes derived from Qing court cuisine, which use gluten, bean curd and potato to mimic the natural attributes of meat, fowl and fish; and **Buddhist cooking**, which often avoids onions, ginger, garlic and other spices considered stimulating.

Having said all this, strict vegetarians visiting China will find their options limited, despite a growing interest in the cuisine. Vegetables might be considered intrinsically healthy, but the Chinese also believe that they lack any physically fortifying properties, and **vegetarian diets** are unusual except for religious reasons. There's also a stigma of poverty attached to not eating meat, and as a foreigner no one can understand why you don't want it when you could clearly afford to gorge yourself on meat on a regular basis. If you really want to be sure that you are being served nothing of animal origin, tell your waiter that you are a Buddhist (see p.1238) – though be aware that cooking fat and stocks in the average dining room are of animal origins.

Things are easiest in big cities such as Beijing, Shanghai and Guangzhou, which have real **vegetarian restaurants**; elsewhere, head for the nearest **temple**, many of which have dining rooms open to the public at lunchtime – some serve extraordinarily good food, worth sampling even if you're not vegetarian. When ordering in these places, note that imitation meat dishes are still called by their usual name, such as West Lake fish, honey pork or roast duck.

in areas with a strong Muslim tradition where it's replaced with mutton or beef. **Fowl** is considered especially good during old age or convalescence, and was quite a luxury in the past (chicken was once the most expensive meat in Beijing), though today most rural people in central and southern China seem to own a couple of hens, and the countryside is littered with duck farms. **Fish and seafood** are highly regarded and can be expensive – partly because local pollution means that they often have to be imported – as are rarer game meats.

Eggs – duck, chicken or quail – are a popular nationwide snack, often flavoured by hard-boiling in a mixture of tea, soy sauce and star anise. There's also the so-called "thousand-year" variety, preserved for a few months in ash and straw – they look gruesome, with translucent brown albumen and green yolks, but actually have a delicate, brackish flavour. **Dairy products** serve limited purposes in China. Goat's cheese and yoghurt are eaten in parts of Yunnan and the Northwest, but milk is considered fit only for children and the elderly and is not used in cooking.

Vegetables accompany nearly every Chinese meal, used in most cases to balance tastes and textures of meat, but also appearing as dishes in their own right. Though the selection can be very thin in some parts of the country, there's usually a wide range on offer, from leafy greens to water chestnuts, mushrooms, bamboo shoots, seaweed and radish – even thin, transparent "glass" noodles, made out of pea starch, which the Chinese regard as vegetables too.

Soya beans are ubiquitous in Chinese cooking, being a good source of protein in a country where meat has often been a luxury. The beans themselves are small and green when fresh, and are sometimes eaten this way in the south. More frequently, however, they are salted and used to thicken sauces, fermented to produce **soy sauce**, or boiled and pressed to make white cakes of **tofu** (bean curd). Fresh tofu is flavourless and as soft as custard, though it can be pressed further to create a firmer texture, or deep-fried until crisp. This is often smoked or cooked in stock, sliced thinly and used as a meat substitute in vegetarian cooking. Regional variations abound: in the west tofu is served heavily spiced; in Hunan they grow mould on it (rather like cheese); in the south it's stuffed with meat; northerners make it spongy by freezing it; and everywhere it gets used in soup. The skin that forms on top of the liquid while tofu is being made is itself skimmed off, dried, and used as a wrapping for spring rolls and the like.

Seasonal availability is smoothed over by a huge variety of **dried**, **salted** and **pickled** vegetables, meats and seafood, which often characterize local cooking styles. There's also an enormous assortment of regional **fruit**, great to clean the palate or fill a space between meals.

When it finally comes to **preparing and cooking** these ingredients, be aware that there's far more on offer than simply chopping everything into small pieces and stir-frying them. A huge number of **spices** are used for their health-giving properties, to mask undesirable flavours or provide a background taste. **Marinating** removes blood (which is generally repugnant to the Chinese, though congealed pig's blood is a common rural dish in the south), and tenderizes and freshens the flavour of meats. Chicken and fish are often cooked whole, though they may be dismembered before serving. Several cooking methods can be used within a single dish to maximize textures or flavours, including crisping by **deep frying** in flour or a batter; **steaming**, which can highlight an ingredient's subtler flavours; **boiling and blanching**, usually to firm meat as a precursor to other cooking methods; and **slow cooking** in a rich stock.

Regional cooking

Not surprisingly, given China's scale, there are a number of distinct **regional cooking styles**, divided into four major traditions. **Northern cookery** was epitomized by the imperial court and so also became known as Mandarin or Beijing cooking, though its influences are far wider than these names suggest. A solid diet of **wheat and millet buns**, noodles, pancakes and dumplings helps to face severe winters, accompanied by the savoury tastes of dark soy sauce and bean paste, white cabbage, onions and garlic. The north's cooking has also been influenced by neighbours and invaders:

Mongols brought their hotpots and grilled and roast meats, and Muslims a taste for mutton, beef and chicken. Combined with exotic items imported by foreign merchants and vassal embassies visiting the court, imperial kitchens turned these rather rough ingredients and cooking styles into sophisticated marvels such as Beijing duck and bird's-nest soup – though most northerners survive on soups of winter pickles, or fried summer greens eaten with a bun.

The central coast provinces produced the **eastern style**, whose cooking delights in seasonal fresh seafood and river fish. Winters can still be cold and summers scorchingly hot, so dried and salted ingredients feature too, pepping up a background of rice noodles and dumplings. Based around Shanghai, eastern cuisine (as opposed to daily fare) enjoys delicate forms and fresh, sweet flavours, though it can tend towards being oily. **Red-cooking**, stewing meat in a sweetened wine and soy-sauce stock, is a characteristically eastern technique.

Western China is dominated by the boisterous cooking of **Sichuan** and **Hunan**, the antithesis of the eastern style. Here, there's a heavy use of chillies and pungent, constructed flavours – vegetables are concealed with "fish-flavoured" sauce, and even normally bland tofu is given enough spices to lift the top off your head. Yet there are still subtleties to enjoy in a cuisine which uses dried orange peel, aniseed, ginger and spring onions, and the cooking methods themselves – such as dry frying and smoking – are refreshingly unusual. Sichuan is also home of the now-ubiquitous **hotpot** (*huoguo*), where you pay a set amount and are served with various raw meats and vegetables which you cook in boiling stock, liberally laced with chillies.

Southern China is fertile and subtropical, a land of year-round plenty. When people say that southerners – specifically the **Cantonese** – will eat anything, they really mean it: fish maw, snake, dog and cane rat are some of the more unusual dishes here, strange even to other Chinese, though there's also a huge consumption of fruit and vegetables, fish and shellfish. Typically, the demand is for extremely fresh ingredients, quickly cooked and only lightly seasoned, though the south is also home to that famous mainstay of Chinese restaurants overseas, sweet-and-sour sauce. The tradition of **dim sum** – "little eats" – reached its pinnacle here, too, where a morning meal of tiny flavoured buns, dumplings and pancakes is washed down with copious tea, satisfying the Chinese liking for a varied assortment of small dishes. Nowadays *dim sum* (*dian xin* in Mandarin) is eaten all over China, but southern restaurants still have the best selection (see p.704 for more details).

Hong Kong's food is heavily biased towards the southern style, though you can eat most regional Chinese cuisines here; while in **Macau** you'll get the chance to try the region's unique mix of Portuguese and Asian food, known as Macanese.

Breakfast, snacks and fast food

Breakfast is not a big event by Chinese standards, more something to line the stomach for a few hours. Much of the country is content with a bowl of **zhou** (also known as congee, rice porridge) or sweetened soy milk, flavoured with pickles and accompanied by a heavy, plain bun or fried dough stick, the latter rather like a straight, savoury doughnut. Another favourite is a plain soup with rice noodles and perhaps a little meat. Most places also have countless small, early-opening **snack stalls**, usually located around markets, train and bus stations. Here you'll get grilled chicken wings; kebabs; spiced noodles; baked yams and potatoes; boiled eggs; various steamed or stewed dishes served in earthenware **sandpots**, grilled corn and countless local treats. Look out also for steamed **buns**, which are either stuffed with meat or vegetables (*baozi*) or plain *(mantou,* literally "bald heads"). The buns originated in the north and are especially warming on a winter's day; a sweeter Cantonese variety is stuffed with barbecued pork. Another northern snack now found everywhere is the ravioli-like **jiaozi**, again with a meat or vegetable filling and either fried or steamed; **shuijiao** are boiled *jiaozi* served in soup. Some small restaurants specialize in *jiaozi*, containing a bewildering range of fillings and always sold by weight.

Western and international food

There's a fair amount of **Western and international food** available in China, though supply and quality vary. Hong Kong, Shanghai and Beijing have the best range, with some excellent restaurants covering everything from Russian to Vietnamese cuisine, and there are international food restaurants in every Chinese city of any size, with Korean and Japanese cuisine the best represented. Elsewhere, upmarket hotels may have Western restaurants, serving expensive but huge **buffet breakfasts** of scrambled egg, bacon, toast, cereal and coffee; and there's a growing number of **cafés** in many cities, offering fresh coffee and tea, along with **set meals** from ¥30–80 – steak hotplates are currently in fashion (the more expensive versions using imported beef), served with a drink, small soup and salad. *Starbucks* have a conspicuous presence in Beijing and Shanghai. **Burger**, **fried-chicken** and **pizza** places are ubiquitous, including domestic chains such as *Dicos* alongside genuine *McDonald's*, *KFC* and *Pizza Hut*.

Where to eat

In itself, getting fed is never difficult as everyone wants your custom. Walk past anywhere that sells cooked food and you'll be hailed by cries of *chi fan* – basically, "come and eat!"

Hotel dining rooms can be very flash affairs, with the most upmarket serving a range of foreign and regional Chinese food at ruinous cost, though mid-range places can often be extremely good value. Advantages include the possibility that staff may speak English, or that they might offer a **set menu** of small local dishes. Elsewhere, **restaurants** are often divided into two or three floors: the first will offer a canteen-like choice, upstairs will be pricier and have more formal dining arrangements, with waitress service and a written menu, while further floors (if they have them) are generally reserved for banquet parties or foreign tour groups and are unlikely to seat individuals. Note that the favoured atmosphere in a Chinese restaurant is *renao*, or "hot and noisy", rather than the often quiet norm in the West.

The cheapest **stalls and canteens** are necessarily basic, with simple food which is often much better than you'd expect from the furnishings. Though foreigners are generally given disposable chopsticks, it's probably worth buying your own set in case these aren't available – washing up frequently involves rinsing everything in a bucket of grey water on the floor and leaving it to dry on the pavement.

While small noodle shops and food stalls around train and bus stations have flexible hours, **restaurant opening times** tend to be early and short: breakfast lasts from around 6–8am; lunch 11am–2pm; and dinner from around 5–9pm, after which the staff will be yawning and sweeping the debris off the tables around your ankles.

Ordering and dining

When **ordering**, unless eating a one-dish meal like Peking duck or a hotpot, try to select items with a range of tastes and textures; it's also usual to include a soup. In cheap places, servings of noodles or rice are huge, but as they are considered basic stomach fillers, quantities decline the more upmarket you go. Note that dishes such as *jiaozi* and some seafood, as well as fresh produce, are sold **by weight**: a *liang* is 50 grams, a *banjin* 250 grams, a *jin* 500 grams, and a *gongjin* one kilo.

Menus are often more of an indication of what's on offer than a definitive list, so don't be afraid to ask for a missing favourite. Note also that English menu translations tend to omit things that the Chinese consider might be unpalatable to foreigners. **Pointing** is all that's required at street stalls and small restaurants, where the ingredients are displayed out the front in buckets, bundles and cages; canteens usually have the fare laid out or will have the selection scrawled illegibly on strips of paper or a board hung on the wall. You either tell the cook directly what you want or buy chits from a cashier, which you exchange at the kitchen hatch for your food and sit down at large communal tables or benches.

When you enter a **proper restaurant** you'll be escorted to a chair and promptly given a pot of tea, along with pickles and nuts in upmarket places. The only tableware provided is a spoon, bowl, and a pair of chopsticks, and at this point the Chinese will ask for a flask of boiling water and a bowl to wash it all in – not usually necessary, but something of a ritual. A menu will be produced, if they have one, but otherwise you might be escorted through to the kitchen to make your choice. Alternatively, have a look at what other diners are eating – the Chinese are often delighted that a foreigner wants to eat Chinese food, and will indicate the best food on their table.

One thing to watch out for is getting the idea across when you want different items cooked together (say *yikuair*) – otherwise you might end up with separate plates of nuts, meat and vegetables when you thought you'd ordered a single dish of chicken with cashews and green peppers. Note also that unless you're specific about how you want your food prepared, it inevitably arrives stir-fried.

Dishes are all **served** at once, placed in the middle of the table for diners to share. To handle **chopsticks**, hold one halfway along its length like a pencil, then slide the other underneath and use them as an extension of your fingers to pick up the food – though note that rice is shovelled in using the chopsticks, with the bowl up against your lips, while soft or slippery foods such as tofu or mushrooms are managed with **spoons**. With some poultry dishes you can crunch up the smaller bones, but anything else is spat out on to the tablecloth or floor, more or less discreetly depending on the establishment – watch what others are doing. Soups tend to be bland and are consumed last (except in the south where they may be served first or as part of the main meal) to wash the meal down, the liquid slurped from a spoon or the bowl once the noodles, vegetables or meat in it have been picked out and eaten. **Desserts** aren't a regular feature in China, though in the south sweet soups and buns are eaten (the latter not confined to main meals), particularly at festive occasions.

Resting your chopsticks together across the top of your bowl means that you've **finished** eating. After a meal the Chinese don't hang around to talk over drinks as in the West, but get up straight away and leave. In canteens you'll **pay** up front, while at restaurants you ask for the bill and pay either the waiter or at the front till. **Tipping** is not expected in mainland China.

Drinking

Water is easily available in China, but never drink what comes out of the tap. **Boiled water** is always on hand in hotels and trains, either provided in large vacuum flasks or an urn, and you can buy **bottled spring water** at station stalls and supermarkets – read the labels and you'll see some unusual substances (such as radon) listed, which you'd probably want to avoid.

Tea

Tea was introduced into China from India around 1800 years ago, and was originally drunk for medicinal reasons. Although its health properties are still important, and some food halls sell nourishing or stimulating varieties by the bowlful, over the centuries a whole social culture has sprung up around this beverage, spawning teahouses which once held the same place in Chinese society that the local pub or bar does in the West. Plantations of neat rows of low tea bushes adorn hillsides across southern China, while the brew is enthusiastically consumed from the highlands of Tibet – where it's mixed with barley meal and butter – to every restaurant and household between Hong Kong and Beijing.

Often the first thing you'll be asked in a restaurant is *he shenme cha* – "what sort of tea would you like?" Chinese tea comes in red, green and flower-scented **varieties**, depending on how it's processed; only Hainan produces Indian-style black tea. Some regional kinds, such as *pu'er* from Yunnan, Fujian's *tie guanyin*, Zhejiang's *longjing*, or Sichuan's *zhuye qing*, are highly sought after – if you like the local style, head for the nearest market and stock up. Though tea is never drunk with milk and only very rarely with sugar, the manner in which it's served also varies from place to place: sometimes it comes in huge mugs with a lid, elsewhere in dainty cups served from a miniature pot; there are also formalized **tea rituals** in parts of Fujian and Guangdong. When drinking in company, it's polite to top up others' cups before your own, whenever they become empty; if someone does this

for you, lightly tap your first two fingers on the table to show your thanks. If you've had enough, leave your cup full, and in a restaurant take the lid off or turn it over if you want the pot refilled during the meal.

It's also worth trying some **Muslim tea**, which involves dried fruit, nuts, seeds, crystallized sugar and tea heaped into a cup with the remaining space filled with hot water, poured with panache from an immensely long-spouted copper kettle. Also known as *babao cha*, or Eight Treasures Tea, it's becoming widely available in upmarket restaurants everywhere, and is sometimes sold in packets from street stalls.

Alcohol

The popularity of **beer** – *pijiu* – in China rivals that of tea, and, for men, is the preferred mealtime beverage (drinking alcohol in public is considered improper for Chinese women, though not for foreigners). The first brewery was set up in the northeastern port of Qingdao by the Germans in the nineteenth century, and now, though the Tsingtao label is widely available, just about every province produces at least one brand of four percent Pilsner. Sold in litre bottles, it's always drinkable, often pretty good, and is actually cheaper than bottled water. Draught beer is becoming available across the country.

Watch out for the term "**wine**" on English menus, which usually denotes **spirits**, made from rice (*mijiu*), sorghum or millet (*baijiu*). Serving spirits to guests is a sign of hospitality, and they're always used for toasting at banquets. Again, local home-made varieties can be quite good, while mainstream brands – especially the expensive, nationally famous Maotai and Wuliangye – are pretty vile to the Western palate. **Imported beers and spirits** are sold in large department stores and in city bars, but are always expensive. China does actually have a couple of commercial **vineyards** producing the mediocre Great Wall and Dynasty labels, more of a status symbol than an attempt to rival Western growers. Far better are the local pressings in Xinjiang province, where the population of Middle Eastern descent takes its grapes seriously.

Western-style bars are found not only in Hong Kong and Macau, but also in the major mainland cities. These establishments serve both local and imported beers and spirits, and are popular with China's middle class as well as foreigners. Mostly, though, the Chinese drink alcohol only with their meals – all restaurants serve at least local beer and *baijiu*.

Soft drinks

Canned products, usually sold unchilled, include various lemonades and colas. **Fruit juices** can be unusual and refreshing, however, flavoured with chunks of lychee, lotus and water chestnuts. **Coffee** is grown and drunk in Yunnan and Hainan, and imported brews are available in cafés; you can buy instant powder in any supermarket. **Milk** is sold in powder form as baby food, and increasingly in bottles for adult consumption as its benefits for invalids and the elderly become accepted wisdom. Sweetened **yoghurt drinks**, available all over the country in little packs of six, are a popular treat for children, though their high sugar content won't do your teeth much good on a regular basis.

Communications

China's communications system is pretty modern and user-friendly, even in some of the more obscure towns. Internet access is cheap and widely available (if sometimes restricted by censorship), and phone and mail services are reliable.

Mail

The Chinese mail service is fast and efficient, with letters taking less than a day to reach destinations in the same city, two or more days to other destinations in China, and up to several weeks to destinations abroad. Overseas postage rates are fairly expensive and vary depending on weight, destination, and also – not so surprising given China's size – where you are in the country. An Express Mail Service (**EMS**) operates to most countries and to most destinations within China; besides cutting delivery times, the service ensures the letter or parcel is sent by registered delivery.

Main **post offices** are open seven days a week between about 8am and 8pm; smaller offices may close earlier or for lunch, or be closed at weekends. As well as at post offices, you can post letters in green **postboxes**, though these are few and far between except in the biggest cities, or at tourist hotels, which usually have a postbox at the front desk. Envelopes can be frustratingly scarce; try the stationery sections of department stores.

To send **parcels**, turn up at the main post office with the goods you want to send and the staff will help you pack them, a service which costs only a few yuan; don't try to do it yourself, as your package will have to be unpacked to ensure it is packed correctly. Boxes must be those issued by the post office. Once packed, but before the parcel is sealed, it must be checked at the customs window. In some parts of the country, especially the south, you'll find separate parcels offices near the post office. Though parcel post from China is reliable, you'll have to complete masses of paperwork, so don't be in a hurry. If you are sending valuable goods bought in China, put the receipt or a photocopy of it in with the parcel, as it may be opened for customs inspection farther down the line.

Poste restante services are available in any city. Mail is kept for several months, and you'll need to present ID when picking it up. Mail is often eccentrically filed – to cut down on misfiling, your name should be printed clearly at the top of the letter and the surname underlined, but it's still worth checking all the other pigeonholes just in case. Have letters addressed to you c/o Poste Restante, GPO, street, town or city, province. You can also leave a message for someone in the poste restante box, but you'll have to buy a stamp.

Phones

Local calls are free from land lines, and long-distance China-wide calls are ¥0.3 a minute. Note that everywhere in China has an **area code** which must be used when phoning from outside that locality; area codes are given for all telephone numbers throughout the guide. International calls cost from ¥3.5 a minute (much cheaper if you use an IP internet phone card – see below).

You can make international calls from offices of the state-run **China Telecom**, usually located next to or within the main post office and usually open 24 hours. You pay a deposit of ¥100 and are told to go to a particular booth. When you have finished, the charge for the call is worked out automatically and you pay at the desk. You may find that a minimum charge for three minutes applies. You can also make IDD calls from streetside telephone shops (generally displaying "IDD" on a sign). These usually charge by the minute, but always check in advance.

Alternatively, tourist hotels offer direct dialling abroad from your room, but will add a surcharge, and a minimum charge equivalent to between one and three minutes will be levied even if the call goes unanswered. The **business centres** you'll find in most big hotels offer fax, telephone, Internet and telex services (as well as photocopying and typing), and you don't have to be a guest to use them – though prices for all these services are typically extortionate. Hotels also charge for receiving faxes, usually around ¥10 per page.

Card phones, widely available in major cities, are the cheapest way to make domestic long-distance calls (¥0.2 for 3min), and can also be used for international calls (under ¥10 for 3min). They take **IC Cards**, which come in units of ¥20, ¥50 and ¥100. There's a fifty percent discount after 6pm and on weekends. You will be cut off when your card value drops below the amount needed for the next minute.

Yet another option is the **IP** (Internet Phone) **card**, which can be used from any phone, and comes in ¥100 units. You dial a local number, then a PIN, then the number you're calling. Rates are as low as ¥2.4 per minute to the US and Canada, ¥3.2 to Europe.

Mobile phones

Your **mobile phone** may already be compatible with the Chinese network (visitors from North America should ensure their phones are GSM/Triband), though note that you will pay a premium to use it abroad, and that

Dialling codes

To call mainland China from abroad, dial your international access code (usually ☎00 in the UK and the Republic of Ireland, ☎011 in the US and Canada, ☎0011 in Australia and ☎00 in New Zealand), then 86 (China's country code), then area code (minus initial zero) followed by the number.

To call Hong Kong, dial your international access code followed by ☎852, then the number; and for Macau dial your international access code, then ☎853 and then the number.

Phoning abroad from China

To call abroad from mainland China, Macau or Hong Kong, dial ☎00, then the country code (see below), then the area code minus initial zero (if any), followed by the number.

UK ☎44	Ireland ☎353	Australia ☎61
New Zealand ☎64	US & Canada ☎1	

Note that all of China is within the same **time zone**; see p.75 for details.

callers within China have to make an international call to reach your phone. For more information, check the manual that came with your phone, or with the manufacturer and/or your telephone service provider. Alternatively, once in China you can buy a GSM SIM card (¥80–200) from any outlet of China Mobile, which gives you a new number for use within China – the SIM card price depends on the amount of "lucky" (and much sought-after) sixes and eights in the number.

Internet

Domestic interest in the Internet is huge, and with personal computer ownership still low, there are cramped **Internet cafés** (*wangba*) throughout the country, crammed with young people surfing (and indulging in networked gaming). A good place to find Net cafés is in the vicinity of colleges and universities, around which there's usually a cluster. In the unlikely event of your being turned away by a Net café, this is generally because many aren't licensed, and don't want the additional responsibility of hosting foreigners on the premises.

While getting online is cheap at ¥2–5 an hour generally, you can't be sure of actually getting at the websites you want. In response to the perceived threat of free access to information, the government has constructed a **firewall** (wryly nicknamed the new Great Wall) to block access to politically sensitive sites. The way this is administered shifts regularly according to the mood among the powers that be – restrictions were loosened, for example, while Beijing was campaigning to be awarded the 2008 summer Olympics (the government was anxious to be seen not to be oppressing its subjects) – but in general you can be pretty sure you won't be able to access the BBC or CNN or the White House, though newspaper websites tend to be left unhindered.

The media

The Chinese news agency, Xinhua, is a state-run organization with an office in every province. Their monopoly on domestic news means that everything you read in newspapers or see on TV will have a pro-Party slant, whatever the content. A few expat-run magazines help to balance the picture slightly, though for serious news you're better off resorting to the Internet.

Newspapers and magazines

The main Chinese-language daily newspaper is the *People's Daily*, which has an online English edition at Ⓦenglish.peopledaily.com.cn. The only English-language newspaper is the *China Daily*, which is scarce outside Beijing, though you can always get it online at Ⓦwww.chinadaily.com.cn. The stories of economic success written in turgid prose may be mind-numbing, but the paper also has a Beijing listings section and articles on uncontroversial aspects of Chinese culture.

Other official English-language publications such as *Beijing Review* and *Business Beijing* are glossy titles, again very difficult to get hold of outside the capital, with articles on investment opportunities, the latest state successes, as well as interesting places to visit.

Despite the heavy **censorship** of the mainland press, stories sometimes break that the Party would rather people didn't know about, such as the appalling conditions of coal-mine workers, or the spread of AIDS through unscreened blood transfusions. It's a brave editor who prints such stuff: in 2004 the editor of the Guangzhou-based *Southern Metropolis Daily* was jailed for reporting the SARS epidemic before the government admitted it existed.

A good range of English-language newspapers and magazines is published in **Hong Kong**, including the *South China Morning Post*, the *Hong Kong Standard*, the *Eastern Express* and the *Far Eastern Economic Review*. Asian editions of a number of international magazines and newspapers are also produced here – *Time*, *Newsweek*, the *Asian Wall Street Journal* and *USA Today*, for example. Surprisingly, all these have so far remained free (and openly critical of Beijing on occasion), despite the former colony's changeover to Chinese control.

It's also worth getting hold of the free English-language **magazines aimed at expats** available in Beijing, Shanghai and Guangzhou, which contain listings of local venues and events, plus classifieds and feature articles; they're closely monitored by the authorities, though this doesn't stop them sailing quite close to the wind at times. In large cities you'll also find copies of (generally uncensored) imported publications such as *Time*, *Newsweek* and the *Far Eastern Economic Review*. Try branches of the Friendship Store (the state-run department store) or big tourist hotels for these.

TV and radio

There is the occasional item of interest on mainland Chinese **television**, though you'd have to be very bored to resort to it for entertainment. Domestic travel and wildlife programmes are common, as are song-and-dance extravaganzas, the most entertaining of which feature dancers performing in fetishistic, tight-fitting military gear while party officials watch with rigor-mortis faces. Soap operas and historical dramas are popular, and often feature a few foreigners; also screened are 20-year-old American thrillers and war films. Chinese war films, in which the Japanese are shown getting mightily beaten, at least have the advantage that you don't need to speak the language to understand what's going on. The same goes for the flirty dating gameshows, where male contestants proudly state their qualifications and height. CCTV, the state broadcaster, has an English-language channel, CCTV9, showing travel, cultural, news and "what's on" shows laced with a dollop of propaganda, which are interesting enough in small doses.

On the **radio** you're likely to hear the latest soft ballads, often from Taiwan or Hong Kong, or versions of Western pop songs sung in Chinese. For news from home, you may want to bring a **short-wave radio** with you; see the websites of the BBC World Service (@www.bbc.co.uk /worldservice), Radio Canada (@www .rcinet.ca), the Voice of America (@www .voa.gov) and Radio Australia (@www.abc. net.au/ra) for schedules and frequencies.

Opening hours, public holidays and festivals

Officially China has a five-day week, with offices – airlines, travel services and the like – enjoying relatively early opening and closing, with long lunch hours. Generalization is difficult, though, as there is no real equivalent to the role that Sunday plays in the West as the day of rest. Post and telecommunications offices open daily, often until late at night. Shops, too, nearly all open daily, keeping long, late hours, especially in big cities. Although banks *usually* close on Sundays – or for the whole weekend – even this is not always the case.

Tourist **sights** such as parks, pagodas and temples open every day, usually between 8am and 5pm and without a lunch break. Most public parks open from about 6am, ready to receive the morning flood of *tai ji* practitioners. Museums, however, tend to have slightly more restricted hours, including lunch breaks and one closing day a week, often Monday or Tuesday. If you arrive at an out-of-the-way place that seems to be closed, however, don't despair – knocking or poking around will often turn up a drowsy doorkeeper. Conversely, you may find other places locked and deserted when they are supposed to be open.

Public holidays and festivals

China celebrates many secular and religious **festivals**, some of which – especially the Spring Festival, Labour Day and National Day – involve public holidays lasting a week or more where businesses may be shut down and half the population go on holiday, making travel impossible or extremely uncomfortable.

Public holidays

A number of **public holidays** have been celebrated since 1949; offices close on these

---

Spring Festival (Chinese New Year)

The **Spring Festival** is two weeks of festivities marking the beginning of the lunar **new year**, usually in late January or early February. In Chinese astrology (see also "Contexts", p.1188), each year is associated with one of twelve animals, and the passing into a new phase is a momentous occasion. The festival sees China at its most colourful, with shops and houses decorated with good-luck messages and stalls and shops selling paper money, drums and costumes. The first day of the festival is marked by a family feast at which *jiaozi* (dumplings) are eaten, sometimes with coins hidden inside. To bring luck, people dress in red clothes (red being a lucky colour) and eat fish, since the Chinese script for fish resembles the script for "surplus", something everyone wishes to enjoy during the year. Firecrackers are let off almost constantly to scare ghosts away and, on the fifth day, to honour **Cai Shen**, god of wealth (in the cities, where fireworks are banned, people play recordings of explosions as a substitute). Another ghost-scaring tradition is the pasting up of images of door gods at the threshold. Outside the home, New Year is celebrated at **temple fairs**, which feature acrobats, drummers, and clouds of smoke as the Chinese light incense sticks to placate the gods. After two weeks, the celebrations end with the **lantern festival**, when the streets are filled with multicoloured paper lanterns, a tradition dating from the Han dynasty. Many places also have flower festivals and street processions with paper dragons and other animals parading through the town. It's customary at this time to eat *tang yuan*, glutinous rice balls stuffed with sweet sesame paste.

dates, though many shops will remain open. The most important of these holidays are January 1 (New Year's Day), May 1 (Labour Day) and October 1 (National Day) – the last two mark the beginning of week-long breaks for many people. There are a few other dates, March 8 (Women's Day), June 1 (Children's Day), July 1 (Chinese Communist Party Day) and August 1 (Army Day), which are celebrated by parades and festive activities by the groups concerned. Businesses and offices tend to operate normally on these dates. A surprising recent introduction is **Christmas**, celebrated here as a secular gift-giving event and more popular each year, primarily in the more Westernized cities.

Traditional festivals

The only traditional Chinese **festival** marked by an official holiday is also the biggest of all, the **Spring Festival** or Chinese New Year. Others, such as the Qingming Festival and the Mid-autumn Festival, aren't marked by holidays, though you may notice a growing tendency for businesses to operate restricted hours at these times.

Most festivals take place according to dates in the Chinese **lunar calendar**, in which the first day of the month is the time when the moon is at its thinnest, with the full moon marking the middle of the month. By the Gregorian calendar used in the West, such festivals fall on a different day every year – check online for the latest dates. Most festivals celebrate the turning of the seasons or auspicious dates, such as the eighth day of the eighth month (eight is a lucky number in China), and are times for gift giving, family reunion and feasting. In the countryside, lanterns are lit and **firecrackers** (banned in the cities) are set off. It's always worth visiting temples on festival days, when the air is thick with incense, and people queue up to kowtow to altars and play games that bring good fortune, such as trying to hit the temple bell by throwing coins.

Aside from the following national festivals, China's **ethnic groups** punctuate the year with their own ritual observances, which are described in the relevant chapters of the Guide. In Hong Kong all the national Chinese festivals are celebrated.

A holidays and festivals calendar

January/February Spring Festival.

February Tiancang Festival. On the twentieth day of the first lunar month Chinese peasants celebrate Tiancang, or Granary Filling Day, in the hope of ensuring a good harvest later in the year.

March Guanyin's Birthday. Guanyin, the Goddess of Mercy, and probably China's most popular deity, is celebrated, most colourfully in Taoist temples, on the nineteenth day of the second lunar month.

April 5 Qingming Festival. This festival, also referred to as Tomb Sweeping Day, is the time to visit the graves of ancestors and burn ghost money in honour of the departed.

April 13–15 Water Splashing Festival. Popular in Yunnan Province. Anyone on the streets is fair game for a soaking.

May 4 Youth Day. Commemorating the student demonstrators in Tian'anmen Square in 1919, which gave rise to the Nationalist "May Fourth Movement". It's marked in most cities with flower displays.

June 1 Children's Day. Most schools go on field trips, so if you're visiting a popular tourist site be prepared for mobs of kids in yellow baseball caps.

June/July Dragon-boat Festival. On the fifth day of the fifth lunar month dragon-boat races are held in memory of the poet Qu Yuan, who drowned himself in 280 BC. Some of the most famous venues for this festival in the country are Yueyang in Hunan province, and Hong Kong. The traditional food to accompany the celebrations is *zongzi* (lotus-wrapped rice packets).

August/September Ghost Festival. The Chinese equivalent of Halloween, this is a time when ghosts from hell are supposed to walk the earth. It's not celebrated so much as observed; it's regarded as an inauspicious time to travel, move house or get married.

September/October Moon Festival. On the fifteenth day of the eighth month of the lunar calendar the Chinese celebrate the Moon Festival, also known as the Mid-autumn Festival, a time of family reunion that is celebrated with fireworks and lanterns. Moon cakes, containing a rich filling of sugar, lotus-seed paste and walnut, are eaten, and plenty of Maotai is consumed. In Hong Kong, the cakes sometimes contain salted duck egg yolks.

September/October Double Ninth Festival. Nine is a number associated with yang, or male energy, and on the ninth day of the ninth lunar month such qualities as assertiveness and strength are celebrated. It's believed to be a good time for the distillation (and consumption) of spirits.

September 28 Confucius Festival. The birthday of Confucius is marked by celebrations at all Confucian temples. It's a good time to visit Qufu, in Shandong province, when elaborate ceremonies are held at the temple there.

October 1 National Day. Everyone has a day off to celebrate the founding of the People's Republic. TV is even more dire than usual as it's full of programmes celebrating Party achievements.

December 25 Christmas. This is marked as a religious event only by the faithful, but for everyone else it's an excuse for a feast and a party.

Crime and personal safety

Despite its new veneer of individual freedom, China remains a police state, with the state interfering with and controlling the lives of its subjects to a degree most Westerners would find hard to tolerate – as indeed many of the Chinese do. This should not affect foreigners much, however, as the state mostly takes a hands-off approach to visitors – they are anxious that you have a good time rather than come away with a bad impression of the country. Indeed, Chinese who commit crimes against foreigners are treated much more harshly than if their victims had been native.

Crime is a growth industry in China, with official corruption and juvenile offences the worst problems. Much of it is put down to spiritual pollution by foreign influences, the result of increasing liberalization. But serious social problems such as mass unemployment are more to blame, as is the get-rich-quick attitude that has become the prevailing ideology.

The police

The police, known as the Public Security Bureau or **PSB** (*gong'an ju* in Chinese), are recognizable by their green uniforms and caps, though there are a lot more around than you might at first think, as plenty are undercover. They have much wider powers than most Western police forces, including establishing the guilt of criminals – trials are used only for deciding the sentence of the accused (though this is changing and China now has the beginnings of an independent judiciary). If the culprit is deemed to show proper remorse, this will result in a more lenient sentence. Laws are harsh, with execution – a bullet in the back of the head – the penalty for a wide range of serious crimes, from corruption to rape.

The PSB also have the job of looking after foreigners, and you'll most likely have to seek them out for **visa extensions**, reporting theft or losses and obtaining permits for otherwise closed areas of the country (mostly in Tibet). On occasion, they might seek you out; it's fairly common for the police to call round to your hotel room if you're staying in an out-of-the-way place that sees few foreigners – they usually just look at your passport and then move on.

While individual police can go out of their way to help foreigners, the PSB itself has all the problems of any police force in a country where corruption is widespread, and it's best to minimize contact with them.

Emergencies

In mainland China dial the following numbers in an emergency:

Police	☏110
Fire	☏119
Ambulance	☏120

In Hong Kong and Macau, dial ☏999 for any of the emergency services.

Crime and petty theft

Violent crime is on the increase in China, and while there is no need for paranoia, you do need to take care. Wandering around cities late at night is as bad an idea in China as anywhere else; similarly, walking alone across the countryside is ill-advised, particularly in remote regions. Both situations have resulted in the murder of foreign tourists in recent years. If anyone does try to rob you, try to stay calm but don't resist.

Less dangerously, you may also see a fair number of **street confrontations**, when huge crowds gather to watch a few protagonists push each other around – though such fights rarely result in violence, just a lot of shouting. Mostly they're just caused by stress, and tend to occur where the crowds are at their most overwhelming, such as at bus stations. Another irritation, particularly in the southern cities, are gangs of **child beggars**, organized by a nearby adult. They target foreigners and can be very hard to shake off; handing over money usually results in increased harassment.

Theft

As a tourist, you are an obvious target for **petty thieves**. Passports and money should be kept in a concealed money belt rather than shoulder or waist bags. Be wary on **buses**, the favoured haunt of pickpockets, and **trains**, particularly in hard-seat class and on overnight journeys. Take a chain and padlock to secure your luggage in the rack.

Hotel rooms are on the whole secure, dormitories much less so, though often it's your fellow travellers who are the problem here. Most hotels should have a safe, but it's not unusual for things to go missing from these. It's a good idea to keep around US$200 separately from the rest of your cash, together with your traveller's-cheque receipts, insurance policy details, and photocopies of your passport and visa.

On the street, try not to be too ostentatious with flashy jewellery or watches, and be discreet when taking out your cash. Not looking obviously wealthy also helps if you want to avoid being ripped off by traders and taxi drivers, as does telling them you are a student – the Chinese have a great respect for education, and much more sympathy for foreign students than for tourists.

If you do have anything stolen, you'll need to get the PSB (locations are given throughout the Guide) to write up a **loss report** in order to claim on your insurance. Though most PSB offices have English-speakers around, take a Chinese-speaker with you if possible, and be prepared to pay a small fee. Make sure they understand that you need a loss report for insurance purposes, otherwise you could spend hours in the station as the police fill out a crime sheet, which is no use either to you or them.

Offences to avoid

With adjacent opium-growing areas in Burma and Laos, and a major Southeast Asian distribution point in Hong Kong, China has a growing **drug** problem. The Chinese are hard on offenders, with dealers and smugglers facing execution, and users forced into rehabilitation. Even so, heroin use has become fairly widespread in the south, particularly in depressed rural areas, and ecstasy is used in clubs and discos – which explains the periodic police raids on these places. In the past, the police have turned a blind eye to foreigners with drugs, as long as no Chinese are involved, but you don't want to test this out. On the annual UN anti-drugs day in June, China regularly holds mass executions of convicted drug offenders.

Visitors are not likely to be accused of **political crimes**, but foreign residents, including teachers or students, may find themselves expelled from the country for talking about politics or religion. The Chinese they talk to will be treated less leniently. In Tibet, and at sensitive border areas, censorship is taken much more seriously; **photographing** military installations (which can include major road bridges), instances of police brutality or gulags is not a good idea.

Sexual attitudes and behaviour

Women travellers usually find incidences of **sexual harassment** less of a problem than in other Asian countries. Chinese men are, on the whole, deferential and respectful. A much more likely complaint is being ignored, as the Chinese will generally assume that any man accompanying a woman will be doing all the talking. White women may get some hassles, however, in Dongbei, where Chinese men may take you for a Russian prostitute, and in Muslim Xinjiang. Women on their own visiting remote temples or sights definitely need to be on their guard – don't assume that all monks and caretakers have impeccable morals. As ever, it pays to be aware of how local women dress and behave accordingly: miniskirts and heels may be fine in the cosmopolitan cities, but fashions are much more conservative in the countryside.

Prostitution, though illegal, has made a big comeback – witness all the "hairdressers", saunas and massage parlours, every one of them a brothel. Single foreign men are likely to be approached inside hotels; it's common practice for prostitutes to phone around hotel rooms at all hours of the night. Bear in mind that China is hardly Thailand – consequences may be dire if you are caught – and that AIDS is on the increase.

Homosexuality is technically illegal, though increasingly tolerated by the authorities and people in general. There are gay bars in most major cities, especially Beijing and Shanghai.

Cultural hints

Some of the culture shock which afflicts foreign visitors to China comes from false expectations, engendered through travel in other parts of Asia. The Chinese are not a "mellow" people, being neither particularly spiritual nor gentle, nor deferential to strangers. However, many of the irritations experienced by foreigners – the sniggers and the unhelpful service – can almost invariably be put down to nervousness and the language barrier, rather than hostility.

Visitors who speak Chinese will encounter an endless series of delighted and amazed interlocutors wherever they go, invariably asking about their age and marital status before anything else. Even if you don't speak Chinese, you will regularly run into locals eager to practise their English.

If such encounters lead to an invitation to someone's home, a **gift** might well be expected, though people will not open it in front of you, nor will they express profuse gratitude for it. The Chinese way to express gratitude is through reciprocal actions rather than words. Indeed, elaborate protestations of thanks can be taken as an attempt to avoid obligation. If you are lucky enough to be asked out to a restaurant, you will discover that **restaurant bills** are not shared out between the guests but instead people will go to great lengths to claim the honour of paying the whole bill by themselves. Normally that honour will fall to the person perceived as the most senior, and as a foreigner dining with Chinese you should make some effort to stake your claim, though it is probable that someone else will grab the bill before you do. Attempting to pay a "share" of the bill may cause serious embarrassment.

Privacy

Another factor that foreign tourists need to note is that the Chinese have almost no concept of **privacy**. People will stare at each other from point-blank range and pluck letters or books out of others' hands for close inspection. Even toilets are built with partitions so low that you can chat with your neighbour while squatting. All leisure activities including visits to natural beauty spots or holy relics are done in large noisy groups, and the desire of some Western tourists to be "left alone" is variously interpreted by locals as eccentric, arrogant or even sinister.

Exotic foreigners inevitably become targets for **blatant curiosity**. People stare and point, voices on the street shout out "helloooo" twenty times a day, or – in rural areas – people even run up and jostle for a better look, exclaiming loudly to each other, *laowai, laowai* ("foreigner"). This is not usually intended to be aggressive or insulting, though the cumulative effects of such treatment can be very alienating. One way to render yourself human again is to address the onlookers in Chinese, if you can. Otherwise, perhaps you should just be grateful that people are showing an interest in you.

Spitting and smoking

Various other forms of behaviour perceived as antisocial in the West are considered perfectly normal in China. Take the widespread habit of **spitting**, for example, which can be observed in buses, trains, restaurants and even inside people's homes. Outside the company of urban sophisticates, it would not occur to people that there was anything disrespectful in delivering a powerful spit while in conversation with a stranger. **Smoking**, likewise, is almost universal among men, and any attempt to stop others from lighting up is met with incomprehension. As in many countries, handing out cigarettes is a basic way of establishing goodwill, and non-smokers should be apologetic about turning down offered cigarettes.

Clothing

Although China would not normally be described as a liberal country, these days restraints on public behaviour are disappearing remarkably fast. **Skimpy clothing** in summer is quite normal in all urban areas, particularly among women (less so in the countryside), and even in potentially sensitive Muslim areas, such as the far west, many Han Chinese girls insist on wearing miniskirts and see-through blouses. Although Chinese men commonly wear short trousers and expose their midriffs in hot weather, Western men who do the same should note that the bizarre sight of hairy flesh in public – chest or legs – will instantly become the focus of giggly gossip. The generally relaxed approach to clothing applies equally when visiting temples, though in **mosques** men and women alike should cover their bodies above the wrists and ankles. As for beachwear, bikinis and briefs are in, but nudity has yet to make its debut.

Skimpy clothing is one thing, but **scruffy clothing** is quite another. If you want to earn the respect of the Chinese – useful for things like getting served in a restaurant or checking into a hotel – you need to make some effort with your appearance. While the average Chinese peasant might reasonably be expected to have wild hair and wear dirty clothes, for a rich foreigner to do so is likely to arouse a degree of contempt.

Meeting people

Another good way to ease your progress when meeting people is to have a name or **business card** to flash around – even better if you can include your name in Chinese characters on it.

Shaking hands is not a Chinese tradition, though it is now fairly common between men. Bodily contact in the form of embraces or back-slapping can be observed between same-sex friends, and these days, in cities, a boy and a girl can walk round arm in arm and even kiss without raising an eyebrow. **Voice level** in China seems to be pitched several decibels louder than in most other countries, though this should not necessarily be interpreted as a sign of belligerence.

Work and study

There are increasing opportunities to work or study in China. Many foreign workers are employed as English-language teachers, and most universities and many private colleges now have a few foreign teachers.

Increasingly on the mainland – and certainly in Guangzhou, Shanghai, Beijing, Kunming and Chengdu – there are no restrictions on where foreigners can **reside**, though either you or your landlord are supposed to seek approval and register your presence with the local PSB. **Property rental** is inexpensive on the whole – two-bedroom flats cost upwards from ¥600 a month – though it's hard to get less than a six-month contract. The easiest way to find accommodation is to go through an agent, who will generally charge one month's rent on the property you choose. There are plenty who advertise in expat magzines and online.

Teaching

There are schemes in operation to place **foreign teachers** in Chinese educational institutions – contact your nearest Chinese embassy (see p.34 for addresses) for details. Some employers ask for a TEFL qualification, though a degree, or simply the ability to speak the language as a native, is usually enough.

Teaching at a **university**, you'll earn about ¥1500 a month, more than a Chinese worker earns, but not enough to allow you to put any aside. The pay is bolstered by subsidised on-campus accommodation – a room in a foreigners' dormitory, usually without a phone. Contracts are generally for one year. Foreign university teachers have a workload of between ten and twenty hours a week – a lot more than their Chinese counterparts have to do. Most teachers find their students keen, hardworking, curious and obedient, and report that it was the contact with them that made the experience worthwhile. That said, avoid talking about religion or politics in the classroom as this can get them to trouble. You'll earn more – up to ¥150 per hour – in a **private school**, though be aware of the risk of being ripped off by a commercial agency; it's possibly best to organize this once you're in China. For **teaching vacancies**, look in the expat magazines or on websites such as Ⓦ www.chinatefl.com, or approach the universities directly.

Studying in China

Many universities in China now host substantial populations of **Western students**, especially in Beijing, Shanghai and Xi'an. Indeed, the numbers of foreigners at these places are so large that in some ways you're shielded from much of a "China experience", and you may find smaller centres like Chengdu and Kunming offer both a mellower pace of life and more contact with Chinese outside the campus.

Most foreign students come to China to study **Mandarin**, though there are many additonal options available – from martial arts to traditional opera or classical literature – once you break the language barrier. Courses cost from US$2400 a year, or US$800 a semester. Hotel-style campus accommodation costs around US$10 a day; most people move out as soon as they speak enough Chinese to rent a flat, which is much cheaper.

Your first resource is the nearest Chinese embassy, which can provide a list of contact details for Chinese universities offering the courses you are interested in. Be aware, however, that universities' promotional material may have little bearing on what is actually provided; though teaching standards are good, university administration departments are often confused or misleading places. Ideally, visit the campus first and be wary of paying course fees up front until you've spoken to a few students.

Commercial opportunities

There are plenty of **white-collar jobs** available for foreigners in mainland China, mostly with foreign firms, though some facility with Chinese is usually required; it's best to turn up in Beijing and Shanghai and trawl around offices or through expat magazines. The job market in Hong Kong is tighter, and specialist skills are usually required if you're going to land employment there; for more information, check the *Rough Guide to Hong Kong and Macau*.

Directory

Addresses Chinese street names often indicate the section of the street concerned, usually by adding the cardinal direction – *bei*, *nan*, *xi* or *dong* for north, south, west and east respectively, or sometimes *zhong* to indicate a central stretch. *Jie* means street; *da* before it simply means big. Thus Jiefang Bei Dajie literally refers to the north section of Liberation Big Street. While street names aren't hard to figure out, the numbering of premises along streets is so random in most Chinese cities that it's little help in finding the address. Note that within buildings, street level is the "First Floor", the next storey is the "Second Floor", and so on.

Admission charges Virtually all tourist sights attract some kind of admission charge, often no more than a few yuan. Usually there is a special student price which you can qualify for if you have a student card.

Airport departure tax Currently ¥50 for internal flights (often incorporated into the price of a ticket) and ¥90 if you're leaving the country.

CDs, VCDs and DVDs Just about every market and bookstore in China has a range of music CDs of everything from Beijing punk to Beethoven, plus VCDs and DVDs of martial-arts movies (often subtitled – check on the back), Hollywood blockbusters, instructional martial-arts or language courses, and computer software. While extremely cheap at ¥2–15, note that most films, foreign music and software are pirated (the discs may be confiscated at customs when you get home). Note also that Chinese DVDs may be region-coded for Asia, so check the label and whether your player at home will handle them. There are no such problems with CDs or VCDs.

Clothes and shoes Clothes are a very good deal in China, with brand stores such as Giordano, Baleno, Meters/Bonwe, Yishion and Hum Phry selling smart-casual jeans, shirts, sweaters, jackets and fleeces for a fraction of what you'd pay at home. Outdoor gear is also increasingly cheap, but tends to look much better than it turns out to be – beware of fake brand labels. Shoes are similarly inexpensive, though sizes are relatively limited.

Contraceptives Condoms are easy to get hold of, with imported brands available in all the big cities.

Deodorant Impossible to buy on the mainland; if it's important, bring it with you.

Disabled travel Mainland China makes no provisions for disabled travellers. In Hong Kong, contact the Hong Kong Tourist Association (ⓦ www.hkta.org) for their free booklet, *Hong Kong Access Guide for Disabled Visitors*.

Electricity The current is 220V on the mainland and most of Macau, and 200V in Hong Kong. Mainland plugs come with two prongs, either round or flattened, while Hong Kong uses the British triple square pin, so a travel conversion plug is useful. A flashlight is also useful, given the erratic power supply.

Laundry Most tourist hotels have a laundry service, though it's not usually cheap. Clothes will be returned the following day.

Left luggage Some hotels will store luggage, and there are always guarded, moderately secure luggage offices at train and bus stations (sometimes open only from dawn to dusk, however) where you can leave your possessions for a few yuan.

Photography Photography is a popular pastime among the Chinese, and all big mainland towns and cities have plenty of places to buy and process 35mm film. In Hong Kong there's likely to be at least as big a range as wherever you've come from; elsewhere, colour print stock is the most widely available. Mainland Chinese brands cost about ¥10 for 36 exposures, scarcer Western varieties are around ¥20. Slide film costs about ¥60 a roll. Processing is very variable in quality and costs about ¥15 per roll. Camera batteries are fairly easy to obtain in big city department stores. Hong Kong has every imaginable type, but it's best to bring a supply with you. Most photo stores can download digital images from your camera onto disc; the service takes an hour or so and costs up to ¥30.

Tampons Tampons can be hard to find, but good sanitary towels are widely available in supermarkets and department stores, and are reasonably cheap.

Things to take Unless you're a big fan of nineteenth-century literature – just about all that is available in English translation – take a few meaty books for the long train rides. Coins and stamps from your country are a good idea – they will cause much excitement and curiosity and make good small presents.

Another aid to bridging the language gap is a few photos of your family and friends, even where you live. China is rarely a quiet place, and for the sake of your sanity as well as comfort, earplugs are a good idea, especially if you're contemplating long bus journeys. It's also advisable to take a set of your own chopsticks, for hygiene reasons. Also worth taking are: a universal plug adaptor and universal sink plug; a flashlight; a multi-purpose penknife; a needle and thread; and a first-aid kit (see p.39). If you'll be travelling in the subtropical south or at high altitudes, bring high-factor sun block and good-quality sunglasses.

Time China occupies a single time zone, eight hours ahead of GMT, sixteen hours ahead of US Pacific Standard Time, thirteen hours ahead of US Eastern Standard Time and two hours behind Australian Eastern Standard Time.

Tipping Not expected on the mainland, but in Hong Kong you might want to tip in restaurants where they don't already levy a ten-percent service charge.

Toilets Chinese toilets can take a lot of getting used to. Apart from the often disgusting standard of hygiene, the lack of privacy can be very off-putting – squat toilets are separated by a low, thin partition or no partition at all. The public kind are typically awful, though any staffed by an attendant should be fairly clean, and you'll have to pay a few jiao before you enter. Probably the best bet is to find a large hotel and use the toilets in the lobby. Most hotel toilets have a wastepaper basket by the side for toilet paper. Don't put paper down the loo as it blocks the primitive sewage system, and staff will get irate with you.

Guide

Guide

CHAPTER 1   # Highlights

✳ **Forbidden City** Imperial magnificence on a grand scale and the centre of the Chinese universe for six centuries. See p.105

✳ **Qianmen area** This tangle of chaotic alleys is a brassy shopping zone, one of the last remnants of the old city. See p.109

✳ **Temple of Heaven** This classic Ming-dynasty building, a picture in stone of ancient Chinese cosmogony, is a masterpiece of architecture and landscpae design. See p.110

✳ **Baiyun Guan** Still functioning, this Taoist temple is ignored by tour groups but is in its way more rewarding than the flashier religious sites. A must during New Year and on festival days,

when it's thronged with worshippers. See p.113

✳ **Summer Palace** Escape the city in this serene and elegant park, dotted with imperial architecture. See p.124

✳ **Hotpot** A northern Chinese classic, a stew of sliced lamb, tofu, cabbage and anything else you fancy boiled up at your table. Specialist restaurants abound, but Neng Ren Ju is one of the best. See p.132

✳ **Acrobatics** The style may be vaudeville, but the stunts, performed by some of the world's greatest acrobats, are breathtaking. See p.136

✳ **The Great Wall** One of the world's most extraordinary engineering achievements, the old boundary between civilizations. See p.143

△ Great Hall of the People, Tian'anmen Square

Beijing and around

The brash modernity of **BEIJING** (the name means "northern capital") comes as a surprise to many visitors. Traversed by freeways (it's the proud owner of more than a hundred flyovers) and spiked with high-rises, this vivid metropolis is China at its most dynamic. For the last thousand years, the drama of China's **imperial history** was played out here, with the emperor sitting enthroned at the centre of the Chinese universe, and though today the city is a very different one, it remains spiritually and politically the heart of the country. Between the swathes of concrete and glass, you'll find some of the lushest temples, and certainly the grandest remnants of the Imperial Age. Unexpectedly, some of the country's most pleasant scenic spots lie within the scope of a day-trip, and, just to the north of the city, is one of China's most famous sights, the old boundary line between civilizations, the **Great Wall**.

First impressions of Beijing are of an almost inhuman vastness, conveyed by the sprawl of apartment buildings in which most of the city's population of fifteen million are housed, and the eight-lane freeways that slice it up. It's an impression that's reinforced on closer acquaintance, from the magnificent **Forbidden City**, with its stunning wealth of treasures, the concrete desert of **Tian'anmen Square** and the gargantuan buildings of the modern executive around it, to the rank after rank of office complexes that line its mammoth roads. Outside the centre, the scale becomes more manageable, with parks, narrow alleyways and ancient sites such as the **Yonghe Gong**, the **Observatory** and, most magnificent of all, the **Temple of Heaven**, offering respite from the city's oppressive orderliness and rampant reconstruction. In the suburbs beyond, the two **Summer Palaces** and the **Western Hills** have been favoured retreats since imperial times.

Beijing is an invaders' city, the capital of oppressive foreign dynasties – the Manchu and the Mongols – and of a dynasty with a foreign ideology – the Communists. As such, it has assimilated a lot of outside influence, and today it is perhaps the most cosmopolitan part of China, with an international flavour reflecting its position as the capital of a major commercial power. As the front line of China's grapple with **modernity** it is being ripped up and rebuilt at a furious pace – attested by the cranes that skewer the skyline and the white character *chai* ("demolish") painted on old buildings. Students in the latest baggy fashions while away their time in Internet cafés and *McDonald's*, hip hop has overtaken the clubs, businessmen are never without their laptops and schoolkids carry mobile phones in their lunchboxes. Red-light districts and gay bars are appearing as the city hits its own sexual revolution. Rising incomes have led not just to a consumer-capitalist society Westerners will feel very familiar with,

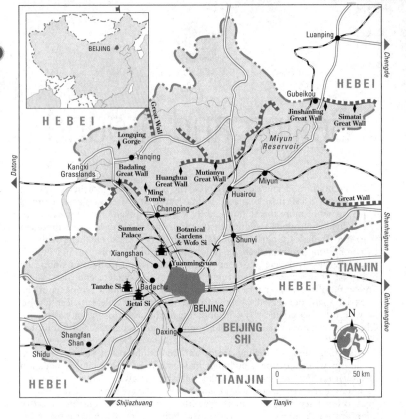

but also to a revival of older **Chinese culture** – witness the re-emergence of the teahouse as a genteel meeting place and the interest in imperial cuisine. In the evening you'll see large groups of the older generation performing the *yangkou* (loyalty dance), Chairman Mao's favourite dance universally learned a few decades ago, and in the *hutongs*, the city's twisted grey stone alleyways, men sit with their pet birds and pipes as they always have done.

Beijing is a city that almost everyone enjoys. For new arrivals it provides a gentle introduction to the country, and for travellers who've been roughing it round outback China, the creature comforts on offer are a delight. It's home to a huge expat population, and it's quite possible to spend years here eating Western food, dancing to Western music and socializing with like-minded foreigners. Beijing is essentially a private city, and one whose surface is difficult to penetrate; sometimes it seems to have the superficiality of a theme park. Certainly there is something mundane about the way tourist groups are efficiently shunted around, plugged from hotel to sight, with little contact with everyday reality. To get deeper into the city, wander what's left of the labyrinthine *hutongs*, "fine and numerous as the hairs of a cow" (as one Chinese guidebook puts it), and check out the little antique markets, the residential shopping districts, the smaller, quirkier sights, and the parks, some of the best in China, where you'll see Beijingers performing *tai ji* and hear birdsong – just

– over the hum of traffic. Take advantage, too, of the city's burgeoning nightlife and see just how far the Chinese have gone down the road of what used to be called spiritual pollution.

If the Party had any control over it, no doubt Beijing would have the best **climate** of any Chinese city; as it is, it has one of the worst. The best time to visit is in autumn, between September and October, when it's dry and clement. In winter it gets very cold, down to minus 20°C, and the mean winds that whip off the Mongolian plains feel like they're freezing your ears off. Summer (June–Aug) is muggy and hot, up to 30°C, and the short spring (April & May) is dry but windy.

Getting to Beijing is no problem. As the centre of China's **transport** network you'll probably wind up here sooner or later, whether you want to or not, and to avoid the capital seems wilfully perverse. On a purely practical level, it's a good place to stock up on visas for the rest of Asia, and to arrange transport out of the country – most romantically, on the Trans-Siberian or Trans-Mongolian trains. To take in its superb sights requires a week, by which time you may well be ready to move on to China proper. Beijing is a fun place, but make no mistake, it in no way typifies the rest of the nation.

Some history

It was in Tian'anmen, on October 1, 1949, that Chairman Mao Zedong hoisted the red flag to proclaim officially the **foundation of the People's Republic**. He told the crowds (the square could then hold only 500,000) that the Chinese had at last stood up, and defined liberation as the final culmination of a 150-year fight against foreign exploitation.

The claim, perhaps, was modest. Beijing's **recorded history** goes back a little over three millennia, to beginnings as a trading centre for Mongols, Koreans and local Chinese tribes. Its predominance, however, dates to the mid-thirteenth century, and the formation of **Mongol China** under Genghis and later **Kublai Khan**. It was Kublai who took control of the city in 1264, and who properly established it as a capital, replacing the earlier power centres of Luoyang and Xi'an. Marco Polo visited him here, working for a while in the city, and was clearly impressed with the level of sophistication; he observed in *The Travels*:

So great a number of houses and of people, no man could tell the number ...
I believe there is no place in the world to which so many merchants come, and dearer things, and of greater value and more strange, come into this town from all sides than to any city in the world ...

The **wealth** came from the city's position at the start of the Silk Road, and Polo described "over a thousand carts loaded with silk" arriving "almost each day", ready for the journey west out of China. And it set a precedent in terms of style and grandeur for the Khans, later known as emperors, with Kublai building himself a palace of astonishing proportions, walled on all sides and approached by great marble stairways.

With the accession of the **Ming dynasty**, who defeated the Mongols in 1368, the capital temporarily shifted to present-day Nanjing, but Yongle, the second Ming emperor, returned, building around him prototypes of the city's two greatest **monuments** – the Imperial Palace and Temple of Heaven. It was in Yongle's reign, too, that the basic **city plan** took shape, rigidly symmetrical, extending in squares and rectangles from the palace and inner-city grid to the suburbs, much as it is today.

Subsequent, post-Ming history is dominated by the rise and eventual collapse of the Manchus – the **Qing dynasty**, northerners who ruled China from Beijing from 1644 to the beginning of the twentieth century. The capital was at its most prosperous in the first half of the eighteenth century, the period in which the Qing constructed the legendary **Summer Palace** – the world's most extraordinary royal garden, with two hundred pavilions, temples and palaces, and immense artificial lakes and hills – to the north of the city. With the central Imperial Palace, this was the focus of endowment and the symbol of Chinese wealth and power. However, in 1860, the Opium Wars brought British and French troops to the walls of the capital, and the Summer Palace was first looted and then burned by the British, more or less entirely to the ground.

While the imperial court lived apart, within what was essentially a separate walled city, conditions for the civilian population, in the capital's suburbs, were starkly different. Kang Youwei, a Cantonese visiting in 1895, described this dual world:

No matter where you look, the place is covered with beggars. The homeless and the old, the crippled and the sick with no one to care for them, fall dead on the roads. This happens every day. And the coaches of the great officials rumble past them continuously.

The indifference, rooted according to Kang in officials throughout the city, spread from the top down. From 1884, using funds meant for the modernization of the nation's navy, the empress Dowager Cixi had begun building a new Summer Palace of her own. The empress's project was really the last grand gesture of **imperial architecture** and patronage – and like its model was also badly burned by foreign troops, in another outbreak of the Opium War in 1900. By this time, with successive waves of occupation by foreign troops, the empire and the imperial capital were near collapse. The **Manchus abdicated** in 1911, leaving the Northern Capital to be ruled by warlords. In 1928 it came under the military dictatorship of Chiang Kaishek's **Guomindang**, being seized by the **Japanese** in 1939, and at the end of **World War II** the city was controlled by an alliance of Guomindang troops and American marines.

The **Communists** took Beijing in January 1949, nine months before Chiang Kaishek's flight to Taiwan assured final victory. The **rebuilding of the capital**, and the erasing of symbols of the previous regimes, was an early priority. The city that Mao Zedong inherited for the Chinese people was in most ways primitive. Imperial laws had banned the building of houses higher than the official buildings and palaces, so virtually nothing was more than one storey high. The roads, although straight and uniform, were narrow and congested, and there was scarcely any industry. The new plans aimed to reverse all except the city's sense of ordered planning, with Tian'anmen Square at its heart – and initially, through the early 1950s, their inspiration was Soviet, with an emphasis on heavy industry and a series of poor-quality high-rise housing programmes.

In the zest to be free from the past and create a modern, people's capital, much of **Old Beijing was destroyed**, or co-opted: the Temple of Cultivated Wisdom became a wire factory and the Temple of the God of Fire produced electric lightbulbs. In the 1940s there were eight thousand temples and monuments in the city; by the 1960s there were only around a hundred and fifty. Even the city walls and gates, relics mostly of the Ming era, were pulled down and their place taken by ring roads and avenues.

Much of the city's **contemporary planning policy** was disastrous, creating more problems than it solved. Most of the traditional courtyard houses which

The Beijing Olympics

The only developing country with the resources to host the Olympic Games, and the narrow loser of the 2000 bid, Beijing was a natural choice for the **2008 Games**, though its lousy human rights record caused plenty of protest at the nomination. Now the city is being energetically transformed into a showcase, and even the cab drivers are studying English in preparation. The focus of the games will be the Olympic Forest Park, a vast arcadia with a boulevard sweeping down the middle, located on the outskirts north of the Forbidden City. Its centrepiece, surrounded by a dragon-shaped canal, is the 80,000-seater National Stadium, built by Swiss firm Herzog de Meuron and designed to resemble a nest. Not all events will take place here; the beach volleyball is slated for Tian'anmen Square. For more information, check out the official website, ⓦ www.beijing-2008.org.

were seen to encourage individualism were destroyed. In their place went anonymous concrete buildings, often with inadequate sanitation and little running water. In 1969, when massive restoration was needed above ground, Mao instead launched a campaign to build a network of subterranean tunnels as shelter in case of war. Millions of man-hours went into constructing a useless labyrinth, built by hand, that would be no defence against modern bombs and served only to lower the city's water table. After the destruction of all the capital's dogs in 1950, it was the turn of sparrows in 1956. A measure designed to preserve grain, its only effect was to lead to an increase in the insect population. To combat this, all the grass was pulled up, which in turn led to dust storms in the windy winter months.

Today, massive urban regeneration projects are underway to prepare the city for the **Olympic Games** in 2008. Attempts have been made to battle pollution, and factories that can't modernize have been closed. A huge reforestation project north of the city, nicknamed the great green wall, has helped stem the annual dust storms. The filthy canals are being dredged. Two more ring roads are being built. And to help with problems of overcrowding, there are ambitious plans for a series of satellite cities. With lots of money washing around for prestige projects, and no geographical constraints or old city to preserve, Beijing has become an architect's playground, with huge, weirdly shaped towers popping up like mushrooms after rain. It gleams like never before, but what little character the city had is fast disappearing. Now the city's main problems are the pressure of migration and traffic – car ownership has rocketed, contributing to the appalling air quality, and the streets are nearing gridlock.

Orientation, arrival and information

There's no doubt that Beijing's initial culture shock owes much to the artificiality of the city's **layout**. The main streets are huge, wide and dead straight, aligned either east–west or north–south, and extend in a series of widening rectangles across the whole thirty square kilometres of the inner capital.

The pivot of the ancient city was a north–south road that led from the entrance of the Forbidden City to the city walls. This remains today as **Qianmen Dajie**, though the main axis has shifted to the east–west road that divides Tian'anmen Square and the Forbidden City, and which changes its name, like all major boulevards, every few kilometres along its length. It's generally referred to as **Chang'an Jie**.

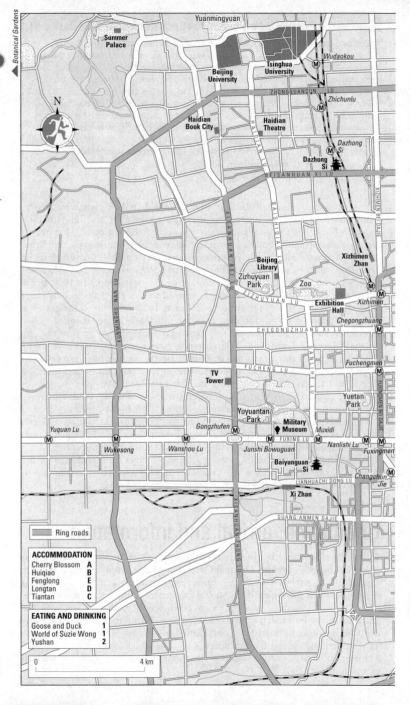

Yuanmingyuan

Summer
Palace

Tsinghua
University

Wudaokou

Beijing
University

ZHONGGUANCUN LU

Zhichunlu

N

Haidian
Book City

Haidian
Theatre

Dazhong
Si

Dazhong
Si

BEISANHUAN XI LU

XIZHIMEN BEI DAJIE

Beijing
Library

Xizhimen
Zhan

Zizhuyuan
Park

Zoo

ZIZHUYUAN LU

Xizhimen

Exhibition
Hall

Chegongzhuang

CHEGONGZHUANG XI LU

XISANHUAN BEI LU

BAISHIQIAO LU

HAIDIAN LU

KUNMINGHU NAN LU

Fuchengmen

FUCHENG LU

TV
Tower

SANLIHE LU

Yuetan
Park

FUXINGMEN BEI DAJIE

Yuyuantan
Park

Gongzhufen

Military
Museum

Muxidi

Yuquan Lu

Wukesong

Wanshou Lu

Junshi Bowuguan

FUXING LU

Nanlishi Lu

Fuxingmen

Baiyunguan
Si

Changchun
Jie

LIANHUACHI DONG LU

Xi Zhan

GUANG'ANMEN DAJIE

XISANHUAN ZHONG LU

Ring roads

ACCOMMODATION

Cherry Blossom   A
Huiqiao   B
Fenglong   E
Longtan   D
Tiantan   C

EATING AND DRINKING

Goose and Duck   1
World of Suzie Wong   1
Yushan   2

0   4 km

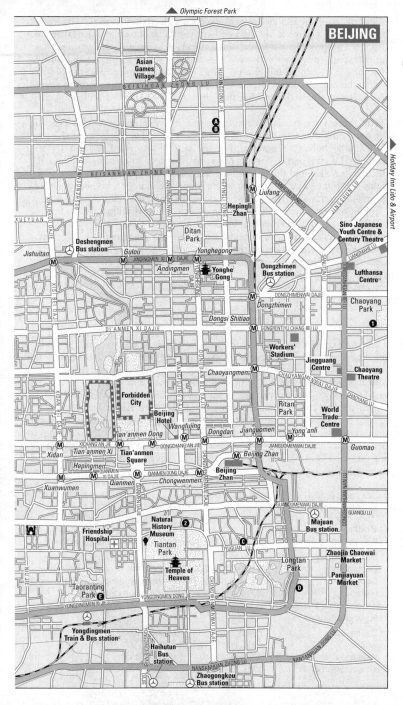

Olympic Forest Park

BEIJING

Holiday Inn Lido & Airport

Asian Games Village

BEISIHUAN ZHONG LU

HUIXINXILU

HUIXIN DONG JIE

A
B

DESHENGMEN WAI DAJIE

BEISANHUAN ZHONG LU

BEISANHUAN DONG LU

JINGSHUN LU

ANDINGMEN WAI DAJIE

HEPINGLI DONG JIE

Liufang

XINJIEKOU DAJIE

XUEYUAN

Hepingli Zhan

Sino Japanese Youth Centre & Century Theatre

LIANGMAHE LU

SANYUANQIAO

Deshengmen Bus station

Ditan Park

Jishuitan

M

Gulou

M Andingmen

M Andingmen Xi

M DAJIE

M Yonghegong

Lufthansa Centre

Andingmen

Yonghe Gong

Dongzhimen Bus station

M

Chaoyang Park

XIS BEI DAJIE

Dongzhimen

DONGZHIMENWAI DAJIE

1

Dongsi Shitiao

M

GONGRENTIYU CHANG BEI LU

WANGFUJING DAJIE

DONGDAN BEI DAJIE

Workers' Stadium

Jingguang Centre

Chaoyang Theatre

M Chaoyangmen

CHAOYANGMENWAI DAJIE

CHAOYANG LU

Forbidden City

Ritan Park

World Trade Centre

DONGSANHUAN ZHONG LU

XIDAN BEI DAJIE

Beijing Hotel

Wangfujing

M Dongdan

M Jianguomen

Yong'anli

M

Tian'anmen Dong

M

XICHANG'AN JIE

DONGCHANG'AN JIE

JIANGUOMENWAI DAJIE

Guomao

M Xidan

M Tian'anmen Xi

Tian'anmen Square

DONGDAN WAI DAJIE

Beijing Zhan

Hepingmen

QIANMEN XI DAJIE

M Qianmen

M

QIANMEN DONG DAJIE

M Chongwenmen

Beijing Zhan

Xuanwumen

Qianmen

QIANMEN DAJIE

CHONGWENMEN WAI DAJIE

GUANGQUMENWAI DAJIE

GUANQU LU

Majuan Bus station

Friendship Hospital

Natural History Museum

2

NU JIE

Tiantan Park

C

TIYUGUAN LU

Zhaojia Chaowai Market

Panjiayuan Market

Temple of Heaven

Longtan Park

CHONGWENMENWAI DAJIE

Taoranting Park

E

YONGDINGMEN DONG JIE

D

YONGDINGMEN XI JIE

NANERHUAN DONG LU

Yongdingmen Train & Bus station

YONGDINGMEN WAI DAJIE

Haihutun Bus station

NANSANHUAN ZHONG LU

NANSANHUAN DONG LU

Zhaogongkou Bus station

Few traces of the old city remain except in the **street names**, which look bewilderingly complex but are not hard to figure out once you realize that they are compounds of a name, plus a direction – *bei, nan, xi, dong* and *zhong* (north, south, west, east and middle) – and the words for inside and outside – *nei* and *wai* – which indicate the street's position in relation to the old city walls which enclosed the centre. Central streets often also contain the word *men* (gate), which indicates that they once had a gate in the wall along their length.

The **three ring roads**, freeways arranged in concentric rectangles centring on the Forbidden City, are rapid-access corridors. The first, running round Tian'anmen Square, is nominal, but the second and third, Erhuan Lu and Sanhuan Lu, are useful, cutting down on journey times but extending the distance travelled and therefore much liked by taxi drivers. While most of the sights are in the city centre, most of the modern buildings – hotels, restaurants, shopping centres and flashy office blocks – are along the ring roads.

You'll soon become familiar with the experience of barrelling along a freeway in a bus or a taxi while identical blocks flicker past, not knowing which direction you're travelling in, let alone where you are. To get some sense of orientation, take fast mental notes on the more obvious and imposing landmarks. The Great Hall of the People in Tian'anmen Square; the *Beijing Hotel*, at the south end of Wangfujing; the oddly shaped *International Hotel* on Dongchang'an Jie; and farther east on the same road, the Friendship Store and World Trade Centre.

Arrival

The first experience most visitors have of China is the smooth ride along the freeway, lined with hoardings and jammed with cars, that leads from the airport into the city. Unless you arrive by train, it's a long way into the centre from either the bus stations or the airport, and even when you get into downtown Beijing you're still a good few kilometres from most hotels, which tend to cluster between the second and third ring roads. It's a good idea to hail a taxi from the centre to get you to your final destination rather than tussle with the buses, as the public transport system is confusing at first and the city layout rather alienating. Walking to your hotel isn't really an option as distances are always long, exhausting at the best of times and unbearable with luggage.

Beijing arrival		
Beijing	北京	*běijīng*
Beijing Capital Airport	北京首都机场	*běijīng shǒudū jīchǎng*
Bus Stations		
Deshengmen	德胜门公共汽车站	*déshèngmén gōnggòng qìchēzhàn*
Dongzhimen	东直门公共汽车站	*dōngzhímén gōnggòng qìchēzhàn*
Haihutun	海户屯公共汽车站	*hǎihùtún gōnggòng qìchēzhàn*
Zhaogongkou bus station	赵公口公共汽车站	*zhàogōngkǒu gōnggòng qìchēzhàn*
Train Stations		
Beijing Zhan	北京站	*běijīng zhàn*
Xi Zhan	西站	*xī zhàn*
Xizhimen Zhan	西直门站	*xīzhímén zhàn*
Yongdingmen Zhan	永定门站	*yǒngdìngmén zhàn*

By plane

The showcase **Beijing Capital Airport** was opened in 1999 on October 1, the fiftieth birthday of communist rule. Twenty-nine kilometres northeast of the centre, it serves both international and domestic flights. There are a couple of banks and an ATM on the right as you exit through customs, and commission rates are the same as everywhere else. Get some small change if you're planning to take any buses. The CAAC office sells tickets for onward domestic flights.

An expressway connects the airport to the city and is one of the best and freest-flowing roads in China. Directly in front of the main exit is the **airport bus** stand, from which comfortable, though rather cramped, air-conditioned buses leave regularly (¥16). There are two routes, A and B. **Route A buses** leave every fifteen minutes from 8am until the last flight arrives, and are the most useful to travellers, stopping at the Lufthansa Centre, Dongzhimen metro stop, and *Swissotel* by Chaoyangmen metro stop before terminating outside the *International Hotel*, just north of Beijing Zhan, the central train station, where there's a taxi rank and a metro station. **Route B buses** leave every hour, from 9.30am until the last flight, and make stops on the north and western sections of the third ring road, Sanhuan Lu, including the Asian Games Village, *Friendship Hotel* and Foreign Language University in Haidian district, before terminating at the *Xinxing Hotel*, at the intersection of Chang'an Jie and Xisanhuan Bei Lu, close to the Gongzhufen metro stop.

Taxis from the airport into the city leave from the taxi rank just outside the main entrance, on the left; don't go with the hustlers who approach new arrivals. Make sure your taxi is registered; it should have a red sticker in the window stating the rate per kilometre and an identity card displayed on the dashboard. A trip to the city centre costs around ¥80 and takes about fifty minutes.

By train

Beijing has two main **train stations**. **Beijing Zhan**, the central station, just south of Dongchang'an Jie, is where trains from destinations north and east of Beijing arrive. There are **left-luggage** lockers as well as a main luggage office here (see p.141 for details). From Beijing Zhan the only hotel within walking distance is the uninspiring *International*. Most arrivals will need to head straight to the **bus terminus**, about 100m east of the station, the **metro stop** at the northwestern edge of the concourse, or to the **taxi rank**, over the road and 50m east. The waiting taxis are supervised by an official with a red armband who makes sure the queue is orderly and that drivers flip their meters on. Don't get a cab from the station concourse, as none of the drivers here will use their meters.

Travellers from the south and west of the capital will arrive at the west station, **Xi Zhan**, Asia's largest rail terminal at the head of the Beijing–Kowloon rail line. A prestige project, the station is ten times the size of Beijing Zhan. The left-luggage office is on the second floor, but at ¥5 an hour, it's expensive. Bus #122 runs between the two main stations, or, if you're heading south to the budget hotels, you can take bus #52 to Qianmen and get another bus from there. However, it's probably easier to take a **taxi** from the taxi rank.

Beijing does have more stations, though you are unlikely to arrive at them unless you have come on a suburban train from, for example, the Great Wall at Badaling or Shidu. Beijing North, also known as **Xizhimen Zhan**, is at the northwestern edge of the second ring road, on the metro. Beijing South, or **Yongdingmen Zhan**, is in the south of the city, just inside the third ring road, a short walk from the *Qiaoyuan Hotel*, with a bus terminus outside.

Moving on from Beijing

From Beijing you can get just about anywhere in China via the extensive air and rail system. You'd be advised to buy a ticket a few days in advance, though, especially in the summer or around Spring Festival. Few visitors travel long-distance by **bus** as it's less comfortable than the train and takes longer, though it has the advantage that you can usually just turn up and get on as services to major cities are frequent. Buy a ticket from the ticket office in the station, or on the bus itself. Tianjin and Chengde are two destinations within easy travelling distance, where the bus and the train have about the same journey time. For details of bus stations and the points they serve, see "By bus", below.

By plane

Domestic **flights** should be booked at least a day in advance. The main outlet for **tickets** is the Aviation Office, at 15 Xichang'an Jie (daily 7am–8pm; information ☏010/66017755, domestic reservations ☏010/66013336, international reservations ☏010/66016667), where most domestic airlines are represented. China Southern Airlines is at 227 Chaoyangmen Dajie (☏010/65533624), and Xinhua Airlines is at 2A Dong Chang'an Jie (☏010/65121587).

Tickets are also available from CITS (see "Listings", p.142), from most hotels and from airline agents dotted around the city (see p.139). You'll often get a cheaper price if you deal with airlines or their agents directly; call the airline to get their agent list.

To get to the airport, **airport buses** run daily from outside the Aviation Office (every 30min; 5.30am–7pm), from the northwest side of the *International Hotel* (cross the road and look for the sign; hourly; 6.30am–4.30pm), and from outside a ticket office on the east side of Wangfujing Dajie, just north of the intersection with Chaoyangmen Dajie (every 30min; 5.30am–6pm). Tickets cost ¥16 and you should allow an hour for the journey, twice this in the rush hour.

A **taxi** to the airport will cost around ¥80, and the journey should take about 45 minutes, at least half an hour longer in rush hour. The information desk at the airport is open 24 hours for enquiries (☏010/64563604).

By domestic train

Trains depart from either **Xi Zhan**, if you're heading south or west, for example to Chengdu or Xi'an, or **Beijing Zhan**, if you're heading north or east, for example to Shanghai or Harbin. You can buy **tickets** with an added surcharge of around ¥40 from large hotels or CITS, though it's little hassle to do it yourself direct. Tickets for

By bus

The **bus system** in Beijing is extensive, but complicated, as there are many terminuses, each one serving buses from only a few destinations. **Dongzhimen**, on the northeast corner of the second ring road, connected by metro, is the largest bus station and handles services from Shenyang and the rest of Dongbei. **Deshengmen**, also called Beijiao, the north station serving Chengde and Datong, is 1km north of the second ring road, on the route of bus #55, which will take you to Xi'anmen Dajie, west of Beihai Park. **Haihutun**, in the south, at the intersection of the third ring road, Nansanhuan Lu, and Yongdingmenwai Dajie, is for buses from Tianjin and cities in southern Hebei. **Private minibuses** are more likely to terminate outside one of the two main train stations.

Information and maps

A large fold-out **map** of the city is vital. There is a wide variety available at all transport connections and from street vendors, hotels and bookshops. The best busy routes should be booked at least a day in advance, and can be booked up to four days ahead. Buy tickets at Beijing Zhan; the Foreigners' Ticket Booking Office is at the back of the station, on the left side as you enter, and is signposted in English. It's open daily 5.30–7.30am, 8am–6.30pm and 7–11pm. There's a timetable in English on the wall. You can also get tickets from separate ticket outlets – as these are little known, there are never any queues. There's one on the first floor in the Wangfujing Department Store at 225 Wangfujing Dajie (daily 9–11am & 1–4pm) and another in the Air China ticket office in the China World Trade Centre at 1 Jianguomenwai Dajie (daily 8am–6pm). For train information (in Chinese only) phone ☎010/65129525.

Trans-Siberian and Trans-Mongolian trains

The International Train Booking Office (Mon–Fri 8.30am–noon & 1.30–5pm; ☎010/65120507) is the best thing about the *International Hotel* at 9 Jianguomenwai Dajie. Here you can buy **tickets to Moscow and Ulan Batur** with the minimum of fuss. Out of season, few people make the journey, but in summer there may well not be a seat for weeks. Allow yourself a week or two for dealing with embassy bureaucracy. After putting down a ¥100 deposit on the ticket at the booking office, you'll be issued with a reservation slip. Take this with you to the embassy when you apply for visas and the process should be fairly painless. A Russian transit visa, valid for a week, costs around US$50, with a surcharge for certain nationalities (mostly African and South American). Transit visas for Mongolia are valid for one week and cost US$30; tourist visas valid for a month cost US$40.

Chinese train #3 to **Moscow via Ulan Batur** leaves every Wednesday from Beijing Zhan and takes five and a half days. A bunk in a second-class cabin with four beds – which is perfectly comfortable – costs ¥1602. First class is ¥2306 (four beds) or ¥2786 (two beds). The Russian train #19, which follows the **Trans-Siberian route**, leaves on Saturdays from Beijing Zhan and takes six days. The cheapest bunk here is ¥1888; first class is ¥3014. A Mongolian train leaves for Ulan Batur every Tuesday and costs ¥606 for one bed in a four-bed berth. Travelling on train #3 is slightly cheaper.

The tour company Monkey Business can organize your trip. Their office is room 35 of the Red House Hotel off Dongzhimenwai Dajie (see Accommodation, p.98; ☎010/65916519, ⓦwww.monkeyshrine.com). A second-class ticket costs US$385 (not including visas), for which you also get an info pack and a ride to the station. Their other packages include stopovers in Ulan Batur, Lake Baikal and Irkutsk.

map to look out for, labelled in English and Chinese, and with bus routes, sights and hotels marked, is the *Beijing Tour Map*. Fully comprehensive A–Z map books are available from bookshops and street vendors outside Beijing Zhan metro stop, but only in Chinese.

BTS – Beijing Travel Service – is an official **tourist information service** with a few central offices (see p.142 for details). They're mostly interested in selling tours and handing out leaflets. There are a number of English-language publications which will help you get the best out of the city. The *China Daily* (¥1), available from the Friendship Store, the Foreign Language Bookstore and the bigger hotels, has a listings section detailing cultural events. The rest of the paper is propaganda written in turgid prose. *Beijing This Month* covers the same ground, with light features aimed at tourists.

Much more useful, though, are the free magazines aimed at the large expat community, which contain up-to-date and fairly comprehensive entertainment and restaurant listings. *City Edition* and *Metro* are aimed at the more upmarket sections of the foreign community, but by far the best is the irreverent and

Warning: Bogus art students and rickshaws

Spend any time in tourist areas of the capital and you will inevitably be approached by youths claiming to be **art students**. They aren't, of course; most are ex-students from teacher-training schools putting their language skills to dubious use. Their aim is to get you to visit a bogus art gallery, and pay ridiculous prices for prints purporting to be paintings, and they'll go to astonishing lengths to befriend foreigners. They're not aggressive, though, and they can be useful if you need directions.

Though there are plenty around, don't ever use **cycle-rickshaws**. Drivers will almost certainly overcharge foreigners, even take them places they don't want to go and then demand more money.

informative monthly *That's Beijing* (ⓦ www.thatsbj.com). You can pick up copies of all three magazines in most bars and other expat hang-outs (the *Metro* chain of restaurants is a good place to look for them if you can't get to the Chaoyang district, where most expat services are).

City transport

The scale of the city militates against taking "bus number 11" – Chinese slang for walking – almost anywhere, and most of the main streets are so straight that going by foot soon gets tedious. The **public transport system** is extensive but somewhat oversubscribed; most visitors tire of the heaving buses pretty quickly and take rather more taxis than they'd planned. The **metro** is speedy but not extensive. **Cycling** is a good alternative, though, with plenty of rental outlets in the city.

Buses

Even though every one of the city's 200-odd **bus and trolleybus services** runs about once a minute, you'll find getting on or off at busy times hard work (rush hours are from 7–9am & 4.30–6pm). The **fare** for ordinary buses depends how far you are going but never exceeds ¥2.5 and is usually ¥0.5 – watch how the Chinese wrap up a one-fen coin in two two-fen notes to make a little origami package to give the conductor. A little more comfortable, if slower, are the **minibuses**, which ply the same routes as the buses and charge ¥2 per journey. There are also five comfortable double-decker bus services, costing ¥2 a trip. **Tourist buses** – which look like ordinary buses but have route numbers written in green – make regular trips (mid-April to mid Oct) between the city centre and certain out-of-town attractions; we've listed useful routes in the text.

Services generally run from 5.30am to 11pm everyday, though some are 24-hour. Buses numbered in the 200s only provide night services. Routes are efficiently organized and easy to understand – an important factor, since stops tend to be a good kilometre apart. Buses numbered in the 800s are modern, air-conditioned, and actually quite pleasant, but more expensive, with fares starting at ¥3 and going up to ¥10.

A word of warning – be very wary of **pickpockets** on buses. Skilful thieves target Westerners, and especially backpackers, looking not just for money but coveted Western passports.

Useful bus routes

Bus routes are indicated by red or blue lines on all good maps; a dot on the line indicates a stop. Next to the stop on the map you'll see tiny characters; that's the stop's name and you need to know it for the conductor to work out your fare. Trying to show the poor man a dot on a map in a swaying, crammed bus is nigh impossible; fortunately, the Beijing Tour Map has stops marked in *pinyin*. The following are some of the most useful services:

Bus #1 and double-decker #1 From Xi Zhan east along the main thoroughfare, Chang'an Jie.

Double-decker #2 From the north end of Qianmen Dajie, north to Dongdan, the Yonghe Gong and the Asian Games Village.

Double-decker #4 From Beijing Zoo to Qianmen via Fuxingmen.

Bus #5 From Deshengmen, on the second ring road in the northwest of the city, south down the west side of the Forbidden City and Tian'anmen to Qianmen Dajie.

Bus #15 From the zoo down Xidan Dajie past Liulichang ending at the Tianqiao area just west of Yongdingmennei Dajie, close to Tiantan Park.

Bus #20 from Beijing Zoo to Yongdingmen Zhan, south of Taoranting Park.

Bus #52 From Xi Zhan east to Lianhuachi Qiao, Xidan Dajie, Tian'anmen Square, then east along Chang'an Jie.

Trolleybus #103 From Beijing Zhan, north up the east side of the Forbidden City, west along Fuchengmennei Dajie, then north up Sanlihe Lu to the zoo.

Trolleybus #104 From Beijing Zhan to Hepingli train station in the north of the city, via Wangfujing.

Trolleybus #105 From the northwest corner of Tiantan Park to Xidan Dajie, then west to the zoo.

Trolleybus #106 From Yongdingmen Zhan to Tiantan Park and Chongwenmen, then up to Dongzhimennei Dajie.

Bus #300 Circles the third ring road.

Bus #332 From Beijing Zoo to Beida (University and the Summer Palace).

Luxury Bus #802 from Xi Zhan to Panjiayuan Market in the southeast.

Luxury Bus #808 From just northwest of Qianmen to the Summer Palace.

The metro

Clean, efficient, and very fast, the **metro** is an appealing alternative to the bus, though it is very crowded during rush hours. Mao Zedong ordered its construction in 1966, and more than 20km were open within three years, but until 1977 it was reserved for the use of senior cadres only, apparently because it was too close to the underground defence network.

The metro operates daily from 5.30am to 11pm and entrances are marked by a logo of a square inside a "C" shape. **Tickets** cost ¥3 per journey; buy them from the ticket offices at the top of the stairs above the platforms. It's worth buying a few at once to save queuing every time you use the system. The tickets are undated slips of paper and an attendant at the station takes one from you before you get on to the platform. All stops are marked in *pinyin*, and announced in English and Chinese over an intercom when the train pulls in, though the system is not taxing to figure out as there are only two lines.

A **loop line** runs around the city, making useful stops at Beijing Zhan, Jianguomen (under the flyover, close to the Ancient Observatory and the Friendship Store), Yonghe Gong (50m north of the temple of the same name),

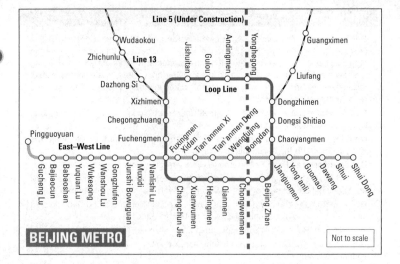

Line 5 (Under Construction)

Wudaokou
Zhichunlu   Line 13
Dazhong Si
Jishuitan
Gulou
Andingmen
Yonghegong
Guangximen
Liufang
Xizhimen
Loop Line
Dongzhimen
Chegongzhuang
Dongsi Shitiao
Pingguoyuan
Fuchengmen
Chaoyangmen
East–West Line
Gucheng Lu
Bajiaocun
Babaoshan
Yuquan Lu
Wukesong
Wanshou Lu
Gongzhufen
Junshi Bowuguan
Nanlishi Lu
Muxidi
Fuxingmen
Xidan
Tian'anmen Xi
Tian'anmen Dong
Wangfujing
Dongdan
Yong'anli
Guomao
Dawang
Sihui
Sihui Dong
Changchun Jie
Xuanwumen
Hepingmen
Qianmen
Chongwenmen
Beijing Zhan
Jianguomen

BEIJING METRO

Not to scale

and Qianmen, at the northern end of Qianmen Dajie. The **east–west line** runs from the western to the eastern suburbs; useful stops are at the Military Museum, Tian'anmen (west and east) and Wangfujing. There are interchanges at Fuxingmen and Jianguomen. The new third line, bafflingly called **Line 13**, serves the far north of the city. In fact it's an overground light rail though the stations use the metro logo. You can get onto it from the loop line at Xizhimen or Dongzhimen though you have to leave the station, walk a short distance and buy a new ticket to do so. The only useful stations for tourists are Dazhong Si – for the Great Bell Temple – and Wudaokou – for Beijing University and the Summer Palaces. A new line, number 5, was being constructed at the time of writing. It will run north-south from Yonghegong to Dongdan.

Taxis

Taxis come in all shapes and sizes, but all have a sticker in the back window which indicates the rate per kilometre. Luxury sedans are the most expensive, at ¥2 per kilometre with a minimum fare of ¥12; the common red "bulletheads" charge ¥1.2 or ¥1.6 per kilometre with a minimum of ¥10. Using a taxi after 11pm will incur a surcharge of twenty percent. Drivers are generally honest (except the ones who hang around transport links), but if they don't put the meter on, you can insist by saying "*da biao*". If you're concerned about being taken on an expensive detour, have a map open on your lap.

Bike rental

As a positive alternative to relying on public transport, it's worth **renting a bike**. Many of the cheaper hotels rent out bikes on a daily basis and will negoti-ate weekly rates. Figure on a daily charge of ¥10–50 and a deposit of ¥200–500. Always test the brakes before riding off, and get the tyres pumped up. If you have any problems, there are plenty of bike repair stalls on the pavement.

Chinese cycling pace is sedate, and with good reason. Chinese roads are unpredictable and at times fairly lawless, with traffic going the wrong way round roundabouts, aggressive trucks that won't get out of the way, impatient taxi drivers in the cycle lane, buses veering suddenly towards the pavement, and jaywalkers aplenty. Still, riding around Beijing is less daunting than riding around many Western cities as there are **bike lanes** on all main roads and you are in the company of plenty of other cyclists, indeed several million at rush hours. Ringing your bell or shouting is rarely effective; urgent noises that would have all other road users scurrying aside in other cities hardly merit a backward glance here. At junctions cyclists cluster together then cross en masse when strength of numbers forces other traffic to give way. If you feel nervous, just dismount and walk the bike across – plenty of Chinese do.

If you have a new bike or a mountain-bike you should get a chain and lock as well, as theft is common. You are supposed to park your bike at the numerous **bike parks**, where you pay ¥0.3 to the attendant, though plenty of people don't, risking a rarely enforced fine by leaving their bicycle propped up against railings or on the pavement.

Tours

Organized **tours** of the city and its outskirts offer a painless if expensive way of seeing all the sights quickly. CITS offers a wide variety of one- and two-day packages, which you can book from their offices or from the information desk in the Friendship Store. However, these tours aren't cheap, at around ¥300 a day.

One good, inexpensive tour that's more imaginative than most is the *hutong* tour (ⓣ010/6615097, ⓦwww.hutongtour.com; ¥180), which offers the opportunity to see a more private side of the city from a rickshaw. Tours leave from 200m west of Beihai Park's north entrance. The one-day tours offered by the classier hotels tend to be expensive; you'll get better value from the cheaper hotels. Worth considering is the day-trip organized from the *Fenglong* hostel, which picks up at all the other budget hotels. It takes you to Jinshanling Great Wall and picks you up later at Simatai (see p.145). They'll also arrange trips to the acrobatics and the opera.

Accommodation

Affordable **accommodation** options in Beijing have much improved of late. There are now several well-run, cheap, well-located hotels and youth hostels – budget travellers no longer have to congregate in soulless suburban dormitories but can stay right in the centre of town. At the **cheapest places** you can expect a bed in a clean but cramped dorm, and all the facilities will be communal. Double rooms almost always come with attached bathrooms. All hostels offer a ¥10 discount for international youth hostel members, and can sell you membership cards for ¥60. In **three-star** places and above, rooms are more spacious, and there are usually facilities such as satellite TV, swimming pools and saunas. Pretty much every hotel has a hairdresser, a restaurant and a business centre. **Luxury hotels** are of an international standard and are generally foreign run and managed, and sometimes offer discounts of up to seventy percent off season.

Hotels in **Qianmen** are close to the centre in a shabby but characterful area. Most of the mid-range and high-class hotels are **east of the centre**, strung out along the international shopping streets of Wangfujing and Jianguomen or clustered around metro stations. Further north, the **Sanlitun district** has some good accommodation options for all budgets, with plenty of places to eat and

Beijing accommodation

Bamboo Garden	竹园宾馆	*zhúyuán bīnguǎn*
Beijing	北京饭店	*běijīng fàndiàn*
Beiwei	北纬饭店	*běiwěi fàndiàn*
Cherry Blossom	樱花宾馆	*yīnghuā bīnguǎn*
Chongwenmen	崇文门饭店	*chóngwénmén fàndiàn*
Far East International Youth Hostel	远东国际青年旅舍	*yuǎndōng guójìqīngnián lǚshè*
Fenglong	凤龙宾馆	*fènglóng bīnguǎn*
Fuhao	富豪宾馆	*fùháo bīnguǎn*
Gongti Youth Hostel	工体国际青年旅舍	*gōngtǐ guójì qīngnián lǚshè*
Great Wall Sheraton	长城饭店	*chángchéng fàndiàn*
Hademen	哈德门饭店	*hādémén fàndiàn*
Haoyuan	好园宾馆	*hǎoyuán bīnguǎn*
Holiday Inn Crowne Plaza	国际艺苑皇冠饭店	*guójìyìyuàn huángguān fàndiàn*
Huiqiao	惠乔饭店	*huìqiáo fàndiàn*
Jianguo	建国饭店	*jiànguó fàndiàn*
Jianguo Qianmen	建国前门饭店	*jiànguó qiánmén fàndiàn*
Jinglun	京伦饭店	*jīnglún fàndiàn*
Kempinski	凯宾斯基饭店	*kǎibīnsījī fàndiàn*
Longtan	龙潭饭店	*lóngtán fàndiàn*
Lüsongyuan	侣松园宾馆	*lǚsōngyuán bīnguǎn*
New Otani	长富宫饭店	*chángfùgōng fàndiàn*
Novotel Xin Qiao	诺富特新桥宾馆	*nuòfùtè xīnqiáo bīnguǎn*
Peninsula Palace	王府饭店	*wángfǔ fàndiàn*
Red House	瑞秀宾馆	*ruìxiù bīnguǎn*
Red Lantern House	红灯笼宾馆	*hóngdēnglóng bīnguǎn*
Ritan	日坛宾馆	*rìtán bīnguǎn*
Saga Youth Hostel	实佳国际青年旅舍	*shíjiā guójì qīngnián lǚshè*
St Regis	国际俱乐部饭店	*guójìjùlèbù fàndiàn*
Tiantan	天坛饭店	*tiāntán fàndiàn*
Youyi Hostel	天坛体育宾馆	*tiāntántǐyù bīnguǎn*
Yuan Dong	远东饭店	*yuǎndōng fàndiàn*
Zhaolong International Youth Hostel	兆龙青年旅舍	*zhàolóngqīngnián lǚshè*

drink nearby. The most characterful places to stay are the small places sunk into *hutongs* **north of the centre**. Finally, a few hotels in the **far north and south** offer good value. Beijing being the size it is, proximity to a metro station is a big advantage.

Except at the cheapest places, you should always **haggle** politely for a room – rack rates are only an indication, and hardly anyone pays those any more. You can often get a worthwhile discount if you book on the Internet (try Ⓦ www .sinohotels.com or www.egochina.com) a few days in advance, or try the airport reservations counter when you arrive.

Qianmen

See map p.100

Beiwei and Tianqiao 13 Xijing Lu
Ⓣ 010/63012266, Ⓕ 010/63011366. This Sino-Japanese joint venture consists of two buildings, one very upmarket, one not; the inexpensive section (*Beiwei*) looks like a barracks compared to the battleship-like superior section (*Tianqiao*) next door. Bus #20 from the main station will get you to Yongdingmennei Dajie, from where the hotel is a one-kilometre walk west. ❻–❾

Far East International Youth Hostel 113 Tieshuxie Jie, Qianmenwai ☎010/63018811, ⓦwww.courtyard@elong.com. A great little place, in a traditional courtyard house. The four- and six-bed dorms are clean and have sinks. There's a kitchen, washing machine and an elegant lounge. The location is fantastic, sunk in one of the city's last earthy *hutong* districts, 1km from Qianmen. The easiest way to find the hostel is to walk south from Hepingmen metro stop and turn left just before the first big junction with Zhushikou Dajie. Then follow the *hutong* and take the first left. Dorm beds ¥45–55, rooms ❸

Jianguo Qianmen 175 Yong'an Lu ☎010/63016688, ⓕ010/63013883. Big, popular three-star hotel with its own theatre, which nightly shows a bastardized version of Beijing Opera, mostly to visiting tour groups (see p.135). ❼

East of the centre

See map p.114

Beijing 33 Dongchang'an Jie ☎010/65137766, ⓦwww.chinabeijinghotel.com. The most central hotel, just east of Tian'anmen Square, and one of the most recognizable buildings in Beijing. The view from the top floors of the west wing, over the Forbidden City, is superb. But it's pricey, the new renovation has expunged the historic feel and service is not up to scratch. The cheapest rooms are US$160. ❾

Chongwenmen 2 Chongwenmen Xi Dajie ☎010/65122211, ⓕ010/65122122. This hotel is a little cramped for space, but well located, close to the Chongwenmen metro stop on the loop line. Rack rates are comparatively high, so barter. ❼

Fuhao 45 Wangfujing Dajie ☎010/65231188, ⓕ010/65131188. A newish three-star place, more affordable than most in the area. ❼

Hademen 2a Chongwenmenwai Dajie ☎010/67012244, ⓕ010/67016865. This two-star place is a little rambling, and staff speak no English, but as one of the few moderately priced, central hotels, close to the Chongwenmen metro stop, it's worth considering. ❻

Haoyuan 53 Shijia Hutong ☎010/65125557, ⓕ010/65253179. A sedate little courtyard hotel just half a kilometre from Wangfujing but very quiet. Rooms are small but cosy and with Ming-style furniture. Head north up Dongdan Bei Dajie and take the last alley to the right before the intersection with Dengshikou Dajie. The hotel is 200m down here on the left, marked by two red lanterns. Often full; book ahead. ❻

Holiday Inn Crowne Plaza 48 Wangfujing Dajie ☎010/65133388. Well-established hotel with artsy pretensions (there's an on-site gallery) that's handy for the shops. US$232. ❾

Jianguo 5 Jianguomen Dajie, next to Yong'an Li metro stop ☎010/65002233, ⓦwww.hoteljianguo .com. Well-run and good-looking, with many of the rooms arranged around cloistered gardens, this place is deservedly very popular with regular visitors. The restaurant, *Justine's*, has some of the best French food in the city. US$190. ❾

Jinglun (Hotel Beijing–Toronto) 3 Jianguomen-wai Dajie ☎010/65002266, ⓕ010/65002022. Bland-looking from the outside, this Japanese-run place is very comfortable and plush inside. A standard double is US$140. ❾

New Otani 26 Jianguomenwai Dajie ☎010/65125555, ⓕ010/65139810. You can get seriously pampered in this five-star, modern, Japanese-run mansion, one of the most luxurious in Beijing, though the fee for the privilege, at least US$212 a night, is hefty. ❾

Novotel Xin Qiao 2 Dong Jiao Min Xiang ☎010/65133366, ⓦwww.novotel.com. A new and decent chain hotel, well located right by Chongwenmen metro stop, that's the best within its range if you want comfort, reliability and familiarity. ❻

Peninsula Palace 8 Jingyu Hutong ☎010/65128899, ⓦwww.beijing.peninsula.com. A discreet and well-located upmarket place with a good shopping centre; it was recently upgraded rather lavishly and is now regularly voted the city's top place to stay. US$300. ❾

Saga Youth Hostel 9 Shijia Hutong, off Chaoy-angmen Nan Xiao Jie ☎010/65272773. In a quiet *hutong* off a busy street, and walkable from the airport bus stop (route B) and the main train station. It's signposted off Chaoyangmen Nan Xiao Jie, just beyond the stop for bus #24. The hostel is clean and utilitarian, with a tour office, bike rental, Internet access, a kitchen and a washing machine. Unusually, some of the otherwise plain dorms have TVs. Dorm beds ¥30–¥60, ❸

St Regis 21 Jianguomen Wai Dajie ☎010/64606688, ⓕ010/64603299. The most expensive hotel in the city, choice of visiting nobs such as President George W. Bush; rooms have a butler thrown in, who'll unpacify your suitcase for you. Rooms start at US$265. ❾

Sanlitun

See map p.131

Gongti Youth Hostel Number 9 Tai, inside the Workers' Stadium (Gongrentiyuchang)

ⓣ010/64164345). A new hostel inside the stadium compound, with decent clean facilities. Well located for the bars and clubs of Chaoyang though hardly an atmospheric place to stay. Fifteen minutes' walk from Dongsishitiao metro station. Dorms ¥55, ❸

Great Wall Sheraton 6 Dongsanhuan Bei Lu ⓣ010/65005566, ⓦwww.sheraton.com/beijing. A very swish, five-star modern compound out on the third ring road. US$160. ❾

Kempinski Lufthansa Centre, 50 Liangmaqiao Lu ⓣ010/64653388, ⓦwww.kempinski-beijing .com. Off the third ring road on the way to the airport, this five-star place is a little out of the way, though with a huge shopping complex attached and an expat satellite town of bars and restaurants nearby there's no shortage of diver-sions on site. ❾

Red House 10 Chunxiu Jie ⓣ010/64167500, ⓦwww.redhouse.com.cn. Head down Dongzhi-menwai Dajie and take the turning opposite *Pizza Hut*. A self-catering hotel with monthly rates, though they will also take guests for short stays. They also have a couple of seven-bed dorms for ¥95 including breakfast. ❼

Youyi Hostel Off Sanlitun Lu ⓣ010/64172632, ⓕ010/64156866, ⓦwww.poachers.com.cn. This place behind the *Poacher's Inn*, just off the Sanlitun bar strip, is clean, though staff are a bit stand-offish. There are dorms, but most of the rooms are doubles. All facilities are communal. There's free laundry and price includes breakfast. To find it, head north up Sanlitun Lu and turn left after 200m, at the sign for the *Cross Bar*. Then follow the road round to the left and it's on the right. Dorm beds ¥70, ❹

Zhaolong International Youth Hostel 2 Gongrentiyuchang Bei Lu ⓣ010/65972299, ⓕ010/65972288, ⓦwww.zhaolonghotel.com.cn. Behind the swanky *Zhaolong Hotel*. Another clean and ably managed hostel, a short stumble from the bars on Sanlitun Lu. Offers free laun-dry, bike rental and Internet access. Dorm beds ¥60–70.

North of the centre

See map p.118

Bamboo Garden 24 Xiaoshiqiao Hutong ⓣ010/64032229, ⓦwww.bbgh.com.cn. A quiet, charming but rather rickety courtyard hotel in a *hutong* close to the Drum and Bell towers. Quiet gardens are its best feature. Brusque service completes the archaic atmos-phere. ❻

Lüsongyuan 22 Banchang Hutong ⓣ010/64040436, ⓕ010/64030418. A charismatic

courtyard hotel converted from a Qing-dynasty mansion. Stylish and elegant rooms in a wide range of categories, including a basement dorm. Pleasant gardens, too. It's popular with tour groups, so you'll probably have to book ahead in season (April–September). The alley is just off Jiaodaokou Nan Dajie. Take bus #104 from the station and get off at Beibingmasi bus stop. Walk south for 50m and you'll see a sign in English pointing down an alley to the hotel. Dorm beds ¥80, ❻

Red Lantern House No.5 Zhengjue Hutong, Xinjie Kou (ⓣ010/63015433). A promising new place, a converted courtyard house in a quiet *hutong*, close to JJs Disco and the Houhai bar area. The alley is east off Xinjie Kou, its entrance marked by a Dairy Queen. Bus #22 from Beijing Zhan. Offers bike rental, Internet and laundry. Two- to four-bed dorms ¥30–60, rooms ❷–❸, breakfast included.

The far south

See map p.86

Fenglong 5 You'anmen Dong Jie ⓣ010/63536413, ⓔsuyuling@etang.com. Best of the old-style backpacker mother ships, with a wide range of dorm rooms – ask to see a selec-tion, as quality, relative fustiness and prices vary widely. Those on the second floor are best. Offers bike rental and even photo developing. Staff are slack but the tourist information office is excel-lent – this is the nerve centre from which the tours from all the other budget places are run. Take bus #122 from Beijing Zhan. Dorm beds ¥25–50, ❸–❹

Longtan 15 Panjiayuan Nan Lu ⓣ010/67712244. Well located and comfortable, with a wide range of rooms. Staff speak little English, though. ❺

Tiantan 1 Tiyuguan Lu ⓣ010/67112277, ⓕ010/67116833. In a quiet area east of Tiantan Park, this is a small but comfortable three-star place, if a little pricey. ❽

The far north

See map p.86

Cherry Blossom 17 Huxing Dong Jie ⓣ010/64934455. Next door to the plusher *Huiqiao* (see below), this place offers slightly cheaper rooms. It's perfectly comfortable, but the restaurant should be avoided. ❺

Huiqiao 19 Huxing Dong Jie ⓣ010/64918811. This place is quiet, with clean, attractive rooms. It's quite far north, but only a ¥10 taxi ride or a short trip on bus #807 from Yonghe Gong, the nearest metro stop. With several universities nearby, the area around the hotel has a lot of good, cheap restaurants, notably Xinjiang and Korean places. ❺

The City

Beijing requires patience and planning to do it justice. Wandering aimlessly around without a destination in mind will rarely be rewarding. The place to start is **Tian'anmen Square**, geographical and psychic centre of the city, where a cluster of important sights can be seen in a day, although the **Forbidden City**, at the north end of the square, deserves a day, or even several, all to itself. **Qianmen**, a noisy market area south of here, is a bit more alive, and ends in style with one of the city's highlights, the **Temple of Heaven** in Tiantan Park. The giant freeway, **Chang'an Jie**, zooming east–west across the city, is a corridor of high-rises with a few museums, shopping centres and even the odd ancient site worth tracking down. **Wangfujing**, running off Chang'an Jie, is the capital's main shopping street. Scattered in the **north** of the city, a section with a more traditional and human feel, are some magnificent **parks, palaces and temples**, some of them in the *hutongs*. The **Sanlitun** area is a ghetto of expat services including some good upscale restaurants and plenty of bars. An expedition to the outskirts is amply rewarded by the **Summer Palace**, the best place to get away from it all.

Tian'anmen Square and the Forbidden City

The first stop for any visitor to Beijing is **Tian'anmen Square**. Physically at the city's centre, symbolically it's the heart of China, and the events it has witnessed have shaped the history of the People's Republic from its inception. Chairman Mao lies here in his marble **mausoleum**, with the **Great Hall of the People** to the west and the **Museum of the Chinese Revolution** to the east. Monumental architecture that's much, much older lies just to the north – the **Forbidden City of the Emperors**, now open to all.

Tian'anmen Square

Covering more than forty hectares, **Tian'anmen Square** must rank as the greatest public square on Earth. It's a modern creation, in a city that traditionally had no squares, as classical Chinese town planning did not allow for places where crowds could gather. Tian'anmen only came into being when imperial offices were cleared from either side of the great processional way that led south from the palace to Qianmen and the Temple of Heaven, and the broad east–west thoroughfare, Chang'an Jie, had the walls across its path removed. In the words of one of the architects: "The very map of Beijing was a reflection of the feudal society, it was meant to demonstrate the power of the emperor. We had to transform it, we had to make Beijing into the capital of socialist China." The square was not enlarged to its present size until ten years after the Communist takeover, when the Party ordained the building of ten new Soviet-style official buildings in ten months. These included the three that dominate Tian'anmen to either side – the Great Hall of the People, and the museums of Chinese History and Revolution. In 1976 a fourth was added in the centre – Mao's mausoleum, constructed (again in ten months) by an estimated million

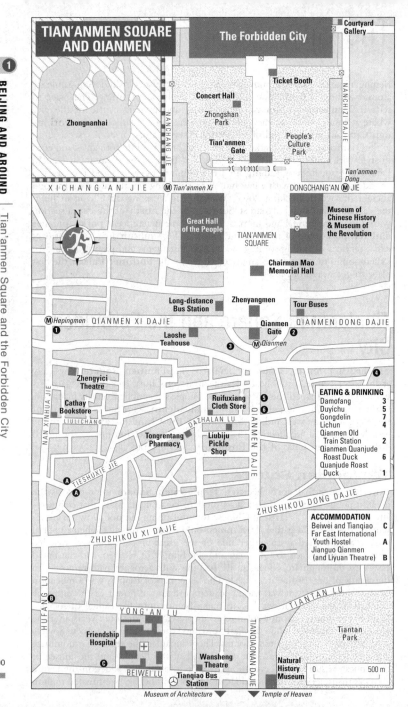

Beijing sights

Ancient Observatory	古观象台	gǔguānxiàngtái
Asian Games Village	亚运村	yàyùncūn
Baita Si	白塔寺	báitǎ sì
Baiyunguan	白云观	báiyúnguàn
Beihai Park	北海公园	běihǎi gōngyuán
Beijing University	北京大学	běijīng dàxué
Beijing Zoo	北京动物园	běijīng dòngwùyuán
China Art Gallery	中国美术馆	zhōngguó měishùguǎn
Confucius Temple	孔庙	kǒngmiào
Dazhong Si	大钟寺	dàzhōng sì
Ditan Park	地坛公园	dìtán gōngyuán
Exhibition Hall	展览馆	zhǎnlǎn guǎn
Forbidden City	故宫	gùgōng
Great Hall of the People	人民大会堂	rénmín dàhuìtáng
Guangji Si	广济寺	guǎngjì sì
Gulou (Drum Tower)	鼓楼	gǔlóu
Jingshan Park	景山公园	jǐngshān gōngyuán
Lu Xun Museum	鲁迅博物馆	lǔxùn bówùguǎn
Mao Memorial Hall	毛主席纪念堂	máozhǔxí jìniàntáng
Military Museum	军事博物馆	jūnshì bówùguǎn
Museum of Ancient Architecture	古代建筑博物馆	gǔdài jiànzhù bówùguǎn
Museum of Chinese History	中国历史博物馆	zhōngguó lìshǐ bówùguǎn
Museum of the Chinese Revolution	中国革命博物馆	zhōngguó gémìng bówùguǎn
Natural History Museum	自然博物馆	zìrán bówùguǎn
Niu Jie	牛街	niújiē
Prince Gong's Palace	恭王府	gōngwángfǔ
Qianmen	前门	qiánmén
Qinghua University	清华大学	qīnghuá dàxué
Ritan Park	日坛公园	rìtán gōngyuán
Song Qingling's Residence	宋庆龄故居	sòngqìnglíng gùjū
Summer Palace	颐和园	yíhéyuán
Taoranting Park	陶然亭公园	táorántíng gōngyuán
Temple of Heaven	天坛	tiāntán
Tian'anmen	天安门	tiān'ānmén
Tian'anmen Square	天安门广场	tiān'ānmén guǎngchǎng
TV Tower	电视塔	diànshì tǎ
World Trade Centre	国际贸易中心	guójìmàoyì zhōngxīn
Xu Beihong Museum	徐悲鸿纪念馆	xúbēihóng jìniànguǎn
Yonghe Gong	雍和宫	yōnghé gōng
Yuanmingyuan	圆明园	yuánmíngyuán
Zhonglou (Bell Tower)	钟楼	zhōnglóu
Zhongnanhai	中南海	zhōngnán hǎi
Zizhuyuan Park	紫竹院公园	zǐzhúyuàn gōngyuán

volunteers. The square is lined with railings (for crowd control) and you can enter or leave only via the gaps at either end or in the middle. Bicycles are not permitted, and the streets either side are one-way; the street on the east side is for traffic going south, the west side for northbound traffic.

Tian'anmen Square unquestionably makes a strong impression, but this concrete plain dotted with worthy statuary and bounded by monumental

Dissent in Tian'anmen Square

Blood debts must be repaid in kind – the longer the delay, the greater the interest.

Lu Xun, writing after the massacre of 1926.

Chinese history is about to turn a new page. Tian'anmen Square is ours, the people's, and we will not allow butchers to tread on it.

Wuer Kaixi, student, May 1989.

It may have been designed as a space for mass declarations of loyalty, but in the twentieth century **Tian'anmen Square** was as often a venue for expressions of popular dissent; against foreign oppression at the beginning of the century, and, more recently, against its domestic form. The first mass protests occurred here on May 4, 1919, when three thousand students gathered in the square to protest at the disastrous terms of the **Versailles Treaty**, in which the victorious allies granted several former German concessions in China to the Japanese. The Chinese, who had sent more than a hundred thousand labourers to work in the supply lines of the British and French forces, were outraged. The protests of May 4, and the movement they spawned, marked the beginning of the painful struggle of Chinese modernization. In the turbulent years of the 1920s the inhabitants of Beijing again occupied the square, first in 1925, to protest over the **massacre in Shanghai** of Chinese demonstrators by British troops, then in 1926, when the public protested after the weak government's capitulation to the Japanese. Demonstrators marched on the government offices and were fired on by soldiers.

In 1976, after the death of popular premier Zhou Enlai, thousands of mourners assembled in Tian'anmen without government approval, to voice their dissatisfaction with their leaders, and again in 1978 and 1979, groups assembled here to discuss new ideas of **democracy and artistic freedom**, triggered by writings posted along Democracy Wall on the edge of the Forbidden City. In 1986 and 1987, people gathered again to show solidarity for the **students** and others protesting at the Party's refusal to allow elections.

But it was in **1989** that Tian'anmen Square became the venue for a massive expression of **popular dissent**, when, from April to June, nearly a million protesters demonstrated against the slowness of reform, lack of freedom and widespread corruption. A giant statue, the Goddess of Liberty, a woman carrying a torch in both hands, was created by art students and set up facing Mao's portrait on Tian'anmen. The government, infuriated at being humiliated by their own people, declared martial law on May 20, and on **June 4** the military moved in. The killing was indiscriminate; tanks ran over tents and machine guns strafed the avenues. No one knows how many died in the massacre – probably thousands. Hundreds were arrested afterwards and many are still in jail. The problems the protesters complained of have not been dealt with, and many, such as corruption, have worsened. Look out for droves of undercover police on the massacre's anniversary.

buildings can seem inhuman. Together with the bloody associations it has for many visitors, it often leaves people cold, especially Westerners unused to such magisterial representations of political power. For many Chinese tourists, though, the square is a place of **pilgrimage**. Crowds of peasants flock to see the corpse of Chairman Mao, others quietly bow their heads before the **Monument to the Heroes**, a thirty-metre-high obelisk commemorating the victims of the revolutionary struggle. Among the visitors is the occasional monk, and the sight of robed Buddhists standing in front of the uniformed sentries outside the Great Hall of the People makes a striking juxtaposition. Others come just to hang out or to fly kites, but the atmosphere is not relaxed and a ¥5 fine for spitting and littering is rigorously enforced. At dawn, the flag at the northern

△ Tian'anmen Square

end of the square is raised in a military ceremony and lowered again at dusk, which is when most people come to see it, though foreigners complain that the regimentation of the crowds is oppressive and reminds them of school. After dark, the square is at its most appealing and, with its sternness softened by mellow lighting, it becomes the haunt of strolling families and lovers.

For an overview of the square, head to the south gate, **Zhenyangmen** (daily 9am–4pm; ¥3), similar to Tian'anmen (the north gate) and 40m high, which gives a good idea of how much more impressive the square would look if Mao's mausoleum hadn't been stuck in the middle of it. A diorama inside shows what the area looked like in 1750.

The Chairman Mao Memorial Hall

At the centre of the centre of China lies a corpse that nobody dare remove.
Tiziano Terzani, Behind the Forbidden Door

The **Chairman Mao Memorial Hall**, home to the pickled corpse of the architect of modern China, is an ugly building, looking like a school gym, which contravenes the principles of *feng shui* (geomancy), presumably deliberately, by interrupting the line from the palace to Qianmen and by facing north. Mao himself wanted to be cremated, and the erection of the mausoleum was apparently no more than a power ploy by his would-be successor, Hua Guofeng. In 1980 Deng Xiaoping said it should never have been built, although he wouldn't go so far as to pull it down.

The memorial hall is open every morning from 8.30am to 11.30am, and also from 2pm to 4pm on Monday, Wednesday and Friday from October to April. After depositing your bag at the offices on the eastern side, you join the orderly queue of Chinese on the northern side. This advances surprisingly quickly, and takes just a couple of minutes to file through the chambers in silence – photography is banned, the atmosphere is reverent and any joking around will cause deep offence. Mao's corpse is draped with a red flag within a crystal coffin. Mechanically raised from a freezer every morning, it looks unreal, like wax or plastic. It is said to have been embalmed with the aid of Vietnamese technicians who had recently worked on Ho Chi Minh (rumour has it that Mao's left ear fell off and had to be stitched back on). Once through the marble halls, you're herded past a splendidly wide array of tacky Chairman Mao souvenirs.

Great Hall of the People and the museums

Taking up almost half the west side of the square is the **Great Hall of the People**. This is the venue of the National People's Congress and hundreds of black Audis with tinted windows are parked outside when it's in session. When it isn't, it's open to the public (daily 8.30am–3pm; ¥20; buy tickets and leave bags at the office on the south side). What you see on the mandatory route is a selection of the 29 reception rooms – all looking like the lobby of a Chinese three-star hotel, with badly fitted red carpet and armchairs lined up against the walls.

On the other side of the square, there are two **museums** (Tues–Sun 8.30am–4.30pm) housed in the same building: the **Museum of Chinese History**, covering everything up to 1919, and the **Museum of the Revolution**. Both are full of propaganda; the latter often closing for refits (for twelve years during the Cultural Revolution, for example) as its curators are faced with the Kafkaesque dilemma of constantly having to reinvent history according to the latest Party line. At the time of writing, it was closed yet again, presumably to be refitted in time for the Olympics. A temporary waxworks show (¥10) has models of superstar communists, if that's your idea of entertainment.

The **Museum of Chinese History** is more interesting, though again it's presently being refitted. A temporary exhibition (¥20) of some of the museum's highlights – a bronze rhino and a figurine of a storyteller banging a drum from the Han, fearsome Tang tomb guardians – should whet the appetite, though they could be better lit and presented. Other themed exhibitions of parts of the collection (¥10–20) occupy other rooms.

Tian'anmen and towards the Forbidden City

Tian'anmen, the "Gate of Heavenly Peace" (daily 8am–5pm; ¥30, students ¥10), is the main entrance to the Forbidden City. The boxy gatehouse is familiar across the world, and occupies an exalted place in Chinese communist iconography, appearing on banknotes, coins, stamps and indeed virtually any piece of state paper you can imagine. As such it's a prime object of pilgrimage, with many visitors milling around waiting to be photographed in front of the large **portrait of Mao** (one of the very few still on public display), which hangs over the central passageway. From the reviewing platform above, Mao delivered the liberation speech on October 1, 1949, declaring that "the Chinese people have now stood up". For the pricey entrance fee you can climb up to this platform yourself, where security is tight – all visitors have to leave their bags, are frisked and have to go through a metal detector, before they can ascend. Inside, the fact that most people cluster around the souvenir stall selling official certificates of their trip reflects the fact that there's not much to look at.

Once through Tian'anmen, you find yourself on a long walkway, with the moated palace complex and massive Wumen gate directly ahead (this is where you buy your ticket to the Forbidden City). The two parks either side, Zhongshan and the People's Culture Park (both daily 6am–9pm), are great places to chill out away from the rigorous formality outside. The **Workers' Culture Palace** (¥5), on the eastern side, which was symbolically named in deference to the fact that only with the Communist takeover in 1949 were ordinary Chinese allowed within this central sector of their city, has a number of modern exhibition halls (sometimes worth checking) and a scattering of original fifteenth-century structures, most of them Ming or Qing ancestral temples. The hall at the back often holds prestigious art exhibitions. The western **Zhongshan Park** (¥1) boasts the remains of the Altar of Land and Grain, a biennial sacrificial site with harvest functions closely related to those of the Temple of Heaven (see p.110).

The Forbidden City

The Gugong, or Imperial Palace, is much better known by its unofficial title, the **Forbidden City**, a reference to its exclusivity. Indeed, for the five centuries of its operation, through the reigns of 24 emperors of the Ming and Qing dynasties, ordinary Chinese were forbidden from even approaching the walls of the palace. The complex, with its maze of eight hundred buildings and reputed nine thousand chambers, was the symbolic and literal heart of the capital, and of the empire too. From within, the **emperors**, the Sons of Heaven, issued commands with absolute authority to their millions of subjects.

Although the earliest structures on the Forbidden City site began with Kublai Khan during the Mongol dynasty, the **plan** of the palace buildings is essentially Ming. Most date to the fifteenth century and the ambitions of the Emperor Yongle, the monarch responsible for switching the capital back to Beijing in 1403. The halls were laid out according to geomantic theories – in accordance to the *yin* and *yang*, the balance of negative and positive – and since they stood at the exact centre of Beijing, and Beijing was considered the centre of the universe, the harmony was supreme. The palace complex constantly reiterates such references, alongside personal symbols of imperial power such as the dragon and phoenix (emperor and empress) and the crane and turtle (longevity of reign).

After the Manchu dynasty fell in 1911, the Forbidden City began to fall into disrepair, exacerbated by looting of artefacts and jewels by the Japanese in the 1930s and again by the Nationalists, prior to their flight to Taiwan, in 1949. A programme of **restoration** has been under way for decades, and today the complex is in better shape than it was for most of the last century.

To do it justice, you should plan to spend a day here, though you can wander the complex for a week and keep discovering new aspects. The central halls, with their wealth of imperial pomp, may be the most magnificent buildings, but for many visitors it's the side rooms, with their displays of the more intimate accoutrements of court life, that bring home the realities of life for the inhabitants of this, the most gilded of cages.

Visiting the Forbidden City

The complex is open to visitors daily 8.30am–5pm in summer, 8.30am–4.30pm in winter, with last admission an hour before closing (¥40, ¥60 including the special exhibitions). Note that the entrance is quite a way after Tian'anmen; just keep on past the souvenir stalls till you can't go any further; as well as the main entrance under Tian'anmen you can also come in through the smaller north and east gates. You have the freedom of most of the hundred-hectare site, though not all of the buildings, which are labelled in English. If you want detailed explanation of everything you see, you can tag on to one of the numerous tour groups or buy one of the many specialist books on sale. The audio tour

---

Life inside the Forbidden City

The emperors rarely left the Foribidden City – perhaps with good reason. Their lives, right down to the fall of the Manchu in the twentieth century, were governed by an extraordinarily developed taste for luxury and excess. It is estimated that a single meal for a Qing emperor could have fed several thousand of his impoverished peasants, a scale obviously appreciated by the last influential occupant, the Empress Dowager Cixi (see box, p.125), who herself would commonly order preparation of a hundred and eight dishes at a single meal. Sex, too, provided startling statistics, with the number of Ming-dynasty **concubines** approaching ten thousand. At night, the emperor chose a girl from his harem by picking out a tablet bearing her name from a pile on a silver tray. She would be delivered to the emperor's bedchamber naked but for a yellow cloth wrapped around her, and carried on the back of a servant, since she could barely walk with her bound feet.

The only other men allowed into the palace were **eunuchs**, to ensure the authenticity of the emperor's offspring. In daily contact with the royals, they often rose to considerable power, but this was bought at the expense of their dreadfully low standing outside the confines of the court. Confucianism held that disfiguration of the body impaired the soul, and eunuchs were buried apart from their ancestors in special graveyards outside the city. In the hope that they would still be buried "whole", they kept and carried around their testicles in bags hung on their belts. They were usually recruited from the poorest families – attracted by the rare chance of amassing wealth other than by birth. Eunuchry was finally banned in 1924 and the remaining 1500 eunuchs were expelled from the palace. An observer described them "carrying their belongings in sacks and crying piteously in high-pitched voices."

(¥30), available by the main gate, is also worth considering. You're provided with a cassette player and headphones and suavely talked through the complex by Roger Moore – though if you do this, it's worth retracing your steps afterwards for an untutored view. Useful **bus routes** serving the Forbidden City are #5 from Qianmen, and #54 from Beijing Zhan, or you could use #1, which passes the complex on its journey along Chang'an Jie. You can get to the back gate on buses #101, #103 or #109. The nearest **metros** are Tian'anmen west and east. If you're in a **taxi**, you can save yourself the walk across Tian'anmen Square by asking to be dropped at the east gate.

From Wumen to Taiheman

The **Wumen** (Meridian Gate) itself is the largest and grandest of the Forbidden City gates and was reserved for the emperor's sole use. From its vantage point, the Sons of Heaven would announce the new year's calendar to their court and inspect the army in times of war. It was customary for victorious generals returning from battle to present their prisoners here for the emperor to decide their fate. He would be flanked, on all such imperial occasions, by a guard of elephants, the gift of Burmese subjects.

Passing through the Wumen you find yourself in a vast paved court, cut east–west by the **Jinshui He**, the Golden Water Stream, with its five marble bridges, decorated with carved torches, a symbol of masculinity. Beyond is a further ceremonial gate, the **Taihemen**, Gate of Supreme Harmony, its entrance guarded by a magisterial row of lions, and beyond this a still greater courtyard where the principal imperial audiences were held. Within this space the entire court, up to one hundred thousand people, could be accommodated. They would have made their way in through the lesser side gates – military men from the west, civilian officials from the east – and waited in total silence as the emperor ascended his throne. Then, with only the Imperial Guard remaining standing, they kowtowed nine times.

The ceremonial halls

The main **ceremonial halls** stand directly ahead, dominating the court. Raised on a three-tiered marble terrace is the first and most spectacular of the three, the **Taihedian**, Hall of Supreme Harmony. This was used for the most important state occasions, such as the emperor's coronation or birthdays and the nomination of generals at the outset of a campaign, and last saw action in an armistice ceremony in 1918. A marble pavement ramp, intricately carved with dragons and flanked by bronze incense burners, marks the path along which the emperor's chair was carried. His golden dragon throne stands within.

Moving on, you enter the **Zhonghedian**, Hall of Middle Harmony, another throne room, where the emperor performed ceremonies of greeting to foreigners and addressed the imperial offspring (the product of several wives and numerous concubines). The hall was used, too, as a dressing room, for the major Taihedian events, and it was here that the emperor examined the seed for each year's crop.

The third of the great halls, the **Baohedian**, Preserving Harmony Hall, was used for state banquets and imperial examinations, graduates from which were appointed to positions of power in what was the first recognizably bureaucratic civil service. Its galleries, originally treasure houses, display various finds from the site, though the most spectacular, a vast block carved with dragons and clouds, stands at the rear of the hall. This is a Ming creation, reworked in the eighteenth century, and it's among the finest carvings in the palace. It's certainly the largest – a 250-tonne chunk of marble transported here from well outside the city by flooding the roads in winter to form sheets of ice.

To the north, paralleling the structure of the ceremonial halls, are the three principal palaces of the **imperial living quarters**. Again, the first chamber, the **Qianqinggong**, Palace of Heavenly Purity, is the most extravagant. It was originally the imperial bedroom – its terrace is surmounted by incense burners in the form of cranes and tortoises (symbols of immortality) – though it later became a conventional state room. Beyond, echoing the Zhonghedian in the ceremonial complex, is the **Jiaotaidian**, Hall of Union, the empress's throne room, and finally the **Kunninggong**, Palace of Earthly Tranquillity, where the emperor and empress traditionally spent their wedding night. By law the emperor had to spend the first three nights of his marriage, and the first day of Chinese New Year, with his wife. This palace is a bizarre building, partitioned in two. On the left is a large sacrificial room with its vats ready to receive offerings (1300 pigs a year under the Ming). The wedding chamber is a small room, off to one side, painted entirely in red, and covered with decorative emblems symbolizing fertility and joy. It was last pressed into operation in 1922 for the child wedding of Pu Yi, the last emperor, who, finding it "like a melted red wax candle", decided that he preferred the Mind Nurture Palace and went back there.

The Mind Nurture Palace, or **Yangxindiang**, is one of a group of palaces to the west where emperors spent most of their time. Several of the palaces retain their furniture from the Manchu times, most of it eighteenth-century; in one, the **Changchundong** (Palace of Eternal Spring), is a series of paintings illustrating the Ming novel, *The Story of the Stone*. To the east is a similarly arranged group of palaces, adapted as **museum galleries** for displays of bronzes, ceramics, paintings, jewellery and Ming and Qing arts and crafts. The atmosphere here is much more intimate, and you can peer into well-appointed chambers full of elegant furniture and ornaments, including English clocks decorated with images of English gentlefolk, which look very odd among the jade trees and ornate fly whisks.

Head over to the other side of the complex to the eastern palace quarters where an extraordinary **Clock Museum** (¥10) is housed, displaying the result of one Qing emperor's collecting passion. Most are English and French explosions of Baroque ornament, though perhaps the most arresting is a rhino-sized Chinese water clock.

Moving away from the palace chambers – and by this stage something of a respite – the Kunningmen leads out from the Inner Court to the **Imperial Garden**. There are a couple of cafés here (and toilets) amid a pleasing network of ponds, walkways and pavilions, the classic elements of a Chinese garden. At the centre is the **Qinandian**, Hall of Imperial Peace, dedicated to the Taoist god of fire, Xuan Wu. You can exit here into Jingshan Park, which provides an overview of the complex – see p.117.

South of Tian'anmen

The **Qianmen** area (see map p.100), to the south of Tian'anmen, offers a tempting antidote to the prodigious grandeurs of the Forbidden City – and a quick shift of scale. The lanes and *hutongs* here comprise a **traditional shopping quarter**, full of small, specialist stores which to a large extent remain grouped according to their particular trades. It's a part of the city to browse in, and a good place to eat, with one of the best selections of snacks available in the capital. Down Qianmen

Dajie, once the Imperial Way, now a clogged road clustered with small shops, the **Museums of Natural History** and **Architecture** are worth a browse, and **Tiantan**, the ravishing Temple of Heaven, perfectly set in one of Beijing's best parks, is an example of imperial architecture at its best.

Qianmen

The entry to this quarter is marked by the imposing, fifteenth-century, double-arched **Qianmen Gate** just south of Tian'anmen Square. Before the city's walls were demolished, this sector controlled the entrance to the inner city from the outer, suburban sector. Shops and places of entertainment were banned from the former in imperial days, and they became concentrated in the Qianmen area.

Qianmen Dajie, the quarter's biggest street, runs immediately south from the gate; off to either side are trading streets and *hutongs*, with intriguing traditional pharmacies and herbalist shops, dozens of clothes shops, silk traders and an impressive array of side-stalls and cake shops selling fresh food and cooked snacks.

Once the district was noisy with opera singers. Today the theatres have been converted to **cinemas** and the area resounds instead with film soundtracks, piped into the street, and with the bips and beeps of the computer games sold at street stalls. For a rather sanitized taste of the district's old delights, visit the *Lao She Tea House* which puts on daily shows of acrobatics and opera (see p.136).

Dazhalan Lu

Cramped **Dazhalan Lu** is the oldest and most interesting of the Qianmen lanes leading west off Qianmen Dajie; the lane's entrance is marked by a white arch opposite the *Qianmen Roast Duck* restaurant on the east side of the road. This was once a major theatre street, now it's a hectic shopping district, with mostly tea shops and clothing stores occupying the genteel old buildings. Go down the first alley on the left, and one of the first shops you'll pass on the right is the Liubiju, a **pickle shop** that's more than a century old. It looks quaint, with pickled vegetables sold out of ceramic jars, but smells awful. Back on Dazhalan, you'll find, at no. 24, Tongrengtang, a famous traditional **Chinese medicine store**, with shelves full of deer horn, bear heart capsules and the like, and a formidable array of aphrodisiacs. At the end of the street, marked by a scattering of Chinese-only hotels, was the old red-light district formerly containing more than three hundred brothels. This is one of the last substantial networks of **hutongs** left in the city, and it's certainly worth wandering (or, better, biking) down random alleyways, though expect to get lost.

Liulichang Jie

Turn north at the western end of Dazhalan, then head west along a *hutong*, then north and west again, to reach **Liulichang Jie**, parallel to Dazhalan Jie. Liulichang, whose name literally means "glaze factory street", after the erstwhile factories here making glazed tiles for the roofs of the Forbidden City, has been rebuilt as a heritage street, using Ming-style architecture; today it's full of **curio stores** (remember to bargain hard, and assume everything is fake) and bookshops.

The Natural History and Architecture museums

It's a long and boring thirty-minute walk from the northern end of Qianmen Dajie down to the **Natural History Museum** (daily 8.30am–5pm; ¥15), a few blocks farther south; take bus #17 or #20. After halls of stuffed wildlife and plastic dinosaurs, check out the gruesome exhibition in the building to the left of the entrance. Pickled human legs, arms, brains and foetuses are arranged around the stars of the show, two adult corpses – a woman wearing socks, gloves and a hood, and a man with all his skin removed, leaving just the fingernails and lips. You can recover in the sedate environs of the **Museum of Architecture** (daily 9am–5pm; ¥15) a short walk to the southwest. Look for the red arch south off Beiwei Lu; the ticket office is just beyond here and the museum itself is further down the road on the right. This was once the Xiannong Temple, where the Emperor ritually ploughed a furrow to ensure a good harvest. You can see the gold-plated plough he used in the Hall of Worship. The Hall of Jupiter has a fantastically ornate ceiling and cutaway models of famous buildings from all over the country. Anyone who has ever wondered how a dougong works – those ornate interlocking brackets seen on temples – can satisfy their curiosity here. A model of the city as it appeared in 1949, before the communists ripped it up, shows how the Imperial buildings that remain today are fragments from an awesome grand design.

The Temple of Heaven – Tiantan

Set in its own large and tranquil park about 2km south of Tian'anmen along Qianmen Dajie, the **Temple of Heaven** (daily 8.30am–8pm, buildings close at 5pm; ¥30 for a ticket that includes access to all buildings; just the park low season ¥10, high season ¥15) is widely regarded as the high point of Ming design. For five centuries it was at the very heart of imperial ceremony and symbolism, and for many modern visitors its architectural unity and beauty remain more appealing – and on a much more accessible scale – than the Forbidden City. There are various bus routes to Tiantan: bus #106 runs from Dongzhimen to the north entrance; #54 passes the west gate on its way from Beijing Zhan; #17 passes the west gate on its way from Qianmen; and #41 from Chongwenmen stops close to the east gate.

The temple was begun during the reign of Emperor Yongle and completed in 1420. It was conceived as the prime meeting point of Earth and Heaven, and symbols of the two are integral to its plan. Heaven was considered round, and Earth square, thus the round temples and altars stand on square bases, while the whole park has the shape of a semicircle sitting beside a square. The intermediary between Earth and Heaven was of course the **Son of Heaven**, the emperor, and the temple was the site of the most important ceremony of the imperial court calendar, when the emperor prayed for the year's harvests at the **winter solstice**. Purified by three days of fasting, he made his way to the park on the day before the solstice, accompanied by his court in all its magnificence. On arrival, he would meditate in the Imperial Vault, ritually conversing with the gods on the details of government, before spending the night in the Hall of Prayer of Good Harvests. The following day, amid exact and numerological ritual, the emperor performed animal sacrifices before the Throne of Heaven at the Round Altar.

It was forbidden for the commoners of old Beijing to catch a glimpse of the great annual procession to the temple and they were obliged to bolt their windows and remain, in silence, indoors. The Tiantan complex remained sacrosanct until it was thrown open to the people on the first Chinese National Day of the Republic in October 1912. Two years after this, the infamous General Yuan Shikai performed the solstice ceremonies himself, as part of his attempt to be proclaimed emperor. He died before the year was out.

The temple buildings

Although you're more likely to enter the actual park from the north or the west, to appreciate the religious ensemble it's best initially to skirt round in order to follow the ceremonial route up from the south entrance, the Zhaohen Gate. The main pathway leads straight to the **Round Altar**, consisting of three marble tiers representing Man, Earth and (at the summit) Heaven. The tiers themselves are composed of blocks in various multiples of nine, which the Chinese saw as cosmologically the most powerful odd number, representing both Heaven and Emperor. The top terrace now stands bare, but the spot at its centre, where the Throne of Heaven was placed, was considered to be the middle of the Middle Kingdom – the very centre of the earth. Various acoustic properties are claimed for the surrounding tiers, and from this point it is said that all sounds are channelled straight upwards. To the east of the fountain, which was reconstructed after fire damage in 1740, are the ruins of a group of buildings used for the preparation of sacrifices.

Directly ahead, the **Imperial Vault of Heaven** is an octagonal structure made entirely of wood, with a dramatic roof of dark blue, glazed tiles. It is preceded by the so-called **Echo Wall**, said to be a perfect whispering gallery, although the unceasing cacophony of tourists trying it out makes it impossible to tell.

The principal temple building – the **Hall of Prayer for Good Harvests**, at the north end of the park – amply justifies all this build-up. It is, quite simply, a wonder. Made entirely of wood, without the aid of a single nail, the circular structure rises from another three-tiered marble terrace, to be topped by three blue-tiled roofs of harmonious proportions. Four compass-point pillars support the vault (in representation of the seasons), enclosed in turn by twelve outer pillars (for the months of the year and the watches of the day). The dazzling colours of the interior, surrounding the central dragon motif, make the pavilion seem ultramodern; it was in fact entirely rebuilt, faithful to the Ming design, after the original was destroyed by lightning in 1889. The official explanation for this appalling omen was that it was divine punishment meted out on a sacrilegious caterpillar, which was on the point of reaching the golden ball on the hall's apex when the lightning struck. Thirty-two court dignitaries were executed for allowing this to happen.

Niu Jie and the Muslim quarter

Some 3km southwest of Qianmen, **Niu Jie** (Ox Street) is a cramped thoroughfare in the city's **Muslim quarter**. The street, a *hutong* leading off Guang'anmenwai Dajie, on the route of bus #6 from the north gate of Tiantan Park, is lined with offal stalls and vendors selling fried dough rings, rice cakes and *shaobang* (muffins). The white hats and the beards worn by the men are what most obviously set these Hui minority people apart from the Han Chinese – there are nearly two hundred thousand of them in the capital. The focus of the street is the **mosque** (daily 8am–5pm; ¥10) at its southern end, an attractive building colourfully decorated in Chinese style with abstract decorations and text in Chinese and Arabic over the doors. You won't get to see the handwritten copy of the Koran, dating back to the Yuan dynasty, without special permission, or be allowed into the main prayer hall if you're not a Muslim, but you can inspect the courtyard, where a copper cauldron, used to cook food for the devotees, sits near the graves of two Persian imams who came here to preach in the thirteenth century.

West of the centre

Heading west from Tian'anmen Square along **Chang'an Jie**, the giant freeway that runs east–west across the city, you pass a string of grandiose buildings, the headquarters of official and corporate power. Though most of the sites and amenities are elsewhere, western Beijing has enough of interest to kill a day or two. There's a good shopping district, Xidan, the Military Museum, and the pleasant **Baiyun Guan** to chill out in.

Zhongnanhai to Xidan

From Tian'anmen Square, the first major building you pass on the right is the **Communist Party Headquarters**, the **Zhongnanhai**. It's not hard to spot as armed sentries stand outside the gates, ensuring that only invited guests actually get inside. This is perhaps the most important and historic building in the country, base since 1949 of the Central Committee and the Central People's Government, and Mao and Zhou Enlai both worked here. Before the Communist takeover it was home to the Empress Dowager Cixi.

Just west, the **Aviation Office**, the place to buy tickets and catch the airport bus, stands on the site of Democracy Wall, and over the road looms the **Beijing Concert Hall**, recessed a little from the street, another uninspiring construction.

Xidan, the street heading north from the next junction, is worth exploring, at least along its initial few blocks, though not at weekends, when it's heaving with people. This is where the locals shop, and the area is a dense concentration of **department stores**. The choice is less esoteric and the shopping experience less earthy than in Qianmen, but if you want to know what the kids are wearing this season, this is the place to go.

It takes persistence to continue much beyond this point, though you might be spurred on by the sight of the **Parkson Building** on the north side of the next junction, a shopping centre for seriously rich Chinese. On the fifth floor of the south building is an exhibition hall (daily 9.30am–4.30pm; ¥15,

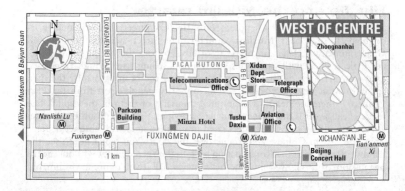

students ¥4) with the air of an exclusive private collection, showing "master-pieces" from the craftwork factories across China – similar to the stuff you'll see in the Friendship Store but of much better quality. Though it's all terribly kitsch – a Red Army meeting in ivory, for example – the craftsmanship in evidence is astonishing. If you're peckish, there's a giant food court on the sixth floor.

Two kilometres west of here, another stern Soviet-style building on Fuxing Lu suits its purpose as the **Military Museum** (daily 8am–4.30pm; ¥5), more exciting than its name suggests. Catch bus #1, which terminates close by, or the metro to Junshi Bowuguan. On entering you are confronted with giant paintings celebrating martial valour, then an enormous rocket stands proud at the centre of the high main hall. With none of the problems that dog other museums of contemporary history in China – the need to tweak the displays with every shift of Party line – the museum does its job of impressing you with China's military might and achievements very well. The exhibits stake out the history of the **People's Liberation Army**, with heavy emphasis, inevitably, on the war against the Nationalists and the Japanese. Curiosities include, in the rear courtyard, a somewhat miscellaneous group of old aircraft – among them the shells of two American spy planes (with Nationalist mark-ings) shot down in the 1950s. Upstairs, there's an exhibition on the Korean War and a "Friendship Hall" which displays gifts from other countries; competition for the most tasteless is fierce, but the gold machine gun from the Lebanon deserves a mention.

The TV Tower and Baiyun Guan

There's little reason to continue west from here – you can visit the four-hundred-metre-high **TV Tower** on Nansanhuan Lu (daily 8am–5pm), which offers a spectacular view over the city, but it costs a steep ¥50. It's more worthwhile to head a little south to the **Baiyun Guan**, White Cloud Temple (daily 8am–5.30pm; ¥10), just off Baiyun Lu and signposted in English. You can get here on bus #212 from Qianmen, or bus #40 from Nansanhuan Lu. Once the most influential Taoist centre in the country, the temple has been extensively renovated after a long spell as a military barracks and is now the location for the China Taoism Association. There are thirty resident monks, and it's become a popular place for pilgrims, with a busy, thriving feel to it, in some ways preferable to the more touristy Lamaist temple, the Yonghe Gong (see p.120). There are three monkeys depicted in relief sculptures around the temple, and it is believed to be lucky to find all three: the first is on the gate, easy to spot as it's been rubbed black, and the other two are in the first courtyard. Though laid out in a similar way to a Buddhist temple, it has a few unusual features, such as the three gateways at the entrance, symbolizing the three worlds of Taoism – Desire, Substance and Emptiness. The attached bookshop has only one text in English, the *Book of Changes*, but plenty of tapes and lucky charms. The place is at its most colourful during the New Year temple fair (see "Festivals", p.67).

East of the centre

As you head east from Tian'anmen Square, the first big billboard opposite Wangfujing marks the abrupt transition from the dour political zone to the upmarket, commercial eastern side of the city. Here you'll find **Wangfujing,**

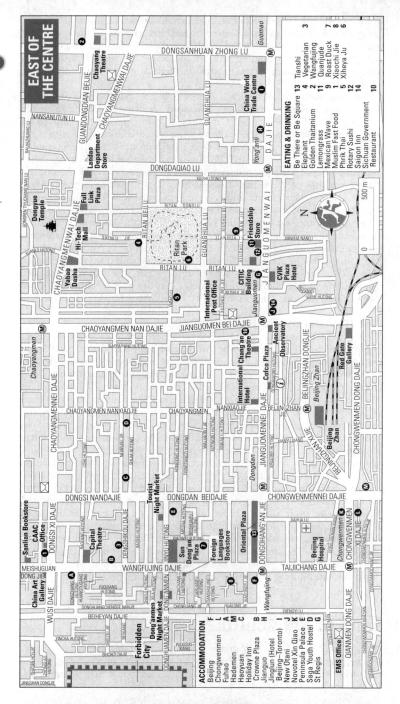

EAST OF THE CENTRE

EATING & DRINKING
Be There or Be Square	13
Elephant	4
Golden Thaitanium	2
Lemongrass	11
Mexican Wave	1
Muslim Fast Food	9
Phrik Thai	5
Rotary Sushi	12
Saigon Inn	14
Sichuan Government Restaurant	10
Tianshi	3
Vegetarian	
Wangfujing	7
Quanjude	8
Roast Duck	6
Xiaochi Jie	
Xiheya Ju	

ACCOMMODATION
Beijing	F
Chongwenmen	L
Fuhao	A
Hademen	M
Haoyuan	C
Holiday Inn	B
Crowne Plaza	
Jianguo	H
Jinglun (Hotel)	J
Beijing–Toronto)	
New Otani	J
Novotel Xin Qiao	K
Peninsula Palace	D
Saga Youth Hostel	E
St Regis	G

the oldest shopping street in the city, and still one of the best, though these days the international zone of Jianguomen, further east, is rather more glamorous. It's not all mindless materialism; the **China Art Gallery**, at the north end of Wangfujing, and the **Ancient Observatory** on Jiangguomen are welcoming oases of culture.

Wangfujing

Wangfujing Dajie (head north from the *Beijing Hotel* on Dongchang'an Jie) is where the capital gets down to the business of **shopping** in earnest. But it does have some decent sights as well, and it's short enough to stroll along its length. For a century the haunt of quality stores, on the western side of the street are plenty of small stores selling clothes. Just before the crossroads with Dong'anmen Jie is the Foreign Language Bookstore, the largest in China and a good resource for travellers (see p.138 for more details). On the other side of the street, the Sun Dong'an Plaza is a glitzy mall; you're better off going for a snack or to change money at the Bank of China (ground floor; Mon–Fri 9am–noon & 1.30–5pm) than to buy any of the very pricey, mostly designer clothes on sale, though the basement stalls are worth a browse if you're after tea or souvenirs.

On the eastern side of the street a number of **hutongs** lead into a quiet area well away from the bustle of the main street. The ten brothers of a Ming-dynasty emperor used to live here, so that he could keep a wary eye on them, and you can still see their palace at the end of Shuaifuyuan Hutong, now converted into a medical college. Continuing east through the *hutongs*, you'll reach **Dongdan Bei Dajie**, parallel to Wangfujing, which is rapidly becoming a shopping centre to rival it, full of clothing boutiques.

The China Art Gallery

When you're tired of shopping, head north for the **China Art Gallery** (Tues–Sun 9am–4pm; entrance fee varies, ¥2–20), at the top end of Wangfujing, on the route of bus #2 which runs north–south between Qianmen and Andingmen Dajie, or trolleybus #104, which runs between Andingmennei Dajie and Beijing Zhan. A huge and draughty building, it usually holds a couple of shows at once, though there's no permanent collection. Shows in the past have included specialist women's and minority exhibitions, even a show of socialist realist propaganda put up not to inspire renewed vigour but as a way to consider past follies. Revolutionary imagery has long had its day and Chinese painting is enjoying a renaissance, with some very interesting work emerging from the Beijing art colleges. You can check their work out in July, when they hold their degree shows here, and it's also a good place to meet some of the most boho Chinese, the art students. Check the listings magazines for what's on.

Jianguomen Dajie

Jianguomen Dajie, the strip beyond the second ring road, is Beijing's rich quarter – a ritzy area with an international flavour thanks to its large contingent of foreigners and staff from the weird Jianguomen embassy compound. Eating and staying around here will soon sap most travellers' budgets (first-time tourists can be heard here expressing disappointment that China is as expensive as New York), but the wide variety of shopping offered – good clothes markets, the Friendship Store, and malls that wouldn't look out of place in Hong Kong – will suit all pockets.

An unexpected survivor marooned amid the high-rises, the **Ancient Observatory** (Mon–Fri 9–11.30am & 1–4.30pm; ¥10) is a delightful surprise, tucked in the southwest corner of the Jianguomen intersection, beside the Jianguomen metro stop. The first observatory on this site was founded under the orders of Kublai Khan, the astronomers' commission being to reform the then faulty calendar. Later it was staffed by Muslim scientists, as medieval Islamic science enjoyed pre-eminence, but, bizarrely, in the early seventeenth century it was placed in the hands of Jesuit Christian missionaries. The Jesuits, a small group led by one Matteo Ricci, arrived in Beijing in 1601 and astonished citizens and emperor by a series of precise astronomical forecasts. They re-equipped the observatory and remained in charge through to the 1830s. Today the building is essentially a shell, and the best features of the complex are the **garden**, a placid retreat, and the eight Ming-dynasty **astronomical instruments** sitting on the roof, stunningly sculptural armillary spheres, theodolites and the like. The small **museum** attached, displaying early astronomy-influenced pottery and navigational equipment, is an added bonus.

Turn up Ritan Lu and you'll hit the **Jianguomenwai Diplomatic Compound**, the first of two embassy complexes (the other is at Sanlitun, well northeast of here), a giant toytown with neat buildings in ordered courtyards and frozen sentries on red and white plinths. **Ritan Park** is a five-minute walk from Jianguomen Dajie. It's popular with embassy staff and courting couples, who make use of its numerous secluded nooks. It also hosts a few upscale restaurants.

Back on Jianguomen Dajie, you'll reach the **Friendship Store**, the Chinese state's idea of a shopping centre, once the only kind allowed, and now overtaken by its commercial competitors. Its top floors are devoted to the usual range of goods – clothes, jewellery and paintings – but its lower floor is more use, with a foreign exchange (open every day), a supermarket selling plenty of foreign goodies, an information desk where you can pick up the *China Daily*, and a bookshop. There's also a photo booth for your visa photographs. Outside is a string of upmarket coffee bars and restaurants, including a pricey *Starbucks*. On the other side of the road, the CVIK Plaza (daily 9am–9pm) is a more modern shopping centre with five floors of clothes and accessories. There's a food court in the basement and a Bank of China on the first floor.

It's a long way, and you may be all shopped out by now, but dedicated consumers who continue to the **World Trade Centre**, just before the intersection with the third ring road, about 3km east of here, are rewarded with Beijing's most exclusive mall, four shining storeys of pricey consumables. As well as boutiques there's a post office (Level B1), a Bank of China (Level 2), another *Starbucks* (Level 1) and a *Sparkice* Internet café (Level 2). The basement has a Wellcome Supermarket (the Hong Kong brand), one of the best supermarkets in the city, though it's not cheap.

North of the centre

The area north of the Forbidden City has a scattered collection of sights, many of them remnants of the imperial past, when this area was the home of princes, dukes and monks. Beyond the imperial parks of **Jingshan** and **Beihai** is the one part of the city that is truly a pleasure to walk around – the well-preserved *hutong* district. Tucked away here you'll find **Prince Gong's Palace**, **Song Qingling's Residence** and the **Bell** and **Drum towers**, all within strolling distance of one another, though expect to get lost. Further west are two thought-provoking museums dedicated to writer Lu Xun and artist Xu Beihong, both important influences on modern cultural life. Beijing's finest temple, the **Yonghe Gong**, is in the northern outskirts of the centre, conveniently beside a metro stop, and the quiet **Confucius Temple** nearby offers an intriguing contrast.

Jingshan and Beihai Parks

Jingshan Park (daily 6am–10pm; ¥3) is a natural way to round off a trip to the Forbidden City. An artificial mound, it was created by the digging of the palace moat and served as a windbreak and a barrier to malevolent spirits (believed to emanate from the north) for the imperial quarter of the city. It takes its name, meaning Coal Hill, from a coal store once sited here. Its history, most momentously, includes the suicide of the last Ming emperor, **Chong Zhen**, in 1644, who hanged himself here from a locust tree after rebel troops broke into the imperial city. The spot, on the eastern side of the park, is easy to find as it is signposted everywhere (underneath signs pointing to a children's playground), though the tree that stands here is not the original.

It's the **views** from the top of the hill that make this park such a compelling target: they take in the whole extent of the Forbidden City – giving a revealing perspective – and a fair swathe of the city outside, a deal more attractive than at ground level. To the west is Beihai with its fat snake lake, in the north Gulou and Zhonglou (the Drum and Bell towers), and to the northeast the Yonghe Gong.

Almost half of **Beihai Park** (daily 6am–8pm; ¥5, buildings ¥10), a few hundred metres west of Jingshan on the route of bus #5 from Qianmen, is water – and a favourite ice-skating spot in the winter months. The park was supposedly created by Kublai Khan, long before any of the Forbidden City structures were conceived, and its scale is suitably ambitious: the lake was man-made, an island being created in its midst with the excavated earth. Emperor Qianlong oversaw its landscaping into a classical garden and Mao's widow, the ill-fated Jiang Qing, was a frequent visitor here. Today its elegance is marred by funfairs and shops among the willows and red-columned galleries, though it's still a grand place to retreat from the city and recharge. Most of the buildings (daily 6am–4pm) lie on the central island, whose summit is marked by a white dagoba, built in the mid-seventeenth century to celebrate a visit by the Dalai Lama, a suitable emblem for a park which contains a curious mixture of religious buildings, storehouses for cultural relics and imperial garden architecture.

Just inside the south gate, the **Round City** encloses a courtyard which holds a jade bowl, said to have belonged to Kublai Khan. The white jade Buddha in the hall behind was a present from Burma. The **island** is accessible by a walkway from here. It's dotted with religious architecture, which you'll come across as you scramble around the rocky paths, including the **Yuegu Lou**, a hall full of steles, and the giant **dagoba** sitting on top with a shrine to the demon-headed, multi-armed Lamaist deity, Yamantaka, nestling inside. An exclusive restaurant, the *Fangshan*, sits off a painted corridor running round the base of the hill. There's a boat dock near here, where you can rent rowing **boats**, or you can rent duck-shaped pedal boats from near the south gate – good ways to explore the lake and its banks. On the north side of the lake an impressive **dragon screen**, in good condition, is one of China's largest at 27m long. The Five Dragon Pavilions nearby are supposedly in the shape of a dragon's spine. Over on the other side of the lake, the gardens and rockeries here were popular with

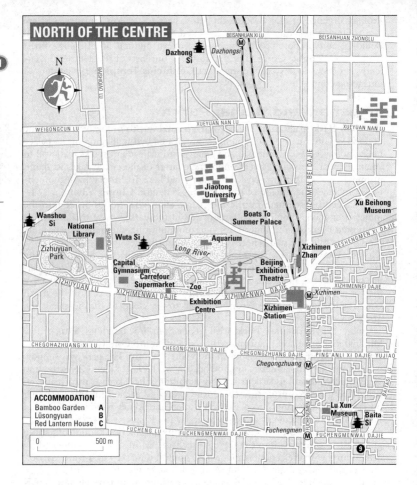

NORTH OF THE CENTRE

Emperor Qianlong, and it's easy to see why – even when the place is crowded at weekends, the atmosphere is tranquil.

The Shicha lake area (Houhai)

The area north of Beihai Park, colloquially known as Houhai, has been subject to very little modernization, and the street plan remains a tangle of alleys, centring on the three artificial **Shicha lakes**, created during the Yuan dynasty, and the port for a canal network that served the capital. The choked, grey alleys show Beijing's other, private, face; here you'll see cluttered courtyards and converted palaces, and come across small open spaces where old men sit with their pet birds. There are also two giant old buildings, the Bell and Drum towers, hidden away among the alleys. The area has recently been prettified, with touristy venues being built and rickshaw tours running from outside the bell tower, but it retains its charm, at least for the moment. It's also become

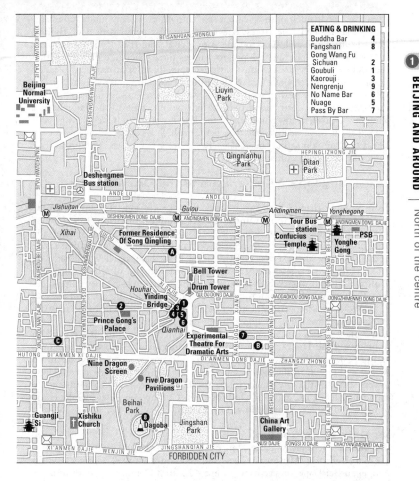

EATING & DRINKING

Buddha Bar	4
Fangshan	8
Gong Wang Fu Sichuan	2
Goubuli	1
Kaorouji	3
Nengrenju	9
No Name Bar	6
Nuage	5
Pass By Bar	7

one of Beijing's hipper hang-outs, with a string of bars and restaurants along the lakeside (see p.133). The best way to get around by yourself is certainly by **bike**. Traffic is light and you're free to dive into any alley you fancy, though you're almost certain to get lost – in which case cycle around until you come to one of the lakes, the only big landmarks around. The best point of entry is the *hutong* nearest the northern entrance to Beihai Park – to get here by bus, take trolleybus #111 from Dondan Bei Dajie, or bus #13 from the Yonghe Gong.

Prince Gong's Palace and around

Residence of the last Qing emperor's father, **Prince Gong's Palace** (daily 9am–4.30pm; ¥10) is the best-kept courtyard house in the city. To get here, follow the curving alley north from Beihai Park's north entrance – Qianhai Hu (the southernmost lake) will be on your right – then take the first left, then the first right on to Qianhai Xi Jie. If you're trying to reach the palace directly by bus, you'll have to get off on Dianmen Xi Dajie and walk the same route. The

119

attractive, leafy garden of the palace is split into discreet compounds and imaginatively landscaped. The largest hall hosts irregular performances of **Beijing Opera** – though you'll have to time your arrival with that of the tour groups, at around 11am, 4pm and 7.30pm, to witness these. There are plenty of other **old palaces** in the area, as this was once something of an imperial pleasure ground and home to a number of high officials and distinguished eunuchs. The Palace of Tao Beile, now a school, is just west of here on Liuyin Jie. Doubling back and heading north along the lake side, you'll come to the humpbacked Yingding Bridge, at the point where the lake is narrowest. Over the bridge is the excellent *Kaorouji Restaurant* (see p.132), which boasts good views over the lake. Opposite you'll find the *Buddha Bar* (among many others), a great place to sit outside with a coffee.

Song Qingling's Residence and the Drum and Bell towers

From Yinding Bridge, head north along the lakeside and loop around to the east and you'll reach **Song Qingling's Residence** (Tues–Sun 9am–4.30pm; ¥8), another Qing mansion, with a delicate, spacious garden. Song Qingling, the wife of Sun Yatsen, commands great respect in China and an exhibition inside details her busy life in a dry, admiring tone. From here, an alley will take you on to Gulou Xi Dajie, a major street, at the eastern end of which squats the **Gulou** (Drum Tower; daily 9am–4.30pm; ¥10), a fifteenth-century Ming creation. From this vantage point drums were beaten to mark the hours of day and night and to call imperial officials to meetings. Every half hour between 10am and noon and from 2pm to 4pm a troupe of drummers whacks cheerfully away at the giant drums inside. They're not, to be blunt, very artful, but it's still an impressive sight. The building's twin, the **Zhonglou** (Bell Tower; same times and prices), is at the other end of the plaza. Originally Ming, it was destroyed by fire and rebuilt in the eighteenth century. It still has its original bell. These towers stand on the city's main north–south axis – head directly south, going round Jingshan Park, and past the Forbidden City, and you'll eventually come to Qianmen Dajie, a route followed by bus #5.

Xu Beihong Museum

Just outside the *hutong* quarter, but easily combined with a visit to Houhai, the **Xu Beihong Museum** (Tues–Sun 9–11am & 1.30–4.30pm; ¥1) at 53 Xinjiekou Bei Dajie, on the route of bus #22 from Qianmen or #38 from the east end of Fuchingmennei Dajie, and five minutes' walk south of Jiushuitan metro stop, is definitely worth the diversion. The son of a wandering portraitist, Xu Beihong (1895–1953) did for Chinese art what his contemporary Lu Xun did for literature. Xu had to look after his whole family from the age of 17 after his father died, and spent much of his early life in semi-destitution before receiving the acclaim he deserved. His extraordinary facility is well in evidence here in seven halls which display a huge collection of his work, including many of the ink paintings of horses he was most famous for, but also oil paintings in a Western style, which he produced when studying in France, and large-scale allegorical images which allude to events in China at the time. But the images it is easiest to respond to are his delightful sketches and studies, in ink and pencil, often of his son.

Yonghe Gong and around

Though it is a little touristy, the colourful **Yonghe Gong**, Tibetan Lama Temple (daily 9am–5pm; ¥25), is well worth a visit; it couldn't be much easier to reach – Yonghe Gong metro stop is right next door. It was built towards the end of the seventeenth century as the residence of Prince Yin Zhen. In 1723, when the prince became the Emperor Yong Zheng and moved into the Forbidden City, the temple was retiled in imperial yellow and restricted thereafter to religious use. It became a lamasery in 1744, housing monks from Tibet and also from Inner Mongolia, over which it had a presiding role, supervising the election of the Mongolian Living Buddha, who was chosen by lot from a gold urn. After the civil war in 1949, the Yonghe Gong was declared a national monument and for thirty years was closed; remarkably, it escaped the ravages of the Cultural Revolution.

Visitors are free to wander through the prayer halls and ornamental gardens, though the experience is largely an aesthetic rather than a spiritual one. As well as the amazing *mandalas* hanging in side halls, there is some notable statuary. In the Third Hall, the **Pavilion of Eternal Happiness**, are **nandikesvras**, representations of Buddha having sex. Once used to educate the emperors' sons, the statues are now completely covered by drapes. The **Hall of the Wheel of Law**, behind it, has a gilded bronze statue of the founder of the Yellow Hat Sect and paintings which depict his life, while the thrones next to it are for the Dalai Lamas when they used to come here to teach. In the last, grandest hall, the **Wanfu Pavilion**, an eighteen-metre-high statue of the Maitreya Buddha, is made from a single trunk of sandalwood, a gift for Emperor Qianlong from the seventh Dalai Lama. The wood is Tibetan and it took three years to ship it to Beijing.

The lamasery also functions as an active **Tibetan Buddhist centre**. It's used basically for propaganda purposes, to show China guaranteeing and respecting the religious freedom of minorities. It's questionable how genuine the monks you see wandering around are – at best, they're state approved. After all, this is where the puppet Panchen Lama chosen by the Chinese government was officially sworn in in 1995. Just before that, the Dalai Lama's own choice for the post, the then 6-year-old Gedhum Choekyi Nyima, "disappeared" (see box, p.1141).

Confucius Temple

Next to the Yonghe Gong, on the west side, is a quiet **hutong** lined with little shops selling religious tapes, incense and images. This street, one of the city's oldest, has been home to scholars since the Yuan dynasty and is lined with *pailous*, decorative arches, which once graced many of Beijing's streets – they were torn down in the 1950s as a hindrance to traffic. On the right, about 100m down, the **Confucius Temple** (daily 8.30am–5pm; ¥10) is a rather dry place, used for decades as a museum. In the courtyard, steles record the names of those who studied here and passed the civil service exams. The last few steles are Qing, paid for by the scholars themselves as the emperor refused to fund them. The Main Hall is a dark, haphazard **museum** holding incense burners and musical instruments. Another, new, museum in a side hall holds a diverse range of artefacts – the Tang pottery, which includes images of pointy-faced foreigners, is the most diverting. At the back, a warehouse-like building holds stele texts of the thirteen Confucian classics, calligraphy which once formed the standard to be emulated by all scholars. But perhaps the best thing to do here is sit on a bench in the peaceful courtyard, among ancient, twisted trees, and enjoy the silence.

Returning to the Yonghe Gong and heading north, **Ditan Park** (daily 6am–9pm; ¥1, buildings ¥5) is just 100m away, more interesting as a place to wander among the trees and spot the odd *tai ji* performance than for its small

museum (¥5) holding the emperor's sedan chair and the enormous altar at which he performed sacrifices to the earth.

Around Fuchengmennei Dajie

Heading west from the south end of Beihai Park along Wenjin Dajie, you'll come to **Fuchengmennei Dajie**, just off Xidan Dajie, the area's shopping district. A couple of places along here make it worth a nose around on the way to the deservedly popular Summer Palace. Bus #101 from the north exit of the Forbidden City, and #13 from the Yonghe Gong, traverse the street. The **Guangji Si**, headquarters of the China Buddhist Association, is a working Buddhist temple near its eastern end, on the north side of the road, with an important collection of painting and sculpture. There's no entrance fee and visitors are free to look around. Farther west along the street you'll come to a temple on the north side that's been converted into a school – the spirit wall now forms one side of a public lavatory. Farther on, the massive white dagoba of the **Baita Si** (Tues–Sun 9am–5pm; ¥10) becomes visible, rising over the rooftops of a labyrinth of *hutongs*; the only access is from Fuchengmennei Dajie. Shaped like an upturned bowl with an ice-cream cone on top, the 35-metre-high dagoba was built to house relics in the Yuan dynasty and designed by a Nepalese architect. The temple is worth a visit just for the collection of small Buddha statues, mostly Tibetan, housed in one hall. Another hall holds a collection of bronze *luohans*, including one with a beak, small bronze Buddhas and other, weirder Lamaist figures, together with silk and velvet priestly garments, which were unearthed from under the dagoba in 1978. Just outside the temple there's a tasty pancake stall.

Lu Xun Museum

Continue west and, just before the giant intersection with Fuchengmen Bei Dajie, you'll see Xisantiao Hutong to the north, which leads to the **Lu Xun Museum** (Tues–Sun 9am–4pm; ¥10), a large and extensively renovated court-yard house. Lu Xun (1881–1936) is widely accepted as the greatest modern Chinese writer, who gave up a promising career in medicine to write books (see p.385).

A hater of pomposity, he might feel a little uneasy in his house now, where the atmosphere is of uncritical admiration. His possessions have been preserved like relics, incidentally giving a good idea of what Chinese interiors looked like at the beginning of last century, and there's a photo exhibition of his life lauding his achievements. A bookshop in the eastern building sells English translations of his work, including his most popular book, *The True Story of Ah Q*.

Beijing Zoo

Beijing Zoo (daily 7.30am–5pm; ¥10), on Xizhimenwei Dajie, marks the edge of the inner city. There's a metro stop, Xizhimen, 1km east of the zoo, and a bus terminus just south of it; bus #7, which you can catch from Fuchingmen Dajie, terminates here. Xizhimen Zhan (Beijing North train station) is north of the metro stop. The zoo itself, flanked on either side by the monumental Capital Gymnasium and Soviet-built Exhibition Centre, is not a great attraction unless you really need to see a panda. You can join the queues to have your photo taken sitting astride a plastic replica, then push your way through to glimpse the living variety – kept in relatively palatial quarters and highly familiar through ritual diplomatic mating exchanges over the last decades. While the pandas lie on their backs in their luxury pad, waving their legs in the air, other animals, less cute or less endangered, slink, pace or flap around their miserable cells. Much the best part of the rest of the zoo is the new **aquarium**, though it's a bit pricey (¥100, ¥50 children).

The summer palaces and far northwest

In the northwest corner of the city is a cluster of attractions which improve the further out you go. The Dazhong Si is worth a poke around on the way to or from more alluring destinations, and the nearby districts of Haidian and Zhongguancun are known for hi-tech shopping and youth culture.

Though it's eclipsed by its newer neighbour, the old summer palace, or **Yuanmingyuan**, is worth checking out for the sobering history it attests to. Nearby **Yiheyuan**, usually known in English as *the* Summer Palace, is an excellent place to get away from the city smog – a recommended escape, summer or winter.

Dazhong Si

The **Dazhong Si** (Great Bell Temple; Tues–Sun 8am–4.30pm; ¥5) is one of Beijing's most interesting little museums, showcasing several hundred **bronze bells** from temples all over the country. It's stuck out on Beisanhuan Lu, the north section of the third ring road, a long way from the centre; buses #302 and #367 go right past, or you can take the metro to Dazhongsi stop and walk 200m west. The best way to visit is on the way to or from the Summer Palace.

The bells here are considerable works of art, their surfaces enlivened with embossed texts in Chinese and Tibetan, abstract patterns, and images of storks and dragons. The odd, scaly, dragon-like creature shown perching on top of each bell is a *pulao*, a legendary animal supposed to shriek when attacked by a whale (the wooden hammers used to strike the bells are carved to look like whales). The smallest bell here is the size of a goblet; the largest, a Ming creation called the **King of Bells**, is as tall as a two-storey house. Hanging in the back hall, it is, at fifty tonnes, the biggest and oldest surviving bell in the world, and can reputedly be heard up to 40km away. You can climb up to a platform above it to get a closer look at some of the 250,000 Chinese characters on its surface, and join Chinese visitors in trying to throw a coin into the small hole in the top. The method of its construction and the history of Chinese bell-making are explained by displays, with English captions, in side halls. Audio tapes and CDs on sale of the bells in action are more interesting than they might appear: the shape of Chinese bells dampens vibrations, so they only sound for a short time and can be effectively used as instruments.

Haidian

It's not an obvious tourist attraction, but the whole of **Haidian district**, northwest of the third ring road, west of the Wudaokou metro stop, bears mentioning: here you'll find the more underground bars and clubs, plenty of Internet cafés, and on Zhongguancun Lu, nicknamed Electronics Street, a hi-tech zone of computer shops. In the north of the area, on the way to the Summer Palace, you'll pass **Beijing University** (or "Beida" as it's known colloquially), China's most prestigious university. Originally established and administered by the Americans at the beginning of the twentieth century, it stood on Coal Hill in Jingshan Park and was moved to its present site in 1953. Now busy with new contingents of foreign students from the West, it was half-deserted during the

Cultural Revolution when both students and teachers, regarded as suspiciously liberal, were dispersed for "re-education". The pleasant campus, with its old buildings and quiet, well-maintained grounds, make it nicer than most of the city's parks. The technical college, Qinghua, not far from here, to the east. Around the gates of both universities you'll find small, inexpensive **restaurants**, **bars** and **Internet cafés** catering for the students.

Yuanmingyuan

Beijing's original Summer Palace, the **Yuanmingyuan** (daily 9am–6pm; ¥15), is a thirty-minute walk north of Beida, or take bus #375 from Xizhimen metro stop, bus #331 from Wudaokou metro stop, or bus #322 from the Zoo. Built by the Qing emperor Kangxi in the early eighteenth century, the palace, nicknamed "China's Versailles" by Europeans, once boasted the largest royal gardens in the world – with some two hundred pavilions and temples set around a series of lakes and natural springs. Marina Warner recreates the scene in *The Dragon Empress*:

Scarlet and golden halls, miradors, follies and gazebos clustered around artificial hills and lakes. Tranquil tracts of water were filled with fan-tailed goldfish with telescopic eyes, and covered with lotus and lily pads; a superabundance of flowering shrubs luxuriated in the gardens; antlered deer wandered through the grounds; ornamental ducks and rare birds nestled on the lakeside.

Today, however, there is little enough to hang your imagination upon. In 1860 the entire complex was burnt and destroyed by British and French troops, ordered by the Earl of Elgin to make the imperial court "see reason" during the Opium Wars. There are plenty of signs around to remind you of this, making the park a tiresome monument to contemporary Chinese xenophobia. The park extends over 350 hectares but the only really identifiable ruins are the **Hall of Tranquillity** in the northeastern section. The stone and marble remains of fountains and columns hint at how fascinating the original must once have been, with its marriage of European Rococo decoration and Chinese motifs. The government is jazzing the place up with a programme of restoration and construction, but this remains an attraction wholly eclipsed by the new Summer Palace.

Yiheyuan (the Summer Palace)

Yiheyuan (daily 8am–7pm, buildings close at 4pm; ¥40) is certainly worth the effort to seek out. This is one of the loveliest spots in Beijing, a vast public park where the latter-day imperial court would decamp during the hottest months of the year. The site is perfect, surrounded by hills, cooled by the lake (which takes up two-thirds of the park's area) and sheltered by garden landscaping. The impressive temples and pleasure houses are spread out along the lakeside and connected by a suitably majestic gallery.

The quickest route to Yiheyuan is to take a taxi from Xizhimen or Wudaokou metro stop (¥15). Alternatively, take the same buses that go to Yuanmingyuan and get off a few stops later, at the terminus, or take bus #808 from Qianmen. There's also an interesting new boat service from the back of the Exhibition Centre, which is just east of the zoo. The boats operate daily between 9am and 3pm, leaving when full, and cost ¥40 single and ¥70 return.

There have been summer imperial pavilions at Yiheyuan since the eleventh century, although the present layout is essentially eighteenth-century, created by

Empress Dowager Cixi

The notorioius Cixi entered the imperial palace at fifteen as Emperor Xianfeng's **concubine**, quickly becoming his favourite and bearing him a son. When the emperor died in 1861 she became regent, ruling in place of her infant boy. For the next 25 years she in effect ruled China, displaying a mastery of intrigue and court politics. When her son died of syphilis, she installed her nephew as puppet regent, imprisoned him, and retained her authority. Her fondness of extravagant gestures (every year she had ten thousand caged birds released on her birthday) drained the state's coffers, and her deeply conservative policies were inappropriate for a time when the nation was calling out for reform.

With foreign powers taking great chunks out of China's borders on and off during the nineteenth century, Cixi was moved to respond in a typically misguided fashion. Impressed by the claims of the xenophobic **Boxer Movement** (whose Chinese title translated as "Righteous and Harmonious fists"), Cixi let them loose on all the foreigners in China in 1899. The Boxers laid seige to the foreign legation's compound in Beijing for nearly two months before a European expeditionary force arrived and, predictably, slaughtered the agitators. Cixi and the emperor escaped the subsequent rout of the capital by disguising themselves as peasants and fleeing the city. On her return, Cixi clung to power, attempting to delay the inevitable fall of her dynasty. One of her last acts, before she died in 1908, was to arrange for the murder of her puppet regent.

the Manchu emperor Qianlong. However, the key character associated with the palace is the **Empress Dowager Cixi**, (see box above). Yiheyuan was very much her pleasure ground. She rebuilt the palaces in 1888 and determinedly restored them in 1902 after foreign troops had ransacked them. Her ultimate flight of fancy was the construction of a magnificent marble boat from the very funds intended for the Chinese navy. Whether her misappropriations had any real effect on the empire's path is hard to determine, but it certainly speeded the decline, with China suffering heavy naval defeats during the war with Japan. To enjoy the site, however, you need know very little of its history – like Beihai, the park, its lake and pavilions form a startling visual array, like a traditional landscape painting brought to life.

The palaces

The **palaces** are built to the north of the lake, on and around Wanshou Shan (Longevity Hill), and many remain intimately linked with Cixi – anecdotes about whom are staple fare of the numerous guides. Most visitors enter through the **East Gate**, where the buses stop, above which is the main palace compound, including the **Renshoudian** (Hall of Benevolence and Longevity), a majestic hall where the empress and her predecessors gave audience. It contains much of the original nineteenth-century furniture, including an imposing throne. Beyond, to the right, is the **Deheyuan** (Palace of Virtue and Harmony), dominated by a three-storey **theatre**, complete with trap doors for the appearances and disappearances of the actors. Theatre was one of Cixi's main passions and she sometimes took part in performances, dressed as Guanyin, the goddess of mercy. The next major building along the path is the **Yulantang** (Jade Waves Palace). This is where the child emperor Guangxu was kept in captivity for ten years, while Cixi exercised his powers. Just to the west is the dowager's own principal residence, the **Leshoutang** (Hall of Joy and Longevity), which houses Cixi's hardwood throne, and the table where she took her notorious 108-course meals. The chandeliers were China's first electric lights, installed in 1903 and powered by the palace's own generator.

From here to the northwest corner of the lake runs the **Long Gallery**, the nine-hundred-metre covered way, painted with mythological scenes and flanked by various temples and pavilions. It is said that no pair of lovers can walk through without emerging betrothed. Near the west end of the gallery is the infamous **marble boat**, completed by Cixi with purloined naval cash and regarded by her acolytes as a suitably witty and defiant gesture. Close by, and the tourist focus of this site, is a jetty with **rowing boats** for rent (¥10 per hour). Boating on the lake is a popular pursuit, with locals as much as foreigners, and well worth the money. You can dock again below Longevity Hill and row out to the two **bridges** – the Jade Belt on the western side and Seventeen Arched on the east. In winter, the Chinese skate on the lake here, an equally spectacular sight, and skates are available for rent.

Eating, drinking, entertainment and shopping

You're spoilt for choice when it comes to food in Beijing. Splurging in classy **restaurants** is a great way to spend your evenings, as prices in even the most luxurious places are very competitive and a lot more affordable than their equivalent in the West. Beijing has a great deal of entertainment options too, with a lively arts scene, and it's well worth seeking them out; remember you won't have much opportunity outside the capital. There is a promising **bar and club scene** worth sampling, if just for the strange cultural juxtapositions it throws up. If you want to check out a Chinese disco or indigenous rock band, this is the place to do it, and again, a night on the town won't break your budget. **Shopping** is another diverting pastime, with the best choice of souvenirs and consumables in the country. In particular, Beijing still has a collection of intriguing little markets offering an appealing and affordable alternative to the new giant malls.

Eating

Nowhere on the Chinese mainland has the culinary wealth of Beijing: every style of **Chinese food** is available, plus just about any Asian and most world cuisines. Amongst all this abundance it's sometimes easy to forget that **Beijing** has its own culinary tradition – specialities well worth trying are **Beijing duck** (*Beijing kaoya*) and **Mongolian hotpot**. Beijing duck appears in Chinese restaurants worldwide and consists of small pieces of meat which you dip in plum sauce, then wrap with chopped onions in a pancake. It's very rich and packs a massive cholesterol count. Mongolian hotpot is healthier, a poor man's

Beijing restaurants

Be There or Be Square	不见不散	*bújiàn búsàn*
Berena's Bistro	伯瑞娜	*bóruì nà*
Bianyifang Roast Duck	便宜坊烤鸭店	*piànyìfáng kǎoyādiàn*
Damofang	大磨坊面包	*dàmòfáng miànbāo*
Dong'anmen night market	东华门夜市	*dōnghuámén yèshì*
Duyichu	都一处烧麦馆	*dūyíchù shāomàiguǎn*
Elephant	大笨象	*dàbènxiàng*
Fangshan	仿膳饭店	*fǎngshàn fàndiàn*
Golden Elephant	金象苑东方餐厅	*jīnxiàngyuàn dōngfāng cāntīng*
Golden Thaitanium	泰合金	*tàihéjīn*
Gong Wang Fu Sichuan	恭王府四川饭店	*gōngwángfǔ sìchuān fàndiàn*
Gongdelin	功德林素菜馆	*gōngdélín sùcàiguǎn*
Goubuli Baozi	狗不理包子铺	*gǒubùlǐ bāozipù*
Hard Rock Café	硬石餐厅	*yìngshí cāntīng*
Kaorouji	烤肉季	*kǎoròujì*
Lichun	利群烤鸭店	*lìqún kǎoyādiàn*
Mexican Wave	墨西哥风味餐	*mòxīgē fēngwèicān*
Nengrenju	能仁居饭庄	*néngrénjū fànzhuāng*
Old Character Hakka	老汉子客家菜馆	*lǎohànzi kèjiācàiguǎn*
One Thousand and One Nights	一千零一夜	*yīqiān língyīyè*
Pass By Bar	过客酒吧	*guòkè jiǔbā*
Phrik Thai	泰辣椒	*tàilàjiāo*
Qianmen Quanjude Roast Duck	前门全聚德烤鸭店	*qiánmén quánjùdé kǎoyādiàn*
Quanjude Roast Duck	全聚德烤鸭店	*quánjùdé kǎoyādiàn*
Rotary Sushi Restaurant	福助回转寿司	*fúzhùhuízhuǎn shòusī*
Saigon Inn	凯莱大酒店	*kǎilái dàjiǔdiàn*
Serve the People	为人民服务	*wèirénmín fúwù*
Shenglinfu	盛林府	*shènglínfǔ*
Sichuan	四川酒楼	*sìchuān jiǔlóu*
Tianshi	绿色天食	*lǜsè tiānshí*
Wangfujing Quanjude Roast Duck	王府井全聚德烤鸭店	*wángfǔjǐng quánjùdé kǎoyādiàn*
Xiaochi Jie	小吃街	*xiǎochījiē*
Xiheya Ju	羲和雅居	*xīhé yǎjū*
Yushan	御膳饭店	*yùshàn fàndiàn*

fondue, involving a large pot of boiling stock, usually heated from underneath the table, into which you dip strips of mutton, cabbage and noodles, then, if you're really committed, drink the rest as soup.

There's ample opportunity to eat **Western food** in Beijing, though it generally costs a little more than Chinese. If you really want the comforts of the familiar, try international places such as the *Hard Rock Café* – everything just like at home, including the prices. **Japanese** and **Korean** cuisine is mainly available from restaurants in upmarket hotels, though it's possible to eat both without breaking your budget, and they're well worth trying.

Fast food comes in two forms: the Chinese version, a canteen-style serving, usually of noodles in a polystyrene packet, which you find in department stores or buy from street stalls; and Western imports such as the ubiquitous *McDonald's*, *Pizza Hut* and *KFC*, which have made a considerable impact and are greatly imitated. **Street food**, mostly noodle dishes, is widely available, though not in the centre, where vendors are shooed away by the police; your best bet is at one of the designated night markets. Avoid the ice-cream vendors who hang around the parks as their home-made wares are often of a dubious standard.

These days, **supermarkets** sell plenty of Western food, though few have any dairy products. The CRC Supermarket in the base of the China World Trade Centre is impressive, though Western goods cost at least twenty percent more here than they do at home. The same is true of the supermarkets in the Friendship Store and Lufthansa Centre. For hard-to-find Western food such as hummus, head to Jenny Lou's outside the west gate of Chaoyang Park.

Breakfast, snacks and fast food

Many visitors find the Chinese **breakfast** of dumplings and glutinous rice served in canteens bland and unappealing, but *jian bing guozi*, the classic Beijing breakfast snack – vegetables wrapped in an omelette wrapped in a pancake – deftly assembled by street vendors in thirty seconds, is definitely worth trying (¥2). Most hotels offer some form of Western breakfast, or alternatively, head for a branch of *Damofang* for cheap croissants or *Starbucks* for cake and a caffeine jolt. For cheap and filling **suppers**, try street food like *huntun*, basically wonton soup, and *xianr bing* – stuffed pancake – or the diverse varieties of noodles. You'll find plenty of street food at the **night markets**, which begin operating around 5pm and start to shut down around 10pm. They're at their best in summer.

It's also worth knowing that every mall and shopping centre has a **food court**, sometimes in the basement but usually on the top floor, which offer inexpensive meals from a variety of outlets. You have to buy a plastic card at a central booth which is debited at the counter when you order. Good food courts can be found at the Parkson Building on Fuxingmennei Dajie, in the Xidan Stores, and, on Wangfujing, on the top floor of the Sun Dong'an Plaza and basement of the Oriental Plaza.

Damofang Qianmen Xi Dajie; basement of the Lufthansa Centre; Level 2, Sun Dong'an Plaza, Wangfujing. This good little French bakery chain has affordable pizzas, fresh croissants and cakes.

Dong'anmen night market Dong'anmen Dajie, off Wangfujing Dajie. Stalls set up along the street offering *xiaochi* (literally, "small food") from all over China. Nothing is more than a few yuan, except the odd delicacy such as scorpion on a stick for ¥10.

Duyichu 36 Qianmen Dajie. This restaurant has been in business for more than a century, though you'd never guess from the bland modern decor, and has built up an enviable reputation for its steamed dumplings, which you can eat on the spot or take away. One of the best places in the area for a light lunch.

Goubuli 155 Dianmenwai Dajie, just south of the Drum Tower. A branch of the Tianjin institution, this place sells delicious dumplings (*baozi*) for a few yuan. You can eat them here – the downstairs canteen is cheaper than upstairs – or take them home, as most of the customers do.

Kempi Deli First Floor, Kempinski Hotel, Lufthansa Centre, 50 Liangmaqiao Lu. Deserves a mention for producing the city's best bread and pastries. Prices halve after 8pm.

Qianmen Old Train Station Qianmen Dong Dajie. Look for the building with the clocktower. The basement foodcourt here has a range of specialities from all over China, most for less than ¥10.

Starbucks First Floor, China World Trade Centre, 1 Jianguomenwai Dajie (just round the corner from the Friendship Store); COFCO building, 8 Jianguomennei Dajie. The caffeine imperialists offer the best, and some of the dearest, coffee in the city – a regular filter coffee costs ¥12, with fancier varieties more expensive.

Xiaochi Jie Xiagongfu Jie, running west off the southern end of Wangfujing. This alley is lined with stalls where pushy vendors sell exotica at fixed prices. It's the perfect place to sample food to freak the folks back home: skewers of fried scorpions, silkworm pupae, crickets and sparrows are all available for less than ¥10 – though none of them, in truth, tastes of much. You can also get good noodles and seafood for a few yuan.

Restaurants

All the expensive **hotels** have several well-appointed restaurants, where the atmosphere is sedate but prices are sometimes not as high as you might expect; look out for their special offers, advertised in the city's listings magazines. Local restaurants, though, are cheaper and livelier. Expect to eat earlier than you would in Western cities: lunch is around noon and dinner around 6 or 7pm. Few places stay open after 11pm. Restaurants usually have two **dining rooms**, sometimes more, which are priced differently – though the food comes from the same kitchen. The cheapest one is usually the open-plan area on the first floor. It's rarely worth phoning ahead to book a table; if you do, you will always end up in the most expensive sections. Telephone numbers have been included in the reviews below only for the more expensive and popular restaurants.

Qianmen

Gongdelin 158 Qianmen Nan Dajie. This odd vegetarian restaurant serves Shanghai dishes with names like "the fire is singeing the snowcapped mountains". The food comprises mostly meat imitations which taste eerily genuine. Try the fish dishes and "dragons' eyes" made of tofu and mushroom. Service and surroundings are a bit lacklustre.

Qianmen Quanjude Roast Duck 32 Qianmen Dajie ☎010/67011379. "The Great Wall and Roast Duck, try both to have a luck," says a ditty by the entrance to this Beijing institution. It's massive, professional and proficient, if obvious and touristy, though there's nothing wrong with the food. Tour groups are shepherded upstairs, but the ground floor is more atmospheric. A whole duck (which feeds two) costs ¥168.

Quanjude Roast Duck 14 Qianmen Xi Dajie ☎010/63018833. The size of this giant eatery – seating more than two thousand – has earned it its "Super Duck" moniker. Prices the same as at the Qianmen branch.

Lichun 11 Bei Xiang Hutong ☎010/67025681. Deep in a *hutong*, this place is tough to find but offers good duck at half the price of the chains (¥80). From Qianmen metro stop walk east along Qianmen Dong Dajie and take the first right into Zhengyi Lu, and at the end turn right. Then follow the English sign to the "Lijun Roast Duck Restaurant" – left, left and it's on the left. You'll probably have to ask. The restaurant is in a shabby old courtyard house, and it's small, so you'd be wise to reserve beforehand.

Yushan 87 Tiantan Lu, 100m west of the north gate of the Temple of Heaven ☎010/67014263. A second branch of the *Imperial Restaurant* in Beihai Park, with the same grand-sounding dishes and banquet setup, but without such an imperial atmosphere. The food, though, is a little cheaper, with the set meals starting at ¥150.

East of the centre

Be There or Be Square Oriental Plaza, Wangfujing Dajie. This fashionable place certainly has something going for it, with simple fast Cantonese food, including lots of chicken and noodle dishes. Dishes labelled "homestyle" are all good, as are the crunchy noodles, deep-fried pork and aubergine and mince. About ¥40 per head.

Elephant 17 Ritan Bei Lu. Home to a Yugoslavian restaurant downstairs and a Russian one upstairs. The Russian restaurant serves a wide variety of soups and salads and the obligatory borscht. Each main dish comes with a generous side of mashed potato. Expect to pay about ¥80 per person, more if you hit the page-long vodka list.

Golden Thaitanium Dongsanhuan Bei Lu, next to the Chaoyang Theatre. Tasty, very spicy and inexpensive Thai food in a relaxed setting. There's a picture menu. Combine with a trip to the acrobatics at the theatre next door (see p.136) for a pleasant evening out; they stay open after the performance finishes at 9pm.

Justine's *Jianguo Hotel*, 5 Jianguomenwai Dajie. An elegant French restaurant with the best wine list in the capital. Try the lobster soup or grilled lamb. Around ¥150 per person.

Lemongrass Jianguomenwai Dajie, just around the corner from the Friendship Store. Small Thai and Indian restaurant, notable for a great lunch buffet – all you can eat for ¥38.

Mexican Wave Dongdaqiao Lu. This cosy bistro-style place is aimed at the expats from the embassy compounds nearby. About the only thing to remind you that you are in China is the barman's accent. The set lunch menu (¥50) changes daily, is tasty and good value, as are the many pizza options.

Muslim Fast Food Head up Wangfujing and just past the crossroads with Wusi Dajie there's a *hutong* full of clothes stalls on the east side of the road. Walk down here about 200m and you'll come to a little square – the restaurant is on the south side, opposite a *McDonald's* (look for the white writing on a green background). This technicolour canteen might not look like much, but the food is both delicious and cheap. Point to the dishes that take your fancy from the wide selection on display at the counters, plenty of vegetarian options among them. The sweets are also especially good.

Nadaman Floor 3, *China World Hotel*, China World Trade Centre ☎010/65052266. Discreet, simple and seriously expensive Japanese restaurant with a set menu priced at ¥300 per person. Most of the ingredients are flown in from Japan.

Phrik Thai Gateway Building, 10 Yabao Lu ☎010/65925236. Elegant Thai restaurant popular with expats. Try the red curry and chicken satay.

Rotary Sushi Restaurant Jianguomen Dajie. Cheap and idiot-proof Japanese fast-food restaurant just outside the Friendship Store: simply choose dishes (colour-coded according to price ¥5–25) from the conveyor belt as they glide past.

Saigon Inn Floor 3, *Gloria Plaza Hotel*, 28 Jianguomenwai Dajie. This restaurant specializes in Vietnamese cuisine, and is pleasingly cheap considering its opulence. You can eat well for less than ¥150 per person, and the set lunch, at ¥50 per person, is very good value.

Sichuan Government Restaurant Gongyun Tou Tiao, off Jianguomennei Dajie. This is the best place for Sichuan food in Beijing, serving the homesick bureaucrats who work in the same building. Head north up the alley that passes the east side of the Chang'an Theatre and after 200m there's an alley to the right with a public toilet opposite. Fifty metres down the alley a set of green and gold gates on the left marks the entrance to the Sichuan Government Building. Pass through the gates and the restaurant is on the left. There's no English menu, but it's superb and inexpensive, and very spicy.

Tianshi Vegetarian Restaurant 57 Dengshi Xikou, just off Wangfujing. All dishes in this bright, modern restaurant are tuber-, legume- or grain-based, low in calories and cholesterol-free, although, this being China, most of it is presented as a meat imitation: try the "chicken" or "eel". About ¥50 per head. No alcohol is served.

Wangfujing Quanjude Roast Duck 13 Shuaifuyuan Hutong ☎010/65253310. Smaller than the others in the chain, with a full roast duck costing ¥160. This one earned its unfortunate nickname, the "Sick Duck", thanks to the proximity of a hospital.

Xiheya Ju Inside Ritan Park, at the northeast corner ☎010/65067643. Sichuan food in an imitation Qing-dynasty mansion. Try the *ganbian rou si*,

dried beef fried with celery and chilli. There's also a Western menu. You'll pay around ¥60 per head.

Sanlitun

Berena's Bistro 6 Gongti Dong Lu. English-speaking waiters, good service and excellent Sichuan food make this a favourite with local expats. Try *gongbao jiding* – pepper chicken.

Golden Elephant Off Sanlitun Jiu Ba Jie. Head north up the west side of the street and turn left after about 200m, at the sign for the *Cross Bar*, and you'll see it. This pleasant place, the haunt of diplomats from the subcontinent, serves Indian and Thai dishes and is recommended if you fancy a change. The menu is in English and has pictures. Try the *palak paneer* and *aloo gobi* with *tandoori* chicken and garlic *nan*. The beer is cheaper here than in the bars around. Figure on about ¥80 per person.

Hard Rock Café 8 Dongsanhuan Bei Lu. American restaurant, with a bar and a disco, the same as every other one, selling T-shirts for the stylistically challenged. A meal will set you back about ¥100. Beers ¥35.

Lufthansa Centre Beisanhuan Dong Lu. There are plenty of upmarket restaurants in this shopping complex including the *Trattoria* (☎010/64653388 ext 5707) for Italian food, or the *Brauhaus* (☎010/64653388 ext 5732) for German fare – their pork and sauerkraut meal for two for ¥135 is about as cheap a meal as you'll get around here. In the basement, *Sorabol* (☎010/64651845) specializes in Korean cuisine.

Old Character Hakka Restaurant Off Sanlitun Jiu Ba Jie, next to the *Cross Bar*. Head north up the west side of Sanlitun, turn off after 200m and follow the signs for the *Cross Bar*. Make sure you don't end up in the pale imitation next door – the real place has a black doorway. It's cramped but atmospheric and the food, Hakka dishes from the south, is delicious and not expensive. There's one English menu. Staff are a bit loud, though.

One Thousand and One Nights 21 Gongrentiyuchang Bei Lu, 200m west of Sanlitun Jiu Ba Jie. Beijing's first Middle Eastern restaurant. Try the hummus as a starter and the baked chicken for a main course, but leave enough room for some baklava, which you can also buy at their sweet shop 100m east of the restaurant. It's open till very late, but some dishes sell out early on.

Serve the People 1 Sanlitun Xiwujie. Trendy Thai restaurant, going for a Soviet look, presumably ironically. Thai staples such as green curry and tom yam seafood soup are all worth trying, and you can ask them to tone down the spices.

Shenglinfu Taiwan Restaurant Off Sanlitun Jiu Ba Jie. Head north up the west side of the street

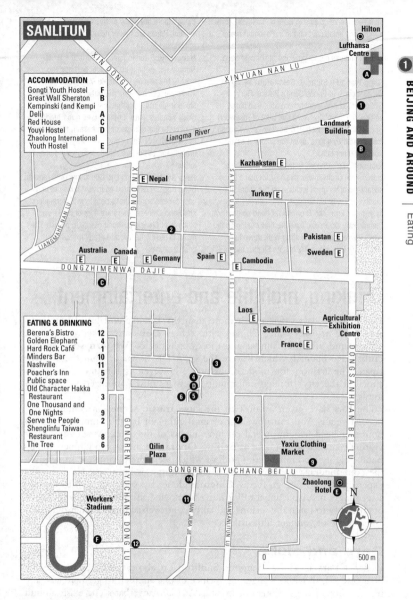

SANLITUN

ACCOMMODATION
Gongti Youth Hostel	F
Great Wall Sheraton	B
Kempinski (and Kempi Deli)	A
Red House	C
Youyi Hostel	D
Zhaolong International Youth Hostel	E

EATING & DRINKING
Berena's Bistro	12
Golden Elephant	4
Hard Rock Café	1
Minders Bar	10
Nashville	11
Poacher's Inn	5
Public space	7
Old Character Hakka Restaurant	3
One Thousand and One Nights	9
Serve the People	2
Shenglinfu Taiwan Restaurant	8
The Tree	6

Hilton
Lufthansa Centre
Landmark Building
Kazhakstan E
Nepal E
Turkey E
Pakistan E
Sweden E
Australia E
Canada E
Germany E
Spain E
Cambodia E
XIN DONGLU
XINYUAN NAN LU
Liangma River
SANLITUN LUJIUBA JIE
DONGZHIMENWAI DAJIE
Laos E
Agricultural Exhibition Centre
South Korea E
France E
DONGSANHUAN BEI LU
Qilin Plaza
Yaxiu Clothing Market
GONGREN TIYUCHANG BEI LU
Zhaolong Hotel E
Workers' Stadium
GONGREN TIYUCHANG DONG LU
NAN JIUBA JIE
NANSANLITUN LU

0   500 m

N

---

and after 200m you'll see a sign for "orthodox Taiwan food" pointing you down an alley. Go down the alley, turn right and look for the place with the red lanterns outside. Inside is an elegant and affordable little restaurant with classical Chinese decor, attentive service and a good claypot chicken in wine. You can also take part in a tea ceremony in an anteroom. A meal will set you back about ¥30 per person.

North of the centre

Fangshan Beihai Park, near the south gate ☎010/64011879. Superbly situated on the central island in Beihai Park, there is no better place to sample imperial cuisine in Beijing. Book first, arrive hungry and splash out on the set banquet menu. Prices range from ¥100 to ¥500 per person as exotica such as camel paw and bird's nest soup appear.

Gong Wang Fu Sichuan Restaurant 14 Liuyin Jie, just north of Prince Gong's Palace. Fiery Sichuan food in a lavishly recreated traditional setting with bamboo chairs and a lot of rosewood. Sees plenty of tourist traffic, so there's an English menu and they'll tone down the spices if asked. About ¥60 per head.

Kaorouji 37 Shichahai. In the northern *hutongs*, close to the Drum Tower, this Muslim place takes advantage of its great location on the shore of Qianhai Hu, with big windows and balcony tables in summer. From the Drum Tower head south down Dianmenwai Dajie, and take the first *hutong* on the right. The restaurant is a short walk down here, just before the bridge. There's no English menu,

though there are a few pictures on the Chinese version. Prices are moderate and you get a sesame roll instead of rice.

Nengrenju 5 Taipingqiao, close to the Baita Temple. An elegant little place, perhaps the best in the capital to sample Mongolian hotpot. There's a lot on the menu, but stick to the classic ingredients – mutton, cabbage, potato and glass noodles – for a guaranteed good feed. It gets quite hot and steamy in here in the evening but it's not geared around the portly banqueting crowd, and tables are small enough for conversation.

Pass By Bar 108 Nan Luo Guo Xiang, off Di'anmen Dong Dajie. A renovated courtyard house turned cosy bar/restaurant that's popular with foreigners and Bobo Chinese. There are a lot of books and pictures of China's far-flung places to peruse. The menu is mostly Italian, and pretty reliable, with good lasagnes.

Drinking, nightlife and entertainment

Beijing these days offers much more than the karaoke and bland hotel bars you'll find in many other Chinese cities. Huge **clubs** are packed every night with young, affluent Chinese, and more sophisticated **Western-style nightclubs** have opened, which feature the latest DJs flown in from the West or Japan. The fashion for modern urbanites, however, is for **bars**. Originally aimed at the city's foreign community, they are now patronized as much by locals.

The bars have given a boost to the city's **music scene**, providing much-needed venues. You can now hear classical zither or bamboo tunes, jazz, deep house, or head-banging metal on most nights of the week. Meanwhile, most visitors take in at least a taste of **Beijing Opera** and the superb Chinese **acrobats** – highly recommended – both of which seem pretty timeless. In contrast, the contemporary theatrical scene is changing fast as home-grown dramatists experiment with foreign forms. **Cinemas** these days are dedicated to feeding a seemingly insatiable appetite for kung fu movies, although there is plenty of opportunity to catch the serious and fairly controversial movies emerging from a new wave of younger film makers.

Bars and clubs

Plenty of **bars** are clustered around **Sanlitun Lu**, also called Jiu Ba Jie (literally "Bar Street"), all within staggering distance of one another. To get here take any bus east from Dongsi Shitiao metro stop. An alternative bar scene exists around the newly prettified **Shicha lakes** (known locally as "Houhai") where lounge bars now proliferate the way pond weed once did. At the time of writing, an embryonic bar scene was starting up around Nan Luo Guo Xiang, 1km or so from here, thanks in large measure to the popularity of the *Pass By Bar* (see "Eating", above) and at Chaoyang Park west gate. A Tsingtao beer is generally ¥15 or more. Phone numbers for those bars that have regular live music have been included below. For up-to-the-minute bar reviews check the expat mags.

Beijing bars and clubs

Buddha Bar	不大	*búdà*
Club Banana	巴那那俱乐部	*bānànà jùlèbù*
Get Lucky Bar	豪运	*háoyùn*
Goose and Duck	鹅和鸭	*éhéyā*
JJ's	川迪斯科	*JJ dísīkē*
Minders Bar	明大酒吧	*míngdà jiǔbā*
Nashville	乡谣	*xiāngyáo*
Nuage	庆云楼	*qìngyúnlóu*
Poacher's Inn	友谊青年酒店	*yǒuyí qīngnián jiǔdiàn*
Public Space	白房子酒吧	*báifángzi jiǔbā*
The Tree	树酒吧	*shù jiǔbā*
Vics	威克斯	*wēikèsī*
What? Bar	什么酒吧	*shénme jiǔbā*
World of Suzie Wong	苏西黄酒吧	*sūxīhuáng jiǔbā*

Sanlitun

Minders Bar Sanlitun Lu. One of the original bars, with an in-house Filipino band that covers seventies and eighties pop and rock.

Nashville Sanlitun Nan Lu. One of the oldest places, where you can hear both kinds of music, country and western. The in-house band plays Wednesdays to Saturdays. A wide variety of draught beers, including Hoegaarten (¥45) and Boddingtons (¥50).

Poachers Inn Off Sanlitun Lu ☏010/64172632 ext 8506. Head north up Sanlitun, then turn left after 200m at the sign for the *Cross Bar* and follow the road round. The only place in the area you can get a beer for ¥5. The dance floor gets busy most nights, and there's live music on Saturdays.

Public Space Sanlitun Lu. Sanlitun's first bar and still one of the most pleasant. Draught beer ¥20.

The Tree Off Sanlitun Lu ☏010/64151954. Popular, cosy bar with a courtyard, and a great selection of draught beers and imported Belgian beers.

Around Chaoyang Park

Goose and Duck Outside the park's west gate. A faux British pub run by an American, this is the place to play pool and darts and not worry too much about what you're wearing. Two drinks for the price of one 4–8pm.

World of Suzie Wong Outside the park's west gate. Striking neo-oriental decor, all lacquer and rose petals, makes this trendy place look like an upmarket opium den. Drinks from ¥25.

Around Houhai Lake

Buddha Bar Shicha Hai, facing the *Kaorouji Restaurant* (see opposite). Charming and trendily ramshackle, with outside seating so you can relax by the lake over a cold one (¥15). Just one of a number of similar bars in the area.

No Name Bar 3 Qianhai Dongyan, next to the Kaorouji Restaurant. The very first bar in the area, its trendy anonymity – there's no sign – and haphazard, bric-a-brac filled interior has been much imitated.

Nuage 22 Qianhai Dong, next to the *Kaorouji Restaurant*. Trendy Vietnamese restaurant upstairs, bar and small disco downstairs (no cover, but drinks ¥30).

Clubs

The trendiest venues – where everyone pretends to know the DJ, wears black, and is willing to pay ¥100 to get in – tend to get closed down quickly. Check listings magazines for what's in with the fickle fashion crowd. Those listed below are reliable stalwarts.

Club Banana CVIK Hotel, 22 Jianguomenwai Dajie. Hot, dark, smoky and packed with an up-for-it local crowd with steam to let off. Daily 8.30pm–2am. Cover ¥50.

JJ's 74–76 Xinjiekou Bei Dajie. This cavernous club has lasers and a sci-fi theme. Silver-clad go-go girls show a high-street crowd how it's done. Take bus #22 from Qianmen. Daily 8pm–2am. Cover ¥20–50.

Vics Inside the Workers' Stadium North Gate. Eighties LA decor, cheap drinks, a sweaty dance floor, and an ambience of numb dissipation. Thursdays is hip hop night. ¥20 cover.

Entertainment and art

There's always a healthy variety of **cultural events** taking place in the city. Check the *China Daily* for listings on officially approved events. For the best rundown of street-level happenings, including gigs, try to track down a copy of *That's Beijing* available at expat bars and restaurants.

Live music

To hear traditional Chinese music, visit the concert halls or the Sanwei Bookstore (see p.136) on a Saturday night. Western classical music is popular and can be heard at any of the concert halls. Mainstream Chinese pop is hard to avoid, much as you may want to, as it pumps out of shops and restaurants. There's also a low-profile rock underground. Good local rock bands to look out for are *Cold Blooded Animal* and *Second hand Roses*; for the latest on who's in, check Ⓦwww.niubi.com.

Beijing Concert Hall 1 Beixinhua Jie, just off Xichang'an Jie ℗010/66055812. Sates the considerable appetite in the capital for classical music, with regular concerts by Beijing's resident orchestra, and visiting orchestras from the rest of China and overseas. Ticket prices vary. You can get tickets at the box office or at the CVIK Plaza.

Fobidden City Concert Hall Zhongshan Park, Xichang'an Jie ℗010/65598285. A stylish new hall, with performances of Western and Chinese classical music.

Get Lucky Bar Tai Yang Gong, 500m east of the Business University (Jingmao Daxue) south gate ℗010/64204249. The main venue for rock and alternative music gigs. Tiny stage and staff are often too cool to work.

Poly Plaza Theatre Poly Plaza, 14 Dongzhimen Nan Dajie ℗010/65001188. A gleaming hall that hosts diverse performances of jazz, ballet, classical music, opera and modern dance for the city's cultural elite. Tickets are on the pricey side, usually starting at ¥100.

Workers' Stadium Gongren Tiyuchang Bei Lu. Giant gigs, mostly featuring Chinese pop stars, though Vanessa Mae and Bjork have played here.

What? Bar 72 Beichang Jie, just north of the west gate of the Forbidden City. A tiny, smoky space, with regular rock gigs.

Beijing entertainment

798 Space	798时态空间	798 shítài kōngjiān
Beijing Concert Hall	音乐厅	yīnyuè tīng
Capital Theatre	首都剧场	shǒudū jùchǎng
Chang'an Theatre	长安大剧院	cháng'ān dàjùchǎng
Chaoyang Theatre	朝阳剧场	cháoyáng jùchǎng
Courtyard Gallery	四合院画廊	sìhéyuàn huàláng
Dahua Cinema	大华电影院	dàhuá diànyǐngyuàn
Forbidden City Concert Hall	中山公园音乐厅	zhōngshāngōngyuán yīnyuètīng
Lao She Tea House	老舍茶馆	lǎoshě cháguǎn
Poly Plaza Theatre	保利大厦国际剧院	bǎolìdàshà guójìjùyuàn
Puppet Theatre	中国木偶剧院	zhōngguó mù'ǒujùyuàn
Red Gate Gallery	红门画廊	hóngmén huàláng
Sanwei Bookstore	三味书屋	sānwèi shūwū
Sino-Japanese Youth Centre	中日青年交流中心	zhōngrì qīngnián jiāoliú zhōngxīn
Tianqiao Tea House	天桥乐茶园	tiānqiáolè cháyuán
Wanfung Art Gallery	云峰画廊	yúnfēng huàláng
Workers' Stadium	工人体育场	gōngrén tǐyùchǎng
Xinrong Theatre	鑫融剧院	xīnróng jùyuàn
Zhengyici Theatre	正义祠剧场	zhèngyìcí jùchǎng

Film

There are plenty of **cinemas** showing Chinese films and subtitled Western films, usually action movies. Around ten Western films are picked by the government for national release every year, and are shown in Beijing first; *Titanic* remains the biggest hit ever in China.

Some of the best are the Capital Cinema at 46 Chang'an Jie, near Xidan (℡010/66055510), the Dahua Cinema at 82 Dongdan Bei Dajie (℡010/65274420) and the Shengli Movie Theatre at 55 Xisi Dong Dajie (℡010/66013130). Tickets cost ¥5–30 and you'll find film listings in *That's Beijing*. For **art films**, try the Tuxin Cinema (℡010/68415566) at 33 Zhongguancun Nan Dajie in Haidian. To see the best in **Chinese films**, with English subtitles, visit the Cherry Lane Cinema (℡010/01134745, ⓦwww.cherry-lanemovies.com.cn), at An Jia Lou, inside the Kent Centre, off Liangmaqiao. Screenings are held every other Friday at 8pm, with a discussion, sometimes featuring the director or actors, afterwards. Tickets cost ¥50.

Traditional opera

Beijing Opera (*jing xi*; see p.1208) is the most celebrated of the country's three hundred and fifty or so regional styles – a unique combination of song, dance, acrobatics and mime, with some similarities to Western pantomime.

Chang'an Theatre 7 Jianguomennei Dajie ℡010/65101309. Tickets from ¥20 up to ¥800 for front seats and a duck dinner. An hour-long performance with a lot of acrobatics.

Liyuan Theatre first floor of the *Qianmen Hotel*, 175 Yong'an Lu. Nightly performances begin at 7.30pm. There's a ticket office in the front courtyard of the hotel (daily 9–11am, noon–4.45pm & 5.30–8pm). Tickets cost ¥30–150; the more expensive seats are at tables at the front where you can sip tea and nibble pastries during the performance. In season you'll need to book tickets a day or two in advance. The opera shown, which lasts for just an hour, is a tourist-friendly bastardization, jazzed up with some martial arts and slapstick.

Zhengyici Theatre 220 Xiheyan Dajie, Qianmen ℡010/63033104. The only surviving wooden Peking opera theatre left, and worth a visit just to check out the architecture. Nightly performances begin at 7.30pm, last two hours and cost ¥150. Dinner – duck, of course – costs an additional ¥110. Check the *China Daily* for listings.

Drama and dance

Spoken drama was only introduced into Chinese theatres in the twentieth century. But the **theatre**, along with most of China's cinemas, was closed down for almost a decade during the Cultural Revolution during which only eight "socially improving" plays were allowed to be performed. The People's Art Theatre company reassembled in 1979, establishing its reputation with a performance of Arthur Miller's *Death of a Salesman*. More recent works include *The Club*, about a football team, performed during the 2002 World Cup. As well as drama, good old-fashioned **song-and-dance** extravaganzas are very popular though a little glitzy for many foreigners' tastes.

Capital Theatre, at 22 Wangfujing Dajie ℡010/65253677. Home to the People's Art Theatre Company, this is the most prestigious, and largest, theatre. Tickets cost at least ¥60.

The Experimental Theatre For Dramatic Arts 45 Mao'er Hutong, just north of the Bell Tower ℡010/64031099. Known for putting on modern and avant-garde performances. Tickets from ¥40.

Beijing Exhibition Theatre 135 Xizhimenwai Dajie ℡010/68354455. For the glitzier end. Musicals at ¥50–100 a ticket are a lot cheaper than at home.

Puppet Theatre Ā Anhua Xi Lu ℡010/64243698. Daily shows at 6.30pm for ¥20. The skilled puppeteers here produce shows pitched at a family audience.

Acrobatics and martial arts

Certainly the most accessible and exciting of the traditional Chinese entertainments, **acrobatics** covers anything from gymnastics and animal tricks to magic and juggling. Professional acrobats have existed in China for two thousand years and the tradition continues at the main training school, Wu Qiao in Hebei province, where students begin training at the age of 5. The style may be vaudeville, but performances are spectacular, with truly awe-inspiring feats.

Chaoyang Theatre 36 Dongsanhuan Bei Lu ☎010/65072421. The easiest place to see a display. Shows are nightly (7.15–9pm; ¥80; it can be cheaper if you book through your hotel). There are plenty of souvenir stalls in the lobby – buy after the show rather than in the interval, as prices go down.

Wansheng Theatre 95 Tianqiao Market, Qianmen. Nightly performances begin at 7.15pm and cost ¥100–150.
Xin Rong Theatre 16 Baizhifang Xi Jie ☎010/83559285; ⓦwww.kungfushow.com. A nightly kung fu show. Performances begin at 7.30pm and cost ¥150.

Teahouse theatres

A few **teahouse theatres**, places to sit and snack and watch performances of Beijing Opera, sedate music and martial arts, have reappeared in the capital.

Lao She Tea House 3rd Floor, Dawancha Building, 3 Qianmen Xi Dajie. You can watch a variety show of opera, martial arts and acrobatics (¥40–130) here. Performances are at 2.30pm and 7.40pm and last an hour and a half; the afternoon performances are cheaper.
Tianqiao Happy Tea House 113 Tianqiao Nan Dajie (closed Mon; performances at 7pm). A

tourist trap that gives a colourful taste of the surface aspects of Chinese culture (¥180). Even the staff are in costume.
Sanwei Bookstore Tea House 60 Fuxingmennei Dajie ☎010/66013204, opposite the *Minzu Hotel*. The haunt of expats and arty Chinese, you can hear performances of light jazz and Chinese folk music (8.30–10pm).

Contemporary art

Beijing is the centre for the vigorous **Chinese arts scene** and there are plenty of interesting new galleries opening up. The best place to find out about new shows is in the expat magazines. For mainstream contemporary art visit the China Art Gallery (see p.115). The places below show quirkier work that's much more hit and miss but more intriguing.

Courtyard Gallery 95 Donghuamen Dajie ☎010/65268882, ⓦwww.courtyard-gallery.com. Located in an old courtyard house opposite the east gate of the Forbidden City. There's also a cigar shop and a very classy restaurant here.
The Red Gate Gallery *China World Hotel* Jianguomenwai Dajie ☎010/65022266. Surprisingly good for a hotel art gallery.
Wanfung 136 Nanchizi Dajie ☎010/65233320, ⓦwww.wanfung.com.cn. In the old archive building of the Forbidden City, showing established

contemporary artists, sometimes from abroad. Can be chintzy.
798 4 Jiuxingqiao Lu ☎010/64384862, ⓦwww.798space.com. A super chic complex of art galleries, artist studios and restaurants in a refurbished factory in the far northeast of the city, beyond the fourth ring road and towards the airport. Also called Beijing Tokyo Art Projects and Dashanzi. Put on your best black clothes and check it out. Hosts an international art festival at the beginning of May.

Shopping

Beijing has a good reputation for shopping, with the widest choice of anywhere in China. **Clothes** are particularly inexpensive, and are one reason for the city's high number of Russians, as smuggling them across the northern border is a lucrative trade. There's also a wide choice of **antiques and handicrafts**, but

Beijing shopping

Army Surplus Store	解放军用品商店	*jiěfàngjūn yòngpǐn shāngdiàn*
Arts and Crafts Store	工艺美术商店	*gōngyìměishù shāng'diàn*
Beijing Curio City	北京古玩城	*běijīng gǔwánchéng*
Cathay Bookstore	中国书店	*zhōngguó shūdiàn*
Dazhalan	大栅栏街	*dàzhàlán jiē*
Foreign Languages Bookstore	外文书店	*wàiwén shūdiàn*
Friendship Store	友谊商店	*yǒuyí shāngdiàn*
Hongqiao Department Store	红桥百货中心	*hóngqiáo bǎihuò zhōngxīn*
Liulichang	琉璃厂	*liúlíchǎng*
Mingxing Clothing Store	明星服饰商店	*míngxīngfúshì shāngdiàn*
Panjiayuan Market	潘家园	*pānjiā yuán*
Parkson Building	百盛购物中心	*bǎishèng gòuwù zhōngxīn*
Sanlian Bookshop	三联书店	*sānlián shūdiàn*
Snowbird Outdoor Equipment	雪鸟野外用品	*xuěniǎoyěwài yòngpǐn*
Sun Dong'an Plaza	新东安	*xīn dōng'ān*
Tushu Daxia	图书大厦	*túshū dàshà*
Yuanlong Silk Corporation	元垄顾绣绸缎商行	*yuánlǒng gùxiù chóuduàn shāngháng*

don't expect to find any bargains or particularly unusual items as the markets are well picked over. Be aware that just about everything that is passed off as antique is fake. Good souvenir buys are **art materials**, particularly brushes and blocks of ink, **chops** carved with a name, small **jade** items and handicraft items such as **kites**, painted snuff bottles and papercuts.

There are four main shopping districts: **Wangfujing**, popular and mainstream; **Xidan**, characterized by giant department stores; **Dongdan**, which mainly sells brand-name clothes; and **Qianmen**, perhaps the area that most rewards idle browsing, with a few oddities among the cheap shoes and clothes stores. In addition, and especially aimed at visitors, **Liulichang** is a good place to get a lot of souvenir buying done quickly. For general goods check the **department stores**, which sell a little of everything, and provide a good index of current Chinese taste. The Beijing Department Store, on Wangfujing, and the Xidan Department Store on Xidan Dajie are prime examples, or check out the newer Landao Store, on Chaoyangmenwai Dajie. The Parkson Building, west of Xidan on Chang'an Jie, is the plushest. Rising living standards for some are reflected in the new giant **malls**, where everything costs as much as it does in the West. Try the Sun Dong'an Plaza, on Wangfujing, the Sea-Sky Plaza, on Chaoyangmenwai Dajie, or the CVIK, COFCO or World Trade Centre plazas on Jianguomen if you don't get enough of this at home.

Shops are open daily from 8.30am to 8pm (7pm in winter), with large shopping centres staying open till 9pm.

Antiques, souvenirs and carpets

If you're a serious antique hunter, go to Tianjin, where the choice is more eclectic and prices cheaper (see p.154). That said, there's no shortage of **antique stores** and **markets** offering opium pipes, jade statues, porcelain Mao figures, mahjong sets and Red Guard alarm clocks. Almost all of the old stuff is fake; even copies of Mao's Little Red Book are new, and aged with tea. It can be hard even for experts to tell what's genuine and what's not, so barter hard, just buy what looks attractive and stay away from jewellery or precious stones (including jade) unless you really know what you're doing. Antiques that date from before 1795 are forbidden for export. Those that date from before 1949 should come with a small red seal and a certificate for export issued by the Cultural Relics Bureau (BCRB), which also serves to authenticate the item. In practice, however, you'll only find these available in shops; anything bought from a stall won't have one – in which case, you can get this service at the Friendship Store (Mon & Fri 2–5pm). Take the object and a receipt along. **Carpets**, made in Xinjiang, Tibet and Tianjin, aren't cheap, but if you're looking to spend at least several hundred dollars, they're pretty good value.

Arts and Crafts Store 293 Wangfujing. A good if predictable selection of expensive objets d'art.

Beijing Curio City Dongsanhuan Nan Lu, west of Huawei Bridge. A giant mall of more than 250 stalls. Visit on a Sunday, when other antique traders come and set up in the streets around. The mall includes a section for duty-free shopping; take your passport and a ticket out of the country along and you can buy goods at the same reduced price as at the airport. Daily 9.30am–6.30pm.

Friendship Store Jianguomenwai Dajie. Tourist souvenirs with a wide range of prices, but more expensive than the markets. Large carpet section.

Hongqiao Department Store Opposite the north-east corner of Tiantan Park. The giant, cramped and humid Hongqiao Department Store can be wearying but has some good bargains. The top floor sells antiques and curios; one stall is given over solely to Cultural Revolution kitsch. The stalls share space, oddly, with a pearl and jewellery market. The second floor sells clothes and accessories and the first is the place to go for small electronic items, including such novelties as watches that speak the time in Russian when you whistle at them.

Liulichang East of Qianmen Dajie (see p.109). This has the densest concentration of curio stores, with a great choice, particularly of art materials and chops, though prices are steep.

Lufthansa Centre Liangmaqiao Lu. A section in this giant mall sells expensive antiques and carpets.

Panjiayuan Market On Panjia Lu, just south of Jinsong Zhong Jie. Beijing's biggest antique market, well worth browsing around, even if you have no intention to buy, for the sheer range of secondhand goods, sometimes in advanced stages of decay, on sale. Open weekdays, but it's at its biggest and best at weekends between 6am and 3pm.

Books

Beijing can claim a better range of **English-language literature** than anywhere else in China. If you're starting a trip of any length, stock up here. The expensive hotels all have bookstores with fairly decent collections, though at off-putting prices. You'll also find copies of foreign **newspapers and magazines**, such as *Time* and *Newsweek*, sold for around ¥40.

Cathay Bookstore 115 Liulichang. An enormous selection including specialist texts, dusty tomes and lavish coffee-table and art books, though not much in English. Mon–Sat 9am–6pm.

Foreign Languages Bookstore 235 Wangfujing Dajie. It might not look like much, but this is the largest foreign-language bookshop in China. Downstairs are textbooks and translations of Chinese classics, and the products of Beijing Foreign Language Press, while upstairs sells pricey imported books including plenty of modern novels. Mon–Sat 9am–7pm.

Friendship Store Jianguomenwai Dajie. As well as a wide variety of books on all aspects of Chinese culture, the bookshop within the store sells foreign newspapers (¥80), a few days out of date. It's all very expensive, though. Daily 9am–8.30pm.

Sanlian Bookshop Wangfujing Dajie (100m beyond the intersection with Chaoyangmennei Dajie, on the east side of the road; look for a blue glass building slightly recessed from the street). This is the most pleasant bookshop in Beijing, though its selection of English fiction, in the basement, is much less extensive than that of the Foreign Languages Bookstore to the south. Upstairs there's a huge variety of art books. Mon–Sat 9am–6pm.

Tushu Daxia Xichang'an Jie. Beijing's biggest bookshop, with the feel of a department store. English fiction is on the third floor. Mon–Sat 9am–7pm.

Clothes

Clothes are a bargain in Beijing; witness all the Russians buying in bulk. The best place to go is Jianguomen Dajie, where the Friendship Store and the CVIK Plaza offer something for every budget (see p.116). The Silk Market that used to stand here – and was the city's third biggest tourist attraction – has been closed down, though no doubt a new venue for cheap knock-offs of branded clothes will reappear elsewhere. Bear in mind that if you're particularly tall or have large feet, you'll have difficulty finding clothes and shoes to fit you. For Chinese street fashion, head to Xidan, and, for designer creations, to the malls.

Army Surplus Store 188 Qianmen Dajie. A wide selection of hats and coats, plus sleeping bags and tents, are sold by the downright abusive staff here.
Mingxing Clothing Store 133 Wangfujing Dajie. Well-made traditional Chinese women's clothing – *cheongsams* and *qipaos* – for slender figures only.
Fou Clothing Company 85 Wangfujing Dajie. Designer *qipaos*; they'll also do custom tailoring.
Ruifuxiang Store 5 Dazhalan. Raw silk and cotton, and a tailoring service.

Snowbird Outdoor Equipment 68 Deshengmen Xi Dajie ☏010/62253630. Quality hiking and mountaineering gear.
Yaxiu Clothing Market 58 Gongrentiyuchang Bei Lu. A two-storey mall of stores selling mostly cheap fakes popular with expats.
Yuanlong Silk Corporation 15 Yongnei Dong Jie, 200m west of the south gate of the Temple of Heaven. A good selection of silk clothes, competitively priced.

Listings

Airline offices Air China, 15 Xi Chang'an Jie ☏010/66013336 for domestic flights, ☏66016667 international; Aeroflot, Hotel Beijing Toronto, Jianguomenwai Dajie ☏010/65002980; Air France, Rm 512, Full Link Plaza, 18 Jianguomenwai Dajie ☏010/65881388; Air Ukraine, Poly Plaza Hotel, Dongsi Shit Tiao ☏010/65010282; Alitalia, Rm 141, *Jianguo Hotel*, 5 Jianguomenwai Dajie ☏010/65918468; All Nippon Airways, Fazhan Dasha, Rm N200, 5 Dongsanhuan Bei Lu ☏010/65909174; Asiana Airlines, Rm 102, Lufthansa Centre ☏010/64684000; Austrian Airlines, Lufthansa Centre, Rm C215, 50 Lianmaqiao Lu ☏010/64622161; British Airways, Rm 210, CVIK Tower, 22 Jianguomenwai Dajie ☏010/65124070; Canadian Airlines, Rm C201, 50 Liangmaqiao Lu, Chaoyang ☏010/64637901; Dragonair, L107, World Trade Centre, 1 Jianguomenwai Dajie ☏010/65182533; Finnair, Rm 204, CVIK Tower, 22 Jianguomenwai Dajie ☏010/65127180; Garuda Indonesia, Poly Plaza, 14 Dongzhimen Nan Dajie ☏010/64157658; Israeli Airlines, Rm 2906, Jing Guang Centre ☏010/65014512; Japan Airlines, 1/F Changfugong Office Building, 26A Jianguomenwai Dajie ☏010/65130888; KLM, W501, West wing, China World Trade Centre, 1 Jianguomenwai Dajie ☏010/65053505; Korean Air, Rm C401 World Trade Centre, 1 Jianguomenwai Dajie ☏010/65050088; Lufthansa, Rm S101, Lufthansa Centre, 50 Liangmaqiao Lu ☏010/64654488; Malaysia Airlines, Lot 115A/B, Level 1, West Wing Office Block, World Trade Centre, 1 Jianguomenwai Dajie ☏010/65052681; Mongolian Airlines, China Golden Bridge Plaza, 1A Jianguomenwai Dajie ☏010/65079297; Pakistan Airlines, Rm 106A, World Trade Centre, 1 Jianguomenwai Dajie ☏010/65052256; Qantas, Lufthansa Centre, 50 Liangmaqiao Lu ☏010/64674794; SAS Scandinavian Airlines, 1403 Henderson Centre, 18 Jianguomennei Dajie ☏010/65183738; Singapore Airlines, L109, World Trade Centre, 1 Jianguomenwai Dajie ☏010/65052233; Swissair, Rm 201, CVIK Tower, 22 Jianguomenwai Dajie ☏010/65123555; Thai International, S102B Lufthansa Centre, 50 Langmaqiao Lu ☏010/64608899; United Airlines, Lufthansa Centre, 50 Liangmaqiao Lu ☏010/64631111.

Banks and exchange The Commercial Bank (Mon–Fri 9am–noon & 1–4pm) in the CITIC Building at 19 Jianguomenwai Dajie, next to the Friendship Store, has the widest service, and the only place that will let you change money into non-Chinese currencies (useful for travellers taking the train to Russia). The main branch of the Bank of China (Mon–Fri 9am–noon & 1.30–5pm) is at 8 Yabuo Lu, off Chaoyangmen Dajie, just north of the International Post Office, but it doesn't do anything the smaller branches won't. You'll find other branches in the CVIK Plaza (Mon–Fri 9am–noon & 1–6.30pm), the World Trade Centre (Mon–Fri 9am–5pm, Sat 9am–noon), the Sun Dong'an Plaza (Mon–Fri 9.30am–noon & 1.30–5pm), and the Lufthansa Centre (Mon–Fri 9–noon & 1–4pm). A foreign exchange office (daily 9am–6.30pm) inside the entrance to the Friendship Store is one of the few places you can change money at the weekend at the standard rate. If you have applied for a visa and only have a photocopy of your passport, some hotels and the Hong Kong and Shanghai Bank in the *Jianguo Hotel* will reluctantly advance cash on traveller's cheques; most banks won't. If you want to wire money, or have it wired to you, go to the International Post Office or the China Courier Service Company at 7 Qianmen Dajie ☎010/63184313. There are ATM machines in the Bright China Chang'an Building, 8 Jianguomen Dajie, in the Dong'an Shopping Centre on Wangfujing, on the east side of Qianmen next to *McDonald's*, on Floor 2 of the Hong Kong-Macau Centre on Chaoyang Bei Dajie and at many other locations.

Bike rental Pretty much all the hotels rent out bikes, at ¥20–50 a day, depending on how classy the hotel is.

Car rental BCNC Car Rental, with seven offices in the city including one at the airport, is open 24hr ☎010/8008109001.

Courier service DHL has a 24hr office at 2 Jiuxian Qiao in the Chaoyang district ☎010/64662211. More convenient are the offices in the New Otani Hotel (daily 8am–8pm; ☎010/65211309) and at L115, China World Trade Centre (daily 8am–8pm).

Embassies Visa departments usually open for a few hours every weekday morning (phone for exact times and to see what you'll need to take); you'll need a Chinese-speaker on standby as not all will have someone who speaks English. Remember that they'll take your passport off you for as long as a week sometimes, and it's very hard to change money without it, so stock up on cash before applying for any visas. You can get passport-size photos from an annexe just inside the front entrance of the Friendship Store. Some embassies require payment in US dollars; you can change traveller's cheques for these at the CITIC Building (see "Banks and exchange" above). Most embassies are either around Sanlitun in the northeast or in Jianguomenwai compound, north of and parallel to Jianguomenwai Dajie: Australia, 21 Dongzhimenwai Dajie, Sanlitun ☎010/65322331; Azerbaijan, 7-2-5-1 Tayuan Building ☎010/65324614; Canada, 19 Dongzhimenwai Dajie, Sanlitun ☎010/65323536; France, 3 Dong San Jie, Sanlitun ☎010/65321331; Germany, 5 Dongzhimenwai Dajie, Sanlitun ☎010/65322161; India, 1 Ritan Dong Lu, Sanlitun ☎010/65321856; Ireland, 3 Ritan Dong Lu, Sanlitun ☎010/65322691; Japan, 7 Ritan Lu, Jianguomenwai ☎010/65322361; Kazakhstan, 9 Dong Liu Jie, Sanlitun ☎010/65326183; Kyrgyzstan, 2-4-1 Tayuan Building ☎010/65326458; Laos, 11 Dong Si Jie, Sanlitun ☎010/65321224; Mongolia, 2 Xiushui Bei Jie, Jianguomenwai ☎010/65321203; Myanmar (Burma), 6 Dongzhimenwai Dajie, Sanlitun ☎010/65321425; New Zealand, 1 Ritan Dong'er Jie, Sanlitun ☎010/65322731; North Korea, Ritan Bei Lu, Jianguomenwai ☎010/65321186; Pakistan, 1 Dongzhimenwai Dajie, Sanlitun ☎010/65322660;

Russian Federation, 4 Dongzhimen Bei Zhong Jie, south off Andingmen Dong Dajie ☎010/65322051; South Korea, Floors 3 & 4, World Trade Centre ☎010/65053171; Thailand, 40 Guanghua Lu, Jianguomenwai ☎010/65321903; UK, 11 Guanghua Lu, Jianguomenwai ☎010/65321961; Ukraine, 11 Dong Lu Jie, Sanlitun ☎010/65324014; US, 3 Xiushui Bei Jie, Jianguomenwai ☎010/65323831; Uzbekistan, 7 Beixiao Jie, Sanlitun ☎010/65326305; Vietnam, 32 Guanghua Lu, Jianguomenwai ☎010/65321155.

English corner Sundays in Zizhuyuan Park.

Spectator sports The Chinese were deliriously happy at qualifying for the World Cup in 2002, and made the team's Yugoslavian coach a national hero. However, they didn't manage to score a goal (under no circumstances bring this up with taxi drivers). Beijing's team, Guo An, plays at the massive Workers' Stadium in the northeast of the city, off Gongren Tiyuchang Bei Lu (bus #110 along Dongdaqiao), usually every other Sunday afternoon at 3.30pm. There's a timetable outside the ticket office, which is just east of the north gate of the stadium. Tickets are cheap (¥15), and you buy them at the ground on the day. Basketball is almost as popular and has thrown up the unlikely hero Yao Ming, a 6'11" Inner Mongolian who plays for the Houston Rockets in the US's NBA. Chinese league teams, including Beijing's Ao Shen, play at the Workers' Stadium.

Hospitals and clinics Most big hotels have a resident medic. If you need a hospital, the following have foreigners' clinics where some English is spoken: Sino-Japanese Friendship Hospital on Heping Dajie ☎010/64221122 (daily 8–11.30am & 1–4.30pm); Friendship Hospital at 95 Yongan Lu, west of Tiantan Park ☎010/63014411; Beijing Hospital at 15 Dahua Lu. For a service run by and for foreigners, try the International Medical Centre at S106 in the Lufthansa Centre, Dong Sanhuan Bei Lu ☎010/64651561, or the Hong Kong International Clinic on the third floor of the Swissotel Hong Kong Macao Centre, Dongsishitiao Qiao ☎010/65012288 ext 2346 (daily 9am–9pm). For real emergencies, the AEA International offers a comprehensive and expensive service at 14 Liangmahe Lu, not far from the Lufthansa Centre (clinic ☎010/64629112, emergencies ☎010/64629100).

Internet access Beijing is one of the few places in China which doesn't abound in Internet cafés, thanks to a mass closure a few years ago. Those still open are heavily regulated – you may be asked to show some identity before being allowed near a computer (take your passport). They're almost all far from the centre in university districts – there's usually one close to the entrance to each college.

Try the Hailetong at 84 Xisi Nan Dajie, Xicheng District or IVNT at 45 Zhongguancun Dajie, Haidian (both 8am–midnight, ¥6 an hour). Beijing National Library on Baishiqiao Lu, just beyond the zoo, has terminals for ¥5 an hour though you'll have to become a temporary member. The only central Internet café is the *Qianyi* on the third floor of "The Station", the shopping centre on the east side of Qianmen; note that there are actually two cafés up here, a cheap one (¥7 an hour) and a pricey one (¥20 an hour), and the obnoxious owners turn foreigners away from the cheap one. All hotels have business centres with Internet available, but it can be ridiculously expensive, especially in the classier places. Your best option is to head for a backpacker hotel or hostel, where Internet access is generally under ¥20 an hour.

Kids Attractions popular with kids include the Beijing Aquarium (see p.123) or the Puppet Theatre (see p.135). Otherwise try the Five Colours Earth Craft Centre at 10 Dongzhimen Nan Lu, just north of the Poly Plaza, where they can try their hand at pottery and tie dyeing. "Explorascience" is a slick interactive science exhibition at the west end of the Orient Plaza, Wangfujing (Mon–Fri 9.30am–5.30pm, weekends 10am–7pm, closed second Mon and Tues of each month; ⓦwww.explorascience.com). There's an amusement park inside Chaoyang Park (daily 8.30am–6pm) with lots of rides – though it's no Disneyland – or they could try ice skating on the basement level 2 of the World Trade Centre (daily 10am–10pm except Tues and Thurs 10am–5.50pm and Sun 10am–8pm; ¥30 an hour) – though be aware that the Chinese kids are very good. Baggily attired skateboarders show off their moves in the plaza at the corner of Xidan Bei Dajie and Xichang'an Jie.

Language courses You can do short courses (from two weeks to two months) in Mandarin Chinese at Beijing Foreign Studies University, 2 Xi Erhuan Lu ☎010/68468167; at the Bridge School in Jianguomenwai Dajie ☎010/64940243, which offers evening classes; or the Cultural Mission at 7 Beixiao Jie in Sanlitun ☎010/65323005, where most students are diplomats. For courses in Chinese lasting six months to a year, apply to Beijing International School at Anzhenxili, Chaoyang ☎010/64433151, Beijing University in Haidian ☎010/62751230; or Beijing Normal University, at 19 Xinjiekouwai ☎010/62207986. Expect to pay around ¥10,000 tuition fees for a year.

Left luggage There's a left-luggage office in the foreigners' waiting room at the back of Beijing Zhan, with lockers for ¥5 or ¥10 a day depending on size, though as these are often full, you are better off going to the main left-luggage office

(daily 5am–midnight; ¥5 a day) at the east side of the station. The left-luggage office at Xi Zhan is downstairs on the left as you enter and costs ¥10 a day.

Libraries The Beijing National Library, at 39 Baishiqiao Lu, just north of Zizhuyuan Park (Mon–Fri 8am–5pm; ☎010/68415566), is one of the largest in the world, with more than ten million volumes, including manuscripts from the Dunhuang Caves and a Qing-dynasty encyclopedia. The oldest texts are Shang-dynasty inscriptions on bone. You'll need to join before they let you in. To take books out, you need to be resident in the city, but you can turn up and get a day pass that lets you browse around. An attached small cinema shows Western films in English at weekends; phone for details. The Library of the British Embassy, on Floor 4 of the Landmark Building at 8 Dong Sanhuan Bei Lu, has a wide selection of books and magazines and anyone can wander in and browse.

Mail The International Post Office is on Chaoyangmen Dajie (Mon–Sat 8am–6pm), just north of the intersection with Jianguomen Dajie. This is where poste restante letters (addressed poste restante, GPO, Beijing) end up, dumped in a box; you have to rifle through them all and pay ¥1.5 for the privilege (you'll also need to bring your passport for identification). Letters are only kept for one month, after which the officious staff are quick to send them back. It's also possible to rent a PO Box here and there's a packing service for parcels and a wide variety of stamps on sale. There are other post offices in the basement of the World Trade Centre, on Xi Chang'an Jie, just east of the Concert Hall, on Wangfujing Dajie near *Dunkin' Donuts*, and at the north end of Xidan Dajie. All are open Mon–Sat 9am–5pm. Express mail can be sent from a counter in the International Post Office or from the EMS office at 7 Qianmen Dajie ☎010/65129948.

Pharmacies There are large pharmacies at 136 Wangfujing and 42 Dongdan Bei Dajie, or you could try the famous Tongrentang Medicine Store on Dazhalan (see p.109), which also has a doctor for on-the-spot diagnosis. For imported non-prescription medicines, try Watsons at the *Holiday Inn Lido*, Shoudujichang Lu.

PSB The Foreigners' Police, at 2 Andingmen Dong Dajie (Mon–Fri 8am–noon & 1.30–4pm; ☎010/84015292), will give you a first visa extension for a fee of ¥160. It will take them up to a week to do it, so make sure you've got plenty of cash before you go as you can't change money without your passport. Apply for a second extension and you'll be told to leave the country: don't, just leave Beijing and apply elsewhere. The nearest place with a friendly PSB office, where your visa will be extended on the spot, is Chengde (see p.172); you can make it there and back in a day. If you have an emergency and require urgent assistance, dial ⓣ110 or ⓣ010/550100, and have a Chinese-speaker handy to help you.

Swimming pool Try the Olympic-size pool in the Asian Games Village, Anding Lu (daily 8am–9pm; ¥50), on the route of trolleybus #108 from Chongwenmennei Dajie, which also boasts some of the city's fiercest showers.

Travel agents CITS is at 103 Fuxingmennei Dajie (daily 8.30–11.30am & 1.30–4.30pm; ⓣ010/66011122. They offer expensive tours, a tour guide and interpreter service, and advance ticket booking for trains, planes and ferries (from Tianjin), with a commission of around ¥20 added. Other CITS offices are in the *Beijing Hotel*, 33 Dongchang'an Jie ⓣ010/65120507 and the *New Century Hotel* (ⓣ010/68491426), opposite the zoo. Good private alternatives to the state monolith, geared at corporate groups, include Sunshine Travel, at 2 Nan Dong Sanhuan Lu ⓣ010/65868069, and the R&R Travel Company, in Room B04, 9 Ritan Dong Lu, inside Ritan Park ⓣ010/65868069. The Tourism Hotline ⓣ010/65130828 is open 24hr for enquiries and complaints; all its staff are English-speaking.

Around Beijing

There are plenty of scenic spots and places of interest scattered in the plains and hills around the capital, and no visit would be complete without a trip to the **Great Wall**, accessible in three places within easy journey time of Beijing. In addition, the Western Hills shouldn't be overlooked, and if you're in the capital for any length of time, this large stretch of densely wooded parkland provides an invigorating breather from the pressures of the city. Further out, the Jietai and Tanzhe temples are pretty in themselves and, unlike the city's other temples, they're attractively situated.

Around Beijing

Badachu	八大处	*bādàchù*
Badaling Great Wall	八达岭长城	*bādálíng chángchéng*
Biyun Si	碧云寺	*bìyún sì*
Botanical Gardens	植物园	*zhíwù yuán*
Great Wall	长城	*chángchéng*
Huairou	怀柔	*huáiróu*
Huanghua Great Wall	黄花长城	*huánghuā chángchéng*
Jietai Si	戒台寺	*jiètái sì*
Jinshanling Great Wall	金山岭长城	*jīnshānlíng chángchéng*
Kangxi Grasslands	康西草原	*kāngxī cǎoyuán*
Longqing Gorge	龙庆峡	*lóngqìng xiá*
Lugou Qiao	卢沟桥	*lúgōu qiáo*
Miyun Reservoir	密云水库	*mìyún shuǐkù*
Mutianyu Great Wall	慕田峪	*mùtiányù*
Shisan Ling	十三陵	*shísān líng*
Simatai Great Wall	司马台	*sīmǎtái*
Tanzhe Si	潭柘寺	*tánzhè sì*
Western Hills	西山	*xīshān*
Wofo Si	卧佛寺	*wòfó sì*
Xiangshan	香山公园	*xiāngshān gōngyuán*

The Great Wall

This is a Great Wall and only a great people with a great past could have a great wall and such a great people with such a great wall will surely have a great future.

Richard M. Nixon

Stretching from Shanhaiguan, by the Yellow Sea, to Jiayuguan Pass in the Gobi Desert, the **Great Wall** is an astonishing feat of engineering. The practice of building walls along China's northern frontier began in the fifth century BC and continued until the sixteenth century. Over time, this discontinuous array of fortifications and ramparts came to be known as **Wan Li Changcheng** (literally, Long Wall of Ten Thousand Li, *li* being a Chinese measure of distance roughly equal to 500m), or "the Great Wall" to English-speakers. Even the most-visited section at **Badaling**, constantly overrun by Chinese and foreign tourists, is still easily one of China's most spectacular sights. The section at **Mutianyu** is somewhat less crowded; distant **Simatai** and **Jinshanling** are much less so, and far more beautiful. To see the wall in all its crumbly glory, head out to **Huanghua**. If you want to make a weekend of it, visit the pretty little town of **Shanhaiguan**, covered on pp.168–172. For other trips to unreconstructed sections, check out Ⓦwww.wildwall.com or contact Beijing Hikers at Ⓦwww .bjhikers.com.

Some history

The Chinese have walled their cities since earliest times and during the Warring States period (around the fifth century BC) simply extended the practice to separate rival territories. The Great Wall's origins lie in these fractured lines of fortifications and in the vision of the first **Emperor Qin Shi Huang** who, having unified the empire in the third century BC, joined and extended the sections to form one continuous defence against barbarians. Under subsequent dynasties – the Han, Wei, Qi and Sui – the wall was maintained and, in response to shifting regional threats, grew and changed course. It did lose importance for a while, with Tang borders extending well to the north, then shrinking back under the Song, but with the emergence of the Ming it again became a priority, and military technicians worked on its reconstruction right through the fourteenth to the sixteenth century.

For much of its history, the wall was hated, and particularly in Qin Shi Huang's time; he wasted the country's wealth and worked thousands to death in building it. It is estimated that he mobilized nearly a million people to construct it, but other dynasties surpassed even that figure. Many of the labourers were criminals, but in the Sui dynasty, when there weren't enough men left for the massive project, widows were pressed into service. A Song-dynasty poem expresses a common sentiment:

The wall is so tall because it is stuffed with the bones of soldiers
The wall is so deep because it is watered with the soldiers' blood.

The irony, of course, is that the seven-metre-high, seven-metre-thick wall, with its 25,000 battlements, did not work. Successive invasions crossed its defences (Genghis Khan is supposed to have merely bribed the sentries), and it was in any case of little use against the sea power of Japan and, later, Europe. But the wall did have significant functions. It allowed the swift passage through the empire of both troops and goods – there is room for five horses abreast most of the way – and, perhaps as important, it restricted the movement of the nomadic peoples in the distant, non-Han minority regions.

During the Qing dynasty, the Manchus let the wall fall into disrepair as it had proved no obstacle to their invasion. Slowly the wall crumbled away, useful only as a source of building material. Now, though, this pointless product of state paranoia does great business – the restored sections are besieged daily by rampaging hordes of tourists – and is touted by the government as a source of national pride. Its image adorns all manner of products, from wine to cigarettes, and is even used – surely rather inappropriately – on visa stickers.

Badaling

The best-known section of the wall is at **BADALING** (daily 9am–4.30pm; ¥35), 70km northwest of Beijing. It was the first section to be restored, in 1957, and opened up to tourists. Here the wall is 6m wide with regular watchtowers dating from the Ming dynasty. It follows the highest contours of a steep range of hills, forming a formidable defence, and this section was never attacked directly but taken by sweeping around from the side after a breach was made in the weaker, lower-lying sections.

It's the easiest part of the wall to get to but it's also the most packaged: you're greeted at the entrance by a giant tourist circus of restaurants, souvenir stalls, even a bank and post office. The **Great Wall Museum** (price included in the main ticket) has plenty of photos, construction tools and models, but is best visited on the way down. On the wall, flanked with guardrails and metal bins and accompanied by hordes of other tourists, it's hard to feel that there's anything genuine about the experience. Indeed, the wall itself is hardly original here, being a modern reconstruction on the ancient foundations. From the entrance you can walk along the wall to the north (left) or south (right). Few people get very far, which gives you a chance to lose the crowds and, generally, things get better the farther you go. Unfortunately, the authorities have recently wised up to the attempts of tourists to escape being herded, and guards will turn you back from unreconstructed sections.

If you head south, which most people do, you'll come to a cable car (¥50), after about 2km, which will take you down to a car park. Head north from the main entrance and you'll shake off the crowds fairly quickly.

Practicalities

As well as CITS, all the more expensive Beijing hotels (and a few of the cheaper ones) run **tours** to Badaling, with prices that are often absurd (¥300 or so). If you come with a tour you'll arrive in the early afternoon, when it's at its busiest, spend an hour or two, then return, which really gives you little time for anything except the most cursory of jaunts, a few photo opportunities, and the purchase of an "I climbed the Great Wall" T-shirt. It's just as easy, and cheaper, to travel under your own steam, and with more time at your disposal you can make for the more deserted sections. The easiest way to get here is on one of the **tourist buses** (¥36–50), which also go to the Shisan Ling Ming Tombs (see p.146). They look like ordinary buses but their numbers are written in green. Tourist buses #1 and #5 go from the north side of Qianmen Dong Dajie, opposite *McDonald's*. Bus #2 goes from Beijing Zhan, bus #4 from Xizhimen, by the zoo. The buses run daily 6–10am, departing every twenty minutes, and the journey takes about an hour and a half. Much cheaper (¥10) is bus #919 from Deshengmen (a two-minute walk east from Jishuitan metro stop).

Mutianyu

Mutianyu Great Wall (daily 8am–4pm; ¥35), 90km northeast of the city, is somewhat less touristy than Badaling. A two-kilometre section of the wall, well endowed with guard towers, built in 1368 and renovated in 1983, it passes along a ridge through some lush, undulating hills. From the entrance, steep steps lead up to the wall; most people turn left, which leads to the cable car (¥35 one-way, ¥50 round trip) for an effortless trip down again. Turn right and you can walk along the wall for about 1km until you come to a barrier – you can't get on to the unreconstructed sections. The atmospheric *Mutianyu Great Wall Guesthouse* (☎010/69626867; ❹), situated in a reconstructed watchtower 500m before this barrier, is a good place for a quiet overnight stay, though there's no plumbing.

To get to Mutianyu, take tourist bus #6 from Xuanwumen, outside the south cathedral (¥43) which also stops at a dull temple and amusement park on the way back. Buses run daily 7–8.30am between April 15 and October 15. Otherwise take a minibus to Huairou from Dongzhimen Station, and change there for a tourist minibus (¥20). Returning to the city shouldn't be a hassle provided you don't leave it too late, as plenty of minibuses wait in the car park to take people back to Beijing. If you can't find a minibus back to Beijing, get one to **Huairou**, from where you can get regular bus #918 back to the capital – the last bus from Huairou leaves at 6.30pm.

Simatai and Jinshanling

Simatai (daily 8am–4pm; ¥32), 110km northeast of the city, though it is geared for mass tourism, with a cable car and toboggan ride, is the most unspoilt of the restored sections of the Great Wall around Beijing. With the wall snaking across purple hills that resemble crumpled velvet from afar, and blue mountains in the distance, it's still beautiful, and fulfils the expectations of most visitors more than the other sections, though it gets a little crowded at weekends. Be aware that it's pretty steep with some vertiginous drops. You will be followed the whole way by locals selling books, drinks and postcards. They'll also make a show of helping you over the difficult sections. Most of the wall here is unrenovated, dating back to the Ming dynasty, and sporting a few late innovations such as spaces for cannons, with its inner walls at right angles to the outer ones to thwart invaders who have already breached the first defence. From the car park, a winding path takes you up to the wall, where most visitors turn right. Regularly spaced watchtowers allow you to measure your progress uphill along the ridge. The less energetic can take the new **cable car** to the eighth tower (¥20). The walk over the ruins is not an easy one, and gets increasingly precipitous after about the tenth watchtower, with sheer drops and steep angles. The views are sublime, though. After about the fourteenth tower (2hr), the wall peters out and the climb becomes quite dangerous, and there's no point going any farther.

Jinshanling (¥25), 10km west of Simatai, is one of the least visited and best preserved parts of the wall, with jutting obstacle walls and oval watchtowers, some with octagonal or sloping roofs. It's presently being reconstructed so expect tourist buses out here some time soon, but for the moment it's not easy to reach without your own transport.

Practicalities

The journey out from the capital to Simatai takes about three hours. **Tours** runs from the backpacker hotels and hostels for around ¥80, generally once a week in the off season, daily in the summer, and sometimes offer overnight stays. Most other hotels can arrange transport too, though expect to pay more. To travel here independently, catch a direct bus from Dongzhimen bus station (¥20) or take a bus to **Miyun** (see p.150) and negotiate for a minibus or taxi to take you the rest of the way (don't pay more than ¥20). The last bus back to Beijing from Miyun is at 4pm. Between mid-April and mid-October tourist bus #12 leaves for Simatai from the #42 bus station south of Domgsishitiao metro stop between 6 and 8am (¥50), and from opposite Xuanwumen metro stop; buses return between 4 and 6pm. A rented **taxi** will cost about ¥300, there and back including a wait. There's a small, reasonably comfortable though pricey **guesthouse** just inside the ticket gate (☎010/69931095; ❻) and plentiful, cheap simple lodgings with local villagers – the small guesthouse behind the car park, for example, isn't bad (❶).

Most people who want to visit both Simatai and Jinshanling visit the latter first, as it's easier to get a lift back to Beijing from Simatai. For Jinshanling, take a bus to Miyun, from where a taxi to the wall will cost around ¥100. It's a three-hour walk from here to Simatai, where there's a suspension bridge (¥30 toll) and they'll try and charge you a second entrance fee. If you start at Simatai, turn left from the path when you reach the wall, and you'll eventually come to the bridge. A popular day-trip from the backpacker hostels takes you to Jinshanling and picks you up at Simatai (¥80 excluding the entrance fee and toll).

Huanghua and Jiugulou

The section of the Great Wall at **Huanghua**, northeast of the capital, is unre-constructed and you can hike along the wall for as long as you feel like, though some sections, among them the first, are a bit of a scramble. At the time of writing it was being heavily restored, so no doubt there'll be a bus service soon. It's worth a visit for its Ming-era ramparts, parapets and beacon towers. Getting here is simple: take bus #916 to the town of **Huairou** (¥8) from Dongzhimen bus station, and from there catch a minibus taxi the remaining 25km, which should cost ¥20, but ask around as drivers may overcharge foreigners. You'll be dropped off on a road that cuts through the wall. Most people head right, over the little reservoir. There's no entrance fee (but locals will attempt to charge you a few yuan). The wall here shouldn't present too many hazards and gets easier, levelling off along a ridge before becoming abruptly precipitous again as it climbs "camel's back" ridge. Most people turn back here, but if you continue over the ridge for about another 500m you come to a path that leads back to the road. You can ascend the left side by heading back down the road about 200m, where you'll find a twisting path that gets you onto the wall.

To get back to Huairou, walk back along the road for five minutes to a bridge where local taxis congregate (¥10), or take a bus from the roadside bus stop. The last bus from Huairou to Beijing is at 6.30pm.

The Ming Tombs (Shisan Ling)

After their deaths, all but three of the sixteen Ming-dynasty emperors were entombed in giant underground vaults, the **Shisan Ling** (literally, thirteen tombs, usually called the **Ming Tombs** in English). Two of the tombs, Chang Ling and Ding Ling, were restored in the 1950s; the latter was also excavated. The tombs are located in and around a valley 40km northwest of Beijing. The location, chosen by the third Ming emperor, Yongle, for its landscape of gentle hills and woods, is undeniably one of the loveliest around the capital, the site marked above ground by grand halls and platforms. That said, the fame of the tombs is overstated in relation to the actual interest of their site, and unless you've a strong archeological bent, a trip here isn't worth making for its own sake. The tombs are, however, very much on the tour circuit, being conveniently placed on the way to Badaling Great Wall (see p.144). The site also makes a nice place to picnic, especially if you just feel like taking a break from the city and its more tangible sights. To get the most out of the place, it's better not to stick to the tourist route between the car park and Ding Ling, but to spend a day here and hike around the smaller tombs farther into the hills. You'll need a map to do this – you'll find one on the back of some Beijing city maps, or you can buy one at the site.

The easiest way to get to the Ming Tombs is to take any of the **tourist buses** that go to Badaling (see p.144), which visit the tombs on the way to and from Beijing. You can get off here, then rejoin another tourist bus later either to continue to Badaling or to return to the city. To get there on ordinary public transport, take bus #845 from Xizhimen to the terminus at Changping, then get bus #345 the rest of the way. All buses drop you at a car park in front of one of the tombs, Ding Ling, where you buy your ticket (¥20).

The Spirit Way and Chang Ling

The approach to the Ming Tombs, the seven-kilometre **Spirit Way**, is Shisan Ling's most exciting feature, well worth backtracking along from the ticket office. The road commences with the **Dahongmen** (Great Red Gate), a triple-entranced triumphal arch, through the central opening of which only the emperor's dead body was allowed to be carried. Beyond, the road is lined with colossal stone statues of animals and men. Startlingly larger than life, they all date from the fifteenth century and are among the best surviving examples of Ming sculpture. Their precise significance is unclear, although it is assumed they were intended to serve the emperors in their next life. The animals depicted include the mythological *qilin* – a reptilian beast with deer's horns and a cow's tail – and the horned, feline *xiechi*; the human figures are stern, military mandarins. Animal statuary reappears at the entrances to several of the tombs, though the structures themselves are something of an anticlimax.

At the end of the Spirit Way stands **Chang Ling** (daily 8.30am–5pm; ¥20), which was the tomb of Yongle himself, the earliest at the site. There are plans to excavate the underground chamber, an exciting prospect since the tomb is contemporary with some of the finest buildings of the Forbidden City in the capital. At present the enduring impression above ground is mainly one of scale – vast courtyards and halls, approached by terraced white marble. Its main feature is the Hall of Eminent Flowers, supported by huge columns consisting of individual tree trunks which, it is said, were imported all the way from Yunnan in the south of the country.

Ding Ling

The main focus of the area is **Ding Ling** (daily 8.30am–5pm; ¥20), the underground tomb-palace of the Emperor Wanli, who ascended the throne in 1573 at the age of ten. Reigning for almost half a century, he began building his tomb when he was 22, in line with common Ming practice, and hosted a grand party within on its completion. The mausoleum, a short distance east of Chang Ling, was opened up in 1956 and found to be substantially intact, revealing the emperor's coffin, flanked by those of two of his empresses, and floors covered with scores of trunks containing imperial robes, gold and silver, and even the imperial cookbooks. Some of the treasures are displayed in the tomb, a huge, musty stone vault, undecorated but impressive for its scale; others have been replaced by replicas. It's a cautionary picture of useless wealth accumulation, as pointed out by the tour guides.

The Western Hills

Like the Summer Palace (see p.124), the **Western Hills** are somewhere to escape urban life for a while, though they're more of a rugged experience. Thanks to their coolness at the height of summer, the hills have long been favoured as a restful retreat by religious men and intellectuals, as well as politicians in the modern times – Mao lived here briefly, and the Politburo assembles here in times of crisis.

The hills are divided into three parks, the nearest to the centre being the Botanical Gardens, 3.5km due west of the Summer Palace. Two kilometres farther west, **Xiangshan** is the largest and most impressive of the parks, but just as pretty is **Badachu**, its eight temples strung out along a hillside 2.5km to the south of Xiangshan.

The hills take roughly an hour to reach on public transport. You can explore two of the parks in one day, but each deserves a day to itself. For a weekend escape and some in-depth exploration of the area, the *Xiangshan Hotel*, close to the main entrance of Xiangshan Park, is a good base (☎010/62591166; ❻). A startling sight, the light, airy hotel is one of the city's more innovative buildings, something between a temple and an airport lounge. It was designed by Bei Yuming (more usually known as I.M. Pei in the West), who also designed the pyramid at the Louvre in Paris and the Bank of China building at Xidan.

The Botanical Gardens

The **Botanical Gardens** (daily 6am–8pm; ¥10) are accessible by bus #333 from the Summer Palace (see Yiheyuan, p.124). Two thousand varieties of trees and plants are arranged in formal gardens (labelled in English) which are at their prettiest in summer, though the terrain is flat and the landscaping is not as original as in the older parks. The impressive new conservatory (¥50) has desert and tropical environments and a lot of fleshy foliage from Yunnan. The main path leads after 1km to the **Wofo Si** (daily 8am–4.30pm; ¥5), whose main hall houses a huge reclining Buddha, more than 5m in length and cast in copper. With two giant feet protruding from the end of his painted robe, and a pudgy, baby face, calm in repose, he looks rather cute, although he is not actually sleeping but dying – about to enter nirvana. Suitably huge shoes, presented as offerings, are on display around the hall. Behind the temple is a bamboo garden, from which paths wind off into the hills. One heads northwest to a pretty cherry valley, just under 1km away, where Cao Xueqiao is supposed to have written *The Dream of Red Mansions* (see p.1224).

Xiangshan Park

Two kilometres west of the gardens lies **Xiangshan** (Fragrant Hills) **Park** (daily 7am–6pm; ¥5; same buses as for the Botanical Gardens, stopping at the main entrance), a range of hills dominated by Incense Burner Peak in the western corner. It's at its best in the autumn (before the sharp November frosts), when the leaves turn red in a massive profusion of colour. Though busy at weekends, the park is too large to appear swamped, and is always a good place for a hike and a picnic.

Northeast from here, the **Zhao Miao** (Temple of Brilliance), one of the few temples in the area that escaped vandalism by Western troops in 1860 and 1900, was built by Qianlong in 1780 in Tibetan style, designed to make visiting Lamas feel at home. From here, follow the path west up to the Peak (1hr) from where, on clear days, there are magnificent views down towards the Summer Palace and as far as distant Beijing. You can hire a horse to take you down again for ¥20, the same price as the cable car (¥20). Both drop you on the northern side of the hill, by the north entrance, a short walk from the superb **Biyun Si** (Azure Clouds Temple), just outside the park gate. A striking building, it's dominated by a north Indian-style dagoba and topped by extraordinary conical stupas. Inside, rather bizarrely, a tomb holds the hat and clothes of Sun Yatsen – his body was held here for a while before being moved in 1924. The giant main hall is now a maze of corridors lined with *arhats*, five hundred in all, and it's a magical place. The benignly smiling golden figures are all different – some have two heads or sit on animals, one is even pulling his face off – and you may see monks moving among them and bowing to each.

Badachu

Badachu, or the Eight Great Sights (daily 8am–5pm; ¥10), is a forested hill 10km south of Xiangshan Park and accessible on bus #347 from the zoo. Along the path that snakes around the hill are eight **temples**, fairly small affairs, but quite attractive on weekdays, when they're not busy. The new pagoda at the base of the path holds a Buddha tooth, which once sat in the second temple. The third, a nunnery, is the most pleasant, with a teahouse in the courtyard. There's a statue of the rarely depicted thunder deity inside, boggle-eyed and grimacing. As well as the inevitable cable car (¥20), it's also possible to slide down the hill on a metal track (¥40).

The Tanzhe and Jietai temples

Due west of Beijing, two splendid temples sit in the wooded country outside the industrial zone that rings the city. Though **Tanzhe Si** and **Jietai Si** are relatively little visited by tourists, foreign residents rate them as among the best places to escape the city smoke. Take a picnic and make a day of it, as getting there and back can be time-consuming.

Tourist bus #7 visits both temples (mid-April to mid-Oct outward journeys 7–8.30am; ¥20 return), giving you ninety minutes at each, before returning to Qianmen. Otherwise, you could ride the east–west metro line all the way to its western terminus at Pingguoyuan, then catch bus #931 (¥3; this bus has two routes, so make sure the driver knows where you're going) to Tanzhe Si. From here you'll be able to find a taxi on to Jietai Si (¥20), from where you'll have to get a cab back to the city. Or you can save yourself some hassle by hiring a taxi to visit both temples, which should cost around ¥180 if you start from the city centre.

Tanzhe Si

Forty kilometres west of the city, the **Tanzhe Si** (daily 8am–6pm; ¥30) occupies the most beautiful and serene temple site anywhere near the city. It's Beijing's largest and one of the oldest, first recorded in the third century as housing a thriving community of monks. Wandering through the complex, past terraces of stupas, you reach an enormous central courtyard, with an ancient towering ginkgo that's more than a thousand years old (christened the "King of Trees" by Emperor Qianlong) at its heart. Across the courtyard, a second, smaller tree is known as "The Emperor's Wife" and is supposed to produce a new branch every time a new emperor is born. From here you can take in the other temple buildings, on different levels up the hillside, or look round the lush bamboo gardens, whose plants are supposed to cure all manner of ailments. The spiky zhe (Cudrania) trees near the entrance apparently "reinforce the essence of the kidney and control spontaneous seminal emission".

Jietai Si

Twelve kilometres back along the road to Beijing, the **Jietai Si** (daily 8am–6pm; ¥30) is a complete contrast to the Tanzhe Si: sitting on a hillside surrounded by forbiddingly tall, red walls it looks more like a fortress than a temple. It's an extremely atmospheric, peaceful place, made slightly spooky by its dramatically shaped pines – eccentric-looking, venerable trees growing in odd directions. Indeed, one, leaning out at an angle of about thirty degrees, is pushing over a pagoda on the terrace beneath it. In the main hall is an enormous Liao-dynasty platform of white marble, 3m high and intricately carved with figures – monks, monsters (beaked and winged) and saints – at which novice monks were ordained. Another, smaller hall, holds a beautiful wooden altar that swarms with dragons in relief.

Miyun and Longqing Gorge

There's not a great deal of lush countryside around Beijing, but the area around the city's reservoirs, **Miyun** and **Longqing**, is well known for its beauty and in summer these are popular local tourist spots. They're best visited on weekdays when it is easier to escape the crowds.

Miyun

The town of **MIYUN** lies some 65km northeast of Beijing, at the foot of the long range of hills along which the Great Wall threads its way. Buses run here from Dongzhimen bus station in the city. The area's claim to fame is the reservoir built in the flat, wide valleys behind the town. Supplying more than half the capital's water, it's a huge lake, scattered with islets and bays, backed by mountains and the deep blue of the Beijing sky. The reservoir has become a favourite destination for Beijing families, who flock out here at weekends to go swimming, fishing, boating and walking. Joining them is half the fun; however, if you're here for a little solitude, it's easy enough to wander off on your own. Behind the reservoir, in the hills, you'll find rock pools big enough to swim in, streams, trees, flowers and a rushing river – and on the hill tops there are outposts of the Great Wall, still in ruins. To make a weekend of it, and perhaps combine your trip with a visit to Simatai, 50km to the northeast, you can stay the night at the three-star *Miyun Yunhu Holiday Resort* (☎010/69044587; ❼), on the shores of the reservoir.

Longqing Gorge

Longqing Gorge is another reservoir and local recreation and beauty spot, 90km northwest of the capital. It's accessible by tourist bus #8 from the #328 bus station near Andingmen metro stop (summer only) or on train #575, which leaves Xizhimen Zhan at 8.30am, arriving two and a half hours later.

The main attraction here is the **ice festival**, similar to the one in Harbin, held in late January and February, sometimes into March. The ice sculptures, with coloured lights inside for a gloriously tacky psychedelic effect, look great at night; unfortunately, the few hotel rooms here are expensive. Not too far from here, the **Kangxi grasslands**, accessible by train from Beijing North station (Xizhimen Zhan) or by minibus from the gorge, is an established summer resort, where you can go horse riding. The nearest decent hotel in this area is the *Yanqing Guesthouse* (☎010/69142363; **⑥**) in **Yanqing.**

Travel details

Trains

Beijing Zhan to: Baotou (daily; 14hr); Beidaihe (3 daily; 5hr); Changchun (daily; 14hr); Chengde (4 daily; 4hr); Dalian (2 daily; 18hr); Dandong (daily; 20hr); Datong (2 daily; 7hr); Fuzhou (daily; 35hr); Hangzhou (daily; 22hr); Harbin (daily; 13hr); Hohhot (2 daily; 12hr); Ji'nan (3 daily; 8hr); Nanjing (daily; 20hr); Qingdao (daily; 18hr); Shanghai (2 express daily; 14hr; otherwise 20hr); Shanhaiguan (3 daily; 4hr); Shenyang (4 daily; 10hr); Tai'an (2 daily; 8hr); Tianjin (frequent; 2hr); Yantai (daily; 20hr).

Xi Zhan to: Changsha (daily; 24hr); Chengdu (one express daily; 27hr; otherwise 2 daily; 35hr); Chongqing (2 daily; 30hr); Guangzhou (3 daily; 25hr); Guilin (1 daily; 25hr); Guiyang (daily; 35hr); Hong Kong (4 weekly; 29hr); Lanzhou (daily; 35hr); Luoyang (daily; 14hr); Kunming (daily; 44hr); Nanchang (daily; 25hr); Nanning (daily; 40hr); Shijiazhuang (daily; 4hr); Taiyuan (daily; 10hr); Ulan Batur (Mongolia; weekly; 90hr); Ürümqi (daily; 50hr); Wuhan (2 daily; 12hr); Xi'an (2 express daily 13hr, otherwise 16hr); Yuncheng (daily; 18hr); Yichang (daily; 19hr); Zhanjiang (daily; 40hr); Zhengzhou (2 daily; 8hr). As well as the above, there are weekly services from Xi Zhan to Moscow and Ulan Batur; see p.91 for details.

Buses

There is little point travelling to destinations far from Beijing by bus; the journey takes longer than the train and is far less comfortable. The following destinations are within bearable travelling distance. Services are frequent, usually hourly during the day, with a few sleeper buses travelling at night. Note that there are also private bus services to Tianjin and Chengde from outside the main train station, Beijing Zhan.

Deshengmen bus station to: Chengde (4hr); Datong (10hr).

Dongzhimen bus station to: Shenyang (18hr).

Haihutun bus station to: Shijiazhuang (10hr); Tianjin (2hr).

Majuan bus station to: Beidaihe (9hr); Shanhaiguan (9hr; express service takes 5hr).

Flights

Beijing to: Baotou (2 daily; 1hr 30min); Beihai (1 daily; 4hr); Changchun (6 daily; 1hr 45min); Changsha (5 daily; 2hr); Chengdu (7 daily; 2hr 30min); Chifeng (3 weekly; 3hr); Chongqing (4–6 daily; 2hr 40min); Dalian (7–9 daily; 1hr 20min); Dandong (3 weekly; 1hr 20min); Fuzhou (4 daily; 2hr 50min); Guangzhou (11 daily; 3hr); Guilin (2–5 daily; 3hr); Guiyang (2–3 daily; 4hr 45min); Haikou (7 daily; 3hr 45min); Hangzhou (5 daily; 1hr 50min); Harbin (5–8 daily; 2hr); Hefei (2 daily; 2hr); Hohhot (0–9 daily; 1hr 10min); Hong Kong (12 daily; 3hr); Huangshan (2 weekly; 2hr); Huangyan (3 weekly; 2hr 40min); Jilin (4 weekly; 1hr 50min); Jiamusi (2 weekly; 2hr); Ji'nan (2–3 daily; 1hr); Jingjinag (daily; 2hr 30min); Jinzhou (2 weekly; 1hr 20min); Kunming (6 daily; 3hr 30min); Lanzhou (2–3 daily; 2hr 20min); Lhasa (2 weekly; 4hr); Lianyungang (2 weekly; 5hr 30min); Linyi (3 weekly; 2hr 30min); Liuzhou (2 weekly; 2hr 45min); Luoyang (weekly; 1hr 40min); Mudanjiang (1 daily; 1hr 50min); Nanchang (2–4 daily; 2hr); Nanjing (4 daily; 1hr 45min); Nanning (2–3 daily; 3hr 30min); Nantong (1 daily; 2hr 30min); Nanyang (2 weekly; 1hr 30min); Ningbo (daily; 2hr 20min); Qingdao (2–3 daily; 1hr 15min); Qiqihar (4 weekly; 2hr); Sanya (2 daily; 5hr 20min); Shanghai (16 daily; 1hr 50min); Shantou (2 daily; 3hr); Shenyang (8 daily; 1hr); Shenzhen (15 daily; 3hr 10min); Taiyuan (2–4 daily; 1hr 10min); Tongliao (2 weekly; 1hr 45min); Ürümqi (2–4 daily; 3hr 50min); Weifang (3 weekly; 1 hr); Wenzhou (2 daily; 2hr 20min); Wuhan (4 daily; 2hr); Wuyishan (daily; 1hr 45min); Xiamen (5 daily; 2hr 50min); Xi'an (10 daily; 1hr 30min); Xuzhou (daily; 1 hr 15min); Xining (4 weekly; 2hr 30min); Yanan (4 weekly; 1hr 20min); Yanji (1–3 daily; 2hr); Yantai (2–3 daily; 1hr); Yibin (3 weekly; 3hr 45min); Yinchuan (1–3 weekly; 2hr); Zhangjiajie (2 weekly; 3hr); Zhanjiang (2 daily; 3hr 30min); Zhengzhou (4 daily; 1hr 20min); Zhuhai (1–2 daily; 3hr 30min).

CHAPTER 2 # Highlights

* **Tianjin** Glimpse dilapidated colonial architecture and browse the souvenir markets of this huge city. See p.154

* **Beidaihe beachfront** Once the pleasure preserve of colonists, then Communists, the summer sands are now chock-a-block with the bikinis of the masses. See p.166

* **Shanhaiguan** A dusty relic of a walled city on the Beihai Gulf, where you can follow the Great Wall to where it disappears dramatically into the sea, and sleep near the First Pass Under Heaven. See p.168

* **Chengde** The summer playground of emperors, whose many palaces and temples have been restored, to the delight of Beijing day-trippers. See p.172

* **Cangyan Shan Si** Make the two-hour walk up to this ancient monastery nestled into the cleft of a mountain. See p.184

△ Chengde

2

Hebei and Tianjin

ebei is a somewhat anonymous province, with two great cities, Beijing and Tianjin, at its heart but administratively outside its domain. In the south, a landscape of flatlands is spotted with heavy industry and mining towns – China at its least glamorous – which are home to the majority of the province's seventy million inhabitants. Most travellers pass through here on their way to or from the capital, though few stop. However, the bleak, sparsely populated tableland to the north, rising from the **Bohai Gulf**, holds more promise. For most of its history this marked China's northern frontier, and was the setting for numerous battles with invading forces; both the **Mongols** and the **Manchus** swept through here. The mark of this bloody history remains in the form of the **Great Wall**, winding across lonely ridges.

The first sections of the wall were built in the fourth century AD, along the Hebei–Shanxi border, by the small state of Zhongshan, in an effort to fortify its borders against its aggressive neighbours. Two centuries later, Qin Shi Huang's Wall of Ten Thousand Li (see p.143) skirted the northern borders of the province. The parts of the wall visible today, however, are the remains of the much later and more extensive Ming-dynasty wall, begun in the fourteenth century as a deterrent against the Mongols. You can see the wall where it meets the sea at **Shanhaiguan**, a relaxing little fortress town only a day's journey from Beijing. If you're in the area, don't miss the strange seaside resort of **Beidaihe**, along the coast to the south, whose beaches and seafood outlets play host to hordes of summertime vacationers and dwindling numbers of Communist Party elite. Well north of the wall, the town of **Chengde** is the province's most visited attraction, an imperial base set amid the wild terrain of the Hachin Mongols, and conceived on a grand scale by the eighteenth-century emperor Kangxi, with temples and monuments to match. All three towns are popular spots with domestic tourists, particularly Beijingers snatching a weekend away from the capital's bustle and stress, and part of the interest of going is in seeing the Chinese at their most carefree. Though the Chinese like their holiday spots the way they like their restaurants – *renao* (literally "hot and noisy") – it's easy to beat the crowds and find some great scenery.

Tianjin, an industrial giant, long ago outgrew its role as the region's capital, and is now a separate municipality. A former concession town with a distinctly Western stamp, it's worth a day-trip from Beijing to see its unique medley of unkempt nineteenth-century European architecture and modern office towers, which loom over the quieter parts of the city. Hebei's new capital, **Shijiazhuang**, in the south, is a major rail junction but a rather dull town. If

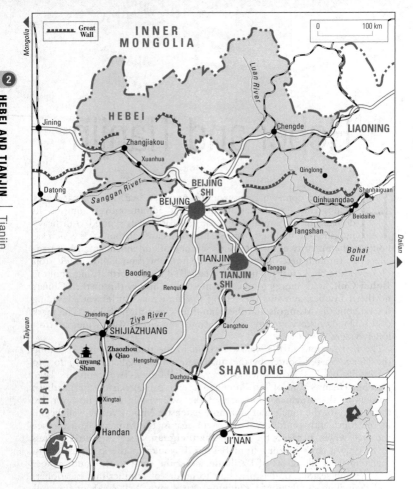

you do find yourself passing through, it's worth checking out the few historical sites scattered in the countryside around.

Good roads link towns in Hebei with Tianjin and Beijing, making long-distance buses a viable alternative to trains. The express buses that run between Beijing and Qinhuangdao, a port town near Shanhaiguan, are actually faster and more convenient than the train.

Tianjin

And there were sections of the city where different foreigners lived – Japanese, white Russians, Americans and Germans – but never together, and all with their own separate habits, some dirty, some clean. And they had houses of all shapes

and colours, one painted in pink, another with rooms that jutted out at every angle like the backs and fronts of Victorian dresses, others with roofs like pointed hats and wood carvings painted white to look like ivory.

Amy Tan, *The Joy Luck Club*

Massive and dynamic, **TIANJIN** is China's third largest city, on the coast some 80km east of Beijing. The city has few actual sights, and it's the streetscapes, an assemblage of ageing nineteenth- and early twentieth-century foreign architecture, mostly European, juxtaposed with the concrete and glass monoliths of wealthy contemporary China, which are its most engrossing attraction. You'll need to enjoy the colonial buildings while you can, however, as wide swaths of the city are being redeveloped. Locals say, not altogether with pride, that the city has become a massive construction site, requiring a new map to be printed every three months. Feng Jicai, one of China's best-known writers and a Tianjin resident, has led a campaign to preserve the old city, noting, "Once a nation has lost its own culture, it faces a spiritual crisis more dreadful than brought on

Tianjin

Tianjin	天津	tiānjīn
Ancient Culture St	古文化街	gǔwénhuà jiē
Antique Market	旧货市场	jiùhuò shìchǎng
Dabei Yuan	大悲院	dàbēi yuàn
Earthquake Memorial	抗震纪念碑	kàngzhèn jìniànbēi
Fine Art Museum	艺术博物馆	yìshù bówùguǎn
Mosque	清真寺	qīngzhēn sì
Passenger ferry booking office	港客轮运输	gǎngkèlún yùnshū
Wanghailou Church	望海楼教堂	wànghǎilóu jiàotáng
Xikai Catholic Church	西开教堂	xīkāi jiàotáng
Zhongxin Park	中心公园	zhōngxīn gōngyuán
Zhou Enlai Memorial Hall	周恩来纪念馆	zhōuēnlái jìniànguǎn

Accommodation

Astor	利顺德饭店	lìshùndé fàndiàn
Friend	富蓝特大酒店	fùlántè dàjiǔdiàn
Friendship	友谊宾馆	yǒuyí bīnguǎn
Jinfang	津纺宾馆	jīnfǎng bīnguǎn
Longmen Guesthouse	龙门旅店	lóngmén lǚdiàn
Nankai University	南开大学	nánkāi dàxué
Sheraton	喜来登大酒店	xǐláidēng dàjiǔdiàn
Tianjin Number One	天津第一饭店	tiānjīn dìyī fàndiàn
Tianjin University	天津大学	tiānjīn dàxué
Xinfang	新纺宾馆	xīnfǎng bīnguǎn

Eating

Erduoyan Fried Cake Shop	耳朵眼炸糕店	ěrduōyǎn zhágāodiàn
Food Street	食品街	shípǐn jiē
Goubuli Stuffed Dumpling Restaurant	狗不理包子铺	gǒubùlǐ bāozipù
Guifaxiang	桂发祥麻花	guìfāxiáng máhuā
Kiessling's	起士林西式餐厅	qǐshìlín xīshì cāntīng
Suiyuan	随园酒家	suíyuán jiǔjiā

Tanggu	塘沽	tánggū
International Seamens' Club	国际海员俱乐部	guójì hǎiyuán jùlèbù
New Harbour Ferry Terminal	新港客运站	xīngǎng kèyùnzhàn

by material poverty. If you regard a city as having a spirit, you will respect it, safeguard it, and cherish it. If you regard it as only matter, you will use it excessively, transform it at will, and damage it without regret." Contemporary Tianjin is an illustration of the latter.

Still, Tianjin has architecture and shopping opportunities, especially for antiques, that make it well worth a day-trip from Beijing. The journey takes just over an hour by train, a journey on which you may well be joined by young Beijingers coming to shop for clubwear, older residents in search of curios, and businesspeople shuttling between deals.

Though today the city is given over to industry and commerce, it was as a **port** that Tianjin first gained importance. When the Ming emperor Yongle moved the capital from Nanjing to Beijing, Tianjin became the dock for vast quantities of imperial tribute rice, transported here from all over the south through the Grand Canal. In the nineteenth century the city caught the attention of the seafaring Western powers, who used the boarding of an English ship by Chinese troops as an excuse to declare war. With well-armed gunboats, they were assured of victory, and the Treaty of Tianjin, signed in 1856, gave the Europeans the right to establish nine concessionary bases on the mainland, from where they could conduct trade and sell opium.

These separate **concessions**, along the banks of the Hai River, were self-contained European fantasy worlds: the French built elegant chateaux and towers, while the Germans constructed red-tiled Bavarian villas. The Chinese were discouraged from intruding, except for servants, who were given pass cards. Tensions between the indigenous population and the foreigners exploded in the **Tianjin Incident** of 1870, when a Chinese mob attacked a French-run orphanage and killed the nuns and priests, in the belief that the Chinese orphans were being kidnapped for later consumption. Twenty Chinese were beheaded as a result, and the prefect of the city was banished. A centre for secretive anti-foreign movements, the city had its genteel peace interrupted again by the **Boxer Rebellion** in 1900 (see p.1162), after which the foreigners levelled the walls around the old Chinese city to enable them to keep an eye on its residents.

Arrival and city transport

The city's huge **main train station** is well organized, and conveniently located just north of the Hai River; the town centre is just under 2km to the south (take bus #24). There are two other stations in town: **North**, which you are likely to arrive at if you have come from northeast China; and **West**, which is on the main line between Beijing and destinations farther south. Trains terminating in Tianjin may call at one of the other stations before reaching the main station. The most stylish way to arrive is on the orange double-decker T-class trains (¥30–40 one way), which leave Beijing every hour, starting before 7am, and take eighty minutes. Public **buses** from Beijing also arrive at the main train station, as do most of the private ones – though the bus trip is comparatively long at nearly three hours (¥20). For details of trains out of Tianjin, see p.185. If you've arrived from Beijing by train and don't fancy returning this way, you could look for the line of unmarked VW Santanas in front of Tianjin's main station; these leave when full and take ninety minutes (¥50/person).

The only buses serving Tianjin's large international **airport**, 15km east of the city, are Air China shuttles coinciding with their flights; a taxi into the centre from the airport should cost around ¥30. If you arrive by **ferry**, you'll find

Moving on by ferry from Tanggu

Much of Tianjin's port activity has shifted to **Tanggu**, 50km east. Every Monday morning a ferry sails from here to **Kobe** in Japan. The cheapest ticket, which gets you a *tatami* mat in a dormitory, costs ¥1600. Another ferry goes to **Inchon**, in South Korea, with departures every Thursday and Sunday; the cheapest tickets are ¥900, rising to ¥1950 for the most comfortable berths. Note that for international ferries you have to check in two hours before departure. CITS in Tianjin sells tickets for international trips, which usually depart at 11am. A **domestic ferry** departs for **Dalian** at 7pm daily from March to October, alternate days the rest of the year (weather depending). Tickets start at ¥155, and can be bought at 1 Pukou Dao (⌕022/24406543), a small street west off Taierzhuang Lu, near Tianjin's *Astor Hotel*.

Frequent **minibuses** to Tanggu run from outside Tianjin main station. Public **buses** leave from the South bus station, or you can catch the #151 which leaves from a small street opposite the main station: cross the bridge to the west, turn left, then take the second right and walk about 100m down the street. Many northbound **trains** out of Tianjin stop in Tanggu, taking half an hour to get there.

Tanggu itself is at least as expensive as Tianjin. One fairly cheap **place to stay** is the *International Seamen's Club* (⌕022/65770518; ⑤), just north of the passenger terminal.

yourself in the port of **Tanggu**, a dull appendage of the city. Buses that take you into the city centre from here congregate around the passenger ferry terminal, and drop you at the **South bus station** near Shuishang Park. The train is quicker, taking just under an hour, but Tanggu South station is inconveniently situated about 2km west of the ferry terminal.

City transport

Downtown and the old concession areas are just small enough to explore on foot, which is fortunate, as the **bus** network is both complicated and overcrowded, though bus maps are widely available around the train stations. Some useful routes include the **#24**, which runs from the West station into town, then doubles back on itself and terminates at the main station; **#1**, which runs from the North station into town, terminating at Zhongxin Park, the northern tip of the downtown area; and **#50**, which meanders into town from the main train station and takes you close to the Xikai Catholic Church. Bus fares around the centre are ¥1.

An alternative to the fiendish bus system is the **subway** (¥2 per journey), which runs south from the West train station, stopping near the Drum Tower and along Nanjing Lu, which is close to the main downtown shopping area. **Taxis** are plentiful – ¥5 is sufficient for most journeys around town.

Accommodation

There are no inexpensive hotels in Tianjin, though hotels do regularly slash their prices, so be sure to ask for a discounted rate and keep pressing until you get one. If you're travelling on a tight budget, the foreign student residences at Tianjin and Nankai Universities, in the south of town (bus #8 from the main train station), are good options, at ¥150 or so for a comfortable double. Of the handful of cut-rate flophouses lining the back of the shopping centre on the train station's western concourse, with signboards in Chinese, the best is the *Longmen Guesthouse* (⌕022/24307611; ②).

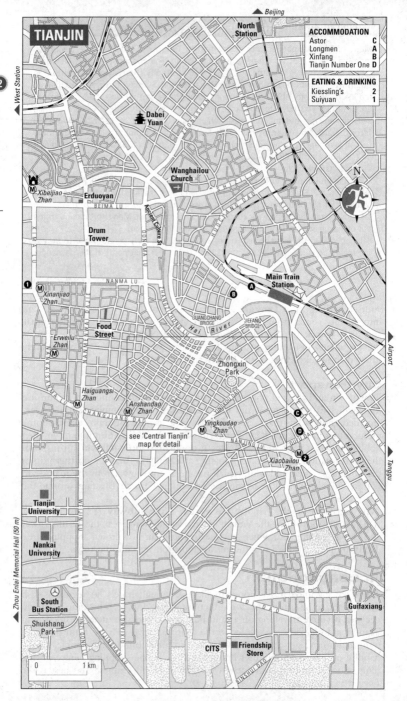

TIANJIN

▲ Beijing

North Station

ACCOMMODATION
Astor   C
Longmen   A
Xinfang   B
Tianjin Number One   D

EATING & DRINKING
Kiessling's   2
Suiyuan   1

◄ West Station

Ⓜ Xibeijiao Zhan
Erduoyan

Dabei Yuan

Wanghailou Church

BEIMA LU

Drum Tower

DONGMA LU

Ancient Culture St.

NANMA LU

N

Main Train Station

Ⓜ
Ⓜ Xinanjiao Zhan

Ⓜ Erweilu Zhan

Food Street

GUANGCHANG BRIDGE
JIEFANG BRIDGE

B
A

Hai River

Zhongxin Park

Ⓜ Haiguangsi Zhan

Ⓜ Anshandao Zhan

see 'Central Tianjin' map for detail

Ⓜ Yingkoudao Zhan

C
D

▲ Airport

NANJING LU

Ⓜ Xiaobailou Zhan 2

Tianjin University

Nankai University

Hai River

▲ Tanggu

◄ Zhou Enlai Memorial Hall (50 m)

South Bus Station

Shuishang Park

Guifaxiang

CITS
Friendship Store

0   1 km

Astor 33 Tai'er Zhuang Lu ☏ 022/23311688, ℱ 23316282. The best of Tianjin's luxury hotels, centrally located in a stylish British mansion more than 100 years old. The management misses no opportunity to remind you of its history: portraits of warlords line the walls, and there are museum-style displays everywhere, including such priceless items as the first Chinese-made light bulbs the hotel ever used. ❾

Friend 231 Xinhua Lu ☏ 022/83326399, ℱ 23125446. Very friendly, clean, and a bargain by Tianjin standards. Across the street from the *Friendship*'s East Building, and much more welcoming. ❺

Friendship 94 Nanjing Lu ☏ 022/23310372, ℱ 23310616. A modern building opposite the earthquake memorial south of the town centre. The cheapest – though rather bland – rooms are around the corner in the East Building on Xinhua Lu. From the main building's entrance turn left, walk to the first intersection, turn left, and the East Building is 50m ahead on the left. East building ❺; main building ❼

Xinfang 10 Sanjing Lu ☏ 022/24463555, ℱ 24468480. Basic, tidy hotel to the west of the main railway station. From the arrival exit, walk straight past the bus stop and taxi stand to the seven-storey building directly across Sanjing Road. ❹

Tianjin Number One Jiefang Bei Lu ☏ 022/23309988, ℱ 23123000. A nice, rambling old colonial building with high ceilings, wide halls and Art Deco touches. ❽

The City

The part of the city of interest to visitors, the dense network of ex-concession streets south and west of the central train station, and south of the Hai River, is fairly compact. Many *pinyin* street signs help in navigating the central grid of streets, as do plenty of distinctive landmarks, notably the T-shaped pedestrian-ized shopping district of **Binjiang Dao** and **Heping Lu** at Tianjin's heart.

The **old city** was strictly demarcated into national zones, and each section of the city centre has retained a hint of its old flavour. The area northwest of the main train station, on the west side of the Hai River, was the old Chinese city. Running from west to east along the north bank of the river were the Austrian, Italian, Russian and Belgian concessions, though most of the old buildings here have been destroyed. Unmistakeable are the chateaux of the French concession, which now make up the downtown district just south of the river, and the haughty mansions the British built east of here. Farther east, also south of the river, the architecture of an otherwise unremarkable district has a sprinkling of stern German constructions. For a waterside view of the entire town all the way to Tanggu, there are marathon daily **boat rides** – popular with Chinese tourists – departing in the morning from the kiosk across from the main train station, just west of Jiefang Bridge (8hr; ¥78).

Downtown Tianjin

The majority of Tianjin's colonial buildings are clustered in the grid of streets on the southern side of the river. From the main train station, you can approach via Jiefang Bridge, built by the French in 1903, which leads south along Jiefang Beilu to an area given an oddly Continental feel by the pastel colours and wrought-iron scrollwork balconies of the French concession. This is at its most appealing around the glorified roundabout known as **Zhongxin Park**. At 77 Jiefang Beilu, the pink **Fine Art Museum** (daily 8.30am–noon & 1.30–5pm; ¥10), a slightly pompous old building, has a broad collection of paintings, kites, Chinese New Year prints and *ni ren*, literally "mud men", clay figurines which became a popular local craft in the nineteenth century. Their greatest exponent was a skilled caricaturist called Zhang who made copies of opera stars and other notables, and some of his work is on display; unfortunately none of his depictions of Tianjin's foreigners, which got him into trouble with the authorities, is on show.

Zhongxin Park marks the southeastern end of the main **shopping district**, an area bounded by Dagu Lu, Jinzhou Dao and Chifeng Dao; Heping Lu and

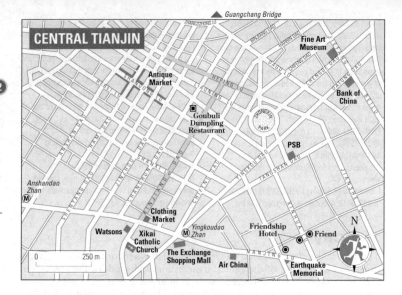

Binjiang Dao are the two busiest streets. Though stuffed with intrepid shoppers (as fashionably dressed as a Beijing crowd), these narrow tree-lined streets have a pleasingly laid-back feel, as traffic is light, and Heping Lu and Binjiang Dao are pedestrianized and lined with sculptures and benches. There are plenty of places for a snack hereabouts. It's hard to avoid Western fast-food chains, though a more traditional form of fast food is available at *Goubuli* (see p.162). Electric trolleybuses run the length of the shopping area (¥2).

The antique market

Just west of here is a shopping district of a very different character, the **antique market** (daily 8am–5pm), centred on Shenyang Jie but spilling over into side alleys. A great attraction even if you have no intention of buying, the alleys are lined with dark, poky shops, pavement vendors with their wares spread out in front of them on yellowed newspapers, and stallholders waving jade and teapots in the faces of passers-by. The market expands and contracts according to the time of year (small in winter, big in the summer) but it's always at its largest on Sundays, swelled by Beijingers here for the weekend. It's generally cheaper than any in the capital, though you will have to look hard for a bargain.

The variety of goods on display is astonishing: among the standard jade jewellery, ceramic teapots, fans and perfume bottles are Russian army watches, opium pipes, snuff boxes, ornate playing cards, old photographs, pornographic paintings, and rimless sunglasses. Look out for the stalls selling picture postcards of revolutionary dramas depicting synchronized ballet dancers performing graceful mid-air leaps with hand grenades. Bargaining is mandatory, and be aware that some of the stuff is fake.

Around Nanjing Lu

At the southern end of Binjiang Lu, the **Xikai Catholic Church** (daily 5.30am–4.30pm) is a useful landmark and one of the most distinctive buildings in the city, with its odd facade of horizontal brown and orange brick stripes topped with three green domes. The diffuse zone of unremarkable buildings east of here, around Nanjing Lu, is notable only for the **Earthquake Memorial** opposite the *Friendship Hotel*. More tasteful than most Chinese public statuary, this hollow pyramid commemorates the 250,000 people who died in the 1976 earthquake in Tangshan to the northeast.

North of the centre

The main sight in the northern part of the city, best reached by taxi, is the **Dabei Yuan**, on a narrow alleyway off Zhongshan Lu (daily 9am–4.30pm; ¥4). Tianjin's major centre for Buddhist worship, it's easy to find as the alleys all around are crammed with stalls selling a colourful mix of religious knick-knacks: incense, tapes of devotional music, mirror-glass shrines, and ceramic Buddhas with flashing lights in their eyes. Large bronze vessels full of water stand outside the buildings, a fire precaution that has been in use for centuries. Outside the first hall, which was built in the 1940s, the devout wrap their arms around a large bronze incense burner before lighting incense sticks and kowtowing. In the smaller, rear buildings – seventeenth-century structures extensively restored after the Tangshan earthquake – you'll see the temple's jovial resident monks, while small antique wood and bronze Buddhist figurines are displayed in a hall in the west of the complex. Before you leave the area, be sure to wander the rapidly diminishing district of alleyways behind the temple.

The stern **Wanghailou Church** (formerly the Notre Dame des Victoires cathedral) stands not far south of Dabei Yuan, over Shizilin Dajie on the north bank of the river. Built in 1904, it has an austere presence thanks to the use of dark stone, and is the third church to stand on this site – the first was destroyed in the massacre of 1870, a year after it was built, and the second was burnt down in 1900 in the Boxer Rebellion. It's possible to visit during the week, but the Sunday-morning Chinese-language services (7am) make a stop here much more interesting.

Ancient Culture Street

A short walk southwest of Wanghailou Church, the more prosaic **Ancient Culture Street** runs off the southern side of Beima Lu, its entrance marked by a colourful arch. Like Liulichang Jie in Beijing, this is a re-creation of a nineteenth-century Chinese street, minus beggars and filth and plus neon "OK Karaoke" signs, designed as a tourist shopping mall. It's all false but is undeniably pretty, with carved balconies and columns decorating the facade of red and green wooden shops topped with curling, tiled roofs. The shops sell pricey antiques and souvenirs, and there's an especially large range of teapots. The first shop on the right after the arch sells fifteen-centimetre-high clay figurines, in the style of Tianjin's master Zhang (see p.159). Look out, too, for the stalls selling *chatang*, soup made with millet and sugar; the stallholders attract customers by demonstrating their skill at pouring boiling soup from a long, dragon-shaped spout into four bowls all held in one hand. About halfway down the street is the entrance to the heavily restored **Sea Goddess Temple** (daily 9am–5pm; ¥3), originally built in 1326 and supposedly the oldest building in Tianjin. There's an exhibition of local crafts in the side halls.

The Drum Tower and around

Just west of Ancient Culture Street, the recently built, characterless **Drum Tower** (daily 9am–4.30pm, ¥10) stands in what was once a quiet network of *hutongs* demarcated by four "horse" (*ma*) streets – **Beima**, **Nanma**, **Dongma** and **Xima**. The original *hutongs* have been swept away, replaced by new pseudo-*hutongs* packed to the rooflines with shops selling souvenirs and antiques, making this one of China's most concentrated tourist shopping areas. The main outlet of the famous **Erduoyan Fried Cake Shop** (see below) is located a short walk north of the Drum Tower development, though the confections and history are poorly showcased by the grubby building.

The **mosque**, farther west, off Dafeng Lu, is an active place of worship, and you're free to wander around the buildings, though only Muslims may enter the prayer halls. It's a fine example of Chinese Muslim architecture, with some striking wood carvings of floral designs in the eaves and around the windows.

Zhou Enlai Memorial Hall

Southwest of the centre is the massive **Zhou Enlai Memorial Hall** (daily 9am–5pm; ¥10), paying tribute to Tianjin's most famous resident. A bunker perched on the northern edge of Shuishang Park, the hall features a few wax figures, Zhou's airplane and limousine, and scattered English explanations of his achievements, though it's not so much an analysis of the difficulties in being Chairman Mao's right-hand man as a paean to his marriage to fellow comrade Deng Yingchao. Try not to crack up when reading the description of the couple's bond: "Cherishing the same ideals, following the same path, and comrade-in-arms affection tied them in love relations." The events around the Cultural Revolution, from which Zhou's legacy derives most of its strength, are curtly summarized thus: "He frustrated the attempts of the Gang of Four." To get here, take bus #8 from the station and get off at Shuishang Park near the statue of Nie Zhongjie, a general who is depicted on horseback.

Eating

Make sure you don't leave Tianjin without sampling some of its speciality cakes and pastries. The **Erduoyan Fried Cake Shop**, Beimen Dajie (just north of Beima Lu), is a century-old institution that specializes in rice-powder cakes fried in sesame oil; don't be put off by the name, which means "ear hole". Another Tianjin institution is the **Guifaxiang** shop, 568 Dagu Nan Lu, renowned for its fried dough twists (*mahua*), a delicious local speciality that makes a good gift – the assistants will wrap and box them for you.

Downtown, the side streets around Heping Lu (close to Zhongxin Park) are home to local restaurants that are often worth sampling, particularly the lively *Goubuli*. Heping Lu itself is rife with Western fast-food chains.

Food Street East of Nanmenwai Dajie on Qingyi Dajie. A cheerful two-storey mall, this is still the best place to eat in Tianjin, though standards have slipped a little over the years, and a *McDonald's* now anchors the ground floor. Yet with over twenty restaurants on each level, there's something to suit all budgets and tastes. Upstairs try the *Zhejiang Restaurant* for Zhejiang cuisine, the *Da Jin Haiwei* for Tianjin seafood, *Penglaichun* for Shandong dishes, and *Haidefu* for Sichuan. A local favourite is the bustling branch of *Goubuli* for *baozi*, also on the second floor. Between the restaurants are stalls and shops selling cakes, biscuits, dried fruit, nuts, chocolates, and dead ducks.

Goubuli Stuffed Dumpling Restaurant 77 Shandong Lu. Handy if you're shopping around Binjiang Dao, this famous Tianjin restaurant has grown from a poky little store to the flagship of a chain with branches in the US and across Asia. Dumplings plus assorted condiments in an airline-food-style tray cost a very reasonable ¥13. The name, which means "dogs wouldn't believe it", is thought to be a reference either to the ugliness of the original proprietor or to the low-class status of dumplings.

Kiessling's 333 Zhejiang Lu. Formerly Austrian-owned, this restaurant has been around for nearly 100 years, and the cafeteria upstairs still serves Western fare: breaded fish fillets, mashed potatoes, pasta and so forth. The beer hall and dining room on the top level is worth a stop, if only for their dark beer, home-brewed.

Suiyuan Huanghe Dao, just west of Xima Lu. A good selection of Shandong-style dishes for around ¥50 per head.

Listings

Airlines Air China's main office is at 103 Nanjing Lu (daily 8am–4.30pm; ☎022/23301543). Airport shuttles (¥10) only run to Tianjin's airport in time for departures of scheduled Air China flights. More convenient are the regular shuttles making the run to and from Beijing's airport (4am, 5am, then 6am–5.30pm every 2hr or so; ¥70).

Banks and exchange The main office of the Bank of China is in a grand colonial edifice at 80 Jiefang Bei Lu (daily 8am–5pm).

Bookshops The Foreign Language Bookstore is at 130 Chifeng Dao.

Internet access Internet cafés are scattered along Baidi Lu, which runs along the west sides of Tianjin and Nankai universities.

Mail and telephones A post office occupies the building just east of the train station (daily 9am–6.30pm), and there's a 24hr telecoms facility here too.

PSB 30 Tangshan Dao.

Shopping As well as the clothes and antique markets in the city centre, Tianjin is renowned for its handmade rugs and carpets, featuring bright, complex, abstract patterns. They're not cheap, and are best bought directly from the factories in the suburbs. Tianjin is also noted for its kites and its bright woodblock prints of domestic subjects, pinned up for good luck at Chinese New Year; the latter are made and sold at the Yangliuqing Picture Studio, which has an outlet on Ancient Culture St,

and another at 111 Sanhe Dao (a small alley west of Youyi Lu and a 15min walk north of the Friendship Store). The Tianjin Antique Company, located fairly centrally at 161 Liaoning Lu (daily 9am–5pm; ☎022/27110308), has a wide selection of antique jade, embroidery, calligraphy and carvings. For pricier souvenirs, try the four-storey Friendship Store, which has a good supermarket, opposite CITS at 21 Youyi Lu.

Trains The majority of trains leave from the main station. A few trains to the northeast leave only from the North station, and some trains to southern destinations, such as Shanghai, that don't originate in Tianjin, call only at the West station. At the time of writing, the last train back to Beijing is the 9.11pm #2141/44, a creeper that pulls into Beijing's West Station around 11pm (the last express departs Tianjin at 4.40pm). Tickets for Beijing are on sale at a special English-labelled kiosk to the right of the escalators of the main station. You can also buy your return ticket on the train from Beijing. To avoid the queues when buying train tickets from the main station, try the soft-sleeper ticket office – go up the escalator, turn left towards the soft-sleeper waiting room, and the office is discreetly located on the left.

Travel agents CITS is at 22 Youyi Lu (☎022/28358866 ext 102), opposite the Friendship Store. They don't impart much information, but they will book train and boat tickets for onward travel.

Beidaihe to Shanhaiguan

On the **Bohai Gulf**, 300km east of Beijing, lies the rather bizarre seaside resort of **Beidaihe**. The coastline, reminiscent of the Mediterranean – rocky, sparsely vegetated, erratically punctuated by beaches – was originally patronized by European diplomats, missionaries and businessmen a hundred years ago, who can only have chosen it out of homesickness. They built villas and bungalows here, and reclined on verandas sipping cocktails after indulging in the new bathing fad. After the Communist takeover, the village became a pleasure resort for Party bigwigs, reaching its height of popularity in the 1970s when seaside trips were no longer seen as decadent and revisionist. Though you'll still see serious men in uniforms and sunglasses licking lollipops, and black Audis with tinted windows (the Party cadre car) cruising the waterfront, most of Beidaihe's visitors nowadays are ordinary, fun-loving tourists, usually well-heeled Beijingers. In season, when the temperature is steady around the mid-20s Celsius and the water warm, it's a fun place to spend the day.

Only 25km or so to the northeast, **Shanhaiguan** is a popular half-day destination with Chinese frolicking at Beidaihe, but isn't much on the backpacker circuit. Small enough to walk around, the town is rapidly being redeveloped, but can still be a peaceful stop, especially if you stay at either of two good hotels

Beidaihe to Shanhaiguan

Beidaihe	北戴河	*běidàihé*
Lianfengshan Park	联峰山公园	*liánfēngshān gōngyuán*
Pigeon Nest Park	鸽子窝公园	*gēziwō gōngyuán*

Accommodation and eating		
Diplomatic Missions Guesthouse	外交人员宾馆	*wàijiāo rényuán bīnguǎn*
Friendship	友谊宾馆	*yǒuyí bīnguǎn*
Jinshan	金山宾馆	*jīnshān bīnguǎn*
Kiessling's	起士林餐厅	*qǐshìlín cāntīng*
Tiger Rock	老虎石宾馆	*lǎohǔshí bīnguǎn*

Nandaihe	南戴河	*nándàihé*

Qinhuangdao	秦皇岛	*qínhuángdǎo*
Haiyue Hotel	海岳大厦	*hǎiyuè dàshà*

Shanhaiguan	山海关	*shānhǎiguān*
First Pass Under Heaven	天下第一关	*tiānxià dìyīguān*
Great Wall Museum	长城博物馆	*chángchéng bówùguǎn*
Jiao Shan	角山	*jiǎo shān*
Lao Long Tou	老龙头	*lǎolóng tóu*
Longevity Mountain	长寿山	*chángshòu shān*
Mengjiangnü Miao	孟姜女庙	*mèngjiāngnǚ miào*
Yansai Hu	燕塞湖	*yànsài hú*

Accommodation and eating		
Dongfang	东方宾馆	*dōngfāng bīnguǎn*
Jingshan	京山宾馆	*jīngshān bīnguǎn*
North Street	北街招待所	*běijiē zhāodàisuǒ*
Sitiao Baozi	四条包子	*sìtiáo bāozi*

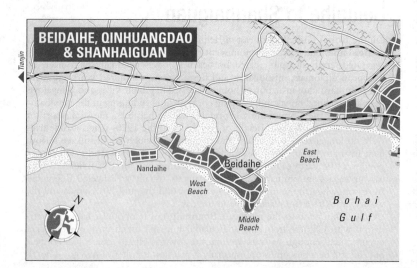

BEIDAIHE, QINHUANGDAO & SHANHAIGUAN

inside the city wall. The surrounding countryside contains some fine sturdy fortifications and remnants of the **Great Wall**.

This part of the Bohai Gulf is more quickly and easily reached from Beijing on the express-bus service to **QINHUANGDAO** than by train. Midway between Beidaihe and Shanhaiguan, Qinhuangdao is an industrial city and charmless modern port. Once you're in the area, it's straightforward to get around by **bus**; local bus services are frequent, usually hourly during the day. Buses #6 and #34 shuttle between Beidaihe and Qinhuangdao (¥2), while buses #25 and #33 run the Qinhuangdao–Shanhaiguan route (same fare). There are also frequent local **minibuses**, which you can catch from any major road, linking Qinhuangdao and Beidaihe (¥4) throughout the day until 6pm. Qinhuangdao used to boast a passenger-ferry service to Dalian, though this wasn't in service at the time of writing. If you do get stuck in Qinhuangdao, you could do worse than stay at the *Haiyue Hotel*, 159 Yingbin Lu (☎0335/3065760; ④); walk south from the train station concourse and the hotel is on the west side of the road.

Beidaihe and around

It wasn't so long ago that **BEIDAIHE** had strict rules ordering where individuals could bathe, according to their rank. West Beach was reserved for foreigners after they were let in in 1979, with guards posted to chase off Chinese voyeurs interested in glimpsing their daringly bourgeois swimming costumes; the Middle Beach was demarcated by rope barriers and reserved for Party officials, with a sandy cove – the best spot – set out for the higher ranks. Dark swimsuits were compulsory, to avoid the illusion of nudity. These days the barriers have gone, along with the inhibitions of the urban Chinese (skimpy bikinis are fashionable now), and the contemporary town is a fascinating mix of the austerely communist and the gaudy kitsch of any busy seaside resort.

The Town
The streets along the seafront are the liveliest – most buildings are either restaurants, with crabs and prawns bobbing about in buckets outside, or shops selling

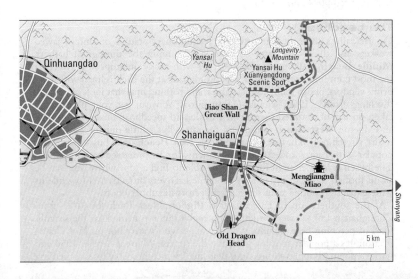

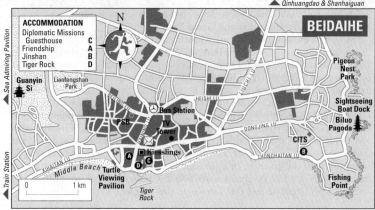

ACCOMMODATION
Diplomatic Missions
  Guesthouse   C
Friendship   A
Jinshan   B
Tiger Rock   D

Day-Glo swimsuits, inflatables, snorkels, souvenirs, even sculptures of chickens made of shells and raffia. Away from the sea, up the hill, the tree-lined streets are much quieter, and many of the buildings are guesthouses, though this is also where you find the **villas** of the Party elite, guarded by discreet soldiers. It's rumoured that every Politburo member once had a residence here, and many probably still do. All around are huge, chunky buildings, often with absurd decorative touches – Roman columns, fake totem poles, Greek porticoes – grafted onto their ponderous facades. These are work-unit hotels and sanatoriums for heroes of the people – factory workers, soldiers and the like – when they are granted the privilege of a seaside holiday.

On the far western side of town, 500m back from the beach, **Lianfengshan Park** is a hill of dense pines with picturesque pavilions and odd little caves, a good place to wander and get away from the crowds for a while. Atop the hill is the **Sea Admiring Pavilion**, which has good views of the coast. Also here is a quiet temple, **Guanyin Si**.

The beaches

On Beidaihe's three beaches, stirring revolutionary statues of lantern-jawed workers and their wives and children stand among the throngs of bathers. **Middle Beach**, really many small beaches with rocky outcrops in between, is the most convenient and popular. The promenade at the back is lined with soft-drink vendors, photo stalls, hoopla games, and bathing huts that look like moon dwellings from a 1950s science-fiction movie. You can get your photograph taken on top of a stuffed tiger or in a cardboard speedboat, or dressed up like an emperor. **West Beach** is more of the same, but a little quieter. East of the resort, stretching 15km to Qinhuangdao, is **East Beach** (take bus #6 or #34), popular with cadres and sanatorium patients for its more sedate atmosphere. The beach is long enough for you to be able to find a spot where you can be alone, though much of the muddy shoreline isn't very attractive. At low tide its wide expanse is dotted with seaweed collectors in rubber boots.

At the southern tip of East Beach is **Pigeon Nest Park** (bus #21 from Zhonghaitan Lu), a twenty-metre-high rocky outcrop named for the seagulls fond of perching here, obviously by someone who wasn't hot on bird identification. It's a popular spot for watching the sunrise. Mao sat here in 1954 and wrote a poem, "Ripples sifting sand/Beidaihe", which probably loses something in translation. Just before Pigeon Nest Park, the bus stops near the dock for Beidaihe's **sightseeing boats**, which in season leave regularly during the day to chug up and down the coast, which isn't really that spectacular (1hr; ¥32).

Practicalities

Beidaihe **train station** is inconveniently located 15km north of the town; bus #5 will take you from here into the centre. If you arrive at night, there'll be private minibuses and taxis waiting; bargain hard to get the fare down below ¥40. If you intend stopping at both Beidaihe and Shanhaiguan, it's far more convenient and interesting to spend your first night in Shanhaiguan (two stops farther down the line, but note that some trains don't stop there), where the station is close to the hotels. From Beidaihe's **bus station**, it's a fifteen-minute downhill walk to Middle Beach.

Taxis around town cost ¥10, but Beidaihe is small enough to get around easily on foot. The Beidaihe **CITS** is located in a very nondescript building at 4 Jinshanzui Lu (☎0335/4041748).

Accommodation and eating

Beidaihe's accommodation is most in demand between May and August; at other times of year, room prices are slashed to half their summer high or less. Few of Beidaihe's many **hotels** are open to foreigners. Of those that are, one of the best is the *Diplomatic Missions Guesthouse* at 1 Baosan Lu (☎0335/4041287, ℱ4041807; ❾), a quiet street ten minutes' walk north of Middle Beach. It's a stylish complex of thirteen villas set among gardens of cypress and pine, with a karaoke bar, a nightclub, a tennis court, a gym and a good outside restaurant where barbecues are held in the summer. Other good options include the *Tiger Rock* (☎0335/4041373; ❺), well located right next to the beach, but a little bland and characterless; and the small *Friendship*, farther north on Haining Lu (☎0335/4041176; ❻). Out of the way in a pleasant, quiet cove on Zhonghaitan Lu is the *Jinshan*, a three-star complex with pool (☎0335/4041338; ❼).

Foodwise, Beidaihe is noted for its crab, cuttlefish and scallops. Try one of the innumerable small **seafood** places on Haining Lu, where you order by pointing to the tastiest looking thing scuttling or slithering around the bucket, or *Kiessling's*, on Dongjing Lu near the *Diplomatic Missions Guesthouse*. Originally Austrian, this restaurant has been serving the foreign community for most of the last century, and still has a few Western dishes on its reasonably priced menu – Western diners are even issued with knives and forks. It's an ideal place for breakfast, offering good pastries and bread.

Around Beidaihe

The countryside around Beidaihe has been designated as a **nature reserve** and is a stopping-off point for Siberian and red-crowned cranes migrating to Dongbei in May; Beidaihe's CITS is a useful point of contact for birders.

Fifteen kilometres west along the coast, **NANDAIHE** is a tourist resort constructed to take advantage of Beidaihe's popularity. With 3km of beach and a few parks and viewpoints, it's the same sort of thing as Beidaihe but more regimented and artificial, and is thus best visited as a day-trip; frequent minibuses come here from the Beidaihe bus station. The main attraction in Nandaihe is **Golden Beach** to the west, where you can go "sand sliding" down the steep sand dunes on a rented sledge – great fun, but remember to keep your feet and elbows in the air. Foreigners can stay here at the *Nandaihe Beach House* resort complex (☎0335/4042807; ❺).

Shanhaiguan and beyond

A town at the northern tip of the Bohai Gulf, **SHANHAIGUAN**, "the Pass Between the Mountains and the Sea", was originally built during the Ming dynasty as a fortress to defend the eastern end of the **Great Wall**. The wall crosses the Yanshan Mountains to the north, forms the east wall of the town and meets the sea a few kilometres to the south. Far from being a solitary castle, Shanhaiguan originally formed the centre of a network of defences: smaller forts, now nothing but ruins, existed to the north, south and east, and beacon towers were dotted around the mountains. Despite its obvious tourist potential, for now the city largely remains a sleepy, dusty little place of low buildings and quiet streets, though some major building projects are pretty obvious in the old town. The best thing to do here is rent a bike and spend a day or two exploring.

The Town

Shanhaiguan is still arranged along its original plan of straight boulevards following the compass points, intersected with a web of alleys. Dominating the

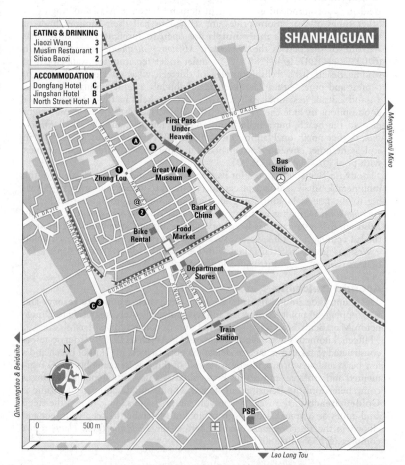

town is a fortified gatehouse in the east wall, the **First Pass Under Heaven**, which for centuries was the entrance to the Middle Kingdom from the barbarian lands beyond. An arch topped by a two-storey tower, the gate is the biggest structure in town, and makes the surrounding buildings look puny in comparison. It must have looked even more formidable when it was built in 1381, with a wooden drawbridge over a moat 18m wide, and three outer walls for added defensive strength. The arch remained China's northernmost entrance until 1644, when it was breached by the Manchus.

These days, the gate (daily 7.30am–6pm; ¥50) is overrun by hordes of marauding tourists, and is at its best in the early morning before most of them arrive. The gate's name is emblazoned in red above the archway, calligraphy attributed to Xiao Xian, a Ming-dynasty scholar who lived in the town. A steep set of steps leads up from Dong Dajie to the impressively thick wall, nearly 30m wide. The tower on top, a two-storey, ten-metre-high building with arrow slits regularly spaced along its walls, is now a **museum**, appropriately containing weapons, armour and costumes, as well as pictures of the nobility, who are so formally dressed they look like puppets. It's possible to stroll a little way along the wall in both directions; the wall is scattered with pay-per-view telescope and binocular stands, which afford a view of tourists on the Great Wall at Jiaoshan several kilometres to the north, where the wall zigzags and dips along vertiginous peaks before disappearing over the horizon. There's plenty of tat for sale at the wall's base, including decorated chopsticks, hologram medallions and jade curios, while in a courtyard to the northern side, a statue of Xu Da, the first general to rule the fort, frowns sternly down on the scene.

Follow the city wall south from the gate and you come to the recently renovated **Great Wall Museum** (daily 8am–6pm; free). A modern, imitation Qing building, it has eight halls showcasing the history of the region in chronological order from Neolithic times. Though there are no English captions, the exhibits themselves are fascinating and well displayed. As well as the tools used to build the wall, the vicious weaponry used to defend and attack it is on display, including mock-ups of siege machines and broadswords that look too big to carry, let alone wield. The last three rooms contain dioramas, plans and photographs of local historic buildings. Inside the final room is a model of the area as it looked in Ming times, giving an idea of the extent of the defences, with many small outposts and fortifications in the district around. It's much better than any CITS map or glossy brochure and should inspire a few bike rides. An annexe outside the museum holds temporary art exhibitions.

Practicalities

Whether you arrive by **train** or **bus**, you'll be greeted by an eager mob of taxi and motor-rickshaw drivers; the ¥5 flagfall covers a ride to any destination in town. **Local buses** from Qinhuangdao and Beidaihe run along Guancheng Nan Lu, with a stop just outside the southern city gate. **Bikes** can be rented from one of many retail bike shops along Nan Dajie (¥10/day, ¥100 deposit).

There are only two **hotels** open to foreigners within the old city walls, but they're both ideally located near the First Pass Under Heaven. The small, friendly *North Street Guesthouse*, at 2 Mujia Hutong (☏0335/5051680; ③), feels like a temple: metal lions guard the gates and, inside, rooms lead off cloisters around a courtyard and garden. It was under renovation at last check, and room rates are likely to rise when it reopens. Nearby on Dong Dajie, the palatial *Jingshan Hotel* (☏0335/5051130; ⑤) was built to imitate a Qing mansion, with high ceilings, decorative friezes, curling roofs and red brick walls and balconies. Rooms, with TV and fan, are off a series of small courtyards. If you can't get into either of these, try the *Dongfang* on Guancheng Nan Lu (℡0335/5151111; ⑤), outside the city's south wall, offering four-person dorms (summer only) and doubles. It's friendly and adequate, but not a patch on the other two, and a long way from the interesting part of town.

As for **eating**, avoid the *Jingshan's* fancy restaurant, which overcharges foreigners; head instead for the small canteens on Bei Dajie and Nan Dajie or, for delicious, plump, steamed Chinese ravioli, there's *Jiaozi Wang*, next to the *Dongfang Hotel*. *Sitiao Baozi* on Nan Dajie turns humble pork and vegetarian *baozi* into the centrepiece of a good meal, along with a range of stir-fries and cold dishes. Just north of the bell tower (Zhong Lou) on Nan Dajie is a tiny Muslim place that's good for breakfast – go for the crispy dumplings, *shao mai*.

The Great Wall beyond Shanhaiguan

You'll see plenty of tourist **minibuses** grouped around the major crossroads in town and at the station, all serving the sights outside Shanhaiguan. Public **buses** also travel these routes, but if you have the time you're best off travelling by **bike**: the roads are quiet, the surrounding countryside is strikingly attractive and there are any number of pretty places off the beaten track where you can escape the crowds.

Intrepid hikers could try and make it to **Yangsai Hu**, a lake in the mountains directly north of Shanhaiguan, or to **Longevity Mountain**, a hill of rugged stones east of the lake, where many of the rocks have been carved with the character *shou* (longevity). There's also a pool here, a good place for a quiet swim.

Lao Long Tou

Follow the remains of the Great Wall south and after 4km you'll reach **Lao Long Tou** (Old Dragon Head, after a large stone dragon's head that used to look out to sea here; daily 7.30am–5pm; ¥50), the point at which the wall hits the coast. Bus #24 heads here from Xinghua Jie, near Shanhaiguan's train station. A miniature fortress with a two-storey temple in the centre stands right at the end of the wall, but unfortunately everything here has been so reconstructed it all looks brand new, and the area is surrounded by a rash of tourist development. The rather dirty beaches either side of the wall are popular bathing spots.

Walk a few minutes past the restaurants west of Lao Long Tou and you'll come to the old British Army **barracks**, on the right; this was the beachhead for the Eight Allied Forces in 1900, when they came ashore to put down the Boxers. A plaque here reminds visitors to "never forget the national humiliation and invigorate the Chinese nation." Do your part by taking care not to trample the lawn.

Mengjiangnü Miao

Some 6.5km northeast of town is **Mengjiangnü Miao** (daily 7.30am–5pm; ¥25), a temple dedicated to a legendary woman whose husband was press-ganged into one of the Great Wall construction squads. He died from exhaustion, and she set out to search for his body to give him a decent burial, weeping as she walked along the wall. So great was her grief, it is said, that the wall crumbled in sympathy, revealing the bones of her husband and many others who had died in its construction. The temple is small and elegant, with good views of the mountains and the sea. Statues of the lady herself and her attendants sit looking rather prim inside. To get here, take bus #23 from outside Shanhaiguan's south gate.

△ The Great Wall near Shanhaiguan

Jiaoshan

A couple of kilometres to the north of Shanhaiguan, it's possible to hike along the worn remains of the Great Wall all the way to the mountains. Head north along Bei Dajie and out of town, and after about 10km you'll come to a reconstructed section known as **Jiao Shan** (daily 8am–4pm; ¥25), passing the ruins of two forts – stone foundations and earthen humps – along the way. A steep path from the reconstructed section takes you through some dramatic scenery into the Yunshan Mountains, or you can cheat and take the cable car (¥15, ¥30 return).

The further along the wall you go the better it gets – the crowds peter out, the views become grander, and once the reconstructed section ends, you're left standing beside – or on top of – the real, crumbly thing. Head a few kilometres further east and you'll discover a trio of passes in the wall, and a beacon tower that's still in good condition. You can keep going into the mountains for as long as you like, so it's worth getting here early and making a day of it. A pedicab or taxi back into town from Jiao Shan's parking lot costs ¥5.

Chengde

CHENGDE, a small country town 250km northeast of Beijing, sits in a river basin on the west bank of the Wulie River, surrounded by the Yunshan mountain range. It's a quiet, unimportant place, rather bland in appearance, but on its outskirts are some of the most magnificent examples of imperial architecture in China, remnants from its glory days as the **summer retreat** of the Manchu emperors. Gorgeous temples punctuate the cabbage fields around town, and a palace-and-park hill complex, **Bishu Shanzhuang**, covers an area nearly as large as the town itself. In recent years Chengde has once more become a

Chengde		
Chengde	承德	*chéngdé*
Anyuan Miao	安远庙	*ānyuǎn miào*
Arhat Hill	罗汉山	*luóhàn shān*
Frog Crag	蛤蟆石	*háma shí*
Bishu Shanzhuang	避暑山庄	*bìshǔ shānzhuāng*
Palace	正宫	*zhèng gōng*
Pule Si	普乐寺	*pǔlè sì*
Puning Si	普宁寺	*pǔníng sì*
Puren Si	溥仁寺	*pǔrén sì*
Putuozongcheng Miao	普陀宗乘之庙	*pǔtuó zōngchéng zhīmiào*
Shuxiang Si	殊像寺	*shūxiàng sì*
Sledgehammer Rock	棒钟山	*bàngzhōng shān*
Xumifushouzhi Miao	须弥福寿之庙	*xūmífúshòu zhīmiào*
Accommodation and eating		
Chengde Binguan	承德宾馆	*chéngdé bīnguǎn*
Chengde Dasha	承德大厦	*chéngdé dàshà*
Huilong Dasha	会龙大厦	*huìlóng dàshà*
Qianlong Jiaoziguan	乾隆饺子馆	*qiánlóng jiǎoziguǎn*
Qiwanglou	绮望楼宾馆	*qǐwànglóu bīnguǎn*
Shanzhuang Binguan	山庄宾馆	*shānzhuāng bīnguǎn*
Yunshan Fandian	云山饭店	*yúnshān fàndiàn*

summer haven, filling up at weekends with Beijingers escaping the hassles of the capital.

Some history

Originally called "Rehe", the town was discovered by the Qing-dynasty emperor **Kangxi** at the end of the seventeenth century, while marching his troops to the Mulan hunting range to the north. He was attracted to the cool summer climate and the rugged landscape, and built small lodges here from where he could indulge in a fantasy Manchu lifestyle, hunting and hiking like his northern ancestors. The building programme expanded when it became diplomatically useful to spend time north of Beijing, to forge closer links with the troublesome Mongol tribes. Kangxi, perhaps the ablest and most enlightened of his dynasty, was known more for his economy – "The people are the foundation of the kingdom, if they have enough then the kingdom is rich" – than for such displays of imperial grandeur. Chengde, however, was a thoroughly pragmatic creation, devised as an effective means of defending the empire by overawing Mongol princes with splendid audiences, hunting parties and impressive military manoeuvres. He firmly resisted all petitions to have the Great Wall repaired, saying this would be an unnecessary burden on the people, and noting that the Wall was a poor means of control, too, as it had posed no obstacle to the founders of his dynasty only a few years before.

Construction of the first palaces started in 1703. By 1711 there were 36 palaces, temples, monasteries and pagodas set in a great walled park, its ornamental pools and islands dotted with beautiful pavilions and linked by bridges. Craftsmen from all parts of China were gathered to work on the project, with Kangxi's grandson, **Qianlong** (1736–96), adding another 36 imperial buildings during his reign, which was considered to be the heyday of Chengde.

In 1786, the **Panchen Lama** was summoned from Tibet by Qianlong for his birthday celebrations. This was an adroit political move to impress the followers of Lamaist Buddhism. The Buddhists included a number of minority groups who were prominent thorns in the emperor's side, such as Tibetans, Mongols, Torguts, Eleuths, Djungars and Kalmucks. Some accounts (notably not Chinese) tell how Qianlong invited the Panchen Lama to sit with him on the Dragon Throne, which was taken to Chengde for the summer season. He was certainly feted with honours and bestowed with costly gifts and titles, but the greatest impression on him and his followers must have been made by the replicas of the Potala and of his own palace, constructed at Chengde to make him feel at home – a munificent gesture, and one that would not have been lost on the Lamaists. However, the Panchen Lama's visit ended questionably when he succumbed to smallpox, or possibly poison, in Beijing and his coffin was returned to Tibet with a stupendous funeral cortege.

The first **British Embassy** to China, under Lord Macartney, visited Qianlong's court in 1793. Having suffered the indignity of sailing up the river to Beijing in a ship whose sails were painted with characters reading "Tribute bearers from the vassal king of England", they were somewhat disgruntled to discover that the emperor had decamped to Chengde for the summer. However, they made the 150-kilometre journey there, in impractical European carriages, arriving at Chengde in September 1793. They were well received by the emperor, despite Macartney's refusal to kowtow, and in spite of Qianlong's disappointment with their gifts, supplied by the opportunist East India Company. Qianlong, at the height of Manchu power, was able to hold out against the British demands, refusing to grant any of the treaties requested and remarking, in reply to a request for trade: "We possess all things. I set no value on objects strange or ingenious, and have no use for your country's manufactures." His letter to the British monarch concluded, magnificently, "O king, Tremblingly Obey and Show No Negligence!"

Chengde gradually lost its imperial popularity when the place came to be seen as unlucky after emperors Jiaqing and Xianfeng died here in 1820 and 1860 respectively. The buildings were left empty and neglected for most of the twentieth century, but largely escaped the ravages of the Cultural Revolution. Restoration, in the interests of tourism, began in the 1980s and is ongoing.

Arrival and transport

The train journey from Beijing to Chengde takes four hours (T-class) through verdant, rolling countryside, passing the Great Wall before arriving at the **train**

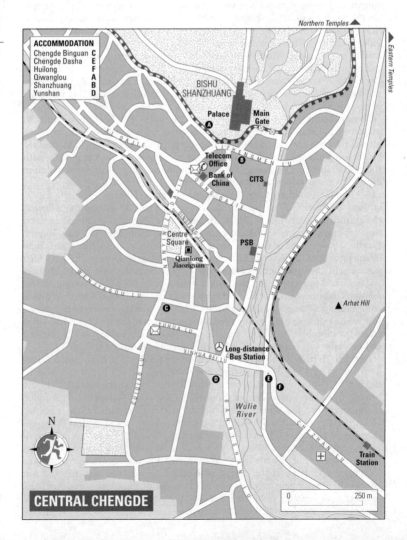

ACCOMMODATION
Chengde Binguan **C**
Chengde Dasha **E**
Huilong **F**
Qiwanglou **A**
Shanzhuang **B**
Yunshan **D**

Northern Temples ▲

▲ Eastern Temples

BISHU SHANZHUANG

Palace
Ⓐ

Main Gate

Telecom Office
Ⓒ Ⓑ

Bank of China

CITS

Centre Square

Qianlong Jiaoziguan

PSB

▲ Arhat Hill

Ⓒ

Long-distance Bus Station

Ⓓ   Ⓔ Ⓕ

Wulie River

N

Train Station

CENTRAL CHENGDE

0   250 m

station in the south of town. Travelling from Beijing by bus takes about the same time, though you run greater risk of traffic and weather delays. Buses terminate at the **long-distance bus station** just off Wulie Lu in the centre of town. Touts wait in ambush at both stations, and can be useful if you already have a hotel in mind, as you won't be charged for the ride there; however, they will hassle you to take a minibus tour with them. Onward train tickets can be booked, with a ¥30 surcharge, from **CITS** at 11 Zhonghua Lu (to the right inside the courtyard; ☏0314/2027483) or from any of the hotels.

Getting around Chengde by public transport isn't easy, as **local buses** are infrequent and always crammed. Buses #5 and #11, which go from the train station to Bishu Shanzhuang, and bus #6, from there to the Puning Si, are the most useful. **Taxis** are easy to find, but the drivers are sometimes unwilling to use their meters – a ride around town should cost ¥5, to an outlying temple ¥10. At peak hours during the summer, the main streets are so congested that it's quicker to walk. The town itself is just about small enough to cover on foot.

If your time is limited, consider a minibus **tour** to cram in all the sights. English-speaking day-tours can be arranged through CITS or through the larger hotels for around ¥50. Chinese tours, which leave sporadically from outside the train station, are slightly cheaper. A day-long organized tour is something of a trial of endurance, however, and the tours tend to overlook the less spectacular temples, which are also the most peaceful. Probably the best way to see everything in a short time is to take a minibus or a bike around the temples one day and explore the mountain resort the next. If you're travelling in a group you can charter a taxi or a minibus for around ¥150 a day (bargain hard) and make up your own itinerary.

Accommodation

There are plenty of hotels in Chengde town itself, plus a couple of expensive places inside Bishu Shanzhuang, although none of them is worth getting excited about. Rates are highly negotiable; the price codes below apply to the peak summer season and weekends. At other times you can get discounts of up to two thirds.

Chengde Binguan 33 Nanyingzi Dajie ☏0314/2023157, ☏2021341. Threadbare and gloomy, this place is only worth it if you can get one of their cheap doubles, which they would rather not tell you about. ❸

Chengde Dasha Chezhan Lu ☏0314/2088808, ☏2024319. This recently renovated fifteen-storey block is convenient for the station, but in an uninteresting area of town. ❼

Huilong Xinjuzhai Building, 1 Chezhan Lu ☏0314/2085369, ☏2082404. Opposite the *Chengde Dasha*, and the better of the two. It's twelve storeys high, with a grand lobby, but the rooms are rather small and merely adequate. ❻

Qiwanglou Around the corner and uphill from the Bishu Shanzhuang main entrance

☏0314/2024385. A well-run three-star hotel in a pleasing imitation Qing-style building. ❽

Shanzhuang 127 Xiaonanmen (entrance on Lizhengmen Lu) ☏0314/2025588. This grand, well-located complex, with huge rooms, high ceilings and a cavernous, gleaming lobby, is good value, and with a wide range of rooms it's Chengde's best bet for most budgets. The large rooms in the main building are nicer but a little more expensive than those in the ugly building round the back. Buses #5 or #11 from the train station will get you here. ❹

Yunshan 2 Banbishan Lu ☏0314/2055588, ☏20558855. This modern block is the most luxurious place to stay in town, and is popular with tour groups. The second-floor restaurant is good, the plushest in town, and not too expensive. A 10min walk from the train station. ❽

The Town

Bishu Shanzhuang lies in the north of the town, while farther north and to the east, on the other side of the river, stand Chengde's eight imposing **temples**. The majority of Chengde's one-million-strong population live in a semi-rural suburban sprawl to the south of the centre, leaving the city itself fairly small-scale, its new high-rises yet to obscure the view of distant mountains and fields. However, hundreds of thousands of visitors come here each year, and on summer weekends especially the town can be packed with tourists, and its main artery, **Nanyingzi Dajie**, clogged with traffic. The street is much more pleasant in the evening, when a **night market** stretches all the way down it. As well as snacks, many vendors sell antiques and curios which are generally cheaper than in Beijing or Tianjin, but you'll have to bargain hard (and don't expect everything to be genuine).

Bishu Shanzhuang

Surrounded by a ten-kilometre wall and larger than the Summer Palace in Beijing, **Bishu Shanzhuang** (also referred to as the Mountain Resort) occupies the northern third of the town's area (daily: summer 7am–5.30pm; winter 8am–4.30pm; ¥60 combined ticket for the park and the palace). This is where, in the summer months, the Qing emperors lived, feasted, hunted, and occasionally dealt with affairs of state. The palace buildings just inside the front entrance are unusual for imperial China as they are low, wooden and unpainted – simple but elegant, in contrast to the opulence and grandeur of Beijing's palaces. It's said that Emperor Kangxi wanted the complex to mimic a Manchurian village, to show his disdain for fame and wealth, though with 120 rooms and several thousand servants he wasn't exactly roughing it. The same principle of idealized naturalness governed the design of the park. With its twisting paths and streams,

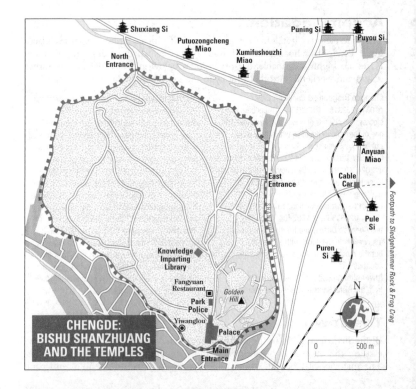

CHENGDE:
BISHU SHANZHUANG
AND THE TEMPLES

rockeries and hills, it's a fantasy re-creation of the rough northern terrain and southern Chinese beauty spots that the emperors would have seen on their tours of inspection. The whole is an attempt to combine water, buildings and plants in graceful harmony. Lord Macartney noted its similarity to the "soft beauties" of an English manor park of the Romantic style.

Covering the whole park and its buildings takes at least a day, and an early start is recommended. It's at its nicest in the early morning anyway, when a vegetable market sets up just outside the front gate, and old people practise *tai ji* or play Go by the palace. The park is simply too big to get overcrowded, and if you head north beyond the lakes, you're likely to find yourself alone.

The palace

The **main gate**, Lizhengmen, is in the south wall, off Lizhengmen Dajie. The **palace quarter**, just inside the complex to the west of the main gate, is built on a slope, facing south, and consists of four groups of dark wooden buildings spread over an area of 100,000 square metres. The first, southernmost group, the Front Palace, where the emperors lived and worked, is the most interesting, as many of the rooms have been restored to their full Qing elegance, decked out with graceful furniture and ornaments. Even the everyday objects are impressive: brushes and ink stones on desks, ornate fly whisks on the arms of chairs, little jade trees on shelves. Other rooms house displays of ceramics, books and exotic martial-art weaponry. The Qing emperors were fine calligraphers, and examples of their work appear throughout the palace.

There are 26 buildings in this group, arranged south to north in nine successive compounds which correspond to the nine levels of heaven. The main gate leads into the **Outer Wumen**, where high-ranking officials waited for a single peal of a large bell, indicating that the emperor was ready to receive them. Next is the **Inner Wumen**, where the emperor would watch his officers practise their archery. Directly behind, the **Hall of Frugality and Sincerity** is a dark, well-appointed room made of cedar wood, imported at great expense from south of the Yangzi River by Qianlong, who had none of his grandfather Kangxi's scruples about conspicuous consumption. Topped with a curved roof, the hall has nine bays, and patterns on the walls include symbols of longevity and good luck. The **Four Knowledge Study Room**, behind, was where the emperor did his ordinary work, changed his clothes and rested. A vertical scroll on the wall outlines the four knowledges required of a gentleman, as written in the Chinese classics: he must be aware of what is small, obvious, soft and strong. It's more spartanly furnished, a little more intimate and less imposing than the other rooms.

The main building in the **Rear Palace** is the **Hall of Refreshing Mists and Waves**, the living quarters of the imperial family, and beautifully turned out in period style. It was in the west room here that Emperor Xianfeng signed the humiliating Beijing Treaty in the 1850s, giving away more of China's sovereignty and territory after their defeat in the Second Opium War. The **Western Apartments** are where the notorious Cixi, better known as the Dowager Empress (see p.125), lived when she was one of Xianfeng's concubines. A door connects the apartments to the hall, and it was through here that she eavesdropped on the dying emperor's last words of advice to his ministers, intelligence she used to force herself into power. The courtyard of the Rear Palace has a good **souvenir shop**, inside an old Buddhist tower reached by climbing a staircase by the rockery.

The other two complexes are much smaller. The **Pine and Crane Residence**, a group of buildings parallel to the front gate, is a more subdued version of the Front Palace, home to the emperor's mother and his concubines. In the **Myriad Valleys of Rustling Pine Trees**, to the north of here, Emperor Kangxi read books and granted audiences, and Qianlong studied as a child. The group of structures southwest of the main palace is the **Ahgesuo**, where during the Manchurian rule, male descendants of the royal family studied; lessons began at 5am and finished at noon. A boy was expected to speak Manchu at 6, Chinese at 12, be competent with a bow by the age of 14, and married at 16.

The grounds

The best way to get around the **lake area** of the park – a network of pavilions, bridges, lakes and waterways – is to rent a **rowing boat** (¥20 an hour). Much of the architecture here is a direct copy of southern Chinese buildings. In the east, the **Golden Hill**, a cluster of buildings grouped on a small island, is notable for a hall and tower modelled after the Golden Hill Monastery in Zhenjiang, Jiangsu Province. The **Island of Midnight and Murmuring Streams**, roughly in the centre of the lake, holds a three-courtyard compound which was used by Kangxi and Qianlong as a retreat, while the compound of halls, towers and pavilions on **Ruyi Island**, the largest, was where Kangxi dealt with affairs of state before the palace was completed.

Just beyond the lake area, on the western side of the park, is the grey-tiled **Wenjinge**, or Knowledge Imparting Library, surrounded by rockeries and pools for fire protection. From the outside, the structure appears to have two storeys. In fact there are three – a central section is windowless to protect the books from the sun. A fine collection is housed in the building, including *The Four Treasures*, a 36,304-volume Qing-dynasty encyclopedia, but sadly you can't go inside.

A vast expanse of **grassland** extends from the north of the lake area to the foothills of the mountains, comprising Wanshun Wan (Garden of Ten Thousand Trees) and Shima Da (Horse Testing Ground). Genuine Qing-dynasty **yurts** sit here, the largest an audience hall where Qianlong received visiting dignitaries from ethnic minorities.

The hilly area in the northwest of the park has a number of rocky valleys, gorges and gullies with a few tastefully placed lodges and pagodas. The deer, which graze on tourist handouts, were reintroduced after being wiped out by imperial hunting expeditions.

The temples and Sledgehammer Rock

The **temples** (daily 8am–5.30pm) in the foothills of the mountains around Chengde were built in the architectural styles of different ethnic nationalities, so that wandering among them is rather like being in a religious theme park. This isn't far from the original intention, as they were constructed by Kangxi and Qianlong less to express religious sentiment than as a way of showing off imperial magnificence, and also to make envoys from anywhere in the empire feel more at home. Though varying in design, all the temples share **Lamaist features** – Qianlong found it politically expedient to promote Tibetan and Mongolian Lamaism as a way of keeping these troublesome minorities in line.

The temples are now in varying states of repair, having been left untended for decades. Originally there were twelve, but two have been destroyed and another two are dilapidated. Present restoration work is being paid for by the high entrance fees charged in the large temples.

The best way to see the temples is to **rent a bicycle** (ask at your hotel; the *Qiwanglou*, for one, has bikes to rent): the roads outside the town are quiet, it's hard to get lost and you can dodge the tour groups. One workable itinerary would be to see the northern cluster in the morning, returning to town for lunch (it's impossible to cross the river to the eastern temples from outside town); in the afternoon, head east for the Pule Si, then take the cable car up to **Sledgehammer Rock**, a bizarre hilltop protuberance that dominates the eastern horizon of the town. Before you head back to the centre, you may want to check out the small, peaceful Anyuan and Puren temples, good places to chill out with a book.

The northern temples

Just beyond the northern border of Bishu Shanzhuang are five temples which were once part of a string of nine. The **Puning Si** (Temple of Universal Peace; ¥40) is a must, if only for the awe-inspiring statue of Guanyin, the largest wooden statue in the world. This is the only working temple in Chengde, with shaven-headed Mongolian monks manning the altars and trinket stalls, though the atmosphere is not especially spiritual. Undergoing restoration at the time of writing, the temple is usually clamorous with day-trippers, some of whom seem to take outrageous liberties, judging by the sign that says "No shooting birds in the temple area". There are rumours that the monks are really paid government employees working for the tourist industry, though the vehemence with which they defend their prayer mats and gongs from romping children suggests otherwise.

The Puning Si was built in 1755 to commemorate the Qing victory over Mongolian rebels at Junggar in northwest China, and is based on the oldest Tibetan temple, the Samye. Like traditional Tibetan buildings, it lies on the slope of a mountain facing south, though the layout of the front is typically Han, with a gate hall, stele pavilions, a bell and a drum tower, a Hall of Heavenly Kings, and the Mahavira Hall. In the **Hall of Heavenly Kings**, the statue of a fat, grinning monk holding a bag depicts Qi Ci, a tenth-century character with a jovial disposition, who is believed to be a reincarnation of the Buddha. Four gaudy *devarajas* (guardian demons) here glare down at you with bulging eyeballs from niches in the walls. In the **West Hall** are statues of Buddha Manjusri, Avalokiteshvara and Samantabhadra. In the **East Hall**, the central statue, flanked by *arhats*, depicts Ji Gong, a Song-dynasty monk who was nicknamed Crazy Ji for eating meat and being almost always drunk, but who was much respected for his kindness to the poor.

The rear section of the temple, separated from the front by a wall, comprises 27 Tibetan-style rooms laid out symmetrically, with the **Mahayana Hall** in the centre. Some of the buildings are actually solid (the doors are false), suggesting that the original architects were more concerned with appearances than function. The hall itself is dominated by the 23-metre-high wooden **statue of Guanyin**, the Goddess of Mercy. She has 42 arms with an eye in the centre of each palm, and three eyes on her face which symbolize her ability to see into the past, the present and the future. The hall has two raised entrances, and it's worth looking at the statue from these upper viewpoints as they reveal new details, such as the eye sunk in her belly button, and the little Buddha sitting on top of her head.

On the thirteenth day of the first lunar month (Jan or Feb), the monks observe the ritual of "**catching the ghost**", during which a ghost made of dough is placed on an iron rack while monks dressed in white dance around it, then divide it into pieces and burn it. The ritual is thought to be in honour of a ninth-century Tibetan Buddhist, Lhalung Oaldor, who assassinated a king who had ordered the destruction of Tibetan Buddhist temples, books and priests. The wily monk entered the palace on a white horse painted black, dressed in a white coat with a black lining. After killing the king, he washed the horse and turned the coat inside out, thus evading capture from the guards who did not recognize him.

Recently restored, the **Xumifushouzhi Miao** (Temple of Sumeru Happiness and Longevity; ¥40), just southwest of Puning Si, was built in 1780 in Mongolian style for the ill-fated sixth Panchen Lama when he came to Beijing to pay his respects to the emperor. The centrepiece is the **Hall of Loftiness and Solemnity**, its finest feature the eight sinuous gold dragons sitting on the roof, each weighing over a thousand kilograms.

The Putuozongcheng Miao and Shuxiang Si

Next door to the Xumifushouzhi Miao, the magnificent **Putuozongcheng Miao** (Temple of Potaraka Doctrine; ¥40) was built in 1771 and is based on the Potala Palace in Lhasa. Covering 220,000 square metres, it's the largest temple in Chengde, with sixty groups of halls, pagodas and terraces. The grand red terrace forms a Tibetan-style facade screening a Chinese-style interior, although many of the windows on the terrace are fake, and some of the whitewashed buildings around the base are merely filled-in shapes. Inside, the West Hall is notable for holding a rather comical copper statue of the Propitious Heavenly Mother, a fearsome woman wearing a necklace of skulls and riding side-saddle on a mule. According to legend, she vowed to defeat the evil demon Raksaka, so she first lulled him into a false sense of security – by marrying him and bearing him two sons – then swallowed the moon and in the darkness crept up on him and turned him into a mule. The two dancing figures at her feet are her sons; their ugly features betray their paternity. The **Hall of All Laws Falling into One**, at the back, is worth a visit for the quality of the decorative religious furniture on display. Other halls hold displays of Chinese pottery and ceramics and Tibetan religious artefacts, an exhibition slanted to portray the gorier side of Tibetan religion and including a drum made from two children's skulls. The roof of the temple has a good view over the surrounding countryside.

The eastern temples

The three **eastern temples** are easily accessible off a quiet road that passes through dusty, rambling settlements, 3–4km from the town centre. From Lizhengmen Lu, cross over to the east bank of the river and head north.

The **Puren Si** (Temple of Universal Benevolence) is the first one you'll reach and the oldest in the complex, but it has been closed to tourists. It was built by Kangxi in 1713, as a sign of respect to the visiting Mongolian nobility, come to congratulate the emperor on the occasion of his sixtieth birthday.

The **Pule Si** (Temple of Universal Happiness; ¥20) farther north was built in 1766 by Qianlong as a place for Mongol envoys to worship, and its style is an odd mix of Han and Lamaist elements. The Lamaist back section, a triple-tiered terrace and hall, with a flamboyantly conical roof and lively, curved surfaces, steals the show from the more sober, squarer Han architecture at the front. The ceiling of the back hall is a wood and gold confection to rival the Temple of Heaven in Beijing. Glowing at its centre is a mandala of Samvara, a Tantric deity, in the form of a cross. The altar beneath holds a Buddha of Happiness, a life-size copper image of sexual congress; more cosmic sex is depicted in two beautiful mandalas hanging outside. In the courtyard, prayer flags flutter while prayer wheels sit empty and unturned. Just north of the temple is the path that leads to **Sledgehammer Rock** and the cable car.

Recently renovated, the unspectacular **Anyuan Miao** (Temple of Appeasing the Borders; ¥20) is the most northerly of the group. It was built in 1764 for a troop of Mongolian soldiers who were moved to Chengde by Qianlong, and has a delightful setting on the tree-lined east bank of the Wulie River.

Sledgehammer Rock and beyond

Of the scenic areas around Chengde, the one that inspires the most curiosity is **Sledgehammer Rock**. Thinner at the base than at the top, the towering column of rock is more than 20m high, and is skirted by stalls selling little metal models of it and Sledgehammer Rock T-shirts. According to legend, the rock is a huge dragon's needle put there to plug a hole in the peak, which was letting the sea through. The rock's obviously phallic nature is tactfully not mentioned in tourist literature, but is acknowledged in local folklore – should the rock fall, it is said, it will have a disastrous effect on the virility of local men.

Sledgehammer Rock (¥20) is a couple of kilometres on foot from the Pule Si, or there's a **cable car** up (¥40), offering impressive views. On the south side of the rock, at the base of a cliff, is **Frog Crag**, a stone that vaguely resembles a sitting frog – the two-kilometre walk here is pleasant, if the frog itself disappoints. Other rocky highlights within walking distance are **Arhat Hill**, on the eastern side of the river, supposed to look like a reclining Buddha, and **Monk's Headgear Peak**, 4km south of town, the highest point in the area and best reached by bike – head south down Chezhan Lu.

Eating and drinking

Chengde is located in Hebei's most fertile area, which mainly produces maize and sorghum but also yields excellent local chestnuts, mushrooms and apricots. This fresh produce, plus the culinary legacy of the imperial cooks, means you can eat very well here. The town is also noted for its **wild game**, particularly deer (*lurou*), hare and pheasant (*shanji*), and its medicinal **juice drinks**: almond juice is said to be good for asthma; date and jujube juice for the stomach; and *jinlianhua* (golden lotus) juice for a sore throat. Date and almond are the sweetest and most palatable. Local **cakes**, such as the glutinous Feng family cakes, once an imperial delicacy but now a casual snack, can be found in the stalls on Yuhua Lu and Qingfeng Jie. Rose cakes – a sweet, crisp pastry cake and a particular favourite of Qianlong – are sold in Chengde's department stores.

There are plenty of **restaurants** catering to tourists on Lizhengmen Lu, around the main entrance to Bishu Shanzhuang. The small places west of the *Shanzhuang* hotel are fine, if a little pricey, and lively on summer evenings, when rickety tables are put on the pavement outside. A meal for two should be about ¥60, and plenty of diners stay on drinking well into the evening. The best *jiaozi* in town are served at *Qianlong Jiaoziguan*, just off Center Square, a park at the heart of the shopping district. Nearby, **Qingfeng Jie** is an old, charmingly seedy street of restaurants and salons, and is a great place to have a satisfying *shaguo* – a veggie claypot costs ¥6, a meat-based one ¥10. Inside Bishu Shanzhuang itself, the *Fangyuan* offers imperial cuisine, including such exotica as "Pingquan Frozen Rabbit", in an attractive environment.

Shijiazhuang and around

Three hours by express train southwest from Beijing, but at least five years behind in development, the capital of Hebei, **SHIJIAZHUANG**, is a major rail junction that you may find yourself passing through if you're heading south to the Yellow River. At the beginning of the last century Shijiazhuang was

Shijiazhuang and around		
Shijiazhuang		
Shijiazhuang	石家庄	*shíjiāzhuāng*
Hebei Hotel	河北市宾馆	*héběi shì bīnguǎn*
Hebei Museum	河北省博物馆	*héběi shěng bówùguǎn*
Hebei Teachers' University	河北师范大学	*héběi shīfàn dàxué*
Martyrs' Memorial	烈士陵园	*lièshì língyuán*
Yanchun Garden Hotel	燕春花园酒店	*yànchūnhuāyuán jiǔdiàn*
Zhongjing Grand Hotel	中京大酒店	*zhōngjīng dàjiǔdiàn*
Around Shijiazhuang		
Cangyan Shan Si	苍岩山寺	*cāngyánshān sì*
Zhaozhou Qiao	赵州桥	*zhàozhōu qiáo*

hardly more than a village, but the building of the rail line made it an important junction town. Having industrialized rapidly, it's now an unglamorous, sprawling place that keeps adding parks, squares and department stores as flourishes. It's known as a centre for medicine and, besides being home to China's largest pharmaceutical factory, is reputedly a good place to study traditional **Chinese medicine**. For tourists, the grave of Canadian surgeon Norman Bethune and the city museum are worth a look, but the best sights – **Cangyan Shan Si** and **Zhaozhou Qiao** – are a couple of hours from town by bus.

The City

Downtown Shijiazhuang is laid out on a grid with long axial roads, which change their names several times along their course, running north–south and east–west. The main street running east–west across town, just north of the train station and served by the #5 bus, is one of the most interesting. Five (rather long) blocks west of the station, along a section called Zhongshan Lu, you'll find the **Martyrs' Memorial** (daily 6am–5pm), an ordered, sober-looking park, containing the graves of the only two foreigners to be honoured as heroes of the Revolution. On the west side of the park, the grave of Canadian doctor **Norman Bethune** is marked by an ornate sarcophagus, a photo exhibition, and a statue, identical to one standing in Bethune Square, Montréal. Bethune (1890–1939), whose remains were moved here from Canada at the request of the Chinese government in 1953, was a brilliant, idealistic surgeon, who came

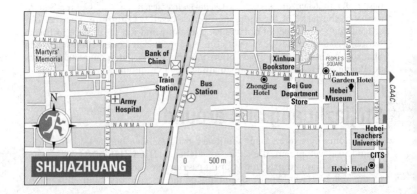

to China to help the Communists in the fight against the Japanese after working on the Republican side in the Spanish Civil War. He was present at most of the major battles of the era, and became a close confidant of Mao when the Red Army was holed up in Yan'an after the Long March. Mao was so impressed with Bethune's devotion to his work that he later exhorted the Chinese to "learn selflessness from Dr Bethune". As one of the most well-known foreigners in China, Bethune is one reason why many Chinese are well disposed towards Canadians. On the east side of the park, identical treatment is given to **Dwarkanath Kotnis** (1900–42), one of five Indian doctors who came to China in the 1930s. Staying in the country for nearly a decade, he joined the Communist Party just before his death. Both doctors are celebrated in a small **museum** at the back of the park; items on display include the exercise books in which they practised writing in Chinese and the crude surgical implements they had to work with. Among the large number of photographs are pictures of Bethune operating by torchlight and chatting with Mao.

East of the station (and, confusingly, behind it), the road becomes Zhongshan Dong Lu, the city's commercial sector, with a few department stores, the largest of which is the ostentatious five-storey **Bei Guo Department Store**. A few blocks further east is the unexpectedly good **Hebei Museum** (Mon–Fri 9–11.30am & 2–5.30pm; ¥10). The downstairs rooms hold temporary exhibitions of local products, while the two rooms upstairs display a fascinating hotchpotch of historic artefacts. The first hall includes a complete mammoth skull and tusk, a miniature terracotta army unearthed in a nearby tomb and a jade burial suit. The second hall, concerned with modern history, has displays of weaponry, photographs of battlefields, and a model village with a network of tunnels underneath – illustrating how the Red Army hid from their enemies.

Practicalities

The large **train station** is conveniently located in the middle of town, and its concourse is the arrival and departure point for **Beijing minibuses**. As you exit, turn right, then right again, to walk west along Zhongshan Lu into the commercial heart of town. The advance booking office for **train tickets** is at 47 Zhongshan Lu (daily 8am–noon & 2–5pm), though buying tickets from the station itself isn't too stressful, and several hotels in town can book train tickets. The **long-distance bus station** stands a block south of the train station, on the eastern side of the road.

Shijiazhuang **airport**, 45km northeast of the city, is served by an airport bus (¥20) which takes you to the **CAAC** office at 471 Zhongshan Lu (☎0311/5054084), far from the centre. If you need to buy air tickets, it's more convenient to do so from an office next to the Hualian Commercial Building, opposite the train station.

Getting around town by bus is straightforward; buses #5 and #6, which run east and west across town, are the most useful. **Taxis** around town have a ¥5 minimum charge, with each subsequent kilometre costing around ¥1.4. Staff at **CITS**, 26 Donggang Lu (☎0311/5827777), can provide information about the whole province, including tours to the surrounding monasteries.

For **changing money**, the Bank of China is at 136 Xinhua Dong Lu (daily 8am–5pm). The **post office** (daily 7am–9pm) and a 24-hour **telephone office** are located in the same building on Gongli Jie, opposite the west side of the train station. **Bikes** can be rented from a stall on the southeast side of the train-station concourse, opposite the Hualian Commercial Building, at the back of a large bike park (daily 8am–8pm; ¥5 per day, plus ¥50 deposit). The Xinhua

Bookstore on the second floor of 13 Jiefang Lu (with a branch opposite the train station's square) sells classic English-language novels on the second floor.

Accommodation and eating

There's not a great choice of hotels in Shijiazhuang, but with Beijing only a few hours' journey away, it's unlikely you'll need to stay more than a night here anyway. For **eating**, the stretch of Zhongshan Dong Lu, between People's Square and the Hebei Museum, features a good mix of Chinese eating places and Western fast-food outlets.

Hebei 168 Yucai Jie ⓣ0311/5266666, ⓕ5814092. This three-star, eight-storey block in the quiet eastern side of town dominates the surrounding low buildings. The hotel has two restaurants, a nightclub and a karaoke lounge, and can book train tickets. ⓺
Hebei Teachers' University Yuhua Lu ⓣ0311/6268347. The foreign teachers' dormitory is a friendly place to stay, offering well-maintained double rooms. Go through the main gate, take the first left and the building is on the right, signposted

in English. Bus #6 comes here from the train station. There are plenty of small restaurants and street stalls in the vicinity. Dorm beds ¥60, ⓷
Yanchun Garden Hotel 195 Zhongshan Donglu, beside People's Square ⓣ0311/6671188, ⓕ6048689. Shijiazhuang's nicest hotel, with all mod cons. ⓻
Zhongjing 176 Zhongshan Donglu ⓣ0311/5116688, ⓕ5116627. This stylish, low-key place has helpful staff and a good location on the main thoroughfare. ⓹

Around Shijiazhuang

Thirty kilometres southwest of Shijiazhuang, **Cangyan Shan Si** (daily 9am–4pm; ¥40), conceived in the Sui dynasty and rebuilt by the Qing, is an elegant monastic complex made beautiful by its dramatic location. Hundreds of feet up, on the steep rocky side of a mountain, the monastery perches on top of a bridge spanning a cleft in the almost vertical face of Cangyan Shan. The two main buildings are Sui in design, with colourful double roofs and attached gardens, and are reached by a pleasant two-hour walk along a twisting cliff path. In summer, **minibuses** run daily from Shijiazhuang to the monastery (¥13; 2hr 30min). Out of season, take a bus from the long-distance bus station to Jingxing County, then hire a motor-rickshaw to take you the last 10km. In winter, the path up to the monastery is sometimes impassable due to snow.

Zhaozhou Qiao (daily 9am–4pm; ¥25), 40km southeast of Shijiazhuang, is a simple, elegant bridge, built at the start of the seventh century, that will impress architects and engineers; the bridge is just outside the town of **Zhaoxian**, served by local buses from Shijiazhuang. Its builder, Li Chun, had to solve some tricky problems: the bridge had to be flat enough for the chariots of the imperial army to use it, yet not so low that it would be destroyed by the frequent floods. It had to rest on soft river banks but still be strong enough to withstand the military and trading convoys. The result of Li's deliberations was a single flattened arch, spanning over 36m, with a rise of just 7m. It's still in use, one of the masterpieces of Chinese architecture, and the model for dozens of northern Chinese stone bridges.

Travel details

Trains

Beidaihe to: Beijing (7 daily; 2hr 30min); Qinhuangdao (frequent; 30min); Shanhaiguan (frequent; 1hr); Shenyang (8 daily; 6hr); Tianjin (frequent; 3–5hr).

Chengde to: Beijing (6 daily; 4hr–6hr 30min); Dandong (daily; 17hr 30min); Shenyang (3 daily; 13–15hr); Tianjin (daily; 9hr).

Qinhuangdao to: Beidaihe (frequent; 20min); Beijing (frequent; 3hr 30min–6hr 15min); Shanhaiguan (frequent; 20min); Shenyang (frequent; 3hr 40min–7hr 15min); Tianjin (frequent; 3hr–4hr 15min).

Shanhaiguan to: Beidaihe (frequent; 1hr); Beijing (frequent; 3–5hr); Qinhuangdao (frequent; 15min); Shenyang (frequent; 4hr–6hr 30min); Tianjin (frequent; 3–4hr).

Shijiazhuang to: Beijing (frequent; 3–5hr); Ji'nan (2 daily; 4hr 20min); Taiyuan (frequent; 5hr); Tianjin (frequent; 4hr 30min–7hr); Zhengzhou (frequent; 4–7hr).

Tianjin to: Beidaihe (frequent; 3hr); Beijing (frequent, including hourly express services; 1–2hr); Chengde (daily; 8hr 50min); Guangzhou (3 daily; 25hr 40min); Jilin (3 daily; 15hr 30min–18hr); Qinhuangdao (frequent; 3–4hr 15min); Shanghai (9 daily; 13hr–19hr 30min); Shanhaiguan (frequent; 3–4hr); Shijiazhuang (frequent; 4hr 30min–7hr); Xi'an (3 daily; 17hr–21hr 30min).

Buses

Beidaihe to: Beijing (4hr); Qinhuangdao (20min); Shanhaiguan (40min); Tianjin (3hr 30min).
Chengde to: Beijing (4–5hr); Tianjin (4hr).

Qinhuangdao to: Beidaihe (20min); Beijing (5hr); Shanhaiguan (20min); Tianjin (4hr).
Shanhaiguan to: Beidaihe (40min); Beijing (5hr 20min); Qinhuangdao (20min); Tianjin (4hr 30min).
Shijiazhuang to: Beijing (4hr).
Tianjin to: Beidaihe (3hr 30min); Beijing (2hr); Chengde (4hr); Qinhuangdao (4hr); Shanhaiguan (4hr 20min).

Ferries

Tianjin (Tanggu) to: Dalian (March–Oct daily; rest of year every other day; 13–15hr); Inchon (South Korea; 2 weekly; 26hr); Kobe (Japan; weekly; 51hr).

Flights

Qinhuangdao to: Dalian (3 weekly; 1hr).
Shijiazhuang to: Chongqing (2 weekly; 2hr); Dalian (3 weekly; 1hr 10min); Guangzhou (6 weekly; 2hr 30min); Kunming (2 weekly; 4hr); Nanjing (4 weekly; 1hr 15 min); Shanghai (daily; 1hr 40min); Xiamen (4 weekly; 3hr 25min); Xi'an (4 weekly; 1hr 10min); Yinchuan (3 weekly; 1hr 20min).

Tianjin to: Changsha (4 weekly; 1hr 40min); Chengdu (daily; 2hr 20min); Dalian (daily; 50min); Fuzhou (3 weekly; 3hr 50min); Guangzhou (4 daily; 3hr); Guilin (2 weekly; 4hr 30min); Haikou (daily; 3hr 15min); Hangzhou (5 weekly; 1hr 30min); Harbin (daily; 3hr); Hong Kong (daily; 3hr 15min); Kunming (8 weekly; 3hr 20min); Nanjing (daily; 1hr 40min); Ningbo (daily; 3hr 10min); Qingdao (daily; 1hr); Shanghai (daily; 1hr 45min); Shenyang (8 weekly; 1hr 20min); Shenzhen (daily; 2hr 45min); Taiyuan (daily; 1hr); Wuhan (7 weekly; 2hr 30min); Xiamen (5 weekly; 2hr 30min); Xi'an (daily; 2hr); Zhengzhou (daily; 1hr 10min).

CHAPTER 3　　Highlights

✳ **The Imperial Palace, Shenyang** Pre-empting Beijing's Forbidden City, this was the historical seat of the Manchus before they seized the capital. See p.193

✳ **Binhai Lu, Dalian** Offering gorgeous views, this cliffside drive winds along the Yellow Sea, past excellent beaches and parks. See p.199

✳ **Old Yalu Bridge, Dandong** Walk halfway to North Korea on this structure, bombed by the US during the Korean War. See p.203

✳ **Puppet Emperor's Palace, Changchun** The second act of the "last emperor" Puyi's life was played out here, where he was installed by the Japanese as leader of Manchuria. See p.207

✳ **Changbai Shan** The north-east's loveliest nature preserve is also its least developed. Root around for wild ginseng, though beware of North Korean border guards. See p.210

✳ **Russian architecture in Harbin** Prettiest in winter, but enjoyable year-round. See p.218

✳ **Winter ice festivals** Most Manchurian metropolises have one, but Harbin's is the biggest and best, where millions pour in to admire carvings by international artists. See p.218

✳ **Zhalong Nature Reserve** Bird-watchers flock to the reedy lakes west of Harbin where the red-crowned crane and thousands of its cousins breed. See p.221

✳ **Yabuli** China's finest ski resort. See p.222

△ Skiing is increasingly popular in Dongbei

Dongbei

Dongbei – or more evocatively Manchuria – may well be the closest thing to the "real" China that visitors vainly seek in the well-travelled central and southern parts of the country. Not many foreign tourists get up to China's northernmost arm, however, due to its reputation as an inhospitable wasteland: "Although it is uncertain where God created paradise," wrote a French priest when he was here in 1846, "we can be sure he chose some other place than this." Yet, with its immense swaths of fertile fields and huge resources of **mineral wealth**, Dongbei is metaphorically a treasure house. Comprising **Liaoning**, **Jilin** and **Heilongjiang** provinces, it is economically and politically among the most important regions of China, and the area has been fiercely contested for much of its history by Manchus, Nationalists, Russians, Japanese and Communists.

With 4000km of sensitive border territory alongside North Korea and Russia, Dongbei is one of China's most vulnerable regions strategically, and also one of the country's most sensitive, with worker protests common and a widening gap between haves and have-nots which is threatening to become a chasm. In the heady days of a planned economy, Dongbei's state-owned enterprises produced more than a third of the country's heavy machinery, half its coal and oil and most of its autos and military equipment. Since market reforms, however, **layoffs** have been rampant, with unofficial statistics suggesting fifty percent unemployment in some areas.

Tourism has become Dongbei's leading growth industry. The region is cashing in on its colourful history, seen most vividly in the preservation of long-ignored Russian and Japanese colonial architecture, some of which you can actually stay in. In Liaoning, the thriving port of **Dalian** sports cleaned-up beaches, a cliffside drive, a restored Russian and Japanese neighbourhood and China's best football club. The country's window on North Korea is **Dandong**, featuring a promenade on the Yalu River and an incredible Korean War Museum. China's other Forbidden City – the restored Manchu Imperial Palace – and the tombs of the men who established the Qing dynasty draw tourists to Liaoning's otherwise bland capital, **Shenyang**. To the north in Jilin province, **Jilin** city's riverfront showcases ice-coated trees in winter, and there are ski resorts on the outskirts of town. In the provincial capital, **Changchun**, the Puppet Emperor's Palace memorializes Puyi's reign as "emperor" of the Japanese state Manchukuo. Evidence of Heilongjiang province's border with Russia can be seen throughout its capital, **Harbin**. A restored central shopping district preserves the city's old architecture, while a history museum set in an Orthodox cathedral ensures China's northernmost metropolis is known for reasons other than its world-famous **ice festival**.

Ferry to Yantai

Visitors to these parts tend to come for quite specific reasons. Dongbei's geography, a terrain of fertile plains, rugged mountains and forests, is itself an attraction, and keen **hunters**, **hikers** and **bird-watchers** will all find places to indulge their passions. Long derided by Han Chinese as "the land beyond the pale", the region "outside" the Great Wall is home to several protected reserves, most famously the mountainous **Changbai Shan Nature Reserve** in Jilin province near the Korean border, where a huge lake, Tian Chi, nestles in jaw-dropping scenery. **Zhalong Nature Reserve**, in Heilongjiang, is a summer breeding ground for thousands of species of birds, including the rare red-crowned crane. Foreign **students** find an environment free of thick accents and perfect for practising Chinese, and fans of recent Chinese **history** couldn't choose a better place to visit: Dongbei's past one hundred years of domestic and international conflicts heavily influenced the shape of the PRC today. Those interested in the **Russo–Japanese War** can follow the route of the Japanese advance; if you can find them, bring copies of Jack London's *Reports*, which contain the columns he wrote on assignment for the *San Francisco Examiner*; and *Thirty Years in Moukden* by Dugald Christie. **Puyi**'s autobiography, *From Emperor to Citizen*, lends insight to Manchukuo, and Ha Jin's *Ocean of Words* shows what life was like patrolling the Heilongjiang–Siberian border in the tense 1970s. CITS has special-interest **tours** to the region, though independent local firms provide better service and a wider selection of trips.

Dongbei's **climate** is one of extremes. In summer it is hot, and in winter it is very, very cold, with temperatures as low as -30°C and howling Siberian gales. But the whole of winter brings excellent, cheap **skiing**, **sledding** and **skating**, while a trip up here in January has the added attraction of **ice festivals** in Jilin and Harbin.

Thanks to Dongbei's export-based economy, there's an efficient **rail** system between the cities and an extensive **highway** network. Dongbei **food** is heavily influenced by neighbouring countries, and every town has a cluster of Korean, Japanese and, up north, Russian restaurants. The cuisine is also diverse, ranging from fresh crabs in Dalian and *luzi* river fish in Dandong, to mushroom dishes and fresh bread in Harbin, to silkworms in the countryside (a mushy, pasty-tasting local delicacy).

Some history

The history of Manchuria proper begins with **Nurhaci**, a tribal leader who in the sixteenth century united the warring tribes of the northeast against the corrupt central rule of Ming-dynasty Liaoning. He introduced an alphabet based on the Mongol script, administered Manchu law and, by 1625, had created a firm and relatively autonomous government that was in constant confrontation with the Chinese. Subsequently Dorgun was able to go a stage further, marching on Beijing with the help of the defeated Ming general, Wu Sangui. In 1644 the **Qing dynasty** was proclaimed and one of Nurhaci's grandsons, Shunzhi, became the first of a long line of Manchu emperors, with his uncle Dorgun as regent.

Keen to establish the Qing over the whole of China, the first **Manchu emperors** – Shunzhi, Kangxi and Qianlong – did their best to assimilate Chinese customs and ideas. They were, however, even more determined to protect their homeland, and so the whole of the northeast was closed to the rest of China. This way they could guard their monopoly on the valuable **ginseng trade**, and keep the Chinese from ploughing up their land and desecrating the graves of their ancestors. But it was a policy that could not last for ever, and the eighteenth century saw increasing migration into Manchuria. By 1878 these laws had been rescinded, and the Chinese were moving into the region by the million, escaping the flood-ravaged plains of the south for the fertile northeast.

All this time, Manchuria was much coveted by its neighbours. The **Sino–Japanese War** of 1894 left the Japanese occupying the Liaodong Peninsula in the south of Liaoning province, and the only way the Chinese could regain it was by turning to **Russia**, also hungry for influence in the area. The deal was that the Russians be allowed to build a rail line linking Vladivostok to the main body of Russia, an arrangement that in fact led to a gradual and, eventually, complete occupation of Manchuria by the imperial Russian armies. This was a bloody affair, marked by atrocities and brutal reprisals, and was followed in 1904 by a Japanese declaration of war in an attempt to usurp the Russians' privileges for themselves.

The Russo–Japanese War ended in 1905 with a convincing Japanese victory, though Japan's designs on Manchuria didn't end there. The Japanese population had almost doubled in the last sixty years, and this, coupled with a disastrous economic situation at home and an extreme militaristic regime, led to their invasion of the region in 1932, establishing the puppet state of **Manchukuo**. This regime was characterized by instances of horrific and violent oppression – not least the secret germ warfare research centre in Pingfang, where experiments were conducted on live human subjects. Rice was reserved for the Japanese, and it was a crime for the locals to eat it. It was only with the establishment of a united front between the **Communists** and the **Guomindang** that Manchuria was finally rid of the Japanese, in 1945, although it was some time (and in spite of a vicious campaign backed by both Russia and the USA against the Communists) before Mao finally took control of the region.

Recent history is dominated by relations with **Russia**. In the brief romance between the two countries in the 1950s, Soviet experts helped the Chinese build efficient, well-designed factories and workshops in exchange for the region's agricultural products. These factories, such as the plant that produces the Liberation Truck in Changchun, remain some of the best in the area today. In the 1960s relations worsened, the Soviets withdrew their technical support, and bitter **border disputes** began, notably around the Wusuli (Ussuri) River, where hundreds of Russian and Chinese troops died fighting over an insignificant island in the world's first military confrontation between communist states. An extensive network of nuclear shelters was constructed in northeastern cities. Following the collapse of the Soviet Union, military build-ups around the border areas and state paranoia have lessened, and the shelters have been turned into underground shopping centres. Russian faces can again be seen on the streets, often **traders**, legal and otherwise, buying up consumer goods to take over the border now that Russia's own manufacturing industry has almost collapsed.

Shenyang

SHENYANG, the capital of Liaoning province and unofficial capital of the northeast, is both a railway junction and banking centre that's served as host to the Manchus, the Russians, the Japanese, the Nationalists and then the Communists. An hour's flight from Beijing, the city likens itself to the capital; any cabby here will tell you, "We have the only other Imperial Palace in China". Shenyang does indeed resemble the capital, but only in its wide, characterless avenues walled by Soviet-style matchbox buildings and glassy bank towers.

In fact, the most remarkable thing about Shenyang is that it isn't remarkable at all. All the ingredients for an interesting visit are here: China's other Forbidden City, constructed by Manchus before their takeover of the Ming dynasty; a stunning monument to Chairman Mao built during the frenzied height of the Cultural Revolution; the tombs of two former emperors; architecture left over from Japan's occupation, including one of China's loveliest hotels. The list goes on and on. And a list is what Shenyang feels like, a collection of curios out of

Shenyang

Shenyang	沈阳	shěnyáng
East Tomb	东陵	dōng líng
Imperial Palace	沈阳故宫	shěnyáng gùgōng
Liaoning Provincial Museum	辽宁省博物馆	liáoníng shěng bówùguǎn
Long-distance bus station	快速客运站	kuàisù kèyùnzhàn
North Pagoda	北塔	běi tǎ
North Tomb	北陵	běi líng
September 18 History Museum	九一八历史博物馆	jiǔyībā lìshǐ bówùguǎn
Zhongshan Square	中山广场	zhōngshān guǎngchǎng
Accommodation and eating		
Courtyard New World Hotel	新世界宾馆	xīnshìjiè bīnguǎn
Dongbei Hotel	东北饭店	dōngběi fàndiàn
Holiday Inn	假日饭店	jiàrì fàndiàn
Laobian Eating House	老边饺子馆	lǎobiān jiǎoziguǎn
Liaoning Hotel	辽宁宾馆	liáoníng bīnguǎn
Meilin Jiudian	美林酒店	měilín jiǔdiàn
Peace Hotel	和平宾馆	hépíng bīnguǎn
Phoenix Hotel	凤凰饭店	fènghuáng fàndiàn
Railway Hotel	沈阳铁路大厦	shěnyáng tiělù dàshà
Traders Hotel	商贸饭店	shāngmào fàndiàn

context in their industrial surroundings, with little to detain you for more than a brief stop.

Though well known in China as an important power base for the more radical hardline factions in Chinese politics (Mao's nephew, Yuanxin, was deputy Party secretary here until he was thrown in jail in 1976), Shenyang had its real heyday in the early seventeenth century. The city (then known as Mukden) was declared first capital of the expanding **Manchu empire** by Nurhaci. He died in 1626, as work on his palace was just beginning, and was succeeded by his eighth son, **Abahai**, who consolidated and extended Manchu influence across northern China. When the Manchus, having defeated the resident Ming, moved to Beijing in 1644 and established the Qing dynasty, Shenyang declined steadily in importance. The city began to take on its modern, industrial role with the arrival of the Russians in the nineteenth century, who made it the centre of their rail-building programme. Years later, the puppets of the Japanese state also set up shop here, exploiting the resources of the surrounding region and building an industrial infrastructure whose profits and products were sent home to Japan.

Arrival and transport

Shenyang's international **airport**, the busiest in the northeast, lies 20km south of the city. It's linked to the CAAC office in the centre by an airport bus (¥15), while a taxi into town costs ¥80.

Five lines converge on Shenyang's two main **train stations**. You'll arrive first at the **South station**, the larger and more central one, if you've come from Beijing or farther south. The newer **North station**, serving destinations to the north of Shenyang (and the terminus for Beijing trains, which continue here from the South station), is out of the centre; take trolleybus #5 from here to Zhongshan Square and the South station (also served from here by bus bus #203). The North station has an upstairs ticket booth, while the booking office

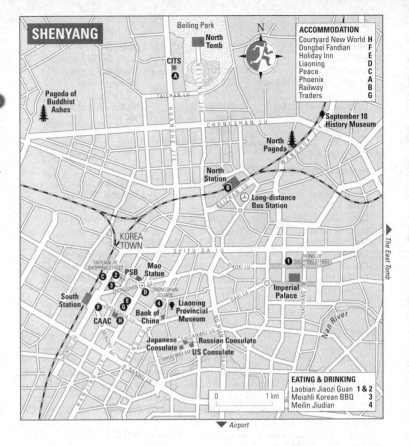

SHENYANG

Beiling Park

North
Tomb

N

ACCOMMODATION
Courtyard New World H
Dongbei Fandian F
Holiday Inn E
Liaoning D
Peace C
Phoenix A
Railway B
Traders G

CITS
A

Pagoda of
Buddhist
Ashes

TAISHAN LU

HUANGHE JIE

CHONGSHAN LU

WANGHUA JIE

September 18
History Museum

North
Pagoda

North
Station
B

BEIZHAN JIE

Long-distance
Bus Station

KOREA
TOWN

SHIFU DA LU

ZHONGJIE
SHOPPING STREET
1

The East Tomb

TAIYUAN JIE
SHOPPING STREET

Mao
Statue

MAOXI LU

DAXI LU

PSB
6 2
3
ZHONGHUA LU

ZHONGSHAN
SQUARE
ZHONGSHAN LU
D

South
Station

G E
F
CAAC H

4

Bank of
China

Liaoning
Provincial
Museum

Imperial
Palace

Nan River

CHAOYANG JIE

QING NAN DAJIE

SHENGLI JIE

MINZHU LU

NANJING JIE

ZHONGSHAN LU

Japanese
Consulate

SUISANWEI LU

Russian Consulate

SHISIWEI LU

US Consulate

NANXUN LU

0   1 km

EATING & DRINKING
Laobian Jiaozi Guan 1 & 2
Meiahli Korean BBQ 3
Meilin Jiudian 4

▼ Airport

for the South station is in a large hall to the left as you face the station. Tickets
for services leaving from the North station can be bought from the South
station, and vice versa; you may need to double-check which station the train
you want actually leaves from. The gleaming, futuristic **long-distance bus
station** (referred to locally as the express-bus station) is near the North
station. To get into the centre from here, catch one of the many minibuses plying the
route, or take a cab (¥10).

If you're entering the city by train and planning on **moving on** immediately
to a major city by bus, get off at the North station, where coaches wait on the
east side of the concourse to depart for Beijing (7–8hr) and Dalian (5hr). For
Jilin (4hr), Changchun (3hr) and Harbin (6hr) services, walk one block south
to the long-distance bus station.

Shenyang is very spread out and trying to walk anywhere is frustrating, especially as bikes have been directed to use the pavements to help alleviate traffic
congestion. **Taxis** are widely available, comprised of new VW Santanas. The
flagfall is ¥7 for 3km; a taxi to or between most of the sights is around ¥15,
though getting to the East Tomb from the South station costs about ¥45. Alternatively, the **local bus** and trolleybus system is extensive and not too crowded.
Bus maps can be bought outside the stations.

Accommodation

Shenyang's **hotels** cater mainly to business travellers, and most respectable establishments in the city centre don't look kindly on haggling over rates. Several no-frills travellers' hotels are gathered around Zhonghua Lu in front of the South station.

Courtyard New World 2 Nanjing Nanjie ☎024/23869888, ⓦwww.courtyard.com. Plush four-star hotel near Taiyuan Jie. **❼**

Dongbei Fandian 6 Zhonghua Lu ☎024/23838120. A somewhat tattered no-frills place in a good location near the South train station (look for the neighbouring *KFC*). If they won't take you, inquire at the facilities next door, which are comparable. **❷**

Holiday Inn 204 Nanjing Beilu ☎024/23341888, ⓕ23341188, ⓦwww.ichotelsgroup.com. New high-rise in the heart of town, and featuring Shenyang's best health club. Rates are slashed in half in the winter months. **❾**

Liaoning Hotel 97 Zhongshan Lu ☎024/23839104, ⓕ23839103. Shenyang's historic lodging, a hotel constructed by the Japanese in 1927, and now overlooking the Chairman Mao statue and Zhongshan Square. Rooms are spacious and light. Stop over if only for a look at the furnishings, wood accents and tiles in the lobby and dining room – this is the closest thing Shenyang has to

a museum. The staff are amenable to bargaining, which can halve the price of rooms. **❾**

Peace Hotel 104 Shengli Beijie ☎024/23833033, ⓕ23837389. The best backpacker place in town. Conveniently near the South train station; turn left as you exit the station's square, and the hotel is a 5min walk ahead on your left. Staff are very friendly, and you can buy train and plane tickets here. Breakfast is included in the rate. Dorm beds from ¥40, **❸**

Phoenix 109 Huanghe Nan Dajie ☎024/86805858, ⓕ86105340, ⓦwww.phoenixhotel.com.cn. Plush behemoth near Beiling Park, recently refurbished but retaining that old Communist group-tour vibe. **❼**

Railway Hotel Located inside the North train station ☎024/22522888. Nothing special, but an adequate place to crash out if arriving late or departing early. **❸**

Traders 68 Zhonghua Lu ☎024/23412288, ⓦwww.shangri-la.com. One of the nicest places to stay in Shenyang; rates include laundry, airport transport and breakfast. **❾**

The City

Shenyang has some great examples of uncompromising Soviet-style building, and you may well find yourself staying in one. The giant **Mao statue** in **Zhongshan Square** at the city's centre, erected in 1969, is by far the most distinctive landmark, its base lined with strident, blocky peasants, Daqing oilmen, PLA soldiers and students, though the Little Red Books they were waving have mostly been chipped off. Above them, the monolithic Mao stands wrapped in an overcoat, a bald superman whose raised hand makes him look as if he's directing the traffic which swarms around him. Head in the direction he's facing, and you'll hit the city's **shopping district**, centred around Zhongshan Lu, Zhonghua Lu and Taiyuan Jie, which abound with department stores.

The **Liaoning Provincial Museum** (Tues–Sun 9am–4pm; ¥8), in the heart of the downtown area, is one of the largest museums in the northeast, the exhibits including paintings, copperware, pottery and porcelain. Perhaps most interesting are the fragments of oracle bones, inscribed with characters and used for divination; these feature some of the earliest extant examples of written Chinese. South of here, the Nan River marks the southern boundary of the downtown area, with the larger Hun River just beyond.

The Imperial Palace

More rewarding than the city centre are the Manchu structures on the outskirts of Shenyang, starting with the **Imperial Palace** (daily: summer 9am–4.30pm; winter 8.30am–4pm; ¥40), begun in 1626, a miniature replica of Beijing's Forbidden City. It's located at the pleasant centre of the old city in the east of town, itself worth pacing around for a few hours (bus #237 comes here from the South station). The complex divides into three sections. The first, the Cong Zhen Dian, is a low, wooden-fronted hall where the Qing dynasty was proclaimed and which was used by ministers to discuss state affairs. Beyond here, in the second courtyard, stands the Phoenix Tower, most formal of the ceremonial halls, and the Qing Ning Lou, which housed bedrooms for the emperor and his concubines. In the eastern section of the complex, the Da Zheng Dian is a squat, octagonal, wooden structure in vivid red and lacquered gold, with two pillars cut with writhing golden dragons in high relief. Here the emperor Shunzhi was crowned before seizing Beijing – and the empire – in 1644. Just in front stand ten square pavilions, the Shi Wang, once used as offices by the chieftains of the Eight Banners (districts) of the Empire, and now housing a collection of bizarrely shaped swords and pikes. Take time to wander away from the groups amid the side palaces, most of which have been restored in the past few years. Note the Manchu dragons in bas-relief, unique to this palace.

Shenyang's other good shopping area, the pedestrianized **Zhong Jie**, can be found just east of here. Dating back to 1636, the street is now fronted by department stores selling Western clothing and also features a branch of a well-known *jiaozi* restaurant chain, *Laobian*.

The tombs

From the palace, bus #213 will get you to the **North Tomb** (daily 9am–4.30pm; ¥13) in **Beiling Park** (park entry ¥3), or you can take bus #220 direct from the South station. The tomb is where Abahai is buried, and though it was his father Nurcahi who was the real pioneering imperialist, Abahai certainly got the better tomb. The well-preserved complex, constructed in 1643, is entered through a gate to the south, either side of which are pavilions; the easternmost was for visiting emperors to wash and refresh themselves, the westernmost for sacrifices of pigs and sheep. A drive flanked with statues of camels, elephants, horses and lions leads to the Long En Hall, which contains an altar for offerings and the spirit tablets of the emperor and his wife. Their tree-covered burial mounds are at the rear, where you'll also see a fine dragon screen. Winter in Beiling Park sees snow sculptures and ice skates available for rent (¥10), as well as *pali* (¥30 for large ones), wooden sleds with blades on the bottom, which you move using two metal ski poles while seated.

The more restrained **East Tomb** (¥10), built in 1629 as the last resting place of Nurhaci, is set among conifers in **Dongling Park** (daily 9am–4.30pm; ¥2) in the east of the city. Bus #218 comes here from the stop one block north and one block east of the Imperial Palace. The tomb is less monumental in layout and shows more signs of age, but it's still an impressive structure, with fortified walls and a three-storey tower. One hundred and eight steps (the number of beads on a Buddhist rosary) lead into the main gate, while all around the tomb are walking trails into the woods covering Mount Tianzhu – a hill, really.

The rest of the city

Shenyang's other sights are hardly worth tracking down unless you have time to spare. Of the four pagodas and four temples which once stood at the limits of the city, one on each side, the only one in a reasonable state is the **North Pagoda** (daily 9am–4.30pm; ¥5), just to the south of the long-distance bus station. The pagoda contains a sky and earth Buddha (Tiandifu), a carnal image of twin Buddhas rarely found in Chinese temples; to see it, you'll have to trouble the lone attendant to unlock the gate. Not far away, the **September 18 History Museum** at 46 Wanghua Nanjie (daily 8.30am–4.30pm; ¥20) focuses on Japan's invasion of Shenyang in 1931, telling the story through a predictable array of black-and-white photos, maps and rusty weapons. It's a "patriotic education base", so the tone of the Chinese-only captions is easy to guess. Bus #213 from the North Tomb stops here, and also near the North Pagoda.

Eating

Eating in Shenyang is a bit of a letdown, though Korean food is a good bargain in the area around the Western Pagoda, on Shifu Da Lu. Another good Korean choice is the *Meiahli Korean BBQ*, 62 Kunming Beijie. Dinner here is good value at around ¥50 for two, and you can wash it down with *zaocha*, a sweet, fruity tea that goes well with platefuls of beef. It's easily spotted as it's next door to a *USA Beef Noodle King*, signed in English. Shenyang's most famous restaurant is *Laobian Jiaozi Guan* at 55 Shengli Beijie, whose excellent *jiaozi* cost ¥5 for a *liang*; try their speciality, and a Dongbei favourite, pork and chives. They have another branch at 6 Zhong Jie, but the service here is poor. Shanghai-style veggie fare is served at *Meilin Jiudian*, 109 Heping Beidajie.

Listings

Airlines CAAC is at 117 Zhonghua Lu (℡024/89392520; daily 8am–6pm). Plane tickets can also be bought from hotels or from CITS.
Banks and exchange Bank of China, 253 Shifu Dalu (Mon–Fri 8.30am–5.30pm, Sat & Sun 9am–3.30pm).
Consulates The Japanese, North Korean, Russian, and US consulates are all in the same road, Shisiwei Lu, in the south of the city. Reports on whether Russian visas can be obtained easily here aren't encouraging; it's better to apply in Beijing.
Internet access Walk from the South train station down Zhonghua Lu, and a block past *KFC*, at no. 25, is a 24hr Internet café – look for the orchid sign reading *wangba*, then head upstairs to the

second floor. Amid the shopping lanes just north of here, *Wanghe Internet Café*, 72 Beier Malu, also stays open around the clock.
Mail and telephones Shenyang's main post office is at 32 Zhongshan Lu (Mon–Fri 8am–6pm), and has a 24hr telephone/fax service.
PSB On Zhongshan Lu, by the Mao statue (Mon–Fri 8am–5pm).
Travel agents The CITS office at 113 Nan Huanghe Lu (℡024/86809383), in the same compound as the *Phoenix Hotel*, is the central branch for Liaoning province, though they offer speciality tours of the northeast only to large groups (twenty or more). The travel service in the *Peace Hotel* is friendlier and more accommodating.

Dalian and around

A modern, sprawling city on the Yellow Sea, **DALIAN** is one of China's most cosmopolitan cities, partly because it has changed hands so often. As the only **ice-free port** in the region it was eagerly sought by the foreign powers who held sway over China in the nineteenth century. The Japanese gained the city in 1895, only to lose it a few years later to the Russians, who saw it as an alternative to ice-bound Vladivostok. In 1905, after decisively defeating the Russian navy, the Japanese wrested it back and remained in control for long enough to complete the construction of the port facilities and city grid – still visible in the many traffic circles and axial roads. After World War II, the Soviet Union occupied the city for ten years, finally withdrawing when Sino–Soviet relations improved.

The "foreign devils" are still here, though they're now invited: Dalian has been designated a Special Economic Zone, one of China's "open-door" cities with regulations designed to attract overseas investment. Today Dalian is busier than ever, the funnel for Dongbei's enormous natural and mineral wealth and an industrial producer in its own right, specializing in petrochemicals and ship-building. Unlike most Chinese metropolises, the city boasts green spaces and an excellent traffic control system, both the handiwork of the high-flying former mayor, **Bo Xilai**, China's Commerce Minister at the time of writing. Locals seem to admire him as much as they do Dalian's football team, **Shide** (formerly Wanda), which has been the champion of the Chinese league more times than not in recent years, and contributed six players to the country's 2002 World Cup squad, facts which explain the large sculptures of footballs you'll see around, including a massive one crowning Laodong Park.

Still, Dalian manages to be a leisurely place, popular with tourists who come here for the scenic spots and **beaches** outside the city, to recover their health in sanatoriums and to stuff themselves on seafood. The city also boasts easy connections to the historical port of **Lüshun**. Tourists looking for relics from Dalian's colonial past will be disappointed, however: unlike other treaty ports such as Shanghai, Dalian is looking firmly forward to the future.

Arrival and transport

Dalian sits at the southern tip of the Liaodong peninsula, filling a piece of land that's shaped like a tiger's head – the result, local legend has it, of a mermaid flattening the animal into land as punishment for eating the fiancé of a beautiful girl. The city has four main sections: **Zhongshan Square**, at the tiger's eye, **Renmin Square**, at his ear, the **beaches**, at his mouth and throat, and **Heishijiao** (Black Coral Reef) across the Malan River to the west of town.

Dalian and around

Dalian	大连	dàlián
Black Coral Reef	黑石礁	hēishí jiāo
Old Russian Quarter	老俄罗斯风景区	lǎoéluósī fēngjǐngqū
People's Square	人民广场	rénmín guǎngchǎng
Sun Asia Ocean World Aquarium	圣亚海洋世界	shèngyà hǎiyáng shìjiè
Tiger Beach	老虎滩	lǎohǔ tān
Zhongshan Square	中山广场	zhōngshān guǎngchǎng

Accommodation and eating		
Dalian Binguan	大连宾馆	dàlián bīnguǎn
Friendship Hotel	友谊饭店	yǒuyí fàndiàn
Furama Hotel	富丽华大酒店	fùlìhuá dàjiǔdiàn
Golden Plaza	大连天富大酒店	dàlián tiānfù dàjiǔdiàn
Huanan Youth Hostel	华南国际青年旅舍	huánán guójìqīngnián lǚshè
Huaneng Hotel	华能饭店	huánéng fàndiàn
Mutual Bar	互情酒吧	hùqíng jiǔbā
Noah's Ark	诺亚方舟酒吧	nuòyà fāngzhōu jiǔbā
People's Culture Guesthouse	人民文化招待所	rénmín wénhuà zhāodàisuǒ
Ramada Hotel	九州华美达酒店	jiǔzhōu huáměidá jiǔdiàn
Tiantian Yugang Jiulou	天天渔港酒楼	tiāntiānyúgǎng jiǔlóu
Yadu Dafandian	亚都大饭店	yàdù dàfàndiàn

Lüshun	旅顺	lǚshùn
Japanese Russian Imperial Prison Site	日俄监狱旧址	rì é jiānyù jiùzhǐ

A taxi to or from the **airport**, 10km northeast of the city, should cost ¥25, or there's a regular airport bus (¥10) to and from the CAAC office. The main **train station** (there are three stations in total) and **ferry terminal** are within 1km of Zhongshan Square. The **long-distance bus station**, served by ancient provincial buses, is located at the terminus of bus #201 west from the train station; if you're on an express bus from Beijing, you'll probably be dropped at the train station. There's also a bus station on Zhongshan Lu near Xinghai Beach in Heishijiao, from where buses to Lüshun depart.

As the city centre is compact, the minimum ¥8 fare in a **taxi** will get you to most places. Alternatively, the tram line, #202 (¥2), runs north–southwest roughly along Zhongshan Lu, beginning in the shopping area around Xi'an Lu, passing Xinghai Square and terminating at Heishijiao.

Accommodation

Dalian is choked with five-star **hotels**, though there are some budget options around Shengli and Zhongshan squares in the heart of the city, and a Hostelling International establishment south of the centre. The good news accommodation-wise is that Dalian is a beach town, so rates out of season are usually half those in summer. Be sure to try bargaining wherever you go, as the city's supply of hotel rooms exceeds demand.

Dalian Binguan 4 Zhongshan Square ☏ 0411/2633111, ℱ 2634363. A stylish old place, built by the Japanese in 1927. Only the location and history make it worthy of consideration – service is indifferent at best, the wallpaper in the rooms is peeling, the furniture musty and the hot water intermittent. ❻

Friendship Third Floor, 91 Renmin Lu ☏ 0411/2634121. Above the Friendship Store. Nobody here speaks English and the place isn't very efficiently run, but the rooms are nice enough. The closest mid-range accommodation to the ferry terminal. Dorm beds ¥160, ❻

Furama 60 Renmin Lu ☏ 0411/2630888, ℱ 2804455. A very upscale Japanese hotel on

CENTRAL DALIAN

OLD RUSSIAN QUARTER

Passenger Ferry Terminal

MINZU SQUARE

International Seamen's Club

Friendship Store

RENMIN LU

Train Station

English Language Bookstore

Bank of China

PSB

Cinema

ZHONGSHAN SQUARE

LUXUN LU

SHENGLI SQUARE

Long-distance Bus Station

CAAC

ZHONGSHAN LU

Night Market

NANSHAN LU

CITS

UNIVERSITY OF FOREIGN LANGUAGES

ZHONGSHAN JIE

CITS

Laodong Park

0   1 km

EATING & DRINKING

Korean BBQs	3
Mutual Bar	1
Tiantan Yugang	2

ACCOMMODATION

Dalian Binguan	E
Friendship	B
Furama	A
People's Culture Guesthouse	C
Ramada	D
Yadu Dafandian	F

▼ *Fujiazhuang Beach*

Renmin Lu, this place has every imaginable facility, a lobby big enough for Shide to play in and palatial rooms. ⑧

Huanan Youth Hostel 1 Yingchun Lu ℡0411/2496830, ℻2496494, ⓦwww.yhachina.com. Dalian's HI representative is 4km from the centre, tucked away in a valley near the zoo and Fujiazhuang Beach. To get here, take bus #702 from the train station and get off at Nanshidao Jie stop; the hostel is on the south side of the road. A taxi costs ¥14 from the centre or ¥18 from the port. Rooms in the hostel range from singles to quads and feature carpeting, a/c, TV, hot water and bathroom. They also provide Internet access facilities, a laundry room and bike rental. Dorm beds from ¥40, ⑤

Huaneng 2 Binhai Lu ℡0411/2401939, ℻2400734. The location is the most noteworthy thing about this two-star affair, overlooking Fujiazhuang Beach. ⑥

People's Culture Guesthouse 8 Zhongshan Square. No-frills doubles, some with a private bathroom. ②

Ramada 18 Shengli Square ℡0411/2808888, ⓦwww.ramada-dalian.com. Four-star luxury in the heart of town next to the train station, overlooking Shengli Square. ⑨

Yadu DaFandian 126 Zhongshan Lu ℡0411/3633560. Conveniently located near Shengli Square and the train station, with half-price discounts in the winter. The doubles have clean bathrooms with reliable hot water. Dorm beds ¥50, ④

The City

The hub of Dalian is Zhongshan Square, really a circle, whose spokes are some of the most interesting streets in the city. Japanese and Russian buildings,

German cars, *KFC* and *McDonald's*, girls in miniskirts and Western dance music blaring from the shops give the area an international flavour. The main **shopping** streets are Shanghai Lu and Tianjin Jie, which at the time of writing were being converted from stalls into massive malls. Continue northwest on Shanghai Lu and cross the railroad tracks to reach the **old Russian quarter**. This neighbourhood used to house Russia's gentry, though today each peeling mansion is home to several families. The pedestrian street takes you past restored pistachio-coloured facades and street vendors selling Russian cigarettes, lighters, vodka and Soviet pins. It's hardly an authentic colonial avenue, but step west into one of the lanes, and you've gone back a century. Ask nicely and you may get to step inside the homes.

Follow Zhongshan Lu west past **Shengli Square**, the train station, and the meandering shopping lanes of Qing Er Jie to reach **Renmin Square**, large, grassy and lit with footlights at night. It's a long walk from the train station, but several buses ply the route, among them #15, #702 and #801. The neighbourhoods to the south of the square retain their Russian colonial architecture and narrow, tree-lined streets, making for excellent wandering.

South of the train station is the Japanese-designed **Laodong Park** (¥3), across from whose Jiefang Lu gate is a good **night market** (daily 5–9.30pm). The hilly neighbourhood across the street east of here, **Nanshan**, was once home to the Japanese community; now the cream-coloured, red-roofed villas are being renovated by nouveau riche Chinese.

The beaches

Dalian's main attraction, its **beaches**, are clean, sandy and packed in the summertime. All are free except for **Xinghai** and **Fujiazhuang** beaches, for which you buy an inexpensive ticket; near Xinghai Beach there's also an unusual attraction in the futuristic **Modern Museum**.

The beaches are hugged by Dalian's scenic drive, **Binhai Lu**, which winds past the villas of Party bigwigs as well as Shide stars. Bus #801 (spring and summer only; ¥20) from the train station circles the entire town and serves all the beaches, though some are reached more directly by trams or other buses from the centre, mentioned below. A taxi from the city centre will cost ¥20–30.

Bangchuidao and Tiger beaches

Bangchuidao beach, next to a golf course, was formerly reserved for cadres but is now open to the public. Highly developed **Tiger Beach**, next along the coast to the west, can be reached from town on buses #2, #4 or #402. The funfair here, which includes a waterborne dodgem ride, has a whopping ¥80 entrance charge, which doesn't cover rides but includes admission to the new **Arctic aquarium**, a navy ship you can board and, west on Binhai Lu, an **aviary** (daily 8am–5pm). Tandem and mountain bikes are available to rent along the waterfront for ¥20 an hour, and there are boat trips out to Bangchui Island and beyond (from ¥40); routes and prices are posted at ticket kiosks.

Yanwoling Park and Fujiazhuang Beach

From Tiger Beach, it's a beautiful, if strenuous, seven-kilometre hike along Binhai Lu to **Fujiazhuang Beach**. The turquoise sea stretches before you to the south, while the north side of the road is green year-round with trees and new grass. You cross Beida Bridge, a suspended beauty, before winding 3km up to **Yanwoling Park** (daily dawn–dusk; ¥5). Once you're past the statue made of shells of a little boy with seagulls, there's a profusion of maintained trails and stairs to take you down to the sea. One particularly nice hike, signed in English, ends up at Sunken Boat Rock, a cove where starfish cling to rocks and the only sounds are those of the waves. Don't attempt to swim here, however, as a strong current 50m out has claimed lives.

Continuing 4km west on Binhai Lu, you wind downhill to **Fujiazhuang Beach** (daily dawn–dusk; ¥5), sheltered from the wind in a rocky bay and less developed than Tiger Beach. You can charter speedboats from here to outlying islands, while a trip west to Xinghai Beach and back costs around ¥40 depending on your bargaining skills. At the back of the beach are plenty of good, open-air **seafood** restaurants; expect to pay around ¥80 for a meal for two.

The Modern Museum and Xinghai Beach

On the northwest shoulder of the massive **Xinghai Square** (tram #202 comes here from the centre), beside the Malan River, the **Modern Museum** (daily 9am–5pm; ¥30) showcases Dalian's idealized future. Visitors can drive unclogged mock streets, steer an oil tanker into the port on a simulator or ride a flying carpet through pollution-free skies. The museum (the brainchild of former mayor Bo Xilai, like so much in Dalian) isn't all pie in the sky – UN awards attest to the success of the city's ongoing urban revamp.

Xinghai Beach (daily 7am–9pm; ¥10) is a long walk or short tram ride (#202) southwest along Zhongshan Lu from the Modern Museum. Besides the usual fairground rides, souvenir stands and restaurants, the beach features the **Sun Asia Ocean World** (Mon–Fri 9am–4pm, Sat & Sun until 4.30pm; adults ¥80, children ¥40), boasting a moving observation platform within an 118-metre underwater tunnel in the main tank. West of the park is **Heishijiao**, the jumping-off point for Lüshun.

Eating, drinking and entertainment

Dalian is full of **restaurants**, especially around Shengli Square, and just south of here on the pedestrian streets bordered by Qing Er Jie and Jiefang Lu, leading south from the train station. The area around Youhao Jie features a pizza parlour and Japanese barbecue place, both brightly signed in English. For simple, affordable fare, head south from Zhongshan Square toward the University of Foreign Languages along Yan'an Lu, lined with restaurants. There's a stretch of **Korean BBQ joints** along Gao Er Ji Lu, a block south of Renmin Square. Simply follow the smoke and bustle, and the touts out front will wave you in.

For **seafood** away from the beaches, don't miss one of Dalian's many branches of *Tiantian Yugang Jiulou*. The one near the university, at 20 Jilin Jie (☏0411/2825198), is usually packed with people enjoying draught beer and fresh steamed crab; dinner for two with drinks comes to around ¥150. You'll have to shell and eat the thing with chopsticks, so wear clothes you don't mind getting splattered with crab.

Dalian has lots of **bars**; among the liveliest is the reliable *Mutual Bar*, 12 Renmin Lu. It has tattooed, English-speaking bartenders, live rock music, bottled beers from around the world and the requisite Russian prostitutes. *Noah's Ark*, 32 Wusi Lu, across the street from Renmin Square, is also a long-standing favourite for live music; look for the wooden wagon out front.

Listings

Airlines CAAC is at 143 Zhongshan Lu (daily 8am–6pm; ☏0411/2818858).
Banks and exchange The Bank of China is at 9 Zhongshan Square (Mon–Fri 8.30am–noon &

1–5pm). Outside office hours you can change money and traveller's cheques at the *Dalian Binguan* opposite.
Buses From the long-distance bus station there

are buses to Shenyang, Dandong and other provincial towns. Tickets can be bought the night before to avoid queues. More convenient are the luxury buses to Shenyang and Beijing, which depart throughout the day from the north and east sides of Shengli Square; tickets can be bought on the bus.

Ferries Services have been greatly reduced, with Yantai now the travel hub for the province. The ferry to Yantai is a full day faster than the train, and cheaper, with a daily express sailing (3hr; ¥190). From Yantai, there are frequent bus connections to Qingdao (4hr). Tickets can be bought in advance from the passenger-ferry terminal on Yimin Jie in the northeast of the city, or from one of the many windows both at and around the train station. A Korean-run ferry departs Wednesday and Saturday for Inchon, South Korea (17hr).

Internet access Many Internet cafés can be found in the area surrounding the University of Foreign Languages, south of Zhongshan Square.

Mail and telephones The post office (Mon–Sat 8am–6pm) is next to the main train station, and there's a 24hr telecoms office next door.

Soccer From late March until October the Physical Stadium, just southwest of Renmin Square on Wusi Lu, is the venue for Dalian Shide matches. Good seats go for ¥40 – buy tickets at the stadium itself.

PSB Centrally located on the northeast side of Zhongshan Square (daily 8am–4.30pm). If you're heading to Lüshun, check here if permits are required.

Trains Tickets are easy to buy at the main train station. The ticket windows are on the ground floor, outside and to the left of the station's main entrance.

Travel agents CITS, Fourth Floor, 1 Changtong Jie (☎0411/3687868; daily 8.30am–4.30pm).

Lüshun

The port city of **LÜSHUN**, a forty-kilometre bus ride south of Dalian, makes up for the latter's lack of attention to the past. It was near Lüshun that the Japanese shocked the world by defeating the Russians in a naval battle in 1904. This was the beginning of a bloody campaign that ended in Shenyang, where the tsar at last surrendered in 1905. Northeast China was subsequently in the hands of the Japanese, who ruled the region for the next forty years.

For tourists interested in the **Russo-Japanese War**, the chief attraction is the town's prison camp turned museum, commemorating those who were interned here. Note that as the authorities have sometimes been known to treat Lüshun as a closed military zone, detaining and heftily fining visiting foreigners, it's essential to ask the **PSB in Dalian** about the current situation if you're thinking of visiting Lüshun.

The Town

Lüshun today is a quiet place, largely unchanged from its colonial role as Port Arthur, with one main square fronted by Japanese-style buildings. The highlight is the **Japanese Russian Imperial Prison Site**, on a small hill in the north of town (daily 9am–5pm; ¥15), a five-minute taxi ride from the bus station. Half the camp was built by the Russians in 1902 as a prison for Chinese; from 1905 to 1945 it was enlarged by Japan, who used it to hold Chinese, Russians and Japanese dissidents opposed to the emperor. Finally, the Communists used the prison to hold Chinese – you can still read, under the neat squares of burgundy paint attempting to block it out, "Mao Ze Dong Live Forever!" The prison also has a torture room, a gallows with skeletons of victims on display, and a 1914 Model T Ford that belonged to the Japanese warden, in front of which you can have your picture taken for ¥15. A Chinese-language tour of the compound is available. Lüshun also has a **Tomb for Russian Martyrs**, in memory of the soldiers who died to liberate the city in 1945, located west of the prison.

Rows of cannon and other fortifications left by the Japanese sit atop **Baiyu Shan** (¥16), a hill overlooking the Yellow Sea near the centre of town. It's not a long walk from the bus station, but the uphill hike is considerable.

Buses from Dalian's Heishijiao bus station make the hour-long run to Lüshun (every 15min; ¥7). From Dalian's centre, take trolleybus #202 or buses #28 or #406, and get off at the *KFC* on the north side of Zhongshan Lu; the bus station is across the road, 50m ahead on your left. The road between Dalian and Lüshun is lined with old Japanese villas since turned into farmhouses or stables, and you can see the sea for some of the ride.

Taxis around Lüshun charge a minimum of ¥5, covering the trip from the bus station to the prison, for example, while a trip up to Baiyun Shan is ¥16. There are no **restaurants** near Lüshun's sights; however, fruit and noodles can be bought around the bus station and the area fronting the central square.

Dandong

Once an obscure port tucked away in the corner of Liaoning province at the confluence of the Yalu River and the Yellow Sea, pleasant **DANDONG** is now a popular weekend destination for Chinese, who come to gaze at the border and North Korea – the listless Korean city of **Sinuiju** (Xinyizhou in Chinese) lies on the other side of the Yalu River. South Koreans, too, come here to look across at their northern neighbour, while foreigners from further afield come also to see the massive memorials to the defence of China's communist neighbour against imperialists during the Korean War. All in all, Dandong makes a worthwhile weekend trip out of Beijing or a stopover while touring the sooty northeast, as well as a convenient departure point for the Changbai Shan Nature Reserve (see p.210).

It's intended that an ambitious highway and undersea tunnel network will pass through Dandong, allowing trains to travel from Beijing, through Korea, all the way to Tokyo. Any plans involving North Korea are, however, speculative at best. For years there has been talk of making Sinuiju a free-trade zone, but while Chinese entrepreneurs are setting up small-scale markets on the other side of the Yalu, the far shore's economy remains moribund.

Dandong

Dandong	丹东	dāndōng
Culture Square	文化广场	wénhuà guǎngchǎng
Museum to Commemorate Aiding Korea Against US Aggression	抗美援朝纪念馆	kàngměi yuáncháo jìniànguǎn
Old Yalu Bridge	鸭绿断桥	yālù duànqiáo
Yalu River Park	鸭绿江公园	yālùjiāng gōngyuán

Accommodation, eating and drinking

Dantiedasha Hotel	丹铁大厦	dāntiě dàshà
Donghai Yucun	东海渔村	dōnghǎi yúcūn
Guolü Hotel	国旅宾馆	guólǚ bīnguǎn
Hong Kong Coffee House	香港咖啡厅	xiānggǎng kāfēitīng
Jinfangzhou Hotel	金方舟酒店	jīnfāngzhōu jiǔdiàn
Taiba Shaokao Dian	太白烧烤店	tàibá shāokǎodiàn
Wooden Guitar Bar	木吉它酒吧	mùjíta jiǔbā
Yalu River Guesthouse	鸭绿江大厦	yālùjiāng dàshà
Zhonglian Hotel	中联大酒店	zhōnglián dàjiǔdiàn

The City

Dandong remains small enough to feel human in scale, and the tree-lined main streets are uncrowded, clean and prosperous. A strong **Korean influence** can be felt in the city: vendors along the riverfront promenade sell North Korean stamps, bearing slogans in Korean like "Become human gun bombs!", and North Korean TV is on view in Dandong hotels.

On foot, the nearest you can get to the North Korean soil without a visa is halfway across the river, on the **Old Yalu Bridge** (daily 8.30am–5pm; ¥15) in the south of town, next to the new bridge. The Koreans have dismantled their half but the Chinese have left theirs as a memorial, replete with thirty framed photos of its original construction by the Japanese in 1911, when the town was called Andong. The bridge ends at a tangled mass of metal resulting from the American bombing in 1950 in response to the Chinese entering the Korean War. Several viewing platforms, with picnic tables, are on site, along with Chinese entrepreneurs who charge ¥1 for a few minutes' staring at Sinuiju through a telescope.

From 8am **boats** set out from all along Dandong's promenade, by the bridge, on 30-minute trips across the river (costing ¥8 in a large boat that leaves when full, or ¥18 per person for a zippy two-seater). The boats take you into North Korean waters to within a metre of shore, where you can do your part for international relations by waving at the teenage soldiers shouldering automatic rifles. Photography is allowed, but most foreign tourists keep their cameras packed away: there isn't much to see on Sinuiju's desultory shore, save for some rusting ships and languid civilians. If you've an interest in visiting

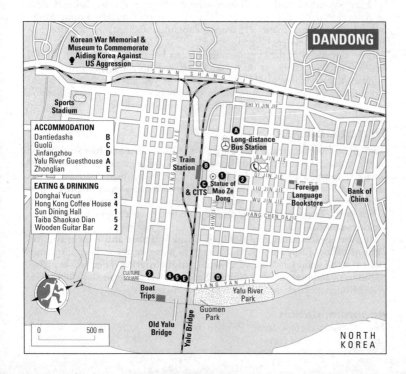

Sinuiju, it's best to check the current situation with Dandong's CITS (see box opposite), who will most likely say all foreigners are forbidden from joining their North Korean tour.

The Dandong side of the river is a boom town in comparison. The riverside by the bridges is the most scenic area, full of strolling tourists, particularly in the early evening. Nearby is **Yalu River Park**, where you can drive bumper cars and pay ¥1 to sit on a patch of downy green grass. At the western end of the riverside promenade, **Culture Square** is a well-lit local evening hangout.

The Museum to Commemorate Aiding North Korea

Built in 1993, the huge, macabre **Museum to Commemorate Aiding Korea Against US Aggression** (daily: summer 8am–4pm; winter 8.30am–3.30pm; ¥20) feels like a relic of the Cold War. It has nine exhibition halls on the Korean War, full of maps, plans, dioramas, machine guns, hand grenades, gory photographs and sculptures of lantern-jawed Chinese and Korean soldiers. Everything is labelled in Chinese; the only English in evidence is on Chinese propaganda which was dropped behind the American lines, in which worried wives wonder what their husbands are fighting for, and on the UN official declaration of war, in the first hall, which is the only written record in the entire museum of the trifling detail that the North Koreans kicked off the war by invading the South.

The opening hall has the catchy ditty "Defeat Wolf-Hearted America" spelled out on marble. Hall five is a trench simulation, while in hall eight, an impressive revolving panorama shows Korean and Chinese soldiers hammering American aggressors. The final hall is a memorial to individual Chinese soldiers, sanctified national heroes whose photographs are printed next to descriptions of their deeds. A gleaming structure on **Huaiyuan Shan**, behind the museum, marks a graveyard containing the remains of more than 10,000 Chinese soldiers.

In the northwest of the city, the museum can be reached on bus #1, #3, #4 or #5 from the station; get off by the sports stadium and walk north for five minutes. If you've developed a thirst by the time you arrive, note the ice-cold Coca-Colas for sale at the entrance to the compound, next to Jiang Zemin's large plaque swearing eternal North Korean–Sino friendship.

Practicalities

Arriving at Dandong **train station**, or at the **long-distance bus station** just to the north, puts you right in the centre of town, a gleaming marble-paved square featuring a statue of Mao Zedong, close to the least expensive hotels and about 1km north of the Yalu River. Dandong has a small **airport** 14km from town, and there's a **ferry terminal** 38km away, where vessels from South Korea dock. **Taxis** in Dandong charge a minimum of ¥5, which is sufficient for rides in town.

Most facilities, including the **Bank of China** and **post and telecommunications offices** (daily 8am–5.30pm), are on Qi Jing Jie, the main road running east from the station and site of a bustling **night market**. There are branches of the bank and post office at Culture Square as well. You can also change US, Hong Kong and Japanese money at the *Yalu River Hotel*.

Accommodation

The poshest accommodation in town faces North Korea and the bombed bridge: the *Zhonglian Hotel* (☎0415/3170666; ℻3170888; ●) on the riverfront

Dandong is well connected to northeast China, with **trains** arriving and departing daily. Tickets are easy enough to get from the train station, and can also be booked through CITS (℡0415/2135854), in front of the *Guolü Hotel*. There are also **flights** to Sanya, Shanghai and Shenzhen; book tickets via CITS or call the airport ticket counter (℡0415/2123427). If you're planning to head off to the **Changbai Shan Nature Reserve**, you'll need to get the 6.30am or 8.45am bus to **Tonghua** (8–10hr; ¥50); buy a ticket the night before from the efficient booking office at the bus station. VW Santanas heading to **Shenyang** ply for passengers on the west side of the station concourse (¥50), which works out faster than taking the train.

CITS run a ten-day **tour** which takes in Sinuiju, Pyongyang and Mount Kumgang in **North Korea**, but note that these tours aren't cheap, and that Westerners are unlikely to be accepted. If you're desperate to visit North Korea, it's better to arrange a tour with the Beijing-based with Koryo Tours (@www.koryogroup.com), run by Englishman Nick Bonner. Note that at the time of writing, US citizens aren't being given visas for North Korea.

By ferry

A Korean company runs the *Oriental Pearl* ferry between Dandong and Seoul; **tickets** for the two-day voyage can be booked via Dandong Ferry Company (℡0415/2100228). Boats leave on Thursday and Sunday at 3pm. A taxi to the ferry terminal takes half an hour (¥40).

promenade. Their lobby travel service is exceedingly helpful in booking tickets. The friendly *Jinfangzhou* at 2 Shi Wei Lu (℡0415/2162009; ❹, dorm beds ¥30) is well located next to the Yalu Bridge, with a view of the river and North Korea (ask for an odd-numbered room on the fourth floor or above, as these look out over the river and North Korea). At 87 Jiu Wei Lu, northeast of the train station, the *Yalu River Guesthouse* (℡0415/2125901; ❻) is a Sino–Japanese hotel that's seen better days; rooms are quite adequate though, with satellite TV, and staff can help with train tickets.

Among the most convenient budget places to stay in Dandong is the CITS-run *Guolü* (℡0415/2122166; ❸, dorm beds ¥50), right next to the train station. It's old but orderly, though skip the downstairs restaurant, and lock your window at night, as thefts have been reported. Another inexpensive option is the *Dantiedasha* (℡0415/2131031; ❷, dorm beds ¥25) in the train station itself.

Eating

Restaurants in Dandong cater to masses of weekenders craving freshwater fish and Korean dishes. Try the local *lu zi yu*, a river fish, at *Donghai Yucun* west of the Yalu Bridge, no. 42, Block E (promenade buildings are labelled with letters). All dishes here are served with glutinous rice, soup, bread and dumplings, and a feast for two is a bargain at ¥70. Also along the promenade, Korean barbecue is plentiful and cheap (¥10) at *Taiba Shaokao Dian*, no. 15, Block B. Opposite the train station, the *Sun Dining Hall #2* is a great experience, hot and boisterous, with excellent, inexpensive noodles and other dishes.

Start your mornings with the latest North Korean TV news at *Hong Kong Coffee House*, no. 32, Block D, where strong Korean coffee is ¥20. For a **beer**, the old standby is the *Wooden Guitar Bar*, around the corner on Qi Jing Jie across from the post office, featuring draught beer (¥15) and frequent live performances.

Changchun and Jilin

The cities of **Jilin province** took the brunt of Japanese, Russian and Chinese communist planning more than anywhere in China. This was a result of Jilin's vast mineral reserves, deposits of coal and iron ore that transformed the area into a network of sprawling industrial hubs, and, for thirteen years, the seat of the Manchukuo government. The closing of state-owned factories has resulted in massive lay-offs, but not all is glum, as tourism has crept in as one of the few growth industries in Jilin. Roads have been improved, the rail network is thorough and easy to use, most hotels are delighted to see foreigners, and winter brings low-cost **skiing and sledding**. Popular with both domestic and South Korean tourists is the **Changbai Shan Nature Reserve** (see p.210), a swath of mountain and forest boasting breathtaking scenery in the far eastern section of the province along the North Korean border. The most convenient jumping-off point for Changbai Shan is **Jilin**, a pleasant little city with little by way of sights, but great winter sports. Some 90km to the west, **Changchun** is the provincial capital and former capital of Manchukuo. The city retains much imperial architecture and design, with straight boulevards and squares throughout.

Jilin Province is famous in its own country for **er ren zhuan**, a form of theatre closer to vaudeville than Beijing opera, incorporating dancing, singing, baton-twirling, costume changes and soliloquies. A typical performance sees a man and woman regaling the audience with a humorous tale of their courtship and love. Tape recordings of the genre are available at stores, and you may be

---

Changchun and Jilin

Changchun	长春	*chángchūn*
Changchun Hotel	长春宾馆	*chángchūn bīnguǎn*
Chunyi Hotel	春谊宾馆	*chūnyí bīnguǎn*
Culture Square	文化广场	*wénhuà guǎngchǎng*
Geological Palace	地质宫博物馆	*dìzhìgōng bówùguǎn*
Maxcourt Hotel	吉隆坡大酒店	*jílóngpō dàjiǔdiàn*
Puppet Emperor's Palace	伪皇宫	*wěihuáng gōng*
Rail Station Hotel	铁路宾馆	*tiělù bīnguǎn*
Shangri-La Hotel	香格里拉饭店	*xiānggélǐlā fàndiàn*
Xiangyangtun Restaurant	向阳屯饭店	*xiàngyángtún fàndiàn*
Jilin	吉林	*jílín*
Angel Hotel	天使宾馆	*tiānshǐ bīnguǎn*
Beidahu Ski Park	北大湖滑雪场	*běidàhú huáxuěchǎng*
Beishan Park	北山公园	*běishān gōngyuán*
Catholic Church	天主堂	*tiānzhǔ táng*
Dongfang Jiaozi Wang	东方饺子王	*dōngfāng jiǎoziwáng*
Dongguan Hotel	东关宾馆	*dōngguān bīnguǎn*
Jiangbei Park	江北公园	*jiāngběi gōngyuán*
Jiangnan Park	江南公园	*jiāngnán gōngyuán*
Jilin Fandian	吉林饭店	*jílín fàndiàn*
Jilin International Hotel	吉林国际大酒店	*jílín guójì dàjiǔdiàn*
Songhua Lake	松花湖	*sōnghuā hú*
Songhuahu Ski Park	松花湖滑雪场	*sōnghuā hú huáxuěchǎng*
Traffic Hotel	交通宾馆	*jiāotōng bīnguǎn*
Zhuque Shan	朱雀山	*zhūquè shān*

able to get into a performance with translation via CITS, or you could just ask a cabby or local to point you to a theatre.

Changchun

CHANGCHUN has a historical notoriety deriving from its role as Hsinking, capital of Manchukuo, the Japanese-controlled state from 1932 to 1945 that had Xuantong (better known as Puyi) as its emperor. Now a huge, sprawling industrial city, it's also renowned for its many colleges, its movie studio and the **Number One Automobile Factory**, producer of the ubiquitous Liberation Truck and Red Flag sedans, though in these joint-venture days the majority of the city's auto production focuses on Volkswagen Santanas.

A good, but long, introduction to the city is to stroll south from the train station down the main artery, Renmin Dajie, past Japan's former Kwangtung Army Headquarters (identifiable by its spiky eaves) to Renmin Square and then west to Wenhua Square. The latter is the second-largest square in the world (after Tian'anmen), and was to be the site of Puyi's palace. Today it's a large paved expanse with statues of a muscular naked man, standing with his arms raised in liberation, and a reclining naked woman marking its centre. All that remains of the planned palace is its foundation, topped today by the so-called **Geological Palace** (daily 8.30am–4.30pm; ¥10). Inside, rows upon rows of minerals attest to Jilin's abundant resources. Bored school groups come to life when they see the pair of dinosaur skeletons, including a "Manchusaurus".

The Puppet Emperor's Palace

Changchun's only notable attraction is the **Puppet Emperor's Palace** (daily 9am–5pm; ¥40), in the east of the city on the route of buses #10, #125, #264 and #268 from the train station. In 1912, at the age of 8, Puyi ascended to the imperial throne in Beijing, at the behest of the dying Dowager Cixi. Although forced to abdicate that same year by the Republican government, he retained his royal privileges, continuing to reside as a living anachronism in the Forbidden City. Outside, the new republic was coming to terms with democracy and the twentieth century, and Puyi's life, circumscribed by court ritual, seems a fantasy in comparison. In 1924, he was expelled by Nationalists uneasy at what he represented, but the Japanese protected him and eventually found a use for him here in Changchun as a figure who lent a symbolic legitimacy to their rule. After the war he was re-educated by the Communists and lived the last years of his life as a gardener. His story was the subject of Bernardo Bertolucci's lavish film, *The Last Emperor*.

Like its former occupant, the palace is really just a shadow of Chinese imperial splendour, a poor miniature of Beijing's Forbidden City. It was meant to be temporary, until his grand abode was completed at Culture Square. Photos of Puyi line the walls, captioned in Chinese only, but you can surmise the tone of the presentation by looking at the mannequins of Puyi and his wife: she reclines on a sofa smoking opium, while her husband gleefully confers with a Japanese general down the hall. Additional photo exhibits in the rear building document Japan's brutal invasion and rule. Be sure to see the restored **Japanese garden**, one of Changchun's most tranquil spots.

Practicalities

Numerous flights connect Changchun with every major city in China. A bus (¥5) from the **airport**, 10km northwest of town, drops you outside the **CAAC** office (☎0431/2988888), next to the train station. Both the **train** and the **bus**

stations are in the north of town, with frequent connections to the rest of the northeast. At the bus station there are also VWs for intercity journeys – negotiate a price and wait for the car to fill with passengers, and you're off. Fares aren't that much higher than taking the bus, and you'll arrive at least an hour earlier. Do expect, however, to be have to change vehicles at some point on the journey. Taxis within the city have a ¥5 flagfall.

The **Bank of China** (Mon–Fri 8.30am–4.30pm) is not far from the *Changchun* and *Shangri-La* hotels, at 1 Tongzhi Lu. **CITS** (☎0431/5388784) is nearby, at 31 Dong Chaoyang Lu. The **PSB** is at 99 Renmin Dajie. The **post office** (daily 8.30am–4.30pm) is next to CAAC, just to the left as you exit the train station. A good **Internet café** can be found on the fifth floor of the building opposite the *Shangri-La* hotel on Xi'an Dalu, while there's a 24-hour one at 47 Tongzhi Jie, across from the Foreign Language Bookstore.

Accommodation, eating and drinking

The most convenient **place to stay** is the *Rail Station Hotel*, right at the train station (☎0431/2703630; ❸, dorm beds ¥30). Across the concourse, to the left as you exit the station, the *Chunyi Hotel* (☎0431/2096888, ☎8960171; ❹) is the province's oldest inn. Built in 1909 by the Japanese, it lacks the charm of similar properties in Shenyang and Dalian, but is good value for cleanliness, location and price. Rooms have cable TV and hot water, and rates include breakfast. Southeast of here and best reached by taxi, the *Changchun Hotel*, 18 Xinghua Lu (☎0431/8929920; ❹), is a large compound with a good travel service and different rates for the rooms in its two blocks. The *Shangri-La* at 9 Xi'an Da Lu (☎0431/8981818, ☎8981919, ☎www.shangri-la.com; ❾) serves as the town's five-star option. They take credit cards and keep free maps of Changchun's sights in the lobby.

The city's main **bar** and **restaurant** area lies between Tongzhi Jie and Renmin Dajie, sandwiched between the zoo and art institute. Here, noodle shops, cafés and pubs pack the three east–west roads – Longli, Guilin and Xikang Lu. Directly across from the *Shangri-La*, *Weiduoqian Lamian* does excellent Xinjiang-style hand-pulled noodles. Consider, too, *Xiangyangtun*, a branch of the Beijing restaurant recalling the privations of the Great Leap Forward. The menu includes griddle cakes, greens fried in batter, even fried scorpions, all of which represent the depths Chinese cooking sank to during lean years. These dishes are merely foils, however, to hearty and well-prepared Dongbei meat and vegetable dishes: here you can sample the region's beloved stewed cabbage (*suan baicai*), which is to Dongbei what duck is to Beijing. To reach *Xiangyangtun*, walk south on Tongzhi Jie from the *Shangri-La* and turn left at Dong Chaoyang Lu; the restaurant is on the left-hand side, at no. 3.

Jilin and around

Known as Kirin during the Manchukuo time, **JILIN** is split in two by the **Songhua River**, with the downtown area spread along its northern shore. The **promenade** along the river was finished in 1998, making for a pretty walk, especially in winter, when the trees are coated in frost – a phenomenon, known as *shugua* in Chinese, that results from condensation from the city's hydroelectric dam at **Songhua Hu**. It's Jilin's claim to fame, along with an **ice festival** in January and three neighbouring **parks** for **skiing and sledding**. This makes winter the ideal time to visit Jilin, though the parks – Beishan, Jiangnan and Jiangbei – are nice enough in summer. Beishan, in the west of town at the terminus of bus route #7 and #107, is the best known of the three (¥5). It's filled with pathways and temples, the most interesting of which is **Yuhuangge** (Jade Emperor's Temple), where rows of fortune tellers gather out front.

A reminder of the past, Jilin's **Catholic church** is the town's prettiest building, built in 1917 at 3 Songjiang Lu, the road bordering the river promenade. Next door is a hospice for the elderly, which explains why the median age of a Jilin Catholic appears to be 80.

Practicalities

Jilin's small **airport** is located 33km northwest of town. A **taxi** into the centre will cost ¥50. Taxi fares begin at ¥5, which covers most rides within town. The central **train and bus station** is near the northern bank of the river; note that departing from Changchun offers many more options. If you're going to Changbai Shan, it's worthwhile talking to the **CITS** office (☏0432/2492978, ⓕ2430690) in front of the *Dongguan Hotel*. The Yintong Tourist Company (☏0432/4842256, ⓕ4842296), on the fifth floor of the *Milky Way* hotel, is even more helpful, with train and airline schedules posted. They also organize tours and skiing packages to the area around town. The main **Bank of China** (daily 8am–5pm) and **post office** are across from each other on opposite sides of Jilin Dajie, just north of the bridge, church and *Dongguan Hotel*. For **Internet access**, Chongqing Jie, a road that runs diagonally northeast from the post office to the train station, has several places to choose from near the intersection with Shanghai Lu.

The *Dongguan* **hotel**, at 2 Jiang Wan Lu (☏0432/2454272; ❹), along the river, is cavernous and frayed but puts you smack in the city centre. More comfortable is the *Jilin International* at 20 Zhongxing Jie (☏0432/2929818, ⓕ2556161; ❻), right in front of the train station. The most luxurious place in town, with its own dance hall, is the *Milky Way*, to the west at 97 Songjiang Lu (☏0432/4841780, ⓕ4841621; ❻). It's also convenient, with a Bank of China branch just next door. Be warned, however, that this establishment fills up with raucous tour groups. Budget accommodation is available at the *Traffic Hotel*, 6 Zhongkang Lu (☏0432/2556859; ❸), located beside the *International*. Better value is the *Angel Hotel*, 2 Nanjing Jie (☏0432/2481848; ❹), located near the Catholic Church, off the main north–south road, Jilin Dajie.

Chongqing Jie is lined with good **restaurants**, including a dumpling place, *Dongfang Jiaozi Wang*, south of the *International Hotel*.

Around Jilin

Twenty kilometres east of Jilin is **Songhua Hu**, a deep, very attractive lake, set in a large forested park and surrounded by hills. A taxi to this popular local beauty spot should cost about ¥40, and there are rowing boats for rent. In 1992 an off-duty soldier reported being attacked by a dragon while boating here – it's a risk you'll just have to take. Unlike most Chinese scenic attractions, Songhua Hu seems big enough to absorb the impact of all its visitors, and even on weekends it's possible to escape to some quiet, peaceful spot.

At the lake's southern end is the huge **Fengman Dam**, a source of great local pride. Although in recent years the Songhua River's level has dropped by half (a result of extensive tree felling in its catchment area), the river floods every year, and at least a couple of the dam's four sluice gates have to be opened. With ruthless Chinese pragmatism, cities in Dongbei have been graded in order of importance in the event that the annual floods ever become uncontrollable. Jilin is judged more important than Harbin, so if the river does ever flood disastrously, Jilin will be spared and Harbin submerged.

In winter, the area around the lake is great for skiing and sledding, and ski packages are available through Jilin's tourist agencies. Closest to Jilin city, on bus routes #9 and #33, is **Zhuque Shan**, a park long known for its hiking and temples but now also for its skiing. It's 14km outside Jilin; a metered taxi costs ¥35 from the train station. After you're dropped off, you have to walk 1km to the park, though entrepreneurs on horseback or dogsled will take you in for ¥10. You then buy an entrance ticket (daily dawn–dusk; ¥5). There are two small slopes here, one for sledding and one for skiing. The sleds are two downhill skis nailed together with a piece of raised plywood, and really fly if you get a running start and bellyflop. It's ¥20 for a day of sledding, or ¥40 for skiing, equipment included (¥100 deposit required). There's a good **restaurant** that seats guests on a *kang*, a heated raised platform which provides a nice vantage point over the hill. Foreigners are a rarity here, and the staff and patrons a lot of fun. Skiing lessons are free; just look helpless and a staffer will come to the rescue.

Jilin also has two first-class ski areas, replete with chairlifts – though transport and lift tickets plus equipment rental at **Songhua Hu Huaxue Chang** (☏0432/4690282) and **Beida Hu Huaxue Chang** (☏0432/42002168) are respectively double and triple the cost at Zhuque Shan. To get to the Songhua Hu resort, take bus #9 or #33 to the small district of **Fengman** (30min) and continue by taxi, or get a taxi all the way from Jilin city (26km) for about ¥50. Transport to the bigger Beida Hu ski area, 56km southeast of Jilin, is easiest by taxi (¥100), though in winter months hourly buses make the trip (1hr 30min; ¥14).

Changbai Shan Nature Reserve

The Changbai mountains run northeast to southwest along the Chinese–Korean border for about a thousand kilometres. With long, harsh winters and humid summers, this is the only mountain range in east Asia to possess alpine tundra, and its highest peak, Baitou Shan (2744m), is the tallest mountain on the eastern side of the continent. The huge lake, **Tian Chi**, high in the Changbai mountains, is one of the highlights of Dongbei, as is the area around, the beautiful **Changbai Shan Nature Reserve**. With jagged peaks emerging from swaths of lush pine forest, this is remote, backwater China, difficult to get to even after recent improvements in tourist infrastructure. Heading a little off

---

Changbai Shan Nature Reserve

Changbai Shan	长白山	*chángbái shān*
Athlete's Village	运动员村宾馆	*yùndòngyuáncūn bīnguǎn*
Baihe	白河	*báihé*
Baiyun Hotel	白云宾馆	*báiyún bīnguǎn*
Changbaishan Hotel	长白山大酒店	*chángbáishān dàjiǔdiàn*
Cuckoo Villas	杜鹃山庄	*dùjuān shānzhuāng*
International Tourist Hotel	长白山国际旅游宾馆	*chángbáishān guójìlǚyóu bīnguǎn*
Tian Chi	天池	*tiānchí*
Tonghua	通化	*tōnghuà*
Yalin Hotel	雅林宾馆	*yǎlín bīnguǎn*
Yanji	延吉	*yánjí*

Ginseng has been collected as a medicinal plant for millennia, and the first Chinese pharmacopoeia, written in the first century, records its ability to nourish the five internal organs, sharpen intelligence, strengthen *yin* (female energy) and invigorate *yang* (male energy).

It is the ginseng **root** that is prized. It's quite conceivable to search for weeks and not find a single specimen, and ginseng hunters have even disappeared, the combination of which has given rise to a host of **superstitions**. The roots are said to be guarded by snakes and tigers, and legend has it that if a hunter should dream of a laughing, white-bearded man or a group of dancing fairies, he must get up, remain silent, and walk off into the forest. His colleagues must follow without speaking to him, and he will lead them to a root.

Changbai **ginseng** is regarded as the finest in China. Ginseng hunters in Changbai work in summer, when the plant can be spotted by its red berries. One way to find it is to listen for the call of the Bangchui sparrow, which becomes hoarse after eating ginseng seeds. When a ginseng is found, a stick is planted in the ground and a red cloth tied to it: according to tradition, the cloth stops the ginseng child – the spirit of the root – from escaping.

Ginseng generally grows in the shade of the Korean pine, and it is said that a plant of real medicinal value takes fifty years to mature. The plants are low-growing, with their roots pointing upwards in the topsoil. Digging one out is a complex, nail-biting operation, because if any of the delicate roots are damaged, the value of the whole is severely diminished. Roots are valued not just by weight, but by how closely the root system resembles a human body, with a head and four limbs. If you find a wild root, you're rich, as Changbai ginseng sells for ¥1000 a gram. Artificially reared ginseng is worth a fraction of this.

DONGBEI | Changbai Shan Nature Reserve

the tourist track into the wilderness is the way to get the most out of the area, though you'll need to come well prepared and patient.

Established in 1961, the nature reserve covers more than 800 square kilometres of luxuriant forest, most of which lies 500–1100m above sea level. At the base of the range, the land is dense with huge Korean pines which can grow up to 50m tall, and mixed broadleaf forest. The rare Manchurian fir is also found here. Higher altitudes are home to the Changbai Scotch pine, recognizable by its yellow bark, and the Japanese yew. As the climate becomes colder and damper higher up, the spruces and firs get hardier before giving way to a layer of sub-alpine grassland with colourful alpine plants and tundra. Animal species on the reserve include the leopard, lynx, black bear and **Siberian tiger**, all now protected, though decades of trapping have made them a rarity. Notable bird species include the golden-rumped swallow, orioles and the ornamental red crossbill. The area is rich in medicinal plants, too, and has been a focus of research since the eleventh century. The Chinese regard the region as the best place in the country for **ginseng** and deer antlers, both prized in traditional remedies, and the reserve's rare lichens have recently been investigated as a treatment for cancer.

Visitors, mostly domestic tourists, South Koreans and Japanese, come here in great numbers, and a tourist village has grown up on the mountain, with the result that the scenery and atmosphere are somewhat marred by litter, souvenir stalls and hawkers. Not all visitors are here for the scenery – plenty come to search for herbs, and many of the Japanese are here to catch butterflies (to keep) and ants (to eat). When the day-trippers have left, though, the reserve is peaceful, and there are ample opportunities to hike far from the crowds.

The **weather** in the region is not kind and can change very suddenly. In summer, torrential rain is common, mist makes it impossible to see far and the buildings at the summit often lose their electricity supply. Chinese-speakers can call the park's tourist office (℡0433/5742016) to check on conditions. Given the climate, the best time to visit is **between June and September**; at other times, heavy snows can close roads and road transport can be limited.

Reaching the reserve

Changbai Shan is a long way from anywhere, and the easiest way to get there is probably by booking one of the three-day, two-night **tours** arranged through CITS or the Yintong agency in Jilin (see p.209). These cost ¥450–600, including park entrance fees and accommodation, and stop at all the major must-sees, including Tian Chi.

At the base of the mountain, **Baihe** village is the rail terminus for Changbai Shan. The most convenient approach is from the north via bus **from Jilin** to Baihe (4hr; ¥50). **From Changchun**, train #N188/189 departs daily at 2.46pm, arriving in Baihe at 5.40am the next day. You can also approach **from Dandong** to the south: two daily buses depart in the early morning for **Tonghua** (¥50), from where you can buy a ticket for the Baihe train. The bus zigzags through rural China along roads that are little better than dirt tracks, a rough but engrossing ride. Service #N188/189 leaves Tonghua at 10.35pm and gets to Baihe at 5.40am; additionally, train #4241 leaves at 8.15am and arrives in Baihe at 2.43pm. **From Beijing**, train #261 departs the city's west station at 9.24am, arriving in Baihe at 5.19am the following day.

The train is the best overland route **back out** of the Changbai Shan region, though there are morning buses from Baihe northeast to **Yanji**, where you can transfer to points beyond.

Baihe

The friendly village of **BAIHE** is a pleasant place to stay, given that village life carries on regardless of the tourists. The *Yanleyuan Restaurant*, opposite the train station, is worthwhile; not only do they serve local specialities such as rare fungi, but the owner is a one-man tourist office – he can get tickets for onward travel, arrange accommodation and sort out transport around the reserve. If you don't plan on staying on the mountain, you can leave your bags at the restaurant.

The *Baiyun Hotel* (℡0433/5712653; ❻, dorm beds ¥60) here has adequate doubles and four-person dorms, as does the *Yalin* (℡0433/5710526; ❹, dorm beds ¥25). Both are on the upper part of the main street, Erdao Baihe Zhen. Tour groups get corralled into the *Changbaishan Hotel* (℡0433/5712422; ❹). A more interesting alternative is to ask around the little family-run restaurants by the station, as many have rooms at the back equipped with *kangs*, where you can stay for as little as ¥10 per person. These rooms can get very hot at night, full of dry, stuffy air, but in winter the warmth is essential. If you do stay in one of these places, the locals appreciate it if you keep as low a profile as possible, as the PSB disapproves.

The reserve

Dramatic and beautiful **Tian Chi** is a deep volcanic crater lake 5km across, surrounded by angular peaks, with waterfalls gushing around it and blue, snow-capped mountains in the distance. The Baihe–Tian Chi bus trip takes two hours (¥35), and regular tourist buses run up and down the mountain during the summer months. The last buses return to Baihe around 4pm. Alternatively, you can charter a **jeep taxi** from Baihe to the lake for ¥80, weather permitting.

At the reserve **entrance** (daily 7.30am–6pm) everyone pays ¥60 to enter, regardless of nationality – though showing a student card cuts the fee in half. The bus from Baihe drops you off in a car park higher up, from where a road leads to the lake; the walk from the entrance itself up the main path takes about an hour. There's a longer western path branching off from the car park, which is more scenic but also rugged, with jagged rocks everywhere. A pretty waterfall lies 500m east of the car park, while a bathhouse just south of the car park offers hot spring baths for ¥40 per person.

Changbai Shan rewards detailed exploration. Head any distance from the obvious paths, and you're quickly swallowed up in the wilderness. Settlements are few and far between, though, and the only roads are dirt tracks, so don't wander too far unless you know what you're doing. Be especially careful when hiking around Tian Chi, as the lake straddles the Chinese–North Korean **border**, and if you stray across you could be liable to arrest. At the height of the Cultural Revolution, Chairman Mao ordered that the line be demarcated, but it isn't clearly marked on the ground.

Among the cluster of new **hotels** in the tourist village, the *Athletes' Village* (☎0433/5712574; ❺) and *Cuckoo Villas* (☎0433/5746099; ❺) both have dorm beds from ¥50, while suites at the latter feature a private hot spring bath. At the upper end of the spectrum, the *International Tourist Hotel* (☎0433/5746001; ❽) has rooms with views of a waterfall. Officially, camping is against the rules, but it's been done.

Harbin and beyond

The capital of Heilongjiang Province, **HARBIN** is probably the northern-most location that's of interest to visitors, the last major city before you hit the

△ Tian Chi

sub-Siberian wilderness and its scattering of oil and mining towns. It's worth a visit for its **winter ice festival** alone, but it's also one of the few northern cities with a distinctive character, the result of colonialism and cooperation with nearby Russia.

Harbin was a small fishing village on the Songhua River until world history intervened. In 1896 the Russians obtained a contract to build a rail line from Vladivostok through Harbin to Dalian, and the town's population swelled to include 200,000 foreigners. More Russians arrived in 1917, this time White Russian refugees fleeing the Bolsheviks, and many stayed on for the rest of their lives. In 1932 the city was briefly captured by the Japanese forces invading Manchuria, then in 1945 it fell again to the Russian army, who held it for a year before Stalin and Chiang Kaishek finally came to an agreement. Harbin

Harbin and around

Harbin	哈尔滨	*hāěrbīn*
Chairman Mao Memorial	毛主席纪念馆	*máozhǔxí jìniànguǎn*
Dongdazhi Jie churches	南岗教堂	*nángǎng jiàotáng*
Flood Control Monument	防洪纪念碑	*fánghóng jìniànbēi*
Harbin Architecture and Art Centre	哈尔滨建筑艺术馆	*hāěrbīn jiànzhù yìshùguǎn*
Ice Lantern Festival	冰灯节	*bīngdēng jié*
Songhua River	松花江	*sōnghuā jiāng*
Stalin Park	斯大林公园	*sīdàlín gōngyuán*
Sun Island	太阳岛	*tàiyáng dǎo*
Zhaolin Park	兆林公园	*zhàolín gōngyuán*
Zhongyang Dajie	中央大街	*zhōngyāng dàjiē*
Accommodation and eating		
Beibei Hotel	北北大酒店	*běiběi dàjiǔdiàn*
Blues Bar	布蓝斯酒吧	*bùlánsī jiǔbā*
Dongcai Dumpling King	东才饺子王	*dōngcái jiǎoziwáng*
French Bakery	巴黎面包房	*bālí miànbāofáng*
Holiday Inn	哈尔滨万达假日饭店	*hāěrbīn wàndájiàrì fàndiàn*
Huamei Hotel	华梅饭店	*huáméi fàndiàn*
Jiachangcai	家常菜饭店	*jiāchángcài fàndiàn*
Longmen Hotel	龙门大厦	*lóngmén dàshà*
Longyun Hotel	龙运宾馆	*lóngyùn bīnguǎn*
Modern Hotel	马达尔宾馆	*mǎdáěr bīnguǎn*
Portman	波特曼西餐厅	*bōtèmàn xīcāntīng*
Russia 1914	俄罗斯 1 9 1 4	*éluósi yìjiǔyìsì*
Shangri-La Hotel	香格里拉大饭店	*xiānggélǐlā dàfàndiàn*
Youlian Hotel	友联宾馆	*yǒulián bīnguǎn*
Daqing	大庆	*dàqìng*
Pingfang	平方	*píngfāng*
Qiqihar	齐齐哈尔	*qíqíhāěr*
Hecheng Binguan	鹤城宾馆	*hèchéng bīnguǎn*
Hubin Binguan	湖滨宾馆	*húbīn bīnguǎn*
Huimin Fandian	回民饭店	*huímín fàndiàn*
Zhalong Nature Reserve	扎龙自然保护区	*zhālóng zìrán bǎohùqū*
Yabuli Ski Resort	亚布力滑雪场	*yàbùlì huáxuěchǎng*

reverted to the Chinese, though when the Russians withdrew, they took with them most of the city's industrial plant. Things haven't been totally peaceful since – Harbin was the scene of fierce factional fighting during the Cultural Revolution, and when relations with the Soviet Union deteriorated, the inhabitants looked anxiously north as fierce border skirmishes took place.

Not surprisingly, the city used to be nicknamed "**Little Moscow**", and though much of the old architecture has been replaced with sterile blocks and skyscrapers, corners of Harbin still look like the last threadbare outpost of imperial Russia. Leafy boulevards are lined with European-style buildings painted in pastel shades, and bulbous onion domes dot the skyline. The city's past is celebrated with a restored shopping street, **Zhongyang Dajie**, as well as in a Russian cathedral that now houses a photographic history of the city. It's possible to eat in Russian restaurants, and the locals have picked up on some of their neighbour's customs: as well as a taste for ice cream and pastries, Harbin residents have a reputation as the hardest drinkers in China.

Attractions beyond here are limited, and journeys can be arduous, though new highways and trains have shortened travel times. Ornithologists will be interested in the **Zhalong Nature Reserve**, home of the rare red-crowned crane, and roughnecks will enjoy **Daqing**, "Big Celebration", home of China's largest petroleum field. Beyond that sits **Qiqihar** and the volcanic spa at **Wudalianchi**, the latter an unattractive place that draws mostly elderly Chinese to its supposedly medicinal hot spa. If you're keen on skiing, you'll find **Yabuli**, the resort southwest of Harbin, the best place in the country to flaunt your skills.

During the summer the **climate** is quite pleasant, but in winter the temperature can plummet to well below -30°C, and the sun sets at 4pm. Local people are accustomed to the dark cold, however, and it is during winter that the city is most alive, with skiing and ice festivals in December and January.

Arrival and transport

Downtown Harbin, the most interesting part for visitors, is laid out on the southern bank of the Songhua River, with the liveliest streets between here and the train station. The urban sprawl farther south is best avoided.

Harbin **airport** is 50km southwest of the town, and served by an airport bus (¥15) which drops you outside the **CAAC** office on Zhongshan Lu. A taxi will cost ¥150. From the central **train station** (shown as Harbin Dong – east – on tickets), a clutch of cheap hotels is a short walk away, or you could head north to the somewhat less seedy and hectic central streets. The **long-distance bus station** is on Songhuajiang Jie, across from the train station. Summertime **ferries** from Jiamusi, a town 200km farther east, use the terminal towards the western end of Stalin Park.

For getting around the city, the most useful **bus** is #103, which runs between Zhongshan Lu and Zhaolin Park just each of Zhongyang Dajie. **Taxi** fares around the city begin at ¥8. Harbin has lots of one-way streets, so don't panic if it seems your driver is lapping the block. In summer there are small boats (¥10–30) across the Songhua, or you can take the ferry (¥5). Good English **maps** of the city are sold in the gift shop at the *Holiday Inn*.

Accommodation

Harbin is one of the less expensive cities of the northeast for accommodation. The choice of **hotels** is better than elsewhere in the region, and the prices almost reasonable. Always ask the front desk if they can lower the price a bit – they usually will, even at the high-end hotels.

The hotels around Zhongyang Dajie are the best option if you're staying for any length of time. There's a cluster of hotels around the train station, but the area is noisy, dirty and crowded. One interesting feature of this area, however, is the row of women sitting in glass-fronted boxes behind the *Longyun Hotel* who bang their combs on the glass as you pass by. The women are, in fact, masseuses, and quote a price of ¥50 for a 45-minute rub, though you can bargain this down.

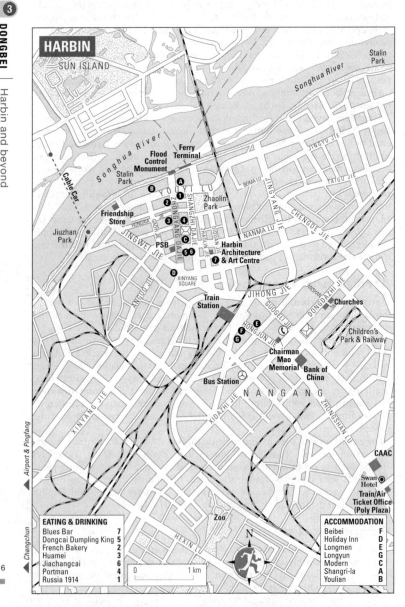

EATING & DRINKING

Blues Bar	7
Dongcai Dumpling King	5
French Bakery	2
Huamei	3
Jiachangcai	6
Portman	4
Russia 1914	1

ACCOMMODATION

Beibei	F
Holiday Inn	D
Longmen	E
Longyun	G
Modern	C
Shangri-la	A
Youlian	B

From northern Heilongjiang, there are a number of crossing points **into Siberia**, of which **Heihe**, a large border town that sees a lot of traffic with the Russian town of Blagoveshchensk, is the best option. From Harbin, take train K485 to Heihe (departs 6.54pm; 12hr), and Russia is a few strides and a mountain of paperwork away. Train K486 returns to Harbin daily, leaving Heihe at 6.53pm. A train connection also exists between Harbin and **Suifenhe** (train K607, leaving at 7.18pm; 11hr), from where it's a four-hour bus ride to Vladivostok. In practice, however, these routes are fraught with difficulties; there is no tourist infrastructure, distances are long and conditions primitive. By far the simplest way to get into Russia from Dongbei is to hop on the **Trans-Siberian train** to Moscow, which passes through Harbin every Friday morning on its way west to the border at Manzhouli.

The biggest problem with crossing from Dongbei into Siberia is getting a **visa**, which you will probably have to sort out in Beijing, although you may get one in Shenyang if you're lucky. To get a two-week tourist visa, all your hotel accommodation in Russia must be booked in advance, and prices are steep – expect to pay at least US$50 a night. A few travellers with connections have managed to get hold of business visas, which last a month and give you more flexibility.

Beibei Directly across from the train station ℡ 0451/83642200. Formerly a seedy dive called the *Beiyuan*, the Beibei has been reincarnated and refurbished under new management – though Russian prostitutes remain in the lobby. That said, the hot water works and rates are reasonable. **④**

Holiday Inn 90 Jingwei Jie ℡ 0451/84226666, Ⓕ 84221661, Ⓦ www.ichotelsgroup.com. Fading a bit, but good value for its location at the head of Zhongyang Dajie, as well as the very helpful English-speaking staff. A breakfast buffet is included in the rate. Enquire about year-round discounts, which can lower rates by as much as a third. **⑨**

Longmen 85 Hongqi Jie ℡ 0451/86791888, Ⓕ 53639700. Built in 1901 as the *Chinese Eastern Railway Hotel*, this restored gem is a snapshot of Harbin's bicultural past. If you don't stay here, pop in to admire the woodwork, sculptures, and English-language captions on the photographs, and ask to see the suite, used by the warlord Zhang Xueliang and then by Chairman Mao. The ordinary rooms are pleasant, and the staff top-notch. Bargaining can lower rates to under ¥300. **⑧**

Longyun ℡ 0451/83634528. A clean, modern place to the right of and behind the *Beibei* as you exit the train station. Dorms from ¥45, **③**

Modern 89 Zhongyang Dajie ℡ 0451/84615846, Ⓕ 84614997. The name is a misnomer, as this place was built in 1906 and survives as Harbin's oldest hotel. An elegant building on one of the city's busiest streets, it's bursting with character, with European- and Russian-style restaurants and 160 rooms. Staff are helpful and speak English. You enter the reception from Zhongyang Dajie via a shop vending leather handbags. **⑥**

Shangri-La 555 Youyi Lu ℡ 0451/84858888, Ⓕ 84621666, Ⓦ www.shangri-la.com. Harbin's only five-star hotel overlooks Stalin Park, Zhongyang Dajie and Zhaolin Park, making it the best place to stay during the Ice Lantern Festival. Book early. **⑨**

Youlian 225 Youyi Lu ℡ 0451/84686106. The friendliest, best-located budget place in Harbin, right near the river and Zhongyang Dajie. Dorms ¥35, **③**

The City

Harbin is more a recreational centre than a cultural mecca, a good place to shop and explore the streets. A good starting point is the **Daoli** district, in the triangle outlined by Diduan Jie and Jingwei Jie, where there are plenty of brand-name clothing boutiques, fur shops and department stores. The smaller streets and alleys around here are the best places to see the city's **Russian architecture**, with its decaying stucco facades and elegant balconies. There's an extensive market selling women's clothes off Xinyang Square, while the best large department stores are on Diduan Jie and **Zhongyang Dajie**.

Harbin festivals

In compensation for the cruel winter weather, the annual **Ice Lantern Festival**, centred on Zhaolin Park, is held from January 5 to February 5 – though with the influx of tourists, the dates extend each year. At this time, the park becomes a fairytale landscape with magnificent sculptures – sometimes entire buildings, complete with slides, stairways, arches and bridges – made of ice, carved with chainsaws and picks, and often with coloured lights inside them to heighten the psychedelic effect. Sculptors, some of them teenagers, work in -20°C December weather, earning ¥20 for a twelve-hour day. Highlights of past festivals have included detailed replicas of St Paul's Cathedral and life-size Chinese temples, though these days cartoon characters outnumber more traditional Chinese subject matter. Over on Sun Island, a snow sculpture display is held, the highlights of which are the toboggan and snow-tube pistes. It's as much fun watching ecstatic Chinese bounce down the slopes as it is sledding. You can walk across the river yourself or take a horse-drawn carriage for ¥10. Festival's end is marked with fireworks and pickaxes; visitors are encouraged to destroy the icy artwork by hand.

In summer, Harbin hosts a classical and traditional **music festival** from the middle to the end of July, during which orchestras and smaller groups play in the city's eight theatres.

Shops along the latter road have all been restored, with plaques out front in English detailing their past lives as colonial homes and stores. Make sure you go in the department store at no. 107, if only to see its spectacular skylight and rendition of a section from Michelangelo's Sistine Chapel mural, which hangs on the back wall. Across the street is another beautiful structure, the Jiaoyu Bookstore, well worth exploring. There are numerous good restaurants and bars along Zhongyang Dajie, which is paved with cobblestones and closed to cars. In winter, ice sculptures line the street, while summer sees pavement cafés set up.

The cathedral and around

The most beautiful and interesting sight in Harbin has to be the Russian Orthodox **cathedral** (formerly St Sofia's, built in 1907) on Zhaolin Jie. Turn east off Zhongyang Dajie on to Xi Shi Er Dao, and carry on until you hit Government Square, which fronts a new department store; the church is right behind the store. Set in its own square and restored to all its onion-domed glory, the cathedral now houses the **Harbin Architecture and Art Centre** (daily 8.30am–5pm; ¥25), with an interesting photographic survey of Harbin's history as a Russian railway outpost. Additional photos are available via touch-screen computers inside, although the captions, like those throughout the hall, are in Chinese.

Due to frosty relations with the Soviet Union in the 1960s and 1970s (subject of Ha Jin's excellent *Ocean of Words*, a book of short stories by a former PLA soldier who was based on the Siberian border), Harbin also boasts a network of **underground bomb shelters** turned marketplaces. You can enter from the train station and walk all the way to Dongdazhi Jie and beyond. The markets sell a huge selection of goods, from pirated video discs to leather jackets.

Along Dongdazhi Jie

Heading southeast from the train station, you can enter a Russian-era mansion, the mansard-roofed **Chairman Mao Memorial** (daily 9am–4pm; ¥10), named for its most famous post-Revolution guest. The home is at the junction of Hongjun Jie and Dondazhi Jie, next to the *Sinoway Hotel*. Just beyond, the junction with **Guogeli Jie** (formerly called Fendou Lu) is an up-and-coming area for drinking and shopping, and is served by a restored tram (¥1). One spin-off of improved Sino-Indian relations is the mall here called India Street, where bemused Indian shopkeepers sell trinkets and curry to camera-wielding Chinese tourists.

Out from the centre, there are some nice old working **churches** in the Nangang District. At 25 Dongdazhi Jie is a German Lutheran chapel built in 1914, while just a little further at no. 268 you can peek inside an onion-domed Russian Orthodox building.

Along the river

The **riverbank** area is another worthwhile district to explore, starting from the **Flood Control Monument** at the bottom of Zhongyang Dajie. Built in 1958, the monument commemorates the many thousands who have died in the Song-hua floods, and has been updated to mark the horrible floods in the summers of 1989 and 1998. The square here is a popular hangout for local people who gather to feed pigeons and fly kites, as is **Stalin Park**, a strip of land along the east bank of the river that's particularly lively on weekends. People come to what must be China's last public memorial to Stalin in order to wash their clothes, meet and chat, even bathe in the river – the last is not a good idea, as mercury levels in the water are so high fish can no longer survive in it. Others cluster around palm-readers and storytellers who relate old Chinese folk legends. Just southeast of the monument, **Zhaolin Park**, unremarkable in summer, is host to the spectacular winter Ice Lantern Festival (see box opposite).

In winter, the **Songhua River** freezes solid and you can take a horse carriage, rent a go-kart or walk across – the ice is so thick it will support a fully loaded bus or lorry and gets used as a road. In summer, ferries (¥5) leave from near the Flood Control Monument for the northern bank of the resort and sanatorium village of **Taiyang (Sun) Island** (daily 8.30am–4.30pm; ¥10). You can also access Taiyang Island by **cable car** during warm months (¥35 one-way). The island is an enormous park and leisure complex, with lakes for boating, swim-ming pools and fairground rides. It's unpleasantly busy on summer weekends, and getting around takes a lot of walking. In winter, the snow sculptures here (¥30) draw tourists from around the world.

Eating, drinking and nightlife

Away from expensive regional delicacies such as bear paw and deer muzzle, available in upmarket hotels, **food** in Harbin is good value. Influenced by Russian cuisine, local cooking is characterized by the exceptionally heavy use of garlic and a lot of potato. A favourite local dish is *xiaoji dunmogu* (chicken and stewed mushrooms).

For **bars**, try Guogeli Jie east of the train station, or along the river, where drinking establishments tend to have a Russian theme. Top draw as regards **nightlife** is the *Blues Bar* on Diduan Jie, where Russian and Chinese students – plus a rogues' gallery of older folks – dance the night away on weekends.

Restaurants and cafés

Dongcai Dumpling King 39 Zhongyang Dajie. The place to be seen in Harbin, with a wait for a table often required. The dumplings here are so good, you may be loath to leave. Everyone else seems to linger for another draught beer, another plate of food.

French Bakery 174 Zhongyang Dajie. Inexpensive espresso, cappuccino, ice cream and pizza, and a good place to chat with locals.

Huamei 142 Zhongyang Jie. Patronized chiefly by tourists, this is Harbin's only authentic Russian restaurant. Though a little pricey – expect to pay at least ¥100 per person – the meals (especially the stroganoff) are good. You can even indulge yourself with caviar.

Jiachangcai Off Zhongyang Dajie and across from the post office, this 24hr restaurant serves cheap eats and beer.

Portman 53 Xi Qidao Jie. A European pub and grill serving dependable pasta, wine and an array of draught beer.

Russia 1914 57 Xi Toudao Jie. A cosy café serving espresso, tea and Russian snacks. Also on sale here is *Paris of the East*, a good primer on the city's historic architecture.

Listings

Airlines CAAC is at 99 Zhongshan Lu (☎0451/2651188). If you're leaving the city by plane, allow an hour to get to the airport through the traffic. An airport bus runs from outside the CAAC office every twenty minutes (1hr; ¥15).
Banks and exchange The Bank of China is on Hongjun Jie (Mon–Fri 8am–noon & 1–5pm). The office for traveller's cheques and credit-card advances is just round the corner. You can also change money at its branch at 37 Zhaolin Jie (same hours).
Internet access The portal at 129 Zhongyang Dajie, near the *Modern Hotel*, leads down to a fast and friendly café. There's another nearby at 20 Xi Shisi Daojie, at the intersection of Zhongyang Dajie.
Mail The main post office is at 51 Jianshe Jie (Mon–Sat 8am–6pm).
PSB 26 Duan Jie, off Zhongyang Dajie (Mon–Fri 8–11am & 2–5pm).

Telephones There's a telecom office (24hr) on Guogeli Jie, east of the train station.
Travel agents Harbin has a number of services that can arrange travel for you. Don't bother with CITS, far out at 82 Yiman Jie, which is focused on domestic tourists. More convenient and useful is Swan Travel (☎0451/2367621), in the grounds of the *Swan Hotel*, 95 Zhongshan Lu. It arranges ski trips and tours to areas farther north, including specialist hunting, fishing, skiing and bird-watching tours. The *Longyun Hotel* does packages to Yabuli. The Heilongjiang New Century International Travel Service, at 49 Hongxia Jie (☎0451/4672888, ☏4612143), runs four- and five-day trips to and over the Russian border. At 93 Zhongshan Lu, in the Poly Plaza building, a small agency based in a booth sells train and airline tickets, and has free timetables, too.

West of Harbin

Harbin's most notorious and macabre attraction is outside the city proper, about 30km southwest, in the tiny village of **PINGFANG**, near the terminus of bus #343 (¥1.5), which you can catch at the train station. This was the home of a secret Japanese research establishment during World War II, now open to the public as a grisly **museum** (daily 9am–4pm; ¥15). Here prisoners of war were injected with deadly viruses, dissected alive and frozen or heated slowly until they died. More than three thousand people from China, Russia and Mongolia were murdered by troops from unit 731 of the Japanese army. After the war, the Japanese tried to hide all evidence of the base, and its existence only came to light through the efforts of Japanese investigative journalists. It was also discovered that, as with scientists in defeated Nazi Germany, the Americans gave the Japanese scientists immunity from prosecution in return for their research findings.

The museum's collection comprises mostly photographs labelled in Chinese. Looking at the displays, which include a painting of bound prisoners being used as bomb targets, you understand why many Chinese mistrust Japan to this day.

Daqing

About two hours' bus journey (¥30) west of Harbin via sleek National Highway 301 (also known as the Ha Da Expressway) sprawls **DAQING**, home of China's largest oil reserve and now Heilongjiang's second city. Daqing is a quirky place to stop for a few hours, with road names such as "Calgary Street" and oil pumps, called *ketouji* (literally, "kowtowing machines"), everywhere. With Western companies operating here as vendors of drilling equipment, foreigners aren't that rare a sight. There's no skyline in Daqing, save for some cooling towers, but the folks are friendly and there are good connections on to Qiqihar and Harbin; trains are frequent and buses leave every fifteen minutes from outside the train station.

Dongbei's minority communities

After forcing **minority communities** to embrace official communist culture during the 1950s and 1960s, the Chinese government now takes a more enlightened – if somewhat patronizing – approach to the minority nations of the north. The **Manchu** people, spread across Inner Mongolia and Dongbei, are the most numerous and assimilated. Having lived so long among the Han, they are now almost identical, though Manchus tend to be slightly taller, and Manchu men have more facial hair. Manchus are noted for an elaborate system of etiquette and will never eat dog, unlike their Korean neighbours who love it. The "three strange things" that the southern Chinese say are found in the northeast are all Manchu idiosyncrasies: paper windows pasted outside their wooden frame, babies carried by their mothers in handbags and women smoking in public (the latter, of course, can be a habit of Han and every other ethnicity in large cities).

In the inhospitable northern margins of Dongbei live small communities such as the **Hezhen**, one of the smallest minority nations in China with an estimated 1400 members. Inhabiting the region where the Songhua, Heilong and Wusuli (Ussuri) rivers converge, they're known to the Han Chinese as the fish tribe, and their culture and livelihood centre around fishing. Indeed, they're the only people in the world to make clothes out of fish skin: the fish is gutted, descaled, then dried and tanned and the skins sewn together to make light, waterproof coats, shoes and gloves. More numerous are the **Daur**, 120,000 of whom live along the Nenjiang River. They are fairly seamlessly assimilated these days, but still retain distinctive marriage and funerary traditions, and have a reputation for being superb at hockey, a form of which they have played since the sixth century.

However, perhaps the most distinctive minority are the **Oroqen**, a tribe of nomadic hunters living in patrilineal clan communes called *wulileng* in the northern sub-Siberian wilderness. Although they have recently adopted a more settled existence, their main livelihood still comes from deer-hunting, while household items, tools and canoes are made from birch bark by Oroqen women. Clothes are fashioned from deer hide, and include a striking hat made of a roe deer head, complete with antlers and leather patches for eyes, which is used as a disguise in hunting.

The town has an older western half and a new, gleaming eastern portion, with a billboard of Deng Xiaoping gracing the entrance to the government offices. Buses #23 and #30 go from the train station to the new section of town, where the *Daqing Hotel* (☏0452/4662073; ❺) lives up to the boomtown image of overpriced rooms, liquor and prostitutes.

Qiqihar and the Zhalong Nature Reserve

Two-and-a-half hours' train or bus journey west of Daqing or four hours' west of Harbin, **QIQIHAR** is one of the northeast's oldest cities, and still a thriving industrial centre. Alas, it's more fun to say the city's name aloud than to stay here for more than a day. The only place of marginal interest is a big park, **Longsha Gongyuan** (¥2), in the south of town, accessible via the main north–south artery, Longhua Lu, which begins in front of the train station; buses #1 and #2 ply the route.

The main reason to come to Qiqihar is to visit the **Zhalong Nature Reserve** (¥20), 30km outside town. This marshy plain abounds in shallow reedy lakes and serves as the summer breeding ground of thousands of species of birds, including white storks, whooper swans, spoonbills, white ibis and – the star attractions – nine of the world's fifteen species of **crane**. Most spectacular of these is the endangered red-crowned crane, a lanky black and white bird over a metre tall, with a scarlet bald patch. It has long been treasured in the East as a paradigm of elegance – the Japanese call it the Marsh God – and is a popular symbol of longevity, as birds can live up to sixty years. The birds mate for life, and the female only lays one or two eggs each season, over which the male stands guard. The best time to visit the reserve is from April to June, when the migrants have just arrived, though the viewing season extends through September. Walking around the reserve, although not forbidden, is not encouraged by the keepers or the murderous swarms of mosquitoes – come prepared. Binoculars are a good idea, too. Dedicated ornithologists might like to spend a few days here, but for most people an afternoon crouched in the reedbeds will be enough.

Practicalities

Buses to the reserve (1hr; ¥5) leave from Qiqihar's **bus station**, 1km south down Longhua Lu, on the left, and also from in front of the **train station**. Splendid though the birds are, it can be difficult to fill the time the bus time-table obliges you to spend in Qiqihar, so consider devoting part of your visit to the flat-bottomed-boat **tour** which leaves from the reserve entrance; book through CITS (☏0452/2712014) at the *Hubin Hotel*.

Visitors to Zhalong have to stay in nearby Qiqihar. The two tourist **hotels** are the two-star *Hecheng* (☏0452/2722540; ❺) and *Hubin* (☏0452/2711711; ❺). They're in the same compound at 4 Wenhua Dajie, on the route of bus #15 from the train station. The *Huimin Fandian*, across the street from the station on the left as you exit, is a good place to eat; a bowl of Muslim-styled pulled noodles is ¥3. Frequent connections out mean you won't get stuck in Qiqihar for a night.

Yabuli

Regarded as the premier ski resort in China, **YABULI** is the place to be for Heilongjiang's **International Ski Festival**, which takes place from December 5 to January 5. The resort's 3800-metre piste spreads across the southern side of Guokui (literally pot-lid) Mountain (1300m), 194km southeast of Harbin. There's also a 2.5-kilometre steel **toboggan run**, built in 1996 when the resort hosted the Asian Winter Games. Six lifts shuttle an average of 10,000 skiers per day during the winter months. Lift tickets and gear rental cost ¥140 for two hours, with half-day and full-day schemes available. Private skiing lessons also run on a sliding scale, with ¥400 buying an entire day with a patient instructor – who may or may not speak English.

In winter, resort buses depart frequently in front of Harbin's **train station** (3hr; ¥80). At Yabuli, the only place to stay is *Windmill Villa* (☏0451/3455168 or 3455088; villas from ¥500, dorms often available). One- or two-day Yabuli packages, including a stay here, are offered by the *Longyun* and other hotels in Harbin.

Travel details

Trains

Changchun to: Beijing (9 daily; 9–11hr); Dandong (3 daily; 10hr); Harbin (27 daily; 3–4hr); Jilin (16 daily; 1hr 30min–3hr); Shenyang (frequent; 3–4hr); Tonghua (2 daily; 7hr 30min).
Dalian to: Beijing (2 daily; 10hr); Dandong (daily; 10hr 30min); Harbin (4 daily; 9–13hr); Shenyang (frequent; 4–6hr).

Dandong to: Beijing (2 daily; 14 hr); Changchun (3 daily; 8hr 30min–10hr); Dalian (daily; 10 hr); Qingdao (daily; 26hr); Shenyang (27 daily; 3–5hr).
Harbin to: Beijing (9 daily; 11–17hr); Changchun (27 daily; 3hr); Daqing (32 daily; 1hr 30min–3hr); Jilin (5 daily; 5–6hr); Moscow (weekly; 6 days); Qiqihar (21 daily; 3–4hr); Shanghai (daily; 33hr); Shenyang (frequent; 5–7hr).
Jilin to: Beijing (daily; 11hr); Changchun (16 daily; 1hr 30min–3hr); Dalian (2 daily; 12hr 30min–14hr

30min); Harbin (3 daily; 5–6hr); Shenyang (18 daily; 5hr 30min–8hr 30min).

Qiqihar to: Bei'an (3 daily; 4hr); Beijing (4 daily; 15–20hr); Hailar (6 daily; 7hr 30min–13hr), Harbin (21 daily; 3–4hr).

Shenyang to: Beijing (20 daily; 6hr 30min–12hr); Changchun (frequent; 3–4hr); Dalian (frequent; 4–6hr); Dandong (27 daily; 3–5hr); Harbin (frequent; 5–7hr); Jilin (18 daily; 5hr 30min–8hr 30min); Tonghua (6 daily; 6hr 30min–10hr).

Tonghua to: Baihe (2 daily; 7hr); Beijing (daily; 16hr 30min); Changchun (2 daily; 7–9hr); Shenyang (6 daily; 6hr 30min–10hr).

Buses

Bus connections are comprehensive and can be picked up at all major towns from the bus station or in front of the train station. For some stretches, buses are faster and more convenient than trains, especially from Harbin to the west and south; Changchun to Jilin and Shenyang; and Shenyang to Dalian. Away from the major cities, however, roads turn rough and the journeys arduous.

Ferries

Dalian to: Inchon (South Korea; 2 weekly; 17hr); Tanggu (for Tianjin; daily or alternate days; 13–15hr); Weihai (daily; 3hr 30min–8hr); Yantai (daily; 3–8hr).
Dandong to: Inchon (South Korea; 3 weekly; 20hr).
Harbin to: Jiamusi (daily in summer; 18hr).

Flights

Besides the domestic services listed, some useful international connections serve this part of China, including flights from Changchun to Seoul; from Dalian to Fukuoka, Hiroshima, Nagoya, Osaka, Seoul, Tokyo and Vladivostok; and from Shenyang to Bangkok, Osaka, Pyongyang, Seoul and Tokyo.
Changchun to: Beijing (11 daily; 1hr 30min); Chengdu (5 weekly; 5hr); Chongqing (3 weekly; 4hr 40min); Dalian (4 daily; 1 hr 10min); Fuzhou (2 weekly; 4hr 20min); Guangzhou (daily; 5hr 40min); Hangzhou (daily; 2hr 50min); Hong Kong (2 weekly; 4hr 20min); Ji'nan (daily; 1hr 55min); Kunming (3 weekly; 6hr); Nanjing (daily; 2hr 15min); Qingdao (daily; 1hr 35min); Shanghai (3 daily; 2hr 30min); Shenzhen (3 daily; 5hr); Xiamen (8 weekly; 5hr); Xi'an (3 weekly; 4hr 10min); Yanji (2 daily; 1hr); Yantai (daily; 2hr 25min).
Dalian to: Beijing (12 daily; 1hr 10min); Changchun (daily; 1hr); Changsha (2 daily; 3hr 40min); Chengdu (daily; 3hr 40min); Chongqing (4 weekly; 3hr); Fuzhou (daily; 3hr 30min); Guangzhou (3 daily; 3hr 15min); Guilin (2 weekly; 4hr 25min); Haikou (daily; 3hr 35min); Hangzhou (2 daily; 2hr); Harbin

(3 daily; 1hr 25min); Hefei (weekly; 1hr 50min); Hong Kong (daily; 3hr 25min); Jilin (3 weekly; 1hr 20min); Ji'nan (2 daily; 1hr); Kunming (daily; 5hr); Luoyang (3 weekly; 1hr 40min); Nanjing (3 daily; 1hr 30min); Ningbo (daily; 1hr 50min); Qingdao (5 daily; 40min); Qinhuangdao (3 weekly; 1hr); Sanya (3 weekly; 6hr 30min); Shanghai (7 daily; 1hr 30min); Shenyang (daily; 50min); Shenzhen (3 daily; 4hr 50min); Taiyuan (daily; 3hr 30min); Tianjin (2 daily; 1hr); Wenzhou (daily; 2hr); Wuhan (8 weekly; 3hr); Xiamen (2 daily; 3hr 35min); Xi'an (daily; 2hr 20min); Yanji (daily; 2hr 30min); Yantai (daily; 35min); Zhengzhou (9 weekly; 1hr 45min).
Dandong to: Sanya (3 weekly; 6hr 25min); Shanghai (3 weekly; 2hr 20min); Shenzhen (3 weekly; 5hr 35min).
Harbin to: Beijing (13 daily; 1hr 50min); Chengdu (daily; 5hr 50min); Chongqing (4 weekly; 3hr 50min); Dalian (4 daily; 1hr 20min); Fuzhou (daily; 4hr 25min); Guangzhou (2 daily; 5hr 35min); Guiyang (3 weekly; 5hr 35min); Haikou (4 weekly; 5hr 30min); Hangzhou (daily; 3hr 10min); Hong Kong (4 weekly; 4hr 40min); Ji'nan (daily; 2hr 10min); Kunming (daily; 7hr); Nanjing (daily; 3hr 50min); Ningbo (4 weekly; 3hr); Qingdao (4 daily; 1hr 50min); Sanya (4 weekly; 7hr); Shanghai (7 daily; 2hr 40min); Shenyang (2 daily; 55min); Shenzhen (daily; 5hr); Tianjin (daily 3hr); Wenzhou (5 weekly; 4hr 30min); Wuhan (daily; 4hr); Xiamen (2 daily; 5hr); Xi'an (daily; 3hr); Zhengzhou (7 weekly; 3hr 40min).
Jilin to: Beijing (4 weekly; 1hr 40min); Dalian (3 weekly; 1hr 20min); Guangzhou (2 weekly; 6hr 35min); Shanghai (2 weekly; 2hr 30min).
Qiqihar to: Beijing (3 weekly; 1hr 50min); Guangzhou (2 weekly; 5hr 55min); Shanghai (2 weekly; 2hr 50min).
Shenyang to: Beijing (7 daily; 1hr 15min); Changsha (daily; 3hr); Chengdu (daily; 4hr 30min); Chongqing (daily; 3hr 15min); Dalian (daily; 50min); Fuzhou (daily; 2hr 50min); Guangzhou (3 daily; 3hr 45min); Guiyang (3 weekly; 4hr 40min); Haikou (daily; 5hr 30min); Hangzhou (daily; 2hr 20min); Harbin (2 daily; 1hr); Hefei (4 weekly; 1hr 45min); Hohhot (3 weekly; 1hr 30min); Hong Kong (4 weekly; 4hr 35min); Ji'nan (daily; 1hr 20min); Kunming (2 daily; 5hr 10min); Lanzhou (7 weekly; 3hr 10min); Nanjing (6 weekly; 1hr 50min); Ningbo (daily; 2hr 10min); Qingdao (2 daily; 1hr 10min); Sanya (daily; 5hr 30min); Shanghai (8 daily; 2hr); Shantou (2 weekly; 4hr); Shenzhen (4 daily; 4hr); Shijiazhuang (4 weekly; 1hr 40min); Taiyuan (2 daily; 1hr 40min); Tianjin (8 weekly; 1hr 20min); Ürümqi (3 weekly; 6hr 30min); Wenzhou (daily; 2hr 35min); Wuhan (daily; 3hr 25min); Xiamen (2 daily; 3hr 10min); Xi'an (daily; 2hr 30min); Yanji (2 daily; 1hr 10min); Yantai (daily; 1hr); Zhengzhou (daily; 2hr); Zhuhai (2 weekly; 6hr 30min).

CHAPTER 4

Highlights

* **Yungang Caves** – See glorious Buddhist statuary from the fifth century, nestling in grottoes near Datong. **See p.236**

* **Walking Wutai Shan** The least developed of China's four Buddhist mountains is actually five flat peaks, perfect for independent exploration. **See p.240**

* **Pingyao** An intact Ming-era walled city, home to winding back alleys and a number of atmospheric hotels and guesthouses. **See p.252**

* **The Terracotta Army** No visit to China is complete without a peek at these warrior figurines, guarding the tomb of Qin Shi Huang near Xi'an. **See p.280**

* **Longmen caves, Luoyang** Walk along a riverside promenade past caves peppering limestone cliff faces, containing more than 100,000 Buddhist carvings. **See p.297**

△ Hukou falls

The Yellow River

The central Chinese provinces of **Shanxi**, **Shaanxi**, **Henan** and **Shandong** are linked and dominated by the **Yellow River** (*huánghé*), which has played a vital role in their history, geography and fortunes. The river is often likened to a dragon, a reference not just to its sinuous course, but also to its uncontrollable nature – by turns benign and malevolent. It provides much-needed irrigation to an area otherwise arid and inhospitable, but as its popular nickname, "China's Sorrow", hints, its floods and changes of course have repeatedly caused devastation, and for centuries helped to keep the delta region in Shandong one of the poorest areas in the nation.

The river's modern name is a reference to the vast quantities of yellow silt – **loess** – it carries, which has clogged and confused its course throughout history, and which has largely determined the region's geography. Loess is a soft soil, prone to vertical fissuring, and in Shanxi and northern Shaanxi it has created one of China's most distinctive landscapes, plains scarred with deep, winding crevasses, in a restricted palette of browns. In southern Shaanxi and Henan, closer to the river, the landscape is flat as a pancake and about the same colour. It may look barren, but where irrigation has been implemented the loess becomes **rich and fertile**, easily tillable with the simplest of tools. It was in this soil, on the Yellow River's flood plain, that Chinese civilization first took root (see p.228).

Of the four provinces, **Shanxi** is the poor relation, relatively underdeveloped and with the least agreeable climate and geography (temperatures regularly drop to -10°C in winter). But it does have some great attractions, most notably the stunning **Yungang cave temples**, and one of the most beautiful – and inaccessible – holy mountains, **Wutai Shan**. Dotted around the small towns along the single rail line leading south to the Yellow River plain are quirky temples and villages that seem stuck in the nineteenth century. **Shaanxi** province is more of the same, yet its wealthy and historically significant capital city, **Xi'an**, is one of China's biggest tourist destinations, with as many temples, museums and tombs as the rest of the province put together, and the **Terracotta Army** deservedly ranking as one of China's premier sights. The city is also home to a substantial Muslim minority, whose cuisine is well worth sampling. Within easy travelling distance of here, following the Yellow River east, are two more holy mountains, **Hua Shan** and **Song Shan** (home of the legendary Shaolin monks), and the city of **Luoyang** in **Henan**, with the superb **Longmen cave temples** and **Baima Si** just outside. Continuing east brings you to the little-visited but appealing town of **Kaifeng**, a mellow lakeside city that provides a refreshing change of scale. Between the two cities lies the provincial capital, **Zhengzhou**, which – conveniently – is also a significant junction on the rail and road

network. The city is home to one of the most impressive provincial museums in the country, whose collection is evidence of Henan's long history and artistic output, chiefly intricate **Shang-dynasty bronzes**. A northward diversion to **Anyang**, capital of the Shang dynasty and site of ongoing excavations, or to the **Red Flag Canal**, a reminder of China's modern history, is possible from here. Farther east lies **Shandong**, a province with less of a distinctive identity, but

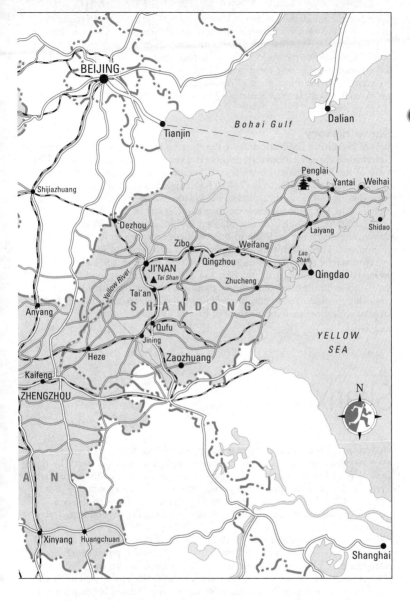

home to more small and intriguing places – **Qufu**, the birthplace of Confucius, with its giant temple and mansion; **Tai Shan**, the most popular holy mountain in the area; and the beautiful coastal city of **Qingdao**, a replica of a Bavarian village built by the Germans in the nineteenth century.

With generally good rail links, a well-developed tourist industry and an agreeable climate outside the winter months, **travel** in the region presents few difficulties, although the rail network in Shanxi and northern Shaanxi is noticeably sparse, and Henan's infrastructure and attitude feels a decade or so behind its progressive neighbours. Sadly, the capricious nature of the river makes river travel impossible in the region. All towns and cities now have hotels offering accommodation catering for a wide range of budgets, with a few travellers' dormitories in the most popular destinations. The best-value hotels, though, are in small towns, such as Kaifeng, Qufu and Wutai Shan, which are anxious to attract visitors.

Some history

Sites of **Neolithic habitation** along the river are common, but the first major conurbation appeared around three thousand years ago, heralding the establishment of the Shang dynasty. For the next few millennia, every Chinese dynasty had its capital somewhere in the Yellow River area, and most of the major cities, from Datong in the north, capital of the Northern Wei, to Kaifeng in the east, capital of the Song, have spent some time as the centre of the Chinese universe, however briefly. With the collapse of imperial China the area sank into provincialism, and it was not until late in the twentieth century that it again came to prominence. The old capitals have today found new leases of life as industrial and commercial centres, and thus present two sides to the visitor: a static history, preserved in the interests of tourism, and a rapidly changing, and sometimes harsh, modernity. It is the remnants of **dynastic history** that provide the most compelling reason to visit, but the region also has much to offer in the way of scenery, with more than its fair share of holy mountains.

Shanxi

Shanxi province, with an average height of 1000m above sea level, is one huge mountain plateau. Strategically important, bounded to the north by the Great Wall and to the south by the Yellow River, it was for centuries a bastion territory against the northern tribes. Today its significance is economic – nearly a third of China's coal reserves are to be found here – and around the two key towns, **Datong** and the capital **Taiyuan**, open-cast mining has obliterated large parts of the countryside.

Physically, Shanxi is dominated by the proximity of the Gobi desert, and wind and water have shifted sand, dust and silt right across the province. The land is farmed, as it has been for millennia, by slicing the hills into steps, creating a plain of ribbed hills that look like the realization of a cubist painting. The dwellings in this terrain often have mud walls, or are simply caves cut into vertical embankments, seemingly a part of the strange landscape. Great tracts of this land, though, are untillable, due to **soil erosion** caused by tree felling, and the uncertainty of rainfall, which has left much of the province fearsomely barren, an endless range of dusty hills cracked by fissures. Efforts are now being made to arrest erosion and the advance of the desert, including a huge tree-planting campaign. Sometimes you'll even see wandering dunes held in place by immense nets of woven straw.

Cave houses

A common sight among the folds and fissures of the dry loess plain of northern Shanxi (and neighbouring Shaanxi) are **cave dwellings**, a traditional form of housing that's been in use for nearly two thousand years. Hollowed into the sides of hills terraced for agriculture, they house more than eighty million people, and are eminently practical – cheap, easy to make, naturally insulated and long-lasting. In fact, a number of intact caves in Hejin, on the banks of the Yellow River in the west of the province, are said to date back to the Tang dynasty. Furthermore, in a region where flat land has to be laboriously hacked out of the hillside, caves don't take up land that could be cultivated.

The **facade** of the cave is usually a wooden frame on a brick base. Most of the upper part consists of a wooden lattice – designs of which are sometimes very intricate – faced with white paper, which lets in plenty of light, but preserves the occupants' privacy. Tiled eaves above protect the facade from rain damage. Inside, the **single-arched chamber** is usually split into a bedroom at the back and a living area in front, furnished with a *kang*, whose flue leads under the bed and then outside to the terraced field that is the roof. Sometimes the first visible indication of a distant village is a set of smoke columns rising from the crops.

Such is the popularity of cave homes that prosperous cave dwellers often prefer to build themselves a new courtyard and another cave rather than move into a house. Indeed, in the suburbs of towns and cities of northern Shaanxi, new **concrete apartment buildings** are built in imitation of caves, with three windowless sides and an arched central door. It is not uncommon even to see soil spread over the roofs of these apartments with vegetables grown on top.

Tourism staff in the province call Shanxi a "museum above the ground", a reference to the many unrestored but still intact **ancient buildings** that dot the region, some from dynasties almost unrepresented elsewhere in China, such as the Song and the Tang. In the same breath they call neighbouring Shaanxi a "museum under the ground", an unfair comment no doubt engendered by that province's greater popularity with tourists. Shanxi's unpopularity, despite its rich crop of historical buildings, can be put down to the grimness of its cities, dominated by the coal industry, and the relative inaccessibility of most of the province's fine constructions. Visitors usually restrict themselves to the main attraction: the **Yungang cave temples** at Datong, seven hours from Beijing, which are easily taken in en route to Hohhot in Inner Mongolia. Anyone who has time to explore the province further, however, is richly rewarded at **Wutai Shan**, a holy mountain in the northeast on the border with Hebei. Formerly difficult to reach (it's now only four hours by private minibus from Taiyuan, the nearest city), Wutai Shan's combination of ancient temples and breathtaking scenery make it one of the best mountain sites in the country, though continued tourism development will only further disturb this serenity. Although **Taiyuan** itself has few historic sights to boast of, the city is accustomed to tourists and a good base from which to move around the region. Farther south, all within a bus ride of the towns spread along the rail line between Taiyuan and Xi'an, are obscure little places, well off the predictable China trails, full of memorable sights. Particularly fine are a couple of superb temples, stuck out in the middle of nowhere, such as the **Shuanglin Si** outside Taiyuan, with its amazing sculptures, and the striking murals of the **Yongle Gong** at Ruicheng. At **Pingyao**, the walled town seems stuck in a time warp, its alleys lined with charming Qing-dynasty architecture. Once you venture far off the arterial rail line, travel becomes hard work, as roads and bus connections aren't good. You'll need to keep this in mind if you wish to make a diversion to the banks of the Yellow River, which runs down the western margin of the province. It's here, at **Hukou Falls**, that the river presents its fiercest aspect, which so impressed the Chinese that they put a picture of the torrent on the back of their fifty-yuan notes, though it's now been replaced by an image of Lhasa's Potala Palace.

❹ Datong and around

Don't be put off by first impressions of contemporary **DATONG**, the second largest city in Shanxi province, situated in the far north, near the border with Inner Mongolia. Amid a blasted landscape of modern industrial China – coal mines, power stations and a huge locomotive factory – are some marvellous ancient sites, remnants of the city's glory days as the capital city of two non-Han Chinese dynasties.

The Turkic Toba people took advantage of the internal strife afflicting central and southern China to establish their own dynasty, the **Northern Wei** (386–534), taking Datong as their capital in 398 AD, by which time they had conquered the whole of the north. Though the period was one of strife and warfare, the Northern Wei, who became fervent Buddhists, made some notable cultural achievements. The finest of these was a magnificent series of **cave temples** at Yungang, just west of the city, still one of the most impressive sights in northern China. Over the course of almost a century, more than one thousand grottoes were completed, containing over fifty thousand statues, before the capital was moved south to Luoyang, where construction began on the similar Longmen Caves.

A second period of greatness came with the arrival of the Mongol **Liao dynasty**, also Buddhists, who made Datong their capital in 907. They were

---

Datong and around

Datong	大同	*dàtóng*
Beijing Hundun	北京馄饨侯	*běijīng húntun hóu*
Datong Binguan	大同宾馆	*dàtóng bīnguǎn*
Feitian Bingguan	飞天宾馆	*fēitiān bīnguǎn*
Hongqi Hotel & Restaurant	红旗大饭店	*hóngqí dàfàndiàn*
Huayan Si	华严寺	*huáyán sì*
Nine Dragon Screen	九龙壁	*jiǔlóng bì*
Railway Binguan	火车宾馆	*huǒchē bīnguǎn*
Shanhua Si	善化寺	*shànhuà sì*
Yonghe Restaurant	永和大酒店	*yǒnghé dàjiǔdiàn*
Yungang Binguan	云冈宾馆	*yúngāng bīnguǎn*
Around Datong		
Yungang Caves	云冈石窟	*yúngāng shíkū*
Hunyuan	浑源	*húnyuán*
Hanging Temple	悬空寺	*xuánkōng sì*
Hengshan	恒山	*héngshān*
Hengshan Binguan	恒山宾馆	*héngshān bīnguǎn*
Yingxian	应县	*yìngxiàn*
Jincheng Binguan	金城宾馆	*jīnchéng bīnguǎn*
Wood Pagoda	应县木塔	*yìngxiàn mùtǎ*

assimilated into the Jin in 1125, but not before leaving a small legacy of statuary and some fine temple architecture, notably in the **Huayan and Shanhua temples** in town, and a **wooden pagoda**, the oldest in China, in the nearby town of Yingxian. Datong remained important to later Chinese dynasties for its strategic position just inside the Great Wall, south of Inner Mongolia, and the tall city walls date from the early Ming dynasty. Though most visitors today are attracted by the Buddhist sites, Datong is also the closest city to **Heng Shan**, one of the five holy mountains of Taoism, whose most spectacular building, the almost unbelievable **Hanging Temple**, is firmly on the tour agenda. It's also possible to use Datong as the jumping-off point for an excursion to the Buddhist centre of **Wutai Shan** (see p.240).

Datong now produces a third of all China's **coal**, enough to fuel the two power stations on the city's outskirts, one of which supplies electricity for Beijing, the other for the whole of Shanxi Province. Coal dominates the modern city – it sits in the donkey carts and lorries that judder up and down the main roads, it stains the buildings black and it swirls in the air you breathe, making Datong one of the most polluted cities in China. Once you have seen the caves and temples there's no reason to stay around, and a day or two here is enough. The city is well connected by rail, and by travelling on the evening sleeper trains Datong's major sights can be seen on a brief daytime stop between Beijing and Taiyuan.

Arrival, information and transport

Downtown Datong, bounded by square walls, is split by **Da Bei Jie** and **Da Xi Jie**, two dead-straight streets on north–south and east–west axes, which intersect at the heart of the city, just north of the old Drum Tower. The tourist sights are all within walking distance of the crossroads, while the two main tourist hotels are considerably farther south. The de facto town centre is at **Hongqi** (Red Flag) **Square**, on the corner of Da Xi Jie and Xinjian Nan Lu.

Datong's **train station** is on the city's northern edge, at the end of Da Bei Jie, far from any of the sights. A major railhead at the intersection of a line to Xi'an and the line between Beijing and Baotou, this is the first stop in China for trains from Mongolia, and it makes a harsh, disorientating introduction to the country. Grimy and cavernous, the station is usually thronged with passengers, many of them peasants migrating in search of construction work, their possessions tied up in grain sacks. Hotel touts wave signs at the crush of arriving passengers emerging from the platform gates on the station's west side. They mostly represent places that won't accept foreigners, though often they'll tell you they do. More usefully, you may be grabbed by a representative of the extremely helpful **station CITS window**, at first indistinguishable from the pushy touts and taxi drivers. If he misses you, the office, just inside the station entrance to the left, is a recommended first stop, a good place to get your bearings and meet other travellers and, unusually, to receive advice and information. **Long-distance buses** terminate just south of the train station on Xinjian Bei Lu, though if you're arriving from Hunyuan or other closer locations, you might be dropped off on a nameless street on the margins of town. The nearest passenger airport is in Taiyuan.

City transport

The train station is the origin of Datong's clutch of **bus routes** (¥1). Annoyingly, no single bus travels the length of the city's north–south axis, along which most places of interest to visitors are located. Bus #4 will get you from

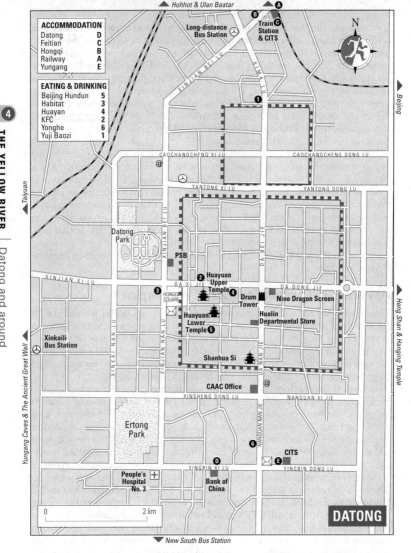

the station to the main crossroads, where it turns west, past the Huayan Si and Hongqi Square before terminating just outside the old city walls. To get from the crossroads to the southern hotels, take bus #17 from its terminus on the east side of Xiao Nan Jie. To get to these hotels direct from the train station, take bus #15, which travels south down Xinjian Nan Lu, then turns east on to Yingbin Xi Lu. For details of buses to places in the vicinity of Datong, see "Listings" p.235.

Taxis cruise the streets; flag fall is ¥5, and either ¥1.8 or ¥1.2 per km after that. A ride within town should be under ¥10. **Walking** around the city is tiring, as it's quite spread out and roads are tediously straight; also the air and noise pollution is astounding.

Accommodation

Budget accommodation is scarce in Datong, and your best bet is to book through the train station CITS (℡0352/7124882), who can book you a discounted rate. More than likely you'll end up at the *Feitian Binguan* (℡0352/2814348, ℱ2813483; ④), on the southeast side of the train-station square. Less than a kilometre north of the station, deep within a complex of railway administration buildings, is the *Railway Binguan* (℡0352/7169118; ④–⑤). From the station walk down the alley to the right as you exit the station and turn left at the second street. Turn right at the first main street and follow it to the end, where the hotel will be to the right. The *Hongqi Hotel* (℡0352/5366111; ⑤), 11 Zhanqian Jie, has a few rooms that are in the same price bracket as the *Railway Binguan* and boasts 24-hour hot water. The rate includes three meals per day in its restaurant, where locals and cadres are drawn to dine. The hotel is the neon-topped tower across the square and to the right as you exit the station.

Two more upmarket hotels are both in the south of the city, a long way from the centre. The refitted *Yungang Binguan*, at 21 Yingbin Dong Lu (℡0352/5021601, ℱ5024927; ⑥), is the most comfortable, and there's a foreign exchange, a post office and a coffee shop on the premises. Also refurbished, the *Datong Binguan* (℡0352/5868222, ℱ5868200; ⑦) is farther west on Yingbin Xi Lu and has similar facilities, catering to Yungang cave tourists. It has nicer surroundings than the *Yungang Hotel*, as it borders a new park and is across the street from a grocery store, bookseller, and several inexpensive restaurants.

The City

The yellow earthen **ramparts** that once bounded the old city are still quite impressive, though they have been heavily cut into and demolished in places as modern Datong has expanded. The best stretches are in the east of the city. Inside the walls, the few treasures that remain of Datong's considerably more prestigious past are off sombre streets lined with utilitarian buildings and walls painted with propaganda slogans. Outside the centre, the streets, along which Mao-suited men ride donkey carts brimming with coal, have a gritty, Dickensian feel which those who don't have to live here might just find appealing.

The Drum Tower and Nine Dragon Screen

Just south of the crossroads of Da Xi Jie and Da Bei Jie, at the heart of the city, Datong's three-storey **Drum Tower** dates back to the Ming dynasty. You can't go inside, but it makes a useful landmark. A little way east from the crossroads, on the south side of Da Dong Jie, the **Nine Dragon Screen** (7.30am–7.30pm; ¥10) stands in a courtyard a few metres back from the road, looking a little out of place without the palace it once stood in front of, which was destroyed by fire in the fifteenth century. Originally the eight-metre-high screen would have stood directly in front of the entrance, an unpassable obstacle to evil spirits which, it was thought, could only travel in straight lines. The raised relief of nine sinuous dragons depicted in 426 glazed tiles along its forty-five-metre surface, rising from the waves and cavorting among suns, is lively and colourful. Underneath, the dragons and other animals, real and imaginary, are depicted in a separate, much smaller, relief. A long, narrow pool in front of the screen is meant to reflect the dragons and give the illusion of movement when you look into its rippling surface.

Huayan Si

About a kilometre west of the Dragon Screen is **Huayan Si**, originally a large temple dating back to 1062 AD during the Liao dynasty, and reached by an alley leading south off Da Xi Jie across from *KFC*; look for the temple's roofs, visible above the surrounding low shops. The remaining buildings, mostly Qing, are split into two complexes. The **Upper Temple** (daily 8am–6.30pm; ¥20), the first one you come to, is a little shabby, but with some interesting details, and the odd monk wandering around. Look for the unusual roof decoration on the first building – elephants carrying pagodas on their backs – and the small handmade shrines that have been placed in the temple courtyard by modern worshippers. Set on a four-metre-high platform and recently restored, the huge twelfth-century **Main Hall** is one of the two largest Buddhist halls in China, and is unusual for facing east – it was originally built by a sect that worshipped the sun. The design at the end of the roof ridge curves inwards like a horn, a rare design peculiar to the region. Inside, five Ming Buddhas, made of stucco or wood and painted gold, sit on elaborate painted thrones, attended by twenty life-size guardians, some of whom look Indian in appearance, gently inclined as if listening attentively. Qing-dynasty frescoes on the walls, depicting Buddha's attainment of nirvana, and nearly one thousand roof panels depicting flowers, Sanskrit letters and dragons, have been repainted in their original gaudy hues. Turn right out of the entrance to this complex and you come to the **Lower Temple** (daily 8am–6.30pm; ¥20), notable for its rugged-looking hall, a rare Liao-dynasty construction from 1038, according to an inscription on a roof beam. Inside, a varied collection of 31 stucco Buddhas and Bodhisattvas, with elegantly carved drapery and delicate features, also Liao, sit gathering dust in the gloom.

Shanhua Si

From Huayan Si, it's an enjoyable twenty-minute meander past shops and restaurants along Da Nan Jie to the **Shanhua Si** (daily 8am–6pm; ¥30). A temple stood here since the Tang dynasty, though what you see is a Ming restoration of a Jin building. The two halls, with little decoration, thick russet walls and huge, chunky wooden brackets in the eaves, have a solid presence very different from the delicate look of later Chinese temples. The Jin-dynasty statues in the main hall, five Buddhas in the centre with 24 *lokapalas* (divine generals) lined up on either side, are exceptionally finely detailed. Look for the Mother of Ghosts, a matronly woman of benign expression, with a small green, impish figure with long teeth, carrying a child on its shoulder, standing at her feet. According to myth, the Mother of Ghosts was an evil woman who ate children until Buddha kidnapped her son. She was so racked with grief that when Buddha returned the child she agreed to devote her life to good deeds; the imp is a depiction of her evil side. A wooden building, in the west of the complex, is Tang in style, with three storeys and a double roof, and is impressive just for its longevity – an inscription on a beam inside records its construction in 1154.

Eating and drinking

Datong is far enough north for mutton hotpot to figure heavily in the local cuisine, along with potatoes, which you can buy, processed into a starchy jelly and seasoned with sauces, from street stalls. Other typically northern dishes available are *zongyi* (glutinous rice dumplings) and *yuanxiao* (sweet dumplings). **Snacks** made from oatmeal are on sale from friendly buskers around Hongqi Square and Da Xi Jie. There are also plenty of cheap eating places north of the train station, serving bowls of noodles and steaming meat dumplings. If you have some extra time, walk down to the *Yuji Baozi* shop on Xima Lu, a packed-out local affair with great food and friendly staff.

You won't find any gourmet food in Datong, but you can sample local fare at the *Huayan Restaurant*, one block east of the temple on Da Xi Jie. *KFC* is nearby, on the same road. Other options in the vicinity are found south of the Drum Tower on Da Nan Jie, where there are noodle and wonton shops near the Hualin department store – *Beijing Hundun* is a popular place. Farther south on Nanguan Nan Jie, the *Yonghe Restaurant*, 2km south of the Drum Tower, is vibrant and plush; expect to pay around ¥30 for two dishes with rice, tea and beer. Wherever you eat, make sure you get there early – restaurants begin closing around 9pm. For a pint and **pub food**, try the expat-oriented *Habitat* on Xinjian Nan Lu, across from Hongqi Square. Datong's latest **clubs** can be found near the Drum Tower on Da Nan Jie and Da Xi Jie.

Listings

Airlines The CAAC office (☏0352/2044039) is on 1 Nanguan Nan Jie (daily 8.30am–5pm), with another office in the *Yungang Binguan*. Note, however, that flights leave from Taiyuan, well to the south.

Banks and exchange The only place to cash traveller's cheques is at the main Bank of China (Mon–Fri 8am–6pm) on Yingbin Xi Lu opposite the *Datong Binguan*. If you're staying at either *Datong Binguan* or the *Yungang Binguan*, you can exchange money or cash traveller's cheques until 7pm – non-guests can only exchange cash.

Buses Buses for most points leave from the bus station on Yantong Xilu, including Taiyuan, Hunyuan, and a direct bus to Hengshan/Hanging Temple that leaves at 7.30am. Regular services to Wutai Shan (3–4 per day) leave from the bus station on Xinjian Bei Lu about 1km from the train station. Buses to Yingxian leave from the new south bus station. Buses to Taiyuan and Wutai Shan also ply the train-station concourse. The public bus station is in Xinkaili, a neighbourhood in the west of town and the terminus of bus #4 from the train station; this is where to catch the #3 bus to the Yungang Caves.

Hospital People's Hospital No. 3 is in the south of the city on Yingbin Xi Lu, just west of the cross-roads with Xinjian Nan Lu.

Internet access Internet cafés can be found on Da Nan Jie, and on the eastern side of Hongqi Square.

Left luggage There's a left-luggage office outside the train station on the western side of the concourse (¥5).

Mail and telephones The large Russian-look-ing stately building fronting Hongqi Square, south of Da Xi Jie, houses both the post office (daily 8am–6pm) and a 24hr telecom office. Droves of laid-off women stand about selling cut-rate IC and IP phone cards.

PSB The police station (Mon–Sat 8.30am–noon & 2.30–6pm) is on Xinjian Bei Lu, 200m north of the post office; take along a Mandarin-speaker since they're not particularly heedful to traveller needs. If you have anything stolen, insist on getting a loss report.

Shopping There's a small antiques mall across from Nine Dragon Screen. Clothing shops line Da Xi Jie. The streets around Huayuan Si are also full with souvenirs and "antiques".

Trains Tickets are straightforward enough to buy at the station, or at the advance ticket office (8am–12.30pm & 2.30–6pm) at the corner of Nanguan Nan Jie and Nanguan Xi Jie. At the back of the station opposite the door, there's a comfortable waiting room (¥5) with armchairs and TV.

Travel agents The main CITS office (daily 6.30am–6pm; ☏0352/7124882), on the eastern side of the concourse of the *Yungang Binguan*, deals with tour groups and provides guides. The more useful train station CITS window (daily 6.30am–6.30pm; ☏0352/5101326), inside the station entrance and to the left, is particularly helpful and they'll book same-day train tickets for a ¥40 charge. Their tours of the major sights out of town are worth considering (¥100 per person to the Hanging Temple and the Wood Pagoda).

Around Datong

The sights outside the city are far more diverting than those within. Apart from the glorious **Yungang Caves**, the ancient buildings dotted around in nearby country towns are worth checking out. Roads in the area are not good (and are often blocked in winter, when transport times can be as much as doubled), but at least journeys are enlivened by great views: the lunar emptiness of the fissured landscape is broken only occasionally by villages whose mud walls seem to grow out of the raw brown earth. Some of the villages in the area still have their beacon towers, left over from when this really was a wild frontier.

To help explore the area around the city, buy a **map** of Datong (¥3) from outside the bus station, as this includes maps of Hunyuan and Yingxian, together with train timetables on the back. Getting around to all the sites on teeth-rattling public buses can be time-consuming, so if time is tight, consider taking a **CITS tour**. They run a combined day excursion from Datong to the **Yungang Caves** and the **Hanging Temple** for ¥145–450, depending upon group size. They also do a daily tour of the caves and the **Hanging Temple**. This leaves daily at 8am and returns in the evening. During the tour, the minibus also stops briefly in a village of squat, mud-walled houses and cave dwellings. Again, costs vary depending on numbers, but expect to pay around ¥150 including an English-speaking guide and lunch but excluding tickets at each sight. Tours are easier to book at the more helpful train station CITS office.

The Yungang Caves

Just twenty-five minutes by bus from Datong, the monumental **Yungang Caves** (daily 8am–6.30pm; ¥60), a set of Buddhist grottoes carved into the side of a sandstone cliff 16km west of the city, are a must. Built around 400 AD at a time of Buddhist revival, the caves were the first and grandest of the three major Buddhist grottoes (the latter two being the Longmen Caves in Luoyang and the Mogao Caves in Gansu); they also remain the best preserved. Access is straightforward: take **bus** #4 from the train station to its terminus at the Xinkaili bus station in the west of the city, then transfer to bus #3 (¥1.5), which terminates at the caves.

Building the Yungang Caves

Construction of the Yungang Caves began in 453 AD, when Datong was the capital of the Wei dynasty, and petered out around 525, after the centre of power moved to Luoyang. The caves were made by first hollowing out a section at the top of the cliff, then digging into the rock, down to the ground and out, leaving two holes, one above the other. As many as forty thousand craftsmen worked on the project, coming from as far as India and Central Asia, and there is much foreign influence in the **carvings**: Greek motifs (tridents and acanthus leaves), Persian symbols (lions and weapons), and bearded figures, even images of the Hindu deities Shiva and Vishnu, are incorporated among the more common dragons and phoenixes of Chinese origin. The soft, rounded modelling of the **sandstone Datong figures** – China's first stone statues – lining the cave interiors has more in common with the terracotta carvings of the Mogao Caves near Dunhuang in Gansu, begun a few years earlier, than with the sharp, more linear features of Luoyang's later limestone work. In addition, a number of the seated Buddhas have sharp, almost Caucasian noses.

The caves' present condition is misleading, as originally the cave entrances would have been covered with wooden facades, and the sculptures would have been faced with plaster and brightly painted; the larger sculptures are pitted with regular holes, which would once have held wooden supports on which the plaster face was built. Over the centuries, some of the caves have inevitably suffered from weathering, though there seems to have been little vandalism, certainly less than at Luoyang.

Arranged in three **clusters** (east, central and west) and numbered east to west from 1–51, the caves originally spread across an area more than 15km long. What you see today is but a small fragment site stretching 1km. If it's spectacle you're after, just wander at will, but to get an idea of the changes of style and the accumulation of influences, you need to move between the three clusters. The earliest group is caves 16–20, followed by 7, 8, 9 and 10, then 5, 6 and 11 – the last to be completed before the court moved to Luoyang. Then followed 4, 13, 14 and 15, with the caves at the eastern end – 1, 2 and 3 – and cave 21 in the west, carved last. Caves 22–50 are smaller and less interesting.

The eastern caves

The easternmost late caves are slightly set apart from, and less spectacular than, the others. **Caves 1 and 2** are constructed around a single square central pillar, elaborately carved in imitation of a wooden stupa but now heavily eroded, around which devotees perambulated. **Cave 3**, 25m deep, is the largest in Yungang; an almost undecorated cavern, it may once have been used as a lecture hall. The three statues at the west end, a ten-metre-high Buddha and his two attendants, are skilfully carved and in good condition. The rounded fleshiness of their faces, with double chins and thick, sensuous lips, hints at their late construction as they are characteristic of Tang-dynasty images. In **Cave 4**, which again has a central pillar carved with images of Buddha, there's a well-preserved, cross-legged Maitreya Buddha on the west wall.

The central caves

The most spectacular caves are numbers 5–13, dense with **monumental sculpture**. Being suddenly confronted and dwarfed by a huge, seventeen-metre-high Buddha as you walk into **cave 5**, his gold face shining softly in the half light, is an awesome, humbling experience. His other-worldly appearance is helped by blue hair and ruby red lips. Other Buddhas of all sizes, a heavenly gallery, are massed in niches which honeycomb the grotto's gently curving walls, and two Bodhisattvas stand attentive at his side.

Cave 6, though very different, is just as arresting. A wooden facade built in 1652 leads into a high, square chamber dominated by a thick central pillar carved with Buddhas and Bodhisattvas in deep relief, surrounded by flying Buddhist angels and musicians. The vertical grotto walls are alive with images, including reliefs depicting incidents from the **life of the Buddha** at just above head height, which were designed to form a narrative when read walking clockwise around the chamber. Easy-to-identify scenes at the beginning include the birth of the Buddha from his mother's armpit, and Buddha's father carrying the young infant on an elephant. The young prince's meeting with a fortune-teller – here an emaciated man with a sharp goatee, who (the story goes) predicted he would become an ascetic if confronted by disease, death and old age – is shown on the north side of the pillar. In an attempt to thwart this destiny, his father kept him in the palace all through his youth. Buddha's first trip out of the palace, which is depicted as a schematic, square Chinese building, is shown on the east wall of the cave, as is his meeting with the grim realities of life, in this case a cripple with two crutches.

Caves 7 and 8 are a pair, both square, with two chambers, and connected by an arch lined with angels and topped with what looks like a sunflower. The figures here, such as the six celestial worshippers above the central arch, are more Chinese in style than their predecessors in caves 16–20, perhaps indicating the presence of craftsmen from Gansu, which the Wei conquered in 439 AD. Two figures on either side of the entrance to cave 8 are some of the best carved and certainly the most blatantly foreign in the complex: a five-headed, six-armed Shiva sits on a bird on the left as you enter, while on the right, a three-headed Vishnu sits on a bull. These Indian figures have distinctly Chinese features, however, and the bird, a garuda in Hindu mythology, is identical to the Chinese phoenix.

The columns and lintels at the entrances of **caves 9, 10 and 12** are awash with sculptural detail in faded pastel colours: Buddhas, dancers, musicians, animals, flowers, angels and abstract, decorative flourishes (which bear a resemblance to Persian art). Parts of cave 9 are carved with imitation brackets to make the interior resemble a wooden building. The tapering columns at the entrance to cave 12 are covered with tiny Buddhas, but look out for the cluster of musicians with strange-looking instruments depicted behind them.

The outstretched right arm of the fifteen-metre-high Buddha inside **cave 13** had to be propped up for stability, so his sculptors ingeniously carved the supporting pillar on his knee into a four-armed mini-Buddha. The badly eroded sculptures of **caves 14 and 15** are stylistically some way between the massive figures of the early western caves and the smaller reliefs of the central caves.

The western caves

Compared to the images in the central caves, the figures in these, the **earliest caves** (nos. 16–20) are simpler and bolder, and though they are perhaps more crudely carved, they are at least as striking. The **giant Buddhas**, with round faces, sharp noses, deep eyes and thin lips, are said to be the representations of five emperors. Constructed between 453 and 462 AD, under the supervision of the monk Tan Hao, all are in the same pattern of an enlarged niche containing a massive Buddha flanked by Bodhisattvas. The Buddha in **cave 16**, whose bottom half has disintegrated, has a knotted belt high on his chest, Korean-style. The Buddhas were carved from the top down, and when the sculptors of the Buddha in **cave 17** reached ground level they needed to dig down to fit his feet in. The same problem was solved in **cave 18** by giving the Buddha shortened legs. Despite the stumpy limbs, this is still one of the finest sculptures in the complex, in which charming details, including the rows of tiny Bodhisattvas carved into his robe, are set off by strong sweeping forms, such as the simplified planes of his face. The fourteen-metre-high Buddha in **cave 20**, sitting open to the elements in a niche that once would have been protected by a wooden canopy, is probably the most famous, and certainly the most photographed. The figure is characteristic of Northern Wei art, with the folds of his garments expressed by an ordered pattern, and his physiognomy and features formed by simple curves and straight lines. His huge ears almost touch his shoulders.

The small caves 20–50, the least spectacular of the set, are not much visited, but the ceiling of **cave 50** is worth a look for its flying elephants, which also appear in cave 48, and in caves 50 and 51 there are sculptures of acrobats.

Heng Shan and the Hanging Temple

Heng Shan (8am–6pm; ¥35, plus ¥20 to enter mountain area) is part of a 250-kilometre-long range curling east to west around northern Shanxi Province and is one of the five holy Taoist mountains in China. The mountain's history as a religious centre stretches back more than two thousand years, and plenty of emperors have put in an appearance here to climb the highest peak, Xuanwu (2000m), a trend begun by the very first emperor, Qin Shi Huang. From the base of the mountain, an easy climb takes you to Heng Shan's main temple, **Hengzong Si**, via switchbacking paths through other smaller temples, about a thirty-minute walk up and twenty minutes down (a cable-car round trip costs

¥42). Hengshan's peak lies another forty minutes uphill from Hengzong Si, and might be the quietest place left on the mountain.

The **Hanging Temple** (Xuankong Si; daily 7am–6pm; ¥50) is on the valley road that runs up to Heng Shan, and you'll probably stop here first if you're on a tour. Clinging perilously halfway up the side of a sheer cliff face, the temple (its name literally translates as "Temple Suspended in the Void") is anchored to the cliff walls with wooden beams set into the rock. There's been a temple on this site since the Northern Wei, though the present structure is mostly Qing. Periodically, the temple buildings were destroyed by the flooding of the Heng River at the base of the cliff (now no longer there, thanks to a dam farther upstream), and at each successive rebuilding, the temple was built higher and higher. It's at its best from a distance, when its dramatic, gravity-defying location can be more fully appreciated. The temple reveals itself as a bit of a tourist trap as you get closer, with the usual gauntlet of souvenir stalls crowding the ticket area; in summer, dense crowds turn the Hanging Temple into a claustrophobe's nightmare. Tall, narrow stairs and plank walkways connect the six halls – natural caves and ledges with wooden facades – in which, uniquely, shrines exist to all three of China's main religions, Confucianism, Buddhism and Taoism, all of whose major figures are represented in nearly eighty statues in the complex, made from bronze, iron and stone. In the Three Religions Hall, at the top of the complex, statues of Confucius, Buddha and Lao Zi are seated happily together.

Practicalities

Contemporary pilgrims usually set out from the small country town of **Hunyuan**, 75km southeast of Datong and 5km north of the Hanging Temple. **Buses** (1hr; ¥10) run from the Datong long-distance bus station and take about an hour, terminating just opposite the expensive *Hengshan Binguan* (T0352/8320925; ❸), where you'll find some mouldy doubles. To get **to Heng Shan** and **to the Hanging Temple**, you can catch a public tourist bus (¥2) from the town to the base of the temple area. Transportation gets more difficult to arrange in low travel seasons, when it might make more sense to book a cab for the round trip (around ¥50 including waiting time).

Be aware that minibus touts at Datong's train station who say they're headed **to the Hanging Temple** will most likely drop you at Hunyuan, where there are also frequent minibuses (¥2) to the gravel road at the temple entrance.

To return to Hunyuan from the Hanging Temple or Heng Shan, be prepared to haggle with the vehicles for hire, which start at ¥20. The last bus back to Datong leaves Hunyuan at 6pm, though note that it's possible to stay the night in Hunyuan and get a ride on to Wutai Shan on the 9am bus from Datong: ask at the Hengshan Binguan.

The Wood Pagoda

At the centre of the small town of **YINGXIAN**, 75km south of Datong, the stately **Wood Pagoda** (daily 8am–6pm; ¥42), built in 1056 in the Liao dynasty, is the oldest wooden building in China, a masterful piece of structural engineering that looks solid enough to stand here for another millennium. The "Woody Tower," as the English sign explains, reaches nearly 70m high and is octagonal in plan, with nine internal storeys, though there are only six layers of eaves on the outside. You can climb up only as far as the second storey, but it's definitely worth going inside to get a closer look at the structure.

The first storey is taller than the rest with extended eaves held up by columns forming a cloister around a mud-and-straw wall. The original pagoda was constructed without a single metal nail, though there are plenty in the floors now. The ceilings and walls of the spacious internal halls are networks of beams held together with huge, intricate **wooden brackets**, called *dougongs*, of which there are nearly sixty different kinds. Interlocking, with their ends carved into curves and layered one on top of another, these give the pagoda a burly, muscular appearance, and as structural supports they perform their function brilliantly – the building has survived seven earthquakes.

Originally each storey had a statue inside, but now only one remains, an eleven-metre-tall Buddha with facial hair and stretched-out earlobes – characteristic of northern ethnic groups, such as the Khitan, who came to power in Shanxi during the Liao dynasty (916–1125 AD). During a recent renovation a cache of treasures was found buried underneath the pagoda, including Buddhist sutras printed using woodblocks dating back to the Liao dynasty.

Local **buses** to Yingxian from Datong (¥10) take two hours and leave from the long-distance bus station. Yingxian's **bus station** is on the western section of the town's main east–west road, about 1km southwest of the pagoda. You can stay the night in Yingxian at the *Jinchen Binguan* (18 Xinjian Nanlu; ℡0349/5022013; ❸), about 2km south of the pagoda on the main north–south road. From Yingxian, there are buses to Hunyuan, about 50km away, for Heng Shan and the Hanging Temple; these leave every hour until 5pm – also the time of the last bus back to Datong. Alternatively, if you start early you can just about manage to see both the Hanging Temple and the Wood Pagoda by public transport in one (long) day.

Wutai Shan

One of China's four Buddhist mountains, the five flat peaks of **Wutai Shan** – the name means "Five-terrace Mountain" – rise around 3000m above sea level in the northeast corner of Shanxi Province, near the border with Hebei. An isolated spot, it rewards the long bus ride it takes to get here with fresh air, superb alpine scenery, some of the best temple architecture in China, decent accommodation and a peaceful, spiritual tone, though these days development has already had a noticeable impact; and once the highway and rail spur into the area are completed in the next two years, it's likely to become a bit of a tourist circus.

However, the mountain's inaccessibility has always given it a degree of protection, and many of the temples survived the Cultural Revolution intact. Most of the forty temples remaining today are in the monastic village of **Taihuai**, which sits in a depression surrounded by the five holy peaks. Highlights are the ninth-century **revolving bookcase** of the Tayuan Si and the **two ancient temples**, the Song-dynasty Foguan and the Tang-dynasty Nanchan. All the temples today are working, and shaven-headed monks in orange and brown robes conducting esoteric ceremonies or perambulating around the stupas are a common sight – as, increasingly, are tour buses and cadres lumbering in to watch them. Developers have taken heed of Jiang Zemin's call to "make Wutai famous" (an order since posted next to an image of the former president on a towering billboard at the entrance to Taihuai) by starting to build massive villas along the valley. So, too, has the local Party branch, which installed a **Mao Zedong Memorial Hall** – housing a ceramic bust of the sworn atheist – at the heart of the main temple, which most visitors tactfully seem to avoid.

Wutai Shan

Wutai Shan	五台山	wǔtái shān
Bishan Si	碧山寺	bìshān sì
Dailuo Ding	黛螺顶	dàiluó dǐng
Falei Si	法雷寺	fǎléi sì
Foguang Si	佛光寺	fóguāng sì
Jinge Si	金阁寺	jīngé sì
Lingying Si	灵应寺	língyīng sì
Longquan Si	龙泉寺	lóngquán sì
Nanchan Si	南禅寺	nánchán sì
Nanshan Si	南山寺	nánshān sì
Puji Si	普济寺	pǔjì sì
Pusa Ding	菩萨顶	púsà dǐng
Shancai Dong	善财洞	shàncái dòng
Shuxiang Si	数象寺	shùxiàng sì
Tayuan Si	塔院寺	tǎyuàn sì
Wanfo Hall	万佛阁	wànfó gé
Wanghai Si	望海寺	wànghǎi sì
Xiantong Si	显通寺	xiǎntōng sì
Yanjiao Si	演教寺	yǎnjiàosì
Zhenhai Si	镇海寺	zhènhǎi sì
Taihuai	台怀	táihuái
China Post Hotel	邮政宾馆	yóuzhèng bīnguǎn
Fudeyuan	福德院	fúdé yuàn
Luohou Si	罗侯寺	luóhóu sì
Number Five Hostel	第五招待所	dìwǔ zhāodàisuǒ
Railway Hostel	铁路招待所	tiělù zhāodàisuǒ

Some history

Wutai Shan was one of the earliest sites where Buddhism took hold in China, and it's been a religious centre at least since the reign of Emperor Ming Di (58–75 AD) when, according to legend, an Indian monk arrived at the mountain and had a vision in which he met the **Manjusri Buddha**. Each Buddhist mountain is dedicated to a particular Bodhisattva, and Wutai Shan became dedicated to Manjusri (also known as the Wenchu Buddha), god of wisdom, who is depicted riding a lion and carrying a manuscript (to represent a sutra) and a sword to cleave ignorance. By the time of the Northern Wei, Wutai Shan was a prosperous Buddhist centre, important enough to be depicted on a mural at the Dunhuang Caves in Gansu. The mountain reached its height of popularity in the Tang dynasty, when there were more than two hundred temples scattered around its peaks, in which monks devoted themselves to the study of the Avatamsaka sutra, which contained references to "a pure and fresh mountain in the northeast" where Manjusri once resided, thought to be Wutai Shan. The number of temples declined in the late Tang, when Buddhism was persecuted, but the mountain enjoyed a second upsurge of popularity in the Ming dynasty, when it found imperial favour; Emperor Kangxi was a frequent visitor. In the fifteenth century, the founder of the Tibetan **Yellow Hat** sect, which emphasizes austerity and rigour over the more indulgent, less doctrinaire, earlier Red Hat sect, came to the area to preach; the Manjusri Buddha is particularly important in Tibetan and Mongolian Buddhism, and Wutai Shan became an important pilgrimage place for Lamaists.

Practicalities

The best way to avoid the crowds is to visit between October and April, when the weather turns cold and domestic tour buses head elsewhere. This does, however, mean banking on the weather holding up. Wutai Shan's remote alpine location means a **winter** trip could well be uncomfortable, and even in **spring**, temperatures can fall well below freezing and transport times can double due to treacherous roads (blizzards occur well into April). Even if you keep a close eye on conditions, you'll need to be prepared for unpredictable weather whatever the time of year. Climbing the peaks shouldn't present many difficulties as there are paths everywhere, but do allow plenty of time for journeys, as the paths are hard to find in the dark and the temperature drops sharply at sundown.

Getting to Wutai Shan

While Wutai Shan is the name of the cultural heritage site, **Taihuai** village, the mountain's tourist and pilgrim settlement, is for transportation purposes your destination. All tourists are charged a mandatory ¥90 **admission fee** upon entering the Wutai Shan area. Your bus tout may claim he can sell you a discounted entrance ticket as part of your fare, but you'll invariably be charged the fee again once you arrive at the checkpoint.

From Beijing

Taihuai is just over an hour's bus ride south from **Shahe**, a town on the Beijing–Taiyuan **rail** line whose train station is named "Wutai Shan". The best train is the overnight #N201, which puts you in Wutai Shan station at around 6.30am, when you can hop on a waiting minibus (¥20) or share a taxi for the ride into Taihuai (¥100–150). Sleeper tickets back to Beijing can be hard to get in Taihuai, so check at Taihuai CITS for help.

From Datong

The bus trip from Datong to Taihuai is a five-hour ride (¥50), climaxing at a mountain pass not far from the northern peak and Wanghai Si; in winter this road is usually impassable, and almost always bumpy and delayed (check with Datong CITS before you leave). Some buses might stop at the Hanging Temple or other sites along the way, so check before buying a ticket. It's worth considering taking a slow overnight train from Datong to Taiyuan, then immediately hopping on a bus bound for Wutai from the Taiyuan train-station concourse. This saves a night's accommodation and puts you at Taihuai well before noon.

From Taiyuan

The road trip from Taiyuan, 240km to the southwest of Taihuai, takes four hours up the lower, southern approach road, passing close to the remote and superb Nanchan and Foguang temples. Cheap local **buses** leave frequently until early afternoon, but the slightly more expensive tourist buses (¥44) are worth seeking out, as they're less likely to troll for extra passengers along the way. You can also make it to Taihuai from **Xinzhou**, which lies on the rail line between Datong and Taiyuan, and from where buses (¥30) take two to three hours, travelling up the southern route. If you've chosen the cheap bus from Taiyuan, your bus may drop passengers here, transferring you to another bus for the final approach.

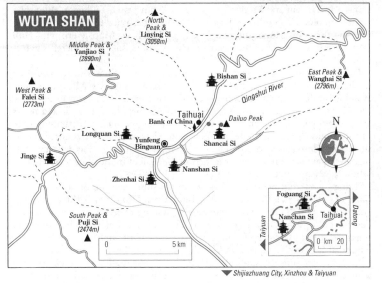

WUTAI SHAN

North
Peak &
Linying Si
(3058m)

Middle Peak &
Yanjiao Si
(2890m)

Bishan Si

East Peak &
Wanghai Si
(2796m)

West Peak &
Falei Si
(2773m)

Qingshui River

Taihuai
Bank of China

Dailuo Peak

Longquan Si

Yunfeng
Binguan

Shancai Si

Jinge Si

Nanshan Si

Zhenhai Si

N

South Peak &
Puji Si
(2474m)

0   5 km

Foguang Si

Nanchan Si   Taihuai

Taiyuan

Datong

0 km 20

Shijiazhuang City, Xinzhou & Taiyuan

Taihuai and around

An unusual little place, **TAIHUAI** is a strip of tourist facilities and temples set along the west bank of a river, surrounded by green hills which rise to the blue mountains of Wutai Shan on the horizon. The village has grown up around a central cluster of temples; the gently curling grey roofs, decorative double eaves and pagodas are so thick on the ground that it's hard to tell where one temple ends and another begins. The surrounding streets are busy with tourist-hectoring stallholders, clusters of slow-moving monks, wandering pilgrims and fortune-tellers sitting at the roadside.

The village temples

A good point of orientation in Taihuai is the chubby statue of Milarepa in the centre square. Facing uphill, to the right, sits the **Luohou Si** (¥4), a Ming-dynasty reconstruction of a Tang temple. Crowds gather to gawk at the spinning round wooden altar in the main hall with a wave design at its base supporting a large wooden lotus with movable petals. A mechanism underneath opens the petals to reveal four Buddhas sitting inside the flower.

Taihuai's most distinctive feature – and the symbol of the village – sits just uphill: the fifty-metre-tall, Tibetan-style **White Stupa** of the **Tayuan Si** (¥4). Its bulbous, whitewashed peak, sitting on a large square base, rises high above the grey roofs, and the chimes of the 250 bells hung from its bronze top can be heard across the town when the wind is strong. The largest of many such bottle-shaped pagodas on Wutai Shan, it testifies to the importance of the mountain to Tibetan and Mongolian Lamaism, which is also represented by the tall wooden poles with bronze caps standing inside many of the temple's entrances.

Inside the temple and behind the pagoda, a Ming-dynasty, two-storey library was built to house a bizarre and beautiful revolving wooden **bookcase**, much older than the rest of the complex and still in use today. Its 33 layers of shelves, split into cubbyholes and painted with decorative designs, hold volumes of sutras – in Tibetan and Mongolian as well as Chinese – including a Ming sutra written in blood, and others whose ink is made of crushed precious stones. Not far from the main gate of the temple is the **Chairman Mao Memorial Hall** (¥2), whose placement at the heart of one of Buddhism's most sacred sights is in decidedly poor taste.

The **Xiantong Si** (¥5), just uphill from the Tayuan Si, is said to date back to the Eastern Han (52 AD), although the present complex is Ming and Qing. Among the four hundred rooms is a hall made entirely of bronze, complete with brackets and hinges in imitation of fine timberwork. Its walls and doors are covered with animal and flower designs on the outside and rank upon rank of tiny Buddhas on the inside, along with an elegant bronze Manjusri Buddha sitting on a human-faced lion. The temple is also known for the delicacy of its brickwork, which can be seen at its best in the Hall of Immeasurable Splendour, whose eaves are built in imitation of wooden brackets.

Sitting on the hill behind Luohou Si atop a stone staircase of 108 steps (the number of beads on a Buddhist rosary) is the **Pusa Ding** (¥5), a Ming and Qing complex in which emperors Kangxi and Qianlong once stayed. This is a great destination for a first day in town, as it affords an aerial view of the valley and is a good way to warm up for longer hikes to higher temples.

Back at the centre square, follow Yanglin Jie to the road and parking lot behind Tayuan Si to the southwest. Here sits **Wanfo Hall** (¥4), which contains a huge number of Buddhist statues. Outside it sit two Tibetan-style stone pagodas. Farther south, the **Shuxiang Si** (¥4) is the largest in Wutai Shan, a Qing restoration of a Tang building, notable for a bronze Manjusri Buddha flanked by five hundred *lohans*.

Practicalities

Buses terminate at the north end of Taihuai, or at the bus station 2km south on Taihuai Jie. If you end up at the bus station, hop on a public bus (6am–9pm; ¥2) into town, or make the 20-minute walk north. If you end up on the street, it's a quick walk downhill to the centre of town. Northbound buses to Datong (¥50) leave from the main street between 7am and 2pm. Buses to Taiyuan (¥44) leave from the bus station. If enough people show up, a one-day tour (¥80, transportation only) to the Hanging Temple, Hengshan and perhaps the Wood Pagoda – ending in Datong – leaves from a guesthouse across the street from the north CITS office. In the same area, you can hire a car and driver for ¥350–400 for the day's trip back to Datong, with stops at any of the sites mentioned north of here – again, entry fees, scenic area fees and parking fees are not included (¥200 for a direct trip to Datong). Buses departing in the morning park at various north-end guesthouses the night before, making it easy to spot the next day's trip out of town (put off buying tickets until you depart).

A good budget **place to stay** near the centre of town is the *Number Five Hostel* (☏0350/6545373; ❸), across the road and just south of the central parking lot (avoid the eastern "karaoke wing"). Across the road to the north from the bus park is the *Railway Hostel* (☏0350/6542041; ❸), a comfortable and quiet place tucked away from the masses; to get here from the bus stop, walk towards Pusa Ding and a few metres on from its entry steps the lane bends right towards the hotel. The *China Post Hotel* (☏0350/6545052; ❻) is counterintuitively comfortable, with clean rooms right in the centre of town, next to the post office on Yanling Jie, just south of Milarepa Square. This area is slated for major redevelopment, but the hotels on the main road are more likely to survive. Many pilgrims stay in the temples themselves, most of which have rudimentary facilities for guests, and this may also be possible for foreigners.

It's less likely you'll be offered a homestay these days, though that still might be worth a shot.

Though **restaurants** are in abundance in Wutai, food here is almost universally expensive and mediocre – expect to pay ¥10 for a vegetarian dish, double that for meat; rice and tea cost extra. The throng of street stalls that sprout around the parking lots after dusk isn't especially hygienic, and it's best to seek out a lively-looking restaurant like the *Fudeyuan* which faces the square on the north side and serves a standard, if overpriced, menu of rice dishes. A number of vegetarian places line the main street north of the square.

Outlying temples

Few of the local tourists get very far out of Taihuai; it's certainly worth the effort, however, as not just the temples, but also the views and the scenery, are gorgeous. The following are all within an easy day's hike from Taihuai. You can also hire a "tour taxi" at the central parking lot for transportation to any combination of sights, ranging from ¥48 for a ten-stop tour to ¥165 for eight of the farthest sights. Posted day rates to hire a car are ¥380 for a half-day, though you can probably negotiate fares well below that on the street.

The **Nanshan Si** (¥4) sits in a leafy spot halfway up the Yangbai Mountain 5km south of Taihuai. It's approached by a steep flight of stairs, its entrance marked by a huge screen wall of cream-coloured brick. More decorated brickwork inside, including fake brackets and images of deities in flowing robes, is the temple's most distinctive feature. Eighteen Ming images of *lohans* in the main hall are unusually lifelike and expressive; one gaunt figure is sleeping with his head propped up on one knee, his skin sagging over his fleshless bones.

Two kilometres southwest of here, the **Zhenhai Si** (¥4), sitting in a beautiful leafy spot at an altitude of 1600m just off the road, seems an odd place to build a temple celebrating the prevention of floods, although legend has it that Manjusri tamed the water of the spring that now trickles past the place. During the Qing dynasty a monk called Zhang Jia, reputed to be the living Buddha, lived here; he is commemorated with a small pagoda south of the temple.

The **Longquan Si** (¥4) is on the west side of the Qingshui River, 5km southwest of Taihuai, just off the main road, and easily accessible by bus from town. Its highlight is the decorated marble entranceway at the top of 108 steps, whose surface is densely packed with images of dragons, phoenixes and foliage buried in a mass of abstract pattern. The rest of the temple seems sedate in comparison, though the Puji Pagoda inside is a similar confection – a fat stupa carved with guardians, surmounted by a fake wooden top and guarded by an elaborate railing. Both structures are fairly late, dating from the beginning of the twentieth century.

The **Bishan Si** (¥4), 2km north of the town, was originally used as a reception house for monks and *upasaka* (lay Buddhists). The Ming building holds many Qing sculptures, including a white jade Buddha donated by Burmese devotees.

For an excellent view of Taihuai, **Dailuo Peak** (¥4), 3km northeast from the bank of the river, can be reached by cable car (¥25 ascent, ¥23 descent). Once you get off, climb up the flight of stairs and you'll arrive at **Shancai Si** (¥10), where there's a small cluster of stalls and telescope stands; for ¥1 you can peer through the latter and get a beautiful view of the mountain range.

The far temples and the peaks

Too far to reach on foot, the following temples and peaks are all served by minibuses which assemble at Taihuai bus station, or run direct from the larger hotels. Taxis and private cars are also available in the village centre (see p.245). Preserved from vandalism by their inaccessibility, the temple complexes include some of the oldest buildings in the country.

The **Jinge Si** (¥4) is 10km southwest of Taihuai, and worth the trip for an impressive seventeen-metre-tall *Guanyin* inside – the largest statue at Wutai Shan. Some of the original Tang structure remains in the inscribed base of the pillars. It's worth inquiring if you can stay in their pilgrims' accommodation, as it's a useful base from which you can walk the trails behind the complex.

The superb Nanchan Si and Foguang Si require a considerable diversion to reach. The **Nanchan Si** (¥5) is about 60km south of Taihuai, a little way off the road from Taiyuan, near the town of **Wutai Xian**. Tour buses from Taiyuan sometimes stop here on their way into Taihuai; otherwise you can catch a bus to Wutai Xian, then get a motor-rickshaw to the village of **Dong Ye**. A large sign here points the way, but it's another 7km along a rough road to the complex. The temple's small main hall, built in 782, is the oldest wooden hall in China, a perfectly proportioned building whose columns and walls slope gently inwards, the sturdiness given by its thick, carved, wooden brackets nicely offset by the slight curves of its wide, flaring roof. Two inward-curving peaks sit at the ends of the roof ridge – all features characteristic of very early Chinese architecture. The hall of the Jin-dynasty **Yanqing Si**, accessible by a short path behind the Nanchan Si and included in the ticket price, is somewhat dilapidated but notable for quirky architectural detail, particularly the carved demons' heads, which sit atop the two columns on either side of its main entrance.

The **Foguang Si** (¥10), 40km west of Taihuai, is a museum complex of more than a hundred buildings, mostly late, but including Wutai Shan's second Tang-dynasty hall, built in 857, whose eaves are impressive for the size and complexity of their interlocking *dougongs*. The walls inside the hall are decorated with lively Tang and Song paintings of Buddhist scenes; most of the images are of saintly figures sitting sedately, but a few ferocious demons are shown, dragging emaciated bodies behind them. To get here, catch a morning bus from Taihuai to **Doucun** (¥10), where you'll be dropped at the junction near a large sign pointing the way to Foguang. It's a five-kilometre walk from here along a dusty road to the temple, or you can negotiate an onward round trip with a vehicle for around ¥150.

The peaks

The five flat **peaks** around Taihuai, north, south, east, west and middle, are all approximately 15km away and considerably higher than Taihuai, with the tallest at over 3000m above sea level. On each summit sits a small temple, and pilgrims endeavour to visit each one, a time-consuming process even with the help of minibuses which go some way up each mountain. In the past, the truly devout took up to two years to reach all the temples on foot, but today most visitors make do with looking at the silhouette of the summit temples through the telescopes of entrepreneurs in town. Set off in any direction out of town for a rewarding walk, although the South Peak is regarded as the most beautiful, its slopes described in a Ming poem as "bedecked with flowers like a coloured silk blanket".

Taiyuan and around

TAIYUAN, industrial powerhouse and the capital of Shanxi Province, lies midway on the rail line between the more appealing Datong and Xi'an, and is the most convenient starting point for a trip to Pingyao or the Wutai Shan

Taiyuan and around

Taiyuan	太原	*tàiyuán*
Chongshan Si	崇善寺	*chóngshàn sì*
Minsu Museum	民俗博物馆	*mínsú bówùguǎn*
Shuangta Si	双塔寺	*shuāngtǎ sì*
Wuyi Square	五一广场	*wǔyī guǎngchǎng*
Yingze Park	迎泽公园	*yíngzé gōngyuán*
Accommodation and eating		
Bingzhou	并州饭店	*bìngzhōu fàndiàn*
Guofang	国防宾馆	*guófáng bīnguǎn*
Huayuan	山西华苑	*shānxī huáyuàn*
Shanshuijian	山水间	*shānshuǐ jiān*
Shanxi Grand	山西大酒店	*shānxī dàjiǔdiàn*
Shipin Jie	食品街	*shípǐn jiē*
Yingze Binguan	迎泽宾馆	*yíngzé bīnguǎn*
Yunshan	云山饭店	*yúnshān fàndiàn*
Around Taiyuan		
Jinci Si	晋祠寺	*jìncí sì*
Shuanglin Si	双林寺	*shuānglín sì*
Xuanzhong Si	玄中寺	*xuánzhōng sì*

mountain area. The glossy new hotels, imposing banks and classy restaurants of **Yingze Dajie**, the showcase street, are perhaps in part an enticement to get travellers to linger a while, and indeed the downtown area, compact enough to explore on foot, rewards wandering with some intriguing alleys and a bustling, pedestrianized food street. If you're breaking your journey here to head for Wutai or Pingyao there's also a scattering of ancient buildings outside town worth a diversion.

Some history

A city never far from shifting frontiers, Taiyuan, or Jinyang as it was originally called, sits in a valley next to the Fen River in the "invasion corridor" between the barbarian lands to the north and the Chinese heartland around the Yellow River to the south. As a result it has suffered even more than most Chinese cities from invaders and the fallout from dynastic collapse. The Mongolian Huns invaded first in 200 BC, ousted when the Tobas, a nomadic Turkish people, swept south in the fourth century and established the Northern Wei dynasty. During the Tang dynasty, the city enjoyed a brief period of prosperity as an important frontier town on the edges of Han Chinese control and the barbarian lands, before becoming one of the major battlefields during the Five Dynasties (907–979), a period of strife following the Tang's collapse. In 976 the expanding Song dynasty razed the city to the ground.

More recently, Taiyuan was the site of one of the worst massacres of the Boxer Rebellion, when all the city's foreign missionaries and their families were killed on the orders of the provincial governor. A habit of playing host to warlike leaders continued when Taiyuan was governed by Yan Xishan between 1912 and 1949. One of the Guomindang's fiercest warlords, he treated the city as a private empire. According to Carl Crow's contemporaneous *Handbook for China*, Xishan's city was a reform-minded place, well known for the suppression of opium and its anti-foot-binding movement. His rule did not stop the city's gradual development by foreign powers, however, and extensive coal mines were constructed by the Japanese in 1940. Industrialization began in earnest after the Communist takeover and today it is the factories that dominate, relentlessly processing the region's coal and mineral deposits.

Arrival, transport and accommodation

Local officials are so proud of Taiyuan's **airport**, 15km southeast of the city (a ¥70 ride away by taxi) that a model of the modernist building sits in Yingze Park in the city centre. The **train station**, on the Beijing–Xi'an line, is likewise the focus of local pride, judging by the number of camera stalls lined up outside catering to those who want to get their photograph taken in front of it. As Chinese stations go, it's a pleasant one: clean, new and efficient, though with the usual chaos of buses and stalls outside. It's conveniently located at the eastern end of **Yingze Dajie**, the city's main thoroughfare, from where bus #16 runs the full length of the street. The **long-distance bus station** is just west of the train station, also on Yingze Dajie.

Although it's a sprawling place, Taiyuan is easy to get around as the majority of places of interest are on or near Yingze Dajie. The street runs east–west

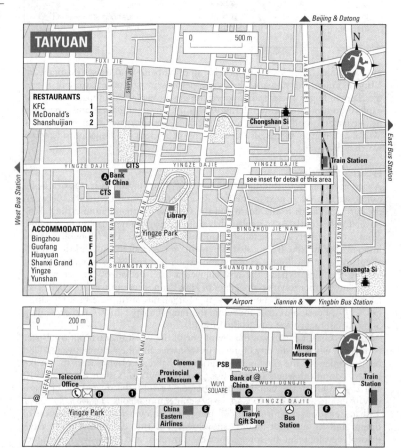

across town, passing the south side of Wuyi Square, the heart of the city, and most sights, hotels and restaurants are within walking distance. Alternatively, bus #804 heads west down Yingze Dajie from the train station, then turns left on to Xinjian Nan Lu; bus #102 begins from a terminus on the west side of Jianshe Bei Lu, just north of the train station, and travels west to Wuyi Square, then turns north up Wuyi Lu. **Taxis** are cheap, with a ¥7 minimum fare, and plentiful.

Accommodation

Most **hotels** are located along Yingze Dajie; the western end is less interesting and farther from the sights, while the eastern end, near the train station, is livelier but noisier.

Bingzhou 118 Yingze Dajie ℡ 0351/8821188, ℻ 4033540. Three-star place, one of the best mid-range options, with a good location opposite Wuyi Square. The cheapest rooms are in a claustrophobic basement – it's worth paying a little more for one of the spacious rooms upstairs. ❻

Guofang 12 Yingze Dajie ℡ 0351/8261166. It may not look like much, but this budget hotel near the station has the largest selection of rooms – though most don't have windows. Clean and friendly. Descend the red-carpeted staircase from the alley off Yingze Dajie. ❸

Huayuan 9 Yingze Dajie ℡ 0351/4046201, ℡ 4646980. Rooms are spacious and clean, though a little noisy. ❺

Shanxi Grand 5 Xinjian Nan Lu ℡ 0351/8829999

ext 3113, ℻ 4043525. The poshest place in town, where tour groups end up, though it's a little far west. Oddly decorated in a mishmash of styles, but very comfortable. ❽

Yingze Binguan 189 Yingze Dajie ℡ 0351/4043211, ℻ 4043784. This stylish four-star hotel consists of two buildings: the western wing is the upmarket section, with excellent facilities; the eastern wing is more down to earth and affordable, but may not take foreign guests. Western wing ❻, eastern wing ❺

Yunshan 99 Yingze Dajie ℡ 0351/4964861. A pleasant and agreeably low-key place with a good location. Singles, doubles and triples available. The westernmost rooms facing the street have balconies and great views of Yingze Dajie. ❸

The City

China's largest stainless-steel sculpture, an image of three noble workers with exaggerated angular features, stands outside Taiyuan train station, and sets the tone for the main city street, **Yingze Dajie**, beyond. New and gleaming, somewhere between a boulevard and a freeway, it has eight lanes and a metal barrier down the middle to prevent you walking across anywhere except at the pedestrian crossing point just east of Wuyi Square and at traffic intersections. Outside the centre, Taiyuan is a dull industrial sprawl, but along Yingze Dajie the city tries its best to live up to its status as provincial capital, with a sprinkling of neon, flashy new buildings, garish statuary and an inordinate number of storefronts proffering massages and marital aids.

About 1km west of the train station, down Yingze Dajie, past numerous hotels and restaurants, you'll find **Wuyi Square**, a concrete plaza marked by a huge sculpture of a man playing a flute, a deer, and a woman with pneumatic breasts; it's lit up in fluorescent green at night. Just west of here, the **Provincial Art Museum** (daily 9am–5pm; ¥5) is housed in a grand Ming temple complex formerly knows as the Chunyanggong. The museum has seen better days, though it is being thoroughly renovated. Once a place to offer sacrifices to the Taoist deity Lu Dongbin, the charming complex of small, multistorey buildings, accessible by steep stairways off small courtyards, seems ill-suited to its present function of housing a motley collection of artefacts and a small natural history collection.

The **Minsu Museum** (daily 9am–noon & 2.30–5pm; ¥2), housed in the former Confucius Temple east of here off Jianshe Bei Lu, mostly comprises displays of photographs and relics concerning Shanxi's modern history, as well as a few Shang bronzes and a large collection of Buddhist sutras. However, the attractive Ming buildings are more engrossing than the exhibits themselves.

Northeast of Wuyi Square, reached along alleys that grow shabbier the farther you go, the **Chongshan Si** (Temple of Veneration of Benevolence; daily 8am–6pm; ¥2) is worth the fifteen-minute walk – look for the fortune-tellers who congregate outside. The temple contains a display of scrolls and books – sutras printed in the Song, Yuan and Ming dynasties, some in Tibetan, and a number of woodcut illustrations. Directly south, with an entrance at its southern end, the monastery complex that it was once attached to has been converted into workshops and warehouses.

The focus for a wander around sparse **Yingze Park** (daily 4.30am–11pm; free) is provided by a Ming-dynasty library south of the park entrance on Yingze Dajie. You can't go inside, but there is some nice eave decoration, including images of pandas. A tour of the city's ancient buildings is completed with a look at the two fifty-metre-tall pagodas of the **Shuangta Si** (Twin Pagoda Temple; daily 8am–8pm; ¥20), south of the train station off Shuangta Bei Lu. These were built by a monk called Fu Deng in the Ming dynasty, under the orders of the emperor, and today have become a symbol of the city. You can climb the thirteen storeys for a panoramic view of Taiyuan.

Eating, drinking and nightlife

Yingze Dajie has a good smattering of **restaurants**, many catering for tourists. The best place to head is **Shipin Jie** (Food Street), which is parallel to and west of Jiefang Lu, and north of Yingze Dajie. The pleasant, pedestrianized row is packed with eating places, from cheap, fast-food-style noodle shops to quiet, upmarket restaurants, as well as stalls selling nuts and fruit, and karaoke bars and hairdressers; it's very busy in the evening (busier usually means better when it comes to which restaurant to pick).

On **Yingze Dajie**, try *Shanshuijian*, which for a hotpot restaurant is surprisingly comfortable; and it looks more expensive than it is – a meal for two here should come to about ¥50. The noodle restaurant just east of the *Yunshan* on the alley is very popular and unusual for serving no rice. Food comes in deep bowls, and last to arrive is a bowl of noodles, which you add to the remains of your other dishes.

Listings

Airlines Most airlines have ticket offices just west of the *Bingzhou* Hotel at 158 Yingze Dajie.

Banks and exchange The main Bank of China is at 288 Yingze Dajie (Mon–Fri 8am–5.30pm, Sat & Sun 8am–5pm).

Buses Taiyuan's new system of satellite bus stations has done wonders for inner-city traffic, but has a steep learning curve. Buses to Datong leave from the long-distance bus station on Yingze Dajie. To Taihuai, go to the east bus station. To Pingyao, head to the Jiannan bus station. To Linfen, Yuncheng and provincial points south, go to the southern Yingbin bus station. (Bus #819 links these stations and the train station.) Many routes will be transferred to the new east station building once it's finished, so be sure to check at any one of the bus station information desks for the latest information.

Cinema Catch the latest dubbed Hollywood blockbusters at the theatre on the west side of Wuyi Square (¥25).

Internet access There's a pleasant Internet café on Wuyi Dongjie (¥4/hr in upstairs café, ¥2 downstairs), just east of Wuyi Square, and others scattered about in the area.

Mail and telephones The white building opposite the train station on the northern side of Yingze Dajie houses an impressively modern and efficient post office (daily 8am–7.30pm). There's a branch office at 215 Yingze Dajie (daily 8am–6pm). The telecom office, open 24hr, is next door.

PSB The PSB office is at 9 Houjia Lane (daily 8am–noon & 2.30–5.30pm) on the northeastern corner of Wuyi Square.

Shopping For either a jade cabbage (¥16,000) or a set of inlaid chopsticks (¥10), browse the Tianyi Gift Shop, underground and across the street from the *Yunshan* hotel (9am–7pm).

Trains Dozens of north–south trains pass through Taiyuan daily, and getting a sleeper is usually not a problem even at the last minute. If need be, opt for *wuzuo* (unreserved) ticket and upgrade on the train, or hang around the returns (*tuipiao*) window and hope your destination becomes available. CITS can book tickets for a ¥5 service fee.

Travel agents CITS is next to the main Bank of China on Yingze Dajie (☎0351/4063562). The CTS office on Xinjian Nanlu (☎351/4946300) is well worth the effort to get to, since the helpful English-speaking staff can arrange discounts on accommodation and a variety of excursions.

Around Taiyuan

Easily reached in the flat countryside around Taiyuan is the very touristy temple complex of **Jinci Si**. A bit farther afield is **Xuanzhong Si**, an active Buddhist temple and a major destination for Zen pilgrims.

Jinci Si

Although **Jinci Si** contains perhaps the finest Song-dynasty buildings in the country, neglect, and its extensive development as a tourist resource, means it is not as impressive as it could be. From Taiyuan, bus #804 from the train station will take you the 25km to the site (daily 8.30am–6pm; ¥40). First impressions don't augur well – after a juddering ride through a stark industrial zone, the bus drops you at the park outside the temple, a charmless fair of souvenir stalls and ragged camels, by a river at the base of a mountain.

A temple has stood on the site since the Northern Wei, and today's buildings are a diverse collection from various dynasties. The open space just inside the gate was once used as a theatre, with the richly ornamented Ming stage, the **Water Mirror Platform**, at its centre. Beyond here, a small river channelled across the complex, now ruined with litter, must have been one of its most pleasant features. Over the bridge behind the stage, four Song-dynasty iron figures of warriors, apparently guardians of the river, stand on a platform looking furious. Inscriptions on their chests record their dates of construction, though parts have been replaced since.

The **Hall of Offerings** beyond and, behind that, the **Hall of the Holy Mother** were originally constructed in the Jin dynasty as places to worship the mother of Prince Shuyu, who founded the dynasty and was attributed with magical powers. They were rebuilt in the Song and today are two of the largest buildings from that dynasty still extant. The Hall of the Holy Mother, one of the earliest wooden halls in China, is the highlight of the complex, its facade a mix of decorative flourishes and the sturdily functional, with wooden dragons curling around the eight pillars that support the ridge of its upward-curving roof. The hall's interior is equally impressive, with some fine, delicate-looking Song-dynasty female figures, posed naturalistically, some with broomsticks, jugs and seals, attendants to a central image of a gracious-looking Holy Mother. Among the buildings to the right of the Hall of the Holy Mother, a Tang-dynasty stele records the visit of Emperor Tai Zong in 647 AD.

Xuanzhong Si

The **Xuanzhong Si** (mountain area ¥8, temple ¥5), 80km southwest of Taiyuan, is famous as one of the birthplaces of Zen Buddhism – the priests Daochuo and Shandao, two of its founders, taught here – and has a history stretching back over 1500 years. Most of the present buildings, however, built on tiers up the side of a hill, are Ming or Qing. A thriving place of worship, today it's a popular pilgrimage spot for the Japanese, some of whom come to hear the contemporary masters preach. Tourist **minibuses** run direct from outside the train station in Taiyuan (¥20–30), or you can take a **bus** from the Xikezhan bus station to **Jiaocheng**, a town 4km northeast of the temple, and hire a motor-rickshaw from there.

Pingyao and Shuanglin Si

The small town of **Pingyao**, 100km south of Taiyuan, and the **Shuanglin Si** nearby are certainly worth making an effort to visit. Despite a burgeoning tourist trade, Pingyao is one of the few towns in this part of China that has retained more than a token of its traditional infrastructure and the buildings of its nineteenth-century heyday. Some of these have been converted into hotels – indeed Pingyao boasts one of the most atmospheric places to stay in China. Spring Festival is an exceptionally good time to visit, when the streets are illuminated by hundreds of red lanterns. Some 5km outside the town walls, Shuanglin Si has a hoard of wood and terracotta sculptures, some lifelike, some ghostly, some comical, which are unparalleled in the region.

Buses to Pingyao from Taiyuan's Jiannan bus station leave every half hour (¥20), and the trip – along the expressway – takes one hour thirty minutes. Regular **trains** also come here from Taiyuan and Xi'an throughout the day and are slightly quicker than the bus.

Pingyao

PINGYAO reached its zenith in the Ming dynasty, when it was a prosperous banking centre, one of the first in China, and its wealthy residents constructed luxurious mansions, adding city walls to defend them. In the course of the twentieth century, however, the town slid rapidly into provincial obscurity,

---

Pingyao and Shuanglin Si

Pingyao	平遥	*píngyáo*
City God Temple	城隍庙	*chénghuáng miào*
Former County Yamen	平遥衙门	*píngyáo yámén*
Former Residence of Lei Lütai	雷履泰故居	*léilǚtài gùjū*
Kuixing Tower	奎星楼	*kuíxīng lóu*
Rishengchang	日升昌	*rìshēngchāng*
Tian Ji Xiang Museum	天吉祥博物馆	*tiānjíxiáng bówùguǎn*
Accommodation and eating		
Dejuyuan Famous Local Snack Shop	德居源地方名吃	*déjūyuán dìfāng míngchī*
Dejuyuan Folk-style Guesthouse	德居源客栈	*déjūyuán kèzhàn*
Minsu Hotel	民俗宾馆	*mínsú bīnguǎn*
Tianyuankui Hotel	天元奎客栈	*tiānyuánkuí kèzhàn*
Yunjincheng Folk Custom Hotel	云锦成民风宾馆	*yúnjīnchéng mínfēng bīnguǎn*
Zhongdu Binguan	中都宾馆	*zhōngdū bīnguǎn*
Shuanglin Si	双林寺	*shuānglín sì*

which has kept it largely unmodernized. Inside the town walls, Pingyao's narrow streets, lined with elegant Qing architecture – no neon, no white tile, no cars – are a revelation, harking back to Pingyao's nineteenth-century heyday. Few buildings are higher than two storeys; most are small shops much more interesting for their appearance than their wares, with ornate wood and painted glass lanterns hanging outside, and intricate wooden latticework holding paper rather than glass across the windows. The similarly designed **Qiao family compound** thirty minutes' drive away was used as a setting by Zhang Yimou for his film *Raise the Red Lantern*, in which the labyrinthine layout of the place symbolizes the woman's restricted life.

Arrival and transport

The plan of Pingyao is very simple. Fifteen-hundred-metre-long walls enclose the city on four sides, with four main streets arranged along the compass points, a typical *feng shui*-influenced design that the Chinese compare to the markings on a tortoise shell. Nan Dajie, these days clogged with lookalike souvenir stalls, actually slopes downward ever so slightly, as it used to transport the city's sewage out of the figurative tortoise's rear end. The central I-shaped pedestrian zone is closed to cars in daylight hours, though it's usually so congested with bicycles and speeding motorcycles that the back alleys make an even more attractive diversion.

Buses terminate outside the tiny **train station** in the northwest of town, which is also where you can catch **buses** to Taiyuan, Jiexiu and Linfen. En route to Xi'an, you can break your journey in Pingyao for the day and then pick up one of the two evening trains that pass through on their way south. Note that Pingyao station is allocated only a dozen or so departing sleeper tickets, which means you may not get that sleeper to Xi'an you hope for. The only tickets usually on sale are for hard seats, though once on the train you should

PINGYAO

ACCOMMODATION
Dejuyuan	B
Minsu	E
Tianyuankui	D
Yunjincheng	C
Zhongdu	A

EATING
Dejuyuan Famous Local Snack Shop	1

be able to upgrade, provided bunks are available (less likely at weekends). Many guesthouses have figured out ways to work around the ticket shortage, so check with yours. Luggage can be left behind the counter at the station shop. If you really get stuck in town during a busy travel time, a taxi to Taiyuan should cost less than ¥300.

Taxis are forbidden from entering the walled town. From the train station or West Gate, you can catch a **bicycle rickshaw** for ¥5, though resist your driver's exhortations that your intended hotel is most certainly full – he's looking for commission to get you to stay elsewhere.

Be aware that Pingyao as yet has no Bank of China. The nearest branch is in Jiexiu, a city about 100km to the south of Pingyao. It's best to arrive with the cash you'll need for your stay.

Accommodation

Staying overnight in Pingyao is recommended, as after twilight the town becomes tranquil after a frenetic day of souvenir selling. There are numerous traditional, renovated guesthouses, most with wooden window screens, traditional furniture and beds raised up on wooden platforms. Pingao's lodging can fill up quickly, so making a reservation is recommended. Also keep in mind that the city packs out on weekends, when discounted rooms evaporate.

Dejuyuan Folk-style Guesthouse 43 Xi Dajie ⊕0354/5685266, ⓕ5685366. Tends to draw larger groups, and often has live-music performances in the courtyard. ④

Minsu Hotel 68 Yamen Jie ⊕0354/5683539, ⓕ5683975. This completely renovated guesthouse just east of the Former County Yamen is a quiet, well-appointed option off bustling Nan Dajie. ③

Tianyuankui Hotel 73 Ming Qing Jie ⊕0354/5680069, ⓕ5683052, ⓦwww.pytyk.com. This is the liveliest of the central guesthouses and tends to draw a younger crowd. ③

Yunjincheng Folk Custom Hotel 62 Ming Qing Jie ⊕0354/5680944, ⓕ5680723, ⓦwww.pyyjc.com. Occupies a superb location in a restored 200-year-old home near the Bell Tower and was the model for the traditional guesthouse boom, though business has suffered from competition. ③

Zhongdu Binguan Opposite the train station ⊕0354/5672618. Sadly, many tour groups still get shunted into this bland building. Though the rooms are clean, staying here takes away most of Pingyao's charm. ⑤

The Town

If you arrive at the train station, Pingyao looks like any other dusty mid-sized Chinese city at first. Walk straight ahead and turn left at the first intersection onto Xiaxiguan Jie, a market street over which the West Gate looms 300m ahead. Through the gate, Xi Dajie leads into the heart of the **old city**, with the buildings becoming lovelier the deeper you go. Between the slender main streets, a lattice of even narrower alleyways links courtyards which are well worth exploring, even by night when the glow from nearby houses shows the way – though small kids stay off the street after dark, haunted by their parents' tales of returning Ming-era ghosts who, it's said, navigate the unchanged alleys with ease. The ghosts of another era can be glimpsed in

To see Pingyao's cultural sites, you have to buy a **¥120 inclusive ticket**: The city's crack tourism authorities will pocket the same cash whether you visit only one site or all. Included in the ticket are the town walls, City God Temple, the Former Residence of Lei Lütai, the Former County Yamen and the Rishengchang. Tickets are sold at any of these sites and are valid for two days, provided you get it stamped the day you purchase it. We've given prices in the text for anything not included.

△ Pingyao town walls

the derelict entrance architecture over old homes and the faded "Long live Chairman Mao" slogans on the walls – Pingyao, the locals say, had "a very bad Cultural Revolution".

Just inside the arch of the West Gate are steps leading up to the Ming **town walls** (daily 8am–6.30pm), 12m high and crenellated, with a watchtower along every 50m of their six-kilometre length. You can walk all the way around them in two hours, and get a good view into some of the many courtyards inside the walls (and at an army training base outside them, where you can watch recruits practising drill and throwing fake hand grenades). The structures where the wall widens out are *mamian* (literally, horse faces), where soldiers could stand and fight. At the southeast corner of the wall, the **Kuixing Tower**, a tall, fortified pagoda with a tiled, upturned roof, is a rather flippant-looking building in comparison to the martial solidity of the battlements.

It's possible to climb the **City Tower** (¥5) on Ming Qing Jie, a charming little building that provides a fantastic rooftop view of the old city. Enter via the camouflaged staircase at the southeast corner. The eave decoration includes colourful reliefs of fish and portly merchants, and guardian statues of Guanyin and Guandi face north and south, respectively. Also on Nan Dajie and a five-minute walk south of the City Tower is the **Tian Ji Xiang Museum** (daily 9am–5pm; ¥10), which holds a collection of coins, paintings and other artefacts from the town's history. At the eastern end of Dong Dajie, you can look around the **Rishengchang** (daily 9am–5pm), a bank established in 1824, the first in the country and one of the first places in the world where cheques were used. During the Qing, more than four hundred financial houses operated in Pingyao, handling over eighty million ounces of silver annually. After the Boxer Rebellion, Dowager Empress Cixi came here to ask for loans to pay the high indemnities demanded by the Eight Allied Forces. Soon after, the court defaulted, then abdicated, and the banks dried up. Hong Kong and Shanghai took over Pingyao's mantle, rendering the city an isolated backwater until now.

South of the Bell Tower, the **Former Residence of Lei Lütai** (daily 8am–7pm), the restored home of Rishengchang's founder, gives an interesting peek into the lives of Pingyao's top brass. Nearby, the **Former County Yamen** (daily 8am–6.30pm) is a massive complex that shows how offices would vary with the rank of the functionaries who used them. Walk east from here on Yamen Jie, which becomes Chenghuang Miao Street at the **City God Temple**. During the Cultural Revolution, the army bivouacked here, which, ironically, kept the place protected from the wrath of the Red Guards. Today it's a ramshackle mix of elderly card players and penitent worshippers.

Eating

While lodging options are great, eating in Pingyao is not nearly as exciting, perhaps because many restaurants are simple guesthouse dining rooms. Look for the crowded spots at dinner times; the *Tianyuankui Hotel* dining room is often full, though it seems to double as a bar in the evening. Traditional Pingyao cuisine includes *ca ge dou*, noodles with tomato; *suan cai chao dou fu*, bean curd with pickles; and *yiya cai*, cold pickled vegetables. Be sure to try the *sanxie shaomai*, an interesting and delicious dumpling variation. A **meal** for two here should cost around ¥40. For cheap eats, head to any one of the places that cluster south of the City Tower, especially the Dejuyuan Famous Local Snack shop, just across the street from the *Tianyuankui*, which has good, cheap local dishes.

Listings

Bike rental Bikes are available from some of the guesthouses, though you can find a fleet of reliable Flying Pigeons at 30 Chenghuangmiao Jie (¥10 per day, ¥100 deposit).

Clinics There is a helpful clinic at 43 Dong Dajie (℡0354/5683732).

Mail The post office is at 1 Xi Dajie (daily 8am–6.30pm).

PSB At 110 Zhoubi Nan Jie, near the Former County Yamen. They might be willing to extend a visa, but it would be better to do this in Taiyuan.

Tours For a guided tour of the locality in English, including a trip to Shuanglin Si, book the services of Wu Qiulian (Julia) at the *Yunjincheng Folk Custom Hotel* (℡wu_qiu_lian@sina.com). She knows a lot of Pingyao history, and her guesthouse was one of the first to accommodate tourist interest in the area.

Trains Sixteen trains pass through Pingyao each day, bound north or south, though tickets can be hard to come by. At busy travel times, you might need to book a ticket through your guesthouse.

Shuanglin Si

The **Shuanglin Si** (daily 8am–6pm; ¥25), with its extraordinary collection of Buddhist sculpture, stands 5km southwest of Pingyao in a stretch of quiet countryside, accessible via a pleasant walk or bike ride along a flat road or by a ten-minute taxi ride (¥25 round trip with wait) from the train station or West Gate. Originally built in the Northern Wei, the present buildings, ten halls arranged around three courtyards, are Ming and Qing. Unfortunately, increased levels of industrial pollution have coated the structures and sculptures with coal dust, and much of the complex is undergoing restoration.

The complex looks more like a fortress from the outside, being protected by high walls and a gate. Once you're inside, the fine architecture pales beside the contents of the halls, a treasury of coloured terracotta and wood **sculptures**, more than 1600 in all, dating from the Song to the Qing dynasties. They're literally arranged behind bars, in tableaux, with backgrounds of swirling water or clouds, turning the dusty wooden halls into rich grottoes. Some of the figures are in bad shape but most still have a good deal of their original paint, although it has lost its gaudy edge. The halls are usually kept padlocked, either for the protection of the figures or simply because visitors are uncommon, and you'll be shown around them one by one by an earnest caretaker who will tell you all about the figures, whether or not you understand his Chinese. It's worth hiring a guide (see "Listings" above), as each hall and each row of statues has intriguing elements, such as the statue of the husband and wife who lived here and protected the temple during the Cultural Revolution.

The horsemen dotted in vertical relief around the **Wushung Hall**, the first on the right, illustrate scenes from the life of Guan Di, the god of war, but the figures in most of the halls are depictions of Buddha or saints and guardians. The eighteen *arhats* in the **second hall**, though unpainted, are eerily lifelike, and somewhat sinister in the gloom with their bulging foreheads, long tapering fingernails and eyes of black glass that follow you round the room. In the **third hall,** the walls are lined with elegant twenty-centimetre-high Bodhisattvas inclined towards a set of larger Buddha figures at the centre. The Bodhisattvas are like so many roosting birds, ranked on shelves carved to represent the levels of existence, with demons on the bottom, clouds and angels at the top. The statue of Guanyin – sitting in a loose, even provocative, pose – is unique in China, and is probably a reflection of the confidence and pride Pingyao enjoyed during its economic heyday. In the **fourth hall**, look out for the monsters hanging above the Buddhas, and, in the **fifth**, for a superb figure of many-armed Guanyin.

Between Pingyao and Xi'an

The small towns between Pingyao and Xi'an, north of the Yellow River, are largely ignored by foreign travellers, though there are some interesting places tucked away here, which should attract anyone who wants to break their journey. About 140km south of Pingyao, **Linfen** is popular with domestic tourists who come here in order to pick up a connection to **Hukou Falls**, which, though regarded by the Chinese as one of their premier beauty spots, fall short of the hype. Farther south, the town of **Yuncheng** is an access point for the **Guan Di Miao**, a fine Qing-dynasty (1644–1911) temple popular with the Taiwanese, and for the town of **Ruicheng** and the nearby **Yongle Gong**, a Taoist temple with some excellent murals, from where Xi'an is only a four-hour bus ride away.

Linfen and around

A provincial town, **LINFEN** is not unpleasant, though there's no point in hanging around. The centre of town is built like a mini-Beijing, with a replica Tian'anmen Square at its centre and a massive amusement park, Yaodu Square, at its edge. There are replicas of Beijing's architectural wonders too, including the Temple of Heaven and the Great Wall, and even a park containing a topographic model of the whole country, to scale, where visitors can play Godzilla, stomping on towns they dislike.

The town's few taxis (¥4 minimum fare) congregate around the **train station**, in the west of town. The **bus station**, for connections to Hukou Falls, is a ten-minute walk from the train station, down the second street on the left. There are frequent buses north to Pingyao (3hr; ¥36). **Accommodation** is available at the *Pingyang Hotel*, at 58 Jiefang Nan Lu (℡0357/2086666; ❸), whose rooms range from the very basic to quite plush.

Hukou Falls

Poetically described by CITS as "giant dragons fighting in a river", **Hukou Falls** (¥37), 150km west of Linfen, is the Yellow River at its most impressively turbulent. At Jinshan Gorge the 400-metre-wide river is suddenly forced into a twenty-metre gap and tumbles down a cliff, where the fierce torrent squirts spray high into the air; the hiss of the water can be heard 2km away, which is what gives it the name "hukou", meaning kettle spout. It's best in the summer

Between Pingyao and Xi'an		
Linfen	临汾	*línfēn*
Pingyang Hotel	平阳宾馆	*píngyáng bīnguǎn*
Hukou Falls	壶口瀑布	*húkǒu pùbù*
Yuncheng	运城	*yùnchéng*
Guan Di Miao	解州关帝庙	*jièzhōu guāndì miào*
Huanghe Hotel	黄河大厦	*huánghé dàshà*
Xinfeng Hotel	鑫丰大酒店	*xīnfēng dàjiǔdiàn*
Jixian	吉县	*jíxiàn*
Hukou Guesthouse	壶口招待所	*húkǒu zhāodàisuǒ*
Ruicheng	芮城	*ruìchéng*
Ruicheng Binguan	芮成宾馆	*ruìchéng bīnguǎn*
Yongle Gong	永乐宫	*yǒnglè gōng*

when the river level is highest. A popular spot with the Chinese, the falls are undoubtedly magnificent, but it's a long way to go, and, with souvenir stalls aplenty, is not exactly a wilderness experience. If you've seen a waterfall or a riotous river, then skip it.

To get here from Linfen, check in first at the Linfen CITS (☎0357/3330281) on the south side of the train-station plaza. They might have tours running, or can recommend where to pick up a **tourist minibus**. To make the trip on your own, take bus #11 from the train station to the Yaomiao bus station in the southwest of town and hop on a long-distance bus to Jixian (¥45); local buses in Jixian make the run to the falls. The bus trip takes between four and six hours, so unless you charter a taxi (¥800 there and back from Linfen) you'll probably have to stay the night; the *Hukou Guesthouse* (❸) is new and quite adequate.

Yuncheng and the Guan Di Miao

YUNCHENG, 140km south of Linfen, is the last major town before Xi'an on the train line south from Datong and the starting point for bus trips west and south to the Guan Di Miao, Ruicheng and the Yongle Gong (see below). The **train station**, with a statue of Guan Di outside glaring at the townspeople, is in the northwest of town, at the north end of Zhan Nan Lu, while the **bus station** is a little farther south on the western side of the same road. Buses for Xi'an (3–4hr; ¥40–60) depart from the train-station concourse or from the bus station. There's an **Internet café** beside the *Railway Hotel* at the train station.

The *Railway Hotel* (☎0359/2068899, ℱ8659168; ❸), to the right as you exit the train station, is a friendly, comfortable place. On the left as you exit the station the *Xinfeng Hotel* (☎0359/2067888, ❸, dorm beds from ¥18–35) is clean and also accepts foreigners. The *Huanghe Hotel* (☎0359/2023135; ❹), east from the station concourse to the end of Zhan Dong Lu, has a wide range of rooms and a decent restaurant.

Guan Di Miao

About 20km west of Yuncheng, the **Guan Di Miao** (daily 8am–6.30pm; ¥25, ¥20 to ascend main hall), the finest temple to the god of war in China, sits in the small country town of **JIEZHOU**, accessible by bus #11 (¥3) from opposite the station concourse. Contemporary Jiezhou, known locally as Haizhou, doesn't look like much – the bus drops you in a muddy square lined with a few stalls and pool tables, which makes the massive temple complex on its western side look quite out of proportion. However, this was the birthplace of **Guan Di** (aka Guan Yu), a general of the Three Kingdoms period (220–280 AD; see box, p.474). Something of a Chinese King Arthur, Guan Di was a popular folk hero who, like many Chinese historical figures who became the stuff of legend, was later deified. As god of war, his temple (founded in 589 AD, though the present structure is eighteenth century) is appropriately robust, looking more like a castle, with high battlements and thick wooden doors. Among the images on the wooden arch at the entrance is a victorious jouster gleefully carrying off the loser's head. The martial theme is carried into the interior, with much smiting of enemies going on in the superb Qing-dynasty friezes and stone carvings in the eaves, and on the pillars of the three halls. Guan Di is a very popular figure in Taiwan, and many Taiwanese come here in winter for the temple fair held between October 18 and 28.

Ruicheng and the Yongle Gong

The bus journey from Yuncheng to **RUICHENG** (¥10, 2.5hrs), 75km south, a town just north of the Yellow River, is an easy trip over the Zhongtiao Mountains, an ochre landscape of loess soil, limestone peaks, cornfields and orchards. While the area is fairly remote, a side trip through Yuncheng and Ruicheng is a straightforward, enjoyable detour on the way to Xi'an. Buses from Yuncheng arrive at the long-distance bus station just west of Ruicheng's main, central intersection. The utilitarian *Ruicheng Binguan* (T0359/3030611, F3030659; ●) is nearby, behind the eastern side of the Tian'anmen Square-like centre square. With frequent bus links to Yuncheng and Xi'an, however, you can probably drop in for a few hours and be on your way.

Yongle Gong

The **Yongle Gong**, Palace of Eternal Joy (daily 8.30am–6pm; ¥30), is a major Taoist temple, 4km north of the village at the terminus of bus #2, most notable for its excellent murals. Its name derives from the position it once held in the village of Yongle, farther south on the banks of the Yellow River. It was moved brick by brick in 1959, when the dam at Sanmenxia was built and Yongle disappeared beneath the water.

There are three halls, three sides of which are covered in vivid **murals**. In the **first hall**, the three major gods of Taoism, sitting on thrones, are surrounded by the pantheon of minor deities, looking like emperors surrounded by courtiers. Each figure is over 2m tall, brightly painted and concisely outlined, but although great attention is paid to an exact rendering of the details of facial expression and costume, the images have no depth. The figures, four deep, are flat, like staggered rows of playing cards. Some have the faces of monsters, others have beards which reach almost to their waists and in which every hair is painted; one man has six eyes. In the **second hall**, elegant robed figures disport themselves in finely observed walled courtyards and temple complexes set among misty, mountainous landscapes. These are images from the life of **Lu Dongbin**, one of the eight Taoist immortals who was born at Yongle, and are arranged in panels like a comic strip. The murals in the **third hall**, showing the life of a Taoist priest, are unfortunately damaged and little remains visible.

Shaanxi and Henan

The provinces of **Shaanxi** and **Henan** are both remarkable for the depth and breadth of their history. The region itself is dusty, harsh and unwelcoming, with a climate of extremes; in winter, strong winds bring yellow dust storms, while summer is hot and officially the rainy season. But, thanks to the Yellow River, this was the cradle of Chinese history, and for millennia the centre of power for a string of dynasties, the remains of whose capital cities are strung out along the southern stretch of the plain.

Of these ancient capitals, none is more impressive today than thriving **Xi'an**, now the capital of Shaanxi Province and perhaps the most cosmopolitan city you will find in China outside the eastern seaboard. It also retains copious evidence of its former glories – most spectacularly in the tomb guards of the great emperor Qin Shi Huang, the renowned **Terracotta Army**, but also in a host of temples and museums. The whole region is crowded with buildings

The Yellow River

The **Yellow River** flows for 6000km through nine provinces, from the Tibetan plateau in the west, through Inner Mongolia, turning abruptly south into Shanxi and then east through the flood plains of Shaanxi, Henan and Shandong to the Bohai Gulf. The upriver section provides much-needed irrigation and power, but in the latter half of its journey the river causes as much strife as it alleviates. The problem is the vast quantity of **silt** the river carries along its twisted length – 1.6 billion tonnes a year – whose choking nature has confused its course throughout history. Sometimes the river has flowed into the sea near Beijing, at other times it has flowed into the lower Yangzi valley, and its unpredictable swings have always brought chaos. From 1194 to 1887 there were fifty major Yellow River **floods**, with three hundred thousand people killed in 1642 alone. A disastrous flood in 1933 was followed in 1937 by another tragedy – this time man-made – when Chiang Kaishek used the river as a weapon against the advancing Japanese, breaching the dykes to cut the rail line. A delay of a few weeks was gained at the cost of hundreds of thousands of Chinese lives.

Attempts to enhance the river's potential for creation rather than destruction began very early, at least by the eighth century BC, when the first **irrigation canals** were cut. In the fifth century BC the Zheng Guo Canal irrigation system stretched an impressive 150km and is still in use today. But the largest scheme was the building of the 1800-kilometre **Grand Canal** in the sixth century, which connected the Yellow and the Yangzi rivers and was used to carry grain to the north. It was built using locks to control water level, an innovation that did not appear in the West for another four hundred years. The more predictable Yangzi soon became the county's main highway for food and trade, leading to a decline in the Yellow River area's wealth.

Dykes, too, have been built since ancient times, and in some eastern sections the river bottom is higher than the surrounding fields, often by as much as 5m. Dyke builders are heroes around the Yellow River, and every Chinese knows the story of Da Yu (Yu the Great), the legendary figure responsible for battling the capricious waters. It is said that he mobilized thousands of people to dredge the riverbed and dig diversionary canals after a terrible flood in 297 BC. The work took thirteen years, and during that period Yu never went home. At work's end, he sank a bronze ox in the waters, a talisman to tame the flow. A replica of the ox guards the shore of Kunming Lake in Beijing's Summer Palace. Today **river control** continues on a massive scale. To stop flooding, the riverbed is dredged, diversion channels are cut and reservoirs constructed on the river's tributaries. Land around the river has been forested to help prevent erosion and so keep the river's silt level down.

For most of its course, the river meanders across a flat flood plain with a horizon sharp as a knife blade. Two good places to see it are at the **Yellow River Viewing Point** in Kaifeng or from the **Yellow River Park** outside Zhengzhou. To see the river in a more tempestuous mood, take a diversion to **Hukou Falls** (see p.258), farther north on the border between Shaanxi and Shanxi provinces.

which reflect the development of **Chinese Buddhism** from its earliest days; one of the finest is the Baima Si in **Luoyang**, a city farther east, thought by the ancient Chinese to be the centre of the universe. The temple is still today a Buddhist centre, and the last resting place of monks who carried sutras back along the road from India. The **Longmen Caves**, just outside the city, are among the most impressive works of art in China, but also rewarding are excursions in the area around, where two holy mountains, **Hua Shan** and **Song Shan**, one Buddhist, one Taoist, offer a welcome diversion from the monumentality of the cities. **Zhengzhou**, farther east, the capital of Henan, has an excellent new provincial museum exhibiting the fruits of ongoing archeological excavations, mostly Shang-dynasty bronzes. East of here, the town of **Kaifeng**, the Song-dynasty capital, is a pretty and quiet little place, though little remains of its past thanks to its proximity to the treacherous Yellow River. North of Kaifeng, near the border with Hebei, the city of **Anyang** remains a backwater with an impressive archeological heritage – you can inspect the current finds from the Shang era in the museum here. If you've had enough of the relics of ancient cultures, get a glimpse of recent history at **Yan'an** in high northern Shaanxi, the isolated base high in the loess plateau to which the Long March led Mao in 1937, or at the **Red Flag Canal** – a flagship project of Mao's self-reliant China of the 1960s – at Linzhou in northern Henan.

Xi'an

The capital of Shaanxi province, **XI'AN** is a manufacturing city of five million inhabitants and holds a key position in the fertile plain between the high loess plateau of the north and the Qingling Mountains to the south. It's one of the more pleasant Chinese cities, more prosperous than anywhere in inland China except Chengdu, with streets full of Japanese cars and consumer goods. As the de facto capital of China's west, Xi'an is also the base of the government's Xibu Da Fazhan (Develop the West) campaign that's sputtering along. Its tourism industry, of course, means Xi'an is already far more developed than the surrounding area, a fact suggested by the large numbers of rural migrants who hang around at informal labour markets near the city gates. Xi'an is also a primer in Chinese history, as between 1000 BC and 1000 AD it served as the **imperial capital** for eleven dynasties. You'll find a wealth of important sites and relics hereabouts: Neolithic Banpo, the Terracotta Army of the Qin emperor, the Han and Tang imperial tombs, and, in the city itself, the **Goose Pagodas** of the Tang, the **Bell and Drum towers** and **Ming city walls**, as well as two excellent **museums** holding a treasury of relics from the most glamorous parts of Chinese history. Despite the drawbacks of **pollution** (many of the locals walk around wearing white face masks) and congestion, common to all rapidly industrializing Chinese cities, Xi'an is very popular with **foreign residents**, and many come here to study, as the colleges are regarded as some of the best places to learn Chinese.

Some history

Three thousand years ago, the western Zhou dynasty, known for their skilled bronzework, built their capital at **Fenghao**, a few miles west of Xi'an – one of their chariot burials has been excavated nearby. When Fenghao was sacked by northwestern tribes, the Zhou moved downriver to **Luoyang** and, as their empire continued to disintegrate into warring chiefdoms, the nearby Qin kingdom expanded. In 221 BC the larger-than-life Qin Shi Huang united the Chinese in a single empire, the Qin, with its capital at **Xianyang**, just north of Xi'an. The underground **Terracotta Army**, intended to guard his tomb, are this tyrant's inadvertent gift to today's tourist prosperity.

His successors, the Han, also based here, ruled from 206 BC to 220 AD. Near-contemporaries of Imperial Rome, they ruled an empire of comparable size and power. Here in Xi'an was the start of the **Silk Road**, along which, among many other things, Chinese silk was carried to dress Roman senators and their wives at the court of Augustus. There was also a brisk trade with south and west Asia; Han China was an outward-looking empire. The emperors built themselves a new, splendid and cosmopolitan capital a few miles northwest of Xi'an which they called **Chang'an** – Eternal Peace. Its size reflected the power of their

Xi'an

Xi'an	西安	xī'ān
Baxian Gong	八仙宫	bāxiān gōng
Bell Tower	钟楼	zhōng lóu
Big Goose Pagoda	大雁塔	dàyàn tǎ
Century Ginwa Department Store	世纪金花百货商店	shìjì jīnhuābǎihuò shāngdiàn
Daci'en Si	大慈恩寺	dàcí'ēn sì
Daxingshan Si	大兴善寺	dàxīngshàn sì
Drum Tower	鼓楼	gǔ lóu
Great Mosque	大清真寺	dàqīngzhēn sì
Shaanxi Beilin Museum	陕西碑林博物馆	shǎnxī bēilín bówùguǎn
Shaanxi History Museum	陕西历史博物馆	shǎnxī lìshǐ bówùguǎn
Small Goose Pagoda	小雁塔	xiǎoyàn tǎ
Tang Dynasty Arts Museum	唐代艺术馆	tángdài yìshùguǎn

Accommodation, eating and drinking

ANA Grand Castle Hotel	长安城堡大酒店	cháng'ān chéngbǎo dàjiǔdiàn
Bell Tower	钟楼饭店	zhōnglóu fàndiàn
Chuanhan Renjia	川汉人家	chuānhàn rénjiā
Flats of Renmin Hotel	人民大厦公寓	rénmín dàshà gōngyù
Foreign Language Guesthouse	西安外语学院外事服务中心	xī'ān wàiyǔxuéyuàn wàishì fúwù zhōngxīn
Grand New World	古都新世界大酒店	gǔdū xīnshìjiè dàjiǔdiàn
Guanzhong Renjia	关中人家	guānzhōng rénjiā
Hotel Royal	西安皇城宾馆	xī'ān huángchéng bīnguǎn
Howard Johnson Plaza	金花豪生国际大饭店	jīnhuā háoshēng guójì dàfàndiàn
Hyatt Regency	凯悦饭店	kǎiyuè fàndiàn
Jiefang	解放饭店	jiěfàng fàndiàn
Laosunjia	老孙家	lǎosūnjiā
May First	五一饭店	wǔyī fàndiàn
Renmin	人民大厦	rénmín dàshà
Shaanxi Local Food	西安饭店	xī'ān fàndiàn
Shanghai Renjia	上海人家	shànghǎi rénjiā
Shuyuan International Hostel	属院青年旅舍	shǔyuàn qīngnián lǚshè
Sushi Restaurant	回转寿司店	huízhuǎn shòusīdiàn
Tang Dynasty	唐乐宫	tánglè gōng
Xi'an	西安宾馆	xī'ān bīnguǎn
Xi'an Roast Duck	西安烤鸭店	xī'ān kǎoyādiàn
Xiang Xiang Da Pan Ji	香香大盘鸡	xiāngxiāng dàpánjī

empire, and records say that its walls were 17km round with twelve great gates. When the dynasty fell, Chang'an was destroyed. Their tombs remain, though, including Emperor Wudi's mound at **Mao Ling**.

It was not until 589 that the Sui dynasty reunited the warring kingdoms into a new empire, but their dynasty hardly lasted longer than the time it took to build a new capital near Xi'an called **Da Xingcheng** – Great Prosperity. The **Tang**, who replaced them in 618, took over their capital, overlaying it with their own buildings in a rational grid plan (taken as the model for many other Chinese cities). During this time the city became one of the biggest in the world, with over a million inhabitants.

The Tang period was a **golden age** for the arts, and ceramics, calligraphy, painting and poetry all reached new heights. Its sophistication was reflected in its religious tolerance – not only was this a great period for Buddhism, with monks at the Jianfu Si busy translating the sutras that the adventurous monk Xuan Zong had brought back from India, but the city's Great Mosque dates from the Tang, and one of the steles in the Provincial Museum bears witness to the founding of a chapel by Nestorian Christians.

After the fall of the Tang, Xi'an went into a long **decline**. It was never again the Imperial capital, though the Ming emperor Hong Wu rebuilt the city as a gift for his son; today's great walls and gates date from this time. Occasionally, though, the city did continue to provide a footnote to history. When the Empress Dowager Cixi had to flee Beijing after the Boxer Rebellion, she set up her court here for two years. In 1911, during the uprising against the Manchu Qing dynasty, the Manchu quarter in Xi'an was destroyed and the Manchus massacred. And in 1936, Chiang Kaishek was arrested at Huaqing Hot Springs nearby in what became known as the Xi'an Incident (see p.279).

Orientation, arrival and city transport

Xi'an is easy to get around as the layout of today's city closely follows the ordered grid plan of the ancient one, with straight, wide streets running along the compass directions. The **centre** is bounded by city walls, with a bell tower marking the crossroads of the four main streets, Bei Dajie, Nan Dajie, Dong Dajie and Xi Dajie – north, south, east and west streets. Another major street runs south from the train station, where it's called Jiefang Lu, across the city, crosses Dong Dajie where it changes its name to Heping Lu, then to Yanta Lu outside the walls and continues all the way to the Big Goose Pagoda in the **southern outskirts**, where many of the city's sights are. The only exception to the grid plan of the central streets is the **Muslim quarter**, northwest of the Bell Tower, around whose unmarked winding alleys it's easy (and not necessarily unpleasurable) to get lost.

The **modern city**, extending far beyond the confines of the walls, in general adheres to the same ordered pattern, with two large highways forming ring roads, the innermost of which goes around the outside of the city walls.

Arrival

The arrivals gate at Xi'an's **airport**, outside the town of Xianyang, 40km northwest of Xi'an, is thronged with taxi drivers, who should charge ¥150 for a ride into town, but you're better off getting the **airport bus** (¥25; buy tickets from an office on the right of the main airport entrance as you exit). The bus journey takes an hour and leaves you outside the *Melody Hotel*, just west of the Bell Tower.

The busy **train station**, in the northeast corner of town, just outside the city walls, is a major terminus on a west–east line which splits just east of the city, one branch going north to Beijing, the other east to Shanghai. City buses leave from the tangled north end of Jiefang Lu, just south of the station, and taxis congregate on the western side of the concourse outside.

Buses supposedly arrive in Xi'an at either the bus station just south of the train station or at the terminus at the southwest corner of the city walls, but in practice where you arrive depends a lot on the bus company, the direction you approach from and the whim of the driver. As most buses arrive at night, it's best to have a destination in mind and hail a taxi.

City transport

The largest concentration of **city buses** is found outside the train station at the northern end of Jiefang Lu. There are other clusters just outside the South

Gate, and at the southern end of Yanta Lu, just north of the Big Goose Pagoda. Normal buses cost ¥1, fancier ones with air conditioning ¥2. Bus #603 and #611 are particularly useful (see box below). Otherwise there are plenty of

Useful bus routes

#9 Train station–*Flats of Renmin Hotel*.
#41 Train station–Heping Lu–Big Goose Pagoda.
#215 South Gate–Chang'an Lu.
#501 Huangcheng Xi Lu, 200m east of the *Flats of Renmin Hotel*–Nan Dajie–Big Goose Pagoda.
#601 Big Goose Pagoda–Dong Dajie–Bei Dajie.
#603 Train station–Jiefang Lu–Bell Tower–Chang'an Lu and Foreign Language Institute.
#611 Train station–Bell Tower–Andingmen–west bus station.

green **taxis** cruising the streets and they can be hailed anywhere. Most destinations within the city fall within the ¥5 flag fall.

As the streets are wide and flat, **cycling** is a good way to get around. All the major streets have cycle lanes, controlled at major intersections by officials with flags. There are, however, few bike parks, and most people run the risk of a (rarely enforced) ¥10 fine by leaving their bikes padlocked to railings. Make sure you have a good security chain, especially if your bike is anything other than a downbeat Flying Pigeon. For rental places, see p.275.

City **maps** (¥8) are available everywhere and hold a lot of information, including bus and tram routes. It's worth picking one up immediately, as bus routes are continually amended.

Accommodation

Xi'an is firmly on the tourist itinerary, and **hotels** abound. The train-station touts offering budget rooms are best avoided, particularly as they may bring you to a place that doesn't take foreigners; if you do decide to go with them, be sure to bargain.

There's no shortage of international luxury hotels, with glossy five-star structures both inside and outside the city walls. Most sights are located around the city centre, so if your budget will stretch to it, it's much more convenient and atmospheric to stay inside the walls, in the thick of things. The mid-range category is also well catered for within the city walls. Cheap rooms can also be had at university foreign student housing, and while the University District in the south of the city is a bit far from the city centre, the Internet cafés, telephone "bars" (*hua ba*), cheap restaurants and good shopping keep the area bustling well after dark.

Inside the walls

Bell Tower 110 Nan Dajie ☎029/87600000, ℱ87218767. Opposite the southwest corner of the Bell Tower, right in the centre of town, this hotel has a great location and is very comfortable. ➑

Grand New World 48 Lianhu Lu ☎029/87216868, ℱ87219754. Quite luxurious (huge marble lobby) with a price tag to match, but in rather a grey part of town. Significant discounts available in low season. ➒

Hotel Royal 334 Dong Dajie ☎029/87235311, ℱ87235887. This deluxe Japanese–Chinese joint venture is well located. ➐

Hyatt Regency 158 Dong Dajie, just east of Heping Lu ☎029/887691234, ℱ87696799. This well-located, steel-and-concrete fortress has a plush interior, populated by tour groups and business folk alike. ➒

Jiefang 181 Jiefang Lu ☎029/87698888, ℱ87422617. Just opposite the train station, this hotel is especially convenient for a short stay, though it's not the most restful spot in town. ➎

May First 351 Dong Dajie ☎029/87681098, ℱ87213824. In a superb location tucked behind its dumpling shop in the centre of town, this little hotel has character and is good value, as well as housing an excellent restaurant. Deservedly

popular and often full. Take bus #611 from the station. ➍

Renmin 319 Dongxin Jie ☎029/87928888, ℱ87928999. The bulbous facade of this quirky building, built in the 1950s to house Russian advisers, looks vaguely eastern European. The inside has been renovated though, and now looks like everywhere else in this price bracket. ➎

Shuyuan International Youth Hostel Just inside and 20m west of the city wall's south gate ☎029/87287721, ℱ87287720. From the train station, take buses #603 or #608 to the south gate. Its location and price are unrivalled, as is its quiet courtyard and friendly staff. Avoid the overflow basement rooms at all costs, however: they're damp, windowless cells. There's a basic restaurant with a backpacker menu, cheap beer and couches. They're also one of the best sources of city information, tours and train ticket bookings. Dorm beds ¥30–50, ➍

Outside the walls

ANA Grand Castle 12 Huancheng Nan Lu Xiduan ☎029/87608888, ℱ87231500. Five-star concrete parody of the Big Goose Pagoda, situated just outside the South Gate. The cavernous atrium-lobby sets the somewhat impersonal tone; caters mainly to tour groups. ➒

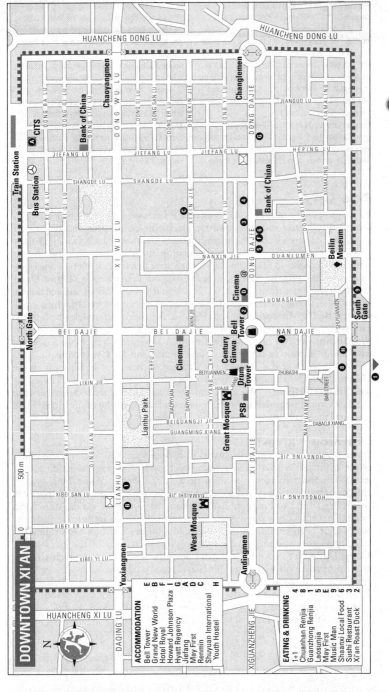

DOWNTOWN XI'AN

HUANCHENG DONG LU

HUANCHENG DONG LU

THE YELLOW RIVER | Xi'an

267

ACCOMMODATION

Bell Tower — E
Grand New World — B
Hotel Royal — F
Howard Johnson Plaza — I
Hyatt Regency — G
Jiefang — A
May First — D
Renmin — C
Shuyuan International Youth Hostel — H

EATING & DRINKING

1+1 — 4
Chuanhan Renjia — 8
Guanzhong Renjia — 1
Laosunjia — 5
May First — E
Music Man — 9
Shaanxi Local Food — 6
Sushi Restaurant — 3
Xi'an Roast Duck — 2

Flats of Renmin 9 Fenghe Lu, 200m west of Xinghuo Lu ☎029/86240349. Most backpackers used to head here, though the *Shuyuan* is far better located. This hostel is on an uninteresting street nine stops west on bus #9 from the train station. If you're getting a taxi (¥10 from the station), make sure the driver doesn't take you to the *Renmin Hotel*. Avoid the older and tattier south block if possible. *Kane's*, the attached restaurant, offers tours, decent travel info, laundry, and bike rentals. ❸

Foreign Language Institute Guesthouse Chang'an Nan Lu ☎029/85309532. Located on a leafy, hip campus popular with expats for Chinese studies. To get here, take bus #603 to the Waiyu

Xueyuan stop, turn into the lane leading east to the campus, turn right at the T-junction, then left along the playing fields. The guesthouse is the white-tiled building on the northeast corner of the fields. Student discounts available. ❹

Howard Johnson Plaza 18 Huancheng Nan Lu Xiduan ☎029/88421111, ☏88429999. With fantastic views of the south city wall, this brand-new five-star hotel makes a convenient, posh base for jaunts to both the inner city and the sights to the south. ❾

Xi'an 58 Chang'an Bei Lu ☎029/85261351, ☏85261796. A large, comfortable place with a huge brown lobby, but a little too far south to warrant the cost. ❼

The City

Xi'an successfully integrates its architectural heritage with the modern city, its imposing walls and ancient geometric street plan, centring on the Bell Tower, giving it a distinct identity missing in the sprawl of most Chinese cities. **Downtown** Xi'an, inside the walls, is just about compact enough to get around on foot, with enough sights to fill a busy day. And it is here that the city's new prosperity is most in evidence, in the variety and prices of goods in the shops on **Dong Dajie**, the main shopping street, where you'll also find the best hotels and restaurants. **Nan Dajie**, to the south, is another shopping district at the end of which you'll find the **Beilin Museum**, which holds a massive collection of steles, next to the **city walls**, more imposing remnants of imperial China. Contrast is provided by the **Muslim quarter** northwest of the Drum Tower, which preserves a different side of old China in its labyrinth of alleys centring on the **Great Mosque**.

The area south of the inner city is scattered with ancient buildings from the Han and Tang dynasties, which predate the Ming-dynasty city walls. The excellent **Shaanxi History Museum** and the small **Daxingshan Si** sit between the two **Goose pagodas** and their temples, which are some of the oldest – and certainly the most distinctive – buildings in the city.

Downtown Xi'an

In the heart of town, the **Bell Tower** (daily 8am–9pm; ¥20) stands at the centre of the crossroads where the four main streets meet. The original building, built in 1384, stood two blocks west of here, at the centre of the Tang-dynasty city; the present triple-eaved wooden structure standing on a brick platform was built in 1582 and restored in 1739. You can enter only via the subway on Bei Dajie, in which you buy your ticket and where you must leave any large bags. Inside is an exhibition of chimes and a bronze bell (not the original). A balcony all the way around the outside provides a view of the city's traffic. **Dong Dajie**, east of here, is the main downtown street, along which you can pick up a pizza, post a letter, get film developed or buy the latest jeans or trainers. There are a number of good restaurants worth checking out, especially the Xi'an fixtures *Laosunjia* and the *Shaanxi Local Fast Food Restaurant* (see p.274). The street is crowded with other fast-food and noodle joints, as well as street food, and after dark a handful of nightclubs come alive.

The Muslim quarter

Just west of the Bell Tower is the **Drum Tower** (daily 8am–6pm, till 10pm summer; ¥20). It's a triple-eaved wooden building atop a fifty-metre-long arch straddling the road. You enter up steps on the western side, though there's not much to see when you're up there, as the building no longer holds the drum which used to be banged at dusk, a complement to the bell in the Bell Tower which heralded the dawn.

North beyond the Drum Tower, the scale of Xi'an's streets constricts, and the narrow alleys lined with cramped half-timbered, two-storey buildings feel more like a village than a sprawling provincial capital. This is the **Muslim quarter**, for centuries the centre for Xi'an's Hui minority who today number around thirty thousand, a people said to be descended from eighth-century Arab soldiers. **Beiyuanmen**, the street that runs north from the Drum Tower gate, is worth browsing, especially if you're in search of a bowl of noodles or *yangrou paomo*. The area is especially lively in the evening, when the restaurants are packed and sidewalks are full of craft tables and souvenir sellers. **Huajue Xiang**, a narrow alley heading west off Beiyuanmen (30m or so north of the Drum Tower), is one of the best spots in Xi'an for "antiques" and other small gifts. In addition to more traditional Chinese cultural artefacts, you can pick up a new carry-on suitcase, some Mao memorabilia, and a machete, though sadly nothing that feels particularly unique to the Muslim quarter.

After Huajue Xiang curves to the north, you'll arrive at the spiritual heart of the district, the **Great Mosque** (daily 8am–6pm; ¥12), the entrance facing a small intersection of alleys. The largest mosque in China, it was originally established in 742, then rebuilt in the Qing dynasty and heavily restored. An east–west facing complex which integrates Arabic features into a familiar Chinese design, it's a calm place, untouched by the hectic atmosphere of the streets outside. On either side of the stone arch at the entrance are two **steles** by two of the most famous calligraphers in China, Mi Fei of the Song dynasty and Dong Qichang of the Ming. The attractive courtyard beyond, which holds a minaret in the form of an octagonal pagoda at its centre, is lined with wooden buildings featuring abstract eave decorations – the usual figurative designs being inappropriate for a mosque. Also here are freestanding steles bearing inscriptions in Chinese, Persian and Arabic. The **main prayer hall**, just beyond the two fountains, has a turquoise roof and some fine carvings on the doors and eaves.

The Muslim quarter extends west from here nearly to the city wall, though redevelopment and the widening of Xi Dajie have begun to encroach on the far end of the quarter. Still, a long walk to the west on Xiyangshi Jie – to the small, still operating **West Mosque** – is enjoyable. The side streets are full of poky dumpling shops with rows of street stalls in front, many of which sell offal. Look out for the sheep skulls – when you buy one the vendor scoops the brains out with a chopstick and wraps them up in paper for you. More palatable, and definitely worth sampling, are the sweets, some stamped with good-luck messages, the mutton cooked on skewers while you wait, and the nuts and seeds heaped on plates outside tiny shopfronts. From here you can double back, continue west to the west gate of the city wall, or walk south to the public bus connections and department stores on Xi Dajie.

The Beilin Museum

Heading south from the Bell Tower along Nan Dajie, a street of department stores and offices, you come to the huge **South Gate**, an arch in the wall topped with a triple-eaved wooden building, not open to the public. A turn east takes you along Shuyuanmen, a pleasant, cobbled street of souvenir shops, art stores and antique shops. This is the heart of Beilin, something of an artists' quarter, though equally geared up for tourists. About 500m east of Nan Dajie along Shuyuanmen, after a quick curve to the south, is an access point for the city wall and the **Beilin Museum** (daily 8.30am–6.30pm; ¥30), a converted Confucian temple. Most of the exhibits are steles, from the Han to the Qing dynasties, which you don't need to understand Chinese to find fascinating – many are marked with maps and drawings.

An annexe on the west side holds an exhibition of small stone **Buddhist images**, a wealth of which have been discovered in Shaanxi. Exhibited chronologically, the sculptures demonstrate the way the physiognomy of Buddha images changed over the centuries. The earliest, from 420 AD, are of plump, Indian-style Buddhas; later images become much more Han-looking, as Buddhism developed Chinese characteristics and absorbed the influence of Confucianism and Taoism. The Sui and Tang figures are particularly good, bearing the most recognizably Chinese characteristics.

The rest of the museum collection consists of six halls containing more than a thousand **steles**. The first hall contains the twelve Confucian classics – texts outlining the Confucian philosophy – carved onto 114 stone tablets, a massive project ordered by the Tang emperor Wenzong in 837 as a way of ensuring the texts were never lost or corrupted by copyists' errors. Like most of the steles in the museum, these are set in a stone wall or secured in a steel frame. The second hall includes the **Daqing Nestorian tablet**, on the left as you go in, recognizable by a cross on the top, which records the arrival of a Nestorian priest in Chang'an in 781 and gives a rudimentary description of Christian doctrine. Condemned as heretical in the West for its central doctrine of the dual nature of Christ, both human and divine, and for refusal to deify the virgin mother, Nestorianism spread to Turkey and the East as its priests fled persecution, and was the first Christian doctrine to appear in China. In the third hall, one stele is inscribed with a **map of Chang'an** at the height of its splendour, when the walls were extensive enough to include the Big Goose Pagoda within their perimeter. Rubbings are often being made in the fourth hall, where the most carved drawings are housed; thin paper is pasted over a stele and a powdered ink applied with a flat stone wrapped in cloth. Among the steles is an image called the "God of Literature Pointing the Dipper", with the eight characters which outline the Confucian virtues – regulate the heart, cultivate the self, overcome selfishness and return propriety – cleverly made into the image of a jaunty figure. "To point the dipper" meant to come first in the exams on Confucian texts which controlled entry to the civil service.

The city walls

Largely intact and imposing enough to act as a physical barrier between the city centre and the suburbs, Xi'an's **walls** were originally built of rammed earth in 1370 on the foundation of the walls of the Tang-dynasty imperial city, though they took their modern form in 1568, when they were faced with brick. Recently restored, the walls are the most distinctive feature of the modern city, forming a twelve-metre-high rectangle whose perimeter is 12km in length. Some 18m wide at the base, they're capped with crenellations, a watchtower at each corner and a fortress-like gate in the centre of each side. Originally the city would have been further defended with a moat and drawbridges, but today the area around the walls is a thin strip of parkland, created after a major restoration in 1983. Few roads pass through the walls, and traffic often has to circle around the outside for some distance before it can gain entry.

You can ascend the wall from most of the major gates in the city (daily: summer 7am–10.30pm; rest of year 8am–6pm; ¥10), though the South Gate is probably the most common starting point. The few remaining breaks in the wall have been restored, which means you can now circumnavigate the city atop the wall. An electric shuttle runs between the South Gate and the East and West Gates (one-way ¥10, return ¥20), but more fun are the rentable bikes (¥20 per hour) – if prepared with food and drinks, you can spend the better part of a day exploring Xi'an from the wall.

The Small Goose Pagoda and the Daxingshan Si

Xiaoyan Ta (Small Goose Pagoda; daily 8am–6pm; ¥28) is southwest of the South Gate on Youyi Lu – from the train station, take bus #603 to the crossroads with Chang'an Lu. A 45-metre-tall, delicate construction, founded in the Tang dynasty in 707 to store sutras brought back from India, the pagoda sits in what remains of the Jianfu Si. Two of the pagoda's original fifteen storeys were damaged in an earthquake, leaving a rather abrupt jagged top to the roof, to which you can ascend for a view of the city. A shop at the back of the complex sells Shaanxi folk arts.

Just south of here on Xingshan Xijie, in Xinfeng Park, accessible down a narrow market street, the small **Daxingshan Si** (daily 8am–5pm; ¥10) is usually overlooked by visitors, but is worth a visit. This is the only working Buddhist temple in Xi'an; it was destroyed in the Tang persecution of Buddhism, and thus today's small, low buildings are mainly Qing and Ming. Monks in baggy orange trousers will write your name on a prayer sheet in the main hall for a donation.

Shaanxi History Museum

One of the city's major highlights, the **Shaanxi History Museum** (summer 8.30am–6pm, winter 9am–5.30pm; ¥35, students ¥15) is an impressive modern building, on the route of buses #5 and #610 from the station, and within walking distance of the Daxingshan Si and the Big Goose Pagoda. The exhibition halls are spacious, well laid out, and have English captions, displaying to full advantage a magnificent collection of more than three thousand relics.

The **lower floor**, which contains a general survey of the development of civilization until the Zhou dynasty, holds mostly weapons, ceramics and simple ornaments – most impressive is a superb set of Western Zhou and Shang **bronze vessels** covered in geometric designs suggestive of animal shapes, used for storing and cooking ritual food. The two **upstairs galleries** display relics from the Han through the Qing dynasties; notable are the Han ceramic funerary objects, particularly the model houses.

Back on the lower floor, two **side halls** hold themed exhibitions. The western hall holds bronzes and ceramics, in which the best-looking artefacts are Tang. Large numbers of ceramic **funerary objects** include superbly expressive and rather vicious-looking camels, guardians, dancers, courtiers and warriors, glazed and unglazed. The eastern hall holds a display of Tang **gold and silver**, mainly finely wrought images of dragons and tiny, delicate flowers and birds, and an exhibition of Tang **costume and ornament**. The hall's introduction states that Tang women led "brisk and liberated lives", though it's hard to imagine how when you see the wigs arranged to show their complex, gravity-defying hairdos, and the tall, thin wooden soles on their shoes.

The Dacien Si, Big Goose Pagoda and Tang Dynasty Arts Museum

The **Dacien Si** (Temple of Grace; daily 8am–6.30pm; ¥25), in the far south of town, 4km from the city wall on the route of buses #5 or #41 from the station, is the largest temple in Xi'an, though when it was established in 647 it was much larger, with nearly two thousand rooms, and a resident population of more than three hundred monks. The original was destroyed in 907, and the present buildings are Qing, as are the garishly repainted figures of *arhats* in the main hall. Other rooms hold shops and exhibitions of paintings. All around the temple you'll see rubbings from a Qing stele in the Xingjiao Si of images of the Tang-dynasty monk **Xuan Zang**, the temple's most famous resident, who spent fifteen years collecting Sanskrit sutras in India before translating them here into 1335 volumes. He is shown with the largest bamboo-frame backpack you're likely to see on your travels.

At Xuan Zang's request, the Big Goose Pagoda (Dayan Ta; daily 8am–6.20pm; ¥20) was built at the centre of the temple as a fireproof store for his precious sutras. No one seems to know where the name "Goose" comes from – perhaps from the tale in which Xuan Zang and Monkey, heroes of the popular classic *Xi You Ji* (*Journey to the West*), are saved by a goose when they get lost in the desert. More impressive than its little brother, the Big Goose Pagoda is sturdy and angular, square in plan, and more than 60m tall. It has been restored and added to many times, though the current design is not far from the original. On the first floor is an exhibition of different pagoda styles, and, at either side of the south entrance, stone tablets hold calligraphy by two Tang emperors, surrounded by bas-relief dragons and flying angels; over the lintel of the west door is a fine Tang carving of Buddha and his disciples sitting in a Chinese building. The pagoda has seven storeys, each with large windows (out of which visitors throw money for luck). The view from the north windows is the most impressive for the rigorous geometry of the streets below, though it's hard to believe that when built the temple was at least 3km inside the Tang city.

A short walk east of here, the **Tang Dynasty Arts Museum** (daily 8.30am–5.30pm; ¥5) is not as good as it could be, considering the wealth of relics from this age, regarded as the high point of Chinese arts. Nevertheless, it does contain some excellent pieces, mostly pottery horses and camels and tricoloured glazed figures, including among the usual range of warriors and courtiers a couple of stuffy-looking bureaucrats in elaborate costumes. The exhibits are dated but have no English captions.

The Baxian Gong

The **Baxian Gong** (also known as Baxian An), at the centre of a shabby area outside the East Gate, is the only Taoist temple in Xi'an, home to around a hundred monks and nuns. Containing an interesting collection of steles, including pictures of local scenic areas and copies of complex ancient medical diagrams of the human body, the temple is the setting for a popular religious festival on the first and fifteenth day of every lunar month. However, it is probably of most interest to visitors for the **antique market** that takes place outside every Wednesday and Sunday (see "Shopping" below).

Shopping

Xi'an is an excellent place to pick up souvenirs and antiques, which are generally cheaper and more varied than in Beijing, though prices have to be bartered down and the standard of goods, especially from tourist shops, is sometimes shoddy. Be aware that many of the antiques sold are fake. Shopping is also an enjoyable evening activity, since the markets and department stores are open until 10pm.

The upmarket **Century Ginwa Department Store**, underground at the northwest corner across from the Drum Tower, offers the usual array of designer labels and has a good coffee bar on the ground floor. The basement supermarket is one of the best in China, with a good selection of reasonably priced imported goods. The **Green Ant outdoors shop** just east of the Shaanxi History Museum has basic travel and backpacking gear. For music, movies, and cheap, gimmicky gifts, take bus #603 to the **University District**, home to a dozen campuses, many of which border Chang'an Lu. Get off at the massive Home Club store and explore the side streets.

The **night markets** in both the Muslim quarter and Beilin make for an entertaining stroll under the stars, where the nocturnal hawkers sell everything from dinner to souvenir silk paintings.

Artwork

Xi'an has a strong artistic pedigree, and the **paintings** available here are much more varied in style than those you see elsewhere. As well as the line and wash paintings of legendary figures, flowers and animals that you see everywhere, look for bright, simple folk paintings, usually of country scenes. A traditional Shaanxi art form, appealing for their decorative, flat design and lush colours, these images were popular in the 1970s in China for their idealistic, upbeat portrayal of peasant life. A good selection is sold in a shop just behind the Small Goose Pagoda and in the temple compound, as well as outside the Banpo Museum (see p.278). For **rubbings** from steles, much cheaper than paintings and quite striking, try the Big Goose Pagoda and the Beilin Museum. The underground pedestrian route at the South Gate includes an interesting diversion down an old bomb shelter tunnel to Nan Shang Jie, where **papercuts** are for sale.

Strong competition means you can pick up a painting quite cheaply if you're prepared to **bargain** – a good, sizeable work can be had for less than ¥150. However, beware the bright young things who introduce themselves as art students whose class happens to be having an exhibition. They're essentially touts who will lead you to a room full of mediocre work at inflated prices.

Souvenirs

Beiyuanmen and Huajue Xiang, the alley that runs off to the Great Mosque, are the places to go for **small souvenirs**, engraved chopsticks, teapots, chiming balls and the like. Another grouping of tourist shops lies scattered along Shuyuanmen, a cobbled street just east of the South Gate. Clusters of stalls and vendors swarm around all the tourist sights, and are often a nuisance, though the stalls around the Great Mosque are worth checking out – you'll see curved Islamic *shabaria* knives among the Mao watches and other tourist knick-knacks. Some stalls sell small figures of terracotta soldiers in a mesh basket; you can bargain them down to just a few yuan, but the figures aren't fired properly, and will leave your hands black whenever you touch them. For better quality, buy them from a department store or more upmarket souvenir shop.

For a personalized souvenir, try the seal engravers along Shuyuanmen, where you'll also find a variety of **artists' materials** – calligraphy sets and the like.

Antiques

The best place to go for **antiques** is the market at the entrance to Baxian Gong, which is biggest on Wednesdays and Sundays, and more of a local affair than a tourist bonanza, so prices are cheaper. Many vendors are villagers from the outlying regions who look as if they are clearing out their attics. You can find much more unusual items here than you will see in the stores, such as books and magazines dating from the Cultural Revolution containing rabid anti-Western propaganda, Qing vases, opium pipes, and even rusty guns.

Clothes and books

A wide range of expensive **clothes** is sold on Dong Dajie, with a good selection of name-brand stores. The old Luomashi street market off Dong Dajie has been destroyed, though a new shopping development should be open soon on the same alley. Hopefully it will provide a home for the old stalls of cheap clothes the street was known for.

For **books** on Xi'an, try the Shaanxi Historical Museum or the shop behind the Small Goose Pagoda. Most are expensive, with more glossy pictures than text, but there are a couple of reasonably priced, well-illustrated paperbacks on sale. Xinhua Bookshop next door has a decent selection of books and music, in Chinese and in English.

Eating

With such a diverse range of ethnic cuisine on offer, it's impossible not to feast in Xi'an. There's a fine selection of restaurants in the centre of town, as well as excellent street food, such as *hele* (buckwheat noodles) and *mianpi* (flat noodles made of refined wheat dough), available from numerous stalls. Try the Muslim quarter, particularly Damaishi Jie (see p.268), or the **night market** on the eastern end of Dongxin Jie. **Muslim cuisine**, featuring skewered kebabs and delicious mutton and beef dishes, is widely available in restaurants, and it's generally true that a restaurant with Arabic above the door can be relied on to be more sanitary than most. There's also the usual **Western fast-food** chains near the Bell Tower.

Restaurants

Chuanhan Renjia 22 Xiangzimiao Jie. An easy walk from the *Shuyuan Hostel*, with cheap Sichuan food.

Guanzhong Renjia 38 Lianhu Lu. Part of a chain of Shaanxi food joints, the Guanzhong's big dining room and platoon of staff are popular with local cadres and tour groups from the Grand New World.

Laosunjia 364 Dong Dajie. Highly recommended multi-floor Muslim restaurant. Most diners come for the house speciality, *yangrou paomo*, meat stew (¥20). You'll be given a hunk of bread, which you break into little pieces and drop into a bowl – a time-consuming process, but it gets you hungry. The bowl, marked with a numbered clothes peg, is then taken to the kitchen and piled with shredded meat and noodles. The beef and oxtail here are also very good.

May First 351 Dong Dajie. Offers steamed buns and dumplings (¥1), which you buy on the street, then take inside to the canteen. The third floor of the hotel upstairs has a restaurant with a more sedate atmosphere specializing in Jiangsui and Anhui cuisine. The speciality Banpo fish is highly recommended.

Pavilion At the *Hyatt Regency*, Dong Dajie. Elegantly decorated Cantonese restaurant, the most exclusive place in town. The food is up to standard: delicacies include abalone and shark, and there's

a speciality tea list. A meal for two costs around ¥350.

Shaanxi Local Food Restaurant 298 Dong Dajie. A Xi'an institution, great for a quick bite at the street-level cafeteria. There are also good views over Dong Dajie from the second-floor dining room, where the atmosphere and food are good; it's not cheap, though – a meal for two is around ¥100.

Shanghai Renjia Zhuque Lu, just north of Naner-huan Lu. An easy walk from the Small Goose Pagoda. Seafood, stews, and other Shanghai and Jiangnan food.

Sushi Restaurant 223 Dong Dajie. Authentic and reasonably priced sushi bar. You can either sit and select from the conveyor belt, or order pricier options from one of the booths.

Tang Dynasty 75 Chang'an Beidajie. Speciality dumplings and a daily Cantonese lunch buffet. Dinner is an imperial-style banquet (arrive 6.30–7pm) followed by a 90min cultural show, which will set you back ¥410, or ¥200 if you only want a cocktail with the performance (8pm). Tickets can be bought in advance from the theatre lobby on the ground floor.

Xi'an Roast Duck 368 Dong Dajie. This other-wise unassuming, two-floor restaurant is usually crowded at lunch. Cafeteria-style downstairs, dining room upstairs.

Xiang Xiang Da Pan Ji 264 Chang'an Nan Lu, opposite the Home Club store. For years this understated eating place, usually packed, has been serving Xi'an's signature dish, *dapanji* (literally "big plate chicken"): an entire chicken is chopped, roasted and served on a plate with hand-pulled noodles poured over the top and an aromatic sauce. Not to be missed, it's especially good with their draught beer.

Drinking and nightlife

Though not as lively as Beijing or Shanghai, Xi'an's large student population and general prosperity make it more exciting at night than most other Chinese cities. By night, red lanterns are lit across the city, and the perimeter of neon along the city walls adds to the evening ambience. Particularly worthwhile are the University District (on the route of bus #603), or the **bar street** area on **Defu Lu**, northwest of the *Shuyuan Hostel*. Just outside the South Gate in an amusement park is *Music Man*, a fun bar with occasional live music.

Tuesday is the most popular night to go out, when women get in free to all the **discos**. A favourite spot with foreign students is *1+1* on Dong Dajie – the music is a typical mix of hip-hop and techno. Things are a lot livelier after 10.30pm, when the music gets faster and only the serious clubbers are left.

The restaurant in the *Tang Dynasty Hotel* has a lavish nightly dinner and **cultural show**, worthwhile if you've not already seen one in Beijing – highlights include opera, acrobatics and classical recitals.

Listings

Airlines CAAC is on the southeast corner of the crossroads with Fenghao Lu (Mon–Sat 8am–9pm; ☏029/88790042). An airport shuttle leaves on the hour from the *Melody Hotel* between 6am and 6pm daily.

Bike rental Bikes usually cost ¥20 a day, with a deposit of up to ¥200. You can rent at many guesthouses and hotels, including the *Shuyuan Hostel* and *Kane's* at the *Flats of Renmin Hotel*.

Banks and exchange Branches of the Bank of China (Mon–Fri 9am–5pm, Sat 9am–3pm) are at 318 Dong Dajie and 233 Jiefang Lu; the branch on Nan Dajie, next to *KFC*, is open on Sun (10am–2pm). An ATM here accepts Western debit cards. You can also exchange cash at the business centres of the larger hotels.

Buses The bus station serves Hua Shan, Yan'an, Ruicheng and Luoyang, among other destinations. Another station just outside the southwest corner of the city walls has a regular service to destinations south and west of the city.

Cinema You can watch Bruce Willis speaking Mandarin at the picture houses at 379 Dong Dajie, where they show the occasional dubbed foreign action movie, a change from all the home-grown action movies. The streets around the Foreign Language Institute have several DVD parlours showing what's playing in America's theatres.

Hospital The Provincial Hospital is on Youyi Xi Lu, just west of the intersection with Lingyuan Lu.

Internet access The *Golden Seahorse* Net bar at 253 Dong Dajie is an air-conditioned refuge with four classes of surfing: common seats ¥2 per hour, soft seats ¥4, and a private room for ¥5. Shida Lu, which runs along the south side of the Foreign Languages University, is a good place to find Net cafés; try Yangguang Yidu at no. 41 (8am–11.30pm; ¥1.5/hr). Take bus #603 from outside the Bell Tower on Chang'an Lu and get off at the Home Club warehouse mart.

Mail and telephones The central post office faces the Bell Tower. There's also one opposite the *Hyatt*, at 161 Dong Dajie (Mon–Fri 9am–7pm), and another opposite the *Grand New World Hotel* on Lianhu Lu (Mon–Fri 9am–noon & 2–5pm). A 24hr telephone service is available in the same building as the central post office; you can also make international phone calls from the business centres of large hotels.

PSB At 138 Xi Dajie (Mon–Sat 8am–noon & 3–5pm).

Trains Xi'an's train station is a frustrating zoo, and outbound train tickets are notoriously difficult to book. If you're trying to get out of town by train and are willing to pay a ¥40–50 service fee, save yourself the headache and book your tickets through your hotel or CITS. The *Shuyuan Hostel* is a very helpful spot for ticket booking and other transportation info. If you really get stuck, consider flying: it's often not that much more expensive

than a soft sleeper ticket, and is available even the same day.
Travel agents The main office of CITS is at 48

Chang'an Lu (daily 8am–6pm; ☏029/85399999) and runs ¥200 guided tours (excluding entrance fees) on eastern and western routes.

Around Xi'an

You could spend days on excursions around Xi'an; look at any tourist map and the area is dense with attractions. Most people see the justifiably famous **Terracotta Army**, **Banpo Museum** and the **Imperial Tombs** at least. Other recommended attractions off the tour-group itinerary are the **Famen Si**, with a superb museum attached, which is a little too remote for most visitors, and **Hua Shan**, the holy mountain (see p.287).

The easiest way to see the sights around Xi'an is to get up early and take one of the many **tours** on offer. There are two routes: the popular **eastern route** covers the Huaqing Pool, the Terracotta Army, Qin Shi Huang's tomb and the Banpo Museum; the **western route**, going to the Imperial Tombs and the Famen Si, is less popular as more travel time is involved, and it's more expensive (it's also harder to find anyone running it off season). Bear in mind that the best tours leave by 8am.

The ticket booths in front of the Jiefang Hotel – with boards outside showing the route and the price – are the civilized faces of the seething mass of **private tour buses** fighting to exit the lot east of the train-station square. Tours should cost about ¥35 for the east route, ¥45 for the west. Tour operators on the western route often skip the remote Famen Temple despite advertising it on their signs: check before you go.

More trustworthy are the tours that operate out of the **hotels and hostels**. The *Shuyuan* offers a one-day east-route tour in a private bus (¥320 including a guide, breakfast and entry fees). *Kane's* runs east-route tours for ¥35, exclusive of entry fees. **CITS** usually deals with larger tour groups, though tours (¥200) covering both routes, with the Big Goose Pagoda conveniently included on the eastern route, leave every morning at 8am from the *Jiefang Hotel*; buy tickets the day before to check the tour is running and ensure a seat.

Around Xi'an

Banpo Museum	半坡博物馆	bànpō bówùguǎn
Famen Si	法门寺	fǎmén sì
Huaqing Pool	华清池	huáqīng chí
Mao Ling	茂陵	màolíng
Princess Yong Tai's Tomb	永泰墓	yǒngtài mù
Qian Ling	乾陵	qián líng
Qin Shi Huang's Tomb	秦始皇陵	qínshǐhuáng líng
Terracotta Army	兵马俑	bīngmǎ yǒng
Xianyang	咸阳	xiányáng
Xianyang Museum	咸阳博物馆	xiányáng bówùguǎn
Zhao Ling	昭陵	zhāo líng
Hua Shan	华山	huáshān
East Peak Guesthouse	东峰饭店	dōngfēng fàndiàn
Hua Shan station	华山站	huáshānzhàn
Yuquan Si	玉泉寺	yùquánsì

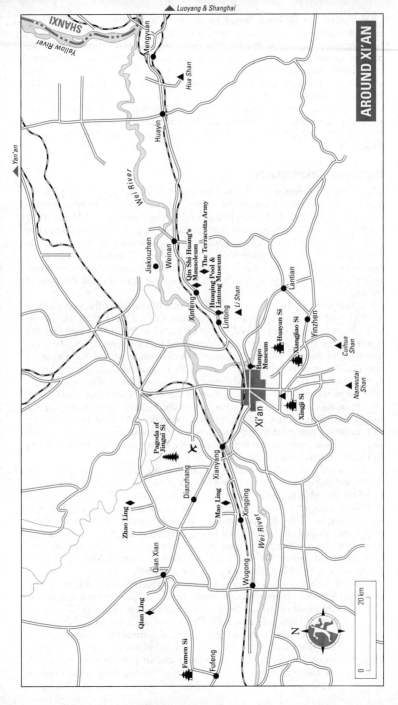

AROUND XI'AN

▲ Luoyang & Shanghai

SHANXI

Yellow River

Mengyuán

Hua Shan

Huayin

Wei River

▲ Yan'an

Jiakouzhen

Weinan

Qin Shi Huang's
Mausoleum

The Terracotta Army

Xinfeng

Huaqing Pool &
Lintong Museum

Lintong

▲ Li Shan

Lantian

Huayan Si

Xiangjiao Si

Yinzhen

▲ Cuihua
Shan

Banpo
Museum

Xi'an

Xingji Si

▲ Nanwutai
Shan

Pagoda of
Jingui Si

Xianyáng

Dianzhang

Mao Ling

Xingping

Wei River

Wugong

Zhao Ling

Qian Xian

Qian Ling

Famen Si

Fufeng

N

20 km

0

277

It's possible to take **local buses** to all the sights. This is a convenient way to get to the eastern attractions, though you'll have to work fast to see them all in one day. Getting to the western sights by local bus is time-consuming but still possible. Three public tourist bus routes leave from the train station every thirty minutes between 7.30am and 5.30pm: the #1 goes to Huashan (2hr; ¥18), #2 to Famen Si (3hr; ¥18), and #3 to Qianling (2hr 30min; ¥18). For the Terracotta Army, buses #306 and #307 leave frequently from the east side of the train-station concourse (1hr; ¥5). Last buses back to the city are around dusk. Chartering a **taxi** for the day will require some agile negotiating to get a price below ¥600. Some hotels can arrange a minibus for the day for ¥300 to ¥500.

Banpo Museum

The **Banpo Museum** on the eastern outskirts of the city, 8km from the station, is the first stop on most eastern tours. If you want to arrive independently, take trolleybus #105, which leaves from a terminus on Bei Dajie, 300m north of the Bell Tower, and get off at the second stop after you cross the river – it's about an hour's ride. The ticket affords access to both the museum (daily 8am–5pm; ¥25) and the model village (same hours), though the latter is a waste of time. The site as a whole is not visually spectacular, so some imagination is required to bring it alive. It was undergoing renovation at the time of writing.

The Banpo Museum is the excavated site of a **Neolithic village**, discovered in 1953, which was occupied between around 4500 BC and 3750 BC. Banpo is the biggest and best-preserved site so far found of **Yangshao culture**, and is named after the village near the eastern bend of the Yellow River where the first relics of this culture were found. A history written around 300 BC states that the Yangshao people "knew their mothers but not their fathers. Living together with the deer they tilled the earth and wove cloth and between themselves there was no strife." This, and the fact that the women's graves have more objects in them than the men's, has led to the Chinese contention that the society was **matriarchal**, and the somewhat questionable claim that theirs was "a primitive communist society", as tourist literature states. From bone hooks and stone tools unearthed, it is more securely known that they farmed, fished and kept domestic animals.

You can walk around the covered excavation site, a lunar landscape of pits, craters and humps, on raised walkways, but it can be hard to relate these to the buildings and objects described on the signs in whimsical English. The village is divided into three areas; the first is a **residential section** bounded by a surrounding trench for defence, which includes the remains of 46 houses, round or pyramid-shaped and constructed half underground around a central fire pit with walls of wood faced with mud and straw. Around the houses are pits, used for storage, and the remains of pens, which would have held domestic animals. A larger, central building was used as a communal hall.

North of here was a **burial ground**, around which are exhibitions of skeletons and funerary objects, mostly ceramic bowls and jade or bone ornaments. One grave, of a young girl, buried in an earthenware jar, contained 76 objects, including jade earrings and stone balls. Other ceramics found at the site, which were made in **six kilns** here, are displayed in the **museum wing**. They are surprisingly sophisticated, made by hand of red clay and decorated with schematic images of fish, deer and heads, or with abstract patterns, sometimes with marks on the rim which appear to be a form of writing. Also in the museum you can see barbed fish hooks with weights, stone tools, spindles and bone needles.

A compound of huts outside the museum, the **Culture Village** is a crude attempt to reconstruct the original village – a Neolithic theme park entered through the nether regions of an enormous fibreglass woman. Little attempt is made at authenticity beyond trying to cover the fire extinguishers with leaves.

Huaqing Pool and the Lintong Museum

Huaqing Pool (daily 8am–5pm; ¥40, students ¥20) is at the foot of Li Shan, 30km east of Xi'an on the road to the Terracotta Army (take bus #306 from the train station). Its springs, with mineral-rich water emerging at a constant and agreeable 43°C, have been attracting people for nearly 2500 years, including many emperors. Qin Shi Huang had a residence here, as did the Han emperors, but its present form, a complex of **bathing houses and pools**, was created in the Tang dynasty. The first Tang emperor, Tai Zong, had a palace at Huaqing, but it was under his successor, **Xuan Zong**, who spent much of the winter here in the company of his favourite concubine, **Yang Guifei** (see box, p.280), that the complex reached its height of popularity as an imperial pleasure resort.

Nowadays Huaqing is a collection of classical buildings, a little less romantic than it sounds – the buildings are nothing special, and the site is always thronged with day-trippers. The old **imperial bathhouses**, at the back of the complex, must once have looked impressive, but today they just resemble half-ruined, drained swimming pools. The largest is Lotus Pool, more than a hundred metres square, once reserved for the use of Xuan Zong; a little smaller is Crabapple Pool, for concubine Yang. As well as the pools, there are a few halls, now housing souvenir shops, and a small **museum**, where fragments of Qin and Tang architectural detail – roof tiles and decorated bricks – hint at past magnificence. A **marble boat**, at the edge of Jiulong Pond, on the left as

THE YELLOW RIVER | Around Xi'an

4

The Xi'an Incident

Huaqing Pool's modern claim to fame is as the setting for the **Xi'an Incident** in 1936, when **Chiang Kaishek** was arrested by his own troops and forced to sign an alliance with the Communists. The story is a little more complicated than this. As Japanese troops continued to advance into China, Chiang insisted on pursuing his policy of national unification – meaning the destruction of the Communists before all else. In December 1936 he flew to Xi'an to overlook another extermination campaign. The area was under the control of **Marshal Zhang Xueliang** and his Manchurian troops. Although GMD supporters, they, like many others, had grown weary of Chiang's policies, a disillusionment fuelled by the failure to make any real impression on the Red Army and by the fact that the Manchurian homeland was now occupied by the Japanese. In secret meetings with Communist leaders, Zhang had been convinced of their genuine anti-Japanese sentiments, and so, on the morning of December 12, Nationalist troops stormed Chiang's headquarters at the foot of Li Shan, capturing most of the headquarters staff. The great leader himself was eventually caught halfway up the slope in a house at the back of the complex, behind the pools – a neo-Grecian pavilion on the lower slopes of the mountain marks the spot. Still in his pyjamas and without his false teeth, he had bolted from his bed at the sound of gunfire. Chiang was forced to pay a heavy ransom but was otherwise unharmed, his captors allowing him to remain in control of China provided that he allied with the Communists against the Japanese. Nowadays, tourists line up at the pavilion to don GMD uniforms and have their pictures taken.

Xuan Zong and Yang Guifei

The tale of Emperor Xuan Zong and his concubine Yang Guifei is one of the great Chinese **tragic romances**, the equivalent to the Western Antony and Cleopatra, and is often depicted in art and drama, most famously in an epic by the great Tang poet Bai Juyi. Xuan Zong took a fancy to Yang Guifei – originally the concubine of his son – when he was over 60, and she was no spring chicken (indeed, accounts of the time describe her as somewhat portly). They fell in love, but his infatuation with her, which led to his neglect of affairs of state, was seen as harmful to the empire by his officials, and in part led to the rebellion of the disgruntled General An Lushan. As An Lushan and his troops approached the capital, the emperor's guards refused to take arms against the invaders unless he order the execution of Yang Guifei; in despair, she hanged herself.

you enter, was constructed in 1956. The **Huaqing Hot Spring Bathhouse** behind it offers you the chance to bathe in the waters; for a steep ¥70 you are shut in a room that looks like a mid-range hotel room (complete with a photo of a glossy tropical paradise on the wall and little plastic bottles of shampoo) with a bath and a shower. Better is the public bathhouse at the front of the complex, on the left of the gate as you go in, where you can bathe in a communal pool for ¥20; you'll need to take your own towel and soap.

The Lintong Museum

The **Lintong Museum** (daily 8am–6pm; ¥25) nearby provides a rewarding diversion while visiting Huaqing Pool; turn right out of the pool complex, then run a gauntlet of souvenir sellers for 150m and you'll see the museum on your right. Though small and relatively expensive, it's worth it for a varied collection that includes silver chopsticks and scissors, a bronze jar decorated with human faces, a crossbow and numerous Han funerary objects, including ceramic figures of horses, dogs, ducks and pigs. The best exhibit, a **Tang reliquary** unearthed nearby, is in the second of the three rooms. Inside a stone stupa about a metre high, decorated with images of everyday life, was found a silver coffin with a steep sloping roof, fussily ornamented with silver spirals, strings of pearls and gold images of monks on the side. Inside this, a gold coffin a few inches long held a tiny glass jar with a handful of dust at the bottom. These delicate relics, and the dust, optimistically labelled "ashes of the Buddha", though crudely exhibited in what look like perspex lunchboxes, are more interesting than anything at Huaqing Pool.

The Terracotta Army and Tomb of Qin Shi Huang

The Terracotta Army – probably the highlight of a trip to Xi'an – and the Tomb of Qin Shi Huang which it guards, are 28km east of Xi'an, just beyond Huaqing Pool. Plenty of tours come here, giving you two hours at the army and twenty minutes at the tomb. Alternatively, it's easy enough to get here by yourself on **bus** #306 from the car park on the east side of the Xi'an train station; the journey, on minor roads, through villages, takes an hour. Slightly more expensive, but a little quicker, are the **minibuses** which leave from right outside the station and take the direct highway. The buses run only to the site of the Terracotta Army; if you want to see the tomb you'll have to walk from there.

Beware of a stop en route to the "Amusement Park of Emperor Qin and the Terracotta Army", 1km before the real thing. Buses sometimes pull in here, and tourists, not seeing the words "amusement park" in small print, hand over ¥20 before realizing they've entered a hall of photographs and torture displays. It's better to remain on the bus until the group finishes its brief, grumbling walkthrough.

The Terracotta Army

No records exist of the **Terracotta Army** (daily 8am–6pm; ¥90, winter ¥65) which was set to guard Qin Shi Huang's tomb, and it was only discovered by peasants sinking a well in 1974. Three rectangular vaults were found, built of earth with brick floors and timber supports. Today, hangars have been built over the excavated site so that the ranks of soldiers – designed never to be seen, but now one of the most popular tourist attractions in China – can be viewed in situ. A guided English tour costs ¥50, but check to see if the electronic audio-guides are back in service (service was suspended at the time of writing) – the

Qin Shi Huang

Though only thirteen when he ascended the throne of the western state of Qin in 246 BC, within 25 years **Qin Shi Huang** had managed to subjugate all the quarrelsome eastern states, thus becoming the first emperor of a **unified China**. "As a silkworm devours a mulberry leaf, so Qin swallowed up the kingdoms of the Empire," or so the first-century BC historian Sima Qian put it. During his eleven years as the sole monarch of the Chinese world, Qin Shi Huang set out to transform it, hoping to create an empire that his descendants would continue to rule for "ten thousand years". His reign was marked by centralized rule, and often **ruthless tyranny**. As well as standardizing weights and measures (even the width of cart wheels) and ordering a unified script to be used, the First Emperor decreed that all books, except those on the history of the Qin and on such practical matters as agriculture, be destroyed, along with the scholars who produced them. It was only thanks to a few Confucian scholars, who hid their books away, that any literature from before this period has survived. Qin Shi Huang himself favoured the strict philosophy of "legalism", a system of thought which taught that human nature was intrinsically bad, and must be reined in by the draconian laws of the state.

As well as overseeing the construction of roads linking all parts of the empire, mainly to aid military operations, Qin Shi Huang began the construction of the **Great Wall**, a project that perhaps more than any of his harsh laws and high taxes turned the populace, drummed into constructing it, against him. Ambitious to the end, Qin Shi Huang died on a journey to the east coast seeking the legendary island of the immortals and the secret drug of longevity they held. His entourage concealed his death – easy to do as he lived in total seclusion from his subjects – and installed an easily manipulated prince on the throne. The empire soon disintegrated into civil war, and within a few years Qin Shi Huang's capital had been destroyed, his palace burnt and his tomb ransacked.

It is possible that Qin Shi Huang, seen as an archetypal tyrant, has been harshly judged by history, as the story of his reign was written in the Han dynasty, when an eastern people whom he subjugated became ascendant. They are unlikely to have been enamoured of him, and the fact that the Terracotta Army faces east, the direction that Qin Shi Huang thought threats to his empire would come from, indicates the animosity that existed. The outstanding artistry of the terracotta figures has revised the accepted view of the Qin dynasty as a time of unremitting philistinism, and his reign has been reassessed since their discovery. Mao Zedong, it is said, was an admirer of his predecessor in revolution.

commentary covers the same topics, and won't badger you to stop taking photographs (despite signs to the contrary, everyone uses their cameras, and most staff have ceased trying to police the flashbulbs).

Vault 1

Vault 1 is the largest, and about a fifth of the area has been excavated, revealing more than a thousand figures (out of an estimated eight thousand) ranked in battle formation. Facing you as you enter the hangar, this is one of the most memorable sights in China; you can inspect the static soldiers at closer range via raised walkways. Averaging 1.8m in height, the figures are hollow from the thighs up; head and hands were modelled separately and attached to the mass-produced bodies. Each soldier has different features and expressions and wears marks of rank; some believe that each is a portrait of a real member of the ancient Imperial Guard. Their hair is tied in buns and they are wearing knee-length battle tunics; the figures on the outside originally wore leather armour, now decayed. Traces of pigment show that their dress was once bright yellow, purple and green, though it's grey now. Originally the troops carried real bows, swords, spears and crossbows, more than ten thousand of which have been found. The metal weapons, made of sophisticated alloys, were still sharp when discovered, and the arrowheads contained lead to make them poisonous.

A central group of terracotta **horses** is all that remains of a set of chariots. These wore harnesses with brass fittings and have been identified as depicting a breed from Gansu and Xinjiang. Each has six teeth, an indication that they are in their prime.

Vaults 2 and 3

Vault 2 is a smaller, L-shaped area, still under excavation; it's thought to hold more warriers than Vault 1. The four groups here – crossbowmen, charioteers, cavalry and infantry – display more variety of posture and uniform than the figures in the main vault, though a large number of smashed and broken figures make the scene look more like the aftermath of a battle than the preparation for one. Four exceptional figures found here are exhibited at the side: a kneeling archer, a cavalryman leading a horse, an officer with a stylish goatee and the magnificent figure of a general, 2m tall, wearing engraved armour and a cap with two tails. Also on show are some of the weapons found at the site, including a huge bronze battle-axe.

The much smaller **vault 3**, where 68 figures and a chariot have been found, seems to have been battle headquarters. Armed with ceremonial *shu*, a short bronze mace with a triangular head, the figures are not in battle formation but form a guard of honour. Animal bones found here provide evidence of ritual sacrifices, which a real army would have performed before going into battle. A photo exhibition of plaster replicas gives some idea of how the figures would have been painted.

The rest of the site

At the side of vault 2 is a small **museum** where two magnificent **bronze chariots**, found in 1982 near Qin Shi Huang's tomb, are displayed in glass cases. They're about half actual size. The front one, depicting the Imperial Fleet leader's chariot, has four horses and a driver, and is decorated with dragon, phoenix and cloud designs, with a curved canopy and a gold-and-silver harness. Behind the driver is a large compartment featuring a silver door-latch and windows that open and close. The chariot at the back was the emperor's and has seats and beds in the rear. Both chariots were made with astonishing attention to detail; even the driver's knuckles, nails and fingerprints are shown. Another museum holds small artefacts found around the area, including a skull with an arrowhead still embedded in it, and a few kneeling pottery attendants, the only female figures depicted.

The complex around the Terracotta Army is a tourist circus, with a souvenir city of industrial proportions; the most popular goods are postcards and slides, as you are not allowed to take pictures inside the halls. They also sell miniature terracotta figures, fur coats and folk crafts. The food is diabolical, and it's best to eat before you go. The shops inside the halls sell souvenirs of slightly better quality, including full-size terracotta figures (¥36,000). At times you'll find a bemused-looking peasant signing postcards in the shop at vault 2. Supposedly, it's Yang Zhifa, the man who discovered it all in 1974.

The Tomb of Qin Shi Huang

The **Tomb of Qin Shi Huang** (daily 8am–5pm; ¥25) is now no more than an artificial hill, nearly 2km west of the Terracotta Army. The burial mound was originally at the southern end of an inner sanctuary with walls 2.5km long, itself the centre of an outer city stretching for 6km, none of which remains. There's not much to see here; hassled at every step by souvenir sellers, you can walk up stone steps to the top of the hill, where you have a view of fields scraped bare for agriculture. According to accounts by Sima Qian in his *Historical Records*, written a century after the entombment, 700,000 labourers took 36 years to create an imperial city below ground, a complex full of wonders: the heavens were depicted on the ceiling of the central chamber with pearls, and the geographical divisions of the earth were delineated on a floor of bronze, with the seas and rivers represented by pools of mercury and made to flow with machinery. Automatic crossbows were set to protect the many gold and silver relics. Abnormally high quantities of mercury have recently been found in the surrounding soil, suggesting that at least parts of the account can be trusted. Secrecy was maintained, as usual, by killing most of the workmen. The tomb has yet to be excavated; digs in the surrounding area have revealed the inner and outer walls, ten gates and four watchtowers.

North and west of the city

Except for the museum at **Xianyang**, the tombs, temples and museums in the north and west of Xi'an are a little far out to be visited conveniently. Trying to get around yourself is a hassle, as **local buses** are slow, routes complex and the country roads, which pass through a stark loess plain, aren't good. At least it's easy to get back into Xi'an – just stand by a road and wave down a minibus. **Tours** start early and get back late, with the sights thinly spread out in a long day of travelling, but the museums are stimulating and it's good to get the feel of the tombs from which so many museum treasures come, even though most are little more than great earth mounds. The farthest, most obscure, sight, the **Famen Si**, is also the most rewarding.

Xianyang

Most travellers who see anything of **XIANYANG**, a nondescript city eclipsed by Xi'an 60km southeast, usually do so only from the window of the CAAC bus, as Xi'an's airport is nearby. A good highway connects the two cities so the bus journey from Xi'an takes only about ninety minutes.

It may be a pale shadow of its southern neighbour, but a couple of millennia ago, Xianyang was the centre of China, the site of the capital of **China's**

first dynasty, the Qin. Little evidence remains of the era, however, except a flat plain in the east of the city that was once the site of Qin Shi Huang's palace. Relics found on the site, mostly unspectacular architectural details of more interest to archeologists – roof tiles, water pipes, bricks and so on – are in the city **museum** on Zhongshan Lu, a converted Confucian temple (daily 8am–5.30pm; ¥20). From the Xianyang bus station the museum is about 2km away: turn left on to Xilan Lu, then immediately left on to Shengli Anding Lu, which turns into Zhongshan Lu when it crosses Leyu Lu – the museum is on Zhongshan Lu, on the left. Star of the collection is a **miniature terracotta army** unearthed from a tomb, probably of a high official, 20km away, a lot less sinister than the real thing as each of the nearly three thousand terracotta figures is about 50cm high. The mass-produced figures are of two types, cavalry and infantry, some of which have heavy armour and a cap; others have light armour and a bun hairstyle. Some also still have traces of their original bright paint scheme, which show that the designs on their shields varied widely. The warriors are fairly crude, but the horses are well done.

The Imperial Tombs

The area around Xi'an was the location of multiple ancient capitals spanning multiple dynasties over more than a thousand years; the result is one of the richest archeological areas in China. Of the many **imperial tombs** scattered along the Wei He river valley, Qin Shi Huang's tomb and its attendant warriors, is the most famous and touristy. But there are others worth exploring that have compelling histories themselves. The imperial tombs to the west of Xi'an are largely Han- and Tang-dynasty structures, less touristy than other sites in Xi'an, and a good way to escape the eastbound crowds and see a bit of the countryside.

Mao Ling

Mao Ling (daily 8am–5pm; ¥20), 40km west of Xi'an, the resting place of the fifth Han emperor Wu Di (157–87 BC), is the largest of the twenty Han tombs in the area. It's a great green mound against the hills, which took more than fifty years to construct and contains, among many treasures, a full **jade burial suit** – jade was believed to protect the corpse from decay and therefore enhanced the possibilities of longevity of the soul. A dozen smaller tombs nearby belong to the emperor's court and include those of his favourite concubine and his generals, including the brilliant strategist Huo Qubing who fought several campaigns against the northern tribes (the Huns) and died at the age of 24. A small **museum** displays some impressive relics, including many massive stone sculptures of animals which once lined the tombs' spirit ways, simplified figures that look appealingly quirky; look for the frogs and a cow, and the horse trampling a demonic-looking Hun with its hooves, a macabre subject made to look almost comical.

Qian Ling

Qian Ling is 80km northwest of Xi'an (daily 8am–5pm; ¥30), and usually the second tomb tour after Mao Ling. To get here under your own steam, take tour bus line #2 (3hr; ¥18) at the Xi'an train station, from across the concourse on the east side in front of the *Jiefang Hotel*. From Xi'an's long-distance bus station, you can go to **Qian Xian**, then hire a rickshaw the rest of the way. This hill tomb, on the slopes of Liang Shan, is where **Emperor Gao Zong** and his empress **Wu Zetian** were buried in the seventh century.

The **Imperial Way** is lined with carved stone figures of men and flying horses, and with two groups of now headless mourners – guest princes and

Empress Wu Zetian

The rise to power of Empress Wu Zetian, in a society that generally regarded women as little better than slaves, is extraordinary. Originally the **concubine** of Emperor Gao Zong's father, she emerged from her mourning to win the affections of the son, bear him sons in turn, and eventually marry him. As her husband ailed, her power over the administration grew until she was strong enough, at his death, to usurp the throne. Seven years later she was declared empress in her own right, and ruled until her death in 705 AD. In later years her reign became notorious for intrigue and bloodshed, but that may be the result of historical bias, as a woman in the position of supreme power (her title was "Emperor", there being no female equivalent for so exalted a position) offended every rule of China's increasingly ossified society. Subsequently, one historian described her as a whore for taking male lovers (while any male emperor would be expected to number his concubines in the hundreds), and the stone mourners along the Imperial Way leading to her tomb were decapitated by unknown later generations.

envoys from tribute states, some with their names on their backs. The tall stele on the left praises Gao Zong; opposite is the uninscribed Wordless Stele, erected by the empress to mark the supreme power that no words could express.

Seventeen **lesser tombs** are contained in the southeast section of the area. Among the five excavated since 1960 here is the tomb of Prince Zhang Huai, second son of Gao Zong, forced to commit suicide by his mother. At this tomb you walk down into a vault frescoed with army and processional scenes, a lovely tiger with a perm in the dip on either side. One fresco shows the court's welcome to visiting foreigners, with a hooknosed Westerner depicted. There are also vivid frescoes of polo playing and, in the **museum** outside, some Tang pottery horses.

Princess Yong Tai's tomb (¥20) is the finest here – she was the emperor's granddaughter, who died at the age of 17. Niches in the wall hold funeral offerings, and the vaulted roof still has traces of painted patterns. The passage walls leading down the ramp into the tomb are covered with murals of animals and guards of honour. The court ladies are still clear, elegant and charming after 1300 years, displaying Tang hairstyles and dress. At the bottom is the great tomb in black stone, lightly carved with human and animal shapes. Some 1300 gold, silver and pottery objects were found here and are now in Xi'an's museum. At the mouth of the tomb is the traditional **stone tablet** into which the life story of the princess is carved – according to this, she died in childbirth, but some records claim that she was murdered by her grandmother, the empress Wu. The **Shun mausoleum** of Wu Zetian's own mother is small, but it's worth a look for the two unusually splendid granite figures that guard it, a lion 3m high and an even bigger unicorn.

Zhao Ling

At **Zhao Ling** (8am–6pm; ¥21), east of Qian Ling and 70km northwest of Xi'an, nineteen **Tang tombs** include that of Emperor Tai Zong. Begun in 636 AD, this took thirteen years to complete. Tai Zong introduced the practice of building his tomb into the hillside instead of as a tumulus on an open plain. From the main tomb, built into the slope of Jiuzou, a great cemetery fans out southeast and southwest, which includes 167 lesser tombs of the imperial family, generals and officials. A small **museum** displays stone carvings, murals and pottery figures from the smaller tombs.

The extraordinary **Famen Si** (8am–6pm; ¥28, relics ¥32), 120km west of Xi'an, home of the finger bone of the Buddha, and the nearby **museum** containing an unsurpassed collection of Tang-dynasty relics, are worth the long trip it takes to get here. The easiest way is to catch tour bus #2 (3hr; ¥18) at the Xi'an train station, across the concourse on the east side in front of the *Jiefang Hotel*. It also stops at Qian Ling. Otherwise, take the hourly bus to **Fufeng**, a small country town of white-tile buildings and cave houses, from Xi'an's long-distance bus station (4hr). From Fufeng bus station take a minibus to the temple (20min).

In 147 AD, King Asoka of India, to atone, it is said, for his warlike life, distributed precious **Buddhist relics** (*sarira*) to Buddhist colonies throughout Asia. One of the earliest places of Buddhist worship in China, the Famen Si was built to house his gift of a **finger**, in the form of three separate bones. The temple enjoyed great fame in the Tang dynasty, when Emperor Tuo Bayu began the practice of having the bones temporarily removed and taken to the court at Chang'an at the head of a procession repeated every thirty years; when the emperor had paid his respects, the finger bones were closed back up in the vault underneath the temple stupa, together with a lavish collection of offerings. After the fall of the Tang, the crypt was forgotten about and the story of the Buddha's finger was dismissed as a legend until 1981, when the stupa collapsed, revealing the crypt beneath, full of the most astonishing array of Tang precious objects, and at the back, concealed in box after box of gold, silver, crystal and jade, the legendary finger of the Buddha.

Today the temple is a popular place of pilgrimage. The stupa has been rebuilt with a large **vault** underneath, around the original crypt, with a shrine holding the finger at its centre. A praying monk is always in attendance, sitting in front of the finger, next to the safe in which it is kept at night (if it's not being exhibited elsewhere, as happens periodically). Indeed, the temple's monks are taking no chances, and the only entrance to the vault is protected by a huge metal door of the kind usually seen in a bank. You can see into the original crypt, at 21m long the largest of its kind ever discovered in China, though there's not much to see in there now.

The museum

The **museum** west of the temple houses the well-preserved Tang relics found in the crypt, and is certainly one of the best small museums in China. Exhibits are divided into sections according to their material, with copious explanations in English. On the lower floor, the **gold and silver** is breathtaking for the quality of its workmanship; especially notable are a silver incense burner with an internal gyroscope to keep it upright, a silver tea basket, the earliest physical evidence of tea-drinking in China, and a gold figure of an elephant-headed man. Some unusual items on display are twenty **glass plates and bottles**, some Persian, with Arabic designs, some from the Roman Empire, including a bottle made in the fifth century. Glassware, imported along the Silk Road, was more highly valued than gold at the time. Also in the crypt were a thousand volumes of Buddhist sutras, pictures of which are shown, and 27,000 **coins**, the most unusual of which, made of tortoiseshell, are on display here. An annexe holds the remains of the silk sheets all the relics were wrapped up in, together with an exhibition on its method of manufacture.

At the centre of the main room is a gilded **silver coffin** which held one of the finger bones, itself inside a copper model of a stupa, inside a marble pagoda. Prominent upstairs is a gold and silver monk's staff which, ironically, would have been used for begging alms, but the main display here is of the **caskets** the other two finger bones were found in – finely made boxes of diminishing size, of silver, sandalwood, gold and crystal, which sat inside each other, while the finger bones themselves were in tiny jade coffins.

South of the city

In the wooded hilly country south of Xi'an, a number of important **temples** serve as worthy focal points for a day's excursion. The **Xingjiao Si**, 24km southeast of the city on a hillside by the Fan River, was founded in 669 AD to house the ashes of the travelling monk Xuan Zang (see p.1050), whose remains are underneath a square stupa at the centre of the temple. The two smaller stupas either side mark the tombs of two of his disciples. Beside the stupa a pavilion holds a charming and commonly reproduced stone carving of Xuan Zang looking cheery despite being laden down under a pack. Little remains of the **Huayan Si**, on the way to the Xingjiao Si, except two small brick pagodas, one of which holds the remains of the monk Dushun, one of the founders of Zen Buddhism. The **Xingji Si**, 5km west of here, has a ten-storey pagoda which covers the ashes of Shandao, founder of the Jingtu sect.

No tours visit the temples, but the sites are accessible on **bus** #215, which leaves from just outside the South Gate. Ride right to the last stop, then take a rickshaw to the temples; you'll have to negotiate a return trip.

Hua Shan

The five peaks of **Hua Shan**, 120km east of Xi'an, are supposed to look like a five-petalled flower, hence the name, Flowery Mountain. Originally it was known as Xiyue, Western Mountain, because it is the westernmost of the five mountains that have been sacred to Taoism for more than two thousand years. It's always been a popular place for pilgrimage, though these days people puffing up the steep, narrow paths or enjoying the dramatic views from the peaks are more likely to be tourists.

There's a Chinese saying, "There is one path and one path only to the summit of Hua Shan", meaning that sometimes the hard way is the only way. This path (¥70 entrance fee) has since been made much easier. The easy way begins at the **east gate**, which leads to a **cable car** (¥110 return, though note that the ride doesn't go to the peak, but does put you above the toughest climbs). The arduous old route starts at the **west gate** and **Yuquan Si** (Jade Fountain Temple), dedicated to the tenth-century monk Xiyi who lived here as a recluse. Starting from here, every few hundred metres you'll come across a wayside refreshment place offering stone seats, a burner, tea, soft drinks, maps and souvenirs – the higher you go, the more attractive the knobbly walking sticks on sale seem. In summer you'll be swept along in a stream of Chinese, mostly young couples, dressed in their fashionable, but often highly impractical, holiday finest, including high-heeled shoes.

Known as the "Eighteen Bends", the deceptively easy-looking climb up the gullies in fact winds for about two hours before reaching the flight of narrow stone steps which ascend to the first summit, **North Peak** (1500m). The mountain was formerly dotted with temples, and there are still half a dozen. Many people turn back at this point, although you can continue to Middle Peak next, then East, West and South peaks (each at around 2000m), which make up an eight-hour circuit trail.

Though the summits aren't that high, the gaunt rocky peaks, twisted pines and rugged slopes certainly look like genuine mountains as they swim in and out of the mist trails. It's quite possible to ascend and descend the mountain in a single day, especially if you use the cable car. The going is rough in places, but chain handrails have been attached at difficult points, such as the evocatively named Thousand Feet Precipice and Green Dragon Ridge, where the path narrows to a ledge with a cliff face on either side. Some people arrive in the evening and climb by moonlight in order to see the sun rise over the Sea of Clouds from Middle or East Peak.

Practicalities

As Hua Shan is a stop on the rail line between Xi'an and Luoyang, you can take in the mountain en route between the two cities, as an excursion from Xi'an, or on the way to Xi'an from Ruicheng in Shanxi. The most direct way to arrive is by **bus**; tour bus #1 from Xi'an's train-station concourse, as well as bus #1, takes two hours to get to the east gate and cable car (¥18). The last buses back to Xi'an leave from each gate at around 5.30pm, but walk to the main road and you'll find private minibuses leaving as late as 8pm.

If you prefer to arrive by **train**, the direct N352 from Xi'an (11:01am; 2hrs) is a comfortable ride, though other trains stop at Hua Shan on their way east. **Hua Shan station** is in a village called Mengyuan, and is about 20km to the east of either of the mountain gates. From the station, public buses (¥3) will drop you at Yuquan Jie, the street that runs uphill to Yuquan Si and the hiking trail. Private minibuses follow the same rule, but go straight to Yuquan Si (¥5). A taxi should cost ¥15–20 to either gate from the train station, and ¥10 to make the trip between the gates if you find yourself in the wrong place. If you plan to climb at night, be sure to take some warm clothes and a flashlight with spare batteries.

There are several **places to stay** (typically ❸, dorm beds ¥40) on Yuquan Jie: the *Huaiying Dajiudian* (standard room ¥80, bed ¥30) is a popular staging point for night ascents. There are also basic hotels about every 5km along the circuit route, where a bed should cost about ¥30, but you'll have to bargain. Don't expect light or heat at these places, and if you plan to stay the night on the mountain it's a good idea to take your own sleeping bag. These places are at least easy to find, and hotel touts waylay travellers along the route. There's a more upmarket place on top of the East Peak, the *East Peak Guesthouse* (❺), catering to the sun watchers.

The nicest thing to be said about the **food** near the east gate and on the mountain is that it's palatable. It's also more expensive the higher you go. If you're on a tight budget, stock up before you go. There is a small convenience store just uphill from the *Huaiying*, and plenty of noodle restaurants nearby as well.

Yan'an

The town of **YAN'AN**, set deep in the bleakly attractive dry loess hills of northern Shaanxi, has very little in common with the other cities of this province. By appearance and temperament it belongs with the industrial cities of Shanxi rather than the ancient capitals of the Yellow River plain; however, the only easy way to get here is on the train or bus from Xi'an, 250km to the south. The town is a quiet backwater, and as you walk its dour streets it's hard to imagine that, as the headquarters of the Communist Party in the 1930s and early 1940s, this was once one of China's most popular tourist spots, a major revolutionary pilgrimage site second only to Mao's

Yan'an

Yan'an	延安	yán'ān
Bao Ta	延安宝塔	yán'ān baŏtǎ
Fenghuangshan Revolutionary HQ	凤凰山革命旧址	fènghuángshān géming jiùzhǐ
Wangjiaping Revolutionary HQ	王家坪革命旧址	wángjiāpíng géming jiùzhǐ
Yan'an Revolutionary Museum	延安革命纪念馆	yán'ān géming jìniànguǎn
Yangjialing Revolutionary HQ	杨家岭革命旧址	yángjiālíng géming jiùzhǐ
Accommodation		
Silver Seas International Hotel	银海国际大饭店	yínhǎi guójì dàjiǔdiàn
Yan'an Binguan	延安宾馆	yán'ān bīnguǎn
Yan'an Jiaoji Binguan	延安交际宾馆	yán'ān jiāojì bīnguǎn
Zhongji	中际大厦	zhōngjì dàshà

birthplace at Shaoshan. In the changed political climate, with enthusiasm for the Party waning (and no longer compulsory), it's now hardly different from any other northern town, rarely visited except by groups of PLA soldiers and the odd ideologue.

There's nothing spectacular about the sights, unless the fact that Mao and Co were once here is enough to inspire awe by itself. The three **revolutionary Communist headquarters** sites are dusty and feel a little forlorn despite their historical importance. The Yangjialing headquarters is the site of the first Central Committee meeting, and is the most popular tourist destination in Yan'an. Some insight into China's modern history is given not just by the **Revolutionary Museum**, but by the town centre, built during the tourist boom, an example of utilitarian 1950s and 1960s **architecture**, and by the slopes around, which are full of traditional Shaanxi **cave houses**. There is something perversely attractive in the town's grimness, which, together with the beauty of the surrounding countryside, makes it worth a day-trip from Xi'an; you could take the overnight train up and a bus back.

The Town

Arranged in a Y-shape around the confluence of the east and west branches of the Yan River, Yan'an is a narrow strip of brutalist breeze-block architecture, about 7km long, hemmed in by steep hills. Ironically, the centre conforms to Cold War clichés of Communist austerity, with streets lined with identical apartment buildings of crumbling grey concrete, plagued by frequent electricity cuts and water shortages. The town's margins are much more attractive, as the dour buildings give way to caves, and windowless houses built to look like caves, on the slopes around.

The Revolutionary Museum

In the northeast corner of town, the **Revolutionary Museum** (daily 8am–6pm; ¥15) has something of the aura of a shrine, and a sculpture depicting revolutionary struggle, opposite the entrance, has offerings of money in front of it. The huge halls hold a massive collection of artefacts including a stuffed white horse that is said to have once carried Mao, and translations of books by Lenin, Stalin and Trotsky in Chinese. Nothing is labelled in English, though; of

The Communists in Yan'an

The arrival of the Communists in Yan'an in October 1935 marked the end of the **Long March**, an astonishing and now semi-mythical journey in which eighty thousand men, women and children of the Red Army fled their mountain bases in Jiangxi Province to escape encirclement and annihilation at the hands of the Nationalists (see box, p.546).

When Mao finally arrived in Yan'an there were only about five thousand still with him, but here they met up with northern Communists who had already established a soviet. Gradually stragglers and those who had been sent on missions to other parts arrived to swell their numbers. The **Yan'an soviet** came to control a vast tract of the surrounding country, with its own economy and banknotes to back the new political system. Soldiers in China usually lived parasitically off the peasants unfortunate enough to be in their way; but Mao's troops, trained to see themselves as defenders of the people, were under orders to be polite and courteous and pay for their supplies. **Mao** wrote some of his most important essays here, including much that was later included in the Little Red Book. As well as most of the major political personalities of Communist China, a number of distinguished foreigners came here, too, including Edgar Snow, whose book *Red Star Over China* includes descriptions of life in Yan'an, and Norman Bethune, the Canadian surgeon who died in the service of the Red Army (see p.182). Both are memorialized at the Fenghuangshan Revolutionary Headquarters.

most interest to non-Chinese-speakers are probably the propaganda pictures, which include wood- and papercuts of Red Army soldiers helping peasants in the fields.

The three revolutionary headquarters

On the #3 bus line northwest along the river is the most impressive, and most touristed, revolutionary site, the **Yangjialing Revolutionary Headquarters** (8am–5.30pm; ¥10). Set in a picturesque gulley, these grounds were home to the Communist leaders in the early 1940s, a time when Mao began to look beyond fighting off the Japanese and Kuomintang, and conceptualized what a Communist Chinese state would be like. The first Central Committee meeting was held in an almost chapel-like hall, with wooden benches and the lyrics to the great revolutionary song *The East is Red* posted on the front wall. Cut into the hillside above are the residences of Mao, Zhou Enlai, Liu Shaoqi, and Zhu De, with plaques marking where The Great Helmsman had a certain conversation, or cultivated vegetables. You half expect to see a tomb with a stone rolled aside.

Back in town, the **Wangjiaping Revolutionary Headquarters** (daily 7am–7pm; ¥10) is a compound of low buildings, just around the corner from the Revolutionary Museum. Turn immediately left as you leave the museum compound and walk 200m to the access road – look for the large traffic sign over the road. The simple, low buildings of white plaster over straw, mud and brick, typical of traditional local architecture, are elegant structures, with wooden lattice windows faced with paper, sometimes incorporating the communist star into their design. Mao and company lived and worked here in the late 1940s. The complex has a rather monastic feel – the arched rooms, with cups sitting on the table and bedding still on the beds, have the simplicity of monks' cells, and the main hall is reminiscent of a prayer hall.

At the end of a side road off Zhongxin Jie between the post office and *Yan'an Binguan*, the unassuming **Fenghuangshan Revolutionary**

Headquarters (daily 8am–5.30pm; ¥7) served as the initial residence of the Communists. In 1937 and 1938, the two main rooms in the western courtyard functioned as Mao's bedroom and study, and still house his wooden bed, desk with chairs and a latrine – as well as a collection of letters and photos of Communist officers, all of which are labelled in Chinese only. Two souvenir shops sell reproductions of anything to do with the period – mostly tacky offerings including singing Mao lighters.

Baota Pagoda

Standing on a hill in the southeast corner of town on the east bank of the river, the Ming-dynasty **Baota Pagoda** (daily 6am–9pm; ¥21, plus ¥10 to ascend the nine flights of stairs) is sometimes used as a symbol of the Communist Party. High above the town and reached by a twisty road, the pagoda commands an impressive view of its angular planes and the ragged hills, pocked with caves, beyond. Outside, tourists can pose for photographs dressed up in the blue and grey military uniforms of the first Communist soldiers, complete with red armband and wooden gun.

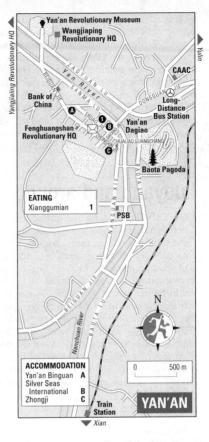

Practicalities

The **train station** is in the far south of town, a long way from anything interesting. Bus #1 goes from the station, up the west fork of Yan'an's Y-shape; bus #2 travels along the opposite bank through the centre of town and past the history museum and the *Yan'an Binguan*. A few taxis, with a ¥5 minimum fare, also cruise the streets. Long-distance **buses**, which are faster than the train, arrive either at the train-station concourse or the **bus station**, about 1km east of the town centre. A service from Linfen in Shanxi and Yulin in the north, close to the border with Inner Mongolia, also arrives here.

Yan'an is notorious for its **lodging restrictions** on foreigners and you may be forced into a higher-end "foreigner" hotel. The brand-new, towering *Silver Seas International Hotel* (☎0911/2139999; ❽) is very well located in the centre of town on Daqiao Jie, and is a far better choice than the ageing *Yan'an Binguan* (☎0911/2113122; ❼) in the north end of town. A better budget option is the *Zhongji* (☎0911/2315666; ❹–❺), at 25 Zhongxin Jie 50m up from the Hualiao Guangchang. **Eating out** in Yan'an can be a problem if you want anything more sophisticated than a bowl of noodles, though the situation has improved in recent years. There is a *KFC* on Hualiao Guangchang, with a sushi place upstairs in the same building, and a Sichuan restaurant in the alley across the street. Still, don't miss the *Xianggumian* noodle shop on Beier Xiang.

To **move on to Xi'an**, there are three daily trains, one in the early afternoon and two in the evening, the best overnight train being #4761 (8hr; ¥76). Hard-sleeper tickets are sold only from the first window of the station ticket office (officially daily 6–7am, 3.30–5pm & 8–9.30pm, but they're often closed). If you arrived from Xi'an by train or are heading for Xi'an for the first time, consider getting the bus, as the views of loess and cave dwellings en route are incredible. Express services to Xi'an leave from the bus station every 30min, beginning at 5.30am and finishing at noon (6hr; ¥69).

Luoyang and around

LUOYANG, in the middle reaches of the Yellow River valley, has two sides. There is industrial Luoyang – established in the 1950s, drab and of little interest except in April when visitors flock to see the peony blossom – and there is the ancient "City of Nine Capitals", occupied from Neolithic times through to 937 AD and now relegated to a few sites on the fringe of the modern city. Ancient Luoyang holds an important place in Chinese history; it is said Confucius studied in the city when it was the Zhou capital from 771 BC and Buddhism was introduced here in 68 AD. However, apart from the exhibits in the diverting museum there is little to be seen of the once glorious palaces and temples. Away from the glossy main boulevards, the streets are rutted and lined with piles of rubble and stacks of identical brown apartment buildings, a marked contrast that illustrates how rapid and uneven the city's development has been.

Beyond the city limits, though, you can still see the **Longmen Caves**, whose Buddhist carvings provide one of the most important artistic sites in China,

---

Luoyang and around

Luoyang	洛阳	*luòyáng*
Arts and Crafts Building	工艺美术楼	*gōngyì měishùlóu*
Luoyang Museum	洛阳博物馆	*luòyáng bówùguǎn*
Wangcheng Park	王成公园	*wángchéng gōngyuán*
Accommodation and eating		
Aviation	航空大厦	*hángkōng dàshà*
Dongbei Fengwei Jiaozi	东北风味饺子	*dōngběi fēngwèi jiǎozi*
Guangzhou	广州酒家	*guǎngzhōu jiǔjiā*
Luoyang Lüshe	洛阳旅社	*luòyáng lǚshè*
Luoyang Restaurant	洛阳酒店	*luòyáng jiǔdiàn*
Luoyang Ying Binguan	洛阳迎宾馆	*luòyáng yíngbīnguǎn*
New Friendship	友谊宾馆	*yǒuyì bīnguǎn*
Peony	牡丹大酒店	*mǔdān dàjiǔdiàn*
Tianxiang	天香旅社	*tiānxiāng lǚshè*
Xuangong	旋宫大厦	*xuángōng dàshà*
Around Luoyang		
Baima Si	白马寺	*báimǎ sì*
Cloud Reaching Pagoda	齐云塔	*qíyún tǎ*
Guanlin Miao	关林庙	*guānlín miào*
Longmen Caves	龙门石窟	*lóngmén shíkū*

and the venerable **Baima and Guanlin temples**. The city also makes a good base for an exploration of **Song Shan**, the holy mountain, and the **Shaolin Si**, home of martial arts.

Arrival and city transport

Luoyang is spread east–west between the Luo River and the rail line, with the old city in the east, the more modern conurbation of factories and residential blocks in the west. **Zhongzhou Zhong Lu** is the main thoroughfare, crossing the length of the city. A T-junction is formed at the centre of town where this street meets the main road heading south from the train station, Jinguyuan Lu.

Luoyang **airport**, 20km north of town, is tiny and served by a bus (¥15) that drops you off at the CAAC office behind the train station. The massive, upgraded **train station**, a busy junction on the line between Xi'an and Zhengzhou, is in the town's northern extremity, a long walk from anywhere exciting. However, the budget hotels are nearby and tours to the sights leave from the concourse of the **bus station** opposite.

The train station is also the place to pick up most **city buses**. From here, trolleybus #103 and bus #2 go south down Jinguyuan Lu, turning west along Zhongzhou Zhong Lu at the central T-junction; bus #5 from the station turns east, passing the Xiguan roundabout in the east of the city. Another clutch of routes begins from the roundabout, too far out to be handy for much, although you can get to the Baima Si from here. **Taxis**, which can be hailed on the streets, are plentiful, with a ¥6 flag fall.

Accommodation

Basing yourself around the train station isn't the bad idea it usually turns out to be in Chinese cities, as in Luoyang most of the attractions are outside the city anyway, and at least here you're conveniently located for all the transport connections. But if you're staying any length of time, and can afford it, stay in town; it's less noisy and cleaner.

Aviation Junction of Fanglin Lu and Kaixuan Xi Lu ☎0379/3944668, ℱ3915552. Take bus #8 from the train station and get off on Wancheng Lu. Staff at this nine-storey place wear the most stylish uniforms of any Luoyang hotel, and the guests – plenty of pilots and flight attendants – are pretty chic, too. The lobby, appropriately, looks like an airport lounge. It's a shame it's stuck in a drab part of town. ❺

Luoyang Lüshe ☎0379/5371573. A shabby building opposite the train station on your left as you exit, this is one of the better budget options. Although it's big, basic and in a noisy place, it's clean inside, and staff are pleasant. Try to get a room at the back, out of earshot of the chiming station clock, and be sure to see your room before paying for it, as some could use renovation. The cosy four-bed dormitories are a bargain. ❷

Luoyang Ying Binguan 6 Renmin Xi Lu ☎0379/3308600, ℱ3919295. A well-located new place on quiet grounds in the city centre. One of the best mid-range options, with its own air ticket office. ❺

New Friendship 6 Xiyuan Lu ☎0379/4686666, ℱ4686667. Bus #8 from the train station. This pleasant red-brick building with a chocolate-coloured lobby is stylish and rather elegant, but perhaps a little far west to be convenient. Faces a park abloom with peonies in springtime. There's a less expensive wing next door, though it's often full with tour groups. ❻

Peony 15 Zhongzhou Zhong Lu ☎0379/4680000, ℱ4857999. The most upmarket place in town, charging up to ¥2400 for the most luxurious rooms. All mod cons provided, and there's a good, though expensive, restaurant. ❼

Tianxiang 56 Jinguyuan Lu ☎0379/3935439, ℱ2561115. Arguably Luoyang's best budget option, with a wide variety of clean and comfort-able – if concrete – rooms. One of Luoyang's best restaurants is downstairs. Across the street from the train and bus stations, so ask for a quieter room at the back. ❹

Xuangong 275 Zhongzhou Zhong Lu ☎0379/3222226. Well located in the thick of things, this is a comfortable hotel with a good restaurant attached; you can't miss it at night when the front door is lit up by neon arches. ❺

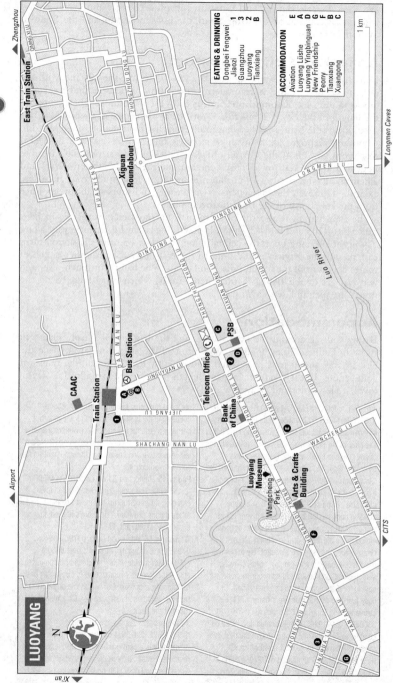

LUOYANG

N

Xi'an

Zhengzhou

East Train Station

Airport

ZHONGZHOU XILU

HUACHENG BEILU

ZHONGZHOU XILU

Xiguan Roundabout

DINGDING LU

DINGDING LU

LONGMEN LU

Luo River

Longmen Caves

ZHONGZHOU ZHONGLU

ZHONGZHOU ZHONGLU

CAAC

Train Station

DAO NAN LU

Bus Station

JINGYUAN LU

JIEFANG LU

SHACHANG NAN LU

Telecom Office

KAIXUAN DONG LU

PSB

Bank of China

KAIXUAN LU

KAIXUAN XILU

WANGCHENG LU

Luoyang Museum

Wangcheng Park

Arts & Crafts Building

ZHONGZHOU ZHONGLU

CHANGCHUN LU

JINGHUA LU

CITS

JINAN LU

0   1 km

The City

There's nothing much to detain you in Luoyang itself; but if you've got time between trips to the attractions outside town, there are a few nice restaurants, a museum and the old city to poke around in.

The main downtown area is around the T-junction where Jinguyuan Lu meets Zhongzhou Zhong Lu. Here you'll find the Department Store, six storeys of shopping with a café in the basement, next door to the *Xuangong Hotel*. Head west down tree-lined Zhongzhou Zhong Lu for 1km, or take bus #9, #2, or trolleybus #102, and you come to **Wangcheng Park** (daily 5.30am–9.30pm; ¥3), at its best in April when the peonies are blooming. Out of season, Wancheng is just another park, with a melancholy zoo, and the river dries up and smells in winter. However, **excavations** undertaken in the park have revealed much of the Zhou capital, including walls, palaces, temples and a marketplace, though none of this can be seen by the public. Across the suspension bridge in the northwest corner of the park there are also two **Han tombs**, which have yet to open to the public, apparently with some good early murals.

Otherwise, almost all that has been left of the city's dynastic importance has been gathered into the **Luoyang Museum** (daily 9am–5.30pm; ¥10), just east of the park. There are five halls arranged chronologically, which look uninspiring at first – there's a surfeit of the bronze vessels that seem to characterize all provincial museum collections, and no English captions. It gets much better as you go on, though. In Hall 2, look for the **Shang bronzes** and an endearing **jade tiger** from the Zhou; Hall 4 has some Indian-influenced **Wei statuary**, as well as a model farm from a Han tomb with a sow and her row of piglets. In Hall 5 you'll find some comical **Tang polychrome figures**, including camels and a travelling merchant keeling over under the weight of his pack. Upstairs is an excellent new hall in which well-presented relics, copiously captioned in English, are grouped by material – bronze, silver and jade – rather than by dynasty, an unusual system that here works very well, allowing direct comparisons across the centuries. As usual, the Tang wins hands down in the pottery section with their expressive camels and a hooknosed, pointy-chinned foreigner, and in **gold and silver**, where their ornate decorative objects show the influence of Persian and Roman styles. There are some strange little animal sculptures in the **jade** section that belong to the Xia and Shang, and in the **bronze** section – particularly extensive as the area around Luoyang entered the Bronze Age before the rest of China – a horse's harness from a Shang chariot.

East of the Xiguan roundabout, the alleyways of the **old city** are a rewarding area to browse around, preferably by bicycle as it's fairly spread out. The best alleys are those south of Zhongzhou Dong Lu, where whitewashed,

---

Luoyang's peonies

It's said that in 800 AD the Tang Empress Wu Zetian, enraged that the **peonies**, alone among flowers, disobeyed her command to bloom in the snow, banished them from her capital at Chang'an. Many were transplanted to Luoyang (the secondary capital) where they flourished, and have since become one of the city's most celebrated attractions, the subject of countless poems and cultivation notes. Luoyang now boasts over 150 varieties of peony, which have found their way on to every available patch or scrap of ground – a splendid sight. The peony motif is also everywhere in the city, from trellises to rubbish bins.

half-timbered buildings house small family shops whose wares include seals (engraved with your name while you wait), tea and art materials.

Eating and drinking

In addition to the restaurants below, there are plenty of noodle places and snack stalls near the station.

Dongbei Fengwei Jiaozi Dao Nan Xi Lu, west of the train station on the south side of the street. This is one of the best lunch spots in the train station area, and not a bad place to kill some time before a train. A full plate of tasty dumplings costs ¥10.

Guangzhou 12 Jinghua Lu. Out of the way but worth the trip, with an English sign so it's easy to spot. Don't walk into the grotty canteen on the lower floor; the real restaurant, boisterous and lively and serving Cantonese food, is upstairs. No English is spoken, nor is there any on the menu,

but the staff are friendly. They'll do half portions for half price, so if there's only one or two of you, you can still have four or five dishes for less than ¥100.

Luoyang Zhongzhou Zhong Lu, near the intersection with Jinguyuan Lu. A quiet place where you can eat cheap, basic dishes.

Tianxiang 56 Jingyuyuan Lu. Sumptuous Sichuan cuisine here at inexpensive prices. Part of the hotel of the same name, and packed out with local diners in the evenings.

Listings

Airlines The main CAAC office is at 196 Dao Bei Lu (℡0379/3935301), 200m north of the station. You can also buy air tickets from the CITS office in the *Peony Hotel* or the CAAC office in the *Luoyang Yingbinguan*.

Banks and exchange The Bank of China is on the corner of Zhongzhou Zhong Lu and Shangchang Nan Lu (daily 8am–5pm).

Bookshops The Xinhua Bookshop, next door to the *Xuangong Hotel* on the western side of Zhongzhou Zhong Lu, has a few novels in English and a good selection of art books.

Buses Luoyang's long-distance bus station is next to the train station on the eastern side of Jinguyuan Lu. Tickets can be bought from the office (daily 8am–5pm) or on the bus itself. Buses for Zhengzhou and Xi'an leave from the lot on the west side of the train-station concourse. Minibuses to local tourist destinations and Shaolin Si leave from the concourse outside the train station.

Mail The post office is tucked on the north side

of Zhongzhou Zhong Lu, near the junction with Jinguyuan Lu (Mon–Sat 8am–6pm).

Shopping Locally made tricolour ceramic copies of Tang sculptures are on sale at the Arts and Crafts Building, at 90 Yan'an Lu. For domestic goods try the Bai Luo Hou Department Store, next to the *Xuangong Hotel* on Zhongzhou Zhong Lu.

Telephones There's a 24hr telecom building next to the post office, on Jinguyuan Lu. For cheap international calls, try the telecom shop across from the bus station and next to the *Luoyang Lüshe*.

Travel agents and tours The main CITS office (℡0379/4313701) is on Changjiang Lu on the first floor of the tourism building. A standard day-tour of the sights in the vicinity of town, including Baima Si and Shaolin Si, costs around ¥35, and can be booked at the *Tianxiang* hotel.

Visa extensions The PSB is at 1 Kaixuan Xi Lu (Mon–Sat 8am–noon & 2–6pm), with gory pictures of traffic accidents displayed outside.

Around Luoyang

The **Longmen Caves** and the **Guanlin Miao** and **Baima Si** can all be visited from Luoyang by **public transport**, and you could just about pack all three into a single day's excursion if you don't have the time to explore at a more leisurely pace. Additionally, tours to **Song Shan** and the **Shaolin Si** usually stop at Baimi Si on the way back. If you're travelling independently to Song Shan, it makes sense to break the four-hour trip at the temple. All the sights are also served by private **tourist minibuses**, which run from outside the station. If you have limited time, the Buddhist carvings at Longmen are the place to head first: however little you know about Buddhism or about sculpture, you cannot help but be impressed by the scale and complexity of the work here and by the extraordinary contrast between the power of the giant figures and the intricate delicacy of the miniatures.

The Longmen Caves

A UNESCO World Heritage Site, the **Longmen Caves** (Dragon Gate Caves) are a spectacular parade of Buddhist figurines and reliefs. You can get to the site (daily 7am–6.30pm; ¥80), 13km south of Luoyang, on bus #81 (¥1), which leaves from the east side of the train station; there's also a stop en route just west of the *Xuangong Hotel*. Bus #60 also goes to the caves from a stop outside the *New Friendship Hotel*, and bus #53 from the Xiguan roundabout. The site is very busy in the summer, overrun with tourists posing in the empty niches for photos. The best times to visit are in the early morning, at lunchtime or in the evening.

Over the years, 1350 caves, 750 niches and 40 pagodas containing 110,000 statues have been carved out of the sheer limestone cliffs bordering the Yi River. The carvings, stretching 1km and mostly found on the west bank, were commissioned by emperors, the imperial family, other wealthy families wanting to buy good fortune, generals hoping for victory and religious groups. The **Toba Wei** began the work in 492 AD, when they moved their capital to Luoyang from Datong, where they had carved the Yungang Caves. At Longmen they adapted their art to the different requirements of a harder, limestone surface. Three sets of caves, **Guyang**, **Bingyang** and **Lianhua**, date from this early period. Work continued for five hundred years and reached a second peak under the **Tang**, particularly under Empress Wu Zetian, a devoted adherent of Buddhism.

There's a clearly visible progression from the early style brought from Datong, of simple, rounded, formally modelled holy figures, to the complex and elaborate, but more linear, Tang carvings, which include women and court characters. In general the Buddhas are simple, but the sculptors were able to show off with the attendant figures and the decorative flourishes around the edges of the caves. Also discernible are traces of vandalism and looting (lots of missing heads and hands) which began with the anti-Buddhist movement in the ninth century, was continued by souvenir-hunting Westerners in the nineteenth and twentieth centuries, and culminated in (surprisingly muted) attacks by Red Guards during the Cultural Revolution.

A tour of the caves

The caves have been beautifully renovated and feature English labelling. Starting from the entrance at the northern end and moving south down the group, the following are the largest and most important carvings, which stand out due to their size. The three **Bingyang** caves are early; the central one, commissioned by Emperor Xuan Wu to honour his parents, supposedly took 800,000 men working from 500 to 523 AD to complete it. The eleven statues of Buddha inside show northern characteristics – long features, thin faces, splayed fishtail robes – and traces of Greek influence. The side caves, completed under the Tang, are more natural and voluptuous, carved in high relief. **Wanfo** (Cave of Ten Thousand Buddhas), just south of here, was built in 680 by Gao Zong and his empress Wu Zetian, and has fifteen thousand Buddhas carved in tiny niches, each one different and the smallest 2cm high. **Lianhua** (Lotus Flower Cave) is another early one, dating from 527, and named after the beautifully carved lotus in its roof. **Fengxian** (Ancestor Worshipping Cave) is the largest and most splendid of all. Made in 672 for Empress Wu Zetian, it has an overwhelming seated figure of Vairocana Buddha, 17m high with two-metre-long ears. On his left a Bodhisattva wears a crown and pearls, and a divine general grinds a malevolent spirit underfoot. This is the highest development of Tang carving and worth studying carefully. **Medical Prescription Cave**, built in 575, details several hundred cures for everything from madness to the common cold. **Guyang** is the earliest of all, begun in 495. Here you can still see traces of the vivid paintwork that originally gave life to these carvings. There's a central Buddha and nineteen of the "Twenty Pieces", important examples of ancient calligraphy.

From the end of the west bank you can cross the bridge to the east bank, for a good view of the caves peppering the opposite bank like rabbit warrens. Up the hill is the **Tomb of Bai Juyi**, the famous Tang poet, who spent his last years in Luoyang as the Retired Scholar of the Fragrant Hill.

The Guanlin Miao

Buses to the Longmen Caves pass through the town of **GUANLIN**, 7km south of the city, and the temple here makes a convenient stop on the way to or from the caves. From Luoyang, don't get off at the main stop in the centre of town, but go to the next stop along, at the end of the red crenellated wall on the east side of the road. The temple is a five-minute walk away at the end of Guanlin Nan Lu, which leads east off from the main road through a wooden archway, by this bus stop.

The Guanlin temple (daily 8am–5pm; ¥20) is dedicated to **Guan Di**, a hero of the Three Kingdoms period and loyal general of Liu Bei, King of Shu. He was defeated and executed by the King of Wu who sent his head to Cao Cao, King of Wei, hoping in this way to divert on to the Wei any revenge that might be coming. Cao Cao neatly sidestepped this grisly game of pass-the-parcel by burying the head with honour in a tomb behind the temple.

Despite its military theme, the temple is strikingly beautiful, the elegant Ming buildings highly carved and richly decorated. Especially fine are the carved stone lionesses lining the path to the Main Hall. Each has a different expression and a different cub, some riding on their mother's back, some hiding coyly behind her paws. In the first hall, look carefully at the eaves for rather comical images of Guan Di fighting – he's the one on the red horse – and leading an army engaged in sacking a city engulfed by carved wooden flames. Inside stands a seven-metre-tall statue of the general, resplendent in technicolour ceremonial robes with a curtain of beads hanging from his hat.

The Baima Si

Historic, leafy **Baima Si** (White Horse Temple; 7.30am–5.30pm; ¥35), 12km east of Luoyang, is attractive for its ancient buildings and devotional atmosphere. You can get to the site on bus #56 (¥1) from the train station. You'll be dropped either on the side of the road or at the car park, from where it's a dash through a gauntlet of souvenir shops to the ticket window.

Founded in 68 AD, the Baima Si has some claim to be the first Buddhist temple in China. Legend says that the Emperor Mingdi of the Eastern Han dreamed of a golden figure with the sun and moon behind its head. Two monks sent to search for the origin of the dream reached India and returned riding white horses with two Indian monks in tow, and a bundle of sutras. This temple was built to honour them, and its layout is in keeping with the legend: there are two stone horses, one on either side of the entrance, and the tombs of the two monks, earthen mounds ringed by round stone walls, lie in the first courtyard.

Home to a thriving community of monks, the Baima Si is primarily a place of worship, and over-inquisitive visitors are tactfully but firmly pointed in the right direction. Inside the temple, out of earshot of the highway and the pushy souvenir sellers with their glazed pottery, you'll find this a placid place, its silence only pricked by the sound of gongs or the tapping of stonemasons carving out a stele. Beyond the Hall of Celestial Guardians, the **Main Hall** holds a statue of Sakyamuni flanked by the figures of Manjusri and Samantabhadra. Near the Great Altar is an ancient bell weighing more than a tonne; as in the days when there were over ten thousand Tang monks here, it is still struck in time with the chanting. The inscription reads: "The sound of the Bell resounds in Buddha's temple causing the ghosts in Hell to tremble with fear." Behind the Main Hall is the Cool Terrace where, it is said, the original sutras were translated. Offerings of fruit on the altars, multicoloured cloths hanging from the ceilings, and lighted candles in bowls floating in basins of water, as well as the heady gusts of incense issuing from the burners in the courtyards, indicate that, unlike other temples in the area, this is the genuine article.

Song Shan

The seventy peaks of the **Song Shan** range stretch over 64km across Dengfeng County, midway between Luoyang and Zhengzhou. When the Zhou ruler Ping moved his capital to Luoyang in 771 BC, it was known as Zhong Yue, Central Peak – being at the axis of the **five sacred Taoist mountains**, with Hua Shan to the west, Tai Shan to the east, Heng Shan to the south and another Heng Shan to the north. The mountains, thickly clad with trees, rise from narrow, steep-sided rocky valleys and appear impressively precipitous, though with the highest peak, Junji, at just 1500m, they're not actually very lofty. When the summits emerge from a swirling sea of cloud, though, and the slopes are dressed in their brilliant autumn colours, they can certainly look the part.

You can visit Song Shan on a **day-trip** from either **Luoyang** or **Zhengzhou**. It's better to visit the area en route from Luoyang to Zhengzhou, though note that the latter offers a much better selection of places to stay. Tours leave from outside both cities' train stations early every morning and take in at least the **Shaolin Si**, the spiritual home of Shaolin kung fu and the **Zhongyue Miao**, a working Daoist temple, though you won't see much of the mountain itself. Tours from Luoyang (¥35 return) usually take in the Baima Si (see opposite) on the way back, too. Alternatively you could stay at **Dengfeng**, a town at the centre of the range, from where there's plenty to occupy two or three days' walking, with numerous paths meandering around the valleys, passing temples, pagodas and guard towers,

Song Shan		
Song Shan	嵩山	*sōngshān*
Observatory	观星台	*guānxīng tái*
Shaolin Si	少林寺	*shàolín sì*
Shaolin Martial Arts Hotel	少林武术宾馆	*shàolín wǔshù bīnguǎn*
Songyang Academy	嵩阳书院	*sōngyáng shūyuàn*
Songyue Temple Pagoda	嵩岳寺塔	*sōngyuèsì tǎ*
Zhongyue Miao	中岳庙	*zhōngyuè miào*
Dengfeng	登封	*dēngfēng*
Shaolin International Hotel	少林国际大酒店	*shàolín guójì dàjiǔdiàn*

and some wonderful views. Unlike at other holy mountains, there is no single set path, and, as the slopes are not steep and the undergrowth is sparse, you can set out in any direction you like. Song Shan's sights aren't close to one another, so you won't be able to do more than one or two a day to count on getting back to Dengfeng before nightfall. **Maps** of the area are included on the back of local maps of Zhengzhou (available in Zhengzhou, and possibly Luoyang), or can be bought for ¥2 from shops around Dengfeng and Shaolin.

Dengfeng and around

The most convenient base for exploring the area is **DENGFENG**, a little town stretched along a valley at the heart of the Song Shan range, 13km from Shaolin and 4km from the Zhongyue Miao. There's nothing much here; it's basically one main street, unusual for having the name and function of every shop written neatly in English under the Chinese characters. Probably the most offbeat outlet is the Dengfeng Legendary Kungfu Weapon Shop, selling curvy swords, pointed sticks, throwing stars and the like, and cheaper than those at the Shaolin Si.

Buses from Luoyang and Zhengzhou both take an hour on the expressway, and arrive at the bus station at the western end of the main street. Here there

Shaolin kung fu

Kung fu was first developed at the Shaolin Si as a form of gymnastics to counterbalance the immobility of meditation. The monks studied the movement of animals and copied them – the way snakes crawled, tigers leapt and mantises danced. As the temple was isolated in fairly lawless territory, it was often prey to bandits, and gradually the monks turned their exercises into a form of self-defence.

The monks owed their strength to rigorous **discipline**. From childhood, monks trained five hours a day, every day. To strengthen their hands, they thrust them into sacks of beans, over and over; when they were older, into bags of sand. To strengthen their fists, they punched a thousand sheets of paper glued to a wall; over the years the paper wore out and the young monks punched brick. To strengthen their legs, they ran around the courtyard with bags of sand tied to their knees, and to strengthen their heads, they hit them with bricks. In the Hall of Wen Shu in the temple, the depressions in the stone floor are caused by monks standing in the same place and practising their stance kicks, year after year.

Only after twenty years of such exercises could someone consider themselves a fully fledged Shaolin monk, by which time they were able to perform incredible feats, examples of which you can see illustrated in the murals at the temple and in photographs of contemporary *wushu* masters in the picture books on sale in the souvenir shops. Apart from such commonplaces as breaking concrete slabs with their fists and iron bars with their heads, the monks could balance on one finger, take a sledgehammer blow to the chest, and hang from a tree by the neck. Just as impressive to watch, though, are the **katas**, a series of movements of balletic grace incorporating kicks and punches, in which the art's origins in animal movements can clearly be seen. Most striking are the exercises called "Drunken Monkey", performed with a pole, and "Praying Mantis", performed almost entirely on one leg.

However, the monks were not just fighters, and their art was also intended as a technique to reach the goal of inner peace, with monks spending as many hours **meditating and praying** as practising. They obeyed a moral code, which included the stricture that only fighting in self-defence was acceptable, and killing your opponent was to be avoided if possible. These rules became a little more flexible over the centuries as emperors and peasants alike sought their help in battles, and are local buses (¥3) to Shaolin Si, though you could also flag down a passing minibus on the main road, Zhongyue Dajie. The only Western-style **hotel** is the *Shaolin International*, 20 Shaolin Lu (☎0371/2866188, ℉2861448; ❻), which offers decent rooms a fifteen-minute walk southeast of the bus station. Head east on Zhongyue Dajie, turn right at the canal, and Dong Shaolin Lu will be on the left; the hotel is on the north side of the road. A motocab should cost ¥3.

Shaolin Si

Venerable and deadly monks are today in pretty short supply at the **Shaolin Si** (daily 8am–6pm; ¥40), the famous home of kung fu (*wushu*). However, this tourist black spot can still be interesting as the prime pilgrimage site of the cult of kung fu that has swept contemporary China.

The approach to the temple, through bleak, mountainous countryside, does nothing to prepare you for the crowds of visitors when you arrive, swarming along the kilometre-long road – jammed with touts, cinemas, food stalls and souvenir shops – that leads from the car park to the temple itself. Most of the shops are full of weapons, everything from throwing stars to cattle prods, or tracksuits, though unfortunately you can't buy the blue tracksuit tops you see

the Shaolin monks became legendary figures for their interventions on the side of righteousness. Well-known Chinese tales include the story of the monk who fought a thousand enemies with a stick while pretending to be drunk, and the tale of the cook who kept a horde at bay with a poker at the temple gates while the other monks continued their meditations undisturbed.

The monks were at the height of their power in the Tang dynasty, though they were still a force to be reckoned with in the Ming, when **weapons** were added to their discipline. The monks did not put up much of a fight in the Cultural Revolution, though, when Red Guards sacked the temple and arrested many of them; others escaped to become peasants. Though their art lived on abroad in **judo**, **karate** and **kendo**, all of which acknowledge Shaolin kung fu as their original form, the teaching of kung fu in China was **banned** for many years until the 1980s, when, partly as a result of the enormously popular film *Shaolin Temple*, there was a **resurgence** of the art. The old masters were allowed to teach again, and the government realized that the temple was better exploited as a tourist resource than left to rot.

Evidence of the popularity of kung fu in China today can be seen not just at the tourist circus of the Shaolin Si, but in any cinema, where **kung-fu films**, often concerning the exploits of Shaolin monks, make up a large proportion of the entertainment on offer. Many young Chinese today want to study kung fu, and to meet demand numerous **schools** have opened around the temple. Few of them want to be monks, though – the dream of many is to be a movie star. It's possible to study at the Shaolin Si itself, but such a distinction does not come cheap; one day of training costs ¥300 – the price for a month at most schools elsewhere in the country.

Though they are undoubtedly skilled fighters, the present residents of the temple cannot be called genuine Shaolin monks as the religious, spiritual side of their discipline is absent. Indeed, the present abbot of the monastery has a reputation for aggression which seems entirely at odds with the Shaolin way, and the temple is vigorously pursuing efforts to trademark the very name "Shaolin", presumably to stop its unauthorized use by everything from martial-arts outfits to beer companies. Genuine Shaolin monks do still exist, however, but they keep a low profile; the last place you will find one is in the Shaolin Si.

worn by the students from the numerous *wushu* schools in the area, which say "Shaolin Monastery" in English and Chinese on the back. You'll forget any plans to steal one when you see them practising at the side of the road, kicking and punching straw-filled dummies. However, if you don't see any kung-fu kicking taking place, there's plenty of evidence of it around in the broken and splintered bark of many of the trees. In September the place is particularly busy, filling up with martial-arts enthusiasts from all over the world who come to attend the international **Wushu Festival**.

The original Shaolin Si was built in 495 AD. Shortly afterwards, according to tradition, **Bodhidarma**, an Indian monk credited with the founding of Zen Buddhism, came to live here, after visiting the emperor in Nanjing, then crossing the Yangzi on a reed (depicted in a tablet at the temple). Very little remains today of the temple's long history, as it has been burnt down on many occasions. The last time was in 1928, when the warlord Shi Yousan ordered its destruction, so the present complex is fairly newly restored and gaudily repainted, with most of the halls now housing souvenir shops. A few shaven-headed kids wander around and man the shops, and will demonstrate their flexibility for a foreign coin.

The first courtyard of the temple holds **steles**, one of which celebrates, in English, the visit of American kung-fu masters. The **murals** in two of the halls at the back are one of the few things here that haven't been repeatedly restored, and they are delightful, though the monks depicted look more comic than frightening. The pictures in the **White Robe Hall**, an illustration of the Rescue of Emperor Tai Zong By Thirteen Monks, are Qing depictions of typical kung-fu moves. In the **Thousand Buddha Hall** is a well-known Ming-dynasty mural of five hundred *arhats*.

Your ticket also gets you into all the other attractions in the area, such as the cinema showing educational films and a hall of modern *arhats*. Most worthwhile is the **Forest of Dagobas**, 200m farther up the hill from the temple, where there are hundreds of stone memorials erected between the ninth and the nineteenth centuries. Up to 10m tall, and with a stepped, recessed top, each one commemorates an individual monk and is inscribed with the names of his disciples. These golden stone structures look particularly impressive against the purple mountain when snow is on the ground, or when the students from the temple are practising here in their orange robes (one of their exercises involves fighting while balanced halfway up the almost vertical sides of the dagobas).

Beyond here the mountain can be ascended by cable car or stone steps, but there is not much to see except the **cave** where Bodhidarma supposedly passed a nine-year vigil, sitting motionless facing a wall in a state of illumination (the mystic knowledge of the Nothingness of Everything). You can save yourself some effort by paying a few yuan to look at it from the road through a high-powered telescope.

Practicalities

Besides minibuses from Dengfeng, it's easy to get here on one of the regular **tourist minibuses** from Luoyang or Zhengzhou (2–3hr; ¥10). They arrive at the top of the market road, where it's a five-minute downhill walk to the temple. Consider hiring a pedicab (¥2), as along the way you will be badgered by middle-aged women as fierce as the *wushu* disciples kicking bricks around you. The women will promise to sneak you in the back of the temple in exchange for the honour of finding you a **room** – for which, of course, they earn a commission. Most will take you east of the temple, up a

steep hill to the *Shaolin Martial Arts Hotel* (℡0371/2749599, ℻2749017; ❸),
a typical Chinese behemoth befitting a tourist trap, though decent enough
as a place to stay.

Zhongyue Miao

The **Zhongyue Miao** (daily 8am–6pm; ¥25), 4km east of Dengfeng on the
route of bus #8, is a huge Taoist temple founded as long ago as 220 BC, and
subsequently rebuilt and considerably extended by the Han emperor, Wu Di.
It was rebuilt again in the Ming, then again in 1986, when damage caused by
Japanese bombs was repaired. Don't be put off by the stuffed tigers and fairground games at the gate – inside it's an attractive place, its broad open spaces
and brilliantly coloured buildings standing out against the grey and green of
the mountain behind. This is a working Taoist monastery, staffed by friendly
monks in characteristic blue robes, their long hair tied tightly on the top of
the head, sticking through a topless blue hat. They live and worship at the
rear of the temple, in old barn-like buildings, while the front is given over to
stallholders.

A series of gateways, courtyards and pavilions leads to the **Main Hall** where
the emperor made sacrifices to the mountain. The Junji Gate, just before the
hall, has two great sentries, nearly 4m high, brightly painted and flourishing
their weapons. The courtyard houses gnarled old cypresses, some of them
approaching the age of the temple itself, and there are four great iron statues
dating from the Song on the eastern side. The Main Hall itself has 45 separate
compartments with red walls and orange tiles, and a well-preserved relief carving of dragons on the terrace steps. The **Bedroom Palace** behind is unusual
for having a shrine that shows a deity lying in bed. Contemporary worshippers
tend to gravitate to the back of the complex, where you may see people burning what look like little origami hats in the iron burners here, or practising *qi
gong*, exercises centring around control of the breath.

If you go right to the back of the complex, past the monks' quarters on the
right, you come to the temple's back exit, where you are charged ¥2 for the
privilege of walking 200m up stone steps to a little **pagoda** on a hill behind
the temple. From here paths take you through pine woods to the craggy peaks
of the mountain, a worthwhile afternoon's excursion and a rare chance for
solitude; the only other person you are likely to see is the odd shepherd.

Other sights around Dengfeng

Three kilometres north of Dengfeng and a good focus for a walk, the **Songyang
Academy** consists of a couple of lecture halls, a library and a memorial hall,
founded in 484 AD, which was one of the great centres of learning under the
Song. Many famous scholars from history lectured here, including Sima Guang
and Cheng Hao. In the courtyard are two enormous cypresses said to be three
thousand years old, as well as a stele from the Tang dynasty. The path beyond
climbs to Junji Peak and branches off to the **Songyue Temple Pagoda**, 5km
north of Dengfeng. Built at the beginning of the sixth century by the Northern Wei, this 45-metre structure is the oldest pagoda in China, rare for having
twelve sides.

Just within a day's walk of Dengfeng, the **Gaocheng Observatory** is 7km
southeast of the town. Built in 1279 and designed by Gui Shou Jing to calculate
the solstices, it's a fascinating, sculptural-looking building, an almost pyramidal
tower with a long straight wall marked with measurements running along the
ground behind it, which would originally have been used to calculate the
solstices.

Zhengzhou and around

Close to the south bank of the Yellow River, **ZHENGZHOU** lies almost midway between Luoyang in the west and Kaifeng to the east. The walled town that existed here 3500 years ago was probably an early capital of the Shang dynasty. Excavations have revealed bronze foundries, bone-carving workshops and sacrificial altars, though there is little evidence of any history above ground except a stretch of the old city walls and artefacts on display in the fantastic provincial museum. Nowadays Zhengzhou is the capital of Henan Province, though this owes nothing to its past and everything to a position astride the meeting of the north–south (Beijing–Guangzhou) and west–east (Xi'an–Shanghai) rail lines. As the most important **rail junction** in China, Zhengzhou has a population of more than three million – and the industry to match.

The modern city is basically a business and transport centre, with no major tourist sights outside the museum, which is worth a day's tour. There is also a good range of hotels and restaurants, which is fortunate as the place is difficult to avoid if you're travelling in central China. From here, Kaifeng and Luoyang are easily accessible, and you can take bus trips to Song Shan.

Arrival and city transport

The **Erqi Pagoda** stands at the heart of the modern city, a roundabout east of the train station from which the main roads radiate out. Zhengzhou **airport** lies well to the east of the city. A taxi into the centre should cost ¥70, while hourly CAAC buses cost ¥15 and drop you at the Aviation Building on Jinshui Lu. The **train station** is fronted by a bustling square dominated by a huge screen showing TV programmes. Most travellers who don't intend spending a lot of time in the city probably won't stray far beyond this area, as the cheap hotels, post and telecom offices and **long-distance bus station** are all located around here. Some buses from western towns, including Luoyang, arrive at the small **western bus station** in the suburbs of the city, from where bus #24 or a ¥8 cab ride will get you to the train station.

There are two clusters of **city bus** terminuses on either side of the square outside the train station. Bus #6, from the southern side, goes to the Erqi Pagoda, then up Erqi Lu; bus #809, from the northern side, goes up Renmin

Zhengzhou and around		
Zhengzhou	郑州	*zhèngzhōu*
Chenghuang Miao	城隍庙	*chénghuáng miào*
Erqi Pagoda	二七塔	*èrqī tǎ*
Henan Provincial Museum	河南省博物馆	*hénánshěng bówùguǎn*
Accommodation and eating		
Cola Planet	可乐星球	*kělè xīngqiú*
Crowne Plaza	中州皇冠假日酒店	*zhōngzhōu huángguān jiàrì jiǔdiàn*
Golden Sunshine	金阳光大酒店	*jīnyángguāng dàjiǔdiàn*
Huayuchuan	华豫川酒家	*huáyùchuān jiǔjiā*
Sofitel	索菲特国际饭店	*suǒfēitè guójì fàndiàn*
Xiaoji	萧记三鲜烩面美食城	*xiāoji sānxiān huìmiàn měishíchéng*
Zhengzhou	郑州饭店	*zhèngzhōu fàndiàn*
Zhongyuan	中原大厦	*zhōngyuán dàshà*
Yellow River Park	黄河公园	*huánghé gōngyuán*

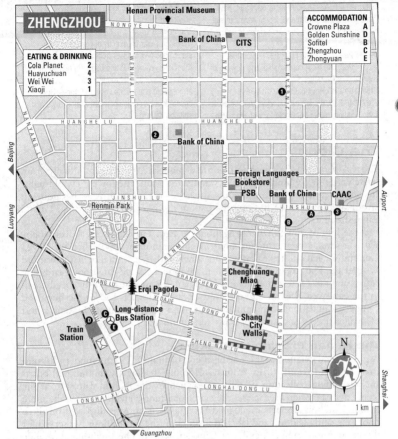

ZHENGZHOU

ACCOMMODATION
Crowne Plaza   A
Golden Sunshine   D
Sofitel   B
Zhengzhou   C
Zhongyuan   E

EATING & DRINKING
Cola Planet   2
Huayuchuan   4
Wei Wei   3
Xiaoji   1

Henan Provincial Museum

NONGYE LU

Bank of China   CITS

WENHUA LU

JINGDU LU

JINGQI LU

JINGWU LU

HUANGHE LU   HUANGHE LU

Bank of China

Foreign Languages
Bookstore
PSB   Bank of China   CAAC

JINSHUI LU   JINSHUI LU

Renmin Park

Erqi Lu

Renmin Lu

Shangcheng Lu

JIEFANG LU

Erqi Pagoda

Chenghuang
Miao

Long-distance
Bus Station

XI DAJIE

DONG DAJIE

NAN DAJIE

Shang
City
Walls

Train
Station

Erhma Lu

Ma Lu

CHENG NAN LU

LONGHAI XI LU   LONGHAI DONG LU

N

0   1 km

Beijing

Luoyang

Airport

Shanghai

Guangzhou

4

THE YELLOW RIVER | Zhengzhou and around

Lu, then Huayan Lu. **Taxis** are plentiful, and have a ¥7 minimum charge, but they aren't allowed to enter the square in front of the station; you can hail them everywhere else. **Maps** in Chinese with details of bus routes are available outside the train station (¥4).

Accommodation

Zhengzhou has a wide range of accommodation to suit all price ranges. If you are just here for a night to pick up a transport connection, the hotels around the **train station** are adequate but noisy. The entire block opposite the station is **dorm accommodation**, where clean rooms can be had for as little as ¥50. Otherwise head up to Jinshui Lu if you're not on a tight budget. Wherever you go, ask for a discount as the glut of rooms in town means rates are often half what's posted.

Crowne Plaza 115 Jinshui Lu ⊕0371/5950055, ⊕5990770. A lobby of cream-coloured marble gives the hotel a palatial look. All mod cons imagi-

nable, including a pool. Located in the east of town in an uninteresting cluster of five-star lodging. ⑧

Golden Sunshine North of the train station at

86 Erma Lu ⊕0371/6969999, ⓕ6999534. New, upmarket place but with a variety of rooms to suit most budgets, from windowless singles to deluxe suites. ❾
Sofitel 289 Chengdong Lu ⊕0371/5950088, ⓕ5950080. The most comfortable, and newest, of Zhengzhou's five-stars. ❾
Zhengzhou 8 Xinglong Jie ⊕0371/6760111, ⓕ6760469. On the left as you leave the station. A huge building, rather bare looking, with staff who require persuasion to allow you the privilege of staying in one of their cheap rooms. ❼
Zhongyuan ⊕0371/6768599, ⓕ6768977. This multistorey warren directly opposite the train station has a very small front door set among the shops selling fruit and bags. There's an enormous stack of budget rooms with an eccentric atmosphere and a wide variety of prices. Huge, cheap doubles come complete with fly swat and spittoon. ❹

The City

Today Zhengzhou is an almost entirely modern city, rebuilt virtually from scratch after heavy bombing in the war against Japan. The town's few old sights are neglected and even the ubiquitous statue of Chairman Mao has gone, in favour of a lovely lawn fronting the park at the intersection of Jinshui Lu and Zijingshan Lu.

At the hub of downtown Zhengzhou, the **Erqi Pagoda** (daily 8.30am–6pm; ¥5) is a seven-storey structure built to commemorate those killed in a 1923 Communist-led rail strike that was put down with great savagery by the warlord Wu Pei Fu. The streets that lead off it are modern, store-lined boulevards, the largest and most interesting being **Erqi Lu** and **Renmin Lu**, which lead north to the east–west **Jinshui Lu**, the most exclusive district. East of the huge and complex roundabout at the junction of Jinshui Lu and Renmin Lu (and a host of smaller streets) is a string of classy restaurants and hotels.

The Henan Provincial Museum

A giant stone pyramid at the northern end of Jing Qi Lu, the modern **Henan Provincial Museum** (daily 8.30am–6.15pm; ¥20; ⓦwww.chnmus.net) boasts an outstanding collection of relics unearthed in the region, dating from the Shang dynasty, when Henan was the cradle of Chinese civilization. Of the more than 1.3 million artefacts catalogued here, just a fraction is displayed on three floors, elegantly laid out and labelled in English (the fourth floor is reserved for the incongruous rubber reptiles of Dinosaur World). The English audio-guide (¥30, plus ¥400 or your passport as a deposit) takes you through Neolithic pottery, oracle bones, Shang bronzes, Silk Road coins, Tang glazed pottery, jade jewellery, and models of Henan's walled cities at the height of their affluence. Ancient musical instruments – some pulled from the ground months before – are displayed in the Huaxia Concert Hall, an additional wing where performances on replicas are often held. Check at the entrance gate for the schedule, usually daily at 10am and 4pm, except Mondays.

The old city

East of the Erqi pagoda, the **old city** is cut through by the **Shang city walls**, rough earthen ramparts 10m high, originally built more than two thousand years ago, though frequently repaired since. There's a path along the top, and you can walk for about 3km along the south and east sections (the west section has been largely destroyed by development). The south section is open to the street, so you can scramble up anywhere. You have to descend to cross Nan Dajie, then walk through an alleyway to pick up the path again, and repeat the process at Shangcheng Lu. Planted with trees, the walls are now used by the locals as a short cut and a park, and in the early evening the path is full of courting couples, kids who slide down the steep sides on metal trays, and old men who hang their cagebirds from the trees and sit around fires cooking sweet potatoes. Indeed, the charm of the wall comes from the way it has been incorporated by the inhabitants – it doesn't seem to occur to anyone to treat the walls as a historical monument.

A short walk from the eastern wall, on the north side of Shangcheng Lu, the **Chenghuang Miao** (Temple of the City God; daily 8am–6pm; free) is worth a look around. The attendants regard visitors as an interruption to their day's knitting and usually keep the doors closed; you have to shout through the gap to gain admittance. Though the temple has the look of an abandoned warehouse, it retains a glimmer of its past glory in the roof decoration. Well-observed images of birds decorate the eaves of the first hall, underneath roof sculptures of dragons and phoenixes. The interior of the Main Hall is modern, with a mural on three walls whose style owes much to 1950s socialist realism. In the centre a sculpture of a stern-looking Chenghuang, magisterial defender of city folk, in a judge's costume, sits flanked by two attendants.

Eating, drinking and entertainment

Zhengzhou has a surprisingly good selection of food. For local dishes head to the *Xiaoji* restaurant on Jingsan Lu. It's a bit out of the way but the place is usually packed for lunch. The *Huayuchuan* restaurant is within walking distance of Erqi Square at 59 Erqi Lu, and is a good spot for a spicy Sichuan fix. If you're missing Western food, go along to either the *Holiday Inn* (behind the *Crowne Plaza*) or *Sofitel*, both of which have reasonably priced coffee shops and lavish weekend brunches (¥100). *Dicos* is the fast-food representative around the concourse, both on the northwest and eastern edges. The typical group of Western fast-food chains centres on the Erqi Pagoda roundabout.

Around the train station there are plenty of small **noodle and snack stalls**, all much the same, and enormous numbers of shops selling travellers' nibbles – walnuts, oranges and dates – which testify to the great number of people passing through here every day.

For an evening drink, *Cola Planet* is styled after a Western pub and has mediocre bar food. For dancing head to *Wei Wei* on Jinshui Lu (cover charge ¥10), across from the CAAC.

Listings

Airlines The main CAAC ticket office is at 3 Jinshui Lu (open 24hrs; ☎0371/5991111). You can also buy tickets from any of the small ticket offices lining the train-station square and from most hotels.

Banks and exchange The main Bank of China is on Jinshui Lu, with another large branch not far from the Provincial Museum (both branches open daily 8am–5pm).

Bookshops The Foreign Language Bookstore (8.30am–6.30pm) is on the block behind the PSB, at 3 Zhengsan Jie.

Buses Zhengzhou's long-distance bus station, opposite the train station, has a computerized ticket office (open 24hrs). Bus stations in the region are generally well organized and easy to navigate.

Buying the most expensive ticket usually means getting on the fastest and most comfortable bus.

Mail and telephones The main post office is next to the train station on the south side (Mon–Fri 8am–8pm). There's a 24hr telecom office next door to the post office.

PSB For visa extensions, apply at 10 Jinshui Lu (Mon–Fri 8am–noon & 3–6pm).

Shopping The Friendship Store is on Erqi Lu, at the north end of Renmin Park. There are also a few pricey antique stores at the eastern end of Jinshui Lu.

Trains The train station has a huge booking office, with more than thirty windows to choose from, and everyone scrambling to press up against them. You can also buy tickets from an advance booking

office at 131 Erqi Lu (Mon–Fri 9am–noon & 2.30–3.30pm).
Travel agents and tours CITS (☎0371/5852326) is situated on the corner of Nongye Lu and Huayuan Lu, on floor 16 of the Yubo Building. There are Chinese-language tours to Song Shan (¥35) leaving every morning between 8am and 10am from a compound on the south side of the train-station concourse.

The Yellow River Park

Twenty-eight kilometres north of Zhengzhou at the terminus of bus #16, which leaves from Minggong Lu just outside Zhengzhou's train station, the **Yellow River Park** (daily 8am–6pm; ¥30) is really a stretch of typical Chinese countryside, incorporating villages and allotments, that you have to pay to get into because it has a view of the Yellow River. There's a pretty hill, Mang Shan, but none of the sights listed on the map which you can buy at the entrance – dilapidated temples and statues, including a huge image of Yu the Great – is worth it. You can spend an afternoon here walking around the hills at the back of the park, or riding – there are plenty of men hiring out horses, and an escorted trot around the hills for an hour or two should cost about ¥20. From the hilltops you have a good view over the river and the plain of mud either side of it. It's hard to imagine that in 1937, when Chiang Kaishek breached the dykes 8km from the city to prevent the Japanese capturing the rail line, the Yellow River flooded this great plain, leaving more than a million dead and countless more homeless.

Anyang and around

The city of **ANYANG**, 200km north of Zhengzhou, is the site of the Shang-dynasty capital and one of the most important archeological sites in China. As the ancient city lies under the ground, however, and the contemporary one is too small for glamour and too big to have much character, it hardly justifies a stop unless you have a special interest or want to break a trip to or from Beijing. From Anyang you can also get to the Red Flag Canal, one of Chinese Communism's sacred sights.

The City

Most of the city is south of the Huan River, but the ancient **Yinxu Ruins** are just north of it, in a grey industrial zone. **Jiefang Lu** and **Honqi Lu** are the liveliest districts of the modern city, with a night and weekend market on

Anyang and around		
Anyang	安阳	*ānyáng*
Anyang Guesthouse	安阳招待所	*ānyáng zhāodàisuǒ*
Anyang Hotel	安阳宾馆	*ānyáng bīnguǎn*
Chenghuang Miao	城隍庙	*chénghuáng miào*
Wenfeng Pagoda	文峰塔	*wénfēng tǎ*
Yinxu Ruins	殷墟博物院	*yīnxū bówùyuàn*
Zhongyuan Hotel	中原宾馆	*zhōngyuán bīnguǎn*
Linzhou	林洲	*línzhōu*
Red Flag Canal	林县红旗运河	*línxiàn hóngqí yùnhé*

Honqi Lu. The most rewarding excursion you can take in central Anyang is a wander around the **old city**, the area around the Bell Tower at the south end of Honqi Lu. Inside the old city, southwest of the Bell Tower, you'll find the **Wenfeng Pagoda** (daily 8am–5pm; ¥10), built in 925 AD and unusually shaped; it gets larger towards the top, ending with a dagoba-shaped peak atop a flat roof – and added Christmas lights. Behind it, a new zone of shops has torn out the heart of the old city, and it's worth perambulating around the remaining alleys to the south before they, too, are razed.

Southeast of the Bell Tower, the **Chenghuang Miao** (daily 8.30am–6pm; free), built in 1451, is an attractive building with stone carvings of dragons and lions around its entrance, well suited to its present purpose as a gallery displaying the work of local artists. On show are papercuts, masks and calligraphy – many of the local calligraphers use the Shang script.

The Yinxu Ruins

The **Yinxu Ruins** (daily 8am–6pm; ¥30) are all that is left of ancient Anyang, a city that vanished into the dusty fields so long ago its very existence had been forgotten. The historian Sima Qian, writing in the first century BC, mentioned the ruins of an early city on the banks of the Huan River, but this was thought to be mere legend until, in 1899, quantities of oracle bones were found. Later, in the 1920s and 1930s, excavations proved beyond doubt that this had been the capital of a historical dynasty, the **Shang**, which flourished from 1711 to 1066 BC, and which is known today for its large decorated bronze vessels.

The easiest way to visit the ruins is by taxi (¥6 from the station). By bus take the #15 from the bus station or #18 from the centre of town, which terminates at the museum. Then walk back up the road to Angang Lu, head west for 100m, cross the rail line and follow the track northwest for about 1km.

At the site, a rough stretch of wasteland, the highlight is a new wing showcasing **six chariots** in pits, the skeletons of horses still attached to them. The find was unearthed in 2000, and is but a sliver of what archeologists believe is a vast trove beneath the soil. Past excavations uncovered the city of Yin, and, most importantly of all, tens of thousands of **oracle bones**, which are the only relics still on display here. Peasants had been digging up these chunks of bone covered with markings and selling them as dragon bones for use in medicine before they were recognized as script and excavations started. The bones were used in divination – the priest or shaman applied heated sticks to them and interpreted the cracks that appeared – and they have provided all sorts of useful information about hunting, war, the harvest and sacrifices as this was scratched on to the bone afterwards. The bones are displayed with a translation into modern Chinese, and the Shang characters they bear are recognizably the more pictorial ancestors of those used today.

Practicalities

Anyang's **bus and train stations** are at the western end of Jiefang Lu, the town's main east–west thoroughfare, at the terminus of a clutch of bus routes. Continuing south **to Zhengzhou** or north **to Shijiazhuang** is easy, as buses and trains ply the route throughout the day. Alternatively, catch a bus (3hr 30min; ¥34) from the bus station. For rides **to Beijing**, there are zippy luxury coaches (6hr; ¥60) from the bus station.

Bus #3 or #4 will get you to the comfortable, though not pretty, *Anyang Hotel*, on Jiefang Lu just east of the crossroads with Zhangde Lu (℡0372/5922219; ❼). Better is the massive *Zhongyuan Hotel* (℡0372/5923235; ❻), a little further east down Jiefang Lu and off an alley to the right, past Honqi Lu. The *Anyang Guest-house*, 23 Xi Huancheng Lu (℡0372/5922266; ❷), is the most friendly and central, located at the western approach to Wenfeng Pagoda. For food, try the **night market** on Bai Dajie, the line of **restaurants** along Jiefang Lu, or the restaurant at the *Anyang Hotel*. **Internet access** is widely available in the alleys around the *Zhongyuan Hotel*, and also at a second-floor shop overlooking the Bell Tower.

The Red Flag Canal

The side-trip from Anyang to the **Red Flag Canal**, in the Taihuang Mountains in the far northwest of Henan Province, makes an unusual diversion. Like Yan'an in the north of Shaanxi, it's one of the holy sites of the Communist legacy. The jumping-off point for the canal is **Linzhou**, 70km west of Anyang. Frequent **buses** (¥7) come here from Anyang's bus station, dropping you off in Linzhou town centre. From Linzhou you can negotiate a jeep tour to the canal for about ¥100.

While most of the province lives under the threat of devastating floods, the problem in this area has been severe **drought**. The ambitious plan to irrigate the area by taking water from the Zhang River in Shanxi, begun in 1960, took more than twelve years to complete, one of the massive engineering feats the Chinese have always excelled at, from the Great Wall onward. Chinese pamphlets for visitors proudly state the figures: over 1000km of channel dug, 1250 hills blasted into, 143 tunnels excavated, thousands of acres of barren land made fertile.

Visitors today are given **tours** that begin at the Youth Tunnel, where the water arrives in the valley through the ridge of a mountain. You then climb up to follow the course of the canal clinging to the hillside high above the valley, where you can see it winding endlessly across spurs running down from the mountain ridges – an impressive sight. The rest of the tour takes in a dam and one of the main aqueducts, with names redolent of the 1960s, among them Hero Branch Canal and Seizing Bumper Harvest Aqueduct.

Kaifeng

Located on the alluvial plains in the middle reaches of the Yellow River, 70km east of Zhengzhou, **KAIFENG** is an ancient capital with a history stretching back over three thousand years. However, unlike other ancient capitals in the area, the city hasn't grown into an industrial monster, and remains pleasingly compact, with all its sights in a fairly small area within the walls. It's been spruced up a lot recently, and today Kaifeng is a thriving town, not at all the sleepy place you might expect, with an ongoing beautification campaign underway to attract tourists. On the downside, this means tourist resources, theme parks and the like have been constructed which, together with the mass influx of visitors, may destroy the charm of the place; but on the plus side the PSB takes a relaxed attitude towards foreign visitors, which means there are no restrictions on where foreigners can stay, and visas can be extended with little hassle. A great night market, a sprinkling of sights – some pretty temples and pagodas – and a calm atmosphere make this a worthwhile place to spend a few days, especially if you've grown weary of the scale and pace of most Chinese cities.

Some history

The city's heyday came under the Northern Song dynasty between 960 and 1127 AD. First heard of as a Shang town around 1000 BC, it served as the

Kaifeng

Kaifeng	开封	kāifēng
Fan Pagoda	繁塔	fán tǎ
Iron Pagoda Park	铁塔公园	tiětǎ gōngyuán
Kaifeng Museum	开封博物馆	kāifēng bówùguǎn
Longting Park	龙亭公园	lóngtíng gōngyuán
Memorial Temple to Lord Bao	包公祠	bāogōng cí
Qingming Park	清明上河园	qīngmíng shànghéyuán
Shanshangan Guild Hall	陕山甘会馆	shǎnshāngān huìguǎn
Song Jie	宋都御街	sòngdū yùjiē
Xiangguo Si	相国寺	xiàngguó sì
Yangjia Hu	杨家湖	yángjiā hú
Yanqing Guan	延庆观	yánqìng guàn
Yellow River Park	黄河公园	huánghé gōngyuán
Yu Terrace	古吹台	gǔchuī tái
Yuwangtai Park	禹王台公园	yǔwángtái gōngyuán
Accommodation and eating		
Bianjing	汴京饭店	biànjīng fàndiàn
Dajintai	大金台旅馆	dàjīntái lǚguǎn
Diyi Lou	第一楼	dìyīlóu
Dongjing	东京大饭店	dōngjīng dàfàndiàn
Gulou Jiaozi Guan	鼓楼饺子馆	gǔlóu jiǎoziguǎn
Kaifeng	开封宾馆	kāifēng bīnguǎn
Shao'e Huang	烧鹅皇酒店	shāo'é huáng jiǔdiàn
Yingbin Fandian	迎宾饭店	yíngbīn fàndiàn
Xinsheng	新生饭庄	xīnshēng fàndiàn

capital of several early kingdoms and minor dynasties, but under the Song the city became the political, economic and cultural centre of the empire. A famous five-metre-long horizontal scroll by Zhang Azheduan, *Riverside Scene at the Qingming Festival*, now in the Forbidden City in Beijing, unrolls to show views of the city at this time, teeming with life, crammed with people, boats, carts and animals. It was a great age for painting, calligraphy, philosophy and poetry, and Kaifeng became famous for the quality of its textiles and embroidery and for its production of ceramics and printed books. It was also the home of the first mechanical clock in history, Su Song's astronomical clock tower of 1092, which worked by the transmission of energy from a huge water wheel.

This Golden Age ended suddenly in 1127 when Jurchen invaders overran the city. Just one royal prince escaped to the south, to set up a new capital out of harm's reach at Hangzhou beyond the Yangzi, but Kaifeng itself never recovered. What survived has been damaged or destroyed by repeated flooding since – between 1194 and 1887 there were more than fifty severe incidents, including one fearful occasion when the dykes were breached during a siege and at least three hundred thousand people are said to have died, among which were many of Kaifeng's Jewish community.

Orientation, arrival and city transport

Central Kaifeng, bounded by walls roughly 3km long at each side, is fairly small, and most places of interest are within walking distance of one another. **Zhongshan Lu** is the main north–south thoroughfare, while **Sihou Jie**, which changes its name to Gulou Jie at the centre and Mujiaqiao Jie in the east, is the

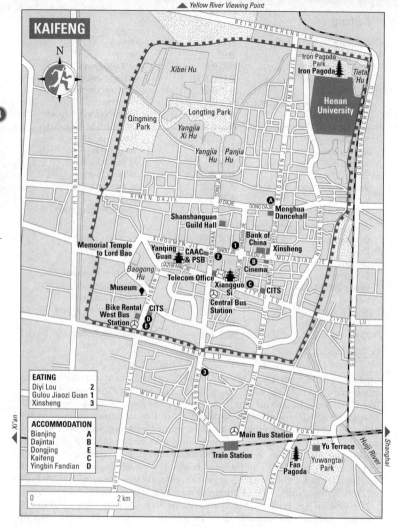

KAIFENG

N

Yellow River Viewing Point

BEIHUANGCHENG LU

Xibei Hu

Iron Pagoda
Park
Iron Pagoda

Tieta
Hu

**Henan
University**

Longting Park

Qingming
Park

Yangjia
Xi Hu

Yangjia
Hu

Panjia
Hu

XIMEN DAJIE

SONG JIE

XI DAJIE

DONG DAJIE

BIANJING JIE

BEIMEN DAJIE

BEIDAONEN JIE

DONGHUANGCHENG LU

NEIHUAN DONG

**Shanshanguan
Guild Hall**

**Memorial Temple
to Lord Bao**

Yanqing
Guan

**CAAC
& PSB**

XIHOUMEN JIE

DAZHIFANG JIE

ZHONGSHAN

SIHOU JIE

GULOU JIE

SHUDIAN JIE

Menghua
Dancehall

Ⓐ

Bank of
China

Ⓑ

Xinsheng

Cinema

Ⓒ

MUJIAQIAO JIE

NANTU JIE

Baogong
Hu

Museum

Telecom Office

Xiangguo
Si

CITS

**Bike Rental
West Bus
Station**

CITS

Ⓓ
Ⓔ

**Central Bus
Station**

ZIYOU LU

GONGYUAN JIE

YONG JIE

BINHE LU

WUYI LU

WUFU XI LU

ZHONGSHAN JIE

XINAN GUAN JIE

TIELEI BU YUAN

GONGXING

ZIYOU LU

Huiji River

Ⓗ **Main Bus Station**

Train Station

Yu Terrace

**Fan
Pagoda**

Yuwangtai
Park

POTA XIJIE

EATING
Diyi Lou   2
Gulou Jiaozi Guan   1
Xinsheng   3

ACCOMMODATION
Bianjing   A
Dajintai   B
Dongjing   E
Kaifeng   C
Yingbin Fandian   D

0   2 km

XIHUANCHENG LU

Xi'an

Shanghai

main east–west road. Kaifeng's heart is the **crossroads** of Sihou Jie and Shudian Jie, where the night market sets up. The town is crisscrossed by canals, once part of a network that connected it to Hangzhou and Yangzhou in ancient times.

The **train station**, on the Xi'an–Shanghai line, is in a dull, utilitarian area outside the walls, about 2km south of the centre. The main long-distance **bus station** is next to the train station, and there's a smaller bus station, for buses to or from western destinations, notably Zhengzhou, on Yingbin Lu, just inside the walls. If coming from Dengfeng or other well-travelled routes, you might end up at a third bus station in the middle of town, on Zhongshan Lu.

Most of the city's **bus routes** begin outside the train station. Bus #1 goes from here north up Yingbin Lu, then along Zhongshan Lu to Panjia Hu, continuing through the centre of town and terminating near the north section of the city wall on Beimen Dajie. Bus #3 is also useful, making a straight north-south run from Iron Pagoda Park to the train station. For a relatively small place, there are a lot of **taxis** cruising the streets and used to dealing with tourists. The minimum fare of ¥5 is sufficient for rides in town. **Cycling** is an ideal way to get around as the streets are wide and flat, though there aren't many spots to rent a bike: the best bet is the bike repair shops across the street from the *Yingbin Hotel* in the south of town. You can get a **map** of Kaifeng (¥2.5) at the bus station.

Accommodation

Despite Kaifeng's small size, it has a wealth of good, cheap **hotels**. As there's no bar here on foreigners staying in Chinese-style hotels, lone travellers may wish to take advantage: staff are generally reluctant to put a Chinese in a room with foreigners, so you'll usually get a room to yourself even though the convention in these places is to charge you for the bed, rather than the room.

The *Dajintai* is the budget hotel of choice in Kaifeng, though if money's tight cheaper rooms might be had at one of several new, inexpensive hotels further east on Gulou Dajie, where you may find a bed on offer for as little as ¥40, a room for ¥80.

Bianjing Corner of Dong Dajie and Beitu Jie ☎0378/2886699. Bus #3 from the station comes here. Go into the large compound and the reception is the first building on the left. The abundance of concrete sets an institutional atmosphere, but it's central, clean and has recently been redecorated. ❺

Dajintai Gulou Dajie ☎0378/2552888. This hotel is about 50m west of the Dazhong Cinema, on the route of bus #4. In the heart of the night market and most interesting section of town, this is the best place to stay, yet not unduly noisy: most pedi-cab drivers know exactly where to go. Haggle hard as they're quite stubborn as regards discounts. ❹

Dongjing 14 Yingbin Lu ☎0378/3989388, ☏3938861. It's a short walk from the west bus station, and buses #1 and #9 come here from the train station. This compound of buildings, set in a

park just inside the walls in the south of the city, looks like a health sanatorium, and is suitably quiet, low-key and comfortable, with a good range of services including a post office. ❹

Kaifeng 66 Ziyou Lu ☎0378/5955589 ext 6119, ☏5953086. Bus #9 from the train station. This central, three-star hotel in a large, attractive compound off the street is where most tour groups end up. It has four buildings and a range of rooms, including triples and quads. Comfortable without being ostentatious, and surprisingly inexpensive. ❺

Yingbin Fandian 96 Yingbin Lu ☎0378/3931943. Just north of the *Dongjing*, to which this brown, institutional-looking building is a budget alterna-tive, decent enough though nothing to write home about. Staff are friendly and game for long negotiations over the price. ❸

The Town

The town **walls**, tamped earth ramparts, have been heavily damaged and there's no path along them, but they are a useful landmark and a boundary line that serves to divide the city into a downtown and a suburban section. Inside the walls, Kaifeng is quite an attractive place, with a sprinkling of good-looking buildings close to each other along streets that have a more human scale and are freer of traffic than most Chinese towns.

Inside the walls

Shudian Jie is a pretty street at the centre of town, lined with two-storey Qing buildings with fancy balconies. Finest is the building on the corner at the intersection with Gulou Jie – inside it's an ordinary dumpling shop, but the architectural detail outside, particularly the stone reliefs at the base, are very fine. Come here in the evening to see this sedate street transformed into a busy

night market, when brightly lit stalls selling mostly underwear, cosmetics and plastic kitchenware line its length. You may find the odd trinket worth bartering for, especially if you collect novelty lighters, but it's really a place to wander in your best clothes, which is what most of the locals do. The stalls on Gulou Jie sell books of all kinds, from art monographs to pulp fiction with lurid covers. Of most interest, though, are the food stalls that set up around the crossroads, huge numbers of them, where for a few yuan you can get food to make the back of the legs quiver (see p.316).

Shanshanguan Guild Hall

An alley, Xufu Jie, too narrow to be marked on some maps, leads west off the northern end of Shudian Jie to the **Shanshanguan Guild Hall** (daily 8am–6.30pm; ¥15), which is worth the effort needed to find it, as it's a superb example of Qing-dynasty architecture at its most lavish. It was established by merchants of Shanxi, Shaanxi and Gansu provinces to provide cheap accommodation and a social centre for visiting merchants. In more recent history, it was part of the school next door, though now it's being pushed as a tourist site and undergoing restoration. With a spirit wall, drum and bell tower, and the Main Hall flanked by smaller side halls, it has the structure of a flashy, ostentatious temple. The wood carvings on the eaves are excellent, including lively and rather wry scenes from the life of a travelling merchant – look for the man being dragged along the ground by his horse in the Eastern Hall. In the eaves of the Main Hall, there are gold bats (a symbol of luck) beneath accurate images of animals and birds frolicking among bunches of grapes. Inside is a model of the modern town next to one of the Song city.

Xiangguo Si and Yanqing Guan

Head back on to Shudian Jie and walk south, past the crossroads, and you'll come to Madao Jie, full of clothing boutiques. At the bottom of this street, turn right and you'll come to the **Xiangguo Si** (daily 8am–6pm; ¥30), which was originally built in 555 AD, though the present structure dates back to 1766. The simple layout of the three buildings is pleasing, though the front courtyard now holds an amusement park. Things get better the farther in you go. At the back of the Main Hall is a colourful, modern frieze of *arhats*, and the Daxiong Baodian (Great Treasure House) has a good early Song bronze Buddha. In an unusual octagonal hall at the back you'll see a magnificent four-sided Guanyin carved in ginkgo wood and covered in gold leaf, about 3m high.

A kilometre west, along Ziyou Lu, is the **Yanqing Guan** (daily 8am–7pm; ¥10), whose rather odd, knobbly central building, the **Pavilion of the Jade Emperor**, is all that remains of a larger complex built at the end of the thirteenth century. The outside of this octagonal structure of turquoise tiles and carved brick is overlaid with ornate decorative touches, such as imitation *dougong* (wooden brackets); inside, a bronze image of the Jade Emperor sits in a room that is by contrast strikingly austere. The rest of the complex at first looks just as old, though the images of kangaroos among the animals decorating the eaves give a clue to its recent construction.

Baogong Hu

Within walking distance of Yanqing Guan is **Baogong Hu**, one of the large lakes inside Kaifeng whose undisturbed space helps give the town its laid-back feel. On a promontory on the western side, and looking very attractive from a distance, the **Memorial Temple to Lord Bao** (daily 7am–7pm; ¥20) is a

Kaifeng's Jews

The origins of Kaifeng's **Jewish community** are something of a mystery. A Song-dynasty stele now in the town museum records that they arrived here in the Zhou dynasty, nearly three thousand years ago, which seems doubtful. It's more likely their ancestors came here from central Asia around 1000 AD, when trade links between the two areas were strong, a supposition given some weight by the characteristics they share with Persian Jews, such as their use of a Hebrew alphabet with 27 rather than 22 letters. The community was never large, but it seems to have flourished until the nineteenth century, when – perhaps as a result of disastrous floods, including one in 1850 which destroyed the synagogue – the Kaifeng Jews almost completely died out. The synagogue, which stood at the corner of Pingdeng Jie and Beixing Jie, on the site of what is now a hospital, was never rebuilt, and no trace of it remains today.

A number of families in Kaifeng trace their lineage back to the Jews, and, following the atmosphere of greater religious tolerance in contemporary China, have begun practising again. You can see a few relics from the synagogue in Kaifeng Museum, including three steles that once stood outside it, but most, such as a Torah in Chinese now in the British Museum, are in collections abroad.

modern imitation of a Song building holding an exhibition of the life of this legendary figure who was Governor of Kaifeng during the Northern Song. Judging from the articles exhibited, including modern copies of ancient guillotines, and the scenes from his life depicted in paintings on the walls, Lord Bao was a harsh but fair judge, who must have had some difficulty getting through doors if he really wore a hat and shoes like the ones on display. A substantial mansion on the south side of the lake, the **Kaifeng Museum** (daily 8.30–11.30am & 2.30–5.30pm; ¥10), holds steles recording the history of Kaifeng's Jewish community that used to stand outside the synagogue, but not much else.

Song Jie, Yangjia Hu, Qingming and Longting parks

Heading back in the general direction of Shanshanguan Guild Hall, you can turn north up Zhongshan Lu and continue on to **Song Jie**, on the site of the Song-dynasty Imperial Palace. This is now a street of tourist shops built to look like Song buildings, and is entered through an arch at the southern end. The shops look impressive from a distance but they're pretty shabbily made, especially the Fan Tower, an entertainments centre at the northern end, which is marked as a major attraction on tourist maps. The shops sell antiques and curios, and there are two good art shops on the eastern side. In the winter, when most of the tourists have gone, many of the shops switch to selling household goods.

At the northern end of Song Jie, **Yangjia Hu** was originally part of the imperial park but is now at the centre of a large warren of carnival-like tourist traps, including an amusement park based on Zhang Zeduan's *Riverside Scene at Qingming Festival*, one China's best-known paintings, a Song-dynasty scroll depicting the city. At **Qingming Park** (daily 9am–5.30pm; ¥30), west of the lake, you can walk through the scenery Zhang painted, wandering to your heart's content past costumed courtesans and ingratiating shopkeepers. **Longting Park** (daily 6am–6.30pm; ¥35), across the causeway and on the northern shore of Yangjia Hu, has a somewhat desolate feel, though it makes for good people-watching when the crowds are out.

From the centre of town, buses #1 and #3 go to the far northeast corner of the rough square formed by the city walls, to **Iron Pagoda Park** (daily 7am–7pm; ¥20), just north of Henan University, and only accessible off Beimen Dajie. At the centre of this leafy park you'll find the 13-storey, 56-metre-high Iron Pagoda that gives it its name, a striking Northern Song (1049 AD) construction so named because its surface of glazed tiles gives the building the russet tones of rusted iron. Its base, like all early buildings in Kaifeng, is buried beneath a couple of metres of silt deposited during floods. Most of the tiles hold relief images, usually of the Buddha, but also of Buddhist angels, animals and abstract patterns. You can climb up the inside, via a gloomy spiral staircase, for an extra ¥10.

Outside the walls

Two kilometres south of town, about 1km east of the train station, you'll find the pleasant **Yuwangtai Park** (daily 7am–7pm; ¥10); buses #8 and #15 will get you close, otherwise its a long and dusty walk through the most run-down part of town. Its main feature is the **Yu Terrace**, an earthen mound now thought to have been a music terrace, that was once the haunt of Tang poets. The park, dotted with pavilions and commemorative steles, is pleasant in summer when the many flower gardens are in bloom.

Not far from here, its top visible from the park, the **Fan Pagoda** (7am–7pm; ¥5) is not in a park as maps say, but sits between a car repair yard and a set of courtyards in a suburbia of labyrinthine alleyways. The only approach is from the western side. The fact that the local inhabitants tie their washing lines to the wall around the base and peel sweetcorn in the courtyard adds to the charm of the place. Built in 997 AD and the oldest standing building in Kaifeng, this dumpy hexagonal brick pagoda was once 80m tall and had nine storeys; three remain today, and you can ascend for a view of rooftops and factories. The carved bricks on the outside are good, though the bottom few layers are new after vandalism in the Cultural Revolution.

From a bus station on the west side of Beimen Dajie, opposite the entrance to the Iron Pagoda Park, it's worth catching bus #6 to the **Yellow River Viewing Point**, 11km north of town, especially if you haven't seen the river before. From the pavilion here you can look out onto a plain of silt that stretches to the horizon, across whose dramatic emptiness the syrupy river meanders. Beside the pavilion is an iron ox, which once stood in a now submerged temple. It's a cuddly-looking beast with a horn on its head that makes it look like a rhino sitting on its hind legs. An inscription on the back reveals its original function – a charm to ward off floods, a tradition begun by the legendary flood-tamer Da Yu (see p.261).

Eating, drinking and nightlife

The best place to eat is the **night market** on Shudian Jie, where the food as well as the ambience is much better than in the few sit-down canteens. Here you'll find not just the usual staples such as *jiaozi*, made in front of you, and skewers of mutton cooked by Uigur pedlars, but also a local **delicacy** consisting of hot liquid jelly, into which nuts, berries, flowers and fruit are poured. You can spot jelly stalls by the huge bronze kettle they all have with a spout in the form of a dragon's head. Another delicious sweet on sale here is slices of banana covered with pancake mix then deep-fried. Wash it all down with a bottle of local Bianjing Beer.

On the south side of Gulou Jie are a couple of **fast-food places**, such as *Dicos*, which has decent coffee. For **dumplings**, don't miss the *Gulou Jiaozi Guan*, probably China's prettiest dumpling shop, in the restored wood structure at the corner of Gulou Jie and Nan Shudian Jie. As for **restaurants**, at 66 Gulou Jie (just down the street from the *Dajintai* hotel) is the *Xinsheng Restaurant*, a clean, comfortable place; otherwise the restaurant in the *Kaifeng Hotel* is pretty good. The swanky *Shao'e Huang Restaurant*, on the southern section of Zhongshan Lu, is where the local elite hang out. There's no English menu, but you can select a variety of vegetable, fish and meat dishes from the display downstairs; expect to pay ¥100 for a meal for two. A variety show of singing, acrobatics and ear-piercing music plays nightly at the *Diyi Lou Restaurant*, 43 Sihou Jie; dinner for two with drinks should come to around ¥60. Aside from the night market, **entertainment** options are poor. Try the Dazhong Cinema at the eastern end of Gulou Jie.

Listings

Airlines Buy air tickets at the CAAC office at the southwest corner of Zhongshan Lu and Sihou Jie (8am–7pm; ☏0378/5955555). The nearest airport is at Zhengzhou (see p.307).

Banks and exchange The Bank of China is on the north side of Gulou Jie (Mon–Fri 8am–5pm).

Bike rental You can rent decent bikes for ¥10 a day, with a ¥100 deposit from the bike repair shops across from the *Yingbin Hotel*. You'll have to ask, as bikes are kept inside, making the stand easy to miss.

Bookshops Shudian Jie is lined with shops catering to most tastes. The Xinhua Bookstore, on the east side of the street just north of Xi Dajie, has a limited selection of English books, but they do sell good maps. More fun is perusing the publications at the large night market that fills the Gulou area.

Buses Both Anyang and Zhengzhou (¥15) are only about ninety minutes away. Most buses departing for major destinations leave from the main station. You can buy tickets from the 24hr booking offices.

Internet A large, clean Internet bar (open 24 hours, ¥1.5/hr) is just down the alley behind the PSB office.

Mail and telephones There's a large, efficient post office on Ziyou Lu (Mon–Fri 8am–noon & 2.30–6pm), with a 24hr telecom office next door.

PSB The main police station is on Zhongshan Lu. The section that deals with visas is windows #3 and #4, where the staff are so laid-back they're almost hip; a visa extension (¥120) can take ten minutes.

Shopping Kaifeng is a good place to find paintings and calligraphy, among the best buys in China. Apart from the shops on Song Jie, there's a good, cheap art shop on the corner of Sihou Jie, not far from the intersection with Shudian Jie.

Trains The train station is small and not too hard to figure out. You can buy tickets at the station booking office or book through CITS.

Travel agents Staff in the CITS office on 68 Ziyou Lu (☏0378/5666456) can be reluctant to help – your reception seems to depend on how much or how little you're willing to spend. They offer one- and two-day tours, sell train tickets (¥40 surcharge) and have a free map in English that is pretty inaccurate. It's east past the *Kaifeng Hotel*.

Shandong

Shandong Province, a fertile plain through which the Yellow River completes its journey, is shaped like an eagle launching itself into the sky – an appropriate image for a province beginning to assert itself after a fraught and stagnant past. For centuries Shandong languished as one of the poorest regions of China, overpopulated and at the mercy of the Yellow River, whose course has continually shifted, its delta swinging over time from the Yellow

Sea in the south to the Bohai Gulf in the north, bringing chaos with every move.

However, the fertility of the flood plain means that human settlements have existed here for more than six thousand years, with **Neolithic remains** found at two sites, Dawenkou and Longshan. Relics such as wheel-made pottery and carved jade indicate a surprisingly highly developed agricultural society. In the Warring States Period (720–221 BC) Shandong included the states of Qi and Lu, and the province is well endowed with **ancient tombs and temples**, the best of which are to be found on **Tai Shan**, China's holiest Taoist mountain near the centre of the province, and its most spectacular tourist site. A second major religious site is the magnificent temple at **Qufu**, home of the province's most illustrious son, **Confucius**.

Shandong's modern history, though, is dominated by **foreign influence** and its ramifications. In 1897 the Germans arrived, occupying the port of **Qingdao** in the south of the province which now looks transplanted from Bavaria (and presides over the best beaches in northern China). The province's ugly contemporary capital, **Ji'nan**, soon followed, and German influence spread as they built a rail system across the province. Their legacy is still visible in the architecture of many of Shandong's train stations. At the beginning of the last century, resentment at foreign interference, exacerbated by floods and an influx of refugees from the south, combined to make Shandong the setting for the **Boxer Rebellion** (see p.1162).

Behind Qingdao's German facade is evidence of a new side to Shandong, and a sprawling mass of factories testifies to the rapid pace of modernization and industrialization. Qingdao is the main industrial town, with Ji'nan second, and most trade is done through the port of **Yantai**. The new **Shengli oilfield**, in the northeast, is China's second largest, and as large oil reserves in the Bohai sea bed have only just begun to be exploited, a massive economic resurgence seems on the cards. Shandong's **tourist industry** is also kicking off. Although the rail network is sparse, travelling around the province is made much easier by new highways which connect the major cities. One welcome feature of the province is the relative laxity of the rules on where foreigners are allowed to stay, and budget travellers will find the main sites, Tai Shan and Qufu, agreeably inexpensive. Another bonus is the friendliness of the people, who are proud of their reputation for hospitality, a tradition that goes right back to Confucius, who declared in *The Analects*, "Is it not a great pleasure to have guests coming from afar?"

Ji'nan

The capital of Shandong and a busy industrial city with three million inhabitants, **JI'NAN** is the province's major transit point and communication centre, and while it's possible to kill a day here, the tourist sights are unspectacular and the hotel situation is poor. The city is best thought of as a stop on the way to or from Qufu and Tai'an.

Ji'nan stands on the site of one of China's **oldest settlements**, and pottery unearthed nearby has been dated to over four thousand years ago. The present town dates from the fourth century AD when Ji'nan was a military outpost and trading centre. The town expanded during the Ming dynasty, when the city walls were built – they're no longer standing but you can see where they were on any map by the moats that once surrounded them. Present development

Ji'nan

Ji'nan	济南	jì'nán
Black Tiger Spring	黑虎泉	hēihǔ quán
Daming Hu	大明湖	dàmíng hú
Quancheng Square	泉城广场	quánchéng guǎngchǎng
Shandong Provincial Museum	山东省博物馆	shāndōng shěng bówùguǎn
Shandong Teachers' University	山东师范大学	shāndōng shīfàn dàxué
Thousand Buddha Mountain	千佛山	qiānfó shān
Wu Longtan Park	舞龙潭公园	wǔlóngtán gōngyuán

Accommodation and eating

Daguan Roast Duck	大观烤鸭店	dàguān kǎoyādiàn
Hongya	泓雅宾馆	hóngyǎ bīnguǎn
Ji'nan Hotel	济南大酒店	jì'nán dàjiǔdiàn
Ji'nan People's Market	人民商场	rénmín shāngchǎng
Oriental Gourmet	东方美食城	dōngfāng měishíchéng
Railway Hotel	铁道大酒店	tiědào dàjiǔdiàn
Shao'ezi	烧鹅仔	shāo'ézi
Sofitel	索菲特银座大酒店	suǒfēitè yínzuò dàjiǔdiàn
Xuelin Hotel	学林大酒店	xuélín dàjiǔdiàn

dates back to 1898, when the Germans obtained the right to build the Shandong rail lines. The city was opened up to foreign trade in 1906, and industrialized rapidly under the Germans, English and Japanese.

Ji'nan is famous in China for its **natural springs**, though these are presently showcased in typical Chinese city parks, and thus actually rather dull. Some of the nineteenth-century German and Japanese architecture remains, but Ji'nan's buildings aren't pretty: the fashion for facing buildings with white bathroom-style tiling seems to have reached its zenith here. Outside the centre, one of the most rewarding ways to spend any time in the city is to stroll through the **parks** with their attractive lakes, or slog your way up **Thousand Buddha Mountain** in the south.

Arrival, city transport and information

Ji'nan's **airport**, with international connections to Japan, South Korea and Hong Kong, is 40km east of the city. A private company operates airport shuttles (6am–6pm, ¥20, 30min ride) which drop you outside the airline ticket office just west of the *Sofitel Silver Plaza* hotel. Taxis from the airport into the city cost ¥100. The large and noisy main **train station**, at the junction of the north–south line between Beijing and Shanghai, and the line that goes east to Yantai and Qingdao, is in the northwest of town; you shouldn't have any problems buying tickets out at the train station itself. The **long-distance bus station** is nearly 2km due north of the train station, though the **Lianyun station** on the train-station square has connections to cities within Shandong, including buses to **Tai'an** and an **express bus** to **Qingdao** (4hr 30min; ¥56).

Most of the city's **bus routes** begin from the train station: bus #3 is the most useful, heading east into town along Quancheng Lu; #K51 goes south from the station to the provincial museum. The mob of **taxi drivers** at the station are some of the most aggressive in China – it's better to walk some distance away and hail one yourself. Taxis are cheap, the ¥6 basic fare just about covering trips around the city centre.

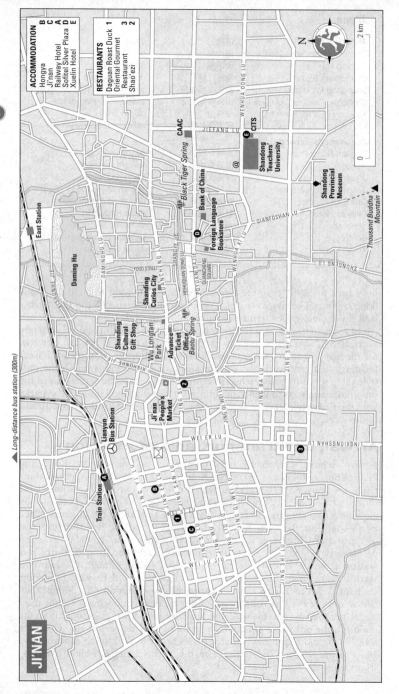

JI'NAN

ACCOMMODATION
Hongya   B
Ji'nan   C
Railway Hotel   A
Sofitel Silver Plaza D
Xuelin Hotel   E

RESTAURANTS
Daguan Roast Duck   1
Oriental Gourmet   3
Restaurant
Shao'ezi   2

N

0   2 km

Long-distance bus station (300m)

East Station

Daming Hu

NASHUNHE JIE

DAMINGHU LU

FOOD STREET

Shanding Curios City

Shanding Cultural Gift Shop

Wu Longtan Park

Advance Ticket Office

Baotu Spring

QUANCHENG LU

HEIHUQUAN XI LU

SHANGYE JIE

BOYUAN DAJIE

QUANCHENG SQUARE

Black Tiger Spring

Bank of China

Foreign Language Bookstore

CAAC

JIEFANG LU

WENHUA DONG LU

@

CITS

Shandong Teachers University

QIANFOSHAN LU

WENHUA XI LU

SHUNGENG LU

Shandong Provincial Museum

Thousand Buddha Mountain

XISHUNHE JIE

Train Station

Lianyun Bus Station

JING YI LU

JING ER LU

JING SAN LU

WEI SI LU

WEI ER LU

Ji'nan People's Market

JING SI LU

JING WU LU

JING QI WU LU

WEI LU JIU

WEI SHI LU

JING BA LU

JING JIU WEI LU

LINGXIONGSHAN LU

JING SHI LU

Accommodation

Ji'nan's **hotel** situation is awful, unless you have a generous budget. Most of the hotels that are allowed to take foreigners are inconveniently located and pricey. It's pretty hard to find a room for less than ¥150, which is the same price as a taxi to Tai'an, a much nicer place altogether.

Hongya 223 Jing'er Lu at Weisi Lu, ⓣ0531/7916789 ext 6188, ⓕ7916789 ext 6006. A serviceable hotel a kilometre from the train station. Not the greatest value, so push for a discount. ⑤

Ji'nan Hotel 240 Jing San Lu ⓣ0531/7938981, ⓕ7932906. Solid but characterless place with a good location and quiet grounds. ④

Railway Hotel On the train-station square ⓣ0531/6328888. Three-star, comfy place attached to the station front, convenient for transport but a

long way from the interesting part of town. Often offers discounts on rooms. ⑥

Sofitel Silver Plaza 66 Luoyuan Dajie ⓣ0531/6068888, ⓕ6066666. The pinnacle of luxury in Ji'nan, right in the heart of the city with views of Quancheng Square. Rates often discounted by half or more. ⑨

Xuelin Hotel 80 Wenhua Dong Lu ⓣ0531/2963388, ⓕ2963358. On the main bustling strip of the University District, southeast of the centre. The best mid-range choice. ⑤

The City

Ji'nan is frustratingly spread out, and there's no real downtown shopping district. The biggest shopping streets are to be found just south of Daming Hu, while a little further south, the enormous rectangular Quancheng Square marks the city centre. The ordered blocks west of here, south of the train station, are among the oldest in town and vaguely atmospheric, though most of the attractions are in the southern suburbs.

There are a few sights in Ji'nan worth checking out while you're waiting for connections. The park around **Daming Hu** (daily 6am–6pm; ¥15), on the route of bus #11 from the train station, is quite pleasant, containing some quaint gardens, pavilions and bridges, and the lake is edged with willow trees and sprinkled with water lilies. Once impressive sights, the area south of Daming Hu is bounded by streams and fed by **springs** which now resemble little more than muddy pools (pollution and droughts seem to have caused the drying up). The most famous is **Black Tiger Spring** on Heihuquan Dong Lu, which rises from a subterranean cave and emerges through tiger-headed spouts. The stone pools here are a popular bathing spot.

Wu Longtan Park (7am–5.30pm; ¥5), southwest of here on the route of bus #3 from the train station, is nice enough, though little remains of its three springs, which were mentioned in the *Spring and Autumn Annals*, government texts of 694 BC. **Luoyuan Pavilion** on the north side was originally constructed in the Song dynasty, and is inscribed with a couplet by Zhao Mengfu, a thirteenth-century artist, which reads: "Clouds and mist in wet vapours, glory unfixed; the sound of the waves thunders in the Lake of Great Brightness." In the east of the park, next to the trickle that is "Gushing from the Ground Spring", is the **Hall to Commemorate Li Qingzhao**, one of China's most famous female poets, born in 1084 in Ji'nan. The modern hall contains portraits, extracts from her work, and poems and paintings by well-known contemporary artists.

Thousand Buddha Mountain and the provincial museum

The other scenic spot worth a trip is **Thousand Buddha Mountain** (daily 8am–6pm; ¥20), to the south of the city, on the route of bus #K51 or #K54, which leaves from a terminus in the southwest corner of Daming Park; the journey is about 5km. The mountainside is leafy and tracked with winding paths, the main one lined with painted opera masks. Most of the original statues that once dotted the slopes, freestanding images of Buddhas and Bodhisattvas, were destroyed by Red Guards, but new ones are being added, largely paid for by donations from Overseas Chinese. It's quite a climb to the summit (2hr), but the sculptures, and the view, get better the higher you go. Behind the **Xingguo Si** near the top are some superb sixth-century Buddhist carvings.

Near the mountain, and accessible on the same bus, the **Shandong Provincial Museum** (Mon–Fri 9–11am & 1–4.30pm, Sat & Sun 9am–4.30pm; ¥10) contains a number of fine Buddhist carvings as well as exhibits from the excavations at Longshan and Dawenkou, two nearby Neolithic sites noted for the delicate black pottery unearthed there. The remains date back to 5000–2000 BC and consist mostly of pottery and stone and shell farming implements. Also on display is China's earliest extant book, found at a Han tomb nearby. Preceding the invention of paper, the book was written with brush and ink on thin strips of bamboo which were then sewn together. It includes a full calendar for the year 134 BC, and a number of military and philosophical texts, including Sun Bin's *Art of War*.

Eating and drinking

To fill up inexpensively, head for **Wenhua Dong Lu**, the road cleaving the University District. Tell the cab driver to take you to the *Shifan Daxue*, the gate of the Teachers' University, around which are a slew of great dumpling and home-style eating places. West of the centre, the Ji'nan People's Market, a shopping mall on Baotuquan Lu, is well stocked with flash restaurants and fast-food places. For duck, the *Daguan Roast Duck* restaurant across from the Pearl Hotel is convenient to the hotels in that area; the *Shao'ezi* dining room across from the People's Market is also a good bet and attracts enough business to support escalators inside. The *Oriental Gourmet Restaurant*, at 188 Yingxiongshan Lu, is also pricey, serving Shandong specialities such as carp and scorpion. For a quick bite in the centre of town, browse the small **food street** just off Quancheng Lu, which is full of snacks and noodle shops.

Listings

Airlines The main CAAC office is at 95 Jiefang Lu (8am–5.30pm; ☎0531/6988777), though it's far easier to get your tickets and airport shuttles from the airline ticket office just west of the *Sofitel*.

Banks and exchange The Bank of China is on Poyuan Dajie, just east of the *Sofitel* (Mon–Fri 8.30am–5pm).

Bookshops The Foreign Language Bookstore is on Chaoshan Jie southwest of the *Sofitel*.

Buses Ji'nan's long-distance bus station has services to Beijing, Tai'an and Qufu. Minibuses for the latter destinations also leave from in front of the train station. Qingdao is an easy trip on one of the luxury coaches (4hr 30min; ¥56).

Internet The third floor of the Tianlong department store on the train-station square has a serviceable Internet café. There are also Internet bars on Wenhua Dong Lu near the Shandong Teachers' University gate.

Mail and telephones Ji'nan's main post office is a red-brick building on Wei Er Lu just west of Jing Er Lu (8am–4.30pm). There's a 24hr telecom office inside.

Shopping The most impressive department store is the Ji'nan People's Market, an enormous mall on Jing Si Lu. There are two good spots for antiques and souvenirs on Quancheng Lu: Shandong Curios City and the higher-end Shandong Cultural Gift Shop at the southeastern corner of Wu Longtan Park.

Trains Besides the train-station ticket windows, there is an advance ticket office (8.30am–5pm) across the street from the main Wu Longtan Park.

Travel agents Dealing mainly with tour groups, CITS (☎0531/2665020) is at the *Xuelin Hotel* on Wehua Dong Lu.

Tai'an and Tai Shan

Tai Shan is not just a mountain, it's a god. Lying 100km south of Ji'nan, it's the easternmost and holiest of China's five holy Taoist mountains (the other four being Hua Shan, the two Heng Shans and Song Shan), and has been worshipped by the Chinese for longer than recorded history. It is justifiably famed for its scenery and the ancient buildings strung out along its slopes. Once host to emperors and the devout, it's now Shandong's biggest tourist attraction. Sections of the walk have suffered from tourist development but the ascent is often engrossing and beautiful – and always hard work.

The town of **Tai'an** lies at the base of the mountain, and for centuries has prospered from the busy traffic of pilgrims coming to pay their respects to the mountain. You'll quickly become aware just how popular the pilgrimage is – on certain holy days ten thousand people might be making their way to the peak, and year-round the town sees over half a million visitors.

Tai'an and Tai Shan

Tai'an	泰安	tài'ān
Dai Miao	岱庙	dài miào
Puzhao Si	普照寺	pǔzhào sì
Accommodation and eating		
A Dong Jiachangcai	阿东家常菜	ādōng jiāchángcài
Lijing Hotel	丽景宾馆	lìjǐng bīnguǎn
Overseas Chinese Hotel	华侨大厦	huáqiáo dàshà
Railway Hotel	铁道大厦	tiědào dàshà
Taishan Binguan	泰山宾馆	tàishān bīnguǎn
Yiheyuan Restaurant	意和园酒楼	yìhéyuán jiǔlóu
Tai Shan	泰山	tàishān
Bixia Ci	碧霞祠	bìxiá cí
Black Dragon Pool	黑龙潭	hēilóng tán
Bridge of the Gods	仙人桥	xiānrén qiáo
Cable car station	索道站	suǒdào zhàn
Cloud Bridge	云步桥	yúnbù qiáo
Dou Mu Convent	斗母宫	dòumǔ gōng
Five Pines Pavilion	五松亭	wǔsōng tíng
Hongmen Gong	红门宫	hóngmén gōng
Jade Emperor's Summit	玉皇顶	yùhuáng dǐng
Nantianmen	南天门	nántiān mén
Pavilion of the Teapot Sky	壶天阁	hútiān gé
Sheng Xian Fang	升仙房	shēngxiān fáng
Stone Sutra Ravine	泾石谷	jīngshí gǔ
Sun Viewing Point	日观峰	rìguān fēng
Tower of Myriad Spirits	万仙楼	wànxiān lóu
Wangmu Chi	王母池	wángmǔ chí
Yitianmen	一天门	yītiān mén
Yuhuang Si	玉皇寺	yùhuáng sì
Zhanlu Terrace	占鲁台	zhànlǔ tái
Zhongtianmen	中天门	zhōngtiān mén
Zhongtianmen Hotel	中天门宾馆	zhōngtiānmén bīnguǎn

Tai'an

TAI'AN is unremarkable but not unpleasant. There's a small-town atmosphere, with buildings that are not too grand and streets not too wide. It's just small enough to cover on foot, though few people pay it much attention; the town is overshadowed, literally, by the great mountain just to the north.

Dongyue Dajie is the largest street, a corridor of new high-rises running east–west across town. Qingnian Lu, the main **shopping street**, runs off its eastern end. The trailhead is reached on Hongmen Lu, which is flanked by a string of souvenir shops selling gnarled walking sticks made from tree roots, and shoes. Just south of Daizhong Dajie, in the north, are some busy **market streets** selling medicinal herbs which grow on the mountain, such as ginseng, the tuber of the multiflower knotweed, and Asian puccoon, along with strange vegetables, bonsai trees and potted plants.

Dai Miao

Tai'an's main sight is the **Dai Miao** (daily 8am–5pm; ¥20), the traditional starting point for the procession up Tai'an, where emperors once made sacrifices and offerings to the mountain. It's a magnificent structure, with yellow-tiled roofs, red walls and towering old trees, one of the largest temples in the country and one of the most celebrated. Though it appears an ordered whole, the temple complex is really a blend of buildings from different belief systems, with veneration of the mountain as the only constant factor.

The Main Hall, **Tiankuangdian** (Hall of the Celestial Gift), is matched in size only by halls in the Forbidden City and at Qufu. The hall's construction started as early as the Qin dynasty (221–206 BC), though construction and renovation have gone on ever since, particularly during the Tang and Song dynasties. Completed in 1009, it was restored in 1956 and is in an excellent state of preservation. Inside is a huge mural fully covering three of the walls. This Song-dynasty masterpiece depicts the God of Tai Shan on an inspection

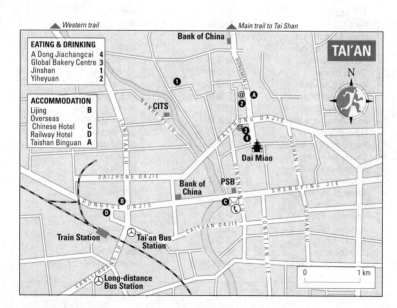

tour and hunting expedition. It's really a massive ego trip as the painting was produced to celebrate the deification of the mountain by Emperor Zhen Zong, and there is a strong resemblance between the God of the Mountain in the painting and Zhen Zong himself. These days the mural isn't in great shape, but some of its original glory remains and you can still see most of the figures of its cast of thousands, each rendered with painstaking attention to the details of facial expression and gesture. There is also a statue of the God of Tai Shan, enthroned in a niche and dressed in flowing robes, holding the oblong tablet which is the insignia of his authority. The five sacrificial vessels laid before him bear the symbols of the five peaks.

Today the courtyards and the temple gardens are used as an open-air museum for **steles**. It's an impressive collection, covering a timespan of over two thousand years. The oldest, inside the Dongyuzuo Hall, celebrates the visit of Emperor Qin and his son in the third century BC. Many of the great calligraphers are represented and even the untrained Western eye can find something to appreciate here. Charcoal rubbings of the steles can be bought from the mercifully discreet souvenir shops inside the temple complex. The courtyard also contains ancient cypresses, ginkgos and acacias, including five cypresses supposedly planted by the Han emperor Wu Di.

The other temple halls are also used as **museums**. One houses a collection of early sacrificial vessels and some exquisite Tang pottery, while another is given over to the Chinese art of cutting and polishing tree roots. The art lies not in what is done to the root, but in its selection; the roots are picked for their abstract beauty and figurative connotations.

In a side courtyard at the back of the complex is the Temple of Yanxi. A Taoist resident on the mountain, Yanxi was linked with the mountain cult of the Tang dynasty. A separate Taoist hall at the rear is devoted to the Wife of the Mountain, a deity who seems somewhat of an afterthought, appearing much later than her spouse.

Practicalities

Arriving at the **train station**, a modern affair on the line south from Ji'nan to Shanghai, you'll be greeted by a mob of eager taxi drivers. The minimum fare of ¥5 is sufficient for rides in town, with no more than ¥7 required to reach the mountain. If you're here on a day-trip, drop your bag at the **left-luggage stand** (¥4–10) beside the ticket office. There is a helpful **tourist info** window (open 24hrs) in front of the train-station exit (bypass the tourist office *inside* the station – they have little in the way of maps or accommodation advice) that sells a very helpful English map (¥5) of the area. Buses from Ji'nan and Qufu terminate at the **long-distance bus station** on Sanlizhuang Lu, south of the train station.

The town's four **bus routes** all leave from or stop at a terminus just north of the train station. Bus #3 is the most useful, looping from the beginning of the main Tai Shan trail head to the train station and north again to the beginning of the western trail route. Bus #2 goes from the south to the north of the town, from Hongmen Lu to Dongyue Dajie, while buses #1 and #4 traverse the east–west axis, both travelling along Shengping Jie.

The **post office** is on Dongyue Dajie (Mon–Fri 8am–6pm), near the junction with Qingnian Lu. The main **Bank of China** is located at #48 Dongyue Lu (8.30am–5pm), though a small branch with an ATM is uphill from the *Taishan Binguan*. The helpful English-speaking branch of **CITS** is a bit out of the way, just off Nanhe Xi Lu (℡0538/8223259). There is an Internet café across the street from the Taishan Binguan, and another not far to the south on Dai Zhong Dajie.

Moving on from Tai'an, buses to most destinations leave from the Tai'an bus station on the east side of the train-station concourse. During daylight hours, minibuses leave every half-hour for Qufu (¥15) and every twenty minutes for Ji'nan (¥15). Trains to either of these destinations are also readily available, though Tai'an is a better place to spend the night than dull Ji'nan.

Accommodation

It's worth considering staying at the hotels **on the mountain** (see p.330), if you can stand slogging up there with your gear, as the surroundings are more pleasant and the prices not unreasonable. Arguably the most worthwhile place to stay in Tai'an itself is the *Taishan Binguan* (☎0538/8225888, ℱ8221432; ❻), a five-storey place conveniently located at the beginning of the main Tai Shan trail on Hongmen Lu. The hotel has a good restaurant, and most of the services you could want are nearby, including the Bank of China, small travel agencies and souvenir shops. Another convenient, though less comfortable, option is the *Railway Hotel* (☎0538/2108000; ❺), which often discounts rooms. Also near the train station is the clean and newly remodelled *Lijing Hotel* (☎0538/8538888 ext 8888, ℱ8538888 ext 8003; ❺).

At the other end of the scale, the four-star *Overseas Chinese Hotel* on Dongyue Dajie is the most exclusive place to stay in town (☎0538/8220001, ℱ8228171; ❻), gleaming like a tiara but with as much character as a plastic cup. It's nineteen storeys high, with a gym, sauna and swimming pool.

Uniquely for a tourist mecca, the **PSB** on Qingnian Lu doesn't seem to care where you stay, so if your budget is really tight, try some of the grotty places round the **station**. They don't have English signs, so look for the characters for *binguan* (see p.1236). You should get a room for around ¥50, less for a dorm, but don't expect anyone to speak English.

Eating and drinking

A speciality of **Tai'an cuisine** is red-scaled carp, fresh from pools on the mountain and fried while it's still alive. Other dishes from the mountain include chicken stewed with *siliquose pelvetia* (a fungus only found within 2m of the ancient pine trees around the Nine Dragon Hill), coral herb and hill lilac. The best **restaurants** are in the *Taishan Binguan* and *Overseas Chinese Hotel*, which serve Western dishes as well as the local specialities; a meal for two at either place, with vegetable and meat dishes as well as drinks, should come to around ¥80.

There are some other good places to eat along Hongmen Lu, with more upmarket tourist restaurants closer to the mountian: try the Sichuan-style *Yiheyuan Restaurant*, which is better value than its neighbours. Don't miss the cheap, local restaurants closer to Tai Miao, however, especially *A Dong Jiachangcai* which serves everything from homestyle Chinese to *jiaozi* and noodles. For seafood try the colourfully decorated *Jinshan Restaurant* in the north of town. Stock up on picnic staples for the ascent of the mountain at the *Global Bakery Centre*.

Tours

Apart from trips up the mountain, which you'd be better off doing under your own steam, CITS runs two **tours** that are worth considering. The **Buyang Village Tour** is a chance to visit a real, dusty, ramshackle Chinese village and get a taste of rural life. You can go fishing with the locals or try your hand at making dumplings, and if you're really interested you can stay the night at a farmer's house. You'll need to get a group of four or five together, and the tour costs ¥120 per person, dinner included.

Another tour (¥50 per person) is by taxi to the **Puzhao Si** to see a venerable old Taoist monk, a *qi gong* master who can apparently swallow needles and thread them with his tongue. Don't expect a performing clown – he only does his stuff when he feels like it. This tour gets mixed reactions, and some visitors have reported feeling intrusive.

Tai Shan

More so than any other holy mountain, **Tai Shan** was the haunt of emperors, and owes its obvious glories – the temples and pavilions along its route – to the patronage of the imperial court. From its summit, a succession of emperors surveyed their empires, made sacrifices and paid tribute. Sometimes their retinues stretched right from the top to the bottom of the mountain, 8km of pomp and ostentatious wealth. In 219 BC, Emperor Qin Shi Huang had **roads** built all over the mountain so that he could ride here in his carriage under escort of the royal guards when he was performing the grand ceremonies of *feng* (sacrifices to heaven) and *chan* (offerings to earth). Various titles were offered to the mountain by emperors keen to bask in reflected glory. As well as funding the temples, emperors had their visits and thoughts recorded for posterity on steles here, and men of letters carved poems and tributes to the mountain on any available rockface. Shandong-native Confucius is also said to have made a trip here, and there is a temple in his honour in the shadow of the highest peak.

In recent years this huge open-air museum has mutated into a religious theme park, and the path is now thronged with a constant procession of **tourists**. There are photo booths, souvenir stalls, soft-drinks vendors and teahouses. You can get your name inscribed on a medal, get your photograph taken and buy fungus and ginseng from vendors squatting on walls. Halfway up there's a **bus station** and **cable car**. Yet somehow, despite all this, Tai Shan retains an atmosphere of grandeur; the buildings and the mountain itself are magnificent enough to survive their trivialization.

It is surprising, though, to see that numbering among the hordes of tourists are a great many genuine **pilgrims**. Taoism, after a long period of Communist proscription, is again alive and flourishing, and you're more than likely to see a bearded Taoist monk on the way up. Women come specifically to pray to **Bixia Yuan Jun**, the Princess of the Rosy Clouds, a Taoist deity believed to be able to help childless women conceive. Tai Shan also plays an important role in the **folk beliefs** of the Shandong peasantry (tradition has it that anyone who has climbed Tai Shan will live to be 100). The other figures you will see are the streams of **porters**, balancing enormous weights on their shoulder poles, moving swiftly up the mountain and then galloping down again for a fresh load; they may make three trips a day, six days a week.

The seriously fit can take part in the annual **Tai Shan Race**, held in early September (check with CITS for dates), which has a prize for the best foreigner competing.

Mountain practicalities

Tai Shan looms at 1545m high, and it's about 8km from the base to the top. There are two main **paths** up the mountain: the grand historical eastern route (¥60), and a quieter, more scenic western route (¥80). The ascent takes about four or five hours, half that if you rush it, and the descent – almost as punishing on the legs – takes two to three hours. The paths converge at **Zhongtianmen**, the midway point (more often than not, climbers using the western route actually

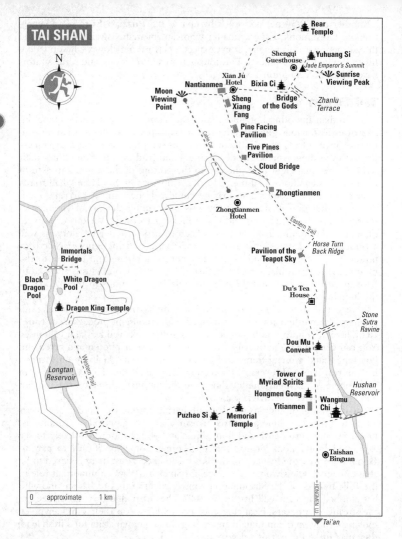

N

Rear Temple

Shengqi Guesthouse

Yuhuang Si

Jade Emperor's Summit

Xian Ju Hotel

Sunrise Viewing Peak

Nantianmen

Bixia Ci

Moon Viewing Point

Sheng Xiang Fang

Bridge of the Gods

Zhanlu Terrace

Pine Facing Pavilion

Cable Car

Five Pines Pavilion

Cloud Bridge

Zhongtianmen

Zhongtianmen Hotel

Eastern Trail

Horse Turn Back Ridge

Immortals Bridge

Pavilion of the Teapot Sky

Black Dragon Pool

White Dragon Pool

Du's Tea House

Dragon King Temple

Stone Sutra Ravine

Dou Mu Convent

Longtan Reservoir

Western Trail

Tower of Myriad Spirits

Hushan Reservoir

Hongmen Gong

Wangmu Chi

Yitianmen

Puzhao Si

Memorial Temple

Taishan Binguan

HONGMEN LU

| 0 | approximate | 1 km |

▼ *Tai'an*

take a **bus** to Zhongtianmen, costing ¥13). The truly sedentary can then complete the journey by **cable car** (¥45 one-way). After Zhongtianmen, the path climbs endless narrow **staircases** (over 6,000 steps) to the summit.

Offically, both path gates are open 24 hours, though evening hikers should bring flashlights and head up by the more travelled eastern route while descending by the western route; this is the circuit we've assumed in the account that follows. For the eastern route, walk uphill on Hongmen Lu from the Taishan Binguan, or catch bus #3 or #9 along the way or from the train station. To reach the western route, take bus #3 (¥1) to the last stop, Tianwaicun, or a taxi (¥5). Cross the street, ascend the stairs dotted with decorated columns, then descend to the bus park.

Whatever the **weather** is in Tai'an, it's usually cold at the top of the mountain and always unpredictable. The average **temperature** at the summit is 18°C in summer, dropping to -9°C in winter. The summit conditions are posted outside the ticket windows at the west route. You should take warm clothing and a waterproof and wear walking shoes, though Chinese tourists ascend dressed in T-shirts and plimsolls, even high heels. The best time to climb is in spring or autumn, outside the humid months. If you can tolerate the cold and want to miss the hordes, there are a number of clear winter days, though fewer hours of daylight in which to climb.

There are plenty of affordable eating places along the eastern route to Zhong-tianmen, but it's a good idea to take your own **food** as well, as the fare on offer past the midway point is unappealing and gets more expensive the higher you go.

If you want to see the sunrise, you can stay at the **guesthouses** on the mountain, or risk climbing at night – take a flashlight and warm clothes. Don't be fooled by the floodlights lining the path – only some of them are ever lit, and in the winter months sunset is around 5pm.

The ascent

Using the eastern route, your ascent will begin from **Daizhong Fang**, a stone arch just to the north of the Dai Miao in Tai'an. North of the arch and on the right is a pool, **Wangmu Chi**, and a small and rather quaint-looking nunnery, from where you can see the whimsically named Hornless Dragon Pool and Combing and Washing River. In the main hall of the nunnery is a statue of Xiwang Mu, Queen Mother of the West, the major female deity in Taoism.

Yitianmen to Zhongtianmen

About 500m up is the official start of the path at **Yitianmen** (First Heavenly Gate). This is followed by a Ming arch, said to mark the spot where Confucius began his climb, and the **Hongmen Gong** (Red Gate Palace), where emperors used to change into sensible clothes for the ascent, and where you buy your ticket, which includes insurance. Built in 1626, Hongmen Gong is the first of a series of temples dedicated to the Princess of the Rosy Clouds. It got its name from the two red rocks to the northwest, which together resemble an arch.

There are plenty of buildings to distract you around here. Just to the north is the Tower of Myriad Spirits, and just below that the Tomb of the White Mule is said to be where the mule that carried the Tang emperor Xuan up and down the mountain finally dropped dead, exhausted. Xuan made the mule a posthumous general and at least it got a decent burial. The next group of buildings is the former **Dou Mu Convent**, a hall for Taoist nuns. Its date of founding is uncertain, but it was reconstructed in 1542. Today there are three halls, a drum tower, a bell tower and a locust tree outside which is supposed to look like a reclining dragon. Like all the temple buildings on the mountain, the walls are painted with a blood-red wash, here interspersed with small grey bricks.

A kilometre north of here, off to the east of the main path, is the **Stone Sutra Ravine** where the text of the Buddhist Diamond Sutra has been carved on the rockface. This is one of the most prized of Tai Shan's many calligraphic works, and makes a worthwhile diversion from the main path as it's set in a charming, quiet spot. It's unsignposted, but the path is wide and well trodden.

Back on the main path, don't miss **Du's Teahouse**, built on the spot where, more than a thousand years ago, General Cheng Yao Jing Tang planted four pines, three of which are still alive. The teahouse and everything in it was built out of polished tree roots, which makes the interior resemble a fairyland – the "maiden tea" is excellent and a speciality of this mountain area.

After a tunnel of cypress trees, and the **Pavilion of the Teapot Sky** (so called because the peaks all around supposedly give the illusion of standing in a teapot), you see a sheer cliff rising in front of you, called **Horse Turn Back Ridge**. This is where Emperor Zhen Zong had to dismount because his horse refused to go any farther. Not far above is **Zhongtianmen** (Halfway Gate to Heaven), the midpoint of the climb. There are some good views here, though the **cable car** will be the most welcome sight if you're flagging. The pleasant *Zhongtianmen Hotel* is situated here (T0538/8226740; ❻), and there's also a collection of rather dull restaurants. Confusingly, you have to descend two staircases and then follow the road round to continue the climb.

Zhongtianmen to the top

The next sight is **Yunbu Qiao** (Step Over the Clouds Bridge), after which you arrive at **Five Pines Pavilion**, where the first Qin Emperor took shelter from a storm under a group of pines. The grateful emperor then promoted the lucky pine trees to ministers of the fifth grade. From here you can see the lesser peaks of Tai Shan: the Mountain of Symmetrical Pines, the Flying Dragon Crag and Hovering Phoenix Ridge.

Farther up you pass under **Sheng Xian Fang** (the Archway to Immortality), which, according to mountain myth, assures your longevity and provides the viewpoint that inspired Tang poet Li Bai to write: "In a long breath by the heavenly gate, the fresh wind comes from a thousand miles away", though by this point most climbers are long past being able to appreciate poetry, let alone compose it.

The **final section** of the climb is the hardest, as the stone stairs are steep and narrow, and climb almost vertically between two walls of rocks (often through thick white mist). Each step towards Nantianmen, standing black against the sky at the top, calls for great effort, and pairs of fit young men offer rides on home-made sedan chairs to the exhausted.

On reaching the top you enter **Tian Jie** (Heaven Street), and the Tai Shan theme park, where you can buy an "I climbed Tai Shan" T-shirt, slurp a pot noodle and get your picture taken dressed as an emperor. There are a couple of **restaurants** here, **hotels** and a few **shops**. This thriving little tourist village on the top of a mountain represents a triumph of the profit motive over the elements; it's often so misty you can hardly see from one souvenir stall to the next. In the middle of the street is Elephant Trunk Peak, which, it's planned, will become the terminal station of a funicular railway. If you want to stay the night, try and negotiate a discount at the expensive three-star *Shenqi Guesthouse* (T0538/8223866; ❾) above the Bixia Ci. There's a restaurant, and an alarm bell that tells you when to get up for the sunrise. At 2 Tian Jie is the *Xian Ju Hotel* (T0538/8226877; ❺, unheated single ¥60).

The **Bixia Ci**, on the southern slopes of the summit, is the final destination for most of the bona fide pilgrims, and offerings are made to a bronze statue of the princess in the main hall. It's a working temple and its guardians enforce strict rules about where the merely curious are allowed to wander. It's also a splendid building, the whole place tiled with iron to resist wind damage, and all the decorations are metal, too. The bells hanging from the eaves, the mythological animals on the roof, and even the two steles outside are bronze. From 1759 until the fall of the Qing, the emperor would send an official here on the eighteenth day of the fourth lunar month each year to make an offering. Just below is a small shrine to Confucius, at the place where he was supposed to have commented, "the world is small".

At the **Yuhuang Si** (Jade Emperor Temple), you have truly arrived at the **highest point** of the mountain, and a rock with the characters for "supreme summit" carved on it stands within the courtyard. In Chinese popular religion, which mixes Taoism and Confucianism with much earlier beliefs, the Jade Emperor is the supreme ruler of heaven, depicted in an imperial hat with bead curtains hanging down his face. Outside the temple is the **Wordless Monument**, thought to have been erected by Emperor Wu more than two thousand years ago. The story goes that Wu wanted to have an inscription engraved that would do justice to his merits. None of the drafts he commissioned came up to scratch, however, so he left the stele blank, leaving everything to the imagination.

Southeast of here is the peak for **watching the sunrise** (4.45am in June, 7am in December). It was here that the Song emperor performed the *feng* ceremony, building an altar and making sacrifices to heaven. On a clear day you can see 200km to the coast, and at night you can see the lights of Ji'nan. There are numerous trails from here to fancifully named scenic spots – Fairy Bridge, Celestial Candle Peak, and the like. If the weather is good, it's a great place for aimless wandering.

The descent

The best way down is along the **western trail**, which is longer, quieter and has some impressive views. It starts at Zhongtianmen, loops round and joins the main trail back at the base of the mountain. Midway is the **Black Dragon Pool**, a dark, brooding pond, home of the Tai Shan speciality dish, red-scaled carp, once so precious that the fish was used as tribute to the court. Near the bottom, the **Puzhao Si** (Temple of Universal Clarity) is a pretty complex, mostly Qing temple, though there has been a temple on this site for more than 1500 years. It's east of the western trail, though access is via the road which runs around the base of the mountain.

Qufu and around

QUFU, a quiet rural town in the south of Shandong, easily accessible by bus or train from Tai'an, 100km north, and Ji'nan, 180km away, has an agreeably sluggish feel despite its great historical and cultural importance. **Confucius** (Kong Zi) was born here around 551 BC, taught here – largely unappreciated – for much

Qufu and around		
Qufu	曲阜	*qǔfù*
Bell Tower	钟楼	*zhōng lóu*
Confucian Forest	孔林	*kǒng lín*
Confucius Mansion	孔府	*kǒng fǔ*
Confucius Temple	孔庙	*kǒng miào*
Drum Tower	鼓楼	*gǔlóu*
Yan Miao	颜庙	*yán miào*
Zhougong Miao	周公庙	*zhōugōng miào*
Accommodation and eating		
Confucius Mansions	孔府宴大酒店	*kǒngfǔyàn dàjiǔdiàn*
Gold Mansion	金府宾馆	*jīnfǔ bīnguǎn*
Great Wall Hotel	长城宾馆	*chángchéng bīnguǎn*
Queli	阙里宾舍	*quèlǐ bīnshè*
Yingshi Binguan	影视宾馆	*yǐngshì bīnguǎn*
Yonghe Doujiang	永和豆浆	*yǒnghé dòujiāng*

of his life, and was buried just outside the town, in what became a sacred burial ground for his clan, the Kong. All around the town, despite a flurry of destructive zeal during the Cultural Revolution, is architectural evidence of the esteem in which he was held by successive dynasties – most monumentally by the Ming, who were responsible for the two dominant sights, the **Confucius Temple** and the **Confucius Mansion**, whose scale seems more suited to Beijing. For more on Confucius and Confucianism, see "Contexts" p.1177.

Qufu is a great place to stop over for a few days, with plenty to see concentrated in a small area. It's small enough to walk everywhere, along unpolluted streets with little traffic – there are benches to sit on and trees full of singing birds. The compactness of the centre, however, also means that it's hard to blend in with the crowd, and you may be the object of the usual tourist hustle. If it all gets too much, remember the words of the master himself: "A gentleman understands what is moral, a base man understands only what is profitable." You could always escape to the Confucius Forest nearby, where you can lose yourself amid the eerie, twisted cypresses. Around the end of September, on Confucius's birthdate in the lunar calendar, the pace of the town picks up when a **festival** is held here and reconstructions of many of the original rituals are performed at the temple.

Arrival, information and city transport

The **nearest train station** is 15km away in the town of Yanzhou, on the line running south from Ji'nan. The direct overnight train from Beijing drops you here, as do three other routes from Tai'an and Ji'nan. Regular buses (¥4) run to Qufu, arriving at the **bus station** to the south of the Star Gate. This is also where long-distance buses pull in, after rattling across flat fertile land where aubergines, beans and potatoes are farmed. Train and airline ticket **advance booking** counters are southwest across the street from the bus station. **CITS** is just south of the Confucius Temple.

Local transport is by **cycle-rickshaw**, whereby the passenger is slung low in the front, giving an uninterrupted dog's-eye view of the street. A ride anywhere in town should cost ¥3–5. There are also horse-drawn gypsy-style carts, strictly for tourists, so not cheap. A **taxi** in town will start at ¥6.

From Qufu's bus station it's easy to get to anywhere in the area. If you want to travel further afield by train, go to Ji'nan (see p.318), which has a wider selection of lines.

Accommodation

Qufu has an abundance of good, inexpensive **hotels**. The following are the most conveniently located.

Confucius Mansions Hotel 6 Gulou Nanjie ☎0537/4487333. Opposite the bus station at the bottom of Gulou Nanjie, this place has a laid-back atmosphere and friendly staff, and is popular with budget travellers. ❻

Gold Mansion 1 Beimen Dajie ☎0537/4413469, ℻4413209. A comfortable, partially foreign-owned hotel a little way out of the centre on the way to the forest. It's not as nice as the *Queli*, but is very popular with Overseas Chinese. ❺

Great Wall Hotel 2 Changqing Lu ☎0537/2287500. One of the better budget hotels,

with large if tattered rooms, hot water (if you let it run long enough) and friendly staff. ❸

Queli 1 Queli Jie ☎0537/4866400, ℻4866660. Located right next to the Confucius Temple and the Mansion. If you can afford it – and you won't mind the tour-group swarms – stay in this impressive modern building: the other guesthouses in town are noticeably grubbier. They have satellite TV, 24hr hot water and English-speaking staff. ❼

Yingshi Binguan 22 Gulou Nan Dajie ☎0537/4412422. Perfectly acceptable, though not quite as good value as the *Great Wall*. ❹

The Town

Orientation is easy, as the centre of town lies at the crossroads of Gulou Dajie and Zhonglou Jie, just east of the temple and mansion. There's not much reason to leave this area except to visit the **Confucian Forest** in the northern suburbs. The centre is a Confucius theme park, with a mass of shopping opportunities clustered between the sights.

Confucius Temple

The **Confucius Temple** (daily 8am–4.30pm; ¥52) ranks with Beijing's Forbidden City and the summer resort of Chengde as one of the three great classical architectural complexes in China. It's certainly big: there are 466 rooms, and it's over 1km long, laid out in the design of an imperial palace, with nine courtyards on a north–south axis. It wasn't always so grand, first established as a three-room temple in 478 BC, containing a few of Confucius's lowly possessions: some hats, a zither and a carriage. In 539, Emperor Jing Di had the complex renovated, starting a trend, and from then on, emperors keen to show their veneration for the sage – and ostentatiously to display their piety to posterity – renovated and expanded the complex for more than two thousand years. Most of the present structure is Ming and Qing.

Entering the complex

The temple's main approach is in the southern section of the temple wall, and this is the best place to enter if you want an ordered impression of the complex (there is also an entrance on Queli Lu, just west of the mansion). Through the gate, flanked by horned creatures squatting on lotus flowers, first views are of clusters of wiry cypresses and monolithic steles, some sitting on the backs of carved *bixi*, stoic-looking turtle-like creatures, in an overgrown courtyard. A succession of gates leads into a courtyard holding the magnificent **Kui Wen Pavilion**, a three-storey wooden building constructed in 1018 with a design unique in Chinese classical architecture – a triple-layered roof with curving eaves and four layers of crossbeams. It was renovated in 1504 and has since withstood an earthquake undamaged, an event recorded on a tablet on the terrace. To the east and west the two pavilions are abstention lodges

Confucianism in modern China

When the **Communists** came to power they saw **Confucianism** as an archaic, feudal system and an anti-Confucius campaign was instigated, with much of its culture being destroyed in the Cultural Revolution. Now, however, it is making something of a **comeback**. Conservatives, perhaps frightened by the pace of change, the growing generation gap, and the new materialism of China, are calling for a return to Confucian values of respect and selflessness, just as their nervous counterparts in the West preach a return to family values. Confucian social morality – obeying authority, regarding family as the seat of morality and emphasizing the mutual benefits of friendship – is sometimes hailed as one of the main reasons for the success of East Asian economies, just as Protestantism provided the ideological complement to the growth of the industrialized West.

Most of the Confucian buildings in Qufu have been recently renovated, but this is strictly in the interests of **tourism**, not worship. Confucianism as a religious force was thought to have died, yet the ability of Chinese traditions to survive modernization and suppression always surprises observers. As one Chinese visitor commented, "Confucius is the one Chinese leader who never let the people down."

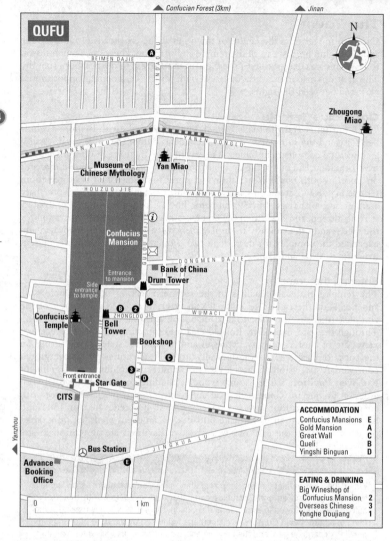

where visiting emperors would fast and bathe before taking part in sacrificial ceremonies.

The **thirteen stele pavilions** in the courtyard beyond are worth checking out, containing 53 tablets presented by emperors to commemorate their visits, and gifts of land and funds for renovations made to the Kong family. The earliest are Tang and the latest are from the Republican period. Continuing north, you come to five gates leading off in different directions. The eastern ones lead to the hall where sacrifices were offered to Confucius's ancestors, the western to the halls where his parents were worshipped, while the central Gate of Great Achievements leads to a large pavilion, the **Apricot Altar**. Tradition has it that

Confucius taught here after travelling the country in search of a ruler willing to implement his ideas. The cypress just inside the gate was supposed to have been planted by Confucius himself, and its state of health is supposed to reflect the fortunes of the Kongs.

The Hall of Great Achievements

The **Hall of Great Achievements**, behind the altar, is the temple's grandest building, its most striking feature being 28 **stone pillars** carved with bas-relief dragons, dating from around 1500. Each pillar has nine gorgeous dragons, coiling around clouds and pearls towards the roof. There is nothing comparable in the Forbidden City in Beijing, and when emperors came to visit, the columns were covered with yellow silk to prevent imperial jealousy. Originally the temple was solely dedicated to the worship of Confucius, but in 72 AD, Emperor Liu Zhuang offered sacrifices to his 72 disciples, too. Five hundred years later, Zhen Guan of the Tang dynasty issued an edict decreeing that 22 eminent Confucians should also be worshipped. Emperors of later dynasties (not wishing to be outdone) added more, until by this century there were 172 "eminent worthies".

Behind the main hall is the inner hall for the worship of Confucius's wife, **Qi Guan**, who also, it seems, merited deification through association. The phoenixes painted on its columns and ceiling are symbols of female power, in the same way as the dragon symbolizes masculinity.

Beyond is the **Hall of the Relics of the Sage**, where 120 carved stone plates made in the sixteenth century from Song paintings depict scenes from Confucius's life. They begin with Confucius's mother praying for a son, and end with his disciples mourning at his grave. The workmanship is excellent but the light in the room is dim and you'll have to squint.

The Hall of Poetry and Rites and the Lu Wall

The **eastern axis** of the temple is entered here, through the Gate of the Succession of the Sage next to the Hall of Great Achievements. Here is the **Hall of Poetry and Rites** where Confucius was supposed to have taught his son, Kong Li, to learn poetry from the *Book of Odes* in order to express himself, and ritual from *The Book of Rites* in order to strengthen his character.

A solitary wall in the courtyard is the famous **Lu Wall**, where Kong Fu, a ninth-generation descendant of Confucius, hid the sage's books when Qin Shi Huang, the first emperor (see p.281), persecuted the followers of Confucius and burned all his books. Several decades later, Liu Yu, prince of Lu and son of the Emperor Jing Di, ordered Confucius's dwelling to be demolished in order to build an extension to his palace, whereupon the books were found, which led to a schism between those who followed the reconstructed version of his last books, and those who followed the teachings in the rediscovered originals. In the east wall of the temple, near the Lu Wall, an unobtrusive gate leads to the legendary site of **Confucius's home**, sandwiched between the spectacular temple and the magnificent mansion, a tiny square of land, just big enough to have held a couple of poky little rooms.

The western section

The **western section** is entered through the Gate of He Who Heralds the Sage, by the Hall of Great Achievements. A paved path leads to a high brick terrace on which stands the five-bay, green-tiled **Hall of Silks and Metals** and the **Hall of He Who Heralds the Sage**, built to venerate Confucius's father, Shu Lianghe. He was originally a minor military official who attained posthumous nobility through his son. Behind is, predictably, the Hall of the Wife of He Who Heralds the Sage, dedicated to Confucius's mother.

Confucius Mansion

The First Family Under Heaven – the descendants of Confucius – lived continuously at the **Confucius Mansion**, accessible off Queli Jie in the centre of town (daily 8am–4.30pm; ¥32), for more than 2500 years, spanning 74 generations. The opulence and size of the mansion testifies to the power and wealth of the **Kong clan** and their head, the Yansheng Duke. Built on a north–south axis, the mansion is loosely divided into living quarters, an administrative area and a garden. In the east is a temple and ancestral hall, while the western wing includes the reception rooms for important guests and the rooms where the rites were learned.

Intricate and convoluted, this complex of twisting alleyways and over 450 rooms (most of them sixteenth century) has something decidedly eccentric about it. Inside the complex lies a central courtyard lined with long, narrow buildings, which were once administrative offices; now they hold a few trinket shops. The **Gate of Double Glory** to the north was opened only on ceremonial occasions or when the emperor dropped in. To its east and west are old **administrative departments**, modelled after the six ministries of the imperial government: the Department of Rites was in charge of ancestor worship; the Department of Seals concerned with jurisdiction and edicts; then followed

---

The Yansheng Duke and the Kong family

The status of the **Yansheng Duke** – the titile given to Confucius's direct male descendant – rose throughout imperial history as emperors granted him increasing **privileges and hereditary titles**; under the Qing dynasty, he enjoyed the unique privilege of being permitted to ride a horse inside the Forbidden City and walk along the Imperial Way inside the palace. Emperors presented the duke with large areas of sacrificial fields (so called because the income from the fields was used to pay for sacrificial ceremonies), as well as exempting him from taxes.

As a family the Kongs remained close-knit, practising a severe interpretation of **Confucian ethics**. For example, any young family member who offended an elder was fined two taels of silver and battered twenty times with a bamboo club. Strict rules governed who could go where within the house, and when a fire broke out in the living quarters in the last century it raged for three days as only twelve of the five hundred hereditary servants were allowed to go into the area to put it out. A female family member was expected to obey her father, her husband and her son. One elderly Kong general, after defeat on the battlefield, cut his throat for the sake of his dignity. When the news reached the mansion, his son hanged himself as an expression of filial piety. After discovering the body, his wife hanged herself out of female virtue. On hearing this, the emperor bestowed the family with a board, inscribed "A family of faithfulness and filiality".

The Kong family enjoyed the good life right up until the beginning of the twentieth century. **Decline** set in rapidly with the downfall of imperial rule, and in the 1920s the family was so poor that when wine was required for entertaining a guest, the servants bought it out of their own pocket, as a favour to their masters. In 1940, the last of the line, **Kong Decheng**, fled to Taiwan during the Japanese invasion, breaking the tradition of millennia. His sister, **Kong Demao**, penned The House of Confucius, a fascinating account of life lived inside this strange family chained to the past; it's available in foreign-language bookstores. Half of Qufu now claims descent from the Kongs, who are so numerous there is an entire local telephone directory dedicated to the letter K.

Music, Letters and Archives, Rent Collection and Sacrificial Fields. Beyond the Gate of Double Glory, the **Great Hall** was where the Yansheng duke sat on a wooden chair covered with a tiger skin and proclaimed edicts. The flags and arrow tokens hanging on the walls are symbols of authority. Signs next to them reading "Make way!" were used to clear the roads of ordinary people when the duke left the mansion.

The next hall was where the duke held examinations in music and rites, and beyond it lies the **Hall of Withdrawal**, where he took tea. The hall contains two sedan chairs; the green one was for trips outside the mansion, the red one for domestic use.

The residential apartments

The **residential apartments** of the mansion are to the north, accessible through gates, which would once have been heavily guarded; no one could enter of their own accord under pain of death. Tiger-tail cudgels, goose-winged pitchforks and golden-headed jade clubs used to hang here to drive the message home. Even the water-carrier was not permitted, and emptied the water into a stone trough outside that runs through the apartment walls. On a screen inside the gates is a painting of a *tan*, an imaginary animal shown eating treasures and greedily eyeing the sun. Feudal officials often had this picture painted in their homes as a warning against avarice.

The first hall is the seven-bay **Reception Hall**, where relatives were received, banquets held and marriage and funeral ceremonies conducted. Today, the only remnants of its once-salubrious past are several golden throne chairs and ornate staffs. Directly opposite the Reception Hall, the central eastern room contains a set of furniture made from tree roots, presented to the mansion by Emperor Qianlong – an original imperial decree lies on the table. Elsewhere in the central eastern room, check out the dinner service; it contains 404 pieces, including plates shaped like fish and deer, for consumption of the appropriate animals. Banquets for honoured guests could stretch to 196 courses.

Past the outbuildings and through a small gate, you reach the **Front Main Building**, an impressive two-storey structure in which are displayed paintings and clothes. The eastern central room was the home of Madame Tao, wife of Kong Lingyi, the seventy-sixth duke. Their daughter, Kong Demao, lived in the far eastern room, while Kong Lingyi's concubine, Wang, originally one of Tao's handmaids, lived in the inner western room. It doesn't sound like an arrangement designed for domestic bliss; indeed, whenever the duke was away, Madame Tao used to beat Wang with a whip she kept for the purpose. When Wang produced a male heir, Tao poisoned her. A second concubine, Feng, was kept prisoner in her rooms by Tao until she died.

The duke himself lived in the **rear building**, which has been left as it was when the last duke fled to Taiwan. Behind that is the garden where, every evening, flocks of crows come to roost noisily. Crows are usually thought to be inauspicious in China, but here they are welcome, and said to be the crow soldiers of Confucius, who protected him from danger on his travels. To the southeast of the inner east wing is a four-storey building called the **Tower of Refuge**, a planned retreat in the event of an uprising or invasion. The first floor was equipped with a movable hanging ladder, and a trap could be set in the floor. Once inside, the refugees could live for weeks on dried food stores.

The temple

In the east of the complex you'll find the family temple, the Ancestral Hall and residential quarters for less important family members. The **temple** is dedicated to the memory of Yu, wife of the seventy-second duke, and daughter of Emperor Qianlong. The princess had a mole on her face which, it was predicted, would bring disaster unless she married into a family more illustrious than either the nobility or the highest of officials. The Kongs were the only clan to fulfil the criteria, but technically the daughter of the Manchu emperor was not allowed to marry a Han Chinese. This inconvenience was got around by first having the daughter adopted by the family of the Grand Secretary Yu, and then marrying her to the duke as Yu's daughter. Her dowry included twenty villages and several thousand trunks of clothing.

The rest of town

Not far to the east of the gate of the Confucius Mansion is the Ming **Drum Tower**, which forms a pair with the **Bell Tower** on Queli Lu. The drum was struck to mark sunset, the bell to mark sunrise, and at major sacrificial ceremonies they would be sounded simultaneously. You can't go inside either.

A little way northeast of the Confucius Temple is **Yan Miao** (8am–5pm; ¥10), a smaller temple dedicated to Yanhui, who was regarded as Confucius's greatest disciple and sometimes called "The Sage Returned". A temple has been situated here since the Han dynasty, though the present structure is Ming. It's attractive, quieter than the Confucius Temple, and contains some impressive architectural details, such as the dragon pillars on the main hall, and a dragon head embedded in the roof. The eastern building now contains a display of locally excavated Neolithic and Zhou pottery.

The **Zhougong Miao** (7.30am–4.30pm; ¥5) in the northeast of the town is dedicated to a Zhou-dynasty duke, a statue of whom stands in the main hall, together with his son Bo Qin and Bo Qin's servant. Legend has it that Bo Qin was a rasher man than his father, and the duke, worried that his son would not act sensibly in state matters, inscribed a pithy maxim from his own political experience on a slate and directed the servant to carry it on his back. Whenever Bo Qin was about to do something foolish, the ever-present servant would turn his back so Bo Qin would think again. The open terrace before the hall, where sacrifices were made to the duke, contains a striking stone incense burner carved with coiling dragons.

Qufu's contemporary attractions don't compare with its historical wealth. The **Museum of Chinese Mythology** (7am–8pm; ¥20), behind the mansion on Houzuo Jie, provides ten minutes of comic relief with its tacky fairground-style show of mechanical dioramas operated by listless guides. One room, the Chinese idea of hell, is quite amusing, with lots of plastic skulls and fake gore. "Heaven" is a room full of half-naked shop-window dummies.

The Confucian Forest

The **Confucian Forest** is in the suburbs 3km north of the town centre (daily 8am–5pm; ¥17), reachable by cycle-rickshaw (¥3), though it's pleasant to walk. On the way, look out for stonemasons chiselling away at sculptures – dragons, lions, eagles, women in bikinis – at the side of the road. The forest is the **burial ground** of the Kongs and, like the temple, it expanded over the centuries from something simple and austere to a grand complex, in this case centring around a single grave – **the tomb of Confucius**. In the Song dynasty, the place was planted with trees, and in 1331 a wall was built around it. Pavilions and halls were added in the Ming dynasty and large-scale reconstructions made in 1730 when Yong Zhen constructed some impressive memorial archways. Confucian disciples collected exotic trees to plant here, and there are now more than a hundred thousand different varieties. Today it's an atmospheric place, sculptures half concealed in thick undergrowth, tombstones standing aslant in groves of ancient trees and wandering paths dappled with sunlight. A great place to spend an afternoon, it's one of the few famous scenic spots in China that it's possible to appreciate unaccompanied by crowds. Just inside the entrance you can board a tram (¥4) to the main sites. There is no bike rental service, which is a shame because the forest is really too large to explore on foot.

Running east from the chunky main gate, the imperial carriageway leads to a gateway and an arched stone bridge, beyond which is the spot where Confucius and his son are buried. The **Hall of Deliberation**, just north of the bridge, was where visitors put on ritual dress before performing sacrifices. An avenue, first of chop carvers and souvenir stalls, then of carved stone animals, leads to the **Hall of Sacrifices**, and behind that to a small grassy mound – the **grave**. Just to the west of the tomb a hut, looking like a potting shed, was where Confucius's disciples each spent three years watching over the grave. Confucius's son is buried just north of here. His unflattering epitaph reads: "He died before his father without making any noteworthy achievements."

According to legend, before his death Confucius told his disciples to bury him at this spot because the *feng shui* was good. His disciples objected, as there was no river nearby. Confucius told them that a river would be dug in the future. After the first Qin emperor, Qin Shi Huang, unified China, he launched an anti-Confucian campaign, burning books and scholars, and tried to sabotage the grave by ordering a river to be dug through the cemetery, thus inadvertently perfecting it.

Eating, drinking and nightlife

Local specialities include fragrant rice and boiled **scorpions** soaked in oil. The Kong family also developed its own cuisine, featuring dishes such as "Going to the Court with the Son" (pigeon served with duck) and "Gold and Silver Fish" (a white and a yellow fish together). It's possible to sample this refined cuisine at the *Queli Hotel*, which does a special **Confucian Mansion Banquet** for (mostly tourist) groups, at a rather extortionate ¥200 per head.

For simpler fare, there are a few **restaurants** on Gulou Dajie, though most near the *Queli* are overpriced and geared for tour groups. The *Yonghe Doujiang* outlet on Gulou Nanjie is open 24 hours, and is a reliable place for rice and noodle dishes anytime or an early-morning soy milk. At night, Wumaci Dajie fills up with open-air **food stalls**, offering tasty-looking hotpots and stews. The food's not bad and the atmosphere is lively, though make sure you know the price before you order anything.

Don't expect much **nightlife** in town. There are a number of sketchy karaoke joints along Gulou Nanjie if you're desperate for entertainment. Think hard before going to the gawdy **Confucius Six Arts City** to see the atrocious revue *Confucius' Dream* (daily April–Oct 8pm; ¥40), advertised all over town. It's doubtful the great sage's mind was filled with feather-headdress-wearing dancing girls and fan-waving martial-arts experts as he slept, as this show depicts.

Shopping

There are plenty of touristy **shops** in the centre of town, and a **night market** on Wumaci Jie. Unsurprisingly, the Confucian connection has been exploited to the hilt, with Confucius fans, beer, sweets and something called the "Confucius Treasure Box", which claims to include an acorn from the Confucian Forest and sand from the great sage's grave. Pick up a book of translated **Confucian sayings** at the *Queli Hotel*, but beware price tags covering the actual printed price on these. While steering clear of Confucian paraphernalia, it's worth checking out the **chops** (which can be carved with your name in a few minutes), rubbings taken from the steles in the temple and locally crafted pistachio carvings.

There's also a charming traditional Chinese **medicine store** on Zhonglou Jie, near the *Queli Hotel*; look for the herbs drying on the pavement. Get your scorpion essence – a local product, advertised as a general tonic – in the department stores on Wumaci Jie.

Qingdao and around

The port city of **QINGDAO** in the east of Shandong province makes a remarkable first impression. Emerging from the train station and walking north with your eyes fixed on the skyline, you could almost believe you had got off at a nineteenth-century Bavarian village, nestling on the Yellow Sea. Once a **German concession**, Qingdao's marriage of European and Chinese architecture has created bizarre juxtapositions, with oriental stone lions sitting in discreet European gardens, and grand, pompous facades now fronting little shops and laundries.

Qingdao and around

Qingdao	青岛	qīngdǎo
Brewery	青岛啤酒厂	qīngdǎo píjiǔ chǎng
Catholic Church	天主教堂	tiānzhǔ jiàotáng
Huilan Ge	回澜阁	huílán gé
Lao Shan	崂山	láoshān
Lu Xun Park	鲁迅公园	lǔxùn gōngyuán
Museum of Marine Products	海产博物馆	hǎichǎn bówùguǎn
Naval Museum	海军博物馆	hǎijūn bówùguǎn
Passenger ferry terminal	港客运站	gǎngkèyùnzhàn
Qingdao Museum	青岛市博物馆	qīngdǎo shì bówùguǎn
Qingdaoshan Park	青岛山公园	qīngdǎoshān gōngyuán
Xiaoqingdao Isle	小青岛	xiǎoqīng dǎo
Xiaoyushan Park	小鱼山公园	xiǎoyúshān gōngyuán
Xinhaoshan Park	信号山公园	xìnhàoshān gōngyuán
Ying Hotel	迎宾馆	yíng bīnguǎn
Zhanqiao Pier	栈桥	zhàn qiáo
Zhongshan Park	中山公园	zhōngshān gōngyuán
Accommodation and eating		
Chunhelou	春和楼饭店	chūnhélóu fàndiàn
Holiday Inn	颐中假日酒店	yízhōng jiàrì jiǔdiàn
Huaneng	华能宾馆	huánéng bīnguǎn
Huiquan Dynasty	汇泉王朝大酒店	huìquán wángcháo dàjiǔdiàn
International Seamen's Club	国际海员俱乐部	guójì hǎiyuán jùlèbù
New Friendship	新友谊宾馆	xīnyǒuyì bīnguǎn
Oceanwide Elite	泛海名人酒店	fànhǎi míngrén jiǔdiàn
Railway	铁道大厦	tiědào dàshà
Shangri-La	青岛香格里拉大酒店	qīngdǎo xiānggélǐlā dàjiǔdiàn
Tianqiao Hotel	天桥宾馆	tiānqiáo bīnguǎn
Xinlongyuan	新龙源大酒店	xīnlóngyuán dàjiǔdiàn
Yushenhu	御神户日本料理	yùshénhù rìběn liàolǐ

Qingdao's distinctive Teutonic stamp dates back to 1897, a legacy of **Kaiser Wilhelm**'s industrious attempts to extend a German sphere of influence in the East. The kaiser's **annexation of Qingdao**, along with the surrounding Jiazhou peninsula, was justified in terms typical of the European actions of the time. It was prompted by concern for "safety", following the murder of two German missionaries during the **Boxer Rebellion** (see p.1162). The kaiser raised the incident to an international crisis, making a near-hysterical speech (which coined the phrase "yellow peril") demanding action from the feeble Manchu government. He got his concession, the Chinese ceding the territory for 99 years, along with the right to build the Shandong rail lines. Previously an insignificant fishing village, Qingdao made an ideal deep-water base for the German navy and was split into a European, a Chinese and a business section, with a garrison of two thousand soldiers to protect its independence. It was to remain German until 1914 when the **Japanese**, anxious to acquire a foothold in China, bombarded Qingdao. The town was taken on November 7, and five thousand prisoners were carted off to Japan. In the Treaty of Versailles, the city was ceded to Japan, which infuriated the Chinese, and led to demonstrations in Beijing – the beginning of the May Fourth Movement (see "Contexts", p.1163). Qingdao was eventually returned to China in 1922.

Modern Qingdao is still a very important **port**, China's fourth largest, and behind the attractive **old town** is an area with a very different character, a sprawling industrial metropolis of high-rises and factories. Of more interest to visitors are the white-sand **beaches** dotted along the shoreline, among the best in northern China; indeed, the city has been chosen to host the sailing events of the **2008 Summer Olympics**. The summer **season** runs from June to September, though many visitors come in late April and early May, when the cherry trees are blooming in Zhongshan Park. Qingdao also produces the world-renowned **Tsingtao Beer** (Tsingtao is the old transliteration of Qingdao) which owes its crisp, clean flavour to the purity of the spring water from **Lao Shan**, one of China's famous peaks, with which it is brewed. Fans of the local brew may be interested in the annual **Beer Festival** (mid- to late Aug).

Arrival, information and city transport

The old concession area and the beachfront are easy to get to know and to get around. Zhongshan Lu, running north–south, is the modern, glitzy shopping district and the heart of the concession district; on the east–west axis, Taiping and Laiyang Lu follow the coastline.

The large city **airport**, 30km north of the city, is served by a regular CAAC bus (¥15), which drops passengers on Zhongshan Lu. Arriving in Qingdao by

---

Ferries from Qingdao

From Qingdao, there are international ferries to Inchon (16hr; ¥750–1090) and Gunsan (22hr; ¥700–1467), South Korea, and to Shimonoseki, Japan (36hr; ¥1200–7000), with multiple departures each week in the high season. **Tickets** can be bought in advance from the passenger ferry terminal on Xinjiang Lu. There are five classes (special, first, second, third and fourth), with severe gradations in price as you move down the scale. Third class is about the same level of comfort as hard sleeper on a train and is probably best unless you're particularly loaded or skint.

For **Dalian**, you'll need to get a ferry from Yantai, three hours north by bus. You can buy tickets in advance from the kiosks on the train-station concourse.

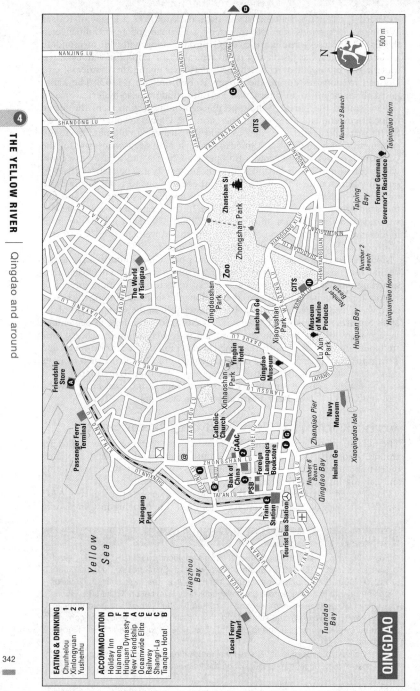

EATING & DRINKING
Chunhelou 1
Xinlongyuan 2
Yushenhu 3

ACCOMMODATION
Holiday Inn D
Huaneng F
Huiquan Dynasty H
New Friendship A
Oceanwide Elite G
Railway E
Shangri-La C
Tianqiao Hotel B

QINGDAO

NANJING LU
SHANDONG LU
NANJING LU
JIANGXI LU
XIANGGANG ZHONG LU
YAN ANSANLU LU
CITS
Number 3 Beach
Taipingjiao Horn
Taiping Bay
Former German Governor's Residence
Zhanshan Si
Zhongshan Park
Zoo
The World of Tsingtao
Qingdaoshan Park
Lanchao Ge
CITS
Museum of Marine Products
Xiaoyushan Park
Lu Xun Park
Number 1 Beach
Number 2 Beach
Huiquan Horn
Huiquanjiao Horn
Huiquan Bay
Taiping Bay
ZHENGYANGGUAN LU
XIANGGANG LU
DAXUE LU
Friendship Store
Passenger Ferry Terminal
Xiaogang Port
Yingbin Hotel
Qingdao Museum
Xinhaoshan Park
Catholic Church
CAAC
Bank of China
Foreign Languages Bookstore
PSB
Zhanqiao Pier
Navy Museum
Zhongshan Lu
Train Station
Tourist Bus Station
Number 6 Beach
Qingdao Bay
Huilan Ge
Xiaoqingdao Isle
Local Ferry Wharf
Jiaozhou Bay
Tuandao Bay
Yellow Sea
HUANGAO LU
WEIHAI LU
LIAONING LU
HEILAN LU
JIAOZHOU LU
SHENXIAN LU
TAI'AN LU
LAIYANG LU
JIANGSU LU
YUNNAN LU
SICHUAN LU
N
0 500 m

train is the easiest option. The station, which is on a single line that splits, one fork leading to Ji'nan, the other to Yantai, is a grand German edifice at the heart of the old town, within walking distance of the beach and the seafront hotels. Convenient **tourist buses** leave from a station just south of the train station; the expressway has now cut the journey time from Ji'nan to under five hours (¥56). The **passenger ferry terminal** is in the grotty north of town, with a cheap hotel nearby. To get **to the seafront** from here, take bus #215 south, get off halfway down Shenxian Lu, opposite Xiaogang Port, walk east to the end of Zhongshan Lu and catch a #6. Or go to the last stop of the #215 route, walk south down to Guizhou Lu and catch bus #25 east. Get off just after Huilange Pavilion, before it turns up Daxue Lu. As this is pretty involved, it's a lot easier just to get a taxi if you are arriving with luggage.

The **Qingdao Tourist Office** (8.30am–5pm; ☏0532/2962000), on the train-station concourse (down the set of stairs in front of the arrivals exit), has helpful staff, touch-screen computers introducing the area and helpful maps.

Bus #6 is a useful service, going from the top of Zhongshan Lu down towards the train station, then heading east along the seafront, getting close to Number 1 beach and terminating near the entrance to Zhongshan Park. Other useful routes are the **#300 series** (#304, #311, #312 & #316), which go between Zhanqiao Pier near the train station along the coast to the eastern sector. Private **minibuses** also run on most bus routes. They're more common, faster, but a little more expensive. **Taxis** to most destinations within the city cost the minimum fare of ¥10, though expect to pay double this to get to the eastern part of town.

Accommodation

Qingdao has a surfeit of top-class international **hotels** well located on the seafront. If you're travelling on a budget, your choices are much more limited, and you'll probably end up some way from the picturesque parts of town. You can trust the touts at the train station to find you a good room in the centre – just tell them how much you want to spend, ask to see the room, then bargain. Good-value places to stay can be found in the area just northeast of the station, on the lanes between Zhongshan Lu and Tai'an Lu.

Holiday Inn 76 Xianggang Zhong Li ☏0532/571888, ℻5777513. Luxury high-rise on the modern east side of town, with all mod cons. ❾

Huaneng 2 Anhui Lu ☏0532/2961310, ℻2860077. With a discounted seaview room, you can hardly do better than the *Huaneng*, which is close to the train station, the beach, important bus lines, and the colonial architecture Qingdao is famous for. ❼

Huiquan Dynasty 9 Nanhai Lu ☏0532/2999888, ℻2871122. A well-located four-star hotel – the beach is directly across a narrow lane. ❾

New Friendship Xinjiang Lu ☏0532/2844888, ℻2834888. This hotel is a long way out in the same building as the Friendship Store, next to the passenger-ferry terminal. The building is bare and ragged, but the rooms are pleasant and popular with budget travellers. It's also notable for having a helpful, English-speaking manager. Try to avoid the

fourth floor as there's a nightclub here which blasts out old Euro-pop till 2am. ❺

Oceanwide Elite 29 Taiping Lu ☏0532/2996699, ℻2891388. In an excellent location opposite Zhanqiao Pier, this new four-star hotel has an impressive interior and all the facilities you'd expect. ❾

Railway 2 Tai'an Lu ☏0532/6067888, ℻2860497. Right next door to the train station, this spartan place is clean though noisy. ❺

Shangri-La 9 Xianggang Zhong Lu ☏0532/3883838, ℻3886868. Another glossy tower, situated 5min from the beach in the plush part of town. It offers all the expected five-star luxuries, and an excellent weekend rate. Buses #223 and #501 come here from the train station. ❾, ❽ at weekends.

Tianqiao Hotel 51 Feicheng Lu ☏0532/2858705. This hotel (and its neighbour the *Jindaiyuan*) has clean rooms that the train-station touts recommend. ❻

The City

Qingdao has plenty of diversions on offer, but the main thing to do here is stroll. The **waterfront** is a place to see and be seen, while the faster-paced **downtown** streets have a definite cosmopolitan feel. Unusually for a city outside Beijing, there's even evidence of the new Chinese youth culture; buskers work the crowds on the esplanade, beach bums recline elegantly on the sands and skateboarders weave down the hills, all adding to Qingdao's generally mellow, trendy feel. As well as the **beaches** and **old German town**, some very pleasant **parks** are an added bonus, ensuring that Qingdao is easily one of the most charismatic of Chinese cities.

The old German town and the brewery

Zhongshan Lu is the main shopping drag, awash with shoe shops and designer clothing stores. Anchoring the area is the fine **Catholic Church** (Mon–Sat 8am–5pm, Sun noon–5pm; ¥5), a German relic whose distinctive double spires can be seen from all over the city. The streets east of here, some cobbled, many lined with pink buildings with black iron balconies overlooking the street, are a good place to wander and take in the flavour of the **old German town**.

The **Qingdao Museum** on Daxue Lu is worth a diversion (Tues–Sun 8.30am–5pm; ¥15). This beautiful building, constructed in 1931, was the headquarters of the sinister-sounding Red Swastika Association, a welfare institute. There's a collection of paintings here from the Yuan through to Qing dynasties, and an archeological section in the courtyard which contains four large standing **Buddhas** dating back to 500–527 AD. They're slim, striking figures with bulbous, smiling heads, one hand pointing upward to heaven, the other down to the earth. The heads were cut off in 1928 by the Japanese and taken away to museums in Japan, though they've now been restored to their rightful shoulders. The museum staff seem proudest, however, of a souvenir collected by Qingdao sailors during the 1985 Chinese expedition to the South Pole – a simple lump of rock – which sits proudly in a specially constructed pavilion in the courtyard.

Fans of **Tsingtao beer** can take a trip into the industrial zone to see the brewery museum known as **The World of Qingdao** (9am–4pm; ¥50). It's on the route of bus #25 and easy enough to spot, but the only way to get inside is to take a tour with CITS (see p.348), which are sporadic. Free samples are available, including an unusual dark brown stout, but you'll have to sit through a lot of statistics first.

The beaches and the waterfront

Qingdao's **beaches**, with fine white sand, are active from very early in the morning, when *tai ji* exponents and beachcombers turn out, to well into the evening, when holidaymakers come for the bars and cafés on the beach and esplanade or just to sit and look out to sea against a backdrop of black Japanese pine trees. Off Nanhai Lu, **Number 1 beach**, flanked by skyscrapers on one side, red-tiled roofs on the other, is the biggest (580m long) and best. In season it's a lively, crowded place, swarming with ice-cream vendors, trinket stalls selling carved shells and a rash of photographers. Fortunately, unlike Beidaihe, the other northern beach resort (see p.165), it doesn't feel overloaded with kitsch. The whole place is very organized, with odd, beachball-shaped changing huts, shower facilities, multicoloured beach umbrellas, and designated swimming areas marked out with buoys and protected by shark nets. The water, however,

△ German-style architecture, Qingdao

is like Chinese soup – murky and warm, with unidentifiable things floating in it – so swimming is not recommended. Sit down and you're not likely to remain alone for long as there are plenty of people around who want to practise their English.

If Number 1 beach feels too crowded, head east to the more sheltered **number 2 and 3 beaches**. These are more sedate, and popular with the older, sanatorium-dwelling crowd. For the liveliest social scene, head to the illogically named **Number 6** beach, at the bottom of Zhongshan Lu; in addition to good swimming, there are plenty of shops here should you choose to stay dry.

Along the waterfront

Above the beaches is the **esplanade**, stretching from the western end of the peninsula all the way to Number 1 beach. Hopeful fishermen with rods line the stretch around Tuandao Bay. Just east of Number 6 beach is **Zhanqiao Pier**, the symbol of the city, with the octagonal **Huilan Ge**, a pavilion where small craft exhibitions are held, at its end. The stretch above Number 6 beach has numerous little stalls selling gaudy swimsuits and cheap souvenirs. This area really comes alive in the evening, when it becomes a crowded thoroughfare and **open-air cinema** with screens on Taiping Lu. It's a great place to wander, though the view out to sea has been compromised; enterprising Chinese advertisers have even found a way to use the ocean as a hoarding and neon characters sit on stilts stuck into the sea bed some way out from the shore.

East of the pier, a decommissioned **submarine** and a **destroyer** sit in the water at the **Navy Museum** (daily 8.30am–7.30pm; ¥25). You're required to leave cameras at the ticket booth, which seems a little oversensitive as both exhibits are virtually antiques. The destroyer is small and rusting, with a display of fearsome weaponry. The submarine is much more interesting and well worth a look. The series of narrow, dark rooms arrayed with masses of chunky old valves, dials, levers and knobs, many of them bearing Russian markings, rewards detailed examination.

Next to the sub, you can tour the military aircraft on display or follow the sandbank leading to **Xiaoqingdao Isle** (¥15). There's a pleasant little park here, a few cafés with good views, and a surprisingly lascivious statue of a sea nymph playing a violin. A white beacon stands at the highest point.

Around the bend is **Lu Xun Park** (daily 6am–7pm; ¥5), a good approach to Number 1 beach. It has green pine trees and cypresses, little winding paths, pavilions, benches and tables, full of couples indulging in what must be the well-heeled Chinese tourists' favourite hobby, photographing your spouse. Inside the park is the **Museum of Marine Products** (daily 7.45am–6pm; ¥30), consisting of two buildings, an aquarium shaped like a castle and a two-storey exhibition hall, with a seal pool in between. Founded in 1932, it's billed as the first aquarium in China, though to Western eyes it's pretty unexciting – lots of exotic marine life swimming about in tanks make it look like an average Chinese restaurant.

The farther east you go, the grander and more exclusive the buildings get. Past the *Huiquan Dynasty Hotel* is the **Badaguan area**, a health resort of sanatoriums and classy guesthouses set among trees. It's a pretty place with a suburban feel, each street lined with a different tree or flower – there are peach blossoms on Shaoguan Lu, crab apples on Ningwuguan Lu, and crab myrtle on Zhengyangguan Lu – and unlike most of the old gardens in Qingdao, the ones here are well looked after. At the eastern end of Number 2 beach stands the **former German Governor's Residence**, a grand castle looking out to sea.

Zhongshan Park and around

Qingdao's **parks**, dotted above the waterfront and serving as a buffer zone between the interesting parts of the city, the waterfront, and the boring industrial bits, are among the best in China. The largest is **Zhongshan Park** (daily 6.30am–5.30pm; ¥3), on the side of Taiping Hill. Within its boundaries sits the Buddhist **Zhanshan Si**, the zoo, a couple of theme parks, a teahouse and the TV Tower, looking as if it's just landed from outer space. A cable car runs from near the entrance to the top of the hill. It's a good place to lose the crowds and hike around, but as it's so enormous you'll need a whole day to explore it thoroughly. The park is famed for its **cherry trees**, which turn the park into a pink forest when they're in bloom in late April and early May; thousands of visitors come just to see the spectacle.

Just west of Zhongshan Park, **Qingdaoshan Park** (7am–5pm; ¥5) contains the small Jingshan Fort. Farther west, the steep but very pleasant **Xinhaoshan Park** holds the **Yingbin Hotel** (daily 8.30am–4.30pm; ¥10), a restored, grand old mansion built in 1905. It's worth a tour, as the German Governor-General, the warlord Yuan Shikai and Chairman Mao have lodged here in their time. The highest point of the park, reached by tortuous winding paths, is a good place to get an overview of the city. **Xiaoyushan Park**, on the top of a hill by the side of Huiquan Bay, is styled like a classical Chinese garden. The main three-storey octagonal structure at the summit is the **Lanchao Ge**, a pavilion traditionally used for watching the tide.

Fans of modern Chinese literature should divert their walk down the hill towards the waterfront past 12 Huangxian Lu. A small plaque in Chinese denotes it as the site where the writer **Lao She** lived from 1934 to 1937.

Eating, drinking and nightlife

Qingdao has plenty of **restaurants** to choose from. The speciality is, unsurprisingly, seafood; mussels and crabs here are particularly good, and not expensive. There are plenty of small **seafood places** along Laiyang Lu, particularly the strip bordering Lu Xun Park. They're all small, noisy and busy, but competition means that standards are high, and, with some exceptions, the food is reasonably cheap. The expensive hotels also have restaurants, and, although they're pricey, the food is very good and the setting is often palatial. The first-floor restaurant in the *Huiquan Dynasty Hotel* is one of the best.

On and around Zhongshan Lu, try the renowned *Chunhelou*, 146 Zhongshan Lu, a quiet little place with discreet service, small tables and ambient lighting which gives it a Continental feel. The food is very good, and portions are more than generous – the spicy chicken is highly recommended. The *Xinlongyuan* at 6 Qufu Lu is an unassuming spot with local food and is a step away from the cathedral. The baozi shop next door is also a good place for a cheap lunch in the middle of town. The *Yushenhu* sushi bar is at 15 Feicheng Lu a few doors down from the intersection with Zhongshan Lu and *McDonald's*. There's a *KFC* on Feixian Lu, across the road at the southern end of the train station.

Strangely, **nightlife** isn't as exciting here as might be expected, and it's easier to find a convenience store with draught beer than it is to find a pub with it on tap. A lot of Chinese visitors end up in karaoke bars or expensive hotel nightclubs near the *Huiquan*. The best place to be in the early evening is around Zhanqiao Pier, where everyone goes for a stroll after eating.

Listings

Airlines The main CAAC office is at 29 Zhongshan Lu (☎0532/2895577). There's another office in the Aviation Building on the east side of town at 30 Xianggang Zhong Lu (☎0532/5775555). Buses to the airport go from here (¥15).

Banks and exchange The main Bank of China is at 62 Zhongshan Lu (Mon–Fri 8.30am–5pm, Sat–Sun 9.30am–4pm).

Boats Kayaks can be rented on the beach across from the *Huiquan Dynasty Hotel* (¥20 single, ¥30 double).

Bookshops The relatively well-stocked Foreign Language Bookstore is at 10 Henan Lu, just south of Hubei Lu.

Buses Qingdao's main bus station is in the north of town, though the tourist bus stop south of the train station is the starting point for the most common intercity routes, including Ji'nan and Yantai.

Internet access A large, comfortable Internet café (¥2 per hr) is at the corner of Zhongshan Lu and Jiaozhou Lu.

PSB The PSB is at 29 Hubei Lu (Mon–Sat 8am–noon & 2–7pm), not far from the train station.

Mail and telephones The main post office and telecom building is at the northern end of Zhongshan Lu (Mon–Sat 8am–6pm).

Travel agents CITS is at 73 Xianggang Xi Lu (☎0532/3893001). As usual, it caters more for domestic groups than independent foreign travellers, and you can get great tourist information at the train station.

Lao Shan

The **Lao Shan** area, 400 square kilometres of rugged coast 40km east of Qingdao, is an easy day-trip from the city. **Minibuses** (¥10) and public buses #304 & #801 (¥8) leave frequently from outside the train station, dropping you off at the foot of Lao Shan itself; they head back to Qingdao from the same location, or you can hail a minibus from any of the three roads inside the area. There are also minibuses travelling between each of the temples and the mountain, so it's not hard to travel from one of the popular scenic spots to another. **Maps** of the area are included on all city maps, and it's a good idea to get one before you set out.

It's a good place to hike around – the whole area is dotted with caves, springs and waterfalls amid striking scenery – and with a bit of effort it's possible to lose the crowds and trinket stalls. The area is also known for being the source of **Lao Shan mineral water**, which gives Tsingtao beer its taste; from Jiushui Valley, to the northeast of the mountain, it's one of the few Chinese mineral waters that doesn't taste of swimming pools. In the Tang dynasty there were 72 Taoist temples in the area; now time, neglect and the Cultural Revolution have reduced most to ruins.

On a clear day, the **coastal road route** from Qingdao is spectacular, winding somewhat precariously along cliff tops. On the way you'll pass the **Stone Old Man**, a ten-metre-high rock standing in the sea, not far from the beach. Legend has it that long ago a beautiful local girl, Mudan, was kidnapped by Longwang, the King of the East Sea. Her distraught father stood so long looking out to sea for his missing daughter that he eventually turned to stone.

Writers have been inspired by the scenery around Lao Shan for centuries – *Strange Stories at Liao's House*, by the Qing-dynasty author Pu Songling, was written here – and have left noble graffiti in the form of poems and sage reflections, cut into rocks all round the area. Throughout the locality you might also see large, distinctive, oddly shaped granite **stones** named after an often tenuous resemblance to an animal or person. They're interesting forms but you need plenty of imagination – or Tsingtao Red – to get the allusion.

Around the mountain

You'll be charged ¥50 entrance (¥30 off season) near Lao Shan village, after which there are three **roads**, each route taking in some magnificent views. The southern road takes you past the Taiqing Gong, Mingxia Cave and Longtan Waterfall. The eastern route goes to Taiqing Gong, and the middle road going southeast takes you to a village at the foot of Lao Shan. From the village, a pathway of stone steps, constructed a century ago by the enterprising German Lao Shan Company to cater for their compatriots' weakness for alpine clambering, runs all the way to the summit and then back down a different route on the other side. The **path** climbs past gullies and woods, streams and pools, and the ascent takes about two hours. There's a temple halfway up, where you can fortify yourself with fruit and tea for the final haul. At the summit, 1133m above sea level, a ruined temple now houses a meteorological station. The view is great, and gets even better as you descend by the alternative route back to the village.

Other scenic spots have a religious connection. On **Naloyan Shan**, 2km northeast of Lao Shan, is a cave in which the Naloyan Buddha was said to have meditated, and on the coast just north of here the **Baiyun Cave** was once the home of a famous monk, Tian Baiyun. Ever since, it has been seen as an auspicious place to meditate. **Mingxia Cave**, 3km farther south down the coast on the slopes of Kunyu Shan, was written about by a famous Taoist, Qiu Changchun. Inside the cave are stones which reflect the rays of the morning sun, and the flat area outside is a good vantage point to watch the sunset.

Well worth a visit is the **Taiqing Gong** (¥15), a temple to the south of Lao Shan, by the coast, and close to the boat dock. It's the oldest and grandest of Lao Shan's temples, consisting of three halls set amid attractive scenery. Outside the first hall are two camellias about which Pu Songling wrote a story. It's a photogenic, leafy place, containing some rare flowers and trees, including Hanbai paleo-cypresses, planted in the Han dynasty, and Tangyu elms dating back to the Tang. There are nine temples nearby, which, though smaller, are quiet, peaceful places.

Yantai and around

YANTAI, on the Yellow Sea in northern Shandong, 240km northeast of Qingdao, is a somewhat battered-looking seaside town, with a burgeoning port and a tourist industry based around its rather average beaches. It's the poor relation of Qingdao, and consequently lost out in the bidding to stage the 2008 Olympic sailing competition despite having better maritime conditions. The main reason to visit is to check out the **temple of Penglai**, 70km west of the city, or to pick up a transport connection; **ferries** leave to Tianjin, Dalian and Shanghai, while pleasant **Weihai**, where you can catch a ferry to South Korea, is a bus ride away.

Yantai means "smoke mound", the name deriving from the ancient practice of lighting fires on the headland to warn of imminent Japanese invasion or (more likely) approaching pirates. Prior to 1949, it was a fishing port called Chefoo, and its recent history, like that of Qingdao, is closely bound up with European colonialism. In 1862, Chefoo was made a **British treaty port** as a prize of the Opium War. Thirty years later the **Germans** arrived, wishing to extend their influence on the peninsula. After World War I it was the turn of the **Americans**, who used the port as a summer station for their entire Asian fleet, then

Yantai and around

Yantai	烟台	*yāntái*
Number One Bathing Beach	第一海水浴场	*dìyī hǎishuǐ yùchǎng*
Number Two Bathing Beach	第二海水浴场	*dì'èr hǎishuǐ yùchǎng*
Yantai Museum	烟台博物馆	*yāntái bówùguǎn*
Yantaishan Park	烟台山公园	*yāntáishān gōngyuán*
Accommodation and eating		
Gangcheng	港城宾馆	*gǎngchéng bīnguǎn*
International Trade Hotel	国贸大酒店	*guómào dàjiǔdiàn*
Shandong Pacific Hotel	太平洋大酒店	*tàipíngyáng dàjiǔdiàn*
Yantai Marina Hotel	滨海假日酒店	*bīnhǎi jiàrì jiǔdiàn*
Penglai	蓬莱	*pénglái*
Weihai	威海	*wēihǎi*
Passenger ferry terminal	港客运站	*gǎngkèyùnzhàn*
Qing Quan Hotel	清泉大酒店	*qīngquán dàjiǔdiàn*
Weihaiwei Hotel	威海威大酒店	*wēihǎiwēi dàjiǔdiàn*

the **Japanese**, who set up a trading establishment here. However, all this foreign influence has not left a distinctive architectural mark – most of the town is of much more recent origin, a product of the rapid industrialization that has taken place since 1949. Yantai is also known for its more than passable **wine**, produced in vineyards set up by Singaporean Chinese in 1893, who learned their skills from French soldiers stationed here.

The City

Plenty of foreigners come to Yantai on the ships that call in at the huge port in the north of town. Mostly Russian sailors, they seldom get much farther than the International Seamen's Club opposite the train station – whose bar is probably the city's most popular attraction – or the well-stocked Friendship Store just around the corner from here, where you can stock up on local wine and brandy. They're not missing much, as there's nothing spirited about the rest of the city, although the museum is worth checking out (the building more so than the exhibits).

Wandering the **seafront** is the most pleasant way to spend any time here. **Yantaishan Park** (¥8) stands at the western end of the seafront, marking the eastern edge of the port area. This steep hill, latticed with twisting paths, is where the locals used to keep an eye out for pirates. It has a modern beacon (¥6), which offers an impressive overview of the port from the top. There are also a few pavilions, a couple of former European consulates and an old Japanese military camp scattered about. The city's two **beaches** are both east of here, but they're not great – littered, windy and hemmed in by unattractive buildings. Number 2 beach, the farther of the two, is the better, though the water is very polluted. Binhai Lu, along the waterfront, has a number of small seafood restaurants.

Yantai Museum

The one sight you shouldn't miss is the **Yantai Museum** on Nan Dajie (daily 8am–5pm; ¥10), housed in the largest and most beautiful of the city's old guild halls, set up for the use of merchants and shipowners. The entrance hall is startling, decorated with an ensemble of more than a hundred stone and wood carvings. The beams are in the shape of a woman lying on her side nursing a baby, and beneath the eaves are Arab figures playing musical instruments. Other panels to the north show scenes from the *Romance of the Three Kingdoms* (see p.1224), the story of the Eight Immortals who Crossed the Sea, and the story of the second-century General Su Wu, condemned to look after sheep for nineteen years as a punishment for refusing to go over to the Huns.

The main building here is the **Temple to the Goddess of the Sea**. Generations of sailors in trouble at sea reported being guided to safety by the vision of a woman. Under the Ming and Qing she became an official deity, and temples in her honour proliferated along the coast. The temple itself, in the style of imperial buildings of the Song dynasty, was brought from Fujian by ship in 1864 and is a unique and beautiful example of southern architecture in northern China, with its double roof and sweeping horns to the eaves, fancifully ornamented with mythical figures in wood, stone and glazed ceramics. Below are stone columns, their deep dragon motif carvings among the finest to be seen in China. The whole temple complex is set in a little garden with pools and a stage (the goddess is said to have been fond of plays). The museum in the side galleries houses a number of Stone-Age cooking pots, axes and arrowheads, believed to be 6000 years old, and some fine seventeenth- and eighteenth-century porcelain.

Practicalities

Yantai's **airport** is 15km south of the city. Taxis into the centre from here cost around ¥50, while the CAAC bus (¥10) drops you at its office on Da Haiyang Lu (☎0535/6669777), near the train station. The **train station**, in the northwest of town, is at the terminus of two lines, one to Qingdao and one to Ji'nan. Ferries arrive at the **passenger-ferry terminal** in the northwest of town, which is packed in summer with peasants beginning their annual migration to Manchuria for the harvest. There are many ferries daily to Dalian;

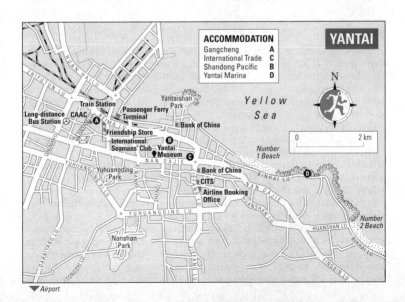

tickets are available at a window on the train-station square. For a ¥20 surcharge, a window at the main booking hall beside the train station sells onward train tickets from Dalian. The bus from Qingdao rockets along an expressway and terminates at the **long-distance bus station** on Qingnian Lu, southwest of the train station.

Taxis are plentiful and cost ¥5, with ¥15 enough to journey to the far eastern beaches. Bus #12 is the most useful around the city, travelling east from the train station along Nan Dajie, the main street, then turning south down Jiefang Lu. Bus #17 travels from the train station east along the coast. Both the **post office** (Mon–Fri 8am–6pm) and the **Bank of China** (Mon–Fri 8am–noon & 2–5pm, Sat 8am–noon) are on its route. The **CITS** office, at 181B Jiefang Lu (☏0535/6617710), isn't good for much.

Accommodation and eating

Yantai's **hotel** situation is not good; we've listed the best of the places to stay below. The city is popular with Chinese tourists and there are many small guesthouses, but many of the cheaper places are not open to foreigners.

The two best **restaurants** in town are the ones at the *Yantai Marina Hotel* on Binhai Lu. Here you can try the seafood stew while averting your eyes from the middle-aged cadres dining with dates young enough to be their daughters. East of here, there are many Korean and dumpling restaurants opposite the train station.

Gangcheng 72 Beima Lu ☏0535/6283888. Tucked off the main road in front of the train station, beside the post office and its hotel. Rooms here are showing their age, but they are cheap and clean. On the downside, note that the place is decidedly seedy.

International Trade Hotel 303 Nan Dajie ☏0535/6587788. A striking new 28-storey tower that looks more expensive than it is. It has all the usual flash amenities, and there's even a bowling alley. **⑥**

Shandong Pacific Hotel 74 Shifu Jie ☏0535/6206888, ℉6205204. A four-star option situated in a bustling neighbourhood; staff are very friendly and speak some English. **⑧**

Yantai Marina Hotel 128 Binhai Bei Lu ☏0535/6669999, ℉6669770. The top choice in Yantai, overlooking the ocean on the scenic drive. **⑧**

Penglai

A temple on a hilltop 70km west of the city, **Penglai** makes for a worthwhile day-trip, as it holds more excitement than anything Yantai can muster. Tourist **minibuses** leave irregularly from outside Yantai's train station (45min; ¥10), or you can get a slower local bus to Penglai town from the long-distance bus station. The temple is 3km beyond the town, but there are plenty of minibuses that ply the last leg of the journey.

Over 1000 years old and in a good state of repair, the temple (¥70, inclusive of all the area's main sights) is a strikingly attractive complex brooding over the cliff face, dominated by a lighthouse-like tower. With crenellated walls making it look more like a castle, it has six main buildings, which have been extensively restored and added to. The Main Hall contains a fine gilt Sea Goddess, behind whose dais is a spectacular mural of sea and cloud dragons disporting themselves. You can swim or catch crabs in the sea – which is a little cleaner here than in Yantai – while you wait for the return bus.

The temple is famous for the **Penglai mirage**, which locals claim appears every few decades. Accounts of it vary widely, from a low-lying sea mist to an island in the sky, complete with people, trees and vehicles. The phenomenon lasts about forty minutes, and if you're not lucky enough to witness it you can watch it on TV in a room set aside for the purpose inside the temple. Staff declare ignorance of any correlation between an increased drive for tourist revenues and the increasing frequency of the apparition.

Weihai

The port of **WEIHAI**, 88km east of Yantai, has nothing specific to recommend it to tourists, but it is a sunny town in which to stroll while waiting for a boat. Weihai's **long-distance bus station** is about ten minutes south of the Bank of China, or 25 minutes' walk from the port. There are sleeper buses to Beijing (¥150 one-way) and Shanghai (¥200 one-way) every afternoon, and frequent services to Yantai (1hr; ¥17) and Qingdao. A thrice-weekly **passenger ferry** leaves Weihai for **Inchon** in South Korea; tickets (¥750–1380) can be booked at the terminal, at the eastern terminus of Kunming Lu, or from the business centre at the *Weihaiwei Dasha*, a **hotel** at 82 Haigang Lu, at the corner of Kunming Lu and Xinwei Lu (☏0631/5285888, ⓕ5285777; ⑧). Cheaper accommodation is offered two blocks west at the *Qing Quan Hotel*, 5 Gongyuan Lu (☏0631/5224112; ⑤). The **Bank of China**, where you can change traveller's cheques, is a few minutes farther west along Kunming Lu from the *Weihaiwei Dasha*.

Travel details

Trains

For short runs between major rail hubs or tourist destinations, trains usually leave at least once per hour, from early morning to evening, if not later. For longer runs or overnight trains, frequencies drop off and can require buying a ticket at least a day in advance.

Hua Shan to: Xi'an (daily; 2hr); Yuncheng (4 daily; 1hr 40min).

Kaifeng to: Shanghai (8 daily; 12hr); Xi'an (13 daily; 8hr); Yanzhou (7 daily; 5hr 30min); Zhengzhou (daily; 50min).

Luoyang to: Beijing (10 daily; 8–11hr); Shanghai (5 daily; 14–16hr); Xi'an (daily; 5hr); Zhengzhou (daily; 1hr 30min).

Xi'an to: Baoji (daily; 2hr); Beijing (10 daily; 12hr 30min); Datong (1 daily; 17hr); Guangzhou (2 daily; 26hr); Hua Shan (daily; 2hr); Lanzhou (daily; 9hr); Linfen (5 daily; 6–7hr); Luoyang (daily; 5hr); Taiyuan (5 daily; 10–12hr); Shanghai (7 daily; 16–21hr); Ürümqi (9 daily; 31–40hr); Xining (4 daily; 13hr); Yuncheng (4 daily; 4hr); Yan'an (3 daily; 7–8hr); Zhengzhou (daily; 7hr).

Yantai to: Beijing (1 daily; 15hr 20min); Ji'nan (7 daily; 9hr); Qingdao (1 daily; 3hr 30min).

Zhengzhou to: Anyang (daily; 2hr); Beijing (daily; 6hr 30min); Guangzhou (11 daily; 16hr); Luoyang (daily; 1hr 30min); Shanghai (11 daily; 10–13hr); Shijiazhuang (daily; 2hr 30min–3hr 30min); Taiyuan (4 daily; 11hr 30min–13hr); Xi'an (many daily; 7hr).

Anyang to: Beijing (daily; 5–7hr); Shijiazhuang (daily; 2hr 30min–3hr 30min); Zhengzhou (daily; 2hr).

Datong to: Baotou (many daily; 6hr); Beijing (many daily; 6–7hr); Hohhot (13 daily; 4hr 20min); Lanzhou (1 daily; 21hr); Linfen (3 daily; 11hr); Taiyuan (5 daily; 7hr); Xi'an (1 daily; 17hr).

Ji'nan to: Beijing (14 daily; 5–8hr); Qingdao (daily; 6–7hr); Shanghai (15 daily, 10–15hr); Taishan (daily; 1hr); Yantai (7 daily; 9hr); Yanzhou, for Qufu (daily; 2hr).

Linfen to: Taiyuan (daily; 4hr 30min); Xi'an (5 daily; 6–7hr); Yuncheng (10 daily; 2hr 30min).

Qingdao to: Beijing (2 daily; 11hr 30min); Ji'nan (daily; 6–7hr); Shenyang (2 daily; 22hr); Tianjin (4 daily, 10–13hr); Yantai (1 daily; 3hr 30min).

Yuncheng to: Linfen (10 daily; 2hr 30min); Taiyuan (9 daily; 5–8hr); Xi'an (4 daily; 4hr).

Taishan to: Beijing (daily; 8–10hr); Ji'nan (daily; 1hr); Yanzhou, for Qufu (daily; 1hr).

Taiyuan to: Beijing (6 daily; 8–10hr); Datong (5 daily; 7hr); Linfen (daily; 4hr 30min); Luoyang (1 daily; 12hr); Pingyao (daily; 2hr); Shijiazhuang (11 daily; 5hr); Xi'an (5 daily; 10–12hr); Yuncheng (9 daily; 5–8hr); Zhengzhou (4 daily; 11hr 30min–13hr).

Buses

With so many services operating in the region, bus frequencies have not been included. To most of the following destinations buses leave at least hourly during the day, with a few buses leaving in the evening and travelling through the night.

Anyang to: Kaifeng (4hr); Linzhou (1hr 30min); Zhengzhou (3hr).

Datong to: Wutai Shan (6hr); Taiyuan (3hr 30min).

Dengfeng to: Gongyi (2hr); Luoyang (1hr 20min); Zhengzhou (1hr 30min).

Gongyi to: Dengfeng (2hr); Luoyang (3hr); Zhengzhou (1hr 30min).

Ji'nan to: Beijing (5hr 30min); Qingdao (4hr 30min); Qufu (2hr 30min); Tai'an (1hr 30min).

Kaifeng to: Anyang (1hr 30min); Zhengzhou (1hr 30min).

Linfen to: Pingyao (3hr); Taiyuan (3hr); Yuncheng (3hr).

Luoyang to: Anyang (5hr); Dengfeng (1hr 20min); Gongyi (3hr); Ruicheng (4hr); Xi'an (4hr 30min); Yuncheng (4hr); Zhengzhou (2hr).

Pingyao to: Linfen (3hr); Taiyuan (2 hr).

Qufu to: Qingdao (6hr); Ji'nan (2hr 30min); Tai'an (1hr).

Tai'an to: Beijing (7hr); Ji'nan (1hr 30min); Qufu (1hr); Zhengzhou (7hr).

Taiyuan to: Datong (3hr 30min); Pingyao (2hr); Shijiazhuang (3hr 30min); Wutai Shan (4hr); Yuncheng (7hr).

Weihai to: Beijing (13hr); Qingdao (4hr); Shanghai (16hr); Yantai (1hr).

Xi'an to: Hua Shan (2hr 30min); Luoyang (4hr); Ruicheng (3hr 30min); Yan'an (6hr); Yuncheng (4hr); Zhengzhou (6hr).

Yantai to: Beijing (12hr); Ji'nan (5hr); Qingdao (3hr 30min); Weihai (1hr).

Yuncheng to: Linfen (3hr); Ruicheng (2hr); Taiyuan (4hr 30min); Xi'an (3hr).

Zhengzhou to: Anyang (3hr); Dengfeng (1hr 30min); Gongyi (1hr 30min); Luoyang (2hr 30min).

Ferries

Qingdao to: Gunsan (South Korea; 3 weekly; 18hr); Inchon (South Korea; 3 weekly; 21hr); Shimonoseki (Japan; 2 weekly; 26hr).

Weihai to: Inchon (South Korea; 3 weekly; 15hr).

Yantai to: Dalian (daily; 7hr, express 3hr).

Flights

Among international connections from this part of China, there are flights from Ji'nan (Seoul, Singapore), Qingdao (Fukuoka, Osaka, Seoul, Singapore, Tokyo), Xi'an (Bangkok, Fukuoka, Nagoya, Niigata, Seoul, Tokyo).

Ji'nan to: Beijing (4–5 daily; 1hr); Changchun (9 weekly; 1hr 30min); Chengdu (2–3 daily; 2hr 20min); Chongqing (1–2 daily; 2hr); Dalian (2–3 daily; 1hr); Fuzhou (1–2 daily; 2hr); Guangzhou (4 daily; 2hr 30min); Haikou (2–3 daily; 4hr 15min); Harbin (1–3 daily; 1hr 45min); Hong Kong (3 weekly; 2hr 50min); Kunming (2–3 daily; 2hr); Nanjing (1–4 daily; 65min); Shanghai (10 daily; 1hr); Shenyang (1–3 daily; 1hr 20min); Shenzhen (3–5 daily; 2hr 30min); Ürümqi (7 weekly; 6hr); Wenzhou (2–3 daily; 1hr 40min); Wuhan (1–3 daily; 1hr 30min); Xiamen (2–4 daily; 2hr); Xi'an (2 daily; 1hr 35min); Yantai (daily; 50min).

Luoyang to: Beijing (daily; 50min); Kunming (3 weekly; 2hr); Guangzhou (daily; 2hr); Shanghai (daily; 50min); Shenzhen (4 weekly; 3hr 20min).

Qingdao to: Beijing (14 daily; 55min); Changchun (2 daily; 1hr 40min); Changsha (4–6 daily; 2hr 10min); Chengdu (2–3 daily; 2hr 30min); Chongqing (2 weekly; 2hr 30min); Dalian (5–8 daily; 40min); Fuzhou (3 daily; 2hr); Guangzhou (3–4 daily; 3hr); Guilin (2 weekly; 3hr); Haikou (daily; 5hr); Hangzhou (8 daily; 1hr 20min); Harbin (3–4 daily; 1hr 30min); Hefei (daily; 70min); Hong Kong (1–2 daily; 3hr 20min); Kunming (2 daily; 3hr 30min); Lanzhou (4 weekly; 3hr 40min); Nanjing (3–5 daily; 65min); Ningbo (6 daily; 1hr 15min); Shanghai (12 daily; 1hr 15min); Shenyang (2 daily; 1hr 10min); Shenzhen (7 daily; 2hr); Ürümqi (daily; 6hr); Wenzhou (3–4 daily; 1hr 45min); Wuhan (2 daily; 1hr 40min); Xiamen (5 daily; 2hr 25min); Xi'an (1–2 daily; 1hr 50min); Zhengzhou (daily; 1hr 15min).

Taiyuan to: Beijing (5 daily; 1hr); Changsha (2 weekly; 1hr 30min); Chengdu (3 weekly; 2hr); Chongqing (1–2 daily; 1hr 40min); Dalian (daily; 2hr 20min); Guangzhou (6 daily; 2hr 40min); Haikou (daily; 4hr 20min); Hangzhou (3 weekly; 3hr); Hohhot (5 daily; 50min); Nanjing (4 weekly; 1hr 50min); Shanghai (4 daily; 1hr 45min); Shenyang (1–3 daily; 2hr 50min); Shenzhen (daily; 3hr); Tianjin (1–2 daily; 1hr); Xi'an (1–3 daily; 55min); Zhengzhou (daily; 55min).

Xi'an to: Beijing (18 daily; 1hr 30min); Changsha (2–3 daily; 1hr 20min); Chengdu (9 daily; 50min); Chongqing (5–6 daily; 1hr), Dalian (1–4 daily; 2hr); Dunhuang (2 daily; 2hr 50min); Fuzhou (1–3 daily; 2hr); Guangzhou (8 daily; 2hr); Guilin (2–3 daily; 1hr 40min); Haikou (3 daily; 2hr 20min); Hangzhou (3–4 daily; 2hr 20min); Harbin (daily; 2hr 40min); Hong Kong (daily; 2hr 30min); Ji'nan (2 daily; 1hr 30min); Kunming (2–3 daily; 2hr); Lanzhou (7 daily; 1hr 10min); Nanjing (2 daily; 1hr 50min); Ningbo (4 weekly; 3hr 10min); Qingdao (1–2 daily; 1hr 40min); Shanghai (8 daily; 1hr 50min); Shenyang (1–3 daily; 2hr); Shenzhen (6 daily; 2hr 20min); Shijiazhuang (4 weekly; 1hr); Taiyuan (1–3 daily; 55min); Tianjin (1–3 daily; 1hr 40min); Ürümqi (5 daily; 3hr 20min); Wenzhou (2–4 daily; 2hr); Wuhan (2–3 daily; 1hr); Xiamen

(1–3 daily; 3hr); Xining (6 daily; 1hr 10min); Yinchuan (5 daily; 1hr).

Yantai to: Beijing (4 daily; 1hr 15min); Changchun (1–2 daily; 1hr 30min); Guangzhou (daily; 3hr); Hong Kong (2 weekly; 3hr 30min); Ji'nan (daily; 50min); Nanjing (4 weekly; 1hr 20min); Shanghai (2–4 daily; 1hr 30min); Shenyang (daily; 70min); Shenzhen (3 weekly; 3hr); Wenzhou (4 weekly; 3hr).

Zhengzhou to: Beijing (7 daily; 65min); Changsha (4 weekly; 1hr 30min); Chengdu (2–3 daily; 1hr 40min); Chongqing (1–2 daily; 1hr 20min); Dalian (daily; 1hr 30min); Fuzhou (daily; 1hr 40min); Guangzhou (4 daily; 2hr); Haikou (5 daily; 2hr 20min); Harbin (7 weekly; 2hr 40min); Hong Kong (daily; 2hr 35min); Kunming (3–4 daily; 2hr 35min); Lanzhou (3 weekly; 1hr 30min); Nanjing (4 weekly; 1hr); Qingdao (daily; 1hr 15min); Shanghai (7 daily; 1hr 40min); Shenyang (daily; 1hr 50min); Shenzhen (3 daily; 2hr); Taiyuan (daily; 50min); Ürümqi (2–3 daily; 4hr); Wenzhou (3 weekly; 2hr 40min); Wuhan (1–2 daily; 50min); Xiamen (1–4 daily; 1hr 50min).

CHAPTER 5

Highlights

✳ **The Bund** Fusty colonial architecture and brash modernity stare each other down over the Huangpu River. See p.372

✳ **Huangpu boat trips** Get out on the river for a sense of the maritime industry that's at the heart of the city's success. See p.375

✳ **Nanjing Lu** One of China's premier consumer cornucopias. See p.377

✳ **Shanghai Museum** A candidate for the best museum in the country, with a wide range of exhibits housed in a building that's shaped like an ancient Chinese pottery vessel. See p.378

✳ **Yuyuan** An elegant Chinese garden with opportunities to snack and sip tea in the vicinity. See p.380

✳ **Shanghai nightlife** Glamorous, raucous, vacuous and often very decadent. See p.390

✳ **Cloud 9 Bar** Sip on a cocktail while taking in the view from the top floor of Shanghai's tallest building. See p.391

△ Shanghai's commercial Pudong district

Shanghai

A fter years of stagnation, the great metropolis of **SHANGHAI** is undergoing one of the fastest economic expansions that the world has ever seen. While shops overflow and the skyline fills with skyscrapers, Shanghai seems certain to recapture its position as East Asia's leading business city, a status it last held before World War II.

And yet, for all the modernization, Shanghai is still known in the West for its infamous role as the base of **European imperialism** in mainland China. Whichever side you were on, life in Shanghai then was rarely one of moderation. China's most prosperous city, in large part European- and American-financed, Shanghai introduced Asia to electric light, boasted more cars than the rest of the country put together, and created for its rich citizens a world of European-style mansions, tree-lined boulevards, chic café society, horse-racing and exclusive gentlemen's clubs. Alongside, and as much part of the legend, lay a city of singsong girls, warring gangsters and millions living in absolute poverty.

When the Communists marched into Shanghai in May 1949, they took control of the most important business and trading centre in Asia, an international port where vast fortunes were made. For most of the Communist period, the central government in Beijing deliberately ran Shanghai down, siphoning off its surplus to other parts of the country, to the point where the city came to resemble a living museum, housing the largest array of **Art Deco architecture** in the world and frozen in time since the 1940s. Parts of the city still resemble a 1920s vision of the future, a grimy metropolis of monolithic Neoclassical facades, threaded with overhead cables and walkways, and choked by vast crowds and rattling trolleybuses.

Yet the Shanghainese never lost their ability to make waves for themselves and, in recent years, China's central government has come to be dominated by individuals from the Shanghai area, who look with favour on the rebuilding of their old metropolis. In the last two decades, city planners have been busy creating a subway network, colossal highways, flyovers and bridges, shopping malls, hotel complexes and a "New Bund" – the Special Economic Zone across the river in Pudong. Significantly, China's main money-printing mint is near here, hence the high proportion of shiny new coins and bills in circulation in the city.

Not that the old Shanghai is set to disappear overnight. Most of the urban area was partitioned between foreign powers until 1949, and their former embassies, banks and official residences still give large areas of Shanghai an early-twentieth-century European flavour. It's still possible to make out the boundaries of what used to be the foreign concessions, with the bewildering tangle of alleyways of the old Chinese city at its heart. Only along the Huangpu waterfront, amid the stolid grandeur of the **Bund**, is there some sense of space – and here you feel the past more strongly than ever, its outward forms very much a working part of the city. It's ironic that the relics of hated foreign imperialism are now protected as city monuments.

Like Hong Kong, its model for economic development, Shanghai does not brim with obvious attractions. Besides the Shanghai Museum, the Suzhou-reminiscent gardens of Yu Yuan, and the Huangpu River cruise, there are few sights with broad appeal. But the beauty of visiting Shanghai lies in less obvious pleasures: strolling the Bund, exploring the pockets of colonial architecture in the old French Concession, sampling the exploding restaurant and nightlife scene, or wandering the shopping streets. Perhaps the greatest fascination is in simply absorbing the nouveau riche splendour of a city wholeheartedly engaged in the quest to appear sophisticated.

Some history

Contrary to Western interpretations, Shanghai's history did not begin with the founding of the British Concession in the wake of the First Opium War. Located at the confluence of the Yangzi River, the Grand Canal and the Pacific Ocean, Shanghai served as a major commercial port from the Song dynasty, channelling the region's extensive cotton crop to Beijing, the hinterland and Japan. By the Qing dynasty, vast **mercantile guilds**, often organized by trade and bearing superficial resemblance to their Dutch counterparts, had established economic and, to some extent, political control of the city. Indeed, the British only chose to set up a treaty port in Shanghai because, in the words of East India Company representative Hugh Lindsay, the city had become "the principal emporium of Eastern Asia" by the 1840s.

After the **Opium Wars**, the British moved in under the Treaty of Nanking in 1842, to be rapidly followed by the French in 1847. These two powers set up the first **foreign concessions** in the city – the British along the Bund and the area to the north of the Chinese city, the French in an area to the south-west on the site of a cathedral a French missionary had founded two centuries earlier. Later the Americans, in 1863, and the Japanese, in 1895, came to tack their own areas onto the British Concession, which expanded into the so-called International Settlement. Traders were allowed to live under their own national laws, policed by their own armed forces, in a series of privileged enclaves which were leased indefinitely. By 1900 the city's favourable position, close to the main trade route to the major silk- and tea-producing regions, had allowed it to develop into a sizeable port and manufacturing centre. At this time it was largely controlled by the "Green Gang", the infamous syndicate founded in the 1700s by unemployed boatmen, which by the 1920s ran the city's vast underworld. Businessmen and criminals who flouted the Green Gang's strict code of behaviour were subject to "knee-capping" punishment – having every visible tendon severed with a fruit knife before being left to die on a busy sidewalk.

Shanghai's cheap workforce was swollen during the Taiping Uprising (see box, p.436) by those who took shelter from the slaughter in the foreign settlements, and by peasants attracted to the city's apparent prosperity. Here China's first urban proletariat emerged, and the squalid living conditions, outbreaks of unemployment and glaring abuses of Chinese labour by foreign investors made Shanghai a natural breeding ground for **revolutionary politics**. The Chinese Communist Party was founded in the city in 1921, only to be driven underground by the notorious massacre of hundreds of strikers in 1927.

Inevitably, after the Communist takeover, the bright lights dimmed. The foreign community may have expected "business as usual", but the new regime was determined that Shanghai should play its role in the radical reconstruction of China. The worst slums were knocked down to be replaced by apartments, the gangsters and whores were taken away for "re-education", and foreign capital was ruthlessly taxed if not confiscated outright (although Chiang Kaishek did manage to spirit away the gold reserves of the Bank of China to Taiwan, leaving the city broke). For 35 years Western influences were forcibly suppressed.

Even since 1949, the city has remained a centre of radicalism – Mao, stifled by Beijing bureaucracy, launched his Cultural Revolution here in 1966. Certain Red Guards even proclaimed a Shanghai Commune, before the whole affair descended into wanton destruction and petty vindictiveness. After Mao's death, Shanghai was the last stronghold of the Gang of Four in their struggle for the succession, though their planned coup never materialized. Today, many key modernizing officials in the central government are from the Shanghai area; Jiang Zemin and Zhu Rongji were both former mayors of the city.

As well as an important power base for the ruling party, Shanghai has always been the most fashion-conscious and **outward-looking** city in China, its people by far the most highly skilled labour force in the country, and renowned for their quick wit and entrepreneurial skills. Many Shanghainese fled to Hong Kong after 1949 and oversaw the colony's economic explosion, while a high proportion of Chinese successful in business elsewhere in the world emigrated from this area. Even during the Cultural Revolution, Western excesses like curled hair and holding hands in public survived in Shanghai. Despite the incomprehensibility of the local Shanghainese dialect to other Chinese, it has always been easier for visitors to communicate with the locals here than anywhere else in the country, because of the excellent level of English spoken and the familiarity with foreigners and foreignness. The city's relative wealth has also allowed a greater interest in **leisure** activities and **nightlife**, with a wide variety of public entertainment on offer as well as a host of new bars and clubs. Not only does Shanghai remain the nation's premier industrial base, it is also the major consumer centre, and the variety and quality of goods in the shops attract people from all over China.

Many problems remain, however. Above all, Shanghai continues to suffer acute **overcrowding**. Though nominally closed to internal migration, and despite the one-child policy and 300,000 abortions annually, Shanghai continues to grow – to the point where a population of more than sixteen million makes it one of the largest (and most congested) cities in the world. Even official statistics give the average inhabitant living space little larger than a double bed, and in practice this often means three generations of a family sleeping in one room. Too many people, rising car ownership and inadequate public transport have combined to bring the city's streets to near **gridlock** at busy times. As a centre of huge oil refineries, chemical and metallurgical plants, Shanghai is also afflicted by air **pollution** pouring from factory chimneys. About four million tons of untreated industrial and domestic waste flow daily into the Huangpu River, the city's main source of drinking water, while the Suzhou Creek is black and foul-smelling. Finally, thanks to all those tall new buildings, Shanghai is **sinking** at the rate of one and a half centimetres a year, which has led to efforts to cap new construction.

Arrival, information and city transport

Shanghai is a surprisingly compact place, considering its enormous population, and it's not hard to find your way around on foot – though you'll certainly need buses or taxis for crossing from one quarter to the next. The area of most interest to visitors is bordered to the east by the **Huangpu River** (which flows from south to north), and to the north by the **Suzhou Creek** (which flows from west to east). A good place to get your bearings is at the southwestern corner of the junction of these two rivers, at the entrance to the small Huangpu Park.

Shanghai: arrival and transport

Shanghai	上海	shànghǎi
Airport Express	飞机场特快汽车	fēijīchǎng tèkuài qìchē
Gongpinglu wharf	公平路码头	gōngpínglù mǎtóu
Hongqiao Airport	虹桥机场	hóngqiáo jīchǎng
International Passenger Quay	国际客运码头	guójì kèyùn mǎtóu
Maglev train	磁悬浮列车	cíxuánfú lièchē
Pudong International Airport	浦东国际机场	pǔdōng guójì jīchǎng
Shanghai Metro	上海地铁	shànghǎi dìtiě
Shanghai Station	上海火车站	shànghǎi huǒchēzhàn
Shanghai West Station	上海西站	shànghǎi xīzhàn
Shiliupu wharf	十六浦码头	shíliùpù mǎtóu

To the north, across the iron Waibaidu Bridge over Suzhou Creek, is the area of the old Japanese Concession. South from Huangpu Park, along the western bank of the Huangpu River, runs the **Bund** – in Chinese, officially **Zhongshan Lu**, unofficially **Wai Tan**. The Bund is in turn overlooked from the east bank by the Oriental Pearl TV Tower, the city's most conspicuous landmark, in the **Pudong** Special Economic Zone.

A hundred metres south from Huangpu Park, the Bund is met by **Nanjing Lu**, one of the city's premier shopping streets, which runs west, past the northern edge of Renmin Park in the centre of the city. (Like all the east–west routes, Nanjing Lu takes its name from that of a city; north–south roads are named after provinces.) A few blocks to the south of Nanjing Lu is another major east–west thoroughfare, Yan'an Lu, which, to the east, leads into a tunnel under the Huangpu River. South of here, just west of the Bund, is the oval-shaped area corresponding to the **Old City**. The most important of the north–south axes is Xizang Lu, cutting through the downtown area just east of **Renmin Park**. Heading south, Xizang Lu runs down to an intersection with **Huaihai Lu**, Shanghai's other main shopping boulevard, which heads west into the heart of the **old French Concession**.

Arrival

Arriving by **air**, you'll touch down either at the new Pudong International Airport, 40km east of the city along the mouth of the Yangzi River, or at the old Hongqiao Airport, 15km west of the city. Pudong handles most international flights, with the smaller Hongqiao servicing domestic flights.

The most romantic way to get into town from Pudong is on the world's only commercial **maglev train** (daily 8.30am–5.30pm; every 20min), suspended above the track and propelled by the forces of magnetism. It whizzes from Pudong to Longyang Lu metro station in eight minutes, accelerating to 430km per hour in the first four minutes, then immediately starting to decelerate. As there's no friction, the ride is completely smooth, and as you near top speed – there's a digital speedometer in each cabin – the view from the windows becomes an impressionistic blur. Built by Siemens, the train is a trial for an even more ambitious project, a maglev line between Beijing and Shanghai. Tickets cost ¥50 one-way, ¥40 if you show a plane ticket. Never mind that the Maglev terminal is five minutes' walk from the airport, and that Longyang Lu metro is still a long way from the centre of town – you may never get another chance to go this fast on land.

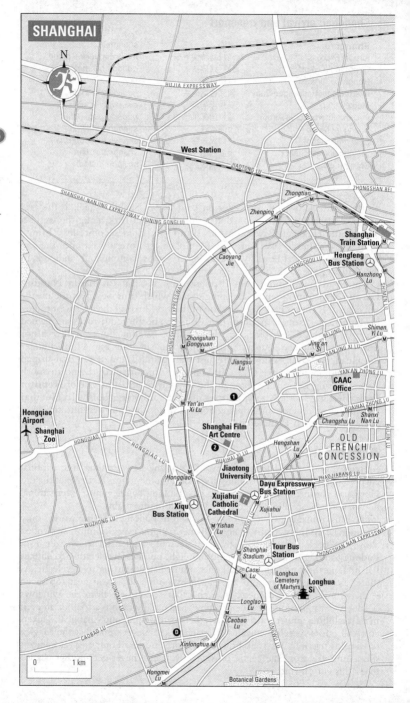

SHANGHAI

N

HUJIA EXPRESSWAY

West Station

JIAOTONG LU

SHANGHAI NANJING EXPRESSWAY (HUNING GONGLU)

ZHONGSHAN BEI

Zhongtian Ⓜ

Zhenping Ⓜ

Shanghai Train Station Ⓜ

Caoyang Jie Ⓜ

CHANGSHOU LU

Hengfeng Bus Station Ⓜ

Hanzhong Lu Ⓜ

ZHONGSHAN XI EXPRESSWAY

Zhongshan Gongyuan Ⓜ

BEIJING XI LU

Shimen Yi Lu Ⓜ

Jiangsu Lu Ⓜ

Jing'an Si Ⓜ

NANJING XI LU

YAN'AN ZHONG LU

CAAC Office

Yan'an Xi Lu Ⓜ

YAN'AN XI LU

Ⓜ

HUAIHAI ZHONG LU

Changshu Lu Ⓜ

Shanxi Nan Lu Ⓜ

RUIJIN LU

①

Hongqiao Airport

✈ **Shanghai Zoo**

HONGQIAO LU

HONGQIAO LU

Shanghai Film Art Centre

②

Hengshan Lu Ⓜ

OLD FRENCH CONCESSION

HUAIHAI XI LU

Jiaotong University

Hongqiao Lu Ⓜ

Dayu Expressway Bus Station Ⓜ

ZHAOJIABANG LU

WUZHONG LU

Xiqu Bus Station Ⓜ

Xujiahui Catholic Cathedral

Xujiahui Ⓜ

Yishan Lu Ⓜ

CAOXI LU

ZHONGSHAN NAN EXPRESSWAY

Shanghai Stadium Ⓜ

Tour Bus Station

LONGMEI LU

Caoxi Lu Ⓜ

Longhua Si 卍

Longhua Cemetery of Martyrs

Longlao Lu Ⓜ Ⓜ

LONGWU LU

CAOBAO LU

Ⓓ

Caobao Lu Ⓜ

Xinlonghua Ⓜ

Hongmei Lu Ⓜ

Botanical Gardens

0 — 1 km

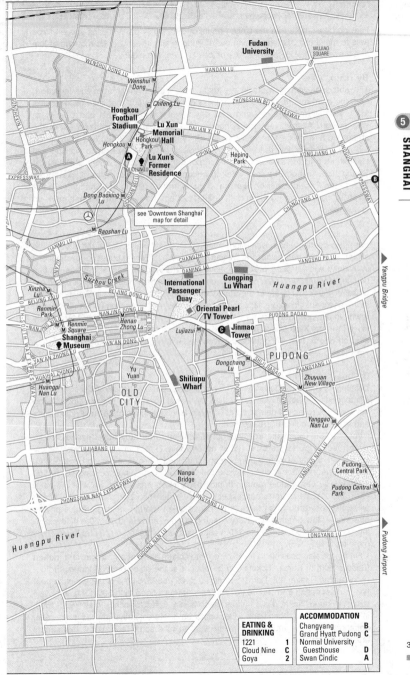

Fudan University
WUJIAO SQUARE
WENSHUI DONG LU
HANDAN LU
Wenshui Dong M
Chifeng Lu M
ZHONGSHAN BEI EXPRESSWAY
Hongkou Football Stadium
DALIAN XI LU
Lu Xun Memorial Hall
SIPING LU
KONGJIANG LU
Hongkou M
Hongkou Park
Heping Park
A
GUOJIV LU
Lu Xun's Former Residence
EXPRESSWAY
CHANGYANG LU
B
Dong Baoxing M Lu
see 'Downtown Shanghai' map for detail
M Baoshan Lu
TIANMU LU
CHANGZHI LU
YANGSHU PU LU
XIKANG LU
Suzhou Creek
DAMING LU
Huangpu River
Xinzha M Lu
BEIJING DONG LU
International Passenger Quay
Gongping Lu Wharf
PUDONG DADAO
Renmin Park
NANJING DONG LU
Oriental Pearl TV Tower
NANJING XI LU
Henan Zhong Lu
Lujiazui
Jinmao Tower
C
Renmin M M Square
YAN AN DONG LU
PUDONG
Shanghai Museum
Dongchang Lu
SHUI DADAO
HUAIHAI ZHONG LU
YAN AN ZHONG LU
Yu Yuan
Zhuyuan New Village
Huangpi M Nan Lu
OLD CITY
Shiliupu Wharf
Yanggao M Nan Lu
LUJIABANG LU
ZHONGSHAN NAN EXPRESSWAY
Nanpu Bridge
Pudong Central Park
Pudong Central M Park
LONGYANG LU
Huangpu River
PUDONG NAN LU
LONGYANG LU

▶ Yangpu Bridge

▶ Pudong Airport

Leaving by air, note that the limited hours of the maglev trains means you won't be able to make use of them if flying out of Pudong airport early in the morning or late in the evening. For details of airline offices in town, see p.395.

By train

The soft-seat waiting room in the main train station (enter from the forecourt, near the eastern end; there's an English sign) has an office that sells **train tickets** (daily 7am–9pm; same-day and next-day travel only), hard seat and sleeper as well as soft. Alternatively, the *Longmen Hotel*, a couple of minutes west of the station square, has a foreigners' ticket office (daily 7am–5.30pm & 6–9pm) in the lobby which sells tickets for up to four days in advance – mainly to Nanjing and Hangzhou, and for sleepers to a few important destinations such as Beijing or Guangzhou. To book up to a week in advance of your journey, buy tickets from CTS in the *Pacific Hotel* on Nanjing Xi Lu, or from CITS, in the Shanghai Centre or at 2 Jinling Dong Lu (both daily 8.30–11.30am & 1–4.45pm); a small mark-up is payable.

By bus

For a few destinations buses might offer a convenient way to leave the city: they're slightly cheaper than trains, and it's easy to get a seat. Private buses for destinations in Jiangsu and Zhejiang provinces leave from the western part of the train-station square, but their fares are nearly as expensive as the train. You can buy tickets there or from a kiosk just south of the Shanghai Museum. The Qiujiang Lu bus station has more reasonable fares, yet less comfortable buses, mainly leaving for Hangzhou and towns in Jiangsu. Services for a few destinations within the Shanghai Municipality leave from the **Xiqu bus station** (bus #113 from the train station) or a nameless bus stop on Shanxi Nan Lu, outside the Wenhua Guangchang, just south of Fuxing Lu. For these buses, you pay on board.

By boat

Leaving by boat also deserves serious consideration, with tickets cheaper and travelling conditions sometimes better than the trains; however, ferries are slowly being cut back due to lack of demand. For Chinese-language information on all ship tickets and schedules, call ☎021/63260050.

You can buy domestic and international tickets from any travel service for an added fee, or go to the **boat ticket office** (daily 7–11.30am & noon–5pm) at the southwest corner of Jinling Dong Lu and the Bund. The office has no English sign, but the entrance is directly opposite the CITS office on Jingling Dong Lu. In first class you'll get a double room with nice beds and a washbasin, while at the other end of the scale patrons can expect a six- or ten-bed berth, and lights left on all night. For Putuo Shan there is a special ticket window belonging to a private operator – slow boats leave every evening at 8pm, arriving at 8am the next morning, with tickets costing ¥100–370. Fast boats, which take four hours, leave every morning (¥195–225).

Finally, it's also possible to travel by boat to **Osaka** and **Kobe** in Japan, and **Inchon** (Seoul's port) in Korea. Tickets can be bought at the office on the eighteenth floor of the Jin'an Dasha, 908 Daming Dong Lu (☎021/63257642). For Japan, each boat has berths costing from ¥1300 (for a tatami mat on a floor) to ¥6500 (for a first-class cabin). A return ticket costs half as much again. Fares to Inchon cost ¥600–1600, in pretty luxurious conditions – all boats have steam baths, discos and clean, comfortable berths, though you might want to take some food as the restaurants are expensive.

A taxi from Pudong to the Bund should cost around ¥80, to Nanjing Xi Lu around ¥100, or you can board an airport bus to the CAAC office on Yan'an Xi Lu (¥15; about 1hr 30min), more or less opposite the Exhibition Centre – very handy for a number of five-star hotels in the vicinity, but still 3km from the Bund. From Hongqiao, a taxi to Nanjing Xi Lu costs about ¥45, and to the Bund about ¥60; there's also an airport bus service to the CAAC office on Yan'an Lu (¥5). In addition, bus #328 departs from a stop in the parking lot directly in front of Hongqiao and runs to Shanghai train station (¥2), while there's another public bus, the **Airport Express**, from Hongqiao to a stop right in front of the Shanghai Museum on Renmin Square (¥3). The latter runs from a bus stop behind Hongqiao's international flight terminal, across the street from the airport's main cargo terminal (ask passers-by for exact directions, as the stop is easily missed). Each of these bus rides from Hongqiao can take up to an hour depending on traffic.

By train

The main **train station – Shanghai Station** – is to the north of Suzhou Creek. Its vast concrete forecourt is a seething mass of encamped peasants at all hours, and it's not a particularly safe place to hang around at night. City buses are not an easy way to get out of the station area; you're better off taking metro line #1 or a taxi, the latter not likely to cost more than ¥15–20. There's an official rank outside the station and no trouble with drivers hustling foreigners. Another station in the remote northwest of town, **Shanghai West**, is the terminus for a few long-distance trains, such as the train from Inner Mongolia. This is linked to the metro and taxi rank at the main station by bus #106.

By bus and boat

Hardly any tourists arrive in Shanghai by **bus**, and one good reason to avoid doing this is that you might be dropped in the remote outskirts of the city. Some services use the **bus station** on Qiujiang Lu, next to the Baoshan Lu metro station, a few private buses terminate at the train station itself, or you may arrive at nearby at Hengfeng Station over the road from the Hanzhong Lu metro station, but generally speaking it's pot luck where you end up.

Probably the nicest way to arrive in Shanghai is by **boat**, whether from Japan, Korea or the towns along the coast or inland up the Yangzi. The Yangzi ferries and coastal boats to and from Ningbo and Putuo Shan sail south right past the Bund to the **Shiliupu wharf**, linked by bus #55 to the northern end of the Bund. Coastal boats to and from Qingdao and Fuzhou use the **Gongping Lu wharf**, which is only about twenty minutes' walk to the northeast of the Bund or a short ride on bus #135, while boats from Japan and South Korea dock at the **International Passenger Quay**, about ten minutes' walk east of the Waibaidu Bridge.

Information

For bland tourist **information** in English, call the tourist hotline ☎021/62520000 (daily 8am–10pm). At the north entrance of the Renmin Square metro station, there's a tourist **kiosk** with free English maps, brochures and advice.

A vital source of English-language information about current events in the city is the excellent monthly **That's Shanghai** (free in print, or check ⓦwww .thatsshanghai.com), available at most hotels, bars and upmarket restaurants. *ShanghaiScene* and *City Weekend* (ⓦwww.cityweekend.com.cn) are also pretty good magazines, offering frank advice on the latest happenings, as do the online-only Ⓦwww.shanghai-ed.com and Ⓦwww.shanghaiexpat.com. The city's official tourism body, the tourist bureau, publishes the English-language papers *Travel China: Shanghai Edition* and *Shanghai Today*, both with an emphasis on news and less on restaurant and nightlife listings.

Various glossy English-language **maps** are available, including the *Shanghai Official Tourist Map*, which is paid for by advertising and is issued free in hotels and in the Renmin Square subway station. Additionally, bus routes can be found on the *Shanghai Communications Map*, which is widely available from street vendors, though this has street names in Chinese only. English maps are available in large hotels, bookshops and from the tourist kiosk at Renmin Square metro station.

City transport

The clean, efficient **Shanghai metro** (daily 5.50am–11pm) currently comprises three lines, with more under construction. Its futuristic design sharply resembles Hong Kong's MTR metro; both systems were created by the same company. Line #1 runs from the main train station (a northward extension may be open by the time you read this), by Renmin Park and the Shanghai Museum, and then turns west along Huaihai Lu. Line #2 starts in Zhongshan in the west (where it connects to line #3), intersects with the first line at Renmin Park, and travels under the Huangpu River to Pudong. Line #3 (aka the Pearl Line) runs overground southwest to northeast, skirting the northwest of the city centre en route. Tickets cost ¥2–3 depending on the distance travelled and are bought from ticket machines, which also sell a card valid for multiple journeys to the tune of ¥50. There's a frustrating lack of English or even *pinyin* signs at stations.

Local buses run everywhere from around 4am to 10.30pm, but they are crowded (especially during rush hour) and slow, stops are far apart, and few lines travel from one side of the city to the other. Fares are generally ¥1 for regular buses and ¥2 for air-conditioned ones; buy your ticket from the conductor on the bus.

Useful Shanghai bus routes

North–south

#18 (trolleybus) From Hongkou Park, across the Suzhou Creek and along Xizang Lu.

#41 Passes Tianmu Xi Lu, in front of the train station and goes down through the French Concession to Longhua Cemetery.

#64 From the train station, along Beijing Lu, then close to the Shiliupu wharf on the south of the Bund. This is the best bus to take from the train station to the hotels just east of Waibaidu Bridge, including the *Pujiang* – get off at the Jiangxi Nan Lu stop.

#65 From the top to the bottom of Zhongshan Lu (the Bund), terminating in the south at the Nanpu Bridge.

East–west

#19 (trolleybus) From near Gongping Lu wharf in the east, passing near the *Pujiang Hotel* and roughly following the course of the Suzhou Creek to Yufo Si.

#20 From Jiujiang Lu (just off the Bund) along Nanjing Lu, past Jing'an Si, then on to Zhongshan Gongyuan in the west of the city.

#42 From Guangxi Lu just off the Bund, then along Huaihai Lu in the French Concession.

#135 From Yangpu Bridge in the east of the city to the eastern end of Huaihai Lu, via the Bund.

Taxis are very easy to get hold of and, if you're not on a very tight budget, they are often the most comfortable way to get around – fares usually come to ¥20–40 for rides within the city, with a flagfall of ¥10 (¥13 at night). Few drivers speak English, so it helps to have your destination written in Chinese. The only hassle you're likely to suffer is from drivers who take you on unnecessarily long detours, but if you sit in the front seat and hold a map on your lap they usually behave themselves. However, very late at night, conventions change – meters are often switched off and you may have to negotiate the fare, or at least tell the driver to use the meter. Drivers also ask if you want to use the elevated expressway – *zou gao jia* – at busy times; it'll be quicker but tends to involve slightly greater distances and is thus more expensive.

Accommodation

Accommodation in Shanghai is plentiful, and in places highly stylish, but prices are generally higher than elsewhere in China. The **grand old-world hotels** that form so integral a part of Shanghai's history cost at least US$120 per night these days, though a short stay in, for example, the famous *Peace Hotel* will give you a memorable flavour of how Shanghai used to be. Even if you're not a resident, however, there's nothing to stop you strolling in to admire some of the finest Art Deco interiors in the world.

Many travellers arrive in Shanghai assuming there is only one really **budget** option in the entire city, the *Pujiang*, which – unsurprisingly – fills up rapidly

Shanghai accommodation		
Captain Hostel	船长青年酒店	*chuánzhǎng qīngnián jiǔdiàn*
Changyang	长阳饭店	*chángyáng fàndiàn*
Chun Shen Jiang	春申宾馆	*chūnshēnjiāng bīnguǎn*
Dong Hu	东湖宾馆	*dōnghú bīnguǎn*
Garden	花园酒店	*huāyuán jiǔdiàn*
Grand Hyatt Pudong	浦东金茂凯悦大酒店	*pǔdōng jīnmàokǎiyuè dàjiǔdiàn*
JC Mandarin	锦沧文华大酒店	*jǐncāngwénhuá dàjiǔdiàn*
Jinjiang	锦江饭店	*jǐnjiāng fàndiàn*
Metropole	新城饭店	*xīnchéng fàndiàn*
New Asia	新亚大酒店	*xīnyà dàjiǔdiàn*
Normal University Guesthouse	师范大学外宾楼	*shīfàn dàxué wàibīnlóu*
Pacific	金门大酒店	*jīnmén dàjiǔdiàn*
Park	国际饭店	*guójì fàndiàn*
Peace	和平饭店	*hépíng fàndiàn*
Portman Ritz-Carlton	波特曼丽思卡尔顿酒店	*bōtèmàn lìsīkǎěrdùn jiǔdiàn*
Pujiang	浦江饭店	*pǔjiāng fàndiàn*
Ruijin Guesthouse	瑞金宾馆	*ruìjīn bīnguǎn*
Seagull	海鸥饭店	*hǎiōu fàndiàn*
Shanghai Conservatory Guesthouse	音乐学院招待所	*yīnyuèxuéyuàn zhāodàisuǒ*
Shanghai Mansions	上海大厦	*shànghǎi dàshà*
Swan Cindic	天鹅宾馆	*tiān'é bīnguǎn*
YMCA Hotel	青年会宾馆	*qīngniánhuì bīnguǎn*

in peak season. However, don't overlook the other quality, inexpensive choices – the guesthouses at the *Shanghai Conservatory of Music* and *Shanghai Normal University* in the southwest of the city, and the *Captain Hostel* on the Bund, all have beds available for less than ¥80 and often have vacancies even into the summer.

Meanwhile, brand-new skyscraper hotels are going up all the time, especially in the business district of Pudong. There are also a number of top-class hotels, including a *Sheraton* and a *Hilton*, in the western part of town, mainly along Nanjing Xi Lu. Prices are often quoted in US dollars, though you can always pay in renminbi.

During the off-season (Nov–April) some good discounts are offered; it's not uncommon to get a discount of up to two-thirds off the rack rate, while foreign students in Chinese universities can get special discounts in many three- and four-star hotels in Shanghai by showing their red foreign student ID card at the front desk. The accommodation reviewed below is shown on the downtown Shanghai map on pp.370–371, except for the places to stay listed under "Outer Shanghai and Pudong", which are marked on the map on pp.362–363.

The Bund and around

Captain Hostel 37 Fuzhou Lu ☎021/63235053, ⓕ63219331, ⓦwww.captainhostel.com.cn. This place has perfectly adequate rooms, but it's the dorms on the floor which functions as a hostel that are most used by foreigners. The nautical theme is carried through with admirable thoroughness – the dorms are made to look like cabins, with portholes for windows, and staff are dressed in sailor suits, though it hasn't made them any jollier. Unusually, dorms are same-sex and Chinese and foreign guests are billeted together. Standards of service are high and the communal facilities very clean. Internet access is available for ¥10/hr, bike rental for ¥2/hr (guests only), and there's free use of the washing machine. Dorm beds ¥50, ❸

Chun Shen Jiang 626 Nanjing Dong Lu, near Fujian Lu ☎021/63515710. Slightly musty and spartan rooms, but the location – almost midway between Renmin Park and the Bund – is hard to beat. Signed in Chinese only. ❺

Metropole 180 Jiangxi Lu ☎021/63213030, ⓕ63217365. Just off the Bund and dating from 1931, this is one of the more affordable of the older hotels. There's a great Art Deco lobby and exterior, but the rooms are plain. ❻

New Asia 422 Tiantong Lu ☎021/63242210, ⓕ63566816. In an old but well-maintained building north of Suzhou Creek, a couple of blocks west of the *Shanghai Mansions*. Good value for the location. ❻

Peace Junction of the Bund and Nanjing Dong Lu ☎021/63216888, ⓕ63290300, ⓦwww.shanghaipeacehotel.com. Occupying both sides of the road, this was formerly the *Cathay Hotel*, the most famous hotel in Shanghai, home to the *Jazz Bar* (see "Entertainment", p.392) and still well worth a visit to admire lobby's Art Deco interiors. The long list of illustrious previous guests includes Charlie Chaplin and Noel Coward. Despite the prices – doubles start at US$160, deluxe suites with original decor at US$520 – the service is definitely not up to five-star standards. Hefty discounts are sometimes available. ❾

Pujiang 15 Huangpu Lu ☎021/63246388, ⓕ63243179, ⓦwww.pujianghotel.com. Located across the Waibaidu Bridge north of the Bund and slightly to the east, opposite the blue Russian Consulate building. Formerly the *Astor Hotel*, and dating back to 1846, this is a pleasingly old-fashioned place with creaky wooden floors and high ceilings and the look of a Victorian school. Good dormitory accommodation is available here, though the communal showers are a long trek away on the third floor. There are also a few cheap doubles, without bathroom, on the attic floor. Dorm beds ¥55, ❹

Seagull 60 Huangpu Lu ☎021/63251500, ⓕ63241263. A smart, modern Chinese hotel aimed at business travellers and foreign tour groups. ❼

Shanghai Mansions 20 Suzhou Bei Lu ☎021/63246260, ⓕ63065147. This is the huge ugly lump of a building on the north bank of the Suzhou Creek, visible from the north end of the Bund. Originally a residential block built in the 1930s, it now offers excellent rooms, larger than those at the *Peace* and with superb views along the length of the Bund. Its most illustrious resident was Jiang Qing (wife of Mao Zedong), who issued a decree during the Cultural Revolution banning barges and sampans from travelling up the Huangpu or Suzhou while she was asleep. If you're not staying here, you can appreciate the views by taking the lift to the eighteenth floor. Rooms get pricier the higher up you go. ❼

YMCA Hotel 123 Xizang Nan Lu ☏ 021/63261040, ⓕ 63201957, ⓦ www.ymcahotel.com. Bright, practical and central; no frills, but well kept. Dorms ¥125, ⑥

Western Shanghai: Nanjing Xi Lu and the old French Concession

Dong Hu 70 Donghu Lu, one block north of Huaihai Zhong Lu ☏ 021/64158158, ⓕ 64157759. Spacious rooms giving no indication that the hotel served as an opium warehouse and the centre of gangland operations in the 1920s and 1930s. ⑦

Garden 58 Maoming Lu ☏ 021/64151111, ⓕ 64158866, ⓦ www.gardenhotelshanghai.com. Japanese-managed luxury mansion constructed in the grounds of the former ultra-exclusive French Club, in the French Concession. Doubles from US$180. ⑨

JC Mandarin 1225 Nanjing Xi Lu ☏ 021/62791888, ⓕ 62791822, ⓦ www .jcmandarin.com. Two blocks east of the Shanghai Centre, this modern five-star hotel has plush rooms and all the amenities you could want. The rack rate is US$300, but discounts of nearly fifty percent are available. ⑨

Jinjiang 59 Maoming Lu ☏ 021/62582582, ⓕ 64150048. A vast place in the French Concession, with many wings, much history, and some of the best facilities in the city. Richard Nixon stayed here on his famous visit in 1972, signing the Shanghai Communiqué in the second-floor auditorium (since renovated). Doubles from ¥1957; major discounts may be available. ⑨

Pacific 108 Nanjing Xi Lu ☏ 021/63276226, ⓕ 63723634. Another historic place, redolent of the 1920s and virtually in the centre of the city, with a grand period lobby. ⑦

Park 170 Nanjing Xi Lu ☏ 021/63275220, ⓕ 63276958. Very central, right opposite Renmin Park, for many years this was the tallest building in Shanghai. Although the hotel dates back to the 1930s, the interiors have been blandly modernized. ⑧

Portman Ritz-Carlton 1376 Nanjing Xi Lu ☏ 021/62798888, ⓕ 021/62798999, ⓦ www. ritzcarlton.com. One of the best hotels in Shanghai, part of the luxury Shanghai Centre complex, which includes restaurants, airline offices and expensive bars and restaurants. Doubles from US$250, with big discounts off season. ⑨

Ruijin Guesthouse 118 Ruijin Er Lu (entrance on Fuxing Lu) ☏ 021/64725222, ⓕ 021/64732277. Comprising eight Tudor-style villa complexes in manicured gardens, complete with a Japanese-style garden and lawn tennis, this hotel was the home of the editor of the *North China Daily News* in the 1920s. It's in a great location, a couple of blocks south of Huaihai Lu, and is home to the trendy *Face* bar. Doubles from US$100. ⑨

Shanghai Conservatory Guesthouse 20 Fen Yang Lu ☏ 021/64372577. Off Huaihai Lu, close to Changshu Lu metro station, the music conservatory's guesthouse offers around thirty dorm beds and eight comfortable but basic doubles, some with their own shower. It's nearly always full in summer. Dorm beds ¥40, ④

Outer Shanghai and Pudong

Changyang 1800 Changyang Lu ☏ 021/65434890. It's a long way out in the university district in the northeast, but this is an excellent, modern place with very reasonably priced doubles. There are a lot of cheap student bars and eating places nearby in Wujiaochang. Bus #22 running from just north of Suzhou Creek passes very close; get off at Linqing Lu bus stop. ③

Grand Hyatt Pudong Jinmao Tower, 177 Lujiazui Lu, Pudong ☏ 021/50491111, ⓦ www.shanghai .grand.hyatt.com. Across the street from the Oriental Pearl TV Tower, this luxury hotel occupies the top 36 floors of one of the tallest buildings in the world, and features a 29-storey atrium. Doubles from US$200. ⑨

Normal University Guesthouse 100 Guilin Lu ☏ 021/64701860, ⓕ 64369249. Far away in the southwest of the city, but well connected via the metro to the centre of town and the train station, this is a quiet and reasonably priced place to stay, offering clean dorm beds and comfortable doubles. To reach it, take the metro to Shanghai Stadium, then bus #43 to the terminus. The guesthouse is through the university's main gate, to the left. Dorms ¥45, ⑤

Swan Cindic 2211 Sichuan Bei Lu ☏ 021/56665666, ⓕ 63248002. A very smart place in a quiet, pleasant area across from Hongkou Park. ⑦

The City

Although most parts of Shanghai that you are likely to visit lie to the west of the **Huangpu River** and its colonial riverfront, the **Bund**, by far the most easily

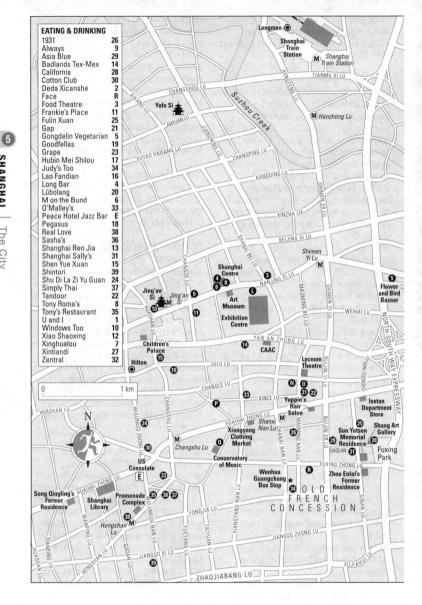

recognizable landmark in the city is on the east side, the rocket-like Oriental Pearl TV Tower, so high its antenna is often shrouded in mist. The best way to check out both banks of the Huangpu River and their sights is to take the splendid **Huangpu River Tour**.

Nanjing Lu, reputedly the busiest shopping street in China, runs through the heart of downtown Shanghai. Headed at its eastern end by the famous

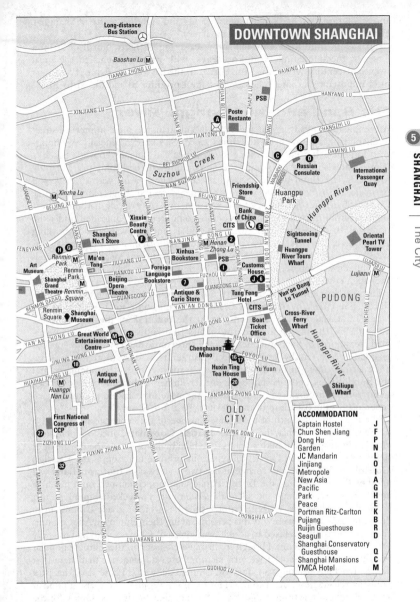

Long-distance
Bus Station

Baoshan Lu Ⓜ

TIANMU ZHONG LU

XINJIANG LU

SICHUAN BEI LU

ZHAPU LU

HAINING LU

HANYANG LU

PSB

Poste
Restante

TIANTONG LU

Ⓐ

CHANGZHI LU

DAMING LU

HENAN BEI LU

Ⓒ

Ⓑ

❶

Ⓓ

Russian
Consulate

WAIBAIDU BRIDGE

International
Passenger
Quay

BEI SUZHOU LU

Creek

Suzhou

NAN SUZHOU LU

ZHEJIANG ZHONG LU

Huangpu
Park

Huangpu River

Ⓜ Xinzha Lu

Friendship
Store

BEIJING DONG LU

FUJIAN BEI LU

SHANXI BEI LU

Bank
of China

Ⓔ

BEIJING XI LU

HUANGHE LU

Ⓜ

CITS

HENAN ZHONG LU

Sightseeing
Tunnel

ZHONGSHAN DONG YI LU (THE BUND)

Oriental
Pearl TV
Tower

FENGYANG LU

Xinxin
Beauty
Centre

NANJING ZHONG LU

Ⓕ

Shanghai
No.1 Store

Ⓖ Ⓗ

Renmin
Park Ⓜ

Mu'en
Tang

JIUJIANG LU

Xinhua
Bookstore

Ⓜ Henan
Zhong Lu

❷

DONG LU

JIANGXI ZHONG LU

PSB

Ⓘ

Customs
House

Huangpu
River Tours
Wharf

Lujiazui Ⓜ

LUJIAZUI LU

YINCHENG LU

PUDONG

Art
Museum

Renmin
Park Ⓜ

Beijing
Opera
Theatre

HANKOU LU

Foreign
Language
Bookstore

FUZHOU LU

Ⓙ Ⓖ

Yan'an Dong
Lu Tunnel

Shanghai
Grand
Theatre

Renmin
Square

GUANGDONG LU

❼

Antique &
Curio Store

GUANGDONG LU

Tung Feng
Hotel

RENMIN DADAO

Renmin
Square

Shanghai
Museum

YAN'AN DONG LU

CITS

Cross-River
Ferry
Wharf

Huangpu River

YAN'AN ZHONG LU

Great World
Entertainment
Centre

Ⓜ ⑫

JINLING DONG LU

Boat
Ticket
Office

YUNNAN LU

JINLING ZHONG LU

⑬

RENMIN LU

Chenghuang
Miao

⑯ ⑰

FUYOU LU

HUAIHAI ZHONG LU

⑱

Antique
Market

Huxin Ting
Tea House

Yu Yuan

Huangpi
Nan Lu

NINGDAJING LU

⑳

ZHONGHUA LU

Shiliupu
Wharf

FANGBANG ZHONG LU

OLD
CITY

First National
Congress of
CCP

HENAN NAN LU

ZHONGHUA LU

FUXING DONG LU

②⑦

ZIZHONG LU

SHUNCHANG LU

FUXING ZHONG LU

ZHONGHUA LU

MADANG LU

HUANGPI NAN LU

③②

ZHIZAOJU LU

XIZANG NAN LU

ZHONGHUA LU

LUJIABANG LU

GUOHUO LU

Peace Hotel, the road leads west to **Renmin Park**, which today houses Shanghai's excellent **museum**. Shanghai's other main sights lie about 1500m south of Nanjing Lu in the **Old City**, the longest continuously inhabited part of the city, with the **Yu Yuan** – a fully restored classical Chinese garden – and bazaars at its heart. To the southwest of here lies the marvellous **old French Concession**, with its cosmopolitan cooking traditions, European-style housing and revolutionary relics. The energetic eating and nightlife centre of Shanghai, **Huaihai Lu**, serves as the area's main artery.

Farther out from the centre remains a scattering of sights. North of Suzhou Creek is the interesting **Hongkou Park**, with its monuments to the great twentieth-century writer, Lu Xun. Finally, in the far west are two of Shanghai's most important surviving religious sites, the **Longhua Si** and the **Yufo Si**.

The Bund and the Huangpu River

A combination of Liverpool and 1920s Manhattan, the most impressive street in Shanghai has always been the **Bund**, since 1949 known officially as Zhong-shan Lu, but better known among locals as Wai Tan (literally "outside beach"). Named after an old Anglo-Indian term, bunding (the embanking of a muddy foreshore), the Bund was old Shanghai's commercial heart, with the river on one side, the offices of the leading banks and trading houses on the other. During Shanghai's riotous heyday it was also a hectic working harbour, where anything from tiny sailing junks to ocean-going freighters unloaded under the watch of British – and later American and Japanese – warships. Everything arrived here, from silk and tea to heavy industrial machinery, and amidst it all, wealthy foreigners disembarked to pick their way to one of the grand hotels through crowds of beggars, hawkers, black marketeers, shoeshine boys and overladen coolies.

The northern end of the Bund starts from the confluence of the Huangpu and the Suzhou Creek, by **Waibaidu Bridge**, and runs south for 1500m to Jinling Dong Lu, formerly Rue du Consulat. At the outbreak of the Sino-Japanese War in 1937 the bridge formed a no-man's-land between the Japanese-occu-pied areas north of Suzhou Creek and the **International Settlement** – it was guarded at each end by Japanese and British sentries. Today, though most ships dock farther downstream, the waterways are still well-used thoroughfares, and the Bund itself is a popular place for an after-dinner stroll or morning exercises, while tourists from all over China patrol the waterfront taking photos of each other against the backdrop of the Oriental Pearl TV Tower.

The first building south of the bridge was one of the cornerstones of British interests in old Shanghai, the **former British Consulate**, once ostentatiously guarded by magnificent Sikh soldiers. The blue building just to the northeast of here across the Suzhou Creek still retains its original function as the **Russian Consulate**. Right on the corner of the two waterways, **Huangpu Park** was another British creation, the British Public Gardens, established on a patch of land formed when mud and silt gathered around a wrecked ship. Here, too, there were Sikh troops, ready to enforce the rules which forbade Chinese from entering, unless they were servants accompanying their employer. After protests the regulations were relaxed to admit "well-dressed" Chinese, who had to apply for a special entry permit. Though it's firmly established in the Chinese popular imagination as a symbol of Western racism, there's no evidence that there ever was a sign here reading "no dogs or Chinese allowed". These days the park contains a stone monument to the "Heroes of the People", and is also a popular spot for citizens practising *tai ji* early in the morning, but it's best simply for the promenade which commands the junction of the two rivers. Underneath the monument lurks a small **museum** (daily 9am–4pm; free) with an informative presentation on Shanghai's history that is worth a few minutes of your time.

Walking down the Bund, you'll pass a succession of grandiose Neoclassical edifices, once built to house the great foreign enterprises. Jardine Matheson, founded by William Jardine – the man who did more than any other individual

Shanghai: The City and around

For entertainment venues, art museums and galleries, see the box on p.391.

Botanical Gardens	植物园	*zhíwù yuán*
Bund	外滩	*wàitān*
Chenghuang Miao	城皇庙	*chénghuáng miào*
Children's Palace	少年宫	*shàonián gōng*
Customs House	海关楼	*hǎiguān lóu*
Dongtai Lu Market	东台路市场	*dōngtáilù shìchǎng*
First National Congress of the CCP	一大会址	*yídà huìzhǐ*
Flower and Bird Bazaar	花鸟市场	*huāniǎo shìchǎng*
Hongkou Park	虹口公园	*hóngkǒu gōngyuán*
Huangpu River	黄浦江	*huángpǔ jiāng*
Huangpu River Tour	黄浦江旅游	*huángpǔjiāng lǚyóu*
Huxin Ting	湖心亭	*húxīn tíng*
Jing'an Si	静安寺	*jìng'ān sì*
Longhua Cemetery of Martyrs	龙华烈士陵园	*lónghuá lièshì língyuán*
Longhua Si	龙华寺	*lónghuá sì*
Lu Xun Memorial Hall	鲁迅纪念馆	*lǔxùn jìniànguǎn*
Lu Xun's Former Residence	鲁迅故居	*lǔxùn gùjū*
Mu'en Tang	沐恩堂	*mù'ēn táng*
Old City	南市区	*nánshì qū*
Oriental Pearl TV Tower	东方明珠广播电视塔	*dōngfāng míngzhū guǎngbō diànshìtǎ*
Pudong	浦东新区	*pǔdōng xīnqū*
Renmin Park	人民公园	*rénmín gōngyuán*
Renmin Square	人民广场	*rénmín guǎngchǎng*
Shanghai Centre	上海商城	*shànghǎi shāngchéng*
Shanghai Exhibition Centre	上海展览中心	*shànghǎi zhǎnlǎn zhōngxīn*
Shanghai Museum	上海博物馆	*shànghǎi bówùguǎn*
Shanghai zoo	上海动物园	*shànghǎi dòngwùyuán*
She Shan	佘山	*shéshān*
Song Qingling's Former Residence	宋庆龄故居	*sòngqìnglíng gùjū*
Sun Yatsen Memorial Residence	孙中山故居	*sūnzhōngshān gùjū*
Tung Feng Hotel	东风饭店	*dōngfēng fàndiàn*
Waibaidu Bridge	外白渡桥	*wàibáidù qiáo*
Xiangyang Market	襄阳服饰市场	*xiāngyáng fúshì shìchǎng*
Xujiahui Cathedral	徐家汇天主教堂	*xújiāhuì tiānzhǔ jiàotáng*
Yu Yuan	豫园	*yùyuán*
Yufo Si	玉佛寺	*yùfó sì*
Zhou Enlai's Former Residence	周恩来故居	*zhōu'ēnlái gùjū*
Zhouzhuang	周庄	*zhōuzhuāng*

to precipitate the Opium Wars and open Shanghai up to foreign trade – was the first foreign concern to buy land in Shanghai. Their former base (they lost all of their holdings in China after 1949), just north of the *Peace Hotel*, is now occupied by the China Textiles Export Corporation.

The Peace Hotel and the Bank of China

Straddling the eastern end of Nanjing Lu is one of the most famous hotels in China, the **Peace Hotel**, formerly the *Cathay Hotel*. The hotel's main building

△ Downtown Shanghai

Even in this age of freeway projects and a sophisticated metro system, the Huangpu is still a vital resource for Shanghai – one third of all China's trade passes through here. The Huangpu is also Shanghai's chief source of drinking water, although, thick and brown, it contains large quantities of untreated waste, including sewage and high levels of mercury and phenol. At least it no longer serves as a burial ground – in the 1930s Chinese too poor to pay for the burial of relatives would launch the bodies into the river in boxes decked in paper flowers.

One highlight of a visit to Shanghai, and the easiest way to view the edifices of the Bund, is to take one of the **Huangpu River tours**. These leave a wharf near the end of Nanjing Dong Lu. You can book tickets at the jetty (daily 8am–4.30pm).

The hour-long round trip to the Yanpu Bridge costs ¥25–35, while the slightly longer trip to Nanpu Bridge costs ¥45 and takes two hours, but the classic cruise here is the sixty-kilometre journey to the mouth of the **Yangzi** and back. On this, you're introduced to the vast amount of shipping which uses the port, and you'll also be able to inspect all the paraphernalia of the shipping industry, from sampans and rusty old Panamanian-registered freighters to sparkling Chinese navy vessels. You'll also get an idea of the colossal construction that is taking place on the eastern shore, before you reach the mouth of the Yangzi River itself, where the wind kicks in and it feels like you're almost in open sea.

Five **ticket classes** are available: the two lower classes (¥35–45) give you crowds of local tourists, a hard seat and a great deal of noise; the next two classes (¥55–70) entitle you to a plastic table outside with endless tea and sweets; while first class (¥100) affords a lounge furnished with great overstuffed armchairs, and usually entertainment in the form of a Chinese juggling act. There are weekday departures in all classes at 9am and 2pm; on Saturday and Sunday boats leave at 11am and 3.30pm. Given that there are sometimes several boats leaving at each of these times you should check your booking carefully. There are also special two-hour-long luxury cruises that include an optional buffet dinner, these boats departing at 7.30pm on weekdays, 8pm on Saturdays and Sundays (¥98–118; ¥53 without buffet). Note that tours do not run in the event of foggy or windy weather (for current information, call ☏021/63744461).

(on the north side of Nanjing Lu) is a relic of another great trading house, **Sassoon's**, and was originally known as Sassoon House. Like Jardine's, the Sassoon business empire was built on opium trading, but by the early years of the last century the family fortune had mostly been sunk into Shanghai real estate, including the *Cathay*. The place to be seen in prewar Shanghai, it offered guests a private plumbing system fed by a spring on the outskirts of town, marble baths with silver taps and vitreous china lavatories imported from Britain. Noel Coward is supposed to have stayed here while writing *Private Lives*. Sassoon lived long enough to see his hotel virtually destroyed by the Japanese, including his rooftop private apartment, with 360-degree views and dark oak panelling (it has recently been restored), but also long enough to get most of his money away to the Bahamas. The *Peace* today is well worth a visit for the **bar**, with its legendary jazz band (see p.391), and for a walk around the lobby and upper floors to take in the faded Art Deco elegance. The smaller wing on the south side of Nanjing Lu was originally the *Palace Hotel*, built around 1906; its first floor now holds the Western-style *Peace Café*, a much used city-centre rendezvous.

Next door to the *Peace*, at no. 19 on the Bund, the **Bank of China** was designed in the 1920s by Shanghai architectural firm Palmer & Turner, who brought in a Chinese architect to make the building "more Chinese" after construction was complete. The architect placed a Chinese roof onto the Art Deco edifice, creating a delightful juxtaposition of styles, an idea which is being endlessly and much less successfully copied across the nation today.

The Customs House and points south

Further down the Bund, the **Customs House** is one of the few buildings to have retained its original function, though its distinctive clock tower was adapted to chime *The East is Red* at six o'clock every morning and evening during the Cultural Revolution (the original clockwork has since been restored). The clock tower was modelled on Big Ben, and after its completion in 1927, local legend had it that the chimes which struck each fifteen minutes confused the God of Fire: believing the chimes were a firebell, the god decided Shanghai was suffering from too many conflagrations, and decided not to send any more. You can step into the downstairs lobby for a peek at some faded mosaics of maritime motifs on the ceiling.

Right next to this, and also with an easily recognizable domed roofline, the former headquarters of the **Hong Kong and Shanghai Bank** (built in 1921) has one of the most imposing of the Bund facades. Each wall of the marble octagonal entrance originally boasted a mural depicting the Bank's eight primary locations: Bangkok, Calcutta, Hong Kong, London, New York, Paris, Shanghai and Tokyo. It's considered lucky to rub the noses of the bronze lions that stand guard outside.

At the corner of the Bund and Yan'an Dong Lu you'll come to the **Tung Feng Hotel**, which until 1949 was home to a bastion of white male chauvinism, the *Shanghai Club*. There's still a strong feel here of the Shanghai of the 1920s and 1930s. The club's showpiece, the 33-metre mahogany Long Bar, where the wealthiest of the city's merchants and their European guests propped themselves at cocktail hour, is unfortunately no more, although the second-floor Seaman's Club, founded in the early 1900s, still functions as a meeting place for sailors.

The east bank of the Huangpu: Pudong district

Historically, **Pudong** has been known as the "wrong side of the Huangpu" – before 1949, the area was characterized by unemployed migrants, prostitution, murders, and the most appalling living conditions in the city. It was here that bankrupt gamblers would *tiao huangpu*, commit suicide by drowning themselves in the river. Shanghai's top gangster, Du Yuesheng, more commonly known as "Big-eared Du", learned his trade growing up in this rough section of town. In 1990, however, fifteen years after China's economic reforms started, it was finally decided to grant the status of Special Economic Zone (SEZ) to this large tract of mainly agricultural land, a decision which, more than any other, is now fuelling Shanghai's rocket-like economic advance. The skyline has since been completely transformed from a stream of rice paddies into a sea of cranes, and ultimately a maze of skyscrapers that seemingly stretches east as far as the eye can see.

Pudong is, above all, an area of **commerce**, with few activities to interest the visitor besides giving your neck a good workout as you gaze upwards at the skyline. Ascending the 457-metre-high **Oriental Pearl TV Tower** (daily 8am–9.30pm; ¥100 to go all the way to the top) to admire the giddying views has become a mandatory pilgrimage for most Chinese visitors to Shanghai, despite the ridiculously high entrance fee and long queue for the lift. You can get a similar view for less by ascending to the observation platform at the top of the **Jinmao Tower** (daily 7am–9.30pm; ¥50). But to observe the panorama in style, put on your best clothes and pay a night-time trip to the hotel bar *Cloud 9*, on the eighty-seventh floor of the same building (see p.391).

The simplest way to reach the area is to catch the subway which whooshes passengers from Renmin Square to downtown Pudong in less than three minutes; otherwise, several minibuses cross under the river using the Yan'an Dong Lu tunnel. For a more picturesque trip, catch the very frequent double-decker **ferry** from the Bund opposite the eastern end of Jinling Lu; buy a plastic token for ¥0.8 at the jetty. The lower deck gives a better feel for how crowded these waterways are. There's also a **tourist tunnel** under the river (entrance in the subway opposite Beijing Dong Lu; ¥20 one-way, ¥30 return), in which you're driven past a silly light show.

Nanjing Lu and around

Stretching west from the Bund through the heart of Shanghai lie the main commercial streets of the city, among them one of the two premier shopping streets, **Nanjing Lu**, with its two major parallel arteries, **Fuzhou Lu** and **Yan'an Lu**. In the days of the foreign concessions, expatriates described Nanjing Lu as a cross between Broadway and Oxford Street. It was also at this time that Nanjing Dong Lu and Fuzhou Lu housed numerous teahouses which functioned as the city's most exclusive brothels. Geisha-like *shuyu* (singer/storyteller girls) would saunter from teahouse to teahouse, performing classical plays and scenes from operas, and host banquets for guests. In a juxtaposition symbolic of prewar Shanghai's extremes, strings of the lowest form of brothel, nicknamed *dingpeng* ("nail sheds" because the sex, at ¥0.3, was "as quick as driving nails"), lay just two blocks north of Nanjing Dong Lu, along Suzhou Creek. The street was dubbed "Blood Alley" for the nightly fights between sailors on leave who congregated here.

Nanjing Dong Lu

On its eastern stretch, **Nanjing Dong Lu**, garish neon lights and expensive window displays of foreign and luxury goods are as prominent as they have ever been, and if any street in mainland China resembles downtown Hong Kong, this is it. Take a stroll among the crowds before things close up in the late evening (9–10pm), and check out the mass of fast-food outlets, fashion boutiques, cinemas, hotels and particularly the huge department stores.

Off the circular overhead walkway at the junction between Nanjing and Xizang Lu, just northeast of Renmin Park, is the grandest of the district's department stores, the venerable **Shanghai No. 1 Store**. Another feature of Nanjing Lu is the innumerable **beauty salons**, where customers are pampered in shop windows for the entertainment of the public on the pavement outside. One of the most famous of these is the Xinxin Beauty Centre, just west of Fujian Lu, which employs no fewer than eighty stylists and masseurs.

Renmin Park and Renmin Square

Immediately west of the junction with Xizang Lu – where Nanjing Dong Lu becomes Nanjing Xi Lu – lies **Renmin Park** and, to the south, **Renmin Square**. This whole area was originally the site of the Shanghai racecourse, which so satisfied the Chinese passion for gambling that by the 1920s the Shanghai Race Club was the third wealthiest foreign corporation in China. It was later converted into a sports arena by Chiang Kaishek, who had decided it was unwise to pander to this passion. During the war the stadium served as a holding camp for prisoners and as a temporary mortuary; afterwards most of it was levelled, and while the north part was landscaped to become the surprisingly intimate Renmin Park, the rest was paved to form a dusty concrete parade ground for political rallies. Only the racecourse's clock tower survives to this day, on the southeast edge of the square. The former area of paving has now been turned over to green grass, fountains and pigeons, while what used to be the bomb shelters beneath have become some of the city's premier shopping malls.

From Renmin Park, a small detour south down Xizang Lu will bring you to the **Mu'en Tang** (Baptized with Mercy Church), a couple of blocks down on the left. Although the service is in Chinese only, visitors are more than welcome and you'll be given a seat in the balcony overlooking the packed congregation – a cross-section of Shanghai society, from old Communists to girls in silver miniskirts. There are services throughout the week – check the Chinese-only board outside.

The Shanghai Grand Theatre and Art Museum

On Renmin Square's northwest corner lies the modern and impressive **Shanghai Grand Theatre** (Ⓦ www.shgtheatre.com), distinguished by its convex roof and transparent walls and pillars. Designed by the same architects who created the Bastille Opera House in Paris, it has pretensions of being a truly world-class theatre. You can stroll around the lobby, stage, auditorium and rehearsal rooms on your own (daily 9–11am & 1–4.30pm; ¥20), or take one of the excellent hour-long tours, given in Chinese and English (¥60).

Just behind the Shanghai Theatre, the **Shanghai Art Museum** (Tues–Sun 9am–5pm; ¥20) occupies a building that was once the racecourse clubhouse. There's no permanent collection, but its shows of contemporary art are always worth a wander round, even if they only leave you quizzical. There's a decent café, and a Western restaurant on the fifth floor.

The Shanghai Museum

The views from Renmin Square are novel, offering an unexpected panorama of the developing city, but, more importantly, the city's showpiece **Shanghai Museum** (Mon–Fri 9am–5pm, Sat 9am–8pm; ¥20, students free Sat 5–7pm, ¥5 at other times) is located here. The museum ranks high on the short must-do list of Shanghai sights. From the outside, the building, shaped like an early Tang vessel, is one of the most impressive constructions in the city, and inside, the presentation, labelling (in English as well as Chinese) and lighting are first-class. The displays give an excellent introduction into the development of all facets of Chinese art and culture, from ceramics to sculpture and seals. Consider the English-language audio guide (¥35) for a more in-depth presentation.

Highlights include watching a live demonstration (seven times daily) of ancient pottery-making techniques, as well as a collection of colourful lacquered opera masks of Guizhou minority groups and a salmon-skin suit, as worn by the Oroqen of Dongbei. There is also an insightful exhibition on the history of Chinese painting, from military souvenirs during the Warring States through literary expressionism during the Song to Westernization under the Qing. You can access the museum's excellent art library by calling ahead and arranging an appointment (☎021/63723500).

Nanjing Xi Lu

The historic **Pacific** and **Park hotels** stand on Nanjing Xi Lu opposite Renmin Park. The *Park Hotel*, for many years the tallest building in Shanghai, once had a reputation for superb food as well as for its dances, when the roof would be rolled back to allow guests to cavort under the stars. Latterly, Mao Zedong always stayed here when he was in Shanghai. Today, however, it has been stripped of most of its old-world charm. The *Pacific*, by contrast, a few metres to the east of the *Park*, is still worth having a look at, both for its mighty and ostentatious facade and for the fabulous plaster reliefs in the lobby. On a small lane called Jiangyin Lu just to the south of here and parallel to the main road, the permanent **Flower and Bird Bazaar** is a superbly earthy little corner, crowded with locals looking at puppies, kittens, goldfish, cagebirds, crickets and a host of plants.

The western end of Nanjing Xi Lu was known to "Shanghailanders" (the Europeans who made their homes here) as Bubbling Well Road, after a spring that used to gush at the far end of the street. Then, as today, it was one of the smartest addresses in the city, leading into tree-lined streets where Westerners' mock-Tudor mansions sheltered behind high walls. Now it's also the location of a number of luxury hotels, including the **Shanghai Centre**, an ultra-modern complex of luxury shops, restaurants and residential flats centred around the five-star *Portman Hotel*.

Opposite the Shanghai Centre, the gigantic Stalinist wedding cake that is the **Exhibition Centre** is worth seeing for its colossal ornate entrance, decorated with columns patterned with red stars and capped by a gilded spire. Constructed by the Russians in 1954, it was originally known as the Palace of Sino-Soviet Friendship and housed a permanent exhibition of industrial produce from the Shanghai area – proof of the advances achieved after 1949. In recent years it has become a vast and vulgar shopping mall selling overpriced furniture and trinkets.

Also at this end of Nanjing Lu, a few hundred metres west of the Shanghai Centre, **Jing'an Si** (daily 5am–5pm; ¥5) is a small active temple nestling beside the tiny Jing'an Park and under looming high-rises. Building work first began on the temple during the Three Kingdoms Period, and its apparent obscurity belies its past as the richest Buddhist foundation in the city, headed by legendary abbot Khi Vehdu, who combined his abbotly duties with a gangster lifestyle. The abbot and his seven concubines were shadowed by White Russian body-guards, each carrying a leather briefcase lined with bulletproof steel, to be used as a shield in case of attack. Today the temple is the primary place of ancestral worship in the city, although an equal number of people come to pray for more material reasons – worshippers eagerly throw coins into incense burners, in the hope that the gods will bestow financial success. Bus #20 runs here from Renmin Square, while the terminus for the metro line #2 lies underneath.

One block southwest of the temple, at the corner of Wulumuqi Bei Lu and Yan'an Zhong Lu, lies the grandiose yet slightly run-down **Children's Palace**. Originally known as Marble Hall, the sprawling estate was built in 1918 as a home by the Kadoories, a Sephardic Jewish family and one of the principal investors in pre-World War II Shanghai. The drab, worn exterior belies the mansion's current function as a children's art centre, with frequent singing and dancing performances on weekday afternoons and at weekends. The only offi-cial way to see them is by arranging a tour with CITS, but you just might find the back gate along Nanjing Xi Lu ajar if you come here on your own. West of the Children's Palace, along Yan'an Zhong Lu, you'll find the flamboyantly Gothic former residence of the GMD minister of transportation.

The Old City

The **Old City** never formed part of the International Settlement and was known by the foreigners who lived in Shanghai, somewhat contemptuously, as the **Chinese City**. Based on the original **walled city** of Shanghai which dated back to the eleventh century, the area was reserved in the nineteenth and early twentieth centuries as a ghetto for vast numbers of Chinese who lived in conditions of appalling squalor, while the foreigners carved out their living space around them. Today it still covers an oval-shaped area of about four square kilometres, circumscribed by Renmin Lu (to the north) and Zhonghua Lu (to the south) and coming to within a couple of hundred metres of the southern Bund on its northeastern side. In modern times it has been slashed down the middle by the main north–south artery, Henan Lu. The easiest approach from Nanjing Dong Lu is to walk due south along Henan Lu or Sichuan Lu.

Tree-lined ring roads had already replaced the original walls and moats as early as 1912, and sanitation has obviously improved vastly since the last century, but to cross the boundaries into the Old City is still to enter a different world. The twisting alleyways are a haven of free enterprise, bursting with makeshift markets selling fish, vegetables, cheap trinkets, clothing and food. Ironically, for a tourist entering the area, the feeling is like entering a Chinatown in a Western city. The centre of activity today is an area known locally as **Chenghuang Miao** (after a local temple), surrounding the two most famous and crowded tourist sights in the whole city, the Yu Yuan and the *Huxin Ting* teahouse, both located right in the middle of a new, touristy bazaar which caters to the Chinese tourists who pour into the area. "Antiques", scrolls and kitsch souvenirs feature prominently, and there are also lots of good places to eat Shanghainese *dianxin*, some more reasonable than others (see "Restaurants", p.389).

Yu Yuan

A classical Chinese garden featuring pools, walkways, bridges and rockeries, the **Yu Yuan** (Jade Garden; daily 8.30am–5pm; ¥25) was created in the sixteenth century by a high official in the imperial court in honour of his father. The Yu Yuan is less impressive than the gardens of nearby Suzhou, but given that it predates the relics of the International Settlement by some three centuries, the Shanghainese are understandably proud of it. Despite fluctuating fortunes, the garden has surprisingly survived the passage of the centuries. It was spared from its greatest crisis – the Cultural Revolution – apparently because the anti-imperialist "Little Sword Society" had used it as their headquarters in 1853 during the Taiping Uprising. Garden connoisseurs today will appreciate the whitewashed walls topped by undulating dragons made of tiles, and the huge, craggy and indented rock in front of the Yuhua Tang (Hall of Jade Magnificence). During the lantern festival on the fifteenth day of the traditional New Year, ten thousand lanterns (and an even larger number of spectators) brighten up the garden.

After visiting the garden, you can step into the delightful **Huxin Ting** (Heart of Lake Pavilion; downstairs daily 5.30am–noon & 1.30–5pm; upstairs daily 8.30am–5pm & 8.30–10pm), where practically every visitor who's ever been to Shanghai, including the Queen of England and Bill Clinton, has dropped in for tea. The teahouse is reached across a zigzag bridge spanning a small ornamental lake, just across from the entrance to Yu Yuan. In the downstairs section, you buy a ticket for ¥10 and can then enjoy endless tea refills while watching the elderly locals – who sit for hours amid the wood panelling – playing cards, chatting or dozing to the music of a venerable Chinese orchestra that occasionally plays here. The daytime charge upstairs is at least ¥25, but you get air conditioning and quails' eggs with your tea, while in the evening (¥65) waitresses perform traditional tea ceremonies. Whenever you come, though, the tea is excellent and the china used is the dark and distinctive Yixing ware.

The antique markets

If you're in Chenghuang Miao early on Sunday morning (8–11am is the best time, though trade continues into mid-afternoon), you can visit a great **Sunday market** on Fuyou Lu, the small street running east to west along the northern edge of Yu Yuan. The market has a raw, entrepreneurial feel about it; all sorts of curios and antiques – mostly fakes – ranging from jade trinkets to Little Red Books can be found here, though you'll have to bargain fiercely if you want to buy.

Just outside the Old City, in a small alley called Dongtai Lu leading west off Xizang Nan Lu, is the largest permanent **antique market** in Shanghai (daily 10am–4pm), and possibly in all China. Even if you're not interested in buying, this is a fascinating area to walk around. The range is vast, from old Buddhas, coins, vases and teapots, to mahjong sets, renovated furniture and Cultural Revolution badges. As with all antique markets in China, the vast majority of goods are fake.

The former French Concession

Established in the mid-nineteenth century, the **former French Concession** lay to the south and west of the International Settlement, abutting the Chinese City. Despite its name, it was never particularly French: before 1949, in fact, it was a low-rent district mainly inhabited by Chinese and White Russians. Other Westerners looked down on the latter as they were obliged to take jobs that, it was felt, should have been left to the Chinese.

The French Concession was notorious for its lawlessness and the ease with which police and French officials could be bribed, in contrast to the well-governed areas dominated by the British. This made it ideal territory for gangsters, including the king of all Shanghai mobsters, Du Yuesheng, the right-hand man of Huang Jinrong. For similar reasons, **political activists** also operated in this sector – the first meeting of the Chinese Communist Party took place here in 1921, and both Zhou Enlai and Sun Yatsen, the first provisional President of the Republic of China after the overthrow of the Qing dynasty, lived here. The preserved former homes of these two in particular (see below) are worth visiting simply because, better than anywhere else in modern Shanghai, they give a sense of how the Westerners, and the Westernized, used to live.

Certain French characteristics have lingered here, in the local chic and in a taste for bread and sweet cakes – exemplified in **Huaihai Lu**, the main street running through the heart of the area. Not as crowded as Nanjing Lu, Huaihai Lu is considerably more upmarket, particularly in the area around **Maoming Lu** and **Shanxi Lu**, where fashion boutiques, extremely expensive department stores and excellent cake shops abound.

The two plushest hotels in town, the *Garden* and the *Jinjiang*, are on Maoming Lu just north of Huaihai Lu, and are worth a visit for glimpses of past luxuries. The *Jinjiang* compound includes the former **Grosvenor Residence** complex, the most fashionable and pricey address in pre-World War II Shanghai. The Grosvenor has recently been modernized, but the VIP Club still retains much of its 1920s architecture and *Great Gatsby* ambience. Non-guests might be able to sneak a peek by taking the elevator to the top floor of the Old Wing of the *Jinjiang*, where the Club is located, although gaining entrance to one of the twenty US$800-a-night VIP mansion rooms on the floors directly below, with astonishingly beautiful, refurbished Art Deco architecture, might prove slightly more difficult.

Some more excellent examples of **Palladian** and **Art Deco architecture** survive in the private residences along Changle Lu and Julu Lu, which run parallel to and several blocks north of Huaihai Zhong Lu. Most notably, the former Russian Orthodox Mission Church still proudly features its blue dome along nearby Xinle Lu.

Several blocks south of this stretch of Huaihai Lu rises the stately **Ruijin Guesthouse**, on Fuxing Zhong Lu. This Tudor-style country manor was home to the Morriss family, owners of the *North China Daily News*; Mr Morriss raised greyhounds for the Shanghai Race Club and the former Canidrome dog track across the street. The house, having miraculously escaped severe damage during the Cultural Revolution because certain high-ranking officials used it as their private residence, has now been turned into a pleasant inn. Even if you're not a guest, you're free to walk around the spacious, quiet grounds, where it's hard to believe you're in the middle of one of the world's most hectic cities.

The French may have long disappeared from the French Concession, but the area's acute sense of style lives on. Nowhere is this more obvious than in the multitude of fashionable boutiques and hair salons lining Huaihai Lu, among them the aptly named **Yuppie's Hair Salon** (☎021/64456640), at no. 819, just east of Maoming Lu. Yuppie's attention to detail and pampering of the customer would put most Western salons to shame. You can be inexpensively spoiled with a haircut, two (pre- and post-haircut) shampoos, and an extended half-body massage, all for around ¥70.

The First National Congress of the Communist Party

If you head west from the Old City, the **First National Congress of the Chinese Communist Party** (daily 9am–5pm, last admission 4pm; ¥4) is the first preserved 1920s relic that you'll come across, south of Huaihai Lu, at the junction of Xingye Lu and Huangpi Nan Lu. The official story of this house is that on July 23, 1921, thirteen representatives of the Communist cells which had developed all over China, including its most famous junior participant Mao Zedong, met here to discuss the formation of a national party. The meeting was discovered by a French police agent (it was illegal to hold political meetings in the French Concession), and on July 30 the delegates fled to Zhejiang province, where they resumed their talks in a boat on Nan Hu. Quite how much of this really happened is unclear, but it seems probable that there were in fact more delegates than the record remembers – the missing names would have been expunged according to subsequent political circumstances. The site today, preserved in its original condition since 1949, contains a little exhibition hall downstairs with the usual propaganda, detailing instances of the oppressions that inspired the Communist movement in the first place. More interesting is the waxwork diorama of Mao and his mates.

The Sun Yatsen and Zhou Enlai residences

West of the gigantic north–south flyover and very close to **Fuxing Park** (daily 5am–5pm; ¥1) is Sinan Lu, where two of the heroes of modern China lived. At no. 39 is the **Sun Yatsen Memorial Residence** (Mon–Sat 9am–4.30pm; ¥8), with its large British-style lawn in the back garden, screened by mature trees and high walls. Sun Yatsen lived here from 1918 to 1924, and inside the house you can see his books, a gramophone, fireplaces and verandas – all rather disorienting in contemporary Shanghai. Sun's widow, Song Qingling, stayed in the house until 1937. Just south of Fuxing Lu is **Zhou Enlai's Former Residence** at 73 Sinan Lu (Mon & Thurs 1–4pm, Tues, Wed & Fri–Sun 8.30–11am & 1–4pm; ¥2). This delightful house has a terrace at the back with rattan chairs and polished wooden floors, and its garden, with hedges and ivy-covered walls, could easily be a part of 1930s suburban London.

Song Qingling's residence

A good deal farther west, at 1843 Huaihai Xi Lu, about twenty minutes' walk northwest from the Hengshan Lu metro station, is **Song Qingling's Former Residence** (daily 9–11am & 1–4.30pm; ¥8). As the wife of Sun Yatsen, Song Qingling was part of a bizarre family coterie – her sister Song Meiling was married to Chiang Kaishek and her brother, known as "TV Soong", was finance minister to Chiang. Song Qingling herself was to remain loyal to China throughout her life, latterly as one of the honorary "Presidents" of the People's Republic, while Meiling – reviled in the People's Republic – moved to New York, where she died in 2003 aged 105. Once again, the house is a charming step back into a residential Shanghai of the past, and although this time the trappings on display – including her official limousines parked in the garage – are largely post-1949, there is some lovely wood panelling and lacquerwork inside the house. Song Qingling lived here on and off from 1948 until her death in 1981.

Western Shanghai

In the west of the city, sights are too distant from one another to walk between. The main attractions are two **temples**, the rambling old Longhua Si to the southwest, and Yufo Si, which has superb statuary, to the northwest.

Due west from the city there is less to see; if you follow Nanjing Lu beyond Jing'an Si, it merges into Yan'an Lu, which (beyond the city ring road) eventually turns into Hongqiao Lu, the road that leads to the airport. Shortly before the airport it passes **Shanghai Zoo** (daily 6.30am–4.30pm; ¥20), a massive affair with more than two thousand animals and birds caged in conditions which, while not entirely wholesome, are better than in most Chinese zoos. The stars, inevitably, are the giant pandas. The zoo grounds used to serve as one of pre-1949 Shanghai's most exclusive golf courses. Next door, at 2409 Hongqiao Lu, stands the mansion that once served as the **Sassoons' home**, and which originally boasted a fireplace large enough to roast an ox; the central room, since renovated, resembled a medieval castle's Great Hall. Victor Sassoon, who used this mansion as a weekend residence (his other house was on the top floor of the *Peace Hotel*), only allowed for the design of two small bedrooms because he wanted to avoid potential overnight guests. It has served since as a Japanese naval HQ, a casino and as the private villa of the Gang of Four, but now suffers the relative ignominy of being rented out as office space. Bus #57 from the western end of Nanjing Lu will bring you out here. The side gate is sometimes open if you wish to take a peek.

The Xujiahui Catholic Cathedral

The **Xujiahui Catholic Cathedral** in the southwest of the city is one of many places of public worship which have received a new lease of life in recent years. Built in 1846 on the grave of Paul Xu Guangqi, Matteo Ricci's personal assistant and first Jesuit convert, it was closed for more than ten years during the Cultural Revolution, reopening in 1979. Most of the cathedral library's 200,000 volumes, as well as the cathedral's meteorological centre (built at the same time as the cathedral and now housing the Shanghai Municipal Meteorology Department), survive on the grounds. The congregations are remarkable for their size and enthusiasm, especially during the early Sunday-morning services and at Christmas or Easter. If you're up in time, take a metro train to Xujiahui station, a short walk from the cathedral. The first service on weekdays starts at 6.30am, while on Sundays it begins at 8am.

The Cemetery of Martyrs, Longhua Si and the Botanical Gardens

Southeast of the Catholic Cathedral, Longhua Park was officially named the **Longhua Cemetery of Martyrs** (daily 6.30am–4pm; ¥1 for the cemetery, ¥5 for the exhibition hall) to commemorate those who died fighting for the cause of Chinese Communism in the decades leading up to the final victory of 1949. In particular, it remembers those workers, activists and students massacred in Shanghai by Chiang Kaishek in the 1920s – the site of the cemetery is said to have been the main execution ground. In the centre is a glass-windowed, pyramid-shaped exhibition hall with a bombastic memorial to 250 Communist martyrs who fought Chiang's forces. Large numbers of commemorative stone sculptures, many bearing a photo and a name, dot the park, including one directly behind the exhibition hall with an eternal flame flickering in front. The fresh flowers brought daily testify to the power these events still hold. The cemetery is a short walk south from the terminus of bus #41, which you can take here from Huaihai Lu near Shanxi Lu, or from Nanjing Xi Lu near the Shanghai Centre.

Right next to the Martyrs' Cemetery is one of Shanghai's main religious sites, the **Longhua Si** (daily 5.30am–4pm; ¥5), and its associated 1700-year-old pagoda. The pagoda itself is an octagonal structure about 40m high (until the feverish construction of bank buildings along the Bund in the 1910s, the pagoda was the tallest edifice in Shanghai), its seven brick storeys embellished with wooden balconies and red lacquer pillars. In 977, a monk installed bronze wind chimes that could be heard on the Huangpu River into the nineteenth century. After a long period of neglect (Red Guards saw the pagoda as a convenient structure to plaster with banners), an ambitious re-zoning project has spruced up the pagoda and created the tea gardens, greenery and shop stalls that now huddle around it.

The **temple complex** is slightly later than the pagoda (345 AD) and is now the most active Buddhist site in the city, with a large number of new monks being trained. Although it has also been reconstructed, it is regarded as a prime specimen of Southern Song architecture. On the right as you enter is a bell tower, where you can strike the bell for ¥10 to bring you good luck. On Chinese New Year a monk bangs the bell 108 times, supposedly to ease the 108 "mundane worries" of Buddhist thought.

Bus #56 south down the main road, Longwu Lu, just to the west of the Longhua Si site, will bring you to the **Botanical Gardens** (daily 7am–4pm; ¥6). Among the more than nine thousand plants on view are two pomegranate trees said to have been planted in the eighteenth century during the reign of Emperor Qianlong, and still bearing fruit despite their antiquity. Take a look as well at the orchid chamber, with more than a hundred different varieties on show.

Yufo Si

Just south of the Suzhou Creek, northwestern Shanghai boasts the second of the city's most important religious sites, the **Yufo Si** (Temple of the Jade Buddha; daily 8.30am–4.30pm; ¥10), a monastery built in 1882 to enshrine two magnificent statues from Burma. Each of these Buddhas is carved from a single piece of white jade: the larger statue, a reclining figure, is displayed downstairs, while the smaller – but far more exquisite – sitting statue is housed in a room upstairs as part of a collection of sutras and paintings. The temple, although closed from 1949 until 1980, is now large and active; a hundred or so monks are in residence, training novices to repopulate the monasteries reopening throughout China and keeping an eye on tourists (photos are not allowed).

The temple is on Anyuan Lu, just south of the intersection of Changshou Lu and Jiangning Lu. Bus #112 from Renmin Square passes here, as does #24 from Huaihai Lu (along Shanxi Lu); alternatively, you can walk from the train station in about 25 minutes.

North of Suzhou Creek

North across the Waibaidu Bridge from the Bund, you enter an area that, before the War, was the Japanese quarter of the International Settlement, and which since 1949 has been largely taken over by housing developments. The obvious interest lies in the Hongkou Park area (also known as Lu Xun Park), and its monuments to the political novelist Lu Xun, although the whole district is lively and architecturally interesting.

Hongkou Park (daily 6am–7pm; ¥1) is one of the best places for observing Shanghainese at their most leisured. Between 6 and 8am, the masses undergo their daily *tai ji* workout; later in the day, amorous couples frolic on paddle boats in the park lagoon and old men teach their grandkids how to fly kites. The park is also home to the pompous **Tomb of Lu Xun**, complete with a seated statue and an inscription in Mao's calligraphy, which was erected here in 1956 to commemorate the fact that Lu Xun had spent the last ten years of his life in this part of Shanghai. The tomb went against Lu Xun's own wishes to be buried simply in a small grave in a western Shanghai cemetery. The novelist is further commemorated in the **Lu Xun Memorial Hall** (daily 9–11am & 1.30–4pm; ¥5), also in the park, to the right of the main entrance. Exhibits include original correspondence, among them letters and photographs from George Bernard Shaw.

A block southeast of the park on Shanyin Lu (Lane 132, House 9), **Lu Xun's Former Residence** (daily 9am–4pm; ¥4) is worth going out of your way to

Lu Xun

The man known by the literary pseudonym **Lu Xun** (his real name was Chou Shujian) was born in 1881 in the small city of Shaoxing. His origins were humble, but he would eventually come to be revered as the greatest of twentieth-century Chinese authors. Writing in a plainer, more comprehensible prose style than any Chinese writer before him – and considered by the Communists as a paragon of Socialist Realism – he sought to understand and portray the lives of the poor and downtrodden elements of Chinese society.

Lu Xun's first chosen career had been as a **doctor** of medicine, which he studied in Japan, under the impression that medicine would be the salvation of humanity. Later, however, horrified at the intractable social problems that beset China, he turned to writing, and published his *Diary of a Madman*, modelled on the work of Gogol, in 1918. This Western-style short story, the first ever written in Chinese, was in reality a scathing satire of Confucian society. Three years later Lu Xun published his most famous short story, **The True Story of Ah Q**, which features a foolish, Panglossian illiterate whose only remedy against the numerous evils which befall him is to rationalize them into spiritual victories – once again, the logic of Confucianism.

Lu Xun's writings soon earned him anger and threats from the ruling Guomindang, and in 1926 he fled his home in Beijing to seek **sanctuary** in the International Settlement of Shanghai. The last ten years of his life he spent living in the then Japanese quarter of the city, where he worked to support the Communist cause. The fact that he refused to join the Party did not stop the Communists from subsequently adopting him as a posthumous icon.

see, especially if you have already visited the former residences of Zhou Enlai and Sun Yatsen in the French Quarter (see p.382). The sparsely furnished house where Lu Xun and his wife and son lived from 1933 until his death in 1936 offers a fascinating glimpse into typical Japanese housing of the period – on the outside, its staid brick facade, tightly packed in among similar houses, strongly resembles the Back Bay District of Boston. Japanese housing of the time was a good deal smaller than European, but still surprisingly comfortable.

No cultural activity would be complete in Shanghai without the chance to go shopping too, and that's provided here at **Duolun Lu**, a new street of antique and bric-a-brac shops housed in elegant imitation Qing buildings. The best thing about it is the *Old Movie Café*, charmingly decorated with film posters.

Outside the city

Shanghai Shi (Shanghai Municipality) covers approximately two thousand square kilometres, comprising ten counties and extending far beyond the limits of the city itself. Surprisingly, very little of this huge area is ever visited by foreign tourists, though there are a couple of interesting sights. Most can be visited by tour bus – services leave from 1111 Caoxi Bei Lu, near Shanghai Stadium.

The most obvious of these is **She Shan** (daily 7.30am–4pm; ¥5), about 30km southwest of the city. Such is the flatness of the surrounding land that the hill, which only rises about 100m, is visible for miles around; it's crowned by a huge and thoroughly impressive **basilica**, a legacy of the nineteenth-century European missionary work. The hill has been under the ownership of a **Catholic** community since the 1850s, though the present church was not built until 1925. Services take place only on Christian festivals; nevertheless, it's a pleasant walk up the hill at any time of year (or you can take the cable car if you prefer), past bamboo groves and the occasional ancient pagoda. Most of the peasants in this area are fervent Catholics and welcoming towards Westerners. Also on the hill is a meteorological station and an old observatory, which contains a small exhibition room displaying an ancient earthquake-detecting device – a dragon with steel balls in its mouth which is so firmly set in the ground that only movement of the earth itself, from the vibrations of distant earthquakes, can cause the balls to drop out. The more balls drop, the more serious the earthquake. To reach She Shan, take a bus from the Wenhua Guangchang bus stop or the Xiqu bus station (see p.364), or take tour bus number 1B (¥12).

Zhouzhuang

Another 20km west, just across the border in Jiangsu Province, is the huddle of Ming architecture that comprises the small canal town of **ZHOUZHUANG**. Lying astride the large Jinghang Canal connecting Suzhou and Shanghai, Zhouzhuang grew prosperous from the area's brisk grain, silk and pottery trade during the Ming dynasty. Many rich government officials, scholars and artisans moved here and constructed beautiful villas, while investing money into developing the stately stone bridges and tree-lined canals that now provide the city's main attractions. Chinese tour groups invade Zhouzhuang in droves on weekends, but if you come on a weekday you should be able to appreciate the town in its serene, original splendour. **Buses** make the two-hour run from outside Shanghai train station at 6.20am & 3.30pm, and from the tour bus stop by Shanghai stadium (line 4; 1hr 30min). There is also the intriguing possibility of travelling by speedboat from here to another canal town farther in Jiangsu, **Tongli** (see p.412), from where frequent buses complete the journey to Suzhou.

Eating

If you are arriving from other areas of China, be prepared to be astounded by the excellent **diversity** of food in Shanghai, with most Chinese regional cuisines represented, as well as an equally impressive range of foreign cuisine including Brazilian, Indian, Japanese and European. It's hard to believe that up until the early 1990s, simply getting a table in Shanghai was a cut-throat business.

Compared to, for example, Sichuan or Cantonese cuisine, **Shanghai cuisine** is not particularly well known or popular among foreigners. Most of the cooking is done with added ginger, sugar and Shaoxing wine, but without heavy

Shanghai eating

1221	一二二一酒家	yī èr èr yī jiǔjiā
1931	一九三一饭店	yījiǔsānyī fàndiàn
Always	奥维斯饭店	àowéi sī fàndiàn
Badlands Tex-Mex	百岚饭店	bǎilán fàndiàn
Bonomi	波诺米饭店	bōnuòmǐ fàndiàn
Deda Xicanshe	德大西餐社	dédà xīcānshè
Ding Xiang Garden	丁香花苑	dīngxiāng huāyuàn
Frankie's Place	法兰奇餐厅	fǎlánqí cāntīng
Fulin Xuan	福临轩饭店	fúlín xuān fàndiàn
Gap	锦亭酒家	jǐntíng jiǔjiā
Gongdelin	功德林素食馆	gōngdélín sùshíguǎn
Grape	葡萄园饭店	pútáo yuán fàndiàn
Huanghe Lu	黄河路饭店	huánghé lù fàndiàn
Hubin Mei Shilou	湖滨美食楼	húbīn měi shí lóu
Lao Fandian	老饭店	lǎo fàndiàn
Lübolang	绿波廊餐厅	lùbōláng cāntīng
M on the Bund	米氏西餐厅	mǐshì xīcāntīng
Manabe	真锅咖啡	zhēnguō kāfēi
Sasha's	萨莎饭店	sàshā fàndiàn
Shanghai Ren Jia	上海人家饭店	shànghǎi rénjiā fàndiàn
Shashi Xiaochi Shijie	沙市小吃世界	shāshì xiǎochī shìjiè
Shen Yue Xuan	申粤轩饭店	shēnyuèxuān fàndiàn
Shintori	新都里餐厅	xīndūlǐ cāntīng
Shu Di La Zi Yu Guan	蜀地辣子鱼馆	shǔdìlàzǐ yúguǎn
Simply Thai	天泰餐厅	tiāntài cāntīng
Tandoor	锦江孟买餐厅	jǐnjiāngmèngmǎi cāntīng
Tony Roma's	多力罗马饭店	duōlì luómǎ fàndiàn
U and I	亚拉餐厅	yàlā cāntīng
Xiao Shaoxing	小绍兴饭店	xiǎo shàoxīng fàndiàn
Xinghualou	杏花楼饭店	xìnghuā lóu fàndiàn
Xintiandi	新天地	xīntiāndì
Yunnan Lu	云南路	yúnnán lù
Zentral	膳趣饭店	shànqù fàndiàn
Zhapu Lu	乍浦路	zhàpǔ lù
Zhejiang Zhong Lu	浙江中路	zhèjiāng zhōnglù

spicing. There are some interesting dishes, especially if you enjoy exotic seafood. Fish and shrimps are considered basic to any respectable meal, and eels and crab may appear as well. In season – between October and December – you may get the chance to try *dazha* crab, the most expensive and supposedly the most delicious. Inexpensive **snack food** is easily available in almost any part of the city at any time of night or day – try *xiao long bao*, a local dumpling speciality.

Unlike many other Chinese, the Shanghainese are famous for their sweet tooth, which is indulged by more than 1800 **bakeries and pastry shops** – a tradition that dates back to the period of the International Settlement. Close to the Bund, **Nanjing Dong Lu** is your best bet for baked goods, confectioneries and pastries. The best bakery in the city is arguably the one in the Japanese Isetan Department Store, at the eastern end of Huaihai Zhong Lu.

Café culture has recently taken off, and every mall and shopping street now boasts a *Starbucks*, or representatives of the better but pricier Italian chain *Bonomi*, or the Taiwanese *Manabe*. A traditional coffee bar, famed for chocolate buns and the like, is *Deda Xicanshe* on Sichuan Lu, which also does Western and Japanese-style meals. All these places are good bets for **breakfast**, as are the bakeries, or you could try the delicious yet very expensive (¥100–150) breakfast buffets at most luxury hotels. Most hotels also have respectable restaurants which serve *dianxin* at breakfast and lunch.

Restaurants

The traditions of Shanghai's cosmopolitan past are still dimly apparent in the city's **restaurants**. Many of the old establishments have continued to thrive, and although the original wood-panelled dining rooms are succumbing to modernization year by year, the growth of private enterprise ensures that the choice of venues is now wider than ever.

Restaurants are more expensive in Shanghai than elsewhere in China, although **prices** remain reasonable by international standards; most dishes at Chinese restaurants are priced at around ¥30, and even many upmarket Western restaurants have meal specials that come to less than ¥80. The reviews give phone numbers for those places where reservations are advisable.

The Bund, Nanjing Dong Lu, Renmin Park and around

The highlight of this area is the presence of a number of specialist **food streets**. In order of proximity to the top end of Nanjing Lu, the first of these is **Shashi Xiaochi Shijie**. A small lane leading south off Nanjing Dong Lu, just west of Jiang Xi Lu, it contains a number of cheap restaurants, good for hotpots or noodle-soup snacks. North of the Suzhou Creek, and just a few minutes' walk west of the *Pujiang Hotel*, runs **Zhapu Lu** – at night it is entirely neon-lit and easily recognizable. There's a large number of Shanghainese restaurants along here, but foreigners need to be very careful not to be overcharged. **Yunnan Lu** is perhaps the most interesting of the food streets, with a number of speciality restaurants, and a huge crowd of outdoor stalls selling snacks at night; it leads south from Nanjing Lu a block to the east of Renmin Park. The stretch of **Zhejiang Zhong Lu** just north of Fuzhou Lu is home to several **Muslim** snack shops offering delicious and filling noodle soups. Finally, **Huanghe Lu**, due north of Renmin Park – in particular the section north of Beijing Lu – contains another large concentration of restaurants, many of them open 24 hours.

The **Bund** itself has few decent options for eating, although this situation is changing quickly with the recent opening of several upmarket restaurants in some of the old Art Deco buildings, most notably *M on the Bund*. The few eating places right along the waterfront are overpriced.

Gongdelin Vegetarian 445 Nanjing Xi Lu. Probably the best vegetarian restaurant in town – the "fish", "meat" and "crab" are actually all made of vegetables and tofu. The "squid" is recommended.

M on the Bund Floor 7, 5 Wai Tan, entrance at Guang Dong Lu ☏ 021/63509988. Worth eating at for the extraordinary view overlooking the Bund. Service could be better, and some complain that this place isn't all it's cracked up to be, but the Mediterranean-style cuisine is some of the classiest (and most expensive) food in town, and the set lunch (¥88) is good value. If you're going to splash out, try the grilled salmon. Reservations recommended.

Shanghai Ren Jia 41 Yunnan Zhong Lu. Huge, bustling restaurant, with interesting twists on standard Shanghainese fare. It's best to come in a large group so you can order and share multiple dishes. Roasted pig's trotter (¥58) is the house speciality.

U and I 108 Daming Lu. A mediocre diner, whose highlight is the ¥16 Western set breakfast – the only such affordable place close to the *Pujiang Hotel*.

Xiao Shaoxing Yunnan Lu (east side), immediately north of Jinling Dong Lu. Famous in Shanghai for its *bai qie ji*, chicken simmered in wine, although adventurous diners might wish to sample the blood soup or chicken feet.

Xinghualou Fuzhou Lu, a couple of blocks west of Henan Lu. Another long-established Cantonese restaurant, popular and not expensive.

The Old City

The Yu Yuan area has traditionally been an excellent place for **snacks** – *xiao long bao* and the like – eaten in unpretentious surroundings. Although the quality is generally excellent and prices very low, there is a drawback, in the long lines which form at peak hours. Try to come outside the main eating times of 11.30am to 1.30pm, or after 5.30pm. Among the snack bars in the alleys around the Yu Yuan, perhaps the best is *Lübolang*, with a large variety of dumplings and noodles. Very close to the Yu Yuan entrance is the *Hubin Mei Shilou*, which serves a delicious sweet bean *changsheng zhou* (long-life soup). The *Lao Fandian*, just north of Yu Yuan at 242 Fuyou Lu, is one of the most famous restaurants in town for local Shanghai food, though prices are slightly inflated. For quick bites, check out the satay, noodle and corn-on-the-cob stands lining the street bordering the western side of Yu Yuan bazaar.

The French Concession and western Shanghai

This is the area where most expatriates eat and correspondingly where prices begin to approach international levels. The compensation is that you'll find menus are almost certainly in English, and English will often be spoken, too. For travellers tired of Chinese food, Huaihai Lu and Maoming Lu brim with **international cuisine** – all-you-can-eat **buffets**, for example, are offered by some of the large hotels, of which the *Hilton's* (at 505 Wulumuqi Bei Lu) is generally reckoned to be the best, though the *Portman's* buffet is much cheaper. The *Hilton* also houses an outstanding Cantonese *dim sum* restaurant that is unlikely to set you back more than ¥100 per person. Many excellent **Shanghainese** and **Sichuanese restaurants** also cluster in the alleys around Huaihai Lu, at prices much lower than for international food. Huaihai Lu itself is lined with fast-food joints, bakeries and snack stalls.

At the junction of Nanjing Xi Lu and Shanxi Lu is the so-called **Food Theatre**, which is, in fact, a mall of immaculately clean Chinese fast-food outlets. East of the French Concession, **Xintiandi** on Taicang Lu is an "olde worlde" renovated courtyard complex of fancy cafés, bars and over 25 restaurants, all rather pricey – you won't get away with paying much less than ¥100 a head. Pick up the handy map at the entrance. Notable are a branch of *Simply Thai* (west side), *Zen* for Cantonese food (south section), *Ye* for Shanghainese (northwest side), *KABB* for American food (northwest side), and a *Paulaner Bräuhaus* (south section) for a hearty German beer afterwards.

1221 1221 Yan'an Xi Lu, by Pan Yu Lu. A little out of the way (though bus #71 stops right outside), this is one of the city's best and most creative Shanghainese restaurants, attracting a mix of locals and expatriates. The drunken chicken and *xiang su ya* (fragrant crispy duck) are excellent, as are the onion cakes. Good choice for vegetarians too.

1931 112 Maoming Nan Lu, just south of Huaihai Zhong Lu ℗ 021/64725264. The right mix of Shanghainese, Japanese and Southeast Asian cuisines and reasonably priced, good-sized portions characterize this civilized little place, with mahogany trim and velvet curtains helping to create the cosy ambience. Try lamb with leek (¥38) or duck pancakes (¥58).

Always 1528 Nanjing Xi Lu. A local institution and very popular, largely thanks to the lunchtime special (served 11.30am–5pm) which costs only ¥20 for a Western meal and includes unlimited coffee.

Badlands Tex-Mex Yan'an Lu, right opposite the Shanghai Exhibition Centre. Good all-you-can-eat buffet of Mexican food for lunch and dinner, and cheap booze available anytime.

Frankie's Place 1477 Gubei Nan Lu. Reasonable Singaporean place serving curries and barbecued stingray.

Fulin Xuan 37 Sinan Lu, two blocks south of Huaihai Lu. Typically massive Cantonese place with an English menu and a good reputation among locals. The abalone and shark's fin are almost like Hong Kong's. The beef with black pepper and Hong Kong-style claypot rice are recommended.

Gap 127 Maoming Nan Lu, just north of Huaihai Zhong Lu; 8 Hengshan Lu, by Wulumuqi Nan Lu. This Shanghainese chain now has six branches – a testament to the superior quality of their cuisine, though they should sack their interior designer. They specialize in seafood, although the *dim sum* is quite good, too. The Maoming Nan Lu branch, in a big converted theatre, has a house band and fashion shows nightly.

Grape 55A Xinle Lu, close to Xiangyang Bei Lu. Unchallenging decor and some English-speaking staff make this Shanghainese place popular with expats, but it's good enough to draw the local crowd too. Try sweet and sour pork (¥15) and make room for a few of their savoury cold dishes.

Sasha's 9 Dong Ping Lu, at Hengshan Lu ℗ 021/64746166. Decent European food and bar snacks served in a charming mansion. The set lunch is the best deal at ¥99.

Shen Yue Xuan 849 Hua Shan Lu ℗ 021/62511166. The best Cantonese place in Shanghai, with scrumptious *dim sum* at lunchtime and pleasant, if cavernous, decor. In warmer weather you can dine al fresco in the garden, a rarity for a Cantonese restaurant. Dinner for two comes to around ¥120 per head, drinks included.

Shintori 288 Wulumuqi Nan Lu, three blocks south of Hengshan Lu ℗ 021/64672459. Take someone you want to impress to this nouvelle Japanese trendsetter: the buffet will set you back around ¥400. Entertaining presentation and great decor and food will give you something to talk about. Finish with green tea tiramisu (¥60).

Shu Di La Zi Yu Guan 187 Anfu Lu, on the corner with Wulumuqi Zhong Lu. Never mind the tacky decor and concentrate on the excellent, inexpensive Sichuan and Hunanese cuisine. The *mala doufu* and "wonderful chicken" (*liang ge xiang ji*) are recommended.

Simply Thai 5-C Dong Ping Lu ℗ 021/64459551. The best of the city's Thai joints, with delicious, eclectic dishes, impressive service and a smart but informal setting, including a leafy courtyard. Try stir-fried asparagus and fish cakes.

Tandoor *Jinjiang Hotel*, New South Building, just north of the Huaihai Lu and Maoming Lu intersection ℗ 021/64725494. First-class Indian food, expensive at ¥150–250 per head including drinks, although at lunchtime there is a ¥76 set menu.

Tony's Restaurant 16 Wulumuqi Nan Lu. Decent, foreigner-friendly Sichuan food at a reasonable price.

Tony Roma's Shanghai Centre, next to the *Portman Ritz-Carlton*. The most American place in Shanghai – so bland, brash and pricey. It's known for its spare ribs and barbecue sauce.

Zentral 567 Huangpi Lu, corner of Fuxing Zhong Lu ⓦ www.zentral.com.cn. Tasteful health-food restaurant behind Xintiandi, with better, cheaper fare than you'll get there. Dishes are very light and generally cost less than ¥20.

Drinking, nightlife and entertainment

Western-style **bars** are found mostly in the Huaihai Lu area, nearly all of which serve food, and some of which have room for dancing. The streets north of Huaihai Lu and south of Yan'an Zhong Lu, most notably Julu Lu and Maoming

Shanghai drinking, nightlife and entertainment

Bars and clubs

California	加州俱乐部	*jiāzhōu jùlèbù*
Cloud Nine	九重天酒吧	*jiǔchóngtiān jiǔbā*
Cotton Club	棉花俱乐部	*miánhuā jùlèbù*
Goodfellas	乌托邦酒吧	*wūtuōbāng jiǔbā*
Goya	戈雅酒吧	*gēyǎ jiǔbā*
Judy's Too	杰迪西餐厅	*jiédí xīcāntīng*
Long Bar	长吧	*chángbā*
O'Malley's	欧玛莉酒吧	*ōumǎli jiǔbā*
Peace Hotel Jazz Bar	和平饭店爵士吧	*hépíng fàndiàn juéshìbā*
Real Love	真爱酒吧	*zhēn'ài jiǔbā*
Shanghai Sally's	上海故乡餐厅	*shànghǎigùxiāng cāntīng*
Windows Too	蕴德诗酒吧	*yùndéshī jiǔbā*

Entertainment venues and art galleries

Art Scene China	艺术景画廊	*yìshùjǐng huàláng*
Biz Art	上海比翼	*shànghǎi bǐyì*
Great World Entertainment Centre	大世界娱乐中心	*dàshìjiè yúlè zhōngxīn*
Jing'an Hotel Auditorium	静安宾馆	*jìngān bīnguǎn*
Lan Xin Theatre	兰馨大戏院	*lánxīn dàxìyuàn*
Shangart	香格纳画廊	*xiānggénà huàláng*
Shanghai Art Museum	艺术展览馆	*yìshù zhǎnlǎnguǎn*
Shanghai Centre	上海商城剧院	*shànghǎi shāngchéng jùyuàn*
Shanghai Concert Hall	上海音乐厅	*shànghǎi yīnyuètīng*
Shanghai Conservatory of Music	上海音乐学院	*shànghǎi yīnyuè xuéyuàn*
Shanghai Grand Theatre	上海大剧院	*shànghǎi dàjùyuàn*
Tianchan Yifu Theatre	逸夫舞台	*yìfū wǔtái*
UME International Cinema	新天地国际影城	*xīntiāndì guójì yīngchéng*
Yong Le Gong Cinema	永乐宫电影院	*yǒnglè gōng diànyǐngyuàn*

Lu, have the greatest concentration of bars in the city, although pockets also exist around Fudan University in the northeast, Tongren Lu (west of the Exhibition Centre) and Hengshan Lu. You'll find the full range of drinks available, though beer is usually bottled rather than draught and prices are on the high side; reckon on ¥30–60 per drink in most places, which is a lot more than what you'll pay in many restaurants. This hasn't stopped the development of a jumping, occasionally sleazy, **nightlife**, though the scene is patently focused on expats and the moneyed Chinese elite.

Bars and clubs

The Bund and Pudong

Cloud Nine 87th floor, *Grand Hyatt Pudong*, Jinmao Tower. There's one reason to come to this classy hotel bar, and that's for the awesome view from the top of the city's tallest building. Each customer has to spend a minimum of ¥100 – which will get you about one and a half cocktails. Pricey but worth it.

Peace Hotel Jazz Bar Junction of the Bund and Nanjing Dong Lu. A dark and cavernous pub inside the north building of the *Peace Hotel*, legendary for its eight-piece dance band whose members played here in the 1930s, suffered persecution during the Cultural Revolution, then re-emerged in the twilight of their years to fame and fortune. Their younger successors now play stately instrumental versions of Fats Domino and Elvis Presley standards, while portly tourists swirl to the nostalgic rhythms and sip cocktails amid the original 1930s decor. Cover charge ¥60. Daily 8pm–1.30am.

The Old French Concession and Western Shanghai

Asia Blue 18 Gao Lan Lu, near Fuxing Park. A straight-friendly gay bar, run by a famous local drag queen. Daily 8pm–2am.

California 2 Gao Lan Lu. Dress up and come to be seen in the company of Shanghai's moneyed set, who sit around this posh nightclub trying to look like they own the place. There's no cover charge though, and it does get lively later on. Mon–Thurs & Sun 7pm–2am, Fri–Sat 9pm–late.

Cotton Club 1428 Huaihai Zhong Lu. *The* place to head for live jazz and blues, every night except Mondays. This is a requisite stop for all the big names doing pan-Asian tours, and there are occasional open-mike nights too. Cover charge ¥25–100 depending on the act. Daily 7.30pm–2am.

Face *Ruijin Guesthouse*, 118 Rui Jin Er Lu. The only hotel bar that's cool. Sip very slowly at your cocktail and admire the old Shanghai decor and the beautiful people. Daily 2pm–2am.

Goodfellas 907 Julu Lu. One of many cheesy dives in the area, with reasonably priced beers and overfriendly girls. Daily 2pm–2am.

Goya 359 Xin Hua Lu, off Huaihai Xi Lu. Sophisticated martini bar with comfy couches to practise raising one eyebrow and jiggling your ice suggestively. Fifty kinds of martini available, from iced to fruit-flavoured. Daily 7pm–2am.

Judy's Too 176 Maoming Nan Lu. A local institution with a raucous reputation. Ugly expat guys, girls with agendas, awful music, scantily clad staff dancing on the bar – is this the antidote to nearby *Face* or is it the other way around? Daily 6pm–2am.

Long Bar 2F, Shanghai Centre, Nanjing Xi Lu. Expat bar for networking and post-work drinks. Beers from ¥35.

O'Malley's 42 Tao Jiang Lu. Comfy Irish theme pub, with the expected expat contingent, but also a sizeable local patronage. Unusually, it's actually run by Irish people. Daily 11am–2am.

Pegasus Floor 2, Golden Bell Plaza, 98 Huaihai Zhong Lu. Cavernous dance club, with Western guest DJs and lively decor. No cover charge and drinks are ¥25. Thursdays are a big, bumping and grinding, hip hop bash. Wed–Fri till 2am, a little later at weekends.

Real Love 10 Hengshan Lu, in the Promenade Complex. Long-running student-friendly meat market for locals. Ladies get in free on Mondays and Wednesdays. ¥40 cover. Daily 8pm–2am.

Shanghai Sally's Corner of Sinan Lu and Xiang-shan Lu opposite Sun Yatsen's Memorial Residence (south of Huaihai Lu). Attempts an approximation of Britishness, including pool, darts and retro posters, though few Brits would stand paying this much for drinks at home (Guinness ¥55). Tues–Sat 4pm–late, Sun 11am–late.

Windows Too J104, Jingan Si Plaza, 1699 Nanjing Xi Lu, by Hua Shan Lu. Packs them in nightly thanks to a revolutionary idea – affordable beer, at ¥10 a bottle. Popular with the bottom of the Shanghai foreigner food chain – students, teachers and backpackers – and those who'll deign to talk to them. No posing, no attitude, no class. Daily 6.30pm–2am.

Entertainment

It's not hard to run away with the impression that, in Shanghai, self-expression means shopping, and culture is something that happens to pearls. There is a cultural scene of sorts out there, though, with theatres featuring **opera** (both Western and Chinese), **dance**, **drama**, **classical music**, **acrobatics** and **puppet shows**. For **jazz**, the most popular venues are the *Cotton Club* (the locals' choice; see above), the touristy *Peace Hotel Jazz Bar* (see p.391) and the auditorium at the *Jing'an Hotel*, covered below. Unlike in Beijing, there's not much of a rock scene.

There are plenty of **cinemas** in Shanghai, some of them dating back to the pre-1949 days, and most foreign films are subtitled in Chinese, not dubbed. The latest blockbusters can be caught at the UME International Cinema in the Xintiandi Complex off Zizhong Lu (☎021/63733333, ⓦwww.ume.com.cn) and the Shanghai Film Art Centre, at 160 Xinhua Lu (☎021/62804088). Artier films can be seen at the Yong Le Gong Cinema (Paradise Theatre) at 308 Anfu Lu (℡021/64312961).

Of late Shanghai has developed a half-decent **visual arts scene**, though not one to rival Beijing. Shanghai's art is bold, brash and sometimes provocative; many works end up abroad, Chinese contemporary art being, for the present, both hot and cheap. To check out contemporary art, visit the much improved Shanghai Art Museum (see p.378), home to the impressive international Shanghai Biennale (ⓦwww.shanghaibiennale.com), held from September to November every two years; the next is in 2006. Good commercial galleries include Biz Art at 610 Huaihai Xi Lu (℡021/32260709, ⓦwww.biz-art.com); Shangart at Ĕ, 2A Gaolan Lu (℡021/63593923, ⓦwww.shangart.com); and Art Scene China, at 37 Fuxing Xi Lu and 50 Moganshan Lu (℡021/64370631; ⓦwww.artscenechina.com).

To find out what's on and where, look in the expat magazines such as *That's Shanghai*, or ask CITS to check the listings in a local newspaper for you. For many events it's worth either booking at the relevant venue in advance (try to have your requirements written out in Chinese) or getting CITS to do it for you for a fee, although you may be lucky just turning up on the night.

Theatres and other venues

Grand Stage Theatre 1111 Cao Xi Bei Lu ℡021/64384952. Occasional performances of traditional Chinese operas and plays.

Great World Entertainment Centre 1 Xizang Nan Lu, just south of the elevated Yan'an Dong Lu expressway. Standing in neon-lit splendour and characterized by its white-and-beige steeple, this began life in the 1920s putting on every conceivable kind of entertainment. It now consists of four floors with two auditoriums on each, surrounding a central well with an open-air stage. Talent shows and puppetry and opera performances are all on offer, along with dodgems and snooker. Getting fusty of late, it's now undergoing renovation to bring its rather quaint attractions up to date. Daily until 8.30pm; ¥25 entry fee includes admission to everything within the complex.

Jing'an Hotel Auditorium 371 Huashan Lu ℡021/62481888 ext 687. Chamber music recitals every Friday evening (¥20) and occasional jazz concerts.

Lan Xin Theatre Opposite the *Jinjiang Hotel* on the northeast corner of Changle Lu and Maoming Lu ℡021/62178530. Both Western and Chinese opera, as well as occasional magic shows, are staged at this imperial-era venue, once the Lyceum Theatre. It was the home of that mainstay of colonial life, the British Amateur Dramatic Society, and the local expatriates' dancing school performed a wildly popular "Follies" revue every year here until 1933, once featuring a promising young ballerina called Margaret Hookham – who grew up to become Margot Fonteyn.

Shanghai Centre Nanjing Xi Lu ℡021/62798663 The huge multipurpose theatre here hosts concerts, ballet, opera and acrobatics of international standard. The nightly acrobatics show by the famous Shanghai Acrobatics Troupe is a superb spectacle – in Western terms it's more of a circus, including tumbling, juggling, clowning, magic and animal acts. Some of these skills – sword swallowing, fire-eating and the amazing balancing stunts – were developed as long ago as the Han dynasty; others have taken on a more trashy look featuring motorbikes, spectacular costumes and even a giant panda driving a car. Tickets (¥70 per show) can be bought on the same day from a window outside the theatre or up to three days in advance at a ticket booth in front of the Shanghai Centre (daily 9am–8pm; ℡021/62798663). Performances begin at 7.30pm.

Shanghai Concert Hall 523 Yan'an Dong Lu ℡021/64604699. Located in an old cinema, this regularly puts on performances by visiting international classical musicians.

Shanghai Conservatory of Music 20 Fenyang Lu, south of Huaihai Lu, quite near the Changshu Lu metro station. Established in 1927 as a college for talented young musicians, it continues to train many of China's infant prodigies, and is one of the most pleasant of Shanghai's venues for Western and Chinese classical music. There are performances here every Sunday evening at around 7pm, for which it's best to book a day or two in advance to be sure of a seat. To find the ticket office, go in through the main entrance and turn immediately right, until you come to a noticeboard; the office is on the third floor of the building opposite here. Tickets are incredibly cheap – just a few yuan (Chinese-speakers can call ℡021/64310334 to make enquiries).

Shanghai Grand Theatre 300 Renmin Dadao ℡021/63728701 or 63723833 for tickets, ⊛www .shgtheatre.com. The state-of-the-art acoustics and large central hall were designed to accommodate all art forms, from Western drama, opera and chamber music recitals to Chinese opera and classical poetry readings. There are two smaller theatres here that host Chinese opera and chamber music productions.

Tianchan Yifu Theatre 701 Fuzhou Lu (south side), one block east of Renmin Park ℡021/63514668. Twice-daily performances of Chinese opera, with Sunday matinees (daily 1.30pm & 7.15pm; ¥20–100).

Shopping

Although Shanghai cannot yet hope to compete with places such as Hong Kong or Bangkok where shopping is concerned – mainly because imported goods are a lot more expensive here – the city's old mercantile and consumerist traditions are reviving fast. **Antiques** shopping can yield fruitful, inexpensive results. The two antique markets at Dongtai Lu and Fuyou Lu in the Old City (see p.381) are the best places for browsing, though be aware that the majority of stuff is fake. If you don't like haggling you might be better off visiting the city's government antique stores, the largest of which, the Shanghai Antique and Curio Store at 218–226 Guangdong Lu (near the Bund), has a large array of modern arts and crafts as well as some large antiques. There's also a much better-value private store, G. E. Tang Antique and Curio Shop, with its head office at 8 Huqingping Gong Lu, which sells extremely attractive restored Chinese furniture and other larger pieces. For secondhand watches, clocks and cameras, including a fair few curiosities, visit Trade and Trust at 73 Shanxi Nan Lu.

For traditional **Chinese art**, pay a visit to the Duoyun Art Gallery, on Nanjing Dong Lu just west of Shanxi Lu, or to any of several galleries along Maoming Bei Lu, just north of Yan'an Zhong Lu. Some superb scrolls (watercolours and calligraphy) are on sale here, as well as art books and all the equipment for producing traditional Chinese art (for galleries selling more modern artwork, see p.393).

One area where Shanghai has pretensions to compete with Hong Kong is in **clothing**. Some of the inexpensive, quality Hong Kong-owned fashion chains such as Giordano have a presence in the city, though large-sized foreigners may have difficulty finding clothes which fit. Every evening Huashan Lu, next to Wujiaochang in the north of the city near Fudan University, fills with a **night market** brimming with decent, inexpensive clothing and souvenirs. To get here from downtown, take bus #55 or #910 from the Bund. **Silk** products, particularly traditional Chinese ladies' wear, are also good value; for these, try department stores such as the monumental No. 1 Store at the junction of Nanjing Lu and Xizang Lu, or – much more upmarket – the swish Huaihai Lu department stores: Printemps at the junction with Shanxi Lu, and the Japanese-run Huating-Isetan Department Store on Huaihai Zhong Lu. Finally, **Xiangyang Clothes Market**, off Huaihai Zhong Lu, is a huge collection of stalls selling fake designer labels, trainers and the like. Everything's a bargain – provided you haggle hard.

Tailored clothes represent one of the best bargains in the city, with bespoke suits, shirts, jackets and trousers costing at least twenty percent less than in the West, with the quality of the workmanship often comparable to the best tailors at home. However, few of the tailors speak English, so you may want to bring a Chinese-speaker along. Among the best tailors are Aijian, at 45 Xianggang Lu (just west of the Bund; ☎021/63299993), and W.W. Chan and Sons at 129B Maoming Nan Lu (☎021/54041469, ⓦwww .wwchan.com).

Listings

Airlines China Eastern Airlines (domestic ☎021/62475953; international ☎021/62472255) is in the CAAC Building at 200 Yan'an Xi Lu, while Shanghai Airlines lies at 212 Jiangning Lu (☎021/62558888). The following foreign carriers have offices in Shanghai (if no address is given, the airline is in the Shanghai Centre, 1376 Nanjing Xi Lu): Aeroflot, *Donghu Hotel*, Donghu Lu ☎021/64158150; Air Canada, Room 702, Central Plaza, 227 Huangpi Bei Lu ☎021/63758899; Air France, Rm 1301, Novel Plaza, 128 Nanjing Xi Lu ☎021/63606688; All Nippon Airways ☎021/62797000; Asiana Airlines, *Rainbow Hotel*, 2000 Yan'an Xi Lu ☎021/62194000; Austrian Airlines, Room 1103, Central Plaza, 227 Huangpi Bei Lu ☎021/63759051; Dragonair, Shanghai Square, 138 Huaihai Zhong Lu ☎021/63756375; Japan Airlines, Room 435, Plaza 66, 1266 Nanjing Xi Lu ☎021/62883000; KLM, Plaza 66, 1266 Nanjing Xi Lu ☎021/62708352; Korean Air, 2099 Yan'an Xi Lu ☎021/62756000; Lufthansa, 24F 480 Pujian Lu ☎021/58304400; Malaysian Airlines ☎021/62798607; Northwest ☎021/68846884; Qantas ☎021/62798660; SAS ☎021/62407003; Singapore Airlines, Rm 105, Kerry Centre, 1515 Nanjing Xi Lu ☎021/62891000; Swissair, Westgate Tower, 1038 Nanjing Xi Lu ☎021/62186810; United Airlines ☎021/62798009; Virgin Atlantic, 12 Zhongshan Dong Lu ☎021/53534600.

American Express Rm 206, Shanghai Centre, 1376 Nanjing Xi Lu (Mon–Fri 9am–5.30pm; ☎021/62798082).

Banks and exchange The head office of the Bank of China is at 23 Zhongshan Lu (The Bund), next to the *Peace Hotel* (Mon–Fri 9am–noon & 1.30–4.30pm, Sat 9am–noon). Next door is a Citibank ATM machine with 24hr access.

Bookshops Fuzhou Lu is nicknamed "Book Street" for its multitude of bookstores, but most outlets here have very limited English sections. By far the best is the Foreign Language Bookstore at no. 390, as it has a good selection of modern and classic English-language fiction and nonfiction; around the corner at 201 Shandong Zhong Lu it has a collection of specialist Chinese literature, translated into English (daily 9am–5.30pm). Western paperbacks

and periodicals can be found at all major hotels and at the Friendship Store.

Consulates Australia, CITIC Square, 1168 Nanjing Xi Lu ☎021/52925500; Austria, Qihua Tower, 1375 Huaihai Zhong Lu ☎021/64740268; Canada, Rm 604 West Tower, Shanghai Centre, 1376 Nanjing Xi Lu ☎021/62798400; Denmark, Floor 6, 1375 Huaihai Lu ☎021/64314301; France, Suite 7A 21/F, Qihua Tower, 1375 Huaihai Zhong Lu ☎021/64377414; Germany, 181 Yongfu Lu ☎021/64336951; Holland, #1403, 250 Hua Shan Lu ☎021/62480000; India, Rm 1008, Shanghai International Trade Center, 2200 Yan'an Lu ☎021/62758885; Israel, #55, Floor 7, Lou Shan Guan Lu ☎021/62098008; Italy, Floor 11, Qihua Tower, 1375 Huaihai Zhong Lu ☎021/64716980; Japan, 8 Wanshan Lu ☎62780788; New Zealand, Floor 15, Qihua Tower, 1375 Huaihai Lu ☎021/64711108; Poland, 618 Jianguo Lu ☎021/64339288; Russia, 20 Huangpu Lu ☎021/63242682; Singapore, 400 Wulumuqi Zhong Lu ☎021/64331362; South Korea, Floor 4, 2200 Yan'an Lu ☎021/62196420; Sweden, 6A Qihua Tower, 1375 Huaihai Zhong Lu ☎021/64741311; Thailand, 3F, 7 Zhongshan Dong Lu ☎021/63219371; UK, Rm 301, Shanghai Centre, 1376 Nanjing Xi Lu ☎021/62797650; USA, 1469 Huaihai Zhong Lu ☎021/64336880.

Football Shanghai's main team, Shenhua (ⓦwww .shenhua.com.cn), were the champions of China in 2003. During the football season (winter), you can see watch them play every other Sun at 3.30pm at the gleaming 35,000-seat Hongkou Football Stadium, 444 Dongjianwan Lu, in the north of town. Tickets are ¥30 and can be bought at the ground on the day.

Hospitals A number of the city's hospitals have special clinics for foreigners, including the Huadong Hospital at 221 Yan'an Xi Lu (☎021/62483180) and the Hua Shan Hospital at 12 Wulumuqi Lu (go to the fifteenth floor; ☎02162489999 ext 2531). You'll find top-notch medical care at World Link Medical and Dental Centres (☎021/62797688, ⓦwww .worldlink-shanghai.com) in Suite 203 of the Shanghai Centre west tower at 1376 Nanjing Xi Lu, but they are pricey at ¥700 per consultation.

Internet access The cheapest Internet connections are in the basement of the Shanghai Library at 1555 Huaihai Zhong Lu (daily 8.30am–8pm; ¥4/hr). Other cafés, charging two to three times as much, include Aztec, 199 Hongqiao Lu (24hr; free drinks served); the second floor of the Shanghai Bookstore, 465 Fuzhou Lu (Mon–Fri 9.30am–6.30pm, Sat & Sun 9.30am–9pm); Hong Tai, second floor, 507 Sichuan Zhong Lu (daily 1–10.30pm); and Worldwide Network Club at 555 Jiangsu Lu (daily 8am–midnight). Cheaper Net places are dotted around Fudan University and other campuses.

Mail The main post office is at 1 Sichuan Bei Lu, just north of and overlooking Suzhou Creek. A stately Art Deco edifice, it offers a very efficient parcel service; the express option can get packages to Britain or the US within two days. Poste restante arrives at the Bei Suzhou Lu office across the street – each separate item is recorded on a little slip of cardboard in a display case near the entrance. Both the main post office and the poste restante service are open daily 9am–5pm. Branch post offices dot the city, with convenient locations

along Nanjing Dong Lu, Huaihai Zhong Lu, in the Portman Centre, and near the Huangpu River ferry jetties at the corner of Jinling Dong Lu and Sichuan Bei Lu. Most hotels, including the *Pujiang*, accept and hold mail for guests.

PSB 210 Hankou Lu, near the corner of Henan Zhong Lu. For visa extensions go to 333 Wusong Lu (☎021/63577925; daily 8.30am–11am & 2–5pm).

Telephones International calls are most easily and cheaply made with phone cards. Otherwise you can call from the second floor of the main post office at 1 Sichuan Bei Lu, or at the China Telecom office three stores down from the north building of the *Peace Hotel* on 30 Nanjing Dong Lu (open 24hr). A large, English-speaking staff can deal with most requests.

Travel agents CITS has a helpful office at 66 Nanjing Dong Lu (☎021/63233384, ℻63290295), providing travel and entertainment tickets, with a small commission added on. There's another CITS branch at 1277 Beijing Xi Lu (☎021/62898899), as well as a transport ticket office just off the Bund at 2 Jinling Dong Lu, opposite the boat ticket office (all branches daily 8.30–11.30am & 1–4.45pm). Most hotels have travel agencies offering the same services.

Travel details

Trains

Shanghai Station to: Beijing (8 daily; 12hr); Changsha (3 daily; 19hr); Changzhou (17 daily; 2–3hr); Chengdu (2 daily; 40–45hr); Chongqing (daily; 44hr); Fuzhou (2 daily; 21hr); Guangzhou (3 daily; 24hr); Guilin (3 daily; 27hr); Hangzhou (16 daily; 2–3hr); Harbin (daily; 33hr); Hefei (5 daily; 9hr); Hong Kong (daily; 24hr); Huangshan (daily; 12hr); Kunming (daily; 48–58hr); Lanzhou (2 daily; 30hr); Nanchang (daily; 12hr); Nanjing (19 daily; 3–4hr); Nanning (2 daily; 15hr); Ningbo (6 daily; 6–9hr); Qingdao (daily; 20hr); Shaoxing (6 daily; 3–5hr); Shenyang (1 daily; 28hr); Suzhou (23 daily; 1hr); Tai'an (for Qufu; 4 daily; 11hr); Tianjin (4 daily; 16hr); Ürümqi (daily; 51hr); Wuxi (16 daily; 2hr); Xiamen (daily; 26hr); Xi'an (7 daily; 18hr); Xining (daily; 41hr); Xuzhou (7 daily; 9hr); Zhenjiang (16 daily; 3hr).
Shanghai West Station to: Baotou (2 daily; 34hr); Hohhot (2 daily; 31hr).

Buses

Shanghai to: Hangzhou (45 daily; 3hr); Lianyungang (5 daily; 8hr); Nanjing (27 daily; 4hr); Shaoxing (6 daily; 4hr); Suzhou (53 daily; 1hr); Wenzhou (3 daily; 12hr); Wuxi (35 daily; 3hr); Yangzhou (13 daily; 5hr); Zhouzhuang (frequent; 1hr 30min–2hr).

Ferries

Shanghai to: Inchon (South Korea; 1–2 weekly; 22hr); Kobe (Japan; 1–2 weekly; 38hr); Osaka (Japan; 1–2 weekly; 36hr); Putuo Shan (4 daily; 4–12hr).

Flights

Shanghai to: Baotou (2 weekly; 2hr 50min); Beijing (16 daily; 1hr 50min); Changsha (daily; 4hr); Changchun (4 daily; 2hr 45min); Chengdu (5 daily; 2hr 45min); Chongqing (5 daily; 2hr 30min); Dalian (5 daily; 1hr 30min); Fuzhou (1 daily; 1hr 30min); Guangzhou (10 daily; 2hr); Guilin (2 daily; 2hr 20min); Haikou (4 daily; 3hr); Harbin (2–4 daily; 2hr

40min); Hefei (daily; 1hr); Hohhot (3 weekly; 2hr 20min); Hong Kong (19 daily; 2hr 10min); Huang-shan (5 weekly; 1hr); Kunming (1–3 daily; 3hr); Lanzhou (1–2 daily; 3hr); Lhasa (2 weekly; 6hr); Lijiang (daily; 4hr 30min); Macau (2 daily; 2hr 20 min); Nanning (daily; 3hr); Ningbo (daily; 40min); Qingdao (daily; 1hr 20min); Shenzhen (10 daily; 2hr); Taiyuan (daily; 2hr); Tianjin (daily; 1hr 30min); Ürümqi (5 weekly; 5hr); Wenzhou (1–3 daily; 1hr); Wuhan (3 daily; 1hr); Xiamen (3 daily; 1hr 30min); Xi'an (6 daily; 2hr 15min); Xining (daily; 4hr); Yichang (6 weekly; 1hr 30min).

CHAPTER 6

Highlights

* **The Grand Canal** The original source of the region's wealth, and a construction feat to rival the Great Wall. See p.402

* **Suzhou** A striking medley of tree-lined canals, ramshackle homes, old stone bridges and hi-tech factories. See p.403

* **Tongli** A quiet, charming town of winding lanes and canals. See p.412

* **The cable car at Zhenjiang** The ride from this sleepy town to the verdant island of Jiao Shan offers a unique view of the Yangzi. See p.421

* **Fuzi Miao, Nanjing** A bustling consumer cornucopia, hot, noisy and earthy. See p.435

* **Xi Hu, Hangzhou** Great vistas are offered by this beautiful lake, best appreciated by cycling the area. See p.451

* **Shaoxing** This charismatic backwater was once home to some cultural heavyweights, such as the writer Lu Xun, whose elegant mansion – now a museum – offers a glimpse into a vanished world. See p.457

* **Putuo Shan** A tranquil island of Buddhist temples and beaches. See p.464

△ Xi Hu

Jiangsu and Zhejiang

China's original heartland may have been the dusty Yellow River basin, but it was the greenness and fertility of the **Yangzi River estuary** that drew the Chinese south, and provided them with the wealth and power needed to sustain a huge empire. The provinces of **Jiangsu** and **Zhejiang**, which today flank the metropolitan area of Shanghai, have played a vital part in the cultural and economic development of China for the last two thousand years. No tour of eastern China would be complete without stopovers in some of their classic destinations.

The story begins in the sixth century BC when the area was part of the state of Wu and had already developed its own distinct culture. The flat terrain, the large crop yield and the superb communications offered by coastal ports and navigable waterways enabled the principal towns of the area to develop quickly into important **trading centres**. These presented an irresistible target for the expanding Chinese empire under the Qin dynasty, and in 223 BC the region was annexed, immediately developing into one of the economic centres of the empire. After the end of the Han dynasty in the third century AD, several regimes established short-lived capitals in southern cities; however, the real boost for southern China came when the Sui (589–618 AD) extended the **Grand Canal** to link the Yangzi with the Yellow River and, ultimately, to allow trade to flow freely between here and the northern capitals. With this, China's centre of gravity took a decisive shift south. Under later dynasties, Hangzhou and then Nanjing became the greatest cities in China.

Visiting the region, you find yourself in a world of **water**. The whole area is intensively drained, canalized, irrigated and farmed, and the rivers, canals and lakes which web the plain give it much of its character. The traditional way to travel here was by **boat**, though passenger traffic has diminished in all but the most touristed areas. One local service inland survives, between Suzhou and Hangzhou, along the canals in among silk farms and tea plantations.

The powerful commercial cities of the waterways have long acted as counterweights to the bureaucratic tendencies of Beijing. Both **Hangzhou** and **Nanjing** have served as capitals of China, the latter having been Sun Yatsen's capital during the brief years of the Chinese Republic after the overthrow of the Qing dynasty. Marco Polo called Hangzhou "the most beautiful and magnificent city in the world", and its Xi Hu (West Lake), still recognizable from classic scroll paintings, is deservedly rated as one of the most scenic spots in China. **Suzhou** and **Yangzhou**, too, should not be missed, for the bustle of life along the canals that crisscross their centres, and the peace of their famous **gardens**. These and other cities – **Zhenjiang**, **Wuxi**, **Ningbo** – have also developed as manufacturing centres, enjoying the boom which

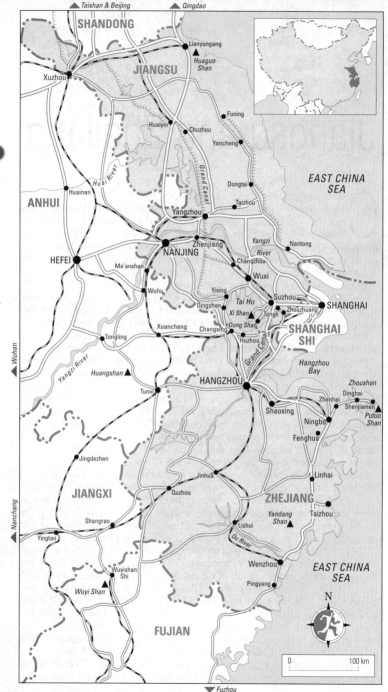

has put Jiangsu and Zhejiang at the forefront of economic development in China.

The downside to relative prosperity in China is chronic overpopulation. Well over 120 million people live in Jiangsu, Shanghai and Zhejiang, and it can seem that the area has been built over from end to end. You'll be hard-pressed to find much that might be classed as countryside here, with the exceptions of the area around charming **Shaoxing**, and, above all, the sacred Buddhist island of **Putuo Shan**, where superb beaches and monasteries are set deep in wooded hillsides.

For visitors, perhaps the most important point is that most foreign tourists who come here are on expensive package tours, and there are few facilities, such as foreigners' dormitories, for independent travellers. **Accommodation** is almost uniformly on the expensive side, with the cheapest hotels dipping only slightly below ¥200 for a double room – often university accommodation is the only budget possibility, though youth hostels are an option in Hangzhou and Suzhou. **Transport** connections are decent, however: comfortable modern buses run along the many intercity expressways, and are often the best way to make relatively short trips, while train connections are also good.

The area around the Yangzi, despite being low-lying and far from the northern plains, is unpleasantly cold and damp in winter, and unbearably hot and sticky during the summer months when most people choose to visit – Nanjing's age-old reputation as one of the "three furnaces" of China is well-justified. If possible, try to visit during the **spring** (mid-April to late May; many residents claim that if you blink you'll miss it), during which a combination of rain showers, sunshine and low humidity gives the terrain a splash of green as well as putting smiles on the faces of residents emerging from the harsh winter.

Jiangsu

Jiangsu is a long, narrow province hugging the coast south of Shandong. Low-lying, flat and wet, it is one of the most fertile and long-inhabited areas of China, dense in population and with plenty of sights of interest. The provincial capital, **Nanjing**, one of the great historical cities of China, was until 1949 the nation's capital. **Suzhou** and **Yangzhou** are ancient cities famous throughout China for their gardens and silk production, while **Wuxi** attracts thousands of tourists to the shores of **Tai Hu** for its scenery, fruit trees and fish, and for the caves of **Yixing** across the lake.

The traditional route across Jiangsu is the **Grand Canal**, which was once navigable all the way from Hangzhou in Zhejiang Province to Beijing, and is still very much alive in the sections that flow through southern Jiangsu. In addition to Suzhou, Yangzhou and Wuxi, **Zhenjiang** is another classic trading centre full of the bustle of canal life. The province's other great water highway – the **Yangzi River** – connects Nanjing with Shanghai, ensuring that trade from both east and west continues to bring wealth to the region.

The northwest has traditionally been the poor and backward part of the province, but even here **Xuzhou** is a major rail junction with modern coal mines, as well as a miniature terracotta army collection. The central parts of Jiangsu have a coast

The **Grand Canal** (Da Yun He), at 1800km the longest canal on earth, ranks alongside the Great Wall of China as the country's greatest engineering achievement. The first sections were dug about 400 BC, probably for military purposes, but the historic task of linking the Yellow and the Yangzi rivers was not achieved until the early seventh century AD under the Sui emperor Yang Di, when as many as six million men may have been pressed into service for its construction.

Locals like to point out that whereas the Great Wall was designed to stop contact and communication, the canal was made to further it. The original function of the canal was specifically to join the fertile rice-producing areas of the Yangzi with the more heavily populated but barren lands of the north, and to alleviate the effects of regular crop failures and famine. Following its completion, however, the canal became a vital element in the expansion of **trade** under the Tang and Song, benefiting the south as much as the north. Slowly the centre of political power drifted south – by 800 AD the Yangzi basin was taking over from the Yellow River as the chief source of the empire's finances, a transformation that would bring an end to the long domination of the old northern capitals, and lead to Hangzhou and Nanjing becoming China's most populous and powerful cities. A Japanese monk, Ennin, who travelled in China from 836 to 847 AD, described the traffic on the water then (in places you might find similar scenes today):

Two water buffalo were tied to more than forty boats, with two or three of the latter joined to form a single raft and with these connected in line by hawsers. Since it was difficult to hear from head to stern there was great shouting back and forth . . . Boats of the salt bureau passed laden with salt, three or four or five boats bound side by side and in line, following one another for several tens of li.

By the twelfth century, the provinces of Jiangsu and Zhejiang had become the economic and political heart of China. The Song dynasty moved south and established a capital at **Hangzhou** and the Ming emperors subsequently based themselves in **Nanjing**. During this period, and for centuries afterwards, the canal was constantly maintained and the banks regularly built up. A Western traveller, Robert Morrison, journeying as late as 1816 from Tianjin all the way down to the Yangzi, described the sophisticated and frequent locks and noted that in places the banks were so high and the country around so low that from the boat it was possible to look down on roofs and treetops.

Not until early in the twentieth century did the canal seriously start falling into **disuse**. Contributing factors included the frequent flooding of the Yellow River, the growth of coastal shipping and the coming of the rail lines. Unused, much of the canal rapidly silted up. But since the 1950s its value has once more been recognized, and renovation undertaken. The stretch **south of the Yangzi**, running from Zhenjiang through Changzhou, Wuxi and Suzhou (and on to Hangzhou in Zhejiang Province), is now navigable all year round, at least by flat-bottomed barges and the cruisers built for the tourist trade. Although most local **passenger boat services** along the canal have been dropped, the surviving services between Hangzhou and Suzhou will probably give you enough of a taste. It's fascinating rather than beautiful – as well as the frenetic loading and unloading of barges, you'll see serious pollution and heavy industry. **North of the Yangzi**, the canal is seasonably navigable virtually up to Jiangsu's northern border with Shandong, and major works are going on to allow bulk carriers access to the coal-producing city of Xuzhou. Beyond here, towards the Yellow River, sadly the canal remains impassable.

too shallow for anchorage, but ideal for salt panning, traditionally the source of its income. Among these flat lands dotted with small towns and lakes, and seamed with canals, the highlight is **Chuzhou**, the attractive hometown of Zhou Enlai.

Jiangsu **cuisine** tends to be on the sweet side and is characterized by an emphasis on flavour rather than texture, and by the use of wine in cooking, though one of the best-known dishes, *yanshui ya* (brine duck), has none of these qualities. The duck is first pressed and salted, then steeped in brine and baked; the skin should be creamy-coloured and the flesh red and tender. Other Jiangsu dishes worth trying include *majiang yaopian* (pig's intestines), *jiwei xia* (a lake crustacean vaguely resembling a lobster, but much better tasting, locals affirm) and *paxiang jiao* (a type of vegetable that resembles banana leaves).

Suzhou and around

Famous for its gardens, beautiful women and silk, the ancient and moated city of **SUZHOU**, just sixty minutes from Shanghai by train, lies at the point where the rail line meets the Grand Canal, about 30km to the east of Tai Hu. The town itself is built on a network of interlocking canals whose waters feed the series of renowned **classical gardens** which are Suzhou's pride and glory.

He Lu, semi-mythical ruler of the Kingdom of Wu, is said to have founded Suzhou in 600 BC as his capital, but it was the arrival of the **Grand Canal** more than a thousand years later that marked the beginning of the city's prosperity. The **silk trade** too was established early here, flourishing under the Tang and thoroughly booming when the whole imperial court moved south under the Song. To this day, silk remains an import source of Suzhou's income.

With the imperial capital close by at Hangzhou, Suzhou attracted an overspill of scholars, officials and merchants, bringing wealth and patronage with them.

△ Classic Chinese scenery at Suzhou

Suzhou and around

Suzhou	苏州	*sūzhōu*
Beisi Ta	北寺塔	*běisì tǎ*
Canglang Ting	沧浪亭	*cānglàng tíng*
Museum of Opera and Theatre	戏曲博物馆	*xìqǔ bówùguǎn*
Ou Yuan	耦园	*ǒuyuán*
Pan Men	盘门	*pánmén*
Ruiguang Ta	瑞光塔	*ruìguāng tǎ*
Shi Lu	石路	*shílù*
Shizi Lin	狮子林	*shīzi lín*
Shuang Ta	双塔	*shuāng tǎ*
Silk Museum	丝绸博物馆	*sīchóu bówùguǎn*
Wangshi Yuan	网师园	*wǎngshī yuán*
Wumen Qiao	吴门桥	*wúmén qiáo*
Xuanmiao Guan	玄妙观	*xuánmiào guàn*
Yi Yuan	怡园	*yíyuán*
Zhuozheng Yuan	拙政园	*zhuōzhèng yuán*

Accommodation and eating

Bamboo Grove	竹辉饭店	*zhúhuī fàndiàn*
Dianyun Fanzhuang	滇云饭庄	*diānyún fànzhuāng*
Dongwu	东吴饭店	*dōngwú fàndiàn*
Korea Restaurant	汉城韩国料理	*hànchénghánguó liàolǐ*
Lexiang	乐乡饭店	*lèxiāng fàndiàn*
Nanlin	南林饭店	*nánlín fàndiàn*
New Century	新世纪大酒店	*xīnshìjì dàjiǔdiàn*
Pub Bar	简妮酒吧	*jiǎnní jiǔbā*
Sheraton	喜来登大酒店	*xǐláidēng dàjiǔdiàn*
Songhelou Caiguan	松鹤楼菜馆	*sōnghèlóu càiguǎn*
Suzhou	苏州饭店	*sūzhōu fàndiàn*
Suzhou International Youth Hostel	苏州国际青年旅社	*sūzhōu guójì qīngnián lǚshè*
Xingjiang Yakexi	新疆亚克西酒楼	*xīnjiāng yàkèxī jiǔlóu*

Around Suzhou

Baodai Qiao	宝带桥	*bǎodài qiáo*
Lingyan Shan	灵岩山	*língyán shān*
Tianchi Shan	天池山	*tiānchí shān*
Tianping Shan	天平山	*tiānpíng shān*
Tongli	同里	*tónglǐ*

In the late thirteenth century, Marco Polo reported "six thousand bridges, clever merchants, cunning men of all crafts, very wise men called Sages and great natural physicians". These were the people responsible for carving out the intricate gardens that now represent Suzhou's primary attractions. When the first Ming emperor founded his capital at Nanjing, the city continued to enjoy a privileged position within the orbit of the court and to flourish as a centre for the production of wood block and the weaving of silk. The business was transformed by the gathering of the workforce into great sheds in a manner not seen in the West until the coming of the Industrial Revolution three centuries later.

Until recently, Suzhou's good fortune had been to avoid the ravages of history, despite suffering brief periods of occupation by the Taipings (see p.436) in the 1860s and by the Japanese during World War II. The 2,500-year-old city walls, however, which even in 1925 were still an effective defence against rampaging

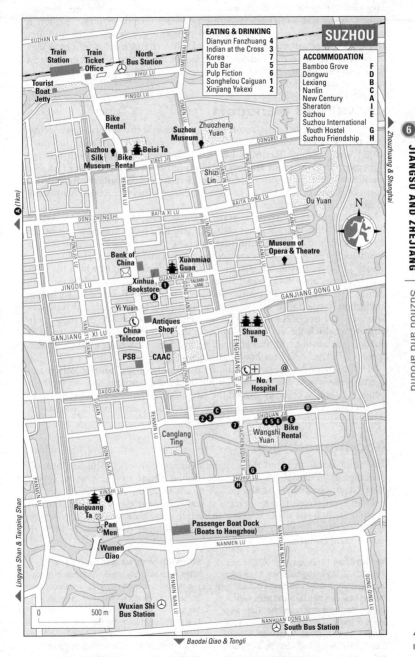

SUZHOU

EATING & DRINKING

Dianyun Fanzhuang	4
Indian at the Cross	3
Korea	7
Pub Bar	5
Pulp Fiction	6
Songhelou Caiguan	1
Xinjiang Yakexi	2

ACCOMMODATION

Bamboo Grove	F
Dongwu	D
Lexiang	B
Nanlin	C
New Century	A
Sheraton	I
Suzhou	E
Suzhou International Youth Hostel	G
Suzhou Friendship	H

Train Station

Train Ticket Office

North Bus Station

Tourist Boat Jetty

SUZHAN LU

XIHUI LU

PINGQI LU

A (1km)

Bike Rental

Suzhou Museum

Zhuozheng Yuan

DONGBEI JIE

Zhouzhuang & Shanghai

Suzhou Silk Museum

Beisi Ta

Bike Rental

XIBEI JIE

Shizi Lin

PINGJIANG LU

YUANLIN LU

DONG ZHONGSHI

BAITA XI LU

BAITA DONG LU

LINDUN LU

Ou Yuan

CANG JIE

N

Bank of China

Xuanmiao Guan

GUANQIAN JIE

Museum of Opera & Theatre

JINGDE LU

Xinhua Bookstore

GONG XIANG

TAIJIAN LANE

PINGJIANG LU

GANJIANG DONG LU

YANGYU XIANG

Yi Yuan

China Telecom

Antiques Shop

GANJIANG XI LU

PSB

CAAC

RENMIN LU

Shuang Ta

FENGHUANG JIE

DAOQIAN JIE

SIQUAN JIE

GANJIANG XI LU

SHIZI JIE

No. 1 Hospital

@

DAICHENGQIAO LU

Lingyan Shan & Tianping Shan

SHIQUAN JIE

D

Canglang Ting

ZHUHUI LU

G

F

Wangshi Yuan

Bike Rental

XINSHI LU

Ruiguang Ta

Pan Men

Wumen Qiao

PANMEN LU

Passenger Boat Dock (Boats to Hangzhou)

NANMEN LU

RENMIN LU

NANYUAN NAN LU

DONG QING LU

Wuxian Shi Bus Station

NANHUAN DONG LU

South Bus Station

0   500 m

Baodai Qiao & Tongli

warlords, were almost entirely demolished after 1949, and the parts of the **old city** that still survive – moats, gates, tree-lined canals, stone bridges, cobble-stoned streets and whitewashed old houses – are disappearing fast. Suzhou is now a boom town, with industrial areas springing up all round the outskirts. But its centre retains enough of its original character to merit a visit of at least several days, while in the immediate vicinity of the city are a number of places which make easy day- or half-day-trips, with Tai Hu (see p.412) a straightforward excursion slightly further afield.

Arrival and transport

Lying within a rectangular moat formed by canals, the historic town's clear grid of streets and waterways makes Suzhou a relatively easy place in which to get your bearings. **Renmin Lu**, the main street, bulldozes south through the centre from the **train station**, which is just to the north of the moat. The traditional commercial centre of the city lies around **Guanqian Jie**, halfway down Renmin Lu, an area of cramped, animated streets thronged with small shops, teahouses and restaurants.

Nearly all travellers arrive by **train**, Suzhou being on the main Shanghai–Nanjing rail line. Buses #1 and #20 take you into town from just east of the train station. Some private **minibuses** also use the train station square as their terminus, for example services to and from Wuxi and points on Tai Hu.

Suzhou has two main bus stations. The **North bus station**, which has half-hourly connections with Shanghai and Wuxi, is directly to the east of the train station. The **South bus station**, which sees arrivals from points south including Hangzhou and Zhouzhuang, is on Nanyuan Nan Lu just south of Nanhuan Dong Lu. Just east of Renmin Lu on the southern stretch of the city moat is the **passenger dock** for canal boats to and from Hangzhou. There's no airport at Suzhou (the nearest is at Shanghai, accessible in about an hour by taxi), though there is a CAAC office for bookings (see p.411).

Directly across the street from the train station exit is a **tourist office** and a small jetty where you can sign up for **boat tours** around Suzhou (¥60 for either Hanshan Si or a ride around the city moat) and to Tongli (day-trip leaves 8am; ¥150). A one-day bus tour of the town can be an excellent way to get round all the main sights; see p.411 for more.

Accommodation

The main **hotel** area, and the heaviest concentration of gardens and historic buildings, is in the south of the city, around **Shiquan Jie**. Out of season (Oct–May), you should be able to get rooms in all the hotels listed below at a discount of ten to twenty percent if you bargain at the front desk. Perhaps because Suzhou is a major tourist destination, hotel touts here are much more aggressive than elsewhere in China – the best strategy to shake them off is to ignore them completely.

Bamboo Grove 168 Zhuhui Jie ☎ 0512/65205601, ⓕ 65208778, ⓦ www.bg-hotel.com. A tour-group favourite, this efficient Japanese-run four-star hotel imitates local style with black and white walls and abundant bamboo in the garden. There are a couple of good restaurants on site. ❾

Dongwu 24 Wu Ya Chang, Shiquan Jie ☎ 0512/65193681, ⓕ 65194590. By far the best budget hotel option, this large place run by Suzhou University is central but quiet, and offers rooms either in the main building or – the cheaper option – in the pleasant foreign students' guesthouse at the back. There's a very cheap canteen on site too. ❹

Lexiang 18 Dajin Xiang, the third lane south of Guanqian Jie, east off Renmin Lu ☎ 0512/65228888, ⓕ 65244165. A very good, friendly, central hotel, one of the best options in its price bracket, with CITS next door and convenient for some good restaurants. The three- or four-bed rooms can work out fairly cheap if you bring enough friends to fill them. ❼

Nanlin 20 Gun Xiu Fang, Shiquan Jie ☏0512/68017888, ℻68015818, ⓦwww.nanlin.com. A big three-star garden-style affair with an immaculate lobby. The new wing has luxury rooms, while the old wing still offers reasonably priced doubles and triples. ❾

New Century 23 Guangji Lu ☏0512/65338888, ℻65335798. Out in the west of the city, beyond the moat (take bus #7 from the train station), with nicely decorated, airy rooms. Handy for the Shi Lu shopping area. ❼

Sheraton 259 Xin Shi Lu, near Pan Men in the southwest of town ☏0512/65103388, ⓦwww.sheraton.com/suzhou. A pastiche Chinese mansion sprawling over two city blocks, Suzhou's best (and most expensive by far) inter-national-standard hotel has double rooms from $200. A stream runs through the middle of the grounds, and there are serene gardens and indoor and outdoor swimming pools. ❾

Suzhou 345 Shiquan Jie ☏0512/65204646, ℻65204015, ⓦwww.suzhou-hotel.com. A huge but relatively characterless place, a favourite of tour groups. The cheapest rooms here are surprisingly dingy but do have clean facilities. ❽

Suzhou International Youth Hostel 186 Zhuhui Lu ☏0512/65180266, ℻65180366. A bit out of the way, but worth it for their decent dorm beds. Stick with the *Dongwu* if you want a room. Dorm beds ¥50, ❺

Suzhou Friendship 349 Zhuhui Lu ☏0512/65291601, ℻65206221. A big city block south of Shiquan Jie, this is large and friendly, with good-value rooms and a nice garden in the central atrium. ❻

The City

Among the Chinese, Suzhou is one of the most highly favoured tourist desti-nations in the country, and the city is packed with visitors from far and wide. This can make for a festive atmosphere, but it also means that you are rarely able to appreciate the **gardens** in the peace for which they were designed. The three most famous gardens – Wangshi Yuan, Shizi Lin and Zhuozheng Yuan – attract a stream of visitors all year round, but many of the equally beautiful yet lesser-known gardens, notably Canglang Ting and Ou Yuan, are compara-tively serene and crowd-free. The best strategy is to visit as much of the three popular gardens as possible before 10am and spend the rest of the day in the smaller gardens. If you can, choose a day with blue sky and a hint of cloud – the gardens need contrast, light and shade, clear shadow and bold reflection. Seasons make surprisingly little difference as the gardens can be appreciated at any time of year, although springtime brings more blossom and brighter colours. The gardens are open daily; note that during the summer and the major public holidays, entry fees are slightly higher than given below.

Suzhou is enjoyable simply **roaming** without special purpose. Stray from the main streets and you'll come across pagodas, temples, lively shopping districts and hectic canal traffic. Distances are a bit too large to rely purely on walking, but **cycling** is an excellent alternative as the terrain is pretty flat (see p.411 for bike rental).

Beisi Ta and the Suzhou Silk Museum

A few minutes' walk south down Renmin Lu from the train station, the **Beisi Ta** (North Temple Pagoda; daily 7.45am–5pm; ¥25) looms up unmistakeably. On the site of the residence of the mother of Wu Kingdom king Sun Quan, the Beisi Ta was first built in the third century AD, and rebuilt in 1582. The pagoda is, at 76m, the tallest Chinese pagoda south of the Yangzi, though it retains only nine of its original eleven storeys. Climbing it gives an excellent view over some of Suzhou's more conspicuous features – the Shuang Ta, the Xuanmiao Guan, and, in the far southwest corner, the Ruiguang Ta. There's also a very pleasant teahouse on site.

Gardens, above all, are what Suzhou is all about. They have been laid out here since the Song dynasty, a thousand years ago, and in their Ming and Qing heyday it is said that the city had two hundred of them. Some half-dozen major gardens have now been restored, as well as a number of smaller ones. Elsewhere in China you'll find grounds – as at Chengde or the Summer Palace outside Beijing – laid out on a grand scale, but the gardens of Suzhou are tiny in comparison, often in small areas behind high compound walls, and thus are far closer to the true essence of a Chinese garden.

Chinese gardens do not set out to improve upon a slice of nature or to look natural, which is why many Western eyes find them hard to accept or enjoy. They are a serious art form, the garden designer working with rock, water, buildings, trees and vegetation in subtly different combinations; as with painting, sculpture and poetry, the aim is to produce for contemplation the **balance**, **harmony**, **proportion** and **variety** which the Chinese seek in life. The wealthy scholars and merchants who built Suzhou's gardens intended them to be enjoyed either in solitude or in the company of friends over a glass of wine and a poetry recital or literary discussion. Their designers used little pavilions and terraces to suggest a larger scale, undulating covered walkways and galleries to give a downward view, and intricate interlocking groups of rock and bamboo to hint at, and half conceal, what lies beyond. Glimpses through delicate lattices, tile-patterned openings or moon gates, and reflections in water created cunning perspectives which either suggested a whole landscape or borrowed outside features (such as external walls of neighbouring buildings) as part of the design, in order to create an illusion of distance.

Among the features of the Suzhou gardens considered essential are the white pine trees, the odd-shaped rocks from Tai Hu and the stone tablets over the entrances. The whole was completed by animals – there are still fish and turtles in some ponds today. **Differences in style** among the various gardens arise basically from the mix and balance of the ingredients; some are dominated by water, others are mazes of contorted rock, yet others are mainly inward-looking, featuring pavilions full of strange furniture. Almost everything you see has some symbolic significance – the pine tree and the crane for long life, mandarin ducks for married bliss, for example.

Virtually opposite, also on Renmin Lu, is the **Suzhou Silk Museum** (daily 9am–5.30pm; ¥7), one of China's better-presented museums, labelled in English throughout. Starting from the legendary inventor of silk, Lei Zu, the concubine of the equally legendary emperor Huang Di, it traces the history of silk production and its use from 4000 BC to the present day. There are displays of looms and weaving machines, and reproductions of early silk patterns, but the most riveting display – and something of a shock – is the room full of silkworms munching mulberry leaves and spinning cocoons, and copulating moths.

Suzhou Museum, the Zhuozheng Yuan and Shizi Lin

Turning east immediately south of Beisi Ta along Xibei Jie (which shortly becomes Dongbei Jie) and continuing beyond the first large intersection brings you to the **Suzhou Museum**. The museum (daily 8.15am–4.15pm; ¥10), housed in the former residence of Taiping leader Li Xiucheng, contains a rather obscure collection of dusty ceramics with no English labels, but the garden next door is compulsory visiting. By far the largest of the Suzhou gardens, covering forty thousand square metres, the **Zhuozheng Yuan** (Humble Administrator's Garden; ¥50) is based on water and set out in three linked sections: the eastern part (just inside the entrance) consists of a small lotus pond and pavilions; the centre is largely water, with two small islands connected by zigzag bridges, while the western part has unusually open green spaces. Built at the time of the Ming by an imperial censor, Wang Xianchen, who had just resigned his post, the garden was named by its creator as an ironic lament on the fact that he could now administer nothing but gardening.

A couple of minutes south of the Zhuozheng Yuan is another must-see garden, the **Shizi Lin** (Lion Grove; daily 7.30am–4.30pm; ¥20). Tian Ru, the monk who laid this out in 1342, named it in honour of his teacher, Zhi Zheng, who lived on Lion Rock Mountain, and the rocks of which it largely consists are supposed to resemble lions in all shapes and sizes. Once chosen, these strange water-worn rocks were submerged for decades in Tai Hu to be further eroded. Part of the rockery takes the form of a convoluted labyrinth, from the top of which you emerge occasionally to gaze down at the water reflecting the green trees and grey stone. Qing emperors Qianlong and Kangxi were said to be so enamoured of these rockeries that they had the garden at the Yuanmingyuan Palace in Beijing modelled on them.

Xuanmiao Guan and Yi Yuan

Moving south from here, you arrive at the **Xuanmiao Guan** (Taoist Temple of Mystery; daily 7.30am–4.30pm; ¥10), just north of Guanqian Jie and rather incongruously at the heart of the modern city's consumer zone. Founded originally during the Jin Dynasty in the third century AD, the temple has been destroyed, rebuilt, burnt down and put back together many times during its history. For centuries it was the scene of a great bazaar where travelling showmen, acrobats and actors entertained the crowds. Nowadays the complex, still an attractive, lively place, basically consists of a vast entrance court full of resting locals with, at its far end, a hall of Taoist deities and symbols; it's all encircled by a newly constructed park.

A few minutes south of Guanqian Jie, on the northwest corner of the Renmin Lu and Ganjiang Lu junction, is one of the lesser gardens, **Yi Yuan** (Joyous Garden; daily 7.30am–11pm; ¥15), laid out by official Gu Wenbin. Late Qing-dynasty, and hence considerably newer than the others, it is supposed to encompass all the key features of a Chinese garden; unusually, it also has formal flowerbeds and arrangements of coloured pebbles.

The Museum of Opera & Theatre and Ou Yuan

A ten-minute walk along narrow lanes due east from Guanqian Jie, the unusual and memorable **Museum of Opera and Theatre** stands on Zhongzhangjia Xiang (daily 8.30am–4.30pm; ¥8). The rooms are filled with costumes, masks, musical instruments, and even a full-sized model orchestra, complete with cups of tea, though the building itself is the star, a Ming-dynasty theatre made of latticed wood. The Suzhou area is the historical home of the 5000-year-old **Kun Opera** style, China's oldest operatic form – Beijing Opera has existed for a mere 3000 years. Kun is distinguished by storytelling and ballad singing, though it can be hard to follow as it is performed in the all-but-unintelligible (even if you speak Chinese) Suzhou dialect. The curators are gold mines of information on the art form as well as on the degradation that opera performers had to endure during the Cultural Revolution – but you'll need to speak Chinese to engage them in conversation.

A five-minute walk northeast of the museum, abutting the outer moat and along a canal, is the **Ou Yuan** (daily 8am–5pm; ¥15), whose greatest asset is its comparative freedom from the loudhailer-toting tour groups that crowd the other gardens. Here a series of hallways and corridors opens onto an intimate courtyard, with a pond in the middle surrounded by abstract rock formations and several relaxing teahouses. The surrounding area houses some of the loveliest architecture, bridges and canals in Suzhou and is well worth an hour-long stroll.

Shuang Ta and Canglang

Several blocks east of Renmin Lu and immediately south of Ganjiang Lu, the **Shuang Ta** (Twin Pagodas; daily 7am–4.30pm; ¥3) are matching slender towers built during the Song dynasty by a group of successful candidates in the imperial examinations who wanted to honour their teacher. Too flimsy to climb, the pagodas sprout from a delightful patch of garden. At the other end is a teahouse crowded in summer with old men fanning themselves against the heat.

A kilometre or so farther southwest of here, just beyond Shiquan Jie, the undervisited but intriguing **Canglang Ting** (Dark Blue Wave Pavilion; daily 8am–5pm; ¥15) is the oldest of the major surviving gardens, at the corner of Renmin Lu and Zhuhui Lu. Originally built in the Song dynasty by scholar Su Zimei around 1044 AD, it's approached through a grand stone bridge and ceremonial marble archway. The central mound inside is designed to look like a forested hill. In the south of the garden (away from the entrance) stands the curious Five Hundred Sage Temple lined with stone tablets recording the names and achievements of great statesmen, heroes and poets of Suzhou.

Wangshi Yuan

Wangshi Yuan (Master of the Nets Garden; daily 7.30am–5pm; ¥20) is on Shiquan Jie, a short walk west from the *Suzhou Hotel* and down a narrow alleyway on the left. So named because the owner, a retired official, decided he wanted to become a fisherman, this tiny and intimate garden was started in 1140, but was later abandoned and not restored to its present layout until 1770. Considered by garden connoisseurs to be the finest of them all, it boasts an attractive central lake, minuscule connecting halls, pavilions with pocket-handkerchief courtyards and carved wooden doors – and rather more visitors than it can cope with. The garden is said to be best seen on moonlit nights, when the moon can be seen three times over from the Moon-watching Pavilion – in the sky, in the water and in a mirror. The garden's other main features are its delicate latticework and fretted windows, through which you can catch a series of glimpses – a glimmer of bamboo, dark interiors, water and a miniature rockery framed in the three windows of a study. Outside the dead winter months the gardens play host to nightly arts performances (see opposite).

Pan Men and around

In the far southwestern corner of the moated area is one of the city's most pleasant areas, centred around **Pan Men** (Coiled Gate) and a stretch of the original city wall, built in 514 BC by King Helu of the Wu Kingdom; the gate is the only surviving one of eight that once surrounded Suzhou. The best approach to this area is from the south, via **Wumen Qiao**, a delightful high-arched bridge (the tallest in Suzhou) with steps built into it; it's a great vantage point for watching the canal traffic (bus #7 from the train station passes the southern edge of the moat). Just inside Pan Men sits the dramatic **Ruiguang Ta** (¥6), a thousand-year-old pagoda now rebuilt from ruins, once housing a rare Buddhist pearl stupa (since moved to the Suzhou Museum).

Eating, drinking and entertainment

Suzhou cooking, with its emphasis on fish from the nearby lakes and rivers, is justly renowned; specialities include *yinyu* ("silver fish") and *kaobing* (grilled pancakes with sweet filling). The town is well stocked with **restaurants** for all budgets, though it holds little in the way of **nightlife** – the city's younger set escapes to Shanghai for serious nights out. That said, there is a slew of touristy bars scattered along Shiquan Jie near Wangshi Yuan; the best are *Pulp Fiction*, 200m west of the *Suzhou Hotel*, and the much smaller *Pub Bar*, 50m farther west.

The best entertainment in town is the nightly **opera extravaganza** at Wangshi Yuan (spring–autumn 7.30–10pm; ¥80 including admission to garden), featuring eight displays of the most prominent forms of Chinese performance arts, from Beijing Opera to folk dancing and storytelling.

Restaurants

Dianyun Fanzhuang 519 Shiquan Jie. A friendly, inexpensive place for rice noodles and other Yunnan specialties – sit by the window for a view of the tourists plying Shiquan Lu. Open 24hr.

Indian at the Cross 758 Shiquan Jie. Relatively cheap curries and friendly staff. Daily 11am–2pm & 5–11pm.

Korea Restaurant 579 Daichengqiao Lu, at the Shiquan Jie intersection. One of the best of a host of unimaginatively named Korean restaurants, with good barbecued beef, cooked at the table.

Songhelou Caiguan On Taijian Lane, 200m east of Renmin Lu. The most famous restaurant in town – it claims to be old enough to have served Emperor Qianlong. The menu is elaborate and long on fish and seafood (crab, eel, squirrel fish and the like), though not cheap at around ¥150 a head.

Taijian Lane Restaurants Flanking *Songhelou* on Taijian Lane are four other restaurants of repute, all claiming more than 100 years of history: the *Dasanyuan*, *Deyuelou*, *Wangsi* and *Laozhengxing*. They're all big, busy and good for a splurge on local dishes, with foreigner-friendly staff and menus.

Xinjiang Yakexi 768 Shiquan Jie. Xinjiang comfort food – pulled noodles with vegetables (*latiaozi*) and *nan* bread, among others – in a bright dining room bustling with local Uigurs and tourists. Open late.

Listings

Airlines The main CAAC reservations and ticketing office is at 943 Renmin Lu, a few minutes' walk south of Ganjiang Lu (⏚0512/65104881; daily 8am–7pm).

Banks and exchange The Bank of China head office is on Renmin Lu right in the centre of town, just north of Guanqian Jie (daily 8.15am–5.15pm).

Bike rental Many gift shops along Shiquan Jie rent bikes; check those just west of the *Suzhou Hotel* main gate. They charge ¥15–25 for a day with a deposit of a few hundred yuan (or a pass-port). A couple of storefronts just north of the Silk Museum also rent bikes.

Boats A nightly boat service operates between Suzhou and Hangzhou in both directions, taking around 10hr, with a bar and karaoke on board. The incoming boat arrives around 7am, and the outbound boat leaves at 5.30pm; fares range from ¥80 to ¥150. Buy tickets at the dock at the passenger boat dock, or at the ticket window (daily 8am–8pm) 50m south of Xuanmiao Guan, on the west side of Gong Xiang.

Bookshops The Xinhua bookstore at 166 Guanqian Jie has a small selection of classic novels.

Hospital The No. 1 Hospital is at the junction of Fenghuang Jie and Shizi Jie.

Internet access The most pleasant place to get online is an unnamed place on Shizi Jie east of the hospital. Alternatively, try the Jinpo Net bar next to China Telecom at 333 Renmin Lu. Places are constantly opening and closing along Shiquan Jie, so check with your hotel for the latest information.

Mail Suzhou's main post office (daily 8am–8pm) is at the corner of Renmin Lu and Jingde Lu.

PSB On Renmin Lu, at the junction with the small lane Dashitou Xiang.

Shopping There are numerous opportunities to shop for silk in Suzhou, although be aware of outrageous prices, especially in the boutiques along Shiquan Jie and Guanyin Jie and the night market on Shi Lu. Bargain hard, as these sellers can quote prices up to ten times the going rate. The King Silk Store next to the Silk Museum has a good selection, including great duvets starting at just over ¥300. The Antique Store (daily 9.30am–9.30pm) along Renmin Lu at Ganjiang Dong Lu is the place to find old furniture, while paintings and embroidery are on hand in a pavilion near the corner of Renmin Lu and Baita Xi Lu and in the shops along Shiquan Jie.

Tours Minibus tours of Suzhou, on which you get ferried to the sights, often without any commentary, depart from the train station square at 7.30am and return at 4.30pm, and cost ¥15 exclusive of admission charges. Air-conditioned bus tours to Suzhou sights or to surrounding areas such as Tongli can be booked at CITS (or other travel services).

Trains The train ticket office is located in a separate building to the left of the station as you emerge. There's also a convenient ticket window 50m south of Xuanmiao Guan on the west side of Gong Xiang (daily 8am–8pm). CITS and most hotels will book tickets for a commission.

Travel agents CITS is next to the *Lexiang Hotel* on Dajing Xiang (☎0512/65155207). Nearly all hotels have their own travel agencies.

Around Suzhou

A short bike ride **south** of the city, out along the canals to the main section of the Grand Canal where it heads off towards Hangzhou, is **Baodai Qiao** (Precious Belt Bridge). With 53 arches, this Tang-dynasty structure is named after Wang Zhongshu, a local prefect who selflessly sold his precious belt to raise money for his subjects. It's not wildly exciting, but does make a tranquil spot for contemplation. To reach it, pedal south along Renmin Lu through Suzhou's southern suburbs, over a roundabout with a re-creation of the Eiffel Tower in the middle, cross the wide Grand Canal, then at Shihu Lu, the first major intersection south of here, turn left (east) and head straight for 2–3km, until the next major junction, where you turn left along a canal.

Much farther south of the bridge, 23km from Suzhou, is **TONGLI**, a superb example of a town built on water – every house backs on to canals, there are 49 stone bridges and nearly all movement takes place by boat. You can reach this small town by minibus from either bus station for ¥7. Tongli's main street has become rather touristy, with overpriced souvenir stands and restaurants, but a little exploration along the back alleys will reveal canals shaded by stately bridges, overhanging willows, lazing elderly folk, put-putting barges and rural splendour. The top sights here include **Tuisi Yuan** (daily 7.45am–5.30pm; ¥25), a late Qing garden that vaguely resembles Suzhou's Ou Yuan, and **Jiayin Hall** (daily 9am–5.15pm; ¥2), the two-storey austere home of Liu Yazi, a Nationalist actor and entertainer renowned for his eccentric collection of gauze caps. Speedboats used to offer an interesting spin across Tongli Lake to the canal town of **Zhouzhuang**, but these days it's best visited as a day-trip from Shanghai (see p.386).

There's more of interest to the **west**, towards Tai Hu. Fifteen and eighteen kilometres respectively from Suzhou, **Lingyan Shan** and **Tianping Shan** both offer tremendous views and together make a good day's outing on a bicycle. At Lingyan Shan (daily 7.30am–5.30pm; ¥10) you climb stone steps past a bell tower to reach a walled enclosure with a temple hall, a seven-storey pagoda and a well. Tianping Shan (daily 8am–5pm; ¥10), 3km beyond, was already a well-known beauty spot under the Song, the hillside cut with streams and dotted with strange rock formations. Wooded paths meander up to the summit past pavilions and small gardens, and in autumn the maples which cover the slopes seem to blaze. Adventurous types can hike from Tianping Shan along a three-to four-kilometre trail that follows a hillcrest to **Tianchi Shan** (¥5), another temple complex set in more remote, scenic surroundings.

Tai Hu and around

One of the four largest freshwater lakes in China, constantly replenished by heavy rains, **Tai Hu** is liberally sprinkled with islands and surrounded by wooded hills. With an average depth of just 2m, it's a natural reservoir of

Tai Hu and around

Tai Hu	太湖	*tàihú*
Ferry pier	陆巷码头	*lùxiàng mǎtóu*
Dong Shan	东山	*dōngshān*
Longtou Shan	龙头山	*lóngtóu shān*
Zijin An	紫金庵	*zǐjīn ān*
Xi Shan	西山	*xīshān*
Donghe	东河	*dōnghé*
Linwu Cave	林屋古洞	*línwūgǔdòng*
Wuxi	无锡	*wúxī*
Hui Shan	惠山	*huìshān*
Lingshan Buddha	灵山大佛	*língshān dàfó*
Mei Yuan	梅园	*méiyuán*
Sanshan Island	三山岛	*sānshān dǎo*
Xihui Park	锡惠公园	*xīhuì gōngyuán*
Yuantou Zhu	鼋头渚	*yuántóuzhǔ*
Accommodation		
CTS Grand	中旅大酒店	*zhōnglǚ dàjiǔdiàn*
Lakeview Park	太湖花园度假村	*tàihú huāyuán dùjiàcūn*
Milido	美丽都	*měilì dū*
Southern Yangzi University Foreign Experts Building	江南大学专家楼	*jiāngnán dàxué zhuānjiālóu*
Taihu	太湖饭店	*tàihú fàndiàn*
Taishan	泰山饭店	*tàishān fàndiàn*
Yixing Town	宜兴市	*yíxīng shì*
Beisite Guoji Hotel	贝斯特国际大酒店	*bèisītè guójì dàjiǔdiàn*
Huating Hotel	华亭大酒店	*huátíng dàjiǔdiàn*
Yixing Hotel	宜兴宾馆	*yíxīng bīnguǎn*
Yixing County	宜兴县	*yíxīngxiàn*
Dingshan (Dingshu)	丁山	*dīngshān*
Linggu Caves	灵谷洞	*línggǔ dòng*
Shanjuan Caves	善卷洞	*shànjuàn dòng*
Zhanggong Caves	张公洞	*zhānggōng dòng*

relatively unpolluted water, where fish are bred, and lotus and water-chestnut are grown in ideal conditions on the islands. Other plant- and wildlife is rich, too, and the shores are clad with tea plantations and orchards of loquat, pear, peach, apricot and plum, particularly on the western side among the caves and potteries of **Yixing County**. The southeastern shore of the lake, particularly the charming rural areas of **Dong Shan** and **Xi Shan**, is most easily visited from Suzhou, but the most famous and popular Tai Hu scenic area, **Yuantou Zhu**, is best visited from the town of **Wuxi** some 40km northwest of Suzhou.

Dong Shan and Xi Shan

Some 35km from Suzhou, and within easy reach of the city, lie two fingers of land projecting into Tai Hu, known as **Dong Shan** (East Hill) and **Xi Shan** (West Hill) respectively; the latter is actually an island, joined to the mainland

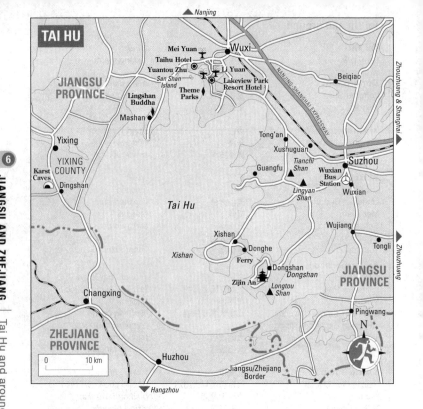

TAI HU

via an artificial causeway. This area of Tai Hu is entirely rural, with small villages of friendly people and green hillsides. Frequent private **minibuses** make their way to Dong Shan, and to Donghe on Xi Shan, from the west side of the train station square in Suzhou and from Wuxian Shi bus station in the south of town. City bus #20 also departs regularly for Dong Shan from in front of Suzhou's train station.

One possible long day-trip from Suzhou involves heading to Dong Shan by minibus, crossing to Xi Shan by boat in the afternoon, then returning to Suzhou by minibus. The minibuses to Dong Shan arrive at a T-junction, the point where the approach road meets the circuit road that runs right around the hill. Take the road south (left) from the T-junction; this passes the ancient **Zijin An** (Purple Gold Nunnery; daily 7.30am–5pm; ¥20), notable for its ancient statuary and its location in a beautiful, secluded wood surrounded by sweet-smelling orange groves. Further along, on the southern side of the peninsula, rises **Longtou Shan** (Dragon's Head Mountain), which, if the peak's not shrouded, rewards the easy hike up with stunning views of the plantations and the lake beyond. The rickshaw drivers all claim that the northern side of Dong Shan holds the best views of Tai Hu, but in fact the southern side of the peninsula, south of Longtou Shan and only accessible on foot, harbours the best vantages.

The pier for **ferries** to Xi Shan (daily 7.30am & 2.30pm; 30min; ¥5) is several kilometres northwest of the T-junction. Once on Xi Shan, you can get around using **motor-rickshaws**; expect to pay ¥30–40, including waiting time for any stopovers, for a day-long excursion. **Linwu Cave** (daily 8am–5pm; ¥20) here is a relatively unspectacular chain of caverns discovered in the tenth century, the cave mouth offering sweeping vistas of Tai Hu below. From **Donghe**, the small settlement on the island, you can pick up a bus back to Suzhou, crossing the four-kilometre-long causeway to the mainland on the way. The last bus leaves around 6pm.

Wuxi

The town of **WUXI**, close by the northern shore of the lake, is not particularly attractive, but it is the most convenient place to base yourself for a visit to the Tai Hu beauty spots. Set in a landscape of water, fertile plains and low hills, Wuxi was allegedly established more than 3500 years ago as the capital of the Wu Kingdom, a role it served for over 600 years until the Han Dynasty, when the neighbouring tin mines were exhausted. At this point, the Wu capital shifted further west to Wuhan (Wuxi means "without tin"). It was the construction of the Grand Canal centuries later that brought importance to local trade and industry, as it did for so many other canal towns.

One place in town to pass a few hours amid trees and small paths is **Xihui Park** (daily 5.30am–5.30pm; ¥25; bus #2 through town from the train station), west of the centre and allegedly once visited by Qin Shi Huang. The path from the main entrance on Huihe Lu leads up to the Dragon Light Pagoda on top of **Xi Shan**; more interesting, though, is the **cable car** (¥28), definitely worth it for panoramic views over to Tai Hu on a clear day. The ride links with

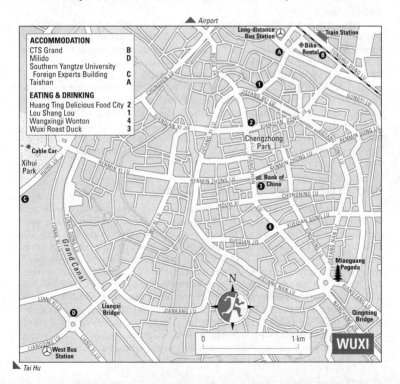

neighbouring **Hui Shan**, the source of a special black clay used for the ugly painted figurines which have been made here since at least the Ming dynasty, and which are sold all over Wuxi.

Practicalities

The old city of Wuxi is roughly oval-shaped, and is surrounded by a ring of canals. Most trains running between Shanghai and Nanjing stop at Wuxi **train station**, outside the canal ring to the northeast. Bus #11 goes right across town from the stop to the east of the *CTS Grand Hotel*, opposite the station. The main **long-distance bus station** faces the train station square, and is served by buses from most nearby cities. On the other side of the city, across the Liangxi Bridge over the Grand Canal, is a smaller bus station from where there are frequent connections with Yixing. Bus #20 and frequent minibuses cross the city from here on their way to the train station.

The best budget place to **stay** is the *Southern Yangtze University Foreign Experts Building*, at 170 Huihe Lu (☎0510/5861034; ❸), with very comfortable singles and doubles, all en suite. If you're heading here on bus #2 from the train station, get off at the second stop (Qingshanwan) after the big bridge over the Grand Canal, cross the road and walk a few metres farther on until you see the English sign. For a cheap room near the train station, try the *Taishan Hotel* (☎0510/2303888, ℱ2301069; ❹), the tallest building across from the station exit. Other options in town include the nondescript *CTS Grand* (☎0510/2300888 ext 1908, ℱ2304561; ❼), directly across the street from the train station; and the upmarket *Milido* at 2 Liang Xi Lu (☎0510/5865665, ℱ5801668; ❼) – though in this price range there are nicer options by the lakeside (see opposite).

There are a few reasonable places to **eat** on Zhongshan Lu, just south of Renmin Lu; among them, the *Wuxi Roast Duck Restaurant* has an English menu. Most restaurants offer the city's most famous contribution to Chinese cuisine, Wuxi spare ribs, cooked in a pungent soy-sauce base. For snacks, try the *Wangxingji Wonton Restaurant*, in the centre of town at the corner of Zhongshan Lu and Xueqian Jie, famous in these parts for its "three-fresh" wonton soup (made with pigs' trotters, shrimp and egg) as well as steamed buns stuffed with crab. Close to the train station – across the bridge and a couple of blocks south on the right – is the *Lou Shang Lou*, serving big bowls of noodles and Shanghai food. For dessert, try the *Huang Ting Delicious Food City* in the Chong'an Temple downtown, with more than 120 years of history, scrumptious plum cake and Yulan pastry.

Mei Yuan and Yuantou Zhu

The shores of Tai Hu closest to Wuxi, fringed with gardens, woods, pagodas and waterside hotels, boast two parks, **Mei Yuan** and **Yuantou Zhu**, where you can spend half a day rambling, though they are expensive to get into and full of tour groups. The two areas are linked by boat, and a circular trip from town taking in both is perhaps the best way to go. In an effort to siphon tourists away from Wuxi's more famous neighbours Suzhou and Hangzhou, many "instant tourism" sights have been built hereabouts in the past few years, most notably a slew of historical theme parks and the pointless **Lingshan Buddha** (daily 6.30am–6pm; ¥68; bus #14 from the train station). At 88m high, this bronze-plated giant is the tallest Buddha in the world, built for the record books and to extract *yuan* from tourists at a spot with no religious significance. You won't miss much if you confine your investigations to the lake itself.

Due west from Wuxi on the slopes of a small hill, looking down through the woods to the spread of fishponds fringing the lake, sits **Mei Yuan** (Plum Garden; daily 6am–10pm; ¥35). Originally established in 1912, the park now offers a springtime sea of blossom from four thousand plum trees, best appreciated from the pagoda at the highest point. In autumn you can enjoy the heady scent of osmanthus blossom, used to flavour the local delicacy, honeyed plums.

From just south of Mei Yuan there are small boats (¥15) to and from **Yuantou Zhu** (Turtle Head Isle; daily 6am–5pm; ¥70), the principal Tai Hu pleasure spot and a relaxing place to stroll around for a few hours, though not worth the steep entrance fee. Capped by a small lighthouse at the western tip, the huge park covers the northwestern end of the peninsula jutting into the lake (which bears little obvious resemblance to a turtle's head), and is scattered with teahouses and pavilions, the former summerhouses of the wealthy.

From a pier on Yuantou Zhu, a little north of the lighthouse, a ferry shuttles tourists regularly to and from the tiny former bandits' lair of **Sanshan Island**, comprising a central knob of land linked by causeways to minuscule outcrops on either side. Neat paths lead up to a teahouse, pavilion and pagoda giving views of tree-clad islands, winding inlets, fishing boats under sail and – if you're lucky enough to catch a sunny day – blue waters.

From another pier, on the northern edge of Yuantou Zhu and facing the mainland, you can catch small, fast boats to the Mei Yuan area, near the #2 bus terminus. Buy your ticket from the kiosk, not on the boat. You arrive at an obscure pier apparently in the middle of nowhere – walk straight ahead, cross a small bridge, then walk along a canal with an entertainment park on the other side, and you'll emerge more or less opposite Mei Yuan.

Practicalities

Bus #1 to Yuantou Zhu and #2 to Mei Yuan both run through Wuxi from the train station square; otherwise it's a pleasant hour's bicycle ride to the lake. The **hotels** here offer great opportunities for enjoying some peace and quiet, particularly after the rush of day-trippers has subsided. Twenty minutes' walk south of the #2 bus terminus, the *Taihu Hotel* (☎0510/5517888; ◐) stands among the fish ponds just south of Mei Yuan. It's a great, secluded place to stay, surrounded by flame trees, with birdsong and green fireflies in the gardens. The hotel restaurant serves excellent Lotus Leaf Chicken, a local speciality of chicken braised in soy sauce and steamed in a lotus leaf wrapping. More luxurious and beautifully located is the opulent *Lakeview Park Resort* (☎0510/5555888, ℱ5556909; ◑), just south of the entrance to Yuantou Zhu on 8 Qitang Lu, with a player-piano in the very stately lobby and an Internet connection in each room.

Yixing County

On the western shores of Tai Hu about 60km from Wuxi, **Yixing County** is a mild, fertile plain crisscrossed by canals and with a smattering of small lakes, making it ideal for the cultivation of tea and bamboo. The most important and traditional of all the local products, however, is the **pottery** from the small town of **Dingshan** (aka Dingshu). The other main attractions of the area are the underground caves that have been hollowed out of the karst hills in a skein running southwest from Yixing Town. The whole area can be visited on a hectic day-trip from Wuxi, though you might choose to spend a night in Yixing Town, perhaps en route from Nanjing to Wuxi or Hangzhou.

Although there's precious little to see in **YIXING TOWN** itself, you'll almost certainly have to pay it a visit, as it's the regional transport and accommodation centre. Travellers arrive by bus, either at the **Shi** (town) **bus station**, or at the smaller **Sheng** (provincial) **bus station**, both of which are in the far northwest of town. Frequent minibuses (¥3) in and out of the stations make the connection with Dingshan to the south.

If you're looking for **accommodation** in Yixing, walk east along Taige Lu from either station, in the direction of the tall Bank of China building, the top of which is clearly visible. About fifteen minutes' walk along here is the *Beisite Guoji Hotel* (⊤0510/7908866, ⒻF7906412; ⑥), offering large, smart doubles. Alternatively, turn south across the bridge (before reaching the *Beisite Guoji*) down the main street, Renmin Lu. A little way down here, on Jiefang Lu to the left, the *Huating Hotel* (⊤0510/7911888, ⒻF7903364; ⑥) has similarly upmarket rooms. Finally, virtually in the centre of the city, farther south down Renmin Lu and on the left through an imposing archway, is the clean, efficient *Yixing Hotel* (⊤0510/7916888, ⒻF7900767; ⑧). Just inside the archway here are a couple of travel services, which will book tours for you and rent cars with drivers.

Dingshan

If you're interested in pottery, or if you simply want to buy a Chinese tea set, head for **DINGSHAN**, a thirty-minute **minibus** ride south of Yixing. There's nothing to see here beyond pots and ceramic artefacts, but it's fascinating to find the products of the **pottery factories** literally crammed into every nook and cranny. Ceramic lampposts line the road into town, pottery shards crunch under your feet on the main street and the walls of buildings are embedded with broken tiles.

Incredibly, this obscure town has been producing pots since the beginning of recorded history. Primitive unglazed pots have been found here which date back to the Shang and Zhou periods, some three thousand years ago. Since the Han dynasty at least, around 200 BC, this has been the most renowned site for glazed wares in China – Dingshan can take a lot of the credit for our use of the word "china" to mean ceramics. In terms of wealth, Dingshan had its heyday under the Ming from the fourteenth century, but manufacturing is still going strong today, in thirty or so ceramics factories. A sandy local clay is used to produce the **purple sand pottery**, a dull brown unglazed ware, heavy in iron, whose properties of retaining the colour, fragrance and flavour of tea supposedly make for incomparable teapots.

All along Dingshan's main street you'll find stalls and pavement displays with **tea sets** on offer at very low prices. If you're interested in buying, first see that the spout, body, knob, handle and lid are all balanced, that the lid fits snugly and that there is a clear sound when the pot is tapped. Feel the texture; a rough texture does not indicate poor quality – in fact pots should be rough, especially on the inside. Also ask to put some water in the teapot; the water should shoot out of the spout, not dribble, when poured. Lastly, don't forget to bargain – as a general rule, you should not pay more than half the shopkeeper's first offer.

Dingshan is also where replacement **roof tiles** and ornamental rocks are manufactured for use in the vast work of reconstructing China's temples. The enormous pots decorated with writhing dragons are extremely fine, as are the round, heavy, blue-glazed tables found in so many Chinese gardens. In the **Pottery Exhibition Centre**, 2km north up the main street from the spot where minibuses arrive, you can see both artistic pieces – from delicate Song-dynasty teapots to flamboyant modern lamps – as well as lavatory bowls and spark-plug insulators.

The Yixing Caves

South and west of Yixing Town and Dingshan are delightful hills, woods, tea plantations and, below ground, several collections of **karst caves** that are worth seeing if you're in the area. All the caves can be reached by buses from Yixing Town – you'll have to ask around both bus stations – and are often connected to each other by private minibuses, so it's easy to spend a pleasant day trundling independently around the area. Alternatively, you can join a group tour from Yixing. Sturdy shoes and some form of waterproof protection against dripping stalactites are a good idea. The caves are all open daily until around 4.30pm and various entrance fees, up to ¥30, are charged.

The nearest and most interesting set of caves, **Zhanggong**, is just forty minutes by bus from Yixing, and only ten minutes north of Dingshan. It consists of 72 separate caves, connected on two levels by more than 1500 steps; you actually climb a hill, but on the inside. Although the stalactites, stalagmites and other rock formations are all named for their resemblance to exotic beasts or everyday objects, you'll need a powerful imagination to work out which is which. Legend has it that Zhang Daolin, the father of Chinese Taoism, and Zhang Guolao, one of the legendary Eight Immortals, both practised their theory here. The real highlight is the **Hall of the Sea Dragon King** where the rock soars upwards in strange contortions and emerges on to the green hillside far above – look up and you'll see an eerie patch of swirling, dripping mist.

A further fifteen minutes on the bus south of the Zhanggong caves takes you through tea plantations to the most recently discovered group, the **Linggu caves**, which feature an underground waterfall. Ancient human remains have been found here, along with Tang inscriptions, many supposedly left by Tang poet Lu Guimeng, who allegedly stumbled upon the cave when he was searching for the perfect tea leaves. The mouth of the cave has great views of Tai Hu, bamboo groves, tea fields, and lush, verdant hills.

The third group, **Shanjuan**, is the most popular cave site, located 25km southwest (an hour on the bus) from Yixing, about halfway on the road to Dingshan. The caves are set on three interconnecting levels, including the snail-shell-shaped upper cave and the more interesting lower Water Cave. From here a boat ferries you through subterranean passages formed by limestone dissolution, the boatman picking out highlights with his flashlight all the way to the exit, humorously named "Suddenly See the Light".

Zhenjiang

Northwest of Wuxi and east of Nanjing, **ZHENJIANG** isn't the most beautiful of cities but does offer three intriguing temples to explore, each perched on top of a hill from which there are some excellent vistas of the Yangzi River. Tourists flock to the temples on weekends, but at most other times, you'll feel blissfully free of the herds that characterize Suzhou and other tourist draws in the area.

For more than two thousand years, Zhenjiang has provided a safe harbour and a strong defensive position at the junction of two of the world's greatest trade routes, the **Yangzi River** and the **Grand Canal**, and protected on three sides by low hills. During the Three Kingdoms period, a Wu ruler built a walled city on this site as his capital; it grew rapidly, boosted over the centuries by the southern branch of the Grand Canal, and by proximity to the Ming capital at Nanjing. Marco Polo remarked on the richness of the local **silks** and gold fabrics, and these are still renowned, as are, less romantically, Zhenjiang

Zhenjiang

Zhenjiang	镇江	*zhènjiāng*
Beigu Shan	北固山	*běigù shān*
Dashikou	大市口	*dàshì kǒu*
Jiao Shan	焦山	*jiāo shān*
Jin Shan	金山	*jīn shān*
Accommodation and eating		
Daniang Shuijiao	大娘水饺	*dàniáng shuǐjiāo*
Great Wall	长城大酒店	*chángchéng dàjiǔdiàn*
Guoji	国际饭店	*guójì fàndiàn*
Jingkou	京口饭店	*jīngkǒu fàndiàn*
Yanchun Jiulou	宴春酒楼	*yànchūn jiǔlóu*
Zhenjiang Binguan	镇江宾馆	*zhènjiāng bīnguǎn*
Zhenjiang Dajiudian	镇江大酒店	*zhènjiāng dàjiǔdiàn*

vinegar and pickles. After the Opium Wars the British and French were granted **concessions** here, intriguing traces of which remain today around the site of the former British Consulate.

Now on the main Shanghai–Nanjing rail line, and still an important Yangzi anchorage, Zhenjiang is an outward-looking city whose prosperity remains assured, with yet more expansion on the way as a new **bridge** across the river – a cornerstone in Jiangsu's massive transportation development plans – creates further trade links with northern Jiangsu.

The City

Zhenjiang is a relatively easy place to get your bearings. Across the north flows the Yangzi; in the south, the rail line forms another barrier; and down through the middle, meandering approximately north–south east of the city centre, is the Grand Canal. The modern downtown area centres on **Dashikou**, the junction of Zhongshan Lu and Jiefang Lu, about 3km east of the train station, and 2km south of the Yangzi. The temples are all close to the riverbank, and can be

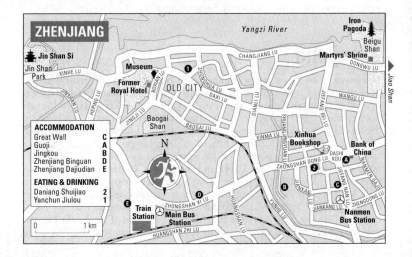

reached by city buses #2 or #4, both of which leave from the square in front of the train station.

The oldest section of town, due north of the train station and just south of the river, around Daxi Lu and Boxian Lu, is a fascinating area for a stroll. You can reach Daxi Lu on the #2 bus which runs here from the train station via Dashikou; get off just as the bus makes a sharp left turn. West along Daxi Lu is the atmospheric former **British Consulate** compound – part British colonial, part Qing-dynasty. Built in the 1890s, the buildings have been refurbished and a new **museum** has been built to house items that used to sit in the consulate. A few minutes' walk south from here brings you to another bizarrely improbable facade, the former **Royal Hotel**, with columns and caryatids on the outside, and a lobby from the 1920s. Disused now, it was until recently the *Mingdu* hotel and a desultory karaoke bar.

Jin Shan Park

In the far northwest of the city at the terminus of bus #2, **Jin Shan Si** is a temple scenically located in its own **park** (daily 6am–6pm; ¥32). At one time a small island in the Yangzi, Jin Shan has silted up over the years to create a low-lying peninsula, with a series of rectangular fish ponds overlooked by a small hill. The temple buildings wrap themselves dramatically around this hill behind a series of heavy yellow-ochre walls. Twisting stairways lead past them to the **Cishou Pagoda** (daily 8.30–6pm; ¥5), built more than 1400 years ago and renovated in 1900 at great expense to celebrate the Dowager Empress Cixi's 65th birthday. The top of this seven-tiered octagonal tower offers a superb view down to the jumbled temple roofs, and across the ponds to the river. The temple itself has recently been restored to something of its former glory and is packed with the usual unselfconscious mix of tourists and worshippers. From a canal in the park you can catch an imitation dragon boat (¥20) around the corner to the **First Spring Under Heaven** at the edge of a small lake.

Beigu Shan and Jiao Shan

Northeast of town and on the route of bus #4, **Beigu Shan** is a refreshing hilltop (daily 8am–5pm; ¥20), described 1400 years ago by an enthusiastic emperor as the "best hill in the world above a river". From the entrance, climb the stairs on the right, then turn left along the rampart to come to the lightning-damaged remains of the 900-year-old **Iron Pagoda** and, on top of the hill, the exquisite **Lingyun Ting** (Soaring Clouds Pavilion), where you can sit in the shade and enjoy the commanding views over the river. Immediately south of Beigu Shan is the modern **Martyrs' Shrine** for victims of the wars that brought communism to China.

Farther east, a few more stops along the bus #4 route, is the most interest-ing place in Zhenjiang, **Jiao Shan** (daily 7.15am–4.15pm; ¥30), still a genuine island, some 5km downstream from the city centre. From the terminus of bus #4, walk a little farther east to the ticket kiosk and small jetty where half-hourly boats take tourists out to the island (the ride is included in the entrance ticket). Alternatively, take the exhilarating **cable-car** ride there from just north of the boat dock (¥20 return), for great views of the Yangzi River on one side and of craggy cliffs rising straight up on the other.

Verdant, rural and lush with bamboo and pine, the island is a great place for just roaming around. For an overall view, climb up to the **Xijiang Lou**, a view-ing tower commanding a glorious stretch of the river and city beyond. Below are the remains of gun batteries used in turn against the British in 1842, the Japanese when they invaded in World War II, and the British again, when HMS *Amethyst* got trapped in the river during the Communist takeover in 1949.

Practicalities

Zhenjiang's **train station**, on Zhongshan Lu, is in the southwest of the city. From here, buses #2 and #4 run to Dashikou and then head north, while buses #10 and #12 run to Dashikou and turn south. Points of arrival by bus are harder to predict: some buses stop very close to the train station, others at the **Nanmen bus station** on Jiefang Nan Lu, 500m south of Dashikou. There are frequent minibuses to Nanjing from the train-station square, and the **main bus station** on the east side of the square is the main point for other bus departures. **Nanjing airport** has a daily bus service to Zhenjiang at 2pm, with the bus from Zhenjiang to the airport leaving 334 Zhongshan Dong Lu at 9am (¥55).

Most facilities are in the Dashikou area, including the **Bank of China** (daily 8am–noon & 2.30–5.30pm), just to the east on Zhongshan Lu, and the **post office** immediately to the north on Jiefang Bei Lu. There's an unhelpful **CITS** office in front of the Zhenjiang Bingguan.

Accommodation

Hotels in Zhenjiang aren't cheap. However, on weekdays and during the September–June off season, you should be able to negotiate a ten- to thirty-percent discount on your room, depending on how hard you bargain with the front desk.

Great Wall Hotel 59 Jiefang Lu ☎0511/5018999. South of Dashikou, this friendly place is signposted in English from the main road, and offers fairly basic double rooms. Convenient for the Nanmen bus station. ❻

Guoji 218 Jiefang Lu, at the corner of Zhongshan Dong Lu ☎0511/5021888, ℻5021777. Right in the city centre, this four-star hotel offers spacious doubles and attentive service. ❼

Jingkou 407 Zhongshan Dong Lu ☎0511/5224866, ℻5230056. A quiet, attractive complex centrally located down a small lane running south from Zhongshan Lu. From the train

station take bus #15; walk right through to the back for the reception. ❻

Zhenjiang Binguan 92 Zhongshan Xi Lu ☎0511/5233888 ext 511, ℻5231055. A 10min walk east of the station square, this is one of the most upmarket places in the city, a little heavy on the marble, with a couple of travel agents based in the lobby. ❼

Zhenjiang Dajiudian Zhongshan Xi Lu ☎0511/5236666, ℻5230130. A smart, modern place, conveniently located right in the train station square – it's to the left as you emerge from the station. ❻

Eating

The most well-known **restaurant** chain locally is *Yanchun Jiulou*, where you'll enjoy the little cold appetizers brought round on a trolley – including salads, stuffed buns and diced pork which melts in the mouth. There's one just north of the *Great Wall Hotel*, and another in an alley just north of Daxi Lu, a short way east of the former British Consulate and opposite a Bank of China. This area of the old town also contains numerous noodle and dumpling shops. One of the ever-reliable *Daniang Shuijiao* outlets can be found on Zhongshan Dong Lu, 500m west of Dashikou.

Yangzhou

YANGZHOU is a leafy and relaxing city straddling the Grand Canal north of the Yangzi, an hour by bus north of Zhenjiang and a couple of hours from Nanjing. Today its proud boast is of having produced ex-President Jiang Zemin, though its origins go back to around 500 BC when the Wu rulers had channels

Yangzhou

Yangzhou	扬州	yángzhōu
Daming Si	大明寺	dàmíng sì
Ershisi Qiao	二十四桥	èrshísì qiáo
He Yuan	何园	héyuán
Shi Kefa Memorial	史可法纪念馆	shǐkěfǎ jìniànguǎn
Shi Ta	石塔	shítǎ
Shou Xihu	瘦西湖	shòu xīhú
Tomb of Puhaddin	普哈丁墓	pǔhādīng mù
Wenfeng Ta	文峰塔	wénfēng tǎ
Wuting Qiao	五亭桥	wǔtíng qiáo
Xianhe Mosque	仙鹤寺	xiānhè sì
Accommodation and eating		
Dongyuan	东园饭店	dōngyuán fàndiàn
Fuchun Tea House	富春茶社	fùchūn cháshè
Grand Metropole	扬州京华大酒店	yángzhōu jīnghuá dàjiǔdiàn
Hongqiao	红桥宾馆	hóngqiáo bīnguǎn
Shita	石塔宾馆	shítǎ bīnguǎn
Xiyuan	西园饭店	xīyuán fàndiàn
Yangzhou Binguan	扬州宾馆	yángzhōu bīnguǎn

dug here, which were later incorporated into the Grand Canal. Thanks to its position on the Grand Canal and sandwiched between the Yangzi and the Huai rivers, Yangzhou rapidly developed into a prosperous city, aided by a monopoly of the lucrative **salt trade**. Under the Tang and later, many foreign merchants, including a community from Persia, lived and traded here, leaving behind a twelfth-century **mosque** and a much-quoted (though wholly unsubstantiated) tale that Marco Polo governed the city for three years. It was a city renowned too for its culture, its storytellers and oral traditions, with stories being handed down through the generations. As such, it frequently attracted the **imperial court** and its entourage, as well as artists and officials moving here in retirement, who endowed temples, created enclosed gardens and patronized local arts.

Despite the industrial belt which now stretches round the south and east of the city, there's still a faint sense of a cosmopolitan, cultured past here, evident in the **gardens**, in the Islamic relics and in the layout of roads, waterways and bridges in the city centre. The two main sights are the **Shou Xihu** and **Daming Si**, a lake and a temple which were part of Emperor Qianlong's regular tourist itinerary in the eighteenth century.

It's possible to visit Yangzhou on a day-trip from Nanjing or Zhenjiang, but note that the last bus back usually goes at around 7pm, and that day-trippers mob the place on weekends and holidays; you'll find things far less hectic if you visit on a weekday.

The City

There's a concentration of sights around the canal to the north and northwest of the city, where you'll find a snaking greenbelt that houses Shou Xihu and Daming Si. It makes sense to visit these two key attractions in conjunction, taking in lesser sights west or north of the centre on the way there or back. If you enter Shou Xihu at the southern end (served by tourist bus #1 and #2) and then exit through the northern end, you're halfway to Daming Si; you can pick up bus #1 from here for the remaining distance, or take a rickshaw.

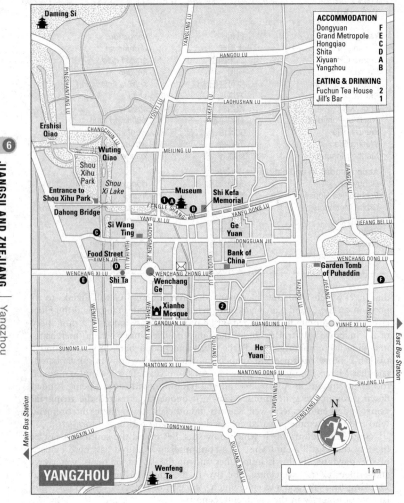

ACCOMMODATION

Dongyuan	F
Grand Metropole	E
Hongqiao	C
Shita	D
Xiyuan	A
Yangzhou	B

EATING & DRINKING

Fuchun Tea House	2
Jill's Bar	1

YANGZHOU

Main Bus Station

East Bus Station

0 — 1 km

The other way to get around both sights is by **tourist boat** – south of the Shou Xihu the canal runs east to Qianlong's old imperial barge landing-place, in front of what is now the *Xiyuan Hotel*. A jetty has been built here so that tourists can travel by mock dragon boats, complete with plush yellow furnishings, through the Shou Xihu and right up as far as Daming Si. The high prices make this only really practicable for large groups, however – reckon on several hundred yuan to rent a twenty-person boat for a couple of hours. Much of the rest of town can be explored on foot, though you'll need city buses for trips across town.

Shou Xihu and Daming Si

The **Shou Xihu**, which winds, snake-like, through an elongated park area (daily 7am–6pm; ¥50), literally translates as "Thin West Lake" – so named to recall the original West Lake at Hangzhou. In some respects it's a typical Chinese park, full of water and melancholy weeping willows, though it does also contain an array of interesting structures: a plain white **dagoba**, modelled after the one in Beihai in Beijing; the **Chui Tai** (Happiness Terrace), whose three moon gates each frame a different scene; and in particular the much-photographed **Wuting Qiao** (Five Pavilion Bridge), an eighteenth-century construction with massive triple-arched and yellow-tiled roofs.

If you walk about fifteen minutes west from the Wuting Qiao, you come to another bridge, the spectacular **Ershisi Qiao** (Twenty-four Bridge), its single hump so high and rounded as to form a virtual circle through which boats could pass. The bridge is so named because there are 24 archways in the design; the designer wanted his masterpiece to be appreciated 24 hours of the day, and in fact there used to be 24 stone bridges spanning the canals of Yangzhou. Near the bridge is a reproduction of Emperor Qianlong's fishing platform, today a favourite spot of photo-taking couples. Legend says that Qianlong's servants would dive into the canal and hook fish to the emperor's fishing line so that he, thinking the town had brought him good luck, would allocate its citizens more funding.

Daming Si

A kilometre or so north of Shou Xihu, and well worth an hour of your time, **Daming Si** (Temple of Great Light; daily 7.20am–6pm; ¥30) occupies a huge area on top of a hill. The temple, originally built in the fifth century, is experiencing a boom – much of what you see today has in fact been reconstructed after damage during the Taiping Uprising (see box, p.436), while the centrepiece, a **Memorial Hall** to honour the Chinese monk Jian Zhen, was only built in 1973. A profound scholar of the eighth century, Jian Zhen was invited to teach in Japan, only to find that on five successive occasions storms and misfortune drove him back to Chinese waters. Finally, on his sixth attempt, at the age of 66, he made it to Japan and sensibly decided against trying the return trip. Credited with having introduced *ritso* Buddhism to Japan, he is still much revered there, and a nine-storey Japanese-funded **pagoda** has been built here to replace a Song-dynasty structure that was razed by fire. There is a Buddhist **vegetarian restaurant** on the premises, though it caters more to the tourists than the monks.

Some way north of the temple itself are parks and gardens laid out in 1751 around a natural spring, the so-called **Fifth Spring under Heaven**. You can sample the waters, and the local tea, from a cool, breezy teahouse overlooking the water, where plump goldfish and carp glide past.

Downtown

Downtown Yangzhou is cut through the middle from north to south by **Guoqing Lu**, which, to the south, turns into Dujiang Lu. Running from east to west across Guoqing Lu are two or three of the main shopping streets.

Cross the canal immediately north of Yanfu Lu and walk a few minutes west to reach Yangzhou's **museum** (daily 8.30–11.30am & 2–5.30pm; ¥12). A delightful group of assorted old pavilions set in large grounds, this is one of China's more interesting provincial museums, featuring a 1000-year-old wooden boat recovered from the Grand Canal, as well as an extraordinary Han dynasty funeral suit made of five hundred pieces of jade, and two wooden tombs from the Han and Song dynasties. An antique market fills the front courtyards of the compound. Next to the museum, to the east, the **Shi Kefa Memorial** (daily 8.30–11.30am & 2.30–5.30pm; ¥10) is a temple devoted to the memory of a local hero who, in the last days of the Ming dynasty, gave his life resisting the advancing Qing armies. It was the victorious Qing who raised this memorial to him, in charming grounds full of flowers and plum trees, in recognition of his courage. West of the museum is a strip along the canal gearing up to become a tourist centre, with "traditional" architecture and souvenir shops, while in front, right on the canal itself, stands the **jetty** from where tourist boats run up to Shou Xihu and Daming Si.

West of the centre

The main surviving testament to the presence of Persian traders in the city in the Middle Ages is the small and austere **Xianhe (Crane) Mosque**, on the small turning to the east of Wenhe Lu; you may have to sign your name in the book before being admitted. The mosque's main feature is one wall covered entirely with Arabic script. The streets in this western quarter conceal several more survivors from different eras of history, scattered thinly in among the traffic and the modern shopping streets. One is the **Shi Ta**, a diminutive Tang-dynasty stone pagoda standing in the shade of a 1000-year-old ginkgo tree, on Wenchang Xi Lu. Also on this road, at the junction with Wenhe Lu, is the round Ming-dynasty **Wenchang Ge** (Flourishing Culture Pavilion), resembling a mini Temple of Heaven, and, one block north, there's the thirteenth-century **Si Wang Ting** (Four View Pavilion), a three-storey octagonal pavilion.

East and south of the centre

For more evidence of the early Muslim presence in Yangzhou, look to the east of the centre, just past the canal. From the west bank of the canal, or from the Jiefang Bridge, just to the north, you'll see a wooded hill and, behind it, a jumble of Muslim architecture. This rather sad, dusty relic from the most cosmopolitan era of China's history is actually the **Garden Tomb of Puhaddin** (or Bulhand-ing; daily 8am–5pm; ¥8), a descendant of the Prophet Mohammed. Puhaddin came to China in the thirteenth century, spent ten years in Yangzhou and adopted the city as his home, to the extent that he insisted on being buried here. His life is chronicled in paintings and artefacts in a small hall next door.

In an old, quiet part of town, just north of Nantong Dong Lu, is the exquisite **He Yuan** (daily 7.45am–5.45pm; ¥30), a tiny garden designed in the nineteenth century. A beautiful little place for a stroll on a sunny morning, it uses trees, shrubs and a raised walkway to give an ingenious illusion of variety and depth. Also here are a couple of charming **teahouses**.

Further south, on Wenfeng Lu, the conspicuous seven-storey **Wenfeng Ta** (daily 6.30am–5.30pm; ¥2) stands by a bend in the Grand Canal, in a small plot crammed with hollyhocks. Built in 1582, it was intended to bring luck to local candidates in the imperial examinations, though the main interest now is in walking up alongside the canal and wharves here for a view of small family boats queuing in vast jams, to be laden with anything from grain and bottled drinks to gravel and truck tyres.

Practicalities

The main **Yangzhou bus station** is about 6km southwest of the centre. If you're heading to Nanjing, you can buy a ticket inside the waiting hall at gate 13 for express buses leaving from gate 0. Buses arriving from the north and east may terminate at the **East station** on Yunhe Xi Lu to the east; bus #33 from the main station passes the Wenchang Pavilion on its way through the city centre, while bus #19 runs between the two stations.

Yangzhou has a relatively new **train station**, though the route is far less travelled than the Nanjing–Shanghai line – buses remain the most convenient way in and out of the city. The nearest airport is at Nanjing, with direct buses from the airport to Yangzhou (see p.422), and plane tickets available at major Yangzhou hotels. There's a **Bank of China** (8.30am–5pm) and a **post office** on Wenchang Zhong Lu. Various **travel agents** have their offices at the *Xiyuan* hotel.

Accommodation

Yangzhou is a rather expensive place to stay unless you can get a room in the *Hongqiao*, the guesthouse of Yangzhou Normal University, or want to stay east of the centre at the *Dongyuan*.

Dongyuan 79 Jiangdu Lu ☏0514/7233003, ℻7221705. Quiet, slightly institutional en-suite rooms in a nondescript area; bus #33 from the centre of town stops right outside. ❺

Grand Metropole 1 Wenchang Xi Lu ☏0514/7322888, ℻7368999, ⓦwww.gmhotel.com. The well-appointed rooms have views of the city, and standards of service are higher than most other places in Yangzhou. ❽

Hongqiao Yangzhou Normal University campus ☏0514/7184276. From the main bus station, take bus #3 to the corner of Yanfu Lu and Huaihai Lu. Walk north, then west and cross Dahong Bridge. Turn left after the bridge and walk 300m south to the university gate – the Hongqiao is the building slightly uphill to the right. The recently renovated

doubles here are among the best deals in town, and the quiet location can't be beaten. ❸

Shita 246 Wenchang Zhong Lu ☏0514/7801188, ℻7314125. Smart rooms and the central location pull in Chinese businessmen by the carload. Conveniently, it's on bus route #33 from the bus station. ❼

Xiyuan 1 Fengle Shang Jie ☏0514/7344888, ℻7233870, ⓦwww.xiyuan-hotel.com. In large grounds just north of the museum, this hotel has a wide range of rooms and is very convenient for the sights. ❼

Yangzhou Binguan 5 Fengle Shang Jie ☏0514/7805888, ℻7343599. An upmarket, high-rise tower located in the north of the city, next to the museum. ❻

Eating and drinking

Eating is a real pleasure in Yangzhou if you know where to look. The best-known restaurant in town is the *Fuchun Tea House*, down a small alley called Dexingqiao running east off Guoqing Lu. It's a bit hard to find, even with the sign suspended at the alley entrance, so look for the alley with hawkers selling knives of all sizes and uses. A plate of ten different kinds of dumplings here costs ¥20; other specialities include *doufu gansi* (dried shreds of tofu) and *qingshao xiaren* (fried shrimps). There are plenty of noodles and dumplings on offer in the area around Ganquan Lu, and every night until 2am street vendors set up a **food street** along Ximen Jie just off Huaihai Lu, offering everything from hotpot to skewered beef and puddings. The restaurant in the *Grand Metropole* is also worth trying for local **Huaiyang cuisine** – the best-known example of which, Yangzhou fried rice, is a staple on restaurant menus countrywide – as well as Cantonese fare.

There's a slither of **nightlife** by the canal near the *Xiyuan* and *Yangzhou Binguan*. Of the bars, *Jill's* is the best and the most foreigner-friendly.

Nanjing

NANJING, formerly known in the West as Nanking, is one of China's greatest cities. Its very name, "Southern Capital", stands as a direct foil to the "Northern Capital" of Beijing, and the city is still considered the rightful capital of China

Nanjing

Nanjing	南京	*nánjīng*
Bailuzhou	白鹭洲	*báilù zhōu*
Chaotian Gong	朝天宫	*cháotiān gōng*
City Wall	城市墙	*chéngshì qiáng*
Dujiang Jinianbei	渡江纪念碑	*dùjiāng jìniànbēi*
Fuzi Miao	夫子庙	*fūzǐ miào*
Gulou	鼓楼	*gǔlóu*
Jinghai Si	静海寺	*jìnghǎi sì*
Linggu Si	灵谷寺	*línggǔ sì*
Meiyuan Xincun	梅园新村	*méiyuán xīncūn*
Memorial to the Nanjing Massacre	南京大屠杀纪念馆	*nánjīngdàtúshā jìniànguǎn*
Ming Xiaoling	明孝陵	*míng xiàolíng*
Mochou Hu Park	莫愁湖公园	*mòchóuhú gōngyuán*
Nanjing Museum	南京博物馆	*nánjīng bówùguǎn*
Presidential Palace	总统府	*zǒngtǒng fǔ*
Qinhuai River	秦淮河	*qínhuái hé*
Qixia Si	栖霞寺	*qīxiá sì*
Shixiang Lu	石象路	*shíxiàng lù*
Taiping Heavenly Kingdom History Museum	太平天国历史博物馆	*tàipíngtiānguólishǐ bówùguǎn*
Tianchao Gong	天朝宫	*tiāncháo gōng*
Xinjiekou	新街口	*xīnjiēkǒu*
Xuanwu Hu Park	玄武湖公园	*xuánwǔhú gōngyuán*
Yangzi River Bridge	长江大桥	*chángjiāng dàqiáo*
Yuejiang Lou	阅江楼	*yuèjiāng lóu*
Yuhuatai Park	雨花台公园	*yǔhuātái gōngyuán*
Zhonghua Men	中华门	*zhōnghuá mén*
Zhongshan Ling	中山陵	*zhōngshān líng*
Zhongshan Men	中山门	*zhōngshān mén*
Zhongyang Men	中央门	*zhōngyāng mén*
Zijin Shan	紫金山	*zǐjīn shān*

by many Overseas Chinese, particularly those from Taiwan. Today, it's a prosperous city, benefiting both from its proximity to Shanghai and from its gateway position on the **Yangzi River**, which stretches away west deep into China's interior. With broad, tree-lined boulevards and balconied houses within Ming walls and gates, Nanjing is also one of the most attractive of the major Chinese cities, and although it has become rather an expensive place to visit, it offers a fairly cosmopolitan range of tourist facilities, as well as a wealth of historic sites that can easily fill several days' exploration.

Some history

Occupying a strategic site on the south bank of the Yangzi River in a beautiful setting of lakes, river, wooded hills and crumbling fortifications, Nanjing has had an important role from the earliest times, though not until 600 BC were there the beginnings of a walled city. By the time the Han empire broke up in 220 AD, Nanjing was the capital of half a dozen local dynasties, and when the Sui reunited China in 589, the building of the **Grand Canal** began considerably to increase the city's economic importance. Nanjing became renowned for its forges, foundries and weaving, especially for the veined **brocade** made

Accommodation

Central	中心大酒店	zhōngxīn dàjiǔdiàn
Daqiao	大桥饭店	dàqiáo fàndiàn
Grand Metro	古南都基店	gǔnán dūjī jiǔdiàn
Hongqiao	虹桥饭店	hóngqiáo fàndiàn
Jinling	金陵饭店	jīnlíng fàndiàn
Longpan	龙蟠饭店	lóngpān fàndiàn
Mandarin Garden	状元大酒店	zhuàngyuán dàjiǔdiàn
Nanjing University Xiyuan	南大西苑	nándà xīyuàn
Nanshan (Normal University)	师范大学南山宾馆	shīfàn dàxué nánshān bīnguǎn
Sheraton Kingsley	金丝利喜来登酒店	jīnsīlì xǐláidēng jiǔdiàn
Shuangmenlou	双门楼宾馆	shuāngménlóu bīnguǎn
Xihuamen	西华门饭店	xīhuámén fàndiàn
Xuanwu	玄武饭店	xuánwǔ fàndiàn
Yuehua	悦华大酒店	yuèhuá dàjiǔdiàn
Zhongshan	中山大厦	zhōngshān dàshà

Eating and drinking

Bella Napoli	贝拉那波利意大利餐厅	bèilā nàbōlì yìdàlì cāntīng
Blue Marlin	蓝枪鱼西餐厅	lánqiāngyú xīcāntīng
Daniang Shuijiao	大娘水饺	dàniáng shuǐjiǎo
Jiangsu	江苏饭店	jiāngsū fàndiàn
Jiaozi Wang	饺子王	jiǎozi wáng
Jinzhu	金竹居	jīnzhú jū
Lao Zhengxing	老正兴菜馆	lǎozhèngxīng càiguǎn
Muslim Restaurant	穆斯林餐厅	mùsīlín cāntīng
Red Balloon Bar	红色气球酒吧	hóngsè qìqiú jiǔbā
Scarlet's	乱世佳人	luànshì jiārén
Shanghai Tan	上海滩	shànghǎi tān
Shizi Qiao	狮子桥	shīzi qiáo
Skyways	云中食品店	yúnzhōng shípǐndiàn
Swede & Kraut	老外乐	lǎowàilè
Xiao Ren Ren	小任任饭店	xiǎorénrén fàndiàn

in noble houses and monasteries. During the Tang and Song periods, the city rivalled nearby Hangzhou as the wealthiest in the country, and in 1368 the first emperor of the Ming dynasty decided to establish Nanjing as the **capital** of all China.

Although Nanjing's claims to be the capital would be usurped by the heavily northern-based Qing dynasty, for centuries thereafter anti-authoritarian movements associated themselves with movements to restore the old capital. For eleven years in the mid-nineteenth century, the **Taiping rebels** (see box, p.436) set up the capital of their Kingdom of Heavenly Peace at Nanjing. The siege and final recapture of the city by the foreign-backed Qing armies in 1864 was one of the saddest and most dramatic events in China's history. After the Opium War, the **Treaty of Nanking** which ceded Hong Kong to Britain was signed here in 1841, and Nanjing itself also suffered the indignity of being a treaty port. Following the overthrow of the Qing dynasty in 1911, however, the city flowered again and became the provisional capital of the new Republic of China, with Sun Yatsen as its first president. Sun Yatsen's mausoleum, **Zhongshan Ling**, on the edge of modern Nanjing, is one of the great centres of pilgrimage of the Chinese.

In 1937, the name Nanjing became synonymous with one of the worst atrocities of World War II, after the so-called **Rape of Nanking**, in which invading Japanese soldiers butchered an estimated 300,000 civilians. Subsequently, Chiang Kaishek's government escaped the Japanese advance by moving west to Chongqing, though after Japan's surrender and Chiang's return, Nanjing briefly resumed its status as the official capital of China. Just four years later, however, in 1949, the victorious Communists decided to abandon Nanjing as capital altogether, choosing instead the ancient – and highly conservative – city of Beijing in which to base the country's first "modern" government. Nowadays capital of Jiangsu Province, Nanjing remains an important rail junction – a great 1960s bridge carries the Beijing–Shanghai line over the Yangzi – and a major river port for large ships.

Orientation

The city's broken and meandering Ming **walls** are still a useful means of orientation, and the main streets run across town between gates in the city wall. The big gate in the north, now marked by a huge traffic circle and massive flyovers, is **Zhongyang Men**. To the northeast of here, outside the city wall, is the **train station**, while inside the wall, running due south from Zhongyang Men, the city's main street (called Zhongyang Lu, then Zhongshan Lu) runs for 8km before emerging through the southern wall west of **Zhonghua Men**. En route, this street passes two of the city's major intersections, first crossing Beijing Lu in the **Gulou** area, before traversing Zhongshan Dong Lu at **Xinjiekou**, from where Zhongshan Dong Lu runs east to **Zhongshan Men**, the major gate in the eastern wall. South of Xinjiekou (a kilometre or two before Zhonghua Men) is another important commercial and tourist centre, recently fashionable, called **Fuzi Miao**. Outside the city wall, many of the historic sites are on **Zijin Shan** to the east, while fringing it to the northwest is the **Yangzi River**, crossed by the Yangzi River Bridge.

Arrival and city transport

Nanjing Lukou Airport lies literally in the middle of rice paddies 42km to the southeast of the city. It is connected to the city by frequent CAAC buses (¥25), which run two services, one terminating at Tianjin Lu Xinghan Building on Hanzhong Lu near Xinjiekou, and the other at the main CAAC office on Ruijin Lu, in the southeast of town. Buses also run direct to Yangzhou (3 daily, at noon, 2.30pm & 5.30pm; ¥60) and Zhenjiang (at 2.30pm; ¥55).

From the **main train station**, bus #1 travels south through the city, via Gulou, Xinjiekou and Fuzi Miao. There's a faint chance of your train terminating at the small **West train station** outside the city walls and near the Yangzi River; from here bus #16 goes to Gulou and Xinjiekou.

The largest and most frequently used **long-distance bus station** is in the north, at **Zhongyang Men**; as a general rule, this is used by buses coming from and departing to points north and east of Nanjing (Shanghai and Yangzhou among them). The remote **East station** to the east of the main train station is mainly used by buses to and from Yangzhou and Yixing. Leaving town, note that the only **bus tickets** on sale are for same- or next-day departures. There are no longer any passenger **ferries** up the Yangzi from Nanjing.

Although **taxis** are a very cheap and easy way to get around Nanjing, you may want to use the **city buses** as well. These make reasonably convenient connections, but are absurdly crowded at rush hours, even by Chinese standards.

A good **map** showing bus routes is pretty much indispensable – an English-language version can be bought at most large hotels and some tourist sights.

Accommodation

Hotels in Nanjing are almost uniformly on the expensive side, and many of them seem almost identical in terms of facilities and cost. Outside the summer months, you should be able to bargain to get a ten to twenty percent discount on rooms. For a cheap place to stay, the best option is university accommodation, with rooms as well as dorms available.

Hotels

Central 75 Zhongshan Lu, west side ☎025/84733888, ℻84733999. A 5min walk north of Xinjiekou and recently renovated, this is one of the most luxurious places in town. ❾

Daqiao 255 Jianning Lu, at the junction with Daqiao Nan Lu ☎025/88801544, ℻8809255. A friendly, if overpriced, place with singles and doubles, about 1km from the West train station. Bus #10 comes here from the train station or Zhongyang Men. ❻

Grand Metro Hotel 22-1 Xuanwumen ☎025/83280000, ℻83280111. A new, low-key hotel with neat, inviting rooms and an excellent location at Xuanwu Hu, and within walking distance of the Shizi Qiao food street. ❺

Hongqiao 202 Zhongshan Bei Lu, just north of Xinmofan Malu ☎025/83400888, ℻83420756. Bus #13 comes here from the train station. A pleasant hotel with very comfortable, spotless doubles. ❼

Jinling Xinjiekou Square ☎025/84711888, ℻84711666. A few steps west of Xinjiekou, this is one of the city's premier hotels, boasting satellite TV, a fitness centre, swimming pool, shops and a choice of restaurants. ❾

Mandarin Garden 9 Zhuang Yuan Jing ☎025/52202555, ℻52201876. A stylish place to stay, with hundreds of rooms and five-star amenities. It's right in the heart of lively Fuzi Miao, on a small lane facing the southern end of Taiping Lu. ❾

Sheraton Kingsley 185 Hanzhong Lu, two blocks west of Xinjiekou ☎025/86668888, ℻86504293, ⓦwww.sheraton.com/nanjing. As plush and luxurious as its sister hotels all over the world. Doubles from ¥1660. ❾

Shuangmenlou 185 Huju Bei Lu, near the intersection with Zhongshan Bei Lu ☎025/58800888

ext 80, ℻58826298. Surrounded by large gardens, this is a perfectly decent place popular with tour groups, though a little far from the interesting parts of town. ❼

Xihuamen 202 Longpan Zhong Lu ☎025/84596221. About 2km east of Xinjiekou. Quite an attractive place set in gardens, and with perfectly decent rooms. ❻

Xuanwu 193 Zhongyang Lu, just north of Hunan Lu ☎025/83358888 ext 10, ℻83369800. A huge place with good views over Xuanwu Hu Park, this has pretentions to being a luxury hotel, and almost makes it. ❾

Zhongshan 200 Zhongshan Lu, at the corner of Zhujiang Lu, midway between Gulou and Xinjiekou ☎025/83361888, ℻83377228. Rooms here are spacious and elegantly furnished, and there's a disco and a travel agency on the premises. ❽

University rooms

Nanjing University Xiyuan Shanghai Lu ☎025/83593589, ℻83594699. Take bus #13 from the train station to Beijing Lu, then it's a short walk south; you'll see the high-rise foreign students' residence building on your left, just down Jinying Jie, a small lane heading east. Excellent two-bed rooms with or without attached bath. ❹

Nanshan 122 Ninghai Lu, ☎025/3716440, ℻3738174. From Beijing Lu (served by bus #13 from the train station), walk south down Shanghai Lu, then cut west down one of the small alleys to Ninghai Lu. Enter the Nanjing Normal University campus through the imposing gate and go straight ahead to the grassy bowl, then bear left up a slope; the *Nanshan* is at the top. A relaxing place with pleasant rooms but no dorms. It's sometimes full (particularly in summer), so book in advance (the telephone operators speak English). ❸

The City

Nanjing is huge, and a thorough exploration of all its sights would take several days. Among the three major **downtown** focal points, Xinjiekou and Fuzi

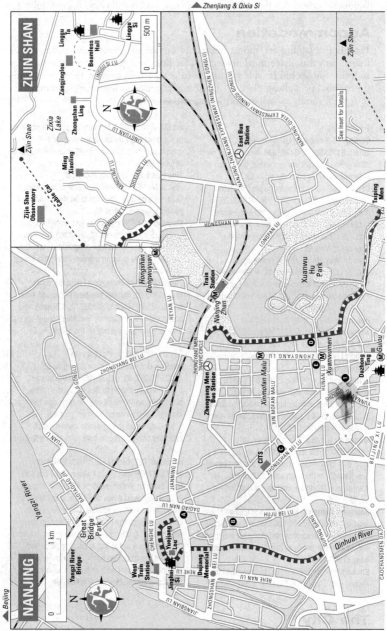

ZIJIN SHAN

▲ Zhenjiang & Qixia Si

Linggu Si
Linggu Ta
Beamless Hall
Linggu

Zangjinglou

Zhongshan Ling

Zixia Lake

Ming Xiaoling

Zijin Shan Observatory

Cable Car

0 — 500 m

LINGGU SI LU

SHIXIANG LU

LINGYUAN LU

MINGLING LU

TAIPINGMEN LU

N

NANJING

Beijing ▲

Yangzi River

Great Bridge Park

Yangzi River Bridge

West Train Station

Jinghai Si

Yuejiang Lou

Dujiang Memorial

0 — 1 km

N

JIANGBIAN LU

ZHONGSHAN LU

REHE LU

REHE NAN LU

CHENGHE LU

YUAN LU

SIGU GONG LU

ZHONGYANG BEI LU

JIANNING LU

DADAO NAN LU

HEYAN LU

Hongshan Dongwuyuan

Zhongyang Men Traffic Circle

Zhongyang Men Bus Station

Train Station

Nanjing Zhan Ⓜ

Ⓜ

Hongshan Lu

HONGSHAN LU

LONGPAN LU

Xuanwu Hu Park

ZHONGYANG MEN

HUNAN LU

Xinmofan Malu

XIN MOFAN MALU

ZHONGSHAN BEI LU

ZHONGYANG LU

ZHONGSHAN DONGLU

CITS Ⓒ

HUJU BEI LU

GUFU GANG

Qinhuai River

CAOCHANGMEN DAJIE

BEIJING XI LU

YUNNAN LU

Xuanwumen Ⓜ Ⓓ Ⓔ

Dazhong Ting

Gulou Ⓜ

Taiping Men

NANJING-QIXIA EXPRESSWAY (NINGZHEN GONGLU)

NANJING-ZHENJIANG EXPRESSWAY (NINGZHEN GONGLU)

East Bus Station

See Inset for Details

Zijin Shan ●

▲ Zijin Shan

Ⓐ Ⓑ Ⓒ Ⓓ Ⓔ ①

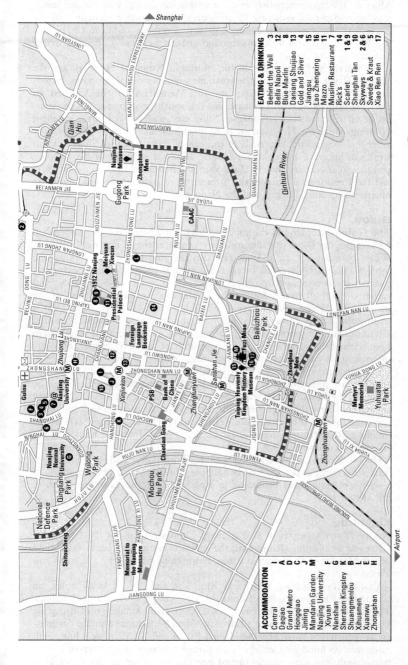

Miao are the most interesting areas for simply wandering, with historic buildings, pedestrianized shopping streets, canals, some good restaurants and the interesting Museum of the Taiping Uprising. A number of bus routes, including #1, #16, #26 and #33, pass through or near these two districts as well as Gulou.

The **north** of the city takes in the enormous **Xuanwu Hu Park** and the **Yangzi River** area, while to the **west** are a number of smaller parks, including the Ming **Chaotian Gong** and the **Memorial to the Victims of the Nanjing Massacre**. The **east** and the **south** contain some of the best-preserved relics of Nanjing's mighty Ming **city wall**, as well as the excellent **Nanjing Museum**. However, the most interesting area of all for tourists is the green hill beyond the city walls to the east of the city, **Zijin Shan**, with its wealth of historical and cultural relics. If you only have a day or two to spare, you should at least try and see Zijin Shan, the Nanjing Museum, the city wall and the **Presidential Palace**, the former seat of government under both the nineteenth-century Taipings and the Nationalists.

Gulou

The **Gulou** area, around the junction between Zhongyang Lu, Zhongshan Lu and Beijing Lu, is the administrative centre in the heart of old Nanjing. When Nanjing became a Treaty Port in the mid-nineteenth century the foreign consulates were all based here, though today it comprises mostly traffic jams overlooked by offices. There are just a couple of relics from earlier times, both rather lost in the bustle. One, immediately west of the main traffic circle, is the 600-year-old Gulou itself (daily 8am–5pm; ¥5), a small, solid **drum tower** on a grassy mound in the road, entered through a traditional-style gateway. Historically, a drum used to call the watch here seven times a day, and sound warnings at times of danger; now the interior holds exhibits of amateur paintings, while the tower itself has been semi-converted into a teahouse. A ghastly legend surrounds the fourteenth-century bell sitting outside – it's said that the emperor ordered the bell be fused by the blood of a virgin. The two daughters of the city's blacksmith apparently threw themselves into the furnace so that their father could obey the emperor and thus escape the death penalty. The large stone stele in the middle of the teahouse commemorates the reign of Emperor Kangxi in the seventeenth century.

The other sight by Gulou is the **Dazhong Ting** (Great Bell Pavilion), immediately northeast of the junction behind the China Telecom building, sitting in a well-kept garden and also home to a pleasant teahouse. Enter just south of the *McDonald's*.

Xinjiekou

Nearly 2km due south of Gulou along Zhongshan Lu lies the geographical centre of Nanjing, **Xinjiekou**, the streets teeming with banks, hotels and department stores. At its heart is a huge traffic circle adorned by a statue of Sun Yatsen.

About fifteen minutes' walk from Xinjiekou and a short block north, on Changjiang Lu (running into Hanfu Jie), are a couple of fascinating buildings. The first of these is an otherwise obscure government building on Changjiang Lu, the **Presidential Palace** (daily 8am–5pm; ¥30), located in the Suzhou-esque garden, Xu Yuan. The Presidential Palace and Xu Yuan were both built more than six hundred years ago as the private residence and gardens of a Ming prince, and were subsequently turned into the seat of the provincial governor under the Qing. In 1853 the building was seized by the armies of the Taiping Heavenly Kingdom and converted into the headquarters of Taiping leader Hong Xiuquan. Later, after the overthrow of the Qing, it became the Guomindang government's Presidential Palace. It was from here, in the early decades of the twentieth century, that first Sun Yatsen and later Chiang Kaishek governed China. Visiting the palace today, you'll see exhibitions on the Taiping Uprising and the life and times of Sun and Chiang.

A short walk east is the **Meiyuan Xincun** (daily 8am–5pm; ¥5), the former office of the Chinese Communist Party, headed by Zhou Enlai, who was based here during the time of the Guomindang government. The Communists and the Guomindang held a failed series of peace talks here in 1946 and 1947, which soon thereafter broke down into civil war. Now a museum, it's worth a visit only to observe the bitterly anti-GMD slant of the explanations (most of which are in English). There are one or two fascinating photos, including a little-known snap of Chiang Kaishek and Mao Zedong standing chatting together.

In the other direction from Xinjiekou on Jianye Lu (bus route #4 from Fuzi Miao) is the former Ming palace, the **Chaotian Gong**, now containing the tiny **Municipal Museum** (daily 8am–5pm; ¥30), which contains a few excellent bronzes. Built in 1384, the Chaotian Gong was used by nobles to worship their ancestors, as well as for audiences with the emperor – hence the name Chaotian, meaning Worshipping Heaven. Later it became a seat of learning and a temple to Confucius. The large square that houses the palace, bounded by a high vermilion wall on one side and a gateway protected by tigers on the other, is supposedly the site of the ancient Ye Cheng (Foundry City), built in the fifth century BC. During the Han dynasty, the square also served as a meeting place where peasants could gather to offer sacrifices to the heavens or ask for a fruitful harvest. Antiques, real and fake, are for sale in the market in the front courtyard.

Fuzi Miao

Two kilometres south of Xinjiekou, near the terminus of bus #1, is the Fuzi Miao (Temple of Confucius) area, which begins south of Jiankang Lu and harbours a noisy welter of street vendors, boutiques, arcades and restaurants. On a hot day, nothing beats slurping on a *lüdou shatou*, a drink made of green beans with shaved ice (¥3), sold by the street-side stalls.

The central **Temple of Confucius** (daily 8am–9.30pm; ¥15) itself resembles a theme park inside, complete with mannequins in fancy dress. The temple is hardly worth bothering about, but there is an attractive waterfront area along the canal here (where the Tang poet Liu Yuxi composed his most famous poem, *Wuyi Lane*), along which you can pick up **leisure boats** (electric ¥20, paddle ¥10; 30min) that trundle south to Zhonghua Men. Cross the canal in front of the temple, and a short walk southeast will bring you to a small park, **Bailuzhou** (Egret Isle). This ancient corner of the city remained the Chinese quarter after the arrival of the Manchu Qing dynasty in the seventeenth century, and the area is still full of traditional houses.

Ten minutes' walk west of the Temple of Confucius and right on the small Zhanyuan Lu, just east of Zhonghua Lu, is the **Taiping Heavenly Kingdom History Museum** (daily 8am–4.30pm; ¥10), well worth a visit. The sad but fascinating story of the Taiping Uprising is told here in pictures and relics, with English captions. The building itself was the residence of Xu Da, a Ming prince, and became the home of one of the rebel generals during the uprising.

The Taiping Uprising

One of the consequences of the weakness of the Qing dynasty in the nineteenth century was the extraordinary **Taiping Uprising**, an event that would lead to the slaughter of millions, and which has been described as the most colossal civil war in the history of the world. The Taipings were led by **Hong Xiuquan**, failed civil-service candidate and Christian evangelist, who, following a fever, declared himself to be the younger brother of Jesus Christ. In 1851, he assembled twenty thousand armed followers at **Jintian village**, near Guiping in Guangxi Province, and established the **Taiping Tianguo**, or Kingdom of Heavenly Peace. This militia routed the local Manchu forces, and by the following year were sweeping up through Hunan into central China. They **captured Nanjing** in 1853, but though the kingdom survived another eleven years, this was its last achievement. Poorly planned expeditions failed to take Beijing or win over western China, and Hong's leadership – originally based on the enfranchisement of the peasantry and the outlawing of opium, alcohol and sexual discrimination – devolved into paranoia and fanaticism. After a gigantic struggle, **Qing forces** finally managed to unseat the Taipings when Western governments sent in assistance, most notably in the person of Queen Victoria's personal favourite, Charles "Chinese" Gordon.

Despite the rebellion's ultimately disastrous failure and its overtly Christian message, the whole episode is seen as a precursor to the arrival of communism in China. Indeed, in its fanatical rejection of Confucianism and the incredible damage it wrought on buildings and sites of historic value, it finds curious echoes in Mao Zedong's Cultural Revolution.

Zhonghua Men and Yuhuatai Park

Zhonghua Men in the far south is now bereft of its wall and isolated in the middle of a traffic island, just inside the river moat on the bus #16 route from Xinjiekou and Gulou. This colossal gate actually comprises four gates, one inside another, and its seven enclosures were designed to hold three thousand men in case of enemy attack, making it one of the biggest of its kind in China. Today you can walk through the central archway and climb up two levels, passing arched recesses which are used for displays and snack stalls, and are beautifully cool in summer. Up above, there's a tremendous view of the gates with the city spread out beyond.

The road south, across the Qinhuai River, between Zhonghua Men and Yuhuatai Park, is an interesting stretch lined with two-storey wooden-fronted houses, many with balconies above, while below are small shops and workshops. The all-purpose trees lining the pavement provide shade as well as room to hang birdcages, pot plants and laundry. Just beyond, the road reaches a small hill, now a park known as **Yuhuatai** (daily 6am–6.45pm; ¥25). In legend it was here that a fifth-century Buddhist monk delivered sermons so moving that flowers rained down from the sky upon him. You still see Chinese tourists grubbing around here for the multicoloured pebbles called *yuhuashi* (literally rain-flower stones), associated with the legend. Sadly, however, the hill also has other very much less pleasant connotations. After 1927 it was used as an execution ground, and the Guomindang is said to have murdered vast numbers of people here. The spot is now marked by a **Martyrs' Memorial**, a colossal composite of nine thirty-metre-high figures, worth seeing as a prime example of gigantic Chinese Socialist Realism. The park itself is pleasantly laid out on a slope thickly forested with pine trees. You can climb the four-storey pagoda on the hillock behind the memorial for excellent views of Nanjing.

Around the Yangzi River

The far northwest of town in the area of the **Yangzi River** offers a modicum of interest. The **Nanjing Treaty Museum**, located in **Jinghai Si** (daily 8am–4.30pm; ¥6), lies very near the West train station off Rehe Lu. It was here in this temple that the British and Chinese negotiated the first of the many unequal treaties in the wake of the Opium War in 1843 (the treaty was later signed on a British naval ship in Nanjing harbour). Unfortunately, the museum's detailed exposition of fractious Sino–British relations throughout the nineteenth and twentieth centuries is in Chinese only, but the temple is a very pleasant place to stroll around nonetheless. It was originally built in the Ming Dynasty by Emperor Chengzu to honour the Chinese Muslim naval hero **Zhenghe**, who led the Chinese fleet on exploratory voyages to East Africa and the Persian Gulf; you'll see his name commemorated throughout the city, with some monuments built for the six-hundredth anniversary of his first voyage, marked in 2005.

Dominating the hilltop above Jinghai Si is **Yuejiang Lou** (daily 8am–5pm; ¥30), created in 2001 as a tourist version of a structure which Zhu Yuanzhang, founder of the Ming dynasty, ordered built to celebrate a key battle he won in the locality. His tower was never actually built, and the modern realization isn't worth the entry fee, though it does have excellent views of the Yangzi.

The streets around Jinghai Si, the West train station (bus #16 from Gulou and Xinjiekou) and the port, just beyond the city wall, are quite atmospheric and a good place to wander, with their crumbling alleys and smelly fish markets. A huge stone monument, **Dujiang Jinianbei**, marks the junction between Rehe Lu and Zhongshan Bei Lu; it was erected in memory of the crossing of the river from the north and the capture of Nanjing by the Communists in 1949.

If you're in this area you should definitely take a look at the 1500-metre-long **double-decker bridge** over the Yangzi, still a source of great pride to the Chinese who built it under their own steam after the Russians pulled out in 1960. Before the bridge was built, it took an hour and a half to ferry trains and road vehicles across the river. For a great view of the structure and the banks of the Yangzi, head for **Great Bridge Park** (daily 7am–4.30pm) on the eastern bank; you can ride in an elevator up to a raised platform above the upper (road) deck of the bridge, for ¥4. Bus #15 heads to the park from Zhongyang Men and Gulou.

Wulong and Mochou Hu parks and the Nanjing Massacre memorial

The west and southwest of the city hold a few minor sights and one major attraction. Arguably the best of the small parks here is the tiny **Wulong Park** off Guangzhou Lu (daily 7am–9pm; ¥4), often full of old musicians who gather to sing opera and play traditional instruments. Farther south, just across the narrow Qinhuai River, lies the entrance to **Mochou Hu Park** (daily 5.30am–10pm; ¥10), which is only worth the rather steep entrance fee during weekdays – at weekends, it's invaded by hordes of loud schoolchildren. An open-air stage juts out into the lake here, with a substantial teahouse behind. Among the clutch of pavilions and walkways is the **Square Pavilion**, with a statue of the legendary maiden, Mochou, after whom the lake is named: her name means "sorrow-free" because her sweet singing could soothe away all unhappiness. Ming emperor Zhu Yuanzhang once played a pivotal game of chess with his first general in the **Winning Chess Building**, next to the Square Pavilion.

West of the park is the must-see **Memorial to the Nanjing Massacre** (Tues–Sun 8.30am–4.30pm; free). This grim, gravelly garden includes a gruesome display of victims' skulls and bones, half-buried in the dirt, as

Nanjing's city walls

Though Nanjing was walled as many as 2500 years ago, the present **city wall** is basically the work of the first Ming emperor, who extended and strengthened the earlier walls in 1369–73. His wall, built of brick and more than 32km long, followed the contours of the country, skirting Xuanwu Hu in the north, fringing Xijin Shan in the east, and tracing the Qinhuai River (which doubled as a moat) to the west and south. The wall was mainly paid for by rich families resettled here by the emperor: one third of it was "donated" by a single native of Wuxiang in Zhejiang Province. Its construction employed 200,000 conscripts, who ensured that the bricks were all the same size and specification, each one bearing the names of the workman and overseer. They were held together, to an average height of 12m and a thickness of 7m, by a mixture of lime and glutinous rice paste.

The original structure, of red rock in places, is still plainly visible along a three-hundred-metre section of the wall at the so-called **Shitoucheng**, in the west of the city between Caochangmen Dajie and Fenghuang Jie. You can see it from bus #18, which runs outside the walls between Xinjiekou and the West train station.

well as a clearly labelled (in English) photographic account of the incredible sufferings endured by the Chinese at the hands of the Japanese army during World War II. One display includes contrite letters written by Japanese schoolchildren.

Xuanwu Hu Park

North of the centre, to the east of Zhongyang Lu and south of the train station, the enormous **Xuanwu Hu Park** (daily 5am–9pm; ¥20) comprises mostly water, with hills on three sides and the city wall skirting the western shore. Formerly a resort for the imperial family and once the site of a naval inspection by Song emperor Xiaowu, it became a park in 1911 and is a pleasant place to stroll and mingle with the locals who come here en masse at weekends. The lake contains five small **islets** linked by causeways and bridges, with restaurants, teahouses, pavilions, rowing boats, paddle boats, places to swim, an open-air theatre and a zoo. The southern end of the park contains one of the better-preserved reaches of the city wall. Xuanwu Gate, on Zhongyang Lu about 1km north of Gulou (bus #1), is the most convenient way to enter the park.

The Nanjing Museum and Zhongshan Men

On Zhongshan Dong Lu about 3km east of Xinjiekou (buses #5 and #9 from Xinjiekou; #20 from Gulou), the huge **Nanjing Museum** (daily 9am–4pm; ¥20) is one of the best provincial museums in China, especially in terms of clarity of explanations – nearly everything is labelled in English. Its highlights include some superb examples of silk-embroidered sedan chairs and several heavy cast bronzes, dating from as early as the Western Zhou (1100–771 BC). The jade and lacquerwork sections, as well as the model Fujian trading ships, are also well worth seeing.

A short walk east of the museum is **Zhongshan Men**, the easternmost gate of the ancient city walls. You can climb up to the top of the wall here, and walk along a little way to the north before the structure crumbles into a small lake, Qian Hu. It's surprisingly spacious and peaceful on the top and affords excellent views. In the morning, you can watch many of Nanjing's elders doing their daily exercises on the top of the wall.

Zijin Shan

Not far outside Zhongshan Men is **Zijin Shan** (Purple Gold Mountain), named after the colour of its rocks. Traditionally, the area has been a cool and shady spot to escape the furnace heat of Nanjing's summer, with beautiful fragrant woods and stretches of long grass, but also here are the three most visited sites in Nanjing. Of these, the centrepiece, right in the middle of the hill, is **Zhongshan Ling**, the magnificent mausoleum of China's first president, Sun Yatsen. To the east of Zhongshan Ling is the **Linggu Si** complex, and to the west are the ancient **Ming Xiaoling**, tombs of the Ming emperors who ruled China from Nanjing.

Visiting the three main sites on Zijin Shan can easily take a full day. Bus #9 goes to Zhongshan Ling via Linggu Si from Xinjiekou, while bus #20 heads to Ming Xiaoling from Gulou. Private minibuses and a host of private operators also make the trek from the train station square. Perhaps the best way to visit all three without backtracking is to catch a bus from town to either Ming Xiaoling or Linggu Si, and then walk to the other two sites. Various half-day **bus tours** are also available from town; ask at any travel service or upmarket hotel. If you're interested in an overview of the whole mountain, you can ride the **cable car** to the peak from a station about 1km east of Taiping Men, the gate by the southern end of Xuanwu Hu Park (one-way ¥25, return ¥45).

Linggu Si

Starting from the eastern side of the hill, farthest from the city, the first if least interesting sight on Zijin Shan is the collection of buildings around **Linggu Si** (daily 8am–5pm; ¥15 entry to the site). If you arrive here by bus, the main building in front of you is the so-called **Beamless Hall**. Completed in 1381, and much restored since, it's unusual for its large size and particularly for its self-supporting brick arch construction, with five columns instead of a central beam. The hall was used to store Buddhist sutras before the Taiping rebels made it a fortress; now it's an exhibition hall.

A couple of minutes' walk southeast from the Beamless Hall is the Linggu Si itself, a very much smaller and much restored version of its original self – and still a thoroughly active temple, attended by monks in yellow robes. North of the hall stands a small pavilion surrounded by beautiful cypresses and pines, and north of this again is the **Linggu Ta**, an octagonal, nine-storey, sixty-metre-high pagoda, dating back to the 1930s and built, rather extraordinarily, as a monument to Guomindang members killed in the fighting against insurgent Communists in 1926–27. It's well worth climbing up for the views over the surrounding countryside.

Although the Linggu buildings and Zhongshan Ling are connected by a shuttle bus, there's also a delightful and fairly clear footpath through the wood between the two, leading northwest from the Linggu buildings. On the way, you'll pass one or two more buildings, including the **Zangjinglou** (Buddhist Library) at the top of a grand stairway, which now houses the rather dull **Sun Yatsen Museum**, a collection of pictures with explanations in Chinese.

Zhongshan Ling

Dr Sun Yatsen, the first president of post-imperial China and the only hero revered by Chinese jointly on both sides of the Taiwan Straits, is, if anything, growing in status as China gropes towards a post-communist future and closer relations with Taiwan. This is reflected in the incredible pulling power of the former leader's mausoleum, the **Zhongshan Ling** (daily 6.30am–6.30pm; ¥40), which, with its famous marble stairway soaring up the green hillside, is one of the most popular sites in the country for Chinese tourists. Walking up the steps is something every tourist to Nanjing has to do once, if nothing else for the great views back down the stairs and across the misty, rolling hills to the south.

An imposing structure of white granite and deep blue tiles (the Nationalist colours), set off by the dark green pine trees, the mausoleum was completed in 1929, four years after Sun Yatsen's death. From the large bronze statue at the bottom, 392 marble steps lead up to the Memorial Hall, dominated by a five-metre-tall seated white marble figure of the great man himself. Beyond the marble figure is the burial chamber with another marble effigy lying on the stone coffin, from where, according to unsubstantiated rumours, the bones were removed to Taiwan by fleeing Guomindang leaders in 1949. The Guomindang ideals – Nationalism, Democracy and People's Livelihood – are carved above the entrance to the burial chamber in gold on black marble.

Ming Xiaoling

A walk of half an hour or so along the road west from Zhongshan Ling brings you to the **Ming Xiaoling** (daily 8am–5.30pm; ¥50), the burial place of Zhu Yuanzhang, founder of the Ming dynasty and the only one of its fourteen emperors to be buried at Nanjing (his thirteen successors are all buried in Beijing; see p.146). So colossal was the task of moving earth and erecting the stone walls that it took two years and a hundred thousand soldiers and conscripts to complete the tomb in 1383. Although the site was originally far larger than the Ming tombs near Beijing, its halls and pavilions, and 22-kilometre-long enclosing vermilion wall, were mostly destroyed by the Taipings. Today what remains is a walled collection of beautiful trees, stone bridges and dilapidated gates leading to the lonely wooded mound at the back containing the (as yet unexcavated) burial site of the emperor and his wife, as well as the fifty courtiers and maids of honour who were buried alive to keep them company.

The Ming Xiaoling actually comprises two parts, the tomb itself and the approach to the tomb, known as Shandao (Sacred Way) or, more commonly, **Shixiang Lu** (Stone Statue Road; daily 8am–6.30pm; ¥10) – which leads to the tomb at an oblique angle as a means of deterring evil spirits, who can only travel in straight lines. It's a strange and magical place to walk through, the road lined with twelve charming pairs of stone animals – including lions, elephants and camels – and four pairs of officials, each statue being carved from a single block of stone. The pairs of animals here are grouped together on a central grass verge, with the road passing either side, while the officials stand among the trees farther off. Most people visit the tomb first and the approach afterwards, simply because the road from Zhongshan Ling arrives immediately outside the tomb entrance. To reach the Sacred Way from the tomb entrance, follow the road right (with the tomb behind you) and then round to the left for about fifteen minutes.

Next to Ming Xiaoling is the entrance to **Zixia Hu** (daily 7am–6pm; ¥10), a small lake whose wooded surroundings are perfect for a comfortable stroll at any time of year. In summer, the lake is open for swimming, although you should avoid the weekends when the place is full of Nanjing residents escaping the heat of the city.

One more sight here is the **Zijin Shan Observatory** (¥15), built in 1929 high on one of the three peaks where the Taipings formerly had a stronghold. For fresh air and good views of Nanjing, try to find a minibus heading this way.

Eating

Nanjing has a wide selection of local, regional Chinese and foreign foods, often at much more reasonable prices than their counterparts in nearby Shanghai. It's an especially great place to sample **Jiangsu cuisine**, the best areas for which are north of Gulou along Zhongyang Lu and northwest along Zhongshan Bei Lu.

The presence of a heavy contingent of foreign students in the city, as well as a growing population of expatriate and home-grown business people, ensures a scattering of highly **Westernized restaurants and bars**, which are not necessarily expensive. There are, in particular, a number of places around the *Nanjing University Xiyuan* that cater to Western palates. Xinjiekou and Fuzi Miao are generally good districts to browse for restaurants, but for a staggering variety of Asian fare – including just about every kind of Chinese cuisine, plus Indian, Japanese and Thai – head for the constellation of restaurants at the pedestrianized **Shizi Qiao**, off Hunan Lu to the west of Xuanwu Hu Park.

Restaurants

Behind the Wall 150 Shanghai Lu. Head a few metres uphill along the alley here, called Nan Xiu Cun, and go up the nondescript staircase on the left, which leads to the patio entrance. Great Mexican-style food, especially the quesadillas and enchiladas. In decent weather, the patio is perfect for quiet lunches and livelier evening barbecues.

Bella Napoli 75 Zhongshan Dong Lu, just east from Xinjiekou. Good if slightly overpriced Italian food; the pizzas are a better bet than the pasta.

Daniang Shuijiao Under the Xinjiekou Department Store, and reached from the pavement facing the traffic circle, this popular chain serves up more than forty varieties of cheap and filling *shuijiao*, most for under ¥5 each.

Jiangsu 26 Jiankang Lu, just east of Zhonghua Lu. One of the most upmarket places to try Jiangsu food – brine duck is a speciality.

Lao Zhengxing 119 Gongyuan Jie, near Fuzi Miao. A favourite of GMD officials in the 1930s, this is a lively place with interesting local dishes, backing onto the river.

Muslim Restaurant Qingwu Lu, near Hankou Xi Lu and the Normal University front gate. Cheap,

filling Xinjiang-style *lamian* (pulled noodles) at this student favourite.

Shanghai Tan On a small alley directly behind the *Central Hotel*, off Guanjia Qiao ☎025/84700010. Excellent Shanghainese cuisine with the odd Jiangsu dish (notably *yanshui ya*) thrown in. The seafood is especially good. Very popular with locals.

Skyways Bakery & Deli 3–6 Hankou Xi Lu, west off Shanghai Lu. The best deli sandwiches in China are served here, though the range of fillings isn't vast: they bake their own baguettes, ciabatta and cookies, and have a caseful of handmade confections and cakes. There's a branch just west of Taiping Men. Daily 9am–9.30pm.

Swede & Kraut 14 Nan Xiu Cun, off Shanghai Lu ☎025/86638798. Sharing management with *Skyways*, this does by far the best Western food in the city, and isn't too pricey either. The pasta and bread are all home-made. The lasagna and fettucini especially are scrumptious, and the steaks are great, too.

Xiao Ren Ren 97 Gongyuan Jie, Fuzi Miao. Friendly place designed in the style of a traditional teahouse, with musicians serenading patrons. You can try a smorgasbord of local delicacies for just ¥40.

Drinking and entertainment

Nanjing **nightlife** is nowhere near as varied as Shanghai's, though there are a few bars and discos that see a regular mix of foreigners and Chinese. The bars are generally pretentious and stiff – for a laid-back drink it's better to hang out at *Behind the Wall*. Clubs are inexpensive for foreigners (for whom cover charges are generally waived) and beers can be as cheap as ¥10 per bottle.

Nanjing's cultural life is sadly lagging far behind Shanghai's, though your visit might coincide with infrequent acrobatics or Chinese opera performances somewhere in town. The expat-oriented **listings** magazine *Map* can be found at most bars and restaurants geared up for foreign custom – *Henry's Home* at the southern end of Shizi Qiao can be relied on to carry it.

Blue Marlin At the north end of the Nanjing 1912 complex, Taiping Bei Lu. Above the restaurant is a dance floor and terrace with occasional Latin dance nights. Staff are often willing to plug your iPod into their sound system.

Mazzo South end of the Nanjing 1912 complex. Good service and comfortable seating make this a great spot to wind down after *Scarlet*. When the music's good (it's distinctly variable), *Mazzo* is also a great place to dance.

Rick's 413 Changbai Lu. A three-level club, with a bar at street level, and dance floor and lounge above. Like the other clubs in Nanjing, hope for a good DJ when you go.

Scarlet 34–1 Hubei Lu, an alley south of Yunnan Lu. Two-storey bar that's the venue of choice with most expat residents, with the occasional Western DJ playing dance sounds and rock. Daily until 2am.

Listings

Airlines The main CAAC reservations and ticketing office is at 52 Ruijin Lu in the southeast of town (☎025/84499378; daily 7.30am–10pm). China Eastern Airlines' head office is at the corner of Changbai Jie and Zhongshan Dong Lu (☎025/84454325; daily 8.30–5.30pm).

Banks and exchange The Bank of China head office (daily 8.30am–5pm) is a few hundred metres due south of Xinjiekou on Zhongshan Nan Lu, and there's a 24hr ATM on site.

Bookshops The best selection of English-language books is in the Foreign Language Bookstore on Zhongshan Dong Lu, 700m east of Xinjiekou.

Hospitals The most central hospital is the Gulou Hospital, on Zhongshan Lu just south of the Gulou intersection.

Internet access A multitude of Internet places are scattered around the Nanjing University area: try the one across from the Muslim Restaurant. There's also a Net bar on the street running along the Gulou post office building's south side.

Mail and telephones Nanjing's main post office (daily 8am–6.30pm), offering international phone and fax calls as well as postal services, faces the Gulou traffic circle. There's also a post office at 19 Zhongshan Lu, just north of Xinjiekou.

Travel agents Nearly all hotels have their own travel agencies. CITS is at 202 Zhongshan Bei Lu (☎025/83538564, ☎83538561; Mon–Fri 8.30am–12noon & 2–5pm, Sat & Sun 9am–4pm), a couple of kilometres northwest of Gulou.

Northern Jiangsu

There's considerably less of interest once you get away from the historic canal towns in the south of Jiangsu province. Although the canal north of the Yangzi is – in season – navigable all the way to the borders of Shandong, and occasionally even as far as the Yellow River, the only thing people are likely to be transporting in this area is coal. There is no tourist traffic along here, and frankly not a great deal to see, though you might want to break a journey between Nanjing and Qingdao here. For the most part, the country is flat and wet, ideal for **salt panning** but little else. Of the towns in the area, none positively demands attention: tiny, rural **Chuzhou**, birthplace of Zhou Enlai, is an attractive old place; and heavily industrial **Xuzhou** is home to the excellent Han Dynasty Tomb.

Chuzhou

CHUZHOU has been a walled town for 1600 years, though these days it's famous throughout China as the birthplace of the much-loved Premier Zhou Enlai. The town has preserved his home as a national monument, as well as constructing a huge mausoleum in his honour.

Chuzhou is one of those pleasant places which you can get around entirely on foot. The main street, Zhenhuailou Lu, cuts from east to west across the middle of the city, with the central **Drum Tower Square** along it; the town's other important commercial street, Nanmen Dajie, leads south from here. The

Northern Jiangsu

Chuzhou	楚州	*chǔzhōu*
Liu E's Former Residence	刘鹗故居	*liú'è gùjū*
Wu Cheng'en's Former Residence	吴承恩故居	*wúchéng'ēn gùjū*
Xiao Hu	肖湖	*xiāohú*
Zhou Enlai's Former Residence	周恩来故居	*zhōu'ēnlái gùjū*
Zhou Enlai Memorial	周恩来纪念馆	*zhōu'ēnlái jìniànguǎn*
Accommodation		
Chuzhou	楚舟宾馆	*chǔzhōu bīnguǎn*
Jingdu	静都大酒店	*jìngdū dàjiǔdiàn*
Youdian	邮电宾馆	*yōudiàn bīnguǎn*
Xuzhou	徐州	*xúzhōu*
Guishan Hanmu	龟山汉墓	*guīshān hànmù*
Hanhua Stone Engravings Museum	汉画像石馆	*hànhuàxiàng shíguǎn*
Railway Hotel	铁路饭店	*tiělù fàndiàn*
Terracotta Army Museum	兵马俑博物馆	*bīngmǎyǒng bówùguǎn*

older part of town lies to the north and northwest of Drum Tower Square, with streets crammed full of little shops, restaurants, fortune-tellers, *daixie* (people who write letters on behalf of the illiterate) and interesting architecture.

Zhou Enlai's Former Residence is the main attraction in the centre of town (daily 7am–6pm; ¥20), signposted up an alley off Zhenhuailou Lu. An attractive house of black brick and heavy roof tiles, it was where Zhou was born in 1898, and has been lovingly restored to its original splendour. Considering the several courtyards within the walls, and the separate rooms for Zhou's stepmother and wet nurse, the family were obviously well off. As well as some interesting old wooden furniture, the house contains a small photo exhibition documenting Zhou's life, and also that of his wife, Deng Yingchao, who occupies a similarly high place in the Chinese people's affections.

Continuing north another ten minutes up Xichang Jie brings you to another former residence, this time of a local intellectual **Liu E**, who died in 1909. The former occupant, known in China for his achievements both as a scientist and novelist, may seem obscure to outsiders, but his house (8am–6pm; ¥5) is a delightful place where, amid the bamboos and goldfish ponds, you can glean an insight into peaceful courtyard living.

The **Zhou Enlai Memorial** (daily 7.30am–5pm; ¥20) stands to the northeast of the centre. There are two entrances, one along Huaijiang Gong Lu, the other just east off Beimen Jie, about 1km north of the Drum Tower. The park, and the memorial itself, built on a small lake, seems to have been modelled on a certain presidential memorial in Washington DC – the seated statue of Zhou is remarkably similar to that of Abraham Lincoln. A small museum downstairs has Chinese-only accounts of the life of this remarkable man.

Northwest of the centre

The west of Chuzhou is delineated along its entire length by an offshoot of the **Grand Canal**, which lies just a bit further on to the west. There's a good two-hour **circular walk** through quiet rural areas here. Begin by heading north along the side canal from the area just west of the *Chuzhou Binguan*. Turn

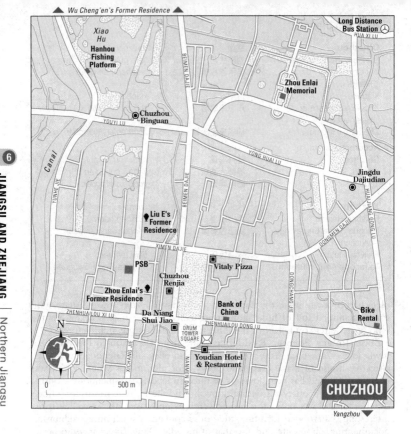

CHUZHOU

Yangzhou ▼

north along the canal; **Xiao Hu** will appear to your right. A stone gateway by this little lake signifies that you've reached **Hanhou Fishing Platform** (daily 8am–5.30pm; ¥5), an attractive walking area by the lakeside amid trees and long grass. Back on the road and farther north from here is an older section of town under redevelopment. Bearing right off the main road at the first intersection, just where the canal begins bending round to the west, continue north to the **Former Residence of Wu Cheng'en** (daily 8am–6pm; ¥10), the sixteenth-century author of the classic *Journey to the West*. It's a charming old house of black brick, with colonnaded walkways and clumps of bamboo in the courtyards, and filled with photos and memorabilia from the *Journey to the West* television series. From here, head east along more country lanes and you'll come out onto Beimen Jie, where you can walk south into town, or catch a pedicab (¥3).

Practicalities

Note that Chuzhou used to be called Huai'an, a name now applied to a town nearby where you may find yourself having to change buses; from here, you can continue to Chuzhou on local bus #8. Chuzhou's **long-distance bus station** is east of the Zhou Enlai Memorial on Hua Xi Lu. The **Bank of China** (daily 8–11am & 2.30–5.30pm) is on the north side of Zhenhuai Lu, with the **post office** nearby, facing the eastern side of Drum Tower Square.

Chuzhou has a handful of **accommodation** options for foreigners. Just southeast of Drum Tower Square is the friendly *Youdian Hotel* (☎0517/5919501; ❸). The *Jingdu Hotel* is a comfortable place just to the southeast of the Zhou Enlai Memorial along Yonghuai Lu (❺). Similar though a little more upmarket is the *Chuzhou Binguan* in the north of town on Xichang Jie (❻).

There are a few places to **eat** around the downtown area, including *Vitaly Pizza*, run by an Italian expat, at the northeast corner of the central square; it does mediocre pizza, but is great for ice cream and espresso. The jumble of lanes around Zhou Enlai's former residence hides several inexpensive family restaurants where a huge bowl of delicious *pingchao dofu* – tofu cooked with black pepper and coriander – costs just a few yuan. For *dianxin*-type snacks, try *Chuzhou Renjia* on the west side of the central park area, or for *jiaozi*, head to *Daniang Shuijiao* on the Drum Tower Square.

Xuzhou

At the intersection of the Beijing–Nanjing–Shanghai and Lianyungang–Zhengzhou rail lines, **XUZHOU** is primarily a coal-mining and food-processing centre, but it hides some interesting attractions that can keep visitors entertained for at least half a day. Southeast of town stands the three-thousand-strong brigade of the **Xuzhou Terracotta Army Museum** (daily 8.30am–4.30pm; ¥25), a miniature (both in size and number) version of its more famous Xi'an counterpart. The army is believed to have protected the grave of a local prince from the Han Dynasty or earlier. Four pits are home to a myriad of archers, foot soldiers, clay horses, chariots and servants, each of whose postures and facial expressions is different. Bus #5 runs here from downtown. Local bus #1 runs from the train station to the centre of town at the intersections of Huaihai Dong Lu and Zhongshan Lu, from where you can pick up bus #37 to take you several kilometres northwest to **Guishan Hanmu**, the tomb of Liu Zhu – the third Duke of Chu – and his wife, and certainly one of provincial China's better-displayed sights (daily 8am–5.30pm; ¥30). Excellent English captions explain the purpose of each of the twenty-plus caverns, which include the stable where live horses were fed by servants sealed in with the duke's body, the treasure room (today filled with replicas) and the coffin rooms themselves.

The **train station** lies in the east of town and has connections to places as far-flung as Guangzhou and Ürümqi. Xuzhou's **accommodation** options for foreigners are limited. The most convenient is the *Railway Hotel* at 2 Fuxing Nan Lu (☎0516/3733596; ❹), across the street from the train station.

Zhejiang

ZHEJIANG, one of China's smallest provinces but also one of the wealthiest, is made up of two quite different areas. The northern part shares its climate, geography, history and the Grand Canal with Jiangsu – the land here is highly cultivated, fertile and netted with waterways, hot in summer and cold in winter. The south, however, mountainous and sparsely populated in the interior, thriving and semitropical on the coast, has much more in common with Fujian province.

Recent excavations have shown, contrary to expectations, that the Yangzi delta had Neolithic settlements every bit as old as those in the Yellow River valley. At Hemudu on the Shaoxing–Ningbo plain, settled farmers were growing rice and building solid, precisely structured two-storey houses as far back as seven thousand years ago, when rhinoceros and elephant still roamed the land. For millennia thereafter the region remained prosperous but provincial, politically in the shadow of the more populous Yellow River basin in northern China. The eventual economic shift to the south slowly worked to the region's advantage, however. The Grand Canal was built and, finally, in the twelfth century AD, the imperial court of the Song moved south and set up capital in Hangzhou. For over two centuries, northern Zhejiang enjoyed a spell of unprecedented power, which ended only when the capital moved back to Beijing.

The whole province has an attractive, prosperous air, but most of the tourist destinations are in the north. **Hangzhou**, the terminus of the Grand Canal, is one of the greenest, most attractive cities in China, with a famous lake, former resort of emperors, and is still a centre for silk, tea and paper-making. Nearby **Shaoxing**, a charming small town threaded by canals, offers the chance to tour its beautiful surroundings by boat, while **Ningbo**, though long superseded by Shanghai as an industrial port, is mainly of interest as a launching pad to the Buddhist island of **Putuo Shan**. With more temples than cars, the island is as fresh, green and tranquil as eastern China ever gets.

Hangzhou

HANGZHOU, capital of the province, southern terminus of the Grand Canal, and one of China's most established tourist attractions, lies in the north of Zhejiang at the head of Hangzhou Bay. The canal has been the instrument of the city's prosperity and fortunes, ensuring it was a place of great wealth and culture for more than a thousand years. As is often the case in China, the modern city is not of much interest in itself, but **Xi Hu** – the lake around which Hangzhou curls – and its shores still offer wonderful Chinese vistas of trees, hills, flowers, old causeways over the lake, fishing boats, pavilions and pagodas. No tour of China would be complete without appreciating the lake's stunning natural beauty – still largely intact despite the ever-increasing flood of tourists – and its subsequent impact on the evolution of Chinese literature and culture.

The city is particularly busy at weekends and in summer, when it's packed with trippers escaping from the concrete jungle of Shanghai. This has pushed up hotel prices, but it also brings advantages: there are plenty of restaurants, the natural environment is being protected and the bulk of the Taiping destruction to the temples and gardens on the lakeside has been repaired. Most of the places to see can be visited on foot or by bicycle.

Some history

Apart from the fact that **Yu the Great**, tamer of floods, is said to have moored his boats here, Hangzhou has little in the way of a legendary past or ancient history, for the simple reason that the present site, on the east shore of Xi Hu, was originally under water. Xi Hu itself started life as a wide shallow **inlet** off the bay, and it is said that Emperor Qin Shihuang sailed in from the sea and moored his boats on what is now the northwestern shore of the lake. Only around the fourth century AD did river currents and tides begin to throw up a barrier of silt, which eventually resulted in the formation of the lake.

Hangzhou

Hangzhou	杭州	*hángzhōu*
Bai Di	白堤	*báidī*
Baopu Daoist Compound	包朴道院	*bāopǔ dàoyuàn*
Baoshu Ta	保淑塔	*bǎoshū tǎ*
Feilai Feng	飞来峰	*fēilái fēng*
Gu Shan	孤山	*gūshān*
Huanglong Dong Park	黄龙洞公园	*huánglóngdòng gōngyuán*
Hupaomeng Quan	虎跑梦泉	*hǔpǎomèng quán*
Huqingyu Tang Museum of Chinese Medicine	胡庆余堂中药博物馆	*húqìngyútáng zhōngyào bówùguǎn*
Jinci Si	净慈寺	*jìngcí sì*
Lingyin Si	灵隐寺	*língyǐn sì*
Liuhe Ta	六和塔	*liùhé tǎ*
Longjing	龙井	*lóngjǐng*
Nine Creeks and Eighteen Gullies Road	九溪十八涧	*jiǔxī shíbājiàn*
Passenger boat dock	市客运码头	*shì kèyùn mǎtóu*
Santanyinyue	三潭印月	*sāntán yìnyuè*
Su Di	苏堤	*sūdī*
Xi Hu	西湖	*xīhú*
Xiling Seal Engravers' Society	西泠印社	*xīlíng yìnshè*
Yuefei Mu	岳飞墓	*yuèfēi mù*
Zhejiang Museum	浙江博物馆	*zhèjiāng bówùguǎn*
Zhongshan Park	中山公园	*zhōngshān gōngyuán*

Accommodation

Chinese Academy of Art	中国美术学院国际教育学院	*zhōngguó měishù xuéyuàn guójì jiàoyù xuéyuàn*
Dahua	大华饭店	*dàhuá fàndiàn*
Dongpo	东坡宾馆	*dōngpō bīnguǎn*
Foreign Students' Building, Zhejiang University	浙大西溪校区留学生楼	*zhèdà xīxī xiàoqū liúxuéshēng lóu*
Holiday Wuyang	五洋假日酒店	*wǔyáng jiàrì jiǔdiàn*
Huaqiao	华侨饭店	*huáqiáo fàndiàn*
Mingtown Hangzhou Garden Youth Hostel	名堂杭州国际青年旅舍	*míngtáng hángzhōu guójì qīngnián lǚshè*
Mingtown Hangzhou Youth Hostel	名堂杭州杨公堤青年旅舍	*míngtáng hángzhōu yánggōngdī qīngnián lǚshè*
Ramada Plaza Hangzhou Haihua	华美达广场杭州海华大酒店	*huáměidá guǎngchǎng hángzhōu hǎihuá dàjiǔdiàn*
Shangri-la	香格里拉饭店	*xiānggélǐlā fàndiàn*
Xinqiao	新桥饭店	*xīnqiáo fàndiàn*
Xinxin	新新饭店	*xīnxīn fàndiàn*
Zhejiang University Guesthouse	浙江大学招待所	*zhèjiāng dàxué zhāodàisuǒ*
Zhonghua	中华饭店	*zhōnghuá fàndiàn*

Eating

Kuiyuan Guan	奎元馆	*kuíyuán guǎn*
Louwailou	楼外楼	*lóuwài lóu*
Tianwaitian	天外天	*tiānwài tiān*
Zhiweiguan	知味馆	*zhīwèi guǎn*

However, Hangzhou rapidly made up for its slow start. The first great impetus came from the building of the **Grand Canal** at the end of the sixth century, and Hangzhou developed with spectacular speed as the centre for trade between north and south, the Yellow and Yangzi river basins. Under the **Tang dynasty** it was a rich and thriving city, but its location between lake and river made it vulnerable to the fierce equinox tides in Hangzhou Bay. When Tang-dynasty governors were building locks and dykes to control the waters round Hangzhou, a contemporaneous writer, describing the beginning of a sea wall in 910 AD, explained that "archers were stationed on the shore to shoot down the waves while a poem was recited to propitiate the King of Dragons and Government of the Waters; the waves immediately left the wall and broke on the opposite bank so the work could go on." The problem of **floods** – and the search for remedies – was to recur down the centuries.

During the **Song dynasty**, Hangzhou received its second great impetus when the encroachment of the Tartars from the north destroyed the northern capital of Kaifeng and sent remnants of the imperial family fleeing south in search of a new base. The result of this upheaval was that from 1138 until 1279 Hangzhou became the **imperial capital**. There was an explosion in the silk and brocade industry, and indeed in all the trades that waited upon the court and their wealthy friends. Marco Polo, writing of Hangzhou towards the end of the thirteenth century, spoke of "the City of Heaven, the most beautiful and magnificent in the world. It has ten principal market places, always with an abundance of victuals, roebuck, stags, harts, hares, partridge, pheasants, quails, hens and ducks, geese … all sorts of vegetables and fruits … huge pears weighing ten pounds apiece. Each day a vast quantity of fish is brought from the ocean. There is also an abundance of lake fish." So glorious was the reputation of the city that it rapidly grew overcrowded. On to its sandbank Hangzhou was soon cramming more than a million people, a population as large as that of Chang'an (Xi'an) under the Tang, but in a quarter of the space – tall wooden buildings up to five storeys high were crowded into narrow streets, creating a ghastly fire hazard.

Hangzhou ceased to be a capital city after the Southern Song dynasty was finally overthrown by the Mongols in 1279, but it remained an important centre of commerce and a place of luxury, with **parks and gardens** outside the ramparts and hundreds of boats on the lake. In later years, the Ming rulers repaired the city walls and deepened the Grand Canal so that large ships could go all the way from Hangzhou to Beijing. Two great Qing emperors, Kangxi and Qianlong, frequented the city and built villas, temples and gardens by the lake. Although the city was largely destroyed by the **Taiping Uprising** (see p.436), it recovered surprisingly quickly, and the **foreign concessions** which were established towards the end of the century – followed by the building of rail lines from Shanghai and Ningbo – stimulated the growth of new industries alongside traditional silk and brocade manufacturing. Since 1949 the city's population has grown to around one million, much the same as under the Song.

Arrival, information and transport

Hangzhou has two halves; to the east and north is **downtown**, with its shops and tourist facilities, while to the west and south the **lake** offers greenery and scenic spots. The area around the Jiefang Lu/Yan'an Lu intersection (including the lake front and the small streets just to the north) is the commercial centre of town where you can shop, stay, eat and catch buses round the lake. On the outskirts of the city, the **Qiantang River**, Hangzhou's gateway to the sea, flows well to the south and west, while the **Grand Canal** runs across to meet it from the north; many travellers to Hangzhou never see either of them.

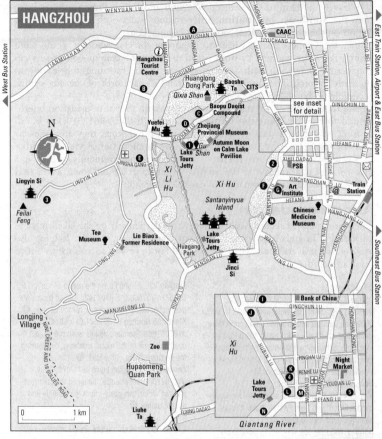

North Bus Station · Suzhou Ferry Jetty

East Train Station, Airport & East Bus Station

Southeast Bus Station

West Bus Station

HANGZHOU

Hangzhou Tourist Centre

Huanglong Dong Park
Qixia Shan
Baoshu Ta
CAAC
CITS

Baopu Daoist Compound

Yuefei Mu
Zhejiang Provincial Museum
Gu Shan
Autumn Moon on Calm Lake Pavilion
Lake Tours Jetty

Lingyin Si
Feilai Feng

Xi Li Hu
Xi Hu
Santanyinyue Island

PSB
Art Institute
Chinese Medicine Museum

Train Station

Tea Museum
Lin Biao's Former Residence
Huagang Park
Lake Tours Jetty
Jinci Si

Longjing Village

Zoo
Hupaomeng Quan Park

Liuhe Ta

Bank of China
Xi Hu
Night Market
Lake Tours Jetty

Qiantang River

NINE CREEKS AND 18 GULLIES ROAD

0 ___ 1 km

ACCOMMODATION		Holiday Wuyang	H	Shangri-La	D	EATING & DRINKING	
Chinese Academy of Art	G	Huaqiao	J	Xinqiao	M	Kuiyuan Guan	5
Dahua		Mingtown Hangzhou		Xinxin	C	Louwailou	1
Dongpo		Youth Hostel	E & F	Zhejiang University		Starbucks	2
Foreign Students' Building,		Ramada Plaza		Guesthouse	B	Tianwaitian	3
Zhejiang University	A	Hangzhou Haihua	I	Zhonghua	L	Zhiweiguan	4

Hangzhou's **airport** is 15km north of town, and connected by CAAC bus (¥5) to the main CAAC office on Tiyuchang Lu. The **train station** is 2km east of the city centre. Reaching the lake from here on foot takes about forty minutes; otherwise, take bus #7 direct to the lake or #151 as far as Yan'an Lu. A few trains stop only at the remote **East train station**; from here, bus #48 goes to the northeastern lakefront.

Buses use a number of stations ringing Hangzhou. Eastern arrivals and departures to Shaoxing, Ningbo and Fuzhou use the **East bus station** in the northeast of town, which is connected by bus #K35 to the centre of town. The **North bus station** (bus #155 runs the 9km to the centre) serves Shanghai and Jiangsu, though frequent private buses on these routes use the train-station square. Huangshan services use the **West bus station** on Tianmushan Lu (bus

#49 travels the 8km to the centre). Wenzhou and Fujian Province buses leave from the **Southeast bus station**, a five-minute walk south of the main train station on the corner of Dongbao Lu and Qiutao Lu.

Since the Grand Canal has been so important for Hangzhou, it would seem appropriate to arrive here by **boat** – and there are still daily passenger services connecting Hangzhou with Suzhou, arriving in the morning and leaving in the early evening. The **dock** is on the Grand Canal north of the city centre, accessible on bus #155.

Hangzhou is one of not many Chinese cities with tourist information booths around town. The **Hangzhou Tourist Centre** (℡0571/96123) has a booth in front of the train station, between the public bus stops; they run one-day tours of Hangzhou and surrounding canal towns and cities, as well as shuttles to Shanghai's Pudong airport. Their main office is inconveniently located at 3 Huanglong Lu, northwest of the lake. As for transport around town, a ¥10 **taxi** ride should cover any destination in central Hangzhou.

Accommodation

There are some excellent **hotels** in Hangzhou, particularly on the lakefront, and a handful of **hostels** have opened in recent years, with inexpensive lodging also available on university campuses. Rooms fill fast in season, so you may want to book in advance.

Hotels

Dahua 171 Nanshan Lu ℡0571/87181888, ℻87061770. On the lakeside, several blocks south of Jiefang Lu. Spacious grounds with comfortable rooms and attentive service justify the prices – this is actually better value than many of its competitors. Mao Zedong and Zhou Enlai stayed here whenever they visited Hangzhou. ❾

Dongpo 52 Renhe Lu ℡0571/87069769, ℻87024266. Smart rooms, a beautiful six-storey central atrium and friendly staff make this just about the best deal in town. ❺

Holiday Wuyang 109 Qingbo Lu, along Xi Hu ℡0571/87655678, ℻87655888. Recently renovated and in a promising location, near the lake but tucked away on a side street. ❽

Huaqiao 39 Hubin Lu ℡0571/87074401, ℻87074978. This four-star offering has good if slightly overpriced rooms, in a great location on the lakefront just south of Qingchun Lu. ❼

Ramada Plaza Hangzhou Haihua 298 Qingchun Lu ℡0571/87215888, ℻87215108, ⌨www.ramadainternational.com. One of the more upmarket offerings from this international hotel chain, with luxurious and tastefully designed rooms. The grand lobby features an imposing staircase. Rooms overlooking the lake command a premium. ❾

Shangri-La Beishan Lu, next to the Yuefei Mu ℡0571/87977951, ℻87073545, ⌨www.shangri-la.com. Total air-conditioned luxury in beautiful, secluded grounds, overhung by trees, on the northern shore of the lake. There's an expensive but scrumptious breakfast buffet. ❾

Xinqiao 226 Jiefang Lu, on the corner of Yan'an Lu ℡0571/87076688, ℻87071428. One of the town's plushest hotels, in an absolutely central location. ❽

Xinxin 58 Beishan Lu ℡0571/87999090, ℻87051898. Standard, mildly worn rooms, but it does have one of the nicest locations, overlooking the northern shore of the lake. ❽

Zhonghua 55 Youdian Lu ℡0571/87027094, ℻87077089. Very central, between the lakefront and Yan'an Lu, this place offers good single and double rooms. ❻

University and hostel lodging

Chinese Academy of Art 218 Nanshan Lu ℡0571/87164713. Inside the left gate as you face the main building: take the first doorway to your left just inside the gate and go to the third floor of building no. 9. The International College here is a well-located place to stay, quieter than the hostels, plus you get to hang out with art students. No dorms. ❹

Foreign Students' Building, Zhejiang University Tianmushan Lu ℡0571/88273784. There are sometimes a few spare beds or double rooms, with communal showers, available here. To find it, head to the university's Xixi campus, turn right inside the main gate, then proceed west for 5min to building no. 3. No dorms. ❷

Mingtown Hangzhou Youth Hostel 101 Nanshan Lu ℡0571/87918948, ℻87922018. Down an alley directly across from the Chinese Academy of Art, with a range of rooms, including a few with lake views and private bathroom. By the time you read this, the management should also be running a second place, the *Mingtown Hangzhou Garden Youth Hostel*, on the west side of the lake off Jinsha Gang. ❸

Zhejiang University Guesthouse 16 Zheda Lu ☎0571/87951211. Just off Yugu Lu near the *Lingfeng Hotel*; take bus #16 from the lakeside. Good value, though with a strong institutional feel. ❹

The City

Unusually for a Chinese city, the municipality of Hangzhou encompasses large areas of greenery which might normally be classified as countryside. This is mainly thanks to Xi Hu itself – so central and dominant a role has the lake played in the city's history that even today a trip right round its shores does not feel like an excursion out of the city.

Within the lake are various **islands** and causeways, while the shores are home to endless **parks** holding Hangzhou's most famous individual sights, ranging from the extravagant and historic **Yuefei Mu** (Tomb of Yuefei) to the ancient hillside Buddhist carvings of **Feilai Feng** and its associated temple, the **Lingyin Si**, one of China's largest and most renowned. Farther afield, beautiful tea plantations nestle around the village of **Longjing**, while south down to the **Qiantang River** are excellent walking opportunities.

With most of Hangzhou's sights located on or near the lake shore, you'll find that the ideal way to get between them is by **bike**; otherwise you can use local buses or simply walk. It's possible to walk round the lake's entire circumference in one day, but you wouldn't have time to do justice to all the sights en route.

Xi Hu

A voyage on this lake offers more refreshment and pleasure than any other experience on earth...

Marco Polo

Xi Hu forms a series of landscapes with rock, trees, grass and lakeside buildings all reflected in the water and backed by luxuriant wooded hills. The lake itself stretches just over 3km from north to south and just under 3km from east to west, though the surrounding parks and associated sights spread far beyond this. On a sunny day the colours are brilliant, but even with grey skies and choppy waters, the lake views are soothing and tranquil; for the Chinese they are also laden with literary and historic associations. Although the crowds and hawkers are sometimes distracting, the area is so large that you can find places to escape the hubbub. A good time to enjoy the lake is sunrise, when mellow *tai ji* practitioners hone their craft against a backdrop of early-morning mists.

As early as the Tang dynasty, work was taking place to control the waters of the lake with dykes and locks, and the two **causeways** which now cross sections of

---

Boat trips on Xi Hu

One of the most pleasant elements of a visit to Hangzhou is a boat trip on the lake. Tourist boats (¥45, including entrance fees for Santanyinyue) launch from the two lake tour jetties and head directly for the **islands**. Then there are the freelance boatmen in small canopied boats, who fish for tourists along major lakeside gathering points, especially the causeways, and charge ¥80 for an hour for up to six people. Also, you can take out a boat of your own – either electric putt-putters for four people (¥30 for 30min; ¥200 deposit), or paddle boats (¥15–20 for 30min).

the lake, Bai Di across the north and Su Di across the west, originated in these ancient embankments. Mainly used by pedestrians and cyclists, the causeways offer instant escape from the noise and smog of the built-up area to the east. Strolling the causeways at any time, surrounded by clean, fresh water and flowering lilies, is a pleasure and a favourite pursuit of Chinese couples. The western end of Bai Di supposedly offers the best vantage point over the lake.

Bai Di and Gu Shan

Bai Di is the shorter and more popular of the two causeways, about 1500m in length. Starting in the northwest of the lake near the *Shangri-La Hotel*, it runs along the outer edge of Gu Shan before crossing back to the northeastern shore, enclosing a small strip known as Beili Hu (North Inner Lake). The little island of **Gu Shan** in the middle of the causeway is one of Hangzhou's highlights, a great place to relax under a shady tree. Bursting with chrysanthemum blossoms in the spring and sprinkled with pavilions and pagodas, this tiny area was originally landscaped under the Tang, but the present style dates from the Qing, when Emperor Qianlong built himself a palace here, surrounded by the immaculate **Zhongshan Park**. Part of the palace itself, facing south to the centre of the lake, is now the **Zhejiang Provincial Museum** (Mon noon–4pm, Tues–Sun 9am–4pm; free), a huge place with clear English captions throughout and a number of different wings. The main building in front of the entrance houses historical relics, including some superb bronzes from the eleventh to the eighth century BC. Another hall centres on coin collections and has specimens of the world's first banknotes, dating to the Northern Song; you'll get an appreciation of the deep conservatism of Chinese society from its coinage, which remained fundamentally unchanged for two thousand years from the Han to the Qing dynasties. New galleries outside hold displays of painting and Tibetan Buddha statues.

The curious **Xiling Seal Engravers' Society** (daily 9am–5pm; ¥5), founded in 1904, occupies the western side of the hill, next to the *Louwailou Restaurant*. Its tiny park encloses a pavilion with a pleasant blend of steps, carved stone tablets, shrubbery, and nearby a small early Buddhist stupa; drop by here in summer and you can often see the engravers at work. On the southeastern side of the hill by the water is another of Qianlong's buildings, the **Autumn Moon on a Calm Lake Pavilion**, which is the perfect place to watch the full moon. It's a teahouse now, very popular after sunset and full of honeymooners. The low stone **Duan Qiao** (Broken Bridge), at the far eastern end of the causeway, gets its name because winter snow melts first on the hump of the bridge, creating the illusion of a gap.

Su Di and Santanyinyue Island

The longer causeway, **Su Di**, named after the Song-dynasty poet-official Su Dong Po, who was governor of Hangzhou, starts from the southwest corner of the lake and runs its full length to the northern shore close to Yuefei Mu. Consisting of embankments planted with banana trees, weeping willows and plum trees, linked by six stone arch bridges, the causeway encloses a narrow stretch of water, **Xili Hu** (West Inner Lake). East of the causeway and in the southern part of the lake is the largest of the islands here, **Xiaoying**, built up in 1607. It's better known as **Santanyinyue** (Three Flags Reflecting the Moon) after the three "flags" in the water – actually stone pagodas, said to control the evil spirits lurking in the deepest spots of the lake. Bridges link across from north to south and east to west so that the whole thing seems like a wheel with four spokes, plus a central hub just large enough for a pavilion, doubling as a shop and a restaurant. The ¥20 admission fee to get onto the island is usually included if you take one of the tourist boat rides here.

The lake shore

The account here assumes you start from the northeast of the lake on Beishan Lu and head anticlockwise, in which case the seven-storey **Baoshu Ta** on Baoshi Shan is the first sight you'll encounter. Looming up on the hillside to your right, the pagoda is a 1933 reconstruction of a Song-dynasty tower, and a nice place to walk to along hillside tracks. From Beishan Lu a small lane leads up behind some buildings to the pagoda. Tracks continue beyond, and you can climb right up to **Qixia Shan** (Mountain Where Rosy Clouds Linger) above the lake. About halfway along this path you'll see a yellow-walled monastery with black roofs lurking below to your left, the **Baopu Daoist Compound**. It's well worth a stop, especially in the late afternoon, if only because you might be able to discreetly watch one of the frequent ancestral worship ceremonies that are held here, with priests clad in colourful garb and widows clutching long black necklaces to pay tribute to their husbands. If you climb the stairs, you will find several smaller halls where old men practise their calligraphy and young women play the *pipa*.

Back on the path along the ridge above the monastery, you can stroll past **Chuyang** (Sunrise Terrace), traditionally the spot for watching the spring sun rise over the lake and Gu Shan. If you continue west, you'll eventually reach some steep stone stairs which will bring you back down to the road, close to the Yuefei Mu at the northwest end of the lake, next to the *Shangri-La Hotel.*

Yuefei Mu and Huanglong Dong Park

The **Yuefei Mu** (Tomb of Yuefei; daily 7.30am–5.30pm; ¥25) is one of Hangzhou's big draws, the twelfth-century Song general Yuefei being considered a hero in modern China thanks to his unquestioning patriotism. Having emerged victorious from a war against barbarian invaders from the north, Yuefei was falsely charged with treachery by a jealous prime minister, and executed at the age of 39. Twenty years later, the subsequent emperor annulled all charges against him and had him reburied here with full honours. Walk through the temple to reach the tomb itself – a tiny bridge over water, a small double row of stone men and animals, steles, a mound with old pine trees and four cast-iron statues of the villains, kneeling in shame with their hands behind their backs. The calligraphy on the front wall of the tomb reads, "Be loyal to your country".

Immediately west of Yuefei's tomb is a lane leading away from the lake and north into the hills behind. Thirty minutes' walk along here eventually leads to the **Huanglong Dong Park** (Yellow Dragon Cave Park; daily 6.30am–4pm; ¥15), to the north of Qixia Shan. The park can also be approached from the roads to the north of here, south of Hangzhou University. The main area of the park is charmingly secretive, sunk down between sharply rising hills with a pond, teahouses, a shrine to Yue Lao (the Chinese god of arranging marriages), cherry blossoms in the early spring, and a pavilion where musicians perform traditional music.

Huagang Park, Jinci Si and the Museum of Chinese Medicine

On a promontory in the southwestern corner of the lake, the small Song-era **Huagang Park** contains a pond full of enormous fish, and there are also wonderful stretches of grass and exotic trees under which to relax. East of here, by the southern shore of Xi Hu, is another temple, **Jinci Si** (daily 7.30am–5pm; ¥10), which has been fully restored; tourist buses #1 and #2 run past.

Finally, a kilometre east of the lake is the **Huqingyu Tang Museum of Chinese Medicine** (daily 8am–5pm; ¥10), which traces the complicated history of Chinese medicine from its roots several thousand years ago. The museum is housed in a traditional medicine shop, an architectural gem hidden down a small alley off Hefang Jie. On Hefang Jie itself, look for the white wall with seven large characters and turn down the first alley along its west side; the museum is on the right after about 30m.

Feilai Feng and Lingyin Si

Three kilometres west, away from the lake (bus #7 from Yuefei Mu to its terminus), are Hangzhou's most famous sights, scattered around **Feilai Feng** (daily 5.30am–5.30pm; ¥25). The hill's bizarre name – "The Hill that Flew Here" – derives from the tale of an Indian Buddhist devotee named Hui Li who, upon arrival in Hangzhou, thought he recognized the hill from one back home in India, and asked when it had flown here. Near the entrance is the **Ligong Pagoda**, constructed for him. If you turn left shortly after entering the site, you'll come to a surprisingly impressive group of fake rock carvings, replicas of giant Buddhas from all over China. To the right of the entrance you'll find a snack bar and beautiful views over the neighbouring tea plantations up the hill.

The main feature of Feilai Feng is the hundreds of **Buddhist sculptures** carved into its limestone rocks. These date from between the tenth and fourteenth centuries and are the most important examples of their type to be found south of the Yangzi. Today the little Buddhas and other figurines are dotted about everywhere, moss-covered and laughing among the foliage. It's possible to follow trails right up to the top of the hill to escape the tourist hubbub.

Deep inside the Feilai Feng tourist area you'll eventually arrive at **Lingyin Si** (Temple of the Soul's Retreat; daily 7.30am–4.30pm; ¥20), one of the biggest temple complexes in China. Founded in 326 AD by Hui Li, who is buried nearby, it was the largest and most important monastery in Hangzhou and once had three thousand monks, nine towers, eighteen pavilions and 75 halls and rooms. Today it is an attractive working temple with daily services, usually in the early morning or after 3pm.

So badly riddled with woodworm was the temple in the 1940s that the main crossbeams collapsed onto the statues; the eighteen-metre-high Tang statue of Sakyamuni is a replica, carved in 1956 from 24 pieces of camphorwood. Elsewhere in the temple, the old frequently brushes against the new – the **Hall of the Heavenly King** contains four large and highly painted Guardians of the Four Directions made in the 1930s, while the Guardian of the Buddhist Law and Order, who shields the Maitreya, was carved from a single piece of wood eight hundred years ago.

Southwest of the lake

Down in the southwestern quarter of the lake, in the direction of the village of Longjing, the dominant theme is **tea production**: gleaming green tea bushes sweep up and down the land, and old ladies pester tourists into buying fresh tea leaves. Fittingly, this is where you'll find the worthwhile **Tea Museum** (daily 8am–5pm; free), a smart place with lots of captions in English, covering themes such as the history of tea and the etiquette of tea drinking. There are displays on different varieties of tea, cultivation techniques, the development of special teaware, and finally, reconstructed tearooms in various ethnic styles, such as Tibetan and Yunnanese. Bus #27 from Pinghai Lu in the town centre comes here; get off more or less opposite the former *Zhejiang Hotel*, then head southwest to the museum along a small lane just to the north of, and parallel to, the main road.

A couple of kilometres further southwest, the village of **LONGJING** ("Dragon Well"), with tea terraces rising on all sides behind the houses, is famous as the origin of **Longjing Tea**, perhaps the finest variety of green tea produced in China. Depending on the season, a stroll around here affords glimpses of leaves in different stages of processing – being cut, sorted or dried. You'll be pestered to sit at an overpriced teahouse or to buy leaves when you get off the bus – have a good look around first, as there is a very complex grading system and a huge range in quality and price. The **Dragon Well** itself is at the end of the village, a group of buildings around a spring, done up in a rather touristy fashion. Bus #27 runs to Longjing from the northwestern lakeshore, near Yuefei Mu; alternatively, you can actually hike up here from the Qiantang River (see below).

South of the lake

The area to the south and southwest of Xi Hu, down to the Qiantang River, is full of trees and gentle slopes. Of all the parks in this area, perhaps the nicest is the **Hupaomeng Quan** (Tiger Running Dream Spring; daily 8am–5pm; ¥15). Bus #504 and tourist bus #5 both run here from the city centre, down the eastern shore of the lake, while tourist bus #3 passes close by on the way down from Longjing. The spring here – according to legend, originally found by a ninth-century Zen Buddhist monk with the help of two tigers – is said to produce the purest water around, the only water that serious connoisseurs use for brewing the best Longjing teas. For centuries, this has been a popular site for hermits to settle and is now a large forested area dotted with teahouses, shrines, waterfalls and pagodas.

A few more stops south on bus #308 takes you to the 1000-year-old **Liuhe Ta** (daily 7am–5.30pm; ¥20, tower ¥10), a pagoda occupying a spectacular site overlooking the Qiantang River, a short way west of the rail bridge. The story goes that a Dragon King used to control the tides of the river, wreaking havoc on farmers' harvests. Once a particularly massive tide swept away the mother of a boy named Liuhe, to the Dragon King's lair. Liuhe threw pebbles into the river, shaking the Dragon Palace violently, which forced the Dragon King to return his mother to him and to promise never again to manipulate the tides. In appreciation villagers built the pagoda, a huge structure of wood and brick, hung with 104 large iron bells on its upturned eaves. Today, ironically, the pagoda is a popular vantage point from which to view the dramatic **tidal bores** during the autumn equinox.

Twenty minutes' walk upriver west from the pagoda, at the #4 bus terminus, a lane known as **Nine Creeks and Eighteen Gullies** runs off at right angles to the river and up to Longjing. This is a delightful narrow way, great for a bike ride or a half-day stroll, following the banks of a stream and meandering through paddy fields and tea terraces with hills rising in swelling ranks on either side. Halfway along the road, a restaurant serving excellent tea and food straddles the stream where it widens into a serene lagoon.

Eating and drinking

As a busy resort for local tourists, Hangzhou has plenty of good **places to eat**, though there's nothing like the cosmopolitan range of either Shanghai or Nanjing. The wedge-shaped neighbourhood between Hubin Lu and Yan'an Lu is home to a number of Chinese restaurants and fast-food joints. Touristy

Hefang Lu is a good spot to make for, with a variety of Chinese restaurants and snacks.

Many Chinese tourists make it a point to visit one of the famous historical restaurants in town: both *Louwailou* (Tower Beyond Tower) and *Tianwaitian* (Sky Beyond Sky) serve local specialities at reasonable prices, while a third, *Shanwaishan* (Mountain Beyond Mountain), has garnered a bad reputation over the years. All three restaurants were named after a line in Southern Song poet Lin Hejin's most famous poem: "Mountain beyond mountain and tower beyond tower/ Could song and dance by West Lake be ended anyhow?"

For a touch of **nightlife**, try the smattering of clubs across from the Chinese Academy of Art, none of which stands out from the pack.

Restaurants and cafés

Kuiyuan Guan Jiefang Lu, just west of Zhongshan Zhong Lu (go through the entrance with Chinese lanterns hanging outside, and it's on the left, upstairs. Specializes in more than forty noodle dishes for all tastes, from the mundane (beef noodle soup) to the acquired (pig intestines and kidneys). Also offers a range of local seafood delicacies.

Louwailou Gu Shan Island. The best-known restaurant in Hangzhou, whose specialities include *dongpo* pork, fish shred soup and beggar's chicken (a whole chicken cooked inside a ball of mud, which is broken and removed at your table). Lu Xun and Zhou Enlai, among others, have dined here. Standard dishes cost ¥30–45.

Starbucks Close to the intersection of Nanshan Lu and Xihu Dadao. In Xihu Tiandi, a restaurant and bar development of bamboo-lined walkways, this is actually an unusually pleasant place to unwind, with views of the lake.

Tianwaitian At the gate to Feiliai Feng and Lingyin Si. Chinese tourists flock here to sample the fresh seafood, supposedly caught from Xi Hu. Not as good as *Louwailou* though. Dishes are ¥40–55 each.

Zhiweiguan Renhe Lu, half a block east of the lake. In a very urbane atmosphere, with piped Western classical music, you can enjoy assorted *dianxin* by the plate for around ¥20, including *xiao long bao* (small, fine stuffed dumplings) and *mao erduo* (fried, crunchy stuffed dumplings). The *huntun tang* (wonton soup) and *jiu miao* (fried chives) are also good.

Listings

Airlines The main CAAC reservations and ticketing office is at 390 Tiyuchang Lu in the north of town (daily 7.30am–8pm; reservations ℡0571/86662391; domestic flight schedules ℡0571/85151397). CAAC buses to the airport (5.45am–8pm; ¥15) leave here every 30min.

Banks and exchange The Bank of China head office is at 140 Yan'an Lu (daily 8am–5pm), immediately north of Qingchun Lu.

Bike rental Hangzhou's Freedom Network Bike Rental is one of the best operations of its kind in China, with locations around the lake and the option to return your bike to any of their outlets. One convenient outlet is the small corner office at 175 Nanshan Lu (℡0571/87131718), in a freestanding grey building 200m south of Jiefang Lu. Rentals cost ¥10/hr or ¥50/day, with a ¥400 deposit.

Hospitals The most central is the Shengzhong, on Youdian Lu three blocks east of the lake.

Internet access There are a number of poky Internet places on Zhongshan Zhong Lu just north of Hefang Jie, as well as outside the gates of both universities.

Mail The main post office is just north of the train station on Huancheng Dong Lu.

PSB For visa extensions, enquire at the PSB in the centre of town, on the southwest corner of the junction between Jiefang Lu and Yan'an Lu.

Shopping The most touristed concentration of souvenir outlets – selling silk, tea and crafts – is along Hefang Jie. An L-shaped night market bends around the western end of Renhe Lu, with street sellers peddling a proletarian jumble of wares, ranging from watches to DVDs to Little Red Books.

Trains The main train station contains a very convenient soft-seat ticket office for foreigners (daily 8am–7pm) on the north side of the station building at street level, left as you enter the station. An equally convenient soft-seat waiting room (daily 6am–midnight) is just around the corner on the station's front facade. The main ticket hall is on the second level; there's also a ticket window next to the tourist info booth.

the left (☎0571/85059033, ℻85059052; daily 8.30am–5pm). Nearly all Hangzhou hotels have their own travel agencies, usually more helpful than CITS.

Shaoxing and around

Located south of Hangzhou Bay in the midst of a flat plain crisscrossed by waterways and surrounded by low hills, **SHAOXING** is one of the oldest cities in Zhejiang, having established itself as a regional centre in the fifth century BC. During the intervening centuries – especially under the Song, when the imperial court was based in neighbouring Hangzhou – Shaoxing remained a flourishing city, though the lack of direct access to the sea has always kept it out of the front line of events.

For the visitor, Shaoxing is a quieter and more intimate version of Suzhou, combining attractive little sights with great opportunities for boating round classic Chinese countryside. It's a small city that seems to have played a disproportionate role in Chinese culture – some of China's more colourful characters came from here, including the mythical tamer of floods Yu the Great, the wife-murdering Ming painter Xin Wei, the female revolutionary hero Qiu Jin, and the great twentieth-century writer Lu Xun, all of whom have left their mark on the city. Although Shaoxing is sometimes recommended as a day-trip from Hangzhou, much of the reason for coming here is to experience the charm and beauty of the surrounding countryside, for which a single day is definitely not enough.

Near Shaoxing is **Jian Hu**, a lake whose unusual clarity has made the city known throughout China for its alcohol. Most famous are the city's sweet **yellow rice wine**, made from locally grown glutinous rice, and its ruby-coloured **nü'er hong wine**, traditionally the tipple brides sipped to toast their

Shaoxing and around

Shaoxing	绍兴	*shàoxīng*
Bazi Qiao	八子桥	*bāzǐ qiáo*
Fushan Park	府山公园	*fǔshān gōngyuán*
Lu Xun's Former Residence	鲁迅故居	*lǔxùn gùjū*
Lu Xun Memorial Hall	鲁迅纪念馆	*lǔxùn jìniànguǎn*
Qingteng Shuwu	青藤书屋	*qīngténg shūwū*
Qiu Jin's Former Residence	秋瑾故居	*qiūjǐn gùjū*
Sanwei Shuwu	三味书屋	*sānwèi shūwū*
Yingtian Pagoda	应天塔	*yìngtiān tǎ*
Accommodation		
Jinyu	金鱼宾馆	*jīnyú bīnguǎn*
Shaoxing Dasha	绍兴大厦	*shàoxīng dàshà*
Shaoxing Fandian	绍兴饭店	*shàoxīng fàndiàn*
Dong Hu	东湖	*dōnghú*
Lanting	兰亭	*lántíng*
Yu Ling	禹陵	*yǔlíng*

new husbands – it was bought when the bride was born, and buried in the backyard to age.

The City and around

Although Shaoxing's immediate centre comprises a standard shopping street, elsewhere there are running streams, black-tiled whitewashed houses, narrow lanes divided by water, alleys paved with stone slabs, and back porches housing tiny kitchens that hang precariously over canals. You can easily explore all of this by bicycle. **Fushan Park** (daily 8am–4.30pm; ¥8), in the west of town south of the *Shaoxing Hotel*, is as good a place as any to get your bearings, with a view over the town's canals and bridges from the top. The main entrance to the park is on Fushanheng Jie – look for the prominent archway guarding its eastern end next to the north–south thoroughfare, Jiefang Lu.

Along Jiefang Lu are the former residences of a number of famous people. The tranquil **Qingteng Shuwu** (Green Vine Study; daily 8am–5pm; ¥5), a perfect

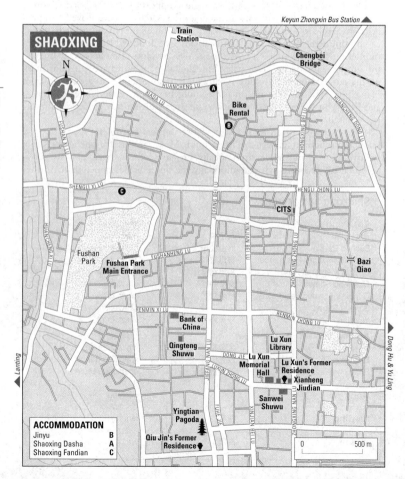

little sixteenth-century black-roofed house, hides 100m south of the Renmin Lu intersection on a small alley, Houguan Xiang, west off the main road. The serenity of the place belies the fact that it was once the home of eccentric Ming painter and dramatist Xu Wei (1521–93), who is notorious for having murdered his wife.

Another 500m south down Jiefang Lu from here, the **Yingtian Pagoda** (daily 8am–5pm; ¥2) crowns a low hill, Tu Shan. Part of a temple founded by the Song, burnt down by the Taiping rebels and subsequently rebuilt, the pagoda repays the stiff climb with splendid views over the town's canals. The black roof tiles, visible a block to the south, belong to the former residence of the radical woman activist **Qiu Jin**, which is situated on a small lane, Hechang Tang (daily 8am–5pm; ¥10). Born here in 1875, Qiu Jin studied in Japan before returning to China and joining Sun Yatsen's clandestine revolutionary party. After editing several revolutionary papers in Shanghai and taking part in a series of abortive coups, she was captured and executed in Hangzhou in 1907 by Qing forces.

East off Jiefang Lu, down Luxun Lu, are several sights associated with the writer **Lu Xun** (see p.385), all open daily from 8am to 5pm; a combined ticket for them costs ¥60. Lu Xun's childhood and early youth were spent in Shaoxing, and local characters populate his books. Supposedly, he based his short story *Kong Yi Ji*, about a village idiot who failed the imperial exams and was thus ostracized from mainstream society, in part on observations in a bar that used to stand on this street. A few minutes farther east from the **Lu Xun Memorial Hall**, beyond the plain **Lu Xun Library**, you'll find **Lu Xun's Former Residence**, now converted into a **Folk Museum**. If you've seen the high, secretive outer walls so many compounds have, you'll find it a refreshing change to get to look at the spacious interior and numerous rooms inside a traditional house; drop in here for a wander through the writer's old rooms and for a stroll in his garden. Immediately across the road from the museum is the **Sanwei Shuwu**, the small school where Lu Xun was taught as a young boy. In the one room to see, there's a small desk on which you'll find a smooth stone and a bowl of water, in former times the only available tools for calligraphy students too poor to buy ink and paper. Visitors are supposed to write their names in water on the stone for luck.

One further sight definitely worth seeking out in Shaoxing predates Lu Xun by several hundred years. A couple of hundred metres to the north of the Lu Xun buildings, in the east of the town – in the heart of one of Shaoxing's most picturesque and traditional neighbourhoods – is the most famous of all the town's old bridges, **Bazi Qiao** (Character Eight Bridge). This thirteenth-century piece of engineering, which acquired its name because it looks like the Chinese character for the number eight, is still very much in use. A small alley called Baziqiao Zhi Jie runs east off Zhongxing Zhong Lu to the bridge.

Dong Hu

Easily accessible from town, the highly photogenic **Dong Hu** (East Lake; daily 7am–5.30pm; ¥25) is a twenty-minute ride away on the #1 bus route. Despite appearances, the lake is not a natural one. In the seventh century the Sui rulers quarried the hard green rock east of Shaoxing for building, and when the hill streams were dammed, the quarry became a lake to which, for picturesque effect, a causeway was added during the Qing. The cliff face and lake are now surrounded by a maze of streams, winding paths, pagodas and stepping-stone bridges. Once inside the site, you can rent a little three-person boat (¥30) to take you around the various caves, nooks and crannies in the cliff face. You can choose to be dropped on the opposite shore, from where a flight of steps leads up to a path running to the clifftop, offering superb views over the surrounding paddy fields.

The last bus back to Shaoxing leaves around 5.30pm, though you can take a **boat** back instead (45min; ¥45 per boat after bargaining), or continue through the network of waterways on to Yu Ling (see below). This is a great trip (1hr 20min; ¥65 per boat after bargaining) in a long, slim, flat-bottomed boat, the boatman steering with a paddle and propelling the boat with his bare feet on the loom of the long oar.

Yu Ling and Lanting

Yu Ling (Tomb of Yu; daily 8am–4pm; ¥50), 6km southeast of Shaoxing and linked to town by bus #2, is a heaped-up chaos of temple buildings in a beautiful setting of trees, mossy rocks and mountains. Yu, the legendary founder of the Xia dynasty, around 2000 BC, earned his title "Tamer of Floods" by tossing great rocks around and dealing with the underwater dragons who caused so many disasters. It took him eight years to control a great flood in the Lower Yangzi. The first temple was probably built around the sixth century AD, while the actual tomb, which seems to predate the temple, may be Han dynasty. The temple today, most recently restored in the 1930s, contains a large painted figure of Yu and scores of inscribed tablets. Outside, the tall, roughly shaped tombstone is sheltered by an elegant open pavilion. The vigorous worshipping you'll see inside the temple shows what a revered figure Yu still is in modern China.

Another wonderfully rural excursion from Shaoxing is 11km southwest to **Lanting**, the Orchid Pavilion (daily 7.30am–5pm; ¥35), named when Goujian, a Yue Kingdom king, planted an orchid here almost three thousand years ago. The fourth-century poet and calligrapher Wang Xizhi allegedly composed the *Orchid Pavilion Anthology* here, today considered one of the masterpieces of Chinese poetry. Wang held a party with 41 friends, sitting along a creek and floating cups full of wine along it. When a cup stopped, the person sitting nearest either had to drink from the cup or compose a poem. Wang later composed the *Anthology* as a preface to all the poems. Today Lanting is considered a shrine, a place of resonance for all Chinese serious about calligraphy and poetry. Inside Wang's ancestral shrine, located on a small island in the middle of spacious gardens, you can watch artists and calligraphers work. Lanting is on the #3 bus route from Jiefang Lu (45min), but you'll have to ask locals where to get off.

Practicalities

Shaoxing's **train station** is in the far north of town – the rail line that comes through here is a spur running between Hangzhou and Ningbo. Bus #2 runs from here along Jiefang Lu to the southern end of the city. If you're coming from Hangzhou or Ningbo by bus, you'll probably arrive at the Keyun Zhongxin, a **bus station** in the far northeast of town, in which case take bus #3 to the city centre.

Bikes can be rented at a stall next to the *Jinyu Hotel* or from other spots nearby on Jiefang Bei Lu. The main **Bank of China** is on Renmin Xi Lu (daily 7.30am–5.30pm). **CITS** at 288 Zhongxing Zhong Lu (☎0575/5200079) can arrange tours of the surrounding area as well as book onward travel.

The most upmarket **hotel** in town is the Ming-style *Shaoxing Fandian* on Shengli Lu (☎0575/5155888; ❼), a huge and charming place in grounds so large that you can travel around them by boat. It's a couple of hundred metres west of Jiefang Lu – bus #30 heads there from the train station. Reasonable air-conditioned doubles are available near the train station at the *Shaoxing Dasha*

(☎0575/5136360; ❹), on the corner of Jiefang Bei Lu and Huancheng Lu. Farther south along Jiefang Bei Lu, the *Jinyu* (☎0575/5126688 ext 2626; ❺) has singles and doubles which are starting to show their age.

You'll find a few **restaurants** around the northern half of Jiefang Bei Lu. The restaurant in the *Jinyu Hotel* is good, serving several dishes in the local Shaoxing *mei* (charcoal-grilled) style, but note that the menu is in Chinese only. Dried freshwater fish is a great speciality in Shaoxing, as is the yellow rice wine that's these days more commonly used for cooking than drinking – *shaoxing ji* (Shaoxing chicken) is a classic dish prepared with it. While walking around town you might be struck by the huge number of stalls selling that malodorous staple of Chinese street life, *chou doufu* (smelly tofu). The recipe was allegedly created by a Shaoxing woman who, tired of her limited cooking prowess, decided to experiment by throwing a variety of spices into a wok with some tofu.

Ningbo and around

The rail spur from Hangzhou through Shaoxing ends at **NINGBO** (Calm Waves), an important economic hub and ocean-going port in the northeast corner of the province. Despite being a port, the city is actually set some 20km inland, at the point where the Yuyao and Yong rivers meet to flow down to the ocean together. All around you'll see flat watery plains and paddy fields, and, along the heavily broken and indented shoreline, the signs of local salt-panning and fishing industries. These would hardly make Ningbo worth a special journey, though the city has one or two features of interest, in the striking Tianyige Library and in the monasteries in the countryside beyond. More importantly, the city is a staging post for the trip to the nearby island of **Putuo Shan** (see p.464).

Ningbo and around		
Ningbo	宁波	*níngbō*
Catholic Church	天主教堂	*tiānzhǔ jiàotáng*
Dongmenkou	东门口	*dōngmén kǒu*
Jiangsha Bridge	江厦桥	*jiāngshà qiáo*
Tianyige Library	天一阁图书馆	*tiānyīgé túshūguǎn*
Xinjiang Bridge	新江桥	*xīnjiāng qiáo*
Yue Hu	月湖	*yuè hú*
Accommodation and eating		
Asia Garden Hotel	亚洲花园宾馆	*yàzhōuhuāyuán bīnguǎn*
Huagang Hotel	华港宾馆	*huágǎng bīnguǎn*
Jianghua Hotel	江花宾馆	*jiānghuā bīnguǎn*
Lao Waitan	老外滩	*làowài tān*
Shipu	石浦大酒店	*shípǔ dàjiǔdiàn*
Yin'an Hotel	银安宾馆	*yín'ān bīnguǎn*
Around Ningbo		
Baoguo Si	保国寺	*bǎoguó sì*
Tiantong Si	天童寺	*tiāntóng sì*
Xikou (Chiang Kaishek's birthplace)	溪口 (蒋介石故居)	*xīkǒu (jiǎngjièshí gùjū)*
Zhenhai	镇海	*zhènhǎi*

Ningbo possesses a short but eventful history. Under the Tang in the seventh century, a complicated system of locks and canals was installed to make the shallow tidal rivers here navigable, and at the end of the twelfth century a breakwater was built to protect the port. From that time onwards, **trade** with Japan and Korea began to develop massively, with silk shipped out in exchange for gold. Under the Ming, Ningbo became China's most important port. There was early European influence, too: by the sixteenth century the Portuguese were using the harbour, building a warehouse downstream and helping to fight pirates, while in the eighteenth century the East India Company began pressing to set up shop. Eventually, in 1843, after the Opium War, Ningbo became a **treaty port** with a British Consulate.

The town was swept briefly into the Taiping Uprising in 1861, but thereafter lost ground to Shanghai very rapidly. Only since 1949 has it begun to expand once more: the river has been dredged, passenger terminals and cargo docks built, bridges completed and facilities generally expanded to handle the output of the local chemicals, food-processing and metals industries.

The City

Downtown Ningbo is divided by the confluence of two rivers. The **Xinjiang Bridge** connects the western part of town, the area of the original walled city, with the northern part, the former foreign concession. The neighbourhoods

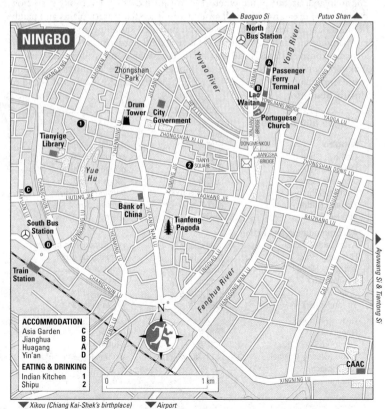

flanking each side of the bridge are the best places in town to soak up a bit of atmosphere; take bus #1 here from the train station. On the northern bank just west of the bridge, you'll find fishing boats, sailors and all the trappings of a busy harbour, while east of the bridge are a few surviving porticoes and verandas of the old **treaty port**, flanked by impromptu waterside fish markets. Also here is a seventeenth-century **Portuguese church**, which still serves the local Christian community. The area surrounding the church has been redeveloped into a bar and restaurant district called **Lao Waitan** (Old Bund), with smart restaurants and nightclubs.

The modern town stretches out south of the Xinjiang Bridge. Two blocks south, the main commercial street, **Zhongshan Lu**, cuts across the big **Dongmenkou** junction from east to west. The eastern section, across the **Jiangsha Bridge**, is an upmarket shopping area, but it's the western stretch that's the heart of the modern city, a broad avenue housing big department stores.

The oldest part of town is an area to the southwest around **Yue Hu** (Moon Lake); bus #20 comes here from just south of the Xinjiang Bridge. Little more than a large village pond, the lake has an enclosed area for swimming and the usual crowd of people doing their washing on the stone steps. Much of the area's charm has gone with the construction of a sprawling new park on the western shores, but Ningbo's best tourist attraction, the **Tianyige Library** (daily 8am–5pm; ¥20), clings on in the middle. Built in 1516 and said to be the oldest surviving library building in China, it's quite a charming place, and the gold-plated, wood-panelled buildings, accompanied by bamboo groves, a pool and rockery, preserve an atmosphere of contemplation and study.

Practicalities

Ningbo's **airport**, with flights to many Chinese cities, is 25km south of the city and connected to the CAAC office in the southeast of downtown via an airport bus. Bus #10 connects the **train station**, in the southwest of the city, with both the CAAC office and the city centre. Minibuses and bus #1 run from the train station through the town centre, north over Xinjiang Bridge and close to the ferry terminal and the **North bus station** across the street, which operates suburban services to the temples and pagodas outside town. Long-distance buses usually arrive at either the **South bus station** next to the train station or the **Keyun Zhongxin** bus station further southwest (bus #369 from train station or #203 from city centre).

The **ferry terminal**, for boats to and from Putuo Shan and Shanghai, is in the northern part of town, north of the Xinjiang Bridge, on Waima Lu; frequent minibuses and bus #1 head to the town centre. If approaching by bus, get off north of Xinjiang Bridge, just after passing beneath an overpass, then walk a couple of minutes northeast. The main **ticket office** here (daily 5.45am–6pm) sells tickets for the daily departures to Putuo Shan and Shanghai. Note that only slow boats – including the 9am Putuo Shan departure – depart from Ningbo itself, leaving from just behind the ticket office. Fast, comfortable services to Shanghai and Putuo Shan leave from **Zhenhai** to the northeast, to which there's a connecting bus from the terminal (1hr; cost included in the price of ferry ticket).

Most of the city's facilities are in the town centre right at the Dongmenkou junction, including the main **post office** and a branch of the **Bank of China**. The main Bank of China office (Mon–Fri 8–11am & 1–4.30pm) is on Jiefang Lu; there's also a branch across from the train station next to the *Jinlong Hotel*. For **visa extensions**, enquire at the City Government headquarters east off Jiefang Bei Lu.

Accommodation and eating

There are two **hotel** areas to consider in Ningbo, one near the train station, the other near the ferry terminal. Eating in Ningbo is dominated by **seafood**, and the *Shipu* restaurant on Tianyi Square is an impressive place to try it – choose your fish from the market-style display and have it cooked to order. The *Indian Kitchen* at 155 Zhongshan Xi Lu is an unlikely combination of tandoori oven and a bar, where you can quaff draught Guinness with your vindaloo or chew aniseed over a game of billiards. These establishments apart, there are upmarket restaurants at Lao Waitan near Xingjiang Bridge, and a cluster of mid-range places on Tianyi Square, 500m southwest of Xinjiang Bridge.

Hotels

Asia Garden 71 Mayuan Lu ⓣ0574/87116888, ⓕ87112138. Ningbo's premier place to stay, with a luxurious lobby and rooms that are almost as impressive. A 10min walk from the train station. ❼

Huagang 154 Zhongma Lu ⓣ0574/87677977, ⓕ27691001. An institutional place right above the ferry terminal; the rooms are comfortable enough. ❺

Jianghua 85 Renmin Lu ⓣ0574/87039858, ⓕ87039988. Well-kept rooms near the ferry terminal, and just across the street from Lao Waitan. ❻

Yin'an 449 Mayuan Lu ⓣ0574/87086088, ⓕ87086066. Good value, with comfortable rooms and a great location opposite the train station. ❹

Around Ningbo

There are numerous temples and pagodas to be visited in the countryside around Ningbo, but they offer few contrasts with their counterparts elsewhere in China. Perhaps the most interesting is **Baoguo Si** (daily 7am–4.30pm; ¥12), some 15km northwest of town on bus #332, the oldest wooden building south of the Yangzi, and one of the oldest of its type in China. Buses run here from the North bus station, out into a landscape of endless paddy fields broken only occasionally by villages with their obligatory duck ponds. Nestling on a hill, the temple itself was built in 1013 and restored under the Qing, but is left bare so that its complex bracket joints – called *dougong* – can be clearly seen.

At the terminus of bus #362 is **Tiantong Si** (daily 5am–5.30pm; ¥5), a splendid collection of buildings at the base of a group of hills, set deep in the forest. Founded in the third century AD, this is one of the largest monasteries in China, with 963 halls and many important Buddhist works of art – the Zen Buddhist sect considers this their second most important pilgrimage site in the country.

A little farther afield, **Chiang Kaishek's birthplace** sits in the delightful small town of **XIKOU**, 35km south of Ningbo, characterized by verdant paddy fields and (increasingly) flotillas of Taiwanese tour groups. The house where Chiang was born no longer stands, but some of his childhood haunts remain, including his grade school and his ancestral graveyard. To get here, take a bus from the East station bound for **Fenghua** (ask the driver where to get off).

Putuo Shan

A few hours by boat north of Ningbo and south of Shanghai lies the island of **Putuo Shan**, just twelve square kilometres in area and divided by a narrow channel from the much larger Zhoushan Island. Putuo Shan is also a peak which rises to 300m at one end of the island, one of the four Chinese mountains sacred to Buddhism. Undoubtedly one of the most charming places in eastern China, the island has no honking cars or department stores, only endless vistas

Putuo Shan

Putuo Shan	普陀山	*pǔtuóshān*
Chaoyang Dong	潮阳洞	*cháoyáng dòng*
Chaoyin Dong	潮音洞	*cháoyīn dòng*
Dacheng An	大乘庵	*dàchèng ān*
Duobao Pagoda	多宝塔	*duōbǎo tǎ*
Fanyin Dong	梵音洞	*fànyīn dòng*
Fayu Si	法雨寺	*fǎyǔ sì*
Foding Shan	佛顶山	*fódǐng shān*
Guanyin Leap	观音跳	*guānyīn tiào*
Huiji Si	慧济寺	*huìjì sì*
Hundred Step Sands	百步沙	*bǎibù shā*
Puji Si	普济寺	*pǔjì sì*
Shenjiamen	沈家门	*shěnjiā mén*
Thousand Step Sands	千步沙	*qiānbù shā*
Zizhu Si	紫竹寺	*zǐzhú sì*
Accommodation		
Fu Quan	福泉山庄	*fúquán shānzhuāng*
Putuoshan Hotel	普陀山大酒店	*pǔtuóshān dàjiǔdiàn*
Putuo Shanzhuang	普陀山庄宾馆	*pǔtuóshānzhuāng bīnguǎn*
Ronglai Yuan	融来院	*rónglái yuàn*
Sanshengtang	三圣堂饭店	*sānshèngtáng fàndiàn*

of blue sea, sandy beaches and lush green hills dotted with ancient monasteries, making it an ideal place to escape the noise, traffic and dirt of the big cities, with endless opportunities for walking. Although bursts of local tourists at weekends and in summer threaten the serenity, and despite the intent of the Chinese travel industry to lure visitors by greatly developing the infrastructure, you should still be able to avoid the hordes if you schedule your visit on a weekday or in the off season; the best times to come are April, May, September and October, when the weather is warm and the island isn't especially busy.

Over the years more than a hundred monasteries and shrines were built at Putuo Shan, with magnificent halls and gardens to match. At one time there were four thousand monks squeezed onto the island, and even as late as 1949 the Buddhist community numbered around two thousand. Indeed, until that date secular structures were not permitted on the island, and nobody lived here who was not a monk. Although there was a great deal of destruction on Putuo Shan during the Cultural Revolution, many treasures survived, some of which are in the Zhejiang Provincial Museum in Hangzhou. Restoration continues steadily, and the number of monks has grown from only 29 in the late 1960s to several hundred. Three principal monasteries survive – **Puji**, the oldest and most central; **Fayu**, on the southern slopes; and **Huiji**, at the summit.

Putuo Shan has been attracting Buddhist pilgrims from all over northeast Asia for at least a thousand years, and there are many tales accounting for the island's status as the centre of the **cult of Guanyin**, Goddess of Mercy. According to one, the goddess attained enlightenment here; another tells how a Japanese monk named Hui'e, travelling home with an image of the goddess, took shelter here from a storm and was so enchanted by the island's beauty that he stayed, building a shrine on the spot. With the old beliefs on the rise again, many people come specifically to ask Guanyin for favours, often to do with producing children or grandchildren. The crowds of Chinese tourists carry identical yellow cotton bags which are stamped with symbols of the goddess at each temple, sometimes in exchange for donations.

Access to the island

Boats to Putuo Shan run frequently from **Ningbo** (see p.463; note that some departures are from Zhenhai near Ningbo) and from **Shanghai** (see p.364). Leaving Putuo Shan, the last ferry to Ningbo goes at 4.30pm (¥58, including bus ride to Ningbo from Zhenhai). There are also several fast ferries to **Shanghai**, plus one or two slow overnight departures (¥80–350). The slow boat back to Shanghai is worth considering, chugging into the city just after sunrise and providing an absorbing and memorable view of the awakening metropolis. Second class on the overnight Shanghai boat affords a tolerably comfortable berth in a three- or four-bed cabin with a washbasin.

Putuo Shan is also linked several times a day with **Shenjiamen** on neighbouring Zhoushan Island, a half-hour boat ride away (¥18). Shenjiamen is an interesting place to spend a few hours, and there are frequent bus connections with Ningbo, via the recently constructed bridge to the mainland.

Arrival

The island is long and thin, with the **ferry jetty**, where all visitors arrive, in the far south; a ¥120 fee is payable when you set foot on the island. About 1km north from here is the main "town", a tiny collection of hotels, shops and restaurants, with a recognizable central square around three ponds, dotted with trees and faced to the north by Puji Si. There are only a few roads, travelled by a handful of minibuses (¥4–6) which connect the port with Puji Si and other sights farther north.

Upon arrival, you can reach the town by following either the road heading west or the one east from the jetty, or by picking up a bus from the car park just east of the arrival gate. The westerly route is slightly shorter and takes you past most of the modern buildings and facilities on the island, including the **Bank of China** (daily 8–11am & 1–4.30pm) and the **CITS** office. A little farther north, up a small lane to the left just before the *Xilin Hotel*, is the **post office** and **China Telecom** office, while in the central square, at the northwestern corner, you'll find a **ticket office** where you can book domestic flights out of Ningbo or Shanghai. The eastern route from the jetty takes you through a ceremonial arch symbolizing the entrance to the mountain and then on to a path that cuts away to the left a few minutes later, with the imposing statue of Guanyin standing on a promontory point straight ahead. When you need to **move on** from Putuo Shan, you can buy tickets for outbound boats from any of the island's hotels or at the jetty office (daily 6am–6pm).

Accommodation

There are several delightful **hotels** on Putuo Shan, including a number of converted monasteries, but be warned that in the peak summer months, and especially during the weekend stampede out of Shanghai, you may face a trek around town to find an empty room, not to mention very expensive rates. The price codes in the reviews represent peak season, outside of which rates fall sharply. Another option, often the only one for budget travellers, is to stay in a private house, standard practice for Chinese tourists on Putuo Shan though technically illegal for foreigners, so use your discretion. It's not hard to find

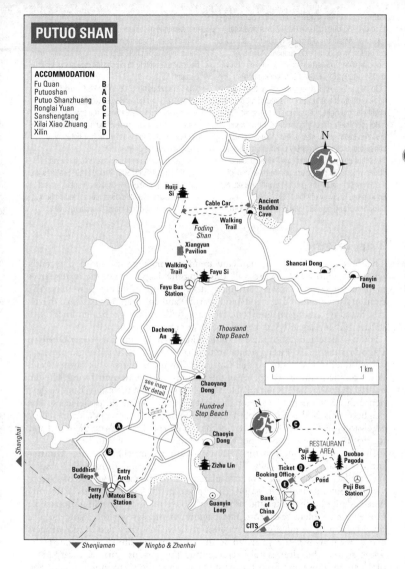

PUTUO SHAN

ACCOMMODATION

Fu Quan	**B**
Putuoshan	**A**
Putuo Shanzhuang	**G**
Ronglai Yuan	**C**
Sanshengtang	**F**
Xilai Xiao Zhuang	**E**
Xilin	**D**

N

Huiji Si

Cable Car

Ancient Buddha Cave

Walking Trail

Foding Shan

Xiangyun Pavilion

Walking Trail

Fayu Si

Shancai Dong

Fanyin Dong

Fayu Bus Station

Dacheng An

Thousand Step Beach

0   1 km

see inset for detail

Chaoyang Dong

Hundred Step Beach

Chaoyin Dong

Zizhu Lin

Buddhist College

Entry Arch

Ferry Jetty

Matou Bus Station

Guanyin Leap

N

RESTAURANT AREA

Puji Si

Duobao Pagoda

Ticket Booking Office

Pond

Puji Bus Station

Bank of China

CITS

◀ Shanghai

▼ Shenjiamen   ▼ Ningbo & Zhenhai

people with houses to let – they congregate at the jetty pier, and you should be able to bargain them down to around ¥100–150 per person, depending on the season. A third option, pursued especially by younger foreign travellers, is to crash on one of the island's two beaches for the night.

Fu Quan Not far from the jetty ☏ 0580/6092069. The sign is only in Chinese and easy to miss. Basic but agreeable rooms. **⑤**

Putuoshan Hotel On the main west road from the jetty to the town ☏ 0580/6092828, ☏ 6091818.

Very easy to spot, thanks to its spacious grounds and opulent design, this is the best hotel on the island, with prices to match. Furniture in the classier rooms and the dining areas is in traditional Chinese style. **⑦**

Putuo Shanzhuang Just south of the *Sansheng-tang* ☎0580/6091530, ℻6091228. A beautiful, relatively isolated and extremely comfortable option set on the wooded hillside opposite Puji Si. ❼

Ronglai Yuan Guesthouse In the middle of town ☎0580/6091262, ℻6091235. Walk past Puji Si to its eastern end, through an arch, then turn left (north) up the first alley. The alley first bends slightly to the right, then seriously to the left (the hotel is actually directly behind Puji Si). Foreigners aren't allowed to stay in the main building, a converted ancient monastery overhung by giant trees, but can use the small annexe across the street, where the rooms are comfortable enough, if slightly cramped. The genteel owner speaks no English but is always helpful. ❼

Sanshengtang ☎0580/6091277, ℻6091140.

On the eastern route from the jetty to town, this is just a couple of minutes due south of the centre on a small path. It's quite an attractive place, styled like a temple, but note that they have an annoying habit of attempting to surcharge foreigners by fifty percent. ❺

Xilai Xiaozhuang ☎0580/6091505 ext 501, ℻6091023. A plain concrete block that's nonetheless a very comfortable hotel, the first choice for many Chinese tour groups. You'll pass it at the northern end of the west route just before you reach the centre of town. ❾

Xilin Right on the central square, to the west of Puji Si ☎0580/6091303, ℻6091199. Features an entrance that makes it look like a temple, plus a good restaurant; a little persuasion should allow you to evade their foreigners' surcharge. ❼

The island

The three main temples on the island are in extremely good condition, recently renovated, with yellow-ochre walls offsetting the deep green of the mature trees in their forecourts. This is particularly true of **Puji Si** (daily 6am–9pm; ¥5), right in the centre of the island, built in 1080 and enlarged by successive dynasties. Standing among magnificent camphor trees, it boasts a bridge lined with statues and an elegantly tall pagoda with an enormous iron bell.

South of here and just to the east of the square ponds is the five-storey **Duobao Pagoda**. Built in 1334 using stones brought over from Tai Hu in Jiangsu province, it has Buddhist inscriptions on all four sides. Twenty minutes' walk farther south down on the southeastern corner of the island is a cave, **Chaoyin Dong**. The din of crashing waves here is remarkable, thought to resemble the call of Buddha (and hence this was a popular spot for monks to commit suicide in earlier days). The neighbouring **Zizhu Si** (Purple Bamboo Temple; daily 6am–6pm; ¥5 including admission to Chaoyin Dong) is one of the less touristed temples on the island and, for that reason alone, a good spot to observe the monks' daily rituals.

On the island's southern tip is Putuo's most prominent sight, the **Guanyintiao** (Guanyin Leap; daily 7am–5pm; ¥6), a headland from which rises a spectacular 33-metre-high bronze-plated statue of the Goddess of Mercy, visible from much of the island. In her left hand, Guanyin holds a steering wheel, symbolically protecting fishermen (not to mention travelling monks like Hui'e) from violent seastorms. The pavilion at the base of the statue holds a small exhibit of wooden murals recounting how Guanyin aided Putuo villagers and fishermen over the years, while in a small room directly underneath the statue sit four hundred statues representing the various spiritual incarnations of Guanyin. The view from the statue's base over the surrounding islands and fishing boats is sublime, especially on a clear day. A small memorial plaque on the coast between Guanyintiao and Chaoyin Dong marks the spot where Hui'e made landfall while escaping a violent storm.

North of the town

The two temples in the northern half of the island, Huiji Si and Fayu Si, make for a pleasant day-trip from town. They're conveniently connected to the southern half by minibuses departing from the bus stop just southeast of the central square, and there are minibuses between the temples as well.

Huiji Si stands near the top of **Foding Shan**, whose summit provides some spectacular views of the sea and the surrounding islands. You can hike up or use the **cable car** from the minibus stand (daily 7am–5pm; ¥25 up, ¥15 down). The temple itself (daily 6.30am–5pm; ¥5), built mainly between 1793 and 1851, occupies a beautiful site just to the northwest of the summit, surrounded by green tea plantations. The halls stand in a flattened area between hoary trees and bamboo groves, the greens, reds, blues and gold of their enamelled tiles gleaming magnificently in the sunshine. There's also a vegetarian restaurant here.

You can head down along a marked path towards the third major temple, Fayu Si, the whole walk taking about an hour. Shortly after setting off, you'll see a secondary track branching away to the left towards the **Ancient Buddha Cave**, a delightfully secluded spot by a sandy beach on the northeastern coast of the island; give yourself a couple of hours to get there and back. Back on the main path, the steep steps bring you to the **Xiangyun Pavilion**, where you can rest and drink tea with the friendly monks.

Thirty minutes farther on you'll reach the **Fayu Si** (daily 6.30am–5.30pm; ¥5), another superb collection of over two hundred halls amid huge green trees, built up in levels against the slope during the Ming. With the mountain behind and the sea just in front, it's a delightful place to sit in peaceful contemplation. The Daxiong Hall has been brilliantly restored, and the Dayuan Hall has a unique beamless arched roof and a dome, around the inside of which squirm nine carved wooden dragons. This hall is said to have been moved here from Nanjing by Emperor Kangxi in 1689. Its great statue of **Guanyin**, flanked by monks and nuns, is the focal point of the goddess's birthday celebrations in early April, when thousands of pilgrims and sightseers crowd onto the island for chanting and ceremonies which last all evening.

Occasional minibuses head out along the promontory immediately east of Fayu Si to **Fanyin Dong** (daily 8am–4.30pm; ¥5), a cave whose name derives from the resemblance of the sound of crashing waves to Buddhist chants. The cave is set in the rocky cliff, with a small shrine actually straddling a ravine. Walking around on the promontory is a pleasure given the absence of crowds and the difficulty of getting lost.

You'll appreciate Putuo's beauty much more by making the trip to Huiji Si and Fayu Si **on foot** via the two excellent **beaches** that line the eastern shore, Qianbu Sha (Thousand Step Beach; ¥12 until 5pm, free afterwards) and Baibu Sha (Hundred Step Beach; ¥10 until 5pm, free afterwards). In summer, it's possible to bring a sleeping bag and camp out on either beach – be sure to bring all your supplies from town as there are no stores or restaurants nearby. The beaches are separated by a small headland hiding the **Chaoyang Dong**. Just inside this little cave there's a teahouse and a seating area overlooking the sea, while from the top of the headland itself you'll get great views. One kilometre south of Fayu Si and directly across from Wanbu Sha, the **Dacheng An** (daily 8am–5.30pm; ¥1) is a nunnery notable for the reclining Buddha downstairs in the main hall, and the thousands of tiny seated Buddhas upstairs.

Eating

Eating is not likely to be the highlight of your trip to Putuo Shan – most food must be brought in from the mainland, and is therefore expensive. The lane running northeast away from Puji Si as well as the road between the jetty departure and arrival points both have a string of dingy-looking eating houses which specialize in **seafood** ranging from fish to molluscs and eel, though they also do standard dishes and noodles.

Travel details

Trains

Hangzhou to: Beijing (4 daily; 10–22hr); Guangzhou (3 daily; 25hr); Nanchang (9 daily; 10–12hr); Nanjing (frequent; 6hr 30min–8hr); Ningbo (frequent; 3hr); Shanghai (frequent; 2–3hr); Shaoxing (frequent; 50min); Suzhou (frequent; 3–4hr); Wenzhou (4 daily; 7–8hr); Wuxi (8 daily; 4hr).

Nanjing to: Beijing (8 daily; 11–16hr); Chengdu (4 daily; 32–36hr); Fuzhou (3 daily; 20–24hr); Hangzhou (frequent; 5hr 30min–7hr 30min); Ma'anshan (frequent; 1hr 30min); Ningbo (4 daily; 9–11hr); Suzhou (frequent; 2hr 30min–4hr); Shanghai (frequent; 3–5hr); Wenzhou (3 daily; 15–16hr); Wuhu (frequent; 2hr); Wuxi (frequent; 2hr); Xi'an (10 daily; 13–19hr); Xuzhou (frequent; 4–7hr); Yangzhou (4 daily; 1hr 45min); Zhenjiang (frequent; 40min–1hr 30min).

Ningbo to: Hangzhou (frequent; 2hr 30min); Shanghai (7 daily; 5–6hr); Shaoxing (frequent; 1hr 30min).

Shaoxing to: Hangzhou (frequent; 50min); Ningbo (frequent; 1hr 30min); Shanghai (7 daily; 4–5hr).

Suzhou to: Hangzhou (frequent; 3–4hr); Nanjing (frequent; 2hr 30min–4hr); Shanghai (frequent; 45min–1hr 20min); Wuxi (frequent; 30min); Yangzhou (1 daily; 4hr); Zhenjiang (frequent; 2hr).

Wuxi to: Hangzhou (8 daily; 4hr); Nanjing (frequent; 2hr); Shanghai (frequent; 1–2hr); Suzhou (frequent; 30min); Zhenjiang (frequent; 1hr 30min–2hr).

Xuzhou to: Beijing (11 daily; 7–11hr); Shanghai (frequent; 6–10hr); Ji'nan (frequent; 4hr); Kaifeng (frequent; 3hr 30min); Nanjing (frequent; 4–7hr); Zhengzhou (frequent; 4hr 30min).

Yangzhou Nanjing (4 daily; 1hr 45min); Shanghai (1 daily; 5hr); Suzhou (1 daily; 4hr)

Zhenjiang to: Nanjing (frequent; 45min–1hr 20min); Shanghai (frequent; 2–4hr); Suzhou (frequent; 2hr); Wuxi (frequent; 1hr 30min–2hr).

Buses

There are frequent departures on many of the routes listed below, though if your journey is a lengthy one, it's advisable to try to set off before midday.

Chuzhou to: Nanjing (2hr); Shanghai (6hr); Xuzhou (3hr 30min); Yangzhou (3hr); Zhenjiang (2 daily; 3hr).

Hangzhou to: Huang Shan (4hr); Nanjing (4hr); Ningbo (2hr 30min); Shanghai (2hr 30min); Shaoxing (1hr 30min); Suzhou (2hr); Wenzhou (4hr 30min); Wuxi (3hr); Yangzhou (4hr 30min).

Nanjing to: Chuzhou (3–4hr); Huang Shan (5hr); Hangzhou (5hr); Hefei (7hr); Ningbo (8hr); Qingdao (12hr); Shanghai (4–5hr); Suzhou (3–4hr); Wenzhou (12hr); Wuhan (19hr); Wuxi (2–3hr); Xuzhou (5–6hr); Yangzhou (2hr); Yixing (4hr); Zhenjiang (1hr).

Ningbo to: Hangzhou (2hr 30min); Nanjing (8hr); Shaoxing (1hr); Wenzhou (7hr).

Shaoxing to: Hangzhou (1hr 30min); Ningbo (1hr).

Suzhou

North station to: Dingshan (3hr); Nanjing (3hr); Shanghai (1–2hr); Wuxi (1hr); Yangzhou (5hr); Yixing (3hr).

South station to: Hangzhou (4hr); Tongli (1hr); Zhouzhuang (2hr).

Wuxi to: Hangzhou (4hr); Nanjing (2hr); Shanghai (2hr); Suzhou (1hr); Yangzhou (2hr 30min); Yixing (2hr); Zhenjiang (1hr 30min).

Xuzhou to: Chuzhou (4hr); Nanjing (5–6hr); Yangzhou (5hr).

Yangzhou to: Hangzhou (7hr); Chuzhou (3hr); Nanjing (1hr 30min); Shanghai (6hr); Suzhou (5hr); Wuxi (2hr 30min); Zhenjiang (1hr).

Yixing to: Hangzhou (4hr); Nanjing (4hr); Wuxi (2hr); Zhenjiang (3hr).

Zhenjiang to: Chuzhou (3hr 30min); Nanjing (1hr 30min); Yangzhou (1hr 30min); Yixing (3hr).

Ferries

Hangzhou to: Suzhou (daily; 10hr).

Ningbo to: Putuo Shan (frequent; 5hr); Shanghai (daily; 9hr).

Putuo Shan to: Ningbo (frequent; 5hr); Shanghai (several daily; 4hr express, 10hr overnight); Shenjiamen (at least 7 daily; 30min); Zhenhai (several daily; 2hr 30min).

Suzhou to: Hangzhou (daily; 10hr).

Zhenhai to: Putuo Shan (several daily; 2hr 30min).

Flights

Hangzhou to: Beijing (frequent; 2hr); Chengdu (5 daily; 2hr 30min); Fuzhou (3 daily; 1hr); Guangzhou (frequent; 2hr); Guilin (2 daily; 2hr); Hong Kong (5 daily; 2hr); Kunming (4 daily; 2hr); Qingdao (6 daily; 1hr 30min); Shanghai (2 daily; 20min); Shenzhen (10 daily; 2hr); Wenzhou (1–3 daily; 40min); Xiamen (4–5 daily; 1hr 10min); Xi'an (3–4 daily; 2hr).

Nanjing to: Beijing (frequent; 1hr 30min); Chengdu (4–5 daily; 2hr 20min); Chongqing (3–4 daily; 2hr 20min); Dalian (3–4 daily; 1hr 30min); Fuzhou (daily; 1hr); Guangzhou (7 daily; 2hr); Guilin (1–3 daily; 2hr); Haikou (3 daily; 2hr 25min); Hong Kong (4 daily; 2hr 20min); Kunming (4 daily; 2hr 40min); Ningbo (2–3 daily; 1hr); Qingdao (3–5 daily; 1hr); Shenzhen (6 daily; 2hr); Wenzhou (daily; 1hr); Xiamen (4–5 daily; 1hr 40min); Xi'an (2 daily; 2hr).

Ningbo to: Beijing (5 daily; 2hr); Guangzhou (5 daily; 2hr); Hong Kong (3 daily; 2hr); Nanjing (2–3 daily; 1hr); Shanghai (5–6 daily; 30min); Shenzhen (2 daily; 2hr).

CHAPTER 7

Highlights

* **Huang Shan** Arguably China's most scenic mountain, wreathed in narrow stone staircases, contorted trees and cloud-swept peaks. See p.490

* **Yixian** An amazing collection of antique Ming villages, used atmospherically in Zhang Yimou's film *Raise the Red Lantern*. See p.490

* **Hubei Provincial Museum, Wuhan** On show here are 2000-year-old relics from the tombs of aristocrats, including a lacquered coffin and an orchestra of 64 giant bronze bells. See p.502

* **Shennongjia Forest Reserve** Wild and remote mountain refuge of the endangered golden monkey and (so it's said) the enigmatic *ye ren*, China's yeti. See p.509

* **Wudang Shan** Temple-covered mountains at the heart of Taoist martial art mythology; it's said this is where *tai ji* originated. See p.511

* **Jingdezhen** China's porcelain capital for the last six centuries, with a fine ceramic history museum and busy street markets. See p.541

△ The Three Gorges Dam

The Yangzi basin

H aving raced out of Sichuan through the narrow Three Gorges, the **Yangzi** (here known as the **Chang Jiang**) widens, slows down, and loops through its flat, low-lying middle reaches, swelled by lesser streams and rivers which drain off the highlands surrounding the four provinces of the Yangzi basin: **Anhui**, **Hubei**, **Hunan** and **Jiangxi**. As well as watering one of China's key rice- and tea-growing areas, this stretch of the Yangzi has long supported trade and transport; back in the thirteenth century, Marco Polo was awed by the "innumerable cities and towns along its banks, and the amount of shipping it carries, and the bulk of merchandise that merchants transport by it". The fact that rural fringes away from the river – including much of Anhui and Jiangxi provinces – remain some of the least developed regions in central China may be redressed by the completion around 2008 of the mighty **Three Gorges Dam** on the border between Hubei and Chongqing, whose hydroelectric output will power a local industrial economy to rival that of the east coast.

The river basin itself is best characterized by the flat expanses of China's two largest freshwater lakes: **Dongting**, which pretty well marks the border between Hunan and Hubei, and **Poyang**, in northern Jiangxi, famed for porcelain produced at nearby **Jingdezhen**. Riverside towns such as **Wuhu** in Anhui are also interesting as working ports, where it's still possible to see traditional river industries – fish farming, grain, rice and bamboo transport – existing alongside newer ventures in manufacturing. Strangely enough, while all four regional capitals are located near water, only **Wuhan**, in Hubei, is actually on the Yangzi itself, a privileged position which has turned the city into central China's liveliest urban conglomeration. By contrast, the other provincial capitals – **Changsha** in Hunan, Anhui's **Hefei** and Jiangxi's **Nanchang** – seem somewhat dishevelled, though long settlement has left a good deal of **history** in its wake, from well-preserved Han-dynasty tombs to whole villages of Ming-dynasty houses, and almost everywhere you'll stumble over sites from the epic of the **Three Kingdoms**, making the tale essential background reading (see box, p.474). Many cities also remain studded with hefty European buildings, a hangover from their being forcibly opened up to foreign traders as **Treaty Ports** in the 1860s, following the Second Opium War. Perhaps partly due to these unwanted intrusions, the Yangzi basin can further claim to be the **cradle of modern China**: Mao Zedong was born in Hunan; Changsha, Wuhan and Nanchang are all closely associated with Communist Party history; while the mountainous border between Hunan and Jiangxi was both a Red refuge during right-wing purges in the late 1920s and the starting point for the subsequent Long March to Shaanxi.

Away from the river, wild mountain landscapes make for some fine **hiking**, the pick of which is undoubtedly at **Huang Shan** in southern Anhui, followed by Hubei's remote **Shennongjia Forest Reserve**, and **Zhangjiajie** in Hunan's far west. Pilgrims also have a selection of Buddhist and Taoist **holy**

Sanguo: The Three Kingdoms

The empire, long divided, must unite; long united, must divide. Thus it has ever been.

So, rather cynically, begins one of China's best-known stories, the fourteenth-century historical novel **Romance of the Three Kingdoms**. Covering 120 chapters and a cast of thousands, the story touches heavily on the Yangzi basin, which, as a buffer zone between the Three Kingdoms, formed the backdrop for many major battles and key events. Some surviving sites are covered in this chapter and elsewhere in the guide.

The *Romance of the Three Kingdoms* is essentially fictionalized, though well founded in historical fact. Opening in 168 AD, the tale recounts the decline of the Han empire, how China was split into three states by competing warlords, and the subsequent (short-lived) reunification of the country in 280 AD under a new dynasty. The main action began in 189 AD. At this point, the two protagonists were the villainous **Cao Cao** and the virtuous **Liu Bei**, whose watery character was compensated for by the strength of his spirited sworn brothers **Zhang Fei** and **Guan Yu** – the latter eventually becoming enshrined in the Chinese pantheon as the red-faced god of war and healing. Having put down the rebellious Yellow Turbans in the name of the emperor, both Cao and Liu felt their position threatened by the other; Cao was regent to the emperor **Xian**, but Liu had a remote blood tie to the throne. Though both claimed to support the emperor's wishes, Cao and Liu began fighting against each other, with Cao being defeated in Hubei at the **Battle of the Red Cliffs** (208 AD) after Liu engaged the aid of the wily adviser **Zhuge Liang**, who boosted Liu's heavily outnumbered forces by enlisting the help of a third warlord, **Sun Quan**.

Consolidating their positions, each of the three formed a private kingdom: Cao Cao retreated north to the Yellow River basin where he established the state of **Wei** around the ailing imperial court; Sun Quan set up **Wu** farther south along the lower Yangzi; while Liu Bei built a power base in the riverlands of Sichuan, the state of **Shu**. The alliance between Shu and Wu fell apart when Sun Quan asked Guan Yu to betray Liu. Guan refused and was assassinated by Sun in 220 AD. At this point Cao Cao died, and his ambitious son, **Cao Pi**, forced the emperor to abdicate and announced himself head of a new dynasty. Fearing retaliation from the state of Shu after Guan Yu's murder, Sun Quan decided to support Cao Pi's claims, while over in Shu, Liu Bei also declared his right to rule.

Against Zhuge Liang's advice, Liu marched against Wu to avenge Guan Yu's death but his troops mutinied, killing Zhang Fei. Humiliated, Liu withdrew to **Baidicheng** in the Yangzi Gorges and died. With him out of the way, Cao Pi attacked Sun Quan, who was therefore forced to renew his uncomfortable alliance with Shu – now governed by Zhuge Liang – to keep the invaders out of his kingdom. By 229 AD, however, things were stable enough for Sun Quan to declare himself as a rival emperor, leaving Zhuge to die five years later fighting the armies of Wei. Wei was unable to pursue the advantage, as a coup against Cao Pi started a period of civil war in the north, ending around 249 AD when the **Sima clan** emerged victorious. Sun Quan died soon afterwards, while Shu abandoned all claim to the empire. Wei's Sima clan founded a new dynasty, the **Jin**, in 265 AD, finally overpowering Wu and uniting China in 280 AD.

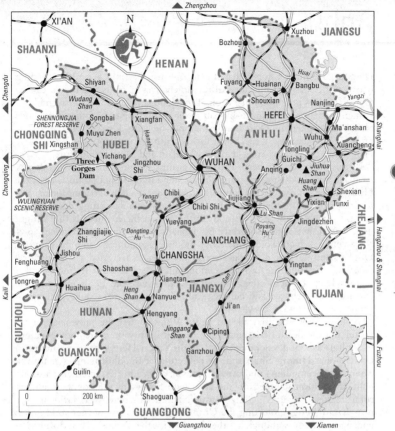

mountains to scale on seemingly unending stone-flagged staircases – Hubei's **Wudang Shan** is outstanding – and less dedicated souls can find pleasant views at the mountain resort town of **Lu Shan** in Jiangxi. As an alternative to the better-known Huang Shan, Anhui's **Jiuhua Shan** has many advantages: it's lower (the highest peak is a little over 1300m), the walking is considerably easier, and there's plenty of interest beyond the scenery.

In theory, **getting around** isn't a problem. **Rail** lines from all over China cross the region, and **buses** and swifter, pricier minibuses link cities to the remotest of corners. **Ferries**, once the principal mode of transport, have been superseded, and passenger services are now limited to the stretch between Wuhan and Chongqing. Autumn is probably the most pleasant time of year, though even winters are generally mild, but near-constant rains and consequential lowland **flooding** plague the summer months. In 1998, the worst floods in living memory claimed four thousand lives, wiped out entire villages, isolated cities and destroyed millions of hectares of crops, with a similar disaster only narrowly averted in 2002.

Anhui

Despite government hopes that it will one day become a wealthy corridor between the coast and interior, **Anhui** largely lives up to its tradition as eastern China's poorest province. It has a long history, however, not all of it bad: million-year-old remains of the proto-human *Homo erectus* have been found here, while Shang-era copper mines in southern Anhui fuelled China's Bronze Age. The province later became well known for its artistic refinements, from decorative Han tombs through to Song-dynasty porcelain and Ming architecture.

All this, however, has been a struggle against Anhui's unfriendly geography. Arid and eroded, the north China plains extend into its upper third as far as the **Huai River**, and while the south is warmer and wetter, allowing for tea and tobacco cultivation, the fertile wooded hills soon climb to rugged mountains, and not much in the way of food can be grown there. But it is the **Yangzi** itself that ensures Anhui's poverty by regularly inundating the province's low-lying centre, which would otherwise produce a significant amount of crops. Until recently, a lack of bridges across the river also created a very physical division, separating the province's mountainous south from its more settled regions. Despite improvements in infrastructure since the 1990s, including the expansion of highways and railways, Anhui seems to remain, rather unfairly, as economically retarded as ever.

For the visitor, this isn't all bad news. While neither the provincial capital, **Hefei**, nor the north have much beyond their history, there are compensations for Anhui's lack of development south of the Yangzi. Here, superlative mountain landscapes at **Huang Shan** and the collection of Buddhist temples at **Jiuhua Shan** have been pulling in droves of sightseers for centuries, and there's a strong cultural tradition stamped on the area, with a substantial amount of antique rural architecture surviving intact around **Tunxi**. Also here is a riverside reserve near **Xuancheng**, protecting the **Chinese alligator**, one of the world's most endangered animals, though another local rarity, the **Yangzi river dolphin**, is heading rapidly towards extinction.

Flooding aside (and there's a near guarantee of this affecting bus travel during the summer months), the main problem with finding your way around Anhui is that many towns have a range of aliases, and can be differently labelled on maps and timetables. **Rail lines** connect Hefei to Nanjing through **Wuhu** – Anhui's major port – with other lines running west towards Changsha, north to Xi'an and Beijing, and south from Tunxi to Jiangxi.

Hefei

Nestled in the heart of the province but generally overlooked in the rush to cross the Yangzi and reach Huang Shan, Anhui's capital, **HEFEI**, gets few chance visitors. An unimportant backwater until being developed as a modest industrial base after 1949, Hefei's sole points of interest are a couple of **historical sites** and an unusually thorough **museum**. However, it's a comfortable place to spend a couple of days, relatively untouched by the ugly building mania sweeping the rest of the country and dignified by a number of important science and technology colleges.

Hefei

Hefei	合肥	héféi
Bao Gong Ci	包公祠	bāogōng cí
Baohe Park	包河公园	bāohé gōngyuán
Li Hongzhang Ju	李鸿章居	lǐhóngzhāng jū
Mingjiao Si	明教寺	míngjiào sì
Provincial Museum	省博物馆	shěng bówùguǎn
Three Kingdoms	三国	sān guó
Xiaoyaojin Park	逍遥津公园	xiāoyáojīn gōngyuán

Accommodation and eating

Chongqing Ba Jiangjun Huoguo	重庆巴将军火锅	chóngqìng bā jiāngjūn huǒguō
Donghai	东海饭店	dōnghǎi fàndiàn
Fuhao	富豪饭店	fùháo fàndiàn
Hainigan	淮上海尼根	huáishànghǎi nígēng
Hao Xiang Lai	豪享来餐厅	háoxiǎnglái cāntīng
Holiday Inn	古井假日饭店	gǔjǐng jiàrì fàndiàn
Huaqiao	华侨饭店	huáqiáo fàndiàn
Jindatang	金大糖宾馆	jīndàtáng bīnguǎn
Luzhou	庐州	lúzhōu
Xinjiyuan	新纪元宾馆	xīnjìyuán bīnguǎn
Xinya	新亚大酒店	xīnyà dàjiǔdiàn
Zhongxi Kafei	中西咖啡	zhōngxī kāfēi

The City

Ringed by parkland and canals – the remains of Ming-dynasty moats – downtown Hefei resembles a suburban high street more than a provincial capital. The **Provincial Museum** on Mengcheng Lu (Tues–Sun 8.30am–5pm; ¥10) provides sound evidence for Anhui's contributions to Chinese culture. A walk-through plaster cave leads on to a cast of the **Homo erectus cranium** from Taodian in the south of the province, proudly displayed in an oversized glass case, while splinters of more immediate history emerge in a few Stone Age items and an exceptional Shang bronze urn decorated with tiger and dragon motifs. Also interesting are the carved blocks taken from **Han-dynasty mausoleums** – Chinese-speakers might be able to decipher the comments about the Cao family (of *Three Kingdoms* fame) incised into the bricks of their Bozhou tomb by construction labourers. Farther on, there's a special exhibition of the "**Four Scholastic Treasures**" for which the province is famed: high-quality ink sticks, heavy carved ink stones, weasel-hair writing brushes and multicoloured papers.

Across town, hyper-modern shopping plazas along the busy, pedestrian eastern half of Huai He Lu seem an unlikely location for **Mingjiao Si** (daily 8am–5.30pm; ¥10), a restored sixteenth-century temple, whose fortress-like walls front the unpretentious halls and peach garden. The temple occupies a Three Kingdoms site where the northern leader **Cao Cao** drilled his crossbowers during the winter of 216–217 AD. Earlier, his general Zhang Liao had routed Wu's armies at the bloody battle of **Xiaoyaojin** – the site is now an unexciting **park** directly north of the temple – where Sun Quan, the leader of Wu, had to flee on horseback by leaping the bridgeless canal. A glassed-in **well** in the temple's main courtyard reputedly dates from this time, and definitely looks ancient, a worn stone ring set close to the ground, deeply scored by centuries of ropes being dragged over the rim. Just west of Mingjiao Si, **Li Hongzhang**

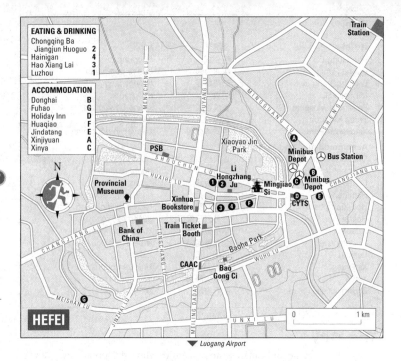

EATING & DRINKING

Chongqing Ba Jiangjun Huoguo	2
Hainigan	4
Hao Xiang Lai	3
Luzhou	1

ACCOMMODATION

Donghai	B
Fuhao	G
Holiday Inn	D
Huaqiao	F
Jindatang	E
Xinjiyuan	A
Xinya	C

HEFEI

0   1 km

▼ Luogang Airport

Ju (daily 8.30am–5.30pm; ¥15) is a similarly anachronistic Qing-era mansion, whose surrounding grey brick wall hides a series of tastefully decorated court-yards and halls embellished with opulently carved wooden furniture.

Down at the southeastern side of town, **Baohe Park** is a nice strip of lake-side willows and arched bridges off Wuhu Lu, where the **Bao Gong Ci** (Lord Bao Memorial Hall; ¥20) identifies Hefei as the birthplace of Bao, the famous Song-dynasty administrator, later governor of Kaifeng. Lord Bao's ability to uncover the truth in complex court cases, and his proverbially unbiased rulings, are the subject of endless tales – he also often appears as a judge in paintings of Chinese hell. Along with gilded statues, a **waxworks** brings a couple of well-known stories to life: look for Lord Bao's dark face, improbably "winged" hat, and the **three choppers** – shaped as a dragon, tiger and dog – he had made for summary executions; the implement used was chosen according to the status of the condemned.

Practicalities

Luogang airport is about 11km from the city, and is connected by an airport bus to the **CAAC office** on Meiling Dadao, whose entrance doubles as a florist's (daily 8am–10pm; ☎0551/2886626, ℻2885553). The **train station** is 3km northeast of the centre at the end of Shengli Lu – bus #119 runs down Shengli Lu and into town along Changjiang Lu – with lines servicing Bozhou, Shanghai, Guangzhou, Chengdu, Xiamen and Beijing. Train tickets are available at the station and at a booth on Meiling Dadao, just south of the Changjiang Lu intersection.

Hefei's **main bus station**, on Minguang Lu, handles traffic to all over Anhui and to adjacent provincial capitals, though there are just as many services from the chaotic clutch of **minibus depots** nearby on Shengli Lu – leaving, you'll have to hunt around stations for the right vehicle.

Changjiang Lu is Hefei's main street, with all essential services in its vicinity, including a huge **Bank of China** (Mon–Fri 8.30am–5pm), a **post office** (daily 8am–6pm) with telephones and upstairs **Internet bar**, and a **hospital** with English-speaking doctors at the junction with Tongchang Lu. For **information** and **tours** concerning Anhui's highlights, the friendly and bilingual **CYTS** (T0551/2206555, Einbound@cyts.ah.cn) is housed on the tenth floor of the *Holiday Inn*. The Xinhua Bookstore on Changjiang Lu has a good range of **books** in English – including translated Chinese novels – on the second floor, as does the Foreign Languages Bookshop on Huai He Lu. The **PSB** is on Shouchun Lu, a few blocks north of Changjiang Lu.

Accommodation

Hefei has a range of unremarkable places to stay. Spoken Chinese may get you into one of the budget **hostels** (dorm beds around ¥35) near the long-distance bus stations.

Donghai Fandian Mingguang Lu T0551/4693004. The best-value budget accommodation in town, with small, comfortable doubles and larger twin rooms. ❸

Fuhao Fandian Meishan Lu T0551/2218888, F2817583. The budget wing of the four-star *Anhui Fandian*, located around the back. Rooms are sparsely furnished but well looked after. ❹

Holiday Inn 1104 Changjiang Dong Lu T0551/2206666, F2201166, Wwww .ichotelsgroup.com. The usual range of facilities, along with a surprisingly inexpensive 24hr noodle bar. Foreign exchange counter for guests only. ❽

Huaqiao Fandian 98 Changjiang Lu T0551/2652221, F2642861. Also known as the *Anhui Overseas Chinese Hotel*, this is arguably overpriced, but has decent facilities and includes a light breakfast in the room tariff. ❻

Jindatang Binguan 1071 Changjiang Dong Lu T0551/4696272. New, good-value place with smart, comfortable rooms. ❹

Xinjiyuan Binguan Mingguang Lu T0551/4297954. Friendly, if slightly past its best, with single and double rooms. ❸

Xinya Dajiudian Near the bus stations on Shengli Lu T0551/2203388, F2203333. The upmarket lobby belies worn furnishings upstairs, but the rooms are large, everything works, and the staff are happy to have you. ❹

Eating, drinking and entertainment

There are plenty of cheap **stalls and canteens** where you can fill up on stir-fries, noodle soups and **river food** – especially little crabs and snails – east of the museum on Huaihe Lu. Near the post office on Changjiang Lu, *Hao Xiang Lai* offers a good, inexpensive range of regional snacks – soups, buns, noodles, cold vegetable and meat dishes – all laid out for you to order by pointing. A few streets back on Suzhou Lu, near the intersection with Huaihe Lu, are a couple of excellent places to tuck in with noisy local crowds: *Luzhou* is a roast-duck restaurant which also serves excellent dumplings, and is so popular you generally have to queue to get in; while *Chongqing Ba Jiangjun Huoguo* is a smarter affair specializing in Chongqing hotpots. For **Western-style** fare, the usual plethora of fast-food outlets are available along Changjiang Lu and Huaihe Lu, or for a steak meal (¥25 upwards) try *Hainigan* near the *Huaqiao Fandian* on Changjiang Lu.

For an evening out, Hefei has something of a reputation for **stage productions** – there are at least two indigenous opera styles and a local acrobatic troupe. Ask at CYTS as to whether there are performances at the Guixiangyuan theatre on Changjiang Lu (tickets cost around ¥100 for a 1hr 30min show).

Northern Anhui

Cynics say that northern Anhui's high points are the roads, which run on flood-proof embankments a few metres above the green, pancake-flat paddy fields. Certainly, about the only geographic features are **rivers** such as the **Huai He**, setting for the rather drab industrial and grain centre of **Bangbu**. The **battle of Huai Hai** took place nearby in 1948, when a million Guomindang and PLA combatants fought a decisive encounter in which the guerrilla-trained Communists overran Chiang Kaishek's less flexible forces. A demoralized GMD surrendered in Beijing in January the next year, and though war resumed when the two sides couldn't agree on terms, it was largely a mopping-up operation by the Communists against GMD bastions.

All this is mainly background for what you'll see along the way, but historians, town planners and anyone interested in Traditional Chinese Medicine will find a smattering of attractions at **Shouxian** – feasible as a day-trip from Hefei – and **Bozhou**, which is worth a day's scrutiny on the long haul into or out of the province. There are **minibuses** throughout the day from Hefei's Shengli Lu depots to Bozhou or Shouxian; make sure with the latter that you don't end up getting herded aboard a bus bound for the more familiar tourist destination of Shexian (the local pronunciation is very similar).

Shouxian

About 100km north of Hefei, **SHOUXIAN** was a regional capital back in 241 BC, during the Warring States Period, and is now a small country seat surrounded by over 6km of dykes and Ming-era **stone walls** which can be climbed for views. Minibuses from Hefei drop you at the virtually defunct bus station about 700m south of the walls; the road bends around to enter the town through the **south gate**'s triple arch, and then you're following Shouxian's die-straight main road through the best surviving example of a Song-dynasty street plan in China. There are a couple of specific sights – an old **theatre** on the eastern axis, and the ruinous **Bao'en Monastery** hidden in the south-western quarter – but there's more fun in just wandering the tiny back lanes,

Northern Anhui		
Bangbu	蚌埠	bàngbù
Bozhou	亳州	bózhōu
Chinese Medicinal Products Marketplace	中药材交易中心	zhōngyàocái jiāoyìzhōngxīn
Cuiwei Dajiudian	翠微大酒店	cuìwēi dàjiǔdiàn
Dixia Yunbing Dao	地下运兵道	dìxià yùnbīng dào
Gujing Dajiudian	古井大酒店	gǔjǐng dàjiǔdiàn
Gu Qian Zhuang	古钱庄	gǔ qián zhuāng
Huaxi Lou	花戏楼	huāxì lóu
Fuyang	阜阳	fùyáng
Huainan	淮南	huáinán
Shouxian	寿县	shòuxiàn
Bao'en Monastery	报恩寺	bào'ēn sì

where you'll frequently come across buildings with dated wooden lintels and bronze detailing on doors. Shouxian was also the home of the Han-dynasty philosopher **Liu An**, who supposedly invented bean curd, and there's an annual September **Tofu Festival** in his honour.

A couple of inexpensive **guesthouses** (¥70) lie along Shouxian's main street, but foreigners are a rare sight in town and attract so much attention that you may feel more comfortable moving on. For destinations further afield than Hefei, catch a minibus-taxi (¥4) from outside the bus station 20km east to the monochrome coal-mining centre of **Huainan**, from where there are irregular buses to Nanjing, Shanghai, Wuhan, and **Fuyang**, on the way to Bozhou.

Bozhou

BOZHOU lies in Anhui's northwestern corner, around five hours from Hefei or three from Shouxian, the journey taking in scenes of river barges loading up with coal, red-brick villages surrounded by pollarded willows, and a level horizon pierced by kiln chimneys. The city's fame rests on its being the largest marketplace in the world for **traditional medicines**; as the birthplace of **Hua Mulan**, heroine of Chinese legend and Disney animation (though there are no monuments to her here); and as the ancestral home of the Three Kingdoms warlord, **Cao Cao**. Portrayed in the *Romance of the Three Kingdoms* as a self-serving villain whose maxim was "Better to wrong the world than have it wrong me", he was nonetheless a brilliant general and respectable poet, whose claims to rule China were just as legitimate as those of his arch-rival, Lu Bei. At any rate, nobody in Bozhou seems ashamed of the connection.

Bozhou's frankly grimy, squalid main streets may have you wondering why you made the journey, but it's worth persevering. About 3km southeast of the centre, the eastern end of Zhan Qian Lu (the train station approach road) sets up from Monday to Friday as a **medicinal market**, attracting something in the region of 60,000 traders daily from all over China and Southeast Asia. The main **Chinese Medicinal Products Marketplace** here is a huge building on the south side of the road, packed to the roof in places with bales of dried plants, fungi – including the bizarre caterpillar fungus, or *cordyceps* – and animals (or bits of them), the rest of the space taken up by enthusiastic crowds. The market's activity and strangely reassuring smell alone justify the trip to town.

The rest of Bozhou is for history buffs. On the south side of Renmin Zhong Lu, **Dixia Yunbing Dao** (¥12) is a one-hundred-metre-long subterranean **tunnel** Cao Cao had installed so his troops could take an invading army by surprise; the arched, claustrophobic brick passages are totally unexpected at street level. North from here, Renmin Bei Jie forms the congested heart of Bozhou's **Muslim** community, full of noodle, bread and mutton kebab vendors, and containing a couple of small **mosques**; the street ends where it passes through the city's solid stone **north gate**. Beyond, the area between Heping Lu and the river is filled by a quiet net of nineteenth-century lanes, a procession of small whitewashed shops and home industries. **Gu Qian Zhuang** (Old Bank; ¥5) on Nanjing Gang here served its original function between 1825 and 1949 and provides great views of surrounding grey-tiled roofs from an upstairs balcony, though otherwise it's rather bare.

Bozhou's architectural masterpiece is **Huaxi Lou** (¥20), a seventeenth-century guild-temple **theatre** some 500m north of Gu Qian Zhuang at the river end of Nanjing Gang. Sporting skilfully carved brick and wood embellishments, the theatre is named after the Han-dynasty doctor **Hua Tuo**, the first person credited with using anaesthetics during surgery, who was bumped off by

Cao Cao after refusing to become the warlord's personal physician. Check out the painted friezes surrounding the stage, where several well-known *Three Kingdoms* set pieces are depicted, including Zhuge Liang's celebrated "Empty City Stratagem": having no troops to defend the key stronghold of Xicheng, Zhuge opened the gates and sat in surrender on the battlements while his men swept the road below. Knowing his cunning, the invading general, Sima Yi, suspected some elaborate trap and fled. The theatre's rear hall contains a collection of Neolithic stone axes and Eastern Han artefacts unearthed nearby, including a **jade burial suit** made of 2400 tiles belonging to Cao Cao's father, Cao Song, who was ignominiously killed by rebels while hiding in a toilet.

Practicalities

Bozhou's centre is a two-kilometre-wide grid just south of the slow-flowing **Wo He**, the main roads being the east–west Renmin Lu and the north–south Qiaoling Lu, which intersect on the eastern side of town. The **train station** is about 3km southeast – best reached by taxi – and has a few services down to Hefei each day. An alternative rail option is to catch a minibus south to **Fuyang** (around 1hr 30min), which is on the Beijing–Jiujiang and Hefei–Zhengzhou lines. The two adjacent **bus stations** on Qiaoling Lu mostly serve Hefei, Fuyang or local destinations, with a few battered and elderly long-distance buses to adjoining provinces.

The intersection of Renmin Lu and Qiaoling Lu, about 500m south of the bus stations, marks a heap of **accommodation** options. *Cuiwei Dajiudian* is an ordinary urban hotel (℡0558/5516604; ❹), while across the road the three-star *Gujing Dajiudian* (℡0558/5521298; ❺) has some pretensions to comfort. The **Bank of China** is also on the crossroads, with the main **post office** 500m west on Renmin Zhong Lu. Hotpot and noodle stalls abound, and the *Gujing Dajiudian's* **restaurant** offers tasty, if pricey, fare.

The Yangzi: Ma'anshan and Xuancheng

The Yangzi flows silt-grey and broad for 350km across Anhui's lower third, forming a very visible geographic boundary. An indication of the province's chronic underdevelopment is the fact that as recently as 1995 the only way to

The Yangzi: Ma'anshan and Xuancheng		
Ma'anshan	马鞍山	*mǎ'ān shān*
Cuiluo Shan	翠螺山	*cuìluó shān*
Great Wall Hotel	长城宾馆	*chángchéng bīnguǎn*
Xuancheng	宣城	*xuānchéng*
Chinese alligator breeding centre	扬子鳄养殖场	*yángzǐ'è yǎngzhíchǎng*
Xuanzhou Binguan	宣州宾馆	*xuānzhōu bīnguǎn*
Tongling	铜岭	*tónglíng*
Wuhu	芜湖	*wúhú*
Yangzi River	长江	*chángjiāng*
River dolphins	白鲫	*báijì*

cross the river was by ferry, though it's now bridged in the east at **Wuhu** and roughly halfway along at **Tongling**. A reserve at the latter was at the forefront of apparently unsuccessful efforts to save the light grey *baiji*, or **Yangzi river dolphin**, from a catastrophic decline – in 2003 there were estimated to be only five animals left, though they were common as recently as the 1970s – linked to the growth of industrial pollution, river traffic and net fishing on the Yangzi. The species seems doomed to linger on only in Tongling's **Baiji beer**, which has the dolphin's Latin name, *Lipotes vexillifer*, stamped on the bottle cap.

Most of the riverside towns are unashamedly functional and don't really justify special trips. **Ma'anshan** and **Xuancheng** offer a modicum of interest in their associations with Tang-dynasty poet Li Bai and the breeding of Chinese alligators, respectively.

Ma'anshan

On the Wuhu–Nanjing rail line, **MA'ANSHAN** is notable for cliffside scenery 7km south at **Cuiluo Shan** (¥40), reached on a twenty-minute crawl through the town's industrial hinterland on bus #4 from the bus or train station. A large parkland, Cuiluo Shan is dotted with a series of halls and pavilions commemorating the itinerant Tang-dynasty romantic poet **Li Bai** (aka Tai Bai, see p.899). Inspired by the scenery at **Caishiji**, considered first among the Yangzi's three famous rock outcrops, Li Bai wrote many of his works here, and it was nearby that he drowned in 762 AD after drunkenly falling out of a boat while trying to touch the moon's reflection. His **tomb** lies amid ancient pines and willows at the foot of Qing Shan.

Ma'anshan's **bus and train stations** are both fairly central on Hongqi Lu, which leads down to the town centre (head left out of the bus station or right out of the train station), set around Yushan Lake Park. You can stay at the *Great Wall Hotel* (☎0555/2479888; ❹), a fifteen-minute walk from the stations down Hongqi Lu and then left along the edge of Yushan Lake on Hubei Lu. The **Bank of China** and **post office** are both on Hubei Lu.

Xuancheng

Chinese-speakers interested in wildlife should make the trip to **XUANCHENG**, two hours by bus to the southeast of Wuhu across low hills patterned by tea plantations – confusingly, you pass another Wuhu, the county town, halfway there. Xuancheng is also reachable by train, as it's on the Hefei–Tunxi (Huang Shan) rail line. An untidy but friendly place, the town is associated with the production of high-quality handmade art paper (though this actually comes from **Jiangxian**, 55km to the southwest), and a **Chinese alligator breeding centre** (daily 8am–5pm; ¥30) lies several kilometres to the south. The centre is worth the effort to reach because wild populations of these timid alligators are few and confined to Anhui, their habitat ever more encroached upon. Since the 1990s a worldwide project coordinated by the US Bronx Zoo has boosted their captive numbers here to ten thousand. The centre offers the opportunity to get very close to the alligators and – inappropriate as it may seem – to enjoy the taste of their meat in its restaurant. To reach the centre, you can negotiate with the minibus drivers at the crossroads near the bus station, or ask travel companies in Tunxi or Hefei to phone ahead and arrange a visit for you.

Surrounded by small rivers, Xuancheng is about 2km across, with the **train station** on the eastern side and the main **bus station** to the southwest. For **accommodation**, there's the *Xuanzhou Binguan* on Zhuangyuan Lu (☎0563/3022957; ❹), near the bus station.

Jiuhua Shan

A place of worship for fifteen hundred years, **Jiuhua Shan** (Nine Glorious Mountains) has been one of China's sacred Buddhist mountains ever since the Korean monk **Jin Qiaojue** (believed to be the reincarnation of the Bodhisattva Dizang, whose doctrines he preached) died here in a secluded cave in 794 AD. Today there are more than sixty temples – some founded back in the ninth century – containing a broad collection of sculptures, religious texts and early calligraphy, though there are also plenty of visitors (many of them overseas Chinese and Koreans) and some outsized building projects threatening to overwhelm Jiuhua Shan's otherwise human scale. Even so, an atmosphere of genuine devotion is clearly evident in the often austere halls with their wisps of incense smoke and distant chanting.

Practicalities

Though it's 60km south of the Yangzi and remote from major transport centres, Jiuhua Shan is straightforward to reach, with direct **buses** at least from Hefei, Tangkou, Taiping (Huang Shan), Tongling and Guichi. Other traffic might drop you 25km to the northeast at **Qingyang**, from where mountain minibuses (¥8) leave when full throughout the day; in case you arrive late, there's a **hotel** (¥75) attached to the bus station here.

The twisting Jiuhua Shan road passes villages scattered through the moist green of rice fields and bamboo stands, white-walled houses built of bricks interlocked in a "herringbone" pattern, with some inspiring views of bald, spiky peaks above and valleys below. The road ends at picturesque **JIUHUA SHAN village**, where the mountain's accommodation, and the most famous temples, huddle around a couple of cobbled streets and squares, all hemmed in by encircling hills. On arrival at the village **gates** you'll have to pay Jiuhua Shan's **entry fee** (March–Nov ¥90; Dec–Feb ¥80). From here the road runs up past a host of market stalls selling postcards, trinkets, and waterproof **maps** and umbrellas for the frequently sodden weather.

Jiuhua Shan

Jiuhua Shan	九华山	jiǔhuá shān
Baisui Gong	百岁宫	bǎisuì gōng
Cable-car station	索道站	suǒdào zhàn
Dabei Lou	大悲楼	dàbēi lóu
Fenghuang Song	凤凰松	fènghuáng sōng
Funicular railway	缆车站	lǎnchē zhàn
Huacheng Si	化城寺	huàchéng sì
Tiantai Zhengding	天台正顶	tiāntái zhèngdǐng
Yingke Song	迎客松	yíngkè sōng
Zhiyuan Si	执园寺	zhíyuán sì

Accommodation

Baisui	百岁宾馆	bǎisuì bīnguǎn
Julong Dajiudian	聚笼大酒店	jùlóng dàjiǔdiàn
Longquan Fandian	龙泉饭店	lóngquán fàndiàn
Taihua Shanzhuang	太华山庄	tàihuá shānzhuāng
Xin Shiji	新世纪大酒店	xīnshìjì dàjiǔdiàn

Qingyang	青阳	qīngyáng

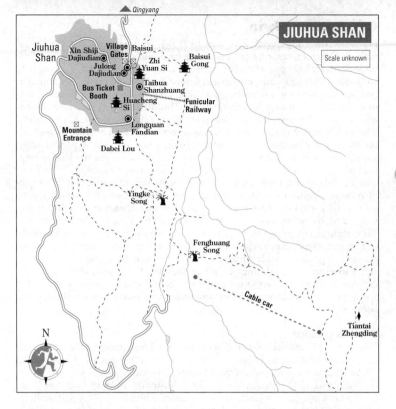

About 100m along, the road divides around the village in a two-kilometre circuit; a booth selling onward **bus tickets** is just down on the right here, while the core of the village lies straight ahead. Long-distance transport to Hefei, Nanjing, Tangkou, Taiping, Tunxi and Shanghai congregates first thing in the morning near the booth, or you can pick up frequent minibuses to Qingyang and look for connections there.

You'll be grabbed on arrival and offered all manner of **accommodation**, most of it decent value. For upmarket facilities try *Julong Dajiudian* (☎0566/5011022, ⓦwww.jiuhuashan.com.cn; ❻) to the right of the village gates behind an illuminated fountain, although they won't bargain and rooms are damp. Next door, the new *Baisui* (☎0566/5011623; ❺) has standard, comfortable rooms, attractively set around a temple-style courtyard. On the other side of the street, Zhiyuan Si has extremely bare beds (¥30) designed for itinerant monks, which may be available to tourists. Up the main street on the left, look for steps and an English sign above a parking lot for *Taihua Shanzhuang* (☎0566/5011340, ⓔjhswwx@163.com; ❹), a hospitable guesthouse with constant hot water; further along on the right you'll find clean rooms and plenty of Chinese tourists at *Longquan Fandian* (☎0566/5011412; ❺). For cheaper lodgings head up the hill past the bus ticket booth, where there are several small hotels such as *Xin Shiji Dajiudian* (☎0566/501174; ❸) with simple, shabby rooms, as well as a few more expensive options. Numerous **places to eat** offer everything from cheap buns to expensive game dishes.

On Jiuhua Shan

Just inside the village gates, **Zhiyuan Si** (¥5) is an imposing Qing monastery built with smooth, vertical walls, upcurving eaves and a yellow-tiled roof nestled up against a cliff. Despite a sizeable exterior, the numerous little halls are cramped and stuffed with sculptures, including a fanged, bearded and hooknosed thunder god bursting out of its protective glass cabinet just inside the gate. Head for the main hall, in which a magnificently gilded **Buddhist trinity** sits solemnly on separate lotus flowers, blue hair dulled by incense smoke, and ringed by *arhat*s. This makes quite a setting for the annual **temple fair**, held in Dizang's honour on the last day of the seventh lunar month, when the hall is packed with worshippers, monks and tourists. Make sure you look behind the altar, where Guanyin statuettes ascend right to the lofty wooden roof beams.

If you follow the main road around through the village, the next temple of note you come to is the new and garish **Dabei Lou** (¥6), which sports some hefty carved stonework; more or less opposite, **Huacheng Si** (¥8) is the mountain's oldest surviving temple, in part possibly dating right back to the Tang, though comprehensively restored. The stone entrance is set at the back of a large cobbled square whose centrepiece is a deep pond inhabited by some gargantuan goldfish. Inside, Huacheng's low-ceilinged, broad main hall doubles as a **museum**, with paintings depicting the life of Jin Qiaojue from his sea crossing to China (accompanied only by a faithful hound) to his death at the age of 90, and the discovery of his miraculously preserved corpse three years later.

To the peaks

The mountain's official "entrance" is marked by a huge ornamental gateway and temple about 500m past Dabei Lou on the main road, though well-concealed, smaller flagstoned paths ascend from behind Zhiyuan Si and at the corners of the main road in the village. There's also a **funicular railway** from the main street near *Longquan Fandian* to the ridge above Zhiyuan Si (¥45). Using these access points, you can take a good, easy **circuit walk** on the ridges just above the village in about an hour, or extend this to a full **day's hike** up around Jiuhua's higher peaks – though again, you can save time by using minibuses and the cable car for part of the way. For the circuit, walk past Dabei Lou to where the road bends sharply right. Steps ascend from here to a moderately-sized temple complex whose entrance-hall atrium contains some gruesomely entertaining, life-size sculptures of **Buddhist hell**. These are so graphic that it's hard not to feel that the artists enjoyed their task of depicting sinners being skewered, pummelled, strangled, boiled and bisected by demons, while the virtuous look down, doubtless exceedingly thankful for their salvation. Beyond the temple, a few minutes' walk brings you to a meeting of several paths at **Yingke Song** (Welcoming Guest Pine). Bear left and it's a couple of kilometres past several pavilions and minor temples to steep views down onto the village at **Baisui Gong** (¥8), a plain, atmospheric monastery whose interior is far from weatherproof, with clouds drifting in and out of the main hall. A rear room contains the mummy of the Ming priest **Wu Xia**, best known for compiling the **Huayan sutras** in gold dust mixed with his own blood; his tiny body is displayed seated in prayer, grotesquely covered in a thick, smooth skin of gold leaf. Steps descend from Baisui Gong to Zhiyuan Si, or you can take the **funicular railway** down to the main street.

To reach the upper peaks, turn right at Yingke Song, and you've a two-hour climb ahead of you via **Fenghuang Song** (Phoenix Pine), more temples, wind-scoured rocks, and superb scenery surrounding the summit area at **Tiantai Zhengding** (Heavenly Terrace). There's also a **cable car** from Fenghuang Song to just below the peaks (¥40); the truly indolent can catch a minibus from the entrance gate to the Fenghuang Song terminus from opposite Dabei Lou in the village – these buses are included in the Jiuhua Shan entry fee. Witnessing the sunrise from here, **Li Bai**, the Tang man of letters, was inspired to bestow Jiuhua Shan with its name by the sight of the major pinnacles rising up out of clouds. In future years, this will also be the place to follow the progress of China's most grandiose religious building project: a 99-metre-high **statue of Dizang** is planned for the mountain, which if completed will be the largest Buddha sculpture in the world.

Tunxi, Shexian and Yixian

The most obvious reason to stop in **Tunxi**, down near Anhui's southernmost borders, is because of the town's transport connections to Huang Shan, 50km off to the northwest (see p.490): Tunxi has the closest **airport** and **train station** to the mountain, while many long-distance buses pass through here as well. However, if you've the slightest interest in classical Chinese **architecture**, then Tunxi and its environs are worth checking out in their own right. Anhui's isolation has played a large part in preserving a liberal sprinkling of seventeenth-century monuments and homes in the area, especially around **Shexian** and **Yixian**, just short bus rides away. The guide fees and other costs associated with spending a day at Yixian make Shexian a better bet if you're on a tight budget.

Tunxi, Shexian and Yixian

Tunxi	屯溪	*túnxī*
Cheng Dawei's House	程大位居	*chéngdàwèi jū*
Cheng Family House	程氏三宅	*chéngshì sānzhái*
Huang Shan Shi	黄山市	*huángshān shì*
Lao Jie	老街	*lǎojiē*
Accommodation and eating		
Hehuachi Zaochi Yitiao Jie	荷花池早吃一条街	*héhuāchí zǎochī yìtiáojiē*
Huashan	华山宾馆	*huáshān bīnguǎn*
Huaxi	花溪饭店	*huāxī fàndiàn*
Huochezhan Tielu	火车站铁路招待所	*huǒchēzhàn tiělù zhāodàisuǒ*
Jingwei	经纬酒店	*jīngwěi jiǔdiàn*
Zhengtong	政通宾馆	*zhèngtōng bīnguǎn*
Shexian	歙县	*shèxiàn*
Doushan Jie	斗山街	*dǒushān jiē*
Nan Lou	南楼	*nánlóu*
Tangyue arches	堂越牌坊	*tángyuè páifǎng*
Xuguo Archway	许国石坊	*xǔguó shífǎng*
Yanghe Men	阳和门	*yánghé mén*
Yixian	黟县	*yīxiàn*
Hongcun	宏村	*hóngcūn*
Nanping	南屏村	*nánpíng cūn*
Xidi	西递	*xīdì*

Any exploration of Shexian and its surroundings will reveal a host of traditional Ming and Qing architectural features, most notably the **paifang** or ornamental archway – there are over eighty of these in She county alone. Of wood or stone, *paifang* can be over 10m in height, and are finely carved, painted or tiled, the central beam often bearing a moral inscription. They were constructed for a variety of reasons, foremost among which, cynics would argue, was the ostentatious display of wealth. This aside, the gateways were built to celebrate or reward virtuous behaviour, family success, important historical events or figures, and to reflect prevailing values such as filial piety; as such, they provide a valuable insight into the mores of the time.

Tunxi

An old trading centre, **TUNXI** (aka **Huang Shan Shi**) is set around the junction of two rivers, with the original part of town along the north bank of the **Xin'an Jiang** at the intersection of Huang Shan Xi Lu and Xin'an Lu, and a newer quarter focused around the train and bus stations a kilometre or so to the northeast. If you've time to spare, try tracking down two **Ming-dynasty houses** in Tunxi's eastern backstreets (neither is well marked). The more easterly house – that of the mathematician Cheng Dawei – is in a sorry state of repair, but both it and the Cheng family house are classic examples of the indigenous **Huizhou style**, of which you'll find plenty more at Shexian or Yixian. Their plan, of two floors of galleried rooms based around a courtyard, proved so popular that it became the benchmark of urban domestic architecture in central and eastern China.

For more, head down to Tunxi's historic, flagstoned **Lao Jie** (Old Street), a westerly continuation of Huang Shan Xi Lu. Here, 500m of **Ming shops**

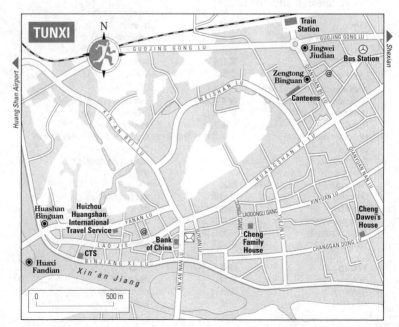

running parallel to the river have been nicely restored for visitors, selling local teas, medicinal herbs and all manner of artistic materials and "antiques" – ink stones, brushes, Mao badges, decadent advertising posters from the 1930s, and carved wooden panels prised off old buildings. A few genuine businesses stand out, notably an apothecary sporting 1920s timber decor, and several small **dumpling houses** filled with local clientele. You'll also see characteristic **horse-head gables** rising out below the rooflines in steps. These originated as fire baffles between adjoining houses, stopping the spread of flames from building to building, but eventually became somewhat decorative affairs.

Practicalities

A taxi into the town centre from busy **Huang Shan airport**, around 10km west of town, should cost around ¥15 on the meter. The **train station** is at the northern city limits on the end of Qianyuan Bei Lu, which runs 250m south to Huang Shan Lu; there are connections to Hefei (via Xuancheng and Wuhu), Nanchang, Shanghai, Xiamen and Beijing, along with useful, though ploddingly slow, trains southwest to Jingdezhen. Tangkou minibuses prowl the station forecourt, while Tunxi's **bus station** occupies an entire block 250m east off Guojing Gong Lu, with frequent services for Shexian, Yixian, Tangkou and Taiping, and long-distance departures to Jiuhua Shan, Wuhu, Hefei, Shanghai, Jiujiang, Nanchang and even Guangzhou. A couple of **city buses** run around Tunxi: from the train station, #6 takes a back road into town, while #12 follows Huang Shan Lu southwest from the bus station – either route is a twenty-minute walk.

A knot of convenient, if mostly dull and overpriced, places to **stay** surrounds the train station, the best of which are the smart *Jingwei Jiudian* (☎0559/2345188, ℉2345098; ❻), which out of season offers fifty-percent discounts; and the nearby *Zengtong Binguan* (☎0559/2112968; ❻) with comfortable, modern rooms. The *Huochezhan Tielu Zhaodaisuo* (☎0559/2113699; ❹) is immediately to the right out of the train station and has acceptable, tidy rooms. Near the old town and next to the bridge on Yanan Lu is the smart *Huashan Binguan* (☎0559/2328888; ❺); on the opposite side of the river the *Huaxi Fandian* is quiet and pleasant (☎0559/2328000, ℉2514990; ❼). For **eating**, there are numerous small restaurants around the Xin'an Lu/Lao Jie intersection. Near the train station, cheap eats can be found at the string of canteens on Hehuachi Zaochi Yitiao Jie, off Qianyuan Lu.

Most services are around the Huang Shan Lu/Xin'an Lu intersection, where, along with markets and department stores, you'll find a **Bank of China** (Mon–Fri 8am–5.30pm) and the main **post office** (Mon–Fri 8am–8pm). For **information**, **plane tickets**, and **permits** for Yixian, try the riverside CTS at 1 Binjiang Xi Lu (☎0559/2522649, ℉2522635) or the Huang Shan Huizhou International Travel Service on Yanan Lu (☎0559/3384556). The latter has day-tours to Shexian and to Yixian. For a cheaper, more foreigner-friendly version of the same, a local man by the name of Stephen Huang (☎13905594053, ℮hshysdn@163.net) offers English-language guided tours using local transport. There are a couple of **Internet** places, one just off Lao Jie and another in the small street on the other side of Qianyuan Bei Lu from Hehuachi Zaochi Yitiao Jie.

Shexian

Anhui owes a good deal to **SHEXIAN**, an easy forty-minute **minibus** ride 25km east of Tunxi up the Xin'an River and once the regional capital – the name "Anhui" is a telescoping of Anqing (a Yangzi town in the southwest) and **Huizhou**, Shexian's former name. The region blossomed in the seventeenth century after local salt merchants started raising elaborate town houses and intricately carved stone archways, some of which survive today, in a showy display of their wealth. The province's opera styles were formalized here, and the town became famous for *hui* inkstones and fine-grained *she* ink sticks, the latter still considered China's best. One of Shexian's charms for the visitor is that most buildings are still in everyday use, not tarted up for tourism, and there's a genuinely dated ambience to soak up.

Shexian's **bus station** is out on the highway, where arrivals are accosted by "guides" and motor-rickshaw drivers. You don't need them: take the bridge over the river and carry straight on past 100m of uninspiring, concrete-and-tile buildings; at the end of the road turn right, then first left, and you're walking up **Jiefang Jie**, off which run the narrow lanes that comprise the older part of town. To the sides you'll see the restored **Nan Lou** and **Yanghe Men** gate towers; straight ahead, however, Jiefang Jie runs under the smaller but highly decorative **Xuguo archway**, one of the finest in the region. Nearby are souvenir stalls and a **bookshop**, where you should pick up a **map** of Shexian (about ¥3) with all the streets and points of interest marked. You could just walk at random, snacking on traditional "pressed buns", but for a detailed look, seek out **Doushan Jie**, a street full of well-preserved Huizhou-style homes, around which you can tour with a Chinese-speaking guide (¥8). When you've had enough, return to the station and get a Tunxi-bound minibus to drop you off around 5km down the highway, then walk or catch a motorbike-rickshaw for the last 3km to where the **Tangyue arches** (¥50, Chinese-speaking guide included) form a strange spectacle of seven ornamental gates standing isolated in a row in a field, albeit with the usual tourist restaurants and shops close at hand.

Yixian

For reasons that have nothing to do with architecture, you need a **police permit** (¥55, most easily arranged through agents in Tunxi for an extra ¥20) to stop off in **YIXIAN**, 60km due west of Tunxi. The town itself is a stepping stone to surrounding villages, for which you'll have to charter a minibus (about ¥30 per stop) and pay fees for compulsory guides (¥10 per person in a group, up to ¥50 if you're on you own) and admission. **Xidi** (entry ¥55) is the pick of these, and hence the most visited, a particularly attractive place comprising some 120 eighteenth-century houses set along a riverbank, now turned into a large antiques market. There are endless examples of carved gilded wooden screens and panels inside the houses, as well as thin line paintings on front walls showing pairs of animals or "double happiness" characters. Mirrors placed above the three-tiered door lintels reflect bad luck or reveal a person's true character – a useful tool for judging the nature of strangers. **Hongcun** (¥55) is another fine spot, whose street plan resembles (with some imagination) the body of a buffalo, complete with horns, body and legs, while **Nanping** (¥35) was used as a set in Zhang Yimou's film *Judou*.

Huang Shan

Rearing over southern Anhui, **Huang Shan** – the Yellow Mountains – are among eastern China's greatest sights. It's said that once you've ascended their peaks you will never want to climb another mountain, and certainly the experience

Huang Shan

Huang Shan	黄山	*huángshān*
Bai'e Feng	白鹅峰	*bái'é fēng*
Banshan Si	半山寺	*bànshān sì*
Beginning-to-Believe Peak	始信峰	*shǐxìn fēng*
Cable-car station	索道站	*suǒdào zhàn*
Ciguang Ge	慈光阁	*cíguāng gé*
Feilai Shi	飞来石	*fēilái shí*
Guangming Ding	光明顶	*guāngmíng dǐng*
Jiyu Bei	鲫鱼背	*jìyú bèi*
Paiyun Ting	排云亭	*páiyún tíng*
Tiandu Feng	天都峰	*tiāndū fēng*
Yingke Song	迎客松	*yíngkèsōng*
Yungu Si	云谷寺	*yúngǔ sì*
Yuping Lou	玉屏楼	*yùpíng lóu*
Accommodation and eating		
Beihai Binguan	北海宾馆	*běihǎi bīnguǎn*
Paiyun Ting Binguan	排云亭宾馆	*páiyúntíng bīnguǎn*
Shilin Dajiudian	石林大酒店	*shílín dàjiǔdiàn*
Tianhai Binguan	天海宾馆	*tiānhǎi bīnguǎn*
Xihai Fandian	西海饭店	*xīhǎi bīnguǎn*
Taiping	太平	*tàipíng*
Tangkou	汤口	*tāngkǒu*
Dazhong Fandian	大众饭店	*dàzhòng fàndiàn*
Fuxing Lou Dajiudian	复兴楼大酒店	*fùxīnglóu dàjiǔdiàn*
Hongdashi Jiudian	洪大师酒店	*hóngdàshī jiǔdiàn*
Zhounan Dajiudian	洲楠大酒店	*zhōunán dàjiǔdiàn*
Wenquan	温泉	*wēnquán*
Huangshan Binguan	黄山宾馆	*huángshān bīnguǎn*
Taoyuan Binguan	桃源宾馆	*táoyuán bīnguǎn*
Wenquan Dajiudian	温泉大酒店	*wēnquán dàjiǔdiàn*

is staggeringly scenic, with pinnacles emerging from thick bamboo forests, above which rock faces dotted with ancient, contorted pine trees growing from narrow ledges disappear into the swirling mists. These views often seem familiar, for Huang Shan's landscape has left an indelible impression on Chinese art, and painters are a common sight on the paths, huddled in padded jackets and sheltering their work from the incipient drizzle beneath umbrellas – the more serious of them spend months at a time up here.

As a pilgrimage site trodden by emperors and Communist leaders alike, Huang Shan is regarded as sacred in China, and it's the ambition of every Chinese to conquer it at least once in their lifetime. Consequently, don't expect to climb alone: noisy multitudes swarm along the neatly paved paths, or crowd out the three cable-car connections to the top. All this can make the experience depressingly like visiting an amusement park, but then you'll turn a corner and come face to face with a huge, smooth monolith topped by a single tree, or be confronted with views of a remote square of forest growing isolated on a rocky platform. Nature is never far away from reasserting itself here.

Accessing Huang Shan

Transport pours into the Huang Shan region from all over eastern China. There are direct buses from Shanghai, Hangzhou and Nanjing, as well as Jiuhua Shan, Wuhu, Hefei and other places within Anhui. Much of this, and all rail and air traffic, passes through **Tunxi** (aka Huang Shan Shi; see p.488), with regular shuttle buses (¥13) connecting the train and bus stations here with Huang Shan's main gateway at **Tangkou**, 50km northwest of Tunxi on the mountain's southern foothills. Alternatively, **Taiping** is a lesser-used access point to the north of the mountain on the Jiuhua Shan–Tangkou road. Be aware that some long-distance buses go directly to Tangkou or Taiping, and might refer to these towns as "Huang Shan" on their timetables.

Tangkou is the starting point for Huang Shan's two **hiking trails** and parallel **cable cars** (daily 8am–4.30pm; April–Oct ¥65, Nov–March ¥55). An additional cable car (same prices) is accessed from Taiping by catching a minibus from the main-street bus station for the 22-kilometre ride to the terminus at **Songgu**. Note that **queues** for peak-bound cable cars can be monumental (there's usually less of a wait to go down), and that services are suspended during windy weather. The Huang Shan **entry fee** (April–Oct ¥130, Nov–March ¥85; ¥65 concessions) is payable at the start of the trails or at the cable-car ticket offices. The cable cars take upwards of twenty minutes, or you'll need between two and eight hours to walk up, depending on whether you follow the easier **eastern route**, or the lengthy and demanding **western route**. Once at the top, there's a half-day of relatively easy hiking around the peaks. Ideally, plan to spend two or three days on the mountain to allow for a steady ascent and circuit, though it's quite feasible to see a substantial part of Huang Shan in a full day.

There's **accommodation** (mostly fairly expensive) and **food** available in Tangkou, Taiping and on the mountain itself, but you'll need to come prepared for steep paths, rain and winter snow – all an essential part of the experience. Note that in winter, hotels either dramatically drop their prices or shut up shop until spring. Hiring guides and porters is something of an extravagance, as paths are easy to follow and accommodation in Tangkou and Taiping will store surplus gear; just bring a day-pack, strong shoes and something warm for the top.

There are branches of the **Bank of China** in Tangkou, Wenquan and on the mountain top, and there's an **Internet café** in Tangkou.

Tangkou and Wenquan

Two hours from Tunxi, **TANG-KOU** is an unattractive jumble

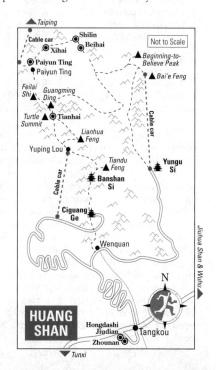

of narrow lanes, hotels and restaurants on the **Taohua Gully**, where roads from Wuhu, Tunxi and Jiuhua Shan meet. From here another road runs up the mountain to further accommodation 3km along at **Wenquan**, where the road divides and continues to the two trailheads.

Minibuses from Tunxi and Jiuhua Shan collect and drop off at Tangkou's central bridge, while the **long-distance bus stop** is 1km up the Wenquan road, by Huang Shan's official entrance. Tangkou's **places to stay** are of most interest to late arrivals: just off the main road, the *Hongdashi Jiudian* (℡0559/5562577; ❻) has clean, comfortable rooms, as does the *Zhounan Dajiudian* (℡0559/5562387; ❽) next door. Alternatively, ask around to find the cheaper Chinese-oriented *Dazhong* (℡0559/5562453; ❺, dorm beds ¥50) or *Fuxing Lou* (℡0559/5563588; ❹).

The cheapest places to **eat** a filling noodle or *baozi* breakfast are at tables under the bridge, with a host of canteens all around the town, whose owners will drag you in as you walk past. Some have bilingual menus offering arresting delights such as squirrel hotpot and scrambled mountain frog, and more conventional soya-braised bamboo shoots and fungi – if there's no price on the menu, agree the cost in advance to avoid being ripped off. You can also pick up umbrellas, walking sticks, warm clothes and mountain **maps** from hawkers and stalls around Tangkou. **Heading up** the mountain, minibuses wait on the Wenquan road, where you'll have to bargain hard for reasonable fares – current rates are ¥5 to Wenquan and ¥10 to the eastern route at **Yungu Si**.

Wenquan

About 3km uphill from Tangkou where the mountain's two main ascent routes diverge, **WENQUAN** is altogether a nicer prospect, surrounded by pine and bamboo forest and perched above the clear blue **Taoyuan Stream** and a noisy waterfall. The first thing you'll see here is the arched bridge over the gully, where the road heads on 8km to the eastern route's trailhead; follow the footpath upstream and it's about half an hour to **Ciguang Ge**, the Merciful Light Pavilion, at the start of the western route. A minibus to either trailhead from Wenquan costs ¥5.

Wenquan's **places to stay** are on either side of the stream. The smartest is the near-side *Taoyuan Binguan* (℡0559/5585666, ℻5585288; ❽), while below the bridge, the *Wenquan Dajiudian* (℡0559/5562198, ℻5562788; ❻) is fine if you avoid the damp cheaper rooms. Across the bridge, the red-roofed *Huangshan Binguan* (℡0559/5585818, ℻5585816; ❻) has tiny rooms but is relatively inexpensive and amenable to bargaining. Near the *Huangshan Binguan*, the trail-weary can take advantage of a **thermal bathhouse** (¥35, or ¥80 for a private spa), though it's a bit grotty. **Eat** at your accommodation or head down to Tangkou.

Huang Shan hikes

Huang Shan barely rises above 1870m, but as you struggle up either of the staircases on the trails it can begin to feel very high indeed. The **eastern route** is by far the easier; the road from Wenquan ends at **Yungu Si** (Cloud Valley Temple), where a **cable car** can whisk you to the summit area at **Bai'e Feng** in twenty minutes – once you've queued two hours for your turn. Alternatively, you can climb the steps to Bai'e Feng in under three hours, though the forest canopy tends to block views and the path is thick with **porters** ferrying laundry, garbage and building materials up and down the slopes.

In contrast, the exceptional landscapes on the fifteen-kilometre **western route** are accompanied by up to eight hours of exhausting legwork – though you can shorten things by catching another gondola between the trailhead at Ciguang Ge and Yuping Lou. There are around two thousand steps from the Ciguang Ge to **Banshan Si**, the misleadingly named Midway Monastery, after which things start to get interesting as you continue up an increasingly steep and narrow gorge, its sides overgrown with witch hazel, azaleas and wild plum. The rocks are huge, their weirdly contorted figures lending some credence to the usual gamut of bizarre names, and the broken hillside is riddled with caves. A steep, hour-long detour from Banshan – not a climb for those nervous of heights – follows steps cut into the cliffs up to **Tiandu Feng** (Heavenly City Peak), where **Jiyu Bei** (Kingfish Ridge), a narrow, ten-metre-long path extending over a precipice towards distant pinnacles surrounded by clouds, provides Huang Shan's most spectacular views.

Back on the main track, the beautifully positioned **Yuping Lou** (Jade Screen Pavilion) is the true halfway house at around three hours into the journey. The vegetation thins out here, exchanged for bare rocks with only the occasional wind-contorted tree, one of which, **Yingke Song** (Welcoming Pine), has been immortalized in countless scroll paintings, photographs, cigarette packets and beer labels. The steps wind on up to a pass where more strange rocks jut out of the mist; bear right for the climb to Huang Shan's apex at **Lianhua Feng** (1864m) or press on to **accommodation** at *Tianhai Binguan* (☎0559/5562201; ¥430). From here, it's just a short climb to where you finally reach the peak circuit at **Guangming Ding** (Brightness Summit), with a TV tower and weather station off to the right, and **Feilai Shi** ahead.

The peak circuit

However you've arrived, it takes around three hours to **circuit the peaks**. North (anticlockwise) from the eastern steps and Bai'e Feng cable-car terminus, the first stop is where a side track leads out to **Shixin Feng**. This cluster of rocky spires makes a wonderful perch to gaze down to lowland woods and rivers, with white-rumped swifts and pine and rock silhouettes moving in and out of shifting silver clouds. Tour groups concentrate on the higher levels, so the lower stairs are more peaceful.

From here, the path continues round to the comfortable *Beihai Binguan* (☎0559/5582555, ℱ5581996; ❽, dorm beds ¥150), where there's also a **Bank of China** with, incredibly, an ATM. Crowds congregate each morning on the terrace nearby to watch the **sunrise** over the "northern sea" of clouds, one of the most stirring sights on the mountain. The views are good even without the dawn, and the area tends to be busy all day. Straight ahead, a side track leads to the cosy *Shilin Dajiudian* (☎0559/5584040, ⓦwww.shilin.com; ❾, dorm beds ¥150), which even has copies of the *China Daily*; while another twenty minutes on the main path brings you to the well-placed *Xihai Fandian* (☎0559/5588888, ⓦwww.hsxihaihotel.com; ❽), the perfect spot to sip drinks on the terrace and watch, in its turn, the sun setting over the "western cloud sea".

It's another ten minutes or so from *Xihai* to where the track splits at the mountain's least expensive accommodation, the *Paiyun Ting Binguan* (☎0559/5581558, ⒺHsxpyl@sohu.com; ❼). Ahead is the **Taiping cable-car station** down to Songgu (p.492). Stay on the main track for **Paiyun Ting**, the Cloud-dispelling Pavilion; on a clear day you'll see a steep gorge squeezed between jagged crags below, all covered in pine trees and magnolias. More views await farther round at the lonely tower of **Feilai Shi**, which after rain looks across at cascades dropping off lesser peaks into infinity. Beyond here, the path undulates along the cliff edge to where the western steps descend on the right (below the TV tower and weather station), then winds back to the Bai'e Feng cable car.

Hubei

HUBEI is Han China's agricultural and geographic centre, mild in climate and well watered. Until 280 BC this was the independent state of **Chu**, whose sophisticated bronzeworking skills continue to astound archeologists, but for the last half-millennium the province's eastern bulk, defined by the low-lying **Jianghan plain** and spliced by waterways draining into the Yangzi and Han rivers, has become an intensely cultivated maze of rice fields so rich that, according to tradition, they alone are enough to supply the national need. More recently, Hubei's central location and mass of transport links into neighbouring regions saw the province becoming the first in the interior to be heavily industrialized. Once the colossal **Three Gorges hydroelectric dam** upstream from **Yichang** is completed (see p.506), car manufacturing – already up and running with the help of foreign investment – and long-established iron and steel plants will provide a huge source of income for central China.

As the "Gateway to Nine Provinces", skirted by mountains and midway along the Yangzi between Shanghai and Chongqing, Hubei has always been of great strategic importance, and somewhere that seditious ideas could easily spread to the rest of the country. The central regions upriver from the capital, **Wuhan**, feature prominently in the *Romance of the Three Kingdoms*, with the ports of **Jingzhou** and **Chibi** retaining their period associations, while Wuhan itself thrives on industry and river trade, and played a key role in China's early twentieth-century revolutions. In the west, the ranges that border Sichuan contain the holy peak of **Wudang Shan**, alive with Taoist temples and martial-arts lore, and the remote and little-visited **Shennongjia Forest Reserve**, said to be inhabited by China's yeti.

Wuhan

One way or the other, almost anyone travelling through central China has to pass through **WUHAN**, Hubei's sprawling capital, most likely cruising in along the Yangzi from Sichuan, or rattling in by rail. The name is a portmanteau label for the original settlements of **Wuchang**, **Hankou** and **Hanyang**, separate across the junction of the Han and Yangzi rivers, but given some sense of unity by three great interconnecting bridges. The city's sheer size, bustle and obvious regional economic importance lend atmosphere, even if Wuhan is more of an administrative and social centre than a tourist magnet. Nonetheless it's an upbeat, characterful metropolis, and Hankou's former role as a **foreign concession** has left a whole quarter of colonial European heritage in its wake, while the **Provincial Museum** in Wuchang is one of China's best. There are also a couple of temples and historical monuments to check out, some connected to the **1911 revolution** which ended two thousand years of Imperial rule. On the downside, Wuhan has a well-deserved reputation – along with Chongqing and Nanjing – as one of China's three summer "furnaces": between May and September you'll find the streets melting and the gasping population surviving on a diet of watermelon and ice lollies.

Wuhan

Wuhan	武汉	wǔhàn
Hankou	汉口	hànkǒu
Hanyang	汉阳	hànyáng
Wuchang	武昌	wǔchāng

The city

Changchun Guan	长春观	chángchūn guàn
Customs House	武汉海关	wǔhàn hǎiguān
Dong Hu Scenic Area	东湖风景区	dōnghú fēngjǐngqū
Electric special #1	电一专路	diànyī zhuānlù
Flood Control Monument	防洪纪念碑	fánghóng jìniànbēi
Great Changjiang Bridge	长江大桥	chángjiāng dàqiáo
Gui Shan Park	龟山公园	guīshān gōngyuán
Guiyuan Si	归元寺	guīyuán sì
Guqin Ta	古琴塔	gǔqín tǎ
Hong Ge	红阁	hóng gé
Hubei Provincial Museum	湖北省博物馆	húběishěng bówùguǎn
She Shan	蛇山	shéshān
Tianhe airport	天河飞机场	tiānhé fēijīchǎng
Workers' Cultural Palace	工人文化宫	gōngrén wénhuàgōng
Wuhan Museum	武汉博物馆	wǔhàn bówùguǎn
Wuhan University	武汉大学	wǔhàn dàxué
Yangzi ferry terminal	武汉港客运站	wǔhàngǎng kèyùnzhàn
Yellow Crane Tower	黄鹤塔	huánghè tǎ
Zhongshan Park	中山公园	zhōngshān gōngyuán

Accommodation

Guansheng Yuan	冠生园大酒店	guānshēngyuán dàjiǔdiàn
Hanghai	航海宾馆	hánghǎi bīnguǎn
Holiday Inn	天安假日酒店	tiān'ānjiàrì jiǔdiàn
Jianghan	江汉饭店	jiānghàn fàndiàn
Jinlun	金轮宾馆	jīnlún bīnguǎn
Kunlun Victory	昆仑胜利饭店	kūnlún shènglì fàndiàn
Linjiang	临江饭店	línjiāng fàndiàn
Mengtian Hu	梦天湖宾馆	mèngtiānhú bīnguǎn
New Oriental Empire	新东方帝豪酒店	xīndōngfāng dìháo jiǔdiàn
Xuangong	璇宫饭店	xuángōng fàndiàn

Eating and drinking

Bordeaux Bar	波尔图酒吧	bō'ěrtú jiǔbā
Changchun Sucai Guan	长春素菜馆	chángchūn sùcàiguǎn
Da Zhonghua	大中华	dà zhōnghuá
Dezhuang Huoguo Guangchang	德庄火锅广场	dézhuāng huǒguō guǎngchǎng
Lao Tongcheng	老通成	lǎotōng chéng
Si Li Mei	四李美	sìlǐměi
Yonghe Dawang	永和大王	yǒnghé dàwáng
Yuanye Jiaozi Guan	原野饺子馆	yuányě jiǎoziguǎn

Arrival and city transport

Wuhan spreads more than 10km across, and, with a choice of transit points all over the place – there are two train stations and at least three long-distance bus stations – it's important to know where you're arriving before you get here; train and bus timetables usually spell out the district where services arrive, rather than just "Wuhan". Most people stay on the northern bank of the Yangzi in **Hankou**, which, as the city's trade and business centre, contains the best of the services and accommodation. South across the smaller Han River is lightly industrial **Hanyang**, while **Wuchang** recedes southeast of the Yangzi into semi-rural parkland.

Tianhe airport lies 30km to the north of Wuhan along a good road, with a **bus link** from here to the China Southern airline office on Hangkong Lu in Hankou. **Rail** services from the north tend to terminate at Hankou's train station, up in the north of the city along Fazhan Dadao, while those from the south favour Wuchang's station, on the other side of town on Zhongshan Lu.

Moving on from Wuhan

Train, plane and ferry tickets can be arranged through some accommodation, and numerous agencies around the Yangzi ferry terminal and Hankou's bus station.

By air

You can **fly** from Wuhan to a host of Chinese cities between Ürümqi and Shenzhen. The main **airline offices** are China Southern (℡ 027/83622000, ℗ 83632264; daily 8am–8pm) and China Eastern (℡ 027/83623820, ℗ 83641320; daily 8am–8pm), either side of the *Ramada Plaza* on Hangkong Lu in Hankou. An **airport bus** from China Southern links up with departures (¥20).

By train

Wuhan's two main **train stations** in Hankou and Wuchang offer direct services to just about everywhere in the country. Hankou is seen as the city's major terminus, but as a rule of thumb, use Hankou for northern destinations, Wuchang if you're heading south. The huge volume of traffic passing through town means that getting tickets isn't difficult, though note that each station sells tickets only for those services which depart from it. You can avoid the lengthy station queues by using agencies or the **advance purchase office** at the southern end of Xinhua Lu. At both stations, ¥5 extra gets you into a smarter waiting room and out to the train earlier.

By bus

Wuhan's biggest and busiest **long-distance bus station** is on Jiefang Dadao in Hankou, handling traffic to most major cities throughout the country. Those in Wuchang and Hanyang are more limited in their coverage, but offer additional useful services south and east at least as far as Nanchang, Changsha and Hefei. Sleeper and standard buses leave from all stations; there's seldom any problem getting a seat wherever you're heading.

By boat

The **Yangzi ferry terminal** is an unmissable white tiled building on Yanjiang Dadao in Hankou: the ticket office (℡ 027/82839546; daily 8.30am–5.30pm) is downstairs at the north end of the building. There are daily departures for the 36hr upriver journey to Chongqing (¥875/580/309), though all other destinations have been superseded by road and rail.

Arriving by bus, you could end up at any one of the major **long-distance bus stations** – on Jiefang Dadao in downtown Hankou, on Hanyang Dadao in Hanyang, and near Wuchang's train station on Zhongshan Lu – irrespective of where you're coming from; there are also several private bus depots outside the Yangzi ferry terminal and along Yanhe Dadao in Hankou. At least there's no confusion with **Yangzi ferries** – passengers arrive at the ferry **terminal** on Yanjiang Dadao in Hankou.

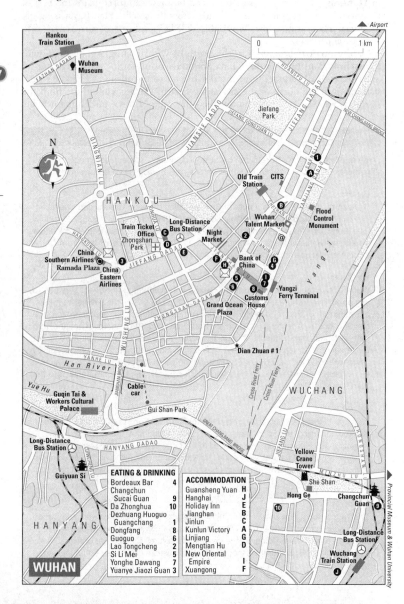

Airport

HANKOU

Hankou Train Station

Wuhan Museum

FAZHAN DADAO

QINGNIAN LU

JIANSHE DADAO

JIEFANG GONGYUAN LU

JIEFANG DADAO

HUANGPU LU

NEW CHANGJIANG BRIDGE

Jiefang Park

Old Train Station   CITS

SHENGLI JIE

YANJIANG DADAO

Flood Control Monument

Long-Distance Bus Station

Train Ticket Office

Zhongshan Park

China Southern Airlines

Ramada Plaza

China Eastern Airlines

XINHUA LU

HANKONG LU

JIEFANG DADAO

Wuhan Talent Market

CHEZHAN LU

Night Market

Bank of China

Grand Ocean Plaza

Customs House

Yangzi Ferry Terminal

Yangzi

WUSHENG LU

ZHONGSHAN DADAO

Dian Zhuan # 1

YANHE LU

Han River

JIANGHAN BRIDGE

Cable car

Cross River Ferry

Cross River Ferry

WUCHANG

Yue Hu

Guqin Tai & Workers Cultural Palace

Gui Shan Park

GREAT CHANGJIANG BRIDGE

Long-Distance Bus Station

HANYANG DADAO

XINGYI LU

Guiyuan Si

HANYANG

JIEFANG LU

Yellow-Crane Tower

She Shan

Hong Ge

Changchun Guan

ZHONGSHAN LU

MINZHU LU

Long-Distance Bus Station

Wuchang Train Station

Provincial Museum & Wuhan University

0   1 km

N

EATING & DRINKING

Bordeaux Bar	4
Changchun Sucai Guan	9
Da Zhonghua	10
Dezhuang Huoguo Guangchang	1
Dongfang	8
Guoguo	6
Lao Tongcheng	2
Si Li Mei	5
Yonghe Dawang	7
Yuanye Jiaozi Guan	3

ACCOMMODATION

Guansheng Yuan	H
Hanghai	J
Holiday Inn	E
Jianghan	B
Jinlun	C
Kunlun Victory	A
Linjiang	G
Mengtian Hu	D
New Oriental Empire	I
Xuangong	F

WUHAN

City transport

Wuhan is too large to consider walking everywhere, though the overloaded **bus and trolleybus** system seldom seems to be much quicker, and stops can be widely separated. The main **city-bus terminuses** are at Hankou and Wuchang train stations, and beside the Yangzi ferry terminal on Yanjiang Dadao. Staff are on hand at each of these to help you find the right vehicle. Services are at least regular and cheap – it only costs ¥2 between Wuchang and Hankou stations – crawling out to almost every corner of the city between around 6am and 10pm.

Taxis are ubiquitous and, at ¥8 for the first 2km, not too expensive. For short hops, haggle with **motorbike** and **motor-rickshaw** drivers who prowl the bus and train depots. During daylight hours, there are **passenger ferries** across the Yangzi between the southern end of Hankou's Yanjiang Dadao and Wuchang's city-bus terminus, below and just north of the Changjiang Bridge; trips cost ¥1.5 and take about twenty minutes.

Maps of Wuhan showing transport routes can be picked up at bus and train stations, but shop around first as many are either painfully detailed or almost abstract. **Bicycles** are difficult to rent and not overly used, partly because of Wuhan's size, but also because of unpredictably enforced regulations banning them from being ridden across the bridges.

Accommodation

Much of Wuhan's **hotel** accommodation is upmarket, but there are a couple of inexpensive options, and mid-range places can be good value. The biggest selection – a sprinkling of which are reviewed below – is in **Hankou**. In Wuchang, the noisy *Hanghai* (☎027/88740122; ❹), on Zhongshan Lu opposite the train station, is only recommended if you arrive late in the day; bus #507 to Hankou runs past the door.

Guansheng Yuan 117 Jianghan Lu ☎027/82779069, ✉guansy@publicwh.hb.cn. Beside a department store of the same name, and just south of the *Xuangong* hotel. Nothing glamorous, but clean, central and the right price. Often full. ❸

Holiday Inn 868 Jiefang Dadao ☎027/85867888, ✆85845353, ⓦwww.ichotelsgroup.com. Reliable comfort and level of service – and surprisingly keen rates – in this smart international hotel. ❼

Jianghan 245 Shengli Jie ☎027/68825888, ⓦwww.jhhotel.com. Wuhan's best, a renovated French colonial mansion, with porphyry floors and wooden panelling throughout the lobby, fairly luxurious rooms and bilingual staff. Polite enquiries often get non-guests the use of exchange and communications facilities. ❾

Jinlun Xinhua Lu ☎027/85807060, ✆85778420. Excellent-value, comfortable twins,

---

Useful bus routes

The most convenient bus for sightseeing is the **Dian Zhuan** (Electric Special) **#1**, not to be confused with any other #1 bus or trolleybus – the characters for *dian zhuan* are displayed either side of the number. It runs from Yanhe Dadao in Hankou, via Hanyang and the Great Changjiang Bridge, and then links the Yellow Crane Tower with Changchun Guan and the Provincial Museum. Other noteworthy services are:

#38 From Hankou train station through the downtown concession area, terminating along the river on Yanjiang Dadao near the Flood Control Monument.

#503 From Wuchang train station to the Yangzi ferry terminal.

#507 Between Hankou and Wuchang train stations, via the Yangzi ferry terminal, taking 45–90 minutes, depending on traffic.

#595 Connects Hankou train station with the Yangzi ferry terminal.

with friendly staff, and well located for the Hankou bus station. ❸

Kunlun Victory 11 Siwei Lu ☎027/82732780, ℱ82721106. Hidden away behind a high wall and difficult to locate, this is a modern, five-storey block with much the same facilities as the nearby *Jianghan*, but none of the panache. ❼

Linjiang 1 Tianjin Lu ☎027/68826185, ℱ68826200. An army-owned hotel with a colonial facade (in 1924, this was the Asian Kerosene Company building), just up the road from the Yangzi ferry terminal. Reasonably priced rooms for town, and good service; discounts are available.

❺**Mengtian Hu** West of the Hankou's bus station,

Jiefang Dadao ☎85772600. Some of the cheapest doubles in town, with shared facilities and certainly past their best; nevertheless, they're still a good deal, as are the slightly pricier en-suite rooms. ❸

New Oriental Empire 136 Yanjiang Dadao ☎027/82211881, ℱ82775912. Another colonial frontage and mid-range urban hotel interior; a notch above the nearby *Linjiang*. ❻

Xuangong 57 Jianghan Lu ☎027/6882258, ⓦwww.xuangonghotel.com. A gloomy but very atmospheric 1920s concession building with comfortable rooms; the entrance is on a side street to the west of the main road. Rates are often hugely reduced. ❼

Hankou

Now the largest of Wuhan's districts, **Hankou** was a simple fishing harbour until being opened up as a **treaty port** in 1861 – a move greatly resented by the Chinese, who took to stoning any foreigners bold enough to walk the streets. Consequently, the Chinese were barred from the riverside concession area, which over the following decades was developed in a grand style, complete with a racetrack and a **Bund** (flood-preventing embankments built by the British in the 1860s) lined with Neoclassical European architecture housing banks, embassies and company headquarters.

The twentieth century was not kind to the city, however. On October 10, 1911, a **bomb** exploded prematurely at the Hankou headquarters of a revolutionary group linked to **Sun Yatsen**'s Tongmen Hui, a society pledged to dismantling Imperial rule in China and replacing it with a democratic government. Imperial troops executed the ringleaders, sparking a savage, city-wide **uprising against the Manchus** which virtually levelled Hankou and soon spread across China. The last emperor, Pu Yi, was forced to abdicate and a Republican government under Sun Yatsen was duly elected in Nanjing the following year. The foreign concession was rebuilt, but anti-Western riots broke out in 1925 and again in 1927, leading to the **handing back** of Hankou's concession areas to China. A few months afterwards, the Guomindang stormed through on their Northern Expedition, and they returned briefly in 1937 to establish a national government in town before being forced farther west by the Japanese. Thirty years later Hankou saw more fighting, this time between the PLA and various Red Guard factions, who had been slugging it out over differing interpretations of Mao's Cultural Revolution.

The district

Bursting with traffic and crowds, Hankou is a place to walk, shop, eat, spend money and watch modern Chinese doing the same. The main thoroughfare is **Zhongshan Dadao**, a packed, three-kilometre-long stretch of restaurants, stores and shopping plazas. Surprisingly, given the city's history, Hankou's **colonial quarter** survives almost in its entirety, restored during a big clean-up project in 2001. Aside from the racetrack, now watery **Zhongshan Park** near the corner of Jiefang Dadao and Qingnian Lu, the colonial core lies mostly between the eastern half of Zhongshan Dadao and the river. The best sections are along the former Bund, renamed **Yanjiang Dadao**, and **Jianghan Lu**. The two roads converge at the mighty **Customs House**, a solid Renaissance edifice with imposing grey-stone portico and Corinthian capitols. The Bund itself is still visible, with the Communists adding a **Flood Control Monument** in 1954 up in Binjiang Park, a tall obelisk embellished with Mao's portrait. Many buildings in the area have plaques in English outlining their history; some to look for include the unusual seven-storey Art Deco/modernist exterior of the former **Siming Bank** at 45 Jianghan Lu, and the brick "Wuhan Talent Market" on Yanjiang Dadao – once the **US Consulate**. The **Bank of China**, at the intersection of Jianghan Lu and Zhongshan Dadao, retains its period interior of wooden panelling and chandeliers, while Hankou's **old train station** on Chezhan Lu sports a derelict French Gothic shell surrounded by a seedy mass of shops and stalls.

If you're up near Hankou's train station, drop in to the **Wuhan Museum** (daily 9am–5pm; ¥20), whose collections of antique bronzes, porcelain, jade, and scrolls of painting and calligraphy are so outstanding that you can begin to appreciate what the Chinese see in these things. In particular, there's a wonderful Ming-dynasty painting of the Yueyang Tower in Hunan (p.524), with a view of gnarled pines and boats riding a turbulent Yangzi; and a 1700-year-old, 15-centimetre-wide bronze mirror decorated with scenes from the Han-dynasty collection of Chinese mythology, the *Book of Songs*.

Hanyang

From Hankou, you cross over the Han River into Hanyang either by bus over the short Jianghan Bridge, or the **cable car** (¥15) between Yanhe Dadao and eastern Hanyang's **Gui Shan Park**. Settled as far back as 600 AD, Hanyang remained insignificant until the late nineteenth century when the viceroy **Zhang Zhidong** built China's first large-scale steel foundry here as part of the "Self-Strengthening Movement" – a last-ditch effort to modernize China during the twilight years of the Qing dynasty.

Hanyang remains Wuhan's principal manufacturing sector, its distinctly shabby streets dotted with small-scale industries. The Jianghan Bridge runs south to a huge **roundabout** below the western end of Gui Shan Park, from whose hills the Xia king Yu is said to have quelled floods four thousand years ago. West of the roundabout, **Guqin Tai** (Ancient Lute Platform; ¥5) was the haunt of legendary strummer **Yu Boya**, who played over the grave of his friend Zhong Ziqi and then smashed his instrument because the one person able to appreciate his music was dead. Infrequent gatherings at the adjacent Workers' Cultural Palace are worth a look, the band performing traditional tunes to a slumbering, elderly audience.

Guiyuan Si (daily 8.30am–5pm; ¥20) is a busy Buddhist monastery a couple of streets southwest of the roundabout on Cuiweiheng Lu, behind Hanyang's long-distance bus station. There's an authoritarian atmosphere to the place, emphasized by blocky, black-and-white brick buildings, though the temple's **scripture collection** – which includes a complete seven-thousand-volume set of the rare *Longcan Sutra* – has made Guiyan famous in Buddhist circles. Of more general interest are several hundred individually styled saintly statues in the Arhat Hall, and the statue of Sakyamuni in the main hall, carved from a single block of white jade, a gift from Burma in 1935.

Wuchang

Wuchang, on the right bank of the Yangzi, was founded as Sun Quan's walled capital of Wu during the Three Kingdoms period. Tang rulers made the city a major port, which, under the Mongols, became the administrative centre of a vast region covering present-day Hunan, Hubei, Guangdong and Guangxi provinces.

During the 1910 insurrection Wuchang hosted appalling scenes when ethnic Han troops mutinied under a banner proclaiming "Long live the Han, Exterminate the Manchu" and accordingly slaughtered a Manchu regiment and over eight hundred civilians here. The city and its bureaucracy survived, though, and today Wuchang comprises government offices and the huge **Wuhan University** campus. Visitor draws out this way include the Taoist **Changchun Guan**, the **Yellow Crane Tower** – the greatest of the Yangzi's many riverside pavilions – and the **Provincial Museum**, close to the lakeside scenery of Dong Hu.

Yellow Crane Tower and around

The road from Hanyang to Wuchang crosses the **Great Changjiang Bridge**, before whose construction in 1957 all traffic – rail included – had to be ferried 1500m across the river. On the far side, Wuluo Lu curves around She Shan (Snake Hill) which, along with the river, is overlooked by the bright tiles and red wooden columns of the fifty-metre-high **Yellow Crane Tower** (¥50). It's no less magnificent for being an entirely modern Qing-style reproduction, and one sited 1km from where the original third-century structure burned down in 1884. Legend has it that She Shan was once home to a Taoist Immortal who paid his bills at a nearby inn by drawing a picture of a crane on the wall, which would fly down at intervals and entertain the guests. A few years later the Immortal flew off on his creation, and the landlord, who doubtless could afford it by then, built the tower in his honour. Climb the internal staircases to the top floor and see Wuhan and the Yangzi at their best.

On the southern slopes of She Shan, **Hong Ge** is a handsome colonial-style red-brick mansion which housed the Hubei Military Government during the 1910 uprising. A bronze statue of Sun Yatsen stands in front, though at the time of the uprising he was abroad raising funds. Follow Wuluo Lu east for 1km from here and you'll be standing outside the russet walls of **Changchun Guan** (¥5), a Taoist complex which made its name through the Yuan-dynasty luminary **Qiu Chuzi**, who preached here and later founded his own sect. Only partially open to the public, the halls are simply furnished with statues of the Three Purities, the Jade Emperor and other Taoist deities. A side wing has been co-opted as a pharmacy, where Chinese-speakers can have their vital signs checked by a traditonal doctor and buy medicines collected, according to the staff, on Wudang Shan. There's also a martial-arts training area, with rusty poleaxes and swords displayed on racks. Next door, Changchun's **vegetarian restaurant** is well worth visiting at lunchtime (see opposite).

Hubei Provincial Museum

From the Yellow Crane Tower, it's around twenty minutes by bus to the **Hubei Provincial Museum** (daily 8.30am–noon & 1.30–5pm; ¥30) on Donghu Lu. The museum's display of items unearthed from the Warring States Period's **tomb of the Marquis Yi** deserves a good hour of your time – especially if you're planning on visiting similar collections at Jingzhou (see p.506) and Changsha (see p.520).

The marquis died in 433 BC and was buried in a huge, multiple-layered, wooden lacquered coffin at nearby Suizhou, then a major city of the state of **Zeng**. His corpse was accompanied by fifteen thousand bronze and wooden artefacts, twenty-one women and one dog. The museum's comprehensive English explanations of contemporary history and photos of the 1978 excavation put everything in perspective. Don't miss the impressive orchestra of **64 bronze bells**, ranging in weight from a couple of kilos to a quarter of a tonne, found in the waterlogged tomb – the largest such set ever discovered – along with the wooden frame from which they once hung in rows. Played with hand-held rods, each bell can produce two notes depending on where it is struck. The knowledge of metals and casting required to achieve this initially boggled modern researchers, who took five years to make duplicates. Souvenir shops outside sell pricey **recordings** of period tunes played on the bells, and there are brief **performances** every hour or so in the museum's auditorium. More than a hundred other musical instruments are also on show, including stone chimes, drums, flutes and zithers, along with spearheads and a very weird brazen crane totem sprouting antlers – an inscription suggests that this was the marquis's steed in the afterlife.

Eating and drinking

Cooking in Wuhan reflects the city's position midway between Shanghai and Chongqing, and restaurants here offer a good balance of eastern-style steamed and braised dishes – particularly **fish and shellfish** – along with some seriously spicy Sichuanese food. There's also a strong **snacking** tradition in town, and many places specialize in designer dumplings: various types of *shaomai*; *tangbao*, soup buns stuffed with jellied stock which burst messily as you bite them, much to the amusement of other diners; and *doupi*, sticky rice packets stuffed with meat and rolled up in a beanpaste skin.

Hankou has the best of the **restaurants**, which are concentrated along Zhongshan Dadao and its offshoots. Even the formal places are inexpensive, and many have first-floor canteens where you can eat local staples very cheaply; the train stations have some good budget places too, serving mostly vegetable and fish dishes. There's also a street of night-market food stalls on Jianghan Yi Lu, which runs east off Jianghan Lu.

An increasing number of Western-style **cafés and bars** – many livening up after dark – are springing up along Yanjiang Dadao and Jianghan Lu. The *Holiday Inn*'s ground-floor coffee shop offers chocolate and cream confections from ¥12 a piece, or you can pay ¥26 per person for afternoon tea. There's also a stack of **cake shops** at the river end of Jianghan Lu.

Restaurants

Hankou

Bordeaux Bar Just west of the *Linjiang* hotel on Yanjiang Dadao. One of many such café-bars in the area, this has a bit of character, with pavement tables and nicely dimmed lighting inside. The Western-style pasta and steak dishes, along with an eclectic range of Chinese fare, are expensive – best to stick to the coffee or beer.

Dezhuang Huoguo Guangchang Corner of Yanjiang Dadao and Sanyang Lu. If you're craving northern-style hotpot, this is the place to come – big, bright, noisy and inexpensive.

Dongfang Near the Customs House on Jianghan Lu. A comfortable and popular place to take a breather from all that strenuous shopping and tuck into some tasty hotpots (¥25).

Guoguo Jiaotong Lu. Seethingly popular canteen serving excellent, inexpensive dumplings. Order at the counter and then wait in line.

Lao Tongcheng Corner of Zhongshan Dadao and Dazhi Lu. Enter through a mobile-phone emporium and head upstairs to reach this canteen-style institution, renowned for its *doupi*, costing around ¥3 a portion. "Three flavoured" are considered best, stuffed with tongue, heart and bamboo shoots, but there are also shrimp and chicken fillings for those not addicted to offal. You order off cards scrawled in Chinese at the front counter. Daily 8am–2.30pm.

Si Li Mei Zhongshan Dadao. It's easy to miss the entrance to this place, which is small and buried behind steamed-bun vendors. Another place to try river food and *tangbao*.

Yonghe Dawang Across from the ferry terminal on Yanjiang Dadao, and elsewhere. Open around the clock, this restaurant chain's logo looks suspiciously like *KFC*'s but the food is very different: big bowls of beef noodle soup or *doujiang*, steamed buns and fried rice.

Yuanye Jiaozi Guan Just west of Zhongshan Park. You'll have no trouble spotting the long glass windows of this extremely popular, comfortable snack house, which offers *jiaozi* by the *jin* (around ¥10), preserved eggs, and cold Sichuan-style vegetable and meat dishes.

Wuchang

Changchun Sucai Guan Changchuan Guan, Wulou Lu. Vegetarian restaurant with Ming decor and a resolutely Chinese menu. The "beef" and "chicken" are made from bean-curd sheets, "prawns" from bean starch, and so on. Portions are huge (ask for small servings if you want to try a variety), liberally laced with chillies and aniseed, and very tasty. Mains from ¥15 or so.

Da Zhonghua Pengliuyang Lu. A four-storey establishment long known for its classic and innovative ways with fish – try the lake fish with red berry sauce. Noodles and soups are served on the first floor, the third floor is a general dining room, with a tea house right on top. Most dishes under ¥30.

Listings

Banks and exchange Bank of China, Zhongshan Dadao, Hankou (Mon–Sat 8.30am–5pm).

Bookshops The Xinhua bookstore, just west of the Jianghan Lu/Zhongshan Dadao intersection, Hankou, has plenty of maps and some English titles, including abridged texts of Chinese classics.

Cinema There are screens in Hankou at Warner Village in Walmart near the Mingcheng Plaza on Zhongshan Dadao, and near the former US Consulate on Yanjiang Dadao.

Hospitals The Tongji, east of the Jiefang Dadao/Qingnian Lu crossroads in Hankou, is considered Wuhan's best. Another good place to go for acupuncture and massage is the hospital attached to the Hubei Traditional Medicine College, just north of She Shan, Wuchang.

Internet access In Hankou, there are Net bars on the second floor of the cinema complex on Yanjiang Dadao, and east of the *Holiday Inn* on Jiefang Dadao. In Wuchang there's one on Wulou Lu, west of Zhongshan Lu.

Left luggage There are booths charging ¥2 a bag at the bus (daily 8am–8pm) and train stations (24hr).

Mail and telephones The main post offices, with IDD phones, are on Zhongshan Dadao and at the junction of Hangkong Lu and Qingnian Lu, Hankou (daily 8am–6pm). There is no GPO as such, so ensure that poste-restante mail addresses use the street name and "Hankou", or it could end up anywhere in the city.

Markets and shopping For "antique" souvenirs, try the shops at the Hubei Provincial Museum, Wuchang. Hankou's old concession area, north of Zhongshan Dadao, has the liveliest market activity, mostly revolving around fruit and vegetables. Like most Chinese cities, Hankou is a very good place to buy clothes – try the new Grand Ocean Plaza or the Walmart Super Centre, both on Zhongshan Dadao, or numerous smaller shops nearby.

Pharmacies In addition to smaller places elsewhere, Hankou's Hangkong Lu has a string of pharmacies stocking traditional and modern medicines, the biggest of which is the Grand Pharmacy, or, according to the English sign, the "Ark of Health".

Travel agents These abound around the Yangzi ferry terminal and Hankou long-distance bus station. Alternatively, CITS here are a well-informed, English-speaking agency geared up to organizing Three Gorges cruises, and trips to Shennongjia and Wudang Shan; they're just north of the *Jianghan Hotel* on Zhongshan Dadao, Hankou (☎027/82811891).

Up the Yangzi: Wuhan to Yichang

The flat, broad river plains west of Wuhan don't seem too exciting at first, but historic remains lend solid character to towns along the way. It takes around 36 hours to navigate upstream from Wuhan via **Chibi** and **Jingzhou** to **Yichang**, from where the exciting journey through the Yangzi Gorges and on to Chongqing begins. As most boats don't stop along the way, however, if you want to see anything it's more convenient – and far quicker – to use the Wuhan–Jingzhou–Yichang **expressway**, which bypasses Chibi but cuts the journey time to Yichang down to less than four hours.

Chibi

The first place of any significance along the river, about 80km southwest of Wuhan, **CHIBI** (Red Cliffs) was the setting for the most important battle

Up the Yangzi: Wuhan to Yichang

Chibi	赤壁	*chìbì*
Baifeng Terrace	拜风台	*bàifēng tái*
Feng Chu An	风雏庵	*fēngchú ān*
Nanping Shan	南屏山	*nánpíng shān*
Wangjiang Pavilion	望江亭	*wàngjiāng tíng*
Wuhou Palace	武侯宫	*wǔhóu gōng*
Jingzhou	荆州	*jīngzhōu*
Jingzhou Museum	荆州博物馆	*jīngzhōu bówùguǎn*
Kaiyuan Guan	开元观	*kāiyuán guàn*
Puqi	蒲圻	*púqí*
Shashi	沙市	*shāshì*
Yichang	宜昌	*yíchāng*
Dagong Bridge Transit Terminal	大公桥水路客运站	*dàgōngqiáo shuǐlù kèyùnzhàn*
Gezhou Dam	葛洲坝	*gězhōu bà*
Happy Hometown	快乐老家	*kuàilè lǎojiā*
Heping Jiari Jiudian	和平假日酒店	*hépíng jiàrì jiǔdiàn*
Hydrofoil port	高速客轮中心	*gāosù kèlún zhōngxīn*
Liujin Suiyue Kafei	流金岁月咖啡	*liújīn suìyuè kāfēi*
Sanxia airport	三峡机场	*sānxiá jīchǎng*
Taohualing Binguan	桃花岭宾馆	*táohuālíng bīnguǎn*
Taozhu Lu	陶珠路	*táozhū lù*
Three Gorges Dam site	三峡大坝区	*sānxiá dàbàqū*
Yichang International Hotel	宜昌国际大酒店	*yíchāng guójì dàjiǔdiàn*
Yunji Fandian	云集饭店	*yúnjí fàndiàn*
Zhenjiangge	镇江阁茶楼	*zhènjiānggé chálóu*

of the Three Kingdoms period, the confrontation at which the competing states defined their final boundaries. It was here in 208 AD that the northern armies of Wei, led by Cao Cao, descended on the combined southern forces of Liu Bei and Sun Quan. Though heavily outnumbered, the southerners had brought two remarkable strategists along – **Zhuge Liang** and **Pang Tong** – who took full advantage of Cao's decision to launch a naval assault across the river. Misled by Pang Tong's spies, Cao chained his ships together on the north bank while preparing for the attack, and Zhuge Liang – using, it's said, Taoist magic – created an unseasonal southeasterly wind and sent a flotilla of burning hulks across the Yangzi, completely incinerating Cao's armada and permanently imprinting the colour of flames on the cliffs. Despite Cao Cao's defeat, neither of the other armies had the strength needed to pursue him, nor to take on each other in a final engagement which might have seen China unified instead of plunged into civil war for most of the following five centuries.

To reach Chibi, clearly visible from the river, take a train or bus to **Chibi Shi** (also known as **Puqi**) about two-thirds of the way between Wuhan and Yueyang in Hunan, from where it's a ninety-minute local bus ride to the site, locally known as **Sanguo Chibi** to distinguish it from Chibi Shi. A flight of steps on the right near the bus stop leads up Jinluan Hill to **Feng Chu An**, a whitewashed hall where Pang Tong studied military strategy and so conceived the plan that defeated Cao. Back below, following the main road to the left brings you to **Nanping Shan**, where two stone lions up on the hill flank the entrance to **Wuhou Palace** and **Baifeng Terrace**. Four statues here commemorate Zhuge Liang and Liu Bei, along with Liu Bei's oath brothers, Guan Yu and Zhang Fei. Farther on towards the river, the small **Wangjiang Pavilion** is a former guard post which still commands broad views of the terraced paddy fields below. Spears, arrowheads and pottery shards in a gloomy museum nearby offer proof that the legends have a historical basis. The cliffs overlooking the Yangzi's southern bank just outside town are carved with the two characters for "*chibi*", supposedly by the triumphant Wu general, **Zhou Yu**.

Jingzhou Shi and around

Around 240km west of Wuhan on the highway to Yichang, or the best part of a day upstream by ferry from Chibi, **JINGZHOU SHI** lies on the north bank of the Yangzi, where the Wuhan–Yichang expressway joins the highway up to Xiangfan in northern Hubei. The city is divided into two separate districts: while the easterly section of **Shashi** is an indifferent modern port, the **Jingzhou** district, 10km west, is ringed by around 8km of moats and well-maintained, seven-metre-high **battlements**, built by the Three Kingdoms hero Guan Yu, who commanded Shu's eastern defences here. Even earlier, the now vanished city of **Jinan**, immediately north of Jingzhou, was the capital of the state of Chu until its destruction by the Qin armies around 278 BC.

From Shashi's long-distance bus station on Taqiao Lu, city bus #1 runs west into Jingzhou through the **east gate**, trundles down past Jingzhou's own long-distance bus station on Jing Nan Lu, turns into **Jingzhong Lu** and finally terminates by the **west gate**. Walls aside, there's not much to be impressed with in this forty-minute trawl, but walk 100m back along Jingzhong Lu from the bus stop and you'll be outside **Jingzhou Museum** (daily 8.30am–4.30pm; ¥20). Skip the lifeless main building, full of dusty cases of unidentified pots and blurred photos, and instead walk around to the back, where ¥10 gets you in to the "Treasure Display" (same hours), a fantastic collection of Western Han **tomb remains**. These were found a few kilometres north at **Fenghuang Shan**, the site of Jinan, which former residents turned into a cemetery after the city's destruction in order to be buried alongside their ancestors. More than 180 tombs dating from the Qin era to the end of the Western Han (221 BC–24 AD) have been found, an impressive range for a single site; the exhibition here focuses on Tomb 168, that of a court official named **Sui**. In many regards the items on display are similar to those in Wuhan's provincial museum (p.502) – the house-like sarcophagi and copious lacquerwork, for example – but the bonus here is Sui's astoundingly well-preserved **corpse**, along with some comfortingly practical household items and wooden miniatures of his servants; either he wasn't powerful enough to have his real attendants buried with him, or else this trend had gone out of style. *Romance of the Three Kingdoms* aficionados should go next door to **Kaiyuan Guan**, a tiny, elderly temple dedicated to Guan Yu and set among overgrown gardens.

There are buses both ways along the expressway until early evening from either Jingzhou's or Shashi's **long-distance bus stations**, with at least eight additional services north to Xiangfan through the day. There's **accommodation** (❾) in the vicinity of both bus stations.

Yichang and the Three Gorges dam

You might well end up spending a night at **YICHANG**, a transport terminus on the Yangzi 120km west from Jingzhou; Yichang marks the start of routes north

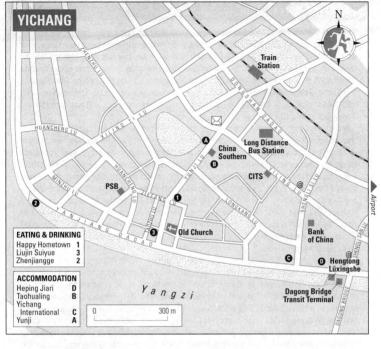

YICHANG

N

Train Station

HUANCHENG LU

Long Distance Bus Station

China Southern

A

B

CITS

@

Airport

PSB

1

Bank of China

LONGKANG LU

3 Old Church

@

C

D Hengtong Lüxingshe

Y a n g z i

Dagong Bridge Transit Terminal

0   300 m

EATING & DRINKING
Happy Hometown   **1**
Liujin Suiyue   **3**
Zhenjiangge   **2**

ACCOMMODATION
Heping Jiari   **D**
Taohualing   **B**
Yichang
  International   **C**
Yunji   **A**

7

THE YANGZI BASIN | Up the Yangzi: Wuhan to Yichang

to Shennongjia (see p.509), and is positioned on the rail line between Xi'an and Hunan. A commercial centre under the Han, it later became an important, if remote, treaty port, fading during the twentieth century. The recent blossoming of Yangzi tourism and the building of the Three Gorges dam just upstream has got the place kicking over again, though in Yichang itself you're limited to tracking down scattered remnants of the colonial era (for instance, the **church** just east off Yujin Lu) or taking in the animated evening river scenery, with water traffic moored up and crowds flying kites, gorging themselves on shellfish at nearby street restaurants, or just cooling off with an ice cream.

The **Three Gorges Dam** (¥68), at which you can watch the progress of the world's most ambitious construction project, is about 35km west of Yichang at **Sandouping**. There's a viewing platform overlooking the locks, ship-lift and the colossus of the dam itself; a visit really brings home just how mind-boggling the project's scale is, though this doesn't deter the hundreds of Chinese tourists from snapping away merrily with their cameras. To reach the site, catch bus #4 from just west of the train station on Dongshan Lu for four stops, then bus #8 (¥10) to the dam – all in all, this takes about an hour. Minibuses are on hand (¥10), or you can just walk out to the viewing area from the bus stop. If you're travelling on a Yangzi cruise boat, the dam may be included on your itinerary, or may be an optional extra, which can make for an easier visit.

Practicalities

Yichang stretches along the Yangzi's northern bank for around 5km, directly below the relatively small **Gezhou dam** (¥20). Arriving at **Sanxia airport**,

The Three Gorges Dam

Through the centuries, the Yangzi's unruly nature has been a source of trauma for China, and conquering the river's tendency to flood extravagantly once a decade or so has been the dream of many Chinese rulers. So far this has only been achieved by the mythical Xia emperor Yu, but by 2009 the river may finally come under human control. After almost a century of planning (the idea was first mooted by Sun Yatsen), the **Three Gorges Dam** will be the largest of its kind in the world, a 1983-metre-long, 185-metre-high wall creating an artificial lake extending back 670km through the Three Gorges to Chongqing.

Investment in the project has been promoted on the back of the dam's **hydroelectric potential** – the eventual output of its 26 generators will be around ten percent of all China's power needs – and the income that the region would receive from both using the generated power and selling it abroad. Financial returns would undoubtedly bring considerable improvements in infrastructure to an otherwise poorly developed part of the country. Yet it's the dam's **flood-controlling** capabilities that blunt-speaking Communist Party front man Zhu Rongji has used to counter protests against the project. For their part, dissenters say that the dam will probably do little to relieve flooding – which occurs along downstream tributaries as much as the Yangzi itself – and claim it would be more effective and cheaper to build a string of lesser dams along these other rivers.

The cost of the project was estimated at around ¥205 billion, but had already overshot that at the time of writing, partly due to developers pocketing funds and then employing inferior materials to make up the shortfall – a practice which resulted in **cracks** appearing in the wall and locks in winter 2001, necessitating expensive repairs. In addition, increased water levels through the Three Gorges are submerging dozens of communities and **historical sites**. Archeologists have frantically scrambled to excavate as much as possible, and nearly two million residents of the area have been **relocated**, a programme which has itself been costly (aggravated by the fact that some of the funds earmarked for it are reckoned to have been embezzled away) and highly controversial; there have been clashes where transmigrants have been resettled on other people's lands. **Ecologically** the project is indefensible – Chongqing, one of China's most heavily industrial cities, pours its effluent directly into the new lake, while even the Chinese government admits that **siltation** will make the dam unusable within seventy years unless they come up with a solution.

10km east of town, you'll need to catch a taxi into the centre (¥60). The **train station** is at the north side of town atop a broad flight of steps leading down to the intersection of Dongshan Dadao and **Yunji Lu**, while the main **long-distance bus station** is 500m east. Buses might terminate south across town at the riverside **Dagong Bridge Transit Terminal**, which is also where **Yangzi ferries** pull in – the bridge in question is an unmistakeable spray of suspension cables and blue and white concrete. Arrival by **hydrofoil** from Chongqing lands you about 5km northwest of town where bus #3 awaits. The train station and Dagong Bridge area are connected by buses #3 and #4 down Yunji Lu and the waterfront. A **taxi** costs a fixed ¥5 in the city centre.

Yichang's **accommodation** is generally a little overpriced in summer, but is a bargain out of season. The *Heping Jiari Jiudian* (℡0717/6254088, ℻8690344; ⑤) offers comfortable new rooms close to the ferry terminal, while nearby is a more upmarket affair, the *Yichang International Hotel* on the corner of Yanjiang Dadao and Shengli Si Lu (℡0717/6222888, ⓦwww.ycinthotel.com; ⑥), which has its own brewery, a revolving restaurant and 24-hour café. Equally smart is the *Taohualing Binguan* (℡0717/6236666, ⓔthlhotel@yc.cninfo.net; ⑦), set

Leaving Yichang, you can arrange plane, ferry and train **tickets** at accommodation tour desks; the one at the *Yichang International Hotel* is the best geared up for foreigners. They also book **tours** of the Three Gorges, Shennongjia, and Zhangjiajie, as do CITS on Yiling Lu (℡0717/6220837, ℻6220973) – a fairly helpful bunch if you can locate an English-speaker – and Hengtong Lüxingshe (℡0717/6222714, ℻6224860) at the Dagong Bridge Transit Terminal.

Ferry departure times upstream to Chongqing are posted on a board beside the Dagong bridge terminal booking office – see pp.923–929 for more about classes and conditions. The **hydrofoil** up through the Three Gorges to Chongqing (11hr; ¥480) departs daily at 7am from above the Gezhou Dam, 5km northwest of town – catch bus #3 or a taxi.

Yichang's **long-distance bus station** has an English-speaking enquiries desk, a **left luggage** office which stays open until 8pm, and departures to almost everywhere between Chongqing and Shanghai. Xingshan, Xiangfan, Jingzhou and Wuhan are also covered by minibuses from the bus-station forecourt.

The **airport** is a ¥60 taxi ride east of town, with flights to Beijing, Chongqing, Guangzhou and Shanghai. China Southern's office (℡0717/6251538) is opposite the *Yunji Fandian* on Yunji Lu. If you're travelling by **train**, it's a smooth ride up to Xiangfan and points north, or south to Zhangjiajie in Hunan; it's easy enough to acquire tickets at the new station.

in quiet grounds off Yunji Lu. A little further up Yunji Lu is the *Yunji Fandian* (℡0717/6443104, ℻6057922; ❹) which has some twin rooms and newer, more comfortable, doubles, some of which enjoy views over the park behind.

There are some good, cheap eating establishments around the Dongshan Dadao/Yunji Lu junction, while street stalls along **Taozhu Lu**, off Yanjiang Dadao, are very popular with locals. For drinks, the Western-style *Liujin Suiyue Kafei* at the river end of Yunji Lu does good coffee, and not far away, *Happy Hometown* on Jiefang Lu is a cosy bar open late and serving imported beers. More traditionally, *Zhenjiangge* is a teahouse set in a pavilion enjoying pleasant views over the river at the western end of the riverside park on Yanjiang Dadao. The main **Bank of China** is on Shengli Lu, while the **post office** is at the junction of Yunji and Yiling Lu. There's a decent place to get **on line** on Shengli San Lu, and smaller possibilities on Yiling Lu.

Shennongjia Forest Reserve

Hidden away 200km north of Yichang in Hubei's far west, **Shennongjia Forest Reserve** encloses a rough crowd of mountains rising to the 3053-metre-high **Da Shennongjia**, the tallest peak in central China. Botanically, this is one of the country's richest corners, famed for its plant life ever since the Taoist immortal and legendary Xia king **Shennong** – also credited with introducing mankind to farming, medicine and tea – scoured these heights for herbs. More recently, the botanist **Ernest Wilson** found several new species for London's Kew Gardens here in the early twentieth century. Intriguingly, Shennongjia has since hosted sightings of the **Chinese wild man**, whose existence seems far from impossible in this stronghold of ancient plants – and even if these elude you, there's a good chance of seeing endangered **golden monkeys** here.

Shennongjia Forest Reserve		
Muyu Zhen	木鱼镇	*mùyú zhèn*
Shennong Resort	神农山庄	*shénnóng shānzhuāng*
Songbo	松柏	*sōngbǎi*
Xingshan	兴山	*xīngshān*
Yumingshan Binguan	玉名山宾馆	*yùmíngshān bīnguǎn*
Shennongjia Forest Reserve	神农架林区	*shénnóngjià línqū*
Banbi Yan	板壁岩	*bǎnbì yán*
Dalong Tan	大龙潭	*dàlóng tán*
Fengjing Ya	风京垭	*fēngjīng yà*
Jinhou Ling	金猴岭	*jīnhóu lǐng*
Reserve Gates	鸭子口	*yāzi kǒu*
Xiaolong Tan	小龙潭	*xiǎolóng tán*
Wildlife		
Giant salamander	娃娃鱼	*wáwáyú*
Golden monkey	金丝猴	*jīnsīhóu*
Golden pheasant	红胸锦鸟	*hóngxiōng jǐnniǎo*
Temminck's tragopan	红胸角雉	*hóngxiōng juézhì*

On few tourist agendas, Shennongjia is easy to reach from Yichang – three days is enough for a quick return trip – though most of the region is actually **off limits to foreigners**. Chinese maps highlight the central **Shennongjia town** (known locally as **Songbai** or **Songbo**) as an access point: arrive here and you will be arrested, fined and booted out by the PSB. Unless the authorities have a change of heart (enquire at Yichang's PSB or CITS about this), it isn't possible for foreigners to continue north to Shiyan and Wudang Shan, however easy this appears on a map. If you stick to the open area around the village of **Muyu Zhen**, however, you'll have a trouble-free trip; just remember that its altitude makes the region very cold in winter, and the reserve can be **snowbound** between November and May.

To Muyu Zhen and the reserve

Minibuses from outside Yichang's bus station leave every thirty minutes between dawn and mid-afternoon for the four-hour run to **XINGSHAN** (¥45), most of this on a decent road climbing through well-farmed, increasingly mountainous country overloaded with hydroelectric stations. Xingshan itself is an unpleasant industrial town; turn right out of the bus station and walk 100m up to a crossroads and you'll find battered **minibuses** to Muyu Zhen (¥10) waiting to fill up with passengers for the final two-hour stretch up the Songbai road.

MUYU ZHEN – also known as **Muyu** or **Yuzhen** – is a service centre 17km south of the reserve, a 500-metre-long street of small stores, guesthouses and canteens leading off the main road. It's a good base for a quick visit, though there's cheaper accommodation inside the reserve if you're planning on staying a while. Muyu's **hotels** are surprisingly upmarket: at the far end of the street, the *Yumingshan Binguan* (☎0719/3453088; ❺) has spacious doubles and a fair restaurant. The exclusive *Shenlong Resort* (☎0719/3452513; ❻) is clearly visible on the hill above. For **maps and tours** of the reserve, drop in on Muyu's **Forestry Office Travel Service** (☎0719/3453213) about 100m before *Yumingshan Binguan* – look for the "Shennongjia Natural Reserve" sign on the left. Some staff here speak English, and can advise on the best places to find unusual plants and animals – hiring a car and interpreter for the day will cost ¥400. To reach the reserve on your own, either flag down Songbai-bound buses on the main road (note that the reserve gates here are as far up this road as foreigners are allowed to travel) or bargain with the Xingshan minibus drivers for a charter (about ¥50 to the reserve gates, or ¥300 for the day), who otherwise run **back to Xingshan** until the afternoon.

Around the reserve

The steep and twisting Songbai road continues north of Muyu to a checkpoint marking the **reserve gates**, where you hand over the ¥60 entry fee and add your name to the list of the few foreigners who make it here each year. From here, 6km of gravel track runs southwest up a once-logged valley to the couple of wooden Forestry Department buildings that comprise **XIAOLONG TAN**, a source of **beds** (¥50), meals and close-up views of golden monkeys – if any have been brought in to the "animal hospital" here. There's also a **Wild Man museum**, where paintings, newspaper clippings, maps and casts of footprints document all known encounters with the gigantic, shaggy, red-haired *ye ren*, first seen in 1924. The creature was most recently spotted in June 2003 by a party of six, including a local reporter, who described the beast as being 1.65 metres tall, of greyish hue, with shoulder-length hair and a footprint measuring some twelve inches.

There are some good **walking tracks** around Xiaolong Tan, though you'll need advice from Forestry staff on current conditions. One route (much of it along a vehicle track) climbs south, in around 2.5km, to a forest of China firs on the slopes of **Jinhou Ling** (Golden Monkey Peak), the prime spot to catch family groups of **golden monkeys** foraging first thing in the morning. Favouring green leaves, stems, flowers and fruit, the monkeys live through the winter on **lichen** and moss, which the trees here are covered in. The males especially are a tremendous sight, with reddish-gold fur, light blue faces, huge lips and no visible nose. A far rougher trail continues to the top of the mountain in four hours, which you'd be ill-advised to tackle without a guide. Alternatively, a relaxed 3km north of Xiaolong Tan is **Dalong Tan**, a cluster of run-down huts by a stream (reputedly inhabited by giant salamanders), from where there's an undemanding eight-kilometre walk up the valley to **Guanyin Cave**. Most of this is through open country with plenty of wildflowers in spring, and the chance for birders to flush out **golden pheasants** and the splendidly coloured, grouse-like **tragopans**.

Worth it for the scenery alone, the gravel road from Xiaolong Tan curves westwards up the valley, climbing almost continually along the ridges and, in clear weather, affording spectacular views. On the way you cross Da Shennongjia, though the rounded peak is barely noticeable above the already high road. Better are the cliffscapes about 10km along at **Fengjing Ya** and **Jinzi Yanya**, and the "forest" of limestone spires where the road finally gives up the ghost 17km due west of Xiaolong Tan at **Banbi Yan**.

Wudang Shan

Hubei's river plains extend well into the province's northwest, where they reluctantly cede to mountain ranges butting up against Henan, Shaanxi and Sichuan. The region's peaks are steeped in legends surrounding **Wudang Shan**, the Military Mountain, known for its Taoist temples and fighting style.

An easy ascent coupled with the mountain's splendid scenery (and the availability of transport from Wuhan, Xi'an and Yichang) really make the journey worthwhile.

Wudang Shan's 72 pinnacles have, since Tang times, been liberally covered in **Taoist temples**. Those that survived a wave of thirteenth-century revolts were restored following proclamations for the development of religion under the Ming emperor **Cheng Zi** in 1413 – the work took three hundred thousand labourers ten years to complete – and the mountain is currently enjoying another bloom of religious fervour, with many of the temples emerging fabulously decorated and busy after decades of neglect.

Wudang Shan is also famous for its **martial arts**, which command as much respect as those of Henan's Shaolin Si (see p.300). It's said that the Song-dynasty monk **Zhang Sanfeng** developed Wudang boxing – from which *tai ji* is derived – after watching a fight between a snake and a magpie, which revealed to him the essence of *neijia*, an internal force used (in typical Taoist manner) to control "action" with "non-action". Fighting skills would also have come in handy considering the vast number of **outlaws** who've inhabited these mountains over the centuries. The rebel peasant **Li Zicheng** massed his forces and rose to depose the last Ming emperor from here, and there's a tablet recording the suppression of the Red Turbans on the mountain by Qing troops in 1856. More recently, the Communist **Third Front Army** found sanctuary here in 1931, after their march from Hong Lake in southern Hubei.

On a more peaceful note, Wudang Shan was also the retreat of emperor **Zhen Wu**, who cultivated his longevity in these mountains during the fifteenth century, and whose portly statue graces many local temples – his **birthday** is celebrated locally on the third day of the third lunar month, a good time to visit the mountain. Wudang's valuable plants later attracted the attention of the sixteenth-century pharmacologist **Li Shizhen**, who included four hundred

Wudang Shan		
Shiyan	十堰	*shíyàn*
Wudang Shan Town	武当山市镇	*wǔdāngshān shìzhèn*
Taishan Miao	泰山庙	*tàishān miào*
Xuanwu Jiudian	玄武酒店	*xuánwǔ jiǔdiàn*
Yuxu Gong	玉虚宫	*yùxū gōng*
Wudang Shan	武当山	*wǔdāng shān*
Feisheng Rock	飞升岩	*fēishēng yán*
Huangjing Hall	皇经堂	*huángjīng táng*
Huanglong Dong	黄龙洞	*huánglóng dòng*
Jindian Gong	金殿宫	*jīndiàn gōng*
Jiulong Villa	九龙山庄	*jiǔlóng shānzhuāng*
Lang Mei Xian Ci	榔梅仙祠	*lángméi xiāncí*
Nanyan Binguan	南岩宾馆	*nányán bīnguǎn*
Nanyan Gong	南岩宫	*nányán gōng*
Santian Men	三天门	*sāntiān mén*
Taihe Gong	太和宫	*tàihé gōng*
Zixiao Gong	紫霄宫	*zǐxiāo gōng*
Xiangfan	襄樊	*xiāngfán*

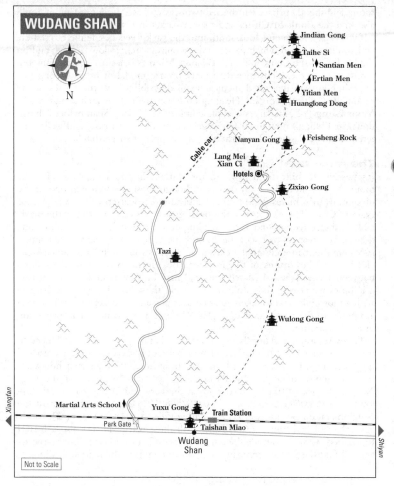

WUDANG SHAN

N

Jindian Gong
Taihe Si
Santian Men
Ertian Men
Yitian Men
Huanglong Dong

Cable car

Nanyan Gong
Feisheng Rock
Lang Mei
Xian Ci
Hotels
Zixiao Gong

Tazi

Wulong Gong

Martial Arts School
Yuxu Gong
Train Station
Park Gate
Taishan Miao
Wudang
Shan

Xiangfan

Shiyan

Not to Scale

local species among the 1800 listed in his *Materia Medica*, still a source work on the medicinal use of Chinese herbs.

Wudang Shan town

About 120km west of **Xiangfan**, a manufacturing town and transport hub on the Hanshui River, road and rail converge at the small market town of **WUDANG SHAN**, with the mountain range rising immediately to the south. There are buses here until late afternoon and daily trains from Xiangfan, or you can leave transport 25km farther west at the city of **Shiyan** and catch a minibus back to Wudang Shan (¥10) from opposite Shiyan's train station.

Wudang Shan town is just a few muddy backstreets south of the 500-metre-long main road. *Xuanwu Jiudian* (☎0719/5666013; ❸), on the main street opposite the bus station, is the pick of the **accommodation**, with some cheaper rooms and slightly pricier refurbished twins, as well as a decent restaurant. You'll also find the **Bank of China** and a supermarket in town.

If you're at a loose end, look south into the backstreets beside the bus station, and you'll see a road which passes under a railway arch; follow it down and on the left before the arch you'll find **Taishan Miao** (¥2), a small temple museum whose eccentric exhibits include a hefty bronze model of Jindian Gong (see opposite), and an illustrated medical scroll describing how the phases of the moon affect different organs. Heading on under the railway arch brings you to **Yuxu Gong** (¥2), the largest temple complex at Wudang Shan before it burnt down in 1745; it's now just a few vegetated pavilions, staircases and wells scattered around a flagstoned area the size of a couple of soccer pitches.

The mountain

It's possible to **hike** from town to the summit in about eight hours – the footpath starts near the train station – though most people catch one of the ubiquitous **minibuses** (¥10) to the roadhead three-quarters of the way up near Nanyan Gong. There's a stop at the **park gates** outside town to pay the inevitable entrance fee (around ¥75, including entry to temples on the mountain), then drivers tear up past stark fields, outlying temples and martial-arts schools to where the road ends amid a cluster of hotels, sword shops and parked vehicles. You can buy **maps** of the area here. Bear in mind that if you're visiting between December and March the road may be snowbound, in which case minibuses won't run, and you'll have to walk the whole lot or try to bargain with a motorbike taxi to take you as far as is possible. Another option is to take a minibus to the cable car at Qiongtai (¥35 each way), which then speeds you up to the summit.

Places to stay are generally expensive for what they offer, and you'll need to thoroughly check out the room and availability of hot water before commencing bargaining. There are several smaller, cheap hotels, though their hot-water situation tends to be sketchy. Reasonable deals can be found at the large *Nanyan Binguan* (☎0719/5689182; ❹) at the very end of the road, or, slightly lower down, *Baihui Shanzhuang* (☎0719/5689191; ❺). At the bottom of the conglomeration lies the welcoming *Jiulong Villa* (☎0718/5689176; ❹). Meals, generally not bad value, are available at all these places. There's also a **hostel** (dorm beds ¥25) just outside the temple gates on Tianzhu Peak; Chinese-speakers will find the monks' company well worth enduring the spartan facilities.

Nanyan Gong and Zixiao Gong

A path from the hotel area leads, via several Tang-dynasty ruins and long views down onto the plains, to **Nanyan Gong**, perched fortress-like on a precipice. The halls are tiny and austere, carved as they are out of the cliff face, but the main sight here is **Dragon Head Rock**, a two-metre-long slab sculpted with swirls and scales, which projects straight out over the void. Before it was walled off, countless people lost their lives trying to walk to the end with a stick of incense. Carry on past the temple to **Feisheng Rock** for far safer views of the scenery.

About 3km downhill from the end of the road – you'll have seen it in passing – is **Zixiao Gong**, the Purple Cloud Palace, an impressively huge early Ming temple complex whose pattern of successively higher platforms appears to mimic the structure of the hills above. Pleasantly active with monks, tourists and the occasional mendicant traveller, the place is becoming the mountain's most important single monastery. Through the gates, a broad stone staircase climbs between boxy Tang pavilions housing massive stone tortoises to the **main hall**, whose exterior is lightened by the graceful sweep of its tiled roof. Inside is a rare wooden spiral cupola and a benevolent statue of the Yellow Emperor; surrounding courtyards are sometimes used for martial-arts displays.

Tianzhu

It takes around two hours to walk from the hotel area to the top of **Tianzhu Peak** (the highest here, at 1600m) along a comfortably paved path (a waterproof or umbrella may come in handy as protection against Wudang Shan's famously changeable weather). One way to keep your mind off the flights of steps is by watching out for the colourful variety of birds in the forest, including boisterous red-billed magpies with graceful blue tails, and magnificent golden pheasants. Almost immediately you arrive at **Lang Mei Xian Ci**, a small shrine dedicated to Zhang Sanfeng and his contribution to Chinese martial arts – there's a statue of him along with a cast-iron halberd in one hall, and Chinese-only accounts of his development of Wudang boxing in adjoining rooms.

Halfway up to Tianzhu the path divides at **Huanglong Dong** (Yellow Dragon Cave) to form an eventual circuit via the peak; continue straight ahead for the least taxing walk and superb views through the canopy of cloud-swept, apparently unscalable cliffs. A surprisingly short time later you'll find yourself on top of them, outside the encircling wall which has turned Tianzhu and its temples into a well-defended citadel. Inside, the Ming-dynasty **Taihe Gong** is impressive for the atmosphere of grand decay enclosed by the thick green tiles and red walls of **Huangjing Hall**, where monks stand around the cramped stone courtyards or pray in the richly decorated, peeling rooms squeezed inside. From here you can ascend the unbelievably steep **Jiuliandeng** (Nine-section Staircase) to where the mountain is literally crowned by **Jindian Gong** (Golden Palace Temple), a tiny shrine decorated with a gilded bronze roof embellished with cranes and deer, whose interior is filled by a statue of armour-clad Zhen Wu sitting behind a desk in judgement. Views from the front terrace (clearest in the morning) look down from the top of the world, with sharp crags dropping away through wispy clouds into the forest below. For an alternative descent, follow the stairs off Jiandian Gong's rear terrace, which return to Huanglong Dong down some very rickety steps via **Santian Men**, the Three Sky Gates.

Hunan

For many travellers, their experience of **Hunan** is a pastiche of the tourist image of rural China – a view of endless muddy tracts or paddy fields rolling past the train window, green or gold depending on the season. But the bland countryside, or rather the lot of the peasants farming it, has greatly affected the country's recent history. Hunan's most famous peasant son, **Mao Zedong**, saw the crushing poverty inflicted on local farmers by landlords and a corrupt government, and the brutality with which any protests were suppressed. Though Mao is no longer accorded his former god-like status, monuments to him litter the landscape around the provincial capital **Changsha**, which is a convenient base for exploring the scenes of his youth. By contrast, the history-laden town of **Yueyang** in northern Hunan, where the Yangzi meanders past **Dongting Hu**, China's second largest lake, offers more genteel attractions. Both Hunan and Hubei – literally "south of the lake" and "north of the lake" respectively – take their names from this vast expanse of water, which is intricately tied to the origins of **dragon-boat racing**. South of Changsha, **Heng Shan** holds a pleasant group of mountain temples, while in the far west there's some inspiringly rugged landscapes to tramp through at **Wulingyuan Scenic Reserve**. A few hours south of here lies the picturesque historic town of **Fenghuang**, where you'll find remnants of the **Southern Great Wall**.

Changsha and around

There's little evidence to show that the site of **CHANGSHA**, Hunan's tidy, nondescript capital, has in fact been inhabited for three thousand years, though it has long been an important river town and, prior to Qin invasions in 280

Changsha and around		
Changsha	长沙	*chángshā*
Aiwan Ting	爱晚亭	*àiwǎn tíng*
Hunan Provincial Museum	湖南省博物馆	*húnánshěng bówùguǎn*
Hunan University	湖南大学	*húnán dàxué*
Juzi Dao	桔子岛	*júzi dǎo*
Martyrs' Park	烈士公园	*lièshì gōngyuán*
Qingshui Tan	清水潭	*qīngshuǐ tán*
Wangxiang Ting	望乡亭	*wàngxiāng tíng*
Yuelu Academy	岳麓书院	*yuèlù shūyuàn*
Yuelu Shan	岳麓山	*yuèlù shān*
Accommodation		
Civil Aviation	民航大酒店	*mínháng dàjiǔdiàn*
Didu	地都大酒店	*dìdū dàjiǔdiàn*
Dolton	通程国际大酒店	*tōngchéng guójì dàjiǔdiàn*
Hunan University Guesthouse	湖南大学专家楼	*húnán dàxué zhuānjiālóu*
Purple Gold Dragon	紫金龙大酒店	*zǐjīnlóng dàjiǔdiàn*
Sanjiu Chunyun	三九楚云大酒店	*sānjiǔchǔyún dàjiǔdiàn*
Taicheng	泰成大酒店	*tàichéng dàjiǔdiàn*
Yinhua	银华大酒店	*yínhuá dàjiǔdiàn*
Eating		
Chaozhou	潮州菜馆	*cháozhōu càiguǎn*
Dong Lai Shun	东来顺	*dōngláishùn*
Fire Palace	火宫饭店	*huǒgōng fàndiàn*
Gaximu	咖稀穆餐厅	*kāxīmù cāntīng*
Xinhua Lou	新华楼	*xīnhuá lóu*
Shaoshan	韶山	*sháoshān*
Dripping Water Cave	滴水洞	*dīshuǐ dòng*
Mao Ancestral Temple	毛氏宗祠	*máoshì zōngcí*
Mao Zedong Exhibition Hall	毛泽东纪念馆	*máozédōng jìniànguǎn*
Mao's Family Home	毛泽东故居	*máozédōng gùjū*
Shaofeng Binguan	韶凤宾馆	*sháofèng bīnguǎn*
Shaoshan Binguan	韶山宾馆	*sháoshān bīnguǎn*

BC, was the southern capital of the kingdom of **Chu**. Changsha was declared a treaty port in 1903, though Europeans found that the Hunanese had a very short fuse (something other Chinese already knew), and, after the British raised the market price of rice during a famine in 1910, the foreign quarter was totally destroyed by rioting. The bulk of the remainder was torched by the Guomindang in 1938, following their "scorched earth" policy as they fled the Japanese advance, and recent modernizations have claimed the rest. While ancient sites and objects occasionally surface nearby – such as Shang-era bronze wine jars, and the magnificently preserved contents of three **Han burial mounds** – their presence is swamped by busy clover-leaf intersections, grey concrete facades and other trappings of modern urban China.

Primarily, though, Changsha is known for its links with **Mao**. Aged 18, he arrived here from his native Shaoshan as nationwide power struggles erupted following the Manchu dynasty's fall in 1911, and soon put aside his university studies to spend six months in the local militia. After he returned to the classroom in 1913, Changsha became a breeding ground for secret political societies and intellectuals, and by 1918 there was a real movement for Hunan to become an independent state. For a time, this idea found favour with the local warlord **Zhao Hendi**, though he soon turned violently on his supporters. Mao, then back in Shaoshan heading a Communist Party branch and leading peasant protests, was singled out and fled to Guangzhou in 1925 to take up a teaching post at the Peasant Movement Training Institute. Within three years he would return to Hunan to organize the abortive **Autumn Harvest Uprising**, and would be establishing guerrilla bases in rural Jiangxi.

Mao was by no means the only young Hunanese caught up in these events, and a number of his contemporaries later surfaced in the Communist government: **Liu Shaoqi**, Mao's deputy until he became a victim of the Cultural Revolution; four Politburo members under Deng Xiaoping, including the former CCP chief, **Hu Yaobang**; and **Hua Guofeng**, Mao's lookalike and briefly empowered successor. Today, several of Changsha's formal attractions involve the Chairman, though there are also a couple of parks to wander around, and a fascinating **Provincial Museum**. Possible day-trips from Changsha include Mao's birthplace at **Shaoshan**, 90km to the southwest, and the famous tower at **Yueyang** (see p.524), 120km to the north, both of which are easily reached by local rail.

Arrival and city transport

The bulk of Changsha is spread east of the **Xiang River**, and the city's name – literally "Long Sand" – derives from a narrow midstream bar, now called **Juzi Dao**, Tangerine Island. The river itself is spanned by the lengthy Xiangjiang Bridge, which links the city to the west-bank suburbs, **Yuelu Academy** and parkland. **Wuyi Dadao** is Changsha's main drag and forms an unfocused downtown district as it runs broad and straight for 4km across the city.

The **airport** is 15km east of town, connected to the airline offices on Wuyi Dadao by a **shuttle bus** (¥15). Changsha's **train station** is conveniently central at the eastern end of Wuyi Dadao, but the three main **long-distance bus stations** are all several kilometres out of town in the suburbs, any one of which you could wind up at: to reach the train station, catch **city bus** #126 from the east bus station (4km), bus #302 from the west bus station (8km), or bus #7 from the south bus station (10km).

Changsha's **city buses** run between about 6am and 9pm and almost all originate, or at least stop, at the train-station square. Chinese **maps** of the city, with the **bus routes** clearly marked, are easily picked up from street vendors at

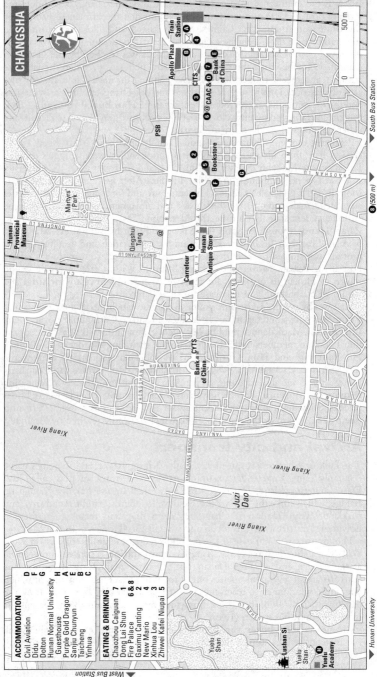

THE YANGZI BASIN | Changsha and around

CHANGSHA

N

▲ Airport & East Bus Station

Train Station

Apollo Plaza

CITS

Bank of China

CAAC & D

PSB

Bookstore

Hunan Provincial Museum

Martyrs' Park

Qingshui Tang

Carrefour

Hunan Antique Store

Bank of China

CYTS

XIANGJIANG BRIDGE

Xiang River

Juzi Dao

Xiang River

Yuelu Shan

Lushan Si

Yuelu Academy

▼ West Bus Station

▼ South Bus Station

8 (500 m) ▼

▼ Hunan University

0   500 m

ACCOMMODATION
Civil Aviation   D
Didu   F
Dolton   G
Hunan Normal University
Guesthouse   H
Purple Gold Dragon   A
Sanju Chunyun   E
Taicheng   B
Yinhua   C

EATING & DRINKING
Chaozhou Caiguan   7
Dong Lai Shun   1
Fire Palace   6 & 8
Gaximu Canting   2
New Mario   4
Xinhua Lou   3
Zhiwei Kafei Niupai   5

Moving on from Changsha

There are **flights** from Changsha to Hefei, Yichang, Zhangjiajie, Shanghai, Beijing, and everywhere else between Hong Kong and Ürümqi. Between 7am and 9pm there are half-hourly buses to the airport from the **airline office**, west of the *Civil Aviation* hotel on Wuyi Dadao (daily 6.30am–8pm; ℡0731/4112222).

Leaving by **bus**, try the east bus station for eastern destinations, the west for western ones, and the south for southern – though the train is a better option for almost all travel. **Trains** head north from Changsha to Yueyang and Hubei province; west to Guizhou, Jishou and Zhangjiajie; east to Nanchang in Jiangxi; and south via Hengyang to Guangdong and Guangxi. There's also a special tourist train daily to Shaoshan. Currently, the fastest train to Zhangjiajie is #T358, which leaves at 6.15am and takes a mere five hours. Ticket offices are on the south side of the square (daily 6am–11pm).

arrival points, which are also good places to hail a **taxi**. These cost ¥6 to hire; you then pay for distance covered in ¥2 increments.

Accommodation

Due to tight controls, **hotels** in Changsha able to accept foreigners are, almost without exception, fairly expensive. The university aside, the following have restaurants and train- and flight-booking agents.

Civil Aviation 75 Wuyi Dadao ℡0731/4170288, ℻4170388. A well-run and tidy airlines-owned operation, though reception staff are harassed and brusque. ❹

Didu 80 Shaoshan Bei Lu ℡0731/4451555, ℻4454483. Inexpensive lodgings in a tatty, renovated 1930s building. Not listed as a foreigners' hotel but – at time of writing – had no qualms about letting them stay. Buses along Wuyi Dadao stop nearby. ❸

Dolton 149 Shaoshan Bei Lu ℡0731/4168888, ⓦwww.dolton-hotel.com. The height of luxury in Changsha, a hugely opulent sprawl of marble and chandeliers, with five-star service. ❾

Hunan Normal University Guesthouse Below Yuelu Shan in western Changsha ℡0731/8872211. Catch bus #202 from the train station, or #305 from the western bus station to its bridge-side terminus, where you can pick up a #202 or #106. The area you need is actually north of the main campus, and it's a good 10min walk uphill to the

guesthouse once you're in the grounds. Rooms are often full, so phone ahead. ❸

Purple Gold Dragon Northeast corner of the train-station square, right next to the arrivals exit ℡0731/2279999, ℻2279978. This popular place is good value and usually full – hang around mid-morning to snap up rooms as they appear. Be firm if the staff try to foist their most expensive rooms on you. ❺

Sanjiu Chunyun Just southwest of the train station, on Chezhan Lu ℡0731/4191999, ℻4191399. Three-star venture with slightly worn but good-quality rooms and enthusiastic staff. ❹

Taicheng Chezhan Lu, opposite the train station ℡0731/2331111. This newish place has passable standard rooms and more comfortable twins for not a lot more. ❸

Yinhua 160 Wuyi Dadao ℡0731/2330000, ℻4429875. A large multistorey complex designed to lure international business folk, with smart rooms and a coffee shop. ❺

The City

While there's little in Changsha to absorb between the sights, it's a clean, well-ordered city and people are noticeably friendly – don't be surprised if you acquire a guide while walking around. If the city's streets seem unusually empty and you're wondering where Changsha's crowds hang out, head down to the main **shopping district** west of the centre at the junction of Wuyi Dadao and **Huangxing Lu**. The latter is pedestrianized between Jiefang Lu and Chengnan

Lu and the area is loaded with shopping plazas, Western fast-food chains, and groups of teenagers orbiting between the two.

Qingshui Tang

North of Wuyi Dadao, on Bayi Lu, is **Qingshui Tang** (Clearwater Pool; daily 8am–4.45pm; ¥10; bus #113 stops outside), Mao's former home in Changsha and the site of the first local Communist Party offices. A white marble statue of Mao greets you at the gate, and the garden walls are covered with stone tablets carved with his epigrams. Near the pool itself is a scruffy vegetable patch and the reconstructed room in which Mao and his second wife, **Yang Kaihui** (daughter of Mao's stoical and influential teacher, Yang Changji), lived after moving here from Beijing following their marriage in 1921. There's also a display of peasant tools – a grindstone, thresher, carrypole and baskets – and a short history of Chinese agriculture. In the same grounds, a brightly tiled **museum** contains a low-key but interesting collection of historical artefacts, including a clay tomb figurine of a bearded horseman and a cannon used for defending the city against Taiping incursions in 1852. These pieces lead through to a depressing photographic record of Guomindang atrocities and eulogies to Mao, Zhou Enlai and others. The three red flags here are those of the Party, the PLA and the nation.

Martyrs' Park and Hunan Provincial Museum

From Qingshui Tang, follow Qingshuitang Lu north and then turn east for 500m to the gates of **Martyrs' Park** (free). Though it's often crowded, plenty of shade and lakes complete with ornamental gardens, bridges and pagodas make the park a nice place to stroll. But the main reason to head up this way is to visit **Hunan Provincial Museum** (daily 9am–6pm; ¥20; bus #126, from the station via Wuyi Dadao, stops outside), whose entrance is on Dongfeng Lu above the park's northwestern corner. One of Changsha's high points, the museum is dedicated solely to the Han-era tomb of **Xin Zui**, the Marquess of Dai. Xin Zui died around 160 BC, and her subterranean tomb – roughly contemporary with similar finds at Jingzhou (see p.506) and Wuhan (see p.502) – was one of three discovered in 1972 during construction work at **Mawangdui**, about 4km northeast (the others contained her husband and son). Thanks to damp-proof rammed walls of clay and charcoal, a triple wooden sarcophagus, and wrappings of linen and silk, the Marquess' **body** was so well preserved that modern pathologists were able to establish that she suffered from tuberculosis, gallstones, arteriosclerosis and bilharzia when she died, aged 50. The sarcophaguses are in a side hall, while access to the mummy (after sealing your dusty shoes in plastic bags) is through a basement display of **embroideries**, lacquered bowls and coffins, musical instruments, wooden tomb figures and other funerary offerings. Taoist texts written on silk were also found in the tomb, and one piece illustrating **qigong postures** is on display. Xin Zui herself lies in a fluid-filled tank below several inches of perspex, a gruesome white doll covered from chin to thigh, with her internal organs displayed in jars.

Around the river

Crossing the river, gaze down on semi-rural midstream **Juzi Dao**, which was settled by the local European community after the events of 1910. Some of their former homes are still standing, though one-time mansions are now partitioned into family apartments. Legend has it that Mao regularly used to swim to shore from the southern tip of the island, a feat he repeated on his 65th birthday as one of his famous river crossings.

Over the river, **Hunan University**'s campus sits south of **Yuelu Shan**, a famous breezy hilltop and beauty spot, reached from the train station on bus #202, which crosses the bridge and heads south to terminate at a square dominated by a Mao statue below **Yuelu Academy**. Paths flanked by food and souvenir stalls lead from here to the park gates (¥20), then meander uphill, making for forty minutes' stroll through pleasant woodland to **Wangxiang Ting**, a pavilion with views over the city. On the way, the small **Aiwan Ting** (Loving the Dusk Pavilion), built in 1792, was one of Mao's youthful haunts, and there's a tablet here bearing his calligraphy. The pavilion's name derives from the verse *Ascending the Hills* by the soulful Tang poet Du Mu:

A stony path winds far up cool hills
Towards cottages hidden deep amongst white clouds
Loving the maple trees at dusk I stop my cart
To sit and watch the frosted leaves
Redder than February flowers

A little west of here, **Lushan Si** dates from the Western Jin dynasty (263–316 AD), making it one of the oldest monasteries in Hunan; the enormous yew tree immediately in front of the temple is said to be of a similar age.

Eating, drinking and entertainment

A predilection for strong flavours and copious chillies places **Hunanese food** firmly inside the Western Chinese cooking belt – Mao himself claimed that it was the fiery food that made locals so (politically) red. Pungent **regional specialities** include air-cured and **chilli-smoked meat**; *dong'an* chicken, where the shredded, poached meat is seasoned with a vinegar-soy dressing; *gualiang fen*, a gelatinous mass of cold, shaved rice noodles covered in a spicy sauce; *chou doufu* (literally "stinking tofu"), a fermented bean-curd dish which actually tastes good; and a mass of less spicy snacks – preserved eggs, pickles, buns and dumplings – that form the regular fare in town. Canteens around the train station are unusually good for these things, as are several upmarket but still inexpensive restaurants.

There's a plethora of **Western-style cafés** with the usual run of set meals and fresh brews, especially along the eastern end of Wuyi Dadao: try *Zhiwei Kafei Niupai*, near the Xinhua bookstore. There are also *New Mario* **cake shops** scattered around the city, including one opposite the train station, which has biscuits, cakes, sponges and Portuguese-style baked custard tarts.

For unknown reasons, tropical **betel nut** (the areca palm's stimulating seed pod) is a popular pick-me-up here, sold either boiled and sliced for chewing, or powdered in cigarettes.

Restaurants

Chaozhou Caiguan Wuyi Dadao. Big, mid-range southern Chinese restaurant with a bias towards seafood.

Dong Lai Shun Wuyi Dadao. Muslim restaurant specializing in lamb hotpot served with pickled garlic dip; their meat is meticulously selected and pretty tasty.

Fire Palace There are at least two branches of this riotously good restaurant: on Shaoshan Lu (bus #7, #202 or #104 from outside the train station), and

Wuyi Dadao. The original on Shaoshan Lu is the best, and a busier, noisier, and more thoroughly enjoyable place to wolf down Hunanese food would be hard to imagine. Get an order card off the waitress, request some dark Baisha beer, and stop trolleys loaded with small plates of goodies as they pass – you could eat here a dozen times and not get through the selection. Stay off the à la carte menu and you'll only pay ¥2–12 a plate at either branch.

Gaximu Canting Wuyi Dadao. Another great Muslim eatery, this one a bit more upmarket and comfortable, but affordable nevertheless. There's a choice of *lamian* (stretched noodles), hefty meat skewers or dumplings. Dishes from ¥5.

Xinhua Lou Eastern end of Wuyi Dadao. Another excellent place for local dishes, with trolleys of smoked tofu and meats, crisp cold vegetables dressed in sesame oil, black-skinned-chicken soup, preserved eggs, and a huge range of dumplings being wheeled around between 6.30am and 1.30am. ¥2–10 a dish.

Listings

Banks and exchange The principal Bank of China is near the train station on Wuyi Dadao (Mon–Sat 8am–noon & 2.30–5pm). Upmarket hotels such as the *Dolton* also change traveller's cheques, and might not mind whether you're staying or not.

Bookshops Xinhua Bookstore, at the Wuyi Dadao/ Shaoshan Lu intersection, has a good art section – including books on painting techniques – but slim pickings in English.

Hospital Changsha Number 2 Medical College, Renmin Lu ☎0731/5550400 or 5550511.

Internet access There are Internet cafés throughout the city, generally charging ¥3 an hour; a convenient option is the one on the second floor of the *Sanjiu Chunyun* hotel, while there are others near the CAAC on Wuyi Dadao and near the entrance to Qingshui Tang on Bayi Lu.

Left luggage Both the train and bus stations have left-luggage offices.

Mail and telephones The most convenient post office – with parcel post and international phones – is in the train-station square.

PSB The Foreign Affairs Department of the PSB is on Bayi Lu at its junction with Chengdao Lu (Mon– Fri 8am–noon & 2.30–5.30pm; ☎0731/4590788).

Shopping As you'll appreciate after visiting the Provincial Museum, Changsha has long had a reputation for silk embroidery, which you can buy at various stores along Wuyi Dadao. The Hunan Antique Store on Wuyi Dadao has a host of old wood carvings, porcelain, inkstones, chops and tourist souvenirs. For day-to-day needs, try Carrefour, on the junction of Furong Lu and Wuyi Dadao.

Travel agents CITS are at 46 Wuyi Dadao (☎0731/2280184, ☎2296270), while CYTS are at the junction of Huangxing Lu and Wuyi Dadao (☎0731/2227111). You can also book Chinese-oriented tours to Heng Shan (¥260), Shaoshan (¥135), Yueyang (¥260) and Zhangjiajie (2–5 days; ¥550–900) at the small bus depot opposite the train station on Chezhan Bei Lu.

Shaoshan

Mao Zedong's birthplace, the hamlet of **SHAOSHAN**, lies 90km to the southwest of Changsha, a fine day-trip from the provincial capital through the Hunanese countryside. Established as a pilgrimage site for idolatrous Red Guards during the Cultural Revolution, Shaoshan today seethes with Chinese tourists, who – following a low point in Mao's reputation through the 1980s – have started to flock back to visit the Great Helmsman's hometown. The best way to get here is on the **special train** from Changsha, which departs daily at 6.45am for the three-hour journey (¥101 return; returns from Shaoshan at 4.55pm). Alternatively, **tour buses** leave from the square outside the train station ticket office at 7am (guided day-tour ¥135).

Shaoshan is two settlements: a knot of hotels and services that have sprung up around the railhead and long-distance bus depot, and **Shaoshan Dong**, the village itself, some 6km distant. Patriotic jingles and a large portrait of Mao greet **arrivals** at the train station, as do **minibuses** heading up to the village. Unless you're planning to stay overnight or are hungry – in which case there's a cheap **hotel** (❸) and several **restaurants** ahead and round to the right near the bus depot – you should hop straight on board the first minibus. The first place to disembark is just before the village proper outside **Mao's Family Home** (daily 8am–5pm; free), a compound of bare adobe buildings next to a lotus-filled pond, where Mao was born on December 26, 1893. The home is neatly preserved, with a few pieces of period furniture, the odd photograph, and wonderfully turgid English explanations completing the spartan furnishings.

Here he led a thoroughly normal childhood, one of four children in a relatively wealthy peasant household which comfortably survived the terrible famines in Hunan during the first decade of the twentieth century. Though a rebellious youth, it was not until he moved to Changsha in his late teens that he became politicized.

Just up the road is the huge **village square** where, next to a bronze statue of an elderly Mao and a swarm of souvenir stalls, stands the **Mao Zedong Exhibition Hall** (daily 8am–5pm; ¥15). Photos and knick-knacks here chart Mao's career, though today there's a great distinction between Mao the heroic revolutionary and the character who inflicted the Great Leap Forward – the disastrous movement which was meant to bring Chinese industrial output up to Western levels – and Cultural Revolution on his country. The exhibition reflects this: noticeable omissions include the Little Red Book, and just about any mention of the years between 1957 and his funeral in 1976. Next door to the museum is the former **Mao Ancestral Temple** (free), now a memorial to the leader's early work among the peasants here.

After his Great Leap Forward had begun to falter, Mao returned to Shaoshan in 1959, interviewing peasants here about the movement's shortcomings. He can't have liked what he heard; on his final visit in 1966 at the start of the Cultural Revolution, he kept himself aloof near the reservoir in a secret retreat, poetically named **Dishui Dong** (Dripping Water Cave; ¥30), to which you can catch a minibus. Alternatively, the elegant pavilion atop of **Shaoshan peak** overlooks the local landscape – not really typical, given the amount of tourist revenue, but a nice scene of healthy fields and bamboo thickets.

There are a few restaurants and **places to stay** in Shaoshan village around the square, including the *Shaoshan Binguan* in the square itself, with a jumble of indifferent rooms around an ornamental pool (℡0732/5685262; ❻), and the welcoming *Shaofeng Binguan* (℡0732/5685073, ℻5685241; ❺), about 100m up a side road from the square.

Yueyang and Dongting Hu

YUEYANG, a major riverside city on the Beijing–Guangzhou rail line and stop for Yangzi ferries, lies 160km southwest of Wuhan and 120km north of Changsha. The city also lies on the eastern shores of **Dongting Hu**, China's second largest freshwater lake, covering 2500 square kilometres. Fringed with reeds and lotus ponds, the lake is surrounded by villages farming rich cane and

Yueyang and Dongting Hu

Yueyang	岳阳	yuèyáng
Chenglingji	城陵矶	chénglíng jī
Junshan Dao	君山岛	jūnshān dǎo
Miluo River	汨罗江	mìluó jiāng
Nanyue Docks	南越码头	nányuè mǎtóu
Yueyang docks	岳阳楼客运站	yuèyánglóu kèyùnzhàn
Yueyang Tower	岳阳楼	yuèyáng lóu
Yunmeng	云梦宾馆	yúnmèng bīnguǎn
Dongting Hu	洞庭湖	dòngtínghú

Dragon boats

The former state of **Chu**, which encompassed northern Hunan, was under siege in 278 BC from the first stirrings of the ambitious Qin armies, who were later to bring all of China under their thumb. At the time, Dongting was the haunt of the exiled poet-governor **Qu Yuan**, a victim of palace politics but nonetheless a great patriot of Chu. Hearing of the imminent invasion, Qu picked up a heavy stone and drowned himself in the nearby **Miluo River** rather than see the state he loved conquered. Distraught locals raced to save him in their boats, but were too late. They returned later to scatter *zongzi* (packets of meat and sticky rice wrapped up in reeds and lotus leaves) into the river as an offering to Qu Yuan's spirit.

The **Dragon-boat Festival**, held throughout China on the fifth day of the fifth lunar month (June or July), commemorates the rowers' hopeless rush – though many historians trace the tradition of food offerings and annual boat races to long before Qu's time. At any rate, it's a festive rather than mournful occasion, with huge quantities of steamed *zongzi* eaten and keen **competition** between local dragon-boat teams, who can be seen practising in their narrow, powerful crafts months before the event, to the steady boom of a pacing drum. It's a lively spectator sport, with crowds cheering their rowers along, and you need to be up early to get the most from the ceremonies – catching, for example, the dedication of the dragon-headed prows – as the race itself lasts only a few minutes. In Yueyang the race is staged on the Miluo River south of town; contact CITS for details.

paddy fields; many locals also earn a livelihood from fishing. Despite accelerating tourism and an unpleasantly down-at-heel new city springing up in the background, the impressive **Yueyang Tower** – frequently packed with Chinese tourists – and historical links to the nationwide sport of **dragon-boat racing** make Yueyang a reasonable place to spend the day in transit between Changsha and Wuhan.

Yueyang's main street, **Baling Lu**, runs west for 5km, bare, broad and numbingly straight right up to **Nanyuepo docks** on the lake shore. Here it's crossed by **Dongting Lu**, with the Yueyang Tower and most of the services close to this junction. On Dongting Bei Lu, the **Yueyang Tower** (daily: summer 7am–6.25pm; winter 7.30am–5.55pm; ¥46) rises from walled ramparts overlooking Dongting Hu, but the site was originally a mere platform where the *Three Kingdoms* general **Lu Su** reviewed his troops. It was through Lu's diplomacy that the armies of his native Wu and those of Shu were united against the overwhelming forces of Wei, who were subsequently defeated in 208 AD at the Battle of the Red Cliffs (p.504). A tower was first built here in 716, but the current timber edifice, 20m tall, is of Qing design. Three upward-curving, yellow-glazed roofs are supported by huge blood-red pillars of *nanmu* ("southernwood"); screens, eaves and crossbeams are decorated with animal carvings, and the tower makes a striking and brilliant spectacle. You can climb up and take in grand views of the lake, which quickly whips up into a stormy sea scene at the first breath of wind.

Flanking the tower are two lesser pavilions: **Xianmei Ting** (Immortal's Plum) – named after the delicately etched blossom design on a Ming stone tablet within – and **Sanzui Ting** (Thrice Drunk). This recalls the antics of **Lu Dongbin**, one of the Taoist Eight Immortals, who regularly visited the pavilion to down a wine gourd or two; there's a comic painting of this inside, warts and all, and an overflowing votive box. Lu is also credited with populating Dongting Hu with shoals of silvery fish by tossing woodshavings into the water. **Xiao Qiao**, the wife of another historic general, lies buried at the northern end of the surrounding gardens, the grassy mound honoured by a tablet bearing the calligraphy of the renowned Song-dynasty poet, **Su Dongpo**.

Stores in Yueyang sell the incredibly expensive **silver needle tea**, the produce of **Jinshan Dao**, an island half an hour away by boat across the lake. Said to impart longevity, the tea was once paid in tribute to the emperor, and has tips that look like pale green twists; pour boiling water over them, inhale the musty vapour and watch them bob up and down in the glass. A spoonful of the tea sells for around ¥5.

Practicalities

Yueyang's **bus and train stations** are on opposite sides of a huge, multi-level roundabout 3km east down Baling Lu, along which you can catch **city bus** #22 to the lake and then north along Dongting Bei Lu to the Yueyang Tower – pick up a **map** on arrival. **Yangzi ferries** stop 17km north of the city at **Chenglingji**, where bus #1 connects with the train station.

The English-speaking **CITS** (daily 9–11.30am & 2–5pm; ☎0730/8232010) is inside the grounds of the *Yunmeng Hotel* on Yunmeng Lu, and can arrange tours to lakeside sights. There's a **post office** on Baling Lu towards the bus and train stations (daily 8am–6pm), and a **Bank of China** just right out of the train station on Zhanqian Lu. There are a range of places to stay around the bus and train stations and the Yueyang Tower, though it isn't worth overnighting here except during the Dragon Boat Festival.

Heng Shan

Some 120km south of Changsha, the **Heng Shan region** is one of China's most holy sites. Spread over 80km or so, the ranges form scores of low peaks dressed in woodland with a smattering of **Buddhist and Taoist temples**, some of which were established more than 1300 years ago. It's somewhere to relax and admire the scenery (frosted in winter, golden in autumn and misty year-round), either tackling the easy walks between shrines on foot, or resorting to local transport to ascend the heights.

Heng Shan		
Heng Shan	衡山	*héngshān*
Danxia Si	丹霞寺	*dānxiá sì*
Huangting Si	黄庭寺	*huángtíng sì*
Shangfeng Si	上封寺	*shàngfēng sì*
Xiufeng Binguan	秀风宾馆	*xiùfēng bīnguǎn*
Xuandu Si	玄都寺	*xuándū sì*
Zhurong Gong	祝融殿	*zhùróng diàn*
Zushi Gong	祖师宫	*zǔshī gōng*
Nanyue	南岳	*nányuè*
Jinsuo Shanzhuang	金稣山庄	*jīnsuǒ shānzhuāng*
Nanyue Damiao	南岳大庙	*nányuè dàmiào*
Xiufeng Binguan	秀风宾馆	*xiùfēng bīnguǎn*
Zhusheng Si	祝圣寺	*zhùshèng sì*
Hengyang	衡阳	*héngyáng*

Confusingly, it's **Nanyue**, not the nearby town of Hengshan, that marks the starting point up into the hills. Early-morning **buses** from Changsha or Shaoshan take around three hours to reach Nanyue via **Xiangtan**. If you're coming up from the south by road or rail from Shaoguan in Guangdong Province, or Guilin in Guangxi, the nearest city is **Hengyang**, where minibuses leave for the hour-long trip from the depot on Jiefang Lu – bus #1 connects Hengyang's nightmarishly busy **train station** with this depot, which is across the river. Alternatively, leave the train farther on at **Hengshan Town**, where regular minibuses cover the twenty-kilometre trip west to Nanyue.

Nanyue

Banners strung across the highway welcome visitors to **NANYUE** (South Mountain), a small but expanding village of old flagstoned streets and new hotels set around Nanyue Damiao and Zhusheng Si, the two largest and most architecturally impressive temple complexes in the area. The Changsha–Hengyang highway runs along the eastern side of the village, with the **bus station** at its southern (Hengyang) end, where map sellers, rickshaw drivers and hotel touts descend on new arrivals. Midway along the highway an ornamental **stone archway** forms the "entrance" to the village proper and leads through to the main street, Dongshan Lu. Here you'll find a mass of **restaurants**, whose staff will call you over as you pass – as always, avoid overcharging by establishing prices as you order. Many of these places also offer basic **accommodation** for about ¥35 a bed, or there are plenty of **hotels** in the vicinity, such as the *Jinsuo Shanzhuang* (☎0734/5666491; ❹) or *Xiufeng Binguan* (☎0734/5666111; ❹).

Off Dongshan Lu, streets lead through the old village centre to **Nanyue Damiao** (¥15). There's been a place of worship at this site since at least 725 AD – some say that it was sanctified in Qin times – but the older buildings succumbed to fire long ago and were replaced in the nineteenth century by a small version of Beijing's Forbidden City. It's a lively place, freshly painted, echoing with bells and thick with smoke from incense and detonating firecrackers – there are actually furnaces in the courtyards to accommodate the huge quantities offered up by the crowds. Seventy-two pillars, representing Heng Shan's peaks, support the massive wooden crossbeams of the **main hall**'s double-staged roof, and gilt phoenixes loom above the scores of kneeling worshippers paying homage to Taoist and Buddhist deities. Other halls in the surrounding gardens are far more humble but sport detailed carvings along their eaves and exterior alcoves.

Far quieter, with fewer tourists and more monks in evidence, is the monastery, **Zhusheng Si**, a short walk left out of the temple gates. A purely Buddhist site originating around the same time as Nanyue, the entire monastery – whose name translates as "Imperial Blessings" – was reconstructed for the anticipated visit of **Emperor Kangxi** in 1705, but he never showed up. The smaller scale and lack of pretence here contrast with Nanyue's extravagances, though there's a series of five hundred engravings of Buddhist *arhat*s set into the wall of the rear hall, and a fine multi-faced and many-handed likeness of **Guanyin** to seek out among the charming courtyards.

In the hills

There's a good day's walking to be had between Nanyue and **Zhurong Gong**, a hall perched 15km from town on Heng Shan's 1290-metre apex. Even major temples along the way are small and unassuming, requiring little time to investigate, and tracks are easy, so around eight hours should be enough for a return hike along the most direct route – though you'd need at least ten hours to see everything on the mountain. **Minibuses** run between Nanyue and Shangfeng Si, below the summit, in under an hour (¥10). **Food stalls** lurk at strategic points, so there's no need to carry much beyond something to keep out any seasonally inclement weather at the top.

Take the main road through Nanyue to the park gates behind Nanyue Damiao, where the **admission fee** (¥102) covers entry to all temples and includes a bilingual **map** of the mountain. The first two hours are spent passing occasional groups of descending tourists and black-clad Taoist mendicants, as the road weaves past rivers and patches of farmland before reaching the temple-like **Martyrs' Memorial Hall**, built to commemorate those killed during the 1911 revolution. Entering pine forests shortly after, you'll find **Xuandu Si** marks the halfway point – it's also known as the Midway Monastery – and is Hunan's Taoist centre, founded around 700 AD. Even so, an occasional Buddhist saint graces side shrines, but the best feature is the unusually domed ceiling in the second hall, watched over by a statue of Lao Zi holding a pill of immortality.

The rest of the ascent is past a handful of functioning, day-to-day temples with monks and nuns wandering around the gardens – **Danxia Si** and **Zushi Gong** are larger than most – before arrival outside **Shangfeng Si**'s red timber halls, which mark the minibus terminus. Overpriced **hotels** here cater for those hoping to catch the dawn from the **sunrise-watching terrace**, a short walk away below a radio tower. On a cloudy day, it's more worthwhile pushing on a further twenty minutes to the summit, where **Zhurong Gong**, a tiny temple built almost entirely of heavy stone blocks and blackened inside from incense smoke, looks very atmospheric as it emerges from the mist. For the descent, there's always the bus, or an alternative track (shown on local maps) from Xuandu Si which takes in Lingzhi spring, the Mirror Grinding Terrace and the bulky Nantai Monastery, before winding back to town past the quiet halls of **Huangting Si**, another sizeable Taoist shrine.

Wulingyuan (Zhangjiajie)

Hidden away in the northwestern extremities of Hunan, **Wulingyuan Scenic Reserve** (widely known as **Zhangjiajie**) protects a mystical landscape of sandstone shelves and fragmented limestone towers, often misted in low cloud and scored by countless streams, with practically every horizontal surface hidden under a primeval, subtropical green mantle. Among the 550–odd tree species (twice Europe's total) within its 370 square kilometres are rare dove trees, ginkgos and **dawn redwoods**, the last identified by their stringy bark and feathery leaves; now popular as an ornamental tree, until 1948 they were believed extinct. The **wildlife** list is impressive, too, including civets, giant salamanders, monkeys and gamebirds. The region is also home to several million ethnic **Tujia**, said by some to be the last descendants of western China's mysterious prehistoric Ba kingdom. On the downside, despite the UNESCO World Heritage listing, a total fire ban (smoking included) and a generous number of erosion-resistant paths, Wulingyuan is definitely beginning to suffer from its popularity – more accessible parts of the reserve are often almost invisible under hordes of litter-hurling tour groups, and the admission fee has reached an exorbitant ¥160.

Practicalities

Most visitors base themselves on the southern boundaries of the reserve at **Zhangjiajie village**, where there's certainly enough to keep you occupied

Wulingyuan (Zhangjiajie)		
Wulingyuan Scenic Reserve	武陵源风景区	*wǔlíngyuán fēngjǐngqū*
Baofeng Hu	宝峰湖	*bǎofēng hú*
Bewitching Terrace	迷魂台	*míhún tái*
Black Dragon Village	黑龙寨	*hēilóng zhài*
Huanglong Cave	黄龙洞	*huánglóng dòng*
Huangshi Village	黄石寨	*huángshí zhài*
Immortal's Bridge	仙人桥	*xiānrén qiáo*
Shentangwan	神堂湾	*shéntángwān*
Suoxi Village	索溪峪镇	*suǒxīyù zhèn*
Ten-li Corridor	十里画廊	*shílǐ huàláng*
Tianzi Feng	天子峰	*tiānzǐ fēng*
Tianzi Shan village	天子山镇	*tiānzǐ shānzhèn*
Zhangjiajie Shi	张家界市	*zhāngjiājiè shī*
Huochezhan Huaihua Binguan	火车站怀化宾馆	*huǒchēzhàn huáihuà bīnguǎn*
Wuling Binguan	武陵宾馆	*wǔlíng bīnguǎn*
Zhangjiajie village	张家界国家森林公园管理处	*zhāngjiājiè guójiā sēnlín gōngyuán guǎnlǐchù*
Minsu Shanzhuang	民俗山庄	*mínsú shānzhuāng*
Xiangdian Shanzhuang	香殿山庄	*xiāngdiàn shānzhuāng*
Zhangjiajie Binguan	张家界宾馆	*zhāngjiājiè bīnguǎn*

for a few days. It's also possible to organize extended walks north to **Tianzi Mountain**, or east to the **Suoxi Valley**. There are villages and stalls along the way supplying accommodation and food, but take water and snacks on long journeys. You'll need comfortable walking shoes and the right seasonal dress – it's humid in summer, cold from late autumn, and the area is often covered in light snow early on in the year.

Note that **accommodation prices** double at weekends and holidays, when crowds are at their worst and train tickets are in short supply – try and avoid these times. If you're on a Chinese package **tour** to Wulingyuan, watch out if they try to sting you an extra ¥50–100 based on a supposedly higher foreigners' entrance fee to the reserve: there's no discriminatory pricing here. If the tour staff won't back down, tell them you'll pay the surcharge yourself at the gates.

Zhangjiajie Shi
ZHANGJIAJIE SHI is the regional hub, 33km south of the reserve. The **bus station** is pretty central, but the **train station** and ticket office are a further 9km south, and the **airport** is a similar distance to the west. **Minibuses** prowl arrival points for the hour-long journey to the reserve at either Zhangjiajie village (¥6) or Suoxi (¥10).

It's only worth staying here if you arrive too late to get the last bus to the park (around 7pm). The *Huochezhan Huaihua Binguan* (☎0744/8512986; ❸) has tolerable doubles next to the train station, and there are a host of mediocre hotels in town – the *Wuling Binguan* is the best of these (☎0744/82226302; ❻).

Leaving, there are regular buses covering the journey to Changsha and down to Jishou for Fenghuang. **Trains** are faster; there are direct services east to Changsha, north to Yichang in Hubei, and south to Jishou and Liuzhou in Guangxi. For Guizhou and points west you'll have to change trains at the junction town of **Huaihua**, four hours to the southwest – sleeper tickets out of Huaihua are virtually impossible to buy at the station, but you can usually upgrade on board. You can also **fly** from Zhangjiajie Shi to Changsha and a half-dozen other provincial capitals.

Zhangjiajie village and around

ZHANGJIAJIE village is simply a couple of streets in the valley at the reserve entrance, overflowing with **map** and souvenir retailers, pricey **restaurants** (meat dishes are particularly expensive), a **post office** and **places to stay**. Note that in winter many of these places close and those that remain open may have water shortages. You can ask around about basic places to stay within the reserve, which are to be recommended if you want to get away from it all.

The best-value hotel in the village is the Tujia-run *Minsu Shanzhuang* (☎0744/5719188; ❹), a wooden building at the bottom of town. Farther up is the village's best hotel, the *Xiangdian Shanzhuang* (☎0744/5712266; ❼). Nearer the park entrance, *Zhangjiajie Binguan* (☎0744/5712388; ❻) has comfy doubles in the new wing, and clean but damp rooms in the older section, arranged around an ornamental pond. Its travel service is fairly helpful with general hiking advice, and can arrange **whitewater rafting** day tours in the Suoxi Valley (¥250 per person).

The reserve

With a closely packed forest of tall, eroded karst pinnacles splintering away from a high plateau, Zhangjiajie's scenery is awesomely poetic – even Chinese tour groups are often hushed by the spectacle. The road through the village leads downhill past a throng of Tujia selling medicinal flora and cheap plastic ponchos to the **reserve entrance**, where you buy your ticket (¥160). You also have your thumbprint scanned to allow you to re-enter for the two days of the ticket's validity. There are also **bicycles** for rent – of dubious value for many of the tracks.

The left path here follows a four-hour circuit along a short valley up to **Huangshi village**, on the edge of a minor, island-like plateau surrounded by views of the area. There's also a cable car to the top (¥45). The right path offers several options, the shortest of which (again, around 4hr) runs along **Golden Whip Stream**, branching off to the right and returning to base through a particularly dense stand of crags below two facing outcrops known as the **Yearning Couple** (engraved tablets along the path identify many other formations). Alternatively, bearing left after a couple of kilometres – consult a map – takes you up past **Bewitching Terrace** into the **Shadao Valley**. From here, basic trails continue through magnificent scenery around the western edge of the plateau to **Black Dragon village**, then circuit back to the park gates. This is a lengthy day's walk, and you won't see many other tourists along the way.

Suoxi Valley and Tianzi Shan

With much the same facilities as Zhangjiajie, **SUOXI village** makes a good base for exploring the east and north of the reserve. Set in the **Suoxi Valley**, it's 10km as the crow flies from Zhangjiajie but the better part of a day away on foot, though it's possible to get between the two by local bus. Attractions here include groups of rhesus monkeys and relatively open riverine gorges where it's possible to **cruise** – or even go whitewater rafting – between the peaks. Around the two-kilometre-long **Baofeng Hu**, a lake accessed by a ladder-like staircase from the valley floor, there's a chance of encountering golden pheasants, the grouse-like tragopans and **giant salamanders** – secretive, red-blotched monsters which reach 2m in length; considered a great delicacy, they're sometimes seen in the early mornings around Baofeng's shore. There's also **Huanglong Dong** (Yellow Dragon Cave), a few kilometres east of Suoxi, a mass of garishly lit limestone caverns linked by a subterranean river, and **Hundred Battle Valley**, where the Song-dynasty Tujia king, Xiang, fought imperial forces.

The **Tianzi Shan** region, which basically covers the north of the park, is named after an isolated 1250-metre-high peak, and contains most of Wulingyuan's caves. It's probably best visited from Suoxi village, where there's a possible circuit of 30km setting off along the **Ten-li Corridor**. High points include the mass of lookouts surrounding **Shentangwan**, a valley thick with needle-like rocks where Xiang is said to have committed suicide after his eventual defeat, and **Immortals' Bridge**, next to the peak itself, an unfenced, narrow strip of rock bridging a deep valley. Instead of returning to Suoxi, you can continue past the mountain to **TIANZI SHAN village**, spend the night in the guesthouse there, and then either hike south to Zhangjiajie or leave Wulingyuan by catching a bus first to **Songzhi** (45km) and then on to **Dayong** (another 60km).

Fenghuang and around

Two hours south of Zhangjiajie by road or rail is **Jishou**, the jumping-off point for the charming town of **FENGHUANG**, with its stilted houses, flagstoned streets and communities of **Miao** and **Tujia** peoples. Fenghuang is a great place to unwind for a couple of days: it's as yet relatively unspoilt (though note that in summer it can be packed out with Chinese visitors), its twelve-hundred-year history is evident in architecture, and there are remnants of the **Southern Great Wall** to explore in the vicinity. However, the best thing about Fenghuang is the chance to meander along its narrow streets, picking up the odd handicraft and stopping for tea or snacks in one of the atmospheric riverside cafés.

The Town

Fenghuang is a small, easily navigable place largely south of the Tuo River, which runs roughly west to east. The old town is bounded on its north side

Fenghuang		
Fenghuang	凤凰	*fènghuáng*
Cuicui Kezhan	翠翠客栈	*cuìcuì kèzhàn*
Dongzheng Jie	东正街	*dōngzhèngjiē*
Government Hotel	政府宾馆	*zhèngfǔ bīnguǎn*
Hong Qiao	虹桥	*hóngqiáo*
Huijiang Binguan	汇江宾馆	*huìjiāng bīnguǎn*
Qinghua Jiudian	庆华酒店	*qìnghuá jiǔdiàn*
Shen Congwen's residence	沈从文故居	*shěncóngwén gùjū*
Shen Congwen's tomb	沈从文墓地	*shěncóngwén mùdì*
Xiaoxiao Kezhan	萧萧客栈	*xiāoxiāo kèzhàn*
Xiong Xiling's residence	熊希龄故居	*xióngxīlíng gùjū*
Around Fenghuang		
Alaying	阿拉营	*ālāyíng*
Huangsi Qiao	黄丝桥	*huángsīqiáo*
Southern Great Wall	南方长城	*nánfāng chángchéng*

by the river, with a restored section of the city's Ming **walls** running along the riverbank, punctuated from west to east by the splendid Nanhua, North and East **gates**, in that order; these respectively give onto a road bridge, a wooden footbridge and adjacent stepping stones, and **Hong Qiao**, a 300-year-old covered bridge. The principal thoroughfare, **Dongzheng Jie**, is a pedestrianized alley squeezing its way northeast between the old houses through the centre to the East gate and Hong Qiao. To the west and south the old town is bounded by Nanhua Lu and Jianshe Lu respectively, the latter curling north from the southeast corner of town to end up at Hong Qiao.

Fenghuang is the home town of many important Chinese, including **Xiong Xiling**, an ethnic Miao who, following the collapse of the Qing dynasty, became the first premier of China's republican government, under Yuan Shikai. You can visit his **former home** near the North Gate (daily 8am–5.30pm; ¥10), a simple affair preserved as it was and holding a few photos, including those of his three wives, with some English captions.

One of China's greatest writers, **Shen Congwen** (1902–88), also Miao, was from Fenghuang and many of his stories centre around the Miao people and the landscapes of Western Hunan (*Recollections of West Hunan* is available in English, published by Chinese Literature). In 1949 Shen's writing was banned in both mainland China and Taiwan after he failed to align with either, and this effectively ended his career, although his works have enjoyed a revival of late. His **former residence** can be found just off Dongzheng Jie (daily 8am–5.30pm; ¥25), while his **tomb** is pleasantly located twenty minutes' stroll east along the south bank at Tingtao Shan. The epitaph on the jagged gravestone translates as "Thinking in my way you can understand me. And thinking in my way you can understand others".

For a different view of the town you could do as the Chinese do and take a **bamboo raft** from the North gate for a forty-minute river ride (¥30 per person), or there are bicycles for rent on Hong Qiao.

Practicalities

Arriving in Jishou by train, take a bus or a taxi (¥4) over the bridge to the **bus station** on Wuling Lu, just off the main Tuan Jie Lu. From here there are plenty of Fenghuang buses until 6pm or so (¥12). If you do need to stay overnight in Jishou, there are a range of **accommodation** options near both the train and bus stations, which are a couple of kilometres apart at opposite ends of Tuanjie Lu, which also has a **Bank of China**, **Internet cafés** and **restaurants**.

Buses from Jishou drop you in Fenghuang on Nanhua Lu near the Nanhua gate, at the meeting point of Fenghuang's old and new towns. If you head downhill away from the gate and then through the stone archway on your left, you'll pass Fenghuang's smartest **accommodation**, the *Government Hotel* (☎0743/3221690, ☏3224091; ❺), where the pricier rooms are better value than the standard twins, which are overpriced. Bearing right a little way from here brings you down to the entrance to the old city. Straight ahead is Dongzheng Jie, which holds some good hotels such as the traditionally styled *Qinghua Jiudian* (☎0743/3221036; ❸) and, on the other side of the street, the less elaborate but equally comfortable and friendly *Huijiang Binguan* (☎0743/3228312; ❸). There are also inexpensive wooden places on both sides of the river, some with balconies enjoying captivating views – on the north bank, try the *Cuicui Kezhan* (☎0743/3261026; ❸) or the slightly more rustic *Xiaoxiao Kezhan* next door (☎0743/3260117; ❸). If the riverside hotels are full, you'll find plenty more on Jianshe Lu, and its continuation after crossing the bridge, Hongqiao Lu.

The main street holds countless small **restaurants** and there's a broad range of tasty street food to be had on Hongqiao Lu next to the bridge. Dongzheng Jie is also a good place to pick up Miao embroidery and jewellery, though you'll find them cheaper out in the surrounding villages or at Alaying (see below), and **maps** in Chinese.

Around Fenghuang

The pretty countryside near Fenghuang has some easily accessible and worthwhile sights, nearest of which is the **Southern Great Wall**, which, astonishingly, wasn't recognized for what it was until 2000. Originally constructed in 1554 as a defence against the Miao, the wall ran for around 190km from Xiqueying in Western Hunan to Tongren in Guizhou. There's several hundred metres of intact wall at a site 13km from Fenghuang, the journey to which takes around half an hour by bus from a roundabout at the western end of Jianshe Lu. Having bought your ticket at the site (¥45), you're free to clamber over what remains of the wall which, while not as rugged as its northern counterpart, is nevertheless impressive and significantly less visited – if you come in winter you'll probably have the place to yourself.

Ten kilometres from the wall, **Huangsi Qiao** (Huang's Silk Bridge) is another ancient settlement which prospered after Huang, a silk merchant, decided to build a bridge to attract people to the town. A smaller version of Fenghuang, with attractive stilted houses, the town is only half a kilometre across and has gate towers to the north, east and west. You can get here by bus from the wall or Fenghuang.

If you want to see more of the Miao or acquire some of their handicrafts, you could head for **Alaying**, 7km west of the Great Wall, where market days (on dates ending with a 2 or 7, as is the local practice) attract the surrounding villagers. Buses head to Alaying from the western end of Jianshe Lu in Fenghuang.

Jiangxi

Stretched between the Yangzi in the north and a mountainous border with Guangdong in the south, **Jiangxi province** has always been a bit of a backwater. Though it has been inhabited for some four thousand years, the first major influx of settlers came as late as the Han dynasty, when its interior offered sanctuary for those dislodged by warfare. The northern half benefited most from these migrants, who began to farm the great plain around China's largest freshwater lake, **Poyang Hu**. A network of rivers covering the province drains into Poyang, and when the construction of the Grand Canal created a route through Yangzhou and the lower Yangzi in the seventh century, Jiangxi's capital, **Nanchang**, became a key point on the great north–south link of inland waterways. The region then enjoyed a long period of quiet prosperity, until coastal shipping and the opening up of treaty ports took business away in the 1840s. The next century saw a complete reversal of Jiangxi's fortunes: the population halved as millions fled competing warlords and, during the 1920s and 1930s, there was protracted fighting between the Guomindang and Communist forces concentrated in the southern **Jinggang Shan** ranges, which eventually led to an evicted Red Army starting on their **Long March** across China.

Despite the troubles, things picked up quickly after the Communist takeover, and a badly battered Nanchang licked its wounds and reinvented itself as a revolutionary city and centre of modern heavy industry. More traditionally, access provided by Poyang and the Yangzi tributaries benefits the hilly areas to the east, where **Jingdezhen** retains its title as China's porcelain capital. North of the lake, **Jiujiang** is a key Yangzi port on the doorsteps of Anhui and Hubei, while the nearby mountain area of **Lu Shan**, also easily visited from Nanchang, offers a pleasant reminder of Jiangxi's better days, having long been a summer retreat for Chinese literati and colonial servants.

Nanchang

Hemmed in by hills, **NANCHANG** sits on Jiangxi's major river, the **Gan Jiang**, some 70km south of where it flows into Poyang Hu. Built on trade,

Nanchang		
Nanchang	南昌	*nánchāng*
August 1 Uprising Museum	八一纪念馆	*bāyī jìniànguǎn*
Bada Shanren Museum	八大山人纪念馆	*bādàshānrén jìniànguǎn*
Bayi Monument	八一纪念塔	*bāyī jìniàntǎ*
Bayi Park	八一公园	*bāyī gōngyuán*
Provincial Museum	省博物馆	*shěng bówùguǎn*
Renmin Square	人民广场	*rénmín guǎngchǎng*
Shengjin Ta	绳金塔	*shéngjīn tǎ*
Taxia Si	塔下寺	*tǎxià sì*
Tengwang Pavilion	滕王阁	*téngwáng gé*
Xiangtan airport	香檀飞机场	*xiāngtán fēijīchǎng*
Youmin Si	佑民寺	*yòumín sì*
Zhu De's Former Residence	朱德旧居	*zhūdé jiùjū*
Accommodation		
Gloria Plaza	凯莱大酒店	*kǎilái dàjiǔdiàn*
Jiaotong	交通宾馆	*jiāotōng bīnguǎn*
Jiujiu Long	九九隆大酒店	*jiǔjiǔlóng dàjiǔdiàn*
Ruidu	瑞都大酒店	*ruìdū dàjiǔdiàn*
Wenhua Gong	文化宫宾馆	*wénhuàgōng bīnguǎn*
Xinhua	新华宾馆	*xīnhuá bīnguǎn*
Youzheng Dasha	邮政大厦	*yóuzhèng dàshà*
Eating and drinking		
Denver 1857	丹佛酒吧	*dānfó jiǔbā*
Fengwei Xiaochi Cheng	风味小吃城	*fēngwèi xiǎochīchéng*
Guhan Feng	古汉风	*gǔhàn fēng*
Jiangnan Fandian	江南饭店	*jiāngnán fàndiàn*
Hao Xiang Lai	豪享来	*háoxiǎnglái*
Hunan Wang Caiguan	湖南王菜馆	*húnán wáng càiguǎn*
Little Sheep Hotpot	小肥羊火锅	*xiǎoféiyáng huǒguō*
Ming Dynasty	明朝铜鼎煨汤府	*míngcháo tóngdǐng wèitāngfǔ*
Wu's Mullet	邬氏乌鱼酒家	*wūshì wūyú jiǔjiā*
Xinghuacun	杏花村	*xìnghuā cūn*

today Nanchang has its position as a rail hub for central-southern China to thank for its character; unfortunately, this mostly reflects its steel and chemical industries and an overbearing, incomplete reconstruction since the 1950s. First impressions of a grey and noisy place afflicted by the usual stifling summer temperatures are slightly moderated by the handful of resurrected older monuments, and the sheer enthusiasm with which locals have grasped free-market principles, crowding every alley with stalls.

Nanchang saw little action until the twentieth century, when the city was occupied by the Guomindang army in December 1926. At the time, the military was still an amalgam of Nationalist and Communist forces, but when Chiang Kaishek broke his marriage of convenience with the Communists the following year, any left-wing elements were expelled from the Party. On August 1, 1927, **Zhou Enlai** and **Zhu De**, two Communist GMD officers, mutinied in Nanchang and took control of the city with thirty thousand troops. Though they were soon forced to flee into Jiangxi's mountainous south, the day is celebrated as the foundation of the **People's Liberation Army**, and the red PLA flag still bears the Chinese characters "8" and "1" (*bayi*) for the month and day.

Arrival, transport and accommodation

Nanchang sprawls away from the east bank of the Gan Jiang into industrial complexes and wasteland, but the centre is a fairly compact couple of square kilometres between the river and **Bayi Dadao**, which runs north through the heart of the city from the huge **Fushan roundabout** and past **Renmin Square**, becoming **Yangming Lu** as it turns east over the Bayi Bridge.

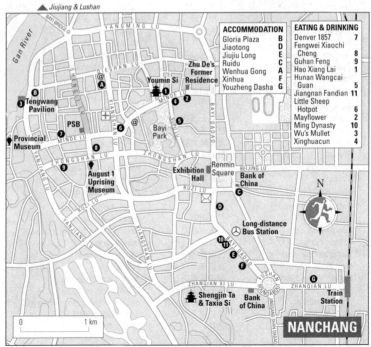

▲ Jiujiang & Lushan

ACCOMMODATION	
Gloria Plaza	B
Jiaotong	D
Jiujiu Long	E
Ruidu	C
Wenhua Gong	A
Xinhua	F
Youzheng Dasha	G

EATING & DRINKING	
Denver 1857	7
Fengwei Xiaochi Cheng	8
Guhan Feng	9
Hao Xiang Lai	1
Hunan Wangcai Guan	5
Jiangnan Fandian	11
Little Sheep Hotpot	6
Mayflower	2
Ming Dynasty	10
Wu's Mullet	3
Xinghuacun	4

NANCHANG

Badashan Ren Studio & Xiangtan Airport ▼

Moving on from Nanchang

You can **fly** from Nanchang to Beijing, Shanghai, Guangzhou and a handful of other cities. Zhanqian Lu is thick with airline agents, and most hotels can book flights. China Eastern (℡0791/8514195) are on Beijing Xi Lu.

Nanchang lies on the Kowloon–Beijing **train** line, and just off the Shanghai–Kunming line, with connections through easterly Yingtan down into Fujian province. Sleeper tickets are pretty easy to obtain, but prepare yourself for some mighty queues; alternatively, the airline agents on Zhanqian Lu also sell train tickets at a slight mark-up. If you're heading to southern Jiangxi, note that "Jinggang Shan" railhead is not Ciping, but a small town 120km further east.

The **bus** station looks huge and crowded, but the ticket office is user-friendly and there's no problem in getting seats. Minibuses and smart coaches run through the day along fast expressways to Jiujiang, Lu Shan and Jingdezhen, with daily services within Jiangxi to Jinggang Shan and Ganzhou, and further afield to Wuyi Shan in Fujian and destinations across central China.

Arriving at **Changbei airport**, forty minutes north of the centre, you'll need to take a taxi into town (¥100). Other transit points are more central. Nanchang's **train station** is 700m east of the Fushan roundabout at the end of Zhanqian Lu; locals consider the huge square hole through the station facade bad *feng shui*, allowing the city's wealth to escape down the tracks. Some buses from Lu Shan, Jinggang Shan and farther afield terminate here, but the main **long-distance bus station** is 1km away on Bayi Dadao. **Taxis** (¥6 standing charge) cruise downtown arrival points, while **city bus** #2 runs from the train station along Bayi Dadao and then makes a circuit of the central area, passing or coming close to all the hotels.

Accommodation

There's a good range of accommodation in town, much of it pretty close to the train and bus stations.

Gloria Plaza 88 Yanjiang Bei Lu ℡0791/6738855, Ⓦwww.gphnanchang.com. Modern, international-style joint-venture hotel, the most foreigner-friendly in Nanchang and worth visiting for its Western food (see p.537). ❾

Jiaotong Just north of the bus station, on Bayi Dadao ℡ & Ⓕ0791/6256918. Clean, well-maintained block of standard hotel rooms, nothing fancy but well priced. Solo travellers might be able to wrangle a half-price double. ❸

Jiujiu Long 122 Bayi Dadao ℡0791/7061199, Ⓕ6295299. Smart three-star venture, good value, with attentive staff. ❹

Ruidu 399 Guangchang Lu ℡0791/6201888, Ⓕ62019999. An upmarket place, nicely located on the southeast corner of Renmin Square. ❼

Wenhua Gong Xiangshan Bei Lu ℡0791/6795180. A peculiar mix of enormous, formerly grand and now slightly shabby rooms and newer, smaller and more functional ones. ❸

Xinhua Bayi Dadao ℡0791/6222152. A little south of its smarter neighbour, *Jiujiu Long*, this place is friendly and has aged but comfortable rooms. ❸

Youzheng Dasha 86 Zhanqian Lu ℡ & Ⓕ0791/7037900. Post-office-run hotel, cheap and convenient for departure points if not wonderfully appealing. Dorm beds ¥50, ❹

The City

Despite slow modernization and a few antiques rising from the rubble, Nanchang's architecture mostly reflects the Civil War years and later Soviet-inspired industrialization. Much of this, such as the overbearing **Exhibition Hall**, is concentrated around the enormous **Renmin Square**, and the strangely shaped red and white stone **Bayi Monument** at the southern end. West of here, **Zhongshan Lu** runs through the core of Nanchang's bustling shopping district, with the water and greenery of **Bayi Park** to the north and, further along, the **August 1 Uprising Museum** (daily 8am–5.30pm; ¥25). Formerly a hotel, this was occupied by the embryonic PLA as their 1927 General Headquarters, and is now of interest mainly as the most complete example of Nanchang's colonial architecture. As a museum, however, it's dull – three floors stuffed with period furniture, weapons, and maps labelled in Chinese. North from here, **pedestrianized** Shengli Lu provides more opportunities to window-shop.

Opposite the top end of Bayi Park and set back off Minde Lu, **Youmin Si** (¥2) is a Buddhist temple dating back to 503 AD, which – perhaps because of the city's revolutionary associations – Nanchang's Red Guards were especially diligent in wrecking during the 1960s. The three restored halls include a striking, ten-metre-high **standing Buddha statue**, which rises out of a lotus flower towards a cupola decorated with a coiled golden dragon. East of here, the austere-looking traditional grey brick house on the corner of Huayuanjiao Jie is **Zhu De's former residence** (daily 8am–5.30pm; ¥2). Inside you'll find a series of Chinese-captioned photographs of Zhu De and Zhou Enlai, Zhu's bedroom and a few personal effects, including his gun.

Tengwang Pavilion and the Provincial Museum

The mighty **Tengwang Pavilion** (summer 7.30am–5.30pm; winter 8am–4.30pm; ¥30) overlooks the river on Yanjiang Lu, 1km or so west of Youmin Si. There have been 26 multistoreyed towers built on this site since the first was raised more than a thousand years ago in memory of a Tang prince; the current "Song-style" building was only completed in 1989. It's impressive to look at, nonetheless, a huge pile isolated by a square of grey paving and a monumental stone base, each floor lightened by a broadly flared roof supported by interlocking wooden beams. Disappointingly, the six-storey interior is a letdown, the upper-level balconies offering only views of a drab cityscape. However, it's worth catching the lift (¥1) to the top floor at weekends, when a tiny indoor **theatre** hosts traditional dances and music sessions; with luck, there may even be a performance of local opera.

South of the pavilion, bridges off Yanjiang Lu cross an inlet to the **Provincial Museum** (Tues–Sun 8.30am–5.30pm; ¥10), a weird, futuristic-looking construction with green glass towers and knife-like side wings. The buildings feel almost deserted, though the collection covers everything from dinosaurs to Jingdezhen **porcelain**.

Southern Nanchang

West of the Fushan roundabout off Zhanqian Lu (bus #5 passes by on its route between the roundabout and Xiangshan Lu), you'll find **Shengjin Ta** (daily 8am–5.30pm; ¥10) which, legend has it, holds the key to Nanchang's survival – apparently the city will fall if the seven-storey pagoda is ever destroyed. The warning is still taken fairly seriously, despite the fact that Shengjin has been knocked down several times, the last time being in the early eighteenth century. At any rate, the pagoda itself is only of moderate interest, but the restored architecture of the surrounding streets and a few **teahouses**, which Nanchang was once famous for – down-to-earth, open-fronted establishments patronized by gregarious old men watching the world go by – make this market quarter worth a wander.

For an easy reprieve from the city, catch bus #20 from Yanjiang Lu 5km south to **Bada Shanren Museum** (Tues–Sun 8.30am–4.30pm; ¥20), a whitewashed

Ming-era compound set in parkland. This was the haunt of the painter Zhu Da, also known as Bada Shanren, a wandering Buddhist monk of royal descent who came to live in this former temple in 1661 and was later buried here. He is said to have painted in a frenzy, often while drunk, and his pictures certainly show great spontaneity. There are a number of originals displayed inside, and some good reproductions on sale.

Eating, drinking and nightlife

Nanchang's **eating** opportunities cover quite a broad range, from dumpling houses and spicy Hunanese restaurants to the regional **Gan cooking** – lightly sauced fresh fish, crayfish, snails and frogs. **Soups** are something of a Jiangxi favourite – egg and pork soup is a typical breakfast – along with communal affairs served up in huge pots at the table. Restaurants are spread all over the city, though the streets around Bayi Park seem to have the highest concentration. All the usual Western fast-food chains are present and there's an increasing number of coffee shops, which also serve some Western and Chinese fare. However, the best **Western-style food** in Nanchang is at the *Gloria Plaza* hotel, serving lunch or dinner buffets where you can stuff your face for ¥80, and coffee and cakes in their *Atrium Café* (¥33).

Minde Lu hosts several **bars and nightclubs**. Try the cosy *Denver 1857* for a drink, or the *Mayflower* if you want to dance as well.

Restaurants

Fengwei Xiaochi Cheng Shengli Lu. Bustling dumpling house, one of several in the area. You order from the range of plastic cards behind the cashier, or point to whatever others are eating. Individual clay-pot casseroles, cold meats, buns and vegetables from around ¥5 a serving.

Guhan Feng Western end of Zhongshan Lu. A modernized "olde worlde" restaurant with repro-duction Ming crockery and heavy chairs, special-izing in local cuisine. There's a proper sit-down dining area plus a separate snack/tea room. Dishes from around ¥20.

Hao Xiang Lai Minde Lu. Good-value, sizzling pepper steaks for ¥25; also trolleyfuls of delicious Chinese snacks, biscuits and dumplings wheeled around *dim sum*-style, from ¥3 a plate. One of the few places in town with an English-language menu.

Hunan Wangcai Guan Supu Lu. Popular, mid-range spicy Hunanese restaurant overlooking Bayi Park.

Little Sheep Hotpot Corner of Zhongshan and Xiangshan Lu. Spicy hotpots from ¥26.

Ming Dynasty Bayi Dadao, next to the *Jiangnan Fandian*. The big bronze cauldron standing outside marks this as a Jiangxi-style soup restaurant. Individual pots from ¥18 or three- to four-person pots from ¥30.

Wu's Mullet Next to the Tengwang Pavilion just off Yanjiang Lu. It's a little touristy, but a fantastic name, reasonable prices, menus in English and – you guessed it – tasty mullet make this estab-lishment worth a visit.

Xinghuacun Minde Lu. Three-storey mid-range restaurant serving good Jiangxi fare, including, of course, soups.

Listings

Bank and exchange The main Bank of China is on Zhanqian Xi Lu just off the Fushan roundabout, and there's another large branch in the south-eastern corner of Renmin Square (both Mon–Fri 8am–5.30pm).

Hospital First City Hospital, Xiangshan Lu ☏0791/6784813.

Internet access There are Net bars scattered across the city, including one on Xiangshan Lu next to the *Wenhua Gong*, and another just west of Bayi Park on Minde Lu.

Left luggage Offices at train and bus stations open roughly 6am–7pm.

Mail and telephones The main post office and the telecommunications building (both daily 8am–6pm) are near each other at the corner of Bayi Dadao and Ruzi Lu.

PSB On Shengli Lu, just north of Minde Lu (☏0791/6742000; daily 8am–noon & 2.30–5.30pm).

Shopping Nanchang Department Store, the city's largest and best-stocked department store, hides behind a 1950s frontage west of Renmin Square along Zhongshan Lu. Zhongshan Lu itself and the pedestrianized southern stretch of Shengli Lu are thick with clothing stores and boutiques. A good supermarket is Walmart, on the second floor of the shopping centre at the northern end of Renmin Square. For a big range of porcelain, chops and paintings, try the Jiangxi Antique Store on Minde Lu.

Travel agents Most accommodation places have travel desks where you can book train and plane tickets.

Jiujiang and Lu Shan

Set on the Yangzi 150km north of Nanchang, **Jiujiang** had its heyday in the nineteenth century as a treaty port, and now serves mostly as a jumping-off point for tourists exchanging the torrid lowland summers for nearby cool hills at **Lu Shan**. Trains on the Kowloon–Beijing line stop at Jiujiang, while fast buses from Nanchang run through the day to both Jiujiang and Lu Shan. On the way, you might consider stopping where the Gan Jiang enters Poyang at the hamlet of **Wucheng**. Between November and March the adjacent **Hou Niao Baohu Reserve** attracts 160 varieties of wintering wildfowl, notably mandarin ducks, storks and a flock of two thousand rare **Siberian cranes**.

Jiujiang

Small but always an important staging post for river traffic, **JIUJIANG** (Nine Rivers) is well named, sited on the south bank of the Yangzi near where Poyang

Jiujiang and Lu Shan		
Jiujiang	九江	*jiǔjiāng*
Bailu Binguan	白鹿宾馆	*báilù bīnguǎn*
Gantang Hu	甘棠湖	*gāntáng hú*
Huifeng Binguan	荟丰宾馆	*huìfēng bīnguǎn*
Xinhua Binguan	新华宾馆	*xīnhuá bīnguǎn*
Xunyang Lou	寻阳楼	*xúnyáng lóu*
Yanshui Pavilion	烟水亭	*yānshuǐ tíng*
Guling	牯岭	*gǔlíng*
Guling Fandian	牯岭饭店	*gǔlíng fàndiàn*
Lushan Binguan	庐山宾馆	*lúshān bīnguǎn*
Lushan Dasha	庐山大厦	*lúshān dàshà*
Lushan Fandian	庐山饭店	*lúshān fàndiàn*
Lushan Villas	庐山别墅	*lúshān biéshù*
Mei Villa	美庐别墅	*měilú biéshù*
Lu Shan	庐山	*lúshān*
Botanical Garden	植物园	*zhíwù yuán*
Five Immortals' Peak	五仙人山	*wǔxiānrén shān*
Lulin Hu	芦林湖	*lúlín hú*
People's Hall	人民剧院	*rénmín jùyuàn*
Ruqin Hu	如琴湖	*rúqín hú*
San Diequan	三叠泉	*sāndié quán*
Xianren Dong	仙人洞	*xiānrén dòng*
Houniao Reserve	鄱阳湖侯鸟保护区	*póyánghú hóuniǎo bǎohùqū*

Hu disgorges itself in a maze of streams. The town grew wealthy during the Ming dynasty through trade in Jingdezhen's porcelain, which was distributed all over China from here. Largely destroyed during the Taiping Uprising, Jiujiang was rebuilt as a treaty port in the 1860s, and today – despite catastrophic flooding through the town centre in 1998 – it's enjoying a low-scale renaissance, the docks and adjacent streets busy from dawn to dusk.

The west side of town between the Yangzi and **Gantang Hu** is the most interesting area, a collection of narrow streets packed with small stores selling bright summer clothing, porcelain and home-made hardware utensils. Completely occupying a tiny islet in the lake is the picturesque **Yanshui Pavilion** (daily 8am–8pm; ¥10), its tastefully proportioned Ming pavilion commemorating the Tang poet-official **Li Bai**, who was responsible for the causeway and the much restored moon-shaped sluice gate.

On Binjiang Lu northeast of Gantang Hu, **Xunyang Lou** (daily 9am till late; ¥6) is an "antique" wooden winehouse facing Anhui and Hubei provinces across the Yangzi. Built in 1986 to replace a previous Tang-dynasty structure, it was the setting for a scene in **Outlaws of the Marsh** (aka *The Water Margin*), China's own Robin Hood legend. This lively story, set mostly farther east in Zhejiang Province, involved 108 rebel heroes who were often more bloodthirsty than the oppressive Song-dynasty officials they fought – the tale was one of Mao's favourites. The winehouse was where the future outlaws' leader Song Jiang imprudently wrote some revolutionary verses on the back wall after downing too much wine; condemned to death, he was dramatically rescued at the last moment. Those familiar with the tale will recognize porcelain figurines of Song Jiang, "Black Whirlwind" Liu Kei (the original axe-wielding maniac) and the other heroes in the lobby. The upstairs **restaurant** is worth visiting at lunchtime for *dongpo rouding* (steamed and braised pork belly), river fish, "Eight Treasure" duck, scrambled eggs and green pepper, or *sunyang dabing* (a pancake invented by one of the outlaws).

Practicalities

Jiujiang's centre is laid out in the narrow space between the north shore of Gantang Hu and the Yangzi: **Xunyang Lu** runs west from the top of the lake out to the highway, while parallel **Binjiang Lu** is 100m farther north and follows the river bank.

The **train station** is 3km southeast of the centre at the bottom end of Gantang Hu – catch #1 to the bus station – and has quick links to Nanchang and Hefei. The **long-distance bus station** is 1500m east down Xunyang Lu, with buses back to Nanchang until 7pm, or earlier for Lu Shan, and others to Wuhan and Nanjing. On Xunyang Lu between here and the lake you'll find a **Bank of China** (Mon–Fri 8am–5pm), and Jiujiang's most convenient **accommodation**. For value, the *Xinhua Binguan* (☎0792/8989222, ℱ8989999; ❺) is the one to look for, slightly past its best but comfortable nevertheless. Nearby, the ultramodern *Huifeng Binguan* (☎0792/8986000; ❻) has chrome fittings and enormous glass-screened bathrooms. More traditional rooms are available at *Bailu Binguan* (☎0792/8980888, ℱ8980866; ❺), a smart place patronized by tour groups.

Summer evenings are too close to spend indoors and everyone heads down Xunyang Lu to window-shop and eat at one of the **pavement cafés** on Gantang's north shore, admiring views of Lu Shan and gorging on fish and crayfish hotpots, sautéed frogs and piles of freshwater snails. There are a number of restaurants, along with cheap street food, in the lanes between the lake and the river; the *Chuanwang* serves tasty, moderately priced hotpots. If you like

Chinese spirits, crack open a bottle of *Jiuling Jiu*, the local firewater, which comes with a clay seal – once opened, you'll have to drink the lot.

Lu Shan

Lu Shan's cluster of wooded hills rises to a sudden 1474m from the level shores of Poyang Hu, its heights a welcome relief from the Yangzi basin's steamy summers. Once covered in temples, Lu Shan was developed in the mid-nineteenth century by **Edward Little**, a Methodist minister turned property speculator, as a resort area for European expatriates. The Chinese elite moved in after the Europeans lost their grip on the region; **Chiang Kaishek** built a summer residence and training school for Guomindang officials up here in the 1930s, and Lu Shan hosted one of the key meetings of the Maoist era twenty years later. Nowadays the place is overrun with proletariat holidaymakers who pack out the restaurants and troop along the paths to enjoy the clean air; former mansions have been converted into hotels and sanatoriums for their benefit. Crowds reach plague proportions between spring and autumn, so winter – though very cold – can be the best season to visit, and a weekend's walking is enough for a good sample of the scenery.

Guling

The thirty-kilometre trip from Jiujiang takes around an hour and a half on the sharply twisting road, with sparkling views back over the great lake and its junction with the Yangzi. There's a pause at the top gates for passengers to pay the steep **entry fee** (¥100), then it's a short way to **GULING** township in Lu Shan's northeastern corner, whose handful of quaintly cobbled streets, European stone villas and bungalows are the base for further exploration. The one "sight" in town is the **Mei Villa** on He Xi Lu (daily 8.30am–5pm; ¥15), former residence of Chiang Kaishek (though it's named after his wife, Song Meiling) and of interest simply because its exhibition is one of the few in China to so much as mention the Generalissimo.

Buses arrive on He Dong Lu immediately after emerging from a tunnel into town (though minibuses from Jiujiang might terminate anywhere). Fifty metres downhill on the right is a pedestrian mall leading through to Guling Jie. Most essential services are either in the mall or on Guling Jie: souvenir shops selling **maps**, a **post office**, **Bank of China** (though larger hotels are a better bet for exchanging traveller's cheques) and a **market** selling vegetables, bananas, peaches and lychees.

Leaving Lu Shan is fairly simple, but it's essential to book long-distance tickets the day before departure. Regular buses head to Jiujiang, Nanchang and beyond; if you can't find direct services, go first to Jiujiang for Wuhan and points east, and Nanchang for southern or westerly destinations.

Accommodation and eating

Summers are very busy – arrive early on in the day to make sure of a room – and expensive, with accommodation raising prices (price codes below apply to summer) and refusing to bargain. Winters see rates tumbling but are cold enough for snow, so check out the availability of heating and hot water.

There are plenty of **restaurants** in Guling, mostly good value, and some post their menus and prices outside. For local flavours – mountain fungus and fish – try the stalls and open restaurants around the market, or the *Wurong Canting*, above a teashop in the mall.

Guling Fandian 104 He Dong Lu ℡0792/8282200, ⓕ8282209. The two wings of this hotel face each other across the road about 100m downhill from the bus stop. Rooms in the newer building are much smarter and thus pricier. ❻

Lushan Binguan 446 He Xi Lu ℡0792/8295203, ⓕ8282843. Ten minutes farther on past the *Guling*, this is a heavy stone mansion with pleasant, comfortable rooms, good-value suites and a fine restaurant. ❽

Lushan Dasha 506 He Xi Lu ℡0792/8282806. Another 5min from the *Lushan Binguan*, a regimental exterior betrays this hotel as the former Guomindang Officers' Training Centre; rooms are well furnished and comfortable. ❼

Lushan Hotel At the bus-stop end of Guling Jie ℡0792/8281813. Acceptable rooms near the centre of town. ❺

Lushan Villas ℡0792/8282927, ⓕ8282387. Nice quiet location off He Xi Lu and next to Meilu Villa. The rooms are in a group of renovated cottage villas named after different historic figures, and there are two excellent restaurants on site. ❽

Into the hills

Covering some 300 square kilometres, Lu Shan's **highlands** form an elliptical platform tilted over to the southwest, comprising a central region of lakes surrounded by pine-clad hills, with superb rocks, waterfalls and views along the vertical edges of the plateau. Freelance minibuses cruise Guling Lu and usually charge a flat fee of ¥10 per person to any site in Lu Shan, while tour buses cover a variety of places on day-trips from the long-distance bus arrival stop.

For an easy walk out from town (3hr there and back), follow the road downhill to the southwest from Guling Lu and the Jiexin Garden to the far end of **Ruqin Hu**, where you can pick up the **Floral Path**. This gives impressive views of the Jinxui Valley as it winds along Lu Shan's western cliff edge past **Xianren Dong**, the Immortal's Cave, once inhabited by an ephemeral Taoist monk and still an active shrine, complete with a slowly dripping spring.

The most spectacular scenery is found on Lu Shan's southern fringes. A full exploration makes a fair day's hike, and even hardened walkers will probably take advantage of transport into the area. About an hour's stroll down He Xi Lu and then left takes you past the unpleasantly crowded **People's Hall** (daily 8am–5pm; ¥15), site of the 1959 Central Committee meeting at which Marshal Peng Dehui openly criticized the Great Leap Forward, and was subsequently denounced as a "Rightist" by Mao – events which ultimately sparked the Cultural Revolution. Next is **Lulin Hu**, a nice lakeside area with its attractive Dragon Pools and elderly Three Treasure trees over to the west. Due east of here – about 5km by road but less along walking tracks – is China's only sub-alpine **botanical garden**, the finest spot in Lu Shan to watch the sunrise. Admittedly, clear days are a rare commodity on Lu Shan, whose peaks are frequently obscured by mist – the local brew is suitably known as "Cloud Fog Tea".

Jingdezhen

JINGDEZHEN, across Poyang Hu from Nanchang and not far from the border with Anhui province, is a scruffy city whose streets labour under the effects of severe pollution caused by the numerous **porcelain factories** dotted throughout the centre. The city was producing ceramics at least two thousand years ago, and, thanks to local geography and national politics, ceramics remain its chief source of income, and the reason Jingdezhen figures on tourist itineraries. You'll find a day-trip here worthwhile even without a specialist interest in porcelain – though given the filthy air, only ceramics buffs will want to hang around longer.

Jingdezhen

Jingdezhen	景德镇	jǐngdézhèn
Ancient Porcelain Workshop	古窑瓷厂	gǔyáo cíchǎng
Jinsheng Dajiudian	金盛大酒店	jīnshèng dàjiǔdiàn
Longzhu Ge	龙珠阁	lóngzhū gé
Museum of Ceramic History	陶瓷历史博物馆	táocí lìshǐ bówùguǎn
Zhongjin Dajiudian	中锦大酒店	zhōngjǐn dàjiǔdiàn
Yingtan	鹰潭	yīngtán

The city lies in a river valley rich not only in clay suitable for firing but also in the feldspar needed to turn it into porcelain, and when the Ming rulers developed a taste for fine ceramics in the fourteenth century, the capital was at Nanjing, conveniently close to Jingdezhen. An **imperial kiln** was built in 1369, and its wares became so highly regarded – "as white as jade, as thin as paper, as bright as a mirror, as tuneful as a bell" – that Jingdezhen retained official favour even after the Ming court shifted to Beijing fifty years later.

As demand grew, workshops experimented with new **glazes** and a classic range of decorative styles emerged: *qinghua*, blue and white; *jihong*, rainbow; *doucai*, a blue and white overglaze; and *fencai*, multicoloured *famille rose*. The first examples reached Europe in the seventeenth century, and became so popular that the English word for China clay – kaolin – derives from its source nearby at **Gaoling**. Factories began to specialize in **export ware** shaped and decorated in European-approved forms, which reached the outside world via the booming Canton markets: the famous **Nanking Cargo**, comprising 150,000 pieces salvaged from the 1752 wreck of the Dutch vessel *Geldermalsen* and auctioned in 1986, was one such shipment. Foreign sales on this scale petered out after European ceramic technologies improved at the end of the eighteenth century, but Jingdezhen survived by sacrificing innovation for a more production-line mentality, and today the town's scores of private and state-owned kilns employ some fifty thousand people.

The Town

The only available vistas of Jingdezhen are from the four-storey **Longzhu**

△ Jingdezhen porcelain

Ge on Zhonghua Bei Lu (daily 8.30am–5.30pm; ¥15), a pleasant construction in wood and orange tiles along the lines of Hunan's Yueyang Tower and which also contains a small porcelain museum. From the top, the town's smoggy horizon, a patchwork of paddy fields and tea terraces, is liberally pierced by tall, thin smokestacks, which fire up by late afternoon.

But porcelain, not views, is the reason Jingdezhen figures on tourist itineraries, and the town is geared towards selling. There are a few tourist shops, but it's more fun – and much cheaper – to head to the **markets** on Jiefang Lu south of the central square, where you'll find pavements clogged by stacks of everything that has ever been made in porcelain, in or out of fashion: metre-high vases, life-sized dogs, Western- and Chinese-style crockery, antique reproductions including yellow and green glazed Tang camels, ugly statuettes of Buddhist and historical figures, and simple porcelain pandas for the mantelpiece. It's a surreal sight, as are the Chinese visitors buying by the cartload.

The Museum of Ceramic History

To experience the manufacturing side of things, either try to join a CITS **factory tour**, or visit the **Museum of Ceramic History** (daily 9am–5pm; ¥50). Normally the museum is a bit quiet, but if a big tour party is expected, the workshops get fired up and it's much more entertaining.

The museum is out of town on the west side of the river – take bus #3 from Zhushan Lu to its terminus on Cidu Dadao, then cross the road and head under the ornamental arch opposite. A fifteen-minute walk through fields leads to a surprising collection of antique buildings divided into two sections. A Ming mansion houses the **museum** itself, and its ornate crossbeams, walled gardens and gilt eave screens are far more interesting than the second-rate **ceramics display**, though this covers everything from 1000-year-old kiln fragments through to the Ming's classic simplicity and overwrought, multicoloured extravagances of the late nineteenth century. Next door, another walled garden conceals the **Ancient Porcelain Workshop**, complete with a Confucian temple and working pottery, where the entire process of throwing, moulding and glazing takes place. Out the back is a rickety two-storey **kiln**, packed with all sizes of the unglazed yellow pottery sleeves commonly seen outside local field kilns – these shield each piece of porcelain from damage in case one explodes during the firing process.

Practicalities

It's only three hours to Jingdezhen from Nanchang, the route following the Jiujiang expressway clockwise around the lake. Arriving from Fujian, you can catch a train to the copper-mining town of **Yingtan**, from where it takes three hours to continue by bus to Jingdezhen, half this for the train (change trains in Yingtan itself). It's also easy to get here by bus or train from Tunxi in Anhui, and there are trains from Nanjing and Shanghai.

The town is concentrated on the east bank of the **Chang Jiang** – not the Yangzi, but a lesser river of the same name. **Zhushan Lu** runs east from the river for a kilometre through to where roads converge at central **Guangchang**, a broad, paved square where children fly kites in windy weather. The **train station** is 1500m southeast of Guangchang on Tongzhan Lu, while the **long-distance bus station** is 3km west across the river – bus #28 connects the two via Zhushan Lu and Guangchang.

For factory tours or ticket booking there's a CITS (Mon–Sat 9am–5.30pm; ☎0798/8629999) in the *Binjiang Hotel* by the river on Zhushan Xi Lu. You'll find the **Bank of China** on the way into town on Ma'anshan Lu; the main

post office is west of the river on Zhushan Lu, and there's a small **Internet bar** (¥2) on Ma'anshan Lu near the junction with Tongzhan Lu.

It's just as well that many visitors treat Jingdezhen as a day-trip, as **accommodation** prospects are mediocre. The best option near the train station is *Zhongjin Dajiudian* on Tongzhan Lu (☎0798/7020777; ❹); around Guangchang, try the comfortable, welcoming *Jinsheng Dajiudian* on the north side of Zhushan Zhong Lu (☎0798/8207818; ❺), west off the square. **Food stalls** offering hotpots and stir-fries can be found east of Guangchang along Tongzhan Lu.

Southern Jiangxi

When Zhou Enlai and Zhu De were driven out of Nanchang after their abortive uprising, they fled to the **Jinggang Shan** ranges, 300km southwest in the mountainous border with Hunan. Here they met up with Mao, whose **Autumn Harvest Uprising** in Hunan had also failed, and the remnants of the two armies joined to form the first real PLA divisions. Their initial base was near the country town of **Ciping**, and, though they declared a Chinese Soviet Republic in 1931 at the Fujian border town of **Ruijin**, Ciping was where the Communists stayed until forced out by the Guomindang in 1934.

Jinggang Shan is reasonably accessible thanks to new roads, though it doesn't attract a great number of tourists. This makes it a pleasant proposition, as there is some good forest scenery and a few hiking trails. Ciping is an eight-hour **bus** trip from Nanchang via the ancient river town of **Ji'an**, whose landmark **Yunzhang Ge** (Cloud Sect Pavilion) is built out on a wooded midstream island. You can also get into the region **by train**, disembarking either at the southern city of **Ganzhou**, or east at **Taihe**, sometimes described as the Jinggang Shan station – either way, you've still got at least 90km to cover by bus.

Ciping and Jinggang Shan

Also known as Jinggang Shan Shi, **CIPING** is, at least in scale, nothing more than a village. Completely destroyed by artillery bombardments during the

---

Southern Jiangxi

Ciping	茨坪	*cípíng*
Former Revolutionary Headquarters	革命旧居群	*géming jiùjūqún*
Jinggang Shan Binguan	井岗山宾馆	*jīnggāngshān bīnguǎn*
Martyrs' Tomb	烈士纪念堂	*lièshì jìniàntáng*
Revolutionary Museum	井岗山博物馆	*jīnggāngshān bówùguǎn*
Jinggang Shan	井岗山	*jīnggāng shān*
Wulong Tan	五龙潭	*wǔlóng tán*
Wuzhi Feng	五指峰	*wǔzhǐ fēng*
Ganzhou	赣州	*gànzhōu*
Bajing Park	八境公园	*bājìng gōngyuán*
Ganzhou Fandian	赣州饭店	*gànzhōu fàndiàn*
Ji'an	吉安	*jí'ān*

1930s, it was rebuilt after the Communist takeover as one enormous revolutionary relic, though recent greening projects have lightened the heavily heroic architecture and monuments, giving the place a dated rural charm. The main streets form a two-kilometre elliptical circuit, the lower half of which is taken up with a lake surrounded by grassy gardens – much appreciated by straying cattle – and a tiny amusement park, complete with a real MiG-style fighter plane to play on.

Ciping's austere historical monuments can be breezed through fairly quickly, as it's the surrounding hills which better recreate a feeling of how the Communist guerrillas might have lived. Five minutes west of the bus station at the top end of town is the squat, angular **Martyrs' Tomb**, positioned at the top of a broad flight of stairs and facing the mountains that the fighters it commemorates died defending. Farther round at the **Revolutionary Museum** (daily 8am–4pm; ¥15), where signs ban smoking, spitting and laughter, the exhibition consists almost entirely of maps showing battle sites and troop movements up until 1930 – after this the Communists suffered some heavy defeats. Paintings of a smiling Mao preaching to peasant armies face cases of the spears, flintlocks and mortars which initially comprised the Communist arsenal. On a more mundane level, a group of mud-brick rooms across the park at the **Former Revolutionary Headquarters** (daily 8am–4pm; ¥15) gives an idea of what Ciping might originally have looked like and, as the site of where Mao and Zhu De coordinated their guerrilla activities and the start of the **Long March**, is the town's biggest attraction as far as visiting cadres are concerned.

Practicalities

Ciping's **bus station** is on the northeastern side of the circuit, served by buses from Nanchang and Ganzhou, and also Hengyang in Hunan province, from where there are transport links into southern and central China. There are a host of budget and mid-range **places to stay** near the bus station. Alternatively, take the first street down the hill on the right, which leads through Ciping's tourist market (a collection of white-tiled shops selling local teas, cloud-ear fungus and bamboo roots carved into faces) to the *Jinggang Shan Binguan* (⌾0796/6552272, ⊕6552221; ⑦), favoured by visiting officials but otherwise a bit grey. There's a **CITS** office here (Mon–Sat 9am–5.30pm; ⌾0796/6552504). Just past the Former Revolutionary Headquarters is a large **Bank of China** only too happy to change traveller's cheques (Mon–Fri 9–11.30am & 2–5pm).

Jinggang Shan

Having waded through the terribly serious displays in town, it's nice to escape from Ciping into Jinggang Shan's surprisingly wild **countryside**. Some of the peaks provide glorious views of the sunrise, or more frequent mists, and there are colourful plants, natural groves of pine and bamboo, deep green temperate cloud forests, and hosts of butterflies and birds. If you want a day-tour of all the local sights, ask CITS to arrange a jeep and driver or use the minibuses which leave from the station.

One problem with **walking** anywhere is that maps of the footpaths are pretty vague, and locals can be shy of foreigners, running off should you stop to ask directions. One of the nicest areas to explore, and relatively easy to find, is **Wulong Tan** (Five Dragon Pools), about 8km north along the road from the Martyrs' Tomb. A footpath from the roadhead leads past some poetically pretty waterfalls dropping into the pools (of which there are actually eight) between a score of pine-covered peaks. The same distance south is **Jinggang Shan** itself, also known as **Wuzhi Feng**, apex of the mountains at 1586m. Follow

The Long March

In 1927, Chiang Kaishek, the new leader of the Nationalist Guomindang (GMD) government, began an obsessive war against the 6-year-old Chinese Communist Party, using a union dispute in Shanghai as an excuse to massacre their leadership. Driven underground, the Communists set up half a dozen remote rural bases, or soviets, across central China. The most important of these were the **Fourth Front army** in northern Sichuan, under the leadership of **Zhang Guotao**; the **Hunan soviet**, controlled by the irrepressible peasant general **He Long**; and the main **Jiangxi soviet** in the Jinggang Mountains, led by **Mao Zedong** and **Zhu De**, the Communist Commander-in-Chief.

Initially poorly armed, the Jiangxi soviet successfully fought off GMD attempts to oust them, acquiring better weapons in the process and swelling their ranks with disaffected peasantry and defectors from the Nationalist cause. But they over-estimated their position and in 1933, abandoning Mao's previously successful guerrilla tactics, they were drawn into several disastrous pitched battles. Chiang, ignoring Japanese incursions into Manchuria in his eagerness to defeat the Communists, blockaded the mountains with a steadily tightening ring of bunkers and barbed wire, systematically clearing areas of guerrillas with artillery bombardments. Hemmed in and facing eventual defeat, the **First Front army**, comprising some eighty thousand Red soldiers, decided to break through the blockade in October 1934 and retreat west to team up with the Hunan soviet – the beginning of the **Long March**.

Covering a punishing 30km a day on average, the Communists moved after dark whenever possible so that the enemy would find it difficult to know their exact position; even so, they faced daily skirmishes. One thing in their favour was that many putative GMD divisions were, in fact, armies belonging to local warlords who owed a token allegiance to Chiang Kaishek, and had no particular reason to fight once it became clear that the Red Army was only crossing their territory. But after severe losses incurred during a battle at the **Xiang River** near Guilin in Guangxi, the marchers found their progress north impeded by massive GMD forces, and were obliged to continue west to Guizhou, where they took the town of **Zunyi** in January 1935. With their power structure in disarray and with no obvious options left, an emergency meeting of the Communist Party hierarchy was called – the **Zunyi Conference**. Mao emerged as the undisputed leader of the Party, with a mandate to "go north to fight the Japanese" by linking up with Zhang Guotao in Sichuan. In subsequent months they circled through Yunnan and Guizhou, trying to shake off the GMD, routing

the road out of town past the Bank of China, then turn right and take the concrete "driveway" uphill past company housing and on to a dirt road. About ten minutes later this forks; go left down to the bridge, cross over and carry on past a huge quarry, where machinery turns boulders into gravel, and on to a **tunnel** leading into the hillside. Ignore the tunnel and follow the steps above up through a small patch of forest full of ginger, ferns and moss-covered trees, to more stairs ascending to Wuzhi Feng's sharp and lightly wooded summit. The last bit of the track is slippery and not overly used, giving a rare opportunity to be on your own, musing on how the Communists must have found things and watching the trees and waterfalls below sliding in and out of the clouds. Examine the bushes and you'll find some extraordinary insects: multicoloured crickets, scarabs with orange antennae, and huge, bushy caterpillars.

Ganzhou

Five hours south of Jinggang Shan and on the Kowloon–Beijing rail line, **GANZHOU** lies on the subtropical side of Jiangxi's mountain ranges, only twenty regiments of the Guangxi provincial army at the **Loushan Pass** in the process; they then suddenly moved up into Sichuan to cross the Jinsha River and, in one of the most celebrated and heroic episodes of the march, took the **Luding Bridge** across the Dadu River (see p.947). Now they had to negotiate **Daxue Shan** (Great Snowy Mountains), where hundreds died from exhaustion, exposure and altitude sickness before the survivors met up on the far side with the Fourth Front army.

The meeting between these two major branches of the Red Army was tense. Mao, with Party backing, wanted to start resistance against the Japanese, but Zhang, who felt that his better-equipped forces and better education gave him superiority, wanted to found a Communist state in Sichuan's far west. Zhang eventually capitulated, and he and Mao took control of separate columns to cross the last natural barrier they faced, the **Aba Grasslands** in northern Sichuan. But here, while Mao was bogged down by swamps, hostile nomads and dwindling food reserves, Zhang's column suddenly retreated to **Garzê**, where Zhang set up an independent government. Mao and what remained of the First Front struggled through southern Gansu, where they suffered further losses through Muslim supporters of the GMD, finally arriving in Communist-held **Yan'an**, Shaanxi province, in October 1935. While the mountains here were to become a Communist stronghold, only a quarter of those who started from Jiangxi twelve months before had completed the 9500-kilometre journey. For his part, Zhang was soon harried out of western Sichuan by Chiang's forces, and after meeting up with He Long, he battled through to Shaanxi, adding another twenty thousand to the Communist ranks. Here he made peace with Mao in October 1936, but later defected to the GMD.

Immediately after the Long March, Mao admitted that in terms of losses and the Red Army's failure to hold their original positions against the Nationalists, the Guomindang had won. Yet in a more lasting sense, the march was an incredible success, uniting the Party under Mao and defining the Communists' aims, while changing the Communists' popular image from simply another rebel group opposing central authority into one of a determined and patriotic movement. After Zunyi, Mao turned the march into a deliberate propaganda mission to spread the Communist faith among the peasantry, opening up prisons in captured GMD towns and promoting tolerance and cooperation with minority groups (though not always successfully). As Mao said, "Without the Long March, how could the broad masses have learned so quickly about the existence of the great truth which the Red Army embodies?"

a short hop from the Guangdong border. The town makes an interesting few hours' break in your journey, and is very different in feel from elsewhere in Jiangxi.

Ganzhou was formerly a strategic port guarding the routes between central and southern China; the town sits on a triangular peninsula where two rivers, the Gong Shui and Zhang Shui, combine to form the **Gan Jiang**, which flows north from here all the way to Nanchang and Poyang Hu. During the 1930s, Chiang Kaishek's son was governor here, doubtless keeping a close watch on the events at Jinggang Shan, and a surprising amount survives from these times. The peninsula's northern end is enclosed by several kilometres of **stone battlements**: at the very tip, **Bajing Park** (¥8) is an untidy arrangement of willows and ponds enlivened by **Bajing Tai**, a platform and tower whose rusting cannon no longer threaten barges negotiating the river junction below. Exiting the park, you can follow the walls southeast down Zhongshan Lu through 1930s streets to the old **east gate**, still with a functioning portcullis; on the far side is a small market, people midstream fishing with cast nets and **cormorants** (see p.744), and villagers wheeling their bicycles to the far bank across a low **pontoon bridge**. Originally built by chaining punts across the river and laying a wooden decking on top (though the mid-section floats are steel), these bridges were common through the region until the 1950s, being cheap to make and easily removed in times of flooding or war. Look back from the middle at the steep walls and appreciate Ganzhou's defences – it wouldn't have taken much time to cut the bridge, drop the portcullis and load the cannon.

Back inside the city, if you head more or less southwest you'll come to more elderly architecture, including narrow side streets of Qing houses, colonial-style colonnaded shop fronts along the main roads, a couple of small temples and a pagoda – nothing of great importance but atmospheric all the same, though demolitions have started to take their toll.

Practicalities

The town is a small place by Chinese standards, with a centre only a couple of kilometres across. The town's focus is **Nanmen Guangchang**, South Gate Square: from here, **Wenqing Lu** runs north through the centre to Bajing Park and the river, lined with clothes shops and restaurants, while **Hongqi Lu** is the town's east–west transport artery.

The **long-distance bus station** is on Bayi Si Dadao 3km from the centre at the southeastern corner of town, a relentlessly unappealing area. The **train station** is farther out in the same direction; from either station, bus #2 will get you to Nanmen Guangchang. **Leaving**, trains head to Jinggang Shan, Nanchang, Jiujiang, Wuhan, Hefei and well beyond, with useful buses south to Shaoguan and Guangzhou in Guangdong Province.

The main **Bank of China** is halfway up Wenqing Lu, with a **post office** on Nanmen Guangchang. There are a few cheap **hotels** north of the bus station on Bayi Si Dadao, but you're better off forking out for a decent room at the *Ganzhou Fandian*, near Nanmen Guangchang at 29 Hongqi Dadao (☎0797/8280188; ❺) – it's not as expensive as you'd think from the exterior. As regards **eating**, head up Wenqing Lu: there's Western-style food and coffee upstairs at *Spring of Taipei*, about 100m along on the west side; 500m along at the intersection with Qingnian Lu you'll find extremely popular hotpots at *Wuzhou Kuaican*, and buns, soya milk and snacks at *Yonghe Doujiang*.

Travel details

Trains

Changsha to: Beijing (14 daily; 14–19hr 30min); Guangzhou (38 daily; 7hr 30min–11hr); Guilin (5 daily; 7–10hr); Guiyang (4 daily; 13hr 30min); Hengyang (40 daily; 2–3hr); Nanchang (daily; 7hr); Shaoshan (daily; 3hr); Shenzhen (7 daily; 9–13hr); Wuhan (41 daily; 3hr 30min–5hr); Yueyang (35 daily; 1hr 30min–2hr 30min); Zhangjiajie (5 daily; 5–6hr).

Ganzhou to: Beijing (daily; 22hr); Guangzhou (3 daily; 8–10hr); Hefei (3 daily; 11–13hr); Jinggang Shan (daily; 1hr 40min); Jiujiang (13 daily; 6–8hr 30min); Nanchang (17 daily; 4hr 30min–6hr); Shenzhen (3 daily; 9hr); Wuhan (daily; 14hr).

Hefei to: Beijing (4 daily; 10–15hr); Bozhou (9 daily; 4hr 30min); Ganzhou (3 daily; 11–13hr); Jingdezhen (2 daily; 9hr 30min); Jiujiang (4 daily; 5hr); Nanchang (5 daily; 6–7hr); Nanjing (5 daily; 4–5hr 30min); Shanghai (3 daily; 7–9hr); Tunxi (3 daily; 6hr 30min–7hr 30min); Wuhu (10 daily; 2–3hr); Xian (3 daily; 15hr 30min–17hr).

Jingdezhen to: Hefei (2 daily; 9–10hr 30min); Nanchang (3 daily; 4hr 30min–6hr); Shanghai (daily; 16hr 30min); Tunxi (11 daily; 3hr 30min).

Jiujiang to: Ganzhou (13 daily; 6–8hr 30min); Hefei (4 daily; 4–5hr); Nanchang (26 daily; 1hr 30min–2hr 30min); Shanghai (daily; 17hr 30min).

Nanchang to: Beijing (7 daily; 13hr 30min–18hr 30min); Changsha (daily; 7hr); Fuzhou (6 daily;

12–13hr 30min); Ganzhou (17 daily; 4hr 30min–
6hr); Guangzhou (6 daily; 11–14hr); Hefei (5 daily;
6–7hr); Jingdezhen (4 daily; 5–6hr); Jinggang Shan
(8 daily; 3hr); Jiujiang (26 daily; 1hr 30min–3hr);
Shanghai (7 daily; 13–16hr); Shenzhen (6 daily;
10–15hr); Tunxi (2 daily; 9hr 30min); Wuhan (14
daily; 6–10hr); Xiamen (4 daily; 17–21hr); Yingtang
(frequent; 2–3hr).
Tunxi to: Beijing (daily; 19hr 30min); Hefei (3 daily;
6–7hr); Jingdezhen (11 daily; 3–5hr); Nanchang
(daily; 9hr); Nanjing (9 daily; 6–10hr); Shanghai (2
daily; 11–12hr 30min).
Wuhan to: Beijing (15 daily; 10–15hr 30min);
Changsha (frequent; 3hr 30min–5hr); Ganzhou (daily;
14hr); Guangzhou (frequent; 11–15hr); Nanchang
(14 daily; 5hr 30min–10hr 30min); Shiyan (8 daily;
5–10hr 30min); Wudang Shan (daily; 7hr 30min);
Xiangfan (12 daily; 3–6hr 30min); Yueyang (frequent;
2–3hr 30min); Xi'an (6 daily; 13hr 30min–19hr).
Wuhu to: Hefei (10 daily; 2hr); Ma'anshan (daily;
40min); Nanjing (18 daily; 2–4hr); Shanghai (4
daily; 5–9hr).
Xiangfan to: Shiyan (19 daily; 2–6hr 30min);
Wudang Shan (3 daily; 2hr–5hr 30min); Wuhan (12
daily; 3hr 30min–6hr 30min); Yichang (8 daily; 4hr);
Zhangjiajie (2 daily; 7–9hr 30min).
Yichang to: Beijing (daily; 20hr); Xi'an (daily; 16hr
30min); Xiangfan (8 daily; 4hr); Zhangjiajie (daily;
5hr 30min).
Yueyang to: Changsha (35 daily; 1hr 30min–2hr
30min); Wuhan (29 daily; 2–3hr 30min).
Zhangjiajie to: Changsha (5 daily; 5–6hr); Huaihua
(for connections to Guiyang or Changsha; 8 daily;
4–6hr 30min); Jishou (for Fenghuang; 6 daily; 2hr);
Xiangfan (2 daily; 7hr 30min–10hr 30min); Yichang
(daily; 6hr).

Buses

Changsha to: Heng Shan (3hr); Jiujiang (13hr);
Nanchang (6hr); Wuhan (4hr); Yichang (6hr);
Yueyang (3hr); Zhangjiajie (7hr).
Ciping (Jinggang Shan Shi) to: Ganzhou (5hr);
Hengyang (8hr); Taihe (for Jinggang Shan; 2hr);
Nanchang (8hr).
Hefei to: Bozhou (5hr); Huainan (2hr); Jiuhua Shan
(5hr); Jiujiang (5hr); Ma'anshan (3hr); Nanchang
(6hr); Nanjing (3hr); Shouxian (2hr); Tongling (3hr);
Tunxi (5hr); Wuhan (6hr); Wuhu (2hr).
Jingdezhen to: Jiujiang (1–2hr); Nanchang (3hr);
Tunxi (3hr 30min); Yingtan (3hr).
Jiuhua Shan to: Hefei (5hr); Qingyang (30min);
Taiping (3hr); Tangkou (4hr); Tongling (2hr); Wuhu
(3hr).
Jiujiang to: Changsha (13hr); Jingdezhen (1–2hr);
Hefei (5hr); Lu Shan (1hr 30min); Nanchang (2hr);
Wuhan (4hr).

Jishou to: Fenghuang (1hr 30min).
Nanchang to: Ciping (8hr); Changsha (6hr); Hefei
(6hr); Jingdezhen (3hr); Jinggang Shan (6hr);
Jiujiang (2hr); Lu Shan (4hr); Wuhan (6hr); Yingtan
(2hr 30min).
Tunxi to: Hefei (5hr); Jingdezhen (3hr 30min);
Jiuhua Shan (5hr); Nanjing (6hr); Shanghai (12hr);
Shexian (1hr); Tangkou (1hr); Tongling (4hr); Wuhu
(3hr); Yixian (2hr).
Wuhan to: Changsha (4hr); Hefei (6hr); Jingzhou
(3hr 30min); Jiujiang (4hr); Nanchang (6hr); Xiang-
fan (5hr); Yichang (4hr); Yueyang (4hr).
Wuhu to: Hefei (2hr); Jiuhua Shan (3hr);
Ma'anshan (1hr); Nanjing (3hr); Tunxi (3hr);
Tongling (2hr); Xuancheng (2hr).
Xiangfan to: Jingzhou (4hr 30min); Wudang Shan
(2hr); Wuhan (5hr); Yichang (5hr).
Yichang to: Changsha (6hr); Jingzhou (1hr 30min);
Jiujiang (12hr); Wuhan (4hr); Xiangfan (5hr); Xing
Shan (4hr).
Zhangjiajie to: Changsha (7hr); Jishou (for Feng-
huang; 2hr).

Ferries

Wuhan to: Chongqing (daily; 5 days).
Yichang to: Chongqing (daily; 11hr by hydrofoil,
otherwise 2–4 days).

Flights

Changsha to: Beijing (6 daily; 2hr); Chongqing
(2 daily; 1hr 15min); Guangzhou (3 daily; 1hr);
Hefei (daily; 1hr 35min); Hong Kong (7 weekly; 1hr
30min); Shanghai (6 daily; 1hr 30min); Shenzhen
(6 daily; 1hr 10min); Tianjin (5 weekly; 1hr 40min);
Zhangjiajie (daily; 40min).
Hefei to: Beijing (3 daily; 1hr 40min); Changsha
(daily; 1hr 35min); Guangzhou (3 daily; 1hr 50min);
Nanchang (2 weekly; 1hr); Shenzhen (2 daily; 2hr);
Tunxi (daily; 40min); Xiamen (daily; 1hr 35min);
Xi'an (daily; 1hr 30min).
Nanchang to: Beijing (5 daily; 2hr); Chengdu
(daily; 2hr); Guangzhou (3 daily; 1hr 10min); Hefei
(2 weekly; 1hr); Kunming (daily; 2hr); Shanghai (5
daily; 1hr); Tunxi (2 weekly; 50min).
Tunxi (Huang Shan) to: Beijing (2 weekly; 2hr);
Guangzhou (2 daily; 1hr 30min–3hr 10min); Hefei
(daily; 40min); Nanchang (2 weekly; 50min);
Shanghai (daily; 1hr).
Wuhan to: Beijing (7 daily; 1hr 50min); Guangzhou
(5 daily; 1hr 30min); Hong Kong (daily; 1hr 50min);
Shanghai (10 daily; 1hr 15min).
Yichang to: Beijing (daily; 2hr); Chongqing (daily;
1hr 20min); Guangzhou (daily; 1hr 45min); Shang-
hai (2 weekly; 1hr 30min).
Zhangjiajie to: Changsha (daily; 40min).

Highlights

✳ **Wuyi Shan** Take a bamboo raft through dramatic gorges or explore hiking trails in this mountain park. See p.558

✳ **Gulangyu Island** Uniquely relaxing island sporting vehicle-free streets, European-style colonial mansions, and sea views. See p.573

✳ **Hakka mansions** These circular mud-brick homes sometimes housing upwards of five hundred people are China's most distinctive traditional architecture. See p.576

✳ **Cantonese food** Sample China's finest cuisine, from *dim sum* to roast goose, in one of Guangzhou's restaurants. See p.599

✳ **Chaozhou** Old town with Ming-dynasty walls, some great street life, the famous Kaiyuan temple, and more good food. See p.627

△ Hakka mansion, Fujian

8

Fujian, Guangdong and Hainan Island

There's something very self-contained about the provinces of **Fujian**, **Guangdong** and **Hainan Island**, which occupy 1200km or so of China's convoluted southern seaboard. Though occasionally taking centre stage in the country's history, the provinces share a sense of being generally isolated from mainstream events by the mountain ranges surrounding Fujian and Guangdong, physically cutting them off from the rest of the empire. Forced to look seawards, the coastal regions have a long history of contact with the outside world, continually importing – or being forced to endure – foreign influences and styles. This is where Islam entered China, and porcelain and tea left it along the **Maritime Silk Road**; where the mid-nineteenth-century theatricals of the Opium Wars, colonialism, the Taiping Uprising and the mass overseas exodus of southern Chinese were played out; and where today you'll find China's most Westernized cities. Conversely, the interior mountains enclose some of the country's wildest, most remote corners, parts of which were virtually in the Stone Age within living memory.

Possibly because its specific attractions are thinly spread, the region receives scant attention from visitors. Huge numbers do pass through Guangdong, in transit between the mainland and Hong Kong and Macau, but only because they have to, and few look beyond the overpowering capital, **Guangzhou**. Yet while the other two regional capitals – **Fuzhou** in Fujian, and Hainan's **Haikou** – share Guangzhou's modern veneer, all three also hide temples and antique architecture that have somehow escaped developers, while other cities and towns have managed to preserve their old, character-laden ambience intact. The pick of these are the Fujian port of **Xiamen**, its streets almost frozen in time since the start of the twentieth century, and **Chaozhou** in eastern Guangdong, a staunchly conservative place consciously preserving its traditions in the face of the modern world.

Indeed, a sense of local tradition and of being different from the rest of the country pervades the whole region, though this feeling is rarely expressed in any tangible way. **Language** is one difference you will notice, however, as the main dialects here are Cantonese and Minnan, whose rhythms are recognizably removed from Mandarin, even if you can't speak a word of Chinese. Southern pronunciation is also very distinct: "h" and "k" replace "f" and "j" respectively, for instance, so that "Fujian" comes out as "Hokkian" in local parlance. Less

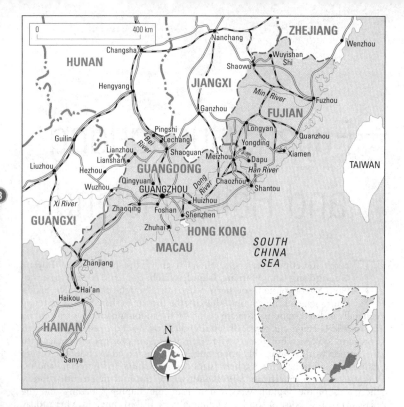

obvious are specific **ethnic groups**, including the **Hakka**, a widely spread Han subgroup whose mountainous Guangdong–Fujian heartland is dotted with fortress-like mansions; the Muslim **Hui**, who form large communities in Guangzhou, coastal Hainan and in **Quanzhou** in Fujian; and the **Li**, Hainan's animistic, original inhabitants.

While a quick look around much of the coastal areas here leaves a gloomy impression of uncontrolled development and its attendant ills (some cities seem to consist of nothing but beggars and building sites), most of this is actually contained within various **Special Economic Zones** (SEZs), specifically created in the mid-1980s as a focus for heavy investment and industrialization. Beyond their boundaries lurk some respectably wild – and some nicely tamed – corners where you can settle back and enjoy the scenery. Over in western Guangdong, the city of **Zhaoqing** sits beside some pleasant lakes and hills, while the **Wuyi Shan** range in northeastern Fujian contains the region's lushest, most picturesque mountain forests. Way down south lie the country's best **beaches** – encouraging the tourist industry to hype Hainan as "China's Hawaii" – and there's also a limited amount of hiking to try, through the island's interior highlands.

Anyone wanting to stop off and explore will find plentiful local and long-distance **transport**, though **accommodation** can be expensive and suffers additional seasonal price hikes in Guangzhou. The **weather** is nicest in spring and autumn, as summer storms from June to August bring daily doses of heavy humidity, thunder and afternoon downpours on the coast, while the higher reaches of the Guangdong–Fujian border can get very cold in winter.

Fujian

FUJIAN, on China's southeastern coast, is well off the beaten track for most Western travellers, which is a pity because the province possesses not only a wild mountainous interior, but also a string of old ports, including **Xiamen**, China's most attractive and interesting coastal city. From Hong Kong, the well-trodden routes head directly west towards Guilin, or north to Shanghai, but a detour to Xiamen makes an excellent introduction to mainland China – boats from Hong Kong come here, as does a spur of China's rail network.

Culturally and geographically, the province splits into distinct halves. One is made up of large, historical seaports and lush, semitropical coastal stretches, whose sophisticated population enjoy warm sun and blossoming trees even in January. The other is the rugged, mountainous and largely inaccessible interior, freezing cold in winter, home to around 140 different local dialects and with a history of poverty and backwardness: when the Red Army arrived in the 1960s they found communities unaware that the Qing dynasty had been overthrown; and even today, the area is wild enough to harbour the last few populations of the **South China tiger**. However, while inland Fujian knew very little of China, contacts between the coastal area and the outside world had been flourishing for centuries. In the Tang dynasty, the port of **Quanzhou** was considered on a par with Alexandria as the most international port in the world, and teemed with Middle Eastern traders, some of whose descendants still live in the area today. So much wealth was brought into the ports here that a population explosion led to mass emigration, and large parts of the Malay Peninsula, the Philippines and Taiwan were colonized by Fujianese. In the early eighteenth century this exodus of able-bodied subjects became so drastic that the imperial court in distant Beijing tried, ineffectually, to ban it.

Today the interior of Fujian remains largely unvisited and unknown, with the exception of the scenic **Wuyi Shan** area in the northwest of the province, and the **Hakka regions** around southwesterly **Yongding**. The coast, however, is booming, with colossal investment pouring in from both Hong Kong and, in particular, neighbouring **Taiwan**, many of whose citizens originate from the province and speak the same dialect, Minnan Hua. The cities of **Fuzhou** and **Xiamen** are among the wealthiest in the country, particularly Xiamen, with its clean beaches, charming streets and shopping arcades that hopefully represent the face of Chinese cities to come. The proximity of Taiwan to Xiamen accounts not only for the rapid economic development and the proliferation of first-class tourist facilities, but also for the occasional outbreak of tension. During the 1996 Taiwanese presidential election, the mainland authorities suddenly decided to hold large-scale military exercises just off the Taiwanese coast, as a gentle reminder to the Taiwanese people not to vote for separatist candidates – despite this, pro-independence Chen Shui-Bian narrowly won a second term. And whilst cross-straits business manages to smooth over the cracks somewhat, the fact that there are hundreds of missiles pointing from the mainland to Taiwan indicates the gravity of the situation.

Getting around Fujian has improved considerably in recent years, with an extremely fast **coastal expressway** linking the main cities with neighbouring Zhejiang and Guangdong provinces. For reaching the interior wilds of Wuyi Shan, you're better off catching a **train**, with separate lines from Fuzhou, Quanzhou and Xiamen; Fuzhou also has a decent link through to Jiangxi province, and there's another track west to Meizhou in Guangdong from Xiamen and Quanzhou. Otherwise, train travel within or beyond the province is circuitous and very slow.

Fuzhou

Capital of Fujian Province, **FUZHOU** is a comfortably modern and clean city, with shiny business skyscrapers looming over the main roads. An important trading centre for over a thousand years, it was visited by Marco Polo during the Yuan dynasty. In the fifteenth century, Fuzhou shipbuilders earned themselves the distinction of having built the world's largest ocean-going ship, the *Baochuan*, sailed by the famous Chinese navigator Zheng He, who used it to travel all around Asia and Africa. One thing Polo noted when he was here was the high-profile presence of Mongol armies to suppress any potential uprisings,

---

Fuzhou

Fuzhou	福州	fúzhōu
Bai Ta	白塔	báitǎ
Changle Airport	长乐机场	chánglè jīchǎng
Fuzhou Provincial Museum	福建省博物馆	fújiànshěng bówùguǎn
Gu Shan	鼓山	gǔshān
Lin Zexu Memorial Hall	林则徐纪念馆	línzéxú jìniànguǎn
Mao Zedong Statue	毛塑像	máo sùxiàng
Min River	闽江	mǐnjiāng
Wu Ta	乌塔	wūtǎ
Wuyi Square	五一广场	wǔyī guǎngchǎng
Xi Hu Park	西湖公园	xīhú gōngyuán
Yu Shan	于山	yúshān

Accommodation and eating

Bifeng Tang	避风塘	bìfēngtáng
Foreign Trade Centre	外宾中心酒店	wàibīnzhōngxīn jiǔdiàn
Galaxy Garden	银河花园大饭店	yínhéhuāyuán dàfàndiàn
Hao Ke Lai	豪客来	háokè lái
Haoyun	好运宾馆	hǎoyùn bīnguǎn
Juchunyuan	聚春园大酒店	jùchūnyuán dàjiǔdiàn
Minhang	民航大厦	mínháng dàshà
Minjiang	闽江饭店	mǐnjiāng fàndiàn
Nanyang	南洋饭店	nányáng fàndiàn
Noble Family	贵族世家牛排	guìzú shìjiā niúpái
Wenquan	温泉大饭店	wēnquán dàfàndiàn
Xinglong Sheng	兴隆盛酒店	xīnglóngshèng jiǔdiàn
Yushan	于山宾馆	yúshān bīnguǎn

and, by coincidence, the city is no less well defended today, forming the heart of Fujian's military opposition to Taiwan. Today, there's precious little to detain casual visitors, and the city is probably best seen as a springboard for reaching the wilds of Wuyi Shan.

Arrival and accommodation

Flowing east–west through the city, the **Min River** roughly delineates the southern border of Fuzhou. The five-kilometre-long main north–south axis, called **Wusi Lu** in the north, and **Wuyi Lu** farther south, cuts right through the city, intersecting with Dong Jie, and farther south with Gutian Lu, marking the centre of the city at **Wuyi Square**. The main shopping areas are **Bayiqi Lu** (parallel with Wuyi Lu), the area around Gutian Lu, and one more much farther south, almost at the river, on Rongcheng Gujie.

Changle airport is 50km south of the city, from where an **airport bus** (¥20) runs to the CAAC office, a few minutes north of Guohuo Lu, on Wuyi Lu, or you can take a taxi (around ¥100). From the **train station**, in the far northeast of town, bus #51 runs straight down Wusi and Wuyi roads to the Min River, while bus #20 runs down Bayiqi Lu. Arriving **by bus**, you'll almost certainly end up at either the **North station**, a few minutes' walk south of the train station, or the **South station** at the junction of Guohuo Lu and Wuyi Lu – both handle arrivals from just about everywhere. There's also an **express bus station** next to the *Minjiang*.

Fuzhou's **PSB** is opposite the sports complex on Beihuan Zhong Lu (℡0591/87821104). The main **post office** is at the southeastern intersection of

Moving on from Fuzhou

For booking **tours** to Wuyi Shan, or plane tickets, approach CTS (℡0591/7536250) next to the *Minjiang*.

By air

You can **fly** from Fuzhou to Wuyi Shan and a host of major cities, including Hong Kong and Macau; the CAAC **ticket office** is on Wuyi Lu (daily 8am–8pm; ℡0591/83340268). Travelling to the **airport**, pick up the bus from inside the courtyard of the *Minhang*, next door – the journey takes an hour and you'll need to get to the airport at least an hour before your departure.

By train

Fuzhou is the terminus for a couple of fairly remote **rail lines**. Heading northwest, trains run to Wuyi Shan, and through into Jiangxi and the rest of China; be aware that most trains to Guangdong province also travel this way and so take much longer than you'd expect. The new line west from Fuzhou, via Longyan to Meizhou in eastern Guangdong, has sparse services at present, and it may well be faster to take a bus for these destinations. The **ticket office** is in the western part of the station (to the left as you face it); you'll almost certainly need to reserve sleeper berths a day in advance.

By bus

Long-distance buses to everywhere in Fujian and neighbouring provinces leave from both bus stations. There are several sleepers daily to Wuyi Shan, and constant departures along the coastal expressway to Quanzhou, Xiamen and Guangdong province; just remember that, if you've a choice, there's a huge price discrepancy between standard and luxury buses. There's also an express bus station next to the *Minjiang*, which serves Guangzhou, Shanghai and a few other distant destinations.

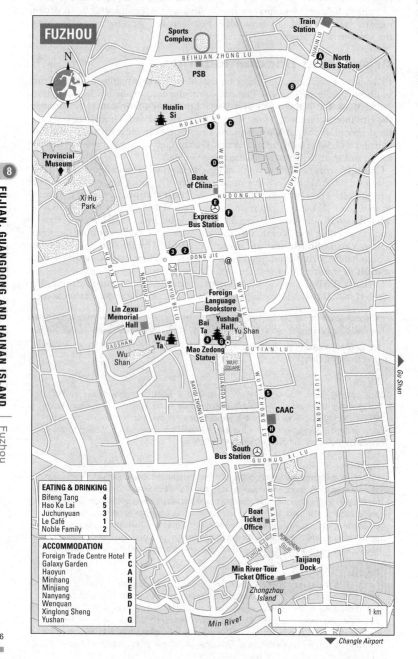

FUZHOU

Sports Complex

BEIHUAN ZHONG LU

PSB

Train Station

North Bus Station

Hualin Si

HUALIN LU

Provincial Museum

Xi Hu Park

WUSI LU

Bank of China

HUDONG LU

Express Bus Station

DONG JIE

Foreign Language Bookstore

Lin Zexu Memorial Hall

HU BIN LU

NANHU JIE

BAYIU BEI LU

DAOSHAN

Wu Ta

Wu Shan

Bai Ta

Yushan Hall

Yu Shan

WUYI LU

Mao Zedong Statue

GUTIAN LU

WUYI SQUARE

GUANGDA LU

BAYIU ZHONG LU

WUYI ZHONG LU

CAAC

South Bus Station

GUOHUO XI LU

LIUYI BEI LU

LIUYI ZHONG LU

RONGCHENG GUJIE

WUYI NAN LU

Boat Ticket Office

Taijiang Dock

YUHAI LU

Min River Tour Ticket Office

Zhongzhou Island

Min River

Gu Shan

Changle Airport

0   1 km

EATING & DRINKING

Bifeng Tang	4
Hao Ke Lai	5
Juchunyuan	3
Le Café	1
Noble Family	2

ACCOMMODATION

Foreign Trade Centre Hotel	F
Galaxy Garden	C
Haoyun	A
Minhang	H
Minjiang	E
Nanyang	B
Wenquan	D
Xinglong Sheng	I
Yushan	G

Dong Jie and Bayiqi Bei Lu and there is a huge **Bank of China** on Wusi Lu. There's an **Internet bar** in a lane south off Dong Jie, near Wuyi Lu.

Accommodation

Most of Fuzhou's accommodation is upmarket, but there are a few budget options that can usually be persuaded to take foreigners, most notably around the train and North bus stations.

Foreign Trade Centre Wusi Lu ☎0591/87523388, ⓕ87550358. Undoubtedly the best hotel in town, but so large it tends to feel rather lonely and empty most of the time. North wing **❽**, South wing **❾**

Galaxy Garden Corner of Hualin Lu and Wusi Lu ☎0591/87831888, ⓕ87843662. New, business-oriented hotel with smart furnishings and attentive staff. **❻**

Haoyun Right beside the North bus station ☎0591/87580888. One of many budget hotels in the vicinity. Beds from ¥38, **❸**

Minhang (aka Fujian Civil Aviation Hotel) Next to CAAC, Wuyi Zhong Lu ☎0591/83343988, ⓕ83341978. New hotel run by CAAC, with spacious, comfortable and clean rooms. A fair deal. **❹**

Minjiang Wusi Lu ☎0591/87557895, ⓔmjht@pub2.fz.fj.cn. Mid-range hotel with sound rooms, well placed just south of Hu Dong Lu on the way into the centre from the train station. **❺**

Nanyang Hualin Lu ☎0591/87579699, ⓕ87577085. A convenient location near the train and North bus stations. Rooms a bit frayed for the price, but staff are helpful. **❹**

Wenquan (aka Hot Spring) Wusi Lu ☎0591/87851818, ⓦwww.hshfz.com. A smart hotel with a cavernous interior full of Pierre Cardin shops and the like. Service is excellent, as you'd expect for the price. **❾**

Xinglong Sheng Wuyi Zhong Lu ☎0591/83371037, ⓕ83370779. A good-value place near the South bus station, with clean, pleasant, slightly tattered rooms and friendly staff. **❸**

Yushan Yushan Lu, off Gutian Lu ☎0591/83351668, ⓕ83357694. An excellent addition to Fuzhou's accommodation options; this hotel enjoys a fine location just below Yushan Park and next to Bai Ta, with large, wooden-floored rooms and helpful staff. **❼**

The City

Almost totally devoid of formal sights – though many small, nondescript temples are secreted away between more modern structures – Fuzhou is centred around **Wuyi Square**, an open expanse dominated by a statue of Mao Zedong looking south. This statue commemorates the Ninth Congress of the Chinese Communist Party in 1969, an event that ratified Maoism as the "state religion" of China, and named the mysterious Lin Biao (subsequently disgraced) as official heir to Mao's throne. Just behind Mao's statue, the large modern building, **Yushan Hall**, is sometimes used for exhibitions – climbing up a path to the west of it lands you at the gates of **Yu Shan** (Jade Hill), a nice place for a stroll. The main sight here is the 1000-year-old **Bai Ta**, a whitewashed pagoda located beside a temple, and a small exhibition of the contents of a local Song-dynasty tomb, which includes the preserved bodies of a man and a woman and some silk garments.

West from Yu Shan is **Bayiqi Lu**, a busy, crowded avenue at the heart of Fuzhou's shopping district. On the far side is another small hill, Wu Shan, currently isolated by a sea of demolitions and roadworks, the net result of which will be an enormous shopping mall. The flat summit, fringed in banyan trees, is capped by a small temple and **Wu Ta**, a black granite pagoda dating back to the same era as the White Tower, and containing some attractive statuary. North from here on Aomen Lu, you'll find the **Lin Zexu Memorial Hall** (daily 8.30am–12.30pm, 1–5pm;¥10), a quiet, attractive couple of halls and courtyards with funereal statues of animals. Lin Zexu (1785–1850) is fondly remembered as the patriotic Qing-dynasty official who fought against the importation of opium by foreigners – even writing persuasive letters to Queen Victoria on the subject – though his destruction of thousands of chests of the drug in 1840 sparked the first Opium War and, rather unfairly, he was exiled to Xinjiang.

The northwest of the city is dominated by **Xi Hu Park** (daily 7am–9pm;¥4), whose entrance is along southerly Hu Bin Lu – you can get here on buses #1 or #2 from the southern end of Bayiqi Lu, or #810 from the train station. The park, mostly comprising an artificial lake formed by excavations some seventeen hundred years ago, is a good spot to go boating or stroll with the masses on a hot day. Within the grounds, the **Fuzhou Provincial Museum** used to include a 3500-year-old coffin-boat removed from a Wuyi Shan cave, though it's currently closed for rebuilding.

Gu Shan

Fuzhou's most-touted tourist attraction is **Gu Shan** (Drum Mountain), about 9km east of the city. To get here, catch one of the regular **minibuses** from the Nanmen terminus on Guangda Lu, just west of Wuyi Square (¥8); it's an attractive 45-minute journey through forested hills, with sweeping views as the road starts climbing. The Gu Shan area offers walks through the woods as well as scattered sights, including the 1000-year-old, heavily restored **Yongquan Si**, which gets phenomenally crowded at weekends. One way to escape the crowds is to climb the 2500 stone steps behind the temple to the wooded summit of Gu Shan.

Eating and drinking

For such a major city, Fuzhou suffers a serious lack of **restaurants**, outside of those in the hotels, though Western and Chinese fast-food chains are omnipresent. For **snacks**, street vendors pedal small, bagel-like "cut buns" (*gua bao*), stuffed with vegetables or a slice of spiced, steamed pork, and hole-in-the-wall operations surround transit points; otherwise, the highest concentration of places to eat is along downtown Dong Jie. You'll find popular hotpot places like the restaurant in the *Juchunyuan*, which does all-you-can-eat for ¥48, and Western-style steakhouses such as the *Noble Family*. North off Wuyi Square on Gutian Lu, *Bifeng Tang* is a three-storey giant, serving tasty Cantonese fare – two can eat well here for ¥50. Another place for inexpensive, good and varied food in a comfortable setting is a branch of *Hao Ke Lai*, which serves Sichuan-style cold spiced meats and vegetables, along with soups, noodles, spring rolls and local buns, all at a few yuan a serve – look for the yellow and green sign spelling out "Houcaller" on Wuyi Zhong Lu. For **nightlife**, there are bars and clubs on Dong Jie, and a Western-style pub, *Le Café*, on Hualin Lu, near the junction with Wusi Lu.

Wuyi Shan

Away in the northeast of the province, 370km from Fuzhou and close to the Fujian–Jiangxi border, the **WUYI SHAN** scenic district contains some of the most picturesque scenery in southern China. It's the only inland part of Fujian regularly visited by tourists, and consists of two principal parts: the **Jiuqu River**, which meanders at the feet of the mountains, and the **Thirty-Six Peaks**, which rise up from the river, mostly to its north. With peaks protruding from low-lying mists, the scenery is classic Chinese scroll-painting material, and the reserve, dotted with small, attractive villages, can be a tremendous place to relax

Wuyi Shan

Wuyi Shan Scenic District	武夷山风景区	*wǔyíshān fēngjǐngqū*
Chishi	赤石	*chìshí*
Chongyang Stream	崇阳溪	*chóngyáng xī*
Dawang Feng	大王峰	*dàwáng fēng*
Dujia Qu	度假区	*dùjiàqū*
Jiuqu River	九曲溪	*jiǔqǔ xī*
Shuilian Cave	水帘洞	*shuǐlián dòng*
Tianyou Feng	天游峰	*tiānyóu fēng*
Wuyigong	武夷宫	*wǔyí gōng*
Wuyishan Shi	武夷山市	*wǔyíshān shì*
Yingzui Yan	鹰嘴岩	*yīngzuǐ yán*
Accommodation		
Aihu	矮胡宾馆	*ǎihú bīnguǎn*
Gu Yue	古越山庄	*gǔyuè shānzhuāng*
Jianyi Mountain Villa	建夷山庄	*jiànyí shānzhuāng*
Sunlight	阳光大酒店	*yángguāng dàjiǔdiàn*
Wuyi Mountain Villa	武夷山庄	*wǔyí shānzhuāng*
Wuyi Shan Manting Villa	武夷山幔亭山房	*wǔyíshān màntíng shānfáng*

for a few days, offering clean mountain air and leisurely walks through scenery of lush green vegetation, deep red sandstone mountains, soaring cliff faces, rock pools, waterfalls and caves. Despite the remoteness, Wuyi is surprisingly full of tourists – especially Taiwanese – in high summer, so a visit off season might be preferable, when you'll also see the mountain tops cloaked with snow. Note that all tourists here are regarded as fair game for some serious overcharging.

Practicalities

The sixty-square-kilometre site is bordered by the **Jiuqu** (Nine-Twisting) **River** to the south, which runs its crooked course for some 8km between **Xingcun** village to the west, and the main village in the area, **WUYIGONG** to the east – where it joins the **Chongyang Stream** running from north to south and demarcates the park's eastern border. There is a strip of tourist hotels, restaurants, shops, and bus- and plane-ticket booking offices, along with a **Bank of China** (daily 8am–5.30pm), immediately east of the stream, just before the bridge. Over the bridge 1km or so, Wuyigong lies in the cleft between the junction of the two waterways and contains a bus stop and some hotels.

Most transport arrives 15km north of the scenic area at **WUYISHAN SHI**, the regional town. You can get here by **train** from Fuzhou, Quanzhou or Xiamen, or by **sleeper bus** (¥80) from Fuzhou. The alternative is to **fly** from Fuzhou (¥380 each way), Xiamen and other cities across China; **Wuyi airport** is at the village of **Chishi**, a few kilometres to the northeast of the scenic area and to the south of Wuyishan Shi. Frequent minibuses connect Wuyishan Shi and the airport with Wuyigong. Fuzhou's CTS (see p.555) also runs **tour buses** direct to Wuyigong.

Accommodation and eating

Dujia Qu, as the new development east of the river is known, holds a plethora of identikit places to stay, many with delusions of grandeur. However, hard bargaining (especially outside of summer or weekends) can bring room prices down as much as fifty percent. Generally, the further south you go on the hotel strip, the

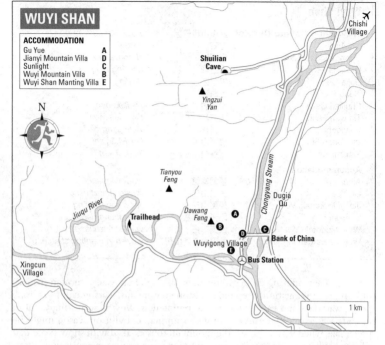

WUYI SHAN

ACCOMMODATION
Gu Yue	A
Jianyi Mountain Villa	D
Sunlight	C
Wuyi Mountain Villa	B
Wuyi Shan Manting Villa	E

Shuilian Cave ▲

Yingzui Yan ▲

N

Tianyou Feng ▲

Chongyang Stream

Jiuqu River

Trailhead

Dawang Feng ▲

Dugia Qu

Ⓐ
Ⓑ

Ⓓ Ⓒ **Bank of China**

Wuyigong Village

Ⓔ

Ⓜ **Bus Station**

Xingcun Village

0 — 1 km

cheaper the accommodation gets; the *Sunlight* (℡0599/5251058; ❹), with its lightly tattered rooms, is one to try if you're looking for a deal. For tranquillity, it's better to cross the river for a couple of quieter, more pleasant options: the *Gu Yue* (℡0599/5252916; ❹) and the *Jianyi Mountain Villa* (℡0599/5252268; ❹). Moving towards Wuyigong, the *Wuyi Mountain Villa* (℡0599/5251888, ℻5252567; ❼) is an upmarket place with a marvellous setting, resting hard under Dawang Feng and built around a Suzhou-style ornamental garden; a little further on, the *Wuyi Shan Manting Villa* (℡0599/5252214, ℻5252763; ❺) is less smart, but enjoys good views. Wuyishan Shi also has several options on Zhanqian Lu near the train station, from budget *Aihu* (℡0559/5196293; ❷) to the smarter *Dengfeng* (℡0599/5101558; ❻) over the road, though there's little point in staying here unless you have to.

Foodwise, it's the local Shilin frogs that make **Wuyi cuisine** special; along with other popular dishes such as bamboo shoots and fungus, they're served almost everywhere. To get out of the hotel restaurants and eat with the locals, try the take-away stalls in the villages – the fried egg and pork cakes are particularly tasty.

The Thirty-Six Peaks

There is a series of trails heading north into the mountains from the main trail-head area at the base of **Tianyou Feng** (Heavenly Tour Peak), about halfway between Xingcun and Wuyigong. Minibuses, motorcycle taxis and taxis all run here. It costs a ruinous ¥62–111 to enter the trails, depending on how much of the area you want to see, though it is possible to avoid this charge by walking

FUJIAN, GUANGDONG AND HAINAN ISLAND

△ Jiuqu River, Wuyi Shan

Bamboo-raft trips

The traditional, and still the best, way to appreciate the Wuyi Shan area is to take a leisurely two-hour **bamboo-raft trip** along the Jiuqu River. The rafts leave daily between 7.30am and 2.30pm all year round, and you can pick one up more or less anywhere on the river. A ticket for the full duration will cost you ¥98, including bus transport. From the first crook in the meandering river right up to the ninth, you'll have stupendous gorge scenery all the way. The odd, boat-shaped **coffins** in caves you can glimpse above the fourth crook are said to be 4000 years old, and appear similar to those in Guangxian and along the Little Three Gorges in Sichuan (see p.917 and p.931).

a little downstream and looking for a path cut into the rock. The **mountains** look quite large and imposing, but in fact are relatively easy to climb. The summit of Tianyou Feng is no more than a thirty-minute clamber away from the ticket office. The best time to get up here is early morning, when you can catch the sunrise and watch the mists clear to reveal a good view of the nine crooks in the Jiuqu River. There are a number of tiny pavilions and **tea gardens** on the lower slopes, should you need sustenance on the way up. **Tea** is a huge institution in Fujian, and Wuyi Shan is famous as the original home of **Oolong**, one of the few types known by name in the West. Leaves for Oolong are picked when mature, then processed by alternate bruising, fermenting and airing before being fire-dried; one of the best varieties is the widely available *tie guanyin cha*, or Iron Buddha Tea.

Another peak well worth the ascent is **Dawang Feng** (King of Peaks) at the easternmost end of the river, north of Wuyigong, and more of a gentle walk than a climb (2hr). If you have time, try to get to the **Shuilian Cave**, about 6km north of the river; you can walk along easy trails or take a minibus from the Tianyou Feng area or from Wuyigong. The cave is about halfway up a cliff of red sandstone, down which a large waterfall cascades in the summer months. You can sit in the adjacent teahouse, cut out of the rock, while the waterfall literally crashes down beside you (watch out for a heavy charge at the entrance to the cave, though). The walk between the cave and river passes tea plantations, more teahouses and all kinds of little sights, including **Yingzui Yan** (Eagle Beak Crag), whose main point of interest is the walkways leading to a set of caves where, during the Taiping Uprising, local bigwigs fled to escape persecution.

Quanzhou and around

I tell you that for one shipload of pepper which may go to Alexandria or to other places, to be carried into Christian lands, there come more than one hundred of them to this port.

Thus wrote Marco Polo when he visited **QUANZHOU**, then called Zaytoun (from the Arabic word for olive, symbol of peace and prosperity), in the late thirteenth century. At this time, Quanzhou was a great port, one of the two largest in the world, exploiting its deep natural harbour and sitting astride trade routes that reached southeast to Indonesian Maluku, and west to Africa and Europe. It became uniquely cosmopolitan, with tens of thousands of Arabs and Persians settling here, some of them to make colossal fortunes – the Arabs of

Quanzhou and around

Quanzhou	泉州	quánzhōu
Fuwen Miao	府文庙	fǔwén miào
Guandi Miao	关帝庙	guāndì miào
Kaiyuan Si	开元寺	kāiyuán sì
Maritime Museum	海外交通史博物馆	hǎiwàijiāotōngshǐ bówùguǎn
Qingjing Mosque	清净寺	qīngjìng sì
Qingyuan Shan	清源山	qīngyuán shān
Sheng Mu	伊斯兰教圣墓	yīsīlánjiào shèngmù
Tianhou Gong	天后宫	tiānhòu gōng

Accommodation, eating and drinking		
Blue & Sea	蓝海餐厅	lánhǎi cāntīng
Coffee Language	尚典啡茶语	shàngdiǎnfēicháyǔ
Great Wall	长城宾馆	chángchéng bīnguǎn
Gucuo Chadian	古厝茶店	gǔcuò chádiàn
Huaqiao Zhijia	华侨之家	huáqiáo zhījiā
Jianfu	建福商务酒店	jiànfú shāngwù jiǔdiàn
Jinquan	金泉酒店	jīnquán jiǔdiàn
Jinzhou	金州大酒店	jīnzhōu dàjiǔdiàn
Korean Restaurant	度彼岸韩国料理	dùbǐ'àn hánguó liàolǐ
Qiwei Yazai	奇味鸭仔	qíwèi yāzǎi
Quanzhou	泉州酒店	quánzhōu jiǔdiàn

Anping Bridge	安平桥	ānpíng qiáo

Chongwu	崇武古城	chóngwǔ gǔchéng

Shishi	石狮	shíshī
Sisters-in-law Tower	姑嫂塔	gūsǎo tǎ

Quanzhou are also believed responsible for introducing to the West the Chinese inventions of the compass, gunpowder and printing.

The Song and Yuan dynasties saw the peak of Quanzhou's fortunes, when the old Silk Road through northwestern China into Central Asia was falling prey to banditry and war, deflecting trade seawards along the **Maritime Silk Road**. Polo was by no means the only European to visit Quanzhou around this time: the Italian **Andrew Perugia**, Quanzhou's third Catholic bishop, died here in 1332, having supervised the building of a cathedral; and fourteen years later the great Moroccan traveller **Ibn Battuta** saw the port bustling with large junks. But by the Qing era, the city was suffering from overcrowding and a decaying harbour, and an enormous **exodus** began, with people seeking new homes in Southeast Asia. According to Chinese government statistics, there are more than two million Quanzhounese living abroad today – which compares to just half a million remaining in the entire municipal area. Despite these depredations of history, Quanzhou today retains several reminders of its glorious past, and it's certainly worth a stopover between Fuzhou and Xiamen.

The Town and around

Quanzhou is a small, prosperous town, located entirely on the northeast bank of the Jin River, and the majority of its sights can be reached on foot. The two major north–south streets are Zhongshan Lu and Wenling Lu. The town centre falls mainly between these two, with the oldest part of town to the west and up along the northern section of Zhongshan Lu, where you'll find attractively restored, colonial-era arcaded streets, lined with trees and packed with pedestrians and cyclists. As in Fuzhou, there are plenty of minor temples scattered around, perhaps the best of which is **Tianhou Gong** (¥4), a large airy hall at the southern end of Zhongshan Lu, crammed with worshippers asking help from southeastern China's most popular deity, the Heavenly Empress.

One of the town centre's most interesting areas lies north off **Tumen Jie**, Quanzhou's main east–west street, which sports a surprisingly well-integrated collection of genuine antique buildings and modern shops with traditional flourishes. Heading northwest up Tumen Jie from its junction with Wenling Lu, you'll first encounter **Guandi Miao**, a splendid temple dedicated to the Three Kingdoms' hero turned god of war and healing, Guan Yu (see p.474). The temple's roofline is typically florid and curly, and the atmospheric interior – guarded by life-sized statues of soldiers on horseback – features low-ceilinged halls, smoke-grimed statues and wall engravings showing scenes from Guan Yu's life.

Almost the next building along, the granite-built **Qingjing Mosque** (daily 8am–5pm; ¥3) provides firm evidence of just how established the Arabs became in medieval Quanzhou. Founded by Arab settlers in 1009 and rebuilt by Persian Muslims three centuries later, Qingjing ranks as one of the oldest mosques in China and is highly unusual in being Middle Eastern in design, though only parts of the original buildings survive. The tall gate tower is said to be an exact copy of a Damascus original, its leaf-shaped archway embellished with

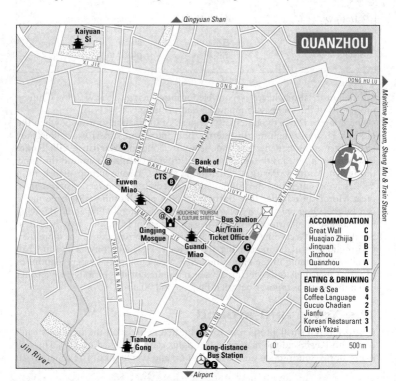

▲ Qingyuan Shan

Kaiyuan Si

XI JIE

DONG JIE

DONG HU LU

ZHONGSHAN ZHONG LU

NANJUN LU

WENLING LU

Bank of China

DAXI JIE

CTS

Fuwen Miao

JIUYI JIE

JIUYI JIE

TUMEN JIE

HOUCHENG TOURISM & CULTURE STREET

Bus Station

Qingjing Mosque

Air/Train Ticket Office

Guandi Miao

ZHONGSHAN NAN LU

QUANZHOU

N

Maritime Museum, Sheng Mu & Train Station

ACCOMMODATION	
Great Wall	C
Huaqiao Zhijia	D
Jinquan	B
Jinzhou	E
Quanzhou	A

EATING & DRINKING	
Blue & Sea	6
Coffee Language	4
Gucuo Chadian	2
Jianfu	5
Korean Restaurant	3
Qiwei Yazai	1

Jin River

Tianhou Gong

Long-distance Bus Station

WENLING LU

0   500 m

▼ Airport

fourteenth-century Arabic calligraphy and designs, while parts of the walls and supporting pillars of the original prayer hall stand alongside. A side room has a detailed account of the Arab presence in Quanzhou, with an English translation; the small tiled building next door is the modern prayer hall. The Houcheng Tourism and Culture Street behind the mosque is a good place to pick up souvenirs.

West between Qingjing Mosque and Zhongshan Lu, an ornamental gateway leads north to a broad paved square, at the back of which is a Confucian temple, **Fuwen Miao**. This isn't of great importance, but the square is dotted with freshly restored examples of Quanzhou's **traditional domestic architecture**, all built of granite blocks and characteristic red bricks marked with dark chevrons, the roof ridges pulled up into projecting forks.

Kaiyuan Si

Quanzhou's most impressive historical remains are at **Kaiyuan Si**, a huge, restful temple dotted with magnificent trees in the northwest of town on Xi Jie (daily 7.30am–5.30pm; ¥10). Bus #2 runs up here from the long-distance bus station, but it's much more interesting to follow the backstreets from the Tumen Jie/Zhongshan Lu intersection, through narrow lanes lined with elderly homes. Founded in 686 AD, Kaiyuan was built, legend has it, after the owner of a mulberry grove dreamed of a Buddhist monk who asked him to erect a place of worship on his land. "Only if my mulberry trees bear lotus flowers," replied the owner dismissively – whereupon the lotus flowers duly appeared. In memory of this, an ancient mulberry in the temple courtyard bears the sign "Mulberry Lotus Tree". The two five-storey **stone pagodas** were added in the thirteenth century, apart from which the whole complex was rebuilt during the Ming dynasty after being destroyed by fire.

The temple is highly regarded architecturally, not least for its details, which include one hundred stone columns supporting the roof of the **main hall**, most of which are carved with delicate musicians holding instruments or sacrificial objects. Surviving everything from earthquakes to the Red Guards, the unimaginably solid pagodas are also carved on each of their eight sides with two images of the Buddha; inside, one of them has forty Buddhist stories inscribed on its walls. The temple grounds also hold a special **exhibition hall** (¥2) housing the hull of a twelfth- or thirteenth-century **wooden sailing vessel** found in 1974 (a series of photos detail the stages of the excavation), still with the herbs and spices it had been carrying, preserved in its hold.

The Maritime Museum

Across on the northeast side of town on Dong Hu Lu, the **Maritime Museum** (Tues–Sun 8.30am–5.30pm; ¥10; bus #19 from the long-distance bus station) recalls Quanzhou's trading history and illustrates how advanced Chinese shipbuilders were, compared to their European contemporaries. Two floors of exhibits track the development of Chinese boatbuilding, reaching as far back as the Warring States period (around 500 BC). A corner devoted to the "Recovery of Taiwan from the Greedy Grasp of the Dutch Invaders and the Development of Foreign Trade" reinterprets **Koxinga**'s exploits (see p.568) in a modern light, but the museum's heart is hundreds of lovingly made **wooden models**, illustrating everything from small, coastal junks to Zheng He's mighty *Baochuan* – possibly the largest wooden vessel ever made – and ornate pleasure boats used by the wealthy for touring China's famous lakes and rivers.

While you're here, don't miss the first-floor collection of **tombstones** dating back to Quanzhou's heyday. Most of these are Muslim, but you'll also find those of Italians and Spaniards, Nestorian Christians from Syria, and the fourteenth-century Bishop, Andrew Perugia. In the back, stone pillars, lintels and statues show that there were also Hindus and Manicheans (followers of a Persian religion that drew on Christianity, Jainism and Buddhism) in Quanzhou, each with their own places of worship – further proof of the city's cosmopolitan heritage.

Qingyuan Shan and Sheng Mu

A few sites just outside the town warrant the effort of reaching them on local buses. The **Qingyuan Shan** scenic area is 3km to the north, with good views over Quanzhou from small crags and pavilions, though most people come out here for the huge stone **Laojun Yan**, a Song-dynasty sculpture of Laozi which is said to aid longevity if you climb onto its back and rub noses. Bus #3 comes up here from Tumen Jie and Zhongshan Zhong Lu.

East of the town centre on Donghu Jie, **Sheng Mu** is a Muslim cemetery housing the graves of two of Mohammed's disciples sent to China in the seventh century to do missionary work – and so presumably the first Muslims in China. There's little to see, but it's a peaceful, semi-forested place; catch bus #7 from Wenling Lu to the Sheng Mu stop. The entrance can be seen to the south of the road – when you glimpse a stone archway, take the alley leading towards it.

Around Quanzhou

Buses from the long-distance station also run to a handful of sights some way out of town. About 60km east of Quanzhou, **CHONGWU** is an old walled city built entirely of stone, now nicely restored as a huge museum piece. The adjacent new town has one of southern China's largest fishing fleets, with just about every man employed in this industry – the women work in local stone quarries, carting huge rocks around on carrypoles and wearing characteristic blue jackets and wide-brimmed straw hats. Slightly closer to the southeast is the town of **SHISHI** (Stone Lion), from where you can pick up a ride for the 5km to the beautiful **Sisters-in-law Tower**, another Song-dynasty monument, overlooking the sea. Finally, 30km south, just off the expressway to Xiamen and outside the town of Anhai, the spectacular two-kilometre-long, 800-year-old **Anping Bridge** actually crosses a section of sea.

Practicalities

You'll most likely arrive in Quanzhou **by bus** along the coastal expressway between Xiamen and Fuzhou. The **long-distance bus station** is down in the newer, southeastern part of town, just east of Wenling Lu. From here there are frequent minibus connections between 8am and 5.30pm with Xiamen (¥15–40) and Fuzhou (¥35–70), as well as long-distance buses for practically anywhere in southern China, from Ningbo and Hangzhou in the north, to Guangzhou and Shenzhen in the south. Quanzhou's new **train station** is about 5km east down Dong Hu Jie; bus #23 from outside will get you to the long-distance bus station. There's a morning departure to Wuyi Shan, and slow services to Longyan, Yongding and Meizhou; a couple of **ticket offices** in town, just north of the *Great Wall* on Wenling Lu and opposite the *Jinquan Dajiudian*, save trekking out to the station. There's also a recently constructed **airport** about 20km southeast of town, from which you'll need to take a taxi. For all bookings, either try your accommodation, or the **CTS office** near the *Jinquan* on Daxi Jie. The **Bank of China** (Mon–Fri 8am–5.30pm) is on Nanjun Lu, while the enormous **post office** (Mon–Sat 8am–8pm) is on Wenling Lu. There are several **Internet cafés** in the lane north of the Qingjing Mosque and more on Haogouqian Lu near the *Quanzhou*.

Accommodation

There's not really any budget accommodation available to foreigners, but the following hotels all offer a good deal.

Great Wall Wenling Lu ☎0595/22171688, ⓕ2288965. Excellent value, good location and friendly staff. ➍

Huaqiao Zhijia Southern end of Wenling Lu ☎0595/22175395, ⓕ22175385. Spacious and comfortable rooms, if slightly threadbare. ➌

Jinquan (aka Golden Fountain) Baiyuan Lu ☎0595/22171361, ⓕ22281676. Situated on a small road leading south from Daxi Jie, this is the budget wing of the adjacent *Huaqiao*

Dasha. The rooms have recently been renovated. ➍

Jinzhou Around the corner from the long-distance bus station, on Quanxiu Lu ☎0595/22586788, ⓕ22581011. Reasonably smart and comfortable place, convenient for the bus station. ➏

Quanzhou Zhuangfu Xiang ☎0595/22289958, ⓦwww.quanzhouhotel.com. Semi-luxurious establishment right in the centre of town, just west of Zhongshan Lu. Old wing ➐, new wing ➑

Eating and drinking

For **food**, northern Zhongshan Lu, the area around Kaiyuan Si, and backstreets off Tumen Jie are thick with cheap noodle stalls and canteens. Light meals can be had at the spotless, good-value *Blue & Sea* canteen, next to the *Jinzhou*, for around ¥12. For something slightly more upmarket, try a barbecue at the *Korean Restaurant* (best in a group), near the *Great Wall* on Wenling Jie, or head north of the Bank of China on Nanjun Lu to *Qiwei Yazai*, a roast-duck restaurant. The *Jianfu* serves weekend all-you-can-eat breakfast *dim sum* (¥15 a person) on the fifth floor.

For Western food, there are the ubiquitous fast-food chains and Tumen Jie hosts several **cafés** serving sandwiches and grills, including a branch of *Coffee Language* at the corner with Wenling Lu, while the *Quanzhou* has a Western-style restaurant. For something more traditional, *Gucuo Chadian* is a **teahouse** in an old brick home, in the lane directly behind Qingjing Mosque.

Xiamen

XIAMEN, traditionally known in the West as **Amoy**, is smaller and much prettier than the provincial capital Fuzhou. It also offers a lot more to see, its streets and buildings, attractive shopping arcades and bustling seafront boasting a nineteenth-century European flavour. One of China's most tourist-friendly cities, Xiamen is, in addition, the cleanest and, perhaps, most tastefully renovated city you'll see anywhere in the country, giving it the feel of a holiday resort, despite the occasional seedy, fishy backstreet. Compounding the resort atmosphere is the wonderful little island of **Gulangyu**, a ten-minute ferry ride to the southwest, the old colonial home of Europeans and Japanese, whose mansions still line the island's traffic-free streets – staying here is highly recommended.

A little history

Xiamen was founded in the mid-fourteenth century and grew in stature under the Ming dynasty, becoming a **thriving port** by the seventeenth century, influenced by a steady and rather secretive succession of Portuguese, Spanish and Dutch fortune-hunters. When invading Manchu armies poured down from

Xiamen and around

Xiamen

Xiamen	厦门	xiàmén
Bailu Dong	白鹿洞	báilù dòng
Huli Shan Paotai	胡里山炮台	húlǐ shān pàotái
Huxiyan	虎溪岩	hǔxī yán
Jinmen	金门	jīnmén
Nanputuo Si	南普陀寺	nánpǔtuó sì
Overseas Chinese Museum	华侨博物馆	huáqiáo bówùguǎn
Wanshi Botanical Gardens	万石植物馆	wànshí zhíwùguǎn
Xiamen University	厦门大学	xiàmén dàxué

Gulangyu

Gulangyu	鼓浪屿	gǔlàng yǔ
Gulangyu Guesthouse	鼓浪屿宾馆	gǔlàngyǔ bīnguǎn
Haoyue Garden	皓月园	hàoyuè yuán
Koxinga Memorial Hall	郑成功纪念馆	zhèngchénggōng jìniànguǎn
Lizhi Dao	丽之岛酒店	lìzhīdǎo jiǔdiàn
Luzhou	绿洲酒店	lǜzhōu jiǔdiàn
Marine Garden	海上花园酒店	hǎishàng huāyuán jiǔdiàn
Piano Museum	鼓浪屿钢琴博物馆	gǔlàngyǔ gāngqín bówùguǎn
Shuzhuang Garden	菽庄花园	shūzhuāng huāyuán
Statue of Koxinga	郑成功塑像	zhèngchénggōng sùxiàng
Sunlight Rock	日光岩	rìguāng yán
Underwater World Xiamen	海底世界	hǎidǐ shìjiè
Yingxiong Shan	英雄山	yīngxióng shān

Downtown accommodation and eating

City	厦门宾馆	xiàmén bīnguǎn
Donghai	东海大厦酒店	dōnghǎi dàshà jiǔdiàn
Gongde Caiguan	功德菜馆	gōngdé càiguǎn
Holiday Inn	假日皇冠海景大酒店	jiàrì huángguàn hǎijǐng dàjiǔdiàn
Huaqiao	华侨宾馆	huáqiáo bīnguǎn
Jiaotong	交通大厦酒店	jiāotōng dàshà jiǔdiàn
Lujiang	鹭江宾馆	lùjiāng bīnguǎn
Wenxinge Café	文心阁	wénxīn gé
Xiamen Spring Sunlight	厦门春光酒店	xiàmén chūnguāng jiǔdiàn
Yoso Café	雅舍咖啡	yǎshè kāfēi
Ze He Huang	黄则和花生汤店	huángzéhé huāshēng tāngdiàn

the north in the seventeenth century, driving out the Ming, Xiamen became a centre of resistance for the old regime. The pirate and self-styled **Prince Koxinga** (also known as Zheng Chenggong) led the resistance before being driven out to set up his last stronghold in Taiwan – incidentally, deposing the Dutch traders who were based there – where he eventually died before Taiwan, too, was taken by the Manchus. Koxinga's exploits have been heavily romanticized and reinterpreted over the years, and today his recapturing of Taiwan from unfriendly forces is used both to justify China's claims on its neighbour, and also to provide an example of how to pursue those claims.

A couple of hundred years later, the **British** arrived, increasing trade and establishing their nerve centre on Gulangyu; the manoeuvre was formalized with the Treaty of Nanjing in 1842. By the start of the twentieth century, Xiamen, with its offshore foreigners, had become a relatively prosperous community, supported partly by a steady turnover in trade and by the trickling back of wealth from the city's emigrants who, over the centuries, had continued to swell in numbers. This happy state of affairs continued until the **Japanese invasion** at the beginning of World War II.

The end of the war did not bring with it a return to the good old days, however. The **arrival of the Communists** in 1949, and the final escape to Taiwan by Chiang Kaishek with the remains of his Nationalist armies, saw total chaos around Xiamen, with thousands of people streaming across the straits in boats to escape the Communist advance. In the following years, the threat of war was constant, as mainland armies manoeuvred in preparation for the final assault on Taiwan, and, more immediately, on the smaller islands of Jinmen and Mazu (known in the West as Quemoy and Matsu), which lie only just off the mainland, within sight of Xiamen.

Today the wheel of history has come full circle. Although Jinmen and Mazu are still in the hands of the Nationalists, the threat of conflict with Taiwan has been subsumed by the promise of colossal economic advantage. In the early 1980s, Xiamen was declared one of China's first **Special Economic Zones** and, like Shenzhen on the border with Hong Kong, the city has entered a period of unprecedented boom. At present, there is a **direct passenger ferry** as well as freight services between Taiwan – they are only for Taiwanese with businesses in China, but in future it appears that domestic tourists may gain more access to Taiwan, albeit within a tightly controlled set of rules, and only arriving by air.

Arrival and transport

Joined to the mainland by a five-kilometre-long causeway, the island on which Xiamen stands is located inside a large inlet on the southeastern coast of Fujian. The built-up area occupies the western part of the island, which faces the mainland, while the eastern part faces onto Taiwanese Jinmen Island. The areas of most interest are the **old town** in the far southwest, and **Gulangyu Island** just offshore. The remainder of the city is the Special Economic Zone, which stretches away to the east and the north, and to the causeway back to the mainland.

The main north–south road, passing through the centre of the old town, is Siming Lu, which is crossed from east to west by Zhongshan Lu, the main shopping street. Xiamen's **train station**, connected by city buses #3 and #7, is on **Xiahe Lu**, about 4km east from the seafront. There are several **long-distance bus stations**; you'll most likely end up either 2km northeast of the centre on Hubin Nan Lu (exit the station, turn right and it's 100m to the stop for city bus #23 to the seafront), or about 200m north of the train station. The most central arrival point, the **Heping Ferry Terminal**, served by boats from Hong Kong, is fifteen minutes' walk south along the seafront from the *Lujiang*. Twelve kilometres to the north of town, Xiamen's **airport** is connected to the waterfront area by bus #27.

Buses cover the city and are fast, regular and cheap – rides cost ¥1–2. **Taxis** are also plentiful, costing upwards of ¥8 to hire. **Maps** of the city (¥5) are sold by vendors near the Gulangyu ferry terminal and outside the stations.

Accommodation

There's a good choice of accommodation in Xiamen, from mid-range to luxurious. Some of the nicest hotels (and the cheapest one that takes foreigners) are on Gulangyu Island, although you'll have to carry your own luggage here, as there are no buses or taxis. The wonderful peace and quiet of the island more

Xiamen is well placed for bus and plane connections; rail lines – as usual in Fujian – are a bit unsatisfactory, though you've also the option of catching a boat to Hong Kong.

By air

Flights link Xiamen with Wuyi Shan, Fuzhou, Guangzhou and several other cities in eastern China; see Listings, p.575, for airline offices and travel agents.

By train

Rail lines run north from Xiamen to **Wuyi Shan** and **Jiangxi province**, and west into **Guangdong province** via **Longyan**. Services to Fuzhou are very circuitous; it's much faster to take the bus. Buying tickets is not too problematic, though queues are often lengthy (ticket office daily 8.10am–noon, 1.40–6.10pm & 7.20–9.30pm).

By bus

Both bus stations have frequent departures to **Fuzhou** and **Quanzhou** between about 6am and 10pm; several daily to **Longyan** and **Yongding**; and services at least daily to **Guangzhou** and **Shantou**. It's possible that your bus might leave from a station other than the one where you buy your ticket; if this is the case, your ticket will be stamped on the back with a message to that effect in Chinese, and a free shuttle bus will be laid on around half an hour before departure.

By boat

There's a weekly (monthly in winter) service to **Hong Kong** from the Heping Ferry Terminal (☎0592/2022517; daily 8–11.15am & 2.30–5.15pm); berths for the eighteen-hour trip cost anything from ¥385 to ¥2180, depending on whether you want a dorm bed, shared cabin or private suite. As yet, there's no regular service to Jinmen Island in Taiwan; group vessels are chartered as necessary and the option isn't open to Westerners.

---

than compensate for this, however. Wherever you stay, make a point of bargaining – off-season discounts can slash forty percent off advertised rates.

Downtown Xiamen

City Huyuan Lu ☎0592/2053333, ⓦwww.cityhotelxm.com. A modern, ultra-smart place to stay, built up a hillside and overhung by trees, yet not too remote. ❾

Donghai (aka East Ocean) Zhongshan Lu ☎0592/2021111, ⓕ2033264. Pretty much behind the *Lujiang*. A good location and nice rooms. ❽

Holiday Inn Zhenhai Lu, at the junction with Siming Nan Lu ☎0592/2023333, ⓦwww.hi592.com. This has all the usual international facilities. ❾

Huaqiao Xinhua Lu ☎0592/2660888, ⓦwww.xmhqhotel.com.cn. Very smart, modern and well-serviced hotel, with airline agents and CTS conveniently located outside. ❾

Jiaotong Siming Bei Lu ☎0592/2024403, ⓕ2022928. Opposite the Siming Bus Station, there's a garage-like entrance with the reception on the right. It may not look like a hotel, but it's a friendly place that has some acceptable, if shabby, doubles. ❹

Lujiang Zhongshan Lu ☎0592/2022922, ⓦwww.Lujiang-Hotel.com. Occupying a prime site on the seafront in a well-maintained colonial building, this is the ideal place to stay for views over Gulangyu Island. Cheaper twins are rather small; an excellent hotel. ❽

Xiamen Spring Sunlight Haihou Lu ☎0592/2021793, ⓕ2071665. Directly opposite the Gulangyu ferry terminal. In a colonial-faced building, though the interior is blandly modern and spotlessly clean. Good value, given the location. ❻

Gulangyu Island

Lizhi Dao (aka Beautiful Island) 133 Longtou Lu ☎0592/2063309, ⓦwww.lzd-hotel.com. Very convenient place, if suffering minor damp problems; the cheapest rooms are small and airless, but get one with a window and it's fair value. ❸

FUJIAN, GUANGDONG AND HAINAN ISLAND | Xiamen

Luzhou Longtou Lu ☎0592/2065390, ☏2065843. Straight ahead and just on the left from the ferry – the hotel faces a green lawn. Nice views from the more expensive rooms, which also have wooden floors; otherwise a clean, ordinary Chinese hotel. ❹

Marine Garden 27 Tianwei Lu ☎0592/2062588, Ⓦwww.MarineGardenHotel.com. Just above Shuzhuang Garden, this new, plush, mildly garish faux-colonial place has quality rooms, a pool, tennis court and good views over the beach. ❽

The City

The main pleasure in Xiamen, apart from visiting Gulangyu Island, is simply walking the streets of the old city. Starting from the Siming and Zhongshan Lu intersection, there's a pleasant mix of early-twentieth-century facades and clean orderly streets, pavements and shops. At the western end of Zhongshan Lu, where the **seafront** opens up, you'll see the island of Gulangyu right in front, across the water. You can organize boat trips around Jinmen from various places, including the waterfront opposite Zhongshan Lu, Heping Ferry Terminal and Gulangyu. Prices start at ¥96 for an hour and forty minutes – for good views of the Guomindang front line, bring binoculars. For a cheaper trip, go to the Gulangyu ferry terminal, from where there are half-hour tours that circle Gulangyu before dropping you on the island (¥10).

Southeast and east from the town centre there's a thin scattering of tourist sights. On Siming Nan Lu, about 2km south of Zhongshan Lu, you'll find the **Overseas Chinese Museum**, which was being renovated at the time of writing, but is due to re-open in late 2005. This houses collections presented by the huge Fujianese diaspora around the world, including pottery and some exceptional bronzes going back as far as the Shang dynasty, three thousand years ago. On the ground floor is a display of paintings, photographs and relics depicting the life of Chinese people abroad over the centuries.

Another kilometre farther southeast (bus #1 to Xiada, Xiamen University) is the **Nanputuo Si** (daily 5am–6pm; ¥3), a temple built more than a thousand years ago on the southern slopes of Wulao Feng. This is one of China's most organized, modern-looking Buddhist temples, its roofs a gaudy jumble of flying dragons, human figures and multicoloured flowers, and containing among its collection of treasures a set of tablets carved by resistance fighters at the time of the early Qing, recording Manchu atrocities. Inside the main hall, behind the Maitreya Buddha, is a statue of Wei Tuo, the deity responsible for Buddhist doctrine, who holds a stick pointing to the ground – signifying that the monastery is wealthy and can provide board and lodging for itinerants. The temple today is very active and has a **vegetarian restaurant** (see p.575).

Immediately south of Nanputuo stands **Xiamen University**, and a few laid-back cafés that cater to students and the odd expat. From here you can cut through to Daxue Lu, the coastal road, which runs past attractive sandy beaches. A kilometre or so southwest is **Huli Shan Paotai** (Huli Mountain Gun Emplacement), at the terminus of bus #2. This nineteenth-century hunk of German heavy artillery had a range of 10km and was used during the Qing dynasty to fend off foreign imperialists. You can rent binoculars here to look across to **Jinmen**, which lies less than 20km to the west. Until 1984, because of the close proximity of Taiwan, this whole area was out of bounds, and the beaches were under a dusk-till-dawn curfew.

A lengthy hike (at least 2hr) from Nanputuo takes you from inside the temple grounds, up and over the forested Wulao Shan behind the temple – otherwise, catch bus #17 from the little street outside Nanputuo's entrance. Either way, you'll arrive at **Wanshi Botanical Gardens** (daily 6.30am–6.30pm; ¥20), where a stock of 4000 varieties of plant life includes a redwood tree brought here by President Nixon on his official visit to China. From the botanical

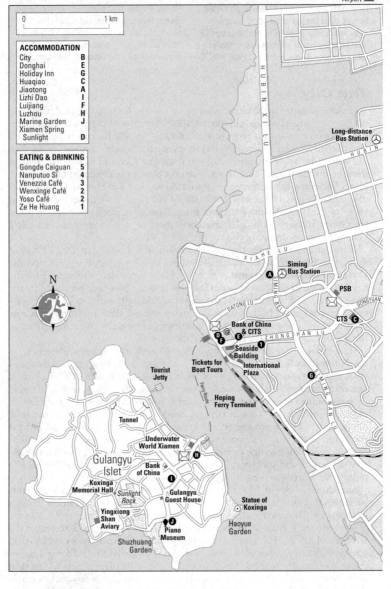

ACCOMMODATION
City   B
Donghai   E
Holiday Inn   G
Huaqiao   C
Jiaotong   A
Lizhi Dao   I
Luijiang   F
Luzhou   H
Marine Garden   J
Xiamen Spring
  Sunlight   D

EATING & DRINKING
Gongde Caiguan   5
Nanputuo Si   4
Venezzia Café   3
Wenxinge Café   2
Yoso Café   2
Ze He Huang   1

gardens' north (main) gate, you cross a rail line to reach the **Revolutionary Martyrs' Memorial**, about 1500m west of the town centre, near the #4 bus route. Southwest of here, along the rail line, is the **Huxiyan** (Tiger Stream Rock) on your right, built up high on a rocky hillside. If you climb up you'll find a great little temple nestling here amid a pile of huge boulders, and you can actually slip through a cave to one side and climb rock-hewn steps to the

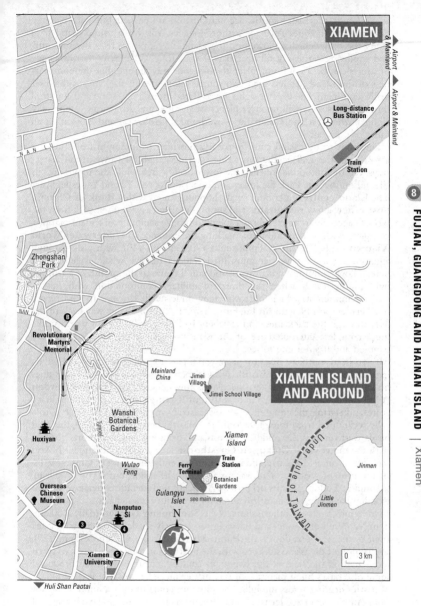

XIAMEN

Airport & Mainland
Airport & Mainland

Long-distance
Bus Station

Train
Station

XIAHE LU

WENYUAN LU

NAN LU

Zhongshan
Park

NAN LU

B

Revolutionary
Martyrs'
Memorial

Wanshi
Botanical
Gardens

Jimei

Huxiyan

Wulao
Feng

Overseas
Chinese
Museum

Nanputuo
Si

2   3   4

Xiamen
University   5

▼ Huli Shan Paotai

**XIAMEN ISLAND
AND AROUND**

Mainland
China   Jimei
Village
Jimei School Village

Xiamen
Island

Under rule of Taiwan

Train
Station

Ferry
Terminal   Botanical
Gardens
Gulangyu
Islet   see main map

Jinmen

Little
Jinmen

N

0   3 km

top of the largest boulder. Right up on the hilltop, a second small temple, **Bailu
Dong**, commands spectacular views over the town and the sea.

Gulangyu Island

Gulangyu Island was Xiamen's foreign concession until World War II, and
architecturally it remains more or less intact from that time. In summer and

at weekends, the island and its accommodation are packed, but with battery-powered golf-buggies (¥10 for a short journey, ¥50 for a round-island trip) being the only vehicles allowed on the island, the atmosphere is always restful, and exploring can easily fill up a day of your time. Gulangyu's narrow tangle of streets can be a confusing place to find your way around, but the compactness of the island (it's less than two square kilometres in size) means this isn't really a problem. The various sights are scattered around the island and any stroll through the streets will uncover plenty of architectural attractions – especially along Fuzhou Lu and Guxin Lu – overhung with flowers and blossom at all times of the year.

The **boat** to the island runs from early morning to midnight from the pier across from the *Lujiang*, the short ride offering delightful views of the waterways. On the outbound journey the lower deck is free while the upper deck is ¥1, and on the way back the lower and upper decks cost ¥3 and ¥4 respectively. The **island centre** – a knot of small shopping streets with a **Bank of China**, a **post office**, a few **restaurants** and shops – is ahead as you disembark from the ferry. Diagonally to your right is a splendid bronze sculpture of a giant octopus, complete with suckers and beak, marking the entrance to **Underwater World Xiamen** (daily 9.30am–4.30pm; adults ¥70, children ¥40), with walk-through aquariums, seal displays, penguins, turtles and a massive whale skeleton. Past here, follow Sanming Lu northwest and you'll come to the mouth of a **tunnel**, built in the 1950s when the threat of military confrontation with Taiwan seemed imminent, which burrows right underneath the hill to Gulangyu's northern end on Neicuo Ao Lu. From here, try and find your way back to the jetty through the backlanes – an excellent half-hour walk. It's not worth walking a complete circumference of the island though, as the northwest is very exposed and has nothing to see.

If you head southeast from the jetty, you'll pass a number of grand old buildings, including the former British and German consulates. The road continues on to the island's rocky eastern headland, now enclosed by **Haoyue Garden** (¥15), containing a gigantic granite **statue of Koxinga** dressed in grand military attire and staring meaningfully out towards Taiwan, the island he once heroically recaptured from foreign colonialists. Shortly beyond the garden, the road heads west towards the middle of the island, bringing you to a sports ground, with the old colonial **Gulangyu Guesthouse** facing onto it. President Nixon stayed here on his 1972 trip, and it was, until recently, the haunt of Chinese VIPs. At the time of writing, there was no access to the inside, but if you do get in, the middle building has its original 1920s decor and furniture intact, with dark wooden panelling, a billiard hall and a terrace with rattan chairs.

Due south, on the southern shore, is the **Shuzhuang Garden** (daily 6.30am–8pm; ¥20), full of flowers and boasting some nicely shaded areas for taking tea right by the sea. Next door is the **Piano Museum** (daily 8.15am–5.15pm; ¥20), a reflection of the island's history with the instrument; foreigners began to teach locals here at the start of the twentieth century and the island has produced some of China's finest pianists – if you stay, chances are you'll hear the tinkling of ivories drifting across the hills. The museum contains over a hundred pianos from Austria, France, Germany and Britain, including the odd Steinway and apparently the world's tallest upright piano.

The clean, sandy **beach** running west from the park is very tempting for swimming when it's not too packed out. It's overlooked to the north by the **Sunlight Rock** (daily 6am–8pm; ¥60 includes cable-car ride), the highest point on Gulangyu (93m) and something of a magnet for the large numbers of local tourists who take a cable car up to the platform for the views right over the entire island. At the foot of the rock (and covered by the same entrance ticket) is the **Koxinga Memorial Hall**, which contains various relics, including Koxinga's own jade belt and bits of his "imperial" robe; unfortunately there are no English captions. Follow the path along the coast from here – a beautiful walk on a bright day – and you pass below **Yingxiong Shan**, the top of which is enclosed in netting as an open-air **aviary** (included in Sunlight Rock ticket price), thick with tropical pigeons, egrets and parrots. You can buy a **multi-ticket** for entry to Haoyue and Shuzhuang Gardens, Sunlight Rock and Yingxiong Shan for ¥80.

Eating and drinking

Food is one of Xiamen's assets, with plenty of fresh **fish and seafood**, particularly oysters, crabs and prawns. The best place to try some is in restaurants around Gulangyu's market area or the backstreets behind the *Donghai*, but make sure you establish a price in advance: the seafood is usually sold by weight, not per portion. Otherwise the city centre is thick with places to eat: for **peanut buns and soups** (another regional speciality) check out *Ze He Huang*, a crowded, noisy canteen on Zhongshan Lu. Nanputuo Si's **vegetarian restaurant** is expensive for what you get, with set meals at ¥30–80, depending on the number of dishes you want; across from the temple and near the University, *Gongde Caiguan* is another, cheaper, vegetarian option. A few student-oriented **cafés** around here offer Chinese and Western food, beers and cocktails, in a relaxed atmosphere with outdoor seating – try *Yoso*, *Wenxinge*, or *Venezzia*. The *Holiday Inn* also has a lobby café charging ¥58 for a pot of coffee, with accompanying cookies.

Listings

Airlines Air China, *Huguang Dasha*, Hubin Dong Lu ☏0592/5084382; Dragon Air, 8 Jianye Lu ☏0592/5117702; China Eastern, 311 Siming Nan Lu ☏0592/2028936; Malaysian Airlines, *Holiday Inn* ☏0592/2023333; Philippine Airlines, *Marco Polo Hotel*, Jianye Lu ☏0592/2394729; Silk Air, International Plaza ☏0592/2053257; Thai Airways, International Plaza ☏0592/2261688.
Banks and exchange There are branches of the Bank of China on Gulangyu Island and on Zhongshan Lu, back from the seafront (Mon–Fri 8.30am–noon & 2.30–5pm, Sat 8am–12.30pm).
Consulates Philippines, near the geographic centre of Xiamen on Lianhua Bei Lu (☏0592/5130355).

Internet access There are several Internet bars in the lane directly north of the *Donghai*, parallel with Datong Lu.
Mail and telephones Xiamen's main post office, where IDD telephone calls can also be made, is on the seafront, just north of the *Xiamen Spring Sunlight*, and there's another large branch on Xinhua Lu, south of the junction with Siming Dong Lu.
PSB Across from the Post Office on Gongyuan Nan Lu ☏0592/2262203.
Travel agents CTS, *Huaqiao Hotel*, Xinhua Lu ☏0592/2025602; Xiamen Tourism Group, *Lujiang* ☏0592/2029933.

Southwestern Fujian: the Hakka homelands

Fujian's hilly southwestern border with Guangdong is an area central to the **Hakka**, a Han subgroup known to locals as *kejia* (guest families) and to nineteenth-century Europeans as "China's gypsies". Originating in the Yangzi basin

Southwestern Fujian		
Yongding	永定	*yǒngdìng*
Dongfu Jiudian	东府酒店	*dōngfǔ jiǔdiàn*
Jiari Lüguan	假日旅馆	*jiàrì lǚguǎn*
Tianhe Lüguan	天河旅馆	*tiānhé lǚguǎn*
Chengqi	乘启	*chéngqǐ*
Gaotou Lou	高头楼	*gāotóu lóu*
Hukeng	湖坑	*húkēng*
Zhencheng Lou	振城楼	*zhènchéng lóu*
Longyan	龙岩	*lóngyán*

during the third century and dislodged ever southward by war and revolution, the Hakka today form large communities both here and in Hong Kong and Hainan Island. They managed to retain their original languages and customs by remaining aloof from their neighbours in the lands in which they settled, a habit that caused resentment and led to their homes being well defended. While towns up this way are mostly unattractive, the countryside is pretty in spring, and villages and hamlets around the focal city of **Yongding** sport fortress-like **Hakka mansions** built of stone and adobe, the largest of which are three storeys high, circular and house entire clans.

If you can't find direct transport from coastal Fujian, aim first for **LONGYAN**, a small city 170km northwest of Xiamen, where roads and separate rail lines from Fuzhou, Quanzhou and Xiamen converge to head west to Meizhou in Guangdong (see p.631). From the **train station** on the eastern edge of town, catch bus #14 over three bridges to Longzhou Xi Lu and the **long-distance bus station**, 2km away and just south of Longyan's centre. Here you'll be mobbed by minibus drivers for the final sixty-kilometre, hour-long run south-west to Yongding (¥10), through several Hakka towns marked by large, mud-brick mansions and inevitably surrounded by cement factories.

Yongding and around

Set on the edge of a flat river basin, **YONGDING** is an old town, today recast as a heavily built-up, typically ugly place, whose residents are nevertheless very friendly towards the few foreigners who make it up here. The road from Longyan ends up at a **roundabout**, where you'll find the **bus station** and decent, if forgettable and slightly noisy, **accommodation** options. The best of these is the *Dongfu Jiudian* (☎0957/5830668; ❸), which has clean, pleasant rooms and helpful staff, while nearby *Jiari Lüguan* (❷) and *Tianhe Lüguan* (☎0597/5835769; ❷) aren't quite as comfortable. From here, the main street runs north over the river and into town; on the far bank, Huangcheng Dong Lu forks left after 100m into a market area, while steps on the right climb a ridge to a park, with views across town and the countryside. If you carry straight on you'll reach the Bank of China. **Places to eat** surround the bus-station area and main streets; you'll find all sorts of rice noodles, snacks, and **kourou**, a Hakka dish made from slices of soya-braised pork belly on a bed of bitter kale. **Leaving**, there are daily buses to Meizhou in Guangdong, and Xiamen, as well as minibuses through the day back to Longyan, and at least as far east as Hukeng village.

Hukeng and Zhencheng Lou

An hour's bus ride east of Yongding via the crossroads town of **Zhiling**, you'll find what is considered the most perfect **Hakka roundhouse**, 5km north of **HUKENG** village. Known as **Zhencheng Lou**, this century-old home is now a well-maintained if slightly sterile tourist attraction (¥25): plain and forbidding on the outside, the huge outer wall encloses three storeys of galleried rooms looking inwards to a central courtyard where guests were entertained, and which contained the clan shrine. The galleries are vertically divided into eight segments by thick **fire walls**, a plan that intentionally turns the building into a giant **bagua**, Taoism's octagonal symbol. This powerful design occurs everywhere in the region, along with demon-repelling **mirrors** and other Taoist motifs. An almost disastrous consequence of roundhouse design – which from above looks like a ring – was that (so locals say) the first US satellite photos of the region identified the houses as missile silos.

The hamlet surrounding Zhencheng is quite attractive in itself, with other, more "authentic", houses (all still lived in) laid out along a small stream. Those worth investigating include a 1920s schoolhouse; **Fuyu Lou**, the old *yamen* building; **Rushen**, one of the smallest multistorey roundhouses; and **Kuijiu**, a splendid, 160-year-old square-sided Hakka mansion, its interior like a temple squeezed into a box. There's also a small, white-tiled roundhouse **hotel** (❷) clearly visible near Zhencheng Lou, and locals may invite you to stay in a room in their home for around ¥40. You might ask about getting 20km farther north to **Chengqi**, where **Gaotou Lou** is the largest roundhouse of them all, built in 1709 and currently home to more than a thousand people in its six hundred rooms.

Heading on **to Guangdong** from Hukeng, catch transport back to Zhiling, which lies on the junction of roads to Guangdong from Longyan and Yongding, from where you should be able to flag down buses for the five-hour trip to Meizhou (see p.631) or Dapu (see p.633) until mid-morning.

Guangdong

Halfway along **Guangdong**'s eight-hundred-kilometre coastline, rivers from all over the province and beyond disgorge themselves into the South China Sea, through the tropically fertile **Pearl River Delta**, one of China's most densely cultivated and developed areas. Perched right at the delta's northern apex and adjacent to both Hong Kong and Macau, the provincial capital **Guangzhou** provides many travellers with their first taste of mainland China. It's not everyone's favourite city, but once you've found your bearings among the busy roads and packed shopping districts, Guangzhou's world-famous **food** merits a stop, as does an assortment of museums, parks and monuments. The Pearl River Delta itself has a few patches of green and some history to pick up in passing, but the major targets are the cities of **Shenzhen** and **Zhuhai**, modern, purpose-built economic buffer zones at the crossings into Hong Kong and Macau.

Farther afield, the rest of the province is more picturesque, with a mass of sights, from Buddhist temples to Stone-Age relics, to slow you down around

Shaoguan, up north by the Hunan and Jiangxi borders. Over in the east near Fujian, the ancient town of **Chaozhou** has well-preserved Ming architecture peppered amongst a warren of narrow streets, while nearby **Meizhou** is a useful stepping stone to the ethnic Hakka heartland, set in the beautiful surrounding countryside. On the way west into Guangxi province, **Zhaoqing** sports pleasant, formalized lakes and hilly landscapes, while those heading towards Hainan need to aim for the ferry port of **Hai'an**, down in Guangdong's southwestern extremities.

Guangdong has a generous quantity of rail and road traffic, and **getting around** is none too difficult, though often requiring some advance preparation. **Rail lines** run north through Shaoguan and up into Hunan and central China, east to Meizhou, Shantou and Fujian, and west through Zhaoqing to Zhanjiang and Guangxi. **River travel** was, until recently, a highlight of the province, though the only easy excursions left are the fast hydrofoils between the Pearl River Delta towns and Hong Kong, and a day-cruise from the northern town of **Qingyuan** to some riverside temples. As for the **climate**, summers can be sweltering across the province, with typhoons along the coast, while winter temperatures get decidedly nippy up in the northern ranges – though it's more likely to be miserably wet than to snow, except around the highest mountain peaks.

Guangzhou

GUANGZHOU, once known to the Western world as **Canton**, was only a decade ago dismissed by many visitors as a nightmare caricature of Hong Kong, one of the most dizzyingly overcrowded, polluted and chaotic places to daunt a newcomer to the country. While the city is still hardly somewhere to come for peace and relaxation, recent improvements have wrought great **changes**: an expanding **metro network** and multiple-layered flyovers are relieving traffic congestion; the waterfront area has been paved and flowerbeds dug wherever possible; old buildings have been scrubbed and restored to public view by demolishing the badly constructed 1950s concrete boxes which obscured them; and the city's **nightlife** is snowballing.

True, Guangzhou's **sights** remain relatively minor, though a fascinating 2000-year-old tomb and palace site complement the obligatory round of temples. Yet the city is an enjoyable place simply to observe the Chinese being themselves. The Cantonese are immediately upfront and, after two thousand years of contact with the outside world, pleasantly indifferent to foreign faces. They're also compulsively garrulous, turning Guangzhou's two famous obsessions – **eating** and **business** – into social occasions, and filling streets, restaurants and buildings with the sounds of *Yueyu*, the Cantonese language. And while the newer districts pass as a blur of chrome and concrete from the inside of your taxi, make your way around on foot through the back lanes and you'll discover a very different city, one of flagstoned residential quarters, tiny collectors' markets, laundry strung on lines between buildings, and homes screened away behind barred wooden gates. Guangzhou has also long been the first place where foreign influences have seeped into the country, often through returning Overseas Chinese, and this is where to watch for the latest fashions and to see how China will interpret alien styles.

It may seem, though, what with the **biannual Trade Fair**, that the emphasis here is towards business rather than tourism – and it's certainly true that commerce is Guangzhou's lifeblood, an ethos inspiring train-station pickpockets and company CEOs alike. In purely practical terms, however, while the city is expensive compared with some parts of China, it's far **cheaper** than Hong Kong, particularly in regard to **onward travel**. Airfares into China are considerably less from Guangzhou than what you'd pay just south of the border, allowing big savings even after you factor in transport from Hong Kong and a night's accommodation.

Some history

Legend tells how Guangzhou was founded by **Five Immortals** riding five rams, each of whom planted a sheaf of rice symbolizing endless prosperity – hence Guangzhou's nickname, **Yang Cheng** (Goat City). Myths aside, a settlement called **Panyu** had sprung up here by the third century BC, when a rogue Qin commander founded the **Nanyue Kingdom** and made it his capital. Remains of a contemporary **shipyard** uncovered in central Guangzhou during the 1970s suggest that the city had contact with foreign lands even then: there were merchants who considered themselves Roman subjects here in 165 AD, and from Tang times, vessels travelled to Middle Eastern ports, introducing **Islam** into China and exporting porcelain to Arab colonies in distant Kenya and Zanzibar. By 1405, Guangzhou's population of foreign traders and Overseas Chinese was so large that the Ming emperor Yongle founded a special quarter for them. When xenophobia later closed the rest of China to outsiders, Guangzhou became the country's main link with the rest of the world.

Restricted though it was, this contact with other nations proved to be Guangzhou's – and China's – undoing. From the eighteenth century, the **British East India Company** used the city as a base from which to purchase silk, ceramics and tea, but became frustrated at the Chinese refusal to accept trade goods instead of cash in return. To even accounts, the company began to import **opium** from India; addiction and demand followed, making colossal profits for the British and the **Co Hong**, their Chinese distributors, but rapidly depleting imperial stocks of silver. In 1839 the Qing government sent the incorruptible Commissioner **Lin Zexu** to Guangzhou with a mandate to stop the drug traffic, which he did by blockading the foreigners into their waterfront quarters and destroying their opium stocks. Britain declared war, and, with a navy partly funded by the opium traders, forced the Chinese to cede five ports (including Guangzhou and Hong Kong) to British control under the **Nanking Treaty** of 1842.

Unsurprisingly, the following century saw Guangzhou develop into a revolutionary cauldron. It was here during the late 1840s that Hong Xiuquan formulated his **Taiping Uprising** (see p.1162), and sixty years later the city hosted a premature attempt by **Sun Yatsen** to kick out China's Qing rulers. When northern China was split by warlords through the 1920s, Sun Yatsen chose Guangzhou as his **Nationalist capital**, while a youthful Mao Zedong and Zhou Enlai flitted in and out between mobilizing rural peasant groups. At the same time, anger at continuing colonial interference in China was channelled by **unionism**, the city's workers becoming notoriously well organized and prone to rioting in the face of outrages perpetrated by the Western powers. However, many of Guangzhou's leftist youth subsequently enrolled in militias and went north to tackle the warlords in the **Northern Expedition**, and so became victims of the 1927 **Shanghai Massacre**, Chiang Kaishek's suppression of the Communists (see p.1163). A Red uprising in Guangzhou that same year, in December, failed, leaving the city's population totally demoralized. Controlled by the Japanese during the war, and the Guomindang afterwards, residents became too apathetic to liberate themselves in 1949, and had to wait for the PLA to do it for them.

Few people would today describe the Cantonese as apathetic, at least when it comes to **business** acumen. Unlike many large, apparently modern Chinese cities, Guangzhou enjoys real wealth and solid infrastructure, its river location and level of development making it in many ways resemble a grittier, rougher-around-the-edges version of Shanghai. Hong Kong's downturn since the handover and Asian financial crisis of the late 1990s has also encouraged southern businesses and wealthy entrepreneurs to relocate to Guangzhou, taking advantage of the mainland's lower costs and better work opportunities. At the same time, Guangzhou is thick with members of China's mobile rural community, many of them living below the poverty line. At any one time, a staggering one million **migrant workers**, many from the backblocks of Jiangxi and Anhui provinces, are based in Guangzhou – forming one fifth of the city's total population.

Orientation

For a city of five million people, Guangzhou is compact and easy to navigate, and readily divides into five uneven areas. **Central** and **Northern Guangzhou** comprise the original city core – still pretty much the geographic centre – north of the river between Renmin Lu in the west and Yuexiu Lu in the east. A modern urban landscape predominates, cut by the city's main arterial roads: **Zhongshan** and **Dongfeng** run east–west, and **Jiefang** and **Renmin** run north–south. These streets are divided up into north, south, east, west and central sections, with the exception of Zhongshan Lu, whose segments are numbered. It's not all relentless modernity and traffic, however: most of Guangzhou's historical sites are located here, along with two sizeable parks, **Yuexiu** and **Liuhua**.

Western Guangzhou, the area west of Renmin Lu, is a thriving shopping and eating district centred on Changshou Lu. This formed a Ming-dynasty overflow from the original city and retains its former street plan, though the narrow back lanes, old houses and markets are also ringed by main roads, such as waterfront **Liuersan Lu**. Right on the river here is the former foreigners' quarter of **Shamian Island**. Over on the south bank, **Honan** was a seedy hotspot during the 1930s, though nowadays it's a smaller version of the Changshou Lu districts, and beginning to grow in popularity.

East of Yuexiu Lu the city opens up, and Zhongshan Lu and Dongfeng Lu are joined by Huanshi Lu as, lined with glassy corporate offices, they run broad and straight through **Eastern Guangzhou** to culminate in the vast, open square and sports stadium at the centre of **Tianhe**. Nightlife is the east's biggest draw – many of Guangzhou's bars are out this way – while a few kilometres to the north is **Baiyun Shan**, a formalized string of hills and parkland just beyond the city proper.

Arrival

The new **Baiyun international airport** lies 20km north of the city centre – there's an **airport bus** to the China Southern offices on Huanshi Zhong Lu for ¥16 and taxis into the centre (¥100). Ferries **from Hong Kong** dock at least a twenty-minute taxi ride southwest of Guangzhou at **Nanhai** (aka Pingzhou), or you can take bus #275 to the main train station.

Currently, the city has two major train stations, although a third, planned to be Asia's largest, is due to be operational in time for the 2008 Olympics. The

Guangzhou arrival and downtown metro stops

Guangzhou	广州	guǎngzhōu
Arrival		
Baiyun Airport	白云机场	báiyún jīchǎng
Guangfo Bus Station	广佛车站	dōngfāng huǒchēzhàn
Guangzhou East Train Station	东方火车站	guǎngzhōu huǒchēzhàn
Guangzhou Train Station	广州火车站	guǎngfó chēzhàn
Liuhua Bus Station	流花客运站	liúhuā kèyùnzhàn
Metro	地铁	dìtiě
Nanhai (Pingzhou) Ferry Terminal	南海（平洲）码头	nánhǎi (píngzhōu) mǎtóu
Provincial Bus Station	省汽车客运站	shěngqìchē kèyùnzhàn
Tianhe Bus Station	天河客运站	tiānhé kèyùnzhàn
Useful metro stops		
Changshou Lu	长寿路	chángshòu lù
Chen Jia Ci	陈家祠	chénjiā cí
Dongshan Kou	东山口	dōngshān kǒu
Gongyuan Qian	公园前	gōngyuán qián
Guangzhou Dong Zhan	广州东站	guǎngzhōu dōngzhàn
Guangzhou Train Station	广州火车站	guǎngzhōu huǒchēzhàn
Haizhu Guangchang	海珠广场	hǎizhū guǎngchǎng
Huang Sha	黄沙	huángshā
Jinian Tang	纪念堂	jìniàntáng
Lieshi Lingyuan	烈士陵园	lièshì língyuán
Nongjiang Suo	农讲所	nóngjiǎng suǒ
Shiergong	市二宫	shì'èrgōng
Yuexiu Park	越秀公园	yuèxiù gōngyuán
Tiyu Xi Lu	体育西路	tǐyù xīlù
Tiyu Zhong Xin	体育中心	tǐyù zhōngxīn
Ximen Kou	西门口	xīmén kǒu
Yangji	杨箕	yángjī

new station is under construction in Shibi, Panyu, and is part of a plan to make Guangzhou capable of handling eighty million passengers a year by 2020.

At the northern end of Renmin Lu, **Guangzhou train station** is the most confrontational place to arrive in town, the vast **square** outside perpetually seething with passengers, hawkers and hustlers. Main-line services from most central, northern and western destinations terminate here. New arrivals exit on the west side of the square, convenient for the metro; for Shamian, take it south three stops to Gongyuan Qian interchange, then catch line #1 south to Huang Sha. **Taxis** and most **city buses** wait over on the east side; buses #5 and #31 will take you down to the Cultural Park near Shamian Island.

Guangzhou's second rail terminus is **Guangzhou East train station**, 5km east of the centre at Tianhe. This is where trains from Shenzhen terminate, along with the Kowloon Express, services from Shantou, Meizhou and western Fujian, and a growing quantity of traffic from central China. From the basement, catch metro line #1 direct to the Huang Sha stop for Shamian Island; for Guangzhou train station, take bus #271 or the metro, changing at Gongyuan Qian. A taxi to the centre costs ¥30–40.

There are several major long-distance bus stations. West of Guangzhou train station on Huanshi Xi Lu, the **provincial bus station** handles arrivals from almost everywhere in the country, with more local traffic often winding up

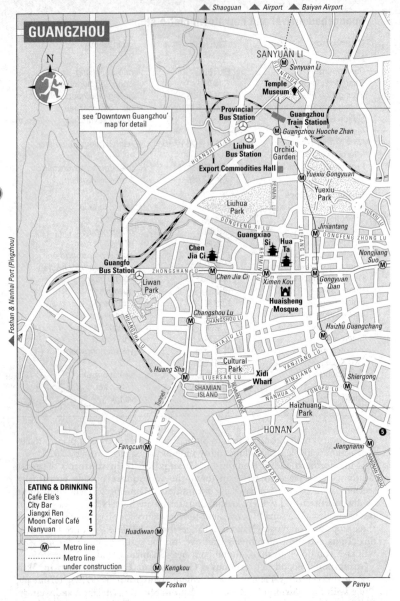

GUANGZHOU

N

▲ Shaoguan   ▲ Airport   ▲ Baiyan Airport

SANYUAN LI

M Sanyuan Li

Temple Museum

Provincial Bus Station

Guangzhou Train Station
M Guangzhou Huoche Zhan

Liuhua Bus Station

Orchid Garden

Export Commodities Hall

Yuexiu Gongyuan

Yuexiu Park

Liuhua Park

DONGFENG XI LU

Jiniantang

DONGFENG ZHONG LU

Guangxiao Si

Chen Jia Ci

Hua Ta

Nongjiang Suo

Guangfo Bus Station

ZHONGSHAN LU M Chen Jia Ci

Ximen Kou

Gongyuan Qian

Liwan Park

Huaisheng Mosque

Changshou Lu M
CHANGSHOU LU

Haizhu Guangchang

XIAJIU LU

Cultural Park

Huang Sha M
LIUERSAN LU

Xidi Wharf

YANJIANG LU

Shiergong

BINJIANG LU

NANHUA LU TONGFU LU

SHAMIAN ISLAND

Haizhuang Park

Tunnel

HONAN

5

Fangcun M

Jiangnanxi

EATING & DRINKING
Café Elle's	3
City Bar	4
Jiangxi Ren	2
Moon Carol Café	1
Nanyuan	5

Huadiwan M

M — Metro line
.... — Metro line under construction

M Kengkou

▼ Foshan   ▼ Panyu

◄ Foshan & Nanhai Port (Pingzhou)

see 'Downtown Guangzhou' map for detail

across the road at one of the number of depots that comprise **Liuhua station**. Buses from eastern Guangdong and central China might terminate out in the northeastern suburbs at **Tianhe bus station**; from here your best bet for reaching the centre is to catch either the shuttle bus to the provincial bus station, or a taxi to Guangzhou East train station and city transport from there – though Tianhe bus station will ultimately also be on a metro line.

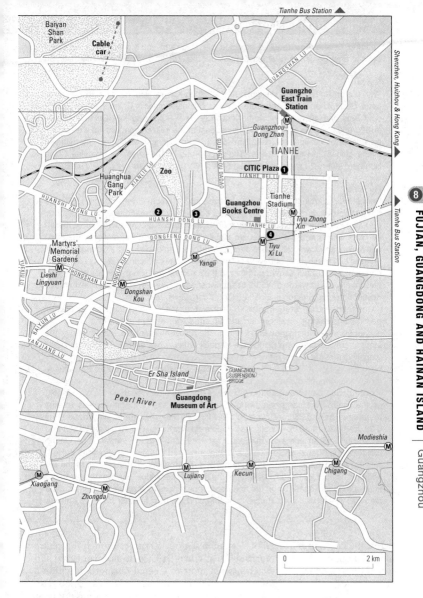

City transport and information

Getting around Guangzhou isn't difficult, though the city is too big to walk everywhere, and bicycles are not recommended because of heavy traffic.

Where possible, it's best to plump for Guangzhou's speedy **metro**. At the time of writing, only **lines #1 and #2** were in operation. Line #1 runs diagonally

Leaving Guangzhou requires advance planning, and you'll generally need a few days to arrange tickets or at least check out the options, especially for the train.

By air

With a brand-new airport designed to rival Hong Kong's, with considerably cheaper fares, Guangzhou is well connected by air to all major cities in China, many in Southeast Asia and increasingly more worldwide. The regional airline, China Southern (℡020/950333), has its headquarters just east of the train station, with its well-organized ticket office upstairs (daily 9am–6pm). See "Listings", p.605, for international airline offices and travel agents. The airport bus (¥16) leaves from outside China Southern (every 20 minutes between 5am and 11pm), or there are taxis (¥100).

By train

Demand for all train tickets out of Guangzhou is very high. Tickets become available three days before departure, but sleepers sell out swiftly, as do even hard seats on popular lines. There are several **advance-ticket offices** around town, where there's no commission and the queues are usually shorter than at the stations: the most convenient are down near the river at the northeastern corner of the Guangzhou Qiyi Lu/Yide Lu intersection; and west of the *Garden* hotel on Huanshi Zhong Lu. Paying an **agent** can cut out so much bother that it's money well spent, despite the service fees involved – upwards of ¥50 a ticket. Most agents, however, deal only with major destinations like Shanghai, Beijing, Hong Kong, Guilin and Xi'an.

Guangzhou train station (bus #5 or #31 from the south of the city) handles all destinations except Kowloon and the Shantou line, though points east are better served from the Guangzhou East station. The **ticket hall** is at the eastern end of the station; crowds are horrendous here at peak times, when entry is through guarded gateways that are closed off when the interior becomes too chaotic. Otherwise, you'll generally get what you want if you've a flexible schedule and are prepared to queue for an hour, though staff can be positively hostile.

Guangzhou East train station (bus #271 from the first floor at Liuhua bus station, or the metro to Guangzhou Dong Zhan) handles the Kowloon express (twelve departures daily 8.35am–9.20pm; ¥198–293), all Shenzhen traffic (fifty departures 6.30am–10.20pm; ¥70) – mostly fast, double-decker trains – eastern lines to Shantou and Fujian, and an increasing number of services north through central China. On the first floor, the **Shenzhen** ticket office is straight ahead of the entrance and to the left, with **Kowloon Express** tickets, customs and the Kowloon departure hall to the left and up one floor. At the time of writing, the **main ticket office** was temporarily to the right of the main entrance on the first floor; once renovations are complete, it should return to the second floor. Before queueing, find the train number from the Chinese

across the city from Guangzhou East train station at Tianhe, through the centre along Zhongshan Lu, then turns south at Chen Jia Ci, past Shamian Island and across the river. Line #2, which has put most of Central Guangzhou within a few minutes' walk of a station, runs south from Sanyuan Li via Guangzhou train station, interchanging with line #1 at Gongyuan Qian, then crossing the river and heading east to Pazhou.

Line #2 should connect to the new airport in the future, and plans are also afoot for a new line (#3) from Tianhe bus station to Panyu, as well as a link from line #1 out to Foshan (see p.613) via the ferry port at Nanhai – all are scheduled to be finished by 2007. **Metro stations** can be hard to locate at street level, but sometimes they will be signposted from nearby roads; keep an eye out timetable on the wall, then match this with the number displayed above each ticket window. The main departure areas are on the third and fourth floors.

A new **high-speed rail** track is also being laid from Guangzhou East to Yichang, Chengdu, Nanyang and Guiyang, which is expected to knock a third to a half off current journey times when it's completed in 2006.

By bus

Leaving Guangzhou by bus can be the cheapest of all exit options, and more comfortable than the average hard-seat experience if you have any distance to travel. Fast, relatively expensive **express buses** are very much the rage at present – especially around the Pearl River Delta and along the expressway to eastern Guangdong – so if money is your prime consideration, check to see whether there are any ordinary buses (*putong che*) to your destination.

The **provincial bus station** on Huanshi Xi Lu is always full of people, but tickets are easy to get – once you've found the right window out of the forty or so available – and there are at least daily departures to everywhere in Guangdong, and as far afield as Guizhou, Anhui, Hainan and Fujian provinces.

Destinations within 100km or so of Guangzhou – including all Delta towns, Qingyuan and Huizhou – are covered from the **Liuhua bus station**, also on Huanshi Xi Lu. In fact, this is a series of depots strung out for 500m along the road; the **main ticket office** is on the second floor at the eastern end of it all, though your bus might leave from anywhere – you'll be herded towards the correct departure point. Buses for Shantou, Meizhou and points east mostly depart from the new **Tianhe bus station**, about 7km east of town. You can buy tickets for these at the provincial bus station – they'll stamp your ticket on the back for a free shuttle bus to the Tianhe station, which takes around thirty minutes.

Express buses to **Hong Kong** and **Macau** run by CTS and others depart from various hotels between 5.30am and 8pm; buy tickets at the departure points. For **Kowloon** – either Hong Kong Airport (3hr; around ¥255) or Kowloon Tong MTR (3hr; around ¥115) – try the *China Marriott* (26 daily), *Landmark* (16), or *White Swan* (5). For **Macau** (3hr 30min; ¥75), the *Landmark* has nine departures daily.

By boat

Guangzhou's **ferry port** is southwest of the city at **Nanhai** (Pingzhou), about halfway to Foshan (see p.613), with two daily speedboats to the China–Hong Kong City Terminal in Hong Kong (2hr 30min; ¥170). To get there, either take the free shuttle bus if you're staying in one of the city's smarter hotels, a taxi or bus #275 from the main train station, although there's a plan to extend Guangzhou's metro line out here by 2007.

for the logo, rather like a "Y" made up of two red (or yellow) lines on a white (or yellow) background. **Fares** are ¥2–7, according to the number of stops from your starting point; ticket machines take ¥1 coins only, with change available from booths at each station. Carriages have bilingual route maps, and each stop is announced in Mandarin and English.

If you can't get there by metro, you'll find yourself using Guangzhou's cheap and slow **bus and trolleybus** network, which covers most of the city from ¥1 a ride.

Taxis are plentiful and can be hailed in the street. Fares start at ¥7, but larger vehicles charge more – all have meters. Drivers rarely try any scams, though the city's complex traffic flows can sometimes make it seem that you're heading in the wrong direction. If you're travelling solo and feeling confident, **motorcycle taxis** are a cheaper way of getting door to door, but you'll probably have to haggle.

Maps of varying detail and quality are sold for around ¥5 by hawkers at the train and bus stations, and at numerous bookshops, hotels and stalls around the city. The current favourite is called *The Tour Map of Guangzhou*, which has many of the sights marked in English, and is kept fairly up to date – though no maps illustrate all of Guangzhou's two-hundred-plus bus routes. For Guangzhou's eating, drinking and bar scene, as well as other expat-related information, you can check out ⓦ www.xianzai.com or ⓦ www.guangzhou.asiaxpat.com, successor to the superior *That's Guangzhou* magazine and website.

Accommodation

Guangzhou's business emphasis means that budget accommodation is limited – even Hong Kong has a better range – so resign yourself to this and plan your finances accordingly. Prices can more than **double** during the three-week Trade Fairs each April and October, when beds will be in short supply, and can be discounted by as much as half in winter, when fewer visitors are about. Every hotel has some sort of travel-booking service, while smarter places have their own banks, post offices, restaurants and shops, and are likely to accept international credit cards.

For anything more than an overnight stop, **Shamian Island** is the best place to hole up. Whatever your budget, it's a pleasant spot with well-tended parks, a bit of peace, and plenty of good places to eat. Otherwise, there are several relatively inexpensive Chinese-style hotels in **central Guangzhou**, mostly near the riverfront, and the bulk of the city's upmarket accommodation in the city's **north and eastern** quarters – though there are two budget options here, near Guangzhou train station.

Shamian Island

The places reviewed below are marked on the map on p.597.

Customs Hotel Shamian Dajie ⓣ 020/81102338, ⓕ 81918552. A new, upmarket venture aimed at Chinese businessmen, inside a former Customs House – though the interior is strictly modern. ❼

Guangzhou Youth Hostel Shamian Si Jie ⓣ 020/81218298, ⓕ 81219079. Across from the lavish *White Swan*, this is one of Guangzhou's cheapest options – there's usually a waiting list for spare beds here, which are distributed at noon. The dorms are a bit damp, but other rooms are modern and clean. There's a left-luggage office and a transport booking service. Despite the name, not an actual IYHF hostel. Dorm beds ¥50, ❹

Overseas Chinese Activity Centre Shamian Dajie ⓣ 020/81218218. Identifiable by the faded Bank of China sign above the door, this place is under-patronized, so they're eager for business and try hard to please. Furnishings are pretty straightforward, in keeping with its reasonable price. ❺

Shamian Shamian Nan Jie ⓣ 020/81218288, ⓦ www.gdshamianhotel.com. Cheaper rooms are small and mostly windowless, but otherwise this

is a very snug and comfortable option, just around the corner from the youth hostel. ❻

Victory (aka Shengli) Shamian Bei Jie and Shamian Si Jie ⓣ 020/81216688, ⓦ www.vhotel .com. Formerly the *Victoria* in colonial days, this is a good-value upmarket choice, with two separate buildings; the annexe (on Si Jie) is a little cheaper, though you may have to walk to the main building for breakfast. There's a good restaurant and store with a coffee bar and trove of imported Western foods. Fifty-percent discounts are available outside of peak season. Bei Jie building ❽, Si Jie building ❼

White Swan Shamian Nan Jie ⓣ 020/81886968, ⓦ www.whiteswanhotel.com. Once Guangzhou's most upmarket place to stay, this hotel is probably still the city's most famous and prestigious, and a favourite with US citizens in town to adopt Chinese orphans. You'll find a waterfall in the lobby, river views, an on-site bakery and countless other services – some reserved for the use of guests alone. ❽

Guangzhou accommodation

Aiqun	爱群大酒店	àiqún dàjiǔdiàn
Baigong	白宫酒店	báigōng jiǔdiàn
Beijing	北京大酒店	běijīng dàjiǔdiàn
China Marriott	中国大酒店	zhōngguó dàjiǔdiàn
CITS Hotel Guangdong	广东国旅酒店	guǎngdōng guólǚ jiǔdiàn
Customs Hotel	海关会议接待中心	hǎiguǎnhuìyì jiēdài zhōngxīn
Dongfang	东方宾馆	dōngfāng bīnguǎn
Garden	花园酒店	huāyuán jiǔdiàn
Guangdong Guesthouse	广东宾馆	guǎngdōng bīnguǎn
Guangzhou Youth Hostel	广州青年招待所	guǎngzhōu qīngnián zhāodàisuǒ
Holiday Inn	文化假日酒店	wénhuà jiārì jiǔdiàn
Landmark	华夏大酒店	huáshà dàjiǔdiàn
Liuhua	流花宾馆	liúhuá bīnguǎn
Overseas Chinese Activity Centre	广东省侨胞活动中心	guǎngdōngshěng qiáobāo huódòng zhōngxīn
Shamian	沙面宾馆	shāmiàn bīnguǎn
Victory	胜利宾馆	shènglì bīnguǎn
White Swan	白天鹅宾馆	báitiān'é bīnguǎn
Yishu	艺术宾馆	yìshù bīnguǎn

Central Guangzhou

Aiqun Yanjiang Lu ⊕020/81866668, ⊕81883519. Slightly gloomy (or possibly atmospheric) 1930s monumental mansion block with good river views and snooty staff; this was the tallest pre-liberation building in Guangzhou. Fair-value doubles and singles available. **❺**

Baigong Renmin Nan Lu ⊕020/81012213, ⓦwww.baigong-hotel.com. Classic urban hotel. Rooms are just past their best and can be noisy, but it's also tidy, friendly and excellent value for the location. **❹**

Beijing Xihao Er Lu ⊕020/81884988, ⊕81861818. Another typical inner-city Chinese

hotel – smart lobby, slightly tarnished rooms, huge restaurant and, of course, a karaoke hall. Also has a travel booking centre. **❹**

Guangdong Guesthouse Jiefang Bei Lu ⊕020/83332950, ⓦwww.ggh.com.cn. A huge complex of square concrete wings, Sinocized with green tiling and flared eaves. Quite comfortable, but fading around the edges. **❻**

Landmark Yanjiang Lu ⊕020/83355988, ⓦwww.hotel-landmark.com.cn. Four-star business centre between a busy roundabout and the river. **❼**

Northern and eastern Guangzhou

China Marriott Liuhua Lu ⊕020/86666888, ⓦwww.marriotthotels.com. Five-star labyrinth of red marble corridors opposite the Export Commodities Hall, with upmarket shopping malls and places to eat. You almost need a map to get around and are expected to pay in foreign currency, but rooms are good despite a stiff price tag. **❾**

CITS Hotel Guangdong Huanshi Xi Lu ⊕020/86666889, ⊕86679787. Right next to the China Southern office and Guangzhou train station, this budget CITS-managed, IYHF-affiliated affair is an excellent deal, offering clean, good-value facilities and a fine restaurant. Often full. Dorm beds ¥60, **❹**

Dongfang Liuhua Lu ⊕020/86669900, ⓦwww.dongfanghotel-gz.com. Literally in the *China Marriott*'s shadow, this is another self-contained five-star maze with a ridiculous number of restaurants housed in smartly remodelled 1950s buildings around a nice garden. **❾**

Garden Huanshi Dong Lu ⊕020/83338989, ⓦwww.gardenhotel-guangzhou.com. The city's most opulent accommodation, this classier version of the *White Swan* – there's even a waterfall – is its superior in every respect but the setting. Pool and gym free for guests. **❾**

Holiday Inn Guangming Lu ⊕020/87766999, ⓦwww.holiday-inn-guangzhou.com. Usual international-standard facilities, including a cinema. **❽**

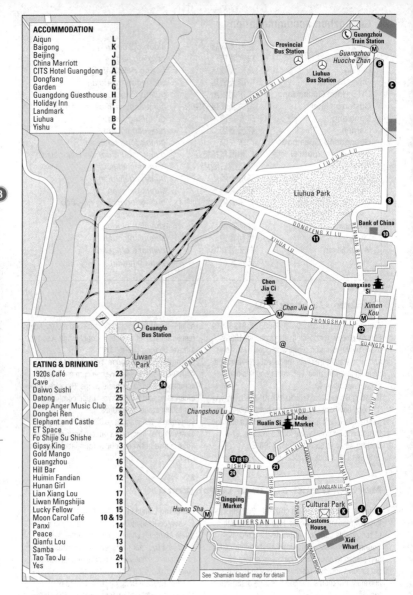

ACCOMMODATION
Aiqun	L
Baigong	K
Beijing	J
China Marriott	D
CITS Hotel Guangdong	A
Dongfang	E
Garden	G
Guangdong Guesthouse	H
Holiday Inn	F
Landmark	I
Liuhua	B
Yishu	C

EATING & DRINKING
1920s Café	23
Cave	4
Daiwo Sushi	21
Datong	25
Deep Anger Music Club	22
Dongbei Ren	8
Elephant and Castle	2
ET Space	20
Fo Shijie Su Shishe	26
Gipsy King	3
Gold Mango	5
Guangzhou	16
Hill Bar	6
Huimin Fandian	12
Hunan Girl	1
Lian Xiang Lou	17
Liwan Mingshijia	18
Lucky Fellow	15
Moon Carol Café	10 & 19
Panxi	14
Peace	7
Qianfu Lou	13
Samba	9
Tao Tao Ju	24
Yes	11

See 'Shamian Island' map for detail

Liuhua Huanshi Xi Lu ☎020/86668800, ⓦwww
.lh.com.cn. Trusty but ageing hotel close to the
train station, with a broad range of rooms – the
cheaper ones are not such good value, however. ⑥

Yishu (aka Art Hotel) Renmin Bei Lu
☎020/86670255, ⓕ86670266. Tucked back from

the street just north of the undistinguished *Friendship Hotel*; look for the English name on a gateway
out front and follow the driveway to the hotel.
Nothing exceptional, with worn carpets and basic
bathrooms, but inexpensive, given its busy location
near to the Export Commodities Hall. ④

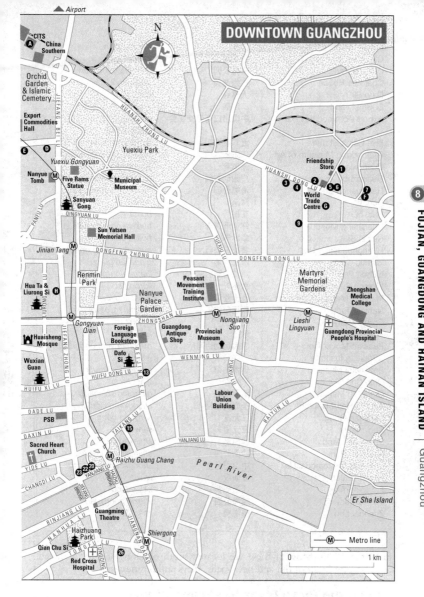

DOWNTOWN GUANGZHOU

▲ Airport

N

CITS
China
Southern
A

Orchid
Garden
& Islamic
Cemetery

Export
Commodities
Hall

E   D

Nanyue
Tomb

Yuexiu Gongyuan

Yuexiu Park

HUANSHI ZHONG LU

HUANSHI DONG LU

Friendship
Store 1

2   5 6
3   World   7
4   Trade   F
Centre G

9

M
Five Rams
Statue   Municipal
Museum

Sanyuan
Gong

QINGYUAN LU

Sun Yatsen
Memorial Hall

M
Jinian Tang

DONGFENG ZHONG LU

YUEXIU LU

DONGFENG DONG LU

Renmin
Park

Peasant
Movement
Training
Institute

Martyrs'
Memorial
Gardens

Zhongshan
Medical
College

Hua Ta &
Liurong Si H

Nanyue
Palace
Garden

M
Gongyuan
Qian

ZHONGSHAN LU

M
Nongjiang
Suo

Lieshi
Lingyuan

M
Guangdong Provincial
People's Hospital

Huaisheng
Mosque

Foreign
Language
Bookstore

Guangdong
Antique
Shop

Provincial
Museum

WENMING LU

Wuxian
Guan

Dafo
Si

13

HUIFU DONG LU

HUIFU XI LU

DADE LU

Labour
Union
Building

BAIYUN LU

PSB

DAXIN LU

15

TAIKANG LU

YANJIANG LU

Sacred Heart
Church

YIDE LU

M
Haizhu Guang Chang

CHANGDI LU

23 22 20
YANJIANG LU

Pearl River

Er Sha Island

BINJIANG LU

NANHUA LU

Guangming
Theatre

Haizhuang
Park

JIANGNAN DADAO

Shiergong

Metro line
M

Qian Chu Si

Red Cross
Hospital

TONGFU LU

26

0   1 km

PANFU LU
JIEFANG BEI LU
JIEFANG ZHONG LU
GONGYUAN
JIEFANG ZHONG LU
BEIJING LU

8

FUJIAN, GUANGDONG AND HAINAN ISLAND | Guangzhou

The City Centre

Central Guangzhou is basically a two-kilometre-wide band running north from the river between Renmin Lu and Yuexiu Lu. As remnants of the **Nanyue Kingdom** illustrate, this was the core of the city from its very foundation around 220 BC, and sports a host of historical monuments from this time right

Guangzhou sights

Baiyun Shan	白云山	*báiyún shān*
Chen Jia Ci	陈家祠	*chénjiā cí*
Cultural Park	文化公园	*wénhuà gōngyuán*
Customs House	广州海关	*guǎngzhōu hǎiguān*
Dafo Si	大佛寺	*dàfó sì*
Er Sha Island	二沙岛	*èrshādǎo*
Export Commodities Hall	中国出口商品交易会	*zhōngguó chūkǒushāngpǐn jiāoyìhuì*
Five Rams Statue	五羊石像	*wǔyáng shíxiàng*
Guangdong Museum of Art	广东美术馆	*guǎngdōng měishùguǎn*
Guangxiao Si	光孝寺	*guāngxiào sì*
Guangzhou Zoo	广州动物园	*guǎngzhōu dòngwùyuán*
Haizhuang Park	海幢公园	*hǎizhuàng gōngyuán*
Honan	河南	*hénán*
Hua Ta	花塔	*huātǎ*
Huaisheng Mosque	怀圣清真寺	*huáishèng qīngzhēn sì*
Hualin Si	华林寺	*huálín sì*
Huanghua Gang Park	黄花岗公园	*huánghuāgǎng gōngyuán*
Islamic Cemetery	清真古墓	*qīngzhēn gǔmù*
Liuhua Park	流花公园	*liúhuā gōngyuán*
Liurong Si	六榕寺	*liùróng sì*
Martyrs' Memorial Gardens	烈士陵园	*lièshì língyuán*
Nanyue Tomb	西汉南越王墓	*xīhàn nányuèwángmù*
Orchid Garden	兰圃	*lánpǔ*
Pearl River	珠江	*zhūjiāng*
Peasant Movement Training Institute	农民运动讲习所	*nóngmín yùndòng jiǎngxí suǒ*
Provincial Museum	省博物馆	*shěng bówùguǎn*
Qian Chu Si	千处寺	*qiānchù sì*
Qingping Market	清平市场	*qīngpíng shìchǎng*
Sacred Heart Church	圣心大教堂	*shèngxīn dàjiàotáng*
Sanyuan Gong	三元宫	*sānyuán gōng*
Sanyuan Li	三元里	*sānyuán lǐ*
Shamian Island	沙面岛	*shāmiàn dǎo*
Shamian Park	沙面公园	*shāmiàn gōngyuán*
Sun Yatsen Memorial Hall	中山纪念堂	*zhōngshān jìniàntáng*
Wuxian Guan	五仙观	*wǔxiān guàn*
Xidi Wharf	西堤码头	*xīdī mǎtóu*
Yuexiu Park	越秀公园	*yuèxiù gōngyuán*
Zhenhai Lou	镇海楼	*zhènhǎi lóu*

up to the 1930s. Most of these are located south of Dongfeng Lu, a mixed, rather scruffy mesh of old and new roads, alleys and businesses.

Around the Pearl River to Wuxian Guan

Yanjiang Lu, the northern promenade along the **Pearl River**, was paved in 2001 as part of a civic smartening campaign coinciding with Guangzhou hosting the China National Games. Lined with trees and a smattering of colonial-era buildings – such as the **Customs House** and **Aiqun Hotel** – it's a good place just to mill about on hot summer evenings.

If you follow Yanjiang Lu to its eastern end you'll find yourself crossing to **Er Sha Island**, the focus of much upmarket housing development and home to

Oily grey and second only to the Yangzi in importance as an industrial channel, the **Pearl River** (Zhu Jiang) originates in eastern Yunnan province and forms one of China's busiest waterways, continually active with ferries and barges loaded down with coal and stone. Its name derives from a legend about a monk named Jiahu, who lost a glowing pearl in its waters, and although it shone on the riverbed night after night, nobody was ever able to recover it.

Several operators run **evening cruises** departing daily between 7.20pm and 9.20pm from **Xidi Wharf**, roughly opposite the Customs House on Yanjiang Lu – tickets cost ¥33 to ¥48 depending on whether you choose the upper or lower deck. These cruises last 75 minutes, but if you want dinner on board, the duration is 90 minutes and costs run from ¥88 to ¥98. On board you can sit back and watch the lights of the city slip slowly past your table, with fine views of Guangzhou's busy waterfront, flanked by ever-higher buildings. The route takes you past the *White Swan* on Shamian Island, back under Renmin Bridge, past Haizhu Bridge and then down to the grand Guangzhou suspension bridge at the far end of Er Sha Island. The largest of the river's mid-stream islands, Er Sha, houses the city's former **boat dwellers** – outcasts who lived on the Pearl River until Liberation, forbidden to settle ashore or marry anyone who lived on land – in a purpose-built estate known as New Riverside Village. From the island, on a clear moonless night you'll be able to see the lights of international freighters at anchor far downstream in **Huangpu**, once the site of a Military Academy where Mao studied under Chiang Kaishek, his future arch enemy and leader of the Guomindang.

the **Guangdong Museum of Art** (Tues–Sun 9am–5pm; ¥15). The museum holds one of China's largest collections of contemporary art, along with special exhibitions reflecting the country's shifting political and social conditions.

Back in the centre, north from the river, **Yide Lu** is stuffed with small shops selling toys, dried marine produce – jellyfish, shark's fin, fish maw and whole salted mackerel – along with sacks of nuts and candied fruit. Set north off the road at the back of a court, the **Sacred Heart Church** – also known as the Stone House – is a Gothic-style cathedral completed in 1888, impressive for its size and unexpected presence, though it's not generally open to the public. Three streets up from here on Huifu Xi Lu is **Wuxian Guan** (Five Immortals' Temple; daily 9am–noon & 1.30–5pm; ¥5). Dating from 1377, the original wooden building is nonfunctional and dusty, but some obviously ancient statues pop up around the place: weathered guardian lions flank the way in, and there are some stylized Ming sculptures out the back, looking like giant chess pieces. The Five Immortals – three men and two women – are depicted too, riding their goatly steeds as they descend through the clouds to found Guangzhou. Also impressive is a fourteenth-century **bell tower** behind the temple, in which hangs a three-metre-high, five-tonne bronze bell, silent since receiving the blame for a plague which broke out shortly after its installation in 1378 – it has been called the "Forbidden Bell" ever since.

Huaisheng Mosque, Liurong Si and Guangxiao Si

A few blocks north of Wuxian Guan, the modern thoroughfare of **Zhong-shan Lu** runs within striking distance of three of Guangzhou's most important **temples** – Ximen Kou or Gongyuan Qian are the closest **metro** stops. South of Zhongshan Liu Lu on Guangta Lu, **Huaisheng Mosque** and its grey, conical tower, **Guangta**, loom over a surrounding wall which bars entry to non-Muslims. Looking like a lighthouse, Guangta is possibly the world's

Chan – known in Japan as **Zen** – believes that an understanding of the true nature of being can be achieved by sudden **enlightenment**, sparked by everyday, banal conversations or events. In this it differs from other forms of Buddhism, with their emphasis on the need for years of study of ritual and religious texts; though also using meditation and little parables to achieve its ends, Chan therefore puts enlightenment within the grasp of even the most secular individual.

The founder of Chan was **Bodhidharma** (known as **Damo** in China), who arrived in Guangzhou from India around 520 AD intending to enrich China's rather formal, stodgy approach to Buddhism with his more lateral slant. After baffling the emperor with his teachings, Bodhidharma ended up at **Shaolin Si** in Henan; while there, exercises he taught the monks, to balance their long hours of meditation, are believed to have formed the basis of Chinese **kung fu** (see p.300 & p.1185). Shaolin subsequently became the centre for Chan Buddhism, spreading from there across China and into Japan and Korea.

Chan's most famous exponent was its Sixth Patriarch, **Huineng** (638–713). Huineng was from Guangzhou, but as a youth heard a wandering monk reciting sutras and was so impressed that he went to **Huangmei** in central China specifically to study Chan under the Fifth Patriarch, Hong Ren. Scorned by his fellow students for his rough southern manners, Huineng nonetheless demonstrated such a deep understanding of Chan that within a mere eight months he had achieved enlightenment on hearing the **Diamond Sutra** (which teaches how to recognize and dispense with illusions), and had been elected by Hong Ren to succeed him as patriarch, though the matter was kept secret at the time. Returning south to Guangzhou in 676, Huineng settled incognito at **Guangxiao Si**, where one day he heard two monks watching a flag and debating whether it was the wind or the flag that was moving. As they couldn't reach a decision, Huineng volunteered that neither was right, it was the mind that moved. His statement so stunned everyone present that he was invited to lecture, thereby revealing himself as the Sixth Patriarch (Hong Ren having died in the meantime). Huineng apparently spent his later years at **Nanhua Si** near Shaoguan in northern Guangdong – see p.624 for more.

oldest minaret outside Mecca and something of a stylistic fossil, said by some to have been built by Abu Waqas in the seventh century (see p.595). During the fifteenth century, Huaisheng's environs were known as **Fanfang**, the foreigners' quarter; today there's a smattering of halal canteens and restaurants in the vicinity, including the famous *Huimin Fandian* (see p.602).

Liurong Si (Temple of the Six Banyan Trees; daily 8am–5pm; ¥1; Flower Pagoda ¥10) lies north of the mosque on Liurong Lu, and is associated with the dissident poet–governor **Su Dongpo**, who named the temple on a visit in 1100 and drew the characters for "Liu Rong" on the two stone steles just inside the gates. Very little of the temple itself survives, and the site is better known for the 57-metre-high **Hua Ta** (Flower Pagoda), a contemporary structure enshrining relics brought from India by Emperor Wu's uncle. Carvings of lions, insects and birds adorn the pagoda's wooden eaves; of its seventeen storeys, nine have balconies and the rest are blind. At the top is a gigantic bronze pillar covered with over a thousand reliefs of meditating figures rising up through the roof, solid enough to support the five-tonne begging bowl and pearl that you can see from ground level.

A narrow lane along Liurong Si's northern boundary leads west through a street market on to Haizhu Bei Lu. Turn south and then west again along Jinghui Lu for the entrance to the spacious and peaceful **Guangxiao Si** (daily

6.30am–5.30pm; ¥4), the oldest of Guangzhou's Buddhist temples. In 113 BC this was the residence of **Zhao Jiande**, last of the Nanyue kings (see p.594), becoming a place of worship only after the 85-year-old Kashmiri monk **Tanmo Yeshe** built the first hall in 401 AD. The temple was later visited by Buddhist luminaries such as the sixth-century monk Zhiyao Sanzang, who planted the fig trees still here today; the Indian founder of Chan (Zen) Buddhism, **Bodhidharma**; and Chan's Sixth Patriarch, **Huineng** (for more on whom, see the box opposite). Though, again, none of the original buildings survives, the grounds are well-ordered and enclose pavilions concealing wells and engraved tablets from various periods, while three halls at the back contain some imposing Buddha images; the westerly one is unusually reclining, while a more ordinary trinity fills the central hall.

The Provincial Museum and around

Around 1500m east of Wuxian Guan on Wenming Lu is the **Provincial Museum** (daily 9am–5pm; ¥15). Walking here from Wuxian Guan, you'll pass the small and unassuming **Dafo Si**, the Big Buddha Temple, and the frenetically crowded shopping district along **Beijing Lu**; coming straight up from the river, look for the yellow 1920s **Labour Union Building** on Yuexiu Lu, later appropriated, somewhat cynically, as the Guomindang headquarters.

The similar-looking buildings inside the Provincial Museum grounds are those of the former **Zhongshan University**; the writer **Lu Xun** lectured here and his life is outlined in photographs. A more modern structure houses the museum proper; its best features are a **natural history display**, incorporating an innovative walk-through "jungle" with spotlit creatures hidden in the undergrowth, as well as several rooms of exquisitely fine porcelain, carved jade and Ming household ornaments. The lack of visitors and explanatory notes somewhat deadens it all, but it's remarkable to see such a high standard of exhibits.

Thanks to the subsequent career of its dean, Mao Zedong, Guangzhou's **Peasant Movement Training Institute**, on Zhongshan Lu (Tues–Sun 9am–4.30pm; ¥5), is the city's most frequented revolutionary site. It still looks like the Confucian Academy it was for six hundred years, before **Peng Pai**, a "rich peasant" from Guangdong, established the Institute in 1924 with Guomindang permission and 38 students. The school lasted just over two years, with Mao, Zhou Enlai and Peng Pai taking the final classes in August 1926, eight months before the Communist and Guomindang alliance ended violently in Shanghai. There's actually little to see; most poignant are the photographs of alumni who failed to survive the Shanghai Massacre and the subsequent **1927 Communist Uprising** in Guangzhou.

The scene of the latter event lies farther east along Zhongshan Lu at the **Martyrs' Memorial Gardens** (daily 6am–9pm; ¥5). It was near here, on December 11, 1927, that a small Communist force under **Zhang Teilai** managed to take the Guangzhou Police Headquarters, announcing the foundation of the **Canton Commune**. Expected support never materialized, however, and on the afternoon of the second day, Guomindang forces moved in; five thousand people were killed outright or later executed for complicity. The grounds contain a small lake, some trees and a lawn, and a strange rifle-like monument beside the grassy mound where the insurgents lie buried.

Northern Guangzhou

The area north between Dongfeng Lu and Guangzhou train station is primarily occupied by two huge **parks**, Liuhua and Yuexiu, with a sole memento of a colonial-era confrontation further out beyond the station at **Sanyuan Li**.

Yuexiu Park

Yuexiu Park is China's biggest spread of urban greenery (daily 6am–9pm; ¥5), encompassing over ninety hectares of sports courts, historic monuments, teahouses and shady groves. On the way here you'll pass a couple of notable buildings, most visibly the large rotunda and blue-tiled roof of the **Sun Yatsen Memorial Hall** on Dongfeng Zhong Lu (daily 8am–6pm; ¥5), built on the spot where the man regarded by Guomindang and Communists alike as the father of modern China took the presidential oath in 1912. Inside it's a plain auditorium with seating for two thousand people, occasionally used as a concert hall. Far less obvious is **Sanyuan Gong** (Three Purities Temple; ¥6) just west of here, whose entrance is virtually unmarked below a broad stone staircase. This is actually the largest Taoist temple in Guangzhou, and the oldest too – it was first consecrated in 319 – though the current arrangement of dark, spartan halls occupied by statues of Taoist deities is Qing. Gloomy furnishings aside, it's a busy place of worship, and there are a few splashes of red and gold in the painted bats, cranes and other Taoist motifs scattered around.

The park

While there are entrances at all points of the compass, Yuexiu's **front gate** is on Jiefang Bei Lu, a ten-minute walk north of San Yuan Gong. To the north of the porcelain dragons here are **Beixiu Hu** and the **Garden of Chinese Idiom**, where many strange stone and bronze sculptures lurk in the undergrowth, illustrating popular sayings. Head south, and you'll wind up at the much-photographed **Five Rams Statue**, commemorating the myth of Guangzhou's foundation – at least one of these is definitely not a ram, however.

Roughly in the middle of the park atop a hill, paths converge at **Zhenhai Lou**, the "Gate Tower Facing the Sea", a wood and rendered-brick building that once formed part of the Ming city walls. Today it houses the **Municipal Museum** (daily 9am–5pm; ¥10), three floors of locally found exhibits ranging from Stone-Age pottery fragments and ivory from Africa found in a Han-dynasty tomb, to fifth-century coins from Persia, a copy of *Good Words for Exhorting the World* (the Christian tract which inspired the Taiping leader, Hong Xiuquan), and nineteenth-century cannons tumbled about in the courtyard (two made by the German company, Krupp). A statue of Lin Zexu and letters from him to the Qing emperor documenting his disposal of the British opium stocks always draws big crowds of tongue-clicking Chinese.

The Nanyue Tomb and Liuhua Park

Five hundred metres north of Yuexiu Park's Jiefang Bei Lu entrance (and reachable on bus #5) is the looming, red sandstone facade of the **Nanyue Tomb** (daily 9am–5.30pm, last admission 4.45pm; ¥12, plus ¥5 to enter the tomb itself). Discovered in 1983 during foundation digging for a residential estate, this houses the 2000-year-old site of the tomb of **Zhao Mo**, grandson of the Nanyue Kingdom's founder Zhao Tuo, and really deserves an hour of your time – there's another English-language **video** and a mass of exhibits.

Zhao Mo made a better job of his tomb than running his kingdom, which disintegrated shortly after his death: excavators found the tomb stacked with gold and priceless trinkets. They're on view in the museum, including a **burial suit** made out of over a thousand tiny jade tiles (jade was considered to prevent decay), and the ash-like remains of slaves and concubines immured with him. Several artefacts show Central Asian influence in their designs, illustrating how even at this early stage in Guangzhou's history there was contact with non-Chinese peoples. It's all fascinating and expertly presented, particularly worthwhile if you plan to visit contemporary grave sites in the Yangzi Basin or at Xi'an. Incidentally, Zhao Tuo's tomb still awaits discovery, though rumours of its fabulous treasures had eager excavators turning Guangzhou inside out as long ago as the Three Kingdoms period (220–280 AD).

West of the Nanyue Tomb between Liuhua Lu and Renmin Bei Lu, **Liuhua Park** (daily 6am–10pm; ¥5) is a large expanse of lakes, purpose-built in 1958 and pleasant enough during the week, though hellishly crowded at weekends. Liuhua means "Flowing Flowers", a name said to date back to the Han period when palace maids tossed petals into a nearby stream while dressing their hair.

To Guangzhou train station

About 1km south of Guangzhou train station and surrounded by business hotels on Liuhua Lu and Renmin Lu, the **Export Commodities Hall** is the venue each April and October for the city's **Trade Fair**, first held in 1957 to encourage Western investments. This isn't the most pleasant area of town but there is one oasis of peace and quiet: Guangzhou's delightful, though fairly small, **Orchid Garden**, off Jiefang Bei Lu (Mon–Fri 8am–6pm, Sat, Sun 8am–7pm; ¥8, or ¥20 including tea in the central pavilion). Besides orchids, there are ponds surrounded by tropical ferns and lilies, winding stone paths, palms and giant figs with drooping aerial roots, and pink-flowering azaleas. Apart from the filtered traffic noise, it's hard to believe that the city lies just outside. Along the western edge of the garden, Guangzhou's **Islamic Cemetery** contains the tomb of **Abu Waqas**, a seventh-century missionary who brought Islam to China. The details are a little sketchy, however, as Abu Waqas supposedly died around 629, three years before Mohammed, and the Quran wasn't collated for another generation afterwards. The cemetery was recently closed to non-Muslims, though it can be glimpsed from inside the garden through a screen of bamboos.

Sanyuan Li

For a return to earth after the Orchid Garden, continue up Jiefang Bei Lu for 1km after it crosses Huanshi Lu – take the metro or bus #58. You're now north of the train station in **Sanyuan Li**, a recently redeveloped part of the city. This was where the **Sanyuan Li Anti-British Movement** formed in 1841 after the British stormed into the area during the First Opium War. Following months of abuse from the invaders, local workers and peasants rose under the farmer **Wei Shaoguang** and attacked the British camp, killing around twenty soldiers in an indecisive engagement before being dispersed by heavy rain. A **temple** 250m along on the south side of Guanghua Lu, built in 1860 on the sight of the battle, is now a **museum** (daily 9am–5pm; ¥15) housing the peasants' armoury of farm tools and ceremonial weapons, though don't take captions – the turgid product of later propaganda – too seriously.

Western Guangzhou

Western Guangzhou, the area west of Renmin Lu and south of Dongfeng Xi Lu, features a charismatic warren of back roads and lanes around Changshou Lu, all stuffed to overflowing with market activity, restaurants and shops, which empty down near the waterfront opposite **Shamian Island**, a quiet haven of colonial mood and huge trees. North of the river, Zhongshan Lu continues westwards through the area, cut by a score of roads running south to parallel **Liuersan Lu**, along the river; south, the main roads are Nanhua Lu and Tongfu Lu.

Chen Jia Ci

Zhongshan Lu's western arm cuts through a new, relatively tidy district before eventually heading over a tributary of the Pearl River and out of the city towards Foshan. About 2.5km from the Jiefang Lu intersection, a pedestrian walkway across the road leads to gardens outside **Chen Jia Ci** (Chen Clan Academy; daily 8.30am–5.30pm, last admission 5pm; ¥10). The story of its founding is unusual; subscriptions were invited from anyone named **Chen** – one of the most common Cantonese surnames – and the money raised went to build this complex, part ancestor temple where Chens could worship, part school where they could receive an education. Though belittled today by tea rooms and souvenir stalls, the buildings remain impressive, forming a series of rooms arranged around open courtyards, all decorated by the most garish tiles and gorgeously carved screens and stonework that money could buy in the 1890s. Have a good look at the extraordinary brick reliefs under the eaves, both inside and out. One of the first, on the right as you enter, features an opera being performed to what looks like a drunken horse, which lies squirming on the floor with mirth. Other cameos feature stories from China's "noble bandit" saga, *Outlaws of the Marsh*, and some of the sights around Guangzhou.

Changshou Lu and around

Below Zhongshan Lu, the ring of part of the old city walls can be traced along **Longjin Lu** in the north, and **Dishifu Lu** and others to the south – you'll actually cross a low mound marking their foundations if you enter the area off Zhongshan Lu down Huagui Lu. Though a couple of wide, modern main roads barge through, most of this district, with east–west **Changshou Lu** at its core, retains its Ming-dynasty street plan and a splash of early-twentieth-century architecture, making for excellent random walks. In addition to some of Guangzhou's biggest shopping plazas and a crowd of markets spreading into each other south from Changshou Lu right down to the river, several **famous restaurants** are here, and the area is particularly busy at night.

Between Xiajiu Lu and Changshou Lu in the vicinity of Hualin Si, shops almost conceal the narrow lanes through into Guangzhou's **jade market** – it's not up to Hong Kong's, but is still worth a browse. The market surrounds an auspiciously red-painted gateway, behind which is the Buddhist temple of **Hualin Si** (daily 8am–5pm; free), founded as a modest nunnery by the Brahman prince **Bodhidharma** in 527 (see box, p.592). After his Chan teachings caught on in the seventeenth century, the main hall was enlarged to house five hundred *arhat* sculptures ranged along the cross-shaped aisles, and Hualin remains the most lively temple in the city – during festivals you'll be crushed, deafened and blinded by the crowds, firecrackers and incense smoke.

From here, the best thing you can do is throw away your map and roam unaided southwards through the maze of alleys and Qing-era homes (some of which are protected historic relics), most likely emerging in the vicinity of the *Guangzhou* restaurant. Two streets lined with restored 1920s facades and pedestrianized at the weekends lie here – **Dishifu Lu** to the west and **Xiajiu Lu** to the east – and places to eat and shop are legion, the pavements always crammed to capacity. South again off Xiajiu Lu, you enter the upper reaches of the infamous **Qingping Market**, with each intersecting east–west lane forming dividing lines for the sale of different goods: dried medicines, spices and herbs, fresh vegetables, livestock, bird and fish. Once one of China's most confronting – not to say gory – markets, this has been scaled down considerably in recent years with the removal of rare animals and large-scale streetside butchering, though it remains a lively and busy affair, amply illustrating the Cantonese demand for fresh and unusual food.

You exit Qingping onto **Liuersan Lu**, a recently widened road given a stack of flyovers to relieve chronic traffic congestion, lined with palms, flowerbeds, and fake colonial frontages mirroring the real thing opposite on Shamian Island. "Liuersan" means "6, 23", referring to June 23, 1925, when fifty people were shot by colonial troops during a demonstration demanding, among other things, the return of Shamian Island to Chinese control. East along Liuersan, the **Cultural Park** (daily 6am–9.30pm; ¥3) is a rather bland area of paving and benches, where gangs of children queue for their turn on arcade games and fairground rides, and theatre and sound stages host weekend performances of anything from local rock to opera. The park also hosts Guangzhou's annual **Food Festival** at the end of November (¥10).

Shamian Island

It's only a short hop across Liuersan Lu and a muddy canal (or head to Huang Sha metro, then cross the bridge) on to **Shamian Island**, but the pace changes instantly, and Guangzhou's busiest quarter is exchanged for its most genteel. A tear-shaped sandbank about 1km long and 500m wide, Shamian was leased to European powers as an Opium War trophy, the French getting the eastern end and the British the rest. Here the colonials recreated their own backyards, planting the now massive **trees** and throwing up solid, Victorian-style **villas**, banks, embassies, churches and tennis courts – practically all of which are still standing. Iron gates on the bridges once excluded the Chinese from Shamian (as the Chinese had once forbidden foreigners to enter within Guangzhou's city walls), leaving the Europeans in self-imposed isolation from the bustle across the water. Shamian retains that atmosphere today, a quiet bolt hole for many long-term travellers in the city. There's restricted traffic flow, and the well-tended architecture, greenery and relative peace make it a refreshing place to visit, even if you're not staying or sampling the restaurants and bars.

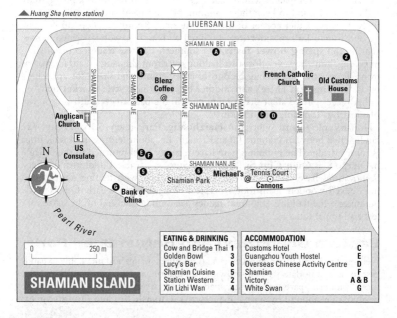

EATING & DRINKING		ACCOMMODATION	
Cow and Bridge Thai	1	Customs Hotel	C
Golden Bowl	3	Guangzhou Youth Hostel	E
Lucy's Bar	6	Overseas Chinese Activity Centre	D
Shamian Cuisine	5	Shamian	F
Station Western	2	Victory	A & B
Xin Lizhi Wan	4	White Swan	G

SHAMIAN ISLAND

The main thoroughfare is east–west **Shamian Dajie**, with five numbered streets running south across the island. Wandering around, you'll find buildings have largely been restored to their original appearance – most were built between the 1860s and early twentieth century – with plaques sketching their history. Though sharing such a tiny area, the British and French seemingly kept themselves to themselves, building separate bridges, churches and customs houses; nothing is particularly worth searching out, but it's all great browsing. Next to the atypically modern *White Swan* on the **Shamian Nan Jie** esplanade, a focus of sorts is provided by **Shamian Park**, where two **cannons**, cast in nearby Foshan during the Opium Wars, face out across the river, and you might catch Cantonese opera rehearsals here on Saturday afternoons. The island's waterfront area is also the venue for Guangzhou's major Spring Festival **fireworks display**, held on the first night at around 9pm; the best seats are at the *White Swan*'s riverside buffet at ¥400 a head, failing which you can join half of the city in the surrounding streets – or watch from your room at the *Youth Hostel*.

Honan

Honan, the area immediately south of the river between westerly **Gongye Dadao** and **Jiangnan Dadao**, 1500m further east, can be reached on any of **three bridges**: Renmin Bridge, which connects Liuersan Lu with Gongye Dadao; and the closely spaced Jiefang and Haizhu bridges off Yanjiang Lu, which become Tongqing Lu and Jiangnan Dadao respectively. Metro line #2 runs along Jiangnan Dadao, with stations at Shiergong and Jiangnanxi, or you can just walk across the nearest bridge and explore on foot.

Prior to 1949, Honan was Guangzhou's red-light district, crawling with opium dens, brothels and gambling houses, none of which survived the Communist takeover. Indeed, in 1984 Honan was chosen as a model of **Hu Yaobang**'s "Civic Spirit" campaign, which called on residents to organize kindergartens, old folks' clubs, and to keep their communities clean and safe. It's still a surprisingly calm and quiet corner of the city, the small flagstoned alleys off Nanhua Lu and Tongfu Lu kept litter-free and lined with austere, wooden-gated homes. During the **spring flower festival** (a southern Chinese tradition originating in Guangzhou), however, florist stalls along riverfront Binjiang Lu attract crowds from all over the city to buy blooms of every colour and shape for good luck in the coming year. There's also another big Cantonese-style **market** here – a rather more spirited affair than Qingping – in the backstreets southwest off the Nanhua Lu/Tongqing Lu junction.

Honan's sole formal sight is in **Haizhuang Park** (daily 6.15am–9pm; ¥2), sandwiched between Nanhua Lu and Tongfu Lu, about ten minutes' walk from Renmin Bridge. The buildings here have recently been returned to their original purpose as **Qian Chu Si** (daily 8am–5pm), a sizeable Buddhist monastery. Renovations have spruced up the broad south hall, with its fine statuary and interlocked wooden beam roof, so typical of south China's early Qing temple buildings – the flashing, coloured "haloes" surrounding several of the statues are less traditional touches.

Eastern Guangzhou and Baiyun Shan Park

Hemmed in on all other flanks by rivers and hills, Guangzhou inevitably expands east to accommodate its ever-growing population, and it's here you'll find the most "modern" parts of the city, shadowed by skyscrapers housing corporate headquarters and cut by several expressways. **Huanshi Lu** and **Dongfeng Lu** are the biggest of these, converging out in the northeastern suburbs at the vast open-plan district of **Tianhe**. Much of the city's **expat community** is based out this way, and there are numerous Western-oriented **restaurants and bars** – if few actual sights – to recommend a visit. One exception is **Baiyun Shan Park**, which lies immediately to the north and offers an unexpectedly thorough escape from the city.

Northeast off Huanshi Dong Lu along Xianlie Lu, **Huanghua Gang Park** (daily 8am–5pm; ¥10) recalls Sun Yatsen's abortive 1911 Canton Uprising in the **Mausoleum to the 72 Martyrs**, a very peculiar monument reflecting the nationalities of numerous donors who contributed to its construction – Buddhist iconography rubbing shoulders with a Statue of Liberty and Egyptian obelisk. Of more general appeal is **Guangzhou Zoo**, about 1km farther out along Xianlie Lu (daily 9am–4pm; ¥20; take bus #6 from Dongfeng Lu, one block east of the Sun Yatsen Memorial Hall). This is the third largest in the country, with the animals kept in relatively decent conditions – though far below what you'll probably consider pleasant. Among the rarities are clouded leopards, several species of wildfowl and, of course, pandas.

You'll most likely find yourself out at **Tianhe**, the area surrounding the train station 2km due east of the zoo, en route to Guangzhou East train station. A planned area of vast spaces of concrete paving, broad roads and glassy towers, where pedestrians are reduced to insignificant specks, Tianhe has as its showpiece a huge **sports stadium** built for the 1987 National Games (Tiyu Zhong Xin metro), all revamped when Guangzhou was the Games' host for the second time in 2001.

Baiyun Shan Park

Just 7km north of downtown, **Baiyun Shan** (White Cloud Mountain) is close enough to central Guangzhou to reach by city bus, but open enough to leave all the city's noise and bustle behind. Once covered with numerous monasteries, Baiyun's heavily reforested slopes now offer lush panoramas out over Guangzhou and the delta region. A **park** here encloses almost thirty square kilometres (¥18), its entrance a thirty-minute ride on bus #24 from the south side of Renmin Park, immediately northeast of the Jiefang Lu/Zhongshan Lu crossroads.

It's a good three-hour walk from the entrance off Luhu Lu to **Moxing Ling** (Star-touching Summit), past strategically placed teahouses and pavilions offering views and refreshments. There's also a **cable car** (¥20) from the entrance as far as the **Cheng Precipice**, a ledge roughly halfway to the top, which earned its name when the Qin-dynasty minister **Cheng Ki** was ordered here by his emperor to find a herb of immortality. Having found the plant, Cheng nibbled a leaf only to see the remainder vanish; full of remorse, he flung himself off the mountain but was caught by a stork and taken to heaven. Sunset views from the precipice are spectacular.

Eating

Eating out is the main recreation in Guangzhou, something the city is famous for and caters to admirably. Guangzhou's restaurants, the best to be found in a province famed for its food, are in themselves justification to spend a few days in the city, and it would be a real shame to leave without having eaten in one of the more elaborate or famous **Cantonese** places – there's nothing to match the experience of tucking into a Cantonese spread while being surrounded by an enthusiastic horde of local diners. Locals are so proud of their cuisine that a

Guangzhou restaurants

Banana Leaf Curry House	蕉叶饮食	jiāoyè yǐnshí
Cow and Bridge Thai	泰国牛桥	tàiguó niúqiáo
Daiwo Sushi	大禾会日本饭店	dàhéhuì rìběn fàndiàn
Datong	大同大酒家	dàtóng dàjiǔjiā
Dongbei Ren	东北人	dōngběi rén
Fo Shijie Su Shishe	佛世界素食社	fóshìjiè sùshíshè
Golden Bowl	金饭碗酒家	jīnfànwǎn jiǔjiā
Guangzhou	广州酒家	guǎngzhōu jiǔjiā
Huimin Fandian	回民饭店	huímín fàndiàn
Hunan Girl	湘妹子	xiāngmèizi
Jiangxi Ren	江西人	jiāngxīrén
Lian Xiang Lou	莲香楼	liánxiāng lóu
Liwan Mingshijia	荔湾名食家	lìwān míngshíjiā
Lucky Fellow	幸运楼酒家	xìngyùnlóu jiǔjiā
Lucy's Bar	露丝吧	lùsī bā
Nanyuan	南园酒店	nányuán jiǔdiàn
Panxi	泮溪酒家	pànxī jiǔjiā
Qianfu Lou	千福楼	qiānfú lóu
Samba	森巴西餐厅	sēnbāxī cāntīng
Shamian Cuisine	沙面咖啡屋美食	shāmiàn kāfēiwū měishí
Station Western	车站西餐酒廊	chēzhàn xīcān jiǔláng
Tao Tao Ju	陶陶居	táotáo jū
Xin Lizhi Wan	新荔枝湾酒楼	xīnlìzhīwān jiǔlóu

few years ago it was hard to find anywhere serving anything else, though now you can also track down a good variety of **Asian**, **European** and even **Indian** food – not to mention **regional Chinese**. Some canteens open as early as 5am, and breakfast – including traditional **dim sum** – is usually served from 7am to 10am, later on Sundays or if the restuarant has a particularly good reputation. Lunch is on offer between 11am and 2pm, and dinner from 5pm to 10pm, though most people eat early rather than late.

Restaurants are pretty evenly spread across the city, though Dishifu Lu in the west, and Shamian Island, have a ridiculous quantity and variety between them. Ordering is a bit easier here than in the average Chinese city, as many restaurants have an **English menu** tucked away somewhere, even if these omit dishes that they believe won't appeal to foreigners. **Prices** have actually fallen somewhat in recent years, though the sociable Cantonese fashion of entertaining (and impressing) family or wealthy clients with food means that you'll pay upwards of ¥40 a head for a good Chinese meal, and ¥60 if you're after more exotic Asian or Western fare.

You can, of course, eat for a fraction of this cost day or night at the city's numerous **food stalls** which, like the restaurants, are never far away (streets off Beijing Lu have the best selection). The usual fare at these places is a few slices of roast duck or pork on rice, meat and chicken dumplings, or noodle soups, and rarely exceeds ¥8–10 a plate. Be sure to try a selection of **cakes** and the fresh tropical **fruits** too; local lychees are so good that the emperors once had them shipped direct to Beijing.

If Chinese dining just isn't for you, there are Western fast-food outlets throughout the city, though there's no need to resort to them – **bars** and **cafés** listed below serve grills, sandwiches, and counter meals as good as anything you'll get at home. Tourist **hotels** have restaurants used to dealing with foreign

Guangdong cooking

Guangdong cooking is one of China's four major regional styles and, despite northern critics decrying it as too uncomplicated to warrant the term "cuisine", it's unmatched in the clarity of its flavours and its appealing presentation. The style subdivides into **Cantonese**, emanating from the Pearl River Delta region; **Chaozhou**, from the city of the same name in the far east of Guangdong; and **Hakka**, from the northeastern border with Fujian, named after the Han subgroup with whom it originated. Though certain Chaozhou and Hakka recipes have been incorporated into the main body of Guangdong cooking – sweet-and-sour pork with fruit, and salt-baked chicken, for instance – it's Cantonese food which has come to epitomize its principles. With many Chinese emigrants leaving through Guangzhou, it's also the most familiar to overseas visitors, though peruse a menu here and you'll soon realize that most dishes served abroad as "Cantonese" would be unrecognizable to a local resident.

Spoiled by good soil and a year-round growing season, the Cantonese demand absolutely **fresh ingredients**, kept alive and kicking in cages, tanks or buckets at the front of the restaurant for diners to select themselves. Westerners can be repulsed by this collection of wildlife, and even other Chinese comment that the Cantonese will eat anything with legs that isn't a piece of furniture, and anything with wings that isn't an aeroplane. The cooking itself is designed to keep **textures** distinct and **flavours** as close to the original as possible, using a minimum amount of mild and complementary seasonings to prevent dishes from being bland. **Fast stir-frying** in a wok is the best known of these procedures, but **slow-simmering** in soy sauce and wine and **roasting** are other methods of teasing out the essential characteristics of the food.

No full meal is really complete without a simple plate of rich green and bitter **choi sam** (cai xin in Mandarin), Chinese broccoli, blanched and dressed with oyster sauce. Also famous is **fish and seafood**, often simply steamed with ginger and spring onions – hairy crabs are a winter treat, sold everywhere – and nobody cooks **fowl** better than the Cantonese, always juicy and flavoursome, whether served crisp-skinned and roasted or fragrantly casseroled. Guangzhou's citizens are also compulsive snackers, and outside canteens you'll see **roast meats**, such as whole goose or strips of cha siu pork, waiting to be cut up and served with rice for a light lunch, or burners stacked with **sandpots** (sai bo), a one-person dish of steamed rice served in the cooking vessel with vegetables and slices of sweet lap cheung sausage. **Cake shops** selling heavy Chinese pastries and filled buns are found everywhere across the region. Some items like **custard tartlets** are derived from foreign sources, while roast-pork buns and flaky-skinned **mooncakes** stuffed with sweet lotus seed paste are of domestic origin.

Perhaps it's this delight in little delicacies that led to the tradition of **dim sum** (dian xin in Mandarin) really blossoming in Guangdong, where it's become an elaborate form of breakfast most popular on Sundays, when entire households pack out restaurants. Also known in Cantonese as **yum cha** – literally, "drink tea" – it involves little dishes of fried, boiled and steamed snacks being stuffed inside bamboo steamers or displayed on plates, then wheeled around the restaurant on trolleys, which you stop for inspection as they pass your table. On being seated, you're given a pot of tea, which is constantly topped up, and a card, which is marked for each dish you select and which is later surrendered to the cashier. Try juk (rice porridge), spring rolls, buns, cakes and plates of thinly sliced roast meats, and small servings of restaurant dishes like spareribs, stuffed capsicum, or squid with black beans. Save most room, however, for the myriad types of little fried and steamed **dumplings** which are the hallmark of a dim sum meal, such as har gau, juicy minced prawns wrapped in transparent rice-flour skins; and siu mai, a generic name for a host of delicately flavoured, open-topped packets.

FUJIAN, GUANGDONG AND HAINAN ISLAND | Guangzhou

palates too, and some are worth checking for special sittings. The daily dessert buffet at the *China Marriott* (3–5pm; ¥46 per person), for example, features an unbelievable array of pastries and cakes served with tea or coffee; the *White Swan* does endless coffee refills (¥40) as well as a buffet breakfast (¥124) before 11am – and has the best riverside views in Guangzhou.

Central Guangzhou

Datong 63 Yanjiang Xi Lu. If you're after an authentically noisy, crowded *dim sum* session with river views, head here to floors 2, 5 or 6 between 7am and noon. They pride themselves on their roast suckling pig. Window seats are in high demand, so arrive early.

Huimin Fandian (aka Five Rams) Southeast corner of the Renmin Lu/Zhongshan Lu crossroads. The city's biggest and most popular Muslim restaurant, serving lamb hotpots, roast duck, lemon chicken and spicy beef. Inexpensive to moderately priced.

Lucky Fellow Sixth floor of a shopping centre on the corner of Taikang Lu and Huilong Lu. This large, smart establishment serves up a range of Chinese cuisines, focusing on Cantonese – both the roast goose and fragrant chicken are excellent. Has an extensive English menu and is reasonably priced, with main dishes starting at ¥18.

Qianfu Lou Corner of Beijing Lu and Yushan Lu. Full-on Cantonese restaurant on three floors, with a take-away roast-meat shop and canteen downstairs, plus more formal arrangements above.

Northern and eastern Guangzhou

Banana Leaf Curry House Fifth floor, World Trade Centre, Huanshi Dong Lu. Good, eclectic mix of Thai, Malaysian and Indonesian fare, all authentically spiced. Not cheap, though; expect upwards of ¥70 a head.

Dongbei Ren Opposite Liuhua Park on Renmin Bei Lu. Nationwide chain serving Manchurian food in comfortable surroundings; sautéed corn kernels with pine nuts, steamed chicken with mushrooms, or eggs and black fungus are all good. Portions from ¥20.

Hunan Girl Taojin Lu. Hunanese restaurant more popular with Guangzhou's expats than Chinese residents – the interior even looks like an average Chinese restaurant overseas – though the cooking is good and prices are reasonable.

Jiangxi Ren 475 Huanshi Dong Lu. It's easy to spot the huge earthenware jars outside this one, and the second-floor restaurant is decked out in Chinese 'folksy' furnishings. The main thing to try here is the Jiangxi-style giant soups, enough for three or four people, at around ¥35–60; the duck and pear variety is excellent.

Samba Jianshe Lu. Excellent evening atmosphere here, with South American music (live, courtesy of the Brazilian staff), a colossal selection of imported booze, and various all-you-can-eat deals for about ¥50–70 – if you're not tempted by the juiciest beef ribs in town.

Western Guangzhou

Daiwo Sushi Shibafu Lu, just south of the *Guangzhou* restaurant. Sit around a central bar and pick up plates of sushi as they pass on a conveyor belt; good fun and very popular. Plates are colour-coded according to a ¥5–15 pricing scheme, and staff tot up your empties at the end.

Guangzhou Corner of Wenchang Nan Lu and Xiajiu Lu; other branches citywide. The oldest, busiest and most famous restaurant in the city, with entrance calligraphy by the Qing emperor Kangxi and a rooftop neon sign flashing "Eating in Guangzhou". The menu is massive, and you won't find better crisp-skinned chicken or pork anywhere – bank on ¥80 a person for a decent feed. Service is offhand, though.

Lian Xiang Lou Dishifu Lu. Established in 1889 and famous for its mooncakes, baked dough confections stuffed with sweet lotus paste and shaped as rabbits and peaches, which you can buy from the downstairs shop. The upstairs restaurant does commendable roast suckling pig, brown-sauced pigeon, and duck fried with lotus flowers for about ¥30 a portion.

Liwan Mingshijia 99 Dishifu Lu. Ming-style canteen and teahouse decked in heavy marble-and-wood furniture, crammed with diners wolfing down *dim-sum*-style snacks. Some of the finest *sheung fan* (stuffed rice rolls), *zongzi* (steamed packets of rice and meat) and *tangyuan* (glutinous riceballs filled with chopped nuts in a sweet soup) you'll find. No English and not much Mandarin spoken, but you can order by pointing to other people's dishes.

Moon Carol Café Dishifu Lu; there are other branches on Dongfeng Zhong Lu and in the CITIC Plaza in Tianhe. Western-style grills, including New Zealand steaks from ¥48, or set meals with coffee from ¥28.

Panxi Longjin Xi Lu, Liwan Park. The best thing about this Cantonese restaurant – a teahouse of poor repute in the 1940s – is the lakeside location and interesting *dim sum* selection. Main meals are undistinguished, however, and the English-language menu is disappointingly perfunctory. Inexplicably popular with tour groups, who apparently haven't discovered the far superior *Tao Tao Ju*.

Tao Tao Ju Dishifu Lu. Looks upmarket, with huge chandeliers, wooden shutters and coloured leadlight windows, but prices are mid-range and very good value. Roast goose is the house speciality, and they also do cracking seafood – plain boiled prawns or fried crab are both excellent – along with crisp-skinned chicken, lily-bud and beef sandpots, and a host of Cantonese favourites. Comprehensive English menu; mains ¥18–80.

Shamian Island

Cow and Bridge Thai Shamian Bei Jie. Very formal place to dine on what is unquestionably the finest Thai food in Guangzhou, if not all China. The food is beautifully presented and the service impeccable, though expect to pay ¥120 a head.

Golden Bowl Shamian Dajie. A new, smart, yet convivial affair serving up tasty Cantonese cuisine for around ¥50 a head; try the Chaozhou pork (¥22).

Lucy's Bar Shamian Nan Jie. Sit outside in the evening at this Westerner-oriented place and eat decent Mexican-, Thai- and Indian-style dishes, along with burgers, pizza and grills – their fish and chips is also nostalgically good. Mains ¥25–70; cheap beer at ¥20 a pint; and afternoon tea for ¥20 per person.

Shamian Cuisine Outside the *White Swan*, Shamian Nan Jie. An inexpensive Chinese canteen with good rice-noodle and pork soups, fried rice,

and bowls of *jiaozi* – nothing to cross town for, but offers the cheapest food on the island.

Station Western Shamian Bei Jie. If you fancy a break from the usual, this mid-range place offers an assortment of cuisines (from Asian to BBQ to Italian), either served in the garden or, if you've got the cash to splash, in a private room aboard one of its two train carriages.

Victory Shamian Bei and Si Jie. Worth a visit for good, if pricey, *dim sum* eaten among the usual cheerful throngs. Daily 7am–5.30pm.

Xin Lizhi Wan Shamian Nan Jie. One of the most highly regarded seafood restaurants in the city, always busy with a mostly upmarket clientele. Not too expensive, however; you can eat well here for ¥80 a head.

South of the river

Fo Shijie Su Shishe South off Tongfu Lu – look for the yellow sign with red characters and green-tiled, temple-like flourishes. Scrumptious vegetarian fare, and huge portions; crispy chicken drumsticks in sweet-and-sour sauce, salt-fried prawns, chicken-ball casserole and the rest are all made from bean curd, with heaps of straightforward vegetable dishes too. Full English menu; most dishes under ¥30.

Nanyuan 142 Qianjin Lu. Possibly the best restaurant in Guangzhou, serving cheapish *dim sum* until about 10am, when it transforms into an upmarket establishment. Superb stewed Chaozhou-style goose, Maotai chicken (steamed in the famous sorghum spirit of that name) and fish with pine nuts. Metro Line #2 to Jiangnanxi or bus #35 from Haizhu Square on Yanjiang Zhong Lu.

Drinking, nightlife and entertainment

By Chinese standards, Guangzhou has good **nightlife**. A scattering of **clubs** in the central and eastern parts of the city ranges from warehouse-sized discos to obscure, almost garage-like affairs, aimed at a mostly Chinese student and yuppie crowd; some have a **cover charge** (usually around ¥30 including a beer) though most get their money through higher-than-average prices for drinks. Expats favour the bars located in Guangzhou's eastern reaches, where the booze is cheaper (around ¥25 a pint), pub-style meals can be had for ¥20–40, and the music is for listening to rather than dancing. Club hours are from 8pm to 2am, bars are open anytime from lunch to 2am, but don't expect much to be happening before 9pm at either. As usual, places open and close without notice, or swing in and out of popularity; one promising up-and-coming area is waterfront **Yanjiang Lu**. The places reviewed overleaf are good starting points, but check out Ⓦ www.guangzhou .asiaxpat.com for the latest.

    Cantonese opera is superficially similar to Beijing's, but more rustic. Virtually extinct by the 1990s, it has recently bounced back in popularity, with *Guangming*, south of the river at the junction of Baogang Dadao and Nanhua

Guangzhou drinking and nightlife

Bars and clubs

Café Elle's	木子吧	mùzǐ bā
Cave	墨西哥餐厅酒吧	mòxīgē cāntīng jiǔbā
City Bar	城市酒吧	chéngshì jiǔbā
Elephant and Castle	大象堡酒吧	dàxiàngbǎo jiǔbā
Gipsy King	万紫千红酒吧	wànzǐqiānhóng jiǔbā
Gold Mango	金芒果酒吧	jīnmángguǒ jiǔbā
Hill Bar	小山吧	xiǎoshān bā
Peace	和平路西餐酒廊	hépínglù xīcānjiǔláng

Opera venues

Guangming	光明剧院	guāngmíng jùyuàn

Lu in Honan (T020/84499721), and *Jiang Nan* at 130 Chang Gang Zhong Lu (T020/84324187) hosting several performances monthly. You might also catch amateur groups performing in the parks at the weekends – Shamian Park on Shamian Island is a good place to look.

Clubs

Café Elle's Floor 2, *Huaxin Dasha*, northeast corner of Huanshi Lu and Shuiyin Lu. Being renovated at the time of writing, but when it re-opens it should continue to be the best jazz and blues venue in the city, with regular international bands and nightly mixes of Latin and dance. It's not easy to find the right entrance, which is the small one on the eastern side of the building.

Cave Huanshi Dong Lu, west from the *Garden* hotel. Italian cantina and dance club, hidden down in a basement, with DJs or drummers playing to an ultraviolet-lit crowd.

Deep Anger Music Club Yanjiang Lu. Vast, Gothic-style venue offering a range of entertainment from disco to live music and floor shows.

ET Space Yanjiang Lu. Next to *Deep Anger*, this place offers more of the same in a space-age setting.

Gipsy King (aka Magic Colours) Huanshi Dong Lu, just west of *Cave*, this place is of a similar ilk, but has nightly shows around 10pm.

Peace Heping Lu. Nightly live music on two floors – everything from Canto-pop to Chinese rock and more offbeat local bands.

Yes Dongfeng Xi Lu, south of Liuhua Park. Huge, popular, full-on house experience at maximum decibels.

Bars

1920s Café Yanjiang Lu. A refined yet relaxed place for a quiet drink. Also has a pleasant outdoor patio.

City Bar City Plaza, Tianhe Lu, Tianhe. Relaxed place to spend an hour or two over a Heineken before your train goes from Guangzhou East. Hard to find, the building is east of the better-signed Teem Plaza.

Elephant and Castle Huanshi Dong Lu. Dim corners and cramped bar make this a favourite with barfly foreigners, though it has a good beer garden and typically gets loud and busy as the evening progresses. Variable happy hours. Opens late afternoon.

Gold Mango Huanshi Dong Lu. Bit of a pick-up joint, but cosy and laid-back atmosphere, welcoming staff and fine beer garden.

Hill Bar Huanshi Dong Lu, across from the *Garden* hotel. Third choice in the trinity of adjacent expat bars, serving cheap beer (¥20 a pint) and bar meals, with occasional live music.

Shopping

Guangzhou's **shopping** ethos is very much towards the practical side of things. The **Changshou Lu** area in western Guangzhou is a mass of shopping plazas, designer clothes shops and boutique stores, with **Beijing Lu** a similar, more central version; both have sections which are pedestrianized at weekends. To see where Guangzhou – and China – is heading, however, make your way over to the shockingly modern and upmarket **Friendship Store**, five floors of expensive imported designer gear and some good-value, domestic formal wear; it's on easterly Taojin Lu, just off Huanshi Dong Lu.

For functional memorabilia, the streets running east off the southern end of Renmin Lu might give you some ideas. Yide Lu has several huge wholesale warehouses stocking **dried foods** and **toys** – action figures from Chinese legends, rockets and all things that rattle and buzz. Other shops in the area deal in home decorations, such as colourful tiling or jigsawed decorative wooden dragons and phoenixes, and at New Year you can buy those red and gold good-luck posters put up outside businesses and homes.

For out-and-out tourist souvenirs, head first to the *White Swan Hotel* on Shamian Island. Their batiks and clothing, carved wooden screens and jade monstrosities are well worth a look, if only to make you realize what a good deal you're getting when you buy elsewhere – such as in the shops just outside on Shamian Si Jie. Wende Lu, running south from Zhongshan Lu, and various small shops in the streets between Dishifu Lu and Liuersan Lu, have varying selections of authenticated **antiques**, jade, lacquerwork, scrolls, chops and cloisonné artefacts, identical to what you'll find in the Yue Hua stores in Hong Kong, but at half the price. The **jade market** near Hualin Si (see p.596) is also worth a snoop.

For **Western groceries**, the Beatrice Supermarket, attached to the *Victory* on Shamian Si Jie, is a treasure trove of imported cheese, olives, pasta and biscuits – and there's also a coffee bar with hearty brews at ¥15 a cup.

Listings

Acupuncture Anyone interested in receiving cheap acupuncture preceded by massage by a blind masseuse should head for the clinic attached to the Zhongshan Medical College, Zhongshan Lu, where students practise.

Airlines China Southern Airlines is at 181 Huanshi Dong Lu (☏22272726), two doors east of the main train station. Japan Airlines are in the *China Marriott* (☏86696688). Malaysia Airlines (☏83358868), Thai Airways (☏38821818) and Vietnam Airlines (☏83867093) all have offices at the *Garden*, Huanshi Dong Lu.

Banks and exchange Two branches of the Bank of China are in the enormous office in the centre of the city on Dongfeng Zhong Lu and outside the *White Swan*, Shamian Island (both open for currency exchange Mon–Fri 9am–noon & 2–5pm). Counters at the *Liuhua*, *China Marriott*, *Landmark* and *Garden* hotels change currency for non-guests; the *White Swan* does not.

Bicycle hire If you want to try a different, if difficult, way of getting around Guangzhou, there's a tandem bike hire shop on Binjiang Zhong Lu, just east of the Haizhu Bridge (two-person bike ¥10 per hour, three-person bike ¥15 per hour).

Bookshops The Xinhua bookstore on Beijing Lu has an unexciting range of English literature and translated Chinese classics. The city's biggest bookstore, Guangzhou Books Centre, is at the southwest corner of Tianhe Square, Tianhe Lu

– four storeys of technical manuals, computer texts and university tomes, but little in English. Otherwise, the main source of reading material is the comprehensive and expensive range of everything from potboilers to coffee-table works and contemporary Chinese fiction paperbacks – along with international newspapers and magazines – available at the *White Swan*.

Consulates Australia, Room 1509, *Guangdong International*, 339 Huanshi Dong Lu ☏83350909, ☏83350718; Canada, Room 801, *China* ☏86660569, ☏86672401; France, Room 803, *Guangdong International*, 339 Huanshi Dong Lu ☏83303405, ☏83303437; Germany, Floor 19, *Guangdong International*, 339 Huanshi Dong Lu ☏83306533, ☏83317033; Italy, Room 5207, CITIC Plaza, 233 Tianhe Bei Lu ☏38770556, ☏38770270; Japan, *Garden*, 368 Huanshi Dong Lu ☏83338972, ☏83878009; Malaysia, Floor 19, CITIC Plaza, 233 Tianhe Bei Lu ☏38770766, ☏38770769; Netherlands, Room 905, *Guangdong International*, 339 Huanshi Dong Lu ☏83302067, ☏83303601; Philippines, Room 709, *Guangdong International*, 339 Huanshi Dong Lu ☏83311461, ☏83330573; Thailand, *Garden*, 368 Huanshi Dong Lu ☏83338967, ☏83889567; UK, Floor 2, *Guangdong International*, 339 Huanshi Dong Lu ☏83351354, ☏83327509; US, Shamian Nan Jie, Shamian Island ☏81218000 ☏81219001; Vietnam, Room 27, *Hua Xia*, Haizhu Square

⊕83305910 ⓕ83305915. Note that consulates' visa sections are usually only open from around 9am to 11.30am, and getting served isn't always easy.

Hospitals Call 120 for emergency services. There's an English-speaking team at SOS, Guangdong Provincial Hospital of Traditional Chinese Medicine, 261 Datong Lu, Er Sha Island, Guangzhou (Mon–Fri 9am–6pm; ⊕87351051). Other options include Guangdong Provincial People's Hospital, 106 Zhongshan Er Lu (⊕83827812) and the Red Cross Hospital, 396 Tongfu Zhong Lu (⊕84412233). There are English-speaking dentists at Sunshine Dental Clinic, 2 Tianhe Bei Lu (24hr English hotline; ⊕33874278). For anything serious, though, you're better off heading to Hong Kong.

Internet access Places come and go very quickly, but can be found for as little as ¥2 an hour. The unnamed Internet café one block south of Chen Jia Ci metro is such a place. However, if you're restricted to Shamian Island, the price will generally be higher. Michael's, at the south end of Shamian Er Jie, Shamian Island, is principally a shop, but offers Internet access for ¥10 an hour (daily 9am–9pm), or if you fancy a caffeine kick with your browsing, Blenz Coffee on Shamian Dajie provides free Internet use for its customers. Many hotels offer Internet access, but this tends to be very expensive.

Interpreters The major hotels can organize interpreters for upwards of ¥600 per day – you're also expected to cover all additional incidental costs such as meals and transport.

Left luggage Offices at the train (24hr) and bus station (daily 8am–6pm).

Mail and telephones There are major post offices with IDD telephones, parcel post and poste restante, on the western side of the square outside Guangzhou train station (daily 8am–8pm), and across from the Cultural Park entrance on Liuersan Lu (daily 8am–6pm). Shamian Island's post counter is open Mon–Sat 9am–5pm for stamps, envelopes and deliveries. All hotels have postal services and international call facilities.

Police For all police matters, such as reporting theft, head to the PSB.

PSB On the corner of Jiefang Lu and Dade Lu (⊕020/83115721); Mon–Fri 8–11.30am & 2.20–5pm).

Travel agents Try the following if hotels can't help with tours and transport reservations: CITS Travel, beside the *CITS Hotel Guangdong*, immediately east of the main train-station square on Huanshi Dong Lu (⊕86666889, ⓦwww.citsgd.cn) can book tours, hotels and tickets within China, whilst STA Travel in the same office (⊕86671445, ⓦwww.statrave.com.cn) is the agent for numerous international airlines and hotels; CTS, at the *Landmark* (⊕83336888, ⓦwww.chinatravelone.com).

The Pearl River Delta

The **Pearl River Delta** initially seems to be entirely a product of the modern age, dominated by industrial complexes and the glossy, high-profile cities of **Shenzhen**, east on the crossing to Hong Kong, and westerly **Zhuhai**, on the Macau border. Back in the 1980s these were marvels of Deng Xiaoping's reforms, rigidly contained **Special Economic Zones** of officially sanctioned free-market activities, which were anathema to Communist ideologies. Their incredible success inspired an invasion of the delta by foreign and domestic companies, obscuring an economic history dating back to the time of Song engineers who constructed irrigation canals through the delta's **five counties** – Nanhai, Panyu, Shunde, Dongguan and Zhongshan. From the Ming dynasty, local crafts and surplus food were exported across Guangdong, artisans flourished and funded elaborate guild temples, while gentlemen of leisure built gardens in which to wander and write poetry.

Today, it's easy to hop on high-speed transport and cut through the delta in a couple of hours, seeing little more than the unattractive urban mantle that surrounds the highways. But spend a little longer on your journey or dip into the region on short trips from Guangzhou, and there's a good deal to discover about China here, especially in the way that everything looks hastily built and temporary – development is clearly happening too fast for any unified planning. The past survives too. Don't miss **Foshan**'s splendid **Ancestral Temple**, or **Lianhua Shan**, a landscaped ancient quarry; historians might also wish to visit **Humen**, where the destruction of British opium in 1839 ignited the first Opium War, and **Cuiheng**, home village of China's revered revolutionary elder statesman, **Sun Yatsen**.

The delta has China's highest density of **expressways**, including the 175-kilometre **Guangshen Expressway**, which runs southeast from Guangzhou to Shenzhen. The delta's western side is covered by a mesh of roads which you can follow more or less directly south between sights to Zhuhai, 155km from Guangzhou. Buses from Guangzhou's Liuhua and Provincial bus stations cover all destinations in the locality. There's also the **Guangzhou–Shenzhen train**, though services don't tend to stop along the way, and there should be a **metro link** to Foshan (from Kengkou metro station, line 1) by 2007.

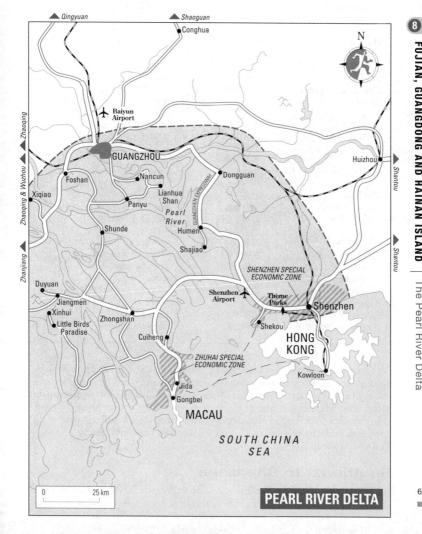

The Pearl River Delta

Cuiheng	翠亨村	*cuìhēng cūn*
Sun Yatsen's Residence	孙中山故居	*sūnzhōngshān gùjù*
Dongguan	东莞	*dōng guǎn*
Keyuan	可园	*kěyuán*
Foshan	佛山	*fóshān*
Huaqiao Dasha	华侨大厦	*huáqiáo dàshà*
Liang Yuan	梁园	*liángyuán*
Mei Yuan Jiujia	梅园酒家	*méiyuán jiǔjiā*
Pearl River Hotel	珠江大酒店	*zhūjiāng dàjiǔdiàn*
Renshou Si	仁受寺	*rénshòu sì*
Zu Miao	祖庙	*zǔmiào*
Humen	虎门	*hǔmén*
Jiangmen	江门	*jiāng mén*
Duyuan	杜院	*dùyuàn*
Little Birds' Paradise	小鸟天堂	*xiǎoniǎo tiāntáng*
Xinhui	薪会	*xīnhuì*
Nancun	南村	*náncūn*
Yuyin Shanfang	余英山房	*yúyīng shānfáng*
Panyu	番禺	*pānyú*
Lianhua Shan	莲花山	*liánhuā shān*
Shajiao	沙角	*shājiǎo*
Shajiao Paotai	沙角炮台	*shājiǎo pàotái*
Lin Zexu Park	林则徐公园	*línzéxú gōngyuán*
Shenzhen	深圳	*shēnzhèn*
Folk Culture Village	民俗文化村	*mínsú wénhuàcūn*
Lizhi Park	荔枝公园	*lìzhī gōngyuán*
Luo Hu Border Crossing	罗湖	*luóhú*
Minsk World	明思克航空世界	*míngsīkè hángkōng shìjiè*
Shekou	蛇口	*shékǒu*
Splendid China	锦绣中华	*jǐnxiù zhōnghuá*
Window on the World	世界之窗	*shìjiè zhīchuāng*

It's worth noting that both Shenzhen and Zhuhai SEZs are surrounded by electric fences and inspection posts to deter smugglers – one of the few times you're likely to see armed police in China – and you'll need to show **passports** to get through, whether you're coming in by bus or, to Shenzhen, by train. Don't confuse these checks with actual border formalities; you'll still have to fill out forms and get your passport inspected again to cross into Macau or Hong Kong from the SEZs.

Southeast to Shenzhen

An hour southeast of Guangzhou down the expressway, **DONGGUAN** is the administrative seat of the delta's most productive county, its factories churning

Downtown metro stops		
Da Ju Yuan	大剧院	*dàjùyuàn*
Guo Mao	国贸	*guómào*
Kexue Guan	科学馆	*kēxuéguǎn*
Lao Jie	老街	*lǎojiē*
Luo Hu	罗湖	*luóhú*
Shijiezhichuang	世界之窗	*shìjièzhīchuāng*

Accommodation		
Airlines	航空大酒店	*hángkōng dàjiǔdiàn*
Dragon	港龙大酒店	*gǎnglóng dàjiǔdiàn*
Far East	远东酒店	*yuǎndōng jiǔdiàn*
Guang Dong	粤海酒店	*yuèhǎi jiǔdiàn*
Landmark	深圳富苑酒店	*shēnzhèn fùyuàn jiǔdiàn*
Petrel	海燕大酒店	*hǎiyàn dàjiǔdiàn*

Shunde	顺德	*shùndé*
Feng Cheng Jiudian	凤城酒店	*fèngchéng jiǔdiàn*
Feng Ling Park	风岭公园	*fēnglǐng gōngyuán*
Marriott Courtyard	顺德新世界万怡酒店	*shùndé xīnshìjiè wànyí jiǔdiàn*
Qinghui Gardens	清晖园	*qīnghuī yuán*
Xishan Gumiao	西山古庙	*xīshān gǔmiào*

Xinhui	薪会	*xīnhuì*

Xiqiao	西樵	*xīqiáo*

Zhongshan	中山	*zhōngshān*

Zhuhai	珠海	*zhūhǎi*
Chang'an Jiudian	昌安酒店	*chāng'ān jiǔdiàn*
Gongbei	拱北	*gǒngběi*
Huaxia Shijie	华夏食街	*huáxià shíjiē*
Jida	吉大	*jídà*
Min'an Jiudian	民安酒店	*mín'ān jiǔdiàn*
Shenjing Canteen	深井烧鹅拱北分店	*shēnjǐng shāo'e gǒngběi fēndiàn*
Taida Jiudian	泰达酒店	*tàidá jiǔdiàn*
Xiangzhou	香州珠海度假村	*xiāngzhōu zhūhǎi dùjiàcūn*
You Yi Jiudian	友谊酒店	*yǒuyí jiǔdiàn*
Yuehai Jiudian	粤海酒店	*yuèhǎi jiǔdiàn*

out textiles, electronic components and pirated VCDs and computer software – an industry which, controlled as it is by the military, Beijing has had no success in suppressing, despite periodic US threats of trade sanctions.

If you're heading to Dongguan's port, **Humen**, famous for its role in the nineteenth-century **Opium Wars**, you may need to stop in Dongguan to change buses, in which case you could take the time to have a look at **Keyuan** (daily 8am–4pm; ¥8), once one of Guangdong's "Four Famous Gardens". Walk north from the **bus station** up Wantai Dadao for 250m, turn west along Keyuan Nan Lu, and it's about 1km away across the river. Laid out for the Qing minister, Zhang Jingxiu, Keyuan puts its very limited space to good use, cramming an unlikely number of passages, rooms, pavilions and devious staircases inside its walls, all built in distinctive, pale blue bricks. There are a few flowerbeds and trees, but Keyuan's most striking aspect is the way it shuts out the rest of the city at ground level – though Dongguan's motorways are only too obvious from the upper storey of the main **Yaoshi Pavilion**.

Humen and Shajiao

Minibuses from Guangzhou or Dongguan land at **HUMEN** (pronounced "Fumen" locally), though some transport drops you 5km short on the Guangshen Expressway, where shuttle buses wait to carry you into town. In 1839, after a six-week siege of the "Foreign Factories" in Guangzhou, the British handed over 1200 tons of **opium** to **Lin Zexu**, the Qing official in charge of stopping the opium trade. Lin brought it to Humen, mixed it with quicklime, and dumped it in two 45-metre pits on the beach 4km south of Humen's centre at **Shajiao**; after three weeks, the remains were flushed out to sea. Incensed at this destruction of their opium, the British massacred the Chinese garrisons at Humen and on nearby **Weiyun Island**, and attacked Guangzhou. Lin got the blame and was exiled to the frontier province of Xinjiang, only to be replaced by the ineffectual Yi Shan, a nephew of the emperor, later a signatory to the humiliating Guangzhou Treaty.

These events are recounted in Chinese documents and heroic sculptures at the **Lin Zexu Park Museum** on Jiefang Lu (daily 9am–5pm; ¥16), a twenty-minute walk between the skyscrapers northwest of Humen's bus station. It's more rewarding, however, to catch a minibus to Shajiao, where the opium pits remain, along with a fortress, **Shajio Paotai** (daily 8am–5.30pm; ¥15). The whole place is thick with poinsettias, banyans and butterflies, all making for a nice couple of hours on the beach.

Shenzhen

If **SHENZHEN** had been around in classical times, poets would doubtless have compared its gleaming downtown towers to mountain peaks, each rising higher than the other. Incredibly, in 1979 this metropolis was a simple rural hamlet and train station called **Baoan**, the first office foundations yet to be dug in its alluvial plains on the Hong Kong border. Within six years, delegations from all over China were pouring in to learn how to remodel their own businesses, cities and provinces on Shenzhen's incentives-based economy. By 1990 the city had four harbours and its manufacturing industries alone were turning over US\$2 billion a year, necessitating the construction of a nuclear power station to deal with local energy needs; fifteen years later, output stood at US\$400 billion a year, and a third power station was under way. Today, a third of Shenzhen's income comes from exporting hi-tech products and almost half the world's watches are made in town.

Shenzhen may not have been the cause of capitalism in the People's Republic, but it was a glorious piece of propaganda for those who promoted its virtues. It's no coincidence that, on his landmark 1992 "**Southern Tour**", Deng Xiaoping chose Shenzhen as the place to make his memorable statement: "Poverty is not Socialism: to get rich is glorious", voicing the Party's shift from Communist dogma to a pragmatic, results-driven approach to economics – and opening the gate for the start of China's financial boom.

Having said all this, Shenzhen isn't so amazing these days, what with similar skylines rearing up all over China; the border area is also a bit grubby, and overrun by beggars and pickpockets. After a quick sniff around, there's little reason to stay any longer than it takes to organize your next move into or out of the mainland.

SHENZHEN

BAOAN

Guangzhou

Airport, Theme Parks, Guangzhou & Shekou

Lizhi Park

Lao Jie

Minsk World

SHENNAN DONG LU

Bank of China

International Trade Centre

Da Ju Yuan

JIEFANG LU

SHENNAN ZHONG LU

Ke Xue Guan

JIABIN LU

Guo Mao

Buses to Shekou

CUNFENG LU

YANHE LU

BINHE LU

Train Station

Luo Hu

Bus & Minibus Station

N

HONG KONG

Luo Hu Border Crossing

Kowloon

ACCOMMODATION

Airlines	B
Dragon	F
Far East	A
Guang Dong	D
Landmark	C
Petrel	E

0   1 km

EATING & DRINKING

Beifang Fengwei	4
KFC	1
Panxi	5
Renren Jiulou	2
Tiecheng	3

The City

For a good glimpse of the city's extremes of wealth and poverty, spend an hour strolling along Renmin Lu, which runs northeast from the train station and **Luo Hu border crossing** (you might see the Cantonese rendering, Lo Wu, on signs) through the centre. The **International Trade Centre** is a three-storey block on the corner of Jiabin Lu, full of people browsing through stocks of upmarket jewellery and perfume. Push on over Jiefang Lu and you're in the tangle of narrow lanes which formed the **old town** of Baoan, now a downmarket selection of stalls selling cheap clothes, shoes and gadgets. There's a historic monument of sorts here in a squat, blue-roofed diner on Qingyuan Lu – China's original *McDonald's* restaurant, now a *KFC* outlet.

For a shot of greenery, take the metro to Da Ju Yuan, or walk 1500m west from the centre along Shennan Zhong Lu, to **Lizhi Park**, a surprisingly refreshing open space, with a nice lake and modern **opera house**, worth checking out for occasional performances of **Chinese theatre**. Alternatively, hop on metro line #1 to its terminus at Shijiezhichuang, or bus #204 from Jianshe Lu for the thirty-minute ride west to Shenzhen's three very professional

theme parks, next to each other on the Guangshen Expressway – look for a miniaturized Golden Gate Bridge spanning the road. Amid limitless souvenir stalls, **Window on the World** (daily 9am–10pm; ¥120) is a collection of scale models of famous world monuments such as the Eiffel Tower and Mount Rushmore, while **Splendid China** (daily 8am–5pm; ¥120) offers the same for China's sights. The latter's ticket also includes the **Folk Culture Village** (daily 8am–5pm), an enjoyably touristy introduction to the nation's ethnic groups – there are yurts, pavilions, huts, archways, rock paintings and mechanical goats, with colourful troupes performing different national dances every thirty minutes (¥35).

If you're after something completely different, jump aboard bus #202 or #205 from the bus depot by the border to **Minsk World** (¥110), a whole Russian aircraft carrier – complete with aircraft – moored up at the docks for your entertainment; allow at least half a day for a full exploration.

Practicalities

A five-kilometre-wide semicircle immediately north of the Hong Kong border, central Shenzhen is evenly bisected by the **rail line** that descends straight down Jianshe Lu to the Luo Hu crossing. The border area itself is defined by the massive Luo Hu **bus station** to the east and similarly-sized **train station** to the west; if you've just crossed from Hong Kong, these are ahead and to your right and left respectively.

The **international airport** is 20km west of town, with a shuttle bus (¥20) operating between here and the *Xinhua* hotel on Shennan Zhong Lu. The **port** lies 15km west at **Shekou**, where ferries from Macau, Zhuhai and Hong Kong pull in, and is served thrice hourly by the #204 bus (¥6) to Jianshe Lu. Taxis and minibuses roam everywhere, and the city has an enviably efficient bus service, as well as a brand new **metro system**; line #1 runs from Luo Hu (and will, in time, connect with Hong Kong's KCR) to Window on the World at Shijiezhichuang, whilst #4 runs south from Shaoniangong to Fumin and when completed it will reach Huanggang on the border with Lok Mau in Hong Kong. Fares are ¥2–5 and trains operate from 6.30am to 10.30pm. There are **banks** at the border crossing, the airport, ferry terminal and some hotels, and a suitably oversized Bank of China on Jianshe Lu (Mon–Fri 9am–5pm).

Moving on from Shenzhen

The **Hong Kong border** is open daily, from 6.30am to midnight. There's a lack of directional signs in the vicinity; you need to get on to the overpass from upstairs at the train station and then head south past souvenir stalls, roasted meat vendors and pet shops. Border formalities on both sides are streamlined, and it shouldn't take more than an hour to find yourself on the other side, purchasing a ticket for the **KCR** (Kowloon–Canton Railway) train into Hong Kong.

Trains to Guangzhou East can take as little as an hour on the new high-speed track; they run between 6.25am and 10.30pm and tickets cost ¥70. There is a designated Guangzhou **ticket office** at street level, and, next door, another sells tickets on direct services to dozens of destinations between Shenzhen and Beijing.

Buses leave regularly from the Luo Hu bus station for the delta, Guangzhou, the rest of Guangdong and many places in central China. **Ferries** depart direct to Macau, Hong Kong and Zhuhai through the day; catch bus #204 from Jianshe Lu to the port at Shekou. For **flights** into the rest of China, contact CAAC on Shennan Zhong Lu.

Accommodation and eating

The cheapest places to **eat** are in the streets immediately north of Jiefang Lu, where Chinese canteens can fill you up with good dumplings, soups and stir-fries. There are dozens of smarter options all through the centre, such as inexpensive casseroles at *Renren Jiulou*, east of the *Airlines* hotel on Shennan Dong Lu; mantis shrimps, stonefish and other seafood at the *Panxi*, on Jianshe Lu; fine northern cooking and an ornate red and gold exterior at the *Beifang Fengwei*, farther up Jianshe Lu; and upmarket snake, cat and wildfowl delights at the *Tiecheng*, west of the tracks on Heping Lu. The **hotels**, a selection of which is reviewed below, have good restaurants, too, along with karaoke bars, interpreters, conference facilities, postal services and the like.

Airlines Shennan Dong Lu ☏0755/82237999, Ⓕ82237866. Good, comfortable rooms, a seafood restaurant and an expensive coffee shop. ❺
Dragon At the train station, Jianshe Lu ☏0755/82329228, Ⓕ82334585. Rooms are smartly furnished and reasonable value and the huge Cantonese restaurant has good *dim sum*. ❺
Far East Shennan Dong Lu ☏0755/82306688, Ⓕ82306539. Well-organized business venue with reasonable rooms, a Sichuanese restaurant and a dance hall. ❺

Guang Dong Shennan Dong Lu ☏0755/82228339, Ⓦwww.gdhhotels.com. A smart, airy, business hotel with three restaurants, including a Japanese. ❼
Landmark Nanhu Lu, corner of Shennan Dong Lu ☏0755/82172288, Ⓕ82290473. Rightly claims to be the best hotel in Shenzhen, boasting a beautifully furnished neo-colonial interior and three restaurants, one of which is described as a "Banquet Hall". ❽
Petrel Jiabin Lu ☏0755/82232828, Ⓕ82221398. Smart, new and friendly option with views of Shenzen's skyline. ❻

The western delta: Foshan

Twenty-five kilometres southwest of Guangzhou, and today a satellite suburb of the city, **FOSHAN** historically was very much a town in its own right, with a history dating back to the seventh century. Along with the nearby village of **Shiwan**, Foshan became famous for its ceramics, silk, metalwork and wood-carving – a reputation it still enjoys – and the splendour of its **temples**, two of which survive on **Zumiao Lu**, a kilometre-long street shaded by office buildings and set in the heart of what was once the old town centre. At the southern end, **Zu Miao** (Ancestral Temple; daily 8.30am–7.30pm; ¥20) is a masterpiece of southern architecture, founded in 1080 as a metallurgist's guild temple. Ahead and to the left of the entrance is an elevated garden fronted by some locally made Opium War **cannons** – sadly for the Chinese, poor casting techniques and a lack of rifling made these inaccurate and liable to explode. Nearby, magnificent glazed **roof tiles** of frolicking lions and characters from local tales were made in Shiwan for temple restorations in the 1830s. The temple's **main hall** is on the left past here, its interior crowded with minutely carved wooden screens, oversized guardian gods leaning threateningly out from the walls, and a three-tonne **statue of Beidi**, God of the North, who in local lore controlled low-lying Guangdong's flood-prone waters – hence this shrine to snare his goodwill.

Opposite the hall is the elaborate masonry of the **Lingying archway**, similar to those at Shexian in Anhui province (see p.489). Foshan is considered the birthplace of Cantonese opera, and beyond the archway you'll find the highly decorative **Wanfu stage**, built in 1685 for autumnal performances given to thank the Divine Emperor for his bountiful harvests. Foshan is also renowned as a martial arts centre, and there are permanent exhibitions to past masters Yip Man, Bruce Lee's instructor, and, in the north of the complex, another to Huang Fei Hong, a doctor and fighter who has been the subject of many a movie.

A few blocks north, **Renshou Si** (Benevolent Longevity Temple; 8am–5pm) is a former Ming monastery whose southern wing, graced by a short seven-storey pagoda, is still consecrated. The rest has been cleaned out and turned into the **Foshan Folk Arts Research Institute** (9am–5pm), a good place to look for souvenirs including excellent **papercuts** with definite Cultural Revolution leanings, showing the modernizing of rural economies. Around the Spring Festival, side halls are also full of celebratory lions, fish and phoenixes constructed from wire and coloured crepe paper.

About 1km due north of here on Songfeng Lu – continue up Zumiao Lu to its end, turn right and then first left – **Liang Yuan** (¥10) is another of the delta's historic **gardens**, built between 1796 and 1850 by a family of famous poets and artists of the period. There are artfully arranged ponds, trees and rocks, and the tastefully furnished residential buildings are worth a look, but the real gem here is the **Risheng Study**, a perfectly proportioned retreat looking out over a tiny, exquisitely designed pond, fringed with willows.

Practicalities

Fenjiang Bei Lu forms the western boundary of the old town, running south for about 2km from the **train station**, over a canal, past the **long-distance bus station** and through to where the skyscrapers, which constitute Foshan's business centre, cluster around a broad roundabout. **Buses** from Guangzhou's Liuhua bus station (¥13) deposit you at **Zumiao station**, just east of the roundabout on Chengmentou Lu; walk 50m east and you're at the bottom end of Zumiao Lu. To reach Zumiao Lu from the other stations, catch bus #1, #6, or #11, or walk down Fenjiang Bei Lu for about 700m, then east for a few minutes along tree-lined Qinren Lu to the intersection with Zumiao Lu. The proposed **metro** from Guangzhou is due for completion by 2007. Foshan's main **Bank of China** (Mon–Fri 8.30am–5pm, Sat 9am–4pm) is between the two temples, as is a post office, whilst a branch of CTS can be found between the two hotels (see below).

Foshan is comfortably visited as a day-trip from Guangzhou; however, if you'd prefer to stay, **accommodation** prospects include the swish *Huaqiao Dasha* (☎0757/82223828, ⓦwww.fshq-hotel.com; ❼), across and a little north from Renshou Si on Zumiao Lu, and the *Pearl River Hotel* a few buildings north (☎0757/82963638, ⓕ82292263; ❺). Both have **restaurants** and bars, and there are Western-style fast-food outlets scattered through the centre; for something more authentic you could try the moderately priced *Mei Yuan Jiujia* just south of Zu Miao, which specializes in Cantonese hotpots.

Around Panyu

A couple of attractive sights surround the town of **PANYU**, about 50km east of Foshan. It's roughly the same distance by road from Guangzhou, with buses departing from the Liuhua station, and there are also direct **ferries** from Hong Kong.

Overlooking the Pearl River 15km east of Panyu, **Lianhua Shan** (daily 8am–4pm; ¥35) is an odd phenomenon, a mountain quarried as long ago as the Han dynasty for its red stone, used in the tomb of the Nanyue king, Zhao Mo. After mining it in such a way as to leave a suspiciously deliberate arrangement of crags, pillars and caves, Ming officials planted the whole thing with trees and turned it into a pleasure garden laid with lotus pools, stone paths and pavilions. A fifty-metre-high pagoda was built in 1612, and the Qing emperor Kangxi added a fortress to defend the river. Still a popular excursion from Guangzhou, it's an interesting spot to while away a few hours, though frequently crowded.

A twenty-kilometre drive north of Panyu is **Nancun**, a fair-sized village where you'll find **Yuyin Shanfang** (daily 8am–5pm; ¥8), a retreat founded by the Qing-dynasty scholar Wu Yantian. He spent a fortune hiring the biggest names in contemporary landscape gardening, and created an artificial mountain, a lake, bamboo clumps, calligraphy walls and an octagonal pavilion. Here, Wu sat listening to flocks of cagebirds, and the muted tones of stringed *zheng* and *pipa*, played upstairs in the ladies' quarters (now a teahouse). The music has gone, and the former ancestral temple has been converted into a dance hall for wedding receptions, but the gardens remain as a nicely nostalgic tribute to a more refined time.

Shunde

Yet another antique garden, **Qinghui Gardens** (daily 8am–5.30pm; ¥15), is one reason to pause in the county town of **SHUNDE**, also known as **Daliang Zhen**, 50km south of Guangzhou on the most direct route to Zhuhai (¥23 from Guangzhou's Liuhua bus station). The well-kept gardens contain a series of square fish ponds surrounded by osmanthus, mulberry bushes and bamboo. The other highlight here is the *Qinghui Yuan* restaurant, in the grounds of the gardens, revered by the gastronomically inclined as the epitome of classic Cantonese cooking. Both the gardens and the restaurant are in the middle of town on Qinghui Lu. The restaurant (daily 7–9am, 11am–2pm & 5–7pm) is expensive – count on at least ¥75 a person – but the dishes are superb, with mild, fresh flavours which have to be taken slowly to be properly appreciated; their braised sea carp with garlic and ginger melts in the mouth. After eating, you can walk off your meal in the restored colonial-style streets behind the gardens off Hua Lu, where the old town centre forms a miniature version of Guangzhou's back lanes, with flagstones, markets and a fully restored street of colonial-era architecture. Alternatively, it's about 1km north across a huge open square and Wenxiu Lu to wooded and hilly **Feng Ling Park**, with the old **Xishan Gumiao** temple on the east side. It might also be worth asking locals to direct you to the Bruce Lee Museum, situated in a teahouse that Bruce supposedly visited once when he was five years old, and which holds memorabilia from China, Hong Kong and the US. Bruce's ancestral home was in nearby Shang village, Jun'an.

Shunde's new **long-distance bus station** is about 3km south of the centre on the highway; catch bus #9 from here to Qinghui Lu and the gardens. For a **place to stay**, there's the plush *Marriott Courtyard* opposite the gardens on Qinghui Lu (☏0757/22218333, Ⓦwww.courtyard.com; ❾); a cheaper option, the *Feng Cheng Jiudian* (☏0757/22331688, ❹), lies between the river and the old town – bus #9 from the station runs here. **Moving on**, if you can't find necessary long-distance transport at the bus station, head to Guangzhou or Zhongshan and pick up services there.

Jiangmen and around

Halfway between Guangzhou and Zhuhai, but slightly off to the west, **JIANGMEN** was formerly a pleasant town on the busy Jiangmen River, birthplace of the Ming poet **Chen Baisha**, and later dressed in cobbled streets and rows of nineteenth-century European-style mansions. Sadly, these have all but vanished, and the city has well and truly sold its soul to the ugliest side of urban development, retaining only its reputation for gymnastic excellence. You'll pass through if you're on the bus between Foshan and Zhuhai; on the way, a fifteen-kilometre stretch of wholesale **furniture warehouses** displaying chairs, beds and tables of every possible shape, style and colour adds a surreal touch to the journey.

While Jiangmen itself holds little appeal, the surrounding countryside might inspire you to stop off long enough to pick up a local minibus from beside the bus station on Jianshe Lu. There are a few very dilapidated Ming villages in the vicinity, some sporting two-storey towers built early last century by returning Overseas Chinese to parade their riches. About 15km southwest, at a spot reached via the town of **Xinhui**, flocks of cranes and waterfowl roost in the huge sprawl of a 500-year-old fig tree in the middle of the Tianma River, known locally as Xiaoniao Tiantang, the **Little Birds' Paradise**; here there are walkways around the tree, and paddle boats for rent. **Duyuan**, 10km west of Jiangmen, sits at the bottom of **Guifeng Shan**, a nicely formalized mountain offering a day's pleasant hiking between temples, trees and waterfalls on the way up to the windswept **Chishi Crag**.

Zhongshan and Cuiheng

Almost every town in China has a park or road named **Zhongshan**, a tribute to China's first Republican president, the remarkable **Dr Sun Yatsen**. Christened with the Cantonese name "Yatsen" (Yixian in Mandarin), he acquired the name Nakayama, meaning "middle mountain", while in exile in Japan, the characters for which are the same in Chinese, but pronounced "Zhongshan". Unless you

Sun Yatsen

Born in 1866, **Sun Yatsen** grew up during a period when China laboured under the humiliation of colonial occupation, a situation justly blamed on the increasingly feeble Qing court. Having spent three years in Hawaii during the 1880s, Sun studied medicine in Guangzhou and Hong Kong, where he became inspired by that other famous Guangdong revolutionary, Hong Xiuquan (see p.436), and began to involve himself in covert anti-Qing activities. Back in Hawaii in 1894, he abandoned his previous notions of reforming the imperial system and founded the **Revive China Society** to "Expel the Manchus, restore China to the people and create a federal government." The following year he incited an uprising in Guangzhou under **Lu Haodong**, notable for being the first time that the green Nationalist flag, painted with a white, twelve-pointed sun (which still appears on the Taiwanese flag), was flown. But the uprising was quashed, Lu Haodong was captured and executed, and Sun fled overseas.

Orbiting between Hong Kong, Japan, Europe and the US, Sun spent the next fifteen years raising money to fund revolts in southern China, and in 1907 his new Alliance Society announced its famous **Three Principles of the People** – Nationalism, Democracy and Livelihood. He was in Colorado when the Manchus finally fell in October 1911; on returning to China he was made provisional president of the Republic of China on January 1, 1912, but was forced to resign in February in favour of the powerful warlord, **Yuan Shikai**. Yuan established a Republican Party, while Sun's supporters rallied to the Nationalist People's Party – **Guomindang** – led by **Song Jiaoren**. Song was assassinated by Yuan's henchmen following Guomindang successes in the 1913 parliamentary elections, and Sun again fled to Japan. Annulling parliament, Yuan tried to set himself up as emperor, but couldn't even control military factions within his own party, who plunged the north into civil war on his death in 1916. Sun, meanwhile, returned to his native Guangdong and established an independent Guomindang government, determined to unite the country eventually. Though unsuccessfull, by the time of his death in 1925 he was greatly respected by both the Guomindang and the four-year-old Communist Party for his life-long efforts to enfranchise the masses.

need to change buses, there's no need to visit Zhongshan itself, a characterless county town 100km from Guangzhou, but 30km east of here on the coastal road to Zhuhai is the good doctor's home village of **CUIHENG**, now the site of a **memorial garden** (daily 8am–5pm; ¥20) celebrating his life and achievements. Transport from Zhongshan town and from Zhuhai (35km south) sets you down right outside, where there are also a few cheap **places to eat** and to buy ice creams; when you need to move on, you'll find that public transport heads in both directions along the highway until at least 6pm.

Along with a banyan tree supposedly brought back from Hawaii and planted by Sun, the grounds incorporate a comprehensive museum of photographs, relics (including the original Nationalist flag) and biographical accounts in English emphasizing the successful aspects of Sun Yatsen's career. There's also the solid, Portuguese-style family home where he lived between 1892 and 1895, "studying, treating patients and discussing national affairs with his friends". Out the back of Sun's home are some rather more typical period buildings belonging to the peasant and landlord classes, restored and furnished with wooden tables and authentic silk tapestries.

Zhuhai

ZHUHAI is an umbrella name for the Special Economic Zone encompassing three separate townships immediately north of **Macau** (Aomen): **Gongbei** on the border itself, and **Jida** and **Xiangzhou**, the port and residential districts 5–10km farther up along the coast. Full of new offices, immensely wide roads and tasty economic incentives, Zhuhai has yet to blossom in the way that Shenzhen has – probably because Zhuhai's neighbour is Macau, not Hong Kong. Sights are also few; the coastline hereabouts is pretty enough on a warm day, but there are few true beaches (Lingjiaozui, in Jida, is the best bet for swimming) and most people have come for the border crossing, or to take advantage of what amounts to a **duty-free enclave** aimed at Macanese day-trippers in Gongbei's backstreets. **Lianhua Lu** is Gongbei's liveliest street, a kilometre of hotels, restaurants, and shops selling cheap clothes, household goods and trinkets you never realized you needed. South across a paved square, the **crossing into Macau** is itself concealed inside a huge shopping plaza – labelled "Gongbei Port" in gold on the red roof – where you can buy more of the same.

Practicalities

If you've just **walked across the border** – which is open 7am to midnight – into Zhuhai from Macau, you exit the customs building at Gongbei with Lianhua Lu and the two adjacent **bus stations** 250m diagonally across to the right. Buses go from both stations to the delta, Guangzhou, and beyond, with the last bus to Guangzhou leaving at 10pm (¥70; 3hr). **Jiuzhou ferry port** is 5km up the road at Jida, with twice-hourly services to Shenzhen between 8am and 6pm (1hr; ¥80), and ten daily departures to Hong Kong from 8am to 9.30pm (1hr; ¥180). Buses #2, #4 and #13 (daily 6.30am–9.30pm) run up to the port from Gongbei, or you can hail a taxi (around ¥20).

For **accommodation**, there are literally dozens of mid-range places in Gongbei with almost identical facilities and prices (which can plummet considerably during the week): on Lianhua Lu, *Min'an Jiudian* (☎0756/8131168; ⑥) is the pick of the moderate bunch, with large, comfortable rooms and attentive staff, whilst the *Changan Jiudian* (☎0756/8118828; ⑥) is nearby and of a similar standard. Nearer the border crossing and bus stations, the *You Yi Jiudian (*aka *Friendship Hotel*; ☎0756/8131818; ⑥) is prone to more substantial discounts

ACCOMMODATION		EATING & DRINKING	
Changan	C	Huaxia Shijie	2
Minan	D	Shen Jing	1
Taida	B		
You Yi	E		
Yuehai	A		

ZHUHAI-GONGBEI

YUEHAI LU

YINGBIN DADAO

LIANHUA LU

YUEHUA LU

SHUIWAN LU

Jida & Xiangzhou

QIAOGUANG LU

Bank of China

SOUTH
CHINA
SEA

**Long-distance
Bus Station**

Bus Station

**Gongbei
Port**

N

MACAU

0   500 m

than the others. There's also the more upmarket *Yuehai Jiudian* (aka *Guangdong Regency*; ☎0756/8888128, ⊛www.gdhhotels.com; ❽) on Yuehai Dong Lu, whose exterior glass lift offers an ear-popping vantage of Macau. Unfortunately, though there are budget hotels around, most of them won't accept foreigners; try the *Taida Jiudian* (☎0755/8877688; ❸) on an unmarked lane between Yuehai Dong Lu and Lianhua Lu – inexplicably, your chances will improve if you have your name written in Chinese.

There are plenty of banks in Gongbei to fuel the shopping needs of visitors, and numerous **places to eat**, to fill their stomachs, from bakeries to street vendors (the spicy beef and mutton skewers are delicious), to fast-food outlets and full-blown restaurants. The following are worthy of note: *Huaxia Shijie*, which faces the border, has a dizzying choice of Chinese, Macanese, Indian and Southeast Asian food which you order direct off the chefs by pointing (try *jiuhua yu*, chrysanthemum fish) – portions are colossal and prices reasonable; the innocuous-looking *Shen Jing* canteen on the other side of the lane from *Huasha Shijie* serves excellent salty chicken and Cantonese roast goose (¥35 for half a kilo) and duck (¥15 for half a kilo).

Northern Guangdong

Guangdong's hilly northern reaches form a watershed between the Pearl River Valley and the Yangzi Basin, guarding the main route through which peoples, armies and culture flowed between central China and the south – there are even remains of the physical road, broad and paved, up near **Meiling** on the Jiangxi border. Its strategic position saw the region occupied as long ago as the Stone Age, and it was later used by the Taiping rebels and the nineteenth-century Wesleyan Church, who founded numerous missions in northern Guangdong. Today, **Qingyuan** and its pretty riverside temples lie only an hour northwest of Guangzhou by bus, while a host of offbeat attractions farther north around the rail town of **Shaoguan** includes the Buddhist shrine of **Nanhua Si** and **Danxia Shan**, a formalized mountain park. For those not continuing up into central China, Shaoguan is also a jumping-off

Northern Guangdong		
Liannan	连南	*liánnán*
Lianzhou	连州	*liánzhōu*
Qingyuan	清远	*qīngyuǎn*
Bei River	北江	*běijiāng*
Docks	水陆客运站	*shuǐlù kèyùnzhàn*
Feilai Si	飞来古寺	*fēilái gǔsì*
Feixia Si	飞霞古寺	*fēixiá gǔsì*
Nandamen Jiudian	南大门酒店	*nándàmén jiǔdiàn*
Sun Hua Yuan	新花园酒店	*xīnhuāyuán jiǔdiàn*
Tianhu Dajiudian	天湖大酒店	*tiānhú dàjiǔdiàn*
Yinglong Lüdian	迎龙旅店	*yínglóng lǚdiàn*
Zhiwei Guan	知味馆	*zhīwèi guǎn*
Shaoguan	韶关	*sháoguān*
Dajian Chan Si	大鉴禅寺	*dàjiànchán sì*
Danxia Shan	丹霞山	*dānxiá shān*
Fengcai Lou	风采楼	*fēngcǎi lóu*
Nanhua Si	南华寺	*nánhuá sì*
Qujiang (Maba)	曲江（马坝）	*qǔjiāng(mǎbà)*
Renhua	仁化	*rénhuà*
Shizi Yan	狮子岩	*shīzi yán*
Wu River	武江	*wǔjiāng*
Zhen River	浈江	*zhēnjiāng*
Accommodation, eating & nightlife		
Focus Bar	焦点酒吧	*jiāodiǎn jiǔbā*
Guests' Hotel	迎宾馆	*yíngbīn guǎn*
Jiaoyu Zhaodaisuo	教育招待所	*jiàoyù zhāodàisuǒ*
Jinhui	金辉食楼	*jīnhuī shílóu*
Lantz	兰芝俱乐部	*lánzhī jùlèbù*
Sanpai	三排	*sānpái*
Shaohua Jiudian	韶华酒店	*sháohuá jiǔdiàn*
Xinglong Jiudian	韶关军分区兴隆酒店	*sháoguān jūnfēnqū xīnglóng jiǔdiàn*
Yuelai Jiudian	悦来酒店	*yuèlái jiǔdiàn*

point for a backwoods trip west **into Guangxi province** through ethnic Yao and Zhuang territories.

Qingyuan and around

Surrounded by countryside thick with rice fields and mud-brick villages, **QINGYUAN** is a busy back-road market town on the north bank of the **Bei River**, about 80km northwest of Guangzhou by bus from the Liuhua station (¥30). Ringed by grimy manufacturing complexes, Qingyuan's centre is none too bad, if crowded by narrow streets and hordes of pedestrians. Its attraction lies in its position as a departure point for day-trips 20km upstream to the poetically isolated, elderly temple complexes of **Feilai and Feixia**, which can be reached only by boat.

Qingyuan's **bus station** is about 3km south of the river in an ugly residential area alongside the highway; from here there are several daily buses to Shaoguan, and masses to Guangzhou, Foshan and Shenzhen. Note, however, that there are unlikely to be any services after 8pm. Heading into the centre, orange bus #6 runs over the Beijiang Bridge and into town, whose kilometre-wide core is centred on the intersection of north–south **Shuguang Lu** and east–west **Xianfeng Lu**. Alternatively, taxis cost around ¥10. Qingyuan's interesting, older quarter is southwest of here along **Beimen Jie** and its disjointed southern extension, **Nanmen Jie**, which runs down to the water. The **docks** – labelled in English "Go to Feilai and Feixia" – are east off the bottom end of Nanmen Jie. There's a collection of noisy, inexpensive **hotels** on the roundabout at the northern end of Beimen Jie: *Sun Hua Yuan* (☎0763/3311138; ❹) is the pick of the bunch, with friendly staff and clean, functional rooms – those on the third floor have pleasant, communal balconies, albeit overlooking the road; *Yinglong Lüdian* (☎0763/3313688; ❸) is the cheapest, with basic, worn rooms. There's also the plush and popular *Tianhu Dajiudian* (☎0763/3820126, ℱ3820333; ❻), on the Shuguang Lu/Xianfeng Lu intersection. Nanmen Jie and Beimen Jie have the best **places to eat**; options include river food at *Nandamen Jiudian*, a café and restaurant in various sections near the dock, as well as countless others to the west along Yanjiang Lu; or at *Zhiwei Guan*, a Cantonese diner on Beimen Jie.

Feilai and Feixia

Ferries to Feilai and Feixia depart daily at 8am from the dock off Nanmen Jie if enough customers show – it's a popular weekend outing with locals – and leave Feixia to return at about 3pm. The ferry costs ¥50 per person, or you can hire a private, six-person boat for ¥300.

The Bei River runs shallow in winter, and the boats oscillate from bank to bank along navigable channels. For the first hour it's a placid journey past a few brick pagodas, bamboo stands screening off villages, and wallowing water buffalo being herded by children. Hills rise up on the right, and then the river bends sharply east into a gorge and past the steps outside the ancient gates of **Feilai Gusi** (¥15), a charmingly positioned Buddhist temple whose ancestry can be traced back 1400 years. Wedged into the base of steep slopes, the current cramped halls date from the Ming dynasty, and manage to look extremely dignified. You'll only need about forty minutes to have a look at the lively ridge tiles and climb up through the thin pine forest to where a modern pavilion offers pretty views of the gorge scenery. If you have time to spare before your boat heads on, the temple gates are a good place to sit and watch the tame cormorants sunbathing on the prows of their owners' tiny sampans, or you can bargain with the local women for freshwater mussels and carp – you'll have a chance to get these cooked for you at Feixia.

Feixia

Some 3km farther upstream from Feilai at the far end of the gorge, **Feixia Gusi** (¥35) is far more recent and much more extensive in the scale and scope of its buildings. The name covers two entirely self-sufficient Taoist monasteries, founded in 1863 and expanded fifty years later, which were built up in the hills in the Feixia and Cangxia grottoes, with hermitages, pavilions and academies adorning the 8km of interlinking, flagstoned paths in between. Chinese visitors initially ignore all this, however, and head straight for the huge collection of **alfresco restaurant shacks** on the riverbank, where they buy and organize the preparation of river food with the numerous, eager wok-wielding cooks – a nice way to have lunch.

A couple of hours is plenty of time to have a look around. A broad and not very demanding set of steps runs up from the riverfront through a pleasant woodland where, after twenty minutes or so, you pass the minute Jinxia and Ligong temples, cross an ornamental bridge, and encounter **Feixia** itself. Hefty surrounding walls and passages connecting halls and courtyards, all built of stone, lend Feixia the atmosphere of a medieval European castle. There's nothing monumental to see – one of the rooms has been turned into a **museum** of holy relics, and you might catch a weekend performance of **traditional temple music** played on bells, gongs and zithers – but the gloom, low ceilings and staircases running off in all directions make it an interesting place to explore. If you walk up through the monastery and take any of the tracks heading uphill, in another ten minutes or so you'll come to the short **Changtian Pagoda** perched right on the top of the ridges, decorated with mouldings picked out in pastel colours, with views down over Feixia and the treetops. Another small temple next door offers food, drink and basic **accommodation** (❻).

Five minutes' walk east along the main track from Feixia brings you to the similar but smaller complex of **Cangxia**. Restorations began here in 1994, but Cangxia remains in a semi-ruinous state, though monks hounded out during the 1960s are back in attendance, and many of the statues and shrines are smudged with incense soot. Look for the garden with its fragrant white magnolia tree, an unusual, life-sized statue of the Monkey God, Sun Wu Kong, and some wonderful **frescoes** – one featuring an immortal crossing the sea on a fish, storm dragons and two golden pheasants.

Shaoguan

Many trains from the Guangzhou train station call in at **SHAOGUAN**, 200km north, and expresses take a mere two and a half hours – not a bad hard-seat experience (¥38). An ancient city, Shaoguan was unfortunately the target of Japanese saturation bombing during the 1930s, which robbed the town of much of its heritage. Since the 1950s, textile mills and steelworks have ensured a moderate prosperity, if not a pretty skyline, but there's plenty to do in the immediate area.

Shaoguan's downtown area fills a south-pointing **peninsula** shaped by the **Zhen River** on the east side and the **Wu River** on the west, which merge at the peninsula's southern tip to form the Bei River. The pedestrianized main street, Fengdu Lu, runs vertically through the centre to the tree-lined **Zhong-shan Park**, crossed by Fengcai Lu at the north end of town, and Jiefang Lu in the south. While there's plenty of activity in the clothing and trinket **markets**

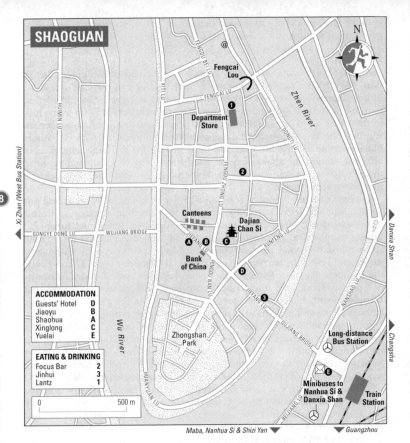

Maba, Nanhua Si & Shizi Yan ▼   ▼ Guangzhou

that fill the side streets off Fengdu Lu, and some crumbling colonial architecture, most of the town is functional and modern. The city sights, such as they are, comprise **Fengcai Lou**, a 1930s reconstruction of the old eastern city gate

West into Guangxi

Though the main transport routes run north and south from Shaoguan, if you're looking for an unusual way into Guangxi province, consider heading west through the mountainous strongholds of Guangdong's **Yao** and **Zhuang** population, a corner of the province virtually untouched by tourism. An early-morning bus leaves Shaoguan's long-distance station daily and takes about six hours to cover the 185km to **Lianzhou**, a Han town established by Emperor Wudi in 111 BC and containing an ancient **hexagonal pagoda** whose base is of Song vintage. Another 15km southwest from Lianzhou is **Liannan**, from where you can catch minibuses 10km out to **Sanpai**, a predominantly Yao village, and 35km beyond Liannan you'll find **Lianshan**, surrounded by Yao and Zhuang hamlets. Continuing through to Guangxi, the road from Lianshan runs a farther 100km over the mountains to **Hezhou**, a small town in Guangxi province from where you can get onward transport to Wuzhou or Guilin.

tower, up along Fengcai Lu; and **Dajian Chan Si**, an insubstantial monastery with ancient heritage – it was founded in 660 AD, and Huineng (see p.592 and p.593) taught here – just east off the bottom end of Fengdu Lu.

Practicalities

Both **arrival points** are immediately east of the centre over the Zhen River, linked to Jiefang Lu by the Qujiang Bridge: the **train station** sits at the back of a big square here, while the **long-distance bus station** is just north of the bridge on the square's edge. Onward train tickets are in short supply, as this is the main line north out of Guangdong and, despite a continuous stream of trains passing through, it's perpetually overcrowded, as is the train station itself. Long-distance buses – heading north to Jiangxi and Hunan, east to Huizhou and Chaozhou, south to Guangzhou and west to Lianshan – leave throughout the day. There are a couple of morning buses to Qingyuan, but for more services you should head to the west station (Xi Zhan) over the Wujiang Bridge on the other side of town. **Taxis** cruise the streets (¥4 within town), with **minibuses** out to nearby attractions leaving from a depot just southwest of the train-station square. There's a **Bank of China** on Jiefang Lu (Mon–Fri 9am–5pm, Sat 10am–3pm), a **post office** on the south side of the train-station square, and several **Internet bars** just north of Fengcai Ta on Dongti Lu.

   Accommodation prospects include: the reasonably modern *Yuelai Jiudian* (☎0751/8222333; ❺), on the south side of the train-station square; the *Guests' Hotel* (☎0751/8188688; ❹) across the river on Xunfeng Lu, a one-time grand option in pleasant grounds, now slightly worn around the edges; the smarter *Shaohua Jiudian* (☎0751/8881870, ☏8881988; ❺) further northwest up Jiefang Lu; the *Xinglong Jiudian* (☎0751/8186028; ❺) which offers substantial discounts, located right next to Dajian Chan Si; and, for the truly budget-conscious, the grubby, but cheap, *Jiaoyu Zhaodaisuo* (☎0751/8885086; ❶) at the northwestern end of Jiefang Lu.

   Shaoguan's **restaurants** are good. The *Jinhui* restaurant on Jiefang Lu offers a range of inexpensive hotpots, from spicy Sichuan style to Cantonese, whilst the *Lantz* restaurant on Fengdu Lu is a five-storey affair serving Cantonese roast meats, *dim sum* and snacks downstairs, and the same in greater comfort up above. There are Western fast-food places on Fengdu Lu and a collection of cheap but filling Chinese meals at canteens on a lane between Jiefang Lu and Fengdu Lu. For **nightlife** you could cause a stir by visiting the *Focus Bar*, east of Jiefang Lu.

Around Shaoguan

Buses and minibuses to the various sights around Shaoguan leave from a depot just southwest of the train-station square whenever full; just approach the area and touts will try to drag you on board. You will almost certainly be asked for at least double the correct fare – even Chinese tourists suffer this – and would be ill-advised to hand over any money without bargaining; nor should you get onto a partially empty vehicle unless you want a long wait. Alternatively, ask at the bus station to see if anything is heading your way.

Shizi Yan

The area's most esoteric attractions are prehistoric human remains uncovered at **Shizi Yan** (Lion Crag; daily 9am–4pm; ¥15), some 18km south of Shaoguan near the town of **Qujiang** (also known as **Maba**) – don't bother with a tour bus for this, just catch a **public bus** to Qujiang (¥3) from near the long-distance bus station. From Qujiang, either hire a cycle-rickshaw (¥20) or simply walk the final 3km – head west along Fuqian Zhong Lu, then turn south down Jiangshe Nan Lu, over a corroded metal footbridge, and follow the rutted main road off into the country.

Once clear of the town, you'll see Shizi Yan not far off, a short limestone hill projecting out of the ground like a tooth; the entrance is marked by a stone archway on the roadside. The crag turns out to be hollow and surrounded by caveman statues, and a Chinese-speaking guide takes you through the small caverns and explains how human remains were first found by the Guomindang when they were caching silver here during the 1930s. More comprehensive investigations twenty years later uncovered animal and human bones in quantities, suggesting that the cave was regularly occupied by *Homo erectus* (here nicknamed Maba Man), our immediate ancestors. A further ¥3 gets you into the **museum** back near the main gate, where there's a second-floor exhibition of stone axes, arrowheads, pottery and other artefacts unearthed from more recent Neolithic burials found in the surrounding fields in 1977. Unfortunately, labelling is scanty and in Chinese only.

Nanhua Si

Nanhua Si (Southern Flower Temple; ¥10) lies southeast of Qujiang, a twenty-five-kilometre, thirty-minute minibus ride from Shaoguan (¥7). Founded in 502 AD by the Indian monk Zhiyao Sanzang, the temple became famous through the activities of the Sixth Patriarch of Chan Buddhism, **Huineng** (see box, p.592), who sat in meditation here for 36 years. The seven halls are rather stark, but look for the **bell tower** in the atrium on the far side of the first hall, whose massive bronze bell was cast in 1167; the room beyond houses a riot of *arhats* and Bodhisattvas cavorting with sea monsters in a sea of papier-mâché. Pick of the sculptures here are those of **Ji Gong**, the Song beggar-monk with a tatty pandanus-leaf fan who became a sort of Robin Hood to China's poor, and an unidentified fat priest waddling on improbable stilts, at the back. A collection of fine **wooden sculptures** and a seventh-century, cast-iron statue of a levitating spirit grace another room, dedicated to Guanyin, while in the back of the final hall is a **model of Huineng** – which some maintain was cast from his corpse – who sits with pendulous ear lobes and sunken eyes, staring at a bhodi tree.

Danxia Shan

Danxia Shan, a formation of vivid red sandstone cliffs lining the **Jin River**, 50km northeast of Shaoguan near the town of **Renhua**, makes a hugely enjoyable day-trip. Buses from Shaoguan's train-station square (¥12) drop you by the main road gates, where you pay the ¥70 **entry fee**, which includes all minibus rides into and around the park – note that these stop around 5pm, and that the **last bus** back to Shaoguan passes the gates in the late afternoon.

The first place to aim for is **Yuan Shan Jing**, 2km inside the gates across the Jin, famous for **Yangyuan Shi**, a rock that – though the description is less suitably applied to outcrops all over China – really does look like the male member. It's a tough climb to the summit of neighbouring (and less phallic) Yuan Shan, after which you can charter a **boat** (¥10 a person) or catch the bus for another couple of kilometres to Danxia Shan itself. The surrounding area is covered in 12km of paths, which rise steeply through woodland, past cliffside nunneries and rock formations, and up the various summits; Chinese tourists stay overnight in the handful of **hotels** here (upwards of ¥100) and rise early to catch the sunrise from the pavilion at the mountain's apex, **Changlao** – only an hour's climb – though the views are great all day long.

Eastern Guangdong

All in one go, it's an arduous six-hundred-kilometre journey east from Guangzhou to Xiamen in Fujian province, but there's a wealth of intrinsically interesting territory to explore on the way. Only three hours away, **Huizhou**'s watery parkland makes it an excellent weekend bolt hole from Guangzhou, while over near the Fujian border, **Chaozhou** is famed for its own cooking style and Ming-era architecture. With enough time, you could spend a few days farther north in the hilly country around **Meizhou**, investigating ethnic **Hakka culture** in its heartland. Getting around is easy: **expressways** from Guangzhou or Shenzhen run via Huizhou along the coast to Shantou and on into Fujian, while the **rail line** from Guangzhou's East train station bends northeast from Huizhou to Meizhou – where a new extension runs up to Yongding in Fujian – then down to Chaozhou and Shantou.

Huizhou and Xi Hu

HUIZHOU, 160km from Guangzhou, is a place of water, caught between five lakes and the confluence of the Dong and Xizhi rivers. It was settled over two thousand years ago and later became capital of the Southern Han court. What saves Huizhou from being just another small, run-of-the-mill Chinese town is the genteel scenery surrounding the two-square-kilometre **Xi Hu** (West Lake). First laid out as a park by Song-dynasty engineers, the lakeside is a pleasant place to spend a day or a few hours strolling around the constructed landscapes and watching crowds of locals do the same.

Huizhou isn't a large place, and Xi Hu covers about the same area as the centre of town. There are several **entrances** (daily 7.30am–9.30pm; ¥16; ¥5 after 6pm), but the main one is next to the *Huizhou Binguan* on Huangcheng Lu. If you want to enjoy the lake from the water, you can hire a boat here from upwards of ¥20 an hour, plus a deposit. From here, the path crosses the lake over a five-hundred-metre causeway, its two sections joined by a small humpbacked bridge made of white marble. It was built in 1096 by a monk named Xigu and funded by the Sichuanese poet-official **Su Dongpo**, then Huizhou's governor and composer of a famous verse extolling the beauty of the full moon seen from this spot. On the far shore there's a thirteen-storey brick pagoda from 1618, whose wobbly wooden stairs can be climbed for fine views north and south across the waters. Next door is a noble statue of Su Dongpo, with an adjacent museum displaying a battered inkstone said to have belonged to this ubiquitous man of letters.

The main path heads off across the lake again from here, this time via a zigzag-ging bridge and a series of strategically placed islets, thick with bamboo groves, to the northern shore forecourt of **Yuan Miao**, an old Taoist nunnery. It's a bizarre place, with an improbable number of tiny rooms and atriums decorated with Taoist symbols and auspicious carvings of bats, tigers and cranes; one hall at the back is dedicated to the Three Kingdoms hero and war god Guan Yu, and a side wing contains a pit full of live tortoises. Walking back down Huangcheng Lu from here, there are a few more islands linked to the footpath, the favoured haunt of weekend street performers who keep crowds entertained with theatre and martial arts displays.

Practicalities

Huizhou's town centre sits immediately below a kink in the 500-metre-wide Dong River, a proportionately thin strip of land hemmed in by the smaller

Eastern Guangdong

Chaozhou 潮州 *cháozhōu*
Confucian Academy 海阳县儒学宫 *hǎiyángxiàn rúxuégōng*
Fenghuang Pagoda 凤凰塔 *fènghuáng tǎ*
Guangji Gate 广济门 *guǎngjì mén*
Hanwen Gong 韩文公 *hánwén gōng*
Kaiyuan Si 开元寺 *kāiyuán sì*
Xiangzi Qiao 湘子桥 *xiāngzǐ qiáo*
Xihu Park 西湖公园 *xīhú gōngyuán*
Xufu Mafu 许驸马府 *xǔfù mǎ fǔ*

Accommodation and eating
Chun Guang Dajiudian 春光大酒店 *chūnguāng dàjiǔdiàn*
Ciyuan Jiujia 瓷苑酒家 *cíyuàn jiǔjiā*
Feng Cheng Binguan 凤城宾馆 *fèngchéng bīnguǎn*
Hongyun Jiujia 鸿运酒家 *hóngyùn jiǔjiā*
Hu Rong Quan 胡荣泉 *húróng quán*
Jinlong Binguan 金龙宾馆 *jīnlóng bīnguǎn*
Xin Banhu Jiulou 新板湖酒楼 *xīnbǎnhú jiǔlóu*
Yunhe Dajiudian 云和大酒店 *yúnhé dàjiǔdiàn*

Dapu 大埔 *dàpǔ*
Gongyuan Binguan 公园宾馆 *gōngyuán bīnguǎn*
Hu Shan 虎山 *hǔshā*

Huizhou 惠州 *huìzhōu*
Daxibei 大西北牛肉拉面 *dàxīběi niúròu lāmiàn*
Gui An Zhou Daxue 贵安州大学 *guì'ānzhōu dàxué*
Hui Hang Binguan 惠航宾馆 *huìháng bīnguǎn*
Huipinglou Lüye 惠平楼旅业 *huìpínglóu lǚyè*
Huizhou Binguan 惠州宾馆 *huìzhōu bīnguǎn*
Xi Hu 西湖 *xīhú*
Xi Hu Dajiudian 西湖大酒店 *xīhú dàjiǔdiàn*
Yuan Miao 元庙 *yuánmiào*

Meizhou 梅州 *méizhōu*
Dongshan Bridge 东山桥 *dōngshān qiáo*
Lingguang Si 灵光寺 *língguāng sì*
Meijiang Bridge 梅江桥 *méijiāng qiáo*
Mei River 梅江 *méijiāng*
Qianfo Si 千佛寺 *qiānfó sì*
Renjinglu 人境庐 *rénjìng lú*
Wenhua Park 文化公园 *wénhuà gōngyuán*
Yinna Shan 阴那山 *yīnnà shān*

Accommodation and eating
Huaqiao Dasha 华侨大厦 *huáqiáo dàshà*
Huihua Jiudian 晖华酒店 *huīhuá jiǔdiàn*
Kejia Fan 客家饭 *kèjiā fàn*
Meizhou Dajiudian 梅州大酒店 *méizhōu dàjiǔdiàn*
Shang's Meatball Store 尚记肉丸店 *shàngjì ròuwándiàn*
Tian Yuan Dajiudian 田园大酒店 *tiányuán dàjiǔdiàn*

Shantou 汕头 *shàntóu*

Xizhi River to the east, and Xi Hu to the west. The **train** pulls in about 3km west, from where a taxi or bus #9 will take you past Huizhou's **long-distance bus station** to Huangcheng Lu. Most buses will take you to the long-distance station; however, some through services between Guangzhou and points further east may drop you near the expressway on Dongjiang Lu – it's best to take a cab to Xi Hu from here (around ¥10). The bus station is on a roundabout below several flyovers 1km south of the lake on Eling Bei Lu, which runs north, away from the roundabout, to Huangcheng Lu, which follows Xi Hu's eastern shore. Take any of the small side streets east off Huangcheng Lu and you'll end up on parallel Shuimen Lu, Huizhou's functional shopping precinct. The town's hotels can **change money**, and the Bank of China has branches opposite the bus station and on Huangcheng Lu (Mon–Fri 8.30am–noon & 2.30–5pm). For **Internet access** head for *Neteasy* on Huangcheng Lu.

There's inexpensive **accommodation** around the bus station; noisy places such as *Huipinglou Lüye* (⊕0752/2662333; ❸) on Eling Bei Lu and *Gui An Zhou Daxue* (⊕0752/2125666; ❷) further along offer basic facilities, but for a little more, you can have a better room near Xi Hu at *Hui Hang Binguan* (⊕0752/2180666; ❹) on Huangcheng Lu, where some rooms have side views of the lake. If you've got more cash to spare, the *Huizhou Binguan* is a very comfortable affair with spacious doubles (⊕0752/2232333, ⊕2231439; ❻), right on Xi Hu's eastern shore, further south on Huangcheng Lu. Alternatively, try the *Xi Hu Dajiudian* just across the road (⊕0752/2226666, ⊛www.hzwest lakehtl.com; ❼), which has plusher rooms, but only the more expensive ones have good views of the lake. For **food**, there are places near the bus station, including tasty and filling stretched beef noodles at spotless and friendly *Daxibei*, and inexpensive restaurants along Huangcheng Lu and Shuicheng Lu. Try the hotels for more upmarket meals – the *Huizhou Binguan* and the *Xi Hu Dajudi-an's Japanese Teppanyaki* restaurant can both rustle up English menus.

Moving on, you can book train tickets through the *Huizhou Binguan's* travel service (daily 8am–8pm); buses run back to Guangzhou and Shenzhen between 6am and 6pm, with several daily onwards at least as far as Chaozhou and Shantou.

Chaozhou

On the banks of the Han River, **CHAOZHOU** is one of Guangdong's most culturally significant towns, yet manages to be overlooked by tourist itineraries and government projects alike – principally through having had its limelight stolen during the nineteenth century by its noisy southern sister, **Shantou**, just 40km away. In response, Chaozhou has become staunchly traditional, proudly preserving the architecture, superstitions and local character which Shantou, a recent, foreign creation, never had, making it a far nicer place to spend some time. However, you may end up passing through Shantou to get to Chaozhou, as more transport finds its way there. There are frequent minibuses for the one-hour journey to Chaozhou from Shantou's long-distance bus station and express bus station. If you get to Shantou and have a few hours to spare, the crumbling **old quarter** around Anping Lu holds a certain seedy charm.

Chaozhou was founded back in antiquity, and by the Ming dynasty it had reached its zenith as a place of culture and refinement; the originals of many of the town's monuments date back to this time. A spate of tragedies followed, however. After an anti-Manchu uprising in 1656, only Chaozhou's monks and their temples were spared the imperial wrath – it's said that the ashes of the 100,000 slaughtered citizens formed several fair-sized hills. The town managed to recover somehow, but was brought down in the nineteenth century by

EATING & DRINKING
Ciyuan Jiujia	1
Hu Rong Quan Bakery	3
Xin Banhu Jiuliu	2

ACCOMMODATION
Chun Guang	D
Feng Cheng	A
Hongyun	C
Jinlong	E
Yunhe	B

0   200 m

CHAOZHOU

Fenghuang Pagoda ▼

famine and the Opium Wars, which culminated in Shantou's foundation. Half a million desperately impoverished locals fled Chaozhou and eastern Guangdong through the new port, many of them **emigrating** to European colonies all over Southeast Asia, where their descendants comprise a large proportion of Chinese communities in Thailand, Malaysia, Singapore and Indonesia. Humiliatingly, Shantou's rising importance saw Chaozhou placed under its administration until becoming an independent municipality in 1983, and there's still real rivalry between the two.

For the visitor, Chaozhou is a splendid place. Among some of the most active and manageable street life in southern China, there are some fine historic **monuments** to tour, excellent shopping for local **handicrafts**, and a nostalgically dated small-town ambience to soak up. Chinese speakers will find that Chaozhou's **language** is related to Fujian's *minnan* dialect, different from either Mandarin or Cantonese, though both of these are widely understood.

Arrival and accommodation

Laid out on the western bank of the Han River, Chaozhou comprises an oval, 1500-metre-long **old town centre**, enclosed by Huangcheng Lu, which, divided into north, south, east and west sections, follows the line of the **Ming-dynasty stone walls**. A stretch of these still faces the river on the centre's eastern side, while Chaozhou's modern fringe spreads west of Huangcheng Lu. The old town's main thoroughfares are Taiping Lu, orientated north–south, crossed by shorter Zhongshan Lu, Xima Lu and Kaiyuan Lu, which all run east from Huangcheng Lu, through arched gates in the walls, and out to the river.

Chaozhou's **long-distance bus station** is just west of the centre on Chaofeng Lu; shuttles from Shantou wind up here too. The **train station** is about 5km northwest; from here, you can walk 100m to the main road and catch city bus #2 (daily 6.30am–8.30pm; ¥2) to Xinqiao Lu, a western extension of Kaiyuan Lu, or take a taxi (around ¥14). **Motor and cycle-rickshaws** – the only vehicles able to negotiate the old town's backstreets – are abundant, though once in town everything is within walking distance, or you can go for the Chinese tourist option and hire a tandem bicycle for ¥4 an hour from just inside the Guanji Gate. The **Bank of China** (Mon–Fri 8.30–11.30am & 2–5pm) is on the southern side of Xihe Lu at the junction with Huangcheng Xi Lu. There are also a few cheap **Internet** places near here.

Moving on from Chaozhou, there are **buses** to Meizhou, Shantou, Guangzhou, Shenzhen and Fujian from the long-distance bus station, and **express coaches** east and west along the coastal road from a private station on Huangcheng Xi Lu. **Trains** (station ticket office daily 6–11.30am & 1.30–5.30pm) run down to Shantou or back to Guangzhou via Meizhou and Huizhou. Shantou is quickest reached by bus, Meizhou by the train.

Places to stay are mostly clustered around the bus station. The cheapest deals are at the equally worn but acceptable *Hongyun Jiujia* (☎0768/2206052; ❹) next to the bus station, and the *Yunhe Dajiudian* (☎0768/2136128; ❸) on Xihe Lu; across the road, the *Chun Guang Dajiudian* (☎0768/2681288; ❹) offers slightly more comfortable, but ageing, rooms. An option closer to the old city is the comfortable, if fractionally shabby, *Feng Cheng Binguan* (☎0768/2223211; ❹) on Taiping Lu. For better rooms, head to the *Jinlong Binguan* (☎0768/2261881, ⓦwww.jinlong-hotel.com; ❻), a smart business hotel at the bottom of the old town on Huangcheng Nan Lu.

The Town

Chaozhou's old centre has none of Shantou's decrepitude. Instead you'll find an endlessly engaging warren of narrow streets packed with a well-maintained mixture of colonial and traditional buildings. In the quieter residential back lanes, look for old wells, Ming-dynasty stone archways, and antique family mansions, protected from the outside world by thick walls and heavy wooden doors, and guarded by mouldings of gods and good luck symbols. Out on the main streets, motorbikes and cycle-rickshaws weave among the shoppers, who are forced off the pavement and into the roads by the piles of goods stacked up outside stores. If you need a target, **Xufu Mafu** is a decaying mansion (undergoing renovation at the time of writing) on a lane just north of Zhongshan Lu; look for the toilet sign. South of here there's a Ming-style memorial archway and a former **Confucian academy** – now a **museum** (daily 8am–5pm; ¥4), full of prewar photos of town. Down in the south of town, **Jiadi Xiang**, a lane west off Taiping Lu, is an immaculate Qing period piece, its flagstones, ornamental porticos and murals (including a life-sized rendition of a lion-like *qilin* opposite no. 16) restored for the benefit of residents, not tourists. For a bit of space, head up to **Xihu Park** (8am–12.30pm; ¥8, ¥3 after 7pm), just north of the old town across a "moat" on Huangcheng Xi Lu, where there's a dwarf pagoda, hillocks, and some vegetated sections of the town walls.

If you bother with only one sight, however, make it **Kaiyuan Si** (daily 8am–6pm; ¥5), a lively Buddhist temple founded in 738 AD, at the eastern end of Kaiyuan Lu. Here, three sets of solid wooden doors open onto courtyards planted with figs and red-flowered phoenix trees, where a pair of Tang-era

stone pillars, topped with lotus buds, symbolically support the sky. The various halls are pleasantly proportioned, with brightly coloured lions, fish and dragons sporting along the sweeping, low-tiled roof ridges. Off to the west side is a **Guanyin pavilion** with a dozen or more statues of this popular Bodhisattva in all her forms. Another room on the east side is full of bearded Taoist saints holding a *yin-yang* wheel, while the interior of the **main hall** boasts a very intricate vaulted wooden ceiling and huge brocade banners almost obscuring a golden Buddhist trinity. At the time of writing, the complex was still being expanded by the construction of a new eastern wing.

The town walls and the east bank

About 250m east past the temple down Kaiyuan Lu you'll pass the 300-year-old **Matsu Miao** set below the **old town walls**. Seven metres high and almost as thick, these were only ever breached twice in Chaozhou's history, and more than 1500m still stand in good condition. The walls run from the **North Pavilion** (daily 8.30am–5pm; ¥4), first constructed by the Song, past Guangji Gate and down as far as Huangcheng Nan Lu. There are access steps at several points along the wall, including above the main **Guangji Gate**, where there's also a guard tower. Pass through the gate and you're standing by the river next to the five-hundred-metre-wide **Xiangzi Qiao**, a bridge whose piles were sunk in the twelfth century. Until the 1950s, the central section was spanned by a row of wooden punts, when they were replaced by an ordinary concrete construction which was under repair at the time of writing, meaning a detour to the next bridge south to get to the other side of the river. Crossing here you'll see the shrub-covered shell of the ancient **Fenghuang Pagoda** and can head north to the gate of **Hanwen Gong** (¥10), a temple complex built in 999 in memory of Han Yu, a Confucian scholar who a century earlier had denounced Buddha as a barbarian and cleared the river of troublesome crocodiles. A flight of broad, steep granite stairs here leads up to three terraces, each with a hall; the uppermost one has numerous ancient stone proclamation tablets and a painted statue of Han Yu.

Eating, drinking and entertainment

Chaozhou's cooking style is becoming ever more popular in China, though thanks to emigrants from the region, it has long been unconsciously appreciated overseas. Seafood is a major feature, while local roast goose, flavoured here with sour plum – the use of fruit is a characteristic feature of the style, as is a garnish of fried garlic chips, a Southeast Asian influence – rivals a good Beijing duck. A string of **restaurants** overlooks Xihu Park on Huangcheng Xi Lu: the *Xin Banhu Jiulou* here serves a decent cold chopped goose and green vegetables, whilst the *Ciyuan Jiujia* has superb goose (around ¥100 for a whole bird), crispy-fried squid, steamed crab, fishball soup, fried spinach and a selection of *dim sum*. For **snacking**, *Hu Rong Quan*, a bakery specializing in mooncakes on Taiping Lu, makes the best spring rolls you'll ever eat, stuffed with spring onions, yellow bean, mushrooms and a little meat.

The local **tea** ritual is called *gongfu cha*, and Chaozhou's residents perform it on the slightest pretext – if nobody offers you a cup, most places to eat serve tea at a couple of yuan a session. First, the distinctive tiny pot and cups arrive on a deep ceramic tray with a grid on top for drainage; the pot is stuffed to the brim with large, coarse Oolong tea leaves, filled with boiling water, and immediately emptied – not into the cups, but the tray. Then the pot is topped up and left to steep for a moment before the cups are filled with a rapid movement which delivers an equal-strength brew to all. For all this effort you have a thimbleful of tea, which has to be swiftly downed before it goes cold, more of a social activity than a source of refreshment.

For **entertainment**, try and track down a performance of *chaoju*, the indigenous **opera** style. It's quite listenable, with little of the warlike clanging and falsetto singing of Beijing's theatre; the plots tend to involve witty cautionary tales about lax sexual morality. Your best bet now is an infrequent show in Xihu Park, most likely during festivals. There's actually an old **opera house** on Yian Lu, parallel with Taiping Lu and one block west, though this has been converted into a **cinema**, sometimes screening videotaped opera performances. For more modern evening entertainment, there are a few **bars and clubs** at the eastern end of Xihe Lu.

Shopping

Adherence to the past has made Chaozhou a centre for **traditional arts and crafts**, and a great place to buy souvenirs. For something a bit unusual, the **hardware market**, just inside the Guangji Gate along Shangdong Ping Lu, has razor-sharp cleavers, kitchenware and old-style brass door rings. **Temple trinkets**, from banners to brass bells, ceramic statues – made at the nearby hamlet of Fengxi – and massive iron incense burners, are sold at numerous stores in the vicinity of Kaiyuan Si, also a good area to find ceramic **tea sets** and **silk embroideries**. The best place to buy **lacework** is at the large store on Huangcheng Xi Lu, opposite Xihu Park. While not dirt cheap, prices for all these items are very reasonable and the quality is high.

Meizhou and around

In the foothills of the Fujian border, 200km north of Chaozhou where rail lines from Guangzhou, Shantou and Fujian converge, **MEIZHOU** is the ancestral home of a huge number of Overseas Chinese, whose descendants have begun to pump an enormous quantity of money back into the region. While not a pretty city, Meizhou is ethnically **Hakka** (see p.575) and is thus a fine place to pick up local background before heading off into their Fujian heartlands, just up the train line around Yongding – if you can't make it out that far, a nearby mountain temple makes a good excuse for a quick trip.

The Town and around

Meizhou is a lightly industrial town, producing handbags and clothing, surrounded by hills and set in the fertile bowl of a prehistoric lake bed through which flows the convoluted **Mei River**. The scruffy centre is a two-square-kilometre spread on the north bank, connected to the neat, newer southern suburbs by the **Meijiang** and **Dongshan bridges**. As in Chaozhou, almost everything is within walking distance or the range of cycle-rickshaws.

Meizhou's social focus and main shopping district surrounds the open **square** at the junction of various main roads immediately north of the **Meijiang Bridge**. The colonial-style shopfronts on Lingfeng Lu, which runs west along the riverfront, are worth a wander, but the tone is set by the Tian'anmen Square-like entrance to the football stadium; you'll certainly know when a game is on, as the entire town descends on the park, the merrymaking kept in order by police. At other times, the park is pleasant enough, and at night, older houses in nearby streets look very atmospheric, lit by tapers and red paper lanterns.

For more local culture, head northeast off the square up Shunfeng Lu, and then follow the lanes and Chinese signs five minutes east to some scummy ponds outside **Renjinglu** (open around 3pm; ¥2), former home of Meizhou's nineteenth

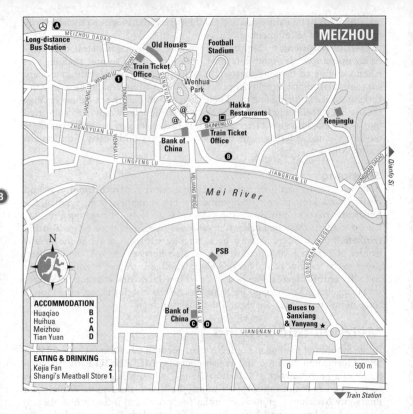

Long-distance Bus Station

MEIZHOU DADAO

Old Houses

Football Stadium

Train Ticket Office

Wenhua Park

Hakka Restaurants

Renjinglu

Train Ticket Office

Bank of China

JIANGBIAN LU

Qianfo Si

Mei River

N

PSB

ACCOMMODATION
Huaqiao	B
Huihua	C
Meizhou	A
Tian Yuan	D

Bank of China

Buses to Sanxiang & Yanyang ★

JIANGNAN LU

EATING & DRINKING
Kejia Fan	2
Shangi's Meatball Store	1

0   500 m

▼ Train Station

-century poet and diplomat, **Huang Zunxian**. The building is the most ornate of several around the ponds, the others being classically austere **Hakka town houses**, with high central gateways and square-sided walls and windows.

Somewhat more attractive, **Qianfo Si** (Thousand Buddha Temple; ¥5) overlooks Meizhou 1km east of the Meijiang Bridge – take Jiangbian Lu east along the river for 700m to the Dongshan Bridge, follow Dongshan Dadao north for another 100m, then bear right over the rail lines and uphill to the gates. Just before you arrive, there's an excellent vegetarian **restaurant** off to the right (see opposite). Above on the hill, the original temple and pagoda were demolished in 1995 in order to be totally rebuilt with expatriate funding and an attention to detail which has to be seen to be believed. The stonework is particularly accomplished, the temple pillars carved in deep relief with heroes and coiling dragons, while the base of the pagoda has finely executed scenes from Buddha's life.

Lingguang Si

One good day-trip from Meizhou is to head 50km east to **Yinna Shan**, sanctified by the elderly temple of **Lingguang Si**, founded in 861, though the present buildings are restored Qing. There are two 1000-year-old trees either side of the gate (a third died 300 years ago), and an extremely unusual wooden spiral ceiling in the main hall, the only other example being in a temple on Wudang Shan in Hubei province.

Unless your hotel can organize you a private jeep and driver (around ¥300), you should start early, as getting there and back is time-consuming. You'll need to take a minibus from the roundabout south of the Dongshan Bridge to either **Sanxiang** or **Yanyang**, two villages in lush rice-growing country on Yinna Shan's eastern side, then hire a tractor for the 7km or so to the walking track leading up to the temple (30min). The last minibuses back go in the mid-afternoon.

Practicalities

Meizhou lies both sides of the Mei River, with the older **town centre** on the north bank, connected to the newer south-bank districts by the central Meijiang Bridge and the Dongshan Bridge 1km to the east. The **long-distance bus station** is 1500m west of the centre on Meizhou Dadao and the number #3 bus route; the **train station** lies 5km south of the river at the end of Binfang Dadao – catch a taxi (around ¥14) or city bus #4 to the centre via the Dongshan Bridge.

To **move on**, there are regular buses to Dapu, Longyan and Xiamen in the east, and everywhere west back to Guangzhou and Shenzhen. Where you've a choice, trains are generally faster, though Fujian-bound services (to Yongding, Longyan, Xiamen and Fuzhou) are surprisingly infrequent. It's easiest to buy train tickets through your hotel. The main **Bank of China** is south of the river on Meijiang Lu and there's another branch at the junction of Gongyuan Lu and Zhongyuan Lu (both Mon–Fri 8am–5pm). The **post office** is on Gingyuan Lu near the road off to the football stadium and there are a couple of **Internet** places next door and over the road.

Accommodation and eating

Places to stay are distributed both sides of the river. South of the Meijiang Bridge on Meijiang Lu, *Huihua Jiudian* (℡0753/2191888; ❸) is an inexpensive option with clean, pleasant rooms; over the road the *Tian Yuan Dajiudian* (℡0753/2163888; ❺) is a plush and modern affair. Across the river on Jiangbian Lu, *Huaqiao Dasha* (℡0753/2192388, ℻2210008; ❺) is an overpriced, upmarket place, but offers good discounts in winter, making it worthwhile; opposite the bus station, the *Meizhou Dajiudian* (℡0753/2355700; ❷) has basic, shabby doubles and is good for early-morning departures, but little else.

Make sure you **eat** at the vegetarian restaurant at Qianfo Si, serving outstanding meals daily at noon, including imitation meat dishes which are virtually indistinguishable from the real thing – it's ¥48 for four dishes, ¥78 for five, and so on. Also try the **Hakka specialities** sold at the smart *Kejia Fan* and numerous family-run restaurants east of the square on Shunfeng Lu – juicy salt-baked chicken, wrapped in greaseproof paper (around ¥40 for a whole bird); little doughy rissoles made with shredded cabbage; and quick-fried cubes of bean curd, stuffed with pork and served in a gluey, rich sauce. For a takeaway, hunt down *Shangi's Meatball Store* on Wenbao Lu in the western backstreets. **Hakka wine** is pretty nice by Chinese standards, similar to a sweet sherry and often served warm with ginger – most places to eat can provide a bottle.

Dapu and beyond

To learn more about the Hakka, you need to head out to settlements north and east of Meizhou, surrounded in summer by some very attractive countryside. The small, dishevelled town of **DAPU**, two hours and 100km east, is a good place to start. A fraction of the size of Meizhou, the town shares the same river valley setting and an unexciting centre, but in the fields just outside, next to a modern sports stadium (another gift from an expatriate investing in his homeland), there's a huge square-sided **weiwu**, a three-storeyed Hakka house with walls as solid as any castle's. The residents, amazed to see a foreign face, will come out to chat if you walk over for a look. Elsewhere are some very nicely constructed low-set family compounds, whose walls enclose several temple-like halls, all with decorated roofs, and at least two small, traditionally circular homesteads. The largest, most highly regarded Hakka mansions anywhere in China, however, are three hours away over the Fujian border around **Yongding** (see p.576) – there are daily buses from Dapu.

The **bus station** is on the northern edge at the corner of Renmin Lu and Hu Shan Lu, which runs south right through Dapu, terminating below steps ascending to the tidy parkland of **Hu Shan** (Tiger Hill). There's **accommodation** at the relatively garish *Gongyuan Binguan* (❸) near the park on Tongren Lu, and plain beds in the peeling **hostel** (❶) 50m west off Hushan Lu on Yanhua Lu.

Western Guangdong

While it's not an unpleasant area, there's very little to delay your passage across western Guangdong on the way to Guangxi or Hainan Island. Buses cover both routes quickly, but the rail line is the most convenient way to get to **Haikou**, although as there's currently only one service daily you may find yourself taking a bus to **Hai'an**, from where there are regular ferries to Hainan. Either way, consider stopping off for a day or two at **Zhaoqing**, a pleasant resort town also connected by a direct ferry to Hong Kong, whose scenery has been a tourist attraction for more than a thousand years.

Western Guangdong		
Zhaoqing	肇庆	*zhàoqìng*
Chongxi Ta	崇禧塔	*chóngxǐ tǎ*
Dinghu Shan	鼎湖山	*dǐnghú shān*
Mosque	清真寺	*qīngzhēn sì*
Plum Monastery	梅庵	*méi'ān*
Qingyun Si	清云寺	*qīngyún sì*
Qixing Yan Park	七星岩公园	*qīxīngyán gōngyuán*
Accommodation and eating		
Dinghu Shan Youth Hostel	鼎湖山国际青年旅馆	*dǐnghúshān guójì qīngnián lǚguǎn*
Duanzhou Dajiudian	端州大酒店	*duānzhōu dàjiǔdiàn*
Dynasty Cake Shop	皇朝西饼	*huángcháo xībǐng*
Huaqiao Dasha	华侨大厦	*huáqiáo dàshà*
Jinye Dasha	金叶大厦	*jīnyè dàshà*
Muslims' Canteen	清真饭店	*qīngzhēn fàndiàn*
Seven Stars Crags Youth Hostel	七星岩国际青年旅馆	*qīxīngyán guójì qīngnián lǚguǎn*
Zhanjiang	湛江	*zhànjiāng*
Hai'an	海安	*hǎi'ān*

Zhaoqing and Dinghu Shan

Road, rail and river converge 110km west of Guangzhou at **ZHAOQING**, a smart, modern city founded as a Qin garrison town to plug a gap in the line of a low mountain range. The first Europeans settled here as early as the sixteenth century, when the Jesuit priest **Matteo Ricci** spent six years in Zhaoqing, using Taoist and Buddhist parallels to make his Christian teachings palatable. Ricci was eventually invited to Beijing by emperor Wanli, where he died in 1610, having published numerous religious tracts. Since the tenth century, however, the Chinese have known Zhaoqing for the limestone hills comprising the adjacent **Qixing Yan**, the Seven Star Crags. Swathed in mists and surrounded by lakes, they lack the scale of Guilin's peaks, but make for an enjoyable wander, as do the surprisingly thick forests at **Dinghu Shan**, just a short local bus ride away from town.

There's quite a bit to see in Zhaoqing itself, though the sights are widely scattered and not of great individual importance. Produced for more than a thousand years, Zhaoqing's **inkstones** are some of the finest in China, and there's a **factory** on Gongnong Lu that turns out some wonderfully executed pieces – you can buy them here and at several craft stores at the start of the causeway at the Duanzhou Lu/Tianning Lu intersection.

Overlooking the river, **Chongxi Ta** (daily 8.30am–5pm; ¥5) is a Ming pagoda at the eastern end of riverfront Jiangbin Lu. Looking much like Guangzhou's Liurong Ta, at 57.5m this is the highest pagoda in the province; views from the top take in sampans, cargo boats and red cliffs across the river surmounted by two more pagodas of similar vintage. A few aged buildings lurk in the backstreets west of here behind Jiangbin Lu – and there's an excellent **market** north off Zhengdong Lu – but Zhaoqing's most interesting quarter is a thirty-minute walk west beyond Renmin Lu. Solid sections of the **ancient city walls** still stand here on Jianshe Lu, which you can climb and follow around to Chengzong Lu; head north from here along Kangle Zhong Lu and enter a tight knot of early twentieth-century lanes, shops and homes – all typically busy and noisy – along with a brightly tiled **mosque**. A further kilometre out on the western

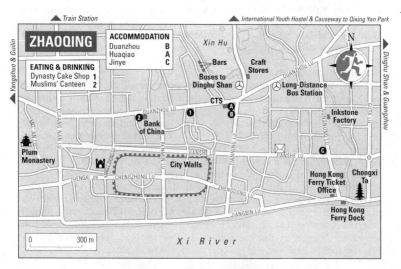

edge of town, the **Plum Monastery** (daily 7am–5.30pm; ¥8), on Mei'an Lu, was established in 996 and has close associations with **Huineng**, founder of Chan Buddhism (see p.592), who is remembered in various paintings and sculptures here.

Arranged in the shape of the Big Dipper and said to be fallen stars, the seven peaks which make up **Qixing Yan Park** (daily 7.30am–5.30pm; ¥50) rise 2km north of town on the far side of **Xin Hu**. To get here, go to the top end of Tianning Lu and cross over busy Duanzhou Lu to the paved area on the lakeshore, from where a **causeway** continues north across Xin Hu. Towards the opposite shore it forks at the park gates. The crags themselves are quite modest, named after objects they imaginatively resemble – **Chanchu** (Toad), **Tianzhu** (Heavenly Pillar), **Shizhang** (Stone Hand). An interlocking network of arched bridges, pathways, graffiti-embellished caves and willows all makes for a pleasantly romantic two-hour stroll.

Practicalities

Set on the north bank of the Xi, Zhaoqing is squashed between the river and the northerly lakes bordering Qixing Yan Park. Jianshe Lu and Duanzhou Lu run right across town east to west in numbered sections, crossed by **Tianning Lu**, which is oriented north–south between Qixing Yan Park's boundaries and the river. Zhaoqing's **train station** lies 5km away to the northwest; the **long-distance bus station** is on Duanzhou Lu, 100m east of the northern end of Tianning Lu; while the **ferry port** lies on the southeastern side of town at the junction of Jiangbin Lu and Gongnong Lu, near Chongxi Ta. **Taxis** can be hailed everywhere (¥5), but otherwise there isn't much in the way of public transport; Zhaoqing is, anyway, somewhere to get about on foot.

There are onward buses to Qingyuan, Shaoguan, Zhanjiang and just about everywhere between Guilin and Guangzhou – check which of Guangzhou's bus stations you're headed for before you board. Trains go to Nanning, Haikou, Guangzhou and through to Shenzhen. A daily ferry for **Hong Kong** (4hr; ¥180) leaves at 2pm from near the ticket office (daily 8–11.30am & 2–5pm; ☎0758/2225736) on the corner of Gongnong Lu and Jiangbin Lu west of Chongxi Ta. If you need help booking any of the above, try the **CTS** (daily 8am–9pm; ☎0758/2229908), just west of the *Huaqiao Dasha* – the transport ticket office is on the ground floor and the tours section is upstairs. The main **Bank of China** is 500m to the west (Mon–Fri 9am–noon & 2.30–5pm), and there's a **post office** (daily 8am–9pm) on Jianshe Lu.

Accommodation and eating

The town has abundant **accommodation**, and there are also places to stay out at Dinghu Shan. Reasonable-value options include the *Duanzhou Dajiudian* (☎07582232281; ❺) and its more upmarket neighbour, the *Huaqiao Dasha* (☎0758/2232650, ℻2231197; ❻) on Duanzhou Lu, and the cosy *Jinye Dasha* on Gongnong Lu (☎0758/2221338, ℻2221368; ❹). Just outside the northern edge of Qixing Yan Park – best reached by taxi from arrival points – *Seven Star Crags International Youth Hostel* (☎0758/2226688, ℻2224155; dorm beds ¥40, ❹) is a well-run, if elderly, place whose manager speaks good English.

There's a shortfall of **restaurants** outside the hotels – where it's worth indulging in *dim sum* at the *Jinye Dasha*'s popular third-floor restaurant – though numerous places along eastern Jianshe Lu and all through the centre sell local *zongzi* (conical rice packets wrapped in a bamboo leaf), sandpots and light Cantonese meals. For something different try *Muslims' Canteen* on Duanzhou Lu, which serves typical Hui fare such as lamb skewers and beef noodles at reasonable prices – note that it closes at 9pm. As well as the usual Western fast-food contingent, the *Dynasty Cake Shop*, next to the hotel of the same name on Duanzhou Lu, sells good sandwiches. For **nightlife** there is a string of bars along Xin Hu's western shore.

Dinghu Shan

Twenty kilometres east of Zhaoqing, the thickly forested mountains at **Dinghu Shan** were declared China's first national park way back in 1956, and have since been incorporated into the UNESCO biosphere programme. With well-formed paths giving access to a waterfall, temple and plenty of trees, the small area open to the public gets crowded at the weekends, but at other times Dinghu Shan makes an excellent half-day out – particularly in summer, when the mountain is cooler than Zhaoqing. The one drawback is another steep **entry fee** (¥50); one way to get the most for your money is to take advantage of Dinghu Shan's fairly inexpensive accommodation and **stay overnight**.

To reach Dinghu Shan, catch public bus #21 from the bottom end of Xin Hu (¥3.6); the bus drops you off about 1km south of the reserve at Dinghu township, from where you can continue on foot or hire a motor-rickshaw uphill to the gates. A further kilometre brings you to a knot of restaurants and souvenir shops, where there's another *International Youth Hostel* (☎0758/2621688; dorm beds ¥40, ❹). Beyond here, the forest proper and walking track start, dividing either to follow a stream or to climb a flight of stairs to **Qingyun Si**, a large temple with an expensive **vegetarian restaurant** open at lunchtime, and with restorations that have decked the exterior in awful green bathroom tiles while providing some accomplished statuary. The track along the stream takes you in ten minutes to a thirty-metre-high **waterfall**, whose plunge pool has been excavated and turned into a swimming hole. A lesser-used track continues up the side of the falls and eventually up to a vehicle road, which you can follow across to the temple. The round trip takes about two hours, and the last bus back to Zhaoqing leaves at 5pm.

Zhanjiang and Hai'an

The only reason to make the long haul to **HAI'AN**, 550km from Guangzhou at the province's southwestern tip, is to catch one of the regular ferries to Hainan Island. There is one direct train from Guangzhou to Haikou each day via Zhaoqing; however, if you haven't managed to get this, or are travelling by bus, you may have to change at **ZHANJIANG** en route to Hai'an; Zhanjiang's southern train station and bus station are next to one another on Jianshe Lu, and buses down to Hai'an take a little under three hours. From Hai'an's ramshackle bus station you can either walk (left out of the station and downhill) or take one of the free buses down to the ferry port. Ferries leave every couple of hours and it costs ¥37 for the ninety-minute journey.

Hainan Island

Rising out of the South China Sea between Guangdong and Vietnam, **Hainan Island** marks the southernmost undisputed limit of Chinese authority, a 300-kilometre-broad spread of beaches, mountain scenery, history, myth and – most

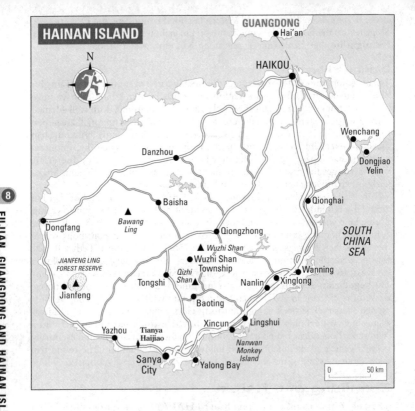

of all – the effects of **exploitation**. Today a province in its own right, Hainan was historically the "Tail of the Dragon", an enigmatic full stop to the Han empire and – in the Han Chinese mind – an area inhabited by unspeakably backward races, only surfacing into popular consciousness when it could be of use. Han settlements were established around the coast in 200 AD, but for millennia the island was only seen fit to be a place of exile. So complete was Hainan's isolation that, as recently as the 1930s, ethnic **Li**, who first settled here more than two thousand years ago, still lived a hunter-gatherer existence in the interior highlands.

Modern Hainan is no primitive paradise, however. After two years of naval bombardments, the island was occupied by the Japanese in 1939, and by the end of the war they had executed a full third of Hainan's male population in retaliation for raids on their forces by Chinese guerrillas. **Ecological decline** began in the 1950s during the Great Leap Forward, and escalated through the 1960s when large numbers of Red Guards were sent over from the mainland to "learn from the peasants", and became involved in the first large-scale **clearing of Hainan's forests** to plant cash crops. Successive governments have continued the process of stripping the island's natural resources and abandoning the inhabitants to fend for themselves, in an appalling example of **economic mismanagement**: while there are skyscrapers and modern factories around the cities, you'll also see country people so poor that they live in lean-tos made of mud and straw, which have to be rebuilt after each wet season. With the exception of ragged remnants clinging to the very tips of Hainan's mountains, rainforest has ceded to eroded plantations given over to experimentation with different crops – rubber, mango, coconuts and coffee – in the hope that a market will emerge. **Tourism** seems to be the sole reliable source of income, and everyone is desperate to be involved. Persistent marketing has made Hainan the place that all Chinese want to come for a holiday, but investment has been wildly overoptimistic, with numerous hotels and entertainment complexes around the place standing empty, unfinished or never used.

For foreign and domestic tourists alike, the most obvious reason to come to Hainan is to flop down on the warm, sandy **beaches** near the southern city of **Sanya** – as a rest cure after months on the mainland, it's a very good one. Initially there doesn't seem much more to get excited about. **Haikou**, Hainan's capital, bears evidence of brief colonial occupation, but its primary importance is as a transit point, while Han towns along the **east coast** have only slightly more character and scenic appeal. Spend a little time and effort elsewhere, however, and things start to get more interesting: the highlands around the town of **Tongshi** are the place to start looking for **Li culture**, and the mountainous southwest hides some forgotten **nature reserves**, where what's left of Hainan's indigenous flora and fauna hangs by a thread. There are even a handful of underwater sites off the southern coast, the only place in provincial China where those with the necessary qualifications can go **scuba diving**.

Hainan's extremely hot and humid **wet season** lasts from June to October. It's better to visit between December and April, when the climate is generally dry and tropically moderate, sunny days peaking around 25°C on the southern coast. **Getting to Hainan** is straightforward, with flights from all over the country to Haikou and Sanya, and regular ferries from Guangzhou and Hai'an in Guangdong province, and Beihai in Guangxi.

Once there, **getting around** is easy: Hainan's highways and roads are covered by a prolific quantity of **local transport**; high-speed buses link Haikou and Sanya in just three hours, while you can easily hop around the rest of the island by bus and minibus. As you move around you'll find that many of Hainan's towns have different local and Mandarin **names**; as the latter occur more frequently on maps and bus timetables, Chinese names are used below in the main text and character boxes, with local names indicated in brackets. Also note that, as a recognized tourist destination, Hainan is more **expensive** than the adjacent mainland – even Chinese tourists grumble about being constantly overcharged.

Haikou and the east coast

Haikou is Hainan's steamy capital, set at the north of the island and separated from Guangdong province by the thirty-kilometre-wide Qiongzhou Channel. Haikou is by no means a bad place to spend a day in transit, and certainly feels more spacious and friendly than the average provincial capital, but nobody would pretend there is much to see or do here. If you can resist heading straight on to Sanya to work on your tan, spend a couple of days hopping down between the towns along Hainan's **east coast**. This is the part of Hainan longest under Han dominion, and it's a good way to get the feel of the island.

Haikou

Business centre, main port and first stop for newly arrived holiday-makers and hopeful migrants alike, **HAIKOU** has all the atmosphere of a typical Southeast

Haikou and the east coast

Haikou 海口 *hǎikǒu*
Central bus station 总站 *zǒngzhàn*
East bus station 汽车东站 *qìchē dōngzhàn*
Hai Rui Mu 海瑞墓 *hǎiruì mù*
Haikou Park 海口公园 *hǎikǒu gōngyuán*
New Port 海口新港 *hǎikǒu xīngǎng*
West bus station 汽车西站 *qìchē xīzhàn*
Wugong Ci 五公祠 *wǔgōng cí*
Xiuying Battery 秀英古炮台 *xiùyīng gǔpàotái*
Xiuying Wharf 秀英港 *xiùyīng gǎng*

Accommodation
Civil Aviation 海南民航宾馆 *hǎinán mínháng bīnguǎn*
Haikou Binguan 海口宾馆 *hǎikǒu bīnguǎn*
Haikou International Commercial 海口国际金融大酒店 *hǎikǒu guójì jīnróng dàjiǔdiàn*
Haiyang 海洋大厦 *hǎiyáng dàshà*
Huaqiao 华侨大厦 *huáqiáo dàshà*
Overseas 海外酒店 *hǎiwài jiǔdiàn*
Post and Telecommunications 邮电大厦 *yóudiàn dàshà*
Songtao 松涛大厦 *sōngtāo dàshà*

Eating
Blue & Sea 蓝海餐厅 *lánhǎi cāntīng*
Ganghai Canting 港海餐厅 *gǎnghǎi cāntīng*
Japanese 香寿司 *xiāngshòusī*
Kuaihuolin 快活林 *kuàihuólín*
Shuihou Doujiang Dawang 水和豆浆大王 *shuǐhé dòujiāng dàwáng*
Xianzong Lin 仙踪林 *Xiānzōnglín*

Lingshui 陵水 *língshuǐ*
Puli Binguan 普利宾馆 *pǔlì bīnguǎn*
Yiyuan Binguan 怡园宾馆 *yíyuán bīnguǎn*

Qionghai 琼海 *qiónghǎi*

Wanning 万宁 *wànníng*
Dongshan Ling 东山岭 *dōngshān lǐng*

Wenchang 文昌 *wénchāng*
Dongjiao Yelin 东郊椰林 *dōngjiāo yēlín*
Prima Resort 百莱玛度假村 *bǎiláimǎ dùjiàcūn*

Xincun 新村 *xīncūn*
Nanwan Monkey Island 南湾猴岛 *nánwān hóudǎo*

Xinglong 兴隆 *xīnglóng*

Asian city. There's a smattering of French colonial architecture, a few parks and monuments, modern skyscrapers, broad streets choked with traffic and pedestrians, and the all-pervading spirit of wilfully glib commerce. An indication of the ethos driving Haikou is that nobody seems to be a local: officials, businessmen and tourists are all from the mainland, while Li, Miao and Hakka flock from southern Hainan to hawk trinkets, as do the Muslim Hui women selling betel nut – all drawn by the opportunities that the city represents. More than anything, Haikou is a truly tropical city: humid, laid-back, pleasantly shabby, and complete with palm-lined streets, something particularly striking if you've just arrived from a miserable northern Chinese winter.

Arrival, city transport and information

Haikou's downtown area forms a compact block south of the waterfront Changti Dadao. The centre is marked by a busy circuit of wide one-way traffic flows and pedestrian overpasses surrounding **Haikou Park**, where much of the accommodation is located, with the most interesting shopping districts in the northerly **old colonial quarter** around Jiefang Lu and Bo'ai Bei Lu.

The **airport** is 2km south of town on Jichang Lu; bus #10 runs up to Haikou Park from outside, or catch the shuttle (¥15) to the CAAC/China Southern office on Haixiu Dong Lu. The **New Port** is north off Changti Dadao on Xingang Lu, where most ferries from Hong Kong and the mainland pull in; those from Beihai in Guangxi sometimes use the **Xiuying Wharf**, 5km farther east along Binhai Dadao – take bus #6 to the centre from either. Buses from the mainland wind up at the **central bus station** south of Haikou Park on Nanbao Lu; those from elsewhere on the island use the **east bus station** 2km down Haifu Dadao (bus #1 or minibus #217 to the Haifu Dadao/Haixiu Dong Lu junction), or the **west bus station** way out on Haixiu Xi Lu (bus #2 or minibus #217 go to Haixiu Dong Lu from here). The **train station** currently

Moving on from Haikou

Flying is the easiest way out of Haikou, with the city connected to Sanya and mainland locations between Harbin, Kunming and Hong Kong. Tickets for all airlines can be reserved at agents (see "Listings", p.645) or one of the numerous China Southern branches – the main office is in the CAAC (daily 8am–9.30pm; ☎0898/66525581, ⓕ6652580), next to the *Civil Aviation* on Haixiu Dong Lu.

Ferries leave Haikou's New Port for Hai'an (¥37) at Guangdong's southernmost tip, where buses meet ferries for the 150-kilometre run to Zhanjiang. There are also ferries from the New Port (and sometimes from the Xiuying Wharf) for Beihai (seat ¥93; cabins from ¥123–333 per person, depending on the number of berths), on which it's worth paying for a cabin rather than spending the trip surrounded by seasick hordes watching nonstop kung fu flicks. Ticket offices at the ports open daily from 9am to 4pm, and there's usually no trouble getting a seat, though rough seas can suspend services. Your accommodation will be able to make bookings for boats and planes if you give them at least a day's notice.

The practicalities of getting out by **bus** depend on where you're heading. All **mainland traffic** leaves from the central bus station, where you'll find standard and luxury buses to destinations as far afield as Chongqing, Nanning, Jiujiang, Shenzhen and Guangzhou; tickets include ferry costs. **Sanya** and the **east coast** are served by the east bus station, from where there are also a few buses to Tongshi; a normal bus to Sanya is ¥50 and takes five hours, while an express is ¥80 and takes three. The west bus station deals mostly with **central and western** destinations, though you can also get to Sanya from here.

There's a new **railway link** from Haikou to Guangzhou – unbelievably, the train goes onto a boat – which leaves daily at 7pm and takes twelve hours to reach Guangzhou; you can book tickets for this train as well as mainland trains departing from Zhanjiang at the CTS office on Haixiu Lu (Mon–Sat 9am–5.30pm; ☎0898/66747268) or at another branch in the *Huaqiao* (same hours; ☎0898/66778455).

◄ Xuiying Wharf & Train Station

◄ West Bus Station, Hai Rui Mu & Xiuying Battery

8

HAIKOU

New Port

PSB

Bookstore

Hospital

Cinema

Bank of China

Cafés
Haikou
Park

Bank of
China

Central
Bus Station

CAAC

CTS

ACCOMMODATION

Civil Aviation	F
Haikou	B
Haikou International Financial	G
Haiyang	C
Huaqiao	A
Overseas	E
Post and Telecommunications	H
Songtao	D

RESTAURANTS

Blue & Sea	6 & 7
Ganghai Canting	1
Japanese	3
Kuaihuolin	4
Shuihe Doujiang Dawang	5
Xianzong Lin	2

Haikou Airport

N

East
Bus Station

0   500 m

Wugong Ci, Wenchang & Sanya ▼

only offers one daily service to Guangzhou and is way out to the northwest – bus #28 heads here from Haixiu Lu.

Haikou's **city bus service** is comprehensive and cheap, with more frequent and crowded private minibuses running the same routes. **Taxis** are so absurdly plentiful that you have only to pause by the kerb for one to pull up instantly, but they're expensive at ¥10 standing charge – New Port to central Haikou costs around ¥20.

There's a total lack of **information** about the island in Haikou, with hotel tour agents only geared to getting you to Sanya as fast as possible. If you plan to explore Hainan's backwaters, pick up a **map** of the island from hawkers or kiosks; some include spreads of Haikou, Sanya and Tongshi, along with detailed road maps of the island including even minor sights marked in English.

Accommodation

There's plenty of central accommodation in Haikou, much of it conveniently located around Haikou Park. Room rates are always flexible; in summer, ensure that air conditioning is part of the bargain. Most hotels handle transport bookings and have their own restaurants.

Civil Aviation Haixiu Dong Lu ☎0898/66772608, ℱ66772610. Smart hotel with light and airy rooms, very central and not bad value for its price. ❼

Haikou Binguan Daying Houlu ☎0898/65351234, ℱ65350232. Formerly Haikou's most prestigious accommodation, recently revamped as a modern outfit, with comfortable rooms and friendly staff. ❼

Haikou International Commercial Datong Lu
⊺0898/66796999, ⊜hkhicc@public.hk.hi.cn.
Luxury, international-standard business affair with
all the trimmings. ❽
Haiyang Jichang Dong Lu ⊺0898/66699558,
⊕66519222. Cheap and not a bad location, but
rooms have definitely seen better days. ❸
Huaqiao Datong Lu ⊺0898/66773288,
⊕66772094. A three-star business centre built in
the early 1990s and beginning to look a bit threadbare, nevertheless comfortable enough and offering
good discounts. ❺

Overseas Jichang Dong Lu ⊺0898/65365999,
⊕65365333. Fairly decent three-star venture, with
tubs in each room taking advantage of a hot spring
located 800m below the hotel. ❺
Post and Telecommunications Nanbao Lu
⊺0898/66778251, ⊕66772452. Hidden away in
the backstreets, this hotel offers fair value, though
the spruced-up lobby is not a reflection of the
rooms. ❸
Songtao Jichang Dong Lu ⊺0898/66729111,
⊕66729006. Currently Haikou's best budget option
with spacious tiled rooms. ❸

The City

The **old quarter**, boxed in by Bo'ai Bei Lu, Datong Lu and pedestrianized
Deshengsha Lu, is the best area to stroll through, with its grid of restored colonial architecture functioning as stores and businesses. **Jiefang Lu** and **Xinhua
Lu** are the main streets here, especially good in the evening when they're
brightly lit and bursting with people out shopping, eating and socializing; there's
also a busy **market** west off Xinhua. Otherwise, **Haikou Park** and the adjacent
lake are small but quite pleasant, the former a venue for extensive early-morning martial-art sessions, and with shrubberies concealing cracked stone statues,
reputedly from a vanished Ming-dynasty temple.

Haikou has just three formal sights, any of which will fill you in on Hainan's position in Han Chinese history. Southeast of the centre along Haifu Lu,
Wugong Ci (Five Officials' Memorial Temple; daily 8.30am–5pm;¥15; bus #1
or minibus #217 down Haifu Lu) is a brightly decorated complex built in 1889
to honour Li Deyu, Li Gang, Li Guang, Hu Chuan and Zhao Ding, Tang men
of letters who were banished here after criticizing their government. Another
hall in the grounds commemorates Hainan's most famous exile, the poet **Su
Dongpo**, who lived in the island's northwest between 1097 and 1100 and died
on his way back to the imperial court the following year. A **museum** in a
new building opposite has photos and Chinese-only captions of historical sites
around the island, though a group of weathered Song-style **stone statues** of
horses and scholars, almost lost in vegetation outside, is more interesting.

About 5km west of the centre, **Xiuying Battery** (daily 8am–7pm;¥10) offers
a different take on the island – to get there, catch bus #1 from Longhua Lu to
its terminus on Jinmao Zhong Lu, then follow it on for ten minutes, or just take
a taxi. Built after the Chinese had apparently beaten off an attempted invasion
by the French in the latter part of the nineteenth century, Xiuying was part
of a string of coastal defences designed to deter foreign incursions along south
China's coastline. A huge fortification, now maintained as a park, it's surrounded
by basalt block walls concealing six twenty-centimetre, naval cannons set in
concrete bunkers, all connected by subterranean passageways. The bunkers are
now camouflaged by fig trees and lit by bare bulbs, with the squat-barrelled,
bezel-mounted guns pointing at high-rises to the north. It must be said that
Xiuying's design and weaponry look suspiciously European – perhaps they were
modernized in 1937 when the fort was dusted off to resist the Japanese.

A kilometre or so southwest of Xiuying off Haixiu Zhong Lu, a park and
stone sculptures of lions surround **Hai Rui Mu**, tomb of the virtuous Ming-
dynasty official Hai Rui (daily 8am–6pm; ¥10) – bus #2 from central Haixiu
Dong Lu comes closest, though again you'll need to walk the last bit. Hai Rui's
honesty, which earned him exile during his lifetime, caused a furore in the

1960s when historian **Wu Han** wrote a play called *The Dismissal of Hai Rui*, a parody of events surrounding the treatment of Marshall Peng Dehui, who had criticized Mao's Great Leap Forward. The play's suppression and the subsequent arrest of Wu Han, who happened to be a friend of Deng Xiaoping, are generally considered to be the opening events of the Cultural Revolution.

Eating

Perhaps because Haikou is essentially a mainland Chinese colony, food here is not as exotic as you'd hope. The ingredients on display at market stalls are promising: green, unhusked coconuts (sold as a drink, but seldom used in cooking); thick fish steaks, mussels, eels, crab and prawns; mangoes, pineapples, bananas, watermelons, guavas, plums, starfruit and jackfruit; and, everywhere, piles of seasonal green vegetables. But Hainan's most famous dishes – Wenchang "white-cut" chicken, steamed duck and glutinous rice, and Dongshan mutton – are nothing extraordinary, though tasty. Compounding this is a current craze for Cantonese and Western-style food, with hotel restaurants trying to out-compete each other in these lines.

Restaurants

The highest concentration of **restaurants** is in the old quarter along Jiefang Lu, with grilled chicken wings, kebabs and other snacks sold outside the cinema and in the market east off Xinhua Lu. A couple of palm-shaded cafés on the northern side of Haikou Park serve light snacks, fruit platters and endless teapots and make a good place to watch the world go by.

Blue & Sea Haixiu Lu and Wuzishan Lu. Two particularly popular branches of this nationwide chain serving a range of inexpensive buffet snacks in a clean, bright and bustling environment.

Cocowind At the *Haikou Binguan*. Best of the hotel restaurants for local favourites, including steamed chicken in coconut milk, and seafood rolls in coconut sauce. Not too expensive either – a whole chicken or duck costs around ¥60, with other dishes starting at ¥20.

Ganghai Canting Jiefang Lu. Locals-oriented teahouse with tiled floor, dated wooden furniture and great *dim sum*.

Japanese Floor 3, Tailongcheng building, Datong Lu. Sushi at ¥5–10 per plate, with set one-dish meals from ¥15.

Kuaihuolin Next door to the *Haiyang*, Jichang Dong Lu. Plates of Cantonese roast meats and steamed chicken, Sichuanese cold spiced noodles, and pickles wheeled around on trolleys for you to point and choose. They also have more complex dishes such as twice-cooked fish, and their *gong-bao jiding* comes with genuine Sichuan peppers. Smart and inexpensive – two can eat well for ¥30–40 – and there's an English menu to boot.

Shuihe Doujiang Dawang Jichang Dong Lu. Open 24hr for excellent *shujiao*, rice packets, *baozi* and soya milk in fast-food-café surroundings.

Xianzong Lin Jiefang Lu. A cute place with swings instead of chairs and a Western/Chinese menu that includes pizza and some weird cold drinks – black sesame-seed milkshakes for one.

Listings

Banks and exchange There are numerous branches of the Bank of China including opposite the *Huaqiao*, and next to the *Haikou International Commercial* on Datong Lu (Mon–Sat 8.30am–5.30pm).

Books There's a big Xinhua bookstore on Jiefang Lu, east of the post office, which has a limited range of English classics on the third floor; the discount bookstore upstairs at the Mingzhu Guangchang shopping centre on Haixiu Dong Lu, west of the bus station, has maps and guides to Hainan, mostly Chinese-only.

Cinema There's a popular screen and entertainment complex behind the snack stalls on Jiefang Lu.

Hospital Hainan Provincial People's Hospital, Longhua Lu ☏0898/6225933.

Internet access There's a Net bar on the second floor of the shopping centre at the junction of Jichang Dong Lu and Daying Lu, near the *Overseas*.

Mail and telephones The main post office, with parcel post service, is opposite the cinema on Jiefang Lu (24hr) and there are IDD phone places throughout the city.

PSB The Foreign Affairs Department is on Changti Dadao, just west of the junction with Longhua Lu.

Shopping Pearls are a good thing to buy while on Hainan, but Sanya is a much better place to find a bargain. Department stores along Haixiu Dong Lu such as Mingzhu Guangchang sell indigenous products such as coconut coffee, coconut powder, coconut wafers, coconut tea, palm sugar and betel nut; clothing sections also stock Hainan shirts, which differ from their Hawaiian counterparts in their use of dragons instead of palm trees on bright backgrounds. Whole shark skins – like sandpaper – dried jellyfish and other maritime curiosities in the shops along Jiefang Lu are also worth a look.

Travel agents *China Travel Air Service*, next to the *Huaqiao* (℡0898/66781735, ℻66706281), are agents for a vast array of domestic and international carriers, including China Southern, Dragonair, Hainan Air, Cathay Pacific, Japan Airlines, Malaysia Airlines and Singapore Airlines. CTS have branches in the *Huaqiao* (℡0898/66778455) and on Haixiu Lu (℡0898/66747268), both of which offer plane and train tickets and coach tours of the island.

The east coast

Most east-coast communities comprise small settlements of ethnic subgroups such as the Hakka, who were shuffled off the mainland by various turmoils, or returning Overseas Chinese deliberately settled here by the government, and many live by fishing, farming cash crops or pearl cultivation. Unless you plan to bask on the beaches at **Dongjiao Yelin**, nowhere here takes more than half a day to look round, with the pick of the bunch being **Lingshui**, a hamlet with a long history, unexpected Communist connections and a nearby wildlife reserve. Everywhere has **accommodation** (often near the bus stations) and places to eat, and **minibuses** are the best way to get around, with shuttle services running between towns from sunrise until after dark. Bear in mind that there are **no banks** capable of foreign currency transactions along the way, so carry enough cash to last until Sanya.

Wenchang and Dongjiao Yelin

WENCHANG, a decent-sized county town 70km southeast of Haikou, is known to the Chinese as the ancestral home of the sisters **Song Qingling** and **Song Meiling**, wives to Sun Yatsen and Chiang Kaishek respectively. Built up as a commercial centre in the nineteenth century by the French, it has now rather gone to seed, but you'll need to pass through to reach the beaches at **DONGJIAO YELIN**, Hainan's first **coconut plantation**. The area is becoming developed in a haphazard way, with a handful of hotels, but remains a relaxing place to laze for a few hours or days, the palms forming a perfect backdrop to acres of white sands.

There are places to stay in Wenchang near the bus station, but you're better off heading straight out to Dongjiao Yelin. Walking downhill from Wenchang's **bus station** you'll come to an acute kink in the road over a **canal** with well-constructed stone embankments; cross over the canal and turn left, and some 500m straight ahead is the **new town** and a far more modern bridge, where you can catch minibuses out to the coastal village of **Qinglan** (20min). From here take the ferry (¥2) or a local boat (¥3) across the small inlet and it's another brief ride in a tractor rickshaw through the plantation to the beaches. Alternatively, you can get a taxi to drive you from Wenchang's bus station to Qinglan (¥20), or the whole way for around ¥80.

In Dongjiao Yelin there are a few **accommodation** choices, best of which is the *Prima Resort* (℡0898/6358222, ⓦwww.bailaima.com; ❹, ❾) with its range of comfortable wooden beachside bungalows, set amidst attractive gardens and coconut palms, though it can get swamped with tour groups at times. The resort has a few cheaper rooms, or there are a couple of less attractive hotels nearby, and you may be approached by locals offering inexpensive lodgings. There's little to do here other than soak up the sun, swim and go for walks through the coconut palms or along the beach with its miles of sand dotted with stilted Chinese fishing nets, although the *Prima Resort* offers activities such as quad-biking, which are popular with domestic tourists. For places to eat, the *Prima Resort* has an English menu and reasonably priced food, including specialities such as Wenchang chicken, or there is a host of small restaurants offering cheaper fare in the village.

Qionghai, Wanning and Xinglong

From Wenchang the road from the modern bridge continues uphill to the outskirts of town and another minibus depot with services 60km south to **Qionghai** (Jiaji), where China's **first Communist cell** was formed in 1924. Qionghai's most famous resident was **Huang Sixiang**, a female guerrilla leader on Hainan during the Japanese occupation, but today it's known for its locally made cane furniture. Ten kilometres east of here, **Boao** is home to a recently constructed statue of Guanyin, the tallest in China.

Another 50km south of Qionghai is **Wanning** (Wancheng), from where motorbike taxis with sidecars can take you 3km southeast to coastal vistas at **Dongshan Ling**, a formation of strangely sculpted and delicately balanced rocks, traced with paths and steps linking strategically placed pavilions and drink vendors. Further south along the highway from town, it's about 20km to **Xinglong**, a dusty little village of interest for its **Tropical Agricultural Research Station**, set up by expatriate Chinese from Vietnam, Malaysia and Indonesia and famed for its coffee, as well as the nearby **hot springs** resort, 3km from town. The cheapest **accommodation** in the area is in Xinglong itself, while the Research Station and hot springs are expensive (❾ and up).

Lingshui

An hour south of Wanning, **LINGSHUI** (Lingcheng) has been around for a long time. They were forging iron tools and making pottery here as far back as the Han dynasty, while uncovered silver tomb ornaments point to the town being an important commercial centre by the Ming dynasty. Lingshui played a part in modern history when, having shifted south from Qionghai, China's **first Communist government** convened here in 1928; it was still functioning when the Japanese stormed Hainan in February 1939, whereupon its members retreated into the hills to wage guerrilla war on the invaders with the help of the local Li population (for more on the Li, see the box on p.655). The Communists never forgot this, and once in power granted the district nominal self-rule as **Lingshui Li Autonomous County**.

Today, Lingshui's dozen or so narrow streets are set back off the highway where it bends sharply past town near the bus station. Around town you'll see remains of a **Qing-dynasty monastery**, the interior still decorated with original frescoes, but now used to store video-game machines; a **Communist Museum** in another building of similar vintage (there's a cannon outside); and several 50-year-old shops with what look like their original fittings. Wander off to Lingshui's fringes and you could be stepping back a hundred years, with lanes twisting into the countryside between walls surrounding family compounds, houses sporting decorative columns topped with lotus-bud motifs, and courtyards thickly planted with slender **areca palms**, often with conical buckets strapped around the trunks. These catch falling **betel nuts** (*binlang*), a crop cultivated as a stimulant by the Li since at least Ming times. Women are the biggest users, but just about everyone in Lingshui seems to have stained their lips and teeth from chewing slices of the palm seed, wrapped inside a heart-shaped pepper vine leaf.

Practicalities

Lingshui's main **bus station**, on a bend in the highway, is where most minibuses from Wanning drop off and where Sanya- and Haikou-bound vehicles depart. If you've arrived on an express bus, you may be dropped just off the express way some 3km out of town from where you'll need to take a motorbike sidecar to the centre (¥5). Coming from the south, you might end up at the **minibus depot** about 1km down the road on the Sanya side of town; this is where you'll also find onward **transport to Xincun**, or a sidecar will take you there for ¥20. For **accommodation**, try the rooms at the *Puli Binguan* (☎0898/83325888; ❹) on the highway, five minutes north of the bus station, or smarter doubles at the *Yiyuan Binguan* (☎0898/83311000; ❹), nearby and just off the main road. The best places to **eat** are around here too, with numerous bustling **teahouses** along the highway and backstreets.

Xincun and Nanwan Monkey Island

About 10km south of Lingshui, **XINCUN** is a small market town with a large Hakka population – you'll see plenty of black-clad women with broad hats and gold and jade jewellery. **Ferries** ply from here across to **Nanwan Monkey Island**, actually a peninsula without overland access. The **research station** based here studies local groups of macaques, small, bronze-haired monkeys with pale eyelids and red backsides, and there's a **visitors' centre** (daily 7.40am–4.30pm; ¥100) where you can feed them.

Minibuses from Lingshui leave you on Xincun's main street. Having pushed your way between market stalls and down to the water, you'll be grabbed by sampan owners to negotiate the cost of the ten-minute ride over to Nanwan – ¥5 per person is a decent price for the return trip, though locals pay far less. Alternatively, there's an oversea cable car (¥45). The inlet here is crammed with Hakka houseboats, all linked by boardwalks, with posts and nets marking their **pearl farms**, a major source of income for the town. When you land on the island, tractors can take you up to the visitors' centre for a small fee, or it's a thirty-minute walk along a well-maintained road – a good option, as you'll almost certainly get your best views of completely wild monkeys along the way. Those that hang out at the visitors' centre itself are technically wild too, but seeing them here can be an awful experience, mainly because Chinese tourists like to intimidate them with big sticks and thrash any monkey they can catch, and the animals have become understandably hostile as a result. Buy peanuts at the gate if you want to feed them, but you'll be mobbed if you show any food and it's much better just to walk through the grounds and climb the hillside for views of family troupes crashing around in the treetops.

Sanya and the southern coast

Across the island from Haikou on Hainan's central southern coast (320km direct down the expressway), **SANYA** is, sooner or later, the destination of every visitor to the island. Though relics at the westerly town of **Yazhou** prove that the area has been settled for close on a thousand years, Sanya City itself is entirely modern, a scruffy fishing port and **naval base** maintained for monitoring events (and staking China's claims) in the South China Sea. These

Sanya and the southern coast

Sanya	三亚	sānyà
Dadonghai	大东海	dàdōng hǎi
Luhuitou Peninsula	鹿回头	lùhuí tóu
Yalong Bay	亚龙湾	yàlóng wān

Accommodation and eating

Cactus Resort	仙人掌度假酒店	xiānrénzhǎng dùjiàjiǔdiàn
Chatterbox Café	话匣子西餐厅	huàxiázi xīcāntīng
Chuanya	川亚宾馆	chuānyà bīnguǎn
Chunfeng Dajiudian	春丰大酒店	chūnfēng dàjiǔdiàn
Dongbei Wang	东北王	dōngběi wáng
Dongjiao Yelin Seafood	东郊椰林海鲜城	dōngjiāoyēlín hǎixiānchéng
Gloria Resort	凯莱度假酒店	kǎilái dùjià jiǔdiàn
Hawaii	夏威夷大酒店	xiàwéiyí dàjiǔdiàn
Holiday Inn	假日酒店	jiàrì jiǔdiàn
Landscape Beach	丽景海湾酒店	lìjǐng hǎiwān jiǔdiàn
Pearl Seaview	明珠海景酒店	míngzhū hǎijǐng jiǔdiàn
Red Coral Seaview	红珊瑚海景度假村	hóngshānhú hǎijǐng dùjiàcūn
South China	南中国大酒店	nánzhōngguó dàjiǔdiàn
Sujingguong Haijing	水晶宫海景酒楼	shuǐjīnggōng hǎijǐng jiǔlóu
Xinghuayuan Seaview	兴华园海景酒店	xīnghuáyuán hǎijǐng jiǔdiàn
Yuhai Binguan	榆海宾馆	yúhǎi bīnguǎn
Dongfang	东方	dōngfāng
Jianfeng	尖峰	jiān fēng
Jiangfeng Ling Forest Reserve	尖峰岭热带原始森林自然保护区	jiānfēnglǐng rèdài yuánshǐ sēnlín zìránbǎohùqū
Tianya Haijiao	天涯海角	tiānyá hǎijiǎo
Yazhou	崖州	yázhōu

unexpectedly came to international attention in 2001, when a **US spyplane** made a forced landing here after colliding with a Chinese fighter jet. Sanya has also hosted two Miss World contests, which put the city in a different international spotlight and has certainly promoted outside investment. Generally, though, what pulls in the crowds – an increasing number of whom are Russian and Korean – are Sanya's surrounding sights, especially **Dadonghai beach**, one of the few places in China where you can unwind in public. The Chinese also flock to legendary landmarks atop the **Luhuitou Peninsula**, a huge granite headland rising immediately south of the city, and west at the scenic spot of **Tianya Haijiao**, while foreigners generally find beach life suffices.

Farther afield, the coastal arc between Sanya and the western industrial port of **Dongfang** sees few visitors. While Dongfang itself doesn't justify a trip, it's emphatically worth getting as far as **Jianfeng Ling**, the most accessible surviving fragment of Hainan's indigenous mountain **rainforest**. If this doesn't appeal, there's plenty of transport north from Sanya to the Li stronghold of Tongshi, and on into the central highlands.

It must be said that though the beaches here are very pleasant, a trip to Sanya can also involve a few **irritations**, especially for those on a budget: rooms can be expensive and poor value; you'll have to watch for scams at cheaper restaurants; and foreign pedestrians are continually mobbed by taxi drivers and touts.

Arrival

The **Sanya area** comprises four sections: Sanya City, Dadonghai, the Luhuitou Peninsula – all fairly closely grouped – and Yalong Bay, a distant satellite tourist development. **Sanya City** occupies a three-kilometre-long peninsula bounded west by the Beibu Gulf and east by the Sanya River. Aligned north–south, Jiefang Lu is the main road, forking at its southern end to run briefly southwest to the cargo wharves as Jiangang Lu, and east to form busy Gangmen Lu. Changing its name several more times, this extends 4km out to **Dadonghai**, a kilometre-long spread of hotels, restaurants and shops backing on to Dadonghai beach, beyond which are the start of routes to Haikou and Tongshi. Accessible by road from Dadonghai, the **Luhuitou Peninsula** is separated from the cargo wharves by the harbour, while **Yalong Bay** is a cluster of insular resorts and nice beaches 20km east of town – note that there's a ¥50 entrance fee to the beach if you're not staying at one of the hotels.

Phoenix **airport** is about 15km to the west, from where you'll need to catch a taxi into the city (¥40). Sanya's main **long-distance bus station** is at the northern end of Jiefang Lu and handles normal and luxury buses to Haikou, and normal services to just about everywhere on the island, including Dongfang, Tongshi and Wenchang. For **getting around**, there's the usual overload of

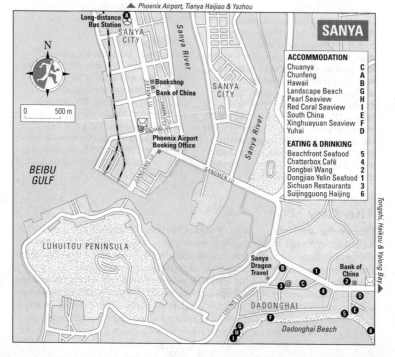

▲ Phoenix Airport, Tianya Haijiao & Yazhou

SANYA

Long-distance Ⓐ
Bus Station
SANYA
CITY
Sanya River
N
0   500 m
JIEFANG LU
■ Bookshop
■ Bank of China
SANYA
CITY
XINJIANG LU
@
JIANG LU
Phoenix Airport
Booking Office
JIANGANG LU
GANGMEN LU
Sanya River
BEIBU
GULF
LUHUITOU PENINSULA
Sanya
Dragon
Travel
LULING LU
Ⓑ ❶ Bank of
@ Ⓒ China ❷
❸ ❹ Ⓓ
Ⓔ
Ⓖ Ⓕ ❺ ❻
Ⓗ Dadonghai Beach
DADONGHAI

ACCOMMODATION	
Chuanya	C
Chunfeng	A
Hawaii	B
Landscape Beach	G
Pearl Seaview	H
Red Coral Seaview	I
South China	E
Xinghuayuan Seaview	F
Yuhai	D

EATING & DRINKING	
Beachfront Seafood	5
Chatterbox Café	4
Dongbei Wang	2
Dongjiao Yelin Seafood	1
Sichuan Restaurants	3
Suijingguong Haijing	6

taxi cabs (who may be reluctant to take you anywhere for less than ¥10) and some motorcycle–and–sidecar assemblies as well as **public buses** – #202 runs regularly from 6am until well after dark between the long-distance bus station and Dadonghai, while bus #102 runs hourly to Yalong Bay, via Jiefang Lu and the highway at Dadonghai.

Accommodation

Sanya's accommodation is increasingly more luxurious, though there are still a few budget options on Dadonghai (bus #202 from the station) as well as in Sanya itself, but the city is a grotty place to stay and you're much better off out at either Dadonghai or at upmarket and secluded, though increasingly developed, Yalong Bay – all accommodation here offers **transfers** from Sanya if you've booked in advance (otherwise, take bus #102 or a taxi for around ¥30).

Sanya and Dadonghai

Chuanya Dadonghai ☎ 0898/88227333. A hastily cobbled-together apartment block, but amenable to bargaining and inexpensive for the area. ❸

Chunfeng Dajiudian ☎ 0898/88276556. Next to the bus station, Jiefang Lu, Sanya. Basic, but one of the few places in town where you'll get exactly what you pay for. ❸

Hawaii Dadonghai ☎ 0898/88227688, Ⓕ 88212210. Unimaginative tower block on the highway, but pretty relaxed and organized, and offers immediate discounts; caters heavily to Russian business visitors. ❼

Landscape Beach Dadonghai ☎ 0898/88228666, Ⓕ 88228555. More characterful than its contemporaries, this low-rise place's atmosphere is enhanced by the thoughtful use of slate tiling. The more expensive rooms have vast terraces. ❾

Pearl Seaview Dadonghai ☎ 0898/88213838, Ⓦ www.pearlhtl.com.cn. International standard four-star resort with all the trimmings. ❽

Red Coral Seaview Dadonghai ☎ 0898/88213665, Ⓦ www.red-coral-diving.com. A handful of low, tiled units in a slightly dishevelled courtyard past the *Pearl Seaview*; ask to see several rooms, as some are a bit tatty; nevertheless, it offers the cheapest accommodation right on the beach. ❹

South China Dadonghai ☎ 0898/8213888, Ⓕ 8214005. Comfortable, beachfront resort with all imaginable facilities, including computers with Internet access in the better rooms, pool, gym and Western and Oriental restaurants. ❾

Xinghuayuan Seaview Dadonghai ☎ 0898/88677666, Ⓕ 88677488. Standard rooms with balconies in a concrete block, or more quirky beachfront apartments subject to good discounts. ❽

Yuhai Binguan Dadonghai ☎ 0898/88223046. On the highway at the eastern edge of town, this place makes no pretences of being a holiday hotel but has excellent-value, immaculate rooms. ❸

Yalong Bay

Cactus Resort ☎ 0898/88568866, Ⓦ www .cactusresort.com. Cheapskate's alternative to sister *Gloria*, and set back from the beach, but it does have a better swimming pool. ❽

Gloria Resort ☎ 0898/88568855, Ⓦ www .gloriaresort.com. Five-star affair with private beach, host of restaurants, pool, bike rental, water-sports hire, travel agent and airport transfers. ❾

Holiday Inn ☎ 0898/88565666, Ⓔ hotel@holiday -inn-sanya.com. Another international effort, with all facilities. ❾

The City

Despite the area's resort image, **Sanya City** itself is not a tourist attraction, its proximity to the beaches only made apparent by the presence of matching short- and shirt-wearing holidaying mainlanders. Recent investment has given the downtown area the appearance of any other mildly prosperous Chinese city, but it has atmosphere, and for seediness you can't beat the **wharf area** along Jiangang Lu, where dubious characters, scantily clad women and an air of lazy indifference fill the untidy teahouses and back alleys. Sanya's **main market**, held in streets parallel to and east of southern Jiefang Lu, is an interesting place to snack on local seafood and shop around the open-fronted stores, many so full that their wares overflow onto tables set up outside. Night or day, you can buy all manner of tropical fruits here, along with clothes, boiled sweets by the kilo, kitchen hardware from coconut graters to giant cleavers and woks, and expensive imported toiletries, cigarettes and spirits smuggled in through Vietnam.

Dadonghai and the Luhuitou Peninsula

Only 150m from the main road, often crowded and seasonally blistering hot, three-kilometre-long **Dadonghai** has pretty well everything you could ask for in a tropical beach: palm trees, white sands, and warm, blue water – a fair reward for making the journey to Hainan. A beachside bar and kiosks renting out beach umbrellas, jet skis, catamarans and rubber rings complete the scene, but on the whole the Chinese appear strangely bemused by beach life, as if they know it should be fun but are unsure of how to go about enjoying themselves. Swimming out farther than waist-deep water may draw disbelieving looks from holidaying mainlanders, many of whom seem uncomfortably self-conscious in swimwear and hardly dare get their ankles wet. While it's all very relaxed for China, don't mellow too much, as unattended valuables will vanish, and women going topless, or any nudity, will lead to arrests.

The **Luhuitou Peninsula** shouldn't take up much of your time. You can catch a motorcycle combi – or bus #101 – from outside the *Hawaii* at Dadonghai to the summit entrance, where ¥50 gains access to a ponderous granite statue depicting a Li legend about a deer transforming into a beautiful girl as it turned to face a young hunter – Luhuitou means "deer turns its head".

Eating and drinking

Given Sanya's tropical climate and location at China's southernmost point, there's something perverse about the bias towards northern and western Chinese food – probably explained by the fact that most of the restaurateurs are migrants from Sichuan and Dongbei. Places of note are all at **Dadonghai** – we've reviewed a selection below – with the best over towards the east; a host of budget Sichuan places with translated menus lurk west of the *Chuanya*, with staff who leap out and try to drag you to a table.

Like accommodation, eating here can be an expensive business, though the excellent **seafood** (almost all from Indonesia and the Philippines – Sanya's marine fauna is long fished out) is reasonably priced. Don't eat anywhere – especially cheaper spots – without getting solid confirmation of **prices**, or you could end up paying ¥30 for a bowl of noodles.

Beachfront Seafood Just above the beach near the *South China*. A surprisingly romantic place to eat in the evening: select fish, crabs, lobster, prawns and other seafood from the live tanks and say how you want it cooked, order a couple of beers, and kick back at outdoor tables under the coconut trees. A *jin* of prawns is about ¥40.

Chatterbox Café On the ground floor of a new shopping centre on the opposite side of the highway to *Dongjiao Yelin*, this new place serves up tasty, if pricey, Asian and Western fare in refined, modern surroundings.

Dongbei Wang On the highway. Lively, enjoyable Manchurian restaurant, with a menu illustrated with photos to help smooth linguistic problems.

Portions are huge and the service good. The fried whole fish with pine nuts is a treat, as are cold beef shreds with aniseed, and a stir-fried mix of peas, pine nuts and corn kernels. ¥60 will feed two.

Dongjiao Yelin Seafood On the highway. A warehouse of a restaurant, offering a glut of seafood and Hainanese dishes in an opulent setting. Expensive.

Suijingguong Haijing At the eastern end of the bay, this place is one of several predominantly catering to sunset groups; however, it enjoys good views and serves reasonably priced fare, specializing in seafood and Hainan specialities such as sweet coconut rice.

Listings

Airlines Most hotels have airline agents on hand. The Phoenix airport booking office is at the junction of Gangmen Lu and Jiefang Lu, Sanya (Mon–Sat 9am–noon & 1.30–5pm; ☎0898/88278221 or 88277409. There's also a major Hainan Air booking office beside the bus station (☎0898/88267988, ℻88252168).

Banks and exchange The main Bank of China, on Jiefang Lu in Sanya (Mon–Fri 9am–5pm), is excruciatingly understaffed and slow. There's another branch opposite the bus station (same hours) as well as a Dadonghai branch (same hours), but it has been known to refuse to cash traveller's cheques.

Internet access There's an Internet café on the third floor of the Haitian bookstore, near the Bank of China on Jiefang Lu, Sanya, and a few more west of the post office on Xinjiang Lu. In Dadonghai the Ultra Speed net café near the *Chuanya* is the place to head for.

Mail There are post offices on Xinjiang Lu, Sanya, and on the highway at Dadonghai (daily 7.30am–6pm).

Scuba diving Low visibility and maximum depths between 10m and 30m don't make Hainan the most exciting location for this, but it can be good fun and there's always the novelty of having dived in China. The three areas are at Yalong Bay, east of Sanya (best for its moderate coral growth, and a variety of fish and lobster); Tianya Haijiao, over to the west (good for molluscs, but extremely shallow); and the coral islands, also west (these are the deepest sites). Staff are NAUI/PADI qualified, hire gear is of reasonable quality, and you'll be expected to flash a C-card or make do with an introductory "resort" dive (¥260). Two shore dives cost ¥410, two boat dives ¥610, or a single dive at Yalong Bay will set you back ¥660. Make bookings at the office by the *South China* pool, or with the beachfront office at the *Red Coral Seaview*.

Shopping Sanya is a good place to pick up pearls, white, pink, yellow or black. The best buys are from local hawkers on Dadonghai beach, who sell strings of "rejects" for ¥40 or less with hard bargaining. Most of these pearls are perfectly genuine, just not of good enough colour, shape or size for commercial jewellery. If in doubt, scratch the surface – flaking indicates a thinly coated plastic bead.

Travel agents Upmarket hotels have their own travel desks, as does the *Red Coral Seaview* (☎0898/88228378) where they speak some English, and can arrange scuba diving, climbing, coral island or fishing trips, whilst Sanya Dragon Travel (daily 8am–10.30pm; ☎0898/88213526), west past the *Hawaii* on Luling Lu, can book air tickets.

Around Sanya

Any westbound bus from Sanya, or tourist bus #101 from the roundabout at the base of the Luhuitou Peninsula at Dadonghai, can cart you 20km out of the city to **Tianya Haijiao** (¥60), a long beach strewn with curiously shaped boulders, whose name roughly translates as the "ends of the earth". This isn't as fanciful as it sounds, for as Hainan's scholarly political exiles this was just about as far as you could possibly be from life's pinnacle at the imperial court. The modern world has unfortunately descended very heavily on the area, however, and a new township with expensive accommodation and restaurants, ever-escalating entry fees to the beach itself and overly persistent hawkers makes for an irritating experience. Chinese come in their thousands to have their photographs taken next to rocks inscribed with big red characters marking them as the "Sweetheart Stones", or "Limit of the Sky, Edge of the Sea".

Another 15km west of here on local transport, past a luxurious golf course, is **YAZHOU**, formerly one of Hainan's biggest towns but now more of a bottleneck for through traffic. It's chiefly known as the place where the thirteenth-century weaver **Huang Daopo** fled from her native Shanghai to escape an arranged marriage. After forty years living with the coastal Li, she returned to northern China in 1295 and introduced their superior textile techniques to the mainland. Get out when you see the reconstructed **Ming city gate**, and walk through it to a tiny **temple museum**, which includes traditional Li clothing and a **Muslim Hui** headstone and mosque oil lamp. The Hui have been on

Chinese maps of the country always show a looped extension of the southern borders reaching 1500km down through the South China Sea to within spitting distance of Borneo, enclosing a host of reefs and minute islands. These sit over what might be major **oil and gas reserves**, and are consequently claimed by every nation in the region – China, Malaysia, the Philippines, Taiwan and Vietnam have all put in their bids, based on historical or geographic associations. Occupied by Japan during the 1940s but unclaimed after World War II, the **Spratly and Paracel islands** are perhaps the most contentious groups. Vietnam and China both declared ownership of the Paracels in the 1970s, coming to blows in 1988 when the Chinese navy sank two Vietnamese gunboats. Then the Philippines stepped in in 1995, destroying Chinese territorial markers erected over the most westerly reefs in the Spratly group and capturing a nearby Chinese trawler. Continuing minor brawls encouraged the nations of the region – including China – to hammer out a landmark agreement in November 2002, which basically allows access for all, while territorial disputes are settled one by one. This is likely to be a relief to companies such as the US conglomerate Exxon, who – despite the fact that guaranteed oil reserves have yet to be found – are already investing in the region.

Hainan for centuries – some say they were originally Song-dynasty refugees from Vietnam, others that they're a relict of the old Maritime Silk Road – and the countryside hereabouts is peppered with their distinctive cylindrical graves. Walk back onto the main road and continue 1km or so west out of town, and you'll find a 400-year-old, seven-storey, brick **pagoda** leaning at a rakish angle next to a school – one of the few genuinely old structures on the island. The last direct transport back to Sanya leaves in the late afternoon.

West to Jianfeng and Dongfang

There are departures from Sanya's long-distance bus station for the 165-kilometre run to the western port of **Dongfang**, up the coast beyond Yazhou, or you could also travel there in stages by minibus. This side of the island is incredibly poor and undeveloped compared with the east, partly because it's too far out of the way to benefit from tourism, also because the main sources of income here are various forms of **mining**, an industry that sees little financial returns for local communities.

The real reason to head out this way is to spend a day at **Jianfeng Ling Forest Reserve**, a small indication of what the whole of southwestern Hainan looked like before the 1960s. Head first for **JIANFENG** township, which lies at the base of the distinctively peaked Jianfeng range some 10km east of the coastal road, about 115km from Sanya. Dongfang-bound transport can drop you at the turning, from where you can walk or wait for the next passing vehicle to pick you up. A dusty little hollow where pigs and dogs roam the streets between the market, Jianfeng has two teahouses and around a hundred homes. The sole **guesthouse** (❸) is a friendly place with a fine **restaurant** (try the chicken with locally grown cashew nuts), functioning plumbing and electric power.

The reserve itself is in the mountains 18km beyond Jianfeng, reached daily by a single scheduled minibus (¥10), although it's possible to hire one (¥70 up, ¥50 down). **Jianfeng Ling** – the mountain range itself – was aggressively logged until 1992, when a UNESCO survey found 400 types of butterfly and 1700 plant species up here and persuaded the Chinese government to establish the reserve, leaving a sharp-edged forested crown above bare lowland slopes.

Though commercial timber stands have since been planted, locals have been left without a livelihood for the time being, a problem slightly eased by aid packages from the Asian Development Bank. The dirt road to the summit ends on the forest's edge at a group of stores, a small restaurant, a botanical research station, and a little-frequented **hotel** (**④**), whose staff will be most surprised to see you. A tiled gateway marks the reserve entrance about 100m back up the road, from where partially paved paths lead off uphill for an hour-long circuit walk taking in some massive trees, vines, orchids, ferns, birds, butterflies and beautiful views from the 1056-metre ridge. After dark, if you're armed with a flashlight and some caution, it's a good place to look for small mammals and reptiles.

Tongshi and the highlands

Occupying the island's central core, **Hainan's highlands** get scant attention from visitors, despite evidence of long association with **Li and Miao** peoples. Just 100km north of Sanya and lying on the main inland route between Haikou and Sanya, **Tongshi**'s quiet pace and large concentration of Li make it the favoured place to start delving into the region.

Tongshi and around

Two hours north of Sanya, **TONGSHI** (Tongza, also known as **Wuzhi Shan Shi**) was voted China's most liveable modern town in 1995, and it still deserves the accolade. Pocket-sized and surrounded by pretty countryside, a lack of heavy traffic or industry makes it a pleasantly unpolluted spot to hang out for a day or two. The town has a well-presented **museum**, and there's the possibility of making local contacts in Tongshi itself, while energetic hikers might want to go scrambling nearby **Qizhi Shan** and **Wuzhi Shan**, whose summits are both steeped in local lore.

Before 1987, Tongshi was also capital of Hainan's autonomous Li government, until it blew a billion-yuan road grant by importing luxury goods from Hong Kong and Vietnam, and building the literally palatial offices, now **Qiongzhou University**, on the hill above town. When Beijing caught up with what was

Tongshi and the highlands		
Tongshi (Wuzhi Shan Shi)	通什(五指山市)	tōngshí (wǔzhǐ shān shì)
Jinyuan Dajiudian	金源大酒店	jīnyuán dà jiǔdiàn
Nationality Museum	民族博物馆	mínzú bówùguǎn
Qiongzhou University	琼州大学	qióngzhōu dàxué
Shang Cheng Chazhuang	山城茶庄	shānchéng cházhuāng
Tongshi Guolü Binguan	通什国旅宾馆	tōngshíguólǚ bīnguǎn
Tongza Resort Hotel	五指山旅游山庄	wǔzhǐshān lǚyóu shānzhuāng
Baisha	白沙	báishā
Baoting	保亭	bǎotíng
Qizhi Shan	七指山	qīzhǐ shān
Qiongzhong	琼中	qióngzhōng
Wuzhi Shan	五指山	wǔzhǐ shān

going on, they sacked the government and put the region under their direct control, a move which, while entirely justified, was greatly resented by the Li.

The Town

Reached via a street running uphill just beyond the bus station, and then past the ostentatious green-tiled **university**, the **Nationality Museum** (daily 8am–5.30pm; ¥10) affords views across town to the aptly named **Nipple Mountain**, 5km away to the west, while the collection itself is excellent. **Historical exhibits** include prehistoric stone tools and a bronze drum decorated with sun and frog motifs, similar to those associated with Guangxi's Zhuang; Ming manuscripts about island life; Qing wine vessels with octopus and frog mouldings; and details of the various modern conflicts culminating in the last pocket of Guomindang resistance being overcome in 1950. Artefacts and photos illustrate Hainan's **cultural heritage**, too – Li looms and textiles, traditional weapons and housing, speckled pottery from Dongfang, and pictures of major festivals. For more views over the town and hills beyond, head uphill from the museum to the deserted Minzhu Hotel.

Back across the river, the town centre is a far less pretentious handful of streets and modern concrete-and-tile buildings, which you can tour in around thirty minutes. **Henan Lu** runs west along the waterfront from the bridge; two blocks back, Tongshi's **public square** is a sociable place to hang out after dark and meet people, full of tables serviced by drink and snack vendors, crowds watching open-air table-tennis tournaments and queuing for the cinema. Nearby, on **Jiefang Lu**, there's a chance to see dark-dressed Miao and the occasional older Li women with tattoos at the daily **market**, whose wares include sweet, milky-white spirit sold in plastic jerrycans, deer and dog meat, and also **rat**, split open like a French roll and grilled.

You can see more of the Li by catching a minibus 2km south to the tacky displays at **Fanmao Mountain Fortress Village**, but there's more to be said for just heading off into the countryside on foot. From the north side of the bridge, follow Hebei Xi Lu west along the river for 150m to a grossly patronizing **statue** of grinning Li, Miao and Han characters standing arm in arm. Take the road uphill from here past the *Tongzha Luyou Shanzhuang* and keep going along the dusty road as long as you want to, through vivid green fields and increasingly poor villages, ultimately built of mud and straw and surrounded by split bamboo pickets to keep livestock in. Among these you'll see more substantial barns with traditional tunnel shapes and carved wooden doors.

Practicalities

Set at the base of low hills, Tongshi's tiny centre sits on the southern bank of a horseshoe bend in the generally unimpressive **Nansheng River**. The main road comes up from the coast as **Haiyu Lu**, skirts the centre, crosses over the river and passes the **post office**, turns sharply left past the **bus station**, and bends off north through the island towards Qiongzhong and Haikou. Buses from the station head to Baoting, Baisha, Qiongzhong, Haikou and Sanya, as well as a couple of daily services to Wuzhi Shan. There are a couple of **Internet cafés** around the bus station, but there's **no Bank of China** in town.

Tongshi's very reasonable **accommodation** prices are a relief after Sanya. Opposite the bus station, *Jinyuan Dajiudian* has clean, tiled rooms (℡0899/86622942; ❸), as does the slightly more upmarket *Tongshi Guolü Binguan* (℡0899/86633158; ❸). Easily the town's best accommodation is the bargainable *Tongza Resort Hotel* (℡0898/86623188, ℻86622201; ❻) on the northeastern edge of town, whose characterful rooms have balconies looking out to the hills, and there's a swimming pool to cool down in after a hike.

Teahouses near the market fill with sociable crowds on most mornings, which is also a good time to eat *dim sum* in *Shan Cheng Chazhuang* on Jiefang Lu – an extraordinary institution whose men's-club atmosphere is compounded by a card-gaming hall out the back; *hainan gau* here are sticky rice packets with coconut and banana. The *Tongza Resort Hotel* has a reasonable **restaurant** with an English menu of sorts or there are plenty of canteens around the bus station.

Wuzhi Shan and Qizhi Shan

Several Li myths explain the formation of **Wuzhi Shan** (Five-Finger Mountain), whose 1867-metre summit rises 30km northeast of Tongshi at Hainan's apex. In one tale, the mountain's five peaks are the fossilized fingers of a dying clan chieftain, while another holds that they represent the Li's five most powerful gods. Either way, Wuzhi Shan was once a holy site drawing thousands of people to animist festivals. Though the mountain is rarely a place of pilgrimage for the Li today, more remote villages in this part of Hainan maintain the old religion, raising archways over their gates, which are occasionally embellished with bull or chicken heads. It's still possible to climb the mountain – take a bus from Tongshi to **Wuzhi Shan township**, then local transport to the *Wuzhi Shan Binguan* (☎0898/86622981; ➋). From here it's a steep and slippery three-hour scramble to the peak, initially through jungly scrub, then pine forests. Although it's often clouded over, the summit offers further contorted pines, begonias and views.

Qizhi Shan (Seven-Finger Mountain), representing seven lesser Li immortals being vanquished by Wuzhi's five, lies about 40km by road southeast of Tongshi via **Baoting** (Baocheng). A sleepy place, Baoting is another good place from which to wander aimlessly off into the countryside, and you can get to the base of the mountain by catching available transport 10km east to **Shiling**, and thence 11km north to **Ba Cun**. The climb is said to be shorter than that at Wuzhi Shan, but much harder.

Travel details

Trains

Chaozhou to: Guangzhou (2 daily; 6hr 30min–8hr); Huizhou (3 daily; 4hr 30min–6hr 30min); Meizhou (3 daily; 2hr); Shantou (5 daily; 30min).
Fuzhou to: Beijing (1 daily; 35hr); Longyan (1 daily; 10hr 30min); Meizhou (1 daily; 13hr 30min); Nanchang (6 daily; 11hr 30min–13hr 30min); Shanghai (2 daily; 19hr); Shenzhen (1 daily; 20hr 30min); Wuyi Shan (4 daily; 5hr 30min–6hr); Yongding (1 daily; 12hr).
Guangzhou to: Beijing (4 daily; 22–23hr); Changsha (38 daily; 7–10hr 30min); Chaozhou (2 daily; 7–8hr 30min); Chengdu (1 daily; 40hr 30min); Foshan (10 daily; 45min); Ganzhou (3 daily; 8–10hr); Guilin (1 daily; 13hr); Guiyang (6 daily; 21–27hr); Haikou (1 daily; 12hr); Huizhou (10 daily; 2hr 30min); Kowloon (3 daily; 2hr); Kunming (2 daily; 25–26hr); Meizhou (3 daily; 6hr); Nanchang (6 daily; 10hr 30min–15hr); Nanning (3 daily; 11–13hr 30min); Shanghai (3 daily; 24–28hr); Shantou (2 daily; 7hr 30min–9hr); Shaoguan (56 daily; 2–4hr); Shenzhen (2 hourly; 1–2hr 30min); Wuhan (25 daily; 10hr 30min–16hr 30min); Xiamen (2 daily; 15hr); Xian (2 daily; 27hr); Zhaoqing (8 daily; 2hr); Zhanjiang (4 daily; 8hr)
Haikou to: Guangzhou (1 daily; 12hr).
Huizhou to: Chaozhou (3 daily; 4hr 30min–6hr 30min); Guangzhou (10 daily; 2–3hr); Meizhou (6 daily; 4hr 30min); Nanchang (13 daily; 8hr 30min–12hr 30min); Shantou (3 daily; 5–7hr); Wuhan (1 daily; 14hr 30min).
Meizhou to: Chaozhou (3 daily; 2hr); Fuzhou (1 daily; 14hr); Guangzhou (3 daily; 6hr 30min); Huizhou (6 daily; 4hr 30min); Longyan (3 daily; 3hr); Shantou (3 daily; 3hr); Yongding (1 daily; 3hr).
Quanzhou to: Wuyi Shan (1 daily; 12hr).

Shantou to: Chaozhou (5 daily; 30 min); Guangzhou (2 daily; 7–8hr 30min); Huizhou (3 daily; 5–7hr); Meizhou (3 daily; 2hr 30min).
Shaoguan to: Changsha (34 daily; 5–7hr 30min); Guangzhou (55 daily; 2–4hr); Hengyang (43 daily; 3hr 30min–5hr).
Shenzhen to: Changsha (7 daily; 9–11hr 30min); Fuzhou (1 daily; 20hr); Ganzhou (3 daily; 9hr); Guangzhou (71 daily; 50min–3hr); Shantou (1 daily; 8hr 30min); Shaoguan (9 daily; 4–5hr 30min); Wuhan (4 daily; 12hr 30min–16hr).
Wuyi Shan to: Fuzhou (4 daily; 6hr); Quanzhou (1 daily; 12hr); Xiamen (3 daily; 13–16hr).
Xiamen to: Guangzhou (2 daily; 14hr 30min); Nanchang (4 daily; 17hr); Nanjing (1 daily; 31hr); Shanghai (1 daily; 26hr 30min); Wuyi Shan (3 daily; 13–16hr); Xi'an (1 daily; 38hr).

Buses

Generally, there are countless services between the places listed below (see the text for exceptions), hence only the duration is noted; however, for longer journeys it is worth arriving early in the day (though conversely there may be overnight buses), and some smaller towns may cease to see any traffic after 8pm.
Chaozhou to: Guangzhou (6hr); Huizhou (4hr); Meizhou (3hr); Shantou (1hr); Shenzhen (5hr); Xiamen (5hr 30min).
Fuzhou to: Guangzhou (12hr); Longyan (7hr); Ningbo (9hr); Quanzhou (2hr 30min); Shantou (7hr); Shenzhen (12hr); Wenzhou (7hr); Wuyi Shan (7hr); Xiamen (4hr).
Guangzhou to: Beihai (24hr); Changsha (20hr); Chaozhou (6hr); Dongguan (1hr); Foshan (45min); Fuzhou (12hr); Ganzhou (11hr); Guilin (13hr); Haikou (12hr); Huizhou (2hr); Jiangmen (3hr); Kowloon (3hr); Meizhou (12hr); Nanning (30hr);

Panyu (1hr); Qingyuan (1hr); Shantou (6hr); Shaoguan (4hr); Shenzhen (3hr); Shunde (1hr 30min); Xiamen (9hr); Zhangjiang (5hr); Zhaoqing (2hr); Zhuhai (3hr).

Haikou to: Chongqing (28hr); Guangzhou (12hr); Lingshui (3hr); Qionghai (2hr 30min); Sanya (3–5hr); Shenzhen (15hr); Tongshi (4hr); Wanning (3hr); Wenchang (1hr); Zhanjiang (5hr).

Huizhou to: Chaozhou (4hr); Guangzhou (2hr); Meizhou (5hr 30min); Shantou (4hr); Shenzhen (2hr).

Meizhou to: Chaozhou (3hr); Dapu (2hr); Guangzhou (12hr); Huizhou (5hr 30min); Longyan (4hr); Shaoguan (12hr); Shantou (4hr); Shenzhen (10hr); Xiamen (9hr); Yongding (4hr).

Quanzhou to: Fuzhou (2hr 30min); Guangzhou (10hr); Hangzhou (11hr); Longyan (5hr); Ningbo (11hr); Shenzen (10hr); Xiamen (1hr 30min).

Qingyuan to: Foshan (2hr); Guangzhou (1hr); Shaoguan (3hr); Shenzen (2hr 30min); Zhaoqing (5hr).

Sanya to: Dongfang (3hr); Haikou (3–5hr); Lingshui (2hr); Qionghai (4hr 30min); Tongshi (2hr); Wanning (3hr); Wenchang (4hr); Yazhou (1hr).

Shantou to: Chaozhou (1hr); Fuzhou (7hr); Guangzhou (6hr); Huizhou (4hr); Meizhou (4hr); Shenzhen (6hr); Xiamen (5hr).

Shaoguan to: Chaozhou (12hr); Ganzhou (4hr); Guangzhou (4hr); Huizhou (4hr); Lianshan (5hr); Meizhou (12hr); Pingshi (4hr); Qingyuan (3hr).

Shenzhen to: Chaozhou (7hr); Dongguan (2hr); Fuzhou (12hr); Guangzhou (3hr); Haikou (15hr); Hong Kong (2hr); Huizhou (2hr); Meizhou (10hr); Shantou (6hr); Zhanjiang (7hr).

Xiamen to: Chaozhou (5hr 30min); Fuzhou (4hr); Guangzhou (9hr); Longyan (5hr); Meizhou (9hr); Quanzhou (1hr 30min); Shantou (5hr 30min); Shenzhen (9hr); Wenzhou (18hr); Yongding (5hr).

Yongding to: Longyan (1hr); Meizhou (4hr); Xiamen (5hr); Zhiling (1hr).

Zhanjiang to: Guangzhou (5hr); Hai'an (3hr); Haikou (5hr); Shenzhen (7hr); Zhaoqing (7hr).

Zhaoqing to: Guangzhou (2hr); Guilin (10hr); Qingyuan (5hr); Yangshuo (8hr 30min); Zhanjiang (7hr).

Zhuhai to: Cuiheng (1hr); Foshan (3hr); Fuzhou (15hr); Guangzhou (3hr); Guilin (13hr); Haikou (15hr); Jiangmen (2hr); Shunde (2hr 30min); Zhongshan (1hr).

Ferries

Guangzhou to: Hong Kong (2 daily; 2hr 30min).
Hai'an to: Haikou (10 daily; 1hr 30min)
Haikou to: Beihai (3 daily; 11hr); Hai'an (10 daily; 1hr 30min); Hong Kong (2 weekly; 25hr).

Shenzhen to: Hong Kong (20 daily; 1hr); Macau (daily; 2hr); Zhuhai (20 daily; 1hr).
Xiamen to: Hong Kong (1 weekly; 18hr).
Zhaoqing to: Hong Kong (daily; 4hr).
Zhuhai to: Hong Kong (10 daily; 1hr); Macau (5 daily; 20min); Shenzhen (20 daily; 1hr).

Flights

Besides the domestic flights listed here, Guangzhou (and, to a lesser extent, Xiamen and Shenzhen) is linked by regular services to major Southeast Asian cities and increasingly more destinations worldwide.

Fuzhou to: Beijing (6 daily; 2hr 30min); Guangzhou (1 daily; 1hr 30min); Haikou (6 weekly; 2hr); Hong Kong (3 daily; 1hr 30min); Shanghai (7 daily; 1hr 10min); Shenzhen (2 daily; 1hr 20min); Wuyi Shan (5 weekly; 30min); Xiamen (1 daily; 30min).

Guangzhou to: Beihai (2 daily; 1hr 20min); Beijing (20 daily; 2hr 45min); Changsha (3 daily; 1hr); Chengdu (10 daily; 2hr); Chongqing (10 daily; 1hr 35min); Dalian (2 daily; 3hr); Fuzhou (1 daily; 1hr 30min); Guilin (4 daily; 1hr); Guiyang (5–6 daily; 1hr 15min); Haikou (7–10 daily; 1hr); Hangzhou (14 daily; 1hr 45min); Harbin (2 daily; 4hr 15min); Hefei (3 daily; 1hr 45min–3hr); Hohhot (3 weekly; 3hr 10min); Hong Kong (7 daily; 40min–1hr); Kunming (6 daily; 2hr); Lanzhou (2 daily; 3hr); Meizhou (1 daily; 50min); Nanchang (3 daily; 1hr); Nanjing (6 daily; 2hr); Nanning (4–5 daily; 1hr 20min); Qingdao (4 daily; 2hr 40min–3hr 20min); Sanya (10 daily; 1hr 20min); Shanghai (25 daily; 1hr 30min); Shantou (2–4 daily; 40min); Tianjin (2 daily; 2hr 30min); Urumqi (3 weekly; 5hr); Wuhan (5 daily; 1hr 30min); Xiamen (4 daily; 1hr); Xi'an (6 daily; 2hr 30min); Yichang (daily; 1hr 45min); Zhengzhou (4 daily; 2hr).

Haikou to: Beijing (6 daily; 3hr 30min); Beihai (1 daily; 40min); Changsha (1–2 daily; 1hr 40min); Chengdu (1 daily; 2hr); Guangzhou (9 daily; 1hr); Guilin (1 daily; 1hr 20min); Hong Kong (1 daily; 1hr); Kunming (2 daily; 1hr 40min); Nanjing (1 daily; 2hr); Shanghai (5 daily; 2hr 20min); Shenzhen (11 daily; 1hr); Wuhan (2–3 daily; 3hr 20min); Xiamen (1–2 daily; 1hr 30min); Xi'an (3 daily; 3hr–3hr 30min); Zhanjiang (2 daily; 30min); Zhuhai (1–2 daily; 1hr).

Sanya to: Beijing (5 daily; 3hr 30min); Guangzhou (10 daily; 1hr 10min); Hong Kong (6 weekly; 1hr 30min); Shanghai (4–5 daily; 2hr 30min–4hr); Shenzhen (3–4 daily; 1hr 15min).

Shenzhen to: Baotou (1daily; 1hr); Beijing (17–19 daily; 3hr); Changsha (5 daily; 1hr); Chengdu (9 daily; 2hr 15min); Chongqing (10 daily; 2hr

35min); Fuzhou (1–2 daily; 1hr); Guilin (3 daily; 1hr); Guiyang (4 daily; 1hr 30min); Haikou (13 daily; 1hr); Hangzhou (8 daily; 1hr 50min); Harbin (1 daily; 4hr); Hefei (2 daily; 2hr); Kunming (3–4 daily; 2hr); Nanchang (1–2 daily; 1hr); Nanjing (5 daily; 2hr); Sanya (3–4 daily; 1hr 15min); Shanghai (many daily; 2hr); Wuhan (5 daily; 1hr 30min); Xiamen (2 daily; 1hr); Xi'an (5 daily; 2hr 20min).

Wuyi Shan to: Fuzhou (5 weekly; 30min), Shanghai (5 weekly; 1hr); Xiamen (5 weekly; 40min).
Xiamen to: Beijing (4–5 daily; 2hr 30min); Fuzhou (1 daily; 30 min); Guangzhou (4 daily; 1hr); Hefei (1 daily; 1hr 35min); Hong Kong (2–3 daily; 1hr); Macau (1–2 daily; 1hr 20min); Shanghai (12–13 daily; 1hr 30min); Shenzhen (3–4 daily; 1hr 10min); Wuyi Shan (4 weekly; 40min).

CHAPTER 9

Highlights

✳ **Hong Kong Island trams** The best way to travel the north shore of Hong Kong Island is by rattling double-decker tram. Ride from North Point to Western, upstairs and at night for the full effect. See p.671

✳ **Star Ferry** The crossing from Tsim Sha Tsui to Hong Kong Island is the cheapest harbour tour on earth and one of the most spectacular. See p.674

✳ **Harbour view from the Peak** Just before dusk, watch the city's dazzling lights slowly brighten across Hong Kong, the harbour and Kowloon. See p.686

✳ **Seafood restaurants** Spend a day hiking the Dragon's Back before tucking in to honey squid at one of Shek O's seafood restaurants. See p.690

✳ **Saikung Peninsula** Get away from the crowds and concrete, amidst beautiful seascapes, beaches and wild countryside in this often overlooked corner of Hong Kong. See p.698

✳ **Dim sum** Book in advance for an authentic *dim sum* lunch alongside enthusiastic families – try the chicken's feet and barbecue pork buns. See p.704

✳ **Old Macau** Hunt for bargain rosewood furniture and traditional clothing in central Macau's cobbled streets. See p.722

✳ **Coffee, tarts and port** Thanks to Macau's Portuguese heritage, most cafés and restaurants serve ink-black coffee, delicious custard tarts and port wine – almost unknown elsewhere in China. See p.726

△ The Peak tram

Hong Kong and Macau

T he handover of **Asia's last two European colonies**, Hong Kong in 1997 and Macau in 1999, opened new eras for both places. While vestiges of their colonial eras are still obvious – the high-tech infrastructure, the buildings, the food and the use of European languages – the essentially Chinese heritage underlying everything is increasingly apparent, as these two "Special Administrative Regions of China" seek to establish identities and roles for themselves.

Under colonial rule such soul-searching was never an issue. The populations in both places had no say in their futures, so they concentrated their efforts on other things, notably making money. They were not the only ones in Asia to take this path, but their economic success – at least Hong Kong's – simply highlighted their anachronistic position as dependent territories, decades after most other colonies had achieved self-rule.

That, understandably, was one of the reasons for the delay in resolving their status. Independence for either was never a serious proposition: in Hong Kong's

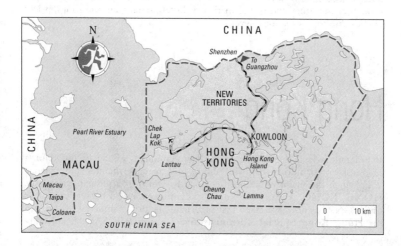

case, this was due to the approach of 1997, when the lease with China over the New Territories – physically, the bulk of the colony - ran out; while in Macau's, it was the desire of the post-revolutionary Portuguese government to get rid of the place. Both entities now find themselves in the unique position of being semi-democratic capitalist enclaves subject to the ultimate control of an unaccountable communist state, under the relatively liberal "**One Country, Two Systems**" policy coined by the late Chinese leader Deng Xiaoping.

It is hard to overstate the symbolic importance that the handovers had for the Chinese as a whole, in sealing the end of centuries of foreign domination with the return of the last pieces of occupied soil to the motherland. The people of Hong Kong and Macau also widely supported the end of colonialism and the transfer of power – if only to see how much leeway they could garner under the new administration. After all, the population of the two territories is 97 percent **Chinese**; they mostly speak only the Cantonese dialect, eat only Cantonese food, pray in Chinese temples and enjoy close ties with the Cantonese population that lives just over the border – even if there is widespread suspicion between them and the mainland Chinese.

Although economic jitters and a succession of health scares have dogged the post-colonial years, life continues as normal in many ways for both territories. With its emphasis on economics and consumerism, **Hong Kong** offers the greatest variety and concentration of **shops and shopping** on earth, along with a colossal range of **cuisines**, and vistas of sea and island, green mountains and futuristic cityscapes. The excellent **infrastructure**, including the efficient public transit system, the helpful tourist offices and all the other facilities of a genuinely international city make this an extremely soft entry into the Chinese world.

While Hong Kong is a place to do business, **Macau**'s reputation is as a mini Las Vegas of the East, a haven for **gambling** and other sins. The marks of its colonial past are more immediately obvious than they are in Hong Kong, in its Mediterranean-style architecture, cheap Portuguese wine, Macanese cooking, and faintly Latin lifestyle, altogether mellower than in other parts of China.

Visitors will spend more **money** here than elsewhere in China, though not necessarily as much as you might expect, considering the cheap public transport and higher quality of service compared to the mainland. Travellers on a tight budget who stay in dormitory accommodation can get by on US$25 a day, though at the other end of the market in hotels, restaurants and shops, prices quickly rise to international levels.

Hong Kong

In its multifaceted role as one of the key economies of the Pacific Rim, a repository of traditional Chinese culture, and an experiment in governance with which the mainland authorities hope to win over a recalcitrant Taiwan, **HONG KONG** is East Asia's most extraordinary city. The territory's per capita GNP has now overtaken that of Britain, its former imperial master, and the **Hong Kong Special Administrative Region** (HK SAR) is currently the largest source of external investment in the People's Republic of China. Yet Hong Kong's famously brash, obsessively materialistic addiction to money and brand names is perhaps nothing more than an outlet for other, unavailable freedoms, and tends to mask the fact that most people work long hours and live in crowded, tiny apartments (Kwun Tong district reputedly possesses the highest population density in the world, at 50,080 people per square kilometre). On the other hand, it's hard not to enjoy the sheer energy of its street- and commercial life, and the population of seven million is sophisticated and well informed compared to their mainland cousins, the result of continuing colonial ties and relatively free press (although self-censorship is a constant and growing concern). The urban panorama of sky-scrapered Hong Kong Island, seen across the harbour from Kowloon, is, frankly, stunning, and you'll find a surprising wealth of undeveloped rural areas within easy commuter range of the hectic centre and its perennial, massive engineering projects.

The Hong Kong SAR comprises an irregularly shaped peninsula abutting the Pearl River Delta to the west, and a number of offshore islands, which cover 1100 square kilometres in total. The bulk of this area, namely the north of the peninsula as well as most of the islands, forms the semi-rural **New Territories**, the land leased to Britain for 99 years in 1898. The southern part of the peninsula, known as **Kowloon**, and the island immediately south of here, **Hong Kong Island**, are the principal urban areas of Hong Kong. Though ceded to Britain in perpetuity, the British government in 1984 saw no alternative but to agree to hand back the entire territory as one piece, returning it to Chinese control from midnight of June 30, 1997.

The island of Hong Kong offers not only traces of the **old colony** – from English place names to ancient, double-decker trams trundling along the shore – but also superb **modern cityscapes** of towering buildings teetering up impossible slopes, as well as opportunities for **hiking** and even bathing on the **beaches** of its southern shore. Kowloon, in particular its southernmost tip, **Tsim Sha Tsui**, is where many visitors end up staying, and it's here you'll find the bulk of the city's budget accommodation. As the territory's principal tourist trap, it also boasts more shops offering a greater variety of goods per square kilometre than anywhere in the world (not necessarily at reasonable prices, though). North of Tsim Sha Tsui, Kowloon stretches away into the New Territories, a varied area of **New Towns** and older villages, secluded beaches and undeveloped country parks. In addition, the **offshore islands** – especially **Lamma** and **Lantau** - are well worth a visit for their seafood restaurants and further rural contrasts to the hubbub of downtown Hong Kong.

Some history

While the Chinese justifiably argue that Hong Kong was always Chinese territory, the development of the city only began with the **arrival of the British** in Guangzhou in the eighteenth century.

The Portuguese had already been based at Macau, on the other side of the Pearl River Delta, since the mid-sixteenth century, and as Britain's sea power grew, so its merchants began casting envious eyes over the Portuguese trade in tea and silk. The initial difficulty was to persuade the Chinese authorities that there was any reason to want to deal with them, but from the 1750s, British traders were allowed to set up their warehouses in Guangzhou, transactions being organized through a Guangzhou merchants' guild called the **Co Hong**.

However, the foreigners soon found that trade was one-way only, and so started to offer **opium**, cheaply supplied by their Indian territories. An explosion of demand for the drug followed, despite edicts from Beijing banning the trade; Co Hong, which received commission on everything bought or sold, had no qualms about distributing opium to its fellow citizens. Before long the balance of trade had been reversed in favour of the British.

The scene for the **Opium Wars** was now set. Alarmed at the outflow of silver, the emperor appointed Lin Zexu as Commissioner of Guangzhou to end the opium trade, which he did by confiscating and destroying the opium stocks in 1840. The British responded by sending gunboats to blockade Chinese ports and raid along the coast, forcing the Chinese government into signing the **Treaty of Nanking** (1842), which gave a small, thinly populated, offshore island – Hong Kong – to Britain. Following more gunboat diplomacy eighteen years later, the **Treaty of Peking** granted Britain the Kowloon peninsula too, and in 1898 Britain secured a 99-year lease on an additional one thousand square kilometres of land north of Kowloon, later known as the New Territories.

Originally a seedy merchants' colony, by 1907 Hong Kong had a large enough manufacturing base to voluntarily drop the drug trade. Up until World War II, the city prospered as turmoils in mainland China drove money and refugees south into the apparently safe confines of the British colony. This confidence proved misplaced in 1941 when **Japanese forces** seized Hong Kong along with the rest of eastern China, though after Japan's defeat in 1945, Britain swiftly reclaimed the colony, stifling putative attempts by the residents to garner some independence. As the mainland fell to the Communists in 1949, a new wave of refugees – many of the wealthier ones from Shanghai – swelled Hong Kong's population threefold to 2.5 million, causing a housing crisis which set in motion themes still current in the SAR: **land reclamation**, the need for efficient infrastructure, and a tendency to save space by building upwards.

The early **Communist era** saw Hong Kong leading a precarious existence. Had China wished, it could have rendered the existence of Hong Kong unviable by a naval blockade, by cutting off water supplies, by a military invasion – or by simply opening its border and inviting the Chinese masses to stream across in search of wealth. That it never wholeheartedly pursued any of these options, even at the height of the Cultural Revolution, was an indication of the huge **financial benefits** that Hong Kong's international trade links, direct investment and technology transfers brought – and still brings – to mainland China.

In the last twenty years of British rule, the spectre of **1997** loomed large. Negotiations on the future of the colony led in 1984 to the **Sino-British Joint Declaration**, paving the way for Britain to hand back sovereignty of the territory in return for Hong Kong maintaining its capitalist system for fifty years. However, it appeared to locals that Hong Kong's lack of democratic institutions – which had suited the British – would in future mean the Chinese could do what they liked. Fears grew that repression and the erosion of freedoms such as travel and speech would follow the handover. The constitutional framework provided by the **Basic Law** of 1988, in theory, answered some of those fears, illustrating how the "One Country, Two Systems" policy would work. But the next year's **crackdown in Tian'anmen Square** only seemed to confirm the most pessimistic views of what might happen following the handover, especially to members of Hong Kong's embryonic **democracy movement**. When **Chris Patten** arrived in 1992 to become the last governor, he controversially – some might say cynically – broadened the voting franchise for the **Legislative Council elections** (Legco) from around 200,000 to around 2.7 million people, infuriating Beijing and ensuring that the road to the handover would be a rough ride.

After the build-up, however, the **handover** was an anticlimax. The British sailed away on HMS *Britannia*, Beijing carried out its threat to disband the elected Legco and reduce the enfranchised population, and Tung Chee-hwa, a shipping billionaire, became the **first chief executive** of the Hong Kong SAR. But his highly unpopular tenure was doomed from the start: within days, the **Asian Financial Crisis** had begun, causing a recession and soaring unemployment as stock and property values crashed. Added to this were the recurrent outbreaks of **avian flu**, involving huge slaughter of chickens amid fears that humans might also contract the potentially deadly virus. Meanwhile, Tung stood unopposed for a second term in 2002, despite his inability to propose or see through any effective policy, alter the public's perception of **increased government corruption**, or hinder a continuously sluggish economy – not helped by Shanghai's rising star as a place to do business. And the worst was yet to come. Previous fears of avian flu soon proved nothing next to the global panic wrought by southern China's **SARS outbreak** of 2003 – some 299 people died and Hong Kong's tourist industry collapsed, causing a third of restaurants to close down. Tung still refused to step down, despite the fact that each June 4 (the anniversary of the Tian'anmen Square crackdown), about half a million people were turning out to **demonstrate** against him.

This last public display of dissatisfaction annoyed the powers in Beijing, who wanted Hong Kong to showcase the benefits of the "One Country, Two Systems" approach to **Taiwan** – which, now that former colonial territories have been reclaimed, remains the last hurdle to China being reunited under one government. In December 2004, Tung was openly chastised by the Chinese leader Hu Jintao, and in March 2005 he **stood down** mid-term to be replaced as chief executive by career civil servant **Donald Tsang**. Despite being a product of the colonial administration (he was even knighted in 1997), Tsang has also promoted ties with the mainland post-handover, and is seen as a neutral character, capable of providing a period of stability and so regaining both investor and public confidence in Hong Kong in the face of the above set backs.

Orientation, arrival and information

Orientation for new arrivals in the main urban areas is relatively easy: if you are "**Hong Kong-side**" – on the northern shore of Hong Kong Island – **Victoria Harbour** lies to your north, while to your south the land slopes upwards steeply to the **Peak**. The heart of this built-up area on Hong Kong Island is known, rather mundanely, as **Central**. Just across the harbour, in the area known as **Tsim Sha Tsui**, you are "**Kowloon-side**", and here all you really need to recognize is the colossal north–south artery, **Nathan Road**, full of shops and budget hotels, that leads down to the harbour, and to the view south over Hong Kong Island. Two more useful points for orientation on both sides of Victoria Harbour are the **Star Ferry terminals**, where the popular cross-harbour ferries dock, in Tsim Sha Tsui (a short walk west of the south end of Nathan Road) and in Central.

Hong Kong phone numbers have no area codes. From outside the territory, dial the normal international access code + ☎852 (the "country" code) + the number. However, **from Macau** you need only dial ☎01 + the number. To call Hong Kong from mainland China, dial ☎00 + 852 + the number.

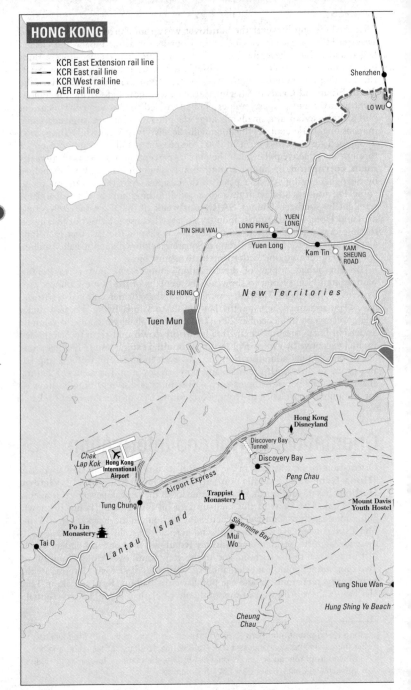

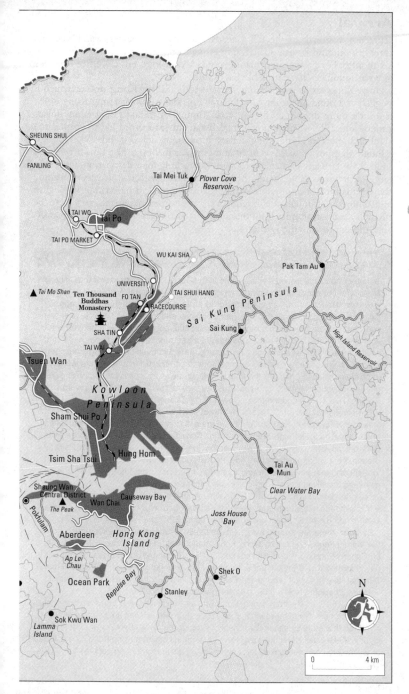

SHEUNG SHUI

FANLING

Tai Mei Tuk • *Plover Cove Reservoir*

TAI WO

Tai Po

TAI PO MARKET

WU KAI SHA

Pak Tam Au •

UNIVERSITY

▲ *Tai Mo Shan*

Ten Thousand
Buddhas
Monastery

FO TAN

TAI SHUI HANG

Sai Kung Peninsula

RACECOURSE

SHA TIN

Sai Kung •

High Island Reservoir

TAI WAI

Tsuen Wan

*Kowloon
Peninsula*

Sham Shui Po

Tai Au
Mun •

Clear Water Bay

Tsim Sha Tsui

• Hung Hom

Sheung Wan
Central District

The Peak ▲

Wan Chai

Causeway Bay

*Joss House
Bay*

Pokfulam

Aberdeen

*Hong Kong
Island*

*Ap Lei
Chau*

Shek O •

Ocean Park

Repulse Bay

• Stanley

N

• Sok Kwu Wan

*Lamma
Island*

0   4 km

Arrival

Currently, nationals of the US, Canada, Australia and New Zealand receive a three-month tourist **visa** on arrival in Hong Kong; British nationals can stay for six months. For present information, contact your local HKTB office or check ⓦ www.immd.gov.hk/ehtml/hkvisas_4.htm.

Hong Kong has its own separate currency, the **Hong Kong dollar**, which is pegged at around $8 to the US dollar. Coincidentally, one Hong Kong dollar is a little more than one Chinese yuan, though yuan and Hong Kong dollars cannot (officially) be used interchangeably in either territory. In this chapter, the symbol $ refers to Hong Kong dollars throughout, unless stated.

Public transport is so convenient and efficient that even first-time arrivals are unlikely to face any particular problems in reaching their destination within the city – apart from the difficulty of communicating with taxi drivers or reading the destinations on minibuses. All signs are supposed to be written in English and Chinese (although the English signs are sometimes so discreet as to be invisible) and travel times from the main international arrival points are reasonable, though road traffic is often heavy.

Moving on: routes into mainland China

To enter China, you'll need a **visa**, issued at the Consulate Department of the Chinese Ministry of Foreign Affairs building on Kennedy Road, in Central (Mon–Fri 9am–4pm). However, it's actually cheaper and faster to arrange a visa through a **travel agency** (see "Listings", p.713) or through your accommodation, many of which offer the service. **Fees** vary between around $200 and $600, according to whether you want a single-entry or double-entry, one-month, three-month, or six-month visa, and whether you want fast (same-day) processing, or two to three days. Bring a passport photo with you. Agents can also arrange hotel accommodation and onward journeys to all major cities in China. At the time of writing, it was also possible to obtain next-day, no-questions-asked, one-year business visas for $1400, from Foreverbright Trading, 707, New Mandarin Plaza, Tower B, 14 Science Museum Road.

The simplest route into China is by **direct train to Guangzhou** from Hung Hom station to Guangzhou East station; there are a dozen trains daily, and the trip takes under three hours (around $200 one-way). Tickets are obtainable in advance from CTS offices (see "Listings", p.714), or on the day from the Hung Hom Railway Station. As a cheaper alternative, ride the KCR up to Lo Wu, cross into Shenzhen on foot and pick up one of the hourly trains to Guangzhou from there – tickets can be purchased easily in Hong Kong dollars and cost about $100.

The other land route is by **bus**. CTS (see "Listings", p.714 for address; ☎2764 9803, ⓦhttp://ctsbus.hkcts.com) runs frequent services to Shenzhen and Guangzhou; the Guangzhou run takes about 3hr 30min and costs $150 one-way.

By **boat**, there are around six fast ferries daily to **Shenzhen** (Shekou), each from the Macau Ferry Terminal on Hong Kong Island, and from the China Ferry Terminal on Canton Road, Kowloon. Tickets cost $105–170 depending on class and time of day, and the crossing takes under an hour. Further departures from the China Ferry Terminal take in towns around the Pearl River Delta – not of much use for tourists – and to **Zhaoqing** (see p.635) in eastern Guangdong province.

Finally, you can **fly** from Hong Kong into all major Chinese cities on regional Chinese carriers. Note, however, that all airfares from Hong Kong are far more expensive than those out of either Shenzhen or Guangzhou, even if you have to spend a night in these cities along the way. Good-value air tickets from Hong Kong, Shenzhen or Guangzhou can be booked through travel agents in Hong Kong such as the CTS or Shoestring Travel.

By plane

The Hong Kong International Airport opened in 1998 in **Chek Lap Kok** on the outlying island of Lantau as part of a $155.3 billion engineering project. The fastest way to get into town from here is by the high-speed, air-conditioned **Airport Express (AEL)** rail service, whose station platforms are joined directly to both the arrival and departure halls. Trains whisk you to Central in 23 minutes ($100) with stops on the way at Tsing Yi (12min; $60) and Kowloon (19min; $90). Services operate daily every eight minutes between 5.50am and 1am. There are taxi ranks, bus stops and hotel shuttle bus stops (operating every twenty minutes) at the AEL stations, and a left-luggage service at Hong Kong and Kowloon stations operates daily from 6am to 1am.

Running alongside the AEL line for much of the way is the **Tung Chung Line**, which also offers services every eight minutes. This is designed as a slower commuter line, stopping at five other stations in addition to the AEL stops. It's handy if you're heading for certain destinations in the New Territories, or as a cheaper means into the centre ($23), but you need to take bus #S51 or #S61 from the airport to Tung Chung first ($4).

Another way from the airport into the city (and to most hotels) is by **bus**. There are eight Airbus routes, and their departure points are clearly signposted in the terminal; the airport customer-service counters sell tickets and give change, while if you pay on the buses themselves you need to have the exact money. All routes have very regular departures between 6am and midnight, and there's plenty of room for luggage. The most useful include the #A11 and #A12 to Causeway Bay on Hong Kong Island via Sheung Wan, Central, Admiralty and Wan Chai; the #A12 continues to Fortress Hill, North Point and Quarry Bay. Bus #A21 goes to Kowloon KCR station via Tsim Sha Tsui, Jordan, Yau Ma Tei and Tai Kok Tsui (and stops off at Chungking Mansions); #A22 to Lam Tin MTR station via Kowloon MTR, Jordan, Hung Hom, To Kwa Wan, Kowloon City, Kowloon Bay, Ngau Tau Kok, and Kwung Tong; #A31 and #A41 go to the New Territories, with #A31 calling at Tsuen Wan MTR station, Kwai Chung Road, Kwai Fong, Tsing Yi Road, and #A41 going to Sha Tin. The average journey time is about an hour. There are also 21 cheaper **city bus** routes, used mainly by local residents, some of which run 24-hour services.

Taxis into the city are metered and reliable (see p.673 for more details). You might want to get the tourist office in the Buffer Hall to write down the name of your destination in Chinese characters for the driver, though they should know the names of the big hotels in English. It costs roughly $290 to get to Tsim Sha Tsui, about $350 for Hong Kong Island. There may be extra charges for luggage and for tunnel tolls – on some tunnel trips the passenger pays the return charge, too. **Rush-hour traffic** can slow down journey times considerably, particularly if you're using one of the cross-harbour tunnels to Hong Kong Island.

The new airport is open 24 hours, but transport for **early or late flights** can be a problem. Between midnight and 5.50am the rail connections are closed. **Night buses** include the #N11 to Causeway Bay and the #N21 to Tsim Sha Tsui, but otherwise you'll have to take a taxi.

By train and bus

The main land route into Hong Kong is by **train**. Express trains from Guangzhou arrive at **Hung Hom Railway Station** east of Tsim Sha Tsui, also known as the **Kowloon–Canton Railway Station** (or **KCR**; ☏2929 3399, ⓦwww.kcrc.com). Signposted walkways lead from here to an adjacent bus terminal, taxi rank and – ten minutes around the harbour – the Hung Hom Ferry Pier to Wan Chai or Central (7am–7pm); for Tsim Sha Tsui, either stay in the station and catch the KCR train for one stop south to its terminus at Tsim Sha Tsui East station, which exits into Middle Road, or take bus #5C to the Star Ferry terminal.

A cheaper alternative is to take a **local train** from Guangzhou to the Chinese border city of Shenzhen, from where you walk across the border to Lo Wu on the Hong Kong side and pick up the regular KCR trains to Kowloon. Queues at PRC customs can tie you up for between ten minutes and two and a half hours, with the longest delays on Fridays, at weekends and public holidays. It's then a fifty-minute ride into central Hong Kong, the trains following the same length of track to Tsim Sha Tsui East via Hung Hom station. By **bus** there are regular daily services from Guangzhou and Shenzhen, operated by CTS and Citybus (see box, p.673); these take about one hour longer than the direct train and arrive in downtown Tsim Sha Tsui (tickets from $100).

By ferry

Arriving by sea is a great way to approach Hong Kong for the first time, though traffic is mostly local. The two terminals both handle regular ferries from Macau and from Shekou (Shenzhen): the **Hong Kong–Macau Ferry Terminal** is in the Shun Tak Centre, on Hong Kong Island, from where the Sheung Wan MTR station is directly accessible; while the **Hong Kong China Ferry Terminal**, which also handles ferries from the Pearl River Delta, is in downtown Tsim Sha Tsui on Canton Road. For more on Macau and Shekou ferries, see p.668 & p.717. There is also a berth for international cruise liners at Ocean Terminal in Tsim Sha Tsui.

Information, maps and the media

The **Hong Kong Tourism Board** or HKTB (daily 8am–6pm ☎2508 1234, ⓦwww.DiscoverHongKong.com) issues more leaflets, pamphlets, brochures and maps than the rest of China put together – and most are free. They have desks at the airport (daily 7am–11pm) and Lo Wu (8am–6pm) arrival halls, where HKTB staff actively seek out newcomers. In downtown Hong Kong, there are two offices staffed by English-speakers: one in Tsim Sha Tsui at the Star Ferry concourse (daily 8am–6pm); the other on the ground floor of The Centre, 99 Queen's Road, Central on Hong Kong Island (daily 8am–6pm). They provide sound, useful advice on accommodation, shopping, restaurants serving specific cuisines, bus routes and hiking trails – or will tell you how to find out yourself. In addition, they organize **free courses** on *tai ji*, Cantonese Opera, tea appreciation, pearl grading, and more, for which you need to sign up a day in advance.

HKTB **maps**, and the maps in this book, should be enough for most purposes, though infuriatingly detailed versions such as the paperback *Hong Kong Guidebook*, which includes all bus routes, can be bought from bookstores (see "Listings", p.712). Free **listings magazines**, providing up-to-date information on restaurants, bars, clubs, concerts and exhibitions, include the trendy *HK Magazine* and acerbic *BC Magazine* (ⓦwww.bcmagazine.net), both available in hotels, cafés and restaurants.

Hong Kong's two English-language **daily papers** are the *South China Morning Post*, whose bland coverage of regional news does its best to toe the party line, and the *Standard*, which is more business-oriented but can be outspoken about politicians' failings. Other international papers, such as the local edition of the *Herald Tribune*, and journals such as *Time* and *Newsweek*, are widely available.

City transport

Hong Kong's public transport system is efficient, extensive and inexpensive – though best avoided during the week-day **rush hours**, which last about 7.30–9am and 5–7pm. If you plan to travel a good deal, get hold of an **Octopus Card** (℡2266 2222 for information), a rechargeable stored-value ticket which can be used for travel on the MTR, KCR, LRT, trams, the Airport Express, most buses, and most ferries (including the Star Ferry and main inter-island services). The card itself costs $50 (refundable only after a three-month period), and you add value to it by feeding it and your money into machines in the MTR. The fare is then electronically deducted each time you use the card by swiping it over yellow sensor pads at station turnstiles or, on a bus, beside the driver. (Octopus cards can also be used to shop at *McDonald's*, Parkn'shop supermarkets, Maxim's restaurants and 7-11 stores.) Another option is to buy a one-day ($50) **tourist pass**, allowing unlimited travel by MTR throughout Hong Kong; the **three-day pass** ($220) includes one AEL journey from the airport to the centre, plus three days' unlimited MTR rides.

Trains

Hong Kong's three train systems all operate on the same principles, and you buy single-journey **tickets** ($4–11) from easy-to-use dispensing machines at the stations.

The underground **MTR** (Mass Transit Railway) comprises five lines, operating from about 6am to 1am. The **Island Line** (marked blue on maps) runs along the north shore of Hong Kong Island, from Sheung Wan in the west to Chai Wan in the east, taking in important stops such as Central, Wan Chai and Causeway Bay. The **Tsuen Wan Line** (red) runs from Central, under the harbour, through Tsim Sha Tsui, and then northwest to the new town of Tsuen Wan. The **Kwun Tong Line** (green) connects with the Tsuen Wan Line at Mong Kok in Kowloon, and then runs east to Yau Tong and Tiu Keng Leng on the Tseung Kwan O Line (see below). The **Tung Chung Line** (yellow) follows much of the same route as the Airport Express, linking Central and Tung Chung. Finally, the **Tseung Kwan O Line** (purple) links the Island Line stations of North Point and Quarry Bay under the harbour to Yau Tong and Tiu Keng Leng on the Kwun Tong Line, then continues northeast to Po Lam.

The other major rail line is the overground **KCR** (Kowloon–Canton Railway), a commuter railway with two sections. The **KCR East** line runs from East Tsim Sha Tsui station in Kowloon, via Hung Hom station, north through the New Territories to the border with mainland China at Lo Wu – though note that unless you have a visa for China, you can only go as far as the penultimate station of Sheung Shui. There is an interchange between the KCR East and MTR at Kowloon Tong station, and a **KCR East extension** northeast from the Sha Tin area, though this is of no interest to tourists. The **KCR West** line runs from Nam Cheong station on the Tung Chung MTR Line to Tuen Mun, useful for bus connections to outlying attractions in the New Territories.

A third transport system, the **LRT** (Light Rail Transit) connects the New Territories towns of Tuen Mun and Yuen Long, though, again, tourists rarely use it.

Trams

Trams have been rattling along Hong Kong Island's north shore since 1904 and, despite being an anachronism in such a hi-tech city, they are as popular as ever with locals and tourists alike, especially for the night-time view from

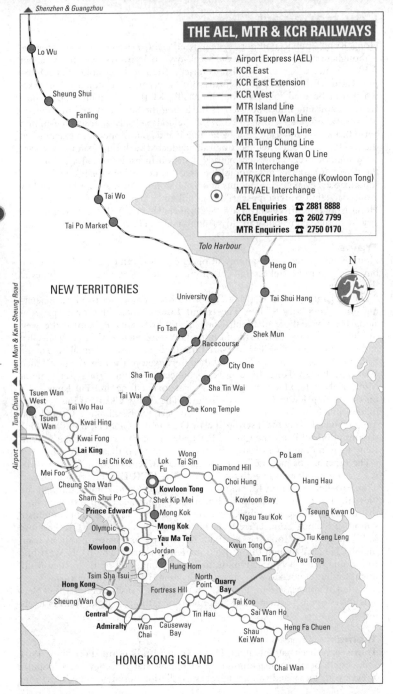

THE AEL, MTR & KCR RAILWAYS

- Airport Express (AEL)
- KCR East
- KCR East Extension
- KCR West
- MTR Island Line
- MTR Tsuen Wan Line
- MTR Kwun Tong Line
- MTR Tung Chung Line
- MTR Tseung Kwan O Line
- MTR Interchange
- MTR/KCR Interchange (Kowloon Tong)
- MTR/AEL Interchange

AEL Enquiries ☎ 2881 8888
KCR Enquiries ☎ 2602 7799
MTR Enquiries ☎ 2750 0170

Shenzhen & Guangzhou

Lo Wu
Sheung Shui
Fanling
Tai Wo
Tai Po Market
Tolo Harbour

NEW TERRITORIES

Heng On
University
Tai Shui Hang
Fo Tan
Shek Mun
Racecourse
City One
Sha Tin
Sha Tin Wai
Tai Wai
Che Kong Temple

Tsuen Wan West
Tai Wo Hau
Tsuen Wan
Kwai Hing
Kwai Fong
Lai King
Lai Chi Kok
Mei Foo
Cheung Sha Wan
Sham Shui Po
Prince Edward
Olympic
Kowloon
Lok Fu
Wong Tai Sin
Diamond Hill
Po Lam
Choi Hung
Hang Hau
Kowloon Tong
Shek Kip Mei
Kowloon Bay
Mong Kok
Ngau Tau Kok
Tseung Kwan O
Yau Ma Tei
Jordan
Kwun Tong
Tiu Keng Leng
Lam Tin
Yau Tong
Hung Hom
Tsim Sha Tsui
North Point
Quarry Bay
Hong Kong
Fortress Hill
Sheung Wan
Tai Koo
Central
Tin Hau
Sai Wan Ho
Admiralty
Wan Chai
Causeway Bay
Heng Fa Chuen
Shau Kei Wan
Chai Wan

HONG KONG ISLAND

N

Tuen Mun & Kam Sheung Road ►
Tung Chung ►
Airport ►

9

HONG KONG AND MACAU | City transport

the upstairs deck. The trams run between Kennedy Town in the west and Shau Kei Wan in the east, via Central, Wan Chai and Causeway Bay (some going via Happy Valley; check the front of the tram). You board the tram at the back, and drop the money in the driver's box ($2; $1 for senior citizens and children; no change given) when you get off.

The so-called **Peak Tram** is, in fact, not a tram but a funicular railway and an essential trip for all visitors to Hong Kong (see p.687).

Buses, taxis and cars

The double-decker **buses** that run around town are comfortable and often air-conditioned, and are essential for many destinations, such as the south of Hong Kong Island, and parts of the New Territories. You pay as you board and exact change is required; the amount is often posted up on the timetables at bus stops and fares range from $1.20 to $45. The HKTB issues up-to-date information on bus routes, including the approximate length of journeys and cost. The **main bus terminal** in Central is at Exchange Square, a few minutes' walk west of the Star Ferry Pier, though some buses also start from right outside the ferry terminal, or from the Outlying Islands Piers, west of the Star Ferry. In Tsim Sha Tsui, Kowloon, the main bus terminal is in front of the Star Ferry Terminal.

As well as the big buses, there are also ubiquitous 16-seater **minibuses** and **maxicabs**, which have set stops but can also be hailed (not on double yellow lines). They cost a little more than regular buses, and you pay the driver as you enter; change – in small amounts – is only given on the minibuses (which have a red rather than a green stripe). The drivers of either are unlikely to speak English.

Taxis in Hong Kong are not expensive, with a minimum fare of $15, although they can be hard to get hold of in rush hours and rainstorms. Note that there is a toll to be paid (around $5–15) on any trips through the cross-harbour tunnel between Kowloon and Hong Kong, and drivers often double this – as they are allowed to do – on the grounds that they have to get back again. Many taxi drivers do not speak English, so be prepared to show the driver the name of your destination written down in Chinese. If you get stuck, gesture to the driver to call his dispatch centre on the two-way radio; someone there will speak English. It is obligatory to wear seat belts in Kowloon and on Hong Kong Island.

Car rental is theoretically possible, though unnecessary, given that taxis are far cheaper and more convenient.

A few important local bus routes

From Central:
#6 and #6A to Stanley via Repulse Bay
#15 to the Peak
#70 to Aberdeen
#629 to Ocean Park

From TsimShat Sui Star Ferry:
#8A and #5C to Hung Hom station
#1 and #1A to Mong Kok
#6A to Lei Cheng Uk Han Tomb Museum
#1, #1A, #2, #6, #7 and #9 to Temple Street Night Market

Ferries

One of the most enjoyable things to do in Hong Kong is to ride the humble **Star Ferry** between Kowloon and Hong Kong Island. The views of the island are superb, particularly at dusk when the lights begin to twinkle through the humidity and the spray. You'll also get a feel for the frenetic pace of life on Hong Kong's waterways, with ferries, junks, hydrofoils and larger ships looming up from all directions. You can ride upper deck ($2.20) or lower deck ($1.70). Ferries run every few minutes between Tsim Sha Tsui and Central (an eight-minute ride; daily 6.30am–11.30pm), and between Tsim Sha Tsui and Wan Chai. There are also similarly cheap and fun ferry crossings between Hung Hom and Central and between Wan Chai and Hung Hom (both $5.30).

In addition, a large array of other boats runs between Hong Kong and the outlying islands, most of which use the **Outlying Islands Piers** in front of the International Finance Centre; see p.699 for details.

Accommodation

Hong Kong boasts a colossal range of **hotels and guesthouses**, particularly in the Tsim Sha Tsui area of Kowloon, and you will always find a room if you are prepared to do some traipsing around. At the upper end of the market are some of the best hotels in the world, costing several thousand dollars a night, though less renowned places offering motel-like facilities start around $500. You'll get the best **deals** on all hotels by **booking ahead**, either by phone or using a website such as the Hong Kong Hotels Association (@ www.hotels-in-hong-kong.com), which features deals, packages and offers for all HKHA properties.

The lower end of the market is served by guesthouses and hostels, the bulk of which are squeezed into blocks at the lower end of Nathan Road – though there are even a few on the outer islands. Always check these rooms for size (many rooms are minuscule), whether the shower is separate, whether it has a window, and whether you have to pay extra for the use of air conditioning.

Even budget hotel accommodation is not that cheap, however – you'll be lucky to find a room for less than $200, though shared **dormitory accommodation** at one of the crowded travellers' hostels will get you down as low as $70–80 a night for a bed. The **Hong Kong Youth Hostels Association** (@2788 1638, @ www.yha.org.hk) also operates seven hostels – mostly a long way from the centre – offering dormitory accommodation at around $30–55 if you've got an IYHF membership card, slightly more if you haven't.

Accommodation price codes

Hong Kong accommodation has been graded according to the following price codes, which represent the cheapest double room available to foreigners, except where the text refers specifically to dorm beds, when the actual price per person is given. Most places have a range of rooms, and staff will usually offer you the more expensive ones – it's always worth asking if they have anything cheaper. The more upmarket hotels will levy an additional ten-percent service charge on top of their quoted room rates. Our price codes are based on the pre-tax rates.

❶ Under $80	❹ $301–500	❼ $1201–2000
❷ $80–200	❺ $501–800	❽ $2001–3000
❸ $201–300	❻ $801–1200	❾ Over $3000

Kowloon

Most of the accommodation listed below is conveniently central, within fifteen minutes' walk of the Tsim Sha Tsui Star Ferry Terminal. For a less claustrophobic atmosphere, however, try locations in Jordan and Yau Ma Tei, which are all located near MTR stations. Places listed represent a fraction of the total on offer, and it is always worth having a look at several options.

Anne Black Guesthouse (YWCA) 5 Man Fuk Rd ⊤2713 9211, ⓦwww.ywca.org.hk. Not far from the Yau Ma Tei MTR, this YWCA pension is surprisingly smart, light and airy. With/without bathroom ④/③

Hotel Miramar 118–130 Nathan Road, Tsim Sha Tsui ⊤2368 1111, ⓦwww.miramarhk.com. The best upmarket deal in Tsim Sha Tsui, with very comfortable rooms and a good location across from Kowloon Park. ⑥

New King's Hotel 473–473A Nathan Rd, Yau Ma Tei ⊤2780 1281, ⓕ2782 1833. Immediately south of the Yau Ma Tei MTR. More than a guesthouse – it occupies the whole building – this is probably the cheapest "real" hotel in town. On-site coffee shop. Single and double rooms. ⑤

Peninsula Hotel Salisbury Rd, Tsim Sha Tsui ⊤2920 2888, ⓦwww.peninsula.com. One of the classiest hotels in the world, which has been overlooking the harbour and Hong Kong Island for nearly eighty years. Even if you're not staying, at least pop in for afternoon tea (see p.706). Rooms start at $2600, but some upmarket package tours offer a better deal. ⑧–⑨

Rent-a-Room Flat A, 2/F, Knight Garden, 7-8 Tak Hing Street, Jordan ⊤2366 3011, ⓦwww.rentaroomhk.com. Fairly spacious self-contained doubles and singles in a residential block, right behind Jordan MTR; there's no sign, so look for "Knight Garden", go up the steps, and bear left, upstairs again, to Flat A. Good rates for stays of a month or more. ④

The Salisbury (YMCA) 41 Salisbury Rd, Tsim Sha Tsui ⊤2268 7888, ⓦwww.ymcahk.org.hk. The location could not be better: right next door to the *Peninsula Hotel* and with views over the harbour and Hong Kong Island, though the atmosphere is sterile. Facilities include indoor pools, fitness centre and a squash court. Four-bed dorms with attached shower are also available, but are relatively expensive and cannot be reserved. Open to both men and women. Dorms $210, rooms ⑤

Star Guesthouse Flat B, 6/F, 21 Cameron Rd, Tsim Sha Tsui ⊤2723 8951, ⓦwww.starguesthouse.com.hk. Very clean and friendly, with good English spoken. The rooms with windows and own bath are bright but slightly pricey for what they are; the cheaper rooms have shared bath. ③

Chungking Mansions

Occupying a prime site towards the southern end of Nathan Road, Chungking Mansions is an ugly monster of a building, as deep and wide as it is tall, looking just about fit for demolition. The lowest two floors form a warren of tiny shops and restaurants with a distinctly Central Asian flavour, while the remaining sixteen floors are crammed with budget guesthouses. Above the second floor, the building is divided into five blocks, lettered A to E, each served by two lifts that can carry only a few people at a time, and which are subject to long queues of people who have decided against using the dim, rank stairwells. Surprisingly, the guesthouses are pleasant and cheap, though overall the building is claustrophobic, and an undoubted safety hazard. The guesthouses listed below are just a handful of the total.

Chungking House Floors 4 & 5, Block A ⊤2366 5362, ⓕ2721 3570. The most upmarket place in the whole building, all things being relative, with carpets, a/c, TV and even bath tubs. ③

Kowloon Guesthouse Floor 10, Block B ⊤2369 9802, ⓕ2739 6635. Fairly standard wooden furnishings, but under good management. ②

New Carlton Guesthouse Floor 15, Block B ⊤2721 0720. Friendly, with good English spoken and spotlessly clean, refurbished rooms on offer. ②

Tai Wan Hotel Floor 3, Block A ⊤9406 2379, ⓔtaiwan_hotel@hotmail.com. New place with bigger rooms than most, and full-time door staff making it feel secure. ②

Tom's Guesthouse Flat 5, Floor 8, Block A ⊤9194 5293. Under very friendly management, the double and triple rooms here are reasonably bright and very good value. *Tom's* has another branch at Flat 1, Floor 16, Block C ⊤2722 6035, ⓕ2366 6706, where the rooms are positively salubrious. ② & ③ respectively.

Welcome Guesthouse Floor 7, Block A ☎ 2721 7793. A recommended first choice, offering a/c doubles with and without shower. Nice clean rooms, luggage storage, laundry service and China visas available. ❷

Yan Yan Guesthouse Floor 8, Block E ☎ 2366 8930. Helpful staff renting out doubles with all facilities; you could sleep three in some at a squeeze, making them pretty good value. ❷

Mirador Mansions

This is the big block at 54–64 Nathan Road, on the east side, in between Carnarvon Road and Mody Road, right next to the Tsim Shat Sui MTR station. Dotted about, in amongst the residential apartments, are large numbers of guesthouses. Mirador Mansions is cleaner and brighter than Chungking Mansions, and queues for the lifts are smaller.

Man Hing Lung Flat F2, Floor 14 ☎ 2722 0678 or 2311 8807. Run by a helpful, friendly man with good English, this is a clean place, offering both singles and doubles, although the rooms are very small. ❷

Mei Lam Guesthouse Flat D1, Floor 5 ☎ 2721 5278. Helpful, English-speaking owner and very presentable singles and doubles, all spick-and-span,

with full facilities. Worth the higher-than-usual prices. ❸

New Garden Hostel Flat F4, Floor 3 ☎ 2311 1183. A scruffy but friendly travellers' hang-out, with washing machines, lockers and even a patio garden. Mixed and women-only dorms; beds get cheaper if you pay by the week. Dorms $80.

Hong Kong Island

Accommodation on the island is mostly upmarket, though there's an emerging budget enclave in Causeway Bay (with prices a tad higher than Kowloon's), and the secluded but excellent *Mount Davis Youth Hostel*.

Bin Man Hotel 1/F, Central Building, 531 Jaffe Road, Causeway Bay ☎ 2833 2063, ℻ 2838 5651. Worth staying here for the name alone, though this budget hotel is also quiet and well located for Causeway Bay's restaurants. ❸

Garden View International House 1 Macdonnell Rd, Central ☎ 2877 3737, ⊛ www.ywca.org.hk. This comfortable YWCA-run hotel is off Garden Road, south of the Zoological and Botanical Gardens. Bus #12A from the Admiralty bus terminal runs past. Prices change considerably depending on demand, but their cheaper rates are a very good deal. ❺–❼

Grand Hyatt 1 Harbour Rd, Wan Chai ☎ 2588 1234, ⊛ www.hongkong.grand.hyatt.com. Part of the Convention and Exhibition Centre complex (along with the neighbouring, cheaper, *Renaissance Harbour View*). The sumptuous lobby needs to be seen to be believed – luxurious rather than tasteful. Regarded by people in the know as one of the poshest places in town. Harbour views from $1600. ❽–❾

Harbour Plaza North Point 665 King's Rd, North Point ☎ 2187 8888, ⊛ www.harbour-plaza.com/hpnp. This very friendly four-star hotel is opposite the Quarry Bay MTR station, exit C, some twenty minutes by MTR from Central. Excellent value, with kitchenettes in each room, large pool and gym

– and they offer visitors a goldfish in their rooms, for company. ❻

King's Hotel 300 Jaffe Road, Wanchai ☎ 3188 2277, ℻ 3188 2626. Quirky boutique hotel with a "cyber" theme resulting in a sort of minimalist sci-fi decor. Rooms come with IDD computers and plasma-screen TVs, and deals can slash rates. ❻, harbour view ❼

Mandarin Oriental 5 Connaught Rd, Central ☎ 2522 0111, ⊛ www.mandarinoriental.com. Unassumingly set in a plain concrete box, this is one of the best hotels in the world, with unmatched service. The hotel lobby is also a great place to people-watch – anyone who's anyone in Hong Kong eats or drinks here. Room rates begin at $3200, but seasonal discounts can cut this by half. ❾

Mount Davis Youth Hostel (Ma Wui Hall) Mt Davis ☎ 2817 5715. Perched on the top of a mountain above Kennedy Town, this self-catering retreat has superb, peaceful views over the harbour. Getting here, however, is a major expedition, unless you catch the infrequent shuttle bus ($10) from the ground floor of the Shun Tak Centre (Macau Ferry Terminal) – phone the hostel for times. Otherwise, catch bus #5 from Admiralty or minibus #54 from the Outlying Islands Ferry Terminal in Central and get off near the junction of Victoria Road and Mount

Davis Path; walk back 100m from the bus stop and you'll see Mt Davis Path branching off up the hill – the hostel is a 35-minute walk. If you have much luggage, get off the bus in Kennedy Town and catch a taxi from there (around $50 plus $5 per item of luggage). Dorms $65, doubles/family rooms ❷

Noble Hostel Floor 17, Patterson Building, 27 Paterson St, Causeway Bay ☎ 2576 6148, ⓦ www .noblehostel.com.hk. A great place to stay, right

in the middle of Causeway Bay, one of the most attractive eating and shopping areas in Hong Kong. Rooms are air-conditioned, clean and good sizes with private bathrooms, and are available as singles, doubles, triples and quads. ❸

The Park Lane 310 Gloucester Rd, Causeway Bay ☎ 2293 8888, ⓦ www.parklane.com.hk. Located slap-bang on Victoria Park, this plush hotel is conveniently sited for the shopping and eating delights of Causeway Bay. Rates start at $2300. ❽

The New Territories and Outlying Islands

Most accommodation in the New Territories and Outlying Islands is rural and low-key, offering an attractive escape from the city's congestion. You won't be the only one who is tempted by the idea, though – always book in advance, especially at weekends and during holidays. Six of Hong Kong's **youth hostels** are here – two on Lantau Island, and four in the New Territories – note that they are self-catering, require you to be a YHA member, and are too remote to be used as a base for exploring the rest of Hong Kong. Commuting from Lamma or Cheung Chau, however, is feasible; guesthouses here raise their rates at weekends but also offer package deals for a week or more – the HKTB can further advise about holiday flats on the islands.

Bella Vista Miami Resort Cheung Chau ☎ 2981 7299, ⓕ 2981 9157. One of several low-key guesthouses on the island; well located in what passes for a main street in a residential block. Weekdays ❷, weekends ❸

Bradbury Lodge 66 Tai Mei Tuk Road, Tai Mei Tuk, Tai Po, New Territories ☎ 2662 5123. Of all the hostels this is about the easiest to get to. Take the KCR train to Tai Po, then bus #75K to Tai Mei Tuk Terminal. Walk south a few minutes, with the sea on your right. Lots of boating, walking and cycling opportunities right by the scenic Plover Cove Reservoir (see p.697). Dorms $35, rooms ❷

Concerto Inn 28 Hung Shing Ye Beach, Yung Shue Wan, Lamma Island ☎ 2982 1668, ⓦ www .concertoinn.com.hk. Near a small and quiet beach, with a delightful terraced restaurant (see p.700). Sun–Fri ❹, Sat ❺

Man Lai Wah Hotel Yung Shue Wan, Lamma Island ☎ 2982 0220 or 2982 0600. Right ahead from the ferry pier, this low-key place has small, double bed flats with balcony and harbour views. ❹

Pak Sha O Hostel Pak Sha O, Hoi Ha Rd, Sai Kung, New Territories ☎ 2328 2327. Take green minibus #7 going to Hoi Ha from Sai Kung (see p.698) and get off at the hostel. Great for access to Hong Kong's cleanest, most secluded snorkelling beaches. Dorms $45.

Regal Airport Hotel 9 Cheong Tat Road, Hong Kong International Airport, Chek Lap Kok

☎ 2286 8888, ⓦ www.RegalHotel.com. Over 1100 sound-proofed rooms with a direct airbridge link to the airport, express check-in, pools and a health club. The website often advertises inexpensive last-minute accommodation deals. ❼

Regal Riverside Hotel 34–36 Tai Chung Kiu Rd, Sha Tin ☎ 2649 7878, ⓦ www.RegalHotel.com. The New Territories' best hotel – though there's not a lot of competition – right in the centre of Sha Tin. This comfortable place often appears in holiday packages; there's a fine Asian lunch buffet served here and a free shuttle bus to Tsim Sha Tsui, too. Again, check their website for discounted rates. ❻

S. G. Davis Hostel Ngong Ping, Lantau Island ☎ 2985 5610. From Mui Wo (see p.701) take bus #2 to the Ngong Ping Terminal and follow the paved footpath south, away from the Tian Tan Buddha and past the public toilets. It's a ten-minute walk and well signposted. This is a great base for hill walking on Lantau, and you can eat at the nearby Po Lin Monastery. It's cold on winter nights, though – bring a sleeping bag. Dorms $45, ❷

Silvermine Beach Hotel 648 Silvermine Bay, Mui Wo, Lantau Island ☎ 2984 8295, ⓦ www.resort .com.hk. Superbly located right on the beachfront, a few minutes' walk from the Mui Wo Ferry Pier. The rooms here are comfortable and quiet, and good value during the week when they are discounted. The restaurant spilling out onto the terraces offers popular barbecues and Thai grub. ❻, sea view ❼

Warwick Hotel East Bay, Cheung Chau ☎ 2981 0081, ⓦ www.warwickhotel.com.hk. Overlooking Tung Wan Beach, this is the most upmarket and expensive of Cheung Chau's accommodation, with a swimming pool and restaurant. Rooms have balconies, private baths, cable TV, and good-value weekly rates. ❺, weekends ❻

Hong Kong Island

As the oldest colonized part of Hong Kong, its administrative and business centre, and site of some of the most expensive real estate in the world, **Hong Kong Island** is naturally the heart of the whole territory. Despite its tiny size, just 15km from east to west and 11km from north to south at the widest points, and despite the phenomenal density of development on its northern shore, the island offers a surprising range of **mountain walks** and attractive **beaches** as well as all the attractions of a great city.

On the northern shore of Hong Kong Island, overlooking **Victoria Harbour** and Kowloon on the mainland opposite, are the major financial and

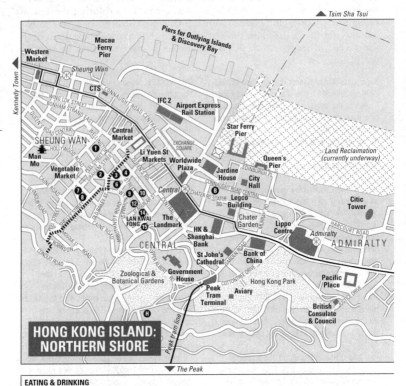

EATING & DRINKING							
2 Sardines	8	East Lake Seafood	11	Luk Yu Tea House	9	Nha Trang	
Chee Kee Wonton Noodle Shop	17	Fook Lam Moon	21	Lulu Shanghai	11	Outback Grill	
Chippy	4	Golden Dynasty	5	M at the Fringe	15	Padang	
Chiu Chow Dynasty	19	Indonesian 1968	23	Man Wah	B	Roof Garden	
Chuan Bar Bar	16	La Pampa	7	Moon	20	SoHo SoHo	
		Lin Heung Tea House	1	Muyu Zigan	3	Thai Lemongrass	

commercial quarters of **Central** and **Wan Chai**, from which sprout several of Asia's tallest and most interesting skyscrapers. To the east is **Causeway Bay**, a shopping and entertainment area, while to the west there's a faintly "traditional" air to **Kennedy Town**, whose streets are lined with shops selling dried fish and Chinese medicines.

The southern shore of the island is more notable for its beaches, greenery and small towns, among them **Aberdeen**, in whose harbour you'll still see the traditional barrel-shaped fishing boats (junks) and the smaller, flat-bottomed sampans, as well as Hong Kong's famous floating restaurants. Meanwhile, the centre of the island rises steeply to a series of wooded peaks. Of these, the most famous, **Victoria Peak**, immediately south of Central district and accessible on the 100-year-old **Peak Tram**, commands superb views of the city and the harbour below.

Central

The area known as **Central** takes in the core of the old city, which was originally called Victoria, after the Queen. It extends out from the Star Ferry

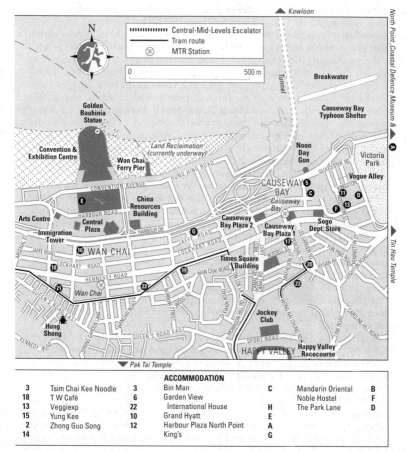

ACCOMMODATION

3	Tsim Chai Kee Noodle	3	Bin Man	C	Mandarin Oriental	B
18	T W Café	6	Garden View		Noble Hostel	F
13	Veggiexp	22	International House	H	The Park Lane	D
15	Yung Kee	10	Grand Hyatt	E		
2	Zhong Guo Song	12	Harbour Plaza North Point	A		
14			King's	G		

Terminal a few hundred metres in all directions, east to the Admiralty MTR, west to the Central Market and south, up the hill, to the Zoological and Botanical Gardens. Moving inland from the shore, the main west–east roads are Connaught Road, Des Voeux Road and Queen's Road respectively, though as Central's busy streets are not ideal for walking, pedestrians are better off concentrating on the extensive system of **elevated walkways** which link many of the buildings.

West from the Star Ferry

Emerging from the **Star Ferry Terminal**, the first things you'll see are a number of ancient, hand-pulled rickshaws and their equally ancient runners, who predate the time when the last licences were issued. Now they are just there for the tourists, so if you take photos, expect to pay for them. This whole waterfront area, from the Star Ferry Terminal east to the Convention and Exhibition Centre in Wanchai (see p.683), is due for an extensive **makeover**, involving plazas, covered walkways and parkland – the plans have yet to be finalized, though reclamation has begun. In this area, just west of the ferry terminal, are the **Outlying Islands Ferry Piers**, in front of which looms the **International Finance Centre** (whose basement station houses the Airport Express terminus), sporting Hong Kong's tallest building, **IFC2**. This 420-metre tower is so beautifully proportioned that it's not until you see the top brushing the clouds that you realize it stands half as high again as any other building in the area.

Before reaching the International Finance Centre, if you take the walkway to the left and follow it inland, you'll pass right between **Jardine House** (the tall building full of portholes) on your left and **Exchange Square** on your right. Exchange Square is home to the three gloriously opulent marble-and-tinted-glass towers which house the **Hong Kong Stock Exchange**. The Exchange Square bus station is located underneath the square. A further branch of the elevated walkway runs northwest from here, parallel with the shore and along the northern edge of Connaught Road, past Exchange Square and all the way to the Macau Ferry Terminal and Sheung Wan MTR; follow this for some great views over the harbour. Otherwise continue across Connaught Road into the heart of an extremely upmarket shopping area, around **Des Voeux Road**.

Easily recognizable from the tramlines that run up and down here, Des Voeux Road used to mark Hong Kong's seafront before the days of reclamation, hence the name of the single smartest shopping mall in the area, the **Landmark**, on the corner with Pedder Street. Of all the shops around here, one definitely worth a visit is **Shanghai Tang**, across Pedder Street from the Landmark, for pricey silver, glass and silk collectibles, and superb designer garments recalling traditional Chinese wear. Continue west down Des Voeux Road for 300m from the Landmark, and you'll reach the multistorey **Central Market** – worth dropping in on during the morning business (if you're not squeamish) for some incredible photo opportunities of poultry, fish and meat being hacked about on a huge scale.

Southwest of Central Market, leading uphill from Queen's Road Central, is Graham Street, a flourishing downtown **fruit and vegetable market**. Also leading uphill from Queen's Road, immediately south of Central Market, is the **Central-Mid-Levels Escalator**, a series of twenty covered escalators rising 800m up the hill as far as Conduit Road, providing easy access to the expensive **Mid-Levels** residential area and spawning an "escalator culture" with the restaurant, bar and café district of **SoHo**. During the morning (6am–10am), when people are setting out to work, the escalators run downwards only; from 10.20am to midnight they run up. It's worth riding up to the top to appreciate

△ Hong Kong trams

this quite unique piece of urban public transport, besides being a great way to explore the old streets that run east and west from the escalator.

East from the Star Ferry

Walk ahead from the Star Ferry Terminal and you'll enter an **underground walkway** which exits into **Statue Square**. This is an oddly empty space, divided from east to west in the middle by Chater Road, which was the heart of the late nineteenth-century colony. Today it is principally used as a picnic area by Hong Kong's tens of thousands of Filipino maids on Sundays, their weekly day off. The 90-year-old domed, granite building to the east of the square, dwarfed and overlooked by the gigantic modern buildings immediately to the south, is the home of the Legislative Council, Hong Kong's equivalent of a parliament – hence its name, the 1898 **Legco Building**.

Immediately south of Statue Square is the magnificently hi-tech **Hong Kong and Shanghai Bank (HSBC)** building designed by Sir Norman Foster. At the time of its construction in 1985, it was reputedly one of the most expensive buildings ever, at a cost of over US$1 billion. At ground level you can see that the whole building is supported on groups of giant pillars and it's possible to walk right under the bank and come out on the other side – a necessity stipulated by the old *feng shui* belief that the centre of power on the island, Government House, which lies directly to the north of the bank, should be accessible in a straight line by foot from the main point of arrival on the island, the Star Ferry. From under the bank, the building's insides are transparent, and you can look up, through the colossal glass atrium, into the heart of the building.

East, a couple of hundred metres down the road from the HSBC, is the three-hundred-metre, 74-floor, blue-glass and steel **Bank of China**, designed by a team led by the internationally renowned I.M. Pei. However, the knife-like profile, pointing skywards, offends all the normal *feng shui* sensitivities, and the building is disliked in Hong Kong. East again from here – reached along the elevated walkways, or by tram – is the curiously bulging **Lippo Centre**, a gleaming office building which you'll pass to the north before reaching the Admiralty MTR station.

South of Queen's Road

South of Queen's Road, the land begins to slope seriously upwards, making walking laborious in hot weather. Head south up D'Aguilar Street (just west of Pedder Street) from Queen's Road, and you'll enter the **Lan Kwai Fong** area, Central's barfly district. Lan Kwai Fong itself is actually an L-shaped lane, jammed with overflowing theme bars, restaurants and flower stalls, which branches southeast off D'Aguilar Street, though several of the neighbouring lanes and small streets boast an interesting range of snack bars and restaurants. Of interest here is the **Luk Yu Tea House** on Stanley Street (just west of D'Aguilar Street), a 1930s-style teahouse (see "Eating, drinking and nightlife", p.705).

In a general southerly direction from Lan Kwai Fong – a short but steep walk along Glenealy Street and under the flyover – are the small **Hong Kong Zoological and Botanical Gardens** (daily 6am–7pm; free), whose collection of birds, monkeys and other beasts makes a pleasant refuge from the hubbub of Central. The gardens are cut down the middle by Albany Street, but an underground walkway connects the two halves. To get here direct from the Star Ferry Terminal area, catch buses #3B or #12 heading east along Connaught Road.

North of the gardens, just across Upper Albert Road, **Government House** was the official residence of fifteen Hong Kong governors, from 1855 until

1997. The house is not open to the public, and the gardens are only open one weekend a year – usually in March. A few hundred metres to the east is **Hong Kong Park** (daily 6.30am–11pm; free). From the eastern exit of the Botanical Gardens you can walk to the park in about ten minutes, along Garden Road. There's also an entrance just to the east of the Peak Tram terminal (see p.687). Otherwise, the main entrance to the park is from the north, on Supreme Court Road; follow signs from Admiralty MTR station, through the Pacific Place shopping mall. The highlight here is the **Edward Youde aviary** (daily 9am–5pm, free), where raised walkways lead you through a re-created rainforest canopy inside a giant meshed enclosure, with rare and colourful birds swooping about, nesting and breeding. Downhill near the Queen's Road entrance, the **Museum of Tea Ware** (daily Thurs–Tues 10am–5pm; free) is housed in Hong Kong's oldest surviving colonial building, Flagstaff House, constructed 1844–46, and today incongruously located right in the shade of the Bank of China tower. It's stuffed with 3000 Chinese artefacts related to tea making.

One other relic of the earliest days of Hong Kong's colonial past is the Anglican **St John's Cathedral**, a little farther north down Garden Road from the Peak Tram terminal. Dating back to 1849, the church is now located in a hillside grove of trees, in the lee of skyscrapers.

Wan Chai and Causeway Bay

Stretching away east of Central, the built-up area on the north shore runs for 6km and comprises a number of localized centres, of which the two most visited by tourists for nightlife, dining and shopping are **Wan Chai** and **Causeway Bay**. The street layout of both districts is similar to Central, with a number of east–west streets running parallel to the shore. The main street, **Hennessy Road**, is a continuation of Queensway from Central, and carries the tramlines right through the whole area (apart from where they temporarily divert south to Johnston Road). Immediately north of Hennessy Road, and parallel with it, is **Lockhart Road**, while farther north still is the principal east–west highway, **Gloucester Road**, a continuation of Connaught Road. South of Causeway Bay, the low-lying area known as **Happy Valley** is home to Hong Kong's racecourse.

MTR trains and trams connect Central with both Wan Chai and Causeway Bay, as do numerous buses, including #2 and #11. Wan Chai is additionally accessible by ferry from Tsim Sha Tsui.

Wan Chai

In the 1950s and 1960s, **Wan Chai** was a thriving red-light district, catering to the needs of US soldiers on leave from Korea and Vietnam, and it was also the setting for Richard Mason's novel about a Wan Chai prostitute, *The World of Suzy Wong*. Nowadays the atmosphere is far less raunchy and the sights few, but Wan Chai's core of **restaurants** and **bars** makes it a good evening destination.

In the far west of the area, just north of Gloucester Road, on the corner of Fenwick Street and Harbour Road, is the **Hong Kong Arts Centre** (ten minutes' walk from Wan Chai MTR), several storeys of galleries, cinemas, art spaces, and two cafés with harbour views. The free monthly magazine, *Artslink*, gives detailed reviews of what's happening here and elsewhere in Hong Kong's art scene.

Immediately to the east of the Arts Centre stands a vast set of imaginatively shaped modern buildings, the most striking of which is the **Hong Kong Convention and Exhibition Centre** on the seafront at 1 Harbour Road, which plausibly resembles a manta ray. This is where the British formally handed Hong Kong back to the Chinese in June 1997, and when there are no events going on, you can visit the hall where the ceremonies took place. Two upmarket hotels, the *Grand Hyatt* and the *Renaissance Harbour View*, are part of the same complex. Outside, there's a daily flag-raising and -lowering ceremony on **Golden Bauhinia Square** opposite, at 8am and 6pm respectively.

Immediately inland, across Harbour Road, soars the 78-storey **Central Plaza**, its golden, glowing cladding, which changes colour every fifteen minutes from 6am to 6pm, visible from far away to the north in Kowloon. For splendid 360-degree views over the city, catch the lift to the (free) public viewing area on the forty-sixth floor. You can reach Central Plaza and the Exhibition Centre by walking along raised walkways from Wan Chai MTR station exit A, or from the ferry terminal immediately in front.

In contrast to these hi-tech marvels near the seafront, inland Wan Chai is a solidly functional area, packed with residential skyscrapers and shopping streets with just a scattering of curiosities. On 129 Queen's Road East, south of the tramlines on Johnston Road, is the little brick, smoke-blackened **Hung Sheng Temple**, built into a hillside and always open. There's a tiny flower and bird market opposite the temple, on Tai Wong Road West. A couple of hundred metres east of the Hung Sheng Temple, you'll pass the quaint, whitewashed, former **Wan Chai Post Office**, in operation between 1912 and 1992. A short walk from here, along Stone Nullah Lane running south from Queen's Road East, is the **Pak Tai Temple**, at 2 Lung On Street (daily 8am–6pm), where you can see craftsmen making fantastic little burial offerings out of bamboo and coloured paper, including cars, houses and aeroplanes.

Causeway Bay

Causeway Bay derives its name from the fact that it used to be a bay, until reclamation in the 1950s. Now it is a crowded, lively district packed with shops and restaurants, centred around the area between the eastern end of Lockhart Road and the western edge of Victoria Park. Trams run just to the south of here, along Yee Wo Street, a continuation of Hennessy Road from Wan Chai. Causeway Bay has an MTR station and is also the point of arrival of the original **cross-harbour tunnel**, which carries vehicle traffic over from Kowloon.

Within a couple of minutes of the MTR station, you'll find several ultra-modern **Japanese department stores**, including Sogo and Mitsukoshi, while slightly to the north is **Vogue Alley**, a lane to the east of and parallel with north–south Paterson Street, whose focus, as its name suggests, is a group of fashion boutiques. South of Yee Wo Street, the atmosphere is slightly more downmarket, but just as busy, particularly around Jardine's Bazaar and Jardine's Crescent, two alleys almost immediately south of Causeway Bay MTR.

Bang on Causeway Bay MTR (exit A), at Matheson Street, lies **Times Square**, two towers constructed in 1993 and packed with themed shopping over sixteen floors. These range from computers to haute couture, a cinema multiplex and four floors of eateries. Look out for the giant outdoor video screen in the piazza, a popular meeting place offering daily news and weather reports.

Wan Chai's sole tourist sights are down at the waterfront; principally, the Causeway Bay Typhoon Shelter, which is always jammed full of yachts, sampans, junks and other boats; and the **Noon Day Gun** – immortalized in Noel Coward's song *Mad Dogs and Englishmen*. This is still fired off with a loud report every day at noon, a habit dating back to the early days of the colony.

The eastern part of Causeway Bay is dominated by **Victoria Park**, an extensive space by Hong Kong's standards, which contains swimming pools and other sports facilities. This has become the location for the annual candle-lit vigil held on June 4 to commemorate the victims of Tian'anmen Square, in addition to hosting one of Hong Kong's largest lunar New Year fairs. Come early in the morning and you'll see dozens of people practising *tai ji*. Down at the south-eastern corner of the park, right by the Tin Hau MTR (exit A), is the 200-year-old **Tin Hau Temple**, a rather dark, gloomy place surrounded unhappily by skyscrapers (daily 7am–7pm). Tin Hau is the name given locally to the Goddess of the Sea, and her temples can be found throughout Hong Kong, originally in prominent positions by the shore but often marooned by land reclamation far inland. You can also reach this Tin Hau Temple on any tram heading for North Point; get off immediately after passing Victoria Park on your left.

Happy Valley

The low-lying area extending inland from the shore south of Wan Chai and Causeway Bay, and known as Happy Valley (or Pau Ma Dei), really means only one thing for the people of Hong Kong: horse racing, or, more precisely, gambling. The **Happy Valley Racecourse**, which dates back to 1846, was, for most of Hong Kong's history, the only one in the territory, until a second course was built at Sha Tin in the New Territories. If you're interested in witnessing Hong Kong at its rawest and most grasping, entrance to the public enclosure is just $10, with races almost every Wednesday during the racing season, which runs from September until June – bus #1M connects Admiralty MTR (East) with the racecourse on race days. Otherwise, enquire at HKTB about their "Come Horse-racing Tour" ($540-790 depending on the event), which includes transportation to and from the track, entry to the Members' Enclosure and a buffet meal at the official Jockey Club – and tips on how to pick a winner. Happy Valley can be reached from Central or Causeway Bay on a spur of the tramline, or on bus #1 from Central.

Western District

West of Central lies a district rather older in character than other parts of Hong Kong. An almost entirely Chinese-inhabited area, its crowded residential streets and traditional shops form a contrast to Central's modernity, though the atmosphere has been somewhat diluted by the building of the road network for the **Western Harbour Crossing**, the third cross-harbour road tunnel from Kowloon. **Sheung Wan** is the largest sub-zone within this area, and, like Central, it comprises straight east–west roads near the shore, and increasingly meandering roads up the hill away from the harbour. **Kennedy Town**, in the far west, is squeezed up against the shore by sharply rising hills, and is served by tramlines that extend from Central along Des Voeux Road, Connaught Road West, Des Voeux Road West, and finally Kennedy Town Praya.

Sheung Wan, immediately adjacent to Central, spreads south up the hill from the seafront at the red-bordered Shun Tak Centre, which houses the Macau Ferry Terminal (for details of travel to Macau, see p.717) and the Sheung Wan MTR station, the last stop on this line. You can reach the Shun Tak Centre by a fifteen-minute walk along the elevated walkway from Exchange Square in Central, though you'll get more flavour of the district by following the tramlines along Des Voeux Road, west from Central Market (see p.680). Extending south from this stretch of Des Voeux Road are a number of interesting lanes: Wing Sing Street specializes in preserved eggs, and Man Wa Lane, very near the Sheung Wan MTR, is where Chinese character chops (name stamps) are carved from stone or wood. Another couple of minutes along Des Voeux Road from here brings you to the back end of **Western Market** (daily 10am–7pm), a brick Edwardian-style building on the outside, but since 1991 no longer a market but a mall full of small, kitschy kiosks, Chinese food joints, arts, crafts and fabric shops.

A short walk south, up the hill from the harbour, is **Bonham Strand**, which specializes in Chinese medicinal products, teas and herbs. This is a fascinating area for poking around, with shop windows displaying items such as snakes, snake-bile wine, birds' nests, antlers and crushed pearls, as well as large quantities of expensive ginseng root. Please avoid the shark's fin, which is also displayed here – it's collected by cutting the flukes off the live animal and throwing it back into the water to drown – besides which, intense fishing is placing many shark species on the endangered list. You'll find medicinal shops scattered along an east–west line extending from Bonham Strand to the small **Ko Shing Street** – the heart of the trade – which is adjacent to, and just south of, Des Voeux Road West. This section of Des Voeux Road boasts another long line of shops specializing in every kind of dried food, including sea slugs, starfish, snakes and flattened ducks, as well as reeds, sacking and salted fish.

A short but stiff walk up from Bonham Strand leads to the scenically located **Hollywood Road**, running west from Wyndham Street in Central (immediately south of Lan Kwai Fong; see p.682) as far as the small Hollywood Park in Sheung Wan, where it runs into Queen's Road West. Bus #26 takes a circular route from Des Voeux Road in Central to the western end of Hollywood Road, then east again along the whole length of the road. The big interest here is the array of **antique, arts and crafts and curio shops**, and you can pick up all sorts of oddities, from tiny embroidered women's shoes to full-size, traditional coffins. The antique shops extend into the small alley, Upper Lascar Row, commonly known as **Cat Street**, which is immediately north of the western end of Hollywood Road and due south of the Sheung Wan MTR. Here you'll find wall-to-wall curiosity stalls with coins, ornaments, jewellery, Chairman Mao badges and chops, all on sale.

Another attraction in the Cat Street area is **Ladder Street**, which runs north–south across Hollywood Road and is, almost literally, as steep as a ladder. This is a relic from the nineteenth century, when a number of such stepped streets existed to help sedan-chair carriers get their loads up the hillsides. On 170 Hollywood Road, adjacent to Ladder Street, the 150-year-old **Man Mo Temple** (daily 10am–6pm) is notable for its great hanging coils of incense, suspended from the ceiling. The two figures on the main altar are the Taoist gods of Literature (Man, or Cheung) and the Martial Arts (Mo, also known as Kwan Tai). Located as it is in a deeply traditional area, this is one of the most atmospheric small temples to visit in Hong Kong.

You'll find a group of smaller temples a few minutes southwest of Hollywood Road on **Tai Ping Shan Street**, which you can reach by climbing a little way south up Ladder Street and taking the second lane on the right. This was one of the first areas of Chinese settlement in Hong Kong, and the temples are still very much part of the fabric of the neighbourhood, and are in daily use.

Finally, back on the shore, trams from Central trundle to a halt at **Kennedy Town**, named after an early governor of the colony. On a clear day there are fine seascapes of barges, ferries and shipping sliding to and from the harbour, but otherwise no reason to linger.

The Peak

The uppermost levels of the 552-metre **Victoria Peak** that towers over Central and Victoria harbour has always been known as **the Peak**. The first path was carved out in 1859, and within twenty years it had become an elite address, the site of numerous summer homes for wealthy British merchants who sought out the higher levels as a way of escaping the heat and malaria of the seafront.

The idea of building a rail link to the top of the Peak was originally scoffed at because of the seemingly impossibly steep gradients, but in 1888 a **funicular railway**, known as the Peak Tram, opened, allowing speedy connections to the harbour. The mountain began to be transformed, with the planting of trees as well as the construction of a regular summer village. By 1924, when the first road to the Peak was built, permanent homes had begun to appear, though Chinese were originally barred. Now, anyone can live here who can afford it – and these days that usually means Chinese tycoons. Aside from its exclusive residential area, the Peak is still a cool, peaceful retreat from the rigours of downtown, and as a vantage point it offers some extraordinary panoramas over the city and harbour below.

Ascending the Peak

Ascending the Peak is half the fun, assuming you plan to ride the **Peak Tram**. The track is incredibly steep, and at times you'll feel that you are practically lying on your back in your seat as the tram climbs the 386 vertical metres to its terminus, a journey that takes about eight minutes.

The **Peak Tram terminal** is on Garden Road in Central, most easily reached via bus #15C (Mon–Sat 10am–11.45pm; $3.50) from outside the Star Ferry Terminal. The Peak Tram itself (daily 7am–midnight; $20 single, $30 return; you can also pay with your Octopus card) runs every ten to fifteen minutes, and you can also use the shuttle bus back to the Star Ferry afterwards, provided you still have your Peak Tram ticket.

You can also catch **bus** #15 (daily 6.15am–midnight; $9.20) to the Peak from Exchange Square – the views are just as good, but it takes thirty minutes. Fitness fanatics can **walk** up too, though for most people walking down is a more realistic option. See below for routes.

On and around the Peak

The Peak Tram drops you right below the ugly, wok-shaped **Peak Tower**, featuring viewing terraces and the Peak Galleria shopping mall, full of souvenir shops and pricey cafés, plus a branch of Madame Tussauds, with wax models ranging from Zhang Zemin to Jacky Chan. Virtually opposite here is the historic **Peak Lookout**, a stone-built colonial place with rattan chairs and fans that, despite having its view blocked by the Peak Tower, still has a great outdoor terrace where you should enjoy at least one cold beer (see "Eating, drinking and nightlife", p.702).

From the Peak Tram terminal area, you'll see four roads leading off to the west and north. Of these, the middle one, Mount Austin Road, leads up to the very top of the Peak, where you'll find the Victoria Peak Garden, formerly the site of the governor's residence. Two of the other roads, however, make a more attractive circuit around the Peak, taking about an hour on foot. Harlech Road (leading due west) is a shady, rural stroll through trees, with a picnic area en route. After half an hour the road runs into Lugard Road, which heads back towards the terminal around the northern rim of the Peak, giving magnificent views over Central and Kowloon. The fourth road, Old Peak Road, leads down to the May Road tram station.

An excellent way to descend the Peak is to walk along one of a number of possible **routes down**, the simplest being to follow the sign pointing to Hatton Road, from opposite the picnic area on Harlech Road. The **walk** is along a very clear path all the way through trees, eventually emerging in Mid-Levels, after about 45 minutes, near the junction between Kotewall Road and Conduit Road. Catch bus #13 from Kotewall Road to Central, or you can walk east for about 1km along Conduit Road until you reach the top end of the Mid-Levels Escalator (see p.680), which will also take you into Central. Another good route down is to take a road leading from Harlech Road, not far from the Peak Tram, signposted to **Pokfulam Reservoir**, a very pleasant spot in the hills. Beyond the reservoir, heading downhill, you'll eventually come out on Pokfulam Road, from where there are plentiful buses to Central, or south to Aberdeen.

Hong Kong Island: the southern and eastern shores

On its south side, Hong Kong Island straggles into the sea in a series of dangling peninsulas and inlets. The atmosphere is far quieter here than on the north shore, and the climate warmer and sunnier. You'll find not only separate towns such as **Aberdeen** and **Stanley**, with a flavour of their own, but also beaches such as that at **Repulse Bay**, and much farther east, at the remote little outpost of **Shek O**. Especially if you're travelling with children, you should consider a visit to **Ocean Park**, a huge adventure theme park with a wonderful aquarium, just beyond Aberdeen, though facing stiff competition from Disney. Buses are plentiful to all destinations on the southern shore, and Aberdeen is linked to Central by a tunnel under the Peak. Nowhere is more than an hour from Central.

Aberdeen
Aberdeen is the largest separate town on Hong Kong Island, with a population of more than sixty thousand living around the narrow harbour – and typhoon shelter – that lies between the main island and the island of Ap Lei Chau. A dwindling minority of Aberdeen's residents still live on **sampans and junks**, and make a living from offering enjoyable harbour tours to tourists. To reach Aberdeen, catch **bus** #70 from Exchange Square in Central (15min), or Admiralty MTR (20min). There's also a **boat** connection between Aberdeen and nearby Lamma Island (see p.700).

You won't get lost in Aberdeen. From the bus stop, just head in the direction of the shore and cross over the main road using the footbridge, where there's a great morning **fish market** and, through the day, women waiting to solicit your custom for a **sampan tour**. Either do a deal with one of these private entrepreneurs, or walk along the ornamental park by the waterfront until you reach a sign advertising "Water Tours" ($50 per head for a thirty-minute ride, irrespective of the number of travellers). The trip offers photogenic views of houseboats jammed together, complete with dogs, drying laundry and outdoor kitchens, as well as endless rags, nets and old tyres. Along the way you'll also pass boat yards and three **floating restaurants**, which are especially spectacular lit up at night (though their food isn't up to much; see "Eating, drinking and nightlife", p.705).

Ocean Park
Ocean Park, a gigantic theme and adventure park (daily 10am–6pm; $185, children aged 3–11 $93, children under 3 free; ⓦwww.oceanpark.com.hk), covers an entire peninsula to the east of Aberdeen. The price of the ticket is all-inclusive, and once you're inside, all rides and shows are free. You could easily spend the best part of a day here, and at weekends in summer you may

find yourself frustrated by queues at the popular attractions, so make sure you arrive early in order to enjoy yourself at a relaxed pace. **Citybus** #629 runs up to Ocean Park from the Star Ferry Pier in Central, or Admiralty MTR (daily approximately every 15min 9am–6.30pm; all-inclusive ticket covers return bus ride and park entrance fee $209, children $105, with one child free for each adult).

In the face of fierce **competition** from Disney over on Lantau, the park is busy repositioning itself, and is scaling back fairground rides in favour of a focus on wildlife and the natural world. Star attractions are An-An and Jia-Jia, two giant pandas, for whom a special $80-million, 2000-square-metre complex has been created, complete with kitchen, clinic, fake mountain slopes and misting machines to mimic a mountain atmosphere.

The first section you will reach is the Lowland section, which includes some life-size moving dinosaur models and a butterfly house – from here, there's a peaceful 1.5-kilometre **cable car ride** to the Headland section at the tip of the peninsula. This is the area where you'll find scary rides such as the Dragon roller coaster and Abyss turbo drop, along with a walk-through **aquarium**, where you can view sharks nose-to-nose through glass, and the Ocean Theatre, where trained **dolphins and sea lions** perform, plus the **Atoll Reef**, a huge coral reef aquarium that contains more than five thousand fish.

Deep Water Bay, Repulse Bay and beyond

Two bays with names ringing of adventure on the high seas, **Deep Water Bay** and **Repulse Bay**, line the coast east of Ocean Park. Unfortunately, the water in this area can be quite polluted, while on summer weekends and public holidays the beaches are jammed with tens of thousands of people. Of all the bays on the south coast, Repulse Bay is the most popular, partly because it contains a number of shops and restaurants, but also because of its **Tin Hau Temple**, which has a longevity bridge, the crossing of which is said to add three days to your life. The backdrop to Repulse Bay is slightly bizarre, with an enormous, garish tower silhouetted against verdant hills, focused around the *Repulse Bay Hotel* – actually a restaurant and shopping complex. South of Repulse Bay, you'll find **Middle Bay** and **South Bay**, fifteen and thirty minutes farther along the coast. These offer more secluded but narrower beaches.

You can reach Repulse Bay on **buses** #6, #61 or #260 from Exchange Square, in Central. Between Aberdeen (to the west) and Stanley (to the east) there are frequent buses that pass all of the bays mentioned above; sit on the right-hand side of the upper deck for the best coastal views along the twisting roads.

Stanley

Straddling the neck of Hong Kong's most southerly peninsula, **Stanley** is a moderately attractive residential village, whose main draw is the bustling covered market, the clutch of pubs and restaurants catering to expatriates, and Hong Kong's largest **Dragon Boat Races**, held on the fifth day of the fifth month of the lunar calendar. Stanley's a tiny place – walk downhill from the bus stop and you'll soon find **Stanley Market** (selling a mishmash of beaded and sequinned outfits, cheap clothing, bed linen, prints and tourist souvenirs), while a little way to the north of here is **Stanley Beach**, which, although not suitable for swimming, has a little row of great seafront restaurants. If you continue walking beyond the restaurants, you'll come to another **Tin Hau Temple**, built in 1767, on the western side of the peninsula. Inside there is a large tiger skin, the remains of an animal bagged near here in 1942 – the last ever shot in Hong Kong. The temple is surrounded by Stanley Plaza, replete with shops, a village square and **Murray House** on the shoreline. One of Hong Kong's oldest colonial buildings, this two-storey mansion was dismantled and removed from its original site in Central to make way for the Bank of China. Today, its colonnades house stylish stores, bars and restaurants, as well as a basement exhibition about its history. In the opposite direction, south down the peninsula along Wong Ma Kok Road, it's about a ten-minute walk to the pleasant St Stephen's Beach, accessible by steps down to the right immediately after a playing field. Beyond here is **Stanley Military Cemetery**, on Wong Ma Kok Road, containing the graves of many of those killed fighting the Japanese in World War II, and also the top-security Stanley Prison. The southern part of the peninsula is a closed military zone. Stanley is accessible on **buses** #6 and #260 from Central, or #73 from Aberdeen or Repulse Bay.

Shek O

In the far east of the island, **Shek O** is Hong Kong's most remote settlement, with an almost Mediterranean flavour in its stone houses, narrow lanes and seafront location. There's a strong surf beating on the wide, white **beach**, which has a shady area of vine trellises at one end for barbecues and, during the week, is more or less deserted. Come for sunbathing and lunch at one of the cheap local restaurants. The surrounding headlands are also popular for hiking; the HKTB can provide you with information about walking part of the Hong Kong Trail along the D'Aguilar peninsula.

You can't miss the beach – it's just a few minutes' walk east from the bus stop, beyond a small roundabout. For a small detour through the village, however, stop at one of the friendly Thai restaurants with outdoor tables and chairs that you see on your left near the roundabout. If you take the small lane left running right through the restaurant area, you'll pass first the local temple and then a variety of shops and stalls.

Reaching Shek O is a great journey in itself for views over hills and seashore. On Sunday afternoons (2.10–6.10pm), bus #309 runs hourly from Exchange Square in Central; otherwise first catch a tram or MTR to **Shau Kei Wan** on Hong Kong's northeastern shore, from where bus #9 continues to Shek O. Shau Kei Wan MTR is also the stopoff for the splendid **Coastal Defence Museum**, located at the 1887 Lei Yue Mui Fort (exit B1, walk ten minutes up Shau Kei Wan Street East, then along Tun Hei Road; daily Fri–Wed 10am–5pm; $10). This offers a history of Hong Kong's coastal defence from the Ming dynasty to the handover.

Kowloon

A four-kilometre strip of the mainland ceded to Britain in perpetuity in 1860 to add to their offshore island, **Kowloon** was accordingly developed with gusto and confidence. With the help of land reclamation and the diminishing significance of the border between Kowloon and the New Territories at Boundary Street, Kowloon has, over the years, just about managed to accommodate the vast numbers of people who have squeezed into it. Today, areas such as Mong Kok, jammed with soaring tenements, are among the most densely populated urban areas in the world.

While Hong Kong Island has mountains and beaches to palliate the effects of urban claustrophobia, Kowloon has just more shops, more restaurants and more

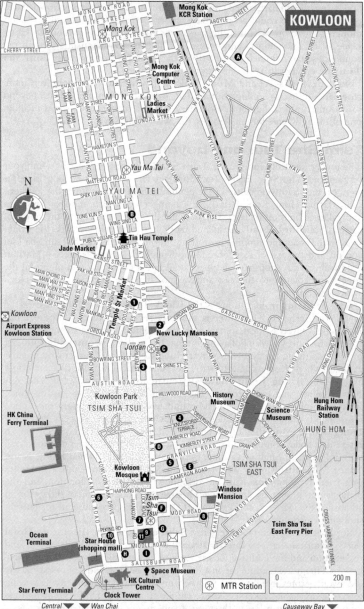

Goldfish Market, Flower Market & Bird Garden

Mong Kok KCR Station

ARGYLE STREET

MONG KOK ROAD

FIFE STREET

TONG MI ROAD

Mong Kok

ARGYLE STREET

NELSON ST

CHERRY STREET

NATHAN ROAD

WATERLOO ROAD

Mong Kok Computer Centre

M O N G   K O K

SAI YEE STREET

TUNG CHOI STREET

FA YUEN STREET

SAI YEUNG CHOI STREET

SHANTUNG STREET

SOY STREET

KAM...

KAM...

KAM...

RECLAMATION STREET

FERRY STREET

PORTLAND STREET

SHANGHAI STREET

CANTON ROAD

Ladies Market

DUNDAS STREET

HAMILTON ST

NTT STREET

CHUN Y LANE

Yau Ma Tei

WATERLOO ROAD

Y A U   M A   T E I

SHEK LUNG ST

MAN LING LA

TUNG KUN ST

WING SING LA

PUBLIC SQUARE ST

KANSU STREET

Tin Hau Temple

MARKET ST

Jade Market

MAN CHONG ST

MAN WAI ST

MAN YUEN ST

MAN WUI ST

PAK HOI ST

SAIGON STREET

NINGPO STREET

WOOSUNG ST

NANKING STREET

RECLAMATION ST

WALCHING ST

CANTON ROAD

FERRY STREET

Temple St Market

NATHAN ROAD

PARKES STREET

SHANGHAI ST

Kowloon
Airport Express
Kowloon Station

JORDAN ROAD

①

② New Lucky Mansions

Jordan

PILKEM ST

TAK SHING ST

③

BOWRING STREET

WOOSUNG ST

KING'S PARK RISE

WYLIE ROAD

WATERLOO ROAD

CHI WO ST

JORDAN ROAD

COX'S ROAD

JORDAN PATH

HO MAN TIN HILL ROAD

WYLIE ROAD

CHUNG HAU STREET

HAU MAN STREET

SHEUNG SHING STREET

SHEUNG LOK STREET

FAT KONG STREET

AUSTIN ROAD

BASCOIGNE ROAD

HK China
Ferry Terminal

Kowloon Park

TSIM SHA TSUI

HILLWOOD ROAD

④ KNUTSFORD TERRACE

KIMBERLEY ROAD

KIMBERLEY STREET

GRANVILLE ROAD

Kowloon
Mosque

History
Museum

OBSERVATORY ROAD

CHONG WAN RD

CHATHAM ROAD

Science
Museum

SCIENCE MUSEUM ROAD

TSIM SHA TSUI EAST

GRANVILLE RD

YUK CHOI ROAD

HONG CHONG RD

Hung Hom
Railway
Station

HUNG HOM

⑤

ⓓ

CAMERON ROAD

⑥

HAIPHONG ROAD

KOWLOON PARK DRIVE

Tsim
Sha
Tsui

ⓕ

Windsor
Mansion

MODY ROAD

⑧

CHATHAM

MODY ROAD

Tsim Sha Tsui
East Ferry Pier

SALISBURY ROAD

CROSS HARBOUR TUNNEL

Ocean
Terminal

⑩

Star House
(shopping mall)

CANTON ROAD

PEKING RD

HANKOW RD

⑦⑨⑪

ⓖ

ⓗ

ⓘ

MIDDLE ROAD

SALISBURY ROAD

Star Ferry Terminal

Space Museum

HK Cultural
Centre

Clock Tower

Central ▼   ▼ Wan Chai

Causeway Bay ▼

0   200 m

⊗ MTR Station

ACCOMMODATION

Anne Black		New King's Hotel	B
Guesthouse (YWCA)	A	Peninsula	I
Chungking Mansions	G	Rent-a-Room	C
Mirador Mansions	F	Salisbury YMCA	H
Miramar	D	Star Guesthouse	E

EATING & DRINKING

Aqua	10	Light Vegetarian	2	Spring Deer	8
Chao Inn	10	Macau Restaurant	1	Tao Heung	6
Felix	I	Mrs Chan	9	Tutto Bene	4
First Cup of Coffee	11	Shadowman	7	Yuan Ji	5
Itamae Sushi	5	Shamrock Seafood	3		

hotels. Initially it's hard to see how such an unmitigatedly built-up, crowded and commercial place could possibly have any cachet among the travelling public, though one reason to visit is the staggering **view** across the harbour to Hong Kong Island's skyscrapers and peaks. This, and its ritzy neon-lit streets in the couple of square kilometres at the tip of the peninsula that make up **Tsim Sha Tsui**, are enough to keep drawing in the crowds.

North, **Yau Ma Tei** and **Mong Kok** are less touristy – though even more crowded – districts teeming with local life, while farther north still, just beyond Kowloon's nominal border at Boundary Street, a scattering of sights includes one of Hong Kong's busiest temples, the **Wong Tai Sin**.

Tsim Sha Tsui and beyond

The tourist heart of Hong Kong, **Tsim Sha Tsui**, is an easy place to find your way around. The **Star Ferry Terminal**, for ferries to Hong Kong Island, is right on the southwestern tip of the peninsula. East of here, along the southern shore, facing Hong Kong Island, are a number of hi-tech, modern museums and galleries built on reclaimed land, while the main road just to the north of these is **Salisbury Road**, dominated by the old colonial landmark, the *Peninsula Hotel*. Broad, and running north right through the middle of Tsim Sha Tsui and on into the rest of Kowloon, Hong Kong's most famous street is **Nathan Road**, alive with shops and shoppers at all hours of the day and night. All the streets immediately to the east and west of here are likewise chock-a-block with small traders.

Tsim Sha Tsui's main antique is the **Clock Tower**, about 100m east of the Star Ferry Terminal. The tower is the only remaining piece of the original Kowloon Railway Station, from where you could once take a train all the way back to Europe, via Mongolia and Russia. The seafront **promenade** runs east from here, giving fantastic views over Hong Kong Island, particularly popular at night when people come to stroll, sit, roller-skate and fish. It's here you'll also find the **Hong Kong Cultural Centre**; its drab, brown-tiled walls, ski-slope roofline, and extraordinary lack of windows – denying anyone inside vistas of the harbour – can only be considered as a wasted opportunity. Inside are concert halls, theatres and galleries including, in an adjacent wing, the **Hong Kong Museum of Art** (Fri–Wed 10am–6pm; $10), which has an interesting collection of Chinese calligraphy, paintings and other antiquities, all with informative English labelling. Immediately east, the domed **Hong Kong Space Museum** (Mon & Wed–Fri 1–9pm, Sat & Sun 10am–9pm; $10) houses user-friendly exhibition halls on astronomy and space exploration, and the planetarium, known as the **Space Theatre**, presents Omnimax shows for an additional fee ($24–32, concessions $16; Ⓦwww.hk.space.museum for current show information).

North of the Cultural Centre across **Salisbury Road**, the **Peninsula Hotel** once commanded a view directly across the harbour to the island, though land reclamation and the Cultural Centre stopped all that. By way of compensation, however, the hotel became the first building in Kowloon allowed to exceed the old twenty-storey height limit imposed on development, with its new wing towering up at the back. Needless to say, rooms are pricey, but it's worth dropping by for afternoon tea in the foyer if you are not looking too scruffy.

The *Peninsula Hotel* sits on the corner of Salisbury Road and **Nathan Road**, which dominates the commercial heart of Kowloon. While by no means a beautiful street, it's one you'll find yourself drawn to again and again for Hong Kong's most concentrated collection of electronics shops, tailors, jewellery stores and fashion boutiques. The variety of goods on offer is staggering, but the southern section of Nathan Road, known as the Golden Mile, is by no means a cheap place to shop, and tourist rip-offs are common (for more details, see "Shopping", p.708). There's also a multicultural flavour provided by the dubious block of **Chungking Mansions**, which, as well as being at the centre of Hong Kong's **budget accommodation**, is an atmospheric shopping arcade where immigrants from the Indian subcontinent rub elbows with Western tourists, businessmen from central and southeastern Asia, and African entrepreneurs. A few hundred metres north of here, **Kowloon Park** (daily 6am–midnight) is marked at its southeastern corner by the white-domed **Kowloon Mosque and Islamic Centre**, which caters to the substantial Muslim population of the area. The park itself provides welcome, green respite from the rest of Tsim Sha Tsui, though you can't see it from the street and have to climb steps up from Nathan Road. There's also an Olympic-size indoor and outdoor **swimming pool complex** (daily 8am–noon, 1.30–6pm & 7.30–10pm; $21), plus an aviary, sculpture walk, and **Kung Fu Corner** (up behind the mosque), where experts in various martial arts give demonstrations every Sunday from 2.30 to 4.30pm.

A few blocks to the east of Nathan Road at no. 100 Chatham Road, you'll find the **Hong Kong Museum of History** (Mon & Wed–Sat 10am–6pm, Sun 10am–7pm; $10), which features "the Hong Kong Story", a permanent history about the SAR's life and times, as well as numerous history-related, temporary exhibitions.

Beyond Chatham Road, the area known as **Tsim Sha Tsui East** is built on entirely reclaimed land and comprises exclusive hotels and shopping malls. From the Star Ferry Terminal, an excellent walk follows the seafront promenade east and then north past this area as far as **Hung Hom**, which is the site of the Kowloon–Canton Railway Station (KCR). The **Hong Kong Science Museum** can also be found in this district, at 2 Science Museum Road (Mon–Wed, and Fri 1–9pm, Sat, Sun & public holidays 10am–9pm; $25). Opened in 1998, its best feature is probably the twenty-metre Energy Machine, although there's also a good children's zone.

Yau Ma Tei and Mong Kok

The Kowloon neighbourhoods north of the tourist ghetto of Tsim Sha Tsui offer more of a Chinese flavour, plus some interesting markets. The first district of interest is **Yau Ma Tei**, which begins north of Jordan Road – it's a twenty-minute walk from Tsim Sha Tsui, otherwise take the MTR to Yau Ma Tei.

Temple Street, running north off Jordan Road, a couple of blocks west of Nathan Road, becomes a very touristy but fun **night market** after 7pm every day, although the market actually opens in the early afternoon. As well as shopping for cheap clothing, watches, DVDs and souvenirs, you can get your fortune told, eat some great seafood from street stalls, and sometimes listen in on impromptu performances of Chinese opera. A minute or two to the north of here is the local **Tin Hau Temple**, just off Nathan Road, tucked away between Public Square Street and Market Street, a couple of minutes south of Jordan MTR. Surrounded by urban hubbub, this old little temple, devoted to the sea, sits in a small, concreted park usually teaming with old men playing mahjong under the banyan trees. East of the Tin Hau Temple, just under the Gascoigne Road flyover at the junction of Kansu and Battery streets, the **Jade Market** (daily 9am–6pm) has 450 stalls in two different sections, offering everything from souvenir trinkets to family heirlooms in jade, crystal, quartz and other stones.

Nearby on Tung Choi Street, between Argyle Street and Dundas Street, is the **Ladies Market**, flogging piles of cheap clothes, jewellery, toys and bags between noon and 10.30pm every day. Follow Tung Choi north to Nelson Street, turn east, and the **Mong Kok Computer Centre** is on the corner of Nelson and Fay Yuen Street. This is a specialist market of a different kind, offering incredible, bargain software on CD – all **pirated** and so, strictly speaking, illegal and not what you want to get caught with at customs on your return home. Further up Tung Choi Street, south of Prince Edward Road, the **Goldfish Market** stocks aquaria, corals, exotic fish and even some dubiously exotic breeds of snake, lizard and turtle. Cross over Prince Edward Road and it's a short walk east to the **Flower Market** (daily from 10am), in Flower Market Street, best on Sundays and in the run-up to Chinese New Year, when many people come to buy narcissi, orange trees and plum blossom to decorate their apartments in order to bring good luck. Flower Market Road runs east to the **Bird Garden** (daily 7am–8pm), where songbird stalls are set in a Chinese-style garden, with trees, seats and elegant carved marble panels showing birds in the wild. As well as the hundreds of birds on sale here, along with their intricately designed bamboo cages, there are also live crickets – food for the birds. Many local men bring their own songbirds here for an airing, and the place gives a real glimpse into a traditional area of Chinese life which is spiritually a thousand miles from Tsim Sha Tsui.

Outer Kowloon

Head a few hundred metres north of Mong Kok and you reach **Boundary Street**, which marks the border between Kowloon and the New Territories – though these days this distinction is pretty meaningless. By far the busiest tourist attraction in this area is well to the northeast at the **Wong Tai Sin Temple** (daily 7am–5.30pm; small donation expected), a huge, thriving Taoist, Buddhist and Confucian temple that's packed with more worshippers than any other in Hong Kong. Big, bright and colourful, it's interesting for a glimpse into the practices of modern, popular Chinese religion: vigorous kneeling, incense burning and the noisy rattling of joss sticks in canisters, as well as the presentation of food and drink to the Taoist deities. Large numbers of fortune-tellers, some of whom speak English, have stands to the right of the entrance and charge around $200 for palm-reading, about half that for a face-reading. The temple can be reached directly from the Wong Tai Sin MTR station, using exit B.

Northwest from Mong Kok, in the opposite direction from Wong Tai Sin, are a couple of places worth a visit. The **Lei Cheng Uk Branch Museum** (Mon–Wed, Fri & Sat 10am–1pm & 2–6pm, Sun 1–6pm; free) is constructed over a 2000-year-old Han-dynasty tomb that was unearthed by workmen in 1955. By far the oldest structure discovered in Hong Kong, the tomb offers some rare proof of the ancient presence of the Chinese in the area. What is really interesting, however, is to compare photos of the site from the 1950s (paddy fields and green hills) with the skyscrapers that surround the area today. You can reach the museum direct on bus #6A from Tsim Sha Tsui's Star Ferry Terminal; alternatively, catch the MTR to Chang Shan Wan, take exit A3, walk for five minutes along Tonkin Street and the museum is on your left.

Further afield, Kowloon also boasts the **Chi Lin Nunnery**, five minutes' walk from exit 2 of the Diamond Hill MTR (daily 9am–3.30pm, free; gardens 6.30am–7pm, free) – you could have a look before catching buses from Diamond Hill to Clearwater Bay or Saikung (see p.697 and p.698). This elegant wooden temple was built without nails in Tang-dynasty style and features pavilions, flower gardens and seven halls over a 30,000-square-metre area, with a large traditional **Chinese garden** under construction at the time of writing.

The New Territories

Many people fly in and out of Hong Kong without even realizing that the territory comprises anything more than the city itself. The mistake is unfortunate, for it is in the **New Territories** that some of the most scenic and traditionally Chinese areas of Hong Kong can be found. Comprising 794 square kilometres of land abutting the southern part of China's Guangdong province, the New Territories come complete with country roads, water buffalo, old villages, valleys and mountains – as well as booming New Towns, which now house well over three million people.

It's the country areas that hold most appeal, and there is a whole series of designated **country parks**, including the amazingly unspoilt **Sai Kung Peninsula** to the east, offering excellent walking trails and secluded beaches. For serious extended hikes, the **MacLehose Trail** runs for 100km, right across the peninsula and beyond; contact the **Country and Marine Parks** (Ⓦwww.parks.afcd.gov.hk/newparks/eng/) for current information on trails and conditions. Some of the towns are also interesting in their own right, either as ordinary residential districts, or as gateways to relics from the past such as the **walled villages** near Kam Tin or the **Heritage Museum** in Sha Tin.

Getting around the New Territories is straightforward – frequent buses connect all towns, while the MTR reaches as far as Tsuen Wan and the KCR runs north through Sha Tin, the Chinese University and Tai Po. There are also a number of boats from Central, including the fast hoverferries that connect with Tuen Mun in only thirty minutes. Tuen Mun is the terminus of the LRT rail line that runs north to Yuen Long. You can get a flavour of the New Territories in just one day's independent exploration, or take the HKTB **Land Between tour** ($395, children $345), which runs every day, takes six hours and includes lunch. Covering such a large distance, this is probably one of their best tours in terms of convenience and value. The HKTB can also advise on forthcoming events or festivals.

The west

Tsuen Wan in the west of the New Territories is one of Hong Kong's **New Towns** – a satellite town, built from scratch in the last 25 years to absorb some of the overflow from Hong Kong's burgeoning population. With a million inhabitants, Tsuen Wan has all the amenities of a large, modern city in its own right, and is easily reached from downtown Hong Kong by MTR or by hoverferries from Central. If you are interested in seeing a New Town (and the way most Hong Kong people live), this is the perfect place to start.

One very attractive sight in Tsuen Wan is the **Sam Tung Uk Museum** (daily Wed–Sun 9am–5pm; free), which is essentially a restored 200-year-old walled village of a type typical of this part of southern China. The village was founded in 1786 by a Hakka clan named Chan, who continued to live here until the 1970s. Now the houses have been restored with period furnishings, and there are various exhibitions on aspects of the lives of the Hakka people. To reach the museum, follow signs out of Tsuen Wan MTR station – it's about a ten-minute walk.

A couple of blocks south of the MTR station (in the direction of the shore), on Shiu Wo Street, maxicab #81 runs up to the nearby Lo Wai Village, where the **Yuen Yuen Institute** is located. This is a large temple complex dedicated to the three main religions practised in Hong Kong – Buddhism, Taoism and Confucianism – and its main structure is a copy of the Temple of Heaven in Beijing. Its chief attractions, however, are the beautiful hillside location and an excellent vegetarian restaurant.

Tai Mo Shan and Kam Tin

Moving on from Tsuen Wan, you can catch the KCR West Rail Line or, from an overpass just north of the MTR, bus #51 north to Kam Tin. The bus ride to Kam Tin is spectacular, running past Hong Kong's highest peak, **Tai Mo Shan**, which at 957m is nearly twice the height of Victoria Peak on Hong Kong Island. If you want to climb the mountain, there's a bus stop on a pass below the peak – get off here and follow a signposted path up to the top, where you can link up with the MacLehose Trail.

At the end of the bus route, or reached from the KCR West Rail line's Kam Sheung Road station, **Kam Tin** is famous in Hong Kong as the site of **Kat Hing Wai**, one of Hong Kong's last inhabited **walled settlements**. Dating back to the late seventeenth century when a clan named Tang settled here, the village ($1 donation to enter) still comprises thick, six-metre-high walls and guard towers, although most traces of the moat have gone. Inside the walls, there's a wide lane running down the middle of the village, with tiny alleys leading off it. A few souvenir sellers and old Hakka ladies in traditional hats pester visitors with cameras for more donations, and most of the buildings are modern and topped with TV aerials, but the atmosphere is as different from Hong Kong as you can possibly imagine. To get here, get off bus #51 in Kam Tin, walk a few minutes farther west (the same direction as the bus), and it's on your left, visible from the main road. From the KCR West station, cross the storm water canal, and follow signs for 250m.

North: the KCR route

There is a whole series of possible outings to be made from the stops dotted along the **Kowloon–Canton Railway** as it wends its way north from Kowloon to the border with mainland China. As well as New Towns, you can still find traces of Hakka communities, the women dressed in conspicuous black baggy trousers and heavy fringed hats. If you're on a day-trip, visits to the New Towns of **Sha Tin** and **Sheung Shui** might be all you have time for, though if you're really keen on getting out into some countryside, the excellent walks around **Plover Cove Country Park** will need a day in themselves.

Sha Tin

The first important stop is at the booming New Town of **Sha Tin**, best known to Hong Kongers as the site of the territory's second **racecourse**, which is packed with fanatical gamblers on race days during the season (for details on the HKTB horse-racing tour, see "Happy Valley", p.685). For tourists, however, the main attraction of Sha Tin is the **Heritage Museum** at 1 Man Lam Road (℡2180 8188, ⓦwww.hk.heritage.museum; Mon & Wed–Sat 10am–6pm, Sun & public holidays 10am–7pm; $10; free admission on Wed). About fifteen minutes' walk from the New Town Plaza at Sha Tin KCR station (it's well signposted), the museum is packed with permanent and temporary exhibitions;

one of the best covers life in the New Territories across the ages and features a mock-up of a traditional fishing village.

Shatin's other attraction is the **Ten Thousand Buddhas Monastery** (daily 9am–5pm; free), dating back to the 1960s, which is probably the single most interesting temple in the whole of the New Territories. To reach the temple, exit Shatin KCR and follow signs to Po Fook Ancestral Worship Halls, then take a lane to the right, between the gate and a building, and you'll find yourself on the temple path. This ascends a steep stairway flanked by 500 gold-painted statues of Buddhist saints, until you reach the temple itself, a garish collection of painted concrete statues and cheaply built halls, the main one of which houses some 13,000 miniature statues of Buddha. It's all rather eccentric and unrestrained compared with other temples in Hong Kong, and you can buy a cheap lunch here at the basic vegetarian restaurant.

Tai Po and the Plover Cove Country Park

Tai Po, a few KCR stops north of Sha Tin, is not in itself an exciting place but it does offer opportunities for escaping into some serious countryside. To reach **Plover Cove Country Park**, take bus #75K from outside Tai Po Market KCR station to its terminus at the small village of **Tai Mei Tuk**, right by the Plover Cove Reservoir. The signposted circular walk around the park takes about an hour. Alternatively, you can stroll or ride a rented bike ($35–60 per day from rental shops in Tai Mei Tuk) along the road to **Bride's Pool**, an attractive picnic and camping site beside pools and waterfalls, or follow on foot the five-kilometre **Pat Sin Leng Nature Trail**, a highly scenic, if slightly circuitous, route from Tai Mei Tuk to the pool. The pool area gets very crowded at weekends, but during the week it is quiet. For more details about the many walks in this area, contact the HKTB.

Sheung Shui

Unless you're planning to cross the border into mainland China, **Sheung Shui** is as far as you can get on the KCR – in fact, it lies just 3km south of the border. There are no special tourist sights as such, but of all the towns in the New Territories, this is one of those least affected by modern development, and casual exploration in the Shek Wu Hui area just outside the KCR station will reward you with a great old market full of haggling Hakka women.

The east

The eastern part of the New Territories, around **Clear Water Bay** and the **Sai Kung Peninsula**, is where you'll find the most secluded beaches and walks in Hong Kong, though at weekends they do begin to fill up. The best way to appreciate the seclusion is to come during the week and bring a picnic – you'll need to put aside a whole day to visit either place. The starting point for buses into both areas is Diamond Hill MTR station.

Clear Water Bay

The forty-minute ride on bus #91 from Choi Hung MTR to Clear Water Bay already gives an idea of the delightful combination of green hills and sea that awaits you. Around the terminus at **Tai Au Mun**, overlooking Clear Water Bay, are a couple of excellent, clean **beaches**, and to the south is the start of a good three- to four-hour walk around the bay. First, follow the road south along the cliff top, as far as the Clear Water Bay Golf and Country Club (to use the tennis, swimming and golf facilities of this luxury club, visitors must join HKTB's "Sports and Recreation Tour", which costs $430 plus pay-as-you-play charges). From the car park outside the club entrance, follow signposts on to the wonderfully located **Tin Hau Temple** in **Joss House Bay**. There is thought to have been a temple to the Taoist goddess of the sea here for more than eight hundred years, and, as one of Hong Kong's few Tin Hau temples actually still commanding the sea, it's of immense significance: on the twenty-third day of the third lunar month each year (Tin Hau's birthday) a colossal seaborne celebration takes place on fishing boats in the bay.

Heading back up the slope, you can take another path which starts from the same car park outside the Golf and Country Club down past **Sheung Lau Wan**, a small village on the western shore of the peninsula. The path skirts the village, and continues on, forming a circular route around the headland back to the Clear Water Bay bus terminal.

Sai Kung Peninsula

Some way to the north of Clear Water Bay, the irregularly shaped Sai Kung Peninsula, jagged with headlands, bluffs and tiny offshore islands, is the least developed area in the whole of Hong Kong, and a haven for lovers of the great outdoors. Recommended **tour operators** specialising in the area are NEI (☎2486 2112, ⓦwww.kayak-and-hike.com), Asiatic Marine (ⓦwww .asiaticmarine.com), and hiking specialists Explore Sai Kung (☎2243 1083, ⓔjudy@accomasia.com).

The only sizeable town in the area, **Sai Kung Town**, accessible on bus #92 from Diamond Hill MTR, lies slightly to the south of the peninsula but is nevertheless the jumping-off point for explorations of Sai Kung. While developed in a laid-back way, it's also obviously a fishing town, the promenade packed with seafood restaurants and fishermen offering their wares, plus additional seafood restaurants, arts and crafts shops, cafés and bars on bustling Sai Kung Hoi Pong Square. Small boats run from the quayside to the various islands, the nearest and most popular of which is **Kiu Tsui Chau** (or Sharp Island), boasting a beach and a short hike to its highest point, although **Tai Long Wan** is also clean, quiet and beautiful.

The highlights of Sai Kung, however, are the **country parks** that cover the peninsula with virgin forest and grassland, leading to perfect sandy beaches, where you can even go snorkelling. Although it is possible to see something of these on a day-trip, the best way really to appreciate them is to bring a tent, rent a junk for the day with a group of friends, join an HKTB junk tour ($350 a day) or consider staying at the youth hostel on Sai Kung (see "Accommodation", p.677). Access to the parks is by bus #94 from Sai Kung Town or #96R (Sundays and public holidays only) from Diamond Hill MTR, which pass through **Pak Tam Chung** on their way to Wong Shek pier in the north of the peninsula. Buses depart once an hour during daylight. Don't come to Pak Tam Chung expecting a town – all you'll find is a **visitors' centre** (daily Wed–Mon 9.30am–4.30pm), which supplies hikers with maps (some are free) and vital information about the trails.

Of the many possible hikes, the MacLehose Trail, liberally dotted with campsites, heads east from here, circumventing the **High Island Reservoir** before heading west into the rest of the New Territories. If you want to follow the trail just a part of the way, the **beaches** at Long Ke, south of the reservoir, and Tai Long, to the northeast, are Hong Kong's finest, though to walk out to them and back from Pak Tam Chung takes several hours. The last bus back from Pak Tam Chung is at 7.30pm.

The Outlying Islands

Officially part of the New Territories, Hong Kong's 260-odd **Outlying Islands** offer visitors a chance to escape downtown's claustrophobic urban hubbub. Covering twenty percent of the land area of the territory but containing just two percent of the population, the islands offer a delightful mix of seascape, low-key fishing villages and rural calm, with not much high-density development. The following three islands of **Lamma**, **Cheung Chau** and **Lantau** are conveniently connected to Central by plentiful **ferries**, and you could even make use of local **accommodation** (see p.677) and base yourself here for your stay in Hong Kong – or just hop over for an evening out at one of the many **fish restaurants**.

Lamma

Lamma is the closest island to Hong Kong Island and the third largest in the SAR, lying just to the southwest of Aberdeen, and conspicuous for the giant chimneys protruding from its power station on the western shore. The tiny population of roughly five thousand includes a number of Western expatriates who have come here in search of a more laid-back existence – although their numbers have dwindled post-1997. Despite the power station and the island's quarrying industry, the air is cleaner than in the main urban areas, there are plenty of cheap, interesting restaurants, no cars and you can walk across green hills to sandy beaches.

Ferries to the islands

The following is a selection of the most useful island ferry services. **Lamma ferries** are operated by HKKF (ⓦ www.hkkf.com.hk), those **to Cheung Chau and Lantau** are run by First Ferry (ⓦ www.nwff.com.hk). Schedules differ slightly on Saturdays and Sundays, when prices also rise.

To Cheung Chau
From Outlying Islands Ferry Piers – 24-hour departures (at least two per hour 6.15am–11.45pm; 1hr; fast ferries 30min). There are also six hoverferries daily from the same piers.

To Sok Kwu Wan, Lamma Island
From Outlying Islands Ferry Piers – first boat out 7.20am, last boat back 10.40pm (10 daily; 50min; fast ferries 35 min).

To Yung Shue Wan, Lamma Island
From Outlying Islands Ferry Piers – first boat out 6.30am, last boat back around 11.30am (at least hourly; 40min; fast ferry 25min). From Aberdeen – first boat out 6.30am, last boat back 9pm (hourly; 25min).

To Discovery Bay, Lantau Island
From Outlying Islands Ferry Pier 3 – 24-hour departures (at least every 30min 6.30am–1am; 25min).

To Mui Wo (Silvermine Bay), Lantau Island
From the Outlying Islands Ferry Piers – 24-hr departures (at least hourly 6.10am–11.50pm; 1hr). There are also four hoverferries daily, all via the adjacent small island of Peng Chau.

There are two possible points of **arrival** on Lamma: either by ferry from Central to Yung Shue Wan, or to Sok Kwu Wan either from Central or from Aberdeen. By far the nicest way to appreciate the island is to take a boat to either Yung Shue Wan or Sok Kwu Wan, then walk to the other and catch the boat back from there.

Yung Shue Wan is a pretty little tree-shaded village, where the bulk of the island's residents live, with one or two hotels and a clustering of small grocery stores, bars and eating places catering for both Chinese and Western palates. There's a very relaxed feel to the place in the evening, when people sit out under the banyan trees. To walk to Sok Kwu Wan from here (1hr), follow the easy-to-find cement path that branches away from the shore by the *Light House Bar*, shortly before the Tin Hau Temple. Make your way through the rather grotty apartment buildings on the outskirts of the village and you'll soon find yourself walking amid butterflies, long grass and trees. After about fifteen minutes you'll arrive at **Hung Shing Yeh Beach**, a nice place if you stick to its northern half; stray a few metres to the south, though, and you'll rapidly find your horizon filling up with power station. There are a couple of places to get a drink or rent a room, including one proper hotel with restaurant (the *Concerto Inn*, see p.677), where you can sit on the outdoor terrace and eat relatively inexpensive sandwiches, noodles and rice dishes. One of Lamma's best restaurants, the *Han Lok Yuen*, is just up the hill behind the beach – its speciality is roast pigeon. On from the beach, the path climbs quite sharply up to the **Youth Hostel** and a little summit with a pavilion commanding views over the island. Continue on for another hour or so and you'll reach **Sok Kwu Wan**, which comprises a row of seafood restaurants built out over the water. The food and the atmosphere are good, and the restaurants are often full of large parties of locals enjoying lavish and noisy meals. Some of the larger places also operate **private boat services** for customers. Many people get the ferry over to Sok Kwu Wan in the evening for dinner, but, if you're not taking a restaurant service, make sure you don't miss the last scheduled boat back around 10pm, because there's nowhere to stay here – your only option would be to hire a sampan back to Aberdeen.

Cheung Chau

Another great little island where you can spend a couple of hours strolling around and then have dinner, hourglass-shaped **Cheung Chau** is just south of Lantau, an hour from Hong Kong by ferry and refreshingly vehicle-free. Despite covering just 2.5 square kilometres, Cheung Chau is the most crowded of all the outer islands, with a population of some 23,000; the difference between here and Lamma is that there are very few expats about. Historically, the island is one of the oldest settled parts of Hong Kong, being notorious as an eighteenth-century base for pirates who enjoyed waylaying the ships that ran between Guangzhou and the Portuguese enclave of Macau. Today, it still gives the impression of being an economically independent little unit, with Pak She Praya Road, the narrow strip between its two headlands, jam-packed with tiny shops, markets and seafront seafood restaurants. As well as romantic dinners and late-night ferry rides home, the island offers **walks** around the old fishing ports and views of traditional junk-building. It also has some interesting temples, including 200-year-old **Pak Tai Temple**, a few hundred metres northwest of the ferry pier, along the interesting Pak She Street, lined with old herbalists and shops selling religious trinkets. Fishermen come to the temple to pray for protection, and beside the statue of Pak Tai, the god of the sea, is an ancient iron sword, discovered by fishermen and supposedly symbolizing good luck. For a few days in late April or early May, the temple is the site of the lively **Tai Chiu (Bun) Festival**.

The main beach on the island, the scenic but crowded **Tung Wan Beach**, is due west of the ferry pier. Windsurfing boards are available for rent at the southern end of the beach, from a centre run by the family of Hong Kong's windsurf champion, Lee Lai Shan, who won a gold medal at the 1996 Olympic Games in Atlanta. The centre also serves beer and snacks on a terrace with a nice sea view.

The southern headland of Cheung Chau contains more walking possibilities, although it can be quite a scrabble up and down rocks and through bays. You can follow the path around the island, with marked trails to the nearby **Tin Hau Temple** and then the **Cheung Po Tsai Cave**, named after Cheung Chau's most famous pirate, who used the cave as a hide-out in the early part of the nineteenth century – it's tightly set into the base of some large granite boulders, and you'll need a torch.

Lantau

Lantau Island is actually twice as big as Hong Kong Island and, despite increasing development, there is considerable scope for getting off the beaten track. More than half the island is designated as a **country park** and remains fairly wild, with trails linking monasteries, old fishing villages and secluded beaches. Serious hikers can also tackle the seventy-kilometre **Lantau Trail**, which links up the popular scenic spots on the island in twelve stages and is dotted along its length by campsites and youth hostels – contact the HKTB or Country Parks (ⓦ www.parks.afcd.gov.hk/newparks/eng/) for current information. However, Lantau's north and northeastern shores are becoming relatively built up, as Hong Kong's airport at Chek Lap Kok and its associated transport links are spawning a range of new commercial and residential developments, including the newly opened Disney World.

Even if you intend doing only a short hike or a quick whip round the main sights, try to set aside a full day for Lantau – or plan to pay two or more visits – as the sights are scattered. If you're pressed for time, you could catch the **Lantau Explorer Bus** trip, operated by New World Fast Ferry ($150 per person, including return ferry trip, bus and guide; lasts five hours and covers the main sights).

The main point of arrival for visitors to Lantau Island is **Mui Wo**, otherwise known as **Silvermine Bay**, about one hour from the Outlying Islands Ferry Piers. Some of the Mui Wo boats stop at the small island of Peng Chau en route. There are also a few ferries daily that connect Mui Wo with Cheung Chau. The other point of arrival is **Discovery Bay**, a residential area connected by frequent high-speed ferries (24hr) from Outlying Islands Ferry Pier 3. You can also catch the MTR to **Tung Chung New Town** on the island's north shore, from where you can catch buses to Discovery Bay or Po Lin Monastery – there's also a **cable car** to the latter under construction.

From Mui Wo to Discovery Bay

Mui Wo itself is just a clutch of restaurants grouped about the ferry pier, with a couple of hotels about 1km north around the beach, and most people head straight for the bus stop right outside. However, the easy walk from here to Discovery Bay (2hr) is worth doing on a clear day. From the pier, head northwest towards the attractive, curving, sandy bay you'll see from the ferry as you approach the island. Keep following the bay around to the end of the beach and continue past the end of the village, until you reach a signposted path bearing steeply uphill to the left. This climbs up through open land to a lookout point with superb views over the mountains, then drops downhill, to the **Trappist Monastery**. Most of the buildings are closed to the public, but it's a pleasant, cool spot – albeit mosquito heaven. From here, follow the road down towards the shore, and a little way down on your left you'll see a signpost pointing you left; take this path and it's about thirty minutes, past a series of sandy bays and **squatters' settlements** – possibly the last in all Hong Kong – to **Discovery Bay**. This nightmarish expatriate settlement of condominiums, blonde kids and golf buggies will leave you wondering whether you've stepped through a time warp into some Orwellian version of middle-America. From Discovery Bay you can catch ferries back to Mui Wo and Peng Chau, or direct to the Outlying Islands Ferry Piers in Central; there are also frequent buses to the airport or **Tung Chung**, from where you can catch the MTR back to town.

Western Lantau

From Mui Wo, several spots in western Lantau are reachable **by bus** from the stop outside the ferry pier – though most of these only run every hour or so, so don't be in too much of a hurry.

The road west from Mui Wo passes along the southern shore, which is where Lantau's best beaches are located. **Cheung Sha Upper and Lower Beaches**, with a couple of cafés and a hotel, are the nicest, and buses #1, #2, #4 and #5 all pass by here. Beaches aside, western Lantau's major draw is the **Po Lin Monastery** (daily 10am–6pm; free; take bus #2 from Mui Wo), which is by far the largest temple in the whole territory of Hong Kong. Located high up on the Ngong Ping Plateau, this was only established in 1927, but is very much a living, breathing temple, dominated by the massive bronze **Tian Tan Buddha**, the largest seated bronze outdoor Buddha in the world and weighing in at 200 tonnes. There's also a huge vegetarian **restaurant** here, serving set meals (daily 11.30am–5pm; meal tickets from $60). The last bus back to Mui Wo leaves at 7.30pm; alternatively, you can catch buses #23 or #11 down to Tung Chung and the MTR, or ride there by **cable car** once it is completed.

Right on the far northwestern shore of Lantau is the interesting fishing village of **Tai O**. This remote place, constructed over salt flats and a tiny offshore island, has become a popular tourist spot, particularly at weekends, but still retains much of its old character. There are some interesting local temples, wooden houses built on stilts, and a big trade in dried fish. You can reach it by bus #41 from Mui Wo (last bus back at 1.30am) and also by the relatively infrequent bus #21 from the Po Lin Monastery (last service at 3pm).

Eating, drinking and nightlife

Hong Kong boasts not only a superb native cuisine – **Cantonese** – but also perhaps the widest range of **international restaurants** of any city outside Europe or North America. This is due in part to the cosmopolitan nature of the population, but more importantly, to the incredible seriousness attached to dining by the local Chinese.

As well as the joys of eating some of the best Cantonese food available anywhere, including that great breakfast institution, **dim sum**, the city offers a variety of regional Chinese restaurants, from Beijing and Shanghai to Sichuan.

You can also choose from curry houses, sushi bars, pub-style food, sophisticated Southeast Asian cuisine, hotel lunchtime buffets, pizzerias, vegetarian, South American, Chinese and Western **fast-food** chains, and cheap noodle houses of no obvious affiliation. The choices listed below are a fraction of the total, with an emphasis on the less expensive end of the market. Free weeklies, *BC* and *HK Magazine*, review places of the moment, or you can fork out $120 for **restaurant guides** by *Hong Kong Tatler* (conservative and upmarket) or *BC* (caustic and more adventurous).

Hong Kong pretty much has more **nightlife** than the rest of China put together. In the **pubs** and **bars** you'll sometimes find **live music and dancing**, but the clutch of restaurant-, bar- and pub-crammed streets known as **Lan Kwai Fong** remain the heart of Hong Kong's party scene and drinking-culture nightlife. Despite its image as a cultural desert, **classical concerts** appear increasingly frequently at several venues and there are a number of art, jazz and other **festivals** year round (check the listings magazines detailed on p.670).

Popular English-language and regional films find their way to Hong Kong's **cinemas** soon after release, either shown in their original versions with Chinese subtitles, or dubbed into Cantonese. Some Chinese-language films are also shown with English subtitles. There's also the two-week-long **Hong Kong International Film Festival**, held each March, with good Southeast Asian representation – see ⓦ www.hkiff.org.hk for information. For main screens, see "Listings", p.712.

Breakfast and snacks

All the bigger hotels serve expensive buffet breakfasts with vast quantities of Chinese and European food. For cheaper, traditional Western breakfasts, head for any of the cafés listed, although *dim sum* with tea or *congee* is a more authentic way to start the morning (see "Restaurants" below). Chains include *DeliFrance*, *Oliver's Super Sandwiches*, *Pacific Coffee* (which has Internet access for patrons), *Starbucks*, *MiX* and *Pret A Manger*, all of which offer muffins, breakfast dishes and sandwiches throughout the day and can be found, amongst other places, in most MTR concourses.

First Cup of Coffee 12 Hankow Road, Tsim Sha Tsui. Open 7am–1am for extremely good coffee, plus home-made croissants, torte, biscuits and toasted sandwiches.

Ge Ming Café 48 Staunton St, SoHo. All-day breakfasts in a cosy, red-walled and tiled hang-out. Fish and veggies also served; cheap and friendly.

Ngan Ki Heung Tea Co Ltd 290 Queen's Rd, Central. A source of a vast range of Chinese teas to drink and buy. The owner is only too happy to serve you teas in the traditional manner and talk you through their various properties.

Shadowman opposite the *Hyatt Regency*, Lock Road, Tsim Sha Tsui. Net bar, café, and light meals with a distinctly Indian flavour served in bright surrounds.

Taichong Bakery 32 Lyndhurst Terrace. Take-away Cantonese roast pork buns and custard tarts, so popular that long queues form as each batch is removed from the oven.

TW Café Lyndhurst Terrace, Central. Not only fine coffee, but also large set breakfasts of egg and toast, fried fillet of sole, or chicken steaks for around $25. Window bar for people-watching.

Restaurants

Eating is an enormously large part of life in Hong Kong, and restaurant dining in particular is a sociable, family affair. Chinese restaurants are large, noisy places where dining takes place under bright lights – not as discreet as the candle-lit ambiences so beloved in the West, but much more fun. Menus in all but the cheapest restaurants should be in English as well as Chinese (although you many not get the full menu translated, and prices have also been known to vary between the two versions). It's worth trying **seasonal dishes**: abalone, garoupa and dried seafood in March to May; melon greens, mushrooms and beancurd from June to August; green, giant, soft-shell and hairy crabs between September and November; and casseroles and hotpots from December to February. On the other hand, please avoid **shark's fin**, which is harvested unethically (see p.686).

The most thoroughly Cantonese dining experience is provided at restaurants serving breakfasts of **dim sum** – snack-sized portions of savoury dumplings, rolls and buns served in bamboo baskets or on small plates. In more traditional places, the selection is wheeled around on trolleys; elsewhere you mark a list given to each table – in which case, you might need to find someone to translate it for you. If you only keep picking things up until you are full, the bill will rarely come to $100 per head.

Hong Kong Island's largest concentration of restaurants is spread between **Wan Chai** and **Causeway Bay**. In Central, the streets around **Lan Kwai Fong** (a small lane branching off D'Aguilar Street), are similarly packed with bars and restaurants, as are the areas of **SoHo** and **NoHo** – respectively south-and north of Hollywood Road, around the Mid-Levels escalators. This whole area is extremely popular with yuppies and expatriates, but is notoriously fickle, with places continually opening and withering away. On the south side of the island, **Stanley** and **Aberdeen** are also popular spots for tourists on dining excursions.

In Kowloon, and especially **Tsim Sha Tsui**, the choice of eateries is hardly less than on the island, though prices are often tourist-inflated; the local equivalent of Lan Kwai Fong is **Knutsford Terrace** off Kimberley Road, where a knot of bars and brasseries is springing up. For Indian food, many of the best-value places are secreted away in the recesses of Chungking Mansions (see box, above). Farther out, the **Outlying Islands** are famous for their seafood restaurants.

Restaurant opening hours are from around 11am to 3pm, and 6pm to late, though cheaper Chinese places open earlier and stay open later, winding down about 9pm. Don't worry too much about **tipping**: expensive restaurants add on a ten-percent service charge anyway, while in cheaper places it's customary to just leave the small change. **Prices** are comparable to those in the West: a bowl of noodles or plate of roast pork on rice will cost around $25; while a full dinner without drinks is unlikely to come in under $100 per head, with that figure climbing above $500 in the plushest venues.

Aberdeen

Jumbo Floating Restaurant Shun Wan Pier, Aberdeen Harbour (℡ 2553 9111, @ www.jumbo .com.hk). This behemoth of a floating restaurant is a Hong Kong institution, though expensive and horrendously touristy – few locals eat here. Daily 11am–11pm; Sunday 7am–11pm. Buses #70 or #75 from Admiralty bus terminal to the Aberdeen ferry pier.

Central

2 Sardines 43 Elgin St, SoHo ℡ 2973 6618. Small restaurant that has built itself a big reputation for reliable, reasonably priced French food.

Café Deco Peak Galleria, 118 Peak Rd, The Peak ℡ 2849 5111. Exceptional views and a stylish Art Deco interior that extends to the rest rooms. The menu ranges over pizzas, curries, noodles, grilled meats and oysters, or just cake and coffee – there's often also live jazz. Book if you want window seats.

Chippy 51A Wellington Street, entrance down the steps on Pottinger. Last authentic British fish and chip shop in Hong Kong; tiny sit-down counter serving great fries, though fish is sometimes a bit mushy. A large plate of battered cod and chips costs $85.

La Pampa 32 Staunton Street, SoHo, Central ℡ 2868 6959. Argentinian restaurant which does what it does – barbecued steak, mainly – exceedingly well. You order by weight, it's grilled just how you want it, and served with nominal quantities of vegetables.

Lin Heung Tea House 160–164 Wellington Street, Central ℡ 2544 4556. This famous place relocated here from Guangzhou around 1950, and they've been so busy since, they haven't had time to change the furnishings or allow their ancient staff to retire. Fantastic atmosphere for *dim sum*, if you like crowded, lively venues with inexpensive food.

Luk Yu Tea House 24–26 Stanley St, just west of D'Aguilar St ℡ 2523 5464. A snapshot from the 1930s, with old wooden furniture and ceiling fans, this self-consciously traditional restaurant offers *dim sum* as the mainstay, though the quality is overrated and barely justifies the tourist-inflated prices. Upwards of $100 a head; reservations essential.

M at the Fringe 2 Lower Albert Rd, Central ℡ 2877 4000. Stylish, high-priced restaurant much favoured by the glitterati for its boldly flavoured, internationally influenced, health-conscious meat, fish and veggie dishes.

Man Wah Floor 25, *Mandarin Oriental*, 5 Connaught Rd, Central ℡ 2522 0111. Subtle and accomplished southern Chinese food at connoisseurs' prices, though the view outperforms the menu. You might also want to try the *Clipper Lounge* for afternoon tea.

Muyu Zigan 26 Cochrane Street, Central. Small English sign over doorway reads "Between Wu Yue". Great Shanghai-style snacks, including spicy noodles, stewed Dongpo pork, little dumplings and marinated cucumber slices. Portions are small, the idea being that you order a selection. Inexpensive.

Nha Trang 88–90 Wellington Street, Central ℡ 2581 9992. First-rate Vietnamese food, whose crisp, clean and sharp flavours make a nice break from more muggy Chinese fare. The grilled prawn and pomelo salad, rice-skin rolls and lemongrass beef are excellent, and two can eat very well for $200.

The Peak Lookout 121 Peak Rd ℡ 2849 1000. This place used to be famous for its views, now cruelly robbed by the ugly Peak Tram terminal. But the stone colonial building with raked ceilings retains plenty of atmosphere inside, and the food, with an Asian–Indian slant, is still reasonable value for brunch, or al fresco dining at night. Reckon on around $200 per head for a full meal.

Roof Garden Top floor at The Fringe Club, 2 Lower Albert Road, Central ℡ 2521 7251. Bar and buffet with rooftop tables attached to a gallery, offering $65 vegetarian all-you-can-eat lunches, and evening tapas from $20.

SoHo SoHo The Workstation, 43–45 Lyndhurst Terrace, Central ℡ 2147 2618. Modern British cooking offering traditional ingredients with a twist, served in chic surrounds with dark walls and glass partitions. The menu changes regularly. Weekday lunchtime specials from $145, and set dinners from $190, are good value.

Thai Lemongrass Floor 3, California Tower, 30 D'Aguilar St, Central ℡ 2905 1688. Authentically spicy – and also complex – flavours in this long-time favourite. Does standards like red curry and *tum yam gaeng* very well, along with less usual dishes such as beef and mango. Mid-range prices; recommended.

Tsim Chai Kee Noodle 98 Wellington Street, Central. You'll find this place by the lunchtime queue tailing downhill; what makes it worth a short wait and being jammed into the packed interior are the bowls of wuntun soup – just about the only dish available – at $11 a serving.

Yung Kee 32–40 Wellington St, on the corner with D'Aguilar St. An enormous place with bright lights, scurrying staff and seating for a thousand, this is one of Hong Kong's institutions. Their roast goose and pigeon are superb, and the *dim sum* is also good. Moderately expensive but highly recommended.

Zhong Guo Song 6 Wo On Lane, Central ☎ 2810 4141. Tiny, with absolutely no decor, but the straightforward home-style Cantonese dishes are fresh, excellently cooked and inexpensive.

Shek O

Happy Garden Vietnamese Thai Shek O. On the way from the main bus stop to the seafront. One of several laid-back places with outdoor tables, luridly coloured drinks, and excellent food – try the morning glory with *blechan* beef, or huge Thai fish cakes. Mains around $60.

Stanley and Repulse Bay

Boathouse 86–88 Stanley Main St ☎ 2813 4467. Popular hang-out, with waterfront views from stylish "Mediterranean" building; food concentrates on fresh, unpretentiously cooked seafood. Booking essential.

Curry Pot Floor 6, 90B Stanley Main St. Very friendly little restaurant with ocean views from its sixth-floor windows and delicately judged Indian food. The set lunch is fair value, but you can't go wrong choosing *à la carte* either.

Spices 109 Repulse Bay Road, Repulse Bay ☎ 2812 2711. Generic "Asian" fare, which means that dishes – from Japanese to Sri Lankan and Indonesian – are tasty but not quite the genuine article. Sea views from outdoor tables compensate on a sunny day.

Verandah The Repulse Bay, 101 Repulse Bay Rd ☎ 2812 2722. Pricey, romantic setting for dinner or indolent Sunday brunch. Jazz, candlelight and views across the bay in a mock-colonial retreat.

Tsim Sha Tsui

Aqua Floor 29 and Penthouse, 1 Peking Road, Tsim Sha Tsui ☎ 3427 2288. Dark wooden floors and superlative harbour views through angled glass windows are the setting for consuming an unexpectedly successful blend of Italian and Japanese dishes. The atmosphere is informal, and the prices high. Reservations essential.

Chao Inn Floor 7, 1 Peking Road ☎ 2369 8819. Need to book window tables for harbour views, and the moderately priced food – cuisine from Chaozhou in Guangdong province – is also a cut above average, especially the roast goose.

Felix Floor 28, *Peninsula Hotel* ☎ 2315 3188. This restaurant was designed by Philippe Starck, and the incredible views of Hong Kong Island in themselves warrant a visit. The Eurasian menu, however, is not as good as it should be, at over $500 a head, but you can just come for a Martini.

Itamae Sushi 14 Granville Road. Open 11.30am–midnight for inexpensive, decent sushi served on a conveyer belt and priced according to colour-coded plates; you'll have to queue at weekends.

Light Vegetarian 13 Jordan Road ☎ 2384 2833. Comprehensive Chinese vegetarian menu, including taro fish, "bird's nest" basket filled with fried vegetables, pumpkin soup served in the shell, vegetarian duck, and a big *dim sum* selection. Nothing stodgy or tasteless; dishes from $35.

Macau Restaurant Ground Floor, 119–127 Parkes St, Jordan MTR ☎ 2270 9166. Dirt-cheap, authentic Macanese cooking; packed out at lunchtime with local workers and office staff.

Mrs Chan Basement, 63 Peking Road, Tsim Sha Tsui ☎ 2368 8706. Singapore-Malay home cooking, very good if you order the right things – including any of the seafood or satay dishes. Moderately priced.

Peninsula Hotel Lobby *Peninsula Hotel* ☎ 2366 6251. The set tea, served in the lobby 2–7pm and accompanied by a string quartet, comes to around $165 – a good way to get a glimpse of a more elegant, civilized and relaxed Hong Kong. Dress is smart casual.

Shamrock Seafood 223 Nathan Road ☎ 2735 6722. Big, busy, unpretentious Cantonese seafood venue, with the menu swimming around in tanks at the front of the establishment. Nothing exceptional, just reliably tasty and filling, at moderate prices.

Spring Deer First Floor, 42 Mody Rd ☎ 2723 3673. Long-established place serving dishes from northeastern China, and noted for its Beijing duck (carved at the table); less conventional dishes such as smoked chicken, and the bean curd with minced pork, are also good.

Tao Heung Floor 3, Silvercord Cinema, 30 Canton Road (entrance on Haiphong Road) ☎ 2375 9128. Opens for *dim sum* daily at 7.30am; come early for a window seat facing Kowloon Park. No trolleys, but they have an English menu, and their selection is first-rate and inexpensive. Recommended.

Tutto Bene 7 Knutsford Terrace ☎ 2316 2116. Located on a small lane just north of Kimberly Road, this popular expatriate hang-out is one of several "Mediterranean" restaurants in the vicinity. Good Italian food in a pleasant atmosphere, with tables spread out on the pavement.

Yuan Ji 16 Granville Road. Cantonese fast-food joint serving noodle soups and rice dishes, whose major assets are that the food is tasty, portions are big, and prices are not geared to tourists.

Wan Chai and Causeway Bay

Chee Kee Wonton Noodle Shop Ground Floor, 52 Russell St, Causeway Bay (Times Square). Noodles are a Hong Kong speciality; this small, low-key haunt (whose sign is in Chinese only) serves some of the tastiest wonton noodles in town amidst "traditional" wooden decor.

Chiu Chow Dynasty Floor 2, Emperor Group Centre, 288 Hennessy Road, Wan Chai ☏ 2832 6628. Sour plum goose, deep-fried duck with taro, dumplings, imitation (vegetarian) cold meat platter, and other Chaozhou classics served in antique-style surrounds.

Chuan Bar Bar 20 Luard Road, Wan Chai ☏ 2527 8388. Essentially a Sichuan restaurant with Ming-style decor, serving hot fish slices, chicken with peanut and chilli sauce, and eggplant with hot garlic sauce, though many come just for the well-stocked bar and some spicy nibbles. Good set lunches at $65 a head; otherwise, around $80 per dish.

East Lake Seafood Floor 4, Pearl City 22–36 Patterson Street, Causeway Bay. Packed with cheerful, noisy Cantonese clientele eating *dim sum* from 7am.

Fook Lam Moon 35–45 Johnston Rd, Wan Chai ☏ 2866 0663. One of the best places in the world to eat Cantonese dishes such as roast suckling pig, crispy-skinned chicken, abalone, and bird's-nest soup, with immaculate presentation. Expensive.

Golden Dynasty 30 Cannon Street, Causeway Bay ☏ 2832 2002. Concrete, minimalist designer decor is the backdrop for Cantonese dishes with slight Shanghai and Japanese leanings. Scrambled eggs with oysters, sautéed eel in sake, stewed gourd with bamboo fungus, and prawn balls are all tasty, but avoid the spareribs with coffee. Inexpensive.

Indonesian 1968 28 Leighton Road, Causeway Bay ☏ 2577 9981. The menu isn't particularly large, but offers outstanding (and often very spicy) Indonesian staples, with top marks going to the char-grilled seafood or satays, along with curries and salad-like *gado-gado*.

Moon 1 Hysan Avenue, Causeway Bay ☏ 3110 2002. Quirky, chic decor, with a giant silver hand holding up a rainbow-coloured, fluoro lighting ring; the Asian-influenced "Australian" menu is tasty and includes fresh oysters, steak and lamb with local herbs and spices.

Lulu Shanghai Floor 3, Pearl City, Paterson Street, Causeway Bay ☏ 2882 2972. Smart Shanghai and northern Chinese dishes, including cold sliced duck, sautéed fish with sweetcorn and pinenuts in a "bird's nest", unusual steamed dumplings, and lightly sautéed shrimps. Expect to pay upwards of $200 for two.

Outback Grill 8–12 Fenwick Street, Wan Chai ☏ 3101 0418. No fine dining here, just gargantuan portions of steak and seafood, grilled to perfection and served with fries.

Padang JP Plaza, 22–36 Paterson Street, Causeway Bay ☏ 2881 5075. A bit overpriced, but very authentic-tasting Indonesian grilled fish, mutton soup and noodle dishes – the highlight, however, is their cake and durian-flavoured dessert selection.

Veggiexp 1/F Ming Fung Building, 140 Wanchai Road ☏ 2155 8880. Exclusively vegetarian fare, from imitation duck and seafood, through to medicinal herb soups, sashimi and desserts. Dishes containing egg are indicated on the menu. Mains around $50, starters from $18.

Bars, pubs and clubs

The most concentrated collection of bars is in the **Lan Kwai Fong** area on Hong Kong Island. A stroll along Lan Kwai Fong Lane, and neighbouring streets, will take you past numerous possibilities for late-night carousing, with drinkers spilling out on to the street. Just up the hill from Lan Kwai Fong, the bars of **SoHo** are also becoming popular, whereas the long-established night scene around **Wan Chai** is more thinly scattered. **Tsim Sha Tsui**'s more limited options are aimed at travellers and expats, and focus around Hart Avenue and Prat Avenue, west from Chatham Road South.

Some venues charge an entrance fee on certain nights (generally Fridays and Saturdays), which ranges from around $50 to as much as $200 in the flashest clubs. In the early evening, on the other hand, a lot of places run **happy hours** – some lasting several hours – serving two drinks for the price of one. Opening times often extend well into the small hours. **Live music**, and sometimes even **raves**, can be found if you look hard, though they are unlikely to match what you're used to back home. For details, consult *HK Magazine*. The **gay scene**, while hardly prominent, is at least more active than in other Chinese cities, given that laws on homosexuality are more liberal here than on the mainland.

Hong Kong Island

Blue Door Floor 5, 37 Cochrane St, Central. Sadly, Hong Kong's only jazz club, following the closure of the eponymous club on D'Aguilar Street. Top-quality live music and jazz Saturday night, 10.30pm–12.30am.

C-Club Basement, California Tower, 30–32 D'Aguilar St, Lan Kwai Fong. Sinfully comfortable basement bar boasting an in-house DJ, VIP zones, velvet and fur decoration, heaped-up cushions and a ground-floor bar dishing out shorts and long drinks.

Caledonia Ground Floor, Hutchinson House, 10 Harcourt Rd, Admiralty. British beer, pub grub and the stuffed heads of various hairy beasts nailed to the walls in a cavernous, clubby pub – plus a "Wall of Whisky", the widest selection available in Asia.

Carnegie's 53–55 Lockhart Rd, Wan Chai. Noise level means conversation here is only possible by flash cards, and once it's packed, hordes of punters, keen to revel the night away, fight for dancing space on the bar. Regular live music.

D26 26 D'Aguilar St. Small, low-key bar; a good place for a warm-up drink or if you actually want a conversation with your companions.

Fringe Club 2 Lower Albert Rd, Central Ⓦwww.hkfringeclub.com. Live acts, drinks, exhibitions and generally alternative culture in a rather bohemian hang-out in the red and white Fringe building. One of the cheaper places, with a regular happy hour.

Insomnia 38-44 D'Aguilar St, Lan Kwai Fong. Street-side bar open from 8am–6pm where, for part of the time at least, conversation is possible. Farther in, the house band plays covers at maximum volume to an enthusiastic dance crowd.

Old China Hand Lockhart Road, Wan Chai. Great food and atmosphere in this dark barfly hangout, full of embittered, seedy expats acting the part.

Post '97 9 Lan Kwai Fong, Central. A disco downstairs and a vaguely arty, bohemian atmosphere in the bar upstairs with a strong gay presence on Friday nights. Serves fry-ups, sandwiches and all-day breakfasts.

Staunton's Bar and Café 10–12 Staunton St, SoHo. Right by the escalator, this rather cavernous bar and fusion-food restaurant quickly fills up in the evening; a good place to gather before checking out neighbouring joints.

Stormy Weather 46 D'Aguilar St. Mellow place for a drink, by local standards, filled with nautical paraphernalia and with 1970s mainstream rock on the sound system.

Kowloon

Bahama Mama's 4–5 Knutsford Terrace, just north of Kimberly Rd. A good atmosphere with a vibrant mix of nationalities, and plenty of space for pavement drinking. There's a beach-bar theme and outdoor terrace that prompts party-crowd antics. On club nights there's a great range of mixed music.

Delaney's Basement, Mary Building, 71–77 Peking Rd. Friendly Irish pub with draught beers, including Guinness; features Irish folk music most nights.

Ned Kelly's Last Stand 11A Ashley Rd. Very popular, long-running venue, which features a nightly performance from an excellent ragtime jazz band.

Stag's Head Hart Avenue, Tsim Sha Tsui. Popular pub attracting expats and tourists alike; almost always has beer, spirit and wine promotions during happy hours.

Shopping

Many visitors come to Hong Kong to go **shopping**. What makes it special is the incredible range of goods on offer, including cutting-edge mobile phones, laptops and cameras, many of which might not yet be available at home. A number of items are indeed cheap, or at least can be good value for money – especially **clothes**, **silk**, **jewellery**, **Chinese arts and crafts**, some **computer accessories** and **pirated goods**. However, before shopping for anything upmarket, you'd be well advised to do some research before coming to Hong Kong; **rip-offs** on electronic gear in particular are all too common. As a rule, know the value of anything you're trying to buy, shop around, check that everything works, and don't let the item out of your sight once you've decided to buy it. The farther you are from touristy Tsim Sha Tsui, the better value your shopping becomes.

Shops stay open late and are open daily. In Tsim Sha Tsui, Causeway Bay and Wan Chai, general hours are 10am–10pm; in Central, it's 10am–7pm.

For more detailed shopping listings, consult the HKTB shopping guide for the latest and greatest, or browse Ⓦ www.qtshk.com for shops and stores listed under the HKTB's Quality Tourism Services Scheme, or check their shopping guide (listed under "Things to do" at Ⓦ www.DiscoverHong Kong.com).

Antiques, arts and crafts

Chinese collectors are far too clued up to make it likely that you'll unearth bargain **antiques** in Hong Kong, but the quality is high and ranges from porcelain through to wooden screens and furniture, sculpture and embroidery. Hollywood Road (see p.686) is at the centre of the trade, a fun place to browse even if you don't intend to buy. Note that "antique" doesn't always mean more than 100 years old – ask to be sure. Hong Kong is also a reasonable place to pick up modern **arts and crafts**, with a couple of big chain stores dealing in Chinese products – prices are cheaper on the mainland, however. For **jade**, the Jade Market in Mong Kok (see p.693) is a good place to look, if you take everything the stallholders say with a pinch of salt.

Some more general stores include:

Banyan Tree 214–218 Prince's Building, Chater Rd, Central (also at 257 Ocean Terminal, Canton Rd, Tsim Sha Tsui, and Horizon Plaza, Ap Lei Chau). Antique and reproduction furniture, and handicrafts from around Asia. Pricey for what it is.

Chinese Arts and Crafts China Resources Building, 26 Harbour Rd, Wan Chai; 230 The Mall, Pacific Place, 88 Queensway, Admiralty; Star House, 3 Salisbury Rd, Tsim Sha Tsui; *Nathan Hotel*, 378 Nathan Rd, Kowloon. Each has a huge selection of fabrics, porcelain, cashmere, clothes, jewellery and jade.

Dragon Culture 184 & 231 Hollywood Rd, Central ⓣ 2545 8098, Ⓦ www.dragonculture.com.hk. More upmarket end of things, covering genuine Tang sculptures and Qing furniture and screens.

Dynasty Antiques Ground Floor, 48–50 Hollywood Rd, Central ⓣ 2851 1389, Ⓦ www.dynastyantiques .com. Finely restored classic Chinese and Tibetan antique furniture in a cavernous store.

Eu Yan Sang Ground Floor, 152–156 Queen's Rd, Central ⓣ 2544 3308, Ⓦ www.euyansang.com. One of the most famous medicine shops in town, said to have been around for over ninety years, this is your source of teas, herbs and Chinese medicines, all carefully weighed and measured.

Karin Weber Gallery 32A Staunton St, SoHo ⓣ 2544 5004, Ⓦ www.karinwebergallery.com. Large selection of mid-price items. Also organizes furniture-buying trips to warehouses on the mainland.

L&E 188 Hollywood Rd ⓣ 2546 9886, Ⓦ www .lneco.com. New decorative porcelain and old Chinese furniture. They have a warehouse in Aberdeen full of old furniture and china. Packing and shipping can be arranged.

Palette Collections Gallery Floor 5, 23 D'Aguilar St, Lan Kwai Fong ⓣ 2522 5928, Ⓦ www .palettecollections.com. Authentic paintings from all over China and the US, in addition to porcelain and antique Chinese furniture.

Shoeni Art Gallery 27 Hollywood Road. Agents for modern Chinese artists such as Chen Yu, who combines Chinese images with Renaissance-era scenery.

Sun Chau Book and Antique Co 32 Stanley Street ⓣ 2522 8268, Ⓦ www.sunchau.com.hk. Quirky shop full of old household bits and pieces such as porcelain, photographs, Cultural Revolution posters and even gramophone records from the 1930s – this is one place where bargains do occasionally surface.

Teresa Coleman 79 Wyndham St ⓣ 2526 2450, Ⓦ www.teresacoleman.com. One of Hong Kong's best-known dealers, with an international reputation for Chinese textiles. In addition, they have a good selection of pictures and prints.

Yue Hwa China Products 301–309 Nathan Road, Kowloon; 1 Kowloon Park Drive, Tsim Sha Tsui; and elsewhere. Chinese medicines, clothing, sports wear, tea, books, spirits, and every conceivable tourist knick-knack produced on the mainland.

Clothes

These are good value in Hong Kong, particularly local fashion brand names such as Gordiano, Baleno, and Bossini, which have branches all over the city. Big-name foreign designer clothes are often more expensive than back home because of the cachet attached to foreign upmarket brands, but sales are worth checking out.

Another potentially cheap way to buy clothes (including designer clothes without the labels) is from **factory outlets**. These places can open and close very quickly, so consult the HKTB brochure, *Factory Outlets*, for addresses, or pick up a locally published guide like *The Smart Shopper in Hong Kong* or *The Complete Guide to Hong Kong Factory Bargains*. Be sure to try things on before you buy – marked sizes mean nothing. If you just want to browse, good places to start include **Granville Road** in Tsim Sha Tsui, the **Pedder Building** on Pedder St in Central and, just round the corner, **Wyndham St** and **D'Aguilar St**. Other places to look include:

Blanc De Chine Floor 2, Pedder Building, 12 Pedder St, Central. Elegant designs loosely based on traditional Chinese clothes, mostly in silk or cashmere.

Joyce Boutique 16 Queen's Rd, Central; Shop 226 & 344 Pacific Place, 88 Queensway, Admiralty. Hong Kong's most fashionable boutique offers its own range of clothing, as well as many top overseas designer brands.

Joyce Warehouse in the Hing Wai Centre, Aberdeen. Where Hong Kong's smartest boutique sends last season's (or last month's) stuff that didn't sell, at discounts of up to eighty percent.

Shanghai Tang Ground Floor, Pedder Building, 12 Pedder St, Central. A must-visit store, beautifully done up in 1930s Shanghai style. It specializes in new versions of traditional Chinese styles like the *cheongsam* split-sided dress – often in vibrant colours – and they can also make to order, although items are far from cheap. The sales are regular and good.

Walter Ma Century Square, 1 D'Aguilar St, Central. One of the best-known local designers, who designs for foreign figures as well as local people. He is particularly well known for his formal wear.

Tailor-made clothes

Tailor-made clothes are a traditional speciality of the Hong Kong tourist trade, and wherever you go in Tsim Sha Tsui you'll be accosted by Indian tailors offering this service. But you may find better work elsewhere, in residential areas and locations like hotels or shopping arcades where the tailors rely on regular clients. Western women in particular should look for someone who understands the Western body shape. Prices are relatively low here, but not rock bottom. Have a long chat with your tailor before committing yourself, and make sure you know exactly what's included. Don't ask for something in 24 hours – it either won't fit or will fall apart, or both. Expect at least two or three fittings over several days if you want a good result. You'll need to pay about fifty percent of the price as deposit.

Johnson & Co 44 Hankow Rd, Kowloon. Does a lot of work for military and naval customers. Mostly male clientele.

Linva Tailor 38 Cochrane St, Central. Well-established ladies' tailor, popular with locals who want *cheongsams* for parties. They work a lot with embroidery.

Margaret Court Tailoress Floor 8, Winner Building, 27 D'Aguilar St, Central. She has lots of local Western female clients, and a solid reputation for good work, although it doesn't come cheaply. A shirt costs around $300 plus fabric.

Pacific Custom Tailors Floor 3, 322 Pacific Place, 88 Queensway, Admiralty. Upmarket suits with a price to match, in one of Hong Kong's snazziest shopping malls.

Punjab House Shop J, Ground Floor, Golden Crown Court, 66–70 Nathan Road, Tsim Sha Tsui. Former favourite of the British Forces and Fire Fighters; good-quality male and female formal wear.

Sam's Tailors 94 Nathan Rd, Tsim Sha Tsui, ⓦwww.samstailor.com. Probably the best-known tailor in Hong Kong, Sam is famous as much for his talent for self-publicity as for his clothes.

Electronic goods

Because of **low tax** on these items – and the fact that locals insist on buying only the latest models, meaning that older stock often attracts discounts – electronic goods and associated items (such as computer software) can work out cheaper in Hong Kong than at home. Check first that it is compatible with your country's electrical mains voltage, and insist on an **international warranty** to make sure items are covered once you have left Hong Kong. To avoid rip-offs, patronize local chains such as Fortress. A good place to check the latest prices and special offers is the Technology supplement in the *South China Morning Post*, published every Tuesday. **Pirated computer software** is also extremely cheap, though if it doesn't work, don't expect a refund – nor should you be surprised if it's taken off you at customs on your way home.

298 Computer Zone 298 Hennessy Road, Wan Chai. Ranging from dodgy pirated stuff to top-notch brands.
Golden Shopping Centre 156 Fuk Wah St, Sham Shui Po, Kowloon (Sham Shui Po MTR exit D2).

Lots of cheap computer goods, including pirated software.
Mong Kok Computer Centre at the corner of Nelson St and Fa Yuen St, Mong Kok. One of the best places for pirated CDs.

Malls and department stores

In summer, the air conditioning in Hong Kong's numerous, glossy shopping malls makes as good a reason as any to visit, and most have nice cafés to boot. Some of the best include Times Square (Causeway Bay MTR), Pacific Place (Admiralty MTR), Lee Gardens (Causeway Bay MTR) and Festival Walk (Kowloon Tong MTR). Department store chains include:

CRC Department Store Chiao Shang Building, 92 Queen's Rd, Central; Lok Sing Centre, 31 Yee Wo St, Causeway Bay. At the cheaper end of the spectrum, but a good supply of Chinese specialities like medicines, foods, porcelain and handicrafts.
Lane Crawford 70 Queen's Rd, Central; One Pacific Place, 88 Queensway, Admiralty; Times Square, 1 Matheson St, Causeway Bay. Hong Kong's oldest Western-style department store.
Mitzukoshi Hennessy Centre, 500 Hennessy Rd, Causeway Bay. If you've never been to Japan, try

this place at least. Possibly the smartest of all the Causeway Bay stores.
SOGO East Point Centre, 555 Hennessy Rd, Causeway Bay. Another of the Japanese contingent. Immaculately presented goods over ten floors, including a Japanese supermarket.
Wing On 26 Des Voeux Rd, Central (and other branches). Another long-established store, with branches throughout Hong Kong SAR. Standard, day-to-day goods rather than luxuries.

Jewellery

Hong Kongers – both men and women – love **jewellery**, and the city sports literally thousands of jewellers. Some offer pieces which look remarkably like the more popular designs of the famous international jewellery houses. Prices are low, so if you've always coveted something like that, it's worth having a look. But shop around, as different shops may ask wildly different prices for the same design. Most places will bargain a little. The HKTB's free *Shopping Guide to Jewellery* is helpful. Some places to start include:

Gallery One 31–33 Hollywood Rd, Central. A huge selection of semi-precious stones and jewellery – amber, amethyst, tiger's eye, crystal and much more. They will string any arrangement you want.
Kai-Yin Lo Ltd Floor 3 Pacific Place; Shop 11A, *Peninsula Hotel*. Hong Kong's best-known jewellery designer, who uses old jade, carved

and semi-precious stones. Expensive, but nice to look.
Peter Choi Gems & Jewellery Shop 224A, *Hong Kong Hotel*, 3 Canton Rd, Kowloon. This shop is just inside the main entrance to Ocean Terminal. It has a lot of nice, simple designs, including some classics, and a wide range of prices. Peter Choi will bargain a little.

Listings

Airlines Aeroflot, Rm 2705, Tower 1, Lippo Centre, 89 Queensway, Central ☎2537 2611; Air Canada, Rm 1608–12, Tower 1, New World Tower, 18 Queen's Road, Central ☎2867 8111; Air India, Unit 01–02, 29/F Vicwood Plaza, 199 Des Voeux Road, Central ☎2522 1176; Air New Zealand, Suite 1701, Jardine House, 1 Connaught Place, Central ☎2862 8988; British Airways, Floor 24, Jardine House, 1 Connaught Place, Central ☎2822 9000; Cathay Pacific, 10/F Peninsula Office Tower, 18 Middle Road, Tsim Sha Tsui ☎2747 1888; China Eastern & China Southern, 4/F CNAC Building, 10 Queen's Road, Central ☎2861 0322; Dragonair, Rm 4611, COSCO Tower, 183 Queen's Road, Central ☎3193 3888; JAL, 30/F, Tower 6, The Gateway, Harbour City, 9 Canton Road, Kowloon ☎2523 0081; KLM, Rm 2201–03, World Trade Centre, 280 Gloucester Rd, Causeway Bay ☎2808 2111; Malaysia Airlines, 23/F, Central Tower, 28 Queen's Rd, Central ☎2521 8181; Qantas, 24/F, Jardine House, 1 Connaught Place, Central ☎2822 9000; Singapore Airlines, Floor 17, United Centre, 95 Queensway, Admiralty ☎2520 2233; Thai International, Floor 24, United Centre, 95 Queensway, Admiralty ☎2876 6888; United Airlines, Floor 29, Gloucester Tower, The Landmark, 11 Pedder St, Central ☎2810 4888.

Banks and exchange Banks generally open Mon–Fri 9am–4.30pm, Sat 9am–12.30pm; almost all have ATMs capable of accepting foreign cards – look for the relevant logos displayed nearby. Most banks also handle foreign exchange, though many levy hefty commissions on traveller's cheques; among those who don't are the Hang Seng, Wing Lung Bank and the Wing On. The licensed money-changers, on the other hand, which open all hours including Sundays, may not charge commission but usually give poor rates, especially in Tsim Sha Tsui – shop around and always establish the exact amount you will receive before handing any money over.

Bookshops The Swindon Book Company is the largest centrally located English-language bookstore, at 13–15 Lock Rd, Tsim Sha Tsui; it is particularly good for books on Hong Kong and for glossy art books. Dymock's bookshop at the Star Ferry, Central, has further paperbacks, travel guides and local interest books. Cosmos Books, at 30 Johnston Road, Wan Chai, and 96 Nathan Road, Tsim Sha Tsui, offers a range of both English- and Chinese-language books on all topics. For an eclectic range of secondhand books, travel guides in both English and Chinese, plus occasional presentations by local travel writers and photographers, visit Traveller's Home, 2/F, 55 Hankow Road, Tsim Sha Tsui ☎2380 8380.

Cinemas Major cinemas include UA Pacific Place at 88 Queensway, Central, and also at Times Square, Causeway Bay; Grand Ocean, 3 Canton Road, Tsim Sha Tsui; and MCL Silvercord, 30 Canton Road, Tsim Sha Tsui. For alternative or art films, including Chinese, try the Hong Kong Arts Centre at 2 Harbour Rd, Wan Chai ⓦwww.hkac .org.hk; Broadway Cinematheque, at Prosperous Garden, 3 Public Square St, Yau Ma Tei ☎2388 3188; or the Cine-Art House, Sun Hung Kai Centre, 30 Harbour Rd, Wan Chai ☎2827 4820.

Embassies and consulates Australia, Floor 23, Harbour Centre, 25 Harbour Rd, Wan Chai ☎2827 8881; Canada, Floor 14, 1 Exchange Square, Central ☎2810 4321; China, 42 Kennedy Road, Central ☎2106 6303; India, 16/F, United Centre, 95 Queensway, Admiralty ☎2528 4028; Ireland, 6/F, Chung Nam Building, 1 Lockhart Road, Wan Chai ☎2527 4897; Japan, Floor 46, One Exchange Square, Central ☎2522 1184; Korea, Floor 5, Far East Finance Centre, 16 Harcourt Rd, Central ☎2529 4141; Malaysia, Floor 23, Malaysia Building, 50 Gloucester Rd, Wan Chai ☎2821 0800; New Zealand, 6501 Central Plaza, 18 Harbour Road, Wan Chai ☎2877 4488; Philippines, 14/F, United Centre, 95 Queensway, Admiralty ☎2823 8500; Singapore, 901–2 Tower 1, Admiralty Centre, Admiralty ☎2527 2212; South Africa, 2706 Great Eagle Centre, 23 Harbour Road, Wan Chai ☎2577 3279; Taiwan, Floor 4, East Tower, Lippo Centre, 89 Queensway, Admiralty ☎2528 8316; Thailand, Floor 8, Fairmont House, 8 Cotton Tree Drive, Central ☎2521 6481; UK, 1 Supreme Court Rd, Admiralty ☎2901 3000; US, 26 Garden Road, Central ☎2523 9011; Vietnam, Floor 15, Great Smart Tower, 230 Wan Chai Rd, Wan Chai ☎2591 4517.

Festivals Festivals specific to Hong Kong include the Tin Hau Festival, in late April or May, in honour of the Goddess of Fishermen. Large seaborne festivities take place, most notably at Joss House Bay on Sai Kung Peninsula (see p.698). Another is the Tai Chiu Festival (known in English as the Bun Festival), held on Cheung Chau Island during May. The Tuen Ng (Dragon-boat) Festival takes place in early June, with races in various places around the territory in long, narrow boats. Other Chinese festivals, such as New Year and Mid-Autumn, are celebrated in Hong Kong with as much, if not more, gusto than on the mainland.

Hospitals Government hospitals have 24-hour casualty wards, where treatment is free. These include the Princess Margaret Hospital, Lai King Hill Rd, Lai Chi Kok, Kowloon ☎2990 1111, and the Queen Mary Hospital, Pokfulam Rd, Hong Kong Island ☎ 2855 3838. For an ambulance dial ☎ 999.

Internet access Many cafés such as *MiX* and *Pacific Coffee* provide 15–30 minutes' free use, provided you purchase something from them.

Laundry There are many laundries in Hong Kong where you pay by dry weight of clothes ($10–20 per kilo) and then pick them up an hour or two later; ask at your accommodation for the nearest.

Left luggage There's an office in the departure lounge at the airport (daily 6.30am–1am), and at the Central and Kowloon stations for the Airport Express. You can usually leave luggage at your guesthouse or hotel, but ensure you're happy with the owners and general security before leaving anything valuable. There are also coin-operated lockers in the HK China Ferry Terminal in Tsim Sha Tsui.

Library The main English-language library is in the City Hall High Block, Edinburgh Place, Central (Mon–Fri 10am–9pm, Sat 10am–5pm, Sun 10am–1pm). The British Council, 1 Supreme Court Rd, Admiralty, also has a library which includes a selection of UK newspapers, videos and talking books (Mon–Fri noon–8pm, Sat 10.30am–5.30pm; ☎ 2913 5100).

Lost property For belongings left in taxis, call ☎ 2389 8288; however, they charge a steep fee in advance to search for lost items, and they don't have a very good record of finding anything. See also the police general enquiries number below.

Mail The general post office is at 2 Connaught Place, Central (Mon–Sat 8am–6pm, Sun 9am–2pm; ☎ 2921 2222), just west of the Star Ferry and north of Jardine House. Poste restante mail is delivered here (you can pick it up Mon–Sat 8am–6pm), unless specifically addressed to "Kowloon". The Kowloon main post office is at 10 Middle Rd, Tsim Sha Tsui ☎ 2366 4111. Both have shops that sell boxes, string and tape, to pack any stuff you want to send home.

Martial arts You can see *tai ji* being practised alongside many other styles early in the morning at Kowloon Park and Victoria Park. If you're serious about studying, contact the Hong Kong Martial Arts Association (☎ 2394 4803) for general advice; C.S. Tang for *tai ji* or *bagua* (☎ 9426 9253, ✉ cstang @i-cable.com); Mr Kong for free-form "propeller hands" (☎ 9450 5882); Donald Mak for *wing chun* (☎ 9132 8162); and William Wan for *choi li fut* and Shaolin (☎ 9885 8336, ⊛ www.kungfuwan.com). All speak English.

Police Crime hotline and taxi complaints ☎ 2527 7177. For general police enquiries call ☎ 2860 2000.

Sport For horse racing, see "Happy Valley", p.685; for martial arts see "Listings" above. Every Easter,

Hong Kong is host to an international Rugby Sevens tournament (information from Hong Kong Rugby Football Union ⊛ www.hkrugby.com). The following activities are also available in the territory: sailing (Hong Kong Yachting Association ⊛ www.sailing .org.hk); windsurfing (try the Windsurf Centre on Kwun Yam Wan Beach, Cheung Chau, for rentals and instruction); marathon-running (the Hong Kong marathon takes place in January, ⊛ www .hkmarathon.com). For tennis courts, contact the Hong Kong Tennis Association (⊛ www.tennishk .org), whose website lists clubs, facilities and events. The easiest way to get a round of golf on the crowded local links is probably by taking the HKTB's golfing tour, which provides transport and entry for around $500. Alternatively, check the Hong Kong Golfing Association's website (⊛ www .hkga.com), which lists contact and access details for all of the SAR's driving ranges and clubs.

Swimming pools One of the most conveniently located public pools is in Kowloon Park on Nathan Rd, Tsim Sha Tsui (daily 6.30am–9pm; adults $19, children $8). Another is in Victoria Park, Causeway Bay (daily 6.30am–10pm; adults $19, children $8). All public pools tend to be very crowded, and the water is sometimes not that clean.

Telephones All local calls are free, and you can usually use any phones in hotel lobbies and restaurants for no charge. Payphones require $1 for five minutes. The cheapest way to make IDD calls is by buying a prepaid discount phone card for the country you want to call; there are heaps of stores selling them inside the Pedder Building on Queen's Road in Central, plus many other shops around town. For directory enquiries in English, call ☎ 1081, and for emergency services, call ☎ 999.

Tours The HKTB runs a series of interesting theme tours, such as the "Sports and Recreation Tour" (see "Clear Water Bay", p.697) and the "Come Horse-racing Tour" (see "Happy Valley", p.685). These tours are fun, but are really for those in a hurry and with plenty of money. Consult HKTB's brochures for details. Other operators offering numerous tours – the harbour, shopping trips to Shenzhen, the New Territories, Kowloon, the Mai Po Wetlands, Hong Kong Dolphinwatch – are advertised in brochures available around the Star Ferry ticket windows.

Travel agents Hong Kong is full of budget travel agents, all able to organize international flights as well as train tickets, tours, flights and visas to mainland China. These include Shoestring Travel Ltd, Flat A, Floor 4, Alpha House, 27–33 Nathan Rd ☎ 2723 2306, ☎ 2721 2085; Hong Kong Student Travel Ltd, Hang Lung Centre, Yee Wo St,

Causeway Bay ☎ 2833 9909; and CTS, Floor 4, CTS House, 78–83 Connaught Rd, Central ☎ 2789 5401, ⓦ www.chinatravel1.com, and 27–33 Nathan Road (entrance in Peking Road) ☎ 2315 7188. Cheaper hostels often have useful up-to-date information and contacts for budget travel as well, or look in the classified ads of the *South China Morning Post*.

TV and radio English-language television channels include Pearl and ATV, although many hotels show satellite and cable TV channels. The BBC World Service is available in Hong Kong on 675kHz AM.

Macau

Sixty kilometres west across the Pearl River estuary from Hong Kong lies the former Portuguese enclave of **MACAU**. Occupying a peninsula and a couple of islands of just twenty-six square kilometres in extent, Macau's unique atmosphere has been unmistakeably shaped by a colonial past – predating Hong Kong's by nearly three hundred years – which has left old fortresses, Baroque churches, faded mansions, public squares, unusual food and Portuguese place names in its wake. As a place to play rather than do business, Macau is also decidedly laid-back compared with Hong Kong, but what really defines the territory – and draws in millions of big-spending tourists from Hong Kong and, increasingly, the mainland – are Macau's abundant **casinos**, the only place in China where they have been legalized. The colossal gambling income generated is currently funding a local economic boom, with the ongoing construction of high-rise hotels, flyovers, bridges and large-scale **land reclamation**, all forever changing Macau's appearance.

Considering that costs are a good deal lower here than in Hong Kong, and the ease of travel between Shenzhen, Hong Kong and Macau, it's a great pity not to drop in on the territory if you are in the region. A day-trip from Hong Kong is possible (tens of thousands do it every weekend), though you really need a couple of nights to do the place justice. Another reason to visit is the extremely **low airfares** to Singapore and Bangkok – what might be the first signs of Macau positioning itself as a bargain gateway to the rest of Asia, next to the expense of travelling from Hong Kong.

The Macau **currency** is the pataca (abbreviated to "MOP$" in this book; also written as "M$" and "ptca"), which is worth fractionally less than the HK dollar, and basically equivalent to the Chinese yuan. HK dollars (but not yuan) are freely accepted as currency in Macau, and a lot of visitors from Hong Kong don't bother changing money at all.

Some history

For more than a thousand years, all **trade** between China and the West had been indirectly carried out overland along the Silk Road through Central Asia. But from the fifteenth century onwards, seafaring European nations started making exploratory voyages around the globe, establishing garrisoned ports along the way and so creating new maritime trade routes over which they had direct control.

In 1557 – having already gained toeholds in India (Goa) and the Malay Peninsula (Malacca) – the **Portuguese** persuaded Chinese officials to rent them a strategically well-placed peninsula at the mouth of the Pearl River Delta, known as **Macao** (or "Aomen" in Mandarin). With their important trade links

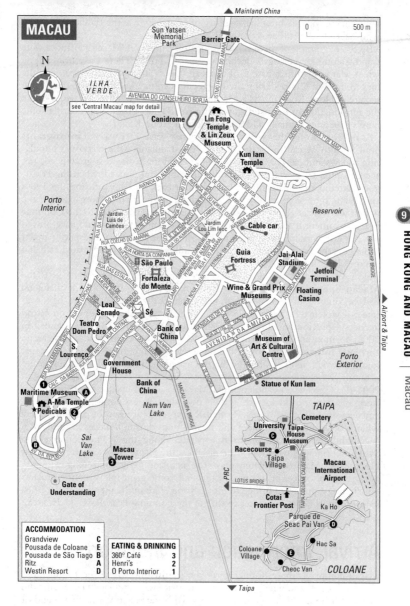

MACAU

▲ *Mainland China*

Sun Yatsen Memorial Park

Barrier Gate

0 — 500 m

N

ILHA VERDE

see 'Central Macau' map for detail

AVENIDA DO CONSELHEIRO BORJA

Canidrome

Lin Fong Temple & Lin Zeux Museum

Kun Iam Temple

Porto Interior

Jardim Luis de Camões

Jardim Lou Lim Ieoc

Cable car

Reservoir

Guia Fortress

Jai-Alai Stadium

São Paulo

Fortaleza do Monte

Wine & Grand Prix Museums

Jetfoil Terminal

Floating Casino

Leal Senado

Sé

Teatro Dom Pedro

Bank of China

S. Lourenço

Museum of Art & Cultural Centre

Porto Exterior

Government House

Bank of China

Statue of Kun Iam

▶ *Airport & Taipa*

Maritime Museum Ⓐ

Nam Van Lake

A-Ma Temple

★**Pedicabs** ❷

❶

TAIPA

University

Taipa House Museum

Cemetery

Ⓒ

Racecourse

Taipa Village

Sai Van Lake

Macau Tower ❸

Ⓑ

Macau International Airport

Gate of Understanding

PRC

LOTUS BRIDGE

Cotai Frontier Post

Ka Ho

Parque de Seac Pai Van Ⓓ

ACCOMMODATION
Grandview	C
Pousada de Coloane	E
Pousada de São Tiago	B
Ritz	A
Westin Resort	D

EATING & DRINKING
360° Café	3
Henri's	2
O Porto Interior	1

Coloane Village

Ⓔ

Hac Sa

Cheoc Van

COLOANE

▼ *Taipa*

with Japan, as well as with India and Malaya, the Portuguese found themselves in the profitable position of being sole agents for merchants across a whole swath of east Asia. Given that the Chinese were forbidden from going abroad to trade themselves, and that other foreigners were not permitted to enter Chinese ports, their trade blossomed and Macau grew immensely wealthy. With the traders came **Christianity**, and among the luxurious homes and churches built during Macau's brief half-century of prosperity was the Basilica of St Paul, whose facade can still be seen today.

By the beginning of the seventeenth century, however, Macau's fortunes were waning alongside Portugal's decline as a marine power. There was a brief respite when Macau became a base for European traders attempting to prize open the locked door of China during the eighteenth century, but following the British seizure of Hong Kong in 1841, Macau's status as a backwater was sealed. Despite the introduction of **licensed gambling** in 1847, as a means of securing some kind of income, virtually all trade was lost to Hong Kong.

As in Hong Kong, the twentieth century saw wave after wave of **immigrants** pouring into Macau to escape strife on the mainland – the territory's population today stands at 470,000 – but, unlike in Hong Kong, this growth was not accompanied by spectacular economic development. Indeed, when the Portuguese attempted unilaterally to hand Macau back to China during the 1960s and 1970s, they were rebuffed: the gambling, prostitution and organized crime which was Macau's lifeblood would only be an embarrassment to the Communist government if they had left it alone, yet cleaning it up would have proved too big a financial drain – after all, half of Macau's GDP and seventy percent of its government revenue comes from gambling, currently estimated at half a billion US dollars annually.

However, by the time China accepted the return of the colony – as the **Macau Special Administrative Region** (MSAR) – in 1999, the mainland had become both richer and more ideologically flexible. A pre-handover spree of violence by Triad gangs was dealt with, then the monopoly on casino licences – previously held by local billionaire **Dr Stanley Ho** – was ended in 2002, opening up this lucrative market. Response has been swift, and there are currently **fourteen casinos** in the territory, including the *Sands*, Macau's first foreign-owned venture. Tourism has increased alongside and the long-torpid economy is heating up to the point – unimaginable just a decade ago – that in 2004 the Chinese government used Macau's pace of change to shame Hong Kong's leaders into kick-starting their own sluggish economy. (An unforeseen embarrassment is that mainland officials have been accused of gambling away billions of yuan of government and public funds during holidays in the SAR.) Meanwhile, Macau's **government** operates along the "One Country, Two Systems" principle, with very little dissent – the reality is that, even more than Hong Kong, Macau desperately needs the mainland for its continuing existence, as it has no resources of its own. To this end, some giant infrastructure projects – including a projected bridge to Hong Kong – are in the pipeline, as the SAR seeks to tie its economy closer to that of the booming Pearl River Delta area.

Arrival, information and transport

Macau comprises three distinct parts: the **peninsula**, where the original, old city was located and where most of the historic sights and facilities remain; the island of **Taipa**, which is linked to it by two bridges; and the former island of

Macau phone numbers have no area codes. From outside the territory, dial the normal international access code + ☎853 (country code) + the number. **To call Hong Kong from Macau** dial ☎01 + the number. To call Macau from mainland China, dial ☎00 + 853 + the number.

Coloane, which – thanks to a further bridge and land reclamation – is virtually contiguous with Taipa. Although Taipa and Coloane are less built-up, the peninsula is entirely developed, right up to the border with China in the north. But it is not large, and it's possible to get around much of it on foot, with public transport available for longer stretches.

Macau's **Jetfoil Terminal** (*Nova Terminal* in Portuguese), for boats to and from Hong Kong, is on the east of the peninsula, from where **Avenida de Amizade** runs down, past many of the casinos and upmarket hotels, to the *Hotel Lisboa*, Macau's most famous casino. From here, the territory's most important road, **Avenida Almeida Ribeiro**, cuts westwards through the historic quarter and budget hotel area, to the Inner Harbour and **Shenzhen ferry port**. City buses #3, #3A and #10A cover this entire route between the two ports.

The international **airport** is on Taipa Island, from where buses #21 or #26 run to Avenida Almeida Ribeiro, or catch #AP1 to the Jetfoil Terminal. If you've walked in **from Zhuhai**, take bus #AP1 to the Jetfoil Terminal, or #2, #3A, #5 or #18 to Avenida Almeida Ribeiro.

Information

The **Macau Government Tourist Office** (MGTO) (Ⓣ315566, Ⓦwww .macautourism.gov.mo) is a helpful organization that provides leaflets on Macau's fortresses, museums, parks, churches and outlying islands as well as a good city **map**. Their free **newspaper**, *Macau Talk*, contains listings of cultural events, plus information on hotels and restaurants.

In Hong Kong, MGTO have an office at the airport's arrivals hall, and in the Macau Ferry Terminal, Room 1303, Shun Tak Centre (Mon–Fri 9am–6pm, Sat 9am–1pm; ☎2857 2287). The Macau main office is at Largo do Senado 9, with counters at the airport, the Jetfoil Terminal, and the Zhuhai border Barrier Gate. All are open daily 9am–6pm; its **tourist information hotline** (☎333000) is staffed 8am–7pm, providing recorded information at other times.

Transport

If you get tired of walking around Macau, **taxis** charge MOP$10 to hire – including surcharges, the one-way fare from downtown to Coloane's Hac Sa beach (the longest trip you can possibly make) costs about MOP$80. **Bus** coverage is comprehensive and costs a flat fare of MOP$2.50 on the peninsula, MOP$3.50 to Taipa, and MOP$4 to Coloane, except that Hac Sa is MOP$5; you need the exact fare as change is not given. Important interchanges include the Jetfoil Terminal; outside the *Hotel Lisboa*; Almeida Ribeiro; Barra (near the A-Ma Temple); and the Barrier Gate (referred to as Porto do Cerco). Useful routes are indicated where necessary in the text.

Finally, **cycling** is a possibility, on the islands at least, though you are not allowed to cycle over the causeway from the mainland to Taipa. For details on rental, see p.726.

Accommodation

Accommodation is a good deal in Macau: the money that would get you a dingy box in Hong Kong here provides a clean room with private shower and a window, while top-end rates are also lower. Note, however, that at weekends, holidays and the Macau Grand Prix (third weekend in November), **prices** can more than double, while winter rates tend to be a little lower overall. It's worth **booking ahead**, too; many mid- and upper-range hotels may offer discounted rates.

The most dense concentration of hotels occurs around the western end of Almeida Ribeiro, spreading out from the Inner Harbour, though one or two places can also be found as far afield as Coloane. Note that addresses are written with the number after the name of the street.

Western Macau

East Asia Hotel Rua da Madeira 1 ☎922433, ℻922430. One of Macau's oldest hotels – a little shabby, but comfortable, with friendly staff and good views from some of the upstairs windows. ❻

Florida Beco do Pa Ralelo 2 ☎923198, ℻923199. Don't be too put off by the density of lobby prostitutes; the rooms are a fair size, clean and reasonably furnished. ❺

Hotel Central Avenida de Almeida Ribeiro 264

Accommodation price codes

All the accommodation in this book has been graded according to price codes, which represent the cheapest double room available. Accommodation in Macau has been given codes from the categories below. Note that accommodation is generally cheaper on weekdays, unless stated otherwise.

❶ Under MOP$75
❷ MOP$75–100
❸ MOP$101–150
❹ MOP$151–200
❺ MOP$201–300
❻ MOP$301–500
❼ MOP$501–700
❽ MOP$701–1000
❾ Over MOP$1000

373888. Hundreds of budget rooms on seven floors in this elderly, gloomy block just around the corner from Largo de Senado. Lower-priced rooms are generally good value, but ask to see a few. **4**

Hotel Sun Sun Praça de Ponte e Horta 14–16 ☏ 939393, ℻ 938822. Good value, though a little drab and with an anonymity reminiscent of mainland hotels. No weekend hike in prices. **7**

Ka Va Calcada de Sao Joao 5 ☏ 323063. On the left as you head uphill from Rua da Se to the Sé church. A good budget choice if you stick to the tidy rear rooms, though those facing the street are windowless and prone to damp. **3**

Ko Wah Rua da Felicidade 71 ☏ 930755. Very pleasant budget hotel in one of Macau's most interesting quarters; furnishings are a little old, and some rooms are windowless, but overall cheerful and welcoming. **4**

Man Va Travessa da Caldeira 30 ☏ 388655, ℻ 342179. New, clean and well-designed rooms with spacious bathrooms, clean carpets and helpful management, though no English spoken. Top value. **5**

Universal Rua Felicidade 73 ☏ 573247. South of Almeida Ribeiro, this is an older, fairly large place, tidy and with spacious rooms. Recommended. **4**

Vong Kong Rua das Lorchas 45 ☏ 574016. This place is one of the last surviving sailors' hostels from the 1950s: dingy, dirty, with ancient furniture and wooden partitions, but it certainly has atmosphere. **1**

Southern and eastern Macau

Hotel Lisboa Avenida de Lisboa 2–4 ☏ 377666, Hong Kong reservations ☏ 800 969130, ⊛ www .hotelisboa.com. This bizarre, cylindrical building, tiled in orange and white, houses Macau's most popular casino, a shopping arcade, an over-the-top exhibition of casino mogul Dr Stanley Ho's jade and porcelain gifts, and numerous restaurants. Double rooms are around MOP$900 on weekdays and up to MOP$1400 at weekends; check the website for current offers. **8**

Hotel Ritz Rua Comendador Kou Ho Neng ☏ 339955, ⊛ www.ritzhotel.com.mo. CTS-run hotel on a steep hillside overlooking the Sai Van Lake; geared to Chinese tour groups, it offers fair value package rates, though the rooms are a bit bland. **9**

Metropole Hotel Avenida Praia Grande 493–501 ☏ 388166, ℻ 330890. A few hundred metres west of the *Hotel Lisboa*; well located and smartly fitted out. **8**

Pousada de São Tiago Avenida da República ☏ 378111, ⊛ www.saotiago.com.mo. Constructed from a seventeenth-century fortress on the southern tip of the peninsula, with walled stairways lined by gushing streams, huge stone archways and 24 rooms with polished wooden furnishings. Popular for local wedding parties. Expect to pay MOP$1650 for a double room. **9**

Taipa

Grandview Hotel Estrada Governador Albano de Oliveria ☏ 837788, ⊛ www.grandview-hotel.com. Glitzy establishment, near the racecourse. Lots of facilities and a shuttle bus to the piers. **8**

Coloane

Pousada de Coloane Praia de Cheoc Van ☏ 828143, ℻ 882251. Great scenery, if somewhat remote, situated by Cheoc Van Beach on the far south shore of the island of Coloane. All rooms have balconies overlooking the beach, there's a swimming pool and an Italian restaurant. If you want a relaxing holiday experience this is the place for it. **7**

Westin Resort Estrada de Hac Sa ☏ 871111, ⊛ www.westin-macau.com. At the far end of Hac Sa's fine beach, this is good for a quiet day or two, midweek, although it fills up with Hong Kong families at the weekend. Three restaurants and excellent sports facilities, including an eighteen-hole golf course, two pools and a Jacuzzi. Doubles from MOP$1625 – although keep your eyes peeled for good weekend special offers. **9**

Macau Peninsula

Macau's older core is centred around **Largo do Senado**, a large cobbled square north off Avenida Almeida Ribeiro and surrounded by unmistakeably European-influenced buildings, with their stucco mouldings, colonnades and shuttered windows. At Largo do Senado's southern side – across Avenida Ribeira – stands the **Leal Senado** (Mon–Sat 1–7pm; free), generally considered the finest Portuguese building in the city. The interior courtyard sports walls decorated with wonderful blue and white Portuguese tiles, while up the staircase from the courtyard is the richly decorated **senate chamber**, still used by the municipal

CENTRAL MACAU

N

Porto
Interior

AVENIDO DO CONSELHEIRO BORJA

Canindrome

Lin Fong
Temple

RUA NORTE DO PATANE

AV. DA CONCORDIA

AV. ENT CASTELO BRANCO

AVENIDO DO ALMIRANTE LACERDA

RUA DO COMANDANTE JOÃO BELO

RUA DA BACIA SUL

AVENIDO DO ALMIRANTE LACERDA

AVENIDA DO CORONEL MESQUITA

AVENIDA DO OUVIDOR ARRIAGA

AVENIDA DE HORTA

RUA DE FERNÃO MENDES PINTO

Jardim
Lou
Lim
Ieoc

Sun
Yatsen
Memorial
House

RUA DA RIBEIRO DO PATANÉ

RUA DA BARCA

ESTRADA DO REPOUSO

Jardim Luis
de Camões

Old Protestant Cemetery

PRAÇA
LUIS DE
CAMÕES

RUA COELHO DO AMARAL

RUA DE TOMAS VEIRA

Cemetério
S. Miguel

ESTRADA DO CEMETERIO

RUA D BELCHIOR CARNEIRO

São
Paulo

Fortaleza do Monte
& Museo de Macau

CALÇADA DO MONTE

RUA DAS ESTALAGENS

Ⓐ

Ⓑ
Ⓒ
Ⓓ

Ⓔ

Ⓕ Market

S. Domingos &
Religious Museum

Police Station

Ⓖ Ⓗ

❷

❸

Ⓘ ❺

❻

Sé

Leal
Senado

S.
Agostinho

São
Lourenço

❼

❿

⓫

Government
Hospital

AVENIDA DO INFANTE D HENRIQUE

❽

❾

Fountain

Bank of
China

Kam Pek
Casino

Nam Van
Lake

HONG KONG AND MACAU ❾

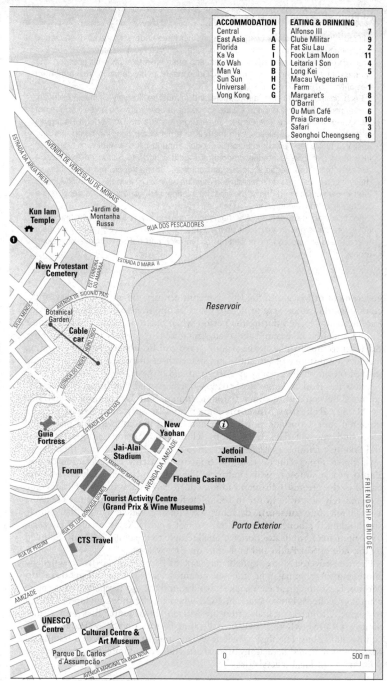

ACCOMMODATION

Central	**F**
East Asia	**A**
Florida	**E**
Ka Va	**I**
Ko Wah	**D**
Man Va	**B**
Sun Sun	**H**
Universal	**C**
Vong Kong	**G**

EATING & DRINKING

Alfonso III	7
Clube Militar	9
Fat Siu Lau	2
Fook Lam Moon	11
Leitaria I Son	4
Long Kei	5
Macau Vegetarian Farm	1
Margaret's	8
O'Barril	6
Ou Mun Café	6
Praia Grande	10
Safari	3
Seonghoi Cheongseng	6

ESTRADA DA AREIA PRETA

AVENIDA DE VENCESLAU DE MORAIS

Kun Iam Temple

Jardim de Montanha Russa

RUA DOS PESCADORES

ESTRADA D MARIA II

New Protestant Cemetery

EST TERRERA DO MARIAA

AVENIDA DE SIDÓNIO PAIS

SILVA MENDES

HENRI TRIGO

Botanical Garden

Cable car

Reservoir

ESTRADA DO ENGENH

ESTRADA DE CACILHAS

Guia Fortress

Jai-Alai Stadium

New Yaohan

AVENIDA DA AMIZADE

Jetfoil Terminal

AV MARGINAL BAPTISTA

Forum

Floating Casino

Tourist Activity Centre (Grand Prix & Wine Museums)

RUA DE LUIS GONZAGA GOMES

Porto Exterior

FRIENDSHIP BRIDGE

CTS Travel

RUA DE PEQUIM

AMIZADE

UNESCO Centre

Cultural Centre & Art Museum

Parque Dr. Carlos d'Assumpção

AVENIDA MARGINAL DA BAÍA NOVA

0		500 m

Airport, Taipa & Coloane ▼

Macau's fourteen **casinos** (with at least another three underway) are all open around the clock and have no clothing restrictions, though you must be at least 18 years of age, are not allowed to bring in cameras, and often have to show your passport and go through a security check at the door. Once inside, many games have a **minimum bet** of MOP$10–100.

Each casino has its own atmosphere and (almost exclusively Chinese) clientele, and a casino crawl will provide a wide scope for people-watching, even if you're not interested in gambling. The *Casino Jai Alai* on Avenida do Dr. Rodrigo Rodrigues is dark and verging on sleazy, with the feel of a hard-core den; the nearby floating casino, the *Macau Palace*, is surprisingly dull, though full of overblown, red good-luck signs and carved golden dragons; the gold-windowed *Sands* on Avenida de Amizade has a Las Vegas slickness and colossal, open interior; and the *Lisboa*, at the junction of Avenida de Amizade and Avenida Infante D. Henrique, is both Macau's best-known casino and one of the most interesting, with pseudo-1930s decor and a loud, noisy, crowded interior.

For information on how to play the various games, ask MGTO for a leaflet; note, however, that signs in tiny print at the entrances to the casinos politely suggest that punters should engage in betting for fun only, and not as a means of making money.

government of Macau. In the late sixteenth century the entire citizenry of the colony would gather here to debate issues of importance, and the senate's title *leal* (loyal) was earned during the period when Spain occupied the Portuguese throne and Macau became the final stronghold of loyalists to the true king. Adjacent to the chamber is the wood-carved **public library**, whose collection includes a repository of fifteenth- and sixteenth-century books, which you can still see on the shelves; you're free to go in and browse.

Across the road at Largo do Senado's northern end, the honey-and-cream-coloured, seventeenth-century Baroque church, **São Domingos**, is adjoined by Macau's **Religious Museum**, containing a treasury of sacred art under a timbered roof. Continue north from here along the cobbled lane and you'll soon find yourself flanked by shops selling reproduction antique furniture, and Macau's famous *patellarias* (cake shops; see p.726). The lane then opens up, a broad stone staircase rising in front to the richly carved facade of **São Paulo**, Macau's most famous landmark. The original church, built in 1602 and hailed as the greatest Christian monument in east Asia, was – the facade aside – completely destroyed by fire in 1835. The former crypt and nave have become a small religious **museum**, detailing the building and design of the church, and holding the bones of the followers of St Francis Xavier (daily Wed–Mon 9am–6pm; free). You'll also notice a small temple to the child god Raja, huddled by the side of São Paulo and built into the city walls.

The tree-covered slope immediately east of São Domingos is crowned by another great colonial relic, the seventeenth-century fortress **Fortaleza do Monte**. For some great views, take a stroll round the old ramparts, whose huge cannons repelled a Dutch attack in 1622, when a lucky shot blew up the Dutch magazine. Up here you'll also find the **Museo de Macau** (Tues–Sun 10am–6pm; MOP$15), whose excellent collection focuses on the SAR's traditions, culture and habits. Highlights include video shows, a mock-up of a traditional Macanese street, and depictions of local arts and crafts, complete with evocative soundtracks of local sellers' cries.

9

HONG KONG AND MACAU | Macau Peninsula

A few hundred metres northwest of São Paulo, Rua de Santo Antonio winds up at a small square, to the north of which is **Jardim Luís de Camões** (6am–10pm), a shady park full of large trees and granite boulders covered in ferns. A grotto in the park was built in honour of the great sixteenth-century Portuguese poet, Luís de Camões, who is thought to have been banished here for part of his life. Immediately east of the square, though, is the real gem, the **Old Protestant Cemetery**, where all the non-Catholic traders, visitors, sailors and adventurers who happened to die in Macau were buried. The gravestones have been restored and are quite legible, recording the last testaments to these mainly British, American and German individuals, who died far from home in the early part of the nineteenth century.

The east

About 1km northeast of the Fortaleza do Monte is another area worth walking around (buses #12 and #22 run up here from the *Hotel Lisboa*, along the Avenida do Conselheiro Ferreira de Almeida). At the junction with Estrada de Adolfo Loureiro, the first site you'll reach, screened off behind a high wall, is the scenic **Jardim Lou Lim Ieoc** (daily dawn–dusk; free), a formal Chinese garden full of bamboos, pavilions, birds in cages and old men playing mahjong. A couple of minutes around the corner from here stands the **Sun Yatsen Memorial House** (Wed–Mon 10am–5pm; free), at the junction of Avenida de Sidonia Pais and the Rua de Silva Mendes. There isn't much to see – basically it's an attractive, rambling old mansion scattered about with mementoes of Sun Yatsen, who spent some time living in Macau in the years before he turned to revolutionary activities.

East of here is **Guia Hill**, Macau's highest and steepest – if you don't want to walk up, catch a **cable car** (MOP$3 one-way, MOP$5 return) from the **Botanical Garden** on Avenida Sidonio Pais. The whole hilltop is one breezy park, planted with trees and shrubs, with outstanding views of the SAR and neighbouring parts of China; the summit is crowned by the seventeenth-century **Guia Fortress**, the dominant feature of which is a whitewashed lighthouse, added in the last century and reputed to be the oldest anywhere on the Chinese coast. The adjacent **Guia chapel** contains original Christian paintings featuring Chinese characters and dragons.

Following the pathway down from the fortress, you'll end up on the south-western side of Guia Hill on Estrada San Fransisco, east of which is a modern grid of lanes and squares where you'll find the **Tourist Activity Centre** (Wed–Mon 10am–6pm) on Rua de Luis Gonzaga Gomes. This houses the dull **Grand Prix Museum** (MOP$10), and more entertaining **Wine Museum** (MOP$15), where you get a free glass of wine to smooth your way around maps, bottles and mannequins, illustrating Portugal's wine industry. Due south of here, a grid of broad streets and plazas built over recent land reclamation is edging into the **Porto Exterior** (Outer Harbour); the *Sands* casino is the most noticeable landmark, concealing the waterfront **Macau Museum of Art** (Tues–Sun 9am–7pm, MOP$15; MOP$8 for children under 11, adults over 60 and students). Its four cavernous levels of gallery space house permanent exhibitions of Chinese calligraphy, China Trade paintings, Shiwan ceramics and historical documents inherited from the Luís de Camões museum, plus a number of temporary exhibitions. West of the building is a twenty-metre-high **bronze statue of Kun Iam**, and clear views of the amazing, ribbon-like and hunchbacked **Taipa Bridge** and **Friendship Bridge**, both crossing to Taipa.

The north

The northern part of the peninsula up to the border with China is largely residential, though it has a couple of points of interest. It's possible to walk the 3km from Almeida Ribeiro to the border, but the streets at this end of town are not particularly atmospheric, so it makes sense to resort to the local buses.

On Avenida do Coronel Mesquita, cutting the peninsula from east to west about 2km north of Almeida Ribeiro, is the enchanting **Kun Iam Temple** (daily 7am–6pm), accessible on bus #12 from the *Hotel Lisboa*. The complex of temples here, dedicated to the Goddess of Mercy, is around 400 years old, but the most interesting fact associated with the place is that here, in 1844, the United States and China signed their first treaty of trade and cooperation – you can still see the granite table they signed it on. Inside the complex, shaded by banyan trees, are a number of small shrines, with the main temple hall approached via a flight of steps. Around the central statue of Kun Iam herself, to the rear, is a crowd of statues representing the eighteen wise men of China, among whom, curiously, is Marco Polo (on the far left), depicted with a curly beard and moustache. The worshippers you'll see here shaking bamboo sticks in cylinders are trying to find out their fortunes.

Bus #17 or a twenty-minute walk from here takes you northwest up Avenida do Almirante Lacerda to the **Canidrome** – Southeast Asia's only greyhound track, with races every Monday, Thursday, Saturday and Sunday from 7.45pm – and Lin Fung Temple, whose main point of interest is its accompanying **Lin Zexu Museum** (Tues–Sun 9am–5pm; MOP$10), China's sole monument to the man who destroyed British opium stocks in Guangzhou and so precipitated the first Opium War (see p.1162). Stay on the bus and you'll wind up at the Portas do Cerco, or **Barrier Gate** (daily 7am–midnight), the nineteenth-century stuccoed archway marking the border with China. These days the old gate itself is redundant – people use the modern customs and immigration complex to one side or choose to cross at the new border gate on the Lotus Bridge. From here, buses #3 or #10 will get you back to Almeida Ribeiro and the *Hotel Lisboa*.

The south

The small but hilly tongue of land south of Almeida Ribeiro is a tight web of lanes, with colonial mansions and their gardens looming up round every corner. The best way to start exploring this area is to walk up the steep Rua Central leading south from Almeida Ribeiro just east of Largo do Senado. After five minutes you can detour off down a small road to your right, which contains the pastel-coloured, early nineteenth-century church of **Santo Agostinho**. Back along Rua Central again will lead you to another attractive church of the same era, the cream and white **São Lourenço**, standing amid palm trees.

Continuing several hundred metres farther south, you'll reach the seafront on the southwestern side of the peninsula, which is known as the **Barra district**. As you face the sea, the celebrated **A-Ma Temple** is immediately to your right. Situated underneath Barra Hill overlooking the Inner Harbour, this temple may be as old as 600 years in parts, and certainly predates the arrival of the Portuguese on the peninsula. Dedicated to the goddess A-Ma, whose identity blurs from Queen of Heaven into Goddess of the Sea (and who seems to be the same as Tin Hau in Hong Kong), the temple is an attractive jumble of altars and little outhouses among the rocks.

On the seafront, immediately across the road from here, stands the twentieth century's votive offering to the sea, the **Maritime Museum** (Wed–Mon

10am–5.30pm; MOP$10, MOP$5 at weekends). This is an excellently presented modern museum, covering old explorers, seafaring techniques, equipment, models and boats. A short walk south along the shore from the museum brings you to the very tip of the peninsula, which is today marked by the *Pousada de São Tiago*, a hotel built into the remains of the seventeenth-century Portuguese fortress, the **Fortaleza de Barra**. Enter the front door and you find yourself walking up a stone tunnel running with water – it's well worth climbing up to the *Pousada's* veranda café for a drink overlooking the sea. The walk from here around the southern headland and back to the north again follows tree-lined Avenida da Republica, the old seafront promenade – today, its views take in **Sai Van Lake** and elegant **Macau Tower** Convention and Entertainment Centre (daily 10am–9pm; various charges, up to MOP$70, depending on level of observation deck). Topping 338m, it boasts a 223-metre observation lounge, plus a decidedly classy revolving restaurant and bar. The continuing walk north up Avenida da Republica to the Praia Grande, near the *Hotel Lisboa*, takes about ten minutes; the shocking pink building on your left shortly before the *Praia Grande* restaurant is the nineteenth-century **Palácio do Governo** (Government House), which is not open to visitors.

The islands

Macau's two islands, **Taipa** and **Coloane**, were originally dots of land supporting a few small fishing villages; now, with the international airport on Taipa, bridges to both the peninsula and mainland, and a large reclamation programme, the islands have become effectively co-joined and things are not as tranquil as before. However, while Taipa is fast acquiring the characteristics of a city suburb, Coloane has a fine beach. Yet both retain quiet pockets of colonial architecture where you can just about imagine yourself in some European village.

From Almeida Ribeiro, buses #11 and #33 go to Taipa Village; buses #21, #21A, #26 and #26A stop outside the *Hyatt Regency* on Taipa before going on to Coloane.

Taipa

Until the eighteenth century, **Taipa** used to be two islands separated by a channel, the silting up of which subsequently caused the two to merge into one. Although Taipa's northern shore is hardly worth a stop, now that it is being subsumed into the general Macau conurbation, tiny **Taipa Village** on the island's south shore, with its old colonial promenade, makes a pleasant place for an extended lunch. The bus drops you off by a modern market, where the hundred-metre-long **Rua do Cunha** (or "food street") leads down to the old covered **market square**, around both of which you'll find several restaurants (see p.727) and snack shops. On the far side of the square, turn right to more restaurants and a **Tin Hau temple**, or left until you see a florid set of tree-lined steps leading up to a ridge above the old colonial promenade, **Avenida da Praia**. Five original, peppermint-green mansions with verandas now form the **Taipa House Museum** (Tues–Sun 10am–6pm; MOP$5 allows entry to all five), which reveals details of early nineteenth-century domestic life for the resident Macanese families: high-ranking civil servants who were highly religious and well-to-do, but not enormously wealthy. Unsurprisingly, the furniture is a Eurasian hybrid, combining features such as statuettes of saints with Chinese dragon motifs on the sofas. House No. 1 can be hired for receptions; No. 2

features an exhibition gallery and archive photographs; No. 3, the House of the Portugal Regions, showcases traditional costumes; No. 4, the House of the Islands, is stuffed with information about Taipa and Coloane but also serves as a temporary exhibition hall; and No. 5 is decorated as a traditional, bourgeois Macanese house.

Coloane

Coloane, at nine square kilometres, is considerably bigger than Taipa and, although it has no outstanding attractions, it is a pleasant place to spend a few hours. After crossing the bridge from Taipa, which also links Macau SAR to mainland China, the buses pass the **Parque de Seac Pai Van** (daily except Mon 9am–7pm; free), a large park with pleasant walks. On top of the hill is a white marble statue of the goddess A-Ma – at 19.99m high, it is the tallest in the world. Once past the park, the buses all stop at the roundabout in pretty **Coloane Village** on the western shore, overlooking mainland China just across the water and home to a fair number of expats – *Lord Stow's Bakery*, at the sea end of the square, offers irresistible **natas**, Portuguese egg tarts. To the north of the village are a few junk-building sheds, while the street leading south from the village roundabout, one block back from the shore, contains a couple of shops selling dried marine products and the unexpected yellow and white **St Francis Xavier Chapel**, where a relic of the saint's arm bone is venerated. A couple of hundred metres beyond this is the **Tam Kung Temple**, housing a metre-long whale bone carved into the shape of a ship.

On the north side of the village roundabout there's a small shop where you can **rent bicycles** for MOP$12 an hour, a good way to travel the 3km farther round to **Hac Sa Beach** (otherwise take bus #21A, #26 or #26A), perhaps dropping in on **Cheoc Van Beach** to the south on the way as well. The beach at Hac Sa, tree-lined and stretching far off round the bay, is without doubt the best in Macau, despite the black colour of its sand, and has cafés, bars, showers and toilets as well as some fine restaurants nearby (see p.728). There's also a sports and swimming pool complex here (Mon–Fri 9am–9pm, Sat & Sun until midnight; MOP$15) although it all gets pretty crowded at weekends. Otherwise, try the **Parque Natural da Barragem de Hac-Sa**; a short hop from Hac-Sa Beach, this features BBQ pits, a kids' playground and maze, boating on a small reservoir and various short trails in the hills (Tues–Fri 2–7pm, Sat, Sun & public holidays 10am–7pm; MOP$10–40 for boat rental).

Eating, drinking and nightlife

Macanese cuisine fuses Chinese with Portuguese elements, further overlaid with tastes from Portugal's Indian and African colonies. Fresh bread, wine and coffee all feature, as well as an array of dishes ranging from *caldo verde* (vegetable soup) to *bacalhau* (dried salted cod). Macau's most interesting Portuguese colonial dish is probably **African chicken**, a concoction of Goan and east African influences, comprising chicken grilled with peppers and spices. The other things worth trying are Portuguese baked **custard tarts** (*natas*), served in many cafés; **almond biscuits**, formed in a wooden mould and baked in a charcoal oven, which can be bought by weight in many *pastellarias* such as **Koi Kei** around São Paulo and Rua da Felicidade; and sheets of pressed **roast meat**, also sold in *pastellarias*. Straightforward **Cantonese restaurants**, often serving *dim sum* for breakfast and lunch, are also plentiful, though you'll find wine on the menus even here; a couple of **regional Chinese** places cater to the increasing number of mainlanders visiting the SAR. Alongside the local dumplings and noodles, Macau's snack bars often offer fresh-milk products such as fruit milkshakes and milk puddings, unusual for China. Thanks to the 24-hour casinos, you'll be able to find something open at any hour of the day or night; **costs** are comparatively low, with bills even in smart venues rarely exceeding MOP$150–250 per head – a bottle of house red will set you back around MOP$90 in a restaurant.

Bars and nightlife include ubiquitous karaoke bars, nightclubs, discos and massage parlours, as most of the drinking is done in restaurants or in the thirty or so bars in the "Macau Lan Kwai Fong", located along the waterfront facing the Outer Harbour, and offering live music and street-side tables.

Cafés

Leitaria I Son Largo do Senado 7. Virtually next door to *Long Kei*, this is an excellent milk bar, offering milk with everything – fruit, chocolate, eggs, ice creams, puddings and breakfasts.

Margaret's Rua Comandante Mata e Oliveira. Surrounded by gloomy apartment blocks, this is an excellent café with first-rate sandwiches and *nata*.

O'Barril Travessa de S. Domingos (off Largo do Senado at *McDonald's*). Difficult to choose between here and adjacent *Ou Mun* (see below) as to which might be best for breakfast or cake and coffee.

Ou Mun Café Fantastic breads, cakes and coffee, and light meals, very popular with Portuguese expats.

Restaurants

Alfonso III Rua Central 11 ☎586272. Genuine and excellent Portuguese food in a Portuguese environment, though the waiters speak English. Centrally located, not far from Largo do Senado.

Clube Militar Avenida de Praia Grande 795 ☎714009. Although this is a private club, the dining room is open to the public. A great way to see inside one of Macau's colonial buildings – which has been beautifully restored – although the food doesn't match the surroundings.

Fat Siu Lau Rua da Felicidade 64 ☎573585. A very popular, traditional old restaurant in an area busy with cafés and restaurants. Pigeon is the speciality.

Fook Lam Mun Avenida Dr Mario Soares 259. Excellent, although expensive, Cantonese seafood.

Henri's Avenida da Republica 4 ☎556251. Order the grilled sardines or African chicken and kick back in the evening with a bottle of red at one of the pavement tables, with views of the Cultural Centre and tower framed by trees. Recommended.

Long Kei Largo do Senado 7B. A 100-year-old, traditional, but inexpensive and excellent Cantonese restaurant, on the left side as you face the square from Almeida Ribeiro. Unsurprisingly, recently granted a tourism award.

Macau Vegetarian Farm opposite the Kun lam temple, Avenida do Coronel Mesquita 11 ☎752824. Warehouse-sized, characterless restaurant offering good-quality Chinese vegetarian cuisine at MOP$30–50 a dish; no English translations but lots of photos of the food on menus.

O Porto Interior Rua da Almirante Sergio 259-B ☎967770. Just by the A-Ma Temple, this features antique Chinese screens, superb old Macanese cuisine such as African chicken, or grilled sardines, plus a splendid wine cellar.

Praia Grande Praca Lobo D'Avila, Rua Praia Grande ☎973022. One of Macau's best restaurants, just outside the city centre. Pleasant staff, excellent food, good value.

Safari Patio do Cotovelo 14 ☎574313. Unpretentious Macanese place offering inexpensive portions of Macanese chicken, cod and scrambled egg, and grilled garoupa; also set meals including soup, main, coffee and/or dessert for MOP$30–55. Not cuisine, but hearty and filling.

Seonghoi Cheongseng across from *Ou Mun Café* on Travessa de S. Domingos. No English sign. Inexpensive – hence perpetually full – Shanghai stir-fry restaurant; good for noodles, steamed buns and seafood dishes.

360° Café Macau Tower ☎9888660. One of Macau's classiest places to dine, serving Indian and Macanese food in a revolving restaurant with unparalleled views. A good way not to bankrupt yourself is to opt for the set buffets at MOP$158 for lunch, and MOP$228 for supper.

Taipa

Galo in the square at Rua da Cunha 45 ☎827423. Cute, blue-shuttered place with low prices and family-run feel; the crab is good.

Mocambique Rua dos Clerigos 28A ☎827471. Probably the most popular restaurant in Taipa Village, serving tasty Portuguese colonial food alongside various dishes from Goa and Africa.

Panda Rua Direita Carlos Eugenio 4–8 ☎827338. On a tiny alley leading east from the southern end of Rua da Cunha in Taipa Village. Reasonably priced Portuguese place, with outdoor tables in good weather.

Pinocchio's Rua do Sol 4 ⊤ 827128. Good Macanese food, including fish cakes, crab, prawns and crispy roast duck. On the square opposite the fire station in Taipa Village.

Portuguesa Rua do Cunha ⊤ 825594. Huge helpings of seafood rice, pork and bean stew, rabbit, roast suckling pig and other Portuguese mainstays from MOP$70.

Tai Lei Lo Kei opposite the Tin Hau temple, Largo Gov Barbosa, Taipa Village. Open-air, cheap noodlery serving Chinese staples, sandwiches, coffee and tea.

Coloane

Caçarola Rua das Gaivotas 8 ⊤ 882226. Welcoming and deservedly popular restaurant with excellent daily specials and very affordable prices. It's off the main village square.

Chan Chi Mei Coloane Village. Right opposite the Chapel of St Francis Xavier. A small, very friendly cheap place with outdoor tables, ideal for lunch or an evening drink; best meals are crab or pork knuckle.

Fernando Hac Sa Beach ⊤ 882531. Not far from the bus stop. An institution amongst expats, its casual, cheerful atmosphere is probably the closest you will get to a Mediterranean bistro without boarding a plane. Add on great Portuguese food and you've got one of the best restaurants in the territory. You might need a taxi to get home, though. Advance booking recommended, and a must at weekends.

Bars and clubs

Crazy Paris Show Mona Lisa Hall, *Hotel Lisboa*, Avenida da Amizade ⊤ 577666. Something of a Macau institution now, this vaguely naughty cabaret-style show of scantily clad dancing girls can be seen nightly at 8pm and 9.30pm (also 11pm Sat; MOP$250).

Embassy Bar *Mandarin Oriental*, Avenida da Amizade, Outer Harbour ⊤ 567888. Rather snazzy indeed, featuring cocktails and live bands, and good value at MOP$30 to enter.

Talkers Rua de Pedro Coutinho 104. A little south of Avenida do Coronel Mesquita, just west of the Kun Iam Temple, this area has several bars and pubs that make up most of Macau's nightlife. *Talkers* tends to get very busy very late.

Listings

Airlines Air Asia ⊛ www.airasia.com; Air Macau ⊤ 396 6888; China Eastern ⊤ 788034; EVA Airways ⊤ 726848; Silk Air ⊤ 323878; Singapore ⊤ 861321; Trans Asia Airways ⊤ 701556; Xiamen Airlines ⊤ 780663.

Banks and exchange Most banks have branches around the junction of Avenida Almeida Ribeiro and Avenida Praia Grande, where you'll also find plenty of attached ATMs. Banks generally open Monday to Friday from 9am until 4 or 4.30pm, but close by lunchtime on Saturdays. There are also licensed moneychangers which exchange traveller's cheques (and which open seven days a week), including a 24-hour one in the basement of the *Hotel Lisboa*, and one near the bottom of the steps leading up to São Paulo.

Bookshops The Portuguese Bookshop, Rua do São Domingos 18–22 (near São Domingos church), has a small English-language section with books on Macau's history, cooking and buildings.

Festivals The normal Chinese holidays are celebrated in Macau, plus some Catholic festivals introduced from Portugal, such as the procession of Our Lady of Fatima from São Domingos church, annually on May 13.

Hospitals There's a 24-hour emergency department at the Centro Hospitalar Conde São Januário, Calçada Visconde São Januário ⊤ 313731; English spoken.

Mail Macau's General Post Office is in Largo do Leal Senado, on the east side (Mon–Fri 9am–6pm, Sat 9am–1pm); poste restante is delivered here. Small red booths all over the territory also dispense stamps from machines.

Police The main police station is at Avenida Dr Rodrigo Rodrigues ⊤ 573333. In an emergency call ⊤ 999.

Telephones Local calls are free from private phones, MOP$1 from payphones. Cardphones work with CTM cards, issued by the Macau State Telecommunication Company, on sale in hotels or at the back of the main post office (open 24hr), where you can also make direct calls.

Travel agencies CITS, Avenida da Praia Grande trav. De Inacio de Carvalho 8–10 ⊤ 715454, ⊕ 715648; CTS Rua de Nagasaki ⊤ 706655, ⊕ 703689. Both can help organize flights, buses, accommodation, and visas for China.

Travel details

Trains

Hong Kong to: Guangzhou (12 daily; 2–3hr); Lo Wu (KCR line, for Shenzhen; frequent; 50min).

Buses

Hong Kong to: Guangzhou (frequent; 3hr); Shenzhen (frequent; 1hr).
Macau to: Guangzhou (several daily; 4hr).

Ferries

Hong Kong to: Macau (frequent; 1hr); Shekou (12 daily; 45min); Zhaoqing (daily; 3hr); Zhuhai (daily; 1hr 10min).
Macau to: Hong Kong (frequent; 1hr); Shenzhen (3 daily; 1hr).

Flights

Hong Kong is a major international gateway for flights both within Asia and beyond. Macau offers international flights to and from Bangkok, Singapore and Taipei.

Hong Kong to: Beijing (many daily; 3hr); Chengdu (2 daily; 2hr 30min); Guangzhou (5 daily; 40min); Guilin (1 daily; 1hr 20min); Haikou (1 daily; 1hr 5min); Hangzhou (4 daily; 2hr); Kunming (2 daily; 2hr); Nanjing (3 daily; 2hr 20min); Ningbo (2 daily; 45min); Shanghai (11 daily; 2hr); Shantou (1 daily; 45min); Tianjin (1 daily; 3hr); Wuhan (1 daily; 2hr); Xiamen (4 daily; 1hr).
Macau to: Bangkok (2 daily; 3hr); Beijing (1 daily; 3hr); Fuzhou (1 daily; 1hr 20min); Hangzhou (3 daily; 1hr 50min); Shanghai (7 daily; 2hr 15min); Shenzhen (2 daily; 30min); Xiamen (2 daily; 1hr); Xi'an (1 daily; 3hr 50min).

CHAPTER 10

Highlights

✳ **Li River** Cruise between Guilin and Yangshuo through a forest of tall, weirdly contorted karst peaks. See p.739

✳ **Dong villages** Communities of wooden houses, bridges and drum towers pepper remote rural highlands along the Guangxi–Guizhou border. See p.751

✳ **Hua Shan** Another boat trip to see a whole cliffside of mysterious rock art flanking Guangxi's Zuo River. See p.766

✳ **Sisters' Meal Festival** Exuberant showpiece of Miao culture, featuring three days of dancing, bull fighting and dragon-boat racing. See p.784

✳ **Zhijin Caves** The largest, most spectacular of China's subterranean limestone caverns, full of creatively named rock formations. See p.791

✳ **Caohai** Spend a day punting around this beautiful lake, a haven for ducks and rare black-necked cranes. See p.793

△ Threshers with a Dong-minority wind-and-rain bridge in the background

Guangxi and Guizhou

I f there's one thing that defines the subtropical southwestern provinces of **Guangxi** and **Guizhou**, it's **limestone**: most of the rivers here are coloured a vivid blue-green by it; everywhere you look are weathered **karst** hills, often worn into poetic collections of tall, sharp peaks; and the ground beneath is riddled with extensive **caverns**, some flooded, others large enough to fit a cathedral inside. Though something of a tourist phenomenon today, historically this topography has proved an immense barrier to communications and, being porous, created some of China's least arable land, with agriculture often confined to the small alluvial plains in between peaks. So poor that it wasn't worth the trouble of invading, for a long while the region was pretty well ignored by Han China, and evolved into a stronghold for **ethnic groups**. But a period of social stability during the early Qing dynasty caused a population explosion in eastern China and an expansion westwards by the Han. Some of the ethnic minorities kept their nominal identity but more or less integrated with the Chinese, while others resisted assimilation by occupying isolated highlands; either way, the new settlers put pressure on available resources and only worsened the region's poverty, creating a hotbed of resentment against both the Han and the government. This finally exploded in central Guangxi's **Taiping Uprising** of 1850 (see p.436), marking the start of a century of devastating civil conflict. Even today, while the minority groups have been enfranchized by the formation of several **autonomous prefectures**, industry and infrastructure remain underdeveloped and few of the cities – including **Nanning** and **Guiyang**, the provincial capitals – have much to offer except transport to more interesting locations.

Despite its bleak history, the region offers a huge range of diversions. The landscape is epitomized by the tall karst towers surrounding the city of **Guilin** in northeastern Guangxi, familiar to Chinese and Westerners alike through centuries of eulogistic poetry, paintings and photographs. Equally impressive are cave systems at **Longgong** and **Zhijin** in western Guizhou, while northern Guizhou has **Chishui**, a wild region of bamboo forests and waterfalls. Most rewarding, perhaps, is the chance of close contact with ethnic groups, particularly the **Miao**, **Dong** and **Zhuang**, whose wooden villages, exuberant festivals, and traces of a prehistoric past are all worth indulging. It's also one of the few places in the country where you can be fairly sure of encountering rare wildlife: notably monkeys at **Chongzuo** in southwestern Guangxi; and cranes at **Caohai** in Guizhou's far west.

While **travel** out to all this can be time-consuming, a reasonable quantity of buses and trains means that remoteness is not the barrier it once was. **Language** is another matter, as many rural people speak only their own dialects or local versions of Mandarin, which can be virtually incomprehensible. With geography

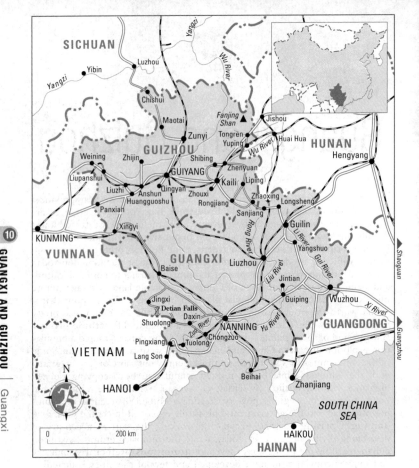

encompassing the South China Sea and some respectable mountains, **weather** is fairly localized, though you should expect warm, wet summers and surprisingly cold winters, especially up in the hills. April and May, and September and October are probably the driest, most pleasant months to visit the region.

Guangxi

Guangxi unfolds south from the cool highlands it shares with Guizhou to a tropical coast and border abutting Vietnam. Up in the northeast, the pick of the province's postcard-perfect peak-and-paddy-field landscape is concentrated along the **Li River**, down which you can cruise between the city of **Guilin** and the travellers' haven of **Yangshuo**. Long famous and easily accessible, this has become a massive tourist draw, but just a few hours north the remoter hills around **Sanjiang** are home to the **Dong** ethnic group, whose architecture and way of life make for a fascinating trip up into Guizhou province, hopping between villages on public buses.

Diagonally across Guangxi, the tropically languid provincial capital **Nanning** has little of interest in itself but provides a base for exploring Guangxi's south-western corner along the open **border with Vietnam**. Actually, since 1958 the province has not been a province at all but the Guangxi Zhuang Autonomous Region, heartland of China's thirteen million-strong Zhuang nationality. They constitute about a third of the regional population and, although largely assimilated into Chinese life today, there's enough archeological evidence to link them with a Bronze-Age culture spread throughout Southeast Asia, including prehistoric **rock friezes** west of Nanning. Nearby are two other major draws: the **Detian Waterfall**, which actually pours over the Vietnamese border; and **Chongzuo Ecology Park**, where it's possible to see the critically endangered white-headed langur, a cliff-dwelling monkey.

Nanning is also something of a springboard for transport heading northwest into Yunnan via the historic town of **Baise**, and south to the coastal port of **Behai**, gateway to Hainan island. **Guiping** is the one place of interest east of Nanning, being central to the origins of the Taiping Uprising, nineteenth-century China's most widespread rebellion against the rotting Qing empire.

Though enjoying fiercely hot, humid summers, Guangxi's **weather** can be deceptive – it actually snows in Guilin about once every ten years. Another thing of note is that the **Zhuang language**, instead of using *pinyin*, follows its own method of rendering Chinese characters into Roman text. This accounts for the novel spellings you'll encounter on street signs and elsewhere – "Minzu Dadao", for example, becomes "Minzcuzdadau".

Guilin

GUILIN has been famous since Tang times for its scenic location amongst a host of gnarled, two-hundred-metre-high rocky hills on the **Li River**, down which you can **cruise** to the village of Yangshuo (for more on which, see p.742). The city rose from a rural backwater in 1372 when emperor Hongwu decided to appoint **Zhou Shouqian**, a minor relative, to govern from here as the **Jinjiang Prince**, and this quasi-royal line ruled for fourteen generations, dying out in the 1650s when the entire city was razed in conflicts between Ming and Manchu forces. Guilin was later resurrected as de facto provincial capital until losing the position to Nanning in 1914; Sun Yatsen planned the Nationalists' "Northern Expedition" here in 1925; the Long Marchers were soundly trounced by Guomindang factions outside the city nine years later; and the war with Japan saw more than a million refugees hiding out here, until the city was occupied by the invaders – events harrowingly recounted in Amy Tan's *Joy Luck Club*. Wartime bombing spared the city's natural monuments but turned the centre into a shabby provincial shell, neatened up since the 1990s by plenty of well-designed landscaping, shady avenues and rocky parkland. Despite being somewhat prone to tourist-driven inflation and hard-sell irritations, the city is a great place to explore while organizing a cruise downstream.

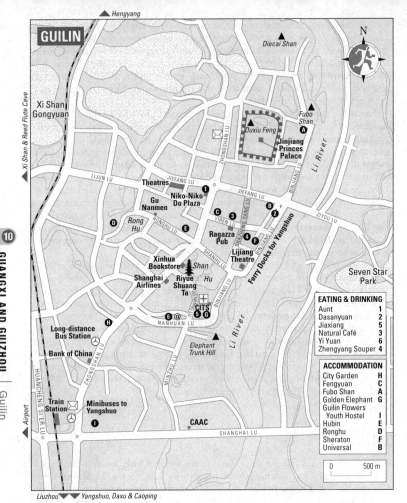

GUILIN

▲ Hengyang

Diecai Shan

N

Xi Shan & Reed Flute Cave ▲

Xi Shan
Gongyuan

Fubo
Shan ▲

▲ Duxiu Feng

Jinjiang
Princes
Palace

Li River

LIJUN LU

Theatres

JIEFANG LU

JIEFANG LU

Gu
Nanmen

Niko-Niko
Do Plaza 1

ZHONGSHAN LU

BINJIANG LU

ZIYOU LU

Rong
Hu

D

RONGHU LU

E

C 3

YIREN LU

SHICHENG YANG LU

B

2

Ferry Docks for Yangshuo

Ragazza
Pub

4 F

SHANHU LU

Lijiang
Theatre

Xinhua
Bookstore

Shan

Seven Star
Park

Shanghai
Airlines

Riyue
Shuang
Ta

Hu

BINJIANG LU

CITS
6 G

Long-distance
Bus Station

H

6 @

WENMING LU

NANHUAN LU

Li River

Bank of China

Elephant
Trunk Hill

MINZHU LU

EATING & DRINKING
Aunt   1
Dasanyuan   2
Jiaxiang   5
Natural Café   3
Yi Yuan   6
Zhengyang Souper 4

ACCOMMODATION
City Garden   H
Fengyuan   C
Fubo Shan   A
Golden Elephant   G
Guilin Flowers
  Youth Hostel   I
Hubin   E
Ronghu   D
Sheraton   F
Universal   B

Train
Station

Minibuses to
Yangshuo

I

CAAC

HUANCHENG SI'ER LU

ZHONGSHAN LU

SHANGHAI LU

Airport ▲

0   500 m

Liuzhou ▼ ▼ Yangshuo, Daxu & Caoping

Arrival and accommodation

Central Guilin lies on the western bank of the Li, with a handful of small,
isolated peaks hemming in the perimeter and riverbanks. Parallel with the river
and about 500m west, Zhongshan Lu is the main street, running north for 4km
or so from the train station past a knot of accommodation and services, the
long-distance bus station and on through the centre. The main roads which
cross it are Nanhuan Lu, Ronghu Lu and adjoining Shanhu Lu, and Jiefang
Lu, all of which stretch for at least 1km west across town from Binjiang Lu, the
riverside promenade.

  Liangjiang International Airport is 20km west of the city, connected to
the CAAC office on Shanghai Lu by airport bus (¥15) and taxi (about ¥75).
The **train station** is centrally set at the back of a large square off Zhongshan
Lu, within striking distance of accommodation and places of interest, with the

Guilin

Guilin	桂林	guìlín
Duxiu Feng	独秀峰	dúxiù fēng
Elephant Trunk Hill	象鼻山	xiàngbí shān
Fubo Shan	伏波山	fúbō shān
Gu Nanmen	古南门	gǔnán mén
Jingjiang Princes' Palace	靖江王府	jìngjiāng wángfǔ
Li River	漓江	líjiāng
Qixing Dong	七星洞	qīxīng dòng
Reed Flute Cave	芦笛岩	lúdí yán
Riyue Shuang Ta	日月双塔	rìyuè shuāngtǎ
Rong Hu	榕湖	róng hú
Seven Star Park	七星公园	qīxīng gōngyuán
Shan Hu	杉湖	shān hú
Xi Shan Park	西山公园	xīshān gōngyuán
Yueya Shan	月牙山	yuèyá shān
Accommodation and eating		
Aunt	好大妈	hǎodàmā
City Garden	城市花园酒店	chéngshì huāyuán jiǔdiàn
Dasanyuan	大三元酒楼	dàsānyuán
Fengyuan	丰源酒店	fēngyuán jiǔdiàn
Fubo Shan	伏波山大酒店	fóbōshān dàjiǔdiàn
Golden Elephant	金象大酒店	jīnxiàng dàjiǔdiàn
Guilin Flowers Youth Hostel	花满楼	huāmǎnlóu
Hubin	湖宾饭店	húbīn fàndiàn
Jiaxiang	家乡菜馆	jiāxiāng càiguǎn
Natural Café	闻莺阁	wényíng gé
Ronghu	榕湖饭店	rónghú fàndiàn
Sheraton	大宇大饭店	dàyǔ dàfàndiàn
Universal	环球大酒店	huánqiú dàjiǔdiàn
Yi Yuan	怡园饭店	yíyuán fàndiàn
Zhengyang Souper Restaurant	正阳汤城	zhèngyáng tāngchéng

long-distance bus station just a couple of hundred metres further north. **Minibuses from Yangshuo** tend to drop passengers west of the long-distance bus station on Huancheng Si'er Lu, though they might also wind up at the depot in front of the train station. Most of Guilin's sights are close enough to walk to, others can be reached easily on public buses, or by taxi (which cost ¥7 to hire).

Accommodation

Guilin's hotels are mostly mid-range and upmarket, but though Chinese hostels won't take foreigners there is a genuine Youth Hostel if you're after a budget bed. The nicest location in town is along the river, with lakeside locations as the next best thing and standard urban hotels there if you need them. Expect a 10–15 percent service charge at upmarket accommodation, though all hotels are desperate for winter custom and often discount rooms by fifty percent or more.

City Garden 75 Zhongshan Nan Lu ☎0773/2861888, ℻3861000. New mid-range place with central location and spacious rooms; a little expensive given the lack of scenic views but not a bad place. ❻

Fengyuan 26 Zhongshan Zhonglu, entrance on Yiren Lu ☎0773/2827262, ℻2827259. This is just a clean, inner-city place with no outstanding features other than being reasonable value for money. ❺

Minibuses to Yangshuo (¥10) leave the train station forecourt (or from the kerb-side across Zhongshan Lu) through the day whenever full. **Buses** from the long-distance station to elsewhere in the province and beyond are easy to book a day in advance: options include heading north to Longsheng, Sanjiang and Guizhou province (pp.747–754); east to the holy peaks at Heng Shan in Hunan; or southeast to Guangzhou – bear in mind you're likely to get a much better seat here than picking the service up at Yangshuo. **Flying** is similarly straightforward, with Guilin linked to cities right across the mainland, as well as to Hong Kong, Thailand, Korea and Japan.

Guilin also has good **rail** links to the rest of China, including direct services east to Shanghai and Beijing, southeast to Guangzhou, west to Chongqing and Kunming, and southeast to Nanning (on a double-decker express which takes just five hours). If you book a few days in advance you should get what you want; the **ticket office** opens daily 7.30–11.30am, 12.30–2.30pm, 3–7pm, and 7.30–9.30pm, and queues are not too bad. Agents in both Guilin and Yangshuo can also sort things out, though they still need three days' notice and charge steep mark-ups for each ticket.

Details for arranging **Li River cruises to Yangshuo** are covered on p.740.

Fubo Shan 121 Binjiang Lu ☎0773/2829988, ℻2822328. An older but well-maintained hotel with endless wings and corridors right next to Fubo Shan and the river, just a little bit over-priced. **❽**

Golden Elephant 36 Binjiang Lu ☎0773/2808888, ℻2809999. Consistently smart and cosy three-star Korean-run affair overlooking Elephant Trunk Hill and the river; most of the rooms have views and, pricewise, this is an excellent deal if you're after something verging on upmarket. **❽**

Guilin Flowers Youth Hostel 6 Shangzhi Lane, Block 2, Zhongshan Lu ☎0773/3839625, ℮yhchina@yahoo.com.cn. A great place, hidden away behind the Plaza Hotel opposite the train station: facing the hotel, follow the building around to the left and you'll see the blue Hostelling International sign; walk through a dreary alley to the back of the hotel, take the equally uninspiring stairs up a flight, and you'll find this delightfully warm and friendly option, very clean with a bar, café, Internet, dorms and doubles. Slight discount for IYHA members. Dorms ¥30, doubles **❸**

Hubin Fandian Ronghu Lu ☎0773/2822837, ℻2811067. Quiet, low-key and slightly run-down option next to the lake (though rooms don't have views); the next best thing pricewise if the youth hostel is full, though nowhere near as comfortable. **❹**

Ronghu 17 Ronghu Bei Lu ☎0773/2823811, ℻2825390. A business-meeting favourite set in huge grounds in a quiet part of town, modern but with a faintly tired atmosphere. **❽**

Sheraton 9 Binjiang Nan Lu ☎0773/2825588, ⓦwww.sheraton.com/guilin. Definitely one of the nicest hotels in town, with the best rooms overlooking the river and across to Seven Star Park, though you pay for the privilege. **❾**

Universal 1 Jiefang Dong Lu ☎0773/2828228, ℻2823868. Fairly swish, three-star Macau-run operation in a pleasant location, with pricier rooms offering river views. **❻**

The City

Look at a map and Guilin's medieval city layout is still clearly visible, defined by the river to the east, Gui Hu to the west, Nanhuan Lu to the south, and protected from the north by Diecai Shan. Separated by Zhongshan Lu, **Rong Hu** and **Shan Hu** are two tree-lined lakes which originally formed a moat surrounding the inner city walls – the last remnant of which is **Gu Nanmen**, the tunnel-like Old South Gate on Ronghu Lu – and are now crossed by attractively hunchbacked stone bridges. Shan Hu is also overlooked by forty-metre-tall twin pagodas named **Riyue Shuang Ta**, one of which is painted gold, the other muted red and green – you can climb to the top of both for ¥30.

Guilin's riverside promenade is Binjiang Lu, shaded from the summer sun by the fragrant **osmanthus trees** after which the city is named Guilin means "osmanthus forest"). Down at the southern end, these also tend to block views of **Elephant Trunk Hill** (7am–7pm; ¥25; the entrance is off Minzhu Lu), said to be the body of a sick imperial baggage elephant who was cared for by locals and turned to stone rather than rejoin the emperor's army. For once the name is not poetically obscure; the jutting cliff with an arched hole at the base really does resemble an elephant taking a drink from the river. There's an easy walk to a podgy pagoda on top, and, at river level, you can have your photo taken holding a parasol while you sit next to a cormorant on a brightly coloured bamboo raft. Two kilometres away at the opposite end of Binjiang Lu, **Fubo Shan** (7am–7pm; ¥15) is a complementary peak, whose grottoes are carved with worn Tang- and Song-dynasty Buddha images. At the base is the "Sword-testing Stone", a stalactite hanging within ten centimetres of the ground which indeed appears to have been hacked through. Steps to Fubo's summit (200m) provide smog-free views of Guilin's low rooftops.

West of Fubo Shan – the entrance is north off Jiefang Lu – **Jinjiang Princes' Palace** (8.30am–5pm; ¥50 includes English-speaking tour guide) is where Guilin's Ming rulers lived between 1372 and 1650. Resembling a miniature Forbidden City in plan (and actually predating Beijing's by 34 years), it is still surrounded by five-metre-high stone walls, though the original buildings were destroyed at the end of the Ming dynasty, and those here today date from the late Qing and house Guangxi's Teachers' Training College. Some older fragments remain, notably a **stone slab** by the entrance embellished with clouds but no dragons, indicating the residence of a prince, not an emperor. The **museum** has abundant historical curios, modern portraits of the fourteen Jinjiang Princes, and remains from one of their **tombs** (most of which lie unexcavated and overgrown about 6km northeast of the city). Out the back – and protecting the buildings from the "unlucky" north direction – is **Duxiu Feng**, another small, sharp pinnacle with 306 steep steps to the summit. Legend has it that the **cave** at hill's base was opened up by the tenth prince, thereby breaking Duxiu Feng's luck and seeding the dynasty's downfall. Get someone to point out the bland, eight-hundred-year-old **inscription** carved on Duxiu's side by the governor Wan Zhengong, which is apparently responsible for the city's fame: *Guilin Shanshui Jia Tianxia* – "Guilin's Scenery is the Best Under Heaven".

Outside the centre

Directly east over the river from the city, Guilin's most extensive limestone formations are at **Seven Star Park** (7am–7pm; ¥20; bus #10 from Zhongshan Lu stops outside). With a handful of small wooded peaks arranged in the shape of the Great Bear (Big Dipper) constellation, a large cavern, and even a few semi-wild monkeys, it's a sort of Guangxi in miniature, worth an hour's wander. The largest mass in the park, dotted with viewing pavilions, is **Putuo**, named after Zhejiang's famous Buddhist mountain, but the most striking formation is **Lutuo Shan**, which doesn't take much lateral thought to see as a kneeling dromedary. Some effort is required to find the entrance to **Qixing Dong**, however, which is a five-hundred-metre-long, thirty-metre-high introduction to the region's limestone caves (and China's romance with coloured lighting). Though a little tame, with most of the inner rock formations cleared to allow easy access, there's a small subterranean waterfall and the entranceway is liberally covered with carved inscriptions – some date back to the Tang dynasty, while a large tablet bears Mao Zedong's distinctive calligraphy.

Two other sights lie west of the centre on the number #3 bus route from opposite the train station on Zhongshan Lu. Around 2km out, **Xi Shan** (¥20), the Western Hills, is an area of long Buddhist associations, whose peaks are named after Buddhist deities. **Xiqinglin Si** here survives as one of Guangxi's major Buddhist temples, filled with hundreds of exquisitely executed statues ranging from 10cm to over 2m in height. There's also a **regional museum** in the park (daily 9am–noon & 2.30–5pm; free), basically a massive collection of ethnic clothing but few explanations.

The #3 bus terminates another 6km north outside **Reed Flute Cave** (daily 8.30am–4.30pm; ¥80), a huge warren eaten into the south side of Guangming Shan which once provided a refuge from banditry and Japanese bombs before being turned into a tourist attraction in the 1950s. The caverns are not huge, but there are some interesting formations and one small underground lake, which makes for some nice reflections. You're meant to follow one of the tours that run every twenty minutes, but you can always linger inside and pick up a later group if you want to spend more time.

Eating, drinking and entertainment

Guilin's **restaurants** are famous for serving exotica, such as pangolins, snakes, turtles, cane rats, game birds, and deer (palm civets, a one-time favourite, are off the menu following their being blamed as the source of SARS). If you want to indulge, look for cages outside restaurants, or try the upmarket hotels; otherwise, there are plenty of places to eat serving more familiar fare. The best concentrations of restaurants are east off Zhongshan Lu along Nanhuan Lu, Wenming Lu, and Yiren Lu, and on pedestrianized Shazheng Yang Lu. Most restaurants have menus – some even with English translations – but check prices to avoid being overcharged. For cheap sandpots and stir-fries, try the side streets and canteens around the long-distance bus station.

Restaurants

Aunt Top floor of Niko-Niko Do Plaza, corner of Jiefang Lu and Zhongshan Lu. A busy place with a huge variety of snacks and light meals from all over China, laid out in front of where chefs are busy preparing more. It works like an upmarket canteen: you get a card and wander round inspecting the food, hand your card over to be stamped when you find something you like, and wait for it to be delivered to your table. Dishes ¥3–20.

Dasanyuan Binjiang Lu. Though fairly low-profile, this place has been in business for over a century, and is a good place to try the local flavour, which is a bit like Cantonese-Sichuan fusion: fresh food simply cooked, but with chillies. Their fish dishes are particularly fine. Around ¥30 a head.

Jiaxiang Wenming Lu. Another fine local-style restaurant featuring popular carp and poultry dishes, along with country-style casseroles such as beef stewed with white raddish, and nice

rice-coated steamed spareribs. Their English menu is useable but not as varied as the Chinese one. Around ¥30 a head.

Natural Café Yiren Lu. Eclectic "foreign" menu including spaghetti, borscht, pizza and Southeast Asian coconut curries from ¥18, and steaks for around ¥50.

Yi Yuan 106 Nanhuan Lu. Real Sichuanese food, comfortable surroundings and friendly, English-speaking staff make this a nice place to dine. Try the strange-flavoured chicken, green beans with garlic or first-rate sweet-and-sour fish; just note that anything marked with three chillies on the menu is seriously spicy. Two or three can eat well for ¥80.

Zhengyang Souper Restaurant Shazheng Yang Lu. Cantonese roast meats, sandpots and steamed greens, with popular pavement tables for hot weather; not expensive at around ¥25 a head.

Drinking and entertainment

For **drinking**, the current place of choice, busy with expat teachers and trendy Chinese, is the *Ragazza Pub*, at the corner of Yiren Lu and Shazheng Yang Lu, though drinks are expensive. Otherwise, your accommodation can tell you if there are any "**minority displays**" being laid on for tour groups, featuring watered-down singing and dancing by the region's various ethnic groups. These can be quite fun, though you'll probably want to avoid occasional specials such as horse fighting – not an edifying spectator sport – which traditionally conclude Lunar New Year festivities. Western-oriented variety, operatic and acrobatic shows are also sometimes held at the Lijiang Theatre on riverfront Binjiang Lu, near the *Sheraton*.

Listings

Airlines CAAC are on Shanghai Lu ☎0773/2834067, open daily 9am–5pm, though offices are scattered all over the place and hotel tour desks can usually make bookings for you.

Banks and exchange The Bank of China (Mon–Fri 9–11.30am & 1.30–5pm) between the bus and train stations on Zhongshan Lu has an ATM and is able to change traveller's cheques. Upmarket hotels have their own currency exchange counters for guests.

Bookshops There's a subterranean Xinhua bookstore just west of Shan Hu on Zhongshan Lu, with a selection of translated Chinese classics, maps, stodgy Victorian potboilers, and even a few cookbooks, plus CDs, VCDs and DVDs.

Hospital Renmin Hospital, off Wenming Lu, is the best place to head if you get sick and your accommodation can't help out.

Internet access There's a very comfortable net bar on Nanhuan Lu, near the corner with Wenming Lu, charging ¥2.5 an hour.

Post and telecommunications The most convenient post office is just north of the train station on Zhongshan Nan Lu, with mail services and post restante downstairs, telephones upstairs (daily 8am–8pm). There's also another major branch about 2.5km farther north on Zhongshan Bei Lu.

Shopping Zhongshan Lu is lined with well-stocked department stores, the best of which is the Niko-Niko Do Plaza on the corner with Jiefang Lu. For local flavour, try osmanthus tea (*guicha*) or osmanthus wine (*guijiu*), both of which are quite pleasant (though some brands of wine are pretty rough). For souvenirs – mostly outright tack and ethnicky textiles – try the shops on Binjiang Lu, though stalls in Yangshuo sell the same stuff at literally a fraction of the price.

Travel agents CITS are at 11 Binjiang Lu, ☎0773/2861623, ⊛www.china4seasons.com or ⊛www.guilintrav.com, with branches at many hotels. They're a helpful bunch if you want to organize a city tour or Li River cruise, or book plane or rail tickets.

The Li River and Yangshuo

The **Li River** meanders south for 85km from Guilin through the finest scenery that this part of the country can provide, the shallow green water flanked by a procession of jutting karst peaks which have been carved by the elements into a host of bizarre shapes, every one of them with a name and associated legend. In between are pretty rural scenes of grazing water buffalo, farmers working their fields in conical hats, locals poling themselves along on half-submerged bamboo rafts and fishing with cormorants, and a couple of small villages with a scattering of old architecture; the densest concentration of peaks is grouped around the middle reaches between the villages of **Caoping** and **Xingping**. A **cruise** through all this is, for some, the highlight of their trip to China, and it would be hard not to be won over by the scenery – though in summer the river can be almost clogged with boats, and there are several ways to do the trip at varying expense and degrees of comfort. At the far end, the village of **Yangshuo** sits surrounded by more exquisite countryside, and is an undemanding place to kick back for a couple of days amongst a host of budget traveller-oriented cafés and guesthouses, and dig a little deeper into the region. The landscape is at its lushest during the wet, humid months between May and September, when

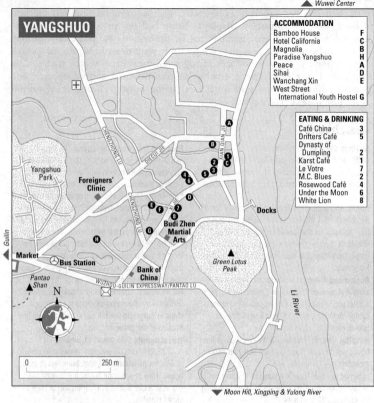

YANGSHUO

ACCOMMODATION
Bamboo House	F
Hotel California	C
Magnolia	B
Paradise Yangshuo	H
Peace	A
Sihai	D
Wanchang Xin	E
West Street International Youth Hostel	G

EATING & DRINKING
Café China	3
Drifters Café	5
Dynasty of Dumpling	2
Karst Café	1
Le Votre	7
M.C. Blues	2
Rosewood Café	4
Under the Moon	6
White Lion	8

Yangshuo Park

Foreigners' Clinic

Docks

Budi Zhen Martial Arts

Green Lotus Peak

Market

Bus Station

Pantao Shan

Bank of China

WUZHOU-GUILIN EXPRESSWAY/PANTAO LU

N

0   250 m

Li River

Guilin

the water is deepest – a serious consideration, as the river can be so shallow in winter that vessels can't make it all the way down to Yangshuo.

Cruising the Li River

The most popular **Li River cruise** covers the whole way between Guilin and Yangshuo, takes about six hours, and can be organized through the CITS or hotel agents in Guilin (see p.739) for upwards of ¥410. This gets you a comfortable seat in a flat-bottomed vessel – all have observation decks – taking around a hundred people, with an ample lunch provided, and a bus back from Yangshuo. In summer, boats depart from the **docks** on Binjiang Lu; when water levels are lower, alternative starting points downstream are used, with buses laid on to get you there. In really dry years, you only spend about an hour cruising around the middle peaks before heading back to the starting point and catching a bus to Yangshuo, though you get charged the same amount and won't be told this beforehand.

Alternatively, you can do the stretch between Caoping (aka Guanyan) and Xingping (25km) in local boats for less money and comfort, though the ninety-minute trip covers the most spectacular scenery and, in winter, may be the only way of seeing this part anyway. **Buses to Caoping** (¥7; one hour) leave every half hour from the depot just on the left inside Guilin's bus station gate, and terminate at the west-bank resort village of **Guanyan**. Go down to the water, find a boat owner – they'll probably grab you anyway – and start bargaining;

The Li River and Yangshuo

Li River　漓江　*líjiāng*
Baxian Guojiang　八仙过江　*bāxiān guòjiāng*
Caoping　草坪　*cǎopíng*
Daxu　大圩　*dàxǔ*
Guanyan　冠岩　*guànyán*
Jilong Shan　鸡笼山　*jīlóng shān*
Jiuma Hua Shan　九马画山　*jiǔmǎ huàshān*
River View Hotel　望江楼饭店　*wàngjiānglóu fàndiàn*
Wangfu Shi　望夫石　*wàngfū shí*
Xingping　兴坪　*xīngpíng*
Yangdi　杨堤　*yángdī*
Yellow Cloth Shoal　黄布滩　*huángbù tān*
Yu Cun　鱼村　*yúcūn*
Yuwei Ling　鱼尾岭　*yúwěi lǐng*

Yangshuo　阳朔　*yángshuò*
Bamboo House　竹林饭店　*zhúlín fàndiàn*
Green Lotus Peak　碧莲峰　*bìlián fēng*
Hotel California　加州饭店　*jiāzhōu fàndiàn*
Magnolia　白玉兰酒店　*báiyùlán jiǔdiàn*
Pantao Shan　蟠桃山　*pántáo shān*
Paradise Yangshuo　阳朔百乐度假饭店　*yángshuò bǎilèdùjià fàndiàn*
Peace　和平客栈　*hépíng kèzhàn*
Sihai　四海饭店　*sìhǎi fàndiàn*
Wanchang Xin　万昌鑫旅馆　*wànchāngxīn lǚguǎn*
West Street International Youth Hostel　西街国际青年旅馆　*xījiē guójì qīngnián lǚguǎn*
Yangshuo Park　阳朔公园　*yángshuò gōngyuán*

Around Yangshuo
Baisha　白沙　*báishā*
Black Buddha New Water Caves　黑佛新水洞　*hēifó xīnshuǐdòng*
Black Dragon Caves　黑龙洞　*hēilóng dòng*
Camel Hill　骆驼山　*luòtuo shān*
Chaoyang　朝阳　*cháoyáng*
Gu Cheng　古诚　*gǔ chéng*
Huang Tu　黄土　*huáng tǔ*
Moon Hill　月亮山　*yuèliàng shān*
Xia Tangzhai　下堂寨　*xià tángzhài*
Yulong River　玉龙河　*yùlóng hé*

¥100 per person is currently a fair deal. The boats seat about 10 people on wooden stools, and the roof peels back for views. Don't be too surprised if you get dropped off upstream from Xingping and have to walk the last kilometre to town – your boatman doesn't want to pay the tax for carrying you. From Xingping, there's heaps of transport through the day to Yangshuo (see p.742). Operators in Yangshuo also offer a slightly shorter version of this trip, starting in Xingping and running upstream to **Yangdi**, for ¥60.

Downstream to Yangshuo

Aside from a few minor peaks, the first place of interest on the Li is around 25km along at the west-bank town of **DAXU**, which features a long, cobbled street, a few old wooden buildings, and a Ming-dynasty arched bridge, though it's all a bit dishevelled – the Guilin-Caoping bus stops here. After this it's a bit flat until a grouping of peaks around **Wangfu Shi**, an east-bank outcrop said to be a wife who turned to stone whilst waiting for her travelling husband to return home. Not far on, **CAOPING** is around 40km from Guilin, marked by **Guan Yan** (Crown Cliff; ¥40), a tiara-shaped rise whose naturally hollowed interior forms a twelve-kilometre-long cavern, garishly lit and complete with escalators and loudspeaker commentaries – access is from the shore (cruise boats don't stop here). Just downstream on the opposite bank, a cliff jutting into the river obstructs footpaths, so that local travellers have to get around it by boat (named the **half-side ferry**, as it stays on the same bank).

South of here is the east-bank settlement of **Yangdi**, where cruises from Guilin actually start in winter, and then you're into the best of the scenery, the hills suddenly tightly packed around the river. Three-pronged **Penholder Peak** drops down sheer into the water, followed by **Jilong Shan** (Chicken-coop Hill), **Yuwei Ling** (Fish-tail Peak), **Baxian Guojiang** (Eight Immortals Crossing the River), before the river squeezes past **Jiuma Hua Shan** (Nine Horses Fresco Hill) – the name referring to a one-hundred-metre-high cliff on whose weathered face you can pick out some horsey patterns. Look into the water past here for **Yellow Cloth Shoal**, a flat, submerged rock at one of the shallowest spots on the river.

XINGPING, 70km from Guilin, is another scruffy, elderly west-bank village of a half-dozen streets laid back from the water. The place is just starting to get its teeth into the tourist industry: down by the docks, the *River View Hotel* (ⓣ0773/8702276; beds ¥30 per person) is the town's first backpacker joint, and faces *One World Café* and *Cottage Café*, displaying English billboard menus. There's a **market** here on calendar dates ending in a 3, 6, or 9, and several **old villages** in the vicinity, including **Yu Cun**, dignified by several stone and wooden buildings. **Buses to Yangshuo** (¥5) leave through the day, while back on the water, the river broadens out for its final twenty-kilometre stretch to Yangshuo's docks beneath Green Lotus Peak.

Yangshuo

Nestled 70km south of Guilin in the thick of China's most spectacular karst scenery, **YANGSHUO**, meaning Bright Moon, rose to prominence during the mid-1980s, when visitors on Li River cruises realized that beyond simply spending an hour here buying souvenirs, the village made a mellow place to settle down and get on intimate terms with the river and its peaks. Yangshuo has grown considerably since then, and today the newer area around the high-way is as noisy, polluted and crowded as anywhere in China. But in the village streets between here and the river the atmosphere remains much calmer, with businesses catering to independent tourists – including many Chinese – who have made Yangshuo their haven. It's an ideal spot to cocoon ruffled nerves: hills surround everything, village lanes swarm with market activity, and there are foreign-oriented restaurants and accommodation everywhere – some of which are surprisingly sophisticated. You can rent a bike and spend a day zipping between hamlets, hike around or go **rock climbing** on nearby peaks, study calligraphy or martial arts, or just relax in the village park.

Arrival, information and accommodation

If you didn't arrive at Yangshuo's docks, you'll most likely find yourself at the **bus station** out on the highway (also known as Pantao Lu), off which Yangshuo's two main streets run northeast to the river; Diecui Jie extends from the bus station through the village centre, while east and parallel is pleasantly cobbled, vehicle-free Xi Jie, extending past cafés and accommodation, plus old wooden shops, down to the **docks**.

There's an unusual quantity of **information** to be had in Yangshuo. All accommodation have tour desks, but many people make all arrangements and bookings by shopping around Yangshuo's ubiquitous **cafés**. Specifically geared to Western travellers, these act as meeting places to swap the latest news – some have noticeboards, others leave journals out for you to write in and read – and offer **book exchanges** (the best being at *Café Too*), Internet access, and deals on everything that it's possible to do during your stay here. One **map** to look out for is the *Trax2.com Free Maps* sheet – many cafés stock it, or you can download it at ⓦ www.trax2.com – which has a clear layout of the village, plus Xingping, the Li River, and surrounding countryside.

Accommodation

Stiff competition means that Yangshuo's accommodation prices are good value. Though there are places to stay everywhere, the nosiy highway end of town is a poor location, and the best selection is concentrated along Xi Jie. At present – aside from a couple of upmarket **hotels** – the bias is towards **guesthouse-style** accommodation, whose lobbies are full of folksy Chinese furnishings and where you can get everything from dorm beds at ¥15 to doubles with bathroom and air conditioning for ¥100–120. Rooms vary greatly in quality, even within individual establishments – Yangshuo's damp climate encourages **mildew** – so have a look at a few before choosing; balconies and wooden floors are nice touches, locations near bars may not be. Rates for rooms halve during the winter low season, when you'll want to check the availability of heating and hot water.

Bamboo House Guihua Xiang ☏0773/8823888, ⓔbamboohouse23@hotmail.com. Laid-back and unpushy owners, rooms a bit on the small side unless you get one with a balcony. Dorm ¥20, ❸
Hotel California 35 Xian Qian Jie ☏ & ⓕ0773/8825559, ⓔhotelcaliforniayangshuo @yahoo.com. Budget favourite, clean and well run, and the only place with air conditioners large enough to cope with both summer and winter temperatures. Dorm beds ¥20, doubles with and without bathroom ❸
Magnolia cnr of Diecui Lu and Xianqian Jie ☏0773/8819288, ⓔlucywhz@hotmail.com. New and pretty smart mid-range place with minimalist decor and huge rooms (though this and tiling make it cold in winter). ❻

Paradise Yangshuo Off Xi Jie ☏0773/8822109, ⓦwww.paradiseyangshuo.com. Yangshuo's longest-running upmarket affair, a series of buildings set in a spacious private garden complete with pond. ❽
Peace Xian Qian Jie, behind the riverfront Bank of China ☏0773/8826262, ⓔJankinLuo@163.net. One of the best deals in town: large rooms with a/c, bathroom, and balconies in a quiet street just off Xi Jie. ❷
Sihai River end of Xi Jie ☏0773/8822013, ⓦwww.sihaihotel.com. Above-average budget hotel, more substantial, cleaner and better organized than most backpacker joints with bigger, mildew-free rooms. Dorm beds ¥20, doubles ¥120, family apartments ❺–❼

Wanchang Xin Guihua Xiang, an alley between Xi Jie and Guihua Lu, ☏0773/8814066. Very friendly management; the building is a bit narrow and slightly claustrophobic, but rooms are spotless and cosy. Dorms ¥25, ❸

West Street International Youth Hostel Xi Jie ☏0773/8820933, ✉stgyp@263.net. Good prices and helpful staff in this slightly sterile, IYHA-affiliated hostel. Dorm beds ¥15, ❷

The village

Yangshuo has few formal attractions – it was a simple country marketplace before tourists arrived – but there's still plenty to explore. West off Diecui Jie is **Yangshuo Park** (¥6), a pleasant place in summer with its colourful formal garden and breezy vantages of town from pavilions lodged on the main rise. Squeezed between the highway and the river directly opposite is **Green Lotus Peak**, the largest in the immediate area – there's a track to the top off the highway east of the post office, but it involves some scrambling. An easier path – leading to better views – ascends **Pantao Shan** from behind the market. Otherwise, just walk upstream from Yangshuo for a kilometre or two and take your pick of the rough trails which scale many other slopes to summits covered in tangled undergrowth and sharp, eroded rocks – again, be prepared for some scrambling, and for safety reasons don't go alone.

The presence of tourists hasn't entirely altered the daily routine of villagers, who spend hours inspecting and buying wares in the **produce market**. There's a good selection of game, fruit (especially a winter glut of pomelos), nuts and mushrooms out on sheets in the street here, including rats and pheasants, fresh straw and needle mushrooms, and spiky water caltrops, which contain a kernel similar to a Brazil nut. It's an interesting place to hang out, especially on **market days** (held on dates ending in a 3, 6, or 9), but foreigners tend to save their money for the shops down at the river end of **Xi Jie** (also signposted as West Street), one of the best places in China to pick up a bargain **souvenir**. There are things from all over the country: silk jackets and T-shirts, outdoor gear and designer-style clothing at absurdly low prices, CDs and DVDs, ethnic textiles, modern and traditional paintings turned out by art students in Guilin, chops, and heaps of elaborately carved wooden screen panels, printing blocks and grotesque theatre masks. Coins and jade are invariably fake. As always in China, buy because you like something, not because it looks valuable – under layers of carefully applied grime most articles are "new antiques". Vigorous, friendly bargaining is essential – about a third of the asking price is recommended – and don't buy anything when tour boats from Guilin pull in unless you want to pay five times the going rate.

Those who find themselves spending weeks in Yangshuo linger not for the sights or shopping but because the village offers a window into the more esoteric

Cormorant fishing

When you've had enough scenery for one day, do something unusual and spend an evening watching **cormorant fishing** (book through cafés; ¥100 for a four-person 90min trip). This involves heading out in a punt at dusk, closely following a tiny wooden fishing boat or bamboo raft from which a group of cormorants fish for their owner. Despite being turned into a tourist activity at Yangshuo, people still make their living from this age-old practice throughout central and southern China, raising young birds to dive into the water and swim back to the boat with full beaks. The birds are prevented from swallowing by rings or ties around their necks, but it's usual practice for the fisherman to slacken these off and let them eat every seventh fish – apparently, the cormorants refuse to work otherwise.

side of Chinese culture. Normally the domain of specialists, for around ¥30–50 an hour you can take **courses** in painting, calligraphy, languages, cooking, massage and many other subjects – cafés (see below) have the current information. There's also the outstanding **Budi Zhen martial arts school** (check the map to find it and turn up at 8.30am; ☏13977350377), run by the irrepressible 80-year-old Mr Gao and his twin sons, whose unique family style is a blend of Shaolin and Wudang kung fu techniques – the sons speak English. Alternatively, the **Wu Wei Center** (1km north along the riverbank; Ⓦwww.wuweicenter .com) is a new riverside retreat where you can study martial arts, yoga, and meditation with foreign and Chinese instructors in beautiful surroundings.

Eating, drinking and nightlife

You'll probably while away the evenings in Yangshuo drinking beer and eating in Xi Jie's numerous **restaurants**. These are relatively upmarket, serving Western-style pizzas, pasta, steak, apple pie and ice cream; many also have decent Chinese menus, including local specialities such as cane rats, fresh bamboo shoots and beer fish. **Cafés** on Xi Jie and Xian Qian Jie – the latter also currently at the core of Yangshuo's **rock-climbing scene** – offer much the same things, though prices are a bit lower and the food more ordinary; most also screen films in the evenings. Both restaurants and cafés open early in the morning for Western breakfasts and coffee, and in fair weather might host outdoor barbecues. Everyone finds their own favourites, and the following recommendations should be treated as a starting point. There are also plenty of inexpensive **Chinese canteens** and **food stalls** selling noodle soups and buns around the bus station.

Eating aside, there are several **bars** around the place, some of which are big enough for **live music** and all getting pretty raucous later on in the evenings – *Bar 98* on Guihua Xiang and *Meiyou's* on Xi Jie are the current picks.

Café China cnr of Xi Jie and Xian Qian Jie. Very snug and serving the best cheesecake, chocolate cake and coffee in Yangshuo, and at very reasonable prices.

Drifters Café Xi Jie. Nostalgic apple crumble and shepherd's pie, good *mapo doufu*, and possibly the best muesli, yoghurt and fruit breakfast in town. Service can be slack, though.

Dynasty of Dumpling Xian Qian Jie. Unusual in its largely Dongbei-based Chinese fare: you can get an acceptable Beijing Duck here for ¥60 and the interestingly named "Tiger Food" (mixed green vegetables), but the house speciality is flavoured *jiaozi* at ¥15 for 16.

Karst Café Xian Qian Jie. A climber-oriented café-bar with an average run of Chinese and Western staples (though their apple pie is amazing) and opportunities to make contacts.

Le Vôtre Xi Jie. Yangshuo's poshest dining, inside a Ming-era building complete with period furnishings. Food is French – snails, pâté, onion soup, steak au

poivre, chocolate mousse – or Chinese seafood. Also, excellent coffee and croissants for breakfast. Expect to pay at least ¥50 a head.

MC Blues at the *Explorer* hotel, Xian Qian Jie. A long-running business, though it keeps changing location, serving toasted sandwiches, bamboo rats, vegetarian hotpots, and much-lauded beer-battered fish.

Rosewood Café Just off Xi Jie. Romantic ambience and extensive Western menu covering pizza, pasta, grills and salads, though perhaps a bit pricey for what you get. Their ice cream (also available in cones outside) is the best in Yangshuo. Two can eat well for ¥80.

Under the Moon Xi Jie. Upstairs dining room with balcony, and slightly over-large first-floor café with the best street tables in town. Western and Chinese food – their lemon sorbet is scrumptious.

White Lion Xi Jie. Big, inexpensive burgers, pepper steak, and fried banana in brandy.

Listings

Bank There's a Bank of China with an ATM on Xi Jie (foreign currency transactions daily 9am–noon & 1–5pm).

English teachers for private lessons are always wanted in Yangshuo; you'll find adverts posted in accommodation and various stores along Xi Jie, or contact Kelly's Yangshuo (☏0773/8814969, ⓦwww.yangshuoenglish.org). Payment is usually in bed and board, rather than cash, but it's a way to conserve funds – you could also swap your services for Chinese lessons.

Internet is available for free at cafés if you have a meal too; otherwise, there are Net bars along the highway charging ¥2 an hour.

Medical There's a Foreigners' Clinic on Diecui Jie; for acupuncture or Chinese massage, contact Dr Lily Li at her clinic on Guihua Xiang (☏0773/8814625).

Post and telephones The Post office (daily 8am–6pm; parcel and post restante services available) is over on the highway. IDD telephones are all around Yangshuo, and at the bigger hotels.

Around Yangshuo

Getting to see the countryside around Yangshuo is no problem, as the land between the hills is flat and perfect for **bicycles** – Xian Qian Jie is thick with rental shops if your accommodation can't help (¥10 a day, plus ¥300 deposit). Various people offer informative **guided bike tours**, too, allowing close contact with villages and locals through an interpreter; costs are subject to negotiation but ¥15 an hour seems about right. **Motor-rickshaws** also cruise around, destinations listed on their windshields in Chinese, but are relatively expensive and the drivers don't speak English.

Except in very dry winters, **boats** depart year round from the dock at the end of Xi Jie; there's a ticket office here and you'll also be mobbed by touts. While the entire reverse Li River cruise to Guilin is an ultimately tedious twelve-hour journey upstream, there are plenty of shorter options, though as Guilin operators have a monopoly on vessels, prices are still relatively high. One way around this is to catch a minibus to **Xingping**, and then hire a boat from there upstream to **Yangdi**, past the thickest, most contorted collection of peaks (¥60; 2hr). From Yangdi, catch transport to either Guilin or Yangshuo along the highway. Agents in Yangshuo can arrange this for you – see p.742 for details of Xingpin and the river scenery.

If you just want to **swim**, take the road southeast of town to **Camel Hill**, turn right down a lane and follow the track to the river – about an hour's cycling time. Villagers turn up to wash at about 6.30pm, and there are clear views of Moon Hill from here.

Climbing Yangshuo's peaks

Yangshuo is one of Asia's fastest-growing **rock-climbing** centres, with an estimated 70,000 pinnacles of up to 200m in height in the area. However, there are only about fifty established climbing routes, many of them under 30m in length – though those at Moon Hill are rated amongst the toughest in China – and, as most are within easy day-trips of Yangshuo, you won't need to plan any mighty expeditions (though camping out on site is fun).

The main **climbing season** lasts from October through to February, as the rest of the year can be uncomfortably hot or wet. There are several sources of local **information** along Xian Qian Jie, notably China Climb (☏0773/8811033, ⓦwww.ChinaClimb .com), the *Karst Café* (☏0773/8828482, ⓔechowoó2@hotmail.com), and Spiderman Climbing (☏0773/8812339, ⓦwww.s-climbing.com) – they also sell copies of *Rock Climbing in Yangshuo* by Paul Collis (who can be contacted at paulcollis@hotmail. com), which gives invaluable information on routes, access, local conditions and grades. The above places can also organize **equipment**, **instruction** and **guides**, of whom the most experienced is probably "Dingo" Han Jun (☏13878373540, ⓔhanjun67@hotmail.com).

The Yulong River and Moon Hill

There's nothing to stop you simply picking a distant hill and heading out there – cycling along the muddy paths between villages takes you through some wonderful scenery – but there are a couple of areas worth focusing on. Paralleling the highway to Guilin, the **Yulong River** west of Yangshuo offers a twelve-kilometre walk or cycle between small hamlets, with a couple of old stone bridges and at least two older-style villages with a few antique buildings. The road from Yangshuo leaves the highway east of the bus station – you might have to ask for directions to **Chaoyang**, the first large settlement along the way – and follows the east side of the Yulong via **Xia Tangzhai**, the old villages of **Huang Tu** and **Gu Cheng**, before rejoining the highway at **Baisha**, whose market runs on dates ending in a 1, 4, or 7 and where you can either cycle or catch a bus back to Yangshuo.

Yangshuo's most famous peak is **Moon Hill**, which lies on the highway 10km southwest of town. Just before you get here, tracks off to the south lead to the **Black Buddha New Water Caves**, whose highlights include an underground river, fossils and bats. Another 3km along the same track are the equally imposing **Black Dragon Caves**, where you take a boat, then have to wade and stagger through the largest regional caverns yet discovered to a fifteen-metre subterranean waterfall and swimming holes inhabited by blind fish. Only open in summer, either system costs about ¥45 for an hour's tour, or ¥65 for a three- or four-hour flashlight exploration – agents in Yangshuo are probably the easiest way to set up a trip. Come prepared to get soaked, cold and muddy.

Moon Hill itself (¥6, plus ¥1 to park your bike) takes an easy thirty minutes to ascend, following stone steps through bamboo and brambles to the summit. A beautiful sight, the hill is named after a large crescent-shaped hole that pierces the peak. Views from the top take in the whole of the Li River valley spread out before you, fields cut into uneven chequers by rice and vegetable plots, and Tolkienesque peaks framed through the hole.

Longsheng, Sanjiang and on to Guizhou

A hundred kilometres northwest of Guilin the road winds steeply through some fine stands of mountain bamboo, and enters the southern limit of a fascinating ethnic **autonomous region**. With a rich landscape of mountains and terraced fields as a backdrop, it's simple to hop on local transport from the county towns of **Longsheng** and **Sanjiang** and head off to tour a very rural corner of China that seemingly remains little affected by the modern world. Day-trips abound, but, with five days or so to spare, you can push right through the mountainous **Dong** heartlands northwest of Sanjiang into Guizhou province, a fabulous journey which takes you to the area around **Kaili**, similarly central to the Miao people (p.777). Before starting, note that there are **no banks** capable of cashing traveller's cheques between Guilin and Kaili.

Longsheng and Longji Titian

Some two hours from Guilin, **LONGSHENG** sits on the torrential **Rongshui River**, known for the tiny quantities of alluvial **gold** found in its tributaries which still entice the occasional Chinese dreamer up into the hills with shovels and pans. It's also a busy marketplace selling those interestingly shaped rocks that end up in miniature gardens and bonsai pots throughout the land, a trade that was illegal until the late 1990s.

Longsheng, Sanjiang and on to Guizhou

Longsheng	龙胜	*lóngshèng*
Longsheng Hotel	龙胜宾馆	*lóngshèng bīnguǎn*
Lüyou Binguan	旅游宾馆	*lǚyóu bīnguǎn*
Longji Titian	龙脊梯田	*lóngjǐ tītián*
Huang Lo	黄洛	*huángluò*
Liqing Guesthouse	丽晴旅社	*líqíng lǚshè*
Longji village	龙脊村	*lóngjǐ cūn*
Ping An	平安	*píng'ān*
Sanjiang	三江	*sānjiāng*
Chengyang Qiao Binguan	程阳桥宾馆	*chéngyángqiáo bīnguǎn*
Department Store Hostel	百货招待所	*bǎihuò zhāodàosuǒ*
Drum tower	鼓楼	*gǔlóu*
Fulu Si	福禄寺	*fúlù sì*
Sanjiang Binguan	三江 宾馆	*sānjiāng bīnguǎn*
Travellers' Home	行旅之家宾馆	*xínglǚzhījiā bīnguǎn*
Chengyang	程阳	*chéngyáng*
Guandong	关东	*guāndōng*
Mapang	马胖	*mǎpàng*
Bajiang	八江	*bājiāng*
Baxie	八协	*bāxié*
Dudong	独峒	*dútóng*
Gaoding	高定	*gāoding*
Hualian	华联	*huálián*
Mengjiang	孟江	*mèngjiāng*
Tongle	同乐	*tónglè*
Zhaoxing	肇兴	*zhàoxīng*
Diping	地坪	*dìpíng*
Fulu	富禄	*fùlù*
Heli	和里	*hélǐ*
Tang An	堂安	*táng'ān*
Liping	黎平	*lípíng*
Baitian Zhaodaisuo	白天招待所	*báitiān zhāodàisuǒ*
Luoxiang	落香	*luòxiāng*
Jitang	纪堂	*jìtáng*
Longtu	龙图	*lóngtú*
Congjiang	丛江	*cóngjiāng*
Basha	八沙	*bāshā*
Jianghu Luguan	江湖旅馆	*jiānghú lǚguǎn*
Yueliang Shan Binguan	月亮山宾馆	*yuèliàng shān bīnguǎn*
Rongjiang	榕江	*róngjiāng*
Qingfeng Binguan	庆丰宾馆	*qìngfēng bīnguǎn*

Longsheng itself is unattractive, but it makes a convenient base for further explorations. The road from Guilin follows the river north into town, then kinks sharply west past the **bus station** and off towards Sanjiang. At the kink, there's a **bridge** east over the river and into Longsheng's centre, just a couple of messy market streets and high-rise buildings parallel to the riverbank. For **accommodation**, the *Riverside Tiger Hotel* (☎0773/7511335; ¥20 per person), is a basic, friendly **hostel** run by an English teacher about 100m south of the bridge on the Guilin road (there's an English sign); more central options include the comfortable *Longsheng Hotel* (☎0773/7517718; ➎) and *Luyou Binguan* (☎0773/7517206, ℱ7516632; ➍). For **food**, there are plenty of hole-in-the-wall options around the bus station; the *Riverside Tiger* does simple Chinese meals; and the *Green Food Restaurant*, north from the town side of the bridge, has an enthusiastic manager and good food.

Scores of daily **buses** run on from Longsheng to Sanjiang (daily 6am–3pm; ¥9) or to Guilin (daily 6am–6pm; ¥11); there are also luxury coaches to Guilin at twice the price. Less frequent services can get you as far south as Liuzhou, or northeast to Congjiang. **Minibuses** for the Longji Titian area (see below) leave at 9.20am, 12.40pm and 4pm (¥6.5); you can leave extra bags at Longsheng's bus station for ¥3 a day.

Longji Titian

The real reason to visit Longsheng is the chance to explore the rest of this splendidly rural county. At **Longji Titian**, a range of hills 20km to the southeast whose name translates as "Dragon's Spine Terraces", you'll find some of the most extraordinarily extreme **rice terracing** that exists in China: the steep-sided and closely packed valleys have been carved over centuries of backbreaking effort to resemble the literal form of a contour map. Most of the people up here are Zhuang, but there are also communities of **Yao**, some of whom still hunt for a living; more aspiring locals in town depict them as rustic savages, happy to own just a gun and a knife. Longji Titian's villages are almost exclusively built of timber in traditional styles, and electricity and telephones are very recent introductions to the region, and still available in only a couple of places.

Tourism is beginning to kick off, however, with a new road making the village of **PING AN** easily accessible in about an hour on minibuses from Longsheng's bus station. Vehicles initially follow the Guilin road south, then turn off up an ever-tightening river valley past the Yao hamlet of **HUANG LO** (from where it's possible to **hike** up to Ping An in an hour), after which the road zigzags steeply uphill to the roadhead. Here all visitors pay the ¥30 **entry fee** before walking the last 500m up stone steps to Ping An itself, a beautiful Zhuang village of wooden homes and cobbled paths squeezed into a steep fold between the terraces. Many places offer **accommodation** at around ¥15 a person in a simple room with shared toilets and showers, with meals extra; the best atmosphere is at family-run businesses such as the *Liqing Guesthouse* (☎0773/7582412; ➊), where some English is spoken, and meals are filling. Ask at your accommodation about the number of **walks** in the region – there's a four-hour round trip to lookouts, or across to the ancient village of **LONGJI** – some offer guides for about ¥25 per person including lunch. Ping An's own **stores** stock only absolute basics, so bring your own snacks or luxuries. **Leaving**, minibuses head back to Longsheng at 7.30am, 10.40am, 2.10pm and 5.30pm.

Sanjiang and the Dong

Two hours west of Longsheng the road crosses a high stone bridge over the Rongshui and lands you at **SANJIANG**, the small, desperately untidy capital of

Sanjiang Dong Autonomous County. Sanjiang's main attraction is the neat, indigo-clad **Dong** themselves, a people renowned for their wooden houses, towers and bridges which dot the countryside hereabouts, and it's well worth roving the region with the help of minibuses and converted tractors known locally as "Dong taxis". There's a scattering of simple hostels and places to eat, and villagers will sometimes offer lodgings and sustenance – characteristically sour hotpots, *douxie cha* or **oil tea** (a bitter, salty soup made from fried tea leaves and puffed rice), and home-made rice wine – though it's polite to offer payment in these circumstances. Just be aware that the only people who have any idea about **local bus departure times** in this region are the drivers themselves – if you're staying the night somewhere remote, track him down to confirm times or risk being stranded for a day.

Sanjiang is split in two by the river, with most of the town on the north bank, and a smaller, newer development on the south. The town's only two sights are also on the south bank, the easiest to locate being the huge **drum tower** (¥5) set on a rise overlooking the water. A special feature of Dong settlements, these towers were once used as lookout posts when the country was at war, the drums inside beaten to rouse the village; today people gather underneath them for meetings and entertainment. Built in 2003, this is the largest one anywhere, at 47m high and with eleven internal levels, all built from pegged cedar and supported by four huge posts; you can climb to the top for views. Behind it, **Fulu Si** is a small Buddhist nunnery dedicated to Guanyin, with separate halls arranged up a slope behind the entrance gateway.

Sanjiang practicalities

Sanjiang's **long-distance bus station** is south of the river on the main road – look for the speed barrier at the entrance on a curve in the road, as it's not otherwise marked – with connections south as far as Guilin and north to Liping and Congjiang. **Local buses** use the depot immediately north of the bridge in the main part of town. Sanjiang is also on the Huaihua–Liuzhou **rail line**; the train station is about 10km northwest of town with minibuses meeting arrivals and landing them immediately north of the bridge.

Places to stay north of the river include the budget *Department Store Hostel* (¥25) – look for the English sign near the local bus station – the *Chengyang Qiao Binguan* (☎0772/8613071; ¥120), 100m west along the road, and the *Sanjiang Binguan* (old wing ¥80; new wing ¥200) on the road uphill from the local bus station. South of the river and about 100m back towards Longsheng from the long-distance station, the *Travellers' Home* (☎0772/8615584; ¥100) is clean, comfortable and good value. For **food**, try the noodle and hotpot stalls north of the bridge, or your accommodation.

Chengyang

Eighteen kilometres north of Sanjiang, **CHENGYANG** sits on the far side of the Linxi River, crossed from the main road by a splendid **wind-and-rain bridge**. There are over a hundred of these in the region, but Chengyang's is the finest and most elaborate. Raised in 1916, five solid stone piers support an equal number of pavilions (whose different roofs illustrate several regional building styles) linked by covered walkways, entirely built from wood – not one nail was used in the bridge's construction. Cool and airy in summer, and protected from downpours, these bridges – **fengyu qiao** in Chinese – are perfect places to sit around and gossip, though they once served a religious purpose, too, and other examples have little shrines grimed with incense smoke in their halfway alcoves. The shrine on Chengyang's is vacant as the bridge is a protected cultural relic and no fire is allowed. Women here hawk pieces of embroidery, cotton blankets boldly patterned in black and white, and the curiously shiny blue-black Dong jackets, dyed indigo and varnished in egg white as a protection against mosquitoes.

Across the bridge, Chengyang itself is a pretty collection of warped, two- and three-storeyed traditional **wooden houses**, overlooked by a square-sided drum tower. By now you'll have noticed that the Dong are not great believers in stone or concrete buildings, as wooden structures can more easily be extended or even shifted as necessary. Fire is a major concern, though, and throughout the year each family takes turns to guard the village from this hazard. There's a trail from the main road up to two pavilions overlooking Chengyang, with some nice views of the dark, gloomy villages nestled among vivid green fields.

Wander out to the fields and you'll find a string of paths connecting Chengyang to visibly poorer hamlets, similar congregations of dark wood and cobbles, many with their own, less elaborate bridges and towers. On the way, look for creaky black **waterwheels** made from plaited bamboo, somehow managing to supply irrigation canals despite dribbling out most of their water in the process.

The last **bus back to Sanjiang** passes by around 5pm, but Chengyang is a better place to stay overnight, with two **hostels**: the *Chengyang National Hostel* (¥15 per person; meals extra) is a traditional wooden building, with simple facilities and nice staff, signposted on the river just outside Chengyang; the similar *Dong Village Hotel* (¥15), run by a local named Michael, is nearby. You can also **hike** from Chengyang to **Mapang** (see below), via the village of **Guandong**, in about six hours, and catch a bus back to Sanjiang from there.

Mapang and the upper Meng River

Feasible as a day-trip from Sanjiang, **MAPANG** lies some 30km north of town via a change of buses in **Bajiang**, and features a huge drum tower with an unusually broad rectangular base. The last buses back to Sanjiang leave late afternoon, though it's also possible to hike from here to Chengyang in about six hours.

The most interesting corner of this land, however, lies northwest across the mountains from Bajiang along the **Meng River**, which ultimately runs down from the north to Chankou on the Sanjiang road (see p.752). Morning buses from Sanjiang to **Dudong** from the local bus station cross these ranges, emerging 33km away above a deep valley containing the tiny, dark-roofed village of **ZHUOLONG**, where Deng Xiaoping rested up during the Long March. There are two drum towers here, but press on a couple of kilometres north to **BAXIE**, whose bright green and yellow bridge was built in 1980 (purists might notice a few nails in the decking). The cobbled village square in front of Baxie's

Longsheng, Sanjiang and on to Guizhou

drum tower also has a small stage carved with monkeys and lions for festival performances. The oldest surviving bridge, built in 1861, is in the next village north, **HUALIAN**, after which comes a unique two-tier example at the village of **BATUAN**, with one lane for people and one for animals. This bridge still has its shrine, a cupboard with a bearded god on a stone slab, and, at the far end, a path leads along the riverbank to where tall trees shade a small new temple.

At the end of the road, **DUDONG** was a centre for guerilla action against the Japanese during the 1940s. There's a store and basic **guesthouse** (¥30) here by the marketplace, which is the only place serving food – though not much of it, and only during daylight hours. An easy hike from here follows a broad, dusty road uphill to a stone bridge, where a smaller track leads to **GAODING**, an attractive Dong village of a hundred homes crammed into a deep fold in the hillside, with six towers, farm animals roaming the lanes, and nothing but wooden buildings (if you ignore the new school on the hill above). The walk takes about two hours each way, and it's best to ask directions off everyone you meet.

After a night in Dudong, either catch the bus back to Sanjiang (the first leaves around daybreak), or the **Tongle** bus as far as **MENGJIANG**, an interesting village only a few kilometres south of Zhuolong. Mengjiang is half Dong, half Miao – the name means "Miao River" – each community settled on opposite banks. After generations of fighting over land, their leaders became reconciled in the 1940s, and together built the traditionally designed **Nationality Union Bridge** across the divide. Today it's hard to distinguish between the two communities, as both dress similarly – women wearing heavy metal earrings or a piece of white cord through their lobes – though the drum tower is, naturally enough, on the Dong side. It's a great place to wander between the large houses and out into the fields, and tractors can be hired for the run down to **TONGLE**. Here you'll find a store, a hostel and an early-morning minibus for the ninety-minute ride back to Sanjiang.

Into Guizhou: Sanjiang to Kaili

The road west of Sanjiang cuts through Dong territory and up to the Miao stronghold of **Kaili** in Guizhou province, a 300km-long run of traditional rural villages, steeply terraced hillsides, lime-blue rivers and windy roads. Daily buses run from Sanjiang to **Zhaoxing** – itself a highlight – from where you can either reach Kaili on regular buses via the northerly town of **Liping**, or by continuing west to **Congjiang**, where you'll find scheduled onward transport – just note that direct Sanjiang-Congjiang buses follow a new road which bypasses most of the villages and scenery. Three days is a likely minimum for the trip, though five would be more realistic and it is, anyway, not a journey to be hurried. Expect frugal facilities and food in villages, and cold, icy winters.

Sanjiang to Zhaoxing

About 20km west from Sanjiang, the **HELI** area is another possible day-trip from town, sporting the semi-ruined **Sanwang Gong** (Three Kings' Palace), a temple to local protective deities, next to three wind-and-rain bridges and a further two drum towers in the nearby village of **Nanzhai**. Another 10km brings you to the junction with the road from Dudong and Tongle at the riverside town of **CHANKOU**, a smattering of modern concrete-and-tile buildings with a huge **banyan tree**, social focus for villages right across tropical Asia.

An hour west of Chankou is the Guangxi–Guizhou border hamlet of **FULU**, known for its **firecracker festival** on the third day of the third lunar month.

Through buses bypass the town, moving north across the border to the scruffy settlement of **DIPING**, which sports plenty of waterwheels, another Dong bridge, a small drum tower and the *Bridge Flower Hotel* (**❶**). Not much farther on, **LONG E** is a similarly dishevelled town with a new drum tower and the mouldy *Concerning Foreign Affairs Hotel* (**❶**) – really just somewhere to pull up for the night.

It's a further ninety minutes from here to **ZHAOXING**, a wonderful place set in a small valley with a generous smattering of old buildings including five square-based **drum towers**, each differently styled and built by separate clans. Some have accompanying wind-and-rain bridges and theatre stages, all decorated with fragments of mirrors and mouldings of actors and animals. Miao and Dong women in town sell embroidery and silver; houses are hung with strings of drying radishes for sour hotpots; the backstreets are full of cruising livestock and the sound of freshly dyed cloth being pounded with wooden mallets to give it a shiny patina; the only downside is a ¥5 **fee** that all visitors to Zhaoxing have to pay. Rice terraces and muddy tracks provide fine country walks; one of the best is 7km uphill from town to **Tang An**, another photogenic collection of wooden buildings.

Zhaoxing has many **guesthouses** (**❶**), all offering pretty much the same comforts – hot water, flush toilets, and even **Internet** access, though this seldom seems to work. There are a couple of places to **eat**, such as the *Sanxiao Fanguan*, which has a partially translated menu, decent food and welcome braziers on a cold day. **Moving on**, several minibuses run daily north to Liping, at least one bus goes via the Liping road to Congjiang, and there are two buses each way to Liping/Sanjiang.

Zhaoxing to Kaili

The easiest road to Kaili heads up to **LIPING** (2hr), famous as the place where the Long Marchers made up their minds to storm Zunyi. While not a traditional town, it's not too unappealing, the streets are lined with trees and the *Baitian Zhaodaisuo* (**❷**) near the central crossroads and **bus station** offers inexpensive, comfy doubles with cable TV. The handful of daily Kaili-bound buses take about eight hours from Liping, travelling southwest through **Rongjiang** (see below); there's also traffic to Sanjiang and Congjiang, and points north on the long road to Sansui and Zhenyuan (see p.785).

A more interesting route heads west from Zhaoxing to Congjiang, Rongjiang and Kaili. You can do this in two ways: either catch a Congjiang-bound bus from Zhaoxing (about 5hr); or walk 7km northwest to **LUOXIANG**, a small, mostly concrete-and-tile place with a big **market** every fifth day, and catch one of the morning minibuses to Congjiang from here (3hr). Either way, the journey passes attractive villages, at least seven drum towers and bridges, and a landscape of broad valleys studded with low limestone bluffs. **Longtu** and **Jitang** are the pick of the places to get off and explore, with formal lodgings at the mid-point town of **Guandong**.

CONGJIANG itself is a drab, relatively large logging town on the Duliu River, with plenty of **accommodation** near the **bus station** – *Yueliang Shan Binguan* (**☎**0855/6418228; **❸**) is a bit dingy and poorly maintained, *Jianghu Lüguan* (**❷**) much cleaner and less pretentious. In common with everywhere else in the region, there are precious few places to eat aside from stir-fry canteens around the station. The town is surrounded by picturesque villages, though – best known is **BASHA**, a Miao village 10km west whose inhabitants grow a long topknot and seem to wear traditionally embroidered clothes, heavy metal jewellery and pleated skirts as a matter of course, not just for festivals.

Heading on, **RONGJIANG** is a reliable two hours away across the mountains, and has a frenetic Sunday **market** where you can watch villagers bargaining the last mao out of a deal. There are comfortable **rooms** at the *Qingfeng Binguan* (❷), beside a small pavilion across from the bus station. From here you can catch a bus **west to Libo** via the small town of Sandu, or it's four hours northwest over steep, thinly settled mountains to Leishan and Kaili. For more about Kaili and the Miao, see pp.777–784.

Nanning

Founded during the Yuan dynasty, **NANNING** was only a medium-sized market town until European traders opened a river route from neighbouring Guangdong in the early twentieth century, starting a period of rapid growth that saw the city supplanting Guilin as the provincial capital. Largely untouched by the civil war and Japanese invasion, it became a centre of supply and command during the **Vietnam War**, when the **Nanning–Hanoi rail line** was used to transport arms shipments via the border town of Pingxiang, 160km away. Nanning saw particularly vicious street fighting after these weapons were looted by rival Red Guard factions during the Cultural Revolution. The military returned for a decade when China and Vietnam came to blows in 1979, but following the resumption of cross-border traffic in the 1990s the city

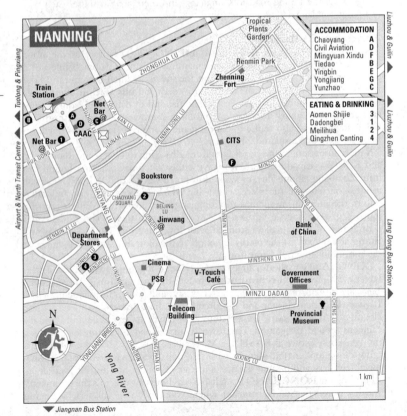

Nanning

Nanning	南宁	nánníng
Chaoyang Square	朝阳广场	cháoyáng guǎngchǎng
Hanoi (Vietnam)	河内	hénèi
Jiangnan bus station	江南汽车站	jiāngnán qìchēzhàn
Langdong bus station	琅东站	lángdōng zhàn
Nanhu Park	南湖公园	nánhú gōngyuán
North Transit Centre	北大客运中心	běidà kèyùn zhōngxīn
Provincial Museum	省博物馆	shěng bówùguǎn
Renmin Park	人民公园	rénmín gōngyuán
Zhonghua Lu bus station	市第二客运中心	dìèr kèyùn zhōngxīn

Accommodation and eating

Aomen Shijie	澳门食街	àomén shíjiē
Chaoyang	朝阳酒店	cháoyáng jiǔdiàn
Civil Aviation	民航饭店	mínháng fàndiàn
Dadongbei	大东北饺子城	dàdōngběi jiǎozichéng
Meilihua	美丽花冰城	měilihuā bīngchéng
Mingyuan Xindu	明园新都酒店	míngyuán xīndū jiǔdiàn
Qingzhen Canting	清真餐厅	qīngzhēn cāntīng
Tiedao	铁道饭店	tiědào fàndiàn
Ying Bin	迎宾饭店	yíngbīn fàndiàn
Yongjiang	邕江宾馆	yōngjiāng bīnguǎn
Yunzhao	运招大酒店	yùnzhāo dàjiǔdiàn

is beginning to capitalize on trade agreements with its neighbour, and recently hosted a meeting of ASEAN, the Southeast Asian trading bloc.

Today, Nanning is a bright, easy-going place with a mild boom-town atmosphere and mix of leafy boulevards, modern architecture and a handful of narrow, colonial-era streets. There's good shopping, decent food, a **museum** strong on regional archeology, and both international and domestic transport connections – in particular, over the nearby **open border with Vietnam**.

Arrival, city transport and accommodation

Well over 5km across, with its downtown area concentrated on the northern bank of the **Yong Jiang**, Nanning is a blandly user-friendly city, its streets dusty, hot and planted with exotic trees. Most of the city's accommodation and attractions are in the vicinity of **Chaoyang Lu**, Nanning's main thoroughfare, which runs for 2km south from the **train station**, through the city centre and down to the **Yongjiang Bridge**. Roughly parallel with Chaoyang Lu but somewhat shorter, easterly **Xinmin Lu** cuts through the more modern part of town, linked to Chaoyang Lu by, amongst others, **Minzhu Lu**, **Minsheng Lu** and **Minzu Dadao**.

Coming from the north or east **by bus** will see you winding up at **Langdong station**, 10km east of the centre on Minzu Dadao – a #6 bus or a taxi (¥25) will get you to Chaoyang Lu. Approaching from the southwest will land you 7km south at **Jiangnan** station, on the #31 bus route to Chaoyang Lu; a taxi will cost ¥20. From the northwest, you'll arrive just 2km from Chaoyang Lu at the **North Transit Centre**, also on the #31 bus route.

The **international airport** is 35km southwest of Nanning, with an **airport bus** (¥15) to the CAAC offices – taking a taxi costs around ¥100. In the city itself, a **taxi** costs ¥7 to hire, and you shouldn't have to pay much more than this for anywhere central.

Apart from destinations within China, including Guilin, Guiyang, Kunming, Guangzhou and Hong Kong, there are also direct **flights** to Bangkok and Hanoi. CAAC (China Southwest) is up near the train station on Chaoyang Lu (℡0771/2095360 or 2431459, ⓦwww.travelsky.com); you can also arrange flights through the CITS (see "Listings" p.758). The airport bus (¥10) leaves from the CAAC office and takes thirty minutes.

There are three main **long-distance bus stations**. The biggest, with departures for east and northern destinations including Beihai, Guiping, and Guilin, as well as Guiyang, is **Langdong station**, 10km out to the east at the end of the number #6 bus route – allow 50 minutes. You can buy tickets for Langdong departures from a booth at the corner of Chaoyang Lu and Huadong Lu; they also have timetables. For destinations around the southwestern border area such as Chongzuo, Ningming, and Pingxiang, as well as Baise, Beihai and Guilin, and inter-provincial buses to Haikou, Guangzhou, and Shenzhen, head 7km south to **Jiangnan station**, on the #31 bus route (around 40 minutes). Jiangnan tickets and timetables can be obtained from a booth on Zhonghua Lu, about 700m west of the train station on the south side of the road. Much closer in, the **North Transit Centre** is about 2km northwest of the train station, also on the #31 bus route, and is of most use for traffic to Baise, Xingyi in Guizhou province, and Kunming. Tickets for direct **buses to Hong Kong** ($HK360) can be bought at the agencies next to the Langdong station booth on Chaoyang Lu.

Where available, you'll find **trains** are a much faster option than the bus. Ticket windows are open 9–11.50am and 12.20–5pm; queues here can be tiring. Services run at least daily northeast to Guilin and central China; southeast to Beihai; northwest via Baise and southwestern Guizhou to Kunming; and southwest via Chongzuo to Tuolong (Ningming) and the Vietnamese border at Pingxiang. The Nanning–Hanoi train also runs every other day, though you still have to get out at Pingxiang, catch a minibus 15km to the border, walk across, and then catch further transport to the Vietnamese railhead at Lang Son – see p.766 for more.

Accommodation

There's plenty of good-value, central accommodation in Nanning for all budgets, and most places also offer at least simple meals.

Chaoyang Corner of Zhonghua Lu & Chaoyang Lu ℡0771/2116388, ⓦwww.cy-hotel.com. A clean hotel with friendly management and a massive permutation of rooms available, from cheap dorms and simple doubles, to more comfy doubles with their own bathrooms. Dorm beds ¥25, ❹

Civil Aviation Chaoyang Lu, between the bus and train stations ℡0771/2099000, ℻2099003. A decent mid-range option, with recently refurbished rooms. The attached restaurant is very reasonable. ❻

Mingyuan Xindu 38 Xinmin Lu ℡0771/2118988, ⓦwww.nn-myxd.com. Almost palatial affair managed by an Overseas Chinese chain, and offers more places to eat than the rest of town combined. ❾

Tiedao Between the train and bus stations on Zhonghua Lu ℡0771/2323188, ℻2422572. Fair value at this railways-run option, though cheaper rooms could use a fresh coat of paint. ❹

Yingbin Diagonally across from the train station, cnr of Chaoyang Lu & Zhonghua Lu ℡0771/2116029, ⓦwww.ybfd.com. Another unpretentious budget option close to the train station, probably the best deal in town – better doubles even come with free Internet. With/without bathroom ❷/❸

Yongjiang Jiangbin Lu ℡0771/2180888, ⓦwww.yjhotel.cn. Set in a mighty 1950s Soviet-style edifice, the last in Nanning, this has recently been revamped into the seriously upmarket league – their suites go for ¥8000 a night – with five-star service and at least three restaurants. ❾

Yunzhao 67 Huadong Lu, on the corner with Suzhou Lu ℡0771/2191918, ℻2191919. Smart, small, almost guesthouse-like hotel; new and so a cut above average for the price. ❺

The City

To get the feel of Nanning's bustle, try wandering around the crowded markets and lanes either west or southeast of Chaoyang Lu. Along with chickens, ducks, turtles and frogs, there's a variety of **tropical fruit**, and the city has some of China's best **longan** (a bit like a spherical lychee). **Chaoyang Lu** itself is mostly modern, colourfully lit up with fairy lights at night. Halfway along at the corner of Renmin Dong Lu, **Chaoyang Square** is an area of tidy paving, park benches and shady trees, popular with *tai ji* enthusiasts, chess players, amateur musicians, groups dancing to country and western tunes, and anyone after a breath of air. West from here and parallel with Chaoyang Lu, pedestrianized **Xingning Lu** and its offshoots sport the city's most attractive older facades, lit with red lanterns around the lunar New Year and always near critical mass with shoppers orbiting between clothing stores.

For a bit of space head to **Renmin Park** (¥2), a couple of square kilometres of waters and woodland about a twenty-minute walk east of the train station on Renmin Dong Lu. Stone causeways zigzag across the lake between islets inhabited by willows and chess players, while on the eastern side, steps ascend to **Zhenning Fort**, a defensive structure built in 1917 to house a six-inch German naval cannon – a serious piece of firepower in such a commanding position, with clear views of the whole city. The **tropical plants garden** (¥2) below has a medicinal herb plot and a carefully constructed undergrowth of philodendrons, palms, heliconias and giant "elephant-ear" taro, bird-nest ferns and cycads – its private recesses are popular with young couples.

The Provincial Museum

Essential viewing for anyone heading southwest to the Zuo River, the **Provincial Museum** on Gucheng Lu (bus #6 from Chaoyang Lu; daily 8.30am–noon & 2.30–5pm; ¥8) provides an insight into the enigmatic **Dongson culture**. Sophisticated metalworkers, the Dongson flourished over two thousand years ago in the Guangxi–Yunnan–Vietnam border area, and their works were ultimately traded as far afield as Burma, Thailand and Indonesia. The characteristic Dongson artefact is a squat, narrow-waisted **bronze drum**, finely chased with lively designs of birds, mythical animals, cattle, dancers and stars, sometimes incorporating dioramas on the lid or human and **frog** figurines sitting on the rim (suitably for a drum, frogs are associated with the thunder god in Zhuang mythology). They seem to have originated as storage vessels, though according to a Ming historian, the drums became a symbol of power: "Those who possess bronze drums are chieftains, and the masses obey them; those who have two or three drums can style themselves king." Drums appeared during the Warring States period and were cast locally right up until the late Qing dynasty; their ceremonial use survives among groups of Zhao, Yi, Miao and Yao in China, and on the eastern Indonesian island of Alor.

The museum has dozens of well-preserved varieties excavated in Guangxi and elsewhere across the region, including a rather gruesome example from Yunnan whose lid sports a diorama of crowds attending what appears to be a human sacrifice – note the "king" up on the platform, surrounded by drums. Check out the museum grounds too, with bamboo and palms growing between full-sized wooden buildings in regional architectural styles: a Zhuang rural theatre, Dong bridge and Miao houses, which are all put to use by Nanning's various communities during festivals.

Eating, drinking and nightlife

Though there are plenty of places to snack in Nanning, real restaurants are a bit thin on the ground. The best place for inexpensive buns, dumplings, noodles, grilled chicken wings, steamed packets of lotus leaf-wrapped *zongzi*, and basic stir-fries are at the handful of open-fronted canteens either side of the *Yingbin* hotel on the corner of Chaoyang Lu and Zhonghua Lu. Aside from the places below, hotels all have restaurants too, mostly serving Cantonese fare – including morning *dim sum* (see p.601). Western fast-food chains are all grouped in the new plaza development north of the corner of Chaoyang Lu and Minzu Dadao.

Aomen Shijie Entrances on Minsheng Lu and Xinhua Lu. One of those popular places serving snacks and dishes from all over the country in smart canteen-like surrounds, with a heavy bias towards Cantonese fare – including a host of dumplings, roast meats and quick-fried greens. You get a card, which is marked by the waitress according to what you order from the counter (or photographs). Dishes ¥5–25.

Dadongbei Cnr Chaoyang Lu and Huadong Lu. *Jiaozi* with big range of stuffings, ordered by the *liang* (50g), cold dishes such as spiced cucumber, spinach with peanuts, whole roasted aubergine, glass noodles, sliced beef with soy dressing, and preserved eggs, plus mammoth servings of mutton. Everything seems to have a hint of aniseed too. A meal for two, plus beer, comes in around ¥35.

Meilihua (aka **Mayflower**) Cnr of Minzhu Lu and Chaoyang Square. English menu, noodle soups, hotpots, fried rice, steak platters, and florid desserts – including refreshing "snow ice", a Southeast Asian treat of shaved ice drizzled with luridly coloured syrups – combined with low prices make this a favourite with expats as well as locals. There's another, more basic, branch near the station on Zhonghua Lu. Most dishes under ¥15.

Qingzhen Canting Minsheng Lu. Inexpensive Muslim restaurant, with a soup-noodle canteen in the front and a dining hall behind. Their English menu is pretty comprehensive; the lemon duck, marinated cucumber, and chicken soup with lily buds are tasty and well presented. Expect to pay ¥25 a head in the dining hall; canteen dishes are mostly ¥5–10.

Listings

Banks and exchange The main Bank of China (foreign exchange Mon–Fri 8–11.30am & 2.30–5.30pm) is on Gucheng Lu, but there are smaller branches with ATMs all over town – the most convenient on Chaoyang Lu being just south of Huadong Lu.

Books Nanning's Foreign Language Bookstore is on the ground floor of the elderly market complex overlooking Chaoyang Park on Minzhu Lu. The surprisingly large selection of pulp paperbacks, as well as English classics, some translated Chinese literature, magazines, maps and art books is above average. The top floors of the building are given over to CD and DVD shops.

Cinema While away a wet afternoon at the multi-screen complex in the new plaza development at the southern end of Chaoyang Lu.

English corner The V-Touch Café on Xinmin Lu hosts a get-together every Saturday from 9–11am for local Chinese and students who want to practise their English with any foreigners who turn up.

Hospital The City First Hospital (Shiyi Yiyuan) is southeast of the centre along Qixing Lu.

Internet access There are several Net bars up around the train station area charging ¥2 an hour – see the Nanning map for their locations.

Mail and telephones The most central post office is on Suzhou Lu (8am–7pm); you can make overseas calls from the main telecom building on Minzu Dadao.

PSB On the roundabout at the south end of Chaoyang Lu. Foreign Affairs Department open Mon–Fri 9am–noon & 2–5pm.

Shopping Nanning is a great place to shop for clothes, either at the three department stores full of good-quality, low-price attire at the junction of Chaoyang Lu and Xinhua Lu or at the brand-label stores along Xingning Lu, such as Giordano, Baleno Meters/Bonwe and Yishion, and Hum Phry. The Nanning Antique Store, next to the museum, has a touristy and expensive selection of batiks, teapots, chops, paintings and jade, on two floors.

Tour agents CITS, 40 Xinmin Lu (daily 8am–noon & 3–5.30pm; ☎0771/284258, ⊛www .citsgx.com) have extensive numbers of staff and offices but take little interest in independent travellers, with the exception of arranging Vietnamese visas (¥450, four working days; you'll need to provide a passport and passport photo). Booths between CAAC and Huadong Lu sell tickets for tours to the cliff paintings at Hua Shan (¥180 day-return) and Detian waterfall (¥180 day-return, ¥380 overnight including accommodation).

East of Nanning

East of Nanning, the country is unremittingly rural and the towns – such as the rail nexus of **Liuzhou**, or **Wuzhou**, right on the Guangdong border – hold little of interest to visitors. The main geographic feature here is, for once, not hills but the **Xi River**, a tiny section of a waterway which, under various names, runs from Yunnan, across central China, and finally flows into the Pearl River and so down to Guangzhou and Hong Kong. The surrounding countryside doesn't look too badly off today, but during the 1840s this corner of China was destitute, wracked by famine and the raising of new taxes to pay off indemnities levied by Britain following the Opium War. Rebellion flared across the region, culminating in the **Taiping Uprising**, a movement which started near the riverside town of **Guiping**, 150km east of Nanning, and ultimately involved millions of participants in the foundation of a rebel capital at Nanjing (see p.436). More recently, a moral famine during the 1960s saw the region involved in one of the more shocking episodes of China's recent history – see the "Cultural Cannibalism" box overleaf. The other place of interest in the area lies 150km southeast of Nanning at **Beihai**, Guangxi's major coastal port and transit point for traffic to Hainan Island.

Guiping and Jintian

GUIPING is a poor, underdeveloped, but busy town at the junction of the Xi and Yu rivers, three hours by bus (¥50) from Nanning's Langdong station. The town centres around **Guangchang**, a public square at the intersection of east–west-oriented Renmin Lu and south-pointing Guinan Lu, where you'll also find the **long-distance bus station**.

East of Nanning		
Guiping	桂平	guìpíng
Changtai Binguan	长泰宾馆	chángtài bīnguǎn
Dianzi	电子宾馆	diànzǐ bīnguǎn
Guiping Binguan	桂平宾馆	guìpíng bīnguǎn
Xi Shan	西山	xīshān
Jintian	金田	jīntián
Taiping Museum	太平博物馆	tàipíng bówùguǎn
Taiping Tianguo	太平天国	tàipíng tiānguó
Beihai	北海	běihǎi
Beihai Binguan	北海宾馆	běihǎi bīnguǎn
Beihai sand beach	北海银滩	běihǎi yíntān
Hainan ferry port	北海港客运站	běihǎigǎng kèyùnzhàn
Taoyuan Dajiudian	桃园大酒店	táoyuán dàjiǔdiàn
Waisha harbour	外沙内港中山公园	wàishā nèigǎng
Zhongshan Park	中山公园	zhōngshān gōngyuán

Cultural cannibalism

It hardly seems credible that in the summer of 1968 – while students were demonstrating in Paris and the anti-war movement was at its height in Washington, DC – the people of the otherwise insignificant rural town of **Wuxuan**, 70km northwest of Guiping, were eating each other. The details are documented in a secret but thorough report compiled by the county government in 1987, which listed the "different forms of eating human flesh"; taboos were eroded by degrees until students ate their teachers and human flesh was being cheerfully served at banquets with wine. When news of the events reached Beijing, the army was swiftly sent in to remove Wuxuan's Red Guard factions and the **ritual cannibalism** ceased – but only after five hundred people had already been eaten. The report listed by name 27 local Party cadres who had been expelled from the Party for cannibalism, as well as a large number of peasant members, only a small proportion of whom were ever jailed. Most of the participants live and prosper in Wuxuan today.

The Chinese government has never admitted that these grotesque events ever occurred, and the details first reached the outside world through the efforts of the dissident writer Zheng Yi. They've since been corroborated in the book *Real China: From Cannibalism to Karaoke* by British journalist John Gittings, who visited Wuxuan in 1995 and spoke to witnesses. These events were certainly part of the wider political conflicts that tore China apart during the Cultural Revolution, but, as far as is known, only in Guangxi did this lead to the killing and eating of "class enemies" – those branded as political undesirables during the Revolution. Certainly there was a tradition, in poorer parts of China, of eating people during times of famine, and so-called "revenge cannibalism" was also noted by the philosopher Menicius in the fourth century BC, and features several times in the fifteenth-century popular novel *Outlaws of the Marsh* (see p.1224). Whatever the answer, an open investigation of the crimes is unlikely during the lifetime of the current regime.

The Chinese come to Guiping to see **Xi Shan**, a typical formalized sacred mountain right on the western outskirts – catch a bus (7am–4.30pm) from Guangchang square or simply walk for twenty minutes along Renmin Xi Lu to the gates (¥15 entry). Far tamer than the country's great holy peaks, Xi Shan is a comfortable introduction to the Chinese obsession with landscaping natural phenomena to turn them into places of pilgrimage and weekend excursions. The two-hour hike to the top follows paved paths leading off into a forest of fish-tailed palms and huge pines, past the usual run of temples – near the entrance, **Xishi Si** has a **vegetarian restaurant** open for lunch – and up to a summit with hazy views of the two rivers snaking across a watery flatland to join at Guiping. **Tea** aficionados should sample the famous Xi Shan brand; rumour has it that temple-bought leaves are superior to anything you'll find in Guiping's shops.

Guiping's **accommodation** includes several hostels around the bus station, though they're not keen on foreign custom. Failing these, there are threadbare rooms at the *Dianzi Binguan* (dorm beds ¥30, rooms with shower and, if you're lucky, functioning air conditioning ❷), on the west side of the square; a few hundred metres east along Renmin Lu, the elderly *Guiping Fandian* (☎0775/3369292, ℱ3380184; ❹) and brand-new *Changtai Binguan* (☎0775/3369988, ℱ3369000; ❺) are more expensive but better value for money – the only **restaurants** are here too, with sandpot and noodle stalls at the bus station as alternatives.

Jintian and Taiping Tianguo

For Taiping historians, Guiping is simply a stop on the way to **JINTIAN**, about 25km and thirty minutes to the north. Catch a minibus (which run whenever full; ¥3) from the western side of Guangchang square. You get dropped off at Jiantian's single, north-pointing street; look for a concrete archway to the west and follow this road for 4km to a small wooded hill and **Taiping Tianguo** (9am–4.30pm, ¥15), the Taiping Uprising's first headquarters – a motorcycle-taxi costs around ¥5. A red sandstone statue of a very heroic-looking Hong Xiuquan, the Taiping leader, faces you as you enter; to the right are the three-metre-high, rammed earth defensive walls of their **barracks**, now a bit worn down and overgrown with pine trees. In the centre of this long rectangular enclosure is the rather ambiguous "pledge rock", supposedly where Hong declared his insurrection to be underway on 11 January 1851. There's also a **museum** here, to the left of the main entrance, though the blurred photos, old coins, and rusty weapons throw little light on what became the world's largest civil revolt – as is often the case, it's the site associations, rather than tangible relics, that justify the journey. Buses run back to Guiping at least until 5pm.

Beihai

BEIHAI, a pleasant town on the Beibu Gulf, is Guangxi's sole seaport. It got going in the late nineteenth century when the British signed the Yantai Trading Agreement with the Qing court, and grew swiftly as Europeans set up schools, churches, offices and banks. A bland four-hour train ride from Nanning or an overnight ride on the **ferry from Hainan Island**, attempts through the 1990s to turn Beihai into a trading centre for the southwest seem to have faltered, leaving the original core of narrow colonial lanes and buildings surrounded by a mesh of pointlessly wide new roads and vacant high-rises.

While the only reason to visit Beihai is in transit to Hainan, there's no problem filling in time between connections. The older part of town is along the seafront and on **Zhongshan Lu**, where mouldering colonial buildings add to the sleepily tropical atmosphere. It's best in the morning when the fresh catches arrive, and there's a fabulous **fish market** here selling every type and part of sea life imaginable. Hop on a #2 bus heading west down **Haijiao Lu** from the end of Zhongshan Lu and you end up a couple of kilometres away at **Waisha harbour**, packed with scores of wooden-hulled junks, motorized and sailless, but otherwise traditionally designed. Most of the vessels here belong to the community of thirteen thousand refugee "**boat people**" living in the adjacent UN-sponsored village. They were victims of an attempt by the Vietnamese authorities to remove ethnic Chinese from their territory, a major cause of the 1979 war between China and Vietnam. China's reciprocal group are the **Jing**, ethnic Vietnamese who settled islands off Beihai in the sixteenth century.

Alternatively, **Beihai Sand Beach** (¥30) is about 5km south of the centre at the end of the #3 bus route (¥3) from Sichuan Lu, a long, broad stretch of grey sand where you can organize a spin in a speedboat or a beach buggy, or just roam – swimming isn't perhaps such a great idea, given that the city lacks a sewerage treatment plant. In all, Hainan's beaches are far better – and free to enter – so don't set aside an extra day for this one if you're in transit.

Practicalities

A hugely sprawling grid of right-angled streets, Beihai is so positioned on a broad peninsula that there is sea to the north and south of town. The centre is marked by **Zhongshan Park**, at the intersection of north–south oriented Beijing Lu, and Beibuwan Lu, which crosses it at right angles. **Arrival points** are widely spread across the city from here: the **train station** is 3km south at the end of Beijing Lu – catch #2 to Zhongshan Park; the **Hainan ferry port** and ticket office is 4km west along Haijiao Lu, also on the #2 bus route; while the **long-distance bus station** is 500m east of the park on Beibuwan Lu (bus #7). **Taxis** cost ¥7 to hire; expect twice this to get between the train and ferry terminals.

One block west of the park, Beibuwan Lu intersects with Sichuan Lu (down which the #3 bus runs south to the beach); 100m south is the **post office**, while the same distance west is the **Bank of China**. Department stores fill the area, and a small booth at the southwestern side of the intersection sells plane, train and ferry **tickets**.

For **accommodation**, try the elderly but reasonable-value *Taoyuan Dajiudian* (ⓣ0779/2020919, ⓕ2020520; ❶), down a lane behind the Xinhua bookstore opposite the bus station on Beibuwan Lu; or the surprisingly inexpensive, colonial-style *Beihai Binguan* (ⓣ0779/2080880, ⓕ2023285; ❷), a short walk west of the bus station on Beibu Lu. **Places to eat** include the string of cheap and filling Cantonese diners east of the bus station – look for the roast meats hanging up in the window – or try the cheap, hole-in-the-wall **seafood** restaurants beside the ferry terminal.

Leaving, there are afternoon ferries to Hainan's capital, Haikou (10hr; seats ¥55; dorms ¥101, very basic private cabins ¥149 per person); all toilets are shared, and hot water urns and a snack shop are the only sources of refreshment. There are also daily trains to Nanning (3hr 15min; ¥55), and buses as far afield as Guilin, Nanning, Baise and Guangzhou.

West to Yunnan and Vietnam

The region **west of Nanning** forms the Zhuang heartlands, consisting of scattered hills surrounded by seas of sugar cane and bananas up against the borders of Vietnam and Yunnan. Unlike many other of southwestern China's ethnic groups, however, there's not much visible difference between the Zhuang and the Han, at least in terms of colourful clothing and festivals, and the towns here are poor and doggedly functional. It's an interesting area nonetheless, especially southwest towards the **Vietnamese border crossing** at **Pingxiang**, where extensive rock art at **Hua Shan** along the Zuo River proves that Zhuang culture goes back a long way; and where you can see the endangered white-headed langur at **Chongzuo Environmental Park**. North of here, there's outstanding scenery at the **Detian Waterfall**, while the historic town of **Baise** is worth a brief look if you're heading up into southwestern Guizhou and Yunnan provinces.

The area has good transport connections: Baise, **Tuolong** (jumping-off point for Hua Shan) and Pingxiang are all easily accessible by train – and, less comfortably, by bus – from Nanning. The Environmental Park and Detian can both be reached by bus, though the latter requires a bit of effort and several changes of vehicles.

Baise

BAISE is a busy, small city set on the junction of the Dengbi and You rivers 220km northwest of Nanning on the Nanning–Kunming rail line. Historically, Baise's fame dates back to 1929: no Chinese government could then seriously lay claim to this remote region, but **Deng Xiaoping** found thousands of willing converts amongst Baise's Zhuang population when he arrived in September with a CCP mandate to spread the Communist message, and on December 11 he declared the formation of the **You Jiang Soviet** here in what became

West to Yunnan and Vietnam

Baise	百色	*bǎisè*
Baise Memorial	百色起义烈士纪念碑	*bǎisè qǐyì lièshì jìniànbēi*
Guixi Dajiudian	桂西大酒店	*guìxī dàjiǔdiàn*
Jindu Dajiudian	金都大酒店	*jīndū dàjiǔdiàn*
Jinfenghua	金丰华咖啡	*jīnfēnghuá kāfēi*
Uprising Museum	粤东会馆	*yuèdōng huìguǎn*
You River Minorities Museum	右江民族博物馆	*yòujiāng mínzú bówùguǎn*
Daxin	大新	*dàxīn*
Chongzuo	崇左	*chóngzuǒ*
Chongzuo Ecology Park	崇左生态 公园	*chóngzuǒ shēngtài gōngyuán*
White-headed langur	白头叶猴	*báitóuyèhóu*
Detian Waterfall	得天瀑布	*détiān pùbù*
Detian Binguan	得天宾馆	*détiān bīnguǎn*
Detian Luguan	得天旅馆	*détiān lǚguǎn*
Detian Shanzhuang	得天山庄	*détiān shānzhuāng*
Hurun	湖润	*húrùn*
Jingxi	靖西	*jìngxī*
Ningming	宁明	*níngmíng*
Pingxiang	凭祥	*píngxiáng*
Friendship Pass	友谊关	*yǒuyíguān*
Hanoi (Vietnam)	河内	*hénèi*
Jinxiangyu Dajiudian	金祥玉大酒店	*jīnxiángyù dàjiǔdiàn*
Shuolong	硕龙	*shuòlóng*
Hongle Lüguan	鸿乐旅馆	*hónglè lǚguǎn*
Tuolong	驮龙	*tuólóng*
Hua Shan	花山	*huāshān*
Zuo River	左江	*zuǒjiāng*
Xialei	下雷	*xiàléi*

known as the **Baise Uprising**. Over-ambitious attempts to raise an army and secure the province against the Nationalists, however, saw the movement falter rapidly, though survivors eventually managed to join up with Mao's Jiangxi Soviet during the Long March in 1934.

The city's **Uprising museum** (8am–5pm; ¥5) is just west of the river on Jiefang Jie, housed in a nineteenth-century Guangdong merchants' guildhall. The building is, in fact, very southern Chinese, with two airy atria flanked by smaller rooms and galleries, built of grey brick and prettied up by some decorative woodwork above the doorways and elaborate roof-ridge ceramic friezes of theatrical costume dramas, made in Foshan near Guangzhou. Aside from a new bronze statue of Deng in the middle of the first atrium, there's almost nothing to betray the building's function as the Uprising's headquarters and barracks, and the intent behind current renovations seems to be to restore it to its Qing-dynasty appearance. Across the river, the revolution is recorded in more concrete terms atop of a broad stairway at the **Baise Memorial**, a stumpy, sharp-tipped spire surrounded by heroic sculptures and an ornamental garden, the latter offering fine views over the city and rivers. Two minutes beyond the memorial, the **You River Minorities Museum** (¥3) provides insight into Zhuang settlement of the region. There are heavy stone tools and photos of cave paintings, including a strikingly fierce creature with dragon's head and cloven paws; bronze drums and an almost comical equestrian statue; textiles featuring loomed cloth and intricate embroideries and tie-dyeing; all rounded out by photos.

Practicalities

Baise is a sprawling place overall, but the centre is concentrated along a kilo-metre-long strip of Zhongshan Lu, with 500-metre-long Xiangyan Lu running north off this to the **bus station**. There's traffic through the day from here to Nanning; minibuses every twenty minutes south to Jingxi, en route to the Detian Waterfall; and daily services to Xingyi in Guizhou province, Guilin and Guangzhou. The **train station** is isolated 5km east, connected to town by bus #1 (¥1); there are several services daily to Nanning (though the bus takes the same time), Xingyi and Kunming.

Baise's best deal on **accommodation** is at the *Jindu Dajiudian* (☏0776/2881188, ℻2881193; ❺), right next to the bus station – the older building's rooms are quiet, however, and often go for a fraction of the listed price. Nearby hostels won't take foreigners, so for anything cheaper, head down to the elderly *Guixi Dajiudian* (❷), at the junction of Zhongshan Lu and Xiangyang Lu. Both places have **restaurants**, with the usual run of cheap eats at the bus station area canteens – an alternative is the *Jinfenghua*, a café-restaurant halfway down Xiangyang Lu, where you can get real coffee, beef and mushrooms steamed with rice in a bamboo tube, and indifferent Southeast Asian curries.

Detian Waterfall

Straddling the Vietnamese border 150km due west of Nanning, or the same distance south by road from Baise, **Detian Waterfall** is worth the trip not just for the falls themselves, but also because it draws you into the Zhuang heart-lands – a world of dark karst hills, grubby towns, water buffalo wallowing in green paddy fields, and Zhuang farmers in broad-sleeved pyjamas and conical hats. Transport operates on a leaves-when-full principle, so you might spend longer on the trip than planned.

The falls

The **Detian falls** repay the effort of reaching them in unexpected ways. The road there winds along a wide river valley to a small congregation of souvenir stalls and **accommodation** at the *Detian Binguan* and *Detian Lüguan* who both offer clean, comfortable rooms (¥80). Just uphill is the **entrance** (¥30), and past here the upmarket *Detian Shanzhuang* (☏0771/3773570, ⓦwww.detian .com; ❼) with views across the river into Vietnam; and then you're looking at the falls themselves, a delightful set of cataracts broader than their thirty-metre height and at their best after the spring rains, framed by peaks and fields. Paths lead down to the base of the falls past a series of pools and bamboo groves; at the bottom you can hire a **bamboo raft** and be punted over to straddle the mid-river borderline. The best part, however, is to follow the road along the top to its end in a field, where you'll find a **stone post** proclaiming the Sino-Vietnamese frontier in French and Chinese, along with a bizarre **border market** – a clutch of trestle tables laden with Vietnamese sweets, cigarettes and stamps in the middle of nowhere. Despite locals crossing as they please, don't try to go any further: Chinese police will spring out from nowhere and stop you.

Practicalities

Tours run to the falls **from Nanning** (see Nanning "Listings", p.759); travelling independently you need to catch a bus from the North Transit Centre to **DAXIN** (3hr; ¥15), from whose bus station there are regular minibuses to **Shuolong** (¥6; 1hr), the nearest settlement to the falls – and, if they get enough customers or you're willing to negotiate an extra fee, to Detian itself. **From Baise**, your first target is **JINGXI** (3hr; ¥35), a strangely stretched, dusty market town surrounded by flat fields and limestone hills which make for some interesting walks. Baise buses wind up at the **north bus station**, from where it's a kilometre through town to the **south station** and minibuses for the ninety-minute ride to tiny **Hurun** (¥5), where you need to change vehicles again for **Xialei** (¥2), a smaller, dustier replay of Jingxi. From here, more minibuses run until mid-afternnon to Shuolong (¥4), or hire a motor-rickshaw (¥15).

    SHUOLONG is a large village under a vertical cliff overhanging the marketplace where traffic running between Daxin and Xialei congregates. A motor-rickshaw for the last 15km to the falls from here costs around ¥10; if you get stuck at Shuolong for the night, *Hongle Lüguan* (beds ¥20, ❷) at the marketplace is the best **place to stay**, with a couple of basic restaurants opposite.

To Vietnam: Chongzuo, Hua Shan and Pingxiang

The **Vietnamese border crossing** lies about 170km southwest of Nanning beyond the town of **Pingxiang**, though it's well worth spending time on the route, taking in the **Chongzuo Ecology Park**'s monkeys, and making the trip up the Zuo River to **Hua Shan**'s prehistoric **rock paintings**. Jumping-off points for these places lie along the Nanning-Pingxiang rail line, with a **train** departing Nanning each morning to the border – though there are also plenty of buses through the day from the Jiangnan station.

Chongzuo Ecology Park

Chongzuo Ecology Park (¥40), a small spread of limestone hills and flat valleys, was created to protect the endangered and endemic **white-headed langur**, whose entire population numbers just 700 animals. The main reason for their decline, which has plummeted since the 1980s, is deforestation for new agricultural land. Their plight was first recognized by renowned panda specialist **Professor Pan** of Beijing University, who turned his attention here in 1996 and set up a permanent study programme, informing villagers of the monkeys' plight, and compensating them for the reserve's creation (which deprived them of potential farmland) by persuading local government to improve schools, water supplies and infrastructure in the area.

    There are 250 monkeys in the reserve, and your chance of seeing some – albeit at a distance, as they spend much of their time bouncing around cliff tops – is good. They form groups of around ten individuals, headed by a single adult male; the black-bodied adults have white heads and tail tips, and spend much of their time eating leaves (though they also like fruit and flowers). The babies, however, are golden all over, darkening during their first two years.

Before turning up, note that this is not a monkey theme park, but primarily a research base. They're happy to have visitors, but the park is fairly wild (cobras are common), and summers are exceedingly hot and wet. The reserve is 15km southeast of **CHONGZUO** city, which is a bit over halfway down the rail line between Nanning and Pingxiang. It's easier, however, to get here **by bus** from Nanning's Jiangnan station (¥35; ninety minutes) – ask the driver to drop you at the park gates. Alternatively, minibuses (¥5) run from Chongzuo's bus station past the park until late afternoon. **Accommodation** at the park is in comfortable air-conditioned cabins (¥100 per person), and they provide ample Chinese meals at around ¥50 per person a day – there's also room to **camp**, if you have the gear, but pack a **flashlight** either way. Staff act as guides, with best viewing times at dawn and dusk, and about 5km of walking trails to explore. For more **information**, contact Mr Qin, the park manager (☎0771/7930222), or ⓔbill@trax2.com. **Moving on**, flag down a minibus from outside the park to Chongzuo, from where there are buses through the day back to Nanning, or on to Tuolong or Ningming (for Hua Shan), and Pingxiang.

Hua Shan and the Zuo River

Set in a beautifully isolated spot where tall karst peaks flank the **Zuo**, the southwest's main river, **Hua Shan**'s waterfront cliffs are daubed with thousands of enigmatic figures believed to be connected with the local Zhuang culture of some 2000 years ago. The main access is by boat from **TUOLONG**, a single-street rail stop for the nearby town of **Ningming**, about two-thirds of the way to Pingxiang from Nanning. You can take a **tour** here from Nanning (see p.759), but it's simple to arrange yourself: if nobody grabs you when you get off the train at Tuolong, walk out of the station and down the street to the river, where you'll find a bridge. Sampans moor up underneath here (there's also a small boatyard), and ask about ¥80 for the run upstream to Hua Shan – allow at least five hours for the return trip, including time viewing the rock art.

It's a placid journey up the Zuo – buffalo wallow in the shallows, people fish from wooden rafts and tend family plots, and the banks are thick with spindly branched kapok trees, flowering red in April. Mountains spring up after a while, flat-faced and sheer by the river, and it's here you'll see the first painted figures, red, stick-like markings, though most are very faded or smeared with age. The boat docks just short of Hua Shan, where you pay the **entrance fee** (¥13) before walking along a track to the paintings. Nobody has worked out a definitive interpretation of the 1900 sharply posed figures, but they include drummers and dancers, dogs and cattle, a dragon-boat race, men with arms bent upwards, a "king" with a sword, and just two women, long-haired and pregnant. The designs are similar to those decorating the Dongson drums, and there's little doubt that they were produced by the same culture, currently identified with the Zhuang people. A few Bronze-Age weapons have also been found here.

Heading on, there's currently only one train a day in each direction from Tuolong, so you'll probably need to head 5km to **NINGMING** (¥1 by three-wheeler), a ghastly market town of cheap concrete construction drowned in exhaust fumes. Regular buses run from Ningming until around 4pm back to Nanning or on to Pingxiang – if you can't get out there are several cheap, nondescript places to stay around the bus station.

Pingxiang and the border crossing

Surrounded by jutting karst hills, **PINGXIANG** is a small, bustling trading town and railhead for the Vietnamese border crossing, 15km away. The **train station** is about 3km outside town on the border road; the **bus station** is in the centre of town on mainstreet Bei Da Lu. Gaggles of motor-rickshaws descend on new arrivals, the drivers engaging in Ben-Hur-like races down to the border – try for around ¥10.

You shouldn't really need to stay in Pingxiang, but almost every building within 100m of the bus station on Bei Da Lu offers **accommodation**: hostels ask ¥15–30 per person; while the *Jinxiangyu Dajiudian* (☎0771/8521303; ❸) is a typically clean, functional hotel, and gives massive discounts. There's a huge produce **market** behind the bus station, a **Bank of China** on Bei Da Lu, and cheap places to eat everywhere. Heading **back to Nanning**, the train currently leaves at 3.20pm – stopping at Tuolong and Chongzuo – with buses running the same route between 7am and 7pm.

The **border crossing**, known here as **Friendship Pass**, is worth a trip even if you're not heading to Vietnam. It's set in a natural gap through a series of steep cliffs and hills all wooded with conifers and bamboo, thick enough to harbour at least one **tiger** – the first spotted in thirty years was seen nearby in May 2002. The Chinese side is marked by lines of imperious black cars with tinted windows, trucks loaded with vehicle chassis, a defunct French colonial Customs House built in 1914, and a huge Chinese **gate tower**. A Ming-era defensive **stone wall** runs off up into the hills to the north of here, which you can follow for a short way; just remember that this is a border area. Back down at the gate tower, walk under the arch and the **customs** are straight ahead. Assuming you have a valid visa, entering Vietnam shouldn't be too complicated, though the border guards examine all documents minutely. The Vietnamese town on the far side is **Dong Dang**, where there's further transport 5km south to **Lang Son**, the railhead for Hanoi.

Guizhou

A traditional saying describes **Guizhou** as a land where there are "no three days without rain, no three hectares without a mountain, and no three coins in any pocket". Superficially this is accurate: Guizhou records the highest rainfall in China and has a poverty ensured by more than eighty percent of its land being covered in untillable mountains or leached limestone soils. The province's recent history is none too happy either, though Guizhou's many **ethnic groups** were, for a long while, left pretty much to themselves. Chinese influence was established here around 100 BC, but it wasn't until the government began settling Han migrants in the province during the seventeenth century that the locals began to fight back, resistance culminating in the **Miao Uprising** of 1854–73, which rivalled the contemporary Taiping insurrection in terms of chaos and bloodshed. Sixty years later the region still hadn't recovered: Red Army soldiers passing through Guizhou in the 1930s found people working naked in the fields and an economy based on opium, and it's only in the last decade that Guizhou's population has exceeded that prior to the uprising.

This being said, ethnic identity and romantic landscapes have become marketable commodities these days in China, and Guizhou is beginning to capitalize on its two major assets. The province's most visible minority groups are the many branches of **Miao**, concentrated in the southeast around **Kaili**; and the **Bouyei**, who are based around the provincial capital, **Guiyang**, and the westerly town of **Anshun**. The Miao in particular indulge in a huge number of **festivals**, some of which attract tens of thousands of participants and are worth any effort to experience. There is also an accomplished artistic tradition to investigate, notably some unusual architecture and exquisite textiles. As for **scenery**, there are truly spectacular **limestone caverns** at **Longgong** and **Zhijin**, both accessed from Anshun; impressive **waterfalls** at **Huangguoshu** – again near Anshun – and **Chishui**, right up on the northern border with Sichuan; Guizhou's single holy mountain, **Fanjing Shan**, reached through the northeastern town of **Tongren**; and everywhere terraced hills, dotted with small villages which tempt hikers. Naturalists will also want to clock up rare **black-necked cranes**, which winter along the northwestern border with Yunnan at **Caohai Lake**.

While Guizhou's often shambolic towns are definitely not a high point of a trip to the region, Guiyang is comfortable enough, and conveniently central to the province. A couple of other places worth a visit in their own right are the historic northern city of **Zunyi**, which is steeped in Long March lore; and the atypically pleasant town of **Zhenyuan**, over on the eastern side of the province, which features some antique buildings squeezed along a beautiful stretch of river.

Guiyang and around

GUIYANG lies in a valley basin, encircled by a range of hills which hems in the city and concentrates its traffic pollution. Established as a capital during the Ming dynasty, Guiyang received little attention until the early 1950s, when the Communist government brought in the rail line and filled the centre with heavy monuments and drab, rectangular apartment blocks. These are gradually being cleared, though enough remain to create something of a patchwork effect as they rub shoulders with glossy new high-rises and department stores, all intercut by a web of wide roads and flyovers. While the result may not be one of China's most beautiful cities – being also overcrowded and glaringly provincial with cheap market stalls clogging the main streets every evening – it's a friendly place, whose unexpected few antique buildings and a surprisingly wild park lend a bit of character. There's enough in Guiyang to fill a day in transit – including a much-neglected Provincial Museum – though it's worth extra time making an easy side-trip to the ancient garrison town of **Qingyan**.

Arrival, city transport and accommodation

Central Guiyang is a concentrated couple of square kilometres around the narrow **Nanming River**, with the downtown area focused along Zhonghua Lu, which runs south through the centre into Zunyi Lu, crosses the river and continues for another kilometre before terminating at the new **train station**. In the large square outside you'll find **taxis** (¥10 to hire), and a **city bus terminus** ahead to the east: two useful services which will get you close to most accommodation are #1, which goes along Zunyi Lu and Zhonghua Lu, turning west along Beijing Lu and back to the train station down Ruijin Lu; and bus #2, which does the same route in reverse.

Guiyang's **airport** lies 15km east of town, a ¥50 taxi ride to the centre. There are several **long-distance bus stations**: coming from anywhere could see you arriving at the main long-distance bus station, west of the centre on Yan'an Lu; from Kaili, Anshun or Zunyi you'll probably arrive at or near the southerly

Guiyang and around

Guiyang
Guiyang	贵阳	*guìyáng*
Cuiwei Yuan	粹惟园	*cuìwéi yuán*
Hebin bus depot	河滨客运站	*hébīn kèyùnzhàn*
Hongfu Si	弘福寺	*hóngfú sì*
Jiaxiu Lou	甲秀楼	*jiǎxiù lóu*
Main bus station	贵阳客运站	*guìyáng kèyùnzhàn*
Provincial Museum	省博物馆	*shěng bówùguǎn*
Qiangling Shan	黔灵山	*qiánlíng shān*
Qianming Si	黔明寺	*qiánmíng sì*
Renmin Plaza	人民广场	*rénmín guǎngchǎng*
Tiyu bus station	体育馆客运站	*tǐyùguǎn kèyùnzhàn*
Wenchang Ge	文昌阁	*wénchāng gé*

Accommodation
Hebin	河滨饭店	*hébīn fàndiàn*
Holiday Inn	神奇假日酒店	*shénqí jiàrì jiǔdiàn*
Jiaoyuan	教苑宾馆	*jiàoyuàn bīnguǎn*
Jinqiao.	金桥饭店	*jīnqiáo fàndiàn*
Nenghui	能辉酒店	*nénghuī jiǔdiàn*
Post Office Hotel	贵州邮电宾馆	*guìzhōu yóudiàn bīnguǎn*
Shunyuan	顺园宾馆	*shùnyuán bīnguǎn*
Trade Point Hotel	柏顿宾馆	*bǎidùn bīnguǎn*

Eating
Beijing Duck	北京烤鸭店	*běijīng kǎoyādiàn*
Beijing Jiaozi Guan	北京饺子馆	*běijīng jiǎoziguǎn*
Gangweitang Guan	缸煨汤馆	*gāngwēi tāngguǎn*
Jue Yuan Sucai Guan	觉园素菜馆	*juéyuán sùcàiguǎn*
Lao Dongzhouhuang	老东粥皇	*lǎodōng zhōuhuáng*
Nantianmen	南天门重庆火锅	*nántiānmén chóngqìng huǒguō*
Tangren Shijie	唐人食街	*tángrén shíjiē*
Yixin Yuan	怡心园	*yíxīn yuán*

Qingyan
Qingyan	青岩	*qīngyán*
Baisui memorial arch	百岁坊	*bǎisuì fāng*
Guzhen Kezhan	古镇客站	*gǔzhèn kèzhàn*
Huaxi	花溪	*huāxī*
Old town	古镇	*gǔzhèn*
South gate	定广门	*dìngguǎngmén*

Tiyu station on Jiefang Lu; while some fast coaches from Zunyi wind up at the Hebin depot on Ruijin Lu.

Accommodation is not a problem, with a range of central places spanning budget to fairly upmarket brackets. Just don't waste your time trying to get in to one of the guesthouses surrounding the train station – they won't take foreigners, and are anyway no cheaper than the *Post Office Hotel* or *Shunyuan*.

Accommodation

Hebin 118 Ruijin Nan Lu ☎0851/5841855, ℗5812988. A fairly new hotel on a busy road but quiet, close to a park, clean and cosy. Bargain and they'll give discounts, but are anyway fair value for a mid-range place. ❹

Holiday Inn Beijing Lu ☎0851/6771888, ⓦwww.holiday-inn.com/guiyangchn. Reasonable option with rooms for ¥920, but badly located on a busy intersection distant from the centre of town. ❾

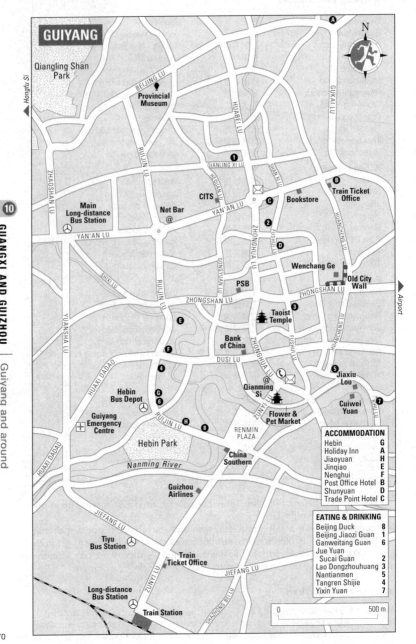

GUIYANG

Qiangling Shan Park

Hongfu Si

Qianling Shan Park

BEIJING LU

Provincial Museum

ZHAOSHAN LU

RUIJIN LU

HUABEI LU

GUKAI LU

QIANLING XI LU

HEQUAN LU

SHAN XI LU

CITS

Net Bar
@

YAN'AN LU

Main Long-distance Bus Station

YAN'AN LU

SHIXI LU

RUIJIN LU

GONGYUAN LU

ZHONGHUA LU

FUSHUI LU

Bookstore

Train Ticket Office

HUANCHENG LU

Wenchang Ge

Old City Wall

ZHONGSHAN LU

PSB

ZHONGSHAN LU

Taoist Temple

Bank of China

DUSI LU

ZHONGHUA LU

FUSHUI LU

Jiaxiu Lou

Cuiwei Yuan

YUANSHA LU

Hebin Bus Depot

Guiyang Emergency Centre

RUIJIN LU

Qianming Si
@

ZUNYI LU

Flower & Pet Market

RENMIN PLAZA

Hebin Park

HUAXI DADAO

Nanming River

China Southern

Guizhou Airlines

JIEFANG LU

Tiyu Bus Station

Train Ticket Office

Long-distance Bus Station

ZUNYI LU

JIEFANG LU

SHAZHONG BELU

Train Station

Airport

N

ACCOMMODATION

Hebin	G
Holiday Inn	A
Jiaoyuan	H
Jinqiao	E
Nenghui	F
Post Office Hotel	B
Shunyuan	D
Trade Point Hotel	C

EATING & DRINKING

Beijing Duck	8
Beijing Jiaozi Guan	1
Ganweitang Guan	6
Jue Yuan Sucai Guan	2
Lao Dongzhouhuang	3
Nantianmen	5
Tangren Shijie	4
Yixin Yuan	7

0   500 m

Guizhou Airlines (☎0851/5982879 or 5981967) and China Southern (☎0851/597777, ⓦwww.cs-air.com) are near each other on Zunyi Lu, open daily 8.30am–5.30pm. At the time of writing there was no airport bus, and taxis charged ¥50 to the airport.

Guiyang's **main bus station**, handling departures to anywhere outside the province, and cities within, is on the corner of Yan'an Xi Lu and Zhaoshan Lu. The **Tiyu station**, on Jiefang Lu near the corner with Zunyi Lu, has more frequent luxury services to Anshun, Zunyi and Kaili; outside on Zunyi Lu between here and the station, you'll find a **kerbside depot** dealing in sleeper buses and coaches to Guangzhou, Nanning, Liupanshui, Xingyi, Anshun and Huangguoshu – the ticket office is made out of a converted bus. This is also where early-morning **day-trips** to Longgong and Huangguoshu depart – come down the afternoon before to sort out times. You can also catch fast buses to Zunyi from the small **Hebin depot** – otherwise dealing in public buses – on Ruijin Lu.

Trains out of Guiyang head east into central China and beyond via Kaili, Zhenyuan and Yuping (the jump-off point for Tongren); north to Zunyi and Chongqing; west to Kunming via Anshun and Liupanshui; and south to Liuzhou and other destinations in Guangxi. Buying tickets at the station is pretty easy, but there are at least two less crowded **advance purchase offices** open 8.30am–noon and 1–4.30pm, and charging a ¥2–5 booking fee per ticket: one signed in Chinese is just north from the train station on Zunyi Lu, set up a level and back from the street; the other is in town at a branch of the Guiyang Commercial Bank on Huancheng Lu, just south off Yan'an Lu.

10

Jiaoyuan Ruijin Lu ☎0851/8129555, ☏5814604. Bright, ordinary budget hotel with slightly overpriced doubles, though no dorms or lifts – a bit problematic if they put you in the upper floors. ❸

Jinqiao 2 Ruijin Nan Lu ☎0851/5829958, ☏5813867. A bulging 1959 exterior immediately sets this mid-range hotel apart from nearby buildings, though it's modern and in a comfortable state of repair inside. ❻

Nenghui 38 Ruijin Nan Lu ☎0851/5898888, ⓦwww.gyspsb.com.cn. New four-star venture where all customers get free use of the gym, and executive suites garner many other discounts. ❼

Post Office Hotel At the eastern end of Yanan Lu ☎0851/5930648, ☏5928668. One of the cheapest places in town but good value – even the dorms are tidy and comfortable. Triples ¥25 per person, doubles with/without bathroom ❷/❹

Shunyuan 76 Fushui Lu ☎0851/5805022. Inexpensive, slightly faded budget hotel in the town centre, which, reluctantly, will take foreigners. Singles ¥30, doubles with/without bathroom ❷/❹

Trade Point Hotel Yanan Dong Lu ☎0851/5827888, ⓦwww.trade-pointhotel.com. Sharp, four-star option with local and Cantonese restaurants and all executive trimmings for ¥850 a night. ❾

The City

Guiyang's social focus is the large open space of **Renmin Plaza**, on the Nanming's south bank between Ruijin Lu, where early-morning crowds indulge in the local craze of spinning wooden tops – all overlooked to the east by a large but inconspicuous statue of Chairman Mao. Just across the river, Guiyang's lively **flower and pet market** sets up in a lane alongside the river, selling a mix of puppies, budgerigars, bonsai and orchids; a few stalls also sell curios such as Mao-era badges, Communist commemorative crockery, pulp comics and the like. Behind all this is **Qianming Si**, a small, cramped and smoky Ming-dynasty nunnery.

Some 500m east of here, a mid-river islet is capped by **Jiaxiu Lou** (¥4), a twenty-nine-metre-high, three-storeyed pavilion reached over an arched stone bridge. Both date back to 1598, when the pavilion was built to inspire students taking imperial examinations. Carefully restored, it holds a teahouse and photos from the 1930s. Continue on across the bridge to the far bank, and you're outside **Cuiwei Yuan** (¥4), a one-time Guanyin temple whose halls were being restored at the time of writing. North up Huancheng Lu, on the corner of Zhongshan Lu, is a restored fragment of Guiyang's **old city wall**, the seven-metre-high battlement capped by **Wenchang Ge**, a gate tower with flared eaves and wooden halls, built in 1596 and now another breezy teahouse.

For a final historical hit, catch northbound bus #1 from central **Zhonghua Lu** around to the **Provincial Museum** (Tues–Sun 9–11.30am & 1–4pm; ¥10), 2.5km north along Beijing Lu. It sits at the back of a truck park; once you've woken up the surprised staff upstairs in the left wing, they'll unlock the place and turn the power on for you. **Ethnic groups** such as the Miao, Dong and Bouyei are represented through costumes, festival photos, and models of their architecture. There are also wooden **ground opera masks** (see p.789), a poster-sized manifesto and armour relating to the nineteenth-century Miao Uprising, and some lively glazed tomb figurines from the Ming dynasty, found near Zunyi.

Qiangling Shan Park and Hongfu Si

About 1km west of the Provincial Museum, **Qiangling Shan Park** (¥5) is a pleasant handful of hills right on the edge of town, thickly forested enough to harbour some colourful birdlife and noisy groups of monkeys. There's a popular funfair, and a large lake with paddle boats to rent, but the highlight is **Hongfu Si**, an important Buddhist monastery up above – follow steps from the gates for thirty minutes to the top. You exit the woods into a courtyard containing the ornamental, four-metre-high **Fahua Pagoda** and a screen showing Buddha being washed at birth by nine dragons. On the right is a **bell tower** with a five-hundred-year-old bell, while bearing left brings you to a new Luohan hall inhabited by 500 glossy, chunky statues of Buddhist saints. The temple's main hall houses a 32-armed Guanyin, each palm displaying an eye, facing a rather benevolent-looking King of Hell.

Eating and drinking

With its predilection for dog meat, chillies and sour soups, Guizhou's cuisine comes under the Western Chinese cooking umbrella, though there's a wide variety of food available in town. Snack stalls selling buns, noodles, chicken wings and the like are scattered through the centre; the block on Fushui Lu north off Zhongshan Lu has several long-established, inexpensive **duck canteens**, serving it crisp-fried in the local style. One local speciality is thin

---

Canine cuisine

Dog meat is widely appreciated not only in Guizhou, Guangxi and Guangdong, but also in nearby culturally connected countries such as Indonesia, the Philippines and Vietnam. Possibly the habit originated in China and was spread through Southeast Asia by tribal migrations. Wherever the practice began, the meat is universally considered to be warming in cold weather and an aid to male virility. As a regional speciality, Chinese tourists to Guizhou generally make a point of trying a dog dish, but for Westerners, eating dog can be a touchy subject. Some find it almost akin to cannibalism, while others are discouraged by the way restaurants display bisected hindquarters in the window, or soaking in a bucket of water on the floor. If you're worried about being served dog by accident, say "wǒ búchì gǒuròu" (I don't eat dog).

crêpes – here called *tianwa*, or "stuffed dolls" – which you fill from a selection of pickled and fresh vegetables to resemble an uncooked spring roll, with the best places just outside Qiangling Shan Park. **Hotpots** are a Guizhou institution offered everywhere, with tables centred round a bubbling pot of slightly sour, spicy stock, in which you cook your own food. **Dog** is a winter dish, usually stir-fried with noodles, soya-braised or part of a hotpot – the southern end of Hequan Lu, opposite CITS, has the best. For **Western food**, there are dozens of **cafés** serving coffee and set meals of steak or burgers, and the *Trade Point Hotel* does a great all-you-can-eat buffet breakfast (7–10.30am; ¥68 a head).

Restaurants

Beijing Duck Ruijin Lu, near the *Jiaoyuan* hotel. Overlooking the river, this place is a bit grubby but cheap – about ¥40 for a full duck – serving exactly what you'd expect from the name.

Beijing Jiaozi Guan Qianling Xi Lu. *Jiaozi* with a bewildering array of stuffings – coriander pork and tofu and egg are good – along with side dishes such as marinated spareribs, garlic cucumber and preserved eggs. You can bloat yourself for ¥15.

Gangweitang Guan Ruijin Lu, near the *Hebin* hotel. Shandong and Sichuanese food, with the speciality being slow-cooked soups (each enough for 2–3 people) served in an earthenware pot – duck with white raddish, and spare ribs with fungus varieties are worth a try. Mains ¥15–40.

Jue Yuan Sucai Guan 51 Fushui Bei Lu. Vegetarian temple restaurant in the town centre (the temple is out the back), whose dishes tend to be liberally laced with chillies. Along with fairly inexpensive stir-fries, they also do some elegant dishes, such as "Lion's Head" stewed rissoles, "Eight Treasure Duck" (stuffed with sweet beanpaste and sticky rice), "Lotus Fish", and Guizhou-style chicken – despite the names, all are made from meat substitutes. There's no English menu, but the staff will help you order. Dishes ¥10–35.

Lao Dongzhouhuang Fushui Lu, south off Zhongshan Lu. Cantonese-style fast-food chain, serving sandpots, steamed spareribs, stuffed bitter gourd slices, prawn dumplings, and even roast duck and pork. Lots of photos and displayed food help smooth language difficulties. Mains around ¥12–20.

Nantianmen Corner of Xihu Lu and Huancheng Lu. Very popular Sichuanese-style hotpot restaurant, with set selections starting at ¥35.

Tangren Shijie Ruijin Lu, near the corner with Dusi Lu. A smart "food street" with both local and nationwide dishes, from dog to Sichuanese spicy tofu, Cantonese *dim sum*, hotpots, Shangdong dumplings, and more – get a card, go up to the counter, and point to what you want. Two can eat well for ¥60.

Yixin Yuan Xihu Lu. An upmarket restaurant near the river and Jiaxiu Lou serving Guizhou, Sichuan and Cantonese food. It's all extremely good, from snacks such as stir-fried potato shreds, crisp-fried sprats in vinegar, and cornmeal steamed in lotus leaves, through to cold sliced meats, noodles or *shuijiao* with dipping sauces, and dried ham and ginkgo nuts. *Zima daming* is another Guizhou speciality you'll find here: a large, circular, bread-like sweet cake. Expensive.

Listings

Banks and exchange The main Bank of China with an ATM is just west off Zhonghua Lu on Dusi Lu; foreign exchange is on the ground floor (Mon–Fri 9–11.30am & 1.30–5pm). There are other branches with ATMs at the eastern end of Yan'an Lu, and opposite the airline offices on Zunyi Lu.

Bookshops The Foreign Language Bookshop, on Yan'an Lu, is well stocked with classics, an eclectic range of children's books, maps of the city and province, and Chinese guidebooks on Guizhou.

Hospital Guiyang Emergency Centre (Guiyang Shi Jijiu Zhan) is on Huaxi Dadao on Guiyang's western side.

Internet access The bright and clean Web Station Net bar is on Yan'an Lu, just east of the intersection with Ruijin Lu – ride the external glass lift to the top floor and pay ¥2 an hour.

PSB The Foreign Affairs Department is in the city centre on Zhongshan Xi Lu.

Post and phones The main post office is on the northeast corner of the Huabei Lu-Yan'an Lu intersection, post code 550001, and is open 8am–7.30pm. There's a smaller branch, and international telephones, at the sprawling telecommunications building on Zhonghua Lu, facing Zunyi Lu.

Travel agents CITS are on Floor 7, Longquan Dasha, 1 Hequan Lu (near the corner with Zhongshan Lu) ⊕0851/6901723, ⓕ6901600, ⓔmajou@citiz.net. The 25-storey yellow tower is easy to find, but the entrance is not, especially as there is no CITS sign outside – you have to cut around to the back from Hequan Lu. Once there, you'll find the staff speak English and are extremely helpful, whether you want to organize a tour or are just after information.

Qingyan

The remains of a Ming-dynasty fortified town 30km south of Guiyang at **QINGYAN** makes for an interesting few hours' excursion. Start by catching bus #201 from the Hebin depot on Ruijin Lu to **Huaxi** (¥1.7; 40 min); at Huaxi, cross the road and pick up a minibus to Qingyan (¥2; 20min). On arrival, don't despair at the shabby main-road junction where the bus pulls up, but head west through the market area into the **old town**, which was founded in 1373 as a military outpost during the first major Han incursions into the region. The old town area forms a kilometre-long elipse, and while by no means comprising pristine period architecture (plenty of concrete and brick buildings put in an appearance), the original street plan is retained along with many temples, guildhalls, homes – even a couple of churches – and narrow, cobbled lanes, all built with skilful stonework and just beginning to be smartened up for tourism. The best area is at the southern end, where a flagstoned street lined with low wooden shops leads to the **Baisui memorial arch**, decorated with crouching lions, and out through the town wall into the fields via the solid stone **south gate**. There are plenty of places to **snack** as you wander – deep-fried balls of tofu are a local speciality – and even an atmospheric **hotel**, the *Guzhen Kezhan* (⊕0851/3200031, ❹), housed in an old guildhall next to the market, if you want to stay. Transport connections back to Guiyang run until late afternoon.

Zunyi and the north

Northern Guizhou's mountainous reaches are famous for *baijiu* **distilleries**, with two interesting stops on the way up to Sichuan or Chongqing: the city of **Zunyi**, pivotal to modern Chinese history; and a wonderful spread of bamboo forests, waterfalls, and atypical red sandstone formations at **Chishui**. Zunyi is on the main road and rail routes, while Chishui lies off the beaten track, right up along the Sichuanese border in the northwestern corner of the province.

Zunyi and around

Some 170km north of Guiyang, **ZUNYI** is surrounded by heavy industry, but the city centre contains a pleasant older quarter surrounded by hilly parkland. It was here that the Communist army arrived on their **Long March** in January 1935, in disarray after months on the run and having suffered two defeats in their attempts to join up with sympathetic forces in Hunan. Having taken the city by surprise, the leadership convened the **Zunyi Conference**, a decision that was to alter China's history in that it saw Mao Zedong emerge as political head of the Communist Party. Previously, the Party had been led by Russian Comintern advisors, who modelled their strategies on urban-based uprisings; Mao felt that China's revolution could only succeed by mobilizing the peasantry, and that the Communist forces should base themselves in the countryside to do this. His opinions carried the day, saving the Red Army from

Zunyi and the north

Zunyi	遵义	*zūnyì*
Fenghuang Shan Park	凤凰山公园	*fènghuángshān gōngyuán*
Monument to the Red Army Martyrs	红军烈士纪念坤	*hóngjūn lièshì jìniànbēi*
Zunyi Conference Hall	遵义会议址	*zūnyì huìyìzhǐ*
Accommodation		
Biyun Binguan	碧云宾馆	*bìyún bīnguǎn*
Xibu Dajiudian	西部大酒店	*xībù dàjiǔdiàn*
Youzheng Binguan	邮政宾馆	*yóuzhèng bīnguǎn*
Chishui	赤水	*chìshuǐ*
Bailong Falls	白龙瀑布	*báilóng pùbù*
Chishui Binguan	赤水宾馆	*chìshuǐ bīnguǎn*
Chishui Dajiudian	赤水大酒店	*chìshuǐ dàjiǔdiàn*
Shizhangdong Falls	十丈洞瀑布	*shízhàngdòng pùbù*
Sidonggou	四洞沟	*sìdòng gōu*
Maotai	茅台	*máotái*

certain annihilation at the hands of the Guomindang and, though its conquest still lay fifteen years away, marking the Communists' first step towards Beijing. (For more on the Long March, see p.546).

The City

The **Zunyi Conference Hall** (daily 8.30am–5pm; ¥40, includes nearby sites covered below) is an attractive grey-brick, European-style house located in the older part of town on Ziyin Lu. It was upstairs, in a room barely big enough to hold the wooden table and chairs for the twenty delegates, that the conference was held from 15–17 January 1935, and where Mao, Zhu De, Zhou Enlai and Lu Shaoqi deposed the Russian Comintern's advisor Otto Braun (aka Li De) and his supporters, placing the course of the revolution in Chinese hands. Through the garden behind here is a small lane with a couple more contemporary buildings filled with period photos, maps and furniture: the former residence of **Bo Gu**, a Communist general criticized by Mao, who held that the Marchers' military defeats were due to Bo's tactics; the **Site of the Red Army Political Department** in the grounds of a French Catholic Church, built in 1866 in an interesting compromise between Chinese and European Gothic styles; and the site of the **China Soviet Republic State Bank** – also known by the Robin Hood-like title of "Commission of Expropriation and Collection" – which funded the Communists by appropriating landlords' property, with cases of period banknotes stamped with the faces of Marx and Lenin displayed.

For a last taste of Red history, cross over the river and up into **Fenghuang Shan Park** (¥15) where the **Monument to the Red Army Martyrs** rises to the west, a reminder that only a quarter of the eighty thousand soldiers who started the Long March actually lived to finish it. However, it's grand rather than maudlin, with four huge red sandstone busts (vaguely resembling Lenin) supporting a floating, circular wall and a pillar topped with the Communist hammer and sickle.

Practicalities

Zunyi is awkwardly laid out around **Fenghuang Shan**, with arrival points and the newer part of town on the eastern side of the hill, and the older streets 2.5km away on the southern side, around the little **Xiang River**. The **bus and train stations** are within 100m of each other in a grimy area on **Beijing Lu**; from here, **Zhonghua Lu** and city buses #1, #6, #23 or #24 run southwest to the river, within walking distance of revolutionary sites – get off the bus at the big, open intersection by the river and cross to the huge **Bank of China** building, from where lanes lead up to the Conference Hall.

There's inexpensive **accommodation** up near the stations, which are surrounded by basic, noisy hostels (¥25 a bed) whose staff have no qualms about foreign custom. For something better, the *Xibu Dajiudian* (☎0852/3191898; ❸), just around from the bus station on Waihuan Lu, is friendly and modern. Options in the nicer part of town include the post office-run *Youzheng Binguan* (☎0852/8221244; ❺), across the intersection on the river; and the *Biyun Binguan* (☎0852/8223671; ❻), a plusher place behind the Conference site on Yujin Lu. The station area has abundant places to get a bowl of noodles or plate of dumplings; otherwise, **eat** at your accommodation. **Leaving**, there are buses to Guiyang 7am–7pm (ordinary/express ¥25/40); three morning buses to Chishui (¥40) and trains through the day to Guiyang and Chongqing.

On to Sichuan: Maotai and Chishui

The rail line continues smoothly north of Zunyi to Chongqing, but there's also a roundabout route out of the province by road, taking in Guizhou's second most impressive waterfalls, near **Chishui**, up on the Sichuanese border some 350km and seven hours from Zunyi on local buses. The region you pass through, besides having some spectacular block-faulted limestone cliffs, positively reeks of brewing, with scores of large ceramic wine jars outside homes and businesses along the way, all sealed with red cloths and stamped with the character "*jiu*" (alcohol). The heart of this local industry is Renhuai County, more specifically the township of **MAOTAI**, nationally famous since a travelling scholar named Zheng Zhen declared it China's finest producer of sorghum spirits in 1704. There's nothing to see as such, but you'll know when you're close – roadside ballustrading is shaped to resemble the Maotai brand's white porcelain bottle with its red diagonal stripe, and signs declare "Zhongguo Jiudu" (China's Spirit Capital). While no banquet would be complete without a bottle, Westerners tend to be of the opinion that Maotai is pretty indistinguishable from the contents of a cigarette lighter.

Chishui

CHISHUI is a small town on the south bank of the **Chishui River**, which marks the border with Sichuan. Geologically, this region belongs not to Guizhou but to Sichuan's **red sandstone** formations: *chishui* means "red water" and during the summer rains the river and its tributaries are coloured a vivid ochre with silt runoff from the surrounding hills. Being an undeveloped corner of the country, there are also some verdant pockets of subtropical **forests** featuring bamboos, three-metre-high *spinulosa* tree ferns, gingers, orchids and moss-covered rocks. The most accessible section is 14km away at **Sidonggou** – minibuses (¥5) run through the day from Renmin Lu to the **park gates** (¥30), from where 6km of flagstoned paths follow either side of a small, bright red river, up through thick forest past three big **waterfalls** – including one split by a large boulder, and several water curtains to walk behind – to the trail's end at thirty-metre-high

Bailong Falls. In addition to the scenery, there's plenty of local life: everywhere people are harvesting **bamboo**, weaving it into mats, and digging up fresh shoots; groups of farmers returning from market with pigs, horses laden with jerrycans of wine, and daily necessities; and several trackside **shrines**, carved with spirits' faces. After heavy rains, it's also worth heading 40km due south of Chishui to where the Fengxi River steps out at the **Shizhangdong Falls**, similar to the more famous Huangguoshu (see p.791) – buses run in summer.

Chishui is a quiet place a kilometre broad, with no real centre; the **bus station** is on Renmin Lu, which runs downhill for 700m to the river. Along the way, there are cheap rooms at the *Chishui Dajiudian* (**②**), the alternative being the new and upmarket *Chishui Binguan* (**⑥**), east down Nanzheng Jie, with many places to **eat** scattered around. **Leaving**, there are three buses daily to Zunyi; for Luzhou and connections to Yibin in Sichuan (see p.916), you might have to cross the river to the township of **Jiuzhi** and pick up services there.

Eastern Guizhou

The journey from Guiyang into **eastern Guizhou** passes through a quintessentially Southeast Asian landscape of high hills cut by rivers, and dotted with dark wooden houses with buffaloes plodding around rice terraces; women working in the fields have babies strapped to their backs under brightly quilted pads, and their long braided hair is coiled into buns secured by fluorescent plastic combs. They are Miao, and the scene marks the border of the **Miao and Dong Autonomous Prefecture**, arguably the best place in China to meet ethnic peoples on their own terms. Miao villages around the district capital, **Kaili**, are noted for their hundred or more annual **festivals**, which though increasingly touristed are anyway such exuberant social occasions that there's no sign yet of their cultural integrity being compromised. Beyond Kaili, the adventurous can head southeast on public buses to the mountainous border with Guangxi province, where **Dong** hamlets sport their unique drum towers and bridges (see p.749), or push on northeast through the pretty countryside surrounding **Zhenyuan** to **Tongren**, jumping-off point for a demanding ascent to cloud forests atop **Fanjing Shan**.

Even if you don't plan anything so energetic, the region is still enjoyable on a daily basis – the attractive home of a friendly people who take pride in their traditions. **Travelling around**, minibuses cover more destinations and leave more frequently than long-distance buses, but to reach more remote corners you'll probably have to aim for the nearest main-road settlement and take pot luck with tractor taxis or whatever else is available – there's also scope for some ad hoc **hiking**.

Kaili and the Miao villages

Surrounded by scores of villages, some lush countryside and a couple of cooling towers for the local power plant, **KAILI**, 170km east from Guiyang, is a moderately industrialized, easy-going focus for China's 7.5 million **Miao**, though migrations and forced resettlements since the Tang dynasty have spread their population from Sichuan right down to Hainan Island. Treated with disdain and forced off their lands by the Qing-dynasty government, rebels such as **Zhang Xiumei** took a lesson from the Taipings in adjacent Guangxi and seeded their own **uprising** in 1854, which – though involving the whole province, and not just ethnic minorities – was centred in the Miao heartlands. The uprising, which at its height saw Guiyang almost fall to the rebels, was only put down in late

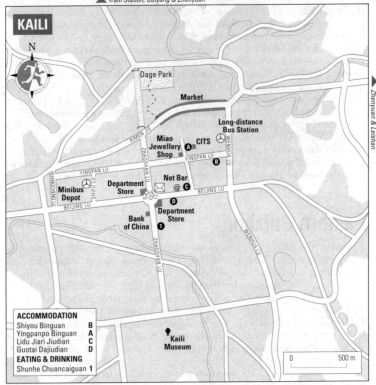

KAILI

N

Dage Park

Market

Long-distance Bus Station

Miao Jewellery Shop   CITS

XIMEN JIE

ZHAOSHAN LU

YINGPAN LU

YINGPAN LU

HUANGCHENG LU

SHIFU LU

Minibus Depot

Department Store

Net Bar @ **G**

Department Store

BEIJING LU

WENHUA LU

WENHUA LU

Bank of China   **1**

DASHIZI

BEIJING LU

ZHAOSHAN LU

▲ Zhenyuan & Leishan

Kaili Museum

ACCOMMODATION
Shiyou Binguan   B
Yingpanpo Binguan   A
Lidu Jiari Jiudian   C
Guotai Dajiudian   D
EATING & DRINKING
Shunhe Chuancaiguan   1

0   500 m

1873 after troops were brought in from neighbouring Sichuan and Hunan provinces, and at the cost of a huge slaughter involving whole towns being obliterated – out of a provincial population of seven million, over half died during the revolt. It wasn't until a century afterwards that the government finally began to make amends – since the 1980s there has been consistent investment in schooling – but Miao culture and traditions are visibly flourishing today.

Arrival, information and accommodation

Functional and compact, Kaili is oriented around the Beijing Lu–Zhaoshan Lu crossroads, known as **Dashizi**. The **train station** is 3km by road to the north,

Moving on from Kaili

Kaili's bus station handles departures through the day to Guiyang (¥40), with frequent departures as far as Rongjiang, Jianhe, Leishan and Taijiang, and fewer services to Xijiang, Shidong, Shibing, Zhenyuan and Congjiang. You can also catch minibuses to Guiyang from the depot about 500m west of Dashizi on Shifu Lu. **Trains** run at intervals through the day to Guiyang (bus is quicker), and northeast to Zhenyuan, Yuping (for Tongren and Fanjing Shan), and into Hunan. **Advance train tickets** can be bought during banking hours from the small branch of the Bank of China just east from the Post Office on Beijing Lu.

Kaili and the Miao villages

Kaili	凯里	*kǎilǐ*
Dage Park	大阁公园	*dàgé gōngyuán*
Dashizi	大十字	*dàshízì*
Kaili Museum	民族博物馆	*mínzú bówùguǎn*
Accommodation and eating		
Guotai Dajiudian	国泰大酒店	*guótài dàjiiǔdiàn*
Lantian Dajiudian	蓝天大酒店	*lántiān dàjiǔdiàn*
Lidu Jiari Jiudian	丽都假日酒店	*lìdū jiàrì jiǔdiàn*
Shiyou Binguan	石油宾馆	*shíyóu bīnguǎn*
Shunhe Chuancaiguan	顺和川菜馆	*shùnhé chuāncài guǎn*
Yingpanpo Binguan	营盘坡宾馆	*yíngpánpō bīnguǎn*
Chong An	重安	*chóng'ān*
Chong An Jiang Binguan	重安江宾馆	*chóng'ānjiāng bīnguǎn*
Xiao Jiangnan	小江南	*xiǎojiāngnán*
Huangping	黄平	*huángpíng*
Feiyun Dong	飞云洞	*fēiyún dòng*
Jianhe	剑河	*jiànhé*
Langde Shang	郎德上	*lángdéshàng*
Leishan	雷山	*léishān*
Matang	麻塘	*mátáng*
Xianglu Shan	香炉山	*xiānglú shān*
Matou	马头	*mǎtóu*
Nanhua	南花	*nánhuā*
Qingman	青曼	*qīngmàn*
Shibing	施秉	*shībǐng*
Shan He Dajiudian	山河大酒店	*shānhé dàjiǔdiàn*
Shidong	施洞	*shīdòng*
Taijiang	台江	*táijiāng*
Lidu Lüguan	丽都旅馆	*lìdū lǚguǎn*
Wenchang Ge	文场阁	*wénchǎng gé*
Xingguang Gongguang	星光公馆	*xīngguāng gōngguǎn*
Xijiang	西江	*xījiāng*

where taxis and buses #1 and #2 meet arrivals, while the **long-distance bus station** is central on Wenhua Bei Lu. The main **Bank of China** and ATM is on Zhaoshan Lu (foreign exchange Mon–Fri 8.30–11am & 2–5pm) – the last branch until you reach Guilin in Guangxi province, if you're heading that way – and the **post office** is right on Dashizi. There's also a convenient **Internet bar** just off the street near the *Lidu* hotel on Beijing Lu. For **information** about village festivals and market days, useful bilingual maps of Kaili and its environs, and even guides, call in on Kaili's **CITS**, just inside the gates at the

Yingpanpo Binguan (daily 8.30–11.30am & 2.30–6pm; ⓣ & ⓕ 0855/8222506, ⓦ www.qdncits.com) – a friendly bunch who know the area backwards.

The cheapest foreign-friendly **accommodation** is at the *Shiyou Binguan* (ⓣ0855/8234331; beds ¥20, doubles with air conditioning and bathroom ❸) near the bus station on Yingpan Lu, otherwise your options are mid-range and include the *Yingpanpo Binguan* (ⓣ0855/3833333, ⓕ3837776; ❺), a renovated 1980s complex just off Yingpan Lu; *Lidu Jiari Jiudian* (ⓣ0855/8266662, ⓕ8266663; ❺), a new business venture offering discounts on Beijing Lu; and the slightly worn *Guotai Dajiudian* (ⓣ0855/8269818; ❺), also on Beijing Lu. For **food**, the two department stores diagonally across from each other on Dashizi both have top-floor "food-street"-style **restaurants**, with a range of regional snacks to order by pointing at around the ¥10 mark. The *Shunhe Chuancaiguan* on Zhaoshan Lu has great Sichuanese fare – garlic beef, spicy tofu, chillied fish – where two can eat well for ¥40, while dog hotpot canteens line the eastern end of Beijing Lu.

The Town

Kaili is more a service centre than a sight in its own right. The most interesting **market area** is along the eastern end of Ximen Jie, a narrow street packed with village-like stalls selling vegetables, trinkets, meat and even livestock. Paths head up from here to **Dage Park**, a tiny hilltop area where old men gather to smoke and decorate the trees with their caged songbirds – there's also a wooden **pagoda** on the summit, home to a mix of incense-blackened Taoist statuary smeared with bloody chicken feathers. The town's only other diversion is the **museum** (¥10) at the far end of Zhaoshan Lu, two dusty floors of bright festival garments and silver jewellery set above a furniture wholesale warehouse.

Around Kaili

The biggest problem around Kaili is deciding which of the area's **Miao villages** to visit. Markets or festivals, both held all over the region, make the choice easier: **markets** operate on a five-day cycle, with the busiest and most interesting at Chong An and Shidong; while **festivals** take place in early spring, early summer and late autumn, when there's little to do in the fields and plenty of food to share. The bigger ones attract as many as fifty thousand people for days of buffalo fights, dances, wrestling, singing, playing the **lusheng** (a long-piped bamboo instrument which accompanies Miao dances), and horse or boat races. Participants dress in multicoloured finery, and the action often crosses over to the spectators – foreigners are rare treats, so don't expect to sit quietly on the sidelines. The biggest events of the year are the springtime **Sisters' Meal**, the traditional time for girls to choose a partner, and **dragon-boat races**, held for a different reason here than others in China – for more on these, see village accounts and the "Sisters' Meal" box on p.784. Major festivals are explosive occasions, while smaller events, where tourists are less expected, can be that much more intimate. If planning a trip to coincide with particular events, be careful of **dates**, as Chinese information sometimes confuses lunar and Gregorian calendars – "9 February", for instance, might mean "the ninth day of the second lunar month".

If there's nothing special going on, the best area to concentrate on is the stretch south of Kaili down to Leishan and Xijiang, which has the most accessible and picturesque **villages**. While some of these are interesting in themselves, outside of the festival season people will be working in the fields, and smaller places may appear completely deserted. With luck, however, you'll be invited

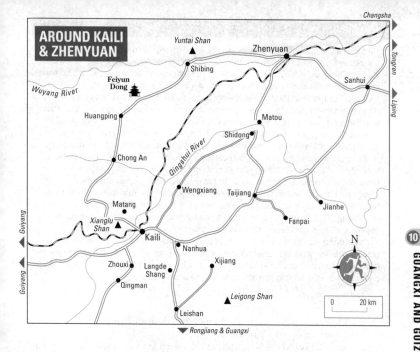

Changsha

Yuntai Shan

Zhenyuan

Shibing

Sanhui

Wuyang River

Feiyun Dong

Huangping

Matou

Shidong

Chong An

Qingshui River

Wengxiang   Taijiang

Matang   Jianhe

Xianglu Shan   Fanpai

Kaili

Nanhua

Zhouxi   Langde Shang   Xijiang

Qingman

Leigong Shan

Leishan

N

0   20 km

Rongjiang & Guangxi

Tongren
Liping
Guiyang
Guiyang

10

to tour the village, look around the distinctive wooden homes, fed – pickled vegetables and sour chicken hotpot, with copious amounts of **nomijiu**, a powerfully soporific rice wine, to wash things down – and asked if you'd like to see some antique wedding garments or have a young woman don full festival regalia for your camera. All this will cost, but it's offered in good humour and worth the price; people often have embroidery or silver to sell, for which bargaining is essential.

CITS **tours** aside, all the villages below are connected by at least daily bus services from Kaili, and also make fine stopovers on the way into the Rongjiang or Zhenyuan regions. Return transport can leave quite early, however, so be prepared to stay the night or hitch back if you leave things too late.

Northwest of Kaili

The 110-kilometre-long road northwest from **Kaili to Shibing** passes a host of interesting villages and gets you much of the way to Zhenyuan (see p.785; note that buses direct from Kaili to Zhenyuan don't generally use this route). Buses leave from Kaili's main bus station, and the whole trip to Shibing costs ¥40 or so.

The first place to aim for is **MATANG**, a village 20km from Kaili, home of the **Gejia** (or Geyi), a Miao sub-group. Tell the bus driver where you're heading; the track to Matang heads off across the paddy fields from below square-topped **Xianglu Shan**, the mountain where rebel leader Zhang Xiumei met his end at the hands of imperial troops in 1873 – there's a big **festival** here each August commemorating the event. It's a twenty-minute walk from the main road to the village, a cluster of muddy fields and dark wooden houses, and you'll be mobbed on arrival to buy jewellery, swirly **batik** cloths and characteristically

"Miao" is a Chinese word; Miao call themselves "Hmong", and their population, while centred in China and Guizhou in particular, is also spread through Vietnam, Laos and Burma. There are three major language groups, though all Miao in eastern Guizhou speak much the same dialect and refer to themselves as "Black Hmong".

Outsiders have found it useful to identify separate Miao communities by their locally distinct ornamentation. Most eye-catching are the detailed **embroideries**: girls start practising with sashes and dress sleeves at an early age, and the more accomplished their work, the higher their social standing. Dresses for festivals and weddings are so intricate that they take years to complete, and often become treasured heirlooms. Patterns are sometimes abstract, sometimes illustrative, incorporating plant designs, butterfly (the bringer of spring and indicating hoped-for change), dragon, fish – a China-wide good luck symbol – and buffalo motifs. Each region produces its own styles, such as the sequinned, curly green-and-red designs from the southerly **Leishan** district, **Chong'an**'s dark geometric work, and the bright, fiery lions and dragons of **Taijiang**. Some places supplement embroidery with other techniques – **batik** from the Gejia villages northwest of Kaili is the best known.

Many of the design themes recur in Miao **silverwork**, the most elaborate pieces being made for wedding assemblages. Women appear at some festivals weighed down with coil necklaces, spiral earrings and huge headpieces, all of which are embossed or shaped into flowers, bells and beasts.

orange-and-yellow embroidery. To move onwards from Matang, return to the main road and flag down a passing vehicle.

Next stop is **CHONG AN**, a dishevelled riverside town about 50km north of Matang with the friendly, basic *Xiao Jiangnan* guesthouse (¥40) or the plusher *Chong An Jiang Binguan* (❷), water-powered mills downstream, and a small **nunnery** just off the Kaili road, reached over a chain-and-plank bridge. Make sure you catch Chong An's fifth-day **market**, where you'll be battered and bruised by crowds of diminutive Miao grandmothers as they bargain for local crafts, or bring in clothes (everything from traditional pleated skirts to denim jeans) for dyeing in boiling vats of indigo. Children around here often wear bright blue "tiger hats", with tufted fabric ears and silver embellishments, which ward off bad luck. There are also some interesting villages near Chong An, and your accommodation may be able to organize guided **walks**.

Some 20km north again on the Shibing road, **HUANGPING** is a larger market town with a few old buildings known for its **silversmiths**. Between here and Shibing you pass **Feiyun Dong** (¥8), a quiet Taoist temple surrounded by trees and rocky outcrops, whose moss-covered main hall houses a **museum** of Miao crafts, a dragon-boat prow and a big bronze drum.

Set in a wide, humid valley 34km from Huangping, **SHIBING** is a busy, ordinary modern town laid out east–west along the south bank of the **Wuyang River**; the bus station is at the west end. If you get stuck between buses, the best bet for **accommodation** is the *Shan He Dajiudian* (❸), across the river by the bridge, or there are cheaper beds at the bus station hostel (❶). **Moving on**, there are buses and minibuses leaving when full back along the Kaili road, and east to Zhenyuan (2hr; ¥8) until late afternoon.

South of Kaili

The prettiest villages and scenery lie **south of Kaili** on the forty-five-kilometre road to **Leishan**, which follows a deep, winding river valley and is a rewarding route if you don't have much time. Buses run back and forth to Leishan through the day, and the best way to travel is simply to ask the driver to stop when you see somewhere you want to check out, then catch another vehicle when you've finished. At Leishan there's further transport northeast to the large village of **Xijiang**, surrounded by some easy walks. Irregular services also run to Xijiang from Kaili – though these often save time by taking entertaining but hair-raising cross-country diversions, avoiding the places below.

Around 13km from Kaili, **NANHUA** is the official "Miao Customs Performance Village", where hornfuls of *no mijiu*, dances and lusheng performances, and souvenirs are all laid on daily for tour buses. It's a nice setting though, with a number of old wooden houses tucked into a fold in the hillside. Far better, however, is 12km further south at **LANGDE SHANG**, a rebel base during the Miao Uprising and still a tremendously photogenic collection of wooden houses, cobbles, fields and chickens set on a terraced hillside capped in pine trees, a twenty-minute walk from the main road. They are also used to tourists, with plenty of silverwork thrust at you as you wander – word gets around if you're not interested, however.

Twenty kilometres south of here, **LEISHAN** is an unselfconsciously grubby town and famous tea-growing region ninety minutes from Kaili, with another recommended market day, and the central *Jianxin Binguan* (❷) as a source of **accommodation**. In a valley 40km (two hours) northeast of Leishan along a dirt road is **XIJIANG**, an incredible collection of closely packed wooden houses built on river stone foundations, all ranged up the side of two adjacent hills. When you've had enough of farmyard smells amongst the narrow, stepped, lanes, walk up through the village and onto the terraced fields above, where you could hike around for hours – views are tremendous. Xijiang has two basic **guesthouses** (❶) – the one above the post office, near where the buses pull up, is best – and a couple of early-closing shops selling rice noodles (boiled or fried). On market days, you can get transport back to Kaili or Leishan until dark; at other times, don't leave it this late, and confirm supposed departure times with bus drivers.

Southeast of Leishan are the fringes of a remote landscape of steep mountain terraces and dark wooden villages dominated by elaborately shaped towers and bridges which spill into Guangxi province: **Dong country**. Your first destination is the town of **Rongjiang**, 100km southeast of Leishan and connected to Kaili by direct buses: for more about the Dong, their architecture, and details of the trip, see pp.749–754.

Northeast of Kaili

The small town of **TAIJIANG** lies 55km northeast of Kaili on the junction of the Sansui and Shidong roads, its sports ground the venue for the big **Sisters' Meal Festival** held on the fifteenth day of the third lunar month (April/May – see p.784). A collection of cheap modern buildings centred on a crossroads about 700m from the main road, there's a daily **market** held behind buildings south of the crossroads, with at least one stall selling the town's renowned **silver**; and **Wenchang Ge**, a recently restored Qing temple at the northern end of town, though it's often locked up. Out on the highway, a paved area surrounds a **statue** of Zhang Xiumei (or "Zangb Xongt Mil" as it's written in Hmong), who was born at the nearby village of Bading Zhai in 1823. Though his role in the Miao Uprising is murky, there's no doubt that Taijiang was a major rebel base from 1855 until November 1870, when imperial troops are said to have killed 10,000 people and destroyed the town. Taijiang's **accommodation** is limited to guesthouses which surround the crossroads, such as *Lidu Lüguan* (❶),

Taijiang's **Sisters' Meal festival**, where Miao teenagers from all over the region meet to choose a partner, is the best one to catch. The town fills beyond capacity for the two-day event, crowds jostling between lottery stalls and markets, buying local produce and, of course, embroidery and silverwork. More of this is being worn by teenage girls from villages around Taijiang, who gamely tramp up and down the streets, sweltering under the weight of their decorated jackets and silver jewellery, jingling as they walk. By nine in the morning there's hardly standing room left in the sports ground, ready for the official opening an hour later; once the necessary speeches are out the way, things formally kick off with two hours of energetic **dancing and lusheng playing**, after which the party breaks up into smaller rings, dancers and musicians practising for bigger things later on in the festivities, or just flirting – this is a teenagers' festival, after all.

Discreet **cockfighting** (not to the death) and much drinking of *mijiu* carries on through the afternoon, then at dusk the **dragon-lantern dances** get underway, a half-dozen teams carrying their wire-and-crepe, twenty-metre-long hollow dragons and accompanying model birds and butterflies into the main street. Candles are lit and placed inside the animals before things begin in earnest, the dragons animated into chasing swirls by the dancers, who charge up and down the street battling with each other; the mayhem is increased by drummers, whooping crowds, and fireworks tossed at leisure into the throng.

Day two sees the action shifting a couple of kilometres west of town to a wide river valley, venue for mid-morning **buffalo fights**. Bloodless trials of strength between two bulls, these draw a good five thousand spectators who assemble around the ill-defined fighting grounds while competitors are paraded up and down, decked out with plaited caps, coloured flags and pheasant tail-feathers, and numbers painted in red on their flanks. The fights each last a few minutes, a skull-cracking charge ending in head-to-head wrestling with locked horns, bulls scrabbling for purchase; the crowds get as close as possible, scattering wildly when one bull suddenly turns tail and bolts, pursued by the victor. Back in town, the **Sisters' Meal** itself is underway, a largely personal affair where young men give parcels of multicoloured **sticky rice** to their prospective partner: a pair of chopsticks buried inside returned rice is an acceptance, a single chopstick or – even worse – a **chilli**, a firm refusal. The festival winds up that night back at the sports ground, the closing dances all held under floodlights, and followed again by much livelier, ad hoc dancing after which couples drift off into the dark.

or the clean *Xingguang Gongguan* (☎0855/5328396; ❸), on the road between town and the highway. **Buses** are a bit hit-and-miss at present – there's no station, just a wooden shack selling tickets on the highway south of town.

Beyond Taijiang, there are two buses daily for the final two-hour, forty-kilometre leg to Shidong, through some of the most beautiful countryside this part of China can provide – there's also transport direct to Shidong from Kaili along a different road. **SHIDONG** itself is a tiny farming town set beside flat fields on a bend in the blue **Qingshui River**, with a single hotel (¥55) and a great **market**, with splendid silverwork and embroideries for sale. The river is the setting of the region's biggest **Dragon–boat Festival**, which follows on from Taijiang's Sisters' Meal celebrations. This riotous occasion commemorates a local hero who battled Han invaders, and not, as in the rest of China, the memory of Qu Yuan's suicide in 280 BC (see p.524). If you're here then you'll be drunk, as a roadblock of young women in festival dress stops arrivals outside town, a draught of *mijiu* from a buffalo horn the price of passage – touch the horn with your hands and you have to drain it. Masses of transport is laid on for the festival, but at other times there are only a couple of buses a day back south from outside the hotel. To continue north **to Zhenyuan**, take a small boat across the river to the hamlet of **Matou** and wait for the midday bus – though in May and June the river may be too high to cross.

Zhenyuan and around

A characterful place on the Guiyang–Changsha rail line, **ZHENYUAN** was founded two thousand years ago, though today's town, occupying a straight, constricted valley 100km northeast of Kaili on the aquamarine **Wuyang River**, sprang up in the Ming dynasty to guard the trade route through to central China. The river runs westwards, with Zhenyuan's tall houses piled together along two narrow, two-kilometre-long streets, one on either bank, the cliffs rising behind. The sole attraction on the south side is a fragment of the **old stone town wall** hidden between houses just west of the main bridge, which you can walk along for 100m. North of the river, **Tianhou Gong** (¥2) is a four-hundred-year-old Taoist complex housing Buddhist statuary at the west end of town, with a balcony overhanging the street. Continuing east, you pass the main bridge and enter Zhenyuan's **old quarter**, about 500m of wood and stone buildings in the Qing style, backed up against stony cliffs. The street eventually crosses the river via a multiple-arch, solid stone span leading to **Qinglong Dong** (¥30), a sixteenth-century temple currently being expanded, whose separate Taoist, Buddhist and Confucian halls appear to grow out of a cliff face, all dripping wet and hung with vines.

Both arrival points are at the west side of town, the **train station** on the south bank, and **bus station** on the north. The best **accommodation** lies on the south side of the river, where the *Jinfenghuang Zhoudaisuo* (¥88), *Lidu Binguan* (☎0855/5726560; ❹) and *Rongfeng Binguan* (with/without bathroom ❸/❷) all offer clean, basic rooms and places to **eat**.

Tongren and Fanjing Shan

The only settlement of any size in far northeastern Guizhou, **TONGREN** is a small, lightly industrial city, situated at a bend on the high banks of the **Jin River**, only a stone's throw from the Hunanese border. In 1981 a nature reserve was formalized at nearby **Fanjing Shan**, a former Buddhist mountain long recognized for the extraordinary diversity of its plants and wildlife, and there's

Zhenyuan and around		
Zhenyuan	镇远	*zhènyuǎn*
Jinfenghuang Zhaodaisuo	金凤凰招待所	*jīnfènghuáng zhāodàisuǒ*
Lidu Binguan	丽都宾馆	*lìdū bīnguǎn*
Miao great wall	苗长城	*miáo chángchéng*
Old town wall	卫城恒	*wèichénghéng*
Qinglong Dong	青龙洞	*qīnglóng dòng*
Rongfeng Binguan	容丰宾馆	*róngfēng bīnguǎn*
Siguan dian	四官店	*sìguān diàn*
Tianhou Gong	天后宫	*tiānhòu gōng*
Wuyang River	舞阳河	*wǔyáng hé*
Sansui	三穗	*sānsuì*

There are several daily **trains** from Zhenyuan southwest to Kaili and Guiyang, and northwest via **Yuping** (1hr; jumping-off point for Tongren) to Huaihua (for Zhangjiajie, p.527) and Changsha. Buy tickets from the station the day before travel if you don't want to stand.

By **bus**, there's plenty of transport through the day west **to Shibing** (2hr; ¥8), and a few services to Kaili, Shidong, Taijiang and Guiyang. If you miss these – or flooding has halted the ferry crossing from Matou to Shidong – head first to **Sansui**, a nondescript town about 40km east of Zhenyuan and connected by frequent minibuses, and catch connections there.

been a steady flow of visitors since access improved in the early 1990s. You need to be fit, but Fanjing Shan's scenery is magnificent and there's always the chance of seeing *jinsi hou*, **golden monkeys**, one of China's prettiest endangered species, whose wild population numbers only a few thousand individuals. Around 170 live on Fanjing Shan's upper reaches and it's easy to recognize their slight build, big lips, tiny nose and, in males, vivid orange-gold fur, should you be lucky enough to spot one.

Tongren is curiously isolated, best reached via **Yuping**, a stop on the Zhenyuan–Huai Hua rail line, from where **minibuses** (¥28) take under two hours to reach town – exit the train station, turn right, and the minibus depot is 400m along the road.

The main part of town is east of the river, where the streets form a compact and unfocused shopping district: Minzhu Lu is a partly pedestrianized collection of clothing and department stores, with a large sculpture of a **bronze drum** halfway along. Overlooking the river to the south is **Dong Shan Park**, where a stone staircase leads up to **Dongshan Si**, China's only official **Nuo temple**. Nuo is an animistic religion, now watered down by Buddhist and Taoist influences but retaining something of its original form in open-air **theatre**, still held at festivals in villages around Tongren. Performing stylized fights to rhythmic drumming, dancers don grotesquely shaped **masks**, each of which is individually named and has a spirit that the wearer is constantly in danger of being overwhelmed by, unless it is propitiated with a sprinkle of chicken's blood. The number of masks owned by a troupe increases their reputation. The temple has more than a hundred arranged in two halls, along with local batiks, a tacky

Tongren and Fanjing Shan

Fanjing Shan	梵净山	*fánjìng shān*
Golden monkey	金丝猴	*jīnsī hóu*
Heiwan	黑湾	*hēiwān*
Jiankou	剑口	*jiànkǒu*
Jinding Si	金顶寺	*jīndǐng sì*
Tongren	铜仁	*tóngrén*
Dong Shan Park	东山公园	*dōngshān gōngyuán*
Dongshan Si	东山寺	*dōngshān sì*
Fanyu Dajiudian	梵宇大酒店	*fányǔ dàjiǔdiàn*
Jin River	锦江	*jǐnjiāng*
Jinlong Binguan	金龙宾馆	*jīnlóng bīnguǎn*
Qiandong Binguan	黔东宾馆	*qiánlóng bīnguǎn*

"Nuo" shrine, and other trappings of the religion. Below, riverside Shuangjiang Lu is lined with elderly wooden stores and homes.

Practicalities

Tongren's **bus station** is west of the river on **Jinjiang Lu**, with regular transport to Yuping (for the Guiyang–Huaihua **train** – ask at the bus station for departure times) and Jiangkou (for Fanjing Shan), and farther afield to Zunyi, Guiyang, and, for some reason, Guangzhou. There's **accommodation** opposite at the dusty *Fanyu Dajiudian* (❹); otherwise, cross the river to the *Jinlong Binguan* (❷) on Huanxi Lu, whose eccentric decor compensates for age; while up along Minzhu Lu is the fairly decent *Qiandong Binguan* (⑦0856/5223636; ❸, dorm beds ¥24). There are a few inexpensive **restaurants** in the centre, including a couple of cake shops serving coffee, plus a large Hui and Uigur population peddling kebabs and grilled chicken wings. Tongren's **Bank of China** is near the *Jinlong* hotel on Huanxi Lu, with several **Internet bars** near the bronze drum on Minzhu Lu.

Fanjing Shan

Some 75km northwest of Tongren, **Fanjing Shan**'s summit rises to 2500m. You should be aware that the climb involves more than seven thousand stairs, long sections of which are narrow, steep, and in a bad state of repair – allow for one day up, one day on the top, and one day to return. There's sufficient **accommodation** and **food** along the route, so copy the Chinese, who carry only a jar of tea with them. Summers are humid lower down, but cold wind and fog often tear across the upper levels, and winters are freezing – take some warm clothing.

From Tongren, minibuses go to **JIANGKOU** (2hr), a single-street town with some uppity urchins, from where jeeps and smaller minibuses bounce along the twenty-five-kilometre dirt track leading up the valley to the mountain. Prices, speed and eventual destination of this latter stage vary according to the vehicle and disposition of the driver; ¥15 should carry you as far as the **park gates** (where you pay the ¥60 entry fee) at **Heiwan**, a collection of basic shops, restaurants and accommodation. A red earth road runs 7km from Heiwan to the foot of the mountain, an enjoyable walk through lowland forests of bamboo and flowering trees, clouds of butterflies and a near-vertical waterfall. At the end is **Dahe** – two teahouses where porters lounge, hoping to carry you up in a bamboo litter, a souvenir shop selling walking sticks and **maps**, and a bridge over the stream – and then you're on the lower stairs, in every respect the worst on the mountain. It's a long ninety minutes to where the steps begin to follow less extreme ridges, through thinner woodland and a dwarf bamboo understorey. This continues pretty well all the way, past a halfway meal shack (they'll let you sleep here if need be) to heath country, basic lodgings and a restaurant five hours from Dahe at **Jinding Si**, the Golden Summit Monastery. The mountain's true apex is up another five hundred stairs to the right past some intriguingly piled rock formations. The general practice is to overnight around the monastery and then climb up to watch the sunrise, but there's also a day's hiking out to minor peaks.

Western Guizhou

Extending for 350km between Guiyang and the **border with Yunnan province**, Western Guizhou is a desperately poor region of beautiful mountainous

Western Guizhou

Anshun	安顺	*ānshùn*
Bai Ta	白塔	*báitǎ*
Beimen bus station	北门客车站	*běimén kèchēzhàn*
Gourou Wang	狗肉王	*gǒuròu wáng*
Huayou Binguan	华油宾馆	*huáyóu bīnguǎn*
Main bus station	客车南站	*kèchē nánzhàn*
Wenhua Miao	文化庙	*wénhuà miào*
West bus station	客车西站	*kèchē xīzhàn*
Xixiu Shan Binguan	西秀山宾馆	*xīxiùshān bīnguǎn*
Shitou Zhai	石头寨	*shítou zhài*
Zhenning	镇宁	*zhènníng*
Tianlong	天龙	*tiānlóng*
Wulong Si	伍龙寺	*wǔlóngsì*
Pingba	平坝	*píngbà*
Longgong and Huangguoshu		
Guanyin Dong	观音洞	*guānyīn dòng*
Huangguoshu Falls	黄果树瀑布	*huángguǒshù pùbù*
Long Gong	龙宫	*lónggōng*
Longgong Caves	龙宫洞	*lónggōng dòng*
Yulong Dong	玉龙洞	*yùlóngdòng*
Liupanshui	六盘水	*liùpánshuǐ*
Weining	威宁	*wēiníng*
Black-necked crane	黑颈鹤	*hēijǐng hè*
Caohai	草海	*cǎohǎi*
Heijing He Binguan	黑颈鹤 宾馆	*hēijǐnghè bīnguǎn*
Jinye Binguan	金叶宾馆	*jīnyè bīnguǎn*
Juhongxuan Zhaodaisuo	聚弘轩招待所	*jùhóngxuān zhāodàisuǒ*
Xingyi	兴义	*xīngyì*
Maling Canyon	马陵峡谷	*mǎlíng xiágǔ*
Panjiang Binguan	盘江宾馆	*pánjiāng bīnguǎn*
Xingyi Binguan	兴义宾馆	*xīngyì bīnguǎn*
Zhijin	织金	*zhījīn*
Zhijin Caves	织金洞	*zhījīndòng*

country and depressingly functional towns drenched in the fallout from coal mining, concrete, and steel operations. About a third of the way along, the town of **Anshun** is a transit hub for visiting **Bouyei villages**; the tourist magnets of **Longgong Caves** and **Huangguoshu Falls**; and remoter, more spectacular **Zhijin Caves**.

Anshun sits on the Guizhou–Yunnan rail line and highway, and all routes west from here can ultimately lead to Kunming, Yunnan's capital: trains head northwest to **Liupanshui**, springboard for a detour through Yi, Hui and Miao settlements to the remote wildfowl sanctuary of **Caohai** – being poled around this shallow lake on a sunny day is one of Guizhou's highlights – while the highway follows a more southerly road into Yunnan through the Yi border town of **Panxian**; and a lesser route snakes southwest from Anshun to further scenic attractions at **Xingyi**. Getting around isn't too tricky if you stick to the main routes, though buying bus tickets for travel along back roads can occasionally be problematic; note that the west has **no banks** capable of changing traveller's cheques.

Anshun

Some 100km west of Guiyang, **ANSHUN** was established as a garrisoned outpost in Ming times to keep an eye on the empire's unruly fringes. Today the town is a healthy but rough-around-the-edges marketplace, whose sole sight is **Wenhua Miao** (¥3), a Ming Confucian hall hidden away in the northeastern backstreets which, while somewhat neglected, has some superbly carved dragon pillars which once must have rivalled those at Qufu's Confucius Mansion (p.331). Anshun's importance is otherwise for its facilities: a useful orientation point is central **Xin Dashizi**, a large crossroads overlooked to the northwest by a hillock topped by **Bai Ta**, a short Ming-dynasty pagoda. South of here, Zhonghua Nan Lu runs for a kilometre past the **main bus station** (handling traffic along the Guiyang-Yunnan road, Xingyi, Liupanshui, and a few local destinations) on the corner with Huangguoshu Dajie, to terminate at the **train station**. North from Xin Dashizi, a 500-metre strip of Zhonghua Lu forms the town's high street, running out of town a kilometre later past the **Beimen bus station** (for Zhijin). You'll need the small **west bus station**, 150m west of Xin Dashizi on Tashan Xi Lu, to reach some local destinations.

Practicalities

For **accommodation**, Anshun's transit-point hostels won't take foreigners – though Chinese-speakers may get lucky – leaving the welcoming *Huayou Binguan* (℡0853/3329164, ℻3226020; ❸), west of Xin Dashizi at 15 Tashan Xi Lu, as the cheapest option (you can bargain a bit with them). Otherwise, the best of the mid-range places is *Xixiu Shan Binguan* (℡0853/2211888, ℻2211801; ❺), diagonally up from the bus station on Zhonghua Nan Lu. Both hotels have **restaurants** – the *Xixiu Shan*'s is Japanese/Korean – with more north of Xin Dashizi on Zhonghua Lu, including a branch of *Dico's*, several hotpot places, and the *Gourou Wang*, a popular spot for dog.

    Leaving, there are several trains daily to Guiyang, and westwards to Yunnan via Liupanshui, jumping-off point for Caohai Hu (see p.793). Buses to Huang-guoshu, Guiyang, Xingyi and Liupanshui depart the main station through the day, with several services to Kunming and Zunyi. You can catch buses to Zhijin from the Beimen station until mid-afternoon.

Around Anshun

The land between the limestone hills **around Anshun** is intensely farmed by blue-skirted **Bouyei** busy planting rice or ploughing muddy flats with buffaloes. The Bouyei number 2.5 million and range throughout southwestern Guizhou, though this is their heartland, their village buildings artfully constructed from split stone and roofed in large, irregularly laid slate tiles. Bouyei specialities include **batik work** and **Ground Opera** or *dixi*, where performers wear brightly painted wooden masks; though native to the region and overlaid with animistic rituals, the current forms are said to have been imported along with Han troops in the Ming dynasty, and are based on Chinese tales such as the *Three Kingdoms*. The Spring Festival period is a good time to see a performance, held in many **villages** around Anshun, a couple of which are reviewed overleaf – Guiyang's CITS can recommend other locations.

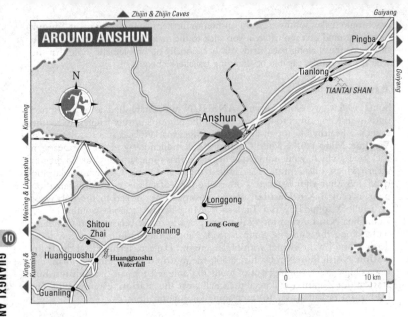

The Anshun area's tourist magnets, however, are **Longgong Caves** and **Huangguoshu Falls**, which can be fitted into a day-trip from either here or Guiyang. The caves are flooded and romantically require boats for some of the route, but Huangguoshu – while impressive on a good day – doesn't quite live up to its reputation. Finally, the trip north to the splendid **Zhijin Caves** requires an overnight stop, though it's well worth the effort.

Shitou Zhai and Tianlong

While there are many Bouyei villages around Anshun, two are within easy striking distance. The first, six-hundred-year-old **SHITOU ZHAI**, lies 30km southwest off the Huangguoshu road past **Zhenning**; tell the driver, and Huangguoshu buses from the west station (¥6; 40min) will drop you at the junction, leaving a two-kilometre walk along a quiet road to the **village gates** (¥20). The fact that there's an entry fee betrays Shitou Zhai's popularity, but it's also a pretty spot, with forty or so stone houses grouped around a rocky hillock, all surrounded by vegetable plots. You'll be offered batik jackets, and might witness the whole process, from drawing the designs in wax, to dyeing in indigo and boiling the wax away to leave a white pattern. You could also walk out to similar surrounding villages, none of which charges admission. To return, walk back to the main road and flag down buses to Huangguoshu, Anshun or Zhenning (for transport to either).

An alternative lies 27km east of Anshun at **TIANLONG**, reached from the main bus station (¥5.5; 30min). The bus leaves you in a narrow, grubby main street choked with stalls, trucks and fumes, but duck south and you're immediately in the **old town**, a small maze of narrow lanes, antique stone and wood buildings with slit windows, running streams and errant livestock. Resemblances to old European villages are enhanced by the nineteenth-century **church-school** at the west end, built by French priests and now housing a collection of

ground opera masks – Tianlong is a *dixi* centre. Three kilometres east down a muddy track, there's also the amazing **Wulong Si**, a fortress-like stone temple which sits atop sheer-sided **Tiantai Shan**. You can catch transport through the day back to Anshun, or on to Guiyang via **Pingba** town.

Longgong and Huangguoshu Falls

Longgong Caves and **Huangguoshu Falls** lie southwest of Anshun, and can be tied together into a day-trip. Tours run from Guiyang, but from Anshun it's just as easy (and cheaper) to do it yourself, either on public transport or – for a group – by hiring a five-person **minibus** (¥300 for the day) at the main station. Note that entry fees top ¥200 in total, and that Longgong requires a bit of walking.

Buses and minibuses to **Longgong** (¥5–10; 1hr) depart Anshun's west station through the morning; the caves are at the end of a country road 28km from town but you could be dropped at either **entrance** (¥120), which are about 5km apart. From the nearer, western gate, you begin by being ferried down a small river between willows and bamboo, to a small knot of houses; walk through the arch, bear left, and it's 250m up some steps to **Guanyin Dong**, a broad cave filled with Buddhist statues. A seemingly minor path continues around the entrance but this is the one you want: it leads through a short cavern lit by coloured lights, then out around a hillside to **Jiujiu Tun** – site of an old guard post – and **Yulong Dong**, a large and spectacular cave system which a guide will take you through (for free). Out the other side, a small river enters **Long Gong** (Dragon's Palace) itself, a two-stage boat ride through tall, flooded caverns picked out with florid lighting, exiting the caves into a broad pool at Longgong's eastern entrance. Transport until late afternoon runs from the car park below to Huangguoshu and, less frequently, back to Anshun.

Huangguoshu Falls lie 64km from Anshun's west or main bus stations (¥10), and about 30km from Longgong, along the Anshun–Xingyi–Yunnan highway. You get dropped off at little Huangguoshu township and walk down to the **entrance** (¥90); at 68m this may not quite rank as China's highest cataract, but in full flood it's the loudest, the thunder rolling way off into the distance. A staircase descends past plagues of souvenir stalls to the blue-green river below the falls, and the most imposing view of Huangguoshu is off to the left where the full weight of its eighty-one-metre span drops into the **Rhino Pool** – expect a good soaking from the spray. **Moving on**, buses run to Anshun and Guiyang through the day; if you're Xingyi or Yunnan bound, first catch a minibus 7km west to the small town of **Guanling** and look for connections there.

Zhijin and Zhijin Caves

About 100km from Anshun (3hrs) or 150km from Guiyang (4.5hrs) – there's direct traffic from either – the dismal country town of **ZHIJIN** sits amongst some gorgeous limestone pinnacles, underneath which are the astounding **Zhijin Caves**, which lie 25km northeast via the township of **Sanyou**. Buses from Zhijin to the caves (¥3; 40min) run through the day and leave you at the **visitors' centre** (open 9am–5pm; ¥80) where you have to hook up with one of the **guided tours** which run whenever they have around ten people. The caves are immensely impressive and absolutely worth the money (though commentary is in Chinese only), lasting a solid two hours and winding through untold numbers of caverns packed with grand and weighty rock formations. The inevitable coloured lighting is actually used creatively, picking out credibly named formations such as "Puxian Riding his Elephant" and "Hermit on Mountain", and the last cavern, **Guanghang Dong**, is 240m long, 170m wide and 60m

△ Huangguoshu Falls

high. If you get here early enough you might not need to spend the night in Zhijin, as buses back to Guiyang or Anshun run until mid-afternoon; failing this, the *Jinye Binguan* (☎0857/7625327; ❸), downhill from the bus station near the market, has acceptable **rooms** and a decent **restaurant**.

The far west

West from Anshun, there are **three routes** to choose between on the way into Yunnan. The Guiyang–Kunming train and fast buses can get you northwest to **Liupanshui**, access point for **Weining** and wintering birdlife at Caohai Lake. Meanwhile, the main Guizhou–Yunnan road runs due west of Anshun to the Yi-dominated border town of **Panxian** – an uneventful journey – while a less direct alternative leads down to **Xingyi** at Guizhou's southwestern extremity, where you can connect with the Nanning–Kunming rail line. Karst mountains and terraced fields are the backdrop wherever you head.

To Liupanshui, Weining and Caohai

The land northwest of Anshun forms a tumultuous barrier of jagged peaks and deep valleys, all masterfully tamed by the new Guiyang–Kunming road and rail line, both masterpieces of engineering. Some 200km from Anshun, **LIUPAN-SHUI** (also known as **Shuicheng**) is generally regarded as the poorest city in China, a mess of broken pavements and dilapidated buildings permanently mired in steel-plant fallout and coal dust. Arrival points are central, with the **train station** on Shuixi Bei Lu and the **bus station** 700m south on parallel Renmin Lu – a taxi between them is ¥7. Buses run up **to Weining** (¥16) until mid-afternoon; there are also expresses to Anshun and Guiyang, and sleepers down **to Xingyi**.

The winding road uphill to Weining takes about three hours (two coming back), emerging above the clouds on the two-thousand-metre-high Weining Plateau, which seems to enjoy a surprisingly mild microclimate. **WEINING** is another small, run-down shell of a town immediately north of reed-fringed **Caohai Lake**, populated by a friendly mix of Muslim Hui, Yi and Dahua Miao, and moderately well known for its Yi torch festival in July/August, sheep farming and **potatoes** – skewers of chilli-dusted potato "kebabs" are sold everywhere. Exit the bus station, turn right, and Weining's most comfy **accommodation** is 100m past the crossroads at the *Heijing He Binguan* (☎0857/6222048, Ⓕ6224438; older doubles with/without bathroom ❸/❷, newer rooms ❹); exit the station, turn left for 50m, and take the street opposite, and you'll find several cheaper options, such as *Juhongxuan Zhaodaisuo* (☎0857/6223480; ❶), which is cleaner than most. **Restaurants** outside the *Hejing He* do inexpensive stir-fries and hotpots.

A ¥1.5 motor-rickshaw ride from the town centre – or a half-hour walk – **Caohai**, the "Grass Sea", fills about twenty-five square kilometres of a shallow lake basin, the core of a regional **nature reserve**. Wintering wildfowl shelter here in huge numbers, including around 400 **black-necked cranes** – almost ten percent of the entire world population – along with golden eagles, white-tailed sea eagles, black storks, Eurasian cranes, spoonbills and assorted ducks. Walk down to the lake and you'll be approached by touts wanting to take you out on **boat trips**: you pay about ¥60 for a three-hour tour being poled around in a four-person punt after wildfowl. The Chinese head first for a meal at the hamlet of **Longjia** on the far shore, famed for its food. On a sunny day, Caohai's overall tranquillity is a complete break with daily life in China; wintering cranes often hang out in the shallows near the shore and are not too hard to photograph.

Moving on from Weining, there are buses to Liupanshui, Anshun, Guiyang, **Zhaotong** (for connections to Xichang in Sichuan) and Kunming (Yunnan).

Xingyi and the Maling Canyon

The scene of sporadic fighting between the Guomindang and locally organized guerrillas before the PLA took control in 1951, **XINGYI** is a small, tidy city surrounded by occasionally dramatic limestone scenery about 250km south-west from Anshun on the Yunnanese border. It's also a stop on the **Nanning–Kunming railway**, making it a more useful place to aim for than you might guess from its otherwise remote location; the town also enjoys a year-round supply of fresh fruit and vegetables as a result.

With low hills rising all around, Xingyi's kilometre-wide centre is south of the insignificant **Wantang stream**, where a small web of lanes converges on **Panjiang Square**, a paved oval surrounded by a two-storey ring of department stores. It's a relaxed place, and you might spot a few Dahua Miao with boldly patterned capes in back-lane markets; mostly the attractions comprise a couple of low-key parks, and a few old teahouses populated by water-pipe-puffing patrons along the Wantang's banks.

Xingyi's **train station** is 10km east of town, connected by minibuses; most trains bound for Kunming, Baise or Nanning pass through either late at night or very early in the morning. The **two long-distance bus stations** are just east of the centre on streamside Hunan Jie, and about a kilometre west on Xihu Lu; both handle sleepers to Anshun, Guizhou, Kunming, Baise and Nanning. For local traffic, there's a **minibus depot** just past the east bus station on Hunan Jie. The best **place to stay** is about 700m south of Panjiang Square at the *Panjiang Binguan*, at the end of Panjiang Xi Lu (T0859/3223456; ❸, dorms ¥25); the similar *Xingyi Binguan* (T0859/3111111; ❹) is 1km east of the centre on Ruijin Lu. The *Panjiang*'s **restaurant** is good and even has an English menu, otherwise look for noodle-soup and dog hotpot kitchens around town.

The area's highlight is the **Maling Canyon**, a tortuous, fifteen-kilometre river gorge northeast of Xingyi featuring rapids, waterfalls, deep cliffs and hanging vegetation. There are two sections: the **upper** part is 25km from town and of most interest for **white-water rafting** (arranged through accommodation); while the **lower section** is 15km away and makes for a good couple of hours' walking – catch an **Anlong**-bound minibus from the Hunan Jie depot (¥3), or charter a taxi (¥15). Entry costs ¥30, with flagstoned paths leading down into the gorge and then heading upstream, and suspension bridges link tracks along both sides of the river. It's all pretty spectacular, with the ice-blue water twisting into ribbon falls and rapids, the high gorge walls green and dripping with moisture – the only downside is agricultural runoff foaming into the gorge from the western side.

Travel details

Trains

Anshun to: Guiyang (10 daily; 1hr 30min); Kunming (8 daily; 10hr); Liupanshui/Shuicheng (10 daily; 2hr).
Baise to: Kunming (4 daily; 11hr); Nanning (5 daily; 4hr); Xingyi (4 daily; 4hr).
Beihai to: Nanning (1 daily; 3hr 30min).
Guilin to: Beijing (3 daily; 28hr); Changsha (5 daily;

8hr); Guangzhou (2 daily; 14hr); Guiyang (2 daily; 15hr); Kunming (2 daily; 22hr); Nanning (7 daily; 5hr 30min–8hr); Shanghai (1 daily; 29hr); Shenzhen (1 daily; 16hr).
Guiyang to: Anshun (10 daily; 1hr 30min); Beijing (3 daily; 29hr); Changsha (3 daily; 14hr); Chengdu (3 daily; 19hr); Chongqing (9 daily; 11hr); Guangzhou (6 daily; 24hr); Guilin (2 daily; 15hr); Huaihua (5 daily; 7hr); Kaili (9 daily; 3hr); Kunming

(8 daily; 13hr); Shanghai (3 daily; 30hr); Liupan-
shui/Shuicheng (10 daily; 4hr); Yuping (5 daily; 6hr);
Zhenyuan (7 daily; 5hr); Zunyi (9 daily; 3hr).
Kaili to: Changsha (3 daily; 12hr); Guiyang (9 daily;
3hr); Huaihua (5 daily; 4hr); Yuping (5 daily; 3hr);
Zhenyuan (7 daily; 1hr 30min).
Liupanshui to: Anshun (10 daily; 2hr); Guiyang (10
daily; 4hr); Kunming (8 daily; 8hr 30min).
Nanning to: Baise (5 daily; 3hr); Beihai (1 daily;
3hr 20min); Beijing (1 daily; 28hr); Chengdu
(1 daily; 10hr 30min); Chongzuo (1 daily; 2hr);
Guangzhou (2 daily; 14hr); Guilin (6 daily; 5–8hr);
Kunming (7 daily; 14hr); Pingxiang (1 daily; 4hr);
Tuolong/Ningming (1 daily; 3hr); Xingyi (7 daily;
7hr 30min).
Pingxiang to: Chongzuo (1 daily; 2hr); Nanning (1
daily; 4hr); Tuolong/Ningming (1 daily; 1hr).
Xingyi to: Baise (4 daily; 4hr); Kunming (6 daily;
5hr); Nanning (7 daily; 7hr 30min).
Zhenyuan to: Guiyang (7 daily; 5hr); Huaihua (7
daily; 3hr 20min); Kaili (7 daily; 1hr 30min); Yuping
(7 daily; 1hr 10min).
Zunyi to: Chongqing (9 daily; 7hr); Guiyang (9
daily; 3hr).

Buses

Anshun to: Guiyang (2hr); Huangguoshu (1hr);
Liupanshui (3hr); Longgong (1hr); Xingyi (8hr).
Baise to: Jingxi (4hr); Kunming (10hr); Nanning
(4hr).
Beihai to: Nanning (3hr 30min).
Guilin to: Guangzhou (19hr); Hengyang (12hr);
Longsheng (2hr); Nanning (6hr); Sanjiang (4hr);
Yangshuo (1hr 30min).
Guiping to: Jintian (30min); Nanning (3hr).
Guiyang to: Anshun (2hr); Huangguoshu (3hr); Kaili
(3hr); Kunming (19hr); Nanning (18hr); Rongjiang
(10hr); Xingyi (9hr); Zunyi (2hr 30min).
Kaili to: Chong An (2hr); Guiyang (5hr); Leishan
(1hr 30min); Rongjiang (6hr); Shibing (3hr); Shidong
(4hr); Taijiang (2hr); Xijiang (2hr); Zhenyuan (6hr).
Liupanshui to: Anshun (3hr); Guiyang (4hr); Wein-
ing (3hr); Xingyi (12hr).

Nanning to: Baise (4hr); Beihai (3hr 30min);
Chongzuo (1hr 30min); Guangzhou (18hr); Guilin
(6hr); Guiping (3hr); Hong Kong (20hr); Ningming
(4hr); Pingxiang (5hr); Yangshuo (6hr).
Pingxiang to: Chongzuo (5hr); Nanning (5hr);
Ningming (1hr).
Sanjiang to: Baxie (1hr 30min); Chengyang
(40min); Diping (2hr); Guilin (4hr); Liping (9hr);
Longsheng (2hr); Mapang (2hr); Zhaoxing (4hr).
Xingyi to: Anshun (8hr); Guiyang (9hr); Kunming
(12hr); Liupanshui (12hr).
Yangshuo to: Guilin (1hr 30min); Nanning (6hr).
Zhaoxing to: Diping (2hr); Liping (4hr); Sanjiang
(4hr).
Zunyi to: Chishui (7hr); Guiyang (2hr 30min).

Ferries

Beihai to: Haikou (2 daily; 10hr).

Flights

In addition to the domestic flights listed, there are
international flights out of Guilin to Korea, Thailand
and Japan, and from Nanning to Thailand and
Vietnam.
Guilin to: Beijing (6 daily; 2hr 15min); Chengdu
(3 daily; 1hr 20min); Guangzhou (6 daily; 50min);
Guiyang (2 daily; 50min); Hong Kong (2 daily; 1hr);
Kunming (2 daily; 1hr 15min); Shanghai (3 daily;
2hr); Shenzhen (2 daily; 1hr); Xi'an (2 daily; 1hr
30min).
Guiyang to: Beijing (2 daily; 2hr 30min); Chengdu
(2 daily; 1hr); Guangzhou (5 daily; 1hr 30min);
Guilin (2 daily; 50min); Hong Kong (1 daily; 1hr
30min); Kunming (1 daily; 55min); Nanning (1 daily;
1hr); Shanghai (1 daily; 2hr); Shenzhen (1 daily;
1hr 30min).
Nanning to: Beijing (4 daily; 3hr); Chengdu (2
daily; 1hr 30min); Chongqing (1 daily; 1hr 20min);
Guangzhou (5 daily; 55min); Guiyang (1 daily; 1hr);
Hanoi (2 weekly; 50min); Haikou (2 daily; 50min);
Hong Kong (1 daily; 1hr); Kunming (at least 1 daily;
1hr); Shanghai (2 daily; 2hr 15min); Shenzhen (2
daily; 55min); Xi'an (1 daily; 2hr).

CHAPTER 11

Highlights

* **Kunming's bars** Check out the laid-back nightlife at one of China's most relaxed cities. See p.809

* **Yuanyang** Base yourself in this attractive town and visit nearby minority villages set in a landscape spectacularly sliced up by rice terraces. See p.818

* **Dali** An ancient town with an enjoyable, laid-back travellers' ghetto, offering café society and lush scenery. See p.822

* **Cycling around Lijiang** Take yourself out of the touristy town centre and cycle round the well-preserved villages at the heart of the Naxi Kingdom. See p.835

* **Tiger Leaping Gorge** Relax for a few days on the ridge of this dramatic gorge, trekking between farmstead home-stays. See p.838

* **Meili Xue Shan** Dramatic jagged scenery in China's remote Shangri-la. See p.845

* **Ruili** A boisterous border town with charming temples and countryside a short bike ride away. See p.855

* **Jungle trekking in Xishuangbanna** Explore a region populated by many different ethnic groups, each with their own distinctive dress and customs. See p.872

△ Pilgrims at Meili Xue Shan

Yunnan

Y unnan has always stood apart from the rest of China, set high on the empire's "barbarous and pestilential" southwestern frontiers and shielded from the rest of the nation by the unruly, mountainous provinces of Sichuan and Guizhou. Within this single province, unmatched in the complexity and scope of its history, landscape and peoples, you'll find a mix of geography, climates and nationalities that elsewhere on Earth takes entire continents to express.

The northeast of the province is fairly flat and productive, seat of the attractive capital, **Kunming**, whose mild climate earned Yunnan its name, meaning literally "South of the Clouds". Increasingly touristed, it's nonetheless a charming area, with enjoyable day-trips to nearby scenic marvels, and easy access to a varied bag of little-visited sights southeast towards the border with **Vietnam**.

West of Kunming, the Yunnan plateau rises to serrated, snowbound peaks extending north **to Tibet** and surrounding the ancient historic towns of **Dali** and **Lijiang**, while farther west is subtropical **Dehong**, a busy trading region and an unlikely Chinese holiday destination on the central **border with Burma**. Yunnan's deep south comprises a further isolated stretch of this frontier, which reaches down to the tropical forests and paddy fields of **Xishuangbanna**, a botanical, zoological and ethnic cornucopia abutting Burma and **Laos** – about as far from Han China as it's possible to be.

Dwelling in this stew of border markets, mountains, jungles, lakes, temples, modern political intrigue and remains of vanished kingdoms are 28 recognized **ethnic groups**, the greatest number in any province. Providing a quarter of the population and a prime reason to visit Yunnan in themselves, the indigenous list includes Dai and Bai, Wa, Lahu, Hani, Jingpo, Nu, Naxi and Lisu plus a host shared with other provinces (such as the Yi; p.912) or adjoining nations. Each minority has its own spoken language, cuisine, distinctive form of dress for women, festivals and belief system. Those in the south often have cultural ties with ethnic cousins in Laos, Burma and Vietnam, while the minorities in the north have strong links with Tibet. Though much of what you'll initially glean of these cultures is put on for tourists, anyone with even a couple of days to spare in Xishuangbanna or Lijiang can begin to flesh out this image. With more time you can look for shyer, remoter groups leading lives less influenced by the modern world.

While all this diversity makes Yunnan as elusive a place for the modern traveller to come to grips with as it was for successive dynasties to govern, the province's obvious charms have in recent years brought about something of a tourist boom. Much of this is associated with the domestic market, but foreigners, too, will find plenty of resources geared up to their needs, from backpacker cafés to companies offering cycling and trekking trips, making Yunnan one of the easiest places to travel in China.

There are international flights into Kunming from Bangkok, Rangoon, Singapore and Vientiane, and to Jinghong – near the border with Burma and Laos – from Chiang Mai and Bangkok. Getting around can be time-consuming given Yunnan's scale, but the province does have one of China's better airlines in Yunnan Air, and the state of country **buses and roads** is often surprisingly good; whatever their condition, it's an undeniable achievement that some routes exist at all. Make sure you travel at least briefly along the famous **Burma Road** between Kunming and the western border, built with incredible determination during the 1930s. There's a limited **rail network** inside Yunnan – one service from Kunming down through the southeast to the Vietnamese border, and a line to Xiaguan, near Dali; Kunming itself is well linked to the rest of the country via Sichuan and Guizhou. The **weather** is generally moderate throughout the year, though northern Yunnan has cold winters and heavy snow up around the Tibetan border, while the south is always warm, with a torrential summer wet season.

In the more remote areas, roads are occasionally closed, usually because of landslides and bad weather, but sometimes thanks to the army looking for illegal

Yunnanese food

Yunnanese food broadly splits into three cooking styles. In the **north**, a cold, pastoral lifestyle produces dried meats and – very unusually for China – dairy products, fused with a Muslim cuisine, a vestige of the thirteenth-century Mongolian invasion. Typical dishes include wind-cured ham (*yuntui* or *huotui*), sweetened, steamed and served with slices of bread; toasted cheese and dried yoghurt wafers (*rushan* and *rubing*); the local version of crisp-skinned duck (*shaoya*), flavoured by basting it with honey and roasting over a pine-needle fire; and *shaguoyu*, a tasty fish claypot.

Southeastern Yunnan produces the most recognizably "Chinese" food. From here comes *qiguo ji*, chicken flavoured with medicinal herbs and stewed inside a specially shaped earthenware steamer, and **crossing-the-bridge noodles** (*guoqiao mian*), a sort of individualized hotpot that is probably the most famous dish in the province. The curious name comes from a tale of a Qing scholar who retired every day to a lakeside pavilion to compose poetry. His wife, an understanding soul, used to cook him lunch, but the food always cooled as she carried it from their home over the bridge to where he studied – until she hit on the idea of keeping the heat in with a layer of oil on top of his soup. It's best sampled in Kunming, where numerous places serve a huge bowl of oily, scalding chicken stock with a platter of noodles, shredded meats and vegetables, which you add along with chilli powder and spices to taste.

Not surprisingly, Yunnan's **southwestern borders** are strongly influenced by Burmese cooking methods, particularly in the use of such un-Chinese ingredients as coconut, palm sugar, cloves and turmeric. Here you'll find a vast range of soups and stews displayed in aluminium pots outside fast-turnover restaurants, roughly recognizable as **curries**, and oddities such as purple rice-flour pancakes sold at street markets. As most of these aren't generally available outside the area, however, their description and a glossary of local names appears in the relevant section (see p.855). The southwest also produces good **coffee** and red *pu'er cha*, Yunnan's best **tea**, both widely appreciated across the province.

Each of Yunnan's minorities has its own culinary specialities, often quite distinctive from mainstream Chinese cuisine; these are described in the relevant accounts.

cross–border traffic in cars, timber, gems and **opiates**. Much of the world's heroin originates in Burma and is funnelled through China to overseas markets. Officially, the Yunnanese government is tough on the drugs trade, executing traffickers and forcibly rehabilitating addicts. All this means that there are military **checkpoints** on many rural roads, where you'll have to show passports. It pays to be polite, and things are often easier if you avoid appearing fluent in Chinese in these circumstances.

Some history

Yunnan has been inhabited for a very long time, with evidence reaching back through galleries of Stone Age rock art to two 1.5-million-year-old teeth found near the northern town of Yuanmou. Records of civilization, however, are far more recent. According to the Han historian Sima Qian, the Chinese warrior prince **Zhuang Qiao** founded the pastoral **Dian Kingdom** in eastern Yunnan during the third century BC, though it's probable that he simply became chief of an existing nation. The Dian were a slave society, who vividly recorded their daily life and ceremonies involving human sacrifice in sometimes gruesome **bronze models**, which have been unearthed from their tombs. In 109 the kingdom was acknowledged by China: the emperor **Wu**, hoping to control the Southern Silk Road through to India, sent its ruler military aid and a golden seal. But in 204 AD the Han empire collapsed, which was followed by the dissolution of Dian into private statelets.

In the eighth century, an aspiring Yunnanese prince named **Piluoge**, favouring Dali for its location near the Silk Road, invited his rivals to dinner in the town, then set fire to the tent with them inside. Subsequently he established the **Nanzhao Kingdom** in Dali, which absorbed these private statelets and was later expanded to include much of modern Burma, Thailand and Vietnam. In 937, the Bai warlord **Duan Siping** toppled the Nanzhao and set up a smaller **Dali Kingdom**, which survived until **Kublai Khan** and his Mongolian hordes descended in 1252, subduing the Bai. Directly controlled by China for the first time, Yunnan served for a while as a remote dustbin for political troublemakers, thereby escaping the population explosions, wars and migrations that plagued central China. However, the Mongol invasion had introduced a large **Muslim population** to the province, who, angered by their deteriorating status under the Chinese, staged a rebellion in 1856. Inspired by the Taipings, **Du Wenxiu** led a **Muslim Uprising** against the Qing empire, and again declared Dali capital of an independent state. But in 1873 the rebellion was crushed with the wholesale massacre of Yunnan's Muslim population, and a wasted Yunnan was left to local bandits and private armies for the following half-century.

Strangely, it was the **Japanese invasion** during the 1930s that sparked a resurgence of the province's fortunes. Blockaded into southwestern China, the **Guomindang government** initiated great programmes of rail and road building through the region, though they never really controlled Yunnan. Moreover, their poor treatment of minority groups made the Red Army's cause all the more attractive when civil war resumed in 1945. Liberation came smoothly, but the **Communists**' good intentions of coexistence with minorities, better hospitals, schools and communications were badly stalled during the Cultural Revolution and then, in the 1980s, by the war with Vietnam. It's only recently that Yunnan has finally benefited from its forced association with the rest of the country. The province, never agriculturally rich (only a tenth of the land is considered arable), looks to mineral resources, tourism and its potential as a future conduit between China and the much discussed – but as yet unformed – trading bloc of **Vietnam**, **Laos**, **Thailand** and **Burma**. Should these countries ever form an unrestricted economic alliance, the amount of trade passing through Yunnan would be immense – a resurrection of the old Silk Road – and highways, rail and air services have already been planned for the day the borders open freely.

Kunming and the southeast

Every visitor to Yunnan finds themselves at some point in **Kunming**, the province's comfortable capital and transport hub. The large population of young foreign expats, mostly students and teachers, testifies to Kunming's appeal as China's Seattle, the most laid-back city in the country and, with Chengdu, the most pleasant provincial capital. The city's immediate face is an ordinary blend of broad, monochrome main roads and glassy modern office blocks, but its character is partly salvaged by the surrounding temples and fine lake-and-limestone-hill landscapes. From Kunming, both road and rail extend southeast all the way down to the **Vietnamese border**, taking you within striking distance of some fine scenery, old architecture, and a few offbeat sights to slow you down en route.

Kunming and around

Basking 2000m above sea level in the fertile heart of the Yunnan plateau, **KUNMING** does its best to live up to its traditional nickname, the City of Eternal Spring. However, until recently it was considered a savage frontier settlement, and the authorities began to realize the city's promise only when people exiled here during the Cultural Revolution refused offers to return home to eastern China, preferring Kunming's climate and more relaxed life. Today, the people remain mellow enough to mix typically Chinese garrulousness with introspective pleasures, such as quietly greeting the day with a stiff hit of Yunnanese tobacco from fat, brass-bound bamboo pipes. There are other novelties – clean pavements enforced by on-the-spot fines, an orderly traffic system, and a low-profile but sizeable gay community – suggesting that Kunming's two million or so residents enjoy a quality of life above that of most urban Chinese.

Though Kunming boasts few specific sights, the countryside around has enough to keep you occupied for a good few days. Extraordinary sculptures make the westerly **Qiongzhu Si** the pick of local holy sites, while immediately south of Kunming is **Dian Chi**, a spectacular 270-square-kilometre spread of deep blue water dotted with the rectangular sails of fishing junks. You can boat across to the lakeside towns, but the lake's colourful sprawl is best absorbed from the nearby heights of Xi Shan, the **Western Hills**. Further afield, **Shilin**, the spectacular Stone Forest, is an enjoyable day-trip if you can accept the fairground atmosphere and the crowds dutifully tagging behind their cosmetically perfect tour guides.

Some history

Historically the domain of Yunnan's earliest inhabitants and first civilization, Kunming long profited from its position on the caravan roads through to Burma and Europe. It was visited in the thirteenth century by Marco Polo, who found the locals of **Yachi Fu** (Duck Pond Town) using cowries for cash, enjoying their meat raw, and inviting guests to sleep with their womenfolk. Little of the city's wealth survived the 1856 Muslim rebellion, when most Buddhist sites in the capital were razed, or events some forty years later, when an uprising against working conditions on the **Kunming–Haiphong rail line** saw 300,000 labourers executed after France shipped in weapons to suppress the revolt. (The line, designed by the French so that they could tap Yunnan's mineral resources for their colonies in Indochina, was only completed in 1911.) Twenty-five years later, **war with Japan** brought a flock of wealthy east-coast refugees to the city, whose money helped establish Kunming as an industrial and manufacturing base for the wartime government in Chongqing. The allies provided essential support for this, importing materials along the Burma Road from British-held Burma and, when that was lost to the Japanese, through the volunteer US-piloted **Flying Tigers**, who flew in supplies over the Himalayas from British bases in India. The city consolidated its position as a supply depot during the Vietnam War and subsequent border clashes, though during the **Cultural Revolution** buildings that escaped the attentions of nineteenth-century vandals perished at the hands of the Red Guards.

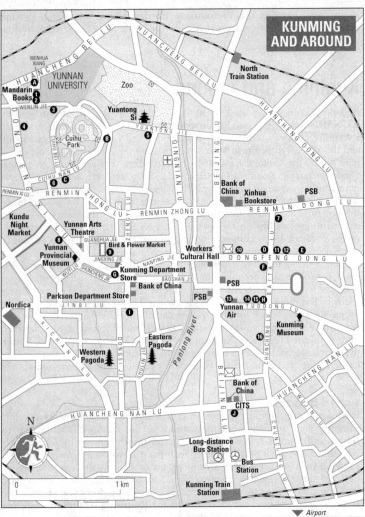

KUNMING AND AROUND

YUNNAN | Kunming and around

EATING & DRINKING		ACCOMMODATION	
Aoma's	16	Camellia	E
Blue Bird	6 & 8	Chuncheng	G
Brothers Jiang	10	Cuihu	B
Camel Bar	14	Golden Dragon	J
French Café	2	Greenland	H
Fuhua Yuan	9	Hump Over	
Hump Over The Himalayas	I	The Himalayas	I
King Dragon		Kunming	D
Regional Cuisine Village	13	Kunming Youth Hostel	C
Mamafu's	12	Sakura	F
Prague Café	3	Yunnan University	
Salvadors	1	Centre for Chinese	
Speakeasy	4	Studies	A
Top One Disco	7		
Vegetarian Restaurant	5		
Wei's Pizza	15		
Zhen Xing	11		

Kunming and around

Kunming
Bird and Flower Market	花鸟市场	*huā niǎo shìchǎng*
Cuihu Park	翠湖公园	*cuìhú gōngyuán*
Daguan Park	大观公园	*dàguān gōngyuán*
Eastern Pagoda	东寺塔	*dōngsì tǎ*
Kunming City Museum	昆明市博物馆	*kūnmíngshì bówùguǎn*
Mosque	南城清真寺	*nánchéng qīngzhēn sì*
Nordica	诺地卡	*nuòdì kǎ*
Western Pagoda	西寺塔	*xīsì tǎ*
Workers' Cultural Hall	工人文化宫	*gōngrén wénhuàgōng*
Yuantong Si	圆通寺	*yuántōng sì*
Yunnan Arts Theatre	艺术剧院	*yìshù jùyuàn*
Yunnan Provincial Museum	云南省博物馆	*yùnnánshěng bówùguǎn*
Zoo	动物园	*dòngwù yuán*

Accommodation
Camellia	茶花宾馆	*cháhuā bīnguǎn*
Chuncheng	春城饭店	*chūnchéng fàndiàn*
Cuihu	翠湖宾馆	*cuìhú bīnguǎn*
Golden Dragon	金龙饭店	*jīnlóng fàndiàn*
Greenland	绿洲大酒店	*lǜzhōu dàjiǔdiàn*
Hump Over the Himalayas	金马碧鸡坊	*jīnmǎ bìjī fǎng*
Kunming	昆明饭店	*kūnmíng fàndiàn*
Kunming Youth Hostel	昆明国际青年旅社	*kūnmíng guójì qīngnián lǚshè*
Sakura	樱花酒店	*yīnghuā jiǔdiàn*
Yunnan University Centre for Chinese Studies	云南大学国际 学术教育交流中心	*yúnnán dàxué guójì xuéshùjiàoyù jiāoliú zhōngxīn*

Eating and drinking
Blue Bird	青鸟饭店	*qīngniǎo fàndiàn*
Brothers Jiang	江氏兄弟	*jiāngshì xiōngdì*
Camel Bar	骆驼酒吧	*luòtuó jiǔbā*
French Café	兰白红	*lánbáihóng*
Fuhua Yuan	福华园饭店	*fúhuá yuán fàndiàn*
King Dragon Regional Cuisine Village	元龙风味城	*yuánlóng fēngwèichéng*
Kundu Night Market	昆都夜市	*kūndū yèshì*
Mamafu's	马马付餐厅	*mǎmǎfù cāntīng*
Speakeasy	说吧	*shuōbā*
Vegetarian restaurant	玉泉斋	*yùquánzhāi*
Zhen Xing	振兴饭店	*zhènxīng fàndiàn*

Around Kunming
Dian Chi	滇池	*diānchí*
Heilong Tan	黑龙滩	*hēilóng tān*
Jin Dian	金殿	*jīndiàn*
Kunyang	昆阳	*kūnyáng*
Lunan	路南	*lùnán*
Qiongzhu Si	筇竹寺	*qióngzhú sì*
Shilin	石林	*shílín*
Tanhua Si	昙华寺	*tánhuá sì*
Western Hills	西山	*xīshān*
Zhenghe Park	郑和公园	*zhènghé gōngyuán*

Since the mid-1980s, Kunming has enjoyed snowballing tourism and foreign investment. Neighbouring nations such as Thailand trace their ancestries back to Yunnan and have proved particularly willing to channel funds into the city, which has become ever more accessible as a result. Virtually all the old architecture that remained was cleared when the city centre was rebuilt in its current "modern" style to impress visitors attending the **1999 World Horticultural Expo**. Survivors include a couple of temples, the long-established university and a Minorities' Institute set up in the 1950s to promote mutual understanding among Yunnan's multifaceted population.

Orientation, arrival and city transport

Kunming has few natural landmarks to help guide you around, but its layout is uncomplicated. The city hangs off two main thoroughfares: **Beijing Lu** forms the north–south axis, passing just east of the centre as it runs for 5km between the city's two train stations, while **Dongfeng Lu** crosses it halfway along. Most

Moving on from Kunming

The **airport bus** (¥5) leaves from outside the Yunnan Air headquarters on Tuodong Lu – check with them inside for bus departure times, and be prepared to take a taxi (at ¥20, possibly the cheapest airport ride in China) if the bus doesn't materialize. The journey takes about forty minutes. Yunnan Air is very helpful and organized, and can also book you on other airlines out of Kunming. Agents around town sometimes have cheaper tickets though.

At the **train station**, the booking office on the west side of the vast station square is open from 6.30am until midnight. When staffed, the ticket service desk here is pretty helpful and will fill you in on which queue to join. Trains run **north to Chengdu** via Xichang in southern Sichuan, **southeast** via Xingyi to Baise and Nanning in Guangxi, and **east through Guizhou**, via Liupanshui, Anshun and Guiyang, into the rest of the country. Tickets can be bought up to three days in advance of travel.

Trains to **Hekou and Vietnam** leave from the **North train station**, and tickets are only available there – take bus #23 up Beijing Lu. The ticket office, hidden away at the northeast corner of the station, advertises hours of 6am to 10.40pm, but don't take this too literally. There's currently one afternoon train, which takes about 16 hours to reach Hekou (a seat is ¥35, berths around ¥90), double that to Hanoi (hard sleeper lower bunk ¥175, upper bunk ¥235). Visas are available from the Vietnamese consulate in Kunming (see p.810).

At Kunming's main **long-distance bus station**, the ticket office is computerized and staff are helpful, with standard, luxury, express and sleeper buses departing for all over Yunnan and neighbouring provinces – but finding the right vehicle out the back can be a protracted business. Keep a tight hold on your luggage, as plenty of people have something stolen either at the station or in transit. Tickets for luxury buses can be bought from an office just inside the entrance, on the right. If you're taking the long road to Jinghong, it's certainly worth considering the luxury bus, which takes 16 hours and costs ¥180; the standard service takes 21 hours and costs ¥120. There's also a useful luxury service to Xiaguan (for Dali), which leaves hourly from 8am to 7pm (¥104), and a morning service to Lijiang (¥152). These buses are new and feature hostesses and even onboard toilets. Another useful service goes to Hekou at 9.45am (¥112).

Leaving for **Vietnam** and **Laos by bus** is possible, through the respective crossings at Hekou in southeastern Yunnan (p.819) or Mo Han in Xishuangbanna (p.872). Foreigners entering **Burma** used to have no choice but to fly to Rangoon, though now an overland route is open to organized tours (see p.811).

of the city's accommodation lies along Dongfeng Dong Lu and the southern half of Beijing Lu, while the majority of sights are north and west of the centre around Dongfeng Xi Lu and **Cuihu Park**. Circling most of this is the first ring road, most of which is known as **Huancheng Lu**.

Arrival and city transport

Kunming's busy **airport** is out in the southeastern suburbs, with the international and domestic terminal buildings next to each other. At the south side of the square outside you'll find a **CAAC bus** which meets arrivals and runs via some of the downtown hotels to the Yunnan Air offices on Tuodong Lu (¥5). There are also slightly cheaper **public minibuses** to various places around the centre (not an option if you have much luggage). **Taxis** should be caught from the rank opposite the entrance; a ride into town costs around ¥20 using the meter.

The **long-distance bus station** and **Kunming train station** are down at the seedy southern end of Beijing Lu. From here, bus #23 runs right up to the **North train station** past hotels and the Dongfeng Lu intersection, where you should alight and head east for further accommodation prospects. You'll end up at the North train station only if you're arriving from the Vietnamese border or southeastern Yunnan. There's also the **Western bus station** on Renmin Xi Lu, of most use for excursions around Kunming, though a few long-distance services also terminate here.

Kunming is not too large to walk around, and **bicycles** are readily rented from several of the hotels. Otherwise, there are plenty of **taxis** (¥8 standing charge) and **public buses** cruising the main streets, and you can stay up to date with the routes by picking up a bus **map** from street sellers.

Accommodation

Kunming has abundant accommodation, mostly mid-range, scattered throughout the city centre. There's also a great range of choice for the many budget travellers who turn up – from old stalwart, the *Camellia*, to party centre the *Hump* (if the police haven't closed it down again).

Camellia 96 Dongfeng Dong Lu ☎0871/3163000 or 3162918, ℻3147033, ⓦwww.kmcamelliahotel.com. Pleasant three-winged affair and a budget travellers' favourite, though it's gone downhill of late. The three-bed dorms represent better value than the rather cramped and overcrowded seven- and eight-bed rooms (the price is the same), and those in building three are better than the ones in the main building. Doubles are universally a good deal. The garden here is a bonus, though watch out for rather predatory students of English. There's also a foreign-exchange counter, an expensive bar and restaurant, ticket booking service, Internet access (¥10/hr), luggage storage and bike rental. Take bus #2 or #23 from the main train station to Dongfeng Dong Lu, then any bus heading east for two stops. Dorm beds ¥35. ❸

Chuncheng Dongfeng Xi Lu, near the junction with Zhengyi Lu ☎0871/3633271. Faded, with a rather oppressive feel, but well positioned for the more interesting western parts of town. Offers basic doubles with bath through to suites. Bus #2 from the train station stops nearby. ❷

Cuihu Cuihu Nan Lu ☎0871/5158888, ℻5153286. Recently spruced up and given a very fancy new lobby, complete with palm trees, this is a long-established and good-value upmarket hotel in pleasant surroundings by Cuihu Park. There's an excellent restaurant, too. Airport transfers can be arranged; all major credit cards are accepted. ❾

Golden Dragon 575 Beijing Lu ☎0871/3133015, ℻3131082. Four-star comforts aimed at the upmarket business traveller, but recent renovations haven't been completely successful in dispelling a tired atmosphere. ❽

Greenland 80 Tuodong Lu ☎0871/3189999, ℻3195888. Hefty discounts of up to fifty percent make this swanky place, on one of the more glamorous streets, worth investigating off season. Complimentary breakfast and late checkouts (3pm) are a nice touch. ❾

Hump Over The Himalayas Jinmabiji Fang, Jinbi Lu ☎0871/3640359. Three hundred police once raided this place to close it down. Now re-opened with a promise of good behaviour, it's basically a set of huge, thirty-bed dorm rooms (and a few doubles, not en suite) above a bar and disco complex, and is aimed squarely at the budget traveller for whom sleep is not a priority. There's a bar, Internet access and pleasant roof terrace with a DVD lounge. Dorms ¥25 including breakfast, ❶

Kunming Dongfeng Dong Lu ☎0871/3162063, ℻3163784, ⊛www.kunminghotel.com.cn. A big, upmarket hotel with reasonable service and a Korean restaurant, and also offering bikes for rent. It's not cheap, though; the less expensive rooms are in the older, south wing. ❼

Kunming Youth Hostel C1 Building, *Zhengxie Hotel*, 94 Cuihu Nan Lu ☎0871/5175395, ℻5167131, ℮youthhostel.km@sohu.com. Well located by Cuihu Park, this efficient hostel offers doubles without bathroom, and four-bed dorms; it also has kitchen facilities and bike rental. It's so low-key it's difficult to find – take bus #2 from the train station, alight at the Wu Yi stop, walk north to Cuihu Nan Lu, and look for the HI triangle on the *Zhengxie Hotel* – the hostel is just behind, down a small alley. There's a small discount for HI members. Dorm beds ¥25, ❷

Sakura Dongfeng Dong Lu ☎0871/3165888, ℻3135189. A tall, distinctive building with decent, mid-range rooms, though the lobby is rather poky. It's also home to a well-reputed Thai restaurant. Large discounts on the rack rate are sometimes available. ❽

Yunnan University Centre for Chinese Studies Wenhua Xiang ☎0871/5033624, ℻5148513. Aimed at long-stay foreign students but open to anyone. It's opposite the university's west gate, in one of the nicest parts of town, with plenty of cafés and bars around. The old wing, to the south, is musty but has a lovely garden and tiled patio. Rooms in the bright new wing are pricier, but still very good value. ❷

The City

Kunming's public focus is the huge square outside the grandiose **Workers' Cultural Hall** at the Beijing Lu/Dongfeng Lu intersection, alive in the mornings with regimented crowds warming up on hip pivots and shuttlecock games. Later in the day it's somewhere to consult a fortune-teller, or receive a shoulder and back massage from the hard-fingered blind practitioners who pounce on passersby; you might catch weekend amateur theatre here, too. Rapidly being modernized, the city's true centre is west of here across the **Panlong River**, outside the modern Kunming Department Store at the Dongfeng Xi Lu/Zhengyi Lu crossroads, a densely crowded shopping precinct packed with clothing and hi-fi stores. The river itself, though black and oily, is at least nicely landscaped – the general impression is that some time, trouble and planning is behind these modernizations, unlike in many Chinese cities. The centre itself is an area of importance to Kunming's Hui population, and **Shuncheng Jie** – the last old street in the city, and an essential wander for as long as it survives – forms a **Muslim quarter**, full of wind-dried beef and sheep carcasses, pitta bread and raisin sellers, and huge woks of roasting coffee beans being earnestly stirred with shovels. Rising behind a supermarket one block north off Zhengyi Lu, **Nancheng Qingzhen Si** is the city's new **mosque**, its green dome and chevron-patterned minaret visible from afar and built on the site of an earlier Qing edifice.

Running west off Zhengyi Jie, **Jingxing Jie** leads into one of the more bizarre corners of the city, with Kunming's huge **bird and flower market** – which sells a much greater range of creatures than its name suggests – convening daily in the streets connecting it with northerly, parallel Guanghua Jie. At least at weekends, this is no run-of-the-mill mix of kittens and grotesque goldfish: rare, multicoloured songbirds twitter and squawk in the wings, while furtive hawkers display geckos, monkey-like lorises and other endangered oddities illegally "liberated" from Xishuangbanna's forests. There are plants here, too, along with **antique and curio** booths – this is somewhere to find coins and Cultural Revolution mementos, bamboo pipes and prayer rugs – as well as plenty of opportunity to sample local snacks. If the crowds get too much, head right up the tiny alley on the right as you come in from Zhengyi Lu, and you'll find a peaceful **teahouse** built in traditional style around a courtyard.

The nearby **grounds of Wen Miao**, a vanished Confucian temple on Renmin Zhong Lu, are worth seeking out. There's an avenue of pines, an ancient pond and pavilion, and beds of bamboo, azaleas and potted palms – a quiet place where old men play chess and drink tea.

Yunnan Provincial Museum

About 500m west of the centre along Dongfeng Xi Lu and the #5 bus route, the **Yunnan Provincial Museum** (daily 9.30am–5.30pm; last entry an hour before the museum closes; ¥15) has its moments, though the building is dim, dusty and largely empty. Best are the **Dian bronzes** on the second floor, dating back more than two thousand years to the Warring States Period and excavated from tombs on the shores of Dian Chi, south of Kunming. The largest pieces include an ornamental plate of a tiger attacking an ox and a **coffin** in the shape of a bamboo house, but lids from **storage drums** used to hold cowries are the most impressive, decorated with dioramas of figurines fighting, sacrificing oxen and men and, rather more peacefully, posing with their families and farmyard animals outside their homes. A replica of the Chinese imperial **gold seal** given to the Dian king early on in the second century implies that his aristocratic slave society had the tacit approval of the Han emperor. Upstairs again is a porcelain gallery and an exhibition of paintings by the Qing-dynasty artist Dan Dang.

Cuihu Park, Yuantong Si and the zoo

Cuihu Park (open from dawn until 10pm) is predominantly lake, a good place to join thousands of others exercising, singing, feeding wintering flocks of **gulls**, or just milling between the plum and magnolia gardens and over the maze of bridges. The park is a twenty-minute walk north of the museum via Dongfeng Xi Lu and Cuihu Nan Lu; alternatively, take bus #5 from the museum or bus #2 from the southern end of Beijing Lu. Immediately northwest, the **Yunnan University** campus offers a glimpse of old Kunming, its partially overgrown 1920s exterior reached up a wide flight of stone steps. **Cafés** and cheap restaurants in the vicinity are the haunt of plenty of expats and students eager to practise their English – see p.809 for details.

East from Cuihu Park along Yuantong Jie is the Qing-vintage **Yuantong Si** (daily 8am–6pm; ¥4), northern Yunnan's major Buddhist site, recently spruced up and an active place of pilgrimage. A bridge over the central pond crosses through an octagonal pavilion dedicated to a multi-armed Guanyin and white marble Sakyamuni, to the threshold of the **main hall**, where two huge central pillars wrapped in colourful, Manga-esque **dragons** support the ornate wooden ceiling. Faded frescoes on the back wall were painted in the thirteenth century, while a new annexe out the back houses a graceful gilded bronze Buddha flanked by peacocks, donated by the Thai government. Cooks in the **vegetarian restaurant** opposite on Yuantong Jie work wonders at lunchtime.

The temple sits on the southern slope of the large Kunming **zoo** (daily 8am–5pm; ¥10), with the entrance at the corner of Yuantong Jie and Qingnian Lu on the #4 bus route. It's not the worst in China, offering nice vignettes of children stroking and feeding the deer, along with views of the city from a hilltop planted with crab-apple groves.

Kunming City Museum

The highlight of the **Kunming City Museum** (Tues–Sun 10am–5pm; ¥5), east off Beijing Lu along Tuodong Lu, is the **Dali Sutra Pillar**. In its own room on the ground floor, it's a 6.5-metre-high, pagoda-like Song-dynasty sculpture, in pink sandstone; an octagonal base supports seven tiers covered in Buddha images, statues of fierce guardian gods standing on subjugated demons, and a mix of Tibetan and Chinese script, part of which is the Dharani Mantra. The rest is a dedication, identifying the pillar as having been raised by the Dali regent, **Yuan Douguang**, in memory of his general **Gao Ming**. The whole thing is topped by a ring of Buddhas carrying a ball – the universe – above them. Formerly part of the defunct Dizang temple, the pillar is a powerful work, full of the energy that later seeped out of the mainstream of Chinese sculpture.

The other exhibits are a well-presented repeat of the Provincial Museum's collection. Enthusiasts for **bronze drums** can examine a range, from the oldest known example to relatively recent castings, to see how the typical decorations – sun and frog designs on top, long-plumed warriors in boats around the sides, tiger handles – became so stylized (for more on bronze drums, see p.757). There are cowrie-drum lids, too, and a host of other bronze pieces worth examining for nit-picking details of birds, animals and people. Other rooms contain two excellent **dioramas** of modern and Ming-dynasty Kunming, accounts (in Chinese) of the voyages of **Zheng He**, the famous Ming eunuch admiral, and five locally found **fossilized dinosaur skeletons** – including a tyrannosaurus-like allosaur, and the bulky *Yunnanosaurus robustus*.

Southern Kunming

Jinbi Lu runs roughly parallel to and south of Dongfeng Lu, and is reached on bus #3 from Beijing Lu. Two large Tang-dynasty **pagodas** rise in the vicinity, each a solid thirteen storeys of whitewashed brick crowned with four jolly iron cockerels. South down Dongsi Jie, past another **mosque**, the entrance to the **Western Pagoda** is along a narrow lane on the right. Paying a few jiao gains you admission to the tiny surrounding courtyard, where sociable idlers while away sunny afternoons playing cards and sipping tea in peaceful, ramshackle surroundings. The **Eastern Pagoda**, a few minutes' walk away on Shulin Jie, is a more cosmetic, slightly tilted duplicate standing in an ornamental garden. The temples associated with both pagodas are closed to the public.

For a change of atmosphere, ride bus #4 from Dongfeng Lu to the terminus at **Daguan Park** (daily 7am–8pm; ¥15) on Kunming's southwestern limits. Originally laid out by the energetic seventeenth-century Qing emperor Kangxi, it has been modified over the years to include a noisy funfair, snack stalls and souvenir emporiums, and is a favourite haunt of Kunming's youth. Among shady walks and pools, Daguan's focal point is **Daguan Ge**, a square, three-storeyed pavilion built to better Kangxi's enjoyment of the distant **Western Hills** and now a storehouse of calligraphy extolling the area's charms. The most famous poem here is a 118-character verse, carved into the gateposts by the Qing scholar Sun Ran; it's reputed to be the longest set of rhyming couplets in China. The park is set on Daguan Stream, which flows south into **Dian Chi** (see p.812), and there are frequent hour-long cruises down the waterway, lined with willows, to points along Dian's northern shore.

Eating

Eating out is the main pleasure in Kunming after dark; the city is stacked with Yunnanese specialities as well as more ordinary Chinese fare. While hotel restaurants have the most refined surroundings, independent restaurants tend to focus their efforts on the food, so don't be discouraged by the outward appearance of some venues. Back lanes running north off **Dongfeng Xi Lu** or **Jinbi Lu** have the best stalls and cheap restaurants where you can battle with the locals over grilled cheese, hotpots, fried snacks rolled in chilli powder, loaves of excellent meat-stuffed soda bread, and rich duck and chicken casseroles. In the same area, **Shuncheng Jie** has endless rows of inexpensive Muslim diners with glazed ducks and fresh ingredients piled up outside; mutton stews, kebabs and *lamian* – pulled noodles – are popular. For Western food and decent coffee, visit one of the many places close to the university, or the Nordica Art Gallery (see p.810).

Restaurants and cafés

Aoma's 20 Chuncheng Lu. Steaks, pasta, pizzas and some local dishes, in an urbane and relaxed atmosphere.

Blue Bird 127 Dongfeng Xi Lu ☏0871/3610478 and 132 Cuihu Nan Lu ☏0871/5315507. The city's finest restaurant; both premises are cosy and have fantastic decor, with mood lighting, plenty of foliage and water features. The larger branch at Dongfeng Xi Lu specializes in Thai and Burmese cuisine; fish with lemon sauce and chicken curry are recommended. The smaller branch on Cuihu Nan Lu does Chinese and Thai cuisine and has a pleasant roof garden. A dinner for two should come to around ¥100.

Brothers Jiang Dongfeng Dong Lu. With several branches around town, this modern-looking fast-food noodle place is certainly one of the best places to try crossing-the-bridge noodles, available for ¥10 or ¥20 depending on the number of ingredients.

French Café Wenlin Jie. There's a large French contingent in Kunming, drawn by the colonial connection perhaps; this café, with its pastries, quiches and air of *hauteur*, must make them feel at home.

Fuhua Yuan Jingxing Jie. Airy, canteen-like affair in one of the most charismatic parts of town, serving crossing-the-bridge noodles and other light meals downstairs, full meals upstairs.

King Dragon Regional Cuisine Village Tuodong Lu. Huge, multi-floored affair with stalls, canteens and sit-down restaurants offering everything from local street snacks through to Cantonese banquet cuisine. Cheaper places are on the ground floor, with posher, private restaurants above. It's good fun at the weekends, when it can get very crowded.

Mamafu's Dongfeng Dong Lu. Owned by the same people as *Aoma's*, this cultivated café is handy for the *Camellia Hotel*.

Prague Café 40 Wenlin Jie. This offshoot of a successful Lijiang enterprise offers very strong coffee and a decent breakfast (¥16), as well as Internet access and book exchange. One of the better cafés in its locality, it's a good place to while away an afternoon.

Salvadors Wenhua Xiang. The best of the foreign-run student cafés, with great home-made ice cream as well as novelties such as hummus and bagels.

Vegetarian restaurant Opposite the Yuantong Si, Yuantong Jie. An excellent place, reasonably priced and with an English menu and pictures of the dishes on the wall. It serves a mix of straight vegetable and imitation-meat dishes – best of the latter are coconut-flavoured "spareribs" (bamboo shoots, celery and fried bean-curd skin), "chicken" and fungus rolls (dried bean curd), and "fish" (deep fried mashed potato served in a rich garlic and vinegar sauce).

Wei's Pizza In an alley north off Tuodong Lu ☏0871/3166189. Long-running, popular expat café with wood-fired pizzas and low prices. Also offered are some unusual Chinese dishes, including river moss with coriander and Hakka bean curd, plus a book exchange. They deliver.

Zhen Xing Corner of Dongfeng Dong Lu and Baita Lu. Inexpensive, unadorned restaurant with brusque staff, a mostly local clientele, and simple fare. Noodles cost ¥3–5; pay at the counter and give the chit to the cook.

Drinking, nightlife and entertainment

Thanks to rising incomes and a big expat population, Kunming is a great place to go out, with plenty of friendly, reasonably priced **bars and clubs** patronized by a good mix of locals and foreigners. *Hump Over The Himalayas* on Jinbi Lu is a complex (or, after a few drinks, a maze) of interlinked bars – stumble out of one and you fall straight into another. The main foreign student hangout is the underground *Speakeasy* at 445 Dongfeng Dong Lu, where beers cost ¥6; there's a Western DJ on Fridays and occasional gigs. The *Camel Bar* on Tuodong Lu is slightly more upmarket, well established and polished, with a lively, mixed clientele. Downstairs there's a dancefloor while the upstairs is more laid-back, a good place to sit over a coffee during the day.

If you can't live without cheesy techno and flashing lights, you can join Kunming's silver-suited and platform-booted finest at the Kundu Night Market on Xinwen Lu, a street of bars and discos, with late-night restaurants and nail and tattoo parlours in between. Everywhere's free to get in but drinks cost at least ¥25. The most popular place with foreigners is the *Top One Disco*. It's probably best visited in an anthropological frame of mind, as it's all fiercely tacky.

Kunming has several **operatic troupes** and indigenous entertainments which include *huadeng*, a lantern dance. Indoor performances are sadly infrequent, but there are often informal shows at the weekend outside the Workers' Cultural Hall and in Cuihu Park. Keep an eye on local newspapers (or ask at your hotel) for similar activities at the Yunnan Arts Theatre on Dongfeng Xi Lu.

Gigs, club nights and talks take place frequently at the Scandinavian-run **Nordica**, 101 Xiba Lu (℡0871/4114692, ⓦwww.tcgnordica.org), an old factory converted into a complex of galleries, cafés and studio spaces. Kunming attracts a lot of artists, and Nordica is also a good place to find them and their work.

Listings

Airlines Yunnan Air, Tuodong Lu (℡0871/3164270 or 3138562; daily 24hr), sells tickets for all Chinese airlines and has discounts on their own flights. Other Chinese airlines with offices here are: China Southern, 433 Beijing Lu, south of the Dongfeng Lu intersection ℡0871/3101831; China Southwest, north of the *King World Hotel* at 160 Beijing Lu ℡0871/3539702; Kunming United Airlines, 13 Dongfeng Xi Lu ℡0871/3628592; Shanghai Airlines, 46 Dongfeng Xi Lu ℡0871/3138502. International airlines in Kunming are: Dragonair, in the *Golden Dragon Hotel* on Beijing Dong Lu ℡0871/3138592; JAL, Floor 25, *Holiday Inn*, Dongfeng Dong Lu ℡0871/3161230; and Thai International, next door to the *King World Hotel*, Beijing Lu ℡0871/3133315.

Banks and exchange The main branch of the Bank of China is at the corner of Beijing Lu and Renmin Dong Lu (Mon–Fri 9–11.45am & 2.30–5.30pm). There's a smaller branch on Huancheng Nan Lu.

Bike rental The *Camellia Hotel*, the *Youth Hostel*, the *Hump* and the *Camel Bar* all rent out bikes for ¥3/hr.

Bookshops The city's best English-language bookshop – in fact one of the best in the country – is Mandarin Books at 52 Wenhua Xiang, near the university, which has many imported novels, obscure academic texts, guidebooks and much that is published in English in China, all of it fairly pricey.

Cinema Kunming's main screen is on the south side of the Dongfeng Lu/Zhengyi Lu intersection. There's another good multiplex, the XJS, at the junction of Wenlin Jie and Dongfeng Xi Lu.

Consulates Burma (Myanmar): in the *Camellia* hotel, Dongfeng Dong Lu, in room 214 (℡0871/3176609; Mon–Fri 8.30am–noon & 1–4.30pm, closed during Burmese public holidays). Tourist visas (28 days) take three working days to issue (¥185). Laos: ground floor, *Camellia* hotel, Dongfeng Dong Lu (℡0871/3176623; Mon–Fri 8.30–11.30am & 1.30–4.30pm); they take three working days to issue visas (costs depend on the applicant's nationality). Thailand: in a building in front of the *Kunming* hotel on Dongfeng Dong Lu (Mon–Fri 9–11.30am; ℡0871/3168916). Vietnam: in the *Zhaxing Hotel*, 157 Beijing Lu (℡0871/3515889; Mon–Fri 9–11.30am). A one-month visa costs ¥400 and takes three working days to process, and requires a date and place of entry to be submitted. Visas for these four countries can also be obtained from travel agents.

Hospital Yunnan Province Red Cross hospital and emergency centre is on Qingnian Lu.

Internet access You can get online in most hotels, and in the foreigner-oriented cafés up near the university, though it's considerably cheaper to do so at one of the many ordinary Internet cafés in the university district.

Mail and telephones The GPO is on the southern stretch of Beijing Lu (daily 8am–8pm). There are phones at the GPO, but the main Telecom building is north at the junction with Dongfeng Lu (Mon–Fri 8am–6.30pm, Sat & Sun 9am–5pm).

PSB The main office is on Beijing Lu, but the Foreign Affairs Department is in Jinxing Huayuan, Jinxing Xiao Lu (℡0871/5717030; daily 8–11am & 1–5pm) in the northeast of the city. They speak good English and are generally helpful with visa extensions.

Shopping The antique store in the grounds of the *Camellia Binguan* on Dongfeng Dong Lu has a collection of wooden panels prised off Qing-dynasty homes, silver hairpins, porcelain and some nice inkstones. For items with a local flavour, try bamboo pipes, home-grown tobacco, and trinkets sold in backstreet markets, such as the curio stalls at the bird and flower market. Yunnan also has a reputation as a source of rare medicines, though prices in Kunming for many of these are grossly inflated – if you're curious, check out the handful of shops south of the Beijing Lu GPO for caterpillar fungus, dragon's blood and other weird items. A "gift pack" selection of these costs ¥680. For hiking gear and travellers' supplies, try On The Tourist's Way at 151 Baoshan Jie. Western culinary staples such as cheese and pasta can be bought at Paul's Shop on Wenhua Xiang, just east of Mandarin Books.

Travel agents CITS has counters at the *Holiday Inn* (☎0871/3165888), *King World*

Hotel (☎0871/3138888), and at Yunnan Air (☎0871/3162214). The *Camellia Binguan*'s agency (☎0871/3166388) is recommended for all independent travellers' needs. Both it and CITS can organize visas and private tours around the city and to Shilin, Dali and Xishuangbanna, and obtain train and plane (and sometimes long-distance bus) tickets. Expect to pay commissions of at least ¥20 for bus or train ticket reservations. The Yunnan Overseas Travel Corporation in room 3104 at the *Camellia Binguan* (☎0871/3184478) will arrange tickets and visas for Vietnam and Laos. Mr Chen at Tibet Travel, in room 3116 in the *Camellia Binguan*, arranges flights from Deqin Airport in Zhongdian to Lhasa, and the necessary permit, for ¥2400. He also arranges overland jeep tours from Zhongdian to Lhasa; these take seven days and cost ¥4500. Ko Wai Lin Travel, in room 221 of the *Camellia Binguan* (☎0871/3137555), offers an intriguing new service, a jeep picking travellers up in Ruili (see p.855) and taking them to Hsipaw, in northern Burma. This day-trip isn't cheap, however, at ¥1350 per person.

Heilong Tan, Jin Dian and Tanhua Si

Three pleasant temple parks are easily visited from Kunming on public buses. Ten kilometres north on bus #10 from the North train station, **Heilong Tan** (Black Dragon Pool; daily 8am–6pm; ¥15) is set in a garden of ancient trees, full of plum blossoms in spring. The two Ming temple buildings are modest Taoist affairs dedicated to the Heavenly Emperor and other deities, while the pool itself is said to be inhabited by a dragon forced by the Immortal, Lu Dongbin, to provide a permanent source of water for the local people. It should also be haunted by a patriotic Ming scholar who zealously drowned himself and his family as a gesture of defiance in the face of invading Qing armies; his tomb stands nearby.

The same distance to the northeast on bus #11 from the North train station, the **Jin Dian** (Golden Temple; daily 8am–5pm; ¥15) has a convoluted history. The original temple, built in 1602 as a copy of the Taihe Gong atop Wudang Shan (see p.515), was shifted to a monastery on Jizu Shan near Dali 35 years later, and the current double-eaved structure was founded by the Qing rebel general Wu Sangui in 1671. Again associated with the mystical Lu Dongbin, who apparently instigated its construction, the temple is supported on a marble base; the lattices, beams and statues in the main hall are made entirely of that thoroughly Yunnanese metal, **bronze**, and house two magical swords used by Taoist warriors. The gardens here are full of fragrant camellias and weekend picnickers, and a tower on the hill behind encloses a large Ming bell from Kunming's demolished southern gates.

Tanhua Si (¥10) is 4km east of the city at the base of the Jinma Hills, over the creek and about 1km north of where the #4 bus from Renmin Dong Lu terminates. There's little to see in the heavily restored Ming Buddhist temple, but the **ornamental gardens** are pleasant, with narrow paths winding around groves of exotic trees, bamboos, peonies and azaleas. *Tanhua* is a type of magnolia which grew here in profusion before the temple was built, though now just one slender, broad-leafed tree survives in a small courtyard next to the scripture hall.

Qiongzhu Si

Facing Kunming in hills 10km to the west, **Qiongzhu Si**, the Bamboo Temple
(¥15), is an essential trip from town thanks to a fantastic array of over-the-top
sculptures. You can get here either on irregular **minibuses** (¥6) from the Western bus station on Renmin Xi Lu, at the end of the #5 bus route; by chartering
a minibus from in front of the Yunnan Arts Theatre on Dongfeng Xi Lu (¥60
for a seven-seater); or on the 8am **tour bus** from the same place, which also
visits the Western Hills (see below).

The temple, a dignified building with black and red woodwork standing on Yuan-dynasty foundations, has been restored continually through the
ages and, late in the nineteenth century, the eminent Sichuanese sculptor **Li
Guangxiu** and his five assistants were engaged to embellish the main halls
with five hundred clay statues of *arhats*. This they accomplished with inspired
gusto, spending ten years creating the comical and grotesquely distorted crew
of monks, goblins, scribes, emperors and beggars which crowds the interior
– some sit rapt with holy contemplation, others smirk, roar with hysteri-
cal mirth or snarl grimly as they ride a foaming sea alive with sea monsters.
Unfortunately it all proved too absurd for Li's conservative contemporaries and
this was his final commission. There's also a fourteenth-century **stone tablet**
to seek out in the main hall recording dealings between imperial China and
Yunnan in Mongolian and Chinese script, and a good **vegetarian restaurant**
open at lunchtime.

Dian Chi and the Western Hills

Kunming has always owed much of its easy living to the well-watered lands
surrounding **Dian Chi** (Dian Lake), which stretches for 50km south from the
city. A road circuits the shore, and you could spend a couple of days hopping
around from Kunming's Western bus station, though the workers' sanatoriums
and recently industrialized lakeside hamlets are not greatly appealing. One
place to aim for is southerly **KUNYANG**, birthplace of China's only famous
navigator, the Ming-dynasty Muslim eunuch **Zheng He**, who commanded
an imperial fleet on fact-finding missions to Southeast Asia, India and Africa
– one of the few times in Chinese history that its rulers showed any interest
in the outside world. A hill outside Kunyang has been set aside as a **park** in
his memory, complete with a temple museum and the mausoleum of Zheng's
pilgrim father, **Hadji Ma**.

Far better, however, are the views of the lake from the top of Xi Shan, the
well-wooded **Western Hills**, which rise to 2500m above the shore, 16km
southwest of Kunming. The easiest way to get here is by catching bus #5 from
Dongfeng Dong Lu to its terminus on Renmin Xi Lu, then transferring to bus
#6 for the township of **GAOYAO** (the last bus back to Kunming goes around
6pm). From Gaoyao you can either slog up to the summit 8km south in about
three hours, pausing for breath and refreshment in temples along the way, or
catch a minibus up. There's also the 8am **tour bus** (¥15) to the top from outside
the Yunnan Arts Theatre on Dongfeng Xi Lu, though walking up makes the trip
far more worthwhile.

The first temple is **Huating Si**, originally designed as a country retreat for
Gao Zhishen, Kunming's eleventh-century ruler, in the form of a pavilion
surrounded by gardens and a small pond. Developed as a Buddhist temple from
the fourteenth century, it was last rebuilt in the 1920s. Today, there are some
fine **statues** – especially the two gate guardians inside the entrance hall – and
a moderately priced **Yunnanese restaurant**.

Winding on through groves of ancient trees, you next reach the halfway **Taihua Si**, a monastery set up by the roving Chan (Zen) sect monk **Xuan Jian** in 1306. It's best known for its carelessly arranged **botanical gardens**; there's a massive ginkgo tree near the entrance claimed to be almost as old as the temple itself. A couple more kilometres bring you to the Taoist complex of **Sanqing Ge**, another former royal villa, set on the Western Hills' highest peak. The nine halls are stacked up the slopes in a fine display of Tao style and Qing architecture, each one dedicated to a particular patriarch.

Less than a kilometre beyond Sanqing Ge, the path runs into the **Dragon Gate Grotto**, a series of chambers and narrow tunnels through the hillside which took the late eighteenth-century monk **Wu Laiqing** and his successors more than seventy years to excavate, and which replaced a set of wooden stairs. It's incredible that anyone could conceive of such a project, far less complete it with enough flair to incorporate the sculptures of Guanyin and the gods of study and righteousness which decorate niches along the way. At the end is **Grand Dragon Gate** (¥20), a precarious balcony offering magnificent views as it overhangs the wide expanse of Dian Chi.

Shilin and Lunan

Yunnan's premier natural wonder is **Shilin**, the **Stone Forest**, an exposed bed of limestone spires weathered and split into intriguing clusters, 60km east of Kunming near the town of **LUNAN**. There are many such "forests" in south-western China, but here the black, house-sized rocks are embellished with trees and vines, steps, paths and pavilions.

It takes about an hour to cover slowly the main circuit through the pinnacles to **Sword Peak Pond**, an ornamental pool surrounded by particularly sharp ridges, which you can climb along a narrow track leading right up across the top of the forest. This is the most frequented part of the park, with large red characters incised into famous rocks, and ethnic **Sani**, a Yi subgroup, in unnaturally clean dresses strategically placed for photographers, but paths heading out towards the perimeter are far quieter and lead out to smaller, separate stone groupings in the fields beyond. You can see a bit more by staying the night, as Shilin is surrounded by Sani villages; furthermore, it's worth catching **market day** – Wednesday – in Lunan (a thirty-minute ride on a motorbike-taxi from outside the park gates), where Sani sell their wares and sport embroidered costumes.

Transport to Shilin is not a problem. Comfortable **day-tours** are run by hotels and travel agents in Kunming (from ¥50), and there are also early-morning **tour minibuses** (about ¥30) from the corner of Huancheng Nan Lu, next to the *King World Hotel* – look for the blue, bilingual sign. Note that the latter are Chinese-oriented, and involve plenty of stops at souvenir shops along the way, giving you only about two hours at Shilin. The cheapest option is the tourist train (1hr 20min; ¥30 return) which leaves from the main station at 8.28am. The *Camellia Binguan* will sell you a ticket for the train and take you to it in a free minibus at 7.50am. The train returns at 3.30pm. By bus, the journey takes around three hours.

Entry to the park costs ¥80, after which you cross the bridge and bear left up the hill for 50m to a basic hostel (❶) in the square. Continue round the lake and you'll find the ageing but comfortable *Stone Forest Hotel* (☎0871/7711405; ❺) and the more modern *Shilin Summer Palace Hotel* (☎0871/7711888; ❻) either side of steps which lead directly down into the forest itself. Keep going around the lake and uphill for the better-value *Yunlin Hotel* (☎0871/7711409;

❸), which offers singles, doubles and triples. All these have decent **restaurants**, and host infrequent but surprisingly enthusiastic evenings of **Sani dancing**. At the park gates themselves, a mess of stalls sell excellent, reasonably priced **food** – roast duck, pheasant, pigeon or fish – as well as poor souvenir embroideries.

Southeastern Yunnan

Off limits until the early 1990s due to the Sino-Vietnamese War, the region between Kunming and Vietnam is a nicely unpackaged corner of the province, and there are plenty of reasons, aside from the border, to head down this way. Closest to Kunming, **Fuxian and Qilu lakes**, while not as scenic as Dian Chi,

Southeastern Yunnan		
Chengjiang	澄江	*chéngjiāng*
Fuxian Hu	抚仙湖	*fŭxiān hú*
Jiangchuan	江川	*jiāngchuān*
Gejiu	个旧	*gèjiù*
Baohua Park	宝华公园	*bǎohuá gōngyuán*
Liangyou Jiudian	良友酒店	*liángyŏu jiŭdiàn*
Shihaolou Binguan	十号楼宾馆	*shíhàolóu bīnguǎn*
Tin Capital Restaurant	锡城饭店	*xīchéng fàndiàn*
Hekou	河口	*hékŏu*
Jianshui	建水	*jiànshuǐ*
Chaoyang Lou	朝阳楼	*cháoyáng lóu*
Confucian Academy	文庙	*wénmiào*
Garden Hotel	花园招待所	*huāyuán zhāodàisuŏ*
Lin'an Jiudian	临安酒店	*lín'ān jiŭdiàn*
Yanzi Dong	燕子洞	*yànzi dòng*
Zhujia Huayuan	朱家花园	*zhūjiā huāyuán*
Kaiyuan	开远	*kāiyuǎn*
Malipo	麻栗坡	*málìpō*
Tonghai	通海	*tōnghǎi*
Liyue Fandian	礼乐饭店	*lǐyuè fàndiàn*
Nanjie Fandian	南街饭店	*nánjiē fàndiàn*
Tonghai Government Guesthouse	通海县政府招待所	*tōnghǎixiàn zhèngfǔ zhāodàisuŏ*
Tong-Print Hotel	通印大酒店	*tōngyìn dàjiŭdiàn*
Xiushan Binguan	秀山宾馆	*xiùshān bīnguǎn*
Xiushan Park	秀山公园	*xiùshān gōngyuán*
Yongjin Si	涌金寺	*yŏngjīn sì*
Wenshan	文山	*wénshān*
Xinmen	薪门	*xīnmén*
Yuanyang	元阳新街镇	*yuányáng xīnjiēzhèn*

have a smattering of historic sites focused on nearby towns, the best of which is **Tonghai**. Farther south, amiable, old-fashioned **Jianshui** has its own complement of Qing architecture, and an unusual attraction in nearby caves, while the surprisingly sophisticated **Gejiu** surrounds an artificial lake, an unintentional consequence of old mining methods. Those with more time should consider side-trips to **Malipo**, a remote Zhuang town reached via the rail town of **Kaiyuan**, or the impressive terraced landscapes of the **Hong He Valley**, best accessed from pretty **Yuanyang**.

There are two ways to cover the 350km between Kunming and the border town of **Hekou**: either on the daily, narrow-gauge **Kunming–Hanoi train**, which stops only at Kaiyuan along the way (see Kunming's "Moving on" box, p.804); or by road, hopping between towns on **public buses** – the better option if you want to have a look around. There's a **Kunming–Hekou highway** too, reaching the border via Lunan and Kaiyuan, with a spur connecting it to Gejiu, but most of the sights lie on smaller roads. Note that you need a Vietnam visa in advance to cross the border.

The lakes and Tonghai

Surrounded by green farmland and russet, mud-block villages, **Fuxian Hu** is a thinner, smaller version of Dian Chi, its blue waters plied by long wooden fishing boats. Around 70km from Kunming along winding country roads, the county capital of **CHENGJIANG** marks Fuxian's northern end, a long-established market town with a sixteenth-century Confucian temple that was used by Guangdong province's Zhongshan University as its campus during the Japanese occupation. The main road from here follows the lake's western shore 50km south via smaller **Xingyun Hu** and **Jiangchuan**. Beyond is little **Qilu Hu**, on the west side of which lies **XINMEN**, home to a community of four thousand **Mongolians**; descendants of an army garrison left behind by Kublai Khan, they're now employed as fishermen and blacksmiths. It's hard to miss the place: by day you'll see Xinmen's huge **mosque**, and by night the town glows in the hellish light of its metal **foundries**, some factory-sized, others just backyard smithies.

Tonghai

Another half hour on the bus brings you to **TONGHAI**, a small town backed by temples arrayed up the slopes of **Xiu Shan**, which makes for a good stopover. Marking Tonghai's centre is a **drum tower**, from where the four main streets, flanked by old wood-fronted shops, run off to the main compass points. Wander around and you'll come across stocky ponies pulling carts, stores selling locally made silver jewellery and copperware, Mongolians upholding their reputation for metalwork by hawking home-made knives, and back-lane markets for tobacco and bamboo pipes. Follow Nan Jie south and uphill onto Wenmiao Lu for 300m, then look for an English sign directing you to **Xiushan Park** (¥15), one of the most charming mountain parks in China. From the entrance, where a useful map is on display, an easy path takes you through pine forests past half-a-dozen unpretentious **temples and pavilions**. All are lovingly decked with bright paint, boast elegant screens and eaves, and are set amid tranquil gardens. Strangely, given the lack of foreign tourists, English signs along the way explain each building's significance; the best building is **Yongjin Si**, whose pride is 400-year-old cypress and fir trees and well-proportioned halls.

Tonghai's core is a 500-metre-wide square grid of streets defined by **Huangcheng Lu**, divided into north, east and west sections. The **bus station** is at the northwest corner of town on the junction of Huangcheng Bei Lu and Huangcheng Xi Lu, with an overflow of private operators in side lanes; between them these manage at least daily runs to Hekou, and more frequent departures to Jiangchuan, Kunming and Jianshui. There's **accommodation** at *Tonghai Government Guesthouse*, whose Chinese-only sign is 100m east of the bus station on Huangcheng Bei Lu; don't let them put you in the musty old building, but go to the new one at the back (➋, dorm beds ¥20). The *Liyue Fandian* (☎0877/3011651; ➋), on Huangcheng Xi Lu 75m south of the bus station, is slightly better value, and has clean communal bathrooms. The *Tong-Print* (☎0877/3021666; ➍), 200m west of the bus station, is the upmarket option, featuring a sauna and fitness room; it had an outdoor swimming pool until it got too dirty and was remodelled as a pond. They'll halve the price of a double for a lone traveller. There are snack stalls throughout the centre; for more substantial **meals** try the cheap portions of red-cooked mutton and vegetable stir-fries at canteens opposite the bus station, or the old-style *Nanjie Fandian*, south of the drum tower, where crossing-the-bridge noodles come in ¥5–20 helpings, and a three-dish meal for two costs around ¥40. The *Iceberg* next door has refreshing rice jelly drinks.

Jianshui and Yanzi Dong

JIANSHUI lies 80km south of Tonghai through some seriously eroded countryside full of short limestone fingers poking out of the soil – a stone forest beginning to sprout. An administrative centre for over a thousand years, the town is full of **historic old buildings**, mostly serving as schools and offices; the grandest are being restored and opened up to the public. The combination of architecture, the town's provincial, kitsch charm and a friendly populace makes Jianshui a fascinating stopover. Get here sooner rather than later, though, as it's all being tarted up for tourists.

First impressions of a parochial Chinese town are dispelled as the huge red **Chaoyang Lou**, the former eastern gate tower in the city's Ming-dynasty walls, looms into view. Chaoyang Lou is locked and the surrounding grounds swarm with loungers, but there's a great **teahouse** at the top, done up in traditional style, where local musicians practise in the evening – a rare opportunity to observe folk traditions. Follow Jianzhong Lu, the main road, for 200m from the gate, then turn north up Jianxin Jie, and you'll arrive shortly at the grand **Zhujia Huayuan**, the Zhu Clan Gardens (¥20); it's a Chinese box of interlocking halls and courtyards in good condition and brightly painted. Back on Jianzhong Lu, a few minutes' walk past more market activity and old shops brings you to the front of a **temple** – don't go in, it's used as a military base – followed shortly afterwards by another, grander, affair, the entrance to Jianshui's venerable **Confucian Academy**. The fee here (¥20) allows you to walk around a small **lake**, haunt of kingfishers and elderly musicians, to **Dacheng Men**, the complex's actual gates. Behind are a school and a series of halls with accomplished interlocking wooden eaves (very good monkeys, as usual) and fine carved screen doors, while in the grounds stand some elderly stone statues of goats, lions and **elephants** – the latter a recurring theme in the academy's decorations.

Practicalities

Buses wind up 100m northwest of Chaoyang Lou on Chaoyang Bei Lu. There are regular departures to Kunming, Tonghai, Gejiu and Kaiyuan, and daily services to Hekou and Yuanyang.

From the bus station, head back to the roundabout and take Jianzhong Lu, the town's main street, which will bring you after 250m to the *Garden Hotel* (**❶**). Rooms with their own bathroom are the best bet as the communal ones, on the fourth floor, are pungent and unlit; the third-floor rooms have balconies and are pleasant enough. The *Lin'an Jiudian* on Chaoyang Bei Lu (**❹**) is a little more classy but is also musty and in a dull part of town. Alternatively, and far more romantically, you can stay at the Zhujia Huayuan's hotel (**☏**0873/7667988; **❹**) – certainly one of China's more imaginative – in a room full of imitation Qing furniture; the four-poster beds are particularly fine.

In food circles, Jianshui's most famous product is the **qiguo** – a casserole whose inverted funnel design simultaneously poaches meat and creates a soup; unfortunately, it's hard to find a restaurant serving the casserole or shops selling *qiguos*. The town's most atmospheric **restaurant** is the *Lin'an Fandian* on Jianzhong Lu, whose lower floor, with beam-and-flagstone decor, offers cheap soups and stir-fries; there are more formal arrangements in the balcony rooms upstairs. Otherwise, you'll fall over swarms of fruit sellers and cheap street kitchens, whose charcoal-grilled, skewered tofu, eggs, meat or veg with chilli relish are the most popular meal in town.

Yanzi Dong

In the karst formations along the forested Lu River Valley are **Yanzi Dong**, the Swallows' Caves (¥30), 30km east of Jianshui on the road to Kaiyuan or Gejiu. Stone tools, animal bones and freshwater mussel middens reveal the caves' use in Neolithic times, but for the last few centuries people have come to see the tens of thousands of swiftlets who nest here – the noise of wheeling birds is deafening during the early summer. Yangzi Dong has become an enjoyable Chinese-style tourist attraction, featuring wooden walkways and underground restaurants selling bird's-nest cakes – swiftlet nests, constructed out of hardened bird spit, are an expensive delicacy for the Chinese. If you can, catch the **Bird Nest Festival** on August 8, the only day of the year that collecting the then-vacant nests is allowed – a very profitable and dangerous task for local Yi men, who scale the sixty-metre-high cliffs as crowds look on. The caves are easy to reach on public buses heading this way from town, or by chartering a minibus from either of the Chaoyang Bei Lu depots. Buses continue along the main road in both directions until mid-afternoon.

Kaiyuan, Malipo, Gejiu and Yuanyang

Kaiyuan, a major stop on both the rail line and highway, is about 50km east of Jianshui and around the same distance north of **Gejiu** on the Hekou road. There's an interesting two-hundred-kilometre side, trip by bus southeast of Kaiyuan via the city of **Wenshan** to **Malipo**, a small town which the authorities may not want you to visit owing to its proximity to a remote section of the Vietnamese border. A number of ethnic groups inhabit the region hereabouts, and there's a collection of **rock paintings** on cliffs about 1km west of town near the Chaoyang River, apparently connected with local Zhuang mythology (for more on which, see p.766).

Gejiu

A more likely target, **GEJIU** is nothing like the towns farther north, owing its character to the **tin mines** above which the city was founded during the late Qing dynasty. These collapsed during a flood in the 1950s, turning the town centre into the kilometre-long **Jin Hu**, a lake now fringed by a shiny and urbane new city whose main streets, along with remnants of the old town, are on the southern shore. There's not really anything to see, but it's a pleasant place to wander. Distant detonations and souvenir shops full of tin trinkets are reminders of the town's *raison d'être*, and you'll probably see village women in semi-traditional blue embroidered clothing in town to trade. There are brilliant vistas from the upper ridges of eastern **Baohua Park** (¥2 entry; cable car ¥20 one-way, ¥30 return).

Gejiu's huge **bus station** is at the north of town, handling transport to neighbouring towns as well as Kunming and Tonghai. From here, **Jinhu Xi Lu** and bus #3, or **Jinhu Dong Lu** and bus #2, head down the west and east sides of the lake respectively, to either end of **Jinhu Nan Lu**, which follows the 300-metre-long southern shore. The town's older quarters, quickly being modernized, are south off here. Gejiu's best-value **accommodation** is the *Shihaolou Binguan* (☎0873/2122514, ℱ2122830; ❸), at the southern end of Jinhu Dong Lu. Of the many places **to eat**, *Liangyou Jiudian*, halfway along Jinhu Nan Lu at the southwest corner of Zhongshan Lu, has excellent all-you-can-eat **hotpots** with sliced meat, fish, seafood and vegetables for ¥35, while the noisy, grubby *Tin Capital Restaurant* on Cailu Jie has cheap steamers of filling dumplings. For street food, visit the covered market on the west side of the lake on Jinhu Xi Lu.

Yuanyang

Hong He, the **Red River**, starts life near Xiaguan in Yunnan's northwest and runs southeast across the province, entering Vietnam at Hekou and flowing through Hanoi before emptying its volcanic-soil-laden waters into the Gulf of Tonkin. For much of its journey the river is straight, channelled by the **Ailao Shan range** into a series of fertile, steep-sided valleys. These have been **terraced** by resident **Hani**, whose mushroom-shaped adobe and thatch houses pepper the hills. The fields stretch as far as the eye can see, and make for one of the greatest sights of the province. In spring and autumn thick mists blanket the area, muting the violent contrast between red soil and brilliant green paddy fields. The best time to see them is between March and May when the paddies are full of water, but they are spectacular at any time.

To take in the scenery, the best place to base yourself is **YUANYANG**, a small town 80km south of Jianshui and 110km southwest of Gejiu. A sleepy hill town, it becomes a hive of activity on market days (every five days), when Hani, Miao, Yi and Yao minorities come into town from the villages around. Head out of Yuanyang in any direction and you'll come across lovely villages precariously perched on hillsides, including **Tuguozhai**, 7km north of town; the Hani village of **Shengcun** a few kilometres further east; and the Yi village of **Mengpin** a further 15km north of Tuguozhai. You can stay with local families in any of these places; expect to pay about ¥10 for a bed, ¥10 for a meal.

Be careful that you get to the right Yuanyang: the dull county seat, **Nansha**, is also called Yuanyang on some maps. You'll probably have to change buses here for the half-hour uphill journey to Yuanyang, also called Xinjiezhen. There are a number of new **places to stay** here catering to the embryonic tourist trade, including the government guesthouse (❶) by the bus station, but the best place to aim for is the *Backpacker Rendezvous*, 250m downhill from the bus station (☎0875/5624625; ❶, dorms ¥20). It has a couple of clean simple doubles and a dorm, and the English-speaking owner Tam Wai is informative and arranges day-trips for ¥200 for a small group. Tours can also be arranged at local hotels, or you can rent a car for the day for around ¥100 (there's nowhere to rent bikes, but in any case the hills are pretty punishing). Walk uphill for 400m from the main bus station and you'll come to a minibus station that serves the villages mentioned above. Moving on from Yuanyang, there are sleeper buses to Kunming at 3.30pm, and wheezy buses making the juddering six-hour ride to Simao, for Xishuangbanna.

Hekou and the border

It's another 150km southeast from either Kaiyuan or Gejiu to where rail and road converge at the border town of **HEKOU**; the border post is only a few minutes' walk from the bus and train station. Across the border in Vietnam, **Lao Cai** has a huge game market, a few despondent hotels, and a **train station** 3km south with two services daily for the ten-hour run to Hanoi. Most travellers take a **bus** or motorbike taxi (US$5) for the hill resort town of **Sa Pa**.

For arrivals from Vietnam, turn right after the border crossing and the train station is 100m away. Trains head up to Kunming at 2.15pm – note that China is one hour ahead of Vietnam – and the station ticket office is open daily from 11am to 1.30pm (you can wait in the *International Hotel* canteen nearby). Alternatively, head 50m up the main road and the bus station is on the left. Here you can get sleepers for Kunming or ordinary buses to Gejiu, Yuanyang and Jianshui. To change money, walk up the main street from the border crossing, turn right after 200m and you'll arrive at the Bank of China (daily 8am–5.30pm; foreign exchange closed Sun).

Northwestern Yunnan

Uplifted vigorously during the last fifty million years as the Indian subcontinent buckled up against China, **northwestern Yunnan** is a geologically unsettled region of subtropical forests, thin pasture, alpine lakes and shattered peaks painted crisply in blue, white and grey. **Xiaguan**, an overnight trip from Kunming, is the regional hub, the start of roads north past the Bai town of **Dali**. Though Dali is firmly on the beaten track, **Er Hai** – the nearby lake – and mountains make a splendid backdrop, while a few hours beyond Dali is the former **Naxi** kingdom of **Lijiang**. The Naxi are still resident, though the old town and surrounding villages endured major renovations following the terrible 1996 earthquake. Here hikers can organize themselves for a two-day trek through **Tiger Leaping Gorge**, where a youthful Yangzi cuts through the deepest chasm on Earth. East is **Lugu Hu**, lakeside home to the matrilineal **Mosuo**, while north again is the Tibetan town of **Zhongdian**, the beginning of trips up to the Tibetan borderlands at **Deqin**, or beyond into Sichuan province. In a completely different direction, heading southwest from Xiaguan to the **Burmese border** takes you to the historic city of **Baoshan** and through the **Dehong region**, a subtropical pocket full of shady traders and ludicrous antics revolving around the border towns of **Ruili** and **Wanding**. Finally, west of Xiaguan is the **Nu Jiang Valley**, one of China's intriguing backwaters, with pristine jungle and isolated minority communities.

Heading up through Dali to Lijiang and Zhongdian, you'll find mild, even warm **weather** from spring through to autumn, though winters are extremely cold, the likelihood of snow between November and April increasing as you move north. Southwest of Xiaguan, however, temperatures are warm year-round, with heavy summer rains and mild winter nights in the hills.

Transport is improving; rough roads – including the famous **Burma Road** between Kunming and Wanding – are being replaced or upgraded to highways, while Kunming is directly connected by **air** to Xiaguan, Lijiang, Zhongdian and **Mangshi** near Wanding, and by **train** to Xiaguan. As far as foreign travellers are concerned, the **Tibet road**, which follows the dramatic upper reaches of the Lancang River to Markam, then turns west towards Lhasa, is at the time of writing open only to groups travelling in a private vehicle, with a driver and a guide; various agencies in Dali, Lijiang and Zhongdian can sort the arrangements out for you.

Chuxiong and Xiaguan

The first 390km of the **Burma Road** run west of Kunming to Xiaguan through a succession of valleys and mountain ranges which would well repay a few days' exploration. But for most, the lure of Dali is too great, an all-too-easy trip from Kunming on a direct bus or train via Xiaguan.

If the leisurely approach suits you, the midpoint town of **CHUXIONG** makes a good base. Inhabited since the Zhou dynasty (700 BC), it's now almost entirely modern and is home to a substantial Yi population, who celebrate their **Torch Festival** on the twenty-fourth day of the sixth lunar month with a fair and night-time revelries. The markets here are known for their silver jewellery, there are a few nearby parks and temples – most notably 20km away at **Zixi Shan**, a wooded mountain dedicated to Buddhism since the twelfth century – and, for historians and paleontologists especially, some interesting associations. In 1975 a huge Zhou mausoleum was discovered on Chuxiong's southern outskirts at **Wanjiaba**, containing farm tools and five of the oldest **bronze drums** yet discovered in Asia, now in the Provincial Museum in Kunming (for more on bronze drum cultures, see p.757). Separate sites surrounding the town of **Lufeng**, 80km east, closer to Kunming, have yielded dinosaur bones and fragments of *ramapithecus* and *sivapithecus* fossils, possible hominid prototypes. For **accommodation** in Chuxiong, try the *Chuxiong Binguan* on Xinshi Jie (❸) or the *Zixi Lüguan* on central Zhong Dalu (❸, dorm beds ¥15), both with fair restaurants.

Chuxiong and Xiaguan		
Chuxiong	楚雄	chǔxióng
Chuxiong Binguan	楚雄宾馆	chǔxióng bīnguǎn
Zixi Lüguan	紫溪旅馆	zǐxī lǚguǎn
Zixi Shan	紫溪山	zǐxī shān
Xiaguan	下关	xiàguān
Binchuan	宾川	bīnchuān
Jizu Shan	鸡足山	jīzú shān
Xiaguan Binguan	下关宾馆	xiàguān bīnguǎn
Xiaguan Fandian	下关饭店	xiàguān fàndiàn

Trade routes through northern Yunnan into **Burma** and beyond were established more than two thousand years ago by merchants carrying goods between the Han empire and Rome along the Southern Silk Road. Travelled by Marco Polo on one of his errands for the Mongol court, it became known as the "Tribute Road" following China's successful eighteenth-century annexation of eastern Burma, but later fell into disuse as the Qing court cut off ties with the outside world. When Japan invaded China during the 1930s they drove the Guomindang government to Sichuan, isolating them from their eastern economic and industrial power base. Turning west for help, the Guomindang found the **British**, who then held Burma and were none too keen to see China's resources in Japanese hands. In fact, there had been plans for a link through to Burma for forty years, and a road had already been built from Kunming to Xiaguan. Britain agreed to help extend this into a 1100-kilometre-long supply line connecting **Kunming** with the Burmese rail head at **Lashio**.

This was to become the **Burma Road**, swiftly completed by three hundred thousand labourers in 1938, an incredible feat considering the basic tools available and the number of mountains along the way. After the Japanese stormed French Indochina in 1940 and halted rail traffic between Vietnam and Kunming, the road became China's only line of communication with the allies, though it was always a tenuous one, cut frequently by landslides and summer monsoons. Lashio fell a year later, however, and the road became redundant once more, remaining so after the war ended through Burma's self-imposed isolation and the chaos of the Cultural Revolution. Now partially sealed and open again as the Yunnan–Burma Highway, the 910-kilometre Chinese stretch between Kunming and the border crossing at **Wanding** remains – like the Great Wall – a triumph of stolid persistence over unfavourable logistics.

Xiaguan and Jizu Shan

XIAGUAN, an increasingly industrialized transport hub, lies on the southern shore of Er Hai Lake. It's also confusingly known as **Dali Shi** (Dali City), and some "Dali" buses from Kunming may actually terminate here. Xiaguan's main drag is **Jianshe Dong Lu**, a 500-metre-long street between Tai'an Lu in the east and Renmin Lu in the west. The **airport** is 15km east of here, for which you'll need a taxi; the ticket office of Yunnan Air is on Jiansghe Lu, at the crossroads with Renmin Lu (℡0872/2166588). The **train station** is 2km east on Dianyuan Lu along the #5 and #6 bus routes. Long-distance buses stop at a number of depots along Jianshe Dong Lu, though the **main bus station** is down towards Renmin Lu. There are daily departures to, among other destinations, **Baoshan** and **Liuku** to the west, Jizu Shan and Lugu Hu to the northeast via **Binchuan**, and south to **Jinghong** in Xishuangbanna, a bumpy 27-hour journey. **For Dali**, catch bus #4, which passes along Jianshe Dong Lu every hour (¥7) and terminates one stop beyond the main bus station. Plentiful minibuses shuttle between Xiaguan and the villages along the western shore of **Er Hai**.

There's a basic **hotel** at the bus station (①), with the upmarket *Xiaguan Fandian* (℡8072/2125859; ⑤), favoured by tour groups and with a CITS desk, about 100m east, and the mid-range *Xiaguan Binguan* (④) on the Jianshe Dong Lu–Renmin Lu corner. Markets and cheap places to eat fill the backstreets. If you've got time to kill, go for a stroll in **Erhai Gongyuan**, a green, hilly park a couple of kilometres northeast of the centre on the lakeshore.

Jizu Shan

From Xiaguan there are buses 60km northeast to **BINCHUAN**, from where it's a short hop to **SHAZHI** at the foot of **Jizu Shan** (Chickenfoot Mountain). This became one of western China's holiest peaks after the legendary monk **Jiaye** – who brought Buddhism from India to southern China – fought here with the wicked Jizu king. By the seventh century both Buddhist and Taoist pilgrims were coming in their thousands to honour his memory. In its heyday, a hundred or more monasteries graced Jizu's heights, including the original Golden Temple transported here from Kunming, though by 1980 all but half a dozen had decayed. Things are now picking up again, and the trip is worth it if you have the time to take in the stunning scenery and some charismatic temples, among them the **Zhusheng Si** and the ninth-century **Lengyan Pagoda** and accompanying **Jinding Si**, a temple splendidly positioned on a cliff edge at the summit. Entry is ¥40, and the steep ascent takes five hours or so, with – of course – a new cable car for the last and steepest section (¥30). There are some basic guesthouses at the halfway point and at the summit (❶), where people stay in order to get up and watch the dawn. Viewed from here, the spurs of the mountain resemble a bird's long toes – hence the name.

Dali and around

A thirty-minute bus ride north of Xiaguan and almost a satellite suburb, **DALI** draws swarms of tourists: Chinese package groups come seeking some colourful history, while foreign backpackers escape China in a Westerner-friendly theme park of beer gardens, massage parlours, language courses and hippified cafés. It might sound grim, but the town and surrounding villages are both pretty and interesting, full of old houses and with an indigenous **Bai** population. To the east lies the great lake, **Er Hai**, while the invitingly green valleys and clouded peaks of the fifty-kilometre-long **Cang Shan range** rear up behind town, the perfect setting for a few days' walking or relaxation.

If you can, visit during the **Spring Fair**, held from the fifteenth day of the third lunar month (April or May). Originally a Buddhist festival, the event has grown into five hectic days of horse trading, wrestling, racing, dancing and singing, attracting thousands of people from all over the region to camp at the fairground just west of town. You'll probably have to follow suit at this time, as beds in Dali will be in short supply.

There's much more to Dali than its modern profile. From the eighth until the thirteenth century, the town was at the centre of the Nanzhao and Dali kingdoms, and in the mid-nineteenth century briefly became capital of the state declared by **Du Wenxiu**, who led the Muslim rebellion against Chinese rule. Millions died in the rebellion's suppression, and Dali was devastated, never to recover its former political position. An earthquake destroyed the town in 1925, but it was rebuilt in its former style. The majority of the regional population today are Bai, though Muslims and Han remain.

Arrival and transport

Dali covers only about four square kilometres, and much of the town is contained by the remains of its Ming-dynasty walls. The main axis of its grid-like street plan is **Fuxing Lu**, cobbled and planted with cherry trees, which runs between the old north and south gates. **Bo'ai Lu** runs parallel and to the west, while the centre hinges around **Huguo Lu**, cutting across both at right angles.

Dali and around

Dali	大理	*dàlǐ*
Dali Museum	大理博物馆	*dàlǐ bówùguǎn*
San Ta Si	三塔寺	*sāntǎ sì*
Yita Si	一塔寺	*yītǎ sì*
Yu'er Park	玉耳公园	*yù'ěr gōngyuán*
Accommodation and eating		
Apricot Flower Restaurant	杏花酒店	*xìnghuā jiǔdiàn*
Bird's Nest Guesthouse/ Bird Bar	鸟吧	*niǎobā*
Café de Jacks	樱花阁	*yīnghuā gégāodì bīnguǎn*
Higherland Inn	高地宾馆	*gāodì bīnguǎn*
Jim's Peace Guesthouse	吉姆和平客楼	*jímǔ hépíng kèlóu*
Jinhua Binguan	金花宾馆	*jīnhuā bīnguǎn*
Marley's	马丽咖啡馆	*mǎlì kāfēiguǎn*
Old Dali Inn	大理四季客栈	*dàlǐ sìjì kèzhàn*
Tibetan Café	西藏餐厅	*xīzàng cāntīng*
Tibetan Lodge	西藏宾馆	*xīzàng bīnguǎn*
Xingyue Hotel	星月宾馆	*xīngyuè bīnguǎn*
Around Dali		
Butterfly Spring	蝴蝶泉	*húdié quán*
Du Wenxiu's tomb	杜文秀之墓	*dùwénxiù zhīmù*
Er Hai	洱海	*ěrhǎi*
Gantong Si	甘通寺	*gāntōng sì*
Guanyin Tang	观音堂	*guānyīn táng*
Jianchun	剑川	*jiànchuān*
Nanzhao Island	南诏岛	*nánzhǎo dǎo*
Shaping	沙坪	*shāpíng*
Shegu Ta	蛇骨塔	*shégǔ tǎ*
Shibao Shan	石宝山	*shíbǎo shān*
Taihe	太河	*tàihé*
Tianzhuang Hotel	田庄宾馆	*tiánzhuāng bīnguǎn*
Wase	挖色	*wāsè*
Xiao Putuo Island	小普陀岛	*xiǎo pǔtuó dǎo*
Xizhou	喜洲	*xīzhōu*
Zhonghe Peak	中和山	*zhōnghé shān*
Zhoucheng	周城	*zhōuchéng*

The #4 bus from Xiaguan drives through the town, but **long-distance buses** either drop off on the highway, which skirts Dali's western side, or deliver to the bus compound just inside the south gates on Fuxing Lu, where there's also a **ticket office**. There's another useful booking office on Bo'ai Lu, with more scattered around. **Leaving**, you might have to pick up long-distance services from the main road, or even proceed to Xiaguan or Lijiang first. **Minibuses** between Xiaguan and sites along Er Hai's western shore can be flagged down on the highway immediately west of Dali, and are a cheaper and more flexible way to get around the vicinity than the **tours** offered by agents – though the latter are convenient and reasonable value. Alternatively, you can rent a **bicycle** from hotels or foreigners' cafés for about ¥20 per day, plus deposit. Always check the condition of the bike, as you are fully responsible for any damage or loss.

Fuxing Lu is where to find the **Bank of China** (foreign exchange daily 8am–7pm) and also the **post office** (where you have to pay for everything,

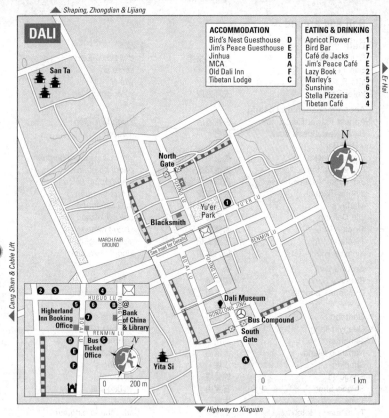

DALI

ACCOMMODATION	
Bird's Nest Guesthouse	D
Jim's Peace Guesthouse	E
Jinhua	B
MCA	A
Old Dali Inn	F
Tibetan Lodge	C

EATING & DRINKING	
Apricot Flower	1
Bird Bar	F
Café de Jacks	7
Jim's Peace Café	E
Lazy Book	2
Marley's	5
Sunshine	6
Stella Pizzeria	3
Tibetan Café	4

San Ta

North Gate

FUXING LU

Yu'er Park ❶

Blacksmith

YU'ER LU

RENMIN LU

MARCH FAIR GROUND

See Inset for Details

BO'AI LU

FUXING LU

❷ ❸   ❹
HUGUO LU

Higherland Inn Booking Office

❺
❼
Bo'ai Lu ❻
RENMIN LU

Bank of China & Library

Dali Museum

HONGLONG JING

Bus Compound

South Gate

Ⓓ Bus Ticket Office Ⓒ

Ⓔ

Ⓕ

Yita Si

Ⓐ

0   200 m

0   1 km

even the overseas postage forms; daily 8am–9pm), which contains Dali's international telephone counter. There's a telecom office with **Internet access** at the corner of Fuxing Lu and Huguo Lu.

Accommodation

Low-pressure touts meet the buses, hoping to escort arrivals to accommodation. During Chinese holidays, rates are at least double those indicated here.

Bird's Nest Guesthouse 22 Renmin Lu ☏0872/2661843. A guesthouse and bar whose lackadaisical attitude is popular with hippified consumers of the local weed and off-putting to everyone else. A bed on the floor in a large dorm is ¥10; no doubles.

Higherland Inn Cang Shan Daorendong ☏0872/2661599, ⊛www.higherland.com. This small guesthouse retreat allows guests to take full advantage of Dali's best feature, the mountains, as it's located high in the Cang Shan range. The best way to get there is to take the cable car to

the Zhonghe Temple (see p.827), then it's a couple of minutes' walk west, uphill; otherwise it's a 2hr slog, which is no fun with luggage. There's a booking office in town, on Bo'ai Lu – call in here or phone before you turn up. Rooms are comfortable, and with a decent garden and restaurant on site, plenty of hiking all around, and cookery and *tai ji* courses, there's little reason to head back down to civilization. Dorms ¥25, ❷

Jim's Peace Guesthouse Bo'ai Lu ☏0872/2671822. Cosy rooms, though ask to see all those available and try to avoid the front of the building overlooking the road. The restaurant is a sociable place and they do plenty of tours. Jim, the likeable half-Tibetan owner, is opening a new, Tibetan-style and slightly more upmarket guesthouse just outside the south gate, on Yuxiu Lu; it should be ready by the time you read this. ❷

Jinhua Binguan Corner of Fuxing Lu and Huguo Lu ℡0872/2673343, ℻2673846. Not bad value, though the rooms are a little musty and full of heavy furniture. The staff are Han Chinese dressed up in minority costume. ❷

MCA Just west off the road, 100m south of the south gate outside the town ℡0872/2673666. A favourite with long-term budget travellers, offering rooms in a self-contained family compound arranged around a garden. There's a nice garden, a small library, even an art studio. Dorm beds ¥15, ❷

Old Dali Inn (No. 5 Guesthouse) Bo'ai Lu ℡0872/2670382. Indifferent staff and basic toilets compensated for by very hot, powerful showers, and a courtyard surrounded by two tiers of wooden "traditional Bai" rooms – check a few out, as some are better than others. Free Internet access and nightly movies. Don't bother with the restaurant. Dorm beds ¥10 or ¥15, ❷

Tibetan Lodge 58 Renmin Lu ℡0872/2664177. A cosy new place that's not Tibetan at all, but at least the Han owners run it competently. It's typical of the new breed of Chinese guesthouses that are popping up all over the province – faux ethnic, a bit chintzy, with a big TV in a little room. Rooms are poky with small bathrooms, but they are some of the best-value doubles in this price range. Free Internet access. ❷

The Town

Dali is small enough to walk around in a morning, though you may be slowed down by the crowds of hawkers, farmers and shoppers who descend for the Friday **market**. Most places of interest are along Fuxing Lu, but the narrow stone side streets are good for a wander. Get your bearings from on top of Dali's old **south gate** (¥2), where you can study Xiaguan, Er Hai, the town and mountains from the comfort of a teahouse. Dali's antique **pagodas** stand as landmarks above the roof lines, **Yita Si** due west, and the trinity of **San Ta** a few kilometres north. Below the gate is a busy **artisans' quarter** where carpenters and masons turn out the heavy and uncomfortable-looking tables and chairs inlaid with streaky grey **Dali marble** that lurk in Chinese emporiums around the world. The marble is mined up in the hills, and smaller pieces of it are worked into all sorts of souvenirs – rolling pins, chopping boards, miniature pagodas – which you can buy from shops and stalls in town.

The **Dali Museum** (Tues–Sun 9am–5pm; ¥5) opposite the bus compound, just 50m or so inside the gate, takes the form of a small Chinese palace with stone lions guarding the gate and cannons in the courtyard. It was built for the Qing governor and appropriated as Du Wenxiu's "Forbidden City" during Du's insurrection. Historic relics include a strange bronze model of two circling dragons, jaws clenched around what might be a tree; a few Buddhist figurines from the Nanzhao period; and some lively statues of an orchestra and serving maids from a Ming noblewoman's tomb – a nice addition to the usual cases of snarling gods and warrior busts. The gardens outside are pleasant, planted with lantana and bougainvillea, with the mountains behind.

North along Fuxing Lu, young and old socialize in the square outside the **library**, playing dominoes or video games according to their interests. Huguo Lu's western arm forms the core of the budget travellers' world, a knot of **cafés**, cheap tailors, bilingual **travel agents** happy to book you on tours or long-distance buses (for a ¥20 commission), and massage clinics advertising their services with couplets like "Painful In, Happy Out". It's also the best place to purchase beautiful jewellery and embroideries (many from Guizhou's Miao), and attractive Bai tie-dyes from hawkers – asking prices are ludicrously high, dropping swiftly once bargaining commences. Don't show any interest unless you really want to buy, or you'll be mercilessly hounded.

Farther north again on the corner of Fuxing Lu and Yu'er Lu, **Yu'er Park** (entrance on Yu'er Lu; ¥1) is a peaceful refuge from Huguo Lu's hard-sell perils, frequented by locals and full of camellias, fruit trees, palms and ponds linked by tidy paths. The backstreets north of the park are some of the nicest in Dali; places to seek out include a stone **church** and a **blacksmith's**, the latter decorated with inventive animal sculptures made from scrap iron. Fuxing Lu itself terminates at the **north gate** (¥2), which can also be climbed.

Yita Si and San Ta Si

Built when the region was a major Buddhist centre, Dali's distinctively tall and elegant **pagodas** are still standing after a millennium of wars and earthquakes. Just west of Dali's south gate is the solitary **Yita Si**, a tenth-century tower and virtually abandoned Ming temple surrounded by ancient trees. Better presented is **San Ta**, the Three Pagodas, a twenty-minute walk north of town in the grounds of the now vanished Chongsheng Monastery (daily 8am–5pm; ¥32). Built around 850, the 69-metre-tall, square-based **Qianxun tower** is some 100 years older than the two smaller octagonal pagodas behind. As the structures are sealed, the stiff entrance fee gives access only to souvenir stalls and a hall at the back containing religious relics discovered during renovations in the 1970s.

Eating and drinking

Two local **specialities** are based on fish from Er Hai: *shaguoyu*, where the fish is fried, then simmered with dried vegetables in a sour stock, and *youdeyu*, a casserole of small oily sprats and tofu. For breakfast, you could take your pick from the sweet buns and noodle soups sold by street stalls and cheap restaurants around the centre. Snacks include pickled vegetables wrapped in a fine pancake, and brittle "fans" of dried yoghurt, which are often fried and crumbled over other dishes – much nicer than it sounds.

Dali's tourist-oriented **cafés and restaurants** serve a mix of Western dishes, Chinese staples and even Bai specialities, and are good places to meet other foreigners and swap news. They're also places where you can use the **Internet** (around ¥15/hr), and get in touch with the latest martial-art, language or painting courses.

Apricot Flower Restaurant Yu'er Lu. Despite a monastic austerity in the stone floors and well-used wooden furniture, this is the best place in town for an inexpensive, accomplished and tasty Chinese dinner. No English menus.

Bird Bar At the *Bird's Nest Guesthouse*, Renmin Lu. A no-frills bar for late-night drinking and "smoking".

Café de Jacks Bo'ai Lu. Popular after dark for its bar and Chinese versions of curries, pizzas, salads and chocolate cake.

Jim's Peace Café Huguo Lu, underneath *Jim's Guesthouse*. A long-termers' hangout, with comfy sofas, a well-stocked bar and a fine yak stew. Get six people together for a Tibetan banquet, cooked by the owner's mother.

Lazy Book Huguo Lu. A little detached from the main strip, and the better for it. It's well titled: a

good library of books and DVDs makes this a prime venue for whiling away an afternoon.

Marley's Huguo Lu. Known for its chocolate cake, good coffee and Western breakfasts, Marley's also organizes "Bai banquets" on Sunday night if they can get the numbers; book before 6pm.

Sunshine Huguo Lu. Hippie-ish hangout, offering baked potatoes, banana splits and hash browns as well as passable curries.

Stella Pizzeria Huguo Lu. The wood-fired clay oven delivers the best pizzas in town, and the laid-back decor is appealing too, with lots of nooks and crannies for privacy.

Tibetan Café Huguo Lu. An upbeat "Tibetan" menu featuring very tasty stews and soups – nothing like what you'd actually get in the Himalayas, which is really no bad thing.

Around Dali

Besides the excursions mentioned below, it's also worth considering a trip out to Jizu Shan, east of Xiaguan (see p.821).

Zhonghe Peak

Due **west** of Dali, **Zhonghe Peak** is one of the tallest in the Cang Shan range, its four-thousand-metre summit often snowcapped until June. For a partial ascent, start at the small bridge on the highway just north of town and walk through the graveyards to the **Shizu stele**, a four-metre-high inscribed tablet planted in 1304 to record Kublai Khan's conquest of Yunnan half a century earlier. The easiest ascent is on the "ropeway" **chairlift** (¥20), but there's a fairly easy, two-hour path up through the pine trees from here to **Zhonghe**

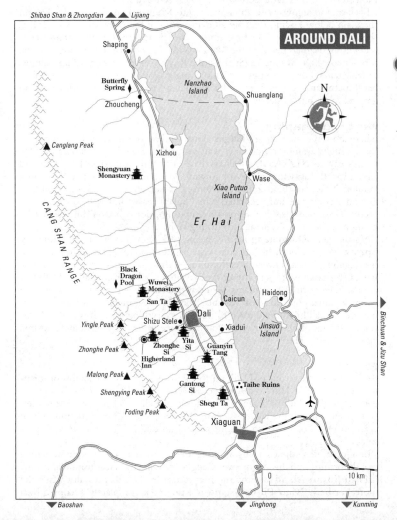

Si – best handled on a windy day, when the chairlift is closed and the temple is therefore free of Chinese tour groups. Views of the lake and the mountains beyond are stupendous in any case. You'll also find the attractive *Higherland Inn* here (see p.824).

South of town

With the exception of **Du Wenxiu's Tomb**, a stone sarcophagus 4km southeast at the lakeside village of **Xiadui**, most of the historic sites south of Dali lie along the highway to Xiaguan. **Guanyin Tang** is about 5km away, a recently rebuilt temple complex with an unusually square and lavishly ornamented pavilion raised to Guanyin, the Goddess of Mercy, who is believed to have routed Dali's enemies during the Han dynasty. Walk west of Guanyin Tang into the hills and it's about an hour's climb to **Gantong Si**, once Dali's most celebrated Buddhist monastery but now reduced to two partially restored halls.

Back on the highway and about halfway to Xiaguan, two ill-defined ridges on the plain below Foding Peak are all that remain of the Nanzhao city of **Taihe**, though a modern pavilion here houses the eighth-century **Nanzhao stele**, recounting dealings between the Nanzhao and Tang courts. Finally, look for the forty-metre-high **Shegu Ta** (Snake-bone Pagoda) at **Yangping village**, almost in Xiaguan's northern suburbs. This Ming pagoda commemorates the fatal battle between a young hero and a menacing serpent demon, both of whom are said to be buried below.

North to Shaping

There are some interesting **villages** along the lake north of Dali. About 20km up the highway, motor-rickshaws wait to carry passengers the couple of kilometres east to **XIZHOU**, a military base during the Nanzhao Kingdom and later a wealthy agricultural town known for the Bai mansions raised by leading families. Ninety of these compounds survive, based on wings of rooms arranged around a courtyard and decorated with "pulled" eaves and wall paintings. The pretty *Tianzhuang Hotel* is a good example (❷, dorm beds ¥10), reached by going past the central square and turning right.

North again, **Zhoucheng** is a tie-dyeing centre, and beyond is the **Butterfly Spring**, a small pond which becomes the haunt of clouds of butterflies when an overhanging acacia flowers in early summer, though there's little to see otherwise. Overlooking the very top of the lake about 30km from Dali, **SHAPING** is definitely worth a visit for its **Monday market**, when what seems like the entire regional population of peasants, labourers, con men and artisans crowds on to the small hill behind town to trade in everything from livestock to hardware and bags of coriander seeds. You'll also see some pretty gruesome ad-hoc dentistry taking place.

Er Hai

An hour's walk east out of Dali's north gate brings you to the shores of forty-kilometre-long **Er Hai**, so called because it's shaped like an ear ("*er*"). You can get out on the water by arranging a **fishing trip** or excursion out to the islets and villages around the lake's east shore (¥25–50), most easily done through an agent in Dali; boats have small cockpits and no canopies against sun and spray, so come prepared.

Besides fishing, there's really nothing to do on the lake beyond watching clouds forming and dissipating over Cang Shan. Directly across from Dali, uninhabited **Jinsuo Island** was the summer retreat for Nanzhao royalty, while the more northerly **Xiao Putuo Island** is a tiny rock completely occupied by a temple whose withered guardian stumbles out after payment. **Nanzhao Island** at the lake's north end is a tourist trap with an overrated castle, but it does also have a pleasant guesthouse (❶).

The east-shore settlements of **HAIDONG** and **WASE** are full of narrow back lanes with crumbling adobe homes and family mansions, their waterfronts thick with fishing gear. You can stay the night in Wase at the government guest-house (❶) and catch the lively Saturday-morning **market**, slightly smaller and less touristed than Shaping's.

Shibao Shan

Shibao Shan is a nature reserve and religious sanctuary that sees few visitors. It's accessible from **Jianchuan**, 75km northwest from Dali on the Zhongdian road. From Jianchuan you'll have to hire a taxi to take you the 20km south to the reserve entrance (¥20). The area is quite spread out, so get a map (available at the entrance) and plan to spend a day or two here. Basic accommodation is available at the Baoxiang and Shizhong (Stone Bell) temples.

There are plenty of temples here, many surprisingly well preserved; some date back to the Nanzhao era, with old-growth forest in between. Don't miss the remarkable Stone Bell temple, in caves in a steep cliff face, and its fantastic, very lifelike stone carvings of Nanzhao kings, Buddha and Guanyin. All the temples here have great frescoes; some show emissaries from India and the Middle East and everyday scenes from the Nanzhao court, and a few are graphically sexual.

Lijiang

Some 150km north of Dali through numerous Bai and Yi hamlets, roads make their final descent from the ridges to a plain dominated by the inspiringly spiky and ice-bound massif of **Yulong Xue Shan**, the Jade Dragon Snow Mountain. Nestled to the southeast of the mountain, among green fields and dwindling pine forests, is **LIJIANG**, capital of the **Naxi Kingdom**, whose centuries-old maze of winding lanes and clean streams, wooden wineshops, weeping willows and rustic stone bridges repay the effort involved in getting here. Lijiang is by no means an entirely traditional, undiscovered haven, however, partly due to a devastating **earthquake** which destroyed a third of the town in 1996. Having invested heavily in rebuilding, the government now aims to profit through tourist development, and while restorations have been largely tasteful, Lijiang's **Naxi** seem marginalized as players in a cultural theme park. Four-fifths of the thirty thousand Naxi inhabitants of 1995 have sold up and moved out, the houses they left behind converted into rank after rank of tacky souvenir shops. Lijiang is still worth visiting for the genuine culture that survives on its fringes, and offers plenty of potential **excursions** (see p.835), but overall the old town is an object lesson in how unregulated mass tourism can rip the heart out of a place.

The Naxi deserve better. Until recently a matriarchal society, they are descended from a race of Tibetan nomads who settled the region before the tenth century, and they brought with them what are still considered some of the sturdiest horses in China, and a shamanistic religion known as **Dongba**. A blend of Tibetan Bon, animist and Taoist tendencies, Dongba's scriptures are written with unique pictograms, and its pantheistic **murals** still decorate temples around Lijiang, a good excuse to explore nearby **villages** by bicycle. For some background reading, try to find the exhaustive, two-volume *Ancient*

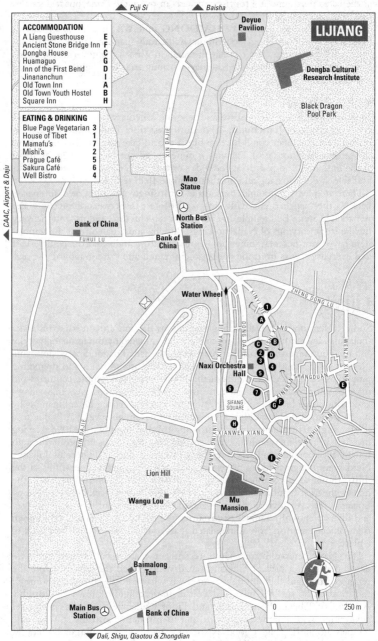

▲ Puji Si ▲ Baisha

LIJIANG

ACCOMMODATION
A Liang Guesthouse .... E
Ancient Stone Bridge Inn ... F
Dongba House C
Huamaguo .... G
Inn of the First Bend .... D
Jinananchun I
Old Town Inn .... A
Old Town Youth Hostel ...... B
Square Inn .... H

EATING & DRINKING
Blue Page Vegetarian 3
House of Tibet 1
Mamafu's 7
Mishi's 2
Prague Café 5
Sakura Café 6
Well Bistro 4

Deyue Pavilion

Dongba Cultural Research Institute

Black Dragon Pool Park

XIN DAJIE

Mao Statue

North Bus Station

Bank of China

Bank of China

FUHUI LU

ZHENG DONG LU

Water Wheel

XINYI

XINHUA JIE

YUNHE JIE

DONG DAJIE

Naxi Orchestra Hall

WENZHI XIANG

SHANGDUAN

XINGREN

SIFANG SQUARE

JINXING

XIANWEN XIANG

XINYI XIANG

WENHUA XIANG

Lion Hill

Wangu Lou

Mu Mansion

Baimalong Tan

Main Bus Station

Bank of China

0   250 m

N

▼ Dali, Shigu, Qiaotou & Zhongdian

Lijiang

Lijiang	丽江	lìjiāng
Baimalong Tan	白马龙潭	báimǎlóng tán
Black Dragon Pool Park	黑龙潭公园	hēilóngtán gōngyuán
Dayan	大研古城	dàyán gǔchéng
Dongba Cultural Research Institute	东巴文化研究室	dōngbā wénhuà yánjiūshì
Five Phoenix Hall	五凤楼	wǔfèng lóu
Lion Hill	狮子山	shīzi shān
Mu Family Mansion	木府	mùfǔ
Sifang	四方	sìfāng

Accommodation

A Liang Guesthouse	阿亮客栈	āliàng kèzhàn
Ancient Stone Bridge Inn	古城大石桥客栈	gǔchéng dàshíqiáo kèzhàn
Dongba House	东巴豪斯	dōngbā háosī
Huamaguo	花吗国客栈	huāmaguó kèzhàn
Inn of the First Bend	一湾酒店	yīwān jiǔdiàn
Jiannanchun	丽江剑南春文苑	lìjiāng jiànnánchūn wényuàn
Old Town Inn	古城客栈	gǔchéng kèzhàn
Old Town Youth Hostel	古城青年旅馆	gǔchéng qīngnián lǚguǎn
Square Inn	四方客栈	sìfāng kèzhàn

Eating and drinking

House of Tibet	西藏咖啡馆	xīzàng kāfēiguǎn
Mamafu's	马马付餐厅	mǎmǎfù cāntīng
Mishi's	密士饭店	mìshì fàndiàn
Prague Café	布拉格咖啡馆	bùlāgé kāfēiguǎn
Well Bistro	井浊餐馆	jǐngzhuó cānguǎn

Nakhi Kingdom of Southwest China by the eccentric botanist-anthropologist **Joseph Rock**, who lived here back in the 1930s.

Arrival and transport

Lijiang is three hours from Dali on the expressway, or five hours if you take the older road (likely if you get a rattletrap country bus). The **airport** lies 20km south along the highway. As a rule of thumb, buses to or from northern destinations use the **North bus station**, while other directions are covered from the **main bus station**, a grey concrete block at the southern edge of town. From the latter, a fifteen-minute walk uphill along Xin Dajie takes you past a shopping centre and the **post office**, then continues north to the **Bank of China**. Note that at the time of writing, you couldn't get a cash advance on a credit card here or anywhere further north of here in Yunnan. There is an ATM, but don't rely on it to work.

Walking and cycling are the main means of getting around – ask at your accommodation about bike rental. The old town is tough to find your way around – look out for prints of the hand-drawn English map, "Roaming in Lijiang", sold in tourist stores (¥5). The best local **tourist agency** is run from the Dongba House (see p.832), which organizes hiking and jeep trips – they also hand out a good cycling map.

As for moving on, buses head in all directions: south as far as Kunming and Baoshan; west to Weixi; north to Qiaotou or Daju (for **Tiger Leaping Gorge**), and Zhongdian; and east to Lugu Hu and Panzhihua in Sichuan province.

△ Locals relaxing in Lijiang

CAAC is in the western part of town on Fuhui Lu (the same road as the **PSB**), or you can buy air tickets from the travel agents outside the bus station; as well as daily services to Kunming, there are also daily flights to Jinghong in Xishuangbanna. All the foreigner-oriented cafés have **Internet access**.

Accommodation

Lijiang has plenty of accommodation, and there are some excellent small family-run guesthouses in the old town. Mid-range hotels in the new town are legion, though there's no reason to stay there – even if you have an early bus, it's a very short cab ride from anywhere in town to the station.

The hotels below are all housed in Naxi-style buildings, some more authentic than others; recently, Han entrepeneurs have been buying up local houses and remodelling them in a faux ethnic style for the domestic tourist market, whose main demand, it seems, is for a giant TV in the room. Addresses are listed but they aren't much help – see the map for locations.

A Liang Guesthouse 110 Wenzhi Xiang ⓣ0888/5129923. One of the best places to stay in Lijiang, this is a snug old Naxi courtyard house – one of a hundred "specially protected" buildings in town – with rooms that the amiable resident family rent out at reasonable rates, though they are pushing it by turning more and more of the rooms into guestrooms. ❶

Ancient Stone Bridge Inn Xingren Shangduan ⓣ0888/5184001. Nice location at the heart of the old town, and, like many such places, has small attractive rooms arranged around a courtyard, with a common bathroom. ❷

Dongba House 16 Xinyi Jie ⓣ0888/5120568. One of the main centres for budget travellers, and run by owners who understand their needs. The simple dorms and doubles are well kept, and the tour agency is the best in town. It's a good place to rent bikes (¥20 a day) as they also hand out a free map. Dorms ¥20, ❶

Huamaguo Xingren Shangduan ⓣ0888/5121688. The best of the new Chinese guesthouses, thanks to a superb location right beside the main canal, which you can appreciate from a charming courtyard. Rooms are a bit dark; facilities are communal. ❷

Inn of the First Bend 43 Mishi Xiang ☎0888/5181688. An old backpacker staple, with friendly, professional staff. Rooms surround a central courtyard, and all facilities are shared. Bike rental available. Dorm beds ¥20, ❷

Jiannanchun 8 Xinyi Xiang ☎0888/5102222. The upmarket option, an imitation Naxi building, in which the mostly Han staff wear Naxi costume all day. The location is good, but it's only worth considering if you absolutely must have your own bathroom. ❼

Old Town Inn Xinyi Jie ☎0888/5189000, ⓕ5126618. Slightly more upmarket than most of the old-town guesthouses, this is a new, quiet, good-looking place offering rooms with or without a bath. ❷

Old Town Youth Hostel 61 Xinhua Jie ☎0888/5188611, ⓦwww.yhachina.com. A new, HI-accredited youth hostel, offering beds in rooms off a central courtyard, plus bike rental. Dorm beds ¥15–50.

Square Inn Off Sifang Square ☎0888/5127487. Small, good value and well located at the heart of the old town. Dorm beds ¥25, ❷

The Town

Oriented north–south, **Xin Dajie** is Lijiang's three-kilometre-long main street. Just about everything west of this line is modern, but east, behind **Lion Hill**'s radio mast, is where you'll find the old town, known locally as **Dayan**. It's not easy to navigate around Dayan's backstreets, but as there are few specific sights this hardly matters. While you wander, try to peek in around the solid wooden gates of **Naxi houses**. These substantial two-storey homes are built around a central paved courtyard, eaves and screens carved with mythological figures and fish, representing good luck. Family houses are very important to the Naxi – Lijiang was formerly organized into clans – and many people spend a large part of their income maintaining and improving them.

All roads into Dayan lead to its core at **Sifang**, the main **marketplace**. Cheap **restaurants** around the square are well geared up to the tourists who come to buy embroidery, hand-beaten copper pots, and wooden carvings of hawks and cockerels, and it is a fine place to stop and watch for older people wearing traditional dark tunics and capes patterned in cream and blue, representing the cosmos. North from here, Dong Dajie is lined with touristy, wooden-fronted souvenir shops; heading south instead takes you right into Dayan's maze, where

---

Naxi music and dancing

The **Naxi Orchestra** is an established part of Lijiang's tourist scene. Using antique instruments, the orchestra performs Song-dynasty tunes derived from the Taoist *Dong Jin* scriptures, a tradition said to have arrived in Lijiang with Kublai Khan, who donated half his court orchestra to the town after the Naxi chieftain helped his army cross the Yangzi. Banned from performing for many years, the orchestra regrouped after the Cultural Revolution under the guidance of **Xuan Ke**, though the deaths of many older musicians have reduced their repertoire from over 60 to just 23 pieces. To counter this, the orchestra's scope has been broadened by including traditional **folk-singing** in their performances.

The orchestra now plays nightly in Lijiang in the well-marked hall just off Dong Dajie (8pm; ¥30–50). The music is haunting, though Xuan Ke's commentaries are too long; it's better to catch the orchestra practising in the afternoon in Black Dragon Pool Park, for free.

A little further north on Dong Dajie, another hall called the "Inheritance and Research Base of China" hosts a song-and-dance troupe who put on spirited nightly performances to a small audience (8–9.30pm; ¥20). Expect to be dragged on stage at the end. Similar audience participation is encouraged in the nightly dances that start around 7pm in Sifang Square.

you'll encounter more locally oriented markets and characterful streets. To the west, cobbled lanes lead up to views of tiled roofs from the fringes of **Lion Hill**, whose forested crown is topped by wooden **Wangu Lou** (¥15), an overbuilt, 22-metre-high pavilion. Below here, the southern part of Dayan didn't survive the earthquake and has been replaced by a complex of weighty Qing-style stone pavilions and ornamental arches, all emphatically Han Chinese and totally inappropriate for the town.

Less at odds with local character is the nearby **Mu Family Mansion** (daily 8.30am–6pm; ¥35). The centre of power for the influential Mu family, the mansion was destroyed in the 1870s but has been painstakingly rebuilt along the lines of the original, with an eclectic mix of Naxi, Bai and Tibetan architecture. The gardens are particularly impressive with their azaleas and orchids, and this is a good place to retreat to if the crowds in the alleys outside become too wearying. The southern boundary of Dayan is marked by **Baimalong Tan**, an old, dragon-headed spring and washing pool in front of a small temple and tangled garden.

When you've had enough of strolling the streets, head up to **Black Dragon Pool Park** (daily 7am–late evening; ¥20) on Lijiang's northern outskirts. The sizeable pool here is also known as **Yuquan** (Jade Spring) after the clear, pale green water which wells up from the base of surrounding hills. With Yulong Xue Shan behind, the elegant mid-pool **Deyue Pavilion** is outrageously photogenic. In the early afternoon, you can watch traditionally garbed musicians performing **Naxi music** in the western halls.

A path runs around the shore between a spread of trees and buildings, passing the cluster of compounds which comprise the **Dongba Cultural Research Institute**. The word *dongba* relates to the Naxi shamans, about thirty of whom are still alive and kept busy here translating twenty thousand rolls of the old Naxi scriptures – *dongba jing* – for posterity. Farther around, and almost at the top end of the pool, is a group of halls imported in the 1970s from the site of what was once Lijiang's major temple, **Fuguo Si**. The best of these is Wufeng Lou, the **Five Phoenix Hall**, a grand Ming-dynasty palace with a triple roof and interior walls embellished with reproductions of the murals at Baisha (see opposite).

Eating

Lijiang's **restaurants** enjoy a good standard of cooking, though local treats are limited to *baba*, a rather stodgy deep-fried flour patty stuffed with meat or vegetables. The old town's **canteens** around Sifang marketplace are interesting places to wolf down claypots, pork stews and dried-ham dishes with locals; some establishments have gone to the trouble of translating their names into English, such as "Welcome to Flourish Snack". There are also plenty of **tourist restaurants** and foreigner-oriented **cafés** in the vicinity of Sifang. In winter, keep an eye open in the markets for the best **walnuts** in Yunnan, and bright orange **persimmons** growing on big, leafless trees around town – these have to be eaten very ripe and are an acquired taste.

Blue Page Vegetarian Mishi Xiang. Provides decent, if slightly pricey, Western, Indian and Chinese dishes. Nice decor and ambience too.

House of Tibet Xinyi Jie. There are a few curiosities on the menu here, such as yak cheese pancakes with honey.

Mamafu's Xinyi Jie. Great outside seating by a stream, and tasty apple pie and Naxi staples such as babas (the local bread) and grilled noodles.

Mishi's Mishi Xiang. Chic modern establishment notable for decent approximations of Western dishes such as shepherd's pie.

Prague Café Xinyi Jie. Scores highly for its location, blueberry cake, DVD collection and menagerie of animals. There's also a "swap two for one" library – shamefully, though, they refuse to take classic works because "no one reads them".

Sakura Café Off Sifang. Actually there are about five places with this name, all next to each other, and all claiming to be the first. All offer reasonably priced beers and coffees, Japanese and Korean food, and get lively in the evening.

Well Bistro Mishi Xiang. Gets universal approval for its pasta, apple cake and chocolate brownies. Service could be better, though.

Around Lijiang

Rich pickings surround Lijiang, with numerous **temples** and villages on the lower slopes of **Yulong Xue Shan** well within bicycle range. Single women should, however, be on their guard when visiting the more remote temples, as the past behaviour of some of the caretakers has been less than exemplary.

There are more ambitious trips to consider from Lijiang: west to the small towns of **Shigu** and **Weixi**, south to **Shibao Shan** (see p.829), or the excellent two-day **hike** through **Tiger Leaping Gorge** along the Yangzi River (here called the **Jinsha**), due north of Lijiang. Those heading further afield, **east into Sichuan** via the rail head at Panzhihua or remote Lugu Lake, have the chance to delve deeper into regional cultures.

Puji Si, Baisha and beyond

The monastery of **Puji Si** is the closest religious site to Lijiang. It's not of great importance, but in summer the journey there takes you through a valley brimming with wild flowers of all descriptions. Head north past the Mao Statue, take the first left and continue about 1500m, then turn left; snake around for a further couple of kilometres and you'll reach **PUJI village**. Ask here for a safe place to leave your bicycle and walk up the hill for thirty minutes or so to where an eccentric caretaker will open the monastery up for you. The temple is new on the inside – like other temples in the area, Puji was destroyed during the Cultural Revolution – and deserted.

More ambitious is a trip to the attractive village of **BAISHA**, about 10km north of Lijiang. From the top of Xin Dajie, take the road left just before Black Dragon Pool Park and follow it for a couple of kilometres until you reach a big reservoir. Keep straight on up the main road for 8km and then take a track left across the fields. Baisha is planted with willows and home to the renowned Doctor Ho who lives at the north end and will doubtless detect your presence, inviting you in to drink one of his

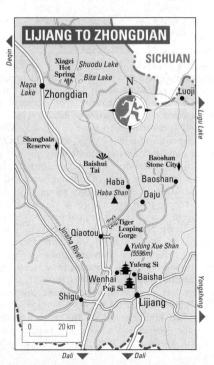

LIJIANG TO ZHONGDIAN

Degin

Xiagei Hot Spring
Shuodu Lake
Bita Lake

Napa Lake
Zhongdian

SICHUAN

N

Luoji

Lugu Lake

Shangbala Reserve

Baishui Tai

Baoshan Stone City

Haba
Haba Shan

Baoshan

Daju

Jinsha River

Qiaotou
Tiger Leaping Gorge

Yulong Xue Shan (5596m)

Yuleng Si

Wenhai
Puji Si
Baisha

Shigu

Lijiang

Yongsheng

0   20 km

Dali   Dali

Around Lijiang

Baisha	白沙	*báishā*
Baoshan Stone City	宝山石头城	*bǎoshān shítouchéng*
Jinjiang	金江	*jīnjiāng*
Panzhihua	攀枝花	*pānzhīhuā*
Shigu	石鼓	*shígǔ*
Weixi	维西	*wéixī*
Wenhai	文海	*wénhǎi*
Yongsheng	永胜	*yǒngshèng*
Yufeng Si	玉峰寺	*yùfēng sì*
Yuhu	玉湖村	*yùhú cūn*
Yulong	玉龙	*yùlóng*
Yulong Xue Shan	玉龙雪山	*yùlóng xuěshān*
Tiger Leaping Gorge	虎跳峡	*hǔtiàoxiá*
Bendiwan	本地湾	*běndiwān*
Daju	大足	*dàzú*
Haba	哈巴村	*hābā cūn*
Margo's Coffee House	玛佳咖啡屋	*mǎjiā kāfēiwū*
Naxi Family Guesthouse	纳西雅阁	*nàxī yǎgé*
Qiaotou	桥头	*qiáotóu*
Sean's Guesthouse	山泉客栈	*shānquán kèzhàn*
Walnut Garden	核桃园	*hétaoyuán*
Lugu Hu	泸沽湖	*lúgū hú*
Dazu	大组	*dàzǔ*
La'ao	落凹	*luò'āo*
Luoshui	落水	*luòshuǐ*
Ninglang	宁蒗	*nínglàng*

cure-all herb teas in return for a donation; prise yourself away and make for the alleyway leading up from the school to **Liuli Dian**, a temple housing wonderful Ming-dynasty **murals** whose strange mix of Taoist, Tibetan and Buddhist influences was the work of local *dongbas*.

It takes around an hour to reach Baisha by bike, and another ten minutes of pedalling north brings you to **YULONG village**. Nearby is **Beiyue Si**, a temple whose eighth-century origins predate the arrival of the Naxi in Lijiang, though it's been managed by descendants of the first Naxi landowners for almost a thousand years and is dedicated to one of their gods, **Sanduo**. There's a mighty statue of him inside, faced by the cringing, life-size image of a peasant – a very feudal tableau. A kilometre farther north again is another village, and here a steep path leads up from the main road to **Yufeng Si**, the Jade Peak Temple (30min). It's not of great interest in itself, but there's an ancient, intertwined **camellia tree** in the top hall representing matrimonial harmony, and in spring the flower-filled courtyard with its mosaic floor is a nice spot for peaceful contemplation. Yufeng Si sits in the foothills of Yulong Xue Shan itself, and higher up there are villages of **Yi** herders and woodcutters, whose women wear oversized black bonnets and three-coloured skirts.

Two kilometres along the main road beyond Yufeng is **Yuhu**, the village where Joseph Rock (see p.831) based himself in the 1920s and 1930s. His house still stands, and a dwindling number of locals can remember him.

Yulong Xue Shan

At 5596m, **Yulong Xue Shan** can't be climbed without proper equipment, though you can ascend on any of three **cable cars**. A special tourist bus running from outside the Black Dragon Pool Park takes you to the base of each (additionally, bus #7 terminates at the first cable car), where you'll pay an entrance fee of ¥85. The first cable car (¥160 one-way) is an impressive 3km long and takes you to an altitude of over 4500m. A short trail leads to a glacier viewing point where tourists shelter from the wind before scuttling back to the relative safety of the cable car. The second cable car (¥40) takes you about a kilometre to another glacier viewing point, the third (¥60) to an alpine meadow. You'll be in the company of plenty of local tourists, but there are endless possibilities for careful and solitary wandering around the trails across the lower slopes – ask at the *Dongba House* in Lijiang about routes.

A great place to base yourself for mountain treks is at **WENHAI**, a beautiful village in the foothills. It's a three-hour trek from Baisha (see p.835), along the road leading northwest out of the village. Otherwise you can reach it by flagging down one of the passing tractors that serve as taxis, or arrange transport with Wenhai's locally run **eco-lodge** (☎0139/08881817, ℰwenhaieco@sina.com; ❶). The converted courtyard house makes a pleasant retreat and has a library and gardens; the management can arrange homestays and guided treks.

Shigu and Weixi

Seventy kilometres west of Lijiang, **SHIGU** (Stone Drum) is a small place named after a tablet raised here in the eighteenth century by one of Lijiang's Mu clan to mark a particularly bloody victory over Han Chinese armies. The Yangzi River makes its first major bend here, deflected sharply to the northeast towards Tiger Leaping Gorge, having flowed uninterrupted in a thousand-kilometre arc from its source away on the Tibet/Qinghai border. Part of the Red Army chose this point to ford the river during the Long March in April 1936, breaking through Nationalist lines under the guidance of the spirited Communist general He Long. There's a small **guesthouse** in Shigu (❷), and it's a pretty area to spend a spring day walking around.

For the adventurous, buses run 100km northwest beyond Shigu through a beautiful, little-explored area which lacks any tourist infrastructure. The road follows the Yangzi to the halfway town of **Judian**, and then bears west past the slopes of **Hengduan Shan** and **Xinzhu Botanical Garden** – basically just a protected natural hillside boasting over three hundred species of trees, some of which are estimated to be a thousand years old. **WEIXI** town marks the end of the road, of interest for nearby villages inhabited by the **Pumi**, a Tibetan race forming one of China's smallest nationalities.

Baoshan Stone City

Sixty kilometres or so north of Lijiang, **Baoshan Stone City**, which gets its name from a karst formation like Kunming's stone forest, is beautiful and unspoilt, and clings to a hillside that invites exploration – though take a guide if you want to go far. A few local families offer accommodation and can arrange horse treks and guides. There is one direct morning bus to Baoshan Shitoucheng ("Stone City") from Lijiang, which leaves when full from outside Black Dragon Pool Park. The trip takes eight hours; don't get off at unremarkable Baoshan but stay on for another hour and a half or so. Alternatively, take a morning bus from Lijiang bus station to Baoshan and then a local bus from there.

Baoshan Stone City is the starting point for a four-day **trek to Lugu Hu** (see p.840), through some remote Naxi and Mosuo territory. The route passes through **Liuqin**, **Fengke**, **Gewa** and **Yongning**, each of which offer simple guesthouse accommodation. Much of the trail is along local footpaths, so a guide is essential.

Tiger Leaping Gorge

About 70km north of Lijiang, and the same distance south of Zhongdian, the Yangzi channels violently through **Tiger Leaping Gorge**. The gorge is so narrow in places that legend has it a tiger once escaped pursuit by leaping across. The drama is heightened by this being the world's deepest canyon, set at an altitude of 2500m with the line of ash-grey mountains forming its southern wall rising for a further 3000m above the rapids. Statistics aside, what makes a **hike** through the gorge so compelling is that for once you're doing something entirely for its own sake: there are no temples to see, the villages along the way are quaint but minute, and the scenery is stark – the gorge's pastoral residents have long since stripped the land of trees and shrubs. Sadly, it looks like the gorge might fall victim to yet another ill-thought-out dam scheme: work had not started at the time of writing, but access roads and test bores had been built in preparation.

There are **two routes** through the gorge between **Daju** in the east and westerly **Qiaotou**, on the Dali–Zhongdian road; both routes take at least two days of walking. No buses run between Qiaotou and Daju, though both are connected by daily services to Lijiang's North bus station. The routes are identical between Daju and the halfway point at the tiny village of **Hutao Yuan**, which has become known to foreign travellers as **Walnut Garden**. From here on to Qiaotou, the forty-kilometre-long **low road** has better views of the river but follows a new vehicle track, especially built for Chinese tour buses; the fifty-kilometre **high road** – actually a trail – offers a rougher and more exciting detour.

Hostel **accommodation and meals** are available along the way, though you need to bring snacks, a solid pair of boots, a flashlight and a first-aid kit. Winter days are often warm enough to hike in a T-shirt and shorts, but nights are cold throughout the year. Plenty of people tackle the trek as if it was a competition, but you'll get more out of it if you take an extra day or two; there are few enough opportunities to stay in attractive villages in China, so take advantage here.

You can tackle the trail in either direction. If you want to head on to Zhongdian afterwards, which has bus connections from Qiaotou, you might prefer to start at Daju – the way described below, and mostly uphill. Alternatively, do a day's hike from Qiaotou (which makes for easier walking) as far as Walnut Garden, where it's easy to hitch a lift back along the low road to Qiaotou; you can leave your luggage in Qiaotou at *Margo's* (see p.840). Yet another possibility is to trek into the gorge from the north, arriving at Walnut Garden from Baishui Tai via the Haba valley; see p.845 for details.

It's best not to walk alone, if only in case something goes wrong along the way. The high road is marked by red and yellow arrows but it's still possible to get lost; try and pick up the home-made **maps** floating around cafés in Lijiang and at the stops on the route. Note that **landslides** are a serious hazard and kill a handful of hikers every year: do not attempt either route in bad weather or during the June–September rainy season. For the latest conditions, check Ⓦwww.tigerleapinggorge.com, run by *Sean's Guesthouse* in Walnut Garden.

Daju to Walnut Garden

The early-morning bus from Lijiang takes an uncomfortable three hours, skirting the base of Yulong Xue Shan and climbing up through patches of primeval forests and open pasture, before finally juddering to a halt at the dusty jumble of stone-walled houses which comprise **DAJU**. There are several restaurants and two simple guesthouses here (➊), along with similar outlying villages to explore; the **bus back to Lijiang** leaves at around 1.30pm.

All things considered, the hike to Walnut Garden is superb. From Daju, it's about an hour's walk, using a well-marked track across the open plateau, to the **ferry across the Yangzi**; the departure point is just short of a small pagoda. Make enough noise and the ferry will turn up, if it isn't there already; foreigners pay a hefty ¥10. Climb the bank on the far side and take any of the tracks towards the gorge, which is clearly visible away to the west. The next hour takes you past a couple of villages before a short, steep descent onto the main path. From here it's steadily uphill around a huge, bowl-shaped depression to rejoin the river at the gorge's mouth, which closes in abruptly, the path now running some 200m above a very fierce Yangzi. A further two hours should see you at the open valley surrounding **WALNUT GARDEN**, where you'll be charged a ¥30 entrance fee at a ticket office. Some people try to avoid this by coming through at night; they only end up getting lost in the dark.

Two establishments here provide good meals, beer and warm beds. The westerly one, *Sean's* (☎0887/8806300; ➊), faces into the gorge and is a favourite for its English-speaking management and front porch, where you can sit after dark and watch an amazing number of satellites zipping through the clear night skies. There's a rare track down to the river here, plus a couple of **guided excursions** that you can arrange: the first is a half-day round trip to a small **cave**, the second a popular two-day trek to **Baishui**, on the way to Zhongdian. The other establishment, *Chateau de Woody* (➊), is in an unattractive building but perfectly comfortable.

Turning northwest after Walnut Grove takes you out of the gorge into the **Haba valley**, for which you'll need a guide as far as **Haba village**, where there's accommodation. Another day's trek and you'll reach **Baishui Tai**, which has charmless guesthouses and a bus on to **Zhongdian**. You might prefer to tackle this trek southwards from Baishui Tai as an alternative route into Tiger Leaping Gorge, as this way you're heading downhill much of the time; for details, see p.845.

Walnut Garden to Qiaotou

The two routes diverge at Walnut Garden. The **low road** is the easier of the two and provides some splendid views: the gorge is tight and steep, the Yangzi fast and rough, and the road narrow, though formerly dangerous stretches now bore through a **tunnel** – but be aware, landslides do still occur along here. You are basically walking along a dusty road, however, and tourist buses will roar back and forth. Expect to take around eight hours to reach Qiaotou.

The **high road** – really a mountain path – is for most the more appealing option. It's a long hike but there are a couple of excellent places to rest up along the way, and it's worth taking your time. From Walnut Garden it's a three-hour, mostly uphill hike to the *Halfway House* (➊) in **Bendiwan village**. You can arrange horse riding and guided walks from here. It's another five hours to the *Naxi Family Guesthouse* (➊), a homely farmhouse with tasty food. Another couple of hours of light trekking takes you to **QIAOTOU**, an ordinary market town. English signs pick out the *Gorge Village Hotel* (❶) on the roadside, but the rooms at the *Youth Hostel* (❶) opposite on the main road are better. *Margo's Coffee House*, just before the bridge, is good for information, and has a pleasant and helpful owner, but the food is pretty poor. There are plenty of buses from here to Zhongdian or Lijiang, either of which is about three hours away; the last bus leaves at around 6pm.

To Sichuan: Panzhihua and Lugu Hu

An increasingly popular route into Sichuan heads 200km due east from Lijiang over the border to Panzhihua, a stop on the Kunming–Chengdu **rail line**. It's about a ten-hour trip – twelve coming the other way – and you're unlikely to forget the early stages of the journey, as the road traverses an almost sheer 1200-metre cliff on the way to the Yangzi crossing and the town of **Yongsheng**, where the bus will probably stop for lunch. It takes about five hours to reach Panzhihua from here, with most of the trip spent above the edges of broad irrigated valleys. **Dukou**'s barren hills and filthy industrial mess appear first, with **PANZHIHUA** – also known as **Jinjiang** – not far beyond. The bus stops right outside the station: try and get on one of the evening trains, as Panzhihua isn't somewhere to stay for long. There's a **hostel** (❷) opposite the train station if you get stuck, and a daybreak bus back to Lijiang.

Lugu Hu

Yongsheng marks the start of a three-hundred-kilometre trail north on public transport to Ninglang, and thence to **Lugu Hu**, a lake right on the provincial border, with transport links to **Xichang** in Sichuan. The shores, partially forested, are inhabited by groups of **Norzu** and **Mosuo**. The former are a branch of the Yi and were once **slave owners**: well into the 1950s, they would raid surrounding lowlands for captives. These were dragged off into the mountains and condemned to live in abject misery while their masters had the power of life and death over them (more of the story is told in Alan Winnington's excellent *Slaves of the Cool Mountains*). For their part, the Mosuo are a Naxi subgroup, still retaining the **matrilineal traditions** lost in Lijiang, such as *axia* marriage, sealed without a specific ceremony and freely broken by either party. Children are automatically adopted by the mother – men have no descendants or property rights. These days, Lugu Lake is being sold to Chinese tourists as the "girl kingdom" and is much visited by single Chinese men looking for a bit of "axia" action – they're inevitably disappointed, and seek solace in the arms of the resident Han prostitutes who wear Mosuo dress. Don't let this put you off, however: it's still a beautiful part of the world, and at least in the villages the locals are in charge of the tourist economy.

It takes five hours to get from Lijiang to **NINGLANG**, where the *Jiamei Binguan* (❷) comes recommended as somewhere **to stay**, and another two hours in a shared taxi from here to lakeside **LUOSHUI**, where you'll be charged ¥30 for a "ticket" you never see. There's plenty of accommodation in Luoshui, or, much more romantically, you can head to one of the lakeside villages where many families rent out beds in their busy farmhouses for around ¥20. The mountains and lake can be stunning, though there's little to do except hire a dugout and be ferried across into Sichuan, landing either at the north-shore village of **Dazu**, or eastern **Lawa** – nicely set at the foot of a 2800-metre peak. From either place, there's local transport east via **Muli** to **Xichang** (9hr), also on the Kunming–Chengdu line (see p.911); roads are really appalling, however.

Zhongdian and around

Six hours from Lijiang, the road northwest climbs out of a steadily narrowing gorge onto a high, barren plateau grazed by shaggy-tailed yaks and ringed by frosted mountains – the borderland between Yunnan, Sichuan and Tibet. The last major town before the high Himalayas is **ZHONGDIAN** (Gyalthang in Tibetan, and often grandiosely called Shangri-la on local maps). It's a commonplace that all over China, traditional houses are being pulled down and ugly modern buildings going up; surely only in Zhongdian is it happening the other way around. In anticipation of a tourist boom, an old town of sturdy Tibetan houses is undergoing massive reconstruction – or rather being built from scratch, making it the newest old town in existence. When it's finished it will be undeniably pretty, a maze of cobbled streets lined with cafés, guesthouses and bars. Add to this limitless possibilities for hiking and horse-riding in the vicinity through forest and alpine meadow, the fact that the road to Tibet – via Deqin and the sublime Meili mountain range – is now open to tour groups, and that new roads are opening up remote areas, and it's clear that Zhongdian is going to be huge. Fortunately, some local entrepreneurs at least are aware that the Lijiang model is one to be avoided. Tour agencies and, more surprisingly, local government are making attempts at sustainable development: logging of old-growth forest, for example, has finally been banned. Among the new arrivals, progressive artsy types outnumber the fast-buck merchants, at least for the moment.

There's a splendid monastery just north of town, and plenty of diverting sights in the countryside around, for which you will have to arrange private transport.

Zhongdian and around

Zhongdian	中甸	*zhōngdiàn*
Songzanlin Monastery	松赞林寺	*sōngzànlín sì*
Accommodation		
Dragon Cloud Inn	龙行客栈	*lóngxíng kèzhàn*
Dukezong	独克宗酒店	*dúkèzōng jiǔdiàn*
Gyalthang Dzong	建格宾馆	*jiàngé bīnguǎn*
Khampa Caravan Eco Lodge	曲及社称尼	*qǔjí shè chēngní*
Rockside Hostel	滇藏驿站	*diānzàng yìzhàn*
YHA	国际青年旅舍	*guójì qīngnián lǚshè*
Eating and drinking		
Cow Pub	牛棚酒吧	*niúpéng jiǔbā*
The Raven	乌鸦酒吧	*wūyā jiǔbā*
Potala Café	布达拉咖啡馆	*bùdálá kāfēiguǎn*
Stupa Book Café	白塔书吧	*báitǎ shūbā*
Tibet Café	西藏咖啡馆	*xīzàng kāfēiguǎn*
Around Zhongdian		
Baishui Tai	白水台	*báishuǐ tái*
Bita Hai	碧塔海	*bìtǎ hǎi*
Haba Snow Mountain Guesthouse	哈巴雪山招待所	*hābāxuěshān zhāodàisuǒ*
Haba Village	哈巴村	*hābā cūn*
Little Zhongdian	小中甸	*xiǎozhōngdiàn*
Napa Lake	纳帕海	*nàpà hǎi*
Shuodu Hai	属都海	*shǔdū hǎi*
Xiagei Hot Springs	下给温泉	*xiàgěi wēnquán*

You can also head much further afield: on the back road into Sichuan, or to mountainous Deqin, and it's even possible to hire a Land Cruiser for the spectacular (if pricey) long road trip to Lhasa.

The Town

Zhongdian is orientated north–south, with most of the mundane business of a grimy frontier town going on in the north, where among cheap concrete and tile buildings you'll find plenty of grisly butchers and the like, and small shops selling knives or rancid yak butter. The tourist facilities and **old town** are all in the far south of town, which is rather more sanitized, and sanitary, and much more attractive. The cobbled alleyways of the old town are lined with sturdy two-storey wooden houses in traditional Tibetan style, mostly new and built with a great deal of skill and care; they look like they'll stand for centuries, which you can't say about much contemporary Chinese building. Actual sights are few, though the **scripture chamber** (daily 8am–6pm;¥10), a reconstructed temple with a couple of exhibition halls showing old photos of the town, is worth a poke around. The huge **chorten** at the centre of the old town is a useful landmark, though it serves no religious function, and locals complain that it's tacky.

The town's star attraction is the splendid **Ganden Sumtseling monastery** just north of town (¥10); catch a northbound bus #3 from the main street. Destroyed during the 1960s but later reactivated, it now houses four hundred Tibetan monks. Among butter sculptures and a forest of pillars, the freshly painted murals in the claustrophobic, windowless main hall are typically gruesome and colourful. Don't forget that you should walk **clockwise** around both the monastery and each hall.

Practicalities

Tiny **Shangri-la Airport** is 7km south of town and there's no bus, so you'll have to take a taxi in (about ¥20). If you're unlucky enough to get stranded – an outside chance if you arrive at night – ring a hotel and they'll pick you up. The new **bus station** is in the north of town; from here bus #2 or #3 will stop on Tuanjie Lu, for the hotels. A couple of the hotels rent out bikes. The **bank** and **post office** are in the north of town.

There is limitless trekking in the area, and a number of **travel**

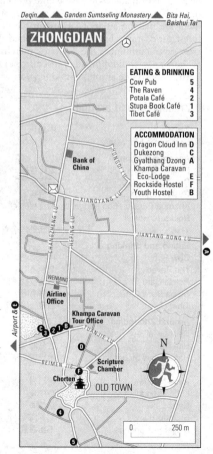

Deqin ▲ ▲ Ganden Sumtseling Monastery ▲ Bita Hai, Baishui Tai

ZHONGDIAN

EATING & DRINKING	
Cow Pub	5
The Raven	4
Potala Café	2
Stupa Book Café	1
Tibet Café	3

ACCOMMODATION	
Dragon Cloud Inn	D
Dukezong	C
Gyalthang Dzong	A
Khampa Caravan Eco-Lodge	E
Rockside Hostel	F
Youth Hostel	B

Bank of China

HONGGU LU

XIANGYANG LU

CHANGZHENG LU

HEPING LU

JIANTANG DONG LU

WENMING JIE

Airline Office

Airport & E

Khampa Caravan Tour Office

TUANJIE LU

BEIMEN JIE

Scripture Chamber

Chorten

OLD TOWN

N

0   250 m

There are daily morning **buses** north to Deqin, the last stop before the Tibetan border. Those taking the rough ride northeast into Sichuan can join the wild-looking guys who reek of yak butter on the 7.30am bus to Litang.

Much of the tourist development in Zhongdian and Deqin is built on the assumption that, sooner or later, the **road to Tibet** will be open to foreign travellers on public transport – though the cartel of travel agents in Chengdu is lobbying to keep the status quo. There is no shortage of agencies that will arrange the journey in private transport, with the requisite guide and driver; recommended in Zhongdian are Khampa Caravan and Haiwei Trails. The Tibet Tourism Bureau in room 2206 of the *Shangbala Hotel* on Changzheng Lu (℡0887/8229028) is the government-approved organization, which means that they are able to organize trips when other agencies might not, for example around politically sensitive anniversaries. The standard price is around ¥4500 per person for a trip to Lhasa, which typically takes a week with stops in the forested Kham area of Tibet; longer trips are also available.

There's also a twice weekly **flight** from Zhongdian to Lhasa, but it is often booked up by tour groups. The only way foreigners can get a ticket is through a tour agency, for around ¥2500, which includes the price of a permit that you'll never see. Flights to Kunming are relatively expensive at ¥700. There are also flights to Chengdu. Buy tickets at the airline office on Wenming Jie (daily 8.30am–noon & 2–6pm; ℡0887/8229555).

agents will help you out with routes and guides. Recommended is the Tibetan-run Khampa Caravan on Tuanjie Lu (℡0887/8288648, Ⓦwww.khampacaravan.com) which works with local communities and offers trips and trekking not just locally but also in Tibet and western Sichuan. Another agency run by local people that prioritizes sustainable development is run from the *Tibet Café* (℡0887/8230282). Foreign-owned Haiwei Trails (℡0887/8289239, Ⓦwww.haiweitrails.com) offer plenty of imaginative treks and mountain biking; though they do a lot of their business on line, by the time you read this their office above the *Raven* bar should be open. If you are looking for other travellers to share a trip, check the noticeboard at the youth hostel. Tour agencies, cafés and accommodation also provide information and can book you on **trips out** from Zhongdian – including the three-day hike via **Baishui** to **Tiger Leaping Gorge** (see p.838).

Accommodation

All the accommodation options are clustered in the far south of town. There are plenty of other Chinese hotels on or just off the main road, but none is very appealing; neither is the *Tibet Longlife Hotel* on Tuanjie Lu, once the only place for backpackers to stay, but now overtaken by the competition.

Dragon Cloud Inn 94 Beimen Jie. A pleasant backpacker hotel at the edge of the old town. The buildings are new and tastefully done, all arranged around a central courtyard and garden. Dorm beds ¥20, ❷

Dukezong Changzheng Lu ℡0887/8230019, Ⓦwww.shangbala.org. This new place behind the *Tibet Café* is the best value in its price range. Dorms have their own bathrooms. Dorms ¥25, ❷

Gyalthang Dzong Hotel ℡0887/8223646,

Ⓦwww.coloursofangsana.com. The perfect place to treat yourself if you've been trekking, this quiet designer hotel at the foot of a hill 3km from town might, very unusually for Chinese accommodation, be somewhere you reminisce about when you get home. The decor, all orange drapes, lacquer and longevity symbols, might best be described as Tibetan minimal. There's a spa and a bar, but no TVs anywhere on site. Substantial discounts available online. ❻

Khampa Caravan Eco Lodge Trinyi Village ℡0887/8288648. A converted Tibetan house 6km southwest of town, just off the airport road, with two rooms, each with seven beds. Call at the Khampa Caravan office when you arrive in town and they'll take you out here. You don't have much choice but to eat in, but the hotpots are delicious. Staff arranges trekking, homestays and horse-riding. Profits help build a school next door. ❶

Rockside Hostel 17 Changfang Jie ℡0887/8288036. In a grand, two-storey Tibetan house in the old town, though rather too many beds have been crammed into the dingy rooms. There's a roofside patio. Definitely worth it if it's not busy, or if you're travelling in a large group. Dorms ¥20, ❷

Youth Hostel 98 Heping Lu ℡0887/8228671. No-frills hostel with a nice bar that serves an inexpensive evening buffet. The affable owner arranges tours into Tibetan villages. Bike rental ¥20 per day; Internet access ¥5 per hour. Dorms ¥20, ❶

Eating and drinking

Don't be put off by the carcasses in the butchers' shops – the yak meat dishes which all the restaurants do are all pretty tasty. Otherwise choice is limited to Chinese staples.

At the time of writing, the old town had thirteen watering holes but only one restaurant. Addresses aren't much use in the old town so phone numbers are provided in case you get lost. As there's no street lighting, mind those cobbles on the way home.

Cow Pub Old town ℡0887/8288774. The first bar to open in the old town, this foreign-owned place has been widely copied. It's a fantastic old Tibetan house full of bric-a-brac, and the bar manager, a Westerner, has a few tales to tell. No *baijiu* is sold, to keep things relatively civilized.

The Raven Old town ℡0887/8289239. The other foreign-owned bar, a little cheaper than the *Cow* but also less atmospheric.

Potala Café Tuanjie Lu. This upstairs café is the most popular place to eat in town. There's a limited menu of Chinese staples but the ambience is pleasant, attracting a good mix of Chinese tourists, grizzly locals and foreigners.

Stupa Book Café Tuanjie Lu. Specializes in Tibetan hotpots – pork soup stewed in a clay pot with ingredients such as yak meat, sausage, lotus root and wild mushroom thrown in. Best if you're in a group of four or more.

Tibet Café Changzheng Lu ℡0887/8238202. Hearty, if somewhat pricey, Western fried break-fasts. They also offer trekking advice and tours, and rent out bikes (¥20 a day).

Around Zhongdian

Popular sights in the area are accessible by car: any taxi in town can be chartered for a day for ¥100 or so, depending on mileage and bargaining skills. **Napa Lake**, 7km north of town, is generally the first stop. It's something of a tourist trap, and only worth a visit in autumn and winter; it dries up almost completely in summer. In winter it's home to a community of rare black-necked cranes.

Ten kilometres east of town are the **Xiagei Hot Springs** (¥10), attractively situated beside a river and below a cave. Spurn the claustrophobic private rooms and swim in the small public pool (¥20); a shop on site sells swimming trunks (¥20). There's also a walking trail, and you can arrange rafting on the river with any of the tour agencies in town (¥200 for an afternoon).

A further hour or so of driving brings you to **Shuodu Hai**, a lake inside the Three Rivers Nature Reserve, acclaimed for its beauty. Plenty of Chinese tour buses come here but their occupants don't seem to get much further than the restaurant and the huge shop in the car park selling traditional medicines such as ginseng and dried ants. Turn right and follow the lake shore for a pleasant, easy walk through old forest. Horses can be hired to take you all the way around the lake for ¥80, which will take about two hours, or you can walk it in four.

Bita Hai, 25km northeast of Zhongdian, is an attractive alpine lake set at an altitude of 3500m and surrounded by lush meadows and unspoilt forest. There are two entrances, south and west, and the best way to explore the place is to ask to be dropped at one and then picked up at the other. Most visitors arrive at the south entrance, from where it's an easy walk down to the lake. Take a rowboat across (a negotiable ¥30 or so per person) to the ferry quay, and you can then walk for two hours or so along a well-marked trail to the west entrance. Horses can be rented at either entrance for ¥50 or so.

Thirty kilometres southeast of Zhongdian, the **Shangbala nature reserve** is a stretch of rugged foothills covered in old-growth forest. A lot of effort is going into keeping tourism sustainable here, and no tour buses turn up. The Shangbala Reserve Project (⊕0887/8238202, ⊜kangbaren@hotmail.com), based in Zhongdian's *Tibet Café*, will arrange a visit, and can also sort out homestays, camping, trekking and horse-riding here.

Baishui Tai and the road to Tiger Leaping Gorge

Over thousands of years, the high carbonic acid content in the water sculpted steps, reminiscent of rice terraces, out of the limestone rocks at **Baishui Tai**. There are plenty of less prosaic local legends concerning their formation, and this is one of the holy sites of the Naxi. It's undeniably pretty, with wooden ladders allowing in-depth exploration of the milky white tiers, which glow orange at sunset. The village at the foot of the site, **Sanba**, is busy transforming itself into a tourist town of guesthouses, all of which offer basic and fairly unattractive rooms.

The limestone terraces provide a scenic break on the trip down the back road to Tiger Leaping Gorge (see p.838). The road is being improved; the trip from Zhongdian took five hours at the time of writing but will soon be down to two, and you should be able to continue by bus all the way to Daju at the eastern end of the gorge, though it would pay to check first in Zhongdian. From Baishui Tai there's a good two-day trek to **Walnut Garden** via the pretty Haba valley and **HABA Village**, for which you'll need a local guide, best arranged in Zhongdian. There's accommodation in Haba at the welcoming *Haba Snow Mountain* Guesthouse (❶) – there's a rudimentary shower and the owner even serves coffee.

Deqin and Meili Xue Shan

Six hours north of Zhongdian across some permanently snowy ranges, and only 80km from Tibet by road, **DEQIN** has traditionally been one of Yunnan's remotest corners. Recently, however, the region was seriously "identified" by the provincial government as **Shangri-la**, the fabled setting for James Hilton's classic tale *Lost Horizon* – an interesting claim considering *Lost Horizon* is fiction. Now the local government is promoting "Shangri-la" tourism for all it is worth as a way to restore revenue lost when logging was outlawed. Hype aside, what really makes the area exciting are the mouthwatering possibilities for hiking around the **Meili Xue mountain range**, whose highest peak is the Kawa Karpo (6740m), of great religious significance to Tibetans; some say it rivals the Annapurna circuit in Nepal for grandeur.

Deqin town itself is nothing special, with a couple of basic accommodation options. The *Deqin Lou* (⊕0887/8412031; ❷, dorms ¥20), just to the north of the bus station, has tolerable rooms. More useful for budget travellers is the

Deqin and Meili Xue Shan

Deqin	德钦	*déqīn*
Dexin Lou	德钦楼	*déqīn lóu*
Feilai Si	飞来寺	*fēilái sì*
Meili Hotel	梅里宾馆	*méilǐ bīnguǎn*
Meili Shanzhuang	梅里山庄	*méilǐ shānzhuāng*
Migrating Bird Café	季候鸟咖啡	*jìhòuniǎo kāfēi*
Meili Xue Shan	梅里雪山	*méilǐ xuěshān*
Hot springs	温泉	*wēnquán*
Kawa Karpa	卡瓦格博	*kǎwǎ gébó*
Lower Yubeng	雨崩下村	*yǔbēng xiàcūn*
Mingyong glacier	明永冰川	*míngyǒng bīngchuān*
Ninong	尼农村	*nínóng cūn*
Upper Yubeng	雨崩上村	*yǔbēng shàngcūn*
Xidang	西当	*xīdāng*
Yubeng Shenpu	雨崩神瀑	*yǔbēng shénpù*

Trekker's Home (℡ 0887/8413966; dorms ¥20); walk north from the bus station for 200m, turn left, and the hostel is on the right. The helpful owner has a lot of information on treks in the area.

However, the most appealing prospect is to skip shabby Deqin town altogether, and, on arrival, jump in a taxi and head 15km north to the viewing point just below the **Feilai Si** (the trip should cost around ¥20), which has sublime views of the mountains and a cluster of guesthouses and cafés. Avoid the overpriced *Meili Hotel* (❷), and plump for the *Meili Shanzhuang* (❸, dorms ¥20) – but wherever you stay, try to get up to see the sunrise over Meili's thirteen peaks. The best place to eat is the *Migrating Bird Café*, which serves as an informal tourist agency and meeting point.

Meili Xue Shan

From the Feilai temple viewing point, it's a further 20km to the entrance to the **Meili Xue Shan reserve**, a trip that costs around ¥30 in a tractor. You could skip the ride, and the ¥63 **entrance fee** too, by walking for three hours along a local footpath to **Xidang village**, a couple of kilometres south of the hot springs (see below); there are details of the route at the *Migrating Bird Café*.

There are two trails from the main entrance. Most people head east for the three-hour ascent to the **Mingyong glacier**, one of the world's lowest at 2700m, and advancing relatively quickly at 500m a year. The road is relatively good for the area, and there are a fair few souvenir shops and guesthouses at the glacier viewing point.

A more interesting option is to head west, into the old forest. Four hours' walk takes you to the **hot springs**, which has a couple of guesthouses – and is irregularly connected to Deqin by bus (officially at 8am and 3pm). The springs are nothing special, but might be the last hot water you'll see for a while. From here there's a gruelling three-hour ascent to Nazongla Pass, or you can go up on a horse for ¥100. A well-marked path then takes you downhill to **Upper Yubeng village**, a Tibetan settlement of considerable charm. You can stay here with a local family, and plenty do (expect to pay ¥10 per night, plus ¥10 for a meal), but it's worth persevering to the even prettier **Lower Yubeng village**

– take the trail to the left as you come into Upper Yubeng and walk for a couple of hours, over a stream and then a bridge. At the end of Lower Yubeng you'll find *Aqinbu's Shenbu Lodge*, the best place to stay in the area, and a handy base for further treks, which the helpful owner can advise on. Be aware that the locals, as well as being fiercely traditional (Tibetan-style polyandrous marriages are common), are desperately poor – one of the few sources of income is picking rare mushrooms for export.

The most popular trip from Lower Yubeng is the straightforward two-hour walk to the dramatic **Yubeng Shenpu**, a sacred waterfall, with bears, snow leopards and the highly endangered Yunnan golden monkey lurking in the nearby forests. If you don't want to retrace your steps back to the reserve entrance, you can hike back via **Ninong**, which skips the Nazongla Pass, but you'll need a local guide.

More ambitious hikers can attempt the full Kawa Karpa pilgrimage trek, three circumnavigations of which will guarantee a beneficial reincarnation, according to Tibetan religious doctrine. The circuit takes twelve days or so, beginning in Deqin and ending in the village of Meili. Much of the route is above 4000m, and is only possible with a local guide – travel agencies in Zhongdian will sort out the arrangements for you.

The Nu Jiang Valley

The **Nu Jiang** (or **Salween River**) flows south through Yunnan from Tibet, skirting the Burmese border to the west. To the east is the Gaoligong mountain range, a huge rock wall that has kept this area an isolated backwater; the only connection with the rest of the province is the road from Xiaguan, which peters out in the far north of the valley. Unless you're a very hardy trekker with a local guide, the culmination of any trip here is the bus ride back down again, as there is no public road from the north end into Deqin.

However, there are some fascinating attractions in this, Yunnan's last true wilderness. The river itself is narrow, fast, full of rapids and crisscrossed by precarious rope bridges, and the settlements clinging to the gorge's sides are most picturesque. Most of the population are Tibetan, Lisu or Dulong, and there are a surprising number of Catholics, the result of French missionary work in the nineteenth century. Tourism is beginning to make inroads, with agencies

The Nu Jiang valley		
Nu Jiang	怒江	*nùjiāng*
Bingzhongluo	丙中洛	*bǐngzhōngluò*
Cizhong	茨中	*cízhōng*
Dimaluo	迪麻洛	*dímáluò*
Fugong	福贡	*fúgòng*
Gongshan	贡山	*gòngshān*
Liuku	六库	*liùkù*

based in Dali, Lijiang and Zhongdian offering **guided treks**, at present the best way to explore the area. Packages organized from Dali and Lijiang are likely to access the river valley via Xiaguan, though agencies in Zhongdian may be able to organize a trek west towards the far north of the area, depending on the time of year. Be wary trekking in winter and spring, however, when high rainfall makes landslides common.

Liuku and Fugong

There's no hardship to spending a day or two in **LIUKU**, the ordinary, fairly laid-back capital of Nu Jiang prefecture – which is just as well, as it's an essential transport stop on the way up the valley. A seven-hour bus trip from Xiaguan, Liuku has a large minority population, but there's not much to do except wander the streets, and nothing to buy unless you're interested in illegally logged Burmese teak or crossbows of dubious efficacy. The sleepy place is at its liveliest around December 20, when the Lisu hold the **Kuoshijie festival** at which, besides singing and dancing, you'll see local men showing off by climbing poles barefoot using swords as steps.

The town straddles both sides of the Nu, with the hotels and **bus station** on the east side. The best budget **place to stay** is the *Minzheng Binguan* (❷); from the bus station, head south back down the Xiaguan road, turn right after 200m and the hotel is a couple of minutes' walk away. Otherwise, try the *Government Guesthouse* (❶) on Renmin Lu, north of the bus station. The more upmarket *Nujiang Binguan* (❹) on Chuancheng Lu, the street east and parallel to this one, isn't that much better. The **bank** and **post office** are along Renmin Lu. For **food**, try the covered night market just south of the intersection of Renmin and Zhenxing Lu, where you'll see game from the surrounding forests as well as Yunnan staples.

Heading north from Liuku, you pass through some very scenic Lisu villages clinging to the steep sides of the gorge, and the river begins to reveal its fierce character, so it's a shame that the next big town, **FUGONG**, five hours from Liuku, is such a dump. Given its vistas of bleak concrete, it's basically a rest stop on the way to the more interesting Gongshan; the *Fugong Binguan* (❷) opposite the bus station is the best place to stay. Every five days there's a **market**, well attended by Lisu, Dulong and Nu people from nearby villages.

Gongshan, Bingzhong, Dimaluo and around

The far north of the Nu valley, being effectively a dead end, is Yunnan's most remote region, and with old forest, waterfalls and thatched roofed villages, it's also one of the prettiest. But it's also very poor, and there is a deal of malnutrition and alcoholism on display from the local minorities, who are nonetheless generally welcoming. Tourism promises to be a lucrative new source of income, though as yet there are fairly few facilities – the only people who get here are intrepid trekkers, most of whom arrive with an agency. Certainly it is not a good idea to venture too far alone, and a local guide is always advised for any ambitious walk.

First stop is the one-street town of **GONGSHAN**, a few hours' bus ride north of Fugong. You'll likely see plenty of Dulong people here: older women have tattooed faces, supposedly for beautification, though the practice seems to have started as a way to dissuade Tibetan slave-traders from kidnapping them. The bus-station **guesthouse** (❷) has hot water.

A bumpy two-hour journey north through dramatic gorge scenery takes you to **BINGZHONGLUO**, a lovely little village at the end of the road, with a couple of basic guesthouses (●). This is the best place to base yourself for treks. One popular walk, simple enough to do by yourself, is to **Dimaluo**, a community of Catholic Tibetans. Board a bus heading south and get off at the footbridge that leads to Pengdang; cross the river and walk south until you reach a bridge and a dirt track, which you follow north to the village. The walk takes about two hours. At Dimaluo, there's accommodation and an intriguing Catholic church built in Tibetan style.

From Dimaluo it's a two-day hike across the Nushan range to **Cizhong**, a village with an impressive 100-year-old stone church; the locals even make their own red wine for communion, though Christianity in this region has been laid on top of much older, animist beliefs, and the result is something of an amalgam. There is a road of sorts from here to **Weixi** (see p.837), though it is treacherous between October and May. Outside these months there is an irregular, fair-weather bus service to Weixi (6hr), from where you can catch a bus to Deqin. Another popular three-day trek, over high passes and through thick forest, runs from Bingzhongluo to **Dulongjihan**. It's also possible to hire a four-wheel drive for this, though again, note that the road is often closed in winter and spring.

Xiaguan to Burma

Southwest of Xiaguan, the last 500km of China's section of the Burma Road continues relentlessly through **Baoshan prefecture** and into the **Dehong Dai/Jingpo Autonomous Region**, cut by the deep watershed gorges of Southeast Asia's mighty **Mekong** and **Salween rivers** (in Chinese, the Lancang Jiang and Nu Jiang respectively). It's impressive country, almost entirely covered by tightly pinched extensions of the dark **Gaoligong Mountains**, and the road forever wobbles across high ridges or descends towards the green fields of rice and sugar cane which occupy the broad valleys in between. Settlements here have large populations of Dai, Burmese, Jingpo and others, and until recently mainstream China never had a great presence. Even after Kublai Khan invaded and left his relatives to govern from inside walled towns, the region was largely left to the pleasure of local **saubwas**, hereditary landowners. They were deposed in the 1950s, but it's still often unclear whether rules and regulations originate in Beijing or with the nearest officer in charge.

The Burma Road itself links the towns of **Baoshan**, **Mangshi** and the border crossing at **Wanding**, around which are some of the most accessible of the Jinpgo settlements. From Wanding – and staying within China – it's only an hour west to weird wonders at the den of iniquity that is **Ruili**. There's also a rougher back road between Baoshan and Ruili, taking in **Tengchong** and some diminishing jungle. Whichever way you travel, roads tend to disintegrate during the subtropically humid **wet season** between May and October, when airports at Baoshan and Mangshi may provide the only access.

Baoshan

BAOSHAN, 120km from Xiaguan, may be dull, but it has its share of history. The region was settled long before Emperor Wu's troops oversaw the paving of stretches of the Southern Silk Road nearby in 109 BC, and the third-century Sichuanese minister **Zhuge Liang** later reached Baoshan in one of his invasive "expeditions" across southwestern China. Kublai Khan fought a massive battle with the Burmese king **Narathihapade** outside the town in 1277, won by the

Xiaguan to Burma

Baoshan 保山 *bǎoshān*
Taibao Shan Park 太保山公园 *tàibǎoshān gōngyuán*
Wuhou Si 武候寺 *wǔhóu sì*
Yu Huang Si 玉皇寺 *yùhuáng sì*

Accommodation
Huacheng 花城宾馆 *huāchéng bīnguǎn*
Yindou 银都大酒店 *yíndū dàjiǔdiàn*
Yongchang 永昌宾馆 *yǒngchāng bīnguǎn*

Mangshi 芒市 *mángshì*
Dehong Binguan 德宏宾馆 *déhóng bīnguǎn*

Ruili 瑞丽 *ruìlì*
Huafeng market 华丰市场 *huáfēng shìchǎng*
Jingcheng Hotel 景成大酒店 *jǐngchéng dàjiǔdiàn*
Limin Hotel 利民宾馆 *lìmín bīnguǎn*
Mandalay Garden Hotel 曼德丽花园 *màndélì huāyuán*
Nanyang Hotel 南洋宾馆 *nányáng bīnguǎn*
Ruili Hotel 瑞丽宾馆 *ruìlì bīnguǎn*

Around Ruili
Denghannong Si 召尚弄寺 *zhāoshàngnòng sì*
Hansha Si 喊沙寺 *hǎnshā sì*
Jiegao 姐告 *jiěgào*
Jiele Jin Ta 姐勒金塔 *jiělè jīntǎ*
Jiexiang 姐相 *jiěxiàng*
Jinya Ta 金鸭塔 *jīnyā tǎ*
Leizhuang Xiang 雷奘相佛寺 *léizhuǎngxiāng fósì*
　Buddhist Temple

Tengchong 腾冲 *téngchōng*
Daying Shan 打应山 *dǎyìng shān*
Heshun Xiang 和顺乡 *héshùn xiāng*
Huoshankou 火山口 *huǒshān kǒu*
Laifeng Shan Park 来风山公园 *láifēngshān gōngyuán*
Leihua Hotel 雷华酒店 *léihuá jiǔdiàn*
Mazhan 马站 *mǎzhàn*
Post Office Hotel 邮政宾馆 *yóuzhèng bīnguǎn*
Rehai 热海 *rèhǎi*
Tengchong Binguan 腾冲宾馆 *téngchōng bīnguǎn*
Tengyun Binguan 腾云宾馆 *téngyún bīnguǎn*
Tonglida Binguan 通利达宾馆 *tōnglìdá bīnguǎn*
Zhonghe 中和 *zhōnghé*

Wanding 畹町 *wǎndīng*
Longlong 弄弄 *nòngnòng*
Manbang 曼棒 *mànbàng*
Wanding Binguan 畹町宾馆 *wǎndīng bīnguǎn*
Wanding Forest Park 畹町国家森林公园 *wǎndīng guójiā sēnlín*
　　gōngyuán
Yufeng Dajiudian 裕丰大酒店 *yùfēng dàjiǔdiàn*

khan after his archers managed to stampede Burmese elephants back through their own lines. Twenty years later the women and slaves of Marco Polo's "Vochan" (today's Baoshan) supported a tattooed, gold-toothed aristocracy – tooth-capping is still practised both here and in Xishuangbanna. Baoshan was again in the front line in the 1940s, when a quarter of a million Chinese troops fought to keep the Japanese from invading through Burma. Today it remains garrisoned, with young army recruits in poorly fitting green fatigues drilling around the parks and parade grounds.

The Town

Baoshan's centre is boxed in by **Huancheng Lu**, whose north, south, east and west sections follow the square lines of the now demolished Ming city walls. Ennobled as a city in 1983, Baoshan is nonetheless very much a provincial town, its streets grubby, half-modernized and full of activity. In the Burma Road's heyday the shops stocked Western goods siphoned off from supply convoys heading through to Kunming, and even now they seem abnormally well provisioned with locally grown "World Number One Arabica" coffee, tins and bottles of imported luxuries, smart suits and shoes. Rural produce gets an airing in the **main marketplace** on Qingzhen Jie, somewhere to browse among Baoshan's older buildings, but it's not especially exciting. A nicer spot to spend a few hours among pine trees, butterflies and twittering birds is **Taibao Shan Park**, about 1500m west of the centre at the end of Baoxiu Lu. Near the entrance is **Yu Huang Si**, a Ming Taoist temple whose slanted pillars support a small octagonal dome. It's no longer a place of worship – it's filled with photos and maps describing local engagements with the Japanese forces – but you'll have to remove your shoes to visit the five alabaster Buddhas in the tiny nunnery next door.

The path climbs farther up to pavilions offering views over town and the surrounding Baoshan Plain, until it reaches **Wuhou Si** on the flattened, wooded summit. The temple commemorates Zhuge Liang, whose huge bearded statue sits between his ministers. Behind the hall are some respectably large trees, and fragments of stone tablets recording imperial proclamations.

Practicalities

Surrounded by dumpling, soup and noodle stalls, the **main bus station** is on the corner of Huancheng Dong Lu and Baoxiu Lu, the latter running due west straight through the city. About 500m along it's crossed by Zhengyang Lu, where there's a **Bank of China** (Mon–Fri 8am–6pm), a department store and a tiny, well-concealed **airline office**. Gradually narrowing in its final kilometre, Baoxiu Lu is further crossed by Qingzhen Jie and Huancheng Xi Lu before ending at a staircase leading up to Taibao Shan Park.

Baoshan has plenty of **accommodation and food**. Just north of the station on Huancheng Dong Lu, *Huacheng Binguan* (☎0875/2203047; ❶) is getting musty round the edges. South along Baoxiu Lu, the smarter *Yindou Dajiudian* (☎0875/2120948; ❷), right next to the bank, is a better bet, though none of its facilities, even the restaurant, ever seems to open. The rooms on the top floor are the best maintained, with good views. The *Yongchang Binguan* (☎0875/2122802; ❷), in a courtyard on the west side of Baoxiu Lu just over Zhengyang Lu, has rooms ranging from spartan to bland in its three buildings. Not counting the hotels, there are a dozen or more restaurants turning out decent stir-fries and casseroles between the bus station and the park, with the yellow-tiled Muslim place on the corner of Qingzhen Jie the best of the bunch – look for the Arabic script.

Moving on, there are direct daily buses to all destinations east and west including Kunming, Tengchong and Ruili, and also a lengthy southern link with Jinghong in Xishuangbanna – see p.000 before undertaking this journey.

Tengchong and the back road to Ruili

The ghost of the former Southern Silk Road runs west of Baoshan, and the bus is initially slowed by police roadblocks and crowded village markets, then by steep hairpin bends as it skirts the dense undergrowth of the **Gaoligong Shan Nature Reserve**. Two valleys along the way are fertilized by the Nu and **Shweli** rivers (the latter a tributary of the Irrawaddy), both of which ultimately empty into the sea several thousand kilometres away in southern Burma. Six hours from Baoshan the bus trundles to a halt at untidy, energetic **TENG-CHONG**. A Han-dynasty settlement which first grew wealthy on Silk Road trade, Tengchong has a high incidence of **earthquakes**, which have left it bereft of large historic monuments or tall buildings, but business still flourishes and there are some unusual geological sights nearby.

Tengchong's premier market is the **Frontier Trade Bazaar**, held every morning along western Guanghua Lu. With business revolving around house-hold goods and food, things are not quite as romantic as they sound, but there's also a small **jewellery and gem market** on the main Fengshan Lu; both markets should whet your appetite for better affairs in Ruili.

For a stroll, head for **Laifeng Shan Park**, several square kilometres of hilly woodland immediately southwest of Tengchong. Paths ascend to **Laifeng Si**, a monastery-turned-museum, and a resurrected, thirteen-storey **pagoda** which will guide you to the park from town.

Practicalities

There are two **bus stations** – one in the eastern outskirts along Huancheng Dong Lu that serves destinations further south such as Ruili, and a new one in the far north of town, serving Kunming, Baoshan and Xiaguan. From the eastern bus station, continue south and then bear west down either Guanghua Lu or parallel Yingjiang Lu to where Tengchong's main street, **Fengshan Lu**, cuts across them at right angles. One kilometre farther south down Fengshan Lu takes you past a **post office** and **bank** to the junction with **Fangshou Lu**, the main road west out of town. Taxis wait at both bus stations, though a walk right across town takes only thirty minutes.

For **accommodation**, try the *Tonglida Binguan* (☎0875/5187787; ❸, dorm beds ¥30), offering huge doubles with bathroom across from the old bus station; the *Post Office Hotel* (❸), next to the post office on Fengshan Lu; or the quiet *Tengchong Binguan* (☎0875/5121044; ❷, dorm beds ¥30) – walk to the western end of Fengshan Lu, cross straight over Fangshou Lu and head uphill, turn left and the hotel is about 100m farther on. Their cheapest rooms are bare, but they can arrange **tours** into the countryside. The *Leihua Binguan* in the south of town on Huancheng Nan Lu is the only upmarket option and, as it's new, is quite good value (❹). Alternatively, take a cab (¥10) to the pretty village of **Heshun Xiang** and stay with a family there (see below). Places to **eat** lurk along Yingjiang Lu and Guanghua Lu, where there are also evening stalls selling charcoal-grilled chicken and fish.

Around Tengchong

Five kilometres west of town along Fangshou Lu, **HESHUN XIANG** is a Qing-style village whose splendid memorial gateways, ornamental gardens and thousand or more houses are tightly packed within a whitewashed perimeter wall. It is trumpeted for the achievements of its former residents, many of whom have led profitable lives after emigrating overseas and have since ploughed money back into the village's upkeep, and you could easily spend half a day here with a camera. In particular, look for **Yuanlong Tan**, a delightful pond surrounded by pavilions and a creaky water mill. There's a nice place to stay here too: go over the bridge, turn left, and on the main track that goes around the hill, look for the sign that says "Inhabitant Hotel". The family that live in this rather grand house have a few rooms (❶), with a shared bathroom.

Geological shuffles over the last fifty million years have opened up a couple of hotspots around Tengchong. The easiest to reach, **Rehai** ("Hot Sea"), is 11km southwest along the Ruili road, where the scalding **Liuhuang** and **Dagung-guo** pools (each ¥20) steam and bubble away, contained by incongruously neat stone paving and ornamental borders. Get there by minibus (¥5) from Huancheng Nan Lu, at the junction with the Ruili road.

Volcano hunters should ask around at the bus station or hotels for transport 10km northwest to **Zhonghe** village and the slopes of 2614-metre-high **Daying Shan**, or 30km north to **Huoshankou**, a large crater near the town of **Mazhan**. These two are the largest of many surrounding cones, dormant but covered in rubble from previous eruptions. Quite a few people do seek out these peaks, but the entrance fee (¥20) might seem a lot of money for the privilege of walking on a flat-topped hill.

On to Ruili

The quickest route from Tengchong to Ruili is to backtrack along the south-easterly road and continue via Mangshi and Wanding (see below), but there's also a direct road running west, towards and then along the Burmese border, a seven-hour trip on a good day. This begins smoothly, cruising through a river valley where the scenery becomes less and less "Chinese" as the bus passes Dai villages with rounded wats, red-leaved poinsettias and huge, shady fig trees. Progress becomes unpredictable after a lunch stop and more officious police checks near **Yingjiang**, where the road turns south to cross the ranges above Ruili. You may well get a close look at the forests here – one downhill stretch is notorious for the house-sized boulders which crash down from the slopes above to block the road completely, causing extended delays. If this happens, go for a walk along the road, as there's birdlife hiding in patches of vegetation and villages which have seen few foreigners.

Mangshi

South of Baoshan the Burma Road makes a grand descent into the Nu River Valley on the five-hour journey to **MANGSHI** (also known as **Luxi**), Dehong's little administrative capital and the site of its airport. Surrounded by Dai and Jingpo villages, the Mangshi region has a reputation for excellent pineapples and silverwork, though the town itself holds enough to occupy only a couple of hours between connections. Hot and grey, the highway runs through as **Tuanjie Dajie**, its eastern end marked by a large roundabout and its western end by a narrow, black canal. Just over this canal, **Yueyi Lu** points north into a jumble of quieter, older streets filled with markets and a fair complement of **Buddhist temples** raised on wooden piles in the ornate Dai style, many of them being restored.

The **airport** is about 7km south off the highway, where taxis and minibuses to town, and also to Ruili and Wanding, meet incoming flights. A minibus to Ruili takes one and a half hours and should cost ¥20. Most Mangshi vehicles will set down at the eastern end of Tuanjie Dajie, either on the roundabout outside the **airline office** (daily 8.30–11.30am & 1.30–5pm; the bus to the airport leaves 2hr before each flight) or about 1km west at the cluster of depots where **long-distance buses** and **minibuses** stop. Note that there is transport southeast along the difficult route to Nansan and on to Xishuangbanna (see p.861). The airline office has a clean and simple **hotel** attached (❷), or there are smart rooms at *Dehong Binguan* (❷), nicely located in large grounds at the top of backstreet Yueyi Lu. The *Dehong* has a good **restaurant**, and there are countless shacks serving buns and curries in almost every lane through the town.

Wanding and around

Two hours south of Mangshi the road crosses the **Long Jiang** (Shweli River) and then finally slaloms down the slopes of a narrow valley to where the shallow Wanding Stream separates Chinese **WANDING** from **Jiugu** over in Burma. Opened in 1938 as the Burma Road's purpose-built border crossing, Wanding was immediately attacked by villagers who suspected that this customs post was connected with Guomindang units who were then busy trying to exterminate Mangshi's Jingpo hill tribes. The tension proved short-lived, but Wanding has never amounted to much – possibly because, aware of its showpiece status as China's official point of entry into Burma, authorities deter the illicit backroom dealings that make neighbouring Ruili such an attractive proposition for traders.

Not that Wanding is uninteresting: the **Wanding Bridge crossing** is a marvel, decked in customs houses, smartly uniformed military, barriers, barbed wire, flags and signs everywhere prohibiting unauthorized passage. The bridge itself – though ridiculously short – is a sturdy concrete span, and there's even a prominent red line painted across the road on the Chinese side. But it's all a sham; walk 100m downstream and you'll find people rolling up their trousers and wading across a ford almost within sight of patrolling soldiers, while farther on some enterprising soul has even set up a bamboo raft (so long it's virtually a bridge) to punt customers over to the far bank. Naturally everyone knows what's happening, but this arrangement spares authorities and locals endless official bother.

Unfortunately, **foreigners wanting to cross** will find the situation very different. At the time of writing, Westerners could enter Burma only by flying to Rangoon or booking a tour (see p.811), and though some have quietly snuck across from Wanding for an hour or two, bear in mind that you'll be very conspicuous and that there's nothing to see in Jiugu apart from a large wat on the hill above.

Practicalities

Wanding stretches thinly for 1500m along the north bank of the Wanding Stream and Minzhu Jie, both of which run west towards Ruili, with Guofang Jie descending from the hills at Minzhu's eastern end to the border checkpoint and Wanding Bridge. There's no **bus station** as such, but local transport and vehicles shuttling between Mangshi (¥10) and Ruili (¥7) stop around the Minzhu Jie/Guofang Jie intersection. Here you'll also find a couple of fairly wholesome **restaurants**, with a **bank** (Mon–Fri 8.30–11.30am & 2–5pm) and **post office** (daily 8am–6pm) nearby on Minzhu Jie. **Accommodation** prospects are limited to the cavernous *Yufeng Dajiudian* on the northeast corner of the intersection (❶), and the surprisingly good *Wanding Binguan* (❷) uphill off Minzhu Jie on Yingbin Lu. Despite the border, the backstreet **markets** along

Wanding Stream are small affairs except on Saturday mornings, when things get pretty enthusiastic. Street hawkers sell herbs and roots and you can pick up presentation packs of **Burmese coins** from shops near the bridge.

Around Wanding

One of the best ways to get a good look at Burma from the Chinese side is to spend an hour in **Wanding Forest Park** (¥3) – walk uphill along Guofang Jie, take the first lane on the left and follow it upwards to the park gates. A few minutes beyond is an amusement area, where a dirt footpath leads into scrub and pine plantations behind the dodgems, eventually ending up at a recently built **temple**, bare inside except for prayer cushions and a large alabaster Buddha. The front entrance looks down across the border at Jiugu, undulating green hills and the red earth continuation of the Burma Road heading south of the crossing towards Lashio.

The **Jingpo** minority live a relatively secluded existence in the Dehong highlands, and a number of their villages are located around Wanding, including **LONGLONG**, 15km west via **Manbang** township. Always considered a primitive spirit-worshipping race by the Han government, the Jingpo are so poor that in the early twentieth century they were forced to grow opium as a cash crop (hence the Guomindang campaign against them). Longlong comes alive for the **Munao festival** on the last day of the lunar new year (usually some time in February), when hundreds of Jingpo take part in an ancient dance said to have been handed down to their ancestors by the children of the sun god. The *Wanding Binguan* sometimes organizes tours of the villages; otherwise, look for minibuses at the intersection in town.

Ruili and around

Yunnan's most westerly town, **RUILI** is barely thirty minutes by road from the sober formalities and polite cross-border sneaking at Wanding, but infinitely

Burmese glossary

Hello (polite)	*Min galaba jinbaya*	Rice	*Htamin*
Thank you	*Jayzu tinbadé*	Sticky rice (in a	*Kauk nyaimn*
I'd like to eat	*Htamin saa gyinbadé*	bamboo tube)	*paung (tauk)*
Beef	*Améda*	Sour sauce	*Achin*
Chicken	*Jeda*	Spoon	*Zone*
Curry	*Hin, tha*	Tea	*La pay-ee*
Cold drink	*A-ay*		
Crushed	*Nanthaung*	One	*Did*
peanuts		Two	*Nhid*
Dhal (split	*Pey hin*	Three	*Dhong*
pea soup)		Four	*Lay*
Fish	*Nga*	Five	*Ngar*
Fish soup with	*Moh hin gha*	Six	*Chauk*
banana stem		Seven	*Khunik*
and noodles		Eight	*Chind*
Fork	*Khayan*	Nine	*Cho*
Milk	*Nwa nou*	Ten	*Desay*
Noodles	*Kaukswe*	Eleven	*Say did*
Pickled	*Lapatoh*		
vegetables			

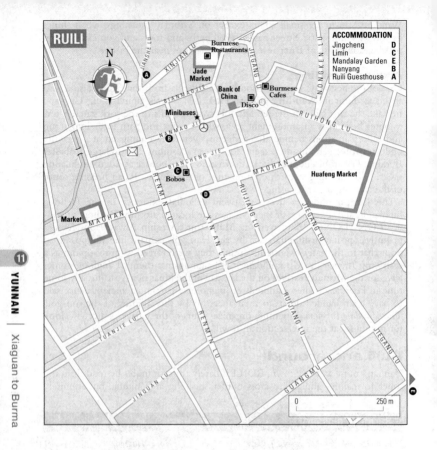

distant in spirit. Once the capital of the Mengmao Dai Kingdom but now an ostentatious boom town, Ruili revels in the possibilities of its proximity to Burma, 5km south over the Shweli. So heavy is the flow of illegal traffic pouring over the dozens of crossing points to **Mu Se**, its Burmese counterpart, that locals quip, "Feed a chicken in China and you get an egg in Burma". Though things along the Burmese side have tightened up considerably in recent years, Ruili is still the main conduit for Burmese **heroin** entering China, reflected in the town's high number of addicts and AIDS patients. Burmese, Pakistani and Bangladeshi nationals wander around in sarongs and thongs, clocks are often set to Rangoon time, and markets display foreign goods. Most Chinese in town are tourists, attracted by the chance to pick up cut-price trinkets and the decadent thrills of drugs, gambling and prostitution. While all this might sound like something to avoid, Ruili is actually a surreal treat at the fringes of the Chinese empire, though take the sleaze seriously – it may be exciting after dark but it's not always safe, especially for women. And don't leave town with any narcotics, as the police search outgoing vehicles. If the town's nightlife appals, the **markets** are unquestionably fascinating; many foreign traders speak good English and make interesting company. Additionally, the surrounding countryside, studded with Dai villages and temples, is only a bike ride away.

The markets

By day Ruili's broad pavements and drab construction pin it down as a typical Chinese town. Fortunately, the **markets** and people are anything but typical. The **Burmese stallholders** in the market off Xinjian Lu can sell you everything from haberdashery and precious stones to birds, cigars, Mandalay rum and Western-brand toiletries; Dai girls powder their faces with yellow talc, young men ask if you'd like to be shown to a backstreet casino and street sellers skilfully assemble little pellets of stimulating **betel nut** dabbed in ash paste and wrapped in pepper-vine leaf, which stains lips red and teeth black.

The Burmese are very approachable, and some are refugees of a sort, as upheavals in Rangoon in 1988 and 1991 saw Muslims slipping over the border to enjoy China's relative religious freedom. Many pedal their wares at the **jade and gem market** on Bianmao Jie, which everyone refers to as "Traveller Street". Chinese dealers come to stock up on ruinously expensive wafers of deep green jade, but most of the rubies, amethysts, sapphires, moonstones and garnets on show are flawed and poorly cut; dealers produce their better stones only for properly appreciative customers. Buying is a protracted process here, and for the newcomer it's safer just to watch the furtive huddles of serious merchants, or negotiate souvenir prices for coloured pieces of sparkling Russian glass "jewels", chunks of polished substandard jade and heavy brass rings.

Dai and Jingpo haunt Ruili's huge **Huafeng market** on Jiegang Lu where, as well as piles of deer meat and wildcat pelts, limes, blocks of jaggery (palm sugar), coconuts, curry pastes and pickles for sale, you'll also find plenty of excellent food stalls, many of them run by minorities.

Practicalities

Ruili's kilometre-long main street is **Nanmao Jie**, which runs west from a tree-shaded roundabout; it passes the Bank of China (foreign exchange Mon–Fri 9–11.30am & 2.30–4.30pm), a **minibus depot** for transport into the immediate area, and the **long-distance bus station**, before crossing Renmin Lu. Turn north here and there's a **post office** 50m away on the corner of Xinjian Lu. Cross over the broad junction here and continue up Jianshe Lu for Ruili Travel Service (Mon–Sat 7.30–11.30am & 3–6.30pm) next to the *Ruili Hotel*. They don't speak English but can organize air tickets, and there's an **airport bus** from here to Mangshi every morning – book the day before. There are minibuses every hour to Wanding and Mangshi (from where there's transport on to **Nansan**, first stop on the rough, three-day haul to Xishuangbanna; see p.861), and **buses** at least daily to everywhere along the highway between here and Kunming.

Accommodation

Jingcheng Maohan Lu, south of and parallel to Nanmao Jie ☏0692/4159999. A four-star place with decent rooms, a swimming pool and gym. ❻

Limin Nanmao Jie, about 300m west of the bus station. Good-value rooms in a well-kept multi-storey block around a courtyard, though finding the staff can be difficult. Bicycles are available to rent. ❷

Mandalay Garden Jiegang Lu ☏0692/9283024. All the staff at this backpacker hangout are laid-back Burmese. It's run by Moe, who is a mine of information about the area. Accommodation is simple – a bed on a floor, in dorms or private rooms – and facilities are shared. There's a very pleasant garden, a DVD lounge, and a restaurant (overpriced). Dorms ¥15.

Nanyang Nanmao Jie, about 200m west of the bus station. Spacious, if a little mildewed, with comfy beds. Dorm beds ¥25, ❸

Ruili Corner of Jianshe Lu and Xinjian Lu ☏0692/4141463 or 4141269. It's set in pleasant grounds, with a palm garden, but the rooms, which share facilities, are overpriced. Scruffy dorm beds ¥25, ❹

Eating and drinking

The **stalls** around the market on Xinjian Lu serve fine grilled meats, hotpots, soups and buns, and you'll also come across some Burmese delicacies. Try *moongsee joh*, a sandwich made from purple glutinous rice pancakes heated over a grill until they puff up, and spread with sugar and peanut powder. Another similar confection involves bamboo tubes stuffed with pleasantly bland, sweetened rice jelly, while *niezi binfang* is a thoroughly Southeast Asian drink made with sago, coconut jelly, condensed milk, sugar, crushed ice and water – quite refreshing on a hot day.

Hotel restaurants have good Chinese fare, but since you're here, try the **Burmese cafés**, which you'll find both north of the roundabout on Jiegang Lu, and in the markets. They don't look up to much, but can produce a platter of a half-dozen small pots of tasty pickles and some basic meat and fish curries for about ¥8. But the most pleasant Burmese place is *Bobos*, on Xin'an Lu, just off Nanmao Jie (look for the sign in English, though not much English is spoken, and not much Chinese either), which sells great juices, including avocado, and snacks such as fried crabs and banana pie. In the far south of town, just beyond the *Mandalay Garden Hotel*, is a pretty decent Dai place – look for the bamboo facing, beyond a dog hotpot restaurant.

Around Ruili

Villages and Buddhist monuments dot the plains around Ruili, easy enough to explore either by renting a bicycle from the *Limin Binguan*, or by minibus from the Nanmao Jie depot – just keep repeating the name of your destination and you'll be shepherded to the right vehicle. Ruili Travel Service can also organize private transport for the day, but tends to be expensive. Most of the destinations below are only of mild interest in themselves, really just excuses to get out into Ruili's attractive countryside. For more about the Dai, see the Xishuangbanna section (p.861).

A few sights lie within walking distance. About 5km east along the Mangshi road is the two-hundred-year-old **Jiele Jin Ta**, a group of seventeen portly **Dai pagodas** painted gold and said to house several of Buddha's bones. Nearby are some open-air hot springs where you can wash away various ailments. Travelling the same distance south takes you past the less expansive **Jinya Ta** (Golden Duck Pagoda) to the busy **bridge over the Shweli River** into Burma, though apart from the volume of traffic, there's little to see.

Another 5km west along the road from Jinya Ta is a small bridge with the region's largest Buddhist temple, the nicely decorated **Hansha Si**, just off to the north. Ten kilometres beyond Hansha Si is the town of **JIEXIANG** and the splendid Tang-era **Leizhuang Xiang**, where the low square hall of a nunnery is dominated by a huge central pagoda and four corner towers, all in white. Another fine temple with typical Dai touches, such as "fiery" wooden eave decorations, **Denghannong Si**, is farther west again, and though the current halls were built only during the Qing dynasty, the site is said to mark where Buddha once stopped to preach.

Finally, those who find Ruili too tame can visit **Jiegao**, the border town a few kilometres further down the road. It's surrounded on all sides by Burma, the Burmese population outnumber the Chinese, and the main strip is almost entirely given over to gambling and prostitution. The town's sole redeeming features are its Burmese restaurants – holes in the wall lurk down most side roads and serve a mean curry. There's a big casino on the island just west of the town. Locals caution that anyone who wins big will end up in the river.

Southwestern Yunnan

The culture and history of southwestern Yunnan are products of adjoining countries. **Transport** into the region has always been a problem for any external power seeking control; even the rivers – historically so important for inter-provincial communications in central China – here run out of the country, and long-promised highways were only completed in the 1990s. Most visitors find their attention fully occupied by the ethnically and environmentally diverse corner of **Xishuangbanna**, barely an hour from Kunming on the flight to the regional capital, **Jinghong**. Coming by road is not such a bad option either, with sleeper buses making the 24-hour incarceration as comfortable as possible, but watch that your luggage doesn't disappear while you slumber – chain bags securely or rest your legs over them. There's also some interesting territory **along the Burmese border** between Yunnan's northwest and Xishuangbanna, though you'll need time and motivation to get the best from landscape and people along the way – and to be impervious to long, tortuous bus rides on extremely rough roads.

The southwest's emphatically tropical **weather** divides into just two main seasons: a drier stretch between November and May, when warm days, cool nights and dense morning mists are the norm, after which high heat and torrential daily rains settle in for the June–October **wet season**. Given the climate, you'll need to take more than usual care of any cuts and abrasions, and to guard against mosquitoes (see "Health" in Basics, p.40). The busiest time of the year here is mid-April, when thousands of tourists flood to Jinghong for the Dai **Water-splashing Festival**, and hotels and flights will be booked solid for a week beforehand. Once you're there, **getting around** Xishuangbanna is easy enough, with well-maintained roads connecting Jinghong to outlying districts. **Place names** can be confusing, though, as the words "Meng-", designating a small town, or "Man-", a village, prefix nearly every destination.

Along the Burmese border

There are a few things to bear in mind before tackling one of the 500-kilometre-long roads probing down **along the Burmese border** between Xiaguan, Baoshan or Ruili in northwestern Yunnan and Jinghong in Xishuangbanna. Whichever route you take, you're in for a tough two- to five-day trip. The roads are often so poor that it can be quicker to travel via Kunming – which is what the PSB will tell you to do if you ask. You'll end up dusty or muddy, and can expect to have your passports and bags searched at regular **army checkpoints** along the way. You'll also penetrate China's untouristed backwaters, zigzagging across cold, thinly inhabited mountain folds between the **Nu** and **Lancang** river systems. What makes it worthwhile is some spellbinding scenery, the chance to glimpse at least three regional ethnic groups, and simply the thrill of travelling through an area which has seen virtually no foreigners.

The most direct way through the region – though still a thirty-hour journey – is to catch a Jinghong-bound sleeper bus from either **Xiaguan** (see p.821) or **Baoshan** (see p.849). These routes converge around 120km into the trip at **Yunxian**, from where there's something approaching a main road all the way

Along the Burmese border

Cangyuan	沧原	cāngyuán
Gengma	耿马	gěngmǎ
Lancang	澜沧	láncāng
Shangye Binguan	商业宾馆	shāngyè bīnguǎn
Mengding	孟定	mèngdìng
Menglian	孟连	mènglián
Nansan	南伞	nánsǎn
Simao	思茅	sīmáo
Yunxian	云县	yúnxiàn

to Jinghong. Around a third of the way into the trip, **LANCANG** is a likely overnight stop, with alternative transport west to Gengma and beyond if you want to explore (see below). Otherwise it's another day to **SIMAO**, briefly a French concession and formerly the site of Xishuangbanna's airport, where the road joins the final 150km of the main Kunming–Jinghong highway.

From Ruili

Beginning at **Ruili** is a much tougher prospect, though there's far more in the way of interest on this route, and the landscape is a spread of intensely cultivated, vastly scaled peaks and deep river valleys, dotted with tiny villages. Start by catching a bus to Mangshi and on to **NANSAN**, basically just a truck stop twelve hours away, with a very basic hostel opposite the bus station (●). You're right on the Burmese border here, though there's a mountain in the way to stop you wandering. From Nansan, the road continues 90km southeast over a seemingly endless succession of serrated ranges to the far more animated market town of **MENGDING**, another possible stop with a range of accommodation options and a host of outlying thatched villages.

GENGMA is a further 30km along, a small, concrete and brick town in a broad valley. Minibuses from Nansan drop off at a depot on the northern edge; walk south down the 250-metre-long main street, past a **guesthouse** (❷) to a roundabout, where you'll find the **long-distance bus station** (with departures to Cangyuan, Lincang, Menghai, Menglian and Jinghong) and a **hotel** (❸) opposite. West off the main street, Gengma's large, every-fifth-day **market** is somewhere to be eyeballed by disbelieving villagers from the hills, and if you're travelling south the town is the first place you'll encounter **Dai** in any quantity – there's even a five-spired Dai pagoda on a hill southeast of the roundabout. A worthwhile detour from Gengma takes you 90km south towards the Burmese border at **CANGYUAN**, a trading centre supplying everything from motor-bikes to betel nut and mushrooms, and surrounded by attractive villages whose population are mostly **Wa**. Though Buddhism was introduced at some point from Burma, several remote **rock painting sites** associated with earlier religious rituals survive in the Awa Mountains northeast of the city. As recently as the 1960s the Wa were head-hunters, also known for their sacred drums, passion for smoking and festivals involving the frenzied dismemberment of live bulls – though such things are rare today.

Lancang

Back on the main Jinghong road, it's 180km to **LANCANG**, the compact capital of **Lahu Autonomous County**. The main reason to pause in the area is to spend a day or two looking at nearby villages, some of which are **Lahu**. Hunters of legendary skill – both men and women hunt – whose name loosely implies "Tiger-eaters", the Lahu probably originated in the Dali area, perhaps driven into this southern refuge by the Mongols. Lahu men shave their heads and wear turbans.

Lancang's main streets form an inverted "Y", the stem pointing north towards Gengma, the arms heading southeast to Jinghong and southwest to **Menglian**, and their junction is at the centre of town. There are scores of places to eat and stay around the centre, a good market at the north end, and separate **long-distance bus stations** on both arms. The best **place to stay** is on the southeastern arm, right behind the Jinghong road bus depot at the friendly *Shangye Binguan* (❷). **From Lancang**, it's just six hours to Jinghong on buses from either station, descending into Xishuangbanna through the westerly town of Menghai (see p.873).

Menglian

Alternatively, try spending a few days 40km southwest of Lancang at **MENG-LIAN**, a pleasant Dai and Lahu town reached on hourly minibuses from the Menglian road bus station. A drab, kilometre-long main street has everything of use, including the **bus station**; head west from here and it's a five-minute walk to a **bank**, and nearby the comfortable *Menglian Binguan* (☎0879/8723020; ❸), next to a **bridge**. Over the road, a simple **restaurant** faces the water, while around 500m south along the river there's another gold-painted Dai **pagoda**. Cross the bridge from the *Menglian Binguan* and bear right (uphill) into the **old town**, and you'll find plenty of winding streets and some fine traditional wooden buildings – including two **temples** and the **Xuanfu Shishu museum**. Menglian also has a busy **market** every fifth day patronized by **Hani** wearing porcupine quills and colourful beetles in their hair, and offers the chance to hitch tractor rides out to Wa settlements, such as **Fu'ai**, 28km northwest.

Xishuangbanna

A lush tropical spread of virgin rainforests, plantations and paddy fields nestled 750km southwest of Kunming along the Burmese and Laotian borders, **Xishuangbanna** has little in common with the rest of provincial China. Despite recent resettlement projects to affirm Han authority, thirteen of Yunnan's ethnic groups constitute a sizeable majority of Xishuangbanna's 500,000-strong population. Foremost are the **Dai**, northern cousins to the Thais, whose distinctive temples, bulbous pagodas and saffron-robed clergy are a common sight down on the plains, particularly around **Jinghong**, Xishuangbanna's sleepy capital. The region's remaining 19,000 square kilometres of hills, farms and forest are split between the administrative townships of **Mengla** in the east and **Menghai** in the west, peppered with villages of Hani, Bulang, Jinuo, Wa and Lahu; remoter tribes are still animistic, and all have distinctive dress and customs. Cultural tourism aside, there are a number of marginally developed **wildlife**

▲ Simao & Kunming

▶ Jianshui & Yuanyang

Lancang ◀

0   40 km

Lancang River

Sancha He
Wildlife
Reserve

Mannanan
Mengyang

Jinghong

Mengzhe   Jingzhen

Xiding   Menghai

Gasa

Jinuo Luoke

Luosuo River

LAOS

Menglun

Menghun

Gelanghe

Ganlanba

Manting

Nana River

Yaoqu

Nanla River

Bupan
Aerial
Walkway

Daluo

Bulangshan   Damenglong

Manguanghan

Mengla

N

BURMA
(MYANMAR)

Mekong River

LAOS

Shangyong

Mo
Han

XISHUANGBANNA

▼ Luang Namtha

reserves inhabited by elephants and other rare beasts, plenty of hiking trails, and China's **open border with Laos** to explore.

Flowing down from the northwest, the Lancang River neatly cuts Xishuang-banna into two regions on either side of Jinghong. To the **east**, there's a choice of roads through highland forests or more cultivated flatlands to the botanic gardens at **Menglun**, down beyond which lies **Mengla**, and the open **Laotian border**. Head **west** and your options are split between the **Damenglong** and **Menghai** regions – linked by a three-day hiking trail – with a more varied bag of ethnic groups and a crossing (firmly closed) into Burma. There are direct public buses and tours to most destinations from Jinghong, but in rural areas the mass of short-range minibuses is far more convenient, with tractors picking up where these won't go. Cycling around is another possibility in the lowlands, though Xishuangbanna's hill roads are steep, twisted and long.

With the exception of Mengla, most main centres can be visited on day-trips from Jinghong, but you won't see more than the superficial highlights unless you stop overnight. The towns are seldom attractive or interesting in them-selves and you'll need to get out to surrounding villages, small temples and the countryside to experience Xishuangbanna's better side. Be prepared for basic accommodation and generally bland, if plentiful, food. Many people are friendly and some villagers may offer meals and a bed for the night in return for a small consideration – or yank you enthusiastically into the middle of a festival, if you're lucky enough to stumble across one – but elsewhere locals are wary of strangers, so don't force your presence while looking around. There have also been a couple of **muggings** in recent years along remoter stretches of the Burmese border – walking alone is ill-advised.

When visiting Dai temples, it's important to **remove your shoes**, as the Dai consider feet to be the most unclean part of the body.

Some history

Historically, there was already a Dai state in Xishuangbanna two thousand years ago, important enough to send ambassadors to the Han court in 69 AD; it was subsequently incorporated into the Nanzhao and Dali kingdoms. A brief period of full independence ended with the Mongols' thirteenth-century conquest of Yunnan. For ease of administration, the Mongols governed Xishuangbanna through Dai chieftains whom they raised in status to **pianling**, hereditary rulers, and the region was later divided into **twelve rice-growing districts** or *sipsawng pa na*, rendered as "Xishuangbanna" in Chinese. The *pianling* wielded enormous power over their fiefdoms, suppressing other minorities and treating people, land and resources as their personal property. This virtual slave system survived well into the twentieth century, when Xishuangbanna came under the thumb of the tyrannical Han warlord, **Ke Shexun**.

Not surprisingly, the **Communists** found Xishuangbanna's populace extremely sceptical of their attempts at reconciliation after taking control of the region in 1950, an attitude eventually softened by the altruistic persistence of medical and educational teams sent by Beijing. But trust evaporated in the violence of the **Cultural Revolution**, and the current atmosphere of apparent cultural freedom is undercut by resentment at what verges on colonial assimilation. More contentious aspects of religion have been banned, and forests are logged to the detriment of semi-nomadic hunter groups, who then have to settle down and plant rice. Many minority people feel that the government would really like them to behave like Han Chinese, except in regard of dress – since the colourful traditional clothing attracts the tourists. It's certainly true that Xishuangbanna is a rather anaemic version of what lies across the border in Laos, though in fairness, Chinese administrators are the first to admit the "terrible mistakes" of the past, and feel that they are now developing the area as sensitively as possible.

Jinghong

It was under the Dai warlord **Bazhen** that **JINGHONG**, Xishuangbanna's small and easy-going "Dawn Capital" (as it's called in Dai), first became a seat of power. Bazhen drove the Bulang and Hani tribes off these fertile central flatlands and founded the independent kingdom of Cheli in 1180, ever since when Jinghong has been maintained as an administrative centre. There was a moment of excitement in the late nineteenth century when a battalion of British soldiers marched in during a foray from Burma, but they soon decided that Jinghong was too remote to be worth defending.

Today the grey edifices of Jinghong's contemporary Han architecture make a suitably colonial backdrop for Dai women in bright sarongs and straw hats meandering along the gently simmering, palm-lined streets, and for the most part the city is an undemanding place to spend a couple of days investigating Dai culture. Aside from energetic excesses during the water-splashing festivities, you'll find the pace of life is set by the tropical heat – though the centre is often full of people, nobody bothers rushing anywhere. Once you've tried the local food and poked around the temples and villages which encroach on the suburbs, there's plenty of transport into the rest of the region. **Menghan**, only 45 minutes away on the bus, is a tempting first target; indeed, as a place to soak up atmosphere for a few days, it's preferable to Jinghong in some respects (see p.870).

Xishuangbanna (Jinghong)

Xishuangbanna	西双版纳	xīshuāngbǎnnà
Jinghong	景洪	jǐnghóng
Chunhuan Park	春欢公园	chūnhuān gōngyuán
Dance Exhibition Hall	勐巴拉娜西	mèngbālā nàxī
Manting	曼听	màntīng
Medicinal Botanic Gardens	药用植物园	yàoyòng zhíwùyuán
Tropical Flowers and Plants Garden	热带花卉园	rèdài huāhuìyuán
Wat Manting	曼听佛寺	màntīng fósì
Accommodation and eating		
Burmese Café	缅甸咖啡馆	miǎndiàn kāfēiguǎn
Crown Hotel	皇冠大酒店	huángguān dàjiǔdiàn
Dai Building Inn	傣家花苑小楼	dǎijiā huāyuàn xiǎolóu
Forest Café	森林咖啡厅	sēnlín kāfēitīng
Mei Mei's	美美咖啡厅	měiměi kāfēitīng
Mengyuan	勐园宾馆	měngyuán bīnguǎn
Namaya Guesthouse	纳木呀招待所	nàmùya zhāodàisuǒ
Thai Restaurant	泰国风味	tàiguó fēngwèi
Wanli Restaurant	婉丽傣味楼	wǎnlì dǎiwèizú
Xinmin International	新门(闵)国际大酒店	xīnmén (mǐn) guójì dàjiǔdiàn
Xishuangbanna Binguan	西双版纳宾馆	xīshuāngbǎnnà bīnguǎn

Arrival and city transport

Jinghong sits on the southwestern bank of the **Lancang River**, which later winds downstream through Laos and Thailand as the Mekong. The city centre is marked by a sculpture of four elephants set where **Jinghong Lu**'s four arms radiate north, south, east and west. A kilometre up along Jinghong Bei Lu is the **Lancang Bridge** and the top of **Galan Lu**, which runs parallel with Jinghong Bei Lu and the river; there's also a **suspension bridge** over the river off the eastern end of Jinghong Dong Lu.

The **airport** lies about 10km southwest of the city, a ten-minute, ¥15–20 taxi ride into the centre along a new expressway, or ¥4 on the bus. There are two **long-distance bus stations**: the main one is Jinghong Banna bus station on Minzu Lu, handling services from all over Xishuangbanna and beyond, including Xiaguan, Kunming and even the Vietnamese border at Hekou (see p.819); the other depot, 500m north on Jinghong Bei Lu, concentrates on minibuses from Menghan and other places around Xishuangbanna. Central Jinghong is too small for a public bus service – nothing is more than a twenty-minute walk away – but there are plenty of taxis, which have a ¥5 basic charge. Watch out for pickpockets at the post office and bus stations.

Accommodation

All but the smallest lodgings have restaurants and tour agencies.

Bai Guesthouse Manting Lu. Very basic rooms but some of the cheapest dorm beds in the city at ¥15. ①

Crown Hotel Jinghong Nan Lu ☎0691/2129888, ℻2127270. One of a number of upmarket places in the area, all aimed at the wealthy Chinese tourist. The swimming pool (¥5) is open to non-residents. ④

Dai Building Inn Manting Lu. Run by a resident Dai family, this offers simple comforts in very popular, spotless bamboo stilt houses with separate toilets and solar heated showers. Dorm beds ¥25, ①

Mengyuan Minhang Lu ☎0691/2123028. Centrally located, tidy Chinese hotel, though nothing stylish, and the cheaper rooms are minimally maintained. Try to get a room on the recently renovated third floor. A range of rooms, from those with shared bath to larger en-suite ones with a/c. ②

Namaya Guesthouse Hualin Lu. A friendly little Korean-owned place, with a Korean restaurant attached. The dorms are the same bargain price as elsewhere around Manting Lu, but with new showers and bathrooms, and touches like pot plants in

the rooms, this place is the best of the cheapies. Head east past the Wat Chienglarn, and it's on the left. Dorms ¥15.

Wanli restaurant Manting Lu. This popular backpacker eating place has a few new, rather bare rooms, with either two or three beds, at the back. Facilities are communal and reasonably maintained. Dorms ¥15, ①

Xinmin International Jingde Dong Lu ☎0691/2126888, ⓕ2132880. Luxury option with gym, sauna, restaurants and business centre, but rather removed from any local flavour. ⑧

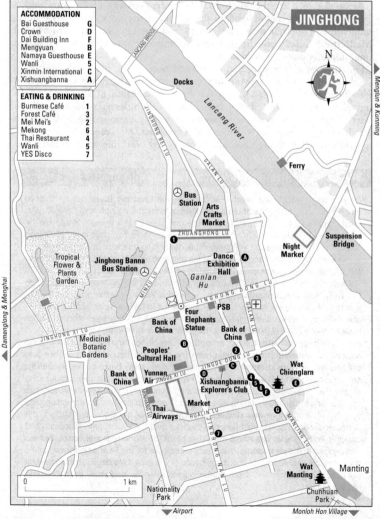

ACCOMMODATION
Bai Guesthouse	G
Crown	D
Dai Building Inn	F
Mengyuan	B
Namaya Guesthouse	E
Wanli	5
Xinmin International	C
Xishuangbanna	A

EATING & DRINKING
Burmese Café	1
Forest Café	3
Mei Mei's	2
Mekong	6
Thai Restaurant	4
Wanli	5
YES Disco	7

JINGHONG

Menglun & Kunming ►

◄ Damenglong & Menghai

Lancang River

Docks

Ferry

Suspension Bridge

Night Market

Bus Station

Arts Crafts Market

ZHUANGHONG LU

Jinghong Banna Bus Station

Tropical Flower & Plants Garden

Dance Exhibition Hall

Ganlan Hu

JINGHONG DONG LU

Four Elephants Statue

PSB

Bank of China

Medicinal Botanic Gardens

JINGHONG XI LU

Peoples' Cultural Hall

Bank of China

Bank of China

Yunnan Air

Xishuangbanna Explorer's Club

JINGDE XI LU

JINGDE DONG LU

Wat Chienglarn

Thai Airways

Market

HUALIN LU

Wat Manting

Manting

Nationality Park

Chunhuan Park

▼ Airport

Monloh Hon Village ▼

0   1 km

Xishuangbanna Binguan (also known as the *Banna Binguan*) Galan Lu ☏0691/2123679, ☎2126501. Large grounds with comfortable doubles and triples and a faded air, which lingers despite a recent renovation. ❸

The City

Right in Jinghong's centre, **Ganlan Hu** is an unexceptional flagstoned park and pond used for early-morning exercises. Much more interesting is the **Tropical Flower and Plants Garden**, 1500m west down Jinghong Xi Lu (daily 8am–6pm; ¥30), where there are palms, fruit trees and brightly flowering shrubs and vines, nicely arranged around a lake. The gardens – aerial flower subgarden, bougainvillea subgarden, and so on – are well worth a visit, and in the early afternoon local dancing is put on for the tour groups. Shops outside the entrance sell local herbal remedies such as **dragon's blood** (see p.870).

Across the road are the **Medicinal Botanic Gardens** (daily 8am–5pm), a quiet grove of gingers and small shrubs growing in the gloom of closely planted, unidentified rainforest trees. The gardens lead through to a large **Traditional Medicine Clinic**, whose friendly staff might invite you in for a cup of tea and impromptu *qi gong* demonstration.

For some more greenery and an introduction to Dai life, head about 1km southeast of the centre to **Manting**, once a separate village but now absorbed into Jinghong's lazy spread. On the way here down Manting Lu is a brisk morning market, outside the temple school of **Wat Chienglarn**. Traditionally, all Dai boys spend three years at such institutions getting a grounding in Buddhism and learning to read and write – skills denied to Dai women. Manting itself is mostly modern, though Neolithic pottery has been dug up here and a few

---

The Lancang River and New Year festivities

Despite its potential as a great river highway, the **Lancang River** has never seen much traffic, and today the docks in the north of town at the junction of Galan Lu and Jinghong Bei Lu are usually moribund. The only vessels you're likely to see are the tour boats to Thailand which leave twice a week and take two days to reach Chiang Saen. Tickets cost between ¥400 and ¥600, depending on the boat. The easiest way to get a ticket is to get a tourist agency, such as one at the *Forest Café*, to sort it out for you; otherwise queue up at the booking office at the ferry port.

Where the river does come into its own, however, is during the highlights of the **Dai New Year celebrations**, of which the famous **Water-splashing Festival** is just a part. The dates were once set by the unpredictable Dai calendar, but are now reliably fixed by the Han authorities for **April 13–16**. The first day sees a **dragon-boat race** on the river, held in honour of a good-natured dragon spirit who helped a local hero outwit an evil king. On the second day everybody in Jinghong gets a good soaking as water-splashing hysteria grips the town, and basinfuls are enthusiastically hurled over friends and strangers alike to wash away bad luck and, hopefully, encourage a good wet season. Manting Park also hosts cockfighting and dancing all day. The finale includes **Diu Bao** (Throwing Pouches) games, where prospective couples fling small, triangular beanbags at each other to indicate their affection, and there's a mammoth **firework display**, when hundreds of bamboo tubes stuffed with gunpowder and good-luck gifts are rocketed out over the river. Nightly carousing and dancing – during which generous quantities of *lajiu*, the local firewater, are consumed – take place in the parks and public spaces. Look out for the **Peacock dance**, a fluid performance said to imitate the movements of the bird, bringer of good fortune in Dai lore, and the **Elephant-drum dance**, named after the instrument used to thump out the rhythm.

older, two-storey wooden Dai houses still lurk in the wings (you'll see entire villages of these elsewhere in the region). Near the end of the road is **Wat Manting** (¥1), Jinghong's main **Buddhist monastery** and the largest in all Xishuangbanna, a simply furnished affair currently being renovated – check out the glossy **jinghua murals**, an art form derived from India, and the roof rafters, full of ceremonial bits and pieces. Dai temples differ from others across the land both in their general shape and the almost exclusive use of wood in their construction, which necessitates their being raised off the ground on low piles to guard against termites and rot. Furthermore, unlike Buddhists elsewhere in China, whose Mahayana (Greater Vehicle) teachings filtered through from India, the Dai follow the **Theravada** (Hinayana, or Lesser Vehicle) school of thought, a sect common to Sri Lanka, Thailand, Laos and Burma.

Next to Wat Manting is the rather more secular **Chunhuan Park** (also known as Manting Park; daily 8am–7.30pm, ¥10; 7.30–11.30pm, ¥2), where the royal slaves were formerly kept. Official tour groups are shown water-splashing highlights every afternoon and there's also a large pen bursting with one hundred **peacocks**, which you can feed. Corners of the park are very pleasant, with paths crossing over one of the Lancang River's tiny tributaries to full-scale copies of Jingzhen's Bajiao Ting (see p.874) and a portly, Dai-style pagoda. Continuing past the park, the road ends at **Manloh Hon village**, which gets its water through the efforts of a large bamboo waterwheel, beyond which is a ferry across the Lancang to paddy fields, more villages and banana groves.

Eating, drinking and entertainment

Jinghong is the best place in Xishuangbanna to try **authentic Dai cooking**, either in restaurants or on the street. **Sticky rice** in various guises is the staple. One type is wrapped in banana leaves, rammed into a bamboo tube and grilled; a prized purple strain is used as the basis of pancakes, stuffed with sugar and chopped nuts. Formal menus often feature meat or fish courses flavoured with sour bamboo shoots or lemon grass, while oddities include **fried moss**, and **pineapple rice** for dessert – the fruit is hollowed out, stuffed with pineapple chunks and sweet glutinous rice, and steamed. Year-round fresh **tropical fruit** is also sold around town – try jackfruit, physically weighty and heavily scented. Sit-down stalls sell bland curries, claypot casseroles, hotpots and huge bowls of noodle soup. The **night market** on Jinghong Nan Lu gets going around 7pm, with the general public roller-skating, playing pool and stuffing their faces at a host of small, low-cost canteens specializing in stewed and simmered dishes. There's a bigger, perpetually full affair just around the corner in Jingde Lu. But the best night market in southern Yunnan is just off Jinghong Dong Lu, under the suspension bridge. It's a great place to try local staples and exotica such as bees and frogs, with nothing costing more than ¥10. Finally, for something different, try the *Burmese Café* at the western end of Zhuanghong Lu, which serves meat and fish curries to the local gem traders.

Unsurprisingly, **tourist cafés** are comparatively expensive, but are good places to pick up local information, rent bikes and arrange tours. Pick of these are *Mei Mei's* on Jingde Dong Lu, and the *Forest Café* over the road, both of which also double as tour agencies. Sarah at the *Forest Café*, in particular, is a mine of information about local treks and a good guide. On Manting Lu, the *Wanli* and the *Mekong*, just north of the *Dai Building Inn* on Manting Lu, are popular places with a standard local menu. The *Thai Restaurant* at 193 Manting Lu is a good inexpensive canteen with an English menu and Chinese and Thai staples.

Entertainment is unpredictable, though there's always something – anything, in fact, from traditional music to huge synchronized dance groups with fans

– going on in the paved square outside the **People's Cultural Hall** between Jinghong Nan Lu and Minhang Lu. Occasionally, tour groups trigger performances of local dances in the hall itself, and elsewhere people just seem to assemble spontaneously in the streets after dark and go through routines. For a kitsch extravaganza of dance routines with a connection to minority culture that's at best tenuous, visit the **Dance Exhibition Hall** on Ganlan Lu (☏0691/2120816). Their nightly performances begin at 8.30pm and go on for two hours (¥120). For more raucous minority dancing, visit the *YES Disco* on Jinghong Nan Lu (open until 3am), which is packed every night with hard-drinking Dai kids. It's free to get in, and a beer costs ¥15.

Listings

Airlines Yunnan Air is on the corner of Jingde Xi Lu and Minhang Lu (☏0691/2124774; daily 8am–8pm), selling tickets for their flights to Kunming and Lijiang. Thai Airways, just around the corner on Minhang Lu (☏0691/2121881; Mon–Fri 9am–6pm), has flights to Chiang Mai and Bangkok.

Banks and exchange Three branches of the Bank of China, on Jinghong Nan Lu, Jingde Xi Lu and Galan Lu, are open for foreign exchange (Mon–Fri 8am–6pm, Sat 8–11.30am & 3–6pm), and all have ATMs. The *Xishuangbanna Binguan* and other larger hotels will cash traveller's cheques outside these hours.

Bike rental *Mei Mei's* and the *Forest Café* have a cluster of city and mountain bikes for rent at ¥20–30 per day, plus whatever they decide is a reasonable deposit.

Hospital The Provincial Hospital is at the lower end of Galan Lu, and there's a clinic and pharmacy attached to the *Xishuangbanna Binguan*.

Internet access There are plenty of Internet cafés along Manting Lu.

Laundry Foreigner cafés offer the least expensive laundry services in town.

Mail and telephones The GPO, with poste restante and international telephones, is on the corner of Jinghong Bei Lu and Jinghong Xi Lu (daily 8am–8.30pm).

Massage White-robed practitioners set up along central Galan Lu in the evening, and there are afternoon foot massage sessions around Ganlan Hu.

PSB At Jinghong Dong Lu, across from Ganlan Hu Park (☏0691/2130366; Mon–Fri 7–11.30am & 3–5.30pm) – look for the English sign.

Shopping For everyday needs, there are plenty of well-stocked department stores around the centre. Zhuanghong Lu, a narrow street between Galan Lu and Jinghong Bei Lu, has a very regulated arts and crafts market run for the most part by Burmese selling gems, jade, colourful curios, elephant carvings and Thai and Burmese food. The most interesting shop, at the eastern end of the street, sells Akha clothing and is run by a personable Akha guy eager to practise his English. The City Produce Market is at the western end of Jingde Lu, near the Yunnan Air office, where there's a massive range of food and clothing, while stores along Manting Lu offer souvenir-quality Dai trinkets and jewellery.

Tour agents Hotel travel services in Jinghong offer much the same range of day-trips to Daluo on the Burmese border, the Botanic Gardens at Menglun, Mandian Waterfall, the Menglong region, the Sunday market at Menghun, and (very rarely) Sancha He Wildlife Reserve. These trips are priced in the ¥100–200 range. Backpackers are better off looking at the choice of guided tours offered by *Mei Mei's* and the *Forest Café*, including boat trips to Menghan and Thailand. For something different, visit the Xishuangbanna Explorers Club on Jingde Dong Lu (☏0691/2120125), which offers a wide range of mountain-bike tours.

The northern route to Menglun

The road to Menglun, 80km east of Jinghong, divides shortly after crossing the Lancang Bridge on the outskirts of town. The **northern route** initially follows the road to Kunming, winding up through forested hills for 35km before levelling out at **MENGYANG**, a market and transport stop surrounded by a host of **Huayao** villages. The Huayao (Flower Belt) form one of three Dai subgroups, though they differ greatly from the lowland "Water Dai", who scorn them for their over-elaborate costumes and the fact that they are not Buddhists. Though you'll see plenty at Mengyang – the women wear turbans draped with thin

Eastern Xishuangbanna

Jinuo Luoke	基诺	*jīnuò*
Mannanan	曼那因	*mànnànān*
Sancha He Wildlife Reserve	三岔河自然保护区听	*sānchàhé zìrán beohùqk*
Manting	曼听	*màntīng*
Dadu Pagoda	大独塔	*dàdútǎ*
Manting Buddhist Temple	曼听佛寺	*màntīng fósì*
Menghan	勐罕	*mènghǎn*
Ganlanba Hotel	橄榄坝宾馆	*gǎnlǎnbà bīnguǎn*
Mengla	勐腊	*mènglà*
Bronze Spire Pagoda	青铜尖顶塔	*qīngtóng jiāndǐng tǎ*
Menglun	勐仑	*mènglún*
Tropical Botanic Garden	热带植物园	*rèdài zhíwùyuán*
Mengyang	勐养	*mèngyǎng*
Mo Han	边贸站	*biānmào zhàn*
Shangyong	尚勇	*shàngyǒng*
Yaoqu	瑶区	*yáoqū*
Bupan Aerial Walkway	补蚌望天树空中索道	*bǔbàng wàngtiānshù kōngzhōngsuǒdào*

silver chains – the village considered most typical is about 10km farther north along the main road at **MANNANAN**.

On a completely different tack, a farther 18km beyond Mannanan (still on the Kunming road) is the **Sancha He Wildlife Reserve** (¥15), a dense chunk of rainforest based around the Sancha Stream. Transport heading north from Mengyang to Dadugang, Puwen or Kunming can drop you at the large stone sign which marks the reserve entrance. There's a resident family of **wild elephants** at Sancha He, frequently seen at dawn from creaky wooden riverside hides, and the jungle gets interesting the farther in you go along the overgrown, partially paved trails – you're sure to encounter elephantine footprints, along with brightly coloured birds, butterflies and snakes. Give the **elephant displays** here a wide berth, however, unless you enjoy watching captive animals perform circus tricks while being jabbed with a spear. **Minibuses** heading in both directions along the Kunming road pass the reserve entrance until well into the afternoon; miss them and you'll have to stay near the reserve entrance at a mildewed **hotel** (④).

The latter 45km of the northern route to Menglun misses all this, however, diverging east off the Kunming road between Mengyang and Mannanan. Twenty kilometres along is **JINUO LUOKE** (Jinuo Shan), home to the independently minded **Jinuo**, who received official recognition of their ethnicity as recently as 1979. An enigmatic group who some say are descended from the remnants of Zhuge Liang's third-century expedition to Yunnan, the Jinuo once lived by hunting and slash-and-burn farming, but now grow tea as a cash crop. Numbering around twenty thousand today, they never got on well with external rulers, describing their highland homeland as *youle* ("hidden from the

Han"), and were almost annihilated by Ke Shexun and the Dai ruling caste after they poisoned a government tax collector in 1942. Jinuo women wear a distinctive white-peaked hood, and both sexes pierce their ears and formerly practised tattooing. Jinuo Luoke is not the most welcoming of places, but there's a **guesthouse** which might let you stay (❶), and a fair amount of through traffic for the final 25-kilometre run to Menglun.

The southern route to Menglun

Because of the time it takes to climb the range to Mengyang, most buses between Jinghong and Menglun follow the **southern road**. This begins across the Lancang Bridge and follows the Lancang River Valley downstream for 30km, between endless neat rows of rubber trees, to **MENGHAN** (also known as **Ganlanba**), the main settlement of the famously fertile "Olive-shaped Flatland", as "Ganlanba" translates. This is one of Xishuangbanna's three major agricultural areas, won by force of arms over the centuries and now vitally important to the Dai (the other two are west at Damenglong and Menghai). You'll see plenty of farming hamlets in the vicinity sporting **traditional wooden houses** completely covered by huge roofs, raised on stilts off the moist earth. However, under "modernization" orders from the regional government, this style is being replaced by absurdly humid brick structures. Menghan itself is pleasantly surrounded by paddy fields and low hills bordering the flatland, and is a great place to stop over and sample regional life for a few days. In the northwest of town, the Dai Minority Park (daily; ¥50), a large and landscaped strip of land incorporating several villages, offers a sanitized version of minority life – and daily water-splashing festivals – to visiting tour groups. Many of the houses here rent out rooms, for around ¥20 a bed – and you should only have to pay the entrance fee once. Otherwise, the most popular **place to stay** is the *Sarlar Restaurant* (☏0691/2410319), 200m on from the bus stop, where you get a mat on the floor in a room off the dining area for ¥10; check their visitors' book for tips. The most upmarket place in town is the *Ganlanba Hotel*, 200m east of the park, but it's expensive for a standard hotel (☏0691/2411233; ❶). You can rent bikes from a shop opposite. There are also plenty of day walks and cycle rides. One popular ride is to take a bike across the Mekong on the local ferry, and then head left for Dai villages.

A couple of kilometres east, at **MANTING**, there's the excellent **Manting Buddhist Temple** and **Dadu Pagoda**, both fine reconstructions of twelfth-century buildings destroyed during the 1960s. Paths lead further east from Manting along and across the river to more pagodas and villages, somewhere to spend a couple of days of easy exploration.

Menglun

Routes from Jinghong meet at **MENGLUN**, a dusty couple of streets overlooking the broad flow of the **Luosuo River**. There's no bus station, so vehicles pull up wherever convenient on the main road, usually among the restaurants and stores on the eastern side of town. Take the side street downhill through the all-day market, and within a couple of minutes you'll find yourself by a large pedestrian **suspension bridge** over the river. Here you pay ¥35 to cross into Menglun's superb **Tropical Botanic Gardens**, founded in 1959 by the botanist **Cai Xitao** who, having carved the gardens out of the jungle, started investigating the lives and medicinal qualities of Xishuangbanna's many little-known plant species. One of his pet projects involved the effects of resin from the **dragon's blood tree**, used as a wound-healing agent in Chinese medicine. The tree itself, which looks like a thin-stemmed yucca with spiky leaves, was believed extinct in China since the Tang dynasty, but Cai located a wild population in Xishuang-banna in 1972 and transplanted some to the gardens. You could spend a good half-day here, as there's masses to see, from dragon's blood trees and rainforest species to a 1000-year-old cycad and groves of palms, bamboos, vines and shrubs. You might also encounter Chinese visitors serenading the undistinguished-look-ing "Singing Plant", which is supposed to nod in time to music.

There's a **guesthouse** inside the gardens (❹) at the side of the pool, which offers the chance of seeing the place at its most charismatic, early in the morning and in the evening. There are plenty of cheap and unremarkable alternatives in town. To catch onward transport you'll need to tramp back onto the main road or out to the rear of the gardens, near the accommodation, where there's an exit on to the Mengla road, where you can flag down buses heading southeast.

Mengla

Having been a patchy affair so far, the jungle really sets in for the hundred-kilo-metre, four-hour trip from Menglun to Mengla. The first part is slow going uphill, then the bus suddenly turns along a ridge giving early-morning passengers a clear view (best in winter) back down on to a "cloud sea" over the treetops below. Farther on are rock outcrops and small roadside settlements carved out of the forest, and though the trees begin to give way to rubber plantations and cultivated land once you're over the mountains, it's all pretty impressive. This is the largest of Xishuangbanna's five wildlife reserves, comprised of relatively untouched tracts which the government has set aside to be protected from development, and full of the plants you'll have seen at the Botanic Gardens up the road.

Doubtless anything would be a disappointment after this, but **MENGLA** seems a deliberately ugly town, quiet and grey. The main point of interest here lies 2km south near the river at the **Bronze Spire Pagoda**, originally founded in antiq-uity by two Burmese monks as a shrine for Buddha relics. With a spire donated by heaven, according to local belief, the pagoda brought lasting peace to the land, though it eventually fell into disrepair and had to be rebuilt in 1759, when Jinghong's Dai ruler contributed thirty thousand silver pieces to cover the pagoda and temple columns in bronze. What happened next is a bit of a mystery, as Mengla was closed to foreign eyes for almost thirty years after the Cultural Revolution, but it's nowhere near this grand today. There are plenty of monks floating around Mengla itself, however, and a smaller temple pagoda on the hill to the west.

Mengla's northern end has a proper **bus station**, with vehicles heading to Menglun throughout the day, and there are also buses to Jinghong. From here Mengla's main street – with the last **bank** before Laos – runs south for 1500m to the far end of town and a **depot** for southbound vehicles. Take your pick of the dozen or so main-street noodle shops, **restaurants** and **hotels** (❷ or ❸). **Plain-clothes police** are everywhere – even among the Uigur running the kebab stalls – as this is the last major town before the Laotian border, 60km southeast.

Around Mengla: to Yaoqu and Laos

An afternoon bus runs from Mengla to the small town of **Yaoqu** (returning the following morning), 40km north along the beautiful farmland and forest scenery flanking the **Nanla He**. Not far off the road, just over halfway, is the **Bupan aerial walkway**, a very insecure-looking metal "sky bridge" running across the forest canopy. **YAOQU** itself is a roadhead for remote highland villages, with two **hostels** (❶) and all sorts of people turning up to trade, including Yao, dressed in dark blue jackets and turbans, and possibly Kumu, one of Xishuang-banna's officially unrecognized nationalities.

Heading down from Mengla's south bus station **towards Laos**, it takes about ninety minutes to reach **SHANGYONG**, the last village before the border. Shangyong is a centre for Xishuangbanna's isolated **Miao** population, more closely allied here with their Hmong relatives in Laos than with other Miao groups in China. The Hmong made the mistake of supporting US forces during the Vietnam War and were savagely repressed in its aftermath, many fleeing into China from their native regions in northern Vietnam and, after the Vietnamese army swarmed into China in 1975, to Laos.

Not much farther, **MO HAN** township (also known as **Bian Mao Zhan**, literally "Frontier Trade Station") is just 6km from the **border crossing**. There's basic **accommodation** at Mo Han, and transport to the relaxed customs post (closes mid-afternoon) where, assuming you already have a visa, the crossing should be free and uncomplicated.

Damenglong and the trail to Bulangshan

Several buses a day make the seventy-kilometre run from Jinghong's Minzu Lu depot south to **DAMENGLONG** (or **Menglong** as it's often marked on maps), one of the many western Xishuangbanna towns worth visiting for its **Sunday market**. It's also an area rich in Buddhism, and just about every village along the way has its own temple and pagoda. One worth closer inspection is **Manguanglong Si** near **Gasa** (15km from Jinghong), a monastery with a wonderful dragon stairway. The most impressive and famous structure in the region is **Manfeilong Sun Ta** (Bamboo Shoot Pagoda), on a hill thirty minutes' walk north of Damenglong. First built in the thirteenth century and now brightly adorned with fragments of evil-repelling mirrors and silver paint, it's a regular place of pilgrimage for Burmese monks, who come to meditate and to worship two footprints left by Sakyamuni in an alcove at the base. The pagoda's unusual name derives from the nine-spired design, which vaguely resembles an emerging cluster of bamboo tips. On a separate rise closer to town, Damenglong's other renowned Buddhist monument is the disappointingly shoddy **Hei Ta** (Black Pagoda), though it looks good from a distance.

While there are plenty of cheap places to eat in Damenglong, high-volume karaoke at the new **bus-station guesthouse** (❶) doesn't always make for a relaxing stay. Instead, head to the main crossroads, turn right, and there's an unmarked hotel 20m up here on the right, where rooms even have a VCD player.

The Bulangshan trail

Most visitors are here for the attractive three-day **hiking trail** which, for 40km, follows the Nana He and its tributaries to **Bulangshan** township, through a region of forests and farmland – there are villagers here who have never been

Western Xishuangbanna

Bulangshan	布朗山	*bùláng shān*
Damenglong	大勐龙	*dàmènglóng*
Manfeilong Sun Ta	曼飞龙笋塔	*mànfēilóng sǔntǎ*
Manguanglong Si	曼光龙寺	*mànguānglóng sì*
Hei Ta	黑塔	*hēitǎ*
Gelanghe	格朗和	*géláng hé*
Jingzhen	景真	*jǐngzhēn*
Baijiao Ting	八角亭	*bājiǎo tíng*
Menghai	勐海	*mènghǎi*
Menghun	勐混	*mènghún*
Mengzhe	勐遮	*mèngzhē*
Manlei Fo Si	曼佛寺	*mànfó sì*
Xiding	西定	*xīdìng*

to Jinghong. However, the route, once all tribal paths, is being earnestly tarmacked, so get here sooner rather than later. Food and camping gear will come in handy, though it is possible to negotiate meals and accommodation in the villages – offer a useful gift or ¥10–15 in these circumstances.

Start by taking any available transport 15km south from Damenglong to **Manguanghan**. Carry on along the road for about 1km, then look for a tractor track to the right leading shortly to **Guanmin**, a riverside Hani settlement. Another 5km takes you past a **thermal spring** to the Bulang village of **Manpo**, beyond which the track becomes a walking path only. In the next 20km you'll pass **Nuna** village before crossing the river and proceeding to **Song'er** (both of which are inhabited by Lahu), then cross back over and re-enter Hani territory at Bangnawan and **Weidong**, the latter one of the nicest villages on the trip. Here the track turns into a new road for the final 10km to the trailhead at **BULANGSHAN**, mountainous headquarters of the dark-clad **Bulang** nationality. There's formal accommodation at Bulangshan (❶), and at least one bus a day 50km north to **Menghun**, on the Menghai–Daluo road.

Menghai and the Hani

MENGHAI is western Xishuangbanna's principal town, centrally placed on the highland plains 55km from Jinghong. The usual grubby assemblage of kilometre-long high street and back lanes, Menghai was once a **Hani** (Aini) settlement until, as elsewhere, they were defeated in battle by the Dai and withdrew into the surrounding hills. They remain there today as Xishuangbanna's second-largest ethnic group and long-time cultivators of Xishuangbanna's **pu'er tea**, the red, slightly musty brew esteemed from Hong Kong to Tibet for its fat-reducing and generally invigorating properties. There's a nice village temple about 2km east off the Jinghong road, and a tea-processing factory in Menghai (Jinghong's CITS can arrange a tour), but otherwise the town is little more than a stop on the way towards outlying Dai and Hani settlements.

The **bus station** is at the eastern end of town along with a **mosque** and Muslim canteens, while the **bank**, **post office** and attached **hotel** (❹), and the basic *Banna Hotel* (❷), are grouped around the central crossroads. The **minibus depot** for western destinations is on the far outskirts.

Beyond Menghai to the Burmese border

The main routes beyond Menghai head southwest down to **Daluo and the Burmese border**, or northwest out of Xishuangbanna towards the Lancang region (see p.861). The most celebrated Buddhist sights around Menghai are within an hour's drive along this latter road, including **Baijiao Ting** (Octagonal Pavilion), 20km away at **JINGZHEN**, and **Manlei Buddhist Temple**, 5km farther on at **MENGZHE**. Both are inferior copies of older buildings, but have important collections of Buddhist manuscripts written on fan-palm fibre. The hilltop Baijiao Ting is a bizarre structure built in the eighteenth century to quell an angry horde of wasps. There's plenty of **minibus** transport to Mengzhe throughout the day, plus a small **guesthouse** (❶) near the marketplace if you want to stay; even better would be to overnight at similar lodgings 10km south-west at **XIDING**, whose busy Thursday **market** is less touristed than some in the region.

One of the best places to come to grips with the Hani is at **GELANGHE** township, 30km southeast of Menghai, where there's hostel accommodation (❶). In fact, many of the people here are Dai and **Akha**, a long-haired Hani subgroup spread as far afield as Menglian and Simao. In common with other Hani, unmarried women have elaborate head ornaments while wives wear cloth caps decorated with silver beads and coins. An excellent walk leads up into the hills above Gelanghe past a lake and plenty of traditional wooden Akha villages, but people are very shy.

Somewhere to meet locals on more even terms is 25km out along the Daluo road at tiny **MENGHUN**, whose **Sunday market**, starting at daybreak and continuing until noon, does a good job of lowering ethnic barriers. It's best to stay in Menghun the night before, as this way you'll already have seen plenty before the tour buses from Jinghong descend around 9am. You'll have to decide which of Menghun's two shabby **guesthouses** (❶) deserves your custom – one is on the main street (look for the English sign), the other 75m on the left down the road leading south into the fields. However, the market is worth a night's discomfort to see Hani women under their silver-beaded headdresses, Bulang in heavy earrings and oversized black turbans, and remote hill-dwellers in plain dress, carrying ancient rifles. Most common, though, are the Dai, who buy rolls of home-made paper and sarongs. Take a look around Menghun itself, too, as there's a dilapidated nineteenth-century **monastery** with a pavilion built in the style of Jingzhen's octagonal effort, and a **pagoda** hidden in the bamboo groves on the hills behind town. Another temple down on the flats to the south is linked to a legend that the stream here changed course at the bidding of Sakyamuni.

Beyond Menghun, the fifty-kilometre-long road takes you past the turning south to Bulangshan (see above) and through a stretch of forest inhabited by a nomadic group only "discovered" in the late 1980s. At the end of the bitumen is the town of **DALUO** (two buses daily between here and Menghai), set just in from the Burmese border. Here there's a multi-trunked, giant **fig tree** whose descending mass of aerial roots form a "forest". You'll find **lodgings** at the newish, white hotel on the far side of the bridge (❶), and a daily **border trade market** is timed for the arrival of Chinese package tours between 11am and 1pm. Chinese nationals can also get a two-hour visa for Burma, ostensibly to shop for jade; in fact, many are really going over to catch transvestite stage shows held for their benefit – check out the photos in the windows of Jinghong's processing labs.

Travel details

Trains

Hekou to: Kaiyuan (2 daily; 8hr); Kunming (daily; 15hr).

Kunming to: Beijing (daily; 48hr); Chengdu (3 daily; 18–21hr); Chongqing (2 daily; 23hr); Hanoi (daily; 28hr); Hekou (daily; 16hr); Guangzhou (2 daily; 45hr); Guilin (2 daily; 30hr); Guiyang (5 daily; 12hr); Kaiyuan (2 daily; 8hr); Nanning (daily; 20hr); Panzhihua (3 daily; 6hr); Shanghai (2 daily; 60hr); Xiaguan (daily; 8hr); Xichang (3 daily; 12hr).

Buses

Baoshan to: Jinghong (48hr); Kunming (12hr); Lancang (12hr); Lijiang (8–12hr); Lincang (12hr); Mangshi (4hr); Ruili (6hr); Tengchong (5hr); Wanding (7hr); Xiaguan (6hr).

Dali to: Kunming (6hr); Lijiang (3hr); Shaping (1hr); Xiaguan (30min); Xizhou (30min); Zhongdian (8hr); Zhoucheng (1hr).

Daluo to: Menghai (2 daily; 2hr).

Deqin to: Weixi (daily; 10hr), Zhongdian (6hr).

Gejiu to: Hekou (6hr); Jianshui (2hr); Kaiyuan (30min); Kunming (5hr); Tonghai (4hr); Yuanyang (8hr).

Hekou to: Gejiu (6hr); Jianshui (9hr); Kaiyuan (9hr 30min); Kunming (15hr); Tonghai (6hr).

Jianshui to: Gejiu (2hr); Hekou (9hr); Kaiyuan (2hr); Kunming (7hr); Tonghai (2hr); Yuanyang (6hr).

Jinghong to: Baoshan (48hr); Daluo (5hr); Damenglong (2hr); Kunming (24hr); Lancang (8hr); Lincang (48hr); Menghai (2hr); Menghun (3hr); Mengla (7hr); Menglun (3hr); Xiaguan (48hr); Yuanyang (11hr).

Kunming to: Anshun (24hr); Baoshan (12hr); Chengdu (36hr); Chuxiong (6hr); Dali (12hr); Gejiu (5hr); Guiyang (72hr); Hekou (11–15hr); Jianshui (5hr); Jinghong (16–21hr); Kaiyuan (5hr); Lijiang (9–11hr); Mangshi (22hr); Nanning (72hr); Panxian (12hr); Ruili (19hr); Shilin (3hr); Tonghai (2hr); Wanding (25hr); Xiaguan (5–7hr); Xichang (24hr); Xingyi (13hr); Yuanyang (13hr).

Lancang to: Gengma (9hr); Jinghong (8hr); Lincang (10hr); Menglian (2hr).

Lijiang to: Baoshan (8–12hr); Daju (4hr); Dali (3hr); Kunming (9–11hr); Ninglang (5hr); Panzhihua (10hr); Qiaotou (4hr); Shigu (2hr); Weixi (5hr); Xiaguan (6hr); Yongsheng (5hr); Zhongdian (5hr).

Ruili to: Baoshan (6hr); Kunming (19hr); Mangshi (hourly; 1–2hr); Nansan (12hr); Tengchong (6hr); Wanding (hourly; 30min–1hr); Xiaguan (14hr).

Tonghai to: Jianshui (2hr); Gejiu (2hr); Hekou (13hr); Kaiyuan (4hr); Kunming (2hr).

Xiaguan to: Baoshan (6hr); Binchuan (2hr); Dali (30min); Jinghong (27hr); Kunming (10hr); Lancang (24hr); Lijiang (6hr); Lincang (12hr); Liuku (7hr); Ruili (14hr); Tengchong (14hr); Wanding (12hr); Zhongdian (11hr).

Yuanyang to: Kunming (13hr); Simao (6hr).

Zhongdian to: Deqin (6hr); Lijiang (10 daily; 5hr); Litang (9hr); Xiaguan (11hr).

Ferries

Jinghong to: Chiang Saen (Thailand; 2 weekly; 40hr).

Flights

Baoshan to: Kunming (3 weekly; 30min).

Dali (Xiaguan) to: Kunming (5 weekly; 30min),

Jinghong to: Kunming (3 daily; 55min); Lijiang (2 weekly; 1hr 20min).

Kunming to: Baoshan (3 weekly; 30min); Beijing (6 daily; 2hr 35min); Changsha (1 or 2 daily; 1hr 30min); Chengdu (6–9 daily; 1hr 5min); Chongqing (4–7 daily; 50min); Dali (5 weekly; 30min); Deqin (3 weekly; 2hr); Guangzhou (5 daily; 1hr 20min); Guilin (1 or 2 daily; 1hr 30min); Guiyang (1 or 2 daily; 1hr 10min); Hong Kong (1 or 2 daily; 2hr 45min); Jinghong (3 daily; 55min); Lijiang (4 weekly, 40min); Mangshi (2 daily; 45min); Nanning (2 daily; 50min); Shanghai (2–3 daily; 2hr 30min); Xi'an (2–4 daily; 1hr 40min).

Lijiang to: Jinghong (daily; 1hr 20min); Kunming (daily; 40min).

Zhongdian to: Chengdu (weekly; 2hr); Kunming (3 weekly; 2hr); Lhasa (2 weekly; 1hr 30min).

CHAPTER 12   # Highlights

* **Teahouses** A central feature of Sichuanese social life. See p.888

* **Huanglongxi** A village of authentic Qing-dynasty shops and temples. See p.896

* **Emei Shan** A tough climb is rewarded with gorgeous scenery and monasteries that make atmospheric places to stay. See p.905

* **The Leshan Buddha** You will never forget the first time you see this gargantuan statue. See p.909

* **Dazu** China's most exquisite collection of Buddhist rock art, illustrating religious parables and cartoon-like scenes from daily life. See p.918

* **Cruising the Yangzi** Relax as the magnificent scenery of the towering Three Gorges glides past your boat. See p.928

* **Wolong Giant Panda Research Base** The best place to see pandas in something resembling their natural habitat. See p.933

* **Horse trekking, Songpan** A chance to get really out into the wild and give your feet – though not your seat – a rest. See p.938

* **Litang** Gritty Tibetan monastery town in the heart of Sichuan's wild west, where monks and cowboys tear around on motorbikes. See p.951

△ A waterside teahouse

Sichuan and Chongqing

Ringed by mountains which, according to the Tang poet Li Bai, made the journey here "harder than the road to heaven", **Sichuan** and **Chongqing** stretch for more than 1000km across China's southwest. Administratively divided in 1997, when **Chongqing municipality** was carved off the eastern end of Sichuan Province, the region has long played the renegade, differing from the rest of China in everything from food to politics and inaccessible enough both to ignore central authority and to provide sanctuary for those fleeing it. Recent divisions aside, Sichuan and Chongqing share a common history, and the area splits more convincingly into very different geographic halves: a densely populated eastern plain, and a mountainous west, emphatically remote.

In the east, peaks surround one of the country's most densely settled areas, the fertile **Red Basin**, whose subtropical climate and rich soil conspire to produce endless green fields turning out three harvests a year. This bounty has created an air of easy affluence in **Chengdu**, Sichuan's relaxed capital, and the southern river towns of **Zigong** and **Yibin**. Elsewhere, visitors have the opportunity of joining pilgrims on **Emei Shan** in a hike up the holy mountain's forested slopes, or of sailing **down the Yangzi** from Chongqing, industrial powerhouse and terminus of one of the world's great river journeys. You'll also find that the influence of **Buddhism** has literally become part of the landscape, most notably at **Leshan**, where a giant Buddha sculpted into riverside cliffs provides one of the most evocative images of China; and farther east at **Dazu**, whose marvellous procession of stone carvings has miraculously escaped desecration.

In contrast, the west is dominated by densely buckled ranges overflowing from the heights of Tibet; this is a wild, thinly populated land of snowcapped peaks, where yaks roam the treeline and roads negotiate hair-raising gradients as they cross ridges or follow deep river valleys. Occupied but untamed by Han China, the west has its appeal in its **Tibetan heritage** – clearly visible in scores of important **monasteries** – and raw, rugged alpine scenery. Nearest to Chengdu, there's a chance to see giant pandas at **Wolong Nature Reserve**, while travelling north towards Gansu takes you through ethnic Hui and Qiang heartlands past the vivid blue lakes and beautiful mountain scenery of **Songpan** and **Jiuzhaigou**, with the tranquil village of **Langmusi** the

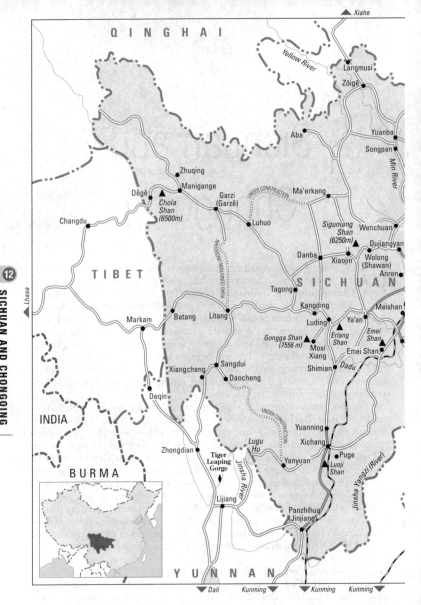

most remote of targets, right on the provincial border. Due west of Chengdu, the real wilds begin beyond **Kangding**, with the monastery towns of **Dêgê** and **Litang** as the pick of destinations – not forgetting an exciting back-road **route to Yunnan**.

   Getting around all this is fairly straightforward, though those heading westwards need to prepare for unpredictably long and uncomfortable journeys.

Rail lines are restricted by geography, and most people use the train only for travel beyond regional borders; the most useful internal route is along the Xi'an–Kunming line, which runs southwest from Chengdu via Emei Shan and Xichang. As for the **weather**, expect warm and wet summers and cold winters, with the north and west frequently buried under snow for three months of the year.

Sichuan cooking

Dominating the southwestern China cooking school, **Sichuanese cooking** is noted for its heavy use of **chilli**, which locals explain as a result of climate – according to Chinese medicine, chillies dispel "wet" illnesses caused by Sichuan's seasonally damp or humid weather. You'll also find that chillies don't simply blast the taste buds, they stimulate them as well, and flavours here are far more complex than they might appear at the initial, eye-watering, mouthful.

Sichuan cuisine's defining taste is described as **mala** – "numb and hot" – created by the potent mix of chillies and **huajiao** (Sichuan pepper), with its soapy perfume and mouth-tingling afterbuzz. One classic *mala* dish is **mapo dofu**, bean curd and minced pork; others include **strange-flavoured chicken** (dressed with sesame paste, soy sauce, sugar and green onions mixed in with the chillies and *huajiao*), and the innocently named **boiled beef slices**, which actually packs more chillies per spoonful than almost any other Sichuanese dish.

A cooking technique unique to Sichuan is **dry-frying**, which involves deep frying to dehydrate the ingredients, followed by sautéeing in a sweet-salty sauce until the liquid has evaporated. **Dry-fried pork shreds**, where the slivers of pork end up dark, chewy and aromatic, is a classic example using meat; a vegetarian counterpart is **dry-fried green beans**, salty and rich with garlic.

Other more general dishes include **hot and sour soup**, flavoured with pepper and vinegar; **double-cooked pork**, where a piece of fatty meat is boiled, sliced thinly and then stir-fried with green chillies; **fish-flavoured pork** (whose "seafood" sauce is made from vinegar, soy sauce, sugar, ginger and sesame oil); **gongbao chicken**, the local version of stir-fried chicken and peanuts; **smoked duck**, a chilli-free cold dish, aromatic and juicy; and **crackling rice**, where a meat soup is poured over a sizzling bed of deep-fried rice crusts. There's also a great number of Sichuanese **snacks** – *xiaochi* – which some restaurants specialize in: green beans with ginger, pork with puréed garlic, cucumber with chilli-oil and sesame seeds, **dandan mian** ("carry-pole" noodles, named after how street vendors used to carry them around), **tiger-skin peppers**, scorched then fried with salt and dark vinegar, five-spiced meat steamed in ground rice (served in the bamboo steamer), and a huge varierty of sweet and savoury dumplings.

One Chongqing speciality now found all over Sichuan (and China) is **huoguo** (hotpot), a social dish eaten everywhere from streetside canteens to specialist restaurants. You get plates or skewers of meat, boiled eggs or vegetables, cooked – by you at the table – in a bubbling pot of stock liberally laced with chillies and cardamom pods. You then season the cooked food in oil spiced with MSG, salt and chilli powder. The effect is powerful, and during a cold winter you may well find that hotpots fast become your favourite food.

Some history

In prehistoric times the region was apparently divided into the eastern **Ba** and western **Shu kingdoms**, which amalgamated during the Shang era (1600–1100 BC). Sites at **Sanxingdui**, near Chengdu, suggest the Ba–Shu was a slave society with highly developed metalworking skills and bizarre aesthetics (see p.895). Agricultural innovations at the end of the third century BC opened up eastern Sichuan to intensive farming, and when the Qin armies stormed through, they found an economic base which financed their unification of China in 221 BC – as did Genghis Khan's forces almost 1500 years later. In between, the area became the Three Kingdoms state of **Shu** – a name by which Sichuan is still sometimes known – and later twice provided refuge for deposed emperors.

Otherwise too distant to play a central role in China's history, the region leapt to prominence in 1911, when government interference in local rail industries sparked the nationwide rebellions that toppled the Qing empire. The next four decades saw rival warlords fighting for control, and, though some stability came when the **Nationalist government** made Chongqing their capital after the Japanese invaded China in 1937, nominally independent states persisted within the former Sichuan's borders as late as 1955: "When the rest of the country is at peace, Sichuan is the last to be brought to heel", went the saying. The province suffered badly during the Cultural Revolution – **Jung Chang**'s autobiography, *Wild Swans*, gives a first-hand account of the vicious arbitrariness of the times in Sichuan – and was left, by the early 1970s, poor and agriculturally devastated. Typically, it was the first province to reject Maoist ideals, when party leader Zhao Ziyang allowed farmers to sell produce on the free market, spearheading the reforms of his fellow native Sichuanese, **Deng Xiaoping**. So effective were these reforms that by the 1990s Sichuan was competing vigorously with the east-coast economy, a situation for which Chongqing – the already heavily industrialized gateway river port between Sichuan and eastern China – claimed a large part of the credit; Chongqing's economic weight secured separate provincial status for the city and its surrounds. Meanwhile, development continues across the region, bringing all the problems of runaway growth: appalling industrial pollution, ecological devastation and an unbelievable scale of urban reconstruction.

Eastern Sichuan and Chongqing

One of the most pleasant areas of China to explore randomly, eastern Sichuan is focused around **Chengdu**, the relaxed provincial capital. Famed not least for its fiery cuisine, the city offers a number of easy excursions to nearby scenic and historic sights, the most unusual of which is a 2000-year-old irrigation scheme at **Dujiangyan**. Northeast is a little-noticed but historically important **route to Shaanxi**, and also **Langzhong**, with its Qing-dynasty architecture; southwest, both road and rail run past Buddhist landmarks at **Emei Shan** and **Leshan** and down to the Yunnanese border via **Xichang**. Southeast of the capital, the historic towns of **Zigong** and **Yibin** offer access to picturesque bamboo forests, and traces of an obscure, long-vanished society. Further Buddhist sites surround the country town of **Dazu** east of Chengdu; beyond, western China's largest city, **Chongqing**, marks the start of the **journey down the Yangzi** to Hubei province, with ferries exiting the region through the dramatic **Three Gorges**.

Chengdu and around

Set on the western side of the Red Basin, **CHENGDU** is a determinedly modern city, its planners furiously converting the last few warrens of leafy lanes and old courtyard houses into ever-larger shopping malls and

Chengdu and around

Chengdu	成都	chéngdū
Baihuatan Park	百花潭公园	bǎihuātán gōngyuán
Cultural Palace	文化宫	wénhuà gōng
Daci Si	大慈寺	dàcí sì
Du Fu Caotang	杜甫草堂	dùfǔ cǎotáng
Giant Panda Breeding Research Base	成都大熊猫繁育研究基地	chéngdū dàxióngmāo fányù yánjiū jīdì
Hospital of Traditional Chinese Medicine College	中医药大学	zhōngyīyào dàxué
Kuan Xiangzi	宽巷子	kuānxiàngzi
Qingyang Gong	青羊宫	qīngyáng gōng
Renmin Park	人民公园	rénmín gōngyuán
Shufeng Yayun	蜀风雅韵	shǔfēng yǎyùn
Shunxing Lao Chaguan	顺兴老茶馆	shùnxīng lǎocháguǎn
Sichuan University Museum	四川大学博物馆	sìchuān dàxué bówùguǎn
Tianfu Square	天府广场	tiānfǔ guǎngchǎng
Wangjiang Lou Park	望江楼公园	wàngjiānglóu gōngyuán
Wenshu Yuan	文殊院	wénshū yuàn
Wuhou Ci	武侯祠	wǔhóu cí
Yong Ling	永陵博物馆	yǒnglíng bówùguǎn

Bus stations

Beimen	北门汽车站	běimén qìchēzhàn
Chadianzi	茶店子客运站	chádiànzi kèyùnzhàn
Chengbei	城北客运中心	chéngběi kèyùn zhōngxīn
Wuguiqiao	五桂桥中心站	wǔguìqiáo zhōngxīnzhàn
Xinnanmen	新南汽车站	xīnnán qìchēzhàn
Zhaojue Si	照觉寺汽车站	zhàojué sì qìchēzhàn

Accommodation

Binjiang	滨江饭店	bīnjiāng fàndiàn
Dragon Town	龙城宽巷子青年旅馆	lóngchéng kuānxiàngzi qīngnián lǚguǎn
Green Bamboo Homestay	新竹家居	xīnzhú jiājū
Holly's Hostel	九龙鼎青酒店	jiǔlóngdǐngqīng jiǔdiàn
Huanhua Shanzhuang	浣花山庄	huànhuā shānzhuāng
Jiaotong	交通饭店	jiāotōng fàndiàn
Jinjiang	锦江宾馆	jīnjiāng bīnguǎn

apartment blocks. Yet despite many of these prestige projects running short of funds, leaving the city with a skeletal skyline, Chengdu remains a cheerful metropolis which takes pride in its appearance. Seasonal floral displays – and ubiquitous **ginkgo trees** – lend colour to its many excellent **parks**, garbage is scrupulously collected, and the formerly dire wastelands which flanked the central riverbanks have been landscaped with willows, lawns and wavy paths. The population is also nicely laid-back, enjoying its **teahouse culture** at every opportunity and unfazed by this being interpreted as laziness by other Chinese.

Chengdu was styled **Brocade City** in Han times, when the urban elite were buried in elegantly decorated tombs, and its silk travelled west along the caravan routes as far as imperial Rome. A refuge for the eighth-century Tang emperor Xuan Zong after his army mutinied over his infatuation with the beautiful concubine Yang Guifei, the city later became a **printing** centre, producing the

Sam's Backpacker House (Rongcheng)	荣城宾馆	róngchéng bīnguǎn
Sim's	观华青年旅舍	guānhuá qīngnián lǚshè
Youyi	友谊宾馆	yǒuyí bīnguǎn
Eating and drinking		
Banmuyuan	半亩苑	bànmǔ yuàn
Beijing Roast Duck	北京烤鸭饭店	běijīng kǎoyā fàndiàn
Cacaja Indian	印度菜菜	yìndù càicài
Chen Mapo Tofu	陈麻婆豆腐	chénmápó dòufù
Chengdu Xiaochi Cheng	成都小吃城	chéngdū xiǎochīchéng
Fiesta Thai	非常泰泰国风味餐厅	fēichángtài tàiguófēngwèi cāntīng
Grandma's Kitchen	祖母的厨房	zǔmǔde chúfáng
Highfly Café	高飞咖啡	gāofēi kāfēi
Lai Tang Yuan	来汤圆	láitāngyuán
Laochuzi Chuancanguan	老厨子川餐馆	lǎochúzi chuāncānguǎn
Long Chaoshou	龙抄手饭店	lóngchāoshǒu fàndiàn
Yanfu Renjia	盐府人家	yánfǔ rénjiā
Zhang Kaoya Jiudian	张烤鸭酒店	zhāngkǎoyā jiǔdiàn
Dujiangyan	都江堰	dūjiāngyàn
Anlan Suspension Bridge	安澜索桥	ānlán suǒqiáo
Erwang Miao	二王庙	èrwáng miào
Fulong Guan	伏龙观	fúlóng guàn
Lidui Park	离堆公园	líduī gōngyuán
Songmao Road	松茂古道	sōngmào gǔdào
Xishu Jiudian	西蜀酒店	xīshǔ jiǔdiàn
Guanghan	广汉	guǎnghàn
Sanxingdui Museum	三星堆博物馆	sānxīngduī bówùguǎn
Huanglongxi	黄龙溪	huánglóng xī
Gulong Si	古龙寺	gǔlóng sì
Qingcheng Shan	青城山	qīngchéng shān
Shangqing Gong	上青宫	shàngqīng gōng
Xindu	新都	xīndū
Baoguang Si	宝光寺	bǎoguāng sì

world's first paper money. Sacked by the Mongols in 1271, Chengdu recovered soon enough to impress Marco Polo with its busy artisans and handsome bridges, since when it has survived similar cycles of war and restoration to become a major industrial, educational and business centre. The city is a mellow spot to spend a few days touring the remaining historical monuments, and spiking your taste buds on one of China's most outstanding cuisines – not to mention getting close-up views of locally-bred **pandas**.

Arrival and city transport

Chengdu's five-kilometre-wide **downtown** area contains a warped grid of streets enclosed on three sides by the canal-like **Fu** and **Jin** rivers, themselves surrounded by three ring roads – the most important of which is innermost **Yihuan Lu**. Broad and lined with plane trees, **Renmin Lu** is the main

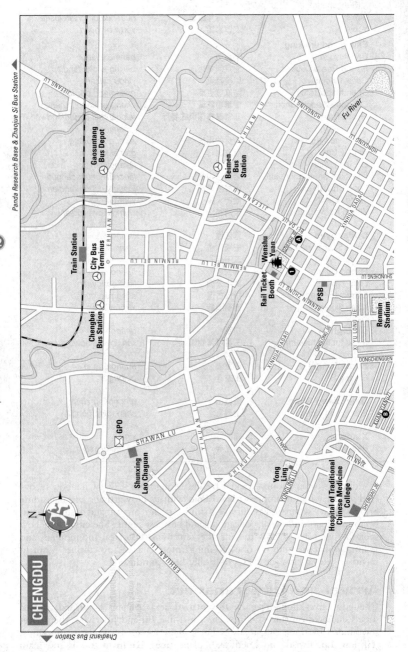

CHENGDU

Panda Research Base & Zhaojue Si Bus Station ◄

Chadianzi Bus Station ◄

Train Station

City Bus Terminus

Gaosuntang Bus Depot

Beimen Bus Station

Chengbei Bus Station

ERHUAN LU

RENMIN BEI LU

YI HUAN LU

HONGXING LU

JIEFANG LU

BEI DAJIE

RENMIN BEI LU

XINHUA DADAO

Wenshu Yuan

Rail Ticket Booth

PSB

RENMIN ZHONG LU

Renmin Stadium

SHUNCHENG LU

XI YU LONG JIE

DONGLONG JIE

DONGCHENGGEN

XINHUA DADAO

YI HUAN LU

SHAWAN LU

GPO

Shunxing Lao Chaguan

Yong Ling

YONGLING LU

Hospital of Traditional Chinese Medicine College

SHI ER QI JIE

RENMIN NAN LU

WUWU

TI YU CHANG LU

WEN WU LU

XI YU JIE

SHI FU JIE

ERHUAN LU

Fu River

HONGXING LU

JIEFANG LU

TI YI AN LU

Fu River

N

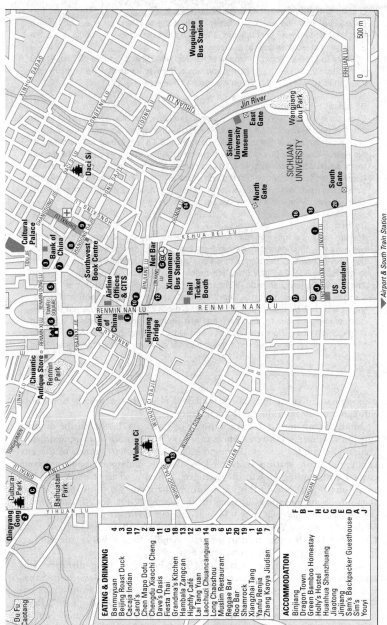

SICHUAN AND CHONGQING

12

885

▶ Airport & South Train Station

EATING & DRINKING

Banmuyuan	4
Beijing Roast Duck	3
Cacaja Indian	10
Carol's	17
Chen Mapo Dofu	8
Chengdu Xiaochi Cheng	2
Dave's Oasis	11
Fiesta Thai	G
Grandma's Kitchen	18
Hambala Zangcan	13
Highfly Café	12
Lai Tang Yuan	5
Laochuzi Chuancanguan	14
Long Chaoshou	9
Muslim Restaurant	6
Reggae Bar	15
Roo Bar	20
Shamrock	19
Xiangzhai Tang	1
Yanfu Renjia	16
Zhang Kaoya Jiudian	7

ACCOMMODATION

Binjiang	F
Dragon Town	B
Green Bamboo Homestay	I
Holly's Hostel	H
Huanhua Shanzhuang	C
Jiaotong	G
Jinjiang	E
Sam's Backpacker Guesthouse	D
Sim's	A
Youyi	J

Outbound **flights** connect Chengdu to major cities across China. The airport bus (¥10) leaves from the lane immediately north of the *Minshan Hotel*, just off Renmin Nan Lu, twice an hour until 6.30pm; it takes half an hour and you should get to the airport with at least an hour to spare.

Flights **to Lhasa** offered by agents at the *Jiaotong*, *Holly's*, and *Sam's* cost ¥1900 and include the airfare, travel permit and airport transfer – note that the length of time you can stay in Tibet is limited only by your Chinese visa.

By train

Chengdu is halfway along the Xi'an–Kunming **rail line**, and also connected to routes into Guizhou and central China through easterly Chongqing. The rail **ticket office** is on the eastern side of the train-station square, but it's less hassle to buy tickets at the nearby Chengbei bus station (ticket window #9) or from various **booths** around town, which open from 8am to 8pm and charge a ¥5 fee per ticket: there's one on Renmin Nan Lu, about one block south of the Binjiang Lu intersection on the east side of the road; and another on Renmin Zhong Lu near the Wenshu temple. Hotel agents generally charge ¥40 or more per person.

By bus

Though there is some overlap of services between Chengdu's many long-distance bus stations, they generally depart from the side of town relevant to the direction they're headed. Details for these and sights surrounding Chengdu are given in the relevant text as indicated. **Northeastern** destinations are handled by the Zhaojue Si station (Jiangyou, Jianmen Guan, and Guanyuan) and Beimen station (Langzhong); the **south** (Emei Shan, Leshan), as well as **Jiuzhaigou** and **Huanglong** (but not Songpan) and **Kangding**, are covered from Xinnanmen; Wuguiqiao is where to find transport for **eastern Sichuan and Chongqing**, including Chongqing, Yibin, Zigong, Gongxian and Dazu – catch bus #58 from outside the north gate of Renmin Park; while buses for all **western Sichuan** depart from Chadianzi.

---

thoroughfare, divided into north, middle and south sections; it runs south through the city from the north train station.

Shuangliu airport is 16km southwest of town, a ¥10 ride on the **airport bus** to the China Southwest Airlines office on Renmin Nan Lu (approximately 2 hourly; 30min); a taxi costs around ¥45. Four kilometres north of the city centre, the **train station** is dwarfed by a square and roundabout out front, packed with jostling crowds of passengers, beggars and hawkers. A **city bus terminus** is just west off this square, from where bus #16 runs the length of Renmin Lu within range of many of the hotels; #28 passes Xinnanmen bus station near the *Jiaotong*; and #34 will get you down to the intersection of Wuhouci Dajie and Yihuan Lu for *Holly's Hostel*. Five kilometres south of town, Chengdu's **South train station** generally handles freight, but if you wind up here, catch bus #16 to the centre.

Otherwise, you'll arrive at one of Chengdu's many **long-distance bus stations**, most of them scattered around the city perimeter. Buses from Songpan and points north terminate at northwesterly **Chadianzi** (from where bus #82 goes to Wuhouci Dajie and Binjiang Lu opposite the *Jiaotong* hotel). Buses from the northeast use **Zhaojue Si** (buses #1 or #302 to Renmin Nan Lu and Wuhouci Dajie) or **Beimen** stations, northeast of the centre. Coming from Kangding or the south will leave you next to the *Jiaotong* hotel at **Xinnanmen**, while buses from Chongqing and the southeast wind up east of the centre at **Wuguiqiao** (bus #58 passes Renmin Park).

City transport

Chengdu's single- and double-decker **buses** run from around 6am until after dark, and charge ¥1 (¥2 for air-conditioned coaches). Fares double after 8pm. **Taxis** are everywhere and cost ¥5 to hire; a trip across town shouldn't cost more than ¥25. Motorbikes are illegal in the downtown area, so **bicycles** (and electric mopeds) remain popular, with cycle lanes and guarded parking throughout the city – see p.894 for rentals.

A **subway** is currently under construction, due for unveiling around 2007; this means that many central roads are being dug up, causing traffic delays and detours.

Accommodation

Chengdu has a great number of **places to stay**, with a choice for every budget. Most are central, though several good-value options to the south and southwest are on convenient bus routes and have places to eat nearby. All **hostels** – as well as the *Jiaotong* hotel – offer Internet access, bike rental, travellers' noticeboards, and good-value **tours** (see "Listings", p.894, for details).

Hostels

Dragon Town 27 Kuan Xiangzi ☎ 028/86648408, ⓦ www.dragontown.com.cn. HI-affiliated operation atmospherically set in a reproduction Qing-era building. Staff are a bit slack, but dorms are inexpensive; the doubles are a little overpriced, though some have their own bathroom. The district, just a short walk from Renmin Park, is quiet and earmarked for restoration to century-old ambience. Dorms ¥30. ❸

Holly's Hostel 246 Wuhouci Dajie ☎ 028/85548131, ⓔ hollyhostelcn@yahoo.com. Sister hostel to *Sam's*, slightly quieter and set in Chengdu's Tibetan quarter. Dorms are a bit cramped, but doubles much more airy. In addition to tours, the hostel also has a book exchange, and a highly recommended Sichuan cooking class. Beds ¥15–30 depending on dorm size, ❸

Sam's Backpacker Guesthouse 130 Shaanxi Jie ☎ 028/86112933 ext 2233, ⓕ 84476823. Reception is a few doors further west of the *Rongcheng Hotel*, set in the hotel's older wing. Popular budget standby, offering down-to-earth advice for independent travellers, and inexpensive dorms – make sure you book in advance between June and October. The rooms are small, gloomy and a bit worn. Dorm beds ¥20, ❸

Sim's 42 Xizhushi Jie ☎ 028/86914422, ⓦ www.gogosc.com. In a quiet lane east of Wenshu temple, though most easily found by heading west off Bei Dajie – take a taxi from arrival points, or phone ahead for a ¥50 pickup from the airport. A 1920s grey-brick Sichuanese/European building,

with a small courtyard garden and a slightly spartan atmosphere. Very friendly and helpful. Dorm beds ¥25–35, ❷

Hotels

Binjiang 16 Binjiang Lu ☎ 028/86651565, ⓕ 86673271. This pink-tiled hotel next to the huge *Sofitel* is in a renovated 1980s building. Prices are surprisingly low: all rooms have showers and toilets, and standards compare favourably with the *Jiaotong's*, though there's no dormitory. ❺

Green Bamboo Homestay Jinxiu Lu ☎ 028/85213513, ⓕ 85254696, ⓔ xinzhu899@sina.com. Gem of a budget hotel, south of the centre near the US Consulate – bus #16 comes within a 10min walk. Single rooms are tiny, but doubles with bathrooms and toilets are immaculate and great value. ❸

Huanhua Shanzhuang 8 Qingyang Zheng Jie ☎ 028/87743636, ⓕ 87779107. Quiet buildings laid out around a series of small Ming-style courtyards and gardens, planted with flowering shrubs and shady trees. Facilities are the usual Chinese urban mid-range sort, perfectly adequate if slightly tarnished. ❼

Jiaotong (Traffic) 77 Jinjiang Lu, near Xinnanmen bus station ☎ 028/85451017, ⓕ 85482777. Well-maintained standby, featuring spotless doubles and three-bed dorms with TV and shared or private bathroom (having the latter doubles the rate). Aside from the drab singles, rooms are good value for money. Bus #34 from the train station stops nearby. Dorm beds ¥30, ❸

Jinjiang 80 Renmin Nan Lu ⊕028/85506666, ⓦwww.jjhotel.com. Chengdu's original tourist hotel, now revamped with some panache to make the International grade and featuring smart rooms (from around ¥1700), bilingual staff, conference and business facilities, and a host of restaurants. ❾

Youyi (Friendship) Lingshiguan Lu ⊕028/85223442, ⓕ85221508. South of the centre opposite the US consulate (bus #16 stops nearby on Renmin Nan Lu), this hotel is past its prime but worth the reasonable price. ❹

The City

Chengdu's centre is marked by **Tianfu Square**, a huge space overlooked by a white statue of Mao Zedong. Turrets and a dome on the western side mark out a **mosque**, built for Chengdu's sizeable Islamic community after the old Muslim quarter was demolished to make the square in 1997. To the east, roads run through the heart of the city's commercial precinct, at the core of which is pedestrianized **Chunxi Lu**, full of clothes shops and upmarket department stores.

Continuing eastwards from here along **Daci Si Lu** brings you to **Daci Si**, a small temple founded in 644 and dedicated to the Tang-dynasty monk **Xuanzang** (see p.1050), who lived briefly in Chengdu before starting on his journey to India. The Qing-style buildings are recent reproductions after the complex was used as a factory during the Cultural Revolution. Of most interest is a side-wing museum, which houses a few pieces of original Tang stonework, along with accounts of Xuanzang's journeys, and a portrait of him carrying a bamboo backpack.

Just west of Tianfu Square, **Renmin Park** (free except during floral exhibitions) offers an introduction to Chengdu's reputedly slack pace of life, comprising a few acres of trees, paved paths, ponds, and ornamental gardens with seasonally varying displays. Near the north entrance there's an ever-busy **teahouse** shaded by wisteria (look for the giant bronze teapot at the gate), and the tall **Monument to the Martyrs**, an obelisk commemorating the 1911 rail disputes which marked the beginning of the end for the Qing empire – hence the unusual motifs of trains and spanners. Behind here is a bizarre subterranean **chamber of horrors** (¥10), with tacky animatronic skeletons, murderers dispatching their victims, and scenes from hell – all suitably gory. Otherwise the park is just a good place to stroll; look for vendors with little burners and a slab of marble along the paths who execute skilful designs of Chinese zodiac

Teahouses

The Sichuanese have a reputation for being particularly garrulous, best experienced at one of the province's many **teahouses**. These hold much the same place in Sichuanese life as a local bar or pub does in the West; some are formal establishments with illuminated signs spelling out *chadian*, *chaguan* or *dachadian* (all meaning "teahouse"); others are just a humble spread of bamboo or plastic chairs in the corner of a park, a temple or indeed any available public space. Whatever the establishment, just sit down to have a waiter come over and ask you what sort of tea you'd like – the standard jasmine-scented variety costs around ¥5 a cup, up to ¥40 or more for a really fine brew. Most are served in the three-piece Sichuanese *gaiwancha*, a squat, handleless cup with lid and saucer. **Refills** are unlimited – either the waiter will give you a top-up on passing your table, or you'll be left with a flask of boiling water. In a country where it's usually difficult to find somewhere to relax in public, teahouses are very welcome: idlers can spend the whole day chatting, playing mahjong, reading or just staring into space, without anyone interrupting.

animals in **toffee**; and, from about 8am at the weekends, huge crowds practising *tai ji* and other martial arts.

About five minutes' walk northwest of Renmin Park off Changshun Shang Jie, traditional homes along **Kuan Xiangzi** (the lane where the *Dragon Town Hostel* is located) and two adjacent alleys are slated for restoration to their Qing-dynasty appearance, though at the time of writing the area is in renovation limbo. If the project succeeds, this will be the sole surviving example of old Chengdu, and well worth investigating.

Wenshu Yuan

Wenshu Yuan (¥1), a bustling, atmospheric Chan (Zen) temple dedicated to **Wenshu**, the Buddhist incarnation of Wisdom, sits 1500m north of Tianfu Square on the #16 bus route, just east off Renmin Zhong Lu. The temple's four elegant single-storey halls were last rebuilt around 1700, each with red-washed walls, wooden pillars and vaulting, and roof corners drawn out into long points. The **first hall** contains a small gilded trinity, not of the usual three aspects of Buddha but of Guanyin, seated on a tiger, flanked by the Bodhisattva Puxian (on an elephant) and Wenshu, riding a **lion**. Wenshu's lion reappears elsewhere through the complex, such as in the cast-iron statue outside the **third hall**, whose interior houses some antique wooden *arhat* statues. The **fourth hall** too has a lion, this time as a mural and looking more like a shaggy, red-haired dog.

If you bear east (right) immediately on entering the temple you'll encounter a narrow, eleven-storey **pagoda**. According to some, the gold-leafed object visible in the base includes **Xuanzang's skull**, though other temples in China also claim to own his mortal remains. Just past here under the ginkgo trees is an open-air maze of bamboo chairs and slurping masses which ranks among Chengdu's best **teahouse** areas, along with a fine **vegetarian restaurant** (see p.892) – both good reasons to visit Wenshu at lunchtime.

Qingyang Gong and around

Sited about 2km west of Renmin Park – buses #19 and #35 stop nearby – **Qingyang Gong** (Green Goat Temple; ¥2) is dedicated to Taoism's mythical proponent, Laozi. The temple's unusual **Bagua Pavilion** is an eight-sided hall with supporting posts wreathed in golden dragons, which houses a statue of **Laozi** astride his buffalo. According to legend, Laozi lost interest in teaching and headed west into the sunset, first baffling posterity by saying that he could be found at the green goat market once his philosophy was understood – hence the temple's unusual name. The tale is again reflected at the main **Three Purities Hall**, built in 1669, where two oversized **bronze goats** have been worn smooth by the caresses of luck-seekers. The right-hand "goat" is weird, being the simultaneous incarnation of all twelve zodiacal animals. Behind them loom the bearded bulks of the Three Purities themselves: **Yuqing Yuan-shi**, holding a pearl representing original chaos; **Shangqing Linghao**, whose *yinyang* symbol represents the origin of form; and **Taiqing Daode**, whose fan symbolizes the beginning of matter. West of here is another excellent **vegetarian restaurant**, open at lunchtime, but for active entertainment head around the back of the next hall, where those after a blessing stumble with eyes shut and arms outstretched towards three large good-luck symbols painted on the bricks, hoping to make contact; onlookers laugh at their efforts before trying themselves.

Next to Qingyang Gong, the **Cultural Park** is only worth a visit for evening theatrical performances (see p.893); east again is **Qintai Lu**, a broad street built in a Qing/Ming style to create a kitsch "Chinatown", full of expensive jewellery shops and restaurants – it's worth a stroll, as is attractive **Baihuatan Park** at Qintai Lu's southern end.

Du Fu Caotang

The line of minibuses pulled up outside **Du Fu Caotang** (Du Fu's Thatched Cottage; daily 9am–5pm; ¥30), located 2km west of Qingyang Gong, attests to the respect the Chinese hold for the Tang-dynasty poet **Du Fu**. His works record the upheavals of his life and times with compassion and humour, and are considered, along with the more romantic imagery of his contemporary Li Bai (see p.899), to comprise the epitome of Chinese poetry. Born in 712, Du Fu struggled for years to obtain a position at the imperial court in Chang'an, succeeding only after one of his sons had died of starvation and just as the empire was struck by the An Lushan rebellion (see p.280). Fleeing the war-ravaged capital for Chengdu in 759, he spent the next five years in a simple grass-roofed dwelling outside the city's west wall, where he wrote some 240 of his 1400 surviving poems. Du Fu spent his later years wandering central China "like a lonely gull between the sea and the sky", dying on a boat in Hunan in 770.

Three centuries after Du Fu's death, a pleasant park was founded at the site of his cottage by fellow poet and admirer Wei Zhuang, and around 1800 it was expanded to its current layout of artfully arranged gardens, bamboo groves, pools, bridges and whitewashed halls. Besides antique and modern statues of Du Fu – depicted as sadly emaciated – there's a small **museum** illustrating his life.

Wuhou Ci and the Tibetan quarter

Wuhou Ci (¥30), southwest of the centre on Wuhouci Dajie (bus #1 from Renmin Nan Lu runs past, as does #82 from outside the *Jiaotong* hotel), is a temple-like complex nominally dedicated to **Zhuge Liang**, the strategist of *Three Kingdoms* fame. As his emperor **Liu Bei** is also buried here, however, the whole site is really a big shrine to the Three Kingdoms era (see p.474).

The site dates to Liu Bei's funeral in 223, though most of the buildings are of early Qing design; as usual in Chengdu, everything is surrounded by gardens. To the left of the entrance, the **Three Kingdoms Culture Exhibition Hall** has contemporary sculptures, lacquered furniture, painted bricks showing daily life (picking mulberry leaves, herding camels, ploughing), and a few martial relics such as arrowheads and copper cavalry figurines. Elsewhere, halls and collonaded galleries house brightly painted **statues** of the epic's heroes, notably a white-faced Liu Bei flanked by his oath-brothers Guan Yu and Zhang Fei; and Zhuge Liang (holding his feather fan) and his son and grandson. Over in the complex's northwestern corner, **Liu Bei's tomb** is a walled mound covered in trees, while right at the rear is a **teahouse theatre** with evening performances of Three Kingdoms episodes and Sichuan opera (see p.893) – buy tickets just inside Wuhou Ci's main entrance.

The district south of Wuhou Ci forms Chengdu's **Tibetan quarter**, full of shops stocked to their roofs with heavy clothes, amber and turquoise jewellery, knives and prayer wheels, conches and other temple accessories – not to mention heavy-duty blenders capable of whipping up a gallon of butter tea in one go. None of this is for tourists; most customers are Tibetan monks, cowboys, and Khampa women with braided hair – all looking decidedly tall and robust next to the local Chinese.

Yong Ling

Northwest of the centre on Yongling Lu and the #46 bus route, **Yong Ling** (daily 8.30am–5pm; ¥5) is the tomb of **Wang Jian**, a member of the Imperial

Guard under the Tang who broke away from the disintegrating dynasty and, in 907 AD, set himself up here as emperor of Shu. After Wang Jian's death in 918, his "fatuous and self-indulgent son" Wang Yan was unable to hold onto the kingdom, which the Tang empire reclaimed in 925. Tomb robbers stripped the site of artefacts centuries before it was excavated during the 1940s, but the brick-lined chambers retain Wang Jian's stone **sarcophagus platform**, richly carved with musicians and twelve very central-Asian-looking bodyguards, and a simply styled, placid **statue**.

Sichuan University Museum and Wangjiang Lou Park

Southeast of the centre, **Sichuan University** merits a visit for its excellent **museum** (¥20), the largest one within the city. Take bus #19, #35 or #335 to the university's **east gate**; the museum is just inside on the right.

The collection, donated in the 1920s by American scholar D.S. Dye, is broad in scope though entirely Sichuanese. Slightly dry **ethnology** exhibits include Qiang, Yi and Miao textiles, and a room devoted to Tibetan religious artefacts – silverwork, paintings and a human thigh-bone flute. Chengdu's once-famous **brocades** also feature, some made into wedding costumes and coverings for an elaborate Qing bridal sedan; there's also a model tearoom with **shadow-puppet theatre** (*piying shi*, "skin-moving theatre" in Chinese), the walls covered with heroes, villains and mythical beasts, all of flat pieces of leather snipped and pierced like paper cutouts.

Continue along the river past the university gates, and you'll soon reach slightly scruffy **Wangjiang Lou Park** (9am–6pm; ¥2), dedicated to the famous Tang poetess **Xue Tao**, who was buried here in 834. She was particularly fond of bamboo as a symbol of virtue and dignity, and the park is planted with many varieties. There's also a **well** where she drew water used to make a special red paper, the small grass mound of her **tomb**, and a Ming-style **pagoda** looking out over the river.

The Giant Panda Breeding Research Base

Some 8km northeast of central Chengdu, the **Giant Panda Breeding Research Base** (daily 8am–6pm; ¥30) offers the best possible views of both giant and arboreal red pandas – housed here in semi-naturalistic, spacious pens – short of your heading off to Wolong (p.933). There's also a **museum**, with bits of panda anatomy in glass jars and, for reasons which remain unexplained, a diorama of a sabre-tooth tiger. Get to the base early, as the pandas slump into a stupor after munching their way through piles of bamboo at around 10am. **Tours** (see "Listings", p.894) to the base are expensive, especially for a group – it's far cheaper to catch bus #1, #45 or #302 to their terminus at Zhaojue Si station, and then take a taxi or rickshaw (about ¥10) the rest of the way.

Eating

Chengdu boasts a colossal number of **restaurants** spread all over the city. As you'd expect, most places are **Sichuanese**, including some famous premises whose modern plastic furnishings disguise both their venerable histories and the quality of their food. **Regional Chinese** and **foreign restaurants** allow a break from chillies and oil, as do **cafés**, which serve a similar run of pizzas, sandwiches, burgers, pasta and desserts. Top of the list are *Highfly Café* on Linjiang Lu; the above-average and inexpensive *Grandma's Kitchen*, near the university on Kehua Bei Lu, a cosy joint favoured by expats and overseas students serving bottomless coffee for ¥10; and the shabby *Dave's Oasis* on Binjiang Lu, popular with backpackers. **Hotpot** places are legion, and your accommodation can point you to the nearest. Sichuanese food tastes especially good with **beer** – try the locally brewed *Xuehua*.

Banmuyuan 98 Jinli Xi Lu, near Baihuatan Gongyuan. Sunken tables, florid tablecloths, bouncy staff, and rice-free, pickle-enhanced Dongbei fare, where even confirmed carnivores might be embarrassed by the quantity of meat you can order in a single serving. A selection of cold vegetable dishes, port stew, a plate of *jiaozi* and beer for two comes in around ¥50.

Beijing Roast Duck Renmin Dong Lu, opposite the *Holiday Inn*. Famous duck served with all the trimmings – including duck soup to wash the cholesterol down. They also do Mongolian hotpot (you need at least two people to get through the mountain of sliced meat, noodles and vegetables) and palate-cleansing side dishes such as tofu-garlic spring rolls and bitter bamboo shoots. Count on ¥40 a head with beer, and be prepared to wait for a table.

Cacaja Indian 18 Binjiang Zhong Lu, near the intersection with Renmin Nan Lu. A vivid escape from China, featuring Bollywood soundtracks and a cosy, orange-painted interior draped in saris and posters of deities. Try any of a selection of curries, bhajis, fresh yoghurt raitas, dal, biryanis and spiced tea – it's all excellent. Plenty of meat-free dishes for vegetarians. Mains ¥15–30.

Chen Mapo Dofu Yihuan Lu, opposite Qingyang Gong. Founded in 1862, this is the original home of Grandma Chen's bean curd, where ¥10 buys a large bowl of tofu glowing with minced meat, chilli oil and *huajiao* sauce. They also do platters of cold dishes and other tofu-based items, including imitation duck, fish, and pork shreds, along with real sweet-and-sour spareribs.

Chengdu Xiaochi Cheng 134 Shandong Dajie. Staff are brusque but the low wooden tables, courtyard fountain and ¥15–30 samplers of classic Sichuanese snacks can't be beaten, and the place is deservedly popular. Dishes include sweet and savoury dumplings, *dandan mian*, small crispy-fried fish, shredded dry-fried beef, rabbit in black bean sauce, shaved rice-jelly noodles, and much more.

Fiesta Thai outside the *Jiaotong Fandian*, Linjiang Lu. Silk-clad staff greet you in Thai, and the food, from green curry chicken, mother-in-law eggs (deep-fried boiled eggs), and pork and glass-noodle salad, through to coconut custard-filled pumpkin and other desserts, is faultless. Worth the ¥50-a-head price.

Hambala Zangcan Wuhouci Dong Jie, near *Holly's Hostel*. Typical of the Tibetan area's diners, and authentic down to the bright colours, grubby walls, DVDs of Tibetan pop, a monk and cowboy clientele, and begging acolytes going round the tables. Expect butter tea in metal teapots, dumplings, fresh yoghurt, and fried, boiled or chopped yak – vegetables have yet to find their way here. Around ¥15 a head.

Lai Tang Yuan Long Bin Jie, the small street running along the east side of the Parkson building. Another one of Chengdu's famous canteens, good for a snack or light lunch. They do a range of Sichuanese snacks, but the house speciality is *tangyuan*, little rice-flour dumplings served with sweet sesame paste – a small bowlful costs just ¥2.

Muslim restaurant At the mosque on Xitu Jie. Catering to Chengdu's large Muslim population, this serves noodles, either in a spicy soup or mixed with a meat and vegetable stir-fry. Stay off the more upmarket dishes, as they're poor value. There are usually Uigurs outside grilling kebabs and bread, if you fancy a take-away.

Long Chaoshou Chunxi Lu. A renowned dumpling house specializing in *long chaoshou*, Sichuanese wonton, and a whole range of famous Sichuanese snacks, with samplers of small dishes for ¥18–28. Eating is most fun downstairs amid the face-stuffing patrons of the ever-rowdy canteen, though slightly better food is available with waitress service upstairs for twice the price.

Laochuzi Chuancanguan 31 Zhimin Lu, 500m east of Xinnanmen bus station. New, four-storey mid-range Sichuanese restaurant with lively atmosphere and hospitable staff. They do excellent sliced steamed pork eaten in delicate "cut" buns, spiced chicken wings packed in sticky rice, sweet taro rolls, and tiger-skin peppers. Around ¥35 a head.

Xiangzhai Tang Wenshu Yuan. The most enjoyable of Chengdu's temple restaurants, where all "meat" dishes are made from gluten, bean curd and potato. For the cheaper public canteen, circle your choices on a tear-off menu (match the Chinese characters with the English shown on a board), pay at the kiosk, then collect food from the kitchen. The more expensive restaurant has an English menu. Two can fill up at the canteen for ¥20, or around ¥60 at the restaurant.

Yanfu Renjia Kehua Bei Lu, near the university – catch bus #45, #59 or #6 heading south from Xinnanmen bus station. Stylish Sichuanese restaurant with jars of layered pickles for decor. They don't drown everything in chilli oil, and pay attention to subtle flavours: the steamed spareribs with mung beans, "beanflower" tofu soup, belly pork slices, and various delicate dumplings have won awards, and the place is always busy. Dishes around ¥25.

Zhang Kaoya Jiudian Qingnian Lu. With a tiny stairway entrance, this comprises a canteen downstairs with horrendous plastic decor and a nicer restaurant above, both serving an array of Sichuanese snacks and dishes; the real treat is their marinated roast duck in an aromatic stock. A plate of garlic cucumber or shredded white radish soup balances the richness of the duck; a meal for two costs around ¥30.

Drinking, nightlife and entertainment

Chengdu has a solid **nightlife**, but venues open and close very rapidly; of the dozen or more **bars** and clubs on Renmin Nan Lu (all within range of bus #16), the following have been around a while and make good starting points. The *Reggae Bar* is a small, dim, smoky barfly joint popular with overseas students and just this side of sleazy, featuring cheap spirits and music as advertised – from Marley to Eek-a-Mouse. A block south, *Carol's* is a lively venue, best Friday and Saturday nights, when they get in a Filipino DJ; the *Shamrock*, just north of the US Consulate, has a lush bar, good food, and loud, live music Wednesday and Sunday, again with a DJ filling in Friday and Saturday. East of the *Shamrock*, the *Roo Bar* at 6 Kehua Jie has nightly happy hours for beer and spirits, cable TV for watching world soccer, and bar meals. As for **entertainment**, you should spend a couple of hours at the theatre, soaking up at least the atmosphere, if not the plots, of *chuanxi*, one of China's main **opera** styles.

Sichuan opera

Sichuan opera – known here as **chuanxi** – is a rustic variant on Beijing's, based on everyday events and local legends. Most pieces are performed in Sichuanese, a rhythmic dialect well suited to theatre, which allows for humour and clever wordplay to shine through. As well as the usual bright costumes, stylized action and glass-cracking vocals, Chuanxi has two specialities: **fire-breathing** and **rapid face-changing**, where the performers – apparently simply by turning around or waving their arms across their faces – completely change their make-up.

Today *chuanxi* has gone into a bit of a decline, at least as a form of popular entertainment, and most locals are not much interested. The most "authentic" big venue is the **Shunxing Lao Chaguan**, in the Chengdu International Convention Centre, Floor 3, 258 Shawan Lu, diagonally across from the post office – enter what looks like a cinema, take escalators up two levels, then bear around the balcony to your right. Performances take place at 8pm most nights (¥48); the venue has ornate antique-style teahouse furnishings, and you can eat here too. There's also a much cheaper, casual teahouse theatre at the **Cultural Palace** on Tidu Jie, just east of the centre, full of octogenarians crunching sunflower seeds, slurping their tea, and breaking off from gossiping to applaud the actors' finer points. Weekend shows begin around 2pm and cost ¥5–10, though staff may try to charge you more; be aware too that performances here are often of Beijing Opera. Otherwise, catch two-hour-long **variety shows** featuring short opera scenes, fire-breathing and face-changing, comedy skits, puppetry, shadow-lantern play and story-telling nightly at **Shufeng Yayun** in the **Cultural Park** (enter off Qintai Lu; 7.30pm; ¥100–120); or at the Ming-style open-air stage in **Wuhou Ci** (8pm; ¥120). Though touristy, they're good fun; you'll get a better deal on **tickets** – around ¥80 – by booking through one of the budget hotel agents (see "Listings", p.894).

Listings

Airlines China Southwest is near the *Minshan Hotel* on Renmin Nan Lu (☏028/86661100).

Banks and exchange The two most useful Bank of China branches, both with ATMs and able to change traveller's cheques, are next to the *Jinjiang* hotel on Renmin Nan Lu, and just east of Tianfu Square on Renmin Dong Lu. There's also an ATM at the entrance to Xinnanmen bus station.

Bike rental Bikes can be rented from the *Jiaotong*, *Sam's*, and *Holly's* for around ¥15 per day, plus a ¥100 deposit.

Bookshops The Southwest Book Centre opposite the south end of Chunxi Lu has a good collection of maps, guidebooks in Chinese, and English-language novels – not all of them Victorian potboilers either.

Camping supplies If you're heading to Tibet, Western Sichuan or elsewhere in China's wilds, there's a clutch of stores such as *Shushanxing* selling good-quality gear at low prices (compared to what you'd pay at home) on Yihuan Lu, just west of the intersection with Renmin Nan Lu.

Chinese medicine Chengdu's Hospital of Traditional Chinese Medicine – one of China's best – is on Shi'er Qiao Lu, 100m east of the intersection with Yihuan Lu. The Foreign Affairs department is signed in English about 70m inside the entrance on the right; they charge ¥30 for an excellent tour with an English-speaking guide. You can also study TCM here.

Consulates US, 4 Lingshiguan Lu, Renmin Nan Lu (☏028/85583992, ℻85583520).

Hospitals People's No. 1 Hospital and Chengdu Municipal Chinese Medicine Research Institute, Chunxi Lu ☏028/86667223; Sichuan Hospital, Yihuan Xi Lu ☏028/85551312 or 85551255.

Internet access There's a huge Net bar above Xinnanmen bus station; enter from the river side, not the station.

Left luggage Accommodation will look after excess gear while you're off in the wilds for around ¥2 per item per day. The train and bus stations also have left-luggage facilities open to anyone who can produce an onward ticket, though you can't generally leave things overnight.

Mail Chengdu's main post office is inconveniently located 2km west of the train station at 73 Shawan Lu; they open daily 8am–7pm and the poste restante counter (marked "International Mail";

the postal code for letters is Chengdu 610031) is ahead and on the right as you enter.

Martial arts The *Renmin Gongyuan Taiji Chuan* association (☏028/86622155), headed by teacher Xiao, meets near the monument in Renmin Park every Saturday and Sunday morning around 9am – you'll need to speak Chinese to take part. *Bagua zhang* is taught by Zhou Huihuan at his studio on Xi Yulong Jie (☏028/86511058), around the corner from the PSB – take the external steps up from beside a branch of the *Chen Mapo Doufu* restaurant chain and look for the yin-yang diagram embedded in the concrete; the northbound bus #16 stops below. Foreigners often train here, though as ever it's useful to be able to speak Chinese.

PSB The branch dealing with visa extensions and foreigners' problems is on Shuncheng Lu (Mon–Fri 9am–noon and 1–5pm), just south of the intersection with Wenwu Lu on the west side of the street. At present, the northbound bus #16 stops directly opposite.

Shopping For clothing, head to Chunxi Lu, where all the Chinese designer brands (and a few Western ones) have stores. There's an interesting, touristy curio market – good for Maomorabilia, wooden screens and all sorts of "new antiques" – on the north side of the road about halfway between the Green Goat Temple and Du Fu Caotang. For genuine antique snuff bottles, jewellery, birdcages, porcelain and the like, try the Chengdu Antique Store, corner of Dongchenggen Lu and Renmin Xi Lu.

Travel agents CITS on Renmin Nan Lu (☏028/86669222, ℻88853655), among a knot of travel agencies outside the *Minshan* hotel, can organize Yangzi cruises, Leshan/Emei Shan tours, and Tibet airfares. The best tour deals are with independent agents at Chengdu's hostels and the *Jiaotong* hotel, who all offer part- and multi-day packages – you don't have to be staying to make bookings. Two-hour Sichuan opera trips visit either a low-key local theatre, where you get a guide to interpret and a look backstage to see the actors get ready (¥70), or the more touristy "Culture Show" at Shufeng Yayun (¥80–100). Other options include three hours at Chengdu's Panda Breeding Centre (¥80); a day-trip to Qingcheng Shan (¥80); four days at Jiuzhaigou and Huanglong (around ¥850); a three-day package to Siguniang Shan (¥480, excluding horse-trekking). Tibet flights work out at around ¥1950 one-way.

Around Chengdu

Chengdu's surrounding diversions are mostly ignored by visitors, lured or sated by grander prospects elsewhere. But the following all make worthy day-trips from the capital, and most can be used as first stops on longer routes. Just to the northeast, **Xindu**'s important Buddhist monastery is just a short hop from the **Sanxingdui museum**, stuffed with inscrutable prehistoric bronzes. Unpretentious Qing architecture graces the picturesque market town of **Huanglongxi** southwest of Chengdu, while northwest, **Dujiangyan** sports a still-functional 2000-year-old irrigation scheme surrounded by wooded parkland, and nearby **Qingcheng Shan** is forested and peppered with Taoist shrines.

Xindu and Baoguang Si

Some 16km northeast of Chengdu, the market town of **XINDU** sits at the start of Shudao, the ancient "Road to Sichuan" (see p.898), to which the cheerful Buddhist monastery Baoguang Si here owes its fame. **Buses** to Xindu (40min; ¥4) depart Chengdu's Gaosuntang depot, 700m east of the train station; once at Xindu, take local bus #8 to the temple.

Hidden away behind a bright red spirit wall at the rear of a large modern plaza, **Baoguang Si** (¥5) had its moment of glory when emperor Xizong fled to Sichuan down Shudao during a rebellion in 880 AD and found sanctuary at the monastery, bestowing its current name (meaning "Bright Treasure"). He later funded rebuilding, but the temple was razed during Ming-dynasty turmoils, and was only restored during the 1830s. Tang traces survive in the thirteen-storey **Sheli Pagoda**, whose upper seven levels have sagged off the perpendicular, and some column supports decorated with imperial dragons at the **Qinfo Hall**. Baoguang's highlight, however, is its **luohan hall**, which houses 518 colourful, surreal statues of Buddhist saints, along with 59 Buddhas and Boddhidarma, founder of the Chan sect (for more on which, see p.592). For lunch, try the airy and cheap **vegetarian restaurant**.

Sanxingdui Museum

In 1986 an archeological team, investigating what appeared to be a Shang-dynasty town 16km northeast of Xindu at **Sanxingdui**, made an extraordinary discovery: a set of rectangular **sacrificial pits** containing a colossal trove of jade, ivory, gold and – especially – **bronze** artefacts, all of which had been deliberately broken up before burial. Subsequent excavation of the area revealed a settlement which, from around 3000 BC until its abandonment for unknown reasons in 800 BC, is believed to have been the capital of the shadowy **Ba-Shu culture**, of which virtually nothing is known.

All this is covered at the excellent **Sanxingdui Museum** (daily 8.30am–5pm; ¥50), with two main halls and English captions. The thousands of artefacts on display are both startling and nightmarish, the products of a very alien view of the world: a two-metre-high bronze figure with a hook nose and oversized,

Luohan halls

Buddhism's original array of eighteen **luohans**, or saints, has since the religion's arrival in China 1900 years ago grown to include over five hundred famous monks, emperors, folk heroes and even the occasional foreigner (look for big noses, curly hair and full beards). This has spawned **luohan halls**, where statues of the five hundred, often grotesquely caricatured, are arranged in a mandala pattern, with an isolated statue of Guanyin at the centre. For an idea of what fate has in store for you, pick any *luohan*, then count off your years of age to a new one (moving left for men, right for women). Note this new statue's number, then go to the front desk and receive a card with that luohan's advice on how to make the most of your future.

grasping hands standing atop four elephants; metre-wide masks with obscene grins and eyes popping out on stalks; a four-metre-high "spirit tree" entwined by a dragon with knives and human hands instead of limbs; and finely detailed bronzes, jade tools and pottery pieces.

To reach Sanxingdui, first catch a bus to **Guanghan**, 8km short of the site, from either Xindu (¥5) or Chengdu's Zhaojue Si station (¥10); to get to Zhaojue Si take a northbound bus #1 or #45 from Renmin Nan Lu, just south of Tianfu Square. From Guanghan, buses for **Xigao** (¥2) serve the museum.

Huanglongxi

HUANGLONGXI, 40km south of Chengdu, is a charming riverside village whose half-dozen understated **Qing-dynasty streets** – all narrow, flagstoned and sided in rickety wooden shops – featured in the martial-arts epic *Crouching Tiger, Hidden Dragon*. The village is popular with Chinese visitors, in particular groups of old ladies coming to pray for grandchildren to Guanyin, to whom all the village's **temples** are dedicated.

Buses (¥11.5) leave for the village until early afternoon, from Xinnanmen bus station; return buses, which run until at least 3.30pm, are marked with the characters for "Xinnanmen". From the highway bus stop, it's 500m through the quiet new settlement to the old village gate; take the left-hand lane, which is almost narrow enough to touch either side as you walk down the middle. All businesses are either shops selling irrelevant souvenirs or restaurants displaying **grindstones** for making one of Huanglongxi's specialities, *douhua* (soft bean curd). You soon reach the 500-metre-long main street; turn left for two tiny **nunneries** (one on the left, the other at the end of the street beside a beribboned banyan tree), both containing brightly painted statues of Guanyin, Puxian and Wenshu.

At the opposite end of town, larger **Gulong Si** (¥1) has two main halls with similar statuary in a wobbly state of repair. There's an ancient banyan supported by posts carved as dragons; the former **governor's court** with a dog-headed guillotine for executing criminals; and an unusually three-dimensional, fifty-armed Guanyin statue in the right-hand hall.

Wandering around will fill an hour, after which you'll want **lunch**; the riverfront restaurants near the nunneries are best, serving *douhua*, fresh fish and crispy deep-fried prawns. You can also buy bamboo-leaf-wrapped packets of *huanglongxi douchi*, smoked salted soya beans, then sit munching them under willows at one of the outdoor **teahouses**.

Dujiangyan

There's enough to hold you for a day at **DUJIANGYAN**, a large town 60km northwest of Chengdu, where in 256 BC the provincial governor, **Li Bing**, set up the **Dujiangyan Irrigation Scheme** to harness the notoriously capricious Min River. Li designed a three-part engineering project using a central dam and artificial islands to split the Min into an inner flow for irrigation and an outer channel for flood control. A spillway directed and regulated the water, while an opening carved through the hillside controlled the flow rate. Completed by Li Bing's son, the scheme has been maintained ever since, the present system of dams, reservoirs and pumping stations irrigating 32,000 square kilometres – even though the project's flood control aspects will become redundant when the **Zipingpu Dam**, 9km upstream, starts operation in 2006.

Buses (¥16) depart for Dujiangyan every few minutes from Chengdu's northwesterly Chadianzi station (the sluggish city bus #82 from outside the *Jiaotong* hotel terminates here). You end up at Dujiangyan's bus station, south of the town centre on Yingbin Dadao; cross the road and catch local bus #4 to the irrigation scheme's **entrance** at **Lidui Park** (daily 8am–6pm; ¥60), which encloses the original heart of the project. An ancient, three-metre-high stone statue of Li Bing found on the riverbed in 1974 graces **Fulong Guan**, a 1600-year-old temple flanked with die-straight *nanmu* trees, which sits right at the tip of the first channel. From here the path crosses to the midstream artificial islands, before arriving at the **Anlan Suspension Bridge**, which spans the whole width of the river. European explorers looked on this bridge as marking the boundary between the settled Chengdu plains and the western wilds, and indeed mountains do rise very abruptly on the western bank. Crossing to the east side brings you to steps ascending to **Erwang Miao**, an ornate Taoist hall dedicated to Li Bing and his son; look for an alcove bust of **Ding Baozhen**, the nineteenth-century governor responsible for renovations, and after whom the Sichuanese dish *gongbao jiding* ("Governor's Chicken Cubes") is named; and also a Qing mural of the whole scheme. Heading back, follow signs for the wooded **Songmao Road**, the ancient route from Dujiangyan to Songpan (p.938), which passes through two stone gateways and the old **Town God's Temple** at the park exit on Xingful Lu, about 500m east of Lidui Park.

For **accommodation** in Dujiangyan, there's a cheap, unnamed hotel (beds ¥30; ❸) next to the bus station where Chinese-speakers might wrangle a bed; otherwise *Xishu Jiudian* (☎028/87131216; ❹), a kilometre away over the stream off central Xingfu Lu, has clean, carpeted rooms with showers. **Restaurants** are everywhere, especially leading up to Lidui Park. **Leaving**, buses head back to Chengdu and on to Qingcheng Shan through the day, with at least daily services west to Wolong and Xiaojin, and north to Wenchuan and Songpan.

Qingcheng Shan

Amazingly fresh after Chengdu's smog, **Qingcheng Shan** (¥60) is a smaller, easier version of Emei Shan, and has been a Taoist site since the Han-dynasty monk **Zhang Ling**, founder of the important Tianshi sect, died here in 157 AD. The walk to the 1200-metre summit takes around three hours, following stone steps through the forest (there's also a **cable car**; ¥50 return). Qingcheng's Taoist **shrines** – they're not really quite temples – are all set in courtyards with open-fronted Qing-dynasty halls, at the back of which are ornate, glassed-in cases containing painted statues of the relevant saints. None gives much protection from the weather (being Taoist, that's probably the point), so reflect the seasons, dripping wet and mossy on a rainy summer day, coated by winter snows, or carpeted in yellow ginkgo leaves in early November. Most have **restaurants**, and though the food isn't great, the mountain's *gong* tea is worth trying.

There are **buses** (¥22) through the morning from Chengdu's Xinnanmen station; you can catch them back until about 5.30pm. The bus leaves you outside the **main gate** at **Jianfu Gong**, whose dark wooden front conceals shrines to Cai Shen, the god of wealth, among others. Once through the gate, it's a half-hour walk to the first major shrine, **Ci Hang Dian**, dedicated to Ci Hang (or **Duomu**), the Taoist version of Guanyin. Next stop is the halfway point of **Tianshi Dong** (Grotto of the Heavenly Teacher), an important complex surrounding a small cave where Zhang Ling lived and meditated before his death at the age of 122.

Beyond here, steps rise steeply to the substantial **Shangqing Gong**, whose attractions include gateway calligraphy by the Guomindang leader Chiang Kaishek, shrines to the Three Purities and the Taoist martial arts mentor Zhang Sanfeng (see p.512), and **accommodation** (❸, dorms ¥15) – the **cable-car terminus** is just beyond. Another ten minutes and you're on Qingcheng's

summit, which is crowned by a six-storey **tower** containing a twelve-metre-high golden statue of Laozi and his buffalo, with views off the balconies of backsloping ridges and lower temples poking out of the forest.

Northeastern Sichuan

The fertile river valleys of **northeastern Sichuan** wind through awkwardly hilly – though still heavily farmed – countryside, all abruptly terminated around 400km from Chengdu by severe escarpments marking the border with Shaanxi. Originally, the sole way through these ranges was provided by **Shudao**, the route linking Chengdu with the former imperial capital Xi'an, along which culture and personalities flowed over the centuries. Aside from the ancient remains at Sanxingdui (see p.895), the region features in *Three Kingdoms* lore; contains the hometowns of **Li Bai**, one of China's greatest poets, and the country's only empress, **Wu Zetian**; and was the escape route down which the Tang

Northeastern Sichuan		
Doutuan Shan	窦团山	*dòutuán shān*
Dongyue Hall	东岳殿	*dōngyuè diàn*
Feitian Scripture Store	飞天藏	*fēitiān cáng*
Qifeng International Hotel	奇峰国际酒店	*qífēng guójì jiǔdiàn*
Yunyan Si	云岩寺	*yúnyán sì*
Guangyuan	广元	*guǎngyuán*
Silian Dajiudian	四联大酒店	*sìlián dàjiǔdiàn*
Zetian Dian	武则天殿	*wǔzétiān diàn*
Zhongsan Binguan	众森鸿福宾馆	*zhòngsēn hóngfú bīnguǎn*
Jianmenguan	剑门关	*jiànmén guān*
Liangshan Si	凉山寺	*liángshān sì*
Jiangyou	江油	*jiāngyóu*
Jiangyou Binguan	江油宾馆	*jiāngyóu bīnguǎn*
Jinxin Binguan	金鑫宾馆	*jīnxīn bīnguǎn*
Libai Museum	李白纪念馆	*lǐbái jìniànguǎn*
Libai's Former Residence	李白故居	*lǐbái gùjū*
Qinglian	青莲	*qīnglián*
Taibai Park	太白公园	*tàibái gōngyuán*
Langzhong	阆中	*lǎngzhōng*
Dafo Si	大佛寺	*dàfó sì*
Daoxiang Cun Jiudian	稻香村酒家	*dàoxiāngcūn jiǔjiā*
Dujia Kezhan	杜家客栈	*dùjiā kèzhàn*
Dunhuang Binguan	敦煌宾馆	*dūnhuáng bīnguǎn*
Gongyuan	贡院	*gòngyuàn*
Huaguang Lou	华光楼	*huáguāng lóu*
Hu's Courtyard	胡家院	*hújiā yuàn*
Kong's Courtyard	孔家大院	*kǒngjiā dàyuàn*
Scholar's Cave	状元洞	*zhuàngyuán dòng*
Zhang Fei Miao	张飞庙	*zhāngfēi miào*
Zhuangyuan Ge	状元阁	*zhuàngyuán gé*

emperor Xuan Zong fled the An Lushan rebellion of 756 AD (see p.280). A Song-dynasty wooden structure and some death-defying martial monks survive at **Doutuan Shan**, while Shudao itself breaks out of the region through a sheer cleft in the ranges known as **Jianmenguan**, the Sword Pass.

The towns of primary interest along Shudao are **Jiangyou** and **Guangyuan**, the latter just 60km short of the Shaanxi border. Both are on the Chengdu–Xi'an **rail line**, and also on a fast expressway – you can get to Guangyuan in around four hours – making the bus the more convenient option, with frequent departures along this route from Chengdu's Zhaojue Si station. Shudao can also serve as the first stage in a journey to **Jiuzhaigou** (see p.941) – in winter, it's sometimes the only viable route.

Well east from Shudao, a large grid of old streets at the pleasant riverside town of **Langzhong** is one of the few places in Sichuan where you can still see substantial areas of urban Qing-dynasty architecture – a welcome refuge from the country's frenzied demolition of its past. Fast buses to Langzhong from Chengdu (¥80) depart little Beimen station, northeast of the centre on the first ring road; you can also get here direct from Chongqing and Guangyuan.

Note that though there are plenty of **banks** in the northeast of Sichuan, none can change traveller's cheques.

Jiangyou and Doutuan Shan

JIANGYOU is a modern, pleasantly leafy town on the north bank of the Fu Jiang some 170km from Chengdu, within sight of the steep line of hills slanting northeast towards the Shaanxi border. It's famed as the hometown of the Tang poet Li Bai, but what really justifies a visit to Jiangyou is a quirky side-trip to nearby **Doutuan Shan**, whose small shrines are curiously shared by Taoist and Buddhist deities, while monks perform some bizarre acrobatic stunts.

Though he grew up near Jiangyou, **Li Bai** – also known as Li Po and Tai Bai – was born in China's far northwest during a period when the country's arts, stimulated by unparalleled contact with the outside world, reached their heights. A swordsman in his youth and famous during his own lifetime, Li Bai is China's most highly regarded romantic poet, his works masterpieces of Taoist, dream-like imagery, often clearly influenced by his notorious **drunkenness** – he drowned in the Yangzi in 762 AD, allegedly while trying to grasp the moon's reflection in the water.

Unsurprisingly perhaps, Jiangyou's Li Bai monuments – such as the dim **Li Bai Museum** (¥30), off Renmin Lu in central **Taibai Park** – fail to capture the great man's spirit. Fans are best off catching bus #9 from near Jiangyou's bus station on Taiping Lu to **Li Bai's Former Residence** (¥40), 10km south on a hillside above **Qinglian** township, which at least has the virtue of being where Li Bai actually lived. Rebuilt many times, the quiet Ming-era halls and courtyards are filled with statues and paintings illustrating his life, and a shrine to his ancestor, the Han-dynasty general Li Xin. An oversized modern **pagoda** marks the hilltop, with a garden below planted with steles of his poems, and the **tomb** of his sister, Li Yueyuan.

Practicalities

Jiangyou's kilometre-wide centre is focused on the north–south Jiefang Lu and its intersections with Renmin Lu and Jinlun Lu; the little **Changming river** flows parallel to Jiefang Lu through town. The **train station** is 5km east of town: city bus #2 will carry you to the main **bus station**, southeast of the centre on Taiping Lu. Here you'll find good-value **accommodation** at the

adjacent *Jinxin Binguan* (☎0816/3262128; ❷) or 500m north on Fujiang Nan
Lu at the new *Jiangyou Binguan* (☎0816/3262221; ❺). Hotel **restaurants** are as
good as anywhere to eat, though there are also cheap stalls outside Taibai Park
on Renmin Lu. **Banks** can be found through the centre.

Doutuan Shan

Doutuan Shan (¥50) is a twin-peaked ridge easily accessible 26km northwest of Jiangyou. **Buses** (¥18 return) depart the little depot opposite Jiangyou's main bus station whenever full; alternatively, the main bus station's **tour
agency** offers the return trip plus entry for a bargain ¥50. There are buses
back to Jiangyou until late afternoon – just how late depends on the number
of visitors.

The mountain's **bus stop** sits below *Qifeng International Hotel* (☎0816/3879999,
Ⓕ3879333; ❽), a four-star country retreat with grand views down towards
Jiangyou. Take the path uphill past the hotel and it's a few minutes to ornate
gates at **Yunyan Si**, the temple's charming eighteenth-century halls filled with
cheerfully cohabiting Taoist and Buddhist statuary, with Doutuan Shan's two
sheer-sided pinnacles behind. The temple's centrepiece is the **Feitian Scripture Store**, built in 1180 and Sichuan's oldest wooden structure; an octagonal,
eight-metre-high revolving drum, it somewhat resembles a pagoda, painted
black and embellished with eight golden dragons.

In a grove behind Yunyan Si, you'll find racks of spiky weapons and a forest
of three-metre-high wooden posts, atop which you can watch **kung-fu** stylist
Luo Kun performing his high-speed boxing routines five times daily. The reason
for this balancing practice becomes clear if you continue uphill – a surprisingly
short, easy ascent on stone steps – to the mountain's main **summit**, which
forms a small terrace outside **Dongyue Hall**, dedicated to Taoism's supreme
deity, the Yellow Emperor. Every twenty minutes, Taoist monks cross from
here to a tiny pavilion on the adjacent peak, using a **chain bridge** slung over
the fifty-metre-deep chasm and performing acrobatics as they go – you won't
begrudge them their safety rope.

Jianmenguan

Jianmenguan, the Sword Pass (¥50), commands a strategic position along
Shudao as the only break through a tall line of hills 100km from Jiangyou and
50km from Guangyuan. Zhuge Liang's forces defended Shu from invasion here
during the Three Kingdoms period, and Jianmenguan – where the main path
runs through a crevice barely half a metre wide – is said to be the origin of the
Chinese phrase "One monkey stops a thousand men" – applied nowadays to
bureaucratic obstruction. **Buses** run here direct from Guangyuan (see opposite);
coming from Jiangyou you'll be dropped 12km short on the hard shoulder, and
you have to walk down the sliproad for a kilometre to waiting minibuses (¥40
for the vehicle).

Jianmenguan forms a narrow slash in the surrounding 500-metre-high cliffs,
which even today present an obstacle to traffic. The pass itself is marked by a
heavy stone **gateway** and watchtower, around which progress is further slowed
by the number of **restaurants** catering to tourists' needs. A **cable car** (¥20)
heads up to a viewing area and tea terrace, or you can get here from the gateway
by following Shudao's original route – a very narrow, steep, and slippery stone
path along the base of the cliffs – for a couple of kilometres, after which you'll
appreciate the sentiment behind Li Bai's poem "Hard is the Road to Shu". Back
at the gateway, buses on **to Guangyuan** (¥10) pass by until late afternoon.

Guangyuan

GUANGYUAN, on the Jialing river halfway between Chengdu and Xi'an, is a sprawling, unattractive manufacturing town of use as a jumping-off point for **Jiuzhaigou** buses, but is also the birthplace of China's only acknowledged empress, the Tang-dynasty ruler **Wu Zetian** (see p.285). About 2km south along the river from the train station, Tang rock sculptures at **Huangze Si** (¥15) offer a reappraisal of her reign after centuries of censure caused by her overturning of Confucian values, in which women had little status. The entranceway is graced by a unique **phoenix tablet**, representing female Imperial power, instead of the usual dragon. Built into the cliffside behind is a two-storey shrine, **Zetian Dian**, whose lower grotto contains a gilded, life-sized statue of Wu Zetian, fashionably portly in the Tang style.

The cliff above has been carved into a four-metre-high trinity of Amidah Buddha flanked by disciples and Bodhisatvas, including a very feminine Guanyin (identifiable by her vase) showing a definite Indian influence. Most other sculptures at the site have been sadly weathered or vandalized, but look for Ming panels depicting the stages of **sericulture**, from picking mulberry leaves to unravelling the silkworms' cocoons.

Guangyuan's two-kilometre-wide core, traversed by the main street, **Shumen Bei Lu**, is bounded by the Jialing river to the west, and the smaller Nan He to the south. The **train station** and **main bus station** share a huge square next to each other over the Jialing, about 1500m from the centre; bus #2 from here runs down Shumen Bei Lu. Coming from Jianmenguan, you'll end up along southern Shumen Bei Lu at the little **Shumen bus station**. The main bus station has dawn departures for the 348-kilometre run **to Jiuzhaigou**, and buses through the day to Jiangyou, Chengdu and Langzhong. For Jianmenguan, buses go when full from the Shumen station, while for Xi'an, trains are your best bet.

Guangyuan's main **Bank of China** is in the new, eastern section of town on Lizhou Dong Lu – take bus #2 and tell the driver where you want to go. There's **accommodation** near the train station, including a host of hostels (beds ¥25) and *Silian Dajiudian* (☎0839/5505788, ℻5505778; ❸); Shumen bus station's nearest option is the *Zhongsen Hongfu Binguan* (☎0839/3218555; ❸), across the road and around 100m up Shumen Bei Lu – the entrance is uninspiring, but rooms are good. For **meals**, hotpot stalls and restaurants fill the town's backstreets.

Langzhong

About 225km northeast of Chengdu, **LANGZHONG** is a small, unassuming town occupying a broad thumb of land around which the Jialing River loops on three sides. Yet appearances are deceptive: Langzhong has long played a pivotal role in provincial history, even becoming the **Sichuanese capital** for seventeen years at the start of the Qing. Notable people associated with the town include the Three Kingdoms general **Zhang Fei**, who is buried here; **Luo Xiahong**, the Han-dynasty inventor of the Chinese calendar and armillary sphere; and no less than four scholars who became officials during the Tang and Song dynasties. In addition, about a quarter of Langzhong comprises a protected **old town**, Sichuan's largest collection of antique architecture, whose streets, houses and temples provide a fascinating wander.

The Town

Langzong's **old town**, which follows a Tang street plan, covers about two square kilometres southwest of the centre. A good place to orient yourself is

near the river at **Huaguang Lou** (¥4), a three-storey, 36-metre-high Tang-style gate tower on Dadong Jie, last reconstructed in 1867. From the top, there are views south over the river, north to the modern town, and down on the grey-tiled roofs and atriums of Langzhong's classical *siheyuan*, or **courtyard houses**. Some are open to the public, but you can just peek at others through open gateways to see a central hall divided up by wooden screens opening into a courtyard, decorated with potted flower gardens. Worth a visit are **Kong's Courtyard** (¥3), built around 1700; **Hu's Courtyard** (¥8), a Ming-era pharmacy full of antique furniture; and **Dujia Kezhan** (¥4), a hotel founded during the Tang dynasty; it claims to have hosted such luminaries as poets Du Fu and Su Dongpo and now, incredibly, it's back in business. Aside from courtyard homes, small industries survive alongside elderly canteens and teahouses, not to mention touristy shops selling antiques, locally-produced Baoning vinegar and preserved Zhangfei beef.

Langzhong's most popular sight, however, is the **Zhang Fei Miao** (¥30), at the end of Xi Jie. This is a shrine to **Zhang Fei**, Liu Bei's foremost general during the Three Kingdoms period (see box, p.474), a ferocious man who was murdered in 221 AD by his own troops while campaigning at Langzhong. Four courtyards of Ming halls, full of painted statuary and interlocking roof brackets, lead through to the grassy mound of his **tomb**, in front of which a finally triumphant Zhang Fei sits between two demons who are holding his cringing assassins **Zhang Da** and **Fan Qiang** by the hair.

Dozens of other historic sites are scattered around Langzhong, all complementing the old town's streets. The most interesting, just east across the river below a prominent Ming-dynasty pagoda – catch a taxi for ¥5 – is **Scholars'**

Cave (¥40), a peaceful grotto laid with ponds and willows where two students, both later court officials, studied in their youth. Behind here, **Dafo Si** protects a ten-metre-high Buddha which was carved into a rockface in Tang times and has survived more or less intact, along with thousands of smaller carvings and reliefs. An unusual target in the north of the old town is the seventeenth-century **Gongyuan** (¥10), one of only two surviving Imperial examination halls in China. Single-storey cells surround a long courtyard where prospective candidates lived and elaborated on their knowledge of the Confucian classics, on which the exams were based and according to which the country was (in principle) governed.

Practicalities

Langzhong's main road, **Zhang Fei Dadao**, runs south for a couple of kilometres to the river, its mid-point marked by a large **equestrian statue** of Zhang Fei; a further block south from here, **Nei Dong Lu** leads west into the heart of the old town.

Langzhong's two **bus stations** are within 200m of each other north of the statue along Zhang Fei Dadao. There are buses to Chengdu, Guangyuan and Chongqing throughout the day – the northern bus station handles most long-distance traffic, and seems to have the better vehicles. Stalls outside both stations sell bilingual **maps** of Langzhong, with all attractions marked. There are a number of **hostels** (dorms ¥30) in the area, or head down to the statue and take your pick from the **hotels**, such as *Dunhuang Binguan* (☏0817/6224959; ❸), a clean, modern place, though rooms are next to a noisy teahouse. Better yet is *Dujia Kezhan* (☏0817/6239789; ⓕ6224436; ❺), in the south of the old town on Shangxin Jie – rooms are simply furnished, but the Tang-style building can't be beaten for atmosphere, and there's a **restaurant** on the premises. The *Daoxiang Cun Jiudian*, 250m west of the Zhang Fei Statue on Xincun Lu, has excellent Sichuanese food and "rustic" furnishings, including a water wheel. You should also check out *Zhuangyuan Ge*, a Tang-style **teahouse** in the old town on Zhangyuan Jie, not far from Gongyuan. **Banks** are grouped west of the Zhang Fei statue on Xincun Lu.

Southern Sichuan

Some 150km southwest of Chengdu lies the edge of the Red Basin and the foothills of mountain ranges which sprawl into Tibet and Yunnan. Fast-flowing rivers converge here at **Leshan**, where more than a thousand years ago sculptors created **Dafo**, a **giant Buddha** overlooking the waters, one of the world's most imposing religious monuments; an hour away, **Emei Shan** rises to more than 3000m, its forested slopes rich in scenery and temples. As Sichuan's most famous sights, Dafo and Emei Shan have become tourist black holes thanks to easy access – don't go near either during holidays, when crowds are so awful that the army is sometimes called in to sort out the chaos – but at other times they are well worth the effort.

As Leshan's accommodation is depressing (either run-down and central, or expensive and out near Pluto), Dafo is best tackled as a day-trip from Baoguo at the base of Emei Shan, just an hour distant. If you're on your way down south to Yunnan, you could treat both Emei Shan and Dafo as a stopover, in which case **Xichang** is also worth a visit, the reward being the chance to visit villages of the **Yi minority**, as well as a research base from where China's Long March

Southern Sichuan

Baoguo 报国 *bàoguó*
Baoguo Si 报国寺 *bàoguó sì*
Emei Shan Dajiudian 峨眉山大酒店 *éméishān dàjiǔdiàn*
Emei Shan Museum 峨眉山博物馆 *éméishān bówùguǎn*
Fuhu Si 伏虎寺 *fúhǔ sì*
Hongzhushan Binguan 红珠山宾馆 *hóngzhūshān bīnguǎn*

Emei Shan 峨眉山 *éméishān*
Chunyang Dian 纯阳殿 *chúnyáng diàn*
Hongchun Ping 洪椿坪 *hóngchūn píng*
Huazang Si 华藏寺 *huázàng sì*
Jieyin Hall 接引殿 *jiēyǐn diàn*
Jinding 金顶 *jīndǐng*
Jinding Dajiudian 金顶大酒店 *jīndǐng dàjiǔdiàn*
Niuxin Si 牛心寺 *niúxīn sì*
Qingyin Ge 清音阁 *qīngyīn gé*
Wanfoding 万佛顶 *wànfó dǐng*
Wannian Si 万年寺 *wànnián sì*
Woyun Nunnery 卧云庵 *wòyún ān*
Xianfeng Si 仙峰寺 *xiānfēng sì*
Xixiang Chi 洗象池 *xǐxiàng chí*

Leshan 乐山 *lèshān*
Dafo 大佛 *dàfó*
Lingyun Shan 凌云山 *língyún shān*
Lingyun Temple Museum 凌云神院博物馆 *língyún shényuàn bówùguǎn*
Taoyuan Binguan 桃园宾馆 *táoyuán bīnguǎn*
Wuyou Si 乌优寺 *wūyōu sì*

Xichang 西昌 *xīchāng*
Old quarter 古城 *gǔchéng*
Qianma Douhua Fanzhuang 千妈豆花饭庄 *qiānmā dòuhuā fànzhuāng*
South gate 南大门 *nándàmén*
Wumao Binguan 物贸宾馆 *wùmào bīnguǎn*
Xingye Binguan 兴业宾馆 *xīngyè bīnguǎn*
XITS 西昌国际旅行社 *xīchāng guójì lǚxíngshè*
Yuechang Plaza 月城广场 *yuèchéng guǎngchǎng*
Yuedu Jiari Jiudian 月都假日酒店 *yuèdū jiàrì jiǔdiàn*

Around Xichang
Huang Shui 黄水 *huángshuǐ*
Liang Shan 凉山 *liángshān*
Lugu Hu 泸沽湖 *lúgū hú*
Luoji Shan 螺髻山 *luójì shān*
Panzhihua 攀枝花 *pānzhīhuā*
Puge 普格 *pǔgé*
Qionghai Hu 邛海湖 *qiónghǎi hú*
Space Flight Centre 航天发射中心 *hángtiān fāshè zhōngxīn*

space rocket is launched (note that you'll need to apply a week in advance for a visitor's permit). Emei and Dafo are best reached on buses, but it's easier to get to Xichang via the Chengdu–Emei–Kunming rail line.

Emei Shan

One of China's most enchanting mountains, **Emei Shan**'s thick forests and dozens of **temples**, all linked by exhausting flights of stone steps, have been pulling in pilgrims and tourists (the latter far more in evidence) for two thousand years. Originally a Taoist retreat, Emei became a sacred Buddhist site following the sixth-century visit of Bodhisattva **Puxian** and his six-tusked elephant – images of whom you'll see everywhere – and extensive Ming-dynasty rebuilding on the mountain converted most of Emei's temples to Buddhism. Religion aside, the pristine natural environment is a major draw, and changes markedly

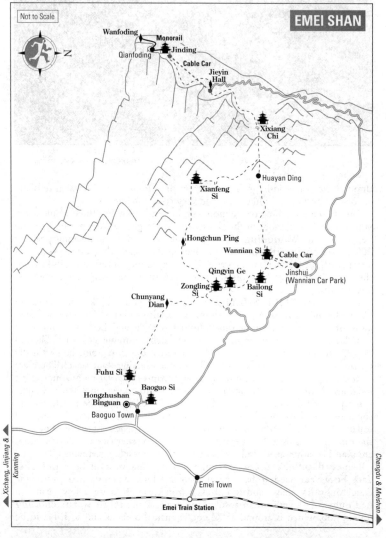

△ Monkeys, sometimes docile, sometimes annoying, are a feature of Emei Shan

through the year – lush, green and wet in the summer; brilliant with reds and yellows in autumn; or white, clear and very cold in winter.

You can see something of the mountain in a single day, but three would allow you to experience more of the forests, spend a night or two in a temple, and perhaps assault **Wanfoding**, the highest of Emei's three undulating peaks at 3099m. It's only worth climbing this high if the weather's good, however: for a richer bag of views, temples, streams and vegetation – everything, in fact, but the satisfaction of reaching the summit – you won't be disappointed with the lower paths.

Access is via **EMEI SHAN** town, a transit point 150km southwest of Chengdu and 7km short of the mountain. **Trains** pull into the station 3.5km away from here, while most **buses** from Chengdu and Leshan terminate at Emei's main street depot, from where you catch a minibus (¥5) or public bus #5 (¥2) from either to the mountain's trailhead at **Baoguo**. Some buses actually terminate at Baoguo, so it's worth asking when buying your ticket. There are **hotels** at Baoguo and the summit area, but **temples** offer far more atmospheric lodgings, charging from ¥10 for a basic dorm bed to more than ¥80 for a double – reception offices display prices. Basic, shared facilities are the norm, though some temples have good rooms with air conditioning, private showers and toilets. Don't leave finding a room too late during the tourist season. **Food** on the mountain tends to be overpriced and ordinary; stir-fries and noodle soups are available either at roadside stalls or vegetarian temple restaurants.

Bring a **flashlight** in case you unexpectedly find yourself on a path after dark. **Footwear** needs to have a firm grip; in winter, when stone steps become dangerously icy, straw sandals and even iron cleats (sold for a few yuan and tied onto your soles) are an absolute necessity. Don't forget **warm clothing** for the top, which is around 15°C cooler than the plains and so liable to be below freezing between October and April. You'll also want an umbrella or other protection against the near certainty of **rain**. A **walking stick** is handy for easing the pressure on thigh muscles during descent – a range is sold along the way. One thing you don't want to take is a heavy backpack – store spare gear at the lower monasteries and hotels, or in Chengdu if you're contemplating a round trip.

Baoguo

BAOGUO is basically one straight kilometre of hotels and restaurants running up past a **bus station** to an ornamental **waterfall**, beyond which are a couple of sights which you can visit without paying the mountain's entry fee. To the right, behind the waterfall, you'll find Emei's **museum** (daily 9am–5pm; free), which has accounts of the development of religion on the mountain, and photos of various rare **plants** found here. There are living examples of these in the surrounding **gardens**, beyond which is **Baoguo Si** (daily 7am–7pm; ¥8), a large and serene temple featuring flagstoned courtyards decorated with potted magnolias and cycads, and high-roofed Ming-style halls. Besides the inevitable Puxian and Guanyin statues, look for the figures of the eight immortals carved into the rear hall's stone staircase, betraying Baoguo's Taoist origins. On a hill opposite Baoguo's entrance, the Ming-dynasty **Shengjishi bell**, encrusted with characters, can be heard 15km away.

If you bear left up the road past the waterfall, it's about 1km to overhanging *zhennan* and **ginkgo trees** outside the charming **Fuhu Si** (Crouching Tiger Temple; daily 6.30am–8pm; ¥6). Emei's largest temple and once associated with the Taoist martial-arts master Zhang Sanfeng, today it's a Guanyin nunnery, with a new five-hundred-luohan hall and the bronze sixteenth-century **Huayan Pagoda**, engraved with 4700 Buddha images.

Practicalities

Mountain buses from Baoguo connect with drop-off points for Qingyin Ge (¥8), Wannian Si (¥11) and Jinding (¥30) from 7am, but they need at least sixteen people to run and so depart infrequently after the early-morning rush. You can also get **long-distance** transport to Chengdu, Chongqing and Leshan from here until late afternoon.

Temples, including the Baoguo Si (❷) and the Fuhu Si (dorms ¥20), offer the best and cheapest **accommodation**. The *Teddy Bear Café* (☏0833/5590135, ✉teddybearcafe@yahoo.com.cn; ❹), just downhill from the bus station, has a helpful manager, doubles and four-bed rooms, and good food (if you stick to their Chinese menu). Just before the waterfall, *Emeishan Dajiudian* (☏0833/5526888, ⓦwww.ems517.com; ❻) is an older hotel in good order, while *Hongzhushan Binguan* (☏0833/5525888, Ⓕ5525666; ❾) is a four-star modern pile past the waterfall and sharp left. All lodgings can make transport bookings, though for a heavy fee.

The mountain

An ascent of Emei can be tackled via two main **routes** from Baoguo: the sixty-kilometre, three-day **southern route**; and the forty-kilometre, two-day **northern route**. Most people knock 15km or so off these by catching **buses** from Baoguo to alternative starting points near either **Qingyin Ge** or **Wannian Si**; leaving early enough, you could make it to the top in one day from either of these via the northern route, descending the next day – though your legs will be like jelly afterwards. If you're really pushed for time, you could get up and down in a single day by catching a minibus between Baoguo Si and **Jieyin Hall**,

Emei Shan flora

Of Emei Shan's three thousand or so plant species, more than a hundred are Chinese endemics, including orchids, primulas, rhododendrons, camellias, cycads and tree ferns. Three unusual trees you'll see growing around temples are the **nanmu**, straight, tall and favoured for temple pillars; the **dove tree**, which has hard spherical fruit, thin pale leaves and a white, two-petalled flower said to resemble a perching bird; and the **ginkgo**, identified by its lobed crescent leaves, which was saved from extinction by its popularity as an ornamental tree in monastery gardens, where it was perhaps grown for the medicinal qualities of its fruit – said to curb desire.

The ginkgo is not the only mountain plant to have benefited from cultivation. Most of Europe's ornamental **roses** are hybrids derived from wild Chinese stock two hundred years ago, and in summer you'll find bushes of their small pink and white ancestors blooming on Emei's lower slopes. The region is also famous for its **tea**, with excellent varieties on offer at Baoguo for around ¥50 per kilo. In addition, the mountain provides a huge range of fungi and **medicinal herbs**, such as gastrodia and fritillary, which you'll see for sale all over the place; make sure you know what you're buying and how to use it, as some are extremely poisonous.

which is located a cable-car ride from the summit, but this way you'll miss out on what makes Emei Shan such a special place. Once past the temples around Baoguo, you'll have to pay Emei's **entry fee** (¥120 for a ticket valid for three days; trails open daily 7am–6pm).

The southern route

From Fuhu Si, the **southern route** passes some minor sights to **Chunyang Dian** (5km from Fuhu Si), a nunnery founded in honour of the Taoist Immortal Lü Dongbin, spookily surrounded by mossy pine trees. From here it's another easy 5km to **Qingyin Ge**, a pavilion built deep in the forest where two streams converge and tumble through a small gorge down **Niuxin Shi**, the ox-heart rock. It's a charming spot, with a small **temple** offering accommodation (en-suite doubles ❸, dorms ¥15), where you can be lulled to sleep by gurgling water and the croaking of Emei's famous **bearded frogs**.

Qingyin Ge is just 3km from Wannian Si (see below), but to continue the southern route, follow the path up past the left side of Qingyin; this takes you along a river bed and past a **monkey-watching area**, before starting to climb pretty steeply through a series of gorges. About 6km further on, **Hongchun Ping** (beds ¥40) is an eighteenth-century temple named after surrounding *hongchun* (toona) trees, and is about as far as you'd make it on the first day. From here it's a very tough 15km of seemingly unending narrow stairs to **Xianfeng Si** (beds ¥40), a strangely unfriendly place, though well forested with pine and dove trees and planted with camellia and rhododendrons. The following 12.5km are slightly easier, heading partly downhill to a dragon-headed bridge, then up again to where the trail joins the north route at **Xixiang Chi** (see opposite), around 43km from Fuhu Si and two-thirds of the way to the summit.

The northern route

Most people start their ascent by catching a bus from Baoguo to Jinshui (Wannian Si car park) at the start of the **northern route**. From here a three-kilometre path or cable car (¥40) leads to **Wannian Si** (daily 7.30am–7pm; ¥6; ❹, dorms ¥20), whose history goes back to the fourth century. Most of the halls burned down in 1945, however, leaving a squat brick **pavilion** out the back, built in 1601, as Emei's oldest structure. Its contents are stunning: three thousand tiny iron Buddhas surround a life-sized enamelled bronze **sculpture of Puxian**, riding a gilt lotus flower astride his great six-tusked white elephant. Weighing 62 tonnes and standing over 7m high, this masterwork was commissioned by the Song emperor Taizu and brought from Chengdu in pieces – note the gold spots on the elephant's knees, which people rub for good luck. Make sure you also visit Wannian's upper halls, which have great views over forested mountain folds.

From Wannian, a steady fourteen-kilometre hike through bamboo and pine groves – you'll pause every now and then to let **mules** ferrying up temple supplies get past – should see you beyond several smaller temples to where the southern and northern routes converge at **Xixiang Chi** (❸, beds ¥20). This eighteenth-century monastery sits on a ridge where Puxian's elephant stopped for a wash, and on cloudy days – being more or less open to the elements and prowled by monkeys – it's amazingly atmospheric, though somewhat run-down and frigid in winter. It's a very popular place to rest up, however, so get in early to be sure of a bed.

On to the summit

Beyond Xixiang Chi the path gets easier, but you'll encounter gangs of aggressive **monkeys** who threaten you for food with teeth bared. They tend to pick on women; showing empty hands and calling their bluff by striding on seems to work, though you will probably feel safer with a stick in your hand and will need to keep a good grip on your bags. The path continues for 9km past some ancient, gnarled rhododendrons to **Jieyin Hall**, where the fifty-kilometre-long road from Baoguo Si, which has snaked its way round the back of the mountain, ends at a **cable car** to the summit (¥40 up, ¥30 down). The area is thick with minibus tour parties fired up for their one-day crack at the peak, and is also somewhere to find a lift back to Baoguo (¥30; 1hr 30min). **Hotels** around Jieyin look good, but they have a reputation for rudeness once they've got your money.

Whether you take the cable car or spend the next couple of hours hoofing it (not to be attempted without cleats in winter), **Jinding**, the Golden Summit (3077m), is the next stop and, for many, the main reason to be up here at all. Just why is a mystery: it's a bleak, windswept area overlooked by a TV antenna, a real disappointment after the mountain's lower reaches. There are two temples: the friendly **Woyun Nunnery** (❹, dorms ¥30) and the oversized **Huazang Si** (❹), whose Ming-dynasty bronze hall was destroyed by lightning in the 1890s, and rebuilt with glazed yellow tiles a century later. It's still being expanded – the present project seems to be installing a pagoda, hopefully with a lightning conductor. There's alternative accommodation nearby at the upmarket *Jinding Dajiudian* (℡0833/55247045; ❻). Jinding has two bright spots: thousands of **padlocks** engraved with couples' names affixed to handrails to symbolize eternal love; and the **sunrise**, which is marvellous on a good day, as it lights up the sea of clouds below the peak. In the afternoon, these clouds sometimes catch rainbow-like rings known as **Buddha's Halo**, which surround and move with your shadow, while in clear conditions you can even make out Gongga Shan (see p.948), 150km to the west. You can also ride a **monorail** (¥50) along the ridge up to **Wanfoding** (Ten Thousand Buddha Summit), Emei's true apex.

Leshan and Dafo

Set beside the wide convergence of the Qingyi, Min and Dadu rivers, 180km from Chengdu and 50km from Emei Shan, **LESHAN** is a spread-out market town with a modern northern fringe and older riverside core, a transit point for visiting the incredible **Dafo**, the Great Buddha, carved deep into a niche in the facing cliffs.

Leshan's main **bus station**, with regular connections to Chengdu, Emei, Xichang, Zigong and Chongqing, is 5km out on the town's northern reaches. If you want to reach Dafo by ferry, catch a taxi (¥8) over to the **ferry terminals** on Binjiang Lu. The best cheap **place to stay** is the *Taoyuan Binguan* (☎0833/231810, ⑤232102; ❸), in two buildings near the ferry docks; make sure you stay in the northern building, as the southern one is pretty musty. There are inexpensive **places to eat** everywhere through the town, with a great **tofu restaurant**, famed for both its plain *douhua* with chilli relish and its stewed bean curd, just up the road from Dafo's north entrance.

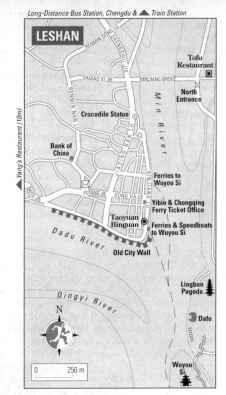

12

SICHUAN AND CHONGQING | Southern Sichuan

Dafo

Impassive and gargantuan, **Dafo** (May–Sept 7.30am–7.30pm; Oct–April 8am–6pm; ¥80) peers out from under half-lidded eyes, oblivious to the sightseers swarming round his head, clambering over his toes and nearly capsizing their boats in their eagerness to photograph his bulk. Tang-dynasty Big Buddha carvings are pretty abundant in Sichuan, but none approaches Dafo's 71-metre height, making him the world's largest Buddhist sculpture. Statistics, however, can't convey the initial impression of this squat icon, comfortably seated with his hands on his knees, looming over you as the ferry nears.

The rough waters below the sandstone cliffs of **Lingyun Shan** had been a problem for shipping since before Qin times, but it wasn't until 713 AD that the monk **Haitong** came up with the idea of filling in the shoals with rubble produced by carving out a giant Buddha image. After Haitong blinded himself to convince the government to hand over funds, the project was continued by various monks and finished by the local governor, Wei Gao, in 803. Once construction started, temples sprang up above the Buddha at Lingyun Shan and on adjacent **Wuyou Shan**, and today you can spend a good three hours walking between the sights.

The site can be accessed from Binjiang Lu either aboard bus #8 to the **north entrance** (where you can hire an English-speaking guide for ¥100) or by ferry (¥30) to Lingyun or Wuyou – the route described below.

Crossing from Leshan jetty to Wuyou Shan, ferries turn in midstream so that both sides get a look at Dafo from beneath – the best view by far – and the vessel tilts alarmingly as people rush to the railings. Ashore, a steep staircase leads up to **Wuyou Si**, a warm pink-walled monastery founded in 742 AD, whose halls occupy the top of Wuyou Shan. The monastery **decorations** are particularly good; look for the splendid gate guardians as you enter, the animated scenes from *Journey to the West* on the second hall (Xuan Zang being carried off by demons, Monkey leaping to the rescue) and the grotesque sculptures inside the Luohan Hall.

Beyond, the path drops down through woodland to the water's edge, where a sturdy covered bridge links Wuyou with **Lingyun Shan**. The gully it crosses was cut in 250 BC on the orders of Li Bing (p.896) to reduce the rapids. On the far side, turn right and follow signs to where **Han-dynasty tomb** chambers at **Maohao Mu** indicate that this may have been a religious site long before the Buddha was carved. Stay on the main path, and you'll find a balustraded terrace offering good views of the river and town, beyond which the five-hundred-metre **Cliff Road**, dating in part to the eighth century, winds down towards Dafo's toes. The upper track continues past minor sights to the terrace around the top of the **Great Buddha** himself. Elbowing your way through the throngs assembling for photos, you'll find yourself up against railings level with Dafo's ear, where you can watch lines descending the slippery **Staircase of Nine Turns** to his feet. You'll begin to appreciate his scale here: Dafo's ears are 7m long, his eyes 10m wide, and around six people at once can stand on his big toenail. There's an insane-looking, modern **statue of Haitong** to one side of the terrace, while the **Lingyun Temple Museum** behind includes accounts of the construction and numerous renovations, and a model of Dafo as he originally appeared, covered in protective pagoda-like roofing.

Past here, the path descends to the **north gate**, from where you can catch bus #8 back to town. On the way down, have a good look at where the three rivers meet – despite Dafo's presence, there are still some vicious currents as brown and black waters mingle over low-lying shoals.

Xichang and around

The long train journey south from Emei Shan town to the Yunnanese border and ultimately Kunming is famous not for the scenery itself, splendid though it is, but for the fact that you rarely catch a glimpse of it. Estimates vary, but there are more than **two hundred tunnels** along the way, some lasting seconds, others several minutes, and you'll soon get fed up trying to get a long look at the peaks and gorges passing the window.

Given its otherwise remote setting in a very undernourished countryside seven hours from Emei Shan by train, **XICHANG**'s friendly bustle and almost prosperous air are surprising. Focus for southwestern China's **Yi community**, and a **satellite launching site** for China's Long March space programme, Xichang is also a staging post for a backroads trip to **Lugu Hu** on the Sichuan/Yunnan border, offering a more interesting alternative to continuing by train to Kunming. In town itself, Xichang's partially walled **old quarter** is just northeast of the centre, a fifteen-minute walk from the bus station via Yuechang Plaza. The old quarter's streets form a cross, of which the southern extension, **Nan Jie**, is the most interesting, running 150m through a busy market and past rickety wooden teahouses to the heavy stone **south gate** and attached battlements.

Practicalities

Xichang's centre forms a kilometre-wide jumble of streets west of the often dry Dong He, with a focus of sorts provided by the open space of **Yuecheng Plaza**, not far from the river on the broad east–west **Chang'an Lu**. Xichang's main **bus station** is 500m west of Yuecheng Plaza on Chang'an Lu, the **train station** around 5km southwest at the end of the #6 bus route. For **accommodation**, turn east out of the bus station to either the *Xingye Binguan* at 60 Chang'an Dong Lu (☏0834/3225570; ➍) or the *Wumao Binguan* opposite at no. 13 (☏0834/3223186; ➋), or head 50m west to the corner of Shengli Lu and the *Yuedu Jiari Jiudian* (☏0834/3234888; ➍). Inexpensive **restaurants** are concentrated around the bus station on Changan Dong Lu and just west of the old south gate on Shangshuncheng Jie, where you'll find excellent Sichuanese snacks at *Qianma Douhua Fanzhuang*.

For **information** on surrounding sights and to organize a space-centre visit, head to **XITS** (☏ & ☏0834/3240007, or ☏13608148339). They're central but hidden away: head 50m west along Chang'an Lu from the bus station, then south down Shengli Lu to the first lane east; XITS are through the gates at the end.

Moving on, it's impossible to get reserved seats on trains here – you'll have to risk upgrading on board. Among the off-the-beaten-track possibilities, **Panzhihua** is five hours south by rail, and has connecting buses west to Lijiang (see p.829). There's also a bus west from Xichang to **Lugu Hu** (see p.840), from where you can take a boat across to the Yunnan side and then a bus to Lijiang; just don't confuse Lugu Hu with Lugu, a small town 50km east of Xichang.

Around Xichang

The area around Xichang, known as **Liang Shan** (the Cool Mountains), is heartland of the Yi community. Minibuses from the Chang'an Lu roundabout head 5km south to **Qionghai Hu**, a large lake where a **museum** exhibits Yi festival clothing and household items, and books written in the Yi script – you'll also see this on official signs around town. For more on the Yi, head 76km south to **PUGE** (buses daily 7am–5pm; ¥15; 2hr), marketplace for surrounding

---

The Yi

Spread through the mountains of southwestern China, the **Yi** form the region's largest – and perhaps China's poorest and most neglected – ethnic group, with a population of around five million. Their shamanistic religion, language and unique, wavy script indicate that the Yi probably originated in northwestern China. Until the 1940s they were farmers with a matriarchal **slave society** divided into a landowning "black" caste, and subordinate tenants and labourers who comprised a "white" caste. Officially, such divisions are gone, but shamanism is certainly still practised and there's a chance of at least a superficial view of the old ways during occasional **festivals**. These can be riotous occasions with heavy drinking sessions, bullfights and wrestling matches interspersed with music and archery displays. Traditionally everyone dressed up, though today this is largely left to the women who don finely embroidered jackets and sometimes twist their hair into bizarre horned shapes, the married women wearing wide, flat black turbans. Best is the **torch festival** at the end of the sixth lunar month, commemorating both an ancient victory over a heavenly insect plague, and the wife of Tang-dynasty chieftain Deng Shan, who starved to death rather than marry the warlord who had incinerated her husband. The Yi new year arrives early, in the tenth lunar month.

hamlets, where you're certain to see people in traditional dress; there's at least one **guesthouse** if you want to delve deeper, though the town is a dump.

To visit the **Space Flight Centre**, 65km north of Xichang, you need a week to arrange a permit and tour through the XITS (which requires your passport number, a photograph and ¥110), though they don't always accept foreigners and the centre closes if a launch is imminent.

To really get off the beaten track, ask XITS to organize a trip 40km south of Xichang to **Luoji Shan**, whose five main peaks rise above 4000m and whose lower slopes are thickly forested. There's some access from Luoji's east side from Puge, but also more adventurous routes around the base of the peaks – requiring horses and at least three days – from the town of **Huang Shui**, south from Xichang on the highway.

Southeastern Sichuan

Surrounding the fertile confluence of the Yangzi and Min rivers 250km from Chengdu, where Sichuan, Yunnan and Guizhou provinces meet, southeastern Sichuan has some intriguing attractions. The town of **Zigong** is a treat, with some well-preserved architecture, dinosaurs and salt mines, especially worth checking out during its Spring Festival lantern displays (though be warned that accommodation doubles in price at this time). Some 80km farther south, **Yibin** offers access to the aptly named **Shunan Bamboo Sea**, and some esoteric **hanging coffins**.

Both Zigong and Yibin are easily accessible **by bus** from Chengdu, Chongqing and Leshan. Approaching from Leshan, you'll encounter yet more monumental religious sculpture at **Rongxian**; the south of town is flanked by carved riverside cliffs, along with an imposing, 36-metre-high **Giant Buddha** protected by a temple frontage. An interesting way out of the region is by bus east to **Luzhou**, and then over to another bamboo forest at **Chishui** in Guizhou province (see p.776).

Zigong and around

ZIGONG, a thriving industrial centre, has long been an important source of **salt**, tapped for thousands of years from artesian basins below the city. In the fourth century the Sichuanese were sinking 300-metre-deep boreholes here using bamboo-fibre cables attached to massive stone bits. By the 1600s, bamboo buckets were drawing brine from wells bored almost a kilometre beneath Zigong, centuries before European technology (which borrowed Chinese techniques) could reach this deep. **Natural gas**, a by-product of drilling, was used from the second century to boil brine in evaporation tanks, and now also powers Zigong's buses and taxis.

Begin a city tour at the splendid **Xiqin Guildhall** on central Jiefang Lu, built in the Qing dynasty by merchants from Shaanxi and now an absorbing **salt museum** (daily 8.30am–5pm; ¥20). Photos and relics chart Zigong's mining history, from pictorial Han-dynasty tomb bricks showing salt panning, to the bamboo piping, frightening metal drills and wooden derricks used until the 1980s. All this is slightly overshadowed by the building itself, whose curled roof corners, flagstone-and-beam halls and gilded woodwork – illustrating Confucian moral tales – were renovated in 1872 by master craftsman Yang Xuesan. Several similar contemporaneous structures survive nearby, most notably **Wangye Miao**, which sits high over the river opposite the *Shawan Binguan* on Binjiang Lu, and **Huanhou Gong**, whose beautifully carved stone gateway overlooks the junction of Jiefang Lu and Zhonghua Lu; both are now highly atmospheric teahouses.

Bus #35 from opposite the *Shawan Binguan* on Binjiang Lu heads northeast to Zigong's suburbs and two other sights. First is **Shenhai Well** (¥8), which in 1835 reached a fraction over 1000m, the deepest ever drilled using traditional methods. Operational until 1966, the twenty-metre-high wooden tripod minehead still overlooks the site, where you can inspect bamboo-fibre cables, stone engravings on the wall detailing the well's development (much of it using buffalo power), and the tiny well shaft itself, corked, reeking of gas, and barely 20cm across. Eight shallow vats in the building behind are evaporation pans, where the muddy brine is purified by mixing in tofu and skimming off the resultant scum as it rises, leaving a thick crust of pure salt when the liquid has been boiled off.

Back on the #35 bus, it's about 45 minutes from Binjiang Lu to the terminus at Zigong's **dinosaur museum** (daily 9am–5pm; ¥40), built over the site of excavations carried out during the 1980s. Near-perfect skeletal remains of dozens of Jurassic fish, amphibians and dinosaurs – including monumental thighbones, and Sichuan's own **Yangchuanosaurus**, a toothy, lightweight velociraptor – have been left partially excavated *in situ*, while others have been fully assembled for easy viewing, posed dramatically against painted backgrounds.

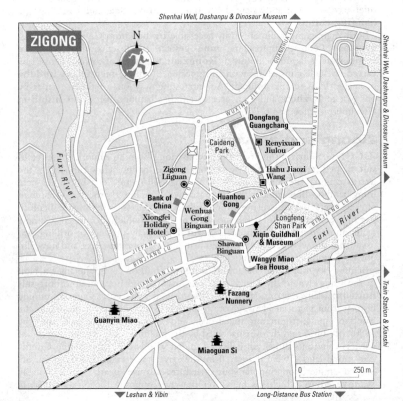

Southeastern Sichuan

One final worthwhile excursion is 15km east from Zigong to the small marketplace of **Xianshi**; buses run from a special stop just short of Zigong's train station. This is one of those unimportant but interesting old villages that Sichuan does so well, comprising a couple of flagstoned streets along a riverbank, full of worn steps, shops selling daily necessities, and a handful of mossy Qing buildings with wavy rooflines and curved firewalls. Best are two weatherbeaten **temples**, both of which are actually bisected by the main street, and the relatively elaborate **Chenjia Citang**, an example of a Sichuanese courtyard building. The last bus back leaves at 4.30pm.

Practicalities

Zigong's compact, hilly centre lies on the north side of the narrow **Fuxi River**. The **long-distance bus station** is about 5km south of town on Dangui Dajie; turn right out of the station and it's 100m to the city bus stop (#35 will drop you outside the central *Shawan Binguan*) – while cabs charge about ¥7. Zigong's **train station** is on Jiaotong Lu, from where bus #33 heads to the *Shawan* hotel. There's no main street in town – all the roads surrounding **Caideng Park** are equally busy, with markets, shops and facilities spread around.

For bedrock **accommodation**, try the *Zigong Lüguan* (**❷**, dorm beds ¥25), which occupies two separate buildings on Ziyou Lu. New and clean is the *Wenhua Gong Binguan* (☎0813/2109999; **❷**), on the pedestrian street behind Huanhou Gong – go up the steps, turn left, and it's 75m along on the right behind a studded red door. Zigong's best mid-range option is the *Shawan Binguan* on Binjiang Lu (☎0813/2208888, ℱ2201168; **❹**), which offers substantial discounts. A touch of luxury is provided by the smart new *Xiongfei Holiday Hotel* at the bottom of Ziyou Lu (☎0813/22118866; **❻**), whose café is the only one in town.

Zigong has an extraordinary density of **teahouses**, even for Sichuan; the most atmospheric are Wangye Miao and Huanhou Gong, with their century-old wood and stonework. Wonton and noodle vendors surround the southern entrance to Caideng Park in a pedestrianized area known as **Dongfang Guangchang**, where you'll also find *Hahu Jiaozi Wang*, which serves thirty excellent types of *jiaozi*, along with Dongbei and Sichuanese snacks. Just east of here, Wangjiatang Lu hosts numerous hotpot restaurants and the mid-range Sichuanese *Renyixuan Jiulou*.

Leaving, there are buses until mid-afternoon to Chengdu, Leshan, Emei Shan, Dazu, Luzhou and Chongqing; twice-hourly departures to Yibin; and daily buses each to Gongxian and Kunming.

Yibin and around

A crowded, grubby port with a modern veneer, the city of **YIBIN** sits where the Jinsha Jiang and Min Jiang combine to form the **Chang Jiang**, the main body of the Yangzi. There's nothing to do here in between organizing transport to surrounding sights, though Yibin produces three substances known for wreaking havoc: enriched plutonium; Wuliangye *bai jiu*, China's second-favourite spirit; and *ranmian*, or burning noodles, whose chilli content has stripped many a stomach lining.

Yibin's kilometre-wide centre focuses on a central **crossroads**, from where Bei Dajie runs north, Minzhu Lu runs south into Nan Jie, Zhongshan Lu heads east to the **docks**, and Renmin Lu runs west. Another orientation point is **Daguan Lou**, an old bell tower just east off Minzhu Lu or south off Renmin Lu, though it's locked up. The main **Beimen bus station** is 250m northwest of the centre off **Zhenwu Lu**, the highway in from Zigong, which skirts the western side of the city. The **Bank of China** (with ATM) and **post office** are next to each other at the bottom of Nan Jie.

Foreigner-friendly budget **accommodation** is scarce; try the *Renhe Binguan* at 69 Renmin Lu (☎0831/8227160; **❸**, dorms ¥25), or the *Shengli Lüguan* on Bei Dajie (**❸**), though you probably won't get into either without some Chinese. Yibin's best mid-range option is the *Xufu Binguan* (☎0831/8189999,

@www.xufugroup.com; ⑤), a comfortable and recently renovated place just north off Renmin Lu. The *Xufu* has a good **restaurant**; otherwise try the canteen-style *Ranmian Fandian*, next to the crossroads on Renmin Lu, where a bowl of cold noodles dressed in chopped nuts, coriander, vinegar and chillies is just ¥2.

Beimen station handles **buses** to, among other places, Chongqing, Chengdu, Zigong and Luzhou (for connections to Chishui in Guizhou province). For regional sights, catch city bus #4 from Nan Jie south over the river to **Nan'an bus station** (15min), from where services to the Shunan Bamboo Sea and the Hanging Coffins depart.

The Shunan Bamboo Sea

Around 75km southeast of Yibin, the extraordinary **Shunan Bamboo Sea** (entry ¥68) covers more than forty square kilometres of mountain slopes with feathery green tufts, and makes for a refreshing few days' rural escape. It's a relatively **expensive** one, however – if you want to see similar scenery at budget rates you're better off heading to Chishui in Guizhou province. The main problem is simply **getting around** within the park; bus services are unpredictable and you'll probably end up having to charter taxis.

Having said all this, Shunan is an undeniably beautiful spot, if a bit spooky given the graceful ten-metre-high stems endlessly repeating into the distance. There's pleasure in just being driven around, but make sure you have at least one walk along any of the numerous paths, and get a look down over the forest to see the bowed tips of bamboo ripple in waves as breezes sweep the slopes. The surreal atmosphere is enhanced by it being a favourite filming location for martial-arts movies and TV series – don't be too surprised if you encounter Song-dynasty warriors galloping along the roads.

Direct **buses to Shunan** are advertised as departing Yibin's Nan'an station, but these may not materialize and it's usually just as quick to catch one of the many buses to **Changning** (¥10), a small town 15km short of Shunan's main **West Gate**, which has bus connections to Chongqing, Chengdu and Luzhou, and minibuses into the park. These go to Shunan's two main settlements of **Wanling** (¥2), 1500m inside the gate, and **Wanli** (¥8), 20km inside, where you'll find plenty of **hotels** – the cheapest charge about ¥50 a bed, though most are mid-range (⑤). Other places to stay are scattered in between; right at the park's centre, *Feicui Binguan* (℡0831/4970111, ⓕ4970155; ④) is a good two-star option.

As for **park transport**, stand by the road and wait for the next bus – they seem to run most frequently in the morning and afternoon, when locals are going to and from their villages – and don't be too surprised if drivers try to overcharge you. Otherwise, ask accommodation to organize a motorbike- or minibus-**taxi**.

The Bo and hanging coffins

Nobody is too sure of the exact history of eastern Sichuan's several **hanging coffin** sites, but they're generally associated with the enigmatic **Bo people**, the ancestors of today's **Tujia** ethnic group, who are scattered through the Three Gorges area into western Hunan and Hubei. The Bo themselves were routed by imperial forces after their leader rashly declared himself emperor during a sixteenth-century rebellion against the local governor. They left behind scores of their cliff-face burials along the broad Dengjia River valley, some 90km south of Yibin near the dispiriting hilltop settlement of **Luobiao**, where transport terminates. Walk downhill for 2km, and you'll see the first wooden coffins

12

above you on the right; **entry** to the site costs ¥10. The coffins are mortised into the cliffs on wooden frames, or placed in shallow caves, with the surrounding rocks daubed in simple ochre designs depicting the sun, people and horses. Locating the coffins high up in the open on wooden galleries, it's believed, was done to aid the return of spirits to the sky.

Buses to the coffins are advertised at Yibin's Nan'an station, but if you can't find direct transport, aim first for **Gongxian** (¥10; 68km), then change to a nearby depot to catch transport to Luobiao (¥7). As it can take up to five hours to make the journey, be aware that this is a very long day-trip from Yibin, and that you'll have to leave Luobiao by mid-afternoon to catch connecting services all the way back.

Dazu and around

About 200km east of Chengdu and 100km west of Chongqing, **Dazu** is the base for viewing some fifty thousand exquisite **Buddhist cliff sculptures** dating back to the Tang and Song dynasties, which are carved into caves and overhangs in the surrounding lush green hills. The two main sites are **Bei Shan**, just outside Dazu, and **Baoding Shan**, 16km to the northeast. What makes these sites so special is not their scale – they cover very small areas compared with more famous works at Datong, Luoyang and Dunhuang – but their quality, state of preservation, and variety of subject and style. Some are small, others huge, many are brightly painted and form comic-strip-like narratives, their characters portraying religious, moral and historical tales. While most are set fairly deeply into rock faces or are protected by galleries, all can be viewed in natural light and are connected by walkways and paths.

The Town and around

DAZU is a small, quiet place whose centre forms a 700-metre-wide rectangle along the north bank of the mild Laixi River. The east side of the rectangle is Longzhong Lu, the north side Beihuan Zhong Lu, and the west side Bei Jie. The **bus station** overlooks the river down at the southeast corner. Right next door, there's **accommodation** at the *Xingyuan Lüguan* (❷, beds ¥30), or three-star comforts another 100m north up Longzhong Lu at the *Dazu Binguan* (☏023/43721888, ℻43722967; ❺), which is either packed with tour groups or empty. A further 500m up Longzhong Lu, the *Jinye Binguan* (☏023/43775566; ❹) is a cosy alternative next to Dazu's tobacco factory. For **food**, cheap noodle and stir-fry places are all over, with a string of inexpensive restaurants on Beihuan Zhong Lu, near the intersection with Bei Jie

Dazu and around		
Dazu	大足	*dàzú*
Baoding Shan	宝顶山	*bǎodǐng shān*
Bei Shan	北山	*běishān*
Dazu Binguan	大足宾馆	*dàzú bīnguǎn*
Guangda Si	广大寺	*guǎngdà sì*
Jinye Binguan	金叶宾馆	*jīnyè bīnguǎn*
Panzhong Can	盘中餐	*pánzhōngcān*
Xingyuan Lüguan	兴源旅馆	*xīngyuán lǚguǎn*

– *Panzhong Can* does great dry-fried green beans, double-cooked pork and stuffed aubergines.

Bei Shan

The carvings at **Bei Shan** (daily 8.30am–5pm; ¥60, students ¥25; joint ticket including Baoding Shan ¥120) include Dazu's earliest works, begun in 892 AD by the Military Governor **Wei Junjing**, who was posted here while campaigning against Sichuanese insurgents. Filling some 264 numbered recesses in two groups and protected by an awning, they are somewhat worn and formal in execution, but offer interesting comparisons with Baoding Shan's livelier carvings. They're easy to reach from town: take the road uphill for 150m from Dazu's northwestern corner at the junction of Bei Jie and Beihuan Zhong Lu, then follow the stone steps and paths ascending Bei Shan for a kilometre or so until you reach the site entrance.

The first, original, group of carvings surrounds a small grotto and features several military pieces – including, tucked away in **niche 1** beside the entrance, a life-sized Wei Junjing in armour, sculpted by a defeated Shu warlord. **Niche 10** here shows a gold-faced Sakyamuni on a lotus surrounded by attendant Bodhisattvas, one of the few examples at Bei Shan showing traces of original paintwork.

Immediately beyond here, Bei Shan's second group of carvings dates from the twelfth century, and decorates a five-metre-high, 500-metre-long overhang. They mostly feature the Bodhisattva of Mercy **Guanyin**, in various incarnations and styles, along with monks, nuns, and private donors who funded the project. **Niche 130** shows an atypically fierce Guanyin as a demon-slayer, each of her many hands holding a weapon (and one severed head); next door in **niche 131** she's in a more usual form, languidly gazing at the moon's reflection. **Niche 136** contains a 4.5-metre-high **prayer wheel**, looking like an octagonal merry-go-round mounted on a coiled dragon, again surrounded by Guanyin images. The Bodhisattva returns seated on a giant peacock in **niche 155**, while the most impressive piece fills **niche 245** with a depiction of the Kingdom of Buddha, showing the trinity surrounded by clouds of Bodhisattvas, with heavenly palaces above and earthly toil below.

Baoding Shan

If you come to Dazu, don't miss **Baoding Shan** (daily 8.30am–6pm; ¥80, students ¥45; joint ticket including Bei Shan ¥120), whose carvings are exciting, comic and realistic by turns. The project was the life work of the monk **Zhao Zhifeng**, who raised the money and designed and oversaw the carving between 1179 and 1245, explaining the unusally cohesive nature of the ten thousand images depicted here. **Buses** (¥2) from Dazu's station leave twice an hour until around 4pm and take thirty minutes for the sixteen-kilometre run.

The bus drops you among a knot of souvenir stalls, with a path bearing right for a kilometre to the main site. Bearing left, however, brings you shortly to **Guangda Si** (¥10), a temple built in honour of Zhao Zhifeng and containing a worn Song-dynasty sculpture of him. Back on the main path is **Dafowan**, the most impressive of several groupings of carvings, whose 31 niches are naturally incorporated into the inner side of a broad, horseshoe-shaped gully. All packed with scenes from Buddhist scriptures and intercut with asides on daily life, they're in amazing condition given that most are unprotected from the weather. Dafowan kicks off with a lion guarding the **Cave of Full Enlightenment**, a deep grotto where twelve life-sized luohans surround the Buddhist trinity, the roof carved with clouds and floating figures. Past here is a smaller work depicting **buffaloes** with their herders, both a symbol of meditation and a tranquil picture of pastoral life, followed by a jutting rock shaped into a spirited **Fierce Tiger Descending a Mountain**. Demonic guardian figures painted in blue, red and green greet you at the overhanging rockface beyond, which follows around to a six-metre-high sculpture of the demon **Anicca** holding the segmented **wheel of predestination** (look for the faint relief near his ankles of a cat stalking a mouse). Next comes a similarly-scaled trinity of **Amidhaba**, **Puxian** and **Wenshu**, Puxian holding a stone pagoda said to weigh half a ton; and then the Dabei Pavilion, housing a magnificent gilded **Guanyin**, whose 1007 arms flicker out behind her like flames, each decorated with an eye and sacred symbol.

By now you're midway around the site, and the cliff wall here is inset with a twenty-metre-long **Reclining Buddha**, fronted by some realistic portraits of important donors, oddly sunk up to their waists into the ground. The following two panels, depicting **Parental Kindness** and **Sakyamuni's Filial Piety**, interestingly use Buddhist themes to illustrate Confucian morals, and feature a mix of monumental busts looming out of the cliff surrounded by miniature figures dressed in Song-dynasty clothing. Next comes the memorable **Eighteen Layers of Hell**, a chamber-of-horrors scene interspersed with amusing cameos such as the Hen Wife and the Drunkard and his Mother. The final panel, illustrating the **Life of Liu Benzun**, a Tang-dynasty ascetic from Leshan, is a complete break from the rest, with the hermit surrounded by multi-faced Tantric figures, showing a very Indian influence.

Chongqing and around

Based around a hilly, comma-shaped peninsula at the junction of the Yangzi and Jialing rivers, **CHONGQING** is southwestern China's dynamo, its largest city both in scale and population. Formerly part of Sichuan province and now the heavily industrialized core of **Chongqing municipality**, the city is also a busy **port**, whose location 2400km upstream from Shanghai at the gateway between eastern and southwestern China has given Chongqing an enviable commercial acumen. While it's not such a bad spot to spend a day or two while arranging **Yangzi river cruises**, in many other respects, however, the **Mountain City** (as locals refer to it) has little appeal. Crowded, fast-paced and not especially welcoming, the city is plagued by oppressive pollution, winter fogs and summer humidity. Nor is there much to illustrate Chongqing's history – as China's wartime capital, it was heavily bombed by the Japanese – though the nearby village of **Ciqi Kou** retains a glimmer of Qing times.

Chongqing has been settled since Ba times (around 1000 BC), with its current name, meaning "Double Celebration", bestowed by former resident **Zhaodun** on his becoming emperor in 1189. The city has a long tradition as a place of defiance against hostile powers, despite being ceded as a nineteenth-century **treaty port** to Britain and Japan. From 1242, Song forces held Mongol invaders at bay for 36 years at nearby **Hechuan**, during the longest continuous campaign on Chinese soil, and it was to Chongqing that the Guomindang government withdrew in 1937, having been driven out of Nanjing by the Japanese. The US military also had a toehold here under **General Stilwell**, who worked alongside the Nationalists until falling out with Chiang Kaishek in 1944. Though still showing a few wartime scars, since the 1990s Chongqing has

Chongqing and around

Chongqing	重庆	chóngqìng
Chaotianmen docks	朝天门码头	cháotiānmén mǎtóu
Chongqing Museum	重庆市博物馆	chóngqìngshì bówùguǎn
Ciqi Kou	磁器口	cíqìkǒu
Hongyan	红岩村	hóngyán cūn
Jiefangbei	解放碑	jiěfàng bēi
Luohan Si	罗汉寺	luóhàn sì
Metropolitan Tower	大都会商厦	dàdūhuì shāngshà
People's Concert Hall	人民大礼堂	rénmín dàlǐtáng
Pipa Shan Park	枇杷山公园	píbāshān gōngyuán
Sanxia Museum	三峡博物馆	sānxiá bówùguǎn
Stilwell Museum	史迪威将军博物馆	shǐdíwēi jiāngjūn bówùguǎn
Zhongjia Yuan	钟家院	zhōngjiā yuàn

Around Chongqing: Hechuan and Diaoyu Cheng

Diaoyu Cheng	钓鱼城	diàoyú chéng
Diaoyu Tai	钓鱼台	diàoyú tái
Hechuan	合川	héchuān
Huguo Si	护国寺	hùguó sì
Pao Tai	炮台	pàotái

Accommodation

Chongqing	重庆宾馆	chóngqìng bīnguǎn
Chung King	重庆饭店	chóngqìng fàndiàn
Huatie	华铁宾馆	huátiě bīnguǎn
Huixian Lou	会仙楼宾馆	huìxiānlóu bīnguǎn
Marriott	重庆JW万豪酒店	chóngqìng JW wànháo jiǔdiàn
Milky Way	银河大酒店	yínhé dàjiǔdiàn
Sanxia	三峡宾馆	sānxiá bīnguǎn

Eating and drinking

Da Paidang	大排挡	dà páidǎng
Lao Sichuan	老四川	lǎosìchuān
Pangzixian Huoguo Cheng	胖子鲜鳝火锅	pàngzi xiānshàn huǒguō
Shi Jie	食街	shíjiē
Xiaobin Lou	小滨楼	xiǎobīnlóu

boomed; now more than two million people rub elbows on the peninsula, with five times that number in the ever-expanding mantle of suburbs and industrial developments spreading away from the river.

Arrival and city transport

Chongqing centres on the four-kilometre-long **peninsula**, whose downtown area and most accommodation prospects surround the eastern **Jiefangbei** commercial district; **Chaotianmen docks**, where Yangzi ferries (see p.929) pull in, are just a short walk away at the eastern tip of the peninsula.

The city's seething **main long-distance bus** and **train stations** are on a complex traffic flow near river level at the western end of the peninsula; to reach the eastern end, either hail a cab or take the underpass below the road and ride the **escalator** up to Zhongshan Er Lu, turn right, and you can catch buses #413 or #405 to Jiefangbei or #114 to Chaotianmen. Some long-distance buses, however, terminate at other depots scattered far out in the suburbs – cabs might be your only option. The **airport** is 30km away, connected to the airlines

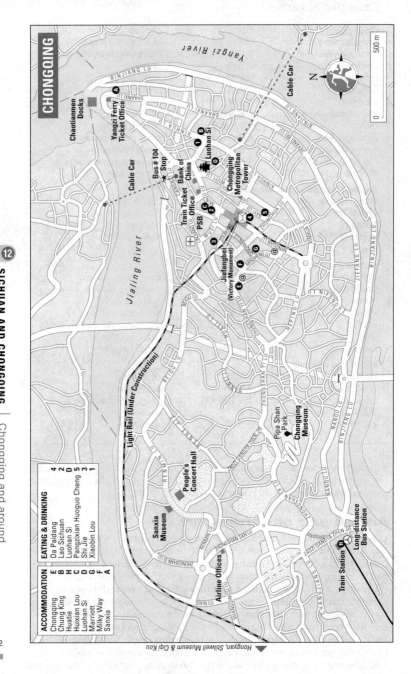

SICHUAN AND CHONGQING | Chongqing and around

CHONGQING

Yangzi River

Cable Car

Cable Car

Chaotianmen Docks

Yangzi Ferry Ticket Office

BINJIANG LU

SHAANXI LU

SHAANXI LU

XINHUA LU

Luohan Si

Bus #104 Stop

Bank of China

Train Ticket Office

PSB

Chongqing Metropolitan Tower

Jialing River

Jiefangbei (Victory Monument)

Light Rail (Under Construction)

RENMIN LU

Sanxia Museum

People's Concert Hall

ZHONGSHAN SAN LU

Pipa Shan Park

Chongqing Museum

Airline Offices

ZHONGSHAN SAN LU

Train Station

Long-distance Bus Station

Hongyan, Stilwell Museum & Ciqi Kou

N

0   500 m

ACCOMMODATION
Chongqing	E
Chung King	B
Huatie	H
Huixian Lou	C
Luohan Si	D
Marriott	G
Milky Way	F
Sanxia	A

EATING & DRINKING
Da Paidang	4
Lao Sichuan	2
Luohan Si	1
Pangxixian Huoguo Cheng	5
Shi Jie	3
Xiaobin Lou	1

Buses to Chengdu, Hechuan, Leshan, Emei town, Dazu, Zigong, Yibin, Changning (for the Shunan Bamboo Sea) and beyond depart through the day from Chongqing's main long-distance station; it's a crowded place, but buying tickets here is easy enough. The adjacent **train station** has a single, overnight service to Chengdu – slower than the bus, but you save the price of a hotel room – and useful links through to Kunming, Guiyang, Xi'an, Beijing, Shanghai, Guangzhou and Ürümqi. Aside from the station, **train tickets** are sold on the ground floor of the building at the corner of Minzu Lu and Wusi Lu, 100m northeast from the *Huixian Lou* hotel – look for the window. They charge a ¥5 mark-up per ticket, sell timetables and are very helpful. By **air**, there are daily departures to Chengdu, Guiyang, Kunming, and provincial capitals across China; buy tickets and catch the **airport bus** (¥15; 6am–6.30pm) at the airlines office on Zhongshan San Lu.

Yangzi ferries

Yangzi ferries, including public services, a hydrofoil and luxury cruise boats, depart daily year-round through the Three Gorges to Yichang and Wuhan in adjacent Hubei province. The main **tourist season**, when you might have trouble getting tickets for next-day travel, is from May through to October.

Luxury cruise ships charge from ¥4000 per person to Wuhan, and need to be booked through a reputable **tour agent**, either overseas, **online** (try ⓦ www.china highlights.com, ⓦ www.orientalroyalcruise.com or ⓦ www.chinaodysseytours.com, all of whom offer seasonal discounts) or through various **travel services** in Chongqing (see "Listings", p.928).

The **public ferry ticket office**, for both ferries and the **hydrofoil** (which runs nonstop to Yichang; ¥352), is at the dock end of Shaanxi Lu at Chaotianmen, on the left as you head downhill. Inside on the right is a board in Chinese showing the next three days' departures, with the **name**, **number** and destination of each ship; the ticket counter is straight ahead. Chongqing has vague docking arrangements, so try to locate your vessel during daylight.

The following **per-person prices** for ferry tickets from Chongqing should be used as a guide only. Note that the bottom bunk is about ten percent cheaper.

	2-berth cabin	3/4-berth	8-berth	16-berth
Yichang	¥1022	¥578	¥270	¥186
Wuhan	¥1644	¥823	¥386	¥277

If you decide to use an agent to set up your tour, establish exactly what the price entails. Many talk of guided tours around sights or trips along the Three Little Gorges as if they're part of an inclusive package, but the price is normally for your cabin only; other agents will try to sell you an all-inclusive ticket that includes tours for all the sights on the way. For further details of on-board conditions, and the boat ride through the Three Gorges to Yichang, see pp.928–931.

office on Zhongshan San Lu by a shuttle (daily 6am–6.30pm; ¥15), from where bus #103 runs via Jiefangbei to Chaotianmen.

Chongqing's gradients mitigate against walking everywhere, and nobody uses bicycles. **City buses** (¥1–2) are comprehensive but bus-stop schedules sometimes bear little resemblance to the route followed – check with drivers if possible. **Taxis** cost ¥5 to hire; drivers aren't too unscrupulous, but it won't hurt to be seen studying a map along the way. There's also a **city rail** line due to start up in 2006, though this will be of more use to residents than tourists.

Accommodation

Chongqing's most convenient area to hole up in is the peninsula's eastern end around Jiefangbei and Chaotianmen, with one option near the train and bus station for late arrivals. There's little budget accommodation, however; most places are mid-range or upmarket – though everywhere discounts during the winter, when few tourists are in town.

Chongqing 235 Minsheng Lu ☏023/63845888, ℻63830643. Business and wedding party venue, with a swimming pool and at least four restaurants. Standard rooms, in an older, separate wing, are not a bad deal, especially if you can wrangle a discount. ⑤

Chung King 41–43 Xinhua Lu ☏023/61609999, ℻63843085. Slightly run-down operation in a 1930s building, but the rooms are in a reasonable state of repair. ⑥

Huatie Between the bus and train stations. This is a well-run budget hotel managed by the railways, but the area is grotty. Dorm beds ¥25, ④

Huixian Lou 186 Minzu Lu ☏023/63845101, ℻63844234. Central, with tidy furnishings and a few English-speaking staff. Doubles are quite a good deal, though bathrooms can be a little musty; the seven-bed dorms, with shared bathroom, are cheap for town. Dorm beds ¥50, ⑤

Luohan Si Xiao Shizi ☏023/63737144. The Luohan temple has rooms available, though these are meant for visiting clergy and they often stick tourists in the basic hostel next door. Dorm beds ¥20–30.

Marriott 77 Qingnian Lu ☏023/63888888, ⓦwww.marriotthotels.com. The best located of Chongqing's many upmarket international chains. Doubles from ¥1200. ⑨

Milky Way 49 Datong Lu ☏023/63808585, ⓦwww.cqyinhe.com. Smart, newly refurbished and very friendly, a favourite with Yangzi tour groups. ⑦

Sanxia 1 Shaanxi Lu, Chaotianmen docks ☏023/63555555. A new two-star hotel opposite the ferry booking hall; rates halve in low season. ¥260

The City and around

During its Qing-dynasty heyday, the **peninsula** *was* Chongqing, described during the 1890s by the Australian journalist George Morrison (who became famous enough to have a Beijing street named after him) as an enormously rich port with mighty walls, temples, pagodas and public buildings. Civil war through the early twentieth century, the Japanese occupation of eastern China, and the subsequent flight to Chongqing of the Chinese government and millions of refugees brought an end to those days, however; after three years of Japanese bombers following the Yangzi upstream to the junction and unloading their cargoes, much of the peninsula was reduced to rubble. Rebuilt in a cheap and cheerless manner during the 1950s, the peninsula as a whole remains grimy and shambolic – most development seems to be targeting Chongqing's newer, western suburbs – though it's gradually being modernized to resemble a miniature Hong Kong, complete with skyscrapers, hills and a profit-hungry populace.

Three worthwhile sights lie west of Chongqing's peninsula along a twelve-kilometre strip of the Jialing river: the wartime US command centre at the **Stilwell Museum**, the Communist headquarters at **Hongyan Cun**, and antique streets at the one-time port town of **Ciqi Kou**. All can be tied together into a single trip – from Cangbai Lu near Jiefangbei, city bus #104 runs past the museum and terminates at Hongyan, where you can catch bus #808 to Ciqi Kou. The journey takes up to ninety minutes in all and costs around ¥4. It's also possible to take a day-trip north to the Song-dynasty fortress of **Diaoyu Cheng** at Hechuan.

Jiefangbei and the east end of the peninsula

Isolated by a broad, paved pedestrian square and glassy modern tower blocks, **Jiefangbei**, the Victory Monument, marks Chongqing's social and commercial heart. The area is always packed to capacity with noisy, well-dressed crowds flitting between restaurants, cafés and the huge covered **market** on adjacent Bayi Lu, or shopping at the surrounding upmarket department stores. The monument itself was a memorial to Sun Yatsen before being appropriated by the Communists in 1949 to celebrate their liberation of the city from seventy years of colonial and right-wing occupation – though you'd expect them to have chosen something more inspiring than this twenty-metre-high clock tower.

Heading northeast along Minzu Lu, you'll find the peninsula's sole surviving temple, **Luohan Si** (daily 8am–6pm; ¥5), hidden just off the street but given away by the incense sellers hanging around the gates. Founded during the Tang dynasty and named for its luohan hall added in 1885, the temple unfortunately took a direct hit from a bomb in 1942 and is still being restored. The luohan hall is intact, however, with a maze of 524 life-sized, grotesque statues of Buddhist saints to wander through – though the most lively, an isolated statue of the inebriated, authority-mocking **Ji Gong**, stands outside on his own. There's a good **vegetarian restaurant** here, too, open at lunchtime.

Across the road and around the corner from the temple, a **cable–car station** on Cangbai Lu offers rides high across the river to northern Chongqing (¥1.5); there's another cable car to the southern suburbs from Xinhua Lu. Views from either cable car take in river traffic, trucks collecting landfill in low-season mud, and distant hills – merely faint grey silhouettes behind the haze.

To spy on more waterfront activity, head down to **Chaotianmen docks**, a five-minute walk downhill from Luohan Si along Xinhua Lu. The paved **viewing area** on the high bank overlooking the tip of the peninsula was built in 1999, and makes a great perch to look down on **Yangzi ferries** and barges moored along the river; funicular trains ferry passengers and the inquisitive to water level from here. The viewing area is also somewhere to appreciate Chongqing's pollution – there are days when you can barely make out the centre of the river, let alone the far bank.

The west end of the peninsula

The peninsula's west end is mostly a business district, but there are a couple of sights to visit in passing. The mighty **Peoples' Concert Hall** on Renmin Lu was built in the 1950s along the lines of Beijing's Temple of Heaven, and accommodates four thousand opera-goers in the circular, green-tiled rotunda (where you can sit for ¥5 outside performance times). You can get here on the #104 bus from opposite the cable-car station on Cangbai Lu. Facing it across a porphyry-paved plaza, the **Sanxia Museum** is due for completion in 2006, and plans to provide historical displays on the city and Three Gorges – presumably incorporating the **Chongqing Museum** (¥5), at the time of writing located on Pipa Shan Zheng Jie on the south side of Pipa Shan Park (catch any bus heading down Zhongshan Lu to the park's north gate). Though dusty and neglected, the museum has a marvellous array of **Eastern Han tomb bricks**, carved in relief with either images of the dragon-bodied sun god Risheng, or scenes of contemporary life – best is a twelve-metre-long depiction of an army drilling with chariots, while the emperor is entertained by acrobats in his tent.

The Stilwell Museum

Just outside the peninsula on Jialingxin Lu (if you're on the #104 bus, get off at the "Liziba" stop, take the set of steps opposite, then turn right and it's 100m uphill), the **Stilwell Museum** (¥5) occupies the former home of General Joseph Stilwell, Chief Commander of the US forces' China, Burma and India operations from 1942 until 1944. Stilwell, who spoke Chinese and had served as a military attaché in China during the 1930s, had to coordinate both the recapture of Burma and re-establishment of overland supply lines into China from India, and the Nationalist–Communist alliance, which had been decidedly shaky since its establishment in 1938. In the end, his insistence that equal consideration be given to both the Guomindang and CCP caused him to fall out with Chiang Kaishek, and he retired in October 1944. The modernist 1930s building has been decked out in period furniture, with informative photo displays charting Stilwell's career. Also featured are the volunteer **Flying Tigers** who flew supplies into China over "the Hump" of the Himalayas after the Burma Road was cut in 1941 – of 1170 flights, 514 crashed. T-shirts of a P-40 Tomahawk fighter plane with tiger's eyes and teeth are sold in the lobby (¥40).

Hongyan

HONGYAN (daily 8.30am–5pm; ¥18), a scattering of European brick buildings set among pretty gardens, is where China's wartime government set up in 1938 – wisely remote from the easily targeted peninsula. Mao was absent most of the time, but he visited under US auspices in August 1945 to negotiate a postwar coalition government with the Nationalists. Chiang's insistence that the Red Army disband led to nothing but a lukewarm agreement, however, described by Mao as mere "words on paper", and nobody was surprised at the subsequent resumption of civil war.

In truth, the Communists had little influence in national affairs during the course of the war, and so Hongyan's focus is on ideology rather than action: signs pick out the room used as the CCP propaganda department, the bed Mao slept in, buildings inhabited by Communist luminaries, without once mentioning the reasons behind their importance. As long as you're after atmosphere rather than information, however, it's interesting enough – and the heroic **waxworks** here of Mao and Zhou Enlai (who spent far more time here than Mao) are worth the entrance fee.

Ciqi Kou

Though well within the modern city's boundaries, **CIQI KOU**, a former porcelain production centre and port, incredibly retains a handful of flagstoned, 100-year-old streets and wooden buildings, and offers an idea what the rest of Chongqing might once have looked like. Bus #808 from Hongyan drops you outside the village gates; on your right, **Zhongjia Yuan** (¥3) is a well-restored *siheyuan*, or courtyard house, built by a Qing official. The English-speaking caretaker provides knowledgeable accounts of the organization of a Chinese household of the time, and the relevance of the antique furniture, clothing and carvings in each room. This is Ciqi Kou's most interesting single structure, but you can spend an enjoyable couple of hours roaming the half-kilometre-long main street and adjacent lanes, thronged with touristy crafts shops (selling local embroideries and romantic paintings of Ciqi Kou), old-style teahouses featuring traditional music recitals, and small restaurants. The #808 bus runs back to Hongyan until at least 5pm.

Hechuan and Diaoyu Cheng

In 1242, invading Mongol forces under Mengge Khan were brought up short by Song defences at **Diaoyu Cheng**, a fortified hilltop just outside the town of **HECHUAN**, some 60km north of Chongqing. Harried by generals Wang Jian and Zhang Yu, the Mongols needed 36 years and two hundred battles to defeat the Chinese, succeeding only after Mengge had been killed by cannon shot in 1259.

Set in pretty, rural surrounds, Diaoyu Cheng's fortifications are still visible, as is the battlefield. Buses to Hechuan (¥25) leave Chongqing's main bus station three times an hour from 8am and take ninety minutes; on arrival, walk across the plaza in front of Hechuan's bus station and you'll find battered minibuses for the eight-kilometre run to Diaoyu Cheng (¥3). Buses back to Chongqing depart until 5pm.

You wind up at a short flight of steps leading up to **Diaoyu Cheng** (¥10); at the top, take the right-hand path until you see a small set of steps down to your right. These lead past some weatherbeaten Buddhist carvings to the remains of the Song observation post of **Diaoyu Tai**, the "Fishing Platform". Opposite is **Huguo Si**, now serving as a museum, with period stonework, paintings and maps illustrating key campaigns, and a useful diorama of the citadel – from which you'll realize that one of the reasons for Diaoyu's strength was the amount of fresh water available up here in ponds. Follow the escarpment from here and you'll come to crenellated **battlements**, parts of which are original. Immediately right is one of the old **gate towers**, from where a long flight of steps descends to the plain below; turning left, it's around 1500m to **Pao Tai**, the cannon emplacement, below which is the 1259 battlefield, now a rather beautiful set of terraced fields hemmed in by the cliffs.

Eating and drinking

Chongqing's centre is alive with canteens and food stalls, and at meal times already busy side streets and markets become obstacle courses of plastic chairs, low tables and wok-wielding cooks. Local tastes lean towards Sichuanese *xiaochi*; a local speciality is the use of puréed garlic as a dressing, which only the Sichuanese could get away with. **Hotpot** is believed to have originated here, with the basic ingredients arriving on plates, not skewers, so the pots are divided up into compartments to prevent everyone's portions getting mixed up.

Bayi Lu off Jiefangbei has been nominated as a "tasty eating street", with numerous places to snack; otherwise, the restaurants below provide a good introduction to Chongqing's culinary potential. At Jiefangbei, **café** chains such as *Shangdao*, and a *KFC*, are your best bets for non-Sichuanese fare. Chongqing Beer is the local brew, served in squat, brown-glass bottles.

Restaurants

Da Paidang Bayi Lu. Great atmosphere, with everything on offer, from *tangbao* dumplings to fresh fish, cold *xiaochi*, stews and rice-coated steamed pork, being cooked or displayed at the front. Either place your order with staff here and sit down in the right-hand canteen to eat, or bear left into the restaurant and use the menu.

Lao Sichuan Minzu Lu, beside the *Huixian Lou* hotel. Do yourself a favour and eat at this Chong-qing institution, featuring not only classic Sichua-nese dishes, such as "wool" beef, *gongbao jiding*, and cold pork with garlic, but also more delicate options including chrysanthemum aubergine, and smoked duck with a steamed rice coating. The English menu is uninspired, so use the Chinese one (with photos). ¥40 a head.

Luohan Si Luohan Si Jie. This sparely furnished vegetarian temple restaurant serves everything from humble *douhua*, soft tofu served with a chilli relish, to imitation spareribs or smoked goose. Order off a Chinese menu board by the entrance, and take your place at the communal tables. You can eat well here for ¥15 a head.

Pangzixian Huoguo Cheng Bayi Lu. An inexpen-sive, noisy hotpot place on the second floor, one of many in this street.

Shi Jie Zourong Lu. Easy to miss, the small entrance – with buns and snacks displayed – is next to a flight of stone steps. It's a good place to sample Chongqing's *xiaochi*, such as sticky rice dumplings, bitter gourd with sesame oil, "shadow-lantern" beef (very thinly sliced and wind-dried), and dry-fried beef in chilli oil. An English menu is available.

Xiaobin Lou Xinhua Lu. Upstairs is a mid-priced Sichuanese restaurant, while downstairs you sit among concrete trees and folksy furnishings to eat set meal samplers of local snacks (mostly dump-lings and noodles) at around ¥10 a person.

Listings

Airlines The China Airlines office is on Zhongshan San Lu (☎023/63660444).

Banks and exchange Two useful branches of the Bank of China are located at 104 Minzu Lu, and next to the *Huixian Lou* hotel; both have ATMs and change traveller's cheques.

Bookshops The Xinhua Bookstore just west of Jiefangbei on Zourong Lu has Chinese-language maps and guides on the first floor, and a small, unusually diverse stock of English-language titles on the fourth floor.

Consulates The Metropolitan Tower on Wuyi Lu has a Canadian consulate in room 1705 (☎023/63738007), and a British one in room 2802 (☎023/63810321).

Internet There are several Net bars scattered through the centre; a convenient option is above the small branch of the Xinhua bookshop on Minsheng Lu, near the *Chongqing* hotel.

Post office The post office is at 5 Minquan Lu 400010 (daily 8.30am–9.30pm).

PSB The foreign affairs department is on Linjiang Lu, just east of Wusi Lu (☎023/63847017).

Travel services Most accommodation has tour desks for booking Three Gorges cruises, many of which are affiliated with the following long-established agents, all located at the eastern end of the peninsula: CTS, 39 Wusi Lu (☎023/63782666, ℱ63803333); CITS, 151 Zourong Lu (☎023/69093333, ⓦwww.citscq.com); Yangtze River Cruise International Travel Service, 99 Zhongshan Er Lu (☎023/63522955, ℱ63505789); CYTS, 109 Zourong Lu (☎023/63709619, ℱ63905408). Alternatively, you can try one of the smaller operators which surround the ferry ticket office on Shaanxi Lu, but be warned that, on the whole, they're a bunch of misleading hustlers. Make exhaustive enquiries about exactly what you're getting before handing any money over, and if you don't like the way you're being treated, go elsewhere.

The Yangzi River: Chongqing to Yichang

Sichuan means "Four Rivers", and of these the most important is the **Yangzi**, once virtually the only route into the province and today still a major link between Sichuan and eastern China. Rising in the mountains above Tibet, the river defines the border with Tibet and Yunnan, and skirts Sichuan's western ranges before running up to Chongqing, from where it becomes navigable year-round to all vessels as it continues east towards Shanghai and the coast. It receives seven hundred tributaries as it sweeps 6400km across the country to spill its muddy waters into the East China Sea, making it the third

The Yangzi river: Chongqing to Yichang

Yangzi River	长江	*cháng jiāng*
Baidi temple	白帝庙	*báidì miào*
Baidicheng	白帝城	*báidì chéng*
Fengdu	丰都	*fēngdū*
Lanruo Dian	兰若殿	*lánruò diàn*
Qutang gorge	瞿塘峡	*qútáng xiá*
Shibaozhai	石宝寨	*shíbǎo zhài*
Three Gorges	三峡	*sānxiá*
Three Little Gorges	小三峡	*xiǎo sānxiá*
Wanzhou	万州	*wànzhōu*
Wu Xia	巫峡	*wūxiá*
Wushan	巫山	*wūshān*
Xiling gorge	西陵峡	*xīlíng xiá*
Zhongxian	中县	*zhōngxiàn*
Zigui	秭归	*zǐguī*

longest flow in the world. Appropriately, one of the Yangzi's Chinese names is **Chang Jiang**, the Long River, though above Yibin it's generally known as **Jinsha Jiang** (River of Golden Sands); the name applied by foreigners to the river as a whole, Yangzi, derives from a ford near Yangzhou in Jiangsu province.

Although people have travelled along the Yangzi since recorded history, it was not, until recently, an easy route – though it was still preferable to traversing Sichuan's difficult, bandit-ridden mountains. The river's most dangerous stretch was the 200-kilometre-long **Three Gorges**, where the waters were squeezed between vertical limestone cliffs over fierce rapids, spread between **Baidicheng** and Yichang in Hubei province. Well into the twentieth century, nobody could negotiate this stretch of river alone; steamers couldn't pass at all, and small boats had to be hauled literally inch by inch through the rapids by teams of **trackers**, in a journey that could take several weeks, if the boat made it at all.

Since the 1950s, however, when the worst of the reefs were cleared, the journey through the Three Gorges' spectacular scenery to Yichang has become one of China's tourist highlights, and is now plied by both **public ferries** and **cruise boats**. It's set to become even easier when the **Three Gorges Dam** above Yichang (see p.508) reaches capacity around 2009, raising water levels through the gorges by over 100m and effectively turning the Chongqing–Yichang stretch into a huge lake. The downside of this is that some of the scenery – not to mention entire towns along the way – is being **submerged**, though the towns have been rebuilt on higher ground, and all the major historical sites will be preserved one way or the other.

Practicalities

Chongqing is the favourite departure point for the two-day cruise downriver through the **Three Gorges** to Yichang, and it's only a day from Yichang to Wuhan. You can do the same trip upriver, but the journey takes twice as long – though the dam may change all this. Many of the towns along the river are also accessible by **road** from Chongqing, so you can shorten the river trip by picking up the ferry along the way. There are two main **cruise options**, both of which run year-round: relatively inexpensive public ferries, which stop along the way to pick up passengers; and upmarket cruise ships, which only stop at tour sites. **Prices** from Chongqing to Yichang and Wuhan, along with practical information on buying both ferry and cruise-ship tickets, are given in the "Moving on from Chongqing" box, p.923.

Public ferries are crowded and noisy, with berths starting at **first class** – a double cabin with bathroom – and descending in varying permutations through triples and quads with shared toilets, to a bed in 12- or 24-person cabins, and, ultimately, a mat on the floor. Don't expect anything luxurious, as even first-class cabins are small and functional. If you're boarding anywhere except the endpoints, vessels are unlikely to arrive on time, so get to the dock early; once aboard, make haste for the purser's office on the mid-deck, where available beds are distributed. It's very unusual for foreigners to be sold anything below cabin class, but if you are, pick up a bamboo mat and get in early to claim some floor space – as the stairwells, decks and toilets are awash with bodies, sacks and phlegm long before the boat pulls out. **Dawn departures** from Chongqing used to be the norm, but an increasing number now leave in the evening to hit the Three Little Gorges (see p.931) early on the third day. Try to avoid leaving between 10am and 12am as you'll hit the first gorge too early and the third too late to see much. Not all ferries pull in at all ports, and some stay longer than others; schedules can change en route to compensate for delays, so it's possible that you'll miss some key sights. At each stop, departure times are announced in Chinese; make sure you have them down correctly before going ashore. Shared toilets fast become vile, and **meals** (buy tickets from the mid-deck office) are cheap, basic and only available for a short time at 7am, 10am and 6pm. Bring plenty of snacks, and in winter, **warm clothing**.

Alternatively, you could travel in style on a **cruise ship**. These vessels verge on five-star luxury, with comfortable cabins, glassed-in observation decks, games rooms and real restaurants. They're usually booked out by tour parties during peak season, though at other times you can often wrangle discounts and get a berth at short notice.

Chongqing to Yichang

The cruise's initial 250km, before the first of the Three Gorges begins at Baidicheng, takes in hilly farmland along the riverbanks, with the first likely stop 172km from Chongqing at **FENGDU**, the "Ghost City". Behind rises **Ming Shan**, covered in shrines and absurdly huge sculptures dedicated to **Tianzi**, King of the Dead, all contained inside a **park** (¥100); the main temple here, **Tianzi Dian**, is crammed full of colourful demon statues and stern-faced judges of hell, as are cheaper fairground-style **sideshows** around town. This is also the first place you'll see white cliffside **markers**, showing how high the water will rise after the dam is fully operational.

A further 70km downstream is **ZHONGXIAN**, famous for its fermented bean curd and, rather more venerably, the **Hall of Four Virtuous Men** where the poet Bai Juyi is commemorated. Next comes the midstream **Shibaozhai**, a 220-metre-high rocky buttress; grafted onto its side is the twelve-storey, bright red **Lanruo Dian** (Orchid Hall), a pagoda built in 1819. The temple above was built in 1750, famed for a hole in its granary wall through which poured just enough rice to feed the monks; greedily, they tried to enlarge it, and the frugal supply stopped forever.

Ferries might pull in overnight 330km from Chongqing at the halfway point of **WANZHOU** (formerly Wanxian), an old city which has been extensively rebuilt above its original site. It's also on a main road, with **buses** running west to Chongqing and southeast to **Enshi** in Hubei, from where there are further services down to the Hunanese town of **Dayong**.

The Three Gorges

The **Three Gorges** themselves begin at **BAIDICHENG**, a town located strategically 450km from Chongqing at the mouth of the first gorge, and

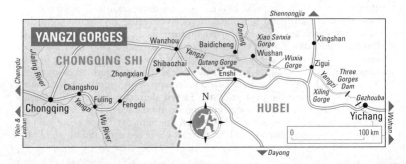

closely associated with events of the *Romance of the Three Kingdoms* (see box, p.474). It was here in 265 AD that **Liu Bei** died after failing to avenge his sworn brother Guan Yu in the war against Wu. These events are recalled at the **Baidi temple** (¥40), where there's a tableau of Liu Bei on his death-bed. The accompanying **Zhang Fei temple**, commemorating Liu's other oath brother, was recently relocated brick by brick to the nearby town of Yunyang.

Beyond Baidicheng, the river pours through a sheer slash in the cliffs and into the first gorge, **Qutang**, the shortest at just 8km long, but also the narrowest and fiercest, its angry waters described by the Song poet Su Dongpo as "a thousand seas in one cup". The vertical cliffs are pocked by **Meng Liang's staircase**, square holes chiselled into the rock as far as a platform halfway up, where legend has it that the Song general **Yang Jiye** was killed by traitors. When his bodyguard climbed the cliff to recover the headless corpse, he was deceived by a monk whom he later hung by the feet from the cliff face. Other man-made features include wooden scaffolds supporting four 2000-year-old **hanging coffins**, similar to those at Gongxian near Yibin (see p.917).

Through Qutang, the small town of **WUSHAN** serves as a likely half-day stopover to detour north up Xiao San Xia, the **Three Little Gorges**, lining the **Daning River**. On a good day, this five-hour, 33-kilometre excursion offers the best scenery of the entire Chongqing–Yichang trip: beautiful countryside, fast, clear water, tiny villages, monkeys, remains of a Qin-era path cut into the cliffs, and the awesome **Longmen Gorge**. When you first arrive in Wushan, bargain with minibuses (¥15) for the ten-minute ride to the Xiao San Xia dock, where you pay ¥150 for a seat in a modern, open-topped canal boat.

Wushan also sits at the mouth of the second set of gorges, **Wu Xia**, 45km of fantastic precipices on the Yangzi where the goddess **Yao Ji** and her eleven sisters quelled some unruly river dragons and then turned themselves into mountains, thoughtfully positioned to help guide ships downriver. Nearby, a rock inscription attributed to Zhuge Liang proclaims: "Wu Xia's peaks rise higher and higher" – words that somehow so frightened an enemy general that on reading them he turned tail and fled with his army.

Farther downstream in Hubei, **ZIGUI** was the birthplace of the poet **Qu Yuan**, whose suicide a couple of millennia ago is commemorated throughout China by dragon-boat races. Zigui is also where 76-kilometre-long **Xiling** gorge begins. The Xiling stretch was always the most dangerous: Westerners passing through in the nineteenth century described the shoals as forming weirs across the river, the boat fended away from threatening rocks by trackers armed with iron-shod bamboo poles, as it rocked through into the sunless, narrow chasm. The scenery hasn't changed a great deal since, but the rocks, rapids and trackers have gone and the boat passes with relative ease, sailing on to a number of smaller gorges, some with splendid names – Sword and Book, Ox Liver and Horse Lung – suggested by the rock formations. At the end, the monstrous **Three Gorges Dam** at **Sandouping** is another possible stopover, with regular minibuses running tourists from the dock to the dam site (see p.507).

Past here are the sheer cliffs and shifting currents of **Nanjin Pass**, and after that the broad gentle plain above **Gezhouba**, an enormous complex of dams, power plants, locks and floodgates. The boat squeezes through the lock, which can take some time, to dock in **Yichang**. Aside from continuing downriver from here to Wuhan, you could take a bus from Yichang to the **Shennongjia** reserve in Hubei's mountainous north – for details, see Chapter 7.

Western Sichuan

Very much on the fringes of modern China despite recent infrastructure improvements, Sichuan's western half, extending north to Gansu, south to Yunnan and west to Tibet, is in every respect an exciting place to travel. The countryside couldn't be farther from the mild Chengdu plains, with the western highlands forming some of China's most imposing scenery – broad grasslands grazed by yaks and horses, ravens tumbling over snowbound gullies and passes, and unforgettable views of mountain ranges rising up against crisp blue skies.

Though larger towns through the west have to a certain extent been settled by Han and Hui (Muslims) – the latter spread between their major populations in adjoining provinces – historically the region was not part of Sichuan at all but was known as **Kham**, a set of small states covering what is now western Sichuan, plus the fringes of Qinghai and Yunnan. The Tibetans who live here, called the **Khampas**, speak their own dialect, and see themselves as distinct from Tibetans further west – it wasn't until the seventeenth century, during the aggressive rule of the **Fifth Dalai Lama**, Lobsang Gyatso (see p.1099), that monasteries here were forcibly converted to the dominant Gelugpa sect and the people brought under Lhasa's thumb. The Khampas retain their tough, independent reputation today, and culturally the region remains emphatically Tibetan, containing not only some of the country's most important lamaseries, but also an overwhelmingly Tibetan population – indeed, statistically a far greater percentage than in Tibet proper.

You're likely to find yourself crossing western Sichuan via one of three areas, depending on your long-term travel plans. For a brief dip into the region, the forested mountains at **Wolong Nature Reserve** are a relatively short trip northwest of Chengdu, where you can see captive **pandas** and then do some exploring below the snowcapped peaks of **Siguniang Shan**. If you're heading north out of the province **to Gansu**, you first want to aim for the walled town of **Songpan**, horse-trekking centre and base for excursions to the nearby scenic reserves of **Huanglong** and **Jiuzhaigou**. Beyond Songpan, the road continues north via a Tibetan monastery at **Langmusi**, and so over into Gansu province.

The immense region due **west of Chengdu** is accessed from the administrative capital **Kangding** – itself worth a stopover for easy access to the nearby

---

Visiting monasteries

Among the draws of many towns in western Sichuan are their Tibetan Buddhist **monasteries**, most of which belong to the yellow-hat **Gelugpa sect** – though other sects are represented, as is **Bon**, Tibet's native religion (see p.940). Monasteries form huge medieval-looking complexes sprawling over hillsides, with a central core of large, red-walled, gold-roofed **temples** surrounded by a maze of smaller buildings housing monks and staff. Monasteries are **free to enter**, except where noted in the text; if there are no signs to the contrary, assume that **photography** is forbidden inside temples. **Monks** are generally friendly, encouraging you to explore, steering you firmly away from closed areas, and sometimes offering **food and accommodation** – though don't take these for granted. Most importantly, remember to orbit **clockwise** around both individual temples and the complex as a whole – the only exception to this rule being at the region's few Bon temples.

Hailuogou glacier and **Tagong grasslands**. Beyond here you have the choice of two routes, both of which head out of the province. The first weaves northwest to Tibet via the monastery towns of **Ganzi** and **Dêgê**, with a faith-inducing mountain pass and Dêgê's **Scripture Printing Hall** as the pick of the sights along the way. The second route runs west of Kangding to the high-altitude seat of **Litang**, site of another monastery, before dividing: the main road continues west to the Tibetan border at **Batang** (at time of writing, crossing **overland into Tibet** from Sichuan was still forbidden for travellers), while the other drops south to scenic valleys surrounding **Daocheng** and **Xiangcheng** and, past them, into Yunnan.

Travel in western Sichuan used to be tough going, but better roads and buses mean that it's not always the severe endurance test that it used to be. You'll still need some stamina, however: journey times between towns remain long, roads twist interminably, breakdowns are far from uncommon, and landslides, ice or heavy snow can block roads for days at a time. One plus is that drivers are careful, as many buses now carry "black box" recorders and speed alarms. It's worth noting that almost all the region rises above 2500m – one pass exceeds 5000m – and you'll probably experience the effects of altitude (see p.42). You'll need to carry enough **cash** to see you through, as there are no banks capable of dealing with traveller's cheques, though there are a few ATMs. Be aware too that **bus fares** are surprisingly high – sometimes double the usual amount. As for the **seasons**, the area looks fantastic from spring through to autumn – though warm, weatherproof clothing is essential whatever the time of year. Once the winter snows have set in, you'll need an infinitely flexible timetable.

Wolong, Siguniang Shan and around

Ideal for those with limited time, the round trip from Chengdu to **Wolong and Siguniang Shan** allows a quick sniff around western Sichuan's highlands, plus the chance to do some trekking and to see pandas in what approximates the wild. **Buses** to Wolong or **Rilong** (for Siguniang Shan) leave early in the morning from Chengdu's Chadianzi station, and also from **Dujiangyan** (see p.896). Three-day **tours** to Siguniang Shan run from the *Jiaotong*, *Sam's* or *Holly's* in Chengdu (see Chengdu Listings, p.894), and you can arrange to leave the tour at Wolong on the return leg and make your own way back. It's also possible to push on from Siguniang Shan further into Sichuan's west.

Wolong

Covering a respectable two thousand square kilometres of high-altitude forest 140km northwest of Chengdu in the Qionglai Shan range, **Wolong Nature Reserve** was established in 1975 as the first region specifically protecting the **giant panda**. Wolong's highland valley and steep mountains, green with undisturbed pine and bamboo forests, are home not just to the panda, but also white- and blue-eared pheasants and the unbelievably coloured, grouse-like Temminck's tragopan; there are also scattered groups of golden monkeys and near-mythical snow leopards. But don't expect to find these rarities ambling down local roads – you'll need to spend months getting worn out in Wolong's dense, wet, rough undergrowth for the chance of encountering any of these animals face to face.

You can, however, see around twenty captive giant pandas easily enough at Wolong's modern **research base** (¥30), where they have been given spacious open-air pens to play or snooze the days away. The base's **breeding programme** has been unusually successful recently, especially given the panda's notorious reluctance to get down to it in captivity, and there are often younger animals on show – far more boisterous creatures than their somnambulistic parents.

Wolong consists of two parts: the research base itself, and a small cluster of buildings 7km further west along the main road at **WOLONG ZHEN**. Much of Wolong Zhen comprises accommodation and inexpensive restaurants, but there's also the new **Panda Museum** (¥20), whose dioramas featuring stuffed pandas, clouded leopards and other beasts are beautifully arranged but uninformative.

Further west again, several marked **walking tracks** head a little way up into the hills, through some tight gorges. None is particularly remote or strenuous, but don't attempt them if the weather looks bad; the best is **Yinchang Gou** (Silver Mine Gully) some 10km from Wolong Zhen.

Practicalities

Wolong is four hours from Chengdu (¥31) and around three from Dujiangyan (¥15). There's **accommodation** just outside the research base at the elderly but tidy *Xiongmao Shanzhuang* (℡0837/6243011, ℱ6243014; ➏), or plenty more up the road at Wolong Zhen: *Wolong Shanzhuang* (℡0837/624688, ℱ6246111;

Wolong, Siguniang Shan and around

Wolong Nature Reserve	卧龙自然保护区	*wòlóng zìrán bǎohùqū*
Giant panda	大熊猫	*dàxióngmāo*
Jiumei Jiujia	九妹酒家	*jiǔmèi jiǔjiā*
Panda Museum	大熊猫博物馆	*dàxióngmāo bówùguǎn*
Red panda	小熊猫	*xiǎoxióngmāo*
Shawan	沙湾	*shāwān*
Sitongyuan Binguan	四通源宾馆	*sìtōngyuán bīnguǎn*
Wolong Shanzhuang	卧龙山庄	*wòlóng shānzhuāng*
Wolong Zhen	卧龙镇	*wòlóng zhèn*
Xiongmao Shanzhuang	熊猫山庄	*xióngmāo shānzhuāng*
Yinchang Gou	银厂沟	*yínchǎng gōu*
Siguniang Shan	四姑娘山	*sìgūniang shān*
Changping Gou	长坪沟	*chángpíng gōu*
Haizi Gou	海子沟	*hǎizi gōu*
Qingnian Lüguan	青年旅馆	*qīngnián lǚguǎn*
Rilong	日隆	*rìlóng*
Shuangqiao Gou	双桥沟	*shuāngqiáo gōu*
Siguniang Binguan	四姑娘宾馆	*sìgūniang bīnguǎn*
Xuequan Binguan	雪泉宾馆	*xuěquán bīnguǎn*
Danba	丹巴	*dānbā*
Ma'erkang	马尔康	*mǎ'ěr kāng*
Ma'erkang Binguan	马尔康宾馆	*mǎ'ěr kāng bīnguǎn*
Tusi Guanzhai	土司官寨	*tǔsì guānzhài*
Zhuokeji	桌克基	*zhuōkè jī*
Xiaojin	小金	*xiǎojīn*
Dianhua Binguan	电话宾馆	*diànhuà bīnguǎn*

Pandas

Two animals share the name panda: the **giant panda**, black-eyed symbol of endangered species worldwide; and the unrelated, racoon-like **red panda**, to which the Nepalese name "panda" was originally applied in the West. The Chinese call the giant panda *da xiongmao*, meaning big bear-cat.

News of giant pandas first reached Europe in the nineteenth century through the French zoologist and traveller **Père Armand David**, who came across a skin in China in 1869. They are decidedly odd creatures, bearlike, endowed with a carnivore's teeth and a digestive tract poorly adapted to their largely vegetarian diet. Though once widespread in southwestern China, they've probably never been very common, and today their endangered status is a result of human encroachment combined with the vagaries of their preferred food – **fountain bamboo** – which periodically flowers and dies off over huge areas, leaving the animals to make do with lesser shrubs and carrion, or starve. Half of Sichuan's panda habitat was lost to logging between 1974 and 1989, which, coupled with the results of a bamboo flowering during the 1980s, reduced the total wild population to a thousand animals, though a recent survey found that their numbers have bounced back to 1200. There are about a hundred at Wolong, with the remainder scattered through twelve other **reserves** in Sichuan, Yunnan and Guizhou.

In response to the international attention their plight garnered, the Chinese government set up a panda study programme at Wolong in association with the **World Wide Fund for Nature**, accompanied by successful **breeding programmes** here and in Chengdu. The government has also arrested (and sometimes executed) anyone found harming pandas. The most serious of the programmes' problems in the past have been that reserves were isolated from each other, leading to inbreeding, and were just too small to obviate the effects of the bamboo's cyclic lifestyle, though the formation of fourteen new interconnected reserves in 1995 was a step towards relieving the situation.

❼) is a plush conference-centre-type operation with huge rooms and soft beds; *Sitongyuan Binguan* (☎0837/6246949, ℉6246772; **❻**) is a standard mid-range place; while just up the hill heading west out of town, *Jiumei* (**❷**) is one of many **restaurants** also offering beds. **Minibus taxis** provide transport between Wolong Zhen and the research base or walking tracks – either will cost about ¥5–10 a person depending on bargaining skills. **Heading on**, ask at your accommodation about where to catch buses back to Dujiangyan and Chengdu or on to Rilong and Siguniang Shan – the latter bus currently calls in to *Jiumei* for a breakfast stop around 9am.

Siguniang Shan

West of Wolong Zhen, there's a twenty-kilometre run up the ever-narrowing valley before you exit a gorge to face an abrupt mountain range blocking the view ahead. Rather than tackling this, the road slaloms northwest up less severe gradients to alpine pastures spotted with yak herds, edelweiss, gentian and daisies, and to a rocky, 4500-metre-high pass, typically draped in Tibetan prayer flags, where you might see **blue poppies** growing in August. On the other side you're out of Wolong Reserve, and the hills are suddenly overgrazed and eroded, but just as you notice this the snowy heights of **Siguniang Shan** pop into view. Siguniang means "Four Girls", and there is indeed a row of **four peaks**, the highest of which touches 6250m and looks most poetic lit by a low sun. The base for exploring the area is **RILONG**, a small Tibetan hamlet and tourist centre which hugs a bend in the road some 50km from Wolong. **Accommodation** possibilities here include the two-star *Siguniang Binguan* (☎0837/2791666; ❺), with a tame vulture and nominally Tibetan architecture; the tidy *Xuequan Binguan* (❸); and the *Qingnian Lüguan* (❷, beds ¥20). These establishments can organize **rental** of horses, camping and climbing gear, and **guides** if wanted.

Rilong sits south of three valleys which run up below the snow-etched peaks; there are thick birch and pine forests draped in strings of "old man's beard", patches of meadow, and wildlife such as marmots, hares, pheasants, and the splendid lammergeier, or bearded vulture. The eastern, shortest, valley is **Haizi Gou**, which features a couple of lakes; **Changping Gou** is the middle option, following steep-sided slopes past Tibetan villages and small temples to three smaller peaks west of Siguniang Shan; and westerly **Shuangqiao Gou**, which has a vehicle track – used by tour buses – and even more peaks. **Hiking** and **horses** are the best ways to get around, but come prepared for very changeable and potentially cold **weather**, even in summer.

Xiaojin and Ma'erkang

Beyond Siguniang Shan, public buses probe deeper into western Sichuan. An hour from Rilong, **XIAOJIN** is a gritty place of tiled box design laid out along hairpin bends above a deep gorge. If you get stuck here – as the Long Marchers did in 1935 after crossing Daxue Shan from Moxi (see p.947) – stay next to the bus station at the *Dianhua Binguan* (☎0837/2782888; ❷) and fill in time tracking down Xiaojin's mosque, defunct nineteenth-century church, Buddhist monastery, and the remains of two ancient iron chain suspension bridges (the latter 5km out of town on the Ma'erkang road).

Kangding (see p.945) is an easy half-day bus ride from Xiaojin via **Danba** (from where you can find direct transport to **Ganzi**; see p.949), but reaching Songpan will most likely take a couple of days with a stopover in the capital of Aba Prefecture, **MA'ERKANG**. This is a litter-free, modern Tibetan town of a dozen streets some four hours north of Xiaojin; the only foreign-friendly **accommodation** is the *Ma'erkang Binguan* (☎0837/2822726, Ⓕ2831508; ❸), one block behind the bus station on Tuanjie Jie. Daily **buses** continue to Songpan (see p.938), and you can use credit cards to recharge your finances at the Agricultural Bank's **ATM** near the hotel. There's a busy **monastery** on the slopes overlooking Ma'erkang, and 7km east, back at the junction with the Xiaojin road (taxis charge ¥15), **Zhuokeji** is a stone-built Tibetan village of some twenty tightly packed houses with brightly-coloured window frames and flower gardens overlooking barley fields; the village gates are guarded by a wooden cannon. On the hill opposite, the sheer, stark walls and watchtower of the unoccupied **Tusi Guanzhai** (Landlord's Fortress) offer a bleak contrast – this was another site utilized by Mao during the Long March.

Chengdu to Songpan and Gansu

The five-hundred-kilometre trip north from Chengdu via **Songpan** to the border with **Gansu** province hauls you through a region that's eminently Tibetan – the border village of **Langmusi** presents a vivid taste of monastic life – yet also underscored by a couple of lower-profile ethnic groups, and faint echoes of Tibet's original animistic religion. Scenically, the mountainous

Chengdu to Songpan and Gansu

Aba Autonomous Prefecture	阿坝自治州	ābà zìzhì zhōu
Huanglong	黄龙	huánglóng
Huanglong Gusi	黄龙古寺	huánglóng gǔsì
Huanglong Shanzhuang	黄龙山庄	huánglóng shānzhuāng
Middle Temple	中寺	zhōngsì
Jiuzhaigou	九寨沟	jiǔzhài gōu
Five-coloured Lake	五彩池	wǔcǎi chí
Long Lake	长海	chánghǎi
Nuorilang	诺日朗	nuòrì lǎng
Pearl Beach Falls	珠滩瀑布	zhū tān pùbù
Primeval Forest	原始森林	yuánshǐ sēnlín
Shuzheng	树正	shùzhèng
Accommodation		
Jinde	金德宾馆	jīndé bīnguǎn
Jiuzhaigou Binguan	九寨沟宾馆	jiǔzhàigōu bīnguǎn
Jiuzhaigou Zhaodaisuo	九寨沟招待所	jiǔzhàigōu zhāodàisuǒ
Longtianyuan	龙天院宾馆	lóngtiānyuàn bīnguǎn
Minzhu	民主饭店	mínzhǔ fàndiàn
Shenshan	神山宾馆	shénshān bīnguǎn
Langmusi	郎木寺	lángmùsì
Maoxian	茂县	màoxiàn
Fengyi Dajiudian	风仪大酒店	fēngyí dà jiǔdiàn
Songpan	松潘	sōngpān
East Gate	东大门	dōngdàmén
Gusong Qiao	古松桥	gǔsōngqiáo
Mosque	古清真寺	gǔ qīngzhēn sì
North Gate	北门	běimén
South Gate	南门	nánmén
Accommodation		
Jiaotong	交通宾馆	jiāotōng bīnguǎn
Gusong Qiao	古松桥宾馆	gǔ sōngqiáo bīnguǎn
Shunjiang Horse Treks	顺江旅游马队	shùnjiāng lǚyóu mǎduì
Songpan	松潘宾馆	sōngpān bīnguǎn
Wenchuan	汶川	wènchuān
Zöigê	诺尔盖	nuòěr gài

backdrop is enhanced by vivid blue waters at **Huanglong** and **Jiuzhaigou** reserves, both accessed from Songpan – just note that these are firmly on the Chinese tourist map, and are subject to severe visitor overload throughout summer and autumn. With this in mind, a few lesser-known reserves, rich in alpine grasslands, waterfalls and views, may be more appealing, and can be reached on **horseback** from Songpan.

Buses to Songpan leave at dawn from Chengdu's Chadianzi bus station – it's on the #82 bus route from outside the *Jiaotong* hotel, but this early in the morning you'll need to arrange a taxi through your accommodation. What with having to go out to Chadianzi a day in advance to buy tickets too, you may find it easier to use an agency, despite their fees, or leave later in the day and aim first for Dujiangyan, Wenchuan or Maoxian; buses for all these places on the Songpan road leave from Chandianzi until around 3pm. Direct buses to Jiuzhaigou or Huanglong – but not Songpan – depart from the Xinnanmen station. Alternatively, the new **Jiuzhai airport**, 30km outside Songpan, has daily flights to and from Chengdu. Arriving from Gansu, you'll enter the region via Langmusi (see p.942).

Tours to Huanglong and Jiuzhaigou are offered by every travel agent in Sichuan, but avoid public holidays if you don't want to pay through the nose. Regional roads are fairly good, though landslides can cause long strandings or detours – some tours from Chengdu actually travel to Jiuzhaigou via Jiangyou (p.899), avoiding Dujiangyan and Songpan altogether.

Wenchuan, Maoxian and the Qiang

Eastern Sichuan's plains end abruptly at Dujiangyan, from where the road twists up into the mountains as it follows the Min river valley past a succession of hydroelectric dams. The main towns along the route are **Wenchuan** and **Maoxian**, which don't offer much reason to stop unless you started late in the day and are looking for a **bed** – Maoxian's *Fengyi Dajiudian* (☏0837/7427188; ❷), on the main road, is one of many offerings. Up in the surrounding stony hills, however, you'll see the flat-roofed, rectangular split stone houses and twenty-metre-high watchtowers of the **Qiang**, who tend the apple and walnut groves lining the roadside. The Qiang themselves are easily identifiable: most rural Sichuanese wear white headscarves – in mourning, they say, for the popular Three Kingdoms minister Zhuge Liang – but the Qiang, who were persecuted by Zhuge, generally wear black turbans instead.

North of Maoxian, the valley narrows considerably while the hills become even starker and more prone to **landslides**. As the road continues to climb towards Songpan, you pass numerous small villages where white yaks, dressed in coloured ribbons and bridles, provide tour-bus photo opportunities.

Songpan

SONGPAN – also known as **Songzhou** – was founded 220km north of Chengdu in Qing times as a garrison town straddling both the Min River and the main road to Gansu. Strategically, it guards the neck of a valley, built up against a stony ridge to the west and surrounded on the remaining three sides by eight-metre-high stone **walls**. These have recently been restored, making it one of Sichuan's few surviving walled towns, though renovations also cleared away the old wooden buildings which gave Songpan so much character. Fortunately the shops, stocked with handmade woolen blankets (¥800–1200), fur-lined jackets (¥320), ornate knives, saddles, stirrups, bridles and all sorts of jewellery, still cater primarily to local Tibetans and Qiang. If you want to see what Songpan used to be like, head east out of town over the river to the **Tibetan quarter**, a low-key assemblage of wooden houses and dusty lanes.

Songpan itself forms a small, easily-navigated rectangle: the main road, partially pedestrianized, runs for about 750m from the **north gate** straight down to the **south gate** – both mighty stone constructions topped with brightly painted wooden pavilions. Around two-thirds of the way down, **Gusong Qiao** is a covered bridge over the Min whose roof, corners drawn out into long points, is embellished with painted dragon, bear and flower carvings. Side roads head off to the **east gate** – another monumental construction – and west into a small grid of market lanes surrounding the town's main **mosque**, an antique wooden affair painted in subdued yellows and greens, catering to the substantial Muslim population. Just outside the south gate is a **second gateway**, with what would originally have been a walled courtyard between the two, where caravans entering the city proper could be inspected for dangerous goods.

The reason most people stop in Songpan is to spend a few days **horse-trekking** through the surrounding hills, which harbour hot springs and waterfalls, grassland plateaus, and permanently icy mountains. **Tours** offered by Shunjiang Horse Treks (☏0837/7231201 or 7233916), on the main road between the bus station and the north gate, work out at around ¥100 a person per day for three to twelve days, including everything except entry fees to reserves. Accommodation is in tents and the guides are attentive, though prepare for extreme cold and tasteless food; some groups have bought and slaughtered a goat (¥400) to bolster rations. Note that the friendly veneer of Shunjiang's staff disappears rapidly if they're presented with a complaint, so be sure to agree beforehand on exactly what your money is buying.

Practicalities

Busy **Jiuzhai airport** is 30km to the northeast, with transport waiting for Songpan, Huanglong and Jiuzhaigou. Songpan's new **bus station** is about 250m outside the north gate on the main road to Huanglong, Jiuzhaigou and Gansu. There's **accommodation** here at the *Jiaotong Binguan* (☏0837/7231818; ❺, dorms ¥30), which, in addition to dorms, provides Songpan's best mid-range deal. Alternatively, there are clean double rooms above Shunjiang Horse Treks (❶); they have toilets and you can shower across the road at the public bathhouse for ¥3. Right by the bridge, *Gusong Qiao Binguan* (☏0837/7232900; ❷) is barely worth the price but is one of the few hotels inside Songpan's walls; the main clutch of tourist hotels, overpriced and under-maintained, is just southeast of town on the Chengdu road and includes the reasonable *Songpan Binguan* (☏0837/7232662; ❻). Songpan's **water** – hot or otherwise – flows at unpredictable times, so use it when available. The Agricultural Bank of China, about 100m south of the north gate, has an **ATM** accepting credit cards.

Songpan's **places to eat** revolve around the numerous noodle joints between the north gate and the bus station; there's a slightly more lavish Muslim restaurant (with English sign and crisp roast duck) some 100m inside the north gate. South of the bus station, *Emma's Kitchen* (☏0837/8802958, ✉emmachina@hotmail .com) is the best of several **foreigners' cafés**, serving a tasty burger or pizza, and – only if asked – offering good **information** about local tours and bus times. *Maoniurou gan* (yak jerky) is sold in shops around town; you should also try *qingke jiu*, local **barley beer**.

There are three early-morning bus departures to Chengdu – miss these, and you can catch buses to Maoxian, Wenquan or Dujiangyan (until around 11am) and look for transport from there. In summer, there are also two buses daily each to Huanglong and Jiuzhaigou, and one each to Ma'erkang (p.936) and Zöigê – where you'll have to change for onward services to Langmusi and Gansu (p.942).

Huanglong and Jiuzhaigou

Northeast of Songpan, the perpetually snow-clad Min Shan range encloses two separate valleys clothed in thick alpine forests and strung with hundreds of impossibly-toned **blue lakes** – said to be the scattered shards of a mirror

Bon

Scattered through Sichuan's northwestern reaches, the **Bonpa** represent the last adherents to Tibet's native religion, **Bon**, before it fused with Buddhist ideas to form Lamaism. A shamanist faith founded by **Gcen-rabs**, one of eighteen saints sent to clear the world of demons, Bon lost influence in Tibet after 755 AD, when the Tibetan royalty began to favour the more spiritual doctrines of Buddhism. As Yellow-hat Sect Lamaism developed and became the dominant faith, the Bonpa were forced out to the borders of Tibet, where the religion survives today.

Though to outsiders Bon is superficially similar to Lamaism – so much so that it's often considered a subsect – the two religions are, in many respects, directly opposed. Bonpa circuit their stupas anti-clockwise, use black where Lamas would use white, and still have rituals reflecting **animal sacrifice**. Because of this last feature, both the Chinese government and Lamas tend to view Bon as a barbaric, backward belief, and Bonpa are often not keen to be approached or identified as such. Bon monasteries survive at Huanglong and several towns in the central Aba Grasslands.

belonging to the Tibetan goddess **Semo**. Closest to Songpan, **Huanglong**, a string of lakes and small ponds in a calcified valley, is relatively small and can be walked around in a few hours; further north on a separate road, **Jiuzhaigou Scenic Reserve** is grander in every respect and requires a couple of days to see properly. Both are targets of intense tourism – except in midwinter, don't come here expecting a quiet commune with nature, as the parks clock up a million or so visitors annually – but beneath this traditional Tibetan life continues: yaks are still herded, prayer wheels turn in the streams, and shrines adorned with prayer flags protect unstable cliffs against further slips.

Aside from direct buses and flights from Chengdu, both reserves can be reached on good roads **by bus** direct from either Songpan or each other – making it possible, for instance, to travel from Songpan to Huanglong, spend a few hours there, and then go on to Jiuzhaigou in a single day; the last buses from Huanglong to either Jiuzhaigou or Songpan depart mid-afternoon. For Huanglong, you can charter a five-person **minibus** from outside Songpan's north gate (¥200 return) – the cafés can set this up if you need help. Note that you can also reach Jiuzhaigou by bus via either **Jiangyou** (see p.899) or **Guangyuan** (see p.901).

Huanglong

Huanglong (¥110, students ¥80) lies 60km northeast of Songpan via the small town of **Chuanzhusi**, with its giant hillside Long March memorial statue of a soldier with upraised arms, and the **Xuebaoding pass** below the red rocks of Hongxing Yan. Xuebaoding itself is the Minshan range's highest peak, a 5588-metre-high white triangle visible to the east on clear days. On the far side, Huanglong reserve covers over a thousand square kilometres of rough terrain, though the accessible section which everyone comes to see is a four-kilometre-long trough at an average altitude of 3000m, carved out by a now-vanished glacier. Limestone-rich waters flowing down the valley have left yellow calcified deposits between hundreds of shallow blue ponds, and their scaly appearance gives Huanglong – "Yellow Dragon" – its name.

An eight-kilometre circuit track – much of it on well-made boardwalks over the fragile formations, but potentially tiring given the altitude – ascends east up the valley from the main-road **park gates**, through surprisingly thick deciduous woodland, pine forest and, finally, rhododondron thickets. On a good day, open stretches give broad views east to 5000-metre-high peaks. Pick of the scenery includes the broad **Golden Flying Waterfall** and the kilometre-long calcified slope **Golden Sand on Earth**, where the shallow flow tinkles over innumerable ridges and pockmarks. Around 3km along, the small **Middle Temple** (the lower one has long gone) was once an important **Bon** shrine; today it seems inactive – even if signs do ask you to circuit to the right in the Bon manner. At the head of the valley, **Huanglong Gusi** is a slightly grander Qing building, featuring an atrium and two small Taoist halls, dedicated to the local guardian deity **Huanglong Zhenren**. Behind here, a 300-metre-long bowl is filled with multihued blue pools, contrasting brilliantly with the drab olive vegetation; the best views are from a small platform on the slopes above.

Huanglong's only **accommodation** is the upmarket *Huanglong Shanzhuang* (☏0837/7249333; ❽) at the park gates. Hotel aside, food is available at a single **canteen** near the Middle Temple. There are **toilets** all along the trail, along with posts offering free **oxygen** should you find things tough going.

Jiuzhaigou Scenic Reserve

Around 100km from Songpan or Huanglong, **Jiuzhaigou Scenic Reserve** (¥145, students ¥115; bus tour around the park ¥90, ticket valid for 2 days) was settled centuries ago by Tibetans, whose fenced villages gave Jiuzhaigou (Nine Stockades' Gully) its name. Hemmed in by high, snowy peaks, the reserve's valleys form a south-orientated Y-shape, with **lakes** descending them in a series of broad steps, fringed in thick forests – spectacular in the autumn when the gold and red leaves contrast brilliantly with the water, or at the onset of winter in early December, when everything is dusted by snow (rather than frozen solid by the end of that month).

Jiuzhaigou's **entrance** is on the highway north of the reserve, surrounded by a small township comprising accommodation, places to eat, and a **bus station**. The pick of the **places to stay** includes the bus station hostel (beds ¥25), which is cheap but lacks any other qualities; the glitzy *Jiuzhaigou Binguan* (☏0837/7734859; ❾); and mid-range *Longtianyuan Binguan* (☏0837/7734336; ❻), *Shenshan Binguan* (☏0837/7735970; ❻) and *Minzhu Fandian* (☏0837/7739926; ❺). **Leaving**, buy return tickets to Songpan well in advance, and note that you can also catch frequent buses 25km east to **Jiuzhaigou township** (try the *Jinde Binguan*, ☏0837/7733168, ¥180 if you get stuck here) and from there on to either Guangyuan or Jiangyou, both on the Xi'an–Chengdu rail line.

It's 14km from the park gates to the centre of the reserve around **Nuorilang**. You can use the bus, but it's a nice four-hour hike past little **Zharu Temple** – brightly decorated inside and out with murals and prayer flags – and the marshy complex of pools at the foot of imposing Dêgê Shan forming **Shuzheng lakes**, the largest group in the reserve and cut part-way along by the twenty-metre **Shuzheng Falls**. Here you'll find touristy **Shuzheng village**, a group of "typical" Tibetan dwellings on the lakeshore with a water-powered millstone and **prayer wheel**, where you can don Tibetan garb and pose on horseback for photos.

Another 4km on, **NUORILANG** consists simply of a restaurant, two stores, basic **beds** at the *Jiuzhaigou Zhaodaisuo* (❶), and Jiuzhaigou's most famous cascades, the **Nuorilang Falls**. They look best from the road, framed by trees as water forks down over the strange, yellow crystalline rock faces. The road forks east and west at Nuorilang, with both forks around 18km long. The **eastern branch** first passes **Pearl Beach Falls**, where a whole hillside has calcified into an ankle-deep cascade ending in a ten-metre waterfall similar to Nuorilang's, then the shallow **Panda-Arrow Bamboo Lake** and **Grass Lake**, before entering the **Primeval Forest**, a dense and very atmospheric belt of conifers. There's less to see along the **western branch** from Nuorilang, but don't miss the stunning **Five-coloured Lake** here which, for sheer intensity, if not scale, is unequalled in the park. Superlatives continue at the road's end, where the mundanely named **Long Lake** is both exactly that and, at 3103m, Jiuzhaigou's highest body of water.

Zöigê, Langmusi and on to Gansu

Songpan sits just east of the vast, marshy **Aba Autonomous Prefecture**, which sprawls over the Sichuan, Gansu and Qinghai borders. Resting at around 3500m and draining directly into the convoluted headwaters of the Yellow River, the **Aba Grasslands** are the domain of the independent-minded **Goloks**, a nomadic group of herders. The region enjoys infamy in China for the losses the Red Army sustained here during their Long March, at the mercy of Golok snipers and the waterlogged, shelterless terrain, but it's also a **Bonpa** stronghold (see box, p.940) and a corridor between Sichuan and **Gansu** province – buses run from Songpan to the grassland town of **Zöigê** and over the border, with the beautiful Tibetan monastery at **Langmusi** offering a prime reason to stop off along the way.

Around 150km northwest of Songpan at the grasslands' northernmost edge, **ZÖIGÊ** is a drab collection of buildings enlivened during the June/July **horse races**, when horsemen set up tents outside the town and show off their riding skills to the crowds. Markets here occasionally display **medicinal oddities**, such as deer musk, the lung- and kidney-strengthening orange caterpillar fungus, and a cough medicine derived from fritillary bulbs, but Zöigê can also be an intimidating place. Dreadlocked, knife-wielding Goloks ride motorcycles down the main street, and people trying to hitch from here to Xiahe have been threatened after turning down the outrageous prices asked by truck drivers. There are several **places to stay** – the *Liangju Binguan* (❷) is recommended – and two **bus stations** with a daily morning bus to Songpan and another to **Hezuo** in Gansu (see p.1012), a couple of hours short of Xiahe. Buy your ticket the day before and get to the station in plenty of time, as schedules are not always respected.

Langmusi

Just off the road to Hezuo, three hours from Zöigê, you'll find the beautiful village of **LANGMUSI**, populated by Hui, Goloks and Tibetans, whose mountain scenery and lamaseries are beginning to attract the attention of travellers – certainly the place gives an easy taster of Tibet. There's no direct bus service; in Zöigê; buy a ticket for "Langmu qiaotou" and the Hezuo-bound bus will drop you at an intersection where jeeps take you to the 3km to the village itself (¥2–5). The jeep drops you at the village square where very basic dorms and rooms at the *Langmusi Hotel, Langmusi Guesthouse* and *White Dragon Hotel* await (¥25). All feature acceptable toilets, warm water in the evening, and monks and kids who show little respect for your personal space.

With two lamaseries, a mosque and good walking in the hills around – though don't anger locals by stumbling through the **sky burial ground** to the west, where the bodies of the dead are left on hilltops for birds of prey to devour – there's plenty to keep you for a few days. Don't leave without eating at *Lesha's*, a small, traveller-style **café** close to the hotels, whose owner whips up a great apple pie. Leaving, there is one direct bus to Hezuo from the village at 7am, though big noses are charged double. Otherwise you'll have to get a ride to the intersection, and hope to catch a bus going your way; one or two pass daily any time between 11am and 2.30pm.

The far west: Kangding and on to Tibet

Sichuan's **far west** begins some six hours over the mountains from Chengdu at **Kangding**, the regional capital. Yet it's only after you leave Kangding, bound northwest to **Ganzi** and **Dêgê** or southwest to **Litang** and **Yunnan**, that you enter what, geographically and ethnically, may as well be Tibet: lowland valleys chequered green and gold with barley fields; flowery grasslands grazed by yaks and dotted with black felt tents, each roped down against the weather and guarded by aggressive, curly-tailed mastiffs; hamlets of square, fortress-like stone or adobe houses; and stark mountain passes draped in coloured flags between wind-scoured peaks. The towns, with accompanying monastic complexes, pilgrims and red-robed clergy, reek of the wild west, with their dusty, bustling streets roamed by livestock, beasts of burden, and cowboys in slouch hats – though like horsemen worldwide, Tibetans are ditching their trusty steeds for motorbikes and four-wheel-drives as fast as they become available. For details on Tibetan food, language and religious thought, see the relevant sections at the start of Chapter 14.

Buses to Kangding and Ganzi depart early in the day from Xinnanmen bus station (and, less conveniently, from Chadianzi; see p.886); all services overnight in Kangding, so look on that as your first destination. Roads beyond are rough in places – mostly due to landslides or roadworks – but on the whole journeys are exhausting due to length rather than physical discomfort. What makes them worthwhile are your fellow passengers, mostly monks and wild-looking Khampa youths, who every time the bus crosses a mountain pass cheer wildly and throw handfuls of paper prayer flags out of the windows. **Buying bus tickets** is frustrating, however – expect to find flexible schedules, early departures, ticket offices open at unpredictable times, and unhelpful station staff.

Though roads west of Dêgê and Litang press right through **to Lhasa**, for the present trying to cross the Tibetan border from Sichuan is a guarantee of being pulled off the bus and booted back the way you came by the PSB. Political considerations aside, these are some of the world's most dangerous roads, high, riven by gorges and permanently snowbound, and the Chinese government is not keen to have tourists extend the list of people killed in bus crashes along the way. What might make the journey worth the risk is that it takes you within sight of the world's highest unclimbed mountain ranges, and even those hardened by stints in the Himalayas have reported the scenery as staggeringly beautiful. If you must attempt the crossing, however, it's probably better to do so from the Lhasa side – authorities are hardly likely to send you back into Tibet if you try to enter Sichuan here, though you may well be fined.

Some history

As a buffer zone between Lhasa and China, control of the fractious states comprising Eastern Tibet, or **Kham** (a region which once included western

The far west: Kangding and on to Tibet

Batang	巴塘	bātáng
Daocheng	稻城	dàochéng
Hot Springs	茹布查卡温泉	rúbùchákǎ wēnquán
Seaburay	喜波热藏庄	xǐbōrè zàngzhuāng
Xianggelila	香格里拉	xiānggé lǐlā
Yading	亚丁	yàdīng
Yading Jiudian	亚丁酒店	yàdīng jiǔdiàn
Dêgê	德格	dégé
Babang Monastery	八帮寺庙	bābāng sìmiào
Dêgê Binguan	德格宾馆	dégé bīnguǎn
Gangqing Monastery	筻庆寺庙	gàngqìng sìmiào
Scripture Printing Hall	印经院	yìnjīng yuàn
Xinquan Xiaochi	心泉小吃	xīnquán xiǎochī
Ganzi	甘孜	gānzǐ
Chengxin Binguan	诚信宾馆	chéngxìn bīnguǎn
Jinmaoniu Jiudian	金牦牛酒店	jīnmáoniú jiǔdiàn
Kandze Monastery	甘孜寺庙	gānzǐ sìmiào
Kangding	康定	kāngdìng
Anjue Si	安觉寺	ānjué sì
Nanmo Si	南甫寺	nánfǔ sì
Old Town Spring	水井子	shuǐjǐngzi
Paoma Shan	跑马山	pǎomǎ shān
Princess Wenchang Bridge	文成公主桥	wénchéng gōngzhǔ qiáo
Accommodation		
Kalaka'er Fandian	卡拉卡尔饭店	kǎlā kǎ'ěr fàndiàn
Sally's Knapsack Inn	背包客栈	bēibāo kèzhàn
Xiangbala Jiudian	香巴拉酒店	xiāngbālā jiǔdiàn
Litang	理塘	lǐtáng
Changqingchun Ke'er Monastery	理塘寺庙	lǐtáng sìmiào
Crane Guesthouse	仙鸿宾馆	xiānhóng bīnguǎn

Sichuan), was long disputed. Chinese claims to the region date back to the betrothal of the Tang **Princess Wenchang** to the Tibetan king Songtsen Gampo and the thirteenth-century Mongol invasions, though the first lasting external influence came when the Fifth Dalai Lama sent the Mongols in to enforce Lhasa's authority in the 1600s. Using the distraction provided by the Younghusband expedition's storming of Tibet in 1904 (see p.1099), China opportunistically invaded Kham, evicting the Dalai Lama who had fled the British. The Qing empire fell soon afterwards, however, and Tibet regained the disputed territory. In 1929 the Nationalists tried once again to claim the region for China by creating **Xikang province**, covering much of Kham. Xikang's presence on paper did little to alter the real situation: divided itself, China was hardly able to counter rival claims from Tibet or even control its own forces in the province. The whole issue was made redundant by China's annexation of Tibet in 1950; five years later, the local warlords whose private fief Xikang had become were evicted by Beijing.

Gaocheng Binguan	高城宾馆	*gāochéng bīnguǎn*
Litang Binguan	理塘宾馆	*lǐtáng bīnguǎn*
Safe and Life International Hotel	平安涉外旅馆	*píng'ān shèwài lǚguǎn*
Tianfu Chuancaiguan	天府川菜馆	*tiānfǔ chuāncàiguǎn*
Luding	泸定	*lúdìng*
Manigange	马尼干戈	*mǎní gāngé*
King Gesar	格萨尔王	*gésà'ěr wáng*
Manigange Pani Fandian	马尼干戈帕尼饭店	*mǎní gāngé pàní fàndiàn*
Xinlu Hai	新路海	*xīnlùhǎi*
Yulong Shenhai Binguan	玉龙神海宾馆	*yùlóng shénhǎi bīnguǎn*
Zhuqing Buddhist College	竹庆佛学院	*zhúqīng fóxuéyuàn*
Moxi	磨西	*móxī*
Gongga Shan	贡嘎山	*gònggā shān*
Hailuo Binguan	海螺宾馆	*hǎiluó bīnguǎn*
Hailuogou Glacier Park	海螺沟公园	*hǎiluógōu gōngyuán*
Minzhu Huayuan Jiudian	明珠花园酒店	*míngzhū huāyuán jiǔdiàn*
Xinfei Fandian	鑫飞饭店	*xīnfēi fàndiàn*
Sangdui	桑堆	*sāngduī*
Benbo Monastery	奔波寺	*bēnbō sì*
Haizi Shan	海子山	*hǎizi shān*
Zhujie Monastery	著杰寺	*zhùjié sì*
Tagong	塔公	*tǎgōng*
Mugecuo	木格措	*mùgé cuò*
Tagong Binguan	塔公宾馆	*tǎgōng bīnguǎn*
Tagong grasslands	塔公草原	*tǎgōng cǎoyuán*
Tagong Si	塔公寺	*tǎgōng sì*
Xiangcheng	乡城	*xiāngchéng*
Bamu Tibetan Guesthouse	巴姆藏庄	*bāmǔ zàngzhuāng*
Coffee Tea Hotel	象泉茶楼	*xiàngquán chálóu*
Chaktreng Gompa	桑披岭寺	*sāngpōlíng sì*

The region's **monasteries** fared badly during the Cultural Revolution, and many are still being repaired or rebuilt outright. Today the number of monks they house is a fraction of the former number – just one of the reasons that the whole far west beyond Kangding was off limits to foreigners as recently as 2000.

Kangding

KANGDING, 250km from Chengdu at the gateway to Sichuan's far west, is likely to be a bit of a disappointment. A crowded, artless collection of modern white-tiled blocks packed along the fast-flowing **Zheduo He**, visually this is a very Chinese town, and though Tibetans are certainly in evidence they are clearly outnumbered by the Hui and Han. But for all this, the deep gorge that Kangding is set in is overlooked by chortens and the frosted peaks of **Daxue Shan** (the Great Snowy Mountains), and, whatever the maps might say, this is where Tibet really begins.

The town was once an important marketplace for **tea**, portered over the mountains from Chengdu in compressed blocks to be exchanged for Tibetan wool, and is now the capital of huge **Ganzi prefecture**. Bus schedules mean that a half-day **stopover** here is likely, but with a couple of temples to check out it's not the worst of fates. In addition, Kangding is a stepping stone for day-trips to the **Hailuogou glacier**, which descends western China's highest peak, and horse-riding excursions across the **Tagong grasslands**.

Kangding's most central temple is **Anjue Si** just off Yanhe Xi Lu; a small affair, it was built in 1654 at the prompting of the Fifth Dalai Lama. The main hall is unusual in being covered in miniature golden Buddha statues instead of the usual gory murals, and features some fine butter sculptures of animals and meditating sages. Following the main road west out of town brings you to the short stone arch of the **Princess Wenchang Bridge**; on the other side, a path runs uphill to **Nanmo Si**, built here in 1639 after the original site was sacked by the Mongols. Present renovations have reached two large side halls containing a large gilded statue of Tsongkhapa and murals of Buddha in all his incarnations – images which, with their typically Tibetan iconography of skulls, demons and fierce expressions, paint a far less forgiving picture of Buddhism than the mainstream Chinese brand.

Kangding's **markets** – mostly selling vegetables and edible

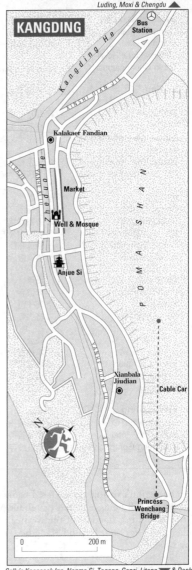

Sally's Knapsack Inn, Nanmo Si, Tagong, Ganzi, Litang ▼ & Danba

autumn fungi of all descriptions – surround the old town **spring** and a dilapidated **mosque** off Yanhe Dong Lu. A lane opposite the mosque heads up to the entrance of pine-clad **Paoma Shan**, the mountain immediately south of town which hosts a **horse-race festival** in the middle of the fourth lunar month. It's a half-hour walk up stone steps to lookouts and the Roman-theatre-style racetrack, or you can catch a **cable car** (¥30 return) from near the Princess Wenchang Bridge.

Practicalities

Kangding sits in a deep Y-shaped valley where the Zheduo River and a minor stream combine to form the east-flowing Kangding He. The kilometre-long downtown area flanks the Zheduo as it flows northeast into the Kangding, with the two main streets – **Yanhe Dong Lu** on the southern side, **Yenhe Xi Lu** on the northern – joined by four bridges. Yanhe Dong Lu continues southwest out of town towards Ganzi and Litang over the Princess Wenchang Bridge.

The **bus station** is a run-down affair at Kangding's western edge; exit the building, turn right, and it's a five-minute walk to Yanhe Dong Lu. The bus station has departures until mid-afternoon to Chengdu, and early-morning runs to Danba (for Siguniang Shan), Ganzi, Dêgê, Litang, Batang, Xiangcheng and Daocheng. For Luding, Moxi or Tagong, catch a cab or minibus-taxi.

Budget accommodation is provided at central Anjue Si (beds ¥20), or 2.5km from the centre at *Sally's Knapsack Inn* (☎0836/2838377; beds ¥20) – catch a cab for ¥5 to the adjacent Jinggang Monastery. Toilets and showers are shared, but staff are helpful and there's a reasonable café. **Hotels** are everywhere, especially around the bus station and Yanhe Dong Lu; in the vicinity of the latter, try the *Xiangbala Jiudian* (☎0836/6691777; ❹) – don't be put off by the drab entrance – or the upmarket *Kalaka'er Fandian* (☎0836/2828888, ℱ2828777; ❼). Your accommodation is probably the best place to seek **food**, though there are hotpot and noodle restaurants all through the backstreets.

Sally's Knapsack Inn offers **tours** of nearby attractions; these can take a few days to organize, so it's best to call in advance. Aside from the Tagong grasslands (see p.948) and **hot springs** just out of town (¥80 per person), they can also get you in to see usually private **sky burials** (¥300 per person; no photographs), the Tibetan way of disposing of corpses.

Luding, Moxi and Hailuogou Glacier Park

A fast road runs 100km from Kangding via Luding to the village of **Moxi**, at the Hailuogou Glacier Park gates; the journey takes two hours. It's possible to cram the trip to the glacier and back into one day if you start early, but better perhaps to overnight either in Moxi or the park itself. The easiest way to travel is to flag down a taxi outside Kangding bus station; they charge around ¥20 for a four-person cab to Luding, or ¥35 to Moxi. There's also a new, direct road from Kangding to Moxi, but at the time of writing cab drivers weren't using it.

Don't be surprised if you have to change vehicles an hour east of Kangding at the market town of **LUDING**, where a few minutes is enough to check out the **Luding Bridge** (¥10), one of the great icons of the Long March. In May 1935, the Red Army reached the Dadu River here to find that a nominal Nationalist force, baulking at destroying the only crossing for hundreds of kilometres, had pulled the decking off the Luding suspension bridge, but left the chains intact. Under heavy fire, 22 Communist soldiers climbed hand-over-hand across the chains and took Guomindang emplacements on the west bank. Official accounts say that only three Long Marchers were killed.

Though substantial by local standards, the bridge is simply a 100-metre-long series of thirteen heavy-gauge chains spanned by planks. The Dadu flows roughly below, while temple-style gates and ornaments at either end lend the bridge an almost religious aspect; a pavilion on the far side houses a **museum** with period photos. For **moving on**, taxis cruise the main road through daylight hours for Kangding (¥20) or Moxi (¥15).

Moxi and Hailuogou Glacier Park

After the action at Luding, Mao and the Red Army recouped at the village of Moxi before heading off on a disastrous 56-kilometre trek north over the mountains to Xiaojin (see p.936), in which Mao nearly joined the hundreds of victims of exposure and altitude sickness. Nobody here today is attempting anything so strenuous, most making an easy tour of **Hailuogou Glacier Park**, whose borders start immediately beyond Moxi. Set among an alpine backdrop of deep valleys forested in pine and rhododendron, Hailuogou is the lowest of four local **glaciers** descending **Gongga Shan** (Minya Konka in Tibetan), western China's highest point at 7556m – a stunning sight on the rare mornings when the near-constant cloud cover and haze of wind-driven snow above the peak suddenly clear. Warm, weatherproof **clothing** is advisable whatever time of year you visit.

The **park entrance** (¥80) is at **MOXI**, a blob of hotels, restaurants and souvenir stalls centred around a crossroads where Luding and Kangding shuttles cluster. Downhill from the crossroads, it's 150m to Moxi's original single street of wooden shops and a small **Catholic church** built in the 1920s. Its colourful bell tower overlooks a European, box-like main building, its eaves pinched as a concession to local aesthetics. Top-notch **accommodation** is provided near the park gates by the *Mingzhu Huayuan Jiudian* (℡0836/3266166, ⓦwww .sctrip.com; ➑), with cheaper options such as the slightly tatty *Hailuo Binguan* (℡0836/3266297; ➌) and friendly *Xinfei Fandian* (℡0836/3266214; ➋) downhill from the crossroads. **Eat** either at your hotel or at any of the scores of stir-fry restaurants nearby.

The **Glacier Park** itself spreads westwards of Moxi, with a **road** running 25km from the gates to the glacier. Most visitors take a **tour bus** from the park gates (¥50 return), though you can also hike, resting up at the three **camps** along the way at the 8-, 15- and 22-kilometre marks. These were once humble campsites, but each now hosts a large hotel (➏), with **hot springs** (¥65) on hand at the first two – camp 2, near where the thicker pine forests begin, is the nicest spot to stay within the park. From camp 3, it's 3.5km to the glacier, from where you can reach a **viewing platform** by cable car (¥160 return) or by simply hiking up along a small path – allow two hours. From the platform, the glacier is revealed as a tongue of blue-white ice scattered with boulders and streaked in crevasses edged in black gravel, with – if you're lucky – Gongga Shan's peak rising in the distance.

The Tagong grasslands

Starting 110km northwest of Kangding, the **Tagong grasslands** occupy a string of flat-bottomed valleys on a 3700-metre-high plateau, all surrounded by magnificent snowy peaks. Horse riding, hiking, and a temple at the Tibetan township of **Tagong** are the attractions here; **riding** is best set up in advance with *Sally's Knapsack Inn* in Kangding, who run day-trips, including food, horses and guide, for ¥120; if it's the scenery and monastery which attract you, simply catch an early-morning minibus to Tagong from outside Kangding's bus station (¥40).

The road from Kangding climbs over a pass at 4300m and then down onto the plateau at **TAGONG**, comprising a single 200-metre-long street below a low ridge which encloses the southern edge of the grasslands. There are several **places to stay** here, from hostels to the *Tagong Binguan* (➌); you may also be invited to stay in a Tibetan home. Basic **restaurants** serve Tibetan and Sichuanese staples.

Thick with monks and pilgrims, Tagong's focus is the dusky **Tagong Si** (¥10), a relatively modest complex built to honour Princess Wenchang. The seventeenth-century main hall houses a sculpture of Sakyamuni as a youth, said to have been brought here by the princess in Tang times. Behind the monastery is **Fotalin**, a forest of a hundred three-metre-high stupas, each built in memory of a monk. Follow the main road 500m past Tagong Si and you'll find a mighty two-storey **golden pagoda** (¥10), fully 20m tall and visible from miles away across the plain, surrounded by a colonnade of prayer wheels – though according to the monks, this recent construction is less of a religious site than an excuse to collect tourist revenue.

The **grasslands** themselves begin at the golden pagoda, a vast sprawl of pasture hemmed in by hillocks and peaks. Hiking and riding possibilities are legion; one recognized **trail** leads 35km southeast to a lake system at **Mugecuo**, below **Dapao Nan Shan** (4900m) – you'll need a guide, best organized through accommodation in Kangding.

To Ganzi and Dêgê

Northwest from Kangding, it's close on 600km across mountains and prairies to Tibet, and the main targets on the way are the people and monasteries at **Ganzi**, about 400km along, and **Dêgê**, not far from the border. The whole region hovers above 3500m, and the passes are considerably higher. **Buses** from Kangding take a full day to reach Ganzi, and two for Dêgê. The halfway point is **LUHUO**, a small junction town where Kangding–Dêgê buses overnight, with well-stocked shops, a mostly Tibetan population and the requisite gold-roofed monastery on a hill. Luhuo's best **accommodation** is near the bus station at the Tibetan-run *Kasa Dajiudian* (☎0836/7322368; ❷, dorm ¥30), whose warm, large rooms have toilets and showers, an incredible luxury if you've spent much time in the far west. Heading on, Ganzi is just three more hours up the road.

Ganzi

GANZI sits at 3500m in a broad, flat-bottomed river valley, with the long, serrated Que'er Shan range rising to the south. The typically dusty, noisy town owes its importance to the adjacent **Kandze monastery**, founded by the Mongols after they invaded in 1642 and once the largest Gelugpa monastery in the Kham region. A bit empty today, it nevertheless remains an important cultural centre, especially for the teaching of religious dances and musical instruments.

Ganzi acts as transport and social focus, with blue trucks rumbling through at all hours, wild crowds cruising the streets and markets throughout the back lanes; the two-kilometre main street is lined with shops selling knives, rugs, silverware, all sorts of jewellery, saddles, religious accessories, copper and tin kitchenware. The **monastery** is 2km north of town – follow the road uphill from the bus station – and for such an obvious structure the entrance is not easy to find, being hidden behind mud-brick homes among medieval backstreets. As with many of the region's monasteries, there's a bit of a ghost-town feel to wandering around the underpopulated complex, though the whole place is being renovated. Aside from the **main hall** – covered in gold, murals and prayer flags, and with an incredible view of the valley and town from its roof – there's not much to see as such. You might encounter monks **debating** (a ritualized but seemingly heated process), and will certainly hear people practising those long Tibetan trumpets. The large adobe walls below the monastery are remains of the Mazur and Khangsar **forts**, built by the Mongols after they took the region.

Back in town, the highway runs through as the east–west main street, with a **crossroads** marking the town centre: the main **bus station** is here (there's another depot at the Kangding side of town), with the **post office** 500m north on the monastery road. There are two good **accommodation** options near the bus station: next door at the *Jinmaoniu Jiudian* (℡0836/7525288, 7525188; ❹, dorms ¥15), which has basic dorms and much better doubles; and opposite at the especially tidy *Chengxin Binguan* (℡0836/7525289; ❸, dorms ¥40). Many other cheap options charge ¥20 per person, all with shared toilets; you shower at public bathhouses for ¥3. Almost every other business is a **restaurant**, though don't expect much beyond noodles and dumplings.

Buses run daily to Luhuo, Dêgê, Kangding and Chengdu. If you've been looking at a map and fancy trying to short-cut south from Ganzi to Litang, note that at the time of writing there were no buses along this route.

Manigange and around

Over a pass and out on the plains 95km northwest from Ganzi, **MANI-GANGE** is a single-street township which was completely disassembled for rebuilding at the time of writing, with at least two places to **stay and eat** – *Manigange Pani Fandian* and *Yulong Shenhai Binguan* – though prices and quality were impossible to gauge. There are two reasons to stop here: Tibetan **horse races** in late August, and the holy lake of **Xinlu Hai** (Yilhun Lhatso), 10km beyond Manigange on the Dêgê road. The kilometre-wide lake sits in a reserve for the elusive **white-lipped deer**, and is partially fed by dusty brown glaciers descending Qu'er Shan, whose slopes hem the shoreline; scores of boulders in the vicinity carved with "om pani padme hum" in Tibetan characters testify to spiritual importance. The area has limitless **hiking potential**, though you need to be fully equipped for the altitude and cold climate, even in summer.

Another possible reason to linger is the **Axu Grasslands** north of Mani-gange, birthplace of the eleventh-century warrior-king **Gesar**, hero of Tibet's longest epic, whose fame for slaughtering his enemies and founding the state of Ling (boundaries unknown) extends from Mongolia to Yunnan. Images of him, inevitably depicted as a fiercely moustached horseman, can be found everywhere through Sichuan's far west. One place to aim for on the grass-lands is **Zhuqing Buddhist College** (Dzongchen Gompa) 50km northwest of Manigange, which is in poor condition but remains the region's major Nyingmapa-sect monastery, established in 1684 and famous for originating an opera version of the Gesar epic.

Dêgê and around

The road from Manigange to Dêgê is the most spectacular – and downright unnerving – in the whole of Sichuan's far west. It first follows a rounded valley below the toothy, snowbound **Chola Shan**, then, at the valley's head, it zigzags back on itself and climbs to just below the peaks, crossing a razor-edged 5050-metre-high pass. As the road hairpins down the even more vertiginous far side, monks in the bus don't help raise expectations of survival by their furious chanting, but with luck you'll be pulling up at Dêgê four hours after leaving Manigange.

DÊGÊ initially appears to be no more than a small cluster of ageing concrete buildings squeezed into a narrow gorge, but was once the most powerful Kham state, and the only one to resist the seventeenth-century Mongol inva-sion – hence the absence of Gelugpa-sect monasteries in the region. The **bus stop** is on the main road, just where Dêgê's single street crosses a stream and rises uphill past shops, a **supermarket** and **Internet bar**, dozens of stir-fry

restaurants – the *Xinquan Xiaochi* is good – to the monastery. The surly river-side *Dêgê Binguan* (❹, dorms ¥20) is the primary source of **beds**, with grubby dorms in an older wing and overpriced newer rooms in the main building; their comfortable tearoom, however, is a treat after the journey.

At the top of the main street is **Gangqing Monastery** (Gongchen Gompa), whose red-walled buildings form one of three hubs of Tibetan culture (the other two are Lhasa and Xiahe in Gansu). The first building encountered is the famous **Bakong** (Scripture Printing Hall; ¥25), encircled by peregrinating pilgrims busy thumbing rosaries, who stick out their tongues in greeting if you join them. Built in 1729, the four-storey hall houses 290,000 **woodblocks** of Tibetan texts, stored in racks on the second floor like books in a library, and covering everything from scriptures to scientific treatises – some seventy percent of all Tibetan literary works. You can watch the **printing process** on the third floor: two printers sit facing each other, with the block in between on a sloping board; one printer inks the block with a pad and lays a fresh page over it; the other rubs a roller over the back of the page and then peels it off, placing it in a pile. Each page takes under six seconds to finish, and it's not unusual to watch ten pairs of printers going full pelt, turning out a hundred pages a minute between them.

The rest of the complex comprises a main hall and associated buildings, and there always seem to be ceremonies going on, which you may or may not be allowed to observe. For an easy walk, follow the stream up past the monastery and into barley fields for about forty minutes to a **swimming hole**.

Some 40km south of Dêgê, the 800-year-old **Babang Monastery** (Palpung Gompa) – also known as the "Little Potala" after its size and general design – is the largest and most important Kagyupa-sect monastery in Sichuan, currently undergoing much-needed repairs. The problem is getting here: there's no public transport so you'll need to hike or ask at the hotel about chartering a jeep.

Leaving, you'll need to buy Ganzi or Kangding tickets a day in advance; the main-road bus ticket booth opens at 7am and 2.30pm. There are also buses to Changdu (**Chamdo**) in Tibet – the border, marked by a youthful **Yangzi River** is about 15km west – if you want to try your luck with the border guards.

Litang and the road to Yunnan

From Kangding, it's 290km west to the monastery town of **Litang**, and a further 150km south from here to **Daocheng**, stepping stone to the scenic wilds of **Yading**; or 200km southwest to the isolated valley hamlet of **Xiangcheng**, and thence down to Yunnan. There are direct Kangding–Litang–Daocheng buses, regular services from Litang or Daocheng to Xiangcheng, and from Daocheng to Zhongdian in Yunnan via Xiangcheng.

The Kangding–Litang road is a real treat, steadily rising to a mountain pass at 4700m. The pass opens onto undulating highlands, whose soft green slopes drop to forests far below – look for **marmots** (prairie dogs) on the ground and wedge-tailed **lammergeiers** (bearded vultures) circling far above. Just as you're wondering whether the road goes on indefinitely, Litang appears below on a flat plain, ringed by mountains.

Litang

LITANG is a lively, outwardly gruff place with a large Tibetan population and an obvious Han presence in its businesses and army barracks. Wild West comparisons are inevitable – you'll soon get used to sharing the pavement with livestock, and watching monks and Khampa toughs with braided hair and

⑫

Litang's horse festival

Litang's week-long **horse festival** kicks off each August 1 on the plains outside town. Thousands of Tibetan horsemen from all over Kham descend to compete, decking their stocky steeds in bells and brightly decorated bridles and saddles. As well as the four daily **races**, the festival features amazing demonstrations of horsemanship, including acrobatics, plucking silk scarves off the ground, and shooting (guns and bows) – all performed at full tilt. In between, you'll see plenty of **dancing**, both religious (the dancers wearing grotesque wooden masks) and for fun, with both men and women gorgeously dressed in heavily embroidered long-sleeved smocks.

boots tearing around the windy, dusty streets on ribboned motorbikes. It's also inescapably **high** – at 4014m above sea level, it actually beats Lhasa by 350m – so don't be surprised if you find even gentle slopes strangely exhausting. As usual, the main distraction here is people-watching; the shops are packed with Tibetans bargaining for temple accessories, solar-power systems for tents, illegal furs, and practical paraphernalia for daily use, while smiths are busy turning out the town's renowned knives and jewellery in backstreet shacks.

Litang's **Changqingchun Ke'er monastery**, founded in 1580 at the behest of the Third Dalai Lama and one of the largest Gelugpa monasteries in China, is today somewhat dilapidated but still populated by over a thousand monks. From the Gesar statue, walk uphill to the intersection, turn left, and follow the road – it's a fifteen-minute walk, or a ¥3 taxi ride. For once, the approach gives a clear view of the complex, entirely encircled by a wall, the two main halls gleaming among an adobe township of monks' quarters. At the entrance is a large stupa and pile of brightly-painted *mani* stones left by pilgrims for good luck, whose inscriptions have been carved to resemble yaks. The **upper temple** (Tsengyi Zhatsang) is the more interesting and older of the two, its portico flanked by aggressively postured statues of guardians of the four directions, along with a typical, finely executed mural of a three-eyed demon wearing tiger skins and skulls, holding the wheel of transmigration. Inside are statues of Tsongkhapa and the Third Dalai Lama, along with photos of the current Dalai Lama and tenth Panchen Lama. Side gates in the wall allow you to hike up onto the hills behind the monastery, sharing the flower-filled pasture with yaks, or join pilgrims circuiting the walls to the **sky burial** ground to the right of the main gates. Don't bother with Litang's paltry **hot springs**, 4km west of town.

The east–west highway forms Litang's 1500-metre main street, with the **bus station** at the eastern side (a new one is under construction at the western end of town). There are daily buses to Kangding, Xiangcheng and Daocheng, with tickets sold around 2.30pm – though the bossy, dismissive staff seem to enjoy making life difficult for passengers. Head uphill from the town's central crossroads and there's a second crossroads with a large equestrian **Gesar statue**, a useful landmark.

The best budget **accommodation** options are across from the bus station at the *Safe & Life International Hotel* (☎0836/5323861; beds ¥20), a friendly, grubby place with tiny rooms; or the efficient and usually full *Crane Guesthouse* 500m further into town (☎0836/5323850; ❶) – showers at either are a few yuan extra. *Litang Binguan* (☎0836/5322163; ❹), on the main road heading west, is an unpretentious mid-range place, though you'll need to speak some Chinese to secure a bed. *Gaocheng Binguan* (☎0836/5322706; ❺), near the Gesar statue, is the town's acme of luxury, with heating and hot water. Stir-fry **restaurants** run by migrants from Chengdu line the main street; the *Tianfuchuan Caiguan* diagonally across from the *Crane Guesthouse* is a cut above average. The *Crane* also runs a very cosy **teahouse** – ask at the guesthouse for directions.

Sangdui, Daocheng and Yading

The main feature of the Litang–Sangdui road is the bleak **Haizi Shan**, a former glacial cap and now a high, boulder-strewn moorland patterned by magenta flowers, small twisting streams, and pale blue tarns. You descend off this past the newly rebuilt **Benbo monastery** to the valley settlement of **SANGDUI**, a scattered hamlet of Tibetan homes surrounding a junction where the routes to Xiangcheng and Daocheng diverge. The latter road follows the west side of a broad, long river valley 30km south to Daocheng; about 7km along, a bridge crosses to a track heading 5km over the valley to **Zhujie monastery**, famed for its meditating monks and beautifully positioned halfway up the facing slope – a good excuse to get off the bus and explore.

DAOCHENG is a small, touristy T-intersection of low buildings and shops, the road from Sangdui running in past the **bus station** to the junction. Turn left (north) and the road runs out into the countryside, degenerating into a track which winds up 5km later at some **hot springs**, set among a tiny village at the head of a valley. **Bathhouses** here ask ¥3 for a soak, and you can cross the valley and hike along a ridge back into town – tiring, given the 3500-metre altitude. Otherwise, the main point of interest lies a 76-kilometre ride south of Daocheng at **Yading**, a beautiful alpine reserve of meadows, lakes and six-thousand-metre peaks. If the **bus** is running, it charges ¥55 return to the reserve gates at **Xianggelila** ("Shangarilla"); otherwise you'll have to arrange a five-person jeep or minibus through your accommodation for ¥500. There's accommodation in Yading, but at present much of the reserve is only accessible on foot or horseback.

Daocheng's best **accommodation** option is the warmly hospitable **Tibetan guesthouses** such as the *Seaburay* (T0836/5728668; ¥30 per person; follow the English signs from near the bus station), where your ability to consume vast amounts of *tsampa*, dumplings and butter tea will be put to the test. Toilets are basic and you shower at the public bathhouse or, more enjoyably, at the hot springs. The town has one big tourist hotel, the *Yading Jiudian* (T0836/8674777;) on the hot-springs road; it's comfortable, but characterless – though there's a useful **foreign exchange** counter.

Daily **buses** depart Daocheng for Litang, Kangding, Xiangcheng, and Zhongdian in Yunnan, all things being equal – but they often aren't. Note that the Zhongdian bus originates here, making it a better place to catch it than Xiangcheng (see below).

Xiangcheng and on to Yunnan

Some 80km over the steep ranges southwest of Sangdui, **XIANGCHENG**'s little core of shops and scattered spread of Tibetan farmhouses and red mud-brick **watchtowers** are set in a deep valley looking south to the mountains marking the Yunnan border. Once capital of a region romantically known as the "White Wolf State", today Xiangcheng is a functional few streets with the flat atmosphere of some long-abandoned outpost, but the small seventeenth-century **monastery** (Chaktreng Gompa; ¥10; photos allowed) is highly unusual and well worth the two-kilometre uphill hike from town. While you're in the portico admiring the scenery, take a look at the wooden support pillars, deeply carved with painted hares, elephants, monkeys and tigers. Inside, the three-storey temple has extraordinary decorations, including murals of mandalas and warrior demons squashing European-looking figures, and sculptures in primary blues and reds showing multi-headed, many-limbed demons cavorting in Tantric postures, fangs bared. Among all this is an eerie seated statue of Tsongkhapa, wreathed in gold filigree and draped in silk scarves.

Xiangcheng's semi-derelict **bus station** is a walled compound dotted with rubble and excrement; the town's short main street stretches beyond. If the owner doesn't meet you, take the small steps uphill from inside the bus station and it's 50m to *Bamu Tibetan Guesthouse* (there's a small English sign; ❶, dorm beds ¥18). This is Xiangcheng's highlight, a traditional three-storey Tibetan home decorated in murals, whose dormitory resembles the interior of a temple (the twin rooms are a bit poky, however). There are great views from the roof, and a basic outdoor shower and toilet – a torch is useful. Another decent option – though with none of *Bamu*'s character – lies just outside the bus station gates at the *Coffee Tea Hotel* (☎0836/8659888; ❸), which also has a good **teahouse** and **bathhouse**.

There are usually daily buses to Litang, Daocheng and Zhongdian in Yunnan. You might be sold a ticket for Litang the day before departure at 2.30pm, but as Xiangcheng is only a brief stop on the Daocheng–Zhongdian run, you'll have to bargain with the driver for a seat to these destinations.

Travel details

Trains

Chengdu to: Beijing (3 daily; 25–30hr); Chongqing (1 daily; 12hr); Emei (10 daily; 2hr); Guangyuan (many daily; 5hr); Guangzhou (1 daily; 38hr); Guiyang (4 daily; 18hr); Jiangyou (many daily; 3hr 30min); Kunming (4 daily; 19hr); Panzhihua (8 daily; 13hr); Shanghai (4 daily; 40hr); Wuhan (3 daily; 17hr); Xi'an (8 daily; 16hr); Xichang (9 daily; 10hr).

Chongqing to: Beijing (2 daily; 25hr); Chengdu (1 daily; 12hr); Guangzhou (5 daily, 36hr); Guiyang (5 daily; 12hr); Shanghai (1 daily; 37hr); Wuhan (2 daily; 13hr); Xi'an (3 daily; 16hr).

Emei Shan to: Chengdu (10 daily; 2hr); Kunming (4 daily; 17hr); Panzhihua (8 daily; 11hr); Xichang (9 daily; 8hr).

Xichang to: Chengdu (9 daily; 10hr); Emei (9 daily; 8hr); Kunming (4 daily; 9hr); Panzhihua (8 daily; 3hr).

Buses

Chengdu to: Chongqing (6hr); Daocheng (2 days); Dazu (4hr); Dujiangyan (1hr); Emei Shan (2hr 30min); Ganzi (2 days); Guanghan (1hr); Guangyuan (4hr); Huanglongxi (1hr); Jiangyou (2hr); Jiuzhaigou (12hr); Kangding (6–8hr); Kunming (24hr); Langzhong (4hr 30min); Leshan (2hr 30min); Luodai (50min); Maoxian (5hr); Siguniang Shan (8hr); Songpan (8hr); Wenchuan (3hr 30min); Wolong (4hr); Xichang (8hr); Xindu (30min); Yibin (8hr); Zöigê (14hr); Zigong (6hr).

Changning to: Chongqing (6hr); Chengdu (10hr); Luzhou (3hr); Yibin (2hr).

Chongqing to: Chengdu (6hr); Dazu (3hr); Langzhong (5hr); Yibin (3hr 30min); Zigong (1hr 30min).

Dazu to: Chengdu (4hr); Chongqing (3hr); Leshan (3hr); Yibin (4hr); Zigong (2hr).

Daocheng to: Litang (5hr); Sangdui (2hr); Xiangcheng (3hr); Zhongdian (12hr).

Dujiangyan to: Chengdu (1hr); Guanghan (1hr 30min); Qingcheng Shan (45min); Songpan (7hr); Wolong (3hr).

Emei Shan to: Chengdu (2hr 30min); Leshan (1hr); Xichang (8hr).

Ganzi to: Chengdu (2 days); Dêgê (8hr); Kangding (12hr); Luhuo (3hr).

Guangyuan to: Chengdu (4hr); Jiangyou (2hr 30min); Jianmenguan (1hr); Jiuzhaigou (8hr); Langzhong (4hr).

Jiangyou to: Chengdu (2hr); Doutuan Shan (1hr); Guangyuan (2hr 30min); Jianmenguan (1hr 30min); Jiuzhaigou (8hr).

Kangding to: Batang (2 days); Chengdu (6–8hr); Danba (4hr); Daocheng (14hr); Dêgê (2 days); Ganzi (12hr); Litang (9hr); Luhuo (9hr); Manigange (15hr); Tagong (3hr); Xichang (8hr).

Langzhong to: Chengdu (5hr); Chongqing (5hr); Guanyuan (4hr).

Leshan to: Chengdu (2hr 30min); Chongqing (5hr); Dazu (3hr); Emei (1hr); Xichang (8hr); Yibin (5hr); Zigong (2hr 30min).

Litang to: Daocheng (5hr); Kangding (9hr); Sangdui (3hr); Xiangcheng (5hr); Zhongdian (12hr).

Songpan to: Chengdu (8hr); Huanglong (2hr); Jiuzhaigou (4hr); Ma'erkang (12hr); Zoige (4–6hr); Langmusi (12hr).

Xiangcheng to: Daocheng (3hr); Litang (5hr); Zhongdian (8hr).

Xichang to: Chengdu (8hr); Kangding (8hr); Kunming (24hr); Panzhihua (3hr); Puge (2hr).

Yibin to: Changning (1hr 30min); Chengdu (4hr); Chongqing (3hr 30min); Dazu (4hr); Gongxian (2hr 15min); Luzhou (3hr); Zigong (1hr 30min).

Zigong to: Chengdu (4hr); Chongqing (4hr); Dazu (2hr); Emei (3hr); Leshan (2hr 30min); Luzhou (5hr); Yibin (1hr 30min).

Ferries

Chongqing to: Wanxian (daily; 12hr); Wuhan (daily; 3 days); Yichang (daily; 13hr by hydrofoil, 48hr conventional ferry).

Flights

Besides the domestic flights listed, there are flights from Chengdu to Bangkok and Singapore.

Chengdu to: Beijing (11 daily; 2hr); Changsha (2 daily; 1hr 30min); Chongqing (2 weekly; 45min); Guangzhou (4 daily; 2hr); Guiyang (2 daily; 1hr); Guilin (1 daily; 1hr 20min); Hong Kong (3 daily; 2hr); Jiuzhai (5 daily; 45min); Kunming (3 daily; 90min); Lhasa (2 daily; 1hr 50min); Shenzhen (3 daily; 1hr 25min); Shanghai (5 daily; 2hr 15min); Wuhan (2 daily; 1hr 20min); Wulumuqi (2 daily; 3hr 30min).

Chongqing to: Beijing (9 daily; 2hr); Chengdu (8 daily; 45min); Guangzhou (10 daily; 90min); Guilin (3 daily; 55min); Hong Kong (5 daily; 1hr 50min); Kunming (8 daily; 1hr 10min); Xi'an (3 daily; 1hr); Shanghai (9 daily; 2hr).

Songpan (Jiuzhai airport) to: Chengdu (daily; 1hr).

CHAPTER 13

Highlights

* **The grasslands** Explore the rolling green horizons of Inner Mongolia's "grass sea" – such as those near Hohhot – and sleep in a Mongol yurt. See p.971

* **Manzhouli** Bustling Sino-Russian border town, littered with century-old architecture from the Trans-Siberian Railway's glory days. See p.975

* **Labrang Monastery** The most imposing Lamaist monastery outside of Tibet, set in a beautiful mountain valley. See p.1009

* **Jiayuguan Fort** Stronghold at the western end of the Great Wall, symbolically marking the end of China proper. See p.1018

* **Mogao Caves** Unbelievable collection of Buddhist grottoes and sculptures, carved into a desert gorge a millennium ago. See p.1025

* **Qinghai Hu** China's largest salt lake is a magnet for waterfowl, including the rare black-necked crane. See p.1039

* **Turpan** Relax under grape trellises or investigate Muslim Uigur culture and ancient Silk Road relics, such as the ruins of Jiaohe. See p.1049

* **Tian Chi** An alpine lake surrounded by meadows and snow-covered mountains, home to a Kazakh population. See p.1062

* **Kashgar's Sunday Market** Join crowds bargaining for goats, carpets, knives and exotic spices in China's most westerly city. See p.1083

△ Id Kah Mosque, Kashgar

13

The Northwest

Reaching across in a giant arc from the fringes of eastern Siberia to the borders of Turkic Central Asia, the provinces of Inner Mongolia, Ningxia, Gansu, Qinghai and Xinjiang account for an entire third of China's land area. Compressing so vast a region into a single chapter of a guidebook may seem something of a travesty – but at least it is based on a perception that originates from China itself, that these territories lie largely beyond the Great Wall. To ancient Chinese thinking the whole region is remote, subject to extremes of weather and populated by non-Chinese-speaking "barbarians" who are, quite literally, the peoples from beyond the pale – *sai wai ren*. It is here, thinly scattered through the vast areas of steppe and grassland, desert and mountain plateau, that the bulk of China's **ethnic minorities** still live. Out of deference to these, Inner Mongolia, Ningxia and Xinjiang are officially not provinces at all, but so-called **Autonomous Regions**, for the Mongol, Hui and Uigur peoples respectively.

However, a **Chinese presence** in the area is not new. Imperial armies were already in control of virtually the whole northwest region by the time of the Han dynasty two thousand years ago, and since then Gansu, Ningxia and the

Staying in a yurt

In regions which still harbour semi-nomadic herders, such as Mongolia's grasslands (p.971) or around Tian Chi (p.1062) in Xinjiang, it's often possible to ask a local family to put you up in their **yurt** (*mengu bao* in Mandarin). The genuine article is a circular felt tent with floor rugs as the only furniture, horsehair blankets, a stove for warmth, and outside toilets. Though it's a well-established custom to offer lodging to travellers, bear in mind that few people in these regions have had much contact with foreigners, and misunderstandings can easily arise. You'll need to haggle over the price with your hosts; around ¥40 should cover bed and simple meals of noodles and vegetables. In addition, it's a good idea to bring a **present** – a bottle of *baijiu*, a clear and nauseatingly powerful vodka-like spirit, rarely goes amiss. Liquor stores, ubiquitous in Chinese cities and towns, are the obvious place to buy the stuff, but you'll also find it on sale at train and bus stations, restaurants, hotel shops and airports. You might also want to bring a flashlight and bug spray for your own comfort.

Note that local tour companies may be able to arrange yurt accommodation, though where Chinese tour groups are commonplace, you may be treated to a very artificial experience – often basically just a concrete cell dolled up in "yurt" fashion, with karaoke laid on in the evenings. If you want something better than this, it's worth at least asking to see photos of the interior when making a booking.

eastern part of Qinghai have become Chinese almost to the core. The uncultivatable plains of Inner Mongolia have been intimately bound up with China since Genghis Khan created his great empire in the early thirteenth century, and even Xinjiang has always found itself drawn back into the Chinese sphere after repeatedly breaking free.

Today the relatively unrestricted use of **local languages and religions** in these areas could be taken as a sign of China's desire to **nurture patriotism** in the minority peoples, and regain some of the sympathy lost during disastrous repressions both under communism and in previous eras. Furthermore, in economic terms, there is a clear transfer of wealth, in the form of industrial and agricultural aid, from the richer areas of eastern China to the poorer, outer fringes of the country. On the other hand, the degree of actual autonomy in the "autonomous" regions is strictly controlled, and relations between Han China and these more remote corners of the empire remain fractious in places.

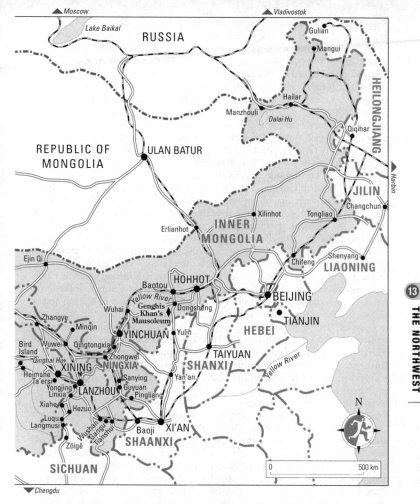

Dissent on the part of the Uigurs of Xinjiang, for example, has shown itself as recently as the 1990s, when there were large-scale city riots in Kashgar.

Organized tourism across the Northwest has boomed in recent years, focusing particularly on the **Silk Road**, a series of historic towns and ruins running from Xi'an in Shaanxi province, through Ningxia, Gansu and Xinjiang, and eventually on into Central Asia. The Northwest also offers possibilities for enjoying the last great remaining **wildernesses** of China – the grasslands, mountains, lakes and deserts of the interior – far from the teeming population centres of the east. For this, there is perhaps no better place to start than **Inner Mongolia**'s famous **grasslands**, on which Genghis Khan trained his cavalry and where nomads on horseback still live today. As well as visiting the supposed **tomb of Genghis Khan**, outside Dongsheng, it's also possible, in places, to catch a glimpse of the Mongols' ancient and unique way of life, packaged for tourists to a greater or lesser degree depending on how far off the beaten track you are willing to travel.

You can sleep in a nomad's yurt, sample Mongol food and ride a horse across the grasslands, all within half a day's train journey from Beijing.

The other great natural feature of Inner Mongolia is the Yellow River, which detours north into the region from tiny, rural **Ningxia**. Here, at the resorts of **Shapotou** and **Sha Hu** you can witness mighty waters running between desert sand dunes. Rarely visited by foreign tourists, Ningxia also offers quiet, attractive cities and a variety of scenery ranging from terraced, abundantly fertile hillsides in the south to pure desert in the north. Extending west from here is **Gansu**, the historic periphery of ancient China. This rugged terrain of high peaks and desert is spliced from east to west by the **Hexi Corridor**, historically the only road from China to the West, and still marked along its length by the Great Wall – terminating magnificently at the fortress of **Jiayuguan** – and a string of Silk Road towns culminating in **Dunhuang**, with its fabulous Buddhist cave art.

South of the Hexi Corridor rise the Kunlun Mountains and, beyond, the high-altitude plateau stretching all the way to India. The ancient borderland between Tibet and China proper is **Qinghai**, perhaps the least-explored province in the whole of the Northwest, which offers monasteries, mountains, the colossal lake of **Qinghai Hu** and, above all, **routes to Tibet** across one of the highest mountain ranges in the world. Originating in this province, too, are the Yellow and Yangzi rivers, the main transport arteries of China throughout recorded history.

Guarding the westernmost passes of the empire is **Xinjiang**, where China ends and another world – once known in the West as Chinese Turkestan – begins. Culturally and geographically this vast, isolated region of searing deserts and snowy mountains, the most arduous and dreaded section of the Silk Road, is a part of Central Asia. Turkic Uigurs outnumber the Han Chinese, mosques replace temples, and lamb kebabs replace steamed dumplings. Highlights of Xinjiang include the desert resort town of **Turpan** and, in the far west, fabled **Kashgar**, a city that until recently few Westerners had ever reached.

Travel in the Northwest can still be hard going, with enormous distances and an extremely harsh continental climate to contend with. **Winter** is particularly severe, with average temperatures as low as -15°C or -20°C in Inner Mongolia, Qinghai and Xinjiang. Conversely, in **summer**, Turpan is China's hottest city, commonly reaching 40°C. Despite the wild, rugged terrain and the great distances, however, facilities for tourists have developed considerably in recent years. In nearly all towns, there are now hotels and restaurants catering for a range of budgets – in general, the price of accommodation is a good deal cheaper here than in eastern China. Where rail lines have not been built, nearly everywhere is accessible by bus, and quite a few towns by plane as well. Finally there is the possibility of **onward travel** to or from China's Asian neighbours – the Republic of Mongolia, Kazakhstan, Kyrgyzstan and Pakistan can all be reached by road or rail from the provinces covered in this chapter (though remember that you may need to acquire visas for these countries in Beijing or elsewhere before setting out).

Inner Mongolia

Mongolia is an almost total mystery to the outside world, its very name being synonymous with remoteness. For hundreds of years, landlocked between the two Asian giants Russia and China, it seems to have been doomed to eternal obscurity, trapped in a hopeless physical environment of fleeting summers and interminable, bitter winters. And yet, seven hundred years ago the people of this benighted land suddenly burst out of their frontiers and for a century subjugated and terrorized virtually the entire Eurasian continent.

Visitors to the **Autonomous Region of Inner Mongolia** will not necessarily find many signs of this today, and if you come here expecting to find something reminiscent of Genghis Khan you are likely to be disappointed. The modern-day heirs of the Mongol hordes are not only placid – quietly going about their business of shepherding, herding horses and entertaining tourists – but, even in their own autonomous region, are vastly outnumbered by the Han Chinese (by seventeen million to two million). In addition, this is, and always has been, a sensitive border area, and there are still restrictions on the movements of tourists here, despite the demise of the Soviet Union.

Nevertheless, there are still traces of the "real" Mongolia out there, in terms of both landscape and people. Dotting the region are enormous areas of **grassland**, gently undulating plains stretching to the horizon and still used by nomadic peoples as pastureland for their horses. Tourists are able to visit the grasslands and even stay with the Mongols in their yurts, though the only simple way to do this is by **organized tour** out of the regional capital **Hohhot** – an experience rather short on authenticity. If you don't find what you are looking for in the Hohhot area, however, don't forget that there is a whole vast swathe of Mongolia stretching up through northeastern China that remains virtually untouched by Western tourists, and here, especially in the areas around **Xilinhot** and **Hailar**, determined independent travellers can manage to glimpse something of the grasslands and their Mongol inhabitants. Finally, Inner Mongolia offers overland connections with China's two northern neighbours, the Republic of Mongolia (Outer Mongolia) and Russia, through the border towns of **Erlianhot** and **Manzhouli** respectively.

Some history

Genghis Khan (1162–1227) was born, ominously enough, with a clot of blood in his hand. Under his leadership, the **Mongols** erupted from their homeland to ravage the whole of Asia, butchering millions, razing cities and laying waste all the land from China to eastern Europe. It was his proud boast that his destruction of cities was so complete that he could ride across their ruins by night without the least fear of his horse stumbling.

Before Genghis exploded onto the scene, the nomadic Mongols had long been a thorn in the side of the city-dwelling Chinese. Construction of the **Great Wall** had been undertaken to keep these two fundamentally opposed societies apart. But it was always fortunate for the Chinese that the early nomadic tribes of Mongolia fought as much among themselves as they did against outsiders. Genghis Khan's achievement was to weld together the warring nomads into a fighting force the equal of which the world had never seen. Becoming Khan of Khans in 1206, he also introduced the Yasak, the first **code of laws** the Mongols had known. Few details of its Draconian tenets survive today (though it was inscribed on iron tablets at Genghis' death), but Tamerlane, at Samarkand, and Baber the Great Mogul in India, were both later to use it as the basis for their authority.

The secret of Genghis Khan's success lay in skilful **cavalry tactics**, acquired from long practice in the saddle on the wide-open Mongolian plains. Frequently his armies would rout forces ten or twenty times their size. Each of his warriors would have light equipment and three or four horses. Food was taken from the

The Silk Road

The passes of Khunjerab and Torugut, linking China with western Asia – and ultimately with the whole of the western world – have only in recent years reopened to a thin and tentative trickle of cross-border traffic. Yet a thousand years ago these were on crucial, well-trodden and incredibly long trade routes between eastern China and the Mediterranean. Starting from Chang'an (Xi'an), the **Silk Road** curved northwest through Gansu to the Yumen Pass, where it split. Leaving the protection of the Great Wall, travellers could follow one of two routes across the deserts of Lop Nor and Taklamakan, braving the attacks from marauding bandits, to Kashgar. The **southern route** ran through Dunhuang, Lop Nor, Miran, Niya, Khotan and Yarkand; the **northern route** through Hami, Turpan, Kuqa and Aqsu. High in the Pamirs beyond Kashgar, the merchants traded their goods with the middlemen who carried them beyond the frontiers of China, either south to Kashmir, Bactria, Afghanistan and India, or north to Ferghana, Tashkent and Samarkand. Then, laden with western goods, the Chinese merchants would turn back down the mountains for the three-thousand-kilometre journey home. **Oases** along the route inevitably prospered as staging posts and watering holes, becoming important and wealthy cities in their own right, with their own garrisons to protect the caravans. When Chinese domination periodically declined, many of these cities turned themselves into self-sufficient city-states, or **khanates**. Today, many of these once powerful cities are now buried in the sands.

The foundations for this famous **road to the West**, which was to become one of the most important arteries of **trade and culture** in world history, were laid over two millennia ago. In the second century BC nothing was known in China of the existence of people and lands beyond its borders, except by rumour. In 139 BC, the imperial court at Chang'an decided to despatch an emissary, a man called Zhang Qiang, to investigate the world to the west and to seek possible allies in the constant struggle against nomadic marauders from the north. Zhang set out with a party of a hundred men; thirteen years later he returned, with only two other members of his original expedition – and no alliances. But the news he brought nevertheless set Emperor Wu Di and his court aflame, including tales of Central Asia, Persia and even the Mediterranean world. Further **expeditions** were soon despatched, initially to purchase horses for military purposes, and from these beginnings trade soon developed.

By 100 BC a dozen immense caravans a year were heading into the desert. From the West came cucumbers, figs, chives, sesame, walnuts, grapes (and wine-making), wool, linen and ivory; from China, jade, porcelain, oranges, peaches, roses, chrysanthemums, cast iron, gunpowder, the crossbow, paper and printing, and **silk**. The silkworm had already been domesticated in China for hundreds of years, but

surrounding country, the troops slept in the open, meat was cooked by being placed under the saddle; and when the going got tough they would slit a vein in the horse's neck and drink the blood while still on the move. There was no supply problem, no camp followers, no excess baggage.

The onslaught that the Mongols unleashed on China in 1211 was on a massive scale. The Great Wall proved no obstacle to Genghis Khan, and with his two hundred thousand men he cut a swathe across northwest China towards Beijing. It was not all easy progress, however – so great was the destruction wrought in northern China that **famine and plague** broke out, afflicting the invader as much as the invaded. Genghis Khan himself died (of injuries sustained in falling from his horse) before the **capture of Beijing** had been completed. His body was carried back to Mongolia by a funeral cortege of ten thousand, who in the West the means by which silk was manufactured remained a total mystery – people believed it was combed from the leaves of trees. The Chinese took great pains to protect their monopoly, punishing any attempt to export silkworms with death. It was only many centuries later that sericulture finally began to spread west, when silkworm larvae were smuggled out of China in hollow walking sticks by Nestorian monks. The first time the **Romans** saw silk, snaking in the wind as the banners of their Parthian enemies, it filled them with terror and resulted in a humiliating rout. They determined to acquire it for themselves, and soon Roman society became obsessed with the fabric which by the first century AD was coming west in such large quantities that the corresponding outflow of gold had begun to threaten the stability of the Roman economy.

As well as goods, the Silk Road carried new ideas in **art and religion**. Nestorian Christianity and Manichaeism trickled east across the mountains, but by far the most influential force was **Buddhism**. The first Buddhist missionaries appeared during the first century AD, crossing the High Pamirs from India, and their creed gained rapid acceptance among the nomads and oasis dwellers of what is now western China. By the fourth century, Buddhism had become the official religion of much of northern China, and by the eighth it was accepted throughout the empire. All along the road, monasteries, chapels, stupas and grottoes proliferated, often sponsored by wealthy traders. The remains of this early flowering of **Buddhist art** along the road are among the great attractions of the Northwest for modern-day travellers. Naturally, history has taken its toll – zealous Muslims, Western archeologists, Red Guards and the forces of nature have all played a destructive part – but some sites have survived intact, above all the cave art at **Mogao** outside Dunhuang.

The Silk Road continued to flourish for centuries, reaching its zenith under the Tang (618–907 AD) and bringing immense wealth to the Chinese nobility and merchants. But it remained a slow, dangerous and expensive route. Predatory tribes to the north and south harried the caravans despite garrisons and military escorts. Occasionally entire regions broke free of Chinese control, requiring years to be "re-pacified". The route was physically arduous, too, taking at least five months from Chang'an to Kashgar, and whole caravans could be lost in the deserts or in the high mountain passes.

There was a brief final flowering of the trade in the thirteenth century, to which **Marco Polo** famously bore witness, when the whole Silk Road came temporarily under Mongol rule. But with the arrival of sericulture in Europe and the opening of sea routes between China and the West, the Silk Road had had its day. The road and its cities were slowly abandoned to the wind and the blowing sands.

murdered every man and beast within ten miles of the road so that news of the Great Khan's death could not be reported before his sons and viceroys had been gathered from the farthest corners of his dominions. The whereabouts of his **tomb** is uncertain, though according to one of the best-known stories his ashes are in a mausoleum near Dongsheng (see p.981), south of Baotou.

In the years after Genghis Khan's death, the fate of both China and of distant Europe teetered together on the brink. Having conquered all of Russia, the Mongol forces were poised in 1241 to make the relatively short final push across Europe to the Atlantic, when a message came from deep inside Asia that the invasion was to be cancelled. The decision to spare western Europe cleared the way for the **final conquest of China** instead, and by 1271 the Mongols had established their own dynasty – the **Yuan**. It was the first time

Kublai Khan

In Xanadu did Kubla Khan
A stately pleasure dome decree ...

Immortalized not only in the poetry of Samuel Coleridge but also in the memoirs of Marco Polo, **Kublai Khan** (1215–94) – known to the Chinese as Yuan Shizu – is the only emperor popularly known by name to the outside world. And little wonder: as well as mastering the subtle statecraft required to govern China as a foreigner, this grandson of Genghis Khan commanded an **empire** that encompassed the whole of China, central Asia, southern Russia and Persia – a larger area of land than perhaps anyone in history has ruled over, before or since. And yet this king of kings had been born into a nomadic tribe which had never shown the slightest interest in political life, and which, until shortly before his birth, was almost entirely illiterate.

From the beginning, Kublai Khan had shown an unusual talent for politics and government. He managed to get himself elected **Khan of the Mongols** in 1260, after the death of his brother, despite considerable opposition from the so-called "steppe aristocracy" who feared his disdain for traditional Mongolian skills. He never learned to read or write Chinese, yet after audaciously establishing himself as **Emperor of China**, proclaiming the Yuan dynasty in 1271, he soon saw the value of surrounding himself with advisers steeped in Confucianism. This was what enabled him to set up one hundred thousand Mongols in power over perhaps two hundred million Chinese. As well as **reunifying China** after centuries of division under the Song, Kublai Khan's contributions include establishing **paper money** as the standard medium of exchange, and fostering the **development of religion**, Lamaist Buddhism in particular. Above all, under his rule China experienced a brief – and uncharacteristic – period of **cosmopolitanism** which saw not only foreigners such as Marco Polo promoted to high positions of responsibility, but also a final flowering of the old Silk Road trade, as well as large numbers of Arab and Persian traders settling in seaports around Quanzhou in southeastern China.

Ironically, however, it was his admiration for the culture, arts, religion and sophisticated bureaucracy of China – as documented so enthusiastically by Marco Polo – that aroused bitter hostility from his own people, the Mongols, who despised what they saw as a betrayal of the ways of Genghis Khan. Kublai Khan was troubled by skirmishing nomads along the Great Wall no less than any of his more authentically Chinese predecessors. The great palace of **Xanadu** (in Inner Mongolia, near the modern city of Duolun), where Kublai Khan kept his legendary summer residence, was abandoned to fall into ruin; today virtually nothing of the site remains.

the Chinese had come under foreign rule. The Yuan is still an era about which Chinese historians can find little good to say, though the boundaries of the empire were expanded considerably, to include Yunnan and Tibet for the first time. The magnificent zenith of the dynasty was achieved under **Kublai Khan**, as documented in Marco Polo's *Travels* (see box, p.1219). Ironically, however, the Mongols were able to sustain their power only by becoming thoroughly Chinese, and abandoning the traditional nomadic Mongol way of life. Kublai Khan and his court soon forgot the warrior skills of their forefathers, and in 1368, less than a hundred years later, the Yuan, a shadow of their former selves, were **driven out of China** by the Ming. The Mongols returned to Mongolia, and reverted to their former ways, hunting, fighting among themselves and occasionally skirmishing with the Chinese down by the Wall. Astonishingly, history had come full circle.

Thereafter, Mongolian history moves gradually downhill, though right into the eighteenth century they maintained at least nominal control over many of the lands to the south and west originally won by Genghis Khan. These included **Tibet**, from where **Lamaist Buddhism** was imported to become the dominant religion in Mongolia. The few Tibetan-style monasteries in Mongolia that survive are an important testimony to this. Over the years, as well, came **settlers** from other parts of Asia: there is now a sizeable Muslim minority in the region, and under the Qing many Chinese settlers moved to Inner Mongolia, escaping overpopulation and famine at home, a trend that has continued under the Communists. The incoming settlers tried ploughing up the grassland with disastrous ecological results – wind and water swept the soil away – and the Mongols withdrew to the hills. Only recently has a serious programme of land stabilization and reclamation been established.

Sandwiched between two imperial powers, Mongolia found its independence constantly threatened. The Russians set up a protectorate over the north, while the rest came effectively under the control of China. In the 1930s, Japan occupied much of eastern Inner Mongolia as part of Manchuguo, and the Chinese Communists also maintained a strong presence. In 1945 Stalin persuaded Chiang Kaishek to recognize the independence of **Outer Mongolia** under Soviet protection as part of the Sino–Soviet anti-Japanese treaty, effectively sealing the fate of what then became the Mongolian People's Republic. In 1947, **Inner Mongolia** was designated the first Autonomous Region of the People's Republic of China.

Hohhot and around

There has been a town at **HOHHOT** (known as Huhehaote, or more commonly Hushi, to the Chinese) since the time of the Ming dynasty four hundred years ago, though it did not become the capital of Inner Mongolia until 1952. Until relatively modern times, it was a small town centred on a number of **Buddhist temples**. The temples are still here, and although it's now a major city, Hohhot manages to be an interesting blend of the old and the new, and a relatively green and leafy place in summer – which is fitting, as the town's Mongolian name means "green city". As well as the shiny new banks and department stores downtown, there's an extensive area in the south of the town with old, narrow streets built of black bricks and heavy roof tiles. These days Hohhot is largely a Han city, though there is also a Hui and a Mongol presence; it's worthwhile tracking down the vanishing **Mongol** areas, not least to try some of their distinctive **food**. The other reason for visiting Hohhot is its proximity to some of the famous Mongolian **grasslands** which lie within a hundred-kilometre radius of the city.

Arrival and accommodation

Hohhot is a fairly easy place to find your way around. The heart of the modern commercial city, including most hotels, lies in the blocks to the south of the **train and bus stations**, while the old city and its flamboyant temples are southwest of the central Qingcheng Park. Hohhot's Baita **airport** lies 35km east of the city, and the airport bus (¥5) drops arriving passengers at the CAAC office on Xilin Guole Lu, the road running south from the bus station. A taxi will cost ¥20.

Travellers arriving by train, in particular, are often subjected to furious and persistent harassment by travel agents trying to sell them grassland tours. The only practical way to escape the melee is to get into a **taxi** – the minimum fare is ¥6, sufficient for most rides within the city.

Hohhot and around

Hohhot	呼和浩特	*hūhé hàotè*
Dazhao	大召	*dàzhào*
Great Mosque	清真大寺	*qīngzhēn dàsì*
Horse racing course	赛马场	*sàimǎ chǎng*
Inner Mongolia Museum	内蒙古博物馆	*nèiménggǔ bówùguǎn*
Jiangjun Yashu	将军衙署	*jiāngjūn yáshǔ*
Mongolian Consulate	蒙古共和国领事馆	*ménggǔ gònghéguó lǐngshìguǎn*
Nationalities Market	民族商场	*mínzú shāngchǎng*
Qingcheng Park	青城公园	*qīngchéng gōngyuán*
Wuta Si	五塔寺	*wǔtǎ sì*
Xilituzhao	席里图召	*xílítú zhào*
Xinhua Square	新华广场	*xīnhuá guǎngchǎng*
Accommodation		
Beiyuan Hotel	北原饭店	*běiyuán fàndiàn*
Holiday Inn	假日大酒店	*jiàrì dàjiǔdiàn*
Railway Hotel	铁路宾馆	*tiělù bīnguǎn*
Tongda	通达饭店	*tōngdá fàndiàn*
Xincheng	新城宾馆	*xīnchéng bīnguǎn*
Zhaojun	昭君大酒店	*zhāojūn dàjiǔdiàn*
Eating		
Beijing Dumpling King	北京饺子王	*běijīng jiǎoziwáng*
Daxue Lu Market	大学路商场	*dàxuélù shāngchǎng*
Malaqin	马拉沁饭店	*mǎlāqìn fàndiàn*
Taiwan Beef Noodle	台湾牛肉面	*táiwān niúròumiàn*
Around Hohhot		
Bai Ta	百塔	*bǎi tǎ*
Erlianhot	二连浩特	*èrlián hàotè*
Gegentala	格根塔拉草原	*gégēntǎlā cǎoyuán*
Huitengxile	辉腾锡勒草原	*huīténgxīlè cǎoyuán*
Tomb of Wang Zhaojun	昭君墓	*zhāojūn mù*
Ulan Batur	乌兰巴托	*wūlán bātuō*
Wusutu Zhao	乌素图召	*wūsùtú zhào*
Xilamuren	希拉穆仁草原	*xīlāmùrén cǎoyuán*
Yurt	蒙古包	*ménggǔ bāo*
Zhaohe	召河	*zhàohé*

Accommodation

Hohhot has a sprinkling of **accommodation**, all fairly good value but not in great locations.

Beiyuan 28 Chezhan Xi Lu ☏0471/6966211. A small, quite salubrious place just opposite the train station offering a wide range of rooms and prices that include breakfast. The double rooms with bathroom are good value for ¥120, and dorm beds begin at ¥30. ❸

Holiday Inn 185 Zhongshan Xi Lu ☏0471/6351888. Hohhot's upmarket option, with a central location and all the amenities. In winter, rates fall as low as ¥280. ❽

Railway Hotel 131 Xilin Guole Lu ☏0471/6933377. Standard budget hotel with attentive staff and clean facilities, far enough south of the train station to escape the attention of touts. Breakfast is included in the rate, and they'll book train tickets. ❸

Tongda Chezhan Dong Lu ☏0471/6968731. Very convenient for the train station – it's straight across the road, and a little to the left as you come out. All rooms – doubles and three- and four-bedded

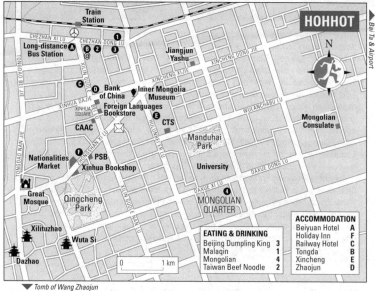

dorms – are clean with private bath. Ask to see the room first, as the photos downstairs are fading. The only drawback about this place is the predatory travel agents, most of whom have offices in the hotel. Dorm beds ¥35, ❷

Xincheng 40 Hulun Nan Lu ☎0471/6292588. In the east of the city near the museum, this was Hohhot's plushest establishment until the Holiday Inn opened in 2004. It feels more like an estate than a hotel, what with a driving range, bowling alley, and sheep grazing the grounds. There's no simple bus route

here, but it only takes about five minutes to get to by taxi (¥6) from the train or bus station. The drawback is there are no restaurants or city bustle nearby. Rooms can be haggled down to ¥400. ❽

Zhaojun Corner of Xilin Guole and Xinhua Dajie ☎0471/6962211. In the centre of town, diagonally across from Xinhua Square, it's worth the price for the location alone; it's also well organized and comfortable. The travel service in the lobby has information in English on their grassland and Genghis Khan mausoleum tours. ❻

The City

The focus of the city is **Xinhua Square**, at the junction of Xilin Guole Lu and the east–west axis Xinhua Dajie; early in the morning the square becomes an exercise ground for hundreds of people. A few blocks to the east of here is the newest shopping street in town, Xincheng Lu, while the busiest shopping area is on Zhongshan Lu, south of Xinhua Lu, around the **Nationalities Market**, a huge department store. Just to the south, **Qingcheng Park** is a fairly standard arrangement of lakes, causeways and pavilions, home to the city zoo.

There is just one historic building marooned in the new city, away to the east on Xincheng Xi Jie. This is the **Jiangjun Yashu** (daily 8am–4.30pm; ¥10), actually the office of a prominent Qing-dynasty general, even though it looks like a temple. Now it's a tiny museum with some bizarre modern Buddhist art mingling with Qing office furniture at the back. The best reason to come here is to see the scale model of ancient Hohhot, back before the city walls and temples were replaced with boulevards and banks. From the train station, bus #3 (¥1) will bring you here.

There are daily trains to the Mongolian border town of **Erlianhot** (see box, p.971), posted "Erlian" on schedules. Train #4602/3 departs Hohhot at 10.30pm, arriving at 7.18am the next day. Alternatively, train #5712/13 leaves Hohhot at 8.10am, pulling in at 7.32pm after rolling through the grasslands. Note that this view of the pastures will be far more relaxing, quiet and comfortable than joining one of many group tours.

To **Baotou**, there are buses running every thirty minutes; you can find them on the main street outside the station, attended by people with loud-hailers. Fast ones (2.5hr) charge ¥26, slower ones (3.5hr) ¥17. (The extra fee is worth it, as the bus drives on the freeway instead of through small towns.) There is also at least one daily (early morning) bus to **Dongsheng** (6hr; ¥60) for Genghis Khan's Mausoleum (see p.981), with increased frequency during the summer. Note that you may have to change buses in Baotou, anyhow – it's much easier to travel there by bus or train, then catch a bus onward.

Hohhot is linked by **train** to **Lanzhou** to the west, **Beijing** to the east and **Hailar** (a 38hr journey via Beijing) to the northeast. There are also trains to **Ulan Batur** in the Republic of Mongolia (see box, p.971). Leaving Hohhot by train, you can seek the help of a travel agent to procure tickets for a small commission. You'll need to give them at least 36 hours' notice for a hard sleeper – or try your luck at the station ticket office, which is sometimes hideously crowded and sometimes empty.

Also on the route of bus #3, the **Inner Mongolia Museum** on the corner of Xinhua Dajie and Hulunbei'er Lu (daily 9am–5pm; ¥10) is well worth a visit. In the downstairs exhibition, there's a large display of ethnic Mongolian items, such as costumes, saddles, long leather coats and cummerbunds, as well as hunting and sporting implements, including some very European-looking hockey sticks and balls. There's also a good paleontology display, with complete fossils of a woolly rhinoceros and a sizeable dinosaur. Upstairs are interesting maps and objects detailing the exploits of Genghis Khan, and the huge Mongol empire of the thirteenth century. While there are some English explanations, if you're truly keen on grasping the significance of the display, check in at the main office behind the ticket desk, where the curator speaks English and may be willing to give you a tour.

A couple of kilometres north of the train station, and served by #13 bus from the centre of town, is the gigantic **Inner Mongolia horse race course**, the biggest in China, built in the shape of two circular Mongolian yurts, adjacent and connected to each other to form the elongated shape of a stadium. It's put to frenzied use during **Naadam**, the summer Mongolian festival that combines horsemanship with wrestling and other games. The dates vary, but Naadam usually falls between late July and early August. Outside the holiday, displays of Mongolian riding and dancing sometimes take place here. It's worth stopping by during the day to see what's scheduled, or try enquiring at hotels and travel agents.

Old Hohhot

Most of the historic buildings of Hohhot are crowded into the interesting – though fast-disappearing – old southwestern part of the city, where you can enjoyably spend a day simply ambling around. From the train station, buses #6, #7 and #8 run here – get off at the Hui Middle School stop. You'll immediately see the Chinese-style minaret (topped with a pagoda roof) of the **Great Mosque**. This attractive black-brick building, situated at the southern end of

Zhongshan Lu, blends traces of Chinese and Arabic style. Some of the Hui people who worship here are extremely friendly, and will probably be delighted if you ask to look round the mosque. The surrounding streets comprise the Muslim area of town, and besides a lot of old men with wispy beards and skull caps, you'll find a fantastic array of noodle and kebab shops if you head down the tight alleyway directly north of the mosque.

Walking south from the mosque for about fifteen minutes along the main road leads to a couple of Buddhist temples. The biggest of these is the **Dazhao**, down a side street west of the main road (daily 8am–5pm; ¥10). Originally constructed in 1579, and recently the subject of a typically gaudy renovation, the structure was dedicated in the late seventeenth century to the famous Qing emperor Kangxi – a gold tablet with the words "Long Live the Emperor" was set before the silver statue of Sakyamuni, and in the main hall murals depicting the visit of the Emperor Kangxi can still be seen.

Just a few minutes from the Dazhao, over on the other side of the main road, is the **Xilituzhao** (daily 8am–5pm; ¥10), another temple of similar scale and layout to the Dazhao, and dating from the same era, though it too has been restored since the destruction of the Cultural Revolution. The dagoba is interesting for featuring Sanskrit writing above Chinese dragons above Tibetan-style murals. Since 1735 this has been the official residence of the reincarnation of the Living Buddha, who is in charge of Buddhist affairs in the city. Friendly and homesick Tibetan monks who speak pretty good English are happy to show you around.

Farther east, via a diverting walk along winding, narrow alleys comprising the last remains of the old city, you'll come to the most attractive piece of architecture in the city, known as the **Wuta Si** (Five Towers Temple; daily 8am–5pm; ¥10). Built in 1727, in pure Indian style, this composite of five pagodas originally belonged to the Ci Deng Temple, which no longer exists. It's relatively small, but its walls are engraved with no fewer than 1563 Buddhas, all in slightly different postures. Currently stored inside the pagoda building is a rare, antique Mongolian cosmological map that marks the position of hundreds of stars.

Eating and drinking

The highlight of eating in Hohhot is the chance to eat **Mongolian food**. Mongolian **hotpot**, or *shuan yangrou*, is best shared with friends and beer. It's a do-it-yourself meal: piles of thinly sliced mutton, ordered by the *jin*, are cooked by being dropped into a cauldron of boiling water at the table, then quickly removed and dipped into a spicy sesame sauce. Tofu, glass noodles, cabbage and mushrooms are common accompaniments which go into the pot too. Many restaurants in Hohhot serve *shuan yangrou* – the most famous being *Malaqin Restaurant* on Xincheng Xi Jie, a few blocks east of Hulunbei'er Lu. Dinner here with plenty of beer shouldn't cost more than ¥40 per head. There's also a branch in the guesthouse of the same name east of the train station, on the north side of Chezhan Donglu.

For an even more exotic meal, however, with the focus on Mongolian dairy products, head for the Mongolian quarter in the southeast of town. Bus #4 comes down here – get off at Daxue Lu just south of the university. During term time, this area is packed with students, and restaurants stay open late. Any restaurant with Mongolian letters above the door is worth trying, in particular the one just 200m down the small street leading south from beside the Daxue Lu Shangchang. For an excellent breakfast or lunch, order a large bowl of sugary milk tea, and *chaomi* (buckwheat), *huangyou* (butter), *nailao* (hard white cheese), and *naipi* (a sweetish, biscuit-like substance formed from the skin of boiled milk). Toss everything into the tea, and eat it with chopsticks – it's surprisingly delicious. To make this into a substantial meal, eat it with *mengu baozi* or *jianbing* – dough stuffed with ground mutton, respectively steamed or fried.

There's plenty of standard **Chinese** food in Hohhot, especially around the train station. *Beijing Dumpling King* is a multi-segmented eating place 100m east of the station on the south side of Chezhan Dongjie; or try the simple *Taiwan Beef Noodle Restaurant*, whose limited menu is written in English – it's a little to the east of the *Tongda Hotel. KFC* nests all across the city, including branches on Tongdao Nan Jie (opposite the mosque) and Zhongshan Xi Lu (at the Nationalities Market).

Listings

Airlines CAAC, Xilinguole Lu, is just south of Xinhua Square (Mon–Sat, 8am–9pm; ☎0471/6963160).

Banks and exchange The easiest place to change money, including traveller's cheques, is inside the *Zhaojun Hotel*, which changes money for non-guests, offers the same rates as the bank and operates at weekends. The head office of the Bank of China (Mon–Fri 8am–noon & 2–5pm, Sat am only) is actually across the road from the hotel.

Bookshops There's a Foreign Language Bookstore on Xilin Guole Lu, across the road from Xinhua Square. Xinhua Bookstore is on Zhongshan Lu, across the road from (and a couple of minutes to the south of) the Nationalities Market.

Consulate The Consulate of the Republic of Mongolia is in the east of the city (Mon, Tues & Thurs 8.30am–noon; ☎0471/4303254), at 5 Wulanzaigu. Visas are fairly easy to obtain, though they cost ¥500 for a month and may take some time to be issued. US citizens do not need visas for stays up to thirty days.

Internet access A cheap Internet café is upstairs in the Telecom Office, next door to the post office

(daily 8am–6pm; ¥8/hr). Walk south from the train station on the left-hand side of Xilin Guole Lu, and a signboard points the way into the recesses of a building, where a grotty but friendly café has fast connections (¥2/hour).

Mail and telephones The main post office is on the south side of Zhongshan Lu, just east of Xilin Guole Lu (Mon–Sat 8am–7pm). The Telecom Centre is adjacent (daily 8am–6pm), with a small 24hr office.

PSB In the government building to the south of the junction between Zhongshan Lu and Xilin Guole Lu.

Travel agents There are numerous travel agents in town, many of whom will find you before you find them. They nearly all have English-speaking employees, and deal in grassland tours as well as booking train tickets. CTS, on the third floor of the back building of the *Inner Mongolia Hotel* (☎0471/6964233), has some pleasant, approachable staff. The *Tongda Hotel* also holds several tour operators, as does the helpful desk in the lobby of the *Holiday Inn* and *Zhaojun Hotel*.

Around Hohhot

There are a few more sights scattered around the outer suburbs of Hohhot, some of which can be reached on city buses. The **Tomb of Wang Zhaojun**, (daily 9am–5pm; ¥18) about 8km to the south of Hohhot, is the burial site of a Tang-dynasty princess sent from present-day Hubei to cement Han–Mongol relations by marrying the king of Mongolia. It isn't spectacular – a huge mound raised from the plain and planted with gardens, in the centre of which is a modern pavilion – but the romantic story it recalls has important implications for modern Chinese politics, signifying the harmonious marrying of the Han with the minority peoples. In the rose garden, among pergolas festooned with gourds, is a tiny museum devoted to Zhaojun, containing some of her clothes, including a tiny pair of shoes, plus jewels, books and a number of steles. You can reach the tomb by the #44 minibus (¥1.5), or by walking due south along the main road from the Great Mosque in the west of town.

Should you require them, visas for the Republic of Mongolia, otherwise known as **Outer Mongolia**, are available in Hohhot and Beijing, and are a lot easier to obtain since the departure of the old Communists from power in the capital, Ulan Batur, in 1996.

There are various ways into the country from China. At the time of writing, CAAC and MIAT (the national airline of the Republic of Mongolian) had suspended **flights** from Hohhot to Ulan Batur. However, Air China and MIAT both fly three times weekly **from Beijing** to Ulan Batur; tickets for the two-hour flight cost around ¥2000 one-way, while the **direct train**, which takes about 36 hours, is cheaper at ¥500.

Alternatively, you can do the journey in stages from Hohhot. The first leg is to get to the border at Erlianhot, shortened to Erlian on timetables. Two **direct trains** run daily (9–11hr; ¥73). Or you can break the trip and soak up more of the grasslands by stopping in Jining (2hr; ¥22), then change to the Erlianhot train (4 daily, 4–7hr; ¥46). If you want to take the **bus** from Hohhot to Erlianhot (9hr), check with the Hohhot PSB if tourists need a permit to travel on it.

Crossing the border at Erlianhot is still something of a hassle if you are not on a through train. Assuming you arrive in the evening you'll certainly have to spend one night here. In the morning there's one local bus that does the seven-kilometre trip across to the Mongolian town of **Zamen Uud**, though you may wait hours for it to leave. From there to Ulan Batur it's an eighteen-hour train journey.

Erlianhot itself is a curious border town in the middle of nowhere, which caters to Mongolian nomads and shepherds coming to town to do their shopping. It's also a famous centre for wool production. Twice a week its train station briefly fills with foreigners as the Trans-Mongolian Express comes through on its way to or from Moscow – there's even a disco and a bar here for their entertainment. Eat all you can here, because the food in Outer Mongolia is notoriously poor.

Not accessible by bus, but well worth the effort to reach, is the **Wusutu Zhao** complex, the only temple in Mongolia to have been designed and built solely by Mongolians. Boasting buildings in Mongolian, Tibetan and Han styles, it lies 12km northwest of Hohhot, south of the Daqing Mountain and in attractive countryside separated from the city by the new expressway. Admission to each of the four neighbouring temples is ¥3, collected by an elderly monk who will probably be surprised to see you. There are still no souvenir stands, no gawdy refurbishments – the complex hasn't made it into the burgeoning Chinese guidebook trade – so take the time to scour the Ming-era murals within and the ornate woodcuts attached to sticks at the base of the Buddhas. The surrounding grasslands and trails into the mountains make for a relaxing day out. To get here from the train station, take bus #5 to its terminus and hire a taxi from there, a ride which shouldn't come to more than ¥20, though unless you're prepared to hire the taxi for a half day, you'll probably have to walk back to the bus stop later, about an hour's hike along a busy road.

Slightly farther out is one more site that you can reach only by taxi: the **Bai Ta**, or White Pagoda (dawn–dusk daily; ¥5), about 17km east of the city, is an attractive, 55-metre-high wood and brick construction, erected in the tenth century and covered in ornate carvings of coiling dragons, birds and flowers on the lower parts of the tower. You can reach it by following Xincheng Xi Jie east out of the city – it's a possible stopoff on the way to the airport.

The grasslands

Mongolia isn't all one giant steppe, but three areas in the vicinity of Hohhot are certainly large enough to give the illusion of endlessness. These are

Xilamuren (which begins 80km north of Hohhot), **Gegentala** (150km north) and **Huitengxile** (120km west). It's hard to differentiate between them, save to say that Xilamuren – the only one of the three that can feasibly be reached independently – is probably the most visited and Gegentala the least. Bear in mind that your grassland experience in the immediate area of the regional capital is likely to be a rather packaged affair, and a visit to a grassland in another, remoter part of the region (such as Hailar – see p.973) may well give you a more authentic flavour of Mongolia.

The most convenient way to visit the grasslands is to take one of the **grassland tours**, which Westerners rarely enjoy but east Asian tourists seem to love – or at least put up with in good humour. The tours always follow a similar pattern, with visitors based at a site comprising a number of **yurts**, plus a dining hall, kitchen and very primitive toilets. The larger sites, at Xilamuren, are the size of small villages. Transport, meals and accommodation are all included in the price, as are various unconvincing "Mongolian entertainments" – wrestling and horse-riding in particular – and visits to typical Mongol families in traditional dress. Only the food is consistently good, though watch out for the local *baijiu*, which you're more or less forced to drink when your Mongolian hosts bring silver bowls of the stuff round to every table during the evening banquet. The banquet is followed by a fairly degenerate evening of drinking, dancing and singing.

If you accept the idea that you are going on a tour of the grasslands primarily to participate in a bizarre social experience, then you'll get much more out of it. Besides, it is perfectly possible to escape from your group if you wish to do so. You can hire your own horse, or head off for a hike. If your stay happens to coincide with a bright moon, you could be in for the most hauntingly beautiful experience of your life.

Practicalities

A two-day tour (with one night in a yurt) is definitely enough – in a group of six or seven people, this should come to between ¥250 and ¥350 each. Some travel services (such as the Inner Mongolia Lüye International Travel Company based in the *Tongda Hotel*, Room 424; ☎0471/6968613) can tack smaller parties onto existing groups. Bear in mind that if you choose this option, you may find yourself sleeping crushed into a small yurt with six others who don't speak your language, and consequently the tour may not be in English, even if you've specifically requested that it should be. That said, if all you really want to do is gaze upon an ocean of grass, consider catching the 7.50am bus for Xilamuren in front of the train station. It ferries the first 20 arrivals out there and back (departing 3pm) for ¥14 each.

Travelling independently to the Xilamuren grassland can work out a good deal cheaper than taking a tour. Store your luggage at your hotel in Hohhot, and catch a bus from the long-distance bus station to the small settlement of **Zhaohe** (2 daily; 2–3hr; ¥8), adjacent to the grassland. When you get off you will be accosted by people offering to take you to their yurts – try to negotiate an all-inclusive daily rate of about ¥50 per person, for food and accommodation, before you accept any offer. You aren't exactly in the wilderness here, but you can wander off into the grass and soon find it.

The northeast of Inner Mongolia

The colossal area of land that comprises Inner Mongolia to the east and north of Hohhot is scarcely visited by tourists, which is reason enough to journey up

The northeast of Inner Mongolia

Pastureland homes	牧场家	*mùchǎngjiā*
Chifeng	赤峰	*chìfēng*
Hailar	海拉尔	*hǎilā'ěr*
Bei'er Hotel	贝尔大酒店	*bè'iěr dàjiǔdiàn*
Beiyuan Hotel	北苑宾馆	*běiyuàn bīnguǎn*
Hulunbeier Hotel	呼伦贝尔宾馆	*hūlúnbèi'ěr bīnguǎn*
Hulunbuir grasslands	呼伦贝尔草原	*hūlúnbèi'ěr cǎoyuán*
Japanese army tunnels	侵华日军海拉尔要塞遗址	*qīnhuá rìjūn hǎilā'ěr yàosài yízhǐ*
Laodong Hotel	劳动宾馆	*láodòng bīnguǎn*
Manzhouli	满洲里	*mǎnzhōulǐ*
Beifang Market	北方市场	*běifāng shìchǎng*
Da Dongbei Nongjia Fanzhuang	大东北农家饭庄	*dàdōngběi nóngjiā fànzhuāng*
Dalai Hu	达赉湖	*dálài hú*
Friendship Hotel	友谊宾馆	*yǒuyí bīnguǎn*
International Hotel	国际大酒店	*guójì dàjiǔdiàn*
Mockba Neon Lights	莫斯科饭店	*mòsīkē fàndiàn*
Tongliao	通辽	*tōngliáo*

here. As an area populated by nomadic sheep-herders since the beginning of history, its attractions lie not in old towns, but in the wilderness. The terrain is hilly, and the farther north you go the wetter it gets and the more trees there are. The grass on the **eastern grasslands** is accordingly longer and more lush, though for only a brief period each year. People are few and far between, the land outside the towns only occasionally punctuated by the sight of **muchang jia** – pastureland homes – comprising groups of yurts in the grass, surrounded by herds of sheep, cattle or horses. Visiting *muchang jia* is exclusively a summertime activity; during the long winters, temperatures can dip to a scary -50°C.

For travellers the area is not an easy one to explore, given the paucity of **transport** connections. As the local authorities have in the past not been keen on foreign travellers crossing the region by **bus** (it's worth checking the current situation with the PSB), flying may turn out to be the only option if you don't want to spend ages on trains – though for rail enthusiasts, the epic train journeys are themselves a possible reason for coming here. The only rail lines are in the far north, offering access to **Hailar** and **Manzhouli** on the Russian border. Hailar lies 38 hours by train from Hohhot, the route first passing east through Datong to Beijing, then moving north back into Inner Mongolia, passing the towns of **Chifeng** and **Tongliao** – both of which are surrounded by their own grasslands which can also be visited. From here the train drifts east into Jilin province in Dongbei (see p.206). Much later the train cuts back into Inner Mongolia at Zhalantun from where it travels northwest to Hailar. For hour after hour there's barely a sign of sentient life, the train traversing hilly, grassy pastures, past misthung rivers and cool, wooded valleys during the last third of the journey.

Hailar

In the far northeast of Inner Mongolia, **HAILAR**, with rail connections as well as an airport, is the main transport hub of the region, and a centre for grassland visits. The town of Hailar itself is of minimal interest, a small, light-industrial and agricultural place on the banks of the Heilongjiang (Amur) River with a small Muslim population as well as the usual Mongol/Han mix. The main attraction in the town itself is the recently reopened **network of tunnels** used by the Japanese army during World War II. Hailar was Japan's westernmost base during the war, the Japanese agreeing to halt their advance at Hailar in exchange for Russia's non-interference in Manchuria, which in turn allowed Russia to concentrate on battling Hitler in the West. The tunnel complex, wrought by Chinese prisoners of war, sits in Hailar's northwest, atop a ridge that affords an excellent vantage point of the river and grasslands. The site can only be reached by a bumpy taxi ride (¥12) from the train station via a rutted track in the grasslands. A plaque at the entrance explains, in English, the wartime history of the area. Enter the rebuilt bunker (¥20) to descend 40m underground into the tunnels themselves. A small Chinese-language exhibit greets you in the chilly depths, after which you're free to wander about with a torch amid the eerie echo of your footsteps. Back above ground, it's a pleasant thirty-minute walk among grasses and dunes back to the train station.

The chief reason most visitors come to Hailar, however, is to see the North Mongolian **Hulunbuir grasslands**, an apparently limitless rolling land of plains and low grassy mountains, traced by slow rivers teeming with fish. Hundreds of thousands of sheep, cattle and horses graze this seemingly inexhaustible pasture, spread over hundreds of kilometres. In summer they occupy the higher pastures and in winter they come down to the lowlands, still often deep in snow. Transport in the area is mostly by camel and pony. Not only is the grass scattered with a variety of flowers and huge fungi, but, as you soon discover, it's also alive with little black toads (which it's virtually impossible to avoid treading on), grasshoppers, birds and insects (**mosquito repellent** is essential).

As elsewhere in Inner Mongolia, there are the CITS-approved villages of Mongol herders, who earn part of their income from occasional groups of tourists, mostly from Japan. Though you could try to strike off independently, it's worth noting that the grassland **tours** here don't attract hordes of people. A day-trip from Hailar to eat a traditional mutton banquet on the grassland, for a group of four people, costs in the region of ¥120 each. If you want to spend a night on the grasslands as well, reckon on around ¥200. Inclusion of an English-speaking guide sends the price soaring to ¥800, so you'll need to be in a large group to make this worth your while. For bookings and more information, contact CITS (☎0470/8246368) at their inconveniently located office on the third floor of the *Beiyuan Hotel* (see p.975).

Practicalities

A compact place, Hailar is divided into two by the Yimin River. The **train station** is on the west bank; to reach the city centre from here, turn left as you exit, continue on for a block and then turn left again to cross the tracks via a pedestrian bridge. Once across the footbridge, you'll find buses #1 and #3 running a little way south to Zhongyang Jie, the city's main artery, passing the **long-distance bus station**, at the junction of Huochezhan Jie and Shanghua Jie, on the way. The bus station is useful only for the frequent service to the Russian border at Manzhouli (3hr; ¥25). Zhongyang Jie turns into Qiaotou Jie at the *Bei'er Dajiudian*; the area between here and Zhongyang Qiao – the river bridge – is filled with shops selling everything from pirated CDs to Mongolian saddles. The district across the bridge, where the road becomes Shengli Dajie, is of minimal interest unless you're staying at one of its cavernous hotels. **CAAC** is off Qiaotou Jie (daily 8am–5pm; ☎0470/8331010), on the small road leading east off the southwestern approach road to the bridge. There's a **bank** that will change money right next to the *Bei'er* hotel.

Hailar offers a range of **accommodation**, so be sure to bargain. One convenient place is the *Binzhou Fandian* (no phone), on the left-hand side of the train-station concourse as you exit the building. Rooms here are simple and clean, and the hot water works. Though it isn't close to the centre, its hourly (¥10) and half-day (¥30) rates make it a good pit stop if you've been out on the grasslands and want to wash up before heading out of town. In the centre, the best option is the *Bei'er Dajiudian* (☎0470/8332511; ❹), 36 Zhongyang Dajie, where the rate includes breakfast. The travel service here is helpful and its grassland tours cost less than those at CITS, though note that you will likely be wedged into a minibus with high-spirited (read: drunk) Chinese tourists. Across the street, at no. 35, the *Laodong Hotel* has three-person dorms as well as doubles (☎0470/8331349; ❸), dorm beds ¥50).

Lurking on the east bank of the river is Hailar's throwback to the bad old days of Chinese tourism, the enormous, impersonal *Hulunbeier Hotel* (☎0470/8211000; ℱ8221123; ❸–❺), with a large range of bland doubles in its many wings, as well as accommodation in cement "yurts" dotting its parking lot. For a better atmosphere at similar rates, head further east to the *Beiyuan Hotel* (☎0471/8235666; ❹), 22 Shengli San Lu, north off Shengli Dajie. Its major drawback is being surrounded by the district government and police offices, meaning street and nightlife congregate elsewhere.

The best area for **eating** is in the pedestrianized commercial district east of the *Bei'er Hotel* and north of Qiaotou Dajie. Be sure to study the menu (or even better, the kitchen), as Hailarites have a taste for **dog**, judging by the number of canine skeletons hanging about. The pedestrian zone has a bazaar atmosphere, and is worth wandering through its sprawl across both sides of Zhongyang Dajie. You'll find bookshops, and **Internet cafés** here as well.

Manzhouli

A few hours to the west of Hailar is the more entertaining **MANZHOULI**, which on arrival feels like the bustling Sino-Russian border town that it was a century ago. Russian engineers of the Trans-Siberian Railway founded the town as Manchuria Station in 1903. Their mark on local architecture can be seen around town, most immediately outside the train station, where today's castle-like Railway Hospital was built as the czar's consulate. Several colonial-era buildings rot on this side of the tracks, so a walk along the dirt lanes is recommended.

Manzhouli proper is on the opposite side of the railyard. From the station, you need to take a taxi (¥10) into town. **Buses** drop off passengers arriving from Hailar in the new city, whose bus station is tucked on the west end, amid wooden cottages and the original, now vacant and peeling, offices of the Trans-Siberian. The city's chequered history gets a good display at the **museum** (daily 9am–5pm; ¥10), at 9 Si Dao Jie.

Manzhouli is compact, with five east–west roads (numbered *yi*, *er*, *san*, *si* and *wu dao jie*) crossed by five north–south avenues (*lu*). The buildings fronting them are either century-old Gothic or modern blocks, meaning that outwardly, Manzhouli looks not even remotely Chinese. Russian cars fill the streets, and it's easier to get a bowl of borscht than a plate of roast duck. The block-size squat marketplaces with squares at their centre look like they rode the train in from Paris, and decided to settle. Largest is the massive **Beifang Market**, at the intersection of Xi Wu Dao Jie and Xinhua Lu. Inside is a warren of Chinese merchants selling everything from ice skates, as well as plungers to eager Russian traders, who began pouring in since the collapse of the Soviet Union and its manufacturing industry. The merchants themselves are migrants too – it's worth asking which province they're from.

Practicalities

For all of Manzhouli's charm, its **hotels** mainly cater to overnight traders but there are reasonable places to stay. The two best centrally located options are the *Friendship Hotel* at 26 Yi Dao Jie (☎0470/6223977; ❻) and the *International*, 35 Er Dao Jie (☎0470/6248188; ❺). At both places, try bargaining down the quoted rate.

Eating is a treat if you love Russian food. The liveliest of the many Russian restaurants is *Mockba Neon Lights*, on Yi Dao Jie, east of the Mingzhu Hotel. At around 10pm, the place begins to resemble a Siberian version of the *Star Wars* cantina, with burly bearded traders knocking back vodkas and Chinese tourists watching the dancers. Over at no. 3 Si Dao Jie, *Da Dongbei Nongjia Fanzhuang* serves great dumplings and Chinese fare.

A **taxi** anywhere in the new town will cost ¥5. **Bank of China** is at 16 Er Dao Jie. The **post office** sits at the corner of Si Dao Jie and Haiguan Lu. **Internet cafés** are common in town; the one directly across from the *Friendship Hotel* is open 24hrs. **PSB** are at 10 Si Dao Jie, directly across from the museum.

Around Manzhouli

The Trans-Siberian train from Beijing to Moscow passes through town once a week in each direction. The tracks cross underneath the **Friendship Gate** on the Sino-Russian border. You can visit, but there's little to see aside from Chinese soldiers, guard dogs, and a very uninspiring cement arch that interrupts an otherwise interminable expanse of grassland. A round-trip cab from town to the gate shouldn't cost more than ¥20. **Steam locomotive** buffs should inquire at the train station or hotels about visiting the opencast mine at Jalainur, 30km east of Manzhouli on the railway. Steam trains are still in operation here, though during freezing months the coal pit gets mothballed.

More appealing, and a similar distance from the south of town, is the great lake **Dalai Hu** (Hulun Nur in Mongolian). The lake is a shallow expanse of water set in marshy grazing country where flocks of swans, geese, cranes and other migratory birds come to nest. The grasslands in this region are said to be the greenest in all Mongolia. Coming here may be the most rewarding – and least expensive – way to see Inner Mongolia's grassland. A taxi from town will cost ¥40 round-trip, and a ticket into the lake preserve only ¥5.

The corner of China north of Hailar and Manzhouli is a **true wilderness**, the final frontier of China. Here are some of the last great areas of untouched primeval forest in the country, a natural habitat for the wolf and the much-threatened Manchurian tiger. There is a rail line that meanders up as far north as Mangui, above the fifty-second parallel, but before attempting to visit this area you should check with the Hailar PSB.

Baotou and beyond

Just three hours to the west of Hohhot by train or bus lies Inner Mongolia's biggest and bleakest city, **BAOTOU**. Its primary significance is as the chief

Baotou and beyond		
Baotou	包头	*bāotóu*
Donghe	东河	*dōnghé*
Kundulun	昆都仑	*kūndūlún*
Qingshan	青山	*qīngshān*
Accommodation		
Aviation	民航大厦	*mínháng dàshà*
Baotou	包头宾馆	*bāotóu bīnguǎn*
Shenhua International	神华国际大酒店	*shénhuá guójì dàjiǔdiàn*
Tianwaitian	天外天大酒店	*tiānwàitiān dàjiǔdiàn*
Dongsheng	东胜	*dōngshèng*
Dongsheng Hotel	东胜宾馆	*dōngshèng bīnguǎn*
Genghis Khan's Mausoleum	成吉思汗陵园	*chéngjísīhàn língyuán*
Jiaotong Hotel	交通宾馆	*jiāotōng bīnguǎn*
Tianjiao Hotel	天骄宾馆	*tiānjiāo bīnguǎn*
Wudangzhao	五当召	*wǔdāng zhào*
Yellow River	黄河	*huánghé*

iron- and steel-producing centre in China: if you're arriving at night from the direction of Yinchuan, your first glimpse of the city is likely to be of satanic fires burning in the great blast furnaces. The sky over the western half of Baotou is a more or less permanent yellow, orange and purple colour. For visitors, there can be something magnificent about ugliness on such a scale, but otherwise, apart from a few minor sights, including **Wudangzhao**, an attractive Tibetan-style monastery outside the town, the city does not have much to offer. One further site of considerable romantic interest (if nothing else), **Genghis Khan's Mausoleum**, lies well to the south of Baotou near the town of **Dongsheng**.

The City

A colossal city stretching for miles in all directions, Baotou comprises three main areas: Donghe, the ramshackle, oldest part of town, to the east, and Qing-shan and Kundulun to the west. Qingshan is a shopping and residential area, while Kundulun includes the iron and steel works on its western edge. The three parts of the city are well connected by frequent buses (#5 and #10; ¥2), which take thirty to forty minutes to travel between the Donghe and Kundu-lun districts. Taxis begin at ¥6 for the first 3km, charging ¥1.2 per additional kilometre. Traversing Baotou, this can add up quickly.

Practicalities

There are two major **train stations**, one in Kundulun (Baotou Zhan) and one in Donghe (Baotou Dong Zhan). All through-trains, including express trains from Beijing and Lanzhou, stop at both stations; trains call at Donghe first if you're approaching from the east (Hohhot, Beijing), while if you're coming from the west or south (Lanzhou, Xi'an) then Kundulun is the first stop. The **bus station** is right opposite the Donghe train station; tickets for Hohhot should be bought on the bus. There are several parked out front on the concourse, so you can choose the level of class and speed you desire. For

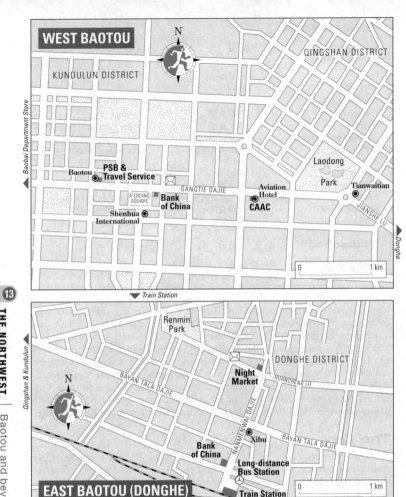

Dongsheng (every 30min), you can buy your ticket inside the bus station, though in warm months the touts will find you before you can say "Genghis Khan". The **airport** is just a couple of kilometres south of the Donghe train station. The **CAAC** office (☏0472/5135492) is across the city in Kundulun, on the south side of Gangtie Dajie between Yinghe Square and Laodong (Labour) Square.

There's a rather unhelpful **CITS** office (☏0472/5154615) in a bunker at the front gate of the *Baotou Hotel*. The **PSB** is also in the *Baotou*, on the first floor. To change traveller's cheques, go to the main office of the **Bank of China** in Kundulun (daily 8am–6pm), on the main road just east of A'erding Square. The Bank of China's branches in Donghe, including the one 50m south of the train station on the western side of Nanmenwai Dajie, change cash only. The main **post and telecommunications office** is in Kundulun near the Bank of China, and there's also a post office in Donghe.

Accommodation, eating and drinking

Of the two ends of town, **Donghe** is the more convenient place **to stay** for embarking to Genghis Khan's mausoleum, though sadly there isn't much choice here. From the train station, walk north straight up the main road, Nanmenwai Dajie. On the right, at no. 10 before the intersection with Bayan Tala Dajie, is the *Xihu (West Lake) Hotel* (℡0472/4187101). It has clean, standard doubles from ¥158, and three-person rooms that begin at ¥31/bed.

If you want to stay in **Kundulun**, be warned that the hotels in this part of town are a long way from the central station, though bus #1 from the station will take you into the centre. A good bet in Kundulun is the enormous *Baotou* (℡0472/5156655, ℻5154641; ❹), on the main east–west Gangtie Dajie, a few hundred metres west of A'erding Square. It's reasonably comfortable, central and home to the city's PSB and CITS offices. The most upmarket hotel in town is the new *Shenhua International*, the tall edifice behind A'erding Square at 17 Shaoxian (℡0472/536888; ❼), with its own pool, sauna and gym. Also fancy, with swimming pool and fitness centre, is the older *Tianwaitian*, on the southern end of Hudemulin Dajie in Qingshan district (℡0472/5361888; ❺), though the cheaper *Aviation Hotel* (℡0472/5135492; ❹), part of the CAAC office, may be more convenient if you're departing by air.

Baotou has a lousy array of **restaurants**. In Kundulun, tell the taxi driver to take you to Baobai, the gleaming shopping district west on Gangtie Dajie; there's a *KFC* and *Goubuli* dumpling franchise here. Across the street is a market with food stalls and small eateries. In Donghe, a summer night market with food stalls sets up near the junction of Nanmenwai Dajie and Huancheng Lu.

Wudangzhao and the Yellow River

The one definite attraction in the Baotou area, **Wudangzhao** is the best-preserved Lamaist monastery still functioning in Inner Mongolia (daily 8am–6pm; ¥35), and is one of the results of the Mongolian conquest of Tibet in the thirteenth century. For centuries afterwards, the roads between Tibet and Mongolia were worn by countless pilgrims and wandering monks, bringing Lamaist Buddhism to Mongolia. This particular monastery, of the Yellow Sect, was established in 1749 and at its height housed twelve hundred lamas; seven generations of Living Buddhas were based here, the ashes of whom are kept in one of the halls. Today, however, the few remaining monks are greatly outnumbered by local tourists from Baotou, and sadly their main duties now seem to involve hanging around at the hall entrances to check tourists' tickets.

Set in a pretty, narrow valley about 70km northeast of Baotou, the monastery can be reached by catching the daily **minibus** (¥7) from outside the Donghe train station at 10am or 4pm. Otherwise, take **bus** #7 (50min; ¥4) from the east side of the station square (on the right as you exit the station) to the terminus at Shiguai. The monastery is another 25km on – if you arrive early enough there are one or two minibuses that go on to it from here, otherwise take a taxi from Shiguai (¥30). Once at the monastery, you can hike off into the surrounding hills and, if you're keen, you should be able to **stay** in the pilgrims' hostel in the monastery as well. Returning to Baotou is fairly easy as there are various minibuses and other tour vehicles plying the route, up to around 5pm. Hiring a taxi for the round-trip to the temple should cost ¥150.

The Yellow River

The other main sight in the Baotou area is the **Yellow River**, worth having a look at, if only to ruminate on its historical significance. When the Chinese built the Great Wall far to the south, the area between the Inner Mongolian loop of the Yellow River and the Wall became known as the **Ordos** and remained the dominion of the nomad. However, to the Chinese the Yellow River seemed like the logical northern limit of China. The Qing eventually decided matters once and for all not only by seizing control of the Ordos, but also by moving north of the river into the heart of Mongolia. Today, the whole Yellow River region from Yinchuan in Ningxia province, up to Baotou and across to Hohhot, is thoroughly irrigated and productive land – without the river, it would be pure desert. You can take a stroll along the northern bank of the Yellow River by taking **bus** #18 (¥2) from in front of Donghe train station for about 6km to the new bridge. The river here is nearly a mile wide, shallow, sluggish and chocolate brown.

Genghis Khan's Mausoleum

The first thing to be said about **Genghis Khan's Mausoleum** (daily 24hrs; ¥35) is that it's not all it's cracked up to be: it probably isn't the tomb of Genghis Khan, and it isn't a particularly attractive place anyway, but can nonetheless be fascinating as an insight into the modern cult of the famous warrior. Note that there are no English captions for the exhibits.

Genghis Khan is known to have died in northern China, but while his funeral cortege may have passed through this region on its way back to Mongolia, the story that the wheels of his funeral cart got stuck in the mud here, resulting in his burial on the spot, is almost certainly apocryphal. At best, scholars believe, the site contains a few relics – perhaps weapons – of Genghis Khan. The real tomb is thought to be on the slopes of Burkhan Khaldun, in the Hentei Mountains, not far to the east of Ulan Batur in Outer Mongolia. The reason why it came to be so strongly believed that the Khan was buried here in China appears to be that the tribe who were charged with guarding the real sepulchre later drifted down across the Yellow River to the Ordos – but continued to claim the honour of being the official guardians of the tomb.

The alleged **relics** here have a murky political history. Several times they have been removed, and later returned, the most recent occasion being during World War II, when the Japanese seized them. Apparently the Japanese had plans to set up a puppet Mongol state, centred around a Genghis Khan shrine. They even drew up plans for an elaborate mausoleum to house them – plans that were then commandeered by the Chinese Communists who, having safely returned the relics from a hiding place in Qinghai, built the mausoleum for themselves in 1955 as a means of currying favour with the Mongolian people.

The site

The main part of the cement mausoleum is formed by three connecting halls, shaped like Mongolian yurts. The corridors connecting the halls are adorned with bizarre murals supposedly depicting the life of Genghis Khan – though note the ladies in Western dress (1890-style). In the middle of the main hall is a five-metre-high marble **statue** of Genghis before a map of his empire. Whatever the truth about the location of his burial place, the popular view among

Mongolians, both in China and in the Republic of Mongolia, is that this is a holy site: the side halls, all very pretty, have ceremonial yurts, altars, burning incense, hanging paintings and Mongolian calligraphy, and offerings as though to a god. Some bring offerings – not the usual apples and bread, but bottles of rotgut *baijiu* on sale in the souvenir shop – and bow in penitence with prayer. Others, including several of the female staff, get drunk early and keep sipping until they're surly – or extremely affectionate; be prepared for anything as the site attracts its fair share of dodgy characters, including about fifteen "hairdressers" just outside. There's a small, free **museum** by the ticket office with a few relics.

Special **sacrificial ceremonies** take place here four times a year on certain days of the lunar calendar – the fifteenth day of the third lunar month, the fifteenth day of the fifth lunar month, the twelfth day of the ninth month and the third day of the tenth month. On these occasions, Mongolian monks lead solemn rituals which involve piling up cooked sheep before the statue of the Khan. The ceremonies are attended not only by local people, but by pilgrims from the Republic of Mongolia itself.

Practicalities

The mausoleum is located in the Ordos, beside a road leading south into Shaanxi province, from where buses originating in the historic walled city **Yulin**, some 200km north of Yan'an, come here. At the time of writing, this route was being improved to an expressway. Presently, however, the most common approach to the site is from dreary Baotou. Take a bus first to the coal-mining town of **DONGSHENG**, 50km from the mausoleum. From Baotou there are frequent **buses** (2hr; ¥12) that leave from outside Donghe district's train station. It would be possible, if you left Baotou very early in the morning, to reach the mausoleum and make it back the same evening – the last bus from Dongsheng to Baotou leaves at about 6pm. It's a tiring trip, though, and spending a night in up-and-coming Dongsheng is the most pleasant way to do it.

For **trains**, inquire at the Baotou or Dongsheng (called Ordos) stations. At the time of writing, a service was planned to start between the two cities, with a connection to Xi'an made possible by transferring at Shenmu.

From Dongsheng to the mausoleum it takes a further hour on a new road by bus (¥7), and outside of summer there are only a few departures a day; you should aim to catch a bus by 12.30pm, otherwise you may have to spend the night there. To return to Dongsheng from the mausoleum, simply stand in the road and flag down a passing minibus.

If you need a bed, you can **stay** either in Dongsheng or at the mausoleum itself. One of the cheapest places to stay **in Dongsheng** is the fading *Jiaotong* (℡0477/8321575; ❷), which is part of the bus station itself – turn right as you exit, then right again. A better bet is a few minutes' walk south down the main street, away from the bus station, to the *Dongsheng* (℡0477/8327333; ❸), which has triples from ¥140. Tour groups stay at the three-star *Tianjiao Hotel*, at 102 Dalate Nan Lu (℡0477/8533888; ❼). For **food**, head for the Hangjin Bei Lu and Yijinhuoluo Xi Jie, as both have Chinese fast food and Lanzhou-style hand-pulled noodle (*lamian*) restaurants; *Maikeni* and *Xin Xin* are popular.

You can also sleep **at the mausoleum** itself, courtesy of the (very) fake yurts on the grounds (¥40–50 per person). Either way, there is no shower (be warned: *baijiu* stings the eyes).

Ningxia

Squeezed between Inner Mongolia, Gansu and Shanxi, **Ningxia Autonomous Hui Region** is the smallest of China's provinces. Historically, the area has never been a secure one for the Chinese: almost every dynasty built its section of **Great Wall** through here and, in the nineteenth century, the Hui people played an active part in the Muslim rebellions, which were subsequently put down with great ferocity by the Qing authorities. Until recent times, Ningxia's very existence as a separate zone remained an open question; having first appeared on the map in 1928, the region was temporarily subsumed by Gansu in the 1950s before finally reappearing again in 1958. It appears that the authorities of the People's Republic could not make up their minds whether the Hui population was substantial enough to deserve its own autonomous region, in the same way as the Uigurs and the Mongols.

Hui is a vague term, applied to followers of the Muslim faith all over China who have no other obvious affiliation; Ningxia's Hui are descended from Middle Eastern traders who arrived here over a thousand years ago. In Ningxia, as with all the autonomous regions of the Northwest, the central government has steadily encouraged **Han immigration** – or colonization – as a way of tying the area to the Chinese nation, but the situation of the Hui people is not comparable with that of the disaffected Uigurs or Tibetans. While remaining Muslim, the Hui have otherwise long since integrated with Han culture; barring a few Persian or Islamic words, they speak Chinese as their mother tongue and, at present, there is little concept of a Hui nation floating round the backstreets of the provincial capital, Yinchuan. Today, the Hui make up about thirty percent of Ningxia's tiny population of four million, the remainder comprising mainly Han. Indeed, most Hui do not live in Ningxia at all, but are scattered around neighbouring regions, to the point where they often seem strangely absent within what is supposed to be their homeland.

Despite a certain degree of industrialization since the Communists came to power, Ningxia remains an underdeveloped area. For visitors, the rural scenes are the charm of the place, but this province is one of the poorest parts of the country. Geographically, the area is dominated by coalfields and the **Yellow River**, without which the hilly south of the province, green and extremely beautiful, would be barren and uninhabitable desert. Unsurprisingly, the science of **irrigation** is at its most advanced here: two thousand years ago, the great founding emperor of China, Qin Shi Huang, sent a hundred thousand men here to dig irrigation channels. To those ancient systems of irrigation, which are still used to farm cereal crops, have now been added ambitious reafforestation and desert reclamation projects. Some of these can be visited, particularly around the city of **Zhongwei**. Other sights include the capital **Yinchuan**, which makes a pleasant stopover, and one relic from an obscure northern branch of the Silk Road, the delightful **Xumi Shan Grottoes**, located well away from the Yellow River in the southern hills.

Yinchuan and around

The capital of Ningxia, **YINCHUAN** is a pleasantly unpolluted and leafy place to spend a couple of days, although the bland modern city possesses little

Yinchuan and around

Yinchuan	银川	yínchuān
Chengtiansi Ta	承天寺塔	chéngtiānsì tǎ
Dawu Kou	大武口	dàwǔ kǒu
Gulou	古楼	gǔlóu
Hai Bao Ta	海宝塔	hǎibǎo tǎ
Jinfeng	金凤区	jīnfèng qū
Nanguan Grand Mosque	南关清真寺	nánguān qīngzhēn sì
Nanmen	南门	nánmén
Regional Museum	宁夏博物馆	níngxià bówùguǎn
Xixia	西夏区	xīxià qū
Xixia Square	西夏广场	xīxià guǎngchǎng
Yuhuang Ge	玉皇阁	yùhuáng gé

Accommodation

Gulou	古楼饭店	gǔlóu fàndiàn
Huatian	华天宾馆	huátiān bīnguǎn
Labour Union	宁夏工会大厦	níngxià gōnghuì dàshà
Longzhong	隆中大酒店	lóngzhōng dàjiǔdiàn
Ningfeng	宁丰宾馆	níngfēng bīnguǎn
Railway Station Hotel	银川铁道宾馆	yínchuān tiědào bīnguǎn
Rainbow Bridge Hotel	宁夏虹桥大酒店	níngxià hóngqiáo dàjiǔdiàn
Xincheng	新城饭店	xīnchéng fàndiàn
Xindu Hotel	新都饭店	xīndū fàndiàn

Eating

Dico's Burger	德克士汉堡	dékèshì hànbǎo
Fugui Lou	富贵楼	fùguì lóu
Hongyuan Shuai	红元帅	hóngyuán shuài
Xianhe Lou	仙鹤楼	xiānhè lóu
Xianhe Shuijiao	仙鹤水饺	xiānhè shuǐjiǎo
Yingbin Lou	迎宾楼	yíngbīn lóu

Around Yinchuan

Baisikou Shuang Ta	拜寺口双塔	bàisìkǒu shuāng tǎ
Gunzhong Pass	滚种口	gǔnzhǒng kǒu
Helan Shan	贺兰山	hèlán shān
Qingtongxia 108 Dagobas	青铜峡一百零八塔	qīngtóngxiá yībǎilíngbā tǎ
Qingtongxia County	青铜峡镇	qīngtóngxiá zhèn
Sha Hu	沙湖	shā hú
Suyu Kou National Park	苏峪口国家公园	sūyù kǒu guójiā gōngyuán
Xixia Wangling	西夏王陵	xīxià wánglíng
Zhenbeibu China West Film Studio	镇北堡中国西部影视城	zhènběibǎo zhōngguó xībù yǐngshìchéng

of tourist interest. From 1038 Yinchuan (then Xingqing) was capital of the **Western Xia kingdom**, an independent state which survived for less than two hundred years (see box on p.988). It was virtually forgotten about until the early twentieth century, when the archeological remains of the kingdom started being recognized for what they were; you should definitely make a visit to their weathered **mausoleums**, some 20km outside the city.

Orientation, arrival and accommodation

Yinchuan is another of China's spread-out cities, divided into three parts from east to west: Xixia, Jinfeng and Xingqing. All the main sights and the main bus

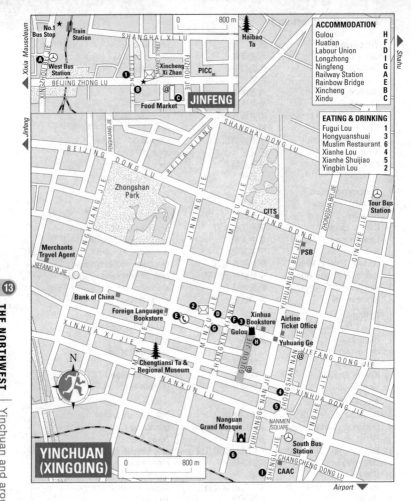

ACCOMMODATION
Gulou	H
Huatian	F
Labour Union	D
Longzhong	I
Ningfeng	G
Railway Station	A
Rainbow Bridge	E
Xincheng	B
Xindu	C

EATING & DRINKING
Fugui Lou	1
Hongyuanshuai	3
Muslim Restaurant	6
Xianhe Lou	4
Xianhe Shuijiao	5
Yingbin Lou	2

YINCHUAN (XINGQING)

station are located in **Xingqing**. The train station, however, lies inconveniently in the west end of **Jinfeng**, some 12km away from Xingqing. Accommodation is adequate in both areas, though Xingqing is certainly the best place to stay. There is no particular reason to stay in **Xixia**, though it is sited close to the mausoleum.

Yinchuan's new **airport** lies 15km southeast of Xingqing. Airport buses (¥15) connect with the CAAC office on Shengli Jie, south of Nanmen Square. Buses from Xi'an, Lanzhou and Baotou arrive at the south long-distance **bus station** (aka Nanmen bus station) at the southeast corner of the square. The **train station** in Jinfeng serves Lanzhou to the west and Beijing (via Inner Mongolia) to the east. Bus #1 (¥1) and private minibuses (negotiable) run from the train station – the stop is in the left part of the station square as you come out – into Jinfeng and on to the south long-distance bus station in Xingqing.

Most of the hotels lie in the vicinity of this route – in Jinfeng you should get off at Xincheng Xi Zhan on Beijing Zhong Lu, while in Xingqing you can get off along Jiefang Jie, the main street which bisects the city. A taxi from the train station to Xingqing costs about ¥20.

Accommodation

Accommodation in Yinchuan can be amazingly tight in midsummer: Chinese tourists flock here and you may end up doing a lot of traipsing around to find a place. Fortunately, however, there are plenty of options in both Jinfeng and Xingqing. The former is more convenient for the train station, but the latter is a far more pleasant place to stay.

Jinfeng

Railway Hotel Off Xinzhou Bei Jie to the east, five minutes' walk from the station ℡0951/3962118. What you might expect from a hotel close to the train staion; staff are efficient if brusque, rooms are spartan though reasonably maintained. **⑤**

Xincheng Beijing Zhong Lu ℡0951/3066010. This simple place is one of the only hotels in the area that doesn't try to charge foreigners double. Doubles with bath **③**

Xindu Fandian Coming from the station, head south down the first intersection east of Xincheng Xi Zhan along a market street. Probably the cheapest option in town, this basic place is still a little nervous of taking foreigners but is friendly enough if you speak some Chinese. The biggest drawback is the lack of hot water. Dorm bed in doubles with bathroom ¥38/person, without ¥17/person. **①**

Xingqing

Gulou Jiefang Dong Jie ℡0951/6024331. Well located beside the Gulou (Drum Tower), this little hotel has comfortable and affordable doubles, though they're very reluctant to rent their cheapest rooms to foreigners. **③**

Huatian West of the Gulou, on Jiefang Dong Jie ℡0951/6035555. Cheap but worn, and you'll need to speak some Chinese to negotiate a room. Discounts are often available throughout the year. **③**

Labour Union Hotel Jiefang Dong Jie ℡0951/6016898, ℻6024931. Comfortable but overpriced, with its own travel service, coffee shop and Muslim restaurant. **⑥**

Longzhong Shengli Bei Jie, opposite the CAAC building ℡0951/7864159. Good value and conveniently near the CAAC office. Doubles with (¥188) or without bath (¥100). Generous discount is available off season. **④**

Ningfeng Jiefang Dong Jie, across the road from Labour Union Hotel ℡0951/6027224. Smart-looking place with good enough standard doubles and pricier newly-furnished rooms. **④**

Rainbow Bridge Jiefang Xi Jie ℡0951/6918888, ℻6918788. Though not as colourful as its name suggests, this four-star block is one of the plushest hotels in town, with a good and expensive restaurant. Rooms range from moderately priced to downright expensive. **⑥**

The City

Yinchuan's sights are all located in Xingqing and can be visited on foot in a single day. The best place to start exploring is the centre of the city, based around the eastern part of Jiefang Jie, which is dominated by a couple of well-restored, traditionally tiered Chinese towers guarding the main intersections. From the west, the first of these is the **Gulou** (Drum Tower) at Gulou Jie, while the second, one block farther east, is the four-hundred-year-old **Yuhuang Ge** (Yuhuang Pavilion, ¥5), at Yuhuangge Jie, which also contains a tiny exhibition room.

Moving south from Jiefang Jie towards the Nanmen bus station takes you through the main **downtown shopping area** of the city. The commercial heart of town centres around pedestrianized Gulou Jie, full of massive department stores and clothing boutiques and crammed to bursting on Sundays. From here it's about another kilometre southeast to **Nanmen Square** at the southern end of Zhongshan Nan Jie near the south bus station, where a mock-up of the front gate of the Forbidden City in Beijing has been erected, complete with Mao Zedong's portrait and tiered seating for dignitaries. Fifteen minutes' walk southwest of Nanmen along Changcheng Dong Lu is the **Nanguan Grand Mosque** (daily 8am–6pm; ¥8). It is the biggest Muslim mosque in Yinchuan and is one of the few places in town you'll find Hui in any appreciable numbers. First built in 1915, it was rebuilt in 1981 after years of damage and neglect during the Cultural Revolution. The mosque is Arabian style with green domes and minarets, which sets it apart from the purely Chinese style of flying eaves and pagoda-style minarets of many mosques farther east.

Moving to the western half of Xingqing, you'll find a couple more sights. At the junction of Jining Jie and Xinhua Xi Jie, a few blocks south of Jiefang Jie, are the **Regional Museum** and **Chengtiansi Ta** pagoda (also known as West Pagoda), together on the same site (daily 9am–6pm; ¥22). The museum contains some interesting English-labelled exhibitions. Relics from the Xixia Mausoleum are displayed, including a 900-year-old Lishi pillar support (Lishi is shown as a squatting troll-like creature). Also presented are Helan Shan pictographs – drawings recording aspects of life and mysterious animals, presumably carved on rocks by nomads some thirty thousand years ago. Outside, the 12-storey pagoda is in classic Chinese style and is a place of worship for Buddhists. It was built around 1050 during the time of the Western Xia with the top six storeys rebuilt during the Qing dynasty. You can climb the octagonal tower right to the top for excellent views.

Look north up Jining Jie from Jiefang Jie and you'll see another tower peering up from the horizon in the distance directly ahead – this is the 1500-year-old **Haibao Ta** (daily 8.30am–6pm; ¥10), otherwise known as the North Pagoda. Brick-built, 54m high and of an unusual, angular shape, with protruding ledges and niches at every level, you can ascend the interior for another view over the city. Walking there from Jiefang Jie takes an hour, or bus #20 from Nanmen Square stops at the north end of Beita Xiang, from where it's a 20-minute walk.

Eating and drinking

Of the three parts of town, it's **Xingqing** that has the better choice of **food**. Just west of the drum tower on Jiefang Dong Jie, *Hongyuan Shuai* is a cheap noodle canteen with shared tables and tasty, Sichuan-style cold snacks; just point at the pictures. For local delicacies, *Yingbin Lou* is a smart, mid-range Muslim restaurant on the east end of Jiefang Xi Jie, serving lamb hotpots, kebabs, noodles and eight-treasure tea; another Muslim eatery can be found in the backstreet of the Nanguan Grand Mosque – look for the giant green dome, which is decorated with fancy neon lights at night. *Xianhe Shuijiao*, down near the bus station on Zhongshan Jie, deals in dumplings – vegetable or various meats – which you order by the *jin* and watch being assembled by an army of cooks in the restaurant window. A half *jin* costs ¥20 and is plenty for one person. Their nearby sister restaurant, *Xianhe Lou*, offers similarly inexpensive hotpots, casseroles and more cold snacks. Be aware that their "vegetable dumplings" also contain meat. For Western-style fare, there are branches of *Dico's Burgers* on Gulou Nan Jie and Xinhua Jie, plus *KFC* have recently set up on Jiefang Xi Jie. The *Labour Union Hotel*'s coffee shop does a decent brew.

In **Jinfeng**, a string of restaurants on Beijing Zhong Lu near the main post office offers spicy grilled lamb kebabs, noodles, dumplings and hotpot.

Walking east from the Beijing Zhong Lu/Tiedong Jie intersection and taking the first right, outside the *Xindu Hotel*, brings you into a market street which has plenty of stands selling fresh and dry fruits as well as local snacks day and night. Otherwise, try *Fugui Lou* next to the south end of Tiedong Bei Jie which serves fairly standard Chinese fare.

Listings

Airline The main CAAC office is at the Changcheng Dong Lu/Shengli Jie intersection ☎0951/6913456 daily 8am–10.30pm. It also has a branch in the main post office of Xingqing, at window 8. Better domestic flight deals can be obtained at a private Airline Ticket office at the northeast corner of the Yuhuang Ge junction.

Banks and exchange The main Bank of China is in the western part of Xingqing, on Jiefang Xi Jie (summer Mon–Fri 8am–noon & 2.30–6.00pm; winter Mon–Fri 8.30am–noon & 2–5.30pm).

Bookshops For English-language novels as well as local maps, the Foreign Language Bookstore (daily 9am–6.30pm) is at the corner of Jiefang Xi Jie and Jining Jie.

Internet access There's an Internet café outside the entrance of the food market on Beijing Zhong Lu in Jinfeng. Others are on Zhongshan Nan Jie and Xinhua Dong Jie in Xingqing. All bars charge ¥2/hour.

Mail and telephones The main post office (daily 8am–5.30pm) in Xingqing is at the junction of Jiefang and Minzu Jie. There's another one on Beijing Zhong Lu, east of Tiedong Jie in Jinfeng. Long-distance calls can be made from the first floor of the China Telecom office (daily 8am–6pm) next to the *Rainbow Bridge* Hotel.

PSB At the corner of Beijing Dong Lu and Yuhuangge Bei Jie ☎0951/6915080; Mon–Thurs 8am–noon & 2.30–6.30pm; closed Fri morning.

Trains Outward-bound tickets can be bought easily from the station, though your hotel will almost certainly be able to arrange this for you, with around ¥30 commission, as long as you give at least 24 hours' notice. Otherwise try a travel agent.

Travel agents The Ningxia CITS is on the first floor of 375 Beijing Dong Lu (☎0951/6717782, ℻6717839). A good alternative is the Ningxia Merchants International Tour at 365 Jiefang Xi Jie (☎0951/5053697, ℠www.cmitnx.com). Both travel agents can provide English-speaking tour guides and organize tours of areas outside the city.

Around Yinchuan

A few interesting spots outside Yinchuan can comfortably be visited as day-trips. The best of these are the **Xixia Wangling** (Mausoleums of the Western Xia; daily 8am–6pm; ¥36) about 10km west of the new city. The mausoleums stand as monuments to the nine kings of Western Xia, whose kingdom was based at Yinchuan (see box, p.988). The site is spectacular and atmospheric, with towering, haystack-shaped piles of brown mud bricks, slowly disintegrating and punctuating the view for miles around the Helan Shan range. The entrance fee includes transport within the complex to the museum, figure gallery and the biggest mausoleum of the nine. Interesting items in the museum include the original pieces of the Lishi pillar support and some terracotta bird ornaments with human faces. From May to October, a tourist bus (daily 9am–6.30pm; ¥6) runs from Nanguan Grand Mosque to the mausoleum. Otherwise, the cheapest way to reach the site is to take **minibus #2** (¥2.5) from the west of Gulou Jie/Xinhua Dong Jie junction to Xixia Square. From here you can take a taxi (¥10) or hire a motor-rickshaw (¥5) for the last 10km.

The **Helan Shan** mountain ranges themselves are also of interest. The **Gunzhong Kou** (Rolling Bell Pass; ¥10), about 25km west of Xixia, where Li Yuanhao built his summer palace, is a pleasant resort with attractive, historic buildings and plenty of opportunities for hiking around the hills and admiring the views. Six or seven kilometres north of here are the **Baisikou Shuang Ta**, a couple of twelve-metre-high pagodas guarding another pass. A few more kilometres to the east is the **Zhenbeibu China West Film Studio** (daily 8am–6pm; ¥40) where the film *Red Sorghum*, directed by Zhang Yimou, was shot. The film depicts village life in northwest China during the period leading up to World War II – in part a rural idyll, in part a brute struggle to survive. The scenes of dry, dusty hillsides alternating with the lush fields of sorghum are a fair record of how Ningxia still looks today. Fairly extensive galleries of engraved **rock art** have been found spread out near here at **Suyu Kou National Park** (¥25); you can also hike to the peak of Helan Shan from here. Merchants International Tour offers a tour of these places from Yinchuan for ¥350 including a car and an English tour guide; otherwise you can hire a taxi on the street for no more than ¥250.

Farther away from town, about 45km north of Yinchuan, is the beautiful **Sha Hu** (Sand Lake; summer ¥80; otherwise ¥20, includes a return trip by boat across the lake). This is a developing summer resort *par excellence*, with swimming, sand dunes, rafting and beautiful scenery. During winter the lake freezes over, making an ideal skating rink, though most tourists arrive in summer to view the expansive lily ponds. Camel rides and caravan trips are also offered in the desert nearby. Accommodation at the comfortable *Qingxin Fandian* (④) is available in summer. You can get there from the Tour Bus Station (also known as North Bus Station) on Qinghe Jie; an hourly direct bus (¥10) leaves from 10.30am till early evening (1hr). Return trips are easy in summer, but in winter the direct bus may stop running completely; if you happen to get stuck, wait at the junction outside the lake entrance and flag down the minibus to Yaofu (¥3.5), where frequent transport back to Yinchuan is available into the late evening.

Finally, about 80km south of Yinchuan, are the **Qingtongxia 108 Dagobas** (¥10). These Buddhist stupas stand in a strange triangular pattern on a slope on the west bank of the Yellow River in Qingtongxia County. The white, bell-shaped dagobas are arranged in twelve rows, tapering from nineteen in the bottom row to a single one at the top. They are thought to have been put there in the fourteenth century during the Yuan dynasty, though their exact significance is not known. To visit the dagobas, take a bus from the **South Bus Station** from Nanmen to Qingtongxia County, 7km east to the site, and catch a motor-rickshaw for about ¥15, or hike.

Zhongwei and Shapotou

A small country town, **ZHONGWEI** is 160km and a few hours by bus to the southwest of Yinchuan. Historically, the old walled city of Zhongwei was said to have had no north gate – simply because there was nothing more to the north of here. The city is still in a potentially awkward location, between the fickle **Yellow River** to the south and the sandy Tenger Desert to the north, but today Zhongwei is surrounded by a rich belt of irrigated fields, and the desert is kept at bay through reafforestation projects. The river outside the town, at **Shapotou**, is a splendid sight and should definitely be visited if you are in the area.

Zhongwei is based around a simple crossroad, with a traditional Gulou (Drum Tower) at the centre. It's small enough to walk everywhere, although there are cycle-rickshaws and taxis available to ferry you around. The town has one intriguing sight, the **Gao Miao** (daily 8am–6pm; ¥15), a quite extraordinary temple catering for a number of different religions, including Buddhism, Confucianism and Taoism. Originally built in the early fifteenth century, and rebuilt many times, the temple is now a magnificent jumble of buildings and styles. From the front entrance you can see dragon heads, columns, stairways and rooftops spiralling up in all directions. The left wing contains vivid sculptures of five hundred *arhats*. The right wing is a mock hell. Altogether, there are more than 250 temple rooms, towers and pavilions. You need a pretty expert eye to distinguish the saints of the various religions – they all look very much alike. To reach the Gao Miao, walk a few minutes north from the crossroads and you'll see the entrance on your left, opposite the *Zhongwei Da Jiudian*.

Practicalities

All trains on the main Lanzhou–Beijing (via Inner Mongolia) rail line call at Zhongwei. Branch lines also serve Wuwei in Gansu province and Baoji in Shaanxi. Zhongwei's **train station** is just off the north arm of the crossroads; the **bus station** is on the east road, with connections to Guyuan farther south and Wuwei in Gansu province. Buses to and from Yinchuan run frequently, but stop at around 3pm.

If you're arriving in Zhongwei by train, you'll find **accommodation** right outside the station at the *Railway Hotel* (℡0955/7011441; ❷), a nice, clean and friendly place offering double rooms with bath, though hot water is only available in the morning and evening. From the train station, it's a short walk into town – crossing Renmin Sqaure as you exit the station will lead you onto Bei

Zhongwei and Shapotou		
Zhongwei	中卫	*zhōngwèi*
Dongguan Hotel	东关饭店	*dōngguān fàndiàn*
Gao Miao	高庙	*gāomiào*
Laomao Shouzhua Meishilou	老毛手抓美食楼	*lǎomáo shǒuzhuā měishílóu*
Railway Hotel	铁路宾馆	*tiělù bīnguǎn*
Xingtuo Fandian	兴拓饭店	*xīngtuò fàndiàn*
Zhongwei Binguan	中卫宾馆	*zhōngwèi bīnguǎn*
Zhongwei Da Jiudian	中卫大酒店	*zhōngwèi dàjiǔdiàn*
Shapotou	沙坡头	*shāpōtóu*
Desert Research Institute	沙坡头沙漠研究所	*shāpōtóu shāmò yánjiūsuǒ*
Shapo Shanzhuang	沙坡山庄	*shāpō shānzhuāng*

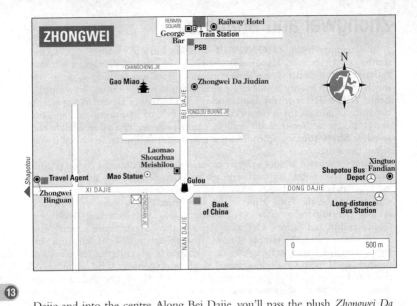

ZHONGWEI

RENMIN SQUARE
Railway Hotel
George Bar
Train Station
PSB
CHANGCHENG JIE
Gao Miao
Zhongwei Da Jiudian
BEI DAJIE
YONGLOU BUXING JIE
Laomao Shouzhua Meishilou
Xingtuo Fandian
Shapotou Bus Depot
Travel Agent
Mao Statue
Zhongwei Binguan
Gulou
XI DAJIE
DONG DAJIE
Bank of China
Long-distance Bus Station
NAN DAJIE
ZHONGSHAN JIE
Shapotou

N

0   500 m

Dajie and into the centre. Along Bei Dajie, you'll pass the plush *Zhongwei Da Jiudian* on the left (℡0955/7012219; ⑤), more or less opposite the entrance to the Gao Miao. An alternative is the faded *Zhongwei Binguan* (℡0955/7012609, Ⓕ7012350; ④), ten minutes' walk west from the centre along the Xi Dajie; the Peace Travel Service (℡0955/7034880, Ⓔxqnlzq@163.com) with friendly English-speaking staff is just outside and offers camel tours and Yellow-River rafting at reasonable prices. East from the centre, on Dong Dajie near the bus station, is the simple *Xingtuo Fandian* (℡0955/7035761; ④); it does not have a permit to take foreigners, but they will anyway – come out of the station, cross the street and walk east for a couple of minutes. The main **Bank of China** is immediately to the southwest of Gulou and there's a **post office** on Zhongshan Jie – a small lane several minutes' walk along the Xi Dajie from the centre; you can also make long-distance phone calls from here. **Internet** access is available from a Net bar on the southeast corner of Renmin Square as you come out of the train station.

There are lots of cheap **noodle shops** along Bei Dajie near the Gao Miao. You'll also find a good-value Muslim restaurant *Laomao Shouzhua Meishilou* northwest of the Gulou (meals around ¥20 including beer). A string of smarter restaurants lies along pedestrianized **Yonglou Buxing Jie**, a few minutes south of the *Zhongwei Da Jiudian*. The recently opened **George Bar**, popular with local trendy youngsters, at the southeast corner of Renmin Square, offers inexpensive cocktails (¥15) and other drinks – an easy place to kill a couple of hours whilst waiting for a train.

Shapotou

SHAPOTOU, 16km west of Zhongwei, is a tourist resort of sorts by the banks of the Yellow River. Most people come on a day-trip, but you can easily spend an enjoyable night or two here. The main pleasure of the place is in the contrast between the leafy, shady banks of the river itself, and the harsh desert that lies just beyond. The **Shapotou Desert Research Centre** has been based here for forty years, working on ways to conquer the sands. Travelling either by bus or train between Zhongwei and Shapotou, you'll see some of the fruits of their labour in the chequerboard grid of straw thatch implanted to hold the sands in place and provide irrigation.

Minibuses (¥3.5) to Shapotou leave from the *Dongguan Hotel*'s parking site opposite the long-distance bus station. Alternatively, there's one daily **train** to Shapotou from Zhongwei that leaves in the early afternoon. Arriving at the train station, facing the river, turn right and walk a few hundred metres along the road to the back entrance of the **tourist resort** (¥60), marked by a couple of kiosks – to get to the main resort area you slide down the huge sand dune. It's quite a charming place, with shady trees, cafés and outdoor restaurants. There are also activities such as camel-riding, zip lines over the Yellow River and, more unusually, **sheepskin rafting** (1hr; ¥60) in traditional rafts of sewn-up sheepskins, pumped full of air and tied together.

A few minutes downstream, the *Shapo Shanzhuang* is a delightful **hotel** (☏0953/7698073; closed Nov–April; ❸) in a very cool and pleasant location, with gardens full of trees and vine trellises. It has nice doubles with bath, and the muffled roar of the neighbouring Yellow River makes for soothing ambient sound.

Southern Ningxia

Located in the remote, impoverished southern part of Ningxia, the town of **Guyuan** has seen very little tourist traffic. Only in 1995 did it finally join the rail network, with the opening of the Zhongwei–Baoji line. Aside from a ruinous stretch of the **Great Wall**, built in the Qin dynasty, 5km north of town (you'll see it in passing), the main interest here is in the Buddhist grottoes at **Xumi Shan**, a major relic of the Silk Road, curiously marooned far to the north of the main route from Lanzhou to Xi'an. The great Taoist temple Kongtang Shan at Pingliang in Gansu is only two hours from Guyuan, another possible day-trip. The hills along the road from Gansu have been terraced for centuries; every inch of land in the vast landscape is under cultivation, with terraces laddering up the slopes and flowing round every tiny hillock and gully in fantastic swirls of colour.

Southern Ningxia		
Liupan Shan	六盘山	liùpán shān
Xumi Shan	须弥山	xūmí shān
Dianli Fandian	电力饭店	diànlì fàndiàn
Haiyuan	海原	huǎiyuán
Sanying	三营	sānyíng
Guyuan	固原	gùyuán
Qingya Xuan	清雅轩	qīngyǎ xuān
Tiedao Binguan	铁道宾馆	tiědào bīnguǎn
Xiaochi Yitiaojie	小吃一条街	xiǎochī yītiáojiē
Xingyuan Da Jiudian	兴源大酒店	xīngyuán dàjiǔdiàn

The high pass on the border with Gansu, **Liupan Shan** (which you cross on the way to or from Tianshui), is also famous for the fact that the Long Marchers managed to elude pursuing Guomindang forces here in the 1930s; a commemorative stone marks the spot.

Guyuan

GUYUAN is a useful place to base yourself for a visit to the Xumi Shan grottoes, but is itself of no special interest. Although trains now pass through Guyuan on their way between Zhongwei and Baoji in Shaanxi province, the **train station** is inconveniently located several kilometres from town. It's easier to rely on long-distance **buses** connecting Guyuan with Xi'an to the east; Lanzhou and Ürümqi to the west. There are also frequent connections to Yinchuan (¥50), leaving every 40 minutes from 8am to 5.30pm. Bus #1 (¥1) links the train station and the bus station in town; wait and flag down the bus at the junction outside the train station as there's no sign post. A taxi to anywhere in town costs ¥4.

Guyuan's **post office** is a short walk east from the bus station – it's on the right just past the roundabout. A **Xinhua Bookstore** is 300m south from the roundabout on your left and there's also an **Internet** café (¥2/hour) down the lane across the way.

Accommodation is available at the recently renovated *Xingyuan Da Jiudian* (☎0954/2022558, ℱ2021556; ●). Come out of the bus station, turn left, and the hotel is about 100m down the road, on the opposite side. The bathrooms are spacious and there's almost 24-hour hot water. If you arrive by train, your best option is *Tiedao Binguan* (●). It's about 100m outside the train station to the right. Hot water is available twice a day and the price includes simple breakfast, though the staff can be unhelpful.

You can find good and cheap Muslim food and cold snacks at the popular *Qingya Xuan*, 500m east of the bus station – look for the grey plate with green characters. Further east from here to the roundabout, turn right and walk a few minutes; an arch gate next to the Xinhua Bookstore on your left will lead you to the lively *Xiaochi Yitiaojie* (Snack Street), where kebabs, noodles and dumplings are all available from dozens of stands.

The Xumi Shan grottoes

The dramatic **Xumi Shan grottoes** (daily; ¥30) lie about 55km northwest of Guyuan and make a worthy day-trip. One hundred and thirty-eight caves have been carved out from the cliff face on five adjoining hillsides, and a large number of statues – primarily from Northern Wei, Sui and Tang dynasties – survive, in a somewhat diminished state. The natural backdrop is beautiful and secluded. At Xumi Shan, the grottoes occupy a huge site of rusty red sandstone cliffs and shining tree-covered slopes commanding panoramic views. The last stage of the journey there takes you through one of the remotest corners of rural China where, at the height of summer, you can see the golden wheat being cut by hand, then spread out over the road to be ground by passing vehicles.

The site takes at least two hours to walk around. After entering the cliffs area, bear left first for Cave no. 5 and the **Dafo Lou**, a statue of a giant twenty-metre-high Maitreya Buddha facing due east. Originally this Buddha was inside a protective wall, but the wall has long since fallen away. Head back to the entrance again and you'll see the five hillocks lined up along an approximate east–west axis, each with one key sight and a cluster of caves. After the Dafo Lou, the second major sight you come to is the **Yuanguang Si**, a temple housing caves 45, 46 and 48, where statues were built in North Zhou and Tang dynasties. You'll need to ask the nun to open the caves. It is hard to imagine that all Buddha statues used to be coated in gold from looking at their now smoky coloured surface. From here you have to cross a bridge and bear left to reach **Xiangguo Si**, centred around the magnificent Cave no. 51 with its five-metre-high Buddha seated around a central pillar. Returning to the bridge, walk underneath it and up the dry river bed towards the cliff, to reach **Taohua Dong** (Peach Blossom Cave).

There's no direct bus to Xumi Shan from Guyuan; the nearest you can get is the small town of **Sanying**, a stop on the Guyuan–Haiyuan bus route (buses leave hourly, 7.30am–4.30pm; ¥5 to Sanying). Tell the driver beforehand that you want to see the grottoes, and you will be dropped off at a junction of Sanying. The trip takes about an hour. From Sanying, hire a minivan for the thirty-minute drive to the caves; a return trip (including 2hr wait while you look around) should cost about ¥50. At the grottoes' car park, there's a kiosk where you can buy **drinks and snacks**, plus a basic **hotel** in the unlikely event that you might need to stay the night, though it's also possible to stay in Sanying at the respectable *Dianli Fandian* (❸).

Gansu

Traditionally, the Chinese have regarded **Gansu** as marking the outer limit of China. During the Han dynasty (206 BC–220 AD), the first serious effort was made to expand into the western deserts, primarily as a means to ensure control over the Silk Road trade. Prefectures were established and, although Gansu did not officially become a Chinese province until the Mongolian Yuan dynasty (1279–1368), it is unquestionably a part of the Chinese heartland. At various

PICC insurance

Irrespective of any other insurance policies you may have, in many rural parts of China foreigners need to be covered by the state insurer, **PICC** (People's Insurance Company of China), in order to travel on buses. This has nothing to do with paying you in the event of an accident, but is a waiver to prevent the authorities from being sued. Generally, insurance for each journey is included in the ticket price, but in Gansu and Western Sichuan you're actually required to **buy** a separate PICC policy before anyone will even sell you a bus ticket. Certificates of two weeks' validity can be bought from PICC offices (in Gansu, all cities have them) for between ¥30 and ¥50, though some offices seem unaware of the regulations and can't understand what you're after. In this case, try hotels, CITS offices, or even bus stations, where you'll have to pay an additional commission.

As is always the case in China, the regulation is erratically enforced: sometimes flashing the policy at the right moment is the only way to get aboard a bus; sometimes nobody cares. If you can't get a policy and nobody will sell you a ticket, try flagging the bus down once it has left the station – often the drivers are happy to take you anyway.

stages over the last two thousand years Chinese control has extended well beyond here into Xinjiang. Nevertheless, right into the nineteenth century the primarily Muslim inhabitants of this province were considered little better than the "barbarian" Uigurs of Xinjiang by central government; the great Muslim revolts of that period were ruthlessly quashed.

A harsh and barren land, subject to frequent droughts, Gansu has always been a better place for travelling through rather than settling down in. The province's geography is remarkable – from the great **Yellow River**, dense with silt, surging through the provincial capital of **Lanzhou**, to the mountains and deserts of the **Hexi Corridor**, a thousand-kilometre route between mountain ranges that narrows at times to as little as fifteen-kilometre-wide bottlenecks. It's the Hexi Corridor that accounts for the curious elongated shape of the province: the Silk Road caravans came down here, the Great Wall was built through here, and today's trains chug through here as well, along what is – until the line from Golmud to Tibet is completed – the only rail line in northwestern China and the only link through Central Asia between China and the West. The towns along the Hexi Corridor are mere dots of life in the desert, sustained by irrigation using water from the mountains. Given that agriculture is barely sustainable here, central government has tried to import a certain amount of industry into the province, particularly in the east. The exploitation of mineral deposits, including oil and coal, has made a tentative beginning. But still the population is relatively small, comprising just twenty million, who continue to display an extraordinary ethnic mix, with Hui, Kazakhs, Mongols and Tibetans all featuring prominently.

The province may be wild and remote by Chinese standards, but it's of enormous historical interest. The **Mogao Caves** at **Dunhuang** in the far west house the finest examples of Buddhist art in all China, and further Silk Road sights are scattered right along the length of the province, ranging from the country's largest reclining Buddha at **Zhangye** to the stunning Buddhist caves at **Bingling Si**, near Lanzhou, and **Maiji Shan**, near **Tianshui** in the far south. The Great Wall, snaking its way west, comes to a symbolic end at the great Ming fortress at **Jiayuguan**, and, in the southwest of the province, right on the edge of the Tibetan plateau, is the fascinating **Labrang Monastery** at the Tibetan town of **Xiahe**.

Eastern Gansu

West of the border with Shaanxi, the first significant Silk Road city is **Tianshui**, with the spectacular **Maiji Shan** complex just a few kilometres to the southeast. Maiji Shan – literally "Wheatstack Mountain", a name derived from its shape – is the fourth largest Buddhist cave complex in China, after Dunhuang, Datong and Luoyang. Set amid stunning wooded hill scenery, the caves are easily accessed from Tianshui, which is located about halfway along on the Lanzhou–Xi'an rail line. You will probably need to spend at least one night at Tianshui, the nearest transport hub to the caves, though in itself of limited interest to tourists. A little way to the west of Tianshui, towards Lanzhou, are some more fascinating Silk Road relics, in and around the towns of **Gangu** and **Wushan**.

Tianshui

The area around **TIANSHUI** was first settled back in Neolithic times, though today the city is an enormous industrial spread with two distinct centres, known

Eastern Gansu

Tianshui	天水	*tiānshuǐ*
Beidao	北道	*běidào*
Fuxi Miao	伏羲庙	*fúxī miào*
Qincheng	秦城	*qínchéng*
Yuquanguan Park	玉泉观公园	*yùquánguàn gōngyuán*
Yuquan Si	玉泉寺	*yùquán sì*
Accommodation		
Golden Sun	阳光饭店	*yángguāng fàndiàn*
Jianxin	建新饭店	*jiànxīn fàndiàn*
Maiji	麦积大酒店	*màijī dàjiǔdiàn*
Tianshui	天水宾馆	*tiānshuǐ bīnguǎn*
Yatai	天水亚太大酒店	*tiānshuǐ yàtài dàjiǔdiàn*
Zhoulin	舟林宾馆	*zhōulín bīnguǎn*
Gangu	甘谷	*gāngǔ*
Daxiang Shan	大像山	*dàxiàng shān*
Maiji Shan	麦积山	*màijī shān*
Pingliang	平凉	*píngliáng*
Kongtong Shan	崆峒山	*kōngtóng shān*
Kongtong Shanzhuang	崆峒山庄	*kōngtóng shānzhuāng*
Pingliang Hotel	平凉宾馆	*píngliáng bīnguǎn*
Pingliang Binguan Fenbu	平凉宾馆分部	*píngliáng bīnguǎn fēnbù*
Taihe Gong	太和宫	*tàihé gōng*
Wushan	武山	*wǔshān*
Lashao Temple	拉稍寺	*lāshāo sì*
Shuilian Dong	水帘洞	*shuǐlián dòng*

as **Qincheng** (West Side) and **Beidao** (East Side), situated some 20km apart. Whether you choose to stay in Beidao or Qincheng will probably be determined by whether you arrive at the Beidao train station or the Qincheng bus station. If your only interest is a trip to Maiji Shan and back, you should stay in Beidao, from where all the Maiji Shan minibuses depart, though this is the grottier of the two ends of town, with the feel of a rural backwater.

In slightly smarter Qincheng, head west from the main square (at the west end of Minzhu Lu) along Jiefang Lu and you'll almost immediately reach an area of crumbling, traditional architecture with low, upward-sweeping roof eaves and heavy tiles now gathering moss. Tiny alleyways lead off in all directions. About fifteen minutes' walk along Jiefang Lu is the Ming-dynasty complex of **Fuxi Miao** (daily 8am–11pm; ¥5) commemorating the mythological Fuxi, credited with introducing the Chinese to fishing, hunting and animal husbandry – there is a statue of him, clad in leaves, in the main hall. The temple is notable for its beautiful cypress trees; as you enter, you pass a thousand-year-old tree on the right. Another interesting temple complex, **Yuquan Si** (daily 8am–7pm; ¥10), in the western part of town, occupies **Yuquanguan Park**, up above Renmin Xi Lu. This is a 700-year-old active Taoist temple, on a hill about ten minutes' walk northwest of the main square. The temple is surrounded by attractive cypress trees and gives good views over the old city. Bus #24 (¥0.5) from Fuxi Miao will take you to the bottom of a path which leads to the entrance.

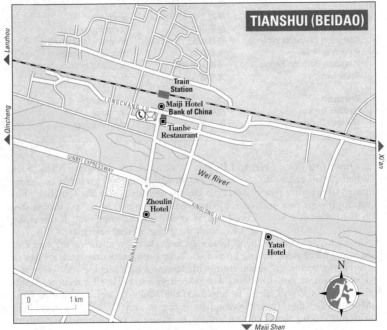

Practicalities

All trains stop at the **train station** in Beidao. **Buses**, including services to and from Lanzhou, Linxia, Pingliang, Guyuan (in Ningxia) and Xi'an, usually use the long-distance **bus station** in Qincheng, or stop and start in front of the train station. **City transport** between the two centres is swift and efficient, with minibuses and bus #1 between the two stations running all day – the run takes about thirty minutes and costs ¥2. Buses become scarce around 10pm at night, and the first bus in the morning leaves at around 6am. A taxi between the two should cost around ¥20.

The Beidao **post office** is just west of the train station, the **Bank of China** just east. About the only decent place to get a **meal** in Beidao is at the *Tianhe* – head south from the station to the first crossroads, then turn left and it's on the corner. The staff are very friendly, and the cook makes an effort to impress.

In Qincheng, the **Bank of China** head office is on Minzhu Lu; look for the twin lions outside. To make long-distance calls, use the main **post office** on Minzhu Lu. The Tianshui **CITS** (℡ 0938/8287337) is on the northwest corner of Hezuo Lu/Minzhu Lu intersection. Staff here can speak English and organize tours to Maiji Shan for a reasonable ¥200.

Accommodation

There's decent accommodation in both Beidao and Qincheng, but as there's little to detain you in town after a visit to Maiji Shan, you might consider getting a late train out.

Beidao

Maiji Opposite the train station ℡ 0938/4920000, ℱ 4929320. Not a bad choice, with elderly furnished rooms, and staff are friendly. Dorm beds ¥40, **❹**
Yatai Xinglong Lu ℡ 0938/2727712. The lobby is a little pretentious given the fairly average rooms, but rates aren't expensive and, usefully, the place is on the minibus route to the caves. **❸**
Zhoulin Bunan Lu ℡ 0938/2738118. Cheap and unattractive, but it's a good place to get away from the crowds in the train station. Dorm beds ¥45, **❷**

Qincheng

Golden Sun On the pedestrianized Zhonghua Lu ℡ 0938/8277777. The most upmarket option in town, with a bar and a restaurant. The staff can speak English. A taxi from the nearby bus station costs ¥3. **❻**
Jianxin A 5min walk west of the bus station ℡ 0938/4985300. This aged hotel is a cheap and hospitable place, with a good restaurant right opposite. **❸**
Tianshui Yingbin Lu ℡ 0938/8212611, ℱ 8213920. From the bus station, walk onto Minzhu Lu and catch bus #1, or any minibus, east to Yingbin Lu. You can also get here with bus #1, or minibuses from Beidao. This is one of the town's earliest hotels, and though a bit frayed and pricey for what you get, renovation is underway, so future prices may bump up accordingly. **❺**

Maiji Shan

The trip to the Buddhist caves on the mountain of **Maiji Shan** is the highlight of eastern Gansu. As is often the case with the Buddhist cave sites in northwest China, the natural setting itself is spectacular: although the whole area is very hilly, the sheer, rocky cliffs of Maiji Shan, rising out of the forest, make this one hill a complete anomaly. The centrepiece of the statuary, the giant **sixteen-metre-high Buddha** (complete with birds nesting in one of its nostrils), is visible from far away, hanging high up on the rock in conjunction with two smaller figures. The combination of rickety walkways on the cliff face with the beautiful wooded, mountain scenery opposite adds charm to the site.

The cliffs were split apart by an earthquake in the eighth century, leaving a total of 194 surviving **caves** on the eastern and western sections, dating from the northern Wei right through to the Qing. The wall paintings are fading due to erosion by rain, but the statues are worth visiting. The western cliff caves are particularly well preserved, and date mainly from the fourth to the sixth century AD: cave no. 133 is considered to be the finest, containing sculptures and engraved stones. You are free to explore on your own, climbing higher and higher up the narrow stairways on the sheer face of the mountain. The caves are all locked, though, and you often find yourself peering into half-lit caverns through wire grilles, but for the non-specialist the view is probably adequate – at least some of the artwork and statuary shows up clearly.

Frequent **minibuses** run to the caves from the square outside Tianshui's train station (45min–1hr); the ride costs ¥10 each way, though they usually try to charge foreigners double. According to some local maps, bus #5 also goes to the caves from Qincheng, but in fact this route is only available on national holidays. When you reach Maiji Shan (daily 8am–6pm), there is a fee of ¥23 per person to enter the mountain area. The minibuses continue for another few hundred metres, after which you have to walk up the hill past the souvenir touts to the ticket office; a ticket without guide costs ¥32. If you ask around at the site, you may be able to find an English-speaking guide to unlock the cave doors and explain the artwork. Another option is to arrange this in advance with the Tianshui CITS before you set out.

Gangu, Wushan and Pingliang

West of Tianshui, on the road and rail line to Lanzhou, are a couple of little-known but fascinating reminders of the Silk Road era. The prime attraction at **GANGU**, 65km west of Tianshui, reached by either train or bus, is **Daxiang Shan** (Giant Statue; ¥10). It gets its name from the giant statue of an unusually moustached Sakyamuni Buddha which was carved out of a cliff during the Tang dynasty. The statue is more than 23m tall, and can be reached in about an hour by foot along a path leading uphill from the town, following a shrine-studded ridge all the way to the temple.

From **Wushan**, 45km farther west from Gangu, you can visit the **Shuilian Dong** (Water Curtain Grottoes; ¥10), which contain a number of important relics, including the **Lashao Temple** (aka Dafo Ya), as well as a Thousand Buddha Cave site. This extraordinary area is all the better preserved for being so inaccessible – the temple, set into a natural cave in a cliff, is not visible from the ground. Digging at the grottoes began during the Sixteen States period (304–439 AD) and continued through the dynasties. The Lashao Temple was built during the Northern Wei (386–534). There is a forty-metre-high statue of Sakyamuni on the mountain cliff, his feet surrounded by wild animals, including lions, deer and elephants. It is a rare design of Hinayana, a branch of Buddhism, in Chinese cave art. The grottoes, about 30km north of Wushan, can only be reached along a dried-up river bed – a new road is being built but it's worth asking about the situation before heading out.

All **buses** – and all **trains** except for express services – running between Tianshui and Lanzhou stop at both Gangu and Wushan. It's also possible to visit Gangu as a day-trip from Tianshui; minibuses run from the Qincheng bus station in the morning. If you want to visit both Gangu and the grottoes in one day from Tianshui you have to rent a vehicle; to handle the rough road from Wushan, it is better to get a small minibus (¥500) rather than a taxi (¥200). It is a long, tiring excursion and might be simpler to stay a night at either Wushan or Gangu, perhaps as a stopover on the way between Tianshui and Lanzhou. Note that access to the Water Curtain Grottoes is dependent on the weather – you won't be able to use the river bed if it has been wet recently.

Pingliang

About 200km northeast of Tianshui, an eight-hour bus ride, lies the modern city of **PINGLIANG**. The surrounding area is a mountainous and beautiful part of Gansu province near the border with Ningxia, and little known to foreigners. The chief local attraction is **Kongtong Shan**, originally a Taoist monastery now combining Buddhism. It is one of China's most venerated, perched precariously on a clifftop, with Guyuan in southern Ningxia a possible day-trip, two hours away by bus. The last bus to Guyuan is at 4pm, and there are trains leaving around midnight to Yinchuan and Xi'an.

If you arrive by bus, the most convenient **place to stay** is at the well-maintained *Tianxing* (℡0933/8713691; ❸, dorm beds ¥20); come out of the bus station, turn left over a bridge and it's about 200m down on the left. Continue down the road and you come to a string of cheap restaurants; try the local *helao mian*, a noodle dish with vegetarian and meat choices (under ¥5). If you arrive at the train station, 2km out of town, the nearest hotel is the *Pingliang Binguan Fenbu* (℡0933/8623711; ❸, dorm beds ¥60), just south of the station, over the bridge and on the right. Continue down this road for 100m and you come to the **east bus station** with sleeper buses to Xi'an (¥50) and Lanzhou (¥63) leaving half-hourly. The plushest hotel in town is the *Pingliang* (℡0933/8253361, ❹) on Xi Dajie, where you can also change foreign currencies. Bus #1 from the train station will get you there. The **west bus station** on the other side of town, also reached by bus #1, is busier with more destinations like Beijing, Ürümqi, Yinchuan, Guyuan, Lanzhou and Tianshui.

Kongtong Shan

Kongtong Shan lies 15km west of the city; a taxi there costs around ¥30 one-way, or tourist buses (¥5) from the west bus station are available in summer. You'll be dropped at the bottom of the mountain, from where you then walk 4km up a winding road to the top, buying a ticket (¥60) on the way. Alternatively, a tourist bus can save you the effort for ¥15. On arrival you'll be rewarded with spectacular views over an azure lake, the surrounding ribbed landscape dotted with Taoist temples. Maps of the area are available from kiosks at the top, and you're free to hike off in any direction – head up for the best buildings, down towards the lake for the best scenery. Accommodation is available at the touristy *Kongtong Shanzhuang* (closed Nov–April; dorm bed ¥60) and a primitive Taoist hostel *Taihe Gong* (dorm bed ¥20) in the resort site. To visit everywhere in Kongtong Shan takes at least three days, and you are free to stay as long as you want once you have purchased the ticket. It is worth staying overnight if you want to avoid the hordes of Chinese tourists.

Lanzhou and around

On the map, **LANZHOU** appears to lie very much in the middle of China, though this is a misleading impression. Culturally and politically it remains remote from the great cities of eastern China, despite being both the provincial capital and the largest industrial centre in the Northwest. At the head of the Hexi Corridor, it was a vital stronghold along the Silk Road and was the principal crossing point of the mighty Yellow River. For centuries it has been a transportation hub, first for caravans, then shallow boats and now rail lines. Not until the Communist era, however, did it become a large population centre as well, in response to the city's burgeoning industry. Now there are nearly three million people in Lanzhou, the vast majority of them Han Chinese.

Lanzhou is a mellow place with an excellent **museum**, tasty food and busy downtown **shopping** areas. The Yellow River, running thick and chocolatey

Lanzhou and around

Lanzhou
Lanzhou	兰州	*lánzhōu*
Baita Shan Park	白塔山公园	*báitǎ shān gōngyuán*
Baiyun Guan	白云观	*báiyún guàn*
City Museum	市博物馆	*shì bówùguǎn*
Dongfanghong Square	东方红广场	*dōngfānghóng guǎngchǎng*
Gansu Provincial Museum	甘肃省博物馆	*gānsùshěng bówùguǎn*
Journey to the West statue	西游记塑像	*xīyóujì sùxiàng*
Lanshan Park	兰山公园	*lánshān gōngyuán*
Wuquan Park	五泉公园	*wǔquán gōngyuán*
Xiguan Shizi	西关十字	*xīguān shízì*
Yellow River	黄河	*huánghé*
Yufo Si	玉佛寺	*yùfó sì*

Arrival
East bus station	汽车东站	*qìchē dōngzhàn*
Main bus station	市长途汽车站	*shì chángtú qìchēzhàn*
South bus station	汽车南站	*qìchē nánzhàn*
West bus station	汽车西站	*qìchē xīzhàn*

Accommodation
Lanshan	兰山宾馆	*lánshān bīnguǎn*
Lanzhou Dasha	兰州大厦	*lánzhōu dàshà*
Lanzhou Fandian	兰州饭店	*lánzhōu fàndiàn*
Lanzhou Legend	飞天大酒店	*fēitiān dàjiǔdiàn*
Longfei	龙飞宾馆	*lóngfēi bīnguǎn*
Shengli	胜利宾馆	*shènglì bīnguǎn*
Youyi	友谊宾馆	*yǒuyì bīnguǎn*

Eating and drinking
Boton Coffee	伯顿餐厅	*bódùn cāntīng*
Hage Fadian	哈格饭店	*hāgé fàndiàn*
Huifeng Lou	惠丰楼	*huìfēng lóu*
Miandian Wang	面点王	*miàndiǎn wáng*
Nongmin Xiang	农民巷美食街	*nóngmínxiàng měishíjiē*
Qianju Lou Huoguo Cheng	千聚楼火锅城	*qiānjùlóu huǒguōchéng*
Zhangye Jie	张掖小吃一条街	*zhāngyè xiǎochī yītiáojiē*

Bingling Si Caves
	炳灵寺千佛洞	*bǐnglíngsì qiānfódòng*
Liujiaxia Reservoir	刘家峡水库	*liújiāxiá shuǐkù*
Liujiaxia Hydro-Electric Dam	刘家峡水电站	*liújiāxiá shuǐdiànzhàn*
Yongjing	永靖	*yǒngjìng*

through the city against a backdrop of hills dim with mist, dust and industrial pollution, is one of China's classic sights, while the major historical and artistic attraction lies just beyond the city at the **Bingling Si** Buddhist Caves. Nearly all travellers on their way to or from Xinjiang will end up stopping in Lanzhou; it's worth staying a day or so.

Arrival and accommodation

Squeezed 1600m up into a narrow valley along the Yellow River, Lanzhou stretches out pencil-thin for nearly 30km, east to west. The eastern part of the city starts at Tianshui Lu and spreads west to the Xiguan Shizi (crossroad) with Dongfanghong Square roughly at the centre; this is the

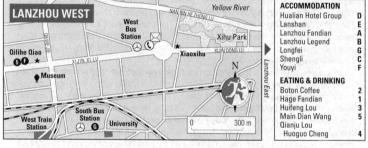

ACCOMMODATION	
Hualian Hotel Group	D
Lanshan	E
Lanzhou Fandian	A
Lanzhou Legend	B
Longfei	G
Shengli	C
Youyi	F

EATING & DRINKING	
Boton Coffee	2
Hage Fandian	1
Huifeng Lou	3
Main Dian Wang	5
Qianju Lou	
Huoguo Cheng	4

oldest part of the town, most interesting for walking, eating and shopping. The western part is relatively quiet, with a provincial museum and the popular *Youyi Hotel*.

Lanzhou's **airport** lies about 70km to the north of the city, at least a 1.5-hour journey, with connections to all major Chinese cities and Dunhuang and Jiayuguan within Gansu province. The airport buses (¥25) terminate conveniently in the eastern part of the city, outside the CAAC office on Donggang Xi Lu, a few minutes west of the *Lanzhou Fandian*.

As the main rail hub of northwest China, Lanzhou is an easy place to travel into or out of by train. Arriving this way, you will almost certainly be dropped off at the massive main **train station** in the far southeast of the city, where there are a number of hotel options in the immediate vicinity. Buses #7, #10 or #34 can take you the 2km north to Tianshui Lu, while western Lanzhou, more than a dozen kilometres away, can be reached on bus #1 and trolleybus #31. Should you arrive from Yinchuan, Jiayuguan, Wuwei or Xining by slow train, you can get off at the **west train station**, from where walking up the Qilihe Lu will take you to the Youyi Hotel. **Taxis** start from ¥7 on the meter – the price per kilometre is pasted on their windscreens.

There are several **long-distance bus stations** in Lanzhou. Buses from **Xiahe** arrive at the **South bus station**; bus #111 outside the station can take you to

Aside from the places mentioned below, plane and train tickets can also be booked through travel agents with 36 hours' notice and around ¥30 commission – see "Listings", p.1005.

There are **flights** to Dunhuang, Ürümqi, Beijing, Xi'an, Shanghai and plenty of other destinations China-wide. Lanzhou's CAAC office is on Donggang Xi Lu (daily 8am–9pm; ☏0931/8411606).

To buy **bus** tickets, you'll need a PICC Travel Insurance Certificate (see box, p.993), available at the bus stations, from travel agents at the *Lanzhou Fandian*, or direct from the PICC office on Qingyang Lu. The **west bus station** isn't of much use except to Liujia Xia, where you can get a boat to Bingling Si (see p.1005). The earliest bus leaves at 7am, and takes about an hour (¥12). Be careful of touts here and buy the tickets only from the window – the station staff are very helpful. The new **south bus station**, at the southwest end of the town, opposite the Lanzhou Science and Technology University, is more useful for tourists. There are three daily (7.30am, 8.30am and 2pm) luxury express buses to Xiahe and frequent buses to Linxia, with the earliest one leaving at 7am and only taking 2.5 hours. There are also other buses to Zhangye, Wuwei, Jiayuguan Dunhuang and Ürümqi. To get to the south bus station, take bus #111 (¥0.5) at Xiaoxi Hu on Xijin Dong Lu, heading west to the end. The **main bus station** on Pingliang Lu is smaller and has frequent departures to Xining, Tianshui, Yinchuan, Guyuan and Pingliang, along with a sleeper to Ürümqi. The chaotic **east bus station**, twenty minutes north of the main station, handles basically the same destinations plus far more long-distance inter-province traffic. Be assertive about where you are going before buying the ticket.

Unless you're heading to Xiahe, Linxia or somewhere similarly remote, the **train** is probably the best way to leave Lanzhou – all main towns along the Hexi Corridor to the northwest have stations, and there are good connections east to Tianshui, north to Yinchuan in Ningxia, and west to Xining over in Qinghai. Even better, you won't need a PICC certificate. **Buying train tickets** is easy enough at the station, though you'll have to queue up. It can be hard to get tickets around the beginning of the year and in summer; in this case, try a travel agent allowing at least 48 hours' notice.

Xiguan Shizi in the centre. Buses from the Hexi Corridor might wind up here too, or – along with traffic from everywhere else – terminate near the train station at the **main bus station** (well hidden on lower Pingliang Lu), or at the larger **East bus station** 1km north.

Accommodation

Most accommodation in Lanzhou is in the vicinity of the train station – an inexpensive but grotty location – though good-value options are emerging rapidly elsewhere.

Lanshan Tianshui Lu ☏0931/8617211 ext 218. Near the station end of Tianshui Lu, look for a blue sign. Very shabby but friendly option with double rooms and three- and four-bed dorms. Dorm beds ¥26, ③

Lanzhou Dasha (Hualian Hotel Group) Tianshui Lu ☏0931/8417210, ⊛www.lzhlbg.com. As you emerge from the train station, you'll see this monolithic hotel opposite and slightly to the left. Chaotic but not bad value, with hot water 7–10am and 6pm–midnight. They are reluctant to rent cheap beds to foreigners. Dorm beds ¥58, ③

Lanzhou Fandian Donggang Xi Lu, northeast on the Panxuan Lu bus stop ☏0931/8416321, ☏8418608. From the train station take bus #1, #7 or #10 due north a couple of stops. A huge complex which looks smart from the front conceals a well-maintained older wing with good–value dorms and doubles ¥180, which the management often discount before you ask. The Western Travel Service is also based here. **⑥**

Lanzhou Legend Panxuan Lu, across the road south from the *Lanzhou Fandian* ℡0931/8532888, ⓦwww.lanzhoulegendhotel .com. This is the plushest hotel in town, with international-standard rooms, three restaurants, a disco, bar and nightclub. **⑦**

Longfei 82 Nangongping Lu, opposite the Lanzhou Science and Technology University ℡0931/2914200. A new budget travellers' option, with a convenient location immediately next to the south bus station. Rooms are clean and comfortable, with 24-hour hot water, dorm beds in quads without bath ¥30. **③**

Shengli (Victory Hotel) Qingyang Lu ℡0931/8465221. Right in between the east and west halves of the city, handily placed for the downtown eating areas. To get here, take trolleybus #31 or bus #1 from the train station (heading west) or bus #111 from the south bus station (heading northeast). Rooms are good value at ¥220; cheaper dorms are in the west wing, but they are reluctant to rent them to foreigners for "security" reasons. Dorm bed ¥46.

Youyi (Friendship Hotel) Xijin Xi Lu ℡0931/2689999, ℻2330304. A good budget option, clean, quiet and with 24hr hot water. It's located opposite the museum, a 15min walk from the West bus station – convenient for Bingling Si. If you're arriving by bus from any point in western Gansu you'll pass in front of the hotel and can ask the driver to let you off. From the train station take bus #1 or trolleybus #31 and get off at Qilihe Qiao; it's a couple of minutes' walk to your left. Economy/standard doubles **②/④**

The City

The best place to start a tour of Lanzhou is the main shopping district, roughly in the middle of the city, in the blocks that lie to the north and east of Xiguan Shizi, along the street of Zhongshan Lu (this street comes south from Zhongshan Bridge, then turns east at the *Shengli Hotel*). There's a downtown feel to the place, with boutiques, Western music, fast food and smart department stores; the city's **Muslim quarter** and accompanying white-tiled mosque is also in the vicinity, at the western end of Zhangye Lu.

Immediately north of here, the city's greatest sight is the **Yellow River**, already flowing thick and fast, although it still has some 1500km to go before it finally reaches the sea at Qingdao. In summer, the water of the river is a rich, muddy brown colour, a legacy of the huge quantities of silt it picks up, and the fast flow helps to create a wind corridor through the city, which both moderates the climate and removes some of the worst effects of the pollution. For boating on the river, try the area just west of Zhongshan Bridge (city side) – there are a few motor boats (¥20) operating brief scenic trips. South-bank Binhe Lu here has a paved promenade from where you can watch the mud slide by, with large *Journey to the West* statues featuring Xuanzang, Monkey, Pigsy, Sandy and the horse (see p.1224); across the road, **Baiyun Guan** (daily 8am–8pm) is a small, semi-ruinous Taoist temple being extensively restored. Over the bridge, **Baita Shan Park** (daily 6am–6pm; ¥5) is ranged up a steep hillside with great views down over the river from stone terraces. A cable-car service (daily 9am–5pm; ¥15 one-way), a few minutes west of Zhongshan Lu from the south bank, can take you over the river and on to a view point in the park among the hills.

Moving east from the central area takes you into the mainly modern part of the city, which has few attractions for tourists. One possible exception, a few minutes southwest of Qingyang Lu, is the **Yufo Si**. The temple is interesting more for the poignancy of its location than anything else; with skyscrapers looming on all sides, it looks as alien as a spaceship. Nearby, a few hundred metres west of the **Dong Fanghong Square** on Qingyang Lu, is an impressive wooden Ming-dynasty stupa, now housing the **City Museum**, which opens irregularly for Chinese art exhibitions.

The Provincial Museum

The west of the city comprises an upmarket shopping and residential area strung out along Xijin Xi Lu; from the centre of town take bus #1, #6 or trolleybus #31. The one sight worth visiting here, the **Gansu Provincial Museum** (Mon–Sat 9am–noon & 2.30–5.30pm; ¥30), occupies a boxy Stalinist edifice opposite the *Youyi* hotel. It has an interesting collection, divided between natural resources of Gansu (including a mammoth skeleton) and historical finds. There are some remarkable **ceramics** dating from the Neolithic age as well as a huge collection of **wooden tablets and carvings** from the Han dynasty – priceless sources for studying the politics, culture and economy of the period. The bronze **Flying Horse of Wuwei**, 2000 years old and still with its accompanying procession of horses and chariots, is the highlight, however – note the stylish chariots for top officials with round seats and sunshades. The fourteen-centimetre-tall horse, depicted with one front hoof stepping on the back of a flying swallow, was discovered in a Han-dynasty tomb in Wuwei some thirty years ago.

Wuquan and Lanshan parks

In the hills bordering the south of the city lie **Wuquan** (daily 6.30am–6.30pm; ¥3) and **Lanshan parks** (daily 6am–6pm; ¥5), just south of the terminus of bus #8 (which you can pick up anywhere on Jiuquan Lu in the centre of town). Wuquan Park is full of mainly Qing pavilions, convoluted stairways twirling up the mountainside interspersed with teahouses, art-exhibition halls and ponds. One of the oldest buildings, the **Jingang Palace**, is Ming and contains a five-metre-high bronze Buddha cast in 1370. The current Buddha was restored after being smashed into pieces in the late 1940s. It's a nice place to wander with the locals at weekends. From Wuquan Park, Lanshan Park can be reached by chair lift (¥10) – it's about twenty minutes to the very top (600m from the city).

Eating and drinking

Lanzhou is famed around China for its beef noodles and there are good places to eat all over the city. The West bus station is surrounded by inexpensive Chinese restaurants, and also in this part of town is *Mian Dian Wang*, west of the *Youyi* hotel, serving cheap Chinese-style breakfasts of steamed or fried dumplings, rice porridge and bowls of soya milk with dough sticks. Around the **centre**, the *Hage Fandian* is a small, family-run Muslim restaurant opposite the post office on Zhongshan Lu; try the *Shaguo* (vegetables or meat with noodles in clay pots) displayed outside the door. The pedestrianized Zhangye Jie, marked by an arch gate and housing numerous stands, sells and a range of foods from kebabs, noodles and Muslim breads to local desserts like *Xingpi Shui* (an apricot drink), egg rolls and cakes.

The Nongmin Xiang north of *Lanzhou Fandian* off Tianshui Lu has a string of inexpensive restaurants, covering different styles of Chinese food. East of the *Lanzhou Fandian*, along Donggang Xi Lu, the almost-smart *Huifeng Lou* is a bright, busy mid-range place serving local delicacies: try *jincheng niangpi* (spiced glass noodles) or *suancai fentiao* (noodles flavoured with pickled vegetables, chillies and aniseed). South on Tianshui Lu, *Qianju Lou Huoguo Cheng* is the place if you like hotpots served while other diners play raucous drinking games in the background; ¥80 buys enough vegetables and meat for two.

For **Western-style food** – and a quiet, low-light environment – try *Boton Coffee*, next to the *Lanzhou* hotel – they have an English menu. Coffee here is ¥25 a pot, and they do pizza (¥30), sandwiches (¥18) and banana pancakes (¥16), as well as set meals and steaks (around ¥40). Finally, Lanzhou is famous for its summer **fruit**; don't leave without trying the melons, watermelons, peaches or grapes.

Listings

Banks and exchange The main Bank of China (Mon–Fri 8.30am–noon & 2.30–6pm) is on Tianshui Lu, just south of the *Lanzhou Legend*; foreign exchange is on the second floor.

Bookshops The Foreign Languages Bookstore, on the south side of Qin'an Lu has a small selection of novels in English. There's an English sign outside the entrance.

Internet access There are several Net bars south of the university on Tianshui Lu, all charging about ¥3 an hour – or try the slightly pricier Green Power Net bar, upstairs through a bar, more or less opposite the *Huifeng Lou*.

Mail and telephones The Post and Telecommunications Office (Mon–Sat 8.30am–7pm) stands at the junction of Pingliang Lu and Minzhu Dong Lu. There's also a post office at the West bus station in the western part of the city, and you can make collect calls at the China Telecom Building on the corner of Qingyang Lu and Jinchang Lu.

PSB Visas can be extended at an office on Wudu Lu, a couple of hundred metres west of Jiuquan Lu.

Shopping Good things to buy in Lanzhou include army surplus clothes – winter coats, waistcoats, hats and boots are all locally produced, tough and cheap. They're made at the 3512 Leather and Garment factory at the west end of Yanchang Lu, north of the river, the largest such factory in China. You can even visit it if you like and buy direct from them (bus #7 from the train station and get off at Caochang Jie).

Travel agents Just about every business remotely connected with travel, from the bus stations and hotels to the Bank of China, seems to have a counter where you can arrange train and plane tickets. The *Lanzhou* hotel's Western Travel Service is highly recommended (℡0931/8820529, ℮wtslzgschina@sina.com, daily 8am–noon & 2.30–6pm), with English-speaking staff; CITS (℡0931/8470918, ℻8817198; daily 9am–6.30pm) has a small office on the first floor of the huge department store northwest of Xiguan Shizi. Aside from transport bookings at commission of about ¥30 per ticket, both run all-inclusive day-trips to Bingling Si (around ¥300–400 per person in a 2- to 3-people group), and whirlwind overnight stays at Xiahe (¥500–600 per person for more than 4 people).

Bingling Si Caves

The trip out from Lanzhou to the Buddhist caves of **Bingling Si** (¥20) is one of the best excursions you can make in all of Gansu province – enough in itself to merit a stay in Lanzhou. Not only does it offer a glimpse of the spectacular **Buddhist cave art** that filtered through to this region along the Silk Road, but it's a powerful introduction to the **Yellow River**.

The caves are carved into a canyon southwest of the **Liujiaxia Reservoir** on the Yellow River, and can be reached only by boat at certain times of the year (see p.1006). From Lanzhou, the first stage of the expedition is a two-hour bus ride through impressively fertile loess fields to the massive **Liujiaxia Hydroelectric Dam**, a spectacular sight poised above the reservoir and surrounded by colourful rocky mountains. At the dam you board a waiting ferry, which takes three hours to reach the caves and offers excellent views en route, of fishermen busy at work and peasants cultivating wheat, sunflowers and rice on the dark, steep banks. During the trip, the ferry enters a tall **gorge** where the river froths and churns; you'll see sections of the bank being whipped away into the waters.

The ferry docks just below the Bingling Si Caves. Cut into sheer cliff, amid stunning scenery above a tributary of the river, the caves number 183 in all. They are among the earliest significant Buddhist monuments in China – started in the Western Jin and subsequently extended by the Northern Wei, the Tang, Song and Ming. Since their inaccessibility spared the caves the attentions of foreign devils in the nineteenth century and the Red Guards in the twentieth, most of the cave sculpture is in good condition, and some impressive restoration work is in progress on the wall paintings. The centrepiece sculpture, approached along a dizzying network of stairs and ramps, is a huge 27-metre **seated Buddha** (cave 172), probably carved under the Tang. The artwork at Bingling Si reached its peak under the Song and Ming dynasties, and though the wall paintings of this period have been virtually washed away, there remain a considerable number of small and exquisite carvings.

Practicalities

The most convenient way to see the caves is on a pre-booked day-trip from Lanzhou. Before booking any tour, note that the water in the reservoir is only high enough to permit **access** between June and October. Some years, however, the caves remain out of bounds through most of the summer as well, and some tour operators have been known to take people all the way to the reservoir before "discovering" that the water level is too low – no fee is refundable. Try to check the situation at the reservoir with other travellers before you book.

Most travel services in Lanzhou can arrange **trips** to the caves (see "Listings", p.1005), though if you are on your own you may have to hunt around in order to tag along with another group. For a maximum car-load of three passengers, an all-inclusive price (car, boat, entry ticket and insurance) usually comes to ¥400–500. There may also be larger (and therefore cheaper) group tours operating out of the *Shengli* – enquire here for details. Lanzhou Western Travel Service (see p.1005) offers a day-trip at ¥300 per person. The standard trip takes up to twelve hours, which includes less than two hours at the caves, but the scenery en route makes it all worthwhile. If you want a detailed guided tour, encompassing all the caves, it's worth asking about the possibility of a private trip.

Alternatively, you could consider travelling **independently** to the reservoir on a public bus. From the West bus station, there are frequent **buses** (¥12) leaving from 7am to Liujia Xia in **Yongjing**, 75km southwest of Lanzhou. At the bus stop there's an arch with a Chinese-only map, and you can join a speedboat for a return trip (about 2–3hr one-way), stopping for one hour, at ¥80 per person, or charter your own motorboat to the caves (around ¥400). On the way back you may end up staying the night in Yongjing, if the last public bus back to Lanzhou (around 5pm) leaves without you.

South from Lanzhou

This mountainous and verdant area to the south and southwest of Lanzhou, bordering on Qinghai to the west and Sichuan to the south, is one of enormous scenic beauty, relatively untouched by the scars of industry and overpopulation. The people who live here are not only few in number, but also display a fascinating cultural and ethnic diversity, with a very strong **Hui** and **Tibetan** presence in the towns of **Linxia** and **Xiahe** respectively. Xiahe, in particular, is a delightful place to visit, housing as it does one of the major Lamaist temples in China, and attracting monks and pilgrims from the whole Tibetan world. South of Xiahe, it's possible to follow an adventurous route into **Sichuan** province.

From Lanzhou to Xiahe

The road southeast from Lanzhou to Xiahe passes by first Yongjing and Liujiaxia, the jumping-off points for Bingling Si, before traversing **Dongxiang**

South from Lanzhou

Dongxiang Autonomous County	东乡自治县	dōngxiāng zìzhìxiàn
Linxia	临夏	línxià
Hehai Dasha	河海大厦	héhǎi dàshà
Nanguan Mosque	南关大寺	nánguān dàsì
Shuiquan Yibu	水泉一部	shuǐquán yībù
South bus station	汽车南站	qìchē nánzhàn
West bus station	汽车西站	qìchē xīzhàn
Xiahe	夏河	xiàhé
Gancha Grassland	甘加草原	gānjiā cǎoyuán
Gongtang Pagoda	贡唐宝塔	gòngtáng bǎotǎ
Hongjiao Si	红教寺	hóngjiào sì
Labrang Monastery	拉卜楞寺	lābùléng sì
Sangke Grasslands	桑科草原	sāngkē cǎoyuán
Accommodation and eating		
Gangjian Longzhu	刚坚龙珠宾馆	gāngjiān lóngzhū bīnguǎn
Gesar Restaurant	格尔萨餐厅	gé'ěrsà cāntīng
Labrang	拉卜楞宾馆	lābùléng bīnguǎn
Tara Guesthouse	才让卓玛旅社	cáiràng zhuómǎ lǚshè
Overseas Tibetan Hotel	华侨宾馆	huáqiáo bīnguǎn
Hezuo	合作	hézuò
Mila'erba Monastery	米拉日巴佛楼阁	mǐlā rìbā fólóugé
Luqu	碌曲	lùqǔ
Qiaotou	桥头	qiáotóu
Langmusi	郎木寺	lángmù sì
Nonghang Zhaodaisuo	农行招待所	nóngháng zhāodàisuǒ

Autonomous County. The Dongxiang minority, numbering nearly two hundred thousand, are Muslims with Mongol origins. These days, to outsiders at least, they are indistinguishable from the Hui except at certain celebrations and festivals when ancient Mongol customs re-emerge. Beyond the pilgrimage centre of Linxia, 60km from Lanzhou, the climb up to Xiahe takes three or four hours (but only two coming down again). The area through which the route passes is a zone of cultural overlap between ancient communities of Islamic and Buddhist peoples. A couple of China's lesser-known minorities also live here, the **Bao'an** and the **Salar**. The Bao'an, who number barely eight thousand, are very similar to the Dongxiang people as they, too, are of Mongolian origins. The Salar are a Turkic-speaking people whose origins lie, it's thought, in Samarkand in Central Asia; they live primarily in Xunhua County in neighbouring Qinghai province.

Linxia

A three-hour bus journey from Lanzhou, **LINXIA** is a very **Muslim** town, full of mosques, most of which have been restored since the depredations of the Cultural Revolution. Nearly everybody here seems to wear a white skull cap, and the women additionally wear a square-shaped veil of fine lace, black if they are married and green if they are not. Linxia is also the place where all the large, fancy eyeglasses that old men wear throughout this region are made. There's not much to see in town; nevertheless, it's an interesting place to stroll around for a few hours if you feel like breaking up your journey from Lanzhou to Xiahe.

Linxia's main street, which runs north–south through town, is called Tuanjie Lu in the north and Jiefang Lu in the south, with a large central square in between the two. Jiefang Lu terminates at a traffic circle at its southern end and is continued further south by Jiefang Nan Lu. The main mosque, **Nanguan Mosque**, is immediately to the south of the central square. There is no train station in Linxia, though there are **two bus stations**. If you're arriving from the west (Xining or Tongren), you may be deposited at the smaller one in the far northwest of the city (known as the West bus station), in which case you'll have to catch a cycle-rickshaw or a minivan (¥4) into town. If you arrive at the main (South) station, on Jiefang Nan Lu a couple of hundred metres south of the Jiefang Lu traffic circle, you'll be able to walk to a **hotel**. The nearest is almost immediately to the north of the station, on the right as you come out – the *Shuiquan Yibu* (T0930/6314968; ❷, dorm beds ¥38). It's the cheapest place around, with doubles and three-bed dorms, but they may try to charge foreigners double. Otherwise, *Hehai Dasha* is the best option available, furnished with western toilet though with filthy carpets (T0930/6235455, F6235476, ❸); it's five minutes' walk west of Hongyuan Lu, which intercepts Tuanjie Lu around 500m north of the large central square. The staff can be rude and are often absent (you need to find them for door keys every time you come back to the room), but the restaurant serves very good food with generous portions. There's also a **travel service** (T0930/6235156, F6210001) just outside the hotel; they organize tours to Xiahe and can also provide English-speaking tour guides in summer. A pleasant **night market**, set around the central square starting from 6pm till late at night, is a good place to stuff yourself on heavy round bread rolls (*bing*) flavoured with curry powder; roast chicken and potatoes are also available, as well as noodles and soups. On terraces overlooking the central square on the south side are a couple of very pleasant teahouses where you can sit out and enjoy the night air.

When trying to **leave** Linxia, be aware that touts for the bus companies can be very aggressive; watch your bags carefully, or they might be grabbed off you and hurled through a minibus window. Bear in mind buses won't leave until the bus is absolutely overloaded with people and goods. There are frequent buses to Lanzhou (via Liujiaxia, for Bingling Si; see p.1005) and several daily to Xiahe leaving in the morning till 4.30pm from the main bus station. There are also buses to Xining, Tianshui and Wuwei (via Lanzhou). You'll need to show your PICC insurance certificate when buying tickets in Linxia; the **PICC office** (daily 8am–noon & 2.30–6pm) is north beyond the central square, along the Hongyuan Xincun road off the Tuanjie Lu. Bus #4 from Haihe Dasha will take you here, or a taxi costs ¥3. The **Bank of China** lies a few minutes south of the Nanguan Mosque, to the west.

Xiahe and around

A tiny, rural town tucked away 3000m up in the remote hills of southern Gansu, right on the edge of the Tibetan plateau, **XIAHE** is an unforgettable place. As well as offering glimpses into the life of the **Tibetan people** – living and working in one of the most beautiful Tibetan monasteries you are likely to see – Xiahe also offers visitors the rare chance to spend some time in open countryside, sited as it is in a sunny, fresh valley surrounded by green hills.

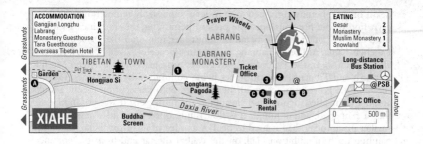

Xiahe is the most important Tibetan monastery town outside Tibet itself, and
the **Labrang Monastery** (Labuleng Si) is one of the six major centres of the
Gelugpa, or Yellow Hat Sect (of the others, four are in Tibet and one, Ta'er Si, is
just outside Xining in Qinghai province; see p.1036). Tibetans from Tibet itself
come here on pilgrimage in traditional dress (equipped with mittens and knee-
pads to cushion themselves during their prostrations), and the constant flow
of monks in bright purple, yellow and red, alongside semi-nomadic herdsmen
wrapped in sheepskins, makes for an endlessly fascinating scene.

The town is essentially built along a single street that stretches 3–4km along
the north bank of the Daxia River, from the bus station in the east, through
the Labrang Monastery in the middle, to the old Tibetan town and finally the
Labrang Hotel in the west. The **eastern end** of town, where the bus station
lies, is predominantly Hui- and Han-populated. It's also the commercial and
administrative part of town, with a couple of banks, a post office and plenty of
shops and markets. The shops round here make interesting browsing, with lots
of Tibetan religious objects on sale, such as hand-printed sutras, little prayer
wheels, bells and jewellery. There's also lots of riding equipment – saddles and
bridles – for the nomads from the nearby grasslands who come striding into
town, spurs jangling.

Beyond the monastery, at the **western end** of town, is the local Tibetan area.
West of the bridge that carries all motorized traffic to the south side of the river,
the road becomes a bumpy dirt track with homes built of mud and wood, and
pigs and cows ambling around. There is one more religious building up here,
the **Hongjiao Si**, or Temple of the Red Hat sect; it's on the right as you walk
west from town. The monks of the Red Hat sect wear red robes with a large
white band, and live in the shadow of their rich and more numerous brethren
from the Yellow Hat sect.

Labrang Monastery

About 1500m up from the bus station, the **monastery** area begins. There's
no wall separating the town from the monastery – the two communities just
merge together and the main road goes right through the middle of both. The
only markers are the long lines of roofed **prayer wheels** stretching out to the
right and left of the road, which together trace a complete circle around the
monastery. To the south side in particular, along the north bank of the river, you
can follow the prayer wheels almost to the other end of the monastery – the
gaps that still exist along the route are being rapidly filled. It's a mesmerizing
experience to walk alongside the pilgrims (clockwise around the monastery),
who turn each prayer wheel they pass.

The monastery was founded in 1709 by a monk called E'Ang Zongzhe, who
thereby became the first-generation Living Buddha, or **Jiemuyang**. Upon the

death of each Jiemuyang, a new one is born, supposedly representing the reincarnation of the previous one. The present Jiemuyang, the sixth incarnation, is third in importance in the Tibetan Buddhist hierarchy after the Dalai Lama and Panchen Lama. Although Labrang may seem a peaceful haven today, it has not always been so. In the 1920s ferocious battles took place here between Muslim warlords and Tibetans, with atrocities being committed by both sides. Then in the Cultural Revolution came further disaster, with persecution for the monks and the virtual destruction (and closure) of the monastery. It was not until 1980 that it reopened, and although it is flourishing once again, it is nevertheless a smaller place today than it used to be. For an idea of its original extent, see the painting in the Exhibition Hall, on the wall at the far end from the entrance. There are now around nine hundred registered lamas, and two thousand unofficial monks, about half their former number.

The vast majority of the important **monastery buildings** are to the north of the main road. The buildings include six colleges, as well as temple halls, Jiemuyang residences and a mass of living quarters for the monks. The institutes, where monks study for degrees, are of Astronomy, Esoteric Buddhism, Law, Medicine and Theology (higher and lower). There are also schools for dance, music and painting. The **Gongtang Pagoda** (daily 7am–11pm; ¥10), built in 1805, is the only major monastery building to the south of the main road – you pass it when following the prayer wheels. You can buy tickets from the lamas inside the pagoda if the outside ticket office is closed. It's worth climbing to the top for a spectacular view over the shining golden roofs of the monastery.

Visiting the monastery

There is nothing to stop you, at any time of day or night, from wandering around the monastery site by yourself. You may even be allowed to wander into the temples – be sensitive and use your discretion, and walk clockwise. On the other hand, given the bewildering wealth of architecture, art and statuary, it's a good idea to take a **guided tour** at some stage during your stay in Xiahe. This can be arranged at the ticket office – take the only sizeable turn off the north side of the road within the monastery area (the right if coming from the station). The hour-long tours including entrance to five buildings, led by English-speaking monks, cost ¥33, and start around 10am and 3.30pm, more frequently in peak season. Or you may be approached by Tibetan students offering guided tours – it is recommended that you settle a price (about ¥20) and route beforehand to avoid future hassles.

Labrang Monastery is the site of some spectacular **festivals** which, as with Chinese festivals, take place according to the lunar calendar. The largest of these is the **Monlam Festival**, three days after the Tibetan new year (late Feb or early March). The opening of the festival is marked by the unfurling of a huge cloth adorned with a holy painting of the Buddha, measuring 20m×30m, on the south side of the Daxia River. Subsequent days see processions, dances and the lighting of butter lamps. You might see activities like these, though on a smaller scale, at any season of the year if you happen to arrive on a special day.

Practicalities

With the construction of Xiahe's airport still at an early stage, practically all travellers will arrive by **bus**, at the station at the far eastern end of town. The station is served by frequent buses from Linxia (¥13.5) and Hezuo (¥9); there are also two buses a day to and from Lanzhou, and one for Tongren in Qinghai (leaves at 7am). For the route to Sichuan, you should take the morning bus to Hezuo and proceed south from there (see p.1012 for more on this route).

Most tourist restaurants and hotels offer **bikes** for hire; the *Monastery Restaurant* and the rental shop opposite have the cheapest rates (¥2/hr, or ¥10 per day) while bikes are annoyingly expensive at the *Labrang Hotel* (¥5/hr). There is no Bank of China in Xiahe (the nearest is in Linxia) and you cannot change traveller's cheques anywhere in town; only cash will do here. There's a **CITS** office (☎0941/7121328) in the *Labrang* hotel. **Internet access** at ¥2.5/hour can be found next to the **PSB** near the long-distance bus station, and opposite to the *Gangjian Longzhu*.

Accommodation

The east end of town has plenty of Chinese-style hotels. However, it's more fun to try one of the charismatic Tibetan-owned guesthouses farther up the road, which attract a mixed clientele of pilgrims and budget travellers.

Gangjian Longzhu A 20min walk west from the long-distance bus station, or hire a motor tricycle (¥2 per person) ☎0941/7123600. A new and clean Chinese-style hotel with freezing rooms. Warm water is available from 9 to 11pm. ❹

Labrang In the fields to the west of the town ☎0941/7121849. It's 4km from the bus station and nearly 1km from the next nearest building; from the station, a cycle-rickshaw here shouldn't cost more than about ¥5, though you might have to get off and push for one or two stretches. Easily Xiahe's best hotel; accommodation ranges from simple three-bed dorms with bath, through plain doubles to rather damp concrete "Tibetan-style" cabins. Prices increase at the height of summer, while in winter the hotel may not be open at all. Dorm beds ¥20, ❻

Monastery Guesthouse In the heart of the monastery area, and run by monks who obviously have more important things on their minds than cleaning. Basic rooms with stoves, spartan as any monk's cell, are arranged around a courtyard. There's an 11pm curfew and no hot water. Dorm beds ¥40, ❶

Overseas Tibetan Hotel A clean and well-maintained building offering the cheapest dorms in town, ☎0941/7122642; the first good place you come to if you head west of the bus station. Dorm beds ¥20, Doubles including breakfast ❹

Tara Guesthouse Signed in English 50m west of the *Overseas Tibetan Hotel*, with its entrance a few doors down in the alley leading off to the south, ☎0941/7121274, ✉t-dolma@yahoo.com. Some find the eccentric Tibetan staff too much to handle, but it's a good place: the lovingly decorated rooms have stoves, some have *kangs*, and there's a stereo instead of a TV in most. Dorm beds ¥30, ❶

Eating

The influx of tourists has given a huge boost to the Xiahe catering trade in recent years. In the eastern part of town there are plenty of **restaurants** offering Tibetan and traveller food – banana pancakes and the like. They usually have either "Tibet" or "Snow" in their titles, and they're all pretty much the same. You won't see many Tibetans in any of them – they tend to eat in the cheaper, unnamed places.

One of two places called *Monastery Restaurant* lies at the monastery's eastern edge; run by a family from the Gancha grasslands, it's a homely place which offers Tibetan staples such as *tsampa*, made from yak butter and coarse flour – you add sugar and turn it into a kind of breakfast cereal. There's an English menu which includes "banana in melted sauce" (actually coated in toffee), and plenty of Wild West characters hanging around. The other popular one with tourists is the *Snowland* over the road, though it may not open in winter. The *Gesar Restaurant* (daily 8am–11pm), a couple of minutes' walk down the street opposite the *Tara Guesthouse*, is also a good place with a cosy environment and English menu. They offer great breakfasts, with yogurt and honey, pancakes, bread and even cream cheese. The other *Monastery Restaurant*, farther west, is a Muslim place serving some pretty decent yak-meat dishes – a lot of meat for very little money. For Chinese food, you can find a string of restaurants along the road west of the long-distance bus station.

Around Xiahe

Even without the monastery, Xiahe would be a delightful place to relax given its rural setting. The hills around the valley offer excellent hiking opportunities, and the views down to the monastery can be breathtaking. About 15km farther west up the valley are the **Sangke grasslands**, which can be reached by motor-rickshaw (about ¥30 return), or by bicycle. If you're cycling you can follow either the dirt track north of the river, or the sealed road to the south. You'll know when you've arrived – a ticket booth (¥5) in the middle of nowhere marks the entrance, beyond which the valley opens out into a vast, grassy pasture, a lovely place to walk in summer. Nomads hang around here offering rides on their horses for ¥20 an hour. You can also stay out here in yurts (¥40) affiliated to the *Labrang Hotel* from July to September – enquire at the hotel reception about these (though the associated garish pink casino labled "Nira Ethnic Paradise Resort" is not an encouraging sign for the future development of this tranquil area). The **Gancha grasslands** (¥15), another 30km to the north, are less touristy and vaster, but harder to get to due to bad road conditions. Tours run in summer from the *Tara Guesthouse* (¥60 for the day) or a return trip by taxi costs ¥180.

The road to Sichuan

South of Xiahe the roads are narrow and traffic irregular; nevertheless, there is a route you can follow by public bus which leads ultimately to Chengdu in Sichuan province. It's a rough trip, which requires several stopovers in remote towns, but a fascinating one – through one of the most beautiful parts of China. Some of the villages en route, notably Langmusi just inside Sichuan, are the most authentically Tibetan settlements most travellers are ever likely to see, given that it can be so hard to travel off the beaten track inside Tibet itself.

Hezuo

From Xiahe, the first stop is **HEZUO**, about 70km to the southeast. It's a trading post for Tibetan nomads and you'll see some fairly wild-looking types in the town. If you get the first morning bus (6.30am; ¥9) from Xiahe, you can move on to Luqu or Langmusi the same day – there's one bus daily from Hezuo at 9.30am. However, getting stuck here for a day is no trial.

Hezuo is centred on a crossroads with a sculpture of a Tibetan antelope in the middle, looking north. The **north bus station**, where you get off coming from Xiahe or Lanzhou, is on the northwest corner of the crossroads. Almost opposite, on the road leading north, is an adequate hotel, the *Gannan Binguan* (☎0931/8213186; ¥38, dorm bed ¥15), kept very clean by its Muslim staff. Look for the blue English sign. The Agricultural Bank, on the southwest corner, is the only place in town that will change foreign currency into yuan. Head east from the crossroads, and you'll find a fascinating little street with a very good two-storey Muslim **restaurant** on the right. Buses heading south leave from the **south bus station**, and a taxi there from the north bus station costs ¥2.

Hezuo also boasts one worthwhile attraction, the **Mila'erba Monastery** (¥20, negotiable), in the north of the city. From the crossroads, head west for 500m then turn north for another 1.5km – you'll see it on the left; you can hardly miss it as the impressive central temple is nine storeys high. The exterior may look stern and robust, but the interior is pure chocolate box, each room gaudy with paintings and sculpture. Provided you take your shoes off at the door, you are free to ascend every storey. From the roof you can gaze at hills dotted with prayer flags.

South of Hezuo

Beyond Hezuo, the road runs **south to Sichuan** via **LUQU**, 80km from Hezuo and served by four to five buses daily from the south bus station. The countryside around Luqu is beautiful and easily accessible for hiking, and a stroll up or down the river is likely to turn up one or two monasteries. In Luqu itself you can stay at the *Nonghang Zhaodaisuo* (☎0941/6621085; ¥50); there's no English sign, but turn right out of the bus station and it's less than five minutes' walk. From Luqu, it's a further 80km south to the charming **Langmusi**, just over the Sichuan border. Buses don't stop in Langmusi itself, but drop you off at *Qiaotou*, 4km away – it's easy to miss the stop marked by an unobvious bridge – ask the driver to remind you beforehand. From Qiaotou jeeps or tractors will take you up the hill to the village for ¥3. For more on Langmusi, see p.942.

The Hexi Corridor

For reasons of simple geography, travellers leaving or entering China to or from Central Asia and the West have always been channelled through this narrow strip of land that runs 1000km northwest of Lanzhou. With the foothills of the Tibetan plateau, in the form of the Qilian Shan range, soaring up to the south, and a merciless combination of waterless desert and mountain to the north, the road known as the **Hexi Corridor** offers the only feasible way through the physical obstacles that crowd in on the traveller west of Lanzhou.

Historically whoever controlled the corridor could operate a stranglehold on the fabulous riches of the Silk Road trade (see box, p.962). Inevitably the Chinese took an interest from the earliest times, and a certain amount of Great Wall-building was already taking place along the Hexi Corridor under Emperor Qin Shi Huang in the third century BC. Subsequently, the powerful Han dynasty succeeded in incorporating the region into their empire, though the influence of central government remained far from constant for many centuries afterwards, as Tibetans, Uigurs and then Mongols vied for control. Not until the Mongol conquests of the thirteenth century did the corridor finally become a settled part of the Chinese empire, with the Ming consolidating the old Great Wall positions and building its magnificent last fort at **Jiayuguan**.

Two other towns along the corridor, **Wuwei** and **Zhangye**, offer convenient means of breaking the long journey from Lanzhou to Dunhuang, and have their own share of historic sights which might justify a stopover.

Wuwei and around

Lying approximately halfway between Lanzhou and Zhangye, **WUWEI** is a small city in the uncomfortable state, rather common in China at present, of being half-demolished and half-rebuilt. Gansu's most famous historical relic, the Han-dynasty **Flying Horse of Wuwei**, was discovered here in 1969 underneath the Leitai Si, a temple just north of town. Now housed in the Lanzhou Museum (see p.1003), the symbol of the horse, depicted in full gallop and stepping on the back of a swallow, can be seen everywhere in Wuwei.

The city is divided into four quadrants by the main north–south road (Bei Dajie and Nan Dajie) and the east–west road (Dong Dajie and Xi Dajie), with the centre of the city at the crossroads, marked by **Wenhua Square**. It is interesting just to wander about the square on a warm day, where people assemble to play traditional musical instruments with snack and trinkets stands peppered

The Hexi Corridor

Hexi Corridor	河西走廊	*héxī zǒuláng*
Jiayuguan	嘉峪关	*jiāyù guān*
First Beacon Tower	第一墩	*dìyī dūn*
Fort	城楼	*chénglóu*
Great Wall Museum	长城博物馆	*chángchéng bówùguǎn*
Heishan rock carvings	黑山岩画	*hēishān yánhuà*
Overhanging Wall	悬壁长城	*xuánbì chángchéng*
Qiyi Bingchuan	七一冰川	*qīyī bīngchuān*
Xincheng Dixia Hualang	新城地下画廊	*xīnchéng dìxià huàláng*
Accommodation and eating		
Changcheng	长城宾馆	*chángchéng bīnguǎn*
Jiayuguan Hotel	嘉峪关宾馆	*jiāyùguān bīnguǎn*
Jincheng Canguan	金城餐馆	*jīnchéng cānguǎn*
Linyuan Jiudian	林苑酒店	*línyuán jiǔdiàn*
Wumao	物贸宾馆	*wùmào bīnguǎn*
Xiongguan	雄关宾馆	*xióngguān bīnguǎn*
Yuanzhongyuan	园中园餐厅	*yuánzhōngyuán cāntīng*
Wuwei	武威	*wǔwēi*
Ancient Bell Tower	大云寺古钟楼	*dàyúnsì gǔzhōnglóu*
Leitai Si	雷台寺	*léitái sì*
Luoshi Pagoda	罗什塔	*luóshí tǎ*
South gate	南门	*nánmén*
Wen Miao	文庙	*wénmiào*
Accommodation		
Liangzhou	凉州宾馆	*liángzhōu bīnguǎn*
Tianma	天马宾馆	*tiānmǎ bīnguǎn*
Ya Ou	亚欧宾馆	*yà'ōu bīnguǎn*
Zhangye	张掖	*zhāngyè*
Dafo Si	大佛寺	*dàfó sì*
Daode Guan	道德观	*dàodé guàn*
Gulou	古楼	*gǔlóu*
Mu Ta	木塔	*mùtǎ*
Tu Ta	土塔	*tǔtǎ*
Xilai Si	西来寺	*xīlái sì*
Accommodation and eating		
Ganzhou	甘州宾馆	*gānzhōu bīnguǎn*
Huachen International	华辰国际大酒店	*huáchén guójì dàjiǔdiàn*
Jindu	金都宾馆	*jīndū bīnguǎn*
Mingqing Jie	明清街	*míngqīng jiē*
Shibazhe Meishilin	十八褶美食林	*shíbāzhě měishílín*
Zhangye	张掖宾馆	*zhāngyè bīnguǎn*

around. There's a trace of the old city near the bus station on Nan Dajie, where the original **south gate** has been impressively reconstructed. Ten minutes' walk north of here, if you take the first road on the right, you'll arrive at the Ming-dynasty-built **Wen Miao** (daily 8am–6pm; ¥31), a delightful museum in the grounds of an old temple with large gardens full of oleanders and singing birds. The most interesting item in the museum is a stone stele with Chinese and Xixia language on both sides, which ultimately deciphered the complicated and extinguished Xixia language (see box p.988).

About twenty minutes due north of here, the **Ancient Bell Tower** in **Dayun Si** (daily 8am–6pm; ¥10) is worth a visit mostly for its grounds, where old men play mah-jong or cards and drink tea under vine trellises and enormous hollyhocks. There are occasional Taoist ceremonies undertaken outside the main hall in the temple, depending upon local demand. A further twenty minutes' walk west brings you to Bei Dajie, near the

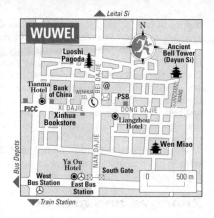

1600-year-old brick **Luoshi Pagoda** (¥10, under renovation at the time of writing), from where you can catch bus #2 a few kilometres or walk 20 minutes north to **Leitai Si** (daily 8am–6pm; ¥50). The temple, built high up on impressive mud ramparts, is unfortunately submerged amongst modern construction projects, but its grounds remain pleasantly calm and shady. Underneath the site, through a separate entrance, a Chinese-speaking tour guide will lead you to the famous Han-dynasty tomb where the Flying Horse statue was discovered. There's not much to see – it's a series of very low passageways, with a mock-up of the tomb contents at the back – but the 2000-year-old brickwork is still in perfect condition and amazingly modern in appearance. Ironically, the bronze Flying Horse, now a prized relic, remained in the tomb long after accompanying items of gold and silver had been stolen.

Practicalities

The **east bus station** lies just outside the old south gates, with several free-lance depots further west. There are frequent **buses** to Zhangye and Lanzhou (7am–8pm); at least one daily bus to Ürümqi (4pm) and Dunhuang if demand is sufficient; and two south to Xining leaving at 7am and 10am. Station staff are rigid in requiring foreigners to have PICC insurance. Ten minutes' walk west from here is the newer **west bus station** with occasional luxury express buses to Lanzhou and Ürümqi. The **train station** is 3km to the south, from where it costs a couple of yuan to take a minibus into the centre. All trains between Ürümqi and the east stop at Wuwei, and there's also a slow train to Zhongwei in Ningxia. It's easy to buy hard-seat tickets at the station – fine for the short hops to Lanzhou or Zhangye – but sleepers are best arranged through a travel agent.

Accommodation in Wuwei for foreigners is increasing though still scarce compared to elsewhere. Just a few minutes west of the bus station is the *Ya Ou* (℡0935/2265700; ❶), which is not allowed to take foreigners, but will, given some persuasion; a few Chinese words may be useful to avoid being charged double. The *Liangzhou* on Dong Dajie (℡0935/2265999; ❹), a couple of minutes east of the central crossroads, has nice doubles with 24-hour hot water. The dull *Tianma*, west on Xi Dajie (℡0935/2212356; ❸), is the official foreigners' hotel, often stacked with Japanese tourist groups. Ask for rooms on the eighth or ninth floor which are cleaner and quieter. For **food**, there are numerous noodle houses around the bus station and on Nan Dajie north of the south gate, serving soups and mutton dishes heavily laced with chilli; the *Liangzhou* also has a decent Chinese restaurant.

The huge China Telecom building (daily 8am–6.30pm), where you can make long-distance phone calls, is immediately east of Wenhua Square, and across Bei Dajie is the **post office**. There's a branch of **CITS** (☏0935/2267239) immediately outside the *Tianma Hotel* which can arrange train tickets (commission ¥15 for hard seat, ¥30 for sleeper); services are frosty to independent budget travellers and staff here pretend not to know the whereabouts of **PICC** (Mon–Fri 8am–noon & 2.30–6pm), which is just a few minutes west of the office, over the crossroads. The **Bank of China**, just to the east of the *Tianma Hotel*, is open Monday to Friday 8.30am to 6pm. The **PSB** office that deals with visa extensions is just a couple of minutes east opposite the *Liangzhou Hotel* – there's a small English sign outside the office.

Zhangye and around

A medium-sized town, about 450km northwest of Lanzhou and 150km southeast of Jiayuguan on the edge of the Loess plateau, **ZHANGYE** has long been an important stopover for caravans and travellers on the Silk Road. Indeed, Marco Polo spent a whole year here. During the Ming period, Zhangye was an important garrison town for soldiers guarding the **Great Wall**, and today the road from Wuwei to Zhangye is still a good place from which to view the

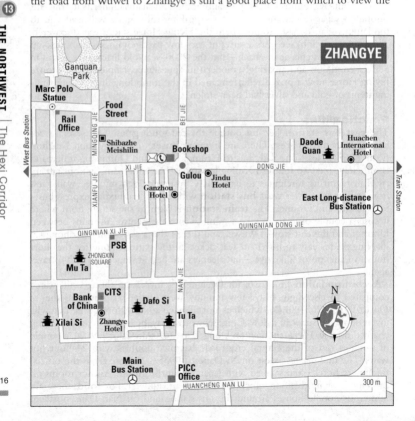

Wall, visible for a large part of the way as a slightly sad and crumbling line of mud ramparts. Initially it runs to the north of the road, until, quite dramatically, the road suddenly cuts right through a hole in the Wall and continues on the other side.

Although Zhangye is not an especially attractive town, there are a number of places that fill at least a day of sightseeing. The centre of the town is marked, as in many Chinese towns, by a **Gulou** (Drum Tower) at the crossroads. The tower, built in 1507 during the Ming dynasty, has two tiers and houses a massive bronze bell. The four streets radiating out from here, Bei Jie, Dong Jie, Nan Jie and Xi Jie, are named after their respective compass points, and most places of interest are in the southwest of town in the vicinity of the *Zhangye Hotel*.

Just east of the *Zhangye*, a central smoke-grimed hall at **Dafo Si** (Big Buddha Temple; daily summer 7.30am–6.30pm & winter 8am–6pm; ¥41) houses a 34-metre-long **reclining Buddha**, easily China's largest, whose calm expression and gentle form make a powerful impression. Immediately behind the Buddha are ten disciples, and grotesque-looking *luohans* (saintly warriors) stand around in the gloom. Unusually, the hall itself, built in 1098 and restored in 1770, is almost entirely made of wood. In the same grounds the **Tu Ta** (Earth Tower; same ticket) is a former Buddhist monastery; now in use as a local Culture Centre (*wenhua guan*), it features a single large stupa 20m in height.

On Xianfu Jie, a few hundred metres north of the *Zhangye*, looms the 31-metre-tall **Mu Ta** (Wooden Tower; daily 8am–6pm; ¥5), built in the sixth century, before being burnt down and then restored in 1925. The octagonal tower is now home to large numbers of jackdaws. A few hundred metres south of here, and one block to the west, the **Xilai Si** is a small Buddhist temple complex, where you can see monks chanting at dusk and dawn.

Much farther away, about fifteen minutes' walk due east from the Drum Tower on the road to the train station, is a charming Taoist monastery, the **Daode Guan**. It's a small, dishevelled place of Ming origins, containing a tiny garden, some vine trellises, and some well-maintained Taoist statues and wall paintings. Monks here are hospitable and seem completely detached from the modern world. The monastery is hidden in a jumble of narrow lanes on the north side of Dong Jie, and can be easily lost among the neighbouring shops – look for the sign with gold characters on a blue background.

Practicalities

Zhangye's **main bus station** is south of the centre on Huancheng Nan Lu, though there's also a newer and bigger **western bus station** about 1km west of Gulou off Xi Jie and a smaller **eastern bus station** about 2km east of Gulou. The **train** station is located about 7km away to the northeast; trains are met by waiting minibuses which take you into town for ¥1.5 or taxi (¥10). No trains actually originate or terminate in Zhangye, though most of the passing trains will stop here and you can buy train tickets (¥5 commission) at the rail office off Mingqing Jie – look for the Marco Polo statue – the office is to its southwest. Moving on **by bus**, the western station handles traffic heading west, as does the main station, which additionally has services to all parts of Gansu province, and also to Xining in Qinghai over a spectacular mountain route, while the eastern station has some faster private services to Lanzhou. Whether you get asked to show a **PICC** certificate depends on who serves you. The PICC office (Mon–Fri 8.30am–noon & 2.30–6pm) is at the northwest corner of Nan Jie/ Huancheng Nan Lu intersection. The **PSB** is on the fourth floor of a building on Qingnian Xi Jie, east of Mu Ta.

Hotels in Zhangye have enjoyed a boom in recent years, and pretty much all of them take foreigners with or without a permit. A couple of minutes south of the Drum Tower, the *Ganzhou* is a bit shabby, but the rooms are fine (T & F 0936/8212402; ❹). Another budget option is the *Jindu* (T 0936/8245088, ❸), with ordinary rooms. The most upmarket place is the brand-new *Huachen International* (T 0936/8257777, ✉ zyhcdh@public.lz.gs.cn; ❻), a few minutes east of the Daode Guan; staff can speak good English and rooms are good value. Finally, *Zhangye* (T 0936/8212601, F 8213806; ❺), recently being renovated by demolition of the budget rooms, is one of the oldest hotels in town; **Bank of China** (Mon–Fri 8am–6pm, Sat & Sun 9am–5pm) and **CITS** (T 0936/8241824, F 8241826) are just outside here to the north. To get here from the main bus station, turn left as you exit, then head north for a few minutes up Xianfu Jie; the hotel is on the right.

The northern end of Xianfu Jie, beyond the junction with Xi Jie, is Mingqing Jie – a mock Ming-dynasty **food street** serving noodle soups, kebabs, hotpots and the like. Several places here specialize in excellent *shuijiao*, stuffed with either vegetables, seafood, beef or more exotic meats, from about ¥10 a *jin*; or try the almost smart *Shibazhe Meishilin*, partway up the east side of the street, which serves an inexpensive range of casseroles, hotpots, and local snacks.

Jiayuguan and beyond

One more cup of wine for our remaining happiness. There will be chilling parting dreams tonight.

Ninth-century poet on a leave-taking at Jiayuguan

To some Chinese the very name **JIAYUGUAN** is synonymous with sorrow and ghastly remoteness. The last **fortress** of the Great Wall was built here by the Ming in 1372, over 5000km from the wall's easternmost point at Shanhaiguan, from which time the town made its living by supplying the needs of the fortress garrison. This was literally the final defence of the empire, the spot where China ended and beyond which lay a terrifying wilderness. The fort, just outside the town and perfectly restored, is one of the great sights of northwestern China, and there are also a number of other forts and beacons scattered around in the desert outside Jiayuguan.

Apart from the great fort, Jiayuguan today is a bleak, lonely place laid out in a regular grid pattern, and sliced through diagonally from east to west by Lanxin Dong Lu. The centre is a large traffic circle, overlooked by the *Jiayuguan Hotel* and the post office; Xinhua Lu is the main street leading southeast from here. In the north of the town is an **Entertainment Park** (daily 8am–10pm), which is a good spot for an evening stroll among the crowds, giant sculptures, pagodas, pleasure boats and dodgem cars. There's also an indoor swimming pool. Head north along Xinhua Bei Lu from the central traffic circle and take the first right along a narrow market street – the park lies at the far end of the street.

Practicalities

Jiayuguan's **train station** is in the far southwest of the city and linked by bus or minibus #1 (¥1) to the centre. All trains running between Ürümqi and eastern China stop here. The **bus station** has a much more convenient location on Lanxin Dong Lu, about 1km southwest of the central roundabout. For tourists, the most useful buses are the frequent connections with Dunhuang or Zhangye. Some services, for example the one running between Hami and Jiuquan, must be flagged down on the highway outside the station. The **airport**, 10km from

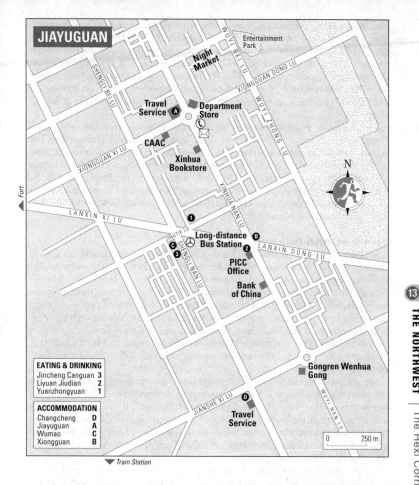

JIAYUGUAN

Entertainment Park

Night Market

WUYI BEI LU

XIONGGUAN DONG LU

WUYI ZHONG LU

SHENGLI BEI LU

Travel Service **A**

Department Store

CAAC

Xinhua Bookstore

XIONGGUAN XI LU

Fort

LANXIN XI LU

XINHUA NAN LU

N

1

JINGTIE LU

SHENGLI NAN LU

Long-distance Bus Station **B**

2

LANXIN DONG LU

C

3

PICC Office

Bank of China

Gongren Wenhua Gong

JIANSHE XI LU

Travel Service **D**

WUYI NAN LU

0   250 m

EATING & DRINKING
Jincheng Canguan   3
Liyuan Jiudian   2
Yuanzhongyuan   1

ACCOMMODATION
Changcheng   **D**
Jiayuguan   **A**
Wumao   **C**
Xiongguan   **B**

▼ Train Station

town, is connected by airport bus (¥10) to *Jiayuguan Hotel*, northwest of the central traffic circle; a taxi costs (¥30).

The **travel agents** in both the *Jiayuguan* and *Changcheng* hotels can supply train tickets for a ¥30 commission and organize local tours. **Train tickets** out of Jiayuguan are hard to come by in peak season – you will almost certainly need the help of a travel service, and may need to resort to soft class if you want a sleeper. When **buying bus tickets**, foreigners without PICC certificates (see p.993) have sometimes managed to sweet-talk the station staff into letting them pay a tiny supplement for single-day cover; if you fail, you can buy certificates at the PICC office (Mon–Fri 8.30am–noon & 2.30–6pm) on Xinhua Nan Lu, just north of Lanxin Dong Lu. The CAAC office (daily 8.30am–6.30pm; ☎0937/6266677) opposite the *Jiayuguan Hotel* to the west sells **flight tickets** to Lanzhou, Xi'an and Beijing.

Accommodation is all fairly central. Just west from the bus station, the *Wumao* is worn (☎0937/6280855; **❹**, dorm beds ¥30), but the friendly staff can arrange bike rental at ¥2 an hour; you can also rent bikes from the outdoor bike shops along Xinhua Nan Lu at the same price. Cleaner rooms are available a few minutes east at the helpful *Xiongguan* (☎0937/6201116, ⓕ6225399; ❸). For something more upmarket, your best bet is the *Jiayuguan Hotel*, right on the central roundabout (☎0937/6226983, ⓕ6227174; ❻), offering smart doubles and a good restaurant. The #1 bus or minibus from the train station stops here. Alternatively, there's the four-star *Changcheng*, south on Jianshe Xi Lu (☎0937/6225213, ⓕ6226016; ¥560), its architecture mimicking a martial theme.

The *Jiayuguan Hotel* **restaurant** serves bland Chinese breakfasts and much better evening meals. Noodles and dumplings are available around the bus station and at the **night market** north from the *Jiayuguan* and along the road to the Entertainment Park. If you want to sit down to standard Chinese fare in a cheerful setting, try either the *Linyuan Jiudian* next to the PICC office or its chain *Yuanzhongyuan* opposite the bus station. The *Jincheng Canguan* on Shengli Nan Lu offers cheap Muslim noodles in a canteen setting; look for the English sign "Lanzhou Beef Noodles".

The fort and beyond

The **fort** (Cheng Lou; daily 8.30am–5.30pm; ¥60) at the Jiayuguan Pass is the biggest sight in the Hexi Corridor. Its location, between the permanently snowcapped Qilian Mountains to the north and the black Mazong (Horse's Mane) Mountains to the south, could not be more dramatic – or more strategically valuable. Everything that travelled between the deserts of central Asia and the fertile lands of China – goods, traders, armies – had to file through this pass. The desolation of the landscape only adds to the melancholy – being forced to leave China altogether was a citizen's worst nightmare, and it was here that disgraced officials and condemned or fleeing criminals had to make their final, bitter farewells.

Some kind of fort may have occupied this site as early as the Han dynasty, but the surviving building is a Ming construction, completed in 1372. Sometimes referred to as the "Impregnable Defile under Heaven", it comprises an outer and an inner wall, the former more than 700m in circumference and about 10m high. At the east and the west of the inner wall stand symbolic gates, the Guanghua Men (Gate of Enlightenment) and the Rouyuan Men (Gate of Conciliation) respectively. Inside each gate are sloping walkways leading to the top of the wall, enabling horses to climb up and patrol the turrets. In between the Gate of Enlightenment and the outer wall stand a pavilion, a temple and a somewhat haunting open-air theatre which was once used to entertain troops. The entrance fee also covers the excellent **Great Wall Museum** (daily 9am–5pm), which reviews the history of the Wall from the Han to the last frenzied spurt of construction under the Ming. The highlights are photos and scale models of the Wall taken from points right across northern China, places that for the most part lie well away from tourist itineraries.

The so-called **Overhanging Wall** (daily 8am–7pm; ¥21), about 8km northwest of the fort, is a section of the Great Wall connecting the fort to the Mazong range, originally built in the sixteenth century and recently restored. From the ramparts there are excellent views of the surrounding land; vast and empty, it's actually much more atmospheric than the fort, especially if you take the scenic cycle route along the crumbling Wall.

Other desert sights

Several other desert attractions around Jiayuguan could also be combined with a trip to the fort and the Wall. About 6km south of Jiayuguan are the ruins of the **First Beacon Tower**. Built on the Great Wall in the sixteenth century, the long-abandoned tower is now crumbling on a cliff top on the northern bank of the Taolai River at the foot of the Qilian Mountains. The desert also harbours a couple of unusual collections of ancient Chinese art. One is the **Xincheng Dixia Hualang** (Underground Gallery; ¥30), about 20km northeast of Jiayuguan. Actually a burial site from the Wei and Jin periods, more than eighteen hundred years ago, the graves are brick-laid and contain vivid paintings depicting contemporary life on each brick. Not far beyond the fort, 9km northwest of Jiayuguan, are the **Heishan rock carvings**. These look more like classic "cave man" art: on the cliffs of the Heishan Mountain are carved more than a hundred pictures of hunting, horse-riding and dancing, all dating back to the Warring States Period (476–221 BC). Finally, one stupendous but rather inaccessible natural sight is the **Qiyi Bingchuan** (July 1st Glacier), located 4300m up in the Qilian Mountains, 120km from Jiayuguan – remarkably close considering what a hot place Jiayuguan is in summer.

Practicalities

The easiest way to reach both the fort and the Wall is to hire a small **minibus** (around ¥50 for the whole trip); visiting the First Beacon Tower and the two art sites in conjunction with a tour of the fort and Overhanging Wall takes a day and costs around ¥100 in a taxi. You can get to the fort itself by public transport in summer – take minibus #4 (¥1) that leaves for the fort from the roundabout outside the *Jiayuguan Hotel*. To **cycle** to the fort, follow Lanxin Dong Lu west from the bus station until you cross the bridge over the rail line. A blue sign pointing right indicates the way to the fort from here. From the Fort to the Overhanging Wall, you go back 50m from the car park and follow the only road to your left with another blue sign not far ahead until reaching a junction, where you take a right, marked by an ugly grey concrete building. Ride straight down this road until you reach the ticket office. It's about thirty minutes to the fort, another thirty to the Overhanging Wall, and forty back into town.

A day-trip to the glacier by taxi costs at least ¥350. Travel agents (see p.1019) in town provide tours with an English guide for around ¥600. The tow involves a three-hour drive, followed by five hours climbing up and down, and three hours driving back.

Dunhuang and the Mogao Caves

An oasis town perched right on the outer periphery of old Chinese Turkestan, **DUNHUANG** has always been literally on the edge of the desert – from downtown you can see giant, spectacular **sand dunes** at the bottom of the street, and winds can whip up abrasive yellow sandstorms. Dunhuang's fame rests on the astonishing artwork at the nearby **Mogao Caves**, and the town has become something of a desert resort for visiting them, with inexpensive hotels, lots of English-language menus in the restaurants and friendly people.

The town itself is nothing more than a few appealing ordinary streets – the centre is marked by a traffic circle with streets radiating out to the north, east, south and west. On the main street east, Yangguan Dong Lu, there's the interesting **Shazhou night market** selling food and **souvenirs** every summer evening, where you can stroll with no pressure to buy. Coins, jade articles, Buddhas, Tibetan bells and horns, leather shadow puppets, scroll paintings and

Dunhuang and the Mogao Caves

Dunhuang	敦煌	dūnhuáng
Baima Ta	白马塔	báimǎ tǎ
Dunhuang City Museum	敦煌市博物馆	dūnhuángshì bówùguǎn
Mingsha Shan	明沙山	míngshā shān
Mogao Caves	莫高窟	mògāo kū
Research and Exhibition Centre	石窟文物研究陈列中心	shíkū wénwù yánjiū chénliè zhōngxīn
Shazhou night market	沙洲夜市	shāzhōu yèshì
Xi Qianfodong	西千佛洞	xī qiānfódòng
Yangguan	阳关	yángguān
Yueya Quan	月牙泉	yuěyá quán
Yumenguan	玉门关	yùmén guān
Accommodation		
Dunhuang Binguan	敦煌宾馆	dūnhuáng bīnguǎn
Dunhuang Fandian	敦煌饭店	dūnhuáng fàndiàn
Feitian	飞天宾馆	fēitiān bīnguǎn
Five Rings	五环宾馆	wǔhuán bīnguǎn
Guangyuan	广源大酒店	guǎngyuán dàjiǔdiàn
International	敦煌国际大酒店	dūnhuáng guójì dàjiǔdiàn
Jinye	金叶宾馆	jīnyè bīnguǎn
Xiyu	西域宾馆	xīyù bīnguǎn
Liuyuan	柳园	liǔyuán

Chinese chops are all on sale. Nearby, the mediocre **Dunhuang City Museum** (daily 8am–6pm; closed Jan–March; ¥10) houses a few of the scrolls left behind after the depredations of the archeologist and adventurer Sir Aurel Stein (see box, p.1026) – there's a much better museum at the caves themselves.

Practicalities

There is no rail line directly to Dunhuang. The nearest **train station** is at Liuyuan (usually labelled as "Dunhuang" on timetables), about 130km away; minibuses wait outside the station to carry passengers to town. The bigger **Dunhuang bus station** lies right in the budget hotel area in the south of town on Mingshan Lu; diagonally opposite is another smaller long-distance bus station, and it's worth asking here if you have no luck at Dunhuang bus station. Dunhuang's **airport** is about 13km southeast of town; the airport bus stops at the **CAAC** office (℡0937/88222389; daily 8am–noon & 3–6pm) on Yangguan Dong Lu; a taxi costs ¥30. Most accommodation has **travel agents**, who arrange local tours, and tickets: *Charley Johng's Café* (✉dhzhzh@public .lz.gs.cn) on Mingshang comes recommended, as well as *John's Information Café* in the *Feitian* hotel (closed in winter; ✉johncafe@hotmail.com); **CITS** are on the second floor in the building facing the *International* hotel (℡0937/8835529) – an English-speaking guide from here costs ¥150 for the day; a car from ¥500. The **Bank of China** (Mon–Fri 8am–noon & 3–6.30pm) is on Yangguan Dong Lu.

You can **rent bikes** from *Shirley's Café* or *Charley Johng's Café* for ¥1 an hour. *Charley Johng's* also offers a laundry service. **Internet bars** abound north of the bus station on Mingshan Lu, and foreign-oriented cafés often have Net access too – connections are good and cost ¥5–10 an hour.

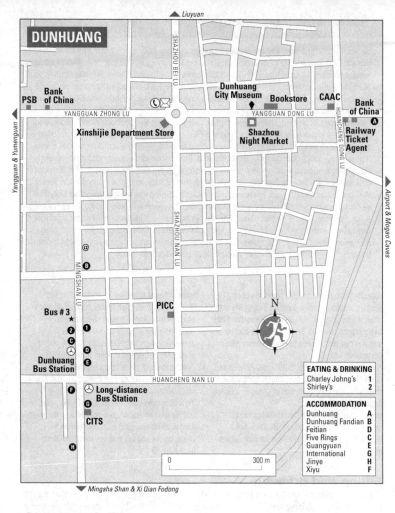

DUNHUANG

Liuyuan

PSB — Bank of China

Dunhuang City Museum — Bookstore — CAAC — Bank of China

YANGGUAN ZHONG LU

Xinshijie Department Store

YANGGUAN DONG LU

Shazhou Night Market

Railway Ticket Agent

SHAZHOU BEI LU

SHAZHOU NAN LU

HUANCHENG DONG LU

Yangguan & Yumenguan

Airport & Mogao Caves

MINGSHAN LU

@

PICC

Bus #3

Dunhuang Bus Station

HUANCHENG NAN LU

Long-distance Bus Station

CITS

N

0 — 300 m

Mingsha Shan & Xi Qian Fodong

EATING & DRINKING

Charley Johng's	1
Shirley's	2

ACCOMMODATION

Dunhuang	A
Dunhuang Fandian	B
Feitian	D
Five Rings	C
Guangyuan	E
International	G
Jinye	H
Xiyu	F

Accommodation

There's a glut of accommodation in Dunhuang, especially at the lower end of the market. Prices rise in peak season (July and August), and are considerably discounted in winter, though you'll need to check on the availability of heating and hot water. Most places offer dorm beds; whether you'll get one depends on the management and how full the hotel is – they won't mix Chinese and Westerners in the same rooms.

Dunhuang Binguan Yangguan Dong Lu ☎0937/8822008, ℱ8859128 Drab 1980s concrete exterior, but smart inside; rooms are comfortable and you can usually get discounts. This place accepts credit cards and is the only place in town where you can change money on Sundays. ❼

Dunhuang Fandian Mingshan Lu ☎0937/8822413, ℮dhfd@public.lz.gs.cn. Recently refurbished to mid-range comforts, though it still has dormitory beds available. Dorm beds ¥40, other room types include breakfast, ❻ **Feitian Hotel** Mingshan Lu, closed in winter, ☎0937/8822337. Very conveniently located

Moving on from Dunhuang

Several standard and luxury-express **buses** depart daily from both the Dunhuang bus station and the long-distance bus station to Jiayuguan (about 5hr; ¥90), and at least one daily to Lanzhou (24hr) and all points in between. There are also buses to Hami in Xinjiang (7hr). The eight-hour bus journey to **Golmud** in Qinghai province (on the road to Tibet) costs ¥78 for hard seat, ¥91 for sleeper bus. Wherever you're heading, nobody seems to be interested in seeing PICC certificates.

At the time of writing, there were **flights** twice a week to Lanzhou (Wed & Sun), and three times a week to Xi'an (Tues, Thurs & Sat). More frequent flights and more destinations (including Ürümqi and Beijing) occur in peak season, while in winter some flights may stop completely. **Train tickets** (hard seat only) are most conveniently bought at a special window in the bus station, or at the rail office next to the **Bank of China**, though other travel agents will insist this is impossible; a commission fee of ¥30 per ticket is charged. Frequent minibuses (¥15) for the **train station at Liuyuan** depart from outside the Dunhuang bus station; the journey takes two to three hours. A four-person taxi (¥30 per person) takes an hour and half. Note that most **accommodation** – and the local branch of *John's Information Café*, inside the *Feitian Hotel*, as well as the CITS in the *International Hotel* – can organize plane and train tickets, though commissions are higher (around ¥50 per person).

opposite the bus station, this place has decent doubles and inexpensive dorms – though the staff often refuse to admit this. *John's Information Café* has a branch here too. Credit cards are accepted and you can also change foreign currency here. Dorm beds ¥40, ❻

Five Rings Mingshan Lu ☏0937/8822276. Just north of the bus station, this hotel is good value if you go for the four-bed dorms or cheaper doubles. Dorm beds ¥40–60, ❷

Guangyuan Huancheng Nan Lu/Mingshan Lu junction ☏0937/8821399, ☏8839008. Not outstanding from the outside, but furnishings are modern. ❻

International Mingshan Lu ☏0937/8828638, ☏8821821, ✉dhgjdjd@public.lz.gs.cn. Modern place, with rooms of a good standard and reasonable prices; CITS are here too. ❼

Jinye Mingshan Lu ☏0937/8821477. A couple of minutes farther to the south from the *Xiyu Hotel*, and much more upmarket though rather overpriced, offering air-conditioned doubles. Credit cards accepted. ❻

Xiyu Mingshan Lu ☏0937/8823017. Very convenient for the bus station, just one block to the south (turn right on emerging from the station). Very cheap dorms and fair doubles with bath. Dorm beds ¥40, ❻

Eating and drinking

There are plenty of good places to **eat** in Dunhuang, especially in the south of town along Mingshan Lu. One block south of the bus station, there are a number of foreigner-oriented places specializing in cheap Western and Chinese dishes with English menus, friendly service and tables on the pavement. *Shirley's* is most popular for its apple pie, coffee and ginger tea; their Chinese food isn't bad either.

A couple of minutes north of the *Feitian Hotel*, on the same side of the road, you'll find *Charley Johng's Café*, opened by Shirley's brother, whose menu includes excellent pancakes, banana fritters and chicken curry, as well as local delicacies. Try the *dunhuang latiaozi* (¥10), a noodle dish with aubergine, tomato and pepper; or *bobing yangrou* (¥18), deep-fried lamb chunks with cumin and chilli wrapped in thin pancakes. The Chinese restaurants farther up Mingshan Lu on the east side of the road from here are more "authentic", but lack English menus and may not suit foreign stomachs.

The most atmospheric place to eat in the evening is the covered **Shazhou night market** located through an imposing gateway off the south side of

Yangguan Dong Lu. Inside you can sit on deck chairs and drink *babao* (also known as "Eight Treasures Tea") containing various dry fruits and herbs, snack on fruit (try the famous *liguang qing*, a local type of apricot), or have a full Muslim or Chinese meal. The *Dunhuang Binguan* has the best of the **hotel restaurants**, including a not-too-expensive Japanese canteen (¥50 per head at least) and a Chinese hotpot restaurant.

The Mogao Caves

The **Mogao Caves**, 25km southeast of Dunhuang, are one of the great archeological discovery stories of the East. The first-known **Buddhist temples** within the boundaries of the Chinese empire, supposedly established in 366 AD by a monk called Lie Zun, they were a centre of culture on the Silk Road right up until the fourteenth century, and today contain religious artworks spanning a thousand years of history. Chinese Buddhism radiated out to the whole Han empire from these wild desert cliffs, and with it – gradually adapting to a Chinese context – came the artistic influences of Central Asia, India, Persia and the West.

Of the original thousand or more **caves**, over six hundred survive in recognizable form, but many are off limits, either no longer considered of significant interest or else containing Tantric murals which the Chinese reckon are too sexually explicit for visitors. Of the thirty main caves open to the public, you are likely to manage only around fifteen in a single day.

Visiting the caves

Getting to the caves from Dunhuang is easy in summer. Step on to the street between eight and nine in the morning and you will instantly be accosted by **minibus** drivers, who charge ¥10 for the one-way fare; the trip takes about thirty minutes. Choose a minibus that is nearly full – they won't leave until the last seat is occupied. In winter, when transport is much less frequent, you can arrange a return trip with any taxi driver in town (half day around ¥80–100, full day ¥200).

The caves are open daily from 8.30am to 11.30am, and from 2.30pm to around 5.30pm. A half-day guided **tour** costs ¥120 (¥100 with a student card) including an English-speaking guide, and entrance to the museum and Research and Exhibition Centre. You cannot take a **camera** into the caves without an extremely expensive permit, and all bags must be left at an office at the gate (¥2). Note that if you're caught taking photos without a permit, your negatives will be confiscated and you will be subjected to a large fine. The caves are not lit, to avoid damage to the murals; your guide will have a **flashlight**, but you are advised to bring one of your own as well – you can hire one for about ¥3 plus a deposit from the ticket office, but they are pretty anaemic.

The guides are well informed, though their English is not always brilliant. There is something of a set route, but you will be able to see more with extra charges depending upon how valuable the cave is (from ¥60 per person per cave up to ¥500 or more). The **museum** has a history in English of the site, plus more scrolls, nineteenth- and twentieth-century photos of Mogao, and reproductions of some of the plundered frescoes, now in Europe.

Before or after your tour, it's worth visiting the **Research and Exhibition Centre** (daily 9am–5pm), the giant modern building opposite the car park. Paid for by Japanese money, it holds eight replica caves – nos. 3, 45, 217, 220, 249, 275, 285 and 419. The big advantage here is that the lights are on, the colours are fresh and you can study the murals close up. The most impressive one is the

The Mogao cave treasures

The story of Mogao's development, then subsequent abandonment and rediscovery, is an intriguing one. Before the arrival of Buddhism from India, the Chinese – Taoist and Confucian – temple tradition had been mainly of buildings in wood, a material well adapted to most Chinese conditions. The idea of cave temples came to China from India, where poverty, lack of building materials and the intense heat had necessitated alternative methods.

The emergence of the complex of cave temples at **Mogao** dominated early Chinese Buddhism, as pilgrims, monks and scholars passing along the Silk Road settled and worked here, translating sutras, or holy texts. Merchants and nobles stopped, too, endowing temples to ensure the success of their caravans or to benefit their souls, as they did in varying degrees all along the Silk Road. Huge numbers of **artists and craftsmen** were employed at Dunhuang, often lying on high scaffoldings in the dim light provided by oil lamps. The workers usually lived in tiny caves in the northern section of Mogao furnished with small brick beds, and were paid a pittance – in a collection of Buddhist scriptures, archeologists have discovered a bill of indenture signed by one sculptor for the sale of his son.

Under the Tang, which saw the establishment of Buddhism throughout the Chinese empire, the monastic community reached its peak, with more than a thousand cave temples in operation. Thereafter, however, as the new ocean-going trading links slowly supplanted the Silk Road, Mogao (and Dunhuang) became increasingly provincial. At some point in the fourteenth century, the caves were **sealed and abandoned**.

Although Mogao's existence remained known to a few Buddhist scholars, it was only in 1900 that a wandering monk, **Wang Yuan Lu**, stumbled upon them by accident and decided to begin the work of excavation. He at once realized their significance, and made it his life's work to restore the site, excavating caves full of sand, touching up the murals, planting trees and gardens and building a guesthouse. This work he undertook with two acolytes and financed through begging expeditions.

The reconstructions might have gone on in relative obscurity were it not for the discovery of a bricked-up hidden chamber (cave no. 17), which Wang opened to reveal an enormous collection of **manuscripts**, **sutras** and **silk and paper paintings** – some 1000 years old and virtually undamaged. News of the cache soon reached the ears of the Dunhuang authorities, who, having appropriated a fair haul for themselves, decided to reseal them in the cave on the grounds that it would be too expensive to transport them. So it remained for a further seven years, until the arrival in 1907 of the Central Asian explorer and scholar **Aurel Stein**. Stein, a Hungarian working for the British and the Indian Survey (in other words, a secret agent),

Bodhisattva statue of the one-thousand-hand and one-thousand-eye Guanyin – the original piece is no longer available for viewing due to the deteriorating conditions. A further cave is not from Mogao at all, but from the Yulin Caves (no. 25) in nearby Anxi County. Upstairs are a few surviving silk scrolls and manuscripts, and there's a film about the Mogao site.

Getting back to Dunhuang is simple in summer: go to the car park and wait for the next minibus; the last one leaves around 4pm. If you get stuck, you could stay on site at the basic **guesthouse**.

The caves

What makes the caves so interesting is that you can trace the **development of Chinese art** over the centuries, from one dynasty to the next. Some grasp of the history of the caves is essential to appreciate them properly, but be warned, restorations and replacements in the modern era have complicated the picture, had heard rumours of the caves and been offered items for sale. In good Howard Carter tradition, he persuaded Wang to reopen the chamber. This is how Stein later described what he saw:

The sight the small room disclosed was one to make my eyes open; heaped up in layers, but without any order, there appeared in the dim light of the priest's little lamp a solid mass of manuscript bundles rising to a height of nearly 10 feet and filling, as subsequent measurement showed, close on 500 cubic feet – an unparalleled archeological scoop.

This was no understatement. Examining the manuscripts, Stein found original sutras brought from India by the Tang monk and traveller **Xuanzang**, along with other Buddhist texts written in Sanskrit, Sogdian, Tibetan, Runic-Turkic, Chinese, Uigur and other languages unknown to the scholar. Amid the art finds, hardly less important were dozens of rare Tang-dynasty paintings on silk and paper – badly crushed but totally untouched by damp.

Eventually Stein, donating the equivalent of £130 to Wang's restoration fund, left Mogao for England with some seven thousand manuscripts and five hundred paintings. Later in the year a Frenchman, Paul Pelliot, negotiated a similar deal, shipping six thousand manuscripts and many paintings back to Paris. And so, virtually overnight, and before the Beijing authorities could put a stop to it, the British Museum and the Louvre had acquired the core of their Chinese manuscript and painting collections. Not all the caves were looted, however; a fresh batch of 248 were only located in 2001, though the scrolls and artefacts they contained have yet to be fully assessed.

Today, fuelled perhaps by Greek claims on the Elgin marbles, the Chinese are pressing for the **return** of all paintings and manuscripts in foreign collections. It is hard to dispute the legitimacy of these claims now, though it was only in 1961 that Mogao was declared a National Monument. Had the treasures not been removed, more would almost certainly have been lost in the chaotic years of the twentieth century. A large party of White Russians used the caves as a barracks in 1920, showing their disregard for history by scrawling their names over the frescoes. Fortunately, despite the massive loss in terms of manuscripts and scrolls, the art work and statuary at the caves themselves are still fabulously preserved. The cave art was not damaged during the Cultural Revolution – protected, it is said, on a personal order from Premier Zhou Enlai.

particularly where statuary is concerned – many of the statues are not original. You may hear your guide blaming the ugly replacements on the Qing dynasty – in other words on the monk Wang Yuan Lu – but some of them are a good deal newer than that. The caves are all clearly labelled with numbers above the doors.

Northern Wei

The earliest caves were hewn out in the fourth and fifth centuries AD during the **Northern Wei** (386–581). This dynasty was formed by Turkic-speaking people known as the Tobas, and as the centuries progressed there was constant friction between the forces of conservatism (who wanted to retain the ancient Toba customs) and those of change (who wanted to adapt Chinese customs).

The Wei caves are relatively small in size, and are often supported in the centre by a large column – a feature imported from India. A statue of the Buddha is usually central, surrounded in tiers on the walls by a **mass of tiny Buddhas** brilliantly painted in black, white, blue, red and green. The statues are in fact made of terracotta: the soft rock inside the caves was not suited to detailed carving, so the craftsmen would first carve a rough outline of the figure, then build it up with clay.

The style of the murals in these caves shows a great deal of **foreign influence**. Faces have long noses and curly hair, and women are large-breasted. **Cave no. 101**, decorated towards the end of the fifth century, provides a good example: the Buddha, enclosed by attendant Bodhisattvas, is essentially a Western figure, recognizably Christ-like, reminiscent of Greek Byzantine frescoes. In **cave 257** the Buddha seems to be dressed in a Roman toga, while the beautiful **cave 428** shows a notably Indian influence in both content (note the peacocks on the ceiling) and style. There are, however, also the beginnings of Chinese influence in the wavy, flower-like angels sometimes seen fluttering above.

Though originally designed as a focus of devotional contemplation, the murals gradually acquired a **narrative purpose** as well, and the paintings soon move towards a wider subject matter, their story sequences arranged in long horizontal strips. **Cave 135** (early sixth century) illustrates a *jataka* story – concerning a former life of Buddha – in which he gave his own body to feed a starving tigress, unable to succour her cubs. The narrative, read from right to left, is broken up by simple landscapes, a frequently used device. **Cave 254** shows the story of Buddha defeating Mara, or Illusion.

Artistic changes, and a shift towards a more distinctive Chinese style, began to appear at the end of the Northern Wei period, around the middle of the sixth century. One of the most strikingly Chinese of the Wei murals is in **cave 120N** and shows, above the devotional niches, a series of battle scenes, interesting for their total lack of perspective. All the figures are drawn as though seen straight on, regardless of their relative positions, a favourite device throughout the history of Chinese painting.

Sui

With the founding of the short-lived but dynamic **Sui dynasty** in 581, Western influences began to decline rapidly. The Chinese empire had been torn apart by civil wars but now there followed a boom in Buddhism, and Buddhist art. In the four decades up to the emergence of the Tang, more than seventy caves were carved at Mogao.

Structurally, they dispense with the central column, while artistically, they show the replacement of the bold, slightly crude Wei brushwork with intricate, flowing lines and an increasingly extravagant use of colour that includes gilding and washes of silver. In **cave 150**, for example, painted in the last year of the Sui, narrative has been dispensed with altogether in favour of a repeated theme of throned Buddhas and Bodhisattvas. In terms of statuary, the Sui period also shows a change, the figures becoming stiff and inflexible and dressed in Chinese robes. **Cave 427** contains some characteristic Sui figures – short legs, long bodies (indicating power and divinity) and big, square heads.

Tang

The **Tang-dynasty** artists (618–906), under whom the caves at Mogao reached their artistic zenith, drew both from past traditions and real life. The classic Tang cave has a square floor, tapering roof and a niche for worship set into the back wall. The statuary includes **warriors** – a new theme – and all figures are carefully detailed, the Bodhisattvas above all, with their pleats and folds clinging softly to undulating feminine figures.

For sheer size, their **Buddhas** are the most famous, notably in **caves 96 and 130**. The astonishing 34-metre-high seated Buddha in cave 96 – dressed in the traditional dragon robe of the emperor – is thought by some to have been designed deliberately to remind pilgrims of the famous Tang empress Wu Zetian. In **cave 148** there is another huge Buddha, this one reclining as though dead, and surrounded by disciples.

The **Tang paintings** range from huge murals depicting scenes from the sutras – now contained within one composition rather than the earlier cartoon-strip convention – to vivid paintings of individuals. One of the most popular and spectacular Tang mural themes was that of the *Visit of the Bodhisattva Manjusri to Vimalakirti*. **Cave 1** contains perhaps the greatest expression of this story. Vimalakirti, on the left, is attended by a great host of heavenly beings, eager to hear the discourse of the ailing old king. Above him the plane is tilted to take in a seemingly limitless landscape, with the Buddha surrounded by Bodhisattvas on an island in the middle. Another version can be seen in **cave 51E**, in a mural that is also especially notable for the subtle shading of its portraiture, which includes a magnificently depicted Central Asian retinue. Other superb Tang murals include a very free, fluid landscape in **cave 70** and, perhaps most developed of all, **cave 139A**'s depiction of the *Western Paradise of the Amitabha Buddha*. This last is a supremely confident painting, working in elaborate displays of architecture and figures within a coherent whole. The theme is the Buddha's promise of paradise: the souls of the reborn rise from lotus flowers in the foreground, with heavenly scenes enclosing the Buddha above.

The later caves

Later work, executed by the **Five Dynasties**, **Song**, **and Western Xia** (906–1227), shows little real progression from the Tang. Much, in any case, is simply restoration or repainting of existing murals. Song work is perhaps the most interesting, tending towards a heavy richness of colour, and with many of its figures displaying the features of minority races.

During the Mongol **Yuan dynasty** (1260–1368), towards the end of which period Mogao seems to have been abandoned, the standard niche in the back wall of the caves gave way to a central altar, creating fresh and uncluttered space for murals. Tibetan-style Lamaist (or Tantric) figures were introduced, and occult diagrams (mandalas) became fashionable. The most interesting Yuan art is in **cave 465**, slightly set apart from the main body of grottoes. You might try asking the guides if they will open this up for you, though they will probably only do so for a huge fee. In the fashion of Indian Buddhist painting, the murals include Tantric figures in the ultimate state of enlightenment, graphically represented by the state of sexual union.

Other sights around Dunhuang

A few kilometres to the south of town are the much-touted **Yueya Quan** (Crescent Moon Lake) and **Mingsha Shan** (Singing Sand Dune), set amid the most impressive sand-dune scenery anywhere in China, with dunes 200–300m high. The sands reportedly make a humming noise in windy weather, hence the name. The Crescent Moon Lake is not much to look at, but is curious for its permanence, despite being surrounded by shifting sands – it was recorded in history at least two thousand years ago. Various activities take place from the tops of the main dune, such as sand-tobogganing and paragliding. The paragliding is great fun and costs ¥30 – you get to try two or three times if your initial flight isn't successful. Tobogganing costs ¥10 and feels a little safer. Climbing the dune in the first place, however, is incredibly hot, exhausting work; if you use the wooden steps you may have to pay a small fee or you can ride up on a camel for ¥30.

Minibus #3 (daily 8am–10pm; ¥1 per person, they sometimes charge foreigners triple) leaves from Mingshan Lu in Dunhuang and will drop you by the gate and **ticket office** – entry is ¥80 in peak season or ¥40. In the summer heat the only sensible time to come here is early in the morning around 8 to 8.30am, or in the evening after 5pm. Otherwise you can walk here in about 45 minutes, or cycle in twenty – just head south out of town. Park your bike somewhere before the entrance or you'll be charged an annoying ¥5 to put it in the bike park. A one way taxi costs ¥10.

About 4km west of town is the **Baima Ta** (White Horse Dagoba; ¥13). This attractive, nine-tiered dagoba was built in honour of the horse belonging to the monk Kumarajiva from Kuqa (see p.1069), which died on this spot in 384 AD. It lies amid corn fields and is a pleasant place to take a breather.

A number of other historical sites lie farther away from Dunhuang but within the scope of a day-trip. One is the **Xi Qianfodong** (Western Thousand Buddha Caves; ¥20; 35km west), another cave site along the lines of Mogao, if incomparably smaller and less significant. If you are a real Buddhist art buff, talk to a travel service about visiting this place: in the past it was open to groups only, and individuals were turned away. A taxi for the return trip costs ¥80. There are also two Han-dynasty gates, **Yumenguan** (¥30) and **Yangguan** (¥40), which for periods of Chinese history marked the western border of China. They lie to the west of Dunhuang, 80km and 75km away respectively, and were originally joined together by a section of the Great Wall before being abandoned as long ago as the sixth century. Both sites today are impressive for their historic resonance and total desolation as much as for anything else. Today, the road to Yangguan is in good condition, but that to Yumenguan is relatively rough – to visit both gates by taxi would take all day and cost more than ¥600. One exciting option, however, is to visit them **by camel**; to see the two gates, and bits of the Han Great Wall (1km), takes around three to four days respectively or up to eight days for both, and in the mild months of the year – early or late summer – this can be an excellent expedition (¥200–300 per day including food and tent accommodation; contact *Charley Johng's Café* for more information).

Qinghai

Qinghai province is for the most part a huge, empty wilderness with a population of just 4.5 million. Geographically and culturally a part of the **Tibetan plateau**, Qinghai has for centuries been a frontier zone, contested between Chinese immigrants and the Tibetans and Muslims who originally dwelt in its pastures and thin snatches of agricultural land. Today, the **minority presence** in Qinghai can still be felt strongly – as well as Tibetans, there are Hui, Salar, Tu, Mongol and Kazakh people all living here.

Only incorporated into the Chinese empire two hundred years ago – and not brought under firm Han control until 1949 when Communist armies defeated those of the Muslim warlord **Ma Bufang** – the area is still perceived by the Han Chinese as a frontier land for pioneers and prospectors, and, on a more sinister note, a dumping ground for criminals and political opponents to the regime. The number of inmates held in Qinghai **prison and labour camps**, including those released but who must remain in the province because they cannot regain residency rights in their home towns, is estimated to reach four hundred thousand – almost one in ten of the population of Qinghai. Of these, a tenth are political prisoners. Several of the prison camps are actually in the outskirts of the capital, Xining, purporting to be ordinary factories.

It is only the eastern part of the province around **Xining** that has a long-established Han presence. With its lush green valleys and plentiful annual rainfall, this is also the only part of Qinghai where sustainable agriculture takes place. To the west and south of here the land rises to a three-thousand-metre plateau which, bitterly cold for half the year, can at best be used as pastureland for cattle and sheep. To the northwest, on the other hand, towards the border with Xinjiang, the land sinks into an arid basin, which was good for little until the Communist era, when mineral deposits and oil were discovered. Now the area supports extensive mining.

For the traveller, the primary point of interest in Qinghai is as an access point **into Tibet**: you can fly from Xining to Lhasa; the road from Golmud to Lhasa is the only officially approved overland route for foreigners; and there's also a rail line under construction which follows this road, due for completion in 2007. Qinghai is in many respects a part of Tibet, and in addition to the substantial Tibetan minority who live here, the splendid **Ta'er Si**, one of the major Tibetan lamaseries in all China, is located just outside Xining.

The province has other attractions, too, chiefly as an unspoilt natural wilderness area. The enormous **Qinghai Hu**, China's biggest lake, in particular, offers opportunities for hikes and bird-spotting. There are also possibilities for longer treks, rafting, hunting and mountaineering. Such activities have to be arranged by local travel agents, who can sometimes manage this at just a few days' notice.

Xining and around

Qinghai's unassuming provincial capital, **XINING** contains few tourist sights in itself, and is usually regarded simply as a base from which to explore the nearby Tibetan monastery of Ta'er Si. Nevertheless, as the only sizeable city in Qinghai, Xining is an interesting place in its own right. Set in a rather extraordinary location, with stark mountains rearing up right behind, the inhospitable terrain immediately beyond gives the city a cosy, reassuring feel. At a height of 2260m, right on the outermost edge of the Tibetan plateau, Xining experiences pleasantly cool weather in summer and bitter cold in winter.

Although definitely a centre of Han population, Xining is also full of minority nationalities, in particular Hui and rather lost-looking Tibetans. It has quite an ancient history, having been established probably as early as the Han dynasty. It even served as a stopover on a minor southern route of the Silk Road and has been a fairly important trading city for the Han since at least the sixteenth century. Today, connected by fast trains to Lanzhou and other Chinese cities, Xining is a firmly established part of the network of Han China.

The city is bordered by steep hills to the north, along the foot of which runs the Huangshui River. The major sight is the **Dongguan Great Mosque** (daily; ¥5), on Dongguan Dajie, one of the most attractive in northwest China. Built

Xining and around

Xining	西宁	*xīníng*
Beishan Si	北山寺	*běishān sì*
Dashizi	大十字	*dàshízi*
Dongguan Great Mosque	东关清真大寺	*dōngguān qīngzhēn dàsì*
Huangshui River	湟水河	*huángshuǐ hé*
Regional Museum	省博物馆	*shěng bówùguǎn*
Ximen	西门	*xīmén*
Accommodation and eating		
Daxinjie night market	大新街夜市	*dàxīnjiē yèshì*
Dico's Burgers	德克士汉堡	*dékèshì hànbǎo*
Longyuan	龙源宾馆	*lóngyuán bīnguǎn*
Meining	美宁宾馆	*měiníng bīnguǎn*
Minzu	民族宾馆	*mínzú bīnguǎn*
Qinghai	青海宾馆	*qīnghǎi bīnguǎn*
Qingzhen Canteen	清真餐厅	*qīngzhēn cāntīng*
Shuijingxiang Food Market	水井巷食品市场	*shuǐjǐngxiàng shípǐn shìchǎng*
UBC Coffee	台湾上岛咖啡	*táiwān shàngdǎo kāfēi*
Xining Guest Hotel	西宁宾馆	*xīníng bīnguǎn*
Yahao Huayuan	雅豪花园宾馆	*yǎháo huāyuán bīnguǎn*
Ledu County	乐都县	*lèdū xiàn*
Nianbo Zhen	碾伯镇	*niǎnbó zhèn*
Qutan Si	瞿昙寺	*qútán sì*
Maduo	玛多	*mǎduō*
Ta'er Si	塔尔寺	*tǎ'ěr sì*
Zongka Hotel	宗喀宾馆	*zōngkā bīnguǎn*
Tongren County	同仁县	*tóngrén xiàn*
Longwu Zhen	隆务镇	*lóngwù zhèn*
Longwu Si	隆务寺	*lóngwù sì*
Shangxia Wutun	上下五屯	*shàngxià wǔtún*
Xunhua County	循化	*xúnhuà*
Jishi Zhen	积石镇	*jīshí zhèn*
Mengda Nature Reserve	孟达自然保护区	*mèngdá zìrán bǎohùqū*

in 1380, it encloses a large public square where worshippers can congregate. The architecture is an interesting combination of green Arabic domes and Chinese-style flying eaves with colourful painted arches. The regional **museum** (daily: May–Sept 9am–5pm, Oct–April 9.30am–4pm, ¥15), southwest of Xining Square, is also worth a look, with artefacts from most dynasties and a display of ethnic minority clothing; the only shame is the lack of English explanations. To get to the museum, take bus #9 from the train station, and get off at Jiaotong Xiang along Wusi Dajie, or it's a forty-minute walk west along Xiguan Dajie from Ximen.

To the north of the Huangshui River, a couple of kilometres west of the train station, it is possible to climb the mountain up to the 1700-year-old Taoist **Beishan Si** (North Mountain Temple; daily; ¥20). You climb hundreds of steps, then walk along a whole series of walkways and bridges connecting together

XINING

N

Beishan Si ▶

Ta'er Si ▶

Airport ▶

QILIAN LU

QILIAN LU

Huangshui River

QILIAN LU

Train Station

Long-distance Bus Station

3 **F**

Airport Bus drop-off ★

BAXI LU

CAAC

GONGHE LU

Bank of China
@ **DONGGUAN DAJIE**
C **E**
A

Dongguan Great Mosque

Daxinjie Night Market

B
2

DONG DAJIE

BEI DAJIE

PSB

Xinhua Bookstore

Airline Ticket Office

Bank of China

Da Shizi

XI DAJIE

NAN DAJIE

NAN RAALKENG LU

@ **A**

Bus Depot to Ta'er Si

1

Ximen

Shuijingxiang Food Market

CHAOJIANG LU

Ertong Park

Xining Gymnasium

HUANGHE LU

Foreign Language Bookstore

CITS **D**

KUNLUN LU

WUSI DAJIE

XIGUAN DAJIE

Jiaotong Xiang ★

XINING SQUARE

Regional Museum

13

ACCOMMODATION

Longyuan	F
Meining	C
Minzu	B
Qinghai	D
Xining	A
Yahao Huayuan	E

EATING & DRINKING

Dico's	2
Muslim Canteen	3 & 4
UBC Coffee	1

0		600 m

little caves decorated with Taoist designs, often packed with people engaged in prayer ceremonies. At the very top is a pagoda, offering fine views over the city on a clear day. Bus #11 from the train station, or #10 from east of the Xining Gymnasium, will take you to Beishan Lu Kou on Qilian Lu, from where 100m east is a tunnel; walk through to the north, passing a bizarrely located Catholic church, and you will eventually reach the entrance of the temple.

Practicalities

Most of the city lies to the south of the river, though the **train station** lies immediately on the north bank, just across the bridge from the long-distance **bus station**. The centre of Xining is located about 3km to the west of here, along the main east–west streets Dong Dajie and then Xi Dajie, which connects **Da Shizi** (Big Crossroads) with the large **Ximen** traffic circle a few hundred metres farther west. Xining's **airport** is 26km east of town; a bus collects arrivals and drops them at the south end of Jianguo Lu or the airline offices on Bayi Lu, about 1500m southeast of the train station – bus #2 runs west up Dongguan Dajie from Bayi Lu, or #28 will get you to the bus and train stations.

Moving on from Xining

Xining's main **airline office** is located a few kilometres east of the centre at 85 Bayi Lu (℡0971/8133333; daily 8.30am–noon & 2–5.30pm), on the #2 bus route (get off at Bayi Lu). An alternative **ticket agent** (℡0971/8250389) is on Da Jie, 10 minutes' walk from Da Shizi; look for the IATA sign. Direct flights are limited, and for most destinations locals advise taking the train to Lanzhou and flying from there. One exception is the biweekly (Tues & Fri) flights from Xining **to Lhasa** as – at the time of writing – the airline office wasn't demanding that foreigners join an expensive tour, but you need to buy a special "Tibet permit" from CITS (¥200) in order to purchase a ticket (see p.1101 for more on visiting Tibet). These things can change very quickly, however, and it's best to ask other travellers about the current situation.

Direct **trains** run to and from most major cities in eastern China, including comfortable, fast double-deckers to Lanzhou in Gansu province (3hr). There are also three services (15hr) west to Golmud, leaving from late evening, for those gravitating towards Tibet; buying tickets at the station is straightforward – window 3 is prioritized for foreigners, and Chinese timetables are on display. Seats to Lanzhou are generally available on the morning of departure. If the mob at the station is too much to deal with, you can purchase tickets leaving within five days through an agent on the first floor of the main post office on Da Shizi (¥5 commission per ticket).

Aside from the obvious smooth rides to Golmud or Lanzhou on the new expressway, there are lots of interesting **bus routes** out of Xining and **tickets** are very cheap. In the direction of **Xiahe**, there are frequent buses to Linxia and one daily to the monastery town of Tongren, from both of which there are connecting services to Xiahe. There are also buses to **Zhangye** (3 daily; ¥43) in Gansu province, via a spectacular ride north across the mountains. An equally exciting possibility is a bus southwest to **Maduo** (¥77), a remote little town 4000m above sea level. From here, very close to the source of the Yellow River, you can continue by bus along a rough route into Sichuan province, though be aware that this route is not officially open to foreigners.

There have been recent reports of bus operators approaching foreigners in Xining offering seats on a **bus to Lhasa** for around ¥1200. While this is substantially cheaper than CITS charges for the Golmud–Lhasa run, foreigners are not officially allowed on the Xining–Lhasa bus; if you're caught along the way – at the checkpoint just outside Golmud, for instance – you'll be kicked off, with no refund available.

The main **Bank of China** is a huge building on Dongguan Dajie near the mosque, though any of the branch offices can also change traveller's cheques – there's one just west of Da Shizi. The main **post office**, where you can make IDD telephone calls, is on the southwest corner of Da Shizi; you enter by climbing the raised pedestrian walkway. You'll find another office for making IDD calls a few minutes east of the train station, next to a smaller post office. **Internet** bars are scattered around the place; there's one 100m west of Xining Binguan, and another along Dongguan Dajie – look for the vertical sign. The **Xinhua bookstore** opposite the main post office sells various local maps. The **Foreign Languages bookstore**, west of Ertong Park on Huanghe Lu, has a surprisingly good selection of English-language classics and Chinese works in translation.

There are several **travel agents** in town that may come in handy for buying train or plane tickets, and for organizing trips to Qinghai Hu (see p.1039) or more remote parts of Qinghai. The most convenient are the Qinghai Jiaotong Lüxingshe (Traffic Travel Service; ☎0971/8133928), based at the front of the long-distance bus station on Jianguo Lu – look for the red English sign; Qinghai Nationality Travel Service at the *Minzu* hotel (☎0971/8225247; closed Nov–March), which can arrange official documents needed into Tibet at an expensive ¥2000 per person; and finally CITS, at 156 Huanghe Lu (☎0971/6130903, Ⓦwww.citsqh.com), which offers trips inside Qinghai.

Accommodation

The amount of foreign-friendly accommodation in Xining is increasing as tourism in Qinghai becomes more established.

Longyuan Jianguo Lu ☎0971/8149499, 500m south of the long-distance bus station. The rooms are cheap but a little worn. They provide 24hr hot water and very warm rooms in winter. They can be nervous about taking foreigners so it helps if you speak a little Chinese. ❸

Meining Across the train-station square on the right ☎0971/8185380. Cheap and good value. Staff speak a little English and prices can always be bartered down. 24hr hot water only available from April to October, otherwise twice a day. Dorm beds ¥30, ❸

Minzu (Nationality Hotel) West of the Dong Dajie/Dongguan Dajie junction ☎0971/8225951, Ⓕ8225892. Buses #1 (6.10am–6.40pm; ¥1) come here (bus-stop name: Huangguang) from the train station. The best feature of this faded place is its central location and 24hr hot water. Staff are friendly and helpful. Dorm beds ¥90, ❸

Qinghai At the south end of Huanghe Lu ☎0971/6144888, Ⓦwww.qhhotel.com. By far the most upmarket place in town with lots of facilities including a pretty decent restaurant. A taxi from the train station costs ¥10. Otherwise take bus #32 (¥1) from the train station which stops outside the hotel – a vast white tower. ❻

Xining Hotel 348 Qiyi Lu ☎0971/8458701. About 1km north of Da Shizi, this is a lifeless, 1950s place which, though recently renovated, still isn't particularly attractive. To get here, take bus #9 (6.10am–6.40pm; ¥1) from the train station and get off at Binguan. Old wings ❸, otherwise ❺

Yahao Huayuan Just west and opposite the mosque on Dongguan Dajie ☎0971/8137994. Clean mid-range choice with friendly staff, though they're not always sure whether foreigners are allowed to stay. ❸

Eating

The hotels all have **restaurants** in keeping with their facilities. For Muslim food, there's a canteen near the bus station, and a large and authentic place across from the mosque on Dongguan Dajie, full of old men sipping tea and chewing their way through lamb and noodle dishes such as *hui yangro*, a lamb stew in spicy soup with tomato and spring onion slices. If you're after vaguely Western fare, head for the branch of *Dico's Burgers* on the Ximen intersection. Alternatively, try the *UBC Coffee* on Changjiang Lu – a Taiwan chain café also serving Western-style set meals.

The best places to eat in Xining, however, are the **markets** downtown; staples here include kebabs, bowls of spicy noodles, mutton hotpots, and *zasui* soup, made with ox and sheep entrails. *Shaguo* – earthenware hotpots full of tofu, mushrooms and meat cooked in broth – are excellent, as are *jiaozi, hundun* soup and other basic dishes prepared on the spot. The covered market, **Shuijingxiang**, off Xi Dajie and very close to Ximen, is a good place to head to – there are more than three thousand fixed stalls of ready-made food and fresh fruits, many of which are open until late at night, their stoves blazing in the dark. Alternatively, you can head to **Daxinjie night market**, a lane off Dong Dajie, ten minutes east from the Xinhua Bookstore, which turns into a fresh-food banquet on summer evenings.

Ta'er Si and beyond

Lying about 25km southeast from Xining, **Ta'er Si**, known as Kumbum in Tibetan, is one of the most important monasteries outside Tibet. Although not as attractive as Labrang in Xiahe, and rather swamped by tourists, Ta'er Si is nevertheless a good introduction for outsiders to Tibetan culture. Both as the birthplace of Tsongkhapa, the founder of the **Yellow Hat Sect**, and as the former home of the current Dalai Lama, the monastery attracts droves of pilgrims from Tibet, Qinghai and Mongolia, who present a startling picture with their rugged features, huge embroidered coats and chunky jewellery.

Aside from the hulking new **military base** built right next to the monastery, installed no doubt to ensure compliance among the monks (though not very successfully – the abbot, considered a puppet of Beijing, recently absconded to the US), the countryside around is beautiful: the views stretch away to distant mountains, and you can ramble through hills of wheat, pastures dotted with cattle or horses, and over ridges and passes strewn with wild flowers. Apart from the large numbers of Han Chinese tourists, the people you meet here are mainly Tibetan horsemen, workers in the fields who will offer an ear of roasted barley by way of hospitality, or pilgrims prostrating their way around the monastery walls.

The monastery

The monastery dates from 1560, when building was begun in honour of **Tsongkhapa**, founder of the reformist Yellow Hat Sect of Tibetan Buddhism, who was born on the Ta'er Si estates. Legend tells how, at Tsongkhapa's birth, drops of blood fell from his umbilical cord causing a tree with a thousand leaves to spring up; on each leaf was the face of the Buddha, and there was a Buddha image on the trunk (now preserved in one of the stupas). During his lifetime, Tsongkhapa's significance was subsequently borne out: his two major disciples were to become the two greatest living Buddhas, one the Dalai Lama, the other the Panchen Lama.

Set in the cleft of a valley, the walled complex (daily: May–Sept 8am–6pm & Oct–April 9am–4pm) is an imposing sight, an active place of worship for about six hundred monks as well as the constant succession of pilgrims. There's a ¥35 **entrance fee**, your ticket providing access to nine temples At the gate, furtive hawkers appear to be selling Dalai Lama pendants which you are strongly advised against buying, since possession of them is illegal and this is doubtless a setup. A stone tablet here, detailing (in English) the restoration of Ta'er Si in the 1980s, contains the worshipful statement that repairs were needed as "400 years of exposure to the elements had taken its toll".

The complex itself defies cynicism, however, and the most beautiful of the **temples** is perhaps the **Great Hall of Meditation** (Da Jingtang; temple no. 5

on your ticket), an enormous, very dimly lit prayer hall, colonnaded by dozens of carpeted pillars and hung with long silk tapestries (*thangkas*). Immediately adjacent to this is the **Great Hall of the Golden Roof**, with its gilded tiles, red-billed choughs nesting under the eaves, wall paintings of scenes from the Buddha's life and a brilliant silver stupa containing a statue of Tsongkhapa. The grooves on the wooden floor in front of the temple have been worn away by the hands of prostrating monks and pilgrims. This hall, built in 1560, is where the monastery began, on the site of the pipal tree that grew with its Buddha imprints. You will still see pilgrims studying fallen leaves here, apparently searching for the face of the Buddha.

Other noteworthy temples include the **Lesser Temple of the Golden Roof** (no. 1) and the **Hall of Butter Sculpture** (no. 7). The former is dedicated to animals, thought to manifest characteristics of certain deities – from the central courtyard you can see stuffed goats, cows and bears on the balcony, wrapped in scarves and flags. The Hall of Butter Sculpture contains a display of colourful painted yak-butter tableaux, depicting Tibetan and Buddhist legends. After touring the temples, you can climb the steep steps visible on one side of the monastery to get a general view over the temples and hills behind.

During the year, four major **festivals** are held at Ta'er Si, each fixed according to the lunar calendar. In January/February, at the end of the Chinese New Year festivities, there's a large ceremony centred around the lighting of yak-butter lamps. In April/May is the festival of Bathing Buddha, during which a giant portrait (*thangka*) of Buddha is unfurled on a hillside facing the monastery. In July/August the birthday of Tsongkhapa is celebrated, and in September/October there's one more celebration commemorating the nirvana of Sakyamuni.

Practicalities

Buses from Xining to Ta'er Si (¥4) depart from a depot on Xiguan Dajie in the west of town; pass the Foreign Languages Bookstore, and the depot is rather well hidden about 150m further west on the north side of the road. Minibuses run frequently from around 7.20am until late afternoon; bear in mind that private tour buses start rolling up at Ta'er Si around 10am, after which the place gets crowded. The ride takes just over thirty minutes through summer scenery of wheat fields, green hills, lush woods and meadows of flowering yellow rape. On arrival, you may be dropped at the bus station 1km short of the monastery, or taken right up to the complex itself. From the bus station, it's a twenty-minute walk uphill past the trinket stalls and rug sellers until you see the row of eight stupas at the monastery entrance. Returning to Xining, exit the monastery and hang around on the street until the bus arrives. Private taxis charge ¥10 per person.

Most travellers just come up to Ta'er Si for a few hours, but by staying the night you can appreciate the monastery unattended by hordes of day-trippers. **Accommodation** is available at the sixteenth-century pilgrims' hostel *Kumbum Motel* (beds ¥15) just inside the monastery entrance, whose basic facilities include an ancient balcony and peeling murals, though it's often full. For something smarter, there's also the *Zongka Hotel* (☎0971/2236761; closed Dec–March; ¥220); the price includes a simple breakfast. It is a large, newish place facing the monastery across a gully to the left of the monastery entrance, as you arrive; ask at the front desk for hot water. You can get **meals** at the *Pilgrim's Hostel*; otherwise, try one of the Muslim restaurants on the road between the town and monastery. These are great value, providing huge, warming bowls of noodles with plenty of vegetables and tea for a few yuan.

Another monastery, **Qutan Si** (¥25), 85km to the east of Xining in Ledu County, is much less visited by tourists. The monastery, started in 1387 during the Ming dynasty, was once among the most important Buddhist centres in China. Today, it is still impressive, with 51 rooms of murals, exceptionally fine examples of their type, illustrating the life story of Sakyamuni. You can reach the town of **Nianbo Zhen** in Ledu County by local train or bus (¥8) from Kunlun Bridge in Xining. From Nianbo Zhen you should be able to find cheap minibuses (¥20 one-way) for the seventeen-kilometre ride to Qutan Si, or you could take a taxi there and back for about ¥80.

About 200km southeast of Xining lies an area of outstanding natural beauty, centred around **Mengda Nature Reserve** (¥30). This part of the province, **Xunhua County**, is the birthplace of the Panchen Lama and the homeland of the Salar people, a Muslim ethnic minority. It has a wet, mild climate conducive to the prolific growth of trees and vegetation. The woods here are full of wild flowers and inhabited by deer and foxes – the highlight of the place is the Heaven Lake – a sacred spot for the Salar. Hardly any foreign tourists come this way, but if you want to try, take a bus from Xining's long-distance bus station to the town of **Jishi Zhen** (¥30) in Xunhua County, from where you can hop on the bus (¥25) to the reserve. **Accommodation** (beds ¥25) is available at the reserve, and it is advisable that you bring along at least one day's food and water.

Approximately 180km south of Xining is the Qinghai Huangnan Tibetan Autonomous Region of **Tongren**, home to the Yuan–dynasty Tibetan lamasery **Longwu Si** (¥10) in the town of Longwu Zhen. The other sight in the region is the intriguing **Shangxia Wutun** (upper and lower Wutun) villages, 8km northeast from Longwu Zhen; these two villages along the Longwu River are known as the "Homeland of Thangkas". It is here that *thangka* painting reaches its peak – strolling through the villages, you can see the colourful tapestries in and outside every household. There are three daily **buses** (¥28) to Longwu Zhen from the Xining long-distance bus station or you can take a bus (2 daily) directly from Jishi Zhen in Xunhua. To reach Shangxia Wutun, you can either walk or hire a taxi (¥10) as you come out of Tongren Longwu bus station in Longwu Zhen. It is about 1km between the two villages; a monastery at the side of the road marks the beginning of the two villages.

West of Xining

West of Xining, Qinghai for the most part comprises a great emptiness. The three-thousand-metre plateau is too high to support any farming, and population centres are almost nonexistent – the only people who traditionally have managed to eke out a living in this environment have been nomadic yak-herders. Not surprisingly, this is where China decided to site its **Nuclear Weapons Research and Design Academy**, where it developed its first atomic and hydrogen bombs in the 1960s and 70s. The centre is on a road and rail line 90km from Xining at **Haiyan** (locally known as "Atom Town") and has recently been opened to visitors – enquire at Xining's travel agents to arrange a tour.

The real highlight of the area, though, is about 150km west of Xining at the huge and virtually unspoilt saline lake of **Qinghai Hu**, the size of a small sea and home to thousands of birds. Beyond here, the solitary road and rail line wind their way slowly to **Golmud**, the only town of any size for hundreds of kilometres

West of Xining

Haiyan	海宴	*hǎiyàn*
Qinghai Hu	青海湖	*qīnghǎi hú*
Bird Island	鸟岛	*niǎodǎo*
Chaka Salt Lake	茶卡盐湖	*chákǎyán hú*
Chaka Zhen	茶卡镇	*chákǎ zhèn*
Dulan	都兰	*dūlán*
Heimahe	黑马河	*hēimǎ hé*
Wulan	乌兰	*wūlán*
Golmud	格尔木	*gé'ěr mù*
Cai Erhan Salt Lake	察尔汗盐湖	*chá'ěrhàn yán hú*
Golmud Hotel	格尔木宾馆	*gé'ěrmù bīnguǎn*
Golmud Mansion	格尔木大厦	*gé'ěrmù dàshà*
Kunlun Mountains	昆仑山	*kūnlún shān*
Qingshui Lou	清水楼	*qīngshuǐ lóu*
Shipin Jie	食品街	*shípǐn jiē*
Tibet bus station	西藏汽车站	*xīzàng qìchēzhàn*

around, and an important crossroads for overland travellers, linked by bus not only to Xining, but also to Lhasa in Tibet and Dunhuang on the Silk Road.

Qinghai Hu and around

Situated 150km west of Xining, high up on the Tibetan plateau, is the extraordinarily remote **Qinghai Hu** (¥60, includes ferry trip). The lake is China's largest, occupying an area of more than 4500 square kilometres, and, at 3200m above sea level, its waters are profoundly cold and salty. They are nevertheless teeming with fish and populated by nesting seabirds, particularly at **Bird Island**, which has long been the main attraction of the lake for visitors. If you don't have time to stop here, you can at least admire the view while travelling between Golmud and Xining. The train spends some hours running along the northern shore; travelling by bus you will pass the southern shore, and it's well worth scheduling your journey to pass the lake during daylight hours.

Apart from a visit to Bird Island – which tends to be a rushed, hectic experience – you can also hike and camp in peaceful solitude around the lake. From the smooth, green, windy shores, grazed by yaks during the brief summer, the blue, icy waters stretch away as far as the eye can see. If you have a tent, and really want a wilderness experience in China, this may be the place to get it. Don't forget to bring warm clothes, sleeping bags and enough drinking water. To get to the lake, you can take any bus bound for Dulan or Wulan (both west of Xining), from Xining's long-distance bus station. Each route passes the lake – one possible place to get off is the **Qinghai Lake Tourist Centre**, where you can stay (❸, dorm beds ¥25) and enjoy boating, fishing and horse riding.

Bird Island

This tiny rocky outcrop, situated at the far western side of the lake, is annually nested upon by literally thousands of birds. An immense variety of seasonal birds spend time here – gulls, cormorants, geese, swans and the rare **black-necked crane**. The main **bird-watching season** is from April to June, though the giant swans are best seen from November to February.

The easiest way to reach Bird Island is on a **day-trip** from Xining; there are **buses** (¥28) from the long-distance bus station in summer. Your best bet, however, is an excursion with one of Xining's **travel services** (see p.1035); foreigners are charged ¥150 excluding food and entrance fees (¥58 including a tourist shuttle bus from the ticket office to the island). It's a very long day out, leaving at 7am and getting back at around 10pm; up to ten hours of the time is spent driving. On the way up onto the plateau you will probably stop at the Riyue Pass, where you can see a Tibetan prayer-flag site and a couple of Chinese towers. One of the highlights is **lunch** – delicious and very cheap fried fish – which you have at a tiny settlement in a beautiful location just outside Bird Island.

Visiting Bird Island **independently** is something of a challenge, but it's possible, as a stopover between Xining and Golmud. Riding any bus between these two cities, make sure you get off at the right place by the lake – a grubby little Tibetan town called **Heimahe**, about four hours from Xining, which has a shop and a basic hotel (❶). From here a road leads up towards Bird Island and you'll have to hitch a ride from a passing tractor or car. Fifty minutes' drive brings you to the *Bird Island Guesthouse* with clean, but very cold, double rooms with bath (❸). You'll be lucky if there's any hot water, but there's always plenty to eat, though dishes are more expensive here (¥20 on average to start).

You need to buy a **ticket** (¥48) at the guesthouse to continue the remaining 15km to the two **observation points**. The first of these is actually a beach, which you view from a hide; the second is Bird Island itself, which you observe from the opposite cliff.

Chaka Salt Lake

Not far beyond Qinghai Hu is the **Chaka Salt Lake** (¥15, or ¥32 including cruise on the lake), which has recently become something of a tourist attraction. It's a potentially beautiful place, with its white gleaming salt crystals forming a perfect mirror-like surface from a distance. At the site, you can ride a small freight train, visit a house of salt, walk on a sixty-kilometre salt bridge – and take a hunk of the stuff home with you afterwards. To visit the lake independently, get on a bus (¥32, 3hr) heading to Dulan or Wulan from the long-distance bus station and get off at the small town of **Chaka Zhen**, near the lake – the earliest bus leaves at 8am. Accommodation is available at the only hotel in town, the *Yanhu Binguan* (❸). To return to Xining, flag down local buses to Heimahe, where there are more frequent buses back to Xining. Alternatively, you can visit the lake on a **tour**, usually in conjunction with Qinghai Hu. A hectic two-day visit to the two lakes (sleeping overnight at one of them) is run by the Qinghai Jiaotong Lüxingshe (see p.1035) for ¥600 per person, inclusive of all food, tickets and accommodation. The tour runs only if there are enough people.

Golmud and the road to Tibet

Nearly 3000m up on the Tibetan plateau, **GOLMUD** is an incredibly isolated city, even by the standards of northwest China. A new airport provides a link to Xining, but otherwise the city lies at least sixteen hours away from the nearest sizeable population centre. In spite of this, it still manages to be the second largest city in Qinghai with around 130,000 mainly Han Chinese residents, workers at the potash plants from which Golmud earns its living. It's hard to imagine that anyone would have come to live in such a cold and arid place otherwise. Geographically, Golmud is located close to the massive **Kunlun Mountains** to the south, and to the **Cai Erhan Salt Lake** to the north. Both are very scenic in parts, though they remain as yet virtually unexplored by foreign tourists.

For travellers, the city is really only interesting as a transit point between Xining in the east, Dunhuang in the north and Lhasa in the south – Golmud is the only place in China from where foreign tourists are officially allowed to cross **by land to Tibet**. At present this means a lengthy bus trip, but the government is also hard at work extending the **rail line to Lhasa**, an incredibly ambitious project due for completion in 2007, which aims to lay 1118km of track, most of it on permanently frozen ground lying at over 4000m above sea level.

Practicalities

Golmud's **train** and **bus** stations sit facing each other, way down in the south of the city. The scene as you exit them is bleak almost beyond belief: a vast emptiness, rimmed by distant buildings. A taxi to anywhere in town costs ¥5. As the demand for tours into Tibet increases, **accommodation** options are growing. Immediately to your right out of the train station is the new but bland *Golmud Mansion* (☎0979/8450876; ❹ dorm beds ¥30). A smarter option is *Qinggang Hotel* (☎0979/8456668, ⓕ8456666; ❺; generous discounts available in off season) – a few minutes up Jiangyuan Lu from the long-distance bus station, it's the glassy building to the east. The rooms are spacious and clean; the only drawback is the irregular hot water. Finally, take minibus #1 from the train station and it'll drop you at the city's oldest hotel, the *Golmud* (☎0979/412066, ⓕ8416484; ❺, dorm beds ¥25), not a bad place, comprising two buildings: the dorms are housed in the building on the left and the double rooms on the right. You can also book train and flight tickets from here by giving three days' notice (¥10 & ¥20 commission respectively).

There is a good range of **food** to be had in town due to the immigrant population. Across the road from the *Golmud* hotel, and a few minutes to the south, is an excellent Sichuan restaurant *Xiangsihai*. You can recognize it from the Chinese character for "Sichuan" on the window – try the old Sichuan favourite, *gongbao jiding*, diced chicken with chillies and peanuts. Nearby, the *Shipin Jie* (Food Street) has numerous restaurants serving hotpot, dumplings, noodles and Muslim food. There's also a lively market with outdoor food stalls and fresh-fruit stands, just east of the Bayi Lu/Kunlun Lu intersection. For local delicacies, try the Muslim restaurant *Qingshui Lou* on Bayi Lu.

CITS (☎0979/8496718; Mon–Fri 9am–noon & 2.30–6pm, Sat 10am–noon & 3–5pm) are at 60 Bayi Zhong Lu – look out for the big building with a flying horse statue on top; you can get here by taking bus #2. As well as Tibet trips, CITS can arrange interesting tours around Golmud. The most excit-

The road to Tibet

Though the **road to Tibet** (The Qingzang Expressway, 1973km) itself is reasonable and sealed to within 50km or so of Lhasa, the fact that it crosses 5000-metre passes and almost continually runs above 4000m makes it one of the toughest in the world for passengers. The journey should take around 30 hours by bus but there are often long delays due to rock slides, and vehicles rarely have adequate heating so take plenty of warm clothing, food and drink.

The regulations concerning travel into Tibet **for foreigners** are constantly changing, but at the time of writing all arrangements must be made through Golmud's **CITS** (see p.1041). There is no other official way of getting a bus ticket or of getting on to the bus into Tibet. The deal here is that you are buying a "**tour**" (¥1700) which covers a Tibet Entry Permit, two-month PICC insurance and one-way sleeper bus. On arrival you also get a guided tour in Lhasa for your money including three nights' dorm-bed accommodation. However, if – having arrived in Tibet – you are not enticed by the idea of a CITS tour, you are free to forfeit it and set off exploring on your own.

There are ways around this situation, though you'll need to be able to speak Chinese. Some people have managed to hook up with Chinese independent travellers renting **jeeps** for the journey; drivers go like maniacs and have been known to reach Lhasa in a mere 16 hours for a fraction of what it costs through CITS. The only other option is to try **hitching**, though note that this is a clandestine operation as drivers carrying foreigners can land themselves in big trouble; given the climate, you'll also have to decide whether you're up to possibly two days exposed to the elements in the back of a truck. Basically, if you hang around the Tibet bus station, you *may* be approached by a truck driver willing to take you. You'll still pay at least ¥800, and run the risk of being caught at police road blocks on the way. In reality, most drivers willing to risk taking you will usually only do so because they have an arrangement with the police – but you can never be sure. If you *are* caught, you will either be fined substantially, or have to pay a bribe, starting from another ¥500.

ing of these is a journey by 4WD to Ruoqiang in Xinjiang over the little-explored western edge of Qinghai; for a small group, expect to pay about US$150 each. **Internet** (¥2/hour) is available from a Net bar on Jiangyuan Lu, fifteen minutes' walk north of *Qinggang Hotel*. There's a **Bank of China** (Mon–Fri 8.30am–noon & 2.30–6pm) on Kunlun Lu, south of the *Golmud* hotel. Ancient **bicycles** (¥1/hour) can be rented from a little compound just behind the *Golmud*; go round the back of the old wing, and you'll see the doorway. About 300m east from the junction along Chaidamu Lu is the **PSB** (Mon–Fri 8.30am–noon & 2.30–6pm) – look for the huge white complex with a red/gold badge on top. The **CAAC** office (☎0979/8423333; 8.30am–noon & 1.30–5.30pm) is another 100m east down Chaidamu Lu. There are biweekly (Wed & Sun) flights to Xining, Xi'an and Qingdao, and airport buses also leave from here (¥10). Bus #2 (¥1) from the train station will get you here.

Heading on to Xining is probably easiest by rail: there are two fast trains daily (14hr) and one slow (16hr). You can only buy tickets from the window at the station on the day of departure, so come early to avoid the queues. **Buses** to Xining take 16 hours; there are also two daily (9am and 6pm) sleeper buses to Dunhuang in Gansu province (8hr; ¥90), a little-trodden route for which you may require a "registration" paper (¥20) from Golmud CITS or the PSB to enable you to buy a ticket at normal price. **Flight** tickets can be purchased through CITS, the *Golmud* hotel or the CAAC office.

Xinjiang

Xinjiang Uigur Autonomous Region is one of the most exciting parts of China, an extraordinary terrain, more than 3000km from any coast, which, despite all the historical upheavals since the collapse of the Silk Road trade, still comprises the same old oasis settlements strung out along the ancient routes, many still producing the silk and cotton for which they were famed in Roman times (see box, p.962).

Geographically, Xinjiang – literally "New Territories" – occupies an area slightly greater than Western Europe or Alaska, and yet its population is just thirteen million. And with the Han population probably comprising more than fifty percent of the whole, Xinjiang is perhaps the least "Chinese" of all parts of the People's Republic. By far the largest minority in Xinjiang is the **Uigur** (pronounced *Weeg-yur*), though there are also some dozen other Central Asian minority populations.

The land of Xinjiang is among the least hospitable in all China, covered for the most part by arid **desert and mountain**. Essentially, it can be thought of as two giant basins, both surrounded on all sides by mountains. Between the two basins are the Tian Shan (Heavenly Mountains), which effectively bisect Xinjiang from west to east. The basin to the north is known as the **Junggar Basin**, or Jungaria. The capital of Xinjiang, and only major city, **Ürümqi**, is here, on the very southern edge of the basin, as is the heavily Kazakh town of **Yining**, right up against the border with Kazakhstan. The Junggar Basin has been subject to fairly substantial Han settlement over the past forty years, with a degree of industrial and agricultural development. It remains largely grassland, with large state farms in the centre and Kazakh and Mongol herdsmen (still partially nomadic) in the mountain pastures on the fringes. The climate is not particularly hot in summer, and virtually Siberian from October through to March. To the south is the **Tarim Basin**, dominated by the scorching Takla-makan Desert, fiercely hot and dry in summer. This is where the bulk of the Uigur population lives, in strings of oases (Turpan and Kashgar among them) scattered along the old routes of the Silk Road. Some of these oasis cities are buried in the desert and long forgotten; others survive on irrigation using water from the various rivers and streams that flow from surrounding mountains. As well as forgotten cities, these sands also cover another buried treasure – **oil**. Chinese estimates reckon that three times the proven US reserves of oil are under the Taklamakan alone, which is one reason that the government is firmly establishing a Han presence in the region.

Xinjiang time

For travellers, the classic illustration of Xinjiang's remoteness from the rest of the country is in the fact that all parts of China set their clocks to Beijing time. The absurdity of this is at its most acute in Xinjiang, 3000–4000km distant from the capital – which means that in Kashgar, in the far west of the region, the summer sun rises at 9am or 10am and sets around midnight. Locally, there is such a thing as unofficial "**Xinjiang time**", a couple of hours behind Beijing time, which is used more frequently the further west you head towards Kashgar; when buying bus, train or plane tickets, you should be absolutely clear about which time is being used.

The Uigur

The Uigur are the easternmost branch of the extended family of **Turkic peoples** who inhabit most of Central Asia. Around 8 million Uigurs live in Xinjiang with another 300,000 in Kazakhstan. Despite centuries of domination by China and some racial mingling along the way, the Uigur remain culturally entirely distinct from the Han Chinese, and many Uigurs look decidedly un-Chinese – stockily built, bearded, with brown hair and round eyes. Although originally Buddhists, the Uigur have been **Muslim** for at least a thousand years and Islam remains the focus of their identity in the face of relentless Han penetration.

As the Uigurs are for the most part unable to speak Chinese and therefore unable to attend university or find well-paid work, their prospects for self-improvement within China are generally bleak. It is also true that many Han Chinese look down on the Uigurs as unsophisticated ruffians, and are frankly scared of their supposedly short tempers and love of knives. Perhaps as a consequence of this, Uigurs seem at times to extend their mistrust of Han Chinese to all foreigners, tourists included. Nevertheless, gestures such as drinking tea with them, or trying a few words of their language, will help to break down the barriers, and invitations to Uigur homes frequently follow.

Traveller's Uigur

The **Uigur language** is essentially an Eastern Turkish dialect, a branch of the Altaic languages from Central Asia (as well as Xinjiang, Uigur is also spoken in parts of Kazakhstan, Kyrgyzstan and Uzbekistan). There are several dialects, of which the Central Uigur (spoken from Ürümqi to Kashgar) is the most popular and hence given here. Unlike Chinese, Uigur is not a tonal language. It involves eight vowels and 24 consonants and uses a slightly modified Arabic script. The only pronunciations you are likely to have difficulties with are **gh** and **kh**, but you can get away by rendering them as **g** and **k** with light h at the end.

Hello	*Yahximusiz*	Thank you	*Rhamat sizge*
Goodbye/Cheers	*Hosh*	Please/Sorry	*kequrung*

Highlights of Xinjiang include the **Tian Shan** mountain pastures outside Ürümqi, where you can hike in rare solitude and stay beside Heaven Lake with Kazakhs in their yurts; but it is the old **Silk Road** that will attract most travellers. The most fascinating of the Silk Road oasis cities are **Turpan** and **Kashgar**, both redolent of old Turkestan, and it is possible to follow not only the Northern Silk Road from Turpan to Kashgar via Aksu and Kuqa, but also the almost forgotten southern route via Khotan. The routes were established over two thousand years ago, but traffic reached its height during the Tang dynasty, when China's most famous Buddhist pilgrim, **Xuanzang**, used them on his seventeen–year voyage to India. There's still the possibility of continuing the Silk Road journey out beyond the borders of China itself – not only over the relatively well-established **Karakoram Highway** into Pakistan, but now also over the less well-known routes into Kazakhstan and Kyrgyzstan (see p.1082). Finally, there exists an exciting if perilous road from Kashgar into western Tibet, a route officially closed to tourists.

Some history

The region's history has been coloured by such personalities as Tamerlane, Genghis Khan, Attila the Hun and even Alexander the Great. More often, though, in counterpoint to the great movements of history, Xinjiang has been at the mercy of its isolation and the feudal warring between the rulers of its oasis kingdoms, or **khanates**.

Yes	*He'e*	Tuesday	*Sixembe*
No	*Yakh*	Wednesday	*Qarxembe*
Very	*Bek*	Thursday	*Peyxembe*
What is your name?	*Ismingiz nime?*	Friday	*Jume*
My name is...	*Mening ismim ...*	Saturday	*Xembe*
How much is it?	*Bahasi khange?*		
OK	*Bolidu*	**Numbers**	
Good	*Yahxi*	1	*bir*
Where is the ...?	*... nede?*	2	*ikki*
toilet	*hajethana*	3	*uq*
hospital	*duhturhana*	4	*tort*
temple	*buthana*	5	*bash*
tomb	*khebre*	6	*alte*
I don't have	*Yenimda yeterlik*	7	*yet'te*
enough money	*pul yokh*	8	*sekkiz*
Please stop here	*Bu yerde tohtang*	9	*tokh'khuz*
This is delicious	*Temlik/lezzetlik*	10	*on*
Cold	*Soghukh*	11	*on bir*
Hot	*Issikh*	12	*on ikki*
Thirsty	*Ussitidighan*	etc	
Hungry	*Ag khusakh*	20	*yigrime*
When?	*Vakhitta?*	30	*ottuz*
Now	*Emdi/hazir*	40	*khirkh*
Today	*Bugun*	50	*ellik*
Yesterday	*Tunogun*	60	*atmix*
Tomorrow	*Ete*	70	*yetmix*
Sunday	*Yekexembe*	80	*seksen*
Monday	*Doxembe*	90	*tokhsen*
		100	*yuz*

The influence of China has been far from constant. The area – commonly referred to in the West as Eastern (or Chinese) Turkestan until 1949 – first passed under Han control in the second century BC, under Emperor Wu Di. But it was only during the **Tang dynasty** (650–850 AD) that this control amounted to more than a military presence. The Tang period for Xinjiang was something of a golden age, with the oases south of the Tian Shan largely populated by a mysterious but sophisticated Indo-European people, and the culture and Buddhist art of the oases at their zenith. Around the ninth century, however, came a change – the gradual rise to dominance of the **Uigurs**, and their conversion to **Islam**.

Subsequent centuries saw the **conquests of the Mongols** under Genghis Khan and later, from the West, of Tamerlane. Both brought havoc and slaughter in their wake, though during the brief period of Mongol rule (1271–1368) the Silk Road trade was hugely facilitated by the fact that, for the first and only time in history, east and west Asia were under a single government.

After the fall of the Mongols, and the final disappearance of the Silk Road, Xinjiang began to split into khanates and suffered a succession of religious and factional wars. Nonetheless, it was an independence of a kind and Qing **reassertion** of Chinese domination in the eighteenth century was fiercely contested. A century later, in 1862, full-scale **Muslim rebellion** broke out, led by the ruler of Kashgaria, **Yakub Beg**, armed and supported by the British who were seeking influence in this buffer zone between India and Russia (for more on which, read Peter Hopkirk's excellent *The Great Game* – see p.1216). Ultimately the revolt failed – Beg became a hated tyrant – and the region remained part of the Chinese empire.

At the beginning of the twentieth century, Xinjiang was still a Chinese backwater controlled by a succession of brutal warlords who acted virtually independently of the central government. The last one of these before World War II, **Sheng Shizai**, seemed momentarily to be a reforming force, instituting religious and ethnic freedoms, and establishing trade with the newly emergent Soviet Union. However, he ended by abandoning his moderate positions. Slamming the door on the Soviets and on leftist influences within Xinjiang itself in 1940, he began a reign of terror resulting in the deaths of more than two hundred thousand Communists, intellectuals, students and Muslim Nationalists.

The drive towards the defeat of the Guomindang in 1949 temporarily united the conflicting forces of Muslim nationalism and Chinese communism. After the Communist victory, however, there could be only one result. The principal Muslim Nationalist leaders were quietly murdered, allegedly killed in a plane crash, and the impetus towards a separate state was lost. The last Nationalist leader, a Kazakh named Osman, was executed in 1951.

Since 1949, the Chinese government has made strenuous attempts to stabilize the region by **settling Han Chinese** from the east, into Ürümqi in particular. The Uigur population of Xinjiang, from being ninety percent of the total in 1949, slipped below fifty percent in the 1980s, and is still slipping, in spite of the minorities' exemption from the One Child Policy. Today, however, the Chinese government remains nervous about Xinjiang, especially given the enormous **economic potential** of the area, in terms of coal mining, oil exploration and tourism, plus its strategic value as a **nuclear test site**. There have been outbursts of **Uigur dissent** in the region, most recently in 1997, when anti-Beijing demonstrations in Yining escalated into full-blown riots with many Uigurs detained and some receiving the death penalty. The situation appears to have calmed in recent years due to the increased presence of Chinese security forces; since the attacks of September 11, 2001 the Chinese government has equated Uigur nationalism with global Islamic terrorism and indulged in its own "war on terror" by monitoring and arresting Uigurs it claims are involved in separatist activities.

Eastern Xinjiang: the road to Turpan

The road from Dunhuang in western Gansu as far as **Hami** and then **Turpan** – the easternmost part of Xinjiang, east of the central area dominated by the Tian Shan – comprises some of the harshest terrain in the whole of China. Little water ever reaches this area of scorching depressions – geographically an extension of the Tarim Basin – which in summer is the hottest part of the country, and which was dreaded by the Silk Road traders as one of the most hazardous sections of the entire cross-Asia trip. Even today, crossing the area is most memorable for its suffocating heat and monotonous gravel and dune landscapes, though ironically Turpan – despite the heat – can be one of the most relaxing and enjoyable places in all China.

Hami

HAMI today is the eastern gateway to Xinjiang, a rich oasis in the midst of a seemingly endless desert, and famous throughout China for its **melons**, the

Eastern Xinjiang

Hami	哈密	*hāmì*
Dianli Hotel	电力宾馆	*diànlì bīnguǎn*
Hami Hotel	哈密宾馆	*hāmì bīnguǎn*
Hui Wang Fen	回王坟	*huíwángfén*
Jiageda Hotel	加格达宾馆	*jiāgédá bīnguǎn*
Maixiang Yuan	麦香园	*màixiāng yuán*
Tomb of Gess	盖斯墓	*gàisī mù*
Turpan	吐鲁番	*tùlǔfān*
Astana Graves	阿斯塔娜古墓区	*āsītǎnà gǔmùqū*
Bezeklik Caves	柏孜克里克石窟	*bǎizīkèlǐkè shíkū*
Daheyan	大河沿	*dàhéyàn*
Emin Minaret	苏公塔	*sūgōng tǎ*
Flaming Mountains	火焰山	*huǒyàn shān*
Gaochang	高昌	*gāochāng*
Grape Valley	葡萄沟	*pútáo gōu*
Iding Lake	艾丁湖	*àidīng hú*
Jiaohe	交河	*jiāohé*
Karez irrigation site	坎儿井	*kǎn'ér jǐng*
Accommodation and eating		
Best Food Burger	百富汉堡	*bǎifù hànbǎo*
Iron Fan Princess Restaurant	铁扇公主餐厅	*tiěshàn gōngzhǔ cāntīng*
Jiaotong	交通宾馆	*jiāotōng bīnguǎn*
Liangmao	粮贸宾馆	*liángmào bīnguǎn*
Oasis	绿洲宾馆	*lǜzhōu bīnguǎn*
Turpan	吐鲁番宾馆	*tùlǔfān bīnguǎn*
Xizhou Grand	西州大酒店	*xīzhōu dàjiǔdiàn*

hami gua. There's not much here to detain the visitor; nevertheless, it's a convenient stopping point along the road between Dunhuang and Turpan – it lies more or less midway between the two.

Historically, Hami has always been an important part of the Silk Road, occupying one of the few fertile spots between Gansu Province and Turpan. Xuanzang, the famous Buddhist pilgrim, nearly died of thirst on his way here, while Marco Polo noted with evident pleasure the locals' habit of not only supplying guests with food and shelter but also allowing them to sleep with their wives.

Kept small by the surrounding inhospitable desert, the town centres around the northern end of Zhongshan Lu. The bus station and hotels are in this area, while the train station is farther out in the north of town. There is just one historical site in Hami – the **Hui Wang Fen**, the Tombs of the Hami Kings (May–Oct 10am–8pm, Nov–April 9am–7pm; ¥10). From 1697 until 1930, Hami was nominally controlled by kings who for a time had obediently sent tribute to the Qing court, before becoming involved in the Muslim revolts that periodically engulfed Xinjiang. Although the kings ruled until 1930, Hami was virtually destroyed at least twice during these revolts. Today the tomb complex is in the south of the city and your ticket covers three mausoleums, a mosque, a small museum and a Chinese-speaking tour guide. The main mausoleum is in appealingly Arabic style, and the two smaller pavilion-shaped mausoleums to the left combine Han, Hui, Mongol and Uigur influences. At the time of writing, a reconstruction of the original Hami Palace was underway next to the mausoleum. You can reach Hui Wang Fen by taking bus #10 along Zhongshan

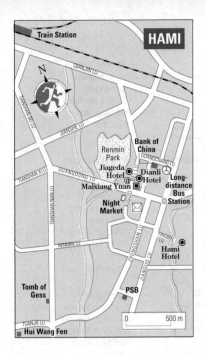

Lu to the end or #1 from the train station heading south to its terminal and then walk another few minutes on from there in the same direction. Alternatively, follow Zhongshan Lu south over the river and right along Tuanjie Lu to the end. It's an engrossing forty-minute walk through the dusty alleys of the Uigur quarter, during which you'll pass some very cheap carpet shops. Nearby is the **Tomb of Gess** (10am–6.30pm; ¥6) – one of the earliest Islamic missionaries in China. The tomb is in a simple wooden structure with a green dome. To get here walk 200m east of Hui Wang Fen then turn left up Tianshan Nan Lu, and it's another 200m to the north.

Practicalities

For most travellers, access to Hami is by **bus** from Dunhuang, Turpan or Ürümqi. There are frequent daily buses to and from Turpan and Jiuquan in Gansu province (via Jiayuguan), two daily buses to Dunhuang and three daily buses to Ürümqi – all leaving in the early morning – journey time to Dunhuang and Turpan is between six and eight hours, while to Ürümqi it's about eleven hours. There's also a daily bus link to Lanzhou from October to February. All **trains** running between Lanzhou and Ürümqi also stop at Hami. The train station is linked to the bus station on Jianguo Lu by bus #3 and to Zhongshan Lu by bus #1. The **Bank of China** (daily 9am–1pm & 4–8pm) is on Guangchang Lu, west of the bus station.

There are various **accommodation** possibilities in the area of the bus station. Take the side exit of the bus station onto Guangchang Lu and walk west until you come to Aiguo Bei Lu, where you'll find the three-star *Jiageda* (☏0902/2232140, ✉jiagedasd@163.com; ❻). Rooms are pricey but clean and smart, with discounts offered in winter. Almost across the road to your left is the cheaper *Dianli Hotel* (☏0902/2260180; ❸), with clean, basic rooms. On the other side of town is the *Hami* (☏0902/2233140 ext1188, ☏2234345; ❹), one of the smartest options in town after a recent refit. Facilities include a gym, swimming pool and two restaurants (the cheapest rooms are in building #1). To get there from the bus station, walk south from the main exit for about fifteen minutes along Jianguo Lu, or take bus #3 for two stops, then turn left down Yingbin Lu. A taxi will cost ¥5.

For **food**, you need go no farther than the excellent **night market** which has a host of stalls (May–Oct) and more permanent canteens selling great kebabs, spicy grilled freshwater fish, noodles and *hundun* soup; it's located on the same road as the *Jiageda* – just head south from the hotel. For approximately Western fare, *Maixiang Yuan* on Aiguo Bei Lu serves cakes, burgers and even steaks. Just opposite is an **Internet** bar (¥2/hour).

Turpan

The small and economically insignificant town of **TURPAN** (**Tulufan** to the Chinese) has in recent years turned itself into one of the major tourist destinations of Xinjiang. Credit for this must go largely to the residents, who have not only covered the main streets and walkways of the town with vine trellises, converting them into shady green tunnels (partly for the benefit of tourists), but have also managed to retain a relatively easy-going manner even in the heady economic climate of modern China.

Today, Turpan is a largely **Uigur-populated** area, and, in Chinese terms, an obscure backwater, but it has not always been so. As early as the Han dynasty, the Turpan oasis was a crucial point along the Northern Silk Road, and the cities of **Jiaohe**, and later **Gaochang** (both of whose ruins can be visited from Turpan), were important and wealthy centres of power. On his way to India, Xuanzang spent more time than he had planned here, when the king virtually kidnapped him in order to have him preach to his subjects. This same king later turned his hand to robbing Silk Road traffic, and had his kingdom annexed by China in 640 as a result. From the ninth to the thirteenth century, a rich intellectual and artistic culture developed in Gaochang, resulting from a fusion between the original Indo-European inhabitants and the (pre-Islamic) Uigurs. It was not until the fourteenth century that the Uigurs of Turpan converted to Islam.

The town is located in a depression 80m below sea level, which accounts for its extreme climate – well above 40°C in summer and well below freezing in winter. In summer the **dry heat** is so soporific that there is little call to do anything but sleep or sip cool drinks in outdoor cafés with other tourists. To ease the consciences of the indolents, there are a number of **ruined cities** and **Buddhist caves** worth visiting in the countryside around the city, testimony to its past role as an important oasis on the Silk Road. Turpan is also an agricultural oasis, famed above all for **grapes**. Today, virtually every household in the town has a hand in the grape business, both in cultivating the vines, and in drying the grapes at the end of the season (a Grape Festival is held at the end of August). Bear in mind that Turpan is very much a summer resort; if you come out of season (Nov–March), the town itself is cold and uninspiring, with the vines cut back and most businesses closed – though the surrounding sights remain interesting, and devoid of other tourists.

The Town

For some travellers, the real draw of Turpan is its absence of sights, enabling total relaxation. The downtown area doesn't amount to much, with most of the services near the bus station on Laocheng Lu; pedestrianized Qingnian Lu is protected from the baking summer sun by

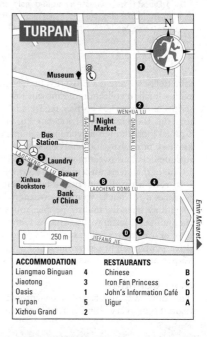

Emin Minaret ▶

ACCOMMODATION		RESTAURANTS	
Liangmao Binguan	4	Chinese	B
Jiaotong	3	Iron Fan Princess	C
Oasis	1	John's Information Café	D
Turpan	5	Uigur	A
Xizhou Grand	2		

Trade goods were not the only things to travel along the Silk Road; it was along this route that **Buddhism** first arrived in China at some point in the first century AD. Cities along the way became bastions of the religion (which in part explains their abandonment and desecration following the introduction of Islam after 1000), and from early on, Chinese pilgrims visited India and brought back a varied bag of Buddhist teachings. The most famous is the Tang-dynasty monk **Xuanzang**, unique for the depth of his learning and the exhaustive quantity of material with which he returned after a seventeen-year journey from the then capital of China, Chang'an (Xi'an), to India.

Born near Luoyang in 602, Xuanzang favoured **Mahayana** Buddhism, which depicts the world as an illusion produced by our senses. Having studied in Luoyang, Chengdu and Chang'an, he became confused by often contradictory teachings, and in 629 he decided to visit India to study Buddhism at its source. But China's new Tang rulers (the dynasty was established in 618) had forbidden foreign travel, so Xuanzang went without official permission, narrowly avoiding arrest in western Gansu. He almost died of thirst before reaching **Hami** and then **Turpan**, at the foot of the Flaming Mountains. Turpan's king detained him for a month to hear him preach but eventually provided a large retinue, money and passports for safe passage through other kingdoms. Despite bandits, Xuanzang reached **Kuqa** unharmed, where he spent two months waiting for the passes north over the Tian Shan to thaw – even so, a great number of his party died traversing the mountains. On the far side in modern Kyrgyzstan, Xuanzang's religious knowledge greatly impressed the Khan of the Western Turks, before he continued, via the great central Asian city of **Samarkand**, through modern-day Afghanistan, over the Hindu Kush and so down into **India**, arriving about a year after he set out. Xuanzang spent fifteen years in India, journeying from the northern mountains, through Assam down the east coast to around Madras, then crossing the centre of the country to northwestern Nasik and Baroda. Everywhere he visited holy sites (including the Ganges and places from Buddha's life), studied major and esoteric forms of Buddhism, lectured, and entered debates – which he often won – with famous teachers on aspects of religious thought.

vine trellises. There is a **museum** on Gaochang Xi Lu (daily 10am–7.30pm; ¥20), with a smallish collection of dinosaur fossils as well as silk fragments, tools, manuscripts and preserved corpses recovered from the nearby Silk Road sites. Other than this, the **bazaars** off Laocheng Lu, almost opposite the bus station, are worth a casual look, though they are not comparable to anything in Kashgar. You'll find knives, clothes, hats and boots on sale, while the most distinctively local products include delicious sweet raisins, as well as walnuts and almonds.

One of the nicest ways to spend an evening after the heat of the day has passed is to **rent a donkey cart** and take a tour of the countryside south of town, a world of dusty tracks, vineyards, wheat fields, shady poplars, running streams and incredibly friendly, smiling people. You are unlikely to encounter many more tranquil rural settings than this in China. It's easy to arrange a tour from any donkey-cart driver around *John's Café*; for a tour lasting an hour or more, two or three people might pay around ¥10–15 each. *John's* also offers **bike rental** for ¥3 per hour, which works out slightly cheaper than the hotels' rates.

Practicalities

The only way to arrive in downtown Turpan is by **bus**. Frequent buses (9am–8pm; every 20min) run between Ürümqi and Turpan, and there's a

If he hoped to find ultimate clarity he was probably disappointed, as the interpretation of Buddhist lore in India was even more varied than in China. However, he did manage to acquire a vast collection of Buddhist statues, relics and – especially – **texts**, and in 644 decided that it was his responsibility to return to China with this trove of knowledge. Given an **elephant** to carry his luggage by the powerful north Indian king Harsha, Xuanzang recrossed the Kush and turned east to travel over the Pamirs to **Tashkurgan** (near where the elephant unfortunately drowned) before heading up to **Kashgar**, then – as now – an outpost of the Chinese empire. From here he turned southeast to the silk and jade emporium of **Khotan**, whose king claimed Indian ancestry and where there were a hundred Buddhist monasteries. Xuanzang spent eight months here, waiting for replacements of Buddhist texts lost in northern India, and a reply from the Tang emperor **Taizong**, to whom he had written requesting permission to re-enter China. When it came, permission was enthusiastic, and Xuanzang lost little time in returning to Chang'an via Minfeng, Miran, Loulan and **Dunhuang**, arriving in the Chinese capital in 645. He had left unknown, alone, and almost as a fugitive; he returned to find tens of thousands of spectators crowding the road to Chang'an. The emperor became his patron, and he spent the last twenty years of his life translating part of the collection of Buddhist texts acquired on his travels.

Xuanzang wrote a biography, but highly coloured accounts of his travels also passed into folklore, becoming the subject of plays and the sixteenth-century novel **Journey to the West**, still a popular tale in China. In it, Xuanzang (known as **Tripitaka**) is depicted as terminally naïve, hopelessly dismayed by the various disasters which beset him. Fortunately, he's aided by the Bodhisattva of Mercy, **Guanyin**, who sends him spirits to protect him in his quest: the vague character of **Sandy**; the greedy and lecherous **Pigsy**; and **Sun Wu Kong**, the brilliant Monkey King. As many of the novel's episodes are similar, varying only in which particular demon has captured Tripitaka, the best parts are the lively exchanges between Pigsy and Monkey, as they endeavour to rescue their master; a good abridgement in English is Arthur Waley's *Monkey* – see "Books", p.1224.

daily bus service to and from Hami and Korla. Turpan's **train station** is 55km away at Daheyan (marked "Tulufan" on timetables) – from where it takes at least an hour to get into town by bus. From Daheyan station, turn right and walk a few hundred metres to reach the bus station, or catch a minibus from the station concourse. The journey costs around ¥8 per person and runs from 9am to 8pm in winter and 8am to 11pm in summer. If you miss the last bus, you'll either have to stay the night in Daheyan or get a taxi (¥50).

Getting around Turpan is best done on foot, or – given the extreme summer heat – by bicycle or donkey cart, for which you should expect to pay around ¥2–3 per journey. All of Turpan's accommodation, regardless of cost, has **air conditioning** – just make sure that yours is working when you check in.

Turpan has two **travel agents**, both of which can help out with transport bookings for around ¥30 commission (including, in the absence of an airport at Turpan, flights out of Ürümqi), as well as local tours. CITS have a branch inside the *Jiaotong* and another at the alley to the *Oasis Hotel*; or try the independent *John's Information Café* (Ⓔjohncafe@hotmail.com) outside the *Turpan Hotel*. "John" is a Chinese entrepreneur who has made a fortune catering to budget travellers – he also has branches of his café in Kashgar and Dunhuang. There's a rumour that he reports on travellers' activities to the authorities, however, so if you are planning anything illegal (such as crossing from Kashgar to Tibet), this is not the place to discuss it. **Internet** access (¥1.5/hr) can be found in the building opposite the museum, where you can also make international phone calls. On Laocheng Xi Lu, from east to west you can find a **Bank of China**, a laundry, which may come in handy in the sweaty temperature, and a Xinhua Bookstore across the road which is also the **post office** (daily 9.30am–8pm).

When you're **leaving Turpan**, the bus (half-hourly 7.30am–8pm) is your best bet to Ürümqi, a journey which takes three hours via the new highway. Otherwise, it's a dusty, gritty ten hours east to Hami or west to Korla, past views of distant snow-ridged mountains. For anything more distant, you definitely want to travel by **train**; travel agents can make bookings in peak season, though it's often possible to buy your own train tickets at Daheyan station at other times.

Accommodation
More and more places in Turpan will take foreigners, resulting in a good range of accommodation options.

Jiaotong At the bus station. Inexpensive, though not the cleanest place in town. ❹

Liangmao (Grain Trade) Laocheng Dong Lu ☏0995/8567449. Staff are reluctant to take foreigners and it's somewhat grotty, but you can find relatively cheap double rooms in peak season. ❸

Oasis North of Qingnian Lu ☏0995/8522491, ℱ8523348, ⓦwww.the-silk-road.com. A pleasant upmarket hotel set in leafy grounds, where occasional performances of local singing and dancing take place. Staff speak English and are very helpful; rooms have clean carpets, modern bathrooms and even mock *kangs* instead of beds. Major discounts available out of season. ❼

Turpan South of Qingnian Lu ☏0995/8568898, ℱ8569299. The best budget option, offering five-bed dorms – primitive and far from the toilets – and smarter doubles. In the hot summer evenings, there are cheerful displays of local singing and dancing in the gardens round the back, which you can join for a small fee. Dorm beds ¥25, ❻

Xizhou Grand 8 Qingnian Lu ☏0995/8554000, ℱ8554068. The newest and plushest in town, rooms are comfortable and clean considering the price, though staff can't speak much English. ❺

Eating and drinking
John's Information Café is the most visible restaurant in Turpan, with **Western breakfasts** available under the trellises, as well as bland Chinese dishes. The outdoor café at the back of the *Turpan* hotel also has an English menu, and is quite a nice place to drink beer in the evenings when you can listen in on the live Uigur singing and dancing performances taking place nearby. Otherwise, the *McDonald's* clone *Best Food Burger* has a chain northwest of Gaochang Lu/Laocheng Lu intersection.

For **Chinese** food, there's a whole series of touristy restaurants with English menus, to the west of the main crossroads north of the *Turpan* hotel on Laocheng Dong Lu. All have outdoor tables and chairs under the vines, and friendly service – though establish prices when ordering to avoid being over-charged. Try *liang ban huang gua*, a delicious cold cucumber salad with garlic and soya sauce. The *Iron Fan Princess Restaurant* just outside the *Turpan* is not bad either, though a little pricey. Around 10am and 7pm are the best times to pick up just-made nan bread along the street, pretty much all less than ¥2 each. The food market a couple of minutes' walk west of the Xinhua Bookstore is an excellent place to sample more **Uigur cuisine** including kebabs, *laghman* and dry and fresh fruits. For more upmarket Chinese and Uigur food, try the restaurants in the *Oasis Hotel*. While you're in Turpan, try to get hold of some

Uigur food

Uigur food, unsurprisingly, has far more of a Central Asian than a Chinese flavour. The most basic staple – which often seems to be the only food available – is **laghman**, known in Chinese as *lamian*, literally "**pulled noodles**". Watching these being made to order is greatly entertaining: the speed at which a skilled cook transforms the raw dough into a bowlful of noodles, banging, pulling, and managing to keep all the strands separate, is incredible. In Xinjiang, *laghman* is served with a stew of mutton, tomatoes, chilli and other vegetables; rather different from the more soupy version sold elsewhere in China. For the same spicy sauce but without the noodles, try *tohogish* (known in Chinese as *dapan ji*), a chicken served chopped up in its entirety, head, feet and all; or *jerkob*, a beef stew – both are served in smarter restaurants. **Coriander leaf** is used as a garnish on everything.

In summer, apart from *laghman,* street vendors also offer endless cold noodle soup dishes, usually very spicy. **Rice** in Xinjiang appears mostly in **pilau** – a fried rice dish with hunks of mutton coloured with saffron. More familiar to foreigners are the skewers of **grilled mutton kebabs**, dusted with chilli and cumin powder – buy several of them at once, as one skewer does not make much more than a mouthful. They are often eaten with delicious glasses of ice-cold yoghurt (known in Chinese as *suannai*), which are available everywhere in Xinjiang. Big chunks of compressed **tea** (*zhuan cha* or literally "brick tea") are sold everywhere in Xinjiang – normally boiled with milk and salt – fancier ones come flavoured with cinnamon, cardamom and rosehips.

Oven-baked **breads** (*nang* in Chinese) are also popular in markets: you'll see bakers apparently plunging their hands into live furnaces, to stick balls of dough on to the brick-lined walls; these are then withdrawn minutes later as bagel-like bread rolls, or simply flat – in villages local people bring their own flour to the bakery shop and make dozens of them for stock – they last for a month. *Permuda* (known in Chinese as *kaobao*) are tasty baked dough packets stuffed with mutton and onions; they can also be fried (*samsa*) or steamed (*manta*); the latter are similar to Chinese dumplings.

A couple of other specialities are worth trying: **madang** is nougat thick with walnuts, raisins and dried fruit, sold by pedlars who carve the amount you want (or usually, more than you want – it's sold by weight) off massive slabs of the stuff. More refreshing is that characteristic Central Asian fruit, the **pomegranate**, known as *shiliu* in Chinese. You can find them whole at markets, or buy the juice from street vendors – look for the piles of skins and the juicing machines, which resemble a large, spiky torture implement.

---

of the **local wine** if you don't mind paying ¥40–50 a bottle. The red is sweet and thick like port, the white fruity and very drinkable.

Around Turpan

Nearly all visitors to Turpan end up taking the customary **tour** of the historical and natural sights outside the town. These are quite fun, as much for the chance to get out into the desert as for the sights in themselves, which usually include the two ancient cities of **Gaochang** and **Jiaohe**, the **Emin Minaret**, the **karez underground irrigation channels**, the **Bezeklik Caves** and **Astana Graves**. Sites are open daily, for most of the hours of daylight.

Assuming you can get together a group of five people – not difficult, as the tourist hotels organize this, as does CITS – a trip to all the above sites will take the best part of a day (with a break for lunch and siesta if you choose) and cost around ¥50 per person for the minibus. CITS also offer a car with driver for ¥200 per day. Alternatively, for places close to town, **cycling** is a good option

△ Making laghman noodles

if you want to avoid a tour. Be aware that, however you travel, you'll be in blistering heat for the whole of the day, so sun cream, a hat, water bottle and sunglasses are essential.

The only downside is the **entry fees**, which are not included in the cost of a tour and have become quite steep recently at ¥20–30 per site (less if you have a Chinese student card). Frankly, the only site which is unquestionably worth the money is Jiaohe: if you're looking to cut costs, the Bezeklik Caves can be skipped, since there is plenty of other Buddhist cave art to visit in China; and you can get good views of Gaocheng and the Emin Minaret without actually entering the sites.

The Emin Minaret, Jiaohe and karez irrigation site

Start off a tour at the eighteenth-century **Emin Minaret** (¥20) just 2km southeast of the city; you can walk there by following Jiefang Jie east out of town for about thirty minutes. Unlike other Islamic architecture, the minaret is built to a very simple style – slightly bulging and potbellied – and erected from sundried brown bricks arranged in differing patterns. The tower tapers its way 40m skyward to a rounded tip adjoining a mosque with an interesting latticework ceiling. You can see the complex without entering the site; otherwise you can ascend the tower or the mosque with good views from each over the green oasis in the foreground and the distant snowy Tian Shan beyond.

About 11km west of Turpan is the ruined city of **Jiaohe** (¥30; signposted in English), just about within bicycle range on a hot day. Although Jiaohe was for large parts of its history under the control of Gaochang (see below), it became the regional administrative centre during the eighth century, and occupies a spectacular defensive setting on top of a two-kilometre-long, steep-sided plateau carved out by the two halves of a forking river. What sets Jiaohe apart from all other ruined cities along the Silk Road is that although most of the buildings comprise little more than crumbling, windswept mud walls, so many survive, and of such a variety – gates, temples, public buildings, graveyards and ordinary dwellings – that Jiaohe's **street plan** is still evident, and there's a real feeling of how great this city must once have been. As with Gaochang, a Buddhist monastery marked the town centre; its foundations – 50m on each side – can still be seen. Another feature is the presence of ancient wells still containing water. Make sure you walk to the far end of the site, where the base of a former tower, dated to around 360 AD, overlooks the river.

Returning from Jiaohe, minibus drivers usually drop you off at a dolled-up **karez irrigation site** (¥20), an intrinsically interesting place unfortunately turned into an ethnic theme park, complete with regular Uigur dance shows, presumably to justify the entry fee. Karez irrigation taps natural underground channels carrying water from source (in this case, glaciers at the base of the Tian Shan) to the point of use. Strategically dug wells then bring water to small surface channels which run around the streets of the town. Many ancient Silk Road cities relied on this system, including those much farther to the west, in areas such as modern Iran, and karez systems are still in use throughout Xinjiang – there are plenty of opportunities to see them for free on the way to Kashgar.

The Bezeklik Caves, Astana Graves and Gaochang ruins

For the other sites, you definitely need a minibus – they are too far to reach by bicycle. The first stop is usually the Bezeklik Caves, but on the way you'll pass the **Flaming Mountains**, made famous in the sixteenth-century Chinese novel *Journey to the West* (see p.1224). The novel depicts these sandstone mountains as walls of flame, and it's not hard to see why, from the red sandstone hillsides, lined and creviced as though flickering with flame in the heat haze. The plains below are dotted with dozens of small "nodding donkey" **oil wells**, all tapping into Xinjiang's vast reserves.

The **Bezeklik Caves** (¥20), in a valley among the Flaming Mountains some 50km northeast of Turpan, are disappointing, offering mere fragments of the former wealth of Buddhist cave art here, dating back to 640 AD. The location is nonetheless strikingly beautiful, with stark orange dunes behind and a deep river gorge fringed in green below, but most of the murals were cut out and removed to Berlin by Albert Von Le Coq at the beginning of the twentieth century, and the remainder painstakingly defaced by Muslim Red Guards during the 1960s. (A good deal of the murals removed by Le Coq were subsequently destroyed by the Allied bombing of Germany in World War II.) Outside the site you can ride camels along the Flaming Mountains for ¥50 per person. Just before the caves is a bizarre theme park (¥25), featuring giant sculptures of characters from *Journey to the West* – a very surreal sight springing up out of the desiccated landscape.

South of here, the **Astana Graves** (¥20) mark the burial site of the imperial dead of Gaochang from the Tang dynasty. Unfortunately, the graves have had most of their interesting contents removed to museums in Ürümqi and Turpan, and little remains beyond a couple of preserved corpses and some murals. The adjacent ruins of **Gaochang** (¥20) are somewhat more impressive, however, especially for their huge scale and despite having suffered from the ravages of both Western archeologists and the local population, who for centuries have been carting off bits of the city's ten-metre-high adobe walls to use as soil for their fields. You can walk, or take a donkey cart (¥20 per person), from the entrance to the centre of the site, which is marked by a large square building, the remains of a monastery. Its outer walls are covered in niches, in each one of which a Buddha was originally seated; just a few bare, broken traces of these Buddhas remain, along with their painted haloes. If you have time, the nicest thing you can do is strike off on your own and listen to the hot wind whistling through the mud-brick walls.

Grape Valley and Iding Lake

Thirteen kilometres north of Turpan, and at the western end of the Flaming Mountains, is the so-called **Grape Valley** (¥60). There's very little point visiting this place out of season, but from mid-July to September it's a pleasant little oasis in the middle of a stark desert, covered in shady trellises bulging with fruit (which you have to pay for if you want to eat). Your ticket covers a Uigur dancing performance and a museum – you can find the locations of both on the map of the valley as you enter. This could be included on your minibus tour, or you could reach it on a very hot bicycle ride, but bear in mind that the scenery here is not much different from that of downtown Turpan.

Finally, about 50km south of Turpan, though not included on any tours, is the bleak but dramatic **Iding Lake**. Located in a natural depression 154m below sea level, this is the second lowest lake in the world after the Dead Sea, though you won't actually see any water here except in spring – the rest of the year the lake is a flat plain of dried salt deposits. The land around the lake is white with crusty salt and dotted with bright yellow-green pools of saturated water that feels like oil on the skin. Locals rub it over themselves enthusiastically, claiming that it's good for you. A car to the lake and back should cost around ¥150 – the road is very rough and expect the one-way trip to take at least two hours. The area around the lake is very muddy so don't take your best shoes.

Ürümqi and Tian Chi

ÜRÜMQI – **Wulumuqi** in Chinese – is the political, industrial and economic capital of Xinjiang, and by far the largest city in the region, with a population of well over one million, the overwhelming majority of whom are Han Chinese. Its name means "Beautiful Pastures" – a misleading description for what has become a drab and functional place, even though the skyline to the east is marked by the graceful snowy peaks of the Tian Shan.

For travellers arriving from western China or Central Asia, this will be the first truly Chinese city on your route, and the first chance to witness the consumer boom that is sweeping the high streets of China, in the shape of smart department stores and designer clothes boutiques. So vital has the city become as China's most westerly industrial outpost that in 1992 it was officially decreed a "port" to enable it to benefit from the special low rates of tax, normally permitted only in port cities such as Shanghai and Xiamen – an unusual distinction, to say the least, for a city located 2000km from the nearest sea.

If you're coming from eastern China, however, the city may not seem particularly exciting given its lack of historical identity, though it's strange to see so many signs written in curly Arabic script and all the non-Chinese faces. Nevertheless, it does have lively bazaars, as well as a certain pioneering feel to it – the

Ürümqi and Tian Chi

Ürümqi		
Ürümqi	乌鲁木齐	wūlǔ mùqí
Erdaoqiao Market	二道桥市场	èrdàoqiáo shìchǎng
Hongshan Park	红山公园	hóngshān gōngyuán
Main bus station	客运站	kèyùn zhàn
Renmin Park	人民公园	rénmín gōngyuán
South bus station	南郊客运站	nánjiāo kèyùnzhàn
Xinjiang Museum	新疆博物馆	xīnjiāng bówùguǎn

Accommodation and eating		
Bogda	博格达宾馆	bógédá bīnguǎn
Junbang Tianshan Fandian	君邦天山饭店	jūnbāng tiānshān fàndiàn
Miram Fandian	米兰饭店	mǐlán fàndiàn
Overseas Chinese	华侨宾馆	huáqiáo bīnguǎn
Ramada	屯河华美达酒店	túnhé huáměidá jiǔdiàn
Shuhan Fengwei Jiulou	蜀汉风味酒楼	shǔhàn fēngwèi jiǔlóu
Xiangyou	湘友酒店	xiāngyǒu jiǔdiàn
Xinjiang	新疆饭店	xīnjiāng fàndiàn
Xinjiang Grand	新疆大酒店	xīnjiāng dàjiǔdiàn

Moving on: foreign cities		
Almaty	阿拉木图	ālā mùtú
Bishkek	比什凯克	bǐshí kǎikè
Islamabad	伊斯兰堡	yīsī lánbǎo
Moscow	莫斯科	mòsīkē
Tashkent	塔什干	tǎshí gàn

Baiyang Gou		
Xi Baiyang Gou	西白杨沟	xī báiyáng gōu
	白杨沟	báiyáng gōu

Tian Chi		
Tian Chi	天池	tiānchí
Dawanzi	大弯子	dàwānzi

Moving on from Ürümqi

There are **flights** from Ürümqi to Kashgar, Korla, Kuqa, Khotan and Yining within Xinjiang (monopolized by China Southern Airlines' Xinjiang branch) and to all major Chinese cities including Hong Kong, and to Almaty (Kazakhstan), Islamabad (Pakistan – a useful fall-back if the Karakoram Highway is closed; see p.1087), Bishkek (Kyrgyzstan), Tashkent (Uzbekistan) and Moscow. Note that you'll probably need to acquire visas from your native country in advance for international destinations; see p.32 for details.

Buses connect Ürümqi with all major towns in Xinjiang province, though in most instances – especially the long crossing to Kashgar – you're far better off taking the train. Exceptions here are the Southern Silk Road, and Yining, neither of which is on the rail line, though Yining is due to be connected to Jinghe soon; Turpan is also to be connected, though it is a relatively easy three hours by bus down the expressway. Ürümqi's **main bus station** serves buses to Hoegs Pass (to Kazakhstan), Yining, Almaty to the west and Altay to the north. Most other traffic – including traffic to points between here along the Northern Silk Road to Kashgar and Turpan – leaves from the **south bus station**, where buying tickets is only complicated by the huge, noisy scrums instead of queues in front of the ticket offices. Beware of pickpockets.

The **rail line** follows the Northern Silk Road west to Kashgar, and heads east via Hami into Gansu and the rest of China. Chaotic crowds make trying to buy tickets at the station difficult, though there's also a hard-seat office at the main bus station – generally, however, you'll save a lot of time by employing an agent (see p.1062).

To Kazakhstan

The opening of the rail link between China and Kazakhstan finally sealed the cross-Asia line that connects the ports of eastern China with those of northwestern Europe – a route that offers a substantial saving of time over the Trans-Siberian route. However, the link is used by just two **trains** a week in both directions connecting Ürümqi and Almaty, departing on Saturday and Monday nights from both ends. In Ürümqi, tickets (sleepers only, from about ¥600) can be bought in the international departure lounge at the north end of the train-station building (daily 10am–1pm & 3.30–7.30pm). Bear in mind that you need to double-check the availability of these trains when planning the trip, since they sometimes stop running without notice.

Buses to Almaty run daily from Ürümqi's long-distance bus station for US$60 and take at least 24 hours; alternatively, you can pick up a bus from Yining everyday except Sunday for only US$30; tickets are sold at a special office inside Yining bus station. The Hoegs Pass to Kazakhstan has a string of interesting souvenir shops selling Turkish chocolates, Russian binoculars and random foreign cigarettes including "American" cigars. Expect protracted delays at the border – upwards of four hours to sort out the paperwork and shift cargo around is usual. There is one **flight** every Wednesday between Ürümqi and Almaty, costing ¥2031 from China Southern Airlines, Xinjiang branch. Nationals of all countries (except Commonwealth of Independent States) require **visas** for Kazakhstan, which at the time of writing had to be obtained from their home country.

shiny, new high-rise office buildings and hotels downtown seem to suggest a great metropolis, until you notice the barren, scrubby hillsides just around the corner. Apart from this, the main reason to visit Ürümqi is to arrange a trip to **Tian Chi** (Heaven Lake), three hours east of the city by bus.

Under the name of Dihua, Ürümqi became the capital of Xinjiang in the late nineteenth century. During the first half of the twentieth century the city was something of a battleground for feuding warlords – in 1916 Governor Yang

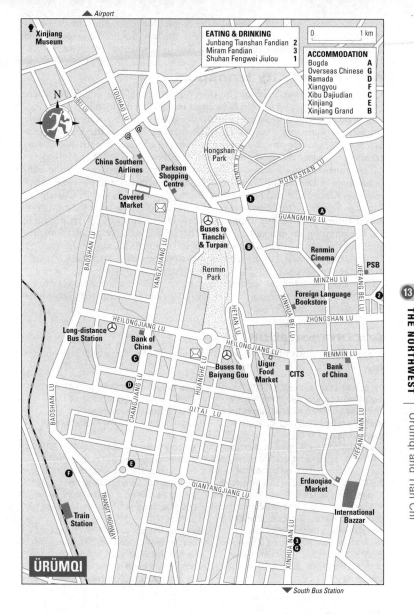

Zengxin invited all his personal enemies to a dinner party here, and then had their heads cut off one by one during the course of the banquet. Later, shortly before the outbreak of World War II, **Soviet troops** entered the city to help quell a Muslim rebellion; they stayed until 1960. Ürümqi began to emerge from its extreme backwardness only with the completion of the Lanzhou–Ürümqi **rail line** in 1963. This more than anything helped to integrate the city, economically and psychologically, into the People's Republic. And with the opening of the Ürümqi–Almaty rail line in 1991, the final link in the long-heralded direct route from China through Central Asia to Europe was complete.

Arrival and city transport

Ürümqi's international **airport** is 15km northwest of the city, from where you can reach town on the CAAC airport bus (¥18), which delivers to various airline offices. Alternatively, take city bus #51 (¥5) from the main road outside the airport, which runs via Xibei Lu, Changjiang Lu (near the long-distance bus station), Qiantanjiang Lu (near the train station) and Xinhua Nan Lu to terminate just past the southern bus station; or hire a taxi (¥30).

The **train station** lies in the southwest of the city, with services arriving from as far afield as Beijing and Shanghai in the east, and Kashgar in the west, not to mention Almaty in Kazakhstan. Bus #8 from the southern end of Changjiang Lu runs northeast to Minzhu Lu, near much of the accommodation. The **main long-distance bus station** is a few blocks north of the train station, on Heilongjiang Lu, but just as many services end up a couple of kilometres south of the centre at the the **south bus station** on Xinhua Nan Lu (bus #1 runs north up Xinhua Lu), and private operators use their own depots, scattered across the city.

Distances within the city are fairly large, so you will need to use **taxis** (starting from ¥6 within the city) and **buses** (¥1–2) – pick up a map with bus routes from hawkers at arrival points.

Accommodation

Ürümqi's **accommodation** options are quite diverse, though budget options have diminished in recent years.

Bogda Guangming Lu ☏0991/8863910, ⓕ8865769. A fair walk away from any site of interest, this is a smart, reasonably priced hotel, though the hot water is on and off. Dorms ¥20, **❻**
Overseas Chinese Xinhua Nan Lu ☏0991/8553512. Slightly remote in the south of the city, but has a pleasant, quiet atmosphere, with one old (cheaper) building and one new one. Take bus #7 south down Xinhua Bei Lu to get here. **❹**
Ramada Changjiang Lu ☏0991/5876688, ⓦwww.ramadahotels.com. Upmarket yet reasonably priced place with all the usual four-star facilities. **❻**
Xiangyou Right in the train station square, to the far left (north) as you come out of the station ☏0991/7770866. Clean, modern doubles and three- and four-bed dorms. The ¥40 dorms have showers. **❺**

Xibu Dajiudian Changjiang Lu ☏0991/5812649. One of the few cheap hotels that still takes foreigners. Rooms are spacious and surprisingly well presented considering the price. **❸**
Xinjiang Grand Xinhua Bei Lu ☏0991/2818788. International standard, with no less than four restaurants, a disco and health club. Even if you're not staying here, foreigners are usually granted the privilege of going up to the lounge on the top floor to watch satellite TV and use the toilets. **❼**
Xinjiang Northeast corner of Changjiang Lu and Qiantangjiang Lu ☏0991/5852511, ⓦwww.xjfd.com.cn. Just a 10min walk from the train station is this lively place full of Pakistani traders. Rooms are somewhat faded. Dorm beds ¥60, **❹**

The City

Ürümqi doesn't really have a well-defined centre as such, being more a collection of districts, though a couple of parks are useful for orientation. One is **Renmin Park** (daily 8am–10.15pm; ¥5), which runs from north to south right through the geographic centre of the city, cooled by various streams and ponds. The other is **Hongshan Park** (daily 7am–11pm; ¥10), clearly visible on a hill to the north of Renmin Park across Guangming Lu; it's a pleasant place with boating, pavilions and pagodas, and a steep hill to climb. At the top it's cool and shady and you can sit and have a drink, or watch the locals clambering about over the rocks. The view over the city from here, with construction cranes rising among the buildings and desert and snowy mountains in the background, is spectacular.

The major sight in Ürümqi is the **Xinjiang Museum** (Mon–Fri 9.30am– 7.30pm, otherwise 10.30am–5.30pm; ¥16), on Xibei Lu in the north of the city. The main building was closed for rebuilding at the time of writing, but exhibits had been moved to a smaller building directly behind the construction site. Exhibits focus on the Silk Road and include an array of tools, fabrics, coins, jade pieces, pots and pictures, along with a number of ancient and particularly well-preserved **corpses** retrieved from the dry desert sands, including the so-called "Loulan Beauty", a woman with long fair hair, allegedly 3800 years old, recovered from the city of Loulan on the Southern Silk Road (p.1074). Of a distinctly non-Chinese appearance, the Loulan Beauty has been taken to heart by some Uigur Nationalists as a symbol of the antiquity (and validity) of their claims for sovereignty over these lands. There are also some antique shops to browse on the museum site. Photos are strictly prohibited, but a few English signs are dotted around the place. To reach the museum, take bus #7 from Xinhua Bei Lu.

Shopping in Ürümqi can be quite an eye-opener – consumerism has reached China's final frontier, with fashion boutiques with pseudo-French and Italian names springing up along Xinhua Bei Lu, the main shopping street. For a taste of something with a more local flavour, head south of here, down Jiefang Nan Lu; the shops become steadily more Uigur-oriented, until you reach the Erdaoqiao Market, a great place for souvenir shopping, selling knives, handmade instruments, jade, carpets, clothes and various ornate crafts (bargain prices down to about one third of the initial cost). The **International Bazaar** complex opposite the Erdaoqiao market sells similar items at a relatively cheaper price and has a more relaxed atmosphere. A string of music shops run by one flank of the bazaar sell CDs of traditional Uigur music (see box, below). The major **mosques** of the city are all located in this area, too, around Jiefang Nan Lu.

Eating and drinking

The Uigur districts of town – principally around the Erdaoqiao Market, streets north off Renmin Lu, and lanes west of the post office – are good areas to snack on **street food**, especially kebabs and breads, the latter often baked in converted

Uigur music – *muqam*

Song and dance is at the core of Uigur cultural identity and is commonly presented at all social gatherings. The most established form of Uigur music, *muqam*, has developed since the sixth century into a unique collection of songs and instrumentals, quite separate from Arabic and Persian influence. A *muqam* must open with a flowing rhythm that complies with strict modal constraints, followed by a suite of pieces that tie into the opening. In the late 16th century scholars and folk musicians gathered to collate this music into a definitive collection of twelve *muqams*. The entire collection takes 24 hours to play and involves around fifteen traditional instruments such as the plucked mandolin-like rawap, metal stringed sitar and large dumbak drums. Sadly, few people can play *muqam* nowadays, but recordings are popular and sold on CD and DVD throughout Xinjiang.

oil-drum ovens, at around ¥2 each. Cheap and cheerful Chinese **restaurants** are all over the town: there's a great place a few doors northwest of the *Xinjiang Grand* serving noodles and buns; and a host of restaurants from pizza places to upmarket Uigur food run the length of Xinhua Lu. *Shuhan Fengwei Jiulou*, in a rounded building near Hongshan Park on Hongshan Lu, serves hotpots, along with good regional Chinese fare and Sichuanese-style cold snacks – portions are huge and cost about ¥15 a dish. Combining dinner and a stage performance appears commonplace in Ürümqi – try an upmarket buffet meal (dinner starts at 8pm and is around ¥60 per person) at the *Junbang Tianshan Fandian*, which includes song and dance performances and dazzling acrobatic displays. To get here, just walk off Xinhua Bei Lu, down the length of Minzhu Lu, and at the opposite end of the square carry on in the same direction for two minutes. To savour the best that Uigur food has to offer, and get a look at traditional dancing, eat at the *Miram Fandian*, two minutes' walk south of the *Overseas Chinese Hotel*. For air-conditioned luxury, the *Xinjiang Grand Hotel* does buffet breakfasts and lunches where you can eat as much as you like for about ¥60; their café makes a good attempt at coffee for ¥18 a cup.

Listings

Airlines China Southern's Xinjiang branch is on Youhao Lu (T0991/4516919 or 4516996, Wwww.cs -air.com); bus #101 heading west along Guangming Lu or #51 north up Changjiang Lu will get you there. Kyrgyzstan Airlines (T0991/2316638 or 2316333) is in the lobby of the *Overseas Chinese Hotel*.

Banks and exchange The main Bank of China is at the junction of Renmin Lu and Jiefang Lu (Mon–Fri 9.30am–1.30pm & 4.30–7.00pm).

Bookshops The Foreign Language Bookstore (daily 9am–6pm) on Xinhua Bei Lu has English novels, plus a few Chinese guidebooks to Xinjiang, on the second floor. Maps of Ürümuqi with English can also be purchased from here.

Cinema There is a modern Renmin cinema (Chinese-language only) in the ornate theatre building on Minzhu Lu.

Internet access There are two smoky Internet bars, charging ¥3/hr, sitting opposite each other past the airline offices on Youhao Lu.

Mail and telephones The main post office (daily 10am–8pm) west of the northern end of Renmin Park is one place to make long-distance calls. More simply, however, you can buy and use telephone cards in the lobbies of upmarket hotels, such as the *Xinjiang Grand*.

Travel agents Just about all places to stay have agents who can book train, bus and plane tickets for about ¥30, though they might need a few days' notice. Ürümqi CITS (T0991/2821427, Wwww.xinjiangtour.com) is located on Xinhua Nan Lu, close to the junction with Heilongjiang Lu, and offers the same services.

Tian Chi and Baiyang Gou

Tian Chi means "Heaven Lake", and this unspoilt natural haven 110km east of Ürümqi – the starting point of Vikram Seth's book *From Heaven Lake* – does almost live up to its name, especially for travellers who have spent long in the deserts of northwest China. At the cool, refreshing height of 2000m, the lake is surrounded by grassy meadows, steep, dense pine forests and jagged snow-covered peaks, including the mighty Bogda Feng, which soars to over 6000m, and the nicest feature of the area is that you can wander at will (you are likely to see eagles flying overhead as you trek towards the far side of the lake). There are no restrictions on accommodation (most people stay in yurts, with the semi-nomadic Kazakh population), and there is virtually limitless hiking. You need only to watch the **weather** – bitterly cold in winter, the lake is really only accessible during the summer months, May to September.

The **Kazakhs**, who lead a semi-nomadic herding existence in these hills, are organized into communes, very loosely managed by the State, which in theory owns both their land and animals and lets them out on fifteen- or thirty-year "contracts". Their traditional livelihood is from sheep, selling lambs in spring if the winter spares them. But it's a hard, unpredictable business – the State sometimes has to bail them out if the winter is a disastrous one – and revenues come increasingly from tourism. As in Inner Mongolia, the Kazakhs have taken to performing at horse shows, mostly for tourists. The extra income from providing visitors with food and accommodation is also welcome.

If you have not pre-booked your accommodation, you can simply set off to find yourself a **yurt**. Staying in one is a well-established custom, and you'll soon find people eager to cater for you. Most tourists lodge by the near side of the lake, but you can climb right up into the remote valleys of the Tian Shan – choose the right-hand main road around the lake to several Kazakh catering points – or you can hire a guide and a horse for the trip (¥50–100 per day), a service which young Kazakhs at the lakeside are happy to provide. Once up at the snowfields, the valleys are yours. Each is dotted with Kazakh yurts, and there's nearly always somewhere you can spend the night. One nice Kazakh stopover is **Dawanzi** close to the lake's edge, and about an hour's walk from the main camps as you approach the lake (look for the map on the way). If you come in May – considered the most beautiful time – you may get to try the alcoholic *kumiss*, fermented mare's milk, a rare delicacy. The rest of the year the Kazakhs make do with a kind of tea, with an infusion of dried snow lily and sheep's milk.

Practicalities

Access to the lake is by **bus** from Ürümqi. Buses leave (9am–3pm) from the northern entrance to Renmin Park, and cost ¥35 for a same-day return (double if you return another day) – try to buy your ticket the day before, from the bus stop. If you miss the last bus, and decide to take a taxi, it will be an expensive ¥200 minimum. The 120-kilometre journey takes around three hours, and the outward trip from Ürümqi is spectacular, initially through flat desert, then climbing through green meadows, conifer forests and along a wild mountain river. There's a ¥60 entrance fee to the lake area, which you pay just before arriving at the small lakeside **village** comprising a bus park, some shops and souvenir stands and a guesthouse – the only place to supply you with fresh water if you stay in the yurts with the Kazakhs. Be aware that if you come by private transport, you are expected to pay an extra ¥10 parking fee when purchasing entrance tickets.

Communication with the Kazakhs can be problematic. Few speak Chinese, let alone English, which sometimes results in unpleasant misunderstandings – you may find yourself being charged extra for every cup of tea. One way to avoid these anxieties is to join a **pre-booked tour**, which will include yurt accommodation as well as transport between Ürümqi and the lake. Agents such as CITS in Ürümqi offer these, but are relatively expensive and of dubious quality; the best people to book through seem to be the independent operators who hang around hotels frequented by budget travellers, as most are touting their own family yurts. Recommended is a Mr Rachit, who speaks a little English and offers two-night tours for ¥100 per person. Included in the price are delightful boat rides on the lake departing from his yurts in Dawanzi.

Baiyang Gou

Seventy-five kilometres south of Ürümqi spreads another natural paradise, the **Baiyang Gou** (Southern Pastures), located in a spur of the Tian Shan. Basically, it's another green valley with a stream and a waterfall, and a backdrop of fir trees and snowy peaks. The Kazakhs and Uzbeks also like to summer here and, accordingly, there are opportunities for tourists to join them. Horse-riding trips to the waterfall take about an hour and cost around ¥50 per person. At the time of writing, the road to the entrance of the pastures was under construction, and no entrance fee was being charged. Commute here by taking the **bus** (¥7) from the depot well hidden in a lane off Heilongjiang Lu. You'll need buses to **Xi Baiyanggou** which run from 9.30am to 4.30pm, four times a day. Accommodation is available at the pasture in summertime.

Yining and around

The pretty **Ili Valley** is centred around the city of **Yining** (known to the Uigurs as Kulja), just 60km east of the border with Kazakhstan, and 400km northwest of Ürümqi. As it is right off the principal Silk Road routes, not many travellers make the detour to get here, but if you have the time, or you're travelling to Kazakhstan, the trip is worthwhile. Ili is one of the three so-called **Kazakh Autonomous Prefectures** within Xinjiang (the other two are Karamay and Altai), which form a block along the northwest frontier. Despite the nominal Kazakh preponderance, the Uigurs are the more dominant minority group in the city, and there have been occasional protests against Beijing's rule here – notably in 1997 when rioting took place. Today, however, after years of Han migration, the "frontier" character of Yining is fast disappearing.

The **climate** in the valley is relatively cool and fresh even at the height of summer (very chilly sometimes – make sure you have warm clothes whatever the time of year), and the views of the Tian Shan – from all routes into Yining, especially if you're coming up from Kuqa to the south – are fabulous. The road climbs the harsh, rocky landscape of the northern Taklamakan, then enters pure alpine scenery with marching forests of pine, azure skies and the glorious blue waters of **Big Dragon Lake**, before drifting into a vast grassland ringed by snowy peaks. At the time of writing, however, a tunnel 130km north of Kuqa had collapsed, forcing an inconvenient 400-kilometre detour in either direction; the road should reopen by the end of 2005. Another draw, north of Yining, is the beautiful **Sayram Lake**, where you can find accommodation in Kazakh yurts.

Yining and around		
Yining	伊宁	*yīníng*
Chapucha'er	察布查尔	*chábù chá'ěr*
Hoegs Pass	霍尔果斯口岸	*huò'ěr guǒsī kǒu'àn*
Huiyuan	惠远	*huìyuàn*
Sayram Lake	赛里木湖	*sàilǐmù hú*
Tomb of Telug Timur	吐虎鲁克铁木尔墓	*tǔhǔ lǔkè tiěmù'ěr mù*
Accommodation		
Ili	伊犁宾馆	*yīlí bīnguǎn*
Yaxiya	亚细亚宾馆	*yàxìyà bīnguǎn*
Yilite Dajiuiian	伊力特大酒店	*yīlìtè dàjiǔdiàn*
Youdian	邮电宾馆	*yóudiàn bīnguǎn*
Youyi	友谊宾馆	*yǒuyí bīnguǎn*
Ili	伊犁	*yīlí*

The **history** of the Ili Valley is one of intermittent Chinese control. At the time of the Han dynasty, two thousand years ago, the area was occupied by the **Wusun kingdom**. The Wusun people, ancestors of today's Kazakhs, kept diplomatic relations with the Han court and were responsible for introducing them to the horse. By the eighth century, however, a Tang-dynasty army had taken control of the region for China – its value as a staging post for a newly developing branch of the Silk Road was too great a temptation. In the thirteenth and fourteenth centuries, the area was controlled first by Genghis Khan from the east, then Tamerlane from the west. This east–west tug of war has gone on ever since, with the Qing seizing the area in the eighteenth century, only for the Russians to march in, in 1871, under the cover of Yakub Beg's Xinjiang rebellion (see p.1045). There remained a significant Russian presence in one form or another until 1949, and traces of this can still be seen in the architecture of Yining. During the 1960s there was a forced mass exodus of sixty thousand Kazakhs and Uigurs to the USSR, an event which has left behind much bitterness.

Yining

YINING today is a booming city and as such has changed almost unrecognizably from the remote backwater it once was. Nevertheless, it's a small, compact place, pleasant for walking, and with an extraordinary amount of food for sale from street vendors. The centre of town isn't readily obvious – most of the action seems to straddle the length of **Jiefang Lu**, though the old city is centred around **Qingnian Park** to the southeast. The **Uigur bazaars**, just south of Qingnian Park, are well worth exploring.

The **bus station** is located in the northwest of the city, miraculously well concealed on Jiefang Lu. Buses depart hourly to Ürümqi from 9am until late (¥120), and two daily buses serve Kashgar (3pm and 3.30pm, 48hr). A daily service to Kuqa also departs at 9am (¥145) – fierce competition between

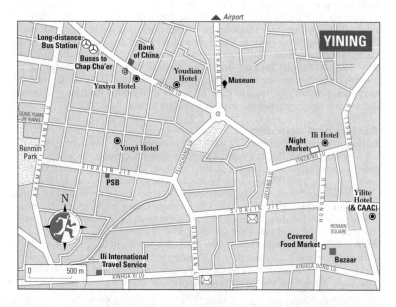

government and private operators drives down prices and ensures that service is good, though private buses leave only when full, despite any guarantees made by their drivers. If you stand still for more than a second at the station, a host of touts will invariably crowd around you, each shouting the name of the place to which his bus departs. Another interesting bus service out of Yining is a daily bus, leaving at 9am, to Almaty (Mon–Sat, 12hr; US$30) through the Hoegs Pass in China and into Kazakhstan, though Kazakhstan visas, now essential, are not available here (see p.1058). There is no train to Yining, though plans to connect it with the nearby rail stop in Qinghe are underway. The only **flights** here are to and from Ürümqi. Yining's **CAAC** office (T0999/8044000) is in the *Yilite Hotel*, but their tickets are hard to book at short notice, so you may prefer to try a **travel service** – for example, the Ili International Travel Service (T0999/8020042), down on Xinhua Xi Lu (bus #1), where a little English is spoken.

Accommodation

A good **place to stay** is the *Ili Hotel* (T0999/8023126, F8024964; ④), an old-fashioned place, in huge leafy grounds. There are a number of buildings offering varying degrees of comfort and different prices – the cheaper no. 4 building, for example, offers respectable, if small, doubles with bath (¥140). To reach the hotel from the bus station, take bus #1 heading east for three stops, cross over the road and it's a few minutes' walk east along Yingbing Lu.

Another long-standing hotel in Yining is the *Youyi* (Friendship Hotel) (T0999/8023901, F8024631; ④), with cheap doubles in the old wing (¥150) and smarter singles and doubles in the new wing (¥250). Dorms do exist, though it may depend upon which member of staff you talk to, whether these are available to foreigners. Also, if you are travelling alone, they might insist you pay for all the beds in the dorm. The hotel is far from any bus route; leaving the bus station, continue right along Jiefang Lu until you pass the **Bank of China** on the left-hand side of the road, take the next street on your right and walk for a good ten minutes to find the hotel. On the way, you'll pass another, smaller, place called the *Yaxiya* (T0999/8031800; ④, dorm beds ¥50). There's no English sign, but you can recognize it from the Greek columns outside; the doubles with bath are clean and modern and breakfast is included in the price. Back on the main road, a little farther down from the bus station, is the *Youdian* (T0999/8023844; ③), offering mid-range doubles, slightly the worse for wear but not bad value. An alternative is the new *Yilite* (T0999/7829000; ⑤) on the crossroads just east of Qingnian Park. It's not in a very interesting part of town, but offers a range of good-size and smart rooms at reasonable prices.

Eating and drinking

Eating in Yining is fun, where bundles of street stalls appear around the town as the sun sets, though this can depend on the weather. Opposite the *Yaxiya Hotel* there is a nice Sichuan restaurant on the first floor where *tangcu liji*, a sweet and sour pork dish, both filling and satisfying, is highly popular. The *Ili Hotel* has a pleasant Chinese restaurant, and an expensive Western restaurant associated with it, and just outside the hotel, on the right, is a busy **Uigur night market**. Roast chickens, *samsa*, kebabs and noodles are all available, and afterwards you can play the locals on the pool tables out the back. This is a good place to try the local **beer**, which is made with honey – the distinctive bottles all have a black rubber cork and cost just ¥2.5, though it is advisable to try no more than one of this sticky and sweet concoction. The street opposite the *Ili*, leading down to Qingnian Park, has lots of **outdoor restaurants** – a whole *dapan ji* costs around

¥40. Immediately south of the Qingnian Park is a covered food market. Here you can get food from all over China, including *baozi*, hotpots and grilled fish. You can also buy the excellent and locally made *kurut* – hard, dry little **cheeses** – from street vendors. Finally, the Ili Valley is famous for its **fruit** – apricots in June, grapes and peaches in July.

Around Yining

There are a couple of obscure and unusual destinations within a day of Yining. About 20km south is the little town of **Chapucha'er**, home to the **Xibo** people, a tiny minority numbering just twenty-eight thousand, who are of Manchu descent despatched to Xinjiang in 1764 as warriors to guard and colonize the area. The Xibo still zealously preserve their own language, script and other customs, including a prowess in archery that is of Olympic standard. Chapucha'er is just thirty minutes by bus from outside Yining's long-distance bus station (or ¥30 by taxi). From the same bus station, there are also buses to **Huiyuan**, 30km west of Yining, a small but historic town with a three-storey **drum tower** (¥6) dating from the nineteenth century. Another 20km north of here is the pretty Persian-style **tomb of Telug Timur** (¥6), a fourteenth-century Muslim leader, located just outside the small town of **Qingshui**. You can climb a staircase to the upper floor and even onto the roof to see the view. Renovations are underway, and a small exhibition room is being built to explain the site. To visit Huiyuan and the tomb of Telug Timur as a combined trip from Yining, rent a car from a travel service – a day with the car will cost about ¥300. Theoretically, foreigners visiting anywhere around Yining other than Chapucha'er require a special permit (¥150), which the Ili International Travel Service can arrange for you. You'll be subject to a fine between ¥500 and ¥5000 if you're unlucky enough to be caught without one.

About 180km out of Yining, on the road east to Ürümqi, **Sayram Lake** occupies a fantastic location between mountains and grassy banks. More than 2000m above sea level and decidedly chilly for most of the year, Sayram is a great place to escape the urban hustle. Tourism here is still very much at a pioneering stage – there are simple **guesthouses** (¥200) at the lakeside, otherwise you can try to find accommodation in a Kazakh or Mongol **yurt**. Every year on July 13–15 thousands of Kazakhs and Mongolian nomads congregate here for traditional games and entertainment. Another interesting venture is to a small pagoda isolated on an island in the middle of the lake. Access to and from the lake is by bus from Yining (3hr) or Ürümqi (15hr); given the frequency of the buses on this route it should be easy to pick one up if you stand on the road.

Korla to Kashgar: the Northern Silk Road

Some 300km southwest of Ürümqi, and 400km southwest of Turpan, the wealthy but dull town of **Korla** marks the start of the most direct route to Kashgar, which follows the ancient Northern Silk Road (see box, p.962). Having crossed the Tian Shan and entered the Tarim Basin, this route skirts round the northern rim of the Taklamakan Desert for more than 1000km, flanked by snowy peaks. The region is largely a barren wilderness, though there are occasional transitions from parched desert to green pasture in the rare places where water from the Tian Shan has found its way down to the plain.

The Northern Silk Road

Korla	库尔勒	*kùěrlè*
Hualing Bus Station	华凌汽车站	*huálíng qìchēzhàn*
Jiaoyuan Binguan	教园宾馆	*jiàoyuán bīnguǎn*
Main bus station	汽车客运总站	*qìchē kèyùn zǒngzhàn*
Silverstar Hotel	银星大酒店	*yínxīng dàjiǔdiàn*
Tiemen Guan	铁门关	*tiěmén guān*
Yumizhixiang	渔米之湘	*yúmǐ zhīxiāng*
Bositun Hu	博斯腾湖	*bósīténg hú*
Bohu Xian	博湖县	*bóhú xiàn*
Yanqi Xian	焉耆县	*yānqí xiàn*
Kuqa	库车	*kùchē*
Kizil Thousand Buddha Caves	克孜尔千佛洞	*kèzī'ěr qiānfódòng*
Qiuci Ruined City	龟兹古城	*qiūcī gǔchéng*
Subashi Ancient Buddhist Complex	苏巴什佛寺遗址	*sūbāshí fósì yízhǐ*
Tomb of Molana Ashidinhan	默拉纳额什丁坟	*mòlānà'é shídīng fén*
Accommodation and eating		
Australian Style Noodles	澳大利亚风情面馆	*àodàlìyà fēngqíng miànguǎn*
Best Food Burger	百富汉堡	*bǎifù hànbǎo*
Kala Kuer Binguan	卡拉库尔宾馆	*kǎlākùěr bīnguǎn*
Kuqa Hotel	库车宾馆	*kùchē bīnguǎn*
Meile Chuancai	美乐川菜馆	*měilè chuāncàiguǎn*
Minmao	民贸宾馆	*mínmào bīnguǎn*
Qiuci	龟兹宾馆	*qiūcī bīnguǎn*

The small oasis towns west of Korla usually comprise brown mud-built houses, perhaps a few vine trellises, and thick muddy water running in trenches beside the streets; **Kuqa**, about a third of the way to Kashgar, is worth a stopover for its Old Town's traditional feel, and a couple of low-key Silk Road relics in the surrounding deserts.

The **road** is in fairly good condition, though given the vast distances involved, it makes much more sense to use the parallel **railway** (completed in 2000), with two services daily running the full distance from Ürümqi, via Korla and Kuqa, to Kashgar; Ürümqi to Kashgar takes 24 hours in an air-conditioned train, instead of at least 36 hours of dust, baking heat and boredom in a bus seat. While epic bus journeys do have their attractions, diehards will find more of interest in the three-day trip to Kashgar via the Southern Silk Road (see p.1072).

Korla

There's been a settlement at **KORLA** (**Kuerle** in Chinese) since at least Tang times, and today the city is capital of the **Bayangol Mongol Autonomous Prefecture**, a vast region that encompasses the eastern side of the Taklamakan as well as better watered areas around the city itself. Despite all this, Mongols themselves are not much in evidence today in a Korla that is termed the "national clean city" and functions mostly as a base for companies – including the US conglomerate Exxon – tapping into the Taklamakan's **oil reserves**. It's also of inescapable interest as a transport nexus: the rail line and roads from

Ürümqi and Turpan converge here; the Northern Silk Road heads due west; and the Southern Silk Road curves down around the eastern side of the Taklamakan via Ruoqiang. The town is also a terminus for buses shortcutting the Southern Silk Road by crossing diagonally southwest across the Taklamakan to Minfeng and Khotan. There isn't anything aside from transport connections to justify a stopover here, though the grey brickwork and red-tiled roof of the Ming-dynasty **Tiemen Guan** (¥6), the Iron Gateway, asserts Korla's age in the face of what is otherwise a relentlessly modern city – you'll see it from the bus to the north of town. In summer, locals spend all their spare time 67km east at **Bositun Hu** (¥30), a huge lake where you can cool off in the water, rent a beach umbrella, and kick back on the sand, admiring distant desert mountain ranges. For Bositun Hu, a taxi return including two hours waiting costs around ¥250. Alternatively, you can take a bus from Korla bus station to **Bohu Xian** or **Yanqi Xian**, which are both quite close to the lake. If you come with a tour, however, you will probably be dropped off at Lianhua Hu (Lotus Lake), a much more touristy resort, 25km from Korla.

Practicalities

Korla's **centre** is only about 1km across, bisected from west to east by the main street, Renmin Lu, home to a massive **Bank of China** (daily 9.30am–1.30pm & 4.30–7.30pm) and lined with upmarket **hotels** – including the four-star *Silverstar Hotel* (℡0996/2028888, ℻2216868; ➍) – and oil-company and mining offices. One cheaper option is the clean and newly-furnished *Jiaoyuan Binguan* (➌, dorm bed ¥30), a few minutes' walk north from the east end of Renmin Lu. The **main bus station** is on Beishan Lu, north off Jiaotong Dong Lu, and has frequent departures through the day to Ürümqi and Turpan. For Kashgar, Khotan via Minfeng, Kuqa and Ruoqiang on the Southern Silk Road, you'll need to go to the **Hualing Bus Station** at the north end of Beishan Lu, about 600m from the main bus station. The **train station**, on the Hami–Ürümqi–Kashgar line, is about 3km east at the end of the #1 bus route from Renmin Lu. Taxis cost ¥5 to anywhere in town. A good place for **food** is the moderately smart *Yumizhixiang*, on the street southeast of *Silverstar Hotel*. The food is in spicy Hunan style; try their *mutong fan* – steamed rice with flavoured vegetables and meat in a bamboo bucket.

Kuqa and around

KUQA (pronounced "ku-cher" and known to the Chinese as **Kuche**) was once a cosmopolitan town full of Silk Road traders and travellers, the "land of jewels" in Xuanzang's journal. It lies about 300km to the west of Korla, past one of the world's largest **wind farms** laid out across the desert. A good place to break the long journey to Kashgar, it's a small town with a long history, and a largely Uigur population. The fourth-century linguist and scholar **Kumarajiva**, one of the most famous of all Chinese Buddhists, came from here. Having travelled to Kashmir for his education, he later returned to China as a teacher and translator of Buddhist documents from Sanskrit into Chinese. It was in large measure thanks to him that Buddhism came to be so widely understood in China and, by the early Tang, Kuqa was a major **centre of Buddhism** in China. The fantastic wealth of the trade caravans subsidized giant monasteries here, and Xuanzang, passing through the city in the sixth century, reported the existence of two huge Buddha statues, 27m high, guarding its entrances. The city even had its own Indo-European language. With the arrival of Islam in the ninth century, however, this era finally began to draw to a close, and today only a few traces of Kuqa's ancient past remain.

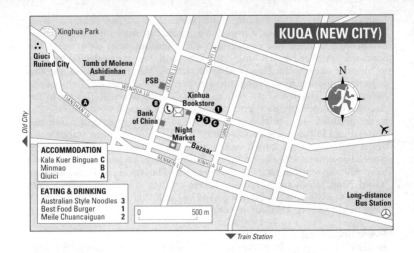

KUQA (NEW CITY)

N

Old City

Train Station

ACCOMMODATION
Kala Kuer Binguan C
Minmao   B
Qiuci   A

EATING & DRINKING
Australian Style Noodles 3
Best Food Burger   1
Meile Chuancaiguan   2

Xinghua Park
Qiuci Ruined City
Tomb of Molena Ashidinhan
PSB
Xinhua Bookstore
Bank of China
Night Market
Bazaar
Long-distance Bus Station

0   500 m

The City

There's little evidence now of Kuqa's past wealth; today the city is dusty and poor. It is effectively in two parts, the old (to the west) and the new (to the east), lying a few kilometres apart. The New City, largely Han-populated, is uninteresting but contains all the facilities you'll need, while the Old City, largely Uigur, is peppered with mosques and bazaars and has a Central Asian atmosphere. To reach the Old City, take any bus heading west along Renmin Lu, the main street on which the bus station is located, until you reach a bridge across the river – the old city lies beyond the river. A **Friday market**, where the Uigur population are out in force in both sections of town, buying and selling leather jackets, carpets, knives, wooden boxes, goats and donkeys, is not to be missed, though it's a much smaller affair than at Kashgar.

From the **New City**, a couple of sights are easily accessible. One is the remains of the ruined city of **Qiuci** (the old name for Kuqa), though there is nothing really to see beyond a solid, weatherbeaten mud wall. If you follow Tianshan Lu from the new city, the ruined city is about ten minutes' walk west of the *Qiuci Hotel*. Across the road from the old wall is the neglected **Xinghua Park** (¥3) – a peaceful place for a picnic. Slightly more interesting is the nearby **Tomb of Molena Ashidinhan**, built in 1867, a simple shrine made of wood, in honour of an Arab missionary who came to the city, probably in the fourteenth century. It's on Wenhua Lu, about fifteen minutes' walk west of the *Minmao Hotel*. There's also a daily **bazaar** in the lane running east for several blocks from the Bank of China, north of and parallel with Xinhua Lu, containing Xinjiang's second-largest **goldsmiths' quarters** (after Kashgar's).

The bridge leading to the **Old City** is really where the main area of interest begins. Right by the bridge, the **bazaar** is the main venue for the Friday market; cattle and sheep are traded on the river banks below. Beyond the bridge, you can soon lose yourself in the labyrinth of narrow streets and mud-brick houses. Right in the heart of this area, fifteen minutes approximately northeast of the bridge, is the **Kuqa Mosque** (¥10), built in 1923. Delightfully neat and compact, with an attractive green-tiled dome, this mosque is of wholly arabesque design, displaying none of the Chinese characteristics of mosques in more eastern parts of the country. Beyond the mosque, on Linji

Lu, is the **museum** (Nov–April 10am–9.30pm & May–Oct 9.30am–8.30pm; ¥15), housing interesting collections of Qiuci relics. The four rooms (labelled in English) exhibit pottery, coins, ancient clothes and a few frescoes – if you don't have time to visit the cave paintings around Kuqa, it's well worth a visit. From the bridge, there are rusty blue English signs indicating the mosque and the museum along the main road, or you can hire a donkey cart for less than ¥1 per person per trip.

Practicalities

Flights connect Kuqa with Ürümqi; the **airport** is a very short taxi ride (¥10) east of the New City. The **bus station** is in the far southeast of the New City with regular services to Korla (10am–6pm, 3.5hr), Ürümqi and Turpan (both 5am–8.30pm, 12hr and 15hr respectively); Kashgar buses don't originate in town – you'll need to take the bus to Aksu (11 daily; 10am–7.30pm) first and change from there. Kuqa's **train station** is 5km southeast of the New City (¥5 in a taxi), with two trains daily west to Kashgar, and three east to Ürümqi (the other eastbound service stops in Korla). You can only buy hard-seat tickets here, and only just before the train pulls in; go to carriage seven to upgrade on board, or try an agent to reserve you something better. Your accommodation will know the current train timetable.

For plane tickets out of Kuqa, and for **booking tours** of the sites outside the city, it's worth paying a call on the friendly Kuqa **CITS** (⊕0997/7136016, ⊕7122524; Mon–Sat 10am–1.30pm & 3.30–7.30pm), in the *Qiuci Hotel*. Commission fee on a plane ticket is ¥40. For train tickets, though, they are reluctant to help independent travellers.

There are a couple of **hotels** right outside the bus station, but this is a rather distant corner of the town to stay in. To reach the more central hotels from here, catch bus #2 from just in front of the station, heading west. Get off at the second stop and take the next road north, Jiefang Lu. Motor-rickshaws also operate from the station, or it's around a twenty-minute walk. The *Minmao* (⊕0997/7122888; ❸), on the southwest side of the intersection between Jiefang Lu and Wenhua Lu, is a convenient place to stay; rooms have old furniture but are reasonably priced. Five minutes' walk farther north up Jiefang Lu is the *Kuqa Hotel* (⊕0997/7122901; ❹) – the rooms are big and bright, offering 24-hour hot water, and the buildings have their own gardens. One block east of the **post office**, the *Kala Kuer Binguan* is clean and neat (⊕0997/7122957; dorm beds ¥50, ❸). The most upmarket accommodation in town is at the secluded *Qiuci Hotel* on Tianshan Lu (⊕0997/7122005, ⊕7129774; ❺), a few minutes west of the New City. For visa extensions, the **PSB** (Mon–Fri 9.30am–7.30pm) is on Jiefang Lu, five minutes' walk north of *Minmao Hotel*. There's also a **Bank of China** (Mon–Fri 9.30am–8pm) south from here.

One thing worth trying in Kuqa is the **giant nan bread** (¥1.5); unlike elsewhere in Xinjiang, the nan bread here is thin and crispy and covered with onion, sesame and carrot bits. Near the new town's market area around the Renmin Lu-Youyi Lu intersection are numerous food stands – hugely busy on Fridays – where you can tuck into delicious baked *kaobao*, *samsa*, bowls of *laghman* and Uigur tea, with great rough sticks and leaves floating in the cup. On Xinhua Lu, a little east of Jiefang Lu, is a busy, smoky **night market** full of the usual kebabs and roast chickens, as well as plenty of fresh fruit in season. Outside the *Kala Kuer* hotel is a string of small Uigur restaurants, where you can sit outside among the locals. Try the canteen-like *Australian Style Noodles* (English sign outside), bizarrely decorated with fake bamboo – the food isn't Aussie – their *dingding chaomian* (¥5) is a cube-shaped noodle dish cooked with tomato sauces, meat and spring onion. A couple of minutes west is a family-run Chinese restaurant, *Meile Chuancaiguan*, serving cheap Sichuan food. If you want something Western, there's a *Best Food Burger* opposite the *Kala Kuer* hotel.

Around Kuqa

Around Kuqa, you can explore a whole series of ruined cities and Buddhist cave sites. Probably the two most significant of these are the **Subashi Ancient Buddhist Complex**, 30km north of Kuqa along a good paved road, and the **Kizil Thousand Buddha Caves**, 75km to the northwest. The Kizil Caves, in particular, were once a Central Asian treasure trove, a mixture of Hellenistic, Indian and Persian styles with not even a suggestion of Chinese influence. Sadly, the caves suffered the ravages of the German archeologist and art thief Albert Von Le Coq (see p.1056) who, at the beginning of the twentieth century, cut out and carried away many of the best frescoes. However, it is still an interesting place to visit and even older than the more extensive Mogao caves in Gansu. Your ticket (¥35) covers eight caves but you can pay extra to be guided round others, including no. 38, the "cave of musicians" – which has Bodhisattvas playing musical instruments on the ceiling.

The **Subashi Ancient Buddhist Complex**, abandoned in the twelfth century, comprises fairly extensive ruins from east to west intercepted by a river. The entrance fee is ¥15 to each side – the west parts of the ruins are more interesting and contain various pagodas and temples, and the remains of some wall paintings. The entire site looks very atmospheric with the bald, pink and black mountain ranges rising up behind. Along the way there, look for the **irrigation channels** carrying runoff from the mountains to villages.

To visit either of these sites, you'll need to rent a car (Kuqa CITS can arrange this – their day-trip tour to both Subashi and Kizil costs ¥300) or simply stop a taxi and start negotiating – ¥1 per kilometre covered is a reasonable rate, so expect to pay ¥150 for the round trip to Kizil, and ¥60 for Subashi.

The Southern Silk Road

Originally, the **Southern Silk Road** split off from the northern route near Dunhuang in Gansu province, crossed to **Ruoqiang** on the eastern edge of the Taklamakan, then skirted the southern rim of the desert before rejoining the northern road at Kashgar. In modern times this route has fallen into almost total obscurity, lacking as it does any major city and connected by poor roads and minimal transport. Of the two branches, however, this route is actually the older and historically more important of the two. The most famous Silk Road travellers used it, including the Chinese Buddhist pilgrims Fa Xian and Xuanzang (see p.1050), as well as Marco Polo, and, in the 1930s, the British journalist and adventurer Peter Fleming. The ancient settlements along the way were oases in the desert, kept alive by streams flowing down from the snowy peaks of the Kunlun Shan, which constitute the outer rim of the Tibetan plateau to the south.

Following what remains of this southern route opens up the prospect of travelling overland from Turpan to Kashgar one way, and returning another way, thus circumnavigating the entire Taklamakan Desert. The southern route is not to everyone's taste, in that it chiefly comprises desert interspersed with extremely dusty oasis towns, with none of the green or the tourist facilities of the northern route; nor is there a rail line to fall back on if bus travel loses its

The Southern Silk Road

Khotan	和田	*hétián*
Carpet factory	地毯厂	*dìtǎn chǎng*
Jade Dragon Kashgar River	玉龙喀什河	*yùlóng kāshíhé*
Jade factory	玉器厂	*yùqì chǎng*
Jiya Xiang	吉亚乡	*jíyà xiāng*
Melikawat	米力克瓦特古城	*mǐlìkèwǎtè gǔchéng*
Silk factory	丝厂	*sīchǎng*
Accommodation and eating		
Hetian	和田宾馆	*hétián bīnguǎn*
Hetian Yingbinguan	和田迎宾馆	*hétián yíngbīnguǎn*
Huimin Fanguan	回民饭馆	*huímín fàndiàn*
Jiaotong	交通宾馆	*jiāotōng bīnguǎn*
Maixiang Yuan Bakery	麦香园蛋糕坊	*màixiāngyuán dàngāofǎng*
Xiangchuan Boziwang	湘川钵子王	*xiāngchuān bōziwáng*
Yurong	玉融宾馆	*yùróng bīnguǎn*
Minfeng	民丰	*mínfēng*
Tarim Desert Expressway	沙漠公路	*shāmò gōnglù*
Xiyu Binguan	西域宾馆	*xīyù bīnguǎn*
Qiemo	且末	*qiěmò*
Qiemo Gucheng	且末古城	*qiěmò gǔchéng*
Muzitage	木孜塔格宾馆	*mùzī tǎgé bīnguǎn*
Ruoqiang	若羌	*ruòqiāng*
Jiaotong Binguan	交通宾馆	*jiāotōng bīnguǎn*
Miran	米兰古城	*mǐlán gǔchéng*
Lop Nor	罗布泊	*luóbù bó*
Loulan	楼兰古城	*loúlán gǔchéng*
Yarkand	莎车	*shāchē*
Altunluq mosque	阿勒屯清真寺	*ālètún qīngzhēnsì*
Amannisahan tomb	阿曼尼莎汗纪念陵	*āmànnísāhàn jìniànlíng*
Meraj Restaurant	米热吉快餐	*mǐrèjì kuàicān*
Shanche Binguan	莎车宾馆	*shāchē bīnguǎn*
Yecheng	叶城	*yèchéng*
Jiaotong	交通宾馆	*jiāotōng bīnguǎn*
Yecheng Dianli	叶城电力宾馆	*yèchéng diànlì bīnguǎn*
Yengisar	英吉沙	*yīngjí shā*
Knife Factory	英吉沙县小刀厂	*yīngjíshā xiàn xiǎodāochǎng*

appeal. Nevertheless, it represents the chance to visit an extremely little-known corner of China, where foreigners are still a rare sight.

Today, there is no sealed road covering the eastern section of the original route between Dunhuang and Ruoqiang, though there are other roads to Ruoqiang from Korla and, less reliably, from Gansu and Qinghai provinces. Once at Ruoqiang – itself 450km from Korla – a decent road runs 1400km around the southern perimeter of the Taklamakan to Kashgar, with the ancient city of **Khotan** the pick of places to get off the bus and explore. You can also reach Khotan more or less directly from Korla, via the splendid 522km-long

Tarim Desert Expressway which traverses the very heart of the Taklamakan and is one of the longest desert roads in the world. For the truly intrepid, it's possible to leave the Southern Silk Road between Khotan and Kashgar and slip south **into Tibet** – for foreigners, an illegal (though regularly travelled) route to Lhasa which will severely test your abilities to travel rough.

From Korla to Khotan

The most painless way to deal with the southern route is to take the desert expressway southwest from Korla **across the Taklamakan** to **Minfeng** and Khotan. It's a very quick road, and the whole one-thousand-kilometre trip between Korla and Khotan takes a mere seventeen hours. Built by the oil companies in the late 1990s, the road gives you a close-up of why the Uigurs call this desert the "Sea of Death". Unfortunately, most buses coming either way make the crossing at night, so you don't get a view of the impressive irrigation grid that provides water for shrubs to protect the road from the ever-shifting desert sands.

For a dustier, rougher, more rewarding trip to Khotan, you'll want to catch a bus southeast from Korla around the eastern edge of the Taklamakan to **Ruoqiang**. It's also theoretically possible to get here from Dunhuang or Golmud along routes which approximately parallel the original Silk Road. One possible route involves negotiating a jeep from Ruoqiang to Shimian Kuang (Mine of Asbestos), then taking a bus from the mine to Huatu Gou where you will find more regular buses into Gansu or Qinghai. Foreigners used to be pulled off buses by policemen and kicked back in the direction they came from, probably due to the proximity of **Lop Nur**, a huge salty marshland covering 3000 square kilometres northeast of Ruoqiang that happens to be China's **nuclear test site**.

Ruoqiang

A small, busy place, **RUOQIANG** (**Charkhlik** to the Uigurs) is most notable for being the jumping-off point for treks by camel or jeep out to two little-known ruined cities of Silk Road vintage. **Accommodation** is available at the primitive *Jiaotong Binguan* (❸, dorm bed ¥30) just north of the bus station. The first of these, **Miran** (¥100) – subject of Christa Paula's book *Voyage to Miran* – is relatively accessible, approximately 75km northeast of Ruoqiang; a far more ambitious trip would be to **Loulan**, at least 250km from town on the western edge of Lop Nor. Loulan is particularly intriguing, as its very existence had been completely forgotten until the Swedish explorer **Sven Anders Hedin** rediscovered the site, which had been buried in sand, in the early twentieth century; it wasn't until the 1980s that the first Chinese archeological surveys were undertaken. Remains include traces of the city walls and huge numbers of collapsed wooden and adobe houses; the site was also littered with wooden bowls and plates. Foundations of a pagoda indicate a Buddhist population, graves yielded mummified corpses of non-Chinese appearance wrapped in silk and wool (see p.1061), and **Han-dynasty coins** reveal the city's age. What little is known about Loulan comes from contemporary records written in Chinese and a northern Indian language found here, which mention that large numbers of people were abandoning the city in the early fourth century – why is a mystery. Certainly by 399, when the Buddhist monk Fa Xian passed through this area, Loulan was depopulated. Unfortunately, the entrance fee to Loulan for foreigners is an absurd ¥3000 (compared to ¥1500 for Chinese), so unless you are an archeological expert this may not be the place for you.

Qiemo and Minfeng

Back on the Kashgar road, the next settlement of any size is **QIEMO** (Cher-chen), another small, surprisingly modern town famed for the frequency of its sandstorms (especially in April), and lying some 360km southwest of Ruoqiang. There are more **ruins** about 10km to the northwest at **Qiemo Gucheng** – dated to at least 2000 years old. A taxi here and back shouldn't cost more than ¥30, though the entrance fee depends upon how well your driver knows the site staff, ranging from ¥15 to ¥300. The *Muzitage* hotel (℡0996/7622687; ℱ7622687; ❹) in the northwest of the city on Yingbin Lu near the airport (closed at the time of writing), is a comfortable place to stay, despite the lack of hot water; they can also arrange trips to Qiemo Gucheng.

From here it's a further 300km west to **MINFENG**, where you meet up with the trans-Taklamakan expressway from Korla. You can stay at the simple *Xiyu Binguan* (❷, dorm beds ¥40), 50m north of Minfeng's bus station. Minfeng comes alive every evening, when long-distance buses converge and the main street becomes one long chaotic strip of kebab, bread and noodle vendors. On the final 300km between here and Khotan, you pass through some of the most vividly empty landscapes you will ever see, an indication of what the centre of the Taklamakan must be like: a formless expanse of sky and desert merging at a vague, dusty yellow horizon.

Khotan and around

KHOTAN (known in Chinese as **Hetian**) has for centuries been famed through-out the country for its **carpets**, **silk** and **white jade**. A bleak and dusty grid of wide streets, the town itself is pretty ordinary, but the substantial Uigur popula-tion is hospitable, and there's ample opportunity to watch the materials for which Khotan is famed being worked in much the same way as they always have been.

The Town

Khotan centres on Tuanjie Square, from where the city is partitioned by two main roads – Beijing Lu (running east–west) and Tanaiyi Lu (north–south). The

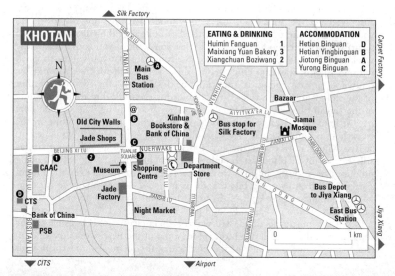

crenelated **old city walls** still dot along the west side of Tanaiyi Bei Lu, east of the river – surrounded by fences in a vain effort to protect them from development. The giant sculpture in the middle of the square is Chairman Mao shaking hands with a local Uigur old man, an actual person who went to Beijing to congratulate the Communist party's victory in the 1950s – the symbol still serves its function, though the hostility of the local Uigurs towards Han Chinese is not a secret. Immediately to the south end of the square is the **jade factory** where you can see craftsmen bent over small lathes. The results of their labour are on sale in the shop above, with prices between ¥30 and ¥30,000, and in shops all over the town, particularly along Beijing Xi Lu.

You can see more hard labour going on at the fascinating **bazaar** which takes place every Friday and Sunday. Silk, carpets, leather jackets, fruit and spices are all on sale, with innumerable blacksmiths, tinsmiths, goldsmiths and carpenters hard at work among the stalls. The bazaar stretches across the whole of the northeast part of town, and the easiest way to reach it is to head east along Aiyitika'er Lu, off Wenhua Lu near the centre. Follow the stalls south towards Jiamai Lu, along where you can see a pretty Jiamai Mosque.

About 4km to the east of town, following Beijing Dong Lu, is the **Jade Dragon Kashgar River** from which, historically, so much jade has been recovered, and which still yields the odd stone for casual searchers. The river flows through a wide, stony plain; it's easy to get down here and forage, but you'll need to find one of the locals – who come here with garden forks to rake the stones – to show you what you are looking for or you may end up with a pocketful of pretty but worthless quartz.

The town **carpet factory** stands just across the river to the left; it's particularly worth a visit if you are interested in making a purchase. Prices here, and in the shop in town, are very cheap (around ¥3500 for a 5m x 2.5m handmade carpet). The atmosphere in the factory workshop is friendly, with the workers, mostly young women, exchanging banter as they weave with incredible dexterity. They encourage visitors to take pictures, and ask to be sent copies.

The Silk factory and Jiya Xiang

If you're interested in the secrets of **silk production**, catch bus #1 north to its last stop along Taibei Xi Lu, on the same road as the long-distance bus station. After you get off, walk back just a few hundred metres towards town and you'll come to the front entrance of the head office of the **silk factory**. The security man there should understand what you want. If you come during the week (avoid the 1–3pm lunch break), the chances are that you will be supplied with an English-speaking employee to show you round for free. You can see the whole process: the initial unpicking of the cocoons, the twisting together of the strands to form a thread (ten strands for each silk thread), the winding of the thread onto reels, and finally the weaving and dying. The women here have it hard compared to those sisters in the carpet factory: the noise in the workshops is immense, and they stand all day long. You can also buy silk designs at **Jiya Xiang**, northeast of the city, a small Uigur village specializing in **atalas silk**. It is an idyllic place just to sample the rural life of locals and see silk being produced traditionally in small workshops. The woman in the exhibition room speaks English and you can buy the silk at around ¥150 per length. To get here, take the minibus (9am–9pm; ¥2.5) from the small courtyard 150m northwest of East Bus Station on Taibei Dong Lu.

To see the nurturing of the **silkworms** themselves – only possible in the summer months – you'll need to explore some of the nearby country lanes in Jiya Xiang or in the vicinity of the silk factory. If you are able to explain your purpose to people (a drawing of a silkworm might do the trick), they will take you to see their silkworms munching away on rattan trays of fresh, cleaned mulberry leaves in cool, dark sheds. Eventually each worm should spin itself a cocoon of pure silk; each cocoon comprises a single strand about 1km in length. The farmers sell the cocoons to the factory for ¥10 per kilo. The hatching and rearing of silkworms is unreliable work, and for most farmers it's a sideline.

Melikawat

Finally, Silk Road specialists should visit the ruined city of **Melikawat** (¥20, plus ¥5 to take photos), out in the desert 30km to the south of town beside the Jade Dragon Kashgar River. This city, formerly an important Buddhist centre on the Silk Road, was abandoned well over a thousand years ago, and the arrival of Islam in the region did nothing to aid its preservation. The site is a fragmentary collection of crumbling walls set among the dunes and tamarisk bushes, thousands of wind-polished pot shards littering the ground – you might find odd fragments of glass or wood poking out of the ruins. For a visit to Melikawat, contact a travel service (see below) or flag down a taxi and start some hard bargaining; ¥60 is a reasonable price for the return trip.

Practicalities

Khotan's **airport**, with daily connections to Ürümqi (¥1300), lies 10km west from town. You can reach the centre either by taxi (¥15–20) or by the airport bus that meets incoming flights. The **bus station** is on the south end of Taibei Xi Lu, north of the city, with daily services to Korla and Ürümqi via the trans-Taklamakan route (prices to Ürümqi in air-con bus are ¥324, and to Korla they vary from ¥190 to ¥300, depending on the vehicle), and to everywhere else along the Southern Silk Road between Kashgar and Qiemo. Other useful bus routes include Yining (¥250) and Turpan (¥283) in the east of Xinjiang. Taxis charge ¥5 to any hotel.

Right beside the bus-station entrance, the *Jiaotong* (❸) is the cleanest of several **hotels** here; more central options include the rather gloomy *Hetian Yingbinguan* (Ⓣ0903/2022824, Ⓕ2023688; ❸ including breakfast, dorm beds ¥20), and the friendly, unpretentious *Yurong Binguan* (Ⓣ0903/2025242; ❹), though be aware of their frequent power cuts. Finally, the *Hetian Binguan* in the southwest of the city (Ⓣ0903/2513564; ❺ including breakfast) is comfortable and good value, despite the slightly aged furniture. The hotel has two large restaurants serving Chinese and Muslim food.

You can purchase flight tickets at the **CAAC office** (daily 10am–8.30pm, Ⓣ0903/2512178) on the Wulumuqi Lu, a few minutes north of the *Hetian Binguan*. South from here, your visa can be extended at the **PSB** (Mon–Fri 10am–2pm & 3.30–7.30pm). All hotels have **travel services** for booking plane and bus tickets and arranging **tours**. Local excursions with a guide taking in the carpet and silk factories should set you back ¥50–100, and it's possible to organize lengthier jeep or camel trips around the region, using routes not necessarily covered by public transport. Expect to pay ¥300 per day for a jeep, ¥100 for a camel; camping gear is around ¥50 per person, and a guide will cost ¥100 a day. If your hotel can't help, try CITS (Ⓣ0903/2516090, Ⓕ2512846), inconveniently located on the third floor of a building at the end of Bositan Lu; or the CTS (Ⓣ0903/2518753) outside the *Hetian Binguan*.

Eating in Khotan is straightforward. *Huimin Fanguan*, just west of the river on Beijing Xi Lu, is a bustling **Muslim restaurant** popular with locals, serving *laghman*, beef noodle soups, kebabs and the like, with nothing over ¥8. There is an excellent Uigur **night market** just south of Tuanjie Square, where you can get roast chickens, pilau, eggs and fish, as well as the customary kebabs, sheep heads and *laghman*. For **Chinese food**, there's an excellent Hunan/Sichuan restaurant *Xiangchuan Boziwang*, on Beijing Xi Lu, a few minutes' walk west of the square; look for the red lanterns outside. The *Maixiang Yuan Bakery* at the northeast corner of the square is a great place if you miss **Western food** – their ground floor sells freshly made cakes, while the upper floor is a stylish café with an extensive menu of pizzas (¥30), pasta (¥15) and coffee (¥20).

Khotan to Kashgar

The last 500km of the Southern Silk Road runs northwest from Khotan to Kashgar through a dusty wasteland interspersed with dunes, groups of camels, mountain ranges to the south, and sudden patches of willows and greenery marking irrigated settlements. Some 200km along, **YECHENG** (Karagilik) is a kind of giant Uigur highway service station, with flashing lights, fires, bubbling cauldrons, overhead awnings and great hunks of mutton hanging from meat hooks. **Accommodation** is available just outside the bus station to the left, at the basic *Jiaotong* (❷, dorm beds ¥30). For a smarter option, try the *Yecheng Dianli* (Yecheng Electricity Hotel, ☎0998/7289800; ❹). Turn right as you come out of the bus station, to the main road, and walk east 500m. It's the light-coloured building with a shiny dome on top to your left.

The road divides at Yecheng, one fork running north towards Kashgar, the other southwest into **Tibet** (see box, below). Heading a further 60km north lands you at **Yarkand**, a miniature version of Kashgar but with minimal tourist infrastructure. That said, the backstreets are possibly the closest you'll come in China to the Central Asia of a hundred years ago.

Yarkand and Yengisar

A strategically important staging post for at least the last thousand years, **YARKAND** (also known as **Shache**) is – now that Kashgar is becoming ever

---

Yecheng to Tibet

The road southeast **from Yecheng** follows the Karakoram mountain ranges for about 1000km to the town of **Ali** in **western Tibet** (see p.1151). Though this route into Tibet is illegal for foreigners, a steady trickle seems to make it through each year. At the time of writing, hitching on trucks was not possible; instead, there are regular local buses whose drivers are willing to take foreigners. The Yecheng–Ali road is dusty and rough and is best tackled between July and October, but can be extremely **cold** even then – adequate water, food, sleeping bags, and warm, windproof clothing are essential. You'll be travelling at over 5000m for most of the duration, with no chance of a speedy descent if you develop **altitude sickness**. There are several **police checkpoints** along the way, and if detected you may be arrested, fined, and sent back. However drivers usually have an arrangement with the police or manage to avoid checkpoints by taking detours.

In Yecheng, you can find **local buses** to Ali in the Ali Banshichu (Ali Representative Office). Bus #2 (¥1.5) from the Yecheng bus station stops right outside the gate to the office – you can see plenty of trucks docking outside. Walk through the gate about 50m to the yellow houses on your left; the buses are hidden away near here. The people here should understand what you are after, and bus drivers will sell you a ticket to Tibet for ¥1000 (you can bargain this down to ¥700–800). The 23-person buses leave for Ali twice a week at around 8 or 9pm, though you may need to wait for a few days if the demand is not sufficient; the trip takes around two days.

13

more developed and sanitized – possibly the best place to soak up the character of Muslim Xinjiang. The town centres on a crossroads, from where Xincheng Lu runs west through the Han-dominated part of town towards Kashgar, while Laocheng Lu runs east into the older, Uigur quarters. The best thing to do here is simply wander the northeastern backstreets, a warren of muddy lanes lined with willows and crowded by donkey carts, artisans' quarters, bazaars and traditional adobe homes with wooden-framed balconies. You'll find the town's major sights here too, close together on a road running north off Laocheng Lu: the **old fort** is opposite the **Altunluq mosque** and **Amannisahan tomb** (¥10), flanked by two narrow towers. The mosque itself is off limits to non-Muslims, but the tomb, built for Amannisahan, the wife of a sixteenth-century khan, is a beautiful white- and blue-tiled affair; Amannisahan was also the most influential contributor to Muqam music (see box, p.1061). The adjacent **cemetery** contains the mausoleums of several of Yarkand's former rulers, including Amannisahan's husband, and is also crowded with more ordinary cylindrical Muslim tombs and truly ancient trees. Sunday would be the best time to visit Yarkand, when a huge rustic **market** along the same lines as the more famous one in Kashgar is held in the main bazaar behind the fort – though this area is pretty good most days.

The **bus station**, with frequent departures through the day to Kashgar and Khotan, is south off Xincheng Lu. You can find the **Bank of China**, post office and China Telecom all around the crossroads. The only **hotel** that accepts foreigners, the *Shache Binguan* (☎0998/8512365; ❹), is a ten-minute walk west along Xincheng Lu from the crossroad; it's a friendly place, but a little overpriced. The best place to eat is the *Meraj Restaurant* on the northeast corner of the cross, extremely popular with local Uigurs. They serve stuffed nan bread and large plates of noodle dishes of all kinds; the delicacy here is one with pigeon meat.

Some 120km further on up the Kashgar road, the town of **YENGISAR** has for centuries been supplying the Uigur people with handcrafted knives. Most of the knives on sale in Xinjiang these days are factory-made, but here at the **Yengisar County Small Knife Factory**, a few craftsmen still ply their old skills, inlaying handles with horn or silver alloy. Some of the more decorative knives take nearly a fortnight to forge. If you want a genuine handmade Yengisar knife, this is definitely the place to come. From here it's a mere 70km or so to Kashgar.

Kashgar

A large part of the excitement of **KASHGAR** lies in the experience of reaching it. Set on the western edge of the Chinese empire astride overland routes to Pakistan and Kyrgyzstan, Kashgar is fantastically remote from eastern China: as the crow flies, it's more than 4000km from Beijing, of which the thousand-plus kilometres from Ürümqi are for the most part sheer desert. As recently as the 1930s, the journey time to and from Beijing ran to a number of months. And yet Kashgar today, an oasis 1200m above sea level, is a remarkably prosperous and pleasant place, despite being, in part, an essentially medieval city.

Kashgar remains a visible bastion of old Chinese Turkestan, though gradually the more "authentic" parts of the town are being cleaned up as tourist attractions, and its residents moved to modern high-rises on the city limits. Nonetheless, despite Han migration into the city, its population is still overwhelmingly Muslim, a fact you can hardly fail to notice with the great **Id Kah**

Kashgar

Kashgar	喀什	kāshí
Hanoi ancient city	罕诺依古城	hànnuòyī gǔchéng
Id Kah Mosque	艾提尕尔清真寺	àitígǎ'ěr qīngzhēnsì
Id Kah Square	艾提尕尔广场	àitígǎ'ěr guǎngchǎng
Kashgar Silk Road Museum	喀什丝绸之路博物馆	kāshí sīchóuzhīlù bówùguǎn
Moor Pagodas	莫尔佛塔	mò'ěr fótǎ
Sunday Market	中西亚市场	zhōngxīyà shìchǎng
Tomb of Abakh Hoja	阿巴克霍加麻扎	abākè huòjiā mázhā
Tomb of Yusup Hazi Hajup	哈撕哈吉南墓	hāsīhájí nán mù

Arrival and international destinations

Ilkshtan Pass	伊尔克什坦口岸	yī'ěrkè shítǎn kǒu'àn
International bus station	国际汽车站	guójì qìchēzhàn
Bishkek	比什凯克	bǐshí kǎikè
Main bus station	客运站	kèyùnzhàn
Narin	那伦	nàlún
Torugut Pass	吐尔尕特口岸	tù'ěr gǎtè kǒu'àn
Wuqia County	乌恰县	wūqià xiàn

Accommodation, eating and drinking

Kashgar	喀什宾馆	kāshí bīnguǎn
Laoding Niurou Mian	老鼎牛肉面	lǎodǐng niúròumiàn
Nanlin Jiucheng	南林酒城	nánlín jiǔchéng
Qiniwak	其尼瓦克宾馆	qíní wǎkè bīnguǎn
Seman	色满宾馆	sèmǎn bīnguǎn
Tianfu Canting	天府餐厅	tiānfǔ cāntīng
Tiannan	天南饭店	tiānnán fàndiàn
Tuman River	吐曼河大饭店	tùmànhé dàfàndiàn

Mosque dominating the central square, the Uigur bazaars and teashops, the smell of grilled lamb and, above all, the faces of the Turkic people around you. If you can choose a time to be here, catch the Uigur Corban **festival** at the end of the Muslim month of Ramadan, and again, exactly two months later, which involves activities such as dancing and goat-tussling. And don't miss Kashgar's extraordinary **Sunday market**, for which half of Central Asia seems to converge on the city and which is as exotic to the average Han Chinese as to the foreign tourist.

Some history

Kashgar's **history** is dominated by its strategic position. There was already a Chinese military governor here when Xuanzang passed through on his way back from India in 644. The city was Buddhist at the time, with hundreds of monasteries; Islam made inroads around 1000 and eventually became the state religion. More recently, the late nineteenth century saw Kashgar at the meeting point of three empires – **Chinese, Soviet and British**. Both Britain and the Soviet Union maintained consulates in Kashgar until 1949: the British with an eye to their interests across the frontier in India, the Soviets (so everyone assumed) with the long-term intention of absorbing Xinjiang into their Central Asian orbit. The conspiracies of this period are brilliantly evoked in Peter Fleming's *News from Tartary* and Ella Maillart's *Forbidden Journey*. At the time of Fleming's visit, in 1935, the city was in effect run by the Soviets, who had brought their rail line to within two days of Kashgar. During World War II, however,

Kashgar swung back under Chinese control, and with the break in Sino-Soviet relations in the early 1960s, the Soviet border (and influence) firmly closed. In the wake of the break-up of the Soviet Union, however, it seemed that Kashgar would resume its status as one of the great travel crossroads of Asia, but this recovery sadly stalled after the events of September 11, 2001 and the ensuing conflict in Afghanistan. The town is still experiencing something of a downturn, with neither traders nor tourists as plentiful as they once were.

Orientation, arrival and accommodation

It's helpful to think of Kashgar as centred on a large cross, with a principal north–south axis, Jiefang Bei Lu and Jiefang Nan Lu, and an east–west axis, Renmin Dong Lu and Renmin Xi Lu. North of Renmin Lu lies the core of the **old town**, containing much of the accommodation, the Id Kah Mosque, former consulates, and interesting streets; south of Renmin Lu the prevailing cityscape is modern Chinese, with grey-fronted department stores and overly wide roads.

The **train station** is 7km east of town, where bus #28 to Jiefang Bei Lu, minibuses and taxis await new arrivals. Just east of centre on Tiannan Lu is the main **long-distance bus station**, handling connections from most parts of

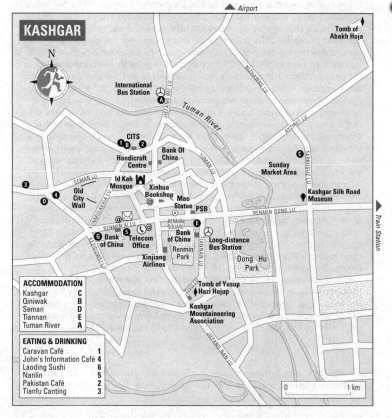

▲ Airport
▶ Train Station

KASHGAR

N

International Bus Station Ⓐ

Tuman River

Tomb of Abakh Hoja

NIZHAWAG LU

AYZIRET LU

CITS ① Ⓑ ②

Bank Of China

Handicraft Centre

Id Kah Mosque

Xinhua Bookshop @

Mao Statue PSB

TARBOGUZI LU

Sunday Market Area Ⓒ

Kashgar Silk Road Museum

SEMAN LU

Old City Wall

Ⓓ ④ ③

YUNMULAKXIA LU

@ ✉

RENMIN XI LU

Ⓖ Bank of China ℂ @ ⑤ Telecom Office

SEMAN DUWEI LU

RENMIN SQUARE

Bank of China Ⓔ

Renmin Park

Xinjiang Airlines

RENMIN DONG LU

Long-distance Bus Station

Dong Hu Park

TIANNAN LU

Tomb of Yusup Hazi Hajup

Kashgar Mountaineering Association

JIEFANG NAN LU

ACCOMMODATION
Kashgar   C
Qiniwak   B
Seman   D
Tiannan   E
Tuman River A

EATING & DRINKING
Caravan Café   1
John's Information Café   4
Laoding Sushi   6
Nanlin   5
Pakistan Café   2
Tianfu Canting   3

0   1 km

There's just one daily **flight** to Ürümqi, so book well ahead in peak season. Three **trains** leave daily, one of which terminates at Korla (where you can pick up buses to Turpan) while the other two continue to Ürümqi; if you can't handle the train station queues, buy tickets through a travel agent.

Buses from the **main bus station** head eastwards, though taking one along the Northern Silk Road via Kuqa to Korla and Ürümqi doesn't make much sense given the availability of the train. For the Southern Silk Road, there's ample traffic through the day as far as Yarkand (¥25), and less frequently to Khotan, Minfeng and Qiemo. The bus-station ticket office is computerized and pretty helpful.

The **international bus station** is where to head for all westbound traffic, via Karakul (¥43) and Tashkurgan (¥63), through the Kunjerab Pass to **Sust in Pakistan** (¥270). Note that the border is open only from May 1 until some point in October – see p.1089 for more. The other option is to travel due north over the Torugut Pass to **Bishkek** (US$50), the capital of **Kyrgyzstan**. Note that you're charged **excess baggage** rates for every kilo over 20kg on international buses, and should get the latest information about **visas** before travelling to either Pakistan or Kyrgyzstan, as they are not reliably available either in Kashgar or at the borders.

The road to Kyrgyzstan

The 720-kilometre-long road due north from Kashgar via the Torugut Pass to **Bishkek** in **Kyrgyzstan** has been open to Westerners since the 1990s, and offers interesting routes overland into Uzbekistan, Kazakhstan and Russia. At the time of writing, however, foreigners had found this route expensive and troublesome. Firstly, you need to contact CITS in Kashgar by faxing them your passport photocopy at least twenty days in advance to acquire a special permit at the charge of US$30. You will then have to pay ¥1200 for a car and a tour guide, which will take you to the border (160km away), across which you'll need to sort out your own transport into Kyrgyzstan (CITS can arrange a US$100 bus to Narin). Going from China to Kyrgyzstan, vehicles are not allowed to **cross the border** until after 1pm; coming the other way, you must cross before 1pm. There are noodle shops on the Chinese side of the pass and you can also change small amounts of money here, apparently at a better rate than in Kashgar. The weather at the 3750-metre pass is very cold, with snow and hail showers frequent even in midsummer. **On the Kyrgyz side** you may be expected to offer **bribes** (try US$20 as a starter); if the guards are happy with you, you'll be through in minutes, though waiting for hours is not uncommon.

An alternative option is to use the southern **Ilkshtan Pass** in Wuqia County, part of the Kizilsu Kirgiz Autonomous Prefecture. The Ilkshtan Pass was officially opened to foreigners in 2002 and is 240km west of Kashgar along rough roads. From the pass to the Kyrgyzstan border, there is another 5km to hitch or walk, though tickets bought in Kashgar to Bishkek (US$50) will include this section. According to the CITS staff, few people choose this pass despite the apparent low costs. This may be due to the harsh road conditions, or simply because the Ilkshtan Pass is so little known – check the situation with local authorities before you go.

Kyrgyzstan visas currently cost US$50 and, in China, are only available through the Beijing consulate (see p.140). In theory, if you have a visa for any CIS country (for example, Kazakhstan, Uzbekistan or Russia) then you can obtain a three-day transit visa (US$25) through Kyrgyzstan at the border; in practice, you may not be able to do so. If you do not have any visa at all, you will not be allowed through the Chinese side.

Xinjiang, including Ürümqi, Kuqa, Korla, Yarkand and Khotan. The **international bus station**, about 1500m north up Jiefang Bei Lu and just over the river beside the *Tuman River* hotel, is terminus for luxury buses from Ürümqi, as well as all traffic from Tashkurgan, Sust in Pakistan, and Bishkek in Kyrgyzstan – bus #2 runs down Jiefang Bei Lu from here. Kashgar's **airport** is to the north of town; the airport bus (¥4) drives straight down Jiefang Lu to the China Southern Airlines' Xinjiang office.

Accommodation

There are some pleasant, inexpensive hotels in Kashgar, catering to Pakistani traders from over the Karakoram Highway and to foreign tourists.

Kashgar Out to the east of town on Tarbogue Lu ⓣ0998/2652369. A pleasant hotel, set aside by trees very near to the Sunday market. Somewhat disappointing double rooms for the price. ❺
Qiniwak (aka Chini Bagh) On Seman Lu ⓣ0998/2982103, ⓕ2982299. A pleasant place conveniently located near the Id Kah Mosque; the friendly staff speak some English. A large variety of rooms is available with bath and a view over Kashgar. Dorms ¥55, ❺–❻
Seman Seman Lu ⓣ0998/2822129. A popular choice, this rambling old complex has a wide range of fully carpeted, clean and comfortable rooms.

Bikes may also be rented here at a price of ¥20 per day. Dorms ¥50, ❹–❻
Tiannan Opposite the long-distance bus station off Tiannan Lu ⓣ0998/2824023. A cheap option with smelly basic rooms; if you are looking for class, turn away. Foreigners are not always welcome in the ¥20 dorms, though if you pay around ¥40 this is sometimes possible. ❷
Tuman River Right beside the international bus station ⓣ0998/2822912. A mid-range option popular with traders, though in a noisy area. Take bus #9 from *Qiniwak*. Dorms ¥20, ❸

The City

There are one or two monuments of note in Kashgar, but the main attractions of this city are the ordinary streets of the old town – principally the bazaars, the restaurants, the teahouses and the people in them. Roads radiate out from the centre of the original Uigur city which is focused on **Id Kah Square**, with its clock tower and huge mosque. A few hundred metres to the south is the modern, commercial centre, at the junction between Jiefang (Bei and Nan)

⓭

THE NORTHWEST | Kashgar

Kashgar's Sunday Market

Known in Chinese as the **Zhongxiya Shichang** (Western-Central Asia Market), or, in Uigur, as the **Yekshenba Bazaar** (Sunday Bazaar), this mother of all markets attracts up to one hundred thousand villagers and nomads, all riding their donkey carts from the surrounding area and gathering in a huge area to the east of town. For the sheer scale of the occasion, it's the number one sight in Kashgar, if not all Xinjiang. Considering the large numbers of minority peoples who come to trade here, all sporting their own particular headwear, it is also an anthropologist's delight. Traffic jams of thousands of donkey carts compete with horsemen and herds of sheep for space in the chaotic dusty alleys. At the animal market, horses are test-driven, sheep are picked over and cattle are paraded before potential buyers. Animals, knives, hats, pots, carpets, and pans, fresh fruit and vegetables, clothes and boots and every kind of domestic and agricultural appliance – often handmade in wood and tin – are all on sale. Some produce, such as Iranian saffron, has come a long way to be sold here. The market goes on all day and into the early evening, and food and drink are widely available on and around the site.

The market is a thirty-minute walk northeast from the town centre, crossing the minor Tuman River on the way. Otherwise, take a donkey cart for a few yuan. If you cycle you will need to find a cycle parking lot well before you reach the confines of the market itself.

Lu and Renmin (Xi and Dong) Lu. The other main landmark is the absurdly colossal **statue of Mao Zedong** hailing a taxi on Renmin Dong Lu, a towering reminder of the ultimate authority of China over the region. Opposite the statue is the bald, stone expanse of Renmin Square with an attached park behind. Finally, scattered around the fringes of the city, are a number of **mausoleums** to Uigur heroes of the past, best reached by bus or bicycle.

Id Kah Square and around

The main historical sight in central Kashgar is the **Id Kah Mosque**, occupying the western side of Id Kah Square, off Jiefang Bei Lu. Originally built in 1442, it has been restored many times, most recently after the Cultural Revolution. It is one of the biggest mosques, and almost certainly the most active, in the country; you can even hear the call to prayer booming around the city centre – a rare sound in China. Although visitors are theoretically allowed in (there is a small entrance fee of ¥10 to the grounds and an additional ¥2 for mosque entry), Western tourists are sometimes shooed away by zealous worshippers – note that visitors of either sex should have their arms and legs fully covered when entering this (or any other) mosque. On Fridays, the main Muslim prayer day, some ten thousand people crowd the mosque and square, and you will not be allowed in at this time; the quietest time, when your presence will cause least disturbance, is probably early to mid-morning of any other day. Inside are pleasant courtyards and tree-lined gardens where the worshippers assemble.

The main Uigur bazaars are in the neighbouring streets, but while you're in the area, keep an eye open for a couple of substantial fragments of Kashgar's **old city walls**, most easily viewed south of Seman Lu and west off Yunmulakxia Lu. And don't miss out on the **old consulates** either: the British had theirs behind the *Qiniwak* hotel, while the Russian headquarters survive as a nicely preserved period piece in the courtyard behind the *Seman* hotel.

The bazaars

The street heading northeast from Id Kah Square is the main **carpet** area. The best carpets of the region are handmade in Khotan, but some good bargains are to be had in the Kashgar bazaars. You should be able to get a nice felt of rolled coloured wool (1.5m x 2.5m) for less than ¥300. A larger hand-knotted carpet, approximately 2m x 3m, should cost around ¥800. The carpets are relatively rough in quality and have geometric designs only, but the prices are about a third of the equivalent in Turkey. Kashgar **kilims**, produced by nomads, are highly sought after and almost impossible to find locally. You can watch people making carpets, musical instruments and jewellery at the *Handicrafts Centre* 200m north of Id Kah Square on Jiefang Lu; here high-quality double-sided silk carpets are woven which cost around ¥1000 per square metre.

A small road east of Id Kah Square, parallel to *Jiefang Lu*, is a big area for Central Asian **hats**. As well as the green and white square-shaped variety so beloved by Uigur old men, there are prayer caps, skullcaps, furry winter hats and plain workmen's caps. Following this lane south, turn right, where a large, semi-underground market occupies the space between the square and hat lane. Here you will find a large selection of **clothes**, carpets and **crockery** as well as Uigur nuts, sweets and spice stands, and the occasional blacksmith also hammers at his trade. Further south down the hat street, you will come to a woodcraft area. North of the square you'll find **jewellery** and high-quality ornate **knives**, produced in Yengisar. The lane directly south of Id Kah Mosque, heading due west, sells a mixture of hats, jewellery, large **chests** overlain with brightly coloured tin (purpose-built for carrying gifts for brides to be), and handmade

instruments. The two-stringed *dutah* is the most common. The *tanber* has an even longer stem and a round bowl shaped like half a gourd, while the *rawupu* has five strings and a snakeskin drum.

In the southern part of the square is the Kashgar **night market**, while to the west – the two roads to the north and south of the Id Kah Mosque – are a few **Uigur teahouses** and small eating establishments, as well as daytime street food.

The outskirts

The historic architecture remaining in Kashgar today chiefly comprises a number of mausoleums to famous Uigur personages. From May to October, a tourist minibus (¥1) runs through the city and covers most sites. At other times, they are accessible by public transport. The most central of these is the **Tomb of Yusup Hazi Hajup** (daily 10am–7pm; ¥10), the eleventh-century Uigur poet and philosopher. It's about 1500m south of Renmin Lu, on Tiyu Lu, a small road located between Jiefang Nan Lu and Tiannan Lu – bus #8 down Jiefang Lu comes within striking distance. The mausoleum, of handsome blue and white wall tiles, was reconstructed in 1986, though with slightly shoddy workmanship – it's worth dropping by if you are in the vicinity.

Within a few kilometres east of the centre, on Tarbogue Lu, the **Kashgar Silk Road Museum** (daily 10am–8pm; ¥6), on the #10 bus route from Renmin Lu, is worth a visit to see an Iron-Age **mummy** recovered from the desert hereabouts, still dressed in felt hat and fur-lined jacket, woollen trousers, leather boots, and a belt with herbs and a knife attached. There are also examples of various ancient **scripts** found at Silk Road sites, including Indian-derived Kharosthi (from Khotan), along with the usual run of pottery, wooden and metal artefacts, some going back to 1000 BC. At the time of writing the museum was undergoing refurbishment and organization but remained open.

The most impressive of all Kashgar's tombs is the **Tomb of Abakh Hoja** (daily 10am–7.30pm; ¥15), 8km northeast of the centre on bus #20 from Renmin Square, or forty minutes by bike through wheat fields and poplar woods. From downtown, head past the Sunday Market site and the turning for the mausoleum is signposted in English after a few kilometres. The mausoleum itself is a large, mosque-like building of blue and white tiles with a green dome and tiled minarets. Built in the seventeenth century, it was the resting place for a large number of people – the most famous being Abakh Hoja and his granddaughter Ikparhan, who is known in Chinese as **Xiang Fei**, "Fragrant Concubine". Having led the Uigurs in revolt against Beijing, she was subsequently seized and married to the Qing emperor Qian Long, later being ordered to commit suicide by the emperor's jealous mother. In both commemorating a local heroine and stirring anti-Qing propaganda in the cruelty she suffered, the story serves the convenient dual purpose of pleasing both the Uigurs and the Han Chinese.

Outside Kashgar and accessible only by car are the **Moor Pagodas** (¥10) at the **ancient city of Hanoi** on a rough road about 30km east of the city. The pagodas have been worn down to rough stumps about a dozen metres high, but the remains of the ruined Tang city walls of Hanoi make quite a dramatic scene in what is a virtual desert. To reach this place, you'll need to rent a car from a travel service, costing around ¥150 through the Mountaineering Association (see p.1086), or deal directly with a taxi yourself – try for ¥60 return.

Eating and drinking

Kashgar has plentiful **places to eat** for all budgets. Westerners tend to gravitate towards the foreigner-friendly restaurants on the roundabout outside the *Seman* hotel; the branch of *John's Information Café* here (see p.1051) offers its usual Sino-Western fare and beer, but is quite expensive. Authentic Sichuan food can be found at the *Tianfu Canting*, a restaurant less than 100m west of the *Seman* hotel. It can get busy here around dinner time, so you may wish to reserve in advance. For a good, cheap breakfast of tea or coffee with bagels, honey and fresh yoghurt, try the *Caravan Café*, outside the *Qiniwak* hotel. Two minutes' walk from here, still on Tuman Lu, stop over in the tiny *Pakistan Café* for cheap and delicious Pakistani food, and a cup of sweet milk tea.

The best place to pick up **Uigur food** is around Id Kah Square. Street vendors sell pilau, kebabs, cold spicy noodles, *kao bao* and *jiaozi*. *Laghman* is available almost everywhere. Other street food worth sampling is the vanilla ice cream, mixed up on the spot in containers encased in lumps of ice, which is delicious, though not obviously hygienic. For a more relaxed atmosphere, try *Laoding Niurou Mian*, a clean canteen on the corner of Renmin Xi Lu and Keziduwei Lu, selling huge bowls of beef noodle soup, along with buns, *laghman* and kebabs; clear noodles with spicy sauce accompany the meal for a mere ¥1 a bowl. For **Chinese food**, *Nanlin Jiucheng* is a well-established hotpot restaurant on Renmin Xi Lu, with occasional music performances. A good place to go **drinking** is at the outdoor seating area at the north end of Jiefang Nan Lu, which is usually open until the small hours. The waitresses bring you beer and nibbles, including such staples as chickens' feet.

Listings

Airline China Southern Xinjiang branch
℡ 0998/2822113, 106 Jiefang Nan Lu (May–Oct 9am–8pm, Nov–April 10am–7.30pm.

Banks and exchange The main Bank of China, in the northeast corner of Renmin Square (daily 9.30am–1.30pm & 4–7.30pm), can change foreign currency. You may have to show proof of purchase for cashing traveller's cheques.

Bike rental Bicycles can be rented from *John's Information Café*, a stall at the front gate of the *Qiniwak*, and from the *Seman Hotel* – all charge ¥20 per day.

Bookshops Xinhua Bookshop is at 32 Jiefang Bei Lu, on the east side of the road and just north of the intersection with Renmin Lu.

Internet access The foreigners' cafés have Internet connections, but they tend to be more expensive than the Internet bars on Renmin Xi Lu (¥2 per hour).

Mail The post office is at 40 Renmin Xi Lu, a short walk west of Jiefang Lu (Mon–Sat 9.30am–8pm).

PSB On Renmin Dong Lu (Mon–Fri 10.30am–2pm and 4–9.30pm), just opposite the Bank of China.

Telephones Direct-dial long-distance calls can be made from an office opposite the post office on Renmin Xi Lu, at China Telecom (daily 9.30am–8pm), or from the *Qiniwak* and *Seman Hotel*. Both charge by the minute.

Travel agents There's little in the way of day-trips around Kashgar, but agents are useful for organizing train tickets (at a ¥30 commission) and longer backroad excursions, and should have the latest advice on international routes out from town. CITS (9.30am–1.30pm & 4–8pm; ℡ 0998/2983316 ℻ 2983087) has a branch on the first floor in a building inside the *Qiniwak*. Staff are friendly and speak English. Independent budget travellers will be better served by the *Caravan Café* outside the *Qiniwak* (ⓔ caravan_cafe@yahoo .com), an excellent place run by American expats; or *John's Information Café* (ⓔ johncafe@hotmail .com). A freelance operator named Elvis Ablimit (ⓔ Elvisablimit@yahoo.com) provides guided camel safaris into the Taklamakan; his English is good, and he knows the surrounding terrain well. There's also the Kashgar Mountaineering Association (daily 9.30am–1.30pm & 4–8pm, ℡ 0998/2523660, ⓦ www.kashgaralpine.com), inside the Kashgar Gymnasium on Jiefang Nan Lu. They're a helpful, English-speaking bunch who can arrange private transport into Ali in Tibet as well as a range of adventure activities including climbing and rafting trips. It is advisable to contact them well in advance if you plan something ambitious, as most activities require some equipment and paperwork preparations.

The Karakoram Highway

For centuries the **Khunjerab Pass**, lying some 400km south of Kashgar, was the key Silk Road crossing point between the Chinese world and the Indian subcontinent – and thence to the whole of the Western world. Today the 4700-metre pass still marks the frontier between China and **Pakistan**, but, while crossing the mountains used to be a highly perilous journey undertaken on horse, camel or foot, modern engineering has blasted a highway right through the pass, opening the route to a seasonal stream of trucks and buses. The entire 1300-kilometre route from Kashgar over the mountains to Rawalpindi in northern Pakistan is known as the **Karakoram Highway**. The highway was formally opened in 1982, and foreign tourists have been travelling through in both directions since 1986. The trip is still not without its perils, but it's hard to think of a more exciting route into or out of China. If the highway is closed for any reason, note that you can also **fly** twice weekly direct from Ürümqi to Islamabad (Wed & Sun; ¥1900).

En route from Kashgar, travellers have to spend a night in **Tashkurgan** on the Chinese side, before crossing over the pass to the Pakistani town of **Sust**. There is also the option of camping out for a night or two by the wintry but beautiful **Lake Karakul**, in the lee of glaciers. The road over the pass is open from the beginning of May until the end of October each year, though it can close without notice when the weather is bad, for days at a time, even in summer. The journey from Kashgar to Rawalpindi/Islamabad, or vice versa, takes a minimum of four days if there are no hold-ups. Most travellers need a **visa to enter Pakistan**; at the time of writing, you'll need to arrange this in your home country – neither Beijing nor Ürümqi supplies the service.

Lake Karakul

Southwest of Kashgar, the road soon leaves the valley, with its mud-brick buildings and irrigated wheat and rice plantations, behind. Climbing through river gorges strewn with giant boulders, it creeps into a land of treeless, bare dunes of sand and gravel, interspersed with pastures scattered with grazing yaks and camels. The sudden appearance of **Lake Karakul** (¥20) by the roadside, some 200km out of Kashgar, is dramatic. Right under the feet of the Pamir Mountains and the magnificent 7546-metre Mount Muztagata, whose vast snowy flanks have been split open by colossal glaciers, the waters of the lake are luminous blue. The opportunities for **hiking** over the surrounding green pasture are virtually limitless, especially if you are equipped with a tent and warm clothing; at 3800m, the weather can be extremely cold even in summer, with snow showers normal well into June. It's

---

The Karakoram Highway

Karakoram Highway	中巴公路	*zhōngbā gōnglù*
Khunjerab Pass	红其拉甫口岸	*hóngqí lāpǔ kǒu'àn*
Lake Karakul	喀拉湖	*kālā hú*
Sust	苏斯特	*sūsī tè*
Tashkurgan	塔什库尔干	*tǎshí kù'ěrgàn*
Ice Mountain	冰山旅店	*bīngshān lǚdiàn*
Jiaotong	交通宾馆	*jiāotōng bīnguǎn*
Pamir	帕米尔宾馆	*pàmǐ'ěr bīnguǎn*
Stone City	石头城	*shítou chéng*

possible to walk round the lake in a day, in which case you will almost certainly encounter some friendly Kyrgyz yurt-dwellers on the way – you may well be able to stay with them if you can communicate your meaning (not easy). Otherwise, if you are without your own tent, you can stay at a rather dull and not particularly enticing tour-group yurt site just off the road, with its own restaurant and local attendants. This costs about ¥60 per head, on the basis of four people in a yurt, plus a rather steep ¥70 per person per day for all meals. The food is good and the local people are friendly. There are very rudimentary washing and toilet facilities, and fresh drinking water originates from the lake, hence swimming is forbidden.

Transport to the lake is simple. From the Kashgar international bus station there are two daily **buses** (¥48) from May to October, leaving at 10am and 4pm. From Tashkurgan you can take the Kashgar bus and get off at the lake. Leaving the lake requires slightly more ingenuity – for either direction you will need to flag down the passing buses or taxis, which may involve standing assertively in the middle of the road; taxis back to Kashgar cost ¥60 or more per person. It's better to ask a local from the yurt for help to avoid rip-offs, or at least check approximate expected times of buses with them. For travellers heading to Pakistan, it is perfectly feasible to travel to Tashkurgan via the lake, and then book yourself onto a bus to Sust from Tashkurgan (contrary to what you may be told in Kashgar).

Tashkurgan

The last town before the border, **TASHKURGAN**, lies 280km southeast of Kashgar, and about 220km north of the Pakistani town of Sust. Its primary importance for travellers is as a staging post between Kashgar and Sust, and all travellers passing through, in either direction, must stay the night here. It's a tiny place, comprising a couple of tree-lined streets, with the bus station and several budget hotels in the northwestern part of town.

The town boasts a long history as well as fantastic mountain scenery. The Chinese Buddhist pilgrim and Silk Road traveller **Xuanzang** stopped here in the seventh century, a time when, as now, it was the last outpost of Chinese rule. Today, Tashkurgan has a peculiar atmosphere. The native population is mainly Tadjik, but there are also groups of melancholy Han Chinese, thousands of miles from home, as well as intrepid Pakistanis setting up shop outside their country – plus, incredibly, a minor entertainment industry involving sex and alcohol for Pakistani tourists. Few travellers bother to stop longer than necessary, but you could pleasantly rest up here for 24 hours or so. Worth a look, especially at sunset, is the 600-year-old, crumbling, mud-brick **Stone City** (¥10, negotiable). If you clamber to the top, the scenes of snowy mountains running parallel on both flanks, and woods and wetland dotted around, are more than picturesque. To reach it, walk east from the bus station right to the end of town passing the *Pamir* hotel, then strike off a few hundred metres to the left.

Practicalities

At the **bus station**, the *Jiaotong Hotel* (open April–Nov, ☎0998/3421192; ❹, dorm beds in triples ¥20) is a simple **place to stay**, hot water is available 24 hours in doubles. Alternatively, you can try the primitive *Ice Mountain* (¥100, dorm beds ¥15–20). As you exit the bus station, turn right and walk 100m to the east along Hongqilapu Lu; it's across the road. The *Pamir* at the east end of the same road is much more upmarket (☎0998/3421085; ❸; April–Oct only), with high ceilings and eclectic decor. Hot water here is available all day, though you may need to double-check with the friendly staff.

The plentiful **beer** in Tashkurgan often comes as a relief to travellers arriving from Pakistan. For **food**, your best bet is to try one of the Chinese restaurants, like *Laochengdu Canting*, a couple of hundred metres east of the bus station. For delicious bread – excellent for breakfast and a snack on long bus journeys – try the bakery south from the east end of Hongqilapu Lu. Keep walking south from here and you will reach the centre cross marked by an eagle statue. The **post office** (daily 10am–2pm & 4–7pm) is at the southeast corner, where you can also make international phone calls. The **PSB office** is diagonally opposite the post office, while the only **bank** (Mon–Fri, 10.30am–2pm & 4–7pm) in town is 150m south of the eagle statue. Cash (and sometimes traveller's cheques) can be changed here at official exchange rates. If arriving from Pakistan, you can easily change your rupees with the locally resident Pakistanis if the banks are closed.

The **entry and exit formalities** for Western tourists are a few hundred metres south from the bank, and are straightforward to the point of being lax. You may or may not be issued with Currency and Valuables Declaration forms – but nobody seems to care what you put on them. If your bus arrives late in the evening, your passports are collected and formalities take place the next morning. Onward connections, in both directions, will wait until everyone is through customs, so there is no need to worry about being left behind.

Travellers heading to Pakistan do not need to buy onward bus tickets – the ticket from Kashgar covers the whole route right through to Sust. Coming from Pakistan, however, you'll find that the only onward transport is the bus to Kashgar (¥60). Buying your ticket requires standing in a long and heated queue, but don't worry – sufficient transport will be laid on for however many people need it. Whichever way you're heading, note that **cyclists** are not allowed to ride their bikes through the pass, but have to bus it between Tashkurgan and Sust. If you plan to get off at Lake Karakul (see p.1087) en route to Kashgar, you may be asked to pay the full Kashgar fare anyway. The alternative to catching buses is to **hitch a ride** on a truck. These often cruise around town in the evening looking for prospective customers to Kashgar (or Karakul) for the day after. You'll pay, but it will be cheaper than travelling by bus.

The Khunjerab Pass

Khunjerab means "River of Blood" in the local Tadjik language – which may refer to the rusty colour of local rivers, or to the long traditions of banditry in these areas. The trip across the border at the **Khunjerab Pass** is not a totally risk-free affair – people are killed almost every year by falling rocks on the highway and you should be aware that if your bus departs in rainy weather, you can almost certainly expect mud slides.

From Tashkurgan, the road climbs into a vast, bright plain, grazed by yaks and camels, with the mountains, clad in snow mantles hundreds of metres thick, pressing in all around. Emerging onto the **top of the pass**, you're greeted by a clear, silent, windswept space of frozen streams, protruding glaciers and glimpses of green pasture under the sunshine. The only creatures that live here are the ginger, chubby Himalayan marmots; a kind of large squirrel or woodchuck, it's easy to spot them from the bus. At these heights (the pass lies at some 4800m) a lot of travellers experience some form of **altitude sickness**, though most people will feel little more than a faintly feverish or nauseous sensation.

The journey time between Tashkurgan and the small town of **Sust**, where Pakistani customs and immigration take place, takes about seven hours. Travellers in both directions have to spend a night here, and accommodation is plentiful. From Sust there are direct daily buses to Gilgit, from where frequent buses cover the sixteen-hour route to **Rawalpindi** and **Islamabad**.

Travel details

Trains

Baotou to: Beijing (10 daily; 12hr); Dongsheng (daily; 4.5hr); Hailar (daily; 40hr); Hohhot (15 daily; 2hr); Lanzhou (2 daily; 14hr); Shanghai (daily; 31hr); Xi'an (daily; 25hr); Yinchuan (4 daily; 7hr).

Daheyan (for Turpan) to: Hami (13 daily; 5–6hr); Jiayuguan (12 daily; 11–16hr); Korla (5 daily; 8hr); Lanzhou (11 daily; 20–28hr); Liuyuan (10 daily; 10–12hr); Tianshui (10 daily; 25–34hr); Ürümqi (16 daily; 2–3hr); Wuwei (20 daily; 17–23hr); Zhangye (12 daily; 14–19hr).

Golmud to: Xining (4 daily; 17–19hr).

Guyuan to: Lanzhou (1 daily; 10hr); Yinchuan (3 daily; 7–9hr); Zhongwei (5 daily; 4hr).

Hailar to: Baotou (daily; 40hr); Beijing (daily; 26hr); Harbin (5 daily; 11hr); Hohhot (daily; 38hr); Manzhouli (5 daily; 2.5hr); Qiqihar (6 daily; 8hr).

Hami to: Daheyan (13 daily; 5hr); Lanzhou (14 daily; 10–13hr); Ürümqi (12 daily; 7–8hr).

Hohhot to: Baotou (15 daily; 2hr); Beijing (12 daily; 10hr); Erlianhot (2 daily; 9–11hr); Hailar (daily; 38hr); Shanghai (daily; 28hr); Taiyuan (2 daily; 12hr); Ulan Batur (daily; 25hr); Xi'an (daily; 22hr).

Jiayuguan to: Daheyan (12 daily; 12–17hr); Lanzhou (10 daily; 11–13hr); Liuyuan (10 daily; 4hr); Tianshui (10 daily; 14–19hr); Ürümqi (11 daily; 13–16hr); Wuwei (10 daily; 5–7hr); Zhangye (16 daily; 2hr 30min–4hr).

Kashgar to: Kuqa (2 daily; 9–11hr); Korla (2 daily; 13–15hr); Ürümqi (2 daily; 24hr or 30hr).

Korla to: Daheyan (5 daily; 8–13hr); Kuqa (3 daily; 3hr 30min–4hr 30min); Kashgar (2 daily; 13–15hr); Ürümqi (4 daily; 11–15hr).

Lanzhou to: Baotou (2 daily; 15hr); Beijing (4 daily; 22hr); Chengdu (3 daily; 22hr); Daheyan (10 daily; 22–28hr); Hami (10 daily; 17–23hr); Hohhot (2 daily; 17hr or 20hr); Guangzhou (1 daily; 35hr); Guyuan (1 daily; 10hr); Jiayuguan (13 daily; 10–14hr); Liuyuan (11 daily; 13–19hr); Shanghai (3 daily; 25hr); Tianshui (25 daily; 5hr); Ürümqi (10 daily; 24–30hr); Wuwei (13 daily; 5hr 30min–8hr); Xi'an (18 daily; 9–11hr); Xining (9 daily; 3hr); Yinchuan (3 daily; 8hr); Zhangye (12 daily; 8–11hr); Zhongwei (4 daily; 6hr).

Liuyuan (for Dunhuang) to: Beijing (1 daily; 35hr); Daheyan (13 daily; 8–9hr); Jiayuguan (12 daily; 4hr); Lanzhou (10 daily; 13–18hr); Tianshui (10 daily; 19hr); Ürümqi (9 daily; 12hr); Wuwei (9 daily; 3–5hr); Zhangye (12 daily; 5–8hr).

Manzhouli to: Beijing (2 daily; 29hr); Hailar (5 daily; 2.5hr); Harbin (3 daily; 13hr); Qiqihar (daily; 11hr).

Tianshui to: Daheyan (10 daily; 28hr); Jiayuguan (10 daily; 14–19hr); Lanzhou (24 daily; 4hr); Liuyuan (10 daily; 17–24hr); Ürümqi (9 daily; 27–36hr); Wuwei (10 daily; 8–12hr); Zhangye (10 daily; 12–16hr).

Ürümqi to: Almaty (Kazakhstan; 2 daily; 36hr); Beijing (1 daily; 46hr); Chengdu (1 daily; 54hr); Daheyan (16 daily; 2–3hr); Hami (12 daily; 7–8hr); Jiayuguan (11 daily; 13–16hr); Kashgar (2 daily; 23hr or 29hr); Korla (4 daily; 10–14hr); Lanzhou (10 daily; 23–30hr); Liuyuan (12 daily; 10–12hr); Shanghai (1 daily; 48hr); Tianshui (9 daily; 28–36hr); Xi'an (9 daily; 32–41hr); Wuwei (11 daily; 19–24hr); Zhangye (11 daily; 15–22hr).

Wuwei to: Daheyan (13 daily; 17–21hr); Jiayuguan (11 daily; 5–10hr); Lanzhou (15 daily; 5–7hr); Liuyuan (12 daily; 8hr 30min–12hr); Tianshui (10 daily; 9–12hr); Ürümqi (13 daily; 19–24hr); Zhangye (11 daily; 3–5hr); Zhongwei (3 daily; 4–6hr).

Xining to: Beijing (1 daily; 25hr); Golmud (4 daily; 14–44hr); Lanzhou (9 daily; 3–5hr); Shanghai (1 daily; 33hr); Xi'an (4 daily; 12–15hr).

Yinchuan to: Baotou (4 daily; 6hr 30min–9hr); Beijing (3 daily; 19hr); Guyuan (3 daily; 6–9hr); Hohhot (4 daily; 9–11hr); Lanzhou (3 daily; 8hr); Xi'an (2 daily; 14hr); Zhongwei (7 daily; 3–4hr).

Zhangye to: Daheyan (12 daily; 5–8hr); Jiayuguan (16 daily; 2–4hr); Lanzhou (13 daily; 8–10hr); Liuyuan (12 daily; 5hr 30min–8hr); Tianshui (9 daily; 12–15hr); Ürümqi (11 daily; 16–20hr); Wuwei (16 daily; 3–5hr); Xi'an (9 daily; 16–21hr).

Zhongwei to: Baotou (3 daily; 9–12hr); Guyuan (5 daily; 4hr); Hohhot (3 daily; 11–14hr); Lanzhou (5 daily; 6hr); Shapotou (1 daily; 30min); Yinchuan (7 daily; 3–5hr); Wuwei (3 daily; 4–6hr).

Buses

Baotou to: Dongsheng (hourly; 2.5hr); Hohhot (every 30min; 2.5hr).

Dongsheng to: Baotou (hourly; 2.5hr); Hohhot (hourly in summer, daily in winter; 4hr).

Dunhuang to: Golmud (8hr); Hami (6hr 30min); Jiayuguan (6hr); Lanzhou (18hr); Liuyuan (2hr); Wuwei (15hr); Zhangye (13hr).

Golmud to: Dunhuang (15hr); Lhasa (36hr); Xining (16hr).

Guyuan to: Lanzhou (7hr); Luoyang (16hr); Pingliang (2hr); Sanying (40min); Tianshui (6hr); Xi'an (7hr); Yinchuan (4.5hr).

Hailar to: Manzhouli (hourly; 3hr).

Hami to: Dunhuang (6hr 30min); Turpan (8hr); Ürümqi (11hr).

Hohhot to: Baotou (every 30min; 2.5hr); Beijing (daily; 12hr); Dongsheng (hourly in summer, daily in winter; 5hr).

Jiayuguan to: Dunhuang (5hr); Lanzhou (16hr); Wuwei (12hr); Zhangye (5hr).

Kashgar to: Khotan (11hr); Kuqa (20hr); Lake Karakul (6hr); Sust (36hr); Tashkurgan (8hr); Korla (30hr); Ürümqi (35hr); Yarkand (2hr 30min); Yecheng (4hr); Yining (40hr).

Khotan to: Kashgar (11hr); Korla (17hr); Minfeng (5hr); Qiemo (12hr); Ürümqi (22hr); Yarkand (5hr).

Korla to: Kashgar (30hr); Khotan (17hr); Kuqa (12hr); Turpan (10hr); Ürümqi (5hr).

Kuqa to: Aksu (12hr); Korla (10hr); Turpan (14hr); Ürümqi (12hr); Yining (24hr).

Lanzhou to: Dunhuang (24hr); Guyuan (7hr); Hezuo (8hr); Jiayuguan (16hr); Linxia (3hr); Tianshui (8hr); Ürümqi (44hr); Wuwei (5hr); Xiahe (8hr); Xi'an (16hr); Xining (5hr); Yinchuan (14hr); Zhangye (11hr).

Linxia to: Lanzhou (3hr); Tianshui (9hr); Wuwei (9hr); Xiahe (5hr); Xining (11hr).

Manzhouli to: Hailar (hourly; 3hr).

Pingliang to: Guyuan (2hr); Lanzhou (5hr); Xi'an (5hr).

Tianshui to: Guyuan (daily; 10hr); Lanzhou (8hr); Linxia (9hr); Pingliang (6hr); Wushan (5hr); Xi'an (9hr).

Turpan to: Hami (6hr 30min); Korla (10hr); Kuqa (12hr); Ürümqi (3hr).

Ürümqi to: Almaty (Kazakhstan; 36hr); Altai (24hr); Hami (11hr); Kashgar (35hr); Khotan (22hr); Korla (10hr); Kuqa (15hr); Liuyuan (daily; 23hr); Lanzhou (44hr); Turpan (3hr); Yining (15hr).

Wuwei to: Dunhuang (14hr 30min); Jiayuguan (10hr); Minqin (1.5hr); Lanzhou (4hr); Zhangye (4hr); Zhongwei (7hr).

Xiahe to: Hezuo (2hr); Lanzhou (6hr); Linxia (4hr); Tongren (6hr).

Xining to: Golmud (16hr); Lanzhou (5hr); Linxia (11hr); Maduo (24hr); Tongren (8hr); Zhangye (24hr).

Yecheng to: Ali (40–50hr); Kashgar (4hr); Ürümqi (24hr); Khotan (2.5hr).

Yinchuan to: Guyuan (7hr); Lanzhou (14hr); Xi'an (12hr); Zhongwei (4hr).

Yining to: Almaty (Kazakhstan; Mon–Sat; 12hr); Kashgar (2 daily; 48hr); Kuqa (24hr); Ürümqi (13hr).

Zhangye to: Dunhuang (8hr); Jiayuguan (5hr); Lanzhou (11hr); Wuwei (6hr).

Zhongwei to: Guyuan (5hr); Shapotou (1hr); Wuwei (7hr); Yinchuan (3hr).

Flights

Besides the domestic services listed below, there are international flights linking Ürümqi with Almaty, Bishkek, Islamabad, Moscow, Novosibirsk and Sharjah.

Baotou to: Beijing (3 daily; 55min); Shanghai (2 daily; 2hr 25min).

Dunhuang to: Beijing (daily; 4hr); Lanzhou (daily; 2hr); Ürümqi (daily; 2hr); Xi'an (daily; 2hr 30min).

Hailar to: Beijing (6 weekly; 2hr); Hohhot (3 weekly; 2hr 25min).

Hohhot to: Beijing (5 daily; 1hr 10min); Chifeng (2 daily; 1hr 10min); Guangzhou (5 weekly; 3hr); Haikou (3 weekly; 6hr 45min); Hailar (3 weekly; 2hr 25min); Qingdao (2 weekly; 2hr 50min); Shanghai (2 daily; 2hr 30min); Shenyang (3 weekly; 1hr 30min); Shenzhen (3 weekly; 3hr); Taiyuan (5 daily; 50min); Tianjin (2 weekly; 1hr); Tongliao (daily; 1hr 40min); Ulanhot (daily; 1hr 40min); Wuhai (daily; 50min); Xi'an (3 weekly; 1hr 30min); Xilinhot (3 weekly; 1hr).

Jiayuguan to: Lanzhou (daily; 1hr 30min).

Kashgar to: Ürümqi (daily; 1hr 20min).

Khotan to: Ürümqi (daily; 1hr 45min).

Kuqa to: Ürümqi (2 weekly; 1hr 50min).

Lanzhou to: Beijing (3 daily; 2hr); Changsha (3 weekly; 2hr); Chengdu (daily; 1hr); Chongqing (1 weekly; 1hr 40min); Dunhuang (1 or 2 daily; 2hr); Xiamen (4 weekly; 4hr); Guangzhou (daily; 3hr); Haikou (daily; 4hr); Jiayuguan (daily; 1hr 30min); Kunming (daily; 1hr 20min); Qingdao (daily; 3hr 30min); Shanghai (1 or 2 daily; 2hr 30min); Shenzhen (daily; 4hr); Ürümqi (daily; 2hr 30min); Xi'an (1 or 2 daily; 1hr); Yinchuan (4 weekly; 50min).

Ürümqi to: Beijing (daily; 3hr 30min); Changsha (daily; 4hr); Chengdu (daily; 3hr 20min); Chongqing (daily; 3hr 30min); Dunhuang (daily; 2hr); Guangzhou (daily; 4hr 40min); Kashgar (daily; 1hr 20min); Khotan (daily; 1hr 45min); Korla (daily; 1hr); Lanzhou (daily; 2hr 30min); Shanghai (daily; 4hr); Xi'an (daily; 2hr 45min); Xining (daily; 2hr 20min); Yinchuan (daily; 3hr); Yining (2 daily; 2hr).

Xining to: Beijing (daily; 2hr 10min); Chengdu (daily; 1hr 20min); Guangzhou (daily; 3hr); Lhasa (2 weekly; 2hr 15min); Shanghai (daily; 2hr 40min); Ürümqi (daily; 2hr 20min); Xi'an (daily; 3hr).

Yinchuan to: Beijing (2 daily; 2hr); Chengdu (1 daily; 2hr); Guangzhou (daily; 4hr); Lanzhou (3 weekly; 50min); Nanjing (daily; 3hr 30min); Shanghai (daily; 3hr 30min); Ürümqi (daily; 3hr); Xi'an (daily; 50min).

Yining to: Ürümqi (2 daily; 2hr).

CHAPTER 14

Highlights

* **The Jokhang, Lhasa**
Wreathed in juniper smoke
and surrounded by prostrating pilgrims, this temple must
be one of the world's most
venerated sites. See p.1116

* **Lake Namtso** Sits bright as
a jewel beneath muscular
peaks. See p.1136

* **The Friendship Highway** The
bumpy winding road between
Lhasa and Nepal passes
some of the region's best
and certainly most accessible
sights. See p.1145

* **Mount Everest Base Camp**
Breathe deep and gaze up at
the jagged, snow-blown top
of the world. See p.1148

* **Mount Kailash** The world's
holiest mountain, its very
remoteness part of its appeal.
See p.1150

△ Samye monastery

Tibet

ibet (Bod to Tibetans, Xizang to the Chinese), the "Roof of the World", has exerted a magnetic pull over travellers for centuries. The scenery has a majesty and grandeur that are spellbinding, the religious monuments and practices are overwhelmingly picturesque and moving, and the Tibetan people are welcoming and wonderful. But look just a little below the surface and it is all too apparent that Tibet's past has been tragic, its present is painful, and the future looks bleak. Tibet today is a sad, subjugated colony of China. While foreign visitors are perhaps more worldly than to expect a romantic Shangri-la, there is no doubt that many are surprised by the heavy military and civilian Chinese presence, the modern apartments and factories alongside traditional Tibetan rural lifestyles and monasteries. All this doesn't mean you should stay away, however: though **tourism** provides legitimacy as well as foreign currency to the Chinese government, many people, the Dalai Lama among them, believe that travellers should visit Tibet to learn all they can of the country and its people.

In reaching Tibet, you'll have entered one of the most isolated parts of the world. The massive **Tibetan plateau**, at an average height of 4500m above sea level, is guarded on all sides by towering **mountain ranges**: the Himalayas separate Tibet from India, Nepal and Bhutan to the south, the Karakoram from Pakistan to the west and the Kunlun from Xinjiang to the north. To the east, dividing Tibet from Sichuan and Yunnan, an extensive series of subsidiary ranges covers almost a thousand kilometres. The plateau is also birthplace to some of the greatest **rivers** of Asia, with the Yangzi, Mekong, Yellow and Salween rising in the east, and the Indus, Brahmaputra, Sutlej and some feeder rivers of the Ganges in the west near Mount Kailash.

Tibet's isolation has long stirred the imagination of the West, yet until the British, under the command of Colonel Younghusband, invaded in 1904, only a trickle of bold eccentrics, adventurers and the odd missionary had succeeded in getting close to Lhasa, and then only at serious risk to their lives, for it was firm Tibetan policy to exclude all influence from the outside world. So great was the uncertainty about the geographical nature of the country even 150 years ago, that the British in India despatched carefully trained spies, known as *pundits*, to walk the length and breadth of the country, counting their footsteps with rosaries and mapping as they went. When Younghusband's invasion force finally reached Lhasa, they were, perhaps inevitably, disappointed. One journalist accompanying them wrote:

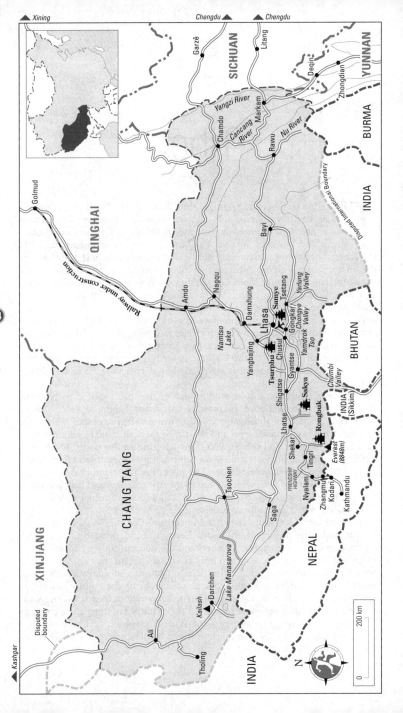

> If one approached within a league of Lhasa, saw the glittering domes of the Potala and turned back without entering the precincts one might still imagine an enchanted city. It was in fact an unsanitary slum. In the pitted streets pools of rainwater and piles of refuse were everywhere: the houses were mean and filthy, the stench pervasive. Pigs and ravens competed for nameless delicacies in open sewers.

Since the Chinese **invasion** in 1950, Tibet has become much more accessible, with approaches eased by plane links with Chengdu and Kathmandu. There has subsequently been heavy Han migration into the region, and although it is impossible to know how many Chinese live here now, it is likely that they outnumber Tibetans. The situation is most marked in the cities, where the greatest opportunities exist: not only are the numbers of Han increasing all the time, but they are becoming economically dominant too – a situation that will be further exacerbated by the completion, due in 2007, of the railway line from Golmud to Lhasa.

Today's **Tibetan Autonomous Region** (TAR), though covering a massive 1.2 million square kilometres, is but a shadow of the former Tibetan lands. The old area, sometimes referred to as Greater Tibet or Ethnographic Tibet, was carved up by the Chinese following their invasion, when the Amdo and Kham regions were absorbed into Qinghai, Sichuan, Gansu and Yunnan provinces. The TAR consists only of the West and Central (U-Tsang) regions of Greater Tibet and divides into four geographical areas. The northern and largest portion is the almost uninhabited **Chang Tang**, a rocky desert at an average altitude of 4000m, where winter temperatures can fall to minus 44°C. South of this is the **mountainous grazing area**, land that cannot support settled agriculture, inhabited by the wide-ranging nomadic people with their herds of yaks, sheep and goats. **Eastern Tibet**, occupying around a quarter of the TAR, is heavily forested. The **southern valleys**, sandwiched between the nomad area and the **Himalayas** along the southern border, are the most hospitable for human habitation. Not surprisingly, this is the most populated area and where visitors spend the majority of their time, particularly in the extensive valley system of the Tsangpo River (Brahmaputra) and its tributaries.

Lhasa, **Shigatse** and **Gyantse** offer the most accessible **monasteries** and **temples** – the Jokhang, Tashilunpo and the Kumbum respectively – and are also tourist-friendly cities with the biggest range of facilities in the region. The **Potala Palace** in Lhasa remains an enduring image of Tibet in the Western mind and should on no account be missed, and there are plenty of smaller sights in the city to keep anyone busy for several days. Farther afield, the **Yarlung** and **Chongye** valleys to the southeast boast temples and ancient monuments, and the ancient walled monastery of **Samye** is easily combined with these. The tourist corridor between Zhangmu on the Nepalese border and Lhasa is relatively well-trodden these days, although by no means overcrowded, and offers side-trips to the huge Mongolian-style monastery at **Sakya** and to **Everest Base Camp**.

While the Chinese prefer easily controllable, high-rolling tour parties rather than the less malleable, less lucrative budget travellers, they are, for the moment, prepared to tolerate both – though the trip is likely to be expensive, as the Chinese authorities are keen to milk tourism by charging for permits to enter the region and restricting accommodation and transport options available to foreigners. **Tibetan organizations** abroad ask that visitors try, wherever possible, to buy from Tibetans and to hire Tibetan guides. At all times, you should avoid putting Tibetans – and yourself – at risk by bringing up **politically sensitive issues**; remember that you (and your emails) are monitored here. It's also advisable not to bring in Dalai Lama pictures to hand out – Tibetans found with them are in serious trouble.

14

TIBET

Finally, remember that the situation here is not black and white. The Han Chinese in Tibet are not demons – most are poor people trying to make a life for themselves and their families, and they may have little knowledge or understanding of the wider political implications of their presence. And don't idealize the pre-Chinese Tibetan administration; it was, after all, a xenophobic religious dictatorship, feudal in outlook, which stifled economic progress and tolerated slavery.

Living Buddhism

There is little ceremony attached to **visiting Buddhist temples** and they are generally open and welcoming places. Most temples are open in the mornings (9am–noon), when pilgrims do the rounds, and usually again after lunch (2– or 3–5pm). Smaller places may well be locked, but ask for the caretaker and the chances are you'll be let in. There is no need to remove your shoes, but when walking inside the chapels or around the complex or building, you should proceed **clockwise**, and you shouldn't eat, drink or smoke inside. It is polite to ask before taking photographs, which isn't always allowed, and if it is, you may be charged for the privilege. The **entrance fees** collected from tourists are taken by the Chinese authorities, so if you want to give to the institution itself, leave an offering on an altar.

The range of **offerings** devout Tibetans make to their gods is enormous. It includes juniper smoke sent skyward in incense burners, prayer flags printed with prayers erected on rooftops and mountains, tiny papers printed with religious images and cast to the wind on bridges and passes (*lungda*), white scarves (*katag*) presented to statues and lamas, butter to keep lamps burning on altars, repetitious *mantras* invoking the gods, and the spinning of prayer wheels that have printed prayers rolled up inside. The idea of each is to gain merit in this life and hence affect your *karma*. If you want to take part, watch what other people do and copy them; nobody is at all precious about religion in Tibet. Giving **alms to beggars** is another way of gaining merit, and most large Tibetan temples have a horde of beggars who survive on charity from pilgrims. Whether or not you give money is up to you, but if you do it's wise to give a few small denomination notes or so, the same amount as Tibetans.

Tibetan Buddhism is divided into several **schools** that have different philosophical emphases rather than fundamental differences. The **Nyingma**, the Old Order, traces its origins back to Guru Rinpoche, Padmasambhava, who brought Buddhism to Tibet. The **Kagyupa**, **Sakya** and **Kadampa** all developed during the eleventh-century revival of Buddhism, while the now dominant **Gelugpa** (Virtuous School) was founded by Tsongkhapa (1357–1419) and numbers the Dalai Lama and Panchen Lama among its adherents. Virtually all monasteries and temples are aligned to one or other of the schools, but, apart from an abundance of statues of revered lamas of that particular school, you'll spot little difference between the temples. Tibetan people are pretty eclectic and will worship in temples which they feel are particularly sacred and seek blessings from lamas they feel are endowed with special powers, regardless of the school they belong to.

Gods and goddesses

Tibetan Buddhism has an overwhelming number of **gods and goddesses**, and matters are complicated by each deity having different manifestations or forms. For example, there are 21 forms of the favourite goddess Tara, and even the most straightforward image has both a Sanskrit and Tibetan name. Below are some of the most common you will encounter:

Amitayus (Tsepame) and **Vijaya** (Namgyelma), often placed with White Tara to form the Three Gods of Longevity.

Avalokiteshvara (Chenresi in Tibetan, Guanyin in Chinese temples), patron god of Tibet, with many forms, most noticeably with eleven faces and a thousand arms.

Some history

According to legend, the **earliest Tibetans** came from the union of the ogress, Sinmo, and a monkey, reincarnation of the god Chenresi, on the mountain of Gangpo Ri near Tsetang. Ethnographers, however, think it likely the Tibetans are descended from the nomadic Ch'iang who roamed eastern Central Asia, to the northwest of China, several thousand years ago. The first Tibetan king,

Maitreya (Jampa), the Buddha of the Future.

Manjusri (Jampelyang), the God of Wisdom.

Padmasambhava, with eight manifestations, most apparent as Guru Rinpoche. You may see him with his consorts, Yeshe Tsogyel and Mandarava.

Sakyamuni, Buddha of the Present.

Tara (Dolma), Goddess of Compassion. Green Tara is associated with protection and White Tara with long life.

Festivals

Festival dates are calculated using the Tibetan lunar calendar and thus correspond to different dates on the Western calendar each year. There is a list of festival dates in the Western calendar at ⓦ www.kalachakranet.org/ta_tibetan_calendar.html.

February/March

Driving out of evil spirits. Twenty-ninth day of the twelfth lunar month, the last day of the year.

Losar, Tibetan New Year. First day of the first lunar month.

Monlam, Great Prayer Festival, Lhasa. Eighth day of the first lunar month.

Butter Lamp Festival, on the final day of Monlam. Fifteenth day of the first lunar month.

May/June

Birth of Buddha. Seventh day of the fourth lunar month.

Saga Dawa (Buddha's Enlightenment). Fifteenth day of the fourth lunar month.

Gyantse Horse Festival. Fifteenth day of the fourth lunar month.

July

Tashilunpo Festival, Shigatse. Fifteenth day of the fifth lunar month.

July/August

Buddha's First Sermon. Fourth day of the sixth lunar month.

Drepung Festival. Thirtieth day of the sixth lunar month.

August/September

Shotun (Yoghurt Festival), Lhasa. First to the seventh day of the seventh lunar month.

Bathing Festival, Lhasa. Twenty-seventh day of the seventh lunar month.

September

Damxhung Horse Festival. Thirtieth day of the seventh lunar month.

September/October

Harvest Festival. First to the seventh day of the eighth lunar month.

November

Lhabab (Buddha's descent from Heaven). Twenty-second day of the ninth lunar month.

November/December

Peldon Lhama Festival, Lhasa. Fifteenth day of the tenth lunar month.

Nyatri Tsenpo, believed to have come to earth via a magical "sky-cord", was the first of a long lineage of 27 kings who ruled in a pre-Buddhist era when the indigenous, shamanistic **Bon religion** held sway throughout the land (see p.940). Each of the **early kings** held power over a small area, the geographical isolation of Tibet making outside contact difficult. Nevertheless, it is apparent that as early as the seventh century there was considerable cultural exchange between Tibet and its neighbours. Pens, ink, silks, jewels and probably tea reached Tibet from China in the seventh century, and for many centuries Tibet looked to India for religious teaching.

It was in the time of **King Songtsen Gampo**, the thirty-third ruler in the dynasty, born in 617 AD, that expansionism began. Songtsen Gampo's twenty-year rule saw the unification of the country and the aggressive spread of his empire from northern India to China. To placate their assertive neighbour, China and Nepal each offered Songtsen Gampo a wife: in 632 he married Princess Bhrikuti (also known as Tritsun) of Nepal, and in 641 Princess Wencheng arrived from the Tang court sent by her father, Emperor Taizong. They both brought their Buddhist faith and magnificent statues of the Buddha, which are now the centrepieces of Ramoche temple and the Jokhang in Lhasa. Songtsen Gampo himself embraced the **Buddhist faith** and established Buddhist temples throughout the country, although the indigenous Bon faith remained the religion of the ordinary people. Following his death in 650, his descendants strengthened the kingdom politically, and in 763, Tibetan armies even took the Chinese capital Chang'an (modern Xi'an). Trisong Detsen (742–797) was another champion of the new faith, who invited two Indian Buddhist teachers to Tibet, Shantarakshita and the charismatic and flamboyant **Padmasambhava**. The latter, who was also known as Guru Rinpoche, is regarded as responsible for overcoming the resistance of the Bon religion and ensuring the spread of Buddhism within Tibet. Although he is closely associated with the Nyingma school of Buddhism, you'll spot his image somewhere in most temples.

In 838, the infamous **Langdarma** came to the throne, having assassinated his brother. A fervent supporter of Bon, he set about annihilating the Buddhist faith. Temples and monasteries were destroyed, monks forced to flee and the previously unified Tibet broke up into a number of small principalities. A Buddhist revival involving monastery construction, the translation of scriptures into Tibetan and the establishment of several of the schools of Tibetan Buddhism was spearheaded by the arrival of **Atisha** (982–1054), the most famous Indian scholar of the time. Politically the country was not united, but the various independent principalities lived largely in harmony and there was little contact with China.

Absorbed in internal events, the Tibetans had largely neglected the outside world, where the Muslim surge across India in the twelfth and thirteenth centuries resulted in the destruction of the great Buddhist centres of teaching to which the Tibetans had looked for generations. And to the north and east of Tibet, the **Mongol leader**, Genghis Khan, was beginning his assault on China. In 1207, Chingis Khan sent envoys to Tibet demanding submission, which was given without a fight, and the territory was largely ignored until Chingis Khan's grandson, Godan, sent raiding parties deep into the country. Hearing from his troops about the spirituality of the Tibetan lamas, Godan invited the head of the Sakya order, Sakya Pandita, to his court. In exchange for peace, Sakya Pandita again offered Tibetan submission and was created regent of Tibet at the Mongolian court, making the Sakya lamas the effective rulers of Tibet under the patronage of the emperor. This lasted through the generations, with Godan's son **Kublai Khan** deeply impressed by Sakya Pandita's nephew, Phagpa.

When the Chinese Ming dynasty overcame the Mongols in the fourteenth century, Tibet began a long period of independence, which ended in 1642 with the Mongols intervening directly in support of the Fifth Dalai Lama, Lobsang Gyatso (1617–82), of the **Gelugpa order**. Often referred to as "**the Great Fifth**", he united the country under Gelugpa rule and within fifteen years, largely neglected by Mongol rulers, established authority from Kham to Kailash – the first time that one religious and political leader had united and ruled the country. He invited scholars to Tibet, restored and expanded religious institutions and began work on the Potala in Lhasa.

One disadvantage of the **reincarnation system** of succession (in which a newborn child is identified as the next manifestation of the dead lama) is that an unstable period of fifteen or twenty years inevitably follows a death while the next reincarnation grows up. Initially, the death of the Fifth Dalai Lama in 1682 was concealed by his regent, Sangye Gyatso, who raised the Sixth Dalai Lama to adulthood while claiming the Fifth Dalai Lama had entered a period of solitary meditation. The following two centuries saw no strong leadership from the Dalai Lamas, and there were repeated incursions by Mongolian factions. The most influential figures in Tibet at this time were the regents and representatives of the Manchu rulers in China, the *ambans*. During the **nineteenth century**, Tibet became increasingly isolationist, fearing Russian plans to expand their empire south and British plans to expand their empire north. Seeing themselves caught in the middle, the Tibetans simply banned foreigners from their land. But at their borders, Tibetans continued trading with Indians, and in 1904 their one-sided trading arrangements exasperated the British, who determined to forge a fair treaty on the subject. The Tibetans refused to negotiate, so an expeditionary force was sent in 1904 under Colonel Younghusband, to obtain satisfaction. Meeting with obfuscation and hostility from Tibet's rulers, the invaders marched further and further into Tibet, and fought a couple of dispiriting battles against peasant soldiers armed with scythes and charms of invulnerability – gifts from their lamas, who stood at the back yelling encouragement. Patching up their poor opponents in improvised field hospitals along the way, the British marched up to Gyantse through the Chumbi Valley and eventually on to Lhasa. A series of British Representatives in Lhasa forged good relationships with Tibet and became a window on the outside world.

The **Thirteenth Dalai Lama**, Tubten Gyatso (1876–1933), was an insightful and capable leader who realized that Tibet's political position needed urgent clarification, but he had a difficult rule, fleeing into exile twice, and was much occupied with border fighting against the Chinese and tensions with conservatives inside the country. Following his death, the **Fourteenth Dalai Lama** was identified in Amdo in 1938 and was still a young man when world events began to close in on Tibet. The British left India in 1947, withdrawing their Representative from Lhasa. In 1949 the Communists, under Mao Zedong, created the People's Republic of China and the following year declared their intention "to liberate the oppressed and exploited Tibetans and reunite them with the great motherland". In October 1950, the People's Liberation Army invaded the Kham region of eastern Tibet before proceeding to Lhasa the following year. Under considerable duress, Tibet signed a seventeen-point treaty in 1951, allowing for the "peaceful integration of Tibet".

The Chinese era

Initially the Chinese offered goodwill and modernization. Tibet had made little headway into the twentieth century; there were few roads, no electricity, and glass windows, steel girders and concrete were all recent introductions. Hygiene and health care were patchy and lay education was unavailable. While some Tibetans viewed modernization as necessary, the opposition was stiff, as many within the religious hierarchy saw changes within the country and overtures to the outside world as a threat to their influence. Throughout the 1950s, an underground resistance operated, which flared into a public confrontation in March 1959, fuelled by mounting distrust and hostility, as refugees from eastern Tibet fled to Lhasa and told of the brutality of Chinese rule. In Lhasa, the Chinese invited the Dalai Lama to a theatrical performance at the Chinese military base. It was popularly perceived as a ploy to kidnap him, and huge numbers of Tibetans mounted demonstrations and surrounded the Norbulingka where the Dalai Lama was staying. On the night of March 17, the Dalai Lama and his entourage escaped, heading into **exile** in India where they were later joined (and are still joined today) by tens of thousands of refugees.

Meanwhile the **uprising in Lhasa** was ferociously suppressed – 87,000 people were killed by the Chinese between March 1959 and September 1960. From that point on, all pretence of goodwill vanished, and a huge military force moved in, with a Chinese bureaucracy replacing Tibetan institutions. Temples and monasteries were destroyed and Chinese **agricultural policies** proved particularly disastrous. During the years of the Great Leap Forward (1959–60) it is estimated that ten percent of Tibetans starved, and it wasn't until the early 1980s that the food situation in Tibet began to improve. Harrowing accounts tell of parents mixing their own blood with hot water and *tsampa* to feed their children.

In September 1965 the U-Tsang and Western areas of Tibet officially became the **Xizang Autonomous Region** of the People's Republic of China, but more significant was the **Cultural Revolution** (1966–76) during which mass destruction of religious monuments and practices took place under the orders of the Red Guards, some of them young Tibetans. In 1959 there were 2700 monasteries and temples in Tibet; by 1978 there were just eight monasteries and fewer than a thousand monks and nuns in the TAR. Liberalization followed Mao's death in 1976, leading to a period of relative openness and peace in the early 1980s when monasteries were rebuilt, religion revived and tourism restored. By the end of the decade repression was again in place following riots in Lhasa in 1988–9, but in the early 1990s foreigners were allowed back.

The current mood is one of apparent openness, with the encouragement of tourism against a background of increased internal control of the Tibetan population. Dissent is ruthlessly quashed and there are currently between six and seven hundred political detainees, more than at any time since 1990. Estimates of three hundred thousand to one million have been given for the number of Tibetans who have perished either directly at the hands of the Chinese or indirectly through starvation and hardship. The International Commission of Jurists in the Hague has held the People's Republic of China to be guilty of genocide.

Meanwhile, the profile of the **Tibetan Government in Exile**, led by the Dalai Lama, continues to increase. Based in Dharamsala in northern India, it represents some 130,000 Tibetan refugees, 100,000 of whom are in India. The world community has refused to take a stand for the Tibetans, yet the Dalai Lama, known to the Tibetans as Gyalwa Rinpoche and regarded as the earthly incarnation of the god Chenresi, has never faltered from advocating a peaceful solution for Tibet, a stance which led to his being awarded the 1989 Nobel Peace Prize. In recent years relations have thawed, as the Dalai Lama wishes to see his homeland before he dies, and the Chinese administration wants to improve their image before the Beijing Olympics in 2008. The terms of the Dalai Lama's return are now being seriously considered. In the meantime, around three thousand young Tibetans every year make the arduous trip to India, though increasingly these days they stay only for a few years before heading home.

For the Tibetans who remain here, the reality of life in Tibet is harsh. China admits that the inhabitants of a quarter of the TAR counties cannot feed or clothe themselves, one third of children do not go to school and Tibet's literacy rate is about thirty percent, the lowest in China. Between 1952 and 1998 it is estimated that China subsidized the TAR to the tune of 40 billion yuan – yet Tibetans are among the poorest people in China and have the lowest life expectancy in the country. As Tibet provides the Chinese with land for their exploding population along with almost untold natural resources, the influx of Han Chinese settlers threatens to swamp the Tibetan population, culture and economy.

The biggest threat to the Tibetan way of life – and the biggest promise of modernization, and therefore rising living standards – comes from the **railway line** being built from Golmud to Lhasa at the cost of four billion US dollars, due for completion in 2007. It makes little economic sense but will allow the Chinese to consolidate their hold over the region and move troops around quickly. It will certainly aid the immigrant Chinese population, who consume huge quantities of expensively imported food – the Tibetans, in contrast, are largely self-sufficient. The project is hugely ambitious, with more than 1200km of new track being built by 11,000 migrant workers, whose toils can be seen if you take the Golmud bus to Lhasa. Most of the track is built at on attitude of over 4000m and on permafrost, in an area susceptible to both earthquakes and landslides, and more than 30km of tunnels are needed. The train carriages themselves will be pressurized, like an aircraft, so passengers will suffer the discomforts of altitude sickness on arrival rather than during their trip.

Tibet practicalities

The **best time to visit** is April to October, outside the coldest months. June to September are the wettest months, when blocked roads and swollen rivers can make travel difficult, but the countryside will be at its greenest. However, health considerations should be taken seriously at any time of the year, and even in relatively balmy Lhasa, temperatures fall below freezing on a regular basis. In winter, as long as you come fully prepared for the cold (most hotels have no heating) and possible delays due to snow-covered passes, the lack of tourists and the preoccupation of the security forces with staying warm can make for a pleasant trip.

It's worth noting that the Chinese authorities are much pricklier around **festival times** (see box, p.1097) and the week before and after certain historically significant dates, when they'll be much more likely to **clamp down** on unregulated travel and demand permits for inspection. Dates to bear in mind include March 5 and 10 (the anniversaries of uprisings in 1988 and 1989), July 6 (the Dalai Lama's birthday), September 27 and October 1 (the anniversary of protests in 1987), and December 10 (International Human Rights Day, and the anniversary of the Dalai Lama's Nobel Peace Prize).

Getting there

Officially you need only a **Chinese visa** to travel to Tibet. However, the authorities control entry into the country by insisting that independent travellers purchase a "**permit**" when they buy travel tickets for the region. You will probably not see this permit and once you are in Tibet nobody is interested in it. **Visa extensions** can be problematic in Tibet; you can apply for extensions

Traveller's Tibetan

Although some people involved in the tourist industry are now conversant in several languages, including English, most Tibetans speak only their native language, with perhaps a smattering of Mandarin. A few words of Tibetan are not only greeted enthusiastically, but are well nigh essential if you're heading off the beaten track or going trekking.

Tibetan belongs to the small Tibeto–Burmese group of languages and has no similarity at all to Mandarin or Hindi. Tibetan script was developed in the seventh century and has thirty consonants and five vowels, which are placed either beside, above or below other letters when written down. There are obvious inaccuracies when trying to render this into the Roman alphabet and the situation is further complicated by the many dialects across the region; the Lhasa dialect is used in the vocabulary below. Word order is back-to-front relative to English, and verbs are placed at the ends of sentences – "this noodle soup is delicious" becomes "tukpa dee shimbo do", literally "noodle soup this delicious is". The only sound you are likely to have trouble with is **ng** at the beginning of words – it is pronounced as in sa**ng**.

Basic Phrases

Hello	tashi delay	Tired	galay ka
Goodbye, to someone staying	kalay shu	I don't understand	nga ha ko ma-song
		What is your name?	kayranggi mingla karay ray?
Goodbye, to someone going	kalay pay	My name is …	ngeye mingla … sa
Thank you	tuk too jay	Where are you from?	kayrang kanay ray?
Sorry	gonda		
Please	coochee	I'm from …	nga … nay yin
How are you?	kusu debo yinbay? or kam sangbo dugay?	Britain	injee
		Australia	otaleeya
I'm …	nga …	America	amerika
Fine	debo yin	How old are you?	kayrang lo katsay ray?
Cold	kya	I'm …	nga lo … yin
Hungry	throko- doe	Where are you going?	kaba drogee yin?
Thirsty	ka gom		

at any PSB but, at best, they will ask to see proof that you are on your way out of the country and then only give you one week.

Tour operators outside Tibet – notably those in Chengdu – will exaggerate the difficulty of independent travel in Tibet; don't believe anything they say and talk to other travellers instead. Once in Tibet, you are fairly independent.

By air

Domestic flights operate daily to Lhasa from Chengdu (¥1550, plus ¥300 for the permit), and there are also services from Beijing (via Chengdu), Xining (see p.1031), Deqin airport in Zhongdian (see p.841; ¥1430, but the permit will cost a further ¥1000 or so) and Kunming (via Zhongdian, ¥1750 for the ticket and the permit will cost ¥1000 or so). There are also flights from Chongqing, but as the PSB there isn't geared up to handing out the required permits, the only time you just might be using this route is when leaving. Note that while ticket prices are reliable, the price and availability of permits fluctuates unpredictably.

The easiest and cheapest option is to fly from Chengdu, where plenty of tour operators, most of them grouped around the *Traffic Hotel*, offer tickets with

English	Tibetan	English	Tibetan
I'm going to ...	nga ... la drogee yin	Friday	sa pasang
		Saturday	sa pemba
Where is the ...?	... kaba doo?	How much is this?	gong kadso ray?
hospital	menkang		
monastery	gompa		
temple/chapel	lhakhang	**Numbers**	
restaurant	sakang	1	chee
convent	ani gompa	2	nyee
caretaker	konyer	3	soom
Is there ... ?	... doo gay?	4	zhee
hot water	chu tsa-bo	5	nga
a candle	yangla	6	droo
I don't have ...	nga ... mindoo	7	doon
Is this OK/ can I do this?	deegee rebay?	8	gyay
		9	goo
It's (not) OK	deegee (ma)ray	10	chew
(Not) Good	yaggo (min)doo	11	chew chee
This is delicious	dee shimbo doo	12	chew nyee
Do you want ... ?	kayrang ... gobay?	etc	
I want tea	nga cha go	20	nyi shoo
I don't want this	dee me-go	21	nyi shoo chee etc
What is this/that?	dee/day karray ray?	30	soom chew
When?	kadoo?	40	shib chew
Now	danta	50	ngab chew
Today	dering	60	drook chew
Yesterday	kezang	70	doon chew
Tomorrow	sangnyee	80	gyay chew
Sunday	sa nima	90	goop chew
Monday	sa dowa	100	gya
Tuesday	sa mingma	200	nyee gya
Wednesday	sa lagba	etc	
Thursday	sa purbur	1000	dong

TIBET | Tibet practicalities

permit (which you'll never see) for ¥1850. They also sell tours, including flight, transport from Gongkar airport into Lhasa, and a few days' accommodation at a budget hotel – a guide can be included, often for not much more. It's simple to arrange, and a ticket for the next day is usually available. Once in Lhasa, you can buy flights back at the standard price.

Flights from **Kathmandu** leave twice weekly (Tues & Sat) but not in the winter (October–March) and can be booked only as part of a tour operated by a travel agent there; expect to pay upwards of US$360 for a flight and a three-day tour. If you don't already have a Chinese visa, you'll only get in as part of a group, on a group visa. You can change this to an individual visa in Lhasa, but the process is expensive (around ¥300) and its success depends on how well connected your travel agent is.

By land
Overland routes to Tibet are well established, although they can be physically taxing. From within China, **Golmud to Lhasa** (1160km, thirty jarring hours) is the only officially permitted land route for foreigners (see p.1040).

CITS charge an outrageous ¥1700 for a return ticket (they won't sell singles). The return leg is dated three days from the date of the inbound trip; you can change your date of return at the bus station in Lhasa, though most people throw the ticket away and fly out – no one wants to do that trip twice. Some travellers have got around the CITS scam by standing on the road outside Golmud, waiting for the bus, and then making a deal with the driver; others make shady deals with characters who hang around the bus station. It's worth trying, if only to avoid enriching CITS. It's also possible to go overland from Yunnan as part of a tour (¥5000 per person, one week to Lhasa – see p.843 for more details).

The overland routes from Sichuan (over 2000km from Chengdu to Lhasa) and Kashgar (1100km to Ali) are officially closed to foreigners, and potentially dangerous, although a few intrepid travellers manage to get through. If you're caught by the authorities you will be fined (around ¥300, after negotiation) and sent back in the direction you came from – so most travellers simply tell the authorities they came from where they're actually headed, and are sent on their way. At the time of writing, foreigners could buy tickets on sleeper buses from Yicheng in Xinjiang to Ali in Tibet for the local price, then in Ali they received a fine and a permit for Kailash – but you can bet this won't last.

If you do try hitchhiking, be aware that you'll need warm clothes and provisions at any time of year – and it can be almost as expensive as flying, with truck drivers charging around ¥1000 – if they're caught, they are fined ten times that much. There's no guarantee of a ride, and conditions out here are tough. A number of foreign hitchhikers have died of hypothermia.

Entering Tibet overland **from Kathmandu** via Kodari on the Nepal side and Zhangmu on the Tibetan side is a popular option, but travellers on this route are vulnerable to snap changes in entry regulations, and also to landslides in summer and snow-blocked passes in winter. The situation in Nepal was highly volatile at the time of writing, with a civil war taking place between government forces and Moaist rebels. Check with your embassy to see what they advise. Under no circumstances should you apply for a Chinese visa in Kathmandu if you want to travel independently to Tibet – the Chinese embassy will not issue these unless you are booked on an organized tour through a Kathmandu travel agent. Independent travellers must have their Chinese visa before arrival in Kathmandu, and even then, Aliens' Travel Permits (see opposite) for the route to Lhasa (which cost US$30 in Kathmandu) were being issued only if an organized tour through to the capital was booked. Expect to pay around US$400 for an organized seven-day overland trip to Lhasa, or around US$250 for a three-day trip. An agency that will group individual travellers together is Nature Trail Trekking at Durbar Marg in Kathmandu (☎977 1 4701925, ⓦwww.allnepal.com), which charges US$330 for a five-day overland "tour" to Lhasa. They will tell you that a ticket out of Tibet is necessary, but some people who don't have one still get in. The best advice is to spend some time in Kathmandu to get a feel for the current situation and check out your options.

At the time of writing, **cyclists** on this route were unable to persuade the authorities to issue a permit without being part of a tour, but this might change. If you're going to attempt cycling in, bear in mind that most of the road between Zhangmu and Shigatse is unpaved and very rough. The altitude gain from Kodari to Zhangmu is 530m in about 9km, then 1450m in the 33km to Nyalam followed by a tough 1300m in the 57-kilometre climb to the Lalung Pass at 5050m. Allow around twenty days to cycle from Kathmandu to Lhasa. You'll need camping equipment, food (plus stove) and adequate warm-weather gear. Dogs are a particular hazard near villages.

Getting around

Aliens' Travel Permits (¥150) are issued by the PSB and give you permission to visit specified places within specified time limits. At the time of writing, the only parts of Tibet where you did not need an Aliens' Travel Permit were Lhasa, Shigatse, Zhangmu, Tsetang and Namtso Lake. For all other areas you need to apply to the PSB for a permit; the best place to apply is at the comparatively lenient and friendly office in Shigatse. You'll be asked what places you want put on the document, and as the price is fixed so you may as well fill it up. Independent travellers will be allowed a permit for all destinations on the Friendship Highway to Nepal, and sights nearby such as Everest, but only those travelling in tour groups with accredited agencies are allowed permits for western or eastern Tibet. There are some areas where a permit will not be given under any circumstances, such as the highly militarized Chumbi Valley. The status of other areas seems to change from one day to the next. Penalties for being caught somewhere without a permit can be fairly heavy: travellers have faced big fines, been harangued at length, and forced to write "confessions".

The **public transport** system in Tibet, such as it is, consists of large public **buses** and the smaller, nippier **minibuses**. For Tibetans these are largely interchangeable, but for foreigners the difference is highly significant. There are, as yet, no problems with foreigners travelling on the public buses, but minibuses come under the label of "private vehicles" and foreigners are banned from travelling on these (although the minibuses that operate within Lhasa itself seem exempt from this ban). This is regardless of the fact that minibuses are often the best, and sometimes the only, public transport between two points. This ban also means foreigners cannot travel in trucks and private cars, which effectively rules out hitchhiking. Drivers face fines and big trouble if they are caught breaking these rules, but the zeal with which the PSB enforces the regulations changes from month to month. The situation with regard to the large **pilgrim buses** which operate daily to Ganden and Tsurphu monasteries is even more

Arranging private transport

For specific excursions, most travellers end up **hiring a jeep** with a driver and perhaps a guide as well (the latter may be obligatory, depending on your destination). There are many private **tour companies** in **Lhasa** who can arrange this: all the hotels have agencies for the purpose, and they adorn Beijing Dong Lu and Mentsikhang Lu. You'll need to decide your exact itinerary, get together five people to fill up the jeep, write a contract detailing timings and costs and pay the deposit (usually half the agreed fee) before you go. You should check that the quoted price includes the cost of permits (which the tour company should arrange), plus fees, lodging and food for the driver and guide, and the cost of fuel – in fact, everything except your own food and lodging and the cost of your admission to monasteries. It pays to be precise in your itinerary (so, for example, don't say Rongbuk Monastery if you mean Everest Base Camp), as well as to work out what the extra cost should be if one of your party falls ill and you are delayed (about ¥200 a day is reasonable). The most popular option, a five-day tour to the Nepalese border, taking in Gyantse, Shigatse and Everest Base Camp, should cost around ¥4400. The cheapest short tour is a trip to Namtso Lake and back (¥425 per person for four days). When rules become more strict, the official agency, FIT, will be able to do things the others won't (see Lhasa listings, p.1122). Hopefully you'll have no problems, but in the event of a misunderstanding, you may wish to **complain** to the Tour Service Inspection Office of Lhasa's **Tibet Tourism Bureau**, 208 Luobulingka Lu (☏0891/6333476 or 6334193).

confused; while most travellers report few problems using them, drivers may be hesitant about taking you when the local situation is particularly tense. Given that the rules as regards travel in Tibet are in a constant state of flux, it's essential to talk to **other travellers** to try to get an up-to-date picture of things.

Long-distance cycling is technically illegal, but the authorities don't seem too bothered, certainly not by those attempting the popular route to Nepal, which takes two to three weeks. The first part of the trip, from Lhasa to Shigatse, is legal, then you'll have to apply for a permit – don't tell them you're on a bike – and hope for the best. Most of the route is level, but the road leaves a lot to be desired, dogs and weather can be a hazard, and there are five 5000-metre passes to contend with – but the last haul is a great three-day downhill. Most of the time, you'll have to camp and cook your own food. The route is covered by a few cycle tour companies, such as the UK-based Exodus (℡0870 240 5550, ⊛www.exodus.co.uk) and HMB Tours in Kathmandu (℡977 1 4700437 ⊛www.bikingnepal.com).

Of the **maps** available, recommended is the English-language *China Tibet Tour Map* and *Lhasa Tour Map*. Both are available at the Xinhua Bookstore, where they cost ¥7, and at most hotels, where they are a little pricier. The *Yak Hotel* has a dated but detailed hand-drawn city map (¥3). See "Basics", p.37, for advice on maps available outside Tibet. The *On This Spot Lhasa Map*, published by the International Campaign for Tibet, shows another side to the city, marking prisons, security facilities and army bases – needless to say, you shouldn't take it there with you.

Health

Tibet poses particular health hazards to travellers. Almost every visitor is affected by **altitude**, as most of Tibet is over 3000m, with plenty of passes over 5000m. For your first two or three days at altitude, rest as much as possible and drink plenty of water. You can buy oxygen canisters in most hotel receptions (¥30), though whether they're much use is debatable. A few painkillers should help to relieve any aches and pains and headaches, but more serious problems can develop; see "Basics", p.42 for more details. The prescription drug Diamox can help, but don't take it as a substitute for descent. Trekkers and anyone travelling long distances in the backs of trucks need also to be particularly aware of the dangers of **hypothermia**.

Travellers to Tibet should have **rabies immunization** before they travel. The dogs here are very aggressive, bites are common and, if you get bitten, Kathmandu is the nearest place stocking rabies serum. A significant number of travellers to Tibet also suffer from **giardiasis**, an unpleasant and debilitating intestinal complaint (see p.40), although there is some controversy over whether it is endemic to the region or brought in from outside. The treatment is Tinadozol or Flagyl, neither or which is reliably available in Lhasa; bring a course along if you are planning an ambitious or lengthy trip.

Accommodation

In most Tibetan towns, simple **guesthouses** offer accommodation to foreigners, pilgrims and truck drivers. You can expect dormitory accommodation with bedding, of variable cleanliness, provided. The communal toilets are usually pit latrines and there are few washing facilities, although most places have bowls. You can expect hot water in vacuum flasks, for drinks and washing, everywhere. Lighting may be by lantern.

There is a greater choice of accommodation in the main tourist centres of Lhasa, Shigatse, Gyantse, Tsetang and Zhangmu, where international-standard hotels provide comfortable rooms with attached bathrooms and at least some hours of hot water. In the administrative centres of Lhasa and Shigatse, foreigners are allowed to stay at **mid-range hotels**, with rooms of a similar quality and generally offering very reasonable value for money.

If you are trekking, you can **camp** wherever the fancy takes you, although many trekkers find accommodation in village houses or with nomadic yak-herders. You should not expect them to feed you, and should pay ¥15 or so per night.

Eating, drinking and nightlife

The traditional **Tibetan diet** – constrained by what little will grow at over 4000m – consists in large part of **butter tea**, a unique mixture of yak butter, tea and salt, all churned into a blend that many Westerners find undrinkable, but which Tibetans consume in huge quantities. Into this is stirred **tsampa**, roasted barley flour, to form a dough with the consistency of raw pastry and a not unpleasant nutty flavour. **Yak meat**, yoghurt and cheese (often dried into bite-sized cubes to preserve it) and sometimes a soup of a few vegetables supplement this. **Thukpa** (pronounced tukpa) is a noodle soup with a few bits and pieces of whatever is available thrown in. If you're lucky, you'll find **momos**, tiny steamed or fried dough parcels containing meat or vegetables (a *thri momo* is a solid dough parcel without a filling). The local brew, **chang**, is a sweet, yellow beer made from a mixture of grains.

Lhasa

Situated in a wide, mountain-fringed valley on the north bank of the Kyichu River, **LHASA** (Ground of the Gods), at 3700m, is a sprawling, rapidly expanding, modern Chinese city with a population of around 200,000. An important settlement for well over a thousand years, it was originally called Rasa, but was

Lhasa		
Lhasa	拉萨	*lāsà*
Barkhor	八角街	*bājiǎo jiē*
Jokhang	大昭寺	*dàzhāosì*
Norbulingka	罗布林卡	*luóbùlínkǎ*
Potala	布达拉宫	*bùdálā gōng*
Tibet Museum	西藏博物馆	*xīzàng bówùguǎn*
Accommodation		
Banak Shol	八朗学旅馆	*bālǎngxué lǚguǎn*
Grand Hotel Tibet	西藏国际大酒店	*xīzàng guójì dàjiǔdiàn*
Hubei Hotel	湖北宾馆	*húběi bīnguǎn*
Kirey	吉日宾馆	*jírì bīnguǎn*
Kyichu	拉萨吉曲饭店	*lāsà jíqǔ fàndiàn*
Lhasa Hotel	拉萨饭店	*lāsà fàndiàn*
Mandala	满斋酒店	*mǎnzhāi jiǔdiàn*
Pentoc Hotel	攀多旅馆	*pānduō lǚguǎn*
Shangbala	香巴拉酒店	*xiāngbālā jiǔdiàn*
Snowlands Hotel	雪域宾馆	*xuěyù bīnguǎn*
Yak Hotel	亚宾馆	*yà bīnguǎn*
Zheng Chang Dong Cuan Cuo Youth Hostel	正昌东措国际青年旅馆	*zhèngchāng dōng cuò guójì qīngnián lǚguǎn*

renamed by King Songtsen Gampo in the seventh century when he moved his capital here from the Yarlung Valley. Following the collapse of the Yarlung dynasty two centuries later, power dispersed among local chieftains, and the city lost its pre-eminence. It was not until the seventeenth century, with the installation of the Fifth Dalai Lama as ruler by the Mongolian emperor, Gushri Khan, that Lhasa once again became the seat of government. It continues now as the capital of the TAR, and while glorious sites from earlier times are spread throughout the area, it is this third period of growth, following the Chinese invasion, which has given the city its most obvious features – wide boulevards and concrete-and-glass blocks. The Chinese population of Lhasa is highly active economically, with two Chinese businesses to every Tibetan one, a ratio that reflects the city's population.

There are plenty of sights in and around the city to keep most visitors occupied for at least a week; the **Potala**, **Jokhang** and **Barkhor** district are not to be missed, and at least one trip to an outlying monastery is a must. It's also worth taking time to see some of the smaller, less showy temples and simply to absorb the atmosphere of the "Forbidden City", which large numbers of explorers died in their vain efforts to reach around a hundred years ago.

Offering tourists better **facilities**, with more choice of accommodation, restaurants and shopping than anywhere else in Tibet, Lhasa is the best place to arrange trips to other parts of the region (see p.1124). Whatever the comforts

ACCOMMODATION
Banak Shol	H
Grand Hotel Tibet	A
Hubei Hotel	B
Kirey	F
Kyichu	E
Lhasa	C
Mandala	L
Pentoc	K
Shangbala	J
Snowlands	I
Yak	D
Zhen Chang Dong	
Cuan Cuo Youth Hostel	G

EATING & DRINKING
Bejing Duck	3
Dunya	5
Gangki	10
Hard Yak Café	2
Lhasa Kitchen	9
Makye Ama	11
Music Kitchen Café	1
Naga	J
Namtso	7
Shangrila	F
Sichuan restaurants	4
Snowlands	8
Tashi 1	6
Tashi 2	F

of Lhasa, remember that the city is just one face of Tibet – 88 percent of the population live in the countryside.

Orientation, arrival and city transport

The **central areas** of Lhasa are along and between three main roads that run east–west, parallel to and north of the Kyichu River: Chingdol Lu, Beijing Lu and Lingkuo Lu. Lhasa is at its most sprawling to the west, where there is very little countryside between the outskirts of the city and the monastery of Drepung, 8km away from the centre of town, and north where the city virtually merges into the Sera monastery complex, 4km distant. So far the river has prevented a spread south, while to the east the city peters out within a couple of kilometres as the road towards Ganden deteriorates quickly. The Potala Palace, on Beijing Zhong Lu, is the major landmark visible throughout the city and, together with the Tibetan enclave around the Jokhang temple, known as the Barkhor, they form the centre of interest for most visitors. The Golden Yaks Statue, at the junction of Beijing Zhong Lu and Luobulingka Lu in the west of the city, erected in 1991 to celebrate the fortieth anniversary of the "liberation" of Tibet, is another useful landmark.

Arriving by air, you'll land at **Lhasa airport** at Gongkhar, a hefty 93km to the southeast of the city. CAAC buses (¥35) bring you to the CAAC office on

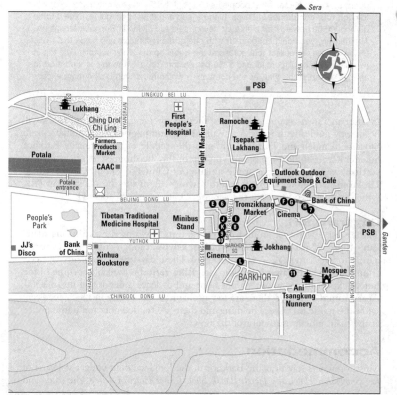

Public bus departures are mostly from the bus station, where it's advisable to buy tickets a day in advance. Pilgrim buses and minibuses leave from various points, but note the possible restrictions on your use of these (p.1105). Further details are given in the accounts of the destinations and in "Travel details" at the end of the chapter. For information on arranging private transport for a customized itinerary, see p.1105.

Leaving Tibet

You can buy **flight** tickets at CAAC in Lhasa or at the ticket agency in the *Tibet Hotel*. Destinations served are: Kathmandu (Tues & Sat; ¥1954), Chengdu (daily; ¥1550), Chongqing (Tues, Thurs, Sat, Sun; ¥1680) and Beijing (daily Tues–Sun; ¥2480). The price includes the departure tax. Airport buses leave from outside the CAAC office in Lhasa, at 1pm and 5pm, and also on Tues at 6am, Thurs and Sat at 10am (¥35). An early-morning jeep-taxi from Lhasa to the airport costs ¥350 for five people plus luggage, or you can arrange a taxi in advance, through the *Pentoc Hotel*, for only ¥200.

At the time of writing, **cycling out** of Tibet was a lot easier than cycling in – you just need to be wary of two checkpoints: one outside Lhatse and one outside Shekar. See "Getting there", p.1101, and "Getting around", p.1105. The only destination outside Tibet that you can reach **by bus** is Golmud, for which buses leave the main bus station daily at 8.30am. There's a choice between luxury buses with reclining seats (¥400) or more basic ones with upright seats (¥210). There's no longer any public service to **Nepal**. Most people heading to Nepal make their own arrangements through **tour companies** in Lhasa, hiring a jeep and driver plus guide. Expect to be quoted ¥4500 upwards for a six-day, seven-night trip taking in Rongbuk Monastery. Alternatively, you could cadge a lift with one of the minibuses and jeeps that leave Lhasa regularly to collect tour parties at the Nepal border. They complete the trip in two days, and it will cost around ¥350 per person. You have to ask around a bit to arrange transport this way, as the companies would rather you took a more expen-

Nyangrain Lu in around two hours, though foreigners coming on tours will be met by guides with jeeps. A few minibuses and pilgrim buses (notably from Shigatse, Ganden and Tsurphu) ply into the middle of town, usually Barkhor Square, if you come by bus, but you'll probably be dropped at the main **bus station**, west of the centre, at the junction of Chingdol Zhong Lu and Minzu Lu. From here, either take a taxi into town (¥10), or use the #2 minibus (¥2), which will take you most of the way (see "City transport", below).

City transport

The easiest way to get around the city and its environs is by **minibus** (daily 7am–10pm; ¥2 flat fare) or on a **cycle-rickshaw**, though you'll have to barter a little for the latter (¥2–4 for most trips). These days there are plenty of **taxis** around too, which have a ¥10 basic rate. **Bike rental** is available at some of the hotels; expect to pay about ¥3 per hour and to leave a deposit of up to ¥300. Apart from the altitude, there are few problems with cycling in Lhasa; roads are wide, the traffic isn't overwhelming and there are traffic lights and traffic police at the main junctions to control the flow.

Accommodation

Most foreigners stay near the Barkhor in the long-standing budget stalwarts of the *Snowlands Hotel*, *Yak Hotel*, *Banak Shol*, *Pentoc Hotel* or *Kirey*. The mid- and upper-range hotels in the outskirts are standard Chinese style. If you're considering a tour that puts you up at the *Tibet Hotel*, think twice – not only is it badly located in the west of the city, it's very shabby and unfriendly.

Banak Shol Beijing Dong Lu ⑦ 0891/6323829. Once clean and homely, this place has gone downhill, crossing the line from appealingly chaotic to just worn out; the staff are lazy, the facilities shoddy. But it's popular with Chinese backpackers. There's a range of rooms with and without bath, but beware the rooms at the front, which can be noisy. The well-established hotel restaurant remains its best feature. It's been renamed the *Namtso* because its previous moniker, the Kailash, has been copyrighted by a new Chinese place. ❷–❹

Grand Hotel Tibet 196 Beijing Zhong Lu ⑦ 0891/6826096, ⑤ 6832195. Shiny, new, and fair value, with good facilities and an oxygen bar. ❺

Hubei Hotel Beijing Xi Lu. A new, Chinese, business-oriented hotel, well run and offering better value than any of its nearby competitors; certainly a better bet than the *Lhasa Hotel*. ❻

Kirey Beijing Dong Lu ⑦ 0891/6323462. Conveniently close to the Barkhor, and with the *Tashi 2* restaurant on the premises. Don't be deterred by the characterless, concrete compound; the rooms are pleasantly furnished, and overall this place represents very good value. As with the other budget places, staff take their duties lightly, but there is a free laundry service. Dorm beds ¥15, ❶

Kyichu 19 Beijing Dong Lu ⑦ 0891/6338824. Centrally located, good-value, with friendly Tibetan staff, this is certainly the best mid-range choice. There's a restaurant on site as well as an antiques shop. ❺

Lhasa Hotel Minzu Lu ⑦ 0891/6324509, ⑤ 6334117. Formerly the *Holiday Inn* (as a sign outside informs you), this is Lhasa's most luxurious hotel, with 460 rooms, a range of restaurants,

including the *Hard Yak Café*, swimming pool (summer only), business centre and in-house doctor. However, the real *Holiday Inn* – which left after pressure by western activists – would never tolerate present lax standards and this place is certainly not value for money. ❽

Mandala 31 Nan Barkhor Jie ⑦ 0891/6324783. Well located, right on the edge of the Jokhang circuit, and a good mid-range option. It's quiet, and rooms are wood panelled. No dorms means no backpackers, which could be considered an advantage. ❺

Pentoc Hotel Mentsikhang Lu ⑦ 0891/6330700. This place gets universal good reports: it's well located, inexpensive and snug, and has good rooms and a range of services – including laundry, bike-hire and nightly videos. Bear in mind that it's owned and run by another form of colonialist, western missionaries (the name is dervied from Pentecostal). Dorm beds ¥30, ❷

Shangbala Mentsikhang Lu. A Chinese, three-star place, well located but lacking character and rather sleazy. ❻

Snowlands Hotel Mentsikhang Lu ⑦ 0891/6323687. Well situated near the Jokhang, and livelier than it used to be, thanks to a renovation. The six-bed dorms are cramped; doubles are better value. Dorm beds ¥15, ❷

Yak Hotel Beijing Dong Lu ⑦ 0891/6323496. A recently renovated budget favourite, offering a range of options from cramped-but-clean dorms to rooms with attached bathroom, all built around two courtyards. The communal bathrooms are the cleanest of any of the budget places. Dorm beds ¥20, ❶–❺

Useful minibus routes in Lhasa

#2 West from the small minibus stand opposite the cinema on Yuthok Lu north up Kharnga Dong Lu and then west along the front of the Potala. Some head west on Beijing Zhong Lu and Beijing Xi Lu and then turn south at the Lhasa, past the Norbulingka, while others follow the old road, Yuan Lin Lu, to the Norbulingka. All pass the bus station and then head west out of the city on Chingdol Xi Lu.

#3 From Beijing Dong Lu at the junction with Dosengge Lu, then loops north at Nyangrain Lu, west along Lingkor Bei Lu, down to the Golden Yaks Statue, then east along Beijing Zhong Lu and Beijing Xi Lu past the Lhasa and out to Drepung and Nechung monasteries.

#5 From the stand opposite the cinema on Yuthok Lu, north up Dosengge Lu, then west along Beijing Dong Lu and north up Nyangrain Lu to Sera Monastery.

Zheng Chang Dong Cuan Cuo Youth Hostel
10 Beijing Dong Lu ☎ 0891/6330683. Promising, well-located new place with six-bed dorms. Clean and well run, with a Korean restaurant attached.

One hour's free Internet a day. Teething problems – such as gas leaks in the shower – will hopefully have been dealt with by the time you read this. ¥25 dorms, ❶–❷

The City

With its mix of ascendar   Chinese modernity set side by side with ancient Tibetan traditions, Lhasa is a vibrant, fast-changing city that throws up some bizarre juxtapositions – witness the pilgrims on their rounds of prostrations passing the ATM machines of the Bank of China. Construction sites abound, but it is still easy to get around to all the major monuments, many of which are within walking distance of the two central landmarks, the **Potala** and **Jokhang**.

The Potala

Perched 130m above Lhasa atop Marpo Ri (Red Mountain), and named after India's Riwo Potala – holy mountain of the god Chenresi – the **Potala Palace** is dazzling both inside and out, an enduring landmark of the city of Lhasa. As you glory in the views from the roof, gaze at the glittering array of gold and jewels and wend your way from chapel to chapel, you'll rub shoulders with excited and awestruck pilgrims from all over ethnic Tibet, making offerings at each of the altars. But be aware that you're in a sad shell of a place: most of the rooms are off limits, part of a UNESCO World Heritage Grant was spent on a CCTV system, and the caretaker monks are not allowed to wear their robes. And don't tackle the Potala on your first day at altitude – the palace is a long climb up, and even the Tibetans huff and puff on the way up; you'll enjoy it more when you've acclimatized.

Rising thirteen dramatic storeys and consisting of over a thousand rooms, the palace complex took a work force of at least seven thousand builders and fifteen hundred artists and craftsmen over fifty years to complete. The main mass of the Potala is the **White Palace** (Potrange Karpo), while the central building rising from the centre of this is the **Red Palace** (Potrang Marpo). There's a huge amount to take in on one visit and a second look helps to put it in perspective, though the **entrance fee** is a painful ¥70, sometimes going up to ¥100 at peak times. The **opening hours** (officially daily 9am–6pm) are a source of major confusion, as they seem to change frequently, so check with other travellers before you set off; occasionally, at peak times you are required to purchase your ticket the day before. At the time of writing, the palace was open to all in the morning, but in the afternoon you could only visit as part of a (loosely) guided tour leaving at 3.30pm. Morning is certainly the best time to come, when the place bustles with excited pilgrims. The policy on **photography** also varies: inside, it's either pricey or banned altogether. However, there seems to be little problem with taking pictures on the roof or on the balconies outside the chapels.

Built for several purposes, the Potala served as administrative centre, seat of government, monastery, fortress and the home of all the Dalai Lamas from the Fifth to the Fourteenth, although from the end of the eighteenth century, when the Norbulingka was built as the summer palace, they stayed here only in winter. It was King Songtsen Gampo who built the first palace on this site in the seventh century, though it was later destroyed by invaders. Today's White Palace (1645–1648) was built during the reign of the Fifth Dalai Lama, who took up residence in 1649, while the Red Palace, begun at the same time, was

△ View of the Potala Palace

completed in 1693. Both survived the Cultural Revolution relatively unscathed; apparently Zhou Enlai ordered their protection.

Into the palace

The #2 minibus passes the gate in the front wall of the massive compound. You enter here and walk through Shol village, once the red-light district of Lhasa, now lined with souvenir shops and vendors, then turn right through the gates and climb to the inner courtyard of the White Palace, the **Deyang Shar**, where you'll find the ticket office. The courtyard is surrounded by monks' rooms and stores, with the **Quarters of the Dalai Lama** at its eastern end. The opulently carved and painted Official Reception Hall beyond is dominated by the bulk of the high throne and hung with fabulous brocade and *thangkas* (embroidered or painted religious scrolls) with a small doorway leading into the private quarters of the Fourteenth Dalai Lama next door. There's a small audience chamber, a chapel, a hallway and finally the bedroom, with an extremely well-painted mural of Tsongkhapa, founder of the Gelugpa school to which the Dalai Lama belongs, over the bed. On the other side of the Official Reception Hall are the private quarters of the previous Dalai Lamas, but these are closed to the public.

Stairs lead from the inner courtyard up into the **Red Palace** and continue straight to the roof, for fabulous views across Lhasa. You can then descend a floor at a time to tour the palace, moving clockwise all the way. The first room on the **upper floor** is the **Maitreya Chapel**, its huge number of fabulously ornate statues setting the tone for the remainder of the chapels. It's dominated by a seated statue of Maitreya, made at the time of the Eighth Dalai Lama and said to contain the brain of Atisha, the eleventh-century Indian scholar responsible for a Buddhist revival in Tibet (see p.1098). On the far left of the Dalai Lama's throne is a statue of the Fifth Dalai Lama, commissioned soon after his death and supposedly containing some of his hair.

The Red Palace is the final resting place of the Fifth to Thirteenth Dalai Lamas, except for the Sixth who died on his way to China and is said to be buried near Qinghai Hu in Qinghai Province. However, not all the tombs are open. Although they vary in size, all are jewel-encrusted golden *chortens* (traditional multi-tiered Tibetan Buddhist monuments that usually contain sacred objects), supporting tier upon tier of fantastic engraving; encased deep within are the bodies of the Dalai Lamas, preserved in dry salt. You should at least be able to see either the Tomb of the Thirteenth Dalai Lama or Tomb of the Eighth Dalai Lama on the upper floor.

Considered the oldest and holiest shrines in the Potala, the **Lokeshvara Chapel**, on the upper floor, and the **Practice Chamber of the Dharma King**, directly below on the **upper middle floor**, date back to Songtsen Gampo's original construction, and are the focus of all Potala pilgrims. It's easy to miss the Practice Chamber, entered from a small corridor from the balcony. King Songtsen Gampo supposedly meditated in this dark, dingy room now dominated by statues of the king and his ministers, Tonmi Sambhota and Gawa. At the base of the main pillar is a stove, apparently used by Songtsen Gampo himself.

Although you pass through the lower middle floor, the chapels here are all closed and the remainder of the open rooms are on the **lower floor** leading off the large, many-columned Assembly Hall. The highlight down here is the grand **Chapel of the Dalai Lamas' Tombs**, containing the awesome golden *chorten* of the Fifth Dalai Lama, which is three storeys high and consists of 3700kg of gold. To the left and right are smaller *chortens* with the remains of the Tenth and Twelfth Dalai Lamas, and the *chortens* on either side of these main ones are believed to contain relics of Buddha himself. Visitors leave the Red Palace by a door behind the altar in the **Chapel of the Holy Born**, from where the path winds down the west side of the hill to the western gate.

Around the Potala

The area around the Potala offers plenty of enjoyable sights. Opposite the front of the palace, on the south side of Beijing Dong Lu, **People's Park** is a mini Tian'anmen Square, seemingly designed to rub the noses of Tibetans in the fact of their occupation; there is a Chinese flag, a monument celebrating "liberation" and even a fighter plane and decorative plastic palm trees. Farther west along Beijing Dong Lu, the new *chorten* in the middle of the road marks the site of the old West Gate to the city. Due south from here, **Chakpori Hill**, the previous site of the medical college, is now topped by a radio transmitter. For a scenic view of the Potala, climb the hill using the path that goes in front of the public toilets just south of the *chorten*; you'll be able to go only as far as a massive tree, laden with prayer flags, before the guards at the transmitter start shouting.

From just east of the public toilets at the *chorten*, a path leads a couple of hundred metres to the fabulously atmospheric **Palhalupuk Temple**, built around an ancient cave. You'll spot the ochre and maroon, and far less interesting, Neten Temple on the cliff first; Palhalupuk is the smaller, white building below. Entered from an ante-chapel, the cave, about 5m square, was King Songtsen Gampo's retreat in the seventh century and is lined with rock carvings, many of which date from that time. The most important altar is in front of the huge rock pillar that supports the roof, the main image here being of Sakyamuni flanked by his chief disciples. At the far right-hand corner stands a jewel- and *katag*-bedecked statue of Pelden Lhamo, the fierce protective deity of Tibet, on a tiny altar. The back wall has been left untouched, and it's said that the jewels of Songtsen Gampo's Nepalese wife, Princess Bhrikuti, are hidden behind. They don't get many tourists here, and the caretaker and monks are welcoming.

The main area of **rock carvings**, numbering around five thousand, is on the west and southern sides of Chakpori Hill. Back on the road, continue west from the *chorten* along the left fork. Just as you get to the junction with Yuan Lin Lu that leads down from the Golden Yaks Statue, you'll find a rough track leading off to the left. Follow it beside a stream for a couple of hundred metres and you'll arrive at the start of the rock paintings and carvings that supposedly represent the visions seen by King Songtsen Gampo during his meditation. The carvers at work here copy ancient texts and prayers or sacred *mantras*; they work partly for alms but also produce work for sale.

North of the Potala

Around the other side of the Potala, the park of **Ching Drol Chi Ling** (¥2) has fine views up to the north facade of the Potala and sports a large area of ill-kept trees and a boating lake formed by the removal of earth during the construction of the palace. The park is entered from the north side of the lake or via the entrance at the end of the Farmers Products Market. On an island in the lake is the small, pleasant **Lukhang**, built by the Sixth Dalai Lama in honour of the *naga* king and for use as a retreat. Legend tells of a pact between the builder of the Potala and the king of the *nagas*, subterranean creatures who resemble dragons – the earth could be used as long as a chapel was built in their honour. The temple is famed for the very old and detailed murals on the middle and top floors, but you'll need a flashlight if you want to study them in detail, and the protective wire in front doesn't help. The top-floor pictures showing the stages of human life, the journey of the soul after death, and various legends, are somewhat esoteric, but the middle-floor murals, depicting the construction of the great monasteries of Sera and Drepung among others, are far more comprehensible.

The Jokhang

The **Jokhang** (daily 8am–6pm, ¥70) – sometimes called Tshuglakhang ("cathedral"), and which is the holiest temple in the Tibetan Buddhist world – can be somewhat unprepossessing from afar, but draw close and you'll get infected by the anticipation of the pilgrims and the almost palpable air of veneration. Inside, you're in for one of the most unforgettable experiences in Tibet; many visitors end up returning day after day.

King Songtsen Gampo built the Jokhang in the seventh century to house the **dowry** brought by his Nepalese bride, Princess Bhrikuti, including the statue known as the Akshobhya Buddha. This later changed places with the Jowo Sakyamuni statue from Princess Wencheng's dowry, which was initially installed in Ramoche temple (see p.1118), and which is now regarded as Tibet's most sacred object. The **site** of the temple was decided by Princess Wencheng after consulting astrological charts, and confirmed by the king following a vision while meditating. However, construction was fraught with problems. Another vision revealed to the king and his queens, was that beneath the land of Tibet lay a huge, sleeping demoness with her head in the east, feet to the west and heart beneath Lhasa. Only by building monasteries at suitable points to pin her to the earth, could construction of the Jokhang succeed. The king embarked on a scheme to construct twelve demon-suppressing temples: four around Lhasa, which included Trandruk (see p.1132), to pin her at hips and shoulders; a set of four farther away, to pin her at elbows and knees; and four even more distant, to pin her hands and feet. When these were complete, construction on the Jokhang began.

The Jokhang stands 1km or so east of the Potala, in the centre of the only remaining Tibetan enclave in the city, the **Barkhor area**, a maze of cobbled alleyways between Beijing Dong Lu and Chingdol Dong Lu. If you're coming from the western side of town, the #2 or #3 minibus may come into Barkhor Square or – more likely – drop you about five minutes' walk away on Dosengge Lu or Beijing Dong Lu.

Pilgrims go in at the front, but the foreign visitor's entrance is on the south east side, and entry – until quite recently free – is now a shocking ¥70. The best time to visit is in the morning, when most pilgrims do the rounds.

Inside the temple

The main entrance to the Jokhang is from **Barkhor Square**, which is to the west of the temple and full of stalls selling prayer flags, white scarves (*katag*) and incense. Two bulbous incense burners in front of the temple send out juniper smoke as an offering to the gods, and the two walled enclosures here contain three ancient engraved pillars. The tallest is inscribed with the Tibetan–Chinese agreement of 821 AD and reads: "Tibet and China shall abide by the frontiers of which they are now in occupation. All to the east is the country of Great China; and all to the west is, without question, the country of Great Tibet. Henceforth on neither side shall there be waging of war nor seizing of territory."

In front of the huge temple doors, a constant crowd of pilgrims prostrate themselves – you can hear the clack of the wooden protectors on their hands and the hiss as the wood moves along the flagstones when they lie flat on the ground. Head round the southern side to the visitor's entrance and you'll enter the main courtyard, where ceremonies and their preparations take place. Rows of tiny butter lamps burn on shelves along the far wall and it's a bustling scene as monks make butter statues and dough offerings and tend the lamps. Through a corridor in the north wall, with small chapels to left and right, you pass into the inner area of the temple. The central section, **Kyilkhor Thil**, houses statues galore, six of them considered particularly important. The most dramatic are the six-metre-high Padmasambhava on the left, which dates from 1955, and the half-seated figure of Maitreya, the Buddha of the Future, to the right.

Devout pilgrims turn left to move clockwise and enter each chapel in turn to pray and make offerings. They don't hang around, though; stand still to admire the statues and you'll get trampled in the rush. Some of the wooden door frames and columns are original – in particular, the door frame of the Chapel of Chenresi, in the north, and the columns in front of the Chapel of Jowo Sakyamuni, in the east, were created by Niwari craftsmen from Nepal during the temple's early years. As with all temples in Tibet, it's often difficult to know exactly what you are looking at. Some of the statues are original, others were damaged during the Cultural Revolution and have been restored either slightly or extensively, and others are replicas. Whatever their age, all are held in deep reverence by the pilgrims.

It's easy to feel overwhelmed, but if you manage only one chapel it should be the **Chapel of Jowo Sakyamuni** in the middle of the eastern, back wall of the temple. The 1.5-metre-high Sakyamuni is depicted at twelve years of age, with a sublimely beautiful golden face. Draped in heavy brocade and jewels, this is the most deeply venerated statue in Tibet. Although the Jokhang was originally built to house the statue, the Jowo Sakyamuni first stood in the temple of Ramoche until rumours of a Tang invasion late in the seventh century led to its removal to a hiding place in the Jokhang. During the reign of Trisong Detsen, the Bon opponents of Buddhism removed the statue and buried it, but it was found and sent out of Lhasa for safety. The statue was again buried during King Langdarma's attempt to annihilate Buddhism, but eventually returned to the Jokhang, where it rests today. Although there is a rumour that the original was destroyed in the eighteenth century by Mongol invaders, neither it nor the chapel was harmed during the Cultural Revolution and the statue is widely regarded as the original. Monks here keep the butter lamps topped up while the pilgrims move around the altar, bowing their heads to Jowo Sakyamuni's right leg and then his left.

By the time you reach the **upper floor** you'll probably be punch-drunk; fortunately perhaps, there is less to detain you up here than down below, although most of the chapels are now open after restoration. Of most interest here is the **Chapel of Songtsen Gampo**, directly above the main entrance in the west wall and featuring a large statue of the king flanked by his two queens. Continue up the stairs in the southwest corner of the chapel to one fierce and one peaceful image of **Pelden Lhamo**, who is regarded as the protective deity of Tibet and is particularly popular with pilgrims.

From the temple **roof**, the views down over Barkhor Square, into the temple courtyard and as far as the Potala in the distance, are wonderful, the golden statues even more impressive. You can get up to the roof using any one of a number of staircases, located just to the right of the main entrance, in the far southeast corner of the temple itself, or at the far end of the side courtyard to the right of the main entrance.

The Barkhor

Traditionally, pilgrims to Lhasa circled the city on two clockwise routes: an outer circuit called the Lingkhor, now vanished under two-lane highways and rebuilding, and the shorter **Barkhor** circuit through the alleyways a short distance from the Jokhang walls. This has survived, a maze of picturesque streets a world away from the rest of Lhasa. It's now lined with the stalls of an outdoor market selling all manner of goods – saddles and stirrups, Chinese army gear, *thangkas*, jewellery, blankets, cassette tapes, carpets, tin trunks and pictures of lamas, to mention a fraction only. The many trinkets and antiques are, of course, fakes made in Nepal. The pilgrims are an amazing sight: statuesque Khampa men with their traditional knives and red-braided hair, decorated with huge chunks of turquoise; Amdo women dripping jewels with their hair in 108 plaits; and old ladies spinning their tiny prayer wheels and intoning *mantras*. The Barkhor circuit is actually at its most interesting in the evening when the stalls clear their tourist junk and vendors start selling what the locals actually want – straw hats, kung-fu T-shirts and abject plastic. The clockwise-strolling masses come here to browse, pray and socialize.

The whole Barkhor area is worth exploring – with huge wooden doors set in long, white walls and leading into hidden courtyards – but try not to miss **Tromzikhang market** to the north of the Jokhang; take the main alleyway into the Barkhor that leads off Beijing Dong Lu just east of Ramoche Lu and it's just down on your left. The two-storey modern building is a bit soulless, but nowhere else in the world can you see (or smell) so much yak butter in one place.

One other sight to seek out here is the **Ani Tsangkung Nunnery** (¥6) to the southeast of the Jokhang; you'll probably need to ask the way (see "Language", p.1102). With over a hundred nuns in residence, several of whom speak good English, there is a lively but devout atmosphere here, especially around prayer time at 11am. The main chapel is dominated by a fabulous Chenresi in a glass case. From the back of the chapel, facing the main door, you can head right, round the outside, to visit the long, narrow room containing King Songtsen Gampo's meditation chamber in a pit at the end. Supposedly, his meditation here altered the course of the Kyichu River when it looked likely to flood the construction of the Jokhang.

Ramoche

The three-storey, robust **Ramoche** (daily 9am–4.30pm; ¥20, plus up to ¥50 per chapel for photographs) is small but intriguing, and second only in importance to the Jokhang. A short walk north of the Barkhor, on Ramoche Lu between Beijing Dong Lu and Lingkor Bei Lu, it was built in the seventh century by Songtsen Gampo's Chinese wife, Princess Wencheng, to house the Jowo Sakyamuni statue that she brought to Tibet. The statue later ended up in the Jokhang and was replaced by the Akshobhya Buddha, a representation of Sakyamuni at the age of 8. This much-revered statue was broken in two during the Cultural Revolution, with one part taken to China and narrowly saved from being melted down, while the other was later discovered on a factory scrapheap in Tibet. The statue in position today in the main shrine, the **Tsangkhang** at the back of the temple, is likely to be a copy.

While you're in the area, call in on the tiny **Tsepak Lakhang** to the south of Ramoche. The little entrance is just beside a huge incense burner, and, once inside, you pass along a small alley lined with a row of prayer wheels. There are two small chapels in this hugely popular temple, and the 55 friendly monks in residence chant their daily prayers around noon. You can walk the small circuit around the walls of Tsepak Lakhang, where the murals have been newly painted.

Norbulingka and museum

Situated in the west of town, on the route of the #2 minibus, the **Norbulingka** (Jewel Park), the Summer Palace of the Dalai Lamas (daily 9am–6.30pm; ¥60), is not in the top league of Lhasa sights, but is worth a look if you've time on your hands and don't object to the steep entrance fee. However, if you're in Lhasa during the festivals of the Worship of the Buddha (July) or during Shotun, the Yoghurt Festival (Aug/Sept), when crowds flock here for picnics and to see masked dances and traditional opera, you should definitely make the trip out here. The forty-hectare park has been used as a recreation area by the Dalai Lamas since the time of the Seventh incarnation. The first palace to be built was the **Palace of the Eighth Dalai Lama**, constructed towards the end of the eighteenth century, and the closest to the entrance. This palace became the official summer residence to which all Dalai Lamas moved, with due ceremony, on the eighteenth day of the third lunar month.

Other buildings open to the public are the **Palace of the Thirteenth Dalai Lama** in the far northwest corner – beyond the appalling zoo – and, the highlight of the visit, the **New Summer Palace**, built in 1956 by the Fourteenth Dalai Lama; it was from here that he fled Lhasa in 1959. Visitors pass through the audience chamber, via an anteroom, to the meditation chamber, on to his bedroom and then into the reception hall dominated by a fabulously carved golden throne, before passing through to the quarters of the Dalai Lama's mother. The Western plumbing and radio sit beside fabulous *thangkas* and religious murals. It's all very sad and amazingly evocative, the forlorn rooms bringing home the reality of exile.

Opposite the Norbulingka, the **Tibet Museum** (daily 9am–6pm; ¥30) offers curiosities to anyone who's had enough of religious iconography; there are some fascinating *thangkas*, illustrating theories from Tibetan medicine as well as stuffed Tibetan wildlife, Neolithic tools and the like. Its primary purpose, however, is propaganda, so it's best to take the captions with a grain of salt.

Eating, drinking and entertainment

Besides the vast number of restaurants in Lhasa, there's a good, cheap **night market** along Dosengge Lu, noodle places near Tromzikhang market, and bakeries outside the mosque selling tasty Muslim bread. For **trekking food** like muesli and chocolate, try the counters at the *Kailash* or *Snowland* restaurants, or one of the **supermarkets** at the west end of Lingkuo Bei Lu. The *Dunya* restaurant does a good picnic lunchbox.

Restaurants and cafés

Beijing Duck Beijing Xi Lu, opposite and a little west of the *Grand Hotel Tibet*; there's a sign in English (but no English menu inside). No prizes for guessing the house speciality here. You'll pay about ¥50 per person.

Dunya Beijing Dong Lu. Run by a Dutch couple, very civilized but not very Tibetan. A diverse range of specials, good Western, Indian and Nepali food and even half-decent Australian wine. Expect to pay around ¥60 a head. The tasty breakfast buffet is ¥25. The upstairs bar is a good place to socialize.

Gangki Corner of Mentsikhang Lu and Barkhor Square. This rooftop place is good value and has great views of the Jokhang. Very popular with Tibetans and often extremely busy. Main dishes cost ¥10–30; Tibetan tea and *tsampa* are also available.

Hard Yak Café *Lhasa Hotel*, Minzu Lu. Offering starched linen, muzak, old magazines and a range of Western food, this place is an expensive retreat for the culture-shocked world. Expect to pay ¥60–80 for a main meal; the Yak Burger (¥68) is the only thing on the menu that's almost worth the price, though it should only be tackled by the seriously hungry.

Lhasa Kitchen Mentsikhang Lu, opposite the *Snowlands Hotel*. Ignore the tacky lampshades and concentrate on the excellent Tibetan cuisine served in this upmarket but inexpensive place. Try soup with *shaphali* (meat and vegetable patties) followed by *deysee* (rice, raisins and yoghurt).

Makye Ama Behind the Jokhang, southeast corner of the Barkhor. The kind of New Age café you might expect to find in the arty quarter of any Western city. Try the Nepali and Indian dishes. The main draw is the great view over the Jokhang perambulators. The restaurant library has a small collection of English-language books you can borrow.

Naga Mentsikhang Lu, opposite the *Snowlands*. A cosy cave of a place that attempts a fusion of Nepalese and French food – *pot au feu de yak*, for example – with variable success. You have to take your shoes off, so don't arrive here immediately after trekking.

Namtso In the *Banak Shol*, Beijing Dong Lu. Their set breakfast includes eggs, toast, hash browns and tomatoes for ¥20. Also on offer are yak burgers, spaghetti and various Israeli and vegetarian options. The Japanese dishes are well done, and the Japanese room at the back is a good place to relax, as it's usually empty.

Oulook Outdoor Café Beijing Dong Lu, opposite the *Kirey*. Notable for a huge collection of National Geographics, and as the only place in town that does real coffee, though you pay at least ¥20 a cup.

Shangrila Restaurant In the courtyard of the *Kirey*. Pleasant Tibetan furnishings, with a large menu, though the food is designed not to tax the palate of any of the tour groups who sometimes take over here. There's some rather lacklustre Tibetan singing and dancing every evening at 7pm.

Sichuan restaurants Beijing Dong Lu, just west of the *Yak Hotel*. Perhaps it's preferable to patronize Tibetan traders, but it has to be admitted that Chinese restaurants make much better food – the three little places here do inexpensive and delicious Sichuan food and hotpots.

Snowlands Restaurant Mentsikhang Lu. Tour-group-friendly, long-established eaterie with bland curries and standard Western and Tibetan dishes.

Tashi 1 Corner of Beijing Dong Lu and Mentsikhang Lu. Along with its sister restaurant, the rather more atmospheric *Tashi 2* in the *Kirey*, this is the mainstay of budget travellers in Lhasa. Both offer the same small and inexpensive menu, including a range of Tibetan *momos* and delicious, tortilla-like *bobis* with sour cream and vegetables or meat, as well as French fries, spaghetti, mashed potatoes and fried yak meat. The cheesecake and the chocolate cake are excellent.

Entertainment

Not many foreigners realize it, but Lhasa is renowned for sleaze – it reputedly has more brothels than any other Chinese city, catering to Chinese sex tourists and the many soldiers billeted here. A wander in the western half of the city at night reveals rashes of karaoke bars and "hairdressers" doing brisk business. For many Tibetans, corruption by Chinese values has become as damaging to their culture as oppression.

A less controversial form of entertainment is the discos. **JJ's**, opposite the Potala on the southwest side of People's Park, is the biggest, and one of the few places you'll see Chinese and Tibetans mixing freely. It's free to get in and best before midnight, when the music and clientele are largely Tibetan. There's also a scattering of **bars** aimed at the well-off Chinese; most are on Beijing Zhong Lu, close to the *Lhasa Hotel*, and charges are comparable to those in the West. Best is the *Music Kitchen Café*, where beers are ¥20.

Sadly, there's not much chance to see **traditional Tibetan** music, dance and opera, unless you happen to be here during a festival. There are occasional shows put on for tourists; ask in your hotel or check for notices in the *Lhasa Hotel* or *Tibet Hotel*, or look in on the *Shangrila Restaurant*. In season, shows of Tibetan opera are sometimes held at the *Potala Hotel*, at the base of the Potala in Shol village. Performances begin at 8pm and 9.30pm and last one hour. Tickets cost ¥100, and should be bought in advance.

The **cinemas** on Yuthok Lu at the junction with Dosengge Lu, and on Beijing Dong Lu between the *Banak Shol* and *Kirey*, have some films from the West, but check whether they've been dubbed in Chinese before you bother; otherwise, it's the staple fare of kung-fu movies. Western videos are shown nightly at 8pm at the *Pentoc Hotel*.

Shopping

A major tourist activity in Lhasa is **shopping**. The main area for browsing is the **Barkhor** (see p.1117), where the better stuff is in the shops behind the stalls, but they're much more expensive than vendors outside. The vendors on the street outside the *Lhasa Hotel* have essentially the same range, but in smaller quantities, and they start off at even higher prices. The shop at the *Pentoc Hotel* has a good range of souvenirs, including **yak-wool jumpers** and socks. A string of gift shops on Mentsikhang Lu sells jewellery, handmade paper and the like. More handicrafts are available at Dropenling, at 11 Chaktsal Gang, just north of the mosque. Profits here go to local charities.

The search for **postcards** can be frustrating and expensive, as sets on offer at the main sights are generally pricey; those at the post office and the Xinhua Bookstore are the best value. For **film**, check out the photography shops on Kharnga Dong Lu opposite People's Park.

Some travellers buy **bikes** here and ride them to Nepal, where they can be sold, sometimes at a profit. The sturdiest bike for this is the Pegasus, which costs ¥700. You can buy it in the department store just east of the intersection of Dosengge Lu and Beijing Dong Lu.

Finally, if you feel like doing some shopping *for* rather than *from* Tibetans, buy notebooks and pens to donate to an orphanage and give them to Neema at the *Snowlands Restaurant*. Alternatively, turn up at the orphanage itself, at 42 Beijing Xi Lu.

Books

If you're very lucky, you might find the odd, classic English novel in one of the two Xinhua Bookstores on Yuthok Lu and on Beijing Xi Lu, just east of the *Tibet Hotel*. Or, for classic Chinese propaganda, search out the comic book in Tibetan about the British invasion in 1904. There are a few pricey English coffee-table books, which you can also get in the lobby of the *Lhasa Hotel*. The best on offer is the paperback *Potala Palace*, with good pictures of many of the treasures in the Potala that either will be closed off when you're there or you'll fail to notice as you're too overwhelmed. The hardback glossies, *Tibet* and *Snowland Tibet*, are both pricey and heavy to carry around, but have evocative photographs taken throughout the country. If you're into Buddhist art, take a look at the even glossier and heavier *Precious True Word Picture Album of the Buddha, Images of Buddhism*.

For a Tibetan **novel**, get hold of *The Secret Tale of Tesur House*, sold in the *Banak Shol* and the shop at the *Pentoc Hotel*. The first fiction translated from Tibetan into English, it's not a bad read, with a plot centring around gory murders and business intrigue, and it's full of fascinating descriptions of Tibetan life and customs – the kind of minutiae that you won't find described anywhere else. Bear in mind, though, that the fact that it's been translated meant it was deemed acceptable by the Chinese authorities. For Western novels, try the library at the *Makye Ama*. You can borrow the books for free, but you have to leave a hefty deposit.

The Guxuna Bookshop, on Mentsikhang Lu, has a Tibetan phrasebook with tape.

Carpets and paintings

If it's **carpets** you're after, visit Khawachen, at 103 Chingdol Xi Lu (Mon–Sat 9am–6.30pm; ℡0891/6333255, ℻6333250), on the route of the #2 minibus. This government-affiliated and US-financed organization offers the best selection of carpets in Lhasa and the chance to watch them being produced, and can also arrange to ship the merchandise home for you. Available in muted, attractive, traditional designs, plus some with a modern slant, the carpets range from 50cm square (US$25) to 2.7m x 3.6m (US$1300). The Lhasa Carpet Factory, Chingdol Dong Lu (Mon–Fri 9am–1pm & 3.30–6pm, Sat 9am–1pm; T0891/6323447), is a bigger operation, where you can watch huge carpets being woven; an extensive range of traditional and modern patterns is available here, costing from ¥140 to ¥32,000. Shipping can also be arranged.

Tibetan **thangkas** (religious scrolls) and religious and secular **paintings** would appear to be obvious souvenirs, but many are of poor quality – best to spend some time browsing before you buy. The least expensive *thangkas* – you'll find masses of these in the Barkhor – have a printed religious picture in the middle, while the better-quality, higher-priced ones have a hand-painted image. Look carefully, though, at the quality of the painting itself: the best ones have finely drawn and highly detailed backgrounds; the less skilled artists leave larger areas of the canvas blank, with less meticulously painted details. The asking prices are high; bargain hard. An excellent range of good-quality, hand-painted *thangkas* is available at the **Tibet Traditional Art Gallery**, just a shop, despite the name, next door to the Ramoche – expect prices starting at ¥3000. Look also in the shops in Shol village just inside the Potala gate and the *Lhasa Hotel* lobby shop (daily 9am–8pm), which has a range of paintings (¥500–2500) and will give you some idea of the top end of the scale.

Clothes and tents

There are plenty of **tailors** in town, both Chinese and Tibetan, who can make traditional Tibetan or Western clothes; look on Beijing Dong Lu west of the *Yak Hotel*. A huge range of materials, from light, summer-weight stuff, to heavier, warmer textiles, is available. Prices depend on the material, but light jackets start around ¥100, while skirts, trousers or a floor-length Tibetan woman's dress (*chuba*) cost ¥80 and up. Many places have samples made up and you can simply shop around until you find the style and material you want. From first measuring, to collecting the finished item, usually takes 24 hours.

Rather like marquees, **Tibetan tents** are used on religious and ceremonial occasions and are usually white with auspicious symbols appliquéd in blue. They're available at the Tibetan Tent Factory, just off the unnamed alley that heads north a couple of hundred metres west of the *Yak Hotel*; take the right fork just inside the alley and the factory is on the left. Expect to start negotiating at around ¥2500 for a tent and ¥100 for a door curtain. Cheaper door curtains of differing qualities are available in the Barkhor.

Trekking equipment

For rucksacks, sleeping bags and serious **hiking gear**, check out Outlook Outdoor Equipment (W www.ontheway.com.cn) on Beijing Dong Lu, opposite the *Kirey*. Export-quality Chinese sleeping bags cost ¥600 to buy (¥20–30 a day to rent), and two- or three-person tents, rucksacks, Karrimats and stoves are ¥30–40 per day to rent. The North Col Mountaineering Shop, opposite the Potala in the northwest corner of People's Park, has a similar selection. You can rent sleeping bags from the *Snowlands Restaurant* for ¥8 a night.

Listings

Airlines CAAC, Nyangrain Lu (open 24hrs; T0891/6833446).

Banks and exchange There are several branches of the *Bank of China* around town, but the main

one on Lingkuo Bei Lu, north of the Golden Yaks Statue (Mon–Fri 9am–1pm & 3.30–6pm), is the only place in Tibet for cash advances on credit cards. The branch on Beijing Dong Lu is

For the experienced walker, Tibet offers plenty of enticing **trekking routes**. The popular Ganden–Samye trek (see p.1128) has the advantages that both the start and finish points are relatively accessible to Lhasa and that it takes only three to four days. Also worth considering are treks to the cave hermitage of **Drak Yerpa** from Lhasa (allow a full day and be prepared to camp), and the five-day trek from Tingri to **Everest Base camp** via Rongbuk. You'd be advised to take a guide for this.

The more challenging options include the sixteen-day mammoth trek to the **Kangshung** face of Everest, exploring the valleys east of the mountain (the trip to second base camp and beyond on the mountain itself should only be tackled by experienced climbers); the 24-day circumnavigation of Namtso Lake, including the arduous exploration of the Shang Valley to the southwest; or the great thirty-day circuit (a Tibetan guide is highly recommended) from Lhatse to **Lake Dangra** up on the Chang Tang plateau.

Spring (April–June) and autumn (September–November) are the best **seasons** in which to trek, though cold-weather threats such as hypothermia and frostbite should be taken seriously even in these months. While trekking is possible at any time in the valleys, high altitudes become virtually impossible in the winter; anyone contemplating trekking at this time should be sure to get local information about the terrain and likely conditions. During the wettest months (June–September), rivers are in flood, and crossing them can be difficult, even impossible.

Once you start trekking, you get off the beaten track extremely quickly and there is no infrastructure to support trekkers and no rescue service; you therefore need to be fit, acclimatized, totally self-reliant and prepared to do some research before you go. There are two essential books: *Tibet Handbook: a Pilgrimage Guide* by Victor Chan (Moon), and *Trekking in Tibet* by Gary McCue (Cordee), which is especially good for shorter day-treks that anyone can do without all the gear.

14

TIBET | Lhasa

---

conveniently located close to the *Banak Shol* (Mon–Fri 9.30am–6pm, Sat & Sun 11am–3pm).

Bike rental The *Snowlands* and *Yak* hotels have the usual clunky bikes for ¥3/hr plus deposit, while the *Pentoc Hotel* has mountain-bikes for ¥6/hr and ¥15/hr, plus deposit.

Consulates The Nepalese Consulate, 13 Norbulingka Lu (Mon–Fri 10am–noon; ☎0891/6830609), has a next-day visa service, for which you'll need to submit one passport photograph. Single-entry visas cost ¥135 for fifteen days, ¥225 for thirty days; multiple-entry visas are ¥360 for thirty days, ¥540 for sixty days. You can get single-entry visas at Kodari (see p.1104), but payment there has to be in US dollars.

Hospital First People's Hospital, Lingkuo Bei Lu (Mon–Fri 10am–12.30pm & 4–6pm; at weekends emergencies only). It's better to go in the morning when more staff are available, and you'll need to take a Chinese translator. There is no dental treatment available in Lhasa, only extraction. Rabies serum is not available (see "Health", p.1106). You could also try the traditional Tibetan Medicine Hospital (Mentsikhang), Yuthok Lu (hours as above). Go upstairs and look for the only sign in English,

which says "Outpatients' Office" – this is where the doctor who deals with foreigners works. Otherwise, as some staff are Tibetan and some Chinese, a translator who speaks both is ideal.

Internet access The cybercafé opposite the *Banakshol* is open 24hr and charges ¥5/hr. There are a couple of smaller places with similar rates on Mentsikhang Lu. Be aware that email from Tibet is monitored, so don't mention any Tibetans by name.

Mail and telephones The main post office is on Beijing Dong Lu, just east of the Potala (daily 9am–8pm). Poste restante and international customs (Mon–Fri 9.30am–1pm & 3.30–6pm) is the counter facing you on the far left as you enter. Mail to be collected here should be addressed Poste Restante, Main Post Office, Lhasa, Tibet, China. Check both the book that lists mail received at the office and ask to see new mail. There's a charge of ¥1.5 per item received. EMS is next door to the post office, and also next door is a 24hr office with direct-dialling facilities and a fax service.

Pharmacies Most are along Yuthok Lu around the junction with Dosengge Lu. There is a pharmacy specializing in Tibetan medicine on the north side of Barkhor Square. Again, you'll need a translator.

Tour Agencies These are all over town, and all offer much the same services, but the official agency FIT, in the courtyards of the *Banak Shol* and *Snowlands*, *Hotel* and next to the *Shang-bala*, is sometimes able to offer trips the others cannot.

Around Lhasa

Not only is Lhasa awash with enough sights to keep even the most energetic visitor busy for several days, but the major monasteries of **Sera**, **Drepung**, **Nechung** and **Ganden** are easily accessible from the city as half-day or day-trips. Indeed, Sera and Drepung have virtually been gobbled up in the urban sprawl that now characterizes Lhasa, while the trip to Ganden is a good chance to get out into the countryside. Morning visits to any of them are likely to be in the company of parties of devout pilgrims who'll scurry around the temples making their offerings before heading on to the next target. Follow on behind them and you'll visit all the main buildings; don't worry too much if you aren't sure what you are looking at – most of the pilgrims haven't a clue either. The monasteries are generally peaceful and atmospheric places where nobody minds you ambling at will, and sooner or later you're bound to come across some monks who want to practise their English. Nearby, the walled, combined village and monastery of **Samye** is not only the most ancient in Tibet, but also a lively and interesting place to spend a day or two.

Sera

To reach **Sera Monastery** (Mon–Sat 9am–noon & 2–4pm; ¥35), 4km north of Lhasa, by public transport, take a #5 **minibus** from the southern end of Nyangrain Lu, or from the small minibus stand, opposite the cinema on Yuthok Lu. You'll either be dropped on the road, about 500m outside the white-walled monastery compound, or be taken along the track to the entrance. To get transport back, it's better to walk back out to the road. The last minibuses leave just after the end of the debating at about 5pm.

Founded in 1419 by Sakya Yeshe, one of the main disciples of Tsongkhapa, founder of the Gelugpa order, Sera is situated below a hermitage where the great man spent many years in retreat. Spared during the Cultural Revolution, the buildings are in good repair, although there is always a fair amount of ongoing building work. Pilgrims proceed on a clockwise circuit, visiting the three main **colleges**, Sera Me, Sera Ngag-Pa and Sera Je, and the main assembly hall, Tsokchen. All are constructed with chapels leading off a central hall and more

Around Lhasa		
Drepung	哲蚌寺	*zhébàng sì*
Ganden	甘丹寺	*gāndān sì*
Samye	桑木耶寺	*sāngmùyē sì*
Sera	色拉寺	*sèlā sì*

Fifty years ago, there were still six great, functioning **Gelugpa monasteries**: Sera, Drepung and Ganden near Lhasa, plus Tashilunpo in Shigatse (see p.1140), Labrang (see p.1009) and Kumbum (see p.1036). They each operated on a similar system to cope with the huge numbers of monks that were drawn to these major institutions from all over Tibet. In their heyday, Sera and Ganden had five thousand residents each and Drepung (possibly the largest monastery the world has ever known) had between eight and ten thousand.

Each monastery was divided into colleges, **dratsang**, which differed from each other in the type of studies undertaken. Each college was under the management of an abbot (*khenpo*), and a monk responsible for discipline (*ge-kor*). Attached to each college were a number of houses or *khangsten*, where the monks lived during their time at the monastery. Usually these houses catered for students from different geographical regions, and admission to the monastery was controlled by the heads of the houses to whom aspirant monks would apply. Each college had its own assembly hall and chapels, but there was also a main assembly hall where the entire community could gather.

Not every member of the community spent their time in scholarly pursuits. Communities the size of these took huge amounts of organization, and the largest monasteries also maintained large estates worked by serfs. About half the monks might be engaged in academic study while the other half worked at administration, the supervision of the estate work and the day-to-day running of what was essentially a small town.

The most obvious feature of these **monasteries today** is their emptiness; hundreds of monks now rattle around in massive compounds built for thousands. Such has been the fate of religious establishments under the Chinese and the flow of lamas into exile that there are now questions about the quality of the Buddhist education available at the monasteries inside Tibet. Monks and nuns nowadays need to be vetted and receive Chinese government approval before they can join a monastery or convent, and although there are persistent rumours of tourists being informed on by monks, it's also apparent that both monks and nuns have been, and continue to be, at the forefront of open political opposition to the Chinese inside Tibet.

chapels on an upper floor. They're great places to linger and watch the pilgrims rushing about their devotions. However, if you just want to catch the flavour of the most dramatic buildings, head straight up the hill from the main entrance. After a couple of hundred metres you'll reach the **Tsokchen**, Sera's largest building, built in 1710. The hall is supported by over a hundred columns and it's here, between statues of the Fifth and Thirteenth Dalai Lamas, that you'll find the main statue of Sakya Yeshe, the founder of the monastery. The Sakya Yeshe statue is a reproduction of the original one in Sera Ngag-Pa college. When there were plans to move the original to the Tsokchen, the story goes that the statue itself said that it wished to stay in the college, so a copy was made.

At the top of the path, the walled and shady **debating courtyard** is definitely worth a visit at 3.30pm, when the monks assemble in small animated groups to practise their highly stylized debating skills, involving much posturing, clapping and stamping. They're used to visitors – indeed, it's hard not to suspect the whole circus is put on for visitors – and there seems to be no problem about taking photographs.

To the left of the courtyard, the college of **Sera Je** is the best college to visit if you manage only one. Its spacious assembly hall is hung with fine *thangkas*, but the focus for pilgrims here is the Hayagriva Chapel (Hayagriva or Tamdrin, "the

Horse-Headed One", is the protective deity of Sera), reached via an entrance in the left-hand wall.

If you're feeling energetic, take the path up the hillside, from behind the Tsokchen (follow the telegraph wires) to **Tsongkhapa's Hermitage** (Chod-ing Khang), which is a reconstruction of the original – his meditation cave is a bit farther up. There are splendid views over Lhasa from here.

Drepung and Nechung

Once the largest monastery in the world, **Drepung** was an immediate success, and a year after opening, there were already two thousand monks in residence, and ten thousand by the time of the Fifth Dalai Lama (1617–82). To reach Drepung, 8km west of Lhasa, catch the #3 **minibus** on Dossenge Lu at the junction with Beijing Dong Lu. It may drop you on the main road (¥2), leaving you with a thirty-minute walk, or carry on up the hill to the entrance of the massive, walled monastery (¥3). Minibuses come back to Lhasa infrequently from the monastery itself, and it's better to walk down the hill to Nechung and then out to the main road to pick up transport there. Easily combined with a trip to Drepung is the eerie **Nechung Monastery** less than 1km southeast of Drepung, and reached by a well-trodden path.

Drepung

Drepung (daily 9am–6pm, chapels closed noon–3pm; ¥35) was founded in 1416 by Jamyang Choje, a leading disciple of Tsongkhapa. Although it has been sacked three times – in 1618 by the king of Tsang, in 1635 by the Mongols and in the early eighteenth century by the Dzungars – there was relatively little damage during the Cultural Revolution.

Drepung is a huge place, and it's easy to attempt to see everything and get overloaded. One thing to make sure to do is to go up on to the **roofs**; the views across the Kyichu Valley are splendid, and it's definitely worth spending a bit of time just wandering the alleyways, courtyards and ancient doorways.

The easiest way to find your way around is to follow the clockwise pilgrim circuit. This leads left from the entrance up to the grand and imposing **Ganden Palace**, built in 1530 by the Second Dalai Lama, and home to the Dalai Lamas until the Fifth incarnation moved to the Potala. The private quarters of the Dalai Lama are behind the balcony at the top right-hand side of the building, but there's little to see inside.

The next stop is the **Tsokchen**, the main assembly hall, its entrance via a small door on the left-hand side, facing the building. Its roof supported by over 180 solid wooden columns, the hall is the highlight of Drepung, a space of awesome size and scale. The *thangkas* and brocade hangings add to the incredible ambience, with dust motes highlighted by the rays of the sun slanting down from the high windows. The main chapel at the rear of the hall is the **Buddha of the Three Ages Chapel**, the most impressive in Drepung, with statues crammed together in such profusion, the mind reels. The central figures are Sakyamuni with his two main disciples, Shariputra and Maudgalyayana.

There are two upper storeys, both definitely worth a visit. On the next floor up, the **Maitreya Chapel** contains the head and shoulders of a massive statue of Maitreya at a young age, commissioned by Tsongkhapa himself, while the **Tara Chapel** contains a version of the *Kanjur*, sacred Buddhist scriptures, dating from the time of the Fifth Dalai Lama. In the middle of the volumes, which are loose leaves stored between wooden planks and wrapped in brocade, sits a statue of Prajnaparamita, the Mother of Buddhas; the amulet on her lap is said to contain a tooth of Tsongkhapa's. Of the three chapels on the top floor, the highlight is the central **Maitreya Chapel** with a stunning statue of the head of Maitreya, boasting exquisite gold ornamentation.

Behind the Tsokchen there's a tiny **Manjusri Temple**, obligatory for the pilgrims who make offerings to the image of the Bodhisattva of Wisdom, carved out of a large rock. The remainder of the circuit is taken up with the **Ngag-Pa College**, to the northwest of the Tsokchen, and **Loseling**, **Gomang and Deyang colleges** to the southeast. They all have items of interest – the stuffed goat at the entrance to the Protector Chapel on the upper storey of Loseling, the cosy Deyang, and the wonderful array of statues in the central chapel of Gomang – but don't feel too bad if you've had enough by now. The main steps of the Tsokchen, looking across the huge courtyard in front of the building, are a good place to sit and admire the view and watch the comings and goings of the other visitors.

Nechung

Nechung Monastery (daily 9am–6pm, chapels closed noon–3pm; ¥10) was, until 1959, the seat of the **state oracle of Tibet**. By means of complex ritual and chanting, an oracle enters a trance and becomes the mouthpiece of a god, in this case Dorje Drakden, the chief minister of the main spiritual protector of Tibet, Pehar Gyalpo; no important decisions are made by the Dalai Lama or government without reference to Drakden. The original shrine on the site was built in the twelfth century, and the Fifth Dalai Lama built the temple later. It was much damaged during the Cultural Revolution, but restoration work is now proceeding quickly. The state oracle fled Tibet in the footsteps of the Dalai Lama in 1959, having questioned Dorje Drakden himself as to what he should do. He died in 1985 in Dharamsala, but a successor has been identified there.

Nechung's spookiness begins outside. The beggars are abject, the villagers seem sullen. Inside you are confronted by a panoply of gore – the doors are decorated with images of flayed human skins and the murals in the courtyard depict torture by devils and people drowning in a sea of blood. In the chapels, unusually subdued supplicants are more likely to offer booze than apples. Bloodshot eyes sunk into the sockets of grinning skulls seem to follow you around.

Upstairs, the main room is the audience chamber, where the Dalai Lama would come to consult the oracle. The inner chapel is dedicated to Tsongkhapa, whose statue is between those of his two main disciples, Gyeltsab Je and Khedrup Je. In the only chapel at roof level is the statue of Padmasambhava which, though it dates from the early 1980s, is gloriously bedecked in old Chinese brocade. It's worth the climb up here, if only to escape from the air of sinister corruption below.

Ganden

Situated farther from Lhasa than the other main temples, **Ganden** (daily 9am–noon & 2–4pm; ¥35) is 45km east of Lhasa, the final 6km of the journey being along a winding track off the Lhasa–Sichuan Highway. It is also the most dramatically situated, high up on the Gokpori Ridge, with excellent views over the surrounding countryside. To get here, take the **pilgrim bus**, which leaves Lhasa daily at 6.30am from the west side of Barkhor Square (3–4hr; ¥20) and returns at 2pm. You can buy tickets in advance from a tin shack just south of the Jokhang.

Founded by Tsongkhapa himself in 1410 on a site associated with King Songtsen Gampo and his queens, the main hall was not completed until 1417, two years before Tsongkhapa died after announcing his disciple, Gyeltsab Je, as the new **Ganden Tripa**, the leader of the Gelugpa order. The appointment is not based on reincarnation but on particular academic qualifications. Ganden has always been particularly targeted by the Chinese, possibly because it is the main seat of the Dalai Lama's order, and what you see today is all reconstruction.

While it is possible, as always, to follow the pilgrims through the various buildings on their circuit, the highlight is the imposing **Serdung Lhakhang**, on the left side as you follow the main path north from the car park. This temple contains a huge gold and silver *chorten*. The original contained the body of Tsongkhapa, who was said to have changed into a 16-year-old youth when he died. The body was embalmed and placed in the *chorten* and, when the Red Guards broke it open during the Cultural Revolution, they supposedly found the body perfectly preserved, with the hair and fingernails still growing. Only a few pieces of skull survived the destruction and they are in the reconstructed *chorten*. Up the hill and to the right, the **Sertrikhang** houses the golden throne of Tsongkhapa and all later Ganden Tripas; the bag on the throne contains the yellow hat of the present Dalai Lama.

Be sure to allow time to walk the **Ganden kora**, the path around the monastery. The views are startling and it takes about an hour to follow round. There is a basic **guesthouse** at the monastery, used mostly by people heading off on the Ganden–Samye **trek** (see below).

Samye

A visit to **SAMYE**, on the north bank of the Tsangpo River, is a highlight of Tibet. A unique monastery and walled village rolled into one, it's situated in wonderful scenery and, however you arrive, the journey is splendid. You can climb the sacred Hepo Ri to the east of the complex for excellent views (1hr); it was here that Padmasambhava is said to have subdued the local spirits and won them over to Buddhism.

The monastery

Tibet's first monastery, **Samye** was founded in the eighth century during King Trisong Detsen's reign, with the help of the Indian masters Padmasambhava and Shantarakshita, whom he had invited to Tibet to help spread the Buddhist faith.

The Ganden–Samye trek

Though popular, the Ganden–Samye trek is no less serious and demanding than other treks. The route, which takes four days to complete, crosses the mountains that divide the **Kyichu Valley** from that of the Tsangpo and travels through high mountain passes and alpine pasture to the dry, almost desert-like countryside around Samye. The trek goes by **Hebu** village (three hours south of Ganden and a good place to hire yaks and guides) and involves camping out or sleeping in caves or nomad encampments, long climbs to the Jooker La and Sukhe La passes, and some deep river wading.

There is also an alternative, ancient pilgrim route from Dechen Dzong, 21km east of Lhasa, to Samye, which takes four days and crosses the same mountain range via Changju nomad camp and Gokar La Pass (the name translates as "white eagle" – apparently these birds also struggle to get over it). A third option is the four-day trek from the Gyama Valley, Songtsen Gampo's birthplace, via two five-hundred-metre passes.

The first Tibetan Buddhist monks were ordained here after examination and are referred to as the "Seven Examined Men". Over the years Samye has been associated with several of the schools of Tibetan Buddhism – Padmasambhava's involvement in the founding of the monastery makes it important in the Nyingma school, and later it was taken over by the Sakya and Gelugpa traditions. Nowadays, followers of all traditions worship here, and Samye is a popular destination for Tibetan pilgrims, some of whom travel for weeks to reach it.

The design of the extensive monastery complex, several hundred metres in diameter, is of a giant **mandala**, a representation of the Buddhist universe, styled after the Indian temple of Odantapuri in Bihar. The main temple, the **utse**, represents Buddha's palace on the summit of Mount Meru, the mythical mountain at the centre of the Buddhist universe. The four continents in the vast ocean around Mount Meru are represented by the *lingshi* temples, a couple of hundred metres away at the cardinal points, each flanked by two smaller temples, *lingtren*, representing islands in the ocean. The utse is surrounded by four giant *chortens*, each several storeys high, at the corners, and there are *nyima* (Sun) and *dawa* (Moon) temples to the north and south respectively. The whole complex is flanked by a newly renovated enclosing wall topped by 1008 tiny *chortens* with gates at the cardinal points. This sounds hugely ordered, but the reality is far more confusing and fun. Samye has suffered much damage and restoration over the years; today, you'll find the temples dotted among houses, barns and animal pens, with only a few of the original 108 buildings on the site remaining in their entirety.

The utse

The **utse** (daily 9am–12.30pm & 3–5pm; ¥35) is a grand, six-storey construction and needs a couple of hours to see thoroughly. Be sure to take a flashlight as there are some good murals tucked away in shadowy corners.

The **first floor** is dominated by the grand, main assembly hall, with fine, old *mandalas* on the high ceiling. On either side of the entrance to the main chapel are statues of historical figures associated with the monastery. Those on the left include Shantarakshita, Padmasambhava (said to be a good likeness of him), Trisong Detsen and Songtsen Gampo. The impressive main chapel, **Jowo Khang**, is reached through three tall doorways and is home to a Sakyamuni statue showing Buddha at the age of 38. To the left of the assembly hall is a small temple, **Chenresi Lhakhang**, housing a gorgeous statue of Chenresi with an eye meticulously painted on the palm of each of his thousand hands – if you look at nothing else in Samye, search this out. To the right of the main assembly hall is the **Gonkhang**, a protector chapel, with all the statues heavily and dramatically draped. Most of the deities here were established as the demons of the Bon religion and were adopted by Buddhism as the fierce protectors – the chapel is an eerie place, imbued with centuries' worth of fear.

Although the first floor is the most impressive, the upper storeys are worth a look. The **second floor** is an open roof area, where monks and local people carry out the craft work needed for the temple. The highlight of the **third floor** is the **Quarters of the Dalai Lama**, consisting of a small anteroom, a throne room and a bedroom. A securely barred, glass-fronted case in the bedroom is stuffed full of fantastic relics, including Padmasambhava's hair and walking stick, a Tara statue that is reputed to speak, and the skull of the Indian master Shantarakshita. The Tibetan pilgrims take this room very seriously and the crush of bodies may mean you can't linger as long as you would like. From the **fourth floor** up, you'll see only recent reconstruction, but the views from the balconies are extensive.

The surrounding buildings

The rest of the buildings in the complex are in varying stages of renovation. Unashamedly modern, the four coloured **chortens** are each slightly different, and visitors love or hate them. There are internal stairs and tiny interior chapels, but generally they are more dramatic from a distance. It's difficult to locate the outer temples accurately and many are still awaiting renovation – some serve as barns and stables, others show the effects of the Cultural Revolution. The most finely worked murals in Samye are in **Mani Lhakhang**, now a chapel in a house compound in the northwest of the complex, but the occupants are happy for visitors to look around.

Practicalities

Permits are needed for Samye, but the PSB in Tsetang will issue them only if you have arranged a tour. That said, the PSB rarely check up on foreigners except at festival times. The Lhasa–Tsetang road runs along the south bank of the Tsangpo and is served by public transport from both ends. To reach the monastery, you'll need to cross the river via the **Samye ferry**, 33km from Tsetang and 150km from Lhasa. Ferries leave when full and are more frequent in the morning, but run until mid-afternoon. The crossing (¥3, although foreigners are charged ¥10) is highly picturesque and takes an hour or more as the boats wind their way among the sand banks inhabited by Brahmini ducks, grebes and plovers. On the other side, tractors (¥5; 45min) and trucks (¥3; 30min) ply the bumpy 8km to Samye through rolling, deforested sand dunes, newly planted here and there with willows. The small, white-painted *chortens* carved out of the hillside about halfway along mark the place where King Trisong Detsen met Padmasambhava when he came to Samye in the eighth century. **Leaving**, a very useful truck departs from the front of the utse each morning at 8am to connect with the ferry and a Lhasa-bound bus on the other side of the river. In addition, local tractors and trucks run until mid-afternoon, but you may well have to wait at the ferry and on the other side of the river for connections.

The only place to stay at Samye is the **guesthouse** next to the utse, which provides comfortable, cheap dorm accommodation (❶). The monastery **restaurant** is just north of the utse, but a better option is the newer establishment opposite the east reception office near the east gate. There's no menu in either place; you negotiate based on what they have. There are several small shops in the monastery complex that are well stocked with tinned goods, beer, confectionery and even Chinese wine.

Tsetang and around

The town of **Tsetang**, southeast of Lhasa and just south of the Tsangpo River, and the nearby valleys of **Yarlung** and **Chongye**, are steeped in ancient history. Legend claims the first Tibetans originated on the slopes of Gongpo Ri to the east of Tsetang, and that the Yarlung Valley was where the first king of Tibet descended from the heavens to earth upon a sky-cord. This king then fathered the first royal dynasty, many members of which are buried in the nearby **Chongye Valley**. The Yarlung Valley was also where, in the fourth century, the first Buddhist scriptures fell from the sky upon the first king's palace at **Yumbulakhang**.

Tsetang is easily accessible via a good road and public transport from Lhasa. However, there is no public transport in the Yarlung and Chongye valleys, although **getting around** by hitching lifts on tractors is feasible for the Yarlung

Chongye	阱结	*jīngjié*
Tsetang	泽当	*zédāng*
Yarlung Valley	雅鲁鲁流域	*yǎlǔlǔ liúyù*
Trandruk Monastery	昌珠寺	*chāngzhū sì*
Yumbulakhang	雍布拉康	*yōngbùlākāng*

Valley. Transport out to Chongye is more limited. The best way to explore is to hire a vehicle and driver in Tsetang to take you to Chongye and Yumbulakhang on a day-trip. For vehicle rental try the *Tsetang Hotel* first, then the *Gesar* restaurant opposite – after hard bargaining expect to pay around ¥350 for the day.

Tsetang is also the starting point for a trip to **Lhamo Lhatso**, a sacred lake 115km northeast of Tsetang where visions on the surface of the water are believed to contain prophecies. Regents searching for the next incarnations of high lamas come here for clues, and Dalai Lamas have traditionally visited for hints about the future. Buses leave the main Tsetang intersection on Monday and Friday for **Gyatsa** (returning the next day), where you have to walk across the bridge and pick up another ride up to Chokorgye Monastery and then trek for around five hours up to the lake. You should bring your own food and be prepared to camp, unless you're intending a long day's walking.

Keep in mind that the **permit** situation here is unclear. The PSB in Tsetang should issue permits to Yarlung, Chongye, Samye and Lhamo Lhatso, but at the time of writing refused to do so unless you were on an organized tour with your own transport and guide – for which purpose, you'll be quoted ¥2000–2500 in Lhasa to rent a jeep for three days and two nights.

Tsetang

There is little to recommend an extended stay in the town of **TSETANG**, administrative centre of Lhoka province, a region stretching from the Tsangpo down to the Bhutan border. However, Tsetang is largely unavoidable as a base for explorations of the area.

Heading south from the main traffic intersection along Naidong Lu, take a narrow left turn through the small, bustling market into the **Tibetan area** of town, a typical jumble of walled compounds swarming with unwelcoming dogs and children scrapping in the dust. The largest monastery and the first you'll come to is **Ganden Chukorlin** (¥5), now bright and gleaming from restoration, having been used as a storeroom for many years. It was founded in the mid-eighteenth century on the site of an earlier monastery, and there are good views of the Tibetan quarter from the roof. At the nearby fourteenth-century **Narchu Monastery** (¥5), restoration is less complete, but it's worth stopping by for the three unusual, brown-painted Sakyamuni statues on the altar. A little farther up the hill, the **Sanarsensky Nunnery** (¥5) was one of the first of its kind in Tibet. It was founded in the fourteenth century in the Sakya tradition but later became a Gelugpa establishment.

Practicalities

Daily **public buses** leave Lhasa between 7am and 8am from Barkhor Square and run as far as the Samye ferry point (4hr; ¥26). You'll then need to pick up another bus or a minibus for the remaining 33km on to Tsetang (¥15) – it's a bit hit-and-miss but you shouldn't have to wait more than an hour or so. Alternatively, direct **minibuses** leave the main bus station in Lhasa for Tsetang from 8am onwards (3hr; ¥35) – they may not be willing to take foreigners, although there are no checkposts between Lhasa and Tsetang. Tsetang's **bus station** is about 500m west of the main traffic intersection in town.

Unfortunately, **accommodation** in Tsetang is not particularly good, and is terribly expensive (typical costing over ¥500 for a double room). Turn right at the intersection on to Naidong Lu past the post office and numerous restaurants and you'll come to the only comparatively cheap hotel that will take foreigners, the *Postal House* (❹), though with dingy rooms and sullied corridors, it's far from a bargain. Continue down the road and you'll come to the grossly overpriced *Tsetang Hotel* (☎0893/21899, ℻21688; ❽). Naidong Lu itself is lined with bars and **restaurants**.

The Yarlung Valley

Though the **Yarlung Valley** is renowned as the seat of the first Tibetan kings, these days it is the dramatically sited and picturesque **Yumbulakhang**, the first Tibetan palace, which draws visitors to the area. The road due south from Naidong Lu in Tsetang to Yumbulakhang is fairly busy, and it's possible to get a lift without too much trouble (there's no public transport).

Trandruk

The small but significant **Trandruk Monastery** (¥25), 7km south of Tsetang, is undergoing reconstruction, although you can still appreciate its grand and imposing structure. One of the earliest Buddhist temples in Tibet, Trandruk was built in the seventh century during the reign of King Songtsen Gampo, and is one of the Twelve Demon-Suppressing Temples (see p.1116) – Trandruk anchors the demon's left shoulder to the earth. Legend tells how the site chosen for Trandruk was covered by a large lake containing a five-headed dragon. King Songtsen Gampo emerged from a period of meditation with such power that he was able to summon a supernatural falcon to defeat the dragon and drink the water of the lake, leaving the earth ready for Trandruk (meaning Falcon-Dragon). Damaged during the Bon reaction against Buddhism in the ninth century, and again by Dzungar invaders in the eighteenth century, the temple then suffered the loss of many highly prized religious relics and objects, following the Chinese invasion. Its remaining glory is the **Pearl Thangka**, an image of King Songtsen Gampo's wife, Princess Wencheng, as the White Tara, created from thousands of tiny pearls meticulously sewn onto a pink background. This is in the central chapel upstairs, which also houses an original statue of Padmasambhava at the age of eight.

Yumbulakhang

From afar, the fortress temple of **Yumbulakhang**, 12km south of Tsetang, appears dwarfed by the scale of the Yarlung Valley. But once you get close, and make the thirty-minute climb up the spur on which it is perched, the drama of the position and the airiness of the site are apparent. Widely regarded as the work of the first king of Tibet, Nyatri Tsenpo, when he arrived in Yarlung, the original Yumbulakhang would have been over 2000 years old and the oldest building in Tibet when it was almost totally destroyed during the Cultural Revolution. The present building is a 1982 reconstruction in two parts, with a small, two-storey chapel and an eleven-metre-high tower. The lower floor of the **chapel** is dedicated to the early Tibetan kings: Nyatri Tsenpo is to the left and Songtsen Gampo to the right of the central Buddha statue. The delightful and unusual upper-storey chapel, with Chenresi as the central image, is built on a balcony. Some of the modern murals up here show legendary events in Tibetan history; look out on the left for Nyatri Tsenpo and for the Buddhist scriptures descending from heaven. The energetic can ascend by ladders almost to the top of the tower where King Nyatri Tsenpo supposedly meditated. The deep, slit windows at knee level mean the views aren't that wonderful, however; for the best scenery, take a walk up to the ridge behind the temple.

The Chongye Valley

From Tsetang it's a bumpy 27km south along unsurfaced roads through the attractive **Chongye Valley** to the village of **CHONGYE**, a sleepy little place currently expanding with plenty of new buildings. There are a couple of restaurants and a basic guesthouse here, but you'll need to ask to find it. The target for most visitors, the **Tombs of the Kings**, is around a kilometre farther south from the village. The entire valley is an agricultural development area and the patchwork of fields is interspersed with irrigation work. There's no **public transport** out here from Tsetang and very little traffic either.

Tangboche

On the east side of the valley, about 20km southeast of Tsetang, **Tangboche Monastery** is situated at the base of the hill and is somewhat difficult to spot among the village houses. It was founded in the eleventh century, and the great Tsongkhapa, founder of the Gelugpa tradition, is thought to have stayed here in the fourteenth century. Take a flashlight so you can really appreciate the most interesting features here – genuine old murals, commissioned in 1915 by the Thirteenth Dalai Lama, are too numerous to list. Look out in particular for Pelden Lhamo on the left as you enter, and, on the right-hand wall, Padmasambhava, Trisong Detsen and Shantarakshita. The artistry and detail of subject and background make an interesting comparison with some of the more modern painting you'll see in Tibet. A couple of hundred metres up the hill is the **hermitage** where the scholar Atisha spent some time in the eleventh century. It's small and recently renovated and, not surprisingly, dominated by rather lurid images of the Indian master. A much-revered statue of Atisha and a set of texts brought by him from India were lost in the Cultural Revolution.

The Tombs of the Kings

One kilometre south of Chongye, the **Tombs of the Kings** are scattered over a vast area on and around the slopes of Mura Ri. Some are huge, up to 200m in length and 30m high. The body of each king was buried along with statues, precious objects and, some sources suggest, live servants. Some of the greatest kings of the Yarlung dynasty were buried here, although there is disagreement over the precise number of tombs – some sources claim it's 21, but far fewer are visible and there is uncertainty about which tomb belongs to which king.

For the best view of the entire area, climb the largest tomb, **Bangso Marpo** (Red Tomb), belonging to **Songtsen Gampo**, just beside the road that heads south along the valley; it's easily identifiable by the chapel on the top. Songtsen Gampo, supposedly embalmed and incarcerated in a silver coffin, was entombed with huge numbers of precious gems, gifts from neighbouring countries (India sent a golden suit of armour), his own jewelled robes and objects of religious significance, all of which were looted long ago. The cosy chapel (¥10), originally built in the twelfth century, has central statues of Songtsen Gampo, his wives and principal ministers, Gar and Thonmi Sambhota.

If you look east from this viewpoint, the large tomb straight ahead belongs to Songtsen Gampo's grandson, Mangsong Mangtsen (646–676), who became king at the age of four. The tomb some distance to the left is that of Tri Ralpachan (805–836), and the nearby enclosure contains an ancient pillar, recording the events of his reign, and constructed on top of a stone turtle symbolizing the foundation of the universe. Originally every tomb had one of these pillars on top, but the others have long since disappeared.

The ruins of **Chingwa Tagste Dzong**, perched high on the mountainside to the west, give an idea of the scale of the fortress and capital of the early Yarlung kings before Songtsen Gampo moved to Lhasa. To the left, the monastery of **Riwo Dechen** is visible, and a rough road means you can drive to within ten minutes' walk of this now thriving Gelugpa community of around eighty monks. Originally founded in the fifteenth century, it was later expanded by the Seventh Dalai Lama and restored in the mid-1980s. There are three main chapels, the central one dominated by a large Tsongkhapa figure.

Tsurphu and Namtso

One of the most rewarding and popular trips in Tibet is to **Namtso Lake**, around 230km northwest of Lhasa, taking in Tsurphu Monastery and Yangba-jing on the way. All these sights can be combined into a two-night/three-day trip in a rented jeep, for which you can expect to pay around ¥1800. There are no checkposts on the roads between Lhasa and Namtso, so you should be all right without a permit, but, as always, check the current situation with other travellers, just in case. If you don't have your own transport, Tsurphu and the town of Damxhung are still reachable, although you may find pilgrim-bus and minibus drivers unwilling to risk carrying you. There is only very infrequent transport (every day or two) from Damxhung across to Namtso Qu on the shores of Namtso.

Tsurphu Monastery

It takes two to three hours by jeep to travel the 70km or so northeast of Lhasa to **Tsurphu Monastery** (daily 9am–1pm; ¥10), at a height of 4480m. A **pilgrim bus** for the monastery leaves Lhasa daily between 7am and 8am (¥25) from the western end of Barkhor Square, returning at 2pm. The monastery is the seat of the **Karmapa Lama**, though it's a seat that's pretty cold these days as the present incumbent, the seventeenth, Urgyen Trinley Dorge, fled to India in 1999. Identi-fied in 1992 at the age of 7, Urgyen is the second holiest Tibetan after the Dalai Lama and seems charismatic and able, and is regarded by many in the government in exile as a natural successor for the role of leader when the Dalai Lama dies.

Tsurphu and Namtso		
Damxhung	当雄	*dāngxióng*
Namtso Lake	纳木错	*nàmù cuò*
Tsurphu Monastery	楚布寺	*chǔbù sì*

Founded in the twelfth century by Dusun Khenyapa, the Karmapa order is a branch of the Kagyupa tradition, where members are known as the **Black Hats** after the Second Karmapa was presented with one by Kublai Khan. Most powerful during the fifteenth century, when they were close to the ruling families of the time, they were eventually eclipsed in 1642 when the Fifth Dalai Lama and the Gelugpa order, aided by the Mongol army, gained the ascendancy. The Karmapa was the first order to institute the system of reincarnated lamas, *tulkus*, a tradition later adopted by the Gelugpa school.

Tsurphu is now undergoing reconstruction after being damaged in the years after the Chinese invasion. The solid **Zhiwa Tratsang** has a splendidly ornate gold roof and houses the main assembly hall, dominated by statues of Sakyamuni and a *chorten* containing the relics of the Sixteenth Karmapa Lama, who played a major part in establishing the order overseas and died in Chicago in 1981. The murals here depict the successive Karmapa lamas. The festival of **Saga Dawa**, on the full moon of the fourth lunar month, usually in May or June, is especially fine at Tsurphu, as the massive new *thangka*, completed in recent years, is displayed at this time.

A visit to the monastery can be exhausting, as it's at a considerably higher altitude than Lhasa. In addition, the clockwise path, the **kora**, climbs steeply up the hill behind the monastery from the left of the temple complex and circles around high above and behind the monastery before descending on the right. The views are great and the truly fit can even clamber to the top of the ridge, but you need to allow two to three hours for the walk.

There's little reason to stay at Tsurphu unless you're trekking in the area, although there is a basic monastery **guesthouse** (❶) – you'll need to take your own sleeping bag, food and candles.

Yangbajing hot springs, Damxhung and Natmso

Don't get carried away by romantic images of the **Yangbajing hot springs** (daily 8am–8pm; ¥10), which flow unspectacularly into a concrete pool (though, at 4270m, this is probably the highest swimming pool you'll ever get to use) at the base of a geothermal power station that provides electricity for Lhasa. **Yangbajing village** itself is 45km northeast of the Tsurphu turn-off along the main Tibet–Qinghai Highway. This is a scenic road with dramatically striated rock formations clearly visible until the valley narrows into impressive gorges. About 1km beyond the village, take a left turn and the pool is 3km farther on the left, opposite the power station, pretty hard to miss and ugly as hell, with chimneys belching steam.

If you're heading up to Namtso, you'll need to continue on the main highway past the Yangbajing turning for another 80km to **DAMXHUNG** (4360m), a bleak truck-stop town. The road is good, and the awesome Nyanchen Tanglha mountain range to the north is dramatically topped by the peak of Nyanchen Tanglha itself (7117m). Minibuses bound here leave Lhasa from just east of the *Yak Hotel* around 7am each morning (3–4hr; ¥30). The turning north to Namtso is about halfway through the town, where a large concrete bridge crosses the river towards the mountains. For **accommodation** in Damxhung, there are several unmemorable places, including the noisy and basic *Tang Shung Shey* (❶), opposite the new petrol station at the far end of town. In front stands the cavernous but atmospheric Muslim restaurant, *Ching Jeng*, and there are plenty of Chinese restaurants around.

Namtso

Set at 4700m and frozen over from November to May, **Namtso** (Sky Lake) is 70km long and 30km wide, the second largest saltwater lake in China (only Qinghai Hu is bigger; see p.1039). The scenery comes straight from a dream image of Tibet, with snowcapped mountains towering behind the massive lake and yaks grazing on the plains around nomadic herders' tents.

From Damxhung, it takes around two hours to pass through the Nyanchen Tanglha mountain range at Lhachen La (5150m) and descend to **NAMTSO QU**, the district centre numbering just a couple of houses at the eastern end of the lake. Here you'll be charged the annoying "entrance fee" of ¥40. The target of most visitors is **Tashi Dor Monastery**, considerably farther west (a hefty 42km from Lhachen La), tucked away behind two massive red rocks on a promontory jutting into the lake. At Tashi Dor (¥10), a small Nyingma monastery is built around a cave and there's a dirt-floored **guesthouse** (❶) between the monastery and lake. It's a glorious site, but facilities are limited – bring your own food and flashlights. Although some bedding is provided, you'll be more comfortable in your own sleeping bag, and your own stove and fuel would be an advantage. You can walk around the rock at the end of the promontory and also climb to the top for even more startling views. For true devotees, a circuit of the lake can be attempted, though this takes twenty days and involves camping on the way.

⑭ The old southern road and Gyantse

The road west from Lhasa divides at the Chusul Bridge and most vehicles follow the paved Friendship Highway along the course of the Yarlung Tsangpo to Shigatse. However, there is an alternative route, the longer but extremely picturesque **old southern road** that heads southwest to the shores of **Yamdrok Tso**, before turning west to **Gyantse** and then northwest to Shigatse.

There is no public transport between Lhasa and Gyantse, and most people rent jeeps to explore the area or include it on the way to or from the border with Nepal. Allow around six or seven hours' driving time from Lhasa to Gyantse in a good jeep. Alternatively, take the public bus to Shigatse, stay the night, then take one of the frequent minibuses to Gyantse. Day-trips to Yamdrok Tso from Lhasa are feasible; you'll start negotiating at about ¥1000 per jeep for these.

Yamdrok Tso

From Chusul Bridge, on the western outskirts of Lhasa, the southern road climbs steeply up to the Kampa La Pass (4794m) with stunning views of the

The old southern road and Gyantse		
Gyantse	江孜	*jiāng zī*
Gyantse Dzong	江孜古堡	*jiāng zī gúbǎo*
Kumbum	千佛塔	*qiānfó tǎ*
Accommodation		
Gyantse Hotel	江孜饭店	*jiāngzī fàndiàn*
Jianzang	建藏饭店	*jiànzàng fàndiàn*
Wutse	乌孜饭店	*wūzī fàndiàn*
Yamdrok Tso	羊卓雍错	*yángzhuó yōngcuò*

turquoise waters of the sacred **Yamdrok Tso**, the third largest lake in Tibet. It is said that if it ever dries up then Tibet itself will no longer support life – a tale of heightened importance now that Yamdrok Tso, which has no inflowing rivers to help keep it topped up, is powering a controversial hydroelectric scheme. From the pass, the road descends to Yamtso village before skirting the northern and western shores amid wild scenery dotted with a few tiny hamlets, yaks by the lakeside and small boats on the water.

On the western side of the lake, 57km beyond the Kampa La Pass, the dusty village of **NAKARTSE** (4500m) is the birthplace of the mother of the Great Fifth Dalai Lama. There is basic **accommodation** in the village (ask for directions), but there have been instances of midnight awakenings here as the PSB move foreigners on. There are several Chinese **restaurants**, but the favourite with visitors is the Tibetan restaurant with tables in a tiny courtyard, hidden away in the middle of the village, where you can eat rice with potato and meat curry (they fish out the meat for vegetarians) under the eyes of the local dogs. Jeep drivers usually come here; otherwise look for the tourist vehicles parked outside.

Yamdrok Tso has many picturesque islands and inlets visible from the road, and there's a seven-day circular **trek** from Nakartse exploring the major promontory into the lake. The climb up from Nakartse to the **Karo La Pass** (5045m) is long and dramatic, with towering peaks on either side as the road heads south and then west towards apparently impenetrable rock faces. From the pass, the road descends gradually, via the mineral mines at Chewang, to the broad, fertile and densely farmed **Nyang Chu Valley** leading to Gyantse.

Gyantse

On the eastern banks of the Nyang Chu at the base of a natural amphitheatre of rocky ridges, **GYANTSE** is an attractive, relaxed town, offering the splendid sights of the **Kumbum** – famous among scholars of Tibetan art throughout the world – and the old **Dzong**. Despite the rapidly expanding Chinese section of town, it has retained a pleasant, laid-back air. It lies 263km from Lhasa on the southern route and 90km southeast of Shigatse.

Little is known about the history of any settlement at Gyantse before the fourteenth century, when it emerged as the capital of a small kingdom ruled by a lineage of princes claiming descent from the legendary Tibetan folk hero, King Gesar of Ling. Hailing originally from northeast Tibet, they allied themselves to the powerful Sakya order. Also at this time, Gyantse operated as a staging post in the **wool trade** between Tibet and India, thanks to its position between Lhasa and Shigatse. By the mid-fifteenth century, the Gyantse Dzong, Pelkor Chode Monastery and the Kumbum had been built, although decline followed as other local families increased their influence.

Gyantse rose to prominence again in 1904 when Younghusband's British expedition, equipped with modern firearms, approached the town via the trade route from Sikkim, routed 1500 Tibetans, killing over half of them, and then marched on Gyantse. In July 1904, the British took the Dzong with four casualties while three hundred Tibetans were killed. From here the British marched on to Lhasa. As part of the ensuing agreement between Tibet and Britain, a British Trade Agency was established in Gyantse and as relations between Tibet and the British in India thawed, the trade route from Calcutta up through Sikkim and on to Gyantse became an effective one.

The Town

The best way to get your bearings in Gyantse is to stand at the main traffic intersection, where, in lieu of a bus station, minibuses drop you off. Heading

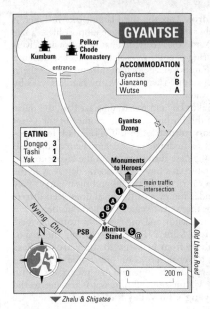

GYANTSE

Kumbum
Pelkor Chode Monastery

entrance

ACCOMMODATION
Gyantse	C
Jianzang	B
Wutse	A

Gyantse Dzong

EATING
Dongpo	3
Tashi	1
Yak	2

Monuments to Heroes

main traffic intersection

❶ Ⓐ Ⓑ ❷ ❸

N

PSB Minibus Stand Ⓒ@

Nyang Chu

Old Lhasa Road

0 ——— 200 m

▼ Zhalu & Shigatse

northeast from here takes you past the cheaper hotels and to the square at the base of the Dzong, where a road leads off to the Kumbum.

The original **Gyantse Dzong** (daily 7am–7pm; ¥30) dates from the mid-fourteenth century, though given the extensive damage caused by the British in 1904, today's remains are a lot more recent. Having climbed up to the fort, visitors are allowed into the **Meeting Hall**, which houses a waxworks tableau, and the **Exhibition Hall**, where weapons, used by the defenders against the British, are on display. Climb higher and you reach the upper and lower chapels of the **Sampal Norbuling Monastery**. A few of the murals in the upper chapel probably date from the early fifteenth century, but most of the other artefacts are modern. The best views are from the top of the tallest tower in the north of the complex. You'll need to clamber up some very rickety ladders, but the scenery is well worth it.

Pelkor Chode and the Gyantse Kumbum

At the northern edge of town, the rather barren monastic compound which now contains Pelkor Chode Monastery and the glorious Kumbum was once home to religious colleges and temples belonging to three schools of Tibetan Buddhism: the Gelugpa, Sakya and Bu (the last of these is a small order whose main centre is at Zhalu; see p.1139).

Constructed around 1440 by Rabten Kunsang, the Gyantse prince most responsible for the town's fine buildings, the **Gyantse Kumbum** (daily 9am–8pm; ¥40, additional ¥10 for photographs) is a remarkable building, a huge *chorten* crowned with a golden dome and umbrella, with chapels bristling with statuary and smothered with paintings at each level. It's a style unique to Tibetan architecture and, while several such buildings have survived, Gyantse is the best preserved (despite some damage in the 1960s) and most accessible. The word *kumbum* means "a hundred thousand images" – which is probably an overestimate, but not by that much. Many of the statues have needed extensive renovation, and most of the murals are very old – take a flashlight if you want a good look.

The structure has eight levels, decreasing in number and size as you ascend; most of the chapels within, except those on the uppermost floors, are open. With almost seventy chapels on the first four levels alone, there's plenty to see. The highlights, with the densest, most lavish decoration, include the two-storey chapels at the cardinal points on the first and third levels and the four chapels on the fifth level. The views of the town and surrounding area get better the higher you go and some of the outside stucco work is especially fine. At the sixth level you'll emerge onto an open platform, level with the eyes of the *chorten* that look in each direction.

The other main building in the compound is **Pelkor Chode Monastery**, also built by Rabten Kunsang, around twenty years earlier than the Kumbum, and used for worship by monks from all the surrounding monasteries. Today the main assembly hall contains two thrones, one for the Dalai Lama and one for the main Sakya lama. The glitter and gold and the sunlight and flickering butter lamps in the chapels make a fine contrast to the gloom of much of the Kumbum. The main chapel, **Tsangkhang**, is at the back of the assembly hall and has a statue of Sakyamuni flanked by deities, amid some impressive wood carvings – look for the two peacocks perched on a beam. The second floor of the monastery contains five chapels, and the top level just one, **Shalyekhang** (the Peak of the Celestial Mansion), with some very impressive, two-metre-wide *mandalas*.

Practicalities

Minibuses operate between the bus station in Shigatse and the main traffic intersection in Gyantse from around 8am to 4pm daily. There are no checkposts between the two towns, but you may still have trouble getting a driver to take you. Most tourists end up paying ¥30 for the two-hour trip.

Accommodation options are all within easy walking distance; north of the main crossroads, the *Jianzang* and the *Wutse* are the two best budget options. Both offer dorms (●) and rooms (¥150-200) and have hot water in the evening. The *Gyantse Hotel*, east of the main crossroads, is the most comfortable place (☎0892/8172222; ●), with a spacious, Tibetan-style lobby and 24-hour hot water and satellite TV. Anyone can hire bikes here for ¥5 an hour.

The most obvious **restaurant** in town is the friendly *Tashi*, just north of the *Wutse*, which does serviceable *momos*; everything here is ¥10–20. On the opposite side of the street, the *Yak*, aimed at tour groups, does decent Nepalese curries. As usual, the best food available is Chinese; in this case at the *Dongpo*, on the main crossroads. There are a couple of Chinese restaurants just west of the *Gyantse Hotel* and, just east, an Internet café.

Zhalu Monastery

Accessible enough for a day-trip from Shigatse, or an easy side-trip between Gyantse and Shigatse, **Zhalu Monastery** is around 22km from Shigatse, 75km from Gyantse and 4km south of the village of Tsungdu between kilo-metre-markers 18 and 19 on the Gyantse–Shigatse road. Originally built in the eleventh century, Zhalu has a finely colonnaded courtyard decorated with luck symbols, but is most remarkable for the green-glazed tiles that line the roof. It rose to prominence as the seat of the Bu tradition of Tibetan Buddhism founded by Buton Rinchendrub in the fourteenth century. Buton's claim to fame is as the scholar who collected, organized and copied the Tengyur commentaries by hand into a coherent whole, comprising 227 thick volumes in all. However, his original work and pen were destroyed during the Cultural Revolution. Although there were once about 3500 monks living here, the tradition never had as many followers as the other schools. But it had a fair degree of influence – Tsongkhapa, among others, was influenced by Buton's teaching. Major renovations are currently underway and chapels have been closed and rearranged, but the monks are friendly and the village is a quiet and pleasant place. For the energetic, it's a one- to two-hour walk up in the hills southwest of Zhalu to the hermitage of **Riphuk**, where Atisha (see p.1098) is supposed to have meditated. You'll need directions or a guide from Zhalu, as you can't see it from the monastery.

About 1km north of Zhalu, **Gyankor Lhakhang** dates from 997. Sakya Pandita, who established the relationship between the Mongol Khans and the Sakya hierarchy in the thirteenth century (see p.1098), was ordained here as a monk, and the stone bowl over which he shaved his head prior to ordination is in the courtyard. Just inside the entrance is a conch shell, said to date from the time of Buton Rinchendrub and be able to sound without human assistance.

Shigatse

Sadly, most people only use **SHIGATSE**, Tibet's second city, as an overnight stop on the way to or from Lhasa. While one day is long enough to see the two main sights, **Tashilunpo Monastery** and **Shigatse Dzong**, it's worth spending at least an extra night here simply to do everything at a more leisurely pace, take in the market and spend a bit of time absorbing the atmosphere and wandering the attractive, tree-lined streets. Basing yourself here also gives you the opportunity to explore some of the sights along the old southern road to Lhasa (see p.1136).

The City

Although the city is fairly spread out, about 2km from end to end, most of the sights and the facilities that you'll need are in or near the north–south corridor around Shanghai Lu and Shandong Lu, extending north along Xue Qiang Lu to the market and Dzong. The main exception is Tashilunpo Monastery, which is a bit of a hike west. Shigatse offers an adequate range of accommodation, a variety of shops and some pleasant restaurants, and the dramatic **Drolma Ridge** rising up on the northern side of town helps you get your bearings easily. The pace of life here is unhurried, but there's a buzz provided by the huge numbers of Tibetan pilgrims and foreign visitors. Although most of the city is modern, you'll find the traditional Tibetan houses concentrated in the area west of the market, where you can explore the narrow alleyways running between high, whitewashed walls.

Tashilunpo Monastery

Something of a showcase for foreign visitors, the large complex of **Tashilunpo Monastery** (Mon–Sat 9.30am–2.30pm & 3.30–6pm; ¥55) is situated on the western side of town just below the Drolma Ridge – the gleaming, golden roofs will lead you in the right direction. The monastery has some of the most fabulous chapels outside Lhasa and it takes several hours to do it justice.

Shigatse		
Shigatse	日喀则	rìkāzé
Shigatse Dzong	日喀则宗	rìkāzé zōng
Tashilunpo Monastery	扎什伦布寺	zhāshílúnbù sì
Accommodation		
Orchard	刚坚宾馆	gāngjiān bīnguǎn
Shigatse Hotel	日喀则饭店	rìkāzé fàndiàn
Tenzin Hotel	旦增宾馆	dànzēng bīnguǎn
Zhufeng Friendship Guesthouse	珠峰友谊宾馆	zhūfēng yǒuyí bīnguǎn

The Panchen Lama controversy

The life of the **Tenth Panchen Lama** (1938–89) was a tragic one. Identified at 11 years of age by the Nationalists in 1949 in Xining, without approval from Lhasa, he fell into Communist hands and was for many years the most high-profile collaborator of the People's Republic of China. His stance changed in 1959 when he openly referred to the Dalai Lama as the true ruler of Tibet. In 1961, in Beijing, the Panchen Lama informed Mao of the appalling conditions in Tibet at that time and pleaded for aid, religious freedom and an end to the huge numbers of arrests. Mao assured the Panchen Lama these would be granted, but nothing changed. Instructed to give a speech condemning the Dalai Lama, he refused and was prevented from speaking in public until the 1964 Monlam Great Prayer Festival in Lhasa. With an audience of ten thousand people, he again ignored instructions and spoke in the Dalai Lama's support, ending with the words, "Long live the Dalai Lama". He was immediately placed under house arrest and the Chinese instituted a campaign to "Thoroughly Smash the Panchen Reactionary Clique". The Panchen Lama's **trial** in August 1964 lasted seventeen days, following which he vanished into prison for fourteen years, where he was tortured and attempted suicide. He was released in 1978, following the death of Zhou Enlai two years earlier, and the Chinese used him as evidence that there was a thawing of their hard-line attitude towards Tibet. He never again criticized the Chinese in public and in private he argued that Tibetan culture must survive at all costs, even if it meant giving up claims for independence. Some Tibetans saw this as a sellout, others worshipped him as a hero when he returned on visits to Tibet. He died in 1989, the Chinese say from a heart attack, others say he was poisoned.

The search for the **Eleventh Panchen Lama** was always likely to be fraught. The central issue is whether the Dalai Lama or the Chinese government have the right to determine the identity of the next incarnation. Stuck in the middle was the abbot of Tashilunpo, Chadrel Rinpoche, who initially led the search according to the normal pattern, with reports of unusual children checked out by high-ranking monks. On January 25, 1995, the Dalai Lama decided that Gendun Choekyi Nyima, the son of a doctor, was the reincarnation, but – concerned for the child's safety – he hesitated about a public announcement. The search committee headed by Chadrel Rinpoche supported the same child.

However, the Chinese decreed that the selection should take place by the drawing of lots from the Golden Urn, an eighteenth-century gold vase, one of a pair used by the Qing emperor Qianlong to resolve disputes in his lands. Chadrel Rinpoche argued against its use. In May, the Dalai Lama, concerned about the delay of an announcement from China, publicly recognized Gendun Choekyi Nyima and the following day Chadrel Rinpoche was arrested while trying to return to Tibet from Beijing. Within days, Gendun Choekyi Nyima and his family were taken from their home by the authorities, put on a plane and disappeared. The Chinese will only admit they are holding them "for protection". Fifty Communist Party officials then moved into Tashilunpo to identify monks still loyal to the Dalai Lama and his choice of Panchen Lama. In July, an open revolt by the monks was quelled by riot police. By the end of 1995 they had re-established enough control to hold the Golden Urn ceremony in the Jokhang in Lhasa, where an elderly monk drew out the name of a boy, Gyaincain Norbu. He was enthroned at Tashilunpo and taken to Beijing for publicity appearances. Meanwhile, the whereabouts of Gendun Choekyi Nyima and his family are still unknown, and hundreds of people have been imprisoned in Tibet for maintaining that he is the true incarnation of the Panchen Lama.

⑭

TIBET | Shigatse

Tashilunpo was founded in 1447 by Gendun Drup, Tsongkhapa's nephew and disciple, who was later recognized as the First Dalai Lama. It rose to prominence in 1642 when the Fifth Dalai Lama declared that Losang Chokyi Gyeltsen,

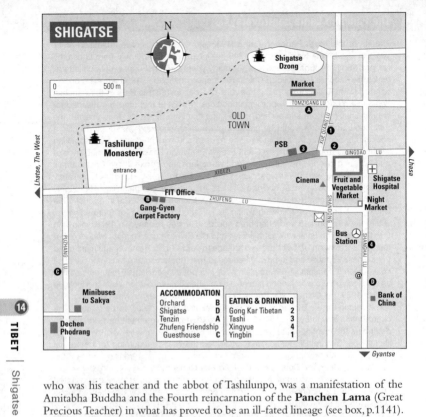

who was his teacher and the abbot of Tashilunpo, was a manifestation of the Amitabha Buddha and the Fourth reincarnation of the **Panchen Lama** (Great Precious Teacher) in what has proved to be an ill-fated lineage (see box, p.1141). The Chinese have consistently sought to use the Panchen Lama in opposition to the Dalai Lama, beginning in 1728 when they gave the Fifth Panchen Lama sovereignty over Western Tibet.

The **temples** and shrines of most interest in Tashilunpo stand in a long line at the northern end of the compound. From the main gate, head uphill and left to the **Jamkhang Chenmo**. Several storeys high, this was built by the Ninth Panchen Lama in 1914 and is dominated by a 26-metre gold, brass and copper statue of Maitreya, the Buddha of the Future. Hundreds of small images of Maitreya and Tsongkhapa and his disciples are painted on the walls.

To the east, the next main building contains the gold and jewel-encrusted **Tomb of the Tenth Panchen Lama**, which was consecrated in 1994 and cost US$8 million. Near the top is a small window cut into a tiny niche, containing his picture. The next building, the **Palace of the Panchen Lamas**, built in the eighteenth century, is closed to the public, but the long building in front houses a series of small, first-floor chapels. The Yulo Drolma Lhakhang, farthest to the right, is worth a look and contains 21 small statues showing each of the 21 manifestations of Tara, the most popular goddess in Tibet.

To the east again, the **Tomb of the Fourth Panchen Lama** contains his eleven-metre-high *chorten*, with statues of Amitayus, White Tara and Vijaya, the so-called Longevity Triad, in front. His entire body was supposedly interred in the *chorten* in a standing position, together with an ancient manuscript and *thangkas* sent by the second Manchu emperor. Next comes the **Kelsang Lhakhang**, the largest, most intricate and confusing building in Tashilunpo, in front of the Tomb of the Fifth Panchen Lama. The Lhakhang consists of a courtyard, the fifteenth-century assembly hall and a whole maze of small chapels, often interconnecting, in the surrounding buildings. The flagged **courtyard** is the setting for all the major temple festivals; the surrounding three-level colonnaded cloisters are covered with murals, many recently renovated. Dominating the **assembly hall** are the huge throne of the Panchen Lama and the hanging *thangkas*, depicting all his incarnations. If you've got the energy, it's worth trying to find the **Thongwa Donden Lhakhang**, one of the most sacred chapels in the complex, containing burial *chortens*, including that of the founder of Tashilunpo, the First Dalai Lama, Gendun Drup, as well as early Panchen Lamas and abbots of Tashilunpo.

Spare an hour or so to walk the three-kilometre **kora**, the pilgrim circuit, which follows a clockwise path around the outside walls of the monastery. Turn right on the main road as you exit the monastery and continue around the walls; a stick is useful, as some of the dogs are aggressive. The highlight of the walk is the view of the glorious golden roofs from above the top wall. The massive, white-painted wall at the top northeast corner is where the forty-metre, giant, appliquéd *thangka* is displayed annually at the festival on the fifteenth day of the fifth lunar month (usually in July). At this point, instead of returning downhill to the main road, you can follow the track that continues on around the hillside above the Tibetan part of town and leads eventually to the old Dzong.

Shigatse Dzong and the market

Shigatse Dzong is now a dramatic pile of ruins. It was built in the seventeenth century by Karma Phuntso Namgyel when he was king of the Tsang region and held sway over much of the country, and it's thought that its design was used as the basis for the later construction of the Potala. The structure was initially ruined by the Dzungars in 1717, and further damage took place in the 1950s. Unlike at Gyantse, there has been no attempt at rebuilding, and the main reason to climb up is for the fantastic views. To get here from town, head west along Tomzigang Lu until the paved surface runs out. A little farther along, a motorable track heads up the hill between some houses to a small pass, from where you can climb right up to the Dzong.

The **market**, opposite the *Tenzin Hotel*, is worth a browse for souvenirs, jewellery, fake antiques and religious objects, but the scale of the place is a bit easier to manage than Lhasa's Barkhor. You'll need to brush up on your bargaining skills and be patient – the stallholders are used to hit-and-run tourists, so the first asking price can be sky-high.

If you're interested in **carpets**, drop into the Tibet Gang-Gyen Carpet Factory (Mon–Fri 9am–12.30pm & 2.30–7pm) on Zhufeng Lu, a few minutes' walk from the entrance of Tashilunpo. Their carpets are made from ninety-percent sheep's wool and ten-percent cotton, and you can watch the whole process, from the winding of the wool through to the weaving and finishing. They have a good range of traditional and modern designs, ranging in price from US$30 up to US$370, and can also arrange shipping.

Practicalities

From Lhasa, public **buses** run to Shigatse from the bus station (¥65), and there are also **minibuses** (¥40) from Beijing Dong Lu, just east of the *Yak Hotel*. Public buses terminate at the **bus station** on Shanghai Lu, returning to Lhasa from here early in the morning. Minibuses to and from **Gyantse** run until

If you are heading independently to the **border with Nepal**, you can get a minibus to Tingri (10hrs) at 8am, and arrange onward transport from there. There is also a daily 8.30am bus service to Lhatse (4hrs) and two morning buses (8am, 9am) to Lhasa (10hrs) from the minibus stand. Buses for Sakya (4hrs) leave from outside the Dechen Phodrang at 8.30am.

For every trip except the ride to Lhasa, you'll need a permit, a document that costs ¥150 and is easily obtained, with only half an hour's wait, at the FIT office on Zhufeng Lu (daily 9am–5.30pm, ☎0892/8991189). At the time of writing, permission was being granted for everywhere west of here, which means independent travel and hiking in, for example, the Sakya or Everest area is easier than it used to be.

around 4pm. There are plenty of taxis (¥10 for a destination in town) or it's about a twenty-minute walk from the bus station to the *Tenzin Hotel*.

Conveniently situated on Xigezi Lu, Shigatse's **PSB** (Mon–Fri 9.30am–1pm & 3.30–7pm) is one of the more friendly offices; they'll send you to FIT for permits, but may extend your visa if you say you are headed to the border and don't have enough time to make it before your existing visa runs out. The **Bank of China** (Mon–Sat 10am–4pm), just beyond the *Shigatse Hotel*, cashes traveller's cheques and gives advances on visa cards. If you're heading west, stock up here on local currency, as there are no more facilities until Zhangmu. At the **post office**, on the corner of Shandong Lu and Zhufeng Lu (daily 9am–7pm), you can send international letters and faxes, but not parcels, and they don't stock postcards – go to the *Shigatse Hotel* for those. There are also international **telephones** here (7am–noon), but no poste restante service. The Shigatse **hospital** on Shanghai Lu has a first-aid post (daily 10am–12.30pm & 4–6pm) – take a Chinese translator with you. There are a couple of Internet cafés opposite the *Shigatse Hotel*.

Accommodation

The long-standing travellers' haunt is the *Tenzin Hotel* (☎0892/8822018; ❷) opposite the market, but a recent renovation has removed its ramshackle charm; it now looks like everywhere else and charges twice as much. Six-bed dorms are ¥35. A better option is the new *Orchard* (☎0892/8820234; ❷–❸) on Zhufeng Lu, which has spotless three-bed dorms for ¥40 – possibly the plushest dorms in China – as well as decent mid-range rooms.

At the other end of the range, the *Shigatse Hotel* is the tour-group hotel, a bit out of the way on Shanghai Lu (☎0892/8822556; ❼), but it's rather cavernous if there aren't plenty of people around. At least you have the choice of taking heavily decorated "Tibetan-style" rooms, which make a change. The lobby shop stocks a good range of books and souvenirs and even oxygen canisters. Another mid-range place is the comfortable *Zhufeng Friendship Guesthouse* (☎0892/8821929; ❻) on Puzhang Lu, but it's a bit out of town.

Eating and drinking

There's no shortage of **restaurants** in Shigatse. Best is the *Tashi* on pedestrianised Xigezi Lu, whose Nepalese cooks whip up standard Chinese, Tibetan and Nepalese food. It's where all the tour groups are herded to, so it's a little pricey. Of the Chinese places lining Xue Qiang Lu, head for the *Yingbin*, which has pretty decent Sichuan food that makes no concessions to wimpy Western palates. Slightly farther away, on Qingdao Lu, the *Gong Kar Tibetan* restaurant has fabulously painted pillars outside and comfortable sofas within. Adventurous carnivores can try yak's heart salad, pig's trotters and ears here, although there are also more mainstream meat and vegetable dishes (¥12–20). Upmarket Chinese food can be had at the *Xingyue*, north of the *Shigatse Hotel*. There's a small **night market** on the corner of Zhufeng Lu and Shanghai Lu, where you can sit on sofas on the pavement and eat spicy kebabs and nourishing bowls of noodles. If you're getting a **picnic** together, visit the **fruit and vegetable market** off Shandong Lu.

The Friendship Highway

From Shigatse, the **Friendship Highway** west to Zhangmu on the Nepalese border is partly surfaced, but generally rough and quite slow. The only public buses in this direction are the Shigatse to Sakya, Lhatse and Tingri services. From the broad plain around Shigatse, the road gradually climbs to the pass of Tsuo La (4500m) before the steep descent to the Sakya Bridge and the turn-off to Sakya village. If you have time, a detour off the Friendship Highway to Sakya is worthwhile; the valleys are picturesque, the villages retain the rhythm of their rural life and **Sakya Monastery** is a dramatic sight, unlike anything you'll encounter elsewhere in Tibet. Further south, the side-trip to Everest Base Camp is a once-in-a-lifetime experience.

Sakya

The small but rapidly growing village of **SAKYA**, set in the midst of an attractive plain, straddles the small Trum River and is highly significant as the centre of the Sakya school of Tibetan Buddhism. The main reason to visit is to see the remaining monastery, a unique, Mongol-style construction dramatically visible from miles away. The village around is now a burgeoning Chinese community, full of ugly concrete, and has been corrupted by tourism; children everywhere will try to sell you quartz or fossils, or sometimes just rocks, and food is very expensive.

Sakya Monastery

Experiences of visiting **Sakya Monastery** (Mon–Sat 9am–noon & 4–6pm; ¥50, photographs inside the chapels ¥80) vary considerably. Some people find the monks rude and offhand, others find them friendly and eager to talk.

Originally there were two monasteries at Sakya, the imposing, Mongol-style structure of the **Southern Monastery** that most visitors come to see today, and the **Northern Monastery** across the river, which was a more typical monastic complex containing 108 chapels; the latter was completely destroyed during the Cultural Revolution and has been largely replaced by housing. Prior to the Chinese occupation, there were around five hundred monks in

---

The Friendship Highway

Everest Base Camp	珠峰大本营	zhūfēng dàběnyíng
Lhatse	拉孜	lāzī
Sakya	萨迦	sàjiā
Tingri	定日	dìngrì
Zhangmu	樟木	zhāngmù

the two monasteries; there are now about a hundred. The Northern Monastery was founded in 1073 by Kong Chogyal Pho, a member of the Khon family, whose son, Kunga Nyingpo, did much to establish Sakya as an important religious centre. He married and had four sons; three became monks but the fourth remained a layman and continued the family line. The Sakya order has remained something of a family affair, and, while the monks take vows of celibacy, their lay brothers ensure the leadership remains with their kin. One of the early leaders was a grandson of Kunga Nyingpo, known as Sakya Pandita. He began the most illustrious era of the order in the thirteenth century when he journeyed to the court of the Mongol emperor, Godan Khan, and established the Sakya lamas as religious advisers to subsequent emperors and effective rulers of Tibet. This state of affairs lasted until the overthrow of the Mongols in 1354.

The Southern Monastery

The **entrance** to the Southern Monastery is in its east wall. On the way there, note the unusual decoration of houses in the area – grey, with white and red vertical stripes; this dates back to a time when it denoted their taxable status within the Sakya principality.

A massive fortress, the Southern Monastery was built in the thirteenth century on the orders of Phagpa, nephew of Sakya Pandita. The five main temples in the complex are surrounded by a huge wall with turrets at each corner. On the left of the entrance is the tall, spacious chapel on the second floor of the **Puntsok Palace**, the traditional home of one of the two main Sakya lamas, who now lives in the US. It is lined with statues – White Tara is nearest to the door and Sakya Pandita farther along the same wall. The central figure of Kunga Nyingpo, the founder of the Northern Monastery, shows him as an old man. The *chortens* contain the remains of early Sakya lamas. As you move clockwise around the courtyard, the next chapel is the **Phurkhang**, with statues of Sakyamuni to the left and Manjusri to the right of Sakya Pandita. The whole temple is stuffed with thousands of small statues and editions of sacred texts with murals on the back wall.

Facing the entrance to the courtyard, the **Great Assembly Hall** is an imposing chapel, with walls 3.5m thick. Its roof is supported by forty solid wooden columns, one of which was said to be a personal gift from Kublai Khan and carried by hand from China; another was supposedly fetched from India on the back of a tiger, a third brought in the horns of a yak and yet another is said to weep the black blood of the *naga* water spirit that lived in the tree used for the column. The chapel is overwhelmingly full of brocade hangings, fine statues, butter lamps, thrones, murals and holy books. The grandest statues, of Buddha, are against a golden, carved background, and contain the remains of previous Sakya lamas.

Next along, the **Silver Chorten Chapel** houses eleven *chortens*, with more in the chapel behind. Completing the circuit, the **Drolma Lhakhang** is on the second floor of the building to the right of the entrance. This is the residence of the other principal Sakya lama, the Sakya Trizin, currently residing in India, where he has established his seat in exile in Rajpur. Be sure to take time to walk around the top of the walls for fine views, both into the monastery and over the surrounding area.

Practicalities

Situated 150km southwest of Shigatse, Sakya is an easy side-trip off the Friendship Highway if you've got your own transport. Public **buses** run here from

Shigatse on weekdays (see box on p.1144), returning from Sakya at 11am the next morning; it's a surprisingly slow trip – allow six hours or more each way. If you want to continue from Sakya to Lhatse, get the bus to drop you at the Friendship Highway turn-off, which it reaches around 1pm. The bus from Shigatse to Lhatse passes here about 1.30pm, so you shouldn't have to wait for long. The **permit** situation is variable: there's a checkpoint just before the village, but some travellers without permits have been waved through by the lazy guards. Don't rely on this, however; if you haven't got a permit and you're trying to get to Nepal, it might be best to give Sakya a miss.

On arrival, avoid the miserable **accommodation** at the bus station; turn right out of the bus-station entrance and walk straight ahead for 150m to the *Tibetan Hotel* opposite the north wall of the monastery; it is marginally better, though electricity is temperamental and pit latrines are the only facilities. The best **restaurant** in Sakya, the *Sichuan Flavour Restaurant*, is just west of the hotel entrance, next to a small shop sporting a *Simone Soda and Cigs* sign. This tiny Chinese restaurant has a surprisingly lengthy menu, written in English, with the usual range of meat, vegetable, rice and noodle dishes (¥10–20); their pancakes make a good breakfast. Alternatively, there is basic accommodation on the Friendship Highway at the turn-off for Sakya (❶) – there's no sign, so ask in the compound there.

Sakya to Everest

Just 24km west of Sakya Bridge (there's no checkpost between the two), the truck-stop town of **Lhatse** (4050m) lines the Friendship Highway and has plenty of restaurants and basic accommodation. There's little to detain you, but most drivers stop here. Another 6km west from Lhatse, there's a checkpoint, after which the road divides: the Friendship Highway continues to the left, and the route to the far west of the region heads right. If you're hitching in to Western Tibet, walk a couple of kilometres along this right fork until you reach the ferry crossing. All the drivers have to stop and wait for the ferry here. If you're hitching to Nepal, walk past the checkpoint and wait there. You are more likely to be picked up by a tour bus heading to the border than by a local.

The continuation of the Friendship Highway is diabolical; allow about four hours in a good jeep, up over the Lhakpa La Pass (5220m) to the checkpost and turn-off to **Shekar** (also known as New Tingri). Avoid the much-advertised but overpriced *Chomolungma Hotel* (❻), a couple of hundred metres towards Shekar off the Friendship Highway, and stay at the new and comfortable, if basic, *Pelbar Family Hotel* (❶), on the highway. There are a few cosy restaurants around here, too. The village itself is 7km farther on, with the Shekar Chode Monastery on the hillside above. There's basic accommodation (❶) in the village, but you'll have to ask, and there's little reason to hang around.

Shekar boasts another checkpost on the highway about 5km from the *Pelbar Family Guesthouse*, and some visitors have reported that the guards here are particularly assiduous in confiscating printed material specifically about Tibet from travellers entering the country (books on China which include Tibet seem to be fine). Just 7km west of this checkpost, the small turning to **Rongbuk Monastery** and on up to **Everest Base Camp** is on the south side of the road. It's a long, bumpy and spellbinding 90km to Rongbuk and worth every tortured minute of the three- or four-hour drive along the rough track. About 3km from the turning, the checkpost at Chay will collect entrance fees (¥400 per jeep, ¥65 per person) for the Everest area.

From Chay, the road zigzags steeply up to the Pang La Pass (5150m), from where the glory of the Everest region is laid out before you – the earlier you go in the day the better the views, as it clouds over later. There's a **lookout** spot with a plan to help you identify individual peaks such as Cho Oyu (8153m), Lhotse (8501m) and Makalu (8463m), as well as the mighty Everest (8848m; Chomolungma in Tibetan, Zhumulangma in Chinese). From here the road descends into a network of fertile valleys with small villages in a patchwork of fields. You'll gradually start climbing again and pass through Peruche (19km from Pang La), Passum (10km farther), where there is accommodation just beside the road at the *Passumpembah Teahouse* (❶), and Chodzom (another 12km), before the scenery becomes rockier, starker and you eventually reach Rongbuk Monastery, 22km farther on.

Rongbuk and Everest Base Camp

Rongbuk Monastery (4980m) – the highest in the world – was founded in 1902 by the Nyingma Lama, Ngawang Tenzin Norbu, although a hardy community of nuns had used meditation huts on the site for about two hundred years before this. The chapels themselves are of limited interest; Padmasambhava is in pride of place and the new murals are attractive, but the position of the monastery, perched on the side of the Rongbuk Valley leading straight towards the north face of Everest, is stunning. Just to sit outside and watch the play of light on the face of the mountain is the experience of a lifetime.

Everest Base Camp (5150m) is a farther 8km due south. The road is driveable, but it's mostly flat, and the walk alongside the river through the boulder-strewn landscape past a small monastery on the cliff is glorious. Base camp is often a bit of a surprise, especially during the climbing seasons (March–May, Sept & Oct), when you'll find a colourful and untidy tent city festooned with Calor gas bottles and satellite dishes. It's possible to camp near the monastery, where there's also a guesthouse offering dorm **accommodation**. Grubby quilts are provided, but you'll be more comfortable with your own sleeping bag. Each room has a stove and pot to boil water (you collect it from up the valley) and the monks will provide fuel (although if you can manage to buy some in the villages on the way, this would be insurance against a shortage – a night here without heat would be grim). There's a small monastery shop selling mostly leftovers from mountaineering expeditions – take your own food. Don't be surprised if you suffer with the **altitude** here. However well you were acclimatized in Lhasa, base camp is around 1500m higher, so be sensible and don't contemplate a trip here soon after arrival up on the Tibetan plateau.

To the border

From the Rongbuk and Everest Base Camp, turning on the Friendship Highway, it's a fast 50km south to **TINGRI** (4342m). The road is good and you should allow about an hour in a jeep. Tingri is the last stop on the public bus service, so if you're headed for Nepal you'll have to hitch from here. A convenient stop before the final day's drive to Zhangmu, Tingri has good views south towards Everest. To get the best of these, climb up to the old fort that stands sentinel over the main part of the village. The three **accommodation** options are on the northern side of the main road. The first, the *Snow Leopard* (❸), is best avoided as it's twice as expensive as the others and has nothing they don't, except carpets. The *Himalaya Hotel* (❶) and *Everest Veo* (❶) are a little farther east, and both offer dorm accommodation, latrines with view, and seats in the sunshine. In both of these, the family's living room doubles as a restaurant, and they produce good, basic fare. For something fancier, try the Sichuan restaurant opposite – look for the red sign.

The road west of Tingri is good quality and lined with ruins of buildings destroyed in an eighteenth-century Gurkha incursion from Nepal. The road climbs gradually for 85km to the double-topped **Lalung La Pass** (5050m), from where the views of the Himalayas are great, especially looking west to the great slab of Shishapangma (8013m). The descent from the pass is steep and startling as the road drops off the edge of the Tibetan plateau and heads down the gorge of the Po Chu River. Vegetation appears and it becomes noticeably warmer as you near Nyalam, around four hours' drive by jeep from Tingri.

Although difficult to spot if you're coming from the north, **Milarepa's Cave** (10km north of Nyalam) is worth a halt – look out for a white *chorten*, to the left of the road on the edge of the gorge. Milarepa (1040–1123) was a much revered Tibetan mystic who led an ascetic, itinerant life in caves and was loved for his religious songs. The Kagyu order of Tibetan Buddhism was founded by his followers and the impressions in the walls and roof are believed to have been made by Milarepa himself. A temple has been built around the cave, the main statue being of Padmasambhava. Perched on the side of the Matsang Zangpo river gorge, **Nyalam** (3750m) is a small village with several Chinese restaurants and a variety of basic accommodation, although there is little to recommend staying the night here rather than continuing to Zhangmu.

The steep descent through the Himalayas continues on a twisty and dramatic road that winds in and out of the forested mountainsides and feels almost tropical as it descends the 33km to the border town of **ZHANGMU** (2300m). This Chinese–Tibetan–Nepalese hybrid clings gamely to the sheer mountain, a collection of tin shacks, construction sites, wooden huts, shops, brothels and offices. It's a great place with a Wild-West-comes-to-Asia atmosphere, although good-quality **accommodation** is limited. The choice is between the *Zhangmu Hotel* (T08074/882272; ❻), at the bottom end of town, with no hot water in the private bathrooms, although there's a shower on the top floor of a building opposite, and the *Himalaya Hotel and Lodge* (❶), on the right heading down through town, offering clean dorms and great views down the valley. There are no washing facilities, but there's a shower operation just up the hill and putrid latrines across the street. The **PSB** is tucked away in an alley close to the *Zhangmu Hotel*. Zhangmu boasts two branches of the **Bank of China** (Mon–Fri 10am–1pm & 3.30–6.30pm, Sat 10am–2pm), one near the border post at the bottom of town and one just above the *Himalaya Hotel and Lodge*. Despite production of exchange certificates, they refuse to change Chinese money into either Nepalese or other hard currency, so if you've got excess, you'll be forced onto the thriving black market. Follow the music and flashing lights for the nightly disco/hostess/**karaoke bar** in the middle of town, where everyone dances the waltz.

Entering Nepal

Border formalities are fairly cursory if you're leaving Tibet for Nepal. The **border posts** (both open daily 9.30am–5pm Chinese time) on the Chinese and Nepalese side, at **Kodari** (1770m), are an extremely steep 9km apart. You can either rent a truck (¥300 for four people), hire a porter (about ¥10 per bag) or carry your own stuff for the ninety-minute walk down (either follow the road or take the short cuts that slice across the zigzags) to the Friendship Bridge, where there is another Chinese checkpost before you cross the bridge into Kodari. The **Nepalese Immigration** post is a couple of hundred metres over the bridge on the left. You can get only single-entry visas here, and you have to pay in US dollars and produce one passport photograph (see p.1123 for details of Nepali visas available in Lhasa). Don't forget to put your watch back (2hr 15min) when you cross into Nepal.

To head to Kathmandu, either take the express bus there or the cheaper local service to Barabise and then change for Kathmandu. Alternatively, there are taxis in Kodari, or you can negotiate for space in a tourist bus that has just dropped its group at the border – bargain hard and you'll end up paying Rp400–600 (US$13 or so) per person for the four-hour trip.

Western Tibet

Travellers in Lhasa spend huge amounts of time and energy plotting and planning trips to the highlights of **Western Tibet**: Mount Kailash, Lake Manasarova, and, less popular but just as enticing, the remains of the tenth-century Guge kingdom, its capital at Tsaparang and main monastery at Thol-ing. However, this is no guarantee of reaching any of these destinations, and it can be dangerous.

Regulations regarding visits to the west change frequently and you shouldn't underestimate the time it will take to set up a trip. Tour companies in Lhasa arrange journeys for trucks of travellers, generally quoting around ¥12,000 per truck for a two- to three-week return trip. Unless you have huge amounts of time and are willing to persevere, there is little realistic alternative to going on an organized tour; there is no public transport beyond the Sakya turning; and plenty more people give up trying to hitchhike than make it. A couple of travellers have died of exposure in the attempt.

The **southern route passes** through Saga, Dongpa and Horpa, a stunningly picturesque journey, parallel to the Himalayas, but with rivers that become swollen and passes that get blocked by snow. This route is most reliable from May through to the beginning of July, and again in October and November, although luck plays a big part. The distance is around 1400km from Lhasa to Mount Kailash. The alternative **northern route** via Tsochen, Gertse and Gakyi is longer; Lhasa to Ali (Shiquanhe) is over 1700km and then it's another 300km or so southeast to Kailash. It is also less scenic but more reliable and there's more traffic using it. Many tours plan to go on one route and return on the other – expect at least a week travelling time on either.

Mount Kailash and around

Top of most itineraries is **Mount Kailash** (6714m), Gang Rinpoche to the Tibetans, the sacred mountain at the centre of the universe for Buddhists, Hindus and Jains. Access is via **DARCHEN**, where there's a guesthouse used as a base by visiting pilgrims. The 58-kilometre tour around the mountain takes around three days; you might consider hiring a porter and/or yak (from about ¥45 per day each) as it's a tough walk and you need to carry all your gear, including a stove, fuel and food. On the first day you should aim to reach Drirapuk Monastery, on the second day you climb over the Dolma La Pass (5636m) to Zutrulpuk Monastery, and the third day you arrive back in Darchen.

After the exertions of Kailash, most tours head south 30km to **Lake Manasarova** (Mapham Yutso), the holiest lake in Asia for Hindus and Tibetan Buddhists alike. For the energetic, it's a four-day, ninety-kilometre trek to get around the lake, but plenty of travellers just relax by the lakeside for a day or two. Travel agencies in Lhasa charge around ¥22,000 for one jeep for a seventeen-day trip. Other agencies might be willing to go for a lot less, though allow plenty of time in Lhasa to sort this trip out.

The third major pilgrimage site in Western Tibet is **Tirthapuri hot springs**, which are closely associated with Padmasambhava; they're situated about 80km northwest of Kailash and accessible by road. Pilgrims here immerse themselves in the pools, visit the monastery containing his footprint and the cave that he used, and dig for small, pearl-like stones that are believed to have healing properties.

The only remains of the tenth-century kingdom of **Guge**, where Buddhism survived while eclipsed in other parts of Tibet, are the main monastery of **Tholing**, 278km from Ali, and the old capital of **Tsaparang**, 26km west of Tholing. Both places are famous for their extensive ruins, some of which are around 1000 years old, and there are many well-preserved murals, but it's all even less accessible than Kailash and Manasarova.

The major town in the area, **ALI** (also known as Shiquanhe), is a modern Chinese-style settlement at the confluence of the Indus and Gar rivers. The only official foreigners' **accommodation** is the overpriced *Ali Hotel* (❸) west of the main crossroads. The PSB here are comparatively decent and, after fining independent travellers ¥300, will sell them permits to Kailash for ¥50.

Travel details

Buses

Gyantse to: Shigatse (frequent minibuses; 2hr).
Lhasa to: Damxhung (daily minibus; 3–4hr); Ganden (daily pilgrim bus; 3hr); Golmud (daily bus; 30hr); Samye ferry crossing (daily bus; 4hr); Shigatse (daily bus; 8hr; frequent minibuses; 9hr); Tsetang (frequent minibuses; 3hr); Tsurphu (daily pilgrim bus; 2–3hr); Xining (daily bus; 40hr).
Sakya to: Shigatse (daily; 7hr).

Shigatse to: Gyantse (frequent minibuses; 2hr); Lhasa (daily bus; 8hr; frequent minibuses; 9hr); Sakya (daily; 5hr); Lhatse (daily; 4hr); Tingri (one daily; 10hr).
Tsetang to: Lhasa (frequent minibuses; 3hr).

Flights

Lhasa to: Beijing (daily Tues–Sun; 4hr 30min); Chengdu (2 daily; 2hr); Chongqing (4 weekly; 2hr); Kathmandu (Mar–Oct, 2 weekly; 1hr).

Contexts

Contexts

History

A s modern archeology gradually confirms ancient records of the country's earliest times, it seems that, however far back you go, China's history is essentially the saga of its autocratic **dynasties**. Although this generalized view is inevitable in the brief account below, bear in mind that, while the concept of being Chinese has been around for over two thousand years, the closer you look, the less "China" seems to exist as an entity – right from the start, **regionalism** played an important part in the country's history. And while concentrating on the great events, it's easy to forget that life for the ordinary people wavered between periods of stability when writers, poets and artisans were at their most creative, to dire times of heavy taxation, war and famine. While the Cultural Revolution, ingrained corruption and clampdowns on political dissent may not be a good track record for the People's Republic, it's also true that since the 1980s – only yesterday in China's immense timescale – the ordinary citizen's quality of life has vastly improved.

Prehistory and the Three Dynasties

Chinese legends hold that the creator, **Pan Ku**, was born from the egg of chaos and grew to fill the space between Yin, the earth, and Yang, the heavens. When he died his body became the soil, rivers and rain, his eyes the sun and moon, while his parasites transformed into human beings. A pantheon of semi-divine rulers known as the **Five Sovereigns** followed, inventing fire, the calendar, agriculture, silk-breeding and marriage. Later a famous triumvirate included **Yao the Benevolent** who abdicated in favour of **Shu**. Shu toiled in the sun until his skin turned black and then he abdicated in favour of **Yu the Great**, tamer of floods and said to be the founder of China's first dynasty, the **Xia**. The Xia was reputed to have lasted 439 years until its last degenerate and corrupt king was overthrown by the **Shang** dynasty. The Shang was in turn succeeded by the **Zhou**, who ended this legendary era by virtue of leaving court histories behind them. Together, the Xia, Shang and Zhou are generally known as the **Three Dynasties**.

As far as archeology is concerned, **homo erectus** remains indicate that China was already broadly occupied by human ancestors well before modern mankind began to emerge 200,000 years ago. Excavations of more recent Stone-Age sites show that agricultural communities based around the fertile Yellow River and Yangzi basins, such as **Banpo** in Shaanxi and **Homudu** in Zhejiang, were producing pottery and silk by 5000 BC. It was along the Yellow River, too, that solid evidence of the bronze-working Three Dynasties first came to light, with the discovery of a series of large rammed-earth palaces at **Erlitou** near Luoyang, now believed to have been the Xia capital in 2000 BC.

Little is known about the Xia, though their territory apparently encompassed Shaanxi, Henan and Hebei. The events of the subsequent Shang dynasty, however, were first documented just before the time of Christ by the historian **Sima Qian**. Shang society, based over much the same area as its predecessors and lasting from roughly 1750 BC to 1040 BC, had a king, a class system and a skilled **bronze**

technology which permeated beyond the borders into Sichuan, and which produced the splendid vessels found in today's museums. Excavations on the site of Yin, the Shang capital, have found tombs stuffed with weapons, jade ornaments, traces of silk and sacrificial victims – indicating belief in **ancestor worship** and an afterlife. The Shang also practised divination by incising questions onto tortoise-shell or bone and then heating them to study the way in which the material cracked around the words. These **oracle bones** provide China's **earliest written records**, covering topics as diverse as rainfall, dreams and ancestral curses.

Around 1040 BC a northern tribe, the **Zhou**, overthrew the Shang, expanded their kingdom west of the Yellow River into Shaanxi and set up a capital at Xi'an. Adopting many Shang customs, the Zhou also introduced the doctrine of the **Mandate of Heaven**, a belief justifying successful rebellion by declaring that heaven grants ruling authority to leaders who are strong and wise, and takes it from those who aren't – still an integral part of the Chinese political perspective. The Zhou consequently styled themselves "Sons of Heaven" and ruled through a hierarchy of vassal lords, whose growing independence led to the gradual dissolution of the Zhou kingdom from around 600 BC.

The decline of the Zhou dynasty

Driven to a new capital at Luoyang, later Zhou rulers exercised only a symbolic role; real power was fought over by some two hundred city states and kingdoms during the four hundred years known as the **Spring and Autumn** and the **Warring States** periods. This time of violence was also a time of vitality and change, with the rise of the ethics of **Confucianism**, **Taoism** and **Legalism** (see pp.1177–1182). As the warring states rubbed up against one another, agriculture and irrigation, trade, transport and diplomacy were all galvanized; iron was first smelted for weapons and tools, and great discoveries were made in medicine, astronomy and mathematics. Three hundred years of war and annexation reduced the competitors to seven states, whose territories, collectively known as Zhong Guo, the **Middle Kingdom**, had now expanded west into Sichuan, south to Hunan and north to the Mongolian border.

The Qin dynasty

The Warring States period came to an end in 221 BC, when the **Qin** armies overran the last opposition and united the Chinese as a single centralized state for the first time, implementing systems of currency and writing that were to last two millennia. The rule of China's first emperor, **Qin Shi Huang**, was absolute: ancient literature and historical records were destroyed to wipe out any ideas that conflicted with his own, and peasants were forced off their land to work as labourers on massive construction projects, which saw thousands of kilometres of roads, canals and an early version of the **Great Wall** laid down across the new empire. Burning with ambition to rule the entire known world, Huang's armies gradually pushed beyond the Middle Kingdom, expanding Chinese rule, if not absolute control, west and southeast. But, though he introduced the basis of China's enduring legacy of bureaucratic government, Huang's 37-year reign was ultimately too self-centred – still apparent in the massive tomb (guarded by the famous **Terracotta Army**) he had built for himself at his capital, Xi'an. When he died in 210 BC the provinces rose in revolt, and his heirs soon proved to lack the personal authority which had held his empire together.

The Han dynasty

In 206 BC the rebel warlord **Liu Bang** took Xi'an and founded the **Han dynasty**. Lasting some four hundred years and larger at its height than imperial Rome of the time, the Han was the first great empire, one that experienced a flowering of culture and a major impetus to push out frontiers and open them to trade, people and new ideas. In doing so it defined the national identity to such an extent that the main body of the Chinese people still style themselves "**Han Chinese**" after this dynasty.

Liu Bang maintained the Qin model of local government, but to prevent others from repeating his own military takeover, he strengthened his position by handing out large chunks of land to his relatives. This secured a period of stability, with effective taxation financing a growing civil service and the building of a huge and cosmopolitan capital, **Chang'an**, at today's Xi'an. Growing revenue also refuelled the expansionist policies of later ruler **Wu**. From 135 to 90 BC he extended his lines of defence well into Xinjiang and Yunnan, opening up the Silk Road for trade in tea, spices and silk with India, west Asia and Rome. At home Wu stressed the Confucian model for his growing civil service, beginning a two-thousand-year institution of Confucianism in government offices.

But by 9 AD the empire's resources and supply lines were stretched to breaking point, increasing taxation led to unrest, and the ruling house was split by political intrigue. Following fifteen years of civil war, the dynasty re-formed as the **Eastern Han** at a new capital, Luoyang, where the classical tradition was reimposed under Emperor **Liu Xiu**. Yet the Han had passed their peak, and were unable to stem the civil strife caused by local authorities setting themselves up as semi-independent rulers. Underneath all this, however, Confucianism's ideology of a centralized universal order had crystallized imperial authority; and **Buddhism**, introduced into the country from India, began to enrich life and thought, especially in the fine arts and literature, while itself being absorbed and changed by native beliefs.

The Three Kingdoms

Nearly four hundred years separate the collapse of the Han in about 220 AD and the return of unity under the Sui in 589. China was under a single government for only about fifty years of that time, though the idea of a unified empire was never forgotten.

From 200 AD the three states of **Wei**, **Wu** and **Shu** struggled for supremacy in a protracted and massively complicated war (later immortalized in the saga *Romance of the Three Kingdoms*; see p.1224) that ruined central China and encouraged mass migrations southwards. The following centuries saw China's regionalism becoming entrenched: the **Southern Empire** suffered weak and short-lived dynasties, but nevertheless there was prosperity and economic growth, with the capital at **Nanjing** becoming a thriving trading and cultural centre. Meanwhile, with the borders unprotected, the north was invaded in 386 by the **Tobas**, who established the northern **Wei dynasty** after their aristocracy adopted Chinese manners and customs – a pattern of assimilation that would recur with other invaders. At their first capital, **Datong**, they created a wonderful series of Buddhist carvings, but in 534 their empire fell apart.

The Three Kingdoms period was a dark age of war, violence and genocide, but it was also a richly formative one and, when the dust had settled, a very different society had emerged. For much of this time many areas produced a **food surplus** which could support a rich and leisured ruling class in the cities and the countryside, as well as large armies and burgeoning Buddhist communities. So culture developed, literature flourished, calligraphy and sculpture – especially Buddhist carvings, all enriched by Indian and central Asian elements – reached unsurpassed levels. This was a rich legacy for the ensuing Sui and Tang dynasties to build on.

The Sui

After grabbing power from his regent in 581, general **Yang Jian** unified the fragmented northern states and then went on to conquer southern China by land and sea, founding the **Sui dynasty**. The Sui get short shrift in historical surveys. Their brief empire was soon eclipsed by their successors, the Tang, but two of the dynasty's three emperors could claim considerable achievements. Until his death in 604 Yang Jian – Emperor **Wen** – was an active ruler who took the best from the past and built on it. He simplified and strengthened the bureaucracy, bought in a new legal code, recentralized civil and military authority and made tax collection more efficient. Near Xi'an his architects designed a new capital, **Da Xing Cheng** (City of Great Prosperity), with an outer wall over 35km round – the largest city in the world at that time.

After Wen's death in 604, **Yang Di** elbowed his elder brother out to become emperor. Yang improved administration, encouraged a revival of Confucian learning and promoted a strong foreign policy. But he is portrayed as a proverbially "Evil Emperor", thanks to the use of forced labour to complete engineering projects, such as the two-thousand-kilometre **Grand Canal** to transport produce from the southern Yangzi to his capital at Xi'an; half the total work force of 5,500,000 died. Yang was assassinated in 618 after popular hatred inspired a military revolt led by General **Li Yuan**.

Medieval China: Tang to Song

The seventh century marks the beginning of the medieval period of Chinese history. This was the age in which Chinese culture reached its peak, a time of experimentation in literature, art, music and agriculture, and one which unified seemingly incompatible elements.

Having changed his name to **Gao Zu**, Li Yuan consolidated his new **Tang dynasty** by spending the rest of his eight-year reign getting rid of rivals. Under his son **Tai Zong**, Tang China broadened its horizons: the Turkic peoples of the Northwest were crushed, the Tibetans brought to heel and relations established with Byzantium. China kept open house for traders and travellers of all races and creeds, who settled in the mercantile cities of Yangzhou and Guangzhou, bringing with them their religions, especially **Islam**, and influencing the arts, cookery, fashion and entertainment. China's goods flowed out to India, Persia, the Near East and many other countries, and her language and religion gained currency in Japan and Korea. At home, **Buddhism** remained the all-pervading foreign influence, with Chinese pilgrims travelling widely in India. The best known of these, **Xuan Zang** (see p.1050), set off in 629 and returned after sixteen years in India with a mass of Buddhist sutras, adding greatly to China's storehouse of knowledge.

The population of Xi'an swelled to over a million and the city became one of the world's great cultural centres, heart of a centralized and powerful state. A decade after Tai Zong's death in 649, his short-lived son **Gao Zong** and China's only empress, **Wu Zetian**, had expanded the Tang empire's direct influence from Korea to Iran, and south into Vietnam. Though widely unpopular, Wu Zetian was a great patron of Buddhism, commissioning the famous Longmen carvings outside Luoyang; she also created a civil service selected on merit rather than birth. Her successor, **Xuan Zong**, began well in 712, but his later infatuation with the beautiful concubine **Yang Guifei** led to the **An Lushan rebellion** of 755, his flight to Sichuan and Yang's ignominious death at the hands of his mutineering army. Xuan Zong's son, **Su Zong**, enlisted the help of Tibetan and Uigur forces and recaptured Xi'an from the rebels; but though the court was re-established, it had lost its authority, and real power was once again shifting to the provinces.

The following two hundred years saw the country split into regional political and military alliances. From 907 to 960 **Five Dynasties** succeeded each other, all too short-lived to be effective. China's northern defences were permanently weakened, while her economic dependence on the south increased and the dispersal of power brought social changes. The traditional elite whose fortunes were tied to the dynasty gave way to a military and merchant class who bought land to acquire status, plus a professional ruling class selected by examination. In the south the **Ten Kingdoms** (some existing side by side) managed to retain what was left of the Tang civilization, their greater stability and economic prosperity sustaining a relatively high cultural level.

Finally, in 960, a disaffected army in the north put a successful general, **Song Tai Zu**, on the throne. His new ruling house, known as the **Northern Song**, made its capital at **Kaifeng** in the Yellow River basin, well placed at the head of the Grand Canal for transport to supply its million people with grain from the south. By skilled politicking rather than military might, the new dynasty consolidated authority over surrounding petty kingdoms and re-established civilian primacy. But in 1115, northern China was occupied by the **Jin**, who pushed the imperial court south to **Hangzhou** where, guarded by the Yangzi River, their culture continued to flourish from 1126 as the **Southern Song**. Developments during their 150-year dynasty included gunpowder, the magnetic compass, fine porcelain and movable type printing. But the Song preoccupation with art and sophistication saw their military might decline and led to them underrating their aggressive "barbarian" neighbours, whose own expansionist policies culminated in the thirteenth-century **Mongol Invasion**.

The Yuan dynasty

In fact, Mongolian influence had first penetrated China in the eleventh century, when the Song emperors paid tribute to separate Mongolian states to keep their armies from invading. But these individual fiefdoms were unified by **Genghis Khan** in 1206 to form an immensely powerful army, which swiftly began the conquest of northern China. Despite Chinese resistance and Mongol infighting, by 1278 the **Yuan dynasty** was on the Chinese throne, with **Kublai**

Khan, Genghis Khan's grandson, at the head of an empire that stretched way beyond China's borders. The Yuan emperors' central control from their capital at Khanbalik (modern **Beijing**) boosted China's economy and helped repair five centuries of civil war. China was thrown wide open to foreign travellers, traders and missionaries; Arabs and Venetians were to be found in Chinese ports, and a Russian came top of the Imperial Civil Service exam of 1341. The Grand Canal was extended from Beijing to Hangzhou, while in Beijing the **Palace of All Tranquillities** was built inside a new city wall, later known as the **Forbidden City**. Descriptions of much of this were brought back to Europe by **Marco Polo**, who put his impressions of Yuan lifestyle and treasures on paper after living in Beijing for several years and serving in the government of Kublai Khan.

The Yuan retained control over all China only until 1368, their power ultimately sapped by a combination of becoming too Chinese for their northern brethren to tolerate, and too aloof from the Chinese to assimilate. After northern tribes had rebelled, and famine and disastrous floods brought a series of uprisings in China, a monk-turned-bandit leader from the south, **Zhu Yuanzhang**, seized the throne from the last boy emperor of the Yuan in 1368.

The Ming dynasty

Zhu Yuanzhang took the name **Hong Wu** and proclaimed himself first emperor of the **Ming dynasty**, with Nanjing as his capital. Zhu's influences on China's history were far-reaching. His extreme despotism saw two appalling purges in which thousands of civil servants and literati died, and he initiated a course of **isolationism** from the outside world which lasted throughout the Ming and Qing eras. Consequently, Chinese culture became inward-looking, and the benefits of trade and connections with foreign powers were lost. Nowhere is this more apparent than in the Ming construction of the current Great Wall, a grandiose but futile attempt to stem the invasion of northern tribes into China, built once military might and diplomacy began to break down in the fifteenth century.

Yet the period also produced fine artistic accomplishments, particularly **porcelain** from the imperial kilns at Jingdezhen, which became famous worldwide. Nor were the Ming rulers entirely isolationist. During the reign of **Yongle**, Zhu's twenty-sixth son, the imperial navy (commanded by the Muslim eunuch, Admiral **Zheng He**) ranged right across the Indian Ocean as far as the east coast of Africa on a fact-finding mission. But stagnation set in after Yongle's death in 1424, and the maritime missions were cancelled as being incompatible with Confucian values, which held contempt for foreigners. Thus initiative for world trade and exploration passed into the hands of the Europeans, with the great period of world voyages by Columbus, Magellan and Vasco da Gama. In 1514, **Portuguese** vessels appeared in the Pearl River at the southern port of Guangzhou (Canton), and though they were swiftly expelled, Portugal was allowed to colonize nearby **Macao** in 1557. Though all dealings with foreigners were officially despised by the imperial court, trade flourished as Chinese merchants and officials were eager to milk the profit from it.

In later years, the Ming produced a succession of less able rulers who allowed power to slip into the hands of the seventy thousand inner court officials, where it was used not to run the empire but for intriguing among the "eunuch bureaucracy". By the early seventeenth century, frontier defences had fallen into decay, and the **Manchu tribes** in the north were already across the Great Wall. A series of peasant and military uprisings against the Ming began in 1627, and when the rebel **Li Zicheng**'s forces managed to break into the capital in 1644, the last Ming emperor fled from his palace and hanged himself – an ignoble end to a 300-year-old dynasty.

The Qing dynasty

The Manchus weren't slow in turning internal dissent to their advantage. Sweeping down on Beijing, they threw out Li Zicheng's army, claimed the capital as their own and founded the **Qing dynasty**. It took a further twenty years for the Manchus to capture the south of the country, but on its capitulation China was once again under foreign rule. Like the Mongol Yuan dynasty before them, the Qing initially did little to assimilate domestic culture, ruling as separate overlords. Manchu became the official language, the Chinese were obliged to wear the Manchu **pigtail** and intermarriage between a Manchu and a Chinese was strictly forbidden. Under the Qing dynasty the distant areas of Inner and Outer Mongolia, Tibet and Turkestan were fully incorporated into the Chinese empire, uniting the Chinese world to a greater extent than during the Tang period.

Soon, however, the Manchus proved themselves susceptible to Chinese culture, and ultimately became deeply influenced by it. Three outstanding Qing emperors also brought an infusion of new blood and vigour to government early on in the dynasty. **Kangxi**, who began his 61-year reign in 1654 at the age of 6, was a great patron of the arts, leaving endless scrolls of famous calligraphy and paintings blotted with his seals stating that he had seen them. He assiduously cultivated his image as the Son of Heaven by making royal progresses throughout the country and by his personal style of leadership. He did much to bring the south under control and by 1683 the southern **Rebellion of Three Federations** (led by three military governors) had been savagely put down. His fourth son, the Emperor **Yungzheng** (1678–1735), ruled over what is considered one of the most efficient and least corrupt administrations ever enjoyed by China. This was inherited by **Qianlong** (1711–99), whose reign saw China's frontiers widely extended and the economy stimulated by peace and prosperity. In 1750 the nation was perhaps at its apex, one of the strongest, wealthiest and most powerful countries in the world.

But during the latter half of the eighteenth century, China began to experience growing economic problems. Settled society had produced a **population explosion**, putting pressure on food resources and causing a land shortage. This in turn saw trouble flaring as migrants from central China tried to settle the country's remoter western provinces, dispossessing the original inhabitants. Meanwhile, expanding European nations were looking for financial opportunities. From about 1660, Portuguese traders in Guangzhou had been joined by British merchants shopping for tea, silk and porcelain, and during the eighteenth century the British **East India Company** moved in, eager for a monopoly. But China's rulers, immensely rich and powerful and convinced of their own superiority, had no wish for direct dealings with foreigners. When **Lord Macartney** arrived in 1793 to propose a political and trade treaty between Britain and China, he found that the emperor rejected totally any idea of alliance with one who, according to Chinese ideas, was a subordinate.

The Opium Wars and the Taiping Uprising

Foiled in their attempts at official negotiations with the Qing court, the East India Company decided to take matters into their own hands and create a clandestine market in China for Western goods. Instead of silver, they began to pay for tea and silk with **opium**, cheaply imported from India. As demand escalated during the early nineteenth century, China's trade surplus became a deficit, as silver drained out of the country to pay for the drug. The emperor intervened in 1840 by ordering the confiscation and destruction of over twenty thousand chests of opium – the start of the first **Opium War**. After two years of British gunboats shelling coastal ports, the Chinese were forced to sign the **Treaty of Nanjing**, whose humiliating terms included a huge indemnity, the opening up of new ports to foreign trade, and the **ceding of Hong Kong**.

To be conquered by foreigners was a crushing blow for the Chinese, who now suffered major internal **rebellions** inspired by anti-Manchu feeling and economic hardship – themselves fuelled by rising taxes to pay off China's war indemnity. While serious uprisings occurred in Guizhou and Yunnan, the most widespread was the **Taiping Uprising**, which stormed through central China in the 1850s to occupy much of the rich Yangzi Valley. Having captured Nanjing as their "Heavenly Capital", the Taipings began to make military forays towards Beijing, and European powers decided to step in, worried that the Taiping's anti-foreign government might take control of the country. With their support, Qing troops defeated the Taipings in 1864, leaving twenty million people dead and five provinces in ruins.

It was during the uprising that the **Empress Dowager Wu Cixi** first took control of the country, ruling from behind various emperors from 1861 until 1908. Ignorant, vain and certain that reform would weaken the Qings' grasp of power, she pursued a deep conservatism at a time when China needed desperately to overhaul its political and economic structure. Her stance saw increased foreign ownership of industry, rising Christian missionary activity which undermined traditional society, and the disintegration of China's **colonial empire**. France took the former vassal states of Laos, Cambodia and Vietnam in 1883–5; Britain gained Burma; and **Tibet**, which had nominally been under China's control since Tang times, began to assert its independence. Even worse, in 1894 a failed military foray into Korea saw China losing control of **Taiwan** to Japan, while a Russian-built rail line into the northeast effectively gave Russia control of Manchuria.

The Boxer Movement – the end of imperial China

By the 1890s China was dissolving into chaos, and popular resentment against the authorities who had allowed the country to be humiliated by foreigners finally crystallized into the **Boxer Rebellion**. The Boxers suffered an initial defeat at the hands of Cixi's troops in 1899, but Cixi's government then decided that the Boxer army might in fact make a useful tool, and set them loose to slaughter missionaries, Christian converts and any other foreigner they could lay their hands on. By the summer of 1900 the Boxers were in Beijing besieging the foreign legation compound, though they were routed when an international relief force arrived on August 14. In the massacre, looting and confusion which followed, Cixi and the emperor disguised themselves as peasants and fled to Xi'an in a cart, leaving her ministers to negotiate a peace.

Though they clung feebly on for another decade, this was the end of the Qing, and internal movements to dismantle the dynastic system and build a new China proliferated. The most influential of these was the **Tong Meng Hui** society, founded in 1905 in Japan by the exile **Sun Yatsen**, a doctor from a wealthy Guangdong family. Cixi died three years later, and, in 1911, opposition to foreigners constructing railways drew events to a head in Wuchang, Hubei province, igniting a popular uprising which finally toppled the dynasty. As two thousand years of dynastic succession ended, Sun Yatsen returned to China to take the lead in the provisional **Republican Government** at Nanjing.

From republic to communism

Almost immediately the new republic was in trouble. Though a **parliament** was duly elected in 1913, the reality was that northern China was controlled by the former leader of the Imperial Army, **Yuan Shikai** (who had forced the abdication of the last emperor, **Pu Yi**). Sun Yatsen, faced with a choice between probable civil war and relinquishing his presidency at the head of the newly formed Nationalist People's Party, the **Guomindang**, stepped down. Yuan promptly dismissed the government, forced Sun into renewed exile, and attempted to establish a new dynasty. But his plans were stalled by his generals, who wanted private fiefdoms of their own, and Yuan's sudden death in 1916 marked the last time in 34 years that China would be united under a single authority. As civil war erupted, Sun Yatsen returned yet again, this time to found a southern Guomindang government.

Thus divided, China was unable to stem the increasingly bold territorial incursions made by Japan and other colonial powers as a result of **World War I**. Siding with the Allies, Japan had claimed the German port of Qingdao and all German shipping and industry in the Shangdong Peninsula on the outbreak of war, and in 1915 presented China with **Twenty-One Demands**, many of which Yuan Shikai, under threat of a Japanese invasion, was forced to accept. After the war, hopes that the 1919 **Treaty of Versailles** would end Japanese aggression (as well as the unequal treaties and foreign concessions) were dashed when the Western powers, who had already signed secret pacts with Japan, confirmed Japan's rights in China. This ignited what became known as the **May 4 Movement**, the first in a series of anti-foreign demonstrations and riots.

The rise of the CCP

As a reflection of these events, the **Chinese Communist Party** (CCP) was formed in Shanghai in 1921, its leadership including the young **Mao Zedong** and **Zhou Enlai**. Though the CCP initially listened to its Russian advisers and supported the Guomindang in its military campaigns against the northern warlords, this alliance began to look shaky after Sun Yatsen died in 1925. He was succeeded by his brother-in-law and military chief **Chiang Kaishek** (better known in China as Jiang Jieshe), an extreme nationalist who had no time for the CCP or its plans to end China's class divisions. In 1927, Communist elements in Shanghai organized a general strike against Chiang, seizing the military arsenal and arming workers. But industry bosses and foreign owners quickly financed a militia for Chiang, which massacred around five thousand workers and Communists, including much of the original Communist hierarchy. Chiang was declared head of a national government in 1928.

Despite attempts at limited social reform, his Guomindang Party quickly came to represent the interests of a social elite. Those Communists who had escaped

while with the bombing of Pearl Harbor two years later all military aid from the United States to Japan ceased. With the country's heavy industry in Japanese hands, China's United Front government, having withdrawn to **Chongqing** in Sichuan province, became dependent on the Americans and British flying in supplies over the Himalayas. Chiang's true allegiances were never far below the surface, however, and after he failed to distribute the arms among the Red Army in 1941, the United Front effectively collapsed.

The end of the war … and the Guomindang

By the time the two atom bombs ended the Japanese empire and World War II in 1945, the Red Army was close on a million strong, with a widespread following throughout the country; Communism in China was established. It wasn't, however, that secure. Predictably, the US sided with Chiang Kaishek and the GMD but, surprisingly, so did the Soviet Union – Stalin believed that with American aid, the GMD would easily destroy the CCP. All the same, **peace negotiations** between the Nationalist and Communist sides were brokered by the US in Chongqing, where Chiang refused to admit the CCP into government, knowing that its policies were uncontrollable while the Red Army still existed. For their part, it was evident to the CCP that without an army, they were nothing. The talks ended in stalemate.

However, buoyed by popular support heightened by Chiang's mishandling of the economy, in 1948 the Communists' newly named **People's Liberation Army** (PLA) rose against the GMD, decisively trouncing them that winter at the massive battle of **Huai Hai** in Anhui province. With Shanghai about to fall before the PLA in early 1949, Chiang Kaishek packed the country's entire gold reserves into a plane and took off for **Taiwan** to form the **Republic of China**. Here he would remain until his death in 1975, forlornly waiting to liberate the mainland with the two million troops and refugees who later joined him. Mopping-up operations against mainland pockets of GMD resistance would continue for several years, but in October 1949 Mao was able to proclaim the formation of the **People's Republic of China** in Beijing. The world's most populous nation was now Communist.

The People's Republic under Mao

With the country laid waste by over a century of economic mismanagement and war, massive problems faced the new republic. Though Russia offered its support, the US refused to recognize Mao's government, siding with Chiang Kaishek. China's infrastructure, industries and agriculture were wrecked, and there were no monetary reserves. But by the mid-1950s all industry had been nationalized and output was back at prewar levels, while, for the first time in China's history, land was handed over to the peasants as their own. A million former landlords were executed, while others were enrolled in "**criticism and self-criticism**" classes, a traumatic re-education designed to prevent elitism or bourgeois deviancy from contaminating the revolutionary spirit.

With all the difficulties on the home front, the **Korean War** of 1950 was a distraction the government could well have done without. After Communist North Korea invaded the south, US forces intervened on behalf of the south and, despite warnings from Zhou Enlai, continued through to Chinese territory. China declared war in June, and sent a million troops to push the Americans back to the thirty-eighth parallel and force peace negotiations. As a boost for the morale of the new nation, the incident could not have been better timed. Meanwhile, China's far western borders were seen to be threatened by an uprising in **Tibet**, and Chinese troops were sent there in 1951, swiftly occupying the entire country and instituting de facto Chinese rule. Eight years later, a failed coup against the occupation by Tibetan monks saw a massive clampdown on religion, and the flight of the **Dalai Lama** and his followers to Nepal.

The Hundred Flowers campaign and the Great Leap Forward

By 1956 China's economy was healthy, but there were signs that the euphoria driving the country was slowing. Mao – whose principles held that constant struggle was part of existence, and thus that acceptance of the status quo was in itself a bad thing – felt that both government and industry needed to be prodded back into gear. To this end, in 1957 he decided to loosen restrictions on public expression, and following the slogan "Let a hundred flowers bloom, and a hundred schools of thought contend", intellectuals were encouraged to voice their complaints. But the plan backfired: instead of picking on inefficient officials as Mao had hoped, the **Hundred Flowers** campaign resulted in attacks on the Communist system itself. As Mao was never one to take personal criticism lightly, those who had spoken out found themselves victims of an **anti-rightist** campaign, confined to jail or undergoing a heavy bout of self-criticism. From this point on, intellectuals as a group were mistrusted and scrutinized.

Agriculture and industry were next to receive a shake-up. In August 1958 it was announced that all farmland was to be pooled into 24,000 self-governing **communes**, with the aim of turning small-scale farming units into hyper-efficient agricultural areas. Industry was to be fired into activity by the co-option of seasonally employed workers, who would construct heavy industrial plants, dig canals and drain marshes. Propaganda campaigns promised eternal well-being in return for initial austerity; in one **Great Leap Forward** China would match British industrial output in ten years, and overtake American in fifteen to twenty years.

From the outset, the Great Leap Forward was a disaster. Having been given their land, the peasants now found themselves losing it once more, and were not eager to work in huge units. This, combined with the problem of ill-trained commune management, led to a slump in agricultural and industrial production. In the face of a stream of ridiculous **quotas** supplied by Beijing – one campaign required that all communes must produce certain quantities of steel, regardless of the availability of raw materials – nobody had time to tend the fields. The 1959 and 1960 harvests both failed, and millions starved. As if this wasn't enough, a thaw in US–USSR relations in 1960 saw the Soviet Union stopping all aid to China.

With the economy in tatters, the commune policy was watered down, and each peasant was given a private house and his own land; by the mid-1960s the country was back on its feet. Politically, though, the incident had ruined Mao's reputation, and set some members of the Communist Party Central Committee against his policies. One of his critics was **Deng Xiaoping**, who had diffused the effects of commune policy by creating a limited free-market economy among the country's traders. Behind this doctrine of material incentives for workers was a large bureaucracy over which Mao held little political sway.

The Cultural Revolution

With his policies discredited, Mao sought to regain his authority. Using a campaign created by Communist Party Vice-Chairman **Lin Biao**, in 1964 he began orchestrating the youth of China against his moderate opponents in what became known as the **Great Proletarian Cultural Revolution**, which in 1966 spread to Beijing University. Under Mao's guidance Beijing's students organized themselves into a political militia – the **Red Guard** – and within weeks were moving out onto the streets.

The enemies of the Red Guard were the **Four Olds**: old ideas, old culture, old customs and old habits. Brandishing copies of the *Quotations of Chairman Mao Zedong* (the famous **Little Red Book**), the Red Guard attacked anything redolent of capitalism, the West or the Soviet Union. Academics were assaulted, books were burned, temples and ancient monuments desecrated. Shops selling anything remotely Western were destroyed along with the gardens of the "decadent bourgeoisie". As under the commune system, quotas were set, this time for unearthing and turning in the "Rightists", "Revisionists" and "Capitalist Roaders" corrupting Communist society. Officials who failed to fill their quotas were likely to become the next victims, as were those who failed to destroy property or denounce others enthusiastically enough. Offenders were paraded through the streets wearing placards carrying humiliating slogans; tens of thousands were ostracized, imprisoned, beaten to death or driven to suicide. On August 5, 1966, Mao proclaimed that reactionaries had reached the highest levels of the CCP: Deng Xiaoping and his followers were dismissed from their posts and imprisoned, condemned to wait on tables at a Party canteen, or given menial jobs.

Meanwhile, the violence was getting completely out of control, with Red Guard factions attacking foreign embassies and even turning on each other. In August 1967 Mao ordered the arrest of several Red Guard leaders and the surrender of all weapons to the army, but was too late to stop nationwide street fighting breaking out, which was halted only after the military stormed the Guard's university strongholds. To clear them out of the way, millions of Red Guards were rounded up and shipped off into the countryside, ostensibly to reinforce the Communist message amongst the rural community. One effect of the Cultural Revolution was the rise of a **personality cult** surrounding Mao Zedong, more a fatalistic acknowledgement of his absolute power over China than a popular seal of approval for his inhuman domestic policies.

Ping-pong diplomacy and the rise of the radicals

The US, its foreign policy determined by business and political interests that stood to gain from the collapse of Communism, had continued to support Chiang Kaishek's Guomindang in the postwar period, while also stirring up paranoia over the chance of a Sino–Soviet pact (despite the split between Khrushchev and Mao in 1960). But in 1964 China exploded its first **atomic bomb**, taking it into the league of nuclear powers not automatically friendly to Washington, and the US began to tread a more pragmatic path. In 1970, envoy Henry Kissinger opened communications between the two countries, cultural and sporting links were formed (sporting engagements gave rise to the phrase **ping-pong diplomacy**), and in 1971 the People's Republic became the official representative at the UN of the nation called China, invalidating claims of Chiang Kaishek for Taiwan. The following year US President **Richard Nixon** was walking on the Great Wall and holding talks with Mao, trade restrictions were lifted and China began commerce with the West. The "bamboo curtain" had parted, and the damage caused by the Cultural Revolution was slowly being repaired.

This new attitude of realistic reform derived from the moderate wing of the Communist Party, headed by Premier Zhou Enlai – seen as a voice of reason – and his protege Deng Xiaoping, now in control of the day-to-day running of the Communist Party Central Committee. Zhou's tact had given him a charmed political existence which for fifty years kept him at Mao's side despite policy disagreements; several holy sites were apparently saved from the Red Guards at Zhou's order. But with Zhou's death early in 1976, the reform movement immediately succumbed to the **Gang of Four**, who, led by Mao's third wife **Jiang Qing**, had become the radical mouthpiece of an increasingly absent Mao. In early April, at the time of the **Qing Ming** festival commemorating the dead, the Heroes Monument in Beijing's Tian'anmen Square was filled with wreaths in memory of Zhou. On April 5 radicals removed the wreaths and moderate supporters flooded into the square in protest; a riot broke out and hundreds were attacked and arrested. The obvious scapegoat for what became known as the **Tian'anmen Incident** was Deng Xiaoping, and he was publicly discredited and thrown out of office for a second time.

The death of Mao

In July 1976 a catastrophic **earthquake** centred on Hebei province killed half a million people. The Chinese hold that natural disasters always foreshadow great events, and no one was too surprised when Mao himself died on September 9. Deprived of their figurehead, and with memories of the Cultural Revolution clear in everyone's mind, his supporters in the Party lost ground to the Right. Just a month after Mao's death, Jiang Qing and the other members of the Gang of Four were arrested. Deng returned to the political scene for the third time and was granted a string of positions that included Vice-Chairman of the Communist Party, Vice-Premier and Chief of Staff to the PLA; titles aside, he was now running the country. The move away from Mao's policies was rapid: in 1978 anti-Maoist **dissidents** were allowed to display wall posters in Beijing and elsewhere, and by 1980 Deng and the moderates were secure enough to sanction officially a cautious condemnation of Mao's actions. His ubiquitous portraits and statues began to come down, and his cult was gradually undermined.

China today: reform and repression

Under **Deng Xiaoping**, China became unrecognizable from the days when Western thought was automatically suspect and the Red Guards enforced ideological purity. Deng's legacy was the "open door" policy, which brought about new social freedoms as well as a huge rise in the trappings of Westernization, especially in the cities. The impetus for such sweeping changes was economic. Deng's statement, "I don't care whether the cat is black or white as long as it catches mice", illustrates the pragmatic approach that he took to the economy, one which has guided policy ever since. In a massive modernization, Deng **decentralized production**, allowing more rational decision-making based

Since 1949 the Chinese state has been controlled by the **Communist Party**, which brooks no dissent or rival, and which, with 66 million members, is the biggest political party in the world. It has a pyramid structure resting on millions of local organizations, and whose apex is formed by a politbureau of 24 members controlled by a nine-man standing committee. The Party's workings are nothing if not opaque; personal relations count more than job titles, and a leader's influence rests on the relations he builds with superiors and proteges, with retired party elders often retaining a great deal of influence; towards the end of Deng Xiaoping's life, for example, he was virtually running the country when his only official title was head of a bridge club. The country's head of the state is its president, while the head of government is the premier. Politbureau members are supposedly chosen by the three thousand delegates of the National People's Congress, officially a parliament though it in fact serves as a rubber stamp for politbureau decisions. In recent years, though, it has displayed a modicum of independence, for instance delaying an unpopular fuel tax in 1999.

The Party owes its success to the **military** of course, and links with the PLA remain close, though it has lost power since Jiang Zemin stripped its huge business empire in the 1990s. There is no PLA representative on the standing committee, but the military has a strong influence on policy issues, particularly over Taiwan and relations with the US, and generally maintains a hard line.

China's law is a mix of legislation based on party priorities and new statutes to haul the economy into line with those of major foreign investors. The National People's Congress is responsible for drafting laws covering taxation and human rights, among other subjects. In other areas, the State Council and local governments can legislate. Even after laws have been passed there is no guarantee they will be respected; provincial governments and state-owned enterprises view court decisions as negotiable, and for the party and the state, the rule of law is not allowed to supersede its own interests.

on local conditions, and the production and allocation of goods according to market forces; factories now contracted with each other instead of with the state. In agriculture, the collective economy was replaced, and farming households, after meeting government targets, were allowed to sell their surpluses on the free market. On the coast, **Special Economic Zones** (SEZ) were set up, where foreign investment was encouraged and Western management practices, such as the firing of unsatisfactory workers, cautiously experimented with.

These economic policies have had a major impact. For a quarter of a century, China's GDP has grown at a rate of nine percent a year on average, and today it's one of the world's largest economies. In the 1970s the "three big buys" – consumer goods that families could realistically aspire to – were a bicycle, a watch and a radio; in the 1980s they were a washing machine, a TV and a refrigerator. The Chinese today can aspire to the same material comforts as their Western counterparts.

Under the rather faceless **Jiang Zemin**, who took power in 1993, China continued its course of controlled liberalization, one which has arguably given the Chinese people two of their most outward-looking and astute governments of any time in the last two thousand years. In particular, **2001** was regarded as an *annus mirabilis*: Beijing secured the summer **Olympics** for 2008, China joined the **World Trade Organization**, and its **football** team made it to the World Cup finals. Even the **9/11** terrorist attacks brought something of a diplomatic dividend for China, which was in the happy position of being seen to support

– or at least not protest against – the subsequent actions of the US government; a war against stateless terrorism suits the Chinese government fine, as it adds justification to its own tough stance on "insurrectionary elements", such as in Xinjiang.

In November 2002, at the sixteenth CCP Congress, Jiang officially stepped down (though he remains a significant force behind the scenes) and passed on power to a new generation of technocrats, led by his protege **Hu Jintao**. Jiang would like his legacy to be his doctrine of the "three represents" – basically the idea that the party should represent all aspects of society rather than just the workers – but is more likely to be remembered for the shift this hints at – the final abandonment of Marxist doctrine. In its pursuit of a "socialist market economy with Chinese characteristics" – whatever that means – the state has continued to retreat from whole areas of life. Mechanisms of control such as the household registration and work-unit systems have largely been abandoned. The private sector now accounts for almost half of the economy, and foreign-funded ventures represent more than half the country's exports.

Economic reform did not precipitate **political reform**, and was really a way of staving it off, with the Party hoping that allowing the populace the right to get rich would halt demands for political rights. However, dissatisfaction with corruption, rising inflation, low wages and the lack of freedom was vividly expressed in the demonstrations in **Tian'anmen Square** in 1989. These started as a mourning service for former Party General Secretary **Hu Yaobang**, who had been too liberal for Deng and was dismissed in 1987; by mid-May there were nearly a million students, workers and even Party cadets around the square, demanding free speech and an end to corruption. On May 20, **martial law** was declared, and by the beginning of June, 350,000 troops were massed around Beijing. In the early hours of June 4 they moved in, crushing barriers with tanks and firing into the crowds, killing hundreds or possibly thousands of the demonstrators. As a result the Party's moral authority has been greatly reduced. Discussion of the event is still contentious in China, particularly as the issues the students identified have not been dealt with.

It's in **Tibet** that China's most serious human-rights abuses are being perpetrated; dissent is ruthlessly suppressed and Tibetan culture is being swamped by Han migration to the region. In 1995, when the exiled Dalai Lama selected a new Panchen Lama following the death of the previous incumbent, the boy he chose was arrested and became one of the world's youngest political prisoners, while the Chinese government enthroned their own representative. Another cause for concern is the Chinese **gulags** – most of them in Xinjiang and Qinghai – in which up to fourteen million prisoners, an estimated ten percent of them political, are kept in punishing conditions and used as slave labour.

Despite hopes for improvement, the government continues to lock up its critics and shows no sign of changing tactics. Recent sufferers have included Xu Wenli and Qin Yongmin, the most prominent dissidents left in China; they were leaders of the Chinese Democratic Party, the first organized opposition to CCP rule. The most daring display of political activism since Tian'anmen, however, came from a very unusual source; in 1999 ten thousand elderly members of **Falun Gong**, a quasi-spiritual sect, sat cross-legged in Beijing on the pavement outside Zhongnanhai, the Communist Party headquarters, to protest perceived oppression. Their reward has been ruthless suppression ever since.

Though most observers agree that the pace of political change is not fast enough, there have been improvements. The National People's Congress has begun to take its task of monitoring government and drafting laws seriously. Under Premier Wen Jiabao, central government has shrunk. More room has been made in government for talented thinkers, including former Tian'anmen protestors. One of the biggest political changes has come at grass roots, where "village" democracy is now practised by two-thirds of the rural population, who have taken with great gusto to their new right to oust incompetent village leaders. No one, though, has yet dared to apply this idea to positions higher up in government.

Stumbling blocks

Short-term gain has become the overriding factor in Chinese planning, with the result that the future is mortgaged for present wealth. Too little thought is given to the environmental effects of modernization, and China now boasts eight of the top ten most **polluted cities** in the world. As success is largely dependent on *guanxi* (connections), the potential for **corruption** is enormous – indeed, graft is thought to be slicing at least a percentage point off growth figures. As in the past, a desperately poor peasantry is at the mercy of corrupt cadres who enrich themselves by setting and purloining local taxes.

A miracle economy?

The spectacular growth of the Chinese economy was one of the great success stories of the late twentieth century and will be one of the most important factors in defining the character of the twenty-first. China is now the world's largest producer of coal and steel and, among other things, makes two-thirds of the world's shoes, DVD players and photocopiers. Chinese production and US consumption together form the engines for global growth. But China is also a massive consumer; in 2004, for instance, the nation bought almost half of the world's cement. Some predict that by 2040 the Chinese economy will overtake that of the US.

But behind the hype there are problems. Even now, more than half China's population lives on less than a dollar a day. Prosperity has been delivered unevenly, and exacerbated regional divisions and social disparities. In the countryside, those who farm unproductive land have become worse off, and with the death of the collective, many of the poorest Chinese lost access to subsidized education or health care. In the cities, with the closure of inefficient state-run factories (whose employees once constituted the Party's core supporters), millions have been thrown out of work into a society that has no welfare provision, while those who have remained in state-sector jobs are on fixed wages and have thus suffered badly from **inflation**. One of the more visible results of rising living costs (coupled with increased agricultural mechanization) has been the mass migration of the working class from the country to the cities, where most remain unemployed or are hired by the day as labourers.

Fifteen million new jobs need to be created every year just to keep up with population growth. Bubbles are forming in property and the steel market. Power generation is running up against capacity constraints. The banking system is inefficient, with US$500 billion of bad loans. Only a high domestic savings rate and uncontrolled exploitation of natural resources make China's growth possible, and neither is sustainable.

The combination of size, growth, stability and potential has set off an avalanche of **foreign investment**. But investing in China is a dangerous game. China's business system is not based on law, respect for property, free markets or patent rights, and the business climate is corrupt. Horror stories about Chinese partners running off with the profits are depressingly common. The rules that do exist are weakly enforced, and local competition is often unfairly subsidized. Foreign investors usually struggle to turn a profit; the most successful foreign firms are those, like Wal-Mart, that largely ignore the domestic market and use China as a cheap base for manufacturing.

The fact that even the government's prestige project, the **Three Gorges Dam**, had to be partially rebuilt because contractors were enriching themselves and using cheap materials illustrates the scale of the problem. To many ordinary Chinese, the price of modernization has become too high, as crime, prostitution and unemployment, formerly seen as Western malaises, have all risen to levels perceived as epidemic.

Perhaps China's biggest problem is its massive **population** (1.3 billion in 2005), which could put unbearable pressure on resources if it continues to rise. Under the country's one-child policy, which began in 1979, couples who have a second child face a cut in wages and restricted access to health care and housing. The policy has been most successful in the cities, but it's not unusual – given heavy prejudice for male children – for female infanticide and the selling off of girls as brides to occur, while there is a growing trend in the kidnapping of male children for ransom or, again, sale. Another side effect of the policy is that a generation of "little emperors" – spoilt only children – is being raised, who will in the future find themselves heavily outnumbered by elderly dependants.

Despite all the gleaming high-rises, little progress has been made on the hallmarks of genuine modernity – investment in education, the rule of law, the freedom of the press and executive accountability. Every year, there are widespread demonstrations by industrial workers who are out of work or owed back pay, by villagers protesting at pollution or corruption, and by homeowners protesting at enforced demolitions. Such actions represent possibly the biggest internal threat to the state. The blame, as well as the credit for creating and managing an economic boom, lies squarely with the Communist Party; designed to change society, it is now incapable of adapting to it. That's fine, as long as economic growth continues apace. But without the safety valves provided by transparency and democracy, if the economy falters, China's political stability is far from assured.

China and the world

Historically, being surrounded by "barbarians" and inhospitable terrain has led China towards insularity. Accordingly, the government's tactic during China's stellar period of economic development has been not to intervene on the world stage. But its explosive expansion is forcing China into engagement. In order to fuel growth, China needs to look elsewhere for raw materials; in Africa and Southeast Asia, China has become the new resource colonizer, striking deals with all comers, including nations shunned by the West such as Zimbabwe and Sudan. China is well regarded by trading partners for its respect for national sovereignty: its deals come with few strings attached. Economic self-interest is pushing China into close alliances with Brazil and with traditional rival India, and together these three nations punch with considerable weight, as they represent more than half the world's population.

China's **human-rights record** is the biggest obstacle to its desire to achieve international respectability, though as China's economic power increases, other nations fast lose their scruples. In 1989, when the Dalai Lama won the Nobel Peace Prize, Western nations were subdued in their congratulations; six years later, President Clinton dropped attempts to make China's application for Most Favoured Nation trading status depend on its human-rights record. The US's support for **Taiwan** remains a cause of contention, as does the artificially low substantially exchange rate for the yuan, which US politicians would like to see revalued. However, the US and China are so tied together economically – not only have US firms invested heavily in manufacturing in China, but China for

Hong Kong and Taiwan

In 1997 China regained control of **Hong Kong**. In the handover agreement between China and the UK, Hong Kong was to retain a high degree of **autonomy** – part of China's avowed "one country, two systems" approach. In practice, the Chinese government quickly reneged on its promise by replacing LEGCO, the democratically elected legislative council, with a group of carefully selected Beijingers. It also interfered with the rule of law (regarded by Hong Kong's people as vital for prosperity) by overturning court judgements and preventing the establishment of a Court of Final Appeal. In 2002 Hong Kong's Chief Executive, **Tung Chee-Hwa**, widely regarded as Beijing's puppet, secured another five-year tenure. He became so disliked that in 2004 half a million people took to Hong Kong's streets to demand his removal, after he backed a law that would have curtailed press freedoms. Beijing finally replaced him in 2005 with **Donald Tsang**, a career civil servant, though as ever calls for greater democracy in the Special Administrative Region are falling on deaf ears.

Events in Hong Kong are keenly watched from **Taiwan**. In 1949 the defeated Guomindang fled to Taiwan and declared itself the legitimate government of China, in opposition to the Communists. Now Taiwan is one of the most successful, and certainly the most democratic, of the Asian tiger economies. Though both Taiwan and China want to be part of the same country, the affluent Taiwanese have no desire to be ruled by Beijing, certainly not after seeing what has happened in Hong Kong.

After years of martial law, Taiwanese politics came alive in 1996, when the country held **presidential elections** for the first time. The favourite, Lee Tenghui, displeased China by pushing for Taiwan's entry into the UN and the WTO, and by having the temerity, in China's view, to treat Taiwan as a separate country. In an attempt to influence the elections, China conducted intimidating missile tests over the island. The US government, as Taiwan's firm ally, responded by parking two aircraft carriers off Taiwan's coast. Lee won the election, despite China's bullying tactics. Elections in 2003 brought even worse news for China, as they returned Chen Shuibian, the first non-GMD president of the island and an avowed supporter of Taiwanese independence. He remains a hate figure in China, where state news organs can hardly bring themselves to call him by name, referring to him as the "arch-splittist".

In 2005 China passed an anti-secession law, authorizing the use of force against Taiwan should it assert its independence. The move brought international condemnation, and resulted in Europe delaying the lifting of a ban on arms sales to China. Conciliatory moves followed in a highly unusual fashion when Lien Chan, the head of the GMD, was invited to meet Hu Jintao in China. Rather cheekily, he took the opportunity to publicly call for democratic reform. Away from the sabre rattling, the two nations have increased their economic ties, with much of Taiwan's industrial production relocating to the mainland. Despite the scaremongering, war looks unlikely; more plausibly, China will continue trying to undermine the independence movement while building up its military power until it could realistically threaten to invade, at which point Taiwan and its allies will baulk at a potential conflict, and some form of reunification process will begin.

its part has bought large quantities of US Treasury bonds – that neither would gain from a change in the status quo.

How China handles its growing influence will determine whether east Asia remains stable enough to continue to prosper, or tumbles back into conflict and rivalry. China's willingness to bind itself to global rules, such as those of the World Trade Organization, has been a welcome way to assimilate it, but an authoritarian, anti-democratic China will never be easy for its neighbours to rub along with, and China's primacy in the Pacific is contested by both Japan and the US.

China's antipathy towards **Japan** stems from Japan's perceived failure to be properly contrite over its crimes in World War II, territorial disputes over some insignificant islands, and simple rivalry. In 2004, anti-Japanese riots followed Japan's soccer victory over China in the final of the Asia Cup, and in 2005, in protests against Japan's bid for a permanent seat at the United Nations, Japanese businesses in several Chinese cities were attacked by mobs. Such demonstrations are awkward for the government: patriotic demonstrations in the last century were often the precursor to pro-democracy unrest, but at the same time the Party would rather not crack down on expressions of nationalism, as such fervour is whipped up by the Party to justify its existence and right to rule.

China today embraces the outside world as never before; witness the passion with which the English language is studied and the fascination with foreign mores, goods, even football teams. Both China and the world have much to gain from Chinese openness. It would be a shame for both should political shakiness lead to a retreat from that.

Chronology

4800 BC ▶ First evidence of **human settlement**. **Banpo** in the Yellow River basin build Bronze-Age town of **Erlitou** in Henan. Excavation at **Yin** in Anyang reveals rich and developed culture.

21C–16C BC ▶ **Xia dynasty**.

16C–11C BC ▶ **Shang dynasty**. First extant writing in China.

11C–771 BC ▶ **Zhou dynasty**. The concept of **Mandate from Heaven** introduced.

770 BC–476 BC ▶ **Spring and Autumn** period. Kong Fuzi or **Confucius** (c. 500 BC) teaches a philosophy of adherence to ritual and propriety.

457 BC–221 BC ▶ **Warring States** period. The **Great Wall** "completed".

221 BC–207 BC ▶ **Qin dynasty**. First centralized empire founded by Emperor **Qin Shi Huang**. **Terra-cotta Army** guard Qin's tomb.

206 BC–220 AD ▶ **Han dynasty**. Han emperors bring stability and great advances in trade; leave **Han tombs** near Xi'an. **Confucianism** and **Buddhism** ascendant. **Silk Road** opens up first trade with central Asia.

220–280 ▶ **Three Kingdoms** period; influence of Buddhist **India** and **Central Asia** enlivens a Dark Age.

265–420 ▶ **Jin dynasty**. Absorption of northern barbarians into Chinese culture.

420–581 ▶ **Southern dynasties and Northern dynasties**: rapid succession of short-lived dynasties brings disunity. Earliest **Longmen caves** near Luoyang.

581–618 ▶ **Sui dynasty**. Centralization and growth under **Wen Di**. Extension and strengthening of **Great Wall**; digging of **Grand Canal**.

618–907 ▶ **Tang dynasty**. Arts and literature reach their most developed stage. **Great Buddha** at Leshan completed.

907–960 ▶ **Five dynasties**. Decline of culture and the northern defences. **Cliff sculptures** of Dazu.

960–1271 ▶ **Song dynasties**. Consolidation of the lesser kingdoms.

1271–1368 ▶ **Yuan dynasty**. **Genghis Khan** invades. Under **Kublai Khan** trade with Europe develops. **Forbidden City** built. **Marco Polo** visits China 1273–92.

1368–1644 ▶ **Ming dynasty**. Imperial investigative fleet under **Admiral Zheng He** reaches Africa. Later isolationist policies restrict contact with rest of world.

1644 ▶ **Qing dynasty** begins. **Manchus** gain control over China and extend its boundaries.

Mid- to late 17C ▶ **Potala Palace** in Lhasa rebuilt by Fifth Dalai Lama.

Late 18C ▶ **East India Company** monopolizes trade with Britain. **Summer Palace** in Beijing completed.

1839–62 ▶ **Opium Wars**. As part of the surrender settlement, Hong Kong is ceded to Britain.

1851–64 ▶ **Taiping Uprising**. Conservative policies of Dowager Empress **Cixi** allow foreign powers to take control of China's industry.

1899 ▶ **Boxer Rebellion**.

1911 ▶ **End of imperial China**. **Sun Yatsen** becomes leader of the **Republic**.

1921 ▶ Chinese Communist Party founded in Beijing.

1927 ▶ **Chiang Kaishek** orders massacre of Communists in Shanghai. **Mao Zedong** organizes first peasant-worker army.

1932 ▶ Japan invades Manchuria.

1936–41 ▶ **United Front**. The Nationalist **Guomindang** and the **People's Liberation Army** collaborate against the Japanese.

1945 ▶ Surrender of Japan. Civil war between the Guomindang and the People's Liberation Army.

1949 ▶ Communist takeover. Chiang Kaishek flees to **Taiwan**. **People's Republic** of China supports the North in the **Korean War**.

1956 ▶ The **Hundred Flowers** campaign unsuccessfully attempts liberalizations.

1958 ▶ Agricultural and industrial reform in the shape of the **commune system** and **Great Leap Forward**. Widespread famine results.

1964 ▶ China explodes its first atomic weapon.

1966–8 ▶ Red Guards purge anti-Maoist elements in the **Cultural Revolution**, along with much "ideologically unsound" art and architecture.

1971 ▶ People's Republic replaces Taiwan at the **United Nations**.

1972 ▶ **US President Nixon** visits Beijing.

1976 ▶ The **Tian'anmen Incident** reveals public support for moderate **Deng Xiaoping**. **Mao Zedong dies**, and the **Gang of Four** are arrested shortly afterwards.

1977 ▶ Deng Xiaoping rises to become **Party Chairman**.

1980 ▶ Beginning of the "open door" policy.

1981 ▶ Trial of the **Gang of Four**.

1986 ▶ Agreement reached on **Hong Kong**'s return to China in 1997.

1989 ▶ Suppression of the democracy movement in **Tian'anmen Square**.

1992 ▶ Major **cabinet reshuffle** puts Deng's men in power.

1995 ▶ Death of Chen Yun, last of the hardline Maoists in the Politburo. Work begins on the **Three Gorges Dam**.

1997 ▶ Return of **Hong Kong** to the mainland. Death of **Deng Xiaoping**.

1999 ▶ Return of **Macau** to the mainland. Persecution of **Falun Gong** begins.

2001 ▶ China admitted to the **World Trade Organization**. Beijing wins bid to host **2008 Olympics**.

2002 ▶ **Hu Jintao** becomes President.

2003 ▶ China puts a man into space.

2004 ▶ **SARS** epidemic; China's population reaches 1.3 billion.

Chinese beliefs

The resilience of ancient beliefs in China, and the ability of the Chinese people to absorb new streams of thought and eventually to dominate them, has been demonstrated again and again over the centuries. While China has been periodically dominated by foreign powers, her belief systems have never been overwhelmed. Instead, conquering invaders, such as the Mongolians in the thirteenth and the Manchus in the seventeenth centuries, have found themselves inexorably **sinicized**. On this strength rests the understandable Chinese confidence in the ultimate superiority of their beliefs, a confidence that has survived through the lowest periods in Chinese history.

Yet the visitor to modern China will find few obvious indications of the traditional beliefs which have underpinned the country's civilization for three thousand years. Certainly, the remains of religious buildings litter the cities and the countryside, yet they appear sadly incongruous amid the furious pace of change all around them. The restored temples – now "cultural relics" with photo booths, concession stands, special foreign tourist shops and cheerful throngs of young Chinese on outings – are garish and evoke few mysteries.

This apparent lack of religion is hardly surprising, however: for decades, the old beliefs have been derided by the authorities as feudal **superstition**, and the oldest and most firmly rooted of them all, Confucianism, has been criticized and repudiated for nearly a century. And in actual fact, the outward manifestations of the ancient beliefs are not essential: the traditions are expressed more clearly in how the Chinese think and act than in the symbols and rituals of overt worship.

The "Three Teachings"

The product of the oldest continuous civilization on earth, Chinese religion actually comprises a number of disparate and sometimes contradictory elements. But at the heart of it all, **three basic philosophies** lie intermingled: Confucianism, Taoism and Buddhism. The way in which a harmonious balance has been created among these three is expressed in the often quoted maxim *san jiao fa yi* – "Three Teachings Flow into One".

Both **Confucianism** and **Taoism** are belief systems rooted in the Chinese soil, and they form as much a part of the Chinese collective unconscious as Platonic and Aristotelian thought does in the West. **Buddhism**, though, was brought to China from India along the Silk Road by itinerant monks and missionaries from about the first century AD onwards. Just as the mutual contradictions of Confucianism and Taoism had been accommodated by the Chinese, however, so Buddhism did not long eclipse other beliefs – as it established itself, its tenets transformed into something very different from what had originally come out of India.

Confucianism

China's oldest and greatest philosopher, Kong Zi, known in the West by his Latinized name **Confucius**, was in his lifetime an obscure and unsuccessful scholar. Born in 551 BC, during the so-called Warring States Period, he lived in an age of petty kingdoms where life was blighted by constant war, feuding and social disharmony. Confucius simply saw that society was something that could be improved if individuals behaved properly. Harking back to an earlier, mythic age of peace and social virtues, he preached adherence to **ritual and propriety** as the supreme answer to the horrifying disorder of the world as he found it. He wandered from court to court attempting to teach rulers a better way to rule, though, like his contemporary Socrates far away in Greece, he was largely ignored by men in power. In the centuries after his death, however, Confucianism, as reflected in the **Analects**, a collection of writings on his life and sayings compiled by disciples, became the most influential and fundamental of Chinese philosophies.

Never a religion in the sense of postulating a higher deity, Confucianism is rather a set of **moral and social values** designed to bring the ways of citizens and governments into harmony with each other, and with their ancestors. Through proper training in the scholarly classics and rigid adherence to the rules of propriety, including ancestor-worship, the superior man could attain a level of moral righteousness which would, in turn, assure a stable and righteous social order. As a political theory, Confucianism called for the "**wisest sage**", the one whose moral sense was most refined, to be ruler. With a good ruler, one who practised the virtuous ways of his ancestors and was exemplary in terms of the **five Confucian virtues** (benevolence, righteousness, propriety, wisdom and trustworthiness), the world and society would naturally be in order. Force, the ultimate sanction, would be unnecessary. As Confucius said:

Just as the ruler genuinely desires the good, the people will be good. The virtue of the ruler may be compared to the wind and that of the common people to the grass. The grass under the force of the wind cannot but bend.

Gods play no part in this structure – man is capable of perfection in his own right, given a superior ruler whose virtues are mirrored in the behaviour of his subjects. Instead of God, **five hierarchical relationships** are the prerequisites for a well-ordered society, and given proper performance of the duties entailed in these, society should be "at ease with itself". The five relationships outline a strict structure of duty and obedience to authority: ruler to ruled, son to father, younger brother to older, wife to husband, and – the only relationship between equals – friend to friend. The intention is to create order and stability through rule by a moral elite, though in practice adherence to the unbending hierarchy of these relationships, as well as to the precepts of filial piety, has been used to justify a form of totalitarian rule throughout Chinese history. The supreme virtue of the well-cultivated man and woman was always **obedience**.

From the time of the Han dynasty (206 BC–220 AD) onwards, Confucianism became institutionalized as a **system of government** which was to prevail in China for two thousand years. With it, and with the notion of the scholar-official as the ideal administrator, came the notorious Chinese **bureaucracy**. Men would study half their lives in order to pass the imperial examinations and attain a government commission. These examinations were rigid tests of the scholar's knowledge of the Confucian classics. Right up until the beginning of the twentieth century, power in China was wielded through a bureaucracy steeped in the classics of rites and rituals written five hundred years before Christ.

The Confucian ideal ruler, of course, never quite emerged (the emperor was not expected to sit the exams) and the scholar-officials often deteriorated into corrupt bureaucrats and exploitative landlords. Furthermore, the Confucian ideals of submission to authority would not seem to have much of a shelf-life at the start of the twenty-first century. On the other hand,

Chiang's purge regrouped in remote areas across the country, principally at **Jinggang Shan** in Jiangxi province, under the leadership of Mao Zedong.

Mao Zedong, the Red Army and the Long March

Son of a well-off Hunanese farmer, **Mao** believed social reform lay in the hands of the peasants who, despite the overthrow of the emperors, still had few rights and no power base. Drawing from Marx's analyses, Mao recognized the parallels between nineteenth-century Europe and twentieth-century China – and that a mass armed rising was the only way the old order could be replaced.

After events in Shanghai, Mao organized the first peasant-worker army in Changsha, in what was later to be called the **Autumn Harvest Uprising**. Moving with other Communist forces to the Hunan–Jiangxi border in 1927, the **Red Army** of peasants, miners and Guomindang deserters achieved unexpected successes against the Nationalist troops sent against them until **Li Lisan**, the Communist leader, ordered Mao out of his mountain base to attack the cities. The ensuing open assaults against the vastly superior Guomindang forces were disastrous, and Chiang Kaishek, following up these defeats, mobilized half a million troops and encircled Jinggang Shan with a ring of concrete blockhouses and barbed-wire entanglements.

Forced between choosing to fight or flee, in October 1934 Mao organized eighty thousand troops in an epic 9500-kilometre retreat which became known as the **Long March**. By the time they reached safety in **Yan'an** in Shaanxi province a year later, the Communists had lost three quarters of their followers to the rigours of the trip, but had also started their path towards victory. The Long March won the Communists immense respect – an army determined enough to do this could do anything. Along the way, Mao had become undisputed leader of the CCP at the **Zunyi Conference**, severing the Party from its Russian advisers.

Japanese invasion and the United Front

Meanwhile, Japan had taken over Chinese Manchuria in 1933 and installed Pu Yi (last emperor of the Qing dynasty) as puppet leader. They were obviously preparing to invade eastern China, and Mao wrote to Chiang Kaishek advocating an end to civil war and a **United Front** against the threat. Chiang's response was to move his Manchurian armies, under **Zhang Xueliang**, down to finish off the Reds in Shaanxi. Zhang, however, saw an alliance as the only way to evict the Japanese from his homeland, and so secretly entered into an agreement with the Communist forces. On December 12, 1936, Chiang was kidnapped by his own troops in what became known as the **Xi'an Incident** and, with Zhou Enlai as a mediator, reluctantly signed an agreement to the United Front on Christmas Day. Briefly, the parties were united, though both sides knew that the alliance would last only as long as the Japanese threat.

Full-scale war broke out in July 1937 when the Japanese attacked Beijing. The GMD, inadequately armed or trained, were forced west and south, and at the end of the year the Japanese had taken most of eastern China between Beijing and Guangzhou. With a capital-in-occupation at Nanjing, the Japanese concentrated their efforts on routing the GMD, leaving a vacuum in the north that the Communists filled, establishing what amounted to stable government of a hundred million people across the North China Plain.

The outbreak of war in Europe in September 1939 soon had repercussions in China. Nazi Germany stopped supplying the weaponry the GMD relied on, with its emphasis on **community and social cohesion**, Confucianism has played an enormous role in keeping China free of the bigotry and religious fanaticism that have been bringing war to Europe for two thousand years. And today it is clear that Confucius does still have a role to play, not least in his new incarnation as the embodiment of the much trumpeted "**Asian values**", exemplified by a non-confrontational system of government – though the old excuse that Confucianism means the Chinese world cannot embrace democracy has been given the lie by developments in Taiwan. On the grass-roots level, too, old practices such as ancestor-worship are making a comeback. Now that the latest foreign religion of Marxism has been thoroughly discredited, it appears that Confucianism is simply reoccupying its rightful position.

Taoism

Tao translates literally as the "Way" and, in its purest form, Taoism is the study and pursuit of this ineffable Way, as outlined in the fundamental text, the **Daodejing** (often written as *Tao Te Ching*) or "The Way of Power". This obscure and mystical text essentially comprises a compilation of the wise sayings of a semi-mythical hermit by the name of **Lao Zi**, who is said to have been a contemporary of Confucius. The Daodejing was not compiled until at least three centuries after his death.

The *Tao* is never really defined – indeed by its very nature it is undefinable. To the despair of the rationalist, the first lines of the Daodejing read:

The Tao that can be told
is not the eternal Tao.
The name that can be named
is not the eternal name.

In essence, however, it might be thought of as the Way of Nature, the underlying principle and source of all being, the bond which unites man and nature. Its central principle is **Wu Wei**, which can crudely be translated as "no action", though it is probably better understood as "no action which runs contrary to nature". Taoism was originally the creed of the recluse. Whereas Confucianism is concerned with repairing social order and social relationships, Taoism is interested in the relationship of the individual with the natural universe. It simply looks at human problems from another, higher plane: having good relations with one's neighbours is of no use if one is not in harmony with nature.

Taoism's second major text is a book of parables written by one ideal practitioner of the Way, **Zhuang Zi**, another semi-mythical figure. Acknowledged in his lifetime as a great sage, he rejected all offers of high rank in favour of a life of solitary reflection. His works – allegorical tales which have delighted Chinese readers for centuries – reveal humour as well as perception; in the famous butterfly parable Zhuang Zi examines the many faces of reality:

Once upon a time Zhuang Zi dreamed he was a butterfly. A butterfly flying around and enjoying itself. It did not know it was Zhuang Zi again. We do not know whether it was Zhuang Zi dreaming that he was a butterfly, or a butterfly dreaming he was Zhuang Zi.

In its affirmation of the irrational and natural sources of life, Taoism has provided Chinese culture with a balance to the rigid social mores of Confucianism. In traditional China it was said that the perfect lifestyle was that of a man who was a Confucian during the day – a righteous and firm administrator, upholding the virtues of the gentleman/ruler – and a Taoist after the duties of the day had been fulfilled. The practice of Taoism affirms the virtues of withdrawing from public duties and giving oneself up to a life of **contemplation and meditation**. If Confucianism preaches duty to family and to society, Taoism champions the sublimity of withdrawal, non-committedness and "dropping out". The **art and literature** of China have been greatly enriched by Taoism's notions of contemplation, detachment and freedom from social entanglement, and the Tao has become embedded in the Chinese soul as a doctrine of yielding to the inevitable forces of nature.

Buddhism

The first organized religion to penetrate China, **Buddhism** enjoyed a glorious, if brief, period of ascendancy under the Tang dynasty (618–906 AD). In the eighth century there were over three hundred thousand Buddhist monks in China. This was also a time which saw the creation of much of the country's **great religious art** – above all the cave shrines at **Luoyang** (Henan), **Datong** (Shaanxi) and **Dunhuang** (Gansu), where thousands of carvings of the Buddha and paintings of holy figures attest to the powerful influence of Indian art and religion.

Gradually, though, Buddhism too was submerged into the native belief system. Most schools of Indian Buddhism of the time taught that life on earth was essentially one of suffering, an endless cycle in which people were born, grew old and died, only to be born again in other bodies; the goal was to break out of this cycle by attaining nirvana, which could be done by losing all desire for things of the world. This essentially individualistic doctrine was not likely to appeal to the highly regimented Chinese, however, and hence it was that the relatively small **Mahayana School** of Buddhism came to dominate Chinese thinking. The Mahayana taught that perfection for the individual was not possible without perfection for all – and that those who had already attained enlightenment would remain active in the world (as **Bodhisattvas**) to help others along the path. In time Bodhisattvas came to be ascribed miraculous powers, and were prayed to in a manner remarkably similar to that of conventional Confucian ancestor-worship. The mainstream of Chinese Buddhism came to be more about maintaining harmonious relations with Bodhisattvas than about attaining nirvana.

Another entirely new sect of Buddhism also arose in China through contact with Taoism. Known in China as **Chan** (and in Japan as Zen) Buddhism, it offered a less extreme path to enlightenment. For a Chan Buddhist it was not necessary to become a monk or a recluse in order to achieve nirvana – instead this ultimate state of being could be reached through life in accord with, and in contemplation of, the Way.

In short, the Chinese managed to marry Buddhism to their pre-existing belief structures with very little difficulty at all. This was facilitated by the general absence of dogma within Buddhist thought. Like the Chinese, the **Tibetans**, too, found themselves able to adapt the new belief system to their old religion, **Bon** (see p.940), rather than simply replacing it. Over the centuries, they established their own schools of Buddhism often referred to as Lamaist Buddhism or Lamaism, which differ from the Chinese versions in minor respects. The now dominant **Gelugpa** (or Yellow Hat) school, of which the Dalai and Panchen Lamas are members, dates back to the teachings of Tsongkhapa (1357–1419). For more on Buddhism in Tibet, see p.1096.

Minority faiths and popular beliefs

Though Buddhism was the only foreign religion to have left a substantial mark on China, it was not the only religion to enter China via the Silk Road. Both **Islam** and **Christianity** also trickled into the country this way, and to this day a significant minority of Chinese, numbering possibly in the tens of millions, are Muslims. Unlike most of the rest of Asia, however, China did not yield wholesale to the tide of Islam – the rigid, all-embracing doctrines of the Koran never stood much of a chance with the flexible Chinese.

When Jesuit missionaries first arrived in China in the sixteenth and seventeenth centuries they were astounded and dismayed by the Chinese **flexibility of belief**. One frustrated Jesuit put it thus: "In China, the educated believe nothing and the uneducated believe everything." For those versed in the classics of Confucianism, Taoism and Buddhism, the normal belief was a healthy and tolerant scepticism. But for the great majority of illiterate peasants, **popular religion** offered a plethora of ghosts, spirits, gods and ancestors who ruled over a capricious nature and protected humanity. If Christian missionaries handed out rice, perhaps Christ too deserved a place alongside them. In popular Buddhism the hope was to reach the "Pure Land", a kind of heaven for believers ruled over by a female deity known as the Mother Ruler. Popular Taoism shared this feminine deity, but its concerns were rather with the sorcerers, alchemists and martial arts aficionados who sought solutions to the riddle of immortality; you may well see some of these figures depicted in Taoist temples.

Modern China

During the twentieth century, confronted by the superior military and technical power of the West, the Chinese have striven to break free from the shackles of superstition. The imperial examinations were abolished at the start of the century and since then Chinese intellectuals have been searching for a modern yet essentially Chinese philosophy. The **Cultural Revolution** can be seen as the culmination of these efforts to repudiate the past. Hundreds of thousands of temples, ancestral halls and religious objects were defaced and destroyed. Monasteries which had preserved their seclusion for centuries were burnt to the ground and their monks imprisoned. The classics of literature and philosophy – the "residue of the reactionary feudal past" – were burned in huge celebratory bonfires. In 1974, towards the end of the Cultural Revolution, a campaign was launched to "criticize Lin Biao and Confucius", pairing the general with the sage to imply that both were equally reactionary in their opposition to the government.

Yet the very fact that Confucius could still be held up as an object for derision in 1974 reveals the tenacity of traditional beliefs. With the Cultural Revolution now long gone, they are once again being accepted as an essential part of the cultural tradition which binds the Chinese people together. The older generation, despite a lifetime of commitment to the Marxist revolution, are comforted and strengthened by their knowledge of the national heritage. The young are rediscovering the classics, the forbidden fruit of their school days. The welcome result is that Chinese temples of all descriptions are prosperous, busy places again, teeming with people who have come to ask for grandchildren or simply for money. The atmosphere may not seem devout or religious, but then perhaps it never did.

Traditional Chinese Medicine

As an agricultural society, the Chinese have long been aware of the importance of the proper **balance** of natural, elemental forces: too much heat causes drought; too much rain, floods; while the correct measure of both encourages farmers' crops to grow. The ancient Chinese saw heaven, earth and humankind existing as an integral whole, such that if people lived in harmony with heaven and earth, then their collective health would be good. The medical treatise *Huang Di Neijing*, attributed to the semi-mythical Yellow Emperor (2500 BC), mentions the importance of spiritual balance, acupuncture and herbal medicine in treating illnesses, and attests to the venerable age of China's medical beliefs – it may well be a compilation of even earlier texts. Acupuncture was certainly in use by the Han period, as tombs in Hebei dated to 113 BC have yielded acupuncture needles made of gold and silver.

The belief in universal balance is known as **Dao** (or Tao) – literally "the Way", but implying "the Way of Nature". As an extension of Daoist principles, life is seen as consisting of opposites – man and woman, sun and moon, right and left, giving and receiving – whereby all things exist as a result of their interaction with their opposites. This is expressed in the black-and-white Daoist diagram which shows two interacting opposites, the **yin** ("female", passive energy) and the **yang** ("male", active energy). At the core of traditional Chinese medicine is the belief that in order for a body to be healthy, its opposites must also be in a state of dynamic balance; there is a constant fluctuation, for example, between the body's heat, depending on its level of activity and the weather, and the amount of water needed to keep the body at the correct temperature. An excess of water in the system creates oedema, too little creates dehydration; too much heat will cause a temperature, and too little cause chills. Chinese medicine therefore views the body as an integrated whole, so that in sickness, the whole body – rather than just the "ill" part of it – requires treatment.

Qi and acupuncture

An underlying feature of Chinese medical philosophy, **qi** (or chi) is the energy of life: in the same way that electricity powers a lightbulb, *qi* enables us to move, see and speak. *Qi* flows along the body's network of **meridians**, or energy pathways, linking the surface tissues to specific internal **organs** which act as *qi* reservoirs; the twelve major meridians are named after the organ to which they are connected. The meridians are further classed as *yin* or *yang* depending on whether they are exposed or protected. In the limbs, for instance, the outer sides' channels are *yang*, and important for resisting disease, while the inner sides' channels are *yin*, and more involved with nourishing the body.

Mental and physical tensions, poor diet, anger or depression, even adverse weather, however, inhibit *qi* flow, causing illness. Needles inserted (and then rotated as necessary) in the body's **acupuncture points**, most of which lie on meridians and so are connected to internal organs, reinforce or reduce the *qi* flow along a meridian, in turn influencing the organs' activities. When the *qi* is balanced and flowing smoothly once more, good health is regained; acupuncture is specifically used to combat inflammation, to regenerate damaged tissue, and to improve the functional power of internal organs.

Herbal medicine

In the 2200 years since the semi-mythical Xia king **Shennong** compiled his classic work on **medicinal herbs**, a vast amount of experience has been gained to help perfect their clinical use. Approximately seven thousand herbs, derived from roots, leaves, twigs and fruit, are today commonly used in Chinese medicine, with another thousand or so of animal or mineral origin (though also classified as "herbs"). Each is first processed by cleaning, soaking, slicing, drying or roasting, or even stir-frying with wine, ginger or vinegar, to influence their effects; the brew is then boiled down and drunk as a tea (typically very bitter and earthy tasting).

Herbs are effective in preventing or combating a wide variety of diseases. Some are used to treat the underlying cause of the complaint, others to treat symptoms and help strengthen the body's own immune system, in turn helping it to combat the problem. An everyday example is in the treatment of flu: the herbal formula would include a "cold action" herb to reduce the fever, a herb to induce sweating and so clear the body-ache, a purgative to clear the virus from the system and a tonic herb to replenish the immune system. In all treatments, the patient is re-examined each week, and as the condition improves the herbal formula is changed accordingly.

In the same way that Western aspirin is derived from willow bark, many Chinese drugs have been developed from herbs. One example is the anti-malarial herb *qinghaosu*, or artemisinin, which has proved effective in treating chloroquine-resistant strains of malaria with minimal side effects.

Chinese versus Western medicine

It's difficult to **compare** Chinese and Western medicine directly, as their approaches are so different. Very broadly, Western medical techniques are superior for treating major physical trauma with surgery; the Chinese approach seems more effective on chronic illness or in maintaining long-term health. In 1974 the World Health Organization recognized the **benefits** of acupuncture, while in 1979 the United Nations accepted that Traditional Chinese Medicine (TCM) worked in the treatment of infections, respiratory, circulatory and neurological conditions, and musculoskeletal traumatic injuries as well as arthritic and inflammatory problems. In addition, the fact that traditional medical schools can be found today in Western cities worldwide, as well as in every province of China, indicates a growing global acceptance.

The martial arts of China

Given China's tumultuous ancient history – of warring clans, warring states and eventually warring dynasties – it's unsurprising that so much energy has been invested in the development and fine-tuning of the **martial arts**. In a society unable to rely on the government for protection, being a capable martial artist was often an essential skill, especially at times of large-scale revolution. Fighting techniques evolved in almost all isolated communities, from Buddhist and Daoist temples down to clan villages, often acquiring unique characteristics which were taught solely to members of that group. It's only in very recent times that outsiders have been able to learn these distinctive styles, though some have now become so popular that even the government has approved formal versions.

Styles and techniques

Thousands of martial arts have evolved in China, but all can be classed into two basic types. **External** or hard styles (*waijia*) concentrate on developing **li**, or physical strength, to literally overpower opponents; for example, conditioning hands by punching plate iron and slapping concrete blocks thousands of times until one is able, by sheer force, to break planks of wood and stones. **Internal** or soft styles (*neijia*) concentrate on developing the internal energy known as **qi**, which supposedly circulates around the body along acupuncture meridians and is also one of the central aspects of Chinese medicine (see p.1183). **Qigong** – which means "breath skills" – is used to build up an awareness of *qi* and an ability to move it around the body, eventually replacing excess muscular action and making all movements fluid and powerful.

In practice, however, such distinctions are blurred, at least for the beginner. Initial internal training tends to be overwhelmingly physical, as it requires years before sufficient awareness of *qi* develops to allow it to be used effectively in fighting. Many external styles also utilize *qigong* techniques, just as most internal styles rely on some brute force. And from the outside, internal and external styles can look very similar, as both use **forms** – pre-arranged sets of movements – to develop the necessary speed, power and timing; both use punches, kicks and open hand strikes as well as a wide variety of **weapons**; and both often incorporate **animal movements** – for instance, in monkey-style kung fu the practitioner behaves and moves like a monkey while fighting. The following gives brief accounts of some of the better-known martial arts, which you might well see being performed in public parks in China.

Shaolin kung fu

One of the most influential people in the development of Chinese external martial arts was the sixth-century Indian Buddhist monk **Boddhidarma**, who spent many years at the **Shaolin temple** (see p.301). Here he taught the monks movement and breathing exercises, which were later combined with indigenous martial arts to form **Shaolin kung fu**. "Shaolin" is a very nebulous term in China today, indiscriminately used to describe a host of fighting styles which probably have very little historical connection with the temple. Nonetheless, it's a vigorous art best known for its powerful kicks and animal styles – especially eagle, mantis and monkey. The classic Shaolin weapon is the **staff**, and there's even a **drunken form**, where the practitioner behaves as if inebriated – an athletic and surprisingly effective technique.

Xingyi quan

Xingyi quan translates awkwardly as "shape through intent boxing", reflecting its guiding principle that the body should act directly from the mind. Believed to have been developed from Shaolin kung fu spear forms by the famous Song-dynasty general **Yue Fei**, *xingyi* is now an internal art, though using *qi* rather differently from either *bagua* or *tai ji*. *Xingyi* schools emphasize **linear** attacks, smashing straight through an opponent's defences and defeating them as directly and effectively as possible. In this uncluttered philosophy, and the use of relatively few techniques, *xingyi* is probably the easiest of the internal arts to learn and use for fighting. The health benefits common to all the internal arts are rarely emphasized in *xingyi*.

Bagua zhang

Bagua zhang's history is murky, but its most famous practitioner and stylist was **Dong Hai Chuan** (1798–1879). The name means "*bagua* palm", referring to the eight-sided symbol used in the Chinese book of divination, the *I Ching*, of which *bagua zhang* is a martial expression, and to the fact that strikes are almost invariably made with the **palm**. *Bagua* is one of the most distinctive martial arts to watch being performed, employing fast footwork and characteristic **twisting movements** to simultaneously evade attacks and place the defender behind the aggressor, and thus in a position to strike back. An internal art, it nonetheless uses some physical force, and tends towards devastating overkill in its response to attacks. The various schools use **circle-walking forms** to develop *qi* – if you see somebody walking endlessly around a tree in a Chinese park, they're practising this – as well as less abstract linear forms to learn fighting skills. Bagua's continuous twisting pumps *qi* from the spine around the body, and bagua practitioners are famous for their health and longevity.

Tai ji quan

Tai ji quan (*yinyang* boxing) is the world's most popular martial art, but it's seldom taught as such. The original form, known as **Chen taiji**, is closely related to Shaolin kung fu though emphasizing *qi* usage; a later form developed by **Yang Luchan** (1799–1872) is entirely internal and the hardest of any style to learn for practical fighting. Despite this, these older forms are effective martial arts, relying on acute sensitivity to anticipate attacks and strike first; counter-strikes are made with the entire body in a state of **minimal tension**, creating *tai ji*'s characteristic "soft" appearance, and increasing *qi* flow and power. Strong *qi* flow means good health, and Yang Luchan's grandson, **Yang Chengfu** (1883–1936) slowed *tai ji* movements and stripped it of obvious martial content in order that the elderly or infirm could learn it and so avoid illness – it's versions of this simplified form which are most widely taught today. A two-person sensitivity training technique common to all *tai ji* styles is *tui shou* (**push hands**), where practitioners alternately attack and yield, learning to absorb and redirect their opponent's force.

Studying martial arts

There's been a considerable watering down of martial arts in China in recent years. Since the 1950s, the Chinese government has produced "official" versions of various fighting styles which are collectively known as **wushu** (literally, "martial arts"). The main intent with *wushu* styles is to promote health and fitness, not fighting ability, and they're taught mainly as competitive sports. In the process, much of what is openly taught today in China is – in martial terms – second-rate. Depending on what you're after, therefore, finding competent **instruction** can be difficult.

Famous martial arts centres, such as Shaolin and the Taoist temples at **Wudang Shan** (see p.511), might seem like the obvious **places to study**, but in practice, their fame has been counter-productive. Shaolin, for example, is surrounded by martial-arts schools all claiming to be the only one to teach the "real" Shaolin techniques. Still, they're used to foreigners turning up, and courses at the schools are very organized; Wudang Shan has yet to become as commercialized, however, and they remain choosy in whom they teach. *Wushu* is widely taught at **sports institutes**, including Beijing University of Physical Education, but serious martial content is lacking. Otherwise, visiting the nearest **park** at dawn to see people practising is a good way of finding an instructor or – if you already know a style – meeting up with others to practise with, though outside of Hong Kong you'll need to speak some Chinese. As a bonus, you may encounter one of the lesser-known **regional styles** such as Southern Mantis, White Crane kung fu, Long boxing or tiger boxing. Unless you practise one of the standardized *wushu* forms, however, expect some **criticism**: nobody performs any one style in exactly the same way, and teachers, having often invested decades in their own training methods, are understandably dogmatic about what you should be doing. Don't be discouraged, but stick to what you know while examining others' techniques and systems with an open mind.

If you can't speak Chinese, you'll be better off considering the travellers' havens of Dali and Yangshuo, which both have martial-arts teachers used to dealing with foreigners; Yangshuo's Budi Zhen school is particularly good (see p.745). For more information on Chinese martial arts, check out **China From Inside** (⊛www.chinafrominside.com), a website run by a Western expatriate living in Shanghai, who regularly posts interviews with martial artists famous and obscure – there's also a message board and links to many other sites.

Astrology

n the **Chinese zodiac**, each **lunar year** (which starts in late January or early February) is represented by one of twelve **animal signs**. These have existed in Chinese folk tradition since the sixth century BC, though it wasn't until the third century BC that they were incorporated into a formal study of astrology and astronomy. (True Chinese astrologers, however, eschew the use of the animal signs in isolation to analyze a person's life, seeing the zodiac signs as mere entertainment.) Quite why animals emerged as the vehicle for Chinese horoscopy is unclear: one story has it that the animals used are the twelve which appeared before the command of Buddha, who named the years in the order in which the animals arrived. Another says that the Jade Emperor held a race to determine the fastest animals. The first twelve to cross a chosen river would be picked to represent the twelve earthly branches which make up the cyclical order of years in the lunar calendar.

Being born under the sign of a particular animal gives a person certain characteristics, ideal partners, lucky and unlucky days. The details below will tell you the basic facts about your character and personality, though to go into your real Chinese astrological self, you need to take your precise date and time of birth along to a Chinese astrologer – in China, you'll find plenty of amateurs plying their trade around city parks. The animals always appear in the same order, so that if you know the animal for the current year you can always work out which one is to influence the following Chinese New Year.

The Rat

Characteristics: Usually generous, intelligent and hard-working, but can be petty and idle; has lots of friends, but few close ones; may be successful, likes challenges and is good at business, but is insecure; generally diplomatic; tends to get into emotional entanglements.

Partners: Best suited to Dragon, Monkey and Ox; doesn't get on with Horse and Goat.

The Ox

Characteristics: Healthy; obstinate; independent; usually calm and cool, but can get stroppy at times; shy and conservative; likes the outdoors and old-fashioned things; always finishes a task.

Partners: Best suited to Snake, Rat or Rooster; doesn't get on with Tiger, Goat or Monkey.

The Tiger

Characteristics: Adventurous; creative and idealistic; confident and enthusiastic; can be diplomatic and practical; fearless and forward, aiming at impossible goals, though a realist with a forceful personality.

Partners: Best suited to Horse for marriage; gets on with Dragon, Pig and Dog; should avoid Snake, Monkey and Ox.

The Rabbit

Characteristics: Peace-loving; sociable but quiet; devoted to family and friends; timid but can be good at business; needs reassurance and affection to avoid being upset; can be vain; long-lived.

Partners: Best suited to Pig, Dog and Goat; not friendly with Tiger and Rooster.

The Dragon

Characteristics: Strong, commanding, a leader; popular; athletic; bright, chivalrous and idealistic, though not always consistent; likely to be a believer in equality.

Partners: Best suited to Snake, Rat, Monkey, Tiger and Rooster; avoid Dog.

Calendar chart

Date of Birth	Animal	Date of Birth	Animal
20.2.1920 – 7.2.1921	Monkey	13.2.1964 – 1.2.1965	Dragon
8.2.1921 – 27.1.1922	Rooster	2.2.1965 – 20.1.1966	Snake
28.1.1922 – 15.2.1923	Dog	21.1.1966 – 8.2.1967	Horse
16.2.1923 – 4.2.1924	Pig	9.2.1967 – 29.1.1968	Goat
5.2.1924 – 23.1.1925	Rat	30.1.1968 – 16.2.1969	Monkey
24.1.1925 – 12.2.1926	Ox	17.2.1969 – 5.2.1970	Rooster
13.2.1926 – 1.2.1927	Tiger	6.2.1970 – 26.1.1971	Dog
2.2.1927 – 22.1.1928	Rabbit	27.1.1971 – 14.2.1972	Pig
23.1.1928 – 9.2.1929	Dragon	15.2.1972 – 2.2.1973	Rat
10.2.1929 – 29.1.1930	Snake	3.2.1973 – 22.1.1974	Ox
30.1.1930 – 16.2.1931	Horse	23.1.1974 – 10.2.1975	Tiger
17.2.1931 – 5.2.1932	Goat	11.2.1975 – 30.1.1976	Rabbit
6.2.1932 – 25.1.1933	Monkey	31.1.1976 – 17.2.1977	Dragon
26.1.1933 – 13.2.1934	Rooster	18.2.1977 – 6.2.1978	Snake
14.2.1934 – 3.2.1935	Dog	7.2.1978 – 27.1.1979	Horse
4.2.1935 – 23.1.1936	Pig	28.1.1979 – 15.2.1980	Goat
24.1.1936 – 10.2.1937	Rat	16.2.1980 – 4.2.1981	Monkey
11.2.1937 – 30.1.1938	Ox	5.2.1981 – 24.1.1982	Rooster
31.1.1938 – 18.2.1939	Tiger	25.1.1982 – 12.2.1983	Dog
19.2.1939 – 7.2.1940	Rabbit	13.2.1983 – 1.2.1984	Pig
8.2.1940 – 26.1.1941	Dragon	2.2.1984 – 19.2.1985	Rat
27.1.1941 – 14.2.1942	Snake	20.2.1985 – 8.2.1986	Ox
15.2.1942 – 4.2.1943	Horse	9.2.1986 – 28.1.1987	Tiger
5.2.1943 – 24.1.1944	Goat	29.1.1987 – 16.2.1988	Rabbit
25.1.1944 – 12.2.1945	Monkey	17.2.1988 – 5.2.1989	Dragon
13.2.1945 – 1.2.1946	Rooster	6.2.1989 – 26.1.1990	Snake
2.2.1946 – 21.1.1947	Dog	27.1.1990 – 14.2.1991	Horse
22.1.1947 – 9.2.1948	Pig	15.2.1991 – 3.2.1992	Goat
10.2.1948 – 28.1.1949	Rat	4.2.1992 – 22.1.1993	Monkey
29.1.1949 – 16.2.1950	Ox	23.1.1993 – 9.2.1994	Rooster
17.2.1950 – 5.2.1951	Tiger	10.2.1994 – 30.1.1995	Dog
6.2.1951 – 26.1.1952	Rabbit	31.1.1995 – 18.2.1996	Pig
27.1.1952 – 13.2.1953	Dragon	19.2.1996 – 6.2.1997	Rat
14.2.1953 – 2.2.1954	Snake	7.2.1997 – 27.1.1998	Ox
3.2.1954 – 23.1.1955	Horse	28.1.1998 – 15.2.1999	Tiger
24.1.1955 – 11.2.1956	Goat	16.2.1999 – 4.2.2000	Rabbit
12.2.1956 – 30.1.1957	Monkey	5.2.2000 – 23.1.2001	Dragon
31.1.1957 – 17.2.1958	Rooster	24.1.2001 – 11.2.2002	Snake
18.2.1958 – 7.2.1959	Dog	12.2.2002 – 30.1.2003	Horse
8.2.1959 – 27.1.1960	Pig	31.1.2003 – 17.2.2004	Goat
28.1.1960 – 14.2.1961	Rat	18.2.2004 – 6.2.2005	Monkey
15.2.1961 – 4.2.1962	Ox	7.2.2005 – 27.1.2006	Rooster
5.2.1962 – 24.1.1963	Tiger	28.1.2006 – 17.2.2007	Dog
25.1.1963 – 12.2.1964	Rabbit	18.2.2007 – 6.2.2008	Pig

The Snake

Characteristics: Charming, but possessive and selfish; private and secretive; strange sense of humour; mysterious and inquisitive; ruthless; likes the nice things in life; thoughtful; superstitious.

Partners: Best suited to Dragon, Rooster and Ox; avoid Snake, Pig and Tiger.

The Horse

Characteristics: Nice appearance and deft; ambitious and quick-witted; favours bold colours; popular, with a sense of humour, gracious and gentle; can be good at business; fickle and emotional.

Partners: Best suited to Tiger, Dog and Goat; doesn't get on with Rabbit and Rat.

The Goat

Characteristics: A charmer and a lucky person who likes money; unpunctual and hesitant; too fond of complaining; interested in the supernatural.

Partners: Best suited to Horse, Pig and Rabbit; avoid Ox and Dog.

The Monkey

Characteristics: Very intelligent and sharp, an opportunist; daring and confident, but unstable and egoistic; entertaining and very attractive to others; inventive; has a sense of humour but little respect for reputations.

Partners: Best suited to Dragon and Rat; doesn't get on with Tiger and Ox.

The Rooster

Characteristics: Frank and reckless, and can be tactless; free with advice; punctual and a hard worker; imaginative to the point of dreaming; likes to be noticed; emotional.

Partners: Best suited to Snake, Dragon and Ox; doesn't get on with Pig, Rabbit and Rooster.

The Dog

Characteristics: Alert, watchful and defensive; can be generous and is patient; very responsible and has good organizational skills; spiritual, home-loving and non-materialistic.

Partners: Best suited to Rabbit, Pig, Tiger and Horse; avoid Dragon and Goat.

The Pig

Characteristics: Honest; vulnerable and not good at business, but still materialistic and ambitious; outgoing and outspoken, but naive; kind and helpful to the point of being taken advantage of; calm and genial.

Partners: Best suited to Dog, Goat, Tiger and Rabbit; avoid Snake and Rooster.

Architecture

After several weeks in China, it seems that – apart from minor regional variations – one temple looks much like another, even that the differences between a palace, a temple or a substantial private house are negligible, and that there is little sign of historical development. Nor does it take even this long to tire of the cheaply built and disappointingly Westernized appearance of the majority of China's cities. But this overall uniformity in no way reflects China's long architectural heritage; it is rather that several factors have conspired to limit variety. For a start, little has survived from different periods to emphasize their individual characteristics: early wooden structures were vulnerable to natural disasters, war and revolutions, while new dynasties often demolished the work of the old to reinforce their takeover. Another reason for the strong streak of conservatism inherent in all traditional Chinese architecture is *feng shui*, a departure from which would risk upsetting the cosmos. And today, with a huge economic boom sweeping the country, a lust for "modernization" is seeing vast new cityscapes being built on the sites of the old.

Compounding these factors is a passion for precedent, which meant that certain basic rules governing building designs were followed from the earliest times, minimizing the variations which separate the works of different periods. This is not to say that it's impossible to tell a Tang pagoda from a Qing one, but it does mean that a certain **homogeneity** pervades traditional Chinese architecture, making it all the more exciting on the occasions when you do come across distinctive temples, dwellings or even towns.

Monumental architecture

Chinese monumental architecture – as represented in temples, palaces and city plans – is notable for constantly repeating **cosmological themes**, the most central of which can be traced right back to the Bronze Age – though the specific details of *feng shui* were only formulated during the Song dynasty.

Feng shui

Whatever the scale of a building project, the Chinese consider divination using **feng shui** an essential part of the initial preparations. Literally meaning "wind and water", *feng shui* is a form of **geomancy**, which assesses how buildings must be positioned so as not to disturb the spiritual attributes of the surrounding landscape. This reflects **Taoist cosmology**, which believes that all components of the universe exist in a balance with one another, and therefore the disruption of a single element can cause potentially dangerous alterations to the whole. It's vital, therefore, that sites – whether for peasant homes, the Hong Kong Bank's skyscraper headquarters, entire cities such as Beijing or the underground tomb of the first Qin emperor – be favourably orientated according to points on the compass and protected from local "unlucky directions" by other buildings, walls, hills, mountain ranges, water or even a Terracotta Army. Geomancy further proposes **ideal forms** for particular types of structure, and carefully arranges spaces and components within a building according to time-honoured formulas.

Whether Buddhist or Taoist, Chinese temples share the same broad **features**. Like cities, they generally **face south** and are surrounded by walls. Gates are sealed by heavy doors, usually guarded by paintings or statues of warrior deities to chase away approaching evil. The doors open on to a courtyard, where further protection is ensured by a **spirit wall** which blocks direct entry; although easy enough for the living to walk around, this foils spirits, who are unable to turn corners. Once inside, you'll find a succession of halls arranged in ornamental courtyards. In case evil influences should manage to get in, the area nearest the entrance contains the least important rooms or buildings, with those of greater significance – living quarters or main halls – set deeper inside the complex.

One way to tell Buddhist and Taoist temples apart is by the colour of the **supporting pillars** – Buddhists use bright red, while Taoists favour black. **Animal carvings** are more popular with Taoists, who use decorative good-luck and longevity symbols such as bats and cranes; some Taoist halls also have distinctive raised octagonal cupolas sporting the black-and-white *yinyang* symbol. Most obviously, however, each religion has its own **deities**. Inside the entrance of a **Buddhist temple** (*si*) you'll be flanked by the Four Heavenly Kings of the Four Directions, and faced by portly **Maitreya**, the Laughing Buddha; there's also likely to be a statue of **Wei Tuo**, the God of Wisdom. The main hall is dominated by three large statues sitting side by side on lotus flowers, representing Buddhas of the past, present and future, while the walls are decorated by often grossly caricatured images of Buddhist saints (*arhats*) – these are sometimes given a separate hall to themselves. Around the back of the Buddhist trinity is a statue of **Guanyin**, the multi-armed, vase-bearing Goddess of Mercy, who likewise is sometimes given her own room. **Taoist temples** (*miao* or *gong*) are similar, but their halls might be dedicated to any number of mythical and legendary figures. Taoism has its own holy trinity, collectively known as the **Three Purities** or Immortals: **Fuxi**, who taught mankind fishing, hunting and animal husbandry; **Shennong** or **Yan Di**, who created farming, tools and medicine; and **Xuan Yuan** or **Huang Di**, the Yellow Emperor and the first Xia king. Other figures include a further Eight Immortals and historical people who were canonized – the Three Kingdoms characters **Guan Yu** (the red-faced God of War and Healing) and **Zhuge Liang** are popular choices, as are local heroes. Strangely, statues to Guanyin are often also found in Taoist halls as her help in childbirth makes her universally popular.

Four thousand years ago, **cities** were already laid out in a spiritually favourable **rectangular pattern**, typically facing south on a north–south axis and surrounded by a defensive **wall**. Aside from the business and residential districts, the central focus (though not necessarily centrally located) was a separately walled quarter; this later became the seat of the emperor or his local representative. This plan, still apparent in the layout of cities such as Xi'an and Beijing, was a representation of the cosmos, with the ruler – the emperor was styled "Son of Heaven" – at the centre. The same general formula is echoed in the ground plan of palaces, temples and even large family mansions, complexes of buildings whose organization in many ways represented a microcosm of city life. All these are surrounded by a wall, and all have their own central spiritual focus: a main hall in temples where statues of deities are displayed; a similar building in palaces, where the emperor or governor would hold court; or an ancestral shrine in a mansion.

As far as individual buildings are concerned, spiritual considerations also ensured that traditional temples and palaces (the two are virtually identical) followed a basic **building structure**, which can be seen in subjects as diverse as 2000-year-old pottery models and the halls of Beijing's Ming–Qing Forbidden City. The foundations formed a raised platform of earth, brick or stone according to the building's importance. Columns rested on separate bases with the heads of the columns linked by beams running lengthways and across. Above this, beams of diminishing length were raised one above the other on short posts set on the beam below, creating an interlocking structure which rose to the point of the roof where single posts at the centre supported the roof ridge. The arrangement produced a characteristic **curved roofline** with upcurled eaves, felt to confer good luck. **Cantilevered brackets**, introduced in the eighth century, allowed the curving eaves to extend well beyond the main pillars and acquire an increasingly decorative value, supplemented by lines of carved animals and figures on the gable ends of the roof. Though scale and space were ultimately limited by a lack of arches, essential in supporting the massive walls found in European cathedrals, this structural design was solid enough to allow the use of heavy **ceramic rooftiles**.

Development of these features reached a peak of elegance and sophistication during the **Tang and Song** eras, never to be entirely recaptured. Though almost nothing survives intact from this time, later restorations of Tang edifices, such as the temples at Wudang Shan in Hubei province, or Xi'an's central bell tower, convey something of the period's spirit. Two **regional styles** also developed: **northern** architecture was comparatively restrained and sober, while that from the **south** eventually exaggerated curves and ornamentation to a high degree; Guangdong's Foshan Ancestral Temple is a classic of the latter type. Inside both, however, spaces between the columns were filled by screens providing different combinations of wall, door and latticework, which could be removed or changed to order differently the spaces within. The columns themselves were sometimes carved in stone, or otherwise painted, with different colours denoting specific religions in temples, or the rank of the occupant in palaces. Similarly, **imperial buildings** might be distinguished by four-sided roofs, by higher platforms reached by wide staircases and by special yellow glazed tiles for the roofs. In rare instances, buildings created their own styles without offending *feng shui*; Beijing's circular Temple of Heaven, for example, manages to break with convention by symbolizing the universe in its overall shape.

Pagodas are another important type of monumental structure, originally introduced from India with **Buddhism**. Intended to house saintly relics, they have intrinsically "positive" attributes, are often used to guard cities or buildings from unlucky directions, or are built along rivers to quell (and indicate) dangerous shoals. Their general design in China was probably influenced by the shape of indigenous wooden watchtowers, though the earliest surviving example, at Shendong Si in Shandong province, is stone and more closely resembles the equivalent Indian stupa. Most, however, are polygonal, with a central stairway rising through an uneven number of storeys – anything from three to seventeen. Buddhism also gave rise to the extraordinary **cave temples** and grottoes, best preserved in the Northwest at Mogao.

Domestic architecture

In general, **domestic architecture** shares many of the guiding principles of temple and palace design: curved rooflines are desirable, and larger groups of buildings might also be walled off and include spirit walls or **mirrors**, the latter placed over external doorways to repulse demons. Older homes with these basic features can be found all over the country, but in many cases, practical considerations – principally the climate – overrode optimum spiritual designs and created very distinctive **local styles**, which are once again most obvious in a basic north–south divide. **Northern** China's intensely cold winters and hot summers have spawned solidly insulated brick walls, while more stable, subtropical **southern** temperatures encourage the use of open eaves, internal courtyards and wooden lattice screens to allow air to circulate freely.

Rural areas are good places to find some of the more traditional or unusual types of residential architecture; aside from the climate, many of these also reflect local cultures. Striking examples exist in the mountainous border areas between Guizhou and Guangxi provinces, where ethnic **Dong** and **Miao** build large, two- or three-storeyed wooden houses from local cedar. The Dong are further known for their wooden **drum towers** and **wind-and-rain bridges**. Another ethnic group building distinctive houses is the **Hakka**, a Han sub-group, whose immense stone circular clan or family mansions – some of which can accommodate hundreds of people – were built for defensive purposes in their Guangdong–Fujian homelands. Extreme adaptation to local conditions can be seen in Shaanxi province, where **underground homes**, cool in summer and warm in winter, have been excavated in prehistoric sedimentary soils deposited by the Yellow River.

Traditional **urban architecture** survives, too, though it tends to be less varied. Wood almost invariably formed at least the framework of these buildings, but if fire hasn't claimed them, demolition and replacement by city authorities – who are either safety-conscious or simply eager to modernize – generally has. Scattered examples of old town houses can still be seen even in large cities such as Beijing, Kunming and Chengdu, however, while the ethnic **Naxi** town of Lijiang in Yunnan sports hundreds of traditional wooden homes, the largest such collection anywhere in China. In the east, the area surrounding Tunxi in Anhui province contains whole villages built in the immensely influential seventeenth-century "**Huizhou style**", which epitomized the basic forms of contemporary east-coast provincial architecture; a house in this style has two storeys and is built around a courtyard.

Modern architecture

China's **modern architecture** tends to reflect political and economic, rather than ethnic or climatic, considerations. From the mid-nineteenth century onwards, treaty ports were built up in the **European** colonial manner by the foreign merchants, banks, shipping firms and missionaries who conducted their affairs there. Today, the former offices, warehouses and churches – often divided up for Chinese use – still give certain cities a distinctive look. Hankou, part of Wuhan, has a Customs House and whole streets of colonial buildings, as do the former east-coast concessions of Shanghai, Qingdao, Yantai, Shantou, Xiamen and Guangzhou. European-inspired building continued on into the 1930s.

After the **Communist takeover**, there were various attempts to unite Chinese styles with modern materials. When employed, this strategy was successful, and many modern rural dwellings still follow traditional designs, simply replacing adobe walls with concrete. But during the 1950s, while Russia was China's ally, a brutally functional **Soviet style** became the urban norm, requiring that everything from factories to hotels be built as identical drab, characterless grey boxes. Since China opened up to the Western world and capitalism in the late 1970s, however, there's been a move towards a more "international" look, as seen in the concrete-and-glass high-rises going up across the country. While brighter than the Russian model, these are, in general, hardly any more inspirational or attractive, and are afflicted by a mania for facing new buildings in bathroom tiles. Perhaps the most distressing aspect of this trend is that any indigenous characteristics are seen as old-fashioned, and yet, compared with similar buildings in the West, these new buildings are very poor imitations. Yet even here there are occasional attempts to marry the traditional Chinese idiom with current needs, and in a few cases you'll see apartment buildings surrounded by walled compounds and topped with curled rooftiles.

In recent years, with a great deal of money and resources washing around (and few planning restrictions), the Chinese urban landscape is set to be ripped up and reconstructed yet again. Eye-catching, prestige projects by the world's most expensive architects have begun springing up, particularly in **Beijing**, which is to be showcased as a dynamic, hip city in time for the Olympics in 2008. The city's residents – three hundred thousand of whom have been relocated to make space for the boom – point out that this much reconstruction would normally only take place after a war. The new **CCTV building** by the radical Dutch firm OMA will be a truly bizarre structure, a double Z with a hole in the middle and no right angles, nicknamed "the Twisted Doughnut". There are plenty who doubt whether it's even possible to build. The **National Theatre** ("the Egg"), three halls under a dome floating at the centre of an artificial lake, has been designed by French architect Paul Anreu, and will be an astonishing sight, especially considering its location at the heart of the staid communist city, just west of Tian'anmen Square. Herzog and de Meuron's **Olympic stadium**, designed to resemble a bird's nest, looks set to be the most popular of the new eyebrow raisers. In **Shanghai**, the **Xintiandi complex** of accommodation and restaurants is a rare example of an extravagant architectural gesture that's still recognizably Chinese, a collection of *shikumen*, houses with stone gateways, painstakingly reconstructed with original materials. Happily, this seems to have started a trend, and Chinese cities may soon start to look a little more Chinese.

Art

his very brief survey aims to reflect what you are likely to see most of in Chinese provincial and city museums – and to an extent *in situ*. In looking at the art displayed in Chinese museums it should be remembered that while for more than two thousand years imperial China produced an incredible wealth of art objects, from the mid-nineteenth century onwards, many of these were acquired – more or less legitimately – by Westerners. Later, too, some of the great imperial collections were removed by the Nationalists to Taiwan, where they are now in the National Palace Museum; perhaps just as well, as most of what was left in the country was destroyed during the Cultural Revolution.

Pottery, bronzes and sculpture

The earliest Chinese objects date back to the Neolithic farmers of the **Yangshao** culture – well-made **pottery** vessels painted in red, black, brown and white with geometric designs. You'll notice that the decoration is usually from the shoulders of the pots upwards; this is because what has survived is mostly from graves and was designed to be seen from above when the pots were placed round the dead. From the same period there are decorated clay heads, perhaps for magic or ritual, and pendants and small ornaments of polished stone or jade, with designs that are sometimes semi-abstract – a simplified sitting bird in polished jade is a very early example of the powerful Chinese tradition of animal sculpture. Rather later is the Neolithic **Longshan** pottery – black, very thin and fine, wheel-turned and often highly polished, with elegant, sharply defined shapes.

The subsequent era, from around 1500 BC, is dominated by **Shang and Zhou bronze** vessels used for preparing and serving food and wine, and for ceremonies and sacrifices. There are many distinct shapes, each with its own name and specific usage. One of the most common is the *ding*, a three- or four-legged vessel which harks back to the Neolithic pots used for cooking over open fires. As you'll see from the museums, these bronzes have survived in great numbers. The **Shang** bronze industry appears already fully developed with advanced techniques and designs and no sign of a primitive stage. Casting methods were highly sophisticated, using moulds, while design was firm and assured and decoration often stylized and linear, with both geometric and animal motifs, as well as grinning masks of humans and fabulous beasts. There are some naturalistic animal forms among the vessels, too – fierce tigers, solid elephants and surly-looking rhinoceroses. Other bronze finds include weapons, decorated horse harnesses and sets of bells used in ritual music. Later, under the **Zhou**, the style of the bronzes becomes more varied and rich: some animal vessels are fantastically shaped and extravagantly decorated; others are simplified natural forms; others again seem to be depicting not so much a fierce tiger, for example, as utter ferocity itself. You'll also see from the Shang and Zhou small objects – ornaments, ritual pieces and jewellery pendants – with highly simplified but vivid forms of tortoises, salamanders and flying birds. From the end of this period there are also painted clay funeral figures and a few carved wooden figures.

The Shang produced a few small sculptured human figures and animals in marble, but **sculptures** and works in stone begin to be found in great quantities in **Han-dynasty** tombs. The decorated bricks and tiles, the bas-reliefs and the terracotta figurines of acrobats, horsemen and ladies-in-waiting placed in the tombs to serve the dead, even the massive stone men and beasts set to guard the Spirit Way leading to the tomb, are all lifelike and reflect concern with everyday activities and material possessions. The scale models of houses with people looking out of the windows and of farmyards with their animals have a spontaneous gaiety and vigour; some of the watchdogs are the most realistic of all. Smaller objects like tiny statuettes and jewellery were also carved, from ivory, jade and wood.

It was the advent of **Buddhism** which encouraged stone carving on a large scale in the round, with mallet and chisel. **Religious sculpture** was introduced from India and in the fourth-century caves at **Datong** (see p.230) and the earlier caves at **Longmen**, near Luoyang (see p.297); the Indian influence is most strongly felt in the stylized Buddhas and attendants. Sometimes of huge size, they have an aloof grace and a rhythmic quality in their flowing robes, but also a smooth, bland and static quality. Not until the **Tang** do you get the full flowering of a native Chinese style, where the figures are rounder, with movement, and the positions, expressions and clothes are more natural and realistic. Some of the best examples are to be seen at **Dunhuang** (see p.1021) and in the later caves at Longmen. The **Song** continued to carve religious figures and at **Dazu** in Sichuan (see p.918) you'll find good examples of a highly decorative style which had broadened its subject matter to include animals, ordinary people and scenes of everyday life; the treatment is down to earth, individual, sometimes even comic. The Dazu carvings are very well preserved and you see them painted, as they were meant to be. In later years less statuary was produced until the **Ming** with their taste for massive and impressive tomb sculptures. You can see the best of these in **Nanjing** and **Beijing**.

Ceramics

From Neolithic painted pottery onwards, China developed a high level of excellence in **ceramics**, based on the availability of high-quality materials. Its pre-eminence was recognized by the fact that for more than four hundred years the English language has used the word "china" to mean fine-quality ceramic ware. In some of the early wares you can see the influence of shapes derived from bronzes, but soon the rise of regional potteries using different materials, and the development of special types for different uses, led to an enormous variety of shapes, textures and colours. This was noticeable by the **Tang dynasty** when an increase in the production of pottery for daily use was partly stimulated by the spread of tea drinking and by the restriction of the use of copper and bronze to coinage. The Tang also saw major technical advances; the production of true **porcelain** was finally achieved and Tang potters became very skilled in the use of polychrome glazing. You can see evidence of this in the *san cai* (three-colour) statuettes of horses and camels, jugglers, traders, polo players, grooms and court ladies, which have come in great numbers from imperial tombs, and which reflect in vivid, often humorous, detail and still brilliant colours so many aspects of the life of the time. It was a cosmopolitan civilization open to foreign influences and this is clearly seen in Tang art.

The **Song** dynasty witnessed a great refinement of ceramic techniques and of regional specialization, many wares being named after the area which produced them. The keynote was simplicity and quiet elegance, both in colour and form. There was a preference for using a **single pure colour** and for incised wares made to look like damask cloth. In the museums you'll see the famous green celadons, the thin white porcelain *ding* ware and the pale grey-green *ju* ware reserved for imperial use. The Mongol **Yuan** dynasty, in the early fourteenth century, enriched Chinese tradition with outside influences – notably the introduction of **cobalt blue underglaze**, early examples of the blue and white porcelain which was to become so famous. The **Ming** saw the flowering of great potteries under imperial patronage, especially **Jingdezhen**. Taste moved away from Song simplicity and returned to the liking for vivid colour which the Tang had displayed – deep **red**, **yellow** and **orange** glazes, with a developing taste for pictorial representation. From the seventeenth century, Chinese export wares flowed in great quantity and variety to the West to satisfy a growing demand for chinoiserie, and the efforts of the Chinese artists to follow what they saw as the tastes and techniques of the West produced a style of its own. The early **Qing** created delicate enamel wares and *famille rose* and *verte*. So precise were the craftsmen that some porcelain includes the instructions for the pattern in the glaze.

You can visit several potteries such as at **Jingdezhen** in Jiangxi province, where both early wares and modern trends are on display. Not so long ago they were turning out thousands of figurines of Mao and Lu Xun sitting in armchairs; now the emphasis is on table lamp bases in the shape of archaic maidens in flowing robes playing the lute, or creased and dimpled Laughing Buddhas.

Painting and calligraphy

While China's famous ceramics were made by craftsmen who remained anonymous, **painting and calligraphy** pieces were produced by famous scholars, officials and poets. It has been said that the four great treasures of Chinese painting are the brush, the ink, the inkstone and the paper or silk. The earliest brush found, from about 400 BC, is made out of animal hairs glued to a hollow bamboo tube. Ink was made from pine soot mixed with glue and hardened into a stick which would be rubbed with water on an inkstone made of non-porous, carved and decorated slate. Silk was used for painting as early as the third century BC and paper was invented by **Cai Lun** in 106 AD. The first known painting on silk was found in a **Han** tomb; records show that there was a great deal of such painting, but in 190 AD the vast imperial collection was destroyed in a civil war – the soldiers used the silk to make tents and knapsacks. All we know of Han painting comes from decorated tiles, lacquer, painted pottery and a few painted tombs, enough to show a great sense of movement and energy. The British Museum has a scroll in ink and colour on silk attributed to **Gu Kaizhi** from around 400 AD and entitled *Admonitions of the Instructress to Court Ladies*, and we know that the theory of painting was already being discussed by this date, as the treatise *The Six Principles of Painting* dates from about 500 AD.

The **Sui–Tang** period, with a powerful stable empire and a brilliant court, was exactly the place for painting to develop, and a great tradition of figure painting grew up, especially of court subjects – portraits and pictures of the emperor receiving envoys and of court ladies were produced, several of which are to be seen in Beijing. Although only a few of these survived, the walls of Tang tombs, such as those near Xi'an, are rich in vivid frescoes which provide a realistic portrayal of court life. Wang Wei in the mid-eighth century was an early exponent of monochrome **landscape** painting, but the great flowering of landscape painting came with the **Song dynasty**. An academy was set up under imperial patronage and different schools of painting emerged which analyzed the natural world with great concentration and intensity; their style has set a mark on Chinese landscape painting ever since. There was also lively **figure painting** – a famous horizontal scroll in Beijing showing the Qing Ming River Festival is the epitome of this. The last emperor of the Northern Song, **Hui Zong**, was himself a painter of some note, which indicates the status of painting in China at the time. The Southern Song preferred a more intimate style and such subjects as flowers, birds and still life grew in popularity.

Under the **Mongols** there were many officials who found themselves unwanted or unwilling to serve the alien Yuan dynasty and who preferred to retire and paint. This produced the **"literati" school**, with many painters harking back to the styles of the tenth century. One of the great masters was **Ni Can**. He, among many others, also devoted himself to the ink paintings of bamboo which became important at this time. In this school, of which there are many extant examples, the highest skills of techniques and composition were applied to the simplest of subjects, such as plum flowers. Both ink painting as well as more conventional media continued to be employed by painters of the next three or more centuries. From the **Yuan** onwards a tremendous quantity of paintings has survived. Under the **Ming** dynasty there was a great interest in collecting the works of previous ages and a linked willingness by painters to be influenced by tradition. There are plenty of examples of bamboo and plum blossom, and bird and flower paintings being brought to a high decorative pitch, as well as a number of schools of land-scape painting firmly rooted in traditional techniques. The arrival of the Manchu **Qing** dynasty did not disrupt the continuity of Chinese painting, but the art became wide open to many influences. It included the Italian **Castiglione** (Lang Shi-ning in Chinese) who specialized in horses, dogs and flowers under imperial patronage, the Four Wangs who reinterpreted Song and Yuan styles in an ortho-dox manner, and the individualists such as the Eight Eccentrics of Yangzhou and some Buddhist monks who objected to derivative art and sought a more distinc-tive approach to subject and style. But on the whole, the weight of tradition was powerful enough to maintain the old approach.

Calligraphy

The word **"calligraphy"** is derived from the Greek for "beautiful writing", and was crystallized into a high art form in China, where the use of the brush saw the development of handwriting of various styles, valued on a par with paint-ing. There are a number of different scripts: the **seal script** is the archaic form found on oracle bones; the **lishu** is the clerical style and was used in inscrip-tions on stone; the **kaishu** is the regular style closest to the modern printed form; and **cao shu** (grass script), a cursive style, is the most individual hand-written style. Emperors, poets and scholars over centuries have left examples of their calligraphy cut into stone at beauty spots, on mountains and in grottoes, tombs and temples all over China; you can see some early examples in the caves at Longmen (see p.297). At one stage during the Tang dynasty, calligraphy was so highly thought of that it was the yardstick for the selection of high officials.

Other arts

Jade and lacquerware have also been constantly in use in China since earliest times. In Chinese eyes, **jade**, in white and shades of green or brown, is the most precious of stones. It was used to make the earliest ritual objects, such as the flat disc **Pi**, symbol of Heaven, which was found in Shang and Zhou graves. Jade was also used as a mark of rank and for ornament, in its most striking form in the jade burial suits which you will see in the country's museums.

Lacquer, made from the sap of the lac tree, is also found as early as the Zhou. Many layers of the stuff were painted on a wood or cloth base which was then carved and inlaid with gold, silver or tortoiseshell, or often most delicately painted. There are numerous examples of painted lacquer boxes and baskets from the Han and, as with jade, the use of this material has continued ever since.

Music

The casual visitor to China could be forgiven for thinking that the only traditional style to compete with bland pop is that of the kitsch folk troupes to be heard in hotels and concert halls. But an earthy traditional music still abounds throughout the countryside; it can be heard at weddings, funerals, temple fairs and New Year celebrations – and even downtown in teahouses. A very different, edgier sound can be heard in certain smoky city bars – the new Chinese rock, energetic expressions of urban angst.

Traditional music

Han music (like Irish music) is heterophonic – the musicians play differently decorated versions of a single melodic line – and its melodies are basically **pentatonic**. Percussion plays a major role, both in instrumental ensembles and as accompaniment to opera, narrative-singing, ritual music and dance.

Chinese musical roots date back millennia – among archeological finds are a magnificent set of 65 bronze bells from the fifth century BC – and its forms can be directly traced to the Tang dynasty, a golden age of great poets such as Li Bai and Bai Juyi, who were also avid musicians. Several *qin* (zithers) from this period are still played today, and there's a good market in fake ones, too. In fact, the industry in fake antiques extends to the music itself, as tourists may be regaled with Hollywood-style routines marketed as the music and dance of the Tang court. In recent years, the rather soulless Confucian rituals of the bygone imperial courts have been revived in Qufu and some other towns like Nanjing, largely for tourists. The reality, of course, is that there are no "living fossils" in music, and most traditional forms in the countryside are the product of gradual accretion over the centuries, and especially over the past hundred years.

After China's humiliation at the hands of foreign imperial powers, and in the turbulent years after 1911, **Western ideas** gained ground, at least in the towns. Some intriguing urban forms sprang up from the meeting of East and West, such as the wonderfully sleazy Cantonese music of the 1920s and '30s. As the movie industry developed, people in Shanghai, colonial Canton (Guangzhou) and nearby Hong Kong threw themselves into the craze for Western-style jazz and dance halls, fusing the local traditional music with jazz, and adding saxophone, violin and xylophone to Chinese instruments such as the *gaohu* (high-pitched fiddle) and the *yangqin* (dulcimer). Composers **Lü Wencheng** and **Qiu Hechou** (Yau Hokchau), the violinist **Yin Zizhong** (Yi Tzuchung), and **He Dasha** ("Thicko He"), guitarist and singer of clown roles in Cantonese opera, made many wonderful commercial 78s during this period. While these musicians kept their roots in Cantonese music, the more Westernized (and even more popular) compositions of **Li Jinhui** and his star singer **Zhou Xuan** subsequently earned severe disapproval from Maoist critics as decadent and pornographic. Today, though, you can still hear these 1930s classics, played in modern arrangements, over street loudspeakers.

New "**revolutionary**" music, composed from the 1930s on, was generally march-like and optimistic, and after the Communist victory of 1949, the whole ethos of traditional music was challenged. Anything "feudal" or "superstitious"

In China it is easier to find good recordings of opera than instrumental music, but authentic recordings of Chinese instrumental and religious music are finally beginning to match the conservatoire-style recordings of souped-up arrangements that used to dominate the market. All the recordings listed are available on CD. If you're interested in finding recordings from the latest hot band on the rock scene, check the recommendations at Ⓦ www.niubi.com.

General traditional

Ⓞ **Li Xiangting** *Chine: L'Art du Qin* (Ocora, France).
Li is professor of *qin* at the Central Conservatoire in Beijing and also a poet, painter and calligrapher. This album is a fine introduction to the refined meditation of the *qin*, though it actually ends with the celebrated "Guangling san", a graphic depiction of the assassination of an evil tyrant, contrasting with the instrument's tranquil image.

Ⓞ **Lin Shicheng** *Chine: L'art du Pipa* (Ocora, France).
Includes not only favourites such as a version of the popular ensemble piece "Spring – River – Flowers – Moon – Night" and the martial piece "The Tyrant Removes his Armour" (also on the Wu Man CD below), but also some rarer intimate pieces.

Ⓞ **The Uyghur Musicians from Xinjiang** *Music From the Oasis Towns of Central Asia* (Globestyle, UK). Enjoyable introduction to the Uigur music of the Northwest, recorded on a spare day during a UK concert tour. Features some fine playing of the long-necked, lute-like *tambur* and *satar*, plus the *surnay*, a small twin-reeded shawm.

Ⓞ **Wu Man** *Traditional and Contemporary Music for Pipa and Ensemble* (Nimbus, UK).
From the southern town of Hangzhou, Wu studied with masters such as Lin Shicheng in Beijing. Since making her home in the US she has championed new music for the instrument.

Ⓞ **Wu Zhaoji** *Wumen Qin Music* (Hugo, Hong Kong).
The late Wu Zhaoji's playing typified the contemplative ethos of the *qin*, eschewing mere technical display. Wumen refers here to the Wu style of the canal city of Suzhou.

Compilations

Ⓞ *An Anthology of Chinese and Traditional Folk Music: A Collection of Music played on the Guqin* (China Record Co., China; Cradle Records, Taiwan).
This is an eight-CD set for serious *qin* enthusiasts, featuring some fantastic reissues of the great masters of the 1950s.

Ⓞ *China: Folk Instrumental Traditions* (VDE-Gallo/AIMP, Switzerland).
A 2-CD set of archive and recent recordings of village ensembles from north and south compiled by Stephen Jones. Includes earthy shawm bands, mystical *shengguan* ritual ensembles, refined silk-and-bamboo, and some awesome percussion. Features some of the master musicians from before the Cultural Revolution, such as the Daoist priests An Laixu on *yunluo* and Zhu Qinfu on drums.

Ⓞ *Chine: musique classique* (Ocora, France).
A selection of solo and ensemble pieces featuring the *qin*, *pipa*, *sheng*, *guanzi* (oboe), *dizi*, *xiao*, *erhu* and *yangqin*, played by outstanding instrumentalists of the 1950s, including Guan Pinghu, Cao Zheng and Sun Yude.

Ⓞ *Songs of the Land in China: Labour Songs and Love Songs* (Wind Records, Taiwan).
Two CDs featuring beautiful archive recordings of folk singing, mostly unaccompanied, from different regions of China, including rhythmic songs of boatmen, Hua'er songs from the Northwest, and the plaintive songs from northern Shaanxi. A surprisingly varied and captivating selection.

Ⓞ *Special Collection of Contemporary Chinese Musicians* (Wind Records, Taiwan).

Ⓒ

CONTEXTS | Music

A more comprehensive 2-CD set of archive recordings of some of the great 1950s instrumentalists, including masters of the *qin*, *zheng*, *pipa*, *suona* and *guanzi*.

Northern traditions

Compilations

○ *Chine: Musique ancienne de Chang'an* (Inédit, France).

The wind pieces on this conservatoire recording are impressive, though lacking the subtlety of tuning, complexity of tempi and sheer guts of the folk ensembles.

○ *China: Music of the First Moon. Shawms from Northeast China Vol. 1* (Musique du Monde, France).

Ear-cleansing shawm and percussion, featuring a succession of groups from the Dalian playing music for New Year festivities. Earthy stuff with good notes.

○ *Xi'an drums music* (Hugo, Hong Kong).

Majestic wind-and-percussion music performed for funerals and calendrical pilgrimages around Xi'an, including some rarely heard vocal hymns (weirdly translated as "rap music").

○ **The Li Family Band** *Shawms from Northeast China Vol. 2* (Musique du Monde, France).

Led by the senior Li Shiren, this band typifies northern shawm and percussion groups. The disc features a spectrum of music from doleful funereal music for large shawms to more popular festive pieces.

Southern traditions

○ **Tsai Hsiao-Yueh** *Nan-kouan: Chant courtois de la Chine du Sud Vol 1* (Ocora, France).

The senior *nanguan* singer Tsai Hsiao-yueh (Cai Xiaoyue), with her group based in Tainan, Taiwan, maintains the proud amateur tradition of this exalted genre originating just across the strait in Fujian. This album features haunting chamber ballads, the female voice accompanied by end-blown flute and plucked and bowed lutes.

Compilations

○ *China: Chuida Wind and Percussive Instrumental Ensembles* (UNESCO/Auvidis, France).

Three traditional ensembles from southern China, including some unusual silk-and-bamboo from Shanghai and ceremonial music for weddings and funerals from Fujian and Zhejiang.

○ *Rain Dropping on the Banana Tree* (Rounder, US).

Taking its title from a popular Cantonese melody, this collection of reissued 78s from 1902 to 1930 features early masters of Cantonese music such as Yau Hokchau, as well as excerpts from Beijing and Cantonese opera.

○ *Sizhu/Silk Bamboo: Chamber music of South China* (Pan, Netherlands).

Several styles of chamber ensemble along the southeastern coast, from silk-and-bamboo from Shanghai to the refined instrumental *nanguan* music from Xiamen, to Chaozhou and Hakka pieces featuring *zheng*, and also examples of the more modern Cantonese style. Excellent notes.

Temple music

Compilations

○ *China: Buddhist Music of the Ming dynasty* (JVC, Japan).

Exquisite music played by the monks of the Zhihua temple, Beijing, in collaboration with musicians from the Central Conservatoire. Features double-reed pipes, flutes, Chinese mouth organs, a frame of pitched gongs and percussion.

● *Tianjin Buddhist Music Ensemble* (Nimbus, UK).

Buddhist ritual *shengguan* music played by a group of musicians in their 70s, with some wonderful *guanzi*. Good notes, too.

Chinese opera

Compilations

● *An Introduction to Chinese Opera* (Hong Kong Records, Hong Kong).
A series of four CDs illustrating the different styles, including Beijing, Cantonese, Shanghai, Huangmei, Henan, Pingju and Qinqiang operas.

● *China: Ka-lé, Festival of Happiness* (VDE-Gallo/AIMP, Switzerland).
Mainly instrumental music from the operas of the Quanzhou Puppet Troupe.

● *Chinese Classical Opera: Kunqu. The Peony Pavilion* (Inédit, France).

A two-CD set featuring excerpts from the great opera by the early-seventeenth-century Tang Xianzu. The vocal sections give a better idea of the tradition than the kitsch harmonized orchestral arrangements.

● *Opera du Sichuan: La Legende de Serpent blanc* (Musique du Monde, France).
A double CD of traditional opera from Sichuan, featuring the distinctive female chorus and ending with the attractive bonus of a "bamboo ballad" on the same theme sung by a narrative-singer.

Contemporary/new wave

● **Wu Man and the Kronos Quartet** *Ghost Opera* by Tan Dun (Nonesuch, US).
An extraordinary multimedia piece "with water, stones, paper and metal", and incorporating traditional shamanistic sounds of the composer's childhood in remote Hunan province, alongside Bach and Shakespeare. Totally original.

● **Yo-Yo Ma** *Symphony 1997* by Tan Dun (Sony Classical).

Yo-Yo Ma's cello provides the narrative element here, blending his classical technique with gliding tones reminiscent of *erhu* music. The theatrical musical panorama includes the 2400-year-old bells, Cantonese opera recorded on the streets of Hong Kong, a dragon dance plus quotations from Beethoven's "Ode to Joy" and Puccini's *Turandot*. Naïve, yet sophisticated and certainly colourful.

– which included a lot of traditional folk customs and music – was severely restricted, while Chinese melodies were "cleaned up" with the addition of rudimentary harmonies and bass lines. The communist anthem "**The East is Red**", which began life as a folksong from the northern Shaanxi province (from where Mao's revolution also sprang), is symptomatic. Its local colour was ironed out as it was turned into a conventionally harmonized hymn-like tune. It was later adopted as the unofficial anthem of the Cultural Revolution, during which time musical life was driven underground, with only eight model operas and ballets permitted on stage.

The **conservatoire style** of **guoyue** (national music), which was about the only Chinese music recorded until recently, was an artificial attempt to create a pan-Chinese style for the concert hall, with composed arrangements in a style akin to Western light music. There are still many conservatoire-style chamber groups – typically including *erhu* (fiddle), *dizi* (flute), *pipa* (lute) and *zheng* (zither) – playing evocatively titled pieces, some of which are newly composed. While the plaintive pieces for solo *erhu* by musicians such as **Liu Tianhua** and the blind beggar **Abing** (also a Daoist priest), or atmospheric tweetings on the *dizi*, have been much recorded by *guoyue* virtuosos like **Min Huifen** or **Lu Chunling** respectively, there is much more to Chinese music than this. Folk music has a life of its own and tends to follow the Confucian ideals of moderation and harmony, in which showy virtuosity is out of place.

The qin and solo traditions

Instrumental music is not as popular as vocal music in China, and many of the short virtuosic pieces that you hear played on the *erhu* or *dizi* are in fact the product of modern composers writing in a pseudo-romantic Western style for the concert hall. The genuine solo traditions going back to the scholar-literati of imperial times, and which live on in the conservatoires today, are for the *pipa*, *zheng* and *qin*.

The **qin** (also known as *guqin*) is the most exalted of these instruments. A seven-string plucked zither, it has been a favourite subject of poets and painters for over a thousand years, and is the most delicate and contemplative instrument in the Chinese palette. It is the most accessible, too, producing expressive slides and ethereal harmonics. Though primarily associated with the moderation of the Confucian scholar, the *qin* is also steeped in the mystical Daoism of ancient philosophy – the contemplative union with nature, where silence is as important as sound. The only instruments which may occasionally blend with the *qin* are the voice of the player, singing ancient poems in an utterly introverted style, or the *xiao* end-blown flute.

With its literate background, *qin* music has been written in a unique and complex notation since the Tang dynasty. The *Shenqi mipu* written by the Ming prince, Zhu Quan, in 1425, which included pieces handed down from earlier dynasties, is still commonly used, though most *qin* pieces today have been transmitted from master to pupil since at least the eighteenth century. Since the 1950s there has been a drive to revive other early pieces, comparable to the early-music movement in the West.

The *qin* is best heard in meetings of aficionados rather than in concert. The **Beijing Qin Association**, led by Li Xiangting of the Central Conservatoire, meets on the first Sunday of each month and is open to visitors. In Shanghai, the professor of *guqin* at the Conservatoire, Lin Youren, will introduce you to any get-togethers of *qin* enthusiasts in the area. Many of the master musicians play instruments dating back to the fifteenth (and in some cases the ninth) century.

Modern traditions of the **pipa** (lute) and **zheng** (zither) also derive from regional styles, transmitted from master to pupil, although "national" repertoires developed during the twentieth century. For the *zheng*, the northern styles of Henan and Shandong and the southern Chaozhou and Hakka schools are best known. The *pipa*, on the other hand, has thrived in the Shanghai region. It makes riveting listening, with its contrast between intimate "civil" pieces and the startlingly modern-sounding martial style of traditional pieces such as "Ambush from All Sides" (*Shimian maifu*), with its frenetic percussive evocation of the sounds of battle.

The poetic titles of many so-called classical solo pieces – like "Autumn Moon in the Han Palace" or "Flowing Streams" – often relate to an identification with nature or to a famous historical scene. Correspondingly, the music is often pictorial, underlining the link with the artistic background of the educated classes of imperial times. The similar titles of the pieces played by folk ensembles, however, are rarely illustrative, serving only as identification for the musicians.

The North: Blowers and Drummers

Today what we might call classical traditions – derived from the elite of imperial times – live on not just with solo instruments but more strongly in **folk ensembles**, which are generally found in the north of the country. The most exciting examples of this music are to be heard at **weddings and funerals**, known as "red and white business" – red being the auspicious colour of the living, white the colour of mourning.

These occasions usually feature raucous **shawm** (a ubiquitous instrument in China, rather like a crude clarinet) and percussion groups called **chuigushou** – "blowers and drummers". While wedding bands naturally tend to use more jolly music, funerals may also feature lively pieces to entertain the guests. The "blowers and drummers" play not only lengthy and solemn suites but also the latest pop hits and theme tunes from TV and films. They milk the audience by sustaining notes, using circular breathing, playing even while dismantling and reassembling their shawms, or by balancing plates on sticks on the end of their instruments while playing. Nobly laying down their lives for their art, shawm players also love to perform while successively inserting cigarettes into both nostrils, both ears, and both corners of the mouth. Some of the more virtuoso shawm bands are found in southwestern Shandong around Heze county.

The **sheng** is one of the oldest Chinese instruments (mentioned as far back as the tenth century BC). It comprises a group of (usually 17) bamboo pipes of different lengths bound in a circle and set in a wooden or metal base into which the player blows. Frequently used for ceremonial music, it adds an incisive rhythmic bite to the music. Long and deafening strings of fire-crackers are another inescapable part of village ceremony. Some processions are led by a Western-style brass band with a shawm-and-percussion group behind, competing in volume, oblivious of key. In northern villages, apart from the blowers and drummers, ritual **shengguan** ensembles are also common, with their exquisite combination of mouth organs and oboes, as well as darting flutes and the shimmering halo of the *yunluo* gong-frame, accompanied by percussion. Apart from this haunting melodic music, they perform some spectacular ritual percussion – the intricate arm movements of the cymbal players almost resemble martial arts.

Around Xi'an, groups performing similar wind and percussion music, misleadingly dubbed **Xi'an Drum Music** (**Xi'an guyue**), are active for temple festivals not only in the villages but also in the towns, especially in the sixth moon, around July. The Xi'an Conservatoire has commercialized these folk traditions, but the real thing is much better. If you remember the tough shawm bands and haunting folksong of Chen Kaige's film *Yellow Earth*, or the harsh falsetto narrative in Zhang Yimou's *The Story of Qiuju*, go for the real thing among the barren hills of northern Shaanxi. This area is home to fantastic folk singers, local opera (such as the Qinqiang and Meihu styles), puppeteers, shawm bands and folk ritual specialists. Even *yangge* dancing, which in the towns is often a geriatric form of conga dancing, has a wild power here, again accompanied by shawms and percussion.

The South: Silk and Bamboo

In southeast China, the best-known instrumental music is that of **sizhu** ("silk and bamboo") ensembles, using flutes (of bamboo) and plucked and bowed strings (until recently of silk). More mellifluous than the outdoor wind bands of the north, these provide perhaps the most accessible Chinese folk music.

There are several regional styles, but the most famous is that of **Shanghai**. In the city's teahouses, old-timers – and some youngsters too – get together in the afternoons, sit round a table and take it in turns to play a set with Chinese fiddles, flutes and banjos. You can't help thinking of an Irish session, with Chinese tea replacing Guinness. The most celebrated teahouse is the **Chenghuang Miao** (see p.380), a picturesque two-storey structure on an island in the old quarter, where there are Monday-afternoon gatherings. The contrasting textures of plucked, bowed and blown sounds are part of the attraction of this music with their individual decorations to the gradually unfolding melody. Many pieces consist of successive decorations of a theme, beginning with the most ornate and accelerating as the decorations are gradually stripped down to a fast and bare final statement of the theme itself. Above the chinking of tea bowls and subdued chatter of the teahouse, enjoy the gradual unravelling of a piece like "Sanliu", or feel the exhilarating dash to the finish of "Xingjie", with its breathless syncopations.

There are amateur *sizhu* clubs throughout the lower Yangzi area including the cities of Nanjing and Hangzhou. Although this music is secular and recreational in its urban form, the *sizhu* instrumentation originated in ritual ensembles and is still so used in the villages and temples of southern Jiangsu. In fact, amateur ritual associations are to be found all over southern China, as far afield as Yunnan, punctuating their ceremonies with sedate music reminiscent of the Shanghai teahouses, although often featuring the *yunluo* gong-frame of northern China.

Another fantastic area for folk music is the coastal region of **southern Fujian**, notably the delightful cities of Quanzhou and Xiamen. Here you can find not only opera, ritual music and puppetry, but the haunting **nanguan ballads**. Popular all along the coast of southern Fujian, as in Taiwan across the strait, *nanguan* features a female singer accompanied by end-blown flute and plucked and bowed lutes. The ancient texts depict the sorrows of love, particularly of women, while the music is mostly stately and the delivery restrained yet anguished.

Still further south, the coastal regions of **Chaozhou** and **Shantou**, and the **Hakka** area (inland around Meixian and Dabu), also have celebrated string ensembles featuring a high-pitched *erxian* (bowed fiddle) and *zheng* (plucked zither), as well as large and imposing ceremonial percussion bands, sometimes accompanied by shrill flutes.

The temples

All over China, particularly on the great religious mountains like **Wutai Shan**, **Tai Shan**, **Qingcheng Shan**, **Wudang Shan** and **Putuo Shan**, temples are not just historical monuments but living sites of worship. Morning and evening services are held daily, and larger rituals on special occasions. The priests mainly perform vocal liturgy accompanied by percussion – few now use melodic instruments. They intone sung hymns with long melismas, alternating with chanted sections accompanied by the relentless and hypnotic beat of the woodblock. Drum, bell, gongs and cymbals also punctuate the service.

Melodic instrumental music tends to be added when priests perform rituals outside the temples. These styles are more earthy and accessible even to ears unaccustomed to Chinese music. The Daoist priests from the Xuanmiao Guan in **Suzhou**, for example, perform wonderful mellifluous pieces for silk-and-bamboo instruments, gutsy blasts on the shawm, music for spectacularly long trumpets and a whole battery of percussion.

Opera and other vocal music

Chinese musical drama dates back at least two thousand years and became an overwhelmingly popular form with both the elite and common people from the Yuan dynasty onwards. There are several hundred types of regional opera, of which **Beijing Opera**, a rather late hybrid form dating from the eighteenth century, is the most widely known – it's now heard throughout China and is the closest thing to a "national" theatre. The rigorous training the form demands – and the heavy hand of ideology which saw it as the most important of "the people's arts" – is graphically displayed in Chen Kaige's film *Farewell My Concubine*. Many librettos now performed date back to the seventeenth century and describe the intrigues of emperors and gods, as well as love stories and comedy. Northern "**clapper operas**" (*bangzi xi*), named after the high-pitched woodblock that insistently runs through them, are earthy in flavour – for example, the "Qinqiang" of Shaanxi province. **Sichuan opera** is remarkable for its female chorus. **Ritual masked opera** may be performed in the countryside of Yunnan, Anhui and Guizhou. Chaozhou and Fujian also have beautiful ancient styles of opera: **Pingju** and **Huangmei Xi** are genteel in style, while **Cantonese opera** is more funky. If you're looking for more music and less acrobatics, try to seek out the classical but now rare **Kunqu**, often accompanied by the sweet-toned *qudi* flute. There are also some beautiful **puppet operas**, often performed for ritual events; Quanzhou in Fujian has a celebrated marionette troupe, and other likely areas include northern Shaanxi and the Tangshan and Laoting areas of eastern Hebei.

While Chinese opera makes a great visual spectacle, musically it is an acquired taste. One must acclimatize to tense, guttural and high-pitched singing styles from both men and women. The music is dominated by the bowed string accompaniment of the *jinghu*, a sort of sawn-off *erhu*. There are also plucked lutes, flutes and – for transitional points – a piercing shawm. The action is driven by percussion, with drum and clappers leading an ensemble of gongs and cymbals in a variety of set patterns. There are professional opera troupes in the major towns, but rural opera performances, which are given for temple fairs and even weddings, tend to be livelier. Even in Beijing you will see groups of old men meeting in parks or, incongruously, at road junctions where the old gateways used to be, going through their favourite Beijing Opera excerpts.

Narrative-singing, sadly neglected in recordings, also features long classical stories. You may find a teahouse full of old people following these story-songs avidly, particularly in Sichuan, where one popular style is accompanied by the *yangqin* (dulcimer). In Beijing, or more often in Tianjin, amateurs sing through traditional *jingyun dagu* ballads, accompanied by drum and sanxian banjo. In Suzhou, *pingtan*, also accompanied by a plucked lute, is a beautiful genre. In Beijing and elsewhere there is also *xiangsheng*, a comic dialogue with a know-all and a straight man, though its subtle parodies of traditional opera may elude the outsider.

Traditional **folk songs** (as opposed to sentimental bel canto arrangements warbled by ball-gowned divas) are more difficult for the casual visitor to find in Han Chinese areas than among the ethnic minorities, but the beautiful songs of areas like northern Shaanxi and Sichuan are thankfully captured on disc.

New-wave composers

One novel angle on traditional music is in the imaginative use being made of it by new-wave Chinese composers (mostly resident in the US) like **Tan Dun** and **Qu Xiaosong**. Part of the talented generation of novelists and film-makers which grew up during the intellectual vacuum of the Cultural Revolution, they have an experience of folk music that is far from the sentimental patriotism of earlier composers, incorporating an uncompromising Chinese spirituality into a radical avant-garde language. Tan Dun composed the vast "Symphony 1997" to celebrate the return of Hong Kong to mainland China. It incorporates the aforementioned set of 65 *bianzhong* bronze bells (with a range of five octaves) found buried in a royal tomb dating to 433 BC.

Chinese rock

China's indigenous rock, although often connected to the Hong Kong/Taiwanese entertainment industry, is a different beast, one which has its traditions in passionate and fiery protest, and which still possesses a cultural and political self-awareness. The rock scene was nonexistent in China until the mid-1980s, when foreign students on cultural exchange brought tapes of their favourite rock and pop music (and their own electric guitars) to the Chinese mainland, and shared them with their fellow students. Their music quickly caught the imagination of Chinese university youths and the urban vanguard.

Chinese **protest–rock** really began with singer-trumpeter-guitarist Cui Jian who was influenced by the Taiwanese singer **Teresa Teng** (known to the Chinese by her original name, Deng Lijun; 1953–95). Teng's singing style can be directly traced to Zhou Xuan and 1930s Shanghai. She was probably the most popular Chinese singer of her time, whose recordings were circulated in China on the black market from the late 1970s, when such music was officially banned.

A Beijinger born of parents of Korean descent, **Cui Jian** studied the trumpet at an early age, trained as a classical musician and joined the Beijing Symphony Orchestra in 1981. After being introduced to Anglo-American rock in the mid-1980s, however, he forged an independent path and his gritty voice became the primary reference point of Chinese rock.

Cui's song "Nothing To My Name", ostensibly a love song, became a democracy movement anthem since its lyrics could be interpreted as a political monologue of the ruled about his ruler:

I used to endlessly ask
When will you go away with me?
You laugh at me always.
I have nothing to my name.
I want to give you my dreams
And also my freedom.
You laugh at me always.
I have nothing to my name.
I must tell you, I have waited too long.
I'll tell you my last request:
I'll hold your two hands
To take you away with me.

This song evoked a memorable complaint from General Wang Zhen, a veteran of the Long March: "What do you mean, you have nothing to your name? You've got the Communist Party, haven't you?"

Even though Cui's lyrics have always been ambiguous, his voice has occasionally been muffled. A nationwide tour was cancelled midway because of his actions on stage (blindfolded in red cloth – the colour of Communism) that mesmerized his fans but enraged officials. He upset the authorities, too, with his recording of *Nanni Wan*, a revolutionary song closely associated with the Communist Party and its ideals, glorifying Chinese peasants and their contribution to society. Cui's rock interpretation was understood by many as a challenge to (or mockery of) authority.

Like most of China's rockers, Cui turned more introspective as the Nineties progressed. His 1994 album *Hongqi Xiade Dan* (*Eggs Under the Red Flag*) reflected the shifting concerns of China's youth from politics to the realities of earning a living. But the powerful title track neatly encapsulated both:

Money floats in the air,
We have no ideals.
Although the air is fresh,
We cannot see into the distance.
Although the chance is here,
We are too timid.
We are wholly submissive,
Like eggs under the red flag.

For the latest on Cui Jian's music and concert dates, check out ⊛www.cuijian .com.

Notable 1980s bands following in Cui Jian's wake include Black Panther *(Hei Bao)* and Tang Dynasty, though their long hair and leathers were perhaps more influential than their soft rock. They were followed by Cobra, China's first all-female rock band, folk-rocker Zhang Chu, bad boy He Yong, Compass, Overload, and Breathing, among others. Unsigned, these bands would perform for very little money as part of vaudeville shows, until 1990, when China's first domestic full-scale rock concert took place. Six bands, including Tang Dynasty and Cobra, played at the Beijing Exhibition Centre Arena and were immediately signed by Japanese and Taiwanese labels, who then brought their music to the mainstream. They paved the way for homegrown labels such as Modern Sky, Scream, New Bees Records, and Zhengda Guoji, which now specialize in Chinese rock, hip hop and alternative music.

These days the rock scene is healthy, though it's largely confined to Beijing and there is a dearth of venues. Punk bands are the most obviously outrageous, if not the most original, element of the indie music scene; try to catch Brain Failure or riot girls Hang on the Box for the most frenzied moshing in Asia. The Nirvana-influenced Cold blooded Animals are another great live act, with some sort of visual affront to the audience pretty much guaranteed. Highly regarded critically are the Second Hand Roses, whose lead singer Liang Long dresses in drag and sings in the vaudevillian style of northeastern opera. Bands to have broken out into commercial success include New Pants and Flower – it helps that both are made up of pretty boys.

Stephen Jones & Joanna Lee,
with additional contributions from Simon Lewis

Film

Film came early to China. The first moving picture was exhibited in 1896 at a "teahouse variety show" in Shanghai, where the country's first cinema was built just twelve years later. By the 1930s, cinema was playing an important role in the cultural life of Shanghai, though the huge number of resident foreigners ensured a largely Western diet of films. Nevertheless, local Chinese films were also being made, mainly by the so-called **May Fourth intellectuals** (middle-class liberals inspired by the uprising of May 4, 1919), who wanted to turn China into a modern country along Western lines. Naturally, Western influence on these films was strong, and they have little to do with the highly stylized, formal world of traditional performance arts such as Beijing Opera or shadow-puppet theatre. Early film showings often employed a "storyteller" who sat near the screen reading out the titles, for the benefit of those who could not read.

The Shanghai studios

Of the few important **studios** in Shanghai operating in the 1920s and 1930s, the most famous was the **Mingxing**, whose films were left-leaning and anti-imperialist. *Sister Flower* (1933) tells the story of twin sisters separated at birth, one of whom ends up a city girl living in Shanghai, while the other remains a poor villager. Another film from the same year, *Spring Silk Worm*, portrays economic decline and hardship in Zhejiang province, and levels the finger of accusation at Japanese imperialism. Finally, *The Goddess* (1934), from the **Lianhua** studio, depicts the struggle of a prostitute to have her son educated. The improbably glamorous prostitute was played by China's own Garbo, the languorous Ruan Lingyu. Despite the liberal pretensions of these films, it was inevitable – given that audiences comprised a tiny elite – that they would later be derided by the Communists as bourgeois.

When the **Japanese occupied** Shanghai in 1937, "subversive" studios such as the Mingxing and Lianhua were immediately closed, and much of the film-making talent fled into the interior. The experience of war put film-makers in touch with their potential future audiences, the Chinese masses. China's great wartime epic, **Spring River Flows East** (1947–8), was the cinematic result of this experience. The story spans the whole duration of the anti-Japanese war – and the ensuing civil war – through the lives of a single family torn apart by the conflict. The heroine, living in poverty, contrasts with her husband, who has abandoned his wife for a decadent existence in Shanghai. Traumatized by a decade of war, the Chinese who saw this film appreciated it as an authentic account of the sufferings through which the nation had lived. Over three quarters of a million people saw the film at its release, a remarkable figure given that the country was still at war.

Communism and the cinema

Chinese film-making under the **Communists** is a story which really dates back to 1938, when Mao Zedong and his fellow Long Marchers set up their base in **Yan'an**. There could have been no world farther removed from the glamour of Shanghai than this dusty, poverty-stricken town, but it was the ideal location for the film-makers of the future People's Republic to learn their skills. Talent escaping through Japanese lines trickled through in search of employment, among them the actress **Jiang Qing**, later to become Mao's wife and self-appointed empress of Chinese culture. One thing that all the leading Communists in Yan'an agreed on was the importance of film as a **centralizing medium**, which could be used to unify the culture of the nation after the war had been won.

The immediate consequence of the Communist victory in 1949 was that the showing of foreign films was curtailed, and the private Shanghai studios wound down. A **Film Guidance committee** was set up to decide upon film output for the entire nation. The first major socialist epic, **Bridge**, appeared in 1949, depicting mass mobilization of workers rushing enthusiastically to construct a bridge in record time. Although predictably dull in terms of character and plot, the cast still contained a number of prewar Shanghai actors to divert audiences. At the end of the film the entire cast gathers to shout "Long live Chairman Mao!", a scene that was to be re-enacted time and again in the coming years.

A year after *Bridge*, one of the very last non-government Shanghai studio films appeared, **The Life of Wu Xun**, a huge project that had started well before 1949, and, surprisingly, was allowed to run to completion. The subject is the famous nineteenth-century entrepreneur, Wu Xun, who started out life as a beggar and rose to enormous riches, whereupon he set out on his lifetime's ambition to educate the peasantry. Despite the addition of a narrator's voice at the end of the film, pointing out that it was revolution and not education that peasants needed, the film was a disaster for the Shanghai film industry. Mao wrote a damning critique of it for idolizing a "Qing landlord", and a campaign was launched against the legacy of the entire Shanghai film world – studios, actors, critics and audiences alike.

The remains of the May Fourth Movement struggled on. The consolation for the old guard was that newer generations of Chinese film-makers had not yet solved the problem of how to portray life in the contemporary era. The 1952 screen adaptation of Lao She's short story *Dragon's Beard Ditch*, for example, was supposed to contrast the miserable pre-1949 life of a poor district of Beijing with the prosperous life that was being lived under the Communists. The only problem, as audiences could immediately see, was that the supposedly miserable pre-1949 scenes actually looked a good deal more heart-warming than the later ones.

Nevertheless, the Communists did achieve some of their original targets during the **1950s**. The promotion of a universal culture and language was one of them. All characters in all films – from Tibetans to Mongolians to Cantonese – were depicted as speaking in flawless **Mandarin Chinese**. Above all, there was an explosion in audiences, from around 47 million tickets sold in 1949, to 600 million in 1956, to over 4 billion in 1959. The latter figure should be understood in the context of the madness surrounding the Great Leap Forward, a time of crazed overproduction in all fields, film included. Film studios began sprouting in every town in China, though with a catastrophic loss of quality – a typical studio in Jiangxi province comprised one man, his bicycle and an antique stills camera. The colossal output of that year included uninspiring titles such as *Loving the Factory as One's Home*.

The conspicuous failure of the Great Leap Forward did, however, bring some short-lived advantages to the film industry. While Mao was forced temporarily into the political sidelines in the late 1950s, the cultural bureaucrats signalled

C

that in addition to "revolutionary realism", a certain degree of "**revolutionary romanticism**" was to be encouraged. Chinese themes and subjects, as opposed to pure Marxism, were looked upon with more favour. A slight blossoming occurred, with improbable films such as *Lin Zexu* (1959), which covered the life of the great Qing-dynasty official who stood up to the British at the time of the Opium Wars. There was even a tentative branching out into comedy, with the film *What's Eating You?* based on the relatively un-socialist antics of a Suzhou waiter. Unusually, the film featured local dialects, as well as a faintly detectable parody of the government's campaign to encourage greater sacrifices by promoting the mythical hero worker Lei Feng.

The Cultural Revolution

Unfortunately, this bright period came to a swift end in 1966 with the Cultural Revolution. Essentially, no interesting work would take place in China for nearly fifteen years, and indeed, no film was produced anywhere in China in the years 1966 to 1970. The few films which did subsequently appear before Mao's death were made under the personal supervision of Jiang Qing, all on the revolutionary model, a kind of ballet with flag waving. Attendance at these dreadful films was virtually **compulsory** for people who did not wish to be denounced for a lack of revolutionary zeal. Ironically, Jiang Qing herself was a big fan of Hollywood productions, which she would watch in secret.

Recovery from the trauma of the Cultural Revolution was bound to take time, but the years 1979 and 1980 saw a small crop of films attempting to assess the horror of what the country had just lived through. The best-known is **The Legend of Tianyun Mountain**, made in Shanghai in 1980, which featured two men, one of whom had denounced the other for "Rightism" in 1958. The subsequent story is one of guilt, love, emotions and human relationships, all subjects that had been banned during the Cultural Revolution. Understandably, the film was an enormous popular success, though before audiences had time to get too carried away, a subsequent film, *Unrequited Love* (1981), was officially criticized for blurring too many issues.

Modern cinema

In **1984** the Chinese film industry was suddenly brought to international attention for the first time by the arrival of the so-called "**Fifth Generation**" of Chinese film-makers. This was the year that director **Chen Kaige** and his cameraman **Zhang Yimou**, both graduates from the first post-Cultural Revolution class (1982) of the Beijing Film School, made the superb art-house film **Yellow Earth.** The story of *Yellow Earth* is a minor feature; the interest is in the images and the colours. Still shots predominate, recalling traditional Chinese scroll painting, with giant landscapes framed by hills and the distant Yellow River. The film was not particularly well received in China, either by audiences, who expected something more modern, or by the authorities, who expected something more optimistic. Nevertheless, the pattern was now set for a series of increasingly foreign-funded (and foreign-watched) films comprising stunning images of a "traditional" China, irritating the censors at home and delighting audiences abroad.

Chen Kaige's protege Zhang Yimou was soon stealing a march on his former boss with his first film **Red Sorghum** in 1987, set in a remote wine-producing village of northern China at the time of the Japanese invasion. This film was not only beautiful, and reassuringly patriotic, but it also introduced the world to **Gong Li**, the actress who was to become China's first international heart-throb. The fact that Gong Li and Zhang Yimou were soon to be lovers added to the general media interest in their work, both in China and abroad. They worked together on a string of hits, including *Judou*, *The Story of Qiu Ju*, *Raise the Red Lantern*, *Shanghai Triads* and *To Live*. None of these could be described as art-house in the way that *Yellow Earth* had been, and the potent mix of Gong Li's sexuality with exotic, mysterious locations in 1930s China was clearly targeted at Western rather than Chinese audiences. Chinese like to point out that the figure-hugging Chinese dresses regularly worn by Gong Li are entirely unlike the period costume they purport to represent.

One of Zhang Yimou's most powerful films is **To Live** (1994), which follows the fortunes of a family from "liberation" to the Great Leap Forward and the Cultural Revolution. The essence of the story is that life cannot be lived to prescription. Its power lies in the fact that it is a very real reflection of the experience of millions of Chinese people. Similarly, Chen Kaige's superb **Fare-well My Concubine** (1994) incorporates the whole span of modern Chinese history, and although the main protagonist – a homosexual Chinese opera singer – is hardly typical of modern China, the tears aroused by the film are wept for the country as a whole.

Zhang Yimou has since been warmly embraced by the authorities, and his films have got worse. **Not One Less** (1998) re-creates the true story of a country teacher who travels to the city to track down a pupil who has run away. All the characters are portrayed by themselves and give magnificent performances, but ultimately the film is sentimental. Zhang's most recent Hollywood-friendly martial arts epics **Hero** (2002) and **The House of Flying Daggers** (2004) are commer-ical successes, and beautifully shot, but are rightly derided for their shallowness.

Contemporary realism

The best Chinese films of the modern age are those that have turned their back on the frigid perfection on offer from Zhang Yimou and are raw, gritty reflec-tions of Chinese life. Inevitably, the fifth generation was followed by a sixth, which produced **underground movies**, generally shot in black and white, depicting what they consider to be the true story of contemporary China – ugly cities, cold flats, broke and depressed people. One of these, **Beijing Bastards** (1993), had a role for the famous rock singer and rebel **Cui Jian**, who is depicted drinking, swearing and playing the guitar.

Many of the best modern movies turn a baleful eye on the recent past. **In the Heat of the Sun** (1995), directed by Jiang Wen, chronicles the antics of a Beijing street gang in the 1970s. It's written by Wang Shuo, the bad boy of contemporary Chinese literature, and displays his characteristic irreverence and earthy humour. **Lei Feng is Gone** (1997) is based on the true story of the man who accidentally killed the iconic hero of Maoist China, the soldier Lei Feng. The potent personal story also works as a metaphor for the state of the nation. **Devils at the Doorstep** (2000) goes a little further back, and its eye is even more jaundiced. Set during the anti-Japanese war, it's a black farce concerning a group of peasants who get a couple of hostages dumped on their farm by the local communists. Unwilling to execute them or release them, they decide to try and return them to the Japanese in return for food.

Many films are simply too controversial for domestic release, but if they garner attention abroad they then become available at home as illegal DVDs.

The most notable film to become popular in this way is **Xiao Wu** (1997), the intimate portrayal of a pickpocket whose life is falling apart, directed by **Jia Zhangke**. Jia's other films revisit similar territory, depicting the moral wasteland of Chinese youth; **The World** (2004), his latest, is set in a world culture theme park in Beijing, where the workers squabble and fail to communicate against a backdrop of tiny replicas of the world's famous monuments. But the best of the banned genre is **Blind Shaft** (2003), directed by Yang Li, about two coal miners who kill colleagues, make it look like an accident, then collect the mine owner's hush money. As well as a telling indictment of runaway capitalism, it's a great piece of film noir. Similar in its clever combination of genre and uncompromising realism is the Tibetan **Ke Ke Xi Li** (2004), a tragic true story about a volunteer gang fighting against ruthless antelope poachers on the high Tibetan plateau. It was filmed using non-professional local actors and has the feel of a western, but is entirely unsentimental.

Hong Kong

The movies which have the least difficulty with the Chinese censors are those produced in **Hong Kong**, the world's third largest movie producer, behind India and the US. Hong Kong film-makers have perfected the high-speed, action-comedy format, and though the films are cheap, unpretentious, and made for domestic consumption, they have been highly influential. Bruce Lee kicked off a whole genre with *Enter the Dragon* (1973), which still hasn't been equalled for kung fu finesse. The hi-octane martial arts frenzy *Dragon Gate Inn* (1992) was what Ang Lee's *Crouching Tiger, Hidden Dragon* wanted to be, and Quentin Tarantino made his career out of ripping off directors like **John Woo**. Woo's breakthrough film in 1985, *A Better Tomorrow*, starred the manly Chow Yun Fat alongside a natural counterpart, the effeminate Leslie Cheung. Woo introduced a whole new class of camera dexterity to the genre, and began specializing in mind-boggling special effects of explosions and scenes of reckless violence. **Hard Boiled** and **Bullet in the Head** are his best creations, masterpieces of relentless, beautiful savagery. The work of kung fu comedian **Jackie Chan** is much more humanistic; some of the best of his many films are *Police Story*, *Miracles* and *Drunken Master* 1 & 2. He has long since sold out and moved to Hollywood; his natural home-grown succesor is Stephen Chow, an actor, director and writer who has churned out a prodigious body of work. Much is awful, but the good ones are really good, the apex of the Hong Kong melange of broad comedy, pastiche, slapstick and kung fu. Look out for *Shaolin Soccer* (surely the world's first kung fu football film), *Monkey King*, *The God of Cookery* and his latest, *Kung Fu Hustle*, set in 1920s Shanghai, in which everyone is a martial artist.

The one "serious" Hong Kong director, **Wong Karwai**, has moved in a totally different direction from that of his mainland counterparts. His extraordinary, if frustrating, films *Chungking Express*, *Fallen Angels*, *Happy Together*, *In the Mood for Love* and *2046*, with their blurred-motion shots, coffee-bar soundtracks and disjointed plots depicting a disjointed society, are right at the cutting edge of modern film-making.

Books

The following is a personal selection of the books that have proved most useful during the preparation of this guide. Bear in mind that, apart from the cheap editions published by the Foreign Languages Press (FLP), there is little in the way of English-language reading available in China, even in Hong Kong, so it's best to locate the following titles before your trip – we've listed publishers throughout. Titles marked ⊡ are particularly recommended, while those marked o/p are out of print.

History

Jasper Becker *The Chinese* (John Murray, UK). An incisive portrait of modern China at both government and individual level by one of the great sinologists. Becker draws intriguing parallels between modern rulers and ancient emperors.

Patricia Ebrey *Cambridge Illustrated History of China* (Cambridge University Press, UK). An up-to-date, easy-going historical overview, excellently illustrated and clearly written.

Peter Fleming *The Siege at Peking* (Oxford University Press, UK). An account of the events which led up to June 20, 1900, when the foreign legations in Beijing were attacked by the Boxers and Chinese imperial troops. The siege, which lasted 55 days, led to a watershed in China's relations with the rest of the world.

⊡ **Larry Gonick** *The Cartoon History of the Universe* vols II and III (W. W. Norton, US). A masterwork setting world history in cartoon format, full of verve, great visuals and awful puns, but also accurate – the bibliography shows how much research has gone into this manic project. About the only textbook that seriously attempts to set China's history (or anyone else's) in a world context.

⊡ **Peter Hopkirk** *Foreign Devils on the Silk Road* and *The Great Game* (Oxford University Press, UK). *Foreign Devils* is the story of the machinations of the various international booty-hunters who operated in Turkestan and the Gobi Desert in the early twentieth century – essential for an appreciation of China's northwest regions. *The Great Game* is a hugely entertaining account of the nineteenth-century struggle between Britain and Russia for control of central Asia. In tracing the roots of the Chinese occupations of Tibet and Xinjiang, and also detailing what has invariably happened to foreign powers who have meddled with Afghanistan, it's also disturbingly topical.

Ann Paludan *Chronicle of the Chinese Emperors* (Thames and Hudson, UK). Lively stories on the lives of all 157 of those strangest of characters, the Chinese emperors. Well illustrated and a good starting point for getting to grips with Chinese history.

Edgar Snow *Red Star Over China* (Penguin, UK; Grove Press, US). Definitive first-hand account of the early days of Mao and the Communist "bandits", written in 1936 after Snow, an American journalist, wriggled through the Guomindang blockade and spent months at the Red base in Yan'an.

Sima Qian *Historical Records* aka *Records of the Historian* (Oxford Paperbacks, UK; Columbia University Press, US). Written by the Han-dynasty court historian, *Records* is a masterpiece, using contemporary court documents and oral tradition to illuminate key characters – everyone from emperors to famous con men – from Chinese history up to that point. Although long discredited, Sima Qian's accounts have now been partially corroborated by recent archeology.

★ **Jonathan Spence** *The Gate of Heavenly Peace* (Penguin, UK & US), *The Search for Modern China* (W.W. Norton, US). The first of these traces the history of twentieth-century China through the eyes of the men and women caught up in it – writers, revolutionaries, poets and politicians. One of the best books for getting to grips with China's complex modern history. *The Search for Modern China* is quite hard for a straight-through read, but it's authoritative and probably the best overall history of China available.

Susan Whitfield *Life along the Silk Road* (John Murray, UK). Using archeological remains and historical sources, the author creates ten fictional characters to illustrate life in northwestern China during its tenth-century Buddhist heyday.

Justin Wintle *Rough Guide Chronicle: China* (Rough Guides, UK & US). Pocket-sized but surprisingly detailed timeline of China's history, the key events and people put neatly into context in a year-by-year format.

Sally Hovey Wriggins *Xuanzang* (Westview Press, US). Accessible biography of the famous Tang-dynasty monk, retracing his epic pilgrimage to India where he studied various Buddhist doctrines at their source, and his subsequent return to Xi'an with a caravan-load of scriptures.

Tibet

John Avedon *In Exile From the Land of Snows* (HarperCollins, UK; Perennial, US). A detailed and moving account of modern Tibetan history, covering both those who remained in the country and those who fled into exile. Required reading for anyone contemplating a trip.

Victor Chan *Tibet Handbook: a Pilgrimage Guide* (Avalon Travel, US). A hugely detailed guide to the pilgrimage sites and treks and how to reach them. Absolutely essential if you're considering a trek.

Graham Coleman (ed) *A Handbook of Tibetan Culture: a Guide to Tibetan Centres and Resources Throughout the World* (Shambhala, UK). The subtitle says it all; the book exhaustively documents cultural organizations, teaching centres and libraries across the globe which have a Tibetan focus. It also includes biographies of major Tibetan lamas, brief histories of the major schools of Tibetan Buddhism and an illustrated glossary.

★ **Heinrich Harrer** *Seven Years In Tibet* (Flamingo, UK; Jeremy P. Tarcher, US). A classic account of a remarkable journey to reach Lhasa and of the years there prior to the Chinese invasion, when Harrer was tutor to the Fourteenth Dalai Lama. The book has some excellent observations of Tibetan life of the time, and has been made into a movie starring Brad Pitt.

Isabel Hilton *The Search for the Panchen Lama* (Penguin, UK & US). Details the whole sorry story of the search for the Eleventh Panchen Lama, and how the Tibetans' choice ended up as the world's youngest political prisoner.

★ **Peter Hopkirk** *Trespassers on the Roof of the World: the Race for Lhasa* (Oxford University Press, UK). Around the turn of the twentieth century, imperial Britain, with the help of a remarkable band of pundits and wallahs from the Indian Survey, was discreetly charting every nook of the most inaccessible part of the earth, the High Tibetan plateau. Peter Hopkirk has researched his subject thoroughly and come up with a highly readable account of this fascinating backwater of history.

Thubten Jigme and Colin Turnbull *Tibet, Its History, Religion and People* (Penguin, UK & US). Co-authored by the brother of the Fourteenth Dalai Lama, this is the best account around of the traditional everyday lives of the Tibetan people.

Culture and society

★ **David Bonavia** *The Chinese: A Portrait* (Penguin, UK & US). A highly readable introduction to contemporary China, focusing on the human aspects as a balance to the socio-political trends.

Ian Baruma *Bad Elements* (Orion, UK; Random House, US). Interviews with dissident exiles abroad tell an (inevitably anti-government) story of modern China.

Gordon Chang *The Coming Collapse of China* (Arrow, UK; Random House, US). A detailed and well-informed overview of what's wrong with contemporary Chinese society by this influential prophet of doom, though the thesis, that a popular revolution will eventually destroy the Communist Party, is overstretched.

Tim Glissold *Mr China* (Constable and Robinson, UK). The well-told and eye-opening story of how the author went to China to make a fortune and lost 400 million dollars. Great first-person account of the eccentric Chinese business environment and a must for anyone thinking of investing there.

Jacques Gernet *Daily Life in China on the Eve of the Mongol Invasion 1250–1276* (Allen and Unwin, UK; Stanford University Press, US). Based on a variety of Chinese sources, this is a fascinating survey of southern China under the Song, focusing on the capital, Hangzhou, then the largest and richest city in the world. Gernet also deals with the daily lives of a cross-section of society, from peasant to leisured gentry, covering everything from cookery to death.

John Gittings *Real China* (Pocket Books, UK; Simon and Schuster, US). A series of essays on rural China, giving a very different picture from the descriptions of the economic miracle that most Western commentators have focused on, though lacking in depth. The chapter on cannibalism during the Cultural Revolution is morbidly fascinating.

Joe Studwell *The China Dream* (Profile, UK; Grove Press, US). Mandatory reading for foreign business people in China, this is a cautionary tale, written in layman's terms, debunking the myth that there's easy money to be made from China's vast markets. A great read for anyone interested in business, economics or human greed.

Xinran *The Good Women of China* (Chatto and Windus, UK; Anchor, US). Tales of the struggles of Chinese women; their stories are heart-warming though the editor (a Beijing journalist) comes across as rather irritating.

Lin Yutang *My Country and My People* (o/p). An expatriate Chinese scholar writes for Western audiences in the 1930s about what it means to be Chinese. Obviously dated in parts, but overall remarkably fresh and accessible.

★ **Zhang Xinxin and Sang Ye** *Chinese Lives* (Penguin, UK; Pan Macmillan, US). This Studs Terkel-like series of first-person narratives from interviews with a broad range of Chinese people is both readable and informative, full of fascinating details of day-to-day existence that you won't read anywhere else.

Travel writing

Charles Blackmore *The Worst Desert on Earth* (John Murray, UK; Trafalgar Square, US). Sergeant-majorly account of an arduous and possibly unique trip across the Takla-makan Desert in northwest China.

Mildred Cable with Francesca French *The Gobi Desert* (Virago Press, UK; Beacon Press, US). Cable and French were missionaries with the China Inland Mission in the early part of the twentieth century. *The Gobi Desert* is a poetic description of their life and travels in Gansu and Xinjiang, without the sanctimonious and patronizing tone adopted by some of their contemporary missionaries.

Peter Fleming *One's Company: a Journey to China* (Pimlico, UK); and *News from Tartary* (Birlinn, UK; Tarcher, US). The first is an amusing account of a journey through Russia and Manchuria to China in the 1930s. En route, Peter Fleming (brother of Ian) encounters a wild assortment of Chinese and Japanese officials and the puppet emperor Henry Pu Yi himself. *News from Tartary* records an epic journey of 3500 miles across the roof of the world to Kashmir in 1935.

Peter Hessler *River Town – Two Years on the Yangtze* (John Murray, UK; Perennial, US). One of the best of the mini-genre "how I taught English for a couple of years in China and survived". The book

accepts China's positive aspects and avoids cynicism when dealing with social problems and contradictions. Especially worth a read if you're planning a lengthy stay in China.

Somerset Maugham *On a Chinese Screen* (Vintage, UK; Arno Press, US). Brief, sometimes humorous, and often biting sketches of the European missionaries, diplomats and business-men whom Maugham encountered in China between 1919 and 1921; worth reading for background detail.

★ **Marco Polo** *The Travels* (Penguin, UK & US). Said to have inspired Columbus, *The Travels* is a fantastic read, full of amazing details picked up during his 26 years of wandering in Asia between Venice and the court of Kublai Khan. It's not, however, a coherent history, having been ghost-written by a novelist from notes supplied by Marco Polo.

Vikram Seth *From Heaven Lake: Travels through Sinkiang and Tibet* (Phoenix, UK; Random House, US). A student for two years at Nanjing University, Seth set out in 1982 to return home to Delhi via Tibet and Nepal. This account of how he hitched his way through four prov-inces, Xinjiang, Gansu, Qinghai and Tibet, is in the best tradition of early travel books.

Colin Thubron *Behind the Wall* (Vintage, UK; HarperCollins, US).

A thoughtful and superbly poetic description of an extensive journey through China just after it opened up in the early 1980s. This is the single best piece of travel writing to have come out of modern China.

Guides and reference books

Kit Chow and Ione Kramer *All the Tea in China* (Sinolingua, UK; China Books, US). Everything you need to know about Chinese teas, from variations in growing and processing techniques to a rundown of fifty of the most famous brews. Good fun and nicely illustrated.

Mackinnon, Showler and Phillipps *A Field Guide to the Birds of China* (Oxford University Press, UK). Over 1300 species illustrated (mostly in colour), with outline text descriptions and distribution maps, making this by far the best book on the subject.

Jessica Rawson *Ancient China: Art and Archaeology* (Icon, UK & US). By an oriental antiquities specialist at the British Museum, this scholarly introduction to Chinese art puts the subject in historical context. Beginning in Neolithic times, the book explores the technology and social organization which shaped its development up to the Han dynasty.

George Schaller *Wildlife of the Tibetan Steppe* (University of Chicago Press, US). Reference book on the mammals – especially the rare Tibetan antelope – inhabiting the inhospitable Chang Tang region, by a zoologist who has spent over thirty years studying China's wildlife.

Mary Tregear *Chinese Art* (Thames and Hudson, UK & US). Authoritative summary of the main strands in Chinese art from Neolithic times, through the Bronze Age and up to the twentieth century. Clearly written and well illustrated.

Cookery

★ **Fuchsia Dunlop** *Sichuan Cookery* (Penguin, UK; W.W. Norton, US). The best available English-language cookbook on Chinese cuisine, from a talented writer who spent three years honing her skills at a Chengdu cookery school. Dishes smell, look and taste exactly as you find them in Sichuan.

Hsiang Ju Lin and Tsuifeng Lin *Chinese Gastronomy* (Tuttle, US). A classic work, relatively short on recipes but strong on cooking methods and philosophy – essential reading for anyone serious about learning the finer details of Chinese cooking. Wavers in and out of print, sometimes under different titles; look for Lin as the author name.

★ **Kenneth Lo** *Chinese Food* (Faber & Faber, US). Good general-purpose cookbook covering a wide range of methods and styles, from Westernized dishes to regional specialities.

Wei Chuan Cultural Education Foundation *Vegetarian Cooking* and *Chinese Dim Sum* (Wei Chuan, Taiwan). Two in a series of excellent, easy-to-follow cookbooks published by the Taiwanese Wei Chuan cooking school; simplified versions of classic dishes produce good results. Not available in China, but easy enough to find in major bookstores in the West.

Martial arts

Paul Brecher *Principles of Tai Chi and Secrets of Energy Work* (Harper-Collins, UK). Two excellent books by a long-time internal martial artist: the first maps out the fundamentals behind *tai ji*, whichever style you practise; the second is a manual on using *qigong* for health.

Kumar Frantzis *The Power of Internal Martial Arts* (North Atlantic Books, US). Trawl through Frantzis' forty years of experience studying the internal martial arts in Japan, China, Taiwan and the US, with personal accounts of different masters and their styles. Articulate and interesting even if you don't know your *li* from your *jing*, though fellow practitioners will find plenty of gems.

Erle Montaigue *Power Taiji* (Paladin Press, US). For those that think *tai ji* is just a series of pretty movements, this book – based on the Yang long form – lifts the lid on an infinitely subtle art that can be used for both healing and combat.

Religion and philosophy

★ *Asiapac* series (Asiapac Books, Singapore). These entertaining titles, available in Hong Kong and Beijing, present ancient Chinese philosophy in comic-book format, making it accessible without losing its complexity. They are all well written and well drawn. Particularly good is the *Book of Zen*, a collection of stories and parables, and the *Sayings of Confucius*.

Kenneth Chen *Buddhism in China* (Princeton University Press, US). Very helpful for tracing the origin of Buddhist thought in China, the development of its many different schools and the four-way traffic of influence between India, Tibet, Japan and China.

Confucius *The Analects* (Penguin, UK & US). Good modern translation of this classic text, a collection of Confucius's teachings focusing on morality and the state.

Lao Zi *Tao Te Ching* (Penguin, UK & US). The collection of mystical thoughts and philosophical speculation that form the basis of Taoist philosophy.

Arthur Waley *Three Ways of Thought in Ancient China* (Routledge-Curzon UK; Stanford University Press US). Translated extracts from the writings of three of the early philosophers – Zhuang Zi, Mencius and Han Feizi. A useful introduction.

Biographies and autobiographies

Anchee Min *Red Azalea* (Orion, UK; Berkley, US). Half-autobiography, half-novel, this beautifully written book is an unusually personal and highly romantic account of surviving the Cultural Revolution.

Dalai Lama *Freedom in Exile* (Abacus, UK; HarperCollins, US). The autobiography of the charismatic, Nobel Prize-winning Fourteenth Dalai Lama.

Richard Evans *Deng Xiaoping* (Penguin, UK and US). The basic handbook to understanding the motives and inspirations behind one of the most influential men in modern China.

Jung Chang *Wild Swans* (Perennial, UK; Touchstone, US). Enormously popular in the West, this family saga covering three generations was unsurprisingly banned in China for its honest account of the horrors of life in turbulent twentieth-century China. It serves as an excellent introduction to modern Chinese history, as well as being a good read. Her latest book is a fiercely critical biography of Mao (Jonathan Cape, UK).

★ **Ma Jian** *Red Dust* (Vintage, UK; Anchor, US). Facing arrest for spiritual pollution, writer and artist Ma Jian fled Beijing to travel around China's remotest corners for three years in the 1980s, living off his wits, often in extreme poverty. This picaresque tale of China in the first phase of its opening up is told in lively prose and offers the kind of insights only an alienated insider could garner. His latest book, the *Noodle Maker*, is a satirical novel about a propagandist and a professional blood donor.

John Man *Genghis Khan* (Bantam, UK). Lively and readable biography of the illiterate nomad who built the biggest empire the world has ever seen, intercut with Man's travels to Mongolia and China to find his tomb.

Naisingoro Pu Yi *From Emperor to Citizen* (FLP). The autobiography of the young boy, born into the Qing imperial family and chosen by the Japanese to become the puppet emperor of the state of Manchukuo in 1931.

Philip Short *Mao: A Life* (John Murray, UK; Owl Books, US). Despite its length, an extremely readable account of Mao and his times – even if the Great Helmsman's ideologies are becoming ever less relevant in contemporary China.

★ **Hugh Trevor-Roper** *Hermit of Peking: the Hidden Life of Sir Edmund Backhouse* (Eland, UK). Sparked by Backhouse's thoroughly obscene memoirs, *Hermit of Peking* uses external sources in an attempt to uncover the facts behind the extraordinarily convoluted life of Edmund Backhouse – Chinese scholar, eccentric recluse and phenomenal liar – who lived in Beijing from the late nineteenth century until his death in 1944.

Marina Warner *The Dragon Empress* (Vintage, UK; Atheneum, US). Exploration of the life of Cixi, one of only two women rulers of China. Warner lays bare the complex personality whose conservatism, passion for power, vanity and greed had such a great impact on the events which culminated in the collapse of the imperial ruling house and the founding of the republic.

Literature

Modern writing

★ **Pearl S. Buck** *The Good Earth* (Simon & Schuster, UK; Washington Square Press, US). The best story from a writer who grew up in China during the early twentieth century, *The Good Earth* follows the fortunes of the peasant Wang Lung from his wedding day to his dotage, as he struggles to hold onto his land for his family through a series of political upheavals.

Chen Yuanbin *The Story of Qiuju* (Panda Books, China). A collection of four tales, of which the title story, about a peasant woman pushing for justice after her husband is assaulted by the village chief, was made into a film by award-winning director Zhang Yimou.

Chun Sue *Beijing Doll* (Abacus Books, UK; Riverhead Books, US). A rambling *roman à clef* about a confused teenage girl who has unsatisfactory sexual encounters with preening rock and rollers – though if it wasn't China it wouldn't be interesting.

Deng Ming-Dao *Chronicles of Tao* (HarperCollins, UK; Harper, US). Pitched as a true story, this is a martial-arts novel aimed at Western audiences, based around the life of a Taoist monk growing up in China during the turbulent years before the Communists came to power.

Guo Xiaolu *The Village of Stone* (Chatto and Windus, UK). A sensitive study of a woman reflecting on her life as a modern metropolitan and her tough country childhood.

James Hilton *Lost Horizon* (Summersdale, UK; Pocket, US). The classic 1930s novel of longevity in a secret Tibetan valley, which gave the world – and the Chinese tourist industry – the myth of Shangri-la.

Robert Van Gulik *The Judge Dee Mysteries* (Perennial, UK; University of Chicago Press, US). Sherlock Holmes-style detective stories set in the Tang dynasty and starring the wily Judge Dee, who gets tough on crime as detective, judge and jury. There are a lot of them; recommended are *The Red Pavilion*, *Murder in Canton*, and *the Chinese Nail Murders*. Fun, informative and unusual.

Lao She *Rickshaw Boy* (FLP). One of China's great modern writers, who was driven to suicide during the Cultural Revolution. The story is a haunting account of a young rickshaw puller in pre-1949 Beijing.

★ **Lu Xun** *The True Story of Ah Q* (FLP). Widely read in China today, Lu Xun is regarded as the father of modern Chinese writing. *Ah Q* is one of his best tales, short, allegorical and cynical, about a simpleton who is swept up in the 1911 revolution.

Mo Yan *The Garlic Ballads* (Penguin, UK & US). Banned in China, this is a hard-hitting novel of rural life by one of China's greatest modern writers.

Amy Tan *The Joy Luck Club* (Vintage, UK; Ivy, US). Uneven but moving story of four Chinese mothers and their first-generation daughters, chronicling the life of American Chinese with a perceptive touch and some brilliant set pieces.

Wang Shuo *Playing For Thrills* (Penguin, UK & US) and *Please Don't Call Me Human* (No Exit Press, UK; Oldcastle, US). Wang Shuo writes in colourful Beijing dialect about the city's wide boys and chancers. *Playing For Thrills* is fairly representative – a mystery story whose boorish narrator spends most of his time drinking, gambling and chasing girls. *Please Don't Call Me Human* is a satire of modern China as a place where greed is everything, as the Party turns a dignified martial artist into a vacuous dancer in order to win an Olympic gold medal.

Wei Hui *Shanghai Baby* (Constable & Robinson, UK; Washington Square Press, US). Salacious chick-lit about a Chinese girl who can't decide between her Western lover and her drug-addled Chinese boyfriend. Notable for the Chinese authorities' attempts to ban it, and for spawning a genre in modern Chinese writing, the urban girl's saucy confessional.

Classics

Asiapac series (Asiapac Books, Singapore). Renders Chinese classics and folk tales into cartoon format. Titles include *Journey to the West*, *Tales of Laozhai* and *Chinese Eunuchs*.

Cyril Birch (ed) *Anthology of Chinese Literature* (Avalon Travel, US). Two volumes covering three thousand years of poetry, philosophy, drama, biography and prose fiction, with interesting variations of translation.

Cao Xueqing and Gao E *Dream of Red Mansions/Story of the Stone* (FLP; Penguin, UK). This intricate eighteenth-century tale of manners follows the fortunes of the Jia Clan through the emotionally charged adolescent lives of Jia Baoyu and his two girl cousins, Lin Daiyu and Xue Baochai. The full translation fills five paperbacks, but there's also a much simplified English version available in China.

Li Bai and Du Fu *Li Po and Tu Fu* (Penguin, UK & US). Fine translations of China's greatest Tang-dynasty poets, with a detailed introduction that puts them in context. Li Bai was a drunken spiritualist, Du Fu a sharp-eyed realist, and their surprisingly accessible and complementary works form an apex of Chinese literature.

 Luo Guanzhong *Romance of the Three Kingdoms* (FLP).

Despite being written 1200 years after the events it portrays, this tale vividly evokes the battles, political schemings and myths surrounding China's turbulent Three Kingdoms period. One of the world's great historical novels.

Shi Nai'an and Luo Guanzhong *Outlaws of the Marsh* aka *The Water Margin* (FLP). A heavy dose of popular legend as a group of Robin Hood-like outlaws takes on the government in feudal times. Wildly uneven, and hard to read right through, but some amazing characters and set pieces.

Sun Zi *The Art of War* (Penguin, UK; Running Press, US). This classic on strategy and warfare, told in short, unambiguous prose, is as relevant today as when it was written around 500 BC. A favourite with the modern business community.

Wu Cheng'en *Journey to the West* (FLP). Absurd, lively rendering of the Buddhist monk Xuanzang's pilgrimage to India to collect sacred scriptures, aided by Sandy, Pigsy and the irrepressible Sun Wu Kong, the monkey king. Arthur Waley's version, *Monkey* (Penguin), retains the tale's spirit while shortening the hundred-chapter opus to paperback length.

Language

Language

Chinese

As the **most widely spoken** language on earth, Chinese can hardly be overlooked. Chinese is, strictly speaking, a series of **dialects** spoken by the dominant ethnic group within China, the Han. Indeed, the term most commonly used by the Chinese themselves to refer to the language is **hanyu**, meaning "Han-language", though *zhongyu*, *zhongwen* and *zhongguohua* are frequently used as well. However, non-Han peoples such as Uigurs and Tibetans speak languages which have little or nothing to do with Chinese.

The dialects of *hanyu* are a complicated story in themselves. Some of them are mutually unintelligible and – where the spoken word is concerned – have about as much in common as, say, German and English. The better-known and most distinct dialects include those spoken around China's coastal fringes, such as **Shanghainese** (*shanghai hua*), **Fujianese** (*minnan hua*) and **Cantonese** (*guangdong hua* or *yueyu*), though even within the areas covered by these dialects you'll find huge local divergences. Cantonese and Fujianese are themselves languages of worldwide significance, being the dialects spoken by the people of Hong Kong and among Overseas Chinese communities, particularly those in Southeast Asia.

What enables Chinese from different parts of the country to converse with each other is **Mandarin Chinese**. Historically based on the language of Han officialdom in the Beijing area, Mandarin has been systematically promoted over the past hundred years to be the official, unifying language of the Chinese people, much as modern French, for example, is based on the original Parisian dialect. It is known in mainland China as **putonghua** – "common language" – and in Taiwan (and also remoter corners of China) as *guoyu* – "national language". As the language of education, government and the media, Mandarin is understood to a greater or lesser extent by the vast majority of Han Chinese, and by many non-Han as well, though there are two caveats to this generalization: first, that knowledge of Mandarin is far more common among the young, the educated and the urban-dwelling; and second, that many people who understand Mandarin cannot actually speak it. For example, the chances of the average Tibetan peasant being able to speak Mandarin are extremely small. In Hong Kong and Macau, likewise, there has been until recently very little Mandarin spoken, though this situation is now changing fast.

Another element tying the various dialects together is the Chinese **script**. No matter how different two dialects may sound when spoken, once they are written down in the form of Chinese characters they become mutually comprehensible again, as the different dialects use the same written characters. A sentence of Cantonese, for example, written down beside a sentence of the same meaning in Mandarin, will look broadly similar except for occasional unusual words or structures. Having said this, it should be added that some non-Han peoples use their own scripts, and apart from Cantonese it is unusual to see Chinese dialects written down at all. Most Chinese people, in fact, associate the written word inextricably with Mandarin.

From the point of view of foreigners, the main distinguishing characteristic of Chinese is that it is a **tonal** language: in order to pronounce a word correctly, it is necessary to know not only its sound but also its correct tone. Despite initial impressions, there is nothing too difficult about learning the basics of communication, however, and being able to speak even a few words of Chinese can mean the difference between a successful trip and a nightmare. Given the way tones affect meaning – and the fact that individual characters are monosyllabic – accuracy in **pronunciation** is particularly important in Chinese, for which an understanding of the **pinyin** phonetic system is vital (see opposite). For advanced **teach-yourself** grounding in spoken Mandarin, try *Hugo's Chinese in Three Months*, which includes *pinyin* transliteration and tapes and, while a bit dry, is wider in its approach than purely business- or travel-oriented alternatives. On the road, the Rough Guide *Mandarin Chinese Dictionary Phrasebook* provides useful words and phrases in both *pinyin* and characters, while Langenscheidt's *Pocket Dictionary Chinese* is – for its size – perhaps the best available **dictionary** of colloquial usage. Once you're in China, you'll find that any bookshop will have a huge range of inexpensive Chinese–English dictionaries, and perhaps livelier teach-yourself texts than are available overseas.

Chinese characters

There are tens of thousands of **Chinese characters**, in use since at least the Shang dynasty (1600–1100 BC), though the vast majority of these are obsolete – you need about 2500 to read a newspaper, and even educated Chinese are unlikely to know more than ten thousand. The characters themselves are **pictograms**, each representing a **concept** rather than a specific pronunciation. This is similar to the use of numerals: there is nothing in the figure "2" which spells out the pronunciation; having learned what the symbol means, we simply know how to say it – whether "two" in English, "deux" in French, and so on. Similarly, Chinese speakers have to memorize the sounds of individual characters, and the meanings attached to them. While the sounds might vary from region to region, the meanings themselves do not – which is how the written word cuts through regional variations in language.

Although to untrained eyes many Chinese characters seem impossibly complex, there is a logic behind their structure which helps in their memorization. Firstly, each character is written using an exact number of brush (or pen) **strokes**: thus the character for "mouth", which forms a square, is always written using only three strokes: first the left side, then the top and right side together, and finally the base. Secondly, characters can very broadly be broken up into two components, which often also exist as characters in their own right: a **main** part, which frequently gives a clue as to the pronunciation; and a **radical**, which usually appears on the left side of the character and which vaguely categorizes the meaning. As an example, the character for "mother" is made up of the character for "horse" (to which it sounds similar), combined with a radical which means "female". In a few cases, it's easy to see the connection between the pictogram and its meaning – the character *mu*, wood, resembles a tree – though others require some lateral thinking or have become so abstract or complex that the meaning is hidden.

Given the time and difficulty involved in **learning characters**, and the negative impact this has had on the general level of literacy, the government of the People's Republic announced in 1954 that a couple of thousand of the most common characters were to be, quite literally, **simplified**, making them not only easier to learn but also quicker to write, as the new characters often use far fewer pen strokes. This drastic measure was not without controversy. Some argued that by interfering with the original structure of the characters, vital clues as to their meaning and pronunciation would be lost, making them harder than ever to learn. These simplified characters were eventually adopted not just in mainland China but also in Singapore; but Hong Kong and Taiwan, as well as many overseas Chinese communities, continue to use the older, traditional forms.

Today, ironically, the traditional forms are also making a **comeback** on the mainland, where they are now seen as sophisticated. Note that some of these traditional forms differ considerably from the simplified forms provided in this book, though their meaning and pronunciation are identical.

Grammar

Chinese **grammar** is relatively simple. There is no need to conjugate verbs, decline nouns or make adjectives agree – being attached to immutable Chinese characters, Chinese words simply cannot have different "endings". Instead, context and fairly rigid rules about word order are relied on to make those distinctions of time, number and gender that Indo-European languages are so concerned with. Instead of cumbersome tenses, the Chinese make use of words such as "yesterday" or "tomorrow"; instead of plural endings they simply state how many things there are, or use quantifier words equivalent to "some" or "many".

Word formation is affected by the fact that the meanings of many Chinese characters have become diffuse over time. For instance, there is a single character, pronounced *ju* with the third tone in Mandarin, which is a verb meaning "to lift", "to start" or "to choose", an adjective meaning "whole" and a noun meaning "deed". In a very dim way we might perhaps see the underlying meaning of *ju* on its own, but to make things clear in practice, many concepts are referred to not by single characters but by combining two or more characters together like building blocks. In the case of *ju* above, the addition of character for "world" creates a word meaning "throughout the world"; and the addition of "eye" creates a word meaning "look".

For English-speakers, **Chinese word order** follows the familiar subject-verb-object pattern, and you'll find that by simply stringing words together you'll be producing fairly grammatical Chinese. Just note that adjectives, as well as all qualifying and describing phrases, precede nouns.

Pronunciation and pinyin

Back in the 1950s it was hoped eventually to replace Chinese characters altogether with a regular alphabet of Roman letters, and to this end the **pinyin** system was devised. Basically, *pinyin* is a way of using the Roman alphabet (except the letter "v") to write out the sounds of Mandarin Chinese, with Mandarin's four tones represented by **accents** above each syllable. Other dialects of Chinese, such as Cantonese – having nine tones – cannot be written in *pinyin*.

The aim of replacing Chinese characters with *pinyin* was abandoned long ago, but in the meantime *pinyin* has one very important function, that of helping foreigners to pronounce Chinese words. However, in *pinyin* the letters do not all have the sounds you would expect, and you'll need to spend an hour or two learning these. You'll often see *pinyin* in China, on street signs and shop displays, but only well-educated locals know the system well. Occasionally, you will come across **other systems** of rendering Mandarin into Roman letters, such as **Wade-Giles**, which writes Mao Zedong as Mao Tse-tung, and Deng Xiaoping as Teng Hsiao-p'ing. These forms are no longer used in mainland China, but you may see them in Western books about China, or in Taiwanese publications.

The Chinese terms in this book have been given both in characters and in *pinyin*; the pronunciation guide below is your first step to making yourself comprehensible. Don't get overly paranoid about your tones: with the help of context, intelligent listeners should be able to work out what you are trying to say. If you're just uttering a single word, however, for example a place name – without a context – you need to hit exactly the right tone, otherwise don't be surprised if nobody understands you.

The tones

There are **four tones** in Mandarin Chinese, and every syllable of every word is characterized by one of them, except for a few syllables which are considered toneless. This emphasis on tones does not make Chinese a particularly musical language – English, for example, uses all of the tones of Chinese and many more. The difference is that English uses tone for effect – exclaiming, questioning, listing, rebuking and so on. In English, to change the tone is to change the mood or the emphasis; in Chinese, to change the tone is to change the word itself.

First or "High" ā ē ī ō ū. In English this level tone is used when mimicking robotic or very boring, flat voices.

Second or "Rising" á é í ó ú. Used in English when asking a question showing surprise, for example "eh?".

Third or "Falling-rising" ǎ ě ǐ ǒ ǔ. Used in English when echoing someone's words with a measure of incredulity. For example, "John's dead." "De-ad?!".

Fourth or "Falling" à è ì ò ù. Often used in English when counting in a brusque manner – "One! Two! Three! Four!".

Toneless A few syllables do not have a tone accent. These are pronounced without emphasis, such as in the English u**pon**.

Note that if there are two consecutive characters with the third tone, the first character is pronounced as though it carries the second tone.

Consonants

Most consonants are pronounced in a similar way to their English equivalents, with the following exceptions:

c as in ha**ts**

g is hard as in **g**od (except when preceded by "n" when it sounds like sa**ng**)

q as in **ch**eese

x has no direct equivalent in English, but you can make the sound by sliding from an "s"

sound to a "sh" sound and stopping midway between the two

z as in su**ds**

zh as in fu**dge**

Vowels and diphthongs

As in most languages, the vowel sounds are rather harder to quantify than the consonants. The examples here give a rough description of the sound of each vowel followed by related combination sounds.

a usually somewhere between f**a**r and m**a**n

ai as in **eye**

ao as in c**ow**

e usually as in f**ur**

ei as in g**ay**

en is an unstressed sound as at the end of hyph**en**

eng as in s**ung**

er as in f**ur** (ie with a stressed "r")

i usually as in t**ea**, except in *zi, ci, si, ri, zhi, chi* and *shi*, when it is a short clipped sound like the American military "s**ir**"

ia as in y**ak**

ian as in y**en**

ie as in **yeah**

o as in b**ore**

ou as in sh**ow**

ü as in the German ü (make an "ee" sound and glide slowly into an "oo"; at the mid-point between the two sounds you should hit the ü-sound)

u usually as in f**oo**l except where *u* follows j, q, x or y, when it is always pronounced **ü**

ua as in s**ua**ve

uai as in **why**

ue as though contracting "you" and "air" together, **you'air**

ui as in **way**

uo as in **wo**re

Useful words and phrases

Chinese put their **family names first** followed by their given names, exactly the reverse of Western convention. The vast majority of Chinese family names comprise a single character, while given names are either one or two characters long. So a man known as Zhang Dawei has the family name of Zhang, and the given name of Dawei.

When asked for their name, the Chinese tend to provide either just their family name, or their whole name. In **formal situations**, you might come across the terms "Mr" (*xiansheng*), "Mrs" (*taitai*, though this is being replaced by the more neutral term *airen*) or "Miss" (*xiaojie*), which are attached after the family name: for example, Mr Zhang is *zhang xiansheng*. In more casual encounters, people use familiar terms such as "old" (*lao*) or "young" (*xiao*) attached in front of the family name, though "old" or "young" are more relative terms of status than indications of actual age in this case: Mr Zhang's friend might call him "Lao Zhang", for instance.

Basics		
I	我	wǒ
You (singular)	你	nǐ
He	他	tā
She	她	tā
We	我们	wǒmén
You (plural)	你们	nǐmén
They	他们	tāmén
I want...	我要	wǒ yào...
No, I don't want...	我不要 ...	wǒ bú yào...
Is it possible...?	可不可以...?	kěbùkěyǐ...?
It is (not) possible.	(不)可以	(bù) kěyǐ
Is there any/Have you got any...?	有没有...?	yǒuméiyǒu...?
There is/I have	有	yǒu

There isn't/I haven't	没有	méiyǒu
Please help me	请帮我忙	qǐng bāng wǒ máng
Mr...	.....先生	xiānshēng
Mrs...	.....太太	tàitài
Miss...	.....小姐	xiǎojiě

Communicating

I don't speak Chinese	我不会说中文	wǒ bú huì shuō zhōngwén
My Chinese is terrible	我的中文很差	wǒ de zhōngwén hěn chà
Can you speak English?	你会说英语吗?	nǐ huì shuō yīngyǔ ma?
Can you get someone who speaks English?	请给我找一个会说英语的人?	qǐng gěi wǒ zhǎo yí ge huì shuō yīngyǔ de rén?
Please speak slowly	请说得慢一点	qǐng shuōde màn yìdiǎn
Please say that again	请再说一遍	qǐng zài shuō yí biàn
I understand	我听得懂	wǒ tīngdedǒng
I don't understand	我听不懂	wǒ tīngbùdǒng
I can't read Chinese characters	我看不懂汉字	wǒ kànbùdǒng hànzì
What does this mean?	这是什么意思?	zhè shì shénme yìsi?
How do you pronounce this character?	这个字怎么念?	zhè ge zì zénme niàn?

Greetings and basic courtesies

Hello/How do you do/ How are you?	你好	nǐ hǎo
I'm fine	我很好	wǒ hěn hǎo
Thank you	谢谢	xièxie
Don't mention it/ You're welcome	不客气	búkèqi
Sorry to bother you...	麻烦你	máfan nǐ
Sorry/I apologize	对不起	duìbùqǐ
It's not important/No problem	没关系	méi guānxi
Goodbye	再见	zài jiàn

Chitchat

What country are you from?	你是哪个国家的?	nǐ shì ná ge guójiā de?
Britain	英国	yīngguó
Ireland	爱尔兰	ài'érlán
America	美国	měiguó
Canada	加拿大	jiānǎdà
Australia	澳大利亚	àodàlìyà
New Zealand	新西兰	xīnxīlán
China	中国	zhōngguó
Outside China	外国	wàiguó
What's your name?	你叫什么名字?	nǐ jiào shénme míngzi?
My name is...	我叫....	wǒ jiào...
Are you married?	你结婚了吗?	nǐ jiéhūn le ma?

I am (not) married	我（没有）结婚（了）	wǒ (méiyou) jiéhun (le)
Have you got (children)?	你有没有孩子？	nǐ yǒu méiyǒu háizi?
Do you like...?	你喜不喜欢.....?	nǐ xǐ bù xǐhuan....?
I (don't) like...	我不喜欢....	wǒ (bù) xǐhuan...
What's your job?	你干什么工作？	nǐ gàn shěnme gōngzuò?
I'm a foreign student	我是留学生	wǒ shì liúxuéshēng
I'm a teacher	我是老师	wǒ shì lǎoshī
I work in a company	我在一个公司工作	wǒ zài yí ge gōngsī gōngzuò
I don't work	我不工作	wǒ bù gōngzuò
Clean/dirty	干净/脏	gānjìng/zāng
Hot/cold	热/冷	rè/lěng
Fast/slow	快/慢	kuài/màn
Pretty	漂亮	piàoliang
Interesting	有意思	yǒuyìsi

Numbers

Zero	零	líng
One	一	yī
Two	二/两	èr/liǎng*
Three	三	sān
Four	四	sì
Five	五	wǔ
Six	六	liù
Seven	七	qī
Eight	八	bā
Nine	九	jiǔ
Ten	十	shí
Eleven	十一	shíyī
Twelve	十二	shíèr
Twenty	二十	èrshí
Twenty-one	二十一	èrshíyī
One hundred	一百	yībǎi
Two hundred	二百	èrbǎi
One thousand	一千	yīqiān
Ten thousand	一万	yīwàn
One hundred thousand	十万	shíwàn
One million	一百万	yībǎiwàn
One hundred million	一亿	yīyì
One billion	十亿	shíyì

*liáng is used when enumerating, for example "two people" liang ge rén. èr is used when counting.

Time

Now	现在	xiànzài
Today	今天	jīntiān
(In the) morning	早上	zǎoshàng

(In the) afternoon	下午	xiàwǔ
(In the) evening	晚上	wǎnshàng
Tomorrow	明天	míngtiān
The day after tomorrow	后天	hòutiān
Yesterday	昨天	zuótiān
Week/month/year	星期/月/年	xīngqī/yuè/nián
Monday	星期一	xīngqī yī
Tuesday	星期二	xīngqī èr
Wednesday	星期三	xīngqī sān
Thursday	星期四	xīngqī sì
Friday	星期五	xīngqī wǔ
Saturday	星期六	xīngqī liù
Sunday	星期天	xīngqī tiān
What's the time?	几点了?	jǐdiǎn le?
10 o'clock	十点钟	shídiǎn zhōng
10.20	十点二十	shídiǎn èrshí
10.30	十点半	shídiǎn bàn

Travelling and getting about town

North	北	běi
South	南	nán
East	东	dōng
West	西	xī
Airport	机场	jīchǎng
Ferry dock	船码头	chuánmǎtóu
Left-luggage office	寄存处	jìcún chù
Ticket office	售票处	shòupiào chù
Ticket	票	piào
Can you buy me a ticket to…?	可不可以给我买到.....的票?	kěbùkěyǐ gěi wǒ mǎi dào… de piào?
I want to go to…	我想到.....去	wǒ xiǎng dào … qù
I want to leave at (8 o'clock)	我想(八点钟)离开	wǒ xiǎng (bā diǎn zhōng) líkāi
When does it leave?	什么时候出发?	shénme shíhòu chūfā?
When does it arrive?	什么时候到?	shénme shíhòu dào?
How long does it take?	路上得多长时间?	lùshàng děi duōcháng shíjiān?
CAAC	中国民航	zhōngguó mínháng
CITS	中国国际旅行社	zhōngguó guójì lǚxíngshè
Train	火车	huǒchē
(Main) Train station	主要火车站	(zhǔyào) huǒchēzhàn
Bus	公共汽车	gōnggòng qìchēzhàn
Bus station	汽车站	qìchēzhàn
Long-distance bus station	长途汽车站	chángtú qìchē
Express train/bus	特快车	tèkuài chē
Fast train/bus	快车	kuài chē
Ordinary train/bus	普通车	pǔtōng chē

Minibus	小车	xiǎo chē
Sleeper bus	卧铺车	wòpù chē
Lower bunk	下铺	xiàpù
Middle bunk	中铺	zhōngpù
Upper bunk	上铺	shàngpù
Hard seat	硬座	yìngzuò
Soft seat	软座	ruǎnzuò
Hard sleeper	硬卧	yìngwò
Soft sleeper	软卧	ruǎnwò
Soft-seat waiting room	软卧候车室	ruǎnwò hòuchēshì
Timetable	时间表	shíjiān biǎo
Upgrade ticket	补票	bǔpiào
Unreserved ticket	无座	wúzuò
Returned ticket window	退票	tuìpiào
Platform	站台	zhàntái

Getting about town

Map	地图	dìtú
Where is…?	……在哪里?	…zài nǎlǐ?
Go straight on	往前走	wǎng qián zǒu
Turn right	往右拐	wǎng yòu guǎi
Turn left	往左拐	wǎng zuǒ guǎi
Taxi	出租车	chūzū chē
Please use the meter	请打开记价器	qǐng dǎkāi jìjiàqì
Underground/Subway station	地铁站	dìtiě zhàn
Rickshaw	三轮车	sānlún chē
Bicycle	自行车	zìxíngchē
I want to rent a bicycle	我想租自行车	wǒ xiǎng zū zìxíngchē
How much is it per hour?	一个小时得多少钱?	yí gè xiǎoshí děi duōshǎo qián?
Can I borrow your bicycle?	能不能借你的自行车?	néng bùnéng jiè nǐ de zìxíngchē?
Bus	公共汽车	gōnggòngqìchē
Which bus goes to…?	几路车到……去?	jǐ lù chē dào … qù?
Number (10) bus	(十)路车	(shí) lù chē
Does this bus go to…?	这车到……去吗?	zhè chē dào … qù ma?
When is the next bus?	下一班车几点开?	xià yì bān chē jǐ diǎn kāi?
The first bus	头班车	tóubān chē
The last bus	末班车	mòbān chē
Please tell me where to get off	请告诉我在哪里下车	qǐng gàosu wǒ zài nǎlǐ xià chē
Museum	博物馆	bówùguǎn
Temple	寺院	sìyuàn
Church	教堂	jiàotáng
Mosque	清真寺	qīngzhēn sì
Toilet (men's)	男厕所	nán cèsuǒ
Toilet (women's)	女厕所	nǚ cèsuǒ

Accommodation

Accommodation	住宿	zhùsù
Hotel (upmarket)	宾馆	bīnguǎn
Hotel (downmarket)	招待所，旅馆	zhāodàisuǒ, lǚguǎn
Hostel	旅社	lǚshè
Foreigner's guesthouse (at a university)	外国专家楼	wàiguó zhuānjiā lóu
Is it possible to stay here?	能不能住在这里?	néng bù néng zhù zài zhèlǐ?
Can I have a look at the room?	能不能看一下房间?	néng bù néng kàn yíxià fángjiān?
I want the cheapest bed you've got	我要你最便宜的床位	wǒ yào nǐ zuì piányi de chuángwèi
Single room	单人房	dānrénfáng
Twin room	双人房	shuāngrénfáng
Three-bed room	三人房	sānrénfáng
Dormitory	多人房	duōrénfáng
Suite	套房	tàofáng
(Large) bed	(大)床	(dà) chuáng
Passport	护照	hùzhào
Deposit	押金	yājīn
Key	钥匙	yàoshi
When is the hot water on?	什么时候有热水?	shénme shíhòu you rèshuǐ?
I want to change my room	我想换一个房间	wǒ xiǎng huàn yí ge fángjiān

Shopping, money and banks, and the police

How much is it?	这是多少钱?	zhè shì duōshǎo qián?
That's too expensive	太贵了	tài guì le
I haven't got any cash	我没有现金	wǒ méiyǒu xiànjīn
Have you got anything cheaper?	有没有便宜一点的?	yǒu méiyǒu piányi yìdiǎn de?
Do you accept credit cards?	可不可以用信用卡?	ke bù keyi yòng xìnyòngka?
Department store	百货商店	bǎihuò shāngdiàn
Market	市场	shìchǎng
¥1 (RMB)	一块(人民币)	yí kuài (rénmínbì)
US$1	一块美金	yí kuài měijīn
£1	一个英磅	yí gè yīngbàng
HK$1	一块港币	yí kuài gǎngbì
Change money	换钱	huàn qián
Bank of China	中国银行	zhōngguó yínháng
Traveller's cheques	旅行支票	lǚxíngzhīpiào
PSB	公安局	gōng'ān jú

Communications

| Post office | 邮电局 | yóudiànjú |
| Envelope | 信封 | xìnfēng |

Stamp	邮票	yóupiào
Airmail	航空信	hángkōngxìn
Surface mail	平信	píngxìn
Poste restante	邮件侯领处	yóujiàn hòulǐngchù
Telephone	电话	diànhuà
International telephone call	国际电话	guójì diànhuà
Reverse charges/collect call	对方付钱电话	duìfāngfùqián diànhuà
Fax	传真	chuánzhēn
Telephone card	电话卡	diànhuàkǎ
I want to make a telephone call to (Britain)	我想给(英国)打电话	wǒ xiǎng gěi (yīngguó) dǎ diànhuà
I want to send a fax to (US)	我想给(美国)发一个传真	wǒ xiǎng gěi (měiguó) fā yí ge chuánzhēn
Can I receive a fax here?	能不能在这里收传真?	néng bù néng zài zhèli shou chuánzhen
Internet café	网吧	wǎngbā

Health

Hospital	医院	yīyuàn
Pharmacy	药店	yàodiàn
Medicine	药	yào
Chinese medicine	中药	zhōngyào
Diarrhoea	腹泻	fùxiè
Vomit	呕吐	ǒutù
Fever	发烧	fāshāo
I'm ill	我生病了	wǒ shēngbìng le
I've got flu	我感冒了	wǒ gǎnmào le
I'm (not) allergic to…	我对…(不)过敏	wǒ duì … (bù) guòmǐn
Antibiotics	抗生素	kàngshēngsù
Quinine	奎宁	kuíníng
Condom	避孕套	bìyùntào
Mosquito coil	蚊香	wénxiāng
Mosquito netting	蚊帐纱	wénzhàngshā

L

LANGUAGE | Useful words and phrases

A food and drink glossary

The following lists should help out in deciphering the characters on a Chinese menu – if they're written clearly. If you know what you're after, try sifting through the staples and cooking methods to create your order, or sample one of the everyday or regional suggestions, many of which are available all over the country. Don't forget to tailor your demands to the capabilities of where you're ordering, however – a street cook with a wok isn't going to be able to whip up anything more complicated than a basic stir-fry. Note that some items, such as seafood and *jiaozi*, are ordered by weight.

General

Restaurant	餐厅	cāntīng
House speciality	拿手好菜	náshǒuhǎocài
How much is that?	多少钱?	duōshǎo qián?
I don't eat (meat)	我不吃(肉)	wǒ bù chī (ròu)
I'm Buddhist/I'm vegetarian	我是佛教徒/我只吃素	wǒ shì fójiàotú/wǒ zhǐ chī sù
I would like....	我想要....	wǒ xiǎng yào...
Local dishes	地方菜	dìfang cài
Snacks	小吃	xiǎochī
Menu/set menu/English menu	菜单/套菜/英文菜单	càidān/tàocài/yīngwén càidān
Small portion	少量	shǎoliàng
Chopsticks	筷子	kuàizi
Knife and fork	刀叉	dāochā
Spoon	勺子	sháozi
Waiter/waitress	服务员/小姐	fúwùyuán/xiǎojiě
Bill/cheque	买单	mǎidān
Cook these ingredients together	一快儿做	yíkuàir zuò
Not spicy/no chilli please	请不要辣椒	qǐng búyào làjiao
Only a little spice/chilli	一点辣椒	yìdiǎn làjiāo
50 grams	两	liǎng
250 grams	半斤	bànjīn
500 grams	斤	jīn
1 kilo	公斤	gōngjīn

Drinks

Beer	啤酒	píjiǔ
Sweet fizzy drink	汽水	qìshuǐ
Coffee	咖啡	kāfēi
Milk	牛奶	niúnǎi
(Mineral) water	(矿泉)水	(kuàngquán) shuǐ
Wine	葡萄酒	pútáojiǔ
Spirits	白酒	báijiǔ
Soya milk	豆浆	dòujiāng
Yoghurt	酸奶	suānnǎi

Teas

Tea	茶	chá
Black tea	红茶	hóng chá
Chrysanthemum	菊花茶	júhuā chá
Eight treasures	八宝茶	bābǎo chá
Green tea	绿茶	lǜ chá
Iron Buddha	铁观音	tiěguānyīn
Jasmine	茉莉花茶	mòlihuā chá
Pu'er	普洱茶	pǔ'ěr chá

Staple foods

Aubergine	茄子	qiézi
Bamboo shoots	笋尖	sǔnjiān
Bean sprouts	豆芽	dòuyá
Beans	豆	dòu
Beef	牛肉	niúròu
Bitter gourd	葫芦	húlu
Black bean sauce	黑豆豉	hēidòuchǐ
Bread	面包	miànbāo
Buns (filled)	包子	bāozi
Buns (plain)	馒头	mántou
Carrot	胡萝卜	húluóbo
Cashew nuts	腰果	yāoguǒ
Cauliflower	菜花	càihuā
Chicken	鸡	jī
Chilli	辣椒	làjiāo
Chocolate	巧克力	qiǎokèlì
Coriander (leaves)	香菜	xiāngcài
Crab	蟹	xiè
Cucumber	黄瓜	huángguā
Dog	狗肉	gǒuròu
Duck	鸭	yā
Eel	鳝鱼	shànyú
Eggs (fried)	煎鸡蛋	jiānjīdàn
Fish	鱼	yú
Fried dough stick	油条	yóutiáo
Frog	田鸡	tiánjī
Garlic	大蒜	dàsuàn
Ginger	姜	jiāng
Green pepper (capsicum)	青椒	qīngjiāo
Green vegetables	绿叶素菜	lǜyè sùcài
Jiaozi (ravioli, steamed or boiled)	饺子	jiǎozi
Lamb	羊肉	yángròu
Lotus root	莲心	liánxīn
MSG	味精	wèijīng

Mushrooms	磨菇	mógū
Noodles	面条	miàntiáo
Omelette	摊鸡蛋	tānjīdàn
Onions	洋葱	yángcōng
Oyster sauce	蚝油	háoyóu
Pancake	摊饼	tānbǐng
Peanut	花生	huāshēng
Pork	猪肉	zhūròu
Potato (stir-fried)	(炒)土豆	(chǎo) tǔdòu
Prawns	虾	xiā
Preserved egg	皮蛋	pídàn
Rice noodles	河粉	héfěn
Rice porridge (aka "congee")	粥	zhōu
Rice, boiled	白饭	báifàn
Rice, fried	炒饭	chǎofàn
Salt	盐	yán
Sesame oil	芝麻油	zhīma yóu
Shuijiao (ravioli in soup)	水饺	shuǐjiǎo
Sichuan pepper	四川辣椒	sìchuān làjiāo
Snails	蜗牛	wōniú
Snake	蛇肉	shéròu
Soup	汤	tāng
Soy sauce	酱油	jiàngyóu
Squid	鱿鱼	yóuyú
Star anise	茴香	huíxiāng
Straw mushrooms	草菇	cǎogū
Sugar	糖	táng
Tofu	豆腐	dòufu
Tomato	蕃茄	fānqié
Vinegar	醋	cù
Water chestnuts	马蹄	mǎtí
White radish	白萝卜	báiluóbo
Wood ear fungus	木耳	mùěr
Yam	芋头	yùtóu

Cooking methods

Boiled	煮	zhǔ
Casseroled (see also "Claypot" opposite)	焙	bèi
Deep-fried	油煎	yóujiān
Fried	炒	chǎo
Poached	白煮	báizhǔ
Red-cooked (stewed in soy sauce)	红烧	hóngshāo
Roast	烤	kǎo
Steamed	蒸	zhēng
Stir-fried	清炒	qīngchǎo

Everyday dishes

Braised duck with vegetables	炖鸭素菜	dùnyā sùcài
Cabbage rolls (stuffed with meat or vegetables)	卷心菜	juǎnxīncài
Chicken and sweetcorn soup	玉米鸡丝汤	yùmǐ jīsī tāng
Chicken with bamboo shoots and babycorn	笋尖嫩玉米炒鸡片	sǔnjiān nènyùmǐ chǎojīpiàn
Chicken with cashew nuts	腰果鸡片	yāoguǒ jīpiàn
Claypot/sandpot (casserole)	沙锅	shāguō
Crispy aromatic duck	香酥鸭	xiāngsūyā
Egg flower soup with tomato	蕃茄蛋汤	fānqié dàn tāng
Egg fried rice	蛋炒饭	dànchǎofàn
Fish ball soup with white radish	萝卜鱼蛋汤	luóbo yúdàn tāng
Fish casserole	焙鱼	bèiyú
Fried shredded pork with garlic and chilli	大蒜辣椒炒肉片	dàsuàn làjiāo chǎoròupiàn
Hotpot	火锅	huǒguō
Kebab	串肉	chuànròu
Noodle soup	汤面	tāngmiàn
Pork and mustard greens	芥末肉片	jièmò ròupiàn
Pork and water chestnut	马蹄猪肉	mǎtí zhūròu
Pork and white radish pie	白萝卜肉馅饼	báiluóbo ròuxiànbǐng
Prawn with garlic sauce	大蒜炒虾	dàsuàn chǎoxiā
"Pulled" noodles	拉面	lāmiàn
Roast duck	烤鸭	kǎoyā
Scrambled egg with pork on rice	滑蛋猪肉饭	huádàn zhūròufàn
Sliced pork with yellow bean sauce	黄豆肉片	huángdòu ròupiàn
Squid with green pepper and black beans	豆豉青椒炒鱿鱼	dòuchǐ qīngjiāo chǎoyóuyú
Steamed eel with black beans	豆豉蒸鳝	dòuchǐ zhēngshàn
Steamed rice packets wrapped in lotus leaves	荷叶蒸饭	héyè zhēngfàn
Stewed pork belly with vegetables	回锅肉	huíguōròu
Stir-fried chicken and bamboo shoots	笋尖炒鸡片	sǔnjiān chǎojīpiàn
Stuffed bean-curd soup	豆腐汤	dòufutāng
Stuffed bean curd with aubergine and green pepper	茄子青椒煲	qiézi qīngjiāobāo
Sweet and sour spare ribs	糖醋排骨	tángcù páigǔ
Sweet bean paste pancakes	赤豆摊饼	chìdòu tānbǐng
White radish soup	白萝卜汤	báiluóbo tāng
Wonton soup	馄饨汤	húntun tāng

Vegetables and eggs

Aubergine with chilli and garlic sauce	大蒜辣椒炒茄子	dàsuàn làjiāo chǎoqiézi
Aubergine with sesame sauce	拌茄子片	bànqiézipiàn
Bean curd and spinach soup	菠菜豆腐汤	bōcài dòufu tāng
Bean-curd slivers	豆腐花	dòufuhuā
Bean curd with chestnuts	马蹄豆腐	mǎtí dòufu
Braised mountain fungus	炖香菇	dùnxiānggū
Monks' vegetarian dish (stir-fry of mixed vegetables and fungi)	罗汉斋	luóhànzhāi
Pressed bean curd with cabbage	卷心菜豆腐	juǎnxīncài dòufu
Egg fried with tomatoes	蕃茄炒蛋	fānqié chǎodàn
Fried bean curd with vegetables	豆腐素菜	dòufu sùcài
Fried bean sprouts	炒豆芽	chǎodòuyá
Spicy braised aubergine	香茄子条	xiāngqiézitiáo
Stir-fried bamboo shoots	炒冬笋	chǎodōngsǔn
Stir-fried mushrooms	炒鲜菇	chǎoxiānggū
Vegetable soup	素菜汤	sùcài tāng

Regional dishes

Northern

Aromatic fried lamb	炒羊肉	chǎoyángròu
Fish with ham and vegetables	火腿素菜鱼片	huǒtuǐ sùcài yúpiàn
Fried prawn balls	炒虾球	chǎoxiāqiú
Mongolian hotpot	蒙古火锅	ménggǔ huǒguō
Beijing (Peking) duck	北京烤鸭	běijīng kǎoyā
Red-cooked lamb	红烧羊肉	hóngshāo yángròu
Lion's head (pork rissoles casseroled with greens)	狮子头	shīzitóu

Eastern

Beggars' chicken (baked)	叫花鸡	jiàohuājī
Brine duck	盐水鸭	yánshuǐ yā
Crab soup	蟹肉汤	xièròu tāng
Dongpo pork casserole (steamed in wine)	东坡焙肉	dōngpō bèiròu
Drunken prawns	醉虾	zuìxiā
Five flower pork (steamed in lotus leaves)	五花肉	wǔhuāròu
Fried crab with eggs	蟹肉鸡蛋	xièròu jīdàn
Pearl balls (rice-grain-coated, steamed rissoles)	珍珠球	zhēnzhūqiú

Shaoxing chicken	绍兴鸡	shàoxīng jī
Soup dumplings (steamed, containing jellied stock)	汤包	tāngbāo
Steamed sea bass	清蒸鲈鱼	qīngzhēnglúyú
Stuffed green peppers	馅青椒	xiànqīngjiāo
West Lake fish (braised in a sour sauce)	西湖醋鱼	xīhúcùyú
"White-cut" beef (spiced and steamed)	白切牛肉	báiqiē niúròu
Yangzhou fried rice	杨州炒饭	yángzhōu chǎofàn

Sichuan and western China

Boiled beef slices (spicy)	水煮牛肉	shuǐzhǔ niúròu
Crackling-rice with pork	爆米肉片	bàomǐ ròupiàn
Crossing-the-bridge noodles	过桥面	guòqiáomiàn
Carry-pole noodles (with a chilli-vinegar-sesame sauce)	担担面	dàndànmiàn
Deep-fried green beans with garlic	大蒜刀豆	dàsuàn dāodòu
Dong'an chicken (poached in spicy sauce)	东安鸡子	dōng'ān jīzi
Doubled-cooked pork	回锅肉	huíguōròu
Dried yoghurt wafers	乳饼	rǔbǐng
Dry-fried pork shreds	油炸肉丝	yóuzhá ròusī
Fish-flavoured aubergine	鱼香茄子	yúxiāng qiézi
Gongbao chicken (with chillies and peanuts)	公保鸡丁	gōngbǎo jīdīng
Green pepper with spring onion and black bean sauce	豆豉青椒	dòuchǐ qīngjiāo
Hot and sour soup (flavoured with vinegar and white pepper)	酸辣汤	suānlà tāng
Hot-spiced bean curd	麻婆豆腐	mápódòufu
Rice-flour balls, stuffed with sweet paste	汤圆	tāngyuán
Smoked duck	熏鸭	xūnyā
Strange flavoured chicken (with sesame-garlic-chilli)	怪味鸡	guàiwèijī
Stuffed aubergine slices	馅茄子	xiànqiézi
Tangerine chicken	桔子鸡	júzijī
"Tiger-skin" peppers (pan-fried with salt)	虎皮炒椒	hǔpí chǎojiāo
Wind-cured ham	火腿	huǒtuǐ

Southern Chinese/Cantonese

| Baked crab with chilli and black beans | 辣椒豆豉焙蟹 | làjiāo dòuchǐ bèixiè |
| Barbecued pork ("char siew") | 叉烧 | chāshāo |

Casseroled bean curd stuffed with pork mince	豆腐煲	dòufubāo
Claypot rice with sweet sausage	香肠饭	xiāngchángfàn
Crisp-skinned pork on rice	脆皮肉饭	cuìpíròufàn
Fish-head casserole	焙鱼头	bèiyútóu
Fish steamed with ginger and spring onion	清蒸鱼	qīngzhēngyú
Fried chicken with yam	芋头炒鸡片	yùtóu chǎojīpiàn
Honey-roast pork	叉烧	chāshāo
Kale in oyster sauce	蚝油白菜	háoyóu báicài
Lemon chicken	柠檬鸡	níngméngjī
Litchi (lychee) pork	荔枝肉片	lìzhīròupiàn
Salt-baked chicken	盐鸡	yánjī
White fungus and wolfberry soup (sweet)	枸杞炖银耳	gǒuqǐ dùnyín'ěr

Dim sum

Dim sum	点心	diǎnxīn
Barbecued pork bun	叉烧包	chāshāo bāo
Chicken feet	凤爪	fèngzhuǎ
Crab and prawn dumpling	蟹肉虾饺	xièròu xiājiǎo
Custard tart	蛋挞	dàntà
Doughnut	炸面饼圈	zhá miànbǐngquān
Pork and prawn dumpling	烧麦	shāomài
Fried taro and mince dumpling	蕃薯糊饺	fānshǔ hújiǎo
Lotus paste bun	莲蓉糕	liánrónggāo
Moon cake (sweet bean paste in flaky pastry)	月饼	yuèbǐng
Paper-wrapped prawns	纸包虾	zhǐbāoxiā
Prawn crackers	虾片	xiāpiàn
Prawn dumpling	虾饺	xiājiǎo
Prawn paste on fried toast	芝麻虾	zhīmaxiā
Shanghai fried meat and vegetable dumpling ("potstickers")	锅帖	guōtiē
Spring roll	春卷	chūnjuǎn
Steamed spare ribs and chilli	排骨	páigǔ
Stuffed rice-flour roll	肠粉	chángfěn
Stuffed green peppers with black bean sauce	豆豉馅青椒	dòuchǐ xiànqīngjiāo
Sweet sesame balls	芝麻球	zhīma qiú
Turnip-paste patty	萝卜糕	luóbo gāo

Fruit

Fruit	水果	shuǐguǒ
Apple	苹果	píngguǒ
Banana	香蕉	xiāngjiāo

Durian	榴莲	liúlián
Grape	葡萄	pútáo
Honeydew melon	哈密瓜	hāmì guā
Longan	龙眼	lóngyǎn
Lychee	荔枝	lìzhī
Mandarin orange	橘子	júzi
Mango	杧果	mángguǒ
Orange	橙子	chéngzi
Peach	桃子	táozi
Pear	梨	lí
Persimmon	柿子	shìzi
Plum	李子	lǐzi
Pomegranate	石榴	shíliú
Pomelo	柚子	yòuzi
Watermelon	西瓜	xīguā

Glossary

General terms

Arhat Buddhist saint.

Bei North.

Binguan Hotel; generally a large one, for tourists.

Bodhisattva A follower of Buddhism who has attained enlightenment, but has chosen to stay on earth to teach rather than enter nirvana; Buddhist god or goddess.

Boxers The name given to an anti-foreign organization which originated in Shandong in 1898. Encouraged by the Qing Empress Dowager Cixi, they roamed China attacking westernized Chinese and foreigners in what became known as the Boxer Movement (see p.125).

Chorten Tibetan stupa.

CITS China International Travel Service. Tourist organization primarily interested in selling tours, though they can help with obtaining train tickets.

CTS China Travel Service. Tourist organization similar to CITS.

Concession Part of a town or city ceded to a foreign power in the nineteenth century.

Cultural Revolution Ten-year period beginning in 1966 and characterized by destruction, persecution and fanatical devotion to Mao (see p.1189).

Dagoba Another name for a stupa.

Dong East.

Dougong Large, carved wooden brackets, a common feature of temple design.

Fandian Restaurant or hotel.

Fen Smallest denomination of Chinese currency – there are one hundred fen to the yuan.

Feng Peak.

Feng shui A system of geomancy used to determine the positioning of buildings (see p.1191).

Gang of Four Mao's widow and her supporters who were put on trial immediately after Mao's death for their role in the Cultural Revolution, for which they were convenient scapegoats.

Ge Pavilion.

Gong Palace; usually indicates a Taoist temple.

Grassland Steppe; areas of land too high or cold to support anything other than grass, and agriculturally useful only as pastureland for sheep or cattle. Found especially in Inner Mongolia, Qinghai and Xinjiang.

Guan Pass; in temple names, usually denotes a Taoist shrine.

Guanxi Literally "connections": the reciprocal favours inherent in the process of official appointments and transactions.

Guanyin The ubiquitous Buddhist Goddess of Mercy, the most popular Bodhisattva in China, who postponed her entry into paradise in order to help ease human misery. Derived from the Indian deity Avalokiteshvara, she is often depicted with up to a thousand arms.

Gulou Drum tower; traditionally marking the centre of a town, this was where a drum was beaten at nightfall and in times of need.

Guomindang (GMD) The Nationalist Peoples' Party. Under Chiang Kaishek, the GMD fought Communist forces for 25 years before being defeated and moving to Taiwan in 1949, where it remains a major political party.

Hai Sea.

Han Chinese The main body of the Chinese people, as distinct from other ethnic groups such as Uigur, Miao, Hui or Tibetan.

He River.

Hu Lake.

Hui Muslim minority, mainly based in Gansu and Ningxia. Visually they are often indistinguishable from Han Chinese.

Hutong A narrow alleyway.

I Ching The Book of Changes, an ancient handbook for divination that includes some of the fundamental concepts of Chinese thought, such as the duality yin and yang.

Inkstones Decoratively carved blocks traditionally used by artists and calligraphers as a palette for mixing ink powder with water. The most famous, smooth-grained varieties come from Anhui and Guangdong provinces.

Jiang River.

Jiao (or mao) Ten fen.

Jiaozi Crescent-shaped, ravioli-like dumpling, usually served fried by the plateful for breakfast.

Jie Street.

Kang A raised wooden platform in a Chinese home, heated by the stove, on which the residents eat and sleep.

Kazakh A minority, mostly nomadic, in Xinjiang.

Lamian "Pulled noodles", a Muslim speciality usually served in a spicy soup.

Legalism In the Chinese context, a belief that humans are intrinsically bad and that strict laws are need to rein in their behaviour.

Ling Tomb.

Little Red Book A selection of "Quotations from Chairman Mao Zedong", produced in 1966 as a philosophical treatise for Red Guards during the Cultural Revolution.

Long March The Communists' 9500-kilometre tactical retreat in 1934–35 from Guomindang troops advancing on their base in the Jinggan Shan ranges, Jiangxi, to Yan'an in Shaanxi province.

Lu Street.

Luohan Buddhist disciple.

Mandala Mystic diagram which forms an important part of Buddhist iconography, especially in Tibet.

Mantou Steamed bread bun (literally "bald head").

Men Gate/door.

Miao Temple, usually Confucian.

Middle Kingdom A literal translation of the Chinese words for China.

Nan South.

PLA The People's Liberation Army, the official name of the Communist military forces since 1949.

PSB Public Security Bureau, the branch of China's police force which deals directly with foreigners.

Pagoda Tower with distinctively tapering structure, often associated with pseudo-science of feng shui.

Pinyin The official system of transliterating Chinese script into Roman characters.

Putonghua Mandarin Chinese; literally "Common Language".

Qianfodong Literally, "Thousand Buddha Cave", the name given to any Buddhist cave site along the Chinese section of the Silk Road.

Qiao Bridge.

RMB Renminbi. Another name for Chinese currency literally meaning "the people's money".

Red Guards The unruly factional forces unleashed by Mao during the Cultural Revolution to find and destroy brutally any "reactionaries" among the populace.

Renmin The people.

SEZ Special Economic Zone. A region in which state controls on production have been loosened and Western techniques of economic management are experimented with.

Sakyamuni Name given to future incarnation of Buddha.

Shan Mountain.

Shi City or municipality.

Shui Water.

Shuijiao Similar to jiaozi but boiled or served in a thin soup.

Si Temple, usually Buddhist.

Siheyuan Traditional courtyard house.

Spirit wall Wall behind the main gateway to a house, designed to thwart evil spirits, which, it was believed, could move only in straight lines.

Spirit Way The straight road leading to a tomb, lined with guardian figures.

Stele Freestanding stone tablet carved with text.

Stupa Multi-tiered tower associated with Buddhist temples that usually contains sacred objects.

Sutra Buddhist texts, often illustrative doctrines arranged in prayer form.

Ta Tower or pagoda.

Taiping Uprising Peasant rebellion against Qing rule during the mid-nineteenth century, which saw over a million troops led by the Christian fanatic Hong Xiuquan establish a capital at Nanjing before their later annihilation at the hands of imperial forces.

Tian Heaven or the sky.

Treaty port A port in which foreigners were permitted to set up residence, for the purpose of trade, under nineteenth-century agreements between China and foreign powers.

Uigur Substantial minority of Turkic people, living mainly in Xinjiang.

Waiguoren Foreigner.

Xi West.

Yuan China's unit of currency. Also a courtyard or garden (and the name of the Mongol dynasty).

Yurt Round, felt tent used by nomads. Also known as *ger*.

Zhan Station.

Zhao Temple; term used mainly in Inner Mongolia.

Zhong Middle; China is referred to as *zhongguo*, the Middle Kingdom.

Zhonglou Bell tower, usually twinned with a Gulou. The bell it contained was rung at dawn and in emergencies.

Zhou Place or region.

Travel
store

Rough Guides travel...

UK & Ireland
Britain
Devon & Cornwall
Dublin DIRECTIONS
Edinburgh DIRECTIONS
England
Ireland
Lake District
London
London DIRECTIONS
London Mini Guide
Scotland
Scottish Highlands & Islands
Wales

Europe
Algarve DIRECTIONS
Amsterdam
Amsterdam DIRECTIONS
Andalucía
Athens DIRECTIONS
Austria
Baltic States
Barcelona
Barcelona DIRECTIONS
Belgium & Luxembourg
Berlin
Brittany & Normandy
Bruges DIRECTIONS
Brussels
Budapest
Bulgaria
Copenhagen
Corfu
Corsica
Costa Brava DIRECTIONS
Crete
Croatia
Cyprus
Czech & Slovak Republics
Dodecanese & East Aegean
Dordogne & The Lot
Europe
Florence & Siena
Florence DIRECTIONS
France
French Hotels & Restos
Germany
Greece
Greek Islands
Hungary
Ibiza & Formentera DIRECTIONS
Iceland
Ionian Islands
Italy
Italian Lakes
Languedoc & Roussillon
Lisbon
Lisbon DIRECTIONS
The Loire
Madeira DIRECTIONS
Madrid DIRECTIONS
Mallorca & Menorca
Mallorca DIRECTIONS
Malta & Gozo DIRECTIONS
Menorca
Moscow
Netherlands
Norway
Paris
Paris DIRECTIONS
Paris Mini Guide
Poland
Portugal
Prague
Prague DIRECTIONS
Provence & the Côte d'Azur
Pyrenees
Romania
Rome
Rome DIRECTIONS
Sardinia
Scandinavia
Sicily
Slovenia
Spain
St Petersburg
Sweden
Switzerland
Tenerife & La Gomera DIRECTIONS
Turkey
Tuscany & Umbria
Venice & The Veneto
Venice DIRECTIONS
Vienna

Asia
Bali & Lombok
Bangkok
Beijing
Cambodia
China
Goa
Hong Kong & Macau
India
Indonesia
Japan
Laos
Malaysia, Singapore & Brunei
Nepal
The Philippines
Singapore
South India
Southeast Asia
Sri Lanka
Taiwan
Thailand
Thailand's Beaches & Islands
Tokyo
Vietnam

Australasia
Australia
Melbourne
New Zealand
Sydney

North America
Alaska
Boston
California
Canada
Chicago
Florida
Grand Canyon
Hawaii
Honolulu
Las Vegas DIRECTIONS
Los Angeles
Maui DIRECTIONS
Miami & South Florida
Montréal
New England
New Orleans DIRECTIONS
New York City
New York City DIRECTIONS
New York City Mini Guide
Orlando & Walt Disney World DIRECTIONS
Pacific Northwest
Rocky Mountains
San Francisco
San Francisco DIRECTIONS
Seattle
Southwest USA
Toronto
USA
Vancouver
Washington DC
Washington DC DIRECTIONS
Yosemite

Caribbean & Latin America
Antigua & Barbuda DIRECTIONS
Argentina
Bahamas
Barbados DIRECTIONS
Belize
Bolivia
Brazil
Cancùn & Cozumel DIRECTIONS
Caribbean
Central America
Chile
Costa Rica
Cuba
Dominican Republic
Dominican Republic DIRECTIONS
Ecuador
Guatemala
Jamaica

TRAVEL STORE

...music & reference

Mexico
Peru
St Lucia
South America
Trinidad & Tobago
Yúcatan

Africa & Middle East
Cape Town & the
  Garden Route
Egypt
The Gambia
Jordan
Kenya
Marrakesh
  DIRECTIONS
Morocco
South Africa, Lesotho
  & Swaziland
Syria
Tanzania
Tunisia
West Africa
Zanzibar

Travel Theme guides
First-Time Around the
  World
First-Time Asia
First-Time Europe
First-Time Latin
  America
Travel Online
Travel Health
Travel Survival
Walks in London & SE
  England
Women Travel

Maps
Algarve
Amsterdam
Andalucia & Costa
  del Sol
Argentina
Athens
Australia
Baja California
Barcelona
Berlin
Boston

Brittany
Brussels
California
Chicago
Corsica
Costa Rica & Panama
Crete
Croatia
Cuba
Cyprus
Czech Republic
Dominican Republic
Dubai & UAE
Dublin
Egypt
Florence & Siena
Florida
France
Frankfurt
Germany
Greece
Guatemala & Belize
Hong Kong
Iceland
Ireland
Kenya
Lisbon
London
Los Angeles
Madrid
Mallorca
Marrakesh
Mexico
Miami & Key West
Morocco
New England
New York City
New Zealand
Northern Spain
Paris
Peru
Portugal
Prague
Rome
San Francisco
Sicily
South Africa
South India
Sri Lanka
Tenerife
Thailand

Toronto
Trinidad & Tobago
Tuscany
Venice
Washington DC
Yucatán Peninsula

Dictionary Phrasebooks
Croatian
Czech
Dutch
Egyptian Arabic
European Languages
  (Czech, French,
  German, Greek,
  Italian, Portuguese,
  Spanish)
French
German
Greek
Hindi & Urdu
Hungarian
Indonesian
Italian
Japanese
Latin American
  Spanish
Mandarin Chinese
Mexican Spanish
Polish
Portuguese
Russian
Spanish
Swahili
Thai
Turkish
Vietnamese

Music Guides
The Beatles
Bob Dylan
Cult Pop
Classical Music
Elvis
Frank Sinatra
Heavy Metal
Hip-Hop
Jazz
Opera
Reggae

Rock
World Music (2 vols)

Reference Guides
Babies
Books for Teenagers
Children's Books, 0–5
Children's Books, 5–11
Comedy Movies
Conspiracy Theories
Cult Fiction
Cult Football
Cult Movies
Cult TV
The Da Vinci Code
Ethical Shopping
Gangster Movies
Horror Movies
iPods, iTunes & Music
  Online
The Internet
James Bond
Kids' Movies
Lord of the Rings
Macs & OS X
Muhammad Ali
Music Playlists
PCs and Windows
Poker
Pregnancy & Birth
Sci–Fi Movies
Shakespeare
Superheroes

Unexplained
  Phenomena
The Universe
Weather
Website Directory

Football
Arsenal 11s
Celtic 11s
Chelsea 11s
Liverpool 11s
Newcastle 11s
Rangers 11s
Tottenham 11s
Man United 11s

TRAVEL STORE

small print and
Index

A Rough Guide to Rough Guides

In the summer of 1981, Mark Ellingham, a recent graduate from Bristol University, was travelling round Greece and couldn't find a guidebook that really met his needs. On the one hand there were the student guides, insistent on saving every last cent, and on the other the heavyweight cultural tomes whose authors seemed to have spent more time in a research library than lounging away the afternoon at a taverna or on the beach.

In a bid to avoid getting a job, Mark and a small group of writers set about creating their own guidebook. It was a guide to Greece that aimed to combine a journalistic approach to description with a thoroughly practical approach to travellers' needs – a guide that would incorporate culture, history and contemporary insights with a critical edge, together with up-to-date, value-for-money listings. Back in London, Mark and the team finished their Rough Guide, as they called it, and talked Routledge into publishing the book.

That first *Rough Guide to Greece*, published in 1982, was a student scheme that became a publishing phenomenon. The immediate success of the book – with numerous reprints and a Thomas Cook Prize shortlisting – spawned a series that rapidly covered dozens of destinations. Rough Guides had a ready market among low-budget backpackers, but soon also acquired a much broader and older readership that relished Rough Guides' wit and inquisitiveness as much as their enthusiastic, critical approach. Everyone wants value for money, but not at any price.

Rough Guides soon began supplementing the "rougher" information about hostels and low-budget listings with the kind of detail on restaurants and quality hotels that independent-minded visitors on any budget might expect, whether on business in New York or trekking in Thailand.

These days the guides – distributed worldwide by the Penguin Group – offer recommendations from shoestring to luxury and cover more than 200 destinations around the globe, including almost every country in the Americas and Europe, more than half of Africa, and most of Asia and Australasia. Our ever-growing team of authors and photographers is spread all over the world, particularly in Europe, the US and Australia.

In 1994, we published the *Rough Guide to World Music* and *Rough Guide to Classical Music*, and a year later the *Rough Guide to the Internet*. All three books have become benchmark titles in their fields – which encouraged us to expand into other areas of publishing, mainly around popular culture. Rough Guides now publish:

- Travel guides to more than 200 worldwide destinations
- Dictionary phrasebooks for 22 major languages
- History guides ranging from Ireland to Islam
- Maps printed on rip-proof and waterproof Polyart™ paper
- Music guides running the gamut from Opera to Elvis
- Restaurant guides to London, New York and San Francisco
- Reference books on topics as diverse as the Weather and Shakespeare
- Sports guides from Formula 1 to Man Utd
- Pop culture books from *Lord of the Rings* to Cult TV
- World Music CDs in association with World Music Network

Visit **www.roughguides.com** to see our latest publications.

Rough Guide credits

Text editors: Richard Lim, Andy Turner and Robin Pridy
Layout: Amit Verma
Cartography: Karobi Gogoi and Jasbir Sandhu
Picture editor: Sarah Smithies
Production: Julia Bovis
Proofreader: Jan McCann
Chinese text compilation and proofing: Frances Feng Dan and Xiaoshan Sun
Editorial: London Kate Berens, Claire Saunders, Geoff Howard, Ruth Blackmore, Polly Thomas, Clifton Wilkinson, Alison Murchie, Sally Schafer, Karoline Densley, Ella O'Donnell, Keith Drew, Edward Aves, Nikki Birrell, Helen Marsden, Joe Staines, Duncan Clark, Peter Buckley, Matthew Milton; **New York** Andrew Rosenberg, Richard Koss, Steven Horak, AnneLise Sorensen, Amy Hegarty, Hunter Slaton
Design & Pictures: London Simon Bracken, Dan May, Diana Jarvis, Mark Thomas, Harriet Mills, Chloë Roberts; **Delhi** Madhulita Mohapatra, Umesh Aggarwal, Ajay Verma, Jessica Subramanian, Ankur Guha

Production: Sophie Hewat, Katherine Owers
Cartography: London Maxine Repath, Ed Wright, Katie Lloyd-Jones; **Delhi** Manish Chandra, Rajesh Chhibber, Jai Prakash Mishra, Ashutosh Bharti, Rajesh Mishra, Animesh Pathak
Online: New York Jennifer Gold, Suzanne Welles, Kristin Mingrone; **Delhi** Manik Chauhan, Narender Kumar, Shekhar Jha, Rakesh Kumar, Lalit Sharma, Chhandita Chakravarty
Marketing & Publicity: London Richard Trillo, Niki Hanmer, David Wearn, Demelza Dallow, Louise Maher; **New York** Geoff Colquitt, Megan Kennedy, Milena Perez; **Delhi** Reem Khokhar
Custom publishing and foreign rights: Philippa Hopkins
Manager India: Punita Singh
Series editor: Mark Ellingham
Reference Director: Andrew Lockett
PA to Managing and Publishing Directors: Megan McIntyre
Publishing Director: Martin Dunford
Managing Director: Kevin Fitzgerald

Publishing information

This 4th edition published October 2005 by
Rough Guides Ltd,
80 Strand, London WC2R 0RL
345 Hudson St, 4th Floor,
New York, NY 10014, US
14 Local Shopping Centre, Panchsheel Park,
New Delhi 110017, India.
Distributed by the Penguin Group
Penguin Books Ltd,
80 Strand, London WC2R 0RL
Penguin Putnam, Inc.,
375 Hudson St, NY 10014, US
Penguin Group (Australia)
250 Camberwell Road, Camberwell,
Victoria 3124, Australia
Penguin Books Canada Ltd,
10 Alcorn Avenue, Toronto, ON,
M4V 1E4 Canada
Penguin Group (New Zealand),
Cnr Rosedale and Airborne Roads,
Albany, Auckland, New Zealand
Typeset in Bembo and Helvetica to an original

design by Henry Iles.
Printed in Italy by LegoPrint S.p.A

© David Leffman, Simon Lewis and Rough Guides 2005

1272pp includes index
A catalogue record for this book is available from the British Library.
ISBN-13: 978-1-84353-479-2
ISBN-10: 1-84353-479-7

The publishers and authors have done their best to ensure the accuracy and currency of all the information in **The Rough Guide to China**; however, they can accept no responsibility for any loss, injury or inconvenience sustained by any traveller as a result of information or advice contained in the guide.

1   3   5   7   9   8   6   4   2

SMALL PRINT

Help us update

We've gone to a lot of effort to ensure that the fourth edition of **The Rough Guide to China** is accurate and up to date. However, things change – places get "discovered", opening hours are notoriously fickle, restaurants and rooms raise prices or lower standards. If you feel we've got it wrong or left something out, we'd like to know, and if you can remember the address, the price, the time, the phone number, so much the better.

We'll credit all contributions, and send a copy of the next edition (or any other Rough Guide if you prefer) for the best letters. Everyone who writes to us and isn't already a subscriber will receive a copy of our full-colour thrice-yearly newsletter. Please mark letters: "**Rough Guide China update**" and send to: Rough Guides, 80 Strand, London WC2R 0RL, or Rough Guides, 4th Floor, 345 Hudson St, New York, NY 10014. Or send an email to **mail@roughguides.com**.

Have your questions answered and tell others about your trip at **www.roughguides.atinfopop.com**.

Acknowledgements

David Leffman thanks Narrell, Paul & Steve, Bonka, Sebastien, Jack, and especially Xiao Laoshi, Lao Li, CS, the Gaos, and everyone else who let me train with them.

Simon Lewis Thanks to Qian Fan, He Kai Yuen, Marsha, Simon, Howard, Rick, Paul, Annie, Noe, and everyone else who helped along the way.

Simon Foster Thanks to Christine, Jasmine and Jo, Jen-woan and Heng, Lu Xinsheng, Pete Mitchell and Hu Ya Lin, Stephen Huang, Susan Lee and Tot.

Travis Klingberg Thanks to Mike Goettig, Peter Hessler, Mike Meyer, Xie Jin and the many others who helped, both on the road and off.

Mike Meyer thanks Frances Feng Dan, Peter Hessler, Michael Goettig and Travis Klingberg for beers and ultimate frisbee at Gulou.

Xiaoshan Sun Many thanks to Chen Lin, Chris Crabtree, Duo Zhenguo, Li Jiang, Li Wenqing, Liu Shulan, Sun Borui, Zang Bing, Zhao Wenting and Zhang Zhihui.

Readers' letters

Thanks to all the readers for taking the trouble to write and email in with comments and suggestions (and apologies to anyone whose name we might have inadvertently misspelt or omitted):

Marco Abate, Zena Yasmin Alkayat, Susie Amann, Andrew Beavan, Boen and Esther, Jon Brain, Nick Bridge, Ana Bush, Sophie Camp, Ryan Clark, Ross Cundy, Carolyn Driver-Burgess, Victoria Durrer, Annabelle Evans, Darren Foy, Aymeric Fraise, Jim Gardiner, Wesley Gibbs, Elizabeth Godfrey, Paul Harris, Philip Harrison, Barbara Hill, Sally Hogbin, Robert Janowsky, Lyn Johnson, Sandra Keogh, Steven King, Mateusz Krzyzosiak, Sebastien Lafortune, Victor Lam, Heather Langendorfer, Alexandre Maier, Angela Marshall, Stacey McDonald, Michelle Merry, Christian Monks, Claire Morsman, Alex & Diane Nikolic, Michelle Noyes, Diana Octafianti, Derek Parkes, Eric Pelzl, Gordon Pickup, Michelle Podmore, Daniel Poon, Kayte Rath, Mandy Renshaw, Allison Rodman, Yves Saint-Pierre, Glenn Sayers, Gary Schiffmiller, Veronica Schmitt, Kristoff Sel, Nigel Singh, Jennifer Steele, Peter Telford, David Thomas, Robin Tilston, Chris Twite, Mark Weston, Isabel Wright, Warren Yeo, Ilona Zatkova.

Photo credits

Cover
Main front picture: Woodwork, Summer Palace, Beijing © Alamy
Small front top picture: Giant Panda, Wolong © Getty
Small front lower picture: Hanging lanterns © Alamy
Back top picture: Shanghai at night © Alamy
Back lower picture: Traditional minority dancers © Alamy

Title page
The Bund (Nanjing Lu), Shanghai © Tibor Bognar/ Alamy

Full page
Meili Xue Shan, Yunnan © Yi, You Wu/China Tourism Photo Library

Introduction
Detail of a lion head, Forbidden City © Jonathan Pile/Impact
Chinese Opera, Beijing © View Stock/Alamy
Corner tower in the Forbidden City © PanoramaStock/Robert Harding
Sichuan food © David Leffman
Panda © David Leffman

New Year calligraphy for sale, Dali, Yunnan © Mark Henley/Impact
Tai ji students, Wudang Shan © David Leffman
Camels in desert © Gao Zhiqiang/ Imaginechina
Sunset at Hong Kong © Justin Yeung/Alamy
Picking vegetables below Yulong Xue Shan, Yunnan © Michael Matthews

Things not to miss
01 The Great Wall – Mutianyu in winter © Li Shaobai/Imaginechina
02 Li River Scenery © K. Cardwell/Trip
03 Meili Xue Shan, Deqin, Yunnan © China Tourism Photo Library
04 Huanglongxi © David Leffman
05 Winter ice festival, Harbin © Zhao Gang/ Imaginechina
06 Colonial architecture, Gulangyu Island, near Xiamen, Fujian © Amar Grover
07 Sisters' Meal festival, Taijiang, Guizhou © David Leffman
08 Skiing at Yabuli © Zhao Gang/Imaginechina
09 Siberian tiger © Zhang Bin/Imaginechina
10 Chengde Temple © Li Shaobai/Imaginechina
11 Mount Everest, Tibet © Zhang Guosheng/ Imaginechina

SMALL PRINT

Index

Map entries are in colour

The following abbreviations are used throughout this index:

AH Anhui	**HEB** Hebei	**QH** Qinghai
BJ Beijing	**HEN** Henan	**SAX** Shaanxi
CQ Chongqing	**HN** Hainan	**SC** Sichuan
DB Dongbei	**HUB** Hubei	**SD** Shandong
FJ Fujian	**HUN** Hunan	**SX** Shanxi
GD Guangdong	**IM** Inner Mongolia	**T** Tibet
GS Gansu	**JS** Jiangsu	**XJ** Xinjiang
GX Guangxi	**JX** Jiangxi	**YN** Yunnan
GZ Guizhou	**NX** Ningxia	**ZJ** Zhejiang

INDEX

INDEX

Map symbols

Maps are listed in the full index using coloured text

-----	International boundary
—----	Provincial boundary
----	Chapter boundary
▬▬▬	Expressway
═══	Major road
▬▬	Minor road
▬▬	Pedestrianized road
⊞⊞⊞	Steps
)······(	Tunnel
------	Path
▬▬	Railway
—Ⓜ—	Metro station & line
— — —	Ferry route
▬▬	Waterway
⊔⊔⊔⊔	Canal
▪▪▪▪	Wall
✈	Airport
◆	Point of interest
🛕	Temple/monastery
♠	Buddhist temple
🌲	Pagoda
🕌	Mosque
⚐	Stupa
♦	Museum
∎	Tower
∴	Ruins
⋎	Viewpoint
⌒	Caves
▲	Mountain peak
⋏⋏	Mountain range
🐜	Waterfall
🐾	Cliffs

〰	Gorge/cutting
⋎	Marshland
⋀⋀	Spring
⚇	Public gardens
🌴	Tree
) (	Bridge
∩	Arch
⚐	Skiing area
♦	Border crossing post
Ⓐ	Bus station/depot
★	Minibus stand/bus stop
E	Embassy/consulate
⊙	Statue
🏛	Monument
⊞	Hospital
@	Internet access
Ⓒ	Telecom office
ⓘ	Information office
⊠	Post office
◉	Hotel
▣	Restaurant
•--•	Cable car
⊠—⊠	Gate
▮	Building
⊞	Church/cathedral
▢	Market
⬭	Stadium
▦	Park
▦	Beach
▧	Forest
⊞	Cemetery

MAP SYMBOLS